ISBN 978-0-260-96499-1
PIBN 11111215

FIFTY-FOURTH ANNUAL

# INSURANCE REPORT

OF THE

## DEPARTMENT OF TRADE AND COMMERCE
## DIVISION OF INSURANCE

OF THE

## STATE OF ILLINOIS

---

GEORGE A. BARR, Director
FRANK E. O'BRYANT, Assistant Director
THOMAS J. HOUSTON, Superintendent of Insurance
GEORGE HUSKINSON, Assistant Superintendent

---

PART II—LIFE INSURANCE

Legal Reserve, Assessment and Fraternal Beneficiary



---

1922

---

[Printed by authority of the State of Illinois.]

ILLINOIS STATE JOURNAL CO.
SPRINGFIELD, ILLINOIS
1 9 2 3

80000—1M

# CONTENTS OF PART II.

(See index at end of volume for list of companies.)

## CONTENTS—Concluded.

FRATERNAL TABLES, FRATERNAL BENEFICIARY SOCIETIES.



ANNUAL STATEMENTS OF LEGAL RESERVE LIFE COMPANIES.



ANNUAL STATEMENTS OF ASSETSSMENT LIFE ASSOCIATIONS.



ANNUAL STATEMENTS OF FRATERNAL BENEFICIARY SOCIETIES.



REPORTS.

# REPORT OF THE DIRECTOR OF TRADE AND COMMERCE OF THE STATE OF ILLINOIS.

## Division of Insurance.

---

### PART II—LIFE.

SPRINGFIELD, *May 31, 1922.*

*To His Excellency, Len Small, Governor of the State of Illinois.*

SIR: Part II of the Fifty-fourth Annual Report of this Department is herewith respectfully submitted.

This part reports the condition and affairs of companies transacting the business of life insurance on the legal reserve, assessment and fraternal plan.

### LEGAL RESERVE COMPANIES.

The number of companies doing business on the legal reserve plan shown herein as authorized to transact business in this State is one hundred four, an increase of one as compared with the number authorized at the date of the last report.

| | |
|---|---|
| Legal reserve life of Illinois | 23 |
| Legal reserve life of other states | 78 |
| Legal reserve life of foreign governments | 3 |
| Total | 104 |

One Illinois company and two companies of other states were licensed during the year 1921:

Liberty Life Insurance Company, Chicago, Illinois, licensed July 25, 1921.

American Life Reinsurance Company, Dallas, Texas, admitted July 1, 1921.

Universal Life Insurance Company, Dubuque, Iowa, admitted May 26, 1921.

Two companies discontinued business in Illinois during 1921:

American Life Insurance Company, Des Moines, Iowa, withdrew August 27, 1921 and was reinsured in the Northern Assurance Company of Detroit, Michigan.

Omaha Life Insurance Company, Omaha, Nebraska, withdrew February 25, 1921.

### CHANGE OF NAME.

Northern Assurance Company of Michigan, Detroit, Michigan. Name changed to American Life Insurance Company, Detroit, Michigan, on August 1, 1921.

## TABLE NO. 1.

### NAME OF STATE OR GOVERNMENT AND NUMBER OF COMPANIES.

|  |  |  |  |
|---|---|---|---|
| California | 1 | Nebraska | 3 |
| Canada | 3 | New Jersey | 2 |
| Colorado | 1 | New York | 10 |
| Connecticut | 5 | Ohio | 5 |
| Illinois | 23 | Pennsylvania | 6 |
| Indiana | 11 | Tennessee | 1 |
| Iowa | 6 | Texas | 1 |
| Louisiana | 1 | Vermont | 1 |
| Maine | 1 | Virginia | 1 |
| Maryland | 1 | Washington | 2 |
| Massachusetts | 6 | Wisconsin | 3 |
| Michigan | 2 | | |
| Minnesota | 2 | Total | 104 |
| Missouri | 6 | | |

## TABLE NO. 2.

### LIFE INSURANCE COMPANIES OF THIS STATE.

| Name of company. | Location. | Paid up capital. |
|---|---|---|
| American Bankers Insurance Co., The | Chicago | $ 118,505 00 |
| Central Life Insurance Co. of Illinois | Ottawa | 300,000 00 |
| Chicago National Life Insurance Co | Chicago | 100,000 00 |
| Cloverleaf Life and Casualty Co | Jacksonville | 200,000 00 |
| Continental Assurance Co | Chicago | 250,000 00 |
| Elgin Life Insurance Co | Elgin | 104,102 95 |
| Federal Life Insurance Co | Chicago | 300,000 00 |
| Franklin Life Insurance Co., The | Springfield | 100,000 00 |
| Illinois Life Insurance Co | Chicago | 1,000,000 00 |
| International Life and Trust Co | Moline | 104,860 00 |
| Liberty Life Insurance Co | Chicago | 100,000 00 |
| Marquette Life Insurance Co | Springfield | 254,742 00 |
| Mutual Life of Illinois | Springfield | 177,907 00 |
| Mutual Trust Life Insurance Co | Chicago | Mutual |
| National Life Insurance Co. of the U. S. A | Chicago | 500,000 00 |
| North American Life Insurance Company of Chicago | Chicago | 700,000 00 |
| Old Colony Life Insurance Co | Chicago | 126,551 87 |
| People's Life Insurance Co., The | Chicago | 101,736 66 |
| Peoria Life Insurance Co | Peoria | 200,000 00 |
| Providers Life Assurance Co | Chicago | 145,960 00 |
| Public Life Insurance Co | Chicago | 200,000 00 |
| Rockford Life Insurance Co | Rockford | 175,650 00 |
| Standard Life Insurance Co | Decatur | 225,000 00 |

### LIFE INSURANCE COMPANIES OF OTHER STATES.

| Name of company. | Location. | Paid up capital. |
|---|---|---|
| Aetna Life Insurance Co | Hartford, Conn | $5,000,000 00 |
| American Central Life Insurance Co | Indianapolis, Ind | 137,000 00 |
| American Life Insurance Co | Detroit, Mich | 100,000 00 |
| American Life Re-insurance Co | Dallas, Tex | 250,000 00 |
| American National Assurance Co | St. Louis, Mo | 200,000 00 |
| Bankers' Life Company | Des Moines, Iowa | Mutual |
| Bankers' Life Insurance Company of Nebraska | Lincoln, Neb | 100,000 00 |
| Bankers' Reserve Life Company, The | Omaha, Neb | 100,000 00 |
| Berkshire Life Insurance Co | Pittsfield, Mass | Mutual |
| Business Men's Assurance Co. of America | Kansas City, Mo | 200,000 00 |
| Capitol Life Insurance Co. of Colorado, The | Denver, Colo | 100,000 00 |
| Central Life Assurance Society of the U. S. (Mutual) | Des Moines, Iowa | Mutual |
| Central States Life Insurance Co | St. Louis, Mo | 400,000 00 |
| Century Life Insurance Company | Indianapolis, Ind | 200,000 00 |
| Cleveland Life Insurance Co., The | Cleveland, Ohio | 250,000 00 |
| Columbia National Life Insurance Co., The | Boston, Mass | 1,000,000 00 |
| Columbus Mutual Life Insurance Co | Columbus, Ohio | 250,000 00 |
| Connecticut General Life Insurance Co | Hartford, Conn | 800,000 00 |
| Connecticut Mutual Life Insurance Co | Hartford, Conn | Mutual |
| Equitable Life Assurance Society of the U. S., The | New York, N. Y | 100,000 00 |
| Equitable Life Insurance Co. of Iowa | Des Moines, Iowa | 500,000 00 |
| Farmers National Life Insurance Company of America | Huntington, Ind | 200,000 00 |
| Federal Union Life Insurance Co., The | Cincinnati, Ohio | 225,000 00 |
| Fidelity Mutual Life Insurance Co., The | Philadelphia, Pa | Mutual |
| Girard Life Insurance Co | Philadelphia, Pa | 419,010 00 |
| Guardian Life Insurance Co. of America, The | New York, N. Y | 200,000 00 |
| Home Life Insurance Co | New York, N. Y | Mutual |
| Indiana National Life Insurance Co | Indianapolis, Ind | 210,000 00 |
| Indianapolis Life Insurance Co | Indianapolis, Ind | Mutual |
| International Life Insurance Co | St. Louis, Mo | 656,250 00 |
| John Hancock Mutual Life Insurance Co | Boston, Mass | Mutual |
| Kansas City Life Insurance Co | Kansas City, Mo | 200,000 00 |
| LaFayette Life Insurance Co | LaFayette, Ind | Mutual |
| Lincoln National Life Insurance Co | Ft. Wayne, Ind | 500,000 00 |
| Manhattan Life Insurance Co., The | New York, N. Y | 100,000 00 |

TABLE NO. 2—Concluded.

| Name of company. | Location. | Paid up capital. |
|---|---|---|
| Maryland Assurance Corporation | Baltimore, Md | $ 500,000 00 |
| Massachusetts Mutual Life Insurance Co | Springfield, Mass | Mutual |
| Merchants Life Insurance Co | Des Moines, Iowa | 400,000 00 |
| Metropolitan Life Insurance Co | New York, N. Y | Mutual |
| Michigan Mutual Life Insurance Co | Detroit, Mich | 250,000 00 |
| Minnesota Mutual Life Insurance Co., The | St. Paul, Minn | Mutual |
| Missouri State Life Insurance Co | St. Louis, Mo | 1,000,000 00 |
| Morris Plan Insurance Society, The | New York, N. Y | 100,000 00 |
| Mutual Benefit Life Insurance Co., The | Newark, N. J | Mutual |
| Mutual Life Insurance Company of New York, The | New York, N. Y | Mutual |
| National Life and Accident Insurance Co., The | Nashville, Tenn | 600,000 00 |
| National Life Insurance Co | Montpelier, Vt | Mutual |
| New England Mutual Life Insurance Co | Boston, Mass | Mutual |
| New World Life Insurance Co | Spokane, Wash | 1,134,500 00 |
| New York Life Insurance Co | New York, N. Y | Mutual |
| Northern States Life Insurance Co | Hammond, Ind | 162,000 00 |
| Northwestern Mutual Life Insurance Co., The | Milwaukee, Wis | Mutual |
| Northwestern National Life Insurance Co | Minneapolis, Minn | Mutual |
| Old Line Insurance Co | Lincoln, Neb | 200,000 00 |
| Old Line Life Insurance Co. of America, The | Milwaukee, Wis | 672,635 00 |
| Pacific Mutual Life Insurance Company of California, The | Los Angeles, Cal | 1,500,000 00 |
| Pan American Life Insurance Co | New Orleans, La | 1,000,000 00 |
| Penn Mutual Life Insurance Co | Philadelphia, Pa | Mutual |
| Peoples Life Insurance Co | Frankfort, Ind | 100,000 00 |
| Philadelphia Life Insurance Co | Philadelphia, Pa | 560,320 00 |
| Phoenix Mutual Life Insurance Co | Hartford, Conn | Mutual |
| Provident Life and Trust Company of Philadelphia, The | Philadelphia, Pa | 2,000,000 00 |
| Prudential Insurance Co. of America, The | Newark, N. J | 2,000,000 00 |
| Reinsurance Life Co. of America | Des Moines, Iowa | 500,000 00 |
| Reliance Life Insurance Company of Pittsburgh | Pittsburgh, Pa | 1,000,000 00 |
| Reserve Loan Life Insurance Co | Indianapolis, Ind | 100,000 00 |
| Security Life Insurance Co. of America | Richmond, Va | 220,000 00 |
| Security Mutual Life Insurance Co | Binghamton, N. Y | Mutual |
| State Life Insurance Co., The | Indianapolis, Ind | Mutual |
| State Mutual Life Assurance Co | Worcester, Mass | Mutual |
| Travelers Insurance Co., The | Hartford, Conn | 7,500,000 00 |
| Union Central Life Insurance Co | Cincinnati, Ohio | 2,500,000 00 |
| Union Mutual Life Insurance Co | Portland, Me | Mutual |
| United States Life Insurance Company in the City of New York, The | New York, N. Y | 264,000 00 |
| Universal Life Insurance Co | Dubuque, Iowa | 369,442 13 |
| Western and Southern Life Insurance Co., The | Cincinnati, Ohio | 1,250,000 00 |
| Western Union Life Insurance Co | Spokane, Wash | 200,000 00 |
| Wisconsin National Life Insurance Co | Oshkosh, Wis | 400,000 00 |

LIFE INSURANCE COMPANIES OF FOREIGN GOVERNMENTS.

| Name of company. | Location. | Paid up capital. |
|---|---|---|
| Canada Life Assurance Co | Toronto, Can | $1,000,000 00 |
| Manufacturers Life Insurance Co., The | Toronto, Can | 300,000 00 |
| North American Life Assurance Co | Toronto, Can | 60,000 00 |

## TABLE NO. 3.

The following table gives the total amount of securities held in trust by the Director of Trade and Commerce, Division of Insurance, for the Life Insurance Companies named therein:

| Name of company. | Location. | Kind of securities. | Deposit value. |
|---|---|---|---|
| American Bankers Insurance Company | Chicago | Capital stock deposit— | |
| | | Mortgages | $88,700 00 |
| | | Commonwealth Edison Co. Bonds | 2,850 00 |
| | | Danville, Champaign & Decatur Ry. & Light Co. Bonds | 11,200 00 |
| | | Portland Gas & Coke Co. Bonds | 8,200 00 |
| | | Columbus, Ohio Ry. Co. Bonds | 3,100 00 |
| | | Little River Drainage District of Mo. Bonds | 920 00 |
| | | Bloomington & Normal Ry. & Light Co. Bonds | 1,600 00 |
| | | North Shore Gas Co. Bonds | 5,600 00 |
| | | United Light & Ry. Co. Bonds | 3,850 00 |
| | | Des Moines Electric Light Co. Bonds | 8,000 00 |
| | | Total | $134,020 00 |

TABLE NO. 3—Continued.

| | | |
|---|---|---|
| tawa | Capital stock deposit— | |
| | Mortgages | $123,500 00 |
| icago | Capital stock deposit— | |
| | Boon Hill Twp., N. C., Road Bonds | $ 5,220 00 |
| | Cass Co., Tex., Road Bonds | 28,000 00 |
| | Shelby Co., Tex., Road Dist. No. 6, Bonds | 27,270 00 |
| | Shelby Co., Tex., Road Dist. No. 2, Bonds | 19,890 00 |
| | Tyler Co., Tex., Road Bonds | 3,000 00 |
| | Cotton Co., Okla., Bonds | 10,800 00 |
| | Chambers Co., Tex., Road Dist. No. 2, Bonds | 2,020 00 |
| | Ashe Co., N. C., Bonds | 16,160 00 |
| | Total | $112,360 00 |
| icago | Capital stock deposit— | |
| | United States Liberty Loan Bonds | $214,400 00 |
| gin | Capital stock deposit— | |
| | Mortgages | $97,700 00 |
| | Pacific Power & Light Co. Bonds | 880 00 |
| | Iowa Ry. & Light Co. Bonds | 1,660 00 |
| | Total | $100,240 00 |
| | Deposit on reserve on registered policies— | |
| | Mortgages | $136,050 00 |
| | Certificate of deposit | 500 00 |
| | United States of America Liberty Loan Bond. | 1,000 00 |
| | Pacific Power & Light Co. Bonds | 880 00 |
| | Detroit Edison Co. Bonds | 1,800 00 |
| | Northern States Power Co. Bonds | 1,780 00 |
| | Total | $142,010 00 |
| icago | Capital stock deposit— | |
| | Mortgages | $173,250 00 |
| | City of Durango, Colo. Bonds | 7,000 00 |
| | Garland Levee Dist. Bonds | 5,300 00 |
| | Waurika, Okla. Bonds | 15,750 00 |
| | Des Moines & Mississippi Levee Bonds | 2,505 00 |
| | Total | $203,805 00 |
| | Deposit on reserve on registered policies (Chicago Life & Northern Life)— | |
| | Mortgages | $553,550 00 |
| | Marshall, Mo., Light, Heat & Power Bonds | 3,650 00 |
| | Poinsett Co., Ark., Drainage Bonds | 42,550 00 |
| | Osceola, Neb., Bonds | 1,000 00 |
| | Caldwell Co., Mo., Drainage Bonds | 9,406 25 |
| | Black Fish Drainage Bonds | 7,970 00 |
| | Durango, Colo., Bonds | 13,000 00 |
| | Pana Gas & Electric Bonds | 3,400 00 |
| | Garland Levee Dist. Bonds | 9,540 00 |
| | Total | $644,066 25 |
| ringfield | Capital stock deposit— | |
| | United States of America Third Liberty Loan Bonds | $100,000 00 |
| | Deposit on reserve on registered policies— | |
| | Mortgages | $7,544,666 00 |
| | Collateral loans | 279,240 00 |
| | United States of America Liberty Loan Bonds | 582,250 00 |
| | Cambridge, Iowa School Bonds | 7,000 00 |
| | Saline Co., Ill., Bonds | 1,000 00 |
| | Spencer, Iowa Funding Bonds | 10,000 00 |
| | Highland Park, Ill., Bonds | 1,010 80 |
| | Marinette, Wis., Insane Asylum Bonds | 10,074 40 |
| | Fayette, Mo., Bonds | 8,000 00 |
| | East St. Louis, Ill., Bonds | 10,309 00 |

TABLE NO. 3—Continued.

| Name of company. | Location. | Kind of securities. | Deposit value. |
|---|---|---|---|
| | | Anamosa, Iowa, Bonds | $ 3,056 70 |
| | | Aberdeen, S. D., Bonds | 10,101 00 |
| | | Anson, Tex., Bonds | 15,097 50 |
| | | Allen, Tex., Bonds | 8,000 00 |
| | | Austin, Tex., Bonds | 15,575 00 |
| | | Louisiana Port Commission Bonds | 8,000 00 |
| | | Chicago West Park Bonds | 4,995 80 |
| | | Jefferson Co., Tex., Bonds | 9,012 60 |
| | | Trinity Co., Tex., Bonds | 13,500 00 |
| | | Navarro Co., Tex., Bonds | 5,300 00 |
| | | Fate, Tex., Bonds | 9,585 50 |
| | | Petty, Tex., Bonds | 8,000 00 |
| | | Gainesville, Tex., Bonds | 50,000 00 |
| | | Collin Co., Tex., Road Bonds | 85,246 10 |
| | | Newman, Ill., Road Bonds | 4,957 10 |
| | | Total | $8,703,977 50 |
| Illinois Life Insurance Company | Chicago | Capital stock deposit— | |
| | | Mortgages | $ 112,250 00 |
| | | Deposit on reserve registered policies— | |
| | | Mortgages | $1,214,800 00 |
| | | Central Trust Co. of Illinois, Chicago, stock | 462,500 00 |
| | | Ft. Dearborn National Bank, Chicago, stock | 225,000 00 |
| | | Continental and Commercial National Banks Chicago, stock | 165,600 00 |
| | | Total | $2,067,900 00 |
| International Life and Trust Company | Moline | Capital stock deposit— | |
| | | Mortgages | $102,500 00 |
| | | United States of America Liberty Loan Bond, | 5,000 00 |
| | | Total | $107,500 00 |
| Liberty Life Insurance Company | Chicago | Capital stock deposit— | |
| | | Mortgages | $98,200 00 |
| | | Certificates of deposit | 1,900 00 |
| | | Total | $100,100 00 |
| Marquette Life Insurance Company | Springfield | Capital stock deposit— | |
| | | Mortgages | $68,135 00 |
| | | Litchfield, Ill., Bonds | 400 00 |
| | | Ft. Smith, Ark., School Bonds | 5,000 00 |
| | | La Trobe, Pa., Bond | 1,000 00 |
| | | Henry Co., Ill., Bonds | 3,010 00 |
| | | Jersey and Greene Counties, Ill., Bonds | 16,500 00 |
| | | Lake Co., Ill., Foss Park Dist., Bonds | 9,060 00 |
| | | Total | $103,105 00 |
| | | Deposit on reserve on registered policies— | |
| | | Mortgages | $783,500 00 |
| | | Ft. Smith, Ark., Water Bonds | 5,000 00 |
| | | Jersey and Greene Counties, Natwood Drainage District Bonds | 24,000 00 |
| | | Total | $812,500 00 |
| Mutual Life of Illinois | Springfield | Capital stock deposit— | |
| | | Mortgages | $107,000 00 |
| | | Deposit on reserve on registered policies— | |
| | | Mortgages | $57,500 00 |
| | | United States of America Liberty Loan Bonds | 41,900 00 |
| | | Total | $99,400 00 |
| Mutual Trust Life Insurance Company | Chicago | Capital stock deposit— | |
| | | Mortgages | $53,500 00 |
| | | Houston, Tex., Bonds | 4,160 00 |

TABLE NO. 3—Continued.

| Name of company. | Location. | Kind of securities. | Deposit value. |
|---|---|---|---|
| | | Chicago City Ry. Bonds | $7,400 00 |
| | | Duluth, Minn., Park Bonds | 4,700 00 |
| | | Jackson, Tenn., Bonds | 5,000 00 |
| | | Pacific Gas and Electric Co., Bonds | 4,450 00 |
| | | Consumers Power Co. Bonds | 9,300 00 |
| | | Wayne Co., Ill., Borah Drainage Dist. Bonds | 6,500 00 |
| | | Hartwell Drainage Dist., Greene Co., Ill., Bonds | 2,550 00 |
| | | Iowa Ry. & Light Co. Bonds | 1,660 00 |
| | | Public Service Co. of Northern Illinois, Bonds | 860 00 |
| | | Total | $100,080 00 |
| | | Deposit on reserve on registered policies— | |
| | | Mortgages | $4,353,000 00 |
| | | Certificates of deposit | 5,000 00 |
| | | United States of America Liberty Loan Bonds | 626,075 50 |
| | | Oklahoma Gas & Electric Co., Bonds | 9,200 00 |
| | | Chicago City Railways Bonds | 7,400 00 |
| | | Peoples Gas Light and Coke Co. Bonds | 8,700 00 |
| | | Commonwealth Edison Co. Bonds | 23,500 00 |
| | | Seattle Lighting Co. Bonds | 8,100 00 |
| | | Consumers Power Co. Bonds | 9,300 00 |
| | | Des Moines Co., Iowa Drainage Bonds | 10,200 00 |
| | | Grand Junction, Colo., Bonds | 5,000 00 |
| | | Memphis, Tenn., Bonds | 2,040 00 |
| | | Bureau Co., Ill., S. D. No. 103 Bonds | 5,100 00 |
| | | Port of Seattle, Wash., Central Water Imp. Bonds | 8,640 00 |
| | | Port of Seattle, Wash., Smith's Cove Imp | 4,800 00 |
| | | Hartwell Drainage & Levee Dist. of Greene Co., Ill., Bonds | 2,550 00 |
| | | Swift & Co. Bonds | 4,650 00 |
| | | Iowa Ry. & Lt. Co. Bonds | 6,640 00 |
| | | Public Service Co. of Northern Ill., Bonds | 7,740 00 |
| | | Northwestern Elev. R. R. Co. Bonds | 3,250 00 |
| | | Bruning, Neb., Water Bonds | 1,000 00 |
| | | Fort Dodge, Des Moines and S. R. R. Co. Bonds | 3,150 00 |
| | | Interborough Rapid Transit Co. Bonds | 5,800 00 |
| | | County of Duval, Tex. Bonds | 9,340 00 |
| | | Armour & Co. Bonds | 4,350 00 |
| | | Madison Ry. Co. Bonds | 7,000 00 |
| | | Wisconsin-Minn. Light & Power Co | 7,900 00 |
| | | McMullen Co., Tex | 5,500 00 |
| | | Koochiching, Minn., Bonds | 9,600 00 |
| | | Seattle, Wash. Ry. Ext. Bonds | 12,480 00 |
| | | Seattle, Wash., Mun. Light Bonds | 4,800 00 |
| | | Seattle, Wash., Salmon Bay Imp. Bonds | 7,680 00 |
| | | Seattle, Wash., East Waterway Imp. Bonds | 960 00 |
| | | Aberdeen, S. D., School Bonds | 23,750 00 |
| | | Clatsop Co., Oregon School Bonds | 5,000 00 |
| | | Cook Co., Ill., Forest Preserve Dist., Bonds | 10,510 00 |
| | | Decatur Co., Tenn., Highway Bonds | 9,800 00 |
| | | Denton Co., Tex., Road Dist. Bonds | 25,000 00 |
| | | Greenlee Co., Ariz., Morenci School Bonds | 10,300 00 |
| | | Houston, Tex., Wharf Bonds | 16,285 00 |
| | | Blackfoot, Idaho, Bonds | 5,300 00 |
| | | Chadron, Neb., School Bonds | 10,700 00 |
| | | State of South Dakota Bonds | 10,800 00 |
| | | South Dakota Soldiers Compensation Bonds | 11,600 00 |
| | | Pueblo Co., Colo., Bonds | 14,550 00 |
| | | Tarrant Co., Tex., School Bonds | 10,000 00 |
| | | Jefferson Co., Tex., Road Bonds | 33,000 00 |
| | | Lamar Co., Tex., Bonds | 10,000 00 |
| | | Little Rock, Hot Springs, Ark., Highway Bonds | 15,150 00 |
| | | State of Louisiana Bonds | 15,000 00 |
| | | Monroe Co., Tenn., Road Bonds | 10,200 00 |
| | | Muscatine, Iowa City Hall Bonds | 25,620 00 |
| | | Paris, Tenn., Water Works Bonds | 4,900 00 |
| | | United Fuel Gas Co. Bonds | 9,500 00 |
| | | City of Vernon, Tex., Imp. Bonds | 9,800 00 |
| | | Oklahoma Gas & Electric Co. Gold Notes | 5,000 00 |
| | | Mishawka, Ind., School Bonds | 10,300 00 |
| | | Dallas, Tex., School Bonds | 10,300 00 |
| | | Allied Packers Bonds | 6,500 00 |
| | | Total | $5,519,310 50 |

TABLE NO. 3—Continued.

| Name of company. | Location. | Kind of securities. | Deposit value. |
|---|---|---|---|
| National Life Insurance Company of the U. S. of A | Chicago | Capital stock deposit— | |
| | | Mortgages | $218,700 00 |
| North American Life Insurance Company | Chicago | Capital stock deposit— | |
| | | Kiefer, Okla., Water Works Bonds | $26,750 00 |
| | | Laurel, Mont., Water Works Bonds | 26,520 00 |
| | | Laurel, Mont., Sewer Bonds | 12,240 00 |
| | | Osyka, Miss., Bonds | 12,600 00 |
| | | City of Ft. Pierce, Fla., Public Utility Bonds | 48,505 00 |
| | | De Soto, Miss., Road Bonds | 36,000 00 |
| | | Andrew, N. C., Water Bonds | 19,620 00 |
| | | Nez Perce, Lewis Co., Idaho, School Bonds | 16,000 00 |
| | | Harlowton, Mont., Town Bonds | 11,000 00 |
| | | Total | $209,235 00 |
| Old Colony Life Insurance Company | Chicago | Capital stock deposit— | |
| | | Mortgages | $96,500 00 |
| | | United States of America Liberty Loan Bonds | 10,000 00 |
| | | Commonwealth Edison Company Bonds | 9,500 00 |
| | | McIntosh Co., Okla., Bonds | 1,000 00 |
| | | Osage Co., Okla., Bonds | 1,000 00 |
| | | Erin, Houston Co., Tenn., Bonds | 1,862 40 |
| | | Adair Co., Okla., Bonds | 700 00 |
| | | Total | $120,562 40 |
| | | Deposit on reserve on registered policies— | |
| | | Mortgages | $27,500 00 |
| | | United States of America Liberty Loan Bonds | 15,000 00 |
| | | Morton Grove, Ill., Bonds | 2,412 50 |
| | | Total | $44,912 50 |
| Peoples Life Insurance Company | Chicago | Capital stock deposit— | |
| | | Mortgages | $94,900 00 |
| | | Certificates of deposit | 5,500 00 |
| | | Total | $100,400 00 |
| Peoria Life Insurance Company | Peoria | Capital stock deposit— | |
| | | Mortgages | $101,000 00 |
| Providers Life Assurance Company | Chicago | Capital stock deposit— | |
| | | Mortgages | $32,400 00 |
| | | Mason City, Iowa, Water Works Bonds | 4,120 00 |
| | | Haywood Co., N. C., Bonds | 8,160 00 |
| | | Lake Cormorant Drainage District Bonds | 5,000 00 |
| | | Northern New York Utilities Inc. Bonds | 7,800 00 |
| | | West Penn. Power Bonds | 5,200 00 |
| | | Santa Crua Co., Ariz., School | 5,000 00 |
| | | Wichita Falls, Tex., Bonds | 5,250 00 |
| | | Tuscon, Ariz., Bonds | 4,800 00 |
| | | Pacific Gas & Electric Bonds | 4,600 00 |
| | | Texas Electric Ry. Bonds | 19,000 00 |
| | | St. Mary's Parish, La., Bonds | 4,750 00 |
| | | Total | $106,080 00 |
| Public Life Insurance Company | Chicago | Capital stock deposit— | |
| | | Mortgage | $ 3,000 00 |
| | | City of Chicago Bonds | 38,300 00 |
| | | City of Jacksonville, Ill., Bonds | 46,000 00 |
| | | Macoupin Co., Ill., Bonds | 7,820 00 |
| | | Chicago Sanitary Dist., Bonds | 3,840 00 |
| | | McLean Co., Ill., School Bonds | 5,200 00 |
| | | Adair Co., Mo., Drainage Bonds | 5,000 00 |
| | | Anderson Co., Tex., Bonds | 5,400 00 |
| | | Akron, Ohio, School Bonds | 9,900 00 |
| | | Total | $124,460 00 |

TABLE NO. 3—Concluded.

| Name of company. | Location. | Kind of securities. | Deposit value. |
|---|---|---|---|
| Rockford Life Insurance Company | Rockford | Capital stock deposit— Mortgages | $106,200 00 |
| Security Life Insurance Company of America | Richmond, Va., principal office Chicago | Reciprocal deposit— United States of America Liberty Loan Bonds | $12,000 00 |
| Standard Life Insurance Company | Decatur | Capital stock deposit— Mortgages | $100,200 00 |

Table No. 4 gives a detailed statement of the assets of each company on December 31, 1921, showing as follows:

| | |
|---|---|
| Real estate | $ 161,704,579 06 |
| Mortgage loans | 2,658,805,858 82 |
| Collateral loans | 29,017,010 20 |
| Premium notes and policy loans | 1,020,777,057 52 |
| Bonds and stocks | 3,509,402,607 55 |
| Cash in office and in bank | 100,560,547 53 |
| Deferred and unpaid premiums | 144,588,682 00 |
| Other admitted assets | 144,875,968 75 |
| Total admitted assets | $7,769,732,311 43 |
| Non admitted assets | $106,214,449 10 |

Table No. 5 gives a detailed statement of the liabilities of each company on December 31, 1921, showing as follows:

| | |
|---|---|
| Policy reserves | $6,617,248,770 62 |
| Policy claims | 41,472,440 55 |
| Other accrued liabilities | 376,383,502 36 |
| Surplus apportioned not yet due | 382,401,035 72 |
| Voluntary contingency reserves | 81,958,526 59 |
| Capital stock paid in | 45,725,149 11 |
| Total liabilities, including surplus apportioned not yet due and contingency reserves, but not including unassigned funds | $7,545,189,424 95 |
| Unassigned funds (surplus) | 224,542,886 48 |

Table No. 6 gives a detailed statement of the income of each company for the year ending December 31, 1921, showing as follows:

| | |
|---|---|
| Premium income | $1,429,369,152 34 |
| Consideration for supplementary contracts, and dividends left on deposit | 28,483,154 21 |
| Gross interest and rents | 360,737,494 29 |
| Adjustment in book value of ledger assets | 6,481,175 89 |
| Increase in capital stock and surplus thereon | 1,726,161 00 |
| Received from other sources | 28,185,065 30 |
| Total income | $1,854,982,203 03 |

Tabe No. 7 gives a detailed statement of the expenditures of each company for the year ending December 31, 1921, showing as follows:

| | |
|---|---|
| Death losses and endowments | $449,614,072 59 |
| Annuities involving life contingencies | 10,211,776 82 |
| Dividends to policyholders | 191,417,624 38 |
| Notes and liens voided by lapse | 1,752,498 06 |
| Surrender value paid in cash, etc | 160,253,756 07 |
| Dividends to stockholders | 3,857,915 88 |
| Supplementary contract payments | 15,478,949 50 |
| Adjustment in book value of ledger assets | 18,734,002 46 |
| All other disbursements | 394,727,799 49 |
| Total disbursements | $1,246,048,395 25 |

Table No. 8 gives a detailed statement showing the policy account of each company for the year 1921.

For the ordinary business, excluding group insurance, it shows as follows:

| | |
|---|---|
| Policies in force at commencement of year | 15,463,529 |
| Amounting to | $31,453,759,229 18 |
| New policies issued, restored and increased | 2,502,050 |
| Amounting to | 6,017,497,829 18 |
| Policies terminated | 1,525,428 |
| Amounting to | $3,326,950,630 23 |
| Policies in force at end of year | 16,440,151 |
| Amounting to | $34,144,306,428 13 |
| Average amount of policy | $2,076 89 |

The group insurance in this table shows as follows:

| | |
|---|---|
| Policies in force at commencement of year | 16,717 |
| Amounting to | $1,621,624,252 00 |
| New policies issued, restored and increased | 4,639 |
| Amounting to | 702,430,354 49 |
| Policies terminated | 5,259 |
| Amounting to | $747,601,461 49 |
| Policies in force at end of year | 16,097 |
| Amounting to | $1,576,453,145 00 |

A statement of the industrial business in the same table shows as follows:

| | |
|---|---|
| Policies in force at commencement of year | 45,448,103 |
| Amounting to | $6,596,487,811 58 |
| New policies issued, restored and increased | 8,384,422 |
| Amounting to | $1,631,431,296 00 |
| Policies terminated | 5,473,082 00 |
| Amounting to | $968,329,778 33 |
| Policies in force at end of year | 48,395,443 |
| Amounting to | $7,259,589,329 25 |
| Average amount of policy | $150 01 |

Table No. 9 gives a detailed statement showing the number and amount of policies terminated during the year 1921, and the cause of termination.

For the ordinary business of each company it shows as follows:

| | |
|---|---|
| By death, number | 113,621 |
| By death, amount | $257,283,263 67 |
| By maturity and disability, number | 81,146 |
| By maturity and disability, amount | $114,689,023 41 |
| By expiry, number | 139,926 |
| By expiry, amount | $269,749,695 24 |
| By surrender, number | 223,933 |
| By surrender, amount | $513,957,056 91 |
| By lapse, decrease and withdrawal, number | 966,802 |
| By lapse, decrease and withdrawal, amount | $2,169,271,591 00 |
| Total number | 1,525,428 |
| Total amount | $3,324,950,630 23 |

Terminations of group insurance given in this table shows as follows:

| | |
|---|---|
| By death, number | 66 |
| By death, amount | $10,708,964 90 |
| By maturity and disability | $648,398 00 |
| By expiry, number | 271 |
| By expiry, amount | 66,011,282 00 |
| By surrender, number | 4,457 |
| By surrender, amount | $5,894,943 00 |
| By lapse, decrease and withdrawal, number | 465 |
| By lapse, decrease and withdrawal, amount | 664,337,873 59 |
| Total number | 5,259 |
| Total amount | $747,601,461 49 |

Terminations of the industrial business are given in the same table, showing as follows:

| | |
|---|---|
| By death, number | 419,080 |
| By death, amount | $55,819,345 15 |
| By maturity and disability, number | 92,938 |
| By maturity and disability, amount | $8,264,012 00 |
| By expiry, number | 102,491 |
| By expiry, amount | $35,082,533 00 |
| By surrender, number | 443,264 |
| By surrender, amount | $72,193,785 68 |
| By lapse and decrease, number | 4,379,309 |
| By lapse and decrease, amount | $796,970,102 50 |
| Total number | 5,437,082 |
| Total amount | $968,329,778 33 |

Table No. 10 gives a detailed statement of business done in this State by all companies during the year 1921.

For ordinary business, excluding group insurance, it shows as follows:

| | |
|---|---|
| Policies issued | 232,820 |
| Amount | $546,337,612 79 |
| Policies terminated | 123,948 |
| Amount | $261,142,396 13 |
| Policies in force at end of year | 1,385,104 |
| Amount | $2,863,542,302 08 |
| Average amount of each policy | $2,067 38 |
| Premiums received | $91,882,127 18 |
| Losses paid | $24,867,493 10 |

The group insurance in this table shows as follows:

| | |
|---|---|
| Policies issued | 93 |
| Amount | $52,823,597 00 |
| Policies terminated | 49 |
| Amount | $47,185,442 00 |
| Policies in force end of year | 396 |
| Amount | $100,858,494 00 |
| Premiums received | $993,126 36 |
| Losses paid | $640,063 02 |

The industrial business in the same table shows as follows:

| | |
|---|---|
| Policies issued | 608,686 |
| Amount | $110,279,845 00 |
| Policies terminated | 347,813 |
| Amount | $60,965,132 33 |
| Policies in force at end of year | 3,621,992 |
| Amount | $520,197,864 75 |
| Average amount of each policy | $143 62 |
| Premiums received | $18,831,840 90 |
| Losses paid | $4,256,269 98 |

## BUSINESS IN ILLINOIS.

*Ordinary.*—Not including industrial business or group insurance, the companies wrote in this State in 1921, 232,800 policies for $546,337,612.79 of insurance, being 41,726 less policies in number, and $71,974,471.34 less insurance than was written in 1920. The premiums received on such business in this State during 1921 amounted to $91,882,127.18, being more than the amount received in 1921 by $8,813,751.50. The losses paid were $268,091.48 less than during the preceding year, being $24,867,493.10.

The business in force in this State at the end of the year 1921 was $284,655,175.78 in excess of the amount in force at the end of the previous year. This net increase in business in force is equal to 52 per cent of the new business written.

*Group.*—The total number of policies of group insurance written in Illinois during 1921 was 93, amounting to $52,823,597.00 of insurance.

At the end of 1921 the companies had in force group insurance on the lives of citizens in this State amounting to $100,858,494.00, represented by 396 policies. The total amount of premiums paid on this class of business by citizens of this State in 1921 was $993,126.36, and the total amount of losses paid in this State by the companies was $640,063.02.

*Industrial.*—The total number of policies of industrial insurance written in Illinois during 1921 was 608,686, amounting to $110,279,845.00 of insurance, being 40,907 policies more in number and $13,682,848.03 more in amount than the insurance written during the preceding year.

At the end of 1921 the companies had in force industrial insurance on the lives of citizens of this State amounting to $520,197,864.75, represented by 3,621,992 policies. The total amount of premiums paid on this class of business by citizens of this State in 1921 was $18,831,840.90, and the total amount of losses paid in this State by the companies was $4,256,269.98.

The following shows the aggregate premiums received and losses paid in the State of Illinois during 1921:

| Class of business. | Premiums received during 1921. | Losses paid during 1921. |
|---|---|---|
| Ordinary | $91,882,127 18 | $24,867,493 10 |
| Group | 993,126 36 | 640,063 02 |
| Industrial | 18,831,840 90 | 4,256,269 98 |
| Aggregate | $111,707,094 44 | $29,763,826 10 |

## GENERAL BUSINESS.

*Ordinary.*—In their general business, not including industrial or group insurance, all the companies reporting to this department for the present year wrote during 1921, 2,502,050 policies, amounting to $6,017,497,829.18 insurance. The net increase in the business of all the companies made during 1921 was $2,666,651,300.55, which is 44 per cent of the new business written.

*Group.*—The general group insurance business of the companies shows the following results:

Total policies written in 1921, 4,639, amounting to $702,430,354.49, of insurance. Net decrease of insurance in force during the year $45,171,107.00.

Total policies written in 1921, 8,384,422, an increase as compared with the number written in 1920 of 981,049. Total insurance written, $1,631,431,-296.00, an increase as compared with the amount written in 1920 of $266,-225,638.03. Net increase of insurance in force during the year, $663,017,467.67, being 41 per cent of the new business written.

A comparison of the number of policies and amount of insurance in force on December 31, 1921, with the same figures for December 31, 1920, in companies licensed in the State of Illinois to transact a life insurance business on the legal reserve plan is as follows, viz:

| Class of business. | Number of policies in force 1920. | Number of policies in force 1921. |
|---|---|---|
| Ordinary | 15,479,051 | 16,440,151 |
| Group | 16,717 | 16,097 |
| Industrial | 45,448,185 | 48,395,443 |
| Total | 60,943,953 | 64,851,691 |

| Class of business. | 1920 Amount of insurance in force. | 1921 Amount of insurance in force. |
|---|---|---|
| Ordinary | $31,477,655,127 58 | $34,144,306,428 13 |
| Group | 1,621,624,252 00 | 1,576,453,145 00 |
| Industrial | 6,596,571,861 58 | 7,259,589,329 25 |
| Total | $39,695,851,241 16 | $42,980,348,902 38 |

The amount of business in force in the State of Illinois shown as follows, viz:

| Class of business. | Number of policies in force 1920. | Number of policies in force, 1921. |
|---|---|---|
| Ordinary | 1,276,527 | 1,385,104 |
| Group | 352 | 396 |
| Industrial | 3,361,119 | 3,621,992 |
| Total | 4,637,998 | 5,007,492 |

| Class of business. | 1920 Amount of insurance in force. | 1921 Amount of insurance in force. |
|---|---|---|
| Ordinary | $2,578,887,126 30 | $2,863,542,302 08 |
| Group | 95,220,339 00 | 100,858,494 00 |
| Industrial | 470,883,089 08 | 520,197,864 75 |
| Total | $3,144,990,554 38 | $3,484,598,660 83 |

## DEPARTMENT EXAMINATIONS.

During the year 1921 the following legal reserve life insurance companies were examined either in the matter of incorporation, upon application for admission, or to ascertain their financial conditions, to-wit:

Liberty Life Insurance Company, Chicago, Illinois.

Peoria Life Insurance Company, Peoria, Illinois.

Public Life Insurance Company, Chicago, Illinois.

National Life and Accident Insurance Company, Nashville, Tennessee.

## LEGAL RESERVE LIFE INSURANCE COMPANIES IN PROCESS OF ORGANIZATION.

By the terms of "An Act in relation to the promotion and organization of insurance corporations and to repeal a certain Act therein named," effective July 1, 1921, capital stock insurance companies in process of organization under the laws of this State were placed under the supervision of the Department of Trade and Commerce and conditions were prescribed as to the form of stock subscription blank to be used for the sale in Illinois of capital stock of any insurance companies in process of organization or already organized. Expenses of organization are also limited thereby to 20 per cent of the selling price of the stock. The organization of a domestic company must be completed within two years from the filing of its declaration of incorporation.

The following shows the names of the life insurance corporations whose organization had not been completed December 31, 1921, but which were still within the two-year period permitted for completing it and also shows the date of filing of their respective declarations of incorporation:

American Union Life Insurance Company, Chicago, Illinois, October 7, 1921.

Columbus Life Insurance Company, Chicago, Illinois, January 12, 1921.

Continental and Commercial National Life Insurance Company, Chicago, Illinois, March 21, 1921.

Economy Life Insurance Company, Chicago, Illinois, March 16, 1921.

National Temperance Life Insurance Company, Chicago, Illinois, April 26, 1921.

Northwetsern Union Life Insurance Company, Ottawa, Illinois, October 17, 1921.

## ASSESSMENT LIFE ASSOCIATIONS.

The last report covered the operations of nineteen assessment life associations reporting to this Department. The Drexel Mutual Life Insurance Company of Chicago, Illinois, was organized under the laws of this State on August 1, 1921. The Commonwealth Life Insurance Company of Chicago was placed in the hands of a receiver December 30, 1921, and the State Council of Catholic Knights of Illinois, Belleville, Illinois, was reinsured in the Catholic Knights and Ladies of Illinois, the reinsurance contract being recorded in this Department on March 30, 1921, making a total of eighteen assessment life associations operating in this State.

### EXAMINATIONS.

During the year 1921, the following assessment life insurance associations were examined to ascertain their financial condition:

Commonwealth Life Insurance Company, Chicago, Illinois.

Globe Mutual Life Insurance Company, Chicago, Illinois.
Hotel Men's Mutual Benefit Association, Chicago, Illinois.
Merchants Reserve Life Insurance Company, Chicago, Illinois.
Swedish Baptist Mutual Aid Association, Chicago, Illinois.
Swedish Methodist Aid Association, Chicago, Illinois.
Swedish Mission Friends Aid Association, Chicago, Illinois.

A comparison of the aggregate results and figures of the business of 1920 and 1921 is here given:

| Classification. | 1920 | 1921 |
|---|---|---|
| Number of companies | 19 | 18 |
| Total admitted assets | $9,656,437 22 | $11,992,157 06 |
| Unadmitted assets | 288,389 93 | 485,235 50 |
| Total liabilities | 1,857,940 17 | 2,075,999 56 |
| Total income | 7,187,847 85 | 8,171,407 63 |
| Total disbursements | 5,901,232 22 | 5,656,639 11 |
| Certificates in force December 31 | 278,245 | 285,184 |
| Insuring | $396,097,421 48 | $402,906,687 91 |
| Received from members | 6,605,333 61 | 7,474,715 91 |
| Received from other sources | 582,514 24 | 696,691 72 |
| Paid for losses | 2,899,788 14 | 2,725,518 28 |
| Paid for expenses | 3,001,444 08 | 2,931,120 83 |
| Certificates written during the year | 74,868 | 71,842 |
| Insuring | $115,622,508 80 | $97,378,989 43 |
| Certificates terminated by death | 2,803 | 2,552 |
| Insuring | $2,979,604 83 | $2,732,062 19 |
| By lapse, surrender, etc | 31,682 | 59,403 |
| Insuring | $42,016,420 99 | $85,554,910 81 |
| Per cent of losses to total income | 40.34 | 33.35 |
| Per cent of expenses to total income | 41.76 | 35.87 |

The amount of business transacted in this State by associations of this character during 1921, and a comparison of the same with the business transacted in 1920, are shown in the following exhibits or summaries:

Summary of assessment life business done in the State of Illinois in 1921, as compared with that done in 1920.

| Classification. | 1920 | 1921 |
|---|---|---|
| Received from members in Illinois for mortuary and expense purposes | $1,511,076 21 | $1,842,210 91 |
| Claims paid | 746,690 25 | 636,877 21 |
| Certificates written during the year | 30,966 | 30,869 |
| Insuring | $23,263,969 80 | $18,433,818 13 |
| Terminated by death | 1,545 | 1,407 |
| Insuring | $731,408 08 | $650,831 19 |
| By lapse, surrender, etc | 15,309 | 23,125 |
| Insuring | $8,776,255 87 | $16,688,687 11 |
| In force December 31 | 124,641 | 129,510 |
| Insuring | $97,312,591 35 | $97,220,141 18 |

The following table gives the total amount and kind of securities held in trust by the Director of Trade and Commerce, Division of Insurance, for the assessment life insurance Companies named:

| Name of company. | Location. | Kind of securities. | Par value. |
|---|---|---|---|
| Bankers Mutual Life Company | Freeport | Savanna, Ill., Water Bonds | $3,000 00 |
| | | Bayard, Neb., School Bonds | 2,000 00 |
| | | Wapella, Ill., School Bonds | 3,000 00 |
| | | Yellowstone, Mont., Bonds | 3,000 00 |
| | | Jacksonville, Ill., Bonds | 2,000 00 |
| | | Jefferson Co., Tenn., Road Bonds | 2,000 00 |
| | | Plum Bayou, Ark., Levee Dist. Bonds | 1,000 00 |
| | | Ft. Bond Co., Tex., Road Bonds | 5,000 00 |
| | | Marion Twp., Ill., School Bonds | 2,000 00 |
| | | Bear Lake, Idaho, Funding Bonds | 2,000 00 |
| | | Geneva Twp., Ill., Park Bond | 500 00 |
| | | Waukegan, Ill., Park Bond | 1,000 00 |
| | | Total | $26,500 00 |

| Name of company. | Location. | Kind of securities. | Par value. |
|---|---|---|---|
| Illinois Bankers Life Association | Monmouth | Mortgages | $448,900 00 |
| | | United States Liberty Loan Bonds | 155,000 00 |
| | | Thurston Co., Neb., School Bonds | 10,000 00 |
| | | La Salle Co., Ill., School Bonds | 15,000 00 |
| | | Franklin Co., Tex., Road Bonds | 25,000 00 |
| | | Burnett Co., Tex., Road Bonds | 36,000 00 |
| | | Collin Co., Tex., Road Bonds | 8,000 00 |
| | | Cooke Co., Tex., Road Bonds | 28,000 00 |
| | | Eastland Co., Tex., Improvement Bonds | 20,000 00 |
| | | Freestone Co., Tex., Road Bonds | 29,000 00 |
| | | Renwick, Iowa, Funding Bonds | 4,000 00 |
| | | Upshur Co., Tex., Road Bonds | 40,000 00 |
| | | Shelby Co., Tex., Road Bonds | 40,000 00 |
| | | Davenport, Iowa, School Bonds | 50,000 00 |
| | | Total | $908,900 00 |
| Merchants Reserve Life Insurance Company | Chicago | Mortgage | $3,300 00 |
| | | Murray Co., Okla., School Bonds | 2,000 00 |
| | | Total | $5,300 00 |

## FRATERNAL BENEFICIARY SOCIETIES.

The statements of 148 fraternal beneficiary societies reporting to this department were included in the last report. During the year 1921 there were no such societies organized under the laws of this State.

The following named societies, located in other states, were licensed to transact business in this State:

Polish Union of America, Buffalo, New York.

Woodmen of Union, Hot Springs, Arkansas.

The following named societies have ceased doing business in Illinois during the year:

Chicago Brith Abraham Order, Chicago, Illinois.

### CHANGES OF NAME.

The Eminent Household of Columbian Woodmen, home office, Memphis, Tennessee, changed its name to Columbian Mutual Life Assurance Society.

The Degree of Honor, Supreme Lodge, of St. Paul, Minnesota, changed its name to Degree of Honor Protective Association.

The Fraternal Mystic Supreme Ruling, of Philadelphia, Pennsylvania, changed its name to Fraternal Home Insurance Society, Supreme Lodge.

These changes leave 149 fraternal societies licensed to carry on business in this State, at the date of this report and statements of their condition will be found herein.

The following societies were examined during the year:

Benefit Association of Railway Employees, Chicago, Illinois.

Bohemian American Union, Chicago, Illinois.

Columbian Circle, Chicago, Illinois.

Concordia Mutual Benefit League, Chicago, Illinois.

Croation League of Illinois, Chicago, Illinois.

Independent Order of Svithiod, Chicago, Illinois.

Independent Order of Vikings, Grand Lodge, Chicago, Illinois.

Knights of Pythias of N. A. S. A. E. A. A. and A., Jurisdiction of Illinois, Grand Lodge, Chicago, Illinois.

Luxemberger Brotherhood of America, Chicago, Illinois.

Mystic Workers of the World, Fulton, Illinois.

National Fraternal Society of the Deaf, Chicago, Illinois.

Order of Mutual Protection, Supreme Lodge, Chicago, Illinois.

Order der Hermans Schwestern, Chicago, Illinois.

Order Sons of St. George, Grand Lodge of the State of Illinois, Chicago, Illinois.

Polish Roman Catholic Union of America, Chicago, Illinois.
Polish Women's Alliance of America, Chicago, Illinois.
Slovenic Progressive Benefit Society, Chicago, Illinois.

Table No. 1 gives a general summary of the assets and liabilities of each society for the year 1921; as compared with 1920, it shows as follows, viz:

| Classification. | 1920 | 1921 |
|---|---|---|
| Number of companies | 148 | 149 |
| Total admitted assets | $311,291,775 61 | $365,837,500 89 |
| Unadmitted assets | 21,635,822 47 | 9,740,724 51 |
| Losses and claims unpaid, including those unadjusted and resisted | $16,856,795 11 | $16,728,956 25 |
| All other liabilities | 70,690,829 34 | 79,467,603 32 |
| Total liabilities | $87,547,624 45 | $96,196,559 57 |

Table No. 2 shows a general summary of the income and disbursements of each society for the year 1921; as compared with 1920, it shows as follows, viz:

| Classification. | 1920 | 1921 |
|---|---|---|
| Number of companies | 148 | 149 |
| Income, membership fees, annual dues and assessments | $142,543,899 45 | $145,366,313 20 |
| Income, all other sources | 16,035,353 25 | 18,674,364 18 |
| Total income | $158,579,252 70 | $164,040,677 38 |
| Paid for losses | $93,412,157 57 | $88,623,902 58 |
| Paid for expenses | 29,022,428 47 | 31,079,696 78 |
| Total disbursements | $122,434,586 04 | $119,703,599 36 |
| Per cent of losses paid to income | | 54.03 |
| Per cent of expenses paid to income | | 18.95 |

Table No. 3 gives a general summary of the business of each society for the year 1921. As compared with 1920, it shows as follows, viz:

| Classification. | 1920 | 1921 |
|---|---|---|
| Number of companies | 148 | 149 |
| Certificates written | 968,582 | 873,505 |
| Amounting to | $1,131,136,198 20 | $989,763,332 00 |
| Terminated by lapse, surrender, death, etc | 7,033,135 | 1,025,642 |
| Amounting to | $1,268,758,377 04 | $1,143,225,381 00 |
| In force December 31 | 1,158,728 | 7,142,600 |
| Amounting to | $8,202,699,969 20 | $8,334,256,935 00 |

Table No. 4 gives a summary of the business of each society in the State of Illinois for the year 1921. As compared with 1920, it shows as follows, viz:

| Classification. | 1920 | 1921 |
|---|---|---|
| Number of companies | 148 | 149 |
| Certificates written | 116,926 | 119,406 |
| Amounting to | $115,353,372 00 | $118,224,682 00 |
| Terminated by lapse, surrender, death, etc | 111,242 | 124,534 |
| Amounting to | $112,961,209 64 | $125,906,671 00 |
| In force December 31 | 1,010,617 | 1,039,204 |
| Amounting to | $1,075,742,326 27 | $1,103,571,915 00 |
| Received from members in Illinois for mortuary, expense purposes, etc | $19,173,614 74 | $20,125,891 97 |
| Claims paid to members in Illinois | $13,515,974 80 | $13,113,273 84 |

The following is a statement of the amount and kind of securities constituting the investment of reserve funds deposited with the Director of Trade and Commerce, Division of Insurance, in trust, by the societies named, under the provisions of the Act of May 14, 1903:

| Name of society. | Location. | Kind of securities. | Par value. |
|---|---|---|---|
| Court of Honor | Springfield | Municipal Bonds | $1,573,160 96 |
| | | Mortgages | 561,305 00 |
| | | Total | $2,134,465 96 |
| North American Union | Chicago | Municipal R. R. and other Bonds | $385,925 00 |

## FINANCIAL REPORT.

Statement of the receipts of the Division of Insurance for the year ending December 31, 1921:

| | |
|---|---|
| Agents' certificates (fire, etc.) | $ 107,886 50 |
| Agents' certificates (life) | 27,229 00 |
| Certificates of compliance, deposit and valuation | 1,722 25 |
| Registering policies | 11,400 00 |
| Annual statements filed (fire, etc.) | 7,415 00 |
| Annual statements filed (life) | 1,885 00 |
| Examinations | 10,126 17 |
| Privilege tax | 2,973,186 62 |
| Fire marshal tax | 141,895 47 |
| District, county and township mutuals | 236 00 |
| Special agents, surplus lines | 2,390 20 |
| Assessment associations, filing statements | 1,554 00 |
| State licenses | 2,513 00 |
| Lloyds and Inter-Insurers | 658 00 |
| Valuing insurance | 24,024 84 |
| Charters filed | 1,230 00 |
| Miscellaneous | 4,027 93 |
| Totals | $3,319,379 98 |
| Less Mid-West Fire check "protested" | 128 53 |
| Total | $3,319,251 45 |
| Amount remitted to State Treasurer by former Director, William H. Boys, on account of protested tax payments withdrawn or released by court decision | 136,443 20 |
| Total | $3,455,694 65 |

Respectfully submitted,

George A. Barr,
*Director of Trade and Commerce.*

Attest:
T. J. Houston, *Superintendent of Insurance.*

—2 L I

# LIFE

## TABLE

SHOWING DETAILED STATEMENT OF ASSETS

| Name of company—location. | Real estate (less incumbrances). | Mortgage loans on real estate. | Loans secured by collateral. | Premium notes and policy loans. |
|---|---|---|---|---|
| I. COMPANIES OF THIS STATE. | | | | |
| The American Bankers Ins. Co., Chicago | $ 314,310 22 | $ 903,559 81 | $ 145,390 39 | $ 287,973 01 |
| Central Life Ins. Co. of Illinois, Ottawa | 175,000 00 | 2,975,074 60 | 30,196 16 | 607,087 96 |
| Chicago National Life Ins. Co., Chicago | | | | |
| Cloverleaf Life and Cas. Co., Jacksonville | 77,493 87 | 387,860 50 | | 32,527 04 |
| Continental Assurance Co., Chicago | | 838,650 00 | | 78,812 83 |
| Elgin Life Ins Co., Elgin | 2,645 09 | 234,656 80 | | 13,863 42 |
| Federal Life, Chicago | 543,805 13 | 2,834,531 98 | 14,246 00 | 1,290,791 31 |
| The Franklin Life, Springfield | 338,841 20 | 7,544,666 00 | 279,940 00 | 3,073,305 08 |
| Illinois Life, Chicago | 1,364,299 93 | 5,589,750 00 | 1,969,572 00 | 2,396,312 32 |
| International Life and Trust Co., Moline | 25,000 00 | 160,750 00 | 94,916 62 | 18,837 55 |
| Liberty Life Ins. Co., Chicago | | 98,200 00 | | |
| Marquette Life, Springfield | 3,000 00 | 938,897 50 | | 113,509 82 |
| Mutual Life of Illinois, Springfield | | 217,500 00 | | 49,912 43 |
| Mutual Trust Life, Chicago | 15,937 78 | 4,707,063 46 | | 819,901 07 |
| National Life of U. S. A., Chicago | 54,424 08 | 8,159,026 91 | | 4,682,899 85 |
| North American Life Ins. Co. of Chicago, Chicago | 108,000 00 | 4,509,216 62 | | 1,110,799 83 |
| Old Colony Life, Chicago | 1,385,788 97 | 154,500 00 | | 254,131 58 |
| Peoples Life, Chicago | 358,750 00 | 190,912 29 | | 69,340 90 |
| Peoria Life, Peoria | 2,457,472 31 | 1,362,445 00 | | 991,207 72 |
| Providers' Life Assurance Co., Chicago | 29,000 00 | 85,630 00 | | 10,780 39 |
| Public Life Ins. Co., Chicago | 148,000 00 | 211,063 00 | | |
| Rockford Life, Rockford | | 727,252 50 | | 63,467 15 |
| Standard Life, Decatur | 466,170 11 | 1,527,829 28 | 138,940 00 | 293,299 74 |
| Totals | $7,867,938 69 | $44,359,036 25 | $2,673,201 17 | $16,258,761 00 |
| II. COMPANIES OF OTHER STATES. | | | | |
| Aetna Life, Hartford, Conn | $1,835,565 92 | $72,063,062 49 | $565,239 00 | $17,572,697 29 |
| American Central Life, Indianapolis, Ind. | 423,958 84 | 5,009,586 25 | | 1,626,241 42 |
| American Life Ins. Co., Detroit, Mich | 500,036 52 | 4,039,142 15 | | 1,188,017 86 |
| American Life Reinsurance Co., Dallas, Tex | | 456,145 57 | | |
| American National Assurance Co., St. Louis, Mo | 57,249 59 | 868,114 40 | | 85,355 50 |
| Bankers Life Co., Des Moines, Ia | 60,116 60 | 40,725,758 71 | | 3,202,643 44 |
| Bankers Life Ins. Co., Lincoln, Neb | 156,654 40 | 15,337,893 87 | | 2,353,327 43 |
| Bankers Reserve Life Co., Omaha, Neb | | 1,129,200 00 | | 2,492,267 93 |
| Berkshire Life, Pittsfield, Mass | 447,543 14 | 8,432,400 00 | 40,700 00 | 5,273,762 11 |
| Business Men's Assurance Co. of America, Kansas City, Mo | | 879,175 00 | | 4,168 98 |
| Capitol Life Ins. Co. of Colorado, Denver, Colo | 18,361 48 | 2,805,846 70 | | 998,486 86 |
| Central Life Assurance Society of U. S. (Mutual), Des Moines, Ia | 273,100 57 | 9,063,340 27 | | 1,903,012 66 |
| Central States Life Ins. Co., St. Louis, Mo | 284,774 06 | 2,636,908 50 | 90,537 42 | 585,048 12 |
| Century Life, Indianapolis, Ind | | 269,034 01 | | 11,005 69 |
| Cleveland Life, Cleveland, Ohio | 302,387 56 | 1,989,765 03 | | 400,238 06 |
| Columbian National Life, Boston, Mass | 997,297 44 | 3,780,830 20 | | 4,002,715 99 |
| Columbus Mutual Life Ins. Co., Columbus, Ohio | 35,000 00 | 2,211,606 50 | | 275,145 68 |
| Connecticut General Life, Hartford, Conn | 610,225 46 | 18,697,678 60 | | 4,388,517 76 |
| Connecticut Mutual Life, Hartford, Conn | 1,891,992 04 | 38,489,354 39 | | 12,410,298 38 |
| Equitable Life Assurance Society of the U. S., New York, N. Y | 14,492,288 27 | 154,033,029 51 | 2,043,800 00 | 99,137,083 43 |

# TABLES.

## NO. 4.

OF EACH COMPANY DECEMBER 31, 1921.

| Book value of bonds and stocks. | Cash in office and in bank. | Deferred and unpaid premiums. | All other assets less assets not admitted. | Total admitted assets. | Ledger and non-ledger items not admitted as assets. |
|---|---|---|---|---|---|
| $ 88,595 00 | $ 125,506 93 | $ 63,020 69 | $ 17,306 97 | $1,945,663 02 | $165,614 91 |
| 14,875 00 | 111,036 77 | 130,018 29 | 96,963 53 | 4,140,252 31 | 103,360 81 |
| 108,731 80 | 10,175 38 | ---------- | 8,335 16 | 127,242 34 | 45,551 56 |
| 12,556 09 | 73,028 73 | 15,033 59 | 37,991 05 | 636,490 87 | 35,093 79 |
| 314,329 21 | 35,076 35 | 94,722 79 | 49,811 29 | 1,411,402 47 | 6,392 33 |
| 8,332 78 | 2,019 10 | 4,755 35 | 5,805 39 | 272,077 93 | 1,382 08 |
| 508,306 25 | 165,926 90 | 126,512 49 | 117,423 48 | 5,601,543 54 | 84,675 90 |
| 1,082,734 58 | 299,184 79 | 309,953 54 | 323,326 88 | 13,251,952 07 | 216,879 29 |
| 7,166,169 33 | 343,866 74 | 577,113 94 | 6,762 46 | 19,413,846 72 | 578,466 19 |
| 71,368 61 | 8,879 63 | 13,142 38 | —11,949 98 | 380,944 81 | 67,548 26 |
| 200 00 | 13,222 75 | 1,665 03 | —4 83 | 113,282 95 | 121,208 62 |
| 73,043 92 | 18,392 16 | 26,244 77 | 3,243 04 | 1,176,331 21 | 31,182 32 |
| 41,900 00 | 72,727 58 | 9,675 98 | —11,663 46 | 380,052 53 | 108,212 81 |
| 1,276,057 00 | 205,128 43 | 301,150 84 | 185,303 17 | 7,510,541 75 | 71,728 79 |
| 6,338,199 13 | 1,057,541 53 | 402,471 76 | 774,289 42 | 21,468,852 68 | 227,014 00 |
| 374,752 42 | 340,197 35 | 179,112 33 | 133,076 81 | 6,755,155 36 | 71,450 11 |
| 74,142 79 | 50,839 17 | 76,680 60 | 151,189 84 | 2,147,272 95 | 38,730 21 |
| 117,330 00 | 24,863 58 | 18,109 19 | 7,473 31 | 786,779 27 | 14,720 24 |
| ---------- | 113,767 19 | 156,320 72 | 5,456 71 | 5,086,669 65 | 134,907 13 |
| 392,501 72 | 20,675 24 | 27,380 98 | 8,569 04 | 574,537 37 | 9,854 70 |
| 277,750 88 | 13,061 06 | 10,845 30 | 15,753 85 | 676,474 09 | 219,387 42 |
| 60,650 00 | 3,424 81 | 31,090 44 | 7,803 27 | 893,688 17 | 23,500 92 |
| 273,538 27 | 284,964 80 | 83,360 67 | 305,435 41 | 3,373,538 28 | 151,897 54 |
| $18,676,064 78 | $3,393,506 97 | $2,658,381 67 | $2,237,701 81 | $98,124,592 34 | $2,528,759 93 |
| $55,438,833 42 | $4,311,195 28 | $3,686,677 16 | $36,244,775 68 | $191,718,046 24 | $ 38,557 32 |
| 882,200 02 | 169,007 03 | 278,522 63 | 216,896 25 | 8,606,412 44 | 39,043 40 |
| 11,967 48 | 437,310 01 | 109,247 12 | 83,017 79 | 6,368,738 93 | 31,707 17 |
| 58,834 00 | 24,544 96 | 42,973 98 | 531 32 | 583,029 83 | 14,561 71 |
| 75,496 27 | 16,266 40 | 39,568 75 | 21,829 03 | 1,163,879 94 | 15,381 19 |
| 3,559,562 87 | 462,237 57 | 1,517,858 63 | 723,632 93 | 50,251,810 75 | 692,683 77 |
| 1,689,366 65 | 151,555 11 | 169,835 42 | 283,977 99 | 20,142,610 87 | ---------- |
| 7,474,073 40 | 461,090 00 | 126,092 22 | 71,545 91 | 11,754,269 46 | 28,735 72 |
| 14,807,431 34 | 471,446 86 | 551,359 77 | 326,967 45 | 30,351,610 67 | 122,922 48 |
| 372,700 00 | 170,474 82 | 11,071 81 | 62,255 72 | 1,499,846 33 | 47,187 83 |
| 677,739 88 | 151,892 03 | 112,151 04 | 55,937 72 | 4,820,415 71 | 34,332 92 |
| 84,362 56 | 128,518 94 | 273,026 51 | 272,124 76 | 11,997,486 27 | 178,556 15 |
| 366,165 78 | 392,965 59 | 98,565 97 | 101,339 75 | 4,556,305 19 | 34,789 54 |
| 19,050 00 | 68,281 45 | 40,010 91 | 669 95 | 408,052 01 | 21,924 15 |
| 1,016,226 93 | 35,184 80 | 115,509 87 | 40,669 00 | 3,899,981 25 | 3,615 48 |
| 12,328,854 08 | 155,046 81 | 462,853 99 | 334,189 27 | 22,061,787 78 | 393,862 07 |
| 545,013 50 | 12,438 61 | 64,152 28 | 77,582 90 | 3,220,939 47 | 30,061 62 |
| 10,350,619 33 | 778,548 46 | 1,566,989 47 | 1,088,935 49 | 37,481,514 57 | 33,891 08 |
| 38,318,573 50 | 1,229,598 75 | 1,650,967 88 | 2,213,985 76 | 96,204,770 70 | 75,649 25 |
| 360,166,986 02 | 6,024,094 44 | 10,233,529 37 | 8,570,207 30 | 655,301,018 34 | 940,426 84 |

TABLE NO. 4—

| Name of company—location. | Real estate (less incumbrances). | Mortgage loans on real estate. | Loans secured by collateral. | Premium notes and policy loans. |
|---|---|---|---|---|
| Equitable Life, Des Moines, Ia | $ 800,000 00 | $ 28,822,579 59 | | $ 4,788,355 07 |
| Farmers National Life, Huntington, Ind. | 74,571 86 | 1,014,263 41 | | 61,349 79 |
| Federal Union Life, Cincinnati, Ohio | 200,000 00 | 154,950 00 | | 30,383 94 |
| The Fidelity Mutual Life, Philadelphia, Pa. | 1,468,937 43 | 17,908,071 27 | $ 101,000 00 | 9,330,151 58 |
| Girard Life, Philadelphia, Pa. | 150,870 75 | 636,000 00 | | 312,711 79 |
| The Guardian Life, New York, N. Y. | 2,558,070 52 | 19,333,461 71 | | 6,196,679 67 |
| Home Life, New York, N. Y. | 1,500,000 00 | 8,230,745 00 | | 7,976,937 06 |
| Indiana National Life, Indianapolis, Ind. | 373,500 00 | 1,212,579 80 | 46,000 00 | 524,686 32 |
| Indianapolis Life, Indianapolis, Ind. | 13,200 00 | 1,473,883 12 | | 328,147 23 |
| International Life, St. Louis, Mo. | 1,192,623 79 | 8,664,960 15 | 1,535,156 86 | 3,984,886 84 |
| John Hancock Mutual Life, Boston, Mass. | 9,950,622 51 | 125,763,854 19 | | 19,380,907 19 |
| Kansas City Life, Kansas City, Mo. | 91,436 91 | 14,031,498 16 | 24,032 00 | 4,067,410 87 |
| LaFayette Life Ins. Co., LaFayette, Ind. | 431,080 38 | 1,326,549 60 | | 424,269 35 |
| Lincoln National Life, Ft. Wayne, Ind. | 321,080 81 | 9,123,379 18 | | 1,677,444 97 |
| Manhattan Life, New York, N. Y. | 4,024,710 22 | 6,586,785 89 | | 4,293,994 69 |
| Maryland Assurance Corp., Baltimore, Md. | | | | 2,074 00 |
| Massachusetts Mutual Life, Springfield, Mass. | 1,029,400 00 | 50,412,804 00 | | 24,157,417 77 |
| Merchants Life, Des Moines, Ia. | 1,500 00 | 3,766,669 13 | | 377,996 99 |
| Metropolitan Life, New York, N. Y. | 28,278,013 67 | 454,517,998 53 | | 75,176,500 08 |
| Michigan Mutual Life, Detroit, Mich. | 458,779 80 | 11,982,967 63 | | 2,476,514 61 |
| Minesota Mutual Life, St. Paul, Minn. | 20,007 65 | 5,292,757 03 | | 1,796,707 19 |
| Missouri State Life, St. Louis, Mo. | 595,115 90 | 22,306,752 53 | | 6,839,269 71 |
| Morris Plan Insurance Society, New York, N. Y. | | | | 377 95 |
| Mutual Benefit Life, Newark, N. J. | 2,626,796 02 | 123,735,785 02 | 5,805,000 00 | 57,066,087 15 |
| Mutual Life, New York, N. Y. | 11,706,467 68 | 111,760,865 78 | | 96,751,667 37 |
| National Life and Accident Ins. Co., Nashville, Tenn. | 135,727 97 | 2,383,943 17 | 178,600 00 | |
| National Life Ins. Co., Montpelier, Vt. | 919,000 00 | 35,567,513 98 | | 12,453,972 41 |
| New England Mutual Life, Boston, Mass. | 3,168,932 00 | 22,588,182 97 | 108,500 00 | 20,604,071 44 |
| New World Life, Spokane, Wash. | 112,666 52 | 2,811,676 68 | | 480,808 79 |
| New York Life, New York, N. Y. | 8,362,881 00 | 183,722,805 92 | 2,301,000 00 | 164,305,881 49 |
| Northern States Life, Hammond, Ind. | | 987,857 59 | | 64,825 74 |
| Northwestern Mutual Life, Milwaukee, Wis. | 2,918,876 95 | 224,503,561 88 | | 78,565,844 13 |
| Northwestern National Life, Minneapolis, Minn. | 72,418 05 | 8,211,902 00 | | 2,007,182 48 |
| Old Line Ins. Co., Lincoln, Neb. | 48,325 19 | 292,034 85 | | 45,770 89 |
| Old Line Life Ins. Co. of America, Milwaukee, Wis. | 8,000 00 | 2,178,190 71 | | 192,912 31 |
| Pacific Mutual Life, Los Angeles, Cal. | 6,812,931 82 | 24,019,442 79 | 5,226,711 53 | 11,255,663 48 |
| Pan American Life, New Orleans, La. | | 5,835,967 59 | 80,000 00 | 1,446,884 79 |
| Penn Mutual Life, Philadelphia, Pa. | 2,041,111 83 | 89,193,596 72 | 1,292,350 00 | 43,588,708 56 |
| Peoples Life, Frankfort, Ind. | 100,000 00 | 1,530,686 00 | | 365,244 90 |
| Philadelphia Life, Philadelphia, Pa. | 353,803 68 | 2,571,850 00 | | 1,564,960 47 |
| Phoenix Mutual Life, Hartford, Conn. | 2,400,989 66 | 34,025,893 04 | | 9,364,589 06 |
| Provident Life and Trust, Philadelphia, Pa. | 807,215 85 | 22,042,100 84 | 4,014,562 50 | 16,093,138 67 |
| Prudential Insurance Co. of America, Newark, N. J. | 15,678,238 17 | 258,732,150 81 | 932,000 00 | 54,169,515 83 |
| Re-insurance Life Co. of America, Des Moines, Ia. | | 676,000 00 | | |
| Reliance Life, Pittsburgh, Pa. | 158,743 86 | 1,220,746 88 | | 3,401,047 38 |
| Reserve Loan Life, Indianapolis, Ind. | 102,795 95 | 3,895,889 00 | | 1,134,060 86 |
| Security Life Ins. Co. of America, Richmond, Va. | 32,681 43 | 1,239,600 00 | 67,423 89 | 1,002,645 22 |
| Security Mutual Life, Binghamton, N. Y. | 743,570 07 | 4,213,541 50 | | 2,267,983 02 |
| State Life, Indianapolis, Ind. | 1,085,879 39 | 12,448,068 68 | | 6,563,474 49 |
| State Mutual Life Assurance, Worcester, Mass. | 1,835,240 00 | 22,304,150 00 | 25,000 00 | 10,628,713 90 |

Continued.

| Book value of bonds and stocks. | Cash in office and in bank. | Deferred and unpaid premiums. | All other assets less assets not admitted. | Total admitted assets. | Ledger and non-ledger items not admitted as assets. |
|---|---|---|---|---|---|
| $ 2,708,440 83 | $ 331,260 17 | $ 736,506 25 | $ 1,047,697 13 | $ 39,234,839 04 | $ 390,030 83 |
| 36,600 00 | 69,662 86 | 119,460 00 | 17,228 28 | 1,393,136 20 | 27,848 44 |
| 444,289 75 | 9,409 97 | 149,259 16 | 10,315 79 | 998,608 61 | 68,152 82 |
| 16,802,613 00 | 722,515 75 | 760,586 19 | 416,713 85 | 47,510,589 07 | 865,911 78 |
| 1,228,068 68 | 122,961 52 | 91,982 90 | —8,541 16 | 2,534,054 48 | 77,011 59 |
| 11,202,013 35 | 449,287 52 | 1,057,668 40 | 354,868 98 | 41,152,050 15 | 321,034 37 |
| 25,098,736 56 | 302,345 86 | 949,919 52 | —836,356 45 | 43,222,327 55 | 1,210,550 87 |
| 36,539 00 | 45,986 28 | 41,907 24 | 168,492 07 | 2,449,690 71 | 37,876 69 |
| 467,808 57 | 131,890 63 | 135,628 45 | 43,930 49 | 2,594,488 49 | 36,477 12 |
| 610,477 95 | 856,490 82 | 252,960 84 | 721,907 59 | 17,819,464 84 | 209,963 10 |
| 72,619,373 74 | 1,904,055 98 | 5,447,435 20 | 4,627,122 16 | 239,693,370 97 | 346,529 36 |
| 1,637,626 35 | 930,550 64 | 865,143 17 | 363,169 14 | 22,010,867 24 | 195,008 81 |
| 91,850 00 | 108,733 66 | 35,107 36 | 33,519 64 | 2,451,109 99 | 8,551 42 |
| 238,460 65 | 796,717 68 | 371,988 99 | 275,007 01 | 12,804,079 29 | 217,873 94 |
| 3,795,716 30 | 578,859 15 | 188,327 09 | 349,811 77 | 19,818,205 11 | 117,649 68 |
| 721,520 75 | 74,839 86 | 38,052 96 | 6,230 00 | 842,717 57 | 4,454 97 |
| 62,816,431 03 | 2,605,910 05 | 3,839,383 86 | 2,229,566 30 | 147,090,913 01 | 437,062 93 |
| 439,930 30 | 233,874 50 | 219,699 02 | 108,474 50 | 5,148,144 44 | 110,404 08 |
| 505,251,586 45 | 10,944,318 69 | 26,578,163 08 | 14,836,444 04 | 1,115,583,024 54 | 4,721,742 79 |
| 362,512 00 | 234,253 69 | 221,219 15 | 257,884 05 | 15,994,130 93 | 14,141 20 |
| 1,356,846 63 | 292,384 83 | 329,790 19 | 155,012 53 | 9,243,506 05 | 228,609 11 |
| 195,592 42 | 1,519,023 22 | 1,186,010 07 | 1,202,739 06 | 33,844,502 91 | 221,547 83 |
| 174,450 57 | 127,013 60 | 2,733 84 | 4,245 66 | 308,821 62 | 251 60 |
| 102,673,339 78 | 2,560,710 06 | 5,358,488 84 | 150,316 75 | 299,976,523 62 | 5,788,558 97 |
| 443,929,767 56 | 7,810,454 52 | 5,319,202 30 | 227,074 06 | 677,505,499 27 | 8,834,620 81 |
| 3,809,549 54 | 479,610 33 | 52,839 05 | 116,734 88 | 7,157,004 94 | 25,076 44 |
| 27,356,613 07 | 1,003,324 84 | 1,469,604 69 | 986,939 71 | 79,756,968 70 | 1,040,381 68 |
| 66,442,700 00 | 1,142,570 53 | 1,748,409 26 | 405,459 50 | 116,208,825 70 | 1,305,940 06 |
| 225,919 60 | 436,819 75 | 100,855 86 | 136,781 26 | 4,305,528 46 | 46,319 73 |
| 610,965,321 26 | 10,238,378 85 | 14,674,443 08 | —41,938,572 80 | 952,632,138 80 | 57,690,505 06 |
| 90,556 25 | 39,362 62 | 63,882 68 | 19,346 34 | 1,265,831 22 | 11,485 50 |
| 182,121,766 05 | 3,763,547 10 | 7,568,659 80 | 7,643,438 41 | 507,085,694 32 | 866,648 82 |
| 858,762 49 | 388,347 93 | 530,278 23 | 382,033 47 | 12,450,924 65 | 167,788 48 |
| 77,871 20 | 380,221 17 | 15,196 60 | 8,925 22 | 868,345 12 | 37,724 95 |
| 1,059,588 13 | 131,158 56 | 90,289 82 | 120,725 22 | 3,780,864 75 | 24,526 31 |
| 8,810,968 22 | 2,212,738 93 | 1,545,454 65 | 5,315,339 74 | 65,199,251 16 | 106,034 33 |
| 1,789,924 77 | 366,863 35 | 214,314 15 | 266,725 05 | 10,000,679 70 | 191,155 62 |
| 90,934,516 18 | 2,460,028 12 | 5,609,914 80 | —1,134,678 38 | 233,985,547 83 | 4,803,414 62 |
| 50,000 00 | 10,181 72 | 93,026 88 | 24,704 57 | 2,173,844 07 | 21,557 52 |
| 2,881,159 80 | 518,652 00 | 148,759 00 | 117,083 44 | 8,156,268 39 | 55,633 04 |
| 13,066,224 25 | 1,145,380 24 | 1,137,085 05 | 1,547,439 62 | 62,687,600 92 | 71,426 09 |
| 71,841,580 46 | 281,673 34 | 2,983,324 76 | 10,335,921 35 | 128,399,517 77 | 296,190 78 |
| 423,983,333 41 | 13,385,313 48 | 12,969,883 99 | 9,657,788 09 | 789,508,223 78 | 5,750,062 77 |
| 138,027 32 | 227,844 12 | 21,472 75 | 16,287 24 | 1,079,631 43 | 10,947 22 |
| 11,253,306 51 | 575,367 32 | 913,794 90 | 426,614 97 | 17,949,621 82 | 243,744 71 |
| 220,301 07 | 124,735 13 | 151,026 52 | 123,861 91 | 5,752,670 44 | 50,850 39 |
| 1,761,242 35 | 175,830 55 | 116,820 87 | 45,825 05 | 4,442,069 36 | 80,415 35 |
| 4,068,573 27 | 229,502 36 | 326,396 62 | 306,562 08 | 12,156,128 92 | 59,529 53 |
| 4,811,293 45 | 495,262 29 | 457,965 70 | 359,611 71 | 26,221,555 71 | 138,851 58 |
| 33,996,010 04 | 919,367 67 | 1,660,960 44 | 849,670 20 | 72,219,112 25 | 273,299 84 |

TABLE NO. 4—

| Name of company—location. | Real estate (less incumbrances). | Mortgage loans on real estate. | Loans secured by collateral. | Premium notes and policy loans. |
|---|---|---|---|---|
| The Travelers Ins. Co., Hartford, Conn. | $7,600,617 76 | $ 53,761,919 45 | | $21,384,906 37 |
| Union Central Life, Cincinnati, Ohio | 2,319,355 24 | 112,469,525 17 | | 30,537,770 52 |
| Union Mutual Life, Portland, Me | 516,168 95 | 705,885 97 | $99,131 00 | 3,157,820 03 |
| United States Life, New York, N. Y | 333,579 55 | 1,831,100 00 | 15,000 00 | 923,324 79 |
| Universal Life Ins. Co., Dubuque, Ia | | 364,800 00 | | 360 40 |
| Western and Southern Life, Cincinnati, Ohio | 550,000 00 | 19,277,765 11 | | 510,727 15 |
| Western Union Life Ins. Co., Spokane, Wash | 141,820 25 | 2,283,415 38 | 28,000 00 | 1,310,992 89 |
| Wisconsin National Life, Oshkosh, Wis | 45,000 00 | 480,100 00 | | 149,554 99 |
| Totals | $149,659,908 93 | $2,569,349,897 55 | $25,219,744 20 | $985,476,321 22 |
| III. COMPANIES OF FOREIGN GOVERNMENTS. | | | | |
| Canada Life Assurance Co., Toronto, Can | $3,812,975 68 | $25,613,457 08 | $1,115,000 00 | $11,339,328 07 |
| Manufacturers Life, Toronto, Can | 215,000 00 | 14,399,524 91 | 9,064 83 | 5,012,452 93 |
| North American Life Assurance Co., Toronto, Can | 148,755 76 | 5,083,943 03 | | 2,690,194 30 |
| Totals | $4,176,731 44 | $45,096,925 02 | $1,124,064 83 | $19,041,975 30 |
| Aggregate | $161,704,579 06 | $2,658,805,858 82 | $29,017,010 20 | $1,020,777,057 52 |

TABLE

SHOWING DETAILED STATEMENT OF LIABILITIES

| Name of company. | Location. | Net reserve on outstanding policies. | Policy claims. | Other accrued liabilities. |
|---|---|---|---|---|
| I. COMPANIES OF THIS STATE. | | | | |
| The American Bankers Ins. Co | Chicago | $ 1,582,299 00 | $ 4,750 00 | $ 217,175 04 |
| Central Life Ins. Co. of Illinois | Ottawa | 3,298,595 00 | | 305,491 41 |
| Chicago National Life Ins. Co | Chicago | | | |
| Cloverleaf Life and Casualty Co | Jacksonville | 351,492 00 | 995 78 | 54,192 90 |
| Continental Assurance Co | Chicago | 939,134 00 | 18,666 81 | 51,086 83 |
| Elgin Life Ins. Co | Elgin | 161,569 00 | 1,500 00 | 3,587 78 |
| Federal Life, Chicago | Chicago | 4,553,016 00 | 63,567 00 | 425,400 73 |
| The Franklin Life | Springfield | 11,665,710 00 | 75,531 04 | 385,104 10 |
| Illinois Life | Chicago | 16,217,279 00 | 89,441 00 | 1,719,469 91 |
| International Life and Trust Co | Moline | 173,472 00 | 3,500 00 | 111,233 03 |
| Liberty Life Ins. Co | Chicago | 2,250 00 | | 2,210 95 |
| Marquette Life | Springfield | 888,583 00 | 9,200 00 | 13,713 12 |
| Mutual Life of Illinois | Springfield | 117,895 00 | | 24,464 32 |
| Mutual Trust Life | Chicago | 6,324,567 00 | 23,481 94 | 370,916 37 |
| National Life of U. S. A | Chicago | 18,702,566 45 | 171,235 70 | 741,973 14 |
| North American Life Ins. Co. of Chicago | Chicago | 5,599,171 00 | 23,913 01 | 226,075 10 |
| Old Colony Life | Chicago | 1,784,181 00 | 17,398 69 | 127,398 31 |
| Peoples Life | Chicago | 662,037 00 | 5,125 00 | 12,886 85 |
| Peoria Life, Peoria | Peoria | 4,343,743 00 | 42,969 48 | 340,243 14 |
| Providers' Life Assurance Co | Chicago | 390,078 00 | 4,450 00 | 5,782 64 |
| Public Life Ins. Co | Chicago | 60,983 00 | 2,000 00 | 7,402 82 |
| Rockford Life | Rockford | 632,925 00 | 1,000 00 | 10,795 67 |
| Standard Life | Decatur | 2,557,768 31 | 48,180 70 | 155,196 73 |
| Totals | | $81,009,313 76 | $606,906 15 | $5,311,800 89 |

Concluded.

| Book value of bonds and stocks. | Cash in office and in bank. | Deferred and unpaid premiums. | All other assets less assets not admitted. | Total admitted assets. | Ledger and non-ledger items not admitted as assets. |
|---|---|---|---|---|---|
| $67,751,557 50 | $3,915,187 97 | $5,639,495 09 | $58,951,998 10 | $219,005,682 24 | $1,055,404 12 |
| 7,298,612 00 | 903,333 01 | 2,148,436 71 | 6,004,718 07 | 161,681,750 72 | 230,955 60 |
| 14,878,411 77 | 187,668 08 | 217,003 59 | —741,390 06 | 19,020,699 33 | 987,132 99 |
| 2,939,995 03 | 67,085 46 | 37,655 57 | 77,333 72 | 6,225,074 12 | 33,693 08 |
| 107,750 00 | 63,416 61 | 4,799 07 | 14,548 21 | 555,674 29 | 246,303 68 |
| 6,947,760 67 | 44,575 68 | 387,383 55 | 577,719 14 | 28,295,931 30 | ---------- |
| 1,854,729 27 | 245,432 17 | 128,678 70 | 83,150 33 | 6,076,218 99 | 8,108 56 |
| 1,311,848 10 | 154,375 42 | 53,171 84 | 142,712 65 | 2,336,763 00 | 7,936 89 |
| $3,428,890,422 28 | $96,128,366 13 | $138,728,873 12 | $138,805,303 22 | $7,532,258,836 65 | $103,208,800 14 |
| $33,553,228 52 | $301,437 87 | $1,518,724 95 | $2,525,126 48 | $79,779,278 65 | ---------- |
| 15,230,920 50 | 462,253 38 | 1,128,280 87 | 1,369,883 95 | 37,827,381 37 | $ 4,156 24 |
| 13,051,971 47 | 274,983 18 | 554,421 39 | —62,046 71 | 21,742,222 42 | 472,732 79 |
| $61,836,120 49 | $1,038,674 43 | $3,201,427 21 | $3,832,963 72 | $139,348,882 44 | $476,889 03 |
| $3,509,402,607 55 | $100,560,547 53 | $144,588,682 00 | $144,875,968 75 | $7,769,732,311 43 | $106,214,449 10 |

## NO. 5.

OF EACH COMPANY DECEMBER 31, 1921.

| Policy dividends apportioned payable 1922. | Surplus apportioned payable subsequent to 1922. | Voluntary contingency reserve fund. | Capital stock paid in. | Unassigned funds. | Total. |
|---|---|---|---|---|---|
| ---------- | ---------- | $ 3,006 47 | $ 118,505 00 | $ 19,927 51 | $ 1,945,663 02 |
| $123,983 39 | $ 1,067 83 | 10,000 00 | 300,000 00 | 101,114 68 | 4,140,252 31 |
| ---------- | ---------- | ---------- | 100,000 00 | 27,242 34 | 127,242 34 |
| ---------- | ---------- | ---------- | 200,000 00 | 29,810 19 | 636,490 87 |
| ---------- | ---------- | 26,389 59 | 250,000 00 | 126,125 24 | 1,411,402 47 |
| ---------- | ---------- | ---------- | 104,102 95 | 1,318 20 | 272,077 93 |
| 44,584 77 | 101,970 09 | 25,000 00 | 300,000 00 | 88,004 95 | 5,601,543 54 |
| 178,973 00 | 211,848 55 | ---------- | 100,000 00 | 634,785 38 | 13,251,952 07 |
| 57,216 33 | 27,795 07 | ---------- | 1,000,000 00 | 302,645 41 | 19,413,846 72 |
| 2,641 85 | ---------- | ---------- | 104,860 00 | —14,762 07 | 380,944 81 |
| ---------- | ---------- | ---------- | 100,000 00 | 8,822 00 | 113,282 95 |
| ---------- | ---------- | ---------- | 254,742 00 | 10,093 09 | 1,176,331 21 |
| 3,986 00 | ---------- | ---------- | 177,853 50 | 55,853 71 | 380,052 53 |
| 90,283 12 | 66,968 80 | ---------- | ---------- | 634,324 52 | 7,510,541 75 |
| 52,246 19 | 505,364 90 | 62,181 99 | 500,000 00 | 733,284 31 | 21,468,852 68 |
| ---------- | ---------- | ---------- | 700,000 00 | 205,996 25 | 6,755,155 36 |
| 1,557 53 | ---------- | 1,016 58 | 126,551 87 | 89,168 97 | 2,147,272 95 |
| 167 81 | 2,340 81 | ---------- | 101,736 66 | 2,485 14 | 786,779 27 |
| 35,971 90 | 73,212 89 | ---------- | 200,000 00 | 50,529 24 | 5,086,669 65 |
| ---------- | ---------- | ---------- | 145,960 00 | 28,266 73 | 574,537 37 |
| ---------- | ---------- | ---------- | 200,000 00 | 406,088 27 | 676,474 09 |
| ---------- | ---------- | ---------- | 175,650 00 | 73,317 50 | 893,688 17 |
| 13,747 37 | 32,262 13 | ---------- | 225,000 00 | 341,383 04 | 3,373,538 28 |
| $605,359 26 | $1,022,831 07 | $127,594 63 | $5,484,961 98 | $3,955,824 60 | $98,124,592 34 |

TABLE NO. 5—

| Name of company. | Location. | Net reserve on outstanding policies. | Policy claims. | Other accrued liabilities. |
|---|---|---|---|---|
| II. COMPANIES OF OTHER STATES. | | | | |
| Aetna Life | Hartford, Conn. | $132,510,267 00 | $1,035,334 38 | $31,349,739 59 |
| American Central Life | Indianapolis, Ind. | 7,612,840 00 | 114,177 70 | 473,658 35 |
| American Life Ins. Co. | Detroit, Mich. | 5,786,784 98 | 27,840 01 | 310,889 19 |
| American Life Re-insurance Co. | Dallas, Tex. | 141,977 00 | 13,788 00 | 17,687 77 |
| American National Assurance Co. | St. Louis, Mo. | 830,721 00 | 19,315 00 | 37,799 44 |
| Bankers Life Co. | Des Moines, Ia. | 31,531,344 00 | 582,214 00 | 15,620,717 46 |
| Bankers Life Ins. Co. | Lincoln, Neb. | 14,330,943 01 | 21,600 00 | 426,183 81 |
| Bankers Reserve Life Co. | Omaha, Neb. | 9,648,616 00 | 17,562 00 | 354,384 09 |
| Berkshire Life | Pittsfield, Mass. | 28,043,501 00 | 125,196 00 | 424,809 45 |
| Business Men's Assurance Co. of America | Kansas City, Mo. | 52,044 35 | 5,000 00 | 1,118,528 01 |
| Capitol Life Ins. Co. of Colorado | Denver, Colo. | 3,815,160 00 | 52,158 58 | 517,070 05 |
| Central Life Assurance Society of U. S. (Mutual) | Des Moines, Ia. | 9,946,530 13 | 118,662 00 | 549,397 44 |
| Central States Life Ins. Co. | St. Louis, Mo. | 3,547,219 09 | 46,990 16 | 488,826 83 |
| Century Life | Indianapolis, Ind. | 178,840 79 | ............ | 10,415 06 |
| Cleveland Life | Cleveland, Ohio. | 3,398,953 00 | 7,490 48 | 157,356 21 |
| Columbian National Life | Boston, Mass. | 19,180,670 00 | 102,041 35 | 938,076 62 |
| Columbus Mutual Life Ins. Co. | Columbus, Ohio. | 2,275,018 00 | 10,340 00 | 255,922 74 |
| Connecticut General Life | Hartford, Conn. | 31,767,139 00 | 175,279 55 | 2,548,930 81 |
| Connecticut Mutual Life | Hartford, Conn. | 84,094,394 00 | 357,461 44 | 4,893,733 84 |
| Equitable Life Assurance Society of the U. S. | New York, N. Y. | 527,435,443 00 | 5,283,324 29 | 23,972,631 61 |
| Equitable Life | Des Moines, Ia. | 33,871,927 00 | 129,189 10 | 1,322,868 22 |
| Farmers National Life | Huntington, Ind. | 909,328 13 | 2,000 00 | 57,636 27 |
| Federal Union Life | Cincinnati, Ohio. | 688,373 00 | 1,500 00 | 42,485 75 |
| The Fidelity Mutual Life | Philadelphia, Pa. | 40,509,209 00 | 299,233 34 | 1,777,499 85 |
| Girard Life | Philadelphia, Pa. | 1,939,327 00 | 15,239 00 | 58,410 90 |
| The Guardian Life | New York, N. Y. | 33,227,498 00 | 511,343 73 | 1,341,637 96 |
| Home Life | New York, N. Y. | 39,849,449 00 | 266,232 90 | 1,245,654 67 |
| Indiana National Life | Indianapolis, Ind. | 2,064,361 84 | 7,000 00 | 157,067 35 |
| Indianapolis Life | Indianapolis, Ind. | 2,314,563 02 | 1,738 73 | 165,023 73 |
| International Life | St. Louis, Mo. | 14,317,984 21 | 118,996 93 | 1,841,174 41 |
| John Hancock Mutual Life | Boston, Mass. | 215,966,588 00 | 584,018 95 | 4,893,477 00 |
| Kansas City Life | Kansas City, Mo. | 18,814,289 00 | 118,707 11 | 1,922,043 89 |
| LaFayette Life Ins. Co. | LaFayette, Ind. | 2,086,087 48 | 6,003 56 | 108,575 41 |
| Lincoln National Life | Ft. Wayne, Ind. | 10,925,822 38 | 106,101 85 | 699,367 20 |
| Manhattan Life | New York, N. Y. | 18,250,542 00 | 116,987 89 | 506,614 16 |
| Maryland Assurance Corp. | Baltimore, Md. | 237,141 56 | 2,720 00 | 42,678 09 |
| Massachusetts Mutual Life | Springfield, Mass. | 127,730,804 00 | 504,170 85 | 9,973,659 26 |
| Merchants Life | Des Moines, Ia. | 3,778,247 00 | 40,489 51 | 778,396 98 |
| Metropolitan Life | New York, N. Y. | 1,025,562,628 00 | 3,951,568 91 | 21,908,145 90 |
| Michigan Mutual Life | Detroit, Mich. | 14,608,788 00 | 82,802 70 | 222,992 35 |
| Minnesota Mutual Life | St. Paul, Minn. | 7,691,042 00 | 105,181 10 | 291,115 00 |
| Missouri State Life | St. Louis, Mo. | 27,904,748 00 | 225,078 69 | 1,668,855 34 |
| Morris Plan Insurance Society | New York, N. Y. | 23,587 93 | 2,210 50 | 5,229 86 |
| Mutual Benefit Life | Newark, N. J. | 268,580,217 00 | 1,058,970 48 | 9,611,178 71 |
| Mutual Life | New York, N. Y. | 567,244,795 00 | 5,398,889 05 | 15,964,363 79 |
| National Life and Accident Ins. Co. | Nashville Tenn. | 2,002,213 23 | 27,328 28 | 3,617,172 34 |
| National Life Ins. Co. | Montpelier, Vt. | 68,384,465 50 | 308,538 44 | 1,513,006 28 |
| New England Mutual Life | Boston, Mass. | 103,632,706 74 | 292,642 63 | 2,914,835 00 |
| New World Life | Spokane, Wash. | 2,466,673 03 | 11,250 00 | 148,086 18 |
| New York Life | New York, N. Y. | 782,811,853 00 | 8,877,764 08 | 42,416,777 81 |
| Northern States Life | Hammond, Ind. | 988,463 95 | 1,015 00 | 28,247 51 |
| Northwestern Mutual Life | Milwaukee, Wis. | 445,125,249 00 | 1,420,437 39 | 40,775,216 30 |
| Northwestern National Life | Minneapolis, Minn. | 10,435,015 00 | 71,464 34 | 508,793 24 |
| Old Line Ins. Co. | Lincoln, Neb. | 507,021 83 | ............ | 116,407 02 |
| Old Line Life Ins. Co. of America | Milwaukee, Wis. | 2,639,762 47 | 11,000 00 | 152,748 13 |

Continued.

| Policy dividends apportioned payable 1922. | Surplus apportioned payable subsequent to 1922. | Voluntary contingency reserve fund. | Capital stock paid in. | Unassigned funds. | Total. |
|---|---|---|---|---|---|
| $1,891,248 08 | $488,988 18 | $2,162,947 00 | $5,000,000 00 | $17,279,522 01 | $191,718,046 24 |
| 3,036 38 | | 25,000 00 | 137,000 00 | 240,700 01 | 8,606,412 44 |
| 4,919 70 | 20,976 00 | | 100,000 00 | 117,329 05 | 6,368,738 93 |
| | | 3,051 92 | 250,000 00 | 156,525 14 | 583,029 83 |
| | | | 200,000 00 | 76,044 50 | 1,163,879 94 |
| 1,100,000 00 | | | | 1,417,535 29 | 50,251,810 75 |
| 623,012 70 | 4,061,838 29 | 219,422 90 | 100,000 00 | 359,610 16 | 20,142,610 87 |
| 193,455 60 | 218,098 50 | | 100,000 00 | 1,222,153 27 | 11,754,269 46 |
| 356,473 92 | 354,465 00 | | | 1,047,165 30 | 30,351,610 67 |
| | | | 200,000 00 | 124,273 97 | 1,499,846 33 |
| 3,332 56 | 46,000 00 | 95,000 00 | 100,000 00 | 191,694 52 | 4,820,415 71 |
| 50,089 79 | 292,997 87 | 15,859 00 | | 1,023,950 04 | 11,997,486 27 |
| 8,737 99 | | 30,000 00 | 400,000 00 | 34,531 12 | 4,556,305 19 |
| | | | 200,000 00 | 18,796 16 | 408,052 01 |
| 20,693 52 | | 15,488 04 | 250,000 00 | 50,000 00 | 3,899,981 25 |
| | 400,000 00 | | 1,000,000 00 | 440,999 81 | 22,061,787 78 |
| 12,196 58 | 350 71 | | 250,000 00 | 417,111 44 | 3,220,939 47 |
| 203,132 46 | | 100,000 00 | 800,000 00 | 1,887,032 75 | 37,481,514 57 |
| 2,060,000 00 | | 750,000 00 | | 4,049,181 42 | 96,204,770 70 |
| 26,148,772 00 | 36,400,411 00 | 254,638 91 | 100,000 00 | 35,705,797 53 | 655,301,018 34 |
| 1,482,128 00 | | 584,000 00 | 500,000 00 | 1,344,726 72 | 39,234,839 04 |
| | | | 200,000 00 | 224,171 80 | 1,393,136 20 |
| | | | 225,000 00 | 41,249 86 | 998,608 61 |
| 1,539,961 38 | 1,479,841 47 | | | 1,904,844 03 | 47,510,589 07 |
| 11,452 54 | 10,102 72 | | 419,040 00 | 80,482 32 | 2,534,054 48 |
| 1,037,909 96 | 1,676,852 66 | 566,303 77 | 200,000 00 | 2,590,504 07 | 41,152,050 15 |
| 750,000 00 | | 130,000 00 | | 980,990 98 | 43,222,327 55 |
| | | | 210,000 00 | 11,261 52 | 2,449,690 71 |
| | | | | 113,163 01 | 2,594,488 49 |
| 38,785 58 | 151 06 | 89,143 12 | 656,250 00 | 756,979 53 | 17,819,464 84 |
| 4,740,000 00 | 176,973 88 | | | 13,332,313 14 | 239,693,370 97 |
| 50,609 34 | 109,708 86 | | 200,000 00 | 795,509 04 | 22,010,867 24 |
| 12,206 94 | 55,997 21 | 26,799 05 | | 155,440 34 | 2,451,109 99 |
| 12,086 95 | 8,738 35 | 51,962 56 | 500,000 00 | 500,000 00 | 12,804,079 29 |
| 19,934 36 | 195,162 91 | 150,000 00 | 100,000 00 | 478,963 79 | 19,818,205 11 |
| | | | 500,000 00 | 60,177 92 | 842,717 57 |
| 2,363,277 38 | | | | 6,519,001 52 | 147,090,913 01 |
| | | | 400,000 00 | 151,010 95 | 5,148,144 44 |
| 15,832,347 72 | 50,984 99 | 1,036,169 52 | | 47,241,179 50 | 1,115,583,024 54 |
| 58,666 55 | 97,697 16 | | 250,000 00 | 673,184 17 | 15,994,130 93 |
| 230,972 42 | 231,954 89 | 125,000 00 | | 568,240 64 | 9,243,506 05 |
| 447,715 04 | 410,637 18 | | 1,000,000 00 | 2,187,468 66 | 33,844,502 91 |
| | | | 100,000 00 | 171,793 27 | 308,821 62 |
| 10,661,048 19 | | 10,065,109 24 | | | 299,976,523 62 |
| 29,831,279 17 | 31,014,585 45 | 28,051,586 81 | | | 677,505,499 27 |
| | | 150,000 00 | 600,000 00 | 760,291 09 | 7,157,004 94 |
| 3,000,442 05 | 2,721,238 81 | 85,342 66 | | 3,743,934 96 | 79,756,968 70 |
| 3,882,491 35 | 244,710 44 | | | 5,241,439 54 | 116,208,825 70 |
| | | | 1,134,500 00 | 545,019 25 | 4,305,528 46 |
| 42,287,368 71 | 59,303,179 00 | 16,935,196 20 | | | 952,632,138 80 |
| 5,000 00 | 309 00 | 14,000 00 | 162,000 00 | 66,795 76 | 1,265,831 22 |
| 19,257,188 63 | 507,603 00 | | | | 507,085,694 32 |
| 267,108 11 | 54,344 43 | 275,000 00 | | 839,199 53 | 12,450,924 65 |
| 3,000 00 | | 2,177 05 | 200,000 00 | 39,739 22 | 868,345 12 |
| | | | 672,635 00 | 304,719 15 | 3,780,864 75 |

TABLE NO. 5—

| Name of company. | Location. | Net reserve on outstanding policies. | Policy claims. | Other accrued liabilities. |
|---|---|---|---|---|
| Pacific Mutual Life | Los Angeles, Cal. | $ 52,879,630 00 | $ 286,329 47 | $ 4,404,373 11 |
| Pan American Life | New Orleans, La. | 7,551,609 00 | 121,711 08 | 850,338 02 |
| Penn Mutual Life | Philadelphia, Pa. | 196,818,790 00 | 773,575 88 | 14,642,070 38 |
| Peoples Life | Frankfort, Ind. | 1,839,001 93 | 4,000 00 | 75,123 56 |
| Philadelphia Life | Philadelphia, Pa. | 6,935,020 00 | 108,935 17 | 269,931 89 |
| Phoenix Mutual Life | Hartford, Conn. | 53,924,044 21 | 173,444 02 | 4,591,508 67 |
| Provident Life and Trust | Philadelphia, Pa. | 112,563,572 00 | 288,191 48 | 3,067,829 24 |
| Prudential Insurance Co. of America | Newark, N. J. | 710,361,811 00 | 3,041,425 33 | 21,830,506 89 |
| Re-insurance Life Co. of America | Des Moines, Ia. | 116,944 06 | 23,611 00 | 45,433 75 |
| Reliance Life | Pittsburgh, Pa. | 15,299,698 00 | 68,758 33 | 830,599 51 |
| Reserve Loan Life | Indianapolis, Ind. | 4,877,818 16 | 65,566 98 | 383,602 41 |
| Security Life Ins. Co. of America | Richmond, Va. | 3,848,029 00 | 39,404 22 | 130,531 07 |
| Security Mutual Life | Binghamton, N. Y. | 11,142,134 00 | 64,437 00 | 274,316 78 |
| State Life | Indianapolis, Ind. | 22,154,322 76 | 113,076 25 | 1,025,851 83 |
| State Mutual Life Assurance | Worcester, Mass. | 62,844,304 00 | 224,013 39 | 2,747,598 10 |
| The Travelers Ins. Co. | Hartford, Conn. | 147,837,943 00 | 595,241 98 | 52,288,354 40 |
| Union Central Life | Cincinnati, Ohio | 137,211,708 00 | 766,873 77 | 5,488,726 99 |
| Union Mutual Life | Portland, Me. | 18,101,434 00 | 68,024 77 | 346,650 69 |
| United States Life | New York, N. Y. | 5,727,042 00 | 54,218 65 | 121,166 93 |
| Universal Life Ins. Co. | Dubuque, Ia. | 28,414 60 | | 2,813 81 |
| Western and Southern Life | Cincinnati, Ohio | 25,807,865 00 | 56,390 12 | 305,288 41 |
| Western Union Life Ins. Co. | Spokane, Wash. | 4,772,125 00 | 18,526 79 | 584,688 28 |
| Wisconsin National Life | Oshkosh, Wis. | 1,614,454 43 | 56,000 00 | 49,966 34 |
| Totals | | $6,418,482,890 86 | $39,805,345 66 | $367,681,471 29 |
| III. COMPANIES OF FOREIGN GOVERNMENTS. | | | | |
| Canada Life Assurance Co. | Toronto, Can. | $68,245,530 00 | $539,605 92 | $1,876,088 68 |
| Manufacturers Life | Toronto, Can. | 31,504,941 00 | 367,599 59 | 1,102,212 92 |
| North American Life Assurance Co. | Toronto, Can. | 18,006,095 00 | 152,983 23 | 411,928 58 |
| Totals | | $117,756,566 00 | $1,060,188 74 | $3,390,230 18 |
| Aggregate | | $6,617,248,770 62 | $41,472,440 55 | $376,383,502 36 |

TABLE

SHOWING DETAILED STATEMENT OF INCOME OF EACH

| Name of company. | Location. | Total premium income. | Consideration for supplementary contracts and dividends left on deposit. |
|---|---|---|---|
| I. COMPANIES OF THIS STATE. | | | |
| American Bankers Ins. Co. | Chicago | $ 538,753 36 | $ 3,683 92 |
| Central Life Insurance Co. of Illinois | Ottawa | 1,106,758 66 | 24,631 54 |
| Chicago National Life Ins. Co. | Chicago | | |
| Cloverleaf Life and Casualty Co. | Jacksonville | 166,080 03 | |
| Continental Assurance Co. | Chicago | 671,639 39 | |
| Elgin Life Ins. Co. | Elgin | 32,919 79 | |
| Federal Life | Chicago | 1,258,942 87 | 11,477 60 |
| The Franklin Life | Springfield | 3,786,256 70 | 644 27 |
| Illinois Life | Chicago | 3,818,060 43 | 41,468 89 |
| International Life and Trust Co. | Moline | 163,794 57 | 1,708 89 |

Concluded.

| Policy dividends apportioned payable 1922. | Surplus apportioned payable subsequent to 1922. | Voluntary contingency reserve fund. | Capital stock paid in. | Unassigned funds. | Total. |
|---|---|---|---|---|---|
| $ 1,228,361 58 | $3,178,967 00 | $ 5,821 32 | $1,500,000 00 | $ 1,715,768 68 | $ 65,199,251 16 |
| 3,229 02 | ----- | 70,249 80 | 1,000,000 00 | 403,542 78 | 10,000,679 70 |
| 9,067,047 04 | 4,592,155 58 | 8,091,908 95 | ----- | ----- | 233,985,547 83 |
| 2,400 00 | ----- | 30,000 00 | 100,000 00 | 123,318 58 | 2,173,844 07 |
| 91,316 00 | 66,265 00 | ----- | 560,320 00 | 124,480 33 | 8,156,268 39 |
| 1,662,721 54 | ----- | 2,335,882 48 | ----- | ----- | 62,687,600 92 |
| 3,296,000 00 | ----- | 7,183,925 05 | 2,000,000 00 | ----- | 128,399,517 77 |
| 11,820,195 00 | 8,931,882 69 | 210,740 00 | 2,000,000 00 | 31,251,662 87 | 789,508,223 78 |
| ----- | ----- | ----- | 500,000 00 | 393,642 62 | 1,079,631 43 |
| 88,578 63 | 197,810 75 | 109,000 00 | 1,000,000 00 | 355,176 60 | 17,949,621 82 |
| 22,868 97 | ----- | 109,478 37 | 100,000 00 | 193,335 55 | 5,752,670 44 |
| ----- | ----- | 50,000 00 | 220,000 00 | 154,105 07 | 4,442,069 36 |
| 82,817 47 | 75,109 57 | ----- | ----- | 517,314 10 | 12,156,128 92 |
| 342,155 23 | ----- | 521,149 64 | ----- | 2,065,000 00 | 26,221,555 71 |
| 2,193,674 00 | 150,993 00 | 43,166 00 | ----- | 4,015,363 76 | 72,219,112 25 |
| 64,216 45 | 503,297 00 | 27,724 00 | 7,500,000 00 | 10,188,905 41 | 219,055,682 24 |
| 6,179,991 92 | 3,717,722 00 | 83,776 35 | 2,500,000 00 | 5,732,951 69 | 161,681,750 72 |
| ----- | ----- | ----- | ----- | 504,589 87 | 19,020,699 33 |
| ----- | ----- | ----- | 264,000 00 | 58,646 54 | 6,225,074 12 |
| ----- | ----- | ----- | 369,442 13 | 155,003 75 | 555,674 29 |
| ----- | ----- | ----- | 1,250,000 00 | 876,387 77 | 28,295,931 30 |
| ----- | ----- | ----- | 200,000 00 | 500,878 92 | 6,076,218 99 |
| ----- | ----- | 20,000 00 | 400,000 00 | 196,342 23 | 2,336,763 00 |
| $206,647,654 50 | $162,049,101 61 | $80,902,019 71 | $38,880,187 13 | $217,810,165 89 | $7,532,258,836 65 |
| $1,850,090 00 | $5,145,716 00 | $334,287 60 | $1,000,000 00 | $ 787,960 45 | $79,779,278 65 |
| 645,076 00 | 2,058,888 00 | 530,000 00 | 300,000 00 | 1,318,663 86 | 37,827,381 37 |
| 509,701 28 | 1,866,618 00 | 64,624 65 | 60,000 00 | 670,271 68 | 21,742,222 42 |
| $3,004,867 28 | $9,071,222 00 | $928,912 25 | $1,360,000 00 | $2,776,895 99 | $139,348,882 44 |
| $210,257,881 04 | $172,143,154 68 | $81,958,526 59 | $45,725,149 11 | $224,542,886 48 | $7,769,732,311 43 |

## NO. 6.

COMPANY FOR THE YEAR ENDING DECEMBER 31, 1921.

| Gross interest and rents. | Adjustment in book value of ledger assets. | Increase in capital stock. | Surplus on capital stock or contributed. | Received from other sources. | Total. |
|---|---|---|---|---|---|
| $106,664 52 | $156,958 00 | $ 13,505 00 | ----- | $127,067 23 | $ 946,632 03 |
| 205,232 79 | ----- | 100,000 00 | ----- | 13,100 00 | 1,449,722 99 |
| 3,888 43 | ----- | ----- | ----- | 166 33 | 4,054 76 |
| 24,045 03 | ----- | ----- | $ 22,400 00 | 10,000 00 | 222,525 06 |
| 48,391 29 | 1,308 91 | 50,000 00 | ----- | 1,912 34 | 773,251 93 |
| 13,198 23 | ----- | ----- | ----- | 23,739 90 | 69,857 92 |
| 331,156 54 | ----- | ----- | ----- | 26,477 61 | 1,628,054 62 |
| 663,330 70 | 16 26 | ----- | ----- | 200,683 00 | 4,650,930 93 |
| 991,613 43 | 3,351 00 | ----- | ----- | 3 16 | 4,854,496 91 |
| 10,026 13 | ----- | 4,860 00 | 2,916 00 | 86,501 86 | 269,807 45 |

TABLE NO. 6—

| Name of company. | Location. | Total premium income. | Consideration for supplementary contracts and dividends left on deposit. |
|---|---|---|---|
| Liberty Life Ins. Co | Chicago | $ 5,471 09 | |
| Marquette Life | Springfield | 234,355 52 | |
| Mutual Life of Illinois | Springfield | 147,578 74 | $ 496 92 |
| Mutual Trust Life | Chicago | 2,383,678 75 | 35,865 89 |
| National Life of U. S. A | Chicago | 4,161,668 51 | 33,103 93 |
| North American Life Ins. Co. of Chicago | Chicago | 1,799,936 22 | |
| Old Colony Life | Chicago | 668,176 66 | 8,588 71 |
| Peoples Life | Chicago | 197,664 34 | |
| Peoria Life | Peoria | 2,101,806 05 | 40,575 30 |
| Providers' Life Assurance Co | Chicago | 225,921 89 | |
| Public Life Ins. Co | Chicago | 84,312 28 | |
| Rockford Life | Rockford | 281,390 20 | |
| Standard Life | Decatur | 1,394 079 32 | 26,596 78 |
| Totals | | $25,229,245 37 | $228,842 64 |
| II. COMPANIES OF OTHER STATES. | | | |
| Aetna Life | Hartford, Conn | $30,874,736 01 | $854,794 63 |
| American Central Life | Indianapolis, Ind | 2,190,377 74 | 45,175 44 |
| American Life Ins. Co | Detroit, Mich | 1,193,321 13 | 36,979 51 |
| American Life Reinsurance Co | Dallas, Tex | 238,768 28 | |
| American National Assurance Co | St. Louis, Mo | 396,827 13 | |
| Bankers Life Co | Des Moines, Iowa | 15,244,742 27 | 124,097 35 |
| Bankers Life Ins. Co | Lincoln, Neb | 2,837,876 39 | 13,000 00 |
| Bankers Reserve Life Co | Omaha, Neb | 2,792,297 78 | 50,916 78 |
| Berkshire Life | Pittsfield, Mass | 4,227,541 60 | 64,317 32 |
| Business Men's Assurance Co. of America | Kansas City, Mo | 92,581 43 | |
| Capitol Life Ins. Co. of Colorado | Denver, Colo | 1,425,244 81 | 96,214 57 |
| Central Life Assur. Society of U. S. (Mutual) | Des Moines, Iowa | 3,613,756 03 | 26,342 41 |
| Central States Life Ins. Co | St. Louis, Mo | 1,611,932 07 | 18,254 19 |
| Century Life | Indianapolis, Ind | 151,135 19 | |
| Cleveland Life | Cleveland, Ohio | 951,564 84 | 19,141 61 |
| Columbian National Life | Boston, Mass | 4,318,964 84 | 15,462 26 |
| Columbus Mutual Life Ins. Co | Columbus, Ohio | 1,290,878 46 | 46,721 88 |
| Connecticut General Life | Hartford, Conn | 9,471,093 40 | 385,751 70 |
| Connecticut Mutual Life | Hartford, Conn | 12,579,523 78 | 785,786 36 |
| Equitable Life Assur. Soc. of the U. S | New York, N. Y | 99,655,588 79 | 3,811,520 35 |
| Equitable Life | Des Moines, Iowa | 9,032,772 28 | 184,200 19 |
| Farmers National Life | Huntington, Ind | 609,132 69 | 6,937 69 |
| Federal Union Life | Cincinnati, Ohio | 529,763 90 | |
| The Fidelity Mutual Life | Philadelphia, Pa | 8,258,244 13 | 161,777 71 |
| Girard Life | Philadelphia, Pa | 604,418 97 | 389 36 |
| The Guardian Life | New York, N. Y | 6,900,003 76 | 89,804 66 |
| Home Life | New York, N. Y | 6,990,547 31 | 94,032 63 |
| Indiana National Life | Indianapolis, Ind | 455,792 78 | 5,987 15 |
| Indianapolis Life | Indianapolis, Ind | 826,303 64 | 18,072 09 |
| International Life | St. Louis, Mo | 4,497,072 76 | 235,335 91 |
| John Hancock Mutual Life | Boston, Mass | 52,611,339 45 | 443,563 06 |
| Kansas City Life | Kansas City, Mo | 6,701,456 75 | 227,887 34 |
| La Fayette Life Ins. Co | La Fayette, Ind | 524,174 24 | 7,650 66 |
| Lincoln National Life | Ft. Wayne, Ind | 5,574,422 54 | 87,345 98 |
| Manhattan Life | New York, N. Y | 2,087,763 30 | 12,345 63 |
| Maryland Assurance Corp | Baltimore, Md | 193,457 68 | |
| Massachusetts Mutual Life | Springfield, Mass | 24,780,361 35 | 2,083,098 47 |
| Merchants Life | Des Moines, Iowa | 1,977,744 19 | 23,815 50 |
| Metropolitan Life | New York, N. Y | 245,858,940 34 | 741,528 16 |
| Michigan Mutual Life | Detroit, Mich | 2,413 347 88 | 22,999 77 |
| Minnesota Mutual Life | St. Paul, Minn | 2,431,669 43 | 8,673 17 |
| Missouri State Life | St. Louis, Mo | 10,217,436 97 | 276,640 28 |
| Morris Plan Insurance Society | New York, N. Y | 178,197 46 | |
| Mutual Benefit Life | Newark, N. J | 47,027,444 23 | 1,241,617 37 |
| Mutual Life | New York, N. Y | 90,309,639 14 | 1,716,849 71 |

Continued.

| Gross interest and rents. | Adjustment in book value of ledger assets. | Increase in capital stock. | Surplus on capital stock or contributed. | Received from other sources. | Total. |
|---|---|---|---|---|---|
| $ 2,164 80 | | $100,000 00 | $200,000 00 | $ 3,109 72 | $ 310,745 61 |
| 57,790 50 | | | | 41,632 75 | 333,778 77 |
| 20,835 03 | | 8,160 00 | 16,320 00 | 15,000 00 | 208,390 69 |
| 302,298 82 | | | | 6,066 26 | 2,727,909 72 |
| 915,241 84 | | | | 27,102 30 | 5,137,116 58 |
| 347,838 60 | $ 6,015 44 | | | 58,970 21 | 2,212,760 47 |
| 239,314 21 | 46,326 24 | | | 20,138 45 | 982,544 27 |
| 60,524 98 | | | | 14,641 42 | 272,830 74 |
| 289,879 44 | | | | 121 54 | 2,432,382 33 |
| 32,775 59 | 10,000 00 | 530 00 | 2,120 00 | 20,391 47 | 291,738 95 |
| 21,840 33 | 49,117 80 | | | 31,283 42 | 186,553 83 |
| 46,480 99 | | | | 2,367 45 | 330,238 64 |
| 195,815 96 | | | | 29,536 02 | 1,646,028 08 |
| $4,930,348 18 | $273,093 65 | $277,055 00 | $243,756 00 | $760,012 44 | $31,942,353 28 |
| $7,496,906 10 | $23,286 47 | | | $ 412,143 47 | $39,661,866 68 |
| 481,097 32 | 195 76 | | | 109,910 92 | 2,826,757 18 |
| 235,024 10 | | | $114,500 00 | 3,145,682 96 | 4,725,507 70 |
| 27,814 71 | | | | | 266,582 99 |
| 57,953 18 | | | | 64,414 58 | 519,194 89 |
| 2,354,159 43 | 1,364 78 | | | 7,044 96 | 17,731,408 79 |
| 1,063,684 58 | | | | 9,309 46 | 3,923,870 43 |
| 565,260 41 | 2,324 25 | | | 237 54 | 3,411,036 76 |
| 1,476,339 79 | 92,972 97 | | | 1,976 73 | 5,863,148 41 |
| 2,929 87 | | $50,000 00 | | | 145,511 30 |
| 275,406 62 | | | | 142,827 39 | 1,939,693 39 |
| 549,868 65 | 3,836 41 | | | 36,105 07 | 4,229,908 57 |
| 192,955 52 | | 65,000 00 | 65,000 00 | 288,947 30 | 2,242,089 08 |
| 20,403 37 | | | | 2,952 34 | 174,490 90 |
| 214,605 90 | | | | 1,036 40 | 1,186,348 75 |
| 1,044,167 42 | 26,784 60 | | | 14,677 42 | 5,420,056 54 |
| 148,303 33 | 2,500 00 | 50,000 00 | 50,000 00 | 326 04 | 1,588,729 71 |
| 1,616,451 09 | 36,563 05 | | | 5,671 08 | 11,515,530 32 |
| 4,542,934 38 | 32,707 25 | | | 5,905 60 | 17,946,857 37 |
| 30,428,743 96 | 466,897 00 | | | 4,358,099 25 | 138,720,849 35 |
| 1,775,657 29 | 4,983 90 | | | 84,545 48 | 11,082,159 14 |
| 71,511 45 | | | | 4,730 64 | 692,312 47 |
| 35,980 72 | 413 40 | | | 82,507 60 | 648,665 62 |
| 2,413,825 69 | 18,214 89 | | | 161,361 16 | 11,013,423 58 |
| 110,125 84 | 2,680 01 | | | 1,154 22 | 718,768 40 |
| 2,164,431 42 | 17,278 62 | | | 14,325 67 | 9,185,844 13 |
| 2,118,591 54 | 31,345 49 | | | 57,020 97 | 9,291,537 94 |
| 107,440 13 | | | | 144,012 83 | 713,232 89 |
| 119,389 75 | 99 28 | —51,500 00 | | 6,654 39 | 919,019 15 |
| 922,118 80 | | 131,250 00 | | 360,261 04 | 6,146,038 51 |
| 10,388,307 86 | 89,295 61 | | | 15,884 73 | 63,548,390 71 |
| 1,070,372 26 | | | | 22,519 25 | 8,022,235 60 |
| 142,316 32 | 43 70 | | | 403 01 | 674,587 93 |
| 623,052 82 | 4 00 | | | 6,258 85 | 6,291,084 19 |
| 1,139,966 59 | 3,866 00 | | | 55,119 91 | 3,299,061 43 |
| 32,323 97 | 1,821 93 | | | 2 70 | 227,606 28 |
| 6,694,046 82 | 96,342 39 | | | 221,461 10 | 33,875,310 13 |
| 255,545 95 | | | | 1,350 36 | 2,258,456 00 |
| 51,938,196 39 | 713,076 46 | | | 2,053,452 40 | 301,305,193 75 |
| 802,510 01 | | | | 12 81 | 3,238,870 47 |
| 415,154 62 | 2,890 00 | | | 100 50 | 2,858,487 72 |
| 1,758,103 97 | | | | 157,526 59 | 12,409,707 81 |
| 10,846 85 | 203 13 | | | 27 53 | 189,274 97 |
| 14,003,099 83 | 14,180 71 | | | 2,155 00 | 62,288,497 14 |
| 32,249,951 41 | 553,078 08 | | | 8,558,684 54 | 133,388,262 88 |

TABLE NO. 6—

| Name of company. | Location. | Total premium income. | Consideration for supplementary contracts and dividends left on deposit. |
|---|---|---|---|
| National Life and Accident Ins. Co. | Nashville, Tenn. | $ 2,247,795 40 | |
| National Life Ins. Co. | Montpelier, Vt. | 11,467,271 85 | $ 191,731 37 |
| New England Mutual Life | Boston, Mass. | 20,042,202 11 | 336,939 21 |
| New World Life | Spokane, Wash. | 962,957 82 | 4,280 80 |
| New York Life | New York, N. Y. | 149,106,548 04 | 3,990,301 56 |
| Northern States Life | Hammond, Ind. | 316,731 34 | 7,938 08 |
| Northwestern Mutual Life | Milwaukee, Wis. | 77,522,978 50 | 1,877 363 18 |
| Northwestern National Life | Minneapolis, Minn. | 3.988,424 36 | 26,059 48 |
| Old Line Ins. Co. | Lincoln, Neb. | 418,161 96 | |
| Old Line Life Ins. Co. of America | Milwaukee, Wis. | 1,220,127 52 | 27,065 00 |
| Pacific Mutual Life | Los Angeles, Cal. | 13,278,804 64 | 237,751 79 |
| Pan American Life | New Orleans, La. | 2,895,333 59 | 105,144 84 |
| Penn Mutual Life | Philadelphia, Pa. | 37,703,496 24 | 1,648,683 74 |
| Peoples Life | Frankfort, Ind. | 583,745 75 | 109 38 |
| Philadelphia Life | Philadelphia, Pa. | 1,880,999 93 | 34,219 28 |
| Phoenix Mutual Life | Hartford, Conn. | 11,105,480 92 | 959,016 94 |
| Provident Life and Trust | Philadelphia, Pa. | 20,490,278 72 | 262,706 78 |
| Prudential Insurance Co. of America | Newark, N. J. | 187,726,376 49 | 1,903,141 14 |
| Reinsurance Life Co. of America | Des Moines, Iowa | 251,510 92 | |
| Reliance Life | Pittsburgh, Pa. | 7,185,299 99 | 108,254 97 |
| Reserve Loan Life | Indianapolis, Ind. | 1,719,037 84 | 480 83 |
| Security Life Ins. Co. of America | Richmond, Va. | 1,090,140 65 | 356 32 |
| Security Mutual Life | Binghamton, N. Y. | 2,361,396 85 | 11,451 60 |
| State Life | Indianapolis, Ind. | 5,132,095 69 | 67,085 51 |
| State Mutual Life Assurance | Worcester, Mass. | 10,781,292 68 | 450,182 17 |
| The Travelers Ins. Co. | Hartford, Conn. | 40,751,948 83 | 1,270,749 86 |
| Union Central Life | Cincinnati, Ohio | 27,412,583 80 | 345,352 04 |
| Union Mutual Life | Portland, Me. | 2,472,909 24 | 32,907 93 |
| United States Life | New York, N. Y. | 616,355 87 | 7,033 00 |
| Universal Life Ins. Co. | Dubuque, Iowa | 68,843 04 | |
| Western and Southern Life | Cincinnati, Ohio | 10,093,994 97 | |
| Western Union Life Ins. Co. | Spokane, Wash. | 1,659,114 71 | 86,435 21 |
| Wisconsin National Life | Oshkosh, Wis. | 581,558 22 | |
| Totals | | $1,381,886,057 62 | $28,077,770 86 |
| III. COMPANIES OF FOREIGN GOVERNMENTS. | | | |
| Canada Life Assurance Co. | Toronto, Can. | $11,173,421 54 | $94,493 91 |
| Manufacturers Life | Toronto, Can. | 7,583,251 23 | 52,158 55 |
| North American Life Assurance Co. | Toronto, Can. | 3,497,176 58 | 29,888 25 |
| Totals | | $22,253,849 35 | $176,540 71 |
| Aggregate | | $1,429,360,152 34 | $28,483,154 21 |

Concluded.

| Gross interest and rents. | Adjustment in book value of ledger assets. | Increase in capital stock. | Surplus on capital stock or contributed. | Received from other sources. | Total. |
|---|---|---|---|---|---|
| $ 160,820 62 | | $300,000 00 | | $ 5,908 06 | $ 2,714,524 08 |
| 3,844,592 78 | $ 52,471 30 | | | 524,359 52 | 16,080,426 82 |
| 5,284,588 30 | 1,006,181 55 | | | 188,014 11 | 26,857,925 28 |
| 259,358 03 | 1,391 50 | | | 66,203 44 | 1,294,191 59 |
| 46,045,917 61 | 1,506,582 68 | | | 2,882,559 85 | 203,531,909 74 |
| 65,534 60 | | | | 10,246 43 | 400,450 45 |
| 23,677,868 21 | 329,044 94 | | | 113,156 08 | 103,520,410 91 |
| 533,596 83 | | | | 5,852 28 | 4,553,932 95 |
| 27,439 68 | 3,259 99 | | | 13,032 64 | 461,894 27 |
| 148,286 11 | 1,127 23 | | | 6,793 90 | 1,403,399 76 |
| 3,353,767 85 | 15,969 07 | | | 37,603 17 | 16,923,896 52 |
| 532,157 68 | | | | 24,947 75 | 3,557,583 86 |
| 11,592,579 50 | | | | 74,171 57 | 51,018,931 05 |
| 117,056 45 | | | | 300 00 | 701,211 58 |
| 412,427 90 | | | | 81,337 93 | 2,408,985 04 |
| 2,917,294 08 | 16,677 50 | | | 56,487 59 | 15,054,957 03 |
| 5,714,411 07 | | | | 223,199 47 | 26,690,596 04 |
| 34,155,647 28 | 515,152 28 | | | 539,409 51 | 224,839,726 70 |
| 58,975 73 | 525 00 | | | | 311,011 65 |
| 756,783 84 | 31,814 96 | | | 4,841 47 | 8,086,995 23 |
| 300,757 31 | 51 71 | | | 38,527 77 | 2,058,855 46 |
| 208,561 10 | | | | 5,606 58 | 1,304,664 65 |
| 620,645 37 | 6,299 81 | | | 8,512 69 | 3,008,306 32 |
| 1,394,357 16 | | | | 6,811 00 | 6,600,349 36 |
| 3,419,189 33 | 31,888 25 | | | 14,064 31 | 14,696,616 74 |
| 7,176,511 15 | 351,354 48 | | | 40,469 90 | 49,591,034 22 |
| 8,496,953 44 | 403 69 | | | 1,268,410 15 | 37,523,703 12 |
| 886,434 14 | 25,128 45 | | | 3,459 36 | 3,420,839 12 |
| 350,433 96 | 861 64 | | | 179,065 00 | 1,153,749 47 |
| 31,932 96 | | —68,900 00 | | 318 76 | 32,194 76 |
| 1,270,359 35 | | 500,000 00 | | 145 86 | 11,864,500 18 |
| 316,070 16 | 987 91 | | | 7,925 93 | 2,070,533 92 |
| 96,091 15 | 1,476 74 | | | 788 13 | 679,914 24 |
| $348,385,278 76 | $6,137,900 82 | $975,850 00 | $229,500 00 | $27,051,332 00 | $1,792,743,690 06 |
| $4,406,994 05 | $51,965 40 | | | $162,066 75 | $15,888,941 65 |
| 1,819,840 77 | 18,216 02 | | | 107,988 63 | 9,581,455 20 |
| 1,195,032 53 | | | | 103,665 48 | 4,825,762 84 |
| $7,421,867 35 | $70,181 42 | | | $373,720 86 | $30,296,159 69 |
| $360,737,494 29 | $6,481,175 89 | $1,252,905 00 | $473,256 00 | $28,185,065 30 | $1,854,982,203 03 |

# TABLE

SHOWING DETAILED STATEMENT OF EXPENDITURES OF

| Name of company. | Location. | Losses and claims. Death losses and endowments. | Losses and claims. Annuities, involving life contingencies. | Dividends to policyholders. |
|---|---|---|---|---|
| I. COMPANIES OF THIS STATE. | | | | |
| The American Bankers Ins. Co. | Chicago | $ 84,504 55 | | |
| Central Life Ins. Co. of Illinois | Ottawa | 164,500 28 | | $ 74,852 08 |
| Chicago National Life Ins. Co. | Chicago | | | |
| Cloverleaf Life and Casualty Co. | Jacksonville | 28,747 30 | | 84 81 |
| Continental Assurance Co. | Chicago | 59,640 10 | $ 223 80 | |
| Elgin Life Ins. Co. | Elgin | 14,300 00 | | 364 61 |
| Federal Life | Chicago | 344,530 65 | | 47,743 80 |
| The Franklin Life | Springfield | 820,685 87 | 1,254 64 | 191,029 95 |
| Illinois Life | Chicago | 1,073,863 06 | 2,716 34 | 79,405 73 |
| International Life and Trust Co. | Moline | 12,000 00 | | 5,500 58 |
| Liberty Life Ins. Co. | Chicago | | | |
| Marquette Life | Springfield | 49,100 00 | | |
| Mutual Life of Illinois | Springfield | 9,000 00 | | 2,244 27 |
| Mutual Trust Life | Chicago | 393,209 62 | 9 52 | 139,224 26 |
| National Life of U. S. A. | Chicago | 1,069,615 66 | 26,334 06 | 110,875 90 |
| North American Life Ins. Co. of Chicago | Chicago | 281,377 66 | 120 00 | |
| Old Colony Life | Chicago | 142,644 74 | | 7,590 74 |
| Peoples Life | Chicago | 34,966 51 | | 1,845 34 |
| Peoria Life | Peoria | 206,419 53 | 1,284 24 | 43,533 30 |
| Providers' Life Assurance Co. | Chicago | 41,676 73 | | 13 31 |
| Public Life Ins. Co. | Chicago | 4,606 50 | | |
| Rockford Life | Rockford | 37,336 34 | | 1,748 21 |
| Standard Life | Decatur | 351,836 24 | | 28,785 14 |
| Totals | | $5,224,561 34 | $31,942 60 | $734,842 03 |
| II. COMPANIES OF OTHER STATES. | | | | |
| Aetna Life | Hartford, Conn. | $12,758,702 93 | $353,262 79 | $1,872,285 37 |
| American Central Life | Indianapolis, Ind. | 572,640 08 | 1,587 00 | 56,163 02 |
| American Life Ins. Co. | Detroit, Mich. | 203,894 32 | | 16,650 14 |
| American Life Re-insurance Co. | Dallas, Tex. | 39,584 63 | | |
| American National Assurance Co. | St. Louis, Mo. | 38,258 19 | | |
| Bankers Life Co. | Des Moines, Ia. | 6,359,667 44 | | 1,174,756 70 |
| Bankers Life Ins. Co. | Lincoln, Neb. | 325,427 91 | 2,489 80 | 468,691 29 |
| Bankers Reserve Life Co. | Omaha, Neb. | 343,668 25 | | 299,712 66 |
| Berkshire Life | Pittsfield, Mass. | 1,800,265 00 | | 644,997 80 |
| Business Men's Assurance Co. of America | Kansas City, Mo. | 5,000 00 | | |
| Capitol Life Ins. Co. of Colorado | Denver, Colo. | 258,421 96 | 533 06 | 104,353 59 |
| Central Life Assurance Society of U. S. (Mutual) | Des Moines, Ia. | 399,331 06 | | 170,584 71 |
| Central States Life Ins. Co. | St. Louis, Mo. | 297,111 81 | | 27,012 17 |
| Century Life | Indianapolis, Ind. | 29,002 33 | | |
| Cleveland Life | Cleveland, Ohio | 190,055 37 | 540 00 | 49,561 25 |
| Columbian National Life | Boston, Mass. | 814,312 55 | 7,617 30 | 37,035 35 |
| Columbus Mutual Life Ins. Co. | Columbus, Ohio | 116,427 29 | 976 34 | 157,792 47 |
| Connecticut General Life | Hartford, Conn. | 2,925,442 52 | 75,898 95 | 497,554 06 |
| Connecticut Mutual Life | Hartford, Conn. | 5,605,265 85 | 75,454 68 | 1,880,740 11 |
| Equitable Life Assurance Society of the U. S. | New York, N. Y. | 46,120,621 46 | 1,791,621 72 | 18,746,160 37 |
| Equitable Life | Des Moines, Ia. | 1,479,625 99 | 4,067 69 | 1,049,857 64 |
| Farmers National Life | Huntington, Ind. | 65,545 01 | | 13,027 46 |
| Federal Union Life | Cincinnati, Ohio | 141,235 04 | 100 00 | |
| The Fidelity Mutual Life | Philadelphia, Pa. | 2,553,593 82 | 31,324 71 | 972,809 03 |
| Girard Life | Philadelphia, Pa. | 72,731 00 | | 58,004 90 |

NO. 7.

EACH COMPANY FOR THE YEAR ENDING DECEMBER 31, 1921.

| On insurance lapsed and surrendered. | | Dividends to stockholders. | Supplementary contract payments, and dividends on deposit surrendered. | Adjustment in book value of ledger assets. | Other disbursements. | Total. |
|---|---|---|---|---|---|---|
| Notes and liens voided by lapse. | Paid in cash etc., including guaranteed dividends and similar allowances. | | | | | |
| $ 920 32 | $ 47,649 82 | | $ 3,218 86 | | $ 460,292 92 | $ 596,586 47 |
| 34,989 88 | 61,645 81 | $116,000 00 | 12,868 32 | | 383,937 32 | 848,793 69 |
| | | | | | 19,072 39 | 19,072 39 |
| 2,578 09 | 7,272 41 | | | | 118,695 26 | 157,377 87 |
| | 13,221 83 | 8,000 00 | 360 00 | $ 44 80 | 284,945 51 | 366,436 04 |
| | 2,472 16 | | 200 00 | | 45,988 99 | 63,325 76 |
| 27,737 57 | 242,331 07 | 24,000 00 | 10,836 21 | | 588,536 35 | 1,285,715 65 |
| 97,706 99 | 533,895 85 | 5,000 00 | 5,601 63 | 82 00 | 1,666,365 32 | 3,321,622 25 |
| | 367,621 84 | 100,000 00 | 36,766 57 | 814 80 | 1,337,318 52 | 2,998,506 86 |
| 5,448 08 | 1,697 73 | | | 1,648 20 | 120,914 12 | 147,208 71 |
| | | | | | 86,789 43 | 86,789 43 |
| 1,238 66 | 16,474 00 | | | 335 92 | 122,310 59 | 189,459 17 |
| 1,353 40 | 127 14 | | | | 119,228 59 | 131,953 40 |
| | 102,218 13 | | 15,311 41 | | 665,932 12 | 1,315,905 06 |
| 8,830 90 | 726,382 06 | 100,000 00 | 16,539 25 | 36,424 99 | 1,367,695 45 | 3,462,698 27 |
| 34,981 51 | 187,615 50 | 139,880 00 | 6,374 72 | | 695,065 48 | 1,345,414 87 |
| 6,999 12 | 68,449 61 | | 3,687 07 | | 471,594 96 | 700,966 24 |
| 16 83 | 23,170 77 | 6,104 20 | | | 137,805 11 | 203,908 76 |
| 36,630 05 | 66,943 35 | 10,000 00 | 13,361 90 | 65 30 | 987,327 77 | 1,365,565 44 |
| | 23,500 96 | | | | 151,498 28 | 216,689 28 |
| | | | | | 211,481 25 | 216,087 75 |
| 3,617 75 | 9,787 49 | | | | 132,568 14 | 185,057 93 |
| 16,477 97 | 84,505 23 | 22,500 00 | 5,071 82 | | 510,773 47 | 1,019,949 87 |
| $279,527 12 | $2,586,982 76 | $531,484 20 | $130,197 76 | $39,416 01 | $10,686,137 34 | $20,245,091 16 |
| $ 49 27 | $3,289,365 15 | $500,000 00 | $502,056 10 | $11,757 29 | $7,254,610 66 | $26,542,089 56 |
| | 355,282 53 | 10,960 00 | 5,356 83 | | 1,018,228 88 | 2,020,218 34 |
| 82,562 24 | 147,196 16 | | 6,593 56 | | 538,063 11 | 994,959 53 |
| | | | | | 100,290 16 | 139,874 79 |
| | 13,363 35 | | 360 00 | | 218,885 06 | 270,866 60 |
| 107,951 97 | 266,843 71 | | 32,573 50 | | 4,373,967 51 | 12,315,760 83 |
| | 551,202 19 | 8,000 00 | 9,877 25 | 7,707 59 | 559,270 70 | 1,932,666 73 |
| 107,098 72 | 411,702 74 | 10,000 00 | 1,465 25 | 11,218 36 | 959,243 10 | 2,144,109 08 |
| | 642,468 80 | | 25,476 91 | 33,483 24 | 1,066,698 66 | 4,213,390 41 |
| | | | | | 61,945 40 | 66,945 40 |
| 24,318 09 | 88,548 66 | | 67,613 61 | 5 10 | 628,248 15 | 1,172,042 22 |
| 29,038 65 | 266,172 90 | | 6,530 19 | | 1,331,182 72 | 2,202,840 23 |
| | 87,751 38 | | 7,696 67 | | 913,140 28 | 1,332,712 31 |
| 263 50 | 3,325 96 | | | | 106,210 79 | 138,802 58 |
| | 50,108 61 | 15,000 00 | 2,370 06 | 50,000 00 | 352,864 88 | 710,500 17 |
| 48,813 57 | 314,259 21 | 70,000 00 | 18,619 71 | 10,326 06 | 1,340,266 89 | 2,661,250 64 |
| 15,432 61 | 31,288 25 | 20,702 80 | 11,908 50 | | 486,059 59 | 840,587 85 |
| | 557,092 98 | 96,000 00 | 189,596 80 | 4,698 31 | 2,401,949 60 | 6,748,233 22 |
| | 1,534,135 17 | | 536,197 41 | 16,196 71 | 3,129,034 32 | 12,777,024 25 |
| | 17,020,360 02 | 7,000 00 | 2,517,388 69 | 2,263,569 00 | 26,026,002 54 | 114,492,723 80 |
| | 601,522 37 | 35,000 00 | 67,332 52 | | 2,370,473 18 | 5,607,879 39 |
| | 14,078 09 | | | | 352,769 91 | 445,420 47 |
| 2,190 58 | 7,602 13 | | | 2,304 93 | 310,118 57 | 463,551 25 |
| | 985,058 63 | | 132,169 34 | 16,275 68 | 2,315,642 78 | 7,006,873 99 |
| | 30,559 66 | | 1,220 66 | 159 48 | 213,798 67 | 376,474 37 |

TABLE NO. 7—

| Name of company. | Location. | Losses and claims. | | Dividends to policyholders. |
|---|---|---|---|---|
| | | Death losses and endowments. | Annuities, involving life contingencies. | |
| The Guardian Life | New York, N. Y. | $ 2,217,976 25 | $ 11,344 87 | $ 1,024,520 60 |
| Home Life | New York, N. Y. | 2,888,245 23 | 46,903 93 | 729,026 77 |
| Indiana National Life | Indianapolis, Ind. | 98,748 11 | | 31,800 57 |
| Indianapolis Life | Indianapolis, Ind. | 83,958 97 | | 79,178 22 |
| International Life | St. Louis, Mo. | 744,630 88 | 760 51 | 371,814 74 |
| John Hancock Mutual Life | Boston, Mass. | 12,589,172 21 | 941 00 | 3,170,929 44 |
| Kansas City Life | Kansas City, Mo. | 1,082,662 28 | 83 50 | 373,438 45 |
| LaFayette Life Ins. Co. | LaFayette, Ind. | 77,442 44 | | 52,126 18 |
| Lincoln National Life | Ft. Wayne, Ind. | 882,213 97 | 2,557 04 | 123,767 50 |
| Manhattan Life | New York, N. Y. | 1,258,572 39 | 10,739 83 | 60,551 58 |
| Maryland Assurance Corp. | Baltimore, Md. | 27,426 00 | | |
| Massachusetts Mutual Life | Springfield, Mass. | 5,941,399 75 | 22,022 77 | 4,834,478 12 |
| Merchants Life | Des Moines, Ia. | 637,102 96 | | |
| Metropolitan Life | New York, N. Y. | 66,842,738 64 | 471,887 63 | 10,838,110 66 |
| Michigan Mutual Life | Detroit, Mich. | 1,113,573 75 | 466 28 | 81,257 31 |
| Minnesota Mutual Life | St. Paul, Minn. | 449,847 31 | 973 60 | 280,244 66 |
| Missouri State Life | St. Louis, Mo. | 1,917,827 02 | 10,211 56 | 547,772 87 |
| Morris Plan Insurance Society | New York, N. Y. | 23,714 16 | | |
| Mutual Benefit Life | Newark, N. J. | 13,973,442 22 | 131,754 44 | 9,471,261 21 |
| Mutual Life | New York, N. Y. | 38,493,063 28 | 2,598,724 03 | 26,090,344 57 |
| National Life and Accident Ins. Co. | Nashville, Tenn. | 706,765 91 | | |
| National Life Ins. Co. | Montpelier, Vt. | 4,145,713 37 | 694,970 93 | 2,704,164 46 |
| New England Mutual Life | Boston, Mass. | 5,624,750 43 | 7,225 17 | 3,403,706 64 |
| New World Life | Spokane, Wash. | 69,646 45 | | 42,825 69 |
| New York Life | New York, N. Y. | 58,499,624 83 | 1,337,944 76 | 38,836,684 89 |
| Northern States Life | Hammond, Ind. | 70,192 00 | | 7,152 10 |
| Northwestern Mutual Life | Milwaukee, Wis. | 26,189,223 22 | 247,203 76 | 17,892,399 43 |
| Northwestern National Life | Minneapolis, Minn. | 776,587 76 | 1,260 08 | 401,002 22 |
| Old Line Ins. Co. | Lincoln, Neb. | 33,204 73 | | |
| Old Line Life Ins. Co. of America | Milwaukee, Wis. | 171,195 19 | | |
| Pacific Mutual Life | Los Angeles, Cal. | 3,359,690 25 | 46,628 47 | 1,330,579 09 |
| Pan American Life | New Orleans, La. | 404,326 50 | 169 33 | 113,409 49 |
| Penn Mutual Life | Philadelphia, Pa. | 13,599,678 47 | 499,184 10 | 7,424,971 64 |
| Peoples Life | Frankfort, Ind. | 83,500 51 | | 17,132 80 |
| Philadelphia Life | Philadelphia, Pa. | 669,355 09 | | 120,948 98 |
| Phoenix Mutual Life | Hartford, Conn. | 3,592,963 63 | 300,106 48 | 1,723,798 61 |
| Provident Life and Trust | Philadelphia, Pa. | 8,229,621 19 | 150,568 62 | 2,934,768 71 |
| Prudential Insurance Co. of America | Newark, N. J. | 42,643,629 77 | 296,402 32 | 16,537,822 39 |
| Re-insurance Life Co. of America | Des Moines, Ia. | 85,298 75 | | |
| Reliance Life | Pittsburgh, Pa. | 1,035,492 49 | 6,322 03 | 513,156 24 |
| Reserve Loan Life | Indianapolis, Ind. | 272,066 76 | | 10,704 97 |
| Security Life Ins. Co. of America | Richmond, Va. | 234,883 29 | 1,191 97 | 356 32 |
| Security Mutual Life | Binghamton, N. Y. | 754,756 09 | 632 31 | 139,779 14 |
| State Life | Indianapolis, Ind. | 1,123,394 03 | 1,656 48 | 771,006 78 |
| State Mutual Life Assurance | Worcester, Mass. | 3,914,197 32 | 46,180 65 | 1,590,450 63 |
| The Travelers Ins. Co. | Hartford, Conn. | 12,080,834 51 | 370,414 84 | 97,162 09 |
| Union Central Life | Cincinnati, Ohio | 10,212,128 81 | 36,627 72 | 4,640,058 68 |
| Union Mutual Life | Portland, Me. | 1,553,764 06 | 6,549 09 | 396,245 95 |
| United States Life | New York, N. Y. | 638,634 46 | 10,656 39 | 93 62 |
| Universal Life Ins. Co. | Dubuque, Ia. | 5,533 59 | | |
| Western and Southern Life | Cincinnati, Ohio | 2,153,920 56 | | |
| Western Union Life Ins. Co. | Spokane, Wash. | 252,390 00 | | 114,641 63 |
| Wisconsin National Life | Oshkosh, Wis. | 63,017 38 | | |
| Totals | | $438,112,571 93 | $9,716,740 53 | $188,223,396 73 |

Continued.

| On insurance lapsed and surrendered. | | Dividends to stockholders. | Supplementary contract payments, and dividends on deposit surrendered. | Adjustment in book value of ledger assets. | Other disbursements. | Total. |
|---|---|---|---|---|---|---|
| Notes and liens voided by lapse. | Paid in cash etc., including guaranteed dividends and similar allowances. | | | | | |
| | $ 1,206,904 10 | $ 24,000 00 | $ 29,938 14 | $ 3,509 97 | $ 2,244,844 63 | $ 6,763,038 56 |
| | 1,076,164 88 | | 63,538 90 | 12,646 00 | 1,761,390 98 | 6,577,916 69 |
| $ 5,769 36 | 56,925 02 | | 540 00 | | 259,821 17 | 453,604 23 |
| | 30,461 76 | 4,908 20 | 4,445 98 | 1,500 00 | 295,829 39 | 500,282 52 |
| | 376,660 45 | 212,129 09 | 110,641 28 | | 2,085,696 00 | 3,902,332 95 |
| | 4,782,872 47 | | 172,938 91 | 37,733 69 | 16,195,871 80 | 36,950,459 52 |
| 98,014 81 | 342,766 94 | 32,000 00 | 41,571 09 | | 1,854,305 45 | 3,824,842 52 |
| 6 58 | 26,245 66 | | 2,237 69 | | 203,892 01 | 361,950 56 |
| 15,229 02 | 210,498 19 | 75,000 00 | 15,436 05 | | 2,546,398 29 | 3,871,100 06 |
| 15,797 27 | 719,528 05 | 13,417 88 | 14,632 39 | 2,178 00 | 974,812 71 | 3,070,230 10 |
| | 314 01 | | | | 134,156 28 | 161,896 29 |
| | 2,344,111 50 | | 1,024,649 43 | 42,257 14 | 5,286,863 28 | 19,495,781 99 |
| 40,889 66 | 53,059 47 | | 3,200 00 | | 741,529 57 | 1,475,781 66 |
| 185,163 11 | 13,010,572 94 | | 463,259 11 | 2,815,119 66 | 76,569,656 18 | 171,196,507 93 |
| 3,556 35 | 369,564 84 | 40,000 00 | 7,922 46 | | 795,413 73 | 2,411,754 72 |
| 2,000 40 | 153,009 25 | | 10,165 19 | 301 00 | 884,280 99 | 1,780,822 40 |
| | 821,066 12 | 100,000 00 | 113,923 28 | 10,903 75 | 3,892,282 30 | 7,413,986 90 |
| | | | | 13 50 | 106,999 23 | 130,726 89 |
| | 5,631,564 91 | | 884,723 77 | 76,850 84 | 7,850,487 22 | 38,023,084 61 |
| | 28,057,106 90 | | 883,175 90 | 6,851,327 05 | 22,802,169 78 | 125,775,911 51 |
| | 332 84 | | | | 1,128,667 54 | 1,835,766 29 |
| | 1,355,054 54 | | 79,923 93 | 316,816 16 | 3,271,644 80 | 12,568,288 19 |
| | 1,782,946 41 | | 189,561 07 | 86,886 10 | 4,330,840 68 | 15,425,916 50 |
| 23,255 23 | 79,913 41 | 90,760 00 | 4,343 62 | 388 27 | 472,833 54 | 783,966 21 |
| | 25,634,154 78 | | 1,982,952 20 | 836,396 53 | 34,837,007 02 | 161,964,765 01 |
| 12 00 | 33,814 47 | 12,960 00 | 1,379 19 | | 136,530 82 | 262,040 58 |
| | 9,581,540 90 | | 917,353 60 | 922,881 73 | 14,007,691 84 | 69,758,294 48 |
| | 221,463 55 | | 9,433 49 | 95 20 | 1,353,307 81 | 2,763,150 11 |
| 31,857 96 | 1,471 48 | | | | 202,446 70 | 268,980 87 |
| 5,276 35 | 30,934 78 | 67,263 50 | 3,820 16 | 17,400 31 | 397,192 28 | 693,082 57 |
| 150 03 | 1,582,281 28 | 73,711 01 | 68,485 19 | 2,315 26 | 4,511,983 75 | 10,975,824 33 |
| 5,565 19 | 272,867 80 | 100,000 00 | 39,941 76 | 67,200 00 | 1,182,845 53 | 2,186,325 60 |
| 137,107 26 | 5,018,113 53 | | 919,624 98 | 170,250 16 | 7,377,566 55 | 35,146,496 69 |
| 3,510 40 | 34,823 81 | 6,000 00 | 1,222 37 | | 217,006 97 | 363,196 86 |
| 29,415 92 | 143,398 48 | 33,619 20 | 2,718 13 | 1,045 46 | 776,303 50 | 1,776,804 76 |
| | 1,120,559 95 | | 312,982 19 | 126,444 77 | 2,894,557 19 | 10,071,412 82 |
| | 2,763,659 29 | | 202,934 09 | 57,012 13 | 4,898,588 03 | 19,237,152 06 |
| | 9,492,658 50 | 400,000 00 | 1,005,724 50 | 3,004,959 92 | 52,354,645 03 | 125,735,842 43 |
| | | 30,000 00 | 889 00 | 50 00 | 81,193 31 | 197,431 06 |
| 32,270 88 | 180,793 25 | 60,000 00 | 13,962 42 | 163,928 67 | 2,625,396 96 | 4,631,322 94 |
| 21,804 91 | 530,851 49 | 8,000 00 | 9,115 77 | 144 50 | 776,950 90 | 1,629,639 30 |
| 20,282 85 | 143,187 68 | | 9,288 54 | | 430,768 67 | 839,959 32 |
| | 459,371 24 | | 10,178 66 | 1,170 30 | 857,350 14 | 2,223,238 78 |
| 71,330 50 | 495,286 94 | | 36,046 53 | | 1,813,272 91 | 4,311,994 17 |
| | 1,334,670 88 | | 222,990 18 | 200,171 09 | 2,400,605 81 | 9,709,266 56 |
| | 2,397,943 55 | | 948,258 66 | 220,160 45 | 11,593,045 22 | 27,707,819 32 |
| 159,017 62 | 2,703,761 15 | 200,000 00 | 261,513 49 | 44,038 67 | 8,240,343 40 | 26,497,489 54 |
| 113,273 10 | 650,348 86 | | 21,781 48 | 20,166 23 | 583,999 74 | 3,346,128 51 |
| 4,912 00 | 389,763 62 | | 6,047 11 | 1,465 20 | 473,136 68 | 1,524,709 08 |
| | | | | | 110,889 71 | 116,423 30 |
| | 222,945 62 | 650,000 00 | | 28,013 40 | 3,647,715 72 | 6,702,595 30 |
| 29,782 98 | 155,910 29 | 16,000 00 | 600 00 | 3,849 68 | 540,293 49 | 1,113,468 07 |
| | 20,334 70 | 24,000 00 | 1,502 50 | 1,918 07 | 197,535 31 | 308,307 96 |
| $1,472,970 94 | $155,373,845 18 | $3,046,431 68 | $15,273,917 94 | $18,577,210 61 | $374,639,824 65 | $1,204,436,910 19 |

TABLE NO. 7—

| Name of company. | Location. | Losses and claims. Death losses and endowments. | Losses and claims. Annuities, involving life contingencies. | Dividends to policyholders. |
|---|---|---|---|---|
| III. COMPANIES OF FOREIGN GOVERNMENTS. | | | | |
| Canada Life Assurance Co. | Toronto, Can. | $3,504,566 55 | $438,139 99 | $1,512,762 87 |
| Manufacturers Life | Toronto, Can. | 1,820,267 08 | 9,776 83 | 489,624 04 |
| North American Life Assurance Co. | Toronto, Can. | 952,105 69 | 15,176 87 | 456,998 71 |
| Totals | | $6,276,939 32 | $463,093 69 | $2,459,385 62 |
| Aggregate | | $449,614,072 59 | $10,211,776 82 | $191,417,624 38 |

TABLE

SHOWING DETAILED STATEMENT OF POLICY

| Name of company—location. | Policies in force at commencement of year. Number. | Policies in force at commencement of year. Amount. | Policies issued, restored and increased during the year. Number. | Policies issued, restored and increased during the year. Amount. |
|---|---|---|---|---|
| I. COMPANIES OF THIS STATE. | | | | |
| The American Bankers Ins. Co., Chicago | 18,415 | $ 18,240,621 00 | 3,041 | $ 4,252,580 00 |
| Central Life Insurance Co. of Ill., Ottawa | 18,010 | 36,055,024 00 | 3,470 | 8,915,081 00 |
| Chicago National Life Ins. Co., Chicago | | | | |
| Cloverleaf Life and Cas. Co., Jacksonville | 4,487 | 6,275,604 00 | 3,177 | 2,564,648 00 |
| Continental Assurance Co., Chicago | 10,451 | 17,727,585 00 | 4,646 | 10,025,293 00 |
| Elgin Life Ins. Co., Elgin | 839 | 1,129,643 00 | 53 | 87,815 00 |
| Federal Life, Chicago | 20,865 | 46,427,362 00 | 3,608 | 12,261,318 00 |
| The Franklin Life, Springfield | 53,870 | 120,754,072 00 | 13,922 | 35,181,914 00 |
| Illinois Life, Chicago | 63,277 | 128,582,376 27 | 9,400 | 26,459,570 20 |
| International Life and Trust Co., Moline | 2,265 | 4,513,450 83 | 885 | 1,926,913 02 |
| Liberty Life Ins. Co., Chicago | | | 184 | 256,500 00 |
| Marquette Life, Springfield | 5,401 | 6,365,399 00 | 890 | 1,298,014 00 |
| Mutual Life of Illinois, Springfield | 2,620 | 5,591,500 00 | 850 | 2,035,212 00 |
| Mutual Trust Life, Chicago | 38,532 | 66,175,685 00 | 6,385 | 14,574,905 00 |
| National Life of U. S. A., Chicago | 70,320 | 134,086,132 00 | 9,021 | 24,486,930 00 |
| North American Life Ins. Co. of Chi., Chicago | 26,373 | 60,064,817 00 | 5,279 | 14,138,951 00 |
| Old Colony Life, Chicago | 16,577 | 22,236,549 85 | 5,638 | 6,410,672 78 |
| Peoples Life, Chicago | 8,553 | 4,417,757 09 | 2,961 | 2,921,677 46 |
| Peoria Life, Peoria | 26,873 | 59,009,042 00 | 5,863 | 15,137,829 00 |
| Providers' Life Assurance Co., Chicago | 18,273 | 6,828,658 00 | 3,923 | 1,590,150 00 |
| Public Life Ins. Co., Chicago | 670 | 1,404,500 00 | 754 | 1,255,500 00 |
| Rockford Life, Rockford | 4,954 | 8,061,836 00 | 1,481 | 3,527,821 00 |
| Standard Life, Decatur | 31,703 | 45,676,720 00 | 2,730 | 6,258,621 00 |
| Totals | 443,328 | $799,624,334 04 | 88,161 | $195,567,915 46 |
| II. COMPANIES OF OTHER STATES. | | | | |
| Aetna Life, Hartford, Conn. | 266,575 | $802,125,276 08 | 38,617 | $175,264,962 27 |
| American Central Life, Indianapolis, Ind. | 38,183 | 101,130,720 00 | 8,097 | 31,942,453 00 |
| American Life Ins. Co., Detroit, Mich. | 13,250 | 30,829,093 00 | 13,858 | 39,167,661 38 |
| American Life Reinsurance Co., Dallas, Tex. | 5,058 | 19,025,345 00 | 2,618 | 15,193,056 00 |
| American National Assur. Co., St. Louis, Mo. | 6,554 | 12,293,285 00 | 1,883 | 3,913,100 00 |

Concluded.

| On insurance lapsed and surrendered. | | Dividends to stockholders. | Supplementary contract payments, and dividends on deposit surrendered. | Adjustment in book value of ledger assets. | Other disbursements. | Total. |
|---|---|---|---|---|---|---|
| Notes and liens voided by lapse. | Paid in cash etc., including guaranteed dividends and similar allowances. | | | | | |
| ---------- | $1,076,296 26 | $250,000 00 | $59,099 83 | $17,328 29 | $5,709,011 05 | $12,567,204 84 |
| ---------- | 675,278 25 | 24,000 00 | 9,274 72 | 98,019 05 | 2,549,014 23 | 5,675,254 20 |
| ---------- | 541,353 62 | 6,000 00 | 6,459 25 | 2,028 50 | 1,143,812 22 | 3,123,934 86 |
| ---------- | $2,292,928 13 | $280,000 00 | $74,833 80 | $117,375 84 | $9,401,837 50 | $21,366,393 90 |
| $1,752,498 06 | $160,253,756 07 | $3,857,915 88 | $15,478,949 50 | $18,734,002 46 | $394,727,799 49 | $1,246,048,395 25 |

# NO. 8.

## ACCOUNTS OF EACH COMPANY FOR THE YEAR 1921.

| Total. | | Policies terminated during the year. | | Policies in force at end of year. | | |
|---|---|---|---|---|---|---|
| Number. | Amount. | Number. | Amount. | Number. | Amount. | Average. |
| 21,456 | $ 22,493,201 00 | 4,391 | $ 3,828,351 00 | 17,065 | $ 18,664,850 00 | $1,093 75 |
| 21,480 | 44,970,105 00 | 2,109 | 5,648,773 00 | 19,371 | 39,321,332 00 | 2,029 91 |
| 7,664 | 8,840,252 00 | 2,674 | 2,355,819 00 | 4,990 | 6,484,433 00 | 1,299 49 |
| 15,097 | 27,752,878 00 | 2,713 | 5,094,044 00 | 12,384 | 22,658,834 00 | 1,829 69 |
| 892 | 1,217,458 00 | 54 | 82,983 00 | 838 | 1,134,475 00 | 1,353 79 |
| 24,473 | 58,688,680 00 | 4,944 | 11,982,544 00 | 19,529 | 46,706,136 00 | 2,391 63 |
| 67,792 | 155,935,986 00 | 10,078 | 26,099,376 00 | 57,714 | 129,836,610 00 | 2,249 66 |
| 72,677 | 155,041,946 47 | 6,680 | 18,556,901 20 | 65,997 | 136,485,045 27 | 2,068 05 |
| 3,150 | 6,440,363 85 | 651 | 1,421,011 28 | 2,499 | 5,019,352 57 | 2,008 54 |
| 184 | 256,500 00 | 2 | 2,000 00 | 182 | 254,500 00 | 1,398 36 |
| 6,291 | 7,663,413 00 | 497 | 696,404 00 | 5,794 | 6,967,009 00 | 1,202 45 |
| 3,470 | 7,626,712 00 | 727 | 1,565,949 00 | 2,743 | 6,060,763 00 | 2,209 54 |
| 44,917 | 80,750,590 00 | 4,377 | 11,057,381 00 | 40,540 | 69,693,209 00 | 1,719 12 |
| 79,341 | 158,573,062 00 | 9,068 | 21,623,346 00 | 70,273 | 136,949,716 00 | 1,948 82 |
| 31,652 | 74,203,768 00 | 4,768 | 14,037,043 00 | 26,884 | 60,166,725 00 | 2,238 01 |
| 22,215 | 28,647,222 63 | 3,725 | 5,708,669 56 | 18,490 | 22,938,553 07 | 1,240 59 |
| 11,514 | 7,339,434 55 | 1,255 | 599,096 78 | 10,259 | 6,740,337 77 | 657 03 |
| 32,736 | 74,146,871 00 | 2,976 | 7,763,006 00 | 29,760 | 66,383,865 00 | 2,230 65 |
| 22,196 | 8,418,808 00 | 4,159 | 1,495,411 00 | 18,037 | 6,923,397 00 | 383 84 |
| 1,424 | 2,660,000 00 | 115 | 226,000 00 | 1,309 | 2,434,000 00 | 1,859 43 |
| 6,435 | 11,589,657 00 | 832 | 1,579,747 00 | 5,603 | 10,009,910 00 | 1,786 53 |
| 34,433 | 51,935,341 00 | 3,924 | 8,082,320 00 | 30,509 | 43,853,021 00 | 1,437 38 |
| 531,489 | $995,192,249 50 | 70,719 | $149,506,175 82 | 460,770 | $845,686,073 68 | $1,835 38 |
| 305,192 | $977,390,238 35 | 24,702 | $91,475,020 44 | 280,490 | $885,915,217 91 | $3,158 46 |
| 46,280 | 133,073,173 00 | 8,432 | 26,742,677 00 | 37,848 | 106,330,496 00 | 2,809 41 |
| 33,108 | 69,996,754 38 | 3,978 | 9,969,238 90 | 29,130 | 60,027,515 48 | 2,060 68 |
| 7,676 | 34,218,401 00 | 1,782 | 7,072,358 00 | 5,894 | 27,146,043 00 | 4,605 71 |
| 8,437 | 16,206,385 00 | 2,168 | 4,209,663 00 | 6,269 | 11,996,722 00 | 1,913 66 |

TABLE NO. 8—

| Name of company—location. | Policies in force at commencement of year. | | Policies issued, restored and increased during the year. | |
|---|---|---|---|---|
| | Number. | Amount. | Number. | Amount. |
| Bankers Life Co., Des Moines, Iowa | 238,792 | $ 555,483,313 00 | 33,258 | $111,683,013 00 |
| Bankers Life Ins. Co., Lincoln, Neb | 55,643 | 95,731,028 23 | 4,139 | 8,056,199 86 |
| Bankers Reserve Life Co., Omaha, Neb | 36,811 | 77,395,695 02 | 8,055 | 18,672,875 53 |
| Berkshire Life, Pittsfield, Mass | 45,514 | 122,898,422 00 | 4,708 | 16,543,549 00 |
| Business Men's Assurance Co. of America, Kansas City, Mo | 637 | 2,007,500 00 | 846 | 2,026,675 00 |
| Capitol Life Ins. Co. of Colo., Denver, Colo. | 20,241 | 40,441,880 19 | 3,772 | 9,813,768 81 |
| Central Life Assur. Society of U. S. (Mutual) Des Moines, Iowa | 54,762 | 105,726,633 00 | 10,118 | 22,721,822 00 |
| Central States Life Ins. Co., St. Louis, Mo | 28,708 | 57,429,868 00 | 5,726 | 15,069,457 00 |
| Century Life, Indianapolis, Ind | 3,067 | 7,337,066 00 | 1,006 | 2,692,793 00 |
| Cleveland Life, Cleveland, Ohio | 17,996 | 29,180,486 00 | 2,691 | 4,942,515 00 |
| Columbian National Life, Boston, Mass | 49,751 | 139,097,910 80 | 7,727 | 28,112,377 15 |
| Columbus Mut. Life Ins. Co., Columbus, Ohio | 15,444 | 28,062,776 00 | 5,221 | 11,364,362 00 |
| Connecticut General Life, Hartford, Conn | 89,160 | 289,611,086 11 | 17,451 | 84,939,779 08 |
| Connecticut Mutual Life, Hartford, Conn | 144,863 | 382,709,528 20 | 18,586 | 62,527,294 29 |
| Equitable Life Assurance Society of the U. S., New York, N. Y | 842,119 | 2,258,013,825 00 | 131,028 | 436,312,658 00 |
| Equitable Life, Des Moines, Iowa | 127,385 | 254,538,407 24 | 20,580 | 55,904,487 32 |
| Farmers National Life, Huntington, Ind | 9,610 | 18,009,454 00 | 3,740 | 8,164,779 00 |
| Federal Union Life, Cincinnati, Ohio | 23,702 | 16,519,737 00 | 6,172 | 4,124,464 00 |
| The Fidelity Mutual Life, Philadelphia, Pa | 83,345 | 203,980,056 00 | 12,464 | 41,850,363 00 |
| Girard Life, Philadelphia, Pa | 6,174 | 15,866,119 00 | 1,665 | 4,559,346 00 |
| The Guardian Life, New York, N. Y | 103,849 | 227,918,950 00 | 13,168 | 37,726,260 00 |
| Home Life, New York, N. Y | 89,427 | 212,483,100 00 | 10,891 | 31,810,915 00 |
| Indiana National Life, Indianapolis, Ind | 9,590 | 16,556,679 00 | 1,191 | 2,448,780 00 |
| Indianapolis Life, Indianapolis, Ind | 14,491 | 26,438,143 90 | 3,612 | 6,948,094 09 |
| International Life, St. Louis, Mo | 57,161 | 130,352,075 00 | 11,783 | 39,597,327 00 |
| John Hancock Mutual Life, Boston, Mass | 529,286 | 766,995,993 00 | 88,634 | 133,767,117 00 |
| Kansas City Life, Kansas City, Mo | 107,600 | 220,336,167 00 | 15,644 | 38,263,787 00 |
| La Fayette Life Ins. Co., La Fayette, Ind | 8,618 | 15,024,714 00 | 1,853 | 3,869,591 00 |
| Lincoln National Life, Ft. Wayne, Ind | 68,675 | 158,574,378 27 | 33,323 | 80,961,063 99 |
| Manhattan Life, New York, N. Y | 34,538 | 69,556,702 00 | 4,503 | 11,616,767 00 |
| Maryland Assurance Corp., Baltimore, Md | 2,113 | 6,108,077 00 | 1,116 | 3,209,043 00 |
| Massachusetts Mutual Life, Springfield, Mass. | 265,671 | 728,743,346 00 | 33,928 | 136,157,351 00 |
| Merchants Life, Des Moines, Iowa | 42,451 | 85,202,044 63 | 5,674 | 15,303,395 76 |
| Metropolitan Life, New York, N. Y | 3,017,410 | 3,220,333,783 00 | 645,125 | 769,742,595 00 |
| Michigan Mutual Life, Detroit, Mich | 48,094 | 85,737,673 48 | 5,215 | 12,935,220 81 |
| Minnesota Mutual Life, St. Paul, Minn | 30,597 | 76,659,380 43 | 5,760 | 18,821,588 91 |
| Missouri State Life, St. Louis, Mo | 134,166 | 293,755,352 00 | 29,412 | 91,536,883 00 |
| Morris Plan Ins. Society, New York, N. Y | 62 | 82,700 00 | 2,928 | 1,402,800 00 |
| Mutual Benefit Life, Newark, N. J | 456,044 | 1,311,052,551 00 | 41,282 | 168,516,755 00 |
| Mutual Life, New York, N. Y | 929,511 | 2,357,973,121 00 | 96,602 | 343,750,863 00 |
| National Life and Accident Ins. Co., Nashville, Tenn | 3,132 | 5,065,100 00 | 4,189 | 9,162,750 00 |
| National Life Ins. Co., Montepelier, Vt | 133,689 | 309,455,304 00 | 16,430 | 50,453,617 00 |
| New England Mutual Life, Boston, Mass | 199,794 | 560,773,236 00 | 20,612 | 82,072,020 00 |
| New World Life, Spokane, Wash | 13,347 | 29,021,090 98 | 3,004 | 7,562,544 75 |
| New York Life, New York, N. Y | 1,605,035 | 3,537,298,756 00 | 207,286 | 603,156,334 00 |
| Northern States Life, Hammond, Ind | 6,513 | 11,310,286 00 | 726 | 2,304,548 00 |
| Northwestern Mutual Life, Milwaukee, Wis | 729,715 | 2,196,673,032 00 | 65,691 | 267,911,313 00 |
| Northwestern Nat. Life, Minneapolis, Minn | 53,307 | 121,232,330 00 | 12,657 | 37,630,265 00 |
| Old Line Ins. Co., Lincoln, Neb | 5,486 | 13,457,500 00 | 1,997 | 5,195,000 00 |
| Old Line Life Ins. Co. of Am., Milwaukee, Wis | 16,351 | 32,988,549 13 | 5,797 | 13,508,325 00 |
| Pacific Mutual Life, Los Angeles, Cal | 149,633 | 350,408,951 00 | 25,131 | 81,184,108 00 |
| Pan American Life, New Orleans, La | 36,784 | 86,558,535 00 | 9,265 | 24,140,154 00 |
| Penn Mutual Life, Philadelphia, Pa | 326,801 | 1,029,203,157 00 | 31,876 | 136,509,538 00 |
| Peoples Life, Frankfort, Ind | 12,223 | 20,541,571 00 | 2,692 | 4,858,746 00 |
| Philadelphia Life, Philadelphia, Pa | 23,550 | 59,723,596 00 | 5,137 | 14,806,955 00 |

Continued.

| Total. | | Policies terminated during the year. | | Policies in force at end of year. | | |
|---|---|---|---|---|---|---|
| Number. | Amount. | Number. | Amount. | Number. | Amount. | Average. |
| 272,050 | $ 667,166,326 00 | 18,294 | $ 56,490,717 00 | 253,756 | $ 610,675,609 00 | $2,406 55 |
| 59,782 | 103,787,228 09 | 4,465 | 8,947,217 03 | 55,317 | 94,840,011 06 | 1,714 48 |
| 44,866 | 96,068,570 55 | 6,387 | 16,089,542 75 | 38,479 | 79,979,027 80 | 2,078 51 |
| 50,222 | 139,441,971 00 | 2,472 | 8,414,909 00 | 47,750 | 131,027,062 00 | 2,744 02 |
| 1,483 | 4,034,175 00 | 164 | 466,000 00 | 1,319 | 3,568,175 00 | 2,705 21 |
| 24,013 | 50,255,649 00 | 4,975 | 11,702,740 00 | 19,038 | 38,552,909 00 | 2,025 05 |
| 64,880 | 128,448,455 00 | 8,447 | 20,207,478 00 | 56,433 | 108,240,977 00 | 1,918 03 |
| 34,434 | 72,499,325 00 | 6,491 | 16,587,243 00 | 27,943 | 55,912,082 00 | 2,000 93 |
| 4,073 | 10,029,859 00 | 1,219 | 2,738,706 00 | 2,854 | 7,291,153 00 | 2,554 71 |
| 20,687 | 34,123,001 00 | 1,917 | 3,436,818 00 | 18,770 | 30,686,183 00 | 1,634 85 |
| 57,478 | 167,210,287 95 | 4,759 | 16,433,436 86 | 52,719 | 150,776,851 09 | 2,860 01 |
| 20,665 | 39,427,138 00 | 2,023 | 4,321,469 00 | 18,642 | 35,105,669 00 | 1,883 15 |
| 106,611 | 374,550;865 19 | 7,616 | 37,409,277 30 | 98,995 | 337,141,587 89 | 3,405 64 |
| 163,449 | 445,236,822 49 | 10,485 | 31,997,818 53 | 152,964 | 413,239,003 96 | 2,701 54 |
| 973,147 | 2,694,326,483 00 | 81,154 | 252,463,120 00 | 891,993 | 2,441,863,363 00 | 2,737 54 |
| 147,965 | 310,442,894 56 | 9,016 | 23,508,278 07 | 138,949 | 286,934,616 49 | 2,065 04 |
| 13,350 | 26,174,233 00 | 1,990 | 4,050,326 00 | 11,360 | 22,123,907 00 | 1,947 53 |
| 29,874 | 20,644,201 00 | 4,080 | 3,489,894 00 | 25,794 | 17,154,307 00 | 665 05 |
| 95,809 | 245,830,419 00 | 7,567 | 23,015,313 00 | 88,242 | 222,815,106 00 | 2,525 05 |
| 7,839 | 20,425,465 00 | 718 | 2,007,400 00 | 7,121 | 18,418,065 00 | 2,586 44 |
| 117,017 | 265,645,210 00 | 9,864 | 67,950,537 00 | 107,153 | 197,694,673 00 | 1,844 98 |
| 100,318 | 244,294,015 00 | 8,117 | 21,177,128 00 | 92,201 | 223,116,887 00 | 2,419,90 |
| 10,781 | 19,005,459 00 | 1,308 | 3,177,087 00 | 9,473 | 15,828,372 00 | 1,670 89 |
| 18,103 | 33,386,237 99 | 1,332 | 3,092,886 11 | 16,771 | 30,293,351 88 | 1,806 29 |
| 68,944 | 169,949,402 00 | 11,331 | 32,476,084 00 | 57,613 | 137,473,318 00 | 2,386 15 |
| 617,920 | 900,763,110 00 | 41,637 | 64,798,624 00 | 576,283 | 835,964,486 00 | 1,450 61 |
| 123,244 | 258,599,954 00 | 13,032 | 31,888,733 00 | 110,212 | 226,711,221 00 | 2,057 05 |
| 10,471 | 18,894,305 00 | 1,198 | 2,589,465 00 | 9,273 | 16,304,840 00 | 1,758 31 |
| 101,998 | 239,535;442 26 | 14,414 | 42,472,024 22 | 87,584 | 197,063,418 04 | 2,249 99 |
| 39,041 | 81,173,469 00 | 4,239 | 10,526,668 00 | 34,802 | 70,646,801 00 | 2,029 96 |
| 3,229 | 9,317,120 00 | 363 | 1,011,837 00 | 2,866 | 8,305,283 00 | 2,897 87 |
| 299,599 | 864,900,697 00 | 13,397 | 47,846,178 00 | 286,202 | 817,054,519 00 | 2,854 82 |
| 48,125 | 100,505,440 39 | 8,615 | 20,070,135 39 | 39,510 | 80,435,305 00 | 2,035 82 |
| 3,662,535 | 3,990,076,378 00 | 374,245 | 387,308,177 00 | 3,288,290 | 3,602,768,201 00 | 1,095 64 |
| 53,309 | 98,672,894 29 | 5,105 | 10,420,401 03 | 48,204 | 88,252,493 26 | 1,830 81 |
| 36,357 | 95,480,969 34 | 5,319 | 18,143,765 90 | 31,038 | 77,337,203 44 | 2,491 69 |
| 163,578 | 385,292,235 00 | 21,439 | 58,913,990 00 | 142,139 | 326,378,245 00 | 2,296 19 |
| 2,990 | 1,485,500 00 | 69 | 65,950 00 | 2,921 | 1,419,550 00 | 485 98 |
| 497,326 | 1,479,569,306 00 | 20,109 | 63,584,557 00 | 477,217 | 1,415,984,749 00 | 2,967 17 |
| 1,026,113 | 2,701,723,984 00 | 78,213 | 229,072,205 00 | 947,900 | 2,472,651,779 00 | 2,608 56 |
| 7,321 | 14,227,850 00 | 1,308 | 4,091,050 00 | 6,013 | 10,136,800 00 | 1,685 81 |
| 150,119 | 359,908,921 00 | 10,120 | 26,014,657 00 | 139,999 | 333,894,264 00 | 2,384 97 |
| 220,406 | 642,845,256 00 | 10,836 | 33,430,174 00 | 209,570 | 609,415,082 00 | 2,907 93 |
| 16,351 | 36,583,635 73 | 2,727 | 7,656,328 00 | 13,624 | 28,927,307 73 | 2,123 26 |
| 1,812,321 | 4,140,455,090 00 | 136,886 | 324,356,566 00 | 1,675,435 | 3,816,098,524 00 | 2,277 68 |
| 7,239 | 13,614,834 00 | 616 | 1,349,675 00 | 6,623 | 12,265,159 00 | 1,851 90 |
| 795,406 | 2,464,584,345 00 | 35,803 | 114,134,047 00 | 759,603 | 2,350,450,298 00 | 3,094 31 |
| 65,964 | 158,862,595 00 | 10,700 | 31,570,024 00 | 55,264 | 127,292,571 00 | 2,303 35 |
| 7,483 | 18,652,500 00 | 2,206 | 6,350,642 50 | 5,277 | 12,301,857 50 | 2,331 22 |
| 22,148 | 46,496,874 13 | 3,224 | 7,928,878 88 | 18,924 | 38,567,995 25 | 2,038 05 |
| 174,764 | 431,593,059 00 | 15,417 | 41,437,016 00 | 159,347 | 390,156,043 00 | 2,448 47 |
| 46,049 | 110,698,689 00 | 9,043 | 23,836,548 00 | 37,006 | 86,862,141 00 | 2,347 24 |
| 358,677 | 1,165,712,695 00 | 21,964 | 74,955,186 00 | 336,713 | 1,090,757,509 00 | 3,239 43 |
| 14,915 | 25,400,317 00 | 1,466 | 3,048,201 00 | 13,449 | 22.352.116 00 | 1,661 99 |
| 28,687 | 74,530,551 00 | 4,939 | 12,506,589 00 | 23,748 | 62,023,962 00 | 2,611 76 |

TABLE NO. 8—

| Name of company—location. | Policies in force at commencement of year. | | Policies issued, restored and increased during the year. | |
|---|---|---|---|---|
| | Number. | Amount. | Number. | Amount. |
| Phoenix Mutual Life, Hartford, Conn | 125,165 | $ 294,348,813 00 | 14,157 | $ 50,462,274 00 |
| Provident Life and Trust, Philadelphia, Pa | 198,417 | 535,003,953 00 | 27,225 | 87,607,287 00 |
| Prudential Ins. Co. of Am., Newark, N. J | 1,799,658 | 2,255,408,186 00 | 296,914 | 436,396,392 00 |
| Reinsurance Life Co. of Am., Des Moines, Ia | 4,718 | 21,969,076 00 | 2,042 | 12,490,444 00 |
| Reliance Life, Pittsburgh, Pa | 90,427 | 196,272,085 00 | 21,555 | 54,830,303 00 |
| Reserve Loan Life, Indianapolis, Ind | 25,600 | 47,178,238 00 | 7,055 | 16,203,215 00 |
| Security Life Ins. Co. of Am., Richmond, Va. | 19,896 | 35,675,435 00 | 5,686 | 11,105,026 00 |
| Security Mutual Life, Binghamton, N. Y | 42,943 | 67,252,413 00 | 5,208 | 9,981,540 00 |
| State Life, Indianapolis, Ind | 64,199 | 146,425,137 00 | 9,699 | 26,566,713 00 |
| State Mutual Life Assur., Worcester, Mass | 112,977 | 315,156,687 00 | 11,317 | 42,796,493 00 |
| The Travelers Ins. Co., Hartford, Conn | 359,640 | 1,142,693,571 00 | 76,013 | 293,379,012 00 |
| Union Central Life, Cincinnati, Ohio | 283,343 | 778,917,578 00 | 28,869 | 112,465,017 00 |
| Union Mutual Life, Portland, Me | 41,576 | 72,248,892 00 | 2,691 | 7,162,832 00 |
| United States Life, New York, N. Y | 14,103 | 24,545,618 00 | 1,439 | 3,144,742 00 |
| Universal Life Ins. Co., Dubuque, Iowa | 379 | 1,191,000 00 | 634 | 1,784,470 00 |
| Western and Southern Life, Cincinnati, Ohio | 53,859 | 52,983,835 00 | 17,977 | 18,721,930 00 |
| Western Union Life Ins. Co., Spokane, Wash. | 24,855 | 61,057,337 00 | 2,605 | 7,423,662 00 |
| Wisconsin National Life, Oshkosh, Wis | 12,434 | 18,794,125 46 | 2,558 | 4,151,982 95 |
| Totals | 14,762,247 | $30,106,162,414 15 | 2,367,804 | $5,701,079,560 95 |
| III. COMPANIES OF FOREIGN GOVERNMENTS. | | | | |
| Canada Life Assurance Co., Toronto, Can | 109,766 | $270,645,799 99 | 17,981 | $59,462,297 77 |
| Manufacturers Life, Toronto, Can | 93,613 | 178,710,411 00 | 18,916 | 42,085,215 00 |
| North American Life Assurance Co., Toronto, Can | 54,575 | 98,616,270 00 | 9,188 | 19,302,840 00 |
| Totals | 257,954 | $547,972,480 99 | 46,085 | $120,850,352 77 |
| Aggregate | 15,463,529 | $31,453,759,229 18 | 2,502,050 | $6,017,497,829 18 |
| I. COMPANIES OF THIS STATE—GROUP INSURANCE. | | | | |
| The American Bankers Ins. Co., Chicago | 3 | $297,250 00 | --------- | --------- |
| The Franklin Life, Springfield | --------- | --------- | 1 | $167,500 00 |
| Totals | 3 | $297,250 00 | 1 | $167,500 00 |
| II. COMPANIES OF OTHER STATES—GROUP INSURANCE. | | | | |
| Aetna Life, Hartford, Conn | 1,301 | $353,464,065 00 | | $149,352,812 00 |
| Capitol Life Ins. Co. of Colo., Denver, Colo. | 19 | 7,798,920 00 | | 6,805,810 00 |
| Connecticut General Life, Hartford, Conn | 268 | 72,776,847 00 | 90<br>42 | 32,982,477 00 |
| Equitable Life Assurance Society of the U. S., New York, N. Y | 1,079 | 398,511,146 00 | 193 | 160,527,802 00 |
| The Guardian Life, New York, N. Y | 2 | 516,578 00 | --------- | 99,867 00 |
| International Life, St. Louis, Mo | 3 | 276,000 00 | 2 | 585,300 00 |
| Lincoln National Life, Ft. Wayne, Ind | 4 | 775,000 00 | --------- | 348,000 00 |
| Maryland Assurance Corp., Baltimore, Md | 4 | 1,458,103 00 | --------- | 581,680 00 |
| Metropolitan Life, New York, N. Y | 1,179 | 280,014,613 00 | 186 | 128,206,617 00 |
| Minnesota Mutual Life, St. Paul, Minn | 8 | 945,100 00 | --------- | 254,093 49 |
| Missouri State Life, St. Louis, Mo | 53 | 8,573,452 00 | 43 | 9,530,063 00 |
| National Life and Accident Ins. Co., Nashville, Tenn | --------- | --------- | 1 | 2,000,000 00 |
| The Northwestern National Life, Minneapolis, Minn | 10,530 | 12,735,249 00 | 3,842 | 4,578,374 00 |
| Pan American Life, New Orleans, La | 6 | 800,050 00 | --------- | 307,450 00 |
| Philadelphia Life, Philadelphia, Pa | 4 | 804,200 00 | --------- | 115,500 00 |
| Prudential Ins. Co. of Am., Newark, N. J | 301 | 45,711,457 00 | 40 | 16,934,161 00 |
| The Travelers Ins. Co., Hartford, Conn | 1,852 | 433,645,422 00 | 173 | 183,744,164 00 |
| United States Life, New York, N. Y | 82 | 150,350 00 | 2 | 31,234 00 |
| Totals | 16,695 | $1,618,056,552 00 | 4,617 | $696,985,404 49 |

Continued.

| Total. | | Policies terminated during the year. | | Policies in force at end of year. | | |
|---|---|---|---|---|---|---|
| Number. | Amount. | Number. | Amount. | Number. | Amount. | Average. |
| 139,322 | $ 344,811,087 00 | 8,063 | $ 22,085,857 00 | 131,259 | $ 322,725,230 00 | $2,458 69 |
| 225,642 | 622,611,240 00 | 13,696 | 47,887,383 00 | 211,946 | 574,723,857 00 | 2,711 65 |
| 2,096,572 | 2,691,804,578 00 | 167,363 | 223,798,582 00 | 1,929,209 | 2,468,005,996 00 | 1,279 28 |
| 6,760 | 34,459,520 00 | 2,014 | 9,294,142 00 | 4,746 | 25,165,378 00 | 5,302 44 |
| 111,982 | 251,102,388 00 | 14,041 | 32,836,350 00 | 97,941 | 218,266,038 00 | 2,228 55 |
| 32,655 | 63,381,453 00 | 6,078 | 13,066,102 00 | 26,577 | 50,315,351 00 | 1,893 19 |
| 25,582 | 46,780,461 00 | 5,119 | 9,679,500 00 | 20,463 | 37,100,961 00 | 1,813 08 |
| 48,151 | 77,233,953 00 | 4,395 | 8,142,844 00 | 43,756 | 69,091,109 00 | 1,579 00 |
| 73,898 | 172,991,850 00 | 8,306 | 22,081,339 00 | 65,592 | 150,910,511 00 | 2,300 75 |
| 124,294 | 357,953,180 00 | 5,997 | 19,676,585 00 | 118,297 | 338,276,595 00 | 2,859 55 |
| 435,653 | 1,436,072,583 00 | 28,049 | 104,026,384 00 | 407,604 | 1,332,046,199 00 | 3,267 99 |
| 312,212 | 891,382,595 00 | 19,861 | 59,510,583 00 | 292,351 | 831,872,012 00 | 2,845 46 |
| 44,267 | 79,411,724 00 | 3,568 | 6,366,734 00 | 40,699 | 73,044,990 00 | 1,794 76 |
| 15,542 | 27,690,360 00 | 1,782 | 3,429,800 00 | 13,760 | 24,260,560 00 | 1,763 12 |
| 1,013 | 2,975,470 00 | 59 | 168,500 00 | 954 | 2,806,970 00 | 2,942 32 |
| 71,836 | 71,705,765 00 | 11,776 | 11,106,000 00 | 60,060 | 60,599,765 00 | 1,008 99 |
| 27,460 | 68,480,999 00 | 4,757 | 15,220,945 00 | 22,703 | 53,260,054 00 | 2,345 95 |
| 14,992 | 22,946,108 41 | 1,418 | 2,352,091 69 | 13,574 | 20,594,016 72 | 1,517 17 |
| 17,130,051 | $35,807,241,975 10 | 1,432,244 | $3,123,228,397 60 | 15,697,807 | $32,684,013,577 50 | $2,082 08 |
| 127,747 | $330,108,097 76 | 7,709 | $20,949,762 81 | 120,038 | $309,158,334 95 | $2,575 50 |
| 112,529 | 220,795,626 00 | 8,452 | 20,444,981 00 | 104,077 | 200,350,645 00 | 1,925 02 |
| 63,763 | 117,919,110 00 | 6,304 | 12,821,313 00 | 57,459 | 105,097,797 00 | 1,829 09 |
| 304,039 | $668,822,833 76 | 22,465 | $54,216,056 81 | 281,574 | $614,606,776 95 | $2,182 75 |
| 17,965,579 | $37,471,257,058 36 | 1,525,428 | $3,326,950,630 23 | 16,440,151 | $34,144,306,428 13 | $2,076 89 |
| 3 | $297,250 00 | 3 | $297,250 00 | ------ | ------ | ------ |
| 1 | 167,500 00 | ------ | ------ | 1 | $167,500 00 | $167,500 00 |
| 4 | $464,750 00 | 3 | $297,250 00 | 1 | $167,500 00 | $167,500 00 |
| 1,391 | $502,816,877 00 | 145 | $184,731,697 00 | 1,246 | $318,085,180 00 | $255,285 05 |
| 22 | 14,604,730 00 | 3 | 4,448,620 00 | 19 | 10,156,110 00 | 53,453 21 |
| 310 | 105,759,324 00 | 31 | 32,652,778 00 | 279 | 73,106,546 00 | 262,030 63 |
| 1,272 | 559,038,948 00 | 93 | 182,931,579 00 | 1,179 | 376,107,369 00 | 319,005 40 |
| 2 | 616,445 00 | 1 | 213,148 00 | 1 | 403,297 00 | 403,297 00 |
| 5 | 861,300 00 | ------ | 94,700 00 | 5 | 766,600 00 | 153,320 00 |
| 4 | 1,123,000 00 | ------ | 211,000 00 | 4 | 912,000 00 | 228,000 00 |
| 4 | 2,039,783 00 | ------ | 273,905 00 | 4 | 1,765,878 00 | 441,469 50 |
| 1,365 | 408,221,230 00 | 170 | 118,722,157 00 | 1,195 | 289,499,073 00 | 242,258 63 |
| 8 | 1,199,193 49 | 2 | 407,193 49 | 6 | 792,000 00 | 132,000 00 |
| 96 | 18,103,515 00 | 3 | 4,064,732 00 | 93 | 14,038,783 00 | 150,954 66 |
| 1 | 2,000,000 00 | 1 | 2,000,000 00 | ------ | ------ | ------ |
| 14,372 | 17,313,623 00 | 4,520 | 4,737,305 00 | 9,852 | 12,576,318 00 | 1,276 52 |
| 6 | 1,107,500 00 | 1 | 320,900 00 | 5 | 786,600 00 | 157,320 00 |
| 4 | 919,700 00 | ------ | 65,900 00 | 4 | 853,800 00 | 213,450 00 |
| 341 | 62,645,618 00 | 45 | 17,263,298 00 | 296 | 45,382,320 00 | 15,331 86 |
| 2,025 | 617,389,586 00 | 230 | 192,945,959 00 | 1,795 | 424,443,627 00 | 236,458 84 |
| 84 | 181,584 00 | 6 | 13,040 00 | 78 | 168,544 00 | 2,160 87 |
| 21,312 | $2,315,941,956 49 | 5,251 | $746,097,911 49 | 16,061 | $1,569,844,045 00 | $97,742 60 |

TABLE NO. 8—

| Name of company—location. | Policies in force at commencement of year. Number. | Amount. | Policies issued, restored and increased during the year. Number. | Amount. |
|---|---|---|---|---|
| III. COMPANIES OF FOREIGN GOVERNMENTS—GROUP INSURANCE. | | | | |
| Canada Life Assurance Co., Toronto, Can | 18 | $2,322,950 00 | 21 | $5,266,650 00 |
| Manufacturers Life, Toronto, Can | 1 | 47,500 00 | | 10,800 00 |
| Totals | 19 | $2,370,450 00 | 21 | $5,277,450 00 |
| Aggregate group | 16,717 | $1,621,624,252 00 | 4,639 | $702,430,354 49 |
| I. COMPANIES OF THIS STATE—INDUSTRIAL BUSINESS. | | | | |
| Federal Life, Chicago | 538 | $85,660 00 | 85 | $7,492 00 |
| Peoples Life, Chicago | 3,645 | 474,138 08 | 11 | 1,902 00 |
| Providers' Life Assurance Co., Chicago | 4,760 | 318,708 00 | 54 | 8,069 00 |
| Public Life Ins. Co., Chicago | 230 | 28,622 00 | 576 | 82,765 00 |
| Totals | 9,173 | $907,128 08 | 726 | $100,228 00 |
| II. COMPANIES OF OTHER STATES—INDUSTRIAL BUSINESS. | | | | |
| Cleveland Life, Cleveland, Ohio | 190 | $27,300 00 | | |
| Columbian National Life, Boston, Mass | 1,220 | 206,469 00 | | |
| Federal Union Life, Cincinnati, Ohio | 23,505 | 3,511,113 00 | 7,328 | $1,019,895 00 |
| The Guardian Life, New York, N. Y | 1,018 | 130,292 00 | | |
| John Hancock Mutual Life, Boston, Mass | 3,472,965 | 642,671,402 00 | 538,676 | 145,019,120 00 |
| Metropolitan Life, New York, N. Y | 20,881,408 | 2,879,664,118 00 | 3,887,051 | 666,840,395 00 |
| Morris Plan Ins. Society, New York, N. Y | 22,201 | 4,305,050 00 | 29,438 | 5,963,400 00 |
| National Life and Accident Ins. Co., Nashville, Tenn | 1,150,728 | 71,527,595 00 | 456,759 | 40,996,495 00 |
| Prudential Ins. Co. of Am., Newark, N. J | 18,662,140 | 2,794,902,131 00 | 3,081,543 | 686,453,679 00 |
| Western and Southern Life, Cincinnati, Ohio | 1,223,418 | 198,610,529 00 | 382,900 | 85,037,535 00 |
| Wisconsin National Life, Oshkosh, Wis | 120 | 22,339 50 | 1 | 549 00 |
| Totals | 45,438,913 | $6,595,578,338 50 | 8,383,696 | $1,631,331,068 00 |
| III. COMPANIES OF FOREIGN GOVERNMENTS—INDUSTRIAL BUSINESS. | | | | |
| North American Life Assurance Co., Toronto, Can | 17 | $2,345 00 | | |
| Aggregate—industrial | 45,448,103 | $6,596,487,811 58 | 8,384,422 | $1,631,431,296 00 |
| Combined—aggregate | 60,928,349 | $39,671,871,292 76 | 10,891,111 | $8,351,359,479 67 |

TABLE

SHOWING DETAILED STATEMENT OF NUMBER AND AMOUNT OF POLICIES TERMI

| Name of company. | Location. | By death. No. | Amount. | By maturity and disability. No. | Amount. |
|---|---|---|---|---|---|
| I. COMPANIES OF THIS STATE. | | | | | |
| The American Bankers Ins. Co | Chicago | 103 | $77,777 00 | 1 | $500 00 |
| Central Life Ins. Co. of Illinois | Ottawa | 67 | 140,634 00 | 4 | 5,109 00 |
| Cloverleaf Life and Casualty Co | Jacksonville | 24 | 38,086 00 | | |
| Continental Assurance Co | Chicago | 46 | 62,800 00 | | |
| Elgin Life Ins. Co | Elgin | 11 | 15,700 00 | 1 | 1,000 00 |

Concluded.

| Total. | | Policies terminated during the year. | | Policies in force at end of year. | | |
|---|---|---|---|---|---|---|
| Number. | Amount. | Number | Amount. | Number. | Amount. | Average. |
| 39 | $7,589,600 00 | 5 | $1,199,900 00 | 34 | $6,389,700 00 | $187,932 35 |
| 1 | 58,300 00 | ........... | 6,400 00 | 1 | 51,900 00 | 51,900 00 |
| 40 | $7,647,900 00 | 5 | $1,206,300 00 | 35 | $6,441,600 00 | $184,045 71 |
| 21,356 | $2,324,054,606 49 | 5,259 | $747,601,461 49 | 16,097 | $1,576,453,145 00 | $97,934 59 |
| 623 | $ 93,152 00 | 142 | $ 26,172 00 | 481 | $ 66,980 00 | $139 25 |
| 3,656 | 476,040 08 | 320 | 38,684 33 | 3,336 | 437,355 75 | 131 10 |
| 4,814 | 326,777 00 | 2,209 | 263,921 00 | 2,605 | 62,856 00 | 24 13 |
| 806 | 111,387 00 | 236 | 32,199 00 | 570 | 79,188 00 | 138 93 |
| 9,899 | $1,007,356 08 | 2,907 | $360,976 33 | 6,992 | $646,379 75 | $92 46 |
| 190 | $ 27,300 00 | 11 | $ 2,050 00 | 179 | $ 25,250 00 | $141 06 |
| 1,220 | 206,469 00 | 83 | 12,160 00 | 1,137 | 194,309 00 | 170 90 |
| 30,833 | 4,531,008 00 | 7,037 | 1,100,768 00 | 23,796 | 3,430,240 00 | 144 15 |
| 1,018 | 130,292 00 | 48 | 6,467 00 | 970 | 123,825 00 | 127 65 |
| 4,011,641 | 787,690,522 00 | 374,532 | 78,066,811 00 | 3,637,109 | 709,623,711 00 | 195 11 |
| 24,768,459 | 3,546,504,513 00 | 2,515,522 | 433,063,948 00 | 22,252,937 | 3,113,440,565 00 | 139 91 |
| 51,639 | 10,268,450 00 | 23,370 | 4,618,275 00 | 28,269 | 5,650,175 00 | 199 87 |
| 1,607,487 | 112,524,090 00 | 610,513 | 45,265,998 00 | 996,974 | 67,258,092 00 | 67 46 |
| 21,743,683 | 3,481,355,810 00 | 1,529,955 | 326,663,256 00 | 20,213,728 | 3,154,692,554 00 | 156 07 |
| 1,606,318 | 283,648,064 00 | 373,094 | 79,166,745 00 | 1,233,224 | 204,481,319 00 | 165 81 |
| 121 | 22,888 50 | 8 | 2,014 00 | 113 | 20,874 50 | 184 73 |
| 53,822,609 | $8,226,909,406 50 | 5,434,173 | $967,968,492 00 | 48,388,436 | $7,258,940,914 50 | $150 01 |
| 17 | $2,345 00 | 2 | $310 00 | 15 | $2,035 00 | $135 67 |
| 53,832,525 | $8,227,919,107 58 | 5,437,082 | $968,329,778 33 | 48,395,443 | $7,259,589,329 25 | $150 01 |
| 71,819,460 | $48,023,230,772 43 | 6,967,769 | $5,042,881,870 05 | 64,851,691 | $42,980,348,902 38 | $662 75 |

# NO. 9.

NATED DURING THE YEAR 1921 BY EACH COMPANY AND CAUSE OF TERMINATION.

| By expiry. | | By surrender. | | By lapse, decrease and withdrawal. | | Total. | |
|---|---|---|---|---|---|---|---|
| No. | Amount. | No. | Amount. | No. | Amount. | No. | Amount. |
| 68 | $ 142,920 00 | 162 | $ 242,550 00 | 4,057 | $ 3,364,604 00 | 4,391 | $ 3,828,351 00 |
| 143 | 242,250 00 | 404 | 1,035,332 00 | 1,491 | 4,225,448 00 | 2,109 | 5.648,773 00 |
| 24 | 30,621 00 | 35 | 43,000 00 | 2,591 | 2,244,112 00 | 2,674 | 2,355,819 00 |
| 25 | 35,059 00 | 63 | 90,500 00 | 2,579 | 4,905,685 00 | 2,713 | 5,094,044 00 |
| 15 | 20,000 00 | 9 | 14,500 00 | 18 | 31,783 00 | 54 | 82,983 00 |

TABLE NO. 9—

| Name of company. | Location. | By death. | | By maturity and disability. | |
|---|---|---|---|---|---|
| | | No. | Amount. | No. | Amount. |
| Federal Life | Chicago | 126 | $311,353 00 | 28 | $ 54,394 00 |
| The Franklin Life | Springfield | 337 | 771,701 00 | 138 | 235,422 00 |
| Illinois Life | Chicago | 476 | 967,357 87 | 141 | 166,387 00 |
| International Life and Trust Co | Moline | 6 | 12,000 00 | | |
| Liberty Life Ins. Co | Chicago | | | | |
| Marquette Life | Springfield | 50 | 56,100 00 | | |
| Mutual Life of Illinois | Springfield | 8 | 9,000 00 | | |
| Mutual Trust Life | Chicago | 261 | 359,259 00 | 21 | 22,565 00 |
| National Life of U. S. A | Chicago | 538 | 958,543 00 | 98 | 152,790 00 |
| North American Life Ins. Co. of Chicago | Chicago | 122 | 303,422 00 | 2 | 4,200 00 |
| Old Colony Life | Chicago | 119 | 172,607 65 | 1 | 1,000 00 |
| Peoples Life | Chicago | 51 | 24,890 00 | 4 | 5,558 00 |
| Peoria Life | Peoria | 82 | 236,620 00 | | |
| Providers' Life Assurance Co | Chicago | 161 | 51,200 00 | | |
| Public Life Ins. Co | Chicago | 3 | 4,000 00 | | |
| Rockford Life | Rockford | 20 | 44,000 00 | | |
| Standard Life | Decatur | 289 | 357,433 00 | | |
| Totals | | 2,900 | $4,974,483 52 | 439 | $648,925 00 |
| II. COMPANIES OF OTHER STATES. | | | | | |
| Aetna Life | Hartford, Conn | 2,711 | $7,393,886 25 | 1,943 | $2,797,240 85 |
| American Central Life | Indianapolis, Ind | 203 | 682,851 00 | 4 | 58,100 00 |
| American Life Ins. Co | Detroit, Mich | 97 | 206,324 39 | 4 | 6,500 00 |
| American Life Re-insurance Co | Dallas, Tex | 16 | 33,517 00 | | |
| American National Assurance Co | St. Louis, Mo | 26 | 52,000 00 | | |
| Bankers Life Co | Des Moines, Ia | 2,853 | 6,218,286 00 | | |
| Bankers Life Ins. Co | Lincoln, Nebr | 175 | 308,623 00 | 644 | 966,200 00 |
| Bankers Reserve Life Co | Omaha, Nebr | 163 | 355,168 25 | 3 | 3,500 00 |
| Berkshire Life | Pittsfield, Mass | 480 | 1,535,139 00 | 162 | 294,272 00 |
| Business Men's Assurance Co. of America | Kansas City, Mo | 2 | 10,000 00 | | |
| Capitol Life Ins. Co. of Colorado | Denver, Col | 106 | 231,715 00 | 6 | 31,500 00 |
| Central Life Assurance Society of U. S. (Mutual) | Des Moines, Ia | 170 | 351,499 00 | 17 | 16,286 00 |
| Central States Life Ins. Co | St. Louis, Mo | 132 | 289,022 00 | 2 | 2,000 00 |
| Century Life | Indianapolis, Ind | 14 | 54,752 00 | | |
| Cleveland Life | Cleveland, Ohio | 96 | 176,250 00 | 6 | 6,500 00 |
| Columbian National Life | Boston, Mass | 250 | 629,695 00 | 35 | 85,106 00 |
| Columbus Mutual Life Ins. Co | Columbus, Ohio | 58 | 94,137 00 | 7 | 7,000 00 |
| Connecticut General Life | Hartford, Conn | 539 | 2,061,421 28 | 374 | 529,357 00 |
| Connecticut Mutual Life | Hartford, Conn | 1,752 | 5,079,502 86 | 292 | 543,356 38 |
| Equitable Life Assurance Society of the U. S | New York, N. Y | 7,968 | 25,352,829 00 | 7,991 | 18,045,734 00 |
| Equitable Life | Des Moines, Ia | 516 | 1,089,256 75 | 282 | 407,474 31 |
| Farmers National Life | Huntington, Ind | 44 | 65,750 00 | | |
| Federal Union Life | Cincinnati, Ohio | 236 | 142,750 00 | | |
| The Fidelity Mutual Life | Philadelphia, Pa | 758 | 2,211,318 00 | 359 | 618,339 00 |
| Girard Life | Philadelphia, Pa | 34 | 101,893 00 | | |
| The Guardian Life | New York, N. Y | 860 | 1,393,183 00 | 1,566 | 902,664 00 |
| Home Life | New York, N. Y | 754 | 1,717,554 00 | 498 | 1,226,079 00 |
| Indiana National Life | Indianapolis, Ind | 55 | 94,824 00 | 1 | 2,000 00 |
| Indianapolis Life | Indianapolis, Ind | 54 | 83,987 50 | 1 | 1,000 00 |
| International Life | St. Louis, Mo | 307 | 798,783 00 | 4 | 10,000 00 |
| John Hancock Mutual Life | Boston, Mass | 3,156 | 5,215,087 00 | 589 | 882,597 00 |
| Kansas City Life | Kansas City, Mo | 453 | 943,441 00 | 15 | 20,498 00 |
| LaFayette Life Ins. Co | LaFayette, Ind | 47 | 79,658 00 | 1 | 1,000 00 |
| Lincoln National Life | Ft. Wayne, Ind | 338 | 822,966 86 | 11 | 15,000 00 |
| Manhattan Life | New York, N. Y | 458 | 1,093,014 00 | 199 | 223,808 00 |
| Maryland Assurance Corp | Baltimore, Md | 9 | 27,000 00 | | |
| Massachusetts Mutual Life | Springfield, Mass | 1,858 | 5,793,896 00 | 258 | 443,727 00 |
| Merchants Life | Des Moines, Ia | 290 | 595,778 00 | 18 | 63,564 00 |
| Metropolitan Life | New York, N. Y | 18,729 | 19,197,040 00 | 21,935 | 12,759,466 00 |
| Michigan Mutual Life | Detroit, Mich | 440 | 795,277 02 | 338 | 436,437 94 |

Continued.

| By expiry. | | By surrender. | | By lapse, decrease and withdrawal. | | Total | |
|---|---|---|---|---|---|---|---|
| No. | Amount. | No. | Amount. | No. | Amount. | No. | Amount. |
| 18 | $ 50,500 00 | 314 | $ 678,959 00 | 4,458 | $10,887,338 00 | 4,944 | $11,982,544 00 |
| 689 | 2,204,368 00 | 997 | 2,244,714 00 | 7,917 | 20,643,171 00 | 10,078 | 26,099,376 00 |
| 281 | 1,120,685 00 | 1,012 | 2,286,335 33 | 4,770 | 14,016,136 00 | 6,680 | 18,556,901 20 |
| -------- | -------------- | 9 | 14,052 28 | 636 | 1,394,959 00 | 651 | 1,421,011 28 |
| -------- | -------------- | ------- | ------------- | 2 | 2,000 00 | 2 | 2,000 00 |
| | | | | | | | |
| 40 | 51,500 00 | 61 | 78,300 00 | 346 | 510,504 00 | 497 | 696,404 00 |
| -------- | -------------- | 1 | 10,000 00 | 718 | 1,546,949 00 | 727 | 1,565,949 00 |
| 80 | 145,031 00 | 482 | 878,079 00 | 3,533 | 9,652,447 00 | 4,377 | 11,057,381 00 |
| 4,846 | 11,198,616 00 | 729 | 1,504,711 00 | 2,857 | 7,808,686 00 | 9,068 | 21,623,346 00 |
| | | | | | | | |
| 143 | 184,110 00 | 399 | 1,311,675 00 | 4,102 | 12,233,636 00 | 4,768 | 14,037,043 00 |
| | | | | | | | |
| 109 | 129,897 15 | 249 | 361,308 59 | 3,247 | 5,043,856 17 | 3,725 | 5,708,669 56 |
| 522 | 172,485 00 | 259 | 204,605 00 | 419 | 191,558 78 | 1,255 | 599,096 78 |
| 101 | 190,611 00 | 260 | 641,776 00 | 2,533 | 6,693,999 00 | 2,976 | 7,763,006 00 |
| 23 | 11,250 00 | 280 | 172,645 00 | 3,695 | 1,260,316 00 | 4,159 | 1,495,411 00 |
| -------- | -------------- | ------- | ------------- | 112 | 222,000 00 | 115 | 226,000 00 |
| 27 | 88,700 00 | 96 | 198,507 00 | 689 | 1,248,540 00 | 832 | 1,579,747 00 |
| 130 | 174,400 00 | 411 | 608,133 00 | 3,094 | 6,942,354 00 | 3,924 | 8,082,320 00 |
| 7,284 | $16,193,003 15 | 6,232 | $12,619,682 20 | 53,864 | $115,070,081 95 | 70,719 | $149,506,175 82 |
| | | | | | | | |
| 1,830 | $1,990,315 00 | 5,435 | $18,371,474 36 | 12,783 | $60,922,103 98 | 24,702 | $91,475,020 44 |
| 148 | 354,935 00 | 529 | 1,104,346 00 | 7,548 | 24,542,445 00 | 8,432 | 26,742,677 00 |
| 333 | 792,109 00 | 357 | 739,460 00 | 3,187 | 8,224,845 51 | 3,978 | 9,969,238 90 |
| -------- | -------------- | ------- | ------------- | 1,766 | 7,038,841 00 | 1,782 | 7,072,358 00 |
| 20 | 30,500 00 | 88 | 203,770 00 | 2,034 | 3,923,393 00 | 2,168 | 4,209,663 00 |
| | | | | | | | |
| 241 | 565,869 00 | 1,047 | 2,515,665 00 | 14,153 | 47,190,897 00 | 18,294 | 56,490,717 00 |
| 95 | 163,000 00 | 540 | 1,000,611 00 | 3,011 | 6,508,783 03 | 4,465 | 8,947,217 03 |
| 18 | 39,000 00 | 580 | 1,817,695 50 | 5,623 | 13,874,179 00 | 6,387 | 16,089,542 75 |
| 105 | 253,454 00 | 719 | 1,902,051 00 | 1,006 | 4,429,993 00 | 2,472 | 8,414,909 00 |
| | | | | | | | |
| -------- | -------------- | ------- | ------------- | 162 | 456,000 00 | 164 | 466,000 00 |
| | | | | | | | |
| 4 | 9,000 00 | 347 | 684,193 00 | 4,512 | 10,746,332 00 | 4,975 | 11,702,740 00 |
| | | | | | | | |
| 476 | 710,200 00 | 688 | 1,241,997 00 | 7,096 | 17,887,496 00 | 8,447 | 20,207,478 00 |
| 221 | 343,159 00 | 133 | 218,607 00 | 6,003 | 15,734,455 00 | 6,491 | 16,587,243 00 |
| 3 | 8,635 00 | 28 | 69,700 00 | 1,174 | 2,605,619 00 | 1,219 | 2,738,706 00 |
| 99 | 159,550 00 | 184 | 305,604 00 | 1,532 | 2,788,914 00 | 1,917 | 3,436,818 00 |
| | | | | | | | |
| 47 | 175,448 71 | 625 | 1,818,366 15 | 3,802 | 13,724,821 00 | 4,759 | 16,433,436 86 |
| 21 | 31,343 00 | 135 | 211,898 00 | 1,802 | 3,977,091 00 | 2,023 | 4,321,469 00 |
| 561 | 1,359,260 00 | 1,628 | 6,293,495 00 | 4,514 | 27,165,744 02 | 7,616 | 37,409,277 30 |
| 347 | 960,890 84 | 2,775 | 8,763,983 45 | 5,319 | 16,650,085 00 | 10,485 | 31,997,818 53 |
| | | | | | | | |
| 7,219 | 25,882,304 00 | 18,132 | 48,487,253 00 | 39,844 | 134,695,000 00 | 81,154 | 252,463,120 00 |
| | | | | | | | |
| 148 | 550,438 00 | 1,482 | 2,532,776 98 | 6,588 | 18,928,332 03 | 9,016 | 23,508,278 07 |
| 13 | 16,264 00 | 65 | 107,000 00 | 1,868 | 3,861,312 00 | 1,990 | 4,050,326 00 |
| 14 | 50,000 00 | 71 | 105,000 00 | 3,759 | 3,192,144 00 | 4,080 | 3,489,894 00 |
| 281 | 650,653 00 | 1,311 | 3,286,956 00 | 4,858 | 16,248,047 00 | 7,567 | 23,015,313 00 |
| 3 | 13,444 00 | 66 | 200,643 00 | 615 | 1,691,420 00 | 718 | 2,007,400 00 |
| | | | | | | | |
| 443 | 1,560,534 00 | 2,201 | 3,758,543 00 | 4,794 | 60,335,613 00 | 9,864 | 67,950,537 00 |
| 362 | 883,570 00 | 2,046 | 4,560,567 00 | 4,457 | 12,789,358 00 | 8,117 | 21,177,128 00 |
| 78 | 116,152 00 | 226 | 577,952 00 | 948 | 2,386,159 00 | 1,308 | 3,177,087 00 |
| 215 | 478,466 38 | 125 | 207,505 65 | 937 | 2,321,926 58 | 1,332 | 3,092,886 11 |
| 245 | 453,119 00 | 1,130 | 2,489,420 00 | 9,645 | 28,724,762 00 | 11,331 | 32,476,084 00 |
| | | | | | | | |
| 287 | 762,273 00 | 6,486 | 9,110,109 00 | 31,119 | 48,828,558 00 | 41,637 | 64,798,624 00 |
| 235 | 458,707 00 | 1,311 | 2,542,193 00 | 11,018 | 27,923,894 00 | 13,032 | 31,888,733 00 |
| 89 | 148,552 00 | 32 | 45,894 00 | 1,029 | 2,314,361 00 | 1,198 | 2,589,465 00 |
| 1,370 | 6,399,800 00 | 3,483 | 10,196,900 00 | 9,212 | 25,037,357 36 | 14,414 | 42,472,024 22 |
| 175 | 422,882 00 | 895 | 1,901,254 00 | 2,512 | 6,885,710 00 | 4,239 | 10,526,668 00 |
| | | | | | | | |
| --------- | 4,830 00 | 4 | 23,500 00 | 350 | 956,507 00 | 363 | 1,011,837 00 |
| 502 | 1,477,291 00 | 4,072 | 13,980,207 00 | 6,707 | 26,151,057 00 | 13,397 | 47,846,178 00 |
| 251 | 1,058,483 00 | 299 | 570,728 00 | 7,757 | 17,781,582 39 | 8,615 | 20,070,135 39 |
| 2,673 | 2,748,367 00 | 34,994 | 34,759,007 00 | 295,914 | 317,844,297 00 | 374,245 | 387,308,177 00 |
| 116 | 201,755 16 | 771 | 1,337,156 87 | 3,440 | 7,649,774 04 | 5,105 | 10,420,401 03 |

TABLE NO. 9—

| Name of company. | Location. | By death. | | By maturity and disability. | |
|---|---|---|---|---|---|
| | | No. | Amount. | No. | Amount. |
| Minnesota Mutual Life | St. Paul, Minn. | 193 | $ 486,666 98 | 2 | $ 3,000 00 |
| Missouri State Life | St. Louis, Mo. | 754 | 1,715,654 00 | 115 | 140,557 00 |
| Morris Plan Insurance Society | New York, N. Y. | | | | |
| Mutual Benefit Life | Newark, N. J. | 3,676 | 11,361,334 00 | 1,184 | 2,557,449 00 |
| Mutual Life | New York, N. Y. | 9,121 | 26,571,083 00 | 5,428 | 10,221,746 00 |
| National Life and Accident Ins. Co. | Nashville, Tenn. | 11 | 14,000 00 | | |
| National Life Ins. Co. | Montpelier, Vt. | 1,193 | 2,758,724 00 | 948 | 1,405,642 00 |
| New England Mutual Life | Boston, Mass. | 1,404 | 4,116,573 00 | 579 | 1,170,562 00 |
| New World Life | Spokane, Wash. | 38 | 74,935 95 | 1 | 1,000 00 |
| New York Life | New York, N. Y. | 13,703 | 32,025,804 00 | 16,114 | 25,048,275 00 |
| Northern States Life | Hammond, Ind. | 45 | 72,115 00 | 2 | 1,060 00 |
| Northwestern Mutual Life | Milwaukee, Wis. | 5,613 | 18,153,939 00 | 3,764 | 7,870,917 00 |
| Northwestern National Life | Minneapolis, Minn. | 330 | 667,647 00 | 16 | 23,267 00 |
| Old Line Ins. Co. | Lincoln, Nebr. | 15 | 42,000 00 | | |
| Old Line Life Ins. Co. of America | Milwaukee, Wis. | 81 | 170,565 00 | 5 | 4,704 00 |
| Pacific Mutual Life | Los Angeles, Cal. | 935 | 2,488,578 00 | 527 | 1,091,056 00 |
| Pan American Life | New Orleans, La. | 181 | 516,821 00 | 4 | 6,500 00 |
| Penn Mutual Life | Philadelphia, Pa. | 2,787 | 9,247,059 00 | 2,225 | 4,098,275 00 |
| Peoples Life | Frankfort, Ind. | 48 | 93,279 00 | 4 | 5,500 00 |
| Philadelphia Life | Philadelphia, Pa. | 213 | 658,957 00 | 19 | 48,173 00 |
| Phoenix Mutual Life | Hartford, Conn. | 1,009 | 2,345,287 00 | 671 | 1,260,912 00 |
| Provident Life and Trust | Philadelphia, Pa. | 1,202 | 4,195,123 00 | 1,657 | 4,011,400 00 |
| Prudential Insurance Co. of America | Newark, N. J. | 11,179 | 14,389,626 00 | 4,863 | 5,236,504 00 |
| Re-insurance Life Co. of America | Des Moines, Ia. | 21 | 97,582 00 | | |
| Reliance Life | Pittsburgh, Pa. | 433 | 1,167,086 00 | 16 | 30,248 00 |
| Reserve Loan Life | Indianapolis, Ind. | 142 | 288,333 00 | | |
| Security Life Ins. Co. of America | Richmond, Va. | 90 | 221,261 00 | 1 | 2,000 00 |
| Security Mutual Life | Binghamton, N. Y. | 363 | 611,304 00 | 125 | 158,851 00 |
| State Life | Indianapolis, Ind. | 376 | 969,731 00 | 36 | 87,797 00 |
| State Mutual Life Assurance | Worcester, Mass. | 909 | 2,868,786 00 | 472 | 1,038,577 00 |
| The Travelers Ins. Co. | Hartford, Conn. | 2,279 | 7,735,902 00 | 722 | 1,658,783 00 |
| Union Central Life | Cincinnati, Ohio | 2,100 | 6,275,650 00 | 1,679 | 2,738,575 00 |
| Union Mutual Life | Portland, Me. | 454 | 882,618 00 | 526 | 556,855 00 |
| United States Life | New York, N. Y. | 209 | 375,592 00 | 177 | 231,547 00 |
| Universal Life Ins. Co. | Dubuque, Ia. | 4 | 14,000 00 | | |
| Western and Southern Life | Cincinnati, Ohio | 342 | 359,978 00 | 13 | 7,638 00 |
| Western Union Life Ins. Co. | Spokane, Wash. | 94 | 259,950 00 | | |
| Wisconsin National Life | Oshkosh, Wis. | 47 | 61,772 45 | 1 | 1,000 00 |
| Totals | | 108,801 | $247,734,391 54 | 79,461 | $112,124,676 48 |
| III. COMPANIES OF FOREIGN GOVERNMENTS. | | | | | |
| Canada Life Assurance Co. | Toronto, Can. | 1,028 | $2,846,102 61 | 442 | $801,538 93 |
| Manufacturers Life | Toronto, Can. | 602 | 1,180,313 00 | 428 | 650,525 00 |
| North American Life Assurance Co. | Toronto, Can. | 290 | 547,973 00 | 376 | 463,358 00 |
| Totals | | 1,920 | $4,574,388 61 | 1,246 | $1,915,421 93 |
| Aggregate | | 113,621 | $257,283,263 67 | 81,146 | $114,689,023 41 |
| I. COMPANIES OF THIS STATE—GROUP INSURANCE. | | | | | |
| The American Bankers Ins. Co. | Chicago | | | | |
| II. COMPANIES OF OTHER STATES—GROUP INSURANCE. | | | | | |
| Aetna Life | Hartford, Conn. | | $2,202,770 00 | | $ 37,217 00 |
| Capitol Life Ins. Co. of Colorado | Denver, Colo. | | 31,274 00 | | |
| Connecticut General Life | Hartford, Conn. | | 471,581 00 | | 33,650 00 |
| Equitable Life Assurance Society of the U. S. | New York, N. Y. | | 2,731,927 00 | | 82,162 00 |
| The Guardian Life | New York, N. Y. | | 4,386 00 | | |

Continued.

| By expiry. | | By surrender. | | By lapse, decrease and withdrawal. | | Total. | |
|---|---|---|---|---|---|---|---|
| No. | Amount. | No. | Amount. | No. | Amount. | No. | Amount. |
| 165 | $ 249,642 00 | 315 | $ 694,941 22 | 4,644 | $ 16,709,515 70 | 5,319 | $ 18,143,765 90 |
| 1,378 | 2,937,913 00 | 2,670 | 6,537,446 00 | 16,522 | 47,582,420 00 | 21,439 | 58,913,990 00 |
| -------- | -------- | -------- | -------- | 69 | 65,950 00 | 69 | 65,950 00 |
| 5,313 | 12,960,638 00 | 5,291 | 17,872,118 00 | 4,645 | 18,833,018 00 | 20,109 | 63,584,557 00 |
| 4,810 | 16,843,941 00 | 26,116 | 76,190,514 00 | 32,738 | 99,244,921 00 | 78,213 | 229,072,205 00 |
| -------- | -------- | -------- | -------- | 1,297 | 2,077,050 00 | 1,308 | 2,091,050 00 |
| 848 | 1,867,536 00 | 1,648 | 4,401,608 00 | 5,483 | 15,581,147 00 | 10,120 | 26,014,657 00 |
| 613 | 1,683,707 00 | 1,957 | 5,202,369 00 | 6,283 | 21,256,963 00 | 10,836 | 33,430,174 00 |
| 49 | 106,250 00 | 223 | 495,753 00 | 2,416 | 6,978,389 05 | 2,727 | 7,656,328 00 |
| 8,321 | 23,197,990 00 | 26,571 | 57,358,785 00 | 72,177 | 186,725,712 00 | 136,886 | 324,356,566 00 |
| 72 | 115,287 00 | 79 | 173,528 00 | 418 | 987,685 00 | 616 | 1,349,675 00 |
| 4,025 | 11,489,369 00 | 7,980 | 23,806,852 00 | 14,421 | 52,812,970 00 | 35,803 | 114,134,047 00 |
| 130 | 239,167 00 | 1,361 | 4,478,578 00 | 8,863 | 26,161,365 00 | 10,700 | 31,570,024 00 |
| 11 | 27,000 00 | 26 | 36,500 00 | 2,154 | 6,245,142 50 | 2,206 | 6,350,642 50 |
| 70 | 230,933 00 | 156 | 486,330 00 | 2,912 | 7,036,346 88 | 3,224 | 7,928,878 88 |
| 5,352 | 14,245,496 00 | 1,999 | 4,800,475 00 | 6,604 | 18,811,411 00 | 15,417 | 41,437,016 00 |
| 440 | 1,359,791 00 | 613 | 1,547,856 00 | 7,805 | 20,405,580 00 | 9,043 | 23,836,548 00 |
| 2,274 | 7,721,668 00 | 4,846 | 18,473,878 00 | 9,832 | 35,414,306 00 | 21,964 | 74,955,186 00 |
| 26 | 27,887 00 | 140 | 229,805 00 | 1,248 | 2,691,730 00 | 1,466 | 3,048,201 00 |
| 196 | 206,005 00 | 187 | 485,578 00 | 4,324 | 11,107,876 00 | 4,939 | 12,506,589 00 |
| 1,125 | 2,173,739 00 | 1,785 | 4,668,852 00 | 3,473 | 11,637,067 00 | 8,063 | 22,085,857 00 |
| 163 | 528,444 00 | 3,963 | 12,599,301 00 | 6,711 | 26,553,115 00 | 13,696 | 47,887,383 00 |
| 71,441 | 88,621,644 00 | 14,409 | 18,555,958 00 | 65,471 | 96,994,850 00 | 167,363 | 223,798,582 00 |
| -------- | -------- | -------- | -------- | 1,993 | 9,196,560 00 | 2,014 | 9,294,142 00 |
| 443 | 1,537,697 00 | 461 | 864,703 00 | 12,688 | 29,236,616 00 | 14,041 | 32,836,350 00 |
| 97 | 161,295 00 | 751 | 1,949,675 00 | 5,088 | 10,666,799 00 | 6,078 | 13,066,102 00 |
| 96 | 127,588 00 | 230 | 463,342 00 | 4,702 | 8,865,309 00 | 5,119 | 9,679,500 00 |
| 191 | 406,759 00 | 660 | 1,058,025 00 | 3,056 | 5,907,905 00 | 4,395 | 8,142,844 00 |
| 372 | 703,406 00 | 881 | 2,168,196 00 | 6,641 | 18,152,209 00 | 8,306 | 22,081,339 00 |
| 367 | 1,068,646 00 | 1,638 | 4,508,560 00 | 2,611 | 10,192,016 00 | 5,997 | 19,676,585 00 |
| 2,179 | 4,191,993 00 | 5,114 | 18,314,017 00 | 17,755 | 72,125,689 00 | 28,049 | 104,026,384 00 |
| 1,646 | 3,730,650 00 | 4,463 | 12,997,206 00 | 9,973 | 33,768,502 00 | 19,861 | 59,510,583 00 |
| 495 | 1,037,996 00 | 1,038 | 1,517,585 00 | 1,055 | 2,371,680 00 | 3,568 | 6,366,734 00 |
| 130 | 201,830 00 | 587 | 1,157,867 00 | 679 | 1,462,964 00 | 1,782 | 3,429,800 00 |
| -------- | -------- | 1 | 5,000 00 | 54 | 149,500 00 | 59 | 168,500 00 |
| 197 | 267,222 00 | 388 | 359,800 00 | 10,836 | 10,111,362 00 | 11,776 | 11,106,000 00 |
| 24 | 166,020 00 | 563 | 1,372,981 00 | 4,076 | 13,421,994 00 | 4,757 | 15,220,945 00 |
| 70 | 104,500 00 | 102 | 137,016 50 | 1,198 | 2,047,802 74 | 1,418 | 2,352,091 69 |
| 132,417 | $252,824,202 09 | 214,252 | $494,014,480 68 | 897,313 | $2,014,530,646 81 | 1,432,244 | $3,121,228,397 60 |
| 80 | $336,875 00 | 1,700 | $4,180,151 03 | 4,459 | $12,785,095 24 | 7,709 | $20,949,762 81 |
| 40 | 150,292 00 | 792 | 1,493,433 00 | 6,590 | 16,970,418 00 | 8,452 | 20,444,981 00 |
| 105 | 245,323 00 | 957 | 1,649,310 00 | 4,576 | 9,915,349 00 | 6,304 | 12,821,313 00 |
| 225 | $732,490 00 | 3,449 | $7,322,894 03 | 15,625 | $39,670,862 24 | 22,465 | $54,216,056 81 |
| 139,926 | $269,749,695 24 | 223,933 | $513,957,056 91 | 966,802 | $2,169,271,591 00 | 1,525,428 | $3,324,950,630 23 |
| -------- | -------- | -------- | -------- | 3 | $297,250 00 | 3 | $297,250 00 |
| -------- | -------- | -------- | -------- | 145 | $182,491,710 00 | 145 | $184,731,697 00 |
| -------- | -------- | -------- | -------- | 3 | 4,417,346 00 | 3 | 4,448,620 00 |
| -------- | -------- | -------- | -------- | 31 | 32,147,547 00 | 31 | 32,652,778 00 |
| 93 | $45,907,957 00 | -------- | -------- | -------- | 134,209,533 00 | 93 | 182,931,579 00 |
| -------- | -------- | 1 | $ 111,000 00 | -------- | 97,762 00 | 1 | 213,148 00 |

TABLE NO. 9—

| Name of company. | Location. | By death. No. | By death. Amount. | By maturity and disability. No. | By maturity and disability. Amount. |
|---|---|---|---|---|---|
| International Life | St. Louis, Mo. | | $ 1,000 00 | | |
| Lincoln National Life | Ft. Wayne, Ind. | | 3,000 00 | | |
| Maryland Assurance Corp. | Baltimore, Md. | | 2,546 00 | | |
| Metropolitan Life | New York, N. Y. | | 1,882,166 00 | | $277,504 00 |
| Minnesota Mutual Life | St. Paul, Minn. | | 5,298 90 | | |
| Missouri State Life | St. Louis, Mo. | | 71,248 00 | | 1,900 00 |
| National Life and Accident Ins. Co. | Nashville, Tenn. | | 3,611 00 | | |
| The Northwestern National Life | Minneapolis, Minn. | 64 | 85,950 00 | | |
| Pan American Life | New Orleans, La. | | 3,200 00 | | |
| Philadelphia Life | Philadelphia, Pa. | | 8,700 00 | | |
| Prudential Ins. Co. of America | Newark, N. J. | | 303,060 00 | | 30,000 00 |
| The Travelers Ins. Co. | Hartford, Conn. | | 2,872,407 00 | | 185,965 00 |
| United States Life | New York, N. Y. | 2 | 5,140 00 | | |
| Totals | | 66 | $10,689,264 90 | | $648,398 00 |
| III. COMPANIES OF FOREIGN GOVERNMENTS—GROUP INSURANCE. | | | | | |
| Canada Life Assurance Co. | Toronto, Can. | | $19,700 00 | | |
| Manufacturers Life | Toronto, Can. | | | | |
| Totals | | | $19,700 00 | | |
| Aggregage group | | 66 | $10,708,964 90 | | $648,398 00 |
| I. COMPANIES OF THIS STATE—INDUSTRIAL BUSINESS. | | | | | |
| Federal Life | Chicago | 4 | $1,000 00 | | |
| Peoples Life | Chicago | 29 | 4,128 15 | | |
| Providers' Life Assurance Co. | Chicago | 4 | 567 00 | | |
| Public Life Insurance Co. | Chicago | 10 | 1,387 00 | | |
| Totals | | 47 | $7,082 15 | | |
| II. COMPANIES OF OTHER STATES—INDUSTRIAL BUSINESS. | | | | | |
| Cleveland Life | Cleveland, Ohio | 5 | $ 850 00 | | |
| Columbian National Life | Boston, Mass. | 46 | 6,658 00 | 2 | $ 64 00 |
| Federal Union Life | Cincinnati, Ohio | 203 | 29,425 00 | | |
| The Guardian Life | New York, N. Y. | 32 | 4,866 00 | | |
| John Hancock Mutual Life | Boston, Mass. | 35,448 | 6,317,837 00 | 462 | 173,850 00 |
| Metropolitan Life | New York, N. Y. | 194,056 | 25,278,010 00 | 88,555 | 7,681,153 00 |
| Morris Plan Insurance Society | New York, N. Y. | 112 | 23,600 00 | | |
| National Life and Accident Ins. Co. | Nashville Tenn. | 12,473 | 825,218 00 | | |
| Prudential Ins. Co. of America | Newark, N. J. | 163,708 | 21,886,893 00 | 99 | 50,875 00 |
| Western and Southern Life | Cincinnati, Ohio | 12,949 | 1,438,706 00 | 3,820 | 358,070 00 |
| Wisconsin National Life | Oshkosh, Wis. | | | | |
| Totals | | 419,032 | $55,812,063 00 | 92,938 | $8,264,012 00 |
| III. COMPANIES OF FOREIGN GOVERNMENTS—INDUSTRIAL BUSINESS. | | | | | |
| North American Life Assurance Co. | Toronto, Can. | 1 | $200 00 | | |
| Aggregate—industrial | | 419,080 | $55,819,345 15 | 92,938 | $8,264,012 00 |
| Combined—aggregate | | 532,767 | $323,811,573 72 | 174,084 | $123,601,433 41 |

Concluded.

| By expiry. | | By surrender. | | By lapse, decrease and withdrawal. | | Total | |
|---|---|---|---|---|---|---|---|
| No. | Amount. | No. | Amount. | No. | Amount. | No. | Amount. |
| | | | | | $ 93,700 00 | | $ 94,700 00 |
| | | | | | 208,000 00 | | 211,000 00 |
| | | | | | 271,359 00 | | 273,905 00 |
| 170 | $14,780,460 00 | | $ 125,074 00 | | 101,656,953 00 | 170 | 118,722,157 00 |
| | | | | 2 | 401,894 59 | 2 | 407,193 49 |
| | 3,060,076 00 | | | 3 | 931,508 00 | 3 | 4,064,732 00 |
| 1 | 1,996,389 00 | | | | | 1 | 2,000,000 00 |
| | | 4,456 | 4,649,855 00 | | 1,500 00 | 4,520 | 4,737,305 00 |
| 1 | 63,000 00 | | | | 254,700 00 | 1 | 320,900 00 |
| | | | | | 57,200 00 | | 65,900 00 |
| | | | | 45 | 16,930,238 00 | 45 | 17,263,298 00 |
| 2 | 195,500 00 | | 1,009,014 00 | 228 | 188,683,073 00 | 230 | 192,945,959 00 |
| 4 | 7,900 00 | | | | | 6 | 13,040 00 |
| 271 | $66,011,282 00 | 4,457 | $5,894,943 00 | 457 | $662,854,023 59 | 5,251 | $746,097,911 49 |
| | | | | 5 | $1,180,200 00 | 5 | $1,199,900 00 |
| | | | | | 6,400 00 | | 6,400 00 |
| | | | | 5 | $1,186;600 00 | 5 | $1,206,300 00 |
| 271 | $66,011,282 00 | 4,457 | $5,894,943 00 | 465 | $664,337,873 59 | 5,259 | $747,601,461 49 |
| | | 8 | $ 800 00 | 130 | $24,372 00 | 142 | $ 26,172 00 |
| 196 | $22,305 00 | 42 | 5,042 68 | 53 | 7,208 50 | 320 | 38,684 33 |
| | | 1,886 | 182,431 00 | 319 | 80,923 00 | 2,209 | 263,921 00 |
| | | | | 226 | 30,812 00 | 236 | 32,199 00 |
| 196 | $22,305 00 | 1,936 | $188,273 68 | 728 | $143,315 50 | 2,907 | $360,976 33 |
| | | | | 6 | $ 1,200 00 | 11 | $ 2,050 00 |
| | | 30 | $ 4,426 00 | 5 | 1,012 00 | 83 | 12,160 00 |
| | | 77 | 11,125 00 | 6,757 | 1,060,218 00 | 7,037 | 1,100,768 00 |
| | | 15 | 1,435 00 | 1 | 166 00 | 48 | 6,467 00 |
| 8,949 | $ 1,963,914 00 | 77,954 | 16,090,083 00 | 251,719 | 53,521,127 00 | 374,532 | 78,066,811 00 |
| 21,073 | 3,168,414 00 | 220,447 | 34,649,971 00 | 1,991,391 | 362,286,400 00 | 2,515,522 | 433,063,948 00 |
| 21,681 | 4,231,825 00 | | | 1,577 | 362,850 00 | 23,370 | 4,618,275 00 |
| | | | | 598,040 | 44,440,780 00 | 610,513 | 45,265,998 00 |
| 50,430 | 25,691,096 00 | 138,655 | 20,857,019 00 | 1,177,063 | 258,177,373 00 | 1,529,955 | 326,663,256 00 |
| 157 | 3,996 00 | 4,148 | 390,903 00 | 352,020 | 76,975,070 00 | 373,094 | 79,166,745 00 |
| 5 | 983 00 | 1 | 440 00 | 2 | 591 00 | 8 | 2,014 00 |
| 102,295 | $35,060,228 00 | 441,327 | $72,005,402 00 | 4,378,581 | $796,826,787 00 | 5,434,173 | $967,968,492 00 |
| | | 1 | $110 00 | | | 2 | $310 00 |
| 102,491 | $35,082,533 00 | 443,264 | $72,193,785 68 | 4,379,309 | $796,970,102 50 | 5,437,082 | $968,329,778 33 |
| 242,688 | $370,843,510 24 | 671,654 | $592,045,785 59 | 5,346.576 | $3,630,579,567 09 | 6,967,769 | $5,040,881,870 05 |

—4 L I

# TABLE NO. 10.

SHOWING DETAILED STATEMENT OF THE BUSINESS TRANSACTED IN THE STATE OF ILLINOIS BY ALL COMPANIES FOR THE YEAR ENDING DECEMBER 31, 1921.

| Name of company—location. | Policies issued. | | Policies terminated. | | Policies in force December 31, 1921. | | | Premiums received. | Losses paid. |
|---|---|---|---|---|---|---|---|---|---|
| | Number. | Amount. | Number. | Amount. | Number. | Amount. | Average amount of each policy. | | |
| I. COMPANIES OF THIS STATE. | | | | | | | | | |
| The American Bankers Ins. Co., Chicago | 640 | $ 929,330 00 | 848 | $ 635,276 00 | 3,145 | $ 2,585,630 00 | $ 822 14 | $ 68,406 55 | $ 24,643 00 |
| Central Life Ins. Co. of Illinois, Ottawa | 1,559 | 3,924,298 00 | 994 | 2,409,738 00 | 14,156 | 26,462,999 00 | 1,869 38 | 794,244 54 | 111,096 00 |
| Cloverleaf Life and Casualty Co., Jacksonville | 371 | 634,783 00 | 257 | 463,529 00 | 758 | 1,294,160 00 | 1,707 34 | 35,859 91 | 10,000 00 |
| Continental Assurance Co., Chicago | 1,228 | 2,731,607 00 | 709 | 1,520,186 00 | 2,684 | 5,600,212 00 | 2,086 52 | 169,109 95 | 10,000 00 |
| Elgin Life Ins. Co., Elgin | 51 | 81,500 00 | 39 | 56,100 00 | 769 | 1,045,217 00 | 1,359 19 | 26,056 19 | 14,700 00 |
| Federal Life, Chicago | 322 | 760,846 00 | 701 | 3,302,811 00 | 4,396 | 7,624,283 00 | 1,734 37 | 248,716 91 | 50,392 97 |
| The Franklin Life, Springfield | 2,539 | 6,947,760 00 | 1,887 | 5,543,026 00 | 16,129 | 39,206,506 00 | 2,430 81 | 1,198,037 08 | 146,774 20 |
| Illinois Life, Chicago | 5,188 | 17,109,825 00 | 3,942 | 12,933,816 00 | 33,589 | 76,703,818 72 | 2,283 60 | 1,925,359 72 | 334,636 67 |
| International Life and Trust Co., Moline | 501 | 1,107,387 00 | 511 | 1,057,459 00 | 1,683 | 3,363,343 00 | 1,998 42 | 109,401 77 | 12,000 00 |
| Liberty Life Ins. Co., Chicago | 179 | 238,500 00 | 2 | 2,000 00 | 177 | 236,500 00 | 1,336 16 | 4,736 67 | |
| Marquette Life, Springfield | 745 | 1,102,664 00 | 270 | 374,350 00 | 3,110 | 3,820,324 00 | 1,228 40 | 129,310 05 | 35,600 00 |
| Mutual Life of Illinois, Springfield | 850 | 2,035,212 00 | 727 | 1,565,949 00 | 2,743 | 6,060,763 00 | 2,209 54 | 147,578 74 | 9,000 00 |
| Mutual Trust Life, Chicago | 1,303 | 2,988,588 00 | 742 | 1,735,722 00 | 11,678 | 18,399,442 00 | 1,575 56 | 667,544 13 | 154,865 00 |
| National Life of U. S. A., Chicago | 1,048 | 5,159,100 97 | 995 | 3,847,771 35 | 12,143 | 29,206,587 87 | 2,405 16 | 902,460 35 | 204,602 64 |
| North American Life Ins. Co. of Chi., Chicago | 244 | 573,914 00 | 113 | 371,579 00 | 2,013 | 4,761,554 00 | 2,365 40 | 149,413 19 | 19,606 82 |
| Old Colony Life, Chicago | 1,855 | 1,931,100 06 | 1,184 | 1,463,823 52 | 7,180 | 7,273,851 05 | 1,013 07 | 235,437 67 | 66,331 48 |
| Peoples Life, Chicago | 2,939 | 2,913,007 46 | 1,105 | 539,231 78 | 8,129 | 5,649,512 65 | 694 98 | 177,410 25 | 22,042 25 |
| Peoria Life, Peoria | 2,735 | 8,166,574 00 | 1,470 | 4,405,309 00 | 15,487 | 35,897,394 00 | 2,317 91 | 1,090,293 11 | 101,904 43 |
| Providers' Life Assurance Co., Chicago | 3,120 | 1,102,350 00 | 4,010 | 1,424,911 00 | 17,383 | 6,506,097 00 | 3,742 79 | 209,689 71 | 44,831 00 |
| Public Life Ins. Co., Chicago | 754 | 1,255,500 00 | 115 | 226,000 00 | 1,309 | 2,434,000 00 | 1,859 43 | 80,692 09 | 4,000 00 |
| Rockford Life, Rockford | 973 | 2,470,900 00 | 708 | 1,362,699 00 | 4,614 | 8,072,924 00 | 1,749 66 | 226,066 83 | 32,334 64 |
| Standard Life, Decatur | 1,214 | 2,355,944 00 | 1,118 | 1,593,434 00 | 14,444 | 18,271,578 00 | 1,264 99 | 587,249 11 | 197,400 00 |
| Totals | 30,358 | $66,520,690 49 | 22,447 | $46,834,720 65 | 177,719 | $310,476,696 29 | $1,747 01 | $9,183,074 52 | $1,606,761 10 |
| II. COMPANIES OF OTHER STATES. | | | | | | | | | |
| Aetna Life, Hartford, Conn | 2,645 | $13,601,907 12 | 863 | $4,605,979 18 | 21,116 | $60,428,649 68 | 2,861 75 | $1,873,132 33 | $612,288 00 |
| American Central Life, Indianapolis, Ind | 261 | 519,043 00 | 310 | 706,862 00 | 1,467 | 2,982,677 00 | 2,033 18 | 78,358 00 | 78,356 00 |

| | | | | | | | | | |
|---|---|---|---|---|---|---|---|---|---|
| American Life Ins. Co., Detroit, Mich | 474 | 757,048 13 | 37 | 93,375 00 | 442 | 727,474 13 | 1,645 87 | 10,091 85 | 2,000 00 |
| American Life Reinsurance Co., Dallas, Tex. | 65 | 471,680 00 | 16 | 75,182 00 | 97 | 563,860 00 | 5,812 99 | 4,083 58 | |
| American Nat. Assur. Co., St. Louis, Mo | 95 | 173,500 00 | 169 | 302,724 00 | 450 | 886,046 00 | 1,968 99 | 29,607 45 | 2,000 00 |
| Bankers Life Co., Des Moines, Iowa | 2,827 | 11,253,753 00 | 1,579 | 5,170,763 00 | 33,461 | 80,833,908 00 | 2,415 76 | 1,805,077 35 | 962,531 00 |
| Bankers Life Ins. Co., Lincoln, Neb | 243 | 506,653 00 | 107 | 217,000 00 | 1,570 | 2,745,417 00 | 1,748 67 | 94,767 22 | 23,500 00 |
| Bankers Reserve Life Co., Omaha, Neb | 527 | 1,422,884 51 | 239 | 1,151,217 50 | 3,380 | 6,431,650 79 | 1,902 86 | 213,164 61 | 44,409 50 |
| Berkshire Life, Pittsfield, Mass | 886 | 2,372,420 00 | 460 | 1,222,625 00 | 7,160 | 16,366,794 00 | 2,285 86 | 509,431 68 | 185,666 00 |
| Business Men's Assurance Co. of America, Kansas City, Mo | 42 | 105,000 00 | 1 | 3,000 00 | 47 | 111,000 00 | 2,361 70 | 2,355 55 | |
| Capitol Life Ins. Co. of Colo., Denver, Colo | 58 | 240,500 00 | 54 | 134,526 00 | 241 | 705,000 00 | 2,925 31 | 22,836 21 | 917 84 |
| Central Life Assur. Society of U. S. (Mutual), Des Moines, Iowa | 301 | 628,998 53 | 193 | 428,150 00 | 1,042 | 1,854,226 53 | 1,779 49 | 65,904 78 | 3,000 00 |
| Central States Life Ins. Co., St. Louis, Mo | 85 | 218,851 00 | 106 | 214,000 00 | 1,049 | 1,579,411 00 | 1,505 63 | 48,181 74 | 1,000 00 |
| Century Life, Indianapolis, Ind | 70 | 226,000 00 | 53 | 103,000 00 | 186 | 528,500 00 | 2,841 40 | 13,805 32 | 5,000 00 |
| Cleveland Life, Cleveland, Ohio | 464 | 798,500 00 | 325 | 700,648 00 | 1,356 | 2,986,501 00 | 2,202 43 | 107,212 78 | 24,018 86 |
| Columbian National Life, Boston, Mass | 1,261 | 5,776,099 00 | 665 | 2,942,855 00 | 5,835 | 22,527,184 00 | 3,860 70 | 664,691 51 | 87,305 98 |
| Columbus Mutual Life Ins. Co., Columbus, Ohio | 204 | 517,000 00 | 5 | 6,000 00 | 217 | 549,000 00 | 2,529 95 | 15,024 53 | |
| Connecticut General Life, Hartford, Conn | 482 | 1,823,531 00 | 233 | 1,025,923 00 | 3,505 | 11,089,648 00 | 3,163 95 | 453,441 32 | 34,848 15 |
| Connecticut Mutual Life, Hartford, Conn | 1,740 | 5,222,126 00 | 1,417 | 4,071,315 00 | 13,751 | 38,734,234 00 | 2,816 83 | 1,169,305 84 | 596,627 00 |
| Equitable Life Assurance Society of the U. S., New York, N. Y | 10,090 | 39,145,107 00 | 4,939 | 18,709,620 00 | 49,577 | 148,157,364 00 | 2,988 43 | 5,526,139 26 | 875,565 41 |
| Equitable Life, Des Moines, Iowa | 2,839 | 7,472,820 00 | 1,244 | 3,323,623 00 | 17,071 | 36,180,250 00 | 2,119 40 | 1,121,374 50 | 147,561 88 |
| Farmers National Life, Huntington, Ind | 939 | 2,248,650 00 | 586 | 1,202,492 00 | 2,788 | 6,297,629 00 | 2,258 83 | 164,005 28 | 8,000 00 |
| Federal Union Life, Cincinnati, Ohio | 940 | 916,387 00 | 756 | 830,800 00 | 2,060 | 1,956,687 00 | 949 85 | 55,754 49 | 24,044 00 |
| The Fidelity Mutual Life, Philadelphia, Pa | 493 | 1,964,213 00 | 242 | 969,937 00 | 3,222 | 8,636,885 00 | 2,680 60 | 322,165 46 | 85,996 50 |
| Girard Life, Philadelphia, Pa | 201 | 693,594 00 | 102 | 465,878 00 | 1,185 | 3,332,611 00 | 2,812 33 | 128,180 00 | 7,299 00 |
| The Guardian Life, New York, N. Y | 657 | 1,855,106 00 | 342 | 884,252 00 | 4,103 | 10,084,843 00 | 2,457 91 | 353,664 08 | 85,793 26 |
| Home Life, New York, N. Y | 641 | 1,736,922 00 | 606 | 1,372,954 00 | 6,871 | 14,432,551 00 | 2,100 50 | 477,434 35 | 245,706 87 |
| Indiana National Life, Indianapolis, Ind | 283 | 442,000 00 | 68 | 218,000 00 | 430 | 652,500 00 | 1,517 44 | 12,898 47 | 1,000 00 |
| Indianapolis Life, Indianapolis, Ind | 1,114 | 1,930,524 01 | 395 | 779,054 65 | 5,234 | 9,028,194 17 | 1,724 91 | 276,136 40 | 25,000 00 |
| International Life, St. Louis, Mo | 1,656 | 5,026,282 00 | 1,177 | 3,564,776 00 | 6,000 | 12,505,163 00 | 2,084 19 | 426,731 21 | 75,897 00 |
| John Hancock Mutual Life, Boston, Mass | 6,818 | 11,156,958 00 | 3,678 | 6,888,181 00 | 41,195 | 65,487,926 00 | 1,589 71 | 1,992,039 54 | 461,583 00 |
| Kansas City Life, Kansas City, Mo | 284 | 617,684 00 | 75 | 150,500 00 | 883 | 1,667,572 00 | 1,888 53 | 60,743 28 | 13,000 00 |
| La Fayette Life Ins. Co., La Fayette, Ind | 164 | 233,822 00 | | | 164 | 233,822 00 | 1,425 74 | 9,089 43 | |
| Lincoln National Life, Ft. Wayne, Ind | 5,023 | 7,111,121 64 | 475 | 1,488,547 00 | 6,423 | 11,079,935 64 | 1,725 04 | 302,583 50 | 35,883 68 |
| Manhattan Life, New York, N. Y | 135 | 464,260 95 | 138 | 285,353 25 | 1,543 | 2,585,044 70 | 1,675 34 | 73,730 41 | 56,878 60 |
| Maryland Assurance Corp., Baltimore, Md | 51 | 240,144 00 | 7 | 20,500 00 | 115 | 549,644 00 | 4,779 51 | 8,085 87 | |
| Massachusetts Mutual Life, Springfield, Mass. | 4,036 | 18,180,485 00 | 1,818 | 6,294,976 00 | 25,167 | 83,489,622 00 | 3,317 42 | 2,730,001 98 | 599,803 94 |
| Merchants Life, Des Moines, Iowa | 313 | 904,400 00 | 315 | 743,939 00 | 3,895 | 8,382,608 00 | 2,152 15 | 196,689 86 | 60,000 00 |
| Metropolitan Life, New York, N. Y | 56,248 | 62,888,887 00 | 27,417 | 25,147,747 00 | 268,344 | 272,032,198 00 | 1,013 74 | 9,171,623 48 | 2,290,963 00 |
| Michigan Mutual Life, Detroit, Mich | 541 | 1,334,268 36 | 328 | 622,921 54 | 3,486 | 7,007,221 83 | 2,010 10 | 194,941 71 | 84,804 17 |

TABLE NO. 10—Continued.

| Name of company—location. | Policies issued. | | Policies terminated. | | Policies in force December 31, 1921. | | | Premiums received. | Losses paid. |
|---|---|---|---|---|---|---|---|---|---|
| | Number. | Amount. | Number. | Amount. | Number. | Amount. | Average amount of each policy. | | |
| Minnesota Mutual Life, St. Paul, Minn | 245 | $ 654,328 0 | 95 | $ 346,675 00 | 986 | $ 2,081,710 58 | $2,111 27 | $ 64,708 57 | $ 30,319 00 |
| Missouri State Life, St. Louis, Mo | 1,855 | 7,548,314 0 | 851 | 2,567,554 00 | 8,540 | 21,316,370 00 | 2,496 06 | 700,346 35 | 70,270 05 |
| Mutual Benefit Life, Newark, N. J | 2,524 | 10,662,079 0 | 1,199 | 4,903,565 00 | 30,943 | 112,750,608 00 | 3,634 82 | 3,727,543 29 | 1,021,197 0 |
| Mutual Life, New York, N. Y | 9,074 | 34,919,214 85 | 5,787 | 16,533,165 92 | 73,323 | 220,575,256 15 | 3,008 27 | 7,383,638 47 | 2,030,757 97 |
| National Life and Accident Ins. Co., Nashville, Tenn | 74 | 135, 0 00 | 21 | 25,000 00 | 101 | 180,000 00 | 1,782 18 | 4,097 90 | |
| National Life Ins. Co., Montpelier, Vt | 678 | 2,464,023 45 | 329 | 985,027 75 | 4,222 | 13,195,741 79 | 3,125 47 | 453,253 95 | 149,514 71 |
| New England Mutual Life, Boston, Mass | 1,288 | 6,961,637 0 | 717 | 2,880,794 0 | 11,277 | 43,850,502 0 | 3,888 49 | 1,400,413 30 | 468,552 00 |
| New World Life, Spokane, Wash | 182 | 357,771 84 | 164 | 297,130 0 | 898 | 1,575,692 05 | 1,754 67 | 45,302 98 | 7, 0 0 |
| New York Life, New York, N. Y | 21,566 | 56,551,466 0 | 10,312 | 23,659,774 0 | 158,995 | 337,614,782 0 | 2,123 43 | 12,234,005 83 | 4,146,386 25 |
| Northern States Life, Hammond, Ind | 121 | 314,500 0 | 273 | 560,179 0 | 3,234 | 4,989,525 0 | 1,542 83 | 154,785 63 | 36,380 0 |
| Northwestern Mutual Life, Milwaukee, Wis | 7,882 | 31,764,447 0 | 3,423 | 12,018,318 00 | 75,729 | 254,697,227 00 | 3,363 27 | 8,185,644 54 | 2,609,270 54 |
| Northwestern Nat. Life, Minneapolis, Minn | 65 | 313,314 0 | 23 | 192,651 00 | 732 | 1,689,863 0 | 2,308 56 | 64,317 99 | 12,883 81 |
| Old Line Ins. Co., Lincoln, Neb | 14 | 29, 0 0 | | | 25 | 46, 0 0 | 1,840 0 | 697 11 | |
| Old Line Life Ins. Co. of Am., Milwaukee, Wis | 311 | 643,884 0 | 109 | 295,590 00 | 980 | 2,187,061 26 | 2,231 70 | 56,747 85 | 3,434 00 |
| Pacific Mutual Life, Los Angeles, Cal | 1,022 | 3,358,520 0 | 496 | 1,209,500 00 | 8,259 | 18,582,635 0 | 2,249 99 | 620,227 41 | 111,213 00 |
| Pan American Life, New Orleans, La | 108 | 205, 0 00 | 172 | 387,634 0 | 867 | 1,490,915 0 | 1,719 63 | 43,810 74 | |
| Penn Mutual Life, Philadelphia, Pa | 1,813 | 9,640,018 00 | 972 | 4,412,874 00 | 15,566 | 70,094,353 0 | 4,503 04 | 2,218,569 48 | 458,055 11 |
| Peoples Life, Frankfort, Ind | 159 | 262,475 0 | 5 | 8,750 0 | 193 | 322,205 0 | 1,669 46 | 8,878 11 | |
| Philadelphia Life, Philadelphia, Pa | 38 | 236,829 0 | 28 | 194,718 0 | 267 | 867,753 0 | 3,250 01 | 29,415 64 | 18,100 0 |
| Phoenix Mutual Life, Hartford, Conn | 472 | 2,698,059 05 | 246 | 828,820 07 | 4,734 | 15,346,796 85 | 3,241 82 | 531,717 73 | 181,514 90 |
| Provident Life and Trust, Philadelphia, Pa | 1,606 | 5,234,698 00 | 964 | 3,160,741 0 | 8,325 | 24,970,211 00 | 2,999 42 | 825,518 58 | 204,566 0 |
| Prudential Ins. Co. of America, Newark, N. J | 28,979 | 36,979,805 00 | 15,401 | 17,871,380 0 | 175,046 | 201,640,018 00 | 1,151 98 | 5,858,538 28 | 1,495,216 55 |
| Reinsurance Life Co. of Am., Des Moines, Ia | 328 | 1,560,187 00 | 199 | 519,732 0 | 577 | 2,691,228 00 | 4,664 17 | 28,233 44 | 475 0 |
| Reliance Life, Pittsburgh, Pa | 1,112 | 2,631,778 00 | 408 | 1,192,217 0 | 3,671 | 8,981,482 00 | 2,446 60 | 312,273 82 | 36,984 16 |
| Reserve Loan Life, Indianapolis, Ind | 184 | 553,000 00 | 173 | 585,810 0 | 315 | 911,008 00 | 2,892 09 | 35,504 77 | 7,500 0 |
| Security Life Ins. Co. of Am., Richmond, Va | 1,053 | 2,063,135 0 | 889 | 1,723,382 0 | 3,355 | 5,816,690 0 | 1,733 74 | 178,617 68 | 13, 0 0 |
| Security Mutual Life, Binghamton, N. Y | 229 | 460,848 20 | 145 | 288,298 20 | 2,051 | 3,111,569 12 | 1,517 10 | 100,593 31 | 10,012 20 |
| State Life, Indianapolis, Ind | 247 | 2,170,259 0 | 87 | 830,204 0 | 1,828 | 9,767,292 00 | 5,343 16 | 295,496 72 | 34, 0 0 |
| State Mutual Life Assur., Worcester, Mass | 938 | 5,010,308 0 | 660 | 2,634,535 0 | 8,463 | 34,022,007 0 | 4,020 09 | 1,145,554 51 | 440,532 55 |
| The Travelers Ins. Co., Hartford, Conn | 5,999 | 25,225,866 0 | 1,322 | 6,058,138 0 | 22,311 | 87,528,900 0 | 3,923,13 | 2,172,220 11 | 608,479 15 |

| | | | | | | | | | |
|---|---|---|---|---|---|---|---|---|---|
| Union Central Life, Cincinnati, Ohio | 2,678 | 9,381,869 00 | 2,251 | 6,922,296 00 | 23,381 | 67,683,321 00 | 2,894 80 | 2,219,552 05 | 955,794 96 |
| Union Mutual Life, Portland, Me | 130 | 291,609 86 | 139 | 303,491 74 | 1,890 | 4,074,733 75 | 2,155 94 | 132,440 12 | 75,693 62 |
| United States Life, New York, N. Y | 201 | 450,846 00 | 189 | 363,515 00 | 1,272 | 2,424,874 00 | 1,906 35 | 58,860 05 | 41,033 33 |
| Universal Life Ins. Co., Dubuque, Iowa | 23 | 63,500 00 | ------ | ------ | 23 | 63,500 00 | 2,760 87 | 1,966 38 | ------ |
| Western and Southern Life, Cincinnati, Ohio | 2,400 | 2,593,250 00 | 1,424 | 1,543,550 00 | 4,260 | 4,485,600 00 | 1,052 96 | 86,996 20 | 18,635 00 |
| Western Union Life Ins. Co., Spokane, Wash | 56 | 94,754 00 | 17 | 30,500 00 | 131 | 216,139 00 | 1,649 92 | 6,564 88 | 15,150 00 |
| Wisconsin National Life, Oshkosh, Wis | 402 | 523,498 80 | 200 | 273,838 68 | 1,272 | 1,670,415 77 | 1,313 22 | 44,587 91 | 6,000 00 |
| Totals | 202,252 | $478,208,222 30 | 101,330 | $213,748,544 48 | 1,204,170 | $2,539,934,437 79 | $2,109 28 | $82,216,127 35 | $23,166,169 50 |
| III. COMPANIES OF FOREIGN GOVERNMENTS. | | | | | | | | | |
| Canada Life Assurance Co., Toronto, Can | 82 | $1,371,817 00 | 64 | $379,796 00 | 1,692 | $10,151,961 00 | $5,999 98 | $368,660 71 | $84,062 50 |
| Manufacturers Life, Toronto, Can | 83 | 133,833 00 | 29 | 50,000 00 | 253 | 997,490 00 | 3,942 65 | 63,594 68 | ------ |
| North Amer. Life Assur. Co., Toronto, Can | 45 | 103,050 00 | 78 | 129,335 00 | 1,270 | 1,981,717 00 | 1,560 41 | 50,669 92 | 10,500 00 |
| Totals | 210 | $1,608,700 00 | 171 | $559,131 00 | 3,215 | $13,131,168 00 | $4,084 34 | $482,925 31 | $94,562 50 |
| Aggregate | 232,820 | $546,337,612 79 | 123,948 | $261,142,396 13 | 1,385,104 | $2,863,542,302 08 | $2,067 38 | $91,882,127 18 | $24,867,493 10 |
| I. COMPANIES OF THIS STATE—GROUP INSURANCE. | | | | | | | | | |
| The American Bankers Ins. Co., Chicago | ------ | ------ | 1 | $208,250 00 | ------ | ------ | ------ | ------ | $1,482 00 |
| II. COMPANIES OF OTHER STATES—GROUP INSURANCE. | | | | | | | | | |
| Aetna Life, Hartford, Conn | 10 | $21,050,064 00 | 12 | $14,847,526 00 | 107 | $35,626,739 00 | $332,960 18 | $258,976 62 | $186,811 00 |
| Capitol Life Ins. Co. of Colo., Denver, Colo | 1 | 1,819,000 00 | ------ | ------ | 1 | 1,819,000 00 | 819,000 00 | 13,781 49 | 500 00 |
| Connecticut General Life, Hartford, Conn | 3 | 475,900 00 | ------ | 275,000 00 | 5 | 763,000 00 | 152,600 00 | 5,475 50 | 3,200 00 |
| Equitable Life Assurance Society of the U. S., New York, N. Y | 40 | 10,200,640 00 | 6 | 11,046,468 00 | 97 | 20,881,208 00 | 215,270 19 | 282,272 60 | 174,048 25 |
| The Guardian Life, New York, N. Y | ------ | 3,250 00 | 1 | 195,000 00 | ------ | ------ | ------ | —281 76 | 750 00 |
| Metropolitan Life, New York, N. Y | 16 | 3,662,500 00 | 7 | 2,462,750 00 | 63 | 6,391,450 00 | 101,451 59 | 67,769 47 | 35,236 00 |
| Missouri State Life, St. Louis, Mo | 6 | 822,900 00 | ------ | 151,900 00 | 8 | 782,500 00 | 97,812 50 | 9,327 66 | 5,500 00 |
| Prudential Ins. Co. of America, Newark, N. J. | 3 | 729,900 00 | 2 | 596,100 00 | 9 | 2,078,100 00 | 230,900 00 | 19,669 97 | 22,900 00 |
| The Travelers Ins. Co., Hartford, Conn | 13 | 13,902,943 00 | 20 | 17,399,198 00 | 105 | 32,363,247 00 | 308,221 40 | 334,641 81 | 209,635 77 |
| Total | 92 | $52,667,097 00 | 48 | $46,973,942 00 | 395 | $100,705,244 00 | $254,949 98 | $991,633 36 | $638,581 02 |
| III. COMPANIES OF FOREIGN GOVERNMENTS—GROUP INSURANCE. | | | | | | | | | |
| Canada Life Assurance Co., Toronto, Can | 1 | $156,500 00 | ------ | $3,250 00 | 1 | $153,250 00 | $153,250 00 | $1,493 00 | ------ |
| Aggregate—group | 93 | $52,823,597 00 | 49 | $47,185,442 00 | 396 | $100,858,494 00 | $254,693 17 | $993,126 36 | $640,063 02 |

TABLE NO. 10—Concluded.

| Name of company—location. | Policies issued. | | Policies terminated. | | Policies in force December 31, 1921. | | | Premiums received. | Losses paid. |
|---|---|---|---|---|---|---|---|---|---|
| | Number. | Amount. | Number. | Amount. | Number. | Amount. | Average amount of each policy. | | |
| I. COMPANIES OF THIS STATE—INDUSTRIAL BUSINESS. | | | | | | | | | |
| Federal Life, Chicago | | | —2 | $ 1,781 00 | 157 | $ 20,421 00 | $130 07 | $ 696 41 | |
| Peoples Life, Chicago | 11 | $1,902 00 | 320 | 38,684 33 | 3,336 | 437,355 75 | 131 10 | 8,958 95 | $4,160 15 |
| Providers' Life Assurance Co., Chicago | 54 | 8,069 00 | 2,209 | 263,921 00 | 2,605 | 62,856 00 | 24 13 | 2,284 05 | 437 00 |
| Public Life Ins. Co., Chicago | 576 | 82,765 00 | 236 | 32,199 00 | 570 | 79,188 00 | 138 93 | 2,889 18 | 606 50 |
| Total | 641 | $92,736 00 | 2,763 | $336,585 33 | 6,668 | $599,820 75 | $89 96 | $14,828 59 | $5,203 65 |
| II. *COMPANIES OF OTHER STATES—INDUSTRIAL BUSINESS. | | | | | | | | | |
| Federal Union Life, Cincinnati, Ohio | 669 | $ 92,285 00 | 1,027 | $ 163,364 00 | 2,528 | $ 370,608 00 | $146 60 | $ 17,206 20 | $ 1,640 00 |
| The Guardian Life, New York, N. Y. | | | | | 11 | 1,544 00 | 140 36 | 18 00 | |
| John Hancock Mutual Life, Boston, Mass. | 26,378 | 7,145,212 00 | 20,128 | 4,122,253 00 | 145,788 | 32,575,245 00 | 223 44 | 946,664 75 | 228,556 85 |
| Metropolitan Life, New York, N. Y. | 280,841 | 42,626,898 00 | 144,051 | 24,428,564 00 | 1,668,255 | 220,214,417 00 | 132 00 | 8,387,282 45 | 2,279,296 39 |
| Morris Plan Ins. Society, New York, N. Y. | 5,204 | 1,062,700 00 | 2,671 | 617,850 00 | 5,190 | 1,059,650 00 | 204 17 | 27,994 25 | 3,050 00 |
| National Life and Accident Ins. Co., Nashville, Tenn. | 18,752 | 1,683,088 00 | 33,767 | 2,421,983 00 | 37,064 | 2,500,419 00 | 67 46 | 96,226 17 | 31,542 42 |
| Prudential Ins. Co. of America, Newark, N. J. | 246,949 | 51,017,520 00 | 119,069 | 23,593,404 00 | 1,721,130 | 255,053,059 00 | 148 18 | 9,059,152 54 | 1,658,382 39 |
| Western and Southern Life, Cincinnati, Ohio | 29,251 | 6,558,857 00 | 24,337 | 5,281,129 00 | 35,355 | 7,822,278 00 | 221 25 | 282,439 95 | 48,598 28 |
| Wisconsin National Life, Oshkosh, Wis. | 1 | 549 00 | | | 3 | 824 00 | 274 66 | 28 00 | |
| Total | 608,045 | $110,187,109 00 | 345,050 | $60,628,547 00 | 3,615,324 | $519,598,044 00 | $143 72 | $18,817,012 31 | $4,251,066 33 |
| Aggregate—industrial | 608,686 | $110,279,845 00 | 347,813 | $60,965,132 33 | 3,621,992 | $520,197,864 75 | $143 62 | $18,831,840 90 | $4,256,269 98 |
| Combined aggregate | 841,599 | $709,441,054 79 | 471,810 | $369,292,970 46 | 5,007,492 | $3,484,598,660 83 | $695 88 | $111,707,094 44 | $29,763,826 10 |

# ASSESSMENT LIFE TABLES.

## TABLE NO. 1.

SHOWING ASSETS AND LIABILITIES OF ASSESSMENT LIFE ASSOCIATIONS TRANSACTING BUSINESS IN THIS STATE FOR THE YEAR ENDING DECEMBER 31, 1921.

| Name of association. | Location. | Assets. | | | | Liabilities. | | |
|---|---|---|---|---|---|---|---|---|
| | | Ledger assets. | Non-ledger assets. | Total unadmitted assets. | Total admitted assets. | Total unpaid claims. | All other liabilities. | Total liabilities. |
| I. ASSOCIATIONS OF THIS STATE. | | | | | | | | |
| Bankers Mutual Life Co. | Freeport | $ 107,605 60 | $ 4,956 74 | | $ 112,562 34 | $ 22,394 90 | $10,195 24 | $ 32,590 14 |
| Chicago Mutual Life Co. | Chicago | 70,328 80 | 218 08 | $43,865 00 | 26,681 88 | | 7,850 11 | 7,850 11 |
| Cloverleaf Mutual Life Ins. Co. | Jacksonville | —1,906 04 | | | —1,906 04 | | | |
| Drexel Mutual Life Ins. Co. | Chicago | 1, 0 0 | | | 1, 0 0 | | | |
| Globe Mutual Life Ins. Co. | Chicago | 329,191 32 | 95,767 07 | 62,152 56 | 362,805 83 | 9,192 00 | 12,695 89 | 21,887 89 |
| Guaranteed Equity Life Co. | Chicago | 17,304 24 | 2,042 17 | 2,042 17 | 17,304 24 | | 10,844 46 | 10,844 46 |
| Hotel Men's Mut. Benefit Assn. of U. S. & Can. | Chicago | 67,297 0 | 1,239 43 | | 68,536 43 | 11,400 00 | 680 98 | 12,080 98 |
| Illinois Bankers Life Assn. | Monmouth | 2,198,597 97 | 53,048 10 | 9,925 61 | 2,241,720 46 | 123,265 80 | 44,991 21 | 168,257 01 |
| Merchants Reserve Life Ins. Co. | Chicago | 105,635 77 | 3,196 28 | 8,258 93 | 100,573 12 | 6,464 79 | 7,233 90 | 13,698 69 |
| Rochdale Life Ins. Co. of Illinois | Chicago | 1,650 35 | 10 80 | 17 72 | 1,643 43 | | 8 09 | 8 09 |
| Swedish Baptists Mutual Aid Assn. of America | Chicago | 183,652 21 | 2,227 62 | 4,418 56 | 181,461 27 | 3,500 00 | 3,651 77 | 7,151 77 |
| Swedish Methodists Aid Assn. | Chicago | 219,847 95 | 2,718 97 | 1,378 44 | 221,188 48 | | 56 50 | 56 50 |
| Swedish Mission Friends Aid Assn. | Chicago | 253,206 41 | 3,765 24 | | 256,971 65 | 9,000 00 | 918 79 | 9,918 79 |
| Western Life Indemnity Co. | Chicago | 165,701 15 | 6,615 71 | 31,578 25 | 140,738 61 | 50,689 55 | 4,688 04 | 55,377 59 |
| Totals | | $3,719,112 73 | $175,806 21 | $163,637 24 | $3,731,281 70 | $235,907 04 | $103,814 98 | $339,722 02 |
| II. ASSOCIATIONS OF OTHER STATES. | | | | | | | | |
| Expressmen's Mutual Benefit Assn. | New York, N. Y. | $1,132,340 35 | $ 63,009 36 | $ 17,323 56 | $1,178,026 15 | $ 5,500 00 | $1,022,387 73 | $1,027,887 73 |
| Guarantee Fund Life Assn. | Omaha, Neb. | 4,945,120 39 | 108,591 82 | 134,039 10 | 4,919,673 11 | 477,986 44 | 47,702 25 | 525,688 69 |
| Knights Templars and Masonic M. A. Assn. | Cincinnati, Ohio | 466,377 39 | 98,937 05 | 17,595 58 | 547,718 86 | 75,500 00 | 1,029 18 | 76,529 18 |
| National Life Assn. | Des Moines, Iowa | 1,525,448 01 | 242,649 25 | 152,640 02 | 1,615,457 24 | 81,666 07 | 24,505 87 | 106,171 94 |
| Totals | | $8,069,286 14 | $513,187 48 | $321,598 26 | $8,260,875 36 | $640,652 51 | $1,095,625 03 | $1,736,277 54 |
| Aggregate | | $11,788,398 87 | $688,993 69 | $485,235 50 | $11,992,157 06 | $876,559 55 | $1,199,440 01 | $2,075,999 56 |

# TABLE NO. 2.

SHOWING INCOME AND DISBURSEMENTS OF ASSESSMENT LIFE ASSOCIATIONS TRANSACTING BUSINESS IN THIS STATE FOR THE YEAR ENDING DECEMBER 31, 1921.

| Name of association. | Location. | Income. | | | Disbursements. | | |
|---|---|---|---|---|---|---|---|
| | | Received from members. | From other sources. | Total receipts. | Paid to members. | Other disbursements. | Total disbursements. |
| I. ASSOCIATIONS OF THIS STATE. | | | | | | | |
| Bankers Mutual Life Co | Freeport | $178,213 34 | $ 9,240 68 | $ 187,454 02 | $ 80,290 43 | $ 98,272 15 | $ 178,562 58 |
| Chicago Mutual Life Co | Chicago | 34,685 17 | 81,420 46 | 116,105 63 | 1,000 00 | 46,663 52 | 47,663 52 |
| Clover Leaf Mutual Life Ins. Co | Jacksonville | 31,389 10 | | 31,389 10 | 5,799 50 | 27,972 88 | 33,772 38 |
| Drexel Mutual Life Ins. Co | Chicago | 3,795 48 | | 3,795 48 | | 2,795 48 | 2,795 48 |
| Globe Mutual Life Ins. Co | Chicago | 409,449 02 | 14,262 39 | 423,711 41 | 92,596 30 | 228,843 73 | 321,440 03 |
| Guaranteed Equity Life Co | Chicago | 27,154 70 | 986 31 | 28,141 01 | 2,452 43 | 16,833 11 | 19,285 54 |
| Hotel Men's Mutual Benefit Assn. of U. S. & Can. | Chicago | 33,298 75 | 2,783 91 | 36,082 66 | 26,178 00 | 6,113 98 | 32,291 98 |
| Illinois Bankers Life Assn | Monmouth | 1,806,431 75 | 121,346 04 | 1,927,777 79 | 625,566 98 | 609,438 74 | 1,235,005 72 |
| Merchants Reserve Life Ins. Co | Chicago | 111,861 88 | 46,108 74 | 157,970 62 | 39,107 27 | 99,468 64 | 138,575 91 |
| Rochdale Life Ins. Co. of Illinois | Chicago | 159 72 | 46 45 | 206 17 | | 31 84 | 31 84 |
| Swedish Baptists Mutual Aid Assn. of America | Chicago | 45,240 66 | 8,599 51 | 53,840 17 | 20,500 00 | 8,383 35 | 28,883 35 |
| Swedish Methodists Aid Assn | Chicago | 75,458 98 | 11,963 80 | 87,422 78 | 59,090 00 | 11,291 35 | 70,381 35 |
| Swedish Mission Friends Aid Assn | Chicago | 37,539 41 | 14,173 48 | 51,712 89 | 13,000 00 | 7,189 26 | 20,189 26 |
| Western Life Indemnity Co | Chicago | 307,764 82 | 9,270 08 | 317,034 90 | 193,236 27 | 74,323 99 | 267,560 26 |
| Totals | | $3,102,442 78 | $320,201 85 | $3,422,644 63 | $1,158,817 18 | $1,237,622 02 | $2,396,439 20 |
| II. ASSOCIATIONS OF OTHER STATES. | | | | | | | |
| Expressmen's Mutual Benefit Assn | New York, N. Y. | $ 515,762 00 | $ 40,149 05 | $ 555,911 05 | $127,640 88 | $ 206,770 67 | $ 334,411 55 |
| Guarantee Fund Life Assn | Omaha, Neb | 2,289,703 57 | 238,759 31 | 2,528,462 88 | 621,879 60 | 1,017,968 57 | 1,639,848 17 |
| Knights Templars and Masonic M. A. Assn | Cincinnati, Ohio | 401,425 40 | 20,565 00 | 421,990 40 | 353,500 00 | 38,679 93 | 392,179 93 |
| National Life Assn | Des Moines, Iowa | 1,165,382 16 | 77,016 51 | 1,242,398 67 | 463,680 62 | 430,079 64 | 893,760 26 |
| Totals | | $4,372,273 13 | $376,489 87 | $4,748,763 00 | $1,566,701 10 | $1,693,498 81 | $3,260,199 91 |
| Aggregate | | $7,474,715 91 | $696,691 72 | $8,171,407 63 | $2,725,518 28 | $2,931,120 83 | $5,656,639 11 |

TABLE

SHOWING A GENERAL SUMMARY OF THE BUSINESS OF EACH ASSESSMENT LIFE DECEMBER

| Name of association. | Location. | Certificates in force December 31, 1920. | | Certificates written, restored, etc. | | Total. |
|---|---|---|---|---|---|---|
| | | No. | Amount. | No. | Amount. | No. |
| I. ASSOCIATIONS OF THIS STATE. | | | | | | |
| Bankers Mutual Life Co. | Freeport | 7,043 | $10,356,500 00 | 2,455 | $3,679,500 00 | 9,498 |
| Chicago Mutual Life Co. | Chicago | 563 | 898,500 00 | 555 | 897,500 00 | 1,118 |
| Cloverleaf Mut. Life Ins. Co. | Jacksonville | 6,027 | 717,958 50 | 3,054 | 687,150 00 | 9,081 |
| Drexel Mutual Life Ins. Co. | Chicago | | | 528 | 520,250 00 | 528 |
| Globe Mutual Life Ins. Co. | Chicago | 59,969 | 15,428,771 00 | 19,432 | 4,833,323 00 | 79,401 |
| Guaranteed Equity Life Co. | Chicago | 550 | 651,000 00 | 305 | 668,000 00 | 855 |
| Hotel Men's Mutual Benefit Assn. of U. S. & Can. | Chicago | 1,216 | 1,185,000 00 | 120 | 73,200 00 | 1,336 |
| Illinois Bankers Life Assn. | Monmouth | 66,830 | 108,021,587 98 | 9,961 | 20,109,125 43 | 76,791 |
| Merchants Reserve Life Ins. Co. | Chicago | 4,451 | 6,367,900 00 | 337 | 755,500 00 | 4,788 |
| Rochdale Life Ins. Co. of Ill. | Chicago | 5 | 5,000 00 | | | 5 |
| Swedish Baptists Mutual Aid Assn. of America | Chicago | 2,174 | 2,207,500 00 | 24 | 28,000 00 | 2,198 |
| Swedish Methodists Aid Assn. | Chicago | 3,817 | 3,525,000 00 | 2 | 2,000 00 | 3,819 |
| Swedish Mission Friends Aid Assn. | Chicago | 2,356 | 1,704,500 00 | 107 | 85,000 00 | 2,463 |
| Western Life Indemnity Co. | Chicago | 17,369 | 9,617,113 00 | 944 | 281,441 00 | 18,313 |
| Totals | | 172,370 | $160,686,330 48 | 37,824 | $32,619,989 43 | 210,194 |
| II. ASSOCIATIONS OF OTHER STATES. | | | | | | |
| Expressmen's Mutual Benefit Assn. | New York, N. Y. | 11,593 | $13,465,341 00 | 12,337 | $13,750,500 00 | 23,930 |
| Guarantee Fund Life Assn. | Omaha, Neb. | 51,154 | 137,071,500 00 | 13,721 | 32,762,500 00 | 64,875 |
| Knights Templars and Masonic M. A. Assn. | Cincinnati, Ohio | 5,086 | 10,209,000 00 | 227 | 566,000 00 | 5,313 |
| National Life Assn. | Des Moines, Iowa | 35,094 | 72,382,500 00 | 7,733 | 17,680,000 00 | 42,827 |
| Totals | | 102,927 | $233,128,341 00 | 34,018 | $64,759,000 00 | 136,945 |
| Aggregate | | 275,297 | $393,814,671 48 | 71,842 | $97,378,989 43 | 347,139 |

## NO. 3.

ASSOCIATION TRANSACTING BUSINESS IN THIS STATE FOR THE YEAR ENDING 31, 1921.

| Total. | Certificates terminated. | | | | | | Certificates in force December 31, 1921. | |
|---|---|---|---|---|---|---|---|---|
| | By death. | | By lapse, surrender, etc. | | Total. | | | |
| Amount. | No. | Amount. | No. | Amount. | No. | Amount. | No. | Amount. |
| $14,036,000 00 | 52 | $ 81,900 00 | 1,782 | $ 2,494,600 00 | 1,834 | $ 2,576,500 00 | 7,664 | $11,459,500 00 |
| 1,796,000 00 | 1 | 1,000 00 | 425 | 638,500 00 | 426 | 639,500 00 | 692 | 1,156,500 00 |
| 1,405,108 50 | 38 | 5,799 50 | 1,695 | 381,375 00 | 1,733 | 387,174 50 | 7,348 | 1,017,934 00 |
| 520,250 00 | ------ | ------------ | 247 | 243,000 00 | 247 | 243,000 00 | 281 | 277,250 00 |
| 20,262,094 00 | 873 | 93,350 00 | 12,727 | 3,465,505 00 | 13,600 | 3,558,855 00 | 65,801 | 16,703,239 00 |
| 1,319,000 00 | 3 | 3,000 00 | 146 | 270,000 00 | 149 | 273,000 00 | 706 | 1,046,000 00 |
| 1,258,200 00 | 27 | 30,000 00 | 96 | 67,800 00 | 123 | 97,800 00 | 1,213 | 1,160,400 00 |
| 128,130,713 41 | 384 | 584,459 02 | 14,165 | 25,345,076 48 | 14,549 | 25,929,535 50 | 62,242 | 102,201,177 91 |
| 7,123,400 00 | 29 | 35,750 00 | 750 | 1,473,000 00 | 779 | 1,508,750 00 | 4,009 | 5,614,650 00 |
| 5,000 00 | ------ | ------------ | ------ | ------------ | ------ | ------------ | 5 | 5,000 00 |
| 2,235,500 00 | 20 | 21,500 00 | 15 | 15,000 00 | 35 | 36,500 00 | 2,163 | 2,199,000 00 |
| 3,527,000 00 | 67 | 56,470 00 | 570 | 556,910 00 | 637 | 613,380 00 | 3,182 | 2,913,620 00 |
| 1,789,500 00 | 28 | 19,000 00 | 54 | 41,500 00 | 82 | 60,500 00 | 2,381 | 1,729,000 00 |
| 9,898,554 00 | 310 | 180,333 67 | 2,530 | 801,194 33 | 2,840 | 981,528 00 | 15,473 | 8,917,026 00 |
| $193,306,319 91 | 1,832 | $1,112,562 19 | 35,202 | $35,793,460 81 | 37,034 | $36,906,023 00 | 173,160 | $156,400,296 91 |
| $ 27,215,841 00 | 85 | $115,000 00 | 2,854 | $ 3,616,950 00 | 2,939 | $ 3,731,950 00 | 20,991 | $23,483,891 00 |
| 169,834,000 00 | 257 | 717,500 00 | 12,781 | 27,221,000 00 | 13,038 | 27,938,500 00 | 51,837 | 141,895,500 00 |
| 10,775,000 00 | 131 | 311,000 00 | 208 | 493,000 00 | 339 | 804,000 00 | 4,974 | 9,971,000 00 |
| 90,062,500 00 | 247 | 476,000 00 | 8,358 | 18,430,500 00 | 8,605 | 18,906,500 00 | 34,222 | 71,156,000 00 |
| $297,887,341 00 | 720 | $1,619,500 00 | 24,201 | $49,761,450 00 | 24,921 | $51,380,950 00 | 112,024 | $246,506,391 00 |
| $491,193,660 91 | 2,552 | $2,732,062 19 | 59,403 | $85,554,910 81 | 61,955 | $88,286,973 00 | 285,184 | $402,906,687 91 |

# TABLE

SHOWING A GENERAL SUMMARY OF THE BUSINESS IN THE STATE OF ILLINOIS OF FOR THE YEAR ENDING

| Name of association. | Location. | Certificates in force December 31, 1920. | | Certificates written restored, etc. | |
|---|---|---|---|---|---|
| | | No. | Amount. | No. | Amount. |
| I. ASSOCIATIONS OF THIS STATE. | | | | | |
| Bankers Mutual Life Co | Freeport | 4,060 | $ 6,024,500 00 | 1,306 | $1,827,000 00 |
| Chicago Mutual Life Co | Chicago | 563 | 898,500 00 | 198 | 429,000 00 |
| Cloverleaf Mutual Life Ins. Co | Jacksonville | 6,027 | 717,958 50 | 3,054 | 687,150 00 |
| Drexel Mutual Life Ins. Co | Chicago | | | 528 | 520,250 00 |
| Globe Mutual Life Ins. Co | Chicago | 59,969 | 15,428,771 00 | 19,432 | 4,833,323 00 |
| Guaranteed Equity Life Co | Chicago | 550 | 651,000 00 | 305 | 668,000 00 |
| Hotel Men's Mutual Benefit Assn. of U. S. & Can | Chicago | 131 | 127,800 00 | 12 | 7,200 00 |
| Illinois Bankers Life Assn | Monmouth | 27,775 | 45,355,595 85 | 2,452 | 4,101,305 13 |
| Merchants Reserve Life Ins. Co | Chicago | 2,344 | 3,308,000 00 | 200 | 424,500 00 |
| Rochdale Life Ins. Co. of Illinois | Chicago | 5 | 5,000 00 | | |
| Swedish Baptists Mutual Aid Assn. of America | Chicago | 2,174 | 2,207,500 00 | 24 | 28,000 00 |
| Swedish Methodists Aid Assn | Chicago | 3,817 | 3,525,000 00 | 2 | 2,000 00 |
| Swedish Mission Friends Aid Assn | Chicago | 2,356 | 1,704,500 00 | 107 | 85,000 00 |
| Western Life Indemnity Co | Chicago | 7,213 | 3,564,125 00 | 668 | 161,181 00 |
| Totals | | 116,984 | $83,518,250 35 | 28,288 | $13,773,909 13 |
| II. ASSOCIATIONS OF OTHER STATES. | | | | | |
| Expressmen's Mutual Benefit Assn | New York, N. Y. | 1,913 | $2,222,091 00 | 1,473 | $1,502,409 00 |
| Guarantee Fund Life Assn | Omaha, Neb | 1,449 | 4,045,500 00 | 555 | 1,677,500 00 |
| Knights Templars and Masonic M. A. Assn | Cincinnati, Ohio | 480 | 785,000 00 | 17 | 44,000 00 |
| National Life Assn | Des Moines, Iowa | 2,347 | 5,555,000 00 | 536 | 1,436,000 00 |
| Totals | | 6,189 | $12,607,591 00 | 2,581 | $4,659,909 00 |
| Aggregate | | 123,173 | $96,125,841 35 | 30,869 | $18,433,818 13 |

# NO. 4.

EACH ASSESSMENT LIFE ASSOCIATION TRANSACTING BUSINESS IN THIS STATE DECEMBER 31, 1921.

| Certificates terminated. | | | | | | Certificates in force December 31, 1921. | | Received from members. | Claims paid. |
|---|---|---|---|---|---|---|---|---|---|
| By death. | | By lapse, surrender, etc. | | Total. | | | | | |
| No. | Amount. | No. | Amount. | No. | Amount. | No. | Amount. | | |
| 38 | $57,900 00 | 627 | $1,004,600 00 | 665 | $1,062,500 00 | 4,701 | $6,789,000 00 | $107,176 35 | $ 47,900 00 |
| ----- | ---------- | 291 | 457,000 00 | 291 | 457,000 00 | 470 | 870,500 00 | 29,571 02 | ---------- |
| 38 | 5,779 50 | 1,695 | 381,375 00 | 1,733 | 387,174 50 | 7,348 | 1,017,934 00 | 31,389 10 | 5,799 50 |
| ----- | ---------- | 247 | 243,000 00 | 247 | 243,000 00 | 281 | 277,250 00 | 3,795 48 | ---------- |
| 873 | 93,350 00 | 12,727 | 3,465,505 00 | 13,600 | 3,558,855 00 | 65,801 | 16,703,239 00 | 415,525 45 | 92,596 30 |
| 3 | 3,000 00 | 146 | 270,000 00 | 149 | 273,000 00 | 706 | 1,046,000 00 | 19,209 89 | 2,452 43 |
| 3 | 3,000 00 | 12 | 14,400 00 | 15 | 17,400 00 | 128 | 117,600 00 | 3,464 00 | 3,000 00 |
| 156 | 241,031 56 | 3,790 | 6,719,729 24 | 3,946 | 6,960,760 80 | 26,281 | 42,496,140 18 | 682,527 68 | 246,501 52 |
| 10 | 16,000 00 | 212 | 447,000 00 | 222 | 463,000 00 | 2,322 | 3,269,500 00 | 37,272 91 | 18,857 27 |
| ----- | ---------- | ----- | ---------- | ----- | ---------- | 5 | 5,000 00 | 159 72 | ---------- |
| 20 | 21,500 00 | 15 | 15,000 00 | 35 | 36,500 00 | 2,163 | 2,199,000 00 | 45,240 66 | 20,500 00 |
| 67 | 56,470 00 | 570 | 556,910 00 | 637 | 613,380 00 | 3,182 | 2,913,260 00 | 75,458 98 | 59,090 00 |
| 28 | 19,000 00 | 54 | 41,500 00 | 82 | 60,500 00 | 2,381 | 1,729,000 00 | 37,539 41 | 13,000 00 |
| 129 | 49,280 13 | 1,469 | 414,167 87 | 1,598 | 463,448 00 | 6,283 | 3,261,858 00 | 93,796 96 | 48,680 19 |
| 1,365 | $566,331 19 | 21,855 | $14,030,187 11 | 23,220 | $14,596,518 30 | 122,052 | $82,695,641 18 | $1,582,127 61 | $558,377 21 |
| 14 | $17,500 00 | 445 | $510,500 00 | 459 | $528,000 00 | 2,927 | $3,196,500 00 | $76,427 92 | $16,500 00 |
| 6 | 16,500 00 | 352 | 861,500 00 | 358 | 878,000 00 | 1,646 | 4,845,000 00 | 72,897 92 | 22,500 00 |
| 5 | 9,000 00 | 34 | 62,000 00 | 39 | 71,000 00 | 458 | 758,000 00 | 14,412 40 | 8,000 00 |
| 17 | 41,500 00 | 439 | 1,224,500 00 | 456 | 1,266,000 00 | 2,427 | 5,725,000 00 | 96,345 06 | 31,500 00 |
| 42 | $84,500 00 | 1,270 | $2,658,500 00 | 1,312 | $2,743,000 00 | 7,458 | $14,524,500 00 | $260,083 30 | $78,500 00 |
| 1,407 | $650,831 19 | 23,125 | $16,688,687 11 | 24,532 | $17,339,518 30 | 129,510 | $97,220,141 18 | $1,842,210 91 | $636,877 21 |

# FRATERNAL TABLES.

## TABLE NO. 1.

SHOWING ASSETS AND LIABILITIES OF FRATERNAL BENEFICIARY SOCIETIES TRANSACTING BUSINESS IN THIS STATE FOR THE YEAR ENDING DECEMBER 31, 1921.

| Name of society. | Assets. | | | | Liabilities. | | |
|---|---|---|---|---|---|---|---|
| | Ledger assets. | Non-ledger assets. | Unadmitted assets. | Total admitted assets. | Losses and claims unpaid, including those unadjusted and resisted. | All other liabilities. | Total liabilities. |
| I. SOCIETIES OF THIS STATE. | | | | | | | |
| American Lithuanian Roman Catholic Women's Alliance | $ 10,925 87 | $ 297 28 | $ 297 28 | $ 10,925 87 | | | |
| Bankers Insurance Corporation | 3,862 88 | 2,924 75 | 600 00 | 6,187 63 | | | |
| Bohemian American Foresters, High Court | 73,517 01 | 30 62 | 591 36 | 72,956 27 | $ 3,000 00 | | $ 3,000 00 |
| Bohemian American Union | 72,786 82 | 1,743 70 | | 74,530 52 | 3,750 00 | | 3,750 00 |
| Bohemian Slavonian Benevolent Society of U. S. | 623,912 62 | 14,295 66 | 8,877 31 | 629,330 97 | 16,750 00 | | 16,750 00 |
| Builders of America | 1,009 41 | | | 1,009 41 | | $ 1,293 50 | 1,293 50 |
| Bohemian Slavonian Union | 129,166 23 | 7,773 13 | | 136,939 36 | 5,750 00 | 835 86 | 6,585 86 |
| Benefit Association of Railway Employees | 547,537 63 | 129,801 15 | 19,902 94 | 657,435 84 | 52,170 40 | 5,748 12 | 57,918 52 |
| Catholic Order of Foresters | 10,510,230 74 | 206,850 52 | 258,474 68 | 10,458,606 58 | 228,910 71 | 634 33 | 229,545 04 |
| Chicago Union of Bohemian Ladies | 1,602 80 | | | 1,602 80 | 1,500 00 | | 1,500 00 |
| Columbian Circle | 506,907 47 | 76,970 21 | | 583,877 68 | 72,793 11 | 110,623 92 | 183,417 03 |
| Concordia Mutual Benefit League | 180,921 59 | 5,753 64 | 2,640 00 | 184,035 23 | 1,725 00 | 168,787 41 | 170,512 41 |
| Confederation of Bohemian American Ladies | 11,993 40 | 5,770 45 | | 17,763 85 | 9,010 93 | 123 31 | 9,134 24 |
| Court of Honor Life Association | 3,080,309 34 | 218,318 68 | 157,038 72 | 3,141,589 30 | 95,908 34 | 3,045,680 96 | 3,141,589 30 |
| Croation League of Illinois | 269,024 12 | 5,875 72 | 2,328 59 | 272,571 25 | 16,833 83 | | 16,833 83 |
| Catholic Knights and Ladies of Illinois | 328,660 87 | 13,460 64 | | 342,121 51 | 1,273 75 | | 1,273 75 |
| Firemen's Mutual Aid and Benefit Association of City of Chicago | 143,158 81 | 2,712 84 | 10,455 87 | 135,415 78 | 6,000 00 | | 6,000 00 |
| German Order of Harugari of the State of Illinois, Grand Lodge | 82,919 58 | 1,633 07 | 400 00 | 84,152 65 | 900 00 | 200 00 | 1,100 00 |
| Grand Carniolian Slovenian Catholic Union | 872,925 88 | 32,293 05 | 7,662 00 | 897,556 93 | 28,866 99 | 639 25 | 29,506 24 |
| Grand Guild of America | | | | | | | |
| Guardian Insurance Corporation | 203 70 | | | 203 70 | 22 50 | | 22 50 |
| Hancock County Mutual Life Association | 6,048 30 | 300 00 | 300 00 | 6,048 30 | 4,000 00 | | 4,000 00 |
| Hibernian Life Insurance Association | 93,840 90 | | | 93,840 90 | 401 53 | | 401 53 |

| | | | | | | | |
|---|---|---|---|---|---|---|---|
| Hlavny Tatranska Slovanska Jednota | 21,917 64 | | | 21,917 64 | 750 00 | | 750 00 |
| Holy Family Society of the U. S. of A | 14,476 33 | | | 14,476 33 | 2,602 75 | | 2,602 75 |
| Independent Order of Svithiod | 485,640 65 | 17,326 37 | 1,140 47 | 501,826 55 | 2,550 00 | 914 48 | 3,464 48 |
| Independent Order of Vikings, Grand Lodge | 274,383 40 | 3,974 05 | 80 00 | 278,277 45 | 1,000 00 | 750 00 | 1,750 00 |
| Independent Western Star Order | 12,484 93 | 8,032 68 | | 20,517 61 | 13,800 00 | 2,281 90 | 16,081 90 |
| Knights of Pythias of N. A. S. A. E. A. A. and A., Jurisdiction of Illinois, Grand Lodge | 77,047 13 | | | 77,047 13 | 2,450 00 | | 2,450 00 |
| Knights of Tabor and Daughters of Tabernacle | 3,821 05 | | | 3,821 05 | 650 00 | | 650 00 |
| Low German Grand Lodge of the U. S. of N. A | 287,541 46 | 9,500 24 | 2,313 00 | 294,728 70 | 8,436 95 | 929 65 | 9,366 60 |
| Loyal American Life Association | 698,638 34 | 61,808 11 | 5,880 00 | 754,566 45 | 26,231 36 | 21,978 00 | 48,209 45 |
| Liberty Life & Casualty Ins. Co | 594 26 | | | 594 26 | 400 00 | 76 56 | 476 56 |
| Luxemberger Brotherhood of America | 46,599 87 | | | 46,599 87 | | | |
| Modern Woodmen of America | 25,983,817 47 | 2,749,745 30 | 498,626 37 | 28,234,936 40 | 2,226,902 73 | 98,612 75 | 2,325,515 48 |
| Mutual Benefit and Aid Society | 104,183 76 | 421 75 | 421 75 | 104,183 76 | 2,750 00 | | 2,750 00 |
| Mystic Workers of the World | 1,682,655 12 | 231,356 83 | 12,803 87 | 1,901,208 08 | 113,240 05 | 91,614 96 | 204,855 01 |
| National Fraternal Society of the Deaf | 353,050 43 | 7,458 69 | | 360,509 12 | 4,110 00 | 1,056 10 | 5,166 10 |
| North American Union | 611,398 46 | 59,138 74 | 17,700 28 | 652,836 92 | 64,497 00 | 80,500 00 | 144,997 00 |
| North Star Benefit Association | 391,856 33 | 17,526 10 | 1,400 00 | 407,982 43 | 8,473 16 | 72,242 59 | 80,715 75 |
| Order of Mutual Protection, Supreme Lodge | 647,311 95 | 14,741 33 | | 662,053 28 | 11,746 35 | | 11,746 35 |
| Order der Hermans Schwestern | 65,492 66 | | | 65,492 66 | 1,133 33 | | 1,133 33 |
| Order Sons of St. George, Grand Lodge of the State of Illinois | 89,449 40 | 5,547 86 | | 94,997 26 | 3,500 00 | | 3,500 00 |
| Pike County Mutual Life Association | 17,761 96 | | | 17,761 96 | | | |
| Polish Alma Mater of U. S. of N. A | 187,179 48 | 4,807 49 | 10,000 00 | 181,986 97 | 3,425 00 | 10,056 39 | 13,481 39 |
| Polish National Alliance of the U. S. of N. A | 6,241,506 32 | 92,036 46 | 173,393 26 | 6,160,149 52 | 286,240 32 | 768 50 | 287,008 82 |
| Polish Roman Catholic Union of America | 3,911,405 25 | 53,288 22 | 87,652 20 | 3,877,041 27 | 138,362 16 | 65,878 07 | 204,240 23 |
| Polish Women's Alliance of America | 573,547 28 | 10,658 59 | 140 00 | 584,065 87 | 30,855 81 | | 30,855 81 |
| Royal League | 3,142,201 09 | 145,844 84 | 11,620 04 | 3,276,425 89 | 77,177 80 | 14,557 97 | 91,735 77 |
| Royal Neighbors of America | 8,882,033 23 | 811,510 77 | | 9,693,544 00 | 421,977 11 | 35,800 00 | 457,777 11 |
| Sicilian Union of Mutual Benefit | 2,142 54 | | | 2,142 54 | | | |
| Supreme Royal Circle of Friends of the World | 6,697 36 | 1,200 00 | 1,200 00 | 6,697 36 | | | |
| Slovak Evangelical Society | 20,105 26 | 176 00 | | 20,281 26 | | | |
| Slovenic National Benefit Society | 1,099,394 98 | 45,009 00 | | 1,144,403 98 | 63,061 95 | | 63,061 95 |
| Slovenic Progressive Benefit Society | 195,490 30 | 11,161 84 | 5,900 75 | 200,751 39 | 12,997 12 | | 12,997 12 |
| Tri-State Counties Mutual Life Association | 9,877 26 | 1,000 00 | 1,000 00 | 9,877 26 | 6,000 00 | | 6,000 00 |
| United Brothers of Friendship and Sisters of the Mysterious Ten | 5,347 09 | | | 5,347 09 | 950 00 | | 950 00 |
| Western Catholic Union, Supreme Council | 516,725 81 | 19,302 01 | 27,308 07 | 508,719 75 | 5,222 22 | 830 02 | 6,052 24 |
| Woman's Catholic Order of Foresters | 4,443,178 34 | 188,693 93 | 10,371 81 | 4,621,500 46 | 161,948 73 | | 161,948 73 |
| Totals | $78,658,420 16 | $5,298,072 31 | $1,338,520 62 | $82,617,971 85 | $4,253,008 99 | $3,833,414 69 | $8,086,423 68 |

TABLE NO. 1—Continued.

| Name of society. | Assets. | | | | Liabilities. | | |
|---|---|---|---|---|---|---|---|
| | Ledger assets. | Non-ledger assets. | Unadmitted assets. | Total admitted assets. | Losses and claims unpaid, including those unadjusted and resisted. | All other liabilities. | Total liabilities. |
| II. SOCIETIES OF OTHER STATES. | | | | | | | |
| Aid Association for Lutherans | $1,658,212 02 | $ 495,764 62 | $430,698 76 | $1,723,277 88 | $ 4,250 00 | $ 34,631 95 | $ 38,881 95 |
| American Insurance Union | 1,140,305 28 | 179,442 08 | | 1,319,747 36 | 168,176 05 | 58,551 50 | 226,727 55 |
| Ancient Order of United Workmen of Iowa | 1,648,180 04 | 125,164 46 | 3,389 31 | 1,769,955 19 | 33,880 77 | | 33,880 77 |
| Ancient Order of Gleaners | 1,412,507 46 | 113,835 99 | 35,913 88 | 1,490,429 57 | 61,188 34 | 3,471 91 | 64,660 25 |
| American Woodmen, Supreme Camp | 793,320 27 | 57,683 18 | 15,950 89 | 835,052 56 | 13,896 25 | 6,959 46 | 20,855 71 |
| Association Canado—Americans | 753,091 60 | 49,329 24 | 12,128 45 | 790,292 39 | 3,570 00 | 1,164 30 | 4,734 30 |
| Beavers National Mutual Benefit | 148,016 42 | 4,414 33 | 500 00 | 151,930 75 | 2,000 00 | 149,930 75 | 151,930 75 |
| Ben Hur, Supreme Tribe | 3,158,135 50 | 133,730 17 | | 3,291,865 67 | 100,519 95 | 19,472 49 | 119,992 44 |
| Bohemian Slavonian Fraternal Beneficiary Union | 75,711 40 | | | 75,711 40 | 230 00 | | 230 00 |
| Bohemian Roman Catholic First Central Union | 417,962 63 | 9,189 40 | | 427,122 03 | 11,400 00 | | 11,400 00 |
| Brotherhood of American Yeoman | 5,290,873 27 | 667,520 39 | 85,407 20 | 5,872,986 46 | 1,780,441 01 | 729,488 33 | 2,509,929 34 |
| Catholic Benevolent Legion, Supreme Council | 882,297 35 | 3,177,703 08 | 16,843 71 | 4,043,156 72 | 29,915 93 | 3,917,808 52 | 3,947,824 45 |
| Catholic Fraternal League | 55,829 08 | 5,169 34 | 14,183 12 | 46,815 30 | 6,495 00 | 1,016 72 | 7,511 72 |
| Catholic Knights of America, Supreme Council | 1,104,761 35 | 30,903 58 | 38,886 25 | 1,096,778 68 | 38,330 97 | 21,163 54 | 59,494 51 |
| Catholic Workman | 517,202 54 | 29,634 21 | 10,693 84 | 536,142 91 | 9,060 75 | 435 00 | 9,495 75 |
| Danish Brotherhood in America | 1,089,541 84 | 41,438 61 | | 1,130,980 45 | 12,000 00 | 729 78 | 12,729 78 |
| Daughters of Norway | 34,483 46 | 649 87 | 500 00 | 34,633 33 | 100 00 | | 100 00 |
| Degree of Honor, Superior Lodge | 2,257,558 31 | 108,785 97 | 8,637 66 | 2,357,706 62 | 10,100 00 | 4,916 32 | 14,916 32 |
| Eminent Household of Columbian Woodmen | 2,141,942 76 | 26,428 88 | 83,139 93 | 2,085,231 71 | 56,573 32 | 1,977,237 40 | 2,033,810 72 |
| Equitable Fraternal Union, Supreme Assembly | 3,396,490 40 | 136,692 21 | 120 00 | 3,533,062 61 | 36,283 24 | | 36,283 24 |
| First Catholic Slovak Union | 2,477,337 49 | 28,637 94 | 89,270 39 | 2,416,705 04 | 42,650 00 | | 42,650 00 |
| Fraternal Aid Union | 3,733,249 31 | 380,858 08 | 3,181 76 | 4,110,925 63 | 299,854 11 | 2,149,836 09 | 2,449,690 20 |
| Fraternal Order of Eagles, Grand Aerie | 45,316 08 | 4,266 90 | | 49,582 98 | 3,000 00 | 6,778 55 | 9,778 55 |
| Fraternal Brotherhood, Supreme Lodge | 2,002,017 29 | 163,461 63 | 11,459 76 | 2,154,019 16 | 575,333 63 | 18,737 74 | 594,071 37 |
| Fraternal Home Insurance Society, Supreme Lodge | 652,236 85 | 147,143 75 | 13,014 36 | 786,366 24 | 50,626 48 | 592,153 58 | 642,780 06 |
| Fraternal Reserve Association | 492,185 88 | 49,228 33 | 8,843 27 | 532,570 94 | 18,369 30 | 47,135 92 | 65,505 22 |
| German Beneficial Union | 2,517,698 75 | 72,214 58 | | 2,589,913 33 | 20,943 42 | 5,000 00 | 25,943 42 |
| Homesteaders | 522,837 82 | 98,013 20 | 29,084 16 | 591,766 86 | 58,694 72 | 35,416 98 | 94,111 70 |

| | | | | | | | |
|---|---|---|---|---|---|---|---|
| Independent Order B'rith Abraham of the U. S. of A. | 1,860,131 66 | 13,018 19 | 29,341 00 | 1,843,208 85 | 220,250 00 | 4,510 85 | 224,760 85 |
| Independent Order of B'rith Sholom | 489,578 40 | 46,730 76 | ---- | 536,309 16 | 53,550 00 | 15,000 00 | 68,550 00 |
| Independent Order Free Sons of Israel, Grand Lodge U. S. | 1,484,015 20 | 68,530 57 | 14,056 57 | 1,538,489 20 | 46,409 55 | 1,089 26 | 47,498 81 |
| Jewish National Workers Alliance of America | 144,835 25 | 8,052 09 | 798 29 | 152,089 05 | 3,858 00 | 10,664 50 | 14,522 50 |
| Junior Order United American Mechanics National Council | 1,003,017 59 | 67,623 50 | ---- | 1,070,641 09 | 35,000 00 | 16,603 46 | 51,603 46 |
| Knights of Columbus | 13,811,868 59 | 259,341 41 | 67,896 51 | 14,003,313 49 | 204,272 86 | 25,000 00 | 229,272 86 |
| Knights and Ladies of Father Mathew | 52,559 86 | 7,669 19 | 2,431 00 | 57,798 05 | 1,000 00 | 2,000 00 | 3,000 00 |
| Knights of Pythias, Supreme Lodge | 13,338,191 85 | 565,874 39 | 8,541 23 | 13,895,525 01 | 182,108 05 | 12,254,544 05 | 12,436,652 10 |
| Ladies Catholic Benevolent Association | 6,301,628 27 | 352,654 63 | 10,500 00 | 6,643,782 90 | 152,551 90 | 4,748 54 | 157,300 44 |
| Ladies of the Maccabees | 1,975,399 34 | 95,563 25 | ---- | 2,070,962 59 | 82,084 31 | 15,581 76 | 97,666 07 |
| Lithuanian Alliance of America | 357,255 50 | 16,609 10 | 16,609 10 | 357,255 50 | 13,077 50 | ---- | 13,077 50 |
| Lithuanian Roman Catholic Alliance of America | 278,047 78 | 18,090 46 | 6,299 71 | 289,838 53 | 5,950 00 | ---- | 5,950 00 |
| L'Union of St. Jean Baptiste d' Amerique | 1,827,442 85 | 76,125 51 | 51,448 39 | 1,852,119 97 | 9,369 34 | 13,627 51 | 22,996 85 |
| Luther Union | 85,158 84 | 15,304 50 | 4,161 11 | 96,302 23 | ---- | 96,302 23 | 96,302 23 |
| Lutheran Mutual Aid Society | 374,925 79 | 12,588 11 | ---- | 387,513 90 | 31,000 00 | 48 01 | 31,048 01 |
| Mosaic Templars of America | 662,548 85 | 9,355 68 | 6,000 00 | 665,904 53 | 82,018 67 | ---- | 82,018 67 |
| The Maccabees | 15,382,281 84 | 5,384,970 75 | 186,127 54 | 20,581,125 05 | 2,561,440 42 | 3,159,794 36 | 5,721,234 78 |
| Masonic Mutual Life Association | 3,676,802 92 | 936,691 65 | 80,796 34 | 4,532,698 23 | 56,026 56 | 4,240,506 74 | 4,296,533 30 |
| Modern Brotherhood of America | 5,288,671 23 | 270,453 68 | 22,987 50 | 5,536,137 41 | 274,860 64 | 22,855 66 | 297,716 30 |
| Modern Order of Praetorians | 3,951,396 04 | 640,699 24 | 70,665 23 | 4,522,030 05 | 54,377 60 | 16,556 78 | 70,934 38 |
| Mutual Benefit Assn. of Pa. R. R. Employees, Inc. | 254,113 57 | 5,150 05 | ---- | 259,263 62 | 1,000 00 | 3,213 91 | 4,213 91 |
| National Benevolent Society | 12,148 00 | 44,496 52 | 44,496 52 | 12,148 00 | 617 00 | 131 00 | 748 00 |
| National Croation Society of the U. S. A. | 1,203,995 13 | 55,124 18 | 47,472 15 | 1,211,647 16 | 54,996 14 | 1,970 24 | 56,966 38 |
| National Protective Legion | 138,760 84 | 88,442 66 | 49,902 04 | 177,301 46 | 8,673 20 | 61,464 27 | 70,137 47 |
| National Slovak Society, U. S. A. | 1,956,956 92 | 223,302 95 | 36,185 18 | 2,144,074 69 | 70,149 71 | 163,925 07 | 234,074 78 |
| National Union Assurance Society | 2,283,262 07 | 1,034,585 56 | ---- | 3,317,847 63 | 328,178 00 | 2,248,035 64 | 2,576,213 64 |
| New Era Association | 152,270 23 | 12,396 38 | 2,497 62 | 162,168 99 | 36,000 00 | 13,751 64 | 49,751 64 |
| Order of B'rith Abraham, U. S. Grand Lodge | 112,402 72 | 58,401 91 | 5,428 07 | 165,376 56 | 70,300 00 | 15,387 87 | 85,687 87 |
| Order of Knights of Joseph | 68,073 27 | 8,918 35 | ---- | 76,991 62 | ---- | ---- | ---- |
| Order Knights of the White Cross, Grand Lodge | 8,532 85 | 785 97 | ---- | 9,318 82 | ---- | ---- | ---- |
| Order of Scottish Clans | 531,318 54 | 70,710 52 | 77,007 50 | 525,021 56 | 15,550 00 | 15,160 18 | 30,710 18 |
| Order Sons of Zion | 160,986 10 | 5,921 84 | 1,875 98 | 165,031 96 | 2,550 00 | 25,613 10 | 28,163 10 |
| Order of United Commercial Travelers of America | 1,363,922 36 | 305,639 34 | 48,243 58 | 1,621,318 12 | 255,075 68 | 901 86 | 255,977 54 |
| Pilgrim Knights of the World, Supreme Lodge | 760 10 | 809 05 | 536 25 | 1,032 90 | 7 00 | 18 36 | 25 36 |
| Polish Association of America | 217,838 47 | 3,998 96 | ---- | 221,837 43 | 4,500 00 | ---- | 4,500 00 |
| Polish Federation of America | 35,672 29 | 4,076 21 | 2,608 14 | 37,140 36 | 300 00 | ---- | 300 00 |
| Polish Union of U. S. of North America | 481,939 93 | 1,986 84 | ---- | 483,926 77 | 24,172 92 | ---- | 24,172 92 |
| Polish Union of America | 378,438 93 | 86,595 77 | 958 00 | 464,076 70 | 4,300 00 | 63,657 60 | 67,957 60 |
| Progressive Order of the West, Grand Lodge | 253,554 37 | 12,569 60 | 6,163 42 | 259,960 55 | 18,494 57 | 100 00 | 18,594 57 |
| Protective Home Circle | 803,978 84 | 27,707 69 | 29,901 22 | 801,785 31 | 177,500 00 | 50,750 00 | 228,250 00 |
| Railway Mail Association | 174,422 91 | 8,616 48 | ---- | 183,039 39 | 9,248 00 | 75 00 | 9,323 00 |
| Royal Arcanum, Supreme Council | 11,800,011 38 | 752,511 54 | 920,468 52 | 11,632,054 40 | 494,690 52 | 3,400 43 | 498,090 95 |

TABLE NO. 1—Concluded.

| Name of society. | Assets. | | | | Liabilities. | | |
|---|---|---|---|---|---|---|---|
| | Ledger assets. | Non-ledger assets. | Unadmitted assets. | Total admitted assets. | Losses and claims unpaid, including those unadjusted and resisted. | All other liabilities. | Total liabilities. |
| Royal Highlanders | $ 2,132,138 64 | $134,227 93 | | $ 2,266,366 57 | $ 20,500 00 | | $ 20,500 00 |
| Scandinavian American Fraternity | 268,849 26 | 11,045 84 | $ 2,129 00 | 277,766 10 | 4,700 00 | | 4,700 00 |
| Slavonic Evangelical Union of America | 429,979 19 | 69,008 98 | 11,450 00 | 487,538 17 | 9,775 00 | $54,936 00 | 64,711 00 |
| Society of the Taborites, National Supreme Lodge | 51,325 54 | 866 72 | | 52,192 26 | | | |
| Security Benefit Association | 2,167,711 47 | 354,607 20 | | 2,522,318 67 | 521,169 26 | 153,175 79 | 674,345 05 |
| Sons of Norway | 418,667 02 | 19,275 53 | 1,998 50 | 435,944 05 | 500 00 | | 500 00 |
| South Slavonic Catholic Union | 464,596 02 | 7,393 89 | | 471,989 91 | | 50,324 27 | 50,324 27 |
| Switchmen's Union of North America | 771,527 38 | 39,147 99 | 40,439 13 | 770,236 24 | 27,783 30 | | 27,783 30 |
| Travelers Protective Assn. of America | 806,592 44 | 16,456 44 | 4,151 98 | 818,896 90 | 113,947 87 | 36,829 47 | 150,737 34 |
| United Order of Foresters | 474,686 04 | 21,739 82 | 2,650 00 | 493,775 86 | 3,500 00 | 5,311 75 | 40,311 75 |
| United Order of the Golden Cross of the World, Supreme Commandery | 131,950 57 | 36,336 29 | 12,189 32 | 156,097 54 | 56,283 34 | 653 96 | 56,937 30 |
| Ukrainian Workingmen's Association | 228,347 79 | 23,963 09 | 896 09 | 251,414 79 | 10,350 00 | | 10,350 00 |
| Woman's Benefit Association of the Maccabees | 15,663,904 00 | 703,067 58 | 168,743 54 | 16,198,228 04 | 194,485 14 | 79,608 66 | 274,093 80 |
| Woman's Bohemian Roman Catholic Central Union, U. S. A. | 344,157 83 | | | 344,157 83 | | | |
| Woodmen Circle, Supreme Forest | 10,312,165 75 | 493,198 95 | 64,844 93 | 10,740,519 77 | 277,190 07 | 43,557 55 | 320,747 62 |
| Woodmen of the World, Sovereign Camp | 47,173,913 20 | 4,523,584 15 | 2,733,219 76 | 48,964,277 59 | 1,664,746 13 | 79,293 40 | 1,744,039 53 |
| Woodmen of Union | 159,889 19 | | | 159,889 19 | | | |
| Workmen's Circle | 1,970,449 13 | 125,798 02 | 137,486 13 | 1,958,761 02 | 64,343 19 | 31,306 38 | 95,649 57 |
| Workmen's Sick and Death Benefit Fund | 1,659,747 98 | 69,511 23 | 43,597 02 | 1,685,662 19 | 51,342 04 | 2,321 54 | 53,663 58 |
| Totals | $220,789,618 36 | $24,665,228 70 | $5,988,645 81 | $239,466,201 25 | $12,145,506 72 | $32,886,345 48 | $88,110,135 89 |
| III. SOCIETIES OF FOREIGN GOVERNMENTS. | | | | | | | |
| Independent Order of Foresters, Supreme Court | $45,202,724 77 | $964,161 10 | $2,413,558 08 | $43,753,327 79 | $330,440 54 | $42,747,843 15 | $43,078,283 69 |
| Aggregate | $344,650,763 29 | $30,927,462 11 | $9,740,724 51 | $365,837,500 89 | $16,728,956 25 | $79,467,603 32 | $96,196,559 57 |

# TABLE NO. 2.

SHOWING INCOME AND DISBURSEMENTS OF FRATERNAL BENEFICIARY SOCIETIES TRANSACTING BUSINESS IN THIS STATE FOR THE YEAR ENDING DECEMBER 31, 1921.

| Name of society. | Income. | | | Disbursements. | | | Business in Illinois. | |
|---|---|---|---|---|---|---|---|---|
| | Paid by members. | From other sources. | Total receipts. | Paid to members. | Expenses. | Total disbursements. | Received from members. | Claims paid. |
| I. SOCIETIES OF THIS STATE. | | | | | | | | |
| American Lithuanian Roman Catholic Women's Alliance | $ 11,656 05 | $ 271 09 | $ 11,927 14 | $ 4,258 22 | $ 3,859 83 | $ 8,118 05 | $ 2,662 90 | $ 2,094 40 |
| Bankers Insurance Corporation | 25,838 00 | 2,091 15 | 27,929 15 | 8,145 60 | 20,016 35 | 28,161 95 | 25,838 00 | 8,145 60 |
| Bohemian American Foresters, High Court | 31,682 67 | 4,414 75 | 36,097 42 | 23,550 00 | 3,499 10 | 27,049 10 | 31,682 67 | 23,550 00 |
| Bohemian American Union | 23,019 21 | 3,815 52 | 26,834 73 | 9,375 00 | 4,261 26 | 13,636 26 | 21,781 51 | 8,250 00 |
| Bohemian Slavonian Benevolent Society of U. S. | 355,534 36 | 31,851 81 | 387,386 17 | 307,540 00 | 22,538 32 | 330,078 32 | 118,820 23 | 113,000 00 |
| Builders of America | 3,786 84 | 1,031 00 | 4,817 84 | 1,450 30 | 2,748 79 | 4,199 09 | 2,885 34 | 1,450 30 |
| Bohemian Slavonian Union | 86,735 58 | 6,908 77 | 93,644 35 | 67,050 00 | 7,017 61 | 74,067 61 | 79,303 48 | 63,300 00 |
| Benefit Association of Railway Employees | 1,039,002 32 | 15,360 29 | 1,054,362 61 | 435,380 52 | 425,354 56 | 860,735 08 | 137,104 17 | 27,542 77 |
| Catholic Order of Foresters | 2,509,383 49 | 511,884 52 | 3,021,268 01 | 1,671,602 61 | 219,048 81 | 1,890,651 42 | 623,212 95 | 584,045 06 |
| Chicago Union of Bohemian Ladies | 9,423 59 | 25 97 | 9,449 56 | 9,000 00 | 183 15 | 9,183 15 | 9,423 59 | 9,000 00 |
| Columbian Circle | 722,672 91 | 98,257 01 | 820,929 92 | 603,434 63 | 288,863 47 | 892,298 10 | 336,686 35 | 291,640 50 |
| Concordia Mutual Benefit League | 65,161 66 | 16,499 49 | 81,661 15 | 20,420 90 | 18,338 75 | 38,759 65 | 56,790 95 | 17,250 00 |
| Confederation of Bohemian American Ladies | 31,459 02 | 769 60 | 32,228 62 | 31,718 57 | 315 41 | 32,033 98 | 32,039 69 | 31,718 57 |
| Court of Honor Life Association | 1,894,733 16 | 154,556 58 | 2,049,289 74 | 1,047,475 69 | 522,838 06 | 1,570,313 75 | 981,659 64 | 560,584 94 |
| Croation League of Illinois | 184,154 13 | 11,255 73 | 195,409 86 | 122,094 00 | 35,604 54 | 157,698 54 | 69,377 31 | 52,846 63 |
| Catholic Knights and Ladies of Illinois | 54,288 68 | 16,371 56 | 70,660 24 | 36,402 35 | 11,000 86 | 47,403 21 | 54,280 18 | 31,858 35 |
| Firemen's Mutual Aid and Benefit Association of City of Chicago | 69,066 30 | 70,469 82 | 139,536 12 | 82,000 00 | 5,690 29 | 87,690 29 | 69,066 30 | 82,000 00 |
| German Order of Harugari of the State of Illinois, Grand Lodge | 21,895 75 | 4,346 25 | 26,242 00 | 21,000 00 | 2,531 83 | 23,531 83 | 21,895 75 | 21,000 00 |
| Grand Carniolian Slovenian Catholic Union | 249,522 63 | 46,911 19 | 296,433 82 | 126,618 13 | 38,220 74 | 164,838 87 | 64,506 31 | 34,440 42 |
| Grand Guild of America | | | | | | | | |
| Guardian Insurance Corporation | 8,960 63 | 305 60 | 9,266 23 | 6,880 46 | 2,380 17 | 9,260 63 | 8,960 63 | 2,380 17 |
| Hancock County Mutual Life Association | 34,681 70 | 26 50 | 34,708 20 | 33,083 34 | 2,265 93 | 35,349 27 | 34,743 03 | 33,083 34 |
| Hibernian Life Insurance Association | 39,983 87 | 4,485 31 | 44,469 18 | 26,507 93 | 4,309 10 | 30,817 03 | 33,931 40 | 25,350 00 |
| Hlavny Tatranska Slovanska Jednota | 10,895 25 | 1,236 03 | 12,131 28 | 4,825 00 | 3,922 40 | 8,747 40 | 9,983 60 | 4,275 00 |
| Holy Family Society of the U. S. of A. | 7,133 21 | 709 65 | 7,842 86 | 4,660 75 | 1,213 25 | 5,874 00 | 5,920 06 | 4,360 75 |

TABLE NO. 2—Continued.

| Name of society. | Income. | | | Disbursements. | | | Business in Illinois. | |
|---|---|---|---|---|---|---|---|---|
| | Paid by members. | From other sources. | Total receipts. | Paid to members. | Expenses. | Total disbursements. | Received from members. | Claims paid. |
| Independent Order of Svithiod | $ 119,532 55 | $ 27,508 02 | $ 147,040 57 | $ 45,500 00 | $ 13,418 54 | $ 58,918 54 | $ 100,255 10 | $ 43,300 00 |
| Independent Order of Vikings, Grand Lodge | 57,183 20 | 16,510 88 | 73,694 08 | 19,947 00 | 15,879 75 | 35,826 75 | 52,116 51 | 18,850 00 |
| Independent Western Star Order | 84,995 65 | 14,452 26 | 99,447 91 | 93,775 00 | 8,865 55 | 102,640 55 | 33,339 44 | 31,300 00 |
| Knights of Pythias of N. A. S. A. E. A. A. and A., Jurisdiction of Illinois, Grand Lodge | 31,767 15 | 4,322 57 | 36,089 72 | 10,900 00 | 3,359 98 | 14,259 98 | 31,767 15 | 10,900 00 |
| Knights of Tabor and Daughters of Tabernacle | 5,384 20 | | 5,384 20 | 3,525 00 | 290 03 | 3,815 03 | 5,384 20 | 3,525 00 |
| Low German Grand Lodge of the U. S. of N. A. | 83,674 95 | 4,804 26 | 88,479 21 | 63,230 00 | 7,495 33 | 70,725 33 | 77,817 45 | 59,290 85 |
| Loyal American Life Association | 439,807 54 | 49,475 96 | 489,283 50 | 206,463 66 | 170,087 21 | 376,550 87 | 299,122 18 | 147,748 86 |
| Liberty Life & Casualty Ins. Co. | 1,746 51 | | 1,746 51 | 650 00 | 2,518 91 | 3,168 91 | 1,303 61 | 450 00 |
| Luxemberger Brotherhood of America | 3,957 00 | 2,506 00 | 6,463 00 | 1,400 00 | 1,635 92 | 3,035 92 | 3,784 50 | 1,200 00 |
| Modern Woodmen of America | 24,652,767 55 | 1,119,476 48 | 25,772,244 03 | 16,741,450 42 | 2,429,093 55 | 19,170,543 97 | 4,346,714 38 | 3,536,754 70 |
| Mutual Benefit and Aid Society | 71,131 65 | 4,470 04 | 75,601 69 | 38,051 75 | 17,629 10 | 55,680 85 | 64,888 90 | 18,500 00 |
| Mystic Workers of the World | 2,115,781 62 | 60,203 70 | 2,175,985 32 | 914,553 74 | 331,381 70 | 1,245,935 44 | 1,126,685 13 | 505,175 36 |
| National Fraternal Society of the Deaf | 103,497 39 | 41,865 18 | 145,362 57 | 22,699 30 | 51,031 74 | 73,731 04 | 9,987 16 | 5,730 00 |
| North American Union | 484,296 01 | 29,065 51 | 513,361 52 | 319,160 28 | 87,401 67 | 406,561 95 | 370,225 27 | 251,797 08 |
| North Star Benefit Association | 98,378 78 | 20,783 95 | 119,162 73 | 54,535 41 | 23,895 55 | 78,430 96 | 70,810 38 | 41,875 00 |
| Order of Mutual Protection, Supreme Lodge | 90,276 34 | 37,342 19 | 127,618 53 | 70,473 48 | 17,526 32 | 87,999 80 | 59,121 62 | 49,267 93 |
| Order der Hermans Schwestern | 12,437 75 | 4,479 22 | 16,916 97 | 7,800 00 | 2,353 22 | 10,153 22 | 12,437 75 | 7,800 00 |
| Order Sons of St. George, Grand Lodge of the State of Illinois | 33,014 86 | 3,434 05 | 36,448 91 | 17,500 00 | 6,236 83 | 23,736 83 | 32,325 32 | 17,000 00 |
| Pike County Mutual Life Association | 50,668 42 | | 50,668 42 | 50,000 00 | 4,580 70 | 54,580 70 | 50,668 42 | 50,000 00 |
| Polish Alma Mater of U. S. of N. A. | 65,776 14 | 20,208 41 | 85,984 55 | 21,400 00 | 14,069 58 | 35,469 58 | 60,759 05 | 20,400 00 |
| Polish National Alliance of the U. S. of N. A. | 1,584,167 85 | 435,702 68 | 2,019,870 53 | 772,460 69 | 357,599 32 | 1,130,060 01 | 327,861 26 | 166,896 43 |
| Polish Roman Catholic Union of America | 1,008,001 35 | 341,454 96 | 1,349,456 31 | 489,803 20 | 249,652 26 | 739,455 46 | 352,317 00 | 161,329 92 |
| Polish Women's Alliance of America | 155,292 05 | 59,233 61 | 214,525 66 | 69,072 51 | 51,769 83 | 120,842 34 | 115,615 54 | 48,830 85 |
| Royal League | 811,636 21 | 161,401 23 | 973,037 44 | 502,611 02 | 128,986 60 | 631,597 62 | 611,321 48 | 385,480 90 |
| Royal Neighbors of America | 6,149,831 20 | 347,728 97 | 6,497,560 17 | 2,641,566 36 | 643,972 26 | 3,285,538 62 | 1,545,960 32 | 639,795 64 |
| Sicilian Union of Mutual Benefit | 57,144 70 | 6,545 72 | 63,690 42 | 66,000 00 | 11,397 95 | 77,397 95 | 57,144 70 | 66,000 00 |
| Supreme Royal Circle of Friends of the World | 32,134 22 | | 32,134 22 | 9,464 75 | 19,360 43 | 28,825 18 | 31,124 22 | 9,464 75 |
| Slovak Evangelical Society | 13,610 22 | 874 97 | 14,485 19 | 4,450 00 | 3,548 78 | 7,998 78 | 12,685 77 | 4,450 00 |
| Slovenic National Benefit Society | 699,753 24 | 262,871 60 | 962,624 84 | 469,644 53 | 116,375 55 | 586,020 08 | 87,006 70 | 57,503 10 |
| Slovenic Progressive Benefit Society | 111,886 04 | 15,621 22 | 127,507 26 | 98,114 72 | 18,283 87 | 116,398 59 | 17,554 85 | 14,946 73 |

| | | | | | | | | |
|---|---|---|---|---|---|---|---|---|
| Tri-State Counties Mutual Life Association | 65,651 58 | 294 70 | 65,946 28 | 55,138 85 | 7,780 56 | 62,919 41 | 65,946 28 | 55,107 92 |
| United Brothers of Friendship and Sisters of the Mysterious Ten | 7,650 43 | | 7,650 43 | 5,400 00 | 1,500 52 | 6,900 52 | 7,650 43 | 6,325 00 |
| Western Catholic Union, Supreme Council | 220,188 87 | 35,757 59 | 255,946 46 | 147,711 23 | 40,674 59 | 188,385 82 | 161,345 23 | 124,205 23 |
| Woman's Catholic Order of Foresters | 1,541,889 71 | 215,259 24 | 1,757,148 95 | 1,104,557 49 | 182,632 40 | 1,287,189 89 | 800,306 37 | 710,744 99 |
| Totals | $48,555,583 94 | $4,347,510 36 | $52,903,094 30 | $29,843,484 39 | $6,688,308 68 | $36,531,793 07 | $13,835,909 71 | $9,305,113 04 |
| II. SOCIETIES OF OTHER STATES. | | | | | | | | |
| Aid Association for Lutherans | $ 554,560 51 | $ 93,438 55 | $ 647,999 06 | $ 170,312 81 | $ 139,945 87 | $ 310,258 68 | $106,148 61 | $11,776 00 |
| American Insurance Union | 2,252,485 31 | 138,008 74 | 2,390,494 05 | 1,545,195 84 | 602,510 56 | 2,147,706 40 | 175,341 13 | 97,245 41 |
| Ancient Order of United Workmen of Iowa | 539,614 40 | 79,161 49 | 618,775 89 | 233,299 35 | 113,597 64 | 346,896 99 | 32,158 19 | 10,159 87 |
| Ancient Order of Gleaners | 723,014 12 | 60,974 63 | 783,988 75 | 480,159 27 | 206,591 15 | 686,750 42 | 186,780 85 | 5,010 00 |
| American Woodmen, Supreme Camp | 487,460 24 | 48,682 68 | 536,142 92 | 131,887 42 | 212,540 82 | 344,428 24 | 7,284 02 | 1,005 00 |
| Association Canado—Americans | 300,219 58 | 36,911 58 | 337,131 16 | 133,293 54 | 46,552 70 | 179,846 24 | 150 47 | |
| Beavers National Mutual Benefit | 139,442 13 | 3,699 58 | 143,141 71 | 29,171 47 | 53,439 64 | 82,611 11 | | |
| Ben Hur, Supreme Tribe | 1,699,775 60 | 169,512 86 | 1,869,288 46 | 899,271 23 | 371,687 62 | 1,270,958 85 | 349,789 18 | 187,203 05 |
| Bohemian Slavonian Fraternal Beneficiary Union | 55,333 72 | 4,624 85 | 59,958 57 | 40,058 34 | 4,772 21 | 44,830 55 | 19,985 18 | 17,650 00 |
| Bohemian Roman Catholic First Central Union | 101,031 24 | 25,131 37 | 126,162 61 | 74,900 00 | 6,818 15 | 81,718 15 | 38,163 27 | 31,700 00 |
| Brotherhood of American Yeoman | 4,445,761 24 | 438,513 36 | 4,884,274 60 | 2,620,789 49 | 1,298,360 27 | 3,919,149 76 | 132,849 56 | 55,572 30 |
| Catholic Benevolent Legion, Supreme Council | 329,958 38 | 41,591 06 | 371,549 44 | 236,626 88 | 21,854 63 | 258,481 51 | 9,938 63 | 4,298 30 |
| Catholic Fraternal League | 35,432 65 | 2,047 60 | 37,480 25 | 19,692 33 | 12,002 07 | 31,694 40 | 1,853 40 | 833 33 |
| Catholic Knights of America, Supreme Council | 469,644 15 | 53,208 80 | 522,852 95 | 400,306 28 | 95,166 51 | 495,472 79 | 35,376 65 | 27,042 45 |
| Catholic Workman | 79,242 50 | 22,364 78 | 101,607 28 | 35,890 67 | 9,831 47 | 45,722 14 | 7,387 55 | 1,500 00 |
| Danish Brotherhood in America | 258,825 45 | 53,958 06 | 312,783 51 | 95,836 64 | 24,260 69 | 120,097 33 | 20,994 39 | 15,000 00 |
| Daughters of Norway | 9,506 90 | 2,162 67 | 11,669 57 | 2,300 00 | 3,363 98 | 5,663 98 | 1,602 82 | 350 00 |
| Degree of Honor, Superior Lodge | 562,641 75 | 319,714 12 | 882,355 87 | 286,443 33 | 124,800 69 | 411,244 02 | 14,168 16 | 11,200 00 |
| Eminent Household of Columbian Woodmen | 804,384 24 | 128,844 20 | 933,228 44 | 394,927 83 | 322,817 83 | 717,745 66 | | |
| Equitable Fraternal Union, Supreme Assembly | 539,517 30 | 181,082 51 | 720,599 81 | 379,465 84 | 146,259 23 | 525,725 07 | 17,931 21 | 9,452 68 |
| First Catholic Slovak Union | 690,699 37 | 154,477 68 | 845,177 05 | 384,507 54 | 155,905 49 | 540,413 03 | 56,975 90 | 31,350 00 |
| Fraternal Aid Union | 3,479,343 58 | 152,915 92 | 3,632,259 50 | 1,973,376 54 | 648,680 37 | 2,622,056 91 | 129,022 08 | 59,782 25 |
| Fraternal Order of Eagles, Grand Aerie | 50,884 32 | 829 96 | 51,714 28 | 5,000 00 | 23,118 65 | 28,118 65 | 8,005 45 | |
| Fraternal Brotherhood, Supreme Lodge | 564,902 92 | 172,773 17 | 737,676 09 | 463,448 17 | 184,747 90 | 648,196 07 | 1,097 30 | |
| Fraternal Home Insurance Society, Supreme Lodge | 468,741 01 | 34,930 86 | 503,671 87 | 259,562 24 | 140,580 22 | 400,142 46 | 11,706 36 | 16,617 33 |
| Fraternal Reserve Association | 413,297 46 | 31,034 89 | 444,332 35 | 271,683 21 | 156,151 99 | 427,835 20 | 15,975 78 | 75 00 |
| German Beneficial Union | 945,914 25 | 127,255 54 | 1,073,169 79 | 576,225 40 | 138,524 63 | 714,750 03 | 53,566 45 | 4,813 76 |
| Homesteaders | 670,977 02 | 21,290 36 | 692,267 38 | 290,291 27 | 286,042 42 | 576,333 69 | 12,790 84 | 6,880 88 |
| Independent Order B'rith Abraham of the U. S. of A. | 1,220,880 00 | 101,917 00 | 1,322,797 00 | 893,350 00 | 92,248 12 | 985,598 12 | 48,015 26 | 39,000 00 |
| Independent Order of B'rith Sholom | 375,937 23 | 54,607 15 | 430,544 38 | 255,064 37 | 108,444 51 | 363,508 88 | 9,293 27 | |

TABLE NO. 2—Concluded.

| Name of society. | Income. | | | Disbursements. | | | Business in Illinois. | |
|---|---|---|---|---|---|---|---|---|
| | Paid by members. | From other sources. | Total receipts. | Paid to members. | Expenses. | Total disbursements. | Received from members. | Claims paid. |
| Independent Order Free Sons of Israel, Grand Lodge U. S. | $ 287,065 70 | $ 78,549 72 | $ 365,615 42 | $ 231,803 21 | $ 40,648 42 | $ 272,451 63 | $ 45,044 78 | $ 16,500 00 |
| Jewish National Workers Alliance of America | 62,270 32 | 19,599 36 | 81,869 68 | 21,031 00 | 51,450 71 | 72,481 71 | 3,509 29 | 2,725 00 |
| Junior Order United American Mechanics National Council | 437,160 32 | 50,227 61 | 487,387 93 | 140,977 70 | 116,899 36 | 257,877 06 | 859 90 | |
| Knights of Columbus | 3,800,231 14 | 669,330 49 | 4,469,561 63 | 1,217,933 41 | 838,651 71 | 2,056,585 12 | 500,244 74 | 161,852 50 |
| Knights and Ladies of Father Mathew | 45,957 42 | 2,467 31 | 48,424 73 | 33,750 00 | 9,400 28 | 43,150 28 | 918 44 | |
| Knights of Pythias, Supreme Lodge | 2,856,388 48 | 666,372 69 | 3,522,761 17 | 1,774,915 98 | 591,991 82 | 2,366,907 80 | 167,521 13 | 93,919 00 |
| Ladies' Catholic Benevolent Association | 2,307,552 33 | 288,082 95 | 2,595,635 28 | 1,395,683 96 | 240,274 57 | 1,635,958 53 | 286,477 45 | 102,150 00 |
| Ladies of the Maccabees | 664,555 01 | 97,868 46 | 762,423 47 | 375,576 37 | 138,837 08 | 514,413 45 | 29,601 20 | 10,944 87 |
| Lithuanian Alliance of America | 158,288 69 | 21,520 00 | 179,808 69 | 83,192 45 | 39,637 77 | 122,830 22 | 42,776 13 | 26,272 00 |
| Lithuanian Roman Catholic Alliance of America | 179,518 42 | 10,558 41 | 190,076 83 | 108,949 21 | 30,832 97 | 139,782 18 | 24,493 69 | 17,118 83 |
| L'Union of St. Jean Baptiste d' Amerique | 441,755 87 | 92,365 40 | 534,121 27 | 172,356 34 | 111,436 81 | 283,793 15 | 14,523 14 | 9,969 97 |
| Luther Union | 80,821 72 | 19,154 75 | 99,976 47 | 4,000 00 | 53,470 26 | 57,470 26 | 3,519 46 | |
| Lutheran Mutual Aid Society | 171,620 93 | 17,101 14 | 188,722 07 | 133,545 60 | 19,731 51 | 153,277 11 | 15,988 11 | 7,000 00 |
| Mosaic Templars of America | 425,097 37 | 22,093 86 | 447,191 23 | 320,367 44 | 129,848 35 | 450,215 79 | 2,821 70 | 1,125 00 |
| The Maccabees | 7,825,628 61 | 831,884 11 | 8,657,512 72 | 5,975,202 79 | 1,765,828 54 | 7,741,031 33 | 423,174 02 | 438,739 49 |
| Masonic Mutual Life Association | 2,600,635 81 | 206,839 89 | 2,807,475 70 | 412,433 03 | 1,192,403 69 | 1,604,836 72 | 364,057 30 | 58,343 00 |
| Modern Brotherhood of America | 1,236,019 88 | 315,732 29 | 1,551,752 17 | 793,906 85 | 212,955 89 | 1,006,862 74 | 45,504 16 | 21,361 52 |
| Modern Order of Praetorians | 1,045,710 58 | 235,634 46 | 1,281,345 04 | 454,774 40 | 371,062 32 | 825,836 72 | 141 25 | |
| Mutual Beneficial Assn. of Pa. R. R. Employees, Inc. | 93,844 03 | 11,418 14 | 105,262 17 | 31,975 00 | 13,888 52 | 45,863 52 | | |
| National Benevolent Society | 41,752 86 | 9,423 15 | 51,176 01 | 19,313 30 | 32,597 14 | 51,910 44 | 1,858 20 | 561 49 |
| National Croation Society of the U. S. A. | 699,637 98 | 93,151 49 | 792,789 47 | 507,829 77 | 173,835 62 | 681,665 39 | 82,979 88 | 57,435 00 |
| National Protective Legion | 283,484 75 | 78,749 81 | 362,234 56 | 189,377 85 | 158,471 74 | 347,849 59 | 57,607 89 | 64,330 65 |
| National Slovak Society, U. S. A. | 496,861 45 | 103,776 27 | 600,637 72 | 294,533 33 | 73,252 42 | 367,785 75 | 47,694 38 | 23,744 00 |
| National Union Assurance Society | 3,272,944 48 | 91,680 39 | 3,364,624 87 | 2,044,612 91 | 787,908 17 | 2,832,521 08 | 866,374 56 | 390,055 00 |
| New Era Association | 493,249 54 | 18,369 47 | 511,619 01 | 383,582 29 | 138,703 90 | 522,286 19 | 26,437 16 | 35,780 25 |
| Order of B'rith Abraham, U. S. Grand Lodge | 335,116 25 | 15,410 74 | 350,526 99 | 298,851 00 | 37,808 47 | 336,659 47 | 38,968 67 | 30,913 17 |
| Order of Knights of Joseph | 101,096 68 | 2,790 72 | 103,887 40 | 99,272 79 | 8,151 72 | 107,424 51 | 25,742 10 | 17,250 00 |
| Order Knights of the White Cross, Grand Lodge | 8,307 37 | 148 12 | 8,455 49 | 3,300 00 | 1,065 00 | 4,365 00 | 5,422 68 | 2,800 00 |
| Order of Scottish Clans | 207,231 48 | 38,690 44 | 245,921 92 | 156,766 00 | 34,909 21 | 191,675 21 | 13,638 60 | 7,650 00 |
| Order Sons of Zion | 41,993 91 | 37,869 26 | 79,863 17 | 8,192 73 | 43,997 59 | 52,190 32 | 449 27 | 422 73 |

| | | | | | | | | |
|---|---|---|---|---|---|---|---|---|
| Order of United Commercial Travelers of America | 1,285,139 00 | 96,739 46 | 1,381,878 46 | 911,092 09 | 287,330 54 | 1,198,422 63 | 63,402 00 | 64,984 50 |
| Pilgrim Knights of the World, Supreme Lodge | 1,508 00 | 41 46 | 1,549 46 | 1,020 00 | 722 44 | 1,742 44 | 410 00 | 535 00 |
| Polish Association of America | 123,184 37 | 17,788 42 | 140,972 79 | 69,075 00 | 19,956 43 | 89,031 43 | 29,198 95 | 15,125 00 |
| Polish Federation of America | 12,322 14 | 3,587 44 | 15,909 58 | 3,271 17 | 5,616 21 | 8,887 38 | 432 48 | |
| Polish Union of U. S. of North America | 230,695 74 | 18,129 32 | 248,825 06 | 120,417 86 | 35,749 31 | 156,167 17 | 20,809 79 | 6,126 23 |
| Polish Union of America | 142,237 66 | 19,847 47 | 162,085 13 | 65,646 35 | 25,919 37 | 91,565 72 | | 1,500 00 |
| Progressive Order of the West, Grand Lodge | 147,084 81 | 12,676 44 | 159,761 25 | 76,590 56 | 20,584 66 | 97,175 22 | 53,874 14 | 24,050 00 |
| Protective Home Circle | 1,531,560 73 | 42,921 38 | 1,574,482 11 | 1,171,895 95 | 412,767 37 | 1,584,663 32 | 19,781 49 | 18,268 06 |
| Railway Mail Association | 150,870 25 | 7,519 86 | 158,390 11 | 39,050 00 | 99,839 80 | 138,889 80 | 14,185 50 | 4,951 00 |
| Royal Arcanum, Supreme Council | 6,367,580 22 | 469,443 42 | 6,837,023 64 | 4,621,348 54 | 408,429 26 | 5,029,777 80 | 566,263 07 | 429,165 18 |
| Royal Highlanders | 698,554 45 | 122,701 76 | 821,256 21 | 388,932 53 | 113,012 54 | 501,945 07 | 135 40 | |
| Scandinavian American Fraternity | 91,354 60 | 13,610 93 | 104,965 53 | 41,118 74 | 22,622 06 | 63,740 80 | | |
| Slavonic Evangelical Union of America | 129,172 44 | 18,867 38 | 148,039 82 | 63,197 65 | 29,255 78 | 92,453 43 | 10,531 08 | 7,565 36 |
| Society of the Taborites, National Supreme Lodge | 23,687 62 | 4,226 02 | 27,913 64 | 16,220 00 | 3,971 94 | 20,191 94 | 15,791 49 | 13,420 00 |
| Security Benefit Association | 3,938,823 08 | 106,571 25 | 4,045,394 33 | 2,764,129 01 | 1,000,325 99 | 3,764,455 00 | 510,614 23 | 360,907 72 |
| Sons of Norway | 107,610 82 | 23,975 31 | 131,586 13 | 31,190 49 | 32,469 05 | 63,659 54 | 4,029 51 | |
| South Slavonic Catholic Union | 237,074 60 | 25,510 24 | 262,584 84 | 157,703 99 | 21,493 86 | 179,197 85 | 17,448 49 | 8,087 33 |
| Switchmen's Union of North America | 284,559 73 | 51,289 43 | 335,849 16 | 143,119 65 | 124,289 41 | 267,409 06 | 39,280 07 | 18,000 00 |
| Travelers Protective Assn. of America | 827,444 24 | 38,995 81 | 866,440 05 | 622,517 25 | 153,161 37 | 775,678 62 | 79,684 00 | 59,682 88 |
| United Order of Foresters | 236,209 96 | 22,597 74 | 258,807 70 | 152,412 50 | 49,870 45 | 202,282 95 | 61,606 82 | 41,900 00 |
| United Order of the Golden Cross of the World, Supreme Commandery | 431,434 19 | 5,269 05 | 436,703 24 | 361,743 28 | 56,217 70 | 417,960 98 | 3,605 70 | 7,500 00 |
| Ukrainian Workingmen's Association | 105,350 89 | 11,081 67 | 116,432 56 | 34,268 53 | 23,461 07 | 57,729 60 | 3,039 54 | 1,020 00 |
| Woman's Benefit Association of the Maccabees | 3,345,898 57 | 644,583 75 | 3,990,482 32 | 1,677,137 79 | 847,970 37 | 2,525,108 16 | 312,197 67 | 192,951 74 |
| Woman's Bohemian Roman Catholic Central Union, U. S. A. | 127,166 16 | 11,314 39 | 138,480 55 | 104,400 00 | 7,593 75 | 111,993 75 | | 57,800 00 |
| Woodmen Circle, Supreme Forest | 2,756,125 17 | 503,055 82 | 3,259,180 99 | 1,238,467 91 | 818,497 28 | 2,056,965 19 | 47,957 38 | 22,383 27 |
| Woodmen of the World, Soverign Camp | 14,272,471 97 | 2,687,017 78 | 16,959,489 75 | 8,080,342 83 | 3,157,486 47 | 11,237,829 30 | 293,144 44 | 1,962 89 |
| Woodmen of Union | 190,335 11 | 67,418 29 | 257,753 40 | 124,854 24 | 79,523 86 | 204,378 10 | 689 00 | 15 00 |
| Workmen's Circle | 1,034,567 31 | 144,740 80 | 1,179,308 11 | 285,607 42 | 459,250 13 | 744,857 55 | 52,650 78 | 20,001 99 |
| Workmen's Sick and Death Benefit Fund | 630,210 35 | 176,102 84 | 806,313 19 | 460,269 50 | 44,853 61 | 505,123 11 | 37,796 95 | 30,306 32 |
| Totals | $93,431,462 13 | $12,270,151 85 | $105,701,613 98 | $55,097,384 84 | $21,573,811 67 | $76,671,196 51 | $6,121,261 23 | $3,652,696 55 |
| III. SOCIETIES OF FOREIGN GOVERNMENT. | | | | | | | | |
| Independent Order of Foresters, Supreme Court | $3,379,267 13 | $2,056,701 97 | $5,435,969 10 | $3,683,033 35 | $2,817,576 43 | $6,500,609 78 | $168,721 03 | $155,464 25 |
| Aggregate | $145,366,313 20 | $18,674,364 18 | $164,040,677 38 | $88,623,902 58 | $31,079,696 78 | $119,703,599 36 | $20,125,891 97 | $13,113,273 84 |

# TABLE NO. 3.

SHOWING A GENERAL SUMMARY OF THE BUSINESS OF EACH FRATERNAL BENEFICIARY SOCIETY TRANSACTING BUSINESS IN THIS STATE FOR THE YEAR ENDING DECEMBER 31, 1921.

| Name of society. | Certificates in force Dec. 31, 1920. | | Certificates written and increased during year. | | Certificates terminated by death, lapse, surrender etc. | | Certificates in force Dec. 31, 1921. | |
|---|---|---|---|---|---|---|---|---|
| | Number. | Amount. | Number. | Amount. | Number. | Amount. | Number. | Amount. |
| I. SOCIETIES OF THIS STATE. | | | | | | | | |
| American Lithuanian Roman Catholic Women's Alliance | 967 | $ 145,050 00 | 269 | $ 40,350 00 | 2 | $ 300 00 | 1,234 | $ 185,100 00 |
| Bankers Insurance Corporation | 1,472 | 678,370 00 | 505 | 213,000 00 | 607 | 257,350 00 | 1,370 | 634,020 00 |
| Bohemian American Foresters, High Court | 2,569 | 1,959,250 00 | 121 | 82,000 00 | 89 | 59,500 00 | 2,601 | 1,981,750 00 |
| Bohemian American Union | 1,679 | 1,291,750 00 | 100 | 70,500 00 | 110 | 67,500 00 | 1,669 | 1,294,750 00 |
| Bohemian Slavonian Benevolent Society of U. S | 22,730 | 15,431,250 00 | 938 | 531,250 00 | 906 | 596,500 00 | 22,762 | 15,366,000 00 |
| Builders of America | 640 | 96,000 00 | 616 | 92,400 00 | 731 | 109,650 00 | 525 | 78,750 00 |
| Bohemian Slavonian Union | 5,812 | 4,367,500 00 | 341 | 196,750 00 | 311 | 194,250 00 | 5,842 | 4,370,000 00 |
| Benefit Association of Railway Employees | 57,047 | 2,827,500 00 | 26,507 | 870,500 00 | 19,398 | 815,000 00 | 64,156 | 2,883,000 00 |
| Catholic Order of Foresters | 161,008 | 160,534,250 00 | 7,030 | 6,141,500 00 | 7,451 | 7,086,250 00 | 160,587 | 159,589,500 00 |
| Chicago Union of Bohemian Ladies | 1,011 | 303,300 00 | 23 | 6,900 00 | 84 | 25,200 00 | 950 | 285,000 00 |
| Columbian Circle | 27,600 | 29,738,250 00 | 2,072 | 1,775,000 00 | 5,242 | 5,583,138 00 | 24,430 | 25,930,112 00 |
| Concordia Mutual Benefit League | 4,123 | 2,086,885 00 | 452 | 370,050 00 | 158 | 82,410 00 | 4,417 | 2,374,525 00 |
| Confederation of Bohemian American Ladies | 1,742 | 871,000 00 | 3 | 1,500 00 | 262 | 131,000 00 | 1,483 | 741,500 00 |
| Court of Honor Life Association | 74,371 | 85,043,195 00 | 4,843 | 5,080,000 00 | 11,413 | 10,379,667 00 | 67,801 | 79,743,528 00 |
| Croation League of Illinois | 9,908 | 7,915,200 00 | 954 | 887,800 00 | 972 | 742,800 00 | 9,890 | 8,060,200 00 |
| Catholic Knights and Ladies of Illinois | 515 | 283,550 00 | 3,162 | 2,473,100 00 | 797 | 560,200 00 | 2,880 | 2,196,450 00 |
| Firemen's Mutual Aid and Benefit Association of City of Chicago | 2,357 | 4,714,000 00 | 118 | 236,000 00 | 55 | 110,000 00 | 2,420 | 4,840,000 00 |
| German Order of Harugari of the State of Illinois, Grand Lodge | 1,184 | 431,200 00 | 100 | 20,300 00 | 103 | 33,800 00 | 1,181 | 417,700 00 |
| Grand Carniolian Slovenian Catholic Union | 12,080 | 10,577,250 00 | 809 | 729,250 00 | 600 | 520,750 00 | 12,289 | 10,785,750 00 |
| Grand Guild of America | 471 | 235,500 00 | 2 | 1,000 00 | 23 | 11,500 00 | 450 | 225,000 00 |
| Guardian Insurance Corporation | 1,125 | | 705 | | 1,229 | | 601 | |
| Hancock County Mutual Life Association | 2,578 | 4,265,500 00 | 68 | 108,500 00 | 48 | 74,000 00 | 2,598 | 4,300,000 00 |
| Hibernian Life Insurance Association | 3,002 | 2,265,600 00 | 111 | 83,062 00 | 230 | 195,312 00 | 2,883 | 2,153,350 00 |
| Hlavny Tatranska Slovanska Jednota | 928 | 780,850 00 | 112 | 85,650 00 | 72 | 48,350 00 | 968 | 818,150 00 |
| Holy Family Society of the U. S. of A | 821 | 337,000 00 | 110 | 55,000 00 | 82 | 38,000 00 | 849 | 354,000 00 |

| | | | | | | | | |
|---|---|---|---|---|---|---|---|---|
| Independent Order of Svithiod | 11,712 | 6,811,400 00 | 1,274 | 603,800 00 | 667 | 296,300 00 | 12,319 | 7,118,900 00 |
| Independent Order of Vikings, Grand Lodge | 8,854 | 2,559,250 00 | 1,058 | 354,950 00 | 1,139 | 302,250 00 | 8,773 | 2,611,950 00 |
| Independent Western Star Order | 7,339 | 3,669,500 00 | 563 | 281,500 00 | 1,253 | 626,500 00 | 6,649 | 3,324,500 00 |
| Knights of Pythias of N. A. S. A. E. A. A. and A., Jurisdiction of Illinois, Grand Lodge | 5,369 | 253,049 00 | 483 | 16,905 00 | 776 | 103,780 00 | 5,076 | 166,174 00 |
| Knights of Tabor and Daughters of Tabernacle | 2,569 | 207,625 00 | 648 | 13,900 00 | 641 | 10,500 00 | 2,576 | 211,025 00 |
| Low German Grand Lodge of the U. S. of N. A. | 6,602 | 3,301,000 00 | 108 | 54,000 00 | 257 | 128,500 00 | 6,453 | 3,226,500 00 |
| Loyal American Life Association | 15,952 | 16,721,304 00 | 2,129 | 2,486,900 00 | 1,919 | 2,355,339 00 | 16,162 | 16,852,865 00 |
| Liberty Life & Casualty Ins. Co. | 390 | 117,800 00 | 40 | 10,000 00 | 90 | 17,800 00 | 340 | 110,000 00 |
| Luxemberger Brotherhood of America | 1,581 | 158,100 00 | 66 | 6,600 00 | 85 | 8,500 00 | 1,562 | 156,200 00 |
| Modern Woodmen of America | 1,059,344 | 1,627,671,000 00 | 73,837 | 93,066,000 00 | 80,076 | 108,389,500 00 | 1,053,105 | 1,612,347,500 00 |
| Mutual Benefit and Aid Society | 3,969 | 1,984,500 00 | 280 | 140,000 00 | 150 | 75,000 00 | 4,099 | 2,043,500 00 |
| Mystic Workers of the World | 95,711 | 114,269,899 00 | 23,543 | 25,792,924 00 | 41,477 | 48,173,033 00 | 77,777 | 91,889,790 00 |
| National Fraternal Society of the Deaf | 4,807 | 3,855,750 00 | 374 | 381,000 00 | 230 | 207,000 00 | 4,951 | 4,029,750 00 |
| North American Union | 17,828 | 18,196,000 00 | 1,336 | 1,205,250 00 | 3,344 | 2,707,386 00 | 15,820 | 16,693,864 00 |
| North Star Benefit Association | 7,478 | 7,053,450 00 | 330 | 263,500 00 | 623 | 577,100 00 | 7,185 | 6,739,850 00 |
| Order of Mutual Protection, Supreme Lodge | 5,797 | 3,864,940 00 | 361 | 252,250 00 | 356 | 210,744 00 | 5,802 | 3,906,446 00 |
| Order der Hermans Schwestern | 4,371 | 874,200 00 | 454 | 90,800 00 | 270 | 54,000 00 | 4,555 | 911,000 00 |
| Order Sons of St. George, Grand Lodge of the State of Illinois | 2,553 | 1,789,000 00 | 72 | 44,750 00 | 234 | 163,750 00 | 2,391 | 1,670,000 00 |
| Pike County Mutual Life Association | 4,191 | 6,197,000 00 | 306 | 491,500 00 | 142 | 174,000 00 | 4,355 | 6,514,500 00 |
| Polish Alma Mater of U. S. of N. A. | 6,893 | 3,675,150 00 | 252 | 154,300 00 | 550 | 285,400 00 | 6,595 | 3,544,050 00 |
| Polish National Alliance of the U. S. of N. A. | 124,225 | 72,830,800 00 | 14,223 | 9,053,400 00 | 16,809 | 9,716,900 00 | 121,639 | 72,167,300 00 |
| Polish Roman Catholic Union of America | 83,993 | 52,092,900 00 | 5,580 | 3,271,200 00 | 10,808 | 6,669,850 00 | 78,765 | 48,694,250 00 |
| Polish Women's Alliance of America | 22,496 | 11,803,300 00 | 1,875 | 1,125,200 00 | 1,432 | 834,100 00 | 22,939 | 12,094,400 00 |
| Royal League | 23,093 | 30,278,750 00 | 1,479 | 1,421,500 00 | 2,230 | 2,463,500 00 | 22,342 | 29,236,750 00 |
| Royal Neighbors of America | 390,185 | 391,341,000 00 | 27,453 | 24,944,000 00 | 22,205 | 21,877,750 00 | 395,433 | 394,407,250 00 |
| Sicilian Union of Mutual Benefit | 2,702 | 4,053,000 00 | 819 | 1,228,500 00 | 1,421 | 2,131,500 00 | 2,100 | 3,150,000 00 |
| Supreme Royal Circle of Friends of the World | 1,255 | 125,300 00 | 4,099 | 625,500 00 | 3,009 | 390,750 00 | 2,345 | 360,050 00 |
| Slovak Evangelical Society | 1,194 | 768,825 00 | 1,271 | 914,850 00 | 1,277 | 815,175 00 | 1,188 | 868,500 00 |
| Slovenic National Benefit Society | 18,981 | 13,172,250 00 | 8,598 | 6,244,250 00 | 966 | 623,200 00 | 26,613 | 18,793,300 00 |
| Slovenic Progressive Benefit Society | 4,776 | 2,720,350 00 | 528 | 392,100 00 | 372 | 215,700 00 | 4,932 | 2,896,750 00 |
| Tri-State Counties Mutual Life Association | 6,608 | 9,808,500 00 | 851 | 1,126,000 00 | 201 | 276,000 00 | 7,258 | 10,658,500 00 |
| United Brothers of Friendship and Sisters of the Mysterious Ten | 3,706 | 370,600 00 | 830 | 83,000 00 | 531 | 53,100 00 | 4,005 | 400,500 00 |
| Western Catholic Union, Supreme Council | 12,580 | 11,214,250 00 | 844 | 576,000 00 | 716 | 610,750 00 | 12,708 | 11,179,500 00 |
| Woman's Catholic Order of Foresters | 81,251 | 77,363,300 00 | 4,705 | 3,753,000 00 | 2,414 | 2,176,100 00 | 83,542 | 78,940,200 00 |
| Totals | 2,448,095 | $2,838,352,242 00 | 230,740 | $200,620,691 00 | 249,645 | $241,443,184 00 | 2,429,190 | $2,797,529,749 00 |

TABLE NO. 3—Continued.

| Name of society. | Certificates in force Dec. 31, 1920. | | Certificates written and increased during year. | | Certificates terminated by death, lapse, surrender, etc. | | Certificates in force Dec. 31, 1921. | |
|---|---|---|---|---|---|---|---|---|
| | Number. | Amount. | Number. | Amount. | Number. | Amount. | Number. | Amount. |
| II. SOCIETIES OF OTHER STATES. | | | | | | | | |
| Aid Association for Lutherans | 17,118 | $14,866,127 00 | 6,842 | $ 6,075,750 00 | 1,268 | $ 1,189,831 00 | 22,692 | $19,752,046 00 |
| American Insurance Union | 110,249 | 114,837,559 00 | 14,687 | 16,168,831 00 | 18,278 | 19,892,424 00 | 106,658 | 111,113,966 00 |
| Ancient Order of United Workmen of Iowa | 12,996 | 18,094,694 00 | 2,512 | 3,635,560 00 | 2,198 | 3,304,929 00 | 13,310 | 18,425,325 00 |
| Ancient Order of Gleaners | 63,427 | 54,701,505 00 | 5,916 | 5,662,900 00 | 4,970 | 4,203,935 00 | 64,373 | 56,160,470 00 |
| American Woodmen, Supreme Camp | 59,356 | 27,805,150 00 | 25,903 | 12,069,250 00 | 32,627 | 15,154,550 00 | 52,632 | 24,719,850 00 |
| Association Canado—Americans | 15,674 | 11,514,800 00 | 438 | 302,950 00 | 1,935 | 1,754,173 00 | 14,177 | 10,063,577 00 |
| Beavers National Mutual Benefit | 5,212 | 5,457,613 00 | 2,926 | 3,263,450 00 | 1,064 | 1,297,983 00 | 7,074 | 7,423,080 00 |
| Ben Hur, Supreme Tribe | 75,624 | 77,479,233 00 | 7,311 | 9,449,415 00 | 12,565 | 14,187,918 00 | 70,370 | 72,740,730 00 |
| Bohemian Slavonian Fraternal Beneficiary Union | 3,465 | 2,319,300 00 | 147 | 73,200 00 | 205 | 130, 0 00 | 3,407 | 2,262,500 00 |
| Bohemian Roman Catholic First Central Union | 5,002 | 3,975,150 00 | 216 | 187,200 00 | 192 | 142,000 00 | 5,026 | 4,020,350 00 |
| Brotherhood of American Yeoman | 285,948 | 367,882,000 00 | 43,643 | 50,997,000 00 | 62,402 | 75,122,500 00 | 267,189 | 343,756,500 00 |
| Catholic Benevolent Legion, Supreme Council | 11,008 | 11,383,750 00 | 145 | 87,500 00 | 647 | 679,750 00 | 10,506 | 10,791,500 00 |
| Catholic Fraternal League | 2,188 | 1,288,450 00 | 302 | 136,500 00 | 336 | 183,650 00 | 2,154 | 1,241,300 00 |
| Catholic Knights of America, Supreme Council | 18,940 | 19,314,426 00 | 972 | 762,250 00 | 984 | 958,138 00 | 18,928 | 19,118,538 00 |
| Catholic Workman | 4,273 | 4,708,500 00 | 365 | 352,500 00 | 93 | 102,500 00 | 4,545 | 4,958,500 00 |
| Danish Brotherhood in America | 19,889 | 13,606,500 00 | 823 | 483,000 00 | 1,270 | 772,500 00 | 19,442 | 13,317,000 00 |
| Daughters of Norway | 4,346 | 434,600 00 | 642 | 64,200 00 | 299 | 29,900 00 | 4,689 | 468,900 00 |
| Degree of Honor, Supreme Lodge | 30,999 | 27,422,001 00 | 9,889 | 9,911,827 00 | 5,050 | 5,531,657 00 | 35,838 | 31,602,171 00 |
| Eminent Household of Columbian Woodmen | 20,802 | 28,055,409 00 | 7,653 | 9,265,508 00 | 5,326 | 6,317,586 00 | 23,129 | 31,003,331 00 |
| Equitable Fraternal Union, Supreme Assembly | 30,143 | 38,540,033 00 | 2,313 | 2,598,500 00 | 2,408 | 2,837,582 00 | 30,048 | 38,300,951 00 |
| First Catholic Slovak Union | 50,567 | 41,219,500 00 | 2,376 | 2,184,000 00 | 2,536 | 2,054,750 00 | 50,407 | 41,348,750 00 |
| Fraternal Aid Union | 81,147 | 90,796,320 00 | 17,606 | 19,165,605 00 | 21,288 | 24,725,358 00 | 77,465 | 85,236,567 00 |
| Fraternal Order of Eagles, Grand Aerie | 1,390 | 1,656,500 00 | 768 | 951,500 00 | 420 | 522,500 00 | 1,738 | 2,085,500 00 |
| Fraternal Brotherhood, Supreme Lodge | 25,346 | 24,595,957 00 | 3,140 | 1,570,000 00 | 3,687 | 3,084,868 00 | 24,799 | 23,081,089 00 |
| Fraternal Home Insurance Society, Supreme Lodge | 19,087 | 12,737,900 00 | 4,383 | 1,982,650 00 | 4,296 | 2,340,722 00 | 19,174 | 12,379,828 00 |
| Fraternal Reserve Association | 15,571 | 17,608,750 00 | 4,889 | 5,821,000 00 | 5,306 | 6,672,250 00 | 15,154 | 16,957,500 00 |
| German Beneficial Union | 45,178 | 30,400,650 00 | 9,941 | 7,034,050 00 | 7,054 | 4,703,650 00 | 48,065 | 32,731,050 00 |
| Homesteaders | 27,018 | 37,587,000 00 | 5,174 | 6,439,000 00 | 7,441 | 10,077,000 00 | 24,751 | 33,949,000 00 |
| Independent Order B'rith Abraham of the U. S. of A | 152,289 | 76,144,500 00 | 6,536 | 3,268,000 00 | 12,256 | 6,128,000 00 | 146,569 | 73,284,500 00 |
| Independent Order of B'rith Sholom | 45,804 | 22,494,500 00 | 2,711 | 1,284,500 00 | 5,535 | 2,736,750 00 | 42,980 | 21,042,250 00 |

| | | | | | | | | |
|---|---|---|---|---|---|---|---|---|
| Independent Order Free Sons of Israel, Grand Lodge U. S. | 7,218 | 6,417,000 00 | 325 | 203,250 00 | 651 | 512,500 00 | 6,892 | 6,107,750 00 |
| Jewish National Workers Alliance of America | 5,705 | 1,952,850 00 | 1,558 | 463,800 00 | 1,492 | 479,950 00 | 5,771 | 1,936,700 00 |
| Junior Order United American Mechanics National Council | 23,023 | 27,675,500 00 | 5,551 | 7,538,000 00 | 4,364 | 6,085,500 00 | 24,210 | 29,128,000 00 |
| Knights of Columbus | 202,359 | 217,224,510 00 | 29,008 | 32,258,000 00 | 11,864 | 12,868,648 00 | 219,503 | 236,613,862 00 |
| Knights and Ladies of Father Mathew | 1,430 | 1,344,050 00 | 8 | 3,000 00 | 121 | 75,400 00 | 1,317 | 1,271,650 00 |
| Knights of Pythias, Supreme Lodge | 81,119 | 108,865,799 00 | 10,792 | 15,688,062 00 | 8,187 | 12,404,918 00 | 83,724 | 112,148,943 00 |
| Ladies' Catholic Benevolent Association | 121,023 | 97,811,500 00 | 2,542 | 2,883,750 00 | 4,389 | 6,332,347 00 | 119,176 | 94,362,901 00 |
| Ladies of the Maccabees | 46,300 | 34,042,750 00 | 3,198 | 2,308,750 00 | 3,723 | 2,590,750 00 | 45,775 | 33,760,750 00 |
| Lithuanian Alliance of America | 12,287 | 4,101,880 00 | 1,598 | 719,800 00 | 1,299 | 389,350 00 | 12,586 | 4,432,330 00 |
| Lithuanian Roman Catholic Alliance of America | 12,118 | 4,399,300 00 | 1,528 | 905,950 00 | 1,206 | 416,500 00 | 12,440 | 4,888,750 00 |
| L'Union of St. Jean Baptiste d' Amerique | 40,164 | 18,516,075 00 | 5,128 | 2,077,000 00 | 3,766 | 1,755,200 00 | 41,526 | 18,837,875 00 |
| Luther Union | 1,329 | 2,193,500 00 | 816 | 1,380,874 00 | 259 | 450,500 00 | 1,886 | 3,123,874 00 |
| Lutheran Mutual Aid Society | 8,296 | 8,966,000 00 | 279 | 275,500 00 | 279 | 297,000 00 | 8,296 | 8,944,500 00 |
| Mosaic Templars of America | 127,958 | 38,387,400 00 | 12,079 | 3,623,700 00 | 6,722 | 2,016,600 00 | 133,315 | 39,994,500 00 |
| The Maccabees | 293,249 | 349,010,268 00 | 14,418 | 16,621,600 00 | 32,246 | 38,402,686 00 | 275,421 | 327,229,182 00 |
| Masonic Mutual Life Association | 39,047 | 71,097,545 00 | 23,689 | 46,739,250 00 | 7,588 | 16,614,500 00 | 55,148 | 101,222,295 00 |
| Modern Brotherhood of America | 50,872 | 58,792,576 00 | 4,322 | 4,863,706 00 | 5,509 | 6,381,832 00 | 49,685 | 57,274,450 00 |
| Modern Order of Praetorians | 36,020 | 44,284,984 00 | 9,880 | 12,676,750 00 | 9,296 | 12,255,992 00 | 36,604 | 44,705,742 00 |
| Mutual Beneficial Assn. of Pa. R. R. Employees, Inc | 5,761 | 3,238,750 00 | 3,669 | 2,008,000 00 | 2,328 | 1,235,250 00 | 7,102 | 4,011,500 00 |
| National Benevolent Society | 5,558 | 238,575 00 | 4,810 | 147,000 00 | 5,528 | 157,750 00 | 4,840 | 227,825 00 |
| National Croation Society of the U. S. A | 38,034 | 29,393,400 00 | 3,057 | 2,814,000 00 | 3,273 | 2,696,600 00 | 37,818 | 29,510,800 00 |
| National Protective Legion | 22,638 | 12,864,385 00 | 3,789 | 2,431,987 00 | 7,125 | 3,526,010 00 | 19,302 | 11,770,362 00 |
| National Slovak Society, U. S. A | 39,473 | 29,439,250 00 | 1,265 | 1,078,750 00 | 1,783 | 1,358,500 00 | 38,955 | 29,159,500 00 |
| National Union Assurance Society | 42,121 | 71,374,580 00 | 1,011 | 1,296,643 00 | 4,789 | 8,771,643 00 | 38,343 | 63,899,580 00 |
| New Era Association | 37,372 | 42,306,500 00 | 4,146 | 5,107,000 00 | 3,891 | 4,294,000 00 | 37,627 | 43,119,500 00 |
| Order of B'rith Abraham, U. S. Grand Lodge | 22,910 | 11,388,750 00 | 468 | 225,750 00 | 5,944 | 2,972,000 00 | 17,434 | 8,642,500 00 |
| Order of Knights of Joseph | 14,384 | 7,192,000 00 | 667 | 333,500 00 | 948 | 474,000 00 | 14,103 | 7,051,500 00 |
| Order Knights of the White Cross, Grand Lodge | 547 | 262,625 00 | 32 | 10,625 00 | 48 | 22,875 00 | 531 | 250,375 00 |
| Order of Scottish Clans | 19,280 | 10,867,050 00 | 1,605 | 892,000 00 | 1,863 | 986,200 00 | 19,022 | 10,772,850 00 |
| Order Sons of Zion | 4,186 | 1,250,300 00 | 208 | 78,900 00 | 434 | 129,550 00 | 3,960 | 1,199,650 00 |
| Order of United Commercial Travelers of America | 99,737 | 498,685,000 00 | 14,773 | 73,865,000 00 | 10,374 | 51,870,000 00 | 104,136 | 520,680,000 00 |
| Pilgrim Knights of the World, Supreme Lodge | 660 | 108,000 00 | 168 | 41,700 00 | 156 | 38,800 00 | 672 | 110,900 00 |
| Polish Association of America | 10,657 | 6,205,050 00 | 478 | 272,100 00 | 861 | 506,100 00 | 10,274 | 5,971,050 00 |
| Polish Federation of America | 1,102 | 541,600 00 | 306 | 188,100 00 | 122 | 64,400 00 | 1,286 | 665,300 00 |
| Polish Union of U. S. of North America | 20,963 | 14,166,835 00 | 919 | 744,150 00 | 1,284 | 801,875 00 | 20,598 | 14,109,110 00 |
| Polish Union of America | | | | | | | | |
| Progressive Order of the West, Grand Lodge | 12,820 | 6,410,000 00 | 1,828 | 914,000 00 | 1,873 | 936,500 00 | 12,775 | 6,387,500 00 |
| Protective Home Circle | 119,743 | 101,769,500 00 | 19,642 | 17,543,750 00 | 17,845 | 15,049,170 00 | 121,540 | 104,264,080 00 |
| Railway Mail Association | 14,372 | 57,488,000 00 | 2,829 | 11,316,000 00 | 963 | 3,852,000 00 | 16,233 | 64,952,000 00 |
| Royal Arcanum, Supreme Council | 135,567 | 220,142,142 00 | 6,362 | 8,123,818 00 | 11,114 | 16,976,126 00 | 130,815 | 211,289,834 00 |

TABLE NO. 3—Concluded.

| Name of society. | Certificates in force Dec. 31, 1920. | | Certificates written and increased during year. | | Certificates terminated by death, lapse, surrender, etc. | | Certificates in force Dec. 31, 1921. | |
|---|---|---|---|---|---|---|---|---|
| | Number. | Amount. | Number. | Amount. | Number. | Amount. | Number. | Amount. |
| Royal Highlanders | 23,412 | $ 32,221,150 00 | 370 | $ 419,000 00 | 1,854 | $ 2,563,150 00 | 21,928 | $ 30,077,000 00 |
| Scandinavian American Fraternity | 7,840 | 5,844,025 00 | 1,281 | 792,125 00 | 898 | 516,500 00 | 8,223 | 6,119,650 00 |
| Slavonic Evangelical Union of America | 7,675 | 6,960,275 00 | 594 | 542,000 00 | 516 | 441,250 00 | 7,753 | 7,061,025 00 |
| Society of the Taborites, National Supreme Lodge | 2,980 | 1,051,500 00 | 308 | 111,300 00 | 160 | 55,300 00 | 3,128 | 1,107,500 00 |
| Security Benefit Association | 233,682 | 277,875,019 00 | 76,304 | 84,470,478 00 | 74,503 | 85,325,226 00 | 235,483 | 277,020,271 00 |
| Sons of Norway | 6,689 | 4,070,600 00 | 1,008 | 910,700 00 | 534 | 371,400 00 | 7,163 | 4,639,900 00 |
| South Slavonic Catholic Union | 7,879 | 6,538,250 00 | 1,172 | 968,000 00 | 778 | 644,000 00 | 8,273 | 6,862,250 00 |
| Switchmen's Union of North America | 9,143 | 11,268,750 00 | 2,027 | 2,349,375 00 | 3,108 | 3,662,625 00 | 8,062 | 9,955,500 00 |
| Travelers Protective Assn. of America | 95,588 | 477,940,000 00 | 21,426 | 107,130,000 00 | 16,610 | 83,050,000 00 | 100,404 | 502,020,000 00 |
| United Order of Foresters | 10,988 | 10,332,300 00 | 1,646 | 1,273,500 00 | 1,745 | 1,453,050 00 | 10,889 | 10,152,750 00 |
| United Order of the Golden Cross of the World, Supreme Commandery | 15,355 | 14,259,975 00 | 1,191 | 879,500 00 | 1,770 | 1,520,100 00 | 14,776 | 13,619,375 00 |
| Ukrainian Workingmen's Association | 5,616 | 4,671,150 00 | 654 | 561,000 00 | 550 | 427,900 00 | 5,720 | 4,804,250 00 |
| Woman's Benefit Association of the Maccabees | 223,108 | 174,780,256 00 | 31,833 | 27,560,350 00 | 21,827 | 17,566,723 00 | 233,114 | 184,773,883 00 |
| Woman's Bohemian Roman Catholic Central Union, U. S. A. | 10,210 | 7,383,200 00 | 504 | 428,100 00 | 248 | 192,600 00 | 10,466 | 7,618,700 00 |
| Woodmen Circle, Supreme Forest | 163,969 | 162,040,999 00 | 12,224 | 13,442,310 00 | 33,068 | 32,632,874 00 | 143,125 | 142,850,435 00 |
| Woodmen of the World, Sovereign Camp | 646,719 | 822,552,903 00 | 52,228 | 61,349,010 00 | 156,437 | 190,830,742 00 | 542,510 | 693,071,171 00 |
| Woodmen of Union | 26,757 | 2,791,940 00 | 14,728 | 989,120 00 | 17,308 | 1,348,850 00 | 24,177 | 2,432,210 00 |
| Workmen's Circle | 81,571 | 21,870,900 00 | 13,338 | 3,265,300 00 | 11,803 | 2,999,600 00 | 83,106 | 22,136,600 00 |
| Workmen's Sick and Death Benefit Fund | 53,738 | 13,434,500 00 | 2,238 | 559,500 00 | 2,455 | 613,750 00 | 53,521 | 13,380,250 00 |
| Totals | 4,670,377 | $5,477,231,848 00 | 624,994 | $769,941,779 00 | 755,615 | $880,104,516 00 | 4,539,756 | $5,367,069,111 00 |
| III. SOCIETIES OF FOREIGN GOVERNMENTS. | | | | | | | | |
| Independent Order of Foresters, Supreme Court | 176,265 | $172,134,894 00 | 17,771 | $19,200,862 00 | 20,382 | $21,677,681 00 | 173,654 | $169,658,075 00 |
| Aggregate | 7,294,737 | $8,487,718,984 00 | 873,505 | $989,763,332 00 | 1,025,642 | $1,143,225,381 00 | 7,142,600 | $8,334,256,935 00 |

# TABLE NO. 4.

SHOWING A GENERAL SUMMARY OF THE BUSINESS IN THE STATE OF ILLINOIS OF EACH FRATERNAL BENEFICIARY SOCIETY TRANSACTING BUSINESS IN THE STATE FOR THE YEAR ENDING DECEMBER 31, 1921.

| Name of society. | Certificates in force Dec. 31, 1920. | | Certificates written and increased during the year. | | Certificates terminated—by death, lapse, surrender, etc. | | Certificates in force Dec. 31, 1921. | |
|---|---|---|---|---|---|---|---|---|
| | Number. | Amount. | Number. | Amount. | Number. | Amount. | Number. | Amount. |
| I. SOCIETIES OF THIS STATE. | | | | | | | | |
| American Lithuanian Roman Catholic Women's Alliance | 444 | $ 66,600 00 | 50 | $ 7,500 00 | 1 | $ 150 00 | 493 | $ 73,950 00 |
| Bankers Insurance Corporation | 1,472 | 678,370 00 | 505 | 213,000 00 | 607 | 257,350 00 | 1,370 | 634,020 00 |
| Bohemian American Foresters, High Court | 2,569 | 1,959,250 00 | 121 | 82,000 00 | 89 | 59,500 00 | 2,601 | 1,981,750 00 |
| Bohemian American Union | 1,582 | 1,221,250 00 | 96 | 68,500 00 | 101 | 60,750 00 | 1,577 | 1,229,000 00 |
| Bohemian Slavonian Benevolent Society of U. S. | 7,523 | 5,358,500 00 | 335 | 188,500 00 | 306 | 210,000 00 | 7,552 | 5,337,000 00 |
| Builders of America | 640 | 96,000 00 | 616 | 92,400 00 | 731 | 109,650 00 | 525 | 78,750 00 |
| Bohemian Slavonian Union | 5,386 | 4,101,750 00 | 315 | 180,000 00 | 283 | 177,750 00 | 5,418 | 4,104,000 00 |
| Benefit Association of Railway Employees | 8,353 | 265,500 00 | 3,376 | 100,500 00 | 2,677 | 38,500 00 | 9,052 | 327,500 00 |
| Catholic Order of Foresters | 38,702 | 39,961,500 00 | 1,333 | 1,033,500 00 | 1,599 | 1,493,000 00 | 38,436 | 39,502,000 00 |
| Chicago Union of Bohemian Ladies | 1,011 | 303,300 00 | 23 | 6,900 00 | 84 | 25,200 00 | 950 | 285,000 00 |
| Columbian Circle | 14,106 | 14,923,000 00 | 2,578 | 2,362,361 00 | 2,110 | 2,243,500 00 | 14,574 | 15,041,861 00 |
| Concordia Mutual Benefit League | 3,738 | 1,921,385 00 | 317 | 220,250 00 | 149 | 76,010 00 | 3,906 | 2,065,625 00 |
| Confederation of Bohemian American Ladies | 1,718 | 859,000 00 | 3 | 1,500 00 | 238 | 119,000 00 | 1,483 | 741,500 00 |
| Court of Honor Life Association | 35,588 | 42,797,200 00 | 1,538 | 1,535,500 00 | 3,671 | 3,401,610 00 | 33,455 | 40,931,090 00 |
| Croation League of Illinois | 3,914 | 3,068,600 00 | 282 | 243,600 00 | 329 | 223,600 00 | 3,867 | 3,088,600 00 |
| Catholic Knights and Ladies of Illinois | 515 | 283,550 00 | 3,162 | 2,473,100 00 | 797 | 560,200 00 | 2,880 | 2,196,450 00 |
| Firemen's Mutual Aid and Benefit Association of City of Chi. | 2,357 | 4,714,000 00 | 118 | 236,000 00 | 55 | 110,000 00 | 2,420 | 4,840,000 00 |
| German Order of Harugari of the State of Illinois, Grand Lodge | 1,184 | 431,200 00 | 100 | 20,300 00 | 103 | 33,800 00 | 1,181 | 417,700 00 |
| Grand Carniolian Slovenian Catholic Union | 3,180 | 2,875,500 00 | 238 | 226,000 00 | 152 | 130,250 00 | 3,266 | 2,971,250 00 |
| Grand Guild of America | 471 | 235,500 00 | 2 | 1,000 00 | 23 | 11,500 00 | 450 | 225,000 00 |
| Guardian Insurance Corporation | 1,125 | | 705 | | 1,229 | | 601 | |
| Hancock County Mutual Life Association | 2,578 | 4,265,500 00 | 68 | 108,500 00 | 48 | 74,000 00 | 2,598 | 4,300,000 00 |
| Hibernian Life Insurance Association | 2,678 | 2,022,300 00 | 101 | 77,512 00 | 213 | 187,362 00 | 2,566 | 1,912,450 00 |
| Hlavny Tatranska Slovanska Jednota | 834 | 656,850 00 | 97 | 75,100 00 | 58 | 43,450 00 | 873 | 688,500 00 |
| Holy Family Society of the U. S. of A. | 694 | 288,500 00 | 83 | 41,500 00 | 54 | 26,000 00 | 723 | 304,000 00 |
| Independent Order of Svithiod | 9,115 | 5,707,700 00 | 894 | 445,400 00 | 461 | 209,800 00 | 9,548 | 5,943,300 00 |
| Independent Order of Vikings, Grand Lodge | 8,010 | 2,317,850 00 | 768 | 264,150 00 | 1,010 | 269,100 00 | 7,768 | 2,312,900 00 |

TABLE NO. 4—Continued.

| Name of society. | Certificates in force Dec. 31, 1920. | | Certificates written and increased during the year. | | Certificates terminated—by death, lapse, surrender, etc. | | Certificates in force Dec. 31, 1921. | |
|---|---|---|---|---|---|---|---|---|
| | Number. | Amount. | Number. | Amount. | Number. | Amount. | Number. | Amount. |
| Independent Western Star Order | 2,708 | $ 1,354,000 00 | 319 | $ 159,500 00 | 499 | $ 249,500 00 | 2,528 | $ 1,264,000 00 |
| Knights of Pythias of N. A. S. A. E. A. A. and A., Jurisdiction of Illinois, Grand Lodge | 5,369 | 253,049 00 | 483 | 16,905 00 | 776 | 103,780 00 | 5,076 | 166,174 00 |
| Knights of Tabor and Daughters of Tabernacle | 2,569 | 207,625 00 | 648 | 13,900 00 | 641 | 10,500 00 | 2,576 | 211,025 00 |
| Low German Grand Lodge of the U. S. of N. A | 6,087 | 3,043,500 00 | 106 | 53,000 00 | 239 | 119,500 00 | 5,954 | 2,977,000 00 |
| Loyal American Life Association | 10,464 | 11,355,635 00 | 809 | 971,908 00 | 961 | 1,185,451 00 | 10,312 | 11,142,092 00 |
| Liberty Life & Casualty Ins. Co | 277 | 95,950 00 | 40 | 10,000 00 | 60 | 13,300 00 | 257 | 92,650 00 |
| Luxemberger Brotherhood of America | 1,425 | 142,500 00 | 66 | 6,600 00 | 76 | 7,600 00 | 1,415 | 141,500 00 |
| Modern Woodmen of America | 173,502 | 289,292,500 00 | 9,686 | 13,540,500 00 | 10,327 | 15,915,000 00 | 172,861 | 286,918,000 00 |
| Mutual Benefit and Aid Society | 3,969 | 1,984,500 00 | 280 | 140,000 00 | 150 | 75,000 00 | 4,099 | 2,049,500 00 |
| Mystic Workers of the World | 48,833 | 60,550,166 00 | 10,965 | 12,504,820 00 | 18,924 | 22,885,842 00 | 40,874 | 50,169,144 00 |
| National Fraternal Society of the Deaf | 426 | 368,500 00 | 49 | 54,750 00 | 26 | 23,250 00 | 449 | 400,000 00 |
| North American Union | 11,293 | 12,175,550 00 | 843 | 750,000 00 | 2,155 | 2,386,267 00 | 9,981 | 10,539,283 00 |
| North Star Benefit Association | 5,128 | 4,878,500 00 | 293 | 237,500 00 | 442 | 432,900 00 | 4,979 | 4,683,100 00 |
| Order of Mutual Protection, Supreme Lodge | 3,700 | 2,572,551 00 | 303 | 217,750 00 | 217 | 139,750 00 | 3,786 | 2,650,551 00 |
| Order der Hermans Schwestern | 4,371 | 874,200 00 | 454 | 90,800 00 | 270 | 54,000 00 | 4,555 | 911,000 00 |
| Order Sons of St. George Grand Lodge of the State of Illinois | 2,503 | 1,759,750 00 | 69 | 43,250 00 | 232 | 163,000 00 | 2,340 | 1,640,000 00 |
| Pike County Mutual Life Association | 4,191 | 6,197,000 00 | 306 | 491,500 00 | 142 | 174,000 00 | 4,355 | 6,514,500 00 |
| Polish Alma Mater of U. S. of N. A | 5,992 | 2,937,775 00 | 165 | 115,600 00 | 454 | 134,420 00 | 5,703 | 2,918,955 00 |
| Polish National Alliance of the U. S. of N. A | 26,368 | 15,176,300 00 | 2,417 | 1,519,300 00 | 3,168 | 1,787,100 00 | 25,617 | 14,908,500 00 |
| Polish Roman Catholic Union of America | 29,328 | 16,983,604 00 | 1,544 | 903,950 00 | 2,979 | 1,320,200 00 | 27,893 | 16,567,354 00 |
| Polish Women's Alliance of America | 14,348 | 7,581,000 00 | 661 | 487,400 00 | 780 | 506,200 00 | 14,229 | 7,562,200 00 |
| Royal League | 16,089 | 19,844,500 00 | 943 | 886,500 00 | 1,389 | 1,554,750 00 | 15,643 | 19,176,250 00 |
| Royal Neighbors of America | 100,103 | 99,019,750 00 | 8,491 | 7,654,000 00 | 6,762 | 6,504,000 00 | 101,832 | 100,169,750 00 |
| Sicilian Union of Mutual Benefit | 2,702 | 4,053,000 00 | 819 | 1,228,500 00 | 1,421 | 2,131,500 00 | 2,100 | 3,150,000 00 |
| Supreme Royal Circle of Friends of the World | 1,255 | 125,300 00 | 4,099 | 625,500 00 | 3,009 | 390,750 00 | 2,345 | 360,050 00 |
| Slovak Evangelical Society | 1,122 | 701,900 00 | 217 | 172,800 00 | 221 | 117,450 00 | 1,118 | 757,250 00 |
| Slovenic National Benefit Society | 2,535 | 1,717,550 00 | 960 | 636,900 00 | 178 | 91,600 00 | 3,317 | 2,262,850 00 |
| Slovenic Progressive Benefit Society | 757 | 420,500 00 | 110 | 62,500 00 | 47 | 22,800 00 | 820 | 460,200 00 |
| Tri-State Counties Mutual Life Association | 6,608 | 9,808,500 00 | 851 | 1,126,000 00 | 201 | 276,000 00 | 7,258 | 10,658,500 00 |
| United Brothers of Friendship and Sisters of the Mysterious Ten | 3,706 | 370,600 00 | 830 | 83,000 00 | 531 | 53,100 00 | 4,005 | 400,500 00 |

| | | | | | | | | |
|---|---|---|---|---|---|---|---|---|
| Western Catholic Union, Supreme Council | 8,599 | 8,265,250 00 | 304 | 213,250 00 | 515 | 484,500 00 | 8,388 | 7,994,000 00 |
| Woman's Catholic Order of Foresters | 41,245 | 4,782,600 00 | 1,308 | 1,132,250 00 | 1,141 | 1,103,500 00 | 41,412 | 4,811,350 00 |
| Totals | 707,059 | $730,273,260 00 | 67,262 | $56,454,706 00 | 76,111 | $70,567,542 00 | 698,210 | $716,160,424 00 |
| II. SOCIETIES OF OTHER STATES. | | | | | | | | |
| Aid Association for Lutherans | 4,160 | $ 3,091,052 00 | 1,834 | $1,544,000 00 | 348 | $ 293,023 00 | 5,646 | $ 4,342,029 00 |
| American Insurance Union | 11,226 | 11,056,324 00 | 1,836 | 1,902,987 00 | 1,584 | 1,784,583 00 | 11,478 | 11,174,728 00 |
| Ancient Order of United Workmen of Iowa | 782 | 948,937 00 | 126 | 178,500 00 | 162 | 226,000 00 | 746 | 901,437 00 |
| Ancient Order of Gleaners | 3,227 | 2,746,485 00 | 309 | 291,500 00 | 440 | 371,000 00 | 3,106 | 2,666,985 0 |
| American Woodmen, Supreme Camp | 997 | 461,050 00 | 1,113 | 543,000 00 | 1,105 | 524,350 00 | 1,005 | 479,700 00 |
| Association Canado—Americans | 10 | 3,000 00 | 1 | 1,000 00 | | | 11 | 4,000 00 |
| Beavers National Mutual Benefit | 49 | 50,500 00 | 8 | 8,000 00 | 11 | 10,500 00 | 46 | 48,000 00 |
| Ben Hur, Supreme Tribe | 15,975 | 16,506,489 00 | 1,754 | 2,210,659 00 | 2,459 | 2,790,177 00 | 15,270 | 15,926,971 00 |
| Bohemian Slavonian Fraternal Beneficiary Union | 1,171 | 833,800 00 | 51 | 28,000 00 | 77 | 51,500 00 | 1,145 | 810,300 0 |
| Bohemian Roman Catholic First Central Union | 1,829 | 1,525,550 00 | 50 | 107,500 00 | 71 | 57,100 00 | 1,808 | 1,575,950 0 |
| Brotherhood of American Yeoman | 9,442 | 10,666,500 00 | 2,859 | 3,268,000 00 | 3,917 | 4,309,000 00 | 8,384 | 9,625,500 00 |
| Catholic Benevolent Legion, Supreme Council | 214 | 297,250 00 | | | 9 | 8,500 0 | 205 | 288,750 00 |
| Catholic Fraternal League | 104 | 79,750 00 | 27 | 24,750 00 | 24 | 19,000 00 | 107 | 85,500 00 |
| Catholic Knights of America, Supreme Council | 1,736 | 1,564,354 0 | 109 | 86,500 00 | 60 | 56,677 00 | 1,785 | 1,594,177 00 |
| Catholic Workman | 443 | 427,500 00 | 37 | 31,000 00 | 15 | 16,000 00 | 465 | 442,500 00 |
| Danish Brotherhood in America | 2,258 | 1,683,500 00 | 84 | 46,750 00 | 81 | 50,250 00 | 2,261 | 1,680,000 00 |
| Daughters of Norway | 698 | 69,800 00 | 122 | 12,200 00 | 41 | 4,100 00 | 779 | 77,900 00 |
| Degree of Honor, Superior Lodge | 1,019 | 763,500 00 | 156 | 118,000 00 | 205 | 142,950 00 | 970 | 738,550 00 |
| Columbian Mutual Life | | | | | | | | |
| Equitable Fraternal Union, Supreme Assembly | 977 | 1,106,500 00 | 340 | 359,500 00 | 296 | 308,723 00 | 1,021 | 1,157,277 00 |
| First Catholic Slovak Union | 4,080 | 3,556,650 0 | 386 | 221,250 00 | 289 | 234,500 00 | 4,177 | 3,543,400 00 |
| Fraternal Aid Union | 3,377 | 3,154,664 0 | 686 | 679,082 00 | 861 | 886,406 00 | 3,202 | 2,947,340 00 |
| Fraternal Order of Eagles, Grand Aerie | 295 | 316,500 00 | 220 | 227,000 00 | 123 | 133,000 00 | 392 | 410,500 00 |
| Fraternal Brotherhood, Supreme Lodge | 56 | 55,480 00 | | | 4 | 4,244 00 | 52 | 51,236 00 |
| Fraternal Home Insurance Society, Supreme Lodge | 454 | 343,764 00 | 41 | 23,200 00 | 60 | 33,829 00 | 435 | 333,135 00 |
| Fraternal Reserve Association | 841 | 903,250 00 | 320 | 448,500 00 | 432 | 555,750 00 | 729 | 796,000 00 |
| German Beneficial Union | 2,343 | 1,563,350 00 | 507 | 408,200 00 | 109 | 66,000 00 | 2,741 | 1,905,550 00 |
| Homesteaders | 552 | 674,500 00 | 235 | 272,500 00 | 230 | 254,500 00 | 557 | 692,500 00 |
| Independent Order B'rith Abraham of the U. S. of A | 5,656 | 2,828,000 00 | 217 | 108,500 00 | 501 | 250,500 00 | 5,372 | 2,686,000 00 |
| Independent Order of B'rith Sholom | | | | | | | | |
| Independent Order Free Sons of Israel, Grand Lodge, U. S. | 1,961 | 1,527,250 0 | 193 | 123,250 00 | 229 | 127,000 00 | 1,925 | 1,523,500 00 |
| Jewish National Workers Alliance of America | 302 | 107,200 00 | 32 | 15,700 00 | 79 | 22,150 00 | 255 | 100,750 00 |
| Junior Order United American Mechanics Nationai Council | 26 | 38,500 00 | | | | 500 00 | 26 | 38,000 00 |
| Knights of Columbus | 32,251 | 33,993,521 00 | 5,124 | 5,473,000 00 | 1,450 | 1,597,200 00 | 35,925 | 37,869,321 00 |
| Knights and Ladies of Father Mathew | 22 | 31,350 00 | | | | | 22 | 31,350 00 |

TABLE NO. 4—Concluded.

| Name of society. | Certificates in force Dec. 31, 1920. | | Certificates written and increased during the year. | | Certificates terminated—by death, lapse, surrender, etc. | | Certificates in force Dec. 31, 1921. | |
|---|---|---|---|---|---|---|---|---|
| | Number. | Amount. | Number. | Amount. | Number. | Amount. | Number. | Amount. |
| Knights of Pythias, Supreme Lodge | 5,508 | $ 6,319,726 00 | 937 | $1,135,250 00 | 527 | $ 636,479 00 | 5,918 | $ 6,818,497 00 |
| Ladies Catholic Benevolent Association | 10,683 | 9,151,750 00 | 277 | 247,250 00 | 254 | 353,317 00 | 10,706 | 9,045,683 00 |
| Ladies of the Maccabees | 2,266 | 1,622,750 00 | 276 | 203,000 00 | 260 | 184,750 00 | 2,282 | 1,641,000 00 |
| Lithuanian Alliance of America | 3,114 | 1,104,050 00 | 815 | 319,250 00 | 475 | 166,000 00 | 3,454 | 1,257,300 00 |
| Lithuanian Roman Catholic Alliance of America | 1,481 | 554,000 00 | 270 | 138,650 00 | 198 | 68,850 00 | 1,553 | 623,800 00 |
| L'Union of St. Jean Baptiste d' Amerique | 1,053 | 681,200 00 | 47 | 33,000 00 | 61 | 39,950 00 | 1,039 | 674,250 00 |
| Lutheran Brotherhood | 41 | 59,000 00 | 47 | 99,220 00 | 19 | 34,000 00 | 69 | 124,220 00 |
| Lutheran Mutual Aid Society | 752 | 816,500 00 | 66 | 68,000 00 | 23 | 24,000 00 | 795 | 860,500 00 |
| Mosaic Templars of America | 748 | 224,400 00 | 224 | 67,200 00 | 69 | 20,700 00 | 903 | 270,900 00 |
| The Maccabees | 20,215 | 23,260,000 00 | 522 | 559,000 00 | 1,133 | 1,274,400 00 | 19,604 | 22,544,600 00 |
| Masonic Mutual Life Association | 5,918 | 11,196,000 00 | 2,561 | 5,217,500 00 | 1,127 | 2,540,750 0 | 7,352 | 13,872,750 00 |
| Modern Brotherhood of America | 2,320 | 2,249,438 00 | 298 | 271,056 00 | 181 | 165,337 00 | 2,437 | 2,355,157 00 |
| Modern Order of Praetorians | 7 | 7,000 00 | | | | | 7 | 7,000 00 |
| Mutual Beneficial Assn. of Pa. R. R. Employees, Inc. | | | | | | | | |
| National Benevolent Society | 77 | 1,925 00 | 120 | 4,550 00 | 38 | 950 00 | 159 | 5,525 00 |
| National Creation Society of the U. S. A. | 4,549 | 3,458,800 00 | 435 | 376,800 00 | 1,139 | 772,400 00 | 3,845 | 3,063,200 00 |
| National Protective Legion | 4,800 | 3,539,825 00 | 1,069 | 910,187 00 | 1,751 | 1,277,550 00 | 4,118 | 3,172,462 00 |
| National Slovak Society, U. S. A. | 3,838 | 2,853,950 00 | 184 | 152,000 00 | 212 | 158,000 00 | 3,810 | 2,847,950 00 |
| National Union Assurance Society | 12,220 | 19,494,412 00 | 707 | 972,743 00 | 1,678 | 2,921,775 00 | 11,249 | 17,545,380 00 |
| New Era Association | 2,385 | 2,444,500 00 | 570 | 646,000 00 | 410 | 386,500 00 | 2,545 | 2,704,000 00 |
| Order of B'rith Abraham, U. S. Grand Lodge | 2,432 | 1,215,750 00 | 77 | 38,500 00 | 707 | 353,500 00 | 1,802 | 900,750 00 |
| Order of Knights of Joseph | 3,689 | 1,844,500 00 | 203 | 101,500 00 | 262 | 131,000 00 | 3,630 | 1,815,000 00 |
| Order Knights of the White Cross, Grand Lodge | 390 | 186,125 00 | 19 | 7,875 00 | 38 | 17,875 00 | 371 | 176,125 00 |
| Order of Scottish Clans | 1,161 | 719,250 00 | 107 | 59,000 00 | 101 | 70,400 00 | 1,167 | 707,850 00 |
| Order Sons of Zion | 47 | 20,500 00 | 5 | 1,850 00 | 12 | 5,950 00 | 40 | 16,400 00 |
| Order of United Commercial Travelers of America | 5,381 | 26,905,000 00 | 683 | 3,415,000 00 | 612 | 3,060,000 00 | 5,452 | 27,260,000 00 |
| Pilgrim Knights of the World, Supreme Lodge | 151 | 32,500 00 | 69 | 18,700 00 | 55 | 17,100 00 | 165 | 34,100 00 |
| Polish Association of America | 2,404 | 1,362,650 00 | 58 | 31,500 00 | 272 | 84,350 00 | 2,190 | 1,309,800 00 |
| Polish Federation of America | 43 | 20,900 00 | 5 | 3,200 00 | 9 | 3,900 00 | 39 | 20,200 00 |
| Polish Union of U. S. of North America | 2,354 | 625,600 00 | 49 | 36,250 00 | 268 | 134,000 00 | 2,135 | 527,850 00 |
| Polish Union of America | | | | | | | | |
| Progressive Order of the West, Grand Lodge | 4,856 | 2,428,000 00 | 888 | 444,000 00 | 859 | 429,500 00 | 4,885 | 2,442,500 00 |

| | | | | | | | | |
|---|---|---|---|---|---|---|---|---|
| Protective Home Circle | 1,436 | 1,215,750 00 | 326 | 296,250 00 | 384 | 346,500 00 | 1,378 | 1,165,500 00 |
| Railway Mail Association | 1,304 | 5,216,000 00 | 332 | 1,328,000 00 | 182 | 728,000 00 | 1,454 | 5,816,000 00 |
| Royal Arcanum, Supreme Council | 14,193 | 21,364,959 00 | 925 | 1,070,743 00 | 1,393 | 1,958,616 00 | 13,725 | 20,477,086 00 |
| Royal Highlanders | 6 | 6,000 00 | 1 | 1,000 00 | | | 7 | 7,000 00 |
| Scandinavian American Fraternity | | | | | | | | |
| Slavonic Evangelical Union of America | 683 | 603,650 00 | 48 | 42,500 00 | 32 | 26,000 00 | 699 | 620,150 00 |
| Society of the Taborites, National Supreme Lodge | 1,914 | 685,400 00 | 198 | 71,800 00 | 98 | 36,500 00 | 2,014 | 720,700 00 |
| Security Benefit Association | 32,944 | 36,023,516 00 | 10,157 | 10,876,004 00 | 8,566 | 9,324,216 00 | 34,535 | 37,575,304 00 |
| Sons of Norway | 183 | 107,500 00 | 40 | 37,250 00 | 18 | 6,900 00 | 205 | 137,850 00 |
| South Slavonic Catholic Union | 652 | 517,000 00 | 19 | 16,250 00 | 7 | 5,000 00 | 664 | 528,250 00 |
| Switchmen's Union of North America | 1,080 | 1,457,250 00 | 203 | 249,000 00 | 265 | 342,000 00 | 1,018 | 1,364,250 00 |
| Travelers Protective Assn. of America | 7,034 | 35,170,000 00 | 1,308 | 6,540,000 00 | 943 | 4,715,000 00 | 7,399 | 36,995,000 00 |
| United Order of Foresters | 3,166 | 2,987,250 00 | 200 | 150,250 00 | 214 | 268,200 00 | 3,152 | 2,869,300 00 |
| United Order of the Golden Cross of the World, Supreme Commandery | 85 | 93,350 00 | | | 8 | 9,000 00 | 77 | 84,350 00 |
| Ukrainian Workingmen's Association | 183 | 127,200 00 | 5 | 3,200 00 | 24 | 13,200 00 | 164 | 117,200 00 |
| Woman's Benefit Association of the Maccabees | 22,294 | 17,387,662 00 | 3,808 | 3,190,050 00 | 1,797 | 1,572,599 00 | 24,305 | 19,005,113 00 |
| Woman's Bohemian Roman Catholic Central Union, U. S. A. | 4,191 | 3,355,300 00 | 130 | 96,800 00 | 97 | 73,800 00 | 4,224 | 3,378,300 00 |
| Woodmen Circle, Supreme Forest | 2,639 | 2,458,155 00 | 499 | 518,600 00 | 592 | 564,100 00 | 2,546 | 2,412,655 00 |
| Woodmen of the World, Sovereign Camp | 11,822 | 13,277,768 00 | 1,446 | 1,550,950 00 | 3,119 | 3,252,151 00 | 10,149 | 11,576,567 00 |
| Woodmen of Union | | | 189 | 17,460 00 | 14 | 1,160 00 | 175 | 16,300 00 |
| Workmen's Circle | 5,744 | 1,547,100 00 | 798 | 219,600 00 | 1,434 | 368,600 00 | 5,108 | 1,398,100 00 |
| Workmen's Sick and Death Benefit Fund | 2,973 | 743,250 00 | 217 | 54,250 00 | 156 | 39,000 00 | 2,034 | 758,500 00 |
| Totals | 327,952 | $371,719,881 00 | 51,214 | $60,670,016 00 | 47,365 | $54,172,837 00 | 331,801 | $378,217,060 00 |
| III. SOCIETIES OF FOREIGN GOVERNMENTS. | | | | | | | | |
| Independent Order of Foresters, Supreme Court | 9,321 | $9,260,817 00 | 930 | $1,099,906 00 | 1,058 | $1,166,292 00 | 9,193 | $9,194,431 00 |
| Aggregate | 1,044,332 | $1,111,253,958 00 | 119,406 | $118,224,682 00 | 124,534 | $125,906,671 00 | 1,039,204 | $1,103,571,915 00 |

# LIFE INSURANCE COMPANIES COMPLYING WITH THE INSURANCE LAWS OF ILLINOIS, FOR THE YEAR 1922.

## Company Statements for the Year Ending December 31, 1921.

## LIFE INSURANCE COMPANIES OF ILLINOIS.

### THE AMERICAN BANKERS INSURANCE COMPANY.

Located at Nos. 43-45 East Ohio Street, Chicago, Illinois; commenced business July 25, 1910.

E. W. SPICER, President. J. O. KARSTROM, Secretary.

CAPITAL.

| | | | |
|---|---|---|---|
| Capital paid up | | $118,505 00 | |
| Amount of ledger assets December 31, of previous year | | $1,663,017 45 | |
| Increase of paid-up capital during year | | 13,505 00 | |
| Extended at | | | $1,676,522 45 |

INCOME.

| | | | |
|---|---|---|---|
| First year's premiums on original policies, less re-insurance | | $110,028 91 | |
| First year's premiums for total and permanent disability benefits | | 1,266 61 | |
| First year's premiums for additional accidental death benefits, less re-insurance | | 172 12 | |
| New premiums | | $111,467 64 | |
| Renewal premiums less re-insurance | $425,320 03 | | |
| Renewal premiums for total and permanent disability benefits | 1,823 24 | | |
| Renewal premiums for additional accidental death benefits, less re-insurance | 142 45 | | |
| Renewal premiums | | 427,285 72 | |
| Total | | | $538,753 36 |
| Coupons left with company to accumulate at interest | | | 3,683 92 |
| Ledger assets other than premiums received from other companies for assuming their risks | | | 42,653 90 |
| Interest on mortgage loans | | $64,657 49 | |
| Interest on collateral loans | | 2,965 00 | |
| Interest on bonds and dividends on stocks | | 3,923 55 | |
| Interest on premium notes, policy loans or liens | | 13,474 88 | |
| Interest on deposits | | 6,024 21 | |
| Interest on other debts due the company | | 1,216 85 | |
| Rents—including $8,800.00 for company's occupancy of its own buildings less $140.00 interest on incumbrances | | 14,402 54 | |
| Total interest and rents | | | 106,664 52 |
| From other sources, viz: Re-insurance, cash surrender, $204.29; depository bond account, $172.02; re-insurance commissions, $261.49; home office printing, $65.37; profit from collateral loan previously written off, $5,000.00; return premiums, fire insurance, $45.84; discount on mortgage loans, $602.50; premiums held in suspense, $61.82 | | | 6,413 33 |
| Borrowed money (gross) | | | 78,000 00 |
| Increase in book value of ledger assets | | | 156,958 00 |
| Total income | | | $933,127 03 |
| Total | | | $2,609,649 48 |

DISBURSEMENTS.

| | | | |
|---|---|---|---|
| Death claims | | $83,729 39 | |
| Matured endowments | | 500 00 | |
| Total and permanent disability claims | | 275 16 | |
| Total death claims and endowments | | | $ 84,504 55 |
| Premium notes and liens voided by lapse | | | 920 32 |
| Surrender values paid in cash, or applied in liquidation of loans or notes | | | 47,649 82 |
| (Total paid policyholders | | $133,074 69) | |
| Expenses of investigation and settlement of policy claims, including legal expenses | | | 2,122 48 |
| Supplementary contracts not involving life contingencies | | | 989 88 |

DISBURSEMENTS—Concluded.

| | |
|---|---|
| Coupons with interest, held on deposit surrendered during the year | $ 2,228 98 |
| Commissions to agents, first year, $83,773.22; renewal, $42,616.16 | 126,389 38 |
| Commuted renewal commissions | 7,750 00 |
| Agency supervision and traveling expenses of supervisors | 8,569 42 |
| Branch office expenses | 9,086 04 |
| Medical examiners' fees and inspection of risks | 9,936 84 |
| Salaries and all other compensation of officers and home office employees | 69,047 63 |
| Rent | 8,800 00 |
| Advertising, printing, stationery, postage, telegraph, telephone, express and exchange | 16,118 19 |
| Legal expense | 6,808 18 |
| Furniture, fixtures and safes | 4,202 84 |
| Repairs and expenses (other than taxes) on real estate | 8,262 81 |
| Taxes on real estate | 1,101 33 |
| State taxes on premiums | 8,113 78 |
| Insurance department licenses and fees | 2,741 79 |
| Federal taxes | 2,653 33 |
| All other licenses, fees and taxes | 165 34 |
| Other disbursements, viz: Actuarial, $234.46; entertainment, $843.97; officers' travel, $6,017.09; real estate appraisals, $768.66; incidental office expense, $1,105.16; commission on real estate sold, $232.50; bonuses and prizes, $546.23; dues and memberships, $668.00; books and periodicals, $1,122.76; officers' and agents' bonds, $1,518.19; war risk premiums, $60.02; loss on mortgage bonds and carried to unlisted assets, $55,447.43 | 68,564 47 |
| Borrowed money repaid (gross) | 80,000 00 |
| Interest on borrowed money | 4,596 84 |
| Agents' balances charged off | 5,070 56 |
| Loss on sale or maturity of ledger assets | 10,191 67 |
| Total disbursements | $596,586 47 |
| Balance | $2,013,063 01 |

LEDGER ASSETS.

| | |
|---|---|
| Book value of real estate | $314,310 22 |
| Mortgage loans on real estate | 903,559 81 |
| Loans secured by collaterals | 145,390 39 |
| Premiums advanced under soldiers' and sailors' civil relief act | 9 94 |
| Loans on company's policies assigned as collateral | 277,137 17 |
| Premium notes on policies in force | 10,825 90 |
| Book value of bonds and stocks | 88,595 00 |
| Cash in office | 2,222 92 |
| Deposits in trust companies and banks not on interest | 26,244 02 |
| Deposits in trust companies and banks on interest | 97,039 99 |
| Bills receivable | 43,224 90 |
| Agents' balances (debit, $105,881.92; credit, $1,379.17) | 104,502 75 |
| Total ledger assets | $2,013,063 01 |

NON-LEDGER ASSETS.

| | | | |
|---|---|---|---|
| Interest due and accrued on mortgages | | $28,989 62 | |
| Interest accrued on bonds | | 1,331 17 | |
| Interest accrued on collateral loans | | 139 25 | |
| Interest accrued on premium notes, loans or liens | | 577 61 | |
| Interest accrued on other assets | | 1,269 55 | |
| Rents due on company's property | | 90 00 | |
| | | | 32,397 20 |
| Market value of real estate over book value | | | 2,797 03 |
| | New business. | Renewals. | |
| Net uncollected and deferred premiums (paid for basis) | $1,898 12 | $61,122 57 | 63,020 69 |
| Gross assets | | | $2,111,277 93 |

DEDUCT ASSETS NOT ADMITTED.

| | | |
|---|---|---|
| Agents' debit balances | $105,881 92 | |
| Bills receivable | 43,224 90 | |
| Book value of bonds and stocks over market value | 11,117 70 | |
| Book value of collateral loan over market value | 5,390 39 | |
| Total | | 165,614 91 |
| Admitted assets | | $1,945,663 02 |

LIABILITIES.

| | | |
|---|---|---|
| Net present value of outstanding policies computed by the Illinois Insurance Department | $1,598,769 00 | |
| Deduct net value of risks re-insured | 16,470 00 | |
| Net reserve (paid for basis) | | $1,582,299 00 |
| Extra reserve for total and permanent disability benefits | | 2,551 00 |
| Present value of supplementary contracts not involving life contingencies | | 7,420 09 |

LIABILITIES—Concluded.

| | |
|---|---|
| Death losses reported for which no proofs have been received | $ 4,750 00 |
| Coupons left with company to accumulate at interest | 18,891 82 |
| Gross premiums paid in advance, including surrender values so applied, less discount, if any | 2,163 63 |
| Unearned interest and rent paid in advance | 6,315 53 |
| Salaries, rents, office expenses, bills, and accounts due or accrued | 2,303 51 |
| Medical examiners' and legal fees due or accrued | 1,069 00 |
| Estimated amount hereafter payable for federal, state and other taxes based upon the business of the year of this statement | 5,296 56 |
| Borrowed money and interest thereon | 30,000 00 |
| Cumulative investment policy reserve fund | 134,159 61 |
| Voluntary extra reserve | 3,006 47 |
| Other liabilities, viz: Premiums held in suspense, $61.82; A. J. Davis contract (settled in full January 11, 1922), $6,942.47 | 7,004 29 |
| Total | $1,807,230 51 |
| Capital paid up | 118,505 00 |
| Unassigned funds (surplus) | 19,927 51 |
| Total | $1,945,663 02 |

EXHIBIT OF POLICIES—ORDINARY.

(Including group insurance.)

ALL BUSINESS PAID FOR.

| | Number. | Amount. | Number. | Amount. |
|---|---|---|---|---|
| Policies in force December 31, 1920 | | | 18,418 | $18,537,871 00 |
| Policies issued, revived, and increased during the year | | | 3,041 | 4,252,580 00 |
| Total | | | 21,459 | $22,790,451 00 |
| Deduct policies which have ceased to be in force during the year— | | | | |
| By death | 103 | $ 77,777 00 | | |
| By maturity | 1 | 500 00 | | |
| By expiry | 68 | 142,920 00 | | |
| By surrender | 162 | 242,550 00 | | |
| By lapse | 4,060 | 3,627,459 00 | | |
| By decrease | -------- | 34,395 00 | | |
| Total | | | 4,394 | 4,125,601 00 |
| Total policies in force December 31, 1921 | | | 17,065 | $18,664,850 00 |
| Re-insured | | | | $834,273 00 |

EXHIBIT OF POLICIES—GROUP INSURANCE.

(Included in ordinary exhibit above).

ALL BUSINESS PAID FOR.

| | Number. | Amount. |
|---|---|---|
| Policies in force December 31, 1920 | 3 | $297,250 00 |
| Deduct policies which have ceased to be in force during the year: By lapse | 3 | 297,250 00 |

BUSINESS IN ILLINOIS—ORDINARY.

(Excluding group insurance).

| | Number. | Amount. |
|---|---|---|
| Policies in force December 31, 1920 | 3,353 | $2,291,576 00 |
| Policies issued during the year | 640 | 929,330 00 |
| Total | 3,993 | $3,220,906 00 |
| Deduct policies ceased to be in force | 848 | 635,276 00 |
| Policies in force December 31, 1921 | 3,145 | $2,585,630 00 |
| Losses and claims unpaid December 31, 1920 | 3 | $ 2,500 00 |
| Losses and claims incurred during the year | 29 | 22,643 00 |
| Total | 32 | $25,143 00 |
| Losses and claims settled during the year | 31 | 24,643 00 |
| Losses and claims unpaid December 31, 1921 | 1 | $500 00 |
| Premiums received | | $68,406 55 |

BUSINESS IN ILLINOIS—GROUP INSURANCE.

| | Number. | Amount. |
|---|---|---|
| Policies in force December 31, 1920 | 1 | $208,250 00 |
| Deduct policies ceased to be in force | 1 | 208,250 00 |
| Losses and claims unpaid December 31, 1920 | 16 | $1,482 00 |
| Losses and claims settled during the year | 16 | 1,482 00 |

## GAIN AND LOSS EXHIBIT.

### INSURANCE EXHIBIT.

| | | Gain in surplus. | Loss in surplus. |
|---|---|---|---|
| Loading on actual premiums of the year (averaging 20.42 per cent of the gross premiums) | $111,834 19 | | |
| Insurance expenses incurred during the year | 292,877 57 | | |
| Loss from loading | | | $181,043 38 |
| Interest earned during the year | $99,296 78 | | |
| Investment expenses incurred during the year | 6,808 18 | | |
| Net income from investments | $92,488 60 | | |
| Interest required to maintain reserve | 52,196 00 | | |
| Gain from interest | | $ 40,292 60 | |
| Expected mortality on net amount at risk | $192,045 00 | | |
| Actual mortality on net amount at risk | 66,068 39 | | |
| Gain from mortality | | 125,976 61 | |
| Total gain during the year from surrendered and lapsed policies | | 14,745 19 | |
| Increase in special funds, and special reserves during the year | | | 29,488 08 |
| Net to loss account | | | 5,070 56 |

### INVESTMENT EXHIBIT.

| | | Gain in surplus. | Loss in surplus. |
|---|---|---|---|
| Total gains from real estate | | 159,755 03 | |
| Total losses from real estate | | | 191 67 |
| Total gains from stocks and bonds | | 90 20 | |
| Total losses from stocks and bonds | | | 20,909 80 |
| Gain from unlisted assets, collateral loan, $5,000.00; discount on mortgages, $602.50 | | 5,602 50 | |
| Loss on mortgage bonds and carried to unlisted assets | | | 55,447 43 |
| Loss from assets not admitted | | | 120,401 67 |
| Net gain on account of total and permanent disability benefits or additional accidental death benefits included in life policies | | 2,652 72 | |
| Gain from National Bankers Re-insurance | | 42,653 90 | |
| Balance unaccounted for | | 10,450 21 | |
| Total gains and losses in surplus during the year | | $402,218 96 | $412,552 59 |
| Surplus December 31, 1920 | $30,261 14 | | |
| Surplus December 31, 1921 | 19,927 51 | | |
| Decrease in surplus | | 10,333 63 | |
| Total | | $412,552 59 | $412,552 59 |

## SCHEDULE D—BONDS AND STOCKS.

| Description. | Book value. | Par value. | Market value. |
|---|---|---|---|
| Chicago City Railways Co., 5s, 1927 | $15,000 00 | $15,000 00 | $10,650 00 |
| Bloomington & Normal Ry. & Light Co., 5s, 1928 | 1,920 00 | 2,000 00 | 1,680 00 |
| North Shore Gas Co., 5s, 1937 | 9,700 00 | 10,000 00 | 6,700 00 |
| Portland Gas & Coke Co., 5, 1940 | 10,000 00 | 10,000 00 | 8,400 00 |
| United Light & Ry. Co., 5s, 1932 | 4,537 50 | 5,000 00 | 4,200 00 |
| Columbus, Ohio, Ry. Co., 4s, 1939 | 4,037 50 | 5,000 00 | 3,000 00 |
| Danville, Champaign & Decatur Ry. & Lt. Co., 5s, 1938 | 14,800 00 | 16,000 00 | 11,680 00 |
| Commonwealth Edison Co., 5s, 1943 | 3,000 00 | 3,000 00 | 2,820 00 |
| Little River Drainage District, 5½s, 1929 | 950 00 | 1,000 00 | 980 00 |
| Des Moines Electric, 5s, 1938 | 9,500 00 | 10,000 00 | 8,700 00 |
| U. S. Second Liberty Bond, 4¼s, 1942 | 150 00 | 150 00 | 145 50 |
| U. S. Third Liberty Bond, 4¼s, 1928 | 700 00 | 700 00 | 686 00 |
| U. S. Fourth Liberty Bond, 4¼s, 1938 | 1,750 00 | 1,750 00 | 1,697 50 |
| U. S. Victory Bonds, 4¾s, 1923 | 550 00 | 550 00 | 550 00 |
| Totals | $76,595 00 | $80,150 00 | $61,889 00 |

## SCHEDULE D—PART 2—STOCKS.

| Description. | Book value. | Par value. |
|---|---|---|
| Bank of Commerce & Savings, Chicago, Ill | $12,000 00 | $10,000 00 |

---

## CENTRAL LIFE INSURANCE COMPANY OF ILLINOIS.

Located at Central Life Building, Ottawa, Illinois; commenced business April 12, 1907.

H. W. JOHNSON, President. S. B. BRADFORD, Secretary.

### CAPITAL.

| | | |
|---|---|---|
| Capital paid up | $300,000 00 | |
| Amount of ledger assets December 31, of previous year | $3,392,279 07 | |
| Increase of paid-up capital during year | 100,000 00 | |
| Extended at | | $3,492,279 07 |

## INCOME.

| | | | |
|---|---|---|---|
| First year's premiums on original policies, less re-insurance | | $227,111 22 | |
| First year's premiums for total and permanent disability benefits | | 1,433 55 | |
| First year's premiums for additional accidental death benefits, less re-insurance | | 4,399 11 | |
| Dividends applied to purchase paid-up additions and annuities | | 17,885 86 | |
| New premiums | | $250,829 74 | |
| Renewal premiums less re-insurance | $813,912 38 | | |
| Renewal premiums for total and permanent disability benefits | 3,889 71 | | |
| Renewal premiums for additional accidental death benefits, less re-insurance | 9,588 51 | | |
| Dividends applied to pay renewal premiums | 28,538 32 | | |
| Renewal premiums | | 855,928 92 | |
| Premium income | | | $1,106,758 66 |
| Dividends left with company to accumulate at interest | | | 24,631 54 |
| Interest on mortgage loans | | $149,192 68 | |
| Interest on collateral loans | | 1,338 14 | |
| Interest on bonds and dividends on stocks | | 940 75 | |
| Interest on premium notes, policy loans or liens | | 24,241 74 | |
| Interest on deposits | | 4,971 45 | |
| Interest on other debts due the company | | 658 03 | |
| Rents—including, $4,800.00 for company's occupancy of its own buildings | | 23,890 00 | |
| Total interest and rents | | | 205,232 79 |
| Receipts from unlisted assets | | | 100 00 |
| Borrowed money (gross) | | | 13,000 00 |
| Total income | | | $1,349,722 99 |
| Total | | | $4,842,002 06 |

## DISBURSEMENTS.

| | | |
|---|---|---|
| Death claims and additions | $151,391 28 | |
| Matured endowments and additions | 5,109 00 | |
| Total and permanent disability claims and additional accidental death benefits | 8,000 00 | |
| Total death claims and endowments | | $164,500 28 |
| Premium notes and liens voided by lapse, less $991.81 restorations | | 34,989 88 |
| Surrender values paid in cash, or applied in liquidation of loans or notes | | 61,645 81 |
| Dividends paid policyholders in cash, or applied in liquidation of loans or notes | | 3,796 36 |
| Dividends applied to pay renewal premiums | | 28,538 32 |
| Dividends applied to purchase paid-up additions and annuities | | 17,885 86 |
| Dividends left with the company to accumulate at interest | | 24,631 54 |
| (Total paid policyholders | $335,988 05) | |
| Expense of investigation and settlement of policy claims, including legal expenses | | 383 58 |
| Supplementary contracts not involving life contingencies | | 2,099 84 |
| Dividends with interest, held on deposit surrendered during the year | | 10,768 48 |
| Dividends to stockholders | | 116,000 00 |
| Commissions to agents, first year, $142,184.20; renewal, $30,173.17 | | 172,357 37 |
| Compensation of managers and agents not paid by commissions on new business | | 29,796 64 |
| Agency supervision and traveling expenses of supervisors | | 13,693 23 |
| Branch office expenses | | 5,817 50 |
| Medical examiners' fees and inspection of risks | | 15,853 16 |
| Salaries and all other compensation of officers and home office employees | | 50,325 28 |
| Rent | | 4,800 00 |
| Advertising, printing, stationery, postage, telegraph, telephone and express | | 17,366 91 |
| Legal expense | | 144 76 |
| Furniture, fixtures and safes | | 6,061 45 |
| Repairs and expenses (other than taxes) on real estate | | 10,579 94 |
| Taxes on real estate | | 3,007 66 |
| State taxes on premiums | | 7,521 13 |
| Insurance department licenses and fees | | 1,905 65 |
| Federal taxes | | 12,542 45 |
| All other licenses, fees and taxes | | 5,602 88 |
| Other disbursements, viz: Agency meetings, $1,387.64; traveling expenses, $2,174.98; agent's and officer's bonds, $183.31; books and supplies, $1,697.25; collection charges, $543.10; impairment service, $299.58; light and power, $331.50; miscellaneous expenses, $91.11 | | 6,708 47 |
| Borrowed money repaid (gross) | | 13,000 00 |
| Interest on borrowed money | | 146 61 |
| Agents' balances charged off | | 6,322 65 |
| Total disbursements | | $848,793 69 |
| Balance | | $3,993,208 37 |

## LEDGER ASSETS.

| | |
|---|---|
| Book value of real estate | $ 175,000 00 |
| Mortgage loans on real estate | 2,975,074 60 |
| Loans secured by collaterals | 30,196 16 |
| Loans on company's policies assigned as collateral | 449,883 84 |
| Premium notes on policies in force | 157,204 12 |
| Book value of bonds and stocks | 14,875 00 |
| Cash in office | 200 00 |
| Deposits in trust companies and banks not on interest | 691 79 |
| Deposits in trust companies and banks on interest | 110,144 98 |
| Bills receivable | 7,080 29 |
| Agents' balances (debit, $74,717.37; credit, $1,859.78) | 72,857 59 |
| Total ledger assets | $3,993,208 37 |

### NON-LEDGER ASSETS.

| | | | |
|---|---|---|---|
| Interest due and accrued on mortgages | | $106,503 82 | |
| Interest due and accrued on collateral loans | | 666 09 | |
| Interest due and accrued on premium notes, loans or liens | | 12,372 99 | |
| Interest due and accrued on other assets | | 843 56 | |
| | | | 120,386 46 |
| | New business. | Renewals. | |
| Net uncollected and deferred premiums (paid for basis) | $1,047 36 | $128,970 93 | 130,018 29 |
| Gross assets | | | $4,243,613 12 |

### DEDUCT ASSETS NOT ADMITTED.

| | | |
|---|---|---|
| Agents' debit balances | $74,717 37 | |
| Bills receivable | 7,080 29 | |
| Premium notes, policy loans and other policy assets in excess of net value and of other policy liabilities on individual policies | 21,463 15 | |
| Book value of bonds and stocks over market value | 100 00 | |
| Total | | 103,360 81 |
| Admitted assets | | $4,140,252 31 |

## LIABILITIES.

| | | |
|---|---|---|
| Net present value of outstanding policies computed by the Illinois Insurance Department | $3,237,051 00 | |
| Same for dividend additions | 79,718 00 | |
| Total | $3,316,769 00 | |
| Deduct net value of risks re-insured | 18,174 00 | |
| Net reserve (paid for basis) | | $3,298,595 00 |
| Extra reserve for total and permanent disability benefits and for additional accidental death benefits included in life policies, less re-insurance | | 12,187 00 |
| Present value of supplementary contracts not involving life contingencies | | 23,772 44 |
| Reserve for guaranteed premium coupons on outstanding policies December 31, 1921 | | 48,353 11 |
| Dividends left with the company to accumulate at interest | | 98,613 42 |
| Gross premiums paid in advance, including surrender values so applied, less discount, if any | | 5,271 93 |
| Unearned interest and rent paid in advance | | 2,479 53 |
| Commissions due agents on premium notes, when paid | | 32,482 65 |
| Salaries, rents, office expenses, bills and accounts due or accrued | | 1,021 22 |
| Estimated amount hereafter payable for federal, state and other taxes based upon the business of the year of this statement | | 42,500 00 |
| Unpaid dividends to stockholders | | 16,000 00 |
| Dividends or other profits due policyholders | | 22,810 11 |
| Dividends declared on or apportioned to annual dividend policies payable to policyholders during 1922 for period to December 31, 1922 | | 123,983 39 |
| Amounts set apart, apportioned, provisionally ascertained, calculated, declared or held awaiting apportionment upon deferred dividend policies | | 1,067 83 |
| Contingent fund | | 10,000 00 |
| Total | | $3,739,137 63 |
| Capital paid up | | 300,000 00 |
| Unassigned funds (surplus) | | 101,114 68 |
| Total | | $4,140,252 31 |

## EXHIBIT OF POLICIES—ORDINARY.

ALL BUSINESS PAID FOR.

| | Number. | Amount. |
|---|---|---|
| Policies in force December 31, 1920 | 18,010 | $36,055,024 00 |
| Policies issued, revived and increased during the year | 3,470 | 8,915,081 00 |
| Total | 21,480 | $44,970,105 00 |

## EXHIBIT OF POLICIES—ORDINARY—Concluded.

ALL BUSINESS PAID FOR.

| | Number. | Amount. | Number. | Amount. |
|---|---|---|---|---|
| Deduct policies which have ceased to be in force during the year— | | | | |
| By death | 67 | $ 140,634 00 | | |
| By maturity | 4 | 5,109 00 | | |
| By expiry | 143 | 242,250 00 | | |
| By surrender | 404 | 1,035,332 00 | | |
| By lapse | 1,491 | 4,210,481 00 | | |
| By decrease | | 14,967 00 | | |
| Total | | | 2,109 | $5,648,773 00 |
| Total policies in force December 31, 1921 | | | 19,371 | $39,321,332 00 |
| Re-insured | | | 346 | $1,459,584 00 |

## BUSINESS IN ILLINOIS—ORDINARY.

| | Number. | Amount. |
|---|---|---|
| Policies in force December 31, 1920 | 13,591 | $24,948,439 00 |
| Policies issued during the year | 1,559 | 3,924,298 00 |
| Total | 15,150 | $28,872,737 00 |
| Deduct policies ceased to be in force | 994 | 2,409,738 00 |
| Policies in force December 31, 1921 | 14,156 | $26,462,999 00 |
| Losses and claims unpaid December 31, 1920 | 1 | $ 1,000 00 |
| Losses and claims incurred during the year | 53 | 110,096 00 |
| Total | 54 | $111,096 00 |
| Losses and claims settled during the year | 54 | 111,096 00 |
| Premiums received | | $794,244 54 |

## GAIN AND LOSS EXHIBIT.

INSURANCE EXHIBIT.

| | | Gain in surplus. | Loss in surplus. |
|---|---|---|---|
| Loading on actual premiums of the year (averaging 23.73 per cent of the gross premiums) | $276,038 67 | | |
| Insurance expenses incurred during the year | 378,215 98 | | |
| Loss from loading | | | $102,177 31 |
| Interest earned during the year | $228,837 88 | | |
| Investment expenses incurred during the year | 13,587 60 | | |
| Net income from investments | $215,250 28 | | |
| Interest required to maintain reserve | 118,664 64 | | |
| Gain from interest | | $ 96,585 64 | |
| Expected mortality on net amount at risk | $329,836 26 | | |
| Actual mortality on net amount at risk | 137,497 04 | | |
| Gain from mortality | | 192,339 22 | |
| Total gain during the year from surrendered and lapsed policies | | 8,922 15 | |
| Dividends paid stockholders | | | 116,000 00 |
| Decrease in surplus on dividend account | | | 113,383 51 |
| Increase in special funds and special reserves during the year | | | 10,000 00 |

INVESTMENT EXHIBIT.

| | | Gain in surplus. | Loss in surplus. |
|---|---|---|---|
| Total losses from stocks and bonds | | | 100 00 |
| Loss from assets not admitted | | | 4,530 17 |
| Net gain on account of total and permanent disability benefits or additional accidental death benefits included in life policies | | 9,570 88 | |
| Loss from agents balances charged off | | | 6,322 65 |
| Gain from unlisted assets | | 100 00 | |
| Loss from premium notes voided by lapse | | | 34,989 88 |
| Balance unaccounted for | | 38 87 | |
| Total gains and losses in surplus during the year | | $307,556 76 | $387,503 52 |
| Surplus December 31, 1920 | $181,061 44 | | |
| Surplus December 31, 1921 | 101,114 68 | | |
| Decrease in surplus | | 79,946 76 | |
| Total | | $387,503 52 | $387,503 52 |

## SCHEDULE D—PART 1.

| Description. | Book value. | Par value. | Market value. |
|---|---|---|---|
| City of Lawton, Okla | $10,000 00 | $10,000 00 | $10,000 00 |

SCHEDULE D—PART 2.

| Description. | Book value. | Par value. | Market value. |
|---|---|---|---|
| Ottawa Banking & Trust Co. | $4,875 00 | $2,500 00 | $5,000 00 |

## CHICAGO NATIONAL LIFE INSURANCE COMPANY.

Located at No. 202 South State Street, Chicago, Illinois; commenced business November 26, 1920.

THOMAS CAREY, President. T. FRANK O'CONNELL, Secretary.

### CAPITAL.

| | | |
|---|---|---|
| Capital paid up | $100,000 00 | |
| Amount of ledger assets December 31, of previous year | | $177,040 19 |

### INCOME.

| | | |
|---|---|---|
| Interest on bonds | $3,261 44 | |
| Interest on other debts due the company | 626 99 | |
| Total interest | | $3,888 43 |
| Profit on sale or maturity of ledger assets | | 166 33 |
| Total income | | $4,054 76 |
| Total | | $181,094 95 |

### DISBURSEMENTS.

| | |
|---|---|
| Salaries and all other compensation of officers and home office employees | $10,114 94 |
| Rent | 1,466 29 |
| Advertising, printing, stationery, postage, telegraph, telephone and express | 2,195 16 |
| Legal expense | 2,050 00 |
| Furniture, fixtures and safes | 887 00 |
| Insurance department licenses and fees | 105 00 |
| Other disbursements, viz: Actuarial expenses, $2,100.00; books, publications and supplies, $154.00 | 2,254 00 |
| Total disbursements | $19,072 39 |
| Balance | $162,022 56 |

### LEDGER ASSETS.

| | |
|---|---|
| Book value of bonds | $108,731 80 |
| Cash in office | 67 65 |
| Deposits in trust companies and banks not on interest | 10,107 73 |
| Bills receivable, including stock notes of $21,409.00 | 42,964 56 |
| War savings stamps | 150 82 |
| Total ledger assets | $162,022 56 |

#### NON-LEDGER ASSETS.

| | |
|---|---|
| Interest due and accrued on bonds | 4,556 14 |
| Market value of bonds over book value | 3,628 20 |
| All other assets, viz: Furniture and fixtures, $887.00; printing and stationery, $1,700.00. | 2,587 00 |
| Gross assets | $172,793 90 |

#### DEDUCT ASSETS NOT ADMITTED.

| | | |
|---|---|---|
| Supplies, printed matter and stationery | $ 1,700 00 | |
| Furniture, fixtures and safes | 887 00 | |
| Stock notes | 21,409 00 | |
| Bills receivable | 21,555 56 | |
| Total | | 45,551 56 |
| Admitted assets | | $127,242 34 |

### LIABILITIES.

| | |
|---|---|
| Capital paid up | $100,000 00 |
| Unassigned funds (surplus) | 27,242 34 |
| Total | $127,242 34 |

### GAIN AND LOSS EXHIBIT.

#### INSURANCE EXHIBIT.

| | Gain in surplus. | Loss in surplus. |
|---|---|---|
| Insurance expenses incurred during the year | | $19,072 39 |
| Interest earned during the year | $ 6,238 25 | |

## GAIN AND LOSS EXHIBIT—Concluded.

### INVESTMENT EXHIBIT.

| | | Gain in surplus. | Loss in surplus. |
|---|---|---|---|
| Total gains from bonds | | $10,791 20 | |
| Loss from assets not admitted | | | $21,744 56 |
| Total gains and losses in surplus during the year | | $17,029 45 | $40,816 95 |
| Surplus December 31, 1920 | $51,029 84 | | |
| Surplus December 31, 1921 | 27,242 34 | | |
| Decrease in surplus | | 23,787 50 | |
| Total | | $40,816 95 | $40,816 95 |

## SCHEDULE D—PART 1—BONDS.

| Description. | Book value. | Par value. | Market value. |
|---|---|---|---|
| Johnston Co., N. C., Boonhull Twp., Rd. Dist. No. 5, 5s, 1946 | $ 5,700 00 | $ 6,000 00 | $ 5,220 00 |
| Tyler Co., Tex., Spec. Rd. No. 5, 5s, 1923 | 2,994 60 | 3,000 00 | 3,000 00 |
| Town of Temple, Cotton Co., Okla., Sewer, 6s, 1945 | 10,000 00 | 10,000 00 | 10,800 00 |
| Chambers Co., Texas, Rd. Dist. No. 2, 5½s, 1949 | 2,000 00 | 2,000 00 | 2,020 00 |
| Asbe Co., N. C., 5½s, 1949 | 16,360 00 | 16,000 00 | 16,160 00 |
| Shelby Co., Tex., Rd. Dist. No. 2, 5s, 1924 | 2,878 08 | 3,000 00 | 3,000 00 |
| Shelby Co., Tex., Rd. Dist. No. 2, 5s, 1925 | 2,878 08 | 3,000 00 | 3,000 00 |
| Shelby Co., Tex., Rd. Dist. No. 2, 5s, 1926 | 2,878 08 | 3,000 00 | 3,000 00 |
| Shelby Co., Tex., Rd. Dist. No. 2, 5s, 1927 | 2,878 08 | 3,000 00 | 2,970 00 |
| Shelby Co., Tex., Rd. Dist. No. 2, 5s, 1934 | 2,878 08 | 3,000 00 | 2,970 00 |
| Shelby Co., Tex., Rd. Dist. No. 2, 5s, 1935 | 2,878 08 | 3,000 00 | 2,970 00 |
| Shelby Co., Tex., Rd. Dist. No. 2, 5s, 1936 | 1,918 72 | 2,000 00 | 1,980 00 |
| Shelby Co., Tex., Rd. Dist. No. 6, 5½s, 1936 | 1,970 00 | 2,000 00 | 2,080 00 |
| Shelby Co., Tex., Rd. Dist. No. 6, 5½s, 1940 | 985 00 | 1,000 00 | 1,040 00 |
| Shelby Co., Tex., Rd. Dist. No. 6, 5½s, 1941 | 985 00 | 1,000 00 | 1,050 00 |
| Shelby Co., Tex., Rd. Dist. No. 6, 5½s, 1942 | 3,940 00 | 4,000 00 | 4,200 00 |
| Shelby Co., Tex., Rd. Dist. No. 6, 5½s, 1943 | 3,940 00 | 4,000 00 | 4,200 00 |
| Shelby Co., Tex., Rd. Dist. No. 6, 5½s, 1944 | 3,940 00 | 4,000 00 | 4,200 00 |
| Shelby Co., Tex., Rd. Dist. No. 6, 5½s, 1945 | 3,940 00 | 4,000 00 | 4,200 00 |
| Shelby County, Tex., Rd. Dist. No. 6, 5½s, 1946 | 3,940 00 | 4,000 00 | 4,200 00 |
| Shelby County, Tex., Rd. Dist. No. 6, 5½s, 1947 | 1,970 00 | 2,000 00 | 2,100 00 |
| Cass Co., Tex., Rd. Dist. No. 8, 5s, 1930 | 960 00 | 1,000 00 | 1,000 00 |
| Cass Co., Tex., Rd. Dist. No. 8, 5s, 1931 | 1,440 00 | 1,500 00 | 1,500 00 |
| Cass Co., Tex., Rd. Dist. No. 8, 5s, 1932 | 1,440 00 | 1,500 00 | 1,500 00 |
| Cass Co., Tex., Rd. Dist. No. 8, 5s,1933 | 1,440 00 | 1,500 00 | 1,500 00 |
| Cass Co., Tex., Rd. Dist. No. 8, 5s, 1934 | 1,440 00 | 1,500 00 | 1,500 00 |
| Cass Co., Tex., Rd. Dist. No. 8, 5s, 1935 | 1,440 00 | 1,500 00 | 1,500 00 |
| Cass Co., Tex., Rd. Dist. No. 8, 5s, 1936 | 1,440 00 | 1,500 00 | 1,500 00 |
| Cass Co., Tex., Rd. Dist. No. 8, 5s, 1937 | 1,440 00 | 1,500 00 | 1,500 00 |
| Cass Co., Tex., Rd. Dist. No. 8, 5s, 1938 | 1,440 00 | 1,500 00 | 1,500 00 |
| Cass Co., Tex., Rd. Dist. No. 8, 5s, 1939 | 1,440 00 | 1,500 00 | 1,500 00 |
| Cass Co., Tex., Rd. Dist. No. 8, 5s, 1940 | 1,440 00 | 1,500 00 | 1,500 00 |
| Cass Co., Tex., Rd. Dist. No. 8, 5s, 1941 | 1,440 00 | 1,500 00 | 1,500 00 |
| Cass Co., Tex., Rd. Dist. No. 8, 5s, 1942 | 1,440 00 | 1,500 00 | 1,500 00 |
| Cass Co., Tex., Rd. Dist. No. 8, 5s, 1943 | 1,440 00 | 1,500 00 | 1,500 00 |
| Cass Co., Tex., Rd. Dist. No. 8, 5s, 1944 | 1,440 00 | 1.500 00 | 1,500 00 |
| Cass Co., Tex., Rd. Dist. No. 8, 5s, 1945 | 1,440 00 | 1,500 00 | 1,500 00 |
| Cass Co., Tex., Rd. Dist. No. 8, 5s, 1946 | 1,440 00 | 1,500 00 | 1,500 00 |
| Cass Co., Tex., Rd. Dist. No. 8, 5s, 1947 | 1,440 00 | 1,500 00 | 1,500 00 |
| Cass Co., Tex., Rd. Dist. No. 8, 5s, 1948 | 1,440 00 | 1,500 00 | 1,500 00 |
| Totals | $108,731 80 | $111,000 00 | $112,360 00 |

---

# CLOVERLEAF LIFE AND CASUALTY COMPANY.

Located at Nos. 306-308 East State Street, Jacksonville, Illinois; commenced business, life, May 24, 1919; casualty, May 22, 1912.

F. H. ROWE, President. R. Y. ROWE, Secretary.

## CAPITAL.

| | | |
|---|---|---|
| Capital paid up | $200,000 00 | |
| Amount of ledger assets December 31, of previous year | | $579,798 59 |

## INCOME.

| | | | |
|---|---|---|---|
| First year's premiums on original policies, less re-insurance | | $69,075 96 | |
| Renewal p less re-insurance | $96,919 26 | | |
| Dividends applied to pay renewal premiums | 84 81 | | |
| Renewal premiums | | 97,004 07 | |
| Premium income | | | $166,080 03 |

## INCOME—Concluded.

| | | |
|---|---|---|
| Interest on mortgage loans | $18,715 67 | |
| Interest on bonds | 636 96 | |
| Interest on premium notes, policy loans or liens | 2,114 36 | |
| Interest on deposits | 119 82 | |
| Interest on other debts due the company | 20 22 | |
| Rents—including, $1,100.00 for company's occupancy of its own buildings | 2,438 00 | |
| Total interest and rents | | $24,045 03 |
| Contributed to surplus | | 22,400 00 |
| Borrowed money (gross) | | 10,000 00 |
| Income, life department | | $222,525 06 |
| Income, casualty department | | 922,079 08 |
| Total income | | $1,144,604 14 |
| Total | | $1,724,402 73 |

## DISBURSEMENTS.

| | | |
|---|---|---|
| Death claims | | $28,747 30 |
| Premium notes and liens voided by lapse | | 2,578 09 |
| Surrender values paid in cash, or applied in liquidation of loans or notes | | 7,272 41 |
| Dividends applied to pay renewal premiums | | 84 81 |
| (Total paid policyholders | $38,682 61) | |
| Expense of investigation and settlement of policy claims | | 30 00 |
| Commissions to agents, first year, $46,121.17; renewal, $2,596.01 | | 48,717 18 |
| Compensation of managers and agents not paid by commissions on new business | | 4,421 23 |
| Branch office expenses | | 1,426 70 |
| Medical examiners' fees and inspection of risks | | 12,152 15 |
| Salaries and all other compensation of officers and home office employees | | 14,005 50 |
| Rent | | 1,792 50 |
| Advertising, printing, stationery, postage, telegraph, telephone and express | | 10,294 85 |
| Legal expense | | 134 00 |
| Furniture, fixtures and safes | | 650 07 |
| Repairs and expenses (other than taxes) on real estate | | 183 42 |
| Taxes on real estate | | 556 80 |
| State taxes on premiums | | 2,902 70 |
| Insurance department licenses and fees | | 1,698 35 |
| Federal taxes | | 2,092 63 |
| All other licenses, fees and taxes | | 3,962 14 |
| Home office expenses (light, heat, repair on equipment, water, etc.) and traveling expenses other than agents | | 2,113 74 |
| Agents' balances charged off | | 1,395 06 |
| Borrowed money repaid (gross) | | 10,000 00 |
| Interest on borrowed money | | 166 24 |
| Disbursements, life department | | $157,377 87 |
| Disbursements, casualty department | | 930,730 84 |
| Total disbursements | | $1,088,108 71 |
| Balance | | $636,294 02 |

## LEDGER ASSETS.

| | | |
|---|---|---|
| Book value of real estate | | $ 77,493 87 |
| Mortgage loans on real estate | | 387,860 50 |
| Loans on company's policies assigned as collateral | | 31,537 50 |
| Premium notes on policies in force | | 989 54 |
| Book value of bonds | | 12,556 09 |
| Cash in office | | 6,360 40 |
| Deposits in trust companies and banks not on interest | | 67 23 |
| Deposits in trust companies and banks on interest | | 66,601 10 |
| Agents' balances (debit, $7,169.65; credit, $50.00) | | 7,119 65 |
| Special assets of casualty department | | 45,708 14 |
| Total ledger assets | | $636,294 02 |

### NON-LEDGER ASSETS.

| | | |
|---|---|---|
| Interest accrued on mortgages | $5,231 77 | |
| Interest accrued on bonds | 47 42 | |
| Interest accrued on premium notes, loans or liens | 12 80 | |
| | | 5,291 99 |
| Net uncollected and deferred premiums (paid for basis) | | 15,033 59 |
| Furniture and fixtures | | 1,692 99 |
| Non-ledger assets of casualty department | | 13,272 07 |
| Gross assets | | $671,584 66 |

## LEDGER ASSETS—Concluded.

DEDUCT ASSETS NOT ADMITTED.

| | | |
|---|---|---|
| Furniture, fixtures and safes | $1,692 99 | |
| Agents' debit balances | 7,169 65 | |
| Premium notes, policy loans and other policy assets in excess of net value and of other policy liabilities on individual policies | 927 93 | |
| Book value of bonds over market value | 1,444 09 | |
| Non-admitted assets of casualty department | 23,859 13 | |
| Total | | $35,093 79 |
| Admitted assets | | $636,490 87 |

## LIABILITIES.

| | | |
|---|---|---|
| Net present value of outstanding policies computed by the Illinois Insurance Department | $357,627 00 | |
| Deduct net value of risks re-insured | 6,135 00 | |
| Net reserve (paid for basis) | | $351,492 00 |
| Extra reserve for total and permanent disability benefits and for additional accidental death benefits included in life policies, less re-insurance | | 838 00 |
| Death losses reported for which no proofs have been received | | 995 78 |
| Premiums paid in advance, including surrender values so applied, less discount, if any | | 504 55 |
| Unearned interest and rent paid in advance | | 888 79 |
| Salaries, rents, office expenses, bills, and accounts due or accrued | | 100 00 |
| Medical examiners' fees due or accrued | | 600 00 |
| Estimated amount hereafter payable for federal, state and other taxes based upon the business of the year of this statement | | 7,200 00 |
| Total | | $362,619 12 |
| Liabilities of casualty department | | 44,061 56 |
| Total | | $406,680 68 |
| Capital paid up | | 200,000 00 |
| Unassigned funds (surplus) | | 29,810 19 |
| Total | | $636,490 87 |

## EXHIBIT OF POLICIES—ORDINARY.

ALL BUSINESS PAID FOR.

| | Number. | Amount. | Number. | Amount. |
|---|---|---|---|---|
| Policies in force December 31, 1920 | | | 4,487 | $6,275,604 00 |
| Policies issued, revived and increased during the year | | | 3,177 | 2,564,648 00 |
| Total | | | 7,664 | $8,840,252 00 |
| Deduct policies which have ceased to be in force during the year— | | | | |
| By death | 24 | $ 38,086 00 | | |
| By expiry | 24 | 30,621 00 | | |
| By surrender | 35 | 43,000 00 | | |
| By lapse | 2,591 | 2,244,112 00 | | |
| Total | | | 2,674 | 2,355,819 00 |
| Total policies in force December 31, 1921 | | | 4,990 | $6,484,433 00 |
| Re-insured | | | 437 | $1,028,065 00 |

## BUSINESS IN ILLINOIS—ORDINARY.

| | Number. | Amount. |
|---|---|---|
| Policies in force December 31, 1920 | 644 | $1,122,906 00 |
| Policies issued during the year | 371 | 634,783 00 |
| Total | 1,015 | $1,757,689 00 |
| Deduct policies ceased to be in force | 257 | 463,529 00 |
| Policies in force December 31, 1921 | 758 | $1,294,160 00 |
| Losses and claims incurred during the year | 3 | $10,000 00 |
| Losses and claims settled during the year | 3 | 10,000 00 |
| Premiums received | | $35,859 91 |

## GAIN AND LOSS EXHIBIT.

INSURANCE EXHIBIT.

| | | Gain in surplus. | Loss in surplus. |
|---|---|---|---|
| Loading on actual premiums of the year (averaging 26.2 per cent of the gross premiums) | $ 45,201 92 | | |
| Insurance expenses incurred during the year | 108,568 67 | | |
| Loss from loading | | | $63,366 75 |

## GAIN AND LOSS EXHIBIT—Concluded.

INSURANCE EXHIBIT.

| | | Gain in surplus. | Loss in surplus. |
|---|---|---|---|
| Interest earned during the year | $22,360 26 | | |
| Investment expenses incurred during the year | 1,537 16 | | |
| Net income from investments | $20,823 10 | | |
| Interest required to maintain reserve | 10,879 75 | | |
| Gain from interest | | $ 9,943 35 | |
| Expected mortality on net amount at risk | $51,267 68 | | |
| Actual mortality on net amount at risk | 26,348 59 | | |
| Gain from mortality | | 24,919 09 | |
| Total gain during the year from surrendered and lapsed policies | | 7,511 37 | |
| Decrease in surplus on dividend account | | | $ 84 81 |
| Net to loss account | | | 3,973 15 |

INVESTMENT EXHIBIT.

| | | Gain in surplus. | Loss in surplus. |
|---|---|---|---|
| Total gain from bonds | | 444 25 | |
| Gain from assets not admitted | | 1,344 66 | |
| Net gain on account of total and permanent disability benefits or additional accidental death benefits included in life policies | | 54 00 | |
| Gain from contributed surplus | | 22,400 00 | |
| Loss, casualty department | | | 311 98 |
| Balance unaccounted for | | | 234 80 |
| Total gains and losses in surplus during the year | | $66,616 72 | $67,971 49 |
| Surplus December 31, 1920 | $31,164 96 | | |
| Surplus December 31, 1921 | 29,810 19 | | |
| Decrease in surplus | | 1,354 77 | |
| Total | | $67,971 49 | $67,971 49 |

## SCHEDULE D—PART 1—BONDS.

| Description. | Book value. | Par value. | Market value. |
|---|---|---|---|
| Life Department— | | | |
| U. S. 2d Liberty Loan, 4¼s | $ 50 00 | $ 50 00 | $ 48 50 |
| U. S. 3d Liberty Loan, 4¼s | 91 96 | 100 00 | 98 00 |
| U. S. 4th Liberty Loan, 4¼s | 2,219 38 | 2,250 00 | 2,182 50 |
| Lenawee Co. Gas & Electric, 1st mortgage, 5½s | 7,000 00 | 7,000 00 | 5,600 00 |
| U. S. Mortgage Bond Co., Real Estate, 1st mortgage 6s | 2,500 00 | 2,500 00 | 2,500 00 |
| Casualty Department— | | | |
| U. S. 2d Liberty Loan, 4¼s | 200 00 | 200 00 | 194 00 |
| U. S. 3d Liberty Loan, 4¼s | 94 75 | 100 00 | 98 00 |
| U. S. 4th Liberty Loan, 4¼s | 300 00 | 300 00 | 291 00 |
| Victory Loan, 4¾s | 100 00 | 100 00 | 100 00 |
| Totals | $12,556 09 | $12,600 00 | $11,112 00 |

---

## CONTINENTAL ASSURANCE COMPANY.

Located at No. 910 South Michigan Avenue, Chicago, Illinois; commenced business May 31, 1911.

H. G. B. ALEXANDER, President. E. G. TIMME, Secretary.

### CAPITAL.

| | | |
|---|---|---|
| Capital paid up | $250,000 00 | |
| Amount of ledger assets December 31, of previous year | $862,122 42 | |
| Increase of paid-up capital during year | 50,000 00 | |
| Extended at | | $912,122 42 |

### INCOME.

| | |
|---|---|
| First year's premiums on original policies, less re-insurance | $247,474 30 |
| First year's premiums for total and permanent disability benefits, less re-insurance | 8,478 13 |
| First year's premiums for additional accidental death benefits, less re-insurance | 4,057 51 |
| Surrender values applied to purchase paid-up insurance and annuities | 101 18 |
| New premiums | $260,111 12 |

## INCOME—Concluded.

| | | | |
|---|---|---|---|
| Renewal premiums less re-insurance | $398,959 43 | | |
| Renewal premiums for total and permanent disability benefits, less re-insurance | 8,324 59 | | |
| Renewal premiums for additional accidental death benefits, less re-insurance | 2,274 02 | | |
| Surrender values applied to pay renewal premiums | 1,970 23 | | |
| Renewal premiums | | 411,528 27 | |
| Premium income | | | $671,639 39 |
| Interest on mortgage loans | | $33,635 65 | |
| Interest on bonds | | 11,024 14 | |
| Interest on premium notes, policy loans or liens | | 3,191 32 | |
| Interest on deposits | | 156 87 | |
| Interest on other debts due the company | | 383 31 | |
| Total interest | | | 48,391 29 |
| From other sources, viz: Suspense items credited to profit and loss, $7.28; increase in ledger liabilities, $1,905.06 | | | 1,912 34 |
| Increase in book value of ledger assets | | | 1,308 91 |
| Total income | | | $723,251 93 |
| Total | | | $1,635,374 35 |

## DISBURSEMENTS.

| | | |
|---|---|---|
| Death claims | $59,300 00 | |
| Total and permanent disability claims | 340 10 | |
| Total death claims | | $59,640 10 |
| Annuities involving life contingencies | | 223 80 |
| Surrender values paid in cash, or applied in liquidation of loans or notes | | 11,150 42 |
| Surrender values applied to pay new and renewal premiums | | 1,970 23 |
| Surrender values applied to purchase paid-up insurance and annuities | | 101 18 |
| (Total paid policyholders | $73,085 73) | |
| Expense of investigation and settlement of policy claims, including legal expenses | | 647 57 |
| Supplementary contracts not involving life contingencies | | 360 00 |
| Dividends to stockholders | | 8,000 00 |
| Commissions to agents, first year, $196,725.79; renewal, $24,952.90 | | 221,678 69 |
| Compensation of managers and agents not paid by commissions on new business | | 1,276 00 |
| Medical examiners' fees and inspection of risks | | 27,813 78 |
| Salaries and all other compensation of officers and home office employees | | 2,410 04 |
| Printing and stationery | | 6,725 21 |
| Legal expense | | 558 50 |
| State taxes on premiums | | 8,125 68 |
| Insurance department licenses and fees | | 2,925 68 |
| Federal taxes | | 7,616 28 |
| All other licenses, fees and taxes | | 125 00 |
| Other disbursements, viz: Home office expense, $4,000.00; general expense, $908.00; miscellaneous items charged to profit and loss, $24.50 | | 4,932 50 |
| Agents' balances charged off | | 110 58 |
| Decrease in book value of ledger assets | | 44 80 |
| Total disbursements | | $366,436 04 |
| Balance | | $1,268,938 31 |

## LEDGER ASSETS.

| | |
|---|---|
| Mortgage loans on real estate | $838,650 00 |
| Loans on company's policies assigned as collateral | 58,613 83 |
| Premium notes on policies in force | 20,199 00 |
| Book value of bonds | 314,329 21 |
| Deposits in trust companies and banks on interest | 35,076 35 |
| Bills receivable | 2,277 44 |
| Agents' balances (debit, $2,295.68; credit, $2,503.20) | —207 52 |
| Total ledger assets | $1,268,938 31 |

### NON-LEDGER ASSETS.

| | | | |
|---|---|---|---|
| Interest accrued on mortgages | | $25,199 90 | |
| Interest accrued on bonds | | 4,781 35 | |
| Interest accrued on premium notes, loans or liens | | 721 86 | |
| | | | 30,703 11 |
| Market value of bonds over book value | | | 23,430 59 |
| | New business. | Renewals. | |
| Net uncollected and deferred premiums (paid for basis) | $12,307 46 | $82,415 33 | 94,722 79 |
| Gross assets | | | $1,417,749 80 |

## LEDGER ASSETS—Concluded.

DEDUCT ASSETS NOT ADMITTED.

| | | |
|---|---|---|
| Agents' debit balances | $2,295 68 | |
| Bills receivable | 2,277 44 | |
| Premium notes, policy loans and other policy assets in excess of net value and of other policy liabilities on individual policies | 1,819 21 | |
| Total | | $6,392 33 |
| Admitted assets | | $1,411,402 47 |

## LIABILITIES.

| | | |
|---|---|---|
| Net present value of outstanding policies computed by the Illinois Insurance Department | $948,748 00 | |
| Same for annuities | 882 00 | |
| Total | $949,630 00 | |
| Deduct net value of risks re-insured | 10,496 00 | |
| Net reserve (paid for basis) | | $939,134 00 |
| Extra reserve for total and permanent disability benefits and for additional accidental death benefits included in life policies, less re-insurance | | 5,795 00 |
| Present value of supplementary contracts not involving life contingencies | | 4,640 35 |
| Present value of amounts incurred but not yet due for total and permanent disability benefits | | 8,315 94 |
| Death losses in process of adjustment | $12,000 00 | |
| Total and permanent disability benefits | 6,666 81 | |
| Total policy claims | | 18,666 81 |
| Gross premiums paid in advance, including surrender values so applied, less discount, if any | | 1,850 58 |
| Unearned interest and rent paid in advance | | 1,153 68 |
| Commissions due agents on premium notes, when paid | | 2,451 83 |
| Cost of collection on uncollected and deferred premiums in excess of loading | | 4,658 29 |
| Salaries, rents, office expenses, bills and accounts due or accrued | | 1,311 11 |
| Medical examiners' and legal fees due or accrued | | 2,467 34 |
| Estimated amount hereafter payable for federal, state and other taxes based upon the business of the year of this statement | | 11,723 00 |
| Special voluntary reserve | | 26,389 59 |
| Survivorship fund | | 4,553 02 |
| Ledger liabilities | | 2,166 69 |
| Total | | $1,035,277 23 |
| Capital paid up | | 250,000 00 |
| Unassigned funds (surplus) | | 126,125 24 |
| Total | | $1,411,402 47 |

## EXHIBIT OF POLICIES—ORDINARY.

ALL BUSINESS PAID FOR.

| | Number. | Amount. | Number. | Amount. |
|---|---|---|---|---|
| Policies in force December 31, 1920 | | | 10,451 | $17,727,585 00 |
| Policies issued, revived and increased during the year | | | 4,646 | 10,025,293 00 |
| Total | | | 15,097 | $27,752,878 00 |
| Deduct policies which have ceased to be in force during the year— | | | | |
| By death | 46 | $ 62,800 00 | | |
| By expiry | 25 | 35,059 00 | | |
| By surrender | 63 | 90,500 00 | | |
| By lapse | 2,579 | 4,804,217 00 | | |
| By decrease | -------- | 101,468 00 | | |
| Total | | | 2,713 | 5,094,044 00 |
| Total policies in force December 31, 1921 | | | 12,384 | $22,658,834 00 |
| Re-insured | | | 452 | $2,166,019 00 |

## BUSINESS IN ILLINOIS—ORDINARY.

| | Number. | Amount. |
|---|---|---|
| Policies in force December 31, 1920 | 2,165 | $4,388,791 00 |
| Policies issued during the year | 1,228 | 2,731,607 00 |
| Total | 3,393 | $7,120,398 00 |
| Deduct policies ceased to be in force | 709 | 1,520,186 00 |
| Policies in force December 31, 1921 | 2,684 | $5,600,212 00 |

## BUSINESS IN ILLINOIS—ORDINARY—Concluded.

| | Number. | Amount. |
|---|---|---|
| Losses and claims unpaid December 31, 1920 | 1 | $ 1,000 00 |
| Losses and claims incurred during the year | 8 | 16,000 00 |
| Total | 9 | $17,000 00 |
| Losses and claims settled during the year | 6 | 10,000 00 |
| Losses and claims unpaid December 31, 1921 | 3 | $7,000 00 |
| Premiums received | | $169,109 95 |

## GAIN AND LOSS EXHIBIT.

### INSURANCE EXHIBIT.

| | | Gain in surplus. | Loss in surplus. |
|---|---|---|---|
| Loading on actual premiums of the year (averaging 23 per cent of the gross premiums) | $159,939 09 | | |
| Insurance expenses incurred during the year | 281,301 20 | | |
| Loss from loading | | | $121,362 11 |
| Interest earned during the year | $60,502 36 | | |
| Investment expenses incurred during the year | 500 04 | | |
| Net income from investments | $60,002 32 | | |
| Interest required to maintain reserve | 28,656 86 | | |
| Gain from interest | | $ 31,345 46 | |
| Expected mortality on net amount at risk | $172,726 54 | | |
| Actual mortality on net amount at risk | 51,686 28 | | |
| Gain from mortality | | 121,040 26 | |
| Expected disbursements to annuitants | $ 65 87 | | |
| Net actual annuity claims incurred | 223 80 | | |
| Loss from annuities | | | 157 93 |
| Total gain during the year from surrendered and lapsed policies | | 30,282 89 | |
| Dividends paid stockholders | | | 8,000 00 |
| Increase in special funds and special reserves during the year | | | 1,171 21 |
| Net to profit account | | 7 28 | |

### INVESTMENT EXHIBIT.

| | | Gain in surplus. | Loss in surplus. |
|---|---|---|---|
| Total gains from bonds | | 24,837 59 | |
| Gain from assets not admitted | | 266 69 | |
| Net loss on account of total and permanent disability benefits or additional accidental death benefits included in life policies | | | 3,189 03 |
| Balance unaccounted for | | 1,333 81 | |
| Total gains and losses in surplus during the year | | $209,113 98 | $133,880 28 |
| Surplus December 31, 1920 | $ 50,891 54 | | |
| Surplus December 31, 1921 | 126,125 24 | | |
| Increase in surplus | | | 75,233 70 |
| Total | | $209,113 98 | $209,113 98 |

## SCHEDULE D—PART 1—BONDS.

| Description. | Book value. | Par value. | Market value. |
|---|---|---|---|
| United States of America, First Liberty Loan, 3½s, 1947 | $ 500 00 | $ 500 00 | $ 500 00 |
| United States of America, Third Liberty Loan, 4¼s, 1928 | 50,000 00 | 50,000 00 | 50,000 00 |
| United States of America, Third Liberty Loan, 4¼s, 1928 | 47,885 00 | 50,000 00 | 48,800 00 |
| United States of America, Fourth Liberty Loan, 4¼s, 1938 | 60,676 00 | 70,000 00 | |
| United States of America, Fourth Liberty Loan, 4¼s, 1938 | 34,196 00 | 40,000 00 | 131,301 00 |
| United States of America, Fourth Liberty Loan, 4¼s, 1938 | 13,393 50 | 15,000 00 | |
| United States of America, Fourth Liberty Loan, 4¼s, 1938 | 8,929 00 | 10,000 00 | |
| United States of America, Third Liberty Loan, 4¼s, 1928 | 22,412 50 | 25,000 00 | 24,400 00 |
| Cook, Kane and McHenry Counties— | | | |
| Community High School Dist. 217, 6s, 1934 | | 7,000 00 | 7,990 50 |
| Community High School Dist. 217, 6s, 1935 | 26,139 60 | 9,000 00 | 10,350 00 |
| Community High School Dist. 217, 6s, 1937 | | 9,000 00 | 10,489 50 |
| Genoa Twp., DeKalb Co., Ill., High School, 5s, 1924 | | 2,000 00 | 2,017 60 |
| Genoa Twp., DeKalb Co., Ill., High School, 5s, 1928 | 9,531 51 | 1,000 00 | 1,020 80 |
| Genoa Twp., DeKalb Co., Ill., High School, 5s, 1931 | | 3,000 00 | 3,085 80 |
| Genoa Twp., DeKalb Co., Ill., High School, 5s, 1933 | | 4,000 00 | 4,132 80 |
| Norfolk, Va., 4½s, 1941 | 10,256 10 | 10,000 00 | 9,700 00 |
| St. Clair School Dist., Mich., 6s, 1935 | 20,410 00 | 20,000 00 | 22,716 00 |
| City of Memphis, Tenn., 5½s, 1954 | | 1,000 00 | 1,122 70 |
| City of Memphis, Tenn., 5½s, 1955 | 10,000 00 | 3,000 00 | 3,373 20 |
| City of Memphis, Tenn., 5½s, 1956 | | 3,000 00 | 3,377 70 |
| City of Memphis, Tenn., 5½s, 1957 | | 3,000 00 | 3,382 20 |
| Totals | $314,329 21 | $335,500 00 | $337,759 80 |

## ELGIN LIFE INSURANCE COMPANY.

Located at Nos. 6-8 North Spring Street, Elgin, Illinois; commenced business April 23, 1909.

E. P. STRANDBERG, President. C. E. BOTSFORD, Secretary.

### CAPITAL.

| | | | |
|---|---|---|---|
| Capital paid up | | $104,102 95 | |
| Amount of ledger assets December 31, of previous year | | | $255,826 43 |

### INCOME.

| | | | |
|---|---|---|---|
| First year's premiums on original policies, less re-insurance | | $2,093 16 | |
| First year's premiums for additional accidental death benefits, less re-insurance | | 20 54 | |
| New premiums | | $ 2,113 70 | |
| Renewal premiums less re-insurance | $30,592 31 | | |
| Renewal premiums for additional accidental death benefits | 6 32 | | |
| Coupons applied to pay renewal premiums | 207 46 | | |
| Renewal premiums | | 30,806 09 | |
| Premium income | | | $32,919 79 |
| Interest on mortgage loans | | $11,924 31 | |
| Interest on bonds | | 444 62 | |
| Interest on premium notes, policy loans or liens | | 826 42 | |
| Interest on renewal premiums | | 2 88 | |
| Total interest | | | 13,198 23 |
| Commissions on loans | | | 539 90 |
| *Borrowed money (gross) | | | 23,200 00 |
| Total income | | | $69,857 92 |
| Total | | | $325,684 35 |

### DISBURSEMENTS.

| | | |
|---|---|---|
| Death claims | $13,200 00 | |
| Matured endowments | 1,000 00 | |
| Total and permanent disability claims | 100 00 | |
| Total death claims and endowments | | $14,300 00 |
| Surrender values paid in cash, or applied in liquidation of loans or notes | | 2,472 16 |
| Coupons paid policyholders in cash, or applied in liquidation of loans or notes | | 157 15 |
| Coupons applied to pay renewal premiums | | 207 46 |
| (Total paid policyholders | $17,136 77) | |
| Supplementary contracts not involving life contingencies | | 200 00 |
| Commissions to agents, first year, $1,605.52; renewal, $452.47 | | 2,057 99 |
| Agency supervision and traveling expenses of supervisors | | 722 00 |
| Medical examiners' fees and inspection of risks | | 261 22 |
| Salaries and all other compensation of officers and home office employees | | 4,597 77 |
| Rent | | 549 13 |
| Advertising, printing, stationery, postage, telegraph, telephone, express and exchange | | 874 44 |
| Insurance department licenses and fees | | 178 79 |
| Federal taxes | | 72 80 |
| All other licenses, fees and taxes | | 2,123 50 |
| Other disbursements, viz: Premium note and policy loan, charged off, $145.73; actuarial fees, $175.00; traveling expense home office, $724.36; home office miscellaneous, $271.07; investment expense, $79.70 | | 1,395 86 |
| Borrowed money repaid (gross) | | 27,750 00 |
| Interest on borrowed money | | 49 26 |
| Interest on trust bonds | | 667 75 |
| Interest on renewal premium loan | | 45 23 |
| Loss on sale or maturity of ledger assets | | 4,643 25 |
| Total disbursements | | $63,325 76 |
| Balance | | $262,358 59 |

### LEDGER ASSETS.

| | |
|---|---|
| Book value of real estate | $ 2,645 09 |
| Mortgage loans on real estate | 234,656 80 |
| Loans on company's policies assigned as collateral | 13,687 15 |
| Premium notes on policies in force | 176 27 |
| Book value of bonds | 8,332 78 |
| Cash in office | 30 00 |
| Deposits in trust companies and banks not on interest | 1,489 10 |
| Deposits in trust companies and banks on interest | 500 00 |
| Bills receivable | 141 40 |
| Agents' balances (debit, $750.00; credit, $50.00) | 700 00 |
| Total ledger assets | $262,358 59 |

* Purchase price of mortgages.

## LEDGER ASSETS—Concluded.

### NON-LEDGER ASSETS.

| | | |
|---|---|---|
| Interest due and accrued on mortgages | $5,814 84 | |
| Interest accrued on bonds | 142 76 | |
| Interest accrued on premium notes, loans or liens | 388 47 | |
| | | $6,346 07 |
| Net uncollected and deferred premiums (paid for basis): Renewals | | 4,755 35 |
| Gross assets | | $273,460 01 |

### DEDUCT ASSETS NOT ADMITTED.

| | | |
|---|---|---|
| Agents' debit balances | $750 00 | |
| Bills receivable | 141 40 | |
| Premium notes, policy loans and other policy assets in excess of net value and of other policy liabilities on individual policies | 61 31 | |
| Book value of real estate over market value | 145 09 | |
| Book value of bonds over market value | 284 28 | |
| Total | | 1,382 08 |
| Admitted assets | | $272,077 93 |

## LIABILITIES.

| | | |
|---|---|---|
| Net present value of outstanding policies computed by the Illinois Insurance Department | $161,798 00 | |
| Deduct net value of risks re-insured | 229 00 | |
| Net reserve (paid for basis) | | $161,569 00 |
| Extra reserve for total and permanent disability benefits included in life policies | | 175 00 |
| Present value of amounts incurred but not yet due for total and permanent disability benefits | | 373 62 |
| Death losses reported for which no proofs have been received | | 1,500 00 |
| Gross premiums paid in advance, including surrender values so applied, less discount, if any | | 160 44 |
| Unearned interest and rent paid in advance | | 158 23 |
| Salaries, rents, office expenses, bills, and accounts due or accrued | | 62 50 |
| Estimated amount hereafter payable for federal, state and other taxes based upon the business of the year of this statement | | 1,200 00 |
| Borrowed money and interest thereon | | 450 00 |
| Accrued interest on trust bonds | | 1,007 99 |
| Total | | $166,656 78 |
| Capital paid up | | 104,102 95 |
| Unassigned funds (surplus) | | 1,318 20 |
| Total | | $272,077 93 |

## EXHIBIT OF POLICIES—ORDINARY.

### ALL BUSINESS PAID FOR.

| | Number. | Amount. | Number. | Amount. |
|---|---|---|---|---|
| Policies in force December 31, 1920 | | | 839 | $1,129,643 00 |
| Policies issued, revived, and increased during the year | | | 53 | 87,815 00 |
| Total | | | 892 | $1,217,458 00 |
| Deduct policies which have ceased to be in force during the year— | | | | |
| By death | 11 | $15,700 00 | | |
| By maturity | 1 | 1,000 00 | | |
| By expiry | 15 | 20,000 00 | | |
| By surrender | 9 | 14,500 00 | | |
| By lapse | 18 | 31,500 00 | | |
| By decrease | | 283 00 | | |
| Total | | | 54 | 82,983 00 |
| Total policies in force December 31, 1921 | | | 838 | $1,134,475 00 |
| Re-insured | | | 18 | $40,500 00 |

## BUSINESS IN ILLINOIS—ORDINARY.

| | Number. | Amount. |
|---|---|---|
| Policies in force December 31, 1920 | 757 | $1,019,817 00 |
| Policies issued during the year | 51 | 81,500 00 |
| Total | 808 | $1,101,317 00 |
| Deduct policies ceased to be in force | 39 | 56,100 00 |
| Policies in force December 31, 1921 | 769 | $1,045,217 00 |

BUSINESS IN ILLINOIS—ORDINARY—Concluded.

| | Number. | Amount. |
|---|---|---|
| Losses and claims unpaid December 31, 1920 | 1 | $ 600 00 |
| Losses and claims incurred during the year | 9 | 14,100 00 |
| Total | 10 | $14,700 00 |
| Losses and claims settled during the year | 10 | 14,700 00 |
| Premiums received | | $26,056 19 |

## GAIN AND LOSS EXHIBIT.

INSURANCE EXHIBIT.

| | | Gain in surplus. | Loss in surplus. |
|---|---|---|---|
| Loading on actual premiums of the year (averaging 9.52 per cent of the gross premiums) | $ 3,092 78 | | |
| Insurance expenses incurred during the year | 10,933 53 | | |
| Loss from loading | | | $7,840 75 |
| Interest earned during the year | $14,901 85 | | |
| Investment expenses incurred during the year | 460 20 | | |
| Net income from investments | $15,362 05 | | |
| Interest required to maintain reserve | 5,549 53 | | |
| Gain from interest | | $9,812 52 | |
| Expected mortality on net amount at risk | $15,340 76 | | |
| Actual mortality on net amount at risk | 12,642 00 | | |
| Gain from mortality | | 2,698 76 | |
| Total gain during the year from surrendered and lapsed policies | | 142 25 | |
| Decrease in surplus on dividend account | | | 364 61 |
| Net to loss account | | | 145 73 |
| INVESTMENT EXHIBIT. | | | |
| Total gains from stocks, bonds and mortgages | | 4,305 50 | |
| Loss on mortgage charged off | | | 4,643 25 |
| Gain from assets not admitted | | 353 86 | |
| Net gain on account of total and permanent disability benefits or additional accidental death benefits included in life policies | | 95 43 | |
| Loss from all other sources: Paid on renewal premium contract, $1,800.00; interest on trust bonds, $1,675.74; interest on premium contract, $45.23 | | | 3,520 97 |
| Balance unaccounted for loss | | | 2,759 39 |
| Total gains and losses in surplus during the year | | $17,408 32 | $19,274 70 |
| Surplus December 31, 1920 | $3,184 58 | | |
| Surplus December 31, 1921 | 1,318 20 | | |
| Decrease in surplus | | 1,866 38 | |
| Total | | $19,274 70 | $19,274 70 |

## SCHEDULE D—PART 1—BONDS.

| Description. | Book value. | Par value. | Market value. |
|---|---|---|---|
| Liberty Loan, 4th, 4¼s, 1938 | $1,050 00 | $1,050 00 | $1,048 50 |
| Iowa Railway and Light Company, first and refunding, 20-yr. gold bonds, 5s, 1932 | 1,872 78 | 2,000 00 | 1,660 00 |
| Pacific Power and Light Company, 1st and refunding, 5s, 1930 | 1,910 00 | 2,000 00 | 1,760 00 |
| Detroit Edison Co., first and refunding, gold bonds, 5s, 1940 | 2,000 00 | 2,000 00 | 1,800 00 |
| Northern States Power Company, first and refunding, 25-yr. gold bonds, 5s, 1941 | 1,500 00 | 2,000 00 | 1,780 00 |
| Totals | $8,332 78 | $9,050 00 | $8,048 50 |

# FEDERAL LIFE INSURANCE COMPANY.

Located at Nos. 166-168 North Michigan Boulevard, Chicago, Illinois; commenced business, life, May 4, 1900; casualty, January 22, 1912.

ISAAC MILLER HAMILTON, President. W. E. BRIMSTIN, Secretary.

## CAPITAL.

| | | |
|---|---|---|
| Capital paid up | $300,000 00 | |
| Amount of ledger assets December 31, of previous year | | $5,037,661 87 |

## INCOME.

| | | | |
|---|---|---|---|
| First year's premiums on original policies less re-insurance | | $255,162 86 | |
| First year's premiums for total and permanent disability benefits | | 998 73 | |
| First year's premiums for additional accidental death benefits | | 1,681 32 | |
| Dividends applied to purchase paid-up additions and annuities | | 65 95 | |
| Surrender values applied to purchase paid-up insurance and annuities | | 2,131 00 | |
| Consideration for original annuities involving life contingencies | | 866 62 | |
| New premiums | | $260,906 48 | |
| Renewal premiums less re-insurance | $963,780 86 | | |
| Renewal premiums for total and permanent disability benefits | 2,615 26 | | |
| Renewal premiums for additional accidental death benefits | 5,642 79 | | |
| Dividends applied to pay renewal premiums | 23,504 15 | | |
| Renewal premiums | | 995,543 06 | |
| Monthly industrial premiums | | 2,493 33 | |
| Premium income | | | $1,258,942 87 |
| Consideration for supplementary contracts not involving life contingencies | | | 2,159 00 |
| Dividends left with company to accumulate at interest | | | 9,318 60 |
| Interest on mortgage loans | | $144,333 32 | |
| Interest on collateral loans | | 80 00 | |
| Interest on bonds and dividends on stocks | | 30,240 76 | |
| Interest on premium notes, policy loans or liens | | 61,325 04 | |
| Interest on deposits | | 1,551 07 | |
| Interest on other debts due the company | | 1,826 90 | |
| Rents—including $25,200.00 for company's occupancy of its own buildings | | 91,799 45 | |
| Total interest and rents | | | 331,156 54 |
| From other sources, viz: Commissions received on mortgage loans, $26,001.50; increase in suspense account, $476.11 | | | 26,477 61 |
| Income—life department | | | $1,628,054 62 |
| Income—casualty department | | | 716,838 08 |
| Total income | | | $2,344,892 70 |
| Total | | | $7,382,554 57 |

## DISBURSEMENTS.

| | | |
|---|---|---|
| Death claims | $280,124 48 | |
| Matured endowments | 59,348 00 | |
| Total and permanent disability claims and additional accidental death benefits | 5,058 17 | |
| Total death claims and endowments | | $344,530 65 |
| Premium notes and liens voided by lapse, less $3,833.82 restorations | | 27,737 57 |
| Surrender values paid in cash, or applied in liquidation of loans or notes | | 239,545 22 |
| Coupons paid in cash | | 654 85 |
| Surrender values applied to purchase paid-up insurance and annuities | | 2,131 00 |
| Dividends paid policyholders in cash, or applied in liquidation of loans or notes | | 14,855 10 |
| Dividends and coupons applied to pay renewal premiums | | 23,504 15 |
| Dividends applied to purchase paid-up additions and annuities | | 65 95 |
| Dividends left with the company to accumulate at interest | | 9,318 60 |
| (Total paid policyholders | $62,343 09) | |
| Expense of investigation and settlement of policy claims, including legal expenses | | 3,756 30 |
| Supplementary contracts not involving life contingencies | | 10,696 67 |
| Dividends with interest, held on deposit surrendered during the year | | 139 54 |
| Dividends to stockholders | | 24,000 00 |
| Commissions to agents, first, $165,687.31; renewal, $55,234.31; industrial, $600.47 | | 221,522 09 |
| Compensation of managers and agents not paid by commissions on new business | | 10,436 98 |
| Agency supervision and traveling expenses of supervisors | | 6,619 18 |
| Branch office expenses | | 31,092 35 |
| Medical examiners' fees and inspection of risks | | 18,484 61 |
| Salaries and all other compensation of officers and home office employees | | 97,367 43 |
| Rent | | 25,200 00 |
| Advertising, printing, stationery, postage, telegraph, telephone, express and exchange | | 55,329 92 |
| Legal expense | | 2,178 64 |
| Furniture, fixtures and safes | | 4,571 48 |
| Repairs and expenses (other than taxes) on real estate | | 60,570 57 |
| Taxes on real estate | | 11,783 48 |
| State taxes on premiums | | 18,312 86 |
| Insurance department licenses and fees | | 3,897 01 |
| Federal taxes | | 11,463 98 |
| All other licenses, fees and taxes | | 1,742 71 |

DISBURSEMENTS—Concluded.

| | | |
|---|---|---|
| Other disbursements, viz: Miscellaneous expenses, $773.20; investment expenses, $1,069.06 | | $1,842 26 |
| Agents' balances charged off | | 2,364 50 |
| Disbursements—life department | | $1,285,715 65 |
| Disbursements—casualty department | | 652,104 21 |
| Total disbursements | | $1,937,819 86 |
| Balance | | $5,444,734 71 |

LEDGER ASSETS.

| | | |
|---|---|---|
| Book value of real estate | | $ 543,805 13 |
| Mortgage loans on real estate | | 2,834,531 98 |
| Loans secured by collaterals | | 14,246 00 |
| Loans on company's policies assigned as collateral | | 1,233,277 50 |
| Premium notes on policies in force | | 57,513 81 |
| Book value of bonds and stocks | | 508,306 25 |
| Cash in office | | 1,488 76 |
| Deposits in trust companies and banks on interest | | 164,438 14 |
| Bills receivable | | 9,028 87 |
| Agents' debit balances | | 5,320 27 |
| Casualty premiums in process of collection | | 72,778 00 |
| Total ledger assets | | $5,444,734 71 |

NON-LEDGER ASSETS.

| | | | |
|---|---|---|---|
| Interest due and accrued on mortgages | | $98,343 61 | |
| Interest due and accrued on bonds | | 9,827 80 | |
| Interest accrued on premium notes, loans or liens | | 6,800 83 | |
| | | | 114,972 24 |
| | New business. | Renewals. | |
| Net uncollected and deferred premiums (paid for basis) | $1,922 13 | $124,590 36 | 126,512 49 |
| Gross assets | | | $5,686,219 44 |

DEDUCT ASSETS NOT ADMITTED.

| | | |
|---|---|---|
| Agents' debit balances | $ 5,320 27 | |
| Bills receivable | 9,028 87 | |
| Premium notes, policy loans and other policy assets in excess of net value and of other policy liabilities on individual policies | 28,342 76 | |
| Overdue and accrued interest on bonds in default | 1,890 00 | |
| Book value of bonds and stocks over market value | 3,568 00 | |
| Book value of other ledger assets over market value, viz— Collateral loan on bank stock | 12,246 00 | |
| Book value of mortgage loans over fifty per cent of the appraised value of the real estate securing the same on individual loans | 24,280 00 | |
| Total | | 84,675 90 |
| Admitted assets | | $5,601,543 54 |

LIABILITIES.

| | | |
|---|---|---|
| Net present value of outstanding policies computed by the Illinois Insurance Department | $4,618,040 00 | |
| Same for dividend additions | 7,366 00 | |
| Same for annuities | 121 00 | |
| Total | $4,625,527 00 | |
| Deduct net value of risks re-insured | 72,511 00 | |
| Net reserve (paid for basis) | | $4,553,016 00 |
| Extra reserve for total and permanent disability benefits and for additional accidental death benefits included in life policies | | 5,933 54 |
| Present value of supplementary contracts not involving life contingencies | | 48,315 17 |
| Present value of amounts incurred but not yet due for total and permanent disability benefits | | 484 98 |
| Death losses in process of adjustment | $17,146 90 | |
| Death losses reported for which no proofs have been received | 41,937 00 | |
| Matured endowments due and unpaid | 1,000 00 | |
| Death losses and other policy claims resisted | 3,483 10 | |
| Total policy claims | | 63,567 00 |
| Dividends left with the company to accumulate at interest | | 31,753 95 |
| Gross premiums paid in advance, including surrender values so applied, less discount, if any | | 6,695 37 |
| Unearned interest and rent paid in advance | | 19,232 12 |
| Commissions due agents on premium notes, when paid | | 1,875 79 |
| Commissions to agents due or accrued | | 207 90 |
| Cost of collection on uncollected and deferred premiums in excess of loading | | 188 39 |

LIABILITIES—Concluded.

| | |
|---|---|
| Salaries, rents, office expenses, bills, and accounts due or accrued | $ 2,800 70 |
| Medical examiners' and legal fees due or accrued | 1,432 50 |
| Estimated amount hereafter payable for federal, state and other taxes based upon the business of the year of this statement | 37,836 26 |
| Dividends declared on or apportioned to annual dividend policies payable to policyholders during 1922 for period to December 31, 1922 | 19,827 44 |
| Dividends declared on orapportioned to deferred dividend policies payable to policyholders during 1922 for period to December 31, 1922 | 24,757 33 |
| Amounts set apart, apportioned, provisionally ascertained, calculated, declared or held awaiting apportionment upon deferred dividend policies | 101,970 09 |
| Contingency reserve for fluctuations, for unusual losses and expenditures and to supplement and build up a fund for apportionment to deferred dividend policies | 25,000 00 |
| Unpaid coupons and interest thereon | 1,749 46 |
| Casualty department | 266,155 84 |
| Suspense | 738 76 |
| Total | $5,213,538 59 |
| Capital paid up | 300,000 00 |
| Unassigned funds (surplus) | 88,004 95 |
| Total | $5,601,543 54 |

## EXHIBIT OF POLICIES—ORDINARY.

ALL BUSINESS PAID FOR.

| | Number. | Amount. | Number. | Amount. |
|---|---|---|---|---|
| Policies in force December 31, 1920 | | | 20,865 | $46,427,362 00 |
| Policies issued, revived, and increased during the year | | | 3,608 | 12,261,318 00 |
| Total | | | 24,473 | $58,688,680 00 |
| Deduct policies which have ceased to be in force during the year— | | | | |
| By death | 126 | $ 311,353 00 | | |
| By maturity | 28 | 54,394 00 | | |
| By expiry | 18 | 50,500 00 | | |
| By surrender | 314 | 678,959 00 | | |
| By lapse | 3,477 | 9,737,591 00 | | |
| By decrease | 981 | 1,149,747 00 | | |
| Total | | | 4,944 | 11,982,544 00 |
| Total policies in force December 31, 1921 | | | 19,529 | $46,706,136 00 |
| Re-insured | | | | $1,802,096 00 |

## EXHIBIT OF POLICIES—INDUSTRIAL.

ALL BUSINESS PAID FOR.

| | Number. | Amount. | Number. | Amount. |
|---|---|---|---|---|
| Policies in force December 31, 1920 | | | 538 | $85,660 00 |
| Policies issued, revived, and increased during the year | | | 85 | 7,492 00 |
| Total | | | 623 | $93,152 00 |
| Deduct policies which have ceased to be in force during the year— | | | | |
| By death | 4 | $ 1,000 00 | | |
| By surrender | 8 | 800 00 | | |
| By lapse | 130 | 24,372 00 | | |
| Total | | | 142 | 26,172 00 |
| Total policies in force December 31, 1921 | | | 481 | $66,980 00 |

## BUSINESS IN ILLINOIS—ORDINARY.

| | Number. | Amount. |
|---|---|---|
| Policies in force December 31, 1920 | 4,775 | $10,166,248 00 |
| Policies issued during the year | 322 | 760,846 00 |
| Total | 5,097 | $10,927,094 00 |
| Deduct policies ceased to be in force | 701 | 3,302,811 00 |
| Policies in force December 31, 1921 | 4,396 | $7,624,283 00 |
| Losses and claims unpaid December 31, 1920 | 3 | $ 7,000 00 |
| Losses and claims incurred during the year | 31 | 73,565 97 |
| Total | 34 | $80,565 97 |
| Losses and claims settled during the year | 27 | 50,392 97 |
| Losses and claims unpaid December 31, 1921 | 7 | $30,173 00 |
| Premiums received | | $248,716 91 |

## BUSINESS IN ILLINOIS—INDUSTRIAL.

| | Number. | Amount. |
|---|---|---|
| Policies in force December 31, 1920 | 155 | $22,202 00 |
| Deduct policies ceased to be in force | 2 | 1,781 00 |
| Policies in force December 31, 1921 | 157 | $20,421 00 |
| Premiums received | | $696 41 |

## GAIN AND LOSS EXHIBIT.

### INSURANCE EXHIBIT.

| | | Gain in surplus. | Loss in surplus. |
|---|---|---|---|
| Loading on actual premiums of the year (averaging 20 per cent of the gross premiums) | $256,529 99 | | |
| Insurance expenses incurred during the year | 521,281 13 | | |
| Loss from loading | | | $264,751 14 |
| Interest earned during the year | $347,955 22 | | |
| Investment expenses incurred during the year | 75,559 66 | | |
| Net income from investments | $272,395 56 | | |
| Interest required to maintain reserve | 165,298 43 | | |
| Gain from interest | | $107,097 13 | |
| Expected mortality on net amount at risk | $478,298 00 | | |
| Actual mortality on net amount at risk | 249,084 58 | | |
| Gain from mortality | | 229,213 42 | |
| Total gain during the year from surrendered and lapsed policies | | 28,439 13 | |
| Dividends paid stockholders | | | 24,000 00 |
| Decrease in surplus on dividend account | | | 62,112 45 |
| Increase in special funds, and special reserves during the year | | | 25,134 89 |

### INVESTMENT EXHIBIT.

| | | Gain in surplus. | Loss in surplus. |
|---|---|---|---|
| Total gains from stocks and bonds | | | 13,041 75 |
| Gain on commissions received on mortgage loans | | 26,001 50 | |
| Loss from mortgage loans in excess of 50 per cent of appraisals | | | 24,280 00 |
| Gain from assets not admitted | | 3,304 25 | |
| Net gain on account of total and permanent disability benefits or additional accidental death benefits included in life policies | | 5,084 41 | |
| Gain from cashalty department | | 9,639 91 | |
| Balance unaccounted for (gain) | | 348 17 | |
| Total gains and losses in surplus during the year | | $409,127 92 | $413,320 23 |
| Surplus December 31, 1920 | $92,197 26 | | |
| Surplus December 31, 1921 | 88,004 95 | | |
| Decrease in surplus | | 4,192 31 | |
| Total | | $413,320 23 | $413,320 23 |

## SCHEDULE D—PART 1—BONDS.

| Description. | Book value. | Par value. | Market value. |
|---|---|---|---|
| City of Durango, Colo., 5s, 1924 | $20,000 00 | $20,000 00 | $20,000 00 |
| Village of Asceola, Neb., 5s, 1925 | 4,000 00 | 4,000 00 | 4,000 00 |
| Waurika, Okla, sewer, 6s, 1933 | 15,000 00 | 15,000 00 | 15,750 00 |
| Dancy Drainage Dist., Wis., 6s, 1921 | 9,000 00 | 9,000 00 | 9,000 00 |
| Poinsett County, Ark., Drain. Dist. No. 3, 6s, 1925 | 12,250 00 | 12,250 00 | 12,250 00 |
| Poinsett County, Ark., Drain. Dist. No. 3, 6s, 1930 | 2,250 00 | 2,250 00 | 2,272 50 |
| Poinsett County, Ark., Drain. Dist. No. 3, 6s, 1931 | 2,000 00 | 2,000 00 | 2,020 00 |
| Poinsett County, Ark., Drain. Dist. No. 3, 6s, 1937 | 10,000 00 | 10,000 00 | 10,100 00 |
| Poinsett County, Ark., Drain. Dist. No. 3, 6s, 1929 | 3,750 00 | 3,750 00 | 3,787 50 |
| Poinsett County Ark., Drain. Dist. No. 3, 6s, 1930 | 3,000 00 | 3,000 00 | 3,030 00 |
| Poinsett County, Ark., Drain. Dist. No. 3, 6s, 1931 | 6,250 00 | 6,250 00 | 6,312 50 |
| Poinsett County, Ark., Drain. Dist. No. 3, 6s, 1932 | 6,000 00 | 6,000 00 | 6,060 00 |
| Poinsett County, Ark., Drain. Dist. No. 3, 6s, 1933 | 1,000 00 | 1,000 00 | 1,010 00 |
| Poinsett County, Ark., Drain. Dist. No. 3, 6s, 1923 | 250 00 | 250 00 | 250 00 |
| Poinsett County, Ark., Drain. Dist. No. 3, 6s, 1926 | 3,750 00 | 3,750 00 | 3,750 00 |
| Poinsett County, Ark., Drain. Dist. No. 3, 6s, 1927 | 6,250 00 | 6,250 00 | 6,312 50 |
| Poinsett County, Ark., Drain. Dist. No. 3, 6s, 1928 | 6,250 00 | 6,250 00 | 6,312 50 |
| Poinsett County, Ark., Drain. Dist. No. 3, 6s, 1929 | 2,500 00 | 2,500 00 | 2,525 00 |
| Poinsett County, Ark., Drain. Dist. No. 3, 6s, 1932 | 250 00 | 250 00 | 252 50 |
| Poinsett County, Ark., Drain. Dist. No. 3, 6s, 1933 | 1,000 00 | 1,000 00 | 1,010 00 |
| Poinsett County, Ark., Drain. Dist. No. 4, 6s, 1927 | 3,500 00 | 3,500 00 | 3,535 00 |
| Poinsett County, Ark., Drain. Dist. No. 4, 6s, 1930 | 5,500 00 | 5,500 00 | 5,555 00 |
| Poinsett County, Ark., Drain. Dist. No. 4, 6s, 1935 | 2,000 00 | 2,000 00 | 2,020 00 |
| Poinsett County, Ark., Drain. Dist. No. 4, 6s, 1928 | 5,500 00 | 5,500 00 | 5,555 00 |
| Poinsett County, Ark., Drain. Dist. No. 4, 6s, 1929 | 5,500 00 | 5,500 00 | 5,555 00 |
| Poinsett County, Ark., Drain. Dist. No. 6, 6s, 1931 | 2,500 00 | 2,500 00 | 2,525 00 |
| Poinsett County, Ark., Drain. Dist. No. 6, 6s, 1932 | 4,500 00 | 4,500 00 | 4,545 00 |
| Poinsett County, Ark., Drain. Dist. No. 6, 6s, 1927 | 5,000 00 | 5,000 00 | 5,050 00 |

SCHEDULE D—PART 1—BONDS—Continued.

| Description. | Book value. | Par value. | Market value. |
|---|---|---|---|
| Poinsett County, Ark., Drain. Dist. No. 6, 6s, 1929 | $ 4,500 00 | $ 4,500 00 | $ 4,545 00 |
| Poinsett County, Ark., Drain. Dist. No. 6, 6s, 1930 | 5,000 00 | 5,000 00 | 5,050 00 |
| Caldwell County, Mo., Drain. Dist. No. 19, 6s, 1922 | 1,000 00 | 1,000 00 | 1,000 00 |
| Caldwell County, Mo., Drain. Dist. No. 19, 6s, 1923 | 1,000 00 | 1,000 00 | 1,000 00 |
| Caldwell County, Mo., Drain. Dist. No. 19, 6s, 1924 | 1,000 00 | 1,000 00 | 1,000 00 |
| Caldwell County, Mo., Drain. Dist. No. 19, 6s, 1925 | 1,000 00 | 1,000 00 | 1,000 00 |
| Caldwell County, Mo., Drain. Dist. No. 19, 6s, 1926 | 1,000 00 | 1,000 00 | 1,000 00 |
| Caldwell County, Mo., Drain. Dist. No. 19, 6s, 1927 | 1,406 25 | 1,406 25 | 1,406 25 |
| Caldwell County, Mo., Drain. Dist. No. 20, 6s, 1921 | 500 00 | 500 00 | 500 00 |
| Caldwell County, Mo., Drain. Dist. No. 20, 6s, 1922 | 500 00 | 500 00 | 500 00 |
| Caldwell County, Mo., Drain. Dist. No. 20, 6s, 1923 | 500 00 | 500 00 | 500 00 |
| Caldwell County, Mo., Drain. Dist. No. 20, 6s, 1924 | 500 00 | 500 00 | 500 00 |
| Caldwell County, Mo., Drain. Dist. No. 20, 6s, 1925 | 500 00 | 500 00 | 500 00 |
| Caldwell County, Mo., Drain. Dist. No. 20, 6s, 1926 | 500 00 | 500 00 | 500 00 |
| Caldwell County, Mo., Drain. Dist. No. 20, 6s, 1927 | 500 00 | 500 00 | 500 00 |
| Blackfish Dr. Dist., Crittenden County, Ark., 6s, 1921 | 1,000 00 | 1,000 00 | 1,000 00 |
| Blackfish Dr. Dist., Crittenden County, Ark., 6s, 1922 | 1,000 00 | 1,000 00 | 1,000 00 |
| Blackfish Dr. Dist., Crittenden County, Ark., 6s, 1923 | 1,000 00 | 1,000 00 | 1,000 00 |
| Blackfish Dr. Dist., Crittenden County, Ark., 6s, 1924 | 1,000 00 | 1,000 00 | 1,000 00 |
| Blackfish Dr. Dist., Crittenden County, Ark., 6s, 1925 | 1,000 00 | 1,000 00 | 1,000 00 |
| Blackfish Dr. Dist., Crittenden County, Ark., 6s, 1926 | 1,000 00 | 1,000 00 | 1,000 00 |
| Blackfish Dr. Dist., Crittenden County, Ark., 6s, 1927 | 1,000 00 | 1,000 00 | 990 00 |
| Blackfish Dr. Dist., Crittenden County, Ark., 6s, 1928 | 1,000 00 | 1,000 00 | 990 00 |
| Blackfish Dr. Dist., Crittenden County, Ark., 6s, 1929 | 1,000 00 | 1,000 00 | 990 00 |
| Des Moines and Miss Levee Dist. No. 1, Clark Co., Mo., 6s, 1922 | 2,000 00 | 2,000 00 | 2,000 00 |
| Des Moines and Miss. Levee Dist. No. 1, Clark Co., Mo., 6s, 1923 | 500 00 | 500 00 | 505 00 |
| Marshall Heat, Light and Power Co., Mo., 5s, 1935 | 5,000 00 | 5,000 00 | 3,650 00 |
| Pana Gas & Electric Co., Pana, Ill., 5s, 1935 | 4,000 00 | 4,000 00 | 3,400 00 |
| Belzoni Drain. Dist., Wash. Co., Miss., 6s, 1933 | 20,000 00 | 20,000 00 | 20,000 00 |
| The Meadows Co., Madison, Wis., 6s, 1924 | 10,000 00 | 10,000 00 | 10,000 00 |
| Garland Levee Dist., Miller Co., Ark., 6s, 1928 | 500 00 | 500 00 | 520 00 |
| Garland Levee Dist., Miller Co., Ark., 6s, 1933 | 14,500 00 | 14,500 00 | 15,370 00 |
| Garland Levee Dist., Miller Co., Ark., 6s, 1934 | 15,500 00 | 15,500 00 | 16,585 00 |
| Cottondale Dr. Dist., Sunflower Co., Miss., 6s, 1922 | 1,300 00 | 1,300 00 | 1,300 00 |
| Cottondale Dr. Dist., Sunflower Co., Miss., 6s, 1923 | 1,400 00 | 1,400 00 | 1,414 00 |
| Cottondale Dr. Dist., Sunflower Co., Miss., 6s, 1924 | 1,500 00 | 1,500 00 | 1,515 00 |
| Cottondale Dr. Dist., Sunflower Co., Miss., 6s, 1925 | 1,600 00 | 1,600 00 | 1,632 00 |
| Cottondale Dr. Dist., Sunflower Co., Miss., 6s, 1926 | 1,600 00 | 1,600 00 | 1,632 00 |
| Cottondale Dr. Dist., Sunflower Co., Miss., 6s, 1927 | 1,700 00 | 1,700 00 | 1,751 00 |
| Cottondale Dr. Dist., Sunflower Co., Miss., 6s, 1928 | 1,700 00 | 1,700 00 | 1,751 00 |
| Cottondale Dr. Dist., Sunflower Co., Miss., 6s, 1929 | 1,800 00 | 1,800 00 | 1,872 00 |
| Cottondale Dr. Dist., Sunflower Co., Miss., 6s, 1930 | 1,900 00 | 1,900 00 | 1 976 00 |
| Cottondale Dr. Dist., Sunflower Co., Miss., 6s, 1931 | 2,000 00 | 2,000 00 | 2,100 00 |
| Cottondale Dr. Dist., Sunflower Co., Miss., 6s, 1932 | 2,000 00 | 2,000 00 | 2,100 00 |
| Cottondale Dr. Dist., Sunflower Co., Miss., 6s, 1933 | 2,200 00 | 2,200 00 | 2,332 00 |
| Cottondale Dr. Dist., Sunflower Co., Miss., 6s, 1934 | 2,200 00 | 2,200 00 | 2,332 00 |
| Loosacoona River Dr. Dist., Calhoun Co., Miss., 6s, 1922 | 1,500 00 | 1,500 00 | 1,500 00 |
| Loosacoona River Dr. Dist., Calhoun Co., Miss., 6s, 1923 | 1,500 00 | 1,500 00 | 1,500 00 |
| Loosacoona River Dr. Dist., Calhoun Co., Miss., 6s, 1924 | 2,000 00 | 2,000 00 | 2,000 00 |
| Loosacoona River Dr. Dist., Calhoun Co., Miss., 6s, 1925 | 3,000 00 | 3,000 00 | 3,000 00 |
| Loosacoona River Dr. Dist., Calhoun Co., Miss., 6s, 1926 | 3,000 00 | 3,000 00 | 3,000 00 |
| Loosacoona River Dr. Dist., Calhoun Co., Miss., 6s, 1927 | 3,000 00 | 3,000 00 | 2,970 00 |
| Loosacoona River Dr. Dist., Calhoun Co., Miss., 6s, 1928 | 3,000 00 | 3,000 00 | 2,970 00 |
| Loosacoona River Dr. Dist., Calhoun Co., Miss., 6s, 1929 | 3,000 00 | 3,000 00 | 2,970 00 |
| Loosacoona River Dr. Dist., Calhoun Co., Miss., 6s, 1930 | 3,000 00 | 3,000 00 | 2,970 00 |
| Loosacoona River Dr. Dist., Calhoun Co., Miss., 6s, 1931 | 4,000 00 | 4,000 00 | 3,960 00 |
| Loosacoona River Dr. Dist., Calhoun Co., Miss., 6s, 1932 | 4,000 00 | 4,000 00 | 3,960 00 |
| Loosacoona River Dr. Dist., Calhoun Co., Miss., 6s, 1933 | 4,000 00 | 4,000 00 | 3,960 00 |
| Loosacoona River Dr. Dist., Calhoun Co., Miss., 6s, 1934 | 4,000 00 | 4,000 00 | 3,960 00 |
| Lick Creek Dr. Dist. No. 3, Hardin and McNairy Cos., Tenn., 6s, 1922 | 1,500 00 | 1,500 00 | 1,500 00 |
| Lick Creek Dr. Dist. No. 3, Hardin and McNairy Cos., Tenn., 6s, 1923 | 1,500 00 | 1,500 00 | 1,500 00 |
| Lick Creek Dr. Dist. No. 3, Hardin and McNairy Cos., Tenn., 6s, 1924 | 1,500 00 | 1,500 00 | 1,500 00 |
| Lick Creek Dr. Dist. No. 3, Hardin and McNairy Cos., Tenn., 6s, 1925 | 1,500 00 | 1,500 00 | 1,500 00 |
| Lick Creek Dr. Dist. No. 3, Hardin and McNairy Cos., Tenn., 6s, 1926 | 1,500 00 | 1,500 00 | 1,500 00 |
| Lick Creek Dr. Dist. No. 3, Hardin and McNairy Cos., Tenn., 6s, 1927 | 500 00 | 500 00 | 505 00 |
| Lick Creek Dr. Dist. No. 3, Hardin and McNairy Cos., Tenn., 6s, 1928 | 500 00 | 500 00 | 505 00 |
| Lick Creek Dr. Dist. No. 3, Hardin and McNairy Cos., Tenn., 6s, 1929 | 500 00 | 500 00 | 505 00 |
| Tippah River Drain. Dist., Benton Co., Miss., 6s, 1922 | 500 00 | 500 00 | 500 00 |
| Tippah River Drain. Dist., Benton Co., Miss., 6s, 1923 | 500 00 | 500 00 | 500 00 |
| Tippah River Drain. Dist., Benton Co., Miss., 6s, 1924 | 500 00 | 500 00 | 500 00 |
| Tippah River Drain. Dist., Benton Co., Miss., 6s, 1925 | 500 00 | 500 00 | 500 00 |
| Tippah River Drain. Dist., Benton Co., Miss., 6s, 1926 | 500 00 | 500 00 | 500 00 |

SCHEDULE D—PART 1—BONDS—Concluded.

| Description. | Book value. | Par value. | Market value. |
|---|---|---|---|
| Tippah River Drain. Dist., Benton Co., Miss., 6s, 1927.. | $ 500 00 | $ 500 00 | $ 500 00 |
| Tippah River Drain. Dist., Benton Co., Miss., 6s, 1928.. | 2,000 00 | 2,000 00 | 2,000 00 |
| Tippah River Drain. Dist., Benton Co., Miss., 6s, 1929.. | 2,000 00 | 2,000 00 | 2,000 00 |
| Tippah River Drain. Dist., Benton Co., Miss., 6s, 1930.. | 2,000 00 | 2,000 00 | 2,000 00 |
| Tippah River Drain. Dist., Benton Co., Miss., 6s, 1931.. | 2,000 00 | 2,000 00 | 2,000 00 |
| Tippah River Drain. Dist., Benton Co., Miss., 6s, 1932.. | 2,000 00 | 2,000 00 | 2,000 00 |
| Tippah River Drain. Dist., Benton Co., Miss., 6s, 1933.. | 3,000 00 | 3,000 00 | 3,000 00 |
| Tippah River Drain. Dist., Benton Co., Miss., 6s, 1934.. | 4,000 00 | 4,000 00 | 4,000 00 |
| Jacks Creek Drain. Dist., No. 2, Chester Co., Tenn., 6s, 1922 | 500 00 | 500 00 | 500 00 |
| Jacks Creek Drain. Dist., No. 2, Chester Co., Tenn., 6s, 1923 | 500 00 | 500 00 | 500 00 |
| Jacks Creek Drain. Dist., No. 2, Chester Co., Tenn., 6s, 1924 | 500 00 | 500 00 | 500 00 |
| Jacks Creek Drain. Dist., No. 2, Chester Co., Tenn., 6s, 1925 | 500 00 | 500 00 | 500 00 |
| Jacks Creek Drain. Dist., No. 2, Chester Co., Tenn., 6s, 1926 | 500 00 | 500 00 | 500 00 |
| Jacks Creek Drain. Dist., No. 2, Chester Co., Tenn., 6s, 1927 | 500 00 | 500 00 | 500 00 |
| Jacks Creek Drain. Dist., No. 2, Chester Co., Tenn., 6s, 1928 | 500 00 | 500 00 | 500 00 |
| Jacks Creek Drain. Dist., No. 2, Chester Co., Tenn., 6s, 1929 | 500 00 | 500 00 | 500 00 |
| Jacks Creek Drain. Dist., No. 2, Chester Co., Tenn., 6s, 1930 | 1,000 00 | 1,000 00 | 1,000 00 |
| Jacks Creek Drain. Dist., No. 2, Chester Co., Tenn., 6s, 1931 | 1,000 00 | 1,000 00 | 1,000 00 |
| Jacks Creek Drain. Dist., No. 2, Chester Co., Tenn., 6s, 1932 | 1,000 00 | 1,000 00 | 1,000 00 |
| Jacks Creek Drain. Dist., No. 2, Chester Co., Tenn., 6s, 1933 | 1,000 00 | 1,000 00 | 1,000 00 |
| Jacks Creek Drain. Dist., No. 2, Chester Co., Tenn., 6s, 1934 | 1,000 00 | 1,000 00 | 1,000 00 |
| Victoria Theater Bldg., 3137 Sheffield Av., Chicago, 6s, 1924 | 21,000 00 | 21,000 00 | 21,000 00 |
| U. S. Government Liberty Bonds, 1st Liberty Loan, 3½s, 1947 | 6,800 00 | 6,800 00 | 6,800 00 |
| U. S. Government Liberty Bonds, 2nd Liberty Loan, conv., 4¼s, 1942 | 25,000 00 | 25,000 00 | 25,000 00 |
| U. S. Government Liberty Bonds, 4th Liberty Loan, 4¼s, 1938 | 100,650 00 | 100,650 00 | 100,650 00 |
| Totals | $502,506 25 | $502,506 25 | $504,738 25 |

SCHEDULE D—PART 2—STOCKS.

| Description. | Book value. | Par value. |
|---|---|---|
| Republic Securities Corporation, Delaware | $5,800 00 | $5,800 00 |

## THE FRANKLIN LIFE INSURANCE COMPANY.

Located at No. 812 South Sixth Street, Springfield, Illinois; incorporated as an assessment association, July 23, 1884; reincorporated as mutual legal reserve company, July 5, 1898; reincorporated as stock legal reserve company, July 29, 1910; commenced business July 23, 1884.

GEORGE B. STADDEN, President. WILL TAYLOR, Secretary.

CAPITAL.

| | | | |
|---|---|---|---|
| Capital paid up | | $100,000 00 | |
| Amount of ledger assets December 31, of previous year | | | $11,490,587 04 |

INCOME.

| | | | |
|---|---|---|---|
| First year's premiums on original policies, less re-insurance | | $851,252 27 | |
| First year's premiums for total and permanent disability benefits, less re-insurance | | 5,070 19 | |
| Surrender values to pay first year's premiums | | 793 33 | |
| Dividends applied to purchase paid-up additions and annuities | | 4,659 36 | |
| Surrender values applied to purchase paid-up insurance and annuities | | 111,415 90 | |
| New premiums | | $ 973,191 05 | |
| Renewal premiums less re-insurance | $2,765,724 48 | | |
| Renewal premiums for total and permanent disability benefits, less re-insurance | 15,215 38 | | |
| Dividends applied to pay renewal premiums | 31,927 21 | | |
| Surrender values applied to pay renewal premiums | 198 58 | | |
| Renewal premiums | | 2,813,065 65 | |
| Premium income | | | 3,786,256 70 |

## INCOME—Concluded.

| | | |
|---|---|---|
| Dividends left with company to accumulate at interest | | $ 644 27 |
| Interest on mortgage loans | $390,139 74 | |
| Interest on collateral loans | 14,342 73 | |
| Interest on bonds | 49,799 80 | |
| Interest on premium notes, policy loans or liens | 137,323 69 | |
| Interest on deposits | 6,710 20 | |
| Interest on other debts due the company | 35,014 54 | |
| Rents—including $30,000.00 for company's occupancy of its own building | 30,000 00 | |
| Total interest and rents | | 663,330 70 |
| Increase in advance premium account | | 535 44 |
| Borrowed money (gross) | | 200,000 00 |
| Agents' balances previously charged off | | 147 56 |
| Increase in book value of ledger assets | | 16 26 |
| Total income | | $4,650,930 93 |
| Total | | $16,141,517 97 |

## DISBURSEMENTS.

| | | |
|---|---|---|
| Death claims and additions | $640,685 42 | |
| Matured endowments | 178,263 00 | |
| Total and permanent disability claims | 1,737 45 | |
| Total death claims and endowments | | $820,685 87 |
| Annuities involving life contingencies | | 1,254 64 |
| Premium notes and liens voided by lapse, less $35,540.22 restorations | | 97,706 99 |
| Surrender values paid in cash, or applied in liquidation of loans or notes | | 421,488 04 |
| Surrender values applied to pay new and renewal premiums | | 991 91 |
| Surrender values applied to purchase paid-up insurance and annutiies | | 111,415 90 |
| Dividends paid policyholders in cash, or applied in liquidation of loans or notes | | 153,799 11 |
| Dividends applied to pay renewal premiums | | 31,927 21 |
| Dividends applied to purchase paid-up additions and annuities | | 4,659 36 |
| Dividends left with the company to accumulate at interest | | 644 27 |
| (Total paid policyholders | $1,644,573 30) | |
| Expense of investigation and settlement of policy claims, including legal expenses | | 1,441 95 |
| Supplementary contracts not involving life contingencies | | 5,501 71 |
| Dividends with interest, held on deposit surrendered during the year | | 99 92 |
| Dividends to stockholders | | 5,000 00 |
| Commissions to agents, first year, $552,089.47; renewal, $146,840.96 | | 698,930 43 |
| Commuted renewal commissions | | 2,250 00 |
| Compensation of managers and agents not paid by commissions on new business | | 50,983 86 |
| Agency supervision and traveling expenses of supervisors | | 93,536 94 |
| Medical examiners' fees and inspection of risks | | 85,968 03 |
| Salaries and all other compensation of officers and home office employees | | 264,027 50 |
| Rent | | 30,000 00 |
| Advertising, printing, stationery, postage, telegraph, telephone, express and exchange | | 83,683 94 |
| Legal expense | | 4,971 90 |
| Furniture, fixtures and safes | | 17,244 22 |
| Repairs and expenses (other than taxes) on real estate | | 11,676 25 |
| Taxes on real estate | | 5,479 52 |
| State taxes on premiums | | 43,297 57 |
| Insurance department licenses and fees | | 11,579 25 |
| Federal taxes | | 23,444 00 |
| All other licenses, fees and taxes | | 13,926 56 |
| Other disbursements, viz: Traveling expenses, $3,461.66; miscellaneous expenses, $14,698.64 | | 18,160 30 |
| Borrowed money repaid (gross) | | 200,000 00 |
| Interest on borrowed money | | 4,895 84 |
| Agents' balances charged off | | 867 26 |
| Decrease in book value of ledger assets | | 82 00 |
| Total disbursements | | $3,321,622 25 |
| Balance | | $12,819,895 72 |

## LEDGER ASSETS.

| | |
|---|---|
| Book value of real estate | $ 338,841 20 |
| Mortgage loans on real estate | 7,544,666 00 |
| Loans secured by collaterals | 279,940 00 |
| Loans on company's policies assigned as collateral | 2,850,231 69 |
| Premium notes on policies in force | 214,073 39 |
| Book value of bonds | 1,082,734 58 |
| Cash in office | 11,103 67 |
| Deposits in trust companies and banks on interest | 288,081 12 |
| Agents' balances (debit, $205,302.00; credit, $4,077.93) | 201,224 07 |
| Total ledger assets | $12,819,895 72 |

## LEDGER ASSETS—Concluded.

### NON-LEDGER ASSETS.

| | | | |
|---|---|---|---|
| Interest accrued on mortgages | | $307,899 52 | |
| Interest accrued on bonds | | 11,947 18 | |
| Interest accrued on collateral loans | | 4,399 56 | |
| Interest accrued on premium notes, loans or liens | | 12,035 27 | |
| Interest accrued on bank deposits | | 516 27 | |
| | | | $336,797 80 |
| Market value of bonds over book value | | | 1,469 92 |
| Due from other companies for losses or claims on policies re-insured | | | 714 38 |
| | New business. | Renewals. | |
| Net uncollected and deferred premiums (paid for basis) | $2,995 61 | $306,957 93 | 309,953 54 |
| Gross assets | | | $13,468,831 36 |

### DEDUCT ASSETS NOT ADMITTED.

| | | |
|---|---|---|
| Agents' debit balances | $205,302 00 | |
| Premium notes, policy loans and other policy assets in excess of net value and of other policy liabilities on individual policies | 11,577 29 | |
| Total | | 216,879 29 |
| Admitted assets | | $13,251,952 07 |

## LIABILITIES.

| | | |
|---|---|---|
| Net present value of outstanding policies computed by the Illinois Insurance department | $11,691,081 00 | |
| Same for dividend additions | 1,293 00 | |
| Same for annuities | 21,844 00 | |
| Total | $11,714,218 00 | |
| Deduct net value of risks re-insured | 48,508 00 | |
| Net reserve (paid for basis) | | $11,665,710 00 |
| Extra reserve for total and permanent disability benefits and included in life policies, less re-insurance | | 23,758 00 |
| Present value of supplementary contracts not involving life contingencies | | 40,823 00 |
| Present value of amounts incurred but not yet due for total and permanent disability benefits | | 7,610 00 |
| Death losses in process of adjustment | $11,534 70 | |
| Death losses reported for which no proofs have been received | 54,727 74 | |
| Reserve for net death losses incurred but unreported | 5,163 60 | |
| Matured endowments due and unpaid | 4,105 00 | |
| Total policy claims | | 75,531 04 |
| Due and unpaid on supplementary contracts not involving life contingencies | | 25 00 |
| Dividends left with the company to accumulate at interest | | 5,838 21 |
| Gross premiums paid in advance, including surrender values so applied, less discount, if any | | 13,995 63 |
| Unearned interest and rent paid in advance | | 67,416 16 |
| Commissions due agents on premium notes, when paid | | 3,025 44 |
| Commissions to agents due or accrued | | 4,142 65 |
| Cost of collection on uncollected and deferred premiums in excess of loading | | 1,520 56 |
| Salaries, rents, office expenses, bills, and accounts due or accrued | | 8,266 49 |
| Medical examiners' and legal fees due or accrued | | 5,841 00 |
| Estimated amount hereafter payable for federal, state and other taxes based upon the business of the year of this statement | | 81,255 33 |
| Dividends or other profits due policyholders | | 3,151 73 |
| Dividends declared on or apportioned to annual dividend policies payable to policyholders during 1922 for period to December 31, 1922 | | 33,549 00 |
| Dividends declared on or apportioned to deferred dividend policies payable to policyholders during 1922 for period to December 31, 1922 | | 145,424 00 |
| Amounts set apart, apportioned, provisionally ascertained, calculated, declared or held awaiting apportionment upon deferred dividend policies | | 211,848 55 |
| Trust fund | | 4,942 60 |
| Fund held for special class of policies | | 112,064 80 |
| Premium suspense account | | 1,427 50 |
| Total | | $12,517,166 69 |
| Capital paid up | | 100,000 00 |
| Unassigned funds (surplus) | | 634,785 38 |
| Total | | $13,251,952 07 |

## EXHIBIT OF POLICIES—ORDINARY.

### ALL BUSINESS PAID FOR.

| | Number. | Amount. |
|---|---|---|
| Policies in force December 31, 1920 | 53,870 | $120,754,072 00 |
| Policies issued, revived and increased during the year | 13,923 | 35,349,414 00 |
| Total | 67,793 | $156,103,486 00 |

## EXHIBIT OF POLICIES—ORDINARY—Concluded.

ALL BUSINESS PAID FOR.

| | Number. | Amount. | Number. | Amount. |
|---|---|---|---|---|
| Deduct policies which have ceased to be in force during the year— | | | | |
| By death | 337 | $ 771,701 00 | | |
| By maturity | 138 | 235,422 00 | | |
| By expiry | 689 | 2,204,368 00 | | |
| By surrender | 997 | 2,244,714 00 | | |
| By lapse | 7,793 | 19,156,377 00 | | |
| By decrease | 124 | 1,486,794 00 | | |
| Total | | | 10,078 | $26,099,376 00 |
| Total policies in force December 31, 1921 | | | 57,715 | $130,004,110 00 |
| Re-insured | | | | $6,304,886 00 |

## EXHIBIT OF POLICIES—GROUP INSURANCE.

ALL BUSINESS PAID FOR.

| | Number. | Amount. |
|---|---|---|
| Policies issued, revived and increased during the year | 1 | $167,500 00 |
| Distribution of business in force at end of year—life | 1 | 167,500 00 |

## BUSINESS IN ILLINOIS—ORDINARY.

| | Number. | Amount. |
|---|---|---|
| Policies in force December 31, 1920 | 15,477 | $37,801,772 00 |
| Policies issued during the year | 2,539 | 6,947,760 00 |
| Total | 18,016 | $44,749,532 00 |
| Deduct policies ceased to be in force | 1,887 | 5,543,026 00 |
| Policies in force December 31, 1921 | 16,129 | $39,206,506 00 |
| Losses and claims unpaid December 31, 1920 | 7 | $ 10,513 25 |
| Losses and claims incurred during the year | 78 | 165,334 85 |
| Total | 85 | $175,848 10 |
| Losses and claims settled during the year | 75 | 146,774 20 |
| Losses and claims unpaid December 31, 1921 | 10 | 29,073 90 |
| Premiums received | | $1,198,037 08 |

## GAIN AND LOSS EXHIBIT.

INSURANCE EXHIBIT.

| | | Gain in surplus. | Loss in surplus. |
|---|---|---|---|
| Loading on actual premiums of the year (averaging 20 per cent of the gross premiums) | $ 769,294 18 | | |
| Insurance expenses incurred during the year | 1,405,719 77 | | |
| Loss from loading | | | $636,425 59 |
| Interest earned during the year | $682,644 21 | | |
| Investment expenses incurred during the year | 77,737 65 | | |
| Net income from investments | $604,906 56 | | |
| Interest required to maintain reserve | 425,275 77 | | |
| Gain from interest | | $179,630 79 | |
| Expected mortality on net amount at risk | $1,269,475 07 | | |
| Actual mortality on net amount at risk | 566,075 75 | | |
| Gain from mortality | | 703,399 32 | |
| Expected disbursements to anuitants | $1,190 24 | | |
| Net actual annuity claims incurred | 1,254 64 | | |
| Loss from annuities | | | 64 40 |
| Total gain during the year from surrendered and lapsed policies | | 38,409 19 | |
| Dividends paid stockholders | | | 5,000 00 |
| Decrease in surplus on dividend account | | | 172,853 17 |
| Decrease in special funds and special reserves during the year | | 353 97 | |

INVESTMENT EXHIBIT.

| | | Gain in surplus. | Loss in surplus. |
|---|---|---|---|
| Total losses from stocks and bonds | | | 449 61 |
| Loss from assets not admitted | | | 126,243 10 |

## GAIN AND LOSS EXHIBIT—Concluded.

### INSURANCE EXHIBIT.

| | | Gain in surplus. | Loss in surplus. |
|---|---|---|---|
| Net gain on account of total and permanent disability benefits or additional accidental death benefits included in life policies | | $11,196 12 | |
| Balance unaccounted for | | 801 98 | |
| Total gains and losses in surplus during the year | | $933,791 37 | $941,035 87 |
| Surplus December 31, 1920 | $642,029 88 | | |
| Surplus December 31, 1921 | 634,785 38 | | |
| Decrease in surplus | | 7,244 50 | |
| Total | | $941,035 87 | $941,035 87 |

## SCHEDULE D—PART 1—BONDS.

| Description. | Book value. | Par value. | Market value. |
|---|---|---|---|
| U. S. Gov., First Liberty Loan, converted, 4¼s, 1947 | $ 1,450 00 | $ 1,450 00 | $ 1,450 00 |
| U. S. Gov., Second Liberty Loan, converted, 4¼s, 1942 | 25,000 00 | 25,000 00 | 25,000 00 |
| U. S. Gov., Second Liberty Loan, converted, 4¼s, 1942 | 99,550 00 | 99,550 00 | 99,550 00 |
| U. S. Gov., Third Liberty Loan, 4¼s, 1928 | 100,000 00 | 100,000 00 | 100,000 00 |
| U. S. Gov., Third Liberty Loan, 4¼s, 1928 | 23,100 00 | 23,100 00 | 23,100 00 |
| U. S. Gov., Fourth Liberty Loan, 4¼s, 1938 | 381,300 00 | 381,300 00 | 381,300 00 |
| U. S. Gov., Fifth Liberty Loan, 4¾s, 1923 | 76,850 00 | 76,850 00 | 76,850 00 |
| Aberdeen, S. D., Sewer, 4½s, 1926 | 10,000 00 | 10,000 00 | 10,101 00 |
| Allen, Tex., School, 5s, 1950 | 8,000 00 | 8,000 00 | 8,000 00 |
| Anamosa, Iowa, Funding, 5s, 1922 | 1,000 00 | 1,000 00 | 1,009 70 |
| Anamosa, Iowa, Funding, 5s, 1923 | 1,000 00 | 1,000 00 | 1,019 00 |
| Anamosa, Iowa, Funding, 5s, 1924 | 1,000 00 | 1,000 00 | 1,028 00 |
| Anson, Tex., School, 5s, 1949 | 15,000 00 | 15,000 00 | 15,097 50 |
| Austin, Tex., Refunding, 4½s, 1924 | 3,000 00 | 3,000 00 | 2,971 50 |
| Austin, Tex., Refunding, 4½s, 1925 | 3,000 00 | 3,000 00 | 2,958 60 |
| Austin, Tex., Refunding, 4½s, 1927 | 1,000 00 | 1,000 00 | 978 10 |
| Austin, Tex., Refunding, 4½s, 1928 | 2,000 00 | 2,000 00 | 1,948 60 |
| Austin, Tex., Refunding, 4½s, 1931 | 2,000 00 | 2,000 00 | 1,928 20 |
| Austin, Tex., Refunding, 4½s, 1933 | 5,000 00 | 5,000 00 | 4,790 00 |
| Cambridge, Iowa, School Funding, 5s, 1924 | 7,000 00 | 7,000 00 | 7,000 00 |
| Chicago, Ill., West Park, 4s, 1922 | 1,995 00 | 2,000 00 | 2,000 00 |
| Chicago, Ill., West Park, 4s, 1925 | 2,992 50 | 3,000 00 | 2,995 80 |
| Collin Co., Tex., Road Dist. No. 7, 5½s, 1925 | 1,000 00 | 1,000 00 | 1,009 50 |
| Collin, Co., Tex., Road Dist. No. 7, 5½s, 1926 | 3,000 00 | 3,000 00 | 3,035 70 |
| Collin Co., Tex., Road Dist. No. 7, 5½s, 1927 | 3,000 00 | 3,000 00 | 3,042 60 |
| Collin Co., Tex., Road Dist. No. 7, 5½s, 1930 | 4,000 00 | 4,000 00 | 4,081 60 |
| Collin Co., Tex., Road Dist. No. 7, 5½s, 1931 | 4,000 00 | 4,000 00 | 4,088 80 |
| Collin Co., Tex., Road Dist. No. 7, 5½s, 1932 | 4,000 00 | 4,000 00 | 4,096 00 |
| Collin Co., Tex., Road Dist. No. 7, 5½s, 1933 | 4,000 00 | 4,000 00 | 4,102 80 |
| Collin Co., Tex., Road Dist. No. 21, 5½s, 1949 | 5,234 40 | 6,000 00 | 5,234 40 |
| Collin Co., Tex., Road Dist. No. 21, 5½s, 1949 | 3,489 60 | 4,000 00 | 3,489 60 |
| Collin Co., Tex., Road Dist. No. 21, 5½s, 1949 | 3,489 60 | 4,000 00 | 3,489 60 |
| Collin Co., Tex., Road Dist. No. 21, 5½s, 1949 | 5,234 40 | 6,000 00 | 5,234 40 |
| Collin Co., Tex., Road Dist. No. 24, 5½s, 1941 | 1,681 76 | 2,000 00 | 1,683 40 |
| Collin Co., Tex., Road Dist. No. 24, 5½s, 1942 | 1,674 48 | 2,000 00 | 1,676 00 |
| Collin Co., Tex., Road Dist. No. 24, 5½s, 1943 | 1,667 62 | 2,000 00 | 1,669 00 |
| Collin Co., Tex., Road Dist. No. 24, 5½s, 1944 | 1,661 24 | 2,000 00 | 1,662 60 |
| Collin Co., Tex., Road Dist. No. 24, 5½s, 1945 | 1,655 22 | 2,000 00 | 1,656 20 |
| Collin Co., Tex., Road Dist. No. 24, 5½s, 1946 | 1,649 68 | 2,000 00 | 1,650 80 |
| Collin Co., Tex., Road Dist. No. 29, 5½s, 1926 | 3,000 00 | 3,000 00 | 3,035 70 |
| Collin Co., Tex., Road Dist. No. 29, 5½s, 1927 | 3,000 00 | 3,000 00 | 3,042 60 |
| Collin Co., Tex., Road Dist. No. 29, 5½s, 1928 | 3,000 00 | 3,000 00 | 3,048 90 |
| Collin Co., Tex., Road Dist. No. 29, 5½s, 1929 | 3,000 00 | 3,000 00 | 3,055 20 |
| Collin Co., Tex., Road Dist. No. 29, 5½s, 1930 | 3,000 00 | 3,000 00 | 3,061 20 |
| Collin Co., Tex., Road Dist. No. 29, 5½s, 1931 | 3,000 00 | 3,000 00 | 3,066 60 |
| Collin Co., Tex., Road Dist. No. 29, 5½s, 1932 | 3,000 00 | 3,000 00 | 3,072 00 |
| Collin Co., Tex., Road Dist. No. 29, 5½s, 1933 | 3,000 00 | 3,000 00 | 3,077 10 |
| Collin Co., Tex., Road Dist. No. 29, 5½s, 1934 | 3,000 00 | 3,000 00 | 3,081 90 |
| Collin Co., Tex., Road Dist. No. 29, 5½s, 1940 | 6,794 20 | 7,000 00 | 6,801 90 |
| East St. Louis, Ill., School, 5s, 1924 | 10,246 00 | 10,000 00 | 10,337 00 |
| East St. Louis, Ill., School, 5s, 1924 | 10,000 00 | 10,000 00 | 10,309 00 |
| Fate, Tex., Independent School, 5s, 1951 | 9,500 00 | 9,500 00 | 9,585 50 |
| Fayette, Mo., Water Works, 4½s, 1926 | 8,000 00 | 8,000 00 | 8,000 00 |
| Gainesville, Tex., Water Works, 5s, 1951 | 50,000 00 | 50,000 00 | 50,000 00 |
| Highland Park, Ill., School, 5s, 1922 | 1,000 00 | 1,000 00 | 1,010 80 |
| Hunt Co., Tex., Road Bonds, 5s, 1959 | 5,000 00 | 5,000 00 | 5,000 00 |
| Hunt Co., Tex., Road Bonds, 5s, 1959 | 2,000 00 | 2,000 00 | 2,000 00 |
| Hunt Co., Tex., Road Bonds, 5s, 1959 | 2,000 00 | 2,000 00 | 2,000 00 |
| Jefferson Co., Tex., School, 5s, 1930 | 9,000 00 | 9,000 00 | 9,012 60 |
| Kaufman Co., Tex., Road Bonds, Prect. No. 3, 5s, 1955 | 30,000 00 | 30,000 00 | 30,189 00 |
| Louisiana Port Commission, Canal Bonds, 5s, 1931 | 8,000 00 | 8,000 00 | 8,000 00 |
| Marinette Co., Wis., Insane Asylum, 4s, 1924 | 3,000 00 | 3,000 00 | 3,017 70 |
| Marinette Co., Wis., Insane Asylum, 4s, 1925 | 7,000 00 | 7,000 00 | 7,056 70 |
| Navarro Co., Tex., School, 5s, 1949 | 5,300 00 | 5,300 00 | 5,300 00 |
| Newman, Ill., Hard Road Bonds, 5s, 1922 | 2,944 20 | 3,000 00 | 2,985 30 |

SCHEDULE D—PART 1—BONDS—Concluded.

| Description. | Book value. | Par value. | Market value |
|---|---|---|---|
| Newman, Ill., Hard Road Bonds, 5s, 1923 | $ 1,945 80 | $ 2,000 00 | $ 1,971 80 |
| Petty, Tex., School, 5s, 1951 | 8,000 00 | 8,000 00 | 8,000 00 |
| Saline Co., Ill., School, 5s, 1922 | 1,000 00 | 1,000 00 | 1,000 00 |
| Spencer, Iowa, Funding, 4½s, 1924 | 10,000 00 | 10,000 00 | 10,000 00 |
| Trinity, Tex., School, 5s, 1930 | 13,500 00 | 13,500 00 | 13,500 00 |
| Wabash Ry. (Toledo & Chicago Div.), 4s, 1941 | 29,828 88 | 30,000 00 | 29,607 00 |
| Totals | $1,082,734 58 | $1,087,550 00 | $1,084,204 50 |

## ILLINOIS LIFE INSURANCE COMPANY.

Located at No. 10 South LaSalle Street, Chicago, Illinois; commenced business August 9, 1899.

JAMES W. STEVENS, President. OSWALD J. ARNOLD, Secretary.

### CAPITAL.

| | | | |
|---|---|---|---|
| Capital paid up | | $1,000,000 00 | |
| Amount of ledger assets December 31, of previous year | | | $17,193,118 86 |

### INCOME.

| | | | |
|---|---|---|---|
| First year's premiums on original policies, less re-insurance | | $684,535 68 | |
| First year's premiums for total and permanent disability benefits | | 9,315 42 | |
| First year's premiums for additional accidental death benefits, less re-insurance | | 1,566 14 | |
| Dividends applied to purchase paid-up additions and annuities | | 5,962 50 | |
| Surrender values applied to purchase paid-up insurance and annuities | | 38,941 22 | |
| New premiums | | $ 740,320 96 | |
| Renewal premiums less re-insurance | $3,034,089 84 | | |
| Renewal premiums for total and permanent disability benefits | 26,379 58 | | |
| Renewal premiums for additional accidental death benefits, less re-insurance | 1,400 24 | | |
| Dividends applied to pay renewal premiums | 8,794 72 | | |
| Dividends applied to shorten the endowment or premium-paying period | 6,964 80 | | |
| Surrender values applied to pay renewal premiums | 49 03 | | |
| Renewal premiums for deferred annuities | 61 26 | | |
| Renewal premiums | | 3,077,739 47 | |
| Premium income | | | $3,818,060 43 |
| Consideration for supplementary contracts involving life contingencies | | | 24,411 00 |
| Consideration for supplementary contracts not involving life contingencies | | | 8,838 60 |
| Dividends left with company to accumulate at interest | | | 8,219 29 |
| Interest on mortgage loans | | $313,612 09 | |
| Interest on collateral loans | | 131,379 34 | |
| Interest on bonds and dividends on stocks | | 359,982 70 | |
| Interest on premium notes, policy loans or liens | | 122,432 51 | |
| Interest on deposits | | 3,556 70 | |
| Interest on other debts due the company | | 22,147 62 | |
| Discount on surrenders paid in advance | | 102 47 | |
| Rents | | 38,400 00 | |
| Total interest and rents | | | 991,613 43 |
| Profit on sale or maturity of ledger assets | | | 3 16 |
| Increase in book value of ledger assets | | | 3,351 00 |
| Total income | | | $4,854,496 91 |
| Total | | | $22,047,615 77 |

### DISBURSEMENTS.

| | | |
|---|---|---|
| Death claims and additions | $907,318 52 | |
| Matured endowments and additions | 166,387 00 | |
| Total and permanent disability claims | 157 54 | |
| Total death claims and endowments | | $1,073,863 06 |
| Annuities involving life contingencies | | 2,716 34 |
| Surrender values paid in cash, or applied in liquidation of loans or notes | | 328,631 59 |
| Surrender values applied to pay new and renewal premiums | | 49 03 |
| Surrender values applied to purchase paid-up insurance and annuities | | 38,941 22 |
| Dividends paid policyholders in cash, or applied in liquidation of loans or notes | | 49,464 42 |
| Dividends applied to pay renewal premiums | | 8,794 72 |
| Dividends applied to shorten the endowment or premium-paying period | | 6,964 80 |

DISBURSEMENTS—Concluded.

| | |
|---|---|
| Dividends applied to purchase paid-up additions and annuities | $ 5,962 50 |
| Dividends left with the company to accumulate at interest | 8,219 29 |
| (Total paid policyholders $1,523,606 97) | |
| Expense of investigation and settlement of policy claims, including legal expenses | 1,582 05 |
| Supplementary contracts not involving life contingencies | 22,116 41 |
| Dividends with interest, held on deposit surrendered during the year | 14,650 16 |
| Dividends to stockholders | 100,000 00 |
| Commissions to agents, first year, $446,902.65; renewal, $234,040.66; bonus, $45,675.97 | 726,619 28 |
| Compensation of managers and agents not paid by commissions on new business | 900 00 |
| Agency supervision and traveling expenses of supervisors | 11,715 35 |
| Branch office expenses | 17,453 87 |
| Medical examiners' fees and inspection of risks | 66,422 28 |
| Salaries and all other compensation of officers and home office employees | 299,916 60 |
| Rent | 30,682 20 |
| Advertising, printing, stationery, postage, telegraph, telephone, express and exchange | 86,947 04 |
| Legal expense | 928 08 |
| Furniture, fixtures and safes | 10,331 16 |
| Repairs and expenses (other than taxes) on real estate | 1,599 38 |
| Taxes on real estate | 2,694 70 |
| State taxes on premiums | 27,851 79 |
| Insurance department licenses and fees | 4,999 73 |
| Federal taxes | 40,236 57 |
| All other licenses, fees and taxes | 1,019 23 |
| Other disbursements, viz: Incidental expense, $2,652.95; investment expense, $432.55; legislative expense, $321.44; association Life Insurance Presidents, $507.18; collection of premiums, $1,505.09 | 5,419 21 |
| Decrease in book value of ledger assets | 814 80 |
| Total disbursements | $2,998,506 86 |
| Balance | $19,049,108 91 |

LEDGER ASSETS.

| | |
|---|---|
| Book value of real estate | $1,364,299 93 |
| Mortgage loans on real estate | 5,589,750 00 |
| Loans secured by collaterals | 1,969,572 00 |
| Loans on company's policies assigned as collateral | 2,396,312 32 |
| Book value of bonds and stocks | 7,166,169 33 |
| Cash in office | 32,167 28 |
| Deposits in trust companies and banks on interest | 311,699 46 |
| Agents' balances (debit, $232,181.23; credit, $13,042.64) | 219,138 59 |
| Total ledger assets | $19,049,108 91 |

NON-LEDGER ASSETS.

| | | | |
|---|---|---|---|
| Interest due and accrued on mortgages | | $101,742 99 | |
| Interest accrued on bonds | | 29,434 81 | |
| Interest accrued on collateral loans | | 22,803 09 | |
| Interest accrued on premium notes, loans or liens | | 5,710 92 | |
| Interest accrued on other assets | | 23 33 | |
| | | | 159,715 14 |
| Market value of real estate over book value | | | 171,000 00 |
| Due from other companies for losses or claims on policies re-insured | | | 35,374 92 |
| | New business. | Renewals. | |
| Net uncollected and deferred premiums (paid for basis) | $4,215 36 | $572,898 58 | 577,113 94 |
| Gross assets | | | $19,992,312 91 |

DEDUCT ASSETS NOT ADMITTED.

| | | |
|---|---|---|
| Agents' debit balances | $232,181 23 | |
| Premium notes, policy loans and other policy assets in excess of net value and of other policy liabilities on individual policies | 29,212 58 | |
| Book value of bonds and stocks over market value | 317,072 38 | |
| Total | | 578,466 19 |
| Admitted assets | | $19,413,846 72 |

LIABILITIES.

| | | |
|---|---|---|
| Net present value of outstanding policies computed by the Illinois Insurance Department | $15,705,236 00 | |
| Same for dividend additions | 507,268 00 | |
| Same for annuities | 73,589 00 | |
| Total | $16,286,093 00 | |
| Deduct net value of risks re-insured | 68,814 00 | |
| Net reserve (paid for basis) | | $16,217,279 00 |
| Extra reserve for total and permanent disability benefits and for additional accidental death benefits included in life policies, less re-insurance | | 48,624 00 |

LIABILITIES—Concluded.

| | | |
|---|---|---|
| Present value of supplementary contracts not involving life contingencies | | $76,348 68 |
| Present value of amounts incurred but not yet due for total and permanent disability benefits | | 1,095 00 |
| Death losses in process of adjustment | $26,000 00 | |
| Death losses reported for which no proofs have been received | 63,441 00 | |
| Total policy claims | | 89,441 00 |
| Dividends left with the company to accumulate at interest | | 37,053 28 |
| Gross premiums paid in advance, including surrender values so applied, less discount, if any | | 27,898 71 |
| Unearned interest and rent paid in advance | | 43,197 16 |
| Commissions to agents due or accrued | | 478 79 |
| Salaries, rents, office expenses, bills and accounts due or accrued | | 17,459 10 |
| Medical examiners' fees and inspections due or accrued | | 4,812 16 |
| Estimated amount hereafter payable for federal, state and other taxes based upon the business of the year of this statement | | 37,999 48 |
| Dividends or other profits due policyholders | | 9,754 05 |
| Dividends declared on or apportioned to annual dividend policies payable to policyholders during 1922 for period to December 31, 1922 | | 25,789 31 |
| Dividends declared on orapportioned to deferred dividend policies payable to policyholders during 1922 for period to December 31, 1922 | | 31,427 02 |
| Amounts set apart, apportioned, provisionally ascertained, calculated, declared or held awaiting apportionment upon optional endowment policies | | 27,795 07 |
| Reserve or surplus funds not otherwise included in liabilities, viz— | | |
| Special reserve liability on account of annuity credits and re-insurance dividend credits on reinsured policies | | 615 54 |
| Deposit on extension notes | | 46,570 45 |
| Aggregate of the survivorship bonus and survivorship investment funds, held awaiting apportionment on survivorship bonus and survivorship investment policies in accordance with the terms thereof | | 1,357,372 91 |
| Additional liability on survivorship investment policies contingent on payment of deferred and uncollected premiums | | 10,190 60 |
| Total | | $18,111,201 31 |
| Capital paid up | | 1,000,000 00 |
| Unassigned funds (surplus) | | 302,645 41 |
| Total | | $19,413,846 72 |

EXHIBIT OF POLICIES—ORDINARY.

ALL BUSINESS PAID FOR.

| | Number. | Amount. | Number. | Amount. |
|---|---|---|---|---|
| Policies in force December 31, 1920 | | | 63,277 | $128,582,376 27 |
| Policies issued, revived and increased during the year | | | 9,400 | 26,459,570 20 |
| Total | | | 72,677 | $155,041,946 47 |
| Deduct policies which have ceased to be in force during the year— | | | | |
| By death | 476 | $ 967,357 87 | | |
| By maturity | 141 | 166,387 00 | | |
| By expiry | 281 | 1,120,685 00 | | |
| By surrender | 1,012 | 2,286,335 33 | | |
| By lapse | 4,753 | 12,742,096 00 | | |
| By decrease | 17 | 1,274,040 00 | | |
| Total | | | 6,680 | 18,556,901 20 |
| Total policies in force December 31, 1921 | | | 65,997 | $136,485,045 27 |
| Re-insured | | | 1,044 | $7,279,433 00 |

BUSINESS IN ILLINOIS—ORDINARY.

| | Number. | Amount. |
|---|---|---|
| Policies in force December 31, 1920 | 32,343 | $72,527,809 72 |
| Policies issued during the year | 5,188 | 17,109,825 00 |
| Total | 37,531 | $89,637,634 72 |
| Deduct policies ceased to be in force | 3,942 | 12,933,816 00 |
| Policies in force December 31, 1921 | 33,589 | $76,703,818 72 |
| Losses and claims unpaid December 31, 1920 | 8 | $ 16,520 00 |
| Losses and claims incurred during the year | 169 | 372,822 67 |
| Total | 177 | $389,342 67 |
| Losses and claims settled during the year | 170 | 334,636 67 |
| Losses and claims unpaid December 31, 1921 | 7 | $54,706 00 |
| Premiums received | | $1,925,359 72 |

## GAIN AND LOSS EXHIBIT.

### INSURANCE EXHIBIT.

| | | Gain in surplus. | Loss in surplus. |
|---|---|---|---|
| Loading on actual premiums of the year (averaging 17.75 per cent of the gross premiums) | $ 706,639 15 | | |
| Insurance expenses incurred during the year | 1,347,086 51 | | |
| Loss from loading | | | $640,447 36 |
| Interest earned during the year | $999,635 08 | | |
| Investment expenses incurred during the year | 7,044 52 | | |
| Net income from investments | $992,590 56 | | |
| Interest required to maintain reserve | 636,316 94 | | |
| Gain from interest | | $356,273 62 | |
| Expected mortality on net amount at risk | $1,339,708 00 | | |
| Actual mortality on net amount at risk | 686,100 01 | | |
| Gain from mortality | | 653,607 99 | |
| Expected disbursements to annuitants | $2,517 00 | | |
| Net actual annuity claims incurred | 2,716 34 | | |
| Loss from annuities | | | 199 34 |
| Total gain during the year from surrendered and lapsed policies | | 80,607 63 | |
| Dividends paid stockholders | | | 100,000 00 |
| Decrease in surplus on dividend account | | | 62,809 40 |
| Increase in special funds and special reserves during the year | | | 14,758 77 |

### INVESTMENT EXHIBIT.

| | | Gain in surplus. | Loss in surplus. |
|---|---|---|---|
| Total gains from real estate | | 93,000 00 | |
| Total gains from stocks and bonds | | 3 16 | |
| Total losses from stocks and bonds | | | 342,977 60 |
| Loss from assets not admitted | | | 37,753 95 |
| Net gain on account of total and permanent disability benefits or additional accidental death benefits included in life policies | | 27,728 84 | |
| Balance unaccounted for | | | 101 39 |
| Total gains and losses in surplus during the year | | $1,211,221 24 | $1,199,047 81 |
| Surplus December 31, 1920 | $290,471 98 | | |
| Surplus December 31, 1921 | 302,645 41 | | |
| Increase in surplus | | | 12,173 43 |
| Total | | $1,211,221 24 | $1,211,221 24 |

## SCHEDULE D—PART 1—BONDS.

| Description. | Book value. | Par value. | Market value. |
|---|---|---|---|
| First Liberty Loan, 3½s, 1947 | $ 1,200 00 | $ 1,200 00 | $ 1,200 00 |
| First Liberty Loan, converted, 4¼s, 1942 | 6,200 00 | 6,200 00 | 6,200 00 |
| Second Liberty Loan, 4¼s, 1942 | 136,000 00 | 136,000 00 | 136,000 00 |
| Third Liberty Loan, 4¼s, 1928 | 145,350 00 | 145,350 00 | 145,350 00 |
| Fourth Liberty Loan, 4¼s, 1928 | 927,800 00 | 927,800 00 | 927,800 00 |
| Victory Loan, 4¾s, 1923 | 359,875 00 | 361,050 00 | 361,050 00 |
| City of Chrisman, Ill., Improvement, 5s | 4,960 00 | 5,000 00 | 5,000 00 |
| City of Kankakee, Ill., Merchant, 5s | 1,987 36 | 2,000 00 | 2,000 00 |
| Atchison, Topeka & Santa Fe Ry., General mortgage, 4s, 1995 | 33,268 78 | 32,000 00 | 27,520 00 |
| Baltimore & Ohio Ry., 4s, 1948 | 1,000 00 | 1,000 00 | 780 00 |
| Buffalo, N. Y., Crosstown Street Ry., 5s, 1932 | 2,175 20 | 2,000 00 | 1,800 00 |
| Chicago, Ill., City Ry. Co., 5s, 1927 | 49,715 00 | 50,000 00 | 35,500 00 |
| Chicago, Ill., Ry. Co., 5s, 1927 | 63,795 00 | 65,000 00 | 46,150 00 |
| Danville, Ill., Street Ry. & Light Co., 5s, 1925 | 15,039 00 | 15,000 00 | 12,150 00 |
| Detroit, Mich., United Ry., 4½s, 1932 | 4,961 00 | 5,000 00 | 3,250 00 |
| Louisville & Nashville R. R., 2d mortgage, 3s, 1980 | 2,105 00 | 3,000 00 | 1,770 00 |
| Louisville Ry. Co., 5s, 1930 | 110,042 50 | 101,000 00 | 87,870 00 |
| Consumers Gas Co., Chicago, 5s, 1936 | 5,216 00 | 5,000 00 | 4,500 00 |
| Louisville, Ky., Board of Trade, 4s, 1924 | 3,044 50 | 3,000 00 | 1,800 00 |
| Stevens Bros. Corporation, Chicago, 6s, 1925 | 380,000 00 | 400,000 00 | 400,000 00 |
| Stevens Building Co., 6s, 1930 | 963,000 00 | 1,000,000 00 | 1,000,000 00 |
| Hotel LaSalle, 6s, 1923-1936 inc | 607,500 00 | 607,500 00 | 607,500 00 |
| Totals | $3,824,234 34 | $3,874,100 00 | $3,815,190 00 |

## SCHEDULE D—PART 2—STOCKS.

| Description. | Book value. | Par value. | Market value. |
|---|---|---|---|
| Central Trust Co. of Illinois, Chicago | $1,492,766 84 | $753,200 00 | $1,446,144 00 |
| *Fort Dearborn National Bank, Chicago | 932,644 00 | 522,400 00 | 522,400 00 |
| Continental & Commercial National Bank, Chicago | 832,524 15 | 352,400 00 | 1,046,628 00 |

*Sold at par January 6, 1922.

SCHEDULE D—PART 2—STOCKS—Concluded.

| Description. | Book value. | Par value. | Market value. |
|---|---|---|---|
| General Liquidation Co., Chicago | $80,000 00 | $20,000 00 | $17,109 95 |
| Chi., No. Shore & Milwaukee R. R., 2d pfd. par. stock | 4,000 00 | 4,000 00 | 1,375 00 |
| Chi., No. Shore & Milwaukee R. R., common stock | | | 250 00 |
| Total | $3,341,934 99 | $1,652,000 00 | $3,033,906 95 |

## INTERNATIONAL LIFE AND TRUST COMPANY.

Located at No. 19 South LaSalle Street, Chicago, Illinois; executive office, Moline, Illinois; commenced business August 5, 1916.

J. O. LAUGMAN, President. A. JOHNSON, Secretary.

### CAPITAL.

| | | | |
|---|---|---|---|
| Capital paid up | | $104,860 00 | |
| Amount of ledger assets December 31, of previous year | | $306,503 78 | |
| Increase of paid-up capital during year | | 4,860 00 | |
| Extended at | | | $311,363 78 |

### INCOME.

| | | | |
|---|---|---|---|
| First year's premiums on original policies, less re-insurance | | $53,182 98 | |
| First year's premiums for total and permanent disability benefits, less re-insurance | | 1,229 93 | |
| First year's premiums for additional accidental death benefits, less re-insurance | | 607 70 | |
| Dividends applied to purchase paid-up additions and annuities | | 698 70 | |
| New premiums | | $55,719 31 | |
| Renewal premiums less re-insurance | $102,743 96 | | |
| Renewal premiums for total and permanent disability benefits | 1,344 11 | | |
| Renewal premiums for additional accidental death benefits, less re-insurance | 894 20 | | |
| Dividends applied to pay renewal premiums | 3,092 99 | | |
| Renewal premiums | | 108,075 26 | |
| Premium income | | | $163,794 57 |
| Dividends left with company to accumulate at interest | | | 1,708 89 |
| Interest on mortgage loans | | $11,585 27 | |
| Interest on collateral loans | | 300 00 | |
| Interest on bonds | | 596 90 | |
| Interest on premium notes, policy loans or liens | | 513 46 | |
| Interest on deposits | | 396 60 | |
| Interest on other debts due the company | | 363 90 | |
| Rents less $4,500.00 interest on incumbrances | | 3,730 00 | |
| Total interest and rents | | | 10,026 13 |
| From other sources, viz: Suspense, $1.33; discount mortgage loans, $1,000.00; surplus from sale of stock, $2,916.00; capital stock subscription suspense account, $12,579.28 | | | 16,496 61 |
| Borrowed money (gross) | | | 72,846 25 |
| Profit on sale or maturity of ledger assets | | | 75 00 |
| Total income | | | $264,947 45 |
| Total | | | $576,311 23 |

### DISBURSEMENTS.

| | | |
|---|---|---|
| Death claims | | $12,000 00 |
| Premium notes and liens voided by lapse, less $420.34 restorations | | 5,448 08 |
| Surrender values paid in cash, or applied in liquidation of loans or notes | | 1,697 73 |
| Dividends applied to pay renewal premiums | | 3,092 99 |
| Dividends applied to purchase paid-up additions and annuities | | 698 70 |
| Dividends left with the company to accumulate at interest | | 1,708 89 |
| (Total paid policyholders | $24,646 39) | |
| Commissions to agents, first year, $36,254.16; renewal, $6,863.89 | | 43,118 05 |
| Compensation of managers and agents not paid by commissions on new business | | 2,014 57 |
| Agency supervision and traveling expenses of supervisors | | 7,373 59 |
| Branch office expenses | | 6,432 00 |
| Medical examiners' fees and inspection of risks | | 2,246 67 |
| Salaries and all other compensation of officers and home office employees | | 15,986 62 |
| Rent | | 1,179 24 |
| Advertising, printing, stationery, postage, telegraph, telephone and express | | 6,156 46 |
| Legal expense | | 1,414 63 |
| Furniture, fixtures and safes | | 298 76 |
| Repairs, and expenses (other than taxes) on real estate | | 145 50 |
| Taxes on real estate | | 789 01 |

DISBURSEMENTS—Concluded.

| | |
|---|---|
| State taxes on premiums | $ 909 14 |
| Insurance department licenses and fees | 566 40 |
| Federal taxes | 1,637 82 |
| All other licenses, fees and taxes | 1,632 00 |
| Other disbursements, viz: War premiums refunded, $375.00; stock notes voided $2,003.52; traveling expense, $2,010.74; books and office supplies, $267.22; entertainment account, $54.70; miscellaneous, $30.80; investment expense, $10.00; collection charge, $104.81; agents' and officers' bond, $67.34 | 4,924 13 |
| Borrowed money repaid (gross) | 21,146 64 |
| Interest on borrowed money | 2,928 35 |
| Agents' balances charged off | 13 94 |
| Decrease in book value of ledger assets | 1,648 20 |
| Total disbursements | $147,208 71 |
| Balance | $429,102 52 |

LEDGER ASSETS.

| | |
|---|---|
| Book value of real estate | $ 25,000 00 |
| Mortgage loans on real estate | 160,750 00 |
| Loans secured by collaterals | 94,916 62 |
| Loans on company's policies assigned as collateral | 6,128 84 |
| Premium notes on policies in force | 12,708 71 |
| Book value of bonds | 71,368 61 |
| Cash in office | 191 99 |
| Deposits in trust companies and banks not on interest | —1,561 76 |
| Deposits in trust companies and banks on interest | 10,249 40 |
| Bills receivable | 3,564 17 |
| Agents' balances (debit, $16,107.67; credit, $292.23) | 15,815 44 |
| Stock notes | 29,970 50 |
| Total ledger assets | $429,102 52 |

NON-LEDGER ASSETS.

| | | | |
|---|---|---|---|
| Interest due and accrued on mortgages | | $2,247 76 | |
| Interest accrued on bonds | | 1,366 47 | |
| Interest due on collateral loans | | 600 00 | |
| Interest accrued on premium notes, loans or liens | | 407 55 | |
| Interest accrued on other assets | | 90 00 | |
| Rents due on company's property | | 150 00 | |
| | | | 4,861 78 |
| Market value of bonds over book value | | | 1,386 39 |
| | New business. | Renewals. | |
| Net uncollected and deferred premiums (paid for basis) | $688 20 | $12,454 18 | 13,142 38 |
| Gross assets | | | $448,493 07 |

DEDUCT ASSETS NOT ADMITTED.

| | | |
|---|---|---|
| Stock notes | $29,970 50 | |
| Agents' debit balances | 16,107 67 | |
| Bills receivable | 3,564 17 | |
| Premium notes, policy loans and other policy assets in excess of net value and of other policy liabilities on individual policies | 2,450 30 | |
| Excess of collateral loan over market value of collateral | 15,455 62 | |
| Total | | 67,548 26 |
| Admitted assets | | $380,944 81 |

LIABILITIES.

| | | |
|---|---|---|
| Net present value of outstanding policies computed by the Illinois Insurance Department | $174,901 00 | |
| Same for dividend additions | 1,620 00 | |
| Total | $176,521 00 | |
| Deduct net value of risks re-insured | 3,049 00 | |
| Net reserve (paid for basis) | | 173,472 00 |
| Extra reserve for total and permanent disability benefits and for additional accidental death benefits included in life policies, less re-insurance | | 2,505 00 |
| Death losses reported for which no proofs have been reported | | 3,500 00 |
| Dividends left with the company to accumulate at interest | | 2,561 37 |
| Gross premiums paid in advance, including surrender values so applied, less discount, if any | | 643 41 |
| Unearned interest and rent paid in advance | | 208 85 |
| Commissions due agents on premium notes, when paid | | 1,443 26 |
| Commissions to agents due or accrued | | 292 23 |
| Salaries, rents, office expenses, bills, and accounts due or accrued | | 1,050 17 |
| Medical examiners' fees due or accrued | | 116 00 |
| Estimated amount hereafter payable for federal, state and other taxes based upon the business of the year of this statement | | 4,447 69 |
| Borrowed money and interest thereon | | 91,825 59 |

LIABILITIES—Concluded.

| | |
|---|---|
| Dividends or other profits due policyholders | $ 414 09 |
| Dividends declared on or apportioned to annual dividend policies payable to policyholders during 1922 for period to June 30, 1922 | 2,641 85 |
| Other liabilities, viz: Suspense, $180.37; interest accrued on real estate incumbrances, $1,875.00; partial payments on capital stock subscriptions, $3,670.00 | 5,725 37 |
| Total | $290,846 88 |
| Capital paid up | 104,860 00 |
| Impairment | 14,762 07 |
| Total | $380,944 81 |

## EXHIBIT OF POLICIES—ORDINARY.

ALL BUSINESS PAID FOR.

| | Number. | Amount. | Number. | Amount. |
|---|---|---|---|---|
| Policies in force December 31, 1920 | | | 2,265 | $4,513,450 83 |
| Policies issued, revived, and increased during the year | | | 885 | 1,926,913 02 |
| Total | | | 3,150 | $6,440,363 85 |
| Deduct policies which have ceased to be in force during the year— | | | | |
| By death | 6 | $ 12,000 00 | | |
| By surrender | 9 | 14,052 28 | | |
| By lapse | 636 | 1,360,891 00 | | |
| By decrease | -------- | 34,068 00 | | |
| Total | | | 651 | 1,421,011 28 |
| Total policies in force December 31, 1921 | | | 2,499 | $5,019,352 57 |
| Re-insured | | | 118 | $510,878 00 |

## BUSINESS IN ILLINOIS—ORDINARY.

| | Number. | Amount. |
|---|---|---|
| Policies in force December 31, 1920 | 1,693 | $3,313,415 00 |
| Policies issued during the year | 501 | 1,107,387 00 |
| Total | 2,194 | $4,420,802 00 |
| Deduct policies ceased to be in force | 511 | 1,057,459 00 |
| Policies in force December 31, 1921 | 1,683 | 3,363,343 00 |
| Losses and claims incurred during the year | 8 | $18,000 00 |
| Losses and claims settled during the year | 6 | 12,000 00 |
| Losses and claims unpaid December 31, 1921 | 2 | $6,000 00 |
| Premiums received | | $109,401 77 |

## GAIN AND LOSS EXHIBIT.

INSURANCE EXHIBIT.

| | | Gain in surplus. | Loss in surplus. |
|---|---|---|---|
| Loading on actual premiums of the year (averaging 35.61 per cent of the gross premiums) | $56,649 92 | | |
| Insurance expenses incurred during the year | 94,880 18 | | |
| Loss from loading | | -------------- | $38,230 26 |
| Interest earned during the year | $6,405 88 | | |
| Investment expenses incurred during the year | 944 51 | | |
| Net income from investments | $5,461 37 | | |
| Interest required to maintain reserve | 6,283 69 | | |
| Loss from interest | | -------------- | 822 32 |
| Expected mortality on net amount at risk | $38,615 90 | | |
| Actual mortality on net amount at risk | 15,189 51 | | |
| Gain from mortality | | $23,426 39 | |
| Total gain during the year from surrendered and lapsed policies | | 3,817 00 | |
| Decrease in surplus on dividend account | | -------------- | 6,483 06 |

INVESTMENT EXHIBIT.

| | Gain in surplus. | Loss in surplus. |
|---|---|---|
| Total losses from real estate | -------------- | 2,636 80 |
| Total gains from bonds | 2,740 79 | |
| Total losses from bonds | -------------- | 386 40 |
| Gain from mortgage loan | 1,000 00 | |
| Loss on account of excess of collateral loan over market value of collateral | -------------- | 15,455 62 |
| Loss from assets not admitted | -------------- | 12,455 13 |
| Net gain on account of total and permanent disability benefits or additional accidental death benefits included in life policies | 3,173 94 | |

GAIN AND LOSS EXHIBIT—Concluded.

INSURANCE EXHIBIT.

| | | Gain in surplus. | Loss in surplus. |
|---|---|---|---|
| Gain from surplus sale of stock, $2,916.00; partial payments on capital stock, $8,909.28 | | $11,825 28 | |
| Loss from war premium refunded | | | $ 375 00 |
| Loss: Stock notes voided, $2,003.52; premium notes voided by lapse, $5,448.08 | | | 7,451 60 |
| Balance unaccounted for | | 1 31 | |
| Total gains and losses in surplus during the year | | $45,984 71 | $84,296 19 |
| Surplus December 31, 1920 | $23,549 41 | | |
| Impairment December 31, 1921 | —14,762 07 | | |
| Decrease in surplus | | 38,311 48 | |
| Total | | $84,296 19 | $84,296 19 |

SCHEDULE D—PART 1—BONDS.

| Description. | Book value. | Par value. | Market value. |
|---|---|---|---|
| Liberty Loan, 3½s, 1947 | $ 50 00 | $ 50 00 | $ 47 50 |
| Liberty Loan, 4¼s, 1947 | 1,000 00 | 1,000 00 | 970 00 |
| Liberty Loan, 4¼s, 1942 | 7,200 00 | 7,200 00 | 6,999 00 |
| Liberty Loan, 4¼s, 1928 | 5,987 78 | 6,000 00 | 5,880 00 |
| Liberty Loan, 4¼s, 1938 | 27,239 33 | 27,350 00 | 26,589 50 |
| Moline, Ill., improvement, 5s, 1923 | 3,740 00 | 4,000 00 | 4,000 00 |
| Moline, Ill., improvement, 5s, 1924 | 3,085 50 | 3,300 00 | 3,333 00 |
| Moline, Ill., improvement, 5s, 1925 | 3,085 50 | 3,300 00 | 3,333 00 |
| Moline, Ill., improvement, 5s, 1926 | 3,085 50 | 3,300 00 | 3,333 00 |
| Moline, Ill., improvement, 5s, 1927 | 3,272 50 | 3,500 00 | 3,535 00 |
| Moline, Ill., improvement, 5s, 1928 | 3,272 50 | 3,500 00 | 3,535 00 |
| Moline, Ill., improvement, 5s, 1929 | 3,272 50 | 3,500 00 | 3,570 00 |
| Moline, Ill., improvement, 5s, 1930 | 2,805 00 | 3,000 00 | 3,060 00 |
| Moline, Ill., improvement, 5s, 1931 | 3,272 50 | 3,500 00 | 3,570 00 |
| Waterloo, Iowa, improvement, 5s, 1921 | 1,000 00 | 1,000 00 | 1,000 00 |
| Totals | $71,368 61 | $73,500 00 | $72,755 00 |

## LIBERTY LIFE INSURANCE COMPANY.

Located at Grand Boulevard at Thirty-fifth Street, Chicago, Illinois; commenced business July 25, 1921.

FRANK L. GILLESPIE, President. W. ELLIS STEWART, Secretary.

CAPITAL.

| | | |
|---|---|---|
| Capital paid up | $100,000 00 | |
| Increase of paid-up capital during the year | | $100,000 00 |

INCOME.

| | | |
|---|---|---|
| First year's premiums on original policies | $5,352 69 | |
| First year's premiums for total and permanent disability benefits | 38 23 | |
| First year's premiums for additional accidental death benefits | 80 17 | |
| Premium income | | $ 5,471 09 |
| Interest on mortgage loans | $2,084 83 | |
| Interest on premium notes, policy loans or liens | 61 | |
| Interest on deposits | 77 54 | |
| Interest on other debts due the company | 1 82 | |
| Total interest | | 2,164 80 |
| From other sources, viz: Contributed to surplus, $200,000.00; deposits on applications, $611.36; deposit on rate books, $269.50; deposit forfeited, $80.35 | | 200,961 21 |
| Borrowed money (gross) | | 2,111 67 |
| Profit on sale or maturity of ledger assets | | 36 84 |
| Total income | | $210,745 61 |
| Total | | $310,745 61 |

DISBURSEMENTS.

| | |
|---|---|
| Commissions to agents, first year | $ 4,127 81 |
| Compensation of managers and agents not paid by commissions on new business | 41 17 |
| Agency supervision and traveling expenses of supervisors | 1,189 99 |
| Branch office expenses | 693 00 |
| Medical examiners' fees and inspection of risks | 1,221 00 |
| Salaries and all other compensation of officers and home office employees | 12,581 63 |
| Rent | 2,730 26 |

## DISBURSEMENTS—Concluded.

| | |
|---|---|
| Advertising, printing, stationery, postage, telegraph, telephone, express and exchange | $10,159 94 |
| Furniture, fixtures and safes | 2,096 61 |
| Insurance department licenses and fees | 31 00 |
| All other licenses, fees and taxes | 1,506 90 |
| Other disbursements, viz: Organization expense (commissions on stock, $47,243.26; miscellaneous expense, $1,739.94; fire insurance, $480.17; investment expense, $372.11 | 48,835 48 |
| Borrowed money repaid (gross) | 1,531 67 |
| Interest on borrowed money | 29 44 |
| Loss on sale or maturity of ledger assets | 13 53 |
| Total disbursements | $86,789 43 |
| Balance | $223,956 18 |

## LEDGER ASSETS.

| | |
|---|---|
| Mortgage loans on real estate | $ 98,200 00 |
| Book value of bonds | 200 00 |
| Cash in office | 637 63 |
| Deposits in trust companies and banks not on interest | 10,685 12 |
| Deposits in trust companies and banks on interest | 1,900 00 |
| Bills receivable | 2,409 03 |
| Agents' credit balances | —1,224 54 |
| Notes receivable on account of capital stock sales | 111,148 94 |
| Total ledger assets | $223,956 18 |

### NON-LEDGER ASSETS.

| | |
|---|---|
| Interest accrued on mortgages | 1,357 58 |
| Net uncollected and deferred premiums (paid for basis): New business | 1,665 03 |
| All other assets, viz: Furniture and fixtures, $2,096.61; stationery and printing, $5,000.00; fire insurance premium paid in advance, $416.17 | 7,512 78 |
| Gross assets | $234,491 57 |

### DEDUCT ASSETS NOT ADMITTED.

| | | |
|---|---|---|
| Supplies, printed matter and stationery | $ 5,000 00 | |
| Furniture, fixtures and safes | 2,096 61 | |
| Bills receivable | 2,409 03 | |
| Premium notes, policy loans and other policy assets in excess of net value and of other policy liabilities on individual policies | 549 04 | |
| Notes receivable on account of capital stock sales | 111,148 94 | |
| Book value of bonds over market value | 5 00 | |
| Total | | 121,208 62 |
| Admitted assets | | $113,282 95 |

## LIABILITIES.

| | |
|---|---|
| Net present value of outstanding policies computed by the Illinois Insurance Department | $2,250 00 |
| Extra reserve for total and permanent disability benefits included in life policies, less reinsurance | 56 00 |
| Salaries, rents, office expenses, bills, and accounts due or accrued | 589 99 |
| Estimated amount hereafter payable for federal, state and other taxes based upon the business of the year of this statement | 253 60 |
| Borrowed money and interest thereon | 580 00 |
| Suspense deposits on applications, $611.36; deposits on rate books, $120.00 | 731 36 |
| Total | 4,460 95 |
| Capital paid up | 100,000 00 |
| Unassigned funds (surplus) | 8,822 00 |
| Total | $113,282 95 |

## EXHIBIT OF POLICIES—ORDINARY.

### ALL BUSINESS PAID FOR.

| | Number. | Amount. |
|---|---|---|
| Policies issued, revived, and increased during the year | 184 | $256,500 00 |
| Deduct policies which have ceased to be in force during the year by lapse | 2 | 2,000 00 |
| Total policies in force December 31, 1921 | 182 | $254,500 00 |

## BUSINESS IN ILLINOIS—ORDINARY.

| | Number. | Amount. |
|---|---|---|
| Policies issued during the year | 179 | $238,500 00 |
| Deduct policies ceased to be in force | 2 | 2,000 00 |
| Policies in force December 31, 1921 | 177 | $236,500 00 |
| Premiums received | | $4,736 67 |

## GAIN AND LOSS EXHIBIT.

### INSURANCE EXHIBIT.

| | | Gain in surplus. | Loss in surplus. |
|---|---|---|---|
| Loading on actual premiums of the year (averaging 68.99 per cent of the gross premiums) | $ 7,509 67 | | |
| Insurance expenses incurred during the year | 41,665 21 | | |
| Loss from loading | | | $34,155 54 |
| Interest earned during the year | $3,492 94 | | |
| Investment expenses incurred during the year | 372 11 | | |
| Net income from investments | $3,120 83 | | |
| Interest required to maintain reserve | 40 04 | | |
| Gain from interest | | $3,080 79 | |
| Expected mortality on net amount at risk | | 1,087 98 | |

### INVESTMENT EXHIBIT.

| | Gain in surplus. | Loss in surplus. |
|---|---|---|
| Total gains from stocks and bonds | 36 84 | |
| Total losses from stocks and bonds | | 18 53 |
| Loss from assets not admitted | | 114,107 01 |
| Net gain on account of total and permanent disability benefits included in life policies | 62 40 | |
| Gain: Surplus realized from sale of capital stock | 200,000 00 | |
| Loss: Organization expense (commission on stock) | | 47,243 26 |
| Balance unaccounted for | 78 33 | |
| Total gains and losses in surplus during the year | $204,346 34 | $195,524 34 |
| Surplus December 31, 1921 | | 8,822 00 |
| Total | $204,346 34 | $204,346 34 |

## SCHEDULE D—PART 1—BONDS.

| Description. | Book value. | Par value. | Market value. |
|---|---|---|---|
| United States of America, 1st Liberty Loan, 4¼s, 1947 | $100 00 | $100 00 | $ 96 06 |
| United States of America, 3d Liberty Loan, 4¼s, 1928 | 100 00 | 100 00 | 100 00 |
| Totals | $200 00 | $200 00 | $196 06 |

---

## MARQUETTE LIFE INSURANCE COMPANY.

Located at Ridgely Farmers' State Bank Building, Springfield, Illinois; commenced business January 15, 1909.

JOSEPH C. BERNARD, President. JULIUS M. GASS, Secretary.

### CAPITAL.

| | | |
|---|---|---|
| Capital paid up | $254,340 00 | |
| Amount of ledger assets December 31, of previous year | | $1,012,147 64 |

### INCOME.

| | | | |
|---|---|---|---|
| First year's premiums on original policies, less re-insurance | | $42,470 09 | |
| First year's premiums for total and permanent disability benefits | | 37 26 | |
| Surrender values applied to purchase paid-up insurance and annuities | | 1,564 25 | |
| New premiums | | $ 44,071 60 | |
| Renewal premiums less re-insurance | $190,094 91 | | |
| Renewal premiums for total and permanent disability benefits | 189 01 | | |
| Renewal premiums | | 190,283 92 | |
| Premium income | | | 234,355 52 |
| Interest on mortgage loans | | $48,247 53 | |
| Interest on bonds | | 3,982 91 | |
| Interest on premium notes, policy loans or liens | | 5,131 82 | |
| Interest on deposits | | 281 85 | |
| Interest on other debts due the company | | 2 39 | |
| Rents | | 144 00 | |
| Total interest and rents | | | 57,790 50 |
| From other sources, viz: Commissions on loans, $1,437.60; stock transfer fees, $50.75; unclaimed dividend, $144.40 | | | 1,632 75 |
| Borrowed money (gross) | | | 40,000 00 |
| Total income | | | $333,778 77 |
| Total | | | $1,345,926 41 |

## DISBURSEMENTS.

| | | |
|---|---|---|
| Death claims | $48,100 00 | |
| Matured endowments | 1,000 00 | |
| Total death claims and endowments | | $49,100 00 |
| Premium notes and liens voided by lapse | | 1,238 66 |
| Surrender values paid in cash, or applied in liquidation of loans or notes | | 14,909 75 |
| Surrender values applied to purchase paid-up insurance and annuities | | 1,564 25 |
| (Total paid policyholders | $66,812 66) | |
| Commissions to agents, first year, $30,049.25; renewal, $10,146.02 | | 40,195 27 |
| Agency supervision and traveling expenses of supervisors | | 3,900 17 |
| Branch office expenses | | 2,354 81 |
| Medical examiners' fees and inspection of risks | | 4,074 16 |
| Salaries and all other compensation of officers and home office employees | | 13,659 24 |
| Rent | | 1,528 00 |
| Advertising, printing, stationery, postage, telegraph, telephone and express | | 4,145 72 |
| Legal expense | | 25 00 |
| Repairs and expenses (other than taxes) on real estate | | 228 15 |
| Taxes on real estate | | 40 65 |
| State taxes on premiums | | 1,628 94 |
| Insurance department licenses and fees | | 967 96 |
| Federal taxes | | 2,141 00 |
| All other licenses, fees and taxes | | 5,006 72 |
| Other disbursements, viz: General expense, $1,061.49; investment expense, $524.49; books and subscription, $489.65; surety bonds, $35.00 | | 2,110 63 |
| Borrowed money repaid (gross) | | 40,000 00 |
| Interest on borrowed money | | 304 17 |
| Decrease in book value of ledger assets | | 335 92 |
| Total disbursements | | $189,459 17 |
| Balance | | $1,156,467 24 |

## LEDGER ASSETS.

| | |
|---|---|
| Book value of real estate | $ 3,000 00 |
| Mortgage loans on real estate | 938,897 50 |
| Loans on company's policies assigned as collateral | 107,304 53 |
| Premium notes on policies in force | 6,205 29 |
| Book value of bonds | 73,043 92 |
| Cash in office | 245 34 |
| Deposits in trust companies and banks not on interest | 250 00 |
| Deposits in trust companies and banks on interest | 17,896 82 |
| Agents' balances (debit, $6,037.04; credit, $790.38) | 5,246 66 |
| Furniture and fixtures, $4,215.15; taxes advanced, $162.03 | 4,377 18 |
| Total ledger assets | $1,156,467 24 |

### NON-LEDGER ASSETS.

| | | | |
|---|---|---|---|
| Interest due and accrued on mortgages | | $23,266 62 | |
| Interest due and accrued on bonds | | 1,407 09 | |
| Interest accrued on premium notes, loans or liens | | 96 08 | |
| Interest accrued on other assets | | 31 73 | |
| | | | 24,801 52 |
| | New business. | Renewals. | |
| Net uncollected and deferred premiums (paid for basis) | $1,498 78 | $24,745 99 | 26,244 77 |
| Gross assets | | | $1,207,513 53 |

### DEDUCT ASSETS NOT ADMITTED.

| | | |
|---|---|---|
| Furniture, fixtures and safes | $ 4,215 15 | |
| Agents' debit balances | 6,037 04 | |
| Premium notes, policy loans and other policy assets in excess of net value and of other policy liabilities on individual policies | 817 53 | |
| Overdue and accrued interest on bonds in default | 112 60 | |
| Book value of mortgage loans in excess of 50 per cent of appraisal of property | 20,000 00 | |
| Total | | 31,182 32 |
| Admitted assets | | $1,176,331 21 |

## LIABILITIES.

| | | |
|---|---|---|
| Net present value of outstanding policies computed by the Illinois Insurance Department | $889,195 00 | |
| Deduct net value of risks re-insured | 612 00 | |
| Net reserve (paid for basis) | | $888,583 00 |
| Extra reserve for total and permanent disability benefits included in life policies | | 321 00 |
| Death losses reported for which no proofs have been received | | 9,200 00 |
| Gross premiums paid in advance, including surrender values so applied, less discount, if any | | 1,693 20 |
| Unearned interest and rent paid in advance | | 1,392 30 |
| Commissions due agents on premium notes, when paid | | 1,110 39 |

LIABILITIES—Concluded.

| | |
|---|---|
| Commissions to agents due or accrued | $ 121 00 |
| Cost of collection on uncollected and deferred premiums in excess of loading | 613 68 |
| Salaries, rents, office expenses, bills and accounts due or accrued | 1,638 51 |
| Estimated amount hereafter payable for federal, state and other taxes based upon the business of the year of this statement | 6,678 64 |
| Unclaimed dividends to stockholders | 144 40 |
| Total | $911,496 12 |
| Capital paid up | 254,742 00 |
| Unassigned funds (surplus) | 10,093 09 |
| Total | $1,176,331 21 |

## EXHIBIT OF POLICIES—ORDINARY.

ALL BUSINESS PAID FOR.

| | Number. | Amount. | Number. | Amount. |
|---|---|---|---|---|
| Policies in force December 31, 1920 | | | 5,401 | $6,365,399 00 |
| Policies issued, revived and increased during the year | | | 890 | 1,298,014 00 |
| Total | | | 6,291 | $7,663,413 00 |
| Deduct policies which have ceased to be in force during the year— | | | | |
| By death | 50 | $ 56,100 00 | | |
| By expiry | 40 | 51,500 00 | | |
| By surrender | 61 | 78,300 00 | | |
| By lapse | 346 | 506,300 00 | | |
| By decrease | -------- | 4,204 00 | | |
| Total | | | 497 | 696,404 00 |
| Total policies in force December 31, 1921 | | | 5,794 | $6,967,009 00 |

## BUSINESS IN ILLINOIS—ORDINARY.

| | Number. | Amount. |
|---|---|---|
| Policies in force December 31, 1920 | 2,635 | $3,092,010 00 |
| Policies issued during the year | 745 | 1,102,664 00 |
| Total | 3,380 | $4,194,674 00 |
| Deduct policies ceased to be in force | 270 | 374,350 00 |
| Policies in force December 31, 1921 | 3,110 | $3,820,324 00 |
| Losses and claims incurred during the year | 32 | $43,600 00 |
| Losses and claims settled during the year | 28 | 35,600 00 |
| Losses and claims unpaid December 31, 1921 | 4 | $8,000 00 |
| Premiums received | | $129,310 05 |

## GAIN AND LOSS EXHIBIT.

INSURANCE EXHIBIT.

| | | Gain in surplus. | Loss in surplus. |
|---|---|---|---|
| Loading on actual premiums of the year (averaging 17.04 per cent of the gross premiums) | $41,759 59 | | |
| Insurance expenses incurred during the year | 72,795 27 | | |
| Loss from loading | | -------------- | $31,035 68 |
| Interest earned during the year | $61,842 67 | | |
| Investment expenses incurred during the year | 8,578 35 | | |
| Net income from investments | $53,264 32 | | |
| Interest required to maintain reserve | 29,631 26 | | |
| Gain from interest | | $23,633 06 | |
| Expected mortality on net amount at risk | $71,974 00 | | |
| Actual mortality on net amount at risk | 46,196 00 | | |
| Gain from mortality | | 25,778 00 | |
| Total gain during the year from surrendered and lapsed policies | | 2,659 74 | |
| INVESTMENT EXHIBIT. | | | |
| Net to loss account | | -------------- | 1,238 66 |
| Loss on mortgages | | -------------- | 7,500 00 |
| Gain from stock transfer fees and commissions on loans | | 1,488 35 | |
| Loss from assets not admitted | | -------------- | 1,987 22 |
| Net gain on account of total and permanent disability benefits or additional accidental death benefits included in life policies | | 175 27 | |
| Balance unaccounted for | | -------------- | 4,441 86 |
| Total gains and losses in surplus during the year | | $53,734 42 | $46,203 42 |

## GAIN AND LOSS EXHIBIT—Concluded.

NVESTMENT EXHIBIT.

| | | Gain in surplus. | Loss in surplus. |
|---|---|---|---|
| Surplus December 31, 1920 | $ 2,562 09 | | |
| Surplus December 31, 1921 | 10,093 09 | | |
| Increase in surplus | | | $7,531 00 |
| Total | | $53,734 42 | $53,734 42 |

## SCHEDULE D—PART 1—BONDS.

| Description. | Book value. | Par value. | Market value. |
|---|---|---|---|
| Jersey and Greene Co., Ill., Nutwood, 6s, 1922 | $7,531 86 | $7,500 00 | $7,500 00 |
| Jersey and Greene Co., Ill., Nutwood, 6s, 1923 | 9,101 23 | 9,000 00 | 9,000 00 |
| Jersey and Greene Co., Ill., Nutwood, 6s, 1925 | 7,169 44 | 7,000 00 | 7,000 00 |
| Jersey and Greene Co., Ill., Nutwood, 6s, 1926 | 13,907 67 | 13,500 00 | 13,500 00 |
| Jersey and Greene Co., Ill., Nutwood, 6s, 1927 | 2,071 77 | 2,000 00 | 2,000 00 |
| Jersey and Greene Co., Ill., Nutwood, 6s, 1929 | 1,569 63 | 1,500 00 | 1,500 00 |
| North Chicago, Ill., Foss Park Dist., 5s, 1922 | 1,503 18 | 1,500 00 | 1,500 00 |
| North Chicago, Ill., Foss Park Dist., 5s, 1923 | 1,512 49 | 1,500 00 | 1,500 00 |
| North Chicago, Ill., Foss Park Dist., 5s, 1924 | 1,521 40 | 1,500 00 | 1,515 00 |
| North Chicago, Ill., Foss Park Dist., 5s, 1925 | 1,529 94 | 1,500 00 | 1,515 00 |
| North Chicago, Ill., Foss Park Dist., 5s, 1926 | 1,538 12 | 1,500 00 | 1,515 00 |
| North Chicago, Ill., Foss Park Dist., 5s, 1927 | 1,545 96 | 1,500 00 | 1,515 00 |
| Latrobe, Pa., School Dist. Refund, 4½s, 1922 | 1,003 10 | 1,000 00 | 1,000 00 |
| School Dist. 70, Henry Co., Ill., 5s, 1922 | 1,004 58 | 1,000 00 | 1,000 00 |
| School Dist. 70, Henry Co., Ill., 5s, 1923 | 1,012 82 | 1,000 00 | 1,000 00 |
| School Dist. 70, Henry Co., Ill., 5s, 1924 | 1,020 73 | 1,000 00 | 1,010 00 |
| Litchfield, Ill., Improvement, 5s, 1922 | 400 00 | 400 00 | 400 00 |
| Ft. Smith, Ark., School Dist., 5s, 1929 | 5,000 00 | 5,000 00 | 5,000 00 |
| Ft. Smith, Ark., Waterworks Imp. Dist. No. 1, 5s, 1923 | 5,000 00 | 5,000 00 | 5,000 00 |
| East St. Louis, Ill., Sewerage and Pumping Sta., 5s, 1928 | 1,500 00 | 1,500 00 | 1,515 00 |
| U. S. Liberty Loan Bond, 2d issue, 4¼s, 1942 | 100 00 | 100 00 | 97 00 |
| U. S. Liberty Loan Bond, 2d issue, 4¼s, 1942 | 1,000 00 | 1,000 00 | 970 00 |
| U. S. Liberty Loan Bond, 2d issue, 4¼s, 1942 | 250 00 | 250 00 | 242 50 |
| U. S. Liberty Loan Bond, 3d issue, 4¼s, 1928 | 4,000 00 | 4,000 00 | 3,920 00 |
| U. S. Liberty Loan Bond, 3d issue, 4¼s, 1928 | 800 00 | 800 00 | 784 00 |
| U. S. Liberty Loan Bond, 4th issue, 4¼s, 1938 | 450 00 | 450 00 | 436 50 |
| Totals | $73,043 92 | $72,000 00 | $71,935 00 |

---

# MUTUAL LIFE OF ILLINOIS.

Located at Southwest corner Fifth Street and Capitol Avenue, Springfield, Illinois; commenced business January 10, 1920.

H. B. HILL, President. J. R. NEAL, Secretary.

## CAPITAL.

| | | | |
|---|---|---|---|
| Capital paid up | | $177,853 50 | |
| Amount of ledger assets December 31, of previous year | | $395,023 32 | |
| Increase of paid-up capital during year | | 8,160 00 | |
| Surplus paid in on capital stock | | 16,320 00 | |
| Extended at | | | $419,503 32 |

## INCOME.

| | | | |
|---|---|---|---|
| First year's premiums on original policies, less re-insurance | | $54,183 28 | |
| First year's premiums for total and permanent disability benefits, less re-insurance | | 1,153 17 | |
| Dividends applied to purchase paid-up additions and annuities | | 153 76 | |
| New premiums | | $55,490 21 | |
| Renewal premiums less re-insurance | $89,175 13 | | |
| Renewal premiums for total and permanent disability benefits, less re-insurance | 1,450 88 | | |
| Dividends applied to pay renewal premiums | 1,462 52 | | |
| Renewal premiums | | 92,088 53 | |
| Premium income | | | $147,578 74 |
| Dividends left with company to accumulate at interest | | | 496 92 |
| Interest on mortgage loans | | $9,789 41 | |
| Interest on bonds | | 1,939 46 | |
| Interest on premium notes, policy loans or liens | | 2,016 16 | |

INCOME—Concluded.

| | | |
|---|---|---|
| Interest on deposits | $ 897 97 | |
| Interest on other debts due the company | 6,192 03 | |
| Total interest | | $20,835 03 |
| Borrowed money (gross) | | 15,000 00 |
| Total income | | $183,910 69 |
| Total | | $603,414 01 |

DISBURSEMENTS.

| | | |
|---|---|---|
| Death claims | | $ 9,000 00 |
| Premium notes and liens voided by lapse | | 1,353 40 |
| Surrender values paid in cash, or applied in liquidation of loans or notes | | 127 14 |
| Dividends paid policyholders in cash, or applied in liquidation of loans or notes | | 131 07 |
| Dividends applied to pay renewal premiums | | 1,462 52 |
| Dividends applied to purchase paid-up additions and annuities | | 153 76 |
| Dividends left with the company to accumulate at interest | | 496 92 |
| (Total paid policyholders | $12,724 81) | |
| Commissions to agents, first year, $30,973.68; renewal, $4,001.50 | | 34,975 18 |
| Compensation of managers and agents not paid by commissions on new business | | 8,711 78 |
| Agency supervision and traveling expenses of supervisors | | 4,362 31 |
| Branch office expenses | | 320 00 |
| Medical examiners' fees and inspection of risks | | 3,419 00 |
| Salaries and all other compensation of officers and home office employees | | 21,072 98 |
| Rent | | 1,800 00 |
| Advertising, printing, stationery, postage, telegraph, telephone, express and exchange | | 5,905 20 |
| Legal expense | | 266 65 |
| Furniture, fixtures and safes | | 1,380 97 |
| Insurance department licenses and fees | | 721 24 |
| Federal taxes | | 1,724 00 |
| All other licenses, fees and taxes | | 2,885 98 |
| Other disbursements, viz: Decrease in premium suspense, $29.21; miscellaneous, $555.88; office supplies, $2,009.79; home office traveling expense, $514.12; investment expenses, $65.00; agency meetings, $2,525.66; association fees, $650.00; commissions on capital stock sales, $9,962.05 | | 16,311 71 |
| Borrowed money repaid (gross) | | 15,000 00 |
| Interest on borrowed money | | 371 59 |
| Total disbursements | | $131,953 40 |
| Balance | | $471,460 61 |

LEDGER ASSETS.

| | |
|---|---|
| Mortgage loans on real estate | $217,500 00 |
| Loans on company's policies assigned as collateral | 1,287 52 |
| Premium notes on policies in force | 48,624 91 |
| Book value of bonds | 41,900 00 |
| Cash in office | 16,130 48 |
| Deposits in trust companies and banks not on interest | 32,322 10 |
| Deposits in trust companies and banks on interest | 24,275 00 |
| Bills receivable | 4,783 28 |
| Agents' balances (debit $21,332.34; credit, $1,614.52) | 19,717 82 |
| Stockholders' notes | 64,919 50 |
| Total ledger assets | $471,460 61 |

NON-LEDGER ASSETS.

| | | | |
|---|---|---|---|
| Interest accrued on mortgages | | $5,208 85 | |
| Interest accrued on bonds | | 338 17 | |
| Interest accrued on premium notes, loans or liens | | 1,266 30 | |
| Interest accrued on other assets | | 315 43 | |
| | | | 7,128 75 |
| | New business. | Renewals. | |
| Net uncollected and deferred premiums (paid for basis) | —$352 15 | $10,028 13 | 9,675 98 |
| Gross assets | | | $488,265 34 |

DEDUCT ASSETS NOT ADMITTED.

| | | |
|---|---|---|
| Agents' debit balances | $21,332 34 | |
| Bills receivable | 4,783 28 | |
| Premium notes, policy loans and other policy assets in excess of net value and of other policy liabilities on individual policies | 16,054 69 | |
| Book value of bonds over market value | 1,123 00 | |
| Stockholders' notes | 64,919 50 | |
| Total | | 108,212 81 |
| Admitted assets | | $380,052 53 |

## LIABILITIES.

| | | |
|---|---|---|
| Net present value of outstanding policies computed by the Illinois Insurance Department | $123,882 00 | |
| Same for dividend additions | 131 00 | |
| Total | $124,013 00 | |
| Deduct net value of risks re-insured | 6,118 00 | |
| Net reserve (paid for basis) | | $117,895 00 |
| Extra reserve for total and permanent disability benefits and for additional accidental death benefits included in life policies, less re-insurance | | 3,894 00 |
| Dividends left with the company to accumulate at interest | | 505 62 |
| Gross premiums paid in advance, including surrender values so applied, less discount, if any | | 295 49 |
| Unearned interest and rent paid in advance | | 52 23 |
| Commissions due agents on premium notes, when paid | | 12,075 50 |
| Salaries, rents, office expenses, bills and accounts due or accrued | | 4,406 52 |
| Medical examiners' fees due or accrued | | 248 00 |
| Estimated amount hereafter payable for federal, state and other taxes based upon the business of the year of this statement | | 1,954 03 |
| Dividends or other profits due policyholders | | 851 92 |
| Dividends declared on or apportioned to annual dividend policies payable to policyholders during 1922 for period to June 30, 1922 | | 3,986 00 |
| Premium suspense account | | 181 01 |
| Total | | $146,345 32 |
| Capital paid up | | 177,853 50 |
| Unassigned funds (surplus) | | 55,853 71 |
| Total | | $380,052 53 |

## EXHIBIT OF POLICIES—ORDINARY.

ALL BUSINESS PAID FOR.

| | Number. | Amount. | Number. | Amount. |
|---|---|---|---|---|
| Policies in force December 31, 1920 | | | 2,620 | $5,591,500 00 |
| Policies issued, revived and increased during the year | | | 850 | 2,035,212 00 |
| Total | | | 3,470 | $7,626,712 00 |
| Deduct policies which have ceased to be in force during the year— | | | | |
| By death | 8 | $ 9,000 00 | | |
| By surrender | 1 | 10,000 00 | | |
| By lapse | 718 | 1,515,500 00 | | |
| By decrease | -------- | 31,449 00 | | |
| Total | | | 727 | 1,565,949 00 |
| Total policies in force December 31, 1921 | | | 2,743 | $6,060,763 00 |
| Re-insured | | | -------- | $1,067,875 00 |

## BUSINESS IN ILLINOIS—ORDINARY.

| | Number. | Amount. |
|---|---|---|
| Policies in force December 31, 1920 | 2,620 | $5,591,500 00 |
| Policies issued during the year | 850 | 2,035,212 00 |
| Total | 3,470 | $7,626,712 00 |
| Deduct policies ceased to be in force | 727 | 1,565,949 00 |
| Policies in force December 31, 1921 | 2,743 | $6,060,763 00 |
| Losses and claims incurred during the year | 8 | $9,000 00 |
| Losses and claims settled during the year | 8 | 9,000 00 |
| Premiums received | | $147,578 74 |

## GAIN AND LOSS EXHIBIT.

INSURANCE EXHIBIT.

| | | Gain in surplus. | Loss in surplus. |
|---|---|---|---|
| Loading on actual premiums of the year (averaging 34.23 per cent of the gross premiums) | $51,278 93 | | |
| Insurance expenses incurred during the year | 94,531 58 | | |
| Loss from loading | | ------------- | $43,252 65 |
| Interest earned during the year | $22,503 01 | | |
| Investment expenses incurred during the year | —263 91 | | |
| Net income from investments | $22,766 92 | | |
| Interest required to maintain reserve | 3,977 00 | | |
| Gain from interest | | $18,789 92 | |

## GAIN AND LOSS EXHIBIT—Concluded.

INSURANCE EXHIBIT.

| | | Gain in surplus. | Loss in surplus. |
|---|---|---|---|
| Expected mortality on net amount at risk | $44,770 00 | | |
| Actual mortality on net amount at risk | 8,935 33 | | |
| Gain from mortality | | $35,834 67 | |
| Total gain during the year from surrendered and lapsed policies | | 7,775 53 | |
| Decrease in surplus on dividend account | | | $7,082 19 |
| Net to loss account | | | 1,353 40 |

INVESTMENT EXHIBIT.

| | | Gain in surplus. | Loss in surplus. |
|---|---|---|---|
| Total gains from bonds | | 5,119 00 | |
| Loss from assets not admitted | | | 17,348 57 |
| Net gain on account of total and permanent disability benefits or additional accidental death benefits included in life policies | | 372 05 | |
| Net gain from capital stock sales | | 30,858 28 | |
| Balance unaccounted for | | 336 45 | |
| Total gains and losses in surplus during the year | | $99,085 90 | $69,036 81 |
| Surplus December 31, 1920 | $25,804 62 | | |
| Surplus December 31, 1921 | 55,853 71 | | |
| Increase in surplus | | | 30,049 09 |
| Total | | $99,085 90 | $99,085 90 |

## SCHEDULE D—PART 1—BONDS.

| Description. | Book value. | Par value. | Market value. |
|---|---|---|---|
| U. S., 1st Liberty Loan, converted, 4¼s, 1947 | $ 1,050 00 | $ 1,050 00 | $ 1,019 00 |
| U. S., 2d Liberty Loan, convertible, 4s, 1942 | 450 00 | 450 00 | 432 00 |
| U. S., 2d Liberty Loan, converted, 4¼s, 1942 | 5,600 00 | 5,600 00 | 5,432 00 |
| U. S., 3d Liberty Loan, 4¼s, 1928 | 4,750 00 | 4,750 00 | 4,655 00 |
| U. S., 4th Liberty Loan, 4¼s, 1938 | 27,050 00 | 27,050 00 | 26,239 00 |
| U. S. Victory Liberty Loan, 4¾s, 1923 | 3,000 00 | 3,000 00 | 3,000 00 |
| Totals | $41,900 00 | $41,900 00 | $40,777 00 |

---

# MUTUAL TRUST LIFE INSURANCE COMPANY.

Located at No. 30 North LaSalle Street, Chicago, Illinois; commenced business December 24, 1904.

EDWIN A. OLSON, President. A. B. SLATTENGREN, Secretary.

| | | | |
|---|---|---|---|
| Amount of ledger assets December 31, of previous year | | | $5,688,011 27 |

## INCOME.

| | | | |
|---|---|---|---|
| First year's premiums on original policies, less re-insurance | | $447,515 99 | |
| First year's premiums for total and permanent disability benefits, less re-insurance | | 10,611 04 | |
| First year's premiums for additional accidental death benefits, less re-insurance | | 9,208 49 | |
| Dividends applied to purchase paid-up additions and annuities | | 1,627 87 | |
| New premiums | | $ 468,963 39 | |
| Renewal premiums less re-insurance | $1,785,901 82 | | |
| Renewal premiums for total and permanent disability benefits, less re-insurance | 23,983 37 | | |
| Renewal premiums for additional accidental death benefits, less re-insurance | 12,462 28 | | |
| Dividends applied to pay renewal premiums | 91,830 18 | | |
| Surrender values applied to pay renewal premiums | 537 71 | | |
| Renewal premiums | | 1,914,715 36 | |
| Premium income | | | $2,383,678 75 |
| Dividends left with company to accumulate at interest | | | 35,865 89 |
| Interest on mortgage loans | | $192,524 93 | |
| Interest on bonds | | 61,517 67 | |
| Interest on premium notes, policy loans or liens | | 39,648 77 | |
| Interest on deposits | | 5,224 09 | |
| Interest on other debts due the company | | 3,383 36 | |
| Total interest | | | 302,298 82 |
| Commissions on loans | | | 5,081 74 |
| Profit on sale or maturity of ledger assets | | | 984 52 |
| Total income | | | $2,727,909 72 |
| Total | | | $8,415,920 99 |

## DISBURSEMENTS.

| | | |
|---|---|---|
| Death claims and additions | $368,296 49 | |
| Matured endowments and additions | 21,109 00 | |
| Total and permanent disability claims and additional accidental death benefits | 3,804 13 | |
| Total death claims and endowments | | $393,209 62 |
| Annuities involving life contingencies | | 9 52 |
| Surrender values paid in cash, or applied in liquidation of loans or notes | | 101,680 42 |
| Surrender values applied to pay new and renewal premiums | | 537 71 |
| Dividends paid policyholders in cash, or applied in liquidation of loans or notes | | 9,900 32 |
| Dividends applied to pay renewal premiums | | 91,830 18 |
| Dividends applied to purchase paid-up additions and annuities | | 1,627 87 |
| Dividends left with the company to accumulate at interest | | 35,865 89 |
| (Total paid policyholders | $634,661 53) | |
| Supplementary contracts not involving life contingencies | | 240 00 |
| Dividends with interest, held on deposit surrendered during the year | | 15,071 41 |
| Commissions to agents, first year, $248,693.12; renewal, $100,456.85 | | 349,149 97 |
| Compensation of managers and agents not paid by commissions on new business | | 13,251 04 |
| Agency supervision and traveling expenses of supervisors | | 12,331 27 |
| Branch office expenses | | 8,919 03 |
| Medical examiners' fees and inspection of risks | | 34,482 04 |
| Salaries and all other compensation of officers and home office employees | | 117,128 42 |
| Rent | | 14,488 72 |
| Advertising, printing, stationery, postage, telegraph, telephone, express and exchange | | 38,917 20 |
| Legal expense | | 1,892 96 |
| Furniture, fixtures and safes | | 9,859 44 |
| Taxes on real estate | | 464 04 |
| State taxes on premiums | | 33,887 44 |
| Insurance department licenses and fees | | 8,501 25 |
| Federal taxes | | 12,065 72 |
| All other licenses, fees and taxes | | 1,355 30 |
| Other disbursements, viz: Auditor, $300.00; bonds, $532.81; books and subscriptions, $924.98; collections, $1,711.62; lights, $799.98; miscellaneous, $2,145.62; investment expenses, $1,171.57 | | 7,586 58 |
| Agents' balances charged off | | 961 53 |
| Loss on sale or maturity of ledger assets | | 690 17 |
| Total disbursements | | $1,315,905 06 |
| Balance | | $7,100,015 93 |

## LEDGER ASSETS.

| | |
|---|---|
| Book value of real estate | $ 6,803 90 |
| Certificate of sale | 9,133 88 |
| Mortgage loans on real estate | 4,707,063 46 |
| Loans on company's policies assigned as collateral | 729,079 94 |
| Premium notes on policies in force | 90,821 13 |
| Book value of bonds | 1,276,057 00 |
| Cash in office | 4,923 85 |
| Deposits in trust companies and banks not on interest | 53,760 14 |
| Deposits in trust companies and banks on interest | 146,444 44 |
| Agents' balances (debit, $63,473.80; credit, $5,108.52) | 58,365 28 |
| War savings stamps, $1,023.20; all others, $16,539.71 | 17,562 91 |
| Total ledger assets | $7,100,015 93 |

### NON-LEDGER ASSETS.

| | | | |
|---|---|---|---|
| Interest due and accrued on mortgages | | $150,984 06 | |
| Interest due and accrued on bonds | | 19,009 22 | |
| Interest due and accrued on premium notes, loans or liens | | 3,323 99 | |
| Interest due and accrued on other assets | | 1,174 93 | |
| | | | 174,492 20 |
| Market value of bonds over book value | | | 6,611 57 |
| | New business. | Renewals. | |
| Net uncollected and deferred premiums (paid for basis) | $23,844 78 | $277,306 06 | 301,150 84 |
| Gross assets | | | $7,582,270 54 |

### DEDUCT ASSETS NOT ADMITTED.

| | | |
|---|---|---|
| Agents' debit balances | $63,473 80 | |
| Premium notes, policy loans and other policy assets in excess of net value and of other policy liabilities on individual policies | 4,929 86 | |
| School warrants, $430.49; and accrued interest thereon, $5.46 | 435 95 | |
| Certificates of deposit | 64 14 | |
| Deposits in banks in receivers hands | 2,825 04 | |
| Total | | 71,728 79 |
| Admitted assets | | $7,510,541 75 |

## LIABILITIES.

| | | |
|---|---|---|
| Net present value of outstanding policies computed by the Illinois Insurance Department | $6,344,939 00 | |
| Same for dividend additions | 6,505 00 | |
| Same for annuities | 50 00 | |
| Total | $6,351,494 00 | |
| Deduct net value of risks re-insured | 26,927 00 | |
| Net reserve (paid for basis) | | $6,324,567 00 |
| Extra reserve for total and permanent disability benefits and for additional accidental death benefits included in life policies | | 126,770 00 |
| Present value of supplementary contracts not involving life contingencies | | 3,100 00 |
| Present value of amounts incurred but not yet due for total and permanent disability benefits | | 9,000 00 |
| Surrender values claimable on policies cancelled | | 322 92 |
| Death losses in process of adjustment | $ 3,376 59 | |
| Death losses reported for which no proofs have been received | 11,567 05 | |
| Reserve for net death losses incurred but unreported | 6,755 30 | |
| Matured endowments due and unpaid | 1,758 00 | |
| Total and permanent disability benefits and for additional accidental death benefits | 25 00 | |
| Total policy claims | | 23,481 94 |
| Dividends left with the company to accumulate at interest | | 116,026 67 |
| Gross premiums paid in advance, including surrender values so applied, less discount, if any | | 9,062 87 |
| Unearned interest and rent paid in advance | | 13,269 14 |
| Cost of collection on uncollected and deferred premiums in excess of loading | | 9,000 00 |
| Salaries, rents, office expenses, bills and accounts due or accrued | | 8,413 15 |
| Medical examiners fees | | 4,864 50 |
| Estimated amount hereafter payable for federal, state and other taxes based upon the business of the year of this statement | | 50,000 00 |
| Dividends or other profits due policyholders | | 21,087 12 |
| Dividends declared on or apportioned to annual dividend policies payable to policyholders during 1922 for period to April 30, 1922 | | 87,475 02 |
| Dividends declared on or apportioned to deferred dividend policies payable to policyholders during 1922 for period to December 31, 1922 | | 2,808 10 |
| Amounts set apart, apportioned, provisionally ascertained, calculated, declared or held awaiting apportionment upon deferred dividend policies | | 66,968 80 |
| Total | | $6,876,217 23 |
| Unassigned funds (surplus) | | 634,324 52 |
| Total | | $7,510,541 75 |

## EXHIBIT OF POLICIES—ORDINARY.

ALL BUSINESS PAID FOR.

| | Number. | Amount. | Number. | Amount. |
|---|---|---|---|---|
| Policies in force December 31, 1920 | | | 38,532 | $66,175,685 00 |
| Policies issued, revived and increased during the year | | | 6,385 | 14,574,905 00 |
| Total | | | 44,917 | $80,750,590 00 |
| Deduct policies which have ceased to be in force during the year— | | | | |
| By death | 261 | $ 359,259 00 | | |
| By maturity | 21 | 22,565 00 | | |
| By expiry | 80 | 145,031 00 | | |
| By surrender | 482 | 878,079 00 | | |
| By lapse | 3,533 | 9,017,935 00 | | |
| By decrease | -------- | 634,512 00 | | |
| Total | | | 4,377 | 11,057,381 00 |
| Total policies in force December 31, 1921 | | | 40,540 | $69,693,209 00 |
| Re-insured | | | 342 | $2,785,333 00 |

## BUSINESS IN ILLINOIS—ORDINARY.

| | Number. | Amount. |
|---|---|---|
| Policies in force December 31, 1920 | 11,117 | $17,146,576 00 |
| Policies issued during the year | 1,303 | 2,988,588 00 |
| Total | 12,420 | $20,135,164 00 |
| Deduct policies ceased to be in force | 742 | 1,735,722 00 |
| Policies in force December 31, 1921 | 11,678 | $18,399,442 00 |

BUSINESS IN ILLINOIS—ORDINARY—Concluded.

| | Number. | Amount. |
|---|---|---|
| Losses and claims unpaid December 31, 1920 | 13 | $ 11,977 00 |
| Losses and claims incurred during the year | 118 | 148,011 00 |
| Total | 131 | $159,988 00 |
| Losses and claims settled during the year | 124 | 154,865 00 |
| Losses and claims unpaid December 31, 1921 | 7 | $5,123 00 |
| Premiums received | | $667,544 13 |

## GAIN AND LOSS EXHIBIT.

INSURANCE EXHIBIT.

| | | Gain in surplus. | Loss in surplus. |
|---|---|---|---|
| Loading on actual premiums of the year (averaging 19 per cent of the gross premiums) | $457,726 66 | | |
| Insurance expenses incurred during the year | 697,602 52 | | |
| Loss from loading | | | $239,875 86 |
| Interest earned during the year | $366,629 47 | | |
| Investment expenses incurred during the year | 1,635 61 | | |
| Net income from investments | $364,993 86 | | |
| Interest required to maintain reserve | 212,777 13 | | |
| Gain from interest | | $152,216 73 | |
| Expected mortality on net amount at risk | $731,547 84 | | |
| Actual mortality on net amount at risk | 326,614 58 | | |
| Gain from mortality | | 404,933 26 | |
| Expected disbursements to annuitants | $9 52 | | |
| Net actual annuity claims incurred | 9 52 | | |
| Total gain during the year from surrendered and lapsed policies | | 150,852 67 | |
| Decrease in surplus on dividend account | | | 207,728 85 |
| Net to loss account | | | 961 53 |

INVESTMENT EXHIBIT.

| | | Gain in surplus. | Loss in surplus. |
|---|---|---|---|
| Total losses from real estate | | | 51 69 |
| Total gains from bonds | | 43,386 32 | |
| Total losses from bonds | | | 638 48 |
| Gain from commission on loans | | 5,081 74 | |
| Loss on account of school warrants deducted as not admitted | | | 430 49 |
| Loss from assets not admitted | | | 20,950 56 |
| Net gain on account of total and permanent disability benefits or additional accidental death benefits included in life policies | | 4,225 61 | |
| Loss: Tabular shortage in assessment net premiums | | | 27,042 00 |
| Balance unaccounted for loss | | | 222 36 |
| Total gains and losses in surplus during the year | | $760,696 33 | $497,901 82 |
| Surplus December 31, 1920 | $371,530 01 | | |
| Surplus December 31, 1921 | 634,324 52 | | |
| Increase in surplus | | | 262,794 51 |
| Total | | $760,696 33 | $760,696 33 |

## SCHEDULE D—PART 1—BONDS.

| Description. | Book value. | Par value. | Market value. |
|---|---|---|---|
| U. S. First Liberty Loan, 3½s, 1947 | $ 15,599 50 | $ 15,600 00 | $ 15,599 50 |
| U. S. First Liberty Loan (converted), 4¼s, 1947 | 1,629 12 | 1,700 00 | 1,649 00 |
| U. S. Second Liberty Loan (converted), 4¼s, 1942 | 24,175 07 | 24,500 00 | 24,175 07 |
| U. S. Third Liberty Loan, 4¼s, 1928 | 103,900 40 | 112,600 00 | 110,348 00 |
| U. S. Fourth Liberty Loan, 4¼s, 1938 | 449,464 03 | 490,600 00 | 475,882 00 |
| U. S. Victory Liberty Loan, 3¾s, 1923 | 240 35 | 250 00 | 250 00 |
| U. S. Victory Liberty Loan, 4¾s, 1923 | 73,232 55 | 73,350 00 | 73,350 00 |
| City of Aberdeen, S. D., Sewer, 4½s, 1935 | 14,790 00 | 15,000 00 | 14,250 00 |
| City of Aberdeen, S. D., Sewer, 4½s, 1936 | 4,927 00 | 5,000 00 | 4,750 00 |
| City of Aberdeen, S. D., Sewer, 4½s, 1937 | 4,924 00 | 5,000 00 | 4,750 00 |
| City of Blackfoot, Idaho, Waterworks, 6s, 1941 | 5,000 00 | 5,000 00 | 5,300 00 |
| Borah Drainage Dist., Wayne Co., Ill., 6s, 1922 | 5,650 97 | 5,500 00 | 5,500 00 |
| Borah Drainage Dist., Wayne Co., Ill., 6s, 1924 | 1,033 85 | 1,000 00 | 1,000 00 |
| Bruning, Neb., Waterworks, 5½s, 1943 | 1,000 00 | 1,000 00 | 1,000 00 |
| Chadron, Neb., School Dist., 6s, 1940 | 9,975 00 | 10,000 00 | 10,700 00 |
| Clatsop Co., Ore., School Dist., 5s, 1934 | 5,000 00 | 5,000 00 | 5,000 00 |
| Cook Co., Ill., Forest Preserve Dist., 4s, 1929 | 960 00 | 1,000 00 | 970 00 |
| Cook Co., Ill., Forest Preserve Dist., 4s, 1933 | 3,720 00 | 4,000 00 | 3,840 00 |
| Cook Co., Ill., Forest Preserve Dist., 4s, 1934 | 5,580 00 | 6,000 00 | 5,700 00 |
| Dallas, Tex., (School Improvement), 5s, 1936 | 9,478 00 | 10,000 00 | 10,300 00 |
| Decatur Co., Tenn., Highway, 5s, 1956 | 995 00 | 1,000 00 | 980 00 |

SCHEDULE D—PART 1—BONDS—Continued.

| Description. | Book value. | Par value. | Market value. |
|---|---|---|---|
| Decatur Co., Tenn., Highway, 5s, 1957 | $ 2,985 00 | $ 3,000 00 | $ 2,940 00 |
| Decatur Co., Tenn., Highway, 5s, 1958 | 2,985 00 | 3,000 00 | 2,940 00 |
| Decatur Co., Tenn., Highway, 5s, 1959 | 2,985 00 | 3,000 00 | 2,940 00 |
| Des Moines Co., Iowa, Drainage, 5½s, 1924 | 10,000 00 | 10,000 00 | 10,200 00 |
| City of Duluth, Minn., Park, 4s, 1939 | 5,000 00 | 5,000 00 | 4,700 00 |
| County of Denton, Tex., Road, 5s, 1949 | 24,875 00 | 25,000 00 | 25,000 00 |
| County of Duval, Tex., Court House, 6s, 1926 | 2,090 00 | 2,000 00 | 2,080 00 |
| County of Duval, Tex., Court House, 6s, 1927 | 3,135 00 | 3,000 00 | 3,150 00 |
| County of Duval, Tex., Court House, 6s, 1928 | 3,135 00 | 3,000 00 | 3,150 00 |
| County of Duval, Tex., Court House, 6s, 1929 | 1,045 00 | 1,000 00 | 1,060 00 |
| City of Grand Junction, Colo., Water, 5s, 1926 | 5,000 00 | 5,000 00 | 5,000 00 |
| Hartwell Drainage and Levee Dist., Green Co., Ill., 6s, 1926 | 5,150 00 | 5,000 00 | 5,100 00 |
| City of Houston, Tex., Waterworks, 5s, 1946 | 4,000 00 | 4,000 00 | 4,160 00 |
| City of Houston, Tex., Wharf, 4½s, 1935 | 2,917 50 | 3,000 00 | 2,940 00 |
| City of Houston, Tex., Wharf, 4½s, 1943 | 962 50 | 1,000 00 | 970 00 |
| City of Houston, Tex., Wharf, 4½s, 1949 | 1,920 00 | 2,000 00 | 1,920 00 |
| City of Houston, Tex., Wharf, 4½s, 1955 | 1,910 00 | 2,000 00 | 1,920 00 |
| City of Houston, Tex., Wharf, 4½s, 1957 | 955 00 | 1,000 00 | 960 00 |
| City of Houston, Tex., Wharf, 5s, 1925 | 7,500 00 | 7,500 00 | 7,575 00 |
| Illinois School Dist., Bureau Co., 5s, 1926 | 1,558 20 | 1,500 00 | 1,530 00 |
| Illinois School Dist., Bureau Co., 5s, 1927 | 1,558 20 | 1,500 00 | 1,530 00 |
| Illinois School Dist., Bureau Co., 5s, 1928 | 1,558 20 | 1,500 00 | 1,530 00 |
| Illinois School Dist., Bureau Co., 5s, 1929 | 519 40 | 500 00 | 510 00 |
| City of Jackson, Tenn., R. R. Refunding, 5s, 1929 | 5,000 00 | 5,000 00 | 5,000 00 |
| Jefferson Co., Tex., Road, Dist. No. 1, 5s, 1932 | 8,000 00 | 8,000 00 | 8,000 00 |
| Jefferson Co., Tex., Road, Dist. No. 1, 5s, 1943 | 9,500 00 | 9,500 00 | 9,500 00 |
| Jefferson Co., Tex., Road, Dist. No. 1, 5s, 1948 | 15,500 00 | 15,500 00 | 15,500 00 |
| County of Koochiching, Minn., Public Drainage Ditch, 4½s, 1932 | 9,563 00 | 10,000 00 | 9,600 00 |
| County of Lamar, Tex., Road, 5s, 1947 | 10,000 00 | 10,000 00 | 10,000 00 |
| Little Rock-Hot Springs, Ark., Highway Dist., 5s, 1939 | 14,981 25 | 15,000 00 | 15,150 00 |
| State of Louisiana, Ports Com., Har. Imp., 5s, 1941 | 4,987 50 | 5,000 00 | 5,000 00 |
| State of Louisiana, Ports Com., Serial Canal, 5s, 1945 | 4,993 75 | 5,000 00 | 5,000 00 |
| State of Louisiana, Ports Com., Serial Canal, 5s, 1950 | 4,993 75 | 5,000 00 | 5,000 00 |
| City of Memphis, Tenn., 5s, 1953 | 2,140 00 | 2,000 00 | 2,040 00 |
| Mishawaka, Ind., School, City of, 5s, 1928 | 8,910 00 | 9,000 00 | 9,270 00 |
| Mishawaka, Ind., School, City of, 5s, 1929 | 990 00 | 1,000 00 | 1,030 00 |
| Monroe Co., Tenn., Road, 5½s, 1926 | 7,156 80 | 7,000 00 | 7,140 00 |
| Monroe Co., Tenn., Road, 5½s, 1927 | 3,075 30 | 3,000 00 | 3,060 00 |
| Morenci School Dist. No. 18, Greenlee Co., Ariz., 5½s, 1930 | 2,067 45 | 2,000 00 | 2,060 00 |
| Morenci School Dist. No. 18, Greenlee Co., Ariz., 5½s, 1931 | 4,134 90 | 4,000 00 | 4,120 00 |
| Morenci School Dist. No. 18, Greenlee Co., Ariz., 5½s, 1932 | 2,067 44 | 2,000 00 | 2,060 00 |
| Morenci School Dist. No. 18, Greenlee Co., Ariz., 5½s, 1934 | 2,067 44 | 2,000 00 | 2,060 00 |
| City of Muscatine, Iowa, City Hall, 5s, 1927 | 1,020 00 | 1,000 00 | 1,020 00 |
| City of Muscatine, Iowa, City Hall, 5s, 1928 | 6,120 00 | 6,000 00 | 6,120 00 |
| City of Muscatine, Iowa, City Hall, 5s, 1929 | 6,120 00 | 6,000 00 | 6,120 00 |
| City of Muscatine, Iowa, City Hall, 5s, 1930 | 6,120 00 | 6,000 00 | 6,180 00 |
| City of Muscatine, Iowa, City Hall, 5s, 1931 | 6,120 00 | 6,000 00 | 6,180 00 |
| McMullen Co., Tex., Bridge Warrants, 6s, 1938 | 1,070 35 | 1,000 00 | 1,000 00 |
| McMullen Co., Tex., Bridge Warrants, 6s, 1939 | 535 17 | 500 00 | 500 00 |
| McMullen Co., Tex., Bridge Warrants, 6s, 1940 | 1,070 35 | 1,000 00 | 1,000 00 |
| McMullen Co., Tex., Bridge Warrants, 2d series, 6s, 1938 | 1,070 35 | 1,000 00 | 1,000 00 |
| McMullen Co., Tex., Bridge Warrants, 2d series, 6s, 1939 | 1,070 35 | 1,000 00 | 1,000 00 |
| McMullen Co., Tex., Bridge Warrants, 2d series, 6s, 1940 | 1,070 36 | 1,000 00 | 1,000 00 |
| City of Paris, Tenn., Waterworks and School, 5s, 1947 | 4,975 00 | 5,000 00 | 4,900 00 |
| County of Pueblo, Colo., Refund. School Dist., 4½s, 1931 | 14,550 00 | 15,000 00 | 14,550 00 |
| City of Seattle, Wash., Ry. Extension, 5s, 1934 | 7,960 00 | 8,000 00 | 8,080 00 |
| City of Seattle, Wash., Ry. Extension, 5s, 1939 | 4,975 00 | 5,000 00 | 5,050 00 |
| City of Seattle, Wash., Municipal Light and Power Plant, 5s, 1931 | 4,875 00 | 5,000 00 | 5,050 00 |
| Port of Seattle, Salmon Bay Improvement, 4½s, 1935 | 7,678 40 | 8,000 00 | 7,680 00 |
| Port of Seattle, Central Water Front, 4½s, 1935 | 3,839 20 | 4,000 00 | 3,840 00 |
| Port of Seattle, East Waterway, 4½s, 1935 | 959 80 | 1,000 00 | 960 00 |
| Port of Seattle, Smith's Cove, 4½s, 1939 | 4,818 50 | 5,000 00 | 4,800 00 |
| Port of Seattle, Central Water Front, 4½s, 1939 | 4,818 50 | 5,000 00 | 4,800 00 |
| State of South Dakota, 6s, 1929 | 10,189 00 | 10,000 00 | 10,800 00 |
| State of South Dakota, (Soldiers' Compensation) 6s, 1941 | 10,478 00 | 10,000 00 | 11,600 00 |
| Tarrant Co., Tex., Wash. Heights, Ind., School Dist., 5s, 1958 | 9,950 00 | 10,000 00 | 9,800 00 |
| City of Vernon, Tex., Street, 5s, 1958 | 10,000 00 | 10,000 00 | 9,800 00 |
| Chicago City Rys. Co., 5s, 1927 | 10,000 00 | 10,000 00 | 7,100 00 |
| Chicago City Rys. Co., 5s, 1927 | 10,000 00 | 10,000 00 | 7,100 00 |
| Ft. Dodge, Des Moines & Southern R. R., 5s, 1938 | 4,700 00 | 5,000 00 | 3,150 00 |
| Interborough Rapid Transit Co., 5s, 1966 | 9,950 00 | 10,000 00 | 5,800 00 |
| Iowa Ry. & Light Co., 5s, 1932 | 9,500 00 | 10,000 00 | 8,300 00 |
| Madison, Wis., Ry. Co., 5s, 1936 | 9,650 00 | 10,000 00 | 7,000 00 |
| Northwestern Elevated R. R. Co., 5s, 1941 | 4,525 00 | 5,000 00 | 3,250 00 |
| Allied Packers, Inc., 6s, 1939 | 9,750 00 | 10,000 00 | 6,500 00 |
| Armour and Co., 4½s, 1939 | 4,650 00 | 5,000 00 | 4,350 00 |
| Consumers Power Co. of Michigan, 5s, 1936 | 9,750 00 | 10,000 00 | 9,000 00 |

SCHEDULE D—PART 1—BONDS—Concluded.

| Description. | Book value. | Par value. | Market value. |
|---|---|---|---|
| Consumers Power Co. of Michigan, 5s, 1936 | $ 4,800 00 | $ 5,000 00 | $ 4,500 00 |
| Consumers Power Co. of Michigan, 5s, 1936 | 4,875 00 | 5,000 00 | 4,500 00 |
| Commonwealth Edison Co. of Illinois, 5s, 1943 | 15,000 00 | 15,000 00 | 14,100 00 |
| Commonwealth Edison Co. of Illinois, 5s, 1943 | 5,000 00 | 5,000 00 | 4,700 00 |
| Commonwealth Edison Co. of Illinois, 5s, 1943 | 5,000 00 | 5,000 00 | 4,700 00 |
| Oklahoma Gas & Electric Co., 5s, 1929 | 9,800 00 | 10,000 00 | 9,200 00 |
| Oklahoma Gas & Electric, 8s, 1931 | 4,806 25 | 5,000 00 | 5,000 00 |
| Pacific Gas & Electric Co., of California, 5s, 1942 | 4,625 00 | 5,000 00 | 4,450 00 |
| Peoples Gas Light & Coke Co. of Chicago, 5s, 1947 | 10,000 00 | 10,000 00 | 8,700 00 |
| Public Service Co. of Northern Illinois, 5s, 1956 | 9,025 00 | 10,000 00 | 8,600 00 |
| Seattle Lighting Co., 5s, 1949 | 9,500 00 | 10,000 00 | 8,100 00 |
| Swift and Co., 5s, 1944 | 4,800 00 | 5,000 00 | 4,650 00 |
| United Fuel Gas Co., S. F. Series "A", 6s, 1936 | 9,900 00 | 10,000 00 | 9,500 00 |
| Wisconsin-Minn. Light & Power Co., La Crosse, Wis., 5s, 1944 | 9,750 00 | 10,000 00 | 7,900 00 |
| Total | $1,276,057 00 | $1,333,100 00 | $1,282,668 57 |

## NATIONAL LIFE INSURANCE COMPANY OF THE UNITED STATES OF AMERICA.

Located at No. 29 South LaSalle Street, Chicago, Illinois; incorporated under federal laws, July 25, 1868; re-incorporated under the laws of Illinois, March 2, 1904; commenced business, life, August 1, 1868; casualty, August 17, 1911.

ALBERT M. JOHNSON, President. ROBERT D. LAY, Secretary.

### CAPITAL.

| | | | |
|---|---|---|---|
| Capital paid up | | $500,000 00 | |
| Amount of ledger assets December 31, of previous year | | | $18,776,231 19 |

### INCOME.

| | | | |
|---|---|---|---|
| First year's premiums on original policies, less re-insurance | | $669,871 90 | |
| First year's premiums for total and permanent disability benefits | | 11,181 21 | |
| First year's premiums for additional accidental death benefits | | 2,907 71 | |
| Surrender values to pay first year's premiums | | 683,960 82 | |
| Dividends applied to purchase paid-up additions and annuities | | 8,050 23 | |
| Surrender values applied to purchase paid-up insurance and annuities | | 80,608 88 | |
| New premiums | | $ 772,619 93 | |
| Renewal premiums less re-insurance | $3,313,194 13 | | |
| Renewal premiums for total and permanent disability benefits, less re-insurance | 21,777 98 | | |
| Renewal premiums for additional accidental death benefits, less re-insurance | 12,599 01 | | |
| Dividends applied to pay renewal premiums | 41,431 76 | | |
| Renewal premiums | | 3,389,002 88 | |
| Premium income | | $4,161,622 81 | |
| Premiums advanced during year under Soldiers' and Sailors' Civil Relief Act | | 45 70 | |
| Total | | | $4,161,668 51 |
| Consideration for supplementary contracts involving life contingencies | | | 1,210 88 |
| Consideration for supplementary contracts not involving life contingencies | | | 31,893 05 |
| Interest on mortgage loans | | $414,456 17 | |
| Interest on bonds and dividends on stocks | | 236,040 24 | |
| Interest on premium notes, policy loans or liens | | 241,093 03 | |
| Interest on deposits | | 20,025 29 | |
| Interest on other debts due the company | | 2,325 50 | |
| Rents | | 1,301 61 | |
| Total interest and rents | | | 915,241 84 |
| From other sources, viz: Federal tax on insurance, $17,072.84; profit and loss, $41.34 | | | 17,114 18 |
| Agents' balances previously charged off | | | 430 62 |
| Profit on sale or maturity of ledger assets | | | 9,557 50 |
| Income, life department | | | $5,137,116 58 |
| Income, casualty department | | | 2,616,948 75 |
| Total income | | | $7,754,065 33 |
| Total | | | $26,530,296 52 |

## DISBURSEMENTS.

| | | |
|---|---|---|
| Death claims and additions | $928,960 83 | |
| Matured endowments and additions | 139,081 35 | |
| Total and permanent disability claims and additional accidental death benefits | 1,573 48 | |
| Total death claims and endowments | | $1,069,615 66 |
| Annuities involving life contingencies | | 26,334 06 |
| Premium notes and liens voided by lapse, less $769.69 restorations | | 8,830 90 |
| Surrender values paid in cash, or applied in liquidation of loans or notes | | 645,773 18 |
| Surrender values applied to purchase paid-up insurance and annuities | | 80,608 88 |
| Dividends paid policyholders in cash, or applied in liquidation of loans or notes | | 61,393 91 |
| Dividends applied to pay renewal premiums | | 41,431 76 |
| Dividends applied to purchase paid-up additions and annuities | | 8,050 23 |
| (Total paid policyholders | $1,942,038 58) | |
| Expense of investigation and settlement of policy claims, including legal expenses | | 5,854 22 |
| Supplementary contracts not involving life contingencies | | 16,539 25 |
| Dividends to stockholders | | 100,000 00 |
| Commissions to agents, first year, $406,838.21; renewal, $212,573.33 | | 619,411 54 |
| Compensation of managers and agents not paid by commissions on new business | | 46,944 71 |
| Agency supervision and traveling expenses of supervisors | | 10,831 05 |
| Branch office expenses | | 33,839 78 |
| Medical examiners' fees and inspection of risks | | 57,200 34 |
| Salaries and all other compensation of officers and home office employees | | 338,245 15 |
| Rent | | 40,789 84 |
| Advertising, printing, stationery, postage, telegraph, telephone, express and exchange | | 51,316 77 |
| Legal expense | | 5,752 53 |
| Furniture, fixtures and safes | | 18,201 16 |
| Taxes on real estate | | 738 71 |
| State taxes on premiums | | 67,893 62 |
| Insurance department licenses and fees | | 8,970 12 |
| Federal taxes | | 20,992 49 |
| All other licenses, fees and taxes | | 4,024 03 |
| Other disbursements, viz: Investment expense, $10,756.66; light, $934.80; periodicals, $3,007.64; Association of Life Ins. Presidents, $1,026.12; American Life Convention, $100.00; profit and loss, $97.74; miscellaneous expense, $4,346.14; cancelled checks, $16.48; insurance and fidelity bonds, $919.80 | | 21,205 38 |
| Agents' balances charged off | | 15,446 51 |
| Loss on sale or maturity of ledger assets | | 37 50 |
| Decrease in book value of ledger assets | | 36,424 99 |
| Disbursements, life department | | $3,462,698 27 |
| Disbursements, casualty department | | 2,573,887 69 |
| Total disbursements | | $6,036,585 96 |
| Balance | | $20,493,710 56 |

## LEDGER ASSETS.

| | |
|---|---|
| Book value of real estate | $ 54,424 08 |
| Mortgage loans on real estate | 8,159,026 91 |
| Premiums advanced under Soldiers' and Sailors' Civil Relief Act | 1,296 51 |
| Loans on company's policies assigned as collateral | 4,131,721 13 |
| Premium notes on policies in force | 549,882 21 |
| Book value of bonds and stocks | 6,338,199 13 |
| Cash in office | 32,783 41 |
| Deposits in trust companies and banks not on interest | 33,072 84 |
| Deposits in trust companies and banks on interest | 991,685 28 |
| Agents' balances (debit, $148,457.08; credit, $12,296.90) | 136,160 18 |
| Partial payments made on death losses that are carried for full amount in liabilities | 8,839 86 |
| Casualty department | 56,619 02 |
| Total ledger assets | $20,493,710 56 |

### NON-LEDGER ASSETS.

| | | | |
|---|---|---|---|
| Interest due and accrued on mortgages | | $356,946 89 | |
| Interest due and accrued on bonds | | 31,532 77 | |
| Interest accrued on premium notes, loans or liens | | 37,747 66 | |
| Interest accrued on deposits | | 1,594 41 | |
| | | | 427,821 73 |
| Market value of bonds and stocks over book value | | | 366,943 63 |
| Due from other companies for losses or claims on policies re-insured | | | 4,919 00 |
| | New business. | Renewals. | |
| Net uncollected and deferred premiums (paid for basis) | $7,094 03 | $395,377 73 | 402,471 76 |
| Gross assets | | | $21,695,866 68 |

### DEDUCT ASSETS NOT ADMITTED.

| | |
|---|---|
| Agents' debit balances | $148,457 08 |
| Premium notes, policy loans and other policy assets in excess of net value and of other policy liabilities on individual policies | 34,557 66 |

## LEDGER ASSETS—Concluded.

DEDUCT ASSETS NOT ADMITTED.

| | | |
|---|---|---|
| Overdue and accrued interest on bonds in default | $ 333 33 | |
| Casualty department | 43,665 93 | |
| Total | | $227,014 00 |
| Admitted assets | | $21,468,852 68 |

## LIABILITIES.

| | | |
|---|---|---|
| Net present value of outstanding policies computed by the Illinois Insurance Department | $18,853,294 11 | |
| Same for dividend additions | 11,214 00 | |
| Same for annuities | 66,238 00 | |
| Total | $18,930,746 11 | |
| Deduct net value of risks re-insured | 228,179 66 | |
| Net reserve (paid for basis) | | $18,702,566 45 |
| Extra reserve for total and permanent disability benefits and for additional accidental death benefits included in life policies, less re-insurance | | 51,674 93 |
| Present value of supplementary contracts not involving life contingencies | | 175,730 77 |
| Present value of amounts incurred but not yet due for total and permanent disability benefits | | 8,021 00 |
| Death losses in process of adjustment | $ 9,495 00 | |
| Death losses reported for which no proofs have been received | 101,887 85 | |
| Reserve for net death losses incurred but unreported | 45,000 00 | |
| Matured endowments due and unpaid | 1,974 00 | |
| Death losses and other policy claims resisted | 5,000 00 | |
| Total and permanent disability benefits and additional accidental death benefits | 1,554 84 | |
| Annuity claims, involving life contingencies, due and unpaid | 6,324 01 | |
| Total policy claims | | 171,235 70 |
| Gross premiums paid in advance, including surrender values so applied less discount, if any | | 17,326 28 |
| Unearned interest and rent paid in advance | | 97,800 62 |
| Commissions due agents on premium notes, when paid | | 6,814 73 |
| Commissions to agents due or accrued | | 10,413 05 |
| Cost of collection on uncollected and deferred premiums in excess of loading | | 3,158 76 |
| Salaries, rents, office expenses, bills and accounts due or accrued | | 15,000 00 |
| Medical examiners | | 3,509 50 |
| Estimated amount hereafter payable for federal, state and other taxes based upon the business of the year of this statement | | 184,041 09 |
| Dividends or other profits due policyholders | | 7,119 22 |
| Dividends declared on or apportioned to annual dividend policies payable fo policyholders during 1922 for period to June 30, 1922 | | 7,051 62 |
| Dividends declared on or apportioned to deferred dividend policies payable to policyholders during 1922 for period to June 30, 1922 | | 45,194 57 |
| Amounts set apart, apportioned, provisionally ascertained, calculated, declared or held awaiting apportionment upon deferred dividend policies | | 505,364 90 |
| Extra premiums for military and naval service permits | | 100 00 |
| Special depreciation reserve | | 62,181 99 |
| Casualty department | | 161,263 19 |
| Total | | $20,235,568 37 |
| Capital paid up | | 500,000 00 |
| Unassigned funds (surplus) | | 733,284 31 |
| Total | | $21,468,852 68 |

## EXHIBIT OF POLICIES—ORDINARY.

ALL BUSINESS PAID FOR.

| | Number. | Amount. | Number. | Amount. |
|---|---|---|---|---|
| Policies in force December 31, 1920 | | | 70,320 | $134,086,132 00 |
| Policies issued, revived and increased during the year | | | 9,021 | 24,486,930 00 |
| Total | | | 79,341 | $158,573,062 00 |
| Deduct policies which have ceased to be in force during the year— | | | | |
| By death | 538 | $ 958,543 00 | | |
| By maturity | 98 | 152,790 00 | | |
| By expiry | 4,846 | 11,198,616 00 | | |
| By surrender | 729 | 1,504,711 00 | | |
| By lapse | 2,859 | 7,146,118 00 | | |
| By decrease | —2 | 662,568 00 | | |
| Total | | | 9,068 | 21,623,346 00 |
| Total policies in force December 31, 1921 | | | 70,273 | $136,949,716 00 |
| Re-insured | | | 1,434 | $9,402,618 00 |

## BUSINESS IN ILLINOIS—ORDINARY.

| | Number. | Amount. |
|---|---|---|
| Policies in force December 31, 1920 | 12,090 | $27,895,258 25 |
| Policies issued during the year | 1,048 | 5,159,100 97 |
| Total | 13,138 | $33,054,359 22 |
| Deduct policies ceased to be in force | 995 | 3,847,771 35 |
| Policies in force December 31, 1921 | 12,143 | $29,206,587 87 |
| Losses and claims unpaid December 31, 1920 | 8 | $ 67,158 00 |
| Losses and claims incurred during the year | 129 | 200,857 55 |
| Total | 137 | $268,015 55 |
| Losses and claims settled during the year | 122 | 204,602 64 |
| Losses and claims unpaid December 31, 1921 | 15 | $63,412 91 |
| Premiums received | | $902,460 35 |

## GAIN AND LOSS EXHIBIT.

### INSURANCE EXHIBIT.

| | | Gain in surplus. | Loss in surplus. |
|---|---|---|---|
| Loading on actual premiums of the year (averaging 18 per cent of the gross premiums) | $ 746,890 75 | | |
| Insurance expenses incurred during the year | 1,363,783 91 | | |
| Loss from loading | | | $616,893 16 |
| Interest earned during the year | $1,005,634 25 | | |
| Investment expenses incurred during the year | 48,418 68 | | |
| Net income from investments | $957,215 57 | | |
| Interest required to maintain reserve | 682,915 10 | | |
| Gain from interest | | $274,300 47 | |
| Expected mortality on net amount at risk | $1,362,128 80 | | |
| Actual mortality on net amount at risk | 738,284 65 | | |
| Gain from mortality | | 623,844 15 | |
| Expected disbursements to annuitants | $25,258 88 | | |
| Net actual annuity claims incurred | 26,536 77 | | |
| Loss from annuities | | | 1,277 89 |
| Total gain during the year from surrendered and lapsed policies | | 83,543 21 | |
| Dividends paid stockholders | | | 100,000 00 |
| Decrease in surplus on dividend account | | | 117,625 97 |
| Increase in special funds and special reserves during the year | | | 9,911 65 |
| Net to loss account | | | 72 88 |

### INVESTMENT EXHIBIT.

| | | Gain in surplus. | Loss in surplus. |
|---|---|---|---|
| Total gains from stocks and bonds | | 77,528 91 | |
| Total losses from stocks and bonds | | | 36,462 49 |
| Loss from assets not admitted | | | 28,650 98 |
| Net gain on account of total and permanent disability benefits or additional accidental death benefits included in life policies | | 34,323 08 | |
| Gain from casualty department | | 32,135 73 | |
| Balance unaccounted for | | | 1,985 29 |
| Total gains and losses in surplus during the year | | $1,125,675 55 | $912,880 31 |
| Surplus December 31, 1920 | $520,489 07 | | |
| Surplus December 31, 1921 | 733,284 31 | | |
| Increase in surplus | | | 212,795 24 |
| Total | | $1,125,675 55 | $1,125,675 55 |

## SCHEDULE D—PART 1—BONDS.

| Description. | Book value. | Par value. | Market value. |
|---|---|---|---|
| Government Bonds— | | | |
| United States Government, 1st Liberty Loan (Orig. Sub.), 3½s, 1947 | $ 30,000 00 | $ 30,000 00 | $ 29,700 00 |
| United States Government, 1st Liberty Loan, (Purchases), 3½s, 1947 | 1,095 40 | 1,100 00 | 1,089 00 |
| United States Government, 1st Liberty Loan Conv., (Purchases), 4¼s, 1947 | 956 21 | 1,000 00 | 950 00 |
| United States Government, 2d Liberty Loan Conv. (Orig. Sub.), 4¼s, 1942 | 91,000 00 | 91,000 00 | 90,090 00 |
| United States Government, 2d Liberty Loan, (Purchases), 4¼s, 1942 | 6,671 41 | 7,100 00 | 6,603 00 |
| United States Government, 3d Liberty Loan (Orig. Sub.), 4¼s, 1928 | 198,500 00 | 198,500 00 | 196,515 00 |

SCHEDULE D—PART 1—BONDS—Continued.

| Description. | Book value. | Par value. | Market value. |
|---|---|---|---|
| United States Government, 3d Liberty Loan, (Purchases), 4¼s, 1928 | $ 17,055 74 | $ 19,250 00 | $ 18,095 00 |
| United States Government, 4th Liberty Loan (Orig. Sub.), 4¼s, 1938 | 581,650 00 | 581,650 00 | 575,833 50 |
| United States Government, 4th Liberty Loan, (Purchases), 4¼s, 1938 | 6,378 97 | 6,800 00 | 6,256 00 |
| United States Government, 5th Victory Loan, (Purchases), 4¾s, 1923 | 697 74 | 700 00 | 693 00 |
| Totals | $934,005 47 | $937,100 00 | $925,824 50 |
| State, Municipal, County and School Bonds— | | | |
| Abbeville, County of, S. C. (Road), 6s, 1941 | $ 1,944 40 | $ 2,000 00 | $ 1,944 40 |
| Abbeville, County of, S. C., (Road), 6s, 1942 | 2,914 50 | 3,000 00 | 2,914 50 |
| Alexander, County of, Ill., (Road), 5s, 1930 | 4,803 50 | 5,000 00 | 4,803 50 |
| Arkansas, State of, 6s, 1935 | 10,000 00 | 10,000 00 | 10,000 00 |
| Avoyelles, Parish of, La., (Road), 5s, 1924 | 946 70 | 1,000 00 | 946 70 |
| Avoyelles, Parish of, La., (Road), 5s, 1925 | 1,862 60 | 2,000 00 | 1,862 60 |
| Avoyelles, Parish of, La., (Road), 5s, 1926 | 1,833 60 | 2,000 00 | 1,833 60 |
| California, State of, (Highway), 5¾s, 1937 | 25,000 00 | 25,000 00 | 25,000 00 |
| Cisco, City of, Tex., (Water Works), 6s, 1941 | 9,771 00 | 10,000 00 | 9,771 00 |
| Coahoma, County of, Miss., (Road and Bridge), 4½s, 1930 | 4,846 05 | 5,500 00 | 4,846 05 |
| Cook, County of, Ill., (Court House), 4s, 1923 | 16,320 00 | 17,000 00 | 16,320 00 |
| Cook, County of, Ill., (Hospital), 4s, 1922 | 960 00 | 1,000 00 | 960 00 |
| Cook, County of, Ill., (Hospital), 4s, 1925 | 13,440 00 | 14,000 00 | 13,440 00 |
| Cook, County of, Ill., (Hospital), 4s, 1935 | 13,160 00 | 14,000 00 | 13,160 00 |
| Cook, County of, Ill., (Hospital), 4s, 1923 | 24,000 00 | 25,000 00 | 24,000 00 |
| Cook, County of, Ill., (Hospital), 4s, 1922 | 6,720 00 | 7,000 00 | 6,720 00 |
| Cook, County of, Ill., (Hospital), 4s, 1928 | 3,840 00 | 4,000 00 | 3,840 00 |
| Cook, County of, Ill., (Hospital), 4s, 1929 | 1,900 00 | 2,000 00 | 1,900 00 |
| Cook, County of, Ill., (Hospital), 4s, 1930 | 1,900 00 | 2,000 00 | 1,900 00 |
| Cook, County of, Ill., (Hospital "K"), 4s, 1923 | 2,880 00 | 3,000 00 | 2,880 00 |
| Cook, County of, Ill., (Hospital "K"), 4s, 1924 | 1,920 00 | 2,000 00 | 1,920 00 |
| Cook, County of, Ill., (Hospital "K"), 4s, 1925 | 4,800 00 | 5,000 00 | 4,800 00 |
| Cook, County of, Ill., (Hospital "K"), 4s, 1926 | 34,560 00 | 36,000 00 | 34,560 00 |
| Cook, County of, Ill., (Hospital "K"), 4s, 1927 | 47,040 00 | 49,000 00 | 47,040 00 |
| Cook, County of, Ill., (Hospital "K"), 4s, 1928 | 4,800 00 | 5,000 00 | 4,800 00 |
| Cook, County of, Ill., (Hospital "K"), 4s, 1929 | 38,400 00 | 40,000 00 | 38,400 00 |
| Cook, County of, Ill., (Hospital "K"), 4s, 1930 | 19,000 00 | 20,000 00 | 19,000 00 |
| Cook, County of, Ill., (Infirmary), 4s, 1928 | 960 00 | 1,000 00 | 960 00 |
| Cook, County of, Ill., (Infirmary "J"), 4s, 1926 | 960 00 | 1,000 00 | 960 00 |
| Cook, County of, Ill., (Infirmary "J"), 4s, 1928 | 960 00 | 1,000 00 | 960 00 |
| Cuyahoga, County of, Ohio (Road), 6s, 1925 | 4,987 50 | 5,000 00 | 4,987 50 |
| Detroit, City of, Mich., (Improvement), 5½s, 1948 | 5,000 00 | 5,000 00 | 5,000 00 |
| Dickson, County of, Tenn., (Road), 6s, 1930 | 4,913 50 | 5,000 00 | 4,913 50 |
| Eastland, County of, Tex., (Highway "C"), 5½s, 1931 | 9,437 05 | 10,000 00 | 9,437 05 |
| Floyd, County of, Iowa, (Road), 5s, 1923 | 8,756 55 | 9,000 00 | 8,756 55 |
| Grainger, County of, Tenn., (Highway), 6s, 1931 | 4,930 25 | 5,000 00 | 4,930 25 |
| Hill, County of, Tex., (Road Dist. No. 3), 5s, 1929 | 9,104 00 | 10,000 00 | 9,104 00 |
| Iron, County of, Utah, (Hospital), 6s, 1936 | 1,968 64 | 2,000 00 | 1,968 64 |
| Iron, County of, Utah, (Hospital), 6s, 1937 | 1,968 64 | 2,000 00 | 1,968 64 |
| Iron, County of, Utah, (Hospital), 6s, 1938 | 1,968 64 | 2,000 00 | 1,968 64 |
| Iron, County of, Utah, (Hospital), 6s, 1939 | 1,968 64 | 2,000 00 | 1,968 64 |
| Iron, County of, Utah, (Hospital), 6s, 1940 | 1,968 64 | 2,000 00 | 1,968 64 |
| Jackson, City of, Tenn., (General Imp.), 6s, 1930 | 9,975 00 | 10,000 00 | 9,975 00 |
| Knoxville, City of, Tenn., (Imp. and Sewer), 4½s, 1937 | 18,000 00 | 20,000 00 | 19,200 00 |
| Livingston, City of, Mont., (Water Works), 5s, 1933 | 4,560 00 | 5,000 00 | 4,560 00 |
| Memphis, City of, Tenn., (Refunding), 4½s, 1939 | 45,000 00 | 50,000 00 | 48,500 00 |
| Michigan, State of, (Soldiers Bonus), 5¼s, 1941 | 60,000 00 | 60,000 00 | 60,000 00 |
| Minneapolis, City of, Minn., (School), 5s, 1923 | 4,930 00 | 5,000 00 | 4,930 00 |
| Minnesota, State of, (Soldier's Bonus), 5s, 1926 | 3,915 20 | 4,000 00 | 3,915 20 |
| Montgomery, County of, Ohio, (Road), 6s, 1930 | 1,000 00 | 1,000 00 | 1,000 00 |
| Montgomery, County of, Ohio, (Road), 6s, 1931 | 4,000 00 | 4,000 00 | 4,000 00 |
| Nashville, City of, Tenn., (Viaduct), 5s, 1942 | 4,621 00 | 5,000 00 | 4,621 00 |
| Oakland, County of, Mich., (Road), 6s, 1926 | 3,000 00 | 3,000 00 | 3,000 00 |
| Oakland, County of, Mich., (Road), 6s, 1927 | 2,000 00 | 2,000 00 | 2,000 00 |
| Oregon, State of, (Highway), 5½s, 1929 | 9,975 00 | 10,000 00 | 9,975 00 |
| Pinal, County of, Ariz., (Road), 5½s, 1932 | 9,577 00 | 10,000 00 | 9,577 00 |
| Pocahontas, County of, Iowa, (Court House), 6s, 1929 | 5,000 00 | 5,000 00 | 5,000 00 |
| Sanders, County of, Mont., (Highway), 6s, 1935 | 1,990 00 | 2,000 00 | 1,990 00 |
| Sanders, County of, Mont., (Highway), 6s, 1936 | 2,985 00 | 3,000 00 | 2,985 00 |
| Sanders, County of, Mont., (Highway), 6s, 1937 | 4,975 00 | 5,000 00 | 4,975 00 |
| Seattle, City of, Wash., (Light and Power Plant, 6s, 1939 | 9,975 00 | 10,000 00 | 9,975 00 |
| South Dakota, State of, (Soldier's Bonus), 6s, 1941 | 5,000 00 | 5,000 00 | 5,000 00 |
| Spartanburg, County of, S. C., (Road), 5s, 1923 | 4,822 50 | 5,000 00 | 4,822 50 |
| Springfield, City of, Ill., (Light and Power Plant), 5s, 1926 | 4,846 00 | 5,000 00 | 4,846 00 |
| Sny Island Levee Drainage District, Pike County, Ill., 6s, 1922 | 6,000 00 | 6,000 00 | 6,000 00 |

SCHEDULE D—PART 1—BONDS—Concluded.

| Description. | Book value. | Par value. | Market value. |
|---|---|---|---|
| Sny Island Levee Drainage District, Pike County, Ill., 6s, 1923 | $ 6,000 00 | $ 6,000 00 | $ 6,000 00 |
| Sny Island Levee Drainage District, Pike County, Ill., 6s, 1924 | 1,000 00 | 1,000 00 | 1,000 00 |
| Sny Island Levee Drainage District, Pike County, Ill., 6s, 1925 | 4,000 00 | 4,000 00 | 4,000 00 |
| Toledo, City of, Ohio, (Sewer), 5½s, 1951 | 5,000 00 | 5,000 00 | 5,000 00 |
| Trumbull, County of, Ohio, (Highway), 6s, 1924 | 3,920 00 | 4,000 00 | 3,920 00 |
| Trumbull, County of, Ohio, (Highway), 6s, 1924 | 4,900 00 | 5,000 00 | 4,900 00 |
| Trumbull, County of, Ohio, (Highway), 6s, 1925 | 4,900 00 | 5,000 00 | 4,900 00 |
| Winnipeg, City of, Manitoba, (School District No. 1), 4s, 1933 | 36,450 00 | 45,000 00 | 36,450 00 |
| Winnipeg, City of, Manitoba, (School District No. 1), 4½s, 1929 | 34,000 00 | 40,000 00 | 35,200 00 |
| Totals | $685,731 10 | $723,500 00 | $691,631 10 |
| Railroad Bonds— | | | |
| At[illegible] Topeka & Santa Fe (Trans. Short Line), [illegible] | $18,750 00 | $25,000 00 | $20,500 00 |
| Atchison, Topeka & Santa Fe (Equip. Trust Notes), 6s, 1934 | 5,000 00 | 5,000 00 | 5,000 00 |
| Chicago City Ry. Co., (1st Mort.), 5s, 1927 | 15,000 00 | 25,000 00 | 17,000 00 |
| Chi., Rock Island & Pacific Ry. Co., (Ref.), 4s, 1934 | 16,250 00 | 25,000 00 | 18,750 00 |
| Great Northern Ry., (Gen. Mort.), 7s, 1936 | 19,200 00 | 20,000 00 | 19,200 00 |
| Interborough Rapid Transit Co., N. Y., (1st and Ref. Mort.), 5s, 1966 | 21,120 00 | 44,000 00 | 24,200 00 |
| Pennsylvania R. R. Co., (General Mort.), 4½s, 1965 | 16,000 00 | 20,000 00 | 17,200 00 |
| Pere Marquette R. R. Co., (L., E. & Det. R. Div.), 4½s, 1932 | 17,500 00 | 25,000 00 | 21,250 00 |
| Rock Island, Arkansas & Louisville R. R. Co., (1st Mort.), 4½s, 1934 | 12,500 00 | 25,000 00 | 19,250 00 |
| Southern Pacific Co., (Conv.), 4s, 1929 | 40,000 00 | 50,000 00 | 43,500 00 |
| Totals | $181,320 00 | $264,000 00 | $205,850 00 |
| Public Utility and Miscellaneous Bonds— | | | |
| Allegheny, Pittsburgh Coal Co., (Guaranteed Mort.) 8s, 1941 | 4,987 50 | 5,000 00 | 4,987 50 |
| Altorfer Brothers Co., (1st Mort.), 8s, 1930 | 10,000 00 | 10,000 00 | 10,000 00 |
| American Hominy Co., (1st Mort.), 7s, 1924 | 4,950 00 | 5,000 00 | 4,950 00 |
| Armour & Co., (Conv. Notes), 7s, 1930 | 9,459 00 | 10,000 00 | 9,459 00 |
| Barchus, Charles (1st Mort.), 7s, 1930 | 7,014 77 | 7,500 00 | 7,014 77 |
| Butte Electric & Power Co., (1st Mort.), 5s, 1951 | 7,650 00 | 9,000 00 | 7,650 00 |
| Calco Chemical Co., (1st Mort.), 8s, 1940 | 8,000 00 | 10,000 00 | 8,000 00 |
| Colorado Power Co., (1st Mort.), 5s, 1953 | 2,960 00 | 4,000 00 | 2,960 00 |
| Columbia Graphophone Mfg. Co., (Notes), 8s, 1925 | 3,500 00 | 10,000 00 | 3,500 00 |
| Commonwealth Edison Co., (1st Mort.), 6s, 1943 | 9,125 00 | 10,000 00 | 9,125 00 |
| Dallas Power & Lt. Co., (1st Mort., Series A), 6s, 1949 | 22,500 00 | 25,000 00 | 24,250 00 |
| Diamond Match Co., (S. F. Debentures), 7½s, 1935 | 9,975 00 | 10,000 00 | 9,975 00 |
| Duquesne Light Co., (1st Mort. Coll. Trust), 6s, 1949 | 22,750 00 | 25,000 00 | 24,250 00 |
| Hines (Edward) Assn. Lumber Interest, (1st Mort.), 8s, 1933 | 9,950 00 | 10,000 00 | 9,950 00 |
| Houston Gas Co., (1st Mort.), 7s, 1923 | 9,712 50 | 10,000 00 | 9,712 50 |
| Interstate Iron & Steel Co., (1st Mort.), 8s, 1941 | 4,950 00 | 5,000 00 | 4,950 00 |
| Kelly Springfield Tire Co., (S. F. Notes), 8s, 1931 | 9,925 00 | 10,000 00 | 9,925 00 |
| Libby, McNeil & Libby, (1st Mort.), 7s, 1931 | 4,762 50 | 5,000 00 | 4,762 50 |
| Lock, Fred G., (1st Mort.), 7s, 1928 | 2,346 24 | 2,500 00 | 2,346 24 |
| Lock, Fred G., (1st Mort.), 7s, 1929 | 2,815 55 | 3,000 00 | 2,815 55 |
| Lock, Fred G., (1st Mort.), 7s, 1930 | 3,754 10 | 4,000 00 | 3,754 10 |
| Mid-Co. Petroleum Co., (1st Mort.), 8s, 1921 | 7,500 00 | 10,000 00 | 7,500 00 |
| Mississippi River Power Co., (1st Mort.), 5s, 1951 | 7,487 50 | 10,000 00 | 7,487 50 |
| Montana River Power Co., (1st and Ref. Mort.), 5s, 1943 | 8,437 50 | 10,000 00 | 8,437 50 |
| National Life Building Co., (1st Mort.), 4s, 1926 | 1,000,000 00 | 1,000,000 00 | 1,000,000 00 |
| Natrona Power Co., (1st Mort.), 8s, 1938 | 4,600 00 | 5,000 00 | 4,600 00 |
| Nebraska Power Co., (1st Mort.), 6s, 1949 | 8,400 00 | 10,000 00 | 8,400 00 |
| Pacific Coast Power Co., (1st Mort.), 5s, 1940 | 7,980 00 | 10,000 00 | 7,980 00 |
| Southern California Edison Co., (General Mort.), 5s, 1939 | 19,500 00 | 25,000 00 | 22,750 00 |
| Spring River Power Co., The, (1st Mort.), 5s, 1922 | 4,587 50 | 5,000 00 | 4,587 50 |
| Standard Bolt Corp., (1st Mort.), 8s, 1923 | 4,950 00 | 5,000 00 | 4,950 00 |
| Toledo Edison Co., (1st Mort.), 7s, 1941 | 4,800 00 | 5,000 00 | 4,800 00 |
| Union Electric Light & Power Co., (Ref. and Ext. Mort.), 5s, 1933 | 20,750 00 | 25,000 00 | 21,500 00 |
| West Penn. Power Co., (1st Mort., Series "D"), 7s, 1946 | 18,800 00 | 20,000 00 | 18,800 00 |
| Winchester Repeating Arms Co., (1st Mort.,.7½s, 1941 | 4,862 50 | 5,000 00 | 4,862 50 |
| Yadkin River Power Co., (1st Mort.), 5s, 1941 | 7,500 00 | 10,000 00 | 7,500 00 |
| Totals | $1,301,242 16 | $1,345,000 00 | $1,308,492 16 |

SCHEDULE D—PART 2—STOCKS.

| Description. | Book value. | Par value. | Market value. |
|---|---|---|---|
| Chicago & Northwestern Ry. Co., (Com.) | $ 26,400 00 | $ 44,000 00 | $ 26,400 00 |
| Central Trust Co. of Illinois, Chicago, Ill. | 34,038 00 | 18,600 00 | 34,410 00 |
| Chicago Title & Trust Co., Chicago, Ill. | 18,576 20 | 15,700 00 | 37,680 00 |
| Continental & Commercial National Bank, Chicago, Ill. | 208,291 70 | 116,300 00 | 319,825 00 |
| Corn Exchange National Bank, Chicago, Ill. | 821,019 83 | 273,900 00 | 972,345 00 |
| Century Trust & Savings Bank, Chicago, Ill. | 31,900 00 | 29,000 00 | 33,350 00 |
| Drexel State Bank, Chicago, Ill. | 9,566 67 | 7,900 00 | 15,010 00 |
| Market Trust & Savings Bank, Chicago, Ill. | 14,000 00 | 14,000 00 | 17,500 00 |
| Noel State Bank, Chicago, Ill. | 26,016 50 | 23,800 00 | 39,270 00 |
| Standard Trust & Savings Bank, Chicago, Ill. | 31,011 50 | 22,600 00 | 35,030 00 |
| The Union Trust Co., Cleveland, Ohio | 15,080 00 | 24,300 00 | 42,525 00 |
| National Life Building Co., Chicago, Ill. | 2,000,000 00 | 1,000,000 00 | 2,000,000 00 |
| Totals | $3,235,900 40 | $1,590,100 00 | $3,573,345 00 |

---

## NORTH AMERICAN LIFE INSURANCE COMPANY OF CHICAGO.

Located at No. 31 South State Street, Chicago, Illinois; commenced business January 27, 1912.

J. H. McNAMARA, President. W. P. KENT, Secretary.

### CAPITAL.

| | | | |
|---|---|---|---|
| Capital paid up | | $700,000 00 | |
| Amount of ledger assets December 31, of previous year | | | $5,625,135 94 |

### INCOME.

| | | | |
|---|---|---|---|
| First year's premiums on original policies, less re-insurance | | $348,532 09 | |
| First year's premiums for total and permanent disability benefits, less re-insurance | | 11,073 29 | |
| First year's premiums for additional accidental death benefits, less re-insurance | | 11,639 97 | |
| Surrender values applied to purchase paid-up insurance and annuities | | 37,150 17 | |
| New premiums | | $ 408,395 52 | |
| Renewal premiums less re-insurance | $1,361,188 67 | | |
| Renewal premiums for total and permanent disability benefits | 19,402 30 | | |
| Renewal premiums for additional accidental death benefits, less re-insurance | 10,949 73 | | |
| Renewal premiums | | 1,391,540 70 | |
| Premium income | | | $1,799,936 22 |
| Interest on mortgage loans | | $234,175 29 | |
| Interest on collateral loans | | 186 16 | |
| Interest on bonds and dividends on stocks | | 21,592 93 | |
| Interest on premium notes, policy loans or liens | | 58,626 40 | |
| Interest on deposits | | 15,526 14 | |
| Interest on other debts due the company | | 2,990 68 | |
| Rents | | 14,741 00 | |
| Total interest and rents | | | 347,838 60 |
| From other sources, viz: Mortgage loan commissions, $45,390.20; war tax collections, $9,213.06 | | | 54,603 26 |
| Profit on sale or maturity of ledger assets | | | 4,366 95 |
| Increase in book value of ledger assets | | | 6,015 44 |
| Total income | | | $2,212,760 47 |
| Total | | | $7,837,896 41 |

### DISBURSEMENTS.

| | | |
|---|---|---|
| Death claims | $270,171 62 | |
| Matured endowments | 1,000 00 | |
| Total and permanent disability claims and additional accidental death benefits | 10,206 04 | |
| Total death claims and endowments | | $281,377 66 |
| Annuities involving life contingencies | | 120 00 |
| Premium notes and liens voided by lapse, less $17,083.07 restorations | | 34,981 51 |
| Surrender values paid in cash, or applied in liquidation of loans or notes | | 150,465 33 |
| Surrender values applied to purchase paid-up insurance and annuities | | 37,150 17 |
| (Total paid policyholders | $504,094 67) | |
| Expense of investigation and settlement of policy claims, including legal expenses | | 586 61 |
| Supplementary contracts not involving life contingencies | | 6,374 72 |
| Dividends to stockholders | | 139,880 00 |
| Commissions to agents, first year, $223,987.97; renewal, $90,817.87 | | 314,805 84 |
| Agency supervision and traveling expenses of supervisors | | 51,748 11 |
| Branch office expenses | | 22,030 22 |
| Medical examiners' fees and inspection of risks | | 30,816 50 |

## DISBURSEMENTS—Concluded.

| | |
|---|---|
| Salaries and all other compensation of officers and home office employees | $118,642 91 |
| Rent | 17,246 39 |
| Advertising, printing, stationery, postage, telegraph, telephone, express and exchange | 41,045 55 |
| Legal expense | 8,259 42 |
| Furniture, fixtures and safes | 5,687 97 |
| Repairs and expenses (other than taxes) on real estate | 4,488 56 |
| Taxes on real estate | 3,215 94 |
| State taxes on premiums | 32,606 36 |
| Insurance department licenses and fees | 4,052 53 |
| Federal taxes | 11,067 77 |
| All other licenses, fees and taxes | 4,035 35 |
| Other disbursements, viz: Traveling expenses, $1,487.89; protest fees, $11.62; photographic supplies, $595.10; medical supplies, $115.63; books and periodicals, $927.00; flowers, $55.55; agency convention, $9,761.11; directors meetings, $702.97; examination and appraisal fees, $6,899.24; premiums on bonds, $1,192.10; association dues, $335.00; suspense items repaid, $2,308.74 | 24,401 95 |
| Loss on sale or maturity of ledger assets | 327 50 |
| Total disbursements | $1,345,414 87 |
| Balance | $6,492,481 54 |

## LEDGER ASSETS.

| | |
|---|---|
| Book value of real estate | $ 108,000 00 |
| Mortgage loans on real estate | 4,509,216 62 |
| Premiums advanced under Soldiers' and Sailors' Civil Relief Act | 19 85 |
| Loans on company's policies assigned as collateral | 1,034,276 37 |
| Premium notes on policies in force | 76,503 61 |
| Book value of bonds and stocks | 374,752 42 |
| Cash in office | 16,017 69 |
| Deposits in trust companies and banks not on interest | 10,224 40 |
| Deposits in trust companies and banks on interest | 313,955 26 |
| Bills receivable | 697 09 |
| Agents' balances (debit, $51,202.29; credit, $5,438.57) | 45,763 72 |
| Cash in branch offices, cashiers under bond, $2,842.83; war savings certificates, ($211.68) | 3,054 51 |
| Total ledger assets | $6,492,481 54 |

### NON-LEDGER ASSETS.

| | | | |
|---|---|---|---|
| Interest due and accrued on mortgages | | $136,552 12 | |
| Interest due and accrued on bonds | | 10,577 50 | |
| Interest accrued on premium notes, loans or liens | | 1,156 62 | |
| Interest accrued on other assets | | 3,829 83 | |
| | | | 152,116 07 |
| Due from other companies for losses or claims on policies re-insured | | | 2,895 53 |
| | New business. | Renewals. | |
| Net uncollected and deferred premiums (paid for basis) | $5,838 75 | $173,273 58 | 179,112 33 |
| Gross assets | | | $6,826,605 47 |

### DEDUCT ASSETS NOT ADMITTED.

| | | |
|---|---|---|
| Agents' debit balances | $51,202 29 | |
| Bills receivable | 697 09 | |
| Premium notes, policy loans and other policy assets in excess of net value and of other policy liabilities on individual policies | 3,775 81 | |
| Overdue and accrued interest on bonds in default | 2,205 00 | |
| Book value of bonds and stocks over market value | 4,769 92 | |
| Reserve on account of deposit in Auburn State Bank | 8,800 00 | |
| Total | | 71,450 11 |
| Admitted assets | | $6,755,155 36 |

## LIABILITIES.

| | | |
|---|---|---|
| Net present value of outstanding policies computed by the Illinois Insurance Department | $5,623,769 00 | |
| Same for annuities | 472 00 | |
| Total | $5,624,241 00 | |
| Deduct net value of risks re-insured | 25,070 00 | |
| Net reserve (paid for basis) | | $5,599,171 00 |
| Extra reserve for total and permanent disability benefits and for additional accidental death benefits included in life policies | | 36,455 00 |
| Present value of supplementary contracts not involving life contingencies | | 71,889 00 |
| Present value of amounts incurred but not yet due for total and permanent disability benefits | | 12,680 00 |
| Death losses in process of adjustment | $ 5,630 01 | |
| Death losses reported for which no proofs have been received | 15,068 00 | |
| Reserve for net death losses incurred but unreported | 3,215 00 | |
| Total policy claims | | 23,913 01 |

## LIABILITIES—Concluded.

| | |
|---|---|
| Gross premiums paid in advance, including surrender values so applied, less discount, if any | $ 2,501 47 |
| Unearned interest and rent paid in advance | 24,736 12 |
| Commissions due agents on premium notes, when paid | 11,717 47 |
| Commissions to agents due or accrued | 756 50 |
| Cost of collection on uncollected and deferred premiums in excess of loading | 5,145 94 |
| Salaries, rents, office expenses, bills and accounts due or accrued | 2,593 00 |
| Medical examiners' and legal fees due or accrued | 1,618 30 |
| Estimated amount hereafter payable for federal, state and other taxes based upon the business of the year of this statement | 51,662 03 |
| Unpaid dividends to stockholders | 310 00 |
| Premium suspense account | 4,010 27 |
| Total | $5,849,159 11 |
| Capital paid up | 700,000 00 |
| Unassigned funds (surplus) | 205,996 25 |
| Total | $6,755,155 36 |

## EXHIBIT OF POLICIES—ORDINARY.

ALL BUSINESS PAID FOR.

| | Number. | Amount. | Number. | Amount. |
|---|---|---|---|---|
| Policies in force December 31, 1920 | | | 26,373 | $60,064,817 00 |
| Policies issued, revived and increased during the year | | | 5,279 | 14,138,951 00 |
| Total | | | 31,652 | $74,203,768 00 |
| Deduct policies which have ceased to be in force during the year— | | | | |
| By death | 122 | $ 303,422 00 | | |
| By maturity | 1 | 1,000 00 | | |
| By disability | 1 | 3,200 00 | | |
| By expiry | 143 | 184,110 00 | | |
| By surrender | 399 | 1,311,675 00 | | |
| By lapse | 4,102 | 12,181,504 00 | | |
| By decrease | -------- | 52,132 00 | | |
| Total | | | 4,768 | 14,037,043 00 |
| Total policies in force December 31, 1921 | | | 26,884 | $60,166,725 00 |
| Re-insured | | | 432 | $2,737,962 00 |

## BUSINESS IN ILLINOIS—ORDINARY.

| | Number. | Amount. |
|---|---|---|
| Policies in force December 31, 1920 | 1,882 | $4,559,219 00 |
| Policies issued during the year | 244 | 573,914 00 |
| Total | 2,126 | $5,133,133 00 |
| Deduct policies ceased to be in force | 113 | 371,579 00 |
| Policies in force December 31, 1921 | 2,013 | $4,761,554 00 |
| Losses and claims unpaid December 31, 1920 | 2 | $ 5,106 82 |
| Losses and claims incurred during the year | 9 | 19,500 00 |
| Total | 11 | $24,606 82 |
| Losses and claims settled during the year | 10 | 19,606 82 |
| Losses and claims unpaid December 31, 1921 | 1 | $5,000 00 |
| Premiums received | | $149,413 19 |

## GAIN AND LOSS EXHIBIT.

INSURANCE EXHIBIT.

| | | Gain in surplus. | Loss in surplus. |
|---|---|---|---|
| Loading on actual premiums of the year (averaging 18.8 per cent of the gross premiums) | $334,095 81 | | |
| Insurance expenses incurred during the year | 679,504 65 | | |
| Loss from loading | | -------------- | $345,408 84 |
| Interest earned during the year | $368,786 36 | | |
| Investment expenses incurred during the year | 28,747 97 | | |
| Net income from investments | $340,038 39 | | |
| Interest required to maintain reserve | 193,838 33 | | |
| Gain from interest | | $146,200 06 | |

GAIN AND LOSS EXHIBIT—Concluded.

INSURANCE EXHIBIT.

| | | Gain in surplus. | Loss in surplus. |
|---|---|---|---|
| Expected mortality on net amount at risk | $562,751 00 | | |
| Actual mortality on net amount at risk | 254,439 53 | | |
| Gain from mortality | | 308,311 47 | |
| Expected disbursements to annuitants | $ 47 05 | | |
| Net actual annuity claims incurred | 120 00 | | |
| Loss from annuities | | | 72 95 |
| Total gain during the year from surrendered and lapsed policies | | 53,357 50 | |
| Dividends paid stockholders | | | 140,000 00 |

INVESTMENT EXHIBIT.

| | | Gain in surplus. | Loss in surplus. |
|---|---|---|---|
| Total gains from real estate | | 11,500 00 | |
| Total gains from stocks and bonds | | 4,507 50 | |
| Total losses from stocks and bonds | | | 327 50 |
| Loss from assets not admitted | | | 17,648 74 |
| Net gain on account of total and permanent disability benefits or additional accidental death benefits included in life policies | | 26,837 25 | |
| Gain from mortgage loans commissions | | 45,390 20 | |
| Balance unaccounted for | | | 1,668 00 |
| Total gains and losses in surplus during the year | | $596,103 98 | $505,126 03 |
| Surplus December 31, 1920 | $115,018 30 | | |
| Surplus December 31, 1921 | 205,996 25 | | |
| Increase in surplus | | | 90,977 95 |
| Total | | $596,103 98 | $596,103 98 |

SCHEDULE D—PART 1—BONDS.

| Description. | Book value. | Par value. | Market value. |
|---|---|---|---|
| Andrew, N. C., Waterworks, 6s, 1941 | $21,600 00 | $20,000 00 | $21,800 00 |
| Bristol, Tenn., Waterworks, 5s, 1931 | 3,204 30 | 3,000 00 | 2,940 00 |
| Butler Co., Mo., Drainage Dist. No. 7, 6s, 1926 | 1,065 50 | 1,000 00 | 1,010 00 |
| Carbon Co., Utah, Wellington Dist. School, 6s, 1931 | 10,300 00 | 10,000 00 | 10,000 00 |
| Cherokee, N. C., School, 6s, 1931 | 3,180 00 | 3,000 00 | 3,030 00 |
| DeFuniak Springs, Walton Co., Fla., Sewer, 6s, 1929 | 18,979 43 | 18,000 00 | 18,900 00 |
| DeSoto Co., Miss., Supervisor's Dist. No. 2, Road, 6s, 1932 | 38,153 27 | 36,000 00 | 36,000 00 |
| Dinwiddie County, Va., Road Improvement, 6s, 1940 | 5,000 00 | 5,000 00 | 5,350 00 |
| Erwin, Town of, Unicoi Co., Tenn., St. and Sewer, 6s, 1931 | 15,885 20 | 15,000 00 | 15,600 00 |
| Fort Pierce, Fla., 6s, 1942 | 15,551 25 | 14,500 00 | 15,805 00 |
| Fort Pierce, Fla., Public Utility, 6s, 1942 | 32,176 80 | 30,000 00 | 32,700 00 |
| Franklin, N. C., Improvement, 6s, 1940 | 4,320 00 | 4,000 00 | 4,280 00 |
| Gunnison, Miss., Waterworks, 6s, 1927 | 5,000 00 | 5,000 00 | 5,000 00 |
| Harlowton, Town of, Mont., 6s, 1930 | 11,330 00 | 11,000 00 | 11,000 00 |
| Harris County, Tex., School, 5s, 1950 | 4,215 60 | 4,000 00 | 4,000 00 |
| Kiefer, Town of, Okla., Waterworks, 6s, 1935 | 25,730 00 | 25,000 00 | 26,750 00 |
| Laurel, Mont., Sewer, 6s, 1930 | 12,480 00 | 12,000 00 | 12,240 00 |
| Laurel, Mont., Water, 6s, 1930 | 27,290 00 | 26,000 00 | 26,520 00 |
| Lewis Co., Ida., Nez Perce Ind., School Dist. No. 1, 5½s, 1932 | 16,288 00 | 16,000 00 | 16,000 00 |
| Moore, Mont., Waterworks, 6s, 1931 | 12,120 00 | 12,000 00 | 12,000 00 |
| Osyka, Town of, Pike County, Miss., 6s, 1930 | 15,852 20 | 15,000 00 | 15,750 00 |
| Overton County, Tenn., 6s, 1926 | 17,652 00 | 17,500 00 | 18,025 00 |
| Overton County, Tenn., 6s, 1925 | 5,402 25 | 5,000 00 | 5,100 00 |
| Parma, Idaho, Waterworks, 6s, 1929 | 7,388 50 | 7,000 00 | 7,420 00 |
| Poinsett County, Ark., Drain. Dist. No. 3, 6s, 1935 | 13,048 12 | 12,250 00 | 12,372 50 |
| Pulaski Co., Va., Waterworks and Elec. Lt., 5s, 1925 | 10,000 00 | 10,000 00 | 10,000 00 |
| Sallisaw, Okla., Waterworks, 6s, 1933 | 5,500 00 | 5,000 00 | 5,300 00 |
| Shelby, N. C., 5s, 1938 | 6,790 00 | 7,000 00 | 6,790 00 |
| Totals | $365,502 42 | $349,250 00 | $361,682 50 |

SCHEDULE D—PART 2—STOCKS.

| Description. | Book value. | Par value. | Market value. |
|---|---|---|---|
| Movi Hotel Co., Preferred | $9,250 00 | $10,000 00 | $8,300 00 |

## OLD COLONY LIFE INSURANCE COMPANY.

Located at No. 166 West Jackson Boulevard, Chicago, Illinois; commenced business June 18, 1907.

B. R. NUESKE, President. R. C. VAN DYKE, Secretary.

CAPITAL.

| | | |
|---|---|---|
| Capital paid up | $126,551 87 | |
| Amount of ledger assets December 31, of previous year | | $1,665,523 44 |

## INCOME.

| | | | |
|---|---|---|---|
| First year's premiums on original policies, less re-insurance | | $151,513 52 | |
| First year's premiums for total and permanent disability benefits, less re-insurance | | 3,784 05 | |
| First year's premiums for additional accidental death benefits, less re-insurance | | 2,432 81 | |
| Surrender values to pay first year's premiums | | 17 75 | |
| Dividends and interest held on deposit, surrendered for paid-up and extended insurance | | 1,074 12 | |
| Surrender values applied to purchase paid-up insurance and annuities | | 31,793 98 | |
| New premiums | | $190,616 23 | |
| Renewal premiums less re-insurance | $461,354 40 | | |
| Renewal premiums for total and permanent disability benefits, less re-insurance | 5,755 68 | | |
| Renewal premiums for additional accidental death benefits, less re-insurance | 7,366 90 | | |
| Dividends applied to pay renewal premiums | 2,996 91 | | |
| Surrender values applied to pay renewal premiums | 86 54 | | |
| Renewal premiums | | 477,560 43 | |
| Premium income | | | $668,176 66 |
| Consideration for supplementary contracts not involving life contingencies | | | 4,343 70 |
| Dividends left with company to accumulate at interest | | | 4,245 01 |
| Interest on mortgage loans | | $ 8,931 05 | |
| Interest on bonds | | 5,047 89 | |
| Interest on premium notes, policy loans or liens | | 10,724 42 | |
| Interest on deposits | | 1,876 34 | |
| Interest on other debts due the company | | 1,606 08 | |
| Rents—including $15,000.00 for company's occupancy of its own buildings less $10,050.00 interest on incumbrances | | 211,128 43 | |
| Total interest and rents | | | 239,314 21 |
| Guaranteed decreasing premium fund | | | 138 45 |
| Borrowed money (gross) | | | 20,000 00 |
| Increase in book value of ledger assets | | | 46,326 24 |
| Total income | | | $982,544 27 |
| Total | | | $2,648,067 71 |

## DISBURSEMENTS.

| | | |
|---|---|---|
| Death claims | $140,644 74 | |
| Matured endowments | 1,000 00 | |
| Total and permanent disability claims and additional accidental death benefits, less re-insurance | 1,000 00 | |
| Total death claims and endowments | | $142,644 74 |
| Premium notes and liens voided by lapse, less $542.18 restorations | | 6,999 12 |
| Surrender values paid in cash, or applied in liquidation of loans or notes | | 36,551 34 |
| Surrender values applied to pay new and renewal premiums | | 104 29 |
| Surrender values applied to purchase paid-up insurance and annuities | | 31,793 98 |
| Dividends paid policyholders in cash, or applied in liquidation of loans or notes | | 348 82 |
| Dividends applied to pay renewal premiums | | 2,996 91 |
| Dividends left with the company to accumulate at interest | | 4,245 01 |
| (Total paid policyholders | $225,684 21) | |
| Expense of investigation and settlement of policy claims | | 230 56 |
| Supplementary contracts not involving life contingencies | | 2,436 01 |
| Dividends with interest, held on deposit surrendered during the year for cash | | 176 94 |
| Dividends with interest held on deposit surrendered during the year for paid up and extended insurance | | 1,074 12 |
| Commissions to agents, first year, $118,945.33; renewal, $21,141.49 | | 140,086 82 |
| Compensation of managers and agents not paid by commissions on new business | | 7,758 33 |
| Branch office expenses | | 3,083 79 |
| Medical examiners' fees and inspection of risks | | 20,741 45 |
| Salaries and all other compensation of officers and home office employees | | 53,840 25 |
| Rent | | 15,000 00 |
| Advertising, printing, stationery, postage, telegraph, telephone, express and exchange | | 24,067 26 |
| Legal expense | | 15,993 71 |
| Furniture, fixtures and safes | | 1,083 63 |
| Repairs and expenses (other than taxes) on real estate | | 97,553 82 |
| Taxes on real estate | | 23,378 77 |
| State taxes on premiums | | 8,569 71 |
| Insurance department licenses and fees | | 2,351 10 |
| Federal taxes | | 5,903 40 |
| All other licenses, fees and taxes | | 1,826 26 |
| Other disbursements, viz: Traveling expense, $4,960.30; incidental expense, $842.37; collection expense, $454.09; books and periodicals, $1,469.49; photographs, applications and documents, $1,381.40; surety bonds, $157.50; contributions and donations, $80.00; discount sale of securities, $747.41; interest on rent paid in advance, $540.00 | | 10,632 56 |
| Borrowed money repaid (gross) | | 20,000 00 |

DISBURSEMENTS—Concluded.

| | |
|---|---|
| Interest on borrowed money | $ 385 11 |
| Agents' balances charged off | 12,716 78 |
| Loss on sale or maturity of ledger assets | 6,391 65 |
| Total disbursements | $700,966 24 |
| Balance | $1,947,101 47 |

LEDGER ASSETS.

| | |
|---|---|
| Book value of real estate | $1,385,788 97 |
| Mortgage loans on real estate | 154,500 00 |
| Loans on company's policies assigned as collateral | 239,348 73 |
| Premium notes on policies in force | 14,782 85 |
| Book value of bonds | 74,142 79 |
| Cash in office | 1,600 00 |
| Deposits in trust companies and banks not on interest | 5,033 23 |
| Deposits in trust companies and banks on interest | 44,205 94 |
| Agents' balances (debit, $32,904.51; credit, $5,205.55) | 27,698 96 |
| Total ledger assets | $1,947,101 47 |

NON-LEDGER ASSETS.

| | | | |
|---|---|---|---|
| Interest accrued on mortgages | | $1,455 95 | |
| Interest accrued on bonds | | 1,028 31 | |
| Interest due and accrued on premium notes, loans or liens | | 259 06 | |
| Interest due and accrued on other assets | | 27 02 | |
| Rents due and accrued on company's property | | 3,200 75 | |
| | | | 5,971 09 |
| Market value of real estate over book value | | | 156,250 00 |
| | New business. | Renewals. | |
| Net uncollected and deferred premiums (paid for basis) | $6,730 47 | $69,950 13 | 76,680 60 |
| Gross assets | | | $2,186,003 16 |

DEDUCT ASSETS NOT ADMITTED.

| | | |
|---|---|---|
| Agents' debit balances | $32,904 51 | |
| Premium notes, policy loans and other policy assets in excess of net value and of other policy liabilities on individual policies | 3,082 64 | |
| Book value of bonds over market value | 1,549 79 | |
| Real estate held without legal authority | 1,193 27 | |
| Total | | 38,730 21 |
| Admitted assets | | $2,147,272 95 |

LIABILITIES.

| | | |
|---|---|---|
| Net present value of outstanding policies computed by the Illinois Insurance Department | $1,810,524 00 | |
| Deduct net value of risks re-insured | 26,343 00 | |
| Net reserve (paid for basis) | | $1,784,181 00 |
| Extra reserve for total and permanent disability benefits and for additional accidental death benefits included in life policies, less re-insurance | | 11,934 00 |
| Present value of supplementary contracts not involving life contingencies | | 15,380 08 |
| Surrender values claimable on policies cancelled | | 59 60 |
| Death losses reported for which no proofs have been received | $12,647 97 | |
| Reserve for net death losses incurred but unreported | 4,002 74 | |
| Death losses and other policy claims resisted | 747 98 | |
| Total policy claims | | 17,398 69 |
| Dividends left with the company to accumulate at interest | | 8,559 02 |
| Gross premiums paid in advance, including surrender values so applied, less discount, if any | | 415 01 |
| Unearned interest on policy loans and rent paid in advance | | 15,494 29 |
| Commissions due agents on premium notes, when paid | | 288 22 |
| Real estate | | 4,756 21 |
| Salaries, rents, office expenses, bills and accounts due or accrued, insurance | | 3,794 39 |
| Medical examiners' and legal fees due or accrued | | 1,408 55 |
| Estimated amount hereafter payable for federal, state and other taxes based upon the business of the year of this statement | | 55,297 66 |
| Dividends or other profits due policyholders | | 266 37 |
| Dividends declared on or apportioned to annual dividend policies payable to policyholders during 1922 for period to March 1, 1922 | | 1,557 53 |
| Guaranteed decreasing premium fund | | 1,547 41 |
| Special voluntary reserve | | 1,016 58 |
| Accrued interest on incumbrances on company's property | | 8,737 50 |
| Total | | $1,931,552 11 |
| Capital paid up | | 126,551 87 |
| Unassigned funds (surplus) | | 89,168 97 |
| Total | | $2,147,272 95 |

## EXHIBIT OF POLICIES—ORDINARY.

ALL BUSINESS PAID FOR.

| | Number. | Amount. | Number. | Amount. |
|---|---|---|---|---|
| Policies in force December 31, 1920 | | | 16,577 | $22,236,549 85 |
| Policies issued, revived and increased during the year | | | 5,638 | 6,410,672 78 |
| Total | | | 22,215 | $28,647,222 63 |
| Deduct policies which have ceased to be in force during the year— | | | | |
| By death | 119 | $ 172,607 65 | | |
| By maturity | 1 | 1,000 00 | | |
| By expiry | 109 | 129,897 15 | | |
| By surrender | 249 | 361,308 59 | | |
| By lapse | 3,247 | 4,885,926 00 | | |
| By decrease | -------- | 157,930 17 | | |
| Total | | | 3,725 | 5,708,669 56 |
| Total policies in force December 31, 1921 | | | 18,490 | $22,938,553 07 |
| Re-insured | | | 885 | $1,690,664 00 |

## BUSINESS IN ILLINOIS—ORDINARY.

| | Number. | Amount. |
|---|---|---|
| Policies in force December 31, 1920 | 6,509 | $6,806,574 51 |
| Policies issued during the year | 1,855 | 1,931,100 06 |
| Total | 8,364 | $8,737,674 57 |
| Deduct policies ceased to be in force | 1,184 | 1,463,823 52 |
| Policies in force December 31, 1921 | 7,180 | $7,273,851 05 |
| Losses and claims unpaid December 31, 1920 | 11 | $ 9,303 97 |
| Losses and claims incurred during the year | 52 | 58,210 27 |
| Total | 63 | $67,514 24 |
| Losses and claims settled during the year | 60 | 66,331 48 |
| Losses and claims unpaid December 31, 1921 | 3 | $1,182 76 |
| Premiums received | | $235,437 67 |

## GAIN AND LOSS EXHIBIT.

INSURANCE EXHIBIT.

| | | Gain in surplus. | Loss in surplus. |
|---|---|---|---|
| Loading on actual premiums of the year (averaging 25.15 per cent of the gross premiums) | $170,932 05 | | |
| Insurance expenses incurred during the year | 321,144 24 | | |
| Loss from loading | | -------------- | $150,212 19 |
| Interest earned during the year | $235,580 42 | | |
| Investment expenses incurred during the year | 145,586 87 | | |
| Net income from investments | $89,993 55 | | |
| Interest required to maintain reserve | 57,871 82 | | |
| Gain from interest | | $32,121 73 | |
| Expected mortality on net amount at risk | $186,499 00 | | |
| Actual mortality on net amount at risk | 120,700 28 | | |
| Gain from mortality | | 65,798 72 | |
| Total gain during the year from surrendered and lapsed policies | | 16,251 84 | |
| Decrease in surplus on dividend account | | -------------- | 7,925 95 |
| Increase in special funds and special reserves during the year | | -------------- | 1,016 58 |
| Net to loss account | | -------------- | 12,716 78 |
| INVESTMENT EXHIBIT. | | | |
| Total gains from real estate | | 46,326 24 | |
| Total gains from bonds | | 715 00 | |
| Total losses from bonds | | -------------- | 6,391 65 |
| Loss account, real estate held without legal authority | | -------------- | 1,193 27 |
| Gain from assets not admitted | | 124 18 | |
| Net gain on account of total and permanent disability benefits or additional accidental death benefits included in life policies | | 19,757 66 | |
| Discount account sale of securities | | -------------- | 747 41 |
| Balance unaccounted for | | -------------- | 641 66 |
| Total gains and losses in surplus during the year | | $181,095 37 | $180,845 49 |
| Surplus December 31, 1920 | $88,919 09 | | |
| Surplus December 31, 1921 | 89,168 97 | | |
| Increase in surplus | | -------------- | 249 88 |
| Total | | $181,095 37 | $181,095 37 |

SCHEDULE D—PART 1—BONDS.

| Description. | Book value. | Par value. | Market value. |
|---|---|---|---|
| City Water Co., East St. Louis and Granite City, Ill., 5s, 1945 | $ 8,937 00 | $10,000 00 | $ 8,400 00 |
| Town of Evin, Tenn., School, 5s, 1931 | 2,000 00 | 2,000 00 | 1,960 00 |
| Adair County, Okla., School, 6s, 1929 | 760 69 | 700 00 | 728 00 |
| Commonwealth Edison Co., 5s, 1943 | 10,275 00 | 10,000 00 | 9,400 00 |
| McIntosh County, Okla., School, 6s, 1929 | 1,088 10 | 1,000 00 | 1,050 00 |
| Osage County, Okla., School, 6s, 1930 | 1,082 00 | 1,000 00 | 1,050 00 |
| Village of Morton Grove, Bridge, Dempster St., 5s, 1923 | 500 00 | 500 00 | 500 00 |
| Village of Morton Grove, Bridge, Dempster St., 5s, 1924 | 500 00 | 500 00 | 500 00 |
| Village of Morton Grove, Bridge, Dempster St., 5s, 1925 | 500 00 | 500 00 | 500 00 |
| Village of Morton Grove, Bridge, Dempster St., 5s, 1926 | 500 00 | 500 00 | 500 00 |
| Village of Morton Grove, Bridge, Dempster St., 5s, 1927 | 500 00 | 500 00 | 505 00 |
| U. S. Liberty Loan, 4th, 4¼s, 1938 | 22,500 00 | 22,500 00 | 22,500 00 |
| U. S. Liberty Loan, 3d, 4¼s, 1928 | 10,000 00 | 10,000 00 | 10,000 00 |
| U. S. Liberty Loan, 2d converted to 3d, 4¼s, 1942 | 15,000 00 | 15,000 00 | 15,000 00 |
| Totals | $74,142 79 | $74,700 00 | $72,593 00 |

## THE PEOPLES LIFE INSURANCE COMPANY.

Located at No. 130 North Wells Street, Chicago, Illinois; commenced business October 8, 1908.

ELON A. NELSON, President. G. L. LUTTERLOH, Secretary.

### CAPITAL.

| | | |
|---|---|---|
| Capital paid up | $101,736 66 | |
| Amount of ledger assets December 31, of previous year | | $696,725 39 |

### INCOME.

| | | | |
|---|---|---|---|
| First year's premiums on original policies, less, re-insurance | | $70,171 24 | |
| First year's premiums for total and permanent disability benefits, less re-insurance | | 56 02 | |
| First year's premiums for additional accidental death benefits, less re-insurance | | 21 25 | |
| Dividends applied to purchase paid-up additions and annuities | | 26 55 | |
| New premiums | | $ 70,275 06 | |
| Renewal premiums less re-insurance | $127,302 65 | | |
| Renewal remiums for total and permanent disability benefitsp | 86 63 | | |
| Renewal premiums | | 127,389 28 | |
| Premium income | | | $197,664 34 |
| Interest on mortgage loans | | $ 9,445 25 | |
| Interest on collateral loans | | 216 67 | |
| Interest on bonds and dividends on stocks | | 5,058 05 | |
| Interest on premium notes, policy loans or liens | | 3,158 69 | |
| Interest on deposits | | 196 03 | |
| Interest on other debts due the company | | 2 92 | |
| Interest from equity in property | | 42,447 37 | |
| Total interest | | | 60,524 98 |
| From other sources, viz: Commission on building loans, $3,990.00; deposits on applications, $151.42 | | | 4,141 42 |
| Borrowed money (gross) | | | 10,500 00 |
| Total income | | | $272,830 74 |
| Total | | | $969,556 13 |

### DISBURSEMENTS.

| | | |
|---|---|---|
| Death claims | $29,408 51 | |
| Matured endowments | 5,558 00 | |
| Total death claims and endowments | | $34,966 51 |
| Premium notes and liens voided by lapse | | 16 83 |
| Surrender values paid in cash, or applied in liquidation of loans or notes | | 23,170 77 |
| Dividends paid policyholders in cash, or applied in liquidation of loans or notes | | 1,818 79 |
| Dividends applied to purchase paid-up additions and annuities | | 26 55 |
| (Total paid policyholders | $59,999 45) | |
| Expense of investigation and settlement of policy claims | | 83 66 |
| Dividends to stockholders | | 6,104 20 |
| Commissions to agents, first year, $58,813.40; renewal, $2,619.15 | | 61,432 55 |
| Compensation of managers and agents not paid by commissions on new business | | 685 41 |
| Agency supervision and traveling expenses of supervisors | | 1,303 29 |
| Medical examiners' fees and inspection of risks | | 4,074 51 |

DISBURSEMENTS—Concluded.

| | | |
|---|---|---|
| Salaries and all other compensation of officers and home office employees | | $30,524 87 |
| Rent | | 5,690 24 |
| Advertising, printing, stationery, postage, telegraph, telephone, express and exchange | | 11,063 86 |
| Legal expense | | 5,232 21 |
| Furniture, fixtures and safes | | 483 01 |
| Taxes on real estate | | 67 71 |
| State taxes on premiums | | 313 26 |
| Insurance department licenses and fees | | 149 76 |
| Federal taxes | | 3,811 68 |
| All other licenses, fees and taxes | | 384 50 |
| Other disbursements, viz: Expense, building loans, $842.00; home office supplies, $1,690.70; officers traveling expense, $301.77; application deposits applied, $43.25 | | 2,877 72 |
| Borrowed money repaid (gross) | | 5,000 00 |
| Interest on borrowed money | | 189 20 |
| Agents' balances charged off | | 3,739 41 |
| Loss on sale or maturity of ledger assets | | 698 26 |
| Total disbursements | | $203,908 76 |
| Balance | | $765,647 37 |

LEDGER ASSETS.

| | | |
|---|---|---|
| Book value of real estate | | $358,750 00 |
| Mortgage loans on real estate | | 190,912 29 |
| Loans on company's policies assigned as collateral | | 68,459 86 |
| Premium notes on policies in force | | 881 04 |
| Book value of bonds and stocks | | 117,330 00 |
| Cash in office | | 300 00 |
| Deposits in trust companies and banks not on interest | | 19,063 58 |
| Deposits in trust companies and banks on interest | | 5,500 00 |
| Bills receivable | | 4,450 60 |
| Total ledger assets | | $765,647 37 |

NON-LEDGER ASSETS.

| | | | |
|---|---|---|---|
| Interest due and accrued on mortgages | | $3,573 21 | |
| Interest accrued on bonds | | 26 25 | |
| Interest accrued on premium notes, loans or liens | | 30 78 | |
| Dividends due and accrued | | 1,812 71 | |
| Interest due and accrued on company's property | | 5,280 00 | |
| | | | 10,722 95 |
| Market value of bonds and stocks over book value | | | 7,020 00 |
| | New business. | Renewals. | |
| Net uncollected and deferred premiums (paid for basis) | $4,016 93 | $14,092 26 | 18,109 19 |
| Gross assets | | | $801,499 51 |

DEDUCT ASSETS NOT ADMITTED.

| | | |
|---|---|---|
| Bills receivable | $4,450 60 | |
| Premium notes, policy loans and other policy assets in excess of net value and of other policy liabilities on individual policies | 200 00 | |
| Second mortgage on real estate | 8,314 64 | |
| Dividends on bank stock due and unpaid | 1,755 00 | |
| Total | | 14,720 24 |
| Admitted assets | | $786,779 27 |

LIABILITIES.

| | | |
|---|---|---|
| Net present value of outstanding policies computed by the Illinois Insurance Department | $664,866 00 | |
| Deduct net value of risks re-insured | 2,829 00 | |
| Net reserve (paid for basis) | | $662,037 00 |
| Extra reserve for total and permanent disability benefits and for additional accidental death benefits included in life policies, less re-insurance | | 52 00 |
| Death losses reported for which no proofs have been received | | 5,125 00 |
| Dividends left with the company to accumulate at interest | | 10 64 |
| Gross premiums paid in advance, including surrender values so applied, less discount, if any | | 3,220 75 |
| Unearned interest and rent paid in advance | | 1,683 77 |
| Salaries, rents, office expenses, bills and accounts due or accrued | | 772 27 |
| Medical examiners' fees due or accrued | | 116 00 |
| Estimated amount hereafter payable for federal, state and other taxes based upon the business of the year of this statement | | 1,380 00 |
| Borrowed money | | 5,500 00 |
| Dividends declared on or apportioned to deferred dividend policies payable to policyholders during 1922 for period to December 31, 1922 | | 167 81 |

LIABILITIES—Concluded.

| | |
|---|---|
| Amounts set apart, apportioned, provisionally ascertained, calculated declared or held awaiting apportionment upon deferred dividend policies | $2,340 81 |
| Deposits on applications | 151 42 |
| Total | $682,557 47 |
| Capital paid up | 101,736 66 |
| Unassigned funds (surplus) | 2,485 14 |
| Total | $786,779 27 |

## EXHIBIT OF POLICIES—ORDINARY.

ALL BUSINESS PAID FOR.

| | Number. | Amount. | Number. | Amount. |
|---|---|---|---|---|
| Policies in force December 31, 1920 | | | 8,553 | $4,417,757 09 |
| Policies issued, revived and increased during the year | | | 2,961 | 2,921,677 46 |
| Total | | | 11,514 | $7,339,434 55 |
| Deduct policies which have ceased to be in force during the year— | | | | |
| By death | 51 | $ 24,890 00 | | |
| By maturity | 4 | 5,558 00 | | |
| By expiry | 522 | 172,485 00 | | |
| By surrender | 259 | 204,605 00 | | |
| By lapse | 419 | 187,558 78 | | |
| By decrease | -------- | 4,000 00 | | |
| Total | | | 1,255 | 599,096 78 |
| Total policies in force December 31, 1921 | | | 10,259 | $6,740,337 77 |
| Re-insured | | | 108 | $312,753 00 |

## EXHIBIT OF POLICIES—INDUSTRIAL.

ALL BUSINESS PAID FOR.

| | Number. | Amount. | Number. | Amount. |
|---|---|---|---|---|
| Policies in force December 31, 1920 | | | 3,645 | $474,138 08 |
| Policies issued, revived and increased during the year | | | 11 | 1,902 00 |
| Total | | | 3,656 | $476,040 08 |
| Deduct policies which have ceased to be in force during the year— | | | | |
| By death | 29 | $ 4,128 15 | | |
| By expiry | 196 | 22,305 00 | | |
| By surrender | 42 | 5,042 68 | | |
| By lapse | 53 | 5,908 18 | | |
| By decrease | -------- | 1,300 32 | | |
| Total | | | 320 | 38,684 33 |
| Total policies in force December 31, 1921 | | | 3,336 | $437,355 75 |

## BUSINESS IN ILLINOIS—ORDINARY.

| | Number. | Amount. |
|---|---|---|
| Policies in force December 31, 1920 | 6,295 | $3,275,736 97 |
| Policies issued during the year | 2,939 | 2,913,007 46 |
| Total | 9,234 | $6,188,744 43 |
| Deduct policies ceased to be in force | 1,105 | 539,231 78 |
| Policies in force December 31, 1921 | 8,129 | $5,649,512 65 |
| Losses and claims unpaid December 31, 1920 | 11 | $ 6,350 00 |
| Losses and claims incurred during the year | 43 | 20,717 25 |
| Total | 54 | $27,067 25 |
| Losses and claims settled during the year | 43 | 22,042 25 |
| Losses and claims unpaid December 31, 1921 | 11 | $5,025 00 |
| Premiums received | | $177,410 25 |

## BUSINESS IN ILLINOIS—INDUSTRIAL.

| | Number. | Amount. |
|---|---|---|
| Policies in force December 31, 1920 | 3,645 | $474,138 08 |
| Policies issued during the year | 11 | 1,902 00 |
| Total | 3,656 | $476,040 08 |
| Deduct policies ceased to be in force | 320 | 38,684 33 |
| Policies in force December 31, 1921 | 3,336 | $437,355 75 |

BUSINESS IN ILLINOIS—INDUSTRIAL—Concluded.

| | Number. | Amount. |
|---|---|---|
| Losses and claims unpaid December 31, 1920 | 1 | $ 132 00 |
| Losses and claims incurred during the year | 29 | 4,128 15 |
| Total | 30 | $4,260 15 |
| Losses and claims settled during the year | 29 | 4,160 15 |
| Losses and claims unpaid December 31, 1921 | 1 | $100 00 |
| Premiums received | | $8,958 95 |

## GAIN AND LOSS EXHIBIT.

INSURANCE EXHIBIT.

| | | Gain in surplus. | Loss in surplus. |
|---|---|---|---|
| Loading on actual premiums of the year (averaging 27.27 per cent of the gross premiums) | $ 58,933 41 | | |
| Insurance expenses incurred during the year | 131,698 22 | | |
| Loss from loading | | | $72,764 81 |
| Interest earned during the year | $41,372 69 | | |
| Investment expenses incurred during the year | 1,179 21 | | |
| Net income from investments | $40,193 48 | | |
| Interest required to maintain reserve | 21,313 28 | | |
| Gain from interest | | $18,880 20 | |
| Expected mortality on net amount at risk | $53,066 75 | | |
| Actual mortality on net amount at risk | 23,349 25 | | |
| Gain from mortality | | 29,717 50 | |
| Total gain during the year from surrendered and lapsed policies | | 12,412 54 | |
| Dividends paid stockholders | | | 6,104 20 |
| Decrease in surplus on dividend account | | | 2,073 41 |
| INVESTMENT EXHIBIT. | | | |
| Total gains from stocks and bonds | | 7,020 00 | |
| Total losses from stocks and bonds | | | 698 26 |
| Gain, commission on building loans | | 3,990 00 | |
| Loss on account of second mortgage on real estate deducted as not admitted | | | 8,314 64 |
| Loss from assets not admitted | | | 811 19 |
| Net gain on account of total and permanent disability benefits or additional accidental death benefits included in life policies | | 121 90 | |
| Balance unaccounted for | | | 1,899 13 |
| Total gains and losses in surplus during the year | | $72,142 14 | $92,665 64 |
| Surplus December 31, 1920 | $23,008 64 | | |
| Surplus December 31, 1921 | 2,485 14 | | |
| Decrease in surplus | | 20,523 50 | |
| Total | | $92,665 64 | $92,665 64 |

## SCHEDULE D—PART 1—BONDS.

| Description. | Book value. | Par value. | Market value. |
|---|---|---|---|
| Building bonds, 1st mortgage, 128 N. Wells St., 7s, 1922 | $1,000 00 | $1,000 00 | $1,000 00 |
| Building bonds, 1st mortgage, 128 N. Wells St., 7s, 1924 | 500 00 | 500 00 | 500 00 |
| Totals | $1,500 00 | $1,500 00 | $1,500 00 |

## SCHEDULE D—PART 2—STOCKS.

| Description. | Book value. | Par value. | Market value. |
|---|---|---|---|
| City State Bank of Chicago | $115,830 00 | $70,200 00 | $122,850 00 |

# PEORIA LIFE INSURANCE COMPANY.

Located at No. 1100 Peoria Life Building, Peoria, Illinois; commenced business February 15, 1908.

EMMET C. MAY, President. G. B. PATTISON, Secretary.

## CAPITAL.

| | | |
|---|---|---|
| Capital paid up | $200,000 00 | |
| Amount of ledger assets December 31, of previous year | | $3,926,497 91 |

## INCOME.

| | | | |
|---|---|---|---|
| First year's premiums on original policies, less re-insurance | | $455,387 65 | |
| First year's premiums for total and permanent disability benefits, less re-insurance | | 20,201 37 | |
| First year's premiums for additional accidental death benefits, less re-insurance | | 8,874 23 | |
| Surrender values to pay first year's premiums | | 440 58 | |
| Dividends applied to purchase paid-up additions and annuities | | 1,944 73 | |
| Surrender values applied to purchase paid-up insurance and annuities | | 13,599 56 | |
| Dividends on deposit applied to purchase paid-up insurance | | 377 86 | |
| New premiums | | $ 500,825 98 | |
| Renewal premiums less re-insurance | $1,540,786 02 | | |
| Renewal premiums for total and permanent disability benefits, less re-insurance | 33,806 97 | | |
| Renewal premiums for additional accidental death benefits, less re-insurance | 9,774 50 | | |
| Dividends applied to pay renewal premiums | 9,770 89 | | |
| G. P. A. coupons applied on premiums | 6,326 45 | | |
| Surrender values applied to pay renewal premiums | 515 24 | | |
| Renewal premiums | | 1,600,980 07 | |
| Premium income | | | $2,101,806 05 |
| Consideration for supplementary contracts not involving life contingencies | | | 22,447 92 |
| Dividends left with company to accumulate at interest | | | 18,127 38 |
| Interest on mortgage loans | | $ 63,524 95 | |
| Interest on premium notes, policy loans or liens | | 45,669 75 | |
| Interest on deposits | | 528 99 | |
| Interest on other debts due the company | | 4,531 44 | |
| Rents—including $21,450.00 for company's occupancy of its own buildings | | 175,624 31 | |
| Total interest and rents | | | 289,879 44 |
| Inspection of mortgage loans | | | 121 54 |
| Total income | | | $2,432,382 33 |
| Total | | | $6,358,880 24 |

## DISBURSEMENTS.

| | | |
|---|---|---|
| Death claims | $194,857 88 | |
| Total and permanent disability claims | 11,561 65 | |
| Total death claims | | $206,419 53 |
| Annuities involving life contingencies | | 1,284 24 |
| Premium notes and liens voided by lapse | | 36,630 05 |
| Surrender values paid in cash, or applied in liquidation of loans or notes | | 52,387 97 |
| Surrender values applied to pay new and renewal premiums | | 955 82 |
| Surrender values applied to puchase paid-up insurance and annuities | | 13,599 56 |
| Dividends paid policyholders in cash, or applied in liquidation of loans or notes | | 5,563 72 |
| Dividends applied to pay renewal premiums | | 9,770 89 |
| G. P. A. coupons applied on premiums | | 8,126 58 |
| Dividends applied to purchase paid-up additions and annuities | | 1,944 73 |
| Dividends left with the company to accumulate at interest | | 18,127 38 |
| (Total paid policyholders | $354,810 47) | |
| Expense of investigation and settlement of policy claims, including legal expenses | | 854 80 |
| Supplementary contracts not involving life contingencies | | 11,205 03 |
| Dividends with interest, held on deposit surrendered during the year | | 2,156 87 |
| Dividends to stockholders | | 10,000 00 |
| Commissions to agents, first year, $343,417.53; renewal, $106,215.58 | | 449,633 11 |
| Compensation of managers and agents not paid by commissions on new business | | 3,120 00 |
| Agency supervision and traveling expenses of supervisors | | 26,298 69 |
| Branch office expenses | | 58,838 62 |
| Medical examiners' fees and inspection of risks | | 34,788 07 |
| Salaries and all other compensation of officers and home office employees | | 139,279 87 |
| Rent | | 21,450 00 |
| Advertising, printing, stationery, postage, telegraph, telephone, express and exchange | | 66,255 18 |
| Legal expense | | 286 50 |
| Furniture, fixtures and safes | | 29,945 51 |
| Repairs, and expenses (other than taxes) on real estate | | 70,186 37 |
| Taxes on real estate | | 6,189 50 |
| State taxes on premiums | | 19,286 04 |
| Insurance department licenses and fees | | 4,432 89 |
| Federal taxes | | 11,252 54 |
| All other licenses, fees and taxes | | 318 29 |
| Decrease in suspense account | | 91 37 |
| Other disbursements, viz: Convention expense, $7,109.05; entertainment, $932.23; home office supplies, $5,899.62; library, $37.75; miscellaneous, $2,731.20; periodicals, $1,754.09; premiums on fire insurance and bond, $537.50; subscriptions and dues, $1,019.15; home office traveling, $4,101.93; agents' traveling, $1,014.04; traveling expense renewals, $1,514.39; $100,000.00 and $200,000.00 clubs, $11,921.33 | | 38,572 28 |

## DISBURSEMENTS—Concluded.

| | | |
|---|---|---|
| Agents' balances charged off | | $6,248 14 |
| Decrease in book value of ledger assets | | 65 30 |
| Total disbursements | | $1,365,565 44 |
| Balance | | $4,993,314 80 |

## LEDGER ASSETS.

| | | |
|---|---|---|
| Book value of real estate | | $2,457,472 31 |
| Mortgage loans on real estate | | 1,362,445 00 |
| Loans on company's policies assigned as collateral | | 627,545 71 |
| Premium notes on policies in force | | 363,662 01 |
| Cash in office | | 1,031 41 |
| Deposits in trust companies and banks not on interest | | 98,189 30 |
| Deposits in trust companies and banks on interest | | 14,546 48 |
| Agents' balances (debit, $73,285.32; credit, $4,862.74) | | 68,422 58 |
| Total ledger assets | | $4,993,314 80 |

### NON-LEDGER ASSETS.

| | | |
|---|---|---|
| Interest due and accrued on mortgages | $33,418 79 | |
| Interest due and accrued on premium notes, loans or liens | 4,520 43 | |
| Interest due and accrued on other assets | 76 24 | |
| Rents due on company's property | 3,536 50 | |
| | | 41,551 96 |
| Due from other companies for losses or claims on policies re-insured | | 25,000 00 |
| Net uncollected and deferred premiums (paid for basis): Renewals | | 156,320 72 |
| All other assets, viz: Cash in Peoria Life Building office, $1,650.00; unearned premiums on miscellaneous insurance, $3,739.30 | | 5,389 30 |
| Gross assets | | $5,221,576 78 |

### DEDUCT ASSETS NOT ADMITTED.

| | | |
|---|---|---|
| Agents' debit balances | $73,285 32 | |
| Premium notes, policy loans and other policy assets in excess of net value and of other policy liabilities on individual policies | 61,621 81 | |
| Total | | 134,907 13 |
| Admitted assets | | $5,086,669 65 |

## LIABILITIES.

| | | |
|---|---|---|
| Net present value of outstanding policies computed by the Illinois Insurance Department | $4,344,023 00 | |
| Same for dividend additions | 7,725 00 | |
| Same for annuities | 8,483 00 | |
| Total | $4,360,231 00 | |
| Deduct net value of risks re-insured | 16,488 00 | |
| Net reserve (paid for basis) | | $4,343,743 00 |
| Extra reserve for total and permanent disability benefits and for additional accidental death benefits included in life policies, less re-insurance | | 34,977 00 |
| Present value of supplementary contracts not involving life contingencies | | 100,874 29 |
| Present value of amounts incurred but not yet due for total and permanent disability benefits | | 16,699 00 |
| Death losses reported for which no proofs have been received | $41,000 00 | |
| Reserve for net death losses incurred but unreported | 1,969 48 | |
| Total policy claims | | 42,969 48 |
| Dividends left with the company to accumulate at interest | | 61,143 15 |
| Gross premiums paid in advance, including surrender values so applied, less discount, if any | | 9,264 01 |
| Unearned interest and rent paid in advance | | 17,273 00 |
| Commissions due agents on premium notes, when paid | | 45,892 09 |
| Salaries, rents, office expenses, bills, and accounts due or accrued | | 5,330 52 |
| Medical examiners' and legal fees due or accrued | | 1,551 00 |
| Estimated amount hereafter payable for federal, state and other taxes based upon the business of the year of this statement | | 46,319 01 |
| Dividends declared on or apportioned to annual dividend policies payable to policyholders during 1922 for period to June 30, 1922 | | 12,750 73 |
| Dividends declared on or apportioned to deferred dividend policies payable to policyholders during 1922 for period to June 30, 1922 | | 23,221 17 |
| Amounts set apart, apportioned, provisionally ascertained, calculated, declared or held awaiting apportionment upon deferred dividend policies | | 73,212 89 |
| Premiums in suspense | | 920 07 |
| Total | | $4,836,140 41 |
| Capital paid up | | 200,000 00 |
| Unassigned funds (surplus) | | 50,529 24 |
| Total | | $5,086,669 65 |

## EXHIBIT OF POLICIES—ORDINARY.

ALL BUSINESS PAID FOR.

| | Number. | Amount. | Number. | Amount. |
|---|---|---|---|---|
| Policies in force December 31, 1920 | | | 26,873 | $59,009,042 00 |
| Policies issued, revived, and increased during the year | | | 5,863 | 15,137,829 00 |
| Total | | | 32,736 | $74,146,871 00 |
| Deduct policies which have ceased to be in force during the year— | | | | |
| By death | 82 | $ 236,620 00 | | |
| By expiry | 101 | 190,611 00 | | |
| By surrender | 260 | 641,776 00 | | |
| By lapse | 2,533 | 6,240,839 00 | | |
| By decrease | -------- | 453,160 00 | | |
| Total | | | 2,976 | 7,763,006 00 |
| Total policies in force December 31, 1921 | | | 29,760 | $66,383,865 00 |
| Re-insured | | | 362 | $2,569,322 00 |

## BUSINESS IN ILLINOIS—ORDINARY.

| | Number. | Amount. |
|---|---|---|
| Policies in force December 31, 1920 | 14,222 | $32,136,129 00 |
| Policies issued during the year | 2,735 | 8,166,574 00 |
| Total | 16,957 | $40,302,703 00 |
| Deduct policies ceased to be in force | 1,470 | 4,405,309 00 |
| Policies in force December 31, 1921 | 15,487 | $35,897,394 00 |
| Losses and claims unpaid December 31, 1920 | 5 | $ 7,193 34 |
| Losses and claims incurred during the year | 41 | 136,766 67 |
| Total | 46 | $143,960 01 |
| Losses and claims settled during the year | 43 | 101,904 53 |
| Losses and claims unpaid December 31, 1921 | 3 | $42,055 48 |
| Premiums received | | $1,090,293 11 |

## GAIN AND LOSS EXHIBIT.

INSURANCE EXHIBIT.

| | | Gain in surplus. | Loss in surplus. |
|---|---|---|---|
| Loading on actual premiums of the year (averaging 23.81 per cent of the gross premiums) | $498,527 20 | | |
| Insurance expenses incurred during the year | 896,437 98 | | |
| Loss from loading | | -------------- | $397,910 78 |
| Interest earned during the year | $295,628 76 | | |
| Investment expenses incurred during the year | 106,787 78 | | |
| Net income from investments | $188,840 98 | | |
| Interest required to maintain reserve | 146,539 29 | | |
| Gain from interest | | $ 42,301 69 | |
| Expected mortality on net amount at risk | $553,616 00 | | |
| Actual mortality on net amount at risk | 189,920 10 | | |
| Gain from mortality | | 363,695 90 | |
| Expected disbursements to annuities | $ 694 58 | | |
| Net actual annuity claims incurred | 1,284 24 | | |
| Loss from annuities | | -------------- | 589 66 |
| Total gain during the year from surrendered and lapsed policies | | 8,911 00 | |
| Dividends paid stockholders | | -------------- | 10,000 00 |
| Decrease in surplus on dividend account | | -------------- | 47,771 62 |
| Net to loss account | | -------------- | 15,281 01 |

INVESTMENT EXHIBIT.

| | | Gain in surplus. | Loss in surplus. |
|---|---|---|---|
| Total losses from real estate | | -------------- | 65 30 |
| Loss from assets not admitted | | -------------- | 25,884 18 |
| Net gain on account of total and permanent disability benefits or additional accidental death benefits included in life policies | | 29,702 42 | |
| Balance unaccounted for | | -------------- | 4,432 24 |
| Total gains and losses in surplus during the year | | $444,611 01 | $501,934 79 |
| Surplus December 31, 1920 | $107,853 02 | | |
| Surplus December 31, 1921 | 50,529 24 | | |
| Decrease in surplus | | 57,323 78 | |
| Total | | $501,934 79 | $501,934 79 |

## PROVIDERS LIFE ASSURANCE COMPANY.

Located at No. 1530 North Robey Street, Chicago, Illinois; commenced business February 18, 1916.

M. F. BOZINCH, President. W. S. MIROSLAWSKI, Secretary.

### CAPITAL.

| | | |
|---|---|---|
| Capital paid up | $145,960 00 | |
| Amount of ledger assets December 31, of previous year | $471,483 92 | |
| Increase of paid-up capital during year | 530 00 | |
| Extended at | | $472,013 92 |

### INCOME.

| | | | |
|---|---|---|---|
| First year's premiums on original policies, less re-insurance | | $41,055 60 | |
| First year's premiums for total and permanent disability benefits | | 27 56 | |
| First year's premiums for additional accidental death benefits, less re-insurance | | 4 00 | |
| Surrender values to pay first year's premiums | | 9,336 35 | |
| New premiums | | $ 50,423 51 | |
| Renewal premiums less re-insurance | $173,173 14 | | |
| Renewal premiums for total and permanent disability benefits | 27 88 | | |
| Dividends applied to pay renewal premiums | 13 31 | | |
| Industrial renewal premiums | 2,284 05 | | |
| Renewal premiums | | 175,498 38 | |
| Premium income | | | $225,921 89 |
| Interest on mortgage loans | | $ 5,505 14 | |
| Interest on bonds | | 22,878 75 | |
| Interest on premium notes, policy loans or liens | | 602 92 | |
| Interest on deposits | | 141 89 | |
| Interest on other debts due the company | | 2 99 | |
| Rents—including $2,250.00 for company's occupancy of its own buildings less $530.10 interest on incumbrances | | 3,643 90 | |
| Total interest and rents | | | 32,775 59 |
| From other sources, viz: Surplus sale of stock, $2,120.00; war tax on insurance, $1,467.85; deposit on rate books, $196.00; suspense, $298.99; rewriting lost policies, $0.95; received for agents' bonds, $292.36 | | | 4,376 15 |
| Borrowed money (gross) | | | 12,000 00 |
| Profit on sale or maturity of ledger assets | | | 6,135 32 |
| Increase in book value of ledger assets | | | 10,000 00 |
| Total income | | | $291,208 95 |
| Total | | | $763,222 87 |

### DISBURSEMENTS.

| | | |
|---|---|---|
| Death claims | | $41,676 73 |
| Surrender values paid in cash, or applied in liquidation of loans or notes | | 14,164 61 |
| Surrender values applied to pay new premiums | | 9,336 35 |
| Dividends applied to pay renewal premiums | | 13 31 |
| (Total paid policyholders | $65,191 00) | |
| Commissions to agents, first year, $32,867.71; renewal, $10,562.12 | | 43,429 83 |
| Commuted renewal commissions | | 2,800 00 |
| Compensation of managers and agents not paid by commissions on new business | | 7,137 05 |
| Agency supervision and traveling expenses of supervisors | | 2,224 01 |
| Branch office expenses | | 4,055 23 |
| Medical examiners' fees and inspection of risks | | 3,783 00 |
| Salaries and all other compensation of officers and home office employees | | 38,433 30 |
| Rent | | 3,878 10 |
| Advertising, printing, stationery, postage, telegraph, telephone, express and exchange | | 13,057 82 |
| Legal expense | | 2,678 92 |
| Furniture, fixtures and safes | | 2,101 29 |
| Repairs and expenses (other than taxes) on real estate | | 4,097 06 |
| Taxes on real estate | | 133 99 |
| State taxes on premiums | | 619 60 |
| Insurance department licenses and fees | | 679 42 |
| Federal taxes | | 1,366 43 |
| All other licenses, fees and taxes | | 30 62 |
| Other disbursements, viz: Expense of remodeling offices, $5,657.24; miscellaneous, $586.79; moving, $478.99; commissions sale of stock, $477.00 | | 7,200 02 |
| Borrowed money repaid (gross) | | 12,000 00 |
| Interest on borrowed money | | 254 33 |
| Agents' balances charged off | | 260 50 |
| Loss on sale or maturity of ledger assets | | 1,277 76 |
| Total disbursements | | $216,689 28 |
| Balance | | $546,533 59 |

## LEDGER ASSETS.

| | | |
|---|---|---|
| Book value of real estate | | $29,000 00 |
| Mortgage loans on real estate | | 85,630 00 |
| Loans on company's policies assigned as collateral | | 10,780 39 |
| Book value of bonds | | 392,501 72 |
| Cash in office | | 50 00 |
| Deposits in trust companies and banks not on interest | | 9,663 21 |
| Deposits in trust companies and banks on interest | | 10,962 03 |
| Bills receivable | | 470 18 |
| Agents' debit balances | | 3,980 57 |
| Securities deposited to cover premiums paid but not remitted to home office | | 3,495 49 |
| Total ledger assets | | $546,533 59 |

### NON-LEDGER ASSETS.

| | | | |
|---|---|---|---|
| Interest due and accrued on mortgages | | $1,413 02 | |
| Interest due and accrued on bonds | | 9,062 19 | |
| Interest due on premium notes, loans or liens | | 2 29 | |
| | | | 10,477 50 |
| | New business. | Renewals. | |
| Net uncollected and deferred premiums (paid for basis) | $941 68 | $26,439 30 | 27,380 98 |
| Gross assets | | | $584,392 07 |

### DEDUCT ASSETS NOT ADMITTED.

| | | |
|---|---|---|
| Agents' debit balances | $3,980 57 | |
| Bills receivable | 470 18 | |
| Premium notes, policy loans and other policy assets in excess of net value and of other policy liabilities on individual policies | 649 23 | |
| Excess premiums not remitted over securities to cover | 1,000 00 | |
| Book value of bonds over market value | 3,754 72 | |
| Total | | 9,854 70 |
| Admitted assets | | $574,537 37 |

## LIABILITIES.

| | | |
|---|---|---|
| Net present value of outstanding policies computed by the Illinois Insurance Department | $390,469 00 | |
| Deduct net value of risks re-insured | 391 00 | |
| Net reserve (paid for basis) | | $390,078 00 |
| Extra reserve for total and permanent disability benefits included in life policies | | 24 00 |
| Death losses due and unpaid | $1,675 00 | |
| Death losses in process of adjustment | 1,000 00 | |
| Death losses reported for which no proofs have been received | 1,775 00 | |
| Total policy claims | | 4,450 00 |
| Gross premiums paid in advance, including surrender values so applied, less discount, if any | | 2,730 84 |
| Unearned interest and rent paid in advance | | 250 31 |
| Salaries, rents, office expenses, bills, and accounts due or accrued | | 148 82 |
| Legal fees due or accrued | | 11 00 |
| Estimated amount hereafter payable for federal, state and other taxes based upon the business of the year of this statement | | 750 00 |
| Other liabilities, viz: Employees' Liberty Bond account, $23.93; deposit on rate books, $196.00; suspense, $1,564.42; war tax on insurance, $83.32 | | 1,867 67 |
| Total | | $400,310 64 |
| Capital paid up | | 145,960 00 |
| Unassigned funds (surplus) | | 28,266 73 |
| Total | | $574,537 37 |

## EXHIBIT OF POLICIES—ORDINARY.

### ALL BUSINESS PAID FOR.

| | | | Number. | Amount. |
|---|---|---|---|---|
| Policies in force December 31, 1920 | | | 18,273 | $6,828,658 00 |
| Policies issued, revived, and increased during the year | | | 3,923 | 1,590,150 00 |
| Total | | | 22,196 | $8,418,808 00 |
| Deduct policies which have ceased to be in force during the year— | Number. | Amount. | | |
| By death | 161 | $ 51,200 00 | | |
| By expiry | 23 | 11,250 00 | | |
| By surrender | 280 | 172,645 00 | | |
| By lapse | 3,349 | 1,022,200 00 | | |
| By decrease | 346 | 238,116 00 | | |
| Total | | | 4,159 | 1,495,411 00 |
| Total policies in force December 31, 1921 | | | 18,037 | $6,923,397 00 |
| Re-insured | | | 35 | $82,000 00 |

## EXHIBIT OF POLICIES—INDUSTRIAL.

ALL BUSINESS PAID FOR.

| | Number. | Amount. | Number. | Amount. |
|---|---|---|---|---|
| Policies in force December 31, 1920 | | | 4,760 | $318,708 00 |
| Policies issued, revived, and increased during the year | | | 54 | 8,069 00 |
| Total | | | 4,814 | $326,777 00 |
| Deduct policies which have ceased to be in force during the year— | | | | |
| By death | 4 | $ 567 00 | | |
| By surrender | 1,886 | 182,431 00 | | |
| By lapse | 319 | 46,368 00 | | |
| By decrease | | 34,555 00 | | |
| Total | | | 2,209 | 263,921 00 |
| Total policies in force December 31, 1921 | | | 2,605 | $62,856 00 |

## BUSINESS IN ILLINOIS—ORDINARY.

| | Number. | Amount. |
|---|---|---|
| Policies in force December 31, 1920 | 18,273 | $6,828,658 00 |
| Policies issued during the year | 3,120 | 1,102,350 00 |
| Total | 21,393 | $7,931,008 00 |
| Deduct policies ceased to be in force | 4,010 | 1,424,911 00 |
| Policies in force December 31, 1921 | 17,383 | $6,506,097 00 |
| Losses and claims unpaid December 31, 1920 | 13 | $ 7,512 00 |
| Losses and claims incurred during the year | 163 | 40,551 00 |
| Total | 176 | $48,063 00 |
| Losses and claims settled during the year | 163 | 43,838 00 |
| Losses and claims unpaid December 31, 1921 | 13 | $4,225 00 |
| Premiums received | | $209,689 71 |

## BUSINESS IN ILLINOIS—INDUSTRIAL.

| | Number. | Amount. |
|---|---|---|
| Policies in force December 31, 1920 | 4,760 | $318,708 00 |
| Policies issued during the year | 54 | 8,069 00 |
| Total | 4,814 | $326,777 00 |
| Deduct policies ceased to be in force | 2,209 | 263,921 00 |
| Policies in force December 31, 1921 | 2,605 | $62,856 00 |
| Losses and claims unpaid December 31, 1920 | 1 | $225 00 |
| Losses and claims incurred during the year | 4 | 437 00 |
| Total | 5 | $662 00 |
| Losses and claims settled during the year | 4 | 437 00 |
| Losses and claims unpaid December 31, 1921 | 1 | $225 00 |
| Premiums received | | $2,284 05 |

## GAIN AND LOSS EXHIBIT.

INSURANCE EXHIBIT.

| | | Gain in surplus. | Loss in surplus. |
|---|---|---|---|
| Loading on actual premiums of the year (averaging 24.85 per cent of the gross premiums) | $ 59,300 05 | | |
| Insurance expenses incurred during the year | 124,465 25 | | |
| Loss from loading | | | $65,165 20 |
| Interest earned during the year | $34,213 09 | | |
| Investment expenses incurred during the year | 9,888 29 | | |
| Net income from investments | $24,324 80 | | |
| Interest required to maintain reserve | 12,782 00 | | |
| Gain from interest | | $11,542 80 | |
| Expected mortality on net amount at risk | $59,237 00 | | |
| Actual mortality on net amount at risk | 36,794 49 | | |
| Gain from mortality | | 22,442 51 | |
| Total gain during the year from surrendered and lapsed policies | | 18,898 75 | |
| Net to loss account | | | 260 50 |

## GAIN AND LOSS EXHIBIT—Concluded.

### INVESTMENT EXHIBIT.

| | | Gain in surplus. | Loss in surplus. |
|---|---|---|---|
| Total gains from real estate | | $10,000 00 | |
| Total gains from bonds | | 13,493 18 | |
| Total losses from bonds | | | $1,277 76 |
| Loss from assets not admitted | | | 4,739 13 |
| Net gain on account of total and permanent disability benefits or additional accidental death benefits included in life policies | | 45 44 | |
| Loss: Commuted commission, $2,800.00; expense of moving, $478.99. Gain: Surplus sale of stock, $1,643.00; war tax on insurance, $18.10; agents' bonds, $292.36; rewriting lost policies, $0.95; net to loss account | | | 1,324 58 |
| Balance unaccounted for | | | 1,084 88 |
| Total gains and losses in surplus during the year | | $76,422 68 | $73,852 05 |
| Surplus December 31, 1920 | $25,696 10 | | |
| Surplus December 31, 1921 | 28,266 73 | | |
| Increase in surplus | | | 2,570 63 |
| Total | | $76,422 68 | $76,422 68 |

## SCHEDULE D—PART 1—BONDS.

| Description. | Book value. | Par value. | Market value. |
|---|---|---|---|
| United States Liberty Bonds, 1st, 4¼s, 1947 | $ 87 74 | $ 100 00 | $ 97 00 |
| United States Liberty Bonds, 2d, 4¼s | 43 84 | 50 00 | 48 50 |
| United States Liberty Bonds, 3d, 4¼s, 1928 | 183 57 | 200 00 | 196 00 |
| United States Liberty Bonds, 4th, 4¼s 1938 | 438 52 | 500 00 | 485 00 |
| United States Liberty Bonds, 5th, 4¾s, 1923 | 789 60 | 800 00 | 800 00 |
| City of Tucson, Ariz., water works, 5s, 1944 | 4,374 50 | 5,000 00 | 5,000 00 |
| Haywood Co., N. C., road and bridge, 6s, 1939 | 3,000 00 | 3,000 00 | 3,060 00 |
| Haywood Co., N. C., road and bridge, 6s, 1941 | 5,000 00 | 5,000 00 | 5,100 00 |
| Lake Carmorant, 6s, 1937 | 5,000 00 | 5,000 00 | 5,000 00 |
| Mason City, Ia., 5½s, 1930 | 3,960 00 | 4,000 00 | 4,280 00 |
| Santa Cruz Co., Ariz., 6s, 1939 | 4,975 00 | 5,000 00 | 5,500 00 |
| St. Mary's Parish, La., 5s, 1933 | 1,827 94 | 2,000 00 | 2,000 00 |
| St. Mary's Parish, La., 5s, 1937 | 897 05 | 1,000 00 | 1,000 00 |
| St. Mary's Parish, La., 5s, 1940 | 886 66 | 1,000 00 | 1,000 00 |
| St. Mary's Parish, La., 5s, 1942 | 880 72 | 1,000 00 | 1,000 00 |
| Wichita Falls, Tex., 6s, 1950 | 4,987 50 | 5,000 00 | 5,650 00 |
| Arkansas Valley Interurban Ry., 5½s, 1936 | 4,000 00 | 5,000 00 | 4,000 00 |
| Arkansas Valley Interurban Ry., 5½s, 1936 | 20,000 00 | 25,000 00 | 20,000 00 |
| Arkansas Valley Interurban Ry., 5½s, 1936 | 800 00 | 1,000 00 | 800 00 |
| Baumont Gas Light Co., 6s, 1944 | 12,375 00 | 15,000 00 | 12,000 00 |
| Brooklyn Edison, 7s, 1940 | 4,868 75 | 5,000 00 | 5,350 00 |
| Central Illinois Public Service Co., 5s, 1952 | 31,412 50 | 35,000 00 | 25,900 00 |
| Columbia Gas & Electric, 5s, 1936 | 15,400 00 | 20,000 00 | 13,800 00 |
| Columbia Railway, Gas & Electric, 5s, 1936 | 4,046 50 | 5,000 00 | 3,450 00 |
| Michigan Northern Power Co., 5s, 1941 | 4,400 00 | 5,000 00 | 4,400 00 |
| North American Light & Power, 6s, 1937 | 1,620 00 | 2,000 00 | 1,700 00 |
| Northern New York Utilities, 5s, 1963 | 22,850 00 | 27,000 00 | 21,060 00 |
| Northwestern Electric Co., 6s, 1935 | 23,400 00 | 26,000 00 | 23,920 00 |
| Oklahoma Gas & Electric Co., 7½s, 1941 | 35,000 00 | 35,000 00 | 35,700 00 |
| Pacific Gas & Electric Co., 6s, 1931 | 4,575 00 | 5,000 00 | 4,600 00 |
| Pacific Gas & Electric Co., 6s, 1931 | 22,500 00 | 25,000 00 | 23,000 00 |
| Pacific Gas & Electric Co., 6s, 1941 | 34,475 00 | 35,000 00 | 34,650 00 |
| Public Service Co. of Northern Illinois, 5s, 1956 | 4,806 25 | 5,000 00 | 4,300 00 |
| Public Service Co. of Northern Illinois, 5s, 1956 | 955 00 | 1,000 00 | 860 00 |
| Salt Lake & Utah R. R. Co., 6s, 1944 | 10,855 00 | 13,000 00 | 10,400 00 |
| Salt Lake & Utah R. R. Co., 6s, 1944 | 177 00 | 200 00 | 160 00 |
| Southern Illinois Light & Power, 6s, 1931 | 5,295 00 | 6,000 00 | 5,400 00 |
| Southern Illinois Light & Power, 6s, 1931 | 176 58 | 200 00 | 180 00 |
| Springfield Railway Co., 5s, 1928 | 810 00 | 1,000 00 | 810 00 |
| Springfield Railway Co., 5s, 1929 | 790 00 | 1,000 00 | 790 00 |
| Springfield Railway Co., 5s, 1930 | 770 00 | 1,000 00 | 770 00 |
| Springfield Railway Co., 5s, 1935 | 576 00 | 800 00 | 560 00 |
| Springfield Railway Co., 5s, 1933 | 3,900 00 | 6,000 00 | 4,200 00 |
| Springfield Railway Co., 5s, 1934 | 1,300 00 | 2,000 00 | 1,400 00 |
| Springfield Railway Co., 5s, 1935 | 11,050 00 | 17,000 00 | 11,900 00 |
| Texas Electric Railway, 5s, 1947 | 18,750 00 | 25,000 00 | 19,000 00 |
| West Pennsylvania Power Co., 7s, 1946 | 4,825 00 | 5,000 00 | 5,250 00 |
| New England Oil Refinery Co., 8s, 1931 | 24,500 00 | 25,000 00 | 24,250 00 |
| New England Oil Refinery Co., 8s, 1931 | 3,920 00 | 4,000 00 | 3,880 00 |
| Robert Gair Co., 7s, 1937 | 19,300 00 | 20,000 00 | 19,400 00 |
| Totals | $391,811 22 | $442,850 00 | $388,056 50 |

## PUBLIC LIFE INSURANCE COMPANY.

Located at No. 108 South LaSalle Street, Chicago, Illinois; commenced business May 5, 1920.

LOUIS NAROWETZ, President. J. W. SINGLETON, Secretary.

### CAPITAL.

| | | |
|---|---|---|
| Capital paid up | $200,000 00 | |
| Amount of ledger assets December 31, of previous year | | $884,796 28 |

### INCOME.

| | | |
|---|---|---|
| First year's premiums on original policies, less re-insurance | $49,284 34 | |
| Renewal premiums less re-insurance | 35,027 94 | |
| Total | | $84,312 28 |
| Interest on mortgage loans | $ 5,216 23 | |
| Interest on bonds and dividends on stocks | 12,054 60 | |
| Interest on deposits | 212 33 | |
| Interest on other debts due the company | 38 75 | |
| Rents—including $250.00 for company's occupancy of its own buildings less $109.08 interest on incumbrances | 4,318 42 | |
| Total interest and rents | | 21,840 33 |
| From other sources, viz: Miscellaneous income, $47.76; refund of commissions on stock, $30,000.00 | | 30,047 76 |
| Profit on sale or maturity of ledger assets | | 1,235 66 |
| Increase in book value of ledger assets | | 49,117 80 |
| Total income | | $186,553 83 |
| Total | | $1,071,350 11 |

### DISBURSEMENTS.

| | | |
|---|---|---|
| Death claims | | $ 4,606 50 |
| (Total paid policyholders | $4,606 50) | |
| Commissions to agents, first year, $37,339.97; renewal, $5,310.58 | | 42,650 55 |
| Compensation of managers and agents not paid by commissions on new business | | 10,412 00 |
| Branch office expenses | | 9,450 55 |
| Medical examiners' fees and inspection of risks | | 3,497 25 |
| Salaries and all other compensation of officers and home office employees | | 63,899 56 |
| Rent | | 8,029 02 |
| Advertising, printing, stationery, postage, telegraph, telephone, express and exchange | | 34,318 18 |
| Legal expense | | 11,775 00 |
| Repairs and expenses (other than taxes) on real estate, $3,208.07; ground lease, $1,125.00 | | 4,333 07 |
| Taxes on real estate | | 312 89 |
| Insurance department licenses and fees | | 1,211 33 |
| Federal taxes | | 946 56 |
| Other disbursements, viz: Traveling expense, $762.45; actuarial expense, $5,685.00; miscellaneous expense, $5,034.89; automobile expense, $1,191.80; managers expense, $1,300.00; medical department expense, $500.00; banquet expense, $4,747.95; auditing, $1,402.50 | | 20,624 59 |
| Loss on sale or maturity of ledger assets | | 20 70 |
| Total disbursements | | $216,087 75 |
| Balance | | $855,262 36 |

### LEDGER ASSETS.

| | |
|---|---|
| Book value of real estate | $148,000 00 |
| Mortgage loans on real estate | 211,063 00 |
| Book value of bonds and stocks | 277,750 88 |
| Deposits in trust companies and banks not on interest | 696 49 |
| Deposits in trust companies and banks on interest | 12,364 57 |
| Bills receivable | 98,238 38 |
| Agents' balances (debit, $15,238.47) | 15,238 47 |
| Public agency | 11,989 03 |
| Capital stock subscription notes, $61,532.72; furniture and fixtures, $18,388.82 | 79,921 54 |
| Total ledger assets | $855,262 36 |

#### NON-LEDGER ASSETS.

| | New business. | Renewals. | |
|---|---|---|---|
| Interest accrued on mortgages | | $3,993 70 | |
| Interest due and accrued on bonds | | 4,811 03 | |
| | | | 8,804 73 |
| Market value of bonds and stocks over book value | | | 7,449 12 |
| Net uncollected and deferred premiums (paid for basis) | $2,659 73 | $8,185 57 | 10,845 30 |
| Stationery, printing and supplies | | | 13,500 00 |
| Gross assets | | | $895,861 51 |

## LEDGER ASSETS—Concluded.

DEDUCT ASSETS NOT ADMITTED.

| | | |
|---|---|---|
| Supplies, printed matter and stationery | $13,500 00 | |
| Furniture, fixtures and safes | 18,388 82 | |
| Agents' debit balances | 15,238 47 | |
| Bills receivable | 98,238 38 | |
| Premium notes, policy loans and other policy assets in excess of net value and of other policy liabilities on individual policies | 500 00 | |
| Accounts receivable | 11,989 03 | |
| Capital stock subscription notes | 61,532 72 | |
| Total | | $219,387 42 |
| Admitted assets | | $676,474 09 |

## LIABILITIES.

| | | |
|---|---|---|
| Net present value of outstanding policies computed by the Illinois Insurance Department | $61,653 00 | |
| Deduct net value of risks re-insured | 670 00 | |
| Net reserve (paid for basis) | | $60,983 00 |
| Extra reserve for total and permanent disability benefits and for additional accidental death benefits included in life policies | | 3,249 00 |
| Death losses reported for which no proofs have been received | | 2,000 00 |
| Gross premiums paid in advance, including surrender values so applied, less discount, if any | | 87 43 |
| Salaries, rents, office expenses, bills and accounts due or accrued | | 2,566 39 |
| Estimated amount hereafter payable for federal, state and other taxes based upon the business of the year of this statement | | 1,500 00 |
| Total | | $ 70,385 82 |
| Capital paid up | | 200,000 00 |
| Unassigned funds (surplus) | | 406,088 27 |
| Total | | $676,474 09 |

## EXHIBIT OF POLICIES—ORDINARY.

ALL BUSINESS PAID FOR.

| | Number. | Amount. | Number. | Amount. |
|---|---|---|---|---|
| Policies in force December 31, 1920 | | | 670 | $1,404,500 00 |
| Policies issued, revived and increased during the year | | | 754 | 1,255,500 00 |
| Total | | | 1,424 | $2,660,000 00 |
| Deduct policies which have ceased to be in force during the year— | | | | |
| By death | 3 | $ 4,000 00 | | |
| By lapse | 112 | 220,000 00 | | |
| By decrease | -------- | 2,000 00 | | |
| Total | | | 115 | 226,000 00 |
| Total policies in force December 31, 1921 | | | 1,309 | $2,434,000 00 |
| Re-insured | | | 5 | $120,000 00 |

## EXHIBIT OF POLICIES—INDUSTRIAL.

ALL BUSINESS PAID FOR.

| | Number. | Amount. | Number. | Amount. |
|---|---|---|---|---|
| Policies in force December 31' 1920 | | | 230 | $28,622 00 |
| Policies issued, revived and increased during the year | | | 576 | 82,765 00 |
| Total | | | 806 | $111,387 00 |
| Deduct policies which have ceased to be in force during the year— | | | | |
| By death | 10 | $ 1,387 00 | | |
| By lapse | 226 | 30,812 00 | | |
| Total | | | 236 | 32,199 00 |
| Total policies in force December 31, 1921 | | | 570 | $79,188 00 |

## BUSINESS IN ILLINOIS—ORDINARY.

| | Number. | Amount. |
|---|---|---|
| Policies in force December 31, 1920 | 670 | $1,404,500 00 |
| Policies issued during the year | 754 | 1,255,500 00 |
| Total | 1,424 | $2,660,000 00 |
| Deduct policies ceased to be in force | 115 | 226,000 00 |
| Policies in force December 31, 1921 | 1,309 | $2,434,000 00 |

## BUSINESS IN ILLINOIS—ORDINARY—Concluded.

| | Number. | Amount. |
|---|---|---|
| Losses and claims incurred during the year | 4 | $6,000 00 |
| Losses and claims settled during the year | 3 | 4,000 00 |
| Losses and claims unpaid December 31, 1921 | 1 | $2,000 00 |
| Premiums received | | $80,692 09 |

## BUSINESS IN ILLINOIS—INDUSTRIAL.

| | Number. | Amount. |
|---|---|---|
| Policies in force December 31, 1920 | 230 | $28,622 00 |
| Policies issued during the year | 576 | 82,765 00 |
| Total | 806 | $111,387 00 |
| Deduct policies ceased to be in force | 236 | 32,199 00 |
| Policies in force December 31, 1921 | 570 | $79,188 00 |
| Losses and claims incurred during the year | 10 | $606 50 |
| Losses and claims settled during the year | 10 | 606 50 |
| Premiums received | | $2,889 18 |

## GAIN AND LOSS EXHIBIT.

### INSURANCE EXHIBIT.

| | | Gain in surplus. | Loss in surplus. |
|---|---|---|---|
| Loading on actual premiums of the year (averaging 36.25 per cent of the gross premiums) | $ 33,005 41 | | |
| Insurance expenses incurred during the year | 200,970 43 | | |
| Loss from loading | | | $167,965 02 |
| Interest earned during the year | $26,782 26 | | |
| Investment expenses incurred during the year | 6,145 96 | | |
| Net income from investments | $20,636 30 | | |
| Interest required to maintain reserve | 1,387 74 | | |
| Gain from interest | | $19,248 56 | |
| Expected mortality on net amount at risk | $11,378 40 | | |
| Actual mortality on net amount at risk | 6,557 44 | | |
| Gain from mortality | | 4,820 96 | |
| Total gain during the year from surrendered and lapsed policies | | 948 25 | |
| **INVESTMENT EXHIBIT.** | | | |
| Total gains from real estate | | 49,117 80 | |
| Total gains from stocks and bonds | | 13,693 28 | |
| Total losses from stocks and bonds | | | 20 70 |
| Loss from assets not admitted | | | 116,472 84 |
| Gain from capital stock account | | 429,572 94 | |
| Gain from Agency Company reimbursed overpayment in 1920 | | 10,236 63 | |
| Gain, miscellaneous income | | 47 76 | |
| Gain, refund of commissions on capital stock | | 30,000 00 | |
| Balance unaccounted for | | | 354 28 |
| Total gains and losses in surplus during the year | | $557,686 18 | $284,812 84 |
| Surplus December 31, 1920 | $133,214 93 | | |
| Surplus December 31, 1921 | 406,088 27 | | |
| Increase in surplus | | | 272,873 34 |
| Total | | $557,686 18 | $557,686 18 |

## SCHEDULE D—PART 1—BONDS.

| Description. | Book value. | Par value. | Market value. |
|---|---|---|---|
| Adair Co., Mo., Salt River Drainage Dist., 6s, 1926 | $ 1,000 00 | $ 1,000 00 | $ 1,020 00 |
| Adair Co., Mo., Salt River Drainage Dist., 6s, 1927 | 2,000 00 | 2,000 00 | 2,040 00 |
| Adair Co., Mo., Salt River Drainage Dist., 6s, 1928 | 2,000 00 | 2,000 00 | 2,040 00 |
| Akron, Ohio, School, 4½s, 1925 | 9,475 00 | 10,000 00 | 9,900 00 |
| Anderson, Tex., Levee Impt., 6s, 1933 | 500 00 | 500 00 | 540 00 |
| Anderson, Tex., Levee Impt., 6s, 1935 | 4,500 00 | 4,500 00 | 4,860 00 |
| Champaign & Pratt Co., High School Dist. 168, community, 5s, 1924 | 4,880 15 | 5,000 00 | 5,000 00 |
| City of Chicago, Judgment Funding, 4s, 1932 | 18,656 00 | 20,000 00 | 19,200 00 |
| City of Chicago, Judgment Funding, 4s, 1933 | 9,286 00 | 10,000 00 | 9,600 00 |
| City of Chicago, Judgment Funding, 4s, 1934 | 9,246 00 | 10,000 00 | 9,500 00 |
| Chicago Sanitary Dist., 4s, 1932 | 3,693 20 | 4,000 00 | 3,840 00 |
| City of Jacksonville, Ill., Funding, 5s, 1925 | 3,910 00 | 4,000 00 | 4,000 00 |
| City of Jacksonville, Ill., Funding, 5s, 1926 | 5,866 80 | 6,000 00 | 6,000 00 |
| City of Jacksonville, Ill., Funding, 5s, 1927 | 5,440 80 | 5,500 00 | 5,500 00 |

SCHEDULE D—PART 1—BONDS—Concluded.

| Description. | Book value. | Par value. | Market value. |
|---|---|---|---|
| City of Jacksonville, Ill., Funding, 5s, 1928 | $ 6,500 00 | $ 6,500 00 | $ 6,500 00 |
| City of Jacksonville, Ill., Funding, 5s, 1929 | 6,500 00 | 6,500 00 | 6,500 00 |
| City of Jacksonville, Ill., Funding, 5s, 1930 | 6,000 00 | 6,000 00 | 6,000 00 |
| City of Jacksonville, Ill., Funding, 5s, 1931 | 6,500 00 | 6,500 00 | 6,500 00 |
| City of Jacksonville, Ill., Funding, 5s, 1932 | 6,500 00 | 6,500 00 | 6,500 00 |
| City of Jacksonville, Ill., Funding, 5s, 1933 | 6,500 00 | 6,500 00 | 6,500 00 |
| City of Jacksonville, Ill., Funding, 5s, 1934 | 1,500 00 | 1,500 00 | 1,500 00 |
| City of Jacksonville, Ill., Funding, 5s, 1937 | 500 00 | 500 00 | 500 00 |
| Decatur, Ill., Sanitary Dist., 5s, 1926 | 14,463 00 | 15,000 00 | 15,300 00 |
| Leesburg, Lee Co., Ga., School Dist., cons., 5s, 1936 | 1,789 50 | 2,000 00 | 2,000 00 |
| Leesburg, Lee Co., Ga., School, Dist., 5s, 1937 | 1,780 70 | 2,000 00 | 2,000 00 |
| Leesburg, Lee Co., Ga., School Dist., 5s, 1938 | 2,658 75 | 3,000 00 | 3,000 00 |
| Leesburg, Lee Co., Ga., School Dist., 5s, 1946 | 2,582 53 | 3,000 00 | 3,000 00 |
| Macoupin Co., Ill., Road Bonds, 4½s, 1927 | 5,908 80 | 6,000 00 | 5,880 00 |
| Macoupin Co., Ill., Road Bonds, 4½s, 1928 | 1,966 20 | 2,000 00 | 1,940 00 |
| Massac Co., Ill., Road Dist. No. 5, Hard Road, 5s, 1927 | 946 80 | 1,000 00 | 1,010 00 |
| Massac Co., Ill., Road Dist. No. 5, Hard Road, 5s, 1928 | 2,820 90 | 3,000 00 | 3,030 00 |
| Massac Co., Ill., Road Dist. No. 5, Hard Road, 5s, 1929 | 2,802 60 | 3,000 00 | 3,060 00 |
| Massac Co , Ill., Road Dist. No. 5, Hard Road, 5s, 1930 | 2,785 20 | 3,000 00 | 3,060 00 |
| McLean & Logan Counties, Ill., School Dist. No. 355, School Bldg., McLean Com. High, 5½s, 1938 | 4,993 75 | 5,000 00 | 5,200 00 |
| Morgan Co., Ill., School Dist., No. 117, Jacksonville, Ill., 5s, 1937 | 9,719 80 | 10,000 00 | 10,000 00 |
| Putnam & LaSalle Co., Ill., Hopkins Twp., High School Dist. No. 536, School Site Bldg., 5½s, 1925 | 1,977 00 | 2,000 00 | 2,040 00 |
| Putnam & LaSalle Co., Ill., Hopkins Twp., High School Dist. No. 536, School Site Bldg., 5½s, 1926 | 2,965 50 | 3,000 00 | 3,060 00 |
| Smithville, Lee Co., Ga., Cons. School Dist., 5s, 1933 | 909 58 | 1,000 00 | 1,000 00 |
| Smithville, Lee Co., Ga., Cons. School Dist., 5s, 1934 | 2,713 05 | 3,000 00 | 3,000 00 |
| Smithville, Lee Co., Ga., Cons. School Dist., 5s, 1935 | 2,698 23 | 3,000 00 | 3,000 00 |
| Smithville, Lee Co., Ga., Cons. School Dist., 5s, 1936 | 1,789 50 | 2,000 00 | 2,000 00 |
| Smithville, Lee Co., Ga., Cons. School Dist., 5s, 1945 | 4,316 95 | 5,000 00 | 5,000 00 |
| Smithville, Lee Co., Ga., Cons. School Dist., 5s, 1946 | 4,304 20 | 5,000 00 | 5,000 00 |
| Smithville, Lee Co., Ga., Cons. School Dist., 5s, 1947 | 3,433 80 | 4,000 00 | 4,000 00 |
| Village of Summit, Cook Co., Ill., Water Works Ext. and Imp., 5s, 1925 | 1,934 00 | 2,000 00 | 2,020 00 |
| Village of Summit, Cook Co., Ill., Water Works, Ext. and Imp., 5s, 1926 | 1,920 00 | 2,000 00 | 2,020 00 |
| Village of Summit, Cook Co., Ill., Water Works Ext. and Imp., 5s, 1927 | 1,904 00 | 2,000 00 | 2,020 00 |
| Village of Summit, Cook Co., Ill., Water Works Ext. and Imp., 5s, 1928 | 1,890 00 | 2,000 00 | 2,020 00 |
| Village of Summit, Cook Co., Ill., Water Works Ext. and Imp., 5s, 1929 | 1,877 50 | 2,000 00 | 2,040 00 |
| Village of Summit, Cook Co., Ill., Water Works Ext. and Imp., 5s, 1930 | 1,865 00 | 2,000 00 | 2,040 00 |
| Continental Iron & Steel, 6s, 1928 | 2,000 00 | 2,000 00 | 2,000 00 |
| Illinois Northern Utilities Co., 1st ref. mortgage, 5s, 1957 | 580 00 | 1,000 00 | 750 00 |
| Woodruff Trust Co., 5s, 1923 | 200 00 | 200 00 | 200 00 |
| Ashland Ave., Apt. Bldg., Chicago, 6s, 1924 | 1,000 00 | 1,000 00 | 1,000 00 |
| Biltimore Apartments, Chicago, 6s, 1924 | 500 00 | 500 00 | 500 00 |
| Chicago Beach Hotels, Chicago, 6s, 1926 | 500 00 | 500 00 | 500 00 |
| Chicago Beach Hotels, Chicago, 6s, 1927 | 500 00 | 500 00 | 500 00 |
| Dorchester Apartments, Chicago, 6s, 1932 | 500 00 | 500 00 | 500 00 |
| Dallas Co., State Bank Bldg., 6s, 1931 | 100 00 | 100 00 | 100 00 |
| Eastwood Apt. Bldg., Chicago, 6s, 1922 | 1,000 00 | 1,000 00 | 1,000 00 |
| LaFayette Apt. Bldg. Corp., Bloomington, 6s, 1922 | 2,500 00 | 2,500 00 | 2,500 00 |
| LaFayette Apt. Bldg. Corp., Bloomington, 6s, 1923 | 2,500 00 | 2,500 00 | 2,500 00 |
| LaFayette Apt. Bldg. Corp., Bloomington, 6s, 1923 | 2,000 00 | 2,000 00 | 2,000 00 |
| LaFayette Apt. Bldg. Corp., Bloomington, 6s, 1924 | 2,000 00 | 2,000 00 | 2,000 00 |
| LaFayette Apt. Bldg. Corp., Bloomington, 6s, 1924 | 3,000 00 | 3,000 00 | 3,000 00 |
| LaFayette Apt. Bldg. Corpl, Bloomington, 6s, 1925 | 500 00 | 500 00 | 500 00 |
| LaFayette Apt. Bldg. Corp., Bloomington, 6s, 1925 | 4,000 00 | 4,000 00 | 4,000 00 |
| LaFayette Apt. Bldg. Corp., Bloomington, 6s, 1927 | 1,000 00 | 1,000 00 | 1,000 00 |
| LaFayette Apt. Bldg. Corp., Bloomington, 6s, 1929 | 1,000 00 | 1,000 00 | 1,000 00 |
| LaFayette Apt. Bldg. Corp., Bloomington, 6s, 1929 | 2,000 00 | 2,000 00 | 2,000 00 |
| LaFayette Apt. Bldg. Corp., Bloomington, 6s, 1930 | 4,000 00 | 4,000 00 | 4,000 00 |
| LaFayette Apt. Bldg. Corp., Bloomington, 6s, 1931 | 1,000 00 | 1,000 00 | 1,000 00 |
| LaFayette Apt. Bldg. Corp., Bloomington, 6s, 1932 | 1,000 00 | 1,000 00 | 1,000 00 |
| Maplewood Business Block, Chicago, 6s, 1924 | 200 00 | 200 00 | 200 00 |
| Melrose Apt. Hotel, Chicago, 7s, 1925 | 100 00 | 100 00 | 100 00 |
| Meriam Apartment, Chicago, 6s, 1923 | 500 00 | 500 00 | 500 00 |
| Oak Forest Apartment Bldg., Chicago, 6s, 1924 | 1,000 00 | 1,000 00 | 1,000 00 |
| Pershing Apt. Bldg., Chicago, 6s, 1926 | 100 00 | 100 00 | 100 00 |
| Randolph Apt. Bldg., Chicago, 6s, 1924 | 500 00 | 500 00 | 500 00 |
| Richmond Apt. Bldg., Chicago, 6s, 1922 | 500 00 | 500 00 | 500 00 |
| Ridgeway Apt. Bldg., Chicago, 6s, 1922 | 500 00 | 500 00 | 500 00 |
| Rockwell Warehouses, Chicago, 6s, 1929 | 500 00 | 500 00 | 500 00 |
| Stores & Apartments (Oldenburg), 6s, 1925 | 500 00 | 500 00 | 500 00 |
| Totals | $250,450 88 | $261,200 00 | $260,230 00 |

SCHEDULE D—PART 2—STOCKS.

| Description. | Book value. | Par value. | Market value. |
|---|---|---|---|
| First National Bank of Oak Park, Ill | $18,750 00 | $15,000 00 | $16,500 00 |
| National City Bank of Chicago, Ill | 8,250 00 | 5,500 00 | 8,470 00 |
| International Life Insurance Co., St. Louis, Mo | 300 00 | 300 00 | 300 00 |
| Totals | $27,300 00 | $20,800 00 | $25,270 00 |

## ROCKFORD LIFE INSURANCE COMPANY.

Located at No. 706 Trust Building, Rockford, Illinois; commenced business March 17, 1910.

P. A. PETERSON, President. FRANCIS L. BROWN, Secretary.

### CAPITAL.

| | | | |
|---|---|---|---|
| Capital paid up | | $175,650 00 | |
| Amount of ledger assets December 31, of previous year | | | $729,065 28 |

### INCOME.

| | | | |
|---|---|---|---|
| First year's premiums on original policies, less re-insurance | | $93,420 59 | |
| First year's premiums for total and permanent disability benefits | | 1,328 31 | |
| First year's premiums for additional accidental death benefits, less re-insurance | | 477 11 | |
| New premiums | | $95,226 01 | |
| Renewal premiums less re-insurance | $185,105 45 | | |
| Renewal premiums for total and permanent disability benefits | 1,003 14 | | |
| Renewal premiums for additional accidental death benefits, less re-insurance | 55 60 | | |
| Renewal premiums | | 186,164 19 | |
| Premium income | | | $281,390 20 |
| Interest on mortgage loans | | $40,308 31 | |
| Interest on bonds | | 2,833 44 | |
| Interest on premium notes, policy loans or liens | | 3,268 09 | |
| Interest on other debts due the company | | 71 15 | |
| Total interest | | | 46,480 99 |
| From other sources, viz: Money received with applications, $190.79; refund by insured of premiums reported to war risk bureau, $27.34; war tax, $2,140.80 | | | 2,358 93 |
| Agents' balances previously charged off | | | 8 52 |
| Total income | | | $330,238 64 |
| Total | | | $1,059,303 92 |

### DISBURSEMENTS.

| | | |
|---|---|---|
| Death claims and additions | | $37,336 34 |
| Premium notes and liens voided by lapse, less $236.97 restorations | | 3,617 75 |
| Surrender values paid in cash, or applied in liquidation of loans or notes | | 9,787 49 |
| Coupons paid policyholders in cash, or applied in liquidation of loans or notes | | 1,748 21 |
| (Total paid policyholders | $52,489 79) | |
| Commissions to agents, first year, $72,660.99; renewal, $7,146.53 | | 79,807 52 |
| Compensation of managers and agents not paid by commissions on new business | | 1,857 78 |
| Agency supervision and traveling expenses of supervisors | | 7,644 51 |
| Branch office expenses | | 446 20 |
| Medical examiners' fees and inspection of risks | | 6,777 48 |
| Salaries and all other compensation of officers and home office employees | | 15,096 70 |
| Rent | | 1,685 27 |
| Advertising, printing, stationery, postage, telegraph, telephone and express | | 7,546 21 |
| Legal expense | | 1,767 60 |
| State taxes on premiums | | 691 63 |
| Insurance department licenses and fees | | 627 43 |
| Federal taxes | | 914 63 |
| All other licenses, fees and taxes | | 4,803 60 |
| Other disbursements, viz: Library, $220.50; membership fees to associations, $150.00; office supplies, $776.41; subscriptions to periodicals, $476.65; sundries, $332.31; traveling expense, home office, $731.79; suspended premiums, $173.92; refund to re-insurance company war hazard premium, $40.00 | | 2,901 58 |
| Total disbursements | | $185,057 93 |
| Balance | | $874,245 99 |

## LEDGER ASSETS.

| | | |
|---|---|---|
| Mortgage loans on real estate | | $727,252 50 |
| Loans on company's policies assigned as collateral | | 51,391 17 |
| Premium notes on policies in force | | 12,075 98 |
| Book value of bonds | | 60,650 00 |
| Cash in office | | 50 00 |
| Deposits in trust companies and banks not on interest | | 3,374 81 |
| Bills receivable | | 3,102 22 |
| Agents' balances (debit, $13,927.45; credit, $1,273.46) | | 12,653 99 |
| Furniture and fixtures | | 3,695 32 |
| Total ledger assets | | $874,245 99 |

### NON-LEDGER ASSETS.

| | | | |
|---|---|---|---|
| Interest due and accrued on mortgages | | $11,145 82 | |
| Interest accrued on bonds | | 388 61 | |
| Interest due and accrued on premium notes, loans or liens | | 318 23 | |
| | | | 11,852 66 |
| | New business. | Renewals. | |
| Net uncollected and deferred premiums (paid for basis) | $48 90 | $31,041 54 | 31,090 44 |
| Gross assets | | | $917,189 09 |

### DEDUCT ASSETS NOT ADMITTED.

| | | |
|---|---|---|
| Furniture, fixtures and safes | $3,695 32 | |
| Agents' debit balances | 13,927 45 | |
| Bills receivable | 3,102 22 | |
| Premium notes, policy loans and other policy assets in excess of net value and of other policy liabilities on individual policies | 2,298 93 | |
| Book value of bonds | 477 00 | |
| Total | | 23,500 92 |
| Admitted assets | | $893,688 17 |

## LIABILITIES.

| | | |
|---|---|---|
| Net present value of outstanding policies computed by the Illinois Insurance Department | $642,168 00 | |
| Deduct net value of risks re-insured | 9,243 00 | |
| Net reserve (paid for basis) | | $632,925 00 |
| Extra reserve for total and permanent disability benefits | | 1,166 00 |
| Death losses reported for which no proofs have been received | | 1,000 00 |
| Gross premiums paid in advance, including surrender values so applied, less discount, if any | | 590 15 |
| Unearned interest and rent paid in advance | | 1,312 97 |
| Commissions due agents on premium notes, when paid | | 570 22 |
| Commissions to agents due or accrued | | 1,273 46 |
| Cost of collection on uncollected and deferred premiums in excess of loading | | 76 45 |
| Salaries, rents, office expenses, bills and accounts due or accrued | | 1,030 25 |
| Medical examiners | | 699 00 |
| Estimated amount hereafter payable for federal, state and other taxes based upon the business of the year of this statement | | 3,706 82 |
| Money received with applications, $190.79; balance in suspense, $179.56 | | 370 35 |
| Total | | $644,720 67 |
| Capital paid up | | 175,650 00 |
| Unassigned funds (surplus) | | 73,317 50 |
| Total | | $893,688 17 |

## EXHIBIT OF POLICIES—ORDINARY.

### ALL BUSINESS PAID FOR.

| | | | Number. | Amount. |
|---|---|---|---|---|
| Policies in force December 31, 1920 | | | 4,954 | $8,061,836 00 |
| Policies issued, revived and increased during the year | | | 1,481 | 3,527,821 00 |
| Total | | | 6,435 | $11,589,657 00 |
| Deduct policies which have ceased to be in force during the year— | Number. | Amount. | | |
| By death | 20 | $44,000 00 | | |
| By expiry | 27 | 88,700 00 | | |
| By surrender | 96 | 198,507 00 | | |
| By lapse | 689 | 1,207,800 00 | | |
| By decrease | | 40,740 00 | | |
| Total | | | 832 | 1,579,747 00 |
| Total policies in force December 31, 1921 | | | 5,603 | $10,009,910 00 |
| Re-insured | | | 155 | $892,200 00 |

BUSINESS IN ILLINOIS—ORDINARY.

| | Number. | Amount. |
|---|---|---|
| Policies in force December 31, 1920 | 4,349 | $6,964,723 00 |
| Policies issued during the year | 973 | 2,470,900 00 |
| Total | 5,322 | $9,435,623 00 |
| Deduct policies ceased to be in force | 708 | 1,362,699 00 |
| Policies in force December 31, 1921 | 4,614 | $8,072,924 00 |
| Losses and claims incurred during the year | 19 | $33,084 64 |
| Losses and claims settled during the year | 19 | 33,084 64 |
| Premiums received | | $226,066 83 |

GAIN AND LOSS EXHIBIT.

INSURANCE EXHIBIT.

| | | Gain in surplus. | Loss in surplus. |
|---|---|---|---|
| Loading on actual premiums of the year (averaging 23.92 per cent of the gross premiums) | $ 69,018 03 | | |
| Insurance expenses incurred during the year | 133,615 51 | | |
| Loss from loading | | | $64,597 48 |
| Interest earned during the year | $46,724 35 | | |
| Investment expenses incurred during the year | 2,382 56 | | |
| Net income from investments | $44,341 79 | | |
| Interest required to maintain reserve | 20,913 37 | | |
| Gain from interest | | $23,428 42 | |
| Expected mortality on net amount at risk | $84,957 33 | | |
| Actual mortality on net amount at risk | 32,404 81 | | |
| Gain from mortality | | 52,552 52 | |
| Total gain during the year from surrendered and lapsed policies | | 6,456 95 | |
| Decrease in surplus on dividend account | | | 1,748 21 |
| Net to loss account | | | 3,609 23 |
| Total gains from bonds | | 2,847 54 | |
| Loss from assets not admitted | | | 11,738 91 |
| Net gain on account of total and permanent disability benefits | | 2,424 16 | |
| Gain from refund by insured of premiums reported to war risk bureau, $27.34; war tax, $2,140.80 | | 2,168 14 | |
| Balance unaccounted for | | 1,420 03 | |
| Total gains and losses in surplus during the year | | $91,297 76 | $81,693 83 |
| Surplus December 31, 1920 | $63,713 57 | | |
| Surplus December 31, 1921 | 73,317 50 | | |
| Increase in surplus | | | 9,603 93 |
| Total | | $91,297 76 | $91,297 76 |

SCHEDULE D—PART 1—BONDS.

| Description. | Book value. | Par value. | Market value. |
|---|---|---|---|
| Liberty Loan of 1917, 3½s, 1947 | $ 50 00 | $ 50 00 | $ 47 50 |
| 1st Liberty Loan, converted, 4¼s, 1947 | 1,000 00 | 1,000 00 | 970 00 |
| 2d Liberty Loan, converted, 4¼s, 1942 | 8,850 00 | 8,850 00 | 8,734 50 |
| 3d Liberty Loan, converted, 4¼s, 1928 | 9,450 00 | 9,450 00 | 9,361 00 |
| 4th Liberty Loan, converted, 4¼s, 1938 | 15,550 00 | 15,550 00 | 15,310 00 |
| Victory Liberty Loan, 4¾s, 1923 | 15,750 00 | 15,750 00 | 15,750 00 |
| A. L. Maxwell Co., 6s, 1927 | 10,000 00 | 10,000 00 | 10,000 00 |
| Totals | $60,650 00 | $60,650 00 | $60,173 00 |

---

## STANDARD LIFE INSURANCE COMPANY.

Located at Standard Life Insurance Building, Decatur, Illinois; commenced business October 29, 1914.

J. R. PAISLEY, President. H. H. NOTTELMANN, Secretary.

CAPITAL.

| | | |
|---|---|---|
| Capital paid up | $225,000 00 | |
| Amount of ledger assets December 31, of previous year | | $2,460,777 11 |

## INCOME.

| | | | |
|---|---|---|---|
| First year's premiums on original policies, less re-insurance | | $214,708 39 | |
| First year's premiums for total and permanent disability benefits | | 1,304 86 | |
| First year's premiums for additional accidental death benefits, less re-insurance | | 451 00 | |
| Surrender values to pay first year's premiums | | 17 00 | |
| Dividends applied to purchase paid-up additions and annuities | | 1,751 14 | |
| Surrender values applied to purchase paid-up insurance and annuities | | 29,736 06 | |
| New premiums | | $ 247,968 45 | |
| Renewal premiums less re-insurance | $1,131,174 12 | | |
| Renewal premiums for total and permanent disability benefits | 8,470 18 | | |
| Renewal premiums for additional accidental death benefits, less re-insurance | 1,523 50 | | |
| Dividends applied to pay renewal premiums | 1,659 83 | | |
| Surrender values applied to pay renewal premiums | 3,283 24 | | |
| Renewal premiums | | 1,146,110 87 | |
| Premium income | | | $1,394,079 32 |
| Consideration for supplementary contracts not involving life contingencies | | | 8,688 71 |
| Dividends left with company to accumulate at interest | | | 17,908 07 |
| Interest on mortgage loans | | $91,069 84 | |
| Interest on collateral loans | | 4,573 93 | |
| Interest on bonds and dividends on stocks | | 7,879 04 | |
| Interest on premium notes, policy loans or liens | | 15,092 06 | |
| Interest on deposits | | 6,039 50 | |
| Interest on other debts due the company | | 132 91 | |
| Rents—including $11,801.52 for company's occupancy of its own buildings less $11,340.62 interest on incumbrances | | 71,028 68 | |
| Total interest and rents | | | 195,815 96 |
| From other sources, viz: Surrender value of re-insurance policies, $506.26; Provident Life Re-insurance, $3,675.89; loss and gain, $353.87 | | | 4,536 02 |
| Borrowed money (gross) | | | 25,000 00 |
| Total income | | | $1,646,028 08 |
| Total | | | $4,106,805 19 |

## DISBURSEMENTS.

| | | |
|---|---|---|
| Death claims and additions | $348,038 93 | |
| Total and permanent disability claims | 3,797 31 | |
| Total death claims | | $351,836 24 |
| Premium notes and liens voided by lapse | | 16,477 97 |
| Surrender values paid in cash, or applied in liquidation of loans or notes | | 54,493 62 |
| Surrender values applied to pay new and renewal premiums | | 275 55 |
| Surrender values applied to purchase paid-up insurance and annuities | | 29,736 06 |
| Dividends paid policyholders in cash, or applied in liquidation of loans or notes | | 4,441 41 |
| Dividends applied to pay renewal premiums | | 4,684 52 |
| Dividends applied to purchase paid-up additions and annuities | | 1,751 14 |
| Dividends left with the company to accumulate at interest | | 17,908 07 |
| (Total paid policyholders | $481,604 58) | |
| Expense of investigation and settlement of policy claims, including legal expenses | | 417 67 |
| Supplementary contracts not involving life contingencies | | 1,185 45 |
| Dividends with interest, held on deposit surrendered during the year | | 3,886 37 |
| Dividends to stockholders | | 22,500 00 |
| Commissions to agents, first year, $132,392.72; renewal, $27,555.65; agents'bonus volume, $17,098.22 | | 177,046 59 |
| Compensation of managers and agents not paid by commissions on new business | | 41,217 84 |
| Agency supervision and traveling expenses of supervisors | | 6,476 19 |
| Branch office expenses | | 12,833 83 |
| Medical examiners' fees and inspection of risks | | 18,695 04 |
| Salaries and all other compensation of officers and home office employees | | 88,965 59 |
| Rent | | 11,801 52 |
| Advertising, printing, stationery, postage, telegraph, telephone, express and collection expense | | 29,949 92 |
| Legal expense | | 265 00 |
| Furniture, fixtures and safes | | 3,084 80 |
| Repairs and expenses (other than taxes) on real estate | | 42,137 01 |
| Taxes on real estate | | 10,080 26 |
| State taxes on premiums | | 15,761 04 |
| Insurance department licenses and fees | | 2,781 30 |
| Federal taxes | | 1,908 85 |
| All other licenses, fees and taxes | | 4,740 10 |
| Other disbursements, viz: Suspense, $456.11; collectors' balances, $1,389.22; investment expense, $6,238.63; office expense, $2,307.09; agents' convention, $2,901.62; supplies, $307.64; war premium refund, $354.11; Standard of Iowa Guarantee Fund, $21.00; bonding account, $24.50 | | 16,770 92 |

DISBURSEMENTS—Concluded.

| | | |
|---|---|---|
| Borrowed money repaid (gross) | | $25,000 00 |
| Interest on borrowed money | | 840 00 |
| Total disbursements | | $1,019,949 87 |
| Balance | | $3,086,855 32 |

LEDGER ASSETS.

| | | |
|---|---|---|
| Book value of real estate | | $ 466,170 11 |
| Mortgage loans on real estate | | 1,527,829 28 |
| Loans secured by collaterals | | 138,940 00 |
| Loans on company's policies assigned as collateral | | 226,430 40 |
| Premium notes on policies in force | | 66,869 34 |
| Book value of bonds and stocks | | 273,538 27 |
| Cash in office | | 17,202 12 |
| Deposits in trust companies and banks not on interest | | 22,126 21 |
| Deposits in trust companies and banks on interest | | 245,636 47 |
| Agents' balances (debit, $104,038.56; credit, $1,925.44 | | 102,113 12 |
| Total ledger assets | | $3,086,855 32 |

NON-LEDGER ASSETS.

| | | | |
|---|---|---|---|
| Interest due and accrued on mortgages | | $50,137 10 | |
| Interest accrued on bonds | | 1,420 34 | |
| Interest due and accrued on collateral loans | | 1,840 17 | |
| Interest due and accrued on premium notes, loans or liens | | 1,326 80 | |
| Interest accrued on certificate of deposit | | 653 43 | |
| Rents due on company's property | | 1,358 70 | |
| | | | 56,736 54 |
| Market value of real estate over book value | | | 260,705 79 |
| Market value of bonds and stocks over book value | | | 5,777 50 |
| | New business. | Renewals. | |
| Net uncollected and deferred premiums (paid for basis) | $590 25 | $82,770 42 | 83,360 67 |
| All other assets, viz: Furniture and fixtures, $20,000.00; printed matter, supplies and stationery, $12,000.00 | | | 32,000 00 |
| Gross assets | | | $3,525,435 82 |

DEDUCT ASSETS NOT ADMITTED.

| | | |
|---|---|---|
| Supplies, printed matter and stationery | $ 12,000 00 | |
| Furniture, fixtures and safes | 20,000 00 | |
| Agents' debit balances | 104,038 56 | |
| Premium notes, policy loans and other policy assets in excess of net value and of other policy liabilities on individual policies | 13,918 40 | |
| Book value of other ledger assets over market value, viz: | | |
| Mortgage loans | 1,500 00 | |
| Due and accrued interest in default | 440 58 | |
| Total | | 151,897 54 |
| Admitted assets | | $3,373,538 28 |

LIABILITIES.

| | | |
|---|---|---|
| Net present value of outstanding policies computed by the Illinois Insurance Department | $2,559,777 00 | |
| Same for dividend additions | 9,457 48 | |
| Total | $2,569,234 48 | |
| Deduct net value of risks re-insured | 11,466 17 | |
| Net reserve (paid for basis) | | $2,557,768 31 |
| Extra reserve for total and permanent disability benefits and for additional accidental death benefits included in life policies, less re-insurance | | 4,887 52 |
| Present value of supplementary contracts not involving life contingencies | | 11,449 32 |
| Death losses due and unpaid | $ 280 70 | |
| Death losses in process of adjustment | 16,000 00 | |
| Death losses reported for which no proofs have been received | 26,100 00 | |
| Death losses and other policy claims resisted | 5,800 00 | |
| Total policy claims | | 48,180 70 |
| Dividends left with the company to accumulate at interest | | 51,092 72 |
| Gross premiums paid in advance, including surrender values so applied, less discount, if any | | 23,411 90 |
| Unearned interest and rent paid in advance | | 6,265 19 |
| Commissions due agents on premium notes, when paid | | 947 23 |
| Commissions to agents due or accrued | | 3,086 43 |
| Salaries, rents, office expenses, bills, and accounts due or accrued | | 1,809 21 |
| Medical examiners' fees accrued | | 990 00 |
| Estimated amount hereafter payable for federal, state and other taxes based upon the business of the year of this statement | | 31,937 50 |

LIABILITIES—Concluded.

| | |
|---|---|
| Dividends or other profits due policyholders | $ 241 28 |
| Dividends declared on or apportioned to annual dividend policies payable to policyholders during 1922 for period to October 31, 1922 | 12,376 23 |
| Dividends declared on or apportioned to deferred dividend policies payable to policyholders during 1922 for period to December 31, 1922 | 1,371 14 |
| Amounts set apart, apportioned, provisionally ascertained, calculated, declared or held awating apportionment upon deferred dividend policies | 32,262 13 |
| Iowa deferred fund, $12,803.61; Iowa guarantee fund, $1,620.00; Iowa trust fund, $488.82 | 14,912 43 |
| Other liabilities, viz: Suspense, $721.17; collectors' balance, $382.33; accrued interest on encumbrance home office building (Powers estate), $3,062.50 | 4,166 00 |
| Total | $2,807,155 24 |
| Capital paid up | 225,000 00 |
| Unassigned funds (surplus) | 341,383 04 |
| Total | $3,373,538 28 |

EXHIBIT OF POLICIES—ORDINARY.

ALL BUSINESS PAID FOR.

| | Number. | Amount. | Number. | Amount. |
|---|---|---|---|---|
| Policies in force December 31, 1920 | | | 31,703 | $45,676,720 00 |
| Policies issued, revived, and increased during the year | | | 2,730 | 6,258,621 00 |
| Total | | | 34,433 | $51,935,341 00 |
| Deduct policies which have ceased to be in force during the year— | | | | |
| By death | 289 | $ 357,433 00 | | |
| By expiry | 130 | 174,400 00 | | |
| By surrender | 411 | 608,133 00 | | |
| By lapse | 3,094 | 6,904,988 00 | | |
| By decrease | | 37,366 00 | | |
| Total | | | 3,924 | 8,082,320 00 |
| Total policies in force December 31, 1921 | | | 30,509 | $43,853,021 00 |
| Re-insured | | | 186 | $938,920 00 |

BUSINESS IN ILLINOIS—ORDINARY.

(Excluding group insurance).

| | Number. | Amount. |
|---|---|---|
| Policies in force December 31, 1920 | 14,348 | $17,509,068 00 |
| Policies issued during the year | 1,214 | 2,355,944 00 |
| Total | 15,562 | $19,865,012 00 |
| Deduct policies ceased to be in force | 1,118 | 1,593,434 00 |
| Policies in force December 31, 1921 | 14,444 | $18,271,578 00 |
| Losses and claims unpaid December 31, 1920 | 15 | $ 17,800 00 |
| Losses and claims incurred during the year | 172 | 194,500 00 |
| Total | 187 | $212,300 00 |
| Losses and claims settled during the year | 173 | 197,400 00 |
| Losses and claims unpaid December 31, 1921 | 14 | $14,900 00 |
| Premiums received | | $587,249 11 |

GAIN AND LOSS EXHIBIT.

INSURANCE EXHIBIT.

| | | Gain in surplus. | Loss in surplus. |
|---|---|---|---|
| Loading on actual premiums of the year (averaging 20.77 per cent of the gross premiums) | $288,561 32 | | |
| Insurance expenses incurred during the year | 426,219 49 | | |
| Loss from loading | | | $137,658 17 |
| Interest earned during the year | $199,026 45 | | |
| Investment expenses incurred during the year | 64,726 06 | | |
| Net income from investments | $134,300 39 | | |
| Interest required to maintain reserve | 77,832 09 | | |
| Gain from interest | | $ 56,468 30 | |
| Expected mortality on net amount at risk | $498,963 07 | | |
| Actual mortality on net amount at risk | 321,707 61 | | |
| Gain from mortality | | 177,255 46 | |
| Total gain during the year from surrendered and lapsed policies | | 38,043 39 | |
| Dividends paid stockholders | | | 22,500 00 |
| Decrease in surplus on dividend account | | | 11,545 05 |
| Decrease in special funds, and special reserves during the year | | 226 67 | |
| Net to profit account | | 353 87 | |

## GAIN AND LOSS EXHIBIT—Concluded.

### INVESTMENT EXHIBIT.

| | | Gain in surplus. | Loss in surplus. |
|---|---|---|---|
| Total gains from stocks and bonds | | $3,027 50 | |
| Loss from assets not admitted | | | $52,473 24 |
| Net gain on account of total and permanent disability benefits or additional accidental death benefits included in life policies | | 8,065 05 | |
| Gain from all other sources: Surrender value re-insurance, $506.26; unearned re-insurance premiums received, $3,675.89 | | 4,182 15 | |
| Balance unaccounted for | | 73 59 | |
| Total gains and losses in surplus during the year | | $287,695 98 | $224,176 46 |
| Surplus December 31, 1920 | $277,863 52 | | |
| Surplus December 31, 1921 | 341,383 04 | | |
| Increase in surplus | | | 63,519 52 |
| Total | | $287,695 98 | $287,695 98 |

## SCHEDULE D—PART 1—BONDS.

| Description. | Book value. | Par value. | Market value. |
|---|---|---|---|
| City of New Orleans, series B, 5s, 1923 | $ 500 00 | $ 500 00 | $ 500 00 |
| City of New Orleans, series A, 5s, 1923 | 2,000 00 | 2,000 00 | 2,000 00 |
| Improvement bonds, City of Des Moines, 6s, 1922 | 1,500 00 | 1,500 00 | 1,500 00 |
| City of Des Moines, 6s, 1923 | 1,900 00 | 1,900 00 | 1,900 00 |
| Sewer bonds, City of Des Moines, 6s, 1922 | 200 00 | 200 00 | 200 00 |
| Improvement bonds, City of Des Moines, 6s, 1922 | 100 00 | 100 00 | 100 00 |
| Improvement bonds, City of Des Moines, 6s, 1923 | 200 00 | 200 00 | 200 00 |
| Improvement bonds, City of Des Moines, 6s, 1922 | 200 00 | 200 00 | 200 00 |
| Improvement bonds, City of Des Moines, 6s, 1922 | 800 00 | 800 00 | 800 00 |
| Improvement bonds, City of Des Moines, 6s, 1923 | 800 00 | 800 00 | 800 00 |
| Improvement bonds, City of Des Moines, 6s, 1924 | 300 00 | 300 00 | 300 00 |
| Improvement bonds, City of Des Moines, 6s, 1923 | 400 00 | 400 00 | 400 00 |
| Improvement bonds, City of Des Moines, 6s, 1924 | 800 00 | 800 00 | 800 00 |
| Improvement bonds, City of Des Moines, 6s, 1922 | 200 00 | 200 00 | 200 00 |
| Improvement bonds, City of Des Moines, 6s, 1923 | 100 00 | 100 00 | 100 00 |
| Improvement bonds, City of Des Moines, 6s, 1924 | 100 00 | 100 00 | 100 00 |
| City of Des Moines, 6s, 1922 | 700 00 | 700 00 | 700 00 |
| City of Des Moines, 6s, 1923 | 1,000 00 | 1,000 00 | 1,000 00 |
| City of Des Moines, 6s, 1924 | 700 00 | 700 00 | 700 00 |
| City of Des Moines, 6s, 1922 | 100 00 | 100 00 | 100 00 |
| City of Des Moines, 6s, 1923 | 600 00 | 600 00 | 600 00 |
| City of Des Moines, 6s, 1924 | 400 00 | 400 00 | 400 00 |
| City of Des Moines, 6s, 1925 | 500 00 | 500 00 | 500 00 |
| City of Des Moines, 6s, 1922 | 200 00 | 200 00 | 200 00 |
| City of Des Moines, 6s, 1923 | 200 00 | 200 00 | 200 00 |
| City of Des Moines, 6s, 1924 | 200 00 | 200 00 | 200 00 |
| City of Des Moines, 6s, 1925 | 200 00 | 200 00 | 200 00 |
| Improvement bonds, City of Des Moines, 6s, 1922 | 100 00 | 100 00 | 100 00 |
| Improvement bonds, City of Des Moines, 6s, 1923 | 100 00 | 100 00 | 100 00 |
| Improvement bonds, City of Des Moines, 6s, 1924 | 200 00 | 200 00 | 200 00 |
| City of Des Moines, 6s, 1922 | 900 00 | 900 00 | 900 00 |
| City of Des Moines, 6s' 1923 | 900 00 | 900 00 | 900 00 |
| City of Des Moines, 6s, 1924 | 900 00 | 900 00 | 900 00 |
| City of Des Moines, 6s, 1925 | 1,100 00 | 1,100 00 | 1,100 00 |
| City of Des Moines, 6s, 1922 | 400 00 | 400 00 | 400 00 |
| City of Des Moines, 6s, 1923 | 400 00 | 400 00 | 400 00 |
| City of Des Moines, 6s, 1925 | 500 00 | 500 00 | 500 00 |
| Valley Junction, Ia., improvement bonds, 6s, 1922 | 2,100 00 | 2,100 00 | 2,100 00 |
| Valley Junction, Ia., improvement bonds, 6s, 1923 | 2,000 00 | 2,000 00 | 2,000 00 |
| City of Ames, series 16043, pav. cert., 6s, 1923 | 869 18 | 869 18 | 869 18 |
| City of Ames, series 16043, 6s, 1923 | 1,339 37 | 1,339 37 | 1,339 37 |
| Street improvement bonds, City of Des Moines, 6s, 1922 | 600 00 | 600 00 | 600 00 |
| Street improvement bonds, City of Des Moines, 6s, 1922 and 1923 | 3,000 00 | 3,000 00 | 3,000 00 |
| Street improvement bonds, City of Des Moines, 6s, 1923 | 3,600 00 | 3,600 00 | 3,600 00 |
| War Savings Stamps | 834 00 | 1,000 00 | 834 00 |
| War Savings Stamps | 678 60 | 780 00 | 678 60 |
| War Savings Stamps | 300 00 | 355 00 | 300 00 |
| Liberty Bonds, Victory, 4¾s | 16,900 00 | 16,900 00 | 16,900 00 |
| Liberty Bonds, 2nd, conv | 5,239 04 | 5,300 00 | 5,239 04 |
| Liberty Bonds, 3d | 1,546 11 | 1,550 00 | 1,546 11 |
| Liberty Bonds, 4th | 10,171 97 | 10,200 00 | 10,171 97 |
| Decatur Water Supply Bonds, 7s | 140 00 | 140 00 | 140 00 |
| Totals | $69,718 27 | $70,133 55 | $69,718 27 |

SCHEDULE D—PART 2—STOCKS.

| Description. | Book value. | Par value. | Market value. |
|---|---|---|---|
| & Trust Co. | $ 1,160 00 | $ 500 00 | $ 1,150 00 |
| ndard Trust Co. | 40,500 00 | 40,500 00 | 43,537 50 |
| ndard Trust Co. | 136,310 00 | 126,800 00 | 136,310 00 |
| ate Bank & Trust Co. | 15,050 00 | 8,900 00 | 17,800 00 |
| ational Bank of St. Louis | 10,800 00 | 9,000 00 | 10,800 00 |
| | $203,820 00 | $185,700 00 | $209,597 50 |

# LIFE INSURANCE COMPANIES OF OTHER STATES.

## AETNA LIFE INSURANCE COMPANY.

Located at No. 650 Main Street, Hartford, Connecticut; incorporated June, 1820; commenced business in Illinois, life, January 18, 1860; casualty, February 12, 1891

M. G. BULKELEY, President. C. E. GILBERT, Secretary.

GEORGE A. BARR, Director of Trade and Commerce, Attorney for service at Springfield.

### CAPITAL.

| | | | |
|---|---|---|---|
| Capital paid up | | $5,000,000 00 | |
| Amount of ledger assets December 31, of previous year | | | $138,656,620 41 |

### INCOME.

| | | | |
|---|---|---|---|
| First year's premiums on original policies, less re-insurance | | $4,822,283 40 | |
| First year's premiums for total and permanent disability benefits | | 102,514 55 | |
| First year's premiums for additional accidental death benefits | | 105,816 07 | |
| Surrender values to pay first year's premiums | | 66,982 67 | |
| Dividends applied to purchase paid-up additions and annuities | | 40,734 03 | |
| Surrender values applied to purchase paid-up insurance and annuities | | 304,272 58 | |
| Consideration for original annuities involving life contingencies | | 518,028 48 | |
| New premiums | | $ 5,960,631 78 | |
| Renewal premiums less re-insurance | $23,233,057 67 | | |
| Renewal premiums for total and permanent disability benefits | 301,973 99 | | |
| Renewal premiums for additional accidental death benefits | 269,079 20 | | |
| Dividends applied to pay renewal premiums | 1,066,520 42 | | |
| Surrender values applied to pay renewal premiums | 5,111 54 | | |
| Renewal premiums for deferred annuities | 38,311 41 | | |
| Renewal premiums | | 24,914,054 23 | |
| Premium income | | $30,874,686 01 | |
| Premiums advanced during year under Soldiers' and Sailors' Civil Relief Act | | 50 00 | |
| Total | | | $30,874,736 01 |
| Consideration for supplementary contracts involving life contingencies | | | 273,471 31 |
| Consideration for supplementary contracts not involving life contingencies | | | 345,119 08 |
| Dividends left with company to accumulate at interest | | | 236,204 24 |
| Interest on mortgage loans | | $3,658,766 84 | |
| Interest on collateral loans | | 28,304 14 | |
| Interest on bonds and dividends on stocks | | 2,501,076 77 | |
| Interest on premium notes, policy loans or liens | | 1,075,623 71 | |
| Interest on deposits | | 128,255 20 | |
| Discount on claims paid in advance | | 47 97 | |
| Rents—including $102,625.00 for company's occupancy of its own buildings | | 134,250 00 | |
| Deduct interest on deposit for re-insurance reserve | | 29,418 53 | |
| Total interest and rents | | | 7,496,906 10 |
| From other sources, viz: Investment expense, $52,447.02; deposit for re-insurance reserve, $292,856.00; cancelled checks missing policy claimants, $1,375.19; federal income taxes refunded, $17,966.19 | | | 364,644 40 |
| Profit on sale or maturity of ledger assets | | | 47,499 07 |
| Increase in book value of ledger assets | | | 23,286 47 |
| Total income | | | $39,661,866 68 |
| Total | | | $178,318,487 09 |

### DISBURSEMENTS.

| | | | |
|---|---|---|---|
| Death claims and additions | | $9,682,697 84 | |
| Matured endowments and additions | | 2,842,035 85 | |
| Total and permanent disability claims and additional accidental death benefits | | 233,969 24 | |
| Total death claims and endowments | | | $12,758,702 93 |
| Annuities involving life contingencies | | | 353,262 79 |
| Premium notes and liens voided by lapse | | | 49 27 |
| Surrender values paid in cash, or applied in liquidation of loans or notes | | | 2,012,998 36 |
| Surrender values applied to pay new and renewal premiums | | | 72,094 21 |

DISBURSEMENTS—Concluded.

| | | |
|---|---|---|
| Surrender values applied to purchase paid-up insurance and annuities | | $ 304,272 58 |
| Dividends and interest paid policyholders in cash, or applied in liquidation of loans or notes | | 528,826 68 |
| Dividends applied to pay renewal premiums | | 1,066,520 42 |
| Dividends applied to purchase paid-up additions and annuities | | 40,734 03 |
| Dividends left with the company to accumulate at interest | | 236,204 24 |
| (Total paid policyholders | $18,273,665 51) | |
| Expense of investigation and settlement of policy claims, including legal expenses | | 35,545 60 |
| Supplementary contracts not involving life contingencies | | 177,025 61 |
| Dividends with interest, held on deposit surrendered during the year | | 325,030 49 |
| Dividends to stockholders | | 500,000 00 |
| Commissions to agents, first year, $2,074,638.59; renewal, $1,354,604.09; annuities (original), $26,870.35; (renewal), $1,825.97) | | 3,457,939 00 |
| Commuted renewal commissions | | 15,500 00 |
| Agency supervision and traveling expenses of supervisors | | 219,134 72 |
| Branch office expenses | | 604,322 81 |
| Medical examiners' fees and inspection of risks | | 225,720 26 |
| Salaries and all other compensation of officers and home office employees | | 857,293 82 |
| Rent | | 204,206 37 |
| Advertising, printing, stationery, postage, telegraph, telephone, express and exchange | | 353,363 80 |
| Legal expense | | 1,653 47 |
| Furniture, fixtures and safes | | 49,698 18 |
| Repairs, and expenses (other than taxes) on real estate and foreclosure expense | | 105,414 05 |
| Taxes on real estate | | 39,806 96 |
| State taxes on premiums | | 436,505 78 |
| Insurance department licenses and fees | | 14,811 14 |
| Federal taxes | | 156,687 64 |
| All other licenses, fees and taxes | | 283,071 54 |
| Other disbursements, viz: Investment expense, $110,762.71; commission on securities, $1,144.19; commission on real estate, $3,000.00; incidentals, $4,238.75; home office travel, $47,516.46; membership Association Life Insurance Presidents, $3,830.92; books, papers and subscriptions, $6,910.31 | | 177,403 34 |
| Agents' balances charged off—loss account | | 38 00 |
| Loss on sale or maturity of ledger assets | | 16,494 18 |
| Decrease in book value of ledger assets | | 11,757 29 |
| Total disbursements | | $26,542,089 56 |
| Balance | | $151,776,397 53 |

LEDGER ASSETS.

| | |
|---|---|
| Book value of real estate | $1,835,565 92 |
| Mortgage loans on real estate | 72,063,062 49 |
| Loans secured by collaterals | 565,239 00 |
| Premiums advanced under Soldiers' and Sailors' Civil Relief Act | 740 53 |
| Loans on company's policies assigned as collateral | 17,508,348 53 |
| Premium notes on policies in force | 63,608 23 |
| Book value of bonds and stocks | 55,438,833 42 |
| Cash in office | 4,164 64 |
| Deposits in trust companies and banks not on interest | 65,110 20 |
| Deposits in trust companies and banks on interest | 4,241,920 44 |
| Bills receivable | 4,293 23 |
| Agents' balances (debit, $21,066.91; credit, $35,556.01) | —14,489 10 |
| Total ledger assets | $151,776,397 53 |

NON-LEDGER ASSETS.

| | | | |
|---|---|---|---|
| Interest due and accrued on mortgages | | $3,614,269 40 | |
| Interest due and accrued on bonds | | 614,665 26 | |
| Interest accrued on collateral loans | | 13,605 54 | |
| Interest due on premium notes, loans or liens | | 187,160 27 | |
| Interest accrued on other assets | | 5,184 98 | |
| | | | 4,434,885 45 |
| Amortized value of bonds and market value of stocks over book value | | | 1,435,586 66 |
| | New business. | Renewals. | |
| Net uncollected and deferred premiums (paid for basis) | $456,936 83 | $3,229,740 33 | 3,686,677 16 |
| Gross assets | | | $161,333,546 80 |

DEDUCT ASSETS NOT ADMITTED.

| | | |
|---|---|---|
| Agents' debit balances | $21,066 91 | |
| Bills receivable | 4,293 23 | |
| Accrued interest on agents' notes | 212 50 | |
| Premium notes, policy loans and other policy assets in excess of net value and of other policy liabilities on individual policies | 3,984 68 | |
| Overdue and accrued interest on bonds in default | 9,000 00 | |
| Total | | 38,557 32 |
| Admitted assets—life department | | $161,294,989 48 |
| Admitted assets—casualty department | | 30,423,056 76 |
| Total admitted assets | | $191,718,046 24 |

## LIABILITIES.

| | | |
|---|---|---|
| Net present value of outstanding policies | $129,600,402 00 | |
| Same for dividend additions | 203,985 00 | |
| Same for annuities and supplementary contracts involving life contingencies | 4,215,094 00 | |
| Total | $134,019,481 00 | |
| Deduct net value of risks re-insured | 1,509,214 00 | |
| Net reserve (paid for basis) | | $132,510,267 00 |
| Extra reserve for total and permanent disability benefits and for additional accidental death benefits included in life policies | | 1,831,463 00 |
| Present value of supplementary contracts not involving life contingencies | | 1,586,960 00 |
| Present value of amounts incurred but not yet due for total and permanent disability benefits | | 50,027 00 |
| Surrender values claimable on policies cancelled | | 8,633 20 |
| Death losses in process of adjustment | $279,208 00 | |
| Death losses reported for which no proofs have been received | 149,628 00 | |
| Reserve for net death losses incurred but unreported | 415,000 00 | |
| Matured endowments due and unpaid | 100,219 00 | |
| Death losses and other policy claims resisted | 41,451 82 | |
| Total and permanent disability benefits and additional accidental death benefits | 41,526 00 | |
| Annuity claims, involving life contingencies, due and unpaid | 8,301 56 | |
| Total policy claims | | 1,035,334 38 |
| Due and unpaid on supplementary contracts not involving life contingencies | | 378 32 |
| Dividends left with the company to accumulate at interest | | 1,485,165 62 |
| Gross premiums paid in advance, including surrender values so applied, less discount, if any | | 93,637 43 |
| Unearned interest and rent paid in advance | | 474,662 81 |
| Commissions due agents on premium notes, when paid and other contingent commissions | | 8,460 33 |
| Commissions to agents due or accrued | | 29,019 43 |
| Cost of collection on uncollected and deferred premiums in excess of loading | | 141,464 75 |
| Salaries, rents, office expenses, bills, and accounts due or accrued | | 56,423 08 |
| Medical examiners' fees due or accrued | | 23,378 25 |
| Estimated amount hereafter payable for federal, state and other taxes based upon the business of the year of this statement | | 901,540 13 |
| Dividends or other profits due policyholders | | 157,711 21 |
| Dividends declared on or apportioned to annual dividend policies payable to policyholders during 1922 for period to December 31, 1922 | | 1,645,410 00 |
| Dividends declared on or apportioned to deferred dividend policies payable to policyholders during 1922 for period to December 31, 1922 | | 245,838 08 |
| Amounts set apart, apportioned, provisionally ascertained, calculated, declared or held awaiting apportionment upon deferred dividend policies | | 488,988 18 |
| Reserve under substandard contracts | | 52,677 00 |
| Reserve under renewable term contracts | | 610,270 00 |
| Special reserve under which note settlements have been accepted by agents | | 72,195 00 |
| Other liabilities, viz: Cancelled checks missing policy claimants, $5,376.58; deposit for re-insurance reserve, $894,523.00; and accrued interest thereon, $39,459.22; special security reserve, $1,000,000.00; special mortality reserve, $500,000.00 | | 2,439,358 80 |
| Liabilities—life department | | $145,949,261 00 |
| Liabilities—casualty department | | 23,489,263 23 |
| Total | | $169,438,524 23 |
| Capital paid up | | 5,000,000 00 |
| Unassigned funds (surplus) | | 17,279,522 01 |
| Total | | $191,718,046 24 |

## EXHIBIT OF POLICIES—ORDINARY.

(Including group insurance).

ALL BUSINESS PAID FOR.

| | Number. | Amount. | Number. | Amount. |
|---|---|---|---|---|
| Policies in force December 31, 1920 | | | 267,876 | $1,155,589,341 08 |
| Policies issued, revived, and increased during the year | | | 38,707 | 324,617,774 27 |
| Total | | | 306,583 | $1,480,207,115 35 |
| Deduct policies which have ceased to be in force during the year— | | | | |
| By death | 2,711 | $ 9,596,656 25 | | |
| By maturity | 1,934 | 2,773,740 85 | | |
| By disability | 9 | 60,717 00 | | |
| By expiry | 1,830 | 1,990,315 00 | | |
| By surrender | 5,435 | 18,371,474 36 | | |
| By lapse | 12,928 | 91,411,735 00 | | |
| By decrease | -------- | 2,410,156 98 | | |
| Withdrawal | -------- | 149,591,922 00 | | |
| Total | | | 24,847 | 276,206,717 44 |
| Total policies in force December 31, 1921 | | | 281,736 | $1,204,000,397 91 |
| Re-insured | | | 1,215 | $26,244,567 12 |

## EXHIBIT OF POLICIES—GROUP INSURANCE.

(Included in ordinary exhibit above).

ALL BUSINESS PAID FOR.

| | Number. | Amount. | Number. | Amount. |
|---|---|---|---|---|
| Policies in force December 31, 1920 | | | 1,301 | $353,464,065 00 |
| Policies issued, revived and increased during the year | | | 90 | 149,352,812 00 |
| Total | | | 1,391 | $502,816,877 00 |
| Deduct policies which have ceased to be in force during the year— | | | | |
| By death | -------- | $ 2,202,770 00 | | |
| By disability | -------- | 37,217 00 | | |
| By lapse | 145 | 32,899,788 00 | | |
| By withdrawal | -------- | 149,591,922 00 | | |
| Total | | | 145 | 184,731,697 00 |
| Total policies in force December 31, 1921 | | | 1,246 | $318,085,180 00 |
| Distribution of business in force at end of year— | | | | |
| One year term | | | 1,240 | $317,361,050 00 |
| Life | | | 6 | 724,130 00 |
| Total | | | 1,246 | $318,085,180 00 |

## BUSINESS IN ILLINOIS—ORDINARY.

(Excluding group insurance.)

| | Number. | Amount. |
|---|---|---|
| Policies in force December 31, 1920 | 19,334 | $51,432,721 74 |
| Policies issued during the year | 2,645 | 13,601,907 12 |
| Total | 21,979 | $65,034,628 86 |
| Deduct policies ceased to be in force | 863 | 4,605,979 18 |
| Policies in force December 31, 1921 | 21,116 | $60,428,649 68 |
| Losses and claims unpaid December 31, 1920 | 58 | $ 14,954 00 |
| Losses and claims incurred during the year | 379 | 646,633 00 |
| Total | 437 | $661,587 00 |
| Losses and claims settled during the year | 375 | 612,288 00 |
| Losses and claims unpaid December 31, 1921 | 62 | $49,299 00 |
| Premiums received | | $1,873,132 33 |

## BUSINESS IN ILLINOIS—GROUP INSURANCE.

| | Number. | Amount. |
|---|---|---|
| Policies in force December 31, 1920 | 109 | $29,424,201 00 |
| Policies issued during the year | 10 | 21,050,064 00 |
| Total | 119 | $50,474,265 00 |
| Deduct policies ceased to be in force | 12 | 14,847,526 00 |
| Policies in force December 31, 1921 | 107 | $35,626,739 00 |
| Losses and claims unpaid December 31, 1920 | -------- | $ 7,600 00 |
| Losses and claims incurred during the year | -------- | 189,711 00 |
| Total | -------- | $197,311 00 |
| Losses and claims settled during the year | -------- | 186,811 00 |
| Losses and claims unpaid December 31, 1921 | -------- | $10,500 00 |
| Premiums received | | $258,976 62 |

## GAIN AND LOSS EXHIBIT.

INSURANCE EXHIBIT.

| | | Gain in surplus. | Loss in surplus. |
|---|---|---|---|
| Loading on actual premiums of the year (averaging 10.87 per cent of the gross premiums) | $3,343,579 93 | | |
| Insurance expenses incurred during the year | 6,949,097 42 | | |
| Loss from loading | | -------------- | $3,605,517 49 |
| Interest earned during the year | $8,100,005 44 | | |
| Investment expenses incurred during the year | 338,526 66 | | |
| Net income from investment | $7,761,478 78 | | |
| Interest required to maintain reserve | 4,436,163 10 | | |
| Gain from interest | | $3,325,315 68 | |

GAIN AND LOSS EXHIBIT—Concluded.

INSURANCE EXHIBIT.

| | | Gain in surplus. | Loss in surplus. |
|---|---|---|---|
| Expected mortality on net amount risk | $13,221,376 00 | | |
| Actual mortality on net amount at risk | 7,225,484 78 | | |
| Gain from mortality | | $5,995,891 22 | |
| Expected disbursements to annuitants | $242,408 00 | | |
| Net actual annuity claims incurred | 254,992 75 | | |
| Loss from annuities | | | $ 12,584 75 |
| Total gain during the year from surrendered and lapsed policies | | 1,379,259 99 | |
| Dividends paid stockholders | | | 500,000 00 |
| Decrease in surplus on dividend account | | | 1,826,828 74 |
| Increase in special funds, and special reserves during the year | | | 1,572,859 00 |
| Net to loss account | | | 38 00 |

INVESTMENT EXHIBIT.

| | | Gain in surplus. | Loss in surplus. |
|---|---|---|---|
| Total gains from real estate | | 376 00 | |
| Total gains from stocks and bonds | | 70,409 54 | |
| Total losses from stocks and bonds | | | 568,969 66 |
| Gain from assets not admitted | | 4,105 47 | |
| Net loss on account of total and permanent disability benefits or additional accidental death benefits included in life policies | | | 111,931 43 |
| Loss—Tax on stock capital | | | 83,854 90 |
| Loss—Surplus applied to maintain the reserve under recoverable term contracts | | | 274,420 00 |
| Gain—Casualty department | | 1,033,751 17 | |
| Total gains and losses in surplus during the year | | $11,809,109 07 | $8,557,003 97 |
| Surplus December 31, 1920 | $14,027,416 91 | | |
| Surplus December 31, 1921 | 17,279,522 01 | | |
| Increase in surplus | | | 3,252,105 10 |
| Total | | $11,809,109 07 | $11,809,109 07 |

## AMERICAN CENTRAL LIFE INSURANCE COMPANY.

Located at No. 8 East Market Street, Indianapolis, Indiana; incorporated February 23, 1899; commenced business in Illinois April 5, 1902.

HERBERT M. WOOLLEN, President. EDWARD A. MEYER, Secretary.

CHARLES P. HITCH, Paris, Attorney for service.

CAPITAL.

| | | |
|---|---|---|
| Capital paid up | $137,000 00 | |
| Amount of ledger assets December 31, of previous year | | $7,301,530 45 |

INCOME.

| | | | |
|---|---|---|---|
| First year's premiums on original policies, less re-insurance | | $490,568 35 | |
| First year's premiums for total and permanent disability benefits, less re-insurance | | 19,472 32 | |
| First year's premiums for additional accidental death benefits | | 15,336 70 | |
| Surrender values to pay first year's premiums | | 998 42 | |
| Dividends applied to purchase paid-up additions and annuities | | 54,185 07 | |
| Surrender values applied to purchase paid-up insurance and annuities | | 34,562 61 | |
| Consideration for original annuities involving life contingencies | | 138 25 | |
| New premiums | | $ 615,261 72 | |
| Renewal premiums less re-insurance | $1,547,132 83 | | |
| Renewal premiums for total and permanent disability benefits, less re-insurance | 19,701 40 | | |
| Renewal premiums for additional accidental death benefits, less re-insurance | 4,384 70 | | |
| Dividends applied to pay renewal premiums | 1,519 13 | | |
| Surrender values applied to pay renewal premiums | 2,377 96 | | |
| Renewal premiums | | 1,575,116 02 | |
| Total | | | $2,190,377 74 |
| Consideration for supplementary contracts involving life contingencies | | | 3,957 99 |
| Consideration for supplementary contracts not involving life contingencies | | | 41,217 45 |
| Interest on mortgage loans | | $281,803 06 | |
| Interest on bonds | | 39,430 91 | |
| Interest on premium notes, policy loans or liens | | 93,008 42 | |
| Interest on deposits | | 5,014 44 | |
| Interest on other debts due the company | | 4,164 82 | |
| Rents—including $22,232.77 for company's occupancy of its own buildings | | 57,675 67 | |
| Total interest and rents | | | 481,097 32 |

INCOME—Concluded.

| | | |
|---|---|---|
| From other sources, viz: Coupons, $102,073.86; insured's personal benefit fund, $6,076.35; reserve on policies reinstated, $364.03; lunch room supplies, $1,202.57; income tax, $109.82 premium extension balance charged off, $84.29 | | $109,910 92 |
| Increase in book value of ledger assets | | 195 76 |
| Total income | | $2,826,757 18 |
| Total | | $10,128,287 63 |

DISBURSEMENTS.

| | | |
|---|---|---|
| Death claims | $508,728 69 | |
| Matured endowments and additions | 57,754 66 | |
| Total and permanent disability claims and additional accidental death benefits, less re-insurance | 6,156 73 | |
| Total death claims and endowments | | $572,640 08 |
| Annuities involving life contingencies | | 1,587 00 |
| Surrender values paid in cash, or applied in liquidation of loans or notes | | 304,863 97 |
| Coupons and interest paid in cash, or applied in liquidation of loans or notes | | 14,964 77 |
| Surrender values applied to pay new and renewal premiums | | 3,376 38 |
| Surrender values applied to purchase paid-up insurance and annuities | | 31,415 56 |
| Coupons applied to purchase paid-up insurance and annuities | | 661 85 |
| Dividends paid policyholders in cash, or applied in liquidation of loans or notes | | 458 82 |
| Dividends applied to pay renewal premiums | | 1,519 13 |
| Dividends applied to purchase paid-up additions and annuities | | 54,185 07 |
| (Total paid policyholders | $985,672 63) | |
| Expense of investigation and settlement of policy claims | | 1,896 99 |
| Supplementary contracts not involving life contingencies | | 5,328 74 |
| Dividends with interest, held on deposit surrendered during the year | | 28 09 |
| Dividends to stockholders | | 10,960 00 |
| Commissions to agents, first year, $365,392.18; renewal, $93,743.75; annuities (original), $106.72 | | 459,242 65 |
| Commuted renewal commissions | | 3,698 31 |
| Agency supervision and traveling expenses of supervisors | | 36,622 11 |
| Branch office expenses | | 16,882 47 |
| Medical examiners' fees and inspection of risks | | 32,774 18 |
| Salaries and all other compensation of officers and home office employees | | 241,750 84 |
| Rent | | 23,032 81 |
| Advertisng, printing, stationery, postage, telegraph, telephone, express and exchange | | 48,913 74 |
| Legal expense | | 9,213 50 |
| Furniture, fixtures and safes | | 11,907 47 |
| Repairs and expenses (other than taxes) on real estate | | 24,544 51 |
| Taxes on real estate | | 9,298 33 |
| State taxes on premiums | | 32,324 42 |
| Insurance department licenses and fees | | 3,925 80 |
| Federal taxes | | 1,385 90 |
| All other licenses, fees and taxes | | 804 75 |
| Other disbursements, viz: Agency meetings and prizes, $11,721.89; insurance societies, $2,647.06; agency and medical inspection, $648.00; investment expense, $9,529.49; medical bureau, $6,493.03; light and heat, $1,787.90; agents literature, $2,334.00; tabulating machine and office supplies, $7,969.82; travel and entertainment, $10,462.40; legislative expense, $1,688.08; surety bonds, $2,009.25; miscellaneous, $2,672.61 | | 59,963 53 |
| Agents' balances charged off | | 53 74 |
| Loss on sale or maturity of ledger assets | | 592 83 |
| Total disbursements | | $2,020,218 34 |
| Balance | | $8,108,069 29 |

LEDGER ASSETS.

| | | |
|---|---|---|
| Book value of real estate | | $ 423,958 84 |
| Mortgage loans on real estate | | 5,009,586 25 |
| Loans on company's policies assigned as collateral | | 1,626,241 42 |
| Book value of bonds | | 882,200 02 |
| Cash in office | | 11,179 49 |
| Deposits in trust companies and banks on interest | | 157,827 54 |
| Agents' balances (debit, $8,069.64; credit, $1,584.74) net, $6,484.90; premium balance (debits, $557.94; credit, $11,123.79) net, —$10,565.85 | | —4,080 95 |
| War savings stamps | | 1,156 68 |
| Total ledger assets | | $8,108,069 29 |

NON-LEDGER ASSETS.

| | | |
|---|---|---|
| Interest due and accrued on mortgages | $144,135 08 | |
| Interest accrued on bonds | 7,097 35 | |
| Interest due on premium notes, loans or liens | 379 35 | |
| Interest accrued on other assets | 87 11 | |
| Rents due on company's property | 555 00 | |
| | | 152,253 89 |
| Market value of real estate over book value | | 76,041 16 |
| Due from other companies for losses or claims on poliies re-insured | | 25,895 40 |

## LEDGER ASSETS—Concluded.

### NON-LEDGER ASSETS.

| | | |
|---|---|---|
| Net uncollected and deferred premiums (paid for basis) | | $278,522 63 |
| All other assets, viz: Cancelled re-insurance premiums due from other companies, $689.14; unearned fire and miscellaneous premiums, $3,984.33 | | 4,673 47 |
| Gross assets | | $8,645,455 84 |

### DEDUCT ASSETS NOT ADMITTED.

| | | |
|---|---|---|
| Agents' debit balances | $ 8,069 64 | |
| Premium notes, policy loans and other policy assets in excess of net value and of other policy liabilities on individual policies | 30,415 82 | |
| Premium debit balance | 557 94 | |
| Total | | 39,043 40 |
| Admitted assets | | $8,606,412 44 |

## LIABILITIES.

| | | |
|---|---|---|
| Net present value of outstanding policies computed by the Indiana Insurance Department | $7,672,200 00 | |
| Same for annuities | 16,180 00 | |
| Total | $7,688,380 00 | |
| Deduct net value of risks re-insured | 75,540 00 | |
| Net reserve (paid for basis) | | $7,612,840 00 |
| Extra reserve for total and permanent disability benefits and for additional accidental death benefits included in life policies, less re-insurance | | 24,839 02 |
| Present value of supplementary contracts not involving life contingencies | | 62,498 58 |
| Present value of amounts incurred but not yet due for total and permanent disability benefits | | 8,081 96 |
| Death losses reported for which no proofs have been received | $107,585 00 | |
| Matured endowments due and unpaid | 345 30 | |
| Death losses and other policy claims resisted | 4,000 00 | |
| Total and permanent disability benefits and additional accidental death benefits | 2,247 40 | |
| Total policy claims | | 114,177 70 |
| Dividends left with the company to accumulate at interest | | 1,091 71 |
| Gross premiums paid in advance, including surrender values so applied, less discount, if any | | 7,327 69 |
| Unearned interest and rent paid in advance | | 42,945 82 |
| Salaries, rents, office expenses, bills and accounts due or accrued | | 7,898 84 |
| Medical examiners' and legal fees due or accrued | | 1,583 00 |
| Estimated amount hereafter payable for federal, state and other taxes based upon the business of the year of this statement | | 43,778 33 |
| Dividends or other profits due policyholders | | 41 22 |
| Dividends declared on or apportioned to annual dividend policies payable to policyholders during 1922 for period to December 31, 1922 | | 3,036 38 |
| Insured's personal benefit fund | | 87,183 63 |
| Coupons | | 176,613 93 |
| General contingencies | | 25,000 00 |
| State, county and municipal taxes | | 9,774 62 |
| Total | | $8,228,712 43 |
| Capital paid up | | 137,000 00 |
| Unassigned funds (surplus) | | 240,700 01 |
| Total | | $8,606,412 44 |

## EXHIBIT OF POLICIES—ORDINARY.

### ALL BUSINESS PAID FOR.

| | Number. | Amount. | Number. | Amount. |
|---|---|---|---|---|
| Policies in force December 31, 1920 | | | 38,183 | $101,130,720 00 |
| Policies issued, revived and increased during the year | | | 8,097 | 31,942,453 00 |
| Total | | | 46,280 | $133,073,173 00 |
| Deduct policies which have ceased to be in force during the year— | | | | |
| By death | 203 | $ 682,851 00 | | |
| By maturity | 4 | 58,100 00 | | |
| By expiry | 148 | 354,935 00 | | |
| By surrender | 529 | 1,104,346 00 | | |
| By lapse | 7,548 | 22,041,122 00 | | |
| By decrease | ------- | 2,501,323 00 | | |
| Total | | | 8,432 | 26,742,677 00 |
| Total policies in force December 31, 1921 | | | 37,848 | $106,330,496 00 |
| Re-insured | | | | $8,815,347 00 |

BUSINESS IN ILLINOIS—ORDINARY.

| | Number. | Amount. |
|---|---|---|
| Policies in force December 31, 1920 | 1,516 | $3,170,496 00 |
| Policies issued during the year | 261 | 519,043 00 |
| Total | 1,777 | $3,689,539 00 |
| Deduct policies ceased to be in force | 310 | 706,862 00 |
| Policies in force December 31, 1921 | 1,467 | $2,982,677 00 |
| Losses and claims unpaid December 31, 1920 | 1 | $1,125 00 |
| Losses and claims inurred during the year | 15 | 77,231 00 |
| Total | 16 | $78,356 00 |
| Losses and claims settled during the year | 16 | 78,356 00 |
| Premiums received | | $78,358 00 |

GAIN AND LOSS EXHIBIT.

INSURANCE EXHIBIT.

| | | Gain in surplus. | Loss in surplus. |
|---|---|---|---|
| Loading on actual premiums of the year (averaging 18.19 per cent of the gross premiums) | $404,890 53 | | |
| Insurance expenses incurred during the year | 949,360 50 | | |
| Loss from loading | | | $544,469 97 |
| Interest earned during the year | $499,504 56 | | |
| Investment expenses incurred during the year | 62,548 78 | | |
| Net income from investments | $436,955 78 | | |
| Interest required to maintain reserve | 286,429 97 | | |
| Gain from interest | | $150,525 81 | |
| Expected mortality on net amount at risk | $955,721 98 | | |
| Actual mortality on net amount at risk | 498,686 69 | | |
| Gain from mortality | | 457,035 29 | |
| Expected disbursements to annuitants | $ 995 34 | | |
| Net actual annuity claims incurred | 1,187 00 | | |
| Loss from annuities | | | 191 66 |
| Total gain during the year from surrendered and lapsed policies | | 27,695 04 | |
| Dividends paid stockholders | | | 10,960 00 |
| Decrease in surplus on dividend account | | | 57,240 73 |
| Increase in special funds and special reserves during the year | | | 5,000 00 |
| Net to profit account | | 1,342 94 | |

INVESTMENT EXHIBIT.

| | | Gain in surplus. | Loss in surplus. |
|---|---|---|---|
| Total losses from real estate | | | 592 83 |
| Total gains from bonds | | 195 76 | |
| Loss on furniture no longer carried as a non-ledger asset | | | 15,000 00 |
| Gain from assets not admitted | | 6,908 55 | |
| Net gain on account of total and permanent disability benefits or additional accidental death benefits included in life policies | | 8,138 39 | |
| Gain from increase in amounts due from re-insurance companies | | 597 15 | |
| Loss from decrease in unearned fire premiums | | | 638 00 |
| Total gains and losses in surplus during the year | | $652,438 93 | $634,093 19 |
| Surplus December 31, 1920 | $222,354 27 | | |
| Surplus December 31, 1921 | 240,700 01 | | |
| Increase in surplus | | | 18,345 74 |
| Total | | $652,438 93 | $652,438 93 |

## AMERICAN LIFE INSURANCE COMPANY.

Located at No. 408 Fort Street West, Detroit, Michigan; incorporated January 24, 1907; commenced business in Illinois July 6, 1921.

CLARENCE L. AYRES, President. MARION O. ROWLAND, Secretary.

GEORGE A. BARR, Director of Trade and Commerce, Attorney for service at Springfield.

CAPITAL.

| | | |
|---|---|---|
| Capital paid up | $100,000 00 | |
| Amount of ledger assets December 31, of previous year | | 2,457,349 32 |

## INCOME.

|  | | | |
|---|---|---|---|
| First year's premiums on original policies, less re-insurance | | $148,135 93 | |
| First year's premiums for total and permanent disability benefits, less re-insurance | | 7,484 92 | |
| First year's premiums for additional accidental death benefits, less re-insurance | | 1,275 09 | |
| Dividends applied to purchase paid-up additions and annuities | | 131 68 | |
| New premiums | | $157,027 62 | |
| Renewal premiums less re-insurance | $1,004,466 02 | | |
| Renewal premiums for total and permanent disability benefits, less re-insurance | 24,427 18 | | |
| Renewal premiums for additional accidental death benefits, less re-insurance | 3,437 68 | | |
| Dividends applied to pay renewal premiums | 3,550 78 | | |
| Surrender values applied to pay renewal premiums | 411 85 | | |
| Renewal premiums | | 1,036,293 51 | |
| Premium income | | | $1,193,321 13 |
| Consideration for supplementary contracts not involving life contingencies | | | 36,671 44 |
| Dividends left with company to accumulate at interest | | | 308 07 |
| Ledger assets other than premiums received from other companies for assuming their risks | | | 3,107,065 85 |
| Interest on mortgage loans | | $160,151 22 | |
| Interest on collateral loans | | 45 00 | |
| Interest on bonds | | 1,272 82 | |
| Interest on premium notes, policy loans or liens | | 37,610 48 | |
| Interest on deposits | | 4,230 75 | |
| Interest on other debts due the company | | 1,623 75 | |
| Rents—including $8,400.00 for company's occupancy of its own buildings | | 30,090 08 | |
| Total interest and rents | | | 235,024 10 |
| From other sources, viz: Contributed surplus, $114,500.00; suspense, $142.81 | | | 114,642 81 |
| Borrowed money (gross) | | | 20,000 00 |
| Agents' balances previously charged off | | | 18,474 30 |
| Total income | | | $4,725,507 70 |
| Total | | | $7,182,857 02 |

## DISBURSEMENTS.

|  | | |
|---|---|---|
| Death claims | $195,972 14 | |
| Matured endowments | 6,500 00 | |
| Total and permanent disability claims | 1,422 18 | |
| Total death claims and endowments | | $203,894 32 |
| Premium notes and liens voided by lapse, less $9,521.99 restorations | | 82,562 24 |
| Surrender values paid in cash, or applied in liquidation of loans or notes | | 146,784 31 |
| Surrender values applied to pay renewal premiums | | 411 85 |
| Dividends paid policyholders in cash, or applied in liquidation of loans or notes | | 12,659 61 |
| Dividends applied to pay renewal premiums | | 3,550 78 |
| Dividends applied to purchase paid-up additions and annuities | | 131 68 |
| Dividends left with the company to accumulate at interest | | 308 07 |
| (Total paid policyholders | $450,302 86) | |
| Expense of investigation and settlement of policy claims, including legal expenses | | 658 11 |
| Supplementary contracts not involving life contingencies | | 6,071 80 |
| Dividends with interest, held on deposit surrendered during the year | | 521 76 |
| Commissions to agents, first year, $92,357.25; renewal, $94,064.44 | | 186,421 69 |
| Commuted renewal commissions | | 4,535 31 |
| Compensation of managers and agents not paid by commissions on new business | | 26,962 88 |
| Agency supervision and traveling expenses of supervisors | | 6,919 70 |
| Branch office expenses | | 10,995 62 |
| Medical examiners' fees and inspection of risks | | 21,451 39 |
| Salaries and all other compensation of officers and home office employees | | 81,255 21 |
| Rent | | 8,854 00 |
| Advertising, printing, stationery, postage, telegraph, telephone, express and exchange | | 35,862 12 |
| Legal expense | | 10,978 19 |
| Furniture, fixtures and safes | | 5,620 13 |
| Repairs and expenses (other than taxes) on real estate | | 13,001 80 |
| Taxes on real estate | | 6,397 85 |
| State taxes on premiums | | 3,013 07 |
| Insurance department licenses and fees | | 4,413 98 |
| Federal taxes | | 5,408 24 |
| All other licenses, fees and taxes | | 3,556 92 |
| Other disbursements, viz: Actuarial expense, $14,423.20; American Life expense, $38,149.78; association assessments, $995.00; collection fees, $1,363.25; officers and directors travel, $4,773.43; premium on bonds, $919.53; expense loan department, $2,743.63; general expense, $1,680.21 | | 65,048 03 |
| Borrowed money repaid (gross) | | 20,000 00 |

## DISBURSEMENTS—Concluded.

| | |
|---|---|
| Interest on borrowed money | $ 180 83 |
| Agents' balances charged off | 15,521 24 |
| Overpaid accounts | 1,006 80 |
| Total disbursements | $994,959 53 |
| Balance | $6,187,897 49 |

## LEDGER ASSETS.

| | |
|---|---|
| Book value of real estate | $ 500,036 52 |
| Mortgage loans on real estate | 4,039,142 15 |
| Loans on company's policies assigned as collateral | 1,073,664 56 |
| Premium notes on policies in force | 114,353 30 |
| Book value of bonds | 11,967 48 |
| Cash in office | 23,486 45 |
| Deposits in trust companies and banks not on interest | 20,735 39 |
| Deposits in trust companies and banks on interest | 393,088 17 |
| Agents' balances (debit, $13,229.28; credit, $8,558.84) | 4,670 44 |
| Tax sale certificates, $4,829.03; travelers check, $500.00; war savings stamps, $824.00; bond held under Soldiers' and Sailors' Relief Act, $600.00 | 6,753 03 |
| Total ledger assets | $6,187,897 49 |

### NON-LEDGER ASSETS.

| | | | |
|---|---|---|---|
| Interest due and accrued on mortgages | | $82,376 41 | |
| Interest accrued on bonds | | 69 26 | |
| Interest accrued on premium notes, loans or liens | | 7,174 38 | |
| Interest accrued on other assets | | 1,132 54 | |
| | | | 90,752 59 |
| Due from other companies for losses or claims on policies re-insured | | | 1,000 00 |
| | New business. | Renewals. | |
| Net uncollected and deferred premiums (paid for basis) | $4,016 52 | $105,230 60 | 109,247 12 |
| All other assets, viz: Loan to policyholders on this companys policies, $2,348.00; due from American Life Insurance Co. of Des Moines on death claims, $9,200.90 | | | 11,548 90 |
| Gross assets | | | $6,400,446 10 |

### DEDUCT ASSETS NOT ADMITTED.

| | | |
|---|---|---|
| Agents' debit balances | $13,229 28 | |
| Cash advanced to or in hands of officers or agents | 500 00 | |
| Premium notes, policy loans and other policy assets in excess of net value and of other policy liabilities on individual policies | 13,320 17 | |
| Book value of real estate over market value | 1,763 05 | |
| Certificates of deposit on closed banks | 2,894 67 | |
| Total | | 31,707 17 |
| Admitted assets | | $6,368,738 93 |

## LIABILITIES.

| | | |
|---|---|---|
| Net present value of outstanding policies computed by the Michigan Insurance Department | $5,830,350 41 | |
| Same for dividend additions | 10,706 00 | |
| Total | $5,841,056 41 | |
| Deduct net value of risks re-insured | 54,271 43 | |
| Net reserve (paid for basis) | | $5,786,784 98 |
| Extra reserve for total and permanent disability benefits and for additional accidental death benefits included in life policies, less re-insurance | | 66,051 69 |
| Present value of supplementary contracts not involving life contingencies | | 122,309 62 |
| Present value of amounts incurred but not yet due for total and permanent disability benefits | | 23,222 27 |
| Death losses reported for which no proofs have been received | 9,740 01 | |
| Death losses and other policy claims resisted | 17,100 00 | |
| Total and permanent disability benefits and additional accidental death benefits | 1,000 00 | |
| Total policy claims | | 27,840 01 |
| Dividends left with the company to accumulate at interest | | 13,842 88 |
| Gross premiums paid in advance, including surrender values so applied, less discount, if any | | 4,415 36 |
| Unearned interest and rent paid in advance | | 19,474 38 |
| Commissions due agents on premium notes, when paid | | 2,287 06 |
| Salaries, rents, office expenses, bills and accounts due or accrued | | 3,801 56 |
| Medical examiners' and legal fees due or accrued | | 1,065 00 |
| Estimated amount hereafter payable for federal, state and other taxes based upon the business of the year of this statement | | 38,348 31 |
| Dividends or other profits due policyholders | | 6,928 62 |
| Dividends declared on or apportioned to annual dividend policies payable to policyholders during 1922 for period to include March 31, 1922 | | 4,919 70 |

## LIABILITIES—Concluded.

| | |
|---|---|
| Amounts set apart, apportioned, provisionally ascertained, calculated, declared or held awaiting apportionment upon deferred dividend policies | $20,976 00 |
| Reserve or surplus funds not otherwise included in liabilities, viz: Contract with Detroit Trust Company, Trustee, $6,405.99; unpaid re-insurance, $1,540.78; claim expense, $641.62 | 8,588 39 |
| Due United States Treasury Department, Soldiers' and Sailors' Relief | 554 05 |
| Total | $6,151,409 88 |
| Capital paid up | 100,000 00 |
| Unassigned funds (surplus) | 117,329 05 |
| Total | $6,368,738 93 |

## EXHIBIT OF POLICIES—ORDINARY.

ALL BUSINESS PAID FOR.

| | Number. | Amount. | Number. | Amount. |
|---|---|---|---|---|
| Policies in force December 31, 1920 | | | 13,250 | $30,829,093 00 |
| Policies issued, revived and increased during the year (including American Life of Des Moines, re-insurance) | | | 19,858 | 39,167,661 38 |
| Total | | | 33,108 | $69,996,754 38 |
| Deduct policies which have ceased to be in force during the year— | | | | |
| By death | 97 | $ 206,324 39 | | |
| By maturity | 4 | 6,500 00 | | |
| By expiry | 333 | 792,109 00 | | |
| By surrender | 357 | 739,460 00 | | |
| By lapse | 3,070 | 7,698,180 00 | | |
| By decrease | 117 | 526,665 51 | | |
| Total | | | 3,978 | 9,969,238 90 |
| Total policies in force December 31, 1921 | | | 29,130 | $60,027,515 48 |

## BUSINESS IN ILLINOIS—ORDINARY.

| | Number. | Amount. |
|---|---|---|
| Policies in force December 31, 1920 | 5 | $ 63,801 00 |
| Policies re-insured | 436 | 686,293 33 |
| Policies issued during the year | 38 | 70,754 80 |
| Total | 479 | $820,849 13 |
| Deduct policies ceased to be in force | 37 | 93,375 00 |
| Policies in force December 31, 1921 | 442 | $727,474 13 |
| Losses and claims incurred during the year | 3 | $3,000 00 |
| Losses and claims settled during the year | 2 | 2,000 00 |
| Losses and claims unpaid December 31, 1921 | 1 | $1,000 00 |
| Premiums received | | $10,091 85 |

## GAIN AND LOSS EXHIBIT.

INSURANCE EXHIBIT.

| | | Gain in surplus. | Loss in surplus. |
|---|---|---|---|
| Loading on actual premiums of the year (averaging 14.48 per cent of the gross premiums) | $179,494 41 | | |
| Insurance expenses incurred during the year | 516,516 26 | | |
| Loss from loading | | | $337,021 85 |
| Interest earned during the year | $249,386 15 | | |
| Investment expenses incurred during the year | 32,285 22 | | |
| Net income from investments | $217,100 93 | | |
| Interest required to maintain reserve | 132,303 68 | | |
| Gain from interest | | $ 84,797 25 | |
| Expected mortality on net amount at risk | $363,871 85 | | |
| Actual mortality on net amount at risk | 152,015 76 | | |
| Gain from mortality | | 211,856 09 | |
| Total gain during the year from surrendered and lapsed policies | | 53,758 89 | |
| Decrease in surplus on dividend account | | | 49,996 22 |
| INVESTMENT EXHIBIT. | | | |
| Total losses from real estate | | | 1,763 05 |
| Net gain on account of total and permanent disability benefits or additional accidental death benefits included in life policies | | 18,300 25 | |
| Contributed surplus | | 114,042 81 | |
| Policy loans in non-ledger assets | | 2,348 00 | |
| Total gains and losses in surplus during the year | | $485,793 29 | $388,781 12 |

GAIN AND LOSS EXHIBIT—Concluded.

INVESTMENT EXHIBIT.

| | | Gain in surplus. | Loss in surplus. |
|---|---|---|---|
| Surplus December 31, 1920 | $ 20,316 88 | | |
| Surplus December 31, 1921 | 117,329 05 | | |
| Increase in surplus | | | $97,012 17 |
| Total | | $485,793 29 | $485,793 29 |

## AMERICAN LIFE RE-INSURANCE COMPANY.

Located at Western Indemnity Building, Dallas, Texas; incorporated February 12, 1919; commenced business in Illinois, July 1, 1921.

A. C. BIGGER, President. FRED D. STRUDELL, Secretary.

GEORGE A. BARR, Director of Trade and Commerce, Attorney for service at Springfield.

CAPITAL.

| | | | |
|---|---|---|---|
| Capital paid up | | $250,000 00 | |
| Amount of ledger assets December 31, of previous year | | | $412,816 33 |

INCOME.

| | | | |
|---|---|---|---|
| First year's premiums on original policies, less re-insurance | | $107,839 13 | |
| First year's premiums for total and permanent disability benefits, less re-insurance | | 1,760 28 | |
| First year's premiums for additional accidental death benefits, less re-insurance | | 16,639 13 | |
| New premiums | | $126,238 54 | |
| Renewal premiums less re-insurance | $110,920 55 | | |
| Renewal premiums for total and permanent disability benefits, less re-insurance | 616 42 | | |
| Renewal premiums for additional accidental death benefits, less re-insurance | 992 77 | | |
| Renewal premiums | | 112,529 74 | |
| Premium income | | | $238,768 28 |
| Interest on mortgage loans | | $24,770 44 | |
| Interest on bonds | | 2,799 92 | |
| Interest on deposits | | 238 92 | |
| Interest on other debts due the company | | 5 43 | |
| Total interest | | | 27,814 71 |
| Total income | | | $266,582 99 |
| Total | | | $679,399 32 |

DISBURSEMENTS.

| | | |
|---|---|---|
| Death claims | $34,584 63 | |
| Additional accidental death benefits, less re-insurance | 5,000 00 | |
| Total death claims | | $39,584 63 |
| (Total paid policyholders | $39,584 63) | |
| Expense of investigation and settlement of policy claims | | 1,474 39 |
| Commissions to agents, first year, $46,420.92; renewal, $345.75 | | 46,766 67 |
| Agency supervision and traveling expenses of supervisors | | 2,275 06 |
| Branch office expenses | | 1,777 49 |
| Inspection of risks | | 9 43 |
| Salaries and all other compensation of officers and home office employees | | 25,973 18 |
| Rent | | 1,466 00 |
| Advertising, printing, stationery, postage, telegraph, telephone and express | | 5,109 21 |
| Legal expense | | 25 00 |
| Furniture, fixtures and safes | | 926 90 |
| State taxes on premiums | | 455 56 |
| Insurance department licenses and fees | | 1,900 00 |
| All other licenses, fees and taxes | | 10,812 88 |
| Other disbursements, viz: Corporation insurance, $846.75; investment expense, $1.50; incidental office expense, $202.39; miscellaneous expense, $267.75 | | 1,318 39 |
| Total disbursements | | $139,874 79 |
| Balance | | $539,524 53 |

## LEDGER ASSETS.

| | | |
|---|---|---|
| Mortgage loans on real estate | | $456,145 57 |
| Book value of bonds | | 58,834 00 |
| Deposits in trust companies and banks not on interest | | 24,544 96 |
| Total ledger assets | | $539,524 53 |

### NON-LEDGER ASSETS.

| | | | |
|---|---|---|---|
| Interest accrued on mortgages | | $12,014 37 | |
| Interest accrued on bonds | | 229 53 | |
| | | | 12,243 90 |
| Market value of bonds over book value | | | 916 00 |
| | New business. | Renewals. | |
| Net uncollected and deferred premiums (paid for basis) | $16,149 74 | $26,824 24 | 42,973 98 |
| Amount due from re-insuring companies as unearned premiums on cancelled policies | | | 1,933 13 |
| Gross assets | | | $597,591 54 |

### DEDUCT ASSETS NOT ADMITTED.

| | |
|---|---|
| Premium notes, policy loans and other policy assets in excess of net value and of other policy liabilities on individual policies | 14,561 71 |
| Admitted assets | $583,029 83 |

## LIABILITIES.

| | | |
|---|---|---|
| Net present value of outstanding policies computed by the Texas Insurance Department | $184,476 00 | |
| Deduct net value of risks re-insured | 42,499 00 | |
| Net reserve (paid for basis) | | $141,977 00 |
| Extra reserve for total and permanent disability benefits and for additional accidental death benefits included in life policies, less re-insurance | | 11,613 54 |
| Surrender values claimable on policies cancelled | | 1,348 32 |
| Death losses reported for which no proofs have been received | $10,788 00 | |
| Additional accidental death benefits | 3,000 00 | |
| Total policy claims | | 13,788 00 |
| Gross premiums paid in advance, including surrender values so applied, less discount, if any | | 364 04 |
| Commissions to agents due or accrued | | 771 89 |
| Salaries, rents, office expenses, bills and accounts due or accrued | | 514 98 |
| Estimated amount hereafter payable for federal, state and other taxes based upon the business of the year of this statement | | 3,075 00 |
| Extra premium reserve on sub-standard risks and mortality fluctuation fund | | 3,051 92 |
| Total | | $176,504 69 |
| Capital paid up | | 250,000 00 |
| Unassigned funds (surplus) | | 156,525 14 |
| Total | | $583,029 83 |

## EXHIBIT OF POLICIES—ORDINARY.

### ALL BUSINESS PAID FOR.

| | Number. | Amount. | Number. | Amount. |
|---|---|---|---|---|
| Policies in force December 31, 1920 | | | 5,058 | $19,025,345 00 |
| Policies issued, revived and increased during the year | | | 2,618 | 15,193,056 00 |
| Total | | | 7,676 | $34,218,401 00 |
| Deduct policies which have ceased to be in force during the year— | | | | |
| By death | 16 | $ 33,517 00 | | |
| By lapse | 1,766 | 6,313,154 00 | | |
| By decrease | | 725,687 00 | | |
| Total | | | 1,782 | 7,072,358 00 |
| Total policies in force December 31, 1921 | | | 5,894 | $27,146,043 00 |
| Re-insured | | | 1,000 | $7,480,322 00 |

## BUSINESS IN ILLINOIS—ORDINARY.

| | Number. | Amount. |
|---|---|---|
| Policies in force December 31, 1920 | 48 | $167,362 00 |
| Policies issued during the year | 65 | 471,680 00 |
| Total | 113 | $639,042 00 |
| Deduct policies ceased to be in force | 16 | 75,182 00 |
| Policies in force December 31, 1921 | 97 | $563,860 00 |
| Premiums received | | $4,083 58 |

## GAIN AND LOSS EXHIBIT.

INSURANCE EXHIBIT.

| | | Gain in surplus. | Loss in surplus. |
|---|---|---|---|
| Loading on actual premiums of the year (averaging 10 per cent of the gross premiums) | $ 26,602 59 | | |
| Insurance expenses incurred during the year | 102,091 50 | | |
| Loss from loading | | | $75,488 91 |
| Interest earned during the year | $30,183 00 | | |
| Investment expenses incurred during the year | 1,191 93 | | |
| Net income from investments | $28,991 07 | | |
| Interest required to maintain reserve | 6,533 00 | | |
| Gain from interest | | $ 22,458 07 | |
| Expected mortality on net amount at risk | $160,440 88 | | |
| Actual mortality on net amount at risk | 32,495 21 | | |
| Gain from mortality | | 127,945 67 | |
| Total gain during the year from surrendered and lapsed policies | | 1,510 92 | |
| Increase in special funds and special reserves during the year | | | 2,771 08 |
| INVESTMENT EXHIBIT. | | | |
| Total gains from bonds | | 916 00 | |
| Loss from assets not admitted | | | 14,561 71 |
| Net gain on account of total and permanent disability benefits or additional accidental death benefits included in life policies | | 1,981 52 | |
| Balance unaccounted for | | 690 76 | |
| Total gains and losses in surplus during the year | | $155,502 94 | $92,821 70 |
| Surplus December 31, 1920 | $ 93,843 90 | | |
| Surplus December 31, 1921 | 156,525 14 | | |
| Increase in surplus | | | 62,681 24 |
| Total | | $155,502 94 | $155,502 94 |

## AMERICAN NATIONAL ASSURANCE COMPANY.

Located at No. 3719 Washington Avenue, St. Louis, Missouri; incorporated March 15, 1912; commenced business in Illinois October 17, 1913.

HARRY M. STILL, President. EARLE E. SALISBURY, Secretary.

GEORGE H. PEAKS, Chicago, Attorney for service.

### CAPITAL.

| | | | |
|---|---|---|---|
| Capital paid up | | $200,000 00 | |
| Amount of ledger assets December 31, of previous year | | | $859,025 38 |

### INCOME.

| | | | |
|---|---|---|---|
| First year's premiums on original policies, less re-insurance | | $90,806 26 | |
| First year's premiums for total and permanent disability benefits, less re-insurance | | 2,076 28 | |
| First year's premiums for additional accidental death benefits, less re-insurance | | 1,960 68 | |
| New premiums | | $ 94,843 22 | |
| Renewal premiums less re-insurance | $294,344 85 | | |
| Renewal premiums for total and permanent disability benefits, less re-insurance | 4,513 37 | | |
| Renewal premiums for additional accidental death benefits, less re-insurance | 3,048 19 | | |
| Surrender values applied to pay renewal premiums | 77 50 | | |
| Renewal premiums | | 301,983 91 | |
| Premium income | | | $396,827 13 |
| Interest on mortgage loans | | $42,483 03 | |
| Interest on bonds | | 3,667 50 | |
| Interest on premium notes, policy loans or liens | | 5,785 66 | |
| Interest on deposits | | 818 28 | |
| Interest on other debts due the company | | 281 21 | |
| Rents—including $4,200.00 for company's occupancy of its own buildings | | 4,917 50 | |
| Total interest and rents | | | 57,953 18 |
| From other sources, viz: Cash in suspense, $241.58; commission on investment, $4,173.00 | | | 4,414 58 |
| Borrowed money (gross) | | | 60,000 00 |
| Total income | | | $519,194 89 |
| Total | | | $1,378,220 27 |

## DISBURSEMENTS.

| | | |
|---|---|---|
| Death claims | $34,523 34 | |
| Total and permanent disability claims and additional accidental death benefits, less re-insurance | 3,734 85 | |
| Total death claims | | $38,258 19 |
| Surrender values paid in cash, or applied in liquidation of loans or notes | | 13,285 85 |
| Surrender values applied to pay new and renewal premiums | | 77 50 |
| (Total paid policyholders | $51,621 54) | |
| Expense of investigation and settlement of policy claims | | 227 22 |
| Supplementary contracts not involving life contingencies | | 360 00 |
| Commissions to agents, first year, $68,716.28; renewal, $29,856.48 | | 98,572 76 |
| Compensation of managers and agents not paid by commissions on new business | | 2,400 00 |
| Agency supervision and traveling expenses of supervisors | | 572 20 |
| Medical examiners' fees and inspection of risks | | 5,165 95 |
| Salaries and all other compensation of officers and home office employees | | 33,441 16 |
| Rent | | 4,200.00 |
| Advertising, printing, stationery, postage, telegraph, telephone, express and exchange | | 7,336 83 |
| Legal expense | | 8 75 |
| Furniture, fixtures and safes | | 375 75 |
| Repairs and expenses (other than taxes) on real estate | | 2,505 90 |
| Taxes on real estate | | 639 70 |
| State taxes on premiums | | 4,225 48 |
| Insurance department licenses and fees | | 1,509 75 |
| Federal taxes | | 1,586 00 |
| All other licenses, fees and taxes | | 309 50 |
| Other disbursements, viz: Incidental expense, $1,245.83; investment expense, $384.26; traveling expense other than agency, $157.91 | | 1,788 00 |
| Borrowed money repaid (gross) | | 50,000 00 |
| Interest on borrowed money | | 553 87 |
| Agents' balances charged off | | 58 44 |
| Loss on sale or maturity of ledger assets | | 3,407 80 |
| Total disbursements | | $270,866 60 |
| Balance | | $1,107,353 67 |

## LEDGER ASSETS.

| | |
|---|---|
| Book value of real estate | $ 57,249 59 |
| Mortgage loans on real estate | 868,114 40 |
| Loans on company's policies assigned as collateral | 72,355 11 |
| Premium notes on policies in force | 13,000 39 |
| Book value of bonds | 75,496 27 |
| Cash in office | 2,036 96 |
| Deposits in trust companies and banks on interest | 14,229 44 |
| Bills receivable | 4,015 59 |
| Agents' balances (debit, $967.73; credit, $111.81) net | 855 92 |
| Total ledger assets | $1,107,353 67 |

### NON-LEDGER ASSETS.

| | | |
|---|---|---|
| Interest due and accrued on mortgages | $25,922 11 | |
| Interest accrued on bonds | 690 29 | |
| Interest accrued on premium notes, loans or liens | 89 27 | |
| Interest accrued on other assets | 9 99 | |
| | | 26,711 66 |
| Net uncollected and deferred premiums (paid for basis) renewals | | 39,568 75 |
| Furniture, fixtures and safes | | 5,627 05 |
| Gross assets | | $1,179,261 13 |

### DEDUCT ASSETS NOT ADMITTED.

| | | |
|---|---|---|
| Furniture, fixtures and safes | $5,627 05 | |
| Agents' debit balances | 967 73 | |
| Bills receivable | 4,015 59 | |
| Premium notes, policy loans and other policy assets in excess of net value and of other policy liabilities on individual policies | 2,215 85 | |
| Book value of bonds over market value | 740 57 | |
| Mortgage loan forgery | 1,814 40 | |
| Total | | 15,381 19 |
| Admitted assets | | $1,163,879 94 |

## LIABILITIES.

| | | |
|---|---|---|
| Net present value of outstanding policies computed by the Missouri Insurance Department | $837,226 00 | |
| Deduct net value of risks re-insured | 6,505 00 | |
| Net reserve (paid for basis) | | $830,721 00 |
| Extra reserve for total and permanent disability benefits and for additional accidental death benefits included in life policies, less re-insurance | | 9,040 58 |
| Present value of supplementary contracts not involving life contingencies | | 4,454 00 |

## LIABILITIES—Concluded.

| | | |
|---|---|---|
| Present value of amounts incurred but not yet due for total and permanent disability benefits | | $ 843 00 |
| Death losses due and unpaid | $ 2,000 00 | |
| Death losses reported for which no proofs have been received | 16,000 00 | |
| Death losses and other policy claims resisted | 1,000 00 | |
| Total and permanent disability benefits and additional accidental death benefits | 315 00 | |
| Total policy claims | | 19,315 00 |
| Gross premiums paid in advance, including surrender values so applied, less discount, if any | | 1,122 99 |
| Unearned interest and rent paid in advance | | 2,613 52 |
| Cost of collection on uncollected and deferred premiums in excess of loading | | 884 32 |
| Salaries, rents, office expenses, bills and accounts due or accrued | | 632 75 |
| Medical examiners and legal inspection fees due or accrued | | 660 50 |
| Estimated amount hereafter payable for federal, state and other taxes based upon the business of the year of this statement | | 6,896 66 |
| Borrowed money | | 10,000 00 |
| Cash in suspense | | 651 12 |
| Total | | $887,835 44 |
| Capital paid up | | 200,000 00 |
| Unassigned funds (surplus) | | 76,044 50 |
| Total | | $1,163,879 94 |

## EXHIBIT OF POLICIES—ORDINARY.

### ALL BUSINESS PAID FOR.

| | Number. | Amount. | Number. | Amount. |
|---|---|---|---|---|
| Policies in force December 31, 1920 | | | 6,554 | $12,293,285 00 |
| Policies issued, revived and increased during the year | | | 1,883 | 3,913,100 00 |
| Total | | | 8,437 | $16,206,385 00 |
| Deduct policies which have ceased to be in force during the year— | | | | |
| By death | 26 | $ 52,000 00 | | |
| By expiry | 20 | 30,500 00 | | |
| By surrender | 88 | 203,770 00 | | |
| By lapse | 2,034 | 3,846,629 00 | | |
| By decrease | | 76,764 00 | | |
| Total | | | 2,168 | 4,209,663 00 |
| Total policies in force December 31, 1921 | | | 6,269 | $11,996,722 00 |
| Re-insured | | | 218 | $1,058,324 00 |

## BUSINESS IN ILLINOIS—ORDINARY.

| | Number. | Amount. |
|---|---|---|
| Policies in force December 31, 1920 | 524 | $1,015,270 00 |
| Policies issued during the year | 95 | 173,500 00 |
| Total | 619 | $1,188,770 00 |
| Deduct policies ceased to be in force | 169 | 302,724 00 |
| Policies in force December 31, 1921 | 450 | $886,046 00 |
| Losses and claims incurred during the year | 2 | $2,000 00 |
| Losses and claims settled during the year | 2 | 2,000 00 |
| Premiums received | | $29,607 45 |

## GAIN AND LOSS EXHIBIT.

### INSURANCE EXHIBIT.

| | | Gain in surplus. | Loss in surplus. |
|---|---|---|---|
| Loading on actual premiums of the year (averaging 22.1 per cent of the gross premiums) | $ 85,934 00 | | |
| Insurance expenses incurred during the year | 159,623 41 | | |
| Loss from loading | | | $73,689 41 |
| Interest earned during the year | $61,477 36 | | |
| Investment expenses incurred during the year | 8,105 36 | | |
| Net income from investments | $53,372 00 | | |
| Interest required to maintain reserve | 27,761 51 | | |
| Gain from interest | | $25,610 49 | |
| Expected mortality on net amount at risk | $118,172 50 | | |
| Actual mortality on net amount at risk | 44,434 35 | | |
| Gain from mortality | | 73,738 15 | |
| Total gain during the year from surrendered and lapsed policies | | 14,123 56 | |
| Net to loss account | | | 58 44 |

GAIN AND LOSS EXHIBIT—Concluded.

INVESTMENT EXHIBIT.

| | | Gain in surplus. | Loss in surplus. |
|---|---|---|---|
| Total gains from bonds | | $3,687 43 | |
| Total losses from bonds | | | $3,407 80 |
| Loss from assets not admitted | | | 2,161 15 |
| Net gain on account of total and permanent disability benefits or additional accidental death benefits included in life policies | | 4,005 97 | |
| Gain from commission on investment | | 4,173 00 | |
| Balance unaccounted for loss | | | 1,668 16 |
| Total gains and losses in surplus during the year | | $125,338 60 | $80,984 96 |
| Surplus December 31, 1920 | $31,690 86 | | |
| Surplus December 31, 1921 | 76,044 50 | | |
| Increase in surplus | | | 44,353 64 |
| Total | | $125,338 60 | $125,338 60 |

## BANKERS LIFE COMPANY.

Located at Fourth and Walnut Streets, Des Moines, Iowa; incorporated as an assessment association, June 24, 1879; re-incorporated as a legal reserve company, October 26, 1911; commenced business in Illinois as an assessment association July 9, 1884; as a legal reserve company, November 11, 1911;

GEORGE KUHNS, President. G. W. FOWLER, Secretary.

GEORGE A. BARR, Director of Trade and Commerce, Attorney for service at Springfield.

| | | | |
|---|---|---|---|
| Amount of ledger assets December 31, of previous year | | | $42,690,219 21 |

### INCOME.

| | | | |
|---|---|---|---|
| First year's premiums on original policies, less re-insurance | | $3,002,600 41 | |
| First year's premiums for total and permanent disability benefits | | 122,208 81 | |
| First year's premiums for additional accidental death benefits | | 82,385 29 | |
| Surrender values to pay first-year's premiums | | 5,436 19 | |
| Dividends applied to purchase paid-up additions and annuities | | 201,911 79 | |
| New premiums | | $3,414,542 49 | |
| Renewal premiums less re-insurance | $10,821,860 26 | | |
| Renewal premiums for total and permanent disability benefits | 81,548 33 | | |
| Renewal premiums for additional accidental death benefits | 64,737 23 | | |
| Dividends applied to pay renewal premiums | 856,735 96 | | |
| Surrender values applied to pay renewal premiums | 5,283 83 | | |
| Renewal premiums | | 11,830,165 61 | |
| Premium income | | $15,244,708 10 | |
| Premiums advanced during year under Soldiers' and Sailors' Civil Relief Act | | 34 17 | |
| Total | | | $15,244,742 27 |
| Consideration for supplementary contracts not involving life contingencies | | | 37,225 32 |
| Dividends left with company to accumulate at interest | | | 86,872 03 |
| Interest on mortgage loans | | $2,060,514 79 | |
| Interest on bonds | | 158,982 68 | |
| Interest on premium notes, policy loans or liens | | 104,992 42 | |
| Interest on deposits | | 20,595 54 | |
| Interest on sundry assets | | 74 00 | |
| Total interest | | | 2,354,159 43 |
| From other sources, viz: Policy fees, $5,587.98; trust fund, $1,456.98 | | | 7,044 96 |
| Increase in book value of ledger assets | | | 1,364 78 |
| Total income | | | $17,731,408 79 |
| Total | | | $60,421,628 00 |

### DISBURSEMENTS.

| | | |
|---|---|---|
| Death claims and additions | $6,297,205 88 | |
| Total and permanent disability claims and additional accidental death benefits | 62,461 56 | |
| Total death claims | | $6,359,667 44 |
| Premium notes and liens voided by lapse, less $23,168.97 restorations | | 107,951 97 |
| Surrender values paid in cash, or applied in liquidation of loans or notes | | 256,123 69 |

## DISBURSEMENTS—Concluded.

| | | |
|---|---|---|
| Surrender values applied to pay new and renewal premiums | | $ 10,720 02 |
| Dividends paid policyholders in cash, or applied in liquidation of loans or notes | | 29,236 92 |
| Dividends applied to pay renewal premiums | | 856,735 96 |
| Dividends applied to purchase paid-up additions and annuities | | 201,911 79 |
| Dividends left with the company to accumulate at interest | | 86,872 03 |
| (Total paid policyholders | $7,909,219 82) | |
| Expense of investigation and settlement of policy claims, including legal expenses | | 6,349 12 |
| Supplementary contracts not involving life contingencies | | 16,130 13 |
| Dividends with interest, held on deposit surrendered during the year | | 16,443 37 |
| Commissions to agents, first year, $1,494,584.10; renewal, $590,280.74 | | 2,084,864 84 |
| Commuted renewal commissions | | 24,107 99 |
| Agency supervision and traveling expenses of supervisors | | 394,064 75 |
| Branch office expenses | | 215,227 82 |
| Medical examiners' fees and inspection of risks | | 198,288 88 |
| Salaries and all other compensation of officers and home office employees | | 520,329 57 |
| Rent | | 43,796 00 |
| Advertising, printing, stationery, postage, telegraph, telephone, express and exchange | | 276,194 85 |
| Legal expense | | 3,096 63 |
| Furniture, fixtures and safes | | 49,580 66 |
| Taxes on real estate | | 1,373 74 |
| State taxes on premiums | | 242,143 27 |
| Insurance department licenses and fees | | 9,380 80 |
| Federal taxes | | 82,718 40 |
| All other licenses, fees and taxes | | 4,747 21 |
| Other disbursements, viz: Office supplies, $6,876.31; expense on loans, $9,287.78; bonds, $10,284.92; publication bureaus, $48,809.23; schools of instructions, $77,535.32; miscellaneous, $3,366.47; travel, $14,775.99; examination, $70.25; audit, $13,271.15 | | 184,277 42 |
| Agents' balances charged off | | 31,139 79 |
| Loss on sale or maturity of ledger assets | | 2,285 77 |
| Total disbursements | | $12,315,760 83 |
| Balance | | $48,105,867 17 |

## LEDGER ASSETS.

| | |
|---|---|
| Book value of real estate | $ 60,116 60 |
| Mortgage loans on real estate | 40,725,758 71 |
| Premiums advanced under Soldiers' and Sailors' Civil Relief Act | 416 47 |
| Loans on company's policies assigned as collateral | 2,441,398 69 |
| Premium notes on policies in force | 760,828 28 |
| Book value of bonds | 3,559,562 87 |
| Deposits in trust companies and banks not on interest | 72,328 16 |
| Deposits in trust companies and banks on interest | 389,909 41 |
| Bills receivable | 1,431 38 |
| Agents' balances (debit, $214,379.10; credit, $120,262.50) net | 94,116 60 |
| Total ledger assets | $48,105,867 17 |

### NON-LEDGER ASSETS.

| | | | |
|---|---|---|---|
| Interest due and accrued on mortgages | | $1,203,781 42 | |
| Interest accrued on bonds | | 37,474 68 | |
| Interest due and accrued on premium notes, loans or liens | | 79,492 94 | |
| Interest accrued on other assets, Soldiers' and Sailors' Civil Relief Act | | 19 68 | |
| | | | 1,320,768 72 |
| | New business. | Renewals. | |
| Net uncollected and deferred premiums (paid for basis) | $281,434 89 | $1,236,423 74 | 1,517,858 63 |
| Gross assets | | | $50,944,494 52 |

### DEDUCT ASSETS NOT ADMITTED.

| | | |
|---|---|---|
| Agents' debit balances | $214,379 10 | |
| Bills receivable | 1,431 38 | |
| Premium notes, policy loans and other policy assets in excess of net value and of other policy liabilities on individual policies | 473,873 29 | |
| Book value of bonds over market value | 3,000 00 | |
| Total | | 692,683 77 |
| Admitted assets | | $50,251,810 75 |

## LIABILITIES.

| | | |
|---|---|---|
| Net present value of outstanding policies computed by the Iowa Insurance Department | $30,946,570 00 | |
| Same for dividend additions | 586,656 00 | |
| Same for annuities | 13,025 00 | |
| Total | $31,546,251 00 | |
| Deduct net value of risks re-insured | 14,907 00 | |
| Net reserve (paid for basis) | | $31,531,344 00 |

## LIABILITIES—Concluded.

| | | |
|---|---|---|
| Extra reserve for total and permanent disability benefits and for additional accidental death benefits included in life policies | | $ 394,749 00 |
| Present value of supplementary contracts not involving life contingencies | | 183,639 00 |
| Present value of amounts incurred but not yet due for total and permanent disability benefits | | 46,716 24 |
| Death losses in process of adjustment | $ 65,137 00 | |
| Death losses reported for which no proofs have been received | 349,031 00 | |
| Reserve for net death losses incurred but unreported | 150,000 00 | |
| Death losses and other policy claims resisted | 17,046 00 | |
| Total and permanent disability benefits | 1,000 00 | |
| Total policy claims | | 582,214 00 |
| Due and unpaid on supplementary contracts not involving life contingencies | | 580 57 |
| Dividends left with the company to accumulate at interest | | 299,549 00 |
| Gross premiums paid in advance, including surrender values so applied, less discount, if any | | 94,220 94 |
| Unearned interest and rent paid in advance | | 42,876 15 |
| Salaries, rents, office expenses, bills and accounts due or accrued | | 40,000 00 |
| Medical examiners' fees due or accrued | | 17,500 00 |
| Estimated amount hereafter payable for federal, state and other taxes based upon the business of the year of this statement | | 380,000 00 |
| Dividends or other profits due policyholders | | 99,239 79 |
| Dividends declared on or apportioned to annual dividend policies payable to policyholders during 1922 for period to October 31, 1922 | | 1,100,000 00 |
| Reserve or surplus funds not otherwise included in liabilities, viz— | | |
| Guarantee fund | | 4,206,051 42 |
| Emergency reserve fund | | 8,313,314 55 |
| Exchange addition fund | | 1,486,819 69 |
| Deposits of members | | 15,461 11 |
| Total | | $48,834,275 46 |
| Contingency reserve | | 1,417,535 29 |
| Total | | $50,251,810 75 |

## EXHIBIT OF POLICIES—ORDINARY.

ALL BUSINESS PAID FOR.

| | Number. | Amount. | Number. | Amount. |
|---|---|---|---|---|
| Policies in force December 31, 1920 | | | 238,792 | $555,483,313 00 |
| Policies issued, revived and increased during the year | | | 33,258 | 111,683,013 00 |
| Total | | | 272,050 | $667,166,326 00 |
| Deduct policies which have ceased to be in force during the year— | | | | |
| By death | 2,853 | $ 6,218,286 00 | | |
| By expiry | 241 | 565,869 00 | | |
| By surrender | 1,047 | 2,515,665 00 | | |
| By lapse | 14,153 | 45,227,719 00 | | |
| By decrease | | 1,963,178 00 | | |
| Total | | | 18,294 | 56,490,717 00 |
| Total policies in force December 31, 1921 | | | 253,756 | $610,675,609 00 |
| Re-insured | | | | $2,327,156 00 |

## BUSINESS IN ILLINOIS—ORDINARY.

| | Number. | Amount. |
|---|---|---|
| Policies in force December 31, 1920 | 32,213 | $74,750,918 00 |
| Policies issued during the year | 2,827 | 11,253,753 00 |
| Total | 35,040 | $86,004,671 00 |
| Deduct policies ceased to be in force | 1,579 | 5,170,763 00 |
| Policies in force December 31, 1921 | 33,461 | $80,833,908 00 |
| Losses and claims unpaid December 31, 1920 | 29 | $ 57,025 00 |
| Losses and claims incurred during the year | 460 | 963,506 00 |
| Total | 489 | $1,020,531 00 |
| Losses and claims settled during the year | 460 | 962,531 00 |
| Losses and claims unpaid December 31, 1921 | 29 | $58,000 00 |
| Premiums received | | $1,805,077 35 |

## GAIN AND LOSS EXHIBIT.

INSURANCE EXHIBIT.

| | | Gain in surplus. | Loss in surplus. |
|---|---|---|---|
| Loading on actual premiums of the year (averaging 20.98 per cent of the gross premiums) | $3,214,060 77 | | |
| Insurance expenses incurred during the year | 4,481,792 12 | | |
| Loss from loading | | | $1,267,731 35 |
| Interest earned during the year | $2,560,737 45 | | |
| Investment expenses incurred during the year | 113,382 09 | | |
| Net income from investments | $2,447,355 36 | | |
| Interest required to maintain reserve | 1,008,492 00 | | |
| Gain from interest | | $1,438,863 36 | |
| Expected mortality on net amount at risk | $9,763,231 30 | | |
| Actual mortality on net amount at risk | 6,000,795 34 | | |
| Gain from mortality | | 3,762,435 96 | |
| Expected disbursements to annuitants | | | 102 72 |
| Total gain during the year from surrendered and lapsed policies | | 331,346 44 | |
| Decrease in surplus on dividend account | | | 1,707,683 18 |
| Decrease in special funds and special reserves during the year | | 1,256,347 98 | |
| Net to loss account | | | 25,551 81 |

INVESTMENT EXHIBIT.

| | | Gain in surplus. | Loss in surplus. |
|---|---|---|---|
| Total gains from bonds | | 3,364 78 | |
| Total losses from bonds | | | 2,285 77 |
| Loss from assets not admitted | | | 191,931 48 |
| Net gain on account of total and permanent disability benefits or additional accidental death benefits included in life policies | | 63,109 17 | |
| Loss from expected mortality in excess of actual assessment certificates | | | 1,573,739 60 |
| Loss from amount paid to beneficiaries from special funds | | | 2,198,188 93 |
| Gain on account of increase in difference between select and ultimate and level premiums valuation | | 489,596 37 | |
| Total gains and losses in surplus during the year | | $7,345,064 06 | $6,967,214 84 |
| Surplus December 31, 1920 | $1,039,686 07 | | |
| Surplus December 31, 1921 | 1,417,535 29 | | |
| Increase in surplus | | | 377,849 22 |
| Total | | $7,345,064 06 | $7,345,064 06 |

---

## BANKERS LIFE INSURANCE COMPANY OF NEBRASKA.

Located at Fourteenth and N Streets, Lincoln, Nebraska; incorporated April 6, 1887; commenced business in Illinois July 14, 1908.

H. S. WILSON, President. M. L. BLACKBURN, Secretary.

E. I. FRANKHAUSER, Chicago, Attorney for service.

### CAPITAL.

| | | |
|---|---|---|
| Capital paid up | $100,000 00 | |
| Amount of ledger assets December 31, of previous year | | $17,678,139 88 |

### INCOME.

| | | |
|---|---|---|
| First year's premiums on original policies, less re-insurance | $226,979 88 | |
| Dividends applied to purchase paid-up additions and annuities | 5,793 85 | |
| Surrender values applied to purchase paid-up insurance and annuities | 41,286 08 | |
| Consideration for original annuities involving life contingencies | 7,338 00 | |
| New premiums | $281,397 81 | |
| Renewal premiums less re-insurance | 2,556,478 58 | |
| Premium income | | $2,837,876 39 |
| Consideration for supplementary contracts not involving life contingencies | | 13,000 00 |
| Interest on mortgage loans | $794,383 32 | |
| Interest on bonds | 83,583 66 | |
| Interest on premium notes, policy loans or liens | 145,719 57 | |
| Interest on deposits | 7,375 73 | |
| Rents—including $15,000.00 for company's occupancy of its own building | 32,622 30 | |
| Total interest and rents | | 1,063,684 58 |

INCOME—Concluded.

| | | |
|---|---|---|
| From other sources, viz: War tax, $6,399.48; bonds for agents, $2,266.52; suspense account, $372.64 | | $9,038 64 |
| Profit on sale or maturity of ledger assets | | 270 82 |
| Total income | | $3,923,870 43 |
| Total | | $21,602,010 31 |

DISBURSEMENTS.

| | | |
|---|---|---|
| Death claims | $317,427 91 | |
| Matured endowments | 8,000 00 | |
| Total death claims and endowments | | $325,427 91 |
| Annuities involving life contingencies | | 2,489 80 |
| Surrender values paid in cash, or applied in liquidation of loans or notes | | 509,916 11 |
| Surrender values applied to purchase paid-up insurance and annuities | | 41,286 08 |
| Dividends paid policyholders in cash, or applied in liquidation of loans or notes | | 462,897 44 |
| Dividends applied to purchase paid-up additions and annuities | | 5,793 85 |
| (Total paid policyholders | $1,347,811 19) | |
| Supplementary contracts not involving life contingencies | | 9,877 25 |
| Dividends to stockholders | | 8,000 00 |
| Commissions to agents, first year, $137,687.60; renewal, $106,573.77; annuities (original), $366.90 | | 244,628 27 |
| Compensation of managers and agents not paid by commissions on new business | | 1,800 00 |
| Agency supervision and traveling expenses of supervisors | | 5,124 45 |
| Branch office expenses | | 9,294 99 |
| Medical examiners' fees and inspection of risks | | 21,435 50 |
| Salaries and all other compensation of officers and home office employees | | 110,880 02 |
| Rent | | 15,000 00 |
| Advertising, printing, stationery, postage, telegraph, telephone, express and exchange | | 41,411 82 |
| Legal expense | | 1,720 70 |
| Furniture, fixtures and safes | | 439 45 |
| Repairs and expenses (other than taxes) on real estate | | 12,039 87 |
| Taxes on real estate | | 5,954 99 |
| State taxes on premiums | | 27,751 80 |
| Insurance department licenses and fees | | 2,975 13 |
| Federal taxes | | 21,165 15 |
| Other disbursements, viz: Sundry expense, $2,434.68; investment expense, $31,292.25; traveling expense, $1,606.27; premiums on new policies not yet issued, $1,711.63 | | 37,044 83 |
| Loss on sale or maturity of ledger assets | | 603 73 |
| Decrease in book value of ledger assets | | 7,707 59 |
| Total disbursements | | $1,932,666 73 |
| Balance | | $19,669,343 58 |

LEDGER ASSETS.

| | |
|---|---|
| Book value of real estate | $ 156,654 40 |
| Mortgage loans on real estate | 15,337,893 87 |
| Loans on company's policies assigned as collateral | 2,353,327 43 |
| Book value of bonds | 1,689,366 65 |
| Cash in office | 7,326 78 |
| Deposits in trust companies and banks not on interest | 1,664 35 |
| Deposits in trust companies and banks on interest | 142,563 98 |
| Agents' credit balances | —19,453 88 |
| Total ledger assets | $19,669,343 58 |

NON-LEDGER ASSETS.

| | | | |
|---|---|---|---|
| Interest accrued on mortgages | | $278,441 22 | |
| Interest accrued on bonds | | 23,435 47 | |
| Interest accrued on premium notes, loans or liens | | 1,555 18 | |
| | | | 303,431 87 |
| | New business. | Renewals. | |
| Net uncollected and deferred premiums (paid for basis) | $10,291 54 | $159,543 88 | 169,835 42 |
| Admitted assets | | | $20,142,610 87 |

LIABILITIES.

| | | |
|---|---|---|
| Net present value of outstanding policies computed by the Nebraska Insurance Department | $14,634,879 71 | |
| Same for annuities | 26,874 79 | |
| Total | $14,661,754 50 | |
| Deduct net value of risks re-insured | 330,811 49 | |
| Net reserve (paid for basis) | | $14,330,943 01 |
| Present value of supplementary contracts not involving life contingencies | | 88,114 10 |
| Death losses reported for which no proofs have been received | | 21,600 00 |
| Dividends left with the company to accumulate at interest | | 7,554 60 |
| Gross premiums paid in advance, including surrender values so applied, less discount, if any | | 69,592 74 |
| Salaries, rents, office expenses, bills and accounts due or accrued | | 13,087 98 |
| Medical examiners' fees due or accrued | | 730 00 |

LIABILITIES—Concluded.

| | |
|---|---|
| Estimated amount hereafter payable for federal, state and other taxes based upon the business of the year of this statement | $ 187,922 38 |
| Dividends or other profits due policyholders | 1,551 52 |
| Dividends declared on or apportioned to annual dividend policies payable to policyholders during 1922 for period to December 31, 1922 | 21,987 42 |
| Dividends declared on or apportioned to deferred dividend policies payable to policyholders during 1922 for period to December 31, 1922 | 601,025 28 |
| Amounts set apart, apportioned, provisionally ascertained, calculated, declared or held awaiting apportionment upon deferred dividend policies | 4,061,838 29 |
| Reserve or surplus funds not otherwise included in liabilities, viz— | |
| Suspense account | 722 36 |
| Reserve for re-instatements and other contingencies | 219,422 90 |
| Dividends and payments on installment policies left with company not on interest | 6,908 13 |
| Reserve for contingent death losses | 50,000 00 |
| Total | $19,683,000 71 |
| Capital paid up | 100,000 00 |
| Unassigned funds (surplus) | 359,610 16 |
| Total | $20,142,610 87 |

EXHIBIT OF POLICIES—ORDINARY.

ALL BUSINESS PAID FOR.

| | Number. | Amount. | Number. | Amount. |
|---|---|---|---|---|
| Policies in force December 31, 1920 | | | 55,643 | $95,731,028 23 |
| Policies issued, revived and increased during the year | | | 4,139 | 8,056,199 86 |
| Total | | | 59,782 | $103,787,228 09 |
| Deduct policies which have ceased to be in force during the year— | | | | |
| By death | 175 | $ 308,623 00 | | |
| By maturity | 644 | 966,200 00 | | |
| By expiry | 95 | 163,000 00 | | |
| By surrender | 540 | 1,000,611 00 | | |
| By lapse | 3,007 | 6,464,283 03 | | |
| By decrease | 4 | 44,500 00 | | |
| Total | | | 4,465 | 8,947,217 03 |
| Total policies in force December 31, 1921 | | | 55,317 | $94,840,011 06 |
| Re-insured | | | 775 | $3,223,860 00 |

BUSINESS IN ILLINOIS—ORDINARY.

| | Number. | Amount. |
|---|---|---|
| Policies in force December 31, 1920 | 1,434 | $2,455,764 00 |
| Policies issued during the year | 243 | 506,653 00 |
| Total | 1,677 | $2,962,417 00 |
| Deduct policies ceased to be in force | 107 | 217,000 00 |
| Policies in force December 31, 1921 | 1,570 | $2,745,417 00 |
| Losses and claims incurred during the year | 11 | $25,500 00 |
| Losses and claims settled during the year | 9 | 23,500 00 |
| Losses and claims unpaid December 31, 1921 | 2 | $2,000 00 |
| Premiums received | | $94,767 22 |

GAIN AND LOSS EXHIBIT.

INSURANCE EXHIBIT.

| | | Gain in surplus. | Loss in surplus. |
|---|---|---|---|
| Loading on actual premiums of the year (averaging 22.89 per cent of the gross premiums) | $662,795 46 | | |
| Insurance expenses incurred during the year | 523,520 02 | | |
| Gain from loading | | $139,275 44 | |
| Interest earned during the year | $1,057,008 40 | | |
| Investment expenses incurred during the year | 49,287 11 | | |
| Net income from investments | $1,007,721 29 | | |
| Interest required to maintain reserve | 530,719 00 | | |
| Gain from interest | | 477,002 29 | |
| Expected mortality on net amount at risk | $814,324 76 | | |
| Actual mortality on net amount at risk | 245,741 71 | | |
| Gain from mortality | | 568,583 05 | |
| Total gain during the year from surrendered and lapsed policies | | 208,038 75 | |
| Dividends paid stockholders | | | 8,000 00 |
| Decrease in surplus on dividend account | | | 952,997 23 |
| Increase in special funds and special reserves during the year | | | 323,861 80 |

GAIN AND LOSS EXHIBIT—Concluded.

INVESTMENT EXHIBIT.

| | | Gain in surplus. | Loss in surplus. |
|---|---|---|---|
| Total losses from real estate | | | $7,707 59 |
| Total gains from stocks and bonds | | $270 82 | |
| Total losses from stocks and bonds | | | 603 73 |
| Total gains and losses in surplus during the year | | $1,393,170 35 | $1,293,170 35 |
| Surplus December 31, 1920 | $259,610 16 | | |
| Surplus December 31, 1921 | 359,610 16 | | |
| Increase in surplus | | | 100,000 00 |
| Total | | $1,393,170 35 | $1,393,170 35 |

## THE BANKERS RESERVE LIFE COMPANY.

Located at Omaha, Nebraska; incorporated January 15, 1908; commenced business in Illinois March 23, 1908.

R. L. ROBISON, President. R. C. WAGNER, Secretary.

THADDEUS H. HOWE, Chicago, Attorney for service.

CAPITAL.

| | | | |
|---|---|---|---|
| Capital paid up | | $100,000 00 | |
| Amount of ledger assets December 31, of previous year | | | $10,306,953 58 |

INCOME.

| | | | |
|---|---|---|---|
| First year's premiums on original policies, less re-insurance | | $591,793 98 | |
| First year's premiums for additional accidental death benefits | | 3,026 26 | |
| Dividends applied to purchase paid-up additions and annuities | | 61,072 53 | |
| Surrender values applied to purchase paid-up insurance and annuities | | 4,406 21 | |
| New premiums | | $ 660,298 98 | |
| Renewal premiums less re-insurance | $1,998,389 34 | | |
| Renewal premiums for additional accidental death benefits | 19 00 | | |
| Dividends applied to pay renewal premiums | 133,590 46 | | |
| Renewal premiums | | 2,131,998 80 | |
| Premium income | | | $2,792,297 78 |
| Dividends left with company to accumulate at interest | | | 50,916 78 |
| Interest on mortgage loans | | $ 60,849 30 | |
| Interest on bonds | | 351,177 99 | |
| Interest on premium notes, policy loans or liens | | 141,279 45 | |
| Interest on deposits | | 11,953 67 | |
| Total interest | | | 565,260 41 |
| Agents' balances previously charged off | | | 237 54 |
| Increase in book value of ledger assets | | | 2,324 25 |
| Total income | | | $3,411,036 76 |
| Total | | | $13,717,990 34 |

DISBURSEMENTS.

| | | |
|---|---|---|
| Death claims and additions | $340,168 25 | |
| Matured endowments | 3,000 00 | |
| Total and permanent disability claims | 500 00 | |
| Total death claims and endowments | | 343,668 25 |
| Premium notes and liens voided by lapse, less $19,732.88 restorations | | 107,098 72 |
| Surrender values paid in cash, or applied in liquidation of loans or notes | | 407,296 53 |
| Surrender values applied to purchase paid-up insurance and annuities | | 4,406 21 |
| Dividends paid policyholders in cash, or applied in liquidation of loans or notes | | 54,132 89 |
| Dividends applied to pay renewal premiums | | 133,590 46 |
| Dividends applied to purchase paid-up additions and annuities | | 61,072 53 |
| Dividends left with the company to accumulate at interest | | 50,916 78 |
| (Total paid policyholders | $1,162,182 37) | |
| Supplementary contracts not involving life contingencies | | 1,465 25 |
| Dividends to stockholders | | 10,000 00 |
| Commissions to agents, first year, $437,440.27; renewal, $51,487.11 | | 488,927 38 |
| Agency supervision and traveling expenses of supervisors | | 127,070 29 |
| Medical examiners' fees and inspection of risks | | 50,955 50 |
| Salaries and all other compensation of officers and home office employees | | 143,302 38 |
| Rent | | 12,542 51 |

DISBURSEMENTS—Concluded.

| | |
|---|---|
| Advertising, printing, stationery, postage, telegraph, telephone, express and exchange | $41,808 11 |
| Legal expense | 5,181 25 |
| Furniture, fixtures and safes | 2,833 62 |
| State taxes on premiums | 48,041 51 |
| Insurance department licenses and fees | 5,830 00 |
| Federal taxes | 1,252 82 |
| All other licenses, fees and taxes | 1,564 67 |
| Other disbursements, viz: Office expense, $4,534.86; suspense account, $4,931.41; investment expense, $6,229.75; premium on fidelity bonds, $5,994.57; loss and gain, $6,850.07; war tax fund, $1,320.40 | 29,861 06 |
| Loss on sale or maturity of ledger assets | 72 00 |
| Decrease in book value of ledger assets | 11,218 36 |
| Total disbursements | $2,144,109 08 |
| Balance | $11,573,881 26 |

LEDGER ASSETS.

| | |
|---|---|
| Mortgage loans on real estate | $1,129,200 00 |
| Loans on company's policies assigned as collateral | 2,276,571 84 |
| Premium notes on policies in force | 215,696 09 |
| Book value of bonds | 7,474,073 40 |
| Cash in office | 148 53 |
| Deposits in trust companies and banks on interest | 460,941 47 |
| Agents' balances (debit, $21,495.47; credit, $4,245.54) net | 17,249 93 |
| Total ledger assets | $11,573,881 26 |

NON-LEDGER ASSETS.

| | | |
|---|---|---|
| Interest accrued on mortgages | $19,743 60 | |
| Interest accrued on bonds | 58,261 86 | |
| Interest accrued on premium notes, loans or liens | 5,026 24 | |
| | | 83,031 70 |
| Net uncollected and deferred premiums (paid for basis) renewals | | 126,092 22 |
| Gross assets | | $11,783,005 18 |

DEDUCT ASSETS NOT ADMITTED.

| | | |
|---|---|---|
| Agents' debit balances | $21,495 47 | |
| Premium notes, policy loans and other policy assets in excess of net value and of other policy liabilities on individual policies | 7,240 25 | |
| Total | | 28,735 72 |
| Admitted assets | | $11,754,269 46 |

LIABILITIES.

| | | |
|---|---|---|
| Net present value of outstanding policies computed by the Nebraska Insurance Department | $9,316,038 00 | |
| Same for dividend additions | 342,440 00 | |
| Total | $9,658,478 00 | |
| Deduct net value of risks re-insured | 9,862 00 | |
| Net reserve (paid for basis) | | $9,648,616 00 |
| Extra reserve for additional accidental death benefits included in life policies | | 1,522 63 |
| Present value of supplementary contracts not involving life contingencies | | 19,741 50 |
| Surrender values claimable on policies cancelled | | 3,250 25 |
| Death losses reported for which no proofs have been received | | 17,562 00 |
| Dividends left with the company to accumulate at interest | | 174,809 74 |
| Gross premiums paid in advance, including surrender values so applied, less discount, if any | | 17,155 19 |
| Unearned interest paid in advance | | 58,348 78 |
| Commissions due agents on premium notes, when paid | | 1,850 00 |
| Salaries, rents, office expenses, bills and accounts due or accrued | | 1,025 00 |
| Medical examiners' fees due or accrued | | 3,972 00 |
| Estimated amount hereafter payable for federal, state and other taxes based upon the business of the year of this statement | | 62,500 00 |
| Dividends or other profits due policyholders | | 9,364 21 |
| Dividends declared on or apportioned to annual dividend policies payable to policyholders during 1922 for period to December 31, 1922 | | 5,782 03 |
| Dividends declared on or apportioned to deferred dividend policies payable to policyholders during 1922 for period to December 31, 1922 | | 187,673 57 |
| Amounts set apart, apportioned, provisionally ascertained, calculated, declared or held awaiting apportionment upon deferred dividend policies | | 218,098 50 |
| Suspense items | | 844 79 |
| Total | | $10,432,116 19 |
| Capital paid up | | 100,000 00 |
| Unassigned funds (surplus) | | 1,222,153 27 |
| Total | | $11,754,269 46 |

## EXHIBIT OF POLICIES—ORDINARY.

ALL BUSINESS PAID FOR.

| | Number. | Amount. | Number. | Amount. |
|---|---|---|---|---|
| Policies in force December 31, 1920 | | | 36,811 | $77,395,695 02 |
| Policies issued, revived and increased during the year | | | 8,055 | 18,672,875 53 |
| Total | | | 44,866 | $96,068,570 55 |
| Deduct policies which have ceased to be in force during the year— | | | | |
| By death | 163 | $ 355,168 25 | | |
| By maturity | 2 | 3,000 00 | | |
| By disability | 1 | 500 00 | | |
| By expiry | 18 | 39,000 00 | | |
| By surrender | 580 | 1,817,695 50 | | |
| By lapse | 5,623 | 13,791,275 00 | | |
| By decrease | -------- | 82,904 00 | | |
| Total | | | 6,387 | 16,089,542 75 |
| Total policies in force December 31, 1921 | | | 38,479 | $79,979,027 80 |
| Re-insured | | | 207 | $1,079,037 00 |

## BUSINESS IN ILLINOIS—ORDINARY.

| | Number. | Amount. |
|---|---|---|
| Policies in force December 31, 1920 | 3,092 | $6,159,983 78 |
| Policies issued during the year | 527 | 1,422,884 51 |
| Total | 3,619 | $7,582,868 29 |
| Deduct policies ceased to be in force | 239 | 1,151,217 50 |
| Policies in force December 31, 1921 | 3,380 | $6,431,650 79 |
| Losses and claims incurred during the year | 15 | $46,409 50 |
| Losses and claims settled during the year | 14 | 44,409 50 |
| Losses and claims unpaid December 31, 1921 | 1 | $2,000 00 |
| Premiums received | | $213,164 61 |

## GAIN AND LOSS EXHIBIT.

INSURANCE EXHIBIT.

| | | Gain in surplus. | Loss in surplus. |
|---|---|---|---|
| Loading on actual premiums of the year (averaging 25.54 per cent of the gross premiums) | $731,132 18 | | |
| Insurance expenses incurred during the year | 964,720 66 | | |
| Loss from loading | | -------------- | $233,588 48 |
| Interest earned during the year | $552,840 93 | | |
| Investment expenses incurred during the year | 6,229 75 | | |
| Net income from investments | $546,611 18 | | |
| Interest required to maintain reserve | 348,185 00 | | |
| Gain from interest | | $198,426 18 | |
| Expected mortality on net amount at risk | $698,948 00 | | |
| Actual mortality on net amount at risk | 269,759 71 | | |
| Gain from mortality | | 429,188 29 | |
| Total gain during the year from surrendered and lapsed policies | | 250,346 35 | |
| Dividends paid stockholders | | -------------- | 10,000 00 |
| Decrease in surplus on dividend account | | -------------- | 336,329 46 |
| Loss on account of increase in reserve Illinois standard | | -------------- | 1,155 00 |
| Net to loss account | | -------------- | 6,850 07 |

INVESTMENT EXHIBIT.

| | | Gain in surplus. | Loss in surplus. |
|---|---|---|---|
| Total gains from bonds | | 103,131 44 | |
| Total losses from bonds | | -------------- | 72 00 |
| Loss from assets not admitted | | -------------- | 23,754 38 |
| Net gain on account of additional accidental death benefits included in life policies | | 1,074 00 | |
| Gain from agents' balances previously charged off | | 237 54 | |
| Loss from premium notes voided by lapse | | -------------- | 107,098 72 |
| Balance unaccounted for | | -------------- | 552 79 |
| Total gains and losses in surplus during the year | | $982,403 80 | $719,400 90 |
| Surplus December 31, 1920 | $ 959,150 37 | | |
| Surplus December 31, 1921 | 1,222,153 27 | | |
| Increase in surplus | | -------------- | 263,002 90 |
| Total | | $982,403 80 | $982,403 80 |

## BERKSHIRE LIFE INSURANCE COMPANY.

Located at Corner of North and West Streets, Pittsfield, Massachusetts; incorporated May, 1851; commenced business in Illinois March 31, 1857.

WILLIAM D. WYMAN, President. ROBERT H. DAVENPORT, Secretary.

FRANKLIN WYMAN, Chicago, Attorney for service.

| | | | |
|---|---|---|---|
| Amount of ledger assets December 31, of previous year | | | $27,883,750 70 |

### INCOME.

| | | | |
|---|---|---|---|
| First year's premiums on original policies, less re-insurance | | $475,353 97 | |
| First year's premiums for total and permanent disability benefits, less re-insurance | | 864 29 | |
| Dividends applied to purchase paid-up additions and annuities | | 337,422 99 | |
| New premiums | | $ 813,641 25 | |
| Renewal premiums less re-insurance | $3,189,226 28 | | |
| Renewal premiums for total and permanent disability benefitspless re-insurance | 1,043 20 | | |
| Dividends applied to pay renewal premiums | 223,630 87 | | |
| Renewal premiums | | 3,413,900 35 | |
| Premium income | | | $4,227,541 60 |
| Consideration for supplementary contracts not involving life contingencies | | | 57,130 57 |
| Dividends left with company to accumulate at interest | | | 7,186 75 |
| Interest on mortgage loans | | $424,475 89 | |
| Interest on collateral loans | | 2,041 29 | |
| Interest on bonds and dividends on stocks | | 722,839 71 | |
| Interest on premium notes, policy loans or liens | | 265,125 14 | |
| Interest on deposits | | 7,582 43 | |
| Interest on other debts due the company | | 2,342 00 | |
| Discount on claims paid in advance | | 13 79 | |
| Rents—including $18,000.00 for company's occupancy of its own buildings | | 51,919 54 | |
| Total interest and rents | | | 1,476,339 79 |
| Refund federal tax of 1917 | | | 90 81 |
| Profit on sale or maturity of ledger assets | | | 1,885 92 |
| Increase in book value of ledger assets | | | 92,972 97 |
| Total income | | | $5,863,148 41 |
| Total | | | $33,746,899 11 |

### DISBURSEMENTS.

| | | |
|---|---|---|
| Death claims and additions | $1,505,314 00 | |
| Matured endowments and additions | 294,951 00 | |
| Total death claims and endowments | | $1,800,265 00 |
| Surrender values paid in cash, or applied in liquidation of loans or notes | | 642,468 80 |
| Dividends paid policyholders in cash, or applied in liquidation of loans or notes | | 76,757 19 |
| Dividends applied to pay renewal premiums | | 223,630 87 |
| Dividends applied to purchase paid-up additions and annuities | | 337,422 99 |
| Dividends left with the company to accumulate at interest | | 7,186 75 |
| (Total paid policyholders | $3,087,731 60) | |
| Expense of investigation and settlement of policy claims, including legal expenses | | 2,057 19 |
| Supplementary contracts not involving life contingencies | | 22,761 71 |
| Dividends with interest, held on deposit surrendered during the year | | 2,715 20 |
| Commissions to agents, first year, $202,588.74; renewal, $221,620.85 | | 424,209 59 |
| Commuted renewal commissions | | 20,000 00 |
| Agency supervision and traveling expenses of supervisors | | 10,300 40 |
| Branch office expenses | | 123,146 33 |
| Medical examiners' fees and inspection of risks | | 31,132 75 |
| Salaries and all other compensation of officers and home office employees | | 169,951 39 |
| Rent | | 68,385 37 |
| Advertising, printing, stationery, postage, telegraph, telephone, express and exchange | | 57,230 58 |
| Legal expense | | 62 08 |
| Furniture, fixtures and safes | | 13,117 69 |
| Repairs and expenses (other than taxes) on real estate | | 28,261 54 |
| Taxes on real estate | | 11,977 40 |
| State taxes on premiums | | 34,748 49 |
| Insurance department licenses and fees | | 4,943 77 |
| Federal taxes | | 15,413 48 |
| All other licenses, fees and taxes | | 34,331 14 |
| Other disbursements, viz:, Subscriptions and law and insurance books, $3,313.67; insurance pamphlets, $182.16; impairment cards, $3,713.41; items of legislative expense, $226.47; Life Insurance Presidents' Association, $510.61; audit by certified accountants, $2,440.70; premium on life insurance policies held as collateral for balance due from ex-agents, $782.40; surety bonds, $150.00; home office traveling, $2,235.68; tabulating machine rental, etc., $1,127.05; pension, $1,000.00; account of expenses National Association of Owners of Railroad Securities, $213.45; compulsory advertising, $369.51; miscellaneous, $909.13 | | 17,174 24 |

DISBURSEMENTS—Concluded.

| | |
|---|---|
| Loss on sale or maturity of ledger assets | $ 255 23 |
| Decrease in book value of ledger assets | 33,483 24 |
| Total disbursements | $4,213,390 41 |
| Balance | $29,533,508 70 |

## LEDGER ASSETS.

| | |
|---|---|
| Book value of real estate | $ 447,543 14 |
| Mortgage loans on real estate | 8,432,400 00 |
| Loans secured by collaterals | 40,700 00 |
| Loans on company's policies assigned as collateral | 5,270,970 05 |
| Premium notes on policies in force | 2,792 06 |
| Book value of bonds and stocks | 14,807,431 34 |
| Cash in office | 50 00 |
| Deposits in trust companies and banks not on interest | 80,233 97 |
| Deposits in trust companies and banks on interest | 391,162 89 |
| Bills receivable | 2,762 01 |
| Agents' balances (debit $8,527.00; credit, $966.33) net | 7,560 67 |
| Cash in transit | 49,902 57 |
| Total ledger assets | $29,533,508 70 |

### NON-LEDGER ASSETS.

| | | | |
|---|---|---|---|
| Interest due and accrued on mortgages | | $116,798 89 | |
| Interest due and accrued on bonds | | 251,223 38 | |
| Interest accrued on collateral loans | | 542 07 | |
| Interest due and accrued on premium notes, loans or liens | | 15,717 52 | |
| Rents due on company's property | | 382 82 | |
| | | | 384,664 68 |
| Due from other companies for losses or claims on policies re-insured | | | 5,000 00 |
| | New business. | Renewals. | |
| Net uncollected and deferred premiums (paid for basis) | $50,731 58 | $500,628 19 | 551,359 77 |
| Gross assets | | | $30,474,533 15 |

### DEDUCT ASSETS NOT ADMITTED.

| | | |
|---|---|---|
| Agents' debit balances | $ 8,527 00 | |
| Bills receivable | 2,762 01 | |
| Overdue and accrued interest on bonds in default | 31,201 67 | |
| Book value of stocks over market value | 80,431 80 | |
| Total | | 122,922 48 |
| Admitted assets | | $30,351,610 67 |

## LIABILITIES.

| | | |
|---|---|---|
| Net present value of outstanding policies | $26,252,259 00 | |
| Same for dividend additions | 2,196,251 00 | |
| Same for annuities | 43,860 00 | |
| Total | $28,492,370 00 | |
| Deduct net value of risks re-insured | 448,869 00 | |
| Net reserve (paid for basis) | | $28,043,501 00 |
| Extra reserve for total and permanent disability benefits included in life policies, less re-insurance | | 1,589 00 |
| Present value of supplementary contracts not involving life contingencies | | 214,706 00 |
| Surrender values claimable on policies cancelled | | 166 52 |
| Death losses reported for which no proofs have been received | $98,026 00 | |
| Reserve for net death losses incurred but unreported | 24,844 00 | |
| Matured endowments due and unpaid | 2,326 00 | |
| Total policy claims | | 125,196 00 |
| Due and unpaid on supplementary contracts not involving life contingencies and interest thereon | | 4,961 67 |
| Dividends left with the company to accumulate at interest | | 22,094 47 |
| Gross premiums paid in advance, including surrender values so applied, less discount, if any | | 28,493 38 |
| Unearned interest and rent paid in advance | | 54,030 47 |
| Salaries, rents, office expenses, bills and accounts due or accrued | | 3,587 45 |
| Medical examiners' fees due or accrued | | 2,201 50 |
| Estimated amount hereafter payable for federal, state and other taxes based upon the business of the year of this statement | | 80,000 00 |
| Dividends or other profits due policyholders | | 12,978 99 |

LIABILITIES—Concluded.

| | |
|---|---|
| Dividends declared on or apportioned to annual dividend policies payable to policyholders during 1922 for period to June 30, 1922 | $257,914 12 |
| Dividends declared on or apportioned to deferred dividend policies payable to policyholders during 1922 for period to June 30, 1922 | 98,559 80 |
| Amounts set apart, apportioned, provisionally ascertained, calculated, declared or held awaiting apportionment upon deferred dividend policies | 354,465 00 |
| Total | $29,304,445 37 |
| Unassigned funds (surplus) | 1,047,165 30 |
| Total | $30,351,610 67 |

## EXHIBIT OF POLICIES—ORDINARY.

ALL BUSINESS PAID FOR.

| | Number. | Amount. | Number. | Amount. |
|---|---|---|---|---|
| Policies in force December 31, 1920 | | | 45,514 | $122,898,422 00 |
| Policies issued, revived and increased during the year | | | 4,708 | 16,543,549 00 |
| Total | | | 50,222 | $139,441,971 00 |
| Deduct policies which have ceased to be in force during the year— | | | | |
| By death | 480 | $1,535,139 00 | | |
| By maturity | 162 | 294,272 00 | | |
| By expiry | 105 | 253,454 00 | | |
| By surrender | 719 | 1,902,051 00 | | |
| By lapse | 1,006 | 3,232,590 00 | | |
| By decrease | | 1,197,403 00 | | |
| Total | | | 2,472 | 8,414,909 00 |
| Total policies in force December 31, 1921 | | | 47,750 | $131,027,062 00 |
| Re-insured | | | 607 | $6,407,370 00 |

## BUSINESS IN ILLINOIS—ORDINARY.

| | Number. | Amount. |
|---|---|---|
| Policies in force December 31, 1920 | 6,734 | $15,216,999 00 |
| Policies issued during the year | 886 | 2,372,420 00 |
| Total | 7,620 | $17,589,419 00 |
| Deduct policies ceased to be in force | 460 | 1,222,625 00 |
| Policies in force December 31, 1921 | 7,160 | $16,366,794 00 |
| Losses and claims unpaid December 31, 1920 | 12 | $46,100 00 |
| Losses and claims incurred during the year | 75 | 146,888 00 |
| Total | 87 | $192,988 00 |
| Losses and claims settled during the year | 79 | 185,666 00 |
| Losses and claims unpaid December 31, 1921 | 8 | $7,322 00 |
| Premiums received | | $509,431 68 |

## GAIN AND LOSS EXHIBIT.

INSURANCE EXHIBIT.

| | | Gain in surplus. | Loss in surplus. |
|---|---|---|---|
| Loading on actual premiums of the year (averaging 19.42 per cent of the gross premiums) | $ 834,630 61 | | |
| Insurance expenses incurred during the year | 1,009,754 89 | | |
| Loss from loading | | | $175,124 28 |
| Interest earned during the year | $1,464,353 10 | | |
| Investment expenses incurred during the year | 75,603 36 | | |
| Net income from investments | $1,388,749 74 | | |
| Interest required to maintain reserve | 980,531 00 | | |
| Gain from interest | | $408,218 74 | |
| Expected mortality on net amount at risk | $1,402,931 00 | | |
| Actual mortality on net amount at risk | 892,939 00 | | |
| Gain from mortality | | 509,992 00 | |
| Total gain during the year from surrendered and lapsed policies | | 53,178 57 | |
| Decrease in surplus on dividend account | | | 656,842 29 |

## GAIN AND LOSS EXHIBIT—Concluded.

INVESTMENT EXHIBIT.

| | | Gain in surplus. | Loss in surplus. |
|---|---|---|---|
| Total gains from stocks and bonds | | $83,935 49 | |
| Total losses from stocks and bonds | | | $13,727 23 |
| Loss from assets not admitted | | | 2,564 34 |
| Net gain on account of total and permanent disability benefits included in life policies | | 547 00 | |
| Balance unaccounted for | | 1,143 46 | |
| Total gains and losses in surplus during the year | | $1,057,015 26 | $848,258 14 |
| Surplus December 31, 1920 | $ 838,408 18 | | |
| Surplus December 31, 1921 | 1,047,165 30 | | |
| Increase in surplus | | | 208,757 12 |
| Total | | $1,057,015 26 | $1,057,015 26 |

## BUSINESS MEN'S ASSURANCE COMPANY OF AMERICA.

Located at Sixth Floor, Gates Building, Kansas City, Missouri; incorporated as an assessment association June 28, 1909; re-incorporated as a legal reserve life insurance company, March 9, 1920; commenced business in Illinois April 27, 1920.

C. S. JOBES, President. W. T. GRANT, Secretary.

GEORGE A. BARR, Director of Trade and Commerce, Attorney for service at Springfield.

### CAPITAL.

| | | | |
|---|---|---|---|
| Capital paid up | | $200,000 00 | |
| Amount of ledger assets December 31, of previous year | | $1,111,811 96 | |
| Increase of paid-up capital during year | | 50,000 00 | |
| Extended at | | | $1,111,811 96 |

### INCOME.

| | | | |
|---|---|---|---|
| First year's premiums on original policies, less re-insurance | | $50,425 29 | |
| First year's premiums for total and permanent disability benefits | | 1,238 60 | |
| First year's premiums for additional accidental death benefits | | 631 53 | |
| New premiums | | $52,295 42 | |
| Renewal premiums less re-insurance | $38,865 98 | | |
| Renewal premiums for total and permanent disability benefits | 965 27 | | |
| Renewal premiums for additional accidental death benefits, less re-insurance | 454 76 | | |
| Renewal premiums | | 40,286 01 | |
| Premium income | | | $92,581 43 |
| Interest on invested assets | | $2,905 91 | |
| Interest on premium notes, policy loans or liens | | 23 96 | |
| Total interest | | | 2,929 87 |
| Income, life department | | | $ 95,511 30 |
| Income, casualty department | | | 2,224,197 72 |
| Total income | | | $2,319,709 02 |
| Total | | | $3,431,520 98 |

### DISBURSEMENTS.

| | | |
|---|---|---|
| Death claims | | $ 5,000 00 |
| (Total paid policyholders | $5,000 00) | |
| Commissions to agents, first year, $35,268.54; renewal, $304.35 | | 35,572 89 |
| Medical examiners' fees and inspection of risks | | 5,252 30 |
| Salaries and all other compensation of officers and home office employees | | 10,687 18 |
| Rent | | 1,772 33 |
| Printing, stationery, postage, telegraph, telephone, express and exchange | | 3,984 89 |
| State taxes on premiums | | 909 96 |
| Insurance department licenses and fees | | 471 75 |
| Federal taxes | | 1,739 40 |
| Disbursements in adjustment of trust fund | | 1,554 70 |
| Disbursements, life department | | $ 66,945 40 |
| Disbursements, casualty department | | 1,855,591 03 |
| Total disbursements | | $1,922,536 43 |
| Balance | | $1,508,984 55 |

## LEDGER ASSETS.

| | |
|---|---|
| Mortgage loans on real estate | $879,175 00 |
| Premium notes on policies in force | 4,168 98 |
| Book value of bonds | 372,700 00 |
| Cash in office | 5,130 34 |
| Deposits in trust companies and banks not on interest | 125,344 48 |
| Deposits in trust companies and banks on interest | 40,000 00 |
| Agents' balances (debit, life, $8,149.98; casualty, $34,429.19; credit, life, $1,079.32, casualty, $4,424.60) net | 37,075 25 |
| Premiums in course of collection, casualty department | 45,390 50 |
| Total ledger assets | $1,508,984 55 |

### NON-LEDGER ASSETS.

| | | | |
|---|---|---|---|
| Interest accrued on mortgages | | $23,288 33 | |
| Interest accrued on bonds | | 3,418 62 | |
| Interest accrued on certificates of deposit | | 239 64 | |
| Interest due and accrued on premium notes, loans or liens | | 31 21 | |
| | | | 26,977 80 |
| | New business. | Renewals. | |
| Net uncollected and deferred premiums (paid for basis) | $3,294 82 | $7,776 99 | 11,071 81 |
| Gross assets | | | $1,547,034 16 |

### DEDUCT ASSETS NOT ADMITTED.

| | | |
|---|---|---|
| Agents' debit balances (life department, $8,149.98; casualty department, $34,429.19) | $42,579 17 | |
| Premium notes, policy loans and other policy assets in excess of net value and of other policy liabilities on individual policies | 1,753 99 | |
| Book value of bonds over market value | 2,854 67 | |
| Total | | 47,187 83 |
| Admitted assets | | $1,499,846 33 |

## LIABILITIES.

| | | |
|---|---|---|
| Net present value of outstanding policies computed by the Missouri Insurance Department | $54,120 13 | |
| Deduct net value of risks re-insured | 2,075 78 | |
| Net reserve (paid for basis) | | $52,044 35 |
| Extra reserve for total and permanent disability benefits included in life policies | | 1,645 08 |
| Death losses and other policy claims resisted | | 5,000 00 |
| Gross premiums paid in advance, including surrender values so applied, less discount, if any | | 91 43 |
| Commissions due agents on premium notes, when paid | | 289 22 |
| Commissions to agents due or accrued | | 1,425 00 |
| Medical examiners' and inspection fees due or accrued | | 953 00 |
| Estimated amount hereafter payable for federal, state and other taxes based upon the business of the year of this statement | | 3,000 00 |
| Liabilities, casualty department | | 1,111,124 28 |
| Total | | $1,175,572 36 |
| Capital paid up | | 200,000 00 |
| Unassigned funds (surplus) | | 124,273 97 |
| Total | | $1,499,846 33 |

## EXHIBIT OF POLICIES—ORDINARY.

### ALL BUSINESS PAID FOR.

| | Number. | Amount. | Number. | Amount. |
|---|---|---|---|---|
| Policies in force December 31, 1920 | | | 637 | $2,007,500 00 |
| Policies issued, revived and increased during the year | | | 846 | 2,026,675 00 |
| Total | | | 1,483 | $4,034,175 00 |
| Deduct policies which have ceased to be in force during the year— | | | | |
| By maturity | 2 | $ 10,000 00 | | |
| By lapse | 162 | 456,000 00 | | |
| Total | | | 164 | 466,000 00 |
| Total policies in force December 31, 1921 | | | 1,319 | $3,568,175 00 |
| Re-insured | | | 95 | $389,500 00 |

BUSINESS IN ILLINOIS—ORDINARY.

| | Number. | Amount. |
|---|---|---|
| Policies in force December 31, 1920 | 6 | $ 9,000 00 |
| Policies issued during the year | 42 | 105,000 00 |
| Total | 48 | $114,000 00 |
| Deduct policies ceased to be in force | 1 | 3,000 00 |
| Policies in force December 31, 1921 | 47 | $111,000 00 |
| Premiums received | | $2,355 55 |

GAIN AND LOSS EXHIBIT.

INSURANCE EXHIBIT.

| | | Gain in surplus. | Loss in surplus. |
|---|---|---|---|
| Loading on actual premiums of the year (averaging 39.78 per cent of the gross premiums) | $41,530 78 | | |
| Insurance expenses incurred during the year | 72,923 83 | | |
| Loss from loading | | | $31,393 05 |
| Interest earned during the year | $2,929 87 | | |
| Interest required to maintain reserve | 1,526 29 | | |
| Gain from interest | | $ 1,403 58 | |
| Expected mortality on net amount at risk | $24,342 47 | | |
| Actual mortality on net amount at risk | 9,854 25 | | |
| Gain from mortality | | 14,488 22 | |
| INVESTMENT EXHIBIT. | | | |
| Loss from assets not admitted | | | 3,844 43 |
| Net gain on account of total and permanent disability benefits or additional accidental death benefits included in life policies | | 3,237 14 | |
| Gain from casualty department | | 47,110 83 | |
| Loss from outstanding and deferred premiums remaining unpaid | | 984 94 | |
| Balance unaccounted for | | 127 72 | |
| Total gains and losses in surplus during the year | | $67,352 43 | $35,237 48 |
| Surplus December 31, 1920 | $ 92,159 02 | | |
| Surplus December 31, 1921 | 124,273 97 | | |
| Increase in surplus | | | 32,114 95 |
| Total | | $67,352 43 | $67,352 43 |

## THE CAPITOL LIFE INSURANCE COMPANY OF COLORADO.

Located at Tabor Opera House Building, Denver, Colorado; incorporated August, 1905; commenced business in Illinois August 1, 1919.

CLARENCE J. DALY, President. PATRICK CROWE, Secretary.

GEORGE A. BARR, Director of Trade and Commerce, Attorney for service at Springfield.

CAPITAL.

| | | | |
|---|---|---|---|
| Capital paid up | | $100,000 00 | |
| Amount of ledger assets December 31, of previous year | | | $3,910,513 68 |

INCOME.

| | | | |
|---|---|---|---|
| First year's premiums on original policies, less re-insurance | | $315,922 01 | |
| First year's premiums for total and permanent disability benefits | | 4,443 25 | |
| First year's premiums for additional accidental death benefits, less re-insurance | | 2,240 80 | |
| Dividends applied to purchase paid-up additions and annuities | | 1,576 73 | |
| New premiums | | $ 324,182 79 | |
| Renewal premiums less re-insurance | $1,077,209 90 | | |
| Renewal premiums for total and permanent disability benefits | 15,095 89 | | |
| Dividends applied to pay renewal premiums | 8,717 37 | | |
| Dividends applied to shorten the endowment or premium-paying period | 38 86 | | |
| Renewal premiums | | 1,101,062 02 | |
| Premium income | | | $1,425,244 81 |

## INCOME—Concluded.

| | | |
|---|---|---|
| Consideration for supplementary contracts not involving life contingencies | | $ 5,210 00 |
| Dividends left with company to accumulate at interest | | 91,004 57 |
| Interest on mortgage loans | $163,695 15 | |
| Interest on bonds | 36,392 27 | |
| Interest on premium notes, policy loans or liens | 61,370 96 | |
| Interest on deposits | 9,275 29 | |
| Interest on other debts due the company | 3,902 95 | |
| Rents | 770 00 | |
| Total interest and rents | | 275,406 62 |
| Miscellaneous suspense items charged off | | 687 39 |
| Borrowed money (gross) | | 140,000 00 |
| Profit on sale or maturity of ledger assets | | 2,140 00 |
| Total income | | $1,939,693 39 |
| Total | | $5,850,207 07 |

## DISBURSEMENTS.

| | | |
|---|---|---|
| Death claims and additions | $224,941 05 | |
| Matured endowments | 31,500 00 | |
| Total and permanent disability claims | 1,980 91 | |
| Total death claims and endowments | | $258,421 96 |
| Annuities involving life contingencies | | 533 06 |
| Premium notes and liens voided by lapse | | 24,318 09 |
| Surrender values paid in cash, or applied in liquidation of loans or notes | | 88,548 66 |
| Dividends paid policyholders in cash, or applied in liquidation of loans or notes | | 3,016 06 |
| Dividends applied to pay renewal premiums | | 8,717 37 |
| Dividends applied to shorten the endowment or premium-paying period | | 38 86 |
| Dividends applied to purchase paid-up additions and annuities | | 1,576 73 |
| Dividends left with the company to accumulate at interest | | 91,004 57 |
| (Total paid policyholders | $476,175 36) | |
| Expense of investigation and settlement of policy claims, including legal expenses | | 1,856 84 |
| Supplementary contracts not involving life contingencies | | 19,783 84 |
| Dividends with interest, held on deposit surrendered during the year | | 47,829 77 |
| Commissions to agents, first year, $225,213.28; renewal, $49,589.24 | | 274,802 52 |
| Agency supervision and traveling expenses of supervisors | | 3,097 25 |
| Branch office expenses | | 21,572 66 |
| Medical examiners' fees and inspection of risks | | 23,984 98 |
| Salaries and all other compensation of officers and home office employees | | 57,208 18 |
| Rent | | 5,991 22 |
| Advertising, printing, stationery, postage, telegraph, telephone, express and exchange | | 21,356 50 |
| Legal expense | | 5,092 04 |
| Furniture, fixtures and safes | | 1,121 58 |
| Repairs and expenses (other than taxes) on real estate | | 241 91 |
| Taxes on real estate | | 289 31 |
| State taxes on premiums | | 19,505 46 |
| Insurance department licenses and fees | | 2,547 55 |
| Federal taxes | | 9,110 56 |
| All other licenses, fees and taxes | | 3,905 38 |
| Other disbursements, viz: Home office traveling expense, $12,156.92; interest paid on surplus contributed, $6,965.00; investment expense, $2,988.10; books and magazines, $1,330.08; miscellaneous expense, $2,129.38; surety bonds, $949.06; bureau earnings, $5,187.91; suspense, $1,492.51 | | 33,198 96 |
| Borrowed money repaid (gross) | | 140,000 00 |
| Interest on borrowed money | | 2,449 17 |
| Agents' balances charged off | | 912 48 |
| Loss on sale or maturity of ledger assets | | 3 60 |
| Decrease in book value of ledger assets | | 5 10 |
| Total disbursements | | $1,172,042 22 |
| Balance | | $4,678,164 85 |

## LEDGER ASSETS.

| | |
|---|---|
| Book value of real estate | $ 18,361 48 |
| Mortgage loans on real estate | 2,805,846 70 |
| Premiums advanced under Soldiers' and Sailors' Civil Relief Act | 235 64 |
| Loans on company's policies assigned as collateral | 934,272 58 |
| Premium notes on policies in force | 63,978 64 |
| Book value of bonds | 677,739 88 |
| Cash in office | 9,556 40 |
| Deposits in trust companies and banks not on interest | 30,251 74 |
| Deposits in trust companies and banks on interest | 112,083 89 |
| Agents' balances (debit, $28,187.32; credit, $2,349.42) | 25,837 90 |
| Total ledger assets | $4,678,164 85 |

## LEDGER ASSETS—Concluded.

NON-LEDGER ASSETS.

| | | |
|---|---|---|
| Interest due and accrued on mortgages | $43,218 87 | |
| Interest accrued on bonds | 6,839 57 | |
| Interest due and accrued on premium notes, loans or liens | 5,950 27 | |
| Interest due and accrued on other assets | 981 03 | |
| Rents due on company's property | 220 00 | |
| | | $ 57,209 74 |
| Due from other companies for losses or claims on policies re-insured | | 7,223 00 |
| Net uncollected and deferred premiums (paid for basis) renewals | | 112,151 04 |
| Gross assets | | $4,854,748 63 |

DEDUCT ASSETS NOT ADMITTED.

| | | |
|---|---|---|
| Agents' debit balances | $28,187 32 | |
| Premium notes, policy loans and other policy assets in excess of net value and of other policy liabilities on individual policies | 6,145 60 | |
| Total | | 34,332 92 |
| Admitted assets | | $4,820,415 71 |

## LIABILITIES.

| | | |
|---|---|---|
| Net present value of outstanding policies computed by the Colorado Insurance Department | $3,856,800 00 | |
| Same for dividend additions | 11,294 00 | |
| Same for annuities | 3,472 00 | |
| Total | $3,871,566 00 | |
| Deduct net value of risks re-insured | 56,406 00 | |
| Net reserve (paid for basis) | | $3,815,160 00 |
| Extra reserve for total and permanent disability benefits and for additional accidental death benefits included in life policies, less re-insurance | | 17,493 36 |
| Present value of supplementary contracts not involving life contingencies | | 15,334 43 |
| Present value of amounts incurred but not yet due for total and permanent disability benefits | | 12,418 00 |
| Death losses due and unpaid | $ 1,152 00 | |
| Death losses in process of adjustment | 10,200 00 | |
| Death losses reported for which no proofs have been received | 35,958 58 | |
| Reserve for net death losses incurred but unreported | 1,000 00 | |
| Death losses and other policy claims resisted | 3,848 00 | |
| Total policy claims | | 52,158 58 |
| Dividends left with the company to accumulate at interest | | 346,461 84 |
| Gross premiums paid in advance, including surrender values so applied, less discount, if any | | 3,360 31 |
| Unearned interest and rent paid in advance | | 27,622 63 |
| Commissions due agents on premium notes, when paid | | 3,198 93 |
| Salaries, rents, office expenses, bills and accounts due or accrued | | 7,459 93 |
| Medical examiners' and legal fees due or accrued | | 1,919 00 |
| Estimated amount hereafter payable for federal, state and other taxes based upon the business of the year of this statement | | 29,519 10 |
| Borrowed money and interest thereon | | 50,000 00 |
| Dividends or other profits due policyholders | | 1,170 62 |
| Dividends declared on or apportioned to annual dividend policies payable to policyholders during 1922 for period to February 28, 1922 | | 1,449 25 |
| Dividends declared on or apportioned to deferred dividend policies payable to policyholders during 1922 for period to December 31, 1922 | | 1,883 31 |
| Amounts set apart, apportioned, provisionally ascertained, calculated, declared or held awaiting apportionment upon deferred dividend policies | | 46,000 00 |
| Special reserve for fluctuations | | 95,000 00 |
| Premiums in suspense | | 1,111 90 |
| Total | | $4,528,721 19 |
| Capital paid up | | 100,000 00 |
| Unassigned funds (surplus) | | 191,694 52 |
| Total | | $4,820,415 71 |

## EXHIBIT OF POLICIES—ORDINARY.

ALL BUSINESS PAID FOR.

| | Number. | Amount. |
|---|---|---|
| Policies in force December 31, 1920 | 20,260 | $48,240,800 19 |
| Policies issued, revived and increased during the year | 3,775 | 16,619,578 81 |
| Total | 24,035 | $64,860,379 00 |

## EXHIBIT OF POLICIES—ORDINARY—Concluded.

ALL BUSINESS PAID FOR.

| | Number. | Amount. | Number. | Amount. |
|---|---|---|---|---|
| Deduct policies which have ceased to be in force during the year— | | | | |
| By death | 106 | $ 262,989 00 | | |
| By maturity | 6 | 31,500 00 | | |
| By expiry | 4 | 9,000 00 | | |
| By surrender | 347 | 684,193 00 | | |
| By lapse | 4,514 | 10,743,135 00 | | |
| By decrease | 1 | 83,997 00 | | |
| Withdrawal | -------- | 4,336,546 00 | | |
| Total | | | 4,978 | $16,151,360 00 |
| Total policies in force December 31, 1921 | | | 19,057 | $48,709,019 00 |
| Re-insured | | | 646 | $2,987,475 00 |

## EXHIBIT OF POLICIES—GROUP INSURANCE.

ALL BUSINESS PAID FOR.

| | Number. | Amount. | Number. | Amount. |
|---|---|---|---|---|
| Policies in force December 31, 1920 | | | 19 | $7,798,920 00 |
| Policies issued, revived and increased during the year | | | 3 | 6,805,810 00 |
| Total | | | 22 | $14,604,730 00 |
| Deduct policies which have ceased to be in force during the year— | | | | |
| By death | -------- | $ 31,274 00 | | |
| By lapse | 3 | 80,800 00 | | |
| By withdrawal | -------- | 4,336,546 00 | | |
| Total | | | 3 | 4,448,620 00 |
| Total policies in force December 31, 1921 | | | 19 | $10,156,110 00 |
| Distribution of business in force at end of year—One year term | | | 19 | $10,156,110 00 |

## BUSINESS IN ILLINOIS—ORDINARY.

| | Number. | Amount. |
|---|---|---|
| Policies in force December 31, 1920 | 237 | $599,026 00 |
| Policies issued during the year | 58 | 240,500 00 |
| Total | 295 | $839,526 00 |
| Deduct policies ceased to be in force | 54 | 134,526 00 |
| Policies in force December 31, 1921 | 241 | $705,000 00 |
| Losses and claims incurred during the year | 1 | $917 84 |
| Losses and claims settled during the year | 1 | 917 84 |

## BUSINESS IN ILLINOIS—GROUP INSURANCE.

| | Number. | Amount. |
|---|---|---|
| Policies issued during the year | 1 | $1,819,000 00 |
| Policies in force December 31, 1921 | 1 | 1,819,000 00 |
| Losses and claims incurred during the year | -------- | $500 00 |
| Losses and claims settled during the year | -------- | 500 00 |

## GAIN AND LOSS EXHIBIT.

INSURANCE EXHIBIT.

| | | Gain in surplus. | Loss in surplus. |
|---|---|---|---|
| Loading on actual premiums of the year (averaging 28.3 per cent of the gross premiums) | $394,767 45 | | |
| Insurance expenses incurred during the year | 468,517 90 | | |
| Loss from loading | | -------------- | $ 73,750 45 |
| Interest earned during the year | $273,038 03 | | |
| Investment expenses incurred during the year | 18,008 64 | | |
| Net income from investments | $255,029 39 | | |
| Interest required to maintain reserve | 137,793 87 | | |
| Gain from interest | | $117,235 52 | |
| Expected mortality on net amount at risk | $429,887 00 | | |
| Actual mortality on net amount at risk | 197,425 55 | | |
| Gain from mortality | | 232,461 45 | |

GAIN AND LOSS EXHIBIT—Concluded.

INSURANCE EXHIBIT.

| | | Gain in surplus. | Loss in surplus. |
|---|---|---|---|
| Expected disbursements to annuitants | $303 06 | | |
| Net actual annuity claims incurred | 533 06 | | |
| Loss from annuities | | | $ 230 00 |
| Total gain during the year from surrendered and lapsed policies | | $10,112 91 | |
| Decrease in surplus on dividend account | | | 128,856 77 |
| Increase in special funds and special reserves during the year | | | 95,000 00 |
| Net to loss account | | | 225 09 |
| **INVESTMENT EXHIBIT.** | | | |
| Total gains from bonds | | 2,140 00 | |
| Total losses from bonds | | | 3 60 |
| Loss from assets not admitted | | | 21,743 39 |
| Net gain on account of total and permanent disability benefits or additional accidental death benefits included in life policies | | 1,120 40 | |
| Interest paid on contributed surplus | | | 6,965 00 |
| Balance unaccounted for | | 10,372 73 | |
| Total gains and losses in surplus during the year | | $373,443 01 | $326,774 30 |
| Surplus December 31, 1920 | $145,025 81 | | |
| Surplus December 31, 1921 | 191,694 52 | | |
| Increase in surplus | | | 46,668 71 |
| Total | | $373,443 01 | $373,443 01 |

## CENTRAL LIFE ASSURANCE SOCIETY OF THE UNITED STATES (MUTUAL).

Located at Seventh and Grand Avenue, Des Moines, Iowa; incorporated May 10, 1919; commenced business in Illinois January 7, 1920.

GEORGE B. PEAK, President. T. C. DENNY, Secretary.

GEORGE A. BARR, Director of Trade and Commerce, Attorney for service at Springfield.

| | | | |
|---|---|---|---|
| Amount of ledger assets December 31, of previous year | | | $9,571,199 23 |

INCOME.

| | | | |
|---|---|---|---|
| First year's premiums on original policies, less re-insurance | | $611,085 06 | |
| First year's premiums for total and permanent disability benefits, less re-insurance | | 19,152 65 | |
| First year's premiums for additional accidental death benefits, less re-insurance | | 20,924 17 | |
| Dividends applied to purchase paid-up additions and annuities | | 15,812 53 | |
| Surrender values applied to purchase paid-up insurance and annuities | | 56,429 39 | |
| New premiums | | $ 723,403 80 | |
| Renewal premiums less re-insurance | $2,729,299 84 | | |
| Renewal premiums for total and permanent disability benefits, less re-insurance | 50,035 29 | | |
| Renewal premiums for additional accidental death benefits, less re-insurance | 51,244 75 | | |
| Dividends applied to pay renewal premiums | 57,415 29 | | |
| Allotments applied to pay renewal premiums | 2,357 06 | | |
| Renewal premiums | | 2,890,352 23 | |
| Premium income | | | $3,613,756 03 |
| Consideration for supplementary contracts not involving life contingencies | | | 5,000 00 |
| Dividends left with company to accumulate at interest | | | 20,871 06 |
| Allotments left with company to accumulate at interest | | | 471 35 |
| Interest on mortgage loans | | $395,594 22 | |
| Interest on bonds | | 15,668 97 | |
| Interest on premium notes, policy loans or liens | | 110,689 87 | |
| Interest on deposits | | 7,815 96 | |
| Interest on other debts due the company | | 20,099 63 | |
| Total interest | | | 549,868 65 |
| From other sources, viz: Commissions on mortgage loans, $27,658.11; bonus on mortgage loans, $4,849.57; expense in connection with mortgage loans in process of foreclosure, $114.65; miscellaneous account, $2,894.92; protested and bad checks, $350.33 | | | 35,867 58 |
| Agents' balances previously charged off | | | 237 49 |
| Increase in book value of ledger assets | | | 3,836 41 |
| Total income | | | $4,229,908 57 |
| Total | | | $13,801,107 80 |

## DISBURSEMENTS.

|  | | |
|---|---|---|
| Death claims and additions | $345,301 94 | |
| Matured endowments | 18,328 12 | |
| Total and permanent disability claims and additional accidental death benefits | 35,701 00 | |
| Total death claims and endowments | | $399,331 06 |
| Premium notes and liens voided by lapse, less $7,274.44 restorations | | 29,038 65 |
| Surrender values paid in cash, or applied in liquidation of loans or notes | | 209,743 51 |
| Surrender values applied to purchase paid-up insurance and annuities | | 56,429 39 |
| Dividends paid policyholders in cash, or applied in liquidation of loans or notes | | 73,541 88 |
| Allotments paid policyholders in cash, or applied in liquidation of loans or notes | | 115 54 |
| Dividends applied to pay renewal premiums | | 57,415 29 |
| Allotments applied to pay renewal premiums | | 2,357 06 |
| Dividends applied to purchase paid-up additions and annuities | | 15,812 53 |
| Dividends left with the company to accumulate at interest | | 20,871 06 |
| Allotments left with the company to accumulate at interest | | 471 35 |
| (Total paid policyholders | $865,127 32) | |
| Expense of investigation and settlement of policy claims | | 1,708 66 |
| Supplementary contracts not involving life contingencies | | 3,559 76 |
| Supplementary contracts involving life contingencies | | 526 80 |
| Dividends with interest, held on deposit surrendered during the year | | 1,136 75 |
| Allotments with interest held on deposit surrendered during the year | | 1,306 88 |
| Commissions to agents, first year, $407,915.59; renewal, $161,784.27 | | 569,699 86 |
| Compensation of managers and agents not paid by commissions on new business | | 20,733 33 |
| Agency conventions, banquets, luncheons, etc | | 2,665 66 |
| Agency supervision and traveling expenses of supervisors | | 14,754 88 |
| Other agents' traveling expenses | | 2,854 70 |
| Branch office expenses | | 33,004 20 |
| Traveling expenses of officers and managers | | 2,222 03 |
| Medical examiners' fees and inspection of risks | | 49,586 11 |
| Salaries and all other compensation of officers and home office employees | | 199,201 04 |
| Rent | | 15,768 00 |
| Advertising, printing, stationery, postage, telegraph, telephone and exchange | | 55,120 11 |
| Legal expense | | 2,683 00 |
| Furniture, fixtures and safes | | 5,667 46 |
| Taxes on real estate | | 252 01 |
| State taxes on premiums | | 71,400 23 |
| Insurance department licenses and fees | | 3,235 27 |
| Federal taxes | | 36,501 16 |
| All other licenses, fees and taxes | | 153 46 |
| Other disbursements, viz: Books, subscriptions, periodicals, etc., $755.71; examination by Insurance Department, $1,394.41; expense of home office alterations, repairs, etc., $2,080.25; fees for collection, $65.13; impairment cards, $4,053.55; incidentals, $7,721.41; interest on liens against reserves on re-insurance, $36.03; interest on reserves deposited with company, $636.28; interest on mortgage payable, $1,593.75; insurance on furniture, fixtures, office records, etc., $455.50; losses on bank accounts, $1,582.91; membership to clubs, etc., $460.00; payments on non-participating business, $209,052.33; prizes awarded to agents, $1,036.33; reserves on re-insurance deposited with company, $1,623.75; reports on agents bonds, $110.00; revenue stamps, $64.25; subscription to Public Welfare Bureau, $1,000.00; sundry mortgage loan expense, $2,339.45 | | 236,061 04 |
| Agents' balances charged off | | 7,657 75 |
| Loss on sale or maturity of ledger assets | | 252 76 |
| Total disbursements | | $2,202,840 23 |
| Balance | | $11,598,267 57 |

## LEDGER ASSETS.

|  | |
|---|---|
| Book value of real estate | $ 273,100 57 |
| Mortgage loans on real estate | 9,062,127 50 |
| Tax certificates | 1,212 77 |
| Premiums advanced under Soldier's and Sailors' Civil Relief Act | 290 60 |
| Loans on company's policies assigned as collateral | 1,834,994 16 |
| Premium notes on policies in force | 67,727 90 |
| Book value of bonds | 84,362 56 |
| Cash in office | 700 00 |
| Deposits in trust companies and banks not on interest | 6,991 34 |
| Deposits in trust companies and banks on interest | 120,827 60 |
| Bills receivable | 89,139 72 |
| Agents' balances (debit, $62,751.12; credit, $6,052.32) net | 56,698 80 |
| School district warrants | 94 05 |
| Total ledger assets | $11,598,267 57 |

### NON-LEDGER ASSETS.

|  | |
|---|---|
| Interest due and accrued on mortgages | $284,108 18 |
| Interest due and accrued on bonds | 3,624 41 |
| Interest due and accrued on premium notes, loans or liens | 1,659 54 |

## LEDGER ASSETS—Concluded.

### NON-LEDGER ASSETS.

| | | | |
|---|---|---|---|
| Interest accrued on other assets | | $4,042 21 | |
| Rent of offices paid in advance | | 1,314 00 | |
| | | | $294,748 34 |
| | New business. | Renewals. | |
| Net uncollected and deferred premiums (paid for basis) | $968 61 | $272,057 90 | 273,026 51 |
| All other assets, viz: Supplies, stationery and printed matter, $4,000.00; furniture, fixtures and safes, $6,000.00 | | | 10,000 00 |
| Gross assets | | | $12,176,042 42 |

### DEDUCT ASSETS NOT ADMITTED.

| | | |
|---|---|---|
| Supplies, printed matter and stationery | $ 4,000 00 | |
| Furniture, fixtures and safes | 6,000 00 | |
| Agents' debit balances | 62,751 12 | |
| Bills receivable | 89,139 72 | |
| Premium notes, policy loans and other policy assets in excess of net value and of other policy liabilities on individual policies | 16,440 40 | |
| Book value of other ledger assets over market value, viz: Certificates of deposit | 224 91 | |
| Total | | 178,556 15 |
| Admitted assets | | $11,997,486 27 |

## LIABILITIES.

| | | |
|---|---|---|
| Net present value of outstanding policies | $9,946,558 00 | |
| Same for dividend additions | 21,429 88 | |
| Present value of amounts involving life contingencies | 9,545 25 | |
| Total | $9,977,533 13 | |
| Deduct net value of risks re-insured | 31,003 00 | |
| Net reserve (paid for basis) | | $9,946,530 13 |
| Extra reserve for total and permanent disability benefits and for additional accidental death benefits included in life policies, less re-insurance | | 175,077 95 |
| Present value of supplementary contracts not involving life contingencies | | 35,121 22 |
| Present value of amounts incurred but not yet due for total and permanent disability benefits | | 30,421 57 |
| Death losses in process of adjustment | $59,662 00 | |
| Reserve for net death losses incurred but unreported | 50,000 00 | |
| Matured endowments due and unpaid | 6,000 00 | |
| Total and permanent disability benefits and additional accidental death benefits | 3,000 00 | |
| Total policy claims | | 118,662 00 |
| Dividends left with the company to accumulate at interest | | 33,714 41 |
| Allotment left with the company to accumulate at interest | | 4,985 57 |
| Gross premiums paid in advance, including surrender values so applied, less discount, if any | | 14,897 50 |
| Unearned interest and rent paid in advance | | 51,530 02 |
| Commissions due agents on premium notes, when paid | | 4,063 67 |
| Commissions to agents due or accrued | | 6,923 62 |
| Salaries, rents, office expenses, bills, and accounts due or accrued | | 10,000 00 |
| Medical examiners' and legal fees due or accrued | | 3,834 00 |
| Estimated amount hereafter payable for federal, state and other taxes based upon the business of the year of this statement | | 135,069 52 |
| Dividends or other profits due policyholders | | 18,827 65 |
| Dividends declared on or apportioned to annual dividend policies payable to policyholders during 1922 for period to March 31, 1922 | | 37,621 59 |
| Dividends declared on or apportioned to deferred dividend policies payable to policyholders during 1922 for period to March 31, 1922 | | 12,468 20 |
| Amounts set apart, apportioned, provisionally ascertained, calculated, declared or held awaiting apportionment upon deferred dividend policies | | 292,997 87 |
| Reserves on business issued but not paid for | | 15,859 00 |
| Other liabilities, viz: Miscellaneous account (renewal premiums in suspense), $5,884.75; excess of cash value over reserves, $4,220.34; reserve deposited with company by Metropolitan Life, $12,515.91; liens against reserves on re-insurance policies in Metropolitan Life, $1,949.33; interest, $360.41 | | 24,930 74 |
| Total | | $10,973,536 23 |
| Unassigned funds (surplus) | | 1,023,950 04 |
| Total | | $11,997,486 27 |

## EXHIBIT OF POLICIES—ORDINARY.

### ALL BUSINESS PAID FOR.

| | Number. | Amount. |
|---|---|---|
| Policies in force December 31, 1920 | 54,762 | $105,726,633 00 |
| Policies issued, revived, and increased during the year | 10,118 | 22,721,822 00 |
| Total | 64,880 | $128,448,455 00 |

## EXHIBIT OF POLICIES—ORDINARY—Concluded.

ALL BUSINESS PAID FOR.

| | Number. | Amount. | Number. | Amount. |
|---|---|---|---|---|
| Deduct policies which have ceased to be in force during the year— | | | | |
| By death | 170 | $ 351,499 00 | | |
| By maturity | 17 | 16,286 00 | | |
| By expiry | 476 | 710,200 00 | | |
| By surrender | 688 | 1,241,997 00 | | |
| By lapse | 7,093 | 17,672,391 00 | | |
| By decrease | 3 | 215,105 00 | | |
| Total | | | 8,447 | $20,207,478 00 |
| Total policies in force December 31, 1921 | | | 56,433 | $108,240,977 00 |
| Re-insured | | | 114 | $923,036 00 |

## BUSINESS IN ILLINOIS—ORDINARY.

| | Number. | Amount. |
|---|---|---|
| Policies in force December 31, 1920 | 934 | $1,653,378 00 |
| Policies issued during the year | 301 | 628,998 53 |
| Total | 1,235 | $2,282,376 53 |
| Deduct policies ceased to be in force | 193 | 428,150 00 |
| Policies in force December 31, 1921 | 1,042 | $1,854,226 53 |
| Losses and claims incurred during the year | 3 | $3,000 00 |
| Losses and claims settled during the year | 3 | 3,000 00 |
| Premiums received | | $65,904 78 |

## GAIN AND LOSS EXHIBIT.

INSURANCE EXHIBIT.

| | | Gain in surplus. | Loss in surplus. |
|---|---|---|---|
| Loading on actual premiums of the year (averaging 24.86 per cent of the gross premiums) | $ 876,327 08 | | |
| Insurance expenses incurred during the year | 1,145,342 72 | | |
| Loss from loading | | | $269,015 64 |
| Interest earned during the year | $642,329 81 | | |
| Investment expenses incurred during the year | 24,419 81 | | |
| Net income from investments | $617,910 00 | | |
| Interest required to maintain reserve | 332,045 98 | | |
| Gain from interest | | $285,864 02 | |
| Expected mortality on net amount at risk | $1,020,930 00 | | |
| Actual mortality on net amount at risk | 337,093 94 | | |
| Gain from mortality | | 683,836 06 | |
| Total gain during the year from surrendered and lapsed policies | | 86,887 43 | |
| Paid stockholders on stock retirement contract | | | 209,052 33 |
| Decrease in surplus on dividend account | | | 168,736 96 |
| Decrease in special funds, and special reserves during the year | | 10,701 00 | |
| Net to loss account | | | 7,420 26 |
| INVESTMENT EXHIBIT. | | | |
| Total gains from bonds | | 18,829 35 | |
| Total losses from bonds | | | 252 76 |
| Loss on bank account | | | 1,582 91 |
| Loss from assets not admitted | | | 41,270 81 |
| Net loss on account of total and permanent disability benefits or additional accidental death benefits included in life policies | | | 26,558 25 |
| Gain from certificates of deposit | | 893 06 | |
| Loss from: Allotments paid in cash, $115.54; allotment applied on premiums, $2,357.06; allotments left at interest, $471.35; excess cash values over reserves, $4,220.34; premium notes voided by lapse, $29,038.65; liens against reserves on re-insurance in Metropolitan Life, $13.33 | | | 36,216 27 |
| Balance unaccounted for | | 3,929 60 | |
| Total gains and losses in surplus during the year | | $1,090,940 52 | $ 760,106 19 |
| Surplus December 31, 1920 | $ 693,115 71 | | |
| Surplus December 31, 1921 | 1,023,950 04 | | |
| Increase in surplus | | | 330,834 33 |
| Total | | $1,090,940 52 | $1,090,940 52 |

## CENTRAL STATES LIFE INSURANCE COMPANY.

Located at No. 3207 Washington Avenue, St. Louis, Missouri; incorporated June 5, 1909; commenced business in Illinois February 4, 1911.

FRANK P. CRUNDEN, President. V. F. LARSON, Secretary.

CYRUS THOMPSON, Belleville, Attorney for service.

### CAPITAL.

| | | | |
|---|---|---|---|
| Capital paid up | | $400,000 00 | |
| Amount of ledger assets December 31, of previous year | | $3,461,715 92 | |
| Increase of paid-up capital during year | | 65,000 00 | |
| Extended at | | | $3,526,715 92 |

### INCOME.

| | | | |
|---|---|---|---|
| First year's premiums on original policies, less re-insurance | | $334,638 90 | |
| First year's premiums for total and permanent disability benefits, less re-insurance | | 22,159 71 | |
| First year's premiums for additional accidental death benefits, less re-insurance | | 4,661 48 | |
| Surrender values to pay first year's premiums | | 244 22 | |
| Dividends applied to purchase paid-up additions and annuities | | 1,228 23 | |
| Surrender values applied to purchase paid-up insurance and annuities | | 9,835 29 | |
| New premiums | | $ 372,767 83 | |
| Renewal premiums less re-insurance | $1,191,418 64 | | |
| Renewal premiums for total and permanent disability benefits | 2,741 03 | | |
| Renewal premiums for additional accidental death benefits, less re-insurance | 24,990 87 | | |
| Dividends applied to pay renewal premiums | 18,798 70 | | |
| Surrender values applied to pay renewal premiums | 1,215 00 | | |
| Renewal premiums | | 1,239,164 24 | |
| Premium income | | | $1,611,932 07 |
| Consideration for supplementary contracts not involving life contingencies | | | 8,000 00 |
| Dividends left with the company to accumulate at interest | | | 6,794 74 |
| Coupons left with company to accumulate at interest | | | 3,459 45 |
| Interest on mortgage loans | | $124,143 77 | |
| Interest on bonds | | 20,141 55 | |
| Interest on premium notes, policy loans or liens | | 35,170 39 | |
| Interest on deposits | | 7,330 72 | |
| Interest on other debts due the company | | 355 65 | |
| Rents—including $5,000.00 for company's occupancy of its own buildings | | 5,813 44 | |
| Total interest and rents | | | 192,955 52 |
| From other sources, viz: Surplus from sale of capital stock of which $15,000.00 was taken credit for in the 1920 statement, $65,000.00; increase in suspense items, $130.05 | | | 65,130 05 |
| Borrowed money (gross) | | | 288,500 00 |
| Agents' balances previously charged off | | | 249 58 |
| From other accounts previously charged off | | | 17 67 |
| Profit on sale or maturity of ledger assets | | | 50 00 |
| Total income | | | $2,177,089 08 |
| Total | | | $5,703,805 00 |

### DISBURSEMENTS.

| | | | |
|---|---|---|---|
| Death claims and additions | | $267,456 11 | |
| Matured endowments | | 2,000 00 | |
| Total and permanent disability claims and additional accidental death benefits | | 27,655 70 | |
| Total death claims and endowments | | | $297,111 81 |
| Surrender values paid in cash, or applied in liquidation of loans or notes | | | 76,456 87 |
| Surrender values applied to pay new and renewal premiums | | | 1,459 22 |
| Surrender values applied to purchase paid-up insurance and annuities | | | 9,835 29 |
| Dividends paid policyholders in cash, or applied in liquidation of loans or notes | | | 190 50 |
| Dividends applied to pay renewal premiums | | | 18,798 70 |
| Dividends applied to purchase paid-up additions and annuities | | | 1,228 23 |
| Dividends left with the company to accumulate at interest | | | 6,794 74 |
| (Total paid policyholders | | $411,875 36) | |
| Expenses of investigation and settlement of policy claims, including legal expenses | | | 2,838 36 |
| Supplementary contracts not involving life contingencies | | | 2,499 55 |
| Dividends with interest, held on deposit surrendered during the year | | | 1,743 49 |
| Coupons with interest held on deposit surrendered during the year | | | 3,453 63 |
| Commissions to agents, first year, $256,855.04; renewal, $82,737.48 | | | 339,592 52 |
| Compensation of managers and agents not paid by commissions on new business | | | 32,498 18 |

## DISBURSEMENTS—Concluded.

| | |
|---|---|
| Agency supervision and traveling expenses of supervisors | $ 5,947 83 |
| Branch office expenses | 7,788 73 |
| Medical examiners' fees and inspection of risks | 30,386 12 |
| Salaries and all other compensation of officers and home office employees | 114,059 01 |
| Rent | 16,372 37 |
| Advertising, printing, stationery, postage, telegraph, telephone, express, exchange and periodicals | 34,252 98 |
| Legal expense | 511 14 |
| Furniture, fixtures and safes | 12,138 19 |
| Repairs and expenses (other than taxes) on real estate | 9,248 04 |
| Taxes on real estate | 458 25 |
| State taxes on premiums | 25,041 38 |
| Insurance department licenses and fees | 5,333 67 |
| Federal taxes | 9,284 37 |
| All other licenses, fees and taxes | 737 77 |
| Other disbursements, viz: Mortgage loan expense, $178.16; Aegis Life stock distribution, $173.03; traveling, $2,120.01; surety bonds, $2,432.03; miscellaneous, $3,076.62 | 7,979 85 |
| Borrowed money repaid (gross) | 160,000 00 |
| Interest on borrowed money | 18,726 59 |
| Repayment of contribution including $7,116.10 interest | 72,916 10 |
| Agents' balances charged off | 21 50 |
| Other assets charged off | 199 88 |
| Loss on sale or maturity of ledger assets | 6,807 45 |
| Total disbursements | $1,332,712 31 |
| Balance | $4,371,092 69 |

## LEDGER ASSETS.

| | |
|---|---|
| Book value of real estate | $ 284,774 06 |
| Mortgage loans on real estate | 2,636,908 50 |
| Loans secured by collaterals | 90,537 42 |
| Premiums advanced under Soldiers' and Sailors' Civil Relief Act | 115 70 |
| Loans on company's policies assigned as collateral | 333,088 78 |
| Premium notes on policies in force | 251,843 64 |
| Book value of bonds | 366,165 78 |
| Cash in office | 1,160 52 |
| Deposits in trust companies and banks not on interest | 2,363 93 |
| Deposits in trust companies and banks on interest | 389,441 14 |
| Bills receivable | 450 00 |
| Agents' balances (debit, $17,266.44; credit, $5,245.33), net | 12,021 11 |
| Protested items, $248.15; taxes, etc. paid in advance on investments, $1,973.96 | 2,222 11 |
| Total ledger assets | $4,371,092 69 |

### NON-LEDGER ASSETS.

| | | |
|---|---|---|
| Interest due and accrued on mortgages | $103,269 72 | |
| Interest due and accrued on bonds | 5,740 38 | |
| Interest accrued on premium notes, loans or liens | 1,658 88 | |
| Interest accrued on other assets | 4,930 31 | |
| | | 115,599 29 |
| Market value of real estate over book value | | 2,836 78 |
| Due from other companies for losses or claims on policies re-insured | | 3,000 00 |
| Net uncollected and deferred premiums (paid for basis): Renewals | | 98,565 97 |
| Gross assets | | $4,591,094 73 |

### DEDUCT ASSETS NOT ADMITTED.

| | | |
|---|---|---|
| Agents' debit balances and interest | $17,451 48 | |
| Bills receivable, $450.00; interest on bills receivable, $49.50; protested items, $248.15 | 747 65 | |
| Premium notes, policy loans and other policy assets in excess of net value and of other policy liabilities on individual policies | 5,416 85 | |
| Book value of bonds over market value | 11,173 56 | |
| Total | | 34,789 54 |
| Admitted assets | | $4,556,305 19 |

## LIABILITIES.

| | | |
|---|---|---|
| Net present value of outstanding policies computed by the Missouri Insurance Department | $3,551,236 43 | |
| Same for dividend additions | 4,364 00 | |
| Same for annuities | 10,455 66 | |
| Total | $3,566,056 09 | |
| Deduct net value of risks re-insured | 18,837 00 | |
| Net reserve (paid for basis) | | $3,547,219 09 |
| Extra reserve for total and permanent disability and surgical benefits and for additional accidental death benefits included in life policies, less re-insurance | | 55,474 65 |

LIABILITIES—Concluded.

| | | |
|---|---|---|
| Present value of supplementary contracts not involving life contingencies | | $ 16,290 00 |
| Present value of amounts incurred but not yet due for total and permanent disability benefits | | 12,458 89 |
| Death losses in process of adjustment | $ 1,000 00 | |
| Death losses reported for which no proofs have been received | 36,400 00 | |
| Death losses and other policy claims resisted | 1,000 00 | |
| Total and permanent disability and surgical benefits and additional accidental death benefits | 8,590 16 | |
| Total policy claims | | 46,990 16 |
| Dividends left with the company to accumulate at interest | | 19,048 15 |
| Coupons left with the company to accumulate at interest | | 33,882 62 |
| Gross premiums paid in advance, including surrender values so applied, less discounts, if any | | 5,212 70 |
| Unearned interest and rent paid in advance | | 11,443 59 |
| Salaries, rents, office expenses, bills, and accounts due or accrued | | 3,364 92 |
| Medical examiners' and inspection fees due or accrued | | 2,284 48 |
| Estimated amount hereafter payable for federal, state and other taxes based upon the business of the year of this statement | | 24,671 80 |
| Borrowed money and interest thereon | | 288,572 22 |
| Dividends or other profits due policyholders | | 2,348 17 |
| Dividends declaredpon or apportioned to annual dividend policies payable to policyholders during 1922 for period to March 31 | | 8,737 99 |
| Reserved on account of contribution fund and investments | | 30,000 00 |
| Central National Mutual surplus and interest thereon | | 8,276 07 |
| Other liabilities, viz: Aegis Life stock distribution, $1,185.19; suspense items, $4,313.38 | | 5,498 57 |
| Total | | $4,121,774 07 |
| Capital paid up | | 400,000 00 |
| Unassigned funds (surplus) | | 34,531 12 |
| Total | | $4,556,305 19 |

## EXHIBIT OF POLICIES—ORDINARY.

ALL BUSINESS PAID FOR

| | Number. | Amount. | Number. | Amount. |
|---|---|---|---|---|
| Policies in force December 31, 1920 | | | 28,708 | $57,429,868 00 |
| Policies issued, revived, and increased during the year | | | 5,726 | 15,069,457 00 |
| Total | | | 34,434 | $72,499,325 00 |
| Deduct policies which have ceased to be in force during the year— | | | | |
| By death | 132 | $ 289,022 00 | | |
| By maturity | 2 | 2,000 00 | | |
| By expiry | 221 | 343,159 00 | | |
| By surrender | 133 | 218,607 00 | | |
| By lapse | 5,998 | 15,587,125 00 | | |
| By decrease | 5 | 147,330 00 | | |
| Total | | | 6,491 | 16,587,243 00 |
| Total policies in force December 31, 1921 | | | 27,943 | $55,912,082 00 |
| Re-insured | | | | $1,986,904 00 |

## BUSINESS IN ILLINOIS—ORDINARY.

| | Number. | Amount. |
|---|---|---|
| Policies in force December 31, 1920 | 1,070 | $1,574,560 00 |
| Policies issued during the year | 85 | 218,851 00 |
| Total | 1,155 | $1,793,411 00 |
| Deduct policies ceased to be in force | 106 | 214,000 00 |
| Policies in force December 31, 1921 | 1,049 | $1,579,411 00 |
| Losses and claims incurred during the year | 1 | $1,000 00 |
| Losses and claims settled during the year | 1 | 1,000 00 |
| Premiums received | | $48,181 74 |

## GAIN AND LOSS EXHIBIT.

INSURANCE EXHIBIT.

| | | Gain in surplus. | Loss in surplus. |
|---|---|---|---|
| Loading on actual premiums of the year (averaging 23.99 per cent of the gross premiums) | $380,196 93 | | |
| Insurance expenses incurred during the year | 636,361 76 | | |
| Loss from loading | | ------------- | $256,164 83 |

## GAIN AND LOSS EXHIBIT—Concluded.

INSURANCE EXHIBIT.

| | | Gain in surplus. | Loss in surplus. |
|---|---|---|---|
| Interest earned during the year | $206,601 59 | | |
| Investment expenses incurred during the year | 26,397 01 | | |
| Net income from investments | $180,204 58 | | |
| Interest required to maintain reserve | 121,968 00 | | |
| Gain from interest | | $ 58,236 58 | |
| Expected mortality on net amount at risk | $507,913 00 | | |
| Actual mortality on net amount at risk | 254,665 50 | | |
| Gain from mortality | | 253,247 50 | |
| Total gain during the year from surrendered and lapsed policies | | 37,059 88 | |
| Decrease in surplus on dividend account | | | $28,469 72 |
| Increase in special funds, and special reserves during the year | | | 26,349 04 |
| INVESTMENT EXHIBIT. | | | |
| Total gains from real estate | | 4,083 89 | |
| Total losses from real estate | | | 6,807 45 |
| Total gains from bonds | | 50 00 | |
| Total losses from bonds | | | 4,547 06 |
| Loss from assets not admitted | | | 5,698 74 |
| Net gain on account of total and permanent disability benefits or additional accidental death benefits included in life policies | | 1,121 00 | |
| Loss from payment of contribution | | | 65,800 00 |
| Gain from sale of capital stock | | 50,000 00 | |
| Total gains and losses in surplus during the year | | $403,798 85 | $393,836 84 |
| Surplus December 31, 1920 | $24,569 11 | | |
| Surplus December 31, 1921 | 34,531 12 | | |
| Increase in surplus | | | 9,962 01 |
| Total | | $403,798 85 | $403,798 85 |

## CENTURY LIFE INSURANCE COMPANY.

Located at No. 827 Occidental Building, Indianapolis, Indiana; incorporated October 20, 1916; commenced business in Illinois February 17, 1917.

THOMAS J. OWENS, President. CLAUDE T. TUCK, Secretary.

GEORGE A. BARR, Director of Trade and Commerce, Attorney for service at Springfield.

### CAPITAL.

| | | | |
|---|---|---|---|
| Capital paid up | | $200,000 00 | |
| Amount of ledger assets December 31, of previous year | | | $343,934 39 |

### INCOME.

| | | | |
|---|---|---|---|
| First year's premiums on original policies, less re-insurance | | $61,022 58 | |
| First year's premiums for total and permanent disability benefits | | 290 56 | |
| First year's premiums for additional accidental death benefits | | 380 98 | |
| New premiums | | $61,694 12 | |
| Renewal premiums less re-insurance | $88,570 01 | | |
| Renewal premiums for total and permanent disability benefits | 346 28 | | |
| Renewal premiums for additional accidental death benefits | 524 78 | | |
| Renewal premiums | | 89,441 07 | |
| Premium income | | | $151,135 19 |
| Interest on mortgage loans | | $16,089 96 | |
| Interest on bonds | | 2,178 27 | |
| Interest on premium notes, policy loans or liens | | 1,642 53 | |
| Interest on deposits | | 492 61 | |
| Total interest | | | 20,403 37 |
| From other sources, viz: survivorship fund, $186.50; coupons deposited, $2,718.83; coupons to purchase extended insurance, $47.01 | | | 2,952 34 |
| Total income | | | $174,490 90 |
| Total | | | $518,425 29 |

## DISBURSEMENTS.

| | | |
|---|---|---|
| Death claims and additions | $27,502 33 | |
| Additional accidental death benefits | 1,500 00 | |
| Total death claims | | $29,002 33 |
| Premium notes and liens voided by lapse | | 263 50 |
| Surrender values paid in cash, or applied in liquidation of loans or notes | | 3,325 96 |
| (Total paid policyholders | $32,591 79) | |
| Expense of investigation and settlement of policy claims, including legal expenses | | 37 57 |
| Commissions to agents, first year, $50,797.93; renewal, $5,207.95 | | 56,005 88 |
| Compensation of managers and agents not paid by commissions on new business | | 1,562 01 |
| Medical examiners' fees and inspection of risks | | 5,394 00 |
| Salaries and all other compensation of officers and home office employees | | 23,002 00 |
| Rent | | 2,400 00 |
| Advertising, printing, stationery, postage, telegraph, telephone and express | | 4,079 93 |
| Legal expense | | 300 00 |
| State taxes on premiums | | 2,311 12 |
| Insurance department licenses and fees | | 1,010 12 |
| Federal taxes | | 2,466 02 |
| All other licenses, fees and taxes | | 4,930 74 |
| Other disbursements, viz: Actuarial expense, $600.00; electric current, $73.09; investment expense, $1,076.60; miscellaneous expense, $728.49; officers traveling expense, $158.91; interest on coupons, $74.31 | | 2,711 40 |
| Total disbursements | | $138,802 58 |
| Balance | | $379,622 71 |

## LEDGER ASSETS.

| | | |
|---|---|---|
| Mortgage loans on real estate | | $269,034 01 |
| Loans on company's policies assigned as collateral | | 9,917 44 |
| Premium notes on policies in force | | 1,088 25 |
| Book value of bonds | | 19,050 00 |
| Cash in office | | 100 00 |
| Deposits in trust companies and banks on interest | | 68,181 45 |
| Agents' balances (debit, $8,564.67; credit, $193.10) | | 8,371 57 |
| Furniture and fixtures | | 3,879 99 |
| Total ledger assets | | $379,622 71 |

### NON-LEDGER ASSETS.

| | | |
|---|---|---|
| Interest due and accrued on mortgages | $5,108 72 | |
| Interest due and accrued on bonds | 177 98 | |
| | | 5,286 70 |
| Net uncollected and deferred premiums (paid for basis) renewals | | 40,010 91 |
| Supplies, printing and stationery | | 5,055 84 |
| Gross assets | | $429,976 16 |

### DEDUCT ASSETS NOT ADMITTED.

| | | |
|---|---|---|
| Supplies, printed matter and stationery | $5,055 84 | |
| Furniture, fixtures and safes | 3,879 99 | |
| Agents' debit balances | 8,564 67 | |
| Premium notes, policy loans and other policy assets in excess of net value and of other policy liabilities on individual policies | 4,423 65 | |
| Total | | 21,924 15 |
| Admitted assets | | $408,052 01 |

## LIABILITIES.

| | | |
|---|---|---|
| Net present value of outstanding policies computed by the Indiana Insurance Department | $228,159 29 | |
| Deduct net value of risks re-insured | 49,318 50 | |
| Net reserve (paid for basis) | | $178,840 79 |
| Gross premiums paid in advance, including surrender values so applied, less discount, if any | | 202 63 |
| Salaries, rents, office expenses, bills and accounts due or accrued | | 352 02 |
| Medical examiners' and inspection fees due or accrued | | 222 00 |
| Estimated amount hereafter payable for federal, state and other taxes based upon the business of the year of this statement | | 3,303 75 |
| Survivorship fund | | 656 00 |
| Coupons deposited | | 5,293 09 |
| Investment expense | | 385 57 |
| Total | | $189,255 85 |
| Capital paid up | | 200,000 00 |
| Unassigned funds (surplus) | | 18,796 16 |
| Total | | $408,052 01 |

## EXHIBIT OF POLICIES—ORDINARY.

ALL BUSINESS PAID FOR.

| | Number. | Amount. | Number. | Amount. |
|---|---|---|---|---|
| Policies in force December 31, 1920 | | | 3,067 | $7,337,066 00 |
| Policies issued, revived and increased during the year | | | 1,006 | 2,692,793 00 |
| Total | | | 4,073 | $10,029,859 00 |
| Deduct policies which have ceased to be in force during the year— | | | | |
| By death | 14 | $ 54,752 00 | | |
| By expiry | 3 | 8,635 00 | | |
| By surrender | 28 | 69,700 00 | | |
| By lapse | 1,174 | 2,543,640 00 | | |
| By decrease | | 61,979 00 | | |
| Total | | | 1,219 | 2,738,706 00 |
| Total policies in force December 31, 1921 | | | 2,854 | $7,291,153 00 |
| Re-insured | | | 549 | $1,822,439 00 |

## BUSINESS IN ILLINOIS—ORDINARY.

| | Number. | Amount. |
|---|---|---|
| Policies in force December 31, 1920 | 169 | $405,500 00 |
| Policies issued during the year | 70 | 226,000 00 |
| Total | 239 | $631,500 00 |
| Deduct policies ceased to be in force | 53 | 103,000 00 |
| Policies in force December 31, 1921 | 186 | $528,500 00 |
| Losses and claims incurred during the year | 1 | $5,000 00 |
| Losses and claims settled during the year | 1 | 5,000 00 |
| Premiums received | | $13,805 32 |

## GAIN AND LOSS EXHIBIT.

INSURANCE EXHIBIT.

| | | Gain in surplus. | Loss in surplus. |
|---|---|---|---|
| Loading on actual premiums of the year (averaging 31 per cent of the gross premiums) | $ 54,356 59 | | |
| Insurance expenses incurred during the year | 104,585 73 | | |
| Loss from loading | | | $50,229 14 |
| Interest earned during the year | $20,383 83 | | |
| Investment expenses incurred during the year | 1,105 21 | | |
| Net income from investments | $19,278 62 | | |
| Interest required to maintain reserve | 5,126 00 | | |
| Gain from interest | | $14,152 62 | |
| Expected mortality on net amount at risk | $57,226 13 | | |
| Actual mortality on net amount at risk | 27,607 30 | | |
| Gain from mortality | | 29,618 83 | |
| Total gain during the year from surrendered and lapsed policies | | 4,104 07 | |
| Net to loss account | | | 263 50 |
| INVESTMENT EXHIBIT. | | | |
| Loss from assets not admitted | | | 7,218 53 |
| Gain from coupons to purchase extended insurance | | 47 01 | |
| Total gains and losses in surplus during the year | | $47,922 53 | $57,711 17 |
| Surplus December 31, 1920 | $28,584 80 | | |
| Surplus December 31, 1921 | 18,796 16 | | |
| Decrease in surplus | | 9,788 64 | |
| Total | | $57,711 17 | $57,711 17 |

## THE CLEVELAND LIFE INSURANCE COMPANY.

Located at No. 1221 Guardian Building, Cleveland, Ohio; incorporated September 26, 1906; commenced business in Illinois August 24, 1918.

WM. H. HUNT, President. H. M. MOORE, Secretary.

J. C. UTTERBACK, Champaign, Attorney for service.

### CAPITAL.

| | | |
|---|---|---|
| Capital paid up | $250,000 00 | |
| Amount of ledger assets December 31, of previous year | | $3,270,245 53 |

## INCOME.

| | | | |
|---|---|---|---|
| First year's premiums on original policies, less re-insurance | | $154,561 63 | |
| First year's premiums for total and permanent disability benefits, less re-insurance | | 5,043 67 | |
| First year's premiums for additional accidental death benefits, less re-insurance | | 5,242 31 | |
| Dividends applied to purchase paid-up additions and annuities | | 2,990 07 | |
| Guaranteed investment credits applied to purchase paid-up additions | | 553 31 | |
| New premiums | | $168,390 99 | |
| Renewal premiums less re-insurance | $740,755 67 | | |
| Renewal premiums for total and permanent disability benefits, less re-insurance | 8,607 91 | | |
| Renewal premiums for additional accidental death benefits, less re-insurance | 5,926 73 | | |
| Dividends applied to pay renewal premiums | 11,045 35 | | |
| Guaranteed income coupons, etc., applied to pay renewal premiums | 15,830 91 | | |
| Renewal monthly premiums | 1,007 28 | | |
| Renewal premiums | | 783,173 85 | |
| Premium income | | | $951,564 84 |
| Guaranteed investment credits and coupons left with company to accumulate at interest | | | 7,606 41 |
| Dividends left with company to accumulate at interest | | | 11,535 20 |
| Interest on mortgage loans | | $116,569 61 | |
| Interest on bonds | | 50,757 26 | |
| Interest on premium notes, policy loans or liens | | 20,428 44 | |
| Interest on deposits | | 1,288 04 | |
| Rents—including $565.40 for company's occupancy of its own buildings | | 25,562 55 | |
| Total interest and rents | | | 214,605 90 |
| Profit on sale or maturity of ledger assets | | | 1,036 40 |
| Total income | | | $1,186,348 75 |
| Total | | | $4,456,594 28 |

## DISBURSEMENTS.

| | | |
|---|---|---|
| Death claims and additions | $178,208 30 | |
| Matured endowments | 6,500 00 | |
| Total and permanent disability claims and additionsl accidental death benefits | 5,347 07 | |
| Total death claims and endowments | | $190,055 37 |
| Annuities involving life contingencies | | 540 00 |
| Surrender values paid in cash, or applied in liquidation of loans or notes | | 50,108 61 |
| Guaranteed investment credits applied to purchase paid-up additions | | 553 31 |
| Guaranteed investment credits and coupons left with company to accumulate at interest | | 7,606 41 |
| Dividends applied to pay renewal premiums | | 11,045 35 |
| Guaranteed income coupons, etc., applied to pay renewal premiums | | 15,830 91 |
| Dividends applied to purchase paid-up additions and annuities | | 2,990 07 |
| Dividends left with the company to accumulate at interest | | 11,535 20 |
| (Total paid policyholders | $290,265 23) | |
| Supplementary contracts not involving life contingencies | | 1,467 24 |
| Dividends with interest, held on deposit surrendered during the year | | 902 82 |
| Dividends to stockholders | | 15,000 00 |
| Commissions to agents, first year, $106,984.04; renewal, $31,598.08; industrial renewed, $202.24 | | 138,784 36 |
| Special renewal commissions | | 25,629 56 |
| Compensation of managers and agents not paid by commissions on new business | | 11,258 88 |
| Agency supervision and traveling expenses of supervisors | | 8,452 00 |
| Branch office expenses | | 19,273 41 |
| Medical examiners' fees and inspection of risks | | 16,000 74 |
| Salaries and all other compensation of officers and home office employees | | 61,579 77 |
| Rent | | 6,000 00 |
| Advertising, printing, stationery, postage, telegraph, telephone, express and exchange | | 19,141 97 |
| Legal expense | | 2,931 01 |
| Furniture, fixtures and safes | | 882 74 |
| Repairs and expenses (other than taxes) on real estate | | 16,744 06 |
| Taxes on real estate | | 1,982 95 |
| State taxes on premiums | | 8,909 28 |
| Insurance department licenses and fees | | 939 08 |
| Federal taxes | | 496 50 |
| All other licenses, fees and taxes | | 5,764 98 |
| Other disbursements, viz: Investment expense, $67.75; miscellaneous expense, $3,562.89; periodicals and books, $1,303.93; officers traveling expenses, $2,790.39 | | 7,724 96 |
| Agents' balances charged off | | 368 63 |
| Decrease in book value of ledger assets | | 50,000 00 |
| Total disbursements | | $710,500 17 |
| Balance | | $3,746,094 11 |

## LEDGER ASSETS.

| | |
|---|---|
| Book value of real estate | $ 302,387 56 |
| Mortgage loans on real estate | 1,989,765 03 |
| Loans on company's policies assigned as collateral | 400,238 06 |
| Book value of bonds | 1,016,226 93 |
| Cash in office | 900 00 |
| Deposits in trust companies and banks not on interest | 4,831 18 |
| Deposits in trust companies and banks on interest | 29,453 62 |
| Agents' balances (debit, $3,615.48; credit, $1,323.75) | 2,291 73 |
| Total ledger assets | $3,746,094 11 |

### NON-LEDGER ASSETS.

| | | | |
|---|---|---|---|
| Interest due and accrued on mortgages | | $21,627 27 | |
| Interest accrued on bonds | | 16,236 49 | |
| Interest due on premium notes, loans or liens | | 1,063 54 | |
| Rents due on company's property | | 565 45 | |
| | | | 39,492 75 |
| | New business. | Renewals. | |
| Net uncollected and deferred premiums (paid for basis) | $2,844 86 | $112,665 01 | 115,509 87 |
| Unearned fire insurance premiums | | | 2,500 00 |
| Gross assets | | | $3,903,596 73 |

### DEDUCT ASSETS NOT ADMITTED.

| | |
|---|---|
| Agents' debit balances | 3,615 48 |
| Admitted assets | $3,899,981 25 |

## LIABILITIES.

| | | |
|---|---|---|
| Net present value of outstanding policies computed by the Ohio Insurance Department | $3,392,235 00 | |
| Same for dividend additions | 13,443 00 | |
| Same for annuities | 3,718 00 | |
| Total | $3,409,396 00 | |
| Deduct net value of risks re-insured | 10,443 00 | |
| Net reserve (paid for basis) | | $3,398,953 00 |
| Extra reserve for total and permanent disability benefits and for additional accidental death benefits included in life policies, less re-insurance | | 16,988 00 |
| Present value of supplementary contracts not involving life contingencies | | 9,791 08 |
| Present value of amounts incurred but not yet due for total and permanent disability benefits | | 4,154 00 |
| Death losses in process of adjustment | $1,000 00 | |
| Death losses reported for which no proofs have been received | 6,490 48 | |
| Total policy claims | | 7,490 48 |
| Dividends and credits left with the company to accumulate at interest | | 42,986 94 |
| Gross premiums paid in advance, including surrender values so applied, less discount, if any | | 3,500 00 |
| Unearned interest and rent paid in advance | | 9,500 00 |
| Medical examiners' fees due or accrued | | 814 00 |
| Estimated amount hereafter payable for federal, state and other taxes based upon the business of the year of this statement | | 22,831 00 |
| Dividends or other profits due policyholders | | 471 00 |
| Guaranteed income coupons, etc., due policyholders | | 599 20 |
| Dividends declared on or apportioned to annual dividend policies payable to policyholders during 1922 for period to June 30, 1922 | | 20,094 32 |
| Reserve for guaranteed income | | 8,578 65 |
| Special investment fund | | 37,404 57 |
| Reserve for special contracts | | 336 97 |
| Security fluctuation fund | | 15,488 04 |
| Total | | $3,599,981 25 |
| Capital paid up | | 250,000 00 |
| Unassigned funds (surplus) | | 50,000 00 |
| Total | | $3,899,981 25 |

## EXHIBIT OF POLICIES—ORDINARY.

### ALL BUSINESS PAID FOR.

| | Number. | Amount. |
|---|---|---|
| Policies in force December 31, 1920 | 17,996 | $29,180,486 00 |
| Policies issued, revived and increased during the year | 2,691 | 4,942,515 00 |
| Total | 20,687 | $34,123,001 00 |

## EXHIBIT OF POLICIES—ORDINARY—Concluded.

ALL BUSINESS PAID FOR.

| | Number. | Amount. | Number. | Amount. |
|---|---|---|---|---|
| Deduct policies which have ceased to be in force during the year— | | | | |
| By death | 96 | $ 176,250 00 | | |
| By maturity | 6 | 6,500 00 | | |
| By expiry | 99 | 159,550 00 | | |
| By surrender | 184 | 305,604 00 | | |
| By lapse | 1,532 | 2,738,910 00 | | |
| By decrease | -------- | 50,004 00 | | |
| Total | | | 1,917 | $3,436,818 00 |
| Total policies in force December 31, 1921 | | | 18,770 | $30,686,183 00 |
| Re-insured | | | 254 | $895,349 00 |

## EXHIBIT OF POLICIES—INDUSTRIAL.

ALL BUSINESS PAID FOR.

| | Number. | Amount. | Number. | Amount. |
|---|---|---|---|---|
| Policies in force December 31, 1920 | | | 190 | $27,300 00 |
| Deduct policies which have ceased to be in force during the year— | | | | |
| By death | 5 | $ 850 00 | | |
| By lapse | 6 | 1,200 00 | | |
| Total | | | 11 | 2,050 00 |
| Total policies in force December 31, 1921 | | | 179 | $25,250 00 |

## BUSINESS IN ILLINOIS—ORDINARY.

| | Number. | Amount. |
|---|---|---|
| Policies in force December 31, 1920 | 1,217 | $2,888,649 00 |
| Policies issued during the year | 464 | 798,500 00 |
| Total | 1,681 | $3,687,149 00 |
| Deduct policies ceased to be in force | 325 | 700,648 00 |
| Policies in force December 31, 1921 | 1,356 | $2,986,501 00 |
| Losses and claims unpaid December 31, 1920 | 2 | $ 4,000 00 |
| Losses and claims incurred during the year | 7 | 20,018 86 |
| Total | 9 | $24,018 86 |
| Losses and claims settled during the year | 9 | 24,018 86 |
| Premiums received | | $107,212 78 |

## GAIN AND LOSS EXHIBIT.

INSURANCE EXHIBIT.

| | | Gain in surplus. | Loss in surplus. |
|---|---|---|---|
| Loading on actual premiums of the year (averaging 23.05 per cent of the gross premiums) | $222,807 57 | | |
| Insurance expenses incurred during the year | 287,729 55 | | |
| Loss from loading | | -------------- | $64,921 98 |
| Interest earned during the year | $224,135 26 | | |
| Investment expenses incurred during the year | 40,958 31 | | |
| Net income from investments | $183,176 95 | | |
| Interest required to maintain reserve | 116,286 15 | | |
| Gain from interest | | $ 66,890 80 | |
| Expected mortality on net amount at risk | $279,435 00 | | |
| Actual mortality on net amount at risk | 135,753 78 | | |
| Gain from mortality | | 143,681 22 | |
| Expected disbursements to annuitants | $373 00 | | |
| Net actual annuity claims incurred | 540 00 | | |
| Loss from annuities | | -------------- | 167 00 |
| Total gain during the year from surrendered and lapsed policies | | 14,200 82 | |
| Dividends paid stockholders | | -------------- | 15,000 00 |
| Decrease in surplus on dividend account | | -------------- | 52,229 53 |
| Increase in special funds and special reserves during the year | | -------------- | 20,943 56 |

GAIN AND LOSS EXHIBIT—Concluded.

INVESTMENT EXHIBIT.

| | | Gain in surplus. | Loss in surplus. |
|---|---|---|---|
| Total losses from real estate | | | $50,000 00 |
| Total gains from bonds | | $1,036 40 | |
| Total losses from bonds | | | 3,459 52 |
| Loss from assets not admitted | | | 1,702 24 |
| Net loss on account of total and permanent disability benefits or additional accidental death benefits included in life policies | | | 3,307 96 |
| Total gains and losses in surplus during the year | | $225,818 24 | $211,731 79 |
| Surplus December 31, 1920 | $35,913 55 | | |
| Surplus December 31, 1921 | 50,000 00 | | |
| Increase in surplus | | | 14,086 45 |
| Total | | $225,818 24 | $225,818 24 |

## THE COLUMBIAN NATIONAL LIFE INSURANCE COMPANY.

Located at No. 77 Franklin Street, Boston, Massachusetts; incorporated June 5, 1902; commenced business in Illinois, life, December 7, 1903; casualty, April 18, 1908.

ARTHUR E. CHILDS, President. WILLIAM H. BROWN, Secretary.

GEORGE A. BARR, Director of Trade and Commerce, Attorney for service at Springfield.

WILLIS W. TATE, Chicago, Attorney for service.

CAPITAL.

| | | | |
|---|---|---|---|
| Capital paid up | | $1,000,000 00 | |
| Amount of ledger assets December 31, of previous year | | | $18,751,833 74 |

INCOME.

| | | | |
|---|---|---|---|
| First year's premiums on original policies, less re-insurance | | $724,438 11 | |
| First year's premiums for total and permanent disability benefits, less re-insurance | | 8,753 75 | |
| Surrender values to pay first year's premiums | | 877 54 | |
| Dividends applied to purchase paid-up additions and annuities | | 23 47 | |
| Surrender values applied to purchase paid-up insurance and annuities | | 31,528 13 | |
| Consideration for original annuities involving life contingencies | | 302 75 | |
| New premiums | | $ 765,923 75 | |
| Renewal premiums less re-insurance | $3,483,340 72 | | |
| Renewal premiums for total and permanent disability, benefits, less re-insurance | 33,374 48 | | |
| Dividends applied to pay renewal premiums | 25,494 83 | | |
| Surrender values applied to pay renewal premiums | 9,791 75 | | |
| Renewal premiums for deferred annuities | 1,039 31 | | |
| Renewal premiums | | 3,553,041 09 | |
| Total | | | $4,318,964 84 |
| Consideration for supplementary contracts involving life contingencies | | | 2,984 00 |
| Consideration for supplementary contracts not involving life contingencies | | | 11,295 38 |
| Dividends left with company to accumulate at interest | | | 1,182 88 |
| Interest on mortgage loans | | $171,689 28 | |
| Interest on bonds and dividends on stocks | | 564,784 35 | |
| Interest on premium notes, policy loans or liens | | 192,705 27 | |
| Interest on deposits | | 9,904 98 | |
| General interest including interest on overdue premiums | | 821 60 | |
| Rents—including $25,620.48 for company's occupancy of its own buildings | | 104,261 94 | |
| Total interest and rents | | | 1,044,167 42 |
| From other sources, viz: Profit on mortgages, $10,659.09; advance deposits with applications, $1,028.97 | | | 11,688 06 |
| Agents' balances previously charged off | | | 426 68 |
| Profit on sale or maturity of ledger assets | | | 2,562 68 |
| Increase in book value of ledger assets | | | 26,784 60 |
| Income, life department | | | $5,420,056 54 |
| Income, casualty department | | | 443,429 30 |
| Total income | | | $5,863,485 84 |
| Total | | | $24,615,319 58 |

## DISBURSEMENTS.

| | | |
|---|---|---|
| Death claims and additions | $728,127 90 | |
| Matured endowments and additions | 84,400 00 | |
| Total and permanent disability claims and additional accidental death benefits | 1,784 65 | |
| Total death claims and endowments | | $814,312 55 |
| Annuities involving life contingencies | | 7,617 30 |
| Premium notes and liens voided by lapse, less $3,930.15 restorations | | 48,813 57 |
| Surrender values paid in cash, or applied in liquidation of loans or notes | | 272,061 79 |
| Surrender values applied to pay new and renewal premiums | | 10,669 29 |
| Surrender values applied to purchase paid-up insurance and annuities | | 31,528 13 |
| Dividends paid policyholders in cash, or applied in liquidation of loans or notes | | 11,457 66 |
| Dividends applied to pay renewal premiums | | 24,371 34 |
| Dividends applied to purchase paid-up additions and annuities | | 23 47 |
| Dividends left with the company to accumulate at interest | | 1,182 88 |
| (Total paid policyholders | $1,222,037 98) | |
| Expense of investigation and settlement of policy claims, including legal expenses | | 6,025 33 |
| Supplementary contracts not involving life contingencies | | 17,496 22 |
| Dividends with interest, held on deposit surrendered during the year | | 1,123 49 |
| Dividends to stockholders | | 70,000 00 |
| Commissions to agents, first year, $291,333.22; renewal, $203,735.76; annuities (original), $15.14; (renewal), $17.14 | | 495,101 26 |
| Branch office expenses | | 278,401 15 |
| Medical examiners' fees and inspection of risks | | 44,092 49 |
| Salaires and all other compensation of officers and home office employees | | 181,725 29 |
| Rent | | 55,571 11 |
| Advertising, printing, stationery, postage, telegraph, telephone, express and exchange | | 65,578 34 |
| Legal expense | | 1,202 82 |
| Furniture, fixtures and safes | | 16,024 85 |
| Repairs and expenses (other than taxes) on real estate | | 38,814 36 |
| Taxes on real estate | | 22,314 04 |
| State taxes on premiums | | 63,978 94 |
| Insurance department licenses and fees | | 6,694 12 |
| Federal taxes | | 19,943 58 |
| All other licenses, fees and taxes | | 1,060 37 |
| Other disbursements, viz: Legislative expenses, $221.44; home office expense, $13,566.94; traveling, $6,302.22; contribution to Life Insurance Presidents' Association, $500.02; American Investment Securities Company, $22,000.00; discount on premiums paid in advance, $235.93; advance deposits with applications, $912.29 | | 43,738 84 |
| Decrease in book value of ledger assets | | 10,326 06 |
| Disbursements, life department | | $2,661,250 64 |
| Disbursements, casualty department | | 436,197 40 |
| Total disbursements | | $3,097,448 04 |
| Balance | | $21,517,871 54 |

## LEDGER ASSETS.

| | |
|---|---|
| Book value of real estate | $ 997,297 44 |
| Mortgage loans on real estate | 3,780,830 20 |
| Premiums advanced under Soldiers' and Sailors' Civil Relief Act | 30 64 |
| Loans on company's policies assigned as collateral | 3,616,020 09 |
| Premium notes on policies in force | 386,665 26 |
| Book value of bonds and stocks | 12,328,854 08 |
| Cash in office | 5,886 70 |
| Deposits in trust companies and banks not on interest | 14,056 07 |
| Deposits in trust companies and banks on interest | 135,103 14 |
| Agents' balances (debit, $102,203.93; credit, $9,096.58) net | 93,107 35 |
| Contingent funds subject to draft by cashiers | 17,650 00 |
| Suspense account | 416 71 |
| Casualty department | 141,952 96 |
| Total ledger assets | $21,517,871 54 |

### NON-LEDGER ASSETS.

| | | | |
|---|---|---|---|
| Interest due and accrued on mortgages | | $ 93,459 21 | |
| Interest due and accrued on bonds | | 212,310 14 | |
| Interest due and accrued on premium notes, loans or liens | | 84,401 96 | |
| Interest due and accrued on bank deposits | | 1,751 03 | |
| Rents accrued on company's property | | 7,288 43 | |
| | | | 399,210 77 |
| Market value of real estate over book value | | | 75,713 55 |
| | New business. | Renewals. | |
| Net uncollected and deferred premiums (paid for basis) | $30,834 48 | $432,019 51 | 462,853 99 |
| Gross assets | | | $22,455,649 85 |

### DEDUCT ASSETS NOT ADMITTED.

| | |
|---|---|
| Agents' debit balances | $102,203 93 |
| Contingent funds | 17,650 00 |

## LEDGER ASSETS—Concluded.

DEDUCT ASSETS NOT ADMITTED.

| | | |
|---|---|---|
| Suspense account | $ 416 71 | |
| Premium notes, policy loans and other policy assets in excess of net value and of other policy liabilities on individual policies (loading on notes) | 46,675 83 | |
| Overdue and accrued interest on bonds in default | 29,509 08 | |
| Book value of bonds and stocks over market value | 188,525 79 | |
| Banks in hands of receivers | 7,514 95 | |
| Casualty department | 1,365 78 | |
| Total | | $393,862 07 |
| Admitted assets | | $22,061,787 78 |

## LIABILITIES.

| | | |
|---|---|---|
| Net present value of outstanding policies computed by the Massachusetts Insurance Department | $18,965,812 00 | |
| Same for dividend additions | 207,606 00 | |
| Same for annuities | 75,810 00 | |
| Total | $19,249,228 00 | |
| Deduct net value of risks re-insured | 68,558 00 | |
| Net reserve (paid for basis) | | $19,180,670 00 |
| Reserve for extra mortality due to overweight | | 3,200 00 |
| Extra reserve for total and permanent disability benefits | | 63,089 00 |
| Present value of supplementary contracts not involving life contingencies | | 183,551 00 |
| Present value of amounts incurred but not yet due for total and permanent disability benefits | | 12,649 00 |
| Surrender values claimable on policies cancelled | | 300 00 |
| Death losses in process of adjustment | $ 1,670 00 | |
| Death losses reported for which no proofs have been received | 56,277 35 | |
| Reserve for net death losses incurred but unreported | 16,000 00 | |
| Matured endowments due and unpaid | 142 00 | |
| Death losses and other policy claims resisted | 27,952 00 | |
| Total policy claims | | 102,041 35 |
| Dividends left with the company to accumulate at interest | | 9,966 62 |
| Gross premiums paid in advance, including surrender values so applied, less discount, if any | | 32,954 51 |
| Unearned interest and rent paid in advance | | 76,239 81 |
| Salaries, rents, office expenses, bills and accounts due or accrued | | 32,147 78 |
| Medical examiners' and legal fees due or accrued | | 6,200 00 |
| Estimated amount hereafter payable for federal, state and other taxes based upon the business of the year of this statement | | 99,824 55 |
| Dividends or other profits due policyholders | | 2,634 96 |
| Amounts set apart, apportioned, provisionally ascertained, calculated, declared or held awaiting apportionment upon deferred dividend policies | | 400,000 00 |
| Other liabilities, viz: Advance deposits with applications, $151.95; casualty department, $325,167.44; American Investment Securities Company, $90,000.00 | | 415,319 39 |
| Total | | $20,620,787 97 |
| Capital paid up | | 1,000,000 00 |
| Unassigned funds (surplus) | | 440,999 81 |
| Total | | $22,061,787 78 |

## EXHIBIT OF POLICIES—ORDINARY.

ALL BUSINESS PAID FOR.

| | Number. | Amount. | Number. | Amount. |
|---|---|---|---|---|
| Policies in force December 31, 1920 | | | 49,751 | $139,097,910 80 |
| Policies issued, revived and increased during the year | | | 7,727 | 28,112,377 15 |
| Total | | | 57,478 | $167,210,287 95 |
| Deduct policies which have ceased to be in force during the year— | | | | |
| By death | 250 | $ 629,695 00 | | |
| By maturity | 35 | 85,106 00 | | |
| By expiry | 47 | 175,448 71 | | |
| By surrender | 625 | 1,818,366 15 | | |
| By lapse | 3,802 | 12,474,988 50 | | |
| By decrease | | 1,249,832 50 | | |
| Total | | | 4,759 | 16,433,436 86 |
| Total policies in force December 31, 1921 | | | 52,719 | $150,776,851 09 |
| Re-insured | | | 739 | $7,935,967 00 |

## EXHIBIT OF POLICIES—INDUSTRIAL.

ALL BUSINESS PAID FOR.

| | Number. | Amount. | Number. | Amount. |
|---|---|---|---|---|
| Policies in force December 31, 1920 | | | 1,220 | $206,469 00 |
| Deduct policies which have ceased to be in force during the year— | | | | |
| By death | 46 | $6,658 00 | | |
| By maturity | 2 | 64 00 | | |
| By surrender | 30 | 4,426 00 | | |
| By lapse | 5 | 574 00 | | |
| By decrease | | 438 00 | | |
| Total | | | 83 | 12,160 00 |
| Total policies in force December 31, 1921 | | | 1,137 | $194,309 00 |

## BUSINESS IN ILLINOIS—ORDINARY.

| | Number. | Amount. |
|---|---|---|
| Policies in force December 31, 1920 | 5,239 | $19,693,940 00 |
| Policies issued during the year | 1,261 | 5,776,099 00 |
| Total | 6,500 | $25,470,039 00 |
| Deduct policies ceased to be in force | 665 | 2,942,855 00 |
| Policies in force December 31, 1921 | 5,835 | $22,527,184 00 |
| Losses and claims unpaid December 31, 1920 | 6 | $22,107 00 |
| Losses and claims incurred during the year | 25 | 75,410 98 |
| Total | 31 | $97,517 98 |
| Losses and claims settled during the year | 29 | 87,305 98 |
| Losses and claims unpaid December 31, 1921 | 2 | $10,212 00 |
| Premiums received | | $664,691 51 |

## GAIN AND LOSS EXHIBIT.

INSURANCE EXHIBIT.

| | | Gain in surplus. | Loss in surplus. |
|---|---|---|---|
| Loading on actual premiums of the year (averaging 10.4 per cent of the gross premiums) | $ 453,375 67 | | |
| Insurance expenses incurred during the year | 1,283,194 57 | | |
| Loss from loading | | | $829,818 90 |
| Interest earned during the year | $1,090,509 07 | | |
| Investment expenses incurred during the year | 110,283 67 | | |
| Net income from investments | $980,225 40 | | |
| Interest required to maintain reserve | 659,514 70 | | |
| Gain from interest | | $320,710 70 | |
| Expected mortality on net amount at risk | $1,440,004 00 | | |
| Actual mortality on net amount at risk | 510,917 44 | | |
| Gain from mortality | | 929,086 56 | |
| Expected disbursements to annuitants | $3,716 30 | | |
| Net actual annuity claims incurred | 5,623 30 | | |
| Loss from annuities | | | 1,907 00 |
| Total gain during the year from surrendered and lapsed policies | | 235,162 92 | |
| Dividends paid stockholders | | | 70,000 00 |
| Decrease in surplus on dividend account | | | 237,112 77 |
| Increase in special funds and special reserves during the year | | | 69,569 00 |
| Net to profit account | | 426 68 | |
| **INVESTMENT EXHIBIT.** | | | |
| Total losses from real estate | | | 3,188 00 |
| Total gains from stocks and bonds | | 16,217 67 | |
| Profit on mortgages | | 10,659 09 | |
| Loss from assets not admitted | | | 41,927 21 |
| Net gain on account of total and permanent disability benefits included in life policies | | 22,069 58 | |
| Loss from premium notes, $48,813.57; American Investment Securities Company, $22,000.00 | | | 70,813 57 |
| Gain, casualty department | | 17,177 53 | |
| Balance unaccounted for | | | 197 14 |
| Total gains and losses in surplus during the year | | 1,551,510 73 | $1,324,533 59 |
| Surplus December 31, 1920 | $214,022 67 | | |
| Surplus December 31, 1921 | 440,999 81 | | |
| Increase in surplus | | | 226,977 14 |
| Total | | $1,551,510 73 | $1,551,510 73 |

## COLUMBUS MUTUAL LIFE INSURANCE COMPANY.

Located at No. 580 East Broad Street, Columbus, Ohio; incorporated January 2, 1907; commenced business in Illinois January 9, 1920.

C. W. BRANDON, President. D. E. BALL, Secretary.

GEORGE A. BARR, Director of Trade and Commerce, Attorney for service at Springfield.

### CAPITAL.

| | | | |
|---|---|---|---|
| Capital paid up | | $250,000 00 | |
| Amount of ledger assets December 31, of previous year | | $2,348,402 89 | |
| Increase of paid-up capital during year | | 50,000 00 | |
| Extended at | | | $2,398,402 89 |

### INCOME.

| | | | |
|---|---|---|---|
| First year's premiums on original policies, less re-insurance | | $365,391 91 | |
| First year's premiums for total and permanent disability benefits, less re-insurance | | 8,540 81 | |
| First year's premiums for additional accidental death benefits, less re-insurance | | 11,683 65 | |
| Dividends applied to purchase paid-up additions and annuities | | 10,809 77 | |
| New premiums | | $396,426 14 | |
| Renewal premiums less re-insurance | $760,129 28 | | |
| Renewal premiums for total and permanent disability benefits, less re-insurance | 22,461 59 | | |
| Renewal premiums for additional accidental death benefits, less re-insurance | 10,990 59 | | |
| Dividends applied to pay renewal premiums | 100,861 44 | | |
| Surrender values applied to pay renewal premiums | 9 42 | | |
| Renewal premiums | | 894,452 32 | |
| Premium income | | | $1,290,878 46 |
| Consideration for supplementary contracts not involving life contingencies | | | 1,764 00 |
| Dividends left with company to accumulate at interest | | | 44,957 88 |
| Interest on mortgage loans | | $112,685 66 | |
| Interest on bonds | | 20,073 19 | |
| Interest on premium notes, policy loans or liens | | 10,904 92 | |
| Interest on deposits | | 772 69 | |
| Interest on other debts due the company | | 1,066 87 | |
| Rents—including $1,400.00 for company's occupancy of its own buildings | | 2,800 00 | |
| Total interest and rents | | | 148,303 33 |
| From other sources, viz: Deposits on abstracts, $100.00; premium on stock, $50,000.00 | | | 50,100 00 |
| Agents' balances previously charged off | | | 226 04 |
| Increase in book value of ledger assets | | | 2,500 00 |
| Income, life department | | | $1,538,729 71 |
| Income, casualty department | | | 66,575 20 |
| Total income | | | $1,605,304 91 |
| Total | | | $4,003,707 80 |

### DISBURSEMENTS.

| | | | |
|---|---|---|---|
| Death claims and additions | | $98,869 73 | |
| Matured endowments and additions | | 5,089 29 | |
| Total and permanent disability claims and additional accidental death benefits | | 12,468 27 | |
| Total death claims and endowments | | | $116,427 29 |
| Annuities involving life contingencies | | | 976 34 |
| Premium notes and liens voided by lapse | | | 15,432 61 |
| Surrender values paid in cash, or applied in liquidation of loans or notes | | | 31,278 83 |
| Surrender values applied to pay new and renewal premiums | | | 9 42 |
| Dividends paid policyholders in cash, or applied in liquidation of loans or notes | | | 1,163 38 |
| Dividends applied to pay renewal premiums | | | 100,861 44 |
| Dividends applied to purchase paid-up additions and annuities | | | 10,809 77 |
| Dividends left with the company to accumulate at interest | | | 44,957 88 |
| (Total paid policyholders | | $321,916 96) | |
| Expense of investigation and settlement of policy claims | | | 3 00 |
| Supplementary contracts not involving life contingencies | | | 1,304 92 |
| Dividends with interest, held on deposit surrendered during the year | | | 10,603 58 |
| Dividends to stockholders | | | 20,702 80 |
| Commissions to agents, first year, $282,177.27; renewal, $39,563.08 | | | 321,740 35 |
| Agency supervision and traveling expenses of supervisors | | | 2,096 83 |
| Medical examiners' fees and inspection of risks | | | 29,742 30 |
| Salaries and all other compensation of officers and home office employees | | | 82,834 66 |
| Rent | | | 1,400 00 |
| Advertising, printing, stationery, postage, telegraph, telephone and express | | | 20,398 23 |

DISBURSEMENTS—Concluded.

| | |
|---|---|
| Furniture, fixtures and safes | $2,582 04 |
| Repairs and expenses (other than taxes) on real estate | 1,519 77 |
| Taxes on real estate | 1,003 02 |
| State taxes on premiums | 704 09 |
| Insurance department licenses and fees | 2,423 63 |
| Federal taxes | 4,417 05 |
| All other licenses, fees and taxes | 8,174 88 |
| Other disbursements, viz: Investment expense, $479.85; miscellaneous expense, $317.04; advance premium payment, $69.34; premium deposit fund, $186.62; fire insurance premium, $152.80; heat, light and water, $1,109.97; dining room, $924.20; returned checks, $333.05; convention, $3,430.00 | 7,002 87 |
| Agents' balances charged off | 16 87 |
| Disbursements, life department | $840,587 85 |
| Disbursements, casualty department | 61,310 84 |
| Total disbursements | $901,898 69 |
| Balance | $3,101,809 11 |

LEDGER ASSETS.

| | |
|---|---|
| Book value of real estate | $ 35,000 00 |
| Mortgage loans on real estate | 2,211,606 50 |
| Loans on company's policies assigned as collateral | 170,847 54 |
| Premium notes on policies in force | 104,298 14 |
| Book value of bonds | 545,013 50 |
| Deposits in trust companies and banks on interest | 12,438 61 |
| Agents' balances (debit, $27,885.59; credit, $5,280.77 | 22,604 82 |
| Total ledger assets | $3,101,809 11 |

NON-LEDGER ASSETS.

| | | | |
|---|---|---|---|
| Interest due and accrued on mortgages | | $47,334 61 | |
| Interest due and accrued on bonds | | 3,109 30 | |
| Interest due and accrued on loans or liens | | 4,557 62 | |
| Interest due and accrued on other assets | | 30 92 | |
| | | | 55,032 45 |
| Market value of bonds over book value | | | 29,924 00 |
| | New business. | Renewals. | |
| Net uncollected and deferred premiums (paid for basis) | $4,921 84 | $59,230 44 | 64,152 28 |
| Casualty department, due premiums | | | 83 25 |
| Gross assets | | | $3,251,001 09 |

DEDUCT ASSETS NOT ADMITTED.

| | | |
|---|---|---|
| Agents' debit balances | $27,885 59 | |
| Premium notes, policy loans and other policy assets in excess of net value and of other policy liabilities on individual policies | 2,176 03 | |
| Total | | 30,061 62 |
| Admitted assets | | $3,220,939 47 |

LIABILITIES.

| | | |
|---|---|---|
| Net present value of outstanding policies computed by the Ohio Insurance Department | $2,230,406 00 | |
| Same for dividend additions | 50,083 00 | |
| Same for annuities | 6,329 00 | |
| Total | $2,286,818 00 | |
| Deduct net value of risks re-insured | 11,800 00 | |
| Net reserve (paid for basis) | | $2,275,018 00 |
| Extra reserve for total and permanent disability benefits and for additional accidental death benefits included in life policies | | 26,838 32 |
| Present value of supplementary contracts not involving life contingencies | | 8,642 64 |
| Present value of amounts incurred but not yet due for total and permanent disability benefits | | 13,327 18 |
| Death losses due and unpaid | $ 340 00 | |
| Death losses reported for which no proofs have been received | 5,000 00 | |
| Reserve for net death losses incurred but unreported | 1,000 00 | |
| Death losses and other policy claims resisted | 1,000 00 | |
| Additional accidental death benefits | 3,000 00 | |
| Total policy claims | | 10,340 00 |
| Dividends left with the company to accumulate at interest | | 158,540 07 |
| Gross premiums paid in advance, including surrender values so applied, less discount, if any | | 6,649 00 |
| Unearned interest paid in advance | | 1,817 99 |
| Commissions due agents on premium notes, when paid | | 5,736 40 |
| Salaries, rents, office expenses, bills and accounts due or accrued | | 1,474 18 |
| Medical examiners' fees due or accrued | | 2,764 00 |

## LIABILITIES—Concluded.

| | |
|---|---|
| Estimated amount hereafter payable for federal, state and other taxes based upon the business of the year of this statement | $ 8,000 00 |
| Dividends or other profits due policyholders | 6,148 24 |
| Dividends declared on or apportioned to annual dividend policies payable to policyholders during 1922 for period to January 31, 1922 | 12,196 58 |
| Amounts set apart, apportioned, provisionally ascertained, calculated declared or held awaiting apportionment upon deferred dividend policies | 350 71 |
| Premium deposit fund | 9,139 93 |
| War revenue tax | 1,485 60 |
| Deposits on abstracts | 225 00 |
| Casualty department | 5,134 19 |
| Total | $2,553,828 03 |
| Capital paid up | 250,000 00 |
| Unassigned funds (surplus) | 417,111 44 |
| Total | $3,220,939 47 |

## EXHIBIT OF POLICIES—ORDINARY.

ALL BUSINESS PAID FOR.

| | Number. | Amount. | Number. | Amount. |
|---|---|---|---|---|
| Policies in force December 31, 1920 | | | 15,444 | $28,062,776 00 |
| Policies issued, revived and increased during the year | | | 5,221 | 11,364,362 00 |
| Total | | | 20,665 | $39,427,138 00 |
| Deduct policies which have ceased to be in force during the year— | | | | |
| By death | 58 | $ 94,137 00 | | |
| By maturity | 5 | 5,000 00 | | |
| By disability | 2 | 2,000 00 | | |
| By expiry | 21 | 31,343 00 | | |
| By surrender | 135 | 211,898 00 | | |
| By lapse | 1,802 | 3,804,647 00 | | |
| By decrease | | 172,444 00 | | |
| Total | | | 2,023 | 4,321,469 00 |
| Total policies in force December 31, 1921 | | | 18,642 | $35,105,669 00 |
| Re-insured | | | 204 | $1,704,101 00 |

## BUSINESS IN ILLINOIS—ORDINARY.

| | Number. | Amount. |
|---|---|---|
| Policies in force December 31, 1920 | 18 | $ 38,000 00 |
| Policies issued during the year | 204 | 517,000 00 |
| Total | 222 | $555,000 00 |
| Deduct policies ceased to be in force | 5 | 6,000 00 |
| Policies in force December 31, 1921 | 217 | $549,000 00 |
| Premiums received | | $15,024 53 |

## GAIN AND LOSS EXHIBIT.

INSURANCE EXHIBIT.

| | | Gain in surplus. | Loss in surplus. |
|---|---|---|---|
| Loading on actual premiums of the year (averaging 33.9 per cent of the gross premiums) | $430,119 72 | | |
| Insurance expenses incurred during the year | 474,352 19 | | |
| Loss from loading | | | $ 44,232 47 |
| Interest earned during the year | $164,597 96 | | |
| Investment expenses incurred during the year | 4,265 41 | | |
| Net income from investments | $160,332 55 | | |
| Interest required to maintain reserve | 81,619 60 | | |
| Gain from interest | | $ 78,712 95 | |
| Expected mortality on net amount at risk | $300,376 94 | | |
| Actual mortality on net amount at risk | 81,719 87 | | |
| Gain from mortality | | 218,657 07 | |
| Expected disbursements to annuitants | $735 96 | | |
| Net actual annuity claims incurred | 976 34 | | |
| Loss from annuities | | | 240 38 |
| Total gain during the year from surrendered and lapsed policies | | 2,686 56 | |
| Dividends paid stockholders | | | 20,702 80 |
| Decrease in surplus on dividend account | | | 162,304 38 |
| Net to gain account | | 209 17 | |

GAIN AND LOSS EXHIBIT—Concluded.

INVESTMENT EXHIBIT.

| | | Gain in surplus. | Loss in surplus. |
|---|---|---|---|
| Total gains from real estate | | $ 2,500 00 | |
| Total gains from bonds | | 45,171 50 | |
| Loss from assets not admitted | | | $15,807 72 |
| Net gain on account of total and permanent disability benefits or additional accidental death benefits included in life policies | | 2,065 38 | |
| Gain: Premium on stock, $50,000.00; casualty department, $5,640.54 | | 55,640 54 | |
| Balance unaccounted for | | | 2,212 20 |
| Total gains and losses in surplus during the year | | $405,643 17 | $245,499 95 |
| Surplus December 31, 1920 | $256,968 22 | | |
| Surplus December 31, 1921 | 417,111 44 | | |
| Increase in surplus | | | 160,143 22 |
| Total | | $405,643 17 | $405,643 17 |

## CONNECTICUT GENERAL LIFE INSURANCE COMPANY.

Located at No. 64 Pearl Street, Hartford, Connecticut; incorporated June, 1865; commenced business in Illinois, life, March 9, 1901; casualty, June 3, 1912.

ROBERT W. HUNTINGTON, President. RICHARD H. COLE, Secretary.

GEORGE A. BARR, Director of Trade and Commerce, Attorney for service at Springfield.

HIRAM C. CASTOR, Chicago, Attorney for service.

CAPITAL.

| | | | |
|---|---|---|---|
| Capital paid up | | $800,000 00 | |
| Amount of ledger assets December 31, of previous year | | | $30,127,914 75 |

INCOME.

| | | | |
|---|---|---|---|
| First year's premiums on original policies, less re-insurance | | $1,844,890 62 | |
| First year's premiums for total and permanent disability benefits, less re-insurance | | 18,214 15 | |
| Surrender values to pay first year's premiums | | 18,186 60 | |
| Dividends applied to purchase paid-up additions and annuities | | 53,522 91 | |
| Surrender values applied to purchase paid-up insurance and annuities | | 8,552 40 | |
| Consideration for original annuities involving life contingencies | | 30,565 10 | |
| New premiums | | $1,973,931 78 | |
| Renewal premiums less re-insurance | $7,032,269 09 | | |
| Renewal premiums for total and permanent disability benefits, less re-insurance | 63,924 02 | | |
| Dividends applied to pay renewal premiums | 375,858 57 | | |
| Dividends applied to shorten the endowment or premium-paying period | 5,803 75 | | |
| Surrender values applied to pay renewal premiums | 2,548 97 | | |
| Renewal premiums for deferred annuities | 16,757 22 | | |
| Renewal premiums | | 7,497,161 62 | |
| Total | | | $9,471,093 40 |
| Consideration for supplementary contracts involving life contingencies | | | 20,207 00 |
| Consideration for supplementary contracts not involving life contingencies | | | 324,775 44 |
| Dividends left with company to accumulate at interest | | | 40,769 26 |
| Interest on mortgage loans | | $827,141 68 | |
| Interest on bonds and dividends on stocks | | 539,128 97 | |
| Interest on premium notes, policy loans or liens | | 194,295 56 | |
| Interest on deposits | | 17,880 64 | |
| Interest on other debts due the company | | 15,818 60 | |
| Discount on claims paid in advance | | 129 14 | |
| Rents | | 22,056 50 | |
| Total interest and rents | | | 1,616,451 09 |
| Profit on sale or maturity of ledger assets | | | 5,671 08 |
| Increase in book value of ledger assets | | | 36,563 05 |
| Income—life department | | | $11,515,530 32 |
| Income—casualty department | | | 994,623 47 |
| Total income | | | $12,510,153 79 |
| Total | | | $42,638,068 54 |

## DISBURSEMENTS.

| | | |
|---|---|---|
| Death claims and additions | $2,341,224 51 | |
| Matured endowments and additions | 551,042 00 | |
| Total and permanent disability claims | 33,176 01 | |
| Total death claims and endowments | | $2,925,442 52 |
| Annuities involving life contingencies | | 75,898 95 |
| Surrender values paid in cash, or applied in liquidation of loans or notes | | 527,805 01 |
| Surrender values applied to pay new and renewal premiums | | 20,735 57 |
| Surrender values applied to purchase paid-up insurance and annuities | | 8,552 40 |
| Dividends paid policyholders in cash, or applied in liquidation of loans or notes | | 21,599 57 |
| Dividends applied to pay renewal premiums | | 375,858 57 |
| Dividends applied to shorten the endowment or premium paying period | | 5,803 75 |
| Dividends applied to purchase paid-up additions and annuities | | 53,522 91 |
| Dividends left with the company to accumulate at interest | | 40,769 26 |
| (Total paid policyholders | $4,055,988 51) | |
| Expense of investigation and settlement of policy claims, including legal expenses | | 1,741 28 |
| Supplementary contracts not involving life contingencies | | 160,195 42 |
| Dividends with interest, held on deposit surrendered during the year | | 29,401 38 |
| Dividends to stockholders | | 96,000 00 |
| Commissions to agents, first year, $772,545.22; renewal, $457,667.22; annuities (original), $6,437.72; (renewal), $1,222.09 | | 1,237,872 25 |
| Commuted renewal commissions | | 1,760 00 |
| Agency supervision and traveling expenses of supervisors | | 11,173 24 |
| Branch office expenses | | 229,334 67 |
| Medical examiners' fees and inspection of risks | | 88,138 34 |
| Salaries and all other compensation of officers and home office employees | | 382,875 48 |
| Rent | | 1,826 25 |
| Advertising, printing, stationery, postage, telegraph, telephone, express and exchange | | 75,430 05 |
| Legal expense | | 3,435 86 |
| Furniture, fixtures and safes | | 14,782 44 |
| Repairs, and expenses (other than taxes) on real estate | | 33,155 65 |
| Taxes on real estate | | 11,822 36 |
| State taxes on premiums | | 93,140 23 |
| Insurance department licenses and fees | | 7,141 59 |
| Federal taxes | | 64,165 79 |
| All other licenses, fees and taxes | | 60,476 23 |
| Other disbursements, viz: Association Life Insurance Presidents, $1,003.65; legislative expense, $442.88; premiums group insurance home office employees, $1,704.00; traveling expense officers and employees, $11,646.32; miscellaneous, $15,448.62; impairment cards, $7,736.73; photographic and machine supplies, $4,592.72; Liberty bond payments, $1,038.00; reserve refunded re-insurance company, $5,054.70; plans for new building, $33,035.84 | | 81,703 46 |
| Loss on sale or maturity of ledger assets | | 1,974 43 |
| Decrease in book value of ledger assets | | 4,698 31 |
| Disbursements—life department | | $6,748,233 22 |
| Disbursements—casualty department | | 874,655 43 |
| Total disbursements | | $7,622,888 65 |
| Balance | | $35,015,179 89 |

## LEDGER ASSETS.

| | |
|---|---|
| Book value of real estate | $ 610,225 46 |
| Mortgage loans on real estate | 18,697,678 60 |
| Loans on company's policies assigned as collateral | 4,169,687 73 |
| Premium notes on policies in force | 218,830 03 |
| Book value of bonds and stocks | 10,350,619 33 |
| Cash in office | 4,545 88 |
| Deposits in trust companies and banks on interest | 774,002 58 |
| Agents' balances (debit, $19,374.41; credit, $558.58) net | 18,815 83 |
| Re-insurance due from other companies, casualty department, $7,365.09; premiums in course of collection, casualty department, $163,409.36 | 170,774 45 |
| Total ledger assets | $35,015,179 89 |

### NON-LEDGER ASSETS.

| | | | |
|---|---|---|---|
| Interest due and accrued on mortgages | | $652,632 42 | |
| Interest due and accrued on bonds | | 168,704 36 | |
| Interest due and accrued on premium notes, loans or liens | | 46,766 84 | |
| Rents due on company's property | | 25 00 | |
| | | | 868,128 62 |
| Market value of bonds in default or not amply secured and stocks over book value | | | 65,107 67 |
| | New business. | Renewals. | |
| Net uncollected and deferred premiums (paid for basis) | $260,563 59 | $1,306,425 88 | 1,566,989 47 |
| Gross assets | | | $37,515,405 65 |

## LEDGER ASSETS—Concluded.

DEDUCT ASSETS NOT ADMITTED.

| | | |
|---|---|---|
| Agents' debit balances | $19,374 41 | |
| Overdue and accrued interest on bonds in default | 14,516 67 | |
| Total | | $33,891 08 |
| Admitted assets | | $37,481,514 57 |

## LIABILITIES.

| | | |
|---|---|---|
| Net present value of outstanding policies | $31,040,337 00 | |
| Same for dividend additions | 486,915 00 | |
| Same for annuities | 750,770 00 | |
| Total | $32,278,022 00 | |
| Deduct net value of risks re-insured | 510,883 00 | |
| Net reserve (paid for basis) | | $31,767,139 00 |
| Extra reserve for total and permanent disability benefits and for additional accidental death benefits included in life policies, less re-insurance | | 241,337 00 |
| Present value of supplementary contracts not involving life contingencies | | 761,984 00 |
| Present value of amounts incurred but not yet due for total and permanent disability benefits | | 14,365 48 |
| Surrender values claimable on policies cancelled | | 2,460 99 |
| Death losses reported for which no proofs have been received | $105,194 00 | |
| Reserve for net death losses incurred but unreported | 31,620 00 | |
| Matured endowments due and unpaid | 1,082 00 | |
| Death losses and other policy claims resisted | 27,500 00 | |
| Total and permanent disability benefits and additional accidental death benefits | 9,883 55 | |
| Total policy claims | | 175,279 55 |
| Dividends left with the company to accumulate at interest | | 234,084 24 |
| Gross premiums paid in advance, including surrender values so applied, less discount, if any | | 67,559 98 |
| Unearned interest and rent paid in advance | | 56,444 90 |
| Salaries, rents, office expenses, bills, and accounts due or accrued | | 2,500 00 |
| Medical examiners, inspection and legal fees due or accrued | | 7,669 14 |
| Estimated amount hereafter payable for federal, state and other taxes based upon the business of the year of this statement | | 200,587 46 |
| Unpaid dividends to stockholders, declared and payable January 2, 1922 | | 24,000 00 |
| Dividends or other profits due policyholders | | 135,394 92 |
| Dividends declared on or apportioned to annual dividend policies payable to policyholders during 1922 for period to May 31, 1922 | | 203,132 46 |
| Surrender values claimable in excess of reserves | | 3,771 40 |
| War service extra premiums re-insurance | | 46 54 |
| Reserves on 3 per cent in excess of 3½ per cent reserves | | 45,715 31 |
| Contingency reserve | | 100,000 00 |
| Liabilities—casualty department | | 751,009 45 |
| Total | | $34,794,481 82 |
| Capital paid up | | 800,000 00 |
| Unassigned funds (surplus) | | 1,887,032 75 |
| Total | | $37,481,514 57 |

## EXHIBIT OF POLICIES—ORDINARY.

(Including group insurance.)

ALL BUSINESS PAID FOR.

| | Number. | Amount. | Number. | Amount. |
|---|---|---|---|---|
| Policies in force December 31, 1920 | | | 89,428 | $362,387,933 11 |
| Policies issued, revived, and increased during the year | | | 17,493 | 117,922,256 08 |
| Total | | | 106,921 | $480,310,189 19 |
| Deduct policies which have ceased to be in force during the year— | | | | |
| By death | 539 | $ 2,533,002 28 | | |
| By maturity | 374 | 529,357 00 | | |
| By disability | -------- | 33,650 00 | | |
| By expiry | 561 | 1,359,260 00 | | |
| By surrender | 1,628 | 6,293,495 00 | | |
| By lapse | 4,545 | 26,945,908 00 | | |
| By decrease | -------- | 5,062,561 02 | | |
| Withdrawal | -------- | 27,304,822 00 | | |
| Total | | | 7,647 | 70,062,055 30 |
| Total policies in force December 31, 1921 | | | 99,274 | $410,248,133 89 |
| Re-insured | | | 1,346 | 18,188,329 00 |

## EXHIBIT OF POLICIES—GROUP INSURANCE.

(Included in ordinary exhibit above.)

ALL BUSINESS PAID FOR.

| | Number. | Amount. | Number. | Amount. |
|---|---|---|---|---|
| Policies in force December 31, 1920 | | | 268 | $72,776,847 00 |
| Policies issued, revived and increased during the year | | | 42 | 32,982,477 00 |
| Total | | | 310 | $105,759,324 00 |
| Deduct policies which have ceased to be in force during the year— | | | | |
| By death | -------- | $ 471,581 00 | | |
| By disability | -------- | 33,650 00 | | |
| By lapse | 31 | 4,842,725 00 | | |
| By withdrawal | -------- | 27,304,822 00 | | |
| Total | | | 31 | 32,652,778 00 |
| Total policies in force December 31, 1921 | | | 279 | $73,106,546 00 |

## BUSINESS IN ILLINOIS—ORDINARY.

(Excluding group insurance.)

| | Number. | Amount. |
|---|---|---|
| Policies in force December 31, 1920 | 3,256 | $10,292,040 00 |
| Policies issued during the year | 482 | 1,823,531 00 |
| Total | 3,738 | $12,115,571 00 |
| Deduct policies ceased to be in force | 233 | 1,025,923 00 |
| Policies in force December 31, 1921 | 3,505 | $11,089,648 00 |
| Losses and claims unpaid December 31, 1920 | 4 | $18,500 00 |
| Losses and claims incurred during the year | 15 | 24,019 15 |
| Total | 19 | $42,519 15 |
| Losses and claims settled during the year | 17 | 34,848 15 |
| Losses and claims unpaid December 31, 1921 | 2 | $7,671 00 |
| Premiums received | | $453,441 32 |

## BUSINESS IN ILLINOIS—GROUP INSURANCE.

| | Number. | Amount. |
|---|---|---|
| Policies in force December 31, 1920 | 2 | $562,100 00 |
| Policies issued during the year | 3 | 475,900 00 |
| Total | 5 | $1,038,000 00 |
| Deduct policies ceased to be in force | -------- | 275,000 00 |
| Policies in force December 31, 1921 | 5 | $763,000 00 |
| Losses and claims incurred during the year | 2 | $3,200 00 |
| Losses and claims settled during the year | 2 | 3,200 00 |
| Premiums received | | $5,475 50 |

## GAIN AND LOSS EXHIBIT.

INSURANCE EXHIBIT.

| | | Gain in surplus. | Loss in surplus. |
|---|---|---|---|
| Loading on actual premiums of the year (averaging 12.3 per cent of the gross premiums) | $1,176,780 10 | | |
| Insurance expenses incurred during the year | 2,275,522 68 | | |
| Loss from loading | | -------------- | $1,098,742 58 |
| Interest earned during the year | $1,862,423 43 | | |
| Investment expenses incurred during the year | 162,480 86 | | |
| Net income from investments | $1,699,942 57 | | |
| Interest required to maintain reserve | 1,111,596 00 | | |
| Gain from interest | | $ 588,346 57 | |
| Expected mortality on net amount at risk | $3,670,752 00 | | |
| Actual mortality on net amount at risk | 2,104,406 46 | | |
| Gain from mortality | | 1,566,345 54 | |
| Expected disbursements to annuitants | $45,931 98 | | |
| Net actual annuity claims incurred | 30,678 17 | | |
| Gain from annuities | | 15,253 81 | |
| Total gain during the year from surrendered and lapsed policies | | 186,054 93 | |
| Dividends paid stockholders | | -------------- | 80,000 00 |
| Decrease in surplus on dividend account | | -------------- | 541,977 82 |
| Increase in special funds, and special reserves during the year | | -------------- | 8,345 26 |

## GAIN AND LOSS EXHIBIT—Concluded.

### INVESTMENT EXHIBIT.

| | | Gain in surplus. | Loss in surplus. |
|---|---|---|---|
| Total gains from stocks and bonds | | $5,671 08 | |
| Total losses from stocks and bonds | | | $62,540 01 |
| Loss from assets not admitted | | | 6,402 50 |
| Net gain on account of total and permanent disability benefits included in life policies | | 17,753 13 | |
| Gain from casualty department | | 1,859 77 | |
| Total gains and losses in surplus during the year | | $2,381,284 83 | $1,798,008 17 |
| Surplus December 31, 1920 | $1,303,756 09 | | |
| Surplus December 31, 1921 | 1,887,032 75 | | |
| Increase in surplus | | | 583,276 66 |
| Total | | $2,381,284 83 | $2,381,284 83 |

## CONNECTICUT MUTUAL LIFE INSURANCE COMPANY.

Located at No. 36 Pearl Street, Hartford, Connecticut; incorporated June 15, 1846; commenced business in Illinois June 6, 1855.

HENRY S. ROBINSON, President. JACOB H. GREENE, Secretary.

SAMUEL T. CHASE, Chicago, Attorney for service

| | | | |
|---|---|---|---|
| Amount of ledger assets December 31, of previous year | | | $87,364,589 27 |

### INCOME.

| | | | |
|---|---|---|---|
| First year's premiums on original policies, less re-insurance | | $1,820,897 01 | |
| First year's premiums for total and permanent disability benefits | | 37,695 81 | |
| Surrender values to pay first year's premiums | | 3,420 90 | |
| Dividends applied to purchase paid-up additions and annuities | | 26,395 22 | |
| Consideration for original annuities involving life contingencies | | 22,477 08 | |
| New premiums | | $1,910,886 02 | |
| Renewal premiums less re-insurance | $9,476,448 43 | | |
| Renewal premiums for total and permanent disability benefits | 60,242 81 | | |
| Dividends applied to pay renewal premiums | 1,112,772 79 | | |
| Renewal premiums for deferred annuities | 19,153 34 | | |
| Renewal premiums | | 10,668,617 37 | |
| Premium income | | $12,579,503 39 | |
| Premiums advanced during year under Soldiers' and Sailors' Civil Relief Act | | 20 39 | |
| Total | | | $12,579,523 78 |
| Consideration for supplementary contracts involving life contingencies | | | 42,396 18 |
| Consideration for supplementary contracts not involving life contingencies | | | 263,259 49 |
| Dividends left with company to accumulate at interest | | | 480,130 69 |
| Interest on mortgage loans | | $2,005,275 70 | |
| Interest on bonds and dividends on stocks | | 1,682,494 00 | |
| Interest on premium notes, policy loans or liens | | 596,512 34 | |
| Interest on deposits | | 31,542 43 | |
| Interest on other debts due the company | | 12,550 12 | |
| Discount on claims paid in advance | | 1,053 52 | |
| Rents—including $50,000.00 for company's occupancy of its own buildings | | 213,506 27 | |
| Total interest and rents | | | 4,542,934 38 |
| Unapplied payments on land contracts (suspense account) | | | 2,229 90 |
| Profit on sale or maturity of ledger assets | | | 3,675 70 |
| Increase in book value of ledger assets | | | 32,707 25 |
| Total income | | | $17,946,857 37 |
| Total | | | $105,311,446 64 |

### DISBURSEMENTS.

| | | | |
|---|---|---|---|
| Death claims and additions | | $5,071,418 91 | |
| Matured endowments | | 529,213 38 | |
| Total and permanent disability claims | | 4,633 56 | |
| Total death claims and endowments | | | $5,605,265 85 |
| Annuities involving life contingencies | | | 75,454 68 |
| Surrender values paid in cash, or applied in liquidation of loans or notes | | | 1,530,714 27 |
| Surrender values applied to pay new and renewal premiums | | | 3,420 90 |
| Dividends paid policyholders in cash, or applied in liquidation of loans or notes | | | 261,441 41 |
| Dividends applied to pay renewal premiums | | | 1,112,772 79 |

## DISBURSEMENTS—Concluded.

| | | |
|---|---|---|
| Dividends applied to purchase paid-up additions and annuities | | $ 26,395 22 |
| Dividends left with the company to accumulate at interest | | 480,130 69 |
| (Total paid policyholders | $9,095,595 81) | |
| Expense of investigation and settlement of policy claims, including legal expenses | | 7,041 06 |
| Supplementary contracts not involving life contingencies | | 102,305 72 |
| Dividends with interest, held on deposit surrendered during the year | | 433,891 69 |
| Commissions to agents, first year, $763,003.35; renewal premiums, $699,904.06; annuities (original), $1,585.40; (renewal), $1,117.51 | | 1,465,610 32 |
| Compensation of managers and agents not paid by commissions on new business | | 29,422 60 |
| Agency supervision and traveling expenses of supervisors | | 19,031 45 |
| Branch office expenses | | 150,684 72 |
| Medical examiners' fees and inspection of risks | | 124,895 00 |
| Salaries and all other compensation of officers and home office employees | | 403,447 31 |
| Rent | | 115,767 69 |
| Advertising, printing, stationery, postage, telegraph, telephone, express and exchange | | 127,384 86 |
| Legal expense | | 8,190 01 |
| Furniture, fixtures and safes | | 29,595 67 |
| Repairs and expenses (other than taxes) on real estate | | 91,502 34 |
| Taxes on real estate | | 68,071 52 |
| State taxes on premiums | | 169,717 49 |
| Insurance department licenses and fees | | 9,348 65 |
| Federal taxes | | 49,968 50 |
| All other licenses, fees and taxes | | 162,749 16 |
| Other disbursements, viz: Traveling expenses, $9,582.34; suspense account of December 31, 1920, $3,469.90; agents' meetings and conventions, $42,578.37; recording and notary fees, $118.29; farm loan inspection, $9,488.42; safe rent, $10.00; lock and vault work, $97.49; premiums on fidelity bonds, $1,969.10; insurance institute, $4.00; investment bureau, $4,453.85; Association of Life Insurance Presidents, $1,511.94 | | 73,283 70 |
| Loss on sale or maturity of ledger assets | | 23,322 27 |
| Decrease in book value of ledger assets | | 16,196 71 |
| Total disbursements | | $12,777,024 25 |
| Balance | | $92,534,422 39 |

## LEDGER ASSETS.

| | |
|---|---|
| Book value of real estate | $ 1,891,992 04 |
| Mortgage loans on real estate | 38,489,354 39 |
| Premiums advanced under Soldiers' and Sailors' Civil Relief Act | 141 55 |
| Loans on company's policies assigned as collateral | 12,336,689 53 |
| Premium notes on policies in force | 73,467 30 |
| Book value of bonds and stocks | 38,318,573 50 |
| Deposits in trust companies and banks on interest | 1,229,598 75 |
| Bills receivable | 79 18 |
| Agents' balances (debit, $15,430.07; credit, $1,351.48) | 14,078 59 |
| Real estate sold under land contract, balance purchase price | 180,447 56 |
| Total ledger assets | $92,534,422 39 |

### NON-LEDGER ASSETS.

| | | | |
|---|---|---|---|
| Interest due and accrued on mortgages | | $1,220,004 83 | |
| Interest due and accrued on bonds | | 454,472 76 | |
| Interest due and accrued on premium notes, loans or liens | | 321,509 95 | |
| Interest due and accrued on other assets | | 2,233 31 | |
| Rents due and accrued on company's property | | 3,079 23 | |
| | | | 2,001,300 08 |
| Market value of bonds and stocks over book value | | | 93,088 50 |
| Due from other companies for losses or claims on policies re-insured | | | 641 10 |
| | New business. | Renewals. | |
| Net uncollected and deferred premiums (paid for basis) | $246,179 43 | $1,404,788 45 | 1,650,967 88 |
| Gross assets | | | $96,280,419 95 |

### DEDUCT ASSETS NOT ADMITTED.

| | | |
|---|---|---|
| Agents' debit balances | $15,430 07 | |
| Bills receivable | 79 18 | |
| Overdue and accrued interest on bonds in default | 60,140 00 | |
| Total | | 75,649 25 |
| Admitted assets | | $96,204,770 70 |

## LIABILITIES.

| | | |
|---|---|---|
| Net present value of outstanding policies computed by the Connecticut Insurance Department | $83,656,584 00 | |
| Same for dividend additions | 125,053 00 | |
| Same for annuities | 711,148 00 | |
| Total | $84,492,785 00 | |
| Deduct net value of risks re-insured | 398,391 00 | |
| Net reserve (paid for basis) | | $84,094,394 00 |

## LIABILITIES—Concluded.

| | | |
|---|---|---|
| Extra reserve for total and permanent disability benefits and for additional accidental death benefits included in life policies | | $ 193,429 00 |
| Present value of supplementary contracts not involving life contingencies | | 1,106,712 00 |
| Present value of amounts incurred but not yet due for total and permanent disability benefits | | 43,802 61 |
| Surrender values claimable on policies cancelled | | 19,201 00 |
| Death losses due and unpaid | $ 16,093 64 | |
| Death losses in process of adjustment | 57,262 00 | |
| Death losses reported for which no proofs have been received | 158,777 00 | |
| Reserve for net death losses incurred but unreported | 100,000 00 | |
| Matured endowments due and unpaid | 2,981 00 | |
| Death losses and other policy claims resisted | 19,535 00 | |
| Total and permanent disability benefits and additional accidental death benefits | 180 00 | |
| Annuity claims, involving life contingencies, due and unpaid | 2,632 80 | |
| Total policy claims | | 357,461 44 |
| Dividends left with the company to accumulate at interest | | 2,654,768 90 |
| Gross premiums paid in advance, including surrender values so applied, less discount, if any | | 93,970 19 |
| Unearned interest and rent paid in advance | | 132,332 79 |
| Commissions to agents due or accrued | | 20,908 42 |
| Salaries, rents, office expenses, bills and accounts due or accrued | | 6,000 00 |
| Medical examiners' and legal fees due or accrued and inspection of risks | | 26,017 40 |
| Estimated amount hereafter payable for federal, state and other taxes based upon the business of the year of this statement | | 400,000 00 |
| Dividends or other profits due policyholders | | 188,426 84 |
| Reserve on account of dividends to be declared on or apportioned to annual dividend policies payable to policyholders to and including December 31, 1922 | | 2,060,000 00 |
| Investment contingency reserve | | 750,000 00 |
| Other liabilities, viz: Surrender values credited, $5,934.79; suspense account (unapplied payments on land contracts,) $2,229.90 | | 8,164 69 |
| Total | | $92,155,589 28 |
| Unassigned funds (surplus) | | 4,049,181 42 |
| Total | | $96,204,770 70 |

## EXHIBIT OF POLICIES—ORDINARY.

ALL BUSINESS PAID FOR.

| | Number. | Amount. | Number. | Amount. |
|---|---|---|---|---|
| Policies in force December 31, 1920 | | | 144,863 | $382,709,528 20 |
| Policies issued, revived, and increased during the year | | | 18,586 | 62,527,294 29 |
| Total | | | 163,449 | $445,236,822 49 |
| Deduct policies which have ceased to be in force during the year— | | | | |
| By death | 1,752 | $ 5,079,502 86 | | |
| By maturity | 288 | 529,274 38 | | |
| By disability | 4 | 14,082 00 | | |
| By expiry | 347 | 960,890 84 | | |
| By surrender | 2,775 | 8,763,983 45 | | |
| By lapse | 5,319 | 15,995,230 00 | | |
| By decrease | -------- | 654,855 00 | | |
| Total | | | 10,485 | 31,997,818 53 |
| Total policies in force December 31, 1921 | | | 152,964 | $413,239,003 96 |
| Re-insured | | | 394 | $7,930,337 00 |

## BUSINESS IN ILLINOIS—ORDINARY.

| | Number. | Amount. |
|---|---|---|
| Policies in force December 31, 1920 | 13,428 | $37,583,423 00 |
| Policies issued during the year | 1,740 | 5,222,126 00 |
| Total | 15,168 | $42,805,549 00 |
| Deduct policies ceased to be in force | 1,417 | 4,071,315 00 |
| Policies in force December 31, 1921 | 13,751 | $38,734,234 00 |
| Losses and claims unpaid December 31, 1920 | 16 | $ 29,505 29 |
| Losses and claims incurred during the year | 194 | 591,004 00 |
| Total | 210 | $620,509 29 |
| Losses and claims settled during the year | 190 | 596,627 00 |
| Losses and claims unpaid December 31, 1921 | 20 | $23,882 29 |
| Premiums received | | $1,169,305 84 |

## GAIN AND LOSS EXHIBIT.

INSURANCE EXHIBIT.

| | | Gain in surplus. | Loss in surplus. |
|---|---|---|---|
| Loading on actual premiums of the year (averaging 18.20 per cent of the gross premiums) | $2,319,691 56 | | |
| Insurance expenses incurred during the year | 2,818,088 49 | | |
| Loss from loading | | | $ 498,396 93 |
| Interest earned during the year | $4,761,532 61 | | |
| Investment expenses incurred during the year | 393,197 25 | | |
| Net income from investments | $4,368,335 36 | | |
| Interest required to maintain reserve | 2,765,883 00 | | |
| Gain from interest | | $1,602,452 36 | |
| Expected mortality on net amount at risk | $4,216,675 00 | | |
| Actual mortality on net amount at risk | 2,442,922 91 | | |
| Gain from mortality | | 1,773,752 09 | |
| Expected disbursements to annuitants | $43,708 45 | | |
| Net actual annuity claims incurred | 64,478 29 | | |
| Loss from annuities | | | 20,769 84 |
| Total gain during the year from surrendered and lapsed policies | | 218,720 97 | |
| Decrease in surplus on dividend account | | | 1,902,916 28 |
| Increase in special funds, and special reserves during the year | | | 900,000 00 |
| INVESTMENT EXHIBIT. | | | |
| Total gains from real estate | | 2,296 05 | |
| Total losses from real estate | | | 2,381 33 |
| Total gains from stocks and bonds | | 1,379 65 | |
| Total losses from stocks and bonds | | | 22,545 82 |
| Gain from assets not admitted | | 20,849 44 | |
| Net loss on account of total and permanent disability benefits or additional accidental death benefits included in life policies | | | 8,825 91 |
| Gain on account of difference between company's reserves and department's reserves | | 10,493 19 | |
| Balance unaccounted for | | | 11,060 36 |
| Total gains and losses in surplus during the year | | $3,629,943 75 | $3,366,896 47 |
| Surplus December 31, 1920 | $3,786,134 14 | | |
| Surplus December 31, 1921 | 4,049,181 42 | | |
| Increase in surplus | | | 263,047 28 |
| Total | | $3,629,943 75 | $3,629,943 75 |

---

# THE EQUITABLE LIFE ASSURANCE SOCIETY OF THE UNITED STATES.

Located at No. 120 Broadway, New York, New York; incorporated, July 26, 1859; commenced business in Illinois, life, October 24, 1859; casualty, July 8, 1919.

W. A. DAY, President. W. ALEXANDER, Secretary.

GEORGE A. BARR, Director of Trade and Commerce, Attorney for service at Springfield.

H. W. HOBBS, Chicago, Attorney for service.

## CAPITAL.

| | | |
|---|---|---|
| Capital paid up | $100,000 00 | |
| Amount of ledger assets December 31, of previous year | | $613,045,780 62 |

## INCOME.

| | | | |
|---|---|---|---|
| First year's premiums on original policies, less re-insurance | | $14,964,186 04 | |
| First year's premiums for total and permanent disability benefits | | 425,428 70 | |
| First year's premiums for additional accidental death benefits | | 292,825 94 | |
| Surrender values to pay first year's premiums | | 26,957 65 | |
| Dividends applied to purchase paid-up additions and annuities | | 1,864,896 08 | |
| Consideration for original annuities involving life contingencies | | 719,279 64 | |
| First year's premiums for total and permanent disability benefits under annuity contracts | | 2,940 39 | |
| New premiums | | $18,296,514 44 | |
| Renewal premiums less re-insurance | $72,768,960 51 | | |
| Renewal premiums for total and permanent disability benefits, less re-insurance | 919,976 33 | | |

INCOME—Concluded.

| | | | |
|---|---|---|---|
| Renewal premiums for additional accidental death benefits, less re-insurance | $ 595,773 32 | | |
| Dividends applied to pay renewal premiums | 5,768,952 38 | | |
| Surrender values applied to pay renewal premiums | 89,784 59 | | |
| Renewal premiums for deferred annuities, less re-insurance $1,411.42 | 1,212,203 61 | | |
| Renewal premiums for total and permanent disability benefits under annuity contracts | 3,302 26 | | |
| Renewal premiums | | $81,358,953 00 | |
| Premium income | | $99,655,467 44 | |
| Premiums advanced during year under Soldiers' and Sailors' Civil Relief Act | | 121 35 | |
| Total | | | $99,655,588 79 |
| Consideration for supplementary contracts involving life contingencies | | | 765,217 50 |
| Consideration for disability claims | | | 1,437 36 |
| Consideration for supplementary contracts not involving life contingencies | | | 2,349,644 87 |
| Dividends left with company to accumulate at interest | | | 608,296 96 |
| Interest, dividend deposits | | | 86,923 66 |
| Interest on mortgage loans | | $ 6,783,106 86 | |
| Interest on collateral loans | | 354,607 97 | |
| Interest on bonds and dividends on stocks | | 16,512,481 62 | |
| Interest on premium notes, policy loans or liens | | 4,885,504 11 | |
| Interest on deposits | | 348,488 66 | |
| Interest on other debts due the company: Agents balances, $5,436.73; premiums, $179.902.18; war liens, $2,615.56; surrender values, $4,336.82; miscellaneous, $3,557.20 | | 195,848 49 | |
| Discount on claims paid in advance | | 2,600 70 | |
| Rents—including $63,792.99 for company's occupancy of its own buildings | | 1,346,105 55 | |
| Total interest and rents | | | 30,428,743 96 |
| From other sources, viz: Foreign exchange and currency adjustment, $4,083,441.65; reports in transit, $122,857.32; dividend suspense, $340.22; policy loan suspense, $7,466.57 surplus purchase policies, $1,166.34; deposits in suspense, $51,627.42; cancelled checks, $10,008.54; U. S. of America Soldiers' and Sailors' Civil Relief Act, $5.03; unclaimed accounts, $6,319.91; dividends on capital stock refunded by trustees, $3,370.96; miscellaneous, $2,686.01 | | | 4,289,280 97 |
| Agents' balances previously charged off | | | 29,918 28 |
| Profit on sale or maturity of ledger assets | | | 38,891 00 |
| Increase in book value of ledger assets | | | 466,897 00 |
| Income, life department | | | $138,720,849 35 |
| Income, casualty department | | | 1,891,735 78 |
| Total income | | | $140,612,585 13 |
| Total | | | $753,658,365 75 |

DISBURSEMENTS.

| | | |
|---|---|---|
| Death claims and additions | $27,973,553 39 | |
| Matured endowments and additions | 17,670,984 17 | |
| Total and permanent disability claims and additional accidental death benefits | 476,083 90 | |
| Total death claims and endowments | | $46,120,621 46 |
| Annuities involving life contingencies | | 1,791,621 72 |
| Surrender values paid in cash, or applied in liquidation of loans or notes | | 16,903,617 78 |
| Surrender values applied to pay new and renewal premiums | | 116,742 24 |
| Reserves applied to consideration for disability claims | | 521 36 |
| Dividends paid policyholders in cash, or applied in liquidation of loans or notes | | 10,503,493 59 |
| Dividends applied to pay renewal premiums | | 5,768,952 38 |
| Dividends applied to purchase paid-up additions and annuities | | 1,864,896 08 |
| Dividends left with the company to accumulate at interest | | 608,296 96 |
| (Total paid policyholders | $83,678,763 57) | |
| Expense of investigation and settlement of policy claims, including legal expenses | | 12,029 40 |
| Supplementary contracts not involving life contingencies | | 2,143,185 44 |
| Dividends with interest, held on deposit surrendered during the year | | 374,203 25 |
| Dividends to stockholders | | 7,000 00 |
| Commissions to agents, first year, $7,054,258.08; renewal, $3,870,068.87; annuities (original) $104,054.78; (renewal), $72,774.28 | | 11,101,156 01 |
| Commuted renewal commissions | | 8,557 55 |
| Compensation of managers and agents not paid by commissions on new business | | 36,186 10 |
| Agency supervision and traveling expenses of supervisors | | 1,103,808 97 |
| Branch office expenses | | 1,471,949 98 |
| Medical examiners' fees and inspection of risks | | 831,378 62 |
| Salaries and all other compensation of officers and home office employees | | 3,285,926 19 |
| Rent | | 1,037,579 39 |
| Advertising, printing, stationery, postage, telegraph, telephone, express and exchange | | 986,287 50 |
| Legal expense | | 66,485 09 |
| Furniture, fixtures and safes | | 346,696 18 |
| Repairs and expenses (other than taxes) on real estate | | 460,999 71 |

DISBURSEMENTS—Concluded.

| | |
|---|---|
| Taxes on real estate | $ 244,184 10 |
| State taxes on premiums | 1,269,035 81 |
| Insurance department licenses and fees | 3,696 27 |
| Federal taxes | 337,218 10 |
| All other licenses, fees and taxes, on surplus and reserve, $48,586.22; on securities, $17,702.61 on income, $34,572.39; stamp taxes, $5,293.04; agents' licenses and fees, $20,801.91; on personal property, $2,208.52; sundry taxes, $34,296.17 | 163,460 86 |
| Other disbursements, viz: Examinations and audits, $36,713.03; conventions and meetings, $146,064.60; fidelity and insurance premiums, $54,890.52; traveling expenses, $152,126.22; safe-keeping of securities, $7,704.53; books, subscriptions, etc., $20,030.81; employees' welfare, $86,134.93; water, ice and other laboratory supplies, $17,146.39; Association of Life Insurance Presidents, $10,722.71; mortgage expenses and appraisals, $9,150.50; legislative expenses, $4,941.64; association dues, $1,540.52; moving expenses, $5,053.17; miscellaneous, $9,137.32; interest: Dividend deposits, $86,923.66; policy claims $40,756.46; miscellaneous, $3,207.16; losses: policy claims, $2,922.31; unclaimed accounts $1,477.85; policy adjustments under French Moratorium, $15,766.17; miscellaneous, $6,905.56; withheld U. S. taxes, $395.90; deposits account insurance, $31,172.05; rent deposits, $27,984.59; premium paid on capital stock acquired under approved plan of mutualization, $5,600.00; liquidation account Russian business, $10,933.12; reserve for depreciation of foreign cash balance released, $815,361.09 | 1,610,762 81 |
| Adjustment arising from adoption of lower standard for conversion of foreign currencies | 1,118,134 00 |
| Agents' balances charged off | 51,232 90 |
| Loss on sale or maturity of ledger assets | 479,237 00 |
| Decrease in book value of ledger assets | 2,263,569 00 |
| Disbursements, life department | $114,492,723 80 |
| Disbursements, casualty department | 1,653,821 42 |
| Total disbursements | $116,146,545 22 |
| Balance | $637,511,820 53 |

LEDGER ASSETS.

| | |
|---|---|
| Book value of real estate | $ 14,492,288 27 |
| Mortgage loans on real estate | 154,033,029 51 |
| Loans secured by collaterals | 2,643,800 00 |
| Premiums advanced under Soldiers' and Sailors' Civil Relief Act | 590 07 |
| Loans on company's policies assigned as collateral | 99,094,474 85 |
| War liens | 42,018 51 |
| Book value of bonds and stocks | 360,166,986 02 |
| Cash in offices | 28,744 26 |
| Deposits in trust companies and banks not on interest | 180,397 35 |
| Deposits in trust companies and banks on interest | 5,402,970 31 |
| Cash in transit | 411,982 52 |
| Bills receivable | 983 46 |
| Agents' balances (debit, $765,128.30; credit, $272,980.32); net | 492,147 98 |
| Supplies | 103,995 33 |
| Par value of capital stock acquired under mutualization plan | 98,100 00 |
| Casualty department | 319,312 09 |
| Total ledger assets | $637,511,820 53 |

NON-LEDGER ASSETS.

| | | | |
|---|---|---|---|
| Interest due and accrued on mortgages | | $2,527,331 68 | |
| Interest due and accrued on bonds | | 4,537,035 76 | |
| Interest accrued on collateral loans | | 3,469 56 | |
| Interest due and accrued on premium notes, loans or liens, including $58.91; interest accrued on premiums reported to war risk insurance bureau | | 1,129,655 51 | |
| Interest due and accrued on other assets | | 30,929 84 | |
| Rents due and accrued on company's property | | 189,474 33 | |
| | | | 8,417,896 68 |
| Market value of stocks and unamortized bonds over book value | | | 77,498 60 |
| Due from other companies for losses or claims on policies re-insured | | | 700 00 |
| | New business. | Renewals. | |
| Net uncollected and deferred premiums (paid for basis) | $1,295,004 57 | $8,938,524 80 | 10,233,529 37 |
| Gross assets | | | $656,241,445 18 |

DEDUCT ASSETS NOT ADMITTED.

| | | |
|---|---|---|
| Supplies, printed matter and stationery | $103,995 33 | |
| Agents' debit balances | 765,128 30 | |
| Bills receivable | 983 46 | |
| Premium notes, policy loans and other policy assets in excess of net value and of other policy liabilities on individual policies | 60,361 01 | |
| Casualty department | 9,958 74 | |
| Total | | 940,426 84 |
| Admitted assets | | $655,301,018 34 |

## LIABILITIES.

| | | |
|---|---|---|
| Net present value of outstanding policies computed by the New York Insurance Department | $493,597,887 00 | |
| Same for dividend additions | 11,696,544 00 | |
| Same for annuities | 22,996,111 00 | |
| Total | $528,290,542 00 | |
| Deduct net value of risks re-insured | 855,099 00 | |
| Net reserve (paid for basis) | | $527,435,443 00 |
| Extra reserve for total and permanent disability benefits and for additional accidental death benefits included in life policies, less re-insurance | | 2,705,410 00 |
| Present value of supplementary contracts not involving life contingencies | | 5,512,090 00 |
| Present value of amounts incurred but not yet due for total and permanent disability benefits | | 1,219,357 00 |
| Surrender values claimable on policies cancelled | | 55,355 01 |
| Death losses due and unpaid | $135,752 20 | |
| Death losses in process of adjustment | 640,372 78 | |
| Death losses reported for which no proofs have been received | 2,141,028 94 | |
| Reserve for net death losses incurred but unreported | 1,000,000 00 | |
| Matured endowments due and unpaid and interest thereon, $21,442.75 | 1,108,275 04 | |
| Death losses and other policy claims resisted | 108,516 33 | |
| Total and permanent disability benefits and additional accidental death benefits | 39,940 32 | |
| Annuity claims, involving life contingencies, due and unpaid | 109,438 68 | |
| Total policy claims | | 5,283,324 29 |
| Due and unpaid on supplementary contracts not involving life contingencies | | 10,726 12 |
| Dividends left with the company to accumulate at interest | | 3,260,024 60 |
| Gross premiums paid in advance, including surrender values so applied, less discount, if any | | 523,249 46 |
| Unearned interest and rent paid in advance | | 2,067,876 59 |
| Commissions to agents due or accrued | | 177,714 07 |
| Salaries, rents, office expenses, bills and accounts due or accrued | | 455,000 00 |
| Medical examiners' and legal fees due or accrued | | 23,593 58 |
| Estimated amount hereafter payable for federal, state and other taxes based upon the business of the year of this statement | | 2,000,000 00 |
| Dividends or other profits due policyholders | | 1,227,712 45 |
| Dividends declared on or apportioned to annual dividend policies payable to policyholders during 1922 for period to December 31 | | 13,900,000 00 |
| Dividends declared on or apportioned to deferred dividend policies payable to policyholders during 1922 for period to December 31 | | 12,248,772 00 |
| Amounts set apart, apportioned, provisionally ascertained, calculated, declared or held awaiting apportionment upon deferred dividend policies | | 36,400,411 00 |
| Reserve for capital stock acquired under mutualization plan | | 26,600 00 |
| Reserve for taxes on business of previous years not finally determined | | 2,200,000 00 |
| Reserve for depreciation of foreign cash balances | | 254,638 91 |
| Other liabilities, viz: Deposits account insurance, $205,187.81; dividend suspense, $7,361.02; policy loan suspense, $21,623.14; deposits in suspense, $51,627.42; cancelled checks outstanding, $44,564.93; U. S. taxes collected, $1,150.16; reports in transit, $522,560.49; real estate superintendents' balances, $5,828.15; U. S. of America Soldiers' and Sailors' Civil Relief Act, $858.74 | | 860,761 86 |
| Contingency reserve, Russian business | | 154,203 01 |
| Casualty department | | 1,492,957 86 |
| Total | | $619,495,220 81 |
| Capital paid up | | 100,000 00 |
| Unassigned funds (surplus) | | 35,705,797 53 |
| Total | | $655,301,018 34 |

## EXHIBIT OF POLICIES—ORDINARY.

ALL BUSINESS PAID FOR.

| | Number. | Amount. | Number. | Amount. |
|---|---|---|---|---|
| Policies in force December 31, 1920 | | | 843,198 | $2,656,524,971 00 |
| Policies issued, revived and increased during the year | | | 131,221 | 596,840,460 00 |
| Total | | | 974,419 | $3,253,365,431 00 |
| Deduct policies which have ceased to be in force during the year— | | | | |
| By death | 7,968 | $28,084,756 00 | | |
| By maturity | 7,991 | 18,045,734 00 | | |
| By disability | -------- | 82,162 00 | | |
| By expiry | 7,312 | 71,790,261 00 | | |
| By surrender | 18,132 | 48,487,253 00 | | |
| By lapse | 39,844 | 126,333,836 00 | | |
| By decrease | -------- | 13,543,115 00 | | |
| By withdrawal | -------- | 129,027,582 00 | | |
| Total | | | 81,247 | 435,394,699 00 |
| Total policies in force December 31, 1921 | | | 893,172 | $2,817,970,732 00 |
| Re-insured | | | 448 | $9,832,773 00 |

## EXHIBIT OF POLICIES—GROUP INSURANCE.

ALL BUSINESS PAID FOR.

| | | | Number. | Amount. |
|---|---|---|---|---|
| Policies in force December 31, 1920 | | | 1,079 | $398,511,146 00 |
| Policies issued, revived and increased during the year | | | 193 | 160,527,802 00 |
| Total | | | 1,272 | $559,038,948 00 |
| Deduct policies which have ceased to be in force during the year— | Number. | Amount. | | |
| By death | -------- | $ 2,731,927 00 | | |
| By disability | -------- | 82,162 00 | | |
| By expiry | 93 | 45,907,957 00 | | |
| By decrease | -------- | 5,181,951 00 | | |
| By withdrawal | -------- | 129,027,582 00 | | |
| Total | | | 93 | 182,931,579 00 |
| Total policies in force December 31, 1921 | | | 1,179 | $376,107,369 00 |
| Distribution of business in force at end of year— | | | | |
| One year term | | | 1,178 | $374,906,869 00 |
| All other | | | 1 | 1,200,500 00 |
| Total | | | 1,179 | $376,107,369 00 |

## BUSINESS IN ILLINOIS—ORDINARY.

| | Number. | Amount. |
|---|---|---|
| Policies in force December 31, 1920 | 44,426 | $127,721,877 00 |
| Policies issued during the year | 10,090 | 39,145,107 00 |
| Total | 54,516 | $166,866,984 00 |
| Deduct policies ceased to be in force | 4,939 | 18,709,620 00 |
| Policies in force December 31, 1921 | 49,577 | $148,157,364 00 |
| Losses and claims unpaid December 31, 1920 | 12 | $ 20,908 81 |
| Losses and claims incurred during the year | 304 | 922,416 50 |
| Total | 316 | $943,325 31 |
| Losses and claims settled during the year | 289 | 875,565 41 |
| Losses and claims unpaid December 31, 1921 | 27 | $67,759 90 |
| Premiums received | | $5,526,139 26 |

## BUSINESS IN ILLINOIS—GROUP INSURANCE.

| | Number. | Amount. |
|---|---|---|
| Policies in force December 31, 1920 | 63 | $21,727,036 00 |
| Policies issued during the year | 40 | 10,200,640 00 |
| Total | 103 | $31,927,676 00 |
| Deduct policies ceased to be in force | 6 | 11,046,468 00 |
| Policies in force December 31, 1921 | 97 | $20,881,208 00 |
| Losses and claims unpaid December 31, 1920 | 9 | $ 13,040 00 |
| Losses and claims incurred during the year | 112 | 164,159 25 |
| Total | 121 | $177,199 25 |
| Losses and claims settled during the year | 118 | 174,048 25 |
| Losses and claims unpaid December 31, 1921 | 3 | $3,151 00 |
| Premiums received | | $282,272 60 |

## GAIN AND LOSS EXHIBIT.

INSURANCE EXHIBIT.

| | | Gain in surplus. | Loss in surplus. |
|---|---|---|---|
| Loading on actual premiums of the year (averaging 20.48 per cent of the gross premiums) | $20,391,207 72 | | |
| Insurance expenses incurred during the year | 22,354,542 47 | | |
| Loss from loading | | ------------- | $ 1,963,334 75 |
| Interest earned during the year | $31,088,405 91 | | |
| Investment expenses incurred during the year | 1,592,824 63 | | |
| Balance | $29,495,581 28 | | |
| Deduct net income from investments on disability and accidental death benefits | 151,135 19 | | |
| Net income from investments | $29,344,446 09 | | |
| Interest required to maintain reserve | 17,230,155 36 | | |
| Gain from interest | | $12,114,290 73 | |

GAIN AND LOSS EXHIBIT—Concluded.

INSURANCE EXHIBIT.

| | | Gain in surplus. | Loss in surplus. |
|---|---|---|---|
| Expected mortality on net amount at risk | $31,116,080 94 | | |
| Actual mortality on net amount at risk | 16,458,315 02 | | |
| Gain from mortality | | $14,657,765 92 | |
| Expected disbursements to annuitants | $1,363,542 60 | | |
| Net actual annuity claims incurred | 1,491,453 97 | | |
| Loss from annuities | | | $ 127,911 37 |
| Total gain during the year from surrendered and lapsed policies | | 2,627,037 89 | |
| Dividends paid stockholders | | | 7,000 00 |
| Decrease in surplus on dividend account | | | 15,503,807 64 |
| Decrease in special funds and special reserves during the year | | 16,533 12 | |
| Net to profit account | | 4,047,432 02 | |

INVESTMENT EXHIBIT.

| | | Gain in surplus. | Loss in surplus. |
|---|---|---|---|
| Total losses from real estate | | | 436,690 00 |
| Total gains from stocks and bonds | | 1,820,111 34 | |
| Total losses from stocks and bonds | | | 3,188,521 00 |
| Loss on investment and miscellaneous profits apportioned to disability and double indemnity business | | | 2,238 05 |
| Loss from assets not admitted | | | 309,005 60 |
| Net loss on account of total and permanent disability benefits or additional accidental death benefits included in life policies | | | 285,673 14 |
| Loss, casualty department | | | 583,574 70 |
| Premium on capital stock | | | 5,600 00 |
| Loss on liquidation account Russian business | | | 10,933 12 |
| Gain on account of decrease in unadmitted re-insurance reserve | | 34,359 00 | |
| Gain on account of reduction in reserve due to change in rate of conversion of foreign currencies | | 484,425 00 | |
| Total gains and losses in surplus during the year | | $35,801,955 02 | $22,424,289 37 |
| Surplus December 31, 1920 | $22,328,131 88 | | |
| Surplus December 31, 1921 | 35,705,797 53 | | |
| Increase in surplus | | | 13,377,665 65 |
| Total | | $35,801,955 02 | $35,801,955 02 |

## EQUITABLE LIFE INSURANCE COMPANY OF IOWA.

Located at Sixth Avenue and Locust Street, Des Moines, Iowa; incorporated January, 1867; commenced business in Illinois August 25, 1883.

H. S. NOLLEN, President. B. F. HADLEY, Secretary.

WM. F. CRAWFORD, Chicago, Attorney for service.

CAPITAL.

| | | |
|---|---|---|
| Capital paid up | $500,000 00 | |
| Amount of ledger assets December 31, of previous year | | $32,345,621 41 |

INCOME.

| | | | |
|---|---|---|---|
| First year's premiums on original policies, less re-insurance | | $1,592,394 13 | |
| First year's premiums for total and permanent disability benefits, less re-insurance | | 41,136 85 | |
| First year's premiums for additional accidental death benefits | | 31,472 18 | |
| Surrender values to pay first year's premiums | | 891 42 | |
| Dividends applied to purchase paid-up additions and annuities | | 237,107 76 | |
| Consideration for original annuities involving life contingencies | | 4,677 62 | |
| New premiums | | $1,907,679 96 | |
| Renewal premiums less re-insurance | $6,369,036 56 | | |
| Renewal premiums for total and permanent disability benefits, less re-insurance | 64,996 88 | | |
| Renewal premiums for additional accidental death benefits | 45,790 45 | | |
| Dividends applied to pay renewal premiums | 618,814 29 | | |
| Surrender values applied to pay renewal premiums | 24,932 69 | | |
| Renewal premiums for deferred annuities | 1,521 45 | | |
| Renewal premiums | | 7,125,092 32 | |
| Premium income | | | $9,032,772 28 |

## INCOME—Concluded.

| | | |
|---|---|---|
| Consideration for supplementary contracts involving life contingencies | | $ 10,533 00 |
| Consideration for supplementary contracts not involving life contingencies | | 36,403 02 |
| Dividends left with company to accumulate at interest | | 137,264 17 |
| Interest on mortgage loans | $1,381,606 88 | |
| Interest on collateral loans | 602 77 | |
| Interest on bonds | 128,966 45 | |
| Interest on premium notes, policy loans or liens | 204,392 91 | |
| Interest on deposits | 7,663 94 | |
| Interest on other debts due the company | 9,499 34 | |
| Rents | 42,925 00 | |
| Total interest and rents | | 1,775,657 29 |
| From other sources, viz: Loan commissions, $64,455.50; refund of 1917 income tax, $140.73; profit from Bankers Trust Building lease, $19,923.25; Bureau War Risk Insurance, $26.00 | | 84,545 48 |
| Increase in book value of ledger assets | | 4,983 90 |
| Total income | | $11,082,159 14 |
| Total | | $43,427,780 55 |

## DISBURSEMENTS.

| | | |
|---|---|---|
| Death claims and additions | $1,039,476 49 | |
| Matured endowments and additions | 400,892 09 | |
| Total and permanent disability claims and additional accidental death benefits | 39,257 41 | |
| Total death claims and endowments | | $1,479,625 99 |
| Annuities involving life contingencies | | 4,067 69 |
| Surrender values paid in cash, or applied in liquidation of loans or notes | | 575,698 26 |
| Surrender values applied to pay new and renewal premiums | | 25,824 11 |
| Dividends paid policyholders in cash, or applied in liquidation of loans or notes | | 56,671 42 |
| Dividends applied to pay renewal premiums | | 618,814 29 |
| Dividends applied to purchase paid-up additions and annuities | | 237,107 76 |
| Dividends left with the company to accumulate at interest | | 137,264 17 |
| (Total paid policyholders | $3,135,073 69) | |
| Expense of investigation and settlement of policy claims, including legal expenses | | 5,152 75 |
| Supplementary contracts not involving life contingencies | | 34,897 39 |
| Dividends with interest, held on deposit surrendered during the year | | 32,435 13 |
| Dividends to stockholders | | 35,000 00 |
| Commissions to agents, first year, $733,700.01; renewal, $412,783.84; annuities (original), $135.77; (renewal), $76.07 | | 1,146,695 69 |
| Compensation of managers and agents not paid by commissions on new business | | 91,012 61 |
| Agency supervision and traveling expenses of supervisors | | 40,047 53 |
| Branch office expenses | | 149,769 93 |
| Medical examiners' fees and inspection of risks | | 125,386 70 |
| Salaries and all other compensation of officers and home office employees | | 354,827 97 |
| Rent | | 68,363 02 |
| Advertising, printing, stationery, postage, telegraph, telephone and express | | 83,387 10 |
| Legal expense | | 2,230 92 |
| Furniture, fixtures and safes | | 27,662 08 |
| Repairs and expenses (other than taxes) on real estate | | 5,141 55 |
| Taxes on real estate | | 17,023 66 |
| State taxes on premiums | | 154,607 41 |
| Insurance department licenses and fees | | 5,958 05 |
| Federal taxes | | 57,521 45 |
| All other licenses, fees and taxes | | 3,394 29 |
| Other disbursements, viz: Association Life Insurance Presidents, $925.85; agency convention, $13,137.85; general expense, $12,554.88; loan expense, $310.60; profit and loss, $4.09; equitable savings fund, $3,072.82; legislative expense, $402.63; special employees emergency fund, $1,881.75 | | 32,290 47 |
| Total disbursements | | $5,607,879 39 |
| Balance | | $37,819,901 16 |

## LEDGER ASSETS.

| | |
|---|---|
| Book value of real estate | $ 800,000 00 |
| Mortgage loans on real estate | 28,822,579 59 |
| Loans on company's policies assigned as collateral | 4,335,703 04 |
| Premium notes on policies in force | 452,652 03 |
| Book value of bonds | 2,708,440 83 |
| Cash in offiee | 350 00 |
| Deposits in trust companies and banks on interest | 330,910 17 |
| Bills receivable | 189,469 44 |
| Agents' balances (debit, $200,561.39; credit, $25,298.11) net | 175,263 28 |
| Tax certificates | 4,532 78 |
| Total ledger assets | $37,819,901 16 |

## LEDGER ASSETS—Concluded.

### NON-LEDGER ASSETS.

| | | | |
|---|---|---|---|
| Interest due and accrued on mortgages | | $922,727 56 | |
| Interest accrued on bonds | | 44,180 40 | |
| Interest due and accrued on premium notes, loans or liens | | 101,358 37 | |
| Rents due on company's property | | 196 13 | |
| | | | 1,068,462 46 |
| | New business. | Renewals. | |
| Net uncollected and deferred premiums (paid for basis) | $84,632 94 | $651,873 31 | 736,506 25 |
| Gross assets | | | $39,624,869 87 |

### DEDUCT ASSETS NOT ADMITTED.

| | | |
|---|---|---|
| Agents' debit balances | $200,561 39 | |
| Bills receivable | 189,469 44 | |
| Total | | 390,030 83 |
| Admitted assets | | $39,234,839 04 |

## LIABILITIES.

| | | |
|---|---|---|
| Net present value of outstanding policies | $32,213,528 00 | |
| Same for dividend additions | 1,583,813 00 | |
| Same for annuities and supplementary contracts involving life contingencies | 100,222 00 | |
| Total | $33,897,563 00 | |
| Deduct net value of risks re-insured | 25,636 00 | |
| Net reserve (paid for basis) | | $33,871,927 00 |
| Extra reserve for total and permanent disability benefits and for additional accidental death benefits included in life policies, less re-insurance | | 180,563 00 |
| Present value of supplementary contracts not involving life contingencies | | 146,924 00 |
| Present value of amounts incurred but not yet due for total and permanent disability benefits | | 19,936 00 |
| Death losses in process of adjustment | $ 6,660 70 | |
| Death losses reported for which no proofs have been received | 74,686 84 | |
| Reserve for net death losses incurred but unreported | 30,000 00 | |
| Matured endowments due and unpaid | 17,841 56 | |
| Total policy claims | | 129,189 10 |
| Dividends left with the company to accumulate at interest | | 474,094 67 |
| Gross premiums paid in advance, including surrender values so applied, less discount, if any | | 94,112 00 |
| Unearned interest and rent paid in advance | | 19,376 19 |
| Commissions due agents on premium notes, when paid | | 34,254 49 |
| Commissions to agents due or accrued | | 28,344 76 |
| Salaries, rents, office expenses, bills and accounts due or accrued | | 936 66 |
| Estimated amount hereafter payable for federal, state and other taxes based upon the business of the year of this statement | | 220,350 00 |
| Dividends or other profits due policyholders | | 100,339 49 |
| Dividends declared on or apportioned to annual dividend policies payable to policyholders during 1922 for period to December 31, 1922 | | 1,482,128 00 |
| Mortality fluctuation fund | | 584,000 00 |
| Other liabilities, viz: Bureau War Risk Insurance, $123.71; special employees emergency fund, $3,513.25 | | 3,636 96 |
| Total | | $37,390,112 32 |
| Capital paid up | | 500,000 00 |
| Unassigned funds (surplus) | | 1,344,726 72 |
| Total | | $39,234,839 04 |

## EXHIBIT OF POLICIES—ORDINARY.

### ALL BUSINESS PAID FOR.

| | | | Number. | Amount. |
|---|---|---|---|---|
| Policies in force December 31, 1920 | | | 127,385 | $254,538,407 24 |
| Policies issued, revived and increased during the year | | | 20,580 | 55,904,487 32 |
| Total | | | 147,965 | $310,442,894 56 |
| Deduct policies which have ceased to be in force during the year— | Number. | Amount. | | |
| By death | 516 | $ 1,089,256 75 | | |
| By maturity | 282 | 407,474 31 | | |
| By expiry | 148 | 550,438 00 | | |
| By surrender | 1,482 | 2,532,776 98 | | |
| By lapse | 6,588 | 16,043,168 03 | | |
| By decrease | -------- | 2,885,164 00 | | |
| Total | | | 9,016 | 23,508,278 07 |
| Total policies in force December 31, 1921 | | | 138,949 | $286,934,616 49 |
| Re-insured | | | | $4,457,240 00 |

BUSINESS IN ILLINOIS—ORDINARY.

| | Number. | Amount. |
|---|---|---|
| Policies in force December 31, 1920 | 15,476 | $32,031,053 00 |
| Policies issued during the year | 2,839 | 7,472,820 00 |
| Total | 18,315 | $39,503,873 00 |
| Deduct policies ceased to be in force | 1,244 | 3,323,623 00 |
| Policies in force December 31, 1921 | 17,071 | $36,180,250 00 |
| Losses and claims unpaid December 31, 1920 | 7 | $ 11,446 25 |
| Losses and claims incurred during the year | 59 | 150,633 48 |
| Total | 66 | $162,079 73 |
| Losses and claims settled during the year | 58 | 147,561 88 |
| Losses and claims unpaid December 31, 1921 | 8 | $14,517 85 |
| Premiums received | | $1,121,374 50 |

GAIN AND LOSS EXHIBIT.

INSURANCE EXHIBIT.

| | | Gain in surplus. | Loss in surplus. |
|---|---|---|---|
| Loading on actual premiums of the year (averaging 20.95 per cent of the gross premiums) | $1,871,230 85 | | |
| Insurance expenses incurred during the year | 2,395,013 09 | | |
| Loss from loading | | | $ 523,782 24 |
| Interest earned during the year | $1,974,801 01 | | |
| Investment expenses incurred during the year | 109,872 21 | | |
| Net income from investments | $1,864,928 80 | | |
| Interest required to maintain reserve | 1,201,831 85 | | |
| Gain from interest | | $ 663,096 95 | |
| Expected mortality on net amount at risk | $2,381,741 00 | | |
| Actual mortality on net amount at risk | 827,392 28 | | |
| Gain from mortality | | 1,554,348 72 | |
| Expected disbursements to annuitants | $2,841 07 | | |
| Net actual annuity claims incurred | —254 31 | | |
| Gain from annuities | | 3,095 38 | |
| Total gain during the year from surrendered and lapsed policies | | 335,271 55 | |
| Dividends paid stockholders | | | 35,000 00 |
| Decrease in surplus on dividend account | | | 1,447,236 40 |
| Increase in special funds and special reserves during the year | | | 365,718 25 |
| INVESTMENT EXHIBIT. | | | |
| Gain on other investments, viz: Loan commissions | | 64,455 50 | |
| Loss from assets not admitted | | | 181,619 12 |
| Net gain on account of total and permanent disability benefits or additional accidental death benefits included in life policies | | 66,827 00 | |
| Gain from all other sources— | | | |
| Bankers Trust Building lease | | 19,923 25 | |
| Refund of income tax | | 140 73 | |
| Balance unaccounted for | | | 3,365 30 |
| Total gains and losses in surplus during the year | | $2,707,159 08 | $2,556,721 31 |
| Surplus December 31, 1920 | $1,194,288 95 | | |
| Surplus December 31, 1921 | 1,344,726 72 | | |
| Increase in surplus | | | 150,437 77 |
| Total | | $2,707,159 08 | $2,707,159 08 |

## FARMERS NATIONAL LIFE INSUANCE COMPANY OF AMERICA.

Located at Huntington, Indiana; executive office, 3401 Michigan Avenue, Chicago, Illinois; incorporated January 17, 1912; commenced business in Illinois May 6, 1913.

JOHN M. STAHL, President. BEN F. BILITER, Secretary.

GEORGE A. BARR, Director of Trade and Commerce, Attorney for service at Springfield.

CAPITAL.

| | | |
|---|---|---|
| Capital paid up | $200,000 00 | |
| Amount of ledger assets December 31, of previous year | | $1,013,137 58 |

## INCOME.

| | | | |
|---|---|---|---|
| First year's premiums on original policies, less re-insurance | | $204,355 65 | |
| First year's premiums for total and permanent disability benefits, less re-insurance | | 3,934 25 | |
| First year's premiums for additional accidental death benefits, less re-insurance | | 4,120 38 | |
| New premiums | | $212,410 28 | |
| Renewal premiums less re-insurance | $373,970 97 | | |
| Renewal premiums for total and permanent disability benefits, less re-insurance | 6,914 12 | | |
| Renewal premiums for additional accidental death benefits, less re-insurance | 11,772 54 | | |
| Dividends applied to pay renewal premiums | 4,064 78 | | |
| Renewal premiums | | 396,722 41 | |
| Premium income | | | $609,132 69 |
| Dividends left with company to accumulate at interest | | | 6,937 69 |
| Interest on mortgage loans | | $47,753 22 | |
| Interest on bonds | | 6,611 33 | |
| Interest on premium notes, policy loans or liens | | 5,698 54 | |
| Interest on deposits | | 2,215 20 | |
| Interest on other debts due the company | | 134 95 | |
| Rents—including $7,800.00 for company's occupancy of its own buildings | | 9,098 21 | |
| Total interest and rents | | | 71,511 45 |
| From other sources, viz: Internal revenue stamps, $0.95; war tax on insurance, $4,696.70 | | | 4,697 65 |
| Agents' balances previously charged off | | | 32 99 |
| Total income | | | $692,312 47 |
| Total | | | $1,705,450 05 |

## DISBURSEMENTS.

| | | |
|---|---|---|
| Death claims | $60,575 48 | |
| Total and permanent disability claims and additional accidental death benefits, less re-insurance | 4,969 53 | |
| Total death claims | | $ 65,545 01 |
| Surrender values paid in cash, or applied in liquidation of loans or notes | | 14,078 09 |
| Dividends paid policyholders in cash, or applied in liquidation of loans or notes | | 2,024 99 |
| Dividends applied to pay renewal premiums | | 4,064 78 |
| Dividends left with the company to accumulate at interest | | 6,937 69 |
| (Total paid policyholders | $92,650 56) | |
| Expense of investigation and settlement of policy claims, including legal expenses | | 100 00 |
| Commissions to agents, first year, $176,553.50; renewal, $34,199.49 | | 210,752 99 |
| Compensation of managers and agents not paid by commissions on new business | | 5,401 35 |
| Agency supervision and traveling expenses of supervisors | | 6,165 84 |
| Branch office expenses | | 2,165 79 |
| Medical examiners' fees and inspection of risks | | 19,714 61 |
| Salaries and all other compensation of officers and home office employees | | 49,695 28 |
| Rent | | 7,800 00 |
| Advertising, printing, stationery, postage, telegraph, telephone and express | | 16,848 73 |
| Legal expense | | 2,520 89 |
| Furniture, fixtures and safes | | 1,074 34 |
| Repairs and expenses (other than taxes) on real estate | | 2,508 07 |
| Taxes on real estate | | 864 51 |
| State taxes on premiums | | 4,328 69 |
| Insurance department licenses and fees | | 1,179 46 |
| Federal taxes | | 419 00 |
| All other licenses, fees and taxes | | 5,181 78 |
| Other disbursements, viz: Tax on capital stock, $6,746.48; office expense, $2,648.94; suspense account, $204.90; entertainment, $486.96; traveling expense, home office, $4,013.32; premiums on surety bonds, $345.95; library expense, $287.03; miscellaneous, $1,299.00 | | 16,032 58 |
| Agents' balances charged off | | 16 00 |
| Total disbursements | | $445,420 47 |
| Balance | | $1,260,029 58 |

## LEDGER ASSETS.

| | |
|---|---|
| Book value of real estate | $ 74,571 86 |
| Mortgage loans on real estate | 1,014,263 41 |
| Loans on company's policies assigned as collateral | 61,349 79 |
| Book value of bonds | 36,600 00 |
| Cash in office | 1,625 40 |
| Deposits in trust companies and banks not on interest | 35,037 46 |
| Deposits in trust companies and banks on interest | 33,000 00 |
| Agents' balances (debit) | 3,581 66 |
| Total ledger assets | $1,260,029 58 |

## LEDGER ASSETS—Concluded.

### NON-LEDGER ASSETS.

| | | |
|---|---|---|
| Interest due and accrued on mortgages | $23,054 09 | |
| Interest accrued on bonds | 329 60 | |
| Interest due and accrued on premium notes, loans or liens | 2,598 10 | |
| Interest accrued on other assets | 146 29 | |
| | | $ 26,128 08 |
| Net uncollected and deferred premiums (paid for basis) renewals | | 119,460 00 |
| All other assets, viz: Furniture and fixtures, $4,527.09; printing and stationery, $10,839.89 | | 15,366 98 |
| Gross assets | | $1,420,984 64 |

### DEDUCT ASSETS NOT ADMITTED.

| | | |
|---|---|---|
| Supplies, printed matter and stationery | $10,839 89 | |
| Furniture, fixtures and safes | 4,527 09 | |
| Agents' debit balances | 3,581 66 | |
| Premium notes, policy loans and other policy assets in excess of net value and of other policy liabilities on individual policies | 8,597 71 | |
| Book value of bonds over market value | 302 09 | |
| Total | | 27,848 44 |
| Admitted assets | | $1,393,136 20 |

## LIABILITIES.

| | | |
|---|---|---|
| Net present values of outstanding policies computed by the Indiana Insurance Department | $916,920 49 | |
| Deduct net value of risks re-insured | 7,592 36 | |
| Net reserve (paid for basis) | | $909,328 13 |
| Extra reserve for total and permanent disability benefits and for additional accidental death benefits included in life policies, less re-insurance | | 13,461 36 |
| Present value of amounts incurred but not yet due for total and permanent disability benefits | | 1,876 80 |
| Death losses in process of adjustment | | 2,000 00 |
| Dividends and coupons left with the company to accumulate at interest | | 27,471 69 |
| Gross premiums paid in advance, including surrender values so applied, less discount, if any | | 2,173 66 |
| Unearned interest and rent paid in advance | | 1,840 49 |
| Medical examiners' fees due or accrued | | 750 00 |
| Estimated amount hereafter payable for federal, state and other taxes based upon the business of the year of this statement | | 4,760 00 |
| Survivorship fund | | 4,142 75 |
| Items in suspense | | 1,159 52 |
| Total | | $968,964 40 |
| Capital paid up | | 200,000 00 |
| Unassigned funds (surplus) | | 224,171 80 |
| Total | | $1,393,136 20 |

## EXHIBIT OF POLICIES—ORDINARY.

### ALL BUSINESS PAID FOR.

| | Number. | Amount. | Number. | Amount. |
|---|---|---|---|---|
| Policies in force December 31, 1920 | | | 9,610 | $18,009,454 00 |
| Policies issued, revived and increased during the year | | | 3,740 | 8,164,779 00 |
| Total | | | 13,350 | $26,174,233 00 |
| Deduct policies which have ceased to be in force during the year— | | | | |
| By death | 44 | $ 65,750 00 | | |
| By expiry | 13 | 16,264 00 | | |
| By surrender | 65 | 107,000 00 | | |
| By lapse | 1,770 | 3,661,750 00 | | |
| By decrease | 98 | 199,562 00 | | |
| Total | | | 1,990 | 4,050,326 00 |
| Total policies in force December 31, 1921 | | | 11,360 | $22,123,907 00 |
| Re-insured | | | 65 | $367,000 00 |

## BUSINESS IN ILLINOIS—ORDINARY.

| | Number. | Amount. |
|---|---|---|
| Policies in force December 31, 1920 | 2,435 | $5,251,471 00 |
| Policies issued during the year | 939 | 2,248,650 00 |
| Total | 3,374 | $7,500,121 00 |
| Deduct policies ceased to be in force | 586 | 1,202,492 00 |
| Policies in force December 31, 1921 | 2,788 | $6,297,629 00 |

BUSINESS IN ILLINOIS—ORDINARY—Concluded.

| | Number. | Amount. |
|---|---|---|
| Losses and claims incurred during the year | 7 | $8,000 00 |
| Losses and claims settled during the year | 7 | 8,000 00 |
| Premiums received | | $164,005 28 |

GAIN AND LOSS EXHIBIT.

INSURANCE EXHIBIT.

| | | Gain in surplus. | Loss in surplus. |
|---|---|---|---|
| Loading on actual premiums of the year (averaging 28.88 per cent of the gross premiums) | $185,561 33 | | |
| Insurance expenses incurred during the year | 342,544 54 | | |
| Loss from loading | | | $156,983 21 |
| Interest earned during the year | $76,332 38 | | |
| Investment expenses incurred during the year | 3,791 58 | | |
| Net income from investments | $72,540 80 | | |
| Interest required to maintain reserve | 26,075 04 | | |
| Gain from interest | | $46,465 76 | |
| Expected mortality on net amount at risk | $149,779 71 | | |
| Actual mortality on net amount at risk | 56,918 82 | | |
| Gain from mortality | | 92,860 89 | |
| Total gain during the year from surrendered and lapsed policies | | 14,424 80 | |
| Decrease in surplus on dividend account | | | 12,627 46 |
| Increase in special funds and special reserves during the year | | | 1,000 00 |
| INVESTMENT EXHIBIT. | | | |
| Total gains from bonds | | 14,716 91 | |
| Loss from assets not admitted | | | 3,564 38 |
| Net gain on account of total and permanent disability benefits or additional accidental death benefits included in life policies | | 21,505 91 | |
| Balance unaccounted for | | | 312 19 |
| Total gains and losses in surplus during the year | | $189,974 27 | $174,487 24 |
| Surplus December 31, 1920 | $208,684 77 | | |
| Surplus December 31, 1921 | 224,171 80 | | |
| Increase in surplus | | | 15,487 03 |
| Total | | $189,974 27 | $189,974 27 |

## THE FEDERAL UNION LIFE INSURANCE COMPANY.

Located at No. 4 East Ninth Street, Cincinnati, Ohio; incorporated August 7, 1914; commenced business in Illinois April 7, 1916.

FRANK M. PETERS, President. CARL SLOUGH, Secretary.

GEORGE A, BARR, Director of Trade and Commerce, Attorney for service at Springfield.

CAPITAL.

| | | |
|---|---|---|
| Capital paid up | $225,000 00 | |
| Amount of ledger assets December 31, of previous year | | $715,572 11 |

INCOME.

| | | |
|---|---|---|
| First year's premiums on original policies, less re-insurance | $114,323 91 | |
| Renewal premiums less re-insurance | 415,439 99 | |
| Premium income | | $529,763 90 |
| Interest on mortgage loans | $ 8,330 40 | |
| Interest on bonds | 12,132 80 | |
| Interest on premium notes, policy loans or liens | 1,494 90 | |
| Interest on deposits | 1 81 | |
| Interest on other debts due the company | 20 75 | |
| Rents—including $9,800.00 for company's occupancy of its own buildings | 14,000 06 | |
| Total interest and rents | | 35,980 72 |
| War tax paid by policyholders | | 2,507 60 |
| *Borrowed money (gross) | | 80,000 00 |
| Increase in book value of ledger assets | | 413 40 |
| Total income | | $648,665 62 |
| Total | | $1,364,237 73 |

* For purchase of liberty bonds.

## DISBURSEMENTS.

| | | |
|---|---|---|
| Death claims | | $141,235 04 |
| Annuities involving life contingencies | | 100 00 |
| Premium notes and liens voided by lapse | | 2,190 58 |
| Surrender values paid in cash, or applied in liquidation of loans or notes | | 7,602 13 |
| (Total paid policyholders | $151,127 75) | |
| Expense of investigation and settlement of policy claims, including legal expenses | | 425 00 |
| Commissions to agents, first year, $61,223.28; renewal, $31,228.15 | | 92,451 43 |
| Compensation of managers and agents not paid by commissions on new business | | 12,927 00 |
| Agency supervision and traveling expenses of supervisors | | 4,688 00 |
| Branch office expenses | | 11,551 85 |
| Medical examiners' fees and inspection of risks | | 11,093 69 |
| Salaries and all other compensation of officers and home office employees | | 47,043 26 |
| Rent | | 9,800 00 |
| Advertising, printing, stationery, postage, telegraph, telephone and express | | 10,645 91 |
| Legal expense | | 1,156 20 |
| Furniture, fixtures and safes | | 1,394 74 |
| Repairs and expenses (other than taxes) on real estate | | 4,170 70 |
| Taxes on real estate | | 1,491 80 |
| State taxes on premiums | | 1,944 02 |
| Insurance department licenses and fees | | 928 71 |
| Federal taxes | | 245 00 |
| All other licenses, fees and taxes | | 2,570 82 |
| Other disbursements, viz: Coupons redeemed, $210.32; miscellaneous expense, $1,618.28; lunch room, $115.64; premiums returned, $649.99; entertainment, $481.94; books and publications, $361.35; decrease in account of items in suspense, $336.58 | | 3,774 10 |
| Borrowed money repaid (gross) | | 76,000 00 |
| Interest on borrowed money | | 1,036 64 |
| Agents' balances charged off | | 14,739 20 |
| Loss on sale or maturity of ledger assets | | 40 50 |
| Decrease in book value of ledger assets | | 2,304 93 |
| Total disbursements | | $463,551 25 |
| Balance | | $900,686 48 |

## LEDGER ASSETS.

| | |
|---|---|
| Book value of real estate | $200,000 00 |
| Mortgages loans on real estate | 154,950 00 |
| Loans on company's policies assigned as collateral | 30,383 94 |
| Book value of bonds | 444,289 75 |
| Cash in office | 2,577 80 |
| Deposits in trust companies and banks not on interest | 6,832 17 |
| Bills receivable | 1,272 22 |
| Agents' debit balances | 60,380 60 |
| Total ledger assets | $900,686 48 |

### NON-LEDGER ASSETS.

| | | | |
|---|---|---|---|
| Interest due and accrued on mortgages | | $4,127 30 | |
| Interest due and accrued on bonds | | 4,733 49 | |
| Interest due and accrued on premium notes, loans or liens | | 1,300 00 | |
| | | | 10,160 79 |
| Due from other companies for losses or claims on policies re-insured | | | 155 00 |
| | New business. | Renewals. | |
| Net uncollected and deferred premiums (paid for basis) | $17,930 52 | $131,328 64 | 149,259 16 |
| All other assets, viz: Supplies, stationery and printed matter, $2,500.00; furniture, fixtures and safes, $4,000.00 | | | 6,500 00 |
| Gross assets | | | $1,066,761 43 |

### DEDUCT ASSETS NOT ADMITTED.

| | | |
|---|---|---|
| Supplies, printed matter and stationery | $ 2,500 00 | |
| Furniture, fixtures and safes | 4,000 00 | |
| Agents' debit balances | 60,380 60 | |
| Bills receivable | 1,272 22 | |
| Total | | 68,152 82 |
| Admitted assets | | $998,608 61 |

## LIABILITIES.

| | | |
|---|---|---|
| Net present value of outstanding policies computed by the Ohio Insurance Department | $699,501 00 | |
| Deduct net value of risks re-insured | 11,128 00 | |
| Net reserve (paid for basis) | | $688,373 00 |
| Extra reserve for total and permanent disability benefits included in life policies | | 2,675 00 |
| Surrender values claimable on policies cancelled | | 1,355 00 |
| Death losses due and unpaid | | 1,500 00 |
| Gross premiums paid in advance, including surrender values so applied, less discount, if any | | 4,961 60 |
| Salaries, rents, office expenses, bills and accounts due or accrued | | 818 05 |
| Medical examiners' fees due or accrued | | 2,206 10 |

LIABILITIES—Concluded.

| | |
|---|---|
| Estimated amount hereafter payable for federal, state and other taxes based upon the business of the year of this statement | $ 2,000 00 |
| Borrowed money | 23,000 00 |
| Commuted value of installment death claims | 5,470 00 |
| Total | $732,358 75 |
| Capital paid up | 225,000 00 |
| Unassigned funds (surplus) | 41,249 86 |
| Total | $998,608 61 |

## EXHIBIT OF POLICIES—ORDINARY.

ALL BUSINESS PAID FOR.

| | Number. | Amount. | Number. | Amount. |
|---|---|---|---|---|
| Policies in force December 31, 1920 | | | 23,702 | $16,519,737 00 |
| Policies issued, revived and increased during the year | | | 6,172 | 4,124,464 00 |
| Total | | | 29,874 | $20,644,201 00 |
| Deduct policies which have ceased to be in force during the year— | | | | |
| By death | 236 | $ 142,750 00 | | |
| By expiy | 14 | 50,000 00 | | |
| By surrender | 71 | 105,000 00 | | |
| By lapse | 3,759 | 3,113,513 00 | | |
| By decrease | -------- | 78,631 00 | | |
| Total | | | 4,080 | 3,489,894 00 |
| Total policies in force December 31, 1921 | | | 25,794 | $17,154,307 00 |
| Re-insured | | | 190 | $641,260 00 |

## EXHIBIT OF POLICIES—INDUSTRIAL.

ALL BUSINESS PAID FOR.

| | Number. | Amount. | Number. | Amount. |
|---|---|---|---|---|
| Policies in force December 31, 1920 | | | 23,505 | $3,511,113 00 |
| Policies issued, revived and increased during the year | | | 7,328 | 1,019,895 00 |
| Total | | | 30,833 | $4,531,008 00 |
| Deduct policies which have ceased to be in force during the year— | | | | |
| By death | 203 | $ 29,425 00 | | |
| By surrender | 77 | 11,125 00 | | |
| By lapse | 6,757 | 1,059,018 00 | | |
| By decrease | -------- | 1,200 00 | | |
| Total | | | 7,037 | 1,100,768 00 |
| Total policies in force December 31, 1921 | | | 23,796 | $3,430,240 00 |

## BUSINESS IN ILLINOIS—ORDINARY.

| | Number. | Amount. |
|---|---|---|
| Policies in force December 31, 1920 | 1,876 | $1,871,100 00 |
| Policies issued during the year | 940 | 916,387 00 |
| Total | 2,816 | $2,787,487 00 |
| Deduct policies ceased to be in force | 756 | 830,800 00 |
| Policies in force December 31, 1921 | 2,060 | $1,956,687 00 |
| Losses and claims unpaid December 31, 1920 | 1 | $ 1,000 00 |
| Losses and claims incurred during the year | 17 | 24,044 00 |
| Total | 18 | $25,044 00 |
| Losses and claims settled during the year | 17 | 24,044 00 |
| Losses and claims unpaid December 31, 1921 | 1 | $1,000 00 |
| Premiums received | | $55,754 49 |

## BUSINESS IN ILLINOIS—INDUSTRIAL.

| | Number. | Amount. |
|---|---|---|
| Policies in force December 31, 1920 | 2,886 | $441,687 00 |
| Policies issued during the year | 669 | 92,285 00 |
| Total | 3,555 | $533,972 00 |
| Deduct policies ceased to be in force | 1,027 | 163,364 00 |
| Policies in force December 31, 1921 | 2,528 | $370,608 00 |
| Losses and claims incurred during the year | 24 | $1,640 00 |
| Losses and claims settled during the year | 24 | 1,640 00 |
| Premiums received | | $17,206 20 |

## GAIN AND LOSS EXHIBIT.

INSURANCE EXHIBIT.

| | | Gain in surplus. | Loss in surplus. |
|---|---|---|---|
| Loading on actual premiums of the year (averaging 26.52 per cent of the gross premiums) | $147,680 92 | | |
| Insurance expenses incurred during the year | 212,292 23 | | |
| Loss from loading | | | $64,611 31 |
| Interest earned during the year | $39,562 25 | | |
| Investment expenses incurred during the year | 5,662 50 | | |
| Net income from investments | $33,899 75 | | |
| Interest required to maintain reserve | 20,530 00 | | |
| Gain from interest | | $13,369 75 | |
| Expected mortality on net amount at risk | $223,989 60 | | |
| Actual mortality on net amount at risk | 134,926 04 | | |
| Gain from mortality | | 89,063 56 | |
| Expected disbursements to annuitants | $ 50 00 | | |
| Net actual annuity claims incurred | 100 00 | | |
| Loss from annuities | | | 50 00 |
| Total gain during the year from surrendered and lapsed policies | | 7,405 00 | |
| Net to loss account | | | 14,739 20 |
| INVESTMENT EXHIBIT. | | | |
| Total gains from bonds | | 413 40 | |
| Total losses from bonds | | | 2,345 43 |
| Loss from assets not admitted | | | 8,157 35 |
| Balance unaccounted for | | 441 88 | |
| Total gains and losses in surplus during the year | | $110,693 59 | $89,903 29 |
| Surplus December 31, 1920 | $20,459 56 | | |
| Surplus December 31, 1921 | 41,249 86 | | |
| Increase in surplus | | | 20,790 30 |
| Total | | $110,693 59 | $110,693 59 |

---

## THE FIDELITY MUTUAL LIFE INSURANCE COMPANY.

Located at Nos. 112-116 North Broad Street, Philadelphia, Pennsylvania; incorporated December 2, 1878; commenced business in Illinois October 6, 1899.

WALTER LE MAR TALBOT, President. CHAS. G. HODGE, Secretary.

MARTIN J. ISAACS, Chicago, Attorney for service.

| | | | |
|---|---|---|---|
| Amount of ledger assets December 31, of previous year | | | $42,565,396 10 |

### INCOME.

| | | | |
|---|---|---|---|
| First year's premiums on original policies, less re-insurance | | $1,451,102 12 | |
| First year's premiums for total and permanent disability benefits, less re-insurance | | 49,554 33 | |
| First year's premiums for additional accidental death benefits, less re-insurance | | 15,524 34 | |
| Surrender values to pay first year's premiums | | 5,347 70 | |
| Dividends applied to purchase paid-up additions and annuities | | 52,857 78 | |
| Surrender values applied to purchase paid-up insurance and annuities | | 349 04 | |
| Consideration for original annuities involving life contingencies | | 7,768 63 | |
| New premiums | | $1,582,503 94 | |
| Renewal premiums less re-insurance | $5,829,228 82 | | |
| Renewal premiums for total and permanent disability benefits, less re-insurance | 148,544 07 | | |
| Renewal premiums for additional accidental death benefits, less re-insurance | 23,682 17 | | |
| Dividends applied to pay renewal premiums | 514,031 29 | | |
| Dividends applied to shorten the endowment or premium-paying period | 111,994 46 | | |
| Surrender values applied to pay renewal premiums | 16,897 30 | | |
| Renewal premiums for deferred annuities | 31,362 08 | | |
| Renewal premiums | | 6,675,740 19 | |
| Total | | | $8,258,244 13 |

INCOME—Concluded.

| | | |
|---|---|---|
| Consideration for supplementary contracts not involving life contingencies | | $ 18,677 30 |
| Dividends left with company to accumulate at interest | | 143,100 41 |
| Interest on mortgage loans | $969,005 39 | |
| Interest on collateral loans | 4,699 47 | |
| Interest on bonds and dividends on stocks | 787,266 87 | |
| Interest on premium notes, policy loans or liens | 475,453 38 | |
| Interest on deposits | 13,928 97 | |
| Interest on other debts due the company | 9,155 78 | |
| Rents—including $60,000.00 for company's occupancy of its own buildings | 159,315 83 | |
| Total interest and rents | | 2,413,825 69 |
| From other sources, viz: Payments on account principal G. M. Parsons mortgage, $500.00; rent 1374 Central Avenue, Memphis, Tenn., $45.83; Oklahoma Central Railway Company, $25,226.25 | | 25,772 08 |
| Profit on sale or maturity of ledger assets | | 135,589 08 |
| Increase in book value of ledger assets | | 18,214 89 |
| Total income | | $11,013,423 58 |
| Total | | $53,578,819 68 |

DISBURSEMENTS.

| | | |
|---|---|---|
| Death claims and additions | $1,908,130 01 | |
| Matured endowments and additions | 630,602 96 | |
| Total and permanent disability claims and additional accidental death benefits | 14,860 85 | |
| Total death claims and endowments | | $2,553,593 82 |
| Annuities involving life contingencies | | 31,324 71 |
| Surrender values paid in cash, or applied in liquidation of loans or notes | | 962,464 59 |
| Surrender values applied to pay new and renewal premiums | | 22,245 00 |
| Surrender values applied to purchase paid-up insurance and annuities | | 349 04 |
| Dividends paid policyholders in cash, or applied in liquidation of loans or notes | | 150,825 09 |
| Dividends applied to pay renewal premiums | | 514,031 29 |
| Dividends applied to shorten the endowment or premium-paying period | | 111,994 46 |
| Dividends applied to purchase paid-up additions and annuities | | 52,857 78 |
| Dividends left with the company to accumulate at interest | | 143,100 41 |
| (Total paid policyholders | $4,542,781 19) | |
| Expense of investigation and settlement of policy claims, including legal expenses | | 5,782 19 |
| Supplementary contracts not involving life contingencies | | 59,017 96 |
| Dividends with interest, held on deposit surrendered during the year | | 73,151 38 |
| Commissions to agents, first year, $594,377.84; renewal, $371,127.37 | | 965,505 21 |
| Compensation of managers and agents not paid by commissions on new business | | 1,300 00 |
| Agency supervision and traveling expenses of supervisors | | 30,686 37 |
| Branch office expenses | | 163,384 72 |
| Medical examiners' fees and inspection of risks | | 89,419 70 |
| Salaries and all other compensation of officers and home office employees | | 366,260 15 |
| Rent | | 118,473 31 |
| Advertising, printing, stationery, postage, telegraph, telephone, express | | 122,667 29 |
| Legal expenses | | 1,458 59 |
| Furniture, fixtures and safes | | 26,259 72 |
| Repairs and expenses (other than taxes) on real estate | | 104,306 52 |
| Taxes on real estate | | 46,899 14 |
| State taxes on premiums | | 122,762 14 |
| Insurance department licenses and fees | | 9,085 69 |
| Federal taxes | | 47,760 80 |
| All other licenses, fees and taxes | | 3,436 08 |
| Other disbursements, viz: Investment expenses, $6,221.19; impairment cards, $4,880.06; agency meetings, $4,280.94; meals employees, $3,434.96; sundry, $1,414.38; tabulating machine, $968.10; surety bonds, $830.22; miscellaneous, $699.55 | | 22,729 40 |
| Loss on sale or maturity of ledger assets | | 67,465 76 |
| Decrease in book value of ledger assets | | 16,275 68 |
| Total disbursements | | $7,006,875 99 |
| Balance | | $46,571,945 69 |

LEDGER ASSETS.

| | |
|---|---|
| Book value of real estate | $ 1,468,037 43 |
| Mortgage loans on real estate | 17,908,071 27 |
| Loans secured by collaterals | 101,000 00 |
| Loans on company's policies assigned as collateral | 8,462,954 27 |
| Premium notes on policies in force | 867,197 31 |
| Book value of bonds and stocks | 16,802,613 00 |
| Cash in office | 1,654 32 |
| Deposits in trust companies and banks not on interest | 1,000 00 |
| Deposits in trust companies and banks on interest | 719,861 43 |
| Bills receivable | 8,982 86 |
| Agents' balances (debit, $250,255.60; credit, $20,581.80), net | 229,673 80 |
| Total ledger assets | $46,571,945 69 |

## LEDGER ASSETS—Concluded.

### NON-LEDGER ASSETS.

| | | | |
|---|---|---|---|
| Interest due and accrued on mortgages | | $368,750 13 | |
| Interest due and accrued on bonds | | 363,606 07 | |
| Interest due and accrued on collateral loans | | 2,536 53 | |
| Interest due and accrued on premium notes, loans or liens | | 71,497 08 | |
| Rents due and accrued on company's property | | 357 50 | |
| | | | 806,747 31 |
| Market value of real estate over book value | | | 237,221 66 |
| | New business. | Renewals. | |
| Net uncollected and deferred premiums (paid for basis) | $81,341 91 | $679,244 28 | 760,586 19 |
| Gross assets | | | $48,376,500 85 |

### DEDUCT ASSETS NOT ADMITTED.

| | | |
|---|---|---|
| Agents' debit balances | $250,255 60 | |
| Bills receivable | 8,982 86 | |
| Premium notes, policy loans and other policy assets in excess of net value and of other policy liabilities on individual policies | 63,551 34 | |
| Overdue and accrued interest on bonds in default | 127,910 00 | |
| Book value of bonds and stocks over market value | 415,211 98 | |
| Total | | 865,911 78 |
| Admitted assets | | $47,510,589 07 |

## LIABILITIES.

| | | |
|---|---|---|
| Net present value of outstanding policies computed by the Pennsylvania Insurance Department | $39,839,138 00 | |
| Same for dividend additions | 262,931 00 | |
| Same for annuities | 466,108 00 | |
| Total | $40,568,177 00 | |
| Deduct net value of risks re-insured | 58,968 00 | |
| Net reserve (paid for basis) | | $40,509,209 00 |
| Extra reserve for total and permanent disability benefits and for additional accidental death benefits included in life policies | | 277,705 00 |
| Present value of supplementary contracts not involving life contingencies | | 425,572 35 |
| Present value of amounts incurred but not yet due for total and permanent disability benefits | | 72,882 00 |
| Surrender values claimable on policies cancelled | | 16,984 50 |
| Death losses in process of adjustment | $31,123 04 | |
| Death losses reported for which no proofs have been received | 164,533 00 | |
| Reserve for net death losses incurred but unreported | 32,703 30 | |
| Matured endowments due and unpaid | 1,000 00 | |
| Death losses and other policy claims resisted | 2,000 00 | |
| Total and permanent disability benefits and additional accidental death benefits | 67,874 00 | |
| Total policy claims | | 299,233 34 |
| Due and unpaid on supplementary contracts not involving life contingencies | | 4,597 31 |
| Dividends left with the company to accumulate at interest | | 402,449 23 |
| Gross premiums paid in advance, including surrender values so applied, less discount, if any | | 27,121 12 |
| Unearned interest and rent paid in advance | | 226,079 54 |
| Commissions due agents on premium notes, when paid | | 65,147 73 |
| Salaries, rents, office expenses, bills, and accounts due or accrued | | 6,727 63 |
| Medical examiners' fees due or accrued | | 6,031 53 |
| Estimated amount hereafter payable for federal, state and other taxes based upon the business of the year of this statement | | 182,224 22 |
| Dividends or other profits due policyholders | | 58,145 59 |
| Dividends declared on or apportioned to annual dividend policies payable to policyholders during 1922 for period to December 31, 1922 | | 1,173,645 00 |
| Dividends declared on or apportioned to deferred dividend policies payable to policyholders during 1922 for period to December 31, 1922 | | 366,316 38 |
| Amounts set apart, apportioned, provisionally ascertained, calculated, declared or held awaiting apportionment upon deferred dividend policies | | 1,479,841 47 |
| Excess interest payable during 1922 on installment claims | | 5,832 10 |
| Total | | $45,605,745 04 |
| Unassigned funds (surplus) | | 1,904,844 03 |
| Total | | $47,510,589 07 |

## EXHIBIT OF POLICIES—ORDINARY.

### ALL BUSINESS PAID FOR.

| | Number. | Amount. |
|---|---|---|
| Policies in force December 31, 1920 | 83,345 | $203,980,056 00 |
| Policies issued, revived, and increased during the year | 12,464 | 41,850,363 00 |
| Total | 95,809 | $245,830,419 00 |

## EXHIBIT OF POLICIES—ORDINARY—Concluded.

ALL BUSINESS PAID FOR.

| | Number. | Amount. | Number. | Amount. |
|---|---|---|---|---|
| Deduct policies which have ceased to be in force during the year— | | | | |
| By death | 758 | $ 2,211,318 00 | | |
| By maturity | 359 | 618,339 00 | | |
| By expiry | 281 | 650,653 00 | | |
| By surrender | 1,311 | 3,286,956 00 | | |
| By lapse | 4,838 | 15,479,276 00 | | |
| By decrease | 20 | 768,771 00 | | |
| Total | | | 7,567 | $23,015,313 00 |
| Total policies in force December 31, 1921 | | | 88,242 | $222,815,105 00 |
| Re-insured | | | 549 | $5,088,652 00 |

## BUSINESS IN ILLINOIS—ORDINARY.

| | Number. | Amount. |
|---|---|---|
| Policies in force December 31, 1920 | 2,971 | $7,642,609 00 |
| Policies issued during the year | 493 | 1,964,213 00 |
| Total | 3,464 | $9,606,822 00 |
| Deduct policies ceased to be in force | 242 | 969,937 00 |
| Policies in force December 31, 1921 | 3,222 | $8,636,885 00 |
| Losses and claims unpaid December 31, 1920 | 1 | $ 1,000 00 |
| Losses and claims incurred during the year | 30 | 85,996 50 |
| Total | 31 | $86,996 50 |
| Losses and claims settled during the year | 30 | 85,996 50 |
| Losses and claims unpaid December 31, 1921 | 1 | $1,000 00 |
| Premiums received | | $322,165 46 |

## GAIN AND LOSS EXHIBIT.

INSURANCE EXHIBIT.

| | | Gain in surplus. | Loss in surplus. |
|---|---|---|---|
| Loading on actual premiums of the year (averaging 21.23 per cent of the gross premiums) | $1,741,241 00 | | |
| Insurance expenses incurred during the year | 2,003,537 28 | | |
| Loss from loading | | | $ 262,296 28 |
| Interest earned during the year | $2,549,732 16 | | |
| Investment expenses incurred during the year | 260,642 61 | | |
| Net income from investments | $2,289,089 55 | | |
| Interest required to maintain reserve | 1,399,407 00 | | |
| Gain from interest | | $889,682 55 | |
| Expected mortality on net amount at risk | $2,232,091 00 | | |
| Actual mortality on net amount at risk | 1,327,097 61 | | |
| Gain from mortality | | 904,993 39 | |
| Expected disbursements to annuitants | $14,419 00 | | |
| Net actual annuity claims incurred | 25,313 11 | | |
| Loss from annuities | | | 10,894 11 |
| Total gain during the year from surrendered and lapsed policies | | 184,269 07 | |
| Decrease in surplus on dividend account | | | 1,220,798 29 |
| INVESTMENT EXHIBIT. | | | |
| Total gains from real estate | | $ 15,299 58 | |
| Total losses from real estate | | | 12,573 76 |
| Total gains from stocks and bonds | | 132,308 61 | |
| Total losses from stocks and bonds | | | 85,802 97 |
| Gain on other investments, viz: Payments on accounts of securities previously written off | | 25,772 08 | |
| Loss from assets not admitted | | | 24,464 77 |
| Net loss on account of total and permanent disability benefits or additional accidental death benefits included in life policies | | | 3,365 98 |
| Loss—special credits, $38,376.00; loss, change in reserve, $65,862.00 | | | 104,238 00 |
| Gain—decrease in surplus interest liabilities | | 228 45 | |
| Balance unaccounted for | | 1,425 48 | |
| Total gains and losses in surplus during the year | | $2,153,979 21 | $1,724,434 16 |
| Surplus December 31, 1920 | $1,475,298 98 | | |
| Surplus December 31, 1921 | 1,904,844 03 | | |
| Increase in surplus | | | 429,545 05 |
| Total | | $2,153,979 21 | $2,153,979 21 |

## GIRARD LIFE INSURANCE COMPANY.

Located Opposite Independence Hall, Philadelphia, Pennsylvania; incorporated January 5, 1909; commenced business in Illinois June 3, 1909.

NATHAN T. FOLWELL, President. ALBERT SHORT, Secretary.

C. L. CONKLING and E. F. IRWIN, Springfield, Attorneys for service.

### CAPITAL.

| | | | |
|---|---|---|---|
| Capital paid up | | $419,040 00 | |
| Amount of ledger assets December 31, of previous year | | | $2,142,969 59 |

### INCOME.

| | | | |
|---|---|---|---|
| First year's premiums on original policies, less re-insurance | | $126,389 31 | |
| First year's premiums for total and permanent disability benefits, less re-insurance | | 601 23 | |
| Dividends applied to purchase paid-up additions and annuities | | 27,156 86 | |
| Surrender values applied to purchase paid-up insurance and annuities | | 5,385 99 | |
| New premiums | | $159,533 39 | |
| Renewal premiums less re-insurance | $442,276 00 | | |
| Renewal premiums for total and permanent disability benefits, less re-insurance | 1,746 15 | | |
| Dividends applied to pay renewal premiums | 829 67 | | |
| Surrender values applied to pay renewal premiums | 33 76 | | |
| Renewal premiums | | 444,885 58 | |
| Total | | | $604,418 97 |
| Dividends left with company to accumulate at interest | | | 389 36 |
| Interest on mortgage loans | | $32,383 68 | |
| Interest on bonds and dividends on stocks | | 51,559 46 | |
| Interest on premium notes, policy loans or liens | | 14,596 50 | |
| Interest on deposits | | 1,586 20 | |
| Rents—including $10,000.00 for company's occupancy of its own buildings | | 10,000 00 | |
| Total interest and rents | | | 110,125 84 |
| Profit on sale or maturity of ledger assets | | | 1,154 22 |
| Increase in book value of ledger assets | | | 2,680 01 |
| Total income | | | $718,768 40 |
| Total | | | $2,861,737 99 |

### DISBURSEMENTS.

| | | |
|---|---|---|
| Death claims and additions | | $ 72,731 00 |
| Surrender values paid in cash, or applied in liquidation of loans or notes | | 25,139 91 |
| Surrender values applied to pay new and renewal premiums | | 33 76 |
| Surrender values applied to purchase paid-up insurance and annuities | | 5,385 99 |
| Dividends paid policyholders in cash, or applied in liquidation of loans or notes | | 29,629 01 |
| Dividends applied to pay renewal premiums | | 829 67 |
| Dividends applied to purchase paid-up additions and annuities | | 27,156 86 |
| Dividends left with the company to accumulate at interest | | 389 36 |
| (Total paid policyholders | $161,295 56) | |
| Supplementary contracts not involving life contingencies | | 952 60 |
| Dividends with interest, held on deposit surrendered during the year | | 268 06 |
| Commissions to agents, first year, $77,788.65; renewal, $23,876.03 | | 101,664 68 |
| Agency supervision and traveling expenses of supervisors | | 3,366 13 |
| Branch office expenses | | 24,527 36 |
| Medical examiners' fees and inspection of risks | | 9,977 71 |
| Salaries and all other compensation of officers and home office employees | | 34,504 56 |
| Rent | | 10,000 00 |
| Advertising, printing, stationery, postage, telegraph, telephone, express | | 7,119 89 |
| Legal expense | | 867 25 |
| Repairs and expenses (other than taxes) on real estate | | 2,567 14 |
| Taxes on real estate | | 2,336 40 |
| State taxes on premiums | | 6,305 76 |
| Insurance department licenses and fees | | 626 83 |
| All other licenses, fees and taxes | | 5,302 18 |
| Other disbursements, viz: Expense, $4,428.92; investment expense, $119.25; unearned extra war premiums returned, $84.61 | | 4,632 78 |
| Decrease in book value of ledger assets | | 159 48 |
| Total disbursements | | $376,474 37 |
| Balance | | $2,485,263 62 |

## LEDGER ASSETS.

| | | |
|---|---|---|
| Book value of real estate | | $ 150,870 75 |
| Mortgage loans on real estate | | 636,000 00 |
| Loans on company's policies assigned as collateral | | 261,040 41 |
| Premium notes on policies in force | | 51,671 38 |
| Book value of bonds and stocks | | 1,228,068 68 |
| Cash in office | | 7,958 12 |
| Deposits in trust companies and banks not on interest | | 1,813 97 |
| Deposits in trust companies and banks on interest | | 113,189 43 |
| Agents' balances (debit, $20,919.18; credit, $1,272.74), net | | 19,646 44 |
| Furniture and fixtures | | 15,004 44 |
| Total ledger assets | | $2,485,263 62 |

### NON-LEDGER ASSETS.

| | | | |
|---|---|---|---|
| Interest due and accrued on mortgages | | $ 8,688 39 | |
| Interest accrued on bonds | | 25,131 16 | |
| | | | 33,819 55 |
| | New business. | Renewals. | |
| Net uncollected and deferred premiums (paid for basis) | $9,879 80 | $82,103 10 | 91,982 90 |
| Gross assets | | | $2,611,066 07 |

### DEDUCT ASSETS NOT ADMITTED.

| | | |
|---|---|---|
| Furniture, fixtures and safes | $15,004 44 | |
| Agents' debit balances | 20,919 18 | |
| Premium notes, policy loans and other policy assets in excess of net value and of other policy liabilities on individual policies | 6,086 18 | |
| Overdue and accrued interest on bonds in default | 3,650 00 | |
| Book value of bonds and stocks over market value | 31,351 79 | |
| Total | | 77,011 59 |
| Admitted assets | | $2,534,054 48 |

## LIABILITIES.

| | | |
|---|---|---|
| Net present value of outstanding policies computed by the Pennsylvania Insurance Department | $1,914,388 00 | |
| Same for dividend additions | 66,563 00 | |
| Total | $1,980,951 00 | |
| Deduct net value of risks re-insured | 41,624 00 | |
| Net reserve (paid for basis) | | $1,939,327 00 |
| Extra reserve for total and permanent disability benefits | | 2,788 10 |
| Present value of supplementary contracts not involving life contingencies | | 10,658 91 |
| Death losses reported for which no proofs have been received | | 15,239 00 |
| Dividends left with the company to accumulate at interest | | 4,067 23 |
| Gross premiums paid in advance, including surrender values so applied, less discount, if any | | 542 35 |
| Unearned interest and rent paid in advance | | 7,298 25 |
| Salaries, rents, office expenses, bills, and accounts due or accrued | | 2,744 17 |
| Medical examiners' fees due or accrued | | 808 50 |
| Estimated amount hereafter payable for federal, state and other taxes based upon the business of the year of this statement | | 11,000 00 |
| Dividends or other profits due policyholders | | 710 78 |
| Dividends declared on or apportioned to annual dividend policies payable to policyholders during 1922 for period to June 30, 1922 | | 4,522 34 |
| Dividends declared on or apportioned to deferred dividend policies payable to policyholders during 1922 for period to December 31, 1922 | | 6,930 20 |
| Amounts set apart, apportioned, provisionally ascertained, calculated, declared or held awaiting apportionment upon deferred dividend policies | | 10,102 72 |
| Reserve for increasing coupon policies | | 17,581 64 |
| Unearned extra war premiums | | 210 97 |
| Total | | $2,034,532 16 |
| Capital paid up | | 419,040 00 |
| Unassigned funds (surplus) | | 80,482 32 |
| Total | | $2,534,054 48 |

## EXHIBIT OF POLICIES—ORDINARY.

### ALL BUSINESS PAID FOR.

| | Number. | Amount. |
|---|---|---|
| Policies in force December 31, 1920 | 6,174 | $15,866,119 00 |
| Policies issued, revived, and increased during the year | 1,665 | 4,559,346 00 |
| Total | 7,839 | $20,425,465 00 |

## EXHIBIT OF POLICIES—ORDINARY—Concluded.

ALL BUSINESS PAID FOR.

| | Number. | Amount. | Number. | Amount. |
|---|---|---|---|---|
| Deduct policies which have ceased to be in force during the year— | | | | |
| By death | 34 | $ 101,893 00 | | |
| By expiry | 3 | 13,444 00 | | |
| By surrender | 66 | 200,643 00 | | |
| By lapse | 615 | 1,691,420 00 | | |
| Total | | | 718 | 2,007,400 00 |
| Total policies in force December 31, 1921 | | | 7,121 | $18,418,065 00 |
| Re-insured | | | 614 | $3,820,912 00 |

## BUSINESS IN ILLINOIS—ORDINARY.

| | Number. | Amount. |
|---|---|---|
| Policies in force December 31, 1920 | 1,086 | $3,104,895 00 |
| Policies issued during the year | 201 | 693,594 00 |
| Total | 1,287 | $3,798,489 00 |
| Deduct policies ceased to be in force | 102 | 465,878 00 |
| Policies in force December 31, 1921 | 1,185 | $3,332,611 00 |
| Losses and claims incurred during the year | 2 | $7,299 00 |
| Losses and claims settled during the year | 2 | 7,299 00 |
| Premiums received | | $128,180 00 |

## GAIN AND LOSS EXHIBIT.

INSURANCE EXHIBIT.

| | | Gain in surplus. | Loss in surplus. |
|---|---|---|---|
| Loading on actual premiums of the year (averaging 29.63 per cent of the gross premiums) | $187,024 60 | | |
| Insurance expenses incurred during the year | 221,019 14 | | |
| Loss from loading | | | $33,994 54 |
| Interest earned during the year | $124,030 93 | | |
| Investment expenses incurred during the year | 6,238 31 | | |
| Net income from investments | $117,792 62 | | |
| Interest required to maintain reserve | 63,944 94 | | |
| Gain from interest | | $53,847 68 | |
| Expected mortality on net amount at risk | $138,890 91 | | |
| Actual mortality on net amount at risk | 60,593 00 | | |
| Gain from mortality | | 78,297 91 | |
| Total gain during the year from surrendered and lapsed policies | | 5,157 70 | |
| Decrease in surplus on dividend account | | | 58,415 78 |
| Increase in special funds, and special reserves during the year | | | 4,845 58 |
| **INVESTMENT EXHIBIT.** | | | |
| Total gains from stocks and bonds | | 1,154 22 | |
| Total losses from stocks and bonds | | | 7,051 75 |
| Loss from assets not admitted | | | 9,880 77 |
| Net gain on account of total and permanent disability benefits or additional accidental death benefits included in life policies | | 1,561 10 | |
| Balance unaccounted for | | | 1,563 53 |
| Total gains and losses in surplus during the year | | $140,018 61 | $115,751 95 |
| Surplus December 31, 1920 | $56,215 66 | | |
| Surplus December 31, 1921 | 80,482 32 | | |
| Increase in surplus | | | 24,266 66 |
| Total | | $140,018 61 | $140,018 61 |

## THE GUARDIAN LIFE INSURANCE COMPANY OF AMERICA.

Located at No. 50 Union Square, New York, New York; incorporated April 10, 1860; commenced business in Illinois September 10, 1860.

CARL HEYE, President.
FRED A. GOECHE and R. C. NEUENDORFFER, Secretaries.

REDMOND D. STEPHENS, Chicago, Attorney for service.

### CAPITAL.

| | | |
|---|---|---|
| Capital paid up | $200,000 00 | |
| Amount of ledger assets December 31, of previous year | $60,287,473 86 | |
| Less adjustment arising from the adoption of a lower standard for conversion of foreign currency | 22,927,579 54 | |
| Extended at | | $37,359,894 32 |

### INCOME.

| | | | |
|---|---|---|---|
| First year's premiums on original policies, less re-insurance | | $1,174,956 51 | |
| First year's premiums for total and permanent disability benefits, less re-insurance | | 36,734 83 | |
| First year's premiums for additional accidental death benefits, less re-insurance | | 27,128 83 | |
| Dividends applied to purchase paid-up additions and annuities | | 89,622 47 | |
| Surrender values applied to purchase paid-up insurance and annuities | | 132,734 83 | |
| Consideration for original annuities involving life contingencies | | 6,842 24 | |
| New premiums | | $1,468,019 71 | |
| Renewal premiums less re-insurance | $4,834,548 40 | | |
| Renewal premiums for total and permanent disability benefits, less re-insurance | 107,933 64 | | |
| Renewal premiums for additional accidental death benefits, less re-insurance | 63,652 97 | | |
| Dividends applied to pay renewal premiums | 424,945 88 | | |
| Renewal premiums for deferred annuities | 874 39 | | |
| Renewal premiums | | 5,431,955 28 | |
| Premium income | | $6,899,974 99 | |
| Premiums advanced during year under Soldiers' and Sailors' Civil Relief Act | | 28 77 | |
| Total | | | $6,900,003 76 |
| Consideration for supplementary contracts involving life contingencies | | | 3,536 65 |
| Consideration for supplementary contracts not involving life contingencies | | | 39,893 64 |
| Dividends left with company to accumulate at interest | | | 46,374 37 |
| Interest on mortgage loans | | $986,786 87 | |
| Interest on collateral loans | | 5,828 57 | |
| Interest on bonds and dividends on stocks | | 481,318 03 | |
| Interest on premium notes, policy loans or liens | | 312,572 61 | |
| Interest on deposits | | 34,243 05 | |
| Interest on other debts due the company | | 11,023 74 | |
| Discount on claims paid in advance | | 1,218 63 | |
| Rents—including $51,503.47 for company's occupancy of its own buildings | | 331,439 92 | |
| Total interest and rents | | | 2,164,431 42 |
| From other sources, viz: Policy fees, $33.45; profit on exchange, $7,035.99; refund of taxes paid, $281.57 | | | 7,351 01 |
| Profit on sale or maturity of ledger assets | | | 6,974 66 |
| Increase in book value of ledger assets | | | 17,278 62 |
| Total income | | | $9,185,844 13 |
| Total | | | $46,545,738 45 |

### DISBURSEMENTS.

| | | |
|---|---|---|
| Death claims and additions | $1,314,191 88 | |
| Matured endowments and additions | 867,983 69 | |
| Total and permanent disability claims and additional accidental death benefits | 35,800 68 | |
| Total death claims and endowments | | $2,217,976 25 |
| Annuities involving life contingencies | | 11,344 87 |
| Surrender values paid in cash, or applied in liquidation of loans or notes | | 1,074,169 27 |
| Surrender values applied to purchase paid-up insurance and annuities | | 132,734 83 |

## DISBURSEMENTS—Concluded.

| | | |
|---|---|---|
| Dividends paid policyholders in cash, or applied in liquidation of loans or notes | | $463,577 88 |
| Dividends applied to pay renewal premiums | | 424,945 88 |
| Dividends applied to purchase paid-up additions and annuities | | 89,622 47 |
| Dividends left with the company to accumulate at interest | | 46,374 37 |
| (Total paid policyholders | $4,460,745 82) | |
| Expense of investigation and settlement of policy claims, including legal expenses | | 6,040 05 |
| Supplementary contracts not involving life contingencies | | 21,066 48 |
| Dividends with interest, held on deposit surrendered during the year | | 8,871 66 |
| Dividends to stockholders | | 24,000 00 |
| Commissions to agents, first year, $557,068.14; renewal, $305,181.21; annuities (original), $1,092.22; (renewal), $68.34 | | 863,409 91 |
| Commuted renewal commissions | | 16,511 31 |
| Agency supervision and traveling expenses of supervisors | | 37,400 49 |
| Branch office expenses | | 286,305 93 |
| Medical examiners' fees and inspection of risks | | 86,642 51 |
| Salaries and all other compensation of officers and home office employees | | 350,569 19 |
| Rent | | 51,503 47 |
| Advertising, printing, stationery, postage, telegraph, telephone, express and exchange | | 90,015 05 |
| Legal expense | | 714 21 |
| Furniture, fixtures and safes | | 13,409 98 |
| Repairs and expenses (other than taxes) on real estate | | 136,125 92 |
| Taxes on real estate | | 53,182 11 |
| State taxes on premiums | | 112,780 93 |
| Insurance department licenses and fees | | 6,094 19 |
| Federal taxes | | 50,873 65 |
| All other licenses, fees and taxes | | 10,344 99 |
| Other disbursements, viz: Traveling expenses, $5,724.11; association dues, $1,547.46; office supplies, $10,034.98; insurance papers and publications, $3,025.99; life extension institute service, $10,152.35; legislative expenses, $457.98; convention expenses, $3,913.62; office repairs, $1,699.62; laundry, ice, spring water and lunches, $1,362.58; premiums on surety bonds, $880.36; expense in connection with mortgage loans, $256.50; medical supplies, $134.57; rent of safe deposit vault, $463.97; rent of tabulating machines, $589.38; sundries, $6,094.78; interest on claims, $711.89; loss on exchange, $2,475.82; loss incurred through compromised settlement of claims, $1,771.07; adjustment on account of loans on Spanish policies transferred from European Branch to Home office, $933.09 | | 52,230 12 |
| Agents' balances charged off | | 2,260 21 |
| Loss on sale or maturity of ledger assets | | 18,430 41 |
| Decrease in book value of ledger assets | | 3,509 97 |
| Total disbursements | | $6,763,038 56 |
| Balance | | $39,782,699 89 |

## LEDGER ASSETS.

| | |
|---|---|
| Book value of real estate | $ 2,558,070 52 |
| Mortgage loans on real estate | 19,333,461 71 |
| Premiums advanced under Soldiers and Sailors' Civil Relief Act | 129 38 |
| Loans on company's policies assigned as collateral | 6,196,550 29 |
| Book value of bonds and stocks | 11,202,013 35 |
| Cash in office | 5,301 26 |
| Deposits in trust companies and banks not on interest | 56,512 93 |
| Deposits in trust companies and banks on interest | 387,473 33 |
| Agents' balances (debit $49,793.37; credit, $7,231.80) net | 42,561 57 |
| Suspense account | 625 55 |
| Total ledger assets | $39,782,699 89 |

### NON-LEDGER ASSETS.

| | | | |
|---|---|---|---|
| Interest due and accrued on mortgages | | $432,334 92 | |
| Interest due and accrued on bonds | | 159,617 50 | |
| Interest due and accrued on premium notes, loans or liens | | 38,423 66 | |
| Interest accrued on bank deposits | | 2,147 35 | |
| Rents due company's property | | 192 80 | |
| | | | 632,716 23 |
| | New business. | Renewals. | |
| Net uncollected and deferred premiums (paid for basis) | $92,966 77 | $964,701 63 | 1,057,668 40 |
| Gross assets | | | $41,473,084 52 |

### DEDUCT ASSETS NOT ADMITTED.

| | | |
|---|---|---|
| Mexican check and currency account | $ 1,785 79 | |
| Agents' debit balances | 49,793 37 | |
| Suspense account | 625 55 | |
| Book value of bonds and stocks over market value | 268,829 66 | |
| Total | | 321,034 37 |
| Admitted assets | | $41,152,050 15 |

## LIABILITIES.

| | | |
|---|---|---|
| Net present value of outstanding policies computed by the New York Insurance Department | $53,534,211 00 | |
| Same for dividend additions | 690,363 00 | |
| Same for annuities | 342,684 00 | |
| Total | $54,567,258 00 | |
| Deduct net value of risks re-insured | 169,900 00 | |
| Net reserve (paid for basis) | $54,397,358 00 | |
| Adjustment arising from the adoption of a lower standard for conversion of foreign currency | 21,169,860 00 | |
| | | $33,227,498 00 |
| Extra reserve for total and permanent disability benefits and for additional accidental death benefits included in life policies | | 237,983 97 |
| Present value of supplementary contracts not involving life contingencies | | 215,496 64 |
| Present value of amounts incurred but not yet due for total and permanent disability benefits | | 105,733 01 |
| Surrender values claimable on policies cancelled | | 2,238 29 |
| Death losses due and unpaid | $ 55,866 61 | |
| Death losses in process of adjustment | 47,684 62 | |
| Death losses reported for which no proofs have been received | 89,899 95 | |
| Reserve for net death losses incurred but unreported | 52,632 12 | |
| Matured endowments due and unpaid | 130,061 73 | |
| Death losses and other policy claims resisted | 22,103 21 | |
| Total and permanent disability benefits and additional accidental death benefits | 112,466 97 | |
| Annuity claims, involving life contingencies, due and unpaid | 628 52 | |
| Total policy claims | | 511,343 73 |
| Due and unpaid on supplementary contracts not involving life contingencies | | 682 36 |
| Dividends left with the company to accumulate at interest | | 144,759 89 |
| Gross premiums paid in advance, including surrender values so applied, less discount, if any | | 35,150 90 |
| Unearned interest and rent paid in advance | | 154,022 27 |
| Commissions to agents due or accrued | | 2,231 91 |
| Salaries, rents, office expenses, bills and accounts due or accrued | | 3,658 60 |
| Medical examiners' and legal fees due or accrued | | 10,372 28 |
| Estimated amount hereafter payable for federal, state and other taxes based upon the business of the year of this statement | | 246,090 60 |
| Dividends or other profits due policyholders | | 178,151 41 |
| Dividends declared on or apportioned to annual dividend policies payable to policyholders during 1922 for period to October 31, 1922 | | 639,497 41 |
| Dividends declared on or apportioned to deferred dividend policies payable to policyholders during 1922 for period to October 31, 1922 | | 398,412 55 |
| Amounts set apart, apportioned, provisionally ascertained, calculated, declared or held awaiting apportionment upon deferred dividend policies | | 1,676,852 66 |
| Additional reserve held by the company for total and permanent disability and accidental death benefits | | 64,880 06 |
| Other liabilities, viz: Reserved for any claims for interest under policy claims awaiting settlement, $2,560.54; reserved for war risks, $105.29; reserved for non-deduction of deferred premiums under policies payable as death claims in full without such deduction, $2,400.00; reserved to provide a fund for any loss by fire in agencies, $1,423.71; special reserve for contingencies, $500,000.00 | | 506,489 54 |
| Total | | $38,361,546 08 |
| Capital paid up | | 200,000 00 |
| Unassigned funds (surplus) | | 2,590,504 07 |
| Total | | $41,152,050 15 |

## EXHIBIT OF POLICIES—ORDINARY.

ALL BUSINESS PAID FOR.

| | Number. | Amount. | Number. | Amount. |
|---|---|---|---|---|
| Policies in force December 31, 1920 | | | 103,851 | $228,435,528 00 |
| Policies issued, revived and increased during the year | | | 13,168 | 37,826,127 00 |
| Total | | | 117,019 | $266,261,655 00 |
| Deduct policies which have ceased to be in force during the year— | | | | |
| By death | 860 | $ 1,397,569 00 | | |
| By maturity | 1,566 | 902,664 00 | | |
| By expiry | 443 | 1,560,534 00 | | |
| By surrender | 2,202 | 3,869,543 00 | | |
| By lapse | 4,794 | 13,808,953 00 | | |
| By decrease | -------- | 46,624,422 00 | | |
| Total | | | 9,865 | 68,163,685 00 |
| Total policies in force December 31, 1921 | | | 107,154 | $198,097,970 00 |
| Re-insured | | | 165 | $1,730,051 00 |

## EXHIBIT OF POLICIES—GROUP INSURANCE.

ALL BUSINESS PAID FOR.

| | Number. | Amount. | Number. | Amount. |
|---|---|---|---|---|
| Policies in force December 31, 1920 | | | 2 | $516,578 00 |
| Policies issued, revived and increased during the year | | | -------- | 99,867 00 |
| Total | | | 2 | $616,445 00 |
| Deduct policies which have ceased to be in force during the year— | | | | |
| By death | -------- | $ 4,386 00 | | |
| By surrender | 1 | 111,000 00 | | |
| By lapse | -------- | 97,762 00 | | |
| Total | | | 1 | 213,148 00 |
| Total policies in force December 31, 1921 | | | 1 | $403,297 00 |
| Distribution of business in force at end of year—One year term | | | 1 | $403,297 00 |

## EXHIBIT OF POLICIES—INDUSTRIAL.

ALL BUSINESS PAID FOR.

| | Number. | Amount. | Number. | Amount. |
|---|---|---|---|---|
| Policies in force December 31, 1920 | | | 1,018 | $130,292 00 |
| Deduct policies which have ceased to be in force during the year— | | | | |
| By death | 32 | $4,866 00 | | |
| By surrender | 15 | 1,435 00 | | |
| By lapse | 1 | 123 00 | | |
| By decrease | -------- | 43 00 | | |
| Total | | | 48 | 6,467 00 |
| Total policies in force December 31, 1921 | | | 970 | $123,825 00 |

## BUSINESS IN ILLINOIS—ORDINARY.

| | Number. | Amount. |
|---|---|---|
| Policies in force December 31, 1920 | 3,788 | $9,113,989 00 |
| Policies issued during the year | 657 | 1,855,106 00 |
| Total | 4,445 | $10,969,095 00 |
| Deduct policies ceased to be in force | 342 | 884,252 00 |
| Policies in force December 31, 1921 | 4,103 | $10,084,843 00 |
| Losses and claims unpaid December 31, 1920 | 6 | $10,829 61 |
| Losses and claims incurred during the year | 47 | 90,197 93 |
| Total | 53 | $101,027 54 |
| Losses and claims settled during the year | 46 | 85,793 26 |
| Losses and claims unpaid December 31, 1921 | 7 | $15,234 28 |
| Premiums received | | $353,664 08 |

## BUSINESS IN ILLINOIS—GROUP INSURANCE.

| | Number. | Amount. |
|---|---|---|
| Policies in force December 31, 1920 | 1 | $191,750 00 |
| Policies issued during the year | -------- | 3,250 00 |
| Total | 1 | $195,000 00 |
| Deduct policies ceased to be in force | 1 | 195,000 00 |
| Losses and claims incurred during the year | 2 | $750 00 |
| Losses and claims settled during the year | 2 | 750 00 |
| Premiums received | | —$281 76 |

## BUSINESS IN ILLINOIS—INDUSTRIAL.

| | Number. | Amount. |
|---|---|---|
| Policies in force December 31, 1920 | 11 | $1,544 00 |
| Policies in force December 31, 1921 | 11 | 1,544 00 |
| Premiums received | | $18 00 |

## GAIN AND LOSS EXHIBIT.

INSURANCE EXHIBIT.

| | | Gain in surplus. | Loss in surplus. |
|---|---|---|---|
| Loading on actual premiums of the year (averaging 19.12 per cent of the gross premiums) | $1,319,663 48 | | |
| Insurance expenses incurred during the year | 1,976,550 53 | | |
| Loss from loading | | ------------- | $656,887 05 |

## GAIN AND LOSS EXHIBIT—Concluded.

INSURANCE EXHIBIT.

| | | Gain in surplus. | Loss in surplus. |
|---|---|---|---|
| Interest earned during the year | $2,226,339 81 | | |
| Investment expenses incurred during the year | 283,503 69 | | |
| Net income from investments | $1,942,836 12 | | |
| Interest required to maintain reserve | 1,035,686 00 | | |
| Gain from interest | | $907,150 12 | |
| Expected mortality on net amount at risk | $1,807,559 00 | | |
| Actual mortality on net amount at risk | 842,248 74 | | |
| Gain from mortality | | 965,310 26 | |
| Expected disbursements to annuitants | $5,440 60 | | |
| Net actual annuity claims incurred | 8,421 69 | | |
| Loss from annuities | | | $ 2,981 09 |
| Total gain during the year from surrendered and lapsed policies | | 243,227 56 | |
| Dividends paid stockholders | | | 24,000 00 |
| Decrease in surplus on dividend account | | | 989,091 45 |
| Decrease in special funds and special reserves during the year | | 308,118 51 | |
| Net to loss account | | | 404 20 |

INVESTMENT EXHIBIT.

| | | Gain in surplus. | Loss in surplus. |
|---|---|---|---|
| Total losses from real estate | | | 2,673 43 |
| Total gains from stocks and bonds | | 152,531 89 | |
| Total losses from stocks and bonds | | | 15,756 98 |
| Loss from assets not admitted | | | 31,155 44 |
| Net loss on account of total and permanent disability benefits or additional accidental death benefits included in life policies | | | 26,398 60 |
| Gain resulting from the adoption of lower standards of conversion of foreign currencies | | 385,912 26 | |
| Balance unaccounted for | | | 25,310 10 |
| Total gains and losses in surplus during the year | | $2,962,250 60 | $1,774,658 34 |
| Surplus December 31, 1920 | $1,402,911 81 | | |
| Surplus December 31, 1921 | 2,590,504 07 | | |
| Increase in surplus | | | 1,187,592 26 |
| Total | | $2,962,250 60 | $2,962,250 60 |

## HOME LIFE INSURANCE COMPANY.

Located at No. 256 Broadway, New York, New York; incorporated April 30, 1860; commenced business in Illinois October 20, 1860.

WILLIAM A. MARSHALL, President. WILLIAM S. GAYLORD, Secretary.

WILLIAM W. BETSCHE, Chicago, Attorney for service.

| | | | |
|---|---|---|---|
| Amount of ledger assets December 31, of previous year | | | $40,397,083 56 |

### INCOME.

| | | | |
|---|---|---|---|
| First year's premiums on original policies, less re-insurance | | $864,669 87 | |
| First year's premiums for total and permanent disability benefits, less re-insurance | | 17,606 44 | |
| First year's premiums for additional accidental death benefits, less re-insurance | | 12,052 64 | |
| Dividends applied to purchase paid-up additions and annuities | | 147,588 17 | |
| Consideration for original annuities involving life contingencies | | 1,151 00 | |
| New premiums | | $1,043,068 12 | |
| Renewal premiums less re-insurance | $5,411,197 93 | | |
| Renewal premiums for total and permanent disability benefits, less re-insurance | 54,034 27 | | |
| Renewal premiums for additional accidental death benefits, less re-insurance | 6,759 01 | | |
| Dividends applied to pay renewal premiums | 471,004 01 | | |
| Dividends applied to shorten the endowment or premium-paying period | 232 02 | | |
| Surrender values applied to pay renewal premiums | 400 46 | | |
| Renewal premiums for deferred annuities | 3,793 79 | | |
| Renewal premiums | | 5,947,421 40 | |
| Premium income | | $6,990,489 61 | |
| Premiums advanced during year under Soldiers' and Sailors' Civil Relief Act | | 57 70 | |
| Total | | | $6,990,547 31 |

## INCOME—Concluded.

|  | | |
|---|---|---|
| Consideration for supplementary contracts involving life contingencies | | $ 7,270 74 |
| Consideration for supplementary contracts not involving life contingencies | | 27,616 45 |
| Dividends left with company to accumulate at interest | | 59,145 44 |
| Interest on mortgage loans | $ 427,763 78 | |
| Interest on bonds and dividends on stocks | 1,077,604 09 | |
| Interest on premium notes, policy loans or liens | 434,333 97 | |
| Interest on deposits | 7,815 96 | |
| Interest on other debts due the company | 13,003 83 | |
| Discount on claims paid in advance | 166 13 | |
| Rents—including $41,000.00 for company's occupancy of its own buildings | 157,903 78 | |
| Total interest and rents | | 2,118,591 54 |
| From other sources, viz: Reserve on policies re-insured deposited with the company, $25,811.92; New York State income tax withheld by the company, $625.46; refund by U. S. Government of taxes paid erroneously or under protest, $13,226.09 | | 39,663 47 |
| Profit on sale or maturity of ledger assets | | 17,357 50 |
| Increase in book value of ledger assets | | 31,345 49 |
| Total income | | $9,291,537 94 |
| Total | | $49,688,621 50 |

## DISBURSEMENTS.

|  | | |
|---|---|---|
| Death claims and additions | $1,652,679 92 | |
| Matured endowments and additions | 1,226,078 71 | |
| Total and permanent disability claims and additional accidental death benefits | 9,486 60 | |
| Total death claims and endowments | | $2,888,245 23 |
| Annuities involving life contingencies | | 46,903 93 |
| Surrender values paid in cash, or applied in liquidation of loans or notes | | 1,075,764 42 |
| Surrender values applied to pay new and renewal premiums | | 400 46 |
| Dividends paid policyholders in cash, or applied in liquidation of loans or notes | | 71,459 69 |
| Dividends applied to pay renewal premiums | | 471,004 01 |
| Dividends applied to shorten the endowment or premium-paying period | | 232 02 |
| Dividends applied to purchase paid-up additions and annuities | | 131,176 07 |
| Dividends left with the company to accumulate at interest | | 55,154 98 |
| (Total paid policyholders | $4,740,340 81) | |
| Expense of investigation and settlement of policy claims, including legal expenses | | 1,030 31 |
| Supplementary contracts not involving life contingencies | | 40,726 52 |
| Dividends with interest, held on deposit surrendered during the year | | 22,812 38 |
| Commissions to agents, first year, $411,464.00; renewal, $384,502.33; annuities (original), $40.29; (renewal), $153.90 | | 796,160 52 |
| Agency supervision and traveling expenses of supervisors | | 51,516 64 |
| Branch office expenses | | 162,144 63 |
| Medical examiners' fees and inspection of risks | | 58,382 36 |
| Salaries and all other compensation of officers and home office employees | | 299,281 58 |
| Rent | | 41,000 00 |
| Advertising, printing, stationery, postage, telegraph, telephone, express and exchange | | 60,286 50 |
| Legal expense | | 6,829 60 |
| Furniture, fixtures and safes | | 6,427 47 |
| Repairs and expenses (other than taxes) on real estate | | 60,252 74 |
| Taxes on real estate | | 29,144 70 |
| State taxes on premiums | | 110,671 09 |
| Insurance department licenses and fees | | 6,187 26 |
| Federal taxes | | 21,743 50 |
| All other licenses, fees and taxes | | 4,932 19 |
| Other disbursements, viz: Traveling expense, home office, $2,338.98; legislative expense, $362.36; Association of Life Insurance Presidents, $795.95; investment expense, $1,836.83; officers' and clerks' bonds and miscellaneous, $7,671.21; New York State income tax withheld, $614.36; interest previously received on bonds deposited with company under the Civil Relief Act now applied to liquidate premiums reported on U. S. monthly difference lists to War Risk Insurance Bureau, $45.20 | | 13,664 89 |
| Loss on sale or maturity of ledger assets | | 31,735 00 |
| Decrease in book value of ledger assets | | 12,646 00 |
| Total disbursements | | $6,577,916 69 |
| Balance | | $43,110,704 81 |

## LEDGER ASSETS.

|  | |
|---|---|
| Book value of real estate | $1,500,000 00 |
| Mortgage loans on real estate | 8,230,745 00 |
| Loans on company's policies assigned as collateral | 7,066,240 16 |
| Premium notes on policies in force | 910,696 90 |
| Book value of bonds and stocks | 25,098,736 56 |
| Cash in office | 722 55 |
| Deposits in trust companies and banks not on interest | 21,959 12 |
| Deposits in trust companies and banks on interest | 279,664 19 |
| Agents' balances (debit, $3,365.22; credit, $1,424.89) net | 1,940 33 |
| Total ledger assets | $43,110,704 81 |

## LEDGER ASSETS—Concluded.

### NON-LEDGER ASSETS.

| | | | |
|---|---|---|---|
| Interest accrued on mortgages | | $ 36,674 11 | |
| Interest accrued on bonds | | 280,154 35 | |
| Interest due and accrued on premium notes, loans or liens | | 53,967 30 | |
| Rents accrued on company's property | | 1,458 33 | |
| | | | $372,254 09 |
| | New business. | Renewals. | |
| Net uncollected and deferred premiums (paid for basis) | $74,280 43 | $875,639 09 | 949,919 52 |
| Gross assets | | | $44,432,878 42 |

### DEDUCT ASSETS NOT ADMITTED.

| | | |
|---|---|---|
| Agents' debit balances | $ 3,365 22 | |
| Premium notes, policy loans and other policy assets in excess of net value and of other policy liabilities on individual policies | 26,255 09 | |
| Book value of bonds and stocks over market value | 1,180,930 56 | |
| Total | | 1,210,550 87 |
| Admitted assets | | $43,222,327 55 |

## LIABILITIES.

| | | |
|---|---|---|
| Net present value of outstanding policies computed by the New York Insurance Department | $37,761,726 00 | |
| Same for dividend additions | 2,453,784 00 | |
| Same for annuities | 476,617 00 | |
| Total | $40,692,127 00 | |
| Deduct net value of risks re-insured | 842,678 00 | |
| Net reserve (paid for basis) | | $39,849,449 00 |
| Extra reserve for total and permanent disability benefits and for additional accidental death benefits included in life policies, less re-insurance | | 109,993 00 |
| Present value of supplementary contracts not involving life contingencies | | 345,255 00 |
| Present value of amounts incurred but not yet due for total and permanent disability benefits | | 18,991 00 |
| Surrender values claimable on policies cancelled | | 13 65 |
| Death losses due and unpaid | $ 5,589 00 | |
| Death losses in process of adjustment | 41,696 82 | |
| Death losses reported for which no proofs have been received | 94,826 28 | |
| Reserve for net death losses incurred but unreported | 45,000 00 | |
| Matured endowments due and unpaid | 73,634 70 | |
| Death losses and other policy claims resisted | 4,519 00 | |
| Annuity claims, involving life contingencies, due and unpaid | 967 10 | |
| Total policy claims | | 266,232 90 |
| Dividends left with the company to accumulate at interest | | 287,331 65 |
| Gross premiums paid in advance, including surrender values so applied, less discount, if any | | 40,106 29 |
| Unearned interest and rent paid in advance | | 231,496 80 |
| Commissions to agents due or accrued | | 8,728 07 |
| Salaries, rents, office expenses, bills and accounts due or accrued | | 10,000 00 |
| Medical examiners' and legal fees due or accrued | | 1,200 00 |
| Estimated amount hereafter payable for federal, state and other taxes based upon the business of the year of this statement | | 140,000 00 |
| Dividends or other profits due policyholders | | 49,572 26 |
| Dividends declared on or apportioned to annual dividend policies payable to policyholders during 1922 for period to 15th day of November, 1922 | | 750,000 00 |
| Reserve for security fluctuations and contingencies | | 130,000 00 |
| Other liabilities, viz: Present value of dividends applied to shorten premium-paying period, $1,091.00; New York State income tax withheld by the company, $625.46; accrued interest on mortgages, $336.05; and bonds, $914.44 held by company under reinsurance agreement | | 2,966 95 |
| Total | | $42,241,336 57 |
| Unassigned funds (surplus) | | 980,990 98 |
| Total | | $43,222,327 55 |

## EXHIBIT OF POLICIES—ORDINARY.

### ALL BUSINESS PAID FOR.

| | Number. | Amount. |
|---|---|---|
| Policies in force December 31, 1920 | 89,427 | $212,483,100 00 |
| Policies issued, revived and increased during the year | 10,891 | 31,810,915 00 |
| Total | 100,318 | $244,294,015 00 |

## EXHIBIT OF POLICIES—ORDINARY—Concluded.

ALL BUSINESS PAID FOR.

| | Number. | Amount. | Number. | Amount. |
|---|---|---|---|---|
| Deduct policies which have ceased to be in force during the year— | | | | |
| By death | 754 | $ 1,717,554 00 | | |
| By maturity | 498 | 1,226,079 00 | | |
| By expiry | 362 | 883,570 00 | | |
| By surrender | 2,046 | 4,560,567 00 | | |
| By lapse | 4,457 | 11,704,261 00 | | |
| By decrease | -------- | 1,085,097 00 | | |
| Total | | | 8,117 | $21,177,128 00 |
| Total policies in force December 31, 1921 | | | 92,201 | $223,116,887 00 |
| Re-insured | | | 942 | $11,709,721 00 |

## BUSINESS IN ILLINOIS—ORDINARY.

| | Number. | Amount. |
|---|---|---|
| Policies in force December 31, 1920 | 6,836 | $14,068,583 00 |
| Policies issued during the year | 641 | 1,736,922 00 |
| Total | 7,477 | $15,805,505 00 |
| Deduct policies ceased to be in force | 606 | 1,372,954 00 |
| Policies in force December 31, 1921 | 6,871 | $14,432,551 00 |
| Losses and claims unpaid December 31, 1920 | 4 | $ 8,072 00 |
| Losses and claims incurred during the year | 124 | 237,774 87 |
| Total | 128 | $245,846 87 |
| Losses and claims settled during the year | 127 | 245,706 87 |
| Losses and claims unpaid December 31, 1921 | 1 | $140 00 |
| Premiums received and premium abatements to policyholders not collected | | $477,434 35 |

## GAIN AND LOSS EXHIBIT.

INSURANCE EXHIBIT.

| | | Gain in surplus. | Loss in surplus. |
|---|---|---|---|
| Loading on actual premiums of the year (averaging 19.67 per cent of the gross premiums) | $1,385,452 50 | | |
| Insurance expenses incurred during the year | 1,627,080 58 | | |
| Loss from loading | | -------------- | $241,628 08 |
| Interest earned during the year | $2,119,444 93 | | |
| Investment expenses incurred during the year | 155,394 27 | | |
| Net income from investments | $1,964,050 66 | | |
| Interest required to maintain reserve | 1,321,412 00 | | |
| Gain from interest | | $642,638 66 | |
| Expected mortality on net amount at risk | $2,005,791 00 | | |
| Actual mortality on net amount at risk | 1,071,870 66 | | |
| Gain from mortality | | 933,920 34 | |
| Expected disbursements to annuitants | $33,175 41 | | |
| Net actual annuity claims incurred | 24,055 78 | | |
| Gain from annuities | | 9,119 63 | |
| Total gain during the year from surrendered and lapsed policies | | 197,776 31 | |
| Decrease in surplus on dividend account | | -------------- | 987,133 52 |
| Increase in special funds and special reserves during the year | | -------------- | 130,000 00 |

INVESTMENT EXHIBIT.

| | | Gain in surplus. | Loss in surplus. |
|---|---|---|---|
| Total gains from stocks and bonds | | 17,357 50 | |
| Total losses from stocks and bonds | | -------------- | 138,776 85 |
| Gain from assets not admitted | | 2,422 18 | |
| Net gain on account of total and permanent disability benefits or additional accidental death benefits included in life policies | | 30,362 76 | |
| Loss on account of method of valuation of dividend endowment accumulations | | -------------- | 2,825 28 |
| Total gains and losses in surplus during the year | | $1,833,597 38 | $1,500,363 73 |
| Surplus December 31, 1920 | $647,757 33 | | |
| Surplus December 31, 1921 | 980,990 98 | | |
| Increase in surplus | | -------------- | 333,233 65 |
| Total | | $1,833,597 38 | $1,833,597 38 |

## INDIANA NATIONAL LIFE INSURANCE COMPANY.

Located at No. 316 North Meridian Street, Indianapolis, Indiana; incorporated June 28, 1906; commenced business in Illinois August 26, 1919.

C. D. RENICK, President. E. E. LEIENDECKER, Secretary.

GEORGE A. BARR, Director of Trade and Commerce, Attorney for service at Springfield.

### CAPITAL.

| | | | |
|---|---|---|---|
| Capital paid up | | $210,000 00 | |
| Amount of ledger assets December 31, of previous year | | | $2,142,711 84 |

### INCOME.

| | | | |
|---|---|---|---|
| First year's premiums on original policies, less re-insurance | | $54,177 88 | |
| Surrender values applied to purchase paid-up insurance and annuities | | 11,263 49 | |
| New premiums | | $65,441 37 | |
| Renewal premiums less re-insurance | $372,396 52 | | |
| Dividends applied to pay renewal premiums | 17,954 89 | | |
| Renewal premiums | | 390,351 41 | |
| Premium income | | | $455,792 78 |
| Dividends left with company to accumulate at interest | | | 5,987 15 |
| Interest on mortgage loans | | $57,006 63 | |
| Interest on collateral loans | | 3,193 33 | |
| Interest on bonds | | 2,873 37 | |
| Interest on premium notes, policy loans or liens | | 22,059 67 | |
| Interest on deposits | | 779 00 | |
| Interest on other debts due the company | | 2,622 38 | |
| Rents—including $5,400.00 for company's occupancy of its own buildings | | 18,905 75 | |
| Total interest and rents | | | 107,440 13 |
| Borrowed money (gross) | | | 143,500 00 |
| Profit on sale or maturity of ledger assets | | | 512 83 |
| Total income | | | $713,232 89 |
| Total | | | $2,855,944 73 |

### DISBURSEMENTS.

| | | |
|---|---|---|
| Death claims | $94,457 24 | |
| Matured endowments | 4,220 26 | |
| Total and permanent disability claims | 70 61 | |
| Total death claims and endowments | | $98,748 11 |
| Premium notes and liens voided by lapse, less $192.41 restorations | | 5,769 36 |
| Surrender values paid in cash, or applied in liquidation of loans or notes | | 45,661 53 |
| Surrender values applied to purchase paid-up insurance and annuities | | 11,263 49 |
| Dividends paid policyholders in cash, or applied in liquidation of loans or notes | | 7,858 53 |
| Dividends applied to pay renewal premiums | | 17,954 89 |
| Dividends left with the company to accumulate at interest | | 5,987 15 |
| (Total paid policyholders | $193,243 06) | |
| Expense of investigation and settlement of policy claims, including legal expenses | | 830 10 |
| Supplementary contracts not involving life contingencies | | 540 00 |
| Commissions to agents, first year, $41,234.49; renewal, $12,073.60 | | 53,308 09 |
| Special renewal commissions | | 18,268 15 |
| Compensation of managers and agents not paid by commissions on new business | | 4,450 00 |
| Agency supervision and traveling expenses of supervisors | | 1,950 05 |
| Branch office expenses | | 633 79 |
| Medical examiners' fees and inspection of risks | | 7,086 95 |
| Salaries and all other compensation of officers and home office employees | | 32,261 50 |
| Rent | | 5,400 00 |
| Advertising, printing, stationery, postage, telegraph, telephone, express and exchange | | 9,772 66 |
| Repairs and expenses (other than taxes) on real estate | | 8,076 94 |
| Taxes on real estate | | 7,073 27 |
| State taxes on premiums | | 2,774 90 |
| Insurance department licenses and fees | | 747 41 |
| Federal taxes | | 2,927 92 |
| All other licenses, fees and taxes | | 285 25 |
| Other disbursements, viz: Actuarial services, $1,862.50; re-insurance contracts, $20,541.97; checks returned, $271.47; certificates of deposit charged off, $2,200.00; investment expense, $284.83; miscellaneous expense, $2,627.87; premiums with application, $58.09; tax on personal property, $497.46; miscellaneous traveling expense, $1,789.58 | | 30,133 77 |
| Borrowed money repaid (gross) | | 65,500 00 |
| Interest on borrowed money | | 8,340 42 |
| Total disbursements | | $453,604 23 |
| Balance | | $2,402,340 50 |

## LEDGER ASSETS.

| | | |
|---|---|---|
| Book value of real estate | | $ 373,500 00 |
| Mortgage loans on real estate | | 1,212,579 80 |
| Loans secured by collaterals | | 46,000 00 |
| Loans on company's policies assigned as collateral | | 476,590 12 |
| Premium notes on policies in force | | 48,096 20 |
| Book value of bonds | | 36,539 00 |
| Cash in office | | 6,962 71 |
| Deposits in trust companies and banks not on interest | | 25,443 40 |
| Deposits in trust companies and banks on interest | | 13,580 17 |
| Bills receivable | | 5,307 02 |
| Agents' balances (debit, $18,913.21; credit, $39.96), net | | 18,873 25 |
| American Service Bureau, $200.00; furniture and fixtures, $11,140.55; judgment vs. Aetna Insurance Company, $11,463.25; Liberal Life Assurance Company, $5,068.89; contracts for sale of real estate, $110,996.14 | | 138,868 83 |
| Total ledger assets | | $2,402,340 50 |

### NON-LEDGER ASSETS.

| | | |
|---|---|---|
| Interest due and accrued on mortgages | $32,625 08 | |
| Interest accrued on bonds | 432 67 | |
| Interest due and accrued on collateral loans | 1,068 78 | |
| Interest accrued on premium notes, loans or liens | 961 92 | |
| Interest due and accrued on other assets | 1,531 21 | |
| | | 36,619 66 |
| Market value of real estate over book value | | 6,700 00 |
| Net uncollected and deferred premiums (paid for basis), renewals | | 41,907 24 |
| Gross assets | | $2,487,567 40 |

### DEDUCT ASSETS NOT ADMITTED.

| | | |
|---|---|---|
| Furniture, fixtures and safes | $11,140 55 | |
| Agents' debit balances | 18,913 21 | |
| Bills receivable | 5,307 02 | |
| Premium notes, policy loans and other policy assets in excess of net value and of other policy liabilities on individual policies | 2,315 91 | |
| American Service Bureau | 200 00 | |
| Total | | 37,876 69 |
| Admitted assets | | $2,449,690 71 |

## LIABILITIES.

| | | |
|---|---|---|
| Net present value of outstanding policies | $2,092,762 76 | |
| Deduct net value of risks re-insured | 28,400 92 | |
| Net reserve (paid for basis) | | $2,064,361 84 |
| Death losses in process of adjustment | $4,500 00 | |
| Death losses reported for which no proofs have been received | 1,500 00 | |
| Death losses and other policy claims resisted | 1,000 00 | |
| Total policy claims | | 7,000 00 |
| Due and unpaid on supplementary contracts not involving life contingencies | | 3,134 00 |
| Dividends left with the company to accumulate at interest | | 54,973 02 |
| Unearned interest and rent paid in advance | | 4,781 60 |
| Commissions to agents due or accrued | | 1,127 11 |
| Salaries, rents, office expenses, bills, and accounts due or accrued | | 1,244 23 |
| Medical examiners' fees due or accrued | | 505 00 |
| Estimated amount hereafter payable for federal, state and other taxes based upon the business of the year of this statement | | 13,000 00 |
| Borrowed money | | 78,000 00 |
| Other liabilities, viz: Premiums paid with application, $52.39; survivorship liens, $250.00 | | 302 39 |
| Total | | $2,228,429 19 |
| Capital paid up | | 210,000 00 |
| Unassigned funds (surplus) | | 11,261 52 |
| Total | | $2,449,690 71 |

## EXHIBIT OF POLICIES—ORDINARY.

### ALL BUSINESS PAID FOR.

| | Number. | Amount. |
|---|---|---|
| Policies in force December 31, 1920 | 9,590 | $16,556,679 00 |
| Policies issued, revived, and increased during the year | 1,191 | 2,448,780 00 |
| Total | 10,781 | $19,005,459 00 |

## EXHIBIT OF POLICIES—ORDINARY—Concluded.

ALL BUSINESS PAID FOR.

| | Number. | Amount. | Number. | Amount. |
|---|---|---|---|---|
| Deduct policies which have ceased to be in force during the year— | | | | |
| By death | 55 | $ 94,824 00 | | |
| By maturity | 1 | 2,000 00 | | |
| By expiry | 78 | 116,152 00 | | |
| By surrender | 226 | 577,952 00 | | |
| By lapse | 873 | 2,061,312 00 | | |
| By decrease | -------- | 106,337 00 | | |
| By withdrawal | 75 | 218,510 00 | | |
| Total | | | 1,308 | 3,177,087 00 |
| Total policies in force December 31, 1921 | | | 9,473 | $15,828,372 00 |
| Re-insured | | | 199 | $818,404 00 |

## BUSINESS IN ILLINOIS—ORDINARY.

| | Number. | Amount. |
|---|---|---|
| Policies in force December 31, 1920 | 215 | $428,500 00 |
| Policies issued during the year | 283 | 442,000 00 |
| Total | 498 | $870,500 00 |
| Deduct policies ceased to be in force | 68 | 218,000 00 |
| Policies in force December 31, 1921 | 430 | $652,500 00 |
| Losses and claims incurred during the year | 1 | $1,000 00 |
| Losses and claims settled during the year | 1 | 1,000 00 |
| Premiums received | | $12,898 47 |

## GAIN AND LOSS EXHIBIT.

INSURANCE EXHIBIT.

| | | Gain in surplus. | Loss in surplus. |
|---|---|---|---|
| Loading on actual premiums of the year (averaging 14.33 per cent of the gross premiums) | $ 66,167 64 | | |
| Insurance expenses incurred during the year | 175,995 65 | | |
| Loss from loading | | ------------- | $109,828 01 |
| Interest earned during the year | $105,265 65 | | |
| Investment expenses incurred during the year | 15,435 04 | | |
| Net income from investments | $89,830 61 | | |
| Interest required to maintain reserve | 67,726 30 | | |
| Gain from interest | | 22,104 31 | |
| Expected mortality on net amount at risk | $182,064 70 | | |
| Actual mortality on net amount at risk | 81,549 76 | | |
| Gain from mortality | | 100,514 94 | |
| Total gain during the year from surrendered and lapsed policies | | 12,315 22 | |
| Decrease in surplus on dividend account | | ------------- | 31,800 57 |
| Decrease in special funds, and special reserves during the year | | 10,613 63 | |
| Net to loss account | | ------------- | 8,240 83 |

INVESTMENT EXHIBIT.

| | | Gain in surplus. | Loss in surplus. |
|---|---|---|---|
| Total gains from bonds | | 512 83 | |
| Total losses from bonds | | ------------- | 1,000 00 |
| Loss from assets not admitted | | ------------- | 2,611 80 |
| Net loss on account of total and permanent disability benefits or additional accidental death benefits included in life policies | | ------------- | 70 61 |
| Total gains and losses in surplus during the year | | $146,060 93 | $153,551 82 |
| Surplus December 31, 1920 | $18,752 41 | | |
| Surplus December 31, 1921 | 11,261 52 | | |
| Decrease in surplus | | 7,490 89 | |
| Total | | $153,551 82 | $153,551 82 |

## INDIANAPOLIS LIFE INSURANCE COMPANY.

Located at No. 300-312 Board of Trade Building, Indianapolis, Indiana; incorporated July 10, 1905; commenced business in Illinois September 8, 1909.

FRANK P. MANLY, President. JOSEPH R. RAUB, Secretary.

NING ELEY, Chicago, Attorney for service.

| | | | |
|---|---|---|---|
| Amount of ledger assets December 31, of previous year | | $2,016,404 99 | |
| Decrease of guaranty capital during year | | 51,500 00 | |
| Extended at | | | $1,964,904 99 |

### INCOME.

| | | | |
|---|---|---|---|
| First year's premiums on original policies, less re-insurance | | $192,382 53 | |
| First year's premiums for total and permanent disability benefits, less re-insurance | | 1,738 45 | |
| First year's premiums for additional accidental death benefits, less re-insurance | | 704 29 | |
| Dividends applied to purchase paid-up additions and annuities | | 458 66 | |
| New premiums | | $195,283 93 | |
| Renewal premiums less re-insurance | $566,278 72 | | |
| Renewal premiums for total and permanent disability benefits, less re-insurance | 1,587 11 | | |
| Renewal premiums for additional accidental death benefits, less re-insurance | 57 74 | | |
| Dividends applied to pay renewal premiums | 62,706 26 | | |
| Surrender values applied to pay renewal premiums | 389 88 | | |
| Renewal premiums | | 631,019 71 | |
| Premium income | | | $826,303 64 |
| Consideration for supplementary contracts not involving life contingencies | | | 2,640 00 |
| Dividends left with company to accumulate at interest | | | 15,432 09 |
| Interest on mortgage loans | | $73,074 49 | |
| Interest on bonds | | 8,522 00 | |
| Interest on premium notes, policy loans or liens | | 19,876 42 | |
| Interest on deposits | | 2,208 60 | |
| Interest on other debts due the company | | 15,354 98 | |
| Rents | | 353 26 | |
| Total interest and rents | | | 119,389 75 |
| From other sources, viz: Increase of unapplied payments on premiums held in suspense, $5,084.80; unapplied payments forfeited to company, $1,049.47; proportional premiums collected on lapse of extension agreements, $507.12 | | | 6,641 39 |
| Agents' balances previously charged off | | | 13 00 |
| Increase in book value of ledger assets | | | 99 28 |
| Total income | | | $970,519 15 |
| Total | | | $2,935,424 14 |

### DISBURSEMENTS.

| | | |
|---|---|---|
| Death claims | $82,935 80 | |
| Matured endowments | 1,000 00 | |
| Total and permanent disability claims | 23 17 | |
| Total death claims and endowments | | $ 83,958 97 |
| Surrender values paid in cash, or applied in liquidation of loans or notes | | 30,071 88 |
| Surrender values applied to pay new and renewal premiums | | 389 88 |
| Dividends paid policyholders in cash, or applied in liquidation of loans or notes | | 581 21 |
| Dividends applied to pay renewal premiums | | 62,706 26 |
| Dividends applied to purchase paid-up additions and annuities | | 458 66 |
| Dividends left with the company to accumulate at interest | | 15,432 09 |
| (Total paid policyholders | $193,598 95) | |
| Supplementary contracts not involving life contingencies | | 1,975 74 |
| Dividends with interest, held on deposit surrendered during the year | | 2,470 24 |
| Interest to scripholders | | 4,908 20 |
| Commissions to agents, first year, $132,433.67; renewal, $14,780.15 | | 147,213 82 |
| Agency supervision and traveling expenses of supervisors | | 15,314 36 |
| Branch office expenses | | 7,097 84 |
| Medical examiners' fees and inspection of risks | | 17,022 26 |
| Salaries and all other compensation of officers and home office employees | | 67,180 21 |
| Rent | | 3,802 20 |
| Advertising, printing, stationery, postage, telegraph, telephone, express and exchange | | 15,797 87 |
| Legal expense | | 32 70 |
| Furniture, fixtures and safes | | 2,090 35 |
| Repairs and expenses (other than taxes) on real estate | | 171 61 |
| Taxes on real estate | | 54 78 |
| State taxes on premiums | | 8,413 92 |

DISBURSEMENTS—Concluded.

| | |
|---|---|
| Insurance department licenses and fees | $ 655 40 |
| Federal taxes | 5,758 14 |
| All other licenses, fees and taxes, state and county taxes | 247 39 |
| Other disbursements, viz: Library expense, $555.73; miscellaneous expense, $3,183.85 | 3,739 58 |
| Agents' balances charged off | 1,202 46 |
| Loss on sale or maturity of ledger assets | 34 50 |
| Decrease in book value of ledger assets | 1,500 00 |
| Total disbursements | $500,282 52 |
| Balance | $2,435,141 62 |

LEDGER ASSETS.

| | |
|---|---|
| Book value of real estate | $ 13,200 00 |
| Mortgage loans on real estate | 1,473,883 12 |
| Loans on company's policies assigned as collateral | 328,147 23 |
| Book value of bonds | 467,808 57 |
| Cash in office | 200 00 |
| Deposits in trust companies and banks not on interest | 39,731 17 |
| Deposits in trust companies and banks on interest | 91,959 46 |
| Bills receivable | 4,076 40 |
| Agents' balances (debit, $16,983.46; credit, $847.79), net | 16,135 67 |
| Total ledger assets | $2,435,141 62 |

NON-LEDGER ASSETS.

| | | | |
|---|---|---|---|
| Interest due and accrued on mortgages | | $40,557 61 | |
| Interest accrued on bonds | | 10,914 44 | |
| Interest accrued on other assets, certificates of deposit, $647.54; bank balance, $45.93 | | 693 47 | |
| | | | 52,165 52 |
| | New business. | Renewals. | |
| Net uncollected and deferred premiums (paid for basis) | $2,631 85 | $132,996 60 | 135,628 45 |
| Furniture, fixtures and safes | | | 8,030 02 |
| Gross assets | | | $2,630,965 61 |

DEDUCT ASSETS NOT ADMITTED.

| | | |
|---|---|---|
| Furniture, fixtures and safes | $ 8,030 02 | |
| Agents' debit balances | 16,983 46 | |
| Bills receivable | 4,076 40 | |
| Premium notes, policy loans and other policy assets in excess of net value and of other policy liabilities on individual policies | 7,387 24 | |
| Total | | 36,477 12 |
| Admitted assets | | $2,594,488 49 |

LIABILITIES.

| | | |
|---|---|---|
| Net present value of outstanding policies computed by the Indiana Insurance Department | $2,327,207 13 | |
| Same for dividend additions | 1,315 38 | |
| Same for annuities | 3,024 11 | |
| Total | $2,331,546 62 | |
| Deduct net value of risks re-insured | 16,983 60 | |
| Net reserve (paid for basis) | | $2,314,563 02 |
| Extra reserve for total and permanent disability benefits and for additional accidental death benefits included in life policies, less re-insurance | | 3,047 14 |
| Present value of supplementary contracts not involving life contingencies | | 30,851 81 |
| Present value of amounts incurred but not yet due for total and permanent disability benefits | | 136 62 |
| Death losses reported for which no proofs have been received | | 1,738 73 |
| Dividends left with the company to accumulate at interest | | 59,258 71 |
| Gross premiums paid in advance, including surrender values so applied, less discount, if any | | 8,010 22 |
| Unearned interest and rent paid in advance | | 7,164 55 |
| Commissions to agents due or accrued | | 7,015 21 |
| Salaries, rents, office expenses, bills, and accounts due or accrued | | 2,069 04 |
| Medical examiners' and legal fees due or accrued | | 2,459 45 |
| Estimated amount hereafter payable for federal, state and other taxes based upon the business of the year of this statement | | 16,497 48 |
| Dividends or other profits due policyholders | | 17,899 56 |
| Unapplied payments on premiums | | 10,613 94 |
| Total | | $2,481,325 48 |
| Outstanding guaranty capital, $56,090.37; not a current liability. | | |
| Unassigned funds (surplus) | | 113,163 01 |
| Total | | $2,594,488 49 |

## EXHIBIT OF POLICIES—ORDINARY.

ALL BUSINESS PAID FOR.

| | Number. | Amount. | Number. | Amount. |
|---|---|---|---|---|
| Policies in force December 31, 1920 | | | 14,491 | $26,438,143 90 |
| Policies issued, revived, and increased during the year | | | 3,612 | 6,948,094 09 |
| Total | | | 18,103 | $33,386,237 99 |
| Deduct policies which have ceased to be in force during the year— | | | | |
| By death | 54 | $ 83,987 50 | | |
| By maturity | 1 | 1,000 00 | | |
| By expiry | 215 | 478,466 38 | | |
| By surrender | 125 | 207,505 65 | | |
| By lapse | 936 | 2,137,024 00 | | |
| By decrease | 1 | 184,902 58 | | |
| Total | | | 1,332 | 3,092,886 11 |
| Total policies in force December 31, 1921 | | | 16,771 | $30,293,351 88 |
| Re-insured | | | 601 | $1,495,177 00 |

## BUSINESS IN ILLINOIS—ORDINARY.

| | Number. | Amount. |
|---|---|---|
| Policies in force December 31, 1920 | 4,515 | $7,876,724 81 |
| Policies issued during the year | 1,114 | 1,930,524 01 |
| Total | 5,629 | $9,807,248 82 |
| Deduct policies ceased to be in force | 395 | 779,054 65 |
| Policies in force December 31, 1921 | 5,234 | $9,028,194 17 |
| Losses and claims unpaid December 31, 1920 | 5 | $ 8,500 00 |
| Losses and claims incurred during the year | 12 | 16,500 00 |
| Total | 17 | $25,000 00 |
| Losses and claims settled during the year | 17 | 25,000 00 |
| Premiums received | | $276,136 40 |

## GAIN AND LOSS EXHIBIT.

INSURANCE EXHIBIT.

| | | Gain in surplus. | Loss in surplus. |
|---|---|---|---|
| Loading on actual premiums of the year (averaging 25.3 per cent of the gross premiums) | $228,045 07 | | |
| Insurance expenses incurred during the year | 317,314 36 | | |
| Loss from loading | | | $89,269 29 |
| Interest earned during the year | $142,540 23 | | |
| Investment expenses incurred during the year | 5,742 84 | | |
| Net income from investments | $136,797 39 | | |
| Interest required to maintain reserve | 78,034 98 | | |
| Gain from interest | | $ 58,762 41 | |
| Expected mortality on net amount at risk | $245,457 43 | | |
| Actual mortality on net amount at risk | 65,744 24 | | |
| Gain from mortality | | 179,713 19 | |
| Net actual annuity claims incurred | | | 19 55 |
| Total gain during the year from surrendered and lapsed policies | | 12,155 19 | |
| Interest paid scripholders | | | 4,908 20 |
| Decrease in surplus on dividend account | | | 87,117 33 |
| Net to gain account | | 367 13 | |

INVESTMENT EXHIBIT.

| | | Gain in surplus. | Loss in surplus. |
|---|---|---|---|
| Total losses from real estate | | | 1,500 00 |
| Total losses from bonds | | | 34 50 |
| Loss from assets not admitted | | | 13,055 44 |
| Net gain on account of total and permanent disability benefits or additional accidental death benefits included in life policies | | 2,917 84 | |
| Decrease in guaranty capital | | | 51,500 00 |
| Balance unaccounted for | | | 517 80 |
| Total gains and losses in surplus during the year | | $253,915 76 | $247,922 11 |
| Surplus December 31, 1920 | $107,169 36 | | |
| Surplus December 31, 1921 | 113,163 01 | | |
| Increase in surplus | | | 5,993 65 |
| Total | | $253,915 76 | $253,915 76 |

## INTERNATIONAL LIFE INSURANCE COMPANY.

Located at No. 722 Chestnut Street, St. Louis, Missouri; incorporated August 19, 1909; commenced business in Illinois September 8, 1909.

MASSEY WILSON, President. W. F. GRANTGES, Secretary.

JUDSON DRENNAN, East St. Louis, Attorney for service.

### CAPITAL.

| | | | |
|---|---|---|---|
| Capital paid up | | $656,250 00 | |
| Amount of ledger assets December 31, of previous year | | $14,680,302 54 | |
| Increase of paid-up capital during year | | 131,250 00 | |
| Extended at | | | $14,811,552 54 |

### INCOME.

| | | | |
|---|---|---|---|
| First year's premiums on original policies, less re-insurance | | $1,005,021 07 | |
| First year's premiums for additional accidental death benefits, less re-insurance | | 1,119 80 | |
| Dividends applied to purchase paid-up additions and annuities | | 32 61 | |
| New premiums | | $1,006,173 48 | |
| Renewal premiums less re-insurance | $3,188,560 25 | | |
| Renewal premiums for total and permanent disability benefits, less re-insurance | 38,063 29 | | |
| Renewal premiums for additional accidental death benefits, less re-insurance | 62,314 58 | | |
| Dividends applied to pay renewal premiums | 148,350 39 | | |
| Dividends applied to shorten the endowment or premium-paying period | 4,989 00 | | |
| Assets received account of reinstatement and re-issue | 48,621 77 | | |
| Renewal premiums | | 3,490,899 28 | |
| Premium income | | | $4,497,072 76 |
| Consideration for supplementary contracts involving life contingencies | | | 10,000 00 |
| Consideration for supplementary contracts not involving life contingencies | | | 17,647 14 |
| Dividends left with company to accumulate at interest | | | 207,688 77 |
| Interest on mortgage loans | | $431,137 08 | |
| Interest on collateral loans | | 5,033 29 | |
| Interest on bonds | | 44,108 64 | |
| Interest on premium notes, policy loans or liens | | 205,096 12 | |
| Interest on deposits | | 25,584 68 | |
| Interest on other debts due the company | | 7,785 18 | |
| Rents—less interest on incumbrances | | 203,373 81 | |
| Total interest and rents | | | 922,118 80 |
| From other sources, viz: Miscellaneous suspense, $3,535.15; received on ledger assets previosuly charged off, $379.78; exchange and collection, $214.50 | | | 4,129 43 |
| Borrowed money (gross) | | | 352,658 27 |
| Agents' balances previously charged off | | | 272 66 |
| Profit on sale or maturity of ledger assets | | | 3,200 68 |
| Total income | | | $6,014,788 51 |
| Total | | | $20,826,341 05 |

### DISBURSEMENTS.

| | | | |
|---|---|---|---|
| Death claims and additions | | $702,484 47 | |
| Matured endowments | | 16,095 91 | |
| Total and permanent disability claims and additional accidental death benefits, less re-insurance | | 26,050 50 | |
| Total death claims and endowments | | | $744,630 88 |
| Annuities involving life contingencies | | | 760 51 |
| Surrender values paid in cash, or applied in liquidation of loans or notes | | | 376,660 45 |
| Dividends paid policyholders in cash, or applied in liquidation of loans or notes | | | 10,753 97 |
| Dividends applied to pay renewal premiums | | | 148,350 39 |
| Dividends applied to shorten the endowment or premium-paying period | | | 4,989 00 |
| Dividends applied to purchase paid-up additions and annuities | | | 32 61 |
| Dividends left with the company to accumulate at interest | | | 207,688 77 |
| (Total paid policyholders | | $1,493,866 58) | |
| Expense of investigation and settlement of policy claims | | | 1,623 71 |
| Supplementary contracts not involving life contingencies | | | 13,447 35 |
| Dividends with interest, held on deposit surrendered during the year | | | 97,193 93 |
| Dividends to stockholders | | | 212,129 09 |

DISBURSEMENTS—Concluded.

| | |
|---|---|
| Commissions to agents, first year, $690,615.57; renewal, $161,609.92 | $852,225 49 |
| Commuted renewal commissions | 970 40 |
| Compensation of managers and agents not paid by commissions on new business | 67,422 16 |
| Agency supervision and traveling expenses of supervisors | 15,806 70 |
| Branch office expenses | 15,070 31 |
| Medical examiners' fees and inspection of risks | 55,600 48 |
| Salaries and all other compensation of officers and home office employees | 229,342 04 |
| Rent | 18,218 15 |
| Advertising, printing, stationery, postage, telegraph, telephone and express | 45,070 46 |
| Legal expense | 13,013 58 |
| Furniture, fixtures and safes | 8,405 39 |
| Repairs and expenses (other than taxes) on real estate | 139,247 34 |
| Taxes on real estate | 29,589 78 |
| State taxes on premiums | 67,296 98 |
| Insurance department licenses and fees | 14,411 75 |
| Federal taxes | 60,658 41 |
| All other licenses, fees and taxes | 3,719 16 |
| Other disbursements, viz: Advance and partial payments, $4,658.29; discount on advance premiums, $90.59; deposit on mortgage loan inspections, $1,118.65; investment expense, $7,038.89; employees' insurance, bonus and pension account, $1,202.19; incidental expense, $1,540.46; paid other companies for assuming our risks, $255.48; traveling expense, $4,326.91; Empire Life expense, $1,297.15; bond premiums, $2,769.31 | 24,297 92 |
| Borrowed money repaid (gross) | 352,658 27 |
| Interest on borrowed money | 32,550 31 |
| Agents' balances charged off | 370 16 |
| Loss on sale or maturity of ledger assets | 38,127 05 |
| Total disbursements | $3,902,332 95 |
| Balance | $16,924,008 10 |

LEDGER ASSETS.

| | |
|---|---|
| Book value of real estate | $1,192,623 79 |
| Mortgage loans on real estate | 8,664,960 15 |
| Loans secured by collaterals | 1,535,156 86 |
| Loans on company's policies assigned as collateral | 3,862,458 47 |
| Premium notes on policies in force | 122,428 37 |
| Book value of bonds | 610,477 95 |
| Cash in office | 6,923 96 |
| Deposits in trust companies and banks not on interest | 21,806 59 |
| Deposits in trust companies and banks on interest | 827,760 27 |
| Agents' balances (debit, $104,862.85; credit, $25,451.16) net | 79,411 69 |
| Total ledger assets | $16,924,008 10 |

NON-LEDGER ASSETS.

| | | |
|---|---|---|
| Interest due and accrued on mortgages | $421,729 81 | |
| Interest accrued on bonds | 10,313 19 | |
| Interest accrued on collateral loans | 85,216 23 | |
| Interest accrued on other assets | 1,234 63 | |
| Rents due on company's property | 20,161 35 | |
| | | 538,655 21 |
| Net uncollected and deferred premiums (paid for basis) renewals | | 252,960 84 |
| All other assets, viz: Empire Life Re-insurance liens, $310,803.79; ground rent paid in advance, $3,000.00 | | 313,803 79 |
| Gross assets | | $18,029,427 94 |

DEDUCT ASSETS NOT ADMITTED.

| | | |
|---|---|---|
| Agents' debit balances | $104,862 85 | |
| Premium notes, policy loans and other policy assets in excess of net value and of other policy liabilities on individual policies | 23,743 06 | |
| Book value of real estate over market value | 26,970 68 | |
| Book value of bonds over market value | 17,059 20 | |
| Book vaule of other ledger assets over market value, viz: Mortgage loan, $14,757.19; interest, $22,570.12 | 37,327 31 | |
| Total | | 209,963 10 |
| Admitted assets | | $17,819,464 84 |

LIABILITIES.

| | | |
|---|---|---|
| Net present value of outstanding policies | $14,372,355 16 | |
| Same for annuities | 16,752 64 | |
| Total | $14,389,107 80 | |
| Deduct net value of risks re-insured | 71,123 59 | |
| Net reserve (paid for basis) | | $14,317,984 21 |
| Extra reserve for total and permanent disability benefits and for additional accidental death benefits included in life policies, less re-insurance | | 189,117 37 |
| Present value of supplementary contracts not involving life contingencies | | 90,705 57 |

LIABILITIES—Concluded.

| | | |
|---|---|---|
| Present value of amounts incurred but not yet due for total and permanent disability benefits | | $ 4,889 69 |
| Surrender values claimable on policies cancelled | | 3,764 30 |
| Death losses in process of adjustment | $17,800 00 | |
| Death losses reported for which no proofs have been received | 55,714 49 | |
| Reserve for net death losses incurred but unreported | 9,000 00 | |
| Death losses and other policy claims resisted | 13,000 00 | |
| Total and permanent disability benefits and additional accidental death benefits | 23,482 44 | |
| Total policy claims | | 118,996 93 |
| Dividends left with the company to accumulate at interest | | 1,161,675 08 |
| Gross premiums paid in advance, including surrender values so applied, less discount, if any | | 31,415 82 |
| Unearned interest and rent paid in advance | | 90,152 77 |
| Commissions due agents on premium notes, when paid | | 6,141 22 |
| Commissions to agents due or accrued | | 3,437 73 |
| Salaries, rents, office expenses, bills and accounts due or accrued | | 22,341 49 |
| Medical examiners' and legal fees due or accrued | | 3,550 91 |
| Estimated amount hereafter payable for federal, state and other taxes based upon the business of the year of this statement | | 177,527 29 |
| Unpaid dividends to stockholders | | 666 87 |
| Dividends or other profits due policyholders | | 17,425 12 |
| Dividends declared on or apportioned to annual dividend policies payable to policyholders during 1922 for period to June 30, 1922 | | 38,413 13 |
| Dividends declared on or apportioned to deferred dividend policies payable to policyholders during 1922 for period to June 30, 1922 | | 372 45 |
| Amounts set apart, apportioned, provisionally ascertained, calculated, declared or held awaiitng apportionment upon deferred dividend policies | | 151 06 |
| Depreciation and contingent reserve account | | 84,143 12 |
| Investment reserve | | 5,000 00 |
| Survivorship fund | | 8,979 57 |
| Other liabilities, viz: Miscellaneous suspense, $7,183.92; accrued interest on real estate incumbrances, $3,322.91; deposit for inspection of mortgage loans, $863.12; advance and partial payments, $2,180.66; Empire Life liability, $15,833.00 | | 29,383 61 |
| Total | | $16,406,235 31 |
| Capital paid up | | 656,250 00 |
| Trust certificates | | 137,605 00 |
| Unassigned funds (surplus) | | 619,374 53 |
| Total | | $17,819,464 84 |

## EXHIBIT OF POLICIES—ORDINARY.

ALL BUSINESS PAID FOR.

| | Number. | Amount. | Number. | Amount. |
|---|---|---|---|---|
| Policies in force December 31, 1920 | | | 57,164 | $130,628,075 00 |
| Policies issued, revived and increased during the year | | | 11,785 | 40,182,627 00 |
| Total | | | 68,949 | $170,810,702 00 |
| Deduct policies which have ceased to be in force during the year— | | | | |
| By death | 307 | $ 799,783 00 | | |
| By maturity | 4 | 10,000 00 | | |
| By expiry | 245 | 453,119 00 | | |
| By surrender | 1,130 | 2,489,420 00 | | |
| By lapse | 9,645 | 27,942,268 00 | | |
| By decrease | -------- | 876,194 00 | | |
| Total | | | 11,331 | 32,570,784 00 |
| Total policies in force December 31, 1921 | | | 57,618 | $138,239,918 00 |
| Re-insured | | | | $8,340,136 00 |

## EXHIBIT OF POLICIES—GROUP INSURANCE.

ALL BUSINESS PAID FOR.

| | Amount. | Number. | Amount. |
|---|---|---|---|
| Policies in force December 31, 1920 | | 3 | $276,000 00 |
| Policies issued, revived and increased during the year | | 2 | 585,300 00 |
| Total | | 5 | $861,300 00 |
| Deduct policies which have ceased to be in force during the year— | | | |
| By death | $ 1,000 00 | | |
| By decrease | 93,700 00 | | |
| Total | | -------- | 94,700 00 |
| Total policies in force December 31, 1921 | | 5 | $766,600 00 |
| Distribution of business in force at end of year—One year term | | 5 | $766,600 00 |

BUSINESS IN ILLINOIS—ORDINARY.

| | Number. | Amount. |
|---|---|---|
| Policies in force December 31, 1920 | 5,521 | $11,043,657 00 |
| Policies issued during the year | 1,656 | 5,026,282 00 |
| Total | 7,177 | $16,069,939 00 |
| Deduct policies ceased to be in force | 1,177 | 3,564,776 00 |
| Policies in force December 31, 1921 | 6,000 | $12,505,163 00 |
| Losses and claims unpaid December 31, 1920 | 4 | $ 8,104 00 |
| Losses and claims incurred during the year | 37 | 97,793 00 |
| Total | 41 | $105,897 00 |
| Losses and claims settled during the year | 34 | 75,897 00 |
| Losses and claims unpaid December 31, 1921 | 7 | $30,000 00 |
| Premiums received | | $426,731 21 |

GAIN AND LOSS EXHIBIT.

INSURANCE EXHIBIT.

| | | Gain in surplus. | Loss in surplus. |
|---|---|---|---|
| Loading on actual premiums of the year (averaging 30.2 per cent of the gross premiums | $1,338,321 96 | | |
| Insurance expenses incurred during the year | 1,468,292 14 | | |
| Loss from loading | | | $129,970 18 |
| Interest earned during the year | $1,050,389 92 | | |
| Investment expenses incurred during the year | 217,072 93 | | |
| Net income from investments | $833,316 99 | | |
| Interest required to maintain reserve | 529,530 79 | | |
| Gain from interest | | $303,786 20 | |
| Expected mortality on net amount at risk | $1,201,279 41 | | |
| Actual mortality on net amount at risk | 620,501 77 | | |
| Gain from mortality | | 580,777 64 | |
| Expected disbursements to annuitants | $932 39 | | |
| Net actual annuity claims incurred | 760 51 | | |
| Loss from annuities | | | 171 88 |
| Total gain during the year from surrendered and lapsed policies | | 86,584 25 | |
| Dividends paid stockholders | | | 209,986 33 |
| Decrease in surplus on dividend account | | | 379,034 07 |
| Increase in special funds and special reserves during the year | | | 39,163 08 |
| Net to loss account | | | 97 50 |

INVESTMENT EXHIBIT.

| | | Gain in surplus. | Loss in surplus. |
|---|---|---|---|
| Total gains from real estate | | 8,841 97 | |
| Total losses from real estate | | | 2,781 97 |
| Total gains from bonds | | 9,079 39 | |
| Total losses from bonds | | | 32,756 24 |
| Gain on mortgage loans, $3,618.86; received on assets charged off, $379.79; loss on collateral loans, $2,588.84 | | 1,409 80 | |
| Gain from assets not admitted | | 6,746 19 | |
| Net gain on account of total and permanent disability benefits or additional accidental death benefits included in life policies | | 17,211 06 | |
| Loss from all other sources: Increase in liability, miscellaneous suspense and partial payments, $852.78; Empire Life liens, $7,982.13 | | | 8,834 91 |
| Balance unaccounted for | | | 4,284 81 |
| Total gains and losses in surplus during the year | | $1,014,436 50 | $807,080 97 |
| Surplus December 31, 1920 | $412,019 00 | | |
| Surplus December 31, 1921 | 619,374 53 | | |
| Increase in surplus | | | 207,355 53 |
| Total | | $1,014,436 50 | $1,014,436 50 |

## JOHN HANCOCK MUTUAL LIFE INSURANCE COMPANY.

Located at No. 178 Devonshire Street, Boston, Massachusetts; incorporated April 21, 1862; commenced business in Illinois August 4, 1865.

WALTON L. CROCKER, President. CHARLES J. DIMAN, Secretary.

JOSEPH H. STRONG, Chicago, Attorney for service.

| | |
|---|---|
| Amount of ledger assets December 31, of previous year | $202,691,568 32 |

## INCOME.

|  | | | |
|---|---|---|---|
| First year's premiums on original policies, less re-insurance | | $3,989,157 62 | |
| First year's premiums for total and permanent disability benefits | | 33,437 98 | |
| First year's premiums for additional accidental death benefits | | 16,763 14 | |
| Dividends applied to purchase paid-up additions and annuities | | 162,230 31 | |
| Surrender values applied to purchase paid-up insurance and annuities | | 494,094 27 | |
| Consideration for original annuities involving life contingencies | | 5,000 00 | |
| New premiums | | $ 4,700,683 32 | |
| Renewal premiums less re-insurance | $45,335,726 95 | | |
| Renewal premiums for total and permanent disability benefits | 101,939 36 | | |
| Renewal premiums for additional accidental death benefits | 1,471 25 | | |
| Dividends applied to pay renewal premiums | 2,471,518 57 | | |
| Renewal premiums | | 47,910,656 13 | |
| Premium income | | | $52,611,339 45 |
| Consideration for certificates of deposit | | | 40,000 00 |
| Consideration for supplementary contracts not involving life contingencies | | | 96,445 00 |
| Dividends left with company to accumulate at interest | | | 307,118 06 |
| Interest on mortgage loans | | $6,318,738 67 | |
| Interest on bonds and dividends on stocks | | 3,151,789 91 | |
| Interest on premium notes, policy loans or liens | | 822,297 16 | |
| Interest on deposits | | 56,214 61 | |
| Interest on other debts due the company | | 12,694 52 | |
| Discount on claims paid in advance | | 4,321 56 | |
| Rents | | 22,251 43 | |
| Total interest and rents | | | 10,388,307 86 |
| From other sources, viz: Accumulation fund, $504.01; unclaimed checks, $5,209.49; received under option of extension, Fort Worth and Denver, City rail road bonds, $4,000.00; conscience money, $147.00 | | | 9,860 50 |
| Agents' balances previously charged off | | | 2,194 42 |
| Profit on sale or maturity of ledger assets | | | 3,829 81 |
| Increase in book value of ledger assets | | | 89,295 61 |
| Total income | | | $63,548,390 71 |
| Total | | | $266,239,959 03 |

## DISBURSEMENTS.

|  | | |
|---|---|---|
| Death claims and additions | $11,515,986 98 | |
| Matured endowments and additions | 1,064,610 13 | |
| Total and permanent disability claims | 8,575 10 | |
| Total death claims and endowments | | $12,589,172 21 |
| Annuities involving life contingencies | | 941 00 |
| Surrender values paid in cash, or applied in liquidation of loans or notes | | 4,288,778 20 |
| Surrender values applied to purchase paid-up insurance and annuities | | 494,094 27 |
| Dividends paid policyholders in cash, or applied in liquidation of loans or notes | | 230,062 50 |
| Dividends applied to pay renewal premiums | | 2,471,518 57 |
| Dividends applied to purchase paid-up additions and annuities | | 162,230 31 |
| Dividends left with the company to accumulate at interest | | 307,118 06 |
| (Total paid policyholders | $20,543,915 12) | |
| Expense of investigation and settlement of policy claims, including legal expenses | | 71,250 19 |
| Supplementary contracts not involving life contingencies | | 90,927 00 |
| Certificates of deposit liqnidated | | 4,000 00 |
| Dividends with interest held on deposit surrendered during the year | | 77,834 08 |
| Net premiums repaid under Soldiers' and Sailors' Civil Relief Act | | 177 83 |
| Commissions to agents, first year, $1,680,059.46; renewal, $1,303,766.99; compensation in industrial branch to assistant superintendents and agents, $6,208,087.06 | | 9,191,913 51 |
| Agency supervision and traveling expenses of supervisors | | 321,888 11 |
| Agency office expenses | | 1,054,456 58 |
| Medical examiners' fees and inspection of risks | | 575,747 33 |
| Salaries and all other compensation of officers and home office employees | | 2,012,905 46 |
| Rent | | 416,625 96 |
| Advertising, printing, stationery, postage, telegraph, telephone, express and exchange | | 669,344 53 |
| Legal expense | | 1,649 76 |
| Legislative expenses | | 5,577 34 |
| Furniture, fixtures and safes | | 196,598 21 |
| Repairs and expenses (other than taxes) on real estate | | 2,273 35 |
| State taxes on premiums | | 477,031 49 |
| Insurance department licenses and fees | | 39,077 98 |
| Federal taxes | | 304,836 20 |
| All other licenses, fees and taxes | | 139,235 59 |
| Other disbursements, viz: Repairs and alterations (other than real estate), $24,064.58; incidental expenses, $71,521.82; lunches for employees, $54,896.31; investment expenses, $310,229.91 | | 460,712 62 |
| Agents' balances charged off | | 177,809 62 |

## DISBURSEMENTS—Concluded.

| | |
|---|---|
| Loss on sale or maturity of ledger assets | $76,937 97 |
| Decrease in book value of ledger assets | 37,733 69 |
| Total disbursements | $36,950,459 52 |
| Balance | $229,289,499 51 |

## LEDGER ASSETS.

| | |
|---|---|
| Book value of real estate | $ 9,950,622 51 |
| Mortgage loans on real estate | 125,763,854 19 |
| Premiums advanced under Soldiers' and Sailors' Civil Relief Act | 828 10 |
| Loans on company's policies assigned as collateral | 18,898,923 00 |
| Premium notes on policies in force | 481,156 09 |
| Book value of bonds and stocks | 72,619,373 74 |
| Cash in office | 30,310 59 |
| Deposits in trust companies and banks not on interest | 63,946 29 |
| Deposits in trust companies and banks on interest | 1,809,799 10 |
| Bills receivable | 659 85 |
| Agents' balances (debit, $87,293.66; credit, $417,267.61) net | —329,973 95 |
| Total ledger assets | $229,289,499 51 |

### NON-LEDGER ASSETS.

| | | | | |
|---|---|---|---|---|
| Interest due and accrued on mortgages | | | $3,967,778 92 | |
| Interest due and accrued on bonds | | | 968,415 73 | |
| Interest due and accrued on premium notes, loans or liens | | | 349,793 15 | |
| Interest accrued on other assets | | | 5,084 95 | |
| Rents due on company's property | | | 11,892 87 | |
| | | | | 5,302,965 62 |
| | Weekly premiums. | New business. | Renewals. | |
| Net uncollected and deferred premiums (paid for basis) | $497,018 73 | $600,255 51 | $4,350,160 96 | 5,447,435 20 |
| Gross assets | | | | $240,039,900 33 |

### DEDUCT ASSETS NOT ADMITTED.

| | | |
|---|---|---|
| Agents' debit balances | $ 87,293 66 | |
| Bills receivable | 659 85 | |
| Overdue and accrued interest on bonds in default | 13,333 34 | |
| Book value of bonds and stocks over market value | 245,242 51 | |
| Total | | 346,529 36 |
| Admitted assets | | $239,693,370 97 |

## LIABILITIES.

| | | |
|---|---|---|
| Net present value of outstanding policies computed by the Massachusetts Insurance Department | $214,563,143 00 | |
| Same for dividend additions | 1,586,294 00 | |
| Same for annuities | 52,970 00 | |
| Total | $216,202,407 00 | |
| Deduct net value of risks re-insured | 235,819 00 | |
| Net reserve (paid for basis) | | $215,966,588 00 |
| Extra reserve for total and permanent disability benefits and for additional accidental death benefits included in life policies | | 217,897 00 |
| Present value of supplementary contracts not involving life contingencies | | 581,826 86 |
| Present value of amounts incurred but not yet due for total and permanent disability benefits | | 53,149 00 |
| Surrender values claimable on policies cancelled | | 269,656 01 |
| Death losses due and unpaid | $ 20,435 00 | |
| Death losses in process of adjustment | 89,585 95 | |
| Death losses reported for which no proofs have been received | 304,732 00 | |
| Reserve for net death losses incurred but unreported | 116,000 00 | |
| Matured endowments due and unpaid | 2,519 00 | |
| Death losses and other policy claims resisted | 50,747 00 | |
| Total policy claims | | 584,018 95 |
| Due and unpaid on supplementary contracts not involving life contingencies | | 40 38 |
| Certificates of deposit not involving life contingencies | | 91,612 68 |
| Dividends left with the company to accumulate at interest | | 1,146,103 80 |
| Gross premiums paid in advance, including surrender values so applied, less discount, if any | | 660,463 61 |
| Unearned interest and rent paid in advance | | 167,045 46 |
| Commissions to agents due or accrued | | 104,200 56 |
| Salaries, rents, office expenses, bills and accounts due or accrued | | 253,624 85 |
| Medical examiners' and legal fees due or accrued | | 41,206 00 |

LIABILITIES—Concluded.

| | |
|---|---|
| Estimated amount hereafter payable for federal, state and other taxes based upon the business of the year of this statement | $ 896,218 03 |
| Dividends or other profits due policyholders | 387,210 25 |
| Dividends declaredpon or apportioned to annual dividend policies payable to policyholders during 1922 for period to December 31, 1922 | 4,648,300 13 |
| Dividends declared on or apportioned to deferred dividend policies payable to policyholders during 1922 for period to December 31, 1922 | 91,699 87 |
| Amounts set apart, apportioned, provisionally ascertained, calculated, declared or held awaiting apportionment upon deferred dividend policies | 176,973 88 |
| Other liabilities, viz: Accumulation fund, $5,116.47; war premiums to be refunded, $154.07; agents deposit in lieu of bonds, $6,733.20; unclaimed checks, $11,218.77 | 23,222 51 |
| Total | $226,361,057 83 |
| Unassigned funds (surplus) | 13,332,313 14 |
| Total | $239,693,370 97 |

EXHIBIT OF POLICIES—ORDINARY.

ALL BUSINESS PAID FOR.

| | Number. | Amount. | Number. | Amount. |
|---|---|---|---|---|
| Policies in force December 31, 1920 | | | 529,286 | $766,995,993 00 |
| Policies issued, revived and increased during the year | | | 88,634 | 133,767,117 00 |
| Total | | | 617,920 | $900,763,110 00 |
| Deduct policies which have ceased to be in force during the year— | | | | |
| By death | 3,156 | $ 5,215,087 00 | | |
| By maturity | 589 | 879,797 00 | | |
| By disability | -------- | 2,800 00 | | |
| By expiry | 287 | 762,273 00 | | |
| By surrender | 6,486 | 9,110,109 00 | | |
| By lapse | 30,411 | 40,021,475 00 | | |
| By decrease | 708 | 8,807,083 00 | | |
| Total | | | 41,637 | 64,798,624 00 |
| Total policies in force December 31, 1921 | | | 576,283 | $835,964,486 00 |
| Re-insured | | | 192 | $4,205,415 00 |

EXHIBIT OF POLICIES—INDUSTRIAL.

ALL BUSINESS PAID FOR.

| | Number. | Amount. | Number. | Amount. |
|---|---|---|---|---|
| Policies in force December 31, 1920 | | | 3,472,965 | $642,671,402 00 |
| Policies issued, revived and increased during the year | | | 538,676 | 145,019,120 00 |
| Total | | | 4,011,641 | $787,690,522 00 |
| Deduct policies which have ceased to be in force during the year— | | | | |
| By death | 35,448 | $ 6,317,837 00 | | |
| By maturity | 462 | 173,850 00 | | |
| By expiry | 8,949 | 1,963,914 00 | | |
| By surrender | 77,954 | 16,090,083 00 | | |
| By lapse | 251,719 | 53,521,127 00 | | |
| Total | | | 374,532 | 78,066,811 00 |
| Total policies in force December 31, 1921 | | | 3,637,109 | $709,623,711 00 |

BUSINESS IN ILLINOIS—ORDINARY.

| | Number. | Amount. |
|---|---|---|
| Policies in force December 31, 1920 | 38,055 | $61,219,149 00 |
| Policies issued during the year | 6,818 | 11,156,958 00 |
| Total | 44,873 | $72,376,107 00 |
| Deduct policies ceased to be in force | 3,678 | 6,888,181 00 |
| Policies in force December 31, 1921 | 41,195 | $65,487,926 00 |
| Losses and claims unpaid December 31, 1920 | 15 | $ 26,566 00 |
| Losses and claims incurred during the year | 236 | 452,041 00 |
| Total | 251 | $478,607 00 |
| Losses and claims settled during the year | 242 | 461,583 00 |
| Losses and claims unpaid December 31, 1921 | 9 | $17,024 00 |
| Premiums received | | $1,992,039 54 |

BUSINESS IN ILLINOIS—INDUSTRIAL.

| | Number. | Amount. |
|---|---|---|
| Policies in force December 31, 1920 | 139,538 | $29,552,286 00 |
| Policies issued during the year | 26,378 | 7,145,212 00 |
| Total | 165,916 | $36,697,498 00 |
| Deduct policies ceased to be in force | 20,128 | 4,122,253 00 |
| Policies in force December 31, 1921 | 145,788 | $32,575,245 00 |
| Losses and claims unpaid December 31, 1920 | 23 | $ 4,710 50 |
| Losses and claims incurred during the year | 1,282 | 234,763 35 |
| Total | 1,305 | $239,473 85 |
| Losses and claims settled during the year | 1,252 | 228,556 85 |
| Losses and claims unpaid December 31, 1921 | 53 | $10,917 00 |
| Premiums received | | $946,664 75 |

GAIN AND LOSS EXHIBIT.

INSURANCE EXHIBIT.

| | | Gain in surplus. | Loss in surplus. |
|---|---|---|---|
| Loading on actual premiums of the year (averaging 28.27 per cent of the gross premiums) | $15,031,032 73 | | |
| Insurance expenses incurred during the year | 15,507,666 45 | | |
| Loss from loading | | | $ 476,633 72 |
| Interest earned during the year | $11,332,128 01 | | |
| Investment expenses incurred during the year | 310,930 95 | | |
| Net income from investments | $11,021,197 06 | | |
| Interest required to maintain reserve | 7,501,387 58 | | |
| Gain from interest | | $3,519,809 48 | |
| Expected mortality on net amount at risk | $15,370,300 40 | | |
| Actual mortality on net amount at risk | 8,690,076 46 | | |
| Gain from mortality | | 6,680,223 94 | |
| Expected disbursements to annuitants | —$139 55 | | |
| Net actual annuity claims incurred | 941 00 | | |
| Loss from annuities | | | 1,080 55 |
| Total gain during the year from surrendered and lapsed policies | | 1,386,637 88 | |
| Decrease in surplus on dividend account | | | 4,642,015 54 |
| Decrease in special funds and special reserves during the year | | 2,800,000 00 | |
| Net to loss account | | | 175,615 20 |

INVESTMENT EXHIBIT.

| | | Gain in surplus. | Loss in surplus. |
|---|---|---|---|
| Total gains from stocks and bonds | | 18,878 67 | |
| Total losses from stocks and bonds | | | 80,937 97 |
| Loss from assets not admitted | | | 18,039 89 |
| Net gain on account of total and permanent disability benefits or additional accidental death benefits included in life policies | | 28,719 00 | |
| Loss from additional reserve required to equalize industrial policy benefits | | | 5,825,071 00 |
| Gain from conscience money and Fort Worth and Denver Railway Co. bonds | | 4,147 00 | |
| Total gains and losses in surplus during the year | | $14,438,415 97 | $11,219,393 87 |
| Surplus December 31, 1920 | $10,113,291 04 | | |
| Surplus December 31, 1921 | 13,332,313 14 | | |
| Increase in surplus | | | 3,219,022 10 |
| Total | | $14,438,415 97 | $14,438,415 97 |

## KANSAS CITY LIFE INSURANCE COMPANY.

Located at Ninth Street and Grand Avenue, Kansas City, Missouri; incorporated May, 1895; commenced business in Illinois April 12, 1915.

J. B. REYNOLDS, President. C. N. SEARS, Secretary.

GEORGE A. BARR, Director of Trade and Commerce, Attorney for service at Springfield.

CAPITAL.

| | | |
|---|---|---|
| Capital paid up | $200,000 00 | |
| Amount of ledger assets December 31, of previous year | | $16,686,715 71 |

## INCOME.

|  | | | |
|---|---|---|---|
| First year's premiums on original policies, less re-insurance | | $1,076,158 44 | |
| First year's premiums for total and permanent disability benefits, less re-insurance | | 12,070 08 | |
| First year's premiums for additional accidental death benefits, less re-insurance | | 11,117 27 | |
| Dividends applied to purchase paid-up additions and annuities | | 10,441 84 | |
| Surrender values applied to purchase paid-up insurance and annuities | | 7,356 71 | |
| Consideration for original annuities involving life contingencies | | 1,516 72 | |
| New premiums | | $1,118,661 06 | |
| Renewal premiums less re-insurance | $5,355,091 46 | | |
| Renewal premiums for total and permanent disability benefits, less re-insurance | 27,181 39 | | |
| Renewal premiums for additional accidental death benefits, less re-insurance | 79,167 60 | | |
| Dividends applied to pay renewal premiums | 113,770 05 | | |
| Dividends applied to shorten the endowment or premium-paying period | 862 16 | | |
| Renewal premiums for deferred annuities | 6,086 07 | | |
| Renewal premiums | | 5,582,158 73 | |
| Premium income | | $6,700,819 79 | |
| Premiums advanced during year under Soldiers' and Sailors' Relief Act | | 636 96 | |
| Total | | | $6,701,456 75 |
| Consideration for supplementary contracts not involving life contingencies | | | 36,150 00 |
| Dividends left with company to accumulate at interest | | | 191,737 34 |
| Interest on mortgage loans | | $743,069 80 | |
| Interest on collateral loans | | 371 37 | |
| Interest on bonds and dividends on stocks | | 74,182 42 | |
| Interest on premium notes, policy loans or liens | | 214,164 40 | |
| Interest on deposits | | 37,018 99 | |
| Rents | | 1,565 28 | |
| Total interest and rents | | | 1,070,372 26 |
| From other sources, viz: Investment expense account, $17,897.78; deposit on abstracts, $23.35 | | | 17,921 13 |
| Agents' balances previously charged off | | | 62 38 |
| Profit on sale or maturity of ledger assets | | | 4,535 74 |
| Total income | | | $8,022,235 60 |
| Total | | | $24,708,951 31 |

## DISBURSEMENTS.

|  | | |
|---|---|---|
| Death claims and additions | $997,005 63 | |
| Matured endowments | 16,500 00 | |
| Total and permanent disability claims and additional accidental death benefits, less re-insurance | 69,156 65 | |
| Total death claims and endowments | | $1,082,662 28 |
| Annuities involving life contingencies | | 83 50 |
| Premium notes and liens voided by lapse | | 98,014 81 |
| Surrender values paid in cash, or applied in liquidation of loans or notes | | 335,410 23 |
| Surrender values applied to purchase paid-up insurance and annuities | | 7,356 71 |
| Dividends paid policyholders in cash, or applied in liquidation of loans or notes | | 56,627 06 |
| Dividends applied to pay renewal premiums | | 113,770 05 |
| Dividends applied to shorten the endowment or premium-paying period | | 862 16 |
| Dividends applied to purchase paid-up additions and annuities | | 10,441 84 |
| Dividends left with the company to accumulate at interest | | 191,737 34 |
| (Total paid policyholders | $1,896,965 98) | |
| Expense of investigation and settlement of policy claims, including legal expenses | | 4,837 00 |
| Supplementary contracts not involving life contingencies | | 13,838 08 |
| Dividends with interest, held on deposit surrendered during the year | | 27,733 01 |
| Dividends to stockholders | | 32,000 00 |
| Commissions to agents, first year, $838,531.77; renewal, $302,051.56; annuities (original), $918.54; (renewal), $444.98 | | 1,141,946 85 |
| Compensation of managers and agents not paid by commissions on new business | | 12,588 07 |
| Agency supervision and traveling expenses of supervisors | | 4,664 56 |
| Branch office expenses | | 95,253 80 |
| Medical examiners' fees and inspection of risks | | 111,395 67 |
| Salaries and all other compensation of officers and home office employees | | 181,430 83 |
| Rent | | 21,425 00 |
| Advertising, printing, stationery, postage, telegraph, telephone, express and exchange | | 48,749 21 |
| Legal expense | | 1,134 21 |
| Furniture, fixtures and safes | | 6,145 10 |
| Repairs and expenses (other than taxes) on real estate | | 2,873 68 |
| Taxes on real estate | | 2,358 49 |
| State taxes on premiums | | 106,802 28 |
| Insurance department licenses and fees | | 13,172 08 |

## DISBURSEMENTS—Concluded.

| | |
|---|---|
| Federal taxes | $43,442 96 |
| All other licenses, fees and taxes | 6,390 23 |
| Other disbursements, viz: Refund extra war service premiums, $731.25; loss and gain account, $6,868.16; miscellaneous expense, $15,274.59; expense branch managers' annual meeting, $6,834.31 | 29,708 31 |
| Official examination | 10,076 26 |
| Loss on sale or maturity of ledger assets | 9,910 86 |
| Total disbursements | $3,824,842 52 |
| Balance | $20,884,108 79 |

## LEDGER ASSETS.

| | |
|---|---|
| Book value of real estate | $ 91,436 91 |
| Mortgage loans on real estate | 14,031,498 16 |
| Loans secured by collaterals | 24,032 00 |
| Loans on company's policies assigned as collateral | 3,519,235 41 |
| Premium notes on policies in force | 548,175 46 |
| Book value of bonds and stocks | 1,637,626 35 |
| Cash in office | 68,493 94 |
| Deposits in trust companies and banks not on interest | 53,607 70 |
| Deposits in trust companies and banks on interest | 808,449 00 |
| Agents' balances (debit, $104,879.06; credit, $3,325.20) net | 101,553 86 |
| Total ledger assets | $20,884,108 79 |

### NON-LEDGER ASSETS.

| | | |
|---|---|---|
| Interest due and accrued on mortgages | $411,640 80 | |
| Interest due and accrued on bonds | 17,306 85 | |
| Interest accrued on collateral loans | 807 30 | |
| Interest accrued on premium notes, loans or liens | 19,023 06 | |
| Interest accrued on other assets | 6,136 08 | |
| | | 454,914 09 |
| Market value of bonds and stocks over book value | | 1,710 00 |
| Net uncollected and deferred premiums (paid for basis), renewals | | 865,143 17 |
| Gross assets | | $22,205,876 05 |

### DEDUCT ASSETS NOT ADMITTED.

| | | |
|---|---|---|
| Agents' debit balances | $104,879 06 | |
| Premium notes, policy loans and other policy assets in excess of net value and of other policy liabilities on individual policies | 80,697 36 | |
| Overdue and accrued interest on bonds in default | 1,311 04 | |
| Book value of bonds and stocks over market value | 8,121 35 | |
| Total | | 195,008 81 |
| Admitted assets | | $22,010,867 24 |

## LIABILITIES.

| | | |
|---|---|---|
| Net present value of outstanding policies | $18,818,953 00 | |
| Same for annuities | 10,520 00 | |
| Total | $18,829,473 00 | |
| Deduct net value of risks re-insured | 15,184 00 | |
| Net reserve (paid for basis) | | $18,814,289 00 |
| Extra reserve for total and permanent disability benefits and for additional accidental death benefits included in life policies | | 54,491 76 |
| Present value of supplementary contracts not involving life contingencies | | 157,356 30 |
| Present value of amounts incurred but not yet due for total and permanent disability benefits | | 17,604 78 |
| Death losses in process of adjustment | $26,064 74 | |
| Death losses reported for which no proofs have been received | 35,642 37 | |
| Death losses and other policy claims resisted | 44,500 00 | |
| Total and permanent disability benefits and additional accidental death benefits | 12,500 00 | |
| Total policy claims | | 118,707 11 |
| Dividends left with the company to accumulate at interest | | 1,363,184 83 |
| Gross premiums paid in advance, including surrender values so applied, less discount, if any | | 24,356 98 |
| Unearned interest and rent paid in advance | | 74,442 28 |
| Commissions due agents on premium notes, when paid | | 29,601 40 |
| Salaries, rents, office expenses, bills, and accounts due or accrued | | 6,344 02 |
| Medical examiners' and legal fees due or accrued | | 9,811 00 |
| Estimated amount hereafter payable for federal, state and other taxes based upon the business of the year of this statement | | 115,000 00 |
| Dividends or other profits due policyholders | | 39,850 54 |
| Dividends declared on or apportioned to annual dividend policies payable to policyholders during 1922 for period to June 30, 1922 | | 49,298 34 |

LIABILITIES—Concluded.

| | |
|---|---|
| Dividends declared on or apportioned to deferred dividend policies payable to policyholders during 1922 for period to June 30, 1922 | $ 1,311 00 |
| Amounts set apart, apportioned, provisionally ascertained, calculated, declared or held awaiting apportionment upon deferred dividend policies | 109,708 86 |
| Accrued agency expense | 30,000 00 |
| Total | $21,015,358 20 |
| Capital paid up | 200,000 00 |
| Unassigned funds (surplus) | 795,509 04 |
| Total | $22,010,867 24 |

## EXHIBIT OF POLICIES—ORDINARY.

ALL BUSINESS PAID FOR.

| | Number. | Amount. | Number. | Amount. |
|---|---|---|---|---|
| Policies in force December 31, 1920 | | | 107,600 | $220,336,167 00 |
| Policies issued, revived, and increased during the year | | | 15,644 | 38,263,787 00 |
| Total | | | 123,244 | $258,599,954 00 |
| Deduct policies which have ceased to be in force during the year— | | | | |
| By death | 453 | $ 943,441 00 | | |
| By maturity | 13 | 16,606 00 | | |
| By disability | 2 | 3,892 00 | | |
| By expiry | 235 | 458,707 00 | | |
| By surrender | 1,311 | 2,542,193 00 | | |
| By lapse | 11,018 | 27,461,231 00 | | |
| By decrease | -------- | 462,663 00 | | |
| Total | | | 13,032 | 31,888,733 00 |
| Total policies in force December 31, 1921 | | | 110,212 | $226,711,221 00 |
| Re-insured | | | 344 | $2,295,500 00 |

## BUSINESS IN ILLINOIS—ORDINARY.

| | Number. | Amount. |
|---|---|---|
| Policies in force December 31, 1920 | 674 | $1,200,388 00 |
| Policies issued during the year | 284 | 617,684 00 |
| Total | 958 | $1,818,072 00 |
| Deduct policies ceased to be in force | 75 | 150,500 00 |
| Policies in force December 31, 1921 | 883 | $1,667,572 00 |
| Losses and claims unpaid December 31, 1920 | 2 | $10,000 00 |
| Losses and claims incurred during the year | 2 | 3,000 00 |
| Total | 4 | $13,000 00 |
| Losses and claims settled during the year | 4 | 13,000 00 |
| Premiums received | | $60,743 28 |

## GAIN AND LOSS EXHIBIT.

INSURANCE EXHIBIT.

| | | Gain in surplus. | Loss in surplus. |
|---|---|---|---|
| Loading on actual premiums of the year averaging 16.382 per cent of the gross premiums) | $1,133,568 50 | | |
| Insurance expenses incurred during the year | 1,932,527 29 | | |
| Loss from loading | | ------------- | $798,958 79 |
| Interest earned during the year | $1,159,410 28 | | |
| Investment expenses incurred during the year | 5,232 17 | | |
| Net income from investments | $1,154,178 11 | | |
| Interest required to maintain reserve | 615,935 81 | | |
| Gain from interest | | $ 538,242 30 | |
| Expected mortality on net amount at risk | $2,092,103 81 | | |
| Actual mortality on net amount at risk | 827,915 64 | | |
| Gain from mortality | | 1,264,188 17 | |
| Expected disbursements to annuitants | $48 29 | | |
| Net actual annuity claims incurred | 83 50 | | |
| Loss from annuities | | ------------- | 35 21 |
| Total gain during the year from surrendered and lapsed policies | | 243,929 87 | |
| Dividends paid stockholders | | ------------- | 32,000 00 |
| Decrease in surplus on dividend account | | ------------- | 422,417 44 |
| Decrease in special funds, and special reserves during the year | | 7,162 30 | |
| Net to loss account | | ------------- | 97,952 43 |

GAIN AND LOSS EXHIBIT—Concluded.

INVESTMENT EXHIBIT.

| | | Gain in surplus. | Loss in surplus. |
|---|---|---|---|
| Total gains from real estate | | $4,535 74 | |
| Total losses from real estate | | | $ 9,910 86 |
| Total losses from stocks and bonds | | | 1,771 35 |
| Gain on investment expense account | | 17,897 78 | |
| Loss from assets not admitted | | | 103,714 12 |
| Net gain on account of total and permanent disability benefits or additional accidental death benefits included in life policies | | 53,982 19 | |
| Balance unaccounted for | | | 6,642 16 |
| Total gains and losses in surplus during the year | | $2,129,938 35 | $1,473,402 36 |
| Surplus December 31, 1920 | $138,973 05 | | |
| Surplus December 31, 1921 | 795,509 04 | | |
| Increase in surplus | | | 656,535 99 |
| Total | | $2,129,938 35 | $2,129,938 35 |

## LA FAYETTE LIFE INSURANCE COMPANY.

Located at Third and Main Streets, Lafayette, Indiana; incorporated December 26, 1905; commenced business in Illinois August 12, 1920.

A. E. WERKHOFF, President. W. W. LANE, Secretary.

GEORGE A. BARR, Director of Trade and Commerce, Attorney for service at Springfield.

Amount of ledger assets December 31, of previous year ... $2,076,575 02

INCOME.

| | | | |
|---|---|---|---|
| First year's premiums on original policies, less re-insurance | | $85,614 16 | |
| First year's premiums for total and permanent disability benefits, less re-insurance | | 820 59 | |
| First year's premiums for additional accidental death benefits, less re-insurance | | 160 18 | |
| Surrender values to pay first year's premiums | | 65 24 | |
| Dividends applied to purchase paid-up additions and annuities | | 983 61 | |
| Dividends left, surrendered and applied to purchase paid-up additions and annuities | | 105 45 | |
| Surrender values applied to purchase paid-up insurance and annuities | | 7,863 49 | |
| New premiums | | $ 95,612 72 | |
| Renewal premiums less re-insurance | $385,393 95 | | |
| Renewal premiums for total and permanent disability benefits | 71 91 | | |
| Renewal premiums for additional accidental death benefits, less re-insurance | 98 55 | | |
| Dividends applied to pay renewal premiums | 42,767 19 | | |
| Surrender values applied to pay renewal premiums | 229 92 | | |
| Renewal premiums | | 428,561 52 | |
| Premium income | | | $524,174 24 |
| Consideration for supplementary contracts not involving life contingencies | | | 1,470 00 |
| Dividends left with company to accumulate at interest | | | 6,180 66 |
| Interest on mortgage loans | | $77,631 47 | |
| Interest on bonds | | 3,904 97 | |
| Interest on premium notes, policy loans or liens | | 22,517 06 | |
| Interest on deposits | | 1,786 34 | |
| Interest on other debts due the company | | 56 00 | |
| Rents—including $3,000.00 for company's occupancy of its own buildings | | 36,420 48 | |
| Total interest and rents | | | 142,316 32 |
| Suspense account, agents' balances | | | 21 32 |
| Agents' balances previously charged off | | | 20 12 |
| Profit on sale or maturity of ledger assets | | | 361 57 |
| Increase in book value of ledger assets | | | 43 70 |
| Total income | | | $674,587 93 |
| Total | | | $2,751,162 95 |

DISBURSEMENTS.

| | | |
|---|---|---|
| Death claims | $76,341 44 | |
| Matured endowments | 1,101 00 | |
| Total death claims and endowments | | $77,442 44 |

DISBURSEMENTS—Concluded.

| | | |
|---|---|---|
| Premium notes and liens voided by lapse | | $ 6 58 |
| Surrender values paid in cash, or applied in liquidation of loans or notes | | 17,096 23 |
| Surrender values of coupon accumulations surrendered | | 990 78 |
| Surrender values applied to pay new and renewal premiums | | 295 16 |
| Surrender values applied to purchase paid-up insurance and annuities | | 7,863 49 |
| Dividends paid policyholders in cash, or applied in liquidation of loans or notes | | 2,194 72 |
| Dividends applied to pay renewal premiums | | 42,767 19 |
| Dividends applied to purchase paid-up additions and annuities | | 983 61 |
| Dividends left with the company to accumulate at interest | | 6,180 66 |
| (Total paid policyholders | $155,820 86) | |
| Expense of investigation and settlement of policy claims, including legal expenses | | 726 46 |
| Supplementary contracts not involving life contingencies | | 1,300 00 |
| Dividends with interest, held on deposit surrendered during the year | | 832 24 |
| Dividends with interest held on deposit surrendered and used to purchase paid-up additional insurance | | 105 45 |
| Commissions to agents, first year, $57,791.98; renewal, $13,836.37 | | 71,628 35 |
| Compensation of managers and agents not paid by commissions on new business | | 10,075 15 |
| Agency supervision and traveling expenses of supervisors | | 4,927 77 |
| Medical examiners' fees and inspection of risks | | 7,714 75 |
| Salaries and all other compensation of officers and home office employees | | 46,334 07 |
| Rent | | 3,180 00 |
| Advertising, printing, stationery, postage, telegraph, telephone and express | | 9,971 53 |
| Furniture, fixtures and safes | | 1,571 22 |
| Repairs and expenses (other than taxes) on real estate | | 20,572 99 |
| Taxes on real estate | | 6,338 46 |
| State taxes on premiums | | 4,650 62 |
| Insurance department licenses and fees | | 1,309 74 |
| Federal taxes | | 3,496 82 |
| All other licenses, fees and taxes | | 3,209 06 |
| Other disbursements, viz: Agency expense other than supervision, $2,664.98; miscellaneous expenses, $855.27; mortgage loan expenses, $413.23; interest on lien (Pittsburg Life and Trust Company), $49.10; light, $1,124.99; papers, subscriptions and books, $1,333.14; suspense account, mortgage loans, $542.61; traveling expenses, home office, $687.26 | | 5,670 58 |
| Agents' balances charged off | | 500 54 |
| Loss on sale or maturity of ledger assets | | 2,013 90 |
| Total disbursements | | $361,950 56 |
| Balance | | $2,389,212 39 |

LEDGER ASSETS.

| | |
|---|---|
| Book value of real estate | $ 431,080 38 |
| Mortgage loans on real estate | 1,326,549 60 |
| Loans on company's policies assigned as collateral | 392,808 45 |
| Premium notes on policies in force | 31,460 90 |
| Book value of bonds | 91,850 00 |
| Cash in office | 200 00 |
| Deposits in trust companes and banks on interest | 108,533 66 |
| Agents' debit balances | 6,378 31 |
| War savings stamps | 351 09 |
| Total ledger assets | $2,389,212 39 |

NON-LEDGER ASSETS.

| | | |
|---|---|---|
| Interest due and accrued on mortgages | $22,629 00 | |
| Interest accrued on bonds | 687 80 | |
| Interest accrued on premium notes, loans or liens | 3,397 42 | |
| Interest accrued on other assets | 2,177 58 | |
| Rents due on company's property | 1,105 51 | |
| | | 29,997 31 |
| Market value of real estate over book value | | 1,413 17 |
| Due from other companies for losses or claims on policies re-insured | | 3,500 00 |
| Due from other companies for refund unearned re-insurance premiums and cash surrender | | 281 65 |
| Net uncollected and deferred premiums (paid for basis), renewals | | 35,107 36 |
| Net amount of uncollected and deferred premiums, less re-insurance on total disability and double indemnity | | 149 53 |
| Gross assets | | $2,459,661 41 |

DEDUCT ASSETS NOT ADMITTED.

| | | |
|---|---|---|
| Agents' debit balances | 6,378 31 | |
| Premium notes, policy loans and other policy assets in excess of net value and of other policy liabilities on individual policies | 1,844 55 | |
| Book value of bonds over market value | 328 56 | |
| Total | | 8,551 42 |
| Admitted assets | | $2,451,109 99 |

## LIABILITIES.

| | | |
|---|---|---|
| Net present value of outstanding policies computed by the Indiana Insurance Department | $2,095,371 64 | |
| Same for dividend additions | 4,725 50 | |
| Same for annuities | 2,093 03 | |
| Total | $2,102,190 17 | |
| Deduct net value of risks re-insured | 16,102 69 | |
| Net reserve (paid for basis) | | $2,086,087 48 |
| Extra reserve for total and permanent disability benefits and for additional accidental death benefits included in life policies, less re-insurance | | 3,199 51 |
| Present value of supplementary contracts not involving life contingencies | | 16,660 82 |
| Death losses in process of adjustment | $ 3 56 | |
| Death losses reported for which no proofs have been received | 3,000 00 | |
| Total and permanent disability benefits and additional accidental death benefits | 3,000 00 | |
| Total policy claims | | 6,003 56 |
| Dividends left with the company to accumulate at interest | | 24,126 98 |
| Gross premiums paid in advance, including surrender values so applied, less discount, if any | | 3,415 95 |
| Unearned interest and rent paid in advance | | 8,842 68 |
| Commissions due agents on premium notes, when paid | | 527 94 |
| Commissions to agents due or accrued | | 2,303 02 |
| Salaries, rents, office expenses, bills, and accounts due or accrued | | 2,439 17 |
| Medical examiners' fees due or accrued | | 410 00 |
| Estimated amount hereafter payable for federal, state and other taxes based upon the business of the year of this statement | | 9,193 81 |
| Dividends or other profits due policyholders | | 4,965 73 |
| Dividends declared on or apportioned to annual dividend policies payable to policyholders during 1922 for period to January and February, 1922 | | 7,209 52 |
| Dividends declared on or apportioned to deferred dividend policies payable to policyholders during 1922 for period to January and February, 1922 | | 4,997 42 |
| Amounts set apart, apportioned, provisionally ascertained, calculated, declared or held awaiting apportionment upon deferred dividend policies | | 55,997 21 |
| Contingent reserve for mortality | | 20,000 00 |
| Reserve for real estate depreciation | | 6,799 05 |
| Coupon accumulation | | 24,623 89 |
| Other liabilities, viz: County taxes, real estate, $6,783.16; personal, $671.95; suspense account mortgage loans, $285.69; suspense account agents' balances, $125.11 | | 7,865 91 |
| Total | | $2,295,669 65 |
| Unassigned funds (surplus) | | 155,440 34 |
| Total | | $2,451,109 99 |

## EXHIBIT OF POLICIES—ORDINARY.

ALL BUSINESS PAID FOR.

| | Number. | Amount. | Number. | Amount. |
|---|---|---|---|---|
| Policies in force December 31, 1920 | | | 8,618 | $15,024,714 00 |
| Policies issued, revived, and increased during the year | | | 1,853 | 3,869,591 00 |
| Total | | | 10,471 | $18,894,305 00 |
| Deduct policies which have ceased to be in force during the year— | | | | |
| By death | 47 | $ 79,658 00 | | |
| By maturity | 1 | 1,000 00 | | |
| By expiry | 89 | 148,552 00 | | |
| By surrender | 32 | 45,894 00 | | |
| By lapse | 1,029 | 2,167,075 00 | | |
| By decrease | -------- | 147,286 00 | | |
| Total | | | 1,198 | 2,589,465 00 |
| Total policies in force December 31, 1921 | | | 9,273 | $16,304,840 00 |
| Re-insured | | | 260 | $890,368 00 |

## BUSINESS IN ILLINOIS—ORDNARY.

| | Number. | Amount. |
|---|---|---|
| Policies issued during the year | 164 | $233,822 00 |
| Policies in force December 31, 1921 | 164 | $233,822 00 |
| Premiums received | | $9,089 43 |

## GAIN AND LOSS EXHIBIT

INSURANCE EXHIBIT.

| | | Gain in surplus. | Loss in surplus. |
|---|---|---|---|
| Loading on actual premiums of the year (averaging 28.68 per cent of the gross premiums) | $153,420 76 | | |
| Insurance expenses incurred during the year | 176,388 89 | | |
| Loss from loading | | | $22,968 13 |
| Interest earned during the year | $145,083 13 | | |
| Investment expenses incurred during the year | 32,309 56 | | |
| Net income from investments | $112,773 57 | | |
| Interest required to maintain reserve | 70,542 79 | | |
| Gain from interest | | $42,230 78 | |
| Expected mortality on net amount at risk | $145,392 86 | | |
| Actual mortality on net amount at risk | 66,837 57 | | |
| Gain from mortality | | 78,555 29 | |
| Total gain during the year from surrendered and lapsed policies | | 12,525 02 | |
| Decrease in surplus on dividend account | | | 107,975 23 |
| Increase in special funds, and special reserves during the year | | | 1,367 13 |
| Coupons surrendered | | | 990 78 |
| Net to loss account | | | 480 42 |

INVESTMENT EXHIBIT.

| | | Gain in surplus. | Loss in surplus. |
|---|---|---|---|
| Total gains from real estate | | 361 57 | |
| Total losses from real estate | | | 2,117 75 |
| Total gains from bonds | | 2,195 99 | |
| Gain from assets not admitted | | 973 51 | |
| Net gain on account of total and permanent disability benefits or additional accidental death benefits included in life policies | | 672 03 | |
| Balance unaccounted for | | | 11 98 |
| Total gains and losses in surplus during the year | | $137,514 19 | $135,911 42 |
| Surplus December 31, 1920 | $153,837 57 | | |
| Surplus December 31, 1921 | 155,440 34 | | |
| Increase in surplus | | | 1,602 77 |
| Total | | $137,514 19 | $137,514 19 |

## LINCOLN NATIONAL LIFE INSURANCE COMPANY.

Located at Nos. 217-219 East Berry Street, Fort Wayne, Indiana; incorporated June 12, 1905; commenced business in Illinois December 8, 1916.

SAMUEL M. FOSTER, President. FRANKLIN B. MEAD, Secretary.

GEORGE A. BARR, Director of Trade and Commerce, Attorney for service at Springfield.

### CAPITAL.

| | | | |
|---|---|---|---|
| Capital paid up | | $500,000 00 | |
| Amount of ledger assets December 31, of previous year | | | $9,811,401 93 |

### INCOME.

| | | | |
|---|---|---|---|
| First year's premiums on original policies, less re-insurance | | $1,828,907 80 | |
| First year's premiums for total and permanent disability benefits | | 24,660 94 | |
| First year's premiums for additional accidental death benefits, less re-insurance | | 33,264 22 | |
| Surrender values to pay first year's premiums | | 61 87 | |
| Dividends applied to purchase paid-up additions and annuities | | 38,210 81 | |
| New premiums | | $1,925,105 64 | |
| Renewal premiums less re-insurance | $3,513,273 48 | | |
| Renewal premiums for total and permanent disability benefits, less re-insurance | 41,878 85 | | |
| Renewal premiums for additional accidental death benefits, less re-insurance | 39,297 35 | | |
| Dividends applied to pay renewal premiums | 52,343 06 | | |
| Surrender values applied to pay renewal premiums | 2,524 16 | | |
| Renewal premiums | | 3,649,316 90 | |
| Premium income | | | $5,574,422 54 |
| Consideration for supplementary contracts involving life contingencies | | | 58,267 07 |
| Dividends left with company to accumulate at interest | | | 29,078 91 |
| Interest on mortgage loans | | $425,621 78 | |
| Interest on bonds | | 15,252 47 | |

INCOME—Concluded.

| | | |
|---|---|---|
| Interest on premium notes, policy loans or liens | $87,735 52 | |
| Interest on deposits | 39,411 36 | |
| Interest on other debts due the company | 4,279 23 | |
| Rents—including $46,660.14 for company's occupancy of its own buildings | 50,752 46 | |
| Total interest and rents | | $623,052 82 |
| From other sources, viz: Sundry receipts, $204.64; return of premium tendered in payment of claim, $115.96; increase in suspense account with Northwest office, $2,420.52 | | 2,741 12 |
| Agents' balances previously charged off | | 289 63 |
| Profit on sale or maturity of ledger assets | | 3,228 10 |
| Increase in book value of ledger assets | | 4 00 |
| Total income | | $6,291,084 19 |
| Total | | $16,102,486 12 |

DISBURSEMENTS.

| | | |
|---|---|---|
| Death claims and additions | $767,985 39 | |
| Matured endowments and additions | 15,230 51 | |
| Total and permanent disability claims and additional accidental death benefits, less re-insurance | 98,998 07 | |
| Total death claims and endowments | | $882,213 97 |
| Annuities involving life contingencies | | 2,557 04 |
| Premium notes and liens voided by lapse, less $1,571.90 restorations | | 15,229 02 |
| Surrender values paid in cash, or applied in liquidation of loans or notes | | 207,912 16 |
| Surrender values applied to pay new and renewal premiums | | 2,586 03 |
| Dividends paid policyholders in cash, or applied in liquidation of loans or notes | | 4,134 72 |
| Dividends applied to pay renewal premiums | | 52,343 06 |
| Dividends applied to purchase paid-up additions and annuities | | 38,210 81 |
| Dividends left with the company to accumulate at interest | | 29,078 91 |
| Total paid policyholders | $1,234,265 72) | |
| Expense of investigation and settlement of policy claims, including legal expenses | | 6,517 98 |
| Supplementary contracts not involving life contingencies | | 1,975 74 |
| Dividends with interest, held on deposit surrendered during the year | | 13,460 31 |
| Dividends to stockholders | | 75,000 00 |
| Commissions to agents, first year, $1,125,020.09; renewal, $156,349.19 | | 1,281,369 28 |
| Commuted renewal commissions | | 7,750 00 |
| Agency supervision aud traveling expenses of supervisors | | 61,290 54 |
| Branch office expenses | | 100,774 71 |
| Medical examiners' fees and inspection of risks | | 105,931 70 |
| Salaries and all other compensation of officers and home office employees | | 356,646 84 |
| Rent | | 46,660 14 |
| Advertising, printing, stationery, postage, telegraph, telephone, express and exchange | | 112,485 24 |
| Legal expense | | 1,301 82 |
| Furniture, fixtures and safes | | 51,204 85 |
| Repairs and expenses (other than taxes) on real estate | | 31,377 58 |
| Taxes on real estate | | 2,905 32 |
| State taxes on premiums | | 69,190 98 |
| Insurance department licenses and fees | | 6,126 47 |
| Federal taxes | | 7,367 62 |
| All other licenses, fees and taxes | | 6,360 00 |
| Other disbursements, viz: Library and subscription, $2,486.86; traveling expenses, $11,361.22; investment expenses, $19,257.49; general expenses, $33,387.45; agency expenses, $24,536.14; expense new building, $147.38; gifts and donations, $570.00; remodeling at home office, $17,998.60; paid on anticipated surplus account, $165,166.00; interest on anticipated surplus account, $8,410.35; loss on account of bank failures, $604.09; decrease in suspense account part paid premiums, $138.82; interest on deferred death claims, $495.18; Extra premiums for military permit returned, $48.84 | | 284,608 42 |
| Agents' balances charged off | | 2,064 30 |
| Loss on sale or maturity of ledger assets | | 4,464 50 |
| Total disbursements | | $3,871,100 06 |
| Balance | | $12,231,386 06 |

LEDGER ASSETS.

| | |
|---|---|
| Book value of real estate | $ 321,080 81 |
| Mortgage loans on real estate | 9,123,379 18 |
| Loans on company's policies assigned as collateral | 1,361,713 68 |
| Premium notes on policies in force | 315,731 29 |
| Book value of bonds | 238,460 65 |
| Cash in office | 28,720 76 |
| Deposits in trust companies and banks on interest | 767,996 92 |
| Agents' balances debit, $86,530.34; credit, $17,933.41) net | 68,596 93 |
| Net amount due from re-insurance companies | 5,705 84 |
| Total ledger assets | $12,231,386 06 |

## LEDGER ASSETS—Concluded.

NON-LEDGER ASSETS.

| | | | |
|---|---|---|---|
| Interest due and accrued on mortgages | | $252,524 10 | |
| Interest accrued on bonds | | 2,253 12 | |
| Interest accrued on premium notes, loans or liens | | 8,843 53 | |
| Interest due and accrued on other assets | | 15,077 69 | |
| Rents due on company's property | | 84 33 | |
| | | | $278,782 77 |
| | New business. | Renewals. | |
| Net uncollected and deferred premiums (paid for basis) | $24,498 10 | $347,490 89 | 371,988 99 |
| All other assets, viz: Furniture and fixtures, $130,010.15; due from other companies on re-insurance cancelled, $2,732.93; re-insurance paid in advance, $1,604.00; fire and miscellaneous insurance premiums paid in advance, $5,448.32 | | | 139,795 41 |
| Gross assets | | | $13,021,953 23 |

DEDUCT ASSETS NOT ADMITTED.

| | | |
|---|---|---|
| Furniture, fixtures and safes | $130,010 15 | |
| Agents' debit balances | 86,530 34 | |
| Overdue and accrued interest on certificates of deposit now in hands of receiver | 1,333 45 | |
| Total | | 217,873 94 |
| Admitted assets | | $12,804,079.29 |

## LIABILITIES.

| | | |
|---|---|---|
| Net present value of outstanding policies computed by the Indiana Insurance Department | $10,723,031 46 | |
| Same for dividend additions | 269,475 86 | |
| Total | $10,992,507 32 | |
| Deduct net value of risks re-insured | 66,684 94 | |
| Net reserve (paid for basis) | | $10,925,822 38 |
| Extra reserve for total and permanent disability benefits and for additional accidental death benefits included in life policies, less re-insurance | | 69,550 69 |
| Present value of supplementary contracts not involving life contingencies | | 66,439 69 |
| Present value of amounts incurred but not yet due for total and permanent disability benefits | | 66,672 11 |
| Surrender values claimable on policies cancelled | | 2,498 39 |
| Death losses reported for which no proofs have been received | $53,015 85 | |
| Reserve for net death losses incurred but unreported | 14,000 00 | |
| Death losses and other policy claims resisted | 39,086 00 | |
| Total policy claims | | 106,101 85 |
| Dividends left with the company to accumulate at interest | | 205,505 90 |
| Gross premiums paid in advance, including surrender values so applied, less discount, if any | | 32,032 67 |
| Unearned interest and rent paid in advance | | 34,775 75 |
| Commissions due agents on premium notes, when paid | | 15,786 56 |
| Salaries, rents, office expenses, bills and accounts due or accrued | | 8,418 20 |
| Medical examiners' and inspection fees due or accrued | | 5,600 25 |
| Estimated amount hereafter payable for federal, state and other taxes based upon the business of the year of this statement | | 113,082 39 |
| Dividends or other profits due policyholders | | 853 97 |
| Dividends declared on or apportioned to deferred dividend policies payable to policyholders during 1922 for period to December 31, 1922 | | 12,086 95 |
| Amounts set apart, apportioned, provisionally ascertained, calculated, declared or held awaiting apportionment upon deferred dividend policies | | 8,738 35 |
| Reserve or surplus funds not otherwise included in liabilities, viz Survivorship fund, $61,150.37; contingency reserve fund, $51,962.56; | | 113,112 93 |
| Other liabilities, viz Extra premiums received for military permits, $376.82; part payments received on premiums, $10,006.38; suspense account with Northwest office, $6,617 06 | | 17,000 26 |
| Total | | $11,804,079 29 |
| Capital paid up | | 500,000 00 |
| Unassigned funds (surplus) | | 500,000 00 |
| Total | | $12,804,079 29 |

## EXHIBIT OF POLICIES—ORDINARY.

ALL BUSINESS PAID FOR.

| | Number. | Amount. |
|---|---|---|
| Policies in force December 31, 1920 | 68,679 | $159,349,378 27 |
| Policies issued, revived and increased during the year | 33,323 | 81,309,063 99 |
| Total | 102,002 | $240,658,442 26 |

## EXHIBIT OF POLICIES—ORDINARY—Concluded.

ALL BUSINESS PAID FOR.

| | Number. | Amount. | Number. | Amount. |
|---|---|---|---|---|
| Deduct policies which have ceased to be in force during the year— | | | | |
| By death | 338 | $ 825,966 86 | | |
| By maturity | 11 | 15,000 00 | | |
| By expiry | 1,370 | 6,399,800 00 | | |
| By surrender | 3,483 | 10,196,900 00 | | |
| By lapse | 9,206 | 22,565,203 89 | | |
| By decrease | 6 | 2,680,153 47 | | |
| Total | | | 14,414 | $42,683,024 22 |
| Total policies in force December 31, 1921 | | | 87,588 | $197,975,418 04 |
| Re-insured | | | 832 | $4,779,777 00 |

## EXHIBIT OF POLICIES—GROUP INSURANCE.

ALL BUSINESS PAID FOR.

| | Amount. | Number. | Amount. |
|---|---|---|---|
| Policies in force December 31, 1920 | | 4 | $775,000 00 |
| Policies issued, revived and increased during the year | | -------- | 348,000 00 |
| Total | | 4 | $1,123,000 00 |
| Deduct policies which have ceased to be in force during the year— | | | |
| By death | $ 3,000 00 | | |
| By decrease | 208,000 00 | | |
| Total | | -------- | 211,000 00 |
| Total policies in force December 31, 1921 | | 4 | $912,000 00 |

## BUSINESS IN ILLINOIS—ORDINARY.

| | Number. | Amount. |
|---|---|---|
| Policies in force December 31, 1920 | 1,875 | $5,457,361 00 |
| Policies issued during the year | 5,023 | 7,111,121 64 |
| Total | 6,898 | $12,568,482 64 |
| Deduct policies ceased to be in force | 475 | 1,488,547 00 |
| Policies in force December 31, 1921 | 6,423 | $11,079,935 64 |
| Losses and claims incurred during the year | 16 | 43,883 68 |
| Losses and claims settled during the year | 14 | 35,883 68 |
| Losses and claims unpaid December 31, 1921 | 2 | $8,000 00 |
| Premiums received | | $302,583 50 |

## GAIN AND LOSS EXHIBIT.

INSURANCE EXHIBIT.

| | | Gain in surplus. | Loss in surplus. |
|---|---|---|---|
| Loading on actual premiums of the year (averaging 21 per cent of the gross premiums) | $1,144,126 46 | | |
| Insurance expenses incurred during the year | 2,351,897 16 | | |
| Loss from loading | | -------------- | $1,207,770 70 |
| Interest earned during the year | $715,457 41 | | |
| Investment expenses incurred during the year | 75,082 65 | | |
| Net income from investments | $640,374 76 | | |
| Interest required to maintain reserve | 377,337 01 | | |
| Gain from interest | | $ 263,037 75 | |
| Expected mortality on net amount at risk | $1,986,585 58 | | |
| Actual mortality on net amount at risk | 746,007 25 | | |
| Gain from mortality | | 1,240,578 33 | |
| Total gain during the year from surrendered and lapsed policies | | 129,467 11 | |
| Dividends paid stockholders | | -------------- | 75,000 00 |
| Decrease in surplus on dividend account | | -------------- | 123,881 74 |
| Decrease in special funds and special reserves during the year | | 25,102 75 | |
| Net to profit account | | 289 63 | |

GAIN AND LOSS EXHIBIT—Concluded.

INVESTMENT EXHIBIT.

| | | Gain in surplus. | Loss in surplus. |
|---|---|---|---|
| Total gains from bonds | | $3,232 50 | |
| Total losses from bonds | | | $ 4,464 50 |
| Loss from assets not admitted | | | 76,305 07 |
| Net loss on account of total and permanent disability benefits or additional accidental death benefits included in life policies | | | 9,120 06 |
| Loss from amounts paid on anticipated surplus account | | | 165,166 00 |
| Total gains and losses in surplus during the year | | $1,661,708 07 | $1,661,708 07 |
| Surplus December 31, 1920 | $500,000 00 | | |
| Surplus December 31, 1921 | 500,000 00 | | |
| Total | | 1,661,708 07 | 1,661,708 07 |

## THE MANHATTAN LIFE INSURANCE COMPANY.

Located at Nos. 64-66-68-70 Broadway, New York, New York; organized, 1850; commenced business in Illinois November 2, 1855.

THOMAS E. LOVEJOY, President. MELVIN DE MOTT, Secretary.

JAMES A. BRADY, Chicago, Attorney for service.

CAPITAL.

| | | |
|---|---|---|
| Capital paid up | $100,000 00 | |
| Amount of ledger assets December 31, of previous year | | $19,072,880 08 |

INCOME.

| | | | |
|---|---|---|---|
| First year's premiums on original policies, less re-insurance | | $351,192 13 | |
| First year's premiums for total and permanent disability benefits, less re-insurance | | 3,408 19 | |
| First year's premiums for additional accidental death benefits | | 3,593 91 | |
| Surrender values to pay first year's premiums | | 50 05 | |
| Dividends applied to purchase paid-up additions and annuities | | 2,974 85 | |
| Consideration for original annuities involving life contingencies | | 20,000 00 | |
| New premiums | | $ 381,219 13 | |
| Renewal premiums less re-insurance | $1,673,662 65 | | |
| Renewal premiums for total and permanent disability benefits, less re-insurance | 3,804 82 | | |
| Renewal premiums for additional accidental death benefits | 7,124 33 | | |
| Dividends applied to pay renewal premiums | 21,425 27 | | |
| Surrender values applied to pay renewal premiums | 26 29 | | |
| Renewal premiums for deferred annuities | 500 81 | | |
| Renewal premiums | | 1,706,544 17 | |
| Premium income | | | $2,087,763 30 |
| Consideration for supplementary contracts involving life contingencies | | | 9,000 00 |
| Consideration for supplementary contracts not involving life contingencies | | | 2,949 18 |
| Dividends left with company to accumulate at interest | | | 396 45 |
| Interest on mortgage loans | | $344,878 95 | |
| Interest on collateral loans | | 74 36 | |
| Interest on bonds and dividends on stocks | | 172,118 95 | |
| Interest on premium notes, policy loans or liens | | 200,977 35 | |
| Interest on deposits | | 23,481 16 | |
| Interest on other debts due the company | | 492 59 | |
| Rents—including $25,000.00 for company's occupancy of its own buildings | | 397,943 23 | |
| Total interest and rents | | | 1,139,966 59 |
| From other sources, viz: Deposits on liberty bond agreements, $34,884.87; deposits account of insurance, $1,588.82; unclaimed checks redeposited, $53.90 | | | 36,527 59 |
| Profit on sale or maturity of ledger assets | | | 18,592 32 |
| Increase in book value of ledger assets | | | 3,866 00 |
| Total income | | | $3,299,061 43 |
| Total | | | $22,371,941 51 |

DISBURSEMENTS.

| | | |
|---|---|---|
| Death claims and additions | $1,032,605 93 | |
| Matured endowments and additions | 225,609 40 | |
| Total and permanent disability claims and additional accidental death benefits | 357 06 | |
| Total death claims and endowments | | $1,258,572 39 |

## DISBURSEMENTS—Concluded.

| | | |
|---|---|---|
| Annuities involving life contingencies | | $ 10,739 83 |
| Premium notes and liens voided by lapse, less $8,696.76 restorations | | 15,797 27 |
| Surrender values paid in cash, or applied in liquidation of loans or notes | | 719,451 71 |
| Surrender values applied to pay new and renewal premiums | | 76 34 |
| Dividends paid policyholders in cash, or applied in liquidation of loans or notes | | 35,755 01 |
| Dividends applied to pay renewal premiums | | 21,425 27 |
| Dividends applied to purchase paid-up additions and annuities | | 2,974 85 |
| Dividends left with the company to accumulate at interest | | 396 45 |
| (Total paid policyholders | $2,065,189 12) | |
| Expense of investigation and settlement of policy claims, including legal expenses | | 423 62 |
| Supplementary contracts not involving life contingencies | | 12,328 84 |
| Supplementary contracts involving life contingencies | | 1,525 00 |
| Dividends with interest, held on deposit surrendered during the year | | 778 55 |
| Interest or dividends to stockholders | | 13,417 88 |
| Commissions to agents, first year, $158,281.70; renewal, $98,889.97; annuities (original), $600.00 | | 257,771 67 |
| Agency supervision and traveling expenses of supervisors and agents | | 27,765 25 |
| Branch office expenses | | 38,131 51 |
| Medical examiners' fees and inspection of risks | | 27,805 55 |
| Salaries and all other compensation of officers and home office employees | | 142,614 93 |
| Rent | | 38,905 75 |
| Advertising, printing, stationery, postage, telegraph, telephone, express and exchange | | 36,565 62 |
| Legal expense | | 8,572 82 |
| Furniture, fixtures and safes | | 2,954 06 |
| Repairs and expenses (other than taxes) on real estate | | 154,243 41 |
| Taxes on real estate | | 113,204 12 |
| State taxes on premiums | | 33,202 95 |
| Insurance department licenses and fees | | 3,675 21 |
| Federal taxes | | 9,721 68 |
| All other licenses, fees and taxes | | 1,469 45 |
| Other disbursements, viz: Auditing Agency accounts, $423.00; books, papers and subscriptions, $1,961.69; expenses, election of directors, $281.86; Holmes Protective Association, $481.00; legislative expenses, $166.08; library bureau, $3,517.98; premiums on fidelity bonds, $622.94; traveling home office employees, $453.52; Association Life Insurance Presidents, $384.25; conventions and meetings, $5,773.36; photographing applications, $78.78; miscellaneous, $3,070.87; commission on real estate sales, $1,887.50; settlement of suit Ramsey vs. Company, $1,000.00; removal violations against real estate (property sold 1919), $300.00; payments of deposits on liberty bond agreements, $38,626.55; payment of New York State income tax withheld at source, $188.54 | | 59,217 92 |
| Loss on sale or maturity of ledger assets | | 18,567 19 |
| Decrease in book value of ledger assets | | 2,178 00 |
| Total disbursements | | $3,070,230 10 |
| Balance | | $19,301,711 41 |

## LEDGER ASSETS.

| | |
|---|---|
| Book value of real estate | $4,024,710 22 |
| Mortgage loans on real estate | 6,586,785 89 |
| Loans on company's policies assigned as collateral | 4,119,418 97 |
| Premium notes on policies in force | 174,575 72 |
| Book value of bonds and stocks | 3,795,716 30 |
| Cash in office | 3,708 72 |
| Deposits in trust companies and banks not on interest | 6,321 07 |
| Deposits in trust companies and banks on interest | 568,829 36 |
| Agents' balances (debit, $25,306.25; credit, $3,661.09) net | 21,645 16 |
| Total ledger assets | $19,301,711 41 |

### NON-LEDGER ASSETS.

| | | | |
|---|---|---|---|
| Interest due and accrued on mortgages | | $129,147 86 | |
| Interest accrued on bonds | | 44,235 23 | |
| Interest due and accrued on premium notes, loans or liens | | 222,591 97 | |
| Interest due and accrued on other assets | | 2,448 25 | |
| Rents due and accrued on company's property | | 17,510 86 | |
| | | | 415,934 17 |
| Due from other companies for losses or claims on policies re-insured | | | 23,089 00 |
| | New business. | Renewals. | |
| Net uncollected and deferred premiums (paid for basis) | $20,579 17 | $167,747 92 | 188,327 09 |
| Prepaid fire insurance premiums | | | 6,793 12 |
| Gross assets | | | $19,935,854 79 |

### DEDUCT ASSETS NOT ADMITTED.

| | | |
|---|---|---|
| Agents' debit balances | $25,306 25 | |
| Premium notes, policy loans and other policy assets in excess of net value and of other policy liabilities on individual policies | 1,092 43 | |
| Book value of bonds and stocks over market value | 91,251 00 | |
| Total | | 117,649 68 |
| Admitted assets | | $19,818,205 11 |

## LIABILITIES.

| | | |
|---|---|---|
| Net present value of outstanding policies computed by the New York Insurance Department | $18,281,066 00 | |
| Same for dividend additions | 48,665 00 | |
| Same for annuities | 83,072 00 | |
| Total | $18,412,803 00 | |
| Deduct net value of risks re-insured | 162,261 00 | |
| Net reserve (paid for basis) | | $18,250,542 00 |
| Extra reserve for total and permanent disability benefits and for additional accidental death benefits included in life policies, less re-insurance | | 7,660 62 |
| Present value of supplementary contracts not involving life contingencies | | 156,532 00 |
| Present value of amounts incurred but not yet due for total and permanent disability benefits | | 1,805 63 |
| Surrender values claimable on policies cancelled | | 1,978 00 |
| Death losses due and unpaid | $58,182 14 | |
| Death losses in process of adjustment | 9,756 00 | |
| Death losses reported for which no proofs have been received | 26,234 50 | |
| Reserve for net death losses incurred but unreported | 15,000 00 | |
| Matured endowments due and unpaid | 4,001 00 | |
| Death losses and other policy claims resisted | 3,500 00 | |
| Annuity claims, involving life contingencies, due and unpaid | 314 25 | |
| Total policy claims | | 116,987 89 |
| Dividends left with the company to accumulate at interest | | 11,786 81 |
| Gross premiums paid in advance, including surrender values so applied, less discount, if any | | 11,175 39 |
| Unearned interest and rent paid in advance | | 83,832 10 |
| Commissions due agents on premium notes, when paid | | 10,422 20 |
| Commissions to agents due or accrued | | 3,005 21 |
| Salaries, rents, office expenses, bills and accounts due or accrued | | 5,092 26 |
| Medical examiners' fees due or accrued | | 3,530 00 |
| Estimated amount hereafter payable for federal, state and other taxes based upon the business of the year of this statement | | 53,676 16 |
| Dividends or other profits due policyholders | | 16,221 04 |
| Dividends declared on or apportioned to annual dividend policies payable to policyholders during 1922 for period to April 15, 1922 | | 8,505 46 |
| Dividends declared on or apportioned to deferred dividend policies payable to policyholders during 1922 for period to April 15, 1922 | | 11,428 90 |
| *Amounts set apart, apportioned, provisionally ascertained, calculated, declared or held awaiting apportionment upon deferred dividend policies | | 195,162 91 |
| Reserve or surplus funds not otherwise included in liabilities, viz— | | |
| Asset fluctuation and general contingency fund | | 150,000 00 |
| Disability benefits, double indemnity and accident and health insurance | | 100,000 00 |
| Other liabilities, viz: Unclaimed checks redeposited, $6,231.86; deposits on liberty bond agreements, $32,076.06; deposits on account of insurance, $1,588.82 | | 39,896 74 |
| Total | | $19,239,241 32 |
| Capital paid up | | 100,000 00 |
| Unassigned funds (surplus) | | 478,963 79 |
| Total | | $19,818,205 11 |

## EXHIBIT OF POLICIES—ORDINARY.

ALL BUSINESS PAID FOR.

| | Number. | Amount. | Number. | Amount. |
|---|---|---|---|---|
| Policies in force December 31, 1920 | | | 34,538 | $69,556,702 00 |
| Policies issued, revived and increased during the year | | | 4,503 | 11,616,767 00 |
| Total | | | 39,041 | $81,173,469 00 |
| Deduct policies which have ceased to be in force during the year— | | | | |
| By death | 458 | $1,093,014 00 | | |
| By maturity | 199 | 223,808 00 | | |
| By expiry | 175 | 422,882 00 | | |
| By surrender | 895 | 1,901,254 00 | | |
| By lapse | 2,512 | 6,623,020 00 | | |
| By decrease | -------- | 262,690 00 | | |
| Total | | | 4,239 | 10,526,668 00 |
| Total policies in force December 31, 1921 | | | 34,802 | $70,646,801 00 |
| Re-insured | | | 429 | $4,590,489 00 |

* Provisionally ascertained and calculated but not a liability in this company.

BUSINESS IN ILLINOIS—ORDINARY.

| | Number. | Amount. |
|---|---|---|
| Policies in force December 31, 1920 | 1,546 | $2,406,137 00 |
| Policies issued during the year | 135 | 464,260 95 |
| Total | 1,681 | $2,870,397 95 |
| Deduct policies ceased to be in force | 138 | 285,353 25 |
| Policies in force December 31, 1921 | 1,543 | $2,585,044 70 |
| Losses and claims unpaid December 31, 1920 | 3 | $ 1,190 00 |
| Losses and claims incurred during the year | 34 | 58,218 60 |
| Total | 37 | $59,408 60 |
| Losses and claims settled during the year | 32 | 56,878 60 |
| Losses and claims unpaid December 31, 1921 | 5 | $2,530 00 |
| Premiums received | | $73,730 41 |

GAIN AND LOSS EXHIBIT.

INSURANCE EXHIBIT.

| | | Gain in surplus. | Loss in surplus. |
|---|---|---|---|
| Loading on actual premiums of the year (averaging 18.05 per cent of the gross premiums) | $378,385 89 | | |
| Insurance expenses incurred during the year | 599,383 07 | | |
| Loss from loading | | | $220,997 18 |
| Interest earned during the year | $1,183,488 70 | | |
| Investment expenses incurred during the year | 312,025 68 | | |
| Net income from investments | $871,463 02 | | |
| Interest required to maintain reserve | 647,638 00 | | |
| Gain from interest | | $223,825 02 | |
| Expected mortality on net amount at risk | $728,733 11 | | |
| Actual mortality on net amount at risk | 515,962 41 | | |
| Gain from mortality | | 212,770 70 | |
| Expected disbursements to annuitants | $7,762 48 | | |
| Net actual annuity claims incurred | 8,879 48 | | |
| Loss from annuities | | | 1.117 00 |
| Total gain during the year from surrendered and lapsed policies | | 113,626 82 | |
| Dividends paid stockholders | | | 13,417 88 |
| Decrease in surplus on dividend account | | | 55,552 48 |
| Increase in special funds and special reserves during the year | | | 100,000 00 |

INVESTMENT EXHIBIT.

| | | Gain in surplus. | Loss in surplus. |
|---|---|---|---|
| Total gains from real estate | | 8,882 92 | |
| Total gains from stocks and bonds | | 6,521 90 | |
| Total losses from stocks and bonds | | | 33,772 00 |
| Gain from assets not admitted | | 3,141 23 | |
| Net gain on account of total and permanent disability benefits or additional accidental death benefits included in life policies | | 12,129 39 | |
| Loss from all other sources: Prepaid fire insurance premiums, $2,139.83; increase in amount set up for estimated federal and state taxes payable 1922, $17,371.20 | | | 19,511 03 |
| Total gains and losses in surplus during the year | | $580,897 98 | $444,367 57 |
| Surplus December 31, 1920 | $342,433 38 | | |
| Surplus December 31, 1921 | 478,963 79 | | |
| Increase in surplus | | | 136,530 41 |
| Total | | $580,897 98 | $580,897 98 |

## MARYLAND ASSURANCE CORPORATION.

Located at Fortieth Street and Cedar Avenue, Baltimore, Maryland; incorporated September 1, 1917; commenced business in Illinois December 26, 1917.

F. HIGHLANDS BURNS, President. E. A. HARTMAN, Jr., Secretary.

GEORGE A. BARR, Director of Trade and Commerce, Attorney for service at Springfield.

CAPITAL.

| | | |
|---|---|---|
| Capital paid up | $500,000 00 | |
| Amount of ledger assets December 31, of previous year | | $738,479 14 |

## INCOME.

| | | | |
|---|---|---|---|
| First year's premiums on original policies, less re-insurance | | $60,355 29 | |
| First year's premiums for total and permanent disability benefits, less re-insurance | | 1,115 94 | |
| First year's premiums for additional accidental death benefits, less re-insurance | | —20 51 | |
| Surrender values to pay first year's premiums | | 7 48 | |
| Surrender values applied to purchase paid-up insurance and annuities | | 167 03 | |
| New premiums | | $ 61,625 23 | |
| Renewal premiums less re-insurance | $129,486 13 | | |
| Renewal premiums for total and permanent disability benefits, less re-insurance | 2,396 47 | | |
| Renewal premiums for additional accidental death benefits, less re-insurance | —50 15 | | |
| Renewal premiums | | 131,832 45 | |
| Premium income | | | $193,457 68 |
| Interest on bonds | | $30,373 61 | |
| Interest on premium notes, policy loans or liens | | 3 27 | |
| Interest on deposits | | 1,875 41 | |
| Interest on other debts due the company | | 71 68 | |
| Total interest | | | 32,323 97 |
| Agents' balances previously charged off | | | 2 70 |
| Increase in book value of ledger assets | | | 1,821 93 |
| Income—life department | | | $227,606 28 |
| Income—casualty department | | | 60,742 46 |
| Total income | | | $288,348 74 |
| Total | | | $1,026,827 88 |

## DISBURSEMENTS.

| | | |
|---|---|---|
| Death claims | | $27,426 00 |
| Surrender values paid in cash, or applied in liquidation of loans or notes | | 139 50 |
| Surrender values applied to pay new and renewal premiums | | 7 48 |
| Surrender values applied to purchase paid-up insurance and annuities | | 167 03 |
| (Total paid policyholders | $27,740 01) | |
| Expense of investigation and settlement of policy claims | | 3 00 |
| Commissions to agents, first year, $22,830.11; renewal, $7,352.85 | | 30,182 96 |
| Commuted renewal commissions | | 316 00 |
| Agency supervision and traveling expenses of supervisors | | 9,408 45 |
| Branch office expenses | | 7,277 68 |
| Medical examiners' fees and inspection of risks | | 8,466 00 |
| Salaries and all other compensation of officers and home office employees | | 43,679 88 |
| Rent | | 1,500 00 |
| Advertising, printing, stationery, postage, telegraph, telephone and express | | 15,654 39 |
| Furniture, fixtures and safes | | 458 84 |
| State taxes on premiums | | 2,465 95 |
| Insurance department licenses and fees | | 6,549 63 |
| Federal taxes | | 2,337 20 |
| All other licenses, fees and taxes | | 1,181 58 |
| Other disbursements, viz: Miscellaneous office expense, $1,707.15; reporting service, $258.50; traveling, $1,768.30; bureaus and associations, $144.00 | | 3,877 95 |
| Agents' balances charged off | | 796 77 |
| Disbursements—life department | | $161,896 29 |
| Disbursements—casualty department | | 61,338 61 |
| Total disbursements | | $223,234 90 |
| Balance | | $803,592 98 |

## LEDGER ASSETS.

| | |
|---|---|
| Loans on company's policies assigned as collateral | $ 2,074 00 |
| Book value of bonds | 721,520 75 |
| Cash in office | 372 39 |
| Deposits in trust companies and banks on interest | 74,467 47 |
| Agents' debit balances | 3,998 93 |
| Casualty department | 1,159 44 |
| Total ledger assets | $803,592 98 |

### NON-LEDGER ASSETS.

| | New business. | Renewals. | |
|---|---|---|---|
| Interest accrued on bonds | | $5,496 87 | |
| Interest due and accrued on premium notes, loans or liens | | 29 73 | |
| | | | 5,526 60 |
| Net uncollected and deferred premiums (paid for basis) | $7,038 61 | $31,014 35 | 38,052 96 |
| Gross assets | | | $847,172 54 |

## LEDGER ASSETS—Concluded.

DEDUCT ASSETS NOT ADMITTED.

| | | |
|---|---|---|
| Agents' debit balances | $3,998 93 | |
| Premium notes, policy loans and other policy assets in excess of net value and of other policy liabilities on individual policies | 29 55 | |
| Casualty department | 426 49 | |
| Total | | $4,454 97 |
| Admitted assets | | $842,717 57 |

## LIABILITIES.

| | | |
|---|---|---|
| Net present value of outstanding policies computed by the Maryland Insurance Department | $284,564 11 | |
| Deduct net value of risks re-insured | 47,422 55 | |
| Net reserve (paid for basis) | | 237,141 56 |
| Extra reserve for total and permanent disability benefits and for additional accidental death benefits included in life policies, less re-insurance | | 3,663 83 |
| Death losses due and unpaid | $1,720 00 | |
| Reserve for net death losses incurred but unreported | 1,000 00 | |
| Total policy claims | | 2,720 00 |
| Gross premiums paid in advance, including surrender values so applied, less discount, if any | | 708 08 |
| Salaries, rents, office expenses, bills and accounts due or accrued | | 1,870 89 |
| Medical examiners' and legal fees due or accrued | | 1,081 82 |
| Estimated amount hereafter payable for federal, state and other taxes based upon the business of the year of this statement | | 6,058 04 |
| Casualty department | | 29,295 43 |
| Total | | $282,539 65 |
| Capital paid up | | 500,000 00 |
| Unassigned funds (surplus) | | 60,177 92 |
| Total | | $842,717 57 |

## EXHIBIT OF POLICIES—ORDINARY.

(Including group insurance.)

ALL BUSINESS PAID FOR.

| | Number. | Amount. | Number. | Amount. |
|---|---|---|---|---|
| Policies in force December 31, 1920 | | | 2,117 | $7,566,180 00 |
| Policies issued, revived, and increased during the year | | | 1,116 | 3,790,723 00 |
| Total | | | 3,233 | $11,356,903 00 |
| Deduct policies which have ceased to be in force during the year— | | | | |
| By death | 9 | $ 29,546 00 | | |
| By expiry | -------- | 4,830 00 | | |
| By surrender | 4 | 23,500 00 | | |
| By lapse | 350 | 947,507 00 | | |
| By decrease | -------- | 9,000 00 | | |
| By withdrawal | -------- | 271,359 00 | | |
| Total | | | 363 | 1,285,742 00 |
| Total policies in force December 31, 1921 | | | 2,870 | $10,071,161 00 |
| Re-insured | | | 323 | $1,980,755 00 |

## EXHIBIT OF POLICIES—GROUP INSURANCE.

(Included in ordinary exhibit above.)

ALL BUSINESS PAID FOR.

| | Number. | Amount. | Number. | Amount. |
|---|---|---|---|---|
| Policies in force December 31, 1920 | | | 4 | $1,458,103 00 |
| Policies issued, revived, and increased during the year | | | -------- | 581,680 00 |
| Total | | | 4 | $2,039,783 00 |
| Deduct policies which have ceased to be in force during the year— | | | | |
| By death | -------- | $ 2,546 00 | | |
| By withdrawal | -------- | 271,359 00 | | |
| Total | | | -------- | 273,905 00 |
| Total policies in force December 31, 1921 | | | 4 | $1,765,878 00 |
| Distribution of business in force at end of year— | | | | |
| One year term | | | 3 | $1,746,878 00 |
| Life | | | 1 | 19,000 00 |
| Total | | | 4 | $1,765,878 00 |

BUSINESS IN ILLINOIS—ORDINARY.

| | Number. | Amount. |
|---|---|---|
| Policies in force December 31, 1920 | 71 | $330,000 00 |
| Policies issued during the year | 51 | 240,144 00 |
| Total | 122 | $570,144 00 |
| Deduct policies ceased to be in force | 7 | 20,500 00 |
| Policies in force December 31, 1921 | 115 | $549,644 00 |
| Premiums received | | $7,597 47 |

GAIN AND LOSS EXHIBIT.

INSURANCE EXHIBIT.

| | | Gain in surplus. | Loss in surplus. |
|---|---|---|---|
| Loading on actual premiums of the year (averaging 15.40 per cent of the gross premiums) | $ 31,286 64 | | |
| Insurance expenses incurred during the year | 136,359 93 | | |
| Loss from loading | | | $105,073 29 |
| Interest earned during the year | $34,397 98 | | |
| Investment expenses incurred during the year | 865 28 | | |
| Net income from investments | $33,532 70 | | |
| Interest required to maintain reserve | 6,451 36 | | |
| Gain from interest | | $27,081 34 | |
| Expected mortality on net amount at risk | $64,946 82 | | |
| Actual mortality on net amount at risk | 23,116 45 | | |
| Gain from mortality | | 41,830 37 | |
| Total gain during the year from surrendered and lapsed policies | | 8,052 94 | |
| INVESTMENT EXHIBIT. | | | |
| Loss from assets not admitted | | | 3,255 53 |
| Net gain on account of total and permanent disability benefits or additional accidental death benefits included in life policies | | 2,405 90 | |
| Gain from casualty department | | 39,941 28 | |
| Balance unaccounted for | | | 15 13 |
| Total gains and losses in surplus during the year | | $119,311 83 | $108,343 95 |
| Surplus December 31, 1920 | $49,210 04 | | |
| Surplus December 31, 1921 | 60,177 92 | | |
| Increase in surplus | | | 10,967 88 |
| Total | | $119,311 83 | $119,311 83 |

## MASSACHUSETTS MUTUAL LIFE INSURANCE COMPANY.

Located at No. 500 Main Street, Springfield, Massachusetts; incorporated May 15, 1851; commenced business in Illinois June 2, 1855.

WM. W. McCLENCH, President. WHEELER H. HALL, Secretary.

WILLIAM C. STONE, Chicago, Attorney for service.

Amount of ledger assets December 31, of previous year $126,642,434 71

INCOME.

| | | | |
|---|---|---|---|
| First year's premiums on original policies, less re-insurance | | $3,378,272 41 | |
| First year's premiums for total and permanent disability benefits, less re-insurance | | 106,060 42 | |
| Dividends applied to purchase paid-up additions and annuities | | 179,478 42 | |
| Consideration for original annuities involving life contingencies | | 67,562 88 | |
| New premiums | | $ 3,731,374 13 | |
| Renewal premiums less re-insurance | $18,362,678 52 | | |
| Renewal premiums for total and permanent disability benefits, less re-insurance | 262,642 59 | | |
| Dividends applied to pay renewal premiums | 2,377,916 56 | | |
| Renewal premiums for deferred annuities | 45,749 55 | | |
| Renewal premiums | | 21,048,987 22 | |
| Premium income | | | $24,780,361 35 |
| Consideration for supplementary contracts involving life contingencies | | | 46,641 11 |
| Consideration for supplementary contracts not involving life contingencies | | | 429,239 51 |
| Dividends left with company to accumulate at interest | | | 1,607,217 85 |
| Interest on mortgage loans | | $2,566,565 02 | |
| Interest on bonds and dividends on stocks | | 2,745,877 32 | |

INCOME—Concluded.

| | | |
|---|---|---|
| Interest on premium notes, policy loans or liens | $1,198,505 82 | |
| Interest on deposits | 71,149 50 | |
| Interest on other debts due the company | 2,231 73 | |
| Discount on claims paid in advance | 27 55 | |
| Rents—including $85,000.00 for company's occupancy of its own buildings | 109,689 88 | |
| Total interest and rents | | $6,694,046 82 |
| From other sources, viz: Commissions on mortgage loans, $210,323.52; refund on account Federal taxes paid in advance in 1913-1914, $6,995.56; protest fees, $23.91 | | 217,342 99 |
| Profit on sale or maturity of ledger assets | | 4,118 11 |
| Increase in book value of ledger assets | | 96,342 39 |
| Total income | | $33,875,310 13 |
| Total | | $160,517,744 84 |

DISBURSEMENTS.

| | | |
|---|---|---|
| Death claims and additions | $5,472,146 21 | |
| Matured endowments and additions | 445,521 00 | |
| Total and permanent disability claims | 23,732 54 | |
| Total death claims and endowments | | $5,941,399 75 |
| Annuities involving life contingencies | | 22,022 77 |
| Surrender values paid in cash, or applied in liquidation of loans or notes | | 2,344,111 50 |
| Dividends paid policyholders in cash, or applied in liquidation of loans or notes | | 669,865 29 |
| Dividends applied to pay renewal premiums | | 2,377,916 56 |
| Dividends applied to purchase paid-up additions and annuities | | 179,478 42 |
| Dividends left with the company to accumulate at interest | | 1,607,217 85 |
| (Total paid policyholders | $13,142,012 14) | |
| Expense of investigation and settlement of policy claims, including legal expenses | | 4,641 21 |
| Supplementary contracts not involving life contingencies | | 259,097 59 |
| Dividends with interest, held on deposit surrendered during the year | | 765,551 84 |
| Commissions to agents, first year, $1,500,345.70; renewal, $1,462.408.68; annuities (original), $3,377.95; (renewal), $2,350.04 | | 2,968,482 37 |
| Compensation of managers and agents not paid by commissions on new business | | 13,205 00 |
| Agency supervision and traveling expenses of supervisors | | 6,346 15 |
| Branch office expenses | | 292,621 73 |
| Medical examiners' fees and inspection of risks | | 213,509 42 |
| Salaries and all other compensation of officers and home office employees | | 686,495 89 |
| Rent | | 174,250 86 |
| Advertising, printing, stationery, postage, telegraph, telephone, express and exchange | | 176,885 94 |
| Legal expense | | 2,928 68 |
| Furniture, fixtures and safes | | 29,076 95 |
| Repairs and expenses (other than taxes) on real estate | | 42,198 00 |
| Taxes on real estate | | 33,945 00 |
| State taxes on premiums | | 317,331 64 |
| Insurance department licenses and fees | | 27,271 10 |
| Federal taxes | | 85,409 34 |
| All other licenses, fees and taxes | | 80,479 00 |
| Other disbursements, viz: Legislative expenses, $1,282.84; home office and agency traveling, $5,873.87; surety bonds and publications, $8,152.04; light and power, alterations and repairs, electrical supplies, $14,267.28; shipping supplies and janitor service, $4,006.85; office furniture, insurance, $325.02; workmen's compensation insurance, $322.66; clerks' lunches, $1,178.50; agents' annual meeting, $12,724.91; directors' meetings, $400.13; rent postoffice boxes, $39.50; photographs, $245.40; legislative information, $470.93; water rent, $26.76; rental of appliances, $2,698.00; funeral expenses, $60.00; moving expenses, $51.87; notary fees, $65.50; agency meetings, $1,012.95; contribution National Association Owners of Railroad securities, $5,359.50; clerks' welfare, $2,015.02; group insurance home office employees, $7,140.67; contribution to the Association of Life Insurance Presidents exclusive of amounts charged to legislative and legal expenses, $2,690.76; Scovell-Wellington and Company, public accountants, 1921, audit, $4,500.00; sundries, $724.86; expenses of mortgage loan agencies, $54,372.87; protest fees, $51.93; commissions on bonds purchased, $45.00 | | 130,105 62 |
| Loss on sale or maturity of ledger assets | | 1,679 38 |
| Decrease in book value of ledger assets | | 42,257 14 |
| Total disbursements | | $19,495,781 99 |
| Balance | | $141,021,962 85 |

LEDGER ASSETS.

| | |
|---|---|
| Book value of real estate | $ 1,029,400 00 |
| Mortgage loans on real estate | 50,412,804 00 |
| Loans on company's policies assigned as collateral | 21,738,754 33 |
| Premium notes on policies in force | 2,418,663 44 |
| Book value of bonds and stocks | 62,816,431 03 |
| Cash in office | 4,545 42 |
| Deposits in trust companies and banks not on interest | 174,698 99 |
| Deposits in trust companies and banks on interest | 2,426,665 64 |
| Total ledger assets | $141,021,962 85 |

## LEDGER ASSETS—Concluded.

### NON-LEDGER ASSETS.

| | | | |
|---|---|---|---|
| Interest due and accrued on mortgages | | $ 910,121 81 | |
| Interest due and accrued on bonds | | 1,040,426 81 | |
| Interest due and accrued on premium notes, loans or liens | | 701,845 50 | |
| Interest due and accrued on other assets | | 4,610 11 | |
| | | | $2,657,004 23 |
| Due from other companies for losses or claims on policies re-insured | | | 9,625 00 |
| | New business. | Renewals. | |
| Net uncollected and deferred premiums (paid for basis) | $530,213 55 | $3,309,170 31 | 3,839,383 86 |
| Gross assets | | | $147,527,975 94 |

### DEDUCT ASSETS NOT ADMITTED.

| | | |
|---|---|---|
| Overdue and accrued interest on bonds in default | $118,250 00 | |
| Book value of bonds and stocks over market value | 318,812 93 | |
| Total | | 437,062 93 |
| Admitted assets | | $147,090,913 01 |

## LIABILITIES.

| | | |
|---|---|---|
| Net present value of outstanding policies | $127,391,157 00 | |
| Same for dividend additions | 1,697,740 00 | |
| Same for annuities | 595,603 00 | |
| Total | $129,684,500 00 | |
| Deduct net value of risks re-insured | 1,953,696 00 | |
| Net reserve (paid for basis) | | $127,730,804 00 |
| Extra reserve for total and permanent disability benefits and for additional accidental death benefits included in life policies, less re-insurance | | 468,389 00 |
| Present value of supplementary contracts not involving life contingencies | | 2,507,471 77 |
| Present value of amounts incurred but not yet due for total and permanent disability benefits | | 150,294 00 |
| Death losses in process of adjustment | $ 57,509 00 | |
| Death losses reported for which no proofs have been received | 352,480 92 | |
| Reserve for net death losses incurred but unreported | 76,834 00 | |
| Matured endowments due and unpaid | 3,125 00 | |
| Death losses and other policy claims resisted | 14,221 93 | |
| Total policy claims | | 504,170 85 |
| Dividends left with the company to accumulate at interest | | 5,876,956 85 |
| Gross premiums paid in advance, including surrender values so applied, less discount, if any | | 169,130 60 |
| Unearned interest and rent paid in advance | | 13,157 07 |
| Commissions to agents due or accrued | | 1,609 59 |
| Salaries, rents, office expenses, bills, and accounts due or accrued | | 19,868 26 |
| Medical examiners' fees due or accrued | | 28,631 50 |
| Estimated amount hereafter payable for federal, state and other taxes based upon the business of the year of this statement | | 540,824 74 |
| Dividends or other profits due policyholders | | 197,325 88 |
| Dividends declared on or apportioned to annual dividend policies payable to policyholders during 1922 for period to May 31, 1922 | | 2,363,277 38 |
| Total | | $140,571,911 49 |
| Unassigned funds (surplus) | | 6,519,001 52 |
| Total | | $147,090,913 01 |

## EXHIBIT OF POLICIES—ORDINARY.

### ALL BUSINESS PAID FOR.

| | | | Number. | Amount. |
|---|---|---|---|---|
| Policies in force December 31, 1920 | | | 265,671 | $728,743,346 00 |
| Policies issued, revived, and increased during the year | | | 33,928 | 136,157,351 00 |
| Total | | | 299,599 | $864,900,697 00 |
| Deduct policies which have ceased to be in force during the year— | Number. | Amount. | | |
| By death | 1,858 | $ 5,793,896 00 | | |
| By maturity | 258 | 443,727 00 | | |
| By expiry | 502 | 1,477,291 00 | | |
| By surrender | 4,072 | 13,980,207 00 | | |
| By lapse | 6,707 | 22,104,957 00 | | |
| By decrease | -------- | 4,046,100 00 | | |
| Total | | | 13,397 | 47,846,178 00 |
| Total policies in force December 31, 1921 | | | 286,202 | $817,054,519 00 |
| Re-insured | | | 4,101 | $36,668,605 00 |

BUSINESS IN ILLINOIS—ORDINARY.

| | Number. | Amount. |
|---|---|---|
| Policies in force December 31, 1920 | 22,949 | $71,604,113 00 |
| Policies issued during the year | 4,036 | 18,180,485 00 |
| Total | 26,985 | $89,784,598 00 |
| Deduct policies ceased to be in force | 1,818 | 6,294,976 00 |
| Policies in force December 31, 1921 | 25,167 | $83,489,622 00 |
| Losses and claims unpaid December 31, 1920 | 6 | $ 8,883 94 |
| Losses and claims incurred during the year | 138 | 596,760 00 |
| Total | 144 | $605,643 94 |
| Losses and claims settled during the year | 136 | 599,803 94 |
| Losses and claims unpaid December 31, 1921 | 8 | $5,840 00 |
| Premiums received | | $2,730,001 98 |

GAIN AND LOSS EXHIBIT.

INSURANCE EXHIBIT.

| | | Gain in surplus. | Loss in surplus. |
|---|---|---|---|
| Loading on actual premiums of the year (averaging 19.9175 per cent of the gross premiums) | $5,011,090 39 | | |
| Insurance expenses incurred during the year | 5,106,780 96 | | |
| Loss from loading | | | $ 95,690 57 |
| Interest earned during the year | $7,073,658 54 | | |
| Investment expenses incurred during the year | 254,528 89 | | |
| Net income from investments | $6,819,129 65 | | |
| Interest required to maintain reserve | 4,510,040 41 | | |
| Gain from interest | | $2,309,089 24 | |
| Expected mortality on net amount at risk | $7,795,965 07 | | |
| Actual mortality on net amount at risk | 3,677,768 27 | | |
| Gain from mortality | | 4,118,196 80 | |
| Expected disbursements to annuitants | $9,337 86 | | |
| Net actual annuity claims incurred | —858 23 | | |
| Gain from annuities | | 10,196 09 | |
| Total gain during the year from surrendered and lapsed policies | | 205,439 50 | |
| Decrease in surplus on dividend account | | | 5,081,393 91 |
| Net to loss account | | | 28 02 |

INVESTMENT EXHIBIT.

| | | Gain in surplus. | Loss in surplus. |
|---|---|---|---|
| Total gains from stocks and bonds | | 41,618 11 | |
| Total losses from stocks and bonds | | | 1,679 38 |
| Net gain on account of total and permanent disability benefits or additional accidental death benefits included in life policies | | 104,958 00 | |
| Balance unaccounted for | | 641 96 | |
| Total gains and losses in surplus during the year | | $6,790,139 70 | $5,178,791 88 |
| Surplus December 31, 1920 | $4,907,653 70 | | |
| Surplus December 31, 1921 | 6,519,001 52 | | |
| Increase in surplus | | | 1,611,347 82 |
| Total | | $6,790,139 70 | $6,790,139 70 |

## MERCHANTS LIFE INSURANCE COMPANY.

Located at Register-Tribune Building, Des Moines, Iowa; incorporated as assessment association, April 4, 1894; re-incorporated as legal reserve company, February 20, 1915; commenced business in Illinois as an assessment association, February 25, 1902; as a legal reserve company March 17, 1915.

WM. A. WATTS, President. FRANK H. DAVIS, Secretary.

GEORGE A. BARR, Director of Trade and Commerce, Attorney for service at Springfield.

CAPITAL.

| | | |
|---|---|---|
| Capital paid up | $400,000 00 | |
| Amount of ledger assets December 31, of previous year | | $4,100,938 00 |

## INCOME.

| | | | |
|---|---|---|---|
| First year's premiums on original policies, less re-insurance | | $355,226 19 | |
| First year's premiums for total and permanent disability benefits, less re-insurance | | 11,437 47 | |
| First year's premiums for additional accidental death benefits, less re-insurance | | 9,286 48 | |
| Surrender values to pay first year's prèmiums | | 4,640 84 | |
| New premiums | | $ 380,590 98 | |
| Renewal premiums less re-insurance | $1,562,638 46 | | |
| Renewal premiums for total and permanent disability benefits, less re-insurance | 17,508 25 | | |
| Renewal premiums for additional accidental death benefits, less re-insurance | 16,931 50 | | |
| Surrender values applied to pay renewal premiums | 75 00 | | |
| Renewal premiums | | 1,597,153 21 | |
| Premium income | | | $1,977,744 19 |
| Consideration for supplementary contracts not involving life contingencies | | | 23,815 50 |
| Interest on mortgage loans | | $200,308 77 | |
| Interest on bonds | | 16,773 25 | |
| Interest on premium notes, policy loans or liens | | 18,026 76 | |
| Interest on deposits | | 20,064 93 | |
| Interest on other debts due the company | | 372 24 | |
| Total interest | | | 255,545 95 |
| From other sources, viz: Special reserve fund, $1,092.12; reserve fund, $1.00; loss by failure of depository banks repaid, $7.44; suspense, $155.78 | | | 1,256 34 |
| Profit on sale or maturity of ledger assets | | | 94 02 |
| Total income | | | $2,258,456 00 |
| Total | | | $6,359,394 00 |

## DISBURSEMENTS.

| | | |
|---|---|---|
| Death claims | $578,970 08 | |
| Matured endowments | 10,375 00 | |
| Total and permanent disability claims and additional accidental death benefits, less re-insurance | 47,757 88 | |
| Total death claims and endowments | | $637,102 96 |
| Prèmium notes and liens voided by lapse, less $5,636.20 restorations | | 40,889 66 |
| Surrender values paid in cash, or applied in liquidation of loans or notes | | 48,343 63 |
| Surrender values applied to pay new and renewal premiums | | 4,715 84 |
| (Total paid policyholders | $731,052 09) | |
| Expense of investigation and settlement of policy claims | | 543 18 |
| Supplementary contracts not involving life contingencies | | 3,200 00 |
| Collection of renewal premiums | | 10,034 08 |
| Commissions to agents, first year, $272,645.20; renewal, $46,510.16 | | 319,155 36 |
| Commuted renewal commissions | | 9,542 40 |
| Compensation of managers and agents not paid by commissions on new business | | 6,195 74 |
| Agency supervision and traveling expenses of supervisors | | 6,015 76 |
| Branch office expenses | | 1,661 88 |
| Medical examiners' fees and inspection of risks | | 32,560 80 |
| Salaries and all other compensation of officers and home office employees | | 124,168 10 |
| Rent | | 9,330 28 |
| Advertising, printing, stationery, postage, telegraph, telephone, express and exchange | | 32,985 56 |
| Legal expense | | 6,215 74 |
| Furniture, fixtures and safes | | 2,170 00 |
| Investment expense | | 11,731 67 |
| State taxes on premiums | | 48,470 40 |
| Insurance department licenses and fees | | 7,649 73 |
| Federal taxes | | 485 00 |
| All other licenses, fees and taxes | | 12,738 42 |
| Other disbursements, viz: Premiums refunded, $2,027.36; premiums on surety bonds, $1,247.14; incidental expense, $5,475.46; traveling expense, $10,014.92; reserve fund applied on legal reserve premiums, $71.44; benefit fund, $148.63; guarantee fund returned, $64.50 | | 19,049 45 |
| Re-insurance, preferred life insurance company | | 25,000 00 |
| Stockholders' contributions | | 52,708 58 |
| Interest on stockholders' contributions | | 1,855 56 |
| Agents' balances charged off | | 475 91 |
| Premiums paid in advance applied | | 785 97 |
| Total disbursements | | $1,475,781 66 |
| Balance | | $4,883,612 34 |

## LEDGER ASSETS.

| | | |
|---|---|---|
| Book value of real estate | | $ 1,500 00 |
| Mortgage loans on real estate | | 3,766,669 13 |
| Loans on company's policies assigned as collateral | | 335,687 52 |
| Premium notes on policies in force | | 42,309 47 |
| Book value of bonds | | 439,930 30 |
| Cash in office | | 8,319 56 |
| Deposits in trust companies and banks on interest | | 225,554 94 |
| Bills receivable | | 12,997 18 |
| Agents' balances (debit, $51,031.07; credit, $1,304.83) | | 49,726 24 |
| War savings stamps | | 918 00 |
| Total ledger assets | | $4,883,612 34 |

### NON-LEDGER ASSETS.

| | | | |
|---|---|---|---|
| Interest due and accrued on mortgages | | $103,051 76 | |
| Interest accrued on bonds | | 2,952 39 | |
| Interest accrued on other assets | | 2,511 57 | |
| | | | 108,515 72 |
| Due from other companies for losses or claims on policies re-insured | | | 939 78 |
| | New business. | Renewals. | |
| Net uncollected and deferred premiums (paid for basis) | $7 49 | $219,691 53 | 219,699 02 |
| Furniture, fixtures and printing plant | | | 45,781 66 |
| Gross assets | | | $5,258,548 52 |

### DEDUCT ASSETS NOT ADMITTED.

| | | |
|---|---|---|
| Furniture, fixtures and safes | $45,781 66 | |
| Agents' debit balances | 51,031 07 | |
| Bills receivable | 12,997 18 | |
| Premium notes, policy loans and other policy assets in excess of net value and of other policy liabilities on individual policies | 594 17 | |
| Total | | 110,404 08 |
| Admitted assets | | $5,148,144 44 |

## LIABILITIES.

| | | |
|---|---|---|
| Net present value of outstanding policies | $3,784,094 00 | |
| Same for dividend additions | 14,729 00 | |
| Total | $3,798,823 00 | |
| Deduct net value of risks re-insured | 20,576 00 | |
| Net reserve (paid for basis) | | $3,778,247 00 |
| Extra reserve for total and permanent disability benefits and for additional accidental death benefits included in life policies | | 26,963 00 |
| Present value of supplementary contracts not involving life contingencies | | 8,448 00 |
| Present value of amounts incurred but not yet due for total and permanent disability benefits | | 21,901 00 |
| Death losses in process of adjustment | $ 7,041 51 | |
| Death losses reported for which no proofs have been received | 33,448 00 | |
| Total policy claims | | 40,489 51 |
| Gross premiums paid in advance, including surrender values so applied, less discount, if any | | 24,227 27 |
| Unearned interest and rent paid in advance | | 9,321 63 |
| Commissions to agents due or accrued | | 2,166 32 |
| Salaries, rents, office expenses, bills and accounts due or accrued | | 4,114 07 |
| Medical examiners' fees due or accrued | | 1,384 00 |
| Estimated amount hereafter payable for federal, state and other taxes based upon the business of the year of this statement | | 42,632 33 |
| Suspense | | 320 68 |
| Future call fund, $1,249.15; guarantee fund, $3,525.51; benefit fund, $149,000.05; reserve fund, $753,391.13; special reserve fund, $1,263.84; less legal reserve on assessment business, $271,541.00 | | 636,888 68 |
| Total | | $4,597,133 49 |
| Capital paid up | | 400,000 00 |
| Unassigned funds (surplus) | | 151,010 95 |
| Total | | $5,148,144 44 |

## EXHIBIT OF POLICIES—ORDINARY.

### ALL BUSINESS PAID FOR.

| | Number. | Amount. |
|---|---|---|
| Policies in force December 31, 1920 | 42,451 | $85,202,044 63 |
| Policies issued, revived and increased during the year | 5,674 | 15,303,395 76 |
| Total | 48,125 | $100,505,440 39 |

## EXHIBIT OF POLICIES—ORDINARY—Concluded.

ALL BUSINESS PAID FOR.

| | Number. | Amount. | Number. | Amount. |
|---|---|---|---|---|
| Deduct policies which have ceased to be in force during the year— | | | | |
| By death | 290 | $ 595,778 00 | | |
| By maturity | 2 | 15,375 00 | | |
| By disability | 16 | 48,189 00 | | |
| By expiry | 251 | 1,058,483 00 | | |
| By surrender | 299 | 570,728 00 | | |
| By lapse | 7,757 | 17,501,017 39 | | |
| By decrease | -------- | 280,565 00 | | |
| Total | | | 8,615 | $20,070,135 39 |
| Total policies in force December 31, 1921 | | | 39,510 | $80,435,305 00 |
| Re-insured | | | 536 | $2,239,996 00 |

## BUSINESS IN ILLINOIS—ORDINARY.

| | Number. | Amount. |
|---|---|---|
| Policies in force December 31, 1920 | 3,897 | $8,222,147 00 |
| Policies issued during the year | 313 | 904,400 00 |
| Total | 4,210 | $9,126,547 00 |
| Deduct policies ceased to be in force | 315 | 743,939 00 |
| Policies in force December 31, 1921 | 3,895 | $8,382,608 00 |
| Losses and claims unpaid December 31, 1920 | 4 | $ 8,000 00 |
| Losses and claims incurred during the year | 22 | 60,000 00 |
| Total | 26 | $68,000 00 |
| Losses and claims settled during the year | 23 | 60,000 00 |
| Losses and claims unpaid December 31, 1921 | 3 | $8,000 00 |
| Premiums received | | $196,689 86 |

## GAIN AND LOSS EXHIBIT.

INSURANCE EXHIBIT.

| | | Gain in surplus. | Loss in surplus. |
|---|---|---|---|
| Loading on actual premiums of the year (averaging 25.89 per cent of the gross premiums) | $415,790 36 | | |
| Insurance expenses incurred during the year | 671,861 37 | | |
| Loss from loading | | -------------- | $256,071 01 |
| Interest earned during the year | $271,403 95 | | |
| Investment expenses incurred during the year | 11,731 67 | | |
| Net income from investments | $259,672 28 | | |
| Interest required to maintain reserve | 160,579 02 | | |
| Gain from interest | | $ 99,093 26 | |
| Expected mortality on net amount at risk | $1,120,271 00 | | |
| Actual mortality on net amount at risk | 552,436 68 | | |
| Gain from mortality | | 567,834 32 | |
| Total gain during the year from surrendered and lapsed policies | | 33,767 43 | |
| Net to loss account | | -------------- | 468 47 |

INVESTMENT EXHIBIT.

| | | Gain in surplus. | Loss in surplus. |
|---|---|---|---|
| Total gains from bonds | | 94 02 | |
| Loss from assets not admitted | | -------------- | 18,189 22 |
| Gain: Commissions on uncollected and deferred premiums | | 11,895 16 | |
| Loss: Excess of net one year term rate over amount from benefit fund, $295,230.14; re-insurance and stockholders' contributions and interest thereon, $78,564.14 | | -------------- | 373,794 28 |
| Balance unaccounted for | | -------------- | 717 78 |
| Total gains and losses in surplus during the year | | $712,684 19 | $649,240 76 |
| Surplus December 31, 1920 | $ 87,567 52 | | |
| Surplus December 31, 1921 | 151,010 95 | | |
| Increase in surplus | | -------------- | 63,443 43 |
| Total | | $712,684 19 | $712,684 19 |

## METROPOLITAN LIFE INSURANCE COMPANY.

Located at No. 1 Madison Avenue, New York, New York; incorporated May, 1866; commenced business in Illinois, life, July 15, 1868; casualty, March 29, 1920.

HALEY FISKE, President. JAMES S. ROBERTS, Secretary.

GEORGE A. BARR, Director of Trade and Commerce, Attorney for service at Springfield.

JOHN O'CONNOR, Chicago, Attorney for service.

| | | | |
|---|---|---|---|
| Amount of ledger assets December 31, of previous year | | | $945,536,128 55 |

### INCOME.

| | | | |
|---|---|---|---|
| First year's premiums on original policies, less re-insurance | | $22,190,771 73 | |
| First year's premiums for total and permanent disability benefits | | 381,524 44 | |
| First year's premiums for additional accidental death benefits | | 175,325 79 | |
| Surrender values to pay first year's premiums | | 153,956 32 | |
| Dividends applied to purchase paid-up additions and annuities | | 126,173 87 | |
| Consideration for original annuities involving life contingencies | | 473,007 37 | |
| New premiums (ordinary) | | $23,500,759 52 | |
| Renewal premiums less re-insurance | $99,757,642 38 | | |
| Renewal premiums for total and permanent disability benefits, less re-insurance | 827,889 33 | | |
| Renewal premiums for additional accidental death benefits, less re-insurance | 234,274 24 | | |
| Dividends applied to pay renewal premiums | 1,894,889 36 | | |
| Surrender values applied to pay renewal premiums | 83,516 77 | | |
| Renewal premiums for deferred annuities | 1,440 49 | | |
| Renewal premiums (ordinary) | | 102,799,652 57 | |
| Total industrial premiums received including $4,493,622.79 dividends applied in payment of premiums and $43,290.16 dividends applied to purchase paid-up additions | | 119,558,062 03 | |
| Premium income | | $245,858,474 12 | |
| Premiums advanced during year under Soldiers' and Sailors' Civil Relief Act (ordinary) | | 466 22 | |
| Total | | | $245,858,940 34 |
| Consideration for supplementary contracts involving life contingencies | | | 71,878 49 |
| Consideration for supplementary contracts not involving life contingencies | | | 573,141 06 |
| Dividends left with company to accumulate at interest | | | 96,508 61 |
| Ledger assets other than premiums received from other companies for assuming their risks | | | 26,197 11 |
| Assets received from policyholders of other companies in exchange for the re-insurance of their policies | | | 31 38 |
| Interest on mortgage loans | | $21,294,983 77 | |
| Interest on bonds and dividends on stocks | | 23,370,195 73 | |
| Interest on premium notes, policy loans or liens | | 2,949,621 51 | |
| Interest on deposits | | 364,887 61 | |
| Interest on other debts due the company | | 140,545 80 | |
| Discount on claims paid in advance | | 1,869 68 | |
| Rents—including $2,085,217.59 for company's occupancy of its own buildings | | 3,816,092 29 | |
| Total interest and rents | | | 51,938,196 39 |
| From other sources, viz: Hegeman memorial fund bequest, $90,541.39; income, $4,623.03; tax refund, $101,917.55; suspense unclaimed checks, etc., $39,721.81; agents deposits, $412.48; New York state income tax withheld at source, $9,151.88; Workmen's Compensation Fund, Ohio, $1,063.78; reserve for depreciation, $404,354.34; printing and binding division, plant and inventory, $734,872.30; fire insurance fund, $52,489.15; miscellaneous income, $3,704.98 | | | 1,442,852 69 |
| Agents' balances previously charged off | | | 2,030 31 |
| Profit on sale or maturity of ledger assets | | | 582,340 91 |
| Increase in book value of ledger assets | | | 713,076 46 |
| Income, life department | | | $301,305,193 75 |
| Income, casualty department | | | 677,505 64 |
| Total income | | | $301,982,699 39 |
| Total | | | $1,247,518,827 94 |

### DISBURSEMENTS.

| | | | |
|---|---|---|---|
| Death claims and additions | | $46,191,338 88 | |
| Matured endowments and additions | | 20,238,817 25 | |
| Total and permanent disability claims and additional accidental death benefits | | 412,582 51 | |
| Total death claims and endowments | | | $66,842,738 64 |

DISBURSEMENTS—Concluded.

| | |
|---|---|
| Annuities involving life contingencies | $ 471,887 63 |
| Premium notes and liens voided by lapse | 185,163 11 |
| Surrender values paid in cash, or applied in liquidation of loans or notes | 12,773,099 85 |
| Surrender values applied to pay new and renewal premiums | 237,473 09 |
| Dividends paid policyholders in cash, or applied in liquidation of loans or notes | 3,365,683 43 |
| Dividends applied to pay renewal premiums | 6,388,512 15 |
| Dividends applied to purchase paid-up additions and annuities | 169,464 03 |
| Dividends left with the company to accumulate at interest | 96,508 61 |
| Sick benefits on assumed policies, $1,348.60; amount returned to policyholders in consideration of direct payment of weekly premiums at home office on district offices, $816,593.84 | 817,942 44 |
| (Total paid policyholders $91,348,472 98) | |
| Expense of investigation and settlement of policy claims, including legal expenses | 64,199 76 |
| Supplementary contracts not involving life contingencies | 427,008 85 |
| Dividends with interest, held on deposit surrendered during the year | 36,250 26 |
| Commissions to agents, first year, $7,792,596.67; renewal, $6,938,810.52; annuities (original), $7,489.19; (renewal), $29.27 | 14,738,925 65 |
| Compensation of managers and agents not paid by commissions on new business | 649 00 |
| Compensation in industrial department to managers assistant managers and agents | 27,903,308 52 |
| Agency supervision and traveling expenses of supervisors | 384,092 03 |
| Branch office expenses | 4,044,555 74 |
| Medical examiners' fees and inspection of risks | 2,280,374 28 |
| Salaries and all other compensation of officers and home office employees | 9,093,060 80 |
| Rent | 2,839,111 27 |
| Advertising, printing, stationery, postage, telegraph, telephone, express and exchange | 1,531,729 42 |
| Legal expense | 40,178 09 |
| Furniture, fixtures and safes | 165,946 53 |
| Repairs and expenses (other than taxes) on real estate | 1,594,655 15 |
| Depreciation of buildings | 404,354 34 |
| Taxes on real estate | 711,199 52 |
| State taxes on premiums | 3,270,597 56 |
| Insurance department licenses and fees | 6,710 47 |
| Federal taxes | 856,340 60 |
| All other licenses, fees and taxes | 231,570 52 |
| Other disbursements, viz: Expense of curative aid to sick industrial policyholders, $1,413,691.48; sick, disabled and inactive agents and clerks, $370,296.12; maintenance and service, company's sanatorium at Mount McGregor, N. Y., $445,704.14; welfare work for employees, $190,149.24; metropolitan staff savings fund, $292,793.34; life extension institute, $73,517.40; employees' group health insurance premiums, $310,648.19; employees' group life insurance premiums, $308,723.18; Madison Co-operative Association of company's employees, $5,079.23; general welfare work, $565,668.50; expense in connection election of directors, 1921, $3,217.74; legislative expense, $19,970.36; Association of Life Insurance Presidents, exclusive of amount charged to legislative and legal expense, $17,063.02; lunches for home office employees, $585,652.97; companys publications, $403,722.70; examinations by departments and public accountants, $3,189.94; handling and shipping field supplies, $81,056.49; outlay on unlisted assets, $63,639.97; miscellaneous interest payments, $33,087.85; law library, $1,719.24; miscellaneous office supplies and furnishings, $21,547.37; storage house expenses, $9,669.24; typewriters, calculating machines, etc., $328,669.97; expenses incident to investigation and care of investments, $52,363.95; conservation and revival of business, $112,155.40; service medals, $31,501.00; pictures and frames, $2,746.54; conventions, $89,158.59; laundry and kitchen improvements—refrigeration and pneumatic service; supplies, materials and labor for account of company's offices, $244,404.08; home office traveling expense, $26,517.42; books, magazines, etc., $4,250.83; medical division expense, $11,023.82; photographic bureau, $37,172.14; laundry, $1,403.00; sundry general expense, $94,957.01 | 6,256,131 46 |
| New York state income tax withheld at source | 8,296 70 |
| Agents' balances charged off, $30,687.38; safe burglary insurance, $2,350.61 | 33,037 99 |
| Agents' deposits returned, $62,219.57; deposit account, interest and rents, $17,549.61 | 79,769 18 |
| Losses—miscellaneous | 4,637 18 |
| Loss on sale or maturity of ledger assets | 26,224 42 |
| Decrease in book value of ledger assets | 2,815,119 66 |
| Disbursements, life department | $171,196,507 93 |
| Disbursements, casualty department | 714,852 62 |
| Total disbursements | $171,911,360 55 |
| Balance | $1,075,607,467 39 |

LEDGER ASSETS.

| | |
|---|---|
| Book value of real estate | $ 28,278,013 67 |
| Mortgage loans on real estate | 454,517,998 53 |
| Premiums advanced under Soldiers' and Sailors' Civil Relief Act | 299 37 |
| Loans on company's policies assigned as collateral | 69,048,544 71 |
| Premium notes on policies in force | 6,127,656 00 |
| Book value of bonds and stocks | 505,251,586 45 |
| Cash in office | 108,232 23 |
| Deposits in trust companies and banks not on interest | 127,050 87 |

## LEDGER ASSETS—Concluded.

| | | |
|---|---|---|
| Deposits in trust companies and banks on interest | | $10,709,035 59 |
| Agents' balances (debit, $53,038.59; credit, $319,631.15) net | | —266,592 56 |
| Cash in transit, $119,062.58; cash in branch office banks, $9,701.06; renting section inventory, $33,839.79; printing and binding division, plant and inventory, $761,461.65; suspense account, unadjusted items, $71,053.58; taxes on mortgaged property, advanced, secured, $8,526.57; contingent reversion, $5,700.00; reserve deposits with re-insured companies, $105,871.20; due from insurance commissioner of Pennsylvania as receiver of Pittsburgh Life and Trust Company in settlement of the re-insurance agreement, $587,650.35 | | 1,702,866 78 |
| Casualty department, premiums in course of collection | | 2,775 75 |
| Total ledger assets | | $1,075,607,467 39 |

### NON-LEDGER ASSETS.

| | | |
|---|---|---|
| Interest due and accrued on mortgages | $7,423,711 21 | |
| Interest due and accrued on bonds | 7,361,400 71 | |
| Interest due and accrued on premium notes, loans or liens | 3,250,089 63 | |
| Rents due and accrued on company's property | 68,220 86 | |
| | | 18,103,422 41 |

| | New business. | Renewals. | |
|---|---|---|---|
| Net uncollected and deferred premiums (paid for basis) | $3,359,674 59 | $20,587,761 75 | 23,947,436 34 |
| Industrial premiums due and unpaid, less loading | | | 2,630,726 74 |
| Checks for annuities issued in advance | | | 14,772 45 |
| Checks for disability annuities issued in advance | | | 942 00 |
| Gross assets | | | $1,120,304,767 33 |

### DEDUCT ASSETS NOT ADMITTED.

| | | |
|---|---|---|
| Agents' debit balances | $ 53,038 59 | |
| Premium notes, policy loans and other policy assets in excess of net value and of other policy liabilities on individual policies | 269,374 10 | |
| Overdue and accrued interest on bonds in default | 614,850 01 | |
| Book value of bonds not subject to amortization and stocks over market value | 2,918,125 07 | |
| Printing and binding division—plant and inventory | 761,461 65 | |
| Renting section inventory | 33,839 79 | |
| Suspense, unadjusted items | 71,053 58 | |
| Total | | 4,721,742 79 |
| Admitted assets | | $1,115,583,024 54 |

## LIABILITIES.

| | | |
|---|---|---|
| Net present value of outstanding policies computed by the New York Insurance Department | $1,019,919,652 00 | |
| Same for dividend additions | 1,644,144 00 | |
| Same for annuities | 4,248,931 00 | |
| Total | $1,025,812,727 00 | |
| Deduct net value of risks re-insured | 250,099 00 | |
| Net reserve (paid for basis) | | $1,025,562,628 00 |
| Extra reserve for total and permanent disability benefits and for additional accidental death benefits included in life policies, less re-insurance | | 1,906,887 34 |
| Extra reserve to pay in full death claims to May 7, 1922 on Pittsburgh Life and Trust Co. policies | | 50,000 00 |
| Present value of supplementary contracts not involving life contingencies | | 1,632,077 50 |
| Present value of amounts incurred but not yet due for total and permanent disability benefits | | 897,252 24 |
| Surrender values claimable on policies cancelled | | 2,910,024 00 |
| Death losses in process of adjustment | $ 325,252 34 | |
| Death losses reported for which no proofs have been received | 775,512 08 | |
| Reserve for net death losses incurred but unreported | 1,914,630 23 | |
| Matured endowments due and unpaid | 218,944 19 | |
| Death losses and other policy claims resisted | 475,725 40 | |
| Total and permanent disability benefits and additional accidental death benefits | 239,778 87 | |
| Annuity claims, involving life contingencies, due and unpaid | 1,725 80 | |
| Total policy claims | | 3,951,568 91 |
| Dividends left with the company to accumulate at interest | | 523,170 52 |
| Gross premiums paid in advance, including surrender values so applied, less discount, if any | | 2,812,813 67 |
| Unearned interest and rent paid in advance | | 88,604 99 |
| Commissions to agents due or accrued | | 183,442 81 |
| Compensation accrued in industrial department to managers and assistant managers | | 527,386 76 |
| Salaries, rents, office expenses, bills and accounts due or accrued | | 477,219 17 |
| Medical examiners' and legal fees due or accrued | | 385,268 75 |
| Estimated amount hereafter payable for federal, state and other taxes based upon the business of the year of this statement | | 4,979,484 00 |
| Dividends or other profits due policyholders | | 864,885 47 |

LIABILITIES—Concluded.

| | |
|---|---|
| Dividends declared on or apportioned to annual dividend policies payable to policyholders during 1922 for period to December 31, 1922 | $11,823,639 00 |
| Dividends declared on or apportioned to deferred dividend policies payable to policyholders during 1922 for period to December 31, 1922 | 3,815 72 |
| Amounts set apart, apportioned, provisionally ascertained, calculated, declared or held awaiting apportionment upon deferred dividend policies | 49,301 52 |
| Present value of annual bonuses to be applied to certain assumed policies | 1,683 47 |
| Reserve for dividends payable in 1922 | 4,004,893 00 |
| Surplus on Pittsburgh Life and Trust Co. business | 2,305,962 62 |
| Due insurance commissioner of Pennsylvania as receiver of Pittsburgh Life and Trust Co. in settlement of the re-insurance agreement | 122,786 16 |
| To cover all other possible items | 150,000 00 |
| Other liabilities, viz: Fire insurance fund, $430,136.17; safe burglary insurance, $1.56; due New York State for income tax withheld at source, $9,036.33; agents cash deposits in lieu of bonds, $150,615.66; accrued interest on deposits, $2,711.51; Hegeman Memorial fund, $154,938.61; suspense, unclaimed checks, etc., $141,737.01; deposit account mortgage interest and rents, $82,633.23; reserve for depreciation $456,031.79; workmans compensation fund, Ohio, $1,063.78; U. S. war Risk Insurance Bureau, $466.22; | 1,429,371 87 |
| Casualty department | 697,677 55 |
| Total | $1,068,341,845 04 |
| Unassigned funds (surplus) | 47,241,179 50 |
| Total | $1,115,583,024 54 |

EXHIBIT OF POLICIES—ORDINARY.

ALL BUSINESS PAID FOR.

| | Number. | Amount. | Number. | Amount. |
|---|---|---|---|---|
| Policies in force December 31, 1920 | | | 3,018,589 | $3,500,348,396 00 |
| Policies issued, revived and increased during the year | | | 645,311 | 897,949,212 00 |
| Total | | | 3,663,900 | $4,398,297,608 00 |
| Deduct policies which have ceased to be in force during the year— | | | | |
| By death | 18,729 | $ 21,079,206 00 | | |
| By maturity | 21,935 | 12,742,741 00 | | |
| By disability | -------- | 294,229 00 | | |
| By expiry | 2,843 | 17,528,827 00 | | |
| By surrender | 34,994 | 34,884,081 00 | | |
| By lapse | 295,914 | 292,774,047 00 | | |
| By decrease | -------- | 25,092,763 00 | | |
| By withdrawal | -------- | 101,634,440 00 | | |
| Total | | | 374,415 | 506,030,334 00 |
| Total policies in force December 31, 1921 | | | 3,289,485 | $3,892,267,274 00 |
| Re-insured | | | 907 | $7,342,582 00 |

EXHIBIT OF POLICIES—GROUP INSURANCE.

ALL BUSINESS PAID FOR.

| | Number. | Amount. | Number. | Amount. |
|---|---|---|---|---|
| Policies in force December 31, 1920 | | | 1,179 | $280,014,613 00 |
| Policies issued, revived and increased during the year | | | 186 | 129,343,264 00 |
| Total | | | 1,365 | $409,357,877 00 |
| Balance of transfers | | | -------- | 1,136,647 00 |
| Total | | | 1,365 | $408,221,230 00 |
| Deduct policies which have ceased to be in force during the year— | | | | |
| By death | -------- | $ 1,882,166 00 | | |
| By disability | -------- | 277,504 00 | | |
| By expiry | 170 | 14,780,460 00 | | |
| By surrender | -------- | 125,074 00 | | |
| By decrease | -------- | 22,513 00 | | |
| By withdrawal | -------- | 101,634,440 00 | | |
| Total | | | 170 | 118,722,157 00 |
| Total policies in force December 31, 1921 | | | 1,195 | $289,499,073 00 |
| Distribution of business in force at end of year— | | | | |
| One year term | | | 1,191 | $284,292,707 00 |
| Life | | | -------- | 983 00 |
| Endowment | | | 4 | 5,205,383 00 |
| Total | | | 1,195 | $289,499,073 00 |

## EXHIBIT OF POLICIES—INDUSTRIAL.

ALL BUSINESS PAID FOR.

| | Number. | Amount. |
|---|---|---|
| Policies in force December 31, 1920 | 20,881,408 | $2,879,664,118 00 |
| Policies issued, revived and increased during the year | 3,887,051 | 666,840,395 00 |
| Total | 24,768,459 | $3,546,504,513 00 |

Deduct policies which have ceased to be in force during the year—

| | Number. | Amount. |
|---|---|---|
| By death | 194,056 | $ 25,278,010 00 |
| By maturity | 88,555 | 7,638,363 00 |
| By disability | -------- | 42,790 00 |
| By expiry | 21,073 | 3,168,414 00 |
| By surrender | 220,447 | 34,649,971 00 |
| By lapse | 1,991,391 | 333,955,381 00 |
| By decrease | -------- | 28,331,019 00 |

| | Number. | Amount. |
|---|---|---|
| Total | 2,515,522 | 433,063,948 00 |
| Total policies in force December 31, 1921 | 22,252,937 | $3,113,440,565 00 |

## BUSINESS IN ILLINOIS—ORDINARY.

| | Number. | Amount. |
|---|---|---|
| Policies in force December 31, 1920 | 239,513 | $234,291,058 00 |
| Policies issued during the year | 56,248 | 62,888,887 00 |
| Total | 295,761 | $297,179,945 00 |
| Deduct policies ceased to be in force | 27,417 | 25,147,747 00 |
| Policies in force December 31, 1921 | 268,344 | $272,032,198 00 |
| Losses and claims unpaid December 31, 1920 | 93 | $ 85,656 66 |
| Losses and claims incurred during the year | 2,957 | 2,305,444 06 |
| Total | 3,050 | $2,391,100 72 |
| Losses and claims settled during the year | 2,925 | 2,290,963 00 |
| Losses and claims unpaid December 31, 1921 | 125 | $100,137 72 |
| Premiums received | | $9,171,623 48 |

## BUSINESS IN ILLINOIS—GROUP INSURANCE.

| | Number. | Amount. |
|---|---|---|
| Policies in force December 31, 1920 | 54 | $5,191,700 00 |
| Policies issued during the year | 16 | 3,662,500 00 |
| Total | 70 | $8,854,200 00 |
| Deduct policies ceased to be in force | 7 | 2,462,750 00 |
| Policies in force December 31, 1921 | 63 | $6,391,450 00 |
| Losses and claims unpaid December 31, 1920 | 2 | $ 1,950 00 |
| Losses and claims incurred during the year | 38 | 35,386 00 |
| Total | 40 | $37,336 00 |
| Losses and claims settled during the year | 37 | 35,236 00 |
| Losses and claims unpaid December 31, 1921 | 3 | $2,100 00 |
| Premiums received | | $67,769 47 |

## BUSINESS IN ILLINOIS—INDUSTRIAL.

| | Number. | Amount. |
|---|---|---|
| Policies in force December 31, 1920 | 1,531,465 | $202,016,083 00 |
| Policies issued during the year | 280,841 | 42,626,898 00 |
| Total | 1,812,306 | $244,642,981 00 |
| Deduct policies ceased to be in force | 144,051 | 24,428,564 00 |
| Policies in force December 31, 1921 | 1,668,255 | $220,214,417 00 |
| Losses and claims unpaid December 31, 1920 | 163 | $ 23,025 69 |
| Losses and claims incurred during the year | 19,609 | 2,306,562 64 |
| Total | 19,772 | $2,329,588 33 |
| Losses and claims settled during the year | 19,365 | 2,279,296 39 |
| Losses and claims unpaid December 31, 1921 | 407 | $50,291 94 |
| Premiums received | | $8,387,282 45 |

## GAIN AND LOSS EXHIBIT.

INSURANCE EXHIBIT.

| | | Gain in surplus. | Loss in surplus. |
|---|---|---|---|
| Loading on actual premiums of the year (averaging 24.01 per cent of the gross premiums) | $59,380,926 57 | | |
| Insurance expenses incurred during the year | 70,828,972 72 | | |
| Loss from loading | | | $11,448,046 15 |
| Interest earned during the year | $55,031,921 26 | | |
| Investment expenses incurred during the year | 2,996,695 96 | | |
| Net income from investments | $52,035,225 30 | | |
| Interest required to maintain reserve | 36,336,822 40 | | |
| Gain from interest | | $15,698,402 90 | |
| Expected mortality on net amount at risk | $63,087,653 00 | | |
| Actual mortality on net amount at risk | 35,530,744 26 | | |
| Gain from mortality | | 27,556,908 74 | |
| Expected disbursements to annuitants | $307,272 67 | | |
| Net actual annuity claims incurred | 313,682 67 | | |
| Loss from annuities | | | 6,410 00 |
| Total gain during the year from surrendered and lapsed policies | | 6,548,444 12 | |
| Decrease in surplus on dividend account | | | 15,168,491 09 |
| Increase in special funds and special reserves during the year | | | 1,222,512 02 |
| INVESTMENT EXHIBIT. | | | |
| Total gains from real estate | | 26,058 51 | |
| Total losses from real estate | | | 2,665,067 61 |
| Total gains from stocks and bonds | | 556,912 91 | |
| Total losses from stocks and bonds | | | 509,573 55 |
| Loss on other investments | | | 63,639 97 |
| Gain from assets not admitted | | 49,819 23 | |
| Net gain on account of total and permanent disability benefits or additional accidental death benefits included in life policies | | 119,296 96 | |
| Loss from sick benefit on assumed policies | | | 1,348 60 |
| Disbursements for health and welfare work | | | 3,976,270 82 |
| Increase in reserve due to change in valuation basis for certain industrial policies | | | 1,267,762 00 |
| Gain from assumed business | | 526 88 | |
| Net loss on account of casualty department | | | 433,921 87 |
| Total gains and losses in surplus during the year | | $50,556,370 25 | $36,763,043 68 |
| Surplus December 31, 1920 | $33,447,852 93 | | |
| Surplus December 31, 1921 | 47,241,179 50 | | |
| Increase in surplus | | | 13,793,326 57 |
| Total | | $50,556,370 25 | $50,556,370 25 |

## MICHIGAN MUTUAL LIFE INSURANCE COMPANY.

Located at No. 105 West Jefferson Avenue, Detroit, Michigan; incorporated November 6, 1867; commenced business in Illinois May 16, 1884.

J. J. MOONEY, President. A. F. MOORE, Secretary.

WILLIAM F. WARRICK, Chicago, Attorney for service.

### CAPITAL.

| | | |
|---|---|---|
| Capital paid up | $250,000 00 | |
| Amount of ledger assets December 31, of previous year | | $14,694,767 28 |

### INCOME.

| | | | |
|---|---|---|---|
| First year's premiums on original policies, less re-insurance | | $344,357 25 | |
| First year's premiums for total and permanent disability benefits | | 4,515 95 | |
| First year's premiums for additional accidental death benefits, less re-insurance | | 764 80 | |
| Dividends applied to purchase paid-up additions and annuities | | 8,845 10 | |
| New premiums | | $358,483 10 | |
| Renewal premiums less re-insurance | $2,040,556 99 | | |
| Renewal premiums for total and permanent disability benefits | 6,377 50 | | |
| Dividends applied to pay renewal premiums | 7,930 29 | | |
| Renewal premiums | | 2,054,864 78 | |
| Premium income | | | $2,413,347 88 |

## INCOME—Concluded.

| | | |
|---|---|---|
| Consideration for supplementary contracts involving life contingencies | | $ 1,368 67 |
| Consideration for supplementary contracts not involving life contingencies | | 21,631 10 |
| Interest on mortgage loans | $642,834 27 | |
| Interest on bonds | 15,337 50 | |
| Interest on premium notes, policy loans or liens | 125,893 13 | |
| Interest on deposits | 6,053 55 | |
| Interest on other debts due the company | 1,888 17 | |
| Discount on claims paid in advance | 503 39 | |
| Rents—including $10,000.00 for company's occupancy of its own buildings | 10,000 00 | |
| Total interest and rents | | 802,510 01 |
| Agents' balances previously charged off | | 12 81 |
| Total income | | $3,238,870 47 |
| Total | | $17,933,637 75 |

## DISBURSEMENTS.

| | | |
|---|---|---|
| Death claims and additions | $749,043 69 | |
| Matured endowments and additions | 363,161 39 | |
| Total and permanent disability claims | 1,368 67 | |
| Total death claims and endowments | | $1,113,573 75 |
| Annuities involving life contingencies | | 466 28 |
| Premium notes and liens voided by lapse, less $576.87 restorations | | 3,556 35 |
| Surrender values paid in cash, or applied in liquidation of loans or notes | | 369,564 84 |
| Dividends paid policyholders in cash, or applied in liquidation of loans or notes | | 64,481 92 |
| Dividends applied to pay renewal premiums | | 7,930 29 |
| Dividends applied to purchase paid-up additions and annuities | | 8,845 10 |
| (Total paid policyholders | $1,568,418 53) | |
| Expense of investigation and settlement of policy claims, including legal expenses | | 1,967 67 |
| Supplementary contracts not involving life contingencies | | 7,922 46 |
| Dividends to stockholders | | 40,000 00 |
| Commissions to agents, first year, $217,570.41; renewal, $92,236.63 | | 309,807 04 |
| Commuted renewal commissions | | 10,000 00 |
| Agency supervision and traveling expenses of supervisors | | 22,534 60 |
| Branch office expenses | | 85,247 79 |
| Medical examiners' fees and inspection of risks | | 47,544 31 |
| Salaries and all other compensation of officers and home office employees | | 157,681 78 |
| Rent | | 35,400 64 |
| Advertising, printing, stationery, postage, telegraph, telephone, express and exchange | | 30,107 48 |
| Legal expense | | 3,541 17 |
| Furniture, fixtures and safes | | 5,087 91 |
| Repairs and expenses (other than taxes) on real estate | | 485 00 |
| Taxes on real estate | | 2,628 49 |
| State taxes on premiums | | 36,587 03 |
| Insurance department licenses and fees | | 3,770 88 |
| Federal taxes | | 18,882 58 |
| All other licenses, fees and taxes | | 7,681 36 |
| Other disbursements, viz: Legislative expense, $181.19; contribution to Association Life Insurance Presidents, exclusive of amounts charged to legislative and legal expense, $415.66; investment expenses, $694.33; subscriptions, $218.50; miscellaneous home office expense, $14,343.83; revenue stamps, $41.00 | | 15,894 51 |
| Agents' balances charged off | | 563 49 |
| Total disbursements | | $2,411,754 72 |
| Balance | | $15,521,883 03 |

## LEDGER ASSETS.

| | |
|---|---|
| Book value of real estate | $ 458,779 80 |
| Mortgage loans on real estate | 11,982,967 63 |
| Loans on company's policies assigned as collateral | 2,324,184 78 |
| Premium notes on policies in force | 152,329 83 |
| Book value of bonds | 362,512 00 |
| Cash in office | 13,559 30 |
| Deposits in trust companies and banks on interest | 220,694 39 |
| Bills receivable | 5,828 20 |
| Agents' balances (debit, $1,187.05; credit, $159.95), net | 1,027 10 |
| Total ledger assets | $15,521,883 03 |

### NON-LEDGER ASSETS.

| | New business. | Renewals. | |
|---|---|---|---|
| Interest due and accrued on mortgages | | $187,817 92 | |
| Interest accrued on bonds | | 2,201 81 | |
| Interest due and accrued on premium notes, loans or liens | | 52,675 88 | |
| Interest accrued on other assets | | 6,254 14 | |
| | | | 248,949 75 |
| Market value of real estate over book value | | | 16,220 20 |
| Net uncollected and deferred premiums (paid for basis) | $11,537 45 | $209,681 70 | 221,219 15 |
| Gross assets | | | $16,008,272 13 |

## LEDGER ASSETS—Concluded.

DEDUCT ASSETS NOT ADMITTED.

| | | |
|---|---|---|
| Agents' debit balances | $1,187 05 | |
| Bills receivable | 5,828 20 | |
| Premium notes, policy loans and other policy assets in excess of net value and of other policy liabilities on individual policies | 7,125 95 | |
| Total | | $14,141 20 |
| Admitted assets | | $15,994,130 93 |

## LIABILITIES.

| | | |
|---|---|---|
| Net present value of outstanding policies computed by the Michigan Insurance Department | $14,718,477 00 | |
| Same for dividend additions | 103,568 00 | |
| Same for annuities | 5,273 00 | |
| Total | $14,827,318 00 | |
| Deduct net value of risks re-insured | 218,530 00 | |
| Net reserve (paid for basis) | | $14,608,788 00 |
| Extra reserve for total and permanent disability benefits and for additional accidental death benefits included in life policies, less re-insurance | | 6,382 10 |
| Present value of supplementary contracts not involving life contingencies | | 84,518 78 |
| Present value of amounts incurred but not yet due for toral and permanent disability benefits | | 7,230 00 |
| Death losses in process of adjustment | $ 154 77 | |
| Death losses reported for which no proofs have been received | 61,938 34 | |
| Reserve for net death losses incurred but unreported | 1,506 93 | |
| Matured endowments due and unpaid | 4,478 66 | |
| Death losses and other policy claims resisted | 14,724 00 | |
| Total policy claims | | 82,802 70 |
| Gross premiums paid in advance, including surrender values so applied, less discount, if any | | 5,174 45 |
| Unearned interest and rent paid in advance | | 28,882 74 |
| Commissions due agents on premium notes, when paid | | 7,557 70 |
| Commissions to agents due or accrued | | 9,615 03 |
| Cost of collection on uncollected and deferred premiums in excess of loading | | 1,361 28 |
| Salaries, rents, office expenses, bills, and accounts due or accrued | | 7,648 43 |
| Medical examiners' and legal fees due or accrued | | 4,589 75 |
| Estimated amount hereafter payable for federal, state and other taxes based upon the business of the year of this statement | | 52,469 69 |
| Dividends or other profits due policyholders | | 7,562 40 |
| Dividends declared on or apportioned to annual dividend policies payable to policyholders during 1922 for period to March 31, 1922 | | 6,411 24 |
| Dividends declared on or apportioned to deferred dividend policies payable to policyholders during 1922 for period to December 31, 1922 | | 52,255 31 |
| Amounts set apart, apportioned, provisionally ascertained, calculated, declared or held awaiting apportionment upon deferred dividend policies | | 97,697 16 |
| Total | | $15,070,946 76 |
| Capital paid up | | 250,000 00 |
| Unassigned funds (surplus) | | 673,184 17 |
| Total | | $15,994,130 93 |

## EXHIBIT OF POLICIES—ORDINARY.

ALL BUSINESS PAID FOR.

| | Number. | Amount. | Number. | Amount. |
|---|---|---|---|---|
| Policies in force December 31, 1920 | | | 48,094 | $85,737,673 48 |
| Policies issued, revived, and increased during the year | | | 5,215 | 12,935,220 81 |
| Total | | | 53,309 | $98,672,894 29 |
| Deduct policies which have ceased to be in force during the year— | | | | |
| By death | 440 | $ 795,277 02 | | |
| By maturity | 338 | 436,437 94 | | |
| By expiry | 116 | 201,755 16 | | |
| By surrender | 771 | 1,337,156 87 | | |
| By lapse | 3,440 | 7,367,905 71 | | |
| By decrease | | 281,868 33 | | |
| Total | | | 5,105 | 10,420,401 03 |
| Total policies in force December 31, 1921 | | | 48,204 | $88,252,493 26 |
| Re-insured | | | 543 | $4,072,947 01 |

BUSINESS IN ILLINOIS—ORDINARY.

| | Number. | Amount. |
|---|---|---|
| Policies in force December 31, 1920 | 3,273 | $6,295,875 01 |
| Policies issued during the year | 541 | 1,334,268 36 |
| Total | 3,814 | $7,630,143 37 |
| Deduct policies ceased to be in force | 328 | 622,921 54 |
| Policies in force December 31, 1921 | 3,486 | $7,007,221 83 |
| Losses and claims unpaid December 31, 1920 | 5 | $ 538 40 |
| Losses and claims incurred during the year | 79 | 84,732 85 |
| Total | 84 | $85,271 25 |
| Losses and claims settled during the year | 78 | 84,804 17 |
| Losses and claims unpaid December 31, 1921 | 6 | $467 08 |
| Premiums received | | $194,941 17 |

GAIN AND LOSS EXHIBIT.

INSURANCE EXHIBIT.

| | | Gain in surplus. | Loss in surplus. |
|---|---|---|---|
| Loading on actual premiums of the year (averaging 11.66 per cent of the gross premiums) | $284,955 99 | | |
| Insurance expenses incurred during the year | 778,512 62 | | |
| Loss from loading | | | $493,556 63 |
| Interest earned during the year | $831,007 43 | | |
| Investment expenses incurred during the year | 38,916 54 | | |
| Net income from investments | $792,090 89 | | |
| Interest required to maintain reserve | 533,305 15 | | |
| Gain from interest | | $258,785 74 | |
| Expected mortality on net amount at risk | $882,617 00 | | |
| Actual mortality on net amount at risk | 498,433 91 | | |
| Gain from mortality | | 384,183 09 | |
| Expected disbursements to annuitants | $394 43 | | |
| Net actual annuity claims incurred | 466 28 | | |
| Loss from annuities | | | 71 85 |
| Loss from charges and restorations made during the year | | | 247 55 |
| Total gain during the year from surrendered and lapsed policies | | 88,363 24 | |
| Dividends paid stockholders | | | 40,000 00 |
| Decrease in surplus on dividend account | | | 41,411 81 |
| Net to loss account | | | 550 68 |

INVESTMENT EXHIBIT.

| | | Gain in surplus. | Loss in surplus. |
|---|---|---|---|
| Loss from assets not admitted | | | 1,929 44 |
| Net gain on account of total and permanent disability benefits or additional accidental death benefits included in life policies | | 8,372 15 | |
| Gained from valuing on combined experience table | | 4,137 97 | |
| Total gains and losses in surplus during the year | | $743,842 19 | $577,767 96 |
| Surplus December 31, 1920 | $507,109 94 | | |
| Surplus December 31, 1921 | 673,184 17 | | |
| Increase in surplus | | | 166,074 23 |
| Total | | $743,842 19 | $743,842 19 |

## THE MINNESOTA MUTUAL LIFE INSURANCE COMPANY.

Located at Commerce Building, Saint Paul, Minnesota; incorporated August 6, 1901; commenced business in Illinois January 15, 1902.

E. W. RANDALL, President. H. W. ALLSTROM, Secretary.

GEORGE A. BARR, Director of Trade and Commerce, Attorney for service at Springfield.

| | |
|---|---|
| Amount of ledger assets December 31, of previous year | $7,828,999 89 |

INCOME.

| | |
|---|---|
| First year's premiums on original policies, less re-insurance | $504,530 80 |
| First year's premiums for total and permanent disability benefits, less re-insurance | 8,526 16 |
| First year's premiums for additional accidental death benefits, less re-insurance | 4,237 06 |
| Dividends applied to purchase paid-up additions and annuities | 21,957 88 |

INCOME—Concluded.

| | | | |
|---|---|---|---|
| Surrender values applied to purchase paid-up insurance and annuities | | $36,879 42 | |
| Consideration for original annuities involving life contingencies | | 6,945 72 | |
| New premiums | | $ 583,(77 04 | |
| Renewal premiums less re-insurance | $1,600,349 95 | | |
| Renewal premiums for total and permanent disability benefits, less re-insurance | 18,387 34 | | |
| Renewal premiums for additional accidental death benefits, less re-insurance | 6,561 50 | | |
| Dividends and annuities applied to pay renewal premiums | 222,185 38 | | |
| Surrender values applied to pay renewal premiums | 1,108 22 | | |
| Renewal premiums | | 1,848,592 39 | |
| Premium income | | | $2,431,669 43 |
| Dividends left with company to accumulate at interest | | | 8,673 17 |
| Interest on mortgage loans | | $245,501 12 | |
| Interest on bonds | | 65,152 51 | |
| Interest on premium notes, policy loans or liens | | 94,222 83 | |
| Interest on deposits | | 6,501 89 | |
| Interest on other debts due the company | | 3,704 27 | |
| Rents | | 72 00 | |
| Total interest and rents | | | 415,154 62 |
| Profit on sale or maturity of ledger assets | | | 100 50 |
| Increase in book value of ledger assets | | | 2,890 00 |
| Total income | | | $2,858,487 72 |
| Total | | | $10,687,487 61 |

DISBURSEMENTS.

| | | |
|---|---|---|
| Death claims and additions | $435,018 86 | |
| Matured endowments | 3,000 00 | |
| Total and permanent disability claims and additional accidental death benefits | 11,828 45 | |
| Total death claims and endowments | | $449,847 31 |
| Annuities involving life contingencies | | 973 60 |
| Premium notes and liens voided by lapse, less $584.39 restorations | | 2,000 40 |
| Surrender values paid in cash, or applied in liquidation of loans or notes | | 115,021 61 |
| Surrender values applied to pay new and renewal premiums | | 1,108 22 |
| Surrender values applied to purchase paid-up insurance and annuities | | 36,879 42 |
| Dividends paid policyholders in cash, or applied in liquidation of loans or notes | | 27,428 23 |
| Dividends applied to pay renewal premiums | | 222,185 38 |
| Dividends applied to purchase paid-up additions and annuities | | 21,957 88 |
| Dividends left with the company to accumulate at interest | | 8,673 17 |
| (Total paid policyholders | $886,075 22) | |
| Expense of investigation and settlement of policy claims, including legal expenses | | 4,649 47 |
| Supplementary contracts not involving life contingencies | | 6,851 05 |
| Dividends with interest, held on deposit surrendered during the year | | 3,314 14 |
| Commissions to agents, first year $311,223.74; renewal, $107,797.49; annuities (original), $347.29 | | 419,368 52 |
| Agency supervision and traveling expenses of supervisors | | 78,399 25 |
| Branch office expenses | | 1,728 46 |
| Medical examiners' fees and inspection of risks | | 40,865 75 |
| Salaries and all other compensation of officers and home office employees | | 128,536 89 |
| Rent | | 10,384 12 |
| Advertising, printing, stationery, postage, telegraph, telephone, express and exchange | | 33,099 82 |
| Legal expense | | 6,398 37 |
| Furniture, fixtures and safes | | 7,844 17 |
| Taxes on real estate | | 77 95 |
| State taxes on premiums | | 52,245 95 |
| Insurance department licenses and fees | | 4,417 12 |
| Federal taxes | | 16,328 90 |
| All other licenses, fees and taxes | | 355 21 |
| Other disbursements, viz: Investment expenses, $24,173.41; traveling expenses, $6,167.42; special examinations, $2,275.00; convention expenses, $9,585.52; sundry expenses, $6,740.45; employees bond payments refunded, $15.00; profit and loss, $49.02 | | 49,005 82 |
| Agents' balances charged off | | 30,575 22 |
| Decrease in book value of ledger assets | | 301 00 |
| Total disbursements | | $1,780,822 40 |
| Balance | | $8,906,665 21 |

LEDGER ASSETS.

| | |
|---|---|
| Book value of real estate | $ 20,007 65 |
| Mortgage loans on real estate | 5,292,757 03 |
| Premiums advanced under Soldiers' and Sailors' Civil Relief Act | 55 07 |
| Loans on company's policies assigned as collateral | 1,615,202 01 |
| Premium notes on policies in force | 181,450 11 |

## LEDGER ASSETS—Concluded.

| | | |
|---|---|---|
| Book value of bonds and stocks | | $1,356,846 63 |
| Cash in office | | 1,000 00 |
| Deposits in trust companies and banks on interest | | 291,384 83 |
| Bills receivable | | 31,152 32 |
| Agents' balances (debit, $77,423.69; credit, $2,345.78), net | | 75,077 91 |
| Bills receivable secured by real estate and other admitted assets | | 41,500 00 |
| Checks in process of collection | | 231 65 |
| Total ledger assets | | $8,906,665 21 |

### NON-LEDGER ASSETS.

| | | |
|---|---|---|
| Interest due and accrued on mortgages | $200,481 77 | |
| Interest accrued on bonds | 18,516 68 | |
| Interest accrued on premium notes, loans or liens | 7,925 31 | |
| Interest accrued on other assets | 1,736 00 | |
| | | 228,659 76 |
| Due from other companies for losses or claims on policies re-insured | | 7,000 00 |
| Net uncollected and deferred premiums (paid for basis): New business. $3,602 78 | Renewals. $326,187 41 | 329,790 19 |
| Gross assets | | $9,472,115 16 |

### DEDUCT ASSETS NOT ADMITTED.

| | | |
|---|---|---|
| Agents' debit balances | $77,423 69 | |
| Bills receivable | 31,152 32 | |
| Premium notes, policy loans and other policy assets in excess of net value and of other policy liabilities on individual policies | 1,975 28 | |
| Book value of bonds over market value | 104,993 27 | |
| Deposits in banks | 12,832 90 | |
| Checks in process of collection | 231 65 | |
| Total | | 228,609 11 |
| Admitted assets | | $9,243,506 05 |

## LIABILITIES.

| | | |
|---|---|---|
| Net present value of outstanding policies computed by the Minnesota Insurance Department | $7,629,195 00 | |
| Same for dividend additions | 95,474 00 | |
| Same for annuities | 12,001 00 | |
| Total | $7,736,670 00 | |
| Deduct net value of risks re-insured | 45,628 00 | |
| Net reserve (paid for basis) | | $7,691,042 00 |
| Extra reserve for total and permanent disability benefits and for additional accidental death benefits included in life policies, less re-insurance | | 36,567 22 |
| Present value of supplementary contracts not involving life contingencies | | 7,151 70 |
| Present value of amounts incurred but not yet due for total and permanent disability benefits | | 614 00 |
| Death losses in process of adjustment | $24,159 96 | |
| Death losses reported for which no proofs have been received | 38,222 14 | |
| Reserve for net death losses incurred but unreported | 25,000 00 | |
| Death losses and other policy claims resisted | 15,000 00 | |
| Total and permanent disability benefits | 2,799 00 | |
| Total policy claims | | 105,181 10 |
| Dividends left with the company to accumulate at interest | | 38,039 99 |
| Gross premiums paid in advance, including surrender values so applied, less discount, if any | | 10,089 21 |
| Unearned interest and rent paid in advance | | 36,521 56 |
| Commissions due agents on premium notes, when paid | | 10,831 46 |
| Commissions to agents due or accrued | | 8,693 99 |
| Salaries, rents, office expenses, bills, and accounts due or accrued | | 15,000 00 |
| Medical examiners' and legal fees due or accrued | | 7,398 00 |
| Estimated amount hereafter payable for federal, state and other taxes based upon the business of the year of this statement | | 65,000 00 |
| Dividends or other profits due policyholders | | 53,790 87 |
| Dividends declared on or apportioned to annual dividend policies payable to policyholders during 1922 for period to August 31, 1922 | | 217,774 83 |
| Dividends declared on or apportioned to deferred dividend policies payable to policyholders during 1922 for period to December 31, 1922 | | 13,197 59 |
| Amounts set apart, apportioned, provisionally ascertained, calculated, declared or held awaiting apportionment upon deferred dividend policies | | 231,954 89 |
| Additional reserve on group policies to cover excess of net premium over gross premium | | 1,417 00 |
| Additional reserve for mortality and security fluctuation | | 125,000 00 |
| Total | | $8,675,265 41 |
| Unassigned funds (surplus) | | 568,240 64 |
| Total | | $9,243,506 05 |

## EXHIBIT OF POLICIES—ORDINARY.

(Including group insurance.)

ALL BUSINESS PAID FOR.

| | Number. | Amount. | Number. | Amount. |
|---|---|---|---|---|
| Policies in force December 31, 1920 | | | 30,605 | $77,604,480 43 |
| Policies issued, revived and increased during the year | | | 5,760 | 19,075,682 40 |
| Total | | | 36,365 | $96,680,162 83 |
| Deduct policies which have ceased to be in force during the year— | | | | |
| By death | 193 | $ 491,965 88 | | |
| By maturity | 2 | 3,000 00 | | |
| By expiry | 165 | 249,642 00 | | |
| By surrender | 315 | 694,941 22 | | |
| By lapse | 4,645 | 16,043,942 43 | | |
| By decrease | 1 | 1,067,467 86 | | |
| Total | | | 5,321 | 18,550,959 39 |
| Total policies in force December 31, 1921 | | | 31,044 | $78,129,203 44 |
| Re-insured | | | | $4,287,731 31 |

## EXHIBIT OF POLICIES—GROUP INSURANCE.

(Included in ordinary exhibit above.)

ALL BUSINESS PAID FOR.

| | Number. | Amount. | Number. | Amount. |
|---|---|---|---|---|
| Policies in force December 31, 1920 | | | 8 | $945,100 00 |
| Policies issued, revived and increased during the year | | | -------- | 254,093 49 |
| Total | | | 8 | $1,199,193 49 |
| Deduct policies which have ceased to be in force during the year— | | | | |
| By death | -------- | $ 5,298 90 | | |
| By lapse | 2 | 141,100 00 | | |
| By decrease | -------- | 260,794 59 | | |
| Total | | | 2 | 407,193 49 |
| Total policies in force December 31, 1921 | | | 6 | $792,000 00 |
| Distribution of business in force at end of year—One year term | | | 6 | $792,000 00 |

## BUSINESS IN ILLINOIS—ORDINARY.

| | Number. | Amount. |
|---|---|---|
| Policies in force December 31, 1920 | 836 | $1,774,057 58 |
| Policies issued during the year | 245 | 654,328 00 |
| Total | 1,081 | $2,428,385 58 |
| Deduct policies ceased to be in force | 95 | 346,675 00 |
| Policies in force December 31, 1921 | 986 | $2,081,710 58 |
| Losses and claims unpaid December 31, 1920 | 2 | $ 5,000 00 |
| Losses and claims incurred during the year | 14 | 40,319 00 |
| Total | 16 | $45,319 00 |
| Losses and claims settled during the year | 15 | 30,319 00 |
| Losses and claims unpaid December 31, 1921 | 1 | $15,000 00 |
| Premiums received | | $64,708 57 |

## GAIN AND LOSS EXHIBIT.

INSURANCE EXHIBIT.

| | | Gain in surplus. | Loss in surplus. |
|---|---|---|---|
| Loading on actual premiums of the year (averaging 30.06 per cent of the gross premiums) | $733,767 67 | | |
| Insurance expenses incurred during the year | 823,905 65 | | |
| Loss from loading | | -------------- | $ 90,137 98 |
| Interest earned during the year | $466,770 79 | | |
| Investment expenses incurred during the year | 24,173 41 | | |
| Net income from investments | $442,597 38 | | |
| Interest required to maintain reserve | 261,944 00 | | |
| Gain from interest | | $180,653 38 | |

GAIN AND LOSS EXHIBIT—Concluded.

INSURANCE EXHIBIT.

| | | Gain in surplus. | Loss in surplus. |
|---|---|---|---|
| Expected mortality on net amount at risk | $789,411 02 | | |
| Actual mortality on net amount at risk | 352,192 22 | | |
| Gain from mortality | | $437,218 80 | |
| Expected disbursements to annuitants | $1,152 21 | | |
| Net actual annuity claims incurred | 1,339 77 | | |
| Loss from annuities | | | $ 187 56 |
| Total gain during the year from surrendered and lapsed policies | | 57,555 13 | |
| Decrease in surplus on dividend account | | | 323,704 44 |
| Increase in special funds, and special reserves during the year | | | 123,626 00 |
| Net to loss account | | | 30,624 24 |

INVESTMENT EXHIBIT.

| | | Gain in surplus. | Loss in surplus. |
|---|---|---|---|
| Total gains from bonds | | 2,990 50 | |
| Total losses from bonds | | | 10,436 80 |
| Gain from assets not admitted | | 13,218 59 | |
| Net gain on account of total and permanent disability benefits or additional accidental death benefits included in life policies | | 2,543 08 | |
| Total gains and losses in surplus during the year | | $694,179 48 | $578,717 02 |
| Surplus December 31, 1920 | $452,778 18 | | |
| Surplus December 31, 1921 | 568,240 64 | | |
| Increase in surplus | | | 115,462 46 |
| Total | | $694,179 48 | $694,179 48 |

## MISSOURI STATE LIFE INSURANCE COMPANY.

Located at Fifteenth and Locust Streets, St. Louis, Missouri; incorporated November 23, 1892; commenced business in Illinois September 11, 1902.

M. E. SINGLETON, President. JAMES J. PARKS, Secretary.

WM. A. SCHWARTZ, Carbondale, Attorney for service.

CAPITAL.

| | | |
|---|---|---|
| Capital paid up | $1,000,000 00 | |
| Amount of ledger assets December 31, of previous year | | $26,656,630 28 |

INCOME.

| | | | |
|---|---|---|---|
| First year's premiums on original policies, less re-insurance | | $2,434,921 02 | |
| First year's premiums for total and permanent disability benefits, less re-insurance | | 50,377 30 | |
| First year's premiums for additional accidental death benefits, less re-insurance | | 34,225 74 | |
| Surrender values to pay first year's premiums | | 1,271 41 | |
| Dividends applied to pay first year premiums | | 482 36 | |
| Dividends applied to purchase paid-up additions and annuities | | 8,778 39 | |
| Consideration for original annuities involving life contingencies | | 7,542 28 | |
| New premiums | | $2,537,598 50 | |
| Renewal premiums less re-insurance | $7,357,085 40 | | |
| Renewal premiums for total and permanent disability benefits, less re-insurance | 53,455 04 | | |
| Renewal premiums for additional accidental death benefits, less re-insurance | 55,646 87 | | |
| Dividends applied to pay renewal premiums | 196,655 67 | | |
| Dividends applied to shorten the endowment or premium-paying period | 170 79 | | |
| Surrender values applied to pay renewal premiums | 16,229 43 | | |
| Renewal premiums | | 7,679,243 20 | |
| Premiums for health and accident riders to life policies, less re-insurance | | 595 27 | |
| Premium income | | | $10,217,436 97 |
| Consideration for supplementary contracts involving life contingencies | | | 5,317 74 |
| Consideration for supplementary contracts not involving life contingencies | | | 71,010 65 |
| Dividends left with company to accumulate at interest | | | 200,311 89 |
| Interest on mortgage loans | | $1,168,270 45 | |
| Interest on bonds | | 51,783 21 | |
| Interest on premium notes, policy loans or liens | | 393,330 11 | |
| Interest on deposits | | 41,644 85 | |
| Interest on other debts due the company | | 7,602 46 | |
| Rents—including $60,000.00 for company's occupancy of its own buildings less $5,250.00 interest on incumbrances | | 95,472 89 | |
| Total interest and rents | | | 1,758,103 97 |

## INCOME—Concluded.

|  | |  |
|---|---|---|
| From other sources, viz: Suspense items, $1,253.49; bonus on mortgage loans paid off prior to maturity, $9,961.37; from mortgage loans previously charged off, $21.00; agents bond premiums, $2,468.13 | | $ 13,703 99 |
| Borrowed money (gross) | | 100,000 00 |
| Agents' balances previously charged off | | 295 19 |
| Profit on sale or maturity of ledger assets | | 43,527 41 |
| Income, life department | | $12,409,707 81 |
| Income, casualty department | | 50,285 41 |
| Total income | | $12,459,993 22 |
| Total | | $39,116,623 50 |

## DISBURSEMENTS.

|  | |  |
|---|---|---|
| Death claims and additions | $1,733,484 92 | |
| Matured endowments | 144,102 20 | |
| Total and permanent disability claims and additional accidental death benefits | 40,239 90 | |
| Total death claims and endowments | | $1,917,827 02 |
| Annuities involving life contingencies | | 10,211 56 |
| Surrender values paid in cash, or applied in liquidation of loans or notes | | 803,565 28 |
| Surrender values applied to pay new and renewal premiums | | 17,500 84 |
| Dividends paid policyholders in cash, or applied in liquidation of loans or notes | | 141,373 77 |
| Dividends applied to pay renewal premiums | | 196,655 67 |
| Dividends applied to pay first year premiums | | 482 36 |
| Dividends applied to shorten the endowment or premium-paying period | | 170 79 |
| Dividends applied to purchase paid-up additions and annuities | | 8,778 39 |
| Dividends left with the company to accumulate at interest | | 200,311 89 |
| (Total paid policyholders | $3,296,877 57) | |
| Expense of investigation and settlement of policy claims, including legal expenses | | 16,507 98 |
| Supplementary contracts not involving life contingencies | | 14,679 79 |
| Dividends with interest, held on deposit surrendered during the year | | 99,243 49 |
| Dividends to stockholders | | 100,000 00 |
| Commissions to agents, first year, $1,558,133.95; renewal, $424,252.80; annuities (original), $377.12; total disability, $38,049.74; accident and double indemnity, $10,287.75; health, $1.25 | | 2,031,102 61 |
| Compensation of managers and agents not paid by commissions on new business | | 149,706 06 |
| Agency supervision and traveling expenses of supervisors | | 35,302 53 |
| Branch office expenses | | 56,878 64 |
| Medical examiners' fees and inspection of risks | | 163,977 68 |
| Salaries and all other compensation of officers and home office employees | | 517,003 77 |
| Rent | | 60,000 00 |
| Advertising, printing, stationery, postage, telegraph, telephone, express and exchange | | 186,342 44 |
| Legal expense | | 13,189 22 |
| Furniture, fixtures and safes | | 70,427 84 |
| Repairs and expenses (other than taxes) on real estate | | 49,307 08 |
| Taxes on real estate | | 13,992 34 |
| State taxes on premiums | | 149,202 89 |
| Insurance department licenses and fees | | 10,953 94 |
| Federal taxes | | 113,722 06 |
| All other licenses, fees and taxes | | 11,306 32 |
| Other disbursements, viz: Premiums on bonds, $2,582.95; investment expense, $23,930.18; commissions on sale of investments, $4,475.92; club conventions, $50,401.49; collection of premiums, $187.06; miscellaneous traveling expense, $6,054.21; incidental office expense, $14,235.31; insurance departments for examination of company, $10,091.18; payment of checks previously cancelled, $3.00 | | 111,961 30 |
| Borrowed money repaid (gross) | | 100,000 00 |
| Interest on borrowed money | | 1,125 00 |
| Agents' balances charged off | | 7,308 12 |
| Loss on sale or maturity of ledger assets | | 22,963 98 |
| Decrease in book value of ledger assets | | 10,903 75 |
| Disbursements, life department | | $7,413,986 90 |
| Disbursements, casualty department | | 92,193 18 |
| Total disbursements | | $7,506,180 08 |
| Balance | | $31,610,443 42 |

## LEDGER ASSETS.

|  |  |
|---|---|
| Book value of real estate | $ 595,115 90 |
| Mortgage loans on real estate | 22,306,752 53 |
| Loans on company's policies assigned as collateral | 6,413,757 99 |
| Premium notes on policies in force | 425,511 72 |
| Book value of bonds | 195,592 42 |
| Cash in office | 47,325 97 |
| Deposits in trust companies and banks not on interest | 77,349 38 |
| Deposits in trust companies and banks on interest | 1,394,347 87 |
| Bills receivable | 54,237 90 |
| Agents' balances (debit, $99,409.31; credit, $11,681.17) | 87,728 14 |
| Casualty department | 12,723 60 |
| Total ledger assets | $31,610,443 42 |

LEDGER ASSETS—Concluded.

NON-LEDGER ASSETS.

| | | | |
|---|---|---|---|
| Interest due and accrued on mortgages | | $1,092,551 71 | |
| Interest accrued on bonds | | 5,409 92 | |
| Interest accrued on premium notes, loans or liens | | 2,936 66 | |
| Interest accrued on other assets | | 2,653 13 | |
| | | | $1,103,551 42 |
| Market value of real estate over book value | | | 166,045 83 |
| | New business. | Renewals. | |
| Net uncollected and deferred premiums (paid for basis) | $37,272 57 | $1,148,737 50 | 1,186,010 07 |
| Gross assets | | | $34,066,050 74 |

DEDUCT ASSETS NOT ADMITTED.

| | | |
|---|---|---|
| Agents' debit balances | $99,409 31 | |
| Bills receivable | 54,237 90 | |
| Premium notes, policy loans and other policy assets in excess of net value and of other policy liabilities on individual policies | 64,068 73 | |
| Book value of bonds over market value | 3,735 14 | |
| Casualty department | 96 75 | |
| Total | | 221,547 83 |
| Admitted assets | | $33,844,502 91 |

LIABILITIES.

| | | |
|---|---|---|
| Net present value of outstanding policies computed by the Missouri Insurance Department | $27,808,098 00 | |
| Same for dividend additions | 32,220 00 | |
| Same for annuities | 143,047 00 | |
| Total | $27,983,365 00 | |
| Deduct net value of risks re-insured | 78,617 00 | |
| Net reserve (paid for basis) | | $27,904,748 00 |
| Extra reserve for total and permanent disability benefits and for additional accidental death benefits included in life policies, less re-insurance | | 332,235 00 |
| Present value of supplementary contracts not involving life contingencies | | 120,881 48 |
| Present value of amounts incurred but not yet due for total and permanent disability benefits | | 48,482 13 |
| Surrender values claimable on policies cancelled | | 699 14 |
| Death losses in process of adjustment | $61,645 28 | |
| Death losses reported for which no proofs have been received | 72,074 05 | |
| Reserve for net death losses incurred but unreported | 48,049 84 | |
| Matured endowments due and unpaid | 787 00 | |
| Death losses and other policy claims resisted | 19,394 81 | |
| Total and permanent disability benefits and additional accidental death benefits | 23,127 71 | |
| Total policy claims | | 225,078 69 |
| Dividends left with the company to accumulate at interest | | 430,981 35 |
| Gross premiums paid in advance, including surrender values so applied, less discount, if any | | 148,109 89 |
| Unearned interest and rent paid in advance | | 160,712 20 |
| Commissions to agents due or accrued | | 1,400 19 |
| Salaries, rents, office expenses, bills and accounts due or accrued | | 28,687 38 |
| Medical examiners' and legal fees due or accrued | | 13,110 00 |
| Estimated amount hereafter payable for federal, state and other taxes based upon the business of the year of this statement | | 247,400 23 |
| Dividends or other profits due policyholders | | 63,657 83 |
| Dividends declared on or apportioned to annual dividend policies payable to policyholders during 1922 for period to June 30, 1922 | | 243,061 03 |
| Dividends declared on or apportioned to deferred dividend policies payable to policyholders during 1922 for period to December 31, 1922 | | 204,654 01 |
| Amounts set apart, apportioned, provisionally ascertained, calculated, declared or held awaiting apportionment upon deferred dividend policies | | 410,637 18 |
| Trust fund, account of trust fund dividend policies | | 2,345 34 |
| Reserve for expense of agency conventions | | 25,000 00 |
| Cash in suspense | | 12,370 90 |
| Liabilities, life department | | $30,624,251 97 |
| Liabilities, casualty department | | 32,782 28 |
| Total | | $30,657,034 25 |
| Capital paid up | | 1,000,000 00 |
| Unassigned funds (surplus) | | 2,187,468 66 |
| Total | | $33,844,502 91 |

## EXHIBIT OF POLICIES—ORDINARY.

ALL BUSINESS PAID FOR.

| | Number. | Amount. | Number. | Amount. |
|---|---|---|---|---|
| Policies in force December 31, 1920 | | | 134,219 | $302,328,804 00 |
| Policies issued, revived and increased during the year | | | 29,455 | 101,066,946 00 |
| Total | | | 163,674 | $403,395,750 00 |
| Deduct policies which have ceased to be in force during the year— | | | | |
| By death | 754 | $ 1,786,902 00 | | |
| By maturity | 115 | 140,557 00 | | |
| By disability | -------- | 1,900 00 | | |
| By expiry | 1,378 | 5,997,989 00 | | |
| By surrender | 2,670 | 6,537,446 00 | | |
| By lapse | 16,513 | 47,975,963 00 | | |
| By decrease | 12 | 537,965 00 | | |
| Total | | | 21,442 | 62,978,722 00 |
| Total policies in force December 31, 1921 | | | 142,232 | $340,417,028 00 |
| Re-insured | | | 1,420 | $12,153,590 00 |

## EXHIBIT OF POLICIES—GROUP INSURANCE.

ALL BUSINESS PAID FOR.

| | Number. | Amount. | Number. | Amount. |
|---|---|---|---|---|
| Policies in force December 31, 1920 | | | 53 | $8,573,452 00 |
| Policies issued, revived and increased during the year | | | 43 | 9,530,063 00 |
| Total | | | 96 | $18,103,515 00 |
| Deduct policies which have ceased to be in force during the year— | | | | |
| By death | -------- | $ 71,248 00 | | |
| By disability | -------- | 1,900 00 | | |
| By expiry | -------- | 3,060,076 00 | | |
| By lapse | 3 | 894,700 00 | | |
| By decrease | -------- | 36,808 00 | | |
| Total | | | 3 | 4,064,732 00 |
| Total policies in force December 31, 1921 | | | 93 | $14,038,783 00 |
| Distribution of business in force at end of year— | | | | |
| One year term | | | 92 | $13,956,383 00 |
| Life | | | 1 | 82,400 00 |
| Total | | | 93 | $14,038,783 00 |

## BUSINESS IN ILLINOIS—ORDINARY.

| | Number. | Amount. |
|---|---|---|
| Policies in force December 31, 1920 | 7,536 | $16,335,610 00 |
| Policies issued during the year | 1,855 | 7,548,314 00 |
| Total | 9,391 | $23,883,924 00 |
| Deduct policies ceased to be in force | 851 | 2,567,554 00 |
| Policies in force December 31, 1921 | 8,540 | $21,316,370 00 |
| Losses and claims unpaid December 31, 1920 | 6 | $ 8,005 00 |
| Losses and claims incurred during the year | 30 | 72,213 32 |
| Total | 36 | $80,218 32 |
| Losses and claims settled during the year | 30 | 70,270 05 |
| Losses and claims unpaid December 31, 1921 | 6 | $9,948 27 |
| Premiums received | | $700,346 35 |

## BUSINESS IN ILLINOIS—GROUP INSURANCE.

| | Number. | Amount. |
|---|---|---|
| Policies in force December 31, 1920 | 2 | $111,500 00 |
| Policies issued during the year | 6 | 822,900 00 |
| Total | 8 | $934,400 00 |
| Deduct policies ceased to be in force | -------- | 151,900 00 |
| Policies in force December 31, 1921 | 8 | $782,500 00 |
| Losses and claims incurred during the year | 8 | $5,500 00 |
| Losses and claims settled during the year | 8 | 5,500 00 |
| Premiums received | | $9,327 66 |

## GAIN AND LOSS EXHIBIT.

INSURANCE EXHIBIT.

| | | Gain in surplus. | Loss in surplus. |
|---|---|---|---|
| Loading on actual premiums of the year (averaging 22 per cent of the gross premiums) | $2,293,418 79 | | |
| Insurance expenses incurred during the year | 3,653,445 81 | | |
| Loss from loading | | | $1,360,027 02 |
| Interest earned during the year | $2,053,784 29 | | |
| Investment expenses incurred during the year | 148,913 85 | | |
| Net income from investments | $1,904,870 44 | | |
| Interest required to maintain reserve | 936,337 00 | | |
| Gain from interest | | $968,533 44 | |
| Expected mortality on net amount at risk | $3,225,946 00 | | |
| Actual mortality on net amount at risk | 1,563,852 26 | | |
| Gain from mortality | | 1,662,093 74 | |
| Expected disbursements to annuitants | $ 750 89 | | |
| Net actual annuity claims incurred | 2,500 00 | | |
| Loss from annuities | | | 1,749 11 |
| Total gain during the year from surrendered and lapsed policies | | 104,476 05 | |
| Dividends paid stockholders | | | 100,000 00 |
| Decrease in surplus on dividend account | | | 658,774 21 |
| Decrease in special funds and special reserves during the year | | 98 78 | |

INVESTMENT EXHIBIT.

| | | Gain in surplus. | Loss in surplus. |
|---|---|---|---|
| Total gains from real estate | | 3,360 62 | |
| Total losses from real estate | | | 105 86 |
| Total gains from bonds | | 56,898 73 | |
| Total losses from bonds | | | 22,858 12 |
| Loss from mortgage loans | | | 921 38 |
| Loss from assets not admitted | | | 16,697 58 |
| Net gain on account of total and permanent disability benefits or additional accidental death benefits included in life policies | | 17,978 85 | |
| Loss: Agents' balances charged off, net, $7,012.93; payment checks previously cancelled, $3.00; casualty department, $74,786.80 | | | 81,802 73 |
| Total gains and losses in surplus during the year | | $2,813,440 21 | $2,242,936 01 |
| Surplus December 31, 1920 | $1,616,964 46 | | |
| Surplus December 31, 1921 | 2,187,468 66 | | |
| Increase in surplus | | | 570,504 20 |
| Total | | $2,813,440 21 | $2,813,440 21 |

# THE MORRIS PLAN INSURANCE SOCIETY.

Located at No. 680 Fifth Avenue, New York, New York; incorporated June 11, 1917; commenced business in Illinois March 2, 1918.

ARTHUR J. MORRIS, President. JOSEPH B. GILDER, Secretary.

GEORGE A. BARR, Director of Trade and Commerce, Attorney for service at Springfield.

## CAPITAL.

| | | |
|---|---|---|
| Capital paid up | $100,000 00 | |
| Amount of ledger assets December 31, of previous year | | $244,045 64 |

## INCOME.

| | | |
|---|---|---|
| First year's premiums on original policies | $177,738 95 | |
| Renewal premiums | 458 51 | |
| Premium income | | $178,197 46 |
| Interest on bonds | $6,949 98 | |
| Interest on premium notes, policy loans or liens | 22 68 | |
| Interest on deposits | 3,611 69 | |
| Interest on other debts due the company | 262 50 | |
| Total interest and rents | | 10,846 85 |
| Amortization of bonds as of January 1, 1921 | | 19 53 |
| Profit on sale or maturity of ledger assets | | 8 00 |
| Increase in book value of ledger assets | | 203 13 |
| Total income | | $189,274 97 |
| Total | | $433,320 61 |

## DISBURSEMENTS.

| | | |
|---|---|---|
| Total death claims | | $23,714 16 |
| (Total paid policyholders | $23,714 16) | |
| Expense of investigation and settlement of policy claims, including legal expenses | | 272 85 |
| Commissions to agents, first year, $51,092.90; renewal, $45.85 | | 51,138 75 |
| Medical examiners' fees | | 3,007 50 |
| Salaries and all other compensation of officers and home office employees | | 28,988 41 |
| Rent | | 5,840 91 |
| Advertising, printing, stationery, postage, telegraph, telephone, express and exchange | | 7,291 65 |
| Legal expense | | 600 00 |
| Furniture, fixtures and safes | | 489 21 |
| State taxes on premiums | | 1,889 97 |
| Insurance department licenses and fees | | 1,499 52 |
| Federal taxes | | 4,058 58 |
| Other disbursements, viz: Expense of examination, $90.65; travel expenses, home office, $1,030.60; supplies advanced to agents, $251.60; general expense, $536.53 | | 1,909 38 |
| Loss on sale or maturity of ledger assets | | 12 50 |
| Decrease in book value of ledger assets | | 13 50 |
| Total disbursements | | $130,726 89 |
| Balance | | $302,593 72 |

## LEDGER ASSETS.

| | |
|---|---|
| Loans on company's policies assigned as collateral | $ 377 95 |
| Book value of bonds | 174,450 57 |
| Cash in office | 10 00 |
| Deposits in trust companies and banks on interest | 127,003 60 |
| Bills receivable | 251 60 |
| Rent prepaid | 500 00 |
| Total ledger assets | $302,593 72 |

### NON-LEDGER ASSETS.

| | | |
|---|---|---|
| Interest due on bonds | $2,792 81 | |
| Interest due on other assets | 952 85 | |
| | | 3,745 66 |
| Net uncollected and deferred premiums (paid for basis), new business | | 2,733 84 |
| Gross assets | | $309,073 22 |

### DEDUCT ASSETS NOT ADMITTED.

| | |
|---|---|
| Bills receivable | 251 60 |
| Admitted assets | $308,821 62 |

## LIABILITIES.

| | |
|---|---|
| Net present value of outstanding policies computed by the New York Insurance Department | $29,587 99 |
| Death losses reported for which no proofs have been received | 2,210 50 |
| Commissions to agents due or accrued | 815 61 |
| Medical examiners' and legal fees due or accrued | 414 25 |
| Estimated amount hereafter payable for federal, state and other taxes based upon the business of the year of this statement | 4,000 00 |
| Total | $ 37,028 35 |
| Capital paid up | 100,000 00 |
| Unassigned funds (surplus) | 171,793 27 |
| Total | $308,821 62 |

## EXHIBIT OF POLICIES—ORDINARY.

### ALL BUSINESS PAID FOR.

| | | | Number. | Amount. |
|---|---|---|---|---|
| Policies in force December 31, 1920 | | | 62 | $ 82,700 00 |
| Policies issued, revived and increased during the year | | | 2,928 | 1,402,800 00 |
| Total | | | 2,990 | $1,485,500 00 |
| Deduct policies which have ceased to be in force during the year— | Number. | Amount. | | |
| By lapse | 69 | $65,950 00 | | |
| Total | | | 69 | 65,950 00 |
| Total policies in force December 31, 1921 | | | 2,921 | $1,419,550 00 |

## EXHIBIT OF POLICIES—INDUSTRIAL.

ALL BUSINESS PAID FOR.

| | Number. | Amount. | Number. | Amount. |
|---|---|---|---|---|
| Policies in force December 31, 1920 | | | 22,201 | $4,305,050 00 |
| Policies issued, revived and increased during the year | | | 29,438 | 5,963,400 00 |
| Total | | | 51,639 | $10,268,450 00 |
| Deduct policies which have ceased to be in force during the year— | | | | |
| By death | 112 | $ 23,600 00 | | |
| By expiry | 21,681 | 4,231,825 00 | | |
| By lapse | 1,577 | 362,850 00 | | |
| Total | | | 23,370 | 4,618,275 00 |
| Total policies in force December 31, 1921 | | | 28,269 | $5,650,175 00 |

## BUSINESS IN ILLINOIS—INDUSTRIAL.

| | Number. | Amount. |
|---|---|---|
| Policies in force December 31, 1920 | 2,657 | $ 614,800 00 |
| Policies issued during the year | 5,204 | 1,062,700 00 |
| Total | 7,861 | $1,677,500 00 |
| Deduct policies ceased to be in force | 2,671 | 617,850 00 |
| Policies in force December 31, 1921 | 5,190 | $1,059,650 00 |
| Losses and claims incurred during the year | 14 | $3,050 00 |
| Losses and claims settled during the year | 14 | 3,050 00 |
| Premiums received | | $27,994 25 |

## GAIN AND LOSS EXHIBIT.

INSURANCE EXHIBIT.

| | | Gain in surplus. | Loss in surplus. |
|---|---|---|---|
| Loading on actual premiums of the year (averaging 52.43 per cent of the gross premiums) | $ 97,109 09 | | |
| Insurance expenses incurred during the year | 107,579 94 | | |
| Loss from loading | | | $10,470 85 |
| Interest earned during the year | $11,576 93 | | |
| Investment expenses incurred during the year | 12 50 | | |
| Net income from investments | $11,589 43 | | |
| Interest required to maintain reserve | 302 95 | | |
| Gain from interest | | $11,286 48 | |
| Expected mortality on net amount at risk | $72,693 58 | | |
| Actual mortality on net amount at risk | 24,117 66 | | |
| Gain from mortality | | 48,575 92 | |
| INVESTMENT EXHIBIT. | | | |
| Total gains from bonds | | 8 00 | |
| Balance unaccounted for | | 348 94 | |
| Total gains and losses in surplus during the year | | $60,219 34 | $10,470 85 |
| Surplus December 31, 1920 | $122,044 78 | | |
| Surplus December 31, 1921 | 171,793 27 | | |
| Increase in surplus | | | 49,748 49 |
| Total | | $60,219 34 | $60,219 34 |

## THE MUTUAL BENEFIT LIFE INSURANCE COMPANY.

Located at No. 750 Broad Street, Newark, New Jersey; incorporated January 31, 1845; commenced business in Illinois October 13, 1855.

FREDERICK FRELINGHUYSEN, President. J. WILLIAM JOHNSON, Secretary.

ALFRED A. DREW, Chicago, Attorney for service.

| | |
|---|---|
| Amount of ledger assets December 31, of previous year | $270,204,117 15 |

## INCOME.

|  | | | |
|---|---|---|---|
| First year's premiums on original policies | | $5,269,214 95 | |
| Surrender values to pay first year's premiums | | 18,436 82 | |
| Dividends applied to purchase paid-up additions and annuities | | 769,076 61 | |
| Consideration for original annuities involving life contingencies | | 20,072 54 | |
| New premiums | | $ 6,076,800 92 | |
| Renewal premiums | $33,168,910 98 | | |
| Dividends applied to pay renewal premiums | 5,380,788 81 | | |
| Dividends applied to shorten the endowment or premium-paying period | 2,337,898 13 | | |
| Surrender values applied to pay renewal premiums | 27,884 32 | | |
| Renewal premiums for deferred annuities | 35,161 07 | | |
| Renewal premiums | | 40,950,643 31 | |
| Premium income | | | $47,027,444 23 |
| Consideration for supplementary contracts involving life contingencies | | | 8,530 47 |
| Consideration for supplementary contracts not involving life contingencies | | | 1,233,086 90 |
| Interest on mortgage loans | | $6,126,097 67 | |
| Interest on collateral loans | | 387,906 45 | |
| Interest on bonds and dividends on stocks | | 4,306,405 12 | |
| Interest on premium notes, policy loans or liens | | 2,851,845 24 | |
| Interest on deposits | | 69,875 20 | |
| Interest on other debts due the company | | 670 56 | |
| Rents—including $112,000.00 for company's occupancy of its own buildings | | 260,299 59 | |
| Total interest and rents | | | 14,003,099 83 |
| Profit on sale or maturity of ledger assets | | | 2,155 00 |
| Increase in book value of ledger assets | | | 14,180 71 |
| Total income | | | $62,288,497 14 |
| Total | | | $332,492,614 29 |

## DISBURSEMENTS.

|  | | |
|---|---|---|
| Death claims and additions | $11,461,611 87 | |
| Matured endowments and additions | 2,514,830 35 | |
| Total death claims and endowments | | $13,976,442 22 |
| Annuities involving life contingencies | | 131,754 44 |
| Surrender values paid in cash, or applied in liquidation of loans or notes | | 5,585,243 77 |
| Surrender values applied to pay new and renewal premiums | | 46,321 14 |
| Dividends paid policyholders in cash, or applied in liquidation of loans or notes | | 983,497 66 |
| Dividends applied to pay renewal premiums | | 5,380,788 81 |
| Dividends applied to shorten the endowment or premium-paying period | | 2,337,898 13 |
| Dividends applied to purchase paid-up additions and annuities | | 769,076 61 |
| (Total paid policyholders | $29,211,022 78) | |
| Expense of investigation and settlement of policy claims | | 900 76 |
| Supplementary contracts not involving life contingencies | | 884,723 77 |
| Commissions to agents' first year, $2,368,135.22; renewal, $2,412,429.79; annuities (original), $1,728.50; ((renewal), $700.09 | | 4,782,993 60 |
| Commuted renewal commissions | | 5,346 42 |
| Agency supervision and traveling expenses of supervisors | | 76,949 39 |
| Agency office expenses | | 41,338 53 |
| Medical examiners' fees and inspection of risks | | 249,453 75 |
| Salaries and all other compensation of officers and home office employees | | 979,345 81 |
| Rent | | 207,183 17 |
| Advertising, printing, stationery, postage, telegraph, telephone, express | | 152,100 77 |
| Legal expense | | 52,606 45 |
| Furniture, fixtures and safes | | 3,587 74 |
| Repairs and expenses (other than taxes) on real estate | | 51,085 98 |
| Taxes on real estate | | 117,943 93 |
| State taxes on premiums | | 617,970 96 |
| Insurance department licenses and fees | | 27,610 70 |
| Federal taxes | | 134,029 62 |
| All other licenses, fees and taxes | | 183,218 83 |
| Other disbursements, viz: Mortgage loan expenses, $4,555.98; Association of Life Insurance Presidents, $6,565.33; heat, light and power, $26,458.66; restaurant, $50,181.25; laundry and extra janitor service, $9,081.79; home office supplies, $37,357.66; home office repairs and alterations, $1,428.15; new index system, $23,721.53; inspection and detective services, $973.50; petty cash, $354.68; miscellaneous, $3,142.28 | | 166,820 81 |
| Decrease in book value of ledger assets | | 76,850 84 |
| Total disbursements | | $38,023,084 61 |
| Balance | | $294,469,529 68 |

## LEDGER ASSETS.

|  | |
|---|---|
| Book value of real estate | $ 2,626,796 02 |
| Mortgage loans on real estate | 123,735,785 02 |
| Loans secured by collaterals | 5,805,000 00 |
| Premiums advanced under Soldiers' and Sailors' Civil Relief Act | 128 30 |
| Loans on company's policies assigned as collateral | 57,065,958 85 |

## LEDGER ASSETS—Concluded.

| | | |
|---|---|---|
| Book value of bonds and stocks | | $102,673,339 78 |
| Cash in office | | 8,265 47 |
| Deposits in trust companies and banks not on interest | | 167,052 74 |
| Deposits in trust companies and banks on interest | | 2,385,391 85 |
| Agents' balances (debit, $10,295.69; credit, $8,484.04) | | 1,811 65 |
| Total ledger assets | | $294,469,529 68 |

NON-LEDGER ASSETS.

| | | | |
|---|---|---|---|
| Interest due and accrued on mortgages | | $3,046,882 99 | |
| Interest due and accrued on bonds | | 1,361,491 88 | |
| Interest due and accrued on premium notes, loans or liens | | 1,528,689 20 | |
| | | | 5,937,064 07 |
| | New business. | Renewals. | |
| Net uncollected and deferred premiums (paid for basis) | $568,385 50 | $4,790,103 34 | 5,358,488 84 |
| Gross assets | | | $305,765,082 59 |

DEDUCT ASSETS NOT ADMITTED.

| | | |
|---|---|---|
| Agents' debit balances | $ 10,295 69 | |
| Overdue and accrued interest on bonds in default | 43,958 33 | |
| Book value of bonds and stocks over market value | 5,734,304 95 | |
| Total | | 5,788,558 97 |
| Admitted assets | | $299,976,523 62 |

## LIABILITIES.

| | | |
|---|---|---|
| Net present value of outstanding policies computed by the New Jersey Insurance Department | $258,415,165 00 | |
| Same for dividend additions | 7,749,879 00 | |
| Same for annuities | 2,415,173 00 | |
| Net reserve (paid for basis) | | $268,580,217 00 |
| Present value of supplementary contracts not involving life contingencies | | 6,540,803 00 |
| Death losses in process of adjustment | $154,668 91 | |
| Death losses reported for which no proofs have been received | 232,552 08 | |
| Reserve for net death losses incurred but unreported | 450,000 00 | |
| Matured endowments due and unpaid | 94,612 08 | |
| Death losses and other policy claims resisted | 126,982 63 | |
| Annuity claims, involving life contingencies, due and unpaid | 154 78 | |
| Total policy claims | | 1,058,970 48 |
| Due and unpaid on supplementary contracts not involving life contingencies | | 3,861 30 |
| Gross premiums paid in advance, including surrender values so applied, less discount, if any | | 726,772 83 |
| Unearned interest and rent paid in advance | | 2,295 75 |
| Commissions to agents due or accrued | | 26,946 05 |
| Cost of collection on uncollected and deferred premiums in excess of loading | | 178,615 14 |
| Salaries, rents, office expenses, bills, and accounts due or accrued | | 50,000 00 |
| Medical examiners' fees due or accrued | | 21,961 00 |
| Estimated amount hereafter payable for federal, state and other taxes based upon the business of the year of this statement | | 964,000 00 |
| Dividends or other profits due policyholders | | 1,095,810 97 |
| Dividends declared on or apportioned to annual dividend policies payable to policyholders during 1922 for period to December 31, 1922 | | 10,661,048 19 |
| Contingency reserve funds; suspended mortality fund | | 8,392,235 23 |
| Dividend and expense equalization fund | | 971,340 76 |
| Security fluctuation and real estate depreciation fund | | 701,533 25 |
| Excess interest paid by U. S. under the Soldiers' and Sailors' Civil Relief Act | | 112 67 |
| Total | | $299,976,523 62 |

## EXHIBIT OF POLICIES—ORDINARY.

ALL BUSINESS PAID FOR.

| | Number. | Amount. | Number. | Amount. |
|---|---|---|---|---|
| Policies in force December 31, 1920 | | | 456,044 | $1,311,052,551 00 |
| Policies issued, revived and increased during the year | | | 41,282 | 168,516,755 00 |
| Total | | | 497,326 | $1,479,569,306 00 |
| Deduct policies which have ceased to be in force during the year— | | | | |
| By death | 3,676 | $11,361,334 00 | | |
| By maturity | 1,184 | 2,557,449 00 | | |
| By expiry | 5,313 | 12,960,638 00 | | |
| By surrender | 5,291 | 17,872,118 00 | | |
| By lapse | 4,631 | 16,742,314 00 | | |
| By decrease | 14 | 2,090,704 00 | | |
| Total | | | 20,109 | 63,584,557 00 |
| Total policies in force December 31, 1921 | | | 477,217 | $1,415,984,749 00 |

BUSINESS IN ILLINOIS—ORDINARY.

| | Number. | Amount. |
|---|---|---|
| Policies in force December 31, 1920 | 29,618 | $106,992,094 00 |
| Policies issued during the year | 2,524 | 10,662,079 00 |
| Total | 32,142 | $117,654,173 00 |
| Deduct policies ceased to be in force | 1,199 | 4,903,565 00 |
| Policies in force December 31, 1921 | 30,943 | $112,750,608 00 |
| Losses and claims unpaid December 31, 1920 | 15 | $ 13,252 00 |
| Losses and claims incurred during the year | 327 | 1,034,842 00 |
| Total | 342 | $1,048,094 00 |
| Losses and claims settled during the year | 323 | 1,021,197 00 |
| Losses and claims unpaid December 31, 1921 | 19 | $26,897 00 |
| Premiums received | | $3,727,543 29 |

GAIN AND LOSS EXHIBIT.

INSURANCE EXHIBIT.

| | | Gain in surplus. | Loss in surplus. |
|---|---|---|---|
| Loading on actual premiums of the year (averaging 18.44 per cent of the gross premiums) | $8,828,250 94 | | |
| Insurance expenses incurred during the year | 7,705,340 06 | | |
| Gain from loading | | $1,122,910 88 | |
| Interest earned during the year | $14,737,386 78 | | |
| Investment expenses incurred during the year | 644,074 22 | | |
| Net income from investments | $14,093,312 56 | | |
| Interest required to maintain reserve | 8,357,186 94 | | |
| Gain from interest | | 5,736,125 62 | |
| Expected mortality on net amount at risk | $14,090,933 70 | | |
| Actual mortality on net amount at risk | 6,861,199 20 | | |
| Gain from mortality | | 7,229,734 50 | |
| Expected disbursements to annuitants | $107,067 72 | | |
| Net actual annuity claims incurred | 100,869 76 | | |
| Gain from annuities | | 6,197 96 | |
| Total gain during the year from surrendered and lapsed policies | | 350,714 83 | |
| Decrease in surplus on dividend account | | | $10,661,048 19 |
| Increase in special funds and special reserves during the year | | | 4,946,786 74 |

INVESTMENT EXHIBIT.

| | Gain in surplus. | Loss in surplus. |
|---|---|---|
| Total gains from real estate | 1,200 00 | |
| Total losses from real estate | | 65,850 84 |
| Total gains from stocks and bonds | 1,236,153 83 | |
| Total losses from stocks and bonds | | 11,000 00 |
| Gain from assets not admitted | 1,648 15 | |
| Total gains and losses in surplus during the year | $15,684,685 77 | $15,684,685 77 |

## THE MUTUAL LIFE INSURANCE COMPANY OF NEW YORK.

Located at No. 34 Nassau Street, New York, New York; incorporated April 12, 1842; commenced business in Illinois, 1855.

CHARLES A. PEABODY, President.

WILLIAM FREDERICK DIX and GEORGE C. KEEFER, Secretaries.

DARBY A. DAY, Chicago, Attorney for service.

| | |
|---|---|
| Amount of ledger assets December 31, of previous year | $664,547,191 07 |

INCOME.

| | | |
|---|---|---|
| First year's premiums on original policies, less re-insurance | | $11,969,808 58 |
| First year's premiums for total and permanent disability benefits | | 359,804 57 |
| First year's premiums for additional accidental death benefits | | 225,880 85 |
| Surrender values to pay first year's premiums | | 22,318 08 |
| Dividends applied to purchase paid-up additions and annuities | | 3,949,020 96 |
| Consideration for original annuities involving life contingencies | | 829,835 87 |
| New premiums | | $17,356,668 91 |
| Renewal premiums less re-insurance | $62,145,463 60 | |
| Renewal premiums for total and permanent disability benefits | 712,632 92 | |

## INCOME—Concluded.

| | | | |
|---|---|---|---|
| Renewal premiums for additional accidental death benefits | $ 424,886 55 | | |
| Dividends applied to pay renewal premiums | 9,020,796 93 | | |
| Surrender values applied to pay renwal premiums | 640,877 91 | | |
| Renewal premiums for deferred annuities | 8,372 32 | | |
| Renewal premiums | | $72,953,030 23 | |
| Premium income | | | $90,309,699 14 |
| Consideration for supplementary contracts involving life contingencies | | | 1,070,199 66 |
| Consideration for supplementary contracts not involving life contingencies | | | 368,230 16 |
| Dividends left with company to accumulate at interest | | | 278,419 89 |
| Interest on mortgage loans | | $ 5,642,906 68 | |
| Interest on bonds and dividends on stocks | | 19,602,879 81 | |
| Interest on premium notes, policy loans or liens | | 4,645,090 85 | |
| Interest on deposits | | 734,412 61 | |
| Interest on other debts due the company | | 215,447 88 | |
| Rents—including $487,878.88 for company's occupancy of its own buildings | | 1,409,213 58 | |
| Total interest and rents | | | 32,249,951 41 |
| From other sources, viz: Premium extension fees, $124,473.55; policy fees, $367.27; profits on settlement of foreign business, $6,427.405.41; collections or deposits received for account of others paid out, $334,945.23; exchange, $2,339.81 | | | 6,889,531 27 |
| Agents' balances previously charged off | | | 7,836 33 |
| Profit on sale or maturity of ledger assets | | | 1,661,316 94 |
| Increase in book value of ledger assets | | | 553,078 08 |
| Total income | | | $133,388,262 88 |
| Total | | | $797,935,453 95 |

## DISBURSEMENTS.

| | | |
|---|---|---|
| Death claims and additions | $27,552,139 06 | |
| Matured endowments and additions | 10,672,005 94 | |
| Total and permanent disability claims and additional accidental death benefits | 268,918 28 | |
| Total death claims and endowments | | $38,493,063 28 |
| Annuities involving life contingencies | | 2,598,724 03 |
| Surrender values paid in cash, or applied in liquidation of loans or notes | | 27,393,910 91 |
| Surrender values applied to pay new and renewal premiums | | 663,195 99 |
| Dividends paid policyholders in cash, or applied in liquidation of loans or notes | | 12,842,106 79 |
| Dividends applied to pay renewal premiums | | 9,020,796 93 |
| Dividends applied to purchase paid-up additions and annuities | | 3,949,020 96 |
| Dividends left with the company to accumulate at interest | | 278,419 89 |
| (Total paid policyholders | $95,239,238 78) | |
| Expense of investigation and settlement of policy claims, including legal expenses | | 94,581 20 |
| Supplementary contracts not involving life contingencies | | 795,030 07 |
| Dividends with interest, held on deposit surrendered during the year | | 88,145 83 |
| Commissions to agents, first year, $5,715,082.70; renewal, $3,609,009.81; annuities (original), $45,286.47; (renewal), $113.99 | | 9,369,492 97 |
| Compensation of managers and agents not paid by commissions on new business | | 696,952 84 |
| Agency supervision and traveling expenses of supervisors | | 957,395 57 |
| Branch office expenses | | 1,130,700 90 |
| Medical examiners' fees and inspection of risks | | 678,315 56 |
| Salaries and all other compensation of officers and home office employees | | 2,386,705 47 |
| Rent | | 812,265 31 |
| Advertising, printing, stationery, postage, telegraph, telephone, express and exchange | | 690,901 71 |
| Legal expense | | 12,708 76 |
| Furniture, fixtures and safes | | 116,955 62 |
| Repairs and expenses (other than taxes) on real estate | | 472,188 51 |
| Taxes on real estate | | 357,588 90 |
| State taxes on premiums | | 1,171,568 43 |
| Insurance department licenses and fees | | 41,793 13 |
| Federal taxes | | 274,382 48 |
| All other licenses, fees and taxes | | 143,259 30 |
| Other disbursements, viz: Sundry investment expenses, $5,414.01; traveling general office employees, $127,370.39; conventions and meetings, $144,605.58; law library, $5,212.57 cost of election and election lists, $83.02; general audit, $1,222.04; office supplies and expenses of home office, $47,393.69; cost of state examinations, $11,873.82; reports to governments, $2,689.03; association memberships, $11,106.96; miscellaneous interest, $24,228.60; disbursed from amounts held for account of sundry parties, $133,446.07 | | 514,645 78 |
| Deposit on account of pending insurance | | 70,731 17 |
| Depreciation in amount of companys deposits with civil court, Budapest, Hungary | | 39,600 00 |
| Agents' balances charged off | | 84,888 59 |
| Loss on sale or maturity of ledger assets | | 2,684,547 58 |
| Decrease in book value of ledger assets | | 6,851,327 05 |
| Total disbursements | | $125,775,911 51 |
| Balance | | $672,159,542 44 |

## LEDGER ASSETS.

| | | |
|---|---|---|
| Book value of real estate | | $ 11,706,467 68 |
| Mortgage loans on real estate | | 111,760,865 78 |
| Premiums advanced under Soldiers' and Sailors' Civil Relief Act | | 1,330 26 |
| Loans on company's policies assigned as collateral | | 96,750,337 11 |
| Book value of bonds and stocks | | 443,929,767 56 |
| Cash in office | | 60,261 58 |
| Cash in transit since received | | 203,663 33 |
| Deposits in trust companies and banks not on interest | | 265,150 27 |
| Deposits in trust companies and banks on interest | | 6,155,422 04 |
| Cash advanced to pay policy claims | | 1,125,957 30 |
| Accounts collectible, $100,358.21; supplies, $75,250.19; cash advanced to or in hands of officers or employees, $24,711.13 | | 200,319 53 |
| Total ledger assets | | $672,159,542 44 |

### NON-LEDGER ASSETS.

| | | |
|---|---|---|
| Interest due and accrued on mortgages | $1,486,278 83 | |
| Interest due and accrued on bonds | 5,694,778 66 | |
| Interest due and accrued on premium notes, loans or liens | 1,598,565 92 | |
| Interest due and accrued on other assets | 41,051 99 | |
| Rents due and accrued on company's property | 40,699 94 | |
| | | 8,861,375 34 |

| | New business. | Renewals. | |
|---|---|---|---|
| Net uncollected and deferred premiums (paid for basis) | $259,337 47 | $5,059,864 83 | 5,319,202 30 |
| Gross assets | | | $686,340,120 08 |

### DEDUCT ASSETS NOT ADMITTED.

| | | |
|---|---|---|
| Supplies, printed matter and stationery | $ 75,250 19 | |
| Cash advanced to or in hands of officers or agents | 24,711 13 | |
| Accounts collectible | 100,358 21 | |
| Book value of bonds and stocks over market value | 8,634,301 28 | |
| Total | | 8,834,620 81 |
| Admitted assets | | $677,505,499 27 |

## LIABILITIES.

| | | |
|---|---|---|
| Net present value of outstanding policies computed by the New York Insurance Department | $512,815,551 00 | |
| Same for dividend additions | 27,135,019 00 | |
| Same for annuities | 27,592,204 00 | |
| Total | $567,542,774 00 | |
| Deduct net value of risks re-insured | 297,979 00 | |
| Net reserve (paid for basis) | | $567,244,795 00 |
| Extra reserve for total and permanent disability benefits and for additional accidental death benefits included in life policies, less re-insurance | | 2,085,538 00 |
| Present value of supplementary contracts not involving life contingencies | | 4,255,926 38 |
| Present value of amounts incurred but not yet due for total and permanent disability benefits | | 474,630 00 |
| Surrender values claimable on policies cancelled | | 371,872 63 |
| Death losses due and unpaid | $ 486,041 92 | |
| Death losses in process of adjustment | 281,938 86 | |
| Death losses reported for which no proofs have been received | 2,270,791 34 | |
| Reserve for net death losses incurred but unreported | 750,000 00 | |
| Matured endowments due and unpaid | 757,373 62 | |
| Death losses and other policy claims resisted | 596,641 40 | |
| Additional accidental death benefits | 56,000 00 | |
| Annuity claims, involving life contingencies, due and unpaid | 200,101 91 | |
| Total policy claims | | 5,398,889 05 |
| Due and unpaid on supplementary contracts not involving life contingencies | | 2,337 21 |
| Dividends left with the company to accumulate at interest | | 1,291,326 60 |
| Gross premiums paid in advance, including surrender values so applied, less discount, if any | | 442,007 40 |
| Unearned interest and rent paid in advance | | 944,154 89 |
| Commissions to agents due or accrued | | 16,118 00 |
| Salaries, rents, office expenses, bills and accounts due or accrued | | 13,970 52 |
| Medical examiners' fees due or accrued, $2,289.24; taxes due and accrued, $224,343.58; unpaid war taxes, $197.31 | | 226,830 13 |
| Estimated amount hereafter payable for federal, state and other taxes based upon the business of the year of this statement | | 3,883,025 10 |
| Dividends or other profits due policyholders | | 971,364 93 |
| Dividends declared on or apportioned to annual dividend policies payable to policyholders during 1922 for period to December 31, 1922 | | 17,282,896 62 |
| Dividends declared on or apportioned to deferred dividend policies payable to to policyholders during 1922 for period to December 31, 1922 | | 12,548,382 55 |
| Amounts set apart, apportioned, provisionally ascertained, calculated, declared or held awaiting apportionment upon deferred dividend policies | | 31,014,585 45 |
| Fund for depreciation of securities and general contingencies | | 28,051,586 81 |
| Other liabilities, viz: Deposits on account of pending insurance, $180,353.54; due sundry parties for collections made or deposits held for their account, $804,908.46 | | 985,262 00 |
| Total | | $677,505,499 27 |

## EXHIBIT OF POLICIES—ORDINARY.

ALL BUSINESS PAID FOR.

| | Number. | Amount. | Number. | Amount. |
|---|---|---|---|---|
| Policies in force December 31, 1920 | | | 929,511 | $2,357,973,121 00 |
| Policies issued, revived and increased during the year | | | 96,602 | 343,750,863 00 |
| Total | | | 1,026,113 | $2,701,723,984 00 |
| Deduct policies which have ceased to be in force during the year— | | | | |
| By death | 9,121 | $26,571,083 00 | | |
| By maturity | 5,428 | 10,221,746 00 | | |
| By expiry | 4,810 | 16,843,941 00 | | |
| By surrender | 26,116 | 76,190,514 00 | | |
| By lapse | 32,157 | 94,149,626 00 | | |
| By decrease | 581 | 5,095,295 00 | | |
| Total | | | 78,213 | 229,072,205 00 |
| Total policies in force December 31, 1921 | | | 947,900 | $2,472,651,779 00 |
| Re-insured | | | 226 | $7,561,905 00 |

## BUSINESS IN ILLINOIS—ORDINARY.

| | Number. | Amount. |
|---|---|---|
| Policies in force December 31, 1920 | 70,036 | $202,189,207 22 |
| Policies issued during the year | 9,074 | 34,919,214 85 |
| Total | 79,110 | $237,108,422 07 |
| Deduct policies ceased to be in force | 5,787 | 16,533,165 92 |
| Policies in force December 31, 1921 | 73,323 | $220,575,256 15 |
| Losses and claims unpaid December 31, 1920 | 15 | $ 20,056 85 |
| Losses and claims incurred during the year | 703 | 2,017,938 13 |
| Total | 718 | $2,037,994 98 |
| Losses and claims settled during the year | 707 | 2,030,757 97 |
| Losses and claims unpaid December 31, 1921 | 11 | $7,237 01 |
| Premiums received | | $7,383,638 47 |

## GAIN AND LOSS EXHIBIT.

INSURANCE EXHIBIT.

| | | Gain in surplus. | Loss in surplus. |
|---|---|---|---|
| Loading on actual premiums of the year (averaging 21.70 per cent of the gross premiums) | $19,344,874 45 | | |
| Insurance expenses incurred during the year | 17,306,084 25 | | |
| Gain from loading | | $ 2,038,790 20 | |
| Interest earned during the year | $33,510,776 47 | | |
| Investment expenses incurred during the year | 1,894,387 26 | | |
| Net income from investments | $31,616,389 21 | | |
| Interest required to maintain reserve | 18,406,323 33 | | |
| Gain from interest | | 13,210,065 88 | |
| Expected mortality on net amount at risk | $25,314,722 71 | | |
| Actual mortality on net amount at risk | 14,289,043 19 | | |
| Gain from mortality | | 11,025,679 52 | |
| Expected disbursements to annuitants | $1,736,624 85 | | |
| Net actual annuity claims incurred | 1,654,656 90 | | |
| Gain from annuities | | 81,967 95 | |
| Total gain during the year from surrendered and lapsed policies | | 2,580,980 93 | |
| Decrease in surplus on dividend account | | | $20,396,598 04 |
| Decrease in special funds and special reserves during the year | | | 5,705,448 56 |
| Net to gain account | | 6,520,482 56 | |

INVESTMENT EXHIBIT.

| | Gain in surplus. | Loss in surplus. |
|---|---|---|
| Total gains from real estate | 35,018 75 | |
| Total gains from stocks and bonds | 1,626,298 19 | |
| Total losses from stocks and bonds | | 10,780,913 31 |
| Gain from assets not admitted | 1,491 08 | |
| Net loss on account of total and permanent disability benefits or additional accidental death benefits included in life policies | | 237,815 15 |
| Total | $37,120,775 06 | $37,120,775 06 |

## THE NATIONAL LIFE AND ACCIDENT INSURANCE COMPANY.

Located at No. 302 Seventh Avenue, North, Nashville, Tennessee; incorporated, 1900; commenced business in Illinois July 31, 1917.

C. A. CRAIG, President. C. R. CLEMENTS, Secretary.

GEORGE A. BARR, Director of Trade and Commerce, Attorney for service at Springfield.

### CAPITAL.

| | | |
|---|---|---|
| Capital paid up | $600,000 00 | |
| Amount of ledger assets December 31, of previous year | $5,663,199 43 | |
| Increase of paid-up capital during year | 300,000 00 | |
| Extended at | | $5,963,199 43 |

### INCOME.

| | | |
|---|---|---|
| First year's premiums on original policies, less re-insurance | $157,475 95 | |
| Surrender values to pay first year's premiums | 320 13 | |
| New premiums | $ 157,796 08 | |
| Renewal premiums less re-insurance | 2,089,999 32 | |
| Premium income | | 2,247,795 40 |
| Interest on mortgage loans | $61,272 51 | |
| Interest on collateral loans | 3,649 64 | |
| Interest on bonds and dividends on stocks | 85,685 40 | |
| Interest on deposits | 3,544 36 | |
| Interest on other debts due the company | 81 25 | |
| Rents—including $5,666.46 for company's occupancy of its own buildings | 6,587 46 | |
| Total interest and rents | | 160,820 62 |
| From other sources, viz: Duplicate policy fees, $93.12; cancelled checks, $39.03; office pay and revival, $3,840.89 | | 3,973 04 |
| Agents' balances previously charged off | | 25 80 |
| Profit on sale or maturity of ledger assets | | 1,909 22 |
| Income, life department | | $2,414,524 08 |
| Income, casualty department | | 8,535,812 24 |
| Total income | | $10,950,336 32 |
| Total | | $16,913,535 75 |

### DISBURSEMENTS.

| | | |
|---|---|---|
| Death claims | $706,740 14 | |
| Total and permanent disability claims | 25 77 | |
| Total death claims | | $706,765 91 |
| Surrender values paid in cash, or applied in liquidation of loans or notes | | 12 71 |
| Surrender values applied to pay new and renewal premiums | | 320 13 |
| (Total paid policyholders $707,098 75) | | |
| Expense of investigation and settlement of policy claims, including legal expenses | | 840 47 |
| Commissions to agents, first year, $56,023.48; renewal, $493,371.30 | | 549,394 78 |
| Agency supervision and traveling expenses of supervisors | | 15,078 42 |
| Branch office expenses | | 266,031 39 |
| Medical examiners' fees and inspection of risks | | 31,812 78 |
| Salaries and all other compensation of officers and home office employees | | 80,461 77 |
| Rent | | 21,410 74 |
| Advertising, printing, stationery, postage, telegraph, telephone, express and exchange | | 46,920 75 |
| Legal expense | | 463 25 |
| Furniture, fixtures and safes | | 20,473 12 |
| Repairs and expenses (other than taxes) on real estate | | 5,395 43 |
| Taxes on real estate | | 4,625 68 |
| State taxes on premiums | | 41,593 20 |
| Insurance department licenses and fees | | 459 32 |
| Federal taxes | | 27,415 89 |
| All other licenses, fees and taxes | | 5,850 26 |
| Other disbursements, viz: Legislative, $95.63; general expense, $8,002.91; agents bank deposits returned, $336.72; agents' bank deposits, $1,441.50 | | 9,876 76 |
| Agents' balances charged off | | 473 53 |
| Loss on sale or maturity of ledger assets | | 90 00 |
| Disbursements, life department | | $1,835,766 29 |
| Disbursements, casualty department | | 8,074,895 65 |
| Total disbursements | | $9,910,661 94 |
| Balance | | $7,002,873 81 |

## LEDGER ASSETS.

| | |
|---|---|
| Book value of real estate | $ 135,727 97 |
| Mortgage loans on real estate | 2,383,943 17 |
| Loans secured by collaterals | 178,600 00 |
| Book value of bonds and stocks | 3,809,549 54 |
| Cash in office and district offices | 69,106 94 |
| Deposits in trust companies and banks not on interest | 25,000 00 |
| Deposits in trust companies and banks on interest | 385,503 39 |
| Agents' balances (debit, $13,546.42; credit, $376.11) | 13,170 31 |
| Accounts, debit, $1,853.89; credit, $1.40 | 1,852 49 |
| Stock and carriage | 420 00 |
| Total ledger assets | $7,002,873 81 |

### NON-LEDGER ASSETS.

| | | | |
|---|---|---|---|
| Interest due and accrued on mortgages | | $20,471 11 | |
| Interest accrued on bonds | | 14,606 83 | |
| Interest accrued on collateral loans | | 95 14 | |
| Interest accrued on other assets, bank deposits | | 228 21 | |
| | | | 35,401 29 |
| | New business. | Renewals. | |
| Net uncollected and deferred premiums (paid for basis) | $14,900 99 | $37,938 06 | 52,839 05 |
| Casualty department | | | 90,967 23 |
| Gross assets | | | $7,182,081 38 |

### DEDUCT ASSETS NOT ADMITTED.

| | | |
|---|---|---|
| Stock and carriage | $ 420 00 | |
| Agents' debit balances | 13,546 42 | |
| Cash advanced to or in hands of officers or agents | 6,330 71 | |
| Loans on personal security | 1,853 89 | |
| Premium notes, policy loans and other policy assets in excess of net value and of other policy liabilities on individual policies | 2,925 42 | |
| Total | | 25,076 44 |
| Admitted assets | | $7,157,004 94 |

## LIABILITIES.

| | | |
|---|---|---|
| Net present value of outstanding policies computed by the Tennessee Insurance Department | $2,002,727 15 | |
| Deduct net value of risks re-insured | 513 92 | |
| Net reserve (paid for basis) | | $2,002,213 23 |
| Extra reserve for total and permanent disability benefits included in life policies | | 2,538 20 |
| Extra premium special hazard | | 495 47 |
| Paid on pending applications | | 1,428 74 |
| Death losses due and unpaid | $23,733 28 | |
| Reserve for net death losses incurred but unreported | 2,500 00 | |
| Death losses and other policy claims resisted | 1,095 00 | |
| Total policy claims | | 27,328 28 |
| Gross premiums paid in advance, including surrender values so applied, less discount, if any | | 56,493 85 |
| Commissions to agents due or accrued | | 8,977 67 |
| Salaries, rents, office expenses, bills and accounts due or accrued | | 6,199 53 |
| Medical examiners' fees due or accrued | | 3,192 00 |
| Estimated amount hereafter payable for federal, state and other taxes based upon the business of the year of this statement | | 45,230 00 |
| Reserve for epidemic | | 150,000 00 |
| Other liabilities, viz: Resisted items other than policy claims, $5,980.00; office pay and revival, $3840.89; agents deposits in lieu of bond, $157,819.37 | | 167,640 26 |
| Casualty department | | 3,324,976 62 |
| Total | | $5,796,713 85 |
| Capital paid up | | 600,000 00 |
| Unassigned funds (surplus) | | 760,291 09 |
| Total | | $7,157,004 94 |

## EXHIBIT OF POLICIES—ORDINARY.

### ALL BUSINESS PAID FOR.

| | Number. | Amount. |
|---|---|---|
| Policies in force December 31, 1920 | 3,132 | $5,065,100 00 |
| Policies issued, revived and increased during the year | 4,190 | 9,162,750 00 |
| Total | 7,322 | $14,227,850 00 |

## EXHIBIT OF POLICIES—ORDINARY—Concluded.

ALL BUSINESS PAID FOR.

| | Number. | Amount. | Number. | Amount. |
|---|---|---|---|---|
| Deduct policies which have ceased to be in force during the year— | | | | |
| By death | 11 | $ 17,611 00 | | |
| By expiry | 1 | 1,996,389 00 | | |
| By lapse | 1,297 | 2,077,050 00 | | |
| Total | | | 1,309 | $4,091,050 00 |
| Total policies in force December 31, 1921 | | | 6,013 | $10,136,800 00 |
| Re-insured | | | 15 | $114,391 00 |

## EXHIBIT OF POLICIES—GROUP INSURANCE.

ALL BUSINESS PAID FOR.

| | Number. | Amount. | Number. | Amount. |
|---|---|---|---|---|
| Policies issued, revived and increased during the year | | | 1 | $2,000,000 00 |
| Deduct policies which have ceased to be in force during the year— | | | | |
| By death | -------- | $ 3,611 00 | | |
| By expiry | 1 | 1,996,389 00 | | |
| Total | | | 1 | 2,000,000 00 |

## EXHIBIT OF POLICIES—INDUSTRIAL.

ALL BUSIBESS PAID FOR.

| | Number. | Amount. | Number. | Amount. |
|---|---|---|---|---|
| Policies in force December 31, 1920 | | | 1,150,728 | $71,527,595 00 |
| Policies issued, revived and increased during the year | | | 456,759 | 40,996,495 00 |
| Total | | | 1,607,487 | $112,524,090 00 |
| Deduct policies which have ceased to be in force during the year— | | | | |
| By death | 12,473 | $ 825,218 00 | | |
| By lapse | 598,040 | 44,440,780 00 | | |
| Total | | | 610,513 | 45,265,998 00 |
| Total policies in force December 31, 1921 | | | 996,974 | $67,258,092 00 |

## BUSINESS IN ILLINOIS—ORDINARY.

| | Number. | Amount. |
|---|---|---|
| Policies in force December 31, 1920 | 48 | $ 70,000 00 |
| Policies issued during the year | 74 | 135,000 00 |
| Total | 122 | $205,000 00 |
| Deduct policies ceased to be in force | 21 | 25,000 00 |
| Policies in force December 31, 1921 | 101 | $180,000 00 |
| Premiums received | | $4,097 90 |

## BUSINESS IN ILLINOIS—INDUSTRIAL.

| | Number. | Amount. |
|---|---|---|
| Policies in force December 31, 1920 | 52,079 | $3,239,314 00 |
| Policies issued during the year | 18,752 | 1,683,088 00 |
| Total | 70,831 | $4,922,402 00 |
| Deduct policies ceased to be in force | 33,767 | 2,421,983 00 |
| Policies in force December 31, 1921 | 37,064 | $2,500,419 00 |
| Losses and claims unpaid December 31, 1920 | 14 | $ 1,187 55 |
| Losses and claims incurred during the year | 504 | 31,503 65 |
| Total | 518 | $32,691 20 |
| Losses and claims settled during the year | 503 | 31,542 42 |
| Losses and claims unpaid December 31, 1921 | 15 | $1,148 78 |
| Premiums received | | $96,226 17 |

## GAIN AND LOSS EXHIBIT.

INSURANCE EXHIBIT.

| | | Gain in surplus. | Loss in surplus. |
|---|---|---|---|
| Loading on actual premiums of the year (averaging 52.53 per cent of the gross premiums) | $1,211,391 50 | | |
| Insurance expenses incurred during the year | 1,083,633 38 | | |
| Gain from loading | | $127,758 12 | |

GAIN AND LOSS EXHIBIT—Concluded.

INSURANCE EXHIBIT.

| | | Gain in surplus. | Loss in surplus. |
|---|---|---|---|
| Interest earned during the year | $149,537 25 | | |
| Investment expenses incurred during the year | 31,775 26 | | |
| Net income from investments | $117,761 99 | | |
| Interest required to maintain reserve | 75,093 83 | | |
| Gain from interest | | $42,668 16 | |
| Expected mortality on net amount at risk | $728,826 93 | | |
| Actual mortality on net amount at risk | 683,788 27 | | |
| Gain from mortality | | 45,038 66 | |
| Total gain during the year from surrendered and lapsed policies | | 53,831 97 | |
| Increase in special funds and special reserves during the year | | | $150,174 70 |
| Net to profit account | | 39 03 | |

INVESTMENT EXHIBIT.

| | | Gain in surplus. | Loss in surplus. |
|---|---|---|---|
| Total gains from real estate | | 1,640 41 | |
| Total gains from stocks and bonds | | 268 81 | |
| Total losses from stocks and bonds | | | 30,861 59 |
| Gain from assets not admitted | | 4,391 82 | |
| Net loss on account of total and permanent disability benefits or additional accidental death benefits included in life policies | | | 1,297 97 |
| Loss from casualty department | | | 41,672 93 |
| Balance unaccounted for | | 234 87 | |
| Total gains and losses in surplus during the year | | $275,871 85 | $224,007 19 |
| Surplus December 31, 1920 | $708,426 43 | | |
| Surplus December 31, 1921 | 760,291 09 | | |
| Increase in surplus | | | 51,864 66 |
| Total | | $275,871 85 | $275,871 85 |

## NATIONAL LIFE INSURANCE COMPANY.

Located at No. 116 State Street, Montpelier, Vermont, incorporated November 13, 1848; commenced business in Illinois October 5, 1860.

FRED A. HOWLAND, President. OSMON D. CLARK, Secretary.

DAVID G. DRAKE, Chicago, Attorney for service.

Amount of ledger assets December 31, of previous year $73,793,547 17

### INCOME.

| | | | |
|---|---|---|---|
| First year's premiums on original policies | | $1,571,211 95 | |
| First year's premiums for total and permanent disability benefits | | 8,684 55 | |
| Surrender values to pay first year's premiums | | 635 88 | |
| Dividends applied to purchase paid-up additions and annuities | | 239,049 29 | |
| Consideration for original annuities involving life contingencies | | 283,906 79 | |
| Dividends held at interest applied to purchase additions | | 184 97 | |
| New premiums | | $2,103,673 43 | |
| Renewal premiums | $8,026,302 83 | | |
| Renewal premiums for total and permanent disability benefits | 16,171 88 | | |
| Dividends applied to pay renewal premiums | 1,313,454 50 | | |
| Dividends applied to shorten the endowment or premium-paying period | 6,375 26 | | |
| Surrender values applied to pay renewal premiums | 234 80 | | |
| Renewal premiums for deferred annuities | 1,059 15 | | |
| Renewal premiums | | 9,363,598 42 | |
| Premium income | | | $11,467,271 85 |
| Consideration for supplementary contracts involving life contingencies | | | 16,480 96 |
| Consideration for supplementary contracts not involving life contingencies | | | 104,965 87 |
| Dividends left with company to accumulate at interest | | | 70,284 54 |
| Interest on mortgage loans | | $1,900,501 53 | |
| Interest on bonds | | 1,241,581 50 | |
| Interest on premium notes, policy loans or liens | | 639,700 09 | |
| Interest on deposits | | 23,898 72 | |
| Interest on other debts due the company | | 5,344 38 | |
| Discount on claims paid in advance | | 106 56 | |
| Rents—including $20,000.00 for company's occupancy of its own buildings | | 33,460 00 | |
| Total interest and rents | | | 3,844,592 78 |

INCOME—Concluded.

| | | |
|---|---|---|
| From other sources, viz: Recovered from over loan, $7.25; profit unclaimed checks, $5.36; unclaimed checks, $1,060.67 | | $ 1,073 28 |
| Borrowed money (gross) | | 500,000 00 |
| Agents' balances previously charged off | | 23,286 24 |
| Increase in book value of ledger assets | | 52,471 30 |
| Total income | | $16,080,426 82 |
| Total | | $89,873,973 99 |

DISBURSEMENTS.

| | | |
|---|---|---|
| Death claims and additions | $2,756,010 32 | |
| Matured endowments and additions | 1,389,703 05 | |
| Total death claims and endowments | | $4,145,713 37 |
| Annuities involving life contingencies | | 694,970 93 |
| Surrender values paid in cash, or applied in liquidation of loans or notes | | 1,354,183 86 |
| Surrender values applied to pay new and renewal premiums | | 870 68 |
| Dividends paid policyholders in cash, or applied in liquidation of loans or notes | | 1,075,000 87 |
| Dividends applied to pay renewal premiums | | 1,313,454 50 |
| Dividends applied to shorten the endowment or premium-paying period | | 6,375 26 |
| Dividends applied to purchase paid-up additions and annuities | | 239,049 29 |
| Dividends left with the company to accumulate at interest | | 70,284 54 |
| (Total paid policyholders | $8,899,903 30) | |
| Expense of investigation and settlement of policy claims, including legal expenses | | 978 85 |
| Supplementary contracts not involving life contingencies | | 62,725 96 |
| Dividends with interest, held on deposit surrendered during the year | | 17,197 97 |
| Commissions to agents' first year, $749.109.73; renewal, $621,032.15; annuities (original), $13,141.94; (renewal), $39.86 | | 1,383,323 68 |
| Compensation of managers and agents not paid by commissions on new business | | 6,116 66 |
| Agency supervision and traveling expenses of supervisors | | 65,322 92 |
| Branch office expenses | | 174,287 56 |
| Medical examiners' fees and inspection of risks | | 106,202 37 |
| Salaries and all other compensation of officers and home office employees | | 336,686 98 |
| Rent | | 91,558 85 |
| Advertising, printing, stationery, postage, telegraph, telephone, express and exchange | | 115,122 13 |
| Legal expense | | 213 86 |
| Furniture, fixtures and safes | | 17,070 08 |
| Repairs and expenses (other than taxes) on real estate | | 15,990 66 |
| Taxes on real estate | | 8,691 51 |
| State taxes on premiums | | 170,905 91 |
| Insurance department licenses and fees | | 9,139 04 |
| Federal taxes | | 39,398 00 |
| All other licenses, fees and taxes | | 77,764 99 |
| Other disbursements, viz: Home office supplies, $53,892.32; home office travel, $1,971.00; investment expenses, $60,809.33; liberty loan withdrawals, $211.08; less unclaimed check account $5.21; error surrender value, $0.90; over-loan policy, $14.87 | | 116,904 71 |
| Borrowed money repaid (gross) | | 500,000 00 |
| Interest on borrowed money | | 20,042 36 |
| Agents' balances charged off | | 1,126 98 |
| Loss on sale or maturity of ledger assets | | 14,796 70 |
| Decrease in book value of ledger assets | | 316,816 16 |
| Total disbursements | | $12,568,288 19 |
| Balance | | $77,305,685 80 |

LEDGER ASSETS.

| | | |
|---|---|---|
| Book value of real estate | | $ 919,000 00 |
| Mortgage loans on real estate | | 35,567,513 98 |
| Loans on company's policies assigned as collateral | | 10,135,097 51 |
| Premium notes on policies in force | | 2,318,874 90 |
| Book value of bonds | | 27,356,613 07 |
| Cash in office | | 3,346 50 |
| Deposits in trust companies and banks not on interest | | 20,000 00 |
| Deposits in trust companies and banks on interest | | 979,978 34 |
| Agents' balances (debit, $5,485.68; credit, $224.18) Net | | 5,261 50 |
| Total ledger assets | | $77,305,685 80 |

NON-LEDGER ASSETS.

| | | | |
|---|---|---|---|
| Interest due and accrued on mortgages | | $1,217,817 47 | |
| Interest accrued on bonds | | 386,468 55 | |
| Interest due and accrued on premium notes, loans or liens | | 414,860 28 | |
| Interest due and accrued on other assets | | 2,396 09 | |
| Rents accrued on company's property | | 517 50 | |
| | | | 2,022,059 89 |
| | New business. | Renewals. | |
| Net uncollected and deferred premiums (paid for basis) | $151,059 85 | $1,318,544 84 | 1,469,604 69 |
| Gross assets | | | $80,797,350 38 |

## LEDGER ASSETS—Concluded.

DEDUCT ASSETS NOT ADMITTED.

| | | |
|---|---|---|
| Agents' debit balances | $ 5,485 68 | |
| Book value of bonds over market value | 1,034,896 00 | |
| Total | | $1,040,381 68 |
| Admitted assets | | $79,756,968 70 |

## LIABILITIES.

| | | |
|---|---|---|
| Net present value of outstanding policies | $61,290,389 50 | |
| Same for dividend additions | 1,022,842 00 | |
| Same for annuities | 6,071,234 00 | |
| Net reserve (paid for basis) | | $68,384,465 50 |
| Express reserve for total and permanent disability benefits and for additional accidental death benefits included in life policies, less re-insurance | | 24,542 50 |
| Present value of supplementary contracts not involving life contingencies | | 680,235 00 |
| Surrender values claimable on policies cancelled | | 4,334 73 |
| Death losses in process of adjustment | $ 32,329 00 | |
| Death losses reported for which no proofs have been received | 100,160 95 | |
| Reserve for net death losses incurred but unreported | 125,000 00 | |
| Matured endowments due and unpaid | 7,034 00 | |
| Death losses and other policy claims resisted | 12,000 00 | |
| Total and permanent disability benefits | 918 00 | |
| Annuity claims, involving life contingencies, due and unpaid | 31,096 49 | |
| Total policy claims | | 308,538 44 |
| Due and unpaid on supplementary contracts not involving life contingencies | | 771 40 |
| Dividends left with the company to accumulate at interest | | 188,994 02 |
| Gross premiums paid in advance, including surrender values so applied, less discount, if any | | 47,994 06 |
| Unearned interest and rent paid in advance | | 3,356 32 |
| Commissions to agents due or accrued | | 85 50 |
| Cost of collection on uncollected and deferred premiums in excess of loading | | 47,771 42 |
| Salaries, rents, office expenses, bills, and accounts due or accrued | | 25,000 00 |
| Medical examiners' and legal fees due or accrued | | 1,390 00 |
| Estimated amount hereafter payable for federal, state and other taxes based upon the business of the year of this statement | | 373,485 74 |
| Dividends or other profits due policyholders | | 105,964 15 |
| Dividends declared on or apportioned to annual dividend policies payable to policyholders during 1922 for period to December 31, 1922 | | 2,113,412 35 |
| Dividends declared on or apportioned to deferred dividend policies payable to policyholders during 1922 for period to December 31, 1922 | | 887,029 70 |
| Amounts set apart, apportioned, provisionally ascertained, calculated, declared or held awaiting apportionment upon deferred dividend policies | | 2,721,238 81 |
| Reserve or surplus funds not otherwise included in liabilities, viz: Life rate endowment extra reserve, $85,342.66; surplus set apart for payment at termination of insurance, $6,792.47 | | 92,135 13 |
| Other liabilities, viz: Unclaimed checks, $1,757.55; agents' and employees' Liberty loan deposit account, $531.42 | | 2,288 97 |
| Total | | $76,013,033 74 |
| Unassigned funds (surplus) | | 3,743,934 96 |
| Total | | $79,756,968 70 |

## EXHIBIT OF POLICIES—ORDINARY.

ALL BUSINESS PAID FOR.

| | Number. | Amount. | Number. | Amount. |
|---|---|---|---|---|
| Policies in force December 31, 1920 | | | 133,689 | $309,455,304 00 |
| Policies issued, revived, and increased during the year | | | 16,430 | 50,453,617 00 |
| Total | | | 150,119 | $359,908,921 00 |
| Deduct policies which have ceased to be in force during the year— | | | | |
| By death | 1,193 | $ 2,758,724 00 | | |
| By maturity | 948 | 1,405,642 00 | | |
| By expiry | 848 | 1,867,536 00 | | |
| By surrender | 1,648 | 4,401,608 00 | | |
| By lapse | 4,352 | 11,779,269 00 | | |
| By decrease | 1,131 | 3,801,878 00 | | |
| Total | | | 10,120 | 26,014,657 00 |
| Total policies in force December 31, 1921 | | | 139,999 | $333,894,264 00 |

BUSINESS IN ILLINOIS—ORDINARY.

| | Number. | Amount. |
|---|---|---|
| Policies in force December 31, 1920 | 3,873 | $11,716,746 09 |
| Policies issued during the year | 678 | 2,464,023 45 |
| Total | 4,551 | $14,180,769 54 |
| Deduct policies ceased to be in force | 329 | 985,027 75 |
| Policies in force December 31, 1921 | 4,222 | $13,195,741 79 |
| Losses and claims unpaid December 31, 1920 | 5 | $ 295 00 |
| Losses and claims incurred during the year | 72 | 159,891 71 |
| Total | 77 | $160,186 71 |
| Losses and claims settled during the year | 68 | 149,514 71 |
| Losses and claims unpaid December 31, 1921 | 9 | $10,672 00 |
| Premiums received | | $453,253 95 |

GAIN AND LOSS EXHIBIT.

INSURANCE EXHIBIT.

| | | Gain in surplus. | Loss in surplus. |
|---|---|---|---|
| Loading on actual premiums of the year (averaging 20.99 per cent of the gross premiums) | $2,445,759 84 | | |
| Insurance expenses incurred during the year | 2,708,464 11 | | |
| Loss from loading | | | $ 262,704 27 |
| Interest earned during the year | $4,058,075 26 | | |
| Investment expenses incurred during the year | 152,935 16 | | |
| Net income from investments | $3,905,140 10 | | |
| Interest required to maintain reserve | 2,221,424 08 | | |
| Gain from interest | | $1,683,716 02 | |
| Expected mortality on net amount at risk | $3,399,211 68 | | |
| Actual mortality on net amount at risk | 1,758,090 27 | | |
| Gain from mortality | | 1,641,121 41 | |
| Expected disbursements to annuitants | $407,423 88 | | |
| Net actual annuity claims incurred | 512,865 34 | | |
| Loss from annuities | | | 105,441 46 |
| Total gain during the year from surrendered and lapsed policies | | 164,854 04 | |
| Decrease in surplus on dividend account | | | 2,431,060 94 |
| Decrease in special funds and special reserves during the year | | 1,142 50 | |
| Net to gain account | | 22,150 89 | |

INVESTMENT EXHIBIT.

| | | Gain in surplus. | Loss in surplus. |
|---|---|---|---|
| Total gains from real estate | | 22,500 00 | |
| Total losses from real estate | | | 310,819 26 |
| Total gains from bonds | | 1,247,888 30 | |
| Total losses from bonds | | | 20,793 60 |
| Gain from assets not admitted | | 5,653 84 | |
| Net gain on account of total and permanent disability benefits or additional accidental death benefits included in life policies | | 10,198 33 | |
| Balance unaccounted for | | 797 44 | |
| Total gains and losses in surplus during the year | | $4,800,022 77 | $3,130,819 53 |
| Surplus December 31, 1920 | $2,074,731 72 | | |
| Surplus December 31, 1921 | 3,743,934 96 | | |
| Increase in surplus | | | 1,669,203 24 |
| Total | | $4,800,022 77 | $4,800,022 77 |

## NEW ENGLAND MUTUAL LIFE INSURANCE COMPANY.

Located at No. 87 Milk Street, Boston, Massachusetts; incorporated April 1, 1835; commenced business in Illinois November 18, 1861.

ALFRED D. FOSTER, President. FRANK T. PARTRIDGE, Secretary.

EDGAR C. FOWLER, Chicago, Attorney for service.

| | |
|---|---|
| Amount of ledger assets December 31, of previous year | $102,631,561 04 |

## INCOME.

|  | | | |
|---|---|---|---|
| First year's premiums on original policies | | $2,702,108 00 | |
| First year's premiums for total and permanent disability benefits | | 53,614 28 | |
| First year's premiums for additional accidental death benefits | | 25,934 12 | |
| Dividends applied to purchase paid-up additions and annuities | | 564,013 57 | |
| New premiums | | $ 3,345,669 97 | |
| Renewal premiums | $13,988,672 90 | | |
| Renewal premiums for total and permanent disability benefits | 160,561 43 | | |
| Renewal premiums for additional accidental death benefits | 60,173 21 | | |
| Dividends applied to pay renewal premiums | 2,486,938 30 | | |
| Renewal premiums | | 16,696,345 84 | |
| Premium income | | $20,042,015 81 | |
| Premiums advanced during year under Soldiers' and Sailors' Civil Relief Act | | 186 30 | |
| Total | | | $20,042,202 11 |
| Consideration for supplementary contracts involving life contingencies | | | 37,195 00 |
| Consideration for supplementary contracts not involving life contingencies | | | 244,418 36 |
| Dividends left with company to accumulate at interest | | | 55,325 85 |
| Interest on mortgage loans | | $1,071,786 75 | |
| Interest on collateral loans | | 8,583 01 | |
| Interest on bonds and dividends on stocks | | 2,907,177 99 | |
| Interest on premium notes, policy loans or liens | | 1,000,057 43 | |
| Interest on deposits | | 38,408 60 | |
| Interest on other debts due the company | | 3,448 79 | |
| Discount on claims paid in advance | | 89 91 | |
| Rents—including $100,000.00 for company's occupancy of its own buildings | | 255,035 82 | |
| Total interest and rents | | | 5,284,588 30 |
| Proceeds of fire insurance on mortgaged property | | | 12,602 11 |
| Profit on sale or maturity of ledger assets | | | 175,412 00 |
| Increase in book value of ledger assets | | | 1,006,181 55 |
| Total income | | | $26,857,925 28 |
| Total | | | $129,489,486 32 |

## DISBURSEMENTS.

|  | | |
|---|---|---|
| Death claims and additions | $4,411,871 25 | |
| Matured endowments and additions | 1,173,293 01 | |
| Total and permanent disability claims and additional accidental death benefits | 39,586 17 | |
| Total death claims and endowments | | $5,624,750 43 |
| Annuities involving life contingencies | | 7,225 17 |
| Surrender values paid in cash, or applied in liquidation of loans or notes | | 1,782,946 41 |
| Dividends paid policyholders in cash, or applied in liquidation of loans or notes | | 297,428 92 |
| Dividends applied to pay renewal premiums | | 2,486,938 30 |
| Dividends applied to purchase paid-up additions and annuities | | 564,013 57 |
| Dividends left with the company to accumulate at interest | | 55,325 85 |
| (Total paid policyholders | $10,818,628 65) | |
| Expense of investigation and settlement of policy claims, including legal expenses | | 2,387 18 |
| Supplementary contracts not involving life contingencies | | 156,099 48 |
| Dividends with interest, held on deposit surrendered during the year | | 33,461 59 |
| Commissions to agents, first year, $1,343,317.92; renewal, $1,009,485.12 | | 2,352,803 04 |
| Commuted renewal commissions | | 1,777 90 |
| Agency supervision and traveling expenses of supervisors | | 4,158 88 |
| Branch office expenses | | 250,516 62 |
| Medical examiners' fees and inspection of risks | | 176,385 27 |
| Salaries and all other compensation of officers and home office employees | | 537,304 87 |
| Rent | | 106,816 60 |
| Advertising, printing, stationery, postage, telegraph, telephone, express and exchange | | 111,786 06 |
| Legal expense | | 148 32 |
| Furniture, fixtures and safes | | 27,953 26 |
| Repairs and expenses (other than taxes) on real estate | | 121,042 50 |
| Taxes on real estate | | 85,315 82 |
| State taxes on premiums | | 297,536 66 |
| Insurance department licenses and fees | | 19,318 82 |
| Federal taxes | | 63,586 26 |
| All other licenses, fees and taxes | | 9,725 76 |
| Other disbursements, viz: Membership in various associations, $7,993.35; home office travel, $5,575.60; protective watch, $881.39; legislative expense, $905.90; vault rentals, $1,502.00; agency and office meetings, $8,180.09; mortgage expense, $4,571.21; magazines and text books, $7,388.79; fidelity bonds, $1,778.43; sundries, $678.79; auditing, $3,516.20; office supplies, $5,708.76; insurance premiums, $1,399.14; typewriters and machines, $5,120.19 | | 55,199 84 |
| To adjust agents' remittances sent in advance | | 6,377 02 |

DISBURSEMENTS—Concluded.

| | |
|---|---|
| Loss on sale or maturity of ledger assets | $100,700 00 |
| Decrease in book value of ledger assets | 86,886 10 |
| Total disbursements | $15,425,916 50 |
| Balance | $114,063,569 82 |

## LEDGER ASSETS.

| | |
|---|---|
| Book value of real estate | $ 3,168,932 00 |
| Mortgage loans on real estate | 22,588,182 97 |
| Loans secured by collaterals | 108,500 00 |
| Premiums advanced under Soldiers' and Sailors' Civil Relief Act | 1,073 60 |
| Loans on company's policies assigned as collateral | 19,024,614 25 |
| Premium notes on policies in force | 1,578,383 59 |
| Book value of bonds and stocks | 66,442,700 00 |
| Cash in office | 15,084 28 |
| Deposits in trust companies and banks on interest | 1,127,486 25 |
| Agents' balances (debit, $9,902.06; credit, $1,289.18) Net | 8,612 88 |
| Total ledger assets | $114,063,569 82 |

NON-LEDGER ASSETS.

| | | | |
|---|---|---|---|
| Interest due and accrued on mortgages | | $ 315,294 35 | |
| Interest accrued on bonds | | 1,015,991 37 | |
| Interest accrued on collateral loans | | 2,035 94 | |
| Interest due and accrued on premium notes, loans or liens | | 344,970 61 | |
| Interest accrued on other assets | | 558 94 | |
| Rents due and accrued on company's property | | 21,886 47 | |
| | | | 1,700,737 68 |
| Market value of real estate over book value | | | 2,049 00 |
| | New business. | Renewals. | |
| Net uncollected and deferred premiums (paid for basis) | $377,520 71 | $1,370,888 55 | 1,748,409 26 |
| Gross assets | | | $117,514,765 76 |

DEDUCT ASSETS NOT ADMITTED.

| | | |
|---|---|---|
| Agents' debit balances | $ 9,902 06 | |
| Book value of bonds and stocks over amortized value | 1,296,038 00 | |
| Total | | 1,305,940 06 |
| Admitted assets | | $116,208,825 70 |

## LIABILITIES.

| | | |
|---|---|---|
| Net present value of outstanding policies | $99,185,531 40 | |
| Same for dividend additions | 3,851,333 82 | |
| Same for annuities | 595,841 52 | |
| Net reserve (paid for basis) | | $103,632,706 74 |
| Extra reserve for total and permanent disability benefits and for additional accidental death benefits included in life policies, less re-insurance | | 321,232 04 |
| Present value of supplementary contracts not involving life contingencies | | 1,495,963 44 |
| Present value of amount incurred but not yet due for total and permanent disability benefits | | 74,464 00 |
| Death losses in process of adjustment | $62,676 11 | |
| Death losses reported for which no proofs have been received | 98,463 00 | |
| Reserve for net death losses incurred but unreported | 54,194 00 | |
| Matured endowments due and unpaid | 64,695 68 | |
| Death losses and other policy claims resisted | 12,613 84 | |
| Total policy claims | | 292,642 63 |
| Dividends left with the company to accumulate at interest | | 114,774 69 |
| Gross premiums paid in advance, including surrender values so applied, less discount, if any | | 193,497 97 |
| Unearned interest and rent paid in advance | | 28,195 93 |
| Commissions due agents on premium notes, when paid | | 86,799 23 |
| Commissions to agents due or accrued | | 5,912 53 |
| Salaries, rents, office expenses, bills, and accounts due or accrued | | 28,231 39 |
| Medical examiners' fees due or accrued | | 3,317 00 |
| Estimated amount hereafter payable for federal, state and other taxes based upon the business of the year of this statement | | 319,695 20 |
| Dividends or other profits due policyholders | | 230,149 47 |
| Dividends declared on or apportioned to annual dividend policies payable to policyholders during 1922 for period to December 31, 1922 | | 3,790,750 00 |
| Dividends declared on or apportioned to deferred dividend policies payable to policyholders during 1922 for period to December 31, 1922 | | 91,741 35 |
| Amounts set apart, apportioned, provisionally ascertained, calculated, declared or held awaiting apportionment upon deferred dividend policies | | 244,710 44 |
| Proceeds of fire insurance on mortgaged property | | 12,602 11 |
| Total | | $110,967,386 16 |
| Unassigned funds (surplus) | | 5,241,439 54 |
| Total | | $116,208,825 70 |

## EXHIBIT OF POLICIES—ORDINARY.

ALL BUSINESS PAID FOR.

| | Number. | Amount. | Number. | Amount. |
|---|---|---|---|---|
| Policies in force December 31, 1920 | | | 199,794 | $560,773,236 00 |
| Policies issued, revived, and increased during the year | | | 20,612 | 82,072,020 00 |
| Total | | | 220,406 | $642,845,256 00 |
| Deduct policies which have ceased to be in force during the year— | | | | |
| By death | 1,404 | $4,116,573 00 | | |
| By maturity | 579 | 1,170,562 00 | | |
| By expiry | 613 | 1,683,707 00 | | |
| By surrender | 1,957 | 5,202,369 00 | | |
| By lapse | 6,283 | 18,625,808 00 | | |
| By decrease | -------- | 2,631,155 00 | | |
| Total | | | 10,836 | 33,430,174 00 |
| Total policies in force December 31, 1921 | | | 209,570 | $609,415,082 00 |

## BUSINESS IN ILLINOIS—ORDINARY.

| | Number. | Amount. |
|---|---|---|
| Policies in force December 31, 1920 | 10,706 | $39,769,659 00 |
| Policies issued during the year | 1,288 | 6,961,637 00 |
| Total | 11,994 | $46,731,296 00 |
| Deduct policies ceased to be in force | 717 | 2,880,794 00 |
| Policies in force December 31, 1921 | 11,277 | $43,850,502 00 |
| Losses and claims unpaid December 31, 1920 | 10 | $ 61,675 00 |
| Losses and claims incurred during the year | 116 | 415,339 00 |
| Total | 126 | 477,014 00 |
| Losses and claims settled during the year | 121 | 468,552 00 |
| Losses and claims unpaid December 31, 1921 | 5 | 8,462 00 |
| Premiums received | | $1,400,413 30 |

## GAIN AND LOSS EXHIBIT.

INSURANCE EXHIBIT.

| | | Gain in surplus. | Loss in surplus. |
|---|---|---|---|
| Loading on actual premiums of the year (averaging 20.71 per cent of the gross premiums) | $4,137,936 22 | | |
| Insurance expenses incurred during the year | 4,001,391 44 | | |
| Gain from loading | | $ 136,544 78 | |
| Interest earned during the year | $5,594,739 61 | | |
| Investment expenses incurred during the year | 340,868 67 | | |
| Net income from investments | $5,253,870 94 | | |
| Interest required to maintain reserve | 3,453,365 93 | | |
| Gain from interest | | 1,800,505 01 | |
| Expected mortality on net amount at risk | $6,005,630 70 | | |
| Actual mortality on net amount at risk | 2,615,015 38 | | |
| Gain from mortality | | 3,390,615 32 | |
| Expected disbursements to annuitants | $ —771 44 | | |
| Net actual annuity claims incurred | —12,432 04 | | |
| Gain from annuities | | 11,660 60 | |
| Total gain during the year from surrendered and lapsed policies | | 233,114 70 | |
| Decrease in surplus on dividend account | | -------------- | $3,867,626 95 |

INVESTMENT EXHIBIT.

| | | Gain in surplus. | Loss in surplus. |
|---|---|---|---|
| Total gains from real estate | | 2,750 00 | |
| Total losses from real estate | | -------------- | 1,450 47 |
| Total gains from stocks and bonds | | 1,178,843 55 | |
| Total losses from stocks and bonds | | -------------- | 460,523 63 |
| Loss from assets not admitted | | -------------- | 9,902 06 |
| Net gain on account of total and permanent disability benefits or additional accidental death benefits included in life policies | | 101,063 71 | |
| Total gains and losses in surplus during the year | | $6,855,097 67 | $4,348,503 11 |
| Surplus December 31, 1920 | $2,734,844 98 | | |
| Surplus December 31, 1921 | 5,241,439 54 | | |
| Increase in surplus | | -------------- | 2,506,594 56 |
| Total | | $6,855,097 67 | $6,855,097 67 |

# NEW WORLD LIFE INSURANCE COMPANY.

Located at Old National Bank Building, Spokane, Washington; incorporated February 21, 1910; commenced business in Illinois February 15, 1913.

JOHN J. CADIGAN, President. RUSSELL C. BURTON, Secretary.

GEORGE A. BARR, Director of Trade and Commerce, Attorney for service at Springfield.

## CAPITAL.

| | | | |
|---|---|---|---|
| Capital paid up | | $1,134,500 00 | |
| Amount of ledger assets December 31, of previous year | | | $3,590,321 38 |

## INCOME.

| | | | |
|---|---|---|---|
| First year's premiums on original policies, less re-insurance | | $203,138 98 | |
| First year's premiums for total and permanent disability benefits | | 1,951 87 | |
| First year's premiums for additional accidental death benefits, less re-insurance | | 1,080 45 | |
| Coupons applied to purchase paid-up additions and annuities | | 35,090 05 | |
| Surrender values applied to purchase paid-up insurance and annuities | | 17,878 06 | |
| New premiums | | $259,139 41 | |
| Renewal premiums less re-insurance | $694,440 18 | | |
| Renewal premiums for total and permanent disability benefits | 4,586 41 | | |
| Renewal premiums for additional accidental death benefits, less re-insurance | 767 90 | | |
| Coupons applied to pay renewal premiums | 3,344 80 | | |
| Surrender values applied to pay renewal premiums | 679 12 | | |
| Renewal premiums | | 703,818 41 | |
| Premium income | | | $962,957 82 |
| Coupons left with company to accumulate at interest | | | 4,280 80 |
| Interest on mortgage loans | | $189,559 46 | |
| Interest on collateral loans | | 22 55 | |
| Interest on bonds | | 23,012 18 | |
| Interest on premium notes, policy loans or liens | | 25,456 86 | |
| Interest on deposits | | 15,396 66 | |
| Interest on other debts due the company | | 4,302 66 | |
| Rents | | 1,607 66 | |
| Total interest and rents | | | 259,358 03 |
| From other sources, viz: Accounts repayable, $25.00; transfer fees, $101.18 | | | 126 18 |
| Borrowed money (gross) | | | 65,000 00 |
| Profit on sale or maturity of ledger assets | | | 1,077 26 |
| Increase in book value of ledger assets | | | 1,391 50 |
| Total income | | | $1,294,191 59 |
| Total | | | $4,884,512 97 |

## DISBURSEMENTS.

| | | |
|---|---|---|
| Death claims | $68,534 80 | |
| Matured endowments | 1,000 00 | |
| Total and permanent disability claims and additional accidental death benefits, less re-insurance | 111 65 | |
| Total death claims and endowments | | $69,646 45 |
| Premium notes and liens voided by lapse | | 23,255 23 |
| Surrender values paid in cash, or applied in liquidation of loans or notes | | 61,356 23 |
| Surrender values applied to pay new and renewal premiums | | 679 12 |
| Surrender values applied to purchase paid-up insurance and annuities | | 17,878 06 |
| Coupons paid policyholders in cash, or applied in liquidation of loans or notes | | 110 04 |
| Coupons applied to pay renewal premiums | | 3,344 80 |
| Coupons applied to purchase paid-up additions and annuities | | 35,090 05 |
| Coupons left with the company to accumulate at interest | | 4,280 80 |
| (Total paid policyholders | $215,640 78) | |
| Expense of investigation and settlement of policy claims, including legal expenses | | 398 02 |
| Supplementary contracts not involving life contingencies | | 2,185 68 |
| Dividends with interest, held on deposit surrendered during the year | | 2,157 94 |
| Dividends to stockholders | | 90,760 00 |
| Commissions to agents, first year, $156,226.46; renewal, $21,354.58 | | 177,581 04 |
| Compensation of managers and agents not paid by commissions on new business | | 1,978 00 |
| Agency supervision and traveling expenses of supervisors | | 6,038 20 |
| Branch office expenses | | 10,584 70 |
| Medical examiners' fees and inspection of risks | | 17,069 96 |
| Salaries and all other compensation of officers and home office employees | | 81,605 28 |
| Rent | | 7,725 00 |
| Advertising, printing, stationery, postage, telegraph, telephone, express and exchange | | 28,617 81 |
| Legal expense | | 1,800 17 |
| Furniture, fixtures and safes | | 3,300 36 |

DISBURSEMENTS—Concluded.

| | |
|---|---|
| Repairs and expenses (other than taxes) on real estate | $ 614 37 |
| Taxes on real estate | 1,794 57 |
| State taxes on premiums | 19,866 00 |
| Insurance department licenses and fees | 4,756 30 |
| Federal taxes | 20,606 75 |
| All other licenses, fees and taxes | 184 24 |
| Other disbursements, viz: Suspense, $356.45; premiums on applications pending, $957.77; profit and loss, $7.45; interest on full-paid bonds, $17.00; commissions paid on mortgage loans, $2,327.00; donations, $1,071.17; depository bonds, $874.82; collection fees, $48.52; periodicals, $124.60; agents' conventions and entertainments, $1,202.92; dues, $306.00; storage, $29.87; motor car, $659.54; traveling expense, $6,854.67; unclassified, $73.65; investment expense, $2,499.96 | 17,411 39 |
| Borrowed money repaid (gross) | 65,000 00 |
| Interest on borrowed money | 792 55 |
| Loss on sale or maturity of ledger assets | 5,108 83 |
| Decrease in book value of ledger assets | 388 27 |
| Total disbursements | $783,966 21 |
| Balance | $4,100,546 76 |

LEDGER ASSETS.

| | |
|---|---|
| Book value of real estate | $ 46,753 84 |
| Contracts for sale of real estate | 65,912 68 |
| Mortgage loans on real estate | 2,811,676 68 |
| Loans on company's policies assigned as collateral | 394,999 45 |
| Premium notes on policies in force | 85,809 34 |
| Book value of bonds | 225,919 60 |
| Cash in office | 400 00 |
| Deposits in trust companies and banks not on interest | 11,930 21 |
| Certificates of deposit | 247,258 08 |
| Deposits in trust companies and banks on interest | 177,231 46 |
| Bills receivable | 3,250 45 |
| Agents' balances (debit, $21,637.41; credit, $5,315.17) | 16,322 24 |
| Tax redemptions | 13,082 73 |
| Total ledger assets | $4,100,546 76 |

NON-LEDGER ASSETS.

| | | |
|---|---|---|
| Interest due and accrued on mortgages | $131,259 55 | |
| Interest accrued on bonds | 1,540 80 | |
| Interest due and accrued on premium notes, loans or liens | 8,493 95 | |
| Interest due and accrued on other assets | 8,144 93 | |
| Rents due and accrued on company's property | 128 50 | |
| | | 149,567 73 |
| Due from other companies for losses or claims on policies re-insured | | 877 84 |
| Net uncollected and deferred premiums (paid for basis): Renewals | | 100,855 86 |
| Gross assets | | $4,351,848 19 |

DEDUCT ASSETS NOT ADMITTED.

| | | |
|---|---|---|
| Agents' debit balances | $21,637 41 | |
| Bills receivable | 3,250 45 | |
| Premium notes, policy loans and other policy assets in excess of net value and of other policy liabilities on individual policies | 10,668 18 | |
| Bank deposits | 392 88 | |
| Book value of real estate over market value | 5,370 81 | |
| Book value of bonds over market value | 5,000 00 | |
| Total | | 46,319 73 |
| Admitted assets | | $4,305,528 46 |

LIABILITIES.

| | | |
|---|---|---|
| Net present value of outstanding policies computed by the Washington Insurance Department | $2,361,741 61 | |
| Same for dividend additions | 116,280 04 | |
| Total | $2,478,021 65 | |
| Deduct net value of risks re-insured | 11,348 62 | |
| Net reserve (paid for basis) | | $2,466,673 03 |
| Extra reserve for total and permanent disability benefits and for additional accidental death benefits included in life policies, less re-insurance | | 28,399 48 |
| Present value of supplementary contracts not involving life contingencies | | 24,118 29 |
| Surrender values claimable on policies cancelled | | 1,793 30 |
| Death losses in process of adjustment | $2,500 00 | |
| Death losses reported for which no proofs have been received | 6,250 00 | |
| Death losses and other policy claims resisted | 2,500 00 | |
| Total policy claims | | 11,250 00 |

LIABILITIES—Concluded.

| | |
|---|---|
| Coupons left with the company to accumulate at interest | $35,480 66 |
| Gross premiums paid in advance, including surrender values so applied, less discount, if any | 5,262 18 |
| Unearned interest and rent paid in advance | 9,549 14 |
| Medical examiners' and legal fees due or accrued | 2,260 73 |
| Estimated amount hereafter payable for federal, state and other taxes based upon the business of the year of this statement | 1,299 13 |
| Advances by officers or others on account of expenses of organization or otherwise | 33,000 00 |
| Other liabilities, viz: Commissions payable to loan agents, $1,219.00; premiums on applications pending, $1,973.83; suspense, $1,323.69; accounts payable, $1,710.50; judgment in excess of face of policy, $696.25 | 6,923 27 |
| Total | $2,626,009 21 |
| Capital paid up | 1,134,500 00 |
| Unassigned funds (surplus) | 545,019 25 |
| Total | $4,305,528 46 |

## EXHIBIT OF POLICIES—ORDINARY.

ALL BUSINESS PAID FOR.

| | Number. | Amount. | Number. | Amount. |
|---|---|---|---|---|
| Policies in force December 31, 1920 | | | 13,347 | $29,021,090 98 |
| Policies issued, revived, and increased during the year | | | 3,004 | 7,562,544 75 |
| Total | | | 16,351 | $36,583,635 73 |
| Deduct policies which have ceased to be in force during the year— | | | | |
| By death | 38 | $ 74,935 95 | | |
| By maturity | 1 | 1,000 00 | | |
| By expiry | 49 | 106,250 00 | | |
| By surrender | 223 | 495,753 00 | | |
| By lapse | 2,416 | 6,873,250 00 | | |
| By decrease | -------- | 105,139 05 | | |
| Total | | | 2,727 | 7,656,328 00 |
| Total policies in force December 31, 1921 | | | 13,624 | $28,927,307 73 |
| Re-insured | | | | $1,941,673 00 |

## BUSINESS IN ILLINOIS—ORDINARY.

| | Number. | Amount. |
|---|---|---|
| Policies in force December 31, 1920 | 880 | $1,515,050 21 |
| Policies issued during the year | 182 | 357,771 84 |
| Total | 1,062 | $1,872,822 05 |
| Deduct policies ceased to be in force | 164 | 297,130 00 |
| Policies in force December 31, 1921 | 898 | $1,575,692 05 |
| Losses and claims unpaid December 31, 1920 | 2 | $3,500 00 |
| Losses and claims incurred during the year | 3 | 7,000 00 |
| Total | 5 | $10,500 00 |
| Losses and claims settled during the year | 3 | 7,000 00 |
| Losses and claims unpaid December 31, 1921 | 2 | $3,500 00 |
| Premiums received | | $45,302 98 |

## GAIN AND LOSS EXHIBIT.

INSURANCE EXHIBIT.

| | | Gain in surplus. | Loss in surplus. |
|---|---|---|---|
| Loading on actual premiums of the year (averaging 16.6 per cent of the gross premiums) | $161,918 10 | | |
| Insurance expenses incurred during the year | 347,218 26 | | |
| Loss from loading | | -------------- | $185,300 16 |
| Interest earned during the year | $281,292 65 | | |
| Investment expenses incurred during the year | 65,267 91 | | |
| Net income from investments | $216,024 74 | | |
| Interest required to maintain reserve | 84,717 48 | | |
| Gain from interest | | $131,307 26 | |
| Expected mortality on net amount at risk | $252,842 21 | | |
| Actual mortality on net amount at risk | 61,003 84 | | |
| Gain from mortality | | 191,838 37 | |
| Total gain during the year from surrendered and lapsed policies | | 26,388 20 | |
| Dividends paid stockholders | | -------------- | 90,760 00 |
| Decrease in special funds, and special reserves during the year | | 29 08 | |

GAIN AND LOSS EXHIBIT—Concluded.

INVESTMENT EXHIBIT.

| | | Gain in surplus. | Loss in surplus. |
|---|---|---|---|
| Total gains from real estate | | $2,235 32 | |
| Total losses from real estate | | | $1,000 00 |
| Total gains from stocks and bonds | | 5,764 61 | |
| Total losses from stocks and bonds | | | 9,108 83 |
| Loss from assets not admitted | | | 8,222 40 |
| Net loss on account of total and permanent disability benefits or additional accidental death benefits included in life policies | | | 652 76 |
| Gain from transfer fees, $101.18; returned re-insurance premiums, $877.84 | | 979 02 | |
| Total gains and losses in surplus during the year | | $358,541 86 | $295,044 15 |
| Surplus December 31, 1920 | $481,521 54 | | |
| Surplus December 31, 1921 | 545,019 25 | | |
| Increase in surplus | | | 63,497 71 |
| Total | | $358,541 86 | $358,541 86 |

## NEW YORK LIFE INSURANCE COMPANY.

Located at No. 346 Broadway, New York, New York; incorporated, 1841; commenced business in Illinois, 1856.

DARWIN P. KINGSLEY, President.
SEYMOUR M. BALLARD, FREDERICK M. CORSE, WILBUR H. PIERSON, Secretaries.

WILLIAM N. MARSHALL, Chicago, Attorney for service.

| | |
|---|---|
| Amount of ledger assets December 31, of previous year | $939,328,504 04 |

### INCOME.

| | | | |
|---|---|---|---|
| First year's premiums on original policies, less re-insurance | | $21,708,716 94 | |
| First year's premiums for total and permanent disability benefits | | 736,984 00 | |
| First year's premiums for additional accidental death benefits | | 484,911 00 | |
| Dividends applied to purchase paid-up additions and annuities | | 3,629,588 11 | |
| Consideration for original annuities involving life contingencies | | 184,580 25 | |
| New premiums | | $ 26,744,780 30 | |
| Renewal premiums less re-insurance | $109,243,816 57 | | |
| Renewal premiums for total and permanent disability benefits | 1,768,343 00 | | |
| Renewal premiums for additional accidental death benefits | 992,260 00 | | |
| Dividends applied to pay renewal premiums | 9,578,664 84 | | |
| Dividends applied to shorten the endowment or premium-paying period | 306,677 00 | | |
| Surrender values applied to pay renewal premiums | 393,906 82 | | |
| Renewal premiums for deferred annuities | 78,099 51 | | |
| Renewal premiums | | 122,361,767 74 | |
| Premium income | | | $149,106,548 04 |
| Consideration for supplementary contracts involving life contingencies | | | 369,636 37 |
| Consideration for supplementary contracts not involving life contingencies | | | 978,236 92 |
| Dividends left with company to accumulate at interest | | | 2,642,428 27 |
| Interest on mortgage loans | | $ 9,127,537 84 | |
| Interest on collateral loans | | 379,381 55 | |
| Interest on bonds and dividends on stocks | | 27,161,018 43 | |
| Interest on premium notes, policy loans or liens | | 7,798,510 90 | |
| Interest on deposits | | 521,985 88 | |
| Discount on claims paid in advance | | 19,950 62 | |
| Rents—including $344,508.60 for company's occupancy of its own buildings | | 1,037,532 39 | |
| Total interest and rents | | | 46,045,917 61 |
| From other sources, viz: Commissions advanced in previous years now repaid, $302.38; policy fees, $2,800.86; New York State income tax, $380.28; doubtful debts recovered, $23,236.69; bonuses received for repayment or extension of mortgage loans, $13,843.79; fire insurance collected, $50.00; exchange, $2,067,275.94; remittances not yet adjusted, $3,233.97; cash received for failure to deliver bonds purchased, $250.00 | | | 2,111,373 91 |
| Profit on sale or maturity of ledger assets | | | 771,185 94 |
| Increase in book value of ledger assets | | | 1,506,582 68 |
| Total income | | | $203,531,909 74 |
| Total | | | $1,142,860,413 78 |

## DISBURSEMENTS.

|  | | |
|---|---|---|
| Death claims and additions | $32,795,646 82 | |
| Matured endowments and additions | 24,800,066 82 | |
| Total and permanent disability claims and additional accidental death benefits | 903,911 19 | |
| Total death claims and endowments | | $58,499,624 83 |
| Annuities involving life contingencies | | 1,337,944 76 |
| Surrender values paid in cash, or applied in liquidation of loans or notes | | 25,240,247 96 |
| Surrender values applied to pay new and renewal premiums | | 393,906 82 |
| Dividends paid policyholders in cash, or applied in liquidation of loans or notes | | 21,247,054 43 |
| Dividends applied to pay renewal premiums | | 9,578,664 84 |
| Dividends applied to shorten the endowment or premium-paying period | | 306,677 00 |
| Dividends applied to purchase paid-up additions and annuities | | 3,629,588 11 |
| Dividends left with the company to accumulate at interest | | 2,201,383 87 |
| Paid on policies transferred to foreign governments and companies | | 1,873,316 64 |
| (Total paid policyholders | $124,308,409 26) | |
| Expense of investigation and settlement of policy claims, including legal expenses | | 66,421 04 |
| Supplementary contracts not involving life contingencies | | 1,034,846 69 |
| Dividends with interest, held on deposit surrendered during the year | | 948,105 51 |
| Commissions to agents, first year, $11,065,944.04; renewal, $4,196,409.82; annuities, (original), $9,883.18; (renewal), $2,277.98 | | 15,274,515 02 |
| Compensation of managers and agents not paid by commissions on new business | | 25,917 62 |
| Agency supervision and traveling expenses of supervisors | | 1,263,065 78 |
| Branch office expenses | | 2,007,133 59 |
| Medical examiners' fees and inspection of risks | | 1,008,092 25 |
| Salaries and all other compensation of officers and home office employees | | 3,635,513 34 |
| Rent | | 848,242 10 |
| Advertising, printing, stationery, postage, telegraph, telephone and express | | 849,862 10 |
| Legal expense | | 10,330 47 |
| Furniture, fixtures and safes | | 268,160 30 |
| Repairs and expenses (other than taxes) on real estate | | 308,437 48 |
| Taxes on real estate | | 179,909 26 |
| State taxes on premiums | | 1,812,251 72 |
| Insurance department licenses and fees | | 30,651 56 |
| Federal taxes | | 3,398,444 72 |
| All other licenses, fees and taxes | | 314,137 85 |
| Other disbursements, viz: Paid agents under Nylie contracts, $1,401,075.61; doubtful debts marked off, $6,640.95; commissions credits Br. Off. agents, $6,128.12; Austrian and Hungarian bonds of unknown value on hand after transfer of company's outstanding business in those countries, transferred to Schedule X, $371,383.07; books, papers and subscriptions, $8,908.38; special inspection reports, $5,769.52; lunch for company's employees, $199,008.70; miscellaneous items of expense, $27,305.75; legislative and departmental expenses, $14,848.92; traveling expenses, $30,457.33; examination and audits of the company's accounts, $3,620.83; foodstuffs sent to European department employees, $759.36; examination by New York State Insurance Department, $10.391.54; association of Life Insurance Presidents, $16,768.88; custom house charges, $995.28; federal income tax, $456.07; annuity mortality investigation, $97.33; expenses directors' election, $426.67; miscellaneous interest payments, $30,321.61; bank charges, $8,814.37; custody of and insurance on securities, $14,530.12; premiums on fidelity bonds, $8,813.28; real estate commissions and fees, $2,600.00; real estate and mortgage department expenses, $12,422.19; National Association of Owners of Railroad Securities, $33,149.57; adjustment arising from the adoption of a lower standard for conversion of foreign currencies,* $636,492.39 | | 2,852,185 84 |
| Loss on sale or maturity of ledger assets | | 683,734 98 |
| Decrease in book value of ledger assets | | 836,396 53 |
| Total disbursements | | $161,964,765 01 |
| Balance | | $980,895,648 77 |

## LEDGER ASSETS.

|  |  |
|---|---|
| Book value of real estate | $ 8,362,881 00 |
| Mortgage loans on real estate | 183,722,805 92 |
| Loans secured by collaterals | 2,301,000 00 |
| Premiums advanced under Soldiers' and Sailors' Civil Relief Act | 740 32 |
| Loans on company's policies assigned as collateral | 157,604,508 43 |
| Premium notes on policies in force | 6,700,632 74 |
| Book value of bonds and stocks | 610,965,321 26 |
| Cash in office | 2,264 20 |
| Deposits in trust companies and banks not on interest | 1,562,196 18 |
| Deposits in trust companies and banks on interest | 8,673,918 47 |
| Bills receivable | 544 50 |
| Branch office debit balances, $170,070.44; credit, $141,482.58; net | 28,587 86 |
| Cash in company's branch offices, $70,308.10; cash in transit, $899,939.79 | 970,247 89 |
| Total ledger assets | $980,895,648 77 |

* This item is not a disbursement but is necessary because in 1921 the company adopted a lower standard for conversion of certain foreign currencies, resulting in a decrease in dollars in its foreign assets and correspondingly in its foreign liabilities.

## LEDGER ASSETS—Concluded.

NON-LEDGER ASSETS.

| | | | |
|---|---|---|---|
| Interest due and accrued on mortgages | | $3,114,787 02 | |
| Interest due and accrued on bonds | | 9,830,325 65 | |
| Interest accrued on collateral loans | | 8,608 15 | |
| Interest accrued on premium notes, loans or liens | | 1,724,912 48 | |
| Interest due and accrued on other assets | | 65,302 08 | |
| Rents due on company's property | | 8,616 63 | |
| | | | $14,752,552 01 |
| | New business. | Renewals. | |
| Net uncollected and deferred premiums (paid for basis) | $1,548,254 50 | $13,126,188 58 | 14,674,443 08 |
| Gross assets | | | $1,010,322,643 86 |

DEDUCT ASSETS NOT ADMITTED.

| | | |
|---|---|---|
| Bills receivable | $ 544 50 | |
| Overdue and accrued interest on bonds in default | 1,472,892 43 | |
| Book value of bonds and stocks over market value | 56,046,997 69 | |
| Branch office debit balances | 170,070 44 | |
| Total | | 57,690,505 06 |
| Admitted assets | | $952,632,138 80 |

## LIABILITIES.

| | | |
|---|---|---|
| Net present value of outstanding policies computed by the New York Insurance Department | $756,884,012 00 | |
| Same for dividend additions | 11,517,440 00 | |
| Same for annuities | 14,660,440 00 | |
| Total | $783,061,892 00 | |
| Deduct net value of risks re-insured | 250,039 00 | |
| Net reserve (paid for basis) | | $782,811,853 00 |
| Extra reserve for total and permanent disability benefits and for additional accidental death benefits included in life policies, less re-insurance | | 4,345,610 00 |
| Present value of supplementary contracts not involving life contingencies | | 6,961,490 95 |
| Present value of amounts incurred but not yet due for total and permanent disability benefits | | 1,858,004 00 |
| Surrender values claimable on policies cancelled | | 624,859 73 |
| Death losses in process of adjustment | $1,265,978 30 | |
| Death losses reported for which no proofs have been received | 2,927,908 44 | |
| Reserve for net death losses incurred but unreported | 2,250 000 00 | |
| Matured endowments due and unpaid | 1,290,515 55 | |
| Death losses and other policy claims resisted | 567,004 22 | |
| Total and permanent disability benefits and additional accidental death benefits | 446,785 28 | |
| Annuity claims, involving life contingencies, due and unpaid | 129,572 29 | |
| Total policy claims | | 8,877,764 08 |
| Due and unpaid on supplementary contracts not involving life contingencies | | 1,023 68 |
| Dividends left with the company to accumulate at interest | | 8,249,320 79 |
| Gross premiums paid in advance, including surrender values so applied, less discount, if any | | 1,800,252 55 |
| Unearned interest and rent paid in advance | | 2,561,742 63 |
| Commissions due agents on premium notes, when paid | | 6,258 23 |
| Commissions to agents due or accrued | | 14,220 37 |
| Salaries, rents, office expenses, bills and accounts due or accrued | | 109,949 03 |
| Medical examiners' inspection and legal fees due or accrued | | 57,433 97 |
| Estimated amount hereafter payable for federal, state and other taxes based upon the business of the year of this statement | | 7,139,815 27 |
| Dividends or other profits due policyholders | | 1,954,561 85 |
| Dividends declared on or apportioned to annual dividend policies payable to policyholders during 1922 for period to December 31, 1922 | | 19,905,256 00 |
| Dividends declared on or apportioned to deferred dividend policies payable to policyholders during 1922 for period to December 31, 1922 | | 22,382,112 71 |
| Amounts set apart, apportioned, provisionally ascertained, calculated, declared or held awaiting apportionment upon deferred dividend policies | | 59,303,179 00 |
| Reserve or surplus funds not otherwise included in liabilities, viz— | | |
| Security fluctuation and general contingency fund, market value basis | | 13,795,156 20 |
| Annual dividend equalization fund | | 2,165,040 00 |
| Reserve for future expenses on paid up annual dividend policies | | 975,000 00 |
| Other liabilities, viz: Due agents under Nylic contracts, $2,262.86; reserve for Nylic contracts, $6,510,874.00; federal and New York State income tax deducted at source, $4,276.23; suspended remittances and unclaimed receipts, $114,071.67; guaranteed deposits on real estate and rents, $750.00; deposited on contracts for sale of real estate, $100,000.00 | | 6,732,234 76 |
| Total | | $952,632,138 80 |

## EXHIBIT OF POLICIES—ORDINARY.

ALL BUSINESS PAID FOR.

| | Number. | Amount. | Number. | Amount. |
|---|---|---|---|---|
| Policies in force December 31, 1920 | | | 1,605,035 | $3,537,298,756 00 |
| Policies issued, revived and increased during the year | | | 207,286 | 603,156,334 00 |
| Total | | | 1,812,321 | $4,140,455,090 00 |
| Deduct policies which have ceased to be in force during the year— | | | | |
| By death | 13,703 | $ 32,025,804 00 | | |
| By maturity | 16,114 | 24,969,475 00 | | |
| By disability | -------- | 78,800 00 | | |
| By expiry | 8,321 | 23,197,990 00 | | |
| By surrender | 26,571 | 57,358,785 00 | | |
| By lapse | 62,035 | 168,329,400 00 | | |
| By decrease | -------- | 11,304,004 00 | | |
| *Other deductions | 10,142 | 7,092,308 00 | | |
| Total | | | 136,886 | 324,356,566 00 |
| Total policies in force December 31, 1921 | | | 1,675,435 | $3,816,098,524 00 |
| Re-insured | | | 298 | $10,536,425 00 |

## BUSINESS IN ILLINOIS—ORDINARY.

| | Number. | Amount. |
|---|---|---|
| Policies in force December 31, 1920 | 147,741 | $304,723,090 00 |
| Policies issued during the year | 21,566 | 56,551,466 00 |
| Total | 169,307 | $361,274,556 00 |
| Deduct policies ceased to be in force | 10,312 | 23,659,774 00 |
| Policies in force December 31, 1921 | 158,995 | $337,614,782 00 |
| Losses and claims unpaid December 31, 1920 | 126 | $ 174,843 49 |
| Losses and claims incurred during the year | 2,318 | 4,209,997 20 |
| Total | 2,444 | $4,384,840 69 |
| Losses and claims settled during the year | 2,284 | 4,146,386 25 |
| Losses and claims unpaid December 31, 1921 | 160 | $238,454 44 |
| Premiums received | | $12,234,005 83 |

## GAIN AND LOSS EXHIBIT.

INSURANCE EXHIBIT.

| | | Gain in surplus. | Loss in surplus. |
|---|---|---|---|
| Loading on actual premiums of the year (averaging 22.64 per cent of the gross premiums) | $33,176,242 50 | | |
| Insurance expenses incurred during the year | 27,329,433 37 | | |
| Gain from loading | | $ 5,846,809 13 | |
| Interest earned during the year | $47,833,164 72 | | |
| Investment expenses incurred during the year | 5,267,312 93 | | |
| Net income from investments | $42,565,851 79 | | |
| Interest required to maintain reserve | 24,100,000 00 | | |
| Gain from interest | | 18,465,851 79 | |
| Expected mortality on net amount at risk | $36,271,100 00 | | |
| Actual mortality on net amount at risk | 20,400,653 71 | | |
| Gain from mortality | | 15,870,446 29 | |
| Expected disbursements to annuitants | $839,985 00 | | |
| Net actual annuity claims incurred | 918,572 38 | | |
| Loss from annuities | | -------------- | $ 78,587 38 |
| Total gain during the year from surrendered and lapsed policies | | 5,078,540 13 | |
| Decrease in surplus on dividend account | | -------------- | 25,186,666 68 |
| Decrease in special funds and special reserves during the year | | 32,723,432 76 | |
| Net to gain account | | 16,895 74 | |

INVESTMENT EXHIBIT.

| | Gain in surplus. | Loss in surplus. |
|---|---|---|
| Total gains from real estate | 100,000 00 | |
| Total losses from real estate | -------------- | 118,217 06 |
| Total gains from stocks and bonds | 1,333,194 94 | |
| Total losses from stocks and bonds | -------------- | 59,170,695 02 |
| Gain on bonuses received for prepayment or extension of mortgage loans | 13,843 79 | |

* This consists of business transferred to foreign governments and companies and decrease on account of changes in standards for conversion of foreign currencies.

GAIN AND LOSS EXHIBIT—Concluded.

INVESTMENT EXHIBIT.

| | Gain in surplus. | Loss in surplus. |
|---|---|---|
| Gain from assets not admitted | $376,710 12 | |
| Net loss on account of total and permanent disability benefits or additional accidental death benefits included in life policies | | $299,928 47 |
| Net gain from exchange, $2,067,275.94; remittances not yet adjusted, $3,233.97; gain from transfers to foreign governments and companies and from changes in standards for conversion of foreign currencies, $2,988,181.62; less miscellaneous interest payments, $30,321.61 | 5,028,369 92 | |
| Total gains and losses in surplus during the year | $84,854,094 61 | $84,854,094 61 |

## NORTHERN STATES LIFE INSURANCE COMPANY.

Located at Citizens National Bank Building, Hammond, Indiana; incorporated May 31, 1910; commenced business in Illinois December 12, 1913.

H. E. SHARRER, President. P. A. PARKER, Secretary.

JOHN R. COCHRAN, Chicago, Attorney for service.

CAPITAL.

| | | | |
|---|---|---|---|
| Capital paid up | | $162,000 00 | |
| Amount of ledger assets December 31, of previous year | | | $1,050,131 15 |

INCOME.

| | | | |
|---|---|---|---|
| First year's premiums on original policies, less re-insurance | | $51,296 33 | |
| First year's premiums for total and permanent disability benefits, less re-insurance | | 1,578 63 | |
| Dividends applied to purchase paid-up additions and annuities | | 1,710 58 | |
| New premiums | | $ 54,585 54 | |
| Renewal premiums less re-insurance | $255,404 41 | | |
| Renewal premiums for total and permanent disability benefits | 2,641 12 | | |
| Dividends applied to pay renewal premiums | 4,100 27 | | |
| Renewal premiums | | 262,145 80 | |
| Premium income | | | $316,731 34 |
| Consideration for supplementary contracts not involving life contingencies | | | 7,500 00 |
| Dividends left with company to accumulate at interest | | | 438 08 |
| Interest on mortgage loans | | $55,288 75 | |
| Interest on bonds | | 5,130 49 | |
| Interest on premium notes, policy loans or liens | | 4,697 19 | |
| Interest on deposits | | 418 17 | |
| Total interest | | | 65,534 60 |
| From other sources, viz: Appraisement fees, $50.12; suspense, $196.31 | | | 246 43 |
| Borrowed money (gross) | | | 10,000 00 |
| Total income | | | $400,450 45 |
| Total | | | $1,450,581 60 |

DISBURSEMENTS.

| | | |
|---|---|---|
| Death claims | $69,132 00 | |
| Matured endowments | 1,060 00 | |
| Total death claims and endowments | | $70,192 00 |
| Premium notes and liens voided by lapse | | 12 00 |
| Surrender values paid in cash, or applied in liquidation of loans or notes | | 33,814 47 |
| Dividends paid policyholders, in cash or applied in liquidation of loans or notes | | 903 17 |
| Dividends applied to pay renewal premiums | | 4,100 27 |
| Dividends applied to purchase paid-up additions and annuities | | 1,710 58 |
| Dividends left with the company to accumulate at interest | | 438 08 |
| (Total paid policyholders | $111,170 57) | |
| Legal expenses | | 309 30 |
| Supplementary contracts not involving life contingencies | | 1,198 85 |
| Dividends with interest, held on deposit surrendered during the year | | 180 34 |
| Dividends to stockholders | | 12,960 00 |
| Commissions to agents, first year, $22,026.46; renewal, $7,225.61 | | 29,252 07 |
| Compensation of managers and agents not paid by commissions on new business | | 4,445 00 |
| Agency supervision and traveling expenses of supervisors | | 2,418 68 |
| Medical examiners' fees and inspection of risks | | 5,162 15 |
| Salaries and all other compensation of officers and home office employees | | 30,734 43 |
| Rent | | 1,301 78 |
| Advertising, printing, stationery, postage, telegraph, telephone, express and exchange | | 6,060 45 |
| Legal expenses | | 1,088 01 |
| Furniture, fixtures and safes | | 797 20 |
| State taxes on premiums | | 3,655 83 |

## DISBURSEMENTS—Concluded.

| | | |
|---|---|---|
| Insurance department licenses and fees | | $ 257 00 |
| Federal taxes | | 2,854 23 |
| All other licenses, fees and taxes | | 1,269 50 |
| Other disbursements, viz: War premiums refunded, $75.00; miscellaneous, $2,076.60 | | 2,151 60 |
| Borrowed money repaid (gross) | | 40,000 00 |
| Interest on borrowed money | | 75 67 |
| Agents' balances charged off | | 4,697 92 |
| Total disbursements | | $262,040 58 |
| Balance | | $1,188,541 02 |

## LEDGER ASSETS.

| | | |
|---|---|---|
| Mortgage loans on real estate | | $987,857 59 |
| Loans on company's policies assigned as collateral | | 60,112 23 |
| Premium notes on policies in force | | 4,713 51 |
| Book value of bonds | | 90,556 25 |
| Cash in office | | 200 00 |
| Deposits in trust companies and banks not on interest | | 9,733 54 |
| Deposits in trust companies and banks on interest | | 29,429 08 |
| Bills receivable | | 3,316 14 |
| Agents' balances (debit, $5,093.76; credit, $2,471.08) | | 2,622 68 |
| Total ledger assets | | $1,188,541 02 |

### NON-LEDGER ASSETS.

| | | | |
|---|---|---|---|
| Interest due and accrued on mortgages | | $19,553 55 | |
| Interest due and accrued on bonds | | 695 01 | |
| Interest due on premium notes, loans or liens | | 509 02 | |
| Interest due on other assets | | 135 44 | |
| | | | 20,893 02 |
| | New business. | Renewals. | |
| Net uncollected and deferred premiums (paid for basis) | $2,825 31 | $61,057 37 | 63,882 68 |
| Rent paid in advance | | | 4,000 00 |
| Gross assets | | | $1,277,316 72 |

### DEDUCT ASSETS NOT ADMITTED.

| | | |
|---|---|---|
| Agents' debit balances | $5,093 76 | |
| Bills receivable | 3,316 14 | |
| Premium notes, policy loans and other policy assets in excess of net value and of other policy liabilities on individual policies | 2,771 16 | |
| Book value of bonds over market value | 169 00 | |
| Interest on notes receivable | 135 44 | |
| Total | | 11,485 50 |
| Admitted assets | | $1,265,831 22 |

## LIABILITIES.

| | | |
|---|---|---|
| Net present value of outstanding policies computed by the Indiana Insurance Department | $1,012,061 81 | |
| Same for dividend additions | 5,909 91 | |
| Total | $1,017,971 72 | |
| Deduct net value of risks re-insured | 29,507 77 | |
| Net reserve (paid for basis) | | $988,463 95 |
| Extra reserve for total and permanent disability benefits and for additional accidental death benefits included in life policies, less re-insurance | | 2,109 88 |
| Present value of supplementary contracts not involving life contingencies | | 6,400 90 |
| Death losses reported for which no proofs have been received | | 1,015 00 |
| Dividends left with the company to accumulate at interest | | 1,996 67 |
| Gross premiums paid in advance, including surrender values so applied, less discount, if any | | 1,121 61 |
| Unearned interest and rent paid in advance | | 1,315 09 |
| Cost of collection on uncollected and deferred premiums in excess of loading | | 125 00 |
| Salaries, rents, office expenses, bills and accounts due or accrued | | 1,206 80 |
| Medical examiners' and legal fees due or accrued | | 735 00 |
| Estimated amount hereafter payable for federal, state and other taxes based upon the business of the year of this statement | | 12,500 00 |
| Dividends declared on or apportioned to annual dividend policies payable to policyholders during 1922 for period to December 31, 1922 | | 5,000 00 |
| Amounts set apart, apportioned, provisionally ascertained, calculated, declared or held awaiting apportionment upon deferred dividend policies | | 309 00 |
| Emergency mortality reserve | | 14,000 00 |
| Suspense | | 736 56 |
| Total | | $1,037,035 46 |
| Capital paid up | | 162,000 00 |
| Unassigned funds (surplus) | | 66,795 76 |
| Total | | $1,265,831 22 |

## EXHIBIT OF POLICIES—ORDINARY.

ALL BUSINESS PAID FOR.

| | Number. | Amount. | Number. | Amount. |
|---|---|---|---|---|
| Policies in force December 31, 1920 | | | 6,513 | $11,310,286 00 |
| Policies issued, revived and increased during the year | | | 726 | 2,304,548 00 |
| Total | | | 7,239 | $13,614,834 00 |
| Deduct policies which have ceased to be in force during the year— | | | | |
| By death | 45 | $ 72,115 00 | | |
| By maturity | 2 | 1,060 00 | | |
| By expiry | 72 | 115,287 00 | | |
| By surrender | 79 | 173,528 00 | | |
| By lapse | 418 | 915,704 00 | | |
| By decrease | -------- | 71,981 00 | | |
| Total | | | 616 | 1,349,675 00 |
| Total policies in force December 31, 1921 | | | 6,623 | $12,265,159 00 |
| Re-insured | | | 465 | $2,453,500 00 |

## BUSINESS IN ILLINOIS—ORDINARY.

| | Number. | Amount. |
|---|---|---|
| Policies in force December 31, 1920 | 3,386 | $5,235,204 00 |
| Policies issued during the year | 121 | 314,500 00 |
| Total | 3,507 | $5,549,704 00 |
| Deduct policies ceased to be in force | 273 | 560,179 00 |
| Policies in force December 31, 1921 | 3,234 | $4,989,525 00 |
| Losses and claims unpaid December 31, 1920 | 3 | $ 3,515 00 |
| Losses and claims incurred during the year | 26 | 33,880 00 |
| Total | 29 | $37,395 00 |
| Losses and claims settled during the year | 28 | 36,380 00 |
| Losses and claims unpaid December 31, 1921 | 1 | $1,015 00 |
| Premiums received | | $154,785 63 |

## GAIN AND LOSS EXHIBIT.

INSURANCE EXHIBIT.

| | | Gain in surplus. | Loss in surplus. |
|---|---|---|---|
| Loading on actual premiums of the year (averaging 14.4 per cent of the gross premiums) | $ 48,801 95 | | |
| Insurance expenses incurred during the year | 104,527 65 | | |
| Loss from loading | | -------------- | $55,725 70 |
| Interest earned during the year | $69,313 04 | | |
| Interest required to maintain reserve | 32,750 00 | | |
| Gain from interest | | $36,563 04 | |
| Expected mortality on net amount at risk | $100,164 00 | | |
| Actual mortality on net amount at risk | 58,896 16 | | |
| Gain from mortality | | 41,267 84 | |
| Total gain during the year from surrendered and lapsed policies | | 3,028 79 | |
| Dividends paid stockholders | | -------------- | 12,960 00 |
| Decrease in surplus on dividend account | | -------------- | 8,770 49 |
| Net to loss account | | -------------- | 4,697 92 |

INVESTMENT EXHIBIT.

| | | Gain in surplus. | Loss in surplus. |
|---|---|---|---|
| Total losses from bonds | | -------------- | 169 00 |
| Gain from assets not admitted | | 405 93 | |
| Net gain on account of total and permanent disability benefits or additional accidental death benefits included in life policies | | 3,864 49 | |
| Gain from all other sources | | 81 87 | |
| Balance unaccounted for | | -------------- | 256 12 |
| Total gains and losses in surplus during the year | | $85,211 96 | $82,579 23 |
| Surplus December 31, 1920 | $64,163 03 | | |
| Surplus December 31, 1921 | 66,795 76 | | |
| Increase in surplus | | -------------- | 2,632 73 |
| Total | | $85,211 96 | $85,211 96 |

## THE NORTHWESTERN MUTUAL LIFE INSURANCE COMPANY.

Located at Milwaukee, Wisconsin; incorporated March, 1857; commenced business in Illinois May 23, 1864.

W. D. VAN DYKE, President. A. S. HATHAWAY, Secretary.

RALPH H. HOBART, Chicago, Attorney for service.

| | | | |
|---|---|---|---|
| Amount of ledger assets December 31, of previous year | | | $458, 132, 002 59 |

### INCOME.

| | | | |
|---|---|---|---|
| First year's premiums on original policies | | $8, 008, 878 86 | |
| First year's premiums for total and permanent disability benefits | | 14, 536 24 | |
| Dividends applied to purchase paid-up additions and annuities | | 2, 427, 162 59 | |
| Consideration for original annuities involving life contingencies | | 2, 072 42 | |
| New premiums | | $10, 452, 650 11 | |
| Renewal premiums | $53, 787, 612 35 | | |
| Renewal premiums for total and permanent disability benefits | 46, 726 03 | | |
| Dividends applied to pay renewal premiums | 13, 141, 316 03 | | |
| Surrender values applied to pay renewal premiums | 60, 946 57 | | |
| Renewal premiums for deferred annuities | 33, 721 88 | | |
| Renewal premiums | | 67, 070, 322 86 | |
| Premium income | | $77, 522, 972 97 | |
| Premiums advanced during year under Soldiers' and Sailors' Civil Relief Act | | 5 53 | |
| Total | | | $77, 522, 978 50 |
| Consideration for supplementary contracts involving life contingencies | | | 80, 172 86 |
| Consideration for supplementary contracts not involving life contingencies | | | 1, 665, 881 76 |
| Dividends left with company to accumulate at interest | | | 131, 308 56 |
| Interest on mortgage loans | | $11, 575, 945 26 | |
| Interest on bonds and dividends on stocks | | 7, 548, 292 03 | |
| Interest on premium notes, policy loans or liens | | 3, 830, 927 22 | |
| Interest on deposits | | 220, 796 17 | |
| Interest on other debts due the company | | 63, 738 41 | |
| Rents—including $325,698.00 for company's occupancy of its own buildings | | 438, 169 12 | |
| Total interest and rents | | | 23, 677, 868 21 |
| From other sources, viz: Federal income tax withheld at the source, $12.35; remittances in advance of agents' reports, December 31, 1921, $88,144.44; conscience money, $700.00 | | | 88, 856 79 |
| Profit on sale or maturity of ledger assets | | | 24, 299 29 |
| Increase in book value of ledger assets | | | 329, 044 94 |
| Total income | | | $103, 520, 410 91 |
| Total | | | $561, 652, 413 50 |

### DISBURSEMENTS.

| | | |
|---|---|---|
| Death claims and additions | $18, 250, 475 07 | |
| Matured endowments and additions | 7, 934, 586 01 | |
| Total and permanent disability claims | 4, 162 14 | |
| Total death claims and endowments | | $26, 189, 223 22 |
| Annuities involving life contingencies | | 247, 203 76 |
| Surrender values paid in cash, or applied in liquidation of loans or notes | | 9, 520, 594 33 |
| Surrender values applied to pay new and renewal premiums | | 60, 946 57 |
| Dividends paid policyholders in cash, or applied in liquidation of loans or notes | | 2, 192, 612 25 |
| Dividends applied to pay renewal premiums | | 13, 141, 316 03 |
| Dividends applied to purchase paid-up additions and annuities | | 2, 427, 162 59 |
| Dividends left with the company to accumulate at interest | | 131, 308 56 |
| (Total paid policyholders | $53, 910, 367 31) | |
| Expense of investigation and settlement of policy claims, including legal expenses | | 6, 433 13 |
| Supplementary contracts not involving life contingencies | | 857, 967 20 |
| Dividends with interest, held on deposit surrendered during the year | | 59, 386 40 |
| Commissions to agents, first year, $3,830,541.85; renewal, $4,744,931.40; annuities (original), $41.45; (renewal), $674.44 | | 8, 576, 189 14 |
| Agency supervision and traveling expenses of supervisors | | 6, 693 76 |
| Medical examiners' fees and inspection of risks | | 374, 621 90 |
| Salaries and all other compensation of officers and home office employees | | 1, 452, 717 56 |
| Rent | | 325, 698 00 |
| Advertising, printing, stationery, postage, telegraph, telephone, express and exchange | | 321, 348 24 |
| Legal expense | | 690 64 |
| Furniture, fixtures and safes | | 35, 470 53 |
| Repairs and expenses (other than taxes) on real estate | | 275, 797 02 |
| Taxes on real estate | | 27, 181 44 |
| State taxes on premiums | | 947, 257 93 |

DISBURSEMENTS—Concluded.

| | |
|---|---|
| Insurance department licenses and fees | $ 40,248 68 |
| Federal taxes | 438,345 01 |
| All other licenses, fees and taxes: State annual license tax, $582,551.19; State tax on policy reserves, $39,418.90; publishing statement as required by lay, $1,414.59; local licenses and taxes on premiums, $7,740.58; federal income tax withheld at the source, $5.24 | 631,130 50 |
| Other disbursements, viz: Mortgage loan and bond investment expense, $200,159.11; traveling expenses, $14,921.74; examination and audit of accounts, $7,123.00; fidelity bond and insurance premiums, $1,072.39; legislative expenses, $2,461.49; expense of trustees' election, $156.48; restaurant, $62,367.38; pensions, $17,073.00; miscellaneous interest payments, $1,505.71; remittances in advance of agents' reports December 31, 1920, allocated in 1921, $213,965.11; amount received on fire loss held in suspense December 31, 1920 disbursed in 1921, $10,000.00 | 530,805 41 |
| Loss on sale or maturity of ledger assets | 17,062 95 |
| Decrease in book value of ledger assets | 922,881 73 |
| Total disbursements | $69,758,294 48 |
| Balance | $491,894,119 02 |

LEDGER ASSETS.

| | |
|---|---|
| Book value of real estate | $ 2,918,876 95 |
| Mortgage loans on real estate | 224,503,561 88 |
| Premiums advanced under Soldiers' and Sailors' Civil Relief Act | 252 12 |
| Loans on company's policies assigned as collateral | 76,182,737 49 |
| Premium notes on policies in force | 2,382,854 52 |
| Book value of bonds and stocks | 182,121,766 05 |
| Cash in office | 9,659 74 |
| Deposits in trust companies and banks on interest | 3,753,887 36 |
| Agents' balances | 20,522 91 |
| Total ledger assets | $491,894,119 02 |

NON-LEDGER ASSETS.

| | | | |
|---|---|---|---|
| Interest due and accrued on mortgages | | $3,253,590 78 | |
| Interest due and accrued on bonds | | 2,843,022 41 | |
| Interest due and accrued on premium notes, loans or liens | | 2,383,897 78 | |
| Interest due and accrued on other assets | | 6,009 18 | |
| Rents due and accrued on company's property | | 3,044 17 | |
| | | | 8,489,564 32 |
| | New business. | Renewals. | |
| Net uncollected and deferred premiums (paid for basis) | $776,356 45 | $6,792,303 35 | 7,568,659 80 |
| Gross assets | | | $507,952,343 14 |

DEDUCT ASSETS NOT ADMITTED.

| | | |
|---|---|---|
| Agents' debit balances | $ 20,522 91 | |
| Premium notes, policy loans and other policy assets in excess of net value and of other policy liabilities on individual policies | 15,002 58 | |
| Overdue and accrued interest on bonds in default | 275,208 33 | |
| Book value over amortized value of bonds and market value of stocks and bonds not amortized | 555,915 00 | |
| Total | | 866,648 82 |
| Admitted assets | | $507,085,694 32 |

LIABILITIES.

| | | |
|---|---|---|
| Net present value of outstanding policies computed by the Wisconsin Insurance Department | $423,096,712 00 | |
| Same for dividend additions | 19,543,330 00 | |
| Same for annuities | 2,485,207 00 | |
| Total | | $445,125,249 00 |
| Extra reserve for total and permanent disability benefits and for additional accidental death benefits included in life policies, less re-insurance | | 66,908 00 |
| Present value of supplementary contracts not involving life contingencies | | 10,879,417 00 |
| Present value of amounts incurred but not yet due for total and permanent disability benefits | | 26,820 00 |
| Surrender values claimable on policies cancelled | | 8,856 23 |
| Death losses due and unpaid | $ 16,518 68 | |
| Death losses in process of adjustment | 182,833 62 | |
| Death losses reported for which no proofs have been received | 555,209 93 | |
| Reserve for net death losses incurred but unreported | 456,262 00 | |
| Matured endowments due and unpaid | 128,409 25 | |
| Death losses and other policy claims resisted | 74,545 25 | |
| Total and permanent disability benefits and additional accidental death benefits | 198 00 | |
| Annuity claims, involving life contingencies, due and unpaid | 6,460 66 | |
| Total policy claims | | 1,420,437 39 |

LIABILITIES—Concluded.

| | |
|---|---|
| Due and unpaid on supplementary contracts not involving life contingencies | $ 98,453 76 |
| Dividends left with the company to accumulate at interest | 439,239 79 |
| Gross premiums paid in advance, including surrender values so applied, less discount, if any | 47,125 33 |
| Unearned interest and rent paid in advance | 576 75 |
| Commissions due agents on premium notes, when paid | 17,946 66 |
| Commissions to agents due or accrued | 57,515 70 |
| Cost of collection on uncollected and deferred premiums in excess of loading | 250,349 74 |
| Salaries, rents, office expenses, bills, and accounts due or accrued | 45,825 80 |
| Medical examiners' and legal fees due or accrued | 45,262 00 |
| Estimated amount hereafter payable for federal, state and other taxes based upon the business of the year of this statement | 2,246,486 45 |
| Dividends or other profits due policyholders | 920,516 63 |
| Dividends declared on or apportioned to annual dividend policies payable to policyholders during 1922 for period to December 31, 1922 | 19,126,000 00 |
| Dividends declared on or apportioned to deferred dividend policies payable to policyholders during 1922 for period to December 31, 1922 | 131,188 63 |
| Amounts set apart, apportioned, provisionally ascertained, calculated, declared or held awaiting apportionment upon deferred dividend policies | 507,603 00 |
| Reserve or surplus funds not otherwise included in liabilities, viz: Reserve for taxes unadjusted, $700,000.00; reserve for contingencies, $24,835,753.67 | 25,535,753 67 |
| Other liabilities, viz: Federal income tax withheld at the source, $12.35; remittances in advance of agents' reports, $88,144.44 | 88,156 79 |
| Total | $507,085,694 32 |

EXHIBIT OF POLICIES—ORDINARY.

ALL BUSINESS PAID FOR.

| | Number. | Amount. | Number. | Amount. |
|---|---|---|---|---|
| Policies in force December 31, 1920 | | | 729,715 | $2,196,673,032 00 |
| Policies issued, revived, and increased during the year | | | 65,691 | 267,911,313 00 |
| Total | | | 795,406 | $2,464,584,345 00 |
| Deduct policies which have ceased to be in force during the year— | | | | |
| By death | 5,613 | $18,153,939 00 | | |
| By maturity | 3,764 | 7,870,917 00 | | |
| By expiry | 4,025 | 11,489,369 00 | | |
| By surrender | 7,980 | 23,806,852 00 | | |
| By lapse | 14,326 | 50,381,203 00 | | |
| By decrease | 95 | 2,431,767 00 | | |
| Total | | | 35,803 | 114,134,047 00 |
| Total policies in force December 31, 1921 | | | 759,603 | $2,350,450,298 00 |

BUSINESS IN ILLINOIS—ORDINARY.

| | Number. | Amount. |
|---|---|---|
| Policies in force December 31, 1920 | 71,270 | $234,951,098 00 |
| Policies issued during the year | 7,882 | 31,764,447 00 |
| Total | 79,152 | $266,715,545 00 |
| Deduct policies ceased to be in force | 3,423 | 12,018,318 00 |
| Policies in force December 31, 1921 | 75,729 | $254,697,227 00 |
| Losses and claims unpaid December 31, 1920 | 25 | $ 43,523 33 |
| Losses and claims incurred during the year | 822 | 2,726,377 96 |
| Total | 847 | $2,769,901 29 |
| Losses and claims settled during the year | 807 | 2,609,270 54 |
| Losses and claims unpaid December 31, 1921 | 40 | $160,630 75 |
| Premiums received | | $8,185,644 54 |

GAIN AND LOSS EXHIBIT.

INSURANCE EXHIBIT.

| | | Gain in surplus. | Loss in surplus. |
|---|---|---|---|
| Loading on actual premiums of the year (averaging 20.40 per cent of the gross premiums) | $15,998,378 05 | | |
| Insurance expenses incurred during the year | 13,741,388 39 | | |
| Gain from loading | | $2,256,989 66 | |
| Interest earned during the year | $24,962,542 48 | | |
| Investment expenses incurred during the year | 1,181,109 60 | | |
| Net income from investments | $23,781,432 88 | | |
| Interest required to maintain reserve | 14,262,120 62 | | |
| Gain from interest | | 9,519,312 26 | |

GAIN AND LOSS EXHIBIT—Concluded.

INSURANCE EXHIBIT.

| | | Gain in surplus. | Loss in surplus. |
|---|---|---|---|
| Expected mortality on net amount at risk | $24,090,441 75 | | |
| Actual mortality on net amount at risk | 11,496,236 29 | | |
| Gain from mortality | | $12,594,205 46 | |
| Expected disbursements to annuitants | $173,905 74 | | |
| Net actual annuity claims incurred | 176,234 59 | | |
| Loss from annuities | | | $ 2,328 85 |
| Total gain during the year from surrendered and lapsed policies | | 675,780 90 | |
| Decrease in surplus on dividend account | | | 18,810,773 82 |
| Increase in special funds, and special reserves during the year | | | 25,035,753 67 |
| Net to profit account | | 700 00 | |
| INVESTMENT EXHIBIT. | | | |
| Total gains from real estate | | 6,817 74 | |
| Total losses from real estate | | | 854,845 70 |
| Total gains from stocks and bonds | | 17,481 55 | |
| Total losses from stocks and bonds | | | 1,126,107 49 |
| Loss from assets not admitted | | | 21,873 97 |
| Net gain on account of total and permanent disability benefits or additional accidental death benefits included in life policies | | 25,987 13 | |
| Total gains and losses in surplus during the year | | $25,097,274 70 | $45,851,683 50 |
| Surplus December 31, 1920 | $20,754,408 80 | | |
| Decrease in surplus | | 20,754,408 80 | |
| Total | | $45,851,683 50 | $45,851,683 50 |

## NORTHWESTERN NATIONAL LIFE INSURANCE COMPANY.

Located at Corner Nicollet Avenue, Minneapolis, Minnesota; incorporated September 15, 1885; commenced business in Illinois October 23, 1919.

J. T. BAXTER, President. M. V. JENNESS, Secretary.

GEORGE A. BARR, Director of Trade and Commerce, Attorney for service at Springfield.

| | | | |
|---|---|---|---|
| Amount of ledger assets December 31, of previous year | | | $9,886,834 67 |

### INCOME.

| | | | |
|---|---|---|---|
| First year's premiums on original policies, less re-insurance | | $809,181 07 | |
| First year's premiums for total and permanent disability benefits | | 16,300 98 | |
| First year's premiums for additional accidental death benefits, less re-insurance | | 16,841 76 | |
| Surrender values to pay first year's premiums | | 85 08 | |
| Dividends applied to purchase paid-up additions and annuities | | 19,482 09 | |
| New premiums | | $ 861,890 98 | |
| Renewal premiums less re-insurance | $2,743,725 17 | | |
| Renewal premiums for total and permanent disability benefits | 40,951 31 | | |
| Renewal premiums for additional accidental death benefits, less re-insurance | 27,916 69 | | |
| Dividends applied to pay renewal premiums | 249,680 82 | | |
| Dividends applied to shorten the endowment or premium-paying period | 63,635 83 | | |
| Surrender values applied to pay renewal premiums | 623 56 | | |
| Renewal premiums | | 3,126,533 38 | |
| Premium income | | | $3,988,424 36 |
| Consideration for supplementary contracts not involving life contingencies | | | 8,087 50 |
| Dividends left with company to accumulate at interest | | | 17,971 98 |
| Interest on mortgage loans | | $349,236 16 | |
| Interest on bonds | | 41,001 60 | |
| Interest on premium notes, policy loans or liens | | 116,138 64 | |
| Interest on deposits | | 14,301 41 | |
| Interest on agents' debit balances | | 11,999 02 | |
| Rents | | 920 00 | |
| Total interest and rents | | | 533,596 83 |
| From other sources, viz: Reserve on re-insured policies deposited by re-insuring companies, $853.12; proceeds of judgment, $134.44; dividends, W. A. Swearingen, banker, Killduff, Iowa, $7.63 | | | 995 19 |
| Agents' balances previously charged off | | | 2,767 39 |
| Profit on sale or maturity of ledger assets | | | 2,089 70 |
| Total income | | | $4,553,932 95 |
| Total | | | $14,440,767 62 |

## DISBURSEMENTS.

| | | |
|---|---|---|
| Death claims and additions | $724,315 96 | |
| Matured endowments and additions | 17,199 00 | |
| Total and permanent disability claims and additional accidental death benefits | 35,072 80 | |
| Total death claims and endowments | | $776,587 76 |
| Annuities involving life contingencies | | 1,260 08 |
| Surrender values paid in cash, or applied in liquidation of loans or notes | | 220,754 91 |
| Surrender values applied to pay new and renewal premiums | | 708 64 |
| Dividends paid policyholders in cash, or applied in liquidation of loans or notes | | 50,231 50 |
| Dividends applied to pay renewal premiums | | 249,680 82 |
| Dividends applied to shorten the endowment or premium-paying period | | 63,635 83 |
| Dividends applied to purchase paid-up additions and annuities | | 19,482 09 |
| Dividends left with the company to accumulate at interest | | 17,971 98 |
| (Total paid policyholders | $1,400,313 61) | |
| Expense of investigation and settlement of policy claims, including legal expenses | | 4,292 69 |
| Supplementary contracts not involving life contingencies | | 2,111 83 |
| Dividends with interest, held on deposit surrendered during the year | | 7,321 66 |
| Commissions to agents, first year, $509,936.35; renewal, $197,200.82 | | 707,137 17 |
| Commuted renewal commissions | | 361 21 |
| Compensation of managers and agents not paid by commissions on new business | | 1,328 30 |
| Agency supervision and traveling expenses of supervisors | | 4,592 20 |
| Branch office expenses | | 46,682 36 |
| Medical examiners' fees and inspection of risks | | 55,317 52 |
| Salaries and all other compensation of officers and home office employees | | 203,136 33 |
| Rent | | 61,955 77 |
| Advertising, printing, stationery, postage, telegraph, telephone, express and exchange | | 56,381 13 |
| Legal expense | | 132 89 |
| Furniture, fixtures and safes | | 13,541 46 |
| Repairs and expenses (other than taxes) on real estate | | 157 59 |
| State taxes on premiums | | 82,268 24 |
| Insurance department licenses and fees | | 5,342 08 |
| Federal taxes | | 20,594 66 |
| All other licenses, fees and taxes | | 24,352 93 |
| Other disbursements, viz: Interest on renewal commissions, $772.84; interest on deposits paid re-insuring companies, $269.98; investment expense, $32,369.44; discount, $260.70; office supplies, $6,391.03; interest on part payment employees' bonds, $6.74; restaurant, $10,200.71; protest fees, $148.83; equipment repairs, $844.95; organization dues, $1,147.87; subscriptions to magazines, $547.76; sundry supplies, $387.32; medical impairment services, $3,987.55; sundry expense, $1,186.90; insurance, $1,274.54 | | 59,797 16 |
| Profit and loss | | 212 60 |
| Bills receivable charged off | | 269 83 |
| Agents' balances charged off | | 4,876 21 |
| Adjustment reserve, deposit Metropolitan Life Insurance Company | | 577 48 |
| Decrease in book value of ledger assets | | 95 20 |
| Total disbursements | | $2,763,150 11 |
| Balance | | $11,677,617 51 |

## LEDGER ASSETS.

| | |
|---|---|
| Book value of real estate | $ 72,418 05 |
| Mortgage loans on real estate | 8,211,902 00 |
| Loans on company's policies assigned as collateral | 2,002,789 64 |
| Premium notes on policies in force | 4,392 84 |
| Book value of bonds | 858,762 49 |
| Cash in office | 37,702 97 |
| Deposits in trust companies and banks on interest | 350,644 96 |
| Bills receivable | 100 00 |
| Agents' balances (debit, $153,626.98; credit, $13,397.68); net, $140,229.30; mortgage loan, tax certificates, $184.76; personal accounts, $330.00; less payments by employees for bonds, $1,839.50 | 138,904 56 |
| Total ledger assets | $11,677,617 51 |

### NON-LEDGER ASSETS.

| | | | |
|---|---|---|---|
| Interest due and accrued on mortgages | | $303,700 25 | |
| Interest accrued on bonds | | 7,652 74 | |
| Interest due on premium notes, loans or liens | | 4,648 16 | |
| Rents due on company's property | | 74 50 | |
| | | | 316,075 65 |
| | New business. | Renewals. | |
| Net uncollected and deferred premiums (paid for basis) | $18,758 17 | $511,520 06 | 530,278 23 |
| All other assets, viz: Reserve liens, $90,464.59; unearned premiums, fire and liability policies, $4,277.15 | | | 94,741 74 |
| Gross assets | | | $12,618,713 13 |

## LEDGER ASSETS—Concluded.

DEDUCT ASSETS NOT ADMITTED.

| | | |
|---|---|---|
| Agents' debit balances | $153,626 98 | |
| Cash advanced to or in hands of officers or agents | 330 00 | |
| Bills receivable | 100 00 | |
| Premium notes, policy loans and other policy assets in excess of net value and of other policy liabilities on individual policies | 3,632 16 | |
| Book value of bonds over market value | 1,655 48 | |
| Certificates of deposit past due on banks in hands of receivers | 8,443 86 | |
| Total | | $167,788 48 |
| Admitted assets | | $12,450,924 65 |

## LIABILITIES.

| | | |
|---|---|---|
| Net present value of outstanding policies computed by the Minnesota Insurance Department | $10,353,378 00 | |
| Same for dividend additions | 186,233 00 | |
| Same for annuities | 7,134 00 | |
| Total | $10,546,745 00 | |
| Deduct net value of risks re-insured | 111,730 00 | |
| Net reserve (paid for basis) | | $10,435,015 00 |
| Extra reserve for total and permanent disability benefits and for additional accidental death benefits included in life policies less re-insurance | | 82,219 00 |
| Present value of supplementary contracts not involving life contingencies | | 22,891 39 |
| Present value of amounts incurred but not yet due for total and permanent disability benefits | | 37,975 00 |
| Surrender values claimable on policies cancelled | | 17,045 49 |
| Death losses reported for which no proofs have been received | 52,052 34 | |
| Reserve for net death losses incurred but unreported | 12,500 00 | |
| Matured endowments due and unpaid | 912 00 | |
| Death losses and other policy claims resisted | 6,000 00 | |
| Total policy claims | | 71,464 34 |
| Dividends left with the company to accumulate at interest | | 64,548 07 |
| Gross premiums paid in advance, including surrender values so applied less discount, if any | | 29,553 82 |
| Unearned interest and rent paid in advance | | 49,877 66 |
| Commissions due agents on premium notes, when paid | | 329 46 |
| Salaries, rents, office expenses, bills and accounts due or accrued | | 8,000 00 |
| Medical examiners' fees due or accrued | | 6,500 00 |
| Estimated amount hereafter payable for federal, state and other taxes based upon the business of the year of this statement | | 100,000 00 |
| Dividends or other profits due policyholders | | 52,659 61 |
| Dividends declared on or apportioned to annual dividend policies payable to policyholders during 1922 for period to June 30, 1922 | | 252,251 81 |
| Dividends declared on or apportioned to deferred dividend policies payable to policyholders during 1922 for period to December 31, 1922 | | 14,856 30 |
| Amounts set apart, apportioned, provisionally ascertained, calculated, declared or held awaiting apportionment upon deferred dividend policies | | 54,344 43 |
| Special reserve | | 30,341 00 |
| Contingent fund | | 275,000 00 |
| Reserve deposited by re-insuring company | | 6,852 74 |
| Total | | $11,611,725 12 |
| Unassigned funds (surplus) | | 839,199 53 |
| Total | | $12,450,924 65 |

## EXHIBIT OF POLICIES—ORDINARY.

ALL BUSINESS PAID FOR.

| | Number. | Amount. | Number. | Amount. |
|---|---|---|---|---|
| Policies in force December 31, 1920 | | | 63,837 | $133,967,579 00 |
| Policies issued, revived and increased during the year | | | 16,499 | 42,208,639 00 |
| Total | | | 80,336 | $176,176,218 00 |
| Deduct policies which have ceased to be in force during the year— | | | | |
| By death | 394 | $ 753,597 00 | | |
| By maturity | 15 | 16,600 00 | | |
| By disability | 1 | 6,667 00 | | |
| By expiry | 130 | 239,167 00 | | |
| By surrender | 5,817 | 9,128,433 00 | | |
| By lapse | 8,863 | 24,904,012 00 | | |
| By decrease | -------- | 1,258,853 00 | | |
| Total | | | 15,220 | 36,307,329 00 |
| Total policies in force December 31, 1921 | | | 65,116 | $139,868,889 00 |
| Re-insured | | | | $5,124,689 00 |

## EXHIBIT OF POLICIES—GROUP INSURANCE.

ALL BUSINESS PAID FOR.

| | Number. | Amount. | Number. | Amount. |
|---|---|---|---|---|
| Policies in force December 31, 1920 | | | 10,530 | $12,735,249 00 |
| Policies issued, revived and increased during the year | | | 3,842 | 4,578,374 00 |
| Total | | | 14,372 | $17,313,623 00 |
| Deduct policies which have ceased to be in force during the year— | | | | |
| By death | 64 | $ 85,950 00 | | |
| By surrender | 4,456 | 4,649,855 00 | | |
| By decrease | -------- | 1,500 00 | | |
| Total | | | 4,520 | 4,737,305 00 |
| Total policies in force December 31, 1921 | | | 9,852 | $12,576,318 00 |
| Distribution of business in force at end of year—One year term | | | 9,852 | $12,576,318 00 |

## BUSINESS IN ILLINOIS—ORDINARY.

| | Number. | Amount. |
|---|---|---|
| Policies in force December 31, 1920 | 690 | $1,569,200 00 |
| Policies issued during the year | 65 | 313,314 00 |
| Total | 755 | $1,882,514 00 |
| Deduct policies ceased to be in force | 23 | 192,651 00 |
| Policies in force December 31, 1921 | 732 | $1,689,863 00 |
| Losses and claims unpaid December 31, 1920 | 1 | $ 500 00 |
| Losses and claims incurred during the year | 9 | 13,633 81 |
| Total | 10 | $14,133 81 |
| Losses and claims settled during the year | 9 | 12,883 81 |
| Losses and claims unpaid December 31, 1921 | 1 | $1,250 00 |
| Premiums received | | $64,317 99 |

## GAIN AND LOSS EXHIBIT.

INSURANCE EXHIBIT.

| | | Gain in surplus. | Loss in surplus. |
|---|---|---|---|
| Loading on actual premiums of the year (averaging 27 per cent of the gross premiums) | $1,104,735 15 | | |
| Insurance expenses incurred during the year | 1,361,369 22 | | |
| Loss from loading | | ------------- | $256,634 07 |
| Interest earned during the year | $634,590 97 | | |
| Investment expenses incurred during the year | 32,132 56 | | |
| Net income from investments | $602,458 41 | | |
| Interest required to maintain reserve | 373,256 00 | | |
| Gain from interest | | $229,202 41 | |
| Expected mortality on net amount at risk | $1,331,038 00 | | |
| Actual mortality on net amount at risk | 587,845 10 | | |
| Gain from mortality | | 743,192 90 | |
| Expected disbursements to annuitants | $1,260 08 | | |
| Net actual annuity claims incurred | 1,260 08 | | |
| Total gain during the year from surrendered and lapsed policies | | 121,013 28 | |
| Decrease in surplus on dividend account | | ------------- | 453,383 12 |
| Increase in special funds and special reserves during the year | | ------------- | 155,341 00 |
| Net to loss account | | ------------- | 340 36 |

INVESTMENT EXHIBIT.

| | | Gain in surplus. | Loss in surplus. |
|---|---|---|---|
| Total gains from bonds | | 8,070 42 | |
| Total losses from bonds | | ------------- | 95 20 |
| Loss from assets not admitted | | ------------- | 64,700 65 |
| Net gain on account of total and permanent disability benefits or additional accidental death benefits included in life policies | | 32,550 00 | |
| Total gains and losses in surplus during the year | | $1,134,029 01 | $930,494 40 |
| Surplus December 31, 1920 | $635,664 92 | | |
| Surplus December 31, 1921 | 839,199 53 | | |
| Increase in surplus | | ------------- | 203,534 61 |
| Total | | $1,134,029 01 | $1,134,029 01 |

## OLD LINE INSURANCE COMPANY.

Located at No. 204 South Eleventh Street, Lincoln, Nebraska; incorporated June 28, 1913; commenced business in Illinois April 1, 1920.

JOHN G. MAHER, President. E. P. MARTIN, Assistant Secretary.

GEORGE A. BARR, Director of Trade and Commerce, Attorney for service at Springfield.

### CAPITAL.

| | | | |
|---|---|---|---|
| Capital paid up | | $200,000 00 | |
| Amount of ledger assets December 31, of previous year | | | $671,675 03 |

### INCOME.

| | | | |
|---|---|---|---|
| First year's premiums on original policies, less re-insurance | | $142,428 61 | |
| First year's premiums for additional accidental death benefits, less re-insurance | | 280 95 | |
| Surrender values to pay first year's premiums | | 23 30 | |
| Surrender values applied to purchase paid-up insurance and annuities | | 357 50 | |
| New premiums | | $143,090 36 | |
| Renewal premiums less re-insurance | $274,085 75 | | |
| Renewal premiums for additional accidental death benefits, less re-insurance | 985 85 | | |
| Renewal premiums | | 275,071 60 | |
| Premium income | | | $418,161 96 |
| Interest on mortgage loans | | $10,235 86 | |
| Interest on bonds | | 1,557 37 | |
| Interest on premium notes, policy loans or liens | | 1,829 46 | |
| Interest on deposits | | 10,062 08 | |
| Interest on other debts due the company | | 864 68 | |
| Rents—including $900.00 for company's occupancy of its own buildings | | 2,890 23 | |
| Total interest and rents | | | 27,439 68 |
| From other sources, viz: War tax, $1,271.00; exchange and collection, $31.11; commission on mortgage loans, $57.35; discount on certificate of deposit, $3,158.35; miscellaneous income, $424.97; special suspense, $241.27 | | | 5,184 05 |
| Borrowed money (gross) | | | 7,500 00 |
| Agents' balances previously charged off | | | 348 59 |
| Increase in book value of ledger assets | | | 3,259 99 |
| Income, life department | | | $461,894 27 |
| Income, casualty department | | | 41,734 48 |
| Total income | | | $503,628 75 |
| Total | | | $1,175,303 78 |

### DISBURSEMENTS.

| | | | |
|---|---|---|---|
| Death claims | | $32,954 73 | |
| Total and permanent disability claims | | 250 00 | |
| Total death claims | | | $33,204 73 |
| Premium notes and liens voided by lapse | | | 31,857 96 |
| Surrender values paid in cash, or applied in liquidation of loans or notes | | | 1,090 68 |
| Surrender values applied to pay new and renewal premiums | | | 23 30 |
| Surrender values applied to purchase paid-up insurance and annuities | | | 357 50 |
| (Total paid policyholders | | $66,534 17) | |
| Expense of investigation and settlement of policy claims, including legal expenses | | | 510 95 |
| Commissions to agents, first year, $128,522.88; renewal, $21,969.07 | | | 150,491 95 |
| Agency supervision and traveling expenses of supervisors | | | 947 09 |
| Medical examiners' fees and inspection of risks | | | 10,154 24 |
| Salaries and all other compensation of officers and home office employees | | | 10,519 23 |
| Rent | | | 900 00 |
| Advertising, printing, stationery, postage, telegraph, telephone, express and exchange | | | 4,250 08 |
| Taxes on real estate | | | 959 38 |
| State taxes on premiums | | | 602 34 |
| Insurance department licenses and fees | | | 2,038 99 |
| Federal taxes | | | 127 50 |
| All other licenses, fees and taxes | | | 356 63 |
| Other disbursements, viz: Insurance premiums, $247.67; agents bonds, $5.00; miscellaneous, $949.50; actuarial expense, $950.10; decrease in suspense, $7,718.45 | | | 9,870 72 |
| Borrowed money repaid (gross) | | | 7,500 00 |
| Agents' balances charged off | | | 3,217 60 |
| Disbursements, life department | | | $268,980 87 |
| Disbursements, casualty department | | | 33,319 48 |
| Total disbursements | | | $302,300 35 |
| Balance | | | $873,003 43 |

## LEDGER ASSETS.

| | | |
|---|---|---|
| Book value of real estate | | $ 48,325 19 |
| Mortgage loans on real estate | | 292,034 85 |
| Loans on company's policies assigned as collateral | | 13,429 04 |
| Premium notes on policies in force | | 32,341 85 |
| Book value of bonds | | 77,871 20 |
| Cash in office | | 44 74 |
| Deposits in trust companies and banks not on interest | | 34,144 80 |
| Deposits in trust companies and banks on interest | | 346,031 63 |
| Bills receivable | | 13,843 17 |
| Agents' balances (debit, $5,097.42; credit, $628.44) | | 4,945 77 |
| Chattel mortgages, $3,545.81; furniture and fixtures, $1,775.23; casualty department, $4,670.15 | | 9,991 19 |
| Total ledger assets | | $873,003 43 |

### NON-LEDGER ASSETS.

| | | |
|---|---|---|
| Interest due and accrued on mortgages | $11,423 33 | |
| Interest accrued on bonds | 646 85 | |
| Interest accrued on premium notes, loans or liens | 435 11 | |
| Interest accrued on other assets | 5,364 75 | |
| | | 17,870 04 |
| Net uncollected and deferred premiums (paid for basis) renewals | | 15,196 60 |
| Gross assets | | $906,070 07 |

### DEDUCT ASSETS NOT ADMITTED.

| | | |
|---|---|---|
| Furniture, fixtures and safes | $ 1,775 23 | |
| Agents' debit balances | 5,097 42 | |
| Loans on personal security | 3,545 81 | |
| Bills receivable | 13,843 17 | |
| Premium notes, policy loans and other policy assets in excess of net value and of other policy liabilities on individual policies | 4,821 69 | |
| Premium notes on policies lapsed | 6,831 31 | |
| Book value of bonds over market value | 1,810 32 | |
| Total | | 37,724 95 |
| Admitted assets | | $868,345 12 |

## LIABILITIES.

| | | |
|---|---|---|
| Net present value of outstanding policies | $511,275 53 | |
| Deduct net value of risks re-insured | 4,253 70 | |
| Net reserve (paid for basis) | | $507,021 83 |
| Extra reserve for total and permanent disability benefits and for additional accidental death benefits included in life policies, less re-insurance | | 4,254 52 |
| Present value of amounts incurred but not yet due for total and permanent disability benefits | | 2,146 28 |
| Unearned interest and rent paid in advance | | 500 00 |
| Commissions due agents on premium notes, when paid | | 1,500 00 |
| Commissions to agents due or accrued | | 10,628 44 |
| Salaries, rents, office expenses, bills, and accounts due or accrued | | 443 35 |
| Medical examiners' fees due or accrued | | 741 00 |
| Estimated amount hereafter payable for federal, state and other taxes based upon the business of the year of this statement | | 5,000 00 |
| Dividends or other profits due policyholders | | 1,000 00 |
| Dividends declared on or apportioned to annual dividend policies payable to policyholders during 1922 for period to December 31, 1922 | | 3,000 00 |
| Mortality fluctuation fund | | 2,177 05 |
| Suspense | | 3,458 81 |
| Liabilities, casualty department | | 86,734 62 |
| Total | | $628,605 90 |
| Capital paid up | | 200,000 00 |
| Unassigned funds (surplus) | | 39,739 22 |
| Total | | $868,345 12 |

## EXHIBIT OF POLICIES—ORDINARY.

### ALL BUSINESS PAID FOR.

| | Number. | Amount. | Number. | Amount. |
|---|---|---|---|---|
| Policies in force December 31, 1920 | | | 5,486 | $13,457,500 00 |
| Policies issued, revived and increased during the year | | | 1,997 | 5,195,000 00 |
| Total | | | 7,483 | $18,652,500 00 |
| Deduct policies which have ceased to be in force during the year— | | | | |
| By death | 15 | $ 42,000 00 | | |
| By expiry | 11 | 27,000 00 | | |
| By surrender | 26 | 36,500 00 | | |

## EXHIBIT OF POLICIES—ORDINARY—Concluded.

ALL BUSINESS PAID FOR.

| | Number. | Amount. | Number. | Amount. |
|---|---|---|---|---|
| Deduct policies which have ceased to be in force during the year— | | | | |
| By lapse | 2,154 | $6,193,142 50 | | |
| By decrease | | 52,000 00 | | |
| Total | | | 2,206 | $6,350,642 50 |
| Total policies in force December 31, 1921 | | | 5,277 | $12,301,857 30 |
| Re-insured | | | 185 | $890,121 85 |

## BUSINESS IN ILLINOIS—ORDINARY.

| | Number. | Amount. |
|---|---|---|
| Policies in force December 31, 1920 | 11 | $17,000 00 |
| Policies issued during the year | 14 | 29,000 00 |
| Policies in force December 31, 1921 | 25 | $46,000 00 |
| Premiums received | | $697 11 |

## GAIN AND LOSS EXHIBIT.

INSURANCE EXHIBIT.

| | | Gain in surplus. | Loss in surplus. |
|---|---|---|---|
| Loading on actual premiums of the year (averaging 30.9 per cent of the gross premiums) | $127,813 03 | | |
| Insurance expenses incurred during the year | 188,522 97 | | |
| Loss from loading | | | $60,709 94 |
| Interest earned during the year | $36,710 96 | | |
| Investment expenses incurred during the year | 959 38 | | |
| Net income from investments | $35,751 58 | | |
| Interest required to maintain reserve | 15,811 60 | | |
| Gain from interest | | $19,939 98 | |
| Expected mortality on net amount at risk | $92,061 26 | | |
| Actual mortality on net amount at risk | 27,511 02 | | |
| Gain from mortality | | 64,550 24 | |
| Total gain during the year from surrendered and lapsed policies | | 5,840 29 | |
| Decrease in surplus on dividend account | | | 4,000 00 |
| Decrease in special funds and special reserves during the year | | 12,822 95 | |

INVESTMENT EXHIBIT.

| | | Gain in surplus. | Loss in surplus. |
|---|---|---|---|
| Total gains from bonds | | 3,259 99 | |
| Total losses from bonds | | | 1,810 32 |
| Loss from assets not admitted | | | 1,194 47 |
| Net gain on account of total and permanent disability benefits or additional accidental death benefits included in life policies | | 532 20 | |
| Gain from casualty department | | 35,531 96 | |
| Gain from war tax, $1,271.00; discount on mortgage and certificate of deposit, $3,215.70; miscellaneous, $456.08 | | 4,942 78 | |
| Loss on account of use of Illinois standard of valuation | | | 67,822 95 |
| Balance unaccounted for | | 942 34 | |
| Total gains and losses in surplus during the year | | $148,362 73 | $135,537 68 |
| Surplus December 31, 1920 | $26,914 17 | | |
| Surplus December 31, 1921 | 39,739 22 | | |
| Increase in surplus | | | 12,825 05 |
| Total | | $148,362 73 | $148,362 73 |

---

## THE OLD LINE LIFE INSURANCE COMPANY OF AMERICA.

Located at No. 425 East Water Street, Milwaukee, Wisconsin; incorporated February 19, 1910; commenced business in Illinois, life, August 8, 1911; casualty, June 27, 1913.

RUPERT F. FRY, President. JOHN E. REILLY, Secretary.

GEORGE A. BARR, Director of Trade and Commerce, Attorney for service at Springfield.

HOWARD G. GRAY, Chicago, Attorney for service.

### CAPITAL.

| | | |
|---|---|---|
| Capital paid up | $672,635 00 | |
| Amount of ledger assets December 31, of previous year | | $2,901,949 52 |

## INCOME.

| | | | |
|---|---|---|---|
| First year's premiums on original policies, less re-insurance | | $307,222 41 | |
| First year's premiums for total and permanent disability benefits | | 949 63 | |
| First year's premiums for additional accidental death benefits, less re-insurance | | 1,552 37 | |
| New premiums | | $309,724 41 | |
| Renewal premiums less re-insurance | $875,746 78 | | |
| Renewal premiums for total and permanent disability benefits | 11,777 55 | | |
| Renewal premiums for additional accidental death benefits | 22,878 78 | | |
| Renewal premiums | | 910,403 11 | |
| Premium income | | | $1,220,127 52 |
| Consideration for supplementary contracts not involving life contingencies | | | 27,065 00 |
| Interest on mortgage loans | | $86,764 85 | |
| Interest on bonds and dividends on stocks | | 50,549 61 | |
| Interest on premium notes, policy loans or liens | | 8,514 53 | |
| Interest on deposits | | 2,457 12 | |
| Total interest | | | 148,286 11 |
| From other sources, viz: Commissions on investments, $437.44; miscellaneous, $9.71 | | | 447 15 |
| Agents' balances previously charged off | | | 38 99 |
| Profit on sale or maturity of ledger assets | | | 6,307 76 |
| Increase in book value of ledger assets | | | 1,127 23 |
| Life department | | | $1,403,399 76 |
| Casualty department | | | 95,991 91 |
| Total income | | | $1,499,391 67 |
| Total | | | $4,401,341 19 |

## DISBURSEMENTS.

| | | |
|---|---|---|
| Death claims | $157,380 22 | |
| Matured endowments | 4,704 00 | |
| Total and permanent disability claims and additional accidental death benefits | 9,110 97 | |
| Total death claims and endowments | | $171,195 19 |
| Premium notes and liens voided by lapse, less $2,955.43 restorations | | 5,276 35 |
| Surrender values paid in cash, or applied in liquidation of loans or notes | | 30,934 78 |
| (Total paid policyholders | $207,406 32) | |
| Expense of investigation and settlement of policy claims | | 363 65 |
| Supplementary contracts not involving life contingencies | | 3,820 16 |
| Dividends to stockholders | | 67,263 50 |
| Commissions to agents, first year, $178,649.47; renewal, $39,587.84 | | 218,237 31 |
| Compensation of managers and agents not paid by commissions on new business | | 13,899 28 |
| Branch office expenses | | 349 58 |
| Medical examiners' fees and inspection of risks | | 27,272 43 |
| Salaries and all other compensation of officers and home office employees | | 61,295 01 |
| Rent | | 5,538 33 |
| Advertising, printing, stationery, postage, telegraph, telephone, express and exchange | | 31,639 43 |
| Legal expense | | 120 50 |
| Furniture, fixtures and safes | | 1,639 98 |
| Repairs and expenses (other than taxes) on real estate | | 70 00 |
| Taxes on real estate | | 118 52 |
| State taxes on premiums | | 5,602 44 |
| Insurance department licenses and fees | | 940 94 |
| Federal taxes | | 14,625 31 |
| All other licenses, fees and taxes | | 452 55 |
| Other disbursements, viz: General travel expenses, $585.88; office expense, $1,381.09; investment expense, $1,259.93; auditing fees, $337.50; miscellaneous, $35.88 | | 3,600 28 |
| Agents' balances charged off | | 1,172 33 |
| Loss on sale or maturity of ledger assets | | 10,254 41 |
| Decrease in book value of ledger assets | | 17,400 31 |
| Life department | | $693,082 57 |
| Casualty department | | 88,049 89 |
| Total disbursements | | $781,132 46 |
| Balance | | $3,620,208 73 |

## LEDGER ASSETS.

| | |
|---|---|
| Book value of real estate | $ 8,000 00 |
| Mortgage loans on real estate | 2,178,190 71 |
| Loans on company's policies assigned as collateral | 180,930 31 |
| Premium notes on policies in force | 11,982 00 |
| Book value of bonds and stocks | 1,059,588 13 |

LEDGER ASSETS—Concluded.

| | | |
|---|---|---|
| Cash in office | | $ 300 00 |
| Deposits in trust companies and banks not on interest | | 6,200 00 |
| Deposits in trust companies and banks on interest | | 124,658 56 |
| Agents' balances (debit, $8,258.31; credit, $4,531.58) | | 3,726 73 |
| Furniture and fixtures | | 14,759 84 |
| Casualty department | | 31,872 45 |
| Total ledger assets | | $3,620,208 73 |

NON-LEDGER ASSETS.

| | | | |
|---|---|---|---|
| Interest due and accrued on mortgages | | $72,662 42 | |
| Interest due and accrued on bonds | | 10,843 11 | |
| Interest accrued on premium notes, loans or liens | | 1,185 11 | |
| Interest accrued on other assets | | 310 71 | |
| | | | 85,001 35 |
| Market value of bonds and stocks over book value | | | 9,633 24 |
| | New business. | Renewals. | |
| Net uncollected and deferred premiums (paid for basis) | $5,913 99 | $84,375 83 | 90,289 82 |
| Casualty department | | | 257 92 |
| Gross assets | | | $3,805,391 06 |

DEDUCT ASSETS NOT ADMITTED.

| | | |
|---|---|---|
| Furniture, fixtures and safes | $14,759 84 | |
| Agents' debit balances | 8,258 31 | |
| Casualty department | 1,508 16 | |
| Total | | 24,526 31 |
| Admitted assets | | $3,780,864 75 |

LIABILITIES.

| | | |
|---|---|---|
| Net present value of outstanding policies computed by the Wisconsin Insurance Department | $2,662,302 14 | |
| Deduct net value of risks re-insured | 22,539 67 | |
| Net reserve (paid for basis) | | $2,639,762 47 |
| Extra reserve for total and permanent disability benefits and for additional accidental death benefits included in life policies | | 43,429 90 |
| Present value of supplementary contracts not involving life contingencies | | 45,008 31 |
| Death losses reported for which no proofs have been received | | 11,000 00 |
| Gross premiums paid in advance, including surrender values so applied, less discount, if any | | 5,016 10 |
| Unearned interest and rent paid in advance | | 2,683 06 |
| Commissions due agents on premium notes, when paid | | 600 00 |
| Salaries, rents, office expenses, bills and accounts due or accrued | | 5,547 34 |
| Medical examiners' and legal fees due or accrued | | 2,458 00 |
| Estimated amount hereafter payable for federal, state and other taxes based upon the business of the year of this statement | | 21,006 64 |
| Casualty department | | 26,998 78 |
| Total | | $2,803,510 60 |
| Capital paid up | | 672,635 00 |
| Unassigned funds (surplus) | | 304,719 15 |
| Total | | $3,780,864 75 |

EXHIBIT OF POLICIES—ORDINARY.

ALL BUSINESS PAID FOR.

| | | | Number. | Amount. |
|---|---|---|---|---|
| Policies in force December 31, 1920 | | | 16,351 | $32,988,549 13 |
| Policies issued, revived and increased during the year | | | 5,797 | 13,508,325 00 |
| Total | | | 22,148 | $46,496,874 13 |
| Deduct policies which have ceased to be in force during the year— | Number. | Amount. | | |
| By death | 81 | $ 170,565 00 | | |
| By maturity | 5 | 4,704 00 | | |
| By expiry | 70 | 230,933 00 | | |
| By surrender | 156 | 486,330 00 | | |
| By lapse | 2,912 | 6,902,141 38 | | |
| By decrease | -------- | 134,205 50 | | |
| Total | | | 3,224 | 7,928,878 88 |
| Total policies in force December 31, 1921 | | | 18,924 | $38,567,995 25 |
| Re-insured | | | 270 | $1,620,114 59 |

BUSINESS IN ILLINOIS—ORDINARY.

| | Number. | Amount. |
|---|---|---|
| Policies in force December 31, 1920 | 778 | $1,838,767 26 |
| Policies issued during the year | 311 | 643,884 00 |
| Total | 1,089 | $2,482,651 26 |
| Deduct policies ceased to be in force | 109 | 295,590 00 |
| Policies in force December 31, 1921 | 980 | $2,187,061 26 |
| Losses and claims incurred during the year | 4 | $3,434 00 |
| Losses and claims settled during the year | 4 | 3,434 00 |
| Premiums received | | $56,747 85 |

GAIN AND LOSS EXHIBIT.

INSURANCE EXHIBIT.

| | | Gain in surplus. | Loss in surplus. |
|---|---|---|---|
| Loading on actual premiums of the year (averaging 19.19 per cent of the gross premiums) | $232,080 79 | | |
| Insurance expenses incurred during the year | 390,960 30 | | |
| Loss from loading | | | $158,879 51 |
| Interest earned during the year | $179,692 02 | | |
| Investment expenses incurred during the year | 8,275 94 | | |
| Net income from investments | $171,416 08 | | |
| Interest required to maintain reserve | 85,329 46 | | |
| Gain from interest | | $ 86,086 62 | |
| Expected mortality on net amount at risk | $339,277 11 | | |
| Actual mortality on net amount at risk | 142,752 81 | | |
| Gain from mortality | | 196,524 30 | |
| Total gain during the year from surrendered and lapsed policies | | 21,296 63 | |
| Dividends paid stockholders | | | 67,263 50 |
| Net to loss account | | | 10,094 02 |

INVESTMENT EXHIBIT.

| | | Gain in surplus. | Loss in surplus. |
|---|---|---|---|
| Total gains from real estate | | 386 39 | |
| Total gains from stocks and bonds | | 15,941 00 | |
| Total losses from stocks and bonds | | | 27,654 72 |
| Gain contracts not involving life contingencies | | 7,859 50 | |
| Loss from assets not admitted | | | 5,634 43 |
| Net gain on account of total and permanent disability benefits or additional accidental death benefits included in life policies | | 9,396 23 | |
| Gain from casualty department | | 10,187 91 | |
| Total gains and losses in surplus during the year | | $347,678 58 | $269,526 18 |
| Surplus December 31, 1920 | $226,566 75 | | |
| Surplus December 31, 1921 | 304,719 15 | | |
| Increase in surplus | | | 78,152 40 |
| Total | | $347,678 58 | $347,678 58 |

## THE PACIFIC MUTUAL LIFE INSURANCE COMPANY OF CALIFORNIA.

Located at No. 501 West Sixth Street, Los Angeles, California; incorporated December 28, 1867; commenced business in Illinois May 11, 1886.

GEORGE I. COCHRAN, President. S. F. McCLUNG, Secretary.

GEORGE A. BARR, Director of Trade and Commerce, Attorney for service at Springfield.

JENS SMITH, Chicago, Attorney for service.

CAPITAL.

| | | |
|---|---|---|
| Capital paid up | $1,500,000 00 | |
| Amount of ledger assets December 31, of previous year | | $52,415,932 18 |

INCOME.

| | |
|---|---|
| First year's premiums on original policies, less re-insurance | $2,652,600 32 |
| First year's premiums for total and permanent disability benefits, less re-insurance | 16,050 26 |
| Surrender values to pay first year's premiums | 1,382 87 |
| Dividends applied to purchase paid-up additions and annuities | 316,560 19 |
| Surrender values applied to purchase paid-up insurance and annuities | 3,351 00 |
| Consideration for original annuities involving life contingencies | 55,926 00 |
| New premiums | $ 3,045,870 64 |

INCOME—Concluded.

| | | | |
|---|---|---|---|
| Renewal premiums less re-insurance | $9,512,211 60 | | |
| Renewal premiums for total and permanent disability benefits, less re-insurance | 81,343 50 | | |
| Dividends applied to pay renewal premiums | 583,902 44 | | |
| Surrender values applied to pay renewal premiums | 55,243 04 | | |
| Renewal premiums for deferred annuities | 233 42 | | |
| Renewal premiums | | $10,232,934 00 | |
| Premium income | | | $13,278,804 64 |
| Consideration for supplementary contracts involving life contingencies | | | 105,630 85 |
| Consideration for supplementary contracts not involving life contingencies | | | 24,961 68 |
| Dividends left wih company to accumulate at interest | | | 107,159 26 |
| Interest on mortgage loans | | $1,531,701 56 | |
| Interest on collateral loans | | 346,872 40 | |
| Interest on bonds | | 457,521 53 | |
| Interest on premium notes, policy loans or liens | | 644,698 85 | |
| Interest on deposits | | 51,173 16 | |
| Interest on other debts due the company | | 7,165 29 | |
| Discount on claims paid in advance | | 168 03 | |
| Rents—including $151,800.00 for company's occupancy of its own buildings | | 314,467 03 | |
| Total interest and rents | | | 3,353,767 85 |
| From other sources, viz: Recovered from collateral loans, $2,789.66; recovered from suspended banks, $105.23; recovered from street improvement bonds, $14.04; refund federal taxes, $3,497.52; sale of Sacramento & Northern Railroad stock, $18,658.40; profit and loss, $1,255.44 | | | 26,320 29 |
| Agents' balances previously charged off | | | 3,010 00 |
| Profit on sale or maturity of ledger assets | | | 8,272 88 |
| Increase in book value of ledger assets | | | 15,969 07 |
| Total income | | | $16,923,896 52 |
| Total | | | $69,339,828 70 |

DISBURSEMENTS.

| | | |
|---|---|---|
| Death claims and additions | $2,395,164 90 | |
| Matured endowments and additions | 906,257 00 | |
| Total and permanent disability claims and additional accidental death benefits | 58,268 35 | |
| Total death claims and endowments | | $3,359,690 25 |
| Annuities involving life contingencies | | 46,628 47 |
| Premium notes and liens voided by lapse | | 150 03 |
| Surrender values paid in cash, or applied in liquidation of loans or notes | | 1,522,304 37 |
| Surrender values applied to pay new and renewal premiums | | 56,625 91 |
| Surrender values applied to purchase paid-up insurance and annuities | | 3,351 00 |
| Dividends paid policyholders in cash, or applied in liquidation of loans or notes | | 322,957 20 |
| Dividends applied to pay renewal premiums | | 583,902 44 |
| Dividends applied to purchase paid-up additions and annuities | | 316,560 19 |
| Dividends left with the company to accumulate at interest | | 107,159 26 |
| (Total paid policyholders | $6,319,329 12) | |
| Expense of investigation and settlement of policy claims, including legal expenses | | 10,379 82 |
| Supplementary contracts not involving life contingencies | | 42,218 57 |
| Dividends with interest, held on deposit surrendered during the year | | 26,266 62 |
| Dividends to stockholders | | 73,711 01 |
| Commissions to agents, first year, $1,690,374.90; renewal, $700,764.16; annuities (original), $2,698.79; (renewal), $6.56 | | 2,393,844 41 |
| Compensation of managers and agents not paid by commissions on new business | | 50,169 38 |
| Agency supervision and traveling expenses of supervisors | | 18,118 27 |
| Medical examiners' fees and inspection of risks | | 138,040 49 |
| Salaries and all other compensation of officers and home office employees | | 643,024 79 |
| Rent | | 142,857 03 |
| Advertising, printing, stationery, postage, telegraph, telephone, express and exchange | | 192,761 09 |
| Legal expense | | 1,086 68 |
| Furniture, fixtures and safes | | 69,493 61 |
| Repairs and expenses (other than taxes) on real estate | | 141,697 57 |
| Taxes on real estate | | 47,844 84 |
| State taxes on premiums | | 220,250 62 |
| Insurance department licenses and fees | | 9,739 99 |
| Federal taxes | | 77,200 95 |
| All other licenses, fees and taxes | | 9,362 79 |
| Other disbursements, viz: Contribution to the Association of Life Insurance Presidents, $1,614.76; home office traveling expenses, $29,519.84; expense, auditing committee, $5,322.04; miscellaneous, $63,117.95; commission on sale of real estate, $406.00; commission on leasing new building, $15,000.00 mortgage loan expense, $16,561.55; disbursement on account of Fontana investment, $141,000.00; renewal bonus, $14,243.15; collateral loans written off, $18,500.00; assessment widening Fifth St., $5,000.00; suspended bank balances written off, $8,000.00 | | 318,285 29 |

DISBURSEMENTS—Concluded.

| | | |
|---|---|---|
| Loss on sale or maturity of ledger assets | | $27,826 13 |
| Decrease in book value of ledger assets | | 2,315 26 |
| Total disbursements | | $10,975,824 33 |
| Balance | | $58,364,004 37 |

## LEDGER ASSETS.

| | | |
|---|---|---|
| Book value of real estate | | $ 6,812,931 82 |
| Mortgage loans on real estate | | 24,019,442 79 |
| Loans secured by collaterals | | 5,226,711 53 |
| Loans on company's policies assigned as collateral | | 9,945,890 31 |
| Premium notes and liens on policies in force | | 1,309,773 17 |
| Book value of bonds | | 8,810,968 22 |
| Cash in office | | 4,500 00 |
| Deposits in trust companies and banks not on interest | | 241,342 06 |
| Deposits in trust companies and banks on interest | | 1,966,896 87 |
| Agents' balances (debit, $37,211.55; credit, $11,663.95) net | | 25,547 60 |
| Total ledger assets | | $58,364,004 37 |

NON-LEDGER ASSETS.

| | | | |
|---|---|---|---|
| Interest due and accrued on mortgages | | $324,615 25 | |
| Interest due and accrued on bonds | | 160,837 44 | |
| Interest due and accrued on collateral loans | | 64,613 26 | |
| Interest due and accrued on premium notes, loans or liens | | 303,670 33 | |
| Interest accrued on other assets | | 5,355 52 | |
| Rents due on company's property | | 3,297 92 | |
| | | | 862,389 72 |
| | New business. | Renewals. | |
| Net uncollected and deferred premiums (paid for basis) | $84,609 23 | $1,460,845 42 | 1,545,454 65 |
| Gross assets | | | $60,771,848 74 |

DEDUCT ASSETS NOT ADMITTED.

| | | |
|---|---|---|
| Agents' debit balances | $37,211 55 | |
| Premium notes, policy loans and other policy assets in excess of net value and of other policy liabilities on individual policies | 37,420 00 | |
| Overdue and accrued interest on bonds in default | 31,402 78 | |
| Total | | 106,034 33 |
| Admitted assets, life department | | $60,665,814 41 |
| Admitted assets, casualty department | | 4,533,436 75 |
| Admitted assets | | $65,199,251 16 |

## LIABILITIES.

| | | |
|---|---|---|
| Net present value of outstanding policies computed by the California Insurance Department | $30,205,767 00 | |
| Same for dividend additions | 2,198,878 00 | |
| Same for annuities | 586,163 00 | |
| Total | $52,990,808 00 | |
| Deduct net value of risks re-insured | 111,178 00 | |
| Net reserve (paid for basis) | | $52,879,630 00 |
| Extra reserve for total and permanent disability benefits and for additional accidental death benefits included in life policies | | 357,800 00 |
| Present value of supplementary contracts not involving life contingencies | | 247,847 00 |
| Present value of amounts incurred but not yet due for total and permanent disability benefits | | 158,951 00 |
| Death losses in process of adjustment | $ 39,524 00 | |
| Death losses reported for which no proofs have been received | 112,326 00 | |
| Reserve for net death losses incurred but unreported | 76,000 00 | |
| Matured endowments due and unpaid | 19,605 00 | |
| Death losses and other policy claims resisted | 38,000 00 | |
| Annuity claims, involving life contingencies, due and unpaid | 874 47 | |
| Total policy claims | | 286,329 47 |
| Dividends left with the company to accumulate at interest | | 349,691 00 |
| Gross premiums paid in advance, including surrender values so applied, less discount, if any | | 81,434 30 |
| Unearned interest and rent paid in advance | | 240,507 85 |
| Commissions due agents on premium notes, when paid | | 5,700 00 |
| Commissions to agents due or accrued | | 4,089 95 |
| Salaries, rents, office expenses, bills and accounts due or accrued | | 29,914 26 |
| Medical examiners' and legal fees due or accrued | | 33,182 32 |
| Estimated amount hereafter payable for federal, state and other taxes based upon the business of the year of this statement | | 255,000 00 |
| Unpaid dividends to stockholders | | 75,000 00 |

LIABILITIES—Concluded.

| | |
|---|---|
| Dividends or other profits due policyholders | $ 16,492 46 |
| Dividends declared on or apportioned to annual dividend policies payable to policyholders during 1922 for period to August 31, 1922 | 842,000 00 |
| Dividends declared on or apportioned to deferred dividend policies payable to policyholders during 1922 for period to December 31, 1922 | 386,361 58 |
| Amounts set apart, apportioned, provisionally ascertained, calculated, declared or held awaiting apportionment upon deferred dividend policies | 3,178,967 00 |
| Renewal bonus fund | 28,586 00 |
| Contingency fund | 5,821 32 |
| Liabilities, life department | $59,463,305 51 |
| Liabilities, casualty department | 2,520,176 97 |
| Total | $61,983,482 48 |
| Capital paid up | 1,500,000 00 |
| Unassigned funds (surplus) | 1,715,768 68 |
| Total | $65,199,251 16 |

## EXHIBIT OF POLICIES—ORDINARY.

ALL BUSINESS PAID FOR.

| | Number. | Amount. | Number. | Amount. |
|---|---|---|---|---|
| Policies in force December 31, 1920 | | | 149,633 | $350,408,951 00 |
| Policies issued, revived and increased during the year | | | 25,131 | 81,184,108 00 |
| Total | | | 174,764 | $431,593,059 00 |
| Deduct policies which have ceased to be in force during the year— | | | | |
| By death | 935 | $ 2,488,578 00 | | |
| By maturity | 506 | 917,661 00 | | |
| By disability | 21 | 173,395 00 | | |
| By expiry | 5,352 | 14,245,496 00 | | |
| By surrender | 1,999 | 4,800,475 00 | | |
| By lapse | 6,604 | 17,670,467 00 | | |
| By decrease | | 1,140,944 00 | | |
| Total | | | 15,417 | 41,437,016 00 |
| Total policies in force December 31, 1921 | | | 159,347 | $390,156,043 00 |
| Re-insured | | | 1,230 | $15,411,034 00 |

## BUSINESS IN ILLINOIS—ORDINARY.

| | Number. | Amount. |
|---|---|---|
| Policies in force December 31, 1920 | 7,733 | $16,433,615 00 |
| Policies issued during the year | 1,022 | 3,358,520 00 |
| Total | 8,755 | $19,792,135 00 |
| Deduct policies ceased to be in force | 496 | 1,209,500 00 |
| Policies in force December 31, 1921 | 8,259 | $18,582,635 00 |
| Losses and claims unpaid December 31, 1920 | 1 | $ 3,023 00 |
| Losses and claims incurred during the year | 41 | 108,685 00 |
| Total | 42 | $111,708 00 |
| Losses and claims settled during the year | 41 | 111,213 00 |
| Losses and claims unpaid December 31, 1921 | 1 | $495 00 |
| Premiums received | | $620,227 41 |

## GAIN AND LOSS EXHIBIT.

INSURANCE EXHIBIT.

| | | Gain in surplus. | Loss in surplus. |
|---|---|---|---|
| Loading on actual premiums of the year (averaging 22.85 per cent of the gross premiums) | $3,119,068 14 | | |
| Insurance expenses incurred during the year | 4,114,627 18 | | |
| Loss from loading | | | $ 995,559 04 |
| Interest earned during the year | $3,382,465 53 | | |
| Investment expenses incurred during the year | 348,030 19 | | |
| Net income from investments | $3,034,435 34 | | |
| Interest required to maintain reserve | 1,774,389 00 | | |
| Gain from interest | | $1,260,046 34 | |
| Expected mortality on net amount at risk | $3,469,819 00 | | |
| Actual mortality on net amount at risk | 1,883,091 90 | | |
| Gain from mortality | | 1,586,727 10 | |

GAIN AND LOSS EXHIBIT—Concluded.

INSURANCE EXHIBIT.

| | | Gain in surplus. | Loss in surplus. |
|---|---|---|---|
| Expected disbursements to annuitants | $34,528 68 | | |
| Net actual annuity claims incurred | 43,168 68 | | |
| Loss from annuities | | | $ 8,640 00 |
| Total gain during the year from surrendered and lapsed policies | | $254,267 53 | |
| Dividends paid stockholders | | | 75,000 00 |
| Decrease in surplus on dividend account | | | 1,646,153 54 |
| Increase in special funds and special reserves during the year | | | 198 00 |
| Carried to reserve | | | 20,094 29 |
| Net to loss account | | | 138,169 71 |

INVESTMENT EXHIBIT.

| | | Gain in surplus. | Loss in surplus. |
|---|---|---|---|
| Total losses from real estate | | | 2,480 82 |
| Total gains from stocks and bonds | | 8,272 88 | |
| Total losses from stocks and bonds | | | 27,545 31 |
| Loss from assets not admitted | | | 24,158 36 |
| Net loss on account of total and permanent disability benefits | | | 59,295 00 |
| Gain from all other sources: Casualty department | | 253,883 39 | |
| Total gains and losses in surplus during the year | | $3,363,197 24 | $2,997,294 07 |
| Surplus December 31, 1920 | $1,349,865 51 | | |
| Surplus December 31, 1921 | 1,715,768 68 | | |
| Increase in surplus | | | 365,903 17 |
| Total | | $3,363,197 24 | $3,363,197 24 |

## PAN-AMERICAN LIFE INSURANCE COMPANY.

Located at Thirteenth Floor, Whitney Building, New Orleans, Louisiana; incorporated March 28, 1911; commenced business in Illinois February 21, 1916.

CRAWFORD H. ELLIS, President. J. E. WOODWARD, Secretary.

GEORGE A. BARR, Director of Trade and Commerce, Attorney for service at Springfield.

### CAPITAL.

| | | | |
|---|---|---|---|
| Capital paid up | | $1,000,000 00 | |
| Amount of ledger assets December 31, of previous year | | | $8,357,374 07 |

### INCOME.

| | | | |
|---|---|---|---|
| First year's premiums on original policies, less re-insurance | | $681,557 73 | |
| First year's premiums for total and permanent disability benefits | | 11,584 59 | |
| Coupons applied to purchase extended insurance and paid-up insurance | | 4,215 29 | |
| Surrender values applied to purchase paid-up insurance and annuities | | 52,415 32 | |
| New premiums | | $ 749,772 93 | |
| Renewal premiums less re-insurance | $2,134,395 42 | | |
| Renewal premiums for additional accidental death benefits, less re-insurance | 10,540 39 | | |
| Dividends applied to pay renewal premiums | 624 85 | | |
| Renewal premiums | | 2,145,560 66 | |
| Premium income | | | $2,895,333 59 |
| Dividends, coupons and reductions left with company to accumulate at interest | | | 105,144 84 |
| Interest on mortgage loans | | $358,378 64 | |
| Interest on collateral loans | | 5,548 67 | |
| Interest on bonds and dividends on stocks | | 73,533 83 | |
| Interest on premium notes, policy loans or liens | | 83,854 48 | |
| Interest on deposits | | 8,594 91 | |
| Interest on other debts due the company | | 2,247 15 | |
| Total interest | | | 532,157 68 |
| From other sources, viz: Internal revenue tax, $13,965.86; Mercury Re-insurance Company, reserve account, $6,643.81; suspense, $3,650.95; miscellaneous profit, $9.68 | | | 24,270 30 |
| Agents' balances previously charged off | | | 446 20 |
| Profit on sale or maturity of ledger assets | | | 231 25 |
| Total income | | | $3,557,583 86 |
| Total | | | $11,914,957 93 |

### DISBURSEMENTS.

| | | | |
|---|---|---|---|
| Death claims | | $392,916 55 | |
| Matured endowments | | 6,529 00 | |
| Total and permanent disability claims and additional accidental death benefits, less re-insurance | | 4,880 95 | |
| Total death claims | | | $404,326 50 |

### DISBURSEMENTS—Concluded.

| | |
|---|---|
| Annuities involving life contingencies | $ 169 33 |
| Premium notes and liens voided by lapse, less $4,559.49 restorations | 5,565 19 |
| Surrender values paid in cash, or applied in liquidation of loans or notes | 219,732 38 |
| Special contract payments | 720 10 |
| Surrender values applied to purchase paid-up insurance and annuities | 52,415 32 |
| Dividends, coupons, reductions paid policyholders in cash, or applied in liquidation of loans or notes | 3,424 51 |
| Dividends applied to pay renewal premiums | 624 85 |
| Dividends applied to purchase paid-up additions and annuities | 4,215 29 |
| Dividends, coupons and reductions left with the company to accumulate at interest | 105,144 84 |
| (Total paid policyholders $796,338 31) | |
| Expense of investigation and settlement of policy claims, including legal expenses | 2,038 80 |
| Supplementary contracts not involving life contingencies | 6,900 55 |
| Dividends, coupons and reductions with interest, held on deposit surrendered during the year | 33,041 21 |
| Dividends to stockholders | 100,000 00 |
| Commissions to agents, first year, $443,177.30; renewal, $125,459.46 | 568,636 76 |
| Compensation of managers and agents not paid by commissions on new business | 60,908 46 |
| Agency supervision and traveling expenses of supervisors | 31,496 55 |
| Branch office expenses | 17,869 91 |
| Medical examiners' fees and inspection of risks | 48,541 21 |
| Salaries and all other compensation of officers and home office employees | 181,865 47 |
| Rent | 24,006 14 |
| Advertisng, printing, stationery, postage, telegraph, telephone, express and exchange | 54,507 83 |
| Legal expense | 2,504 45 |
| Furniture, fixtures and safes | 5,544 24 |
| Repairs and expenses (other than taxes) on real estate | 13 00 |
| Taxes on real estate | 74 41 |
| State taxes on premiums | 49,474 55 |
| Insurance department licenses and fees | 1,588 08 |
| All other licenses, fees and taxes | 25,500 32 |
| Other disbursements, viz: Suspense, $1,523.29; interest on Mercury re-insurance reserve account, $2,468.64; traveling expenses, $6,792.73; loan appraisement and expenses, $1,781.46; employees' bonds, $291.45; agents' bonds, $882.10; examination cost, $2,500.00; expenses of re-instatement and renewals, $6,839.90; convention expense, $15,842.81; commission on sale of bank stock, $250.00; contributions, $475.00; loss, account defunct Banco Nacional de Cuba, Havana, Cuba, $301.26; balance loss account defunct Banco Nacional de Cuba, Havana, Cuba, $294.26; excess cash value loaned policyholders charged off, $123.00; renewal premiums collected by collector at Chaparra, Cuba, who died before remitting, $370.59; electric light, ice, subscription to Life Underwriters, laundry, towels, etc., $6,384.91 | 47,121 40 |
| Agents' balances charged off | 3,477 84 |
| Loss on sale or maturity of ledger assets | 57,676 11 |
| Decrease in book value of ledger assets | 67,200 00 |
| Total disbursements | $2,186,325 60 |
| Balance | $9,728,632 33 |

### LEDGER ASSETS.

| | |
|---|---|
| Mortgage loans on real estate | $5,835,967 59 |
| Loans secured by collaterals | 80,000 00 |
| Loans on company's policies assigned as collateral | 1,261,356 11 |
| Premium notes on policies in force | 185,528 68 |
| Book value of bonds and stocks | 1,789,924 77 |
| Cash in office | 400 00 |
| Deposits in trust companies and banks not on interest | 13,743 11 |
| Deposits in trust companies and banks on interest | 352,720 24 |
| Bills receivable | 7,097 80 |
| Agents' balances (debit, $127,879.74; credit, $6,418.50) | 121,461 24 |
| Re-insuring companies accounts, $1,664.76; automatic premium liens, $20,905.42; furniture and fixtures, $49,898.25; law library, $890.36; disability premium liens, $1,824.00; American Service Bureau, $5,250.00 | 80,432 79 |
| Total ledger assets | $9,728,632 33 |

#### NON-LEDGER ASSETS.

| | | | |
|---|---|---|---|
| Interest due and accrued on mortgages | | $172,319 15 | |
| Interest accrued on bonds | | 31,983 02 | |
| Interest accrued on collateral loans | | 4,690 14 | |
| Interest accrued on premium notes, loans or liens | | 2,478 59 | |
| Interest accrued on other assets | | 527 44 | |
| | | | 211,998 34 |
| Market value of bonds and stocks over book value | | | 2,924 00 |
| Due from other companies for losses or claims on policies re-insured | | | 30,000 00 |
| | New business. | Renewals. | |
| Net uncollected and deferred premiums (paid for basis) | $5,057 89 | $209,256 26 | 214,314 15 |
| Refunds due from other companies | | | 3,966 50 |
| Gross assets | | | $10,191,835 32 |

## LEDGER ASSETS—Concluded.

DEDUCT ASSETS NOT ADMITTED.

| | | |
|---|---|---|
| Furniture, fixtures and safes | $ 50,788 61 | |
| Agents' debit balances | 127,879 74 | |
| Bills receivable | 7,097 80 | |
| Premium notes, policy loans and other policy assets in excess of net value and of other policy liabilities on individual policies | 5,389 47 | |
| Total | | $191,155 62 |
| Admitted assets | | $10,000,679 70 |

## LIABILITIES.

| | | |
|---|---|---|
| Net present value of outstanding policies computed by the Louisiana Insurance Department | $7,801,246 00 | |
| Same for dividend additions | 6,091 00 | |
| Total | $7,807,337 00 | |
| Deduct net value of risks re-insured | 255,728 00 | |
| Net reserve (paid for basis) | | $7,551,609 00 |
| Extra reserve for total and permanent disability benefits and for additional accidental death benefits included in life policies, less re-insurance | | 41,192 72 |
| Present value of supplementary contracts not involving life contingencies | | 51,948 70 |
| Present value of amounts incurred but not yet due for total and permanent disability benefits | | 15,607 73 |
| Death losses reported for which no proofs have been received | $72,082 57 | |
| Reserve for net death losses incurred but unreported | 31,128 51 | |
| Death losses and other policy claims resisted | 18,500 00 | |
| Total policy claims | | 121,711 08 |
| Gross premiums paid in advance, including surrender values so applied, less re-insurance premiums paid on policies not in force | | 2,626 93 |
| Unearned interest and rent paid in advance | | 30,164 45 |
| Cost of collection of uncollected and deferred premiums in excess of loading | | 2,781 83 |
| Salaries, rents, office expenses, bills and accounts due or accrued | | 8,266 45 |
| Medical examiners' fees due or accrued | | 2,414 50 |
| Estimated amount herafter payable for federal, state and other taxes based upon the business of the year of this statement | | 76,500 00 |
| Dividends or other profits due plicyholders | | 738 00 |
| Dividends declared on or apportioned to deferred dividend policies payable to policyholders during 1922 for period to December 31, 1922 | | 3,229 02 |
| Surplus apportioned for contingencies not otherwise provided for | | 45,249 80 |
| Coupons on deposit and interest thereon, $351,483.31; persistency bonus funds, $201,066.78 Mercury Re-insurance Company reserve account, $61,502.55; special contracts, $700.00; surplus apportioned for general agents meeting and district agency conventions, $25,000.00 | | 639,752 64 |
| Other liabilities, viz: Suspense, $129.72; re-insurance premiums due other companies, $46.58; Pittsburgh Life liens, $3,167.77 | | 3,344 07 |
| Total | | $8,597,136 92 |
| Capital paid up | | 1,000,000 00 |
| Unassigned funds (surplus) | | 403,542 78 |
| Total | | $10,000,679 70 |

## EXHIBIT OF POLICIES—ORDINARY.

ALL BUSINESS PAID FOR.

| | Number. | Amount. | Number. | Amount. |
|---|---|---|---|---|
| Policies in force December 31, 1920 | | | 36,790 | $87,358,585 00 |
| Policies issued, revived and increased during the year | | | 9,265 | 24,447,604 00 |
| Total | | | 46,055 | $111,806,189 00 |
| Deduct policies which have ceased to be in force during the year— | | | | |
| By death | 181 | $ 520,021 00 | | |
| By maturity | 4 | 6,500 00 | | |
| By expiry | 441 | 1,422,791 00 | | |
| By surrender | 613 | 1,547,856 00 | | |
| By lapse | 7,805 | 19,813,522 00 | | |
| By decrease | | 846,758 00 | | |
| Total | | | 9,044 | 24,157,448 00 |
| Total policies in force December 31, 1921 | | | 37,011 | $87,648,741 00 |
| Re-insured | | | 1,484 | $7,705,088 00 |

## EXHIBIT OF POLICIES—GROUP INSURANCE.

ALL BUSINESS PAID FOR.

| | Number. | Amount. | Number. | Amount. |
|---|---|---|---|---|
| Policies in force December 31, 1920 | | | 6 | $800,050 00 |
| Policies issued, revived and increased during the year | | | -------- | 307,450 00 |
| Total | | | 6 | $1,107,500 00 |
| Deduct policies which have ceased to be in force during the year— | | | | |
| By death | -------- | $ 3,200 00 | | |
| By expiry | 1 | 63,000 00 | | |
| By decrease | -------- | 254,700 00 | | |
| Total | | | 1 | 320,900 00 |
| Total policies in force December 31, 1921 | | | 5 | $786,600 00 |
| Distribution of business in force at end of year—One year term | | | 5 | $786,600 00 |

## BUSINESS IN ILLINOIS—ORDINARY.

| | Number. | Amount. |
|---|---|---|
| Policies in force December 31, 1920 | 931 | $1,673,549 00 |
| Policies issued during the year | 108 | 205,000 00 |
| Total | 1,039 | $1,878,549 00 |
| Deduct policies ceased to be in force | 172 | 387,634 00 |
| Policies in force December 31, 1921 | 867 | $1,490,915 00 |
| Premiums received | | $43,810 74 |

## GAIN AND LOSS EXHIBIT.

INSURANCE EXHIBIT.

| | | Gain in surplus. | Loss in surplus. |
|---|---|---|---|
| Loading on actual premiums of the year (averaging 28.04 per cent of the gross premiums) | $ 805,100 10 | | |
| Insurance expenses incurred during the year | 1,111,589 12 | | |
| Loss from loading | | -------------- | $306,489 02 |
| Interest earned during the year | $523,383 63 | | |
| Investment expenses incurred during the year | 17,127 37 | | |
| Net income from investments | $506,256 26 | | |
| Interest required to maintain reserve | 266,904 47 | | |
| Gain from interest | | $239,351 79 | |
| Expected mortality on net amount at risk | $774,581 96 | | |
| Actual mortality on net amount at risk | 368,836 81 | | |
| Gain from mortality | | 405,745 15 | |
| Expected disbursements to annuitants | $ 89 95 | | |
| Net actual annuity claims incurred | —3,893 44 | | |
| Gain from annuities | | 3,983 39 | |
| Total gain during the year from surrendered and lapsed policies | | 143,712 29 | |
| Dividends paid stockholders | | -------------- | 100,000 00 |
| Decrease in surplus on dividend account | | -------------- | 114,449 30 |
| Increase in special funds and special reserves during the year | | -------------- | 22,477 27 |
| Net to loss account | | -------------- | 1,079 43 |
| INVESTMENT EXHIBIT. | | | |
| Total losses from real estate | | -------------- | 781 36 |
| Total gains from stocks and bonds | | 51,202 65 | |
| Total losses from stocks and bonds | | -------------- | 124,094 75 |
| Loss from assets not admitted | | -------------- | 55,318 14 |
| Net gain on account of total and permanent disability benefits or additional accidental death benefits included in life policies | | 2,915 12 | |
| Decrease in refunds due from other companies less re-insurance premiums due other companies | | -------------- | 4,510 29 |
| Balance unaccounted for | | -------------- | 70 97 |
| Total gains and losses in surplus during the year | | $846,910 39 | $729,270 53 |
| Surplus December 31, 1920 | $285,902 92 | | |
| Surplus December 31, 1921 | 403,542 78 | | |
| Increase in surplus | | -------------- | 117,639 86 |
| Total | | $846,910 39 | $846,910 39 |

## PENN MUTUAL LIFE INSURANCE COMPANY.

Located at Sixth and Walnut Streets, Philadelphia, Pennsylvania; incorporated February 24, 1847; commenced business in Illinois September 30, 1865.

GEORGE K. JOHNSON, President. SYDNEY A. SMITH, Secretary.

CLYDE J. McCARY, Chicago, Attorney for service.

| | | | |
|---|---|---|---|
| Amount of ledger assets December 31, of previous year | | | $213,717,432 68 |

### INCOME.

| | | | |
|---|---|---|---|
| First year's premiums on original policies | | $4,105,594 41 | |
| First year's premiums for total and permanent disability benefits | | 63,054 10 | |
| Surrender values to pay first year's premiums | | 40,840 15 | |
| Dividends applied to purchase paid-up additions and annuities | | 314,799 27 | |
| Surrender values applied to purchase paid-up insurance and annuities | | 444,804 13 | |
| Consideration for original annuities involving life contingencies | | 180,662 70 | |
| New premiums | | $5,149,754 76 | |
| Renewal premiums less re-insurance | $28,162,469 84 | | |
| Renewal premiums for total and permanent disability benefits | 263,104 22 | | |
| Dividends applied to pay renewal premiums | 4,112,464 09 | | |
| Surrender values applied to pay renewal premiums | 7,218 67 | | |
| Renewal premiums for deferred annuities | 8,484 66 | | |
| Renewal premiums | | 32,553,741 48 | |
| Premium income | | | $37,703,496 24 |
| Consideration for supplementary contracts involving life contingencies | | | 10,880 05 |
| Consideration for supplementary contracts not involving life contingencies | | | 724,777 01 |
| Dividends left with company to accumulate at interest | | | 913,026 68 |
| Interest on mortgage loans | | $4,841,991 34 | |
| Interest on collateral loans | | 59,727 09 | |
| Interest on bonds and dividends on stocks | | 4,241,535 59 | |
| Interest on premium notes, policy loans or liens | | 2,091,881 35 | |
| Interest on deposits | | 78,735 62 | |
| Interest on other debts due the company | | 6,323 96 | |
| Rents—including $200,000.00 for company's occupancy of its own buildings | | 272,384 55 | |
| Total interest and rents | | | 11,592,579 50 |
| Bonuses on mortgages | | | 21,874 67 |
| Profit on sale or maturity of ledger assets | | | 52,296 90 |
| Total income | | | $51,018,931 05 |
| Total | | | $264,736,363 73 |

### DISBURSEMENTS.

| | | |
|---|---|---|
| Death claims and additions | $9,485,644 73 | |
| Matured endowments and additions | 4,103,472 20 | |
| Total and permanent disability claims | 10,561 54 | |
| Total death claims and endowments | | $13,599,678 47 |
| Annuities involving life contingencies | | 499,184 10 |
| Premium notes and liens voided by lapse, less $15,889.51 restorations | | 137,107 26 |
| Surrender values paid in cash, or applied in liquidation of loans or notes | | 4,525,250 58 |
| Surrender values applied to pay new and renewal premiums | | 48,058 82 |
| Surrender values applied to purchase paid-up insurance and annuities | | 444,804 13 |
| Dividends paid policyholders in cash, or applied in liquidation of loans or notes | | 2,022,878 52 |
| Dividends applied to pay renewal premiums | | 4,112,464 09 |
| Dividends applied to purchase paid-up additions and annuities | | 314,799 27 |
| Dividends left with the company to accumulate at interest | | 913,026 68 |
| Interest paid under installment policies | | 61,803 08 |
| (Total paid policyholders | $26,679,055 00) | |
| Expense of investigation and settlement of policy claims, including legal expenses | | 5,874 41 |
| Supplementary contracts not involving life contingencies | | 669,075 24 |
| Dividends with interest, held on deposit surrendered during the year | | 250,549 74 |
| Commissions to agents, first year, $1,950,566.16; renewal, $2,004,301.47; annuities (original) $7,612.29; (renewal), $316.45 | | 3,962,796 37 |
| Commuted renewal commissions | | 272,873 86 |
| Agency supervision and traveling expenses of supervisors | | 56,605 75 |
| Branch office expenses | | 254,268 22 |
| Medical examiners' fees and inspection of risks | | 228,498 24 |
| Salaries and all other compensation of officers and home office employees | | 888,661 18 |
| Rent | | 349,767 14 |
| Advertising, printing, stationery, postage, telegraph, telephone, express and exchange | | 217,357 50 |
| Legal expense | | 20,444 48 |
| Furniture, fixtures and safes | | 31,923 19 |
| Repairs and expenses (other than taxes) on real estate | | 120,914 64 |

## DISBURSEMENTS—Concluded.

| | |
|---|---|
| Taxes on real estate | $ 45,245 44 |
| State taxes on premiums | 582,353 98 |
| Insurance department licenses and fees | 30,467 55 |
| Federal taxes | 97,864 65 |
| All other licenses, fees and taxes | 114,859 02 |
| Other disbursements, viz: Investment inspections, $17,220.09; election expenses, $1,536.10 home office expenses, supplies, $76,784.74 | 95,540 93 |
| Loss on sale or maturity of ledger assets | 1,250 00 |
| Decrease in book value of ledger assets | 170,250 16 |
| Total disbursements | $35,146,496 69 |
| Balance | $229,589,867 04 |

## LEDGER ASSETS.

| | |
|---|---|
| Book value of real estate | $ 2,041,111 83 |
| Mortgage loans on real estate | 89,193,596 72 |
| Loans secured by collaterals | 1,292,350 00 |
| Premiums advanced under Soldiers' and Sailors' Civil Relief Act | 655 60 |
| Loans on company's policies assigned as collateral | 35,028,042 47 |
| Premium notes on policies in force | 8,560,010 49 |
| Book value of bonds and stocks | 90,934,516 18 |
| Cash in office | 329,057 93 |
| Deposits in trust companies and banks on interest | 2,130,970 19 |
| Bills receivable | 28,651 10 |
| Agents' balances (debit, $58,036.42; credit, $7,131.89) net | 50,904 53 |
| Total ledger assets | $229,589,867 04 |

### NON-LEDGER ASSETS.

| | | | |
|---|---|---|---|
| Interest due and accrued on mortgages | | $1,754,239 88 | |
| Interest accrued on bonds | | 1,247,985 31 | |
| Interest accrued on collateral loans | | 13,005 22 | |
| Interest due and accrued on premium notes, loans or liens | | 573,719 28 | |
| Interest due and accrued on other assets | | 200 92 | |
| Rents due on company's property | | 30 00 | |
| | | | 3,589,180 61 |
| | New business. | Renewals. | |
| Net uncollected and deferred premiums (paid for basis) | $312,496 82 | $5,297,417 98 | 5,609,914 80 |
| Gross assets | | | $238,788,962 45 |

### DEDUCT ASSETS NOT ADMITTED.

| | | |
|---|---|---|
| Agents' debit balances | $ 58,036 42 | |
| Bills receivable | 28,852 02 | |
| Book value of bonds and stocks over market value | 4,716,526 18 | |
| Total | | 4,803,414 62 |
| Admitted assets | | $233,985,547 83 |

## LIABILITIES.

| | | |
|---|---|---|
| Net present value of outstanding policies | $188,871,160 00 | |
| Same for dividend additions | 2,555,995 00 | |
| Same for annuities | 5,431,490 00 | |
| Total | $196,858,645 00 | |
| Deduct net value of risks re-insured | 39,855 00 | |
| Net reserve (paid for basis) | | $196,818,790 00 |
| Extra reserve for total and permanent disability benefits and for additional accidental death benefits included in life policies | | 464,302 00 |
| Present value of supplementary contracts not involving life contingencies | | 6,109,078 42 |
| Present value of amounts incurred but not yet due for total and permanent disability benefits | | 144,538 00 |
| Death losses in process of adjustment | $146,650 98 | |
| Death losses reported for which no proofs have been received | 439,308 88 | |
| Reserve for net death losses incurred but unreported | 150,000 00 | |
| Death losses and other policy claims resisted | 37,616 02 | |
| Total policy claims | | 773,575 88 |
| Dividends left with the company to accumulate at interest | | 5,040,266 60 |
| Gross premiums paid in advance, including surrender values so applied, less discount, if any | | 206,391 08 |
| Unearned interest and rent paid in advance | | 474,038 25 |
| Commissions to agents due or accrued | | 6,370 27 |
| Salaries, rents, office expenses, bills and accounts due or accrued | | 7,987 34 |
| Medical examiners' fees due or accrued | | 17,800 00 |
| Estimated amount hereafter payable for federal, state and other taxes based upon the business of the year of this statement | | 985,000 00 |
| Dividends or other profits due policyholders | | 1,163,876 42 |

LIABILITIES—Concluded.

| | |
|---|---|
| Dividends declared on or apportioned to annual dividend policies payable to policyholders during 1922 for period to December 31, 1922 | $7,100,000 00 |
| Dividends declared on or apportioned to deferred dividend policies payable to policyholders during 1922 for period to December 31, 1922 | 1,967,047 04 |
| Amounts set apart, apportioned, provisionally ascertained, calculated, declared or held awaiting apportionment upon deferred dividend policies | 4,592,155 58 |
| Reserve or surplus funds not otherwise included in liabilities, viz— | |
| Reserve for mortality fluctuation | 5,251,960 00 |
| Reserve for asset fluctuation and other contingencies | 2,839,948 95 |
| Matured credits awaiting proof | 22,422 00 |
| Total | $233,985,547 83 |

EXHIBIT OF POLICIES—ORDINARY.

ALL BUSINESS PAID FOR.

| | Number. | Amount. | Number. | Amount. |
|---|---|---|---|---|
| Policies in force December 31, 1920 | | | 326,801 | $1,029,203,157 00 |
| Policies issued, revived and increased during the year | | | 31,876 | 136,509,538 00 |
| Total | | | 358,677 | $1,165,712,695 00 |
| Deduct policies which have ceased to be in force during the year— | | | | |
| By death | 2,787 | $ 9,247,059 00 | | |
| By maturity | 2,225 | 4,098,275 00 | | |
| By expiry | 2,274 | 7,721,668 00 | | |
| By surrender | 4,846 | 18,473,878 00 | | |
| By lapse | 7,820 | 26,175,250 00 | | |
| By decrease | 2,012 | 9,239,056 00 | | |
| Total | | | 21,964 | 74,955,186 00 |
| Total policies in force December 31, 1921 | | | 336,713 | $1,090,757,509 00 |
| Re-insured | | | | $594,500 00 |

BUSINESS IN ILLINOIS—ORDINARY.

| | Number. | Amount. |
|---|---|---|
| Policies in force December 31, 1920 | 14,725 | $64,867,209 00 |
| Policies issued during the year | 1,813 | 9,640,018 00 |
| Total | 16,538 | $74,507,227 00 |
| Deduct policies ceased to be in force | 972 | 4,412,874 00 |
| Policies in force December 31, 1921 | 15,566 | $70,094,353 00 |
| Losses and claims unpaid December 31, 1920 | 22 | $ 78,136 00 |
| Losses and claims incurred during the year | 95 | 401,444 11 |
| Total | 117 | $479,580 11 |
| Losses and claims settled during the year | 108 | 458,055 11 |
| Losses and claims unpaid December 31, 1921 | 9 | $21,525 00 |
| Premiums received | | $2,218,569 48 |

GAIN AND LOSS EXHIBIT.

INSURANCE EXHIBIT.

| | | Gain in surplus. | Loss in surplus. |
|---|---|---|---|
| Loading on actual premiums of the year (averaging 19.59 per cent of the gross premiums) | $7,429,321 68 | | |
| Insurance expenses incurred during the year | 6,621,161 07 | | |
| Gain from loading | | $ 808,160 61 | |
| Interest earned during the year | $11,868,138 31 | | |
| Investment expenses incurred during the year | 730,010 78 | | |
| Net income from investments | $11,138,127 53 | | |
| Interest required to maintain reserve | 5,972,584 00 | | |
| Gain from interest | | 5,165,543 53 | |
| Expected mortality on net amount at risk | $11,780,473 00 | | |
| Actual mortality on net amount at risk | 6,249,459 63 | | |
| Gain from mortality | | 5,531,013 37 | |
| Expected disbursements to annuitants | $305,943 45 | | |
| Net actual annuity claims incurred | 313,107 20 | | |
| Loss from annuities | | | $ 7,163 75 |
| Total gain during the year from surrendered and lapsed policies | | 503,862 03 | |
| Decrease in surplus on dividend account | | | 7,277,507 05 |
| Increase in special funds and special reserves during the year | | | 5,154,289 87 |

GAIN AND LOSS EXHIBIT—Concluded.

INVESTMENT EXHIBIT.

| | Gain in surplus. | Loss in surplus. |
|---|---|---|
| Total gains from stocks and bonds | $782,261 49 | |
| Total losses from stocks and bonds | | $171,500 16 |
| Gain on bonuses on mortgages | 21,874 67 | |
| Loss from assets not admitted | | 1,380 38 |
| Net gain on account of total and permanent disability benefits or additional accidental death benefits included in life policies | 31,916 88 | |
| Loss from all other sources: Interest paid under installment policies, $61,803.08; accrued interest included in liability item, $170,988.29 | | 232,791 37 |
| Total | $12,844,632 58 | $12,844,632 58 |

## PEOPLES LIFE INSURANCE COMPANY.

Located at Peoples Life Building, Frankfort, Indiana; incorporated April 4, 1910; commenced business in Illinois August 14, 1917.

ANDREW A. LAIRD, President. EUGENE O. BURGET, Secretary.

GEORGE A. BARR, Director of Trade and Commerce, Attorney for service at Springfield.

CAPITAL.

| | | | |
|---|---|---|---|
| Capital paid up | | $100,000 00 | |
| Amount of ledger assets December 31, of previous year | | | $1,731,395 15 |

INCOME.

| | | | |
|---|---|---|---|
| First year's premiums on original policies, less re-insurance | | $120,962 96 | |
| First year's premiums for total and permanent disability benefits | | 2,042 15 | |
| First year's premiums for additional accidental death benefits, less re-insurance | | 668 83 | |
| New premiums | | $123,673 94 | |
| Renewal premiums less re-insurance | $440,327 67 | | |
| Renewal premiums for total and permanent disability benefits | 2,213 15 | | |
| Renewal premiums for additional accidental death benefits, less re-insurance | 507 57 | | |
| Dividends applied to pay renewal premiums | 1,984 81 | | |
| Coupons applied to pay renewal premiums | 15,038 61 | | |
| Renewal premiums | | 460,071 81 | |
| Premium income | | | $583,745 75 |
| Dividends left with company to accumulate at interest | | | 109 38 |
| Interest on mortgage loans | | $84,285 68 | |
| Interest on bonds | | 2,125 00 | |
| Interest on premium notes, policy loans or liens | | 19,773 77 | |
| Rents—including $1,500.00 for company's occupancy of its own buildings | | 10,872 00 | |
| Total interest and rents | | | 117,056 45 |
| Agents' balances previously charged off | | | 300 00 |
| Total income | | | $701,211 58 |
| Total | | | $2,432,606 73 |

DISBURSEMENTS.

| | | |
|---|---|---|
| Death claims | $79,305 17 | |
| Matured endowments | 2,000 00 | |
| Total and permanent disability claims | 2,195 34 | |
| Total death claims and endowments | | $ 83,500 51 |
| Premium notes and liens voided by lapse, less $786.89 restorations | | 3,510 40 |
| Surrender values paid in cash, or applied in liquidation of loans or notes | | 34,823 81 |
| Dividends applied to pay renewal premiums | | 1,984 81 |
| Coupons applied to pay renewal premiums | | 15,038 61 |
| Dividends left with the company to accumulate at interest | | 109 38 |
| (Total paid policyholders | $138,967 52) | |
| Expense of investigation and settlement of policy claims, including legal expenses | | 50 00 |
| Dividends with interest, held on deposit surrendered during the year | | 1,222 37 |
| Dividends to stockholders | | 6,000 00 |
| Commissions to agents, first year, $96,867.97; renewal, $17,249.39 | | 114,117 36 |
| Compensation of managers and agents not paid by commissions on new business | | 9,314 70 |
| Agency supervision and traveling expenses of supervisors | | 6,305 11 |
| Medical examiners' fees and inspection of risks | | 13,208 70 |
| Salaries and all other compensation of officers and home office employees | | 29,680 00 |

DISBURSEMENTS—Concluded.

| | | |
|---|---|---|
| Rent | | $ 1,500 00 |
| Advertising, printing, stationery, postage, telegraph, telephone and express | | 12,714 42 |
| Legal expense | | 25 00 |
| Repairs and expenses (other than taxes) on real estate | | 6,934 50 |
| Taxes on real estate | | 1,989 50 |
| State taxes on premiums | | 67 62 |
| Insurance department licenses and fees | | 351 57 |
| Federal taxes | | 9,830 72 |
| All other licenses, fees and taxes | | 1,046 50 |
| Other disbursements, viz: Actuarial services, $2,881.83; officers' traveling expenses, $769.26; office and miscellaneous expense, $1,733.88; investment expense, $17.20 | | 5,402 17 |
| Trust fund under policy contract | | 4,038 00 |
| Agents' balances charged off | | 431 10 |
| Total disbursements | | $363,196 86 |
| Balance | | $2,069,409 87 |

LEDGER ASSETS.

| | | |
|---|---|---|
| Book value of real estate | | $ 100,000 00 |
| Mortgage loans on real estate | | 1,530,686 00 |
| Loans on company's policies assigned as collateral | | 340,880 00 |
| Premium notes on policies in force | | 24,364 90 |
| Book value of bonds | | 50,000 00 |
| Cash in office | | 2,840 52 |
| Deposits in trust companies and banks not on interest | | 7,341 20 |
| Bills receivable | | 1,116 21 |
| Agents' debit balances | | 12,181 04 |
| Total ledger assets | | $2,069,409 87 |
| NON-LEDGER ASSETS. | | |
| Interest accrued on mortgages | $25,739 14 | |
| Interest accrued on bonds | 442 70 | |
| Interest accrued on premium notes, loans or liens | 4,783 00 | |
| | | 30,964 84 |
| Net uncollected and deferred premiums (paid for basis) renewals | | 93,026 88 |
| Furniture and fixtures | | 2,000 00 |
| Gross assets | | $2,195,401 59 |
| DEDUCT ASSETS NOT ADMITTED. | | |
| Furniture, fixtures and safes | $ 2,000 00 | |
| Agents' debit balances | 12,181 04 | |
| Bills receivable | 1,116 21 | |
| Premium notes, policy loans and other policy assets in excess of net value and of other policy liabilities on individual policies | 6,260 27 | |
| Total | | 21,557 52 |
| Admitted assets | | $2,173,844 07 |

LIABILITIES.

| | | |
|---|---|---|
| Net present value of outstanding policies computed by the Indiana Insurance Department | $1,871,364 97 | |
| Deduct net value of risks re-insured | 32,363 04 | |
| Net reserve (paid for basis) | | $1,839,001 93 |
| Extra reserve for total and permanent disability benefits | | 2,208 96 |
| Death losses reported for which no proofs have been received | | 4,000 00 |
| Dividends left with the company to accumulate at interest | | 1,407 53 |
| Gross premiums paid in advance, including surrender values so applied, less discount, if any | | 2,792 42 |
| Unearned interest and rent paid in advance | | 8,257 32 |
| Commissions to agents due or accrued | | 2,334 23 |
| Salaries, rents, office expenses, bills and accounts due or accrued | | 3,277 17 |
| Medical examiners' fees due or accrued, including inspection fees | | 417 75 |
| Estimated amount hereafter payable for federal, state and other taxes based upon the business of the year of this statement | | 12,538 56 |
| Dividends declared on or apportioned to annual dividend policies payable to policyholders during 1922 for period to December 31, 1922 | | 2,400 00 |
| Coupons deposited with the company and interest thereon | | 41,889 62 |
| Contingent reserve for mortuary fluctuations | | 30,000 00 |
| Total | | $1,950,525 49 |
| Capital paid up | | 100,000 00 |
| Unassigned funds (surplus) | | 123,318 58 |
| Total | | $2,173,844 07 |

## EXHIBIT OF POLICIES—ORDINARY.

ALL BUSINESS PAID FOR.

| | Number. | Amount. | Number. | Amount. |
|---|---|---|---|---|
| Policies in force December 31, 1920 | | | 12,223 | $20,541,571 00 |
| Policies issued, revived and increased during the year | | | 2,692 | 4,858,746 00 |
| Total | | | 14,915 | $25,400,317 00 |
| Deduct policies which have ceased to be in force during the year— | | | | |
| By death | 48 | $ 93,279 00 | | |
| By maturity | 2 | 2,000 00 | | |
| By disability | 2 | 3,500 00 | | |
| By expiry | 26 | 27,887 00 | | |
| By surrender | 140 | 229,805 00 | | |
| By lapse | 1,248 | 2,521,035 00 | | |
| By decrease | | 170,695 00 | | |
| Total | | | 1,466 | 3,048,201 00 |
| Total policies in force December 31, 1921 | | | 13,449 | $22,352,116 00 |
| Re-insured | | | 333 | $1,296,034 00 |

## BUSINESS IN ILLINOIS—ORDINARY.

| | Number. | Amount. |
|---|---|---|
| Policies in force December 31, 1920 | 39 | $ 68,480 00 |
| Policies issued during the year | 159 | 262,475 00 |
| Total | 198 | $330,955 00 |
| Deduct policies ceased to be in force | 5 | 8,750 00 |
| Policies in force December 31, 1921 | 193 | $322,205 00 |
| Premiums received | | $8,878 11 |

## GAIN AND LOSS EXHIBIT.

INSURANCE EXHIBIT.

| | | Gain in surplus. | Loss in surplus. |
|---|---|---|---|
| Loading on actual premiums of the year (averaging 21.3 per cent of the gross premiums) | $128,987 88 | | |
| Insurance expenses incurred during the year | 208,903 73 | | |
| Loss from loading | | | $79,915 85 |
| Interest earned during the year | $118,427 79 | | |
| Investment expenses incurred during the year | 8,941 20 | | |
| Net income from investments | $109,486 59 | | |
| Interest required to maintain reserve | 60,942 70 | | |
| Gain from interest | | $48,543 89 | |
| Expected mortality on net amount at risk | $168,465 64 | | |
| Actual mortality on net amount at risk | 69,227 66 | | |
| Gain from mortality | | 99,237 98 | |
| Total gain during the year from surrendered and lapsed policies | | 18,893 31 | |
| Dividends paid stockholders | | | 6,000 00 |
| Decrease in surplus on dividend account | | | 2,099 05 |
| Increase in special funds and special reserves during the year | | | 30,000 00 |
| Net to loss account | | | 3,641 50 |

INVESTMENT EXHIBIT.

| | | Gain in surplus. | Loss in surplus. |
|---|---|---|---|
| Gain on federal taxes assessed in 1917 | | 6,002 54 | |
| Loss from coupon account | | | 24,217 07 |
| Loss from assets not admitted | | | 6,704 80 |
| Net gain on account of total and permanent disability benefits or additional accidental death benefits included in life policies | | 3,158 42 | |
| Gain from dividends left to accumulate | | 60 71 | |
| Total gains and losses in surplus during the year | | $175,896 85 | $152,578 27 |
| Surplus December 31, 1920 | $100,000 00 | | |
| Surplus December 31, 1921 | 123,318 58 | | |
| Increase in surplus | | | 23,318 58 |
| Total | | $175,896 85 | $175,896 85 |

## PHILADELPHIA LIFE INSURANCE COMPANY.

Located at No. 111 North Broad Street, Philadelphia, Pennsylvania; incorporated April 17, 1906; commenced business in Illinois September 7, 1906.

CLIFTON MALONEY, President. FRANK G. COMBES, Secretary.

GEORGE A. BARR, Director of Trade and Commerce, Attorney for service at Springfield.

### CAPITAL.

| | | | |
|---|---|---|---|
| Capital paid up | | $560,320 00 | |
| Amount of ledger assets December 31, of previous year | | | $7,281,990 01 |

### INCOME.

| | | | |
|---|---|---|---|
| First year's premiums on original policies, less re-insurance | | $377,406 56 | |
| First year's premiums for total and permanent disability benefits | | 9,792 98 | |
| First year's premiums for additional accidental death benefits, less re-insurance | | 6,363 92 | |
| Dividends applied to purchase paid-up additions and annuities | | 10,286 31 | |
| Surrender values applied to purchase paid-up insurance and annuities | | 11,545 67 | |
| New premiums | | $ 415,395 44 | |
| Renewal premiums less re-insurance | $1,353,682 19 | | |
| Renewal premiums for total and permanent disability benefits | 13,404 96 | | |
| Renewal premiums for additional accidental death benefits, less re-insurance | 4,865 83 | | |
| Dividends applied to pay renewal premiums | 92,858 24 | | |
| Surrender values applied to pay renewal premiums | 793 27 | | |
| Renewal premiums | | 1,465,604 49 | |
| Premium income | | | $1,880,999 93 |
| Consideration for supplementary contracts not involving life contingencies | | | 25,060 28 |
| Dividends left with company to accumulate at interest | | | 9,159 00 |
| Interest on mortgage loans | | $155,128 30 | |
| Interest on bonds and dividends on stocks | | 116,122 85 | |
| Interest on premium notes, policy loans or liens | | 77,148 32 | |
| Interest on deposits | | 24,982 16 | |
| Interest on other debts due the company | | 3,246 23 | |
| Rents—including $27,800.00 for company's occupancy of its own buildings | | 35,800 04 | |
| Total interest and rents | | | 412,427 90 |
| Borrowed money (gross) | | | 75,000 00 |
| Agents' balances previously charged off | | | 445 38 |
| Profit on sale or maturity of ledger assets | | | 5,892 55 |
| Total income | | | $2,408,985 04 |
| Total | | | $9,690,975 05 |

### DISBURSEMENTS.

| | | |
|---|---|---|
| Death claims and additions | $613,303 97 | |
| Matured endowments and additions | 48,274 00 | |
| Total and permanent disability claims and additional accidental death benefits | 7,777 12 | |
| Total death claims and endowments | | $669,355 09 |
| Premium notes and liens voided by lapse, less $1,101.45 restorations | | 29,415 92 |
| Surrender values paid in cash, or applied in liquidation of loans or notes | | 131,059 54 |
| Surrender values applied to pay new and renewal premiums | | 793 27 |
| Surrender values applied to purchase paid-up insurance and annuities | | 11,545 67 |
| Dividends paid policyholders in cash, or applied in liquidation of loans or notes | | 8,645 43 |
| Dividends applied to pay renewal premiums | | 92,858 24 |
| Dividends applied to purchase paid-up additions and annuities | | 10,286 31 |
| Dividends left with the company to accumulate at interest | | 9,159 00 |
| (Total paid policyholders | $963,118 47) | |
| Expense of investigation and settlement of policy claims, including legal expenses | | 4,492 89 |
| Supplementary contracts not involving life contingencies | | 2,718 13 |
| Dividends to stockholders | | 33,619 20 |
| Commissions to agents, first year, $269,442.96; renewal, $86,067.11 | | 355,510 07 |
| Agency supervision and traveling expenses of supervisors | | 3,400 57 |
| Branch office expenses | | 12,281 05 |
| Medical examiners' fees and inspection of risks | | 48,506 21 |

## DISBURSEMENTS—Concluded.

| | |
|---|---|
| Salaries and all other compensation of officers and home office employees | $148,589 16 |
| Rent | 27,800 00 |
| Advertising, printing, stationery, postage, telegraph, telephone and express | 35,713 69 |
| Legal expenses | 3,063 02 |
| Furniture, fixtures and safes | 2,183 72 |
| Repairs and expenses (other than taxes) on real estate | 9,864 45 |
| Taxes on real estate | 8,197 06 |
| State taxes on premiums | 23,593 87 |
| Insurance department licenses and fees | 2,492 11 |
| Federal taxes | 11,309 33 |
| All other licenses, fees and taxes | 2,157 34 |
| Interest and discount paid | 1,078 11 |
| Borrowed money repaid (gross) | 75,000 00 |
| Interest on borrowed money | 1,070 85 |
| Decrease in book value of ledger assets | 1,045 46 |
| Total disbursements | $1,776,804 76 |
| Balance | $7,914,170 29 |

## LEDGER ASSETS.

| | |
|---|---|
| Book value of real estate | $ 353,803 68 |
| Mortgage loans on real estate | 2,571,850 00 |
| Loans on company's policies assigned as collateral | 1,485,521 26 |
| Premium notes on policies in force | 79,439 21 |
| Book value of bonds and stocks | 2,881,159 80 |
| Cash in office | 18,339 07 |
| Deposits in trust companies and banks on interest | 500,312 93 |
| Agents' balances (debit, $23,884.04; credit, $6,051.99) net | 17,832 05 |
| Due from other companies for premiums on re-insurance | 5,412 29 |
| Special deposit with insurance department of Alabama | 500 00 |
| Total ledger assets | $7,914,170 29 |

### NON-LEDGER ASSETS.

| | | | |
|---|---|---|---|
| Interest due and accrued on mortgages | | $41,230 00 | |
| Interest accrued on bonds | | 50,348 00 | |
| Interest accrued on premium notes, loans or liens | | 43,869 00 | |
| Interest due and accrued on other assets | | 5,174 00 | |
| | | | 140,621 00 |
| Market value of bonds and stocks over book value | | | 4,212 14 |
| Due from other companies for losses or claims on policies re-insured | | | 4,139 00 |
| | New business. | Renewals. | |
| Net uncollected and deferred premiums (paid for basis) | $6,225 00 | $142,534 00 | 148,759 00 |
| Gross assets | | | $8,211,901 43 |

### DEDUCT ASSETS NOT ADMITTED.

| | | |
|---|---|---|
| Agents' debit balances | $23,884 04 | |
| Premium notes, policy loans and other policy assets in excess of net value and of other policy liabilities on individual policies | 31,749 00 | |
| Total | | 55,633 04 |
| Admitted assets | | $8,156,268 39 |

## LIABILITIES.

| | | |
|---|---|---|
| Net present value of outstanding policies computed by the Pennsylvania Insurance Department | $6,870,997 00 | |
| Same for dividend additions | 66,792 00 | |
| Total | $6,937,789 00 | |
| Deduct net value of risks re-insured | 2,769 00 | |
| Net reserve (paid for basis) | | $6,935,020 00 |
| Extra reserve for total and permanent disability benefits and for additional accidental death benefits included in life policies, less re-insurance | | 34,091 00 |
| Present value of supplementary contracts not involving life contingencies | | 35,823 13 |
| Present value of amounts incurred but not yet due for total and permanent disability benefits | | 6,500 00 |
| Surrender values claimable on policies cancelled | | 6,339 14 |
| Death losses in process of adjustment | $ 4,623 77 | |
| Death losses reported for which no proofs have been received | 55,939 00 | |
| Reserve for net death losses incurred but unreported | 10,275 00 | |
| Death losses and other policy claims resisted | 37,500 00 | |
| Total and permanent disability benefits and additional accidental death benefits | 597 40 | |
| Total policy claims | | 108,935 17 |

LIABILITIES—Concluded.

| | |
|---|---|
| Dividends left with the company to accumulate at interest | $93,928 00 |
| Gross premiums paid in advance, including surrender values so applied, less discount, if any | 5,122 00 |
| Unearned interest and rent paid in advance | 38,131 02 |
| Commissions due agents on premium notes, when paid | 5,938 00 |
| Salaries, rents, office expenses, bills and accounts due or accrued | 3,630 00 |
| Medical examiners' fees due or accrued | 1,545 00 |
| Estimated amount hereafter payable for federal, state and other taxes based upon the business of the year of this statement | 38,884 60 |
| Dividends declared on or apportioned to annual dividend policies payable to policyholders during 1922 for period to December 31, 1922 | 89,784 00 |
| Dividends declared on or apportioned to deferred dividend policies payable to policyholders during 1922 for period to December 31, 1922 | 1,532 00 |
| Amounts set apart, apportioned, provisionally ascertained, calculated, declared or held awaiting apportionment upon deferred dividend policies | 66,265 00 |
| Total | $7,471,468 06 |
| Capital paid up | 560,320 00 |
| Unassigned funds (surplus) | 124,480 33 |
| Total | $8,156,268 39 |

## EXHIBIT OF POLICIES—ORDINARY.

ALL BUSINESS PAID FOR.

| | Number. | Amount. | Number. | Amount. |
|---|---|---|---|---|
| Policies in force December 31, 1920 | | | 23,554 | $60,527,796 00 |
| Policies issued, revived and increased during the year | | | 5,137 | 14,922,455 00 |
| Total | | | 28,691 | $75,450,251 00 |
| Deduct policies which have ceased to be in force during the year— | | | | |
| By death | 213 | $ 667,657 00 | | |
| By maturity | 19 | 48,173 00 | | |
| By expiry | 196 | 206,005 00 | | |
| By surrender | 187 | 485,578 00 | | |
| By lapse | 4,324 | 10,333,294 00 | | |
| By decrease | | 831,782 00 | | |
| Total | | | 4,939 | 12,572,489 00 |
| Total policies in force December 31, 1921 | | | 23,752 | $62,877,762 00 |
| Re-insured | | | | $544,128 00 |

## EXHIBIT OF POLICIES—GROUP INSURANCE.

ALL BUSINESS PAID FOR.

| | Amount. | Number. | Amount. |
|---|---|---|---|
| Policies in force December 31, 1920 | | 4 | $804,200 00 |
| Policies issued, revived and increased during the year | | | 115,500 00 |
| Total | | 4 | $919,700 00 |
| Deduct policies which have ceased to be in force during the year— | | | |
| By death | $ 8,700 00 | | |
| By decrease | 57,200 00 | | |
| Total | | | 65,900 00 |
| Total policies in force December 31, 1921 | | 4 | $853,800 00 |

## BUSINESS IN ILLINOIS—ORDINARY.

| | Number. | Amount. |
|---|---|---|
| Policies in force December 31, 1920 | 257 | $825,642 00 |
| Policies issued during the year | 38 | 236,829 00 |
| Total | 295 | $1,062,471 00 |
| Deduct policies ceased to be in force | 28 | 194,718 00 |
| Policies in force December 31, 1921 | 267 | $867,753 00 |
| Losses and claims incurred during the year | 4 | $19,100 00 |
| Losses and claims settled during the year | 3 | 18,100 00 |
| Losses and claims unpaid December 31, 1921 | 1 | $1,000 00 |
| Premiums received | | $29,415 64 |

## GAIN AND LOSS EXHIBIT.

INSURANCE EXHIBIT.

| | | Gain in surplus. | Loss in surplus. |
|---|---|---|---|
| Loading on actual premiums of the year (averaging 25.7 per cent of the gross premiums) | $480,971 24 | | |
| Insurance expenses incurred during the year | 670,426 13 | | |
| Loss from loading | | | $189,454 89 |
| Interest earned during the year | $425,269 63 | | |
| Investment expenses incurred during the year | 38,134 82 | | |
| Net income from investments | $387,134 81 | | |
| Interest required to maintain reserve | 204,889 10 | | |
| Gain from interest | | $182,245 71 | |
| Expected mortality on net amount at risk | $658,882 21 | | |
| Actual mortality on net amount at risk | 502,570 66 | | |
| Gain from mortality | | 156,311 55 | |
| Total gain during the year from surrendered and lapsed policies | | 37,653 61 | |
| Dividends paid stockholders | | | 33,619 20 |
| Decrease in surplus on dividend account | | | 145,906 40 |
| Decrease in special funds and special reserves during the year | | 716 00 | |
| Net to profit account | | 445 38 | |

INVESTMENT EXHIBIT.

| | | Gain in surplus. | Loss in surplus. |
|---|---|---|---|
| Total gains from real estate | | 2,491 85 | |
| Total gains from stocks and bonds | | 3,709 15 | |
| Loss from assets not admitted | | | 12,044 08 |
| Net gain on account of total and permanent disability benefits or additional accidental death benefits included in life policies | | 15,211 87 | |
| Total gains and losses in surplus during the year | | $398,785 12 | $381,024 57 |
| Surplus December 31, 1920 | $106,719 78 | | |
| Surplus December 31, 1921 | 124,480 33 | | |
| Increase in surplus | | | 17,760 55 |
| Total | | $398,785 12 | $398,785 12 |

## PHOENIX MUTUAL LIFE INSURANCE COMPANY.

Located at No. 79 Elm Street, Hartford, Connecticut; incorporated May, 1851; commenced business in Illinois April 2, 1862.

JOHN M. HOLCOMBE, President. HARRY E. JOHNSON, Secretary.

JULES GIRARDIN, Chicago, Attorney for service.

Amount of ledger assets December 31, of previous year $55,035,599 99

### INCOME.

| | | | |
|---|---|---|---|
| First year's premiums on original policies, less re-insurance | | $1,530,943 18 | |
| First year's premiums for total and permanent disability benefits | | 43,210 14 | |
| First year's premiums for additional accidental death benefits | | 31,601 57 | |
| Surrender values to pay first year's premiums | | 17,850 02 | |
| Dividends applied to purchase paid-up additions and annuities | | 180,291 00 | |
| Surrender values applied to purchase paid-up insurance and annuities | | 133,729 00 | |
| Consideration for original annuities involving life contingencies | | 271,991 71 | |
| New premiums | | $2,209,616 62 | |
| Renewal premiums less re-insurance | $7,857,073 12 | | |
| Renewal premiums for total and permanent disability benefits | 102,987 74 | | |
| Renewal premiums for additional accidental death benefits | 72,701 71 | | |
| Dividends applied to pay renewal premiums | 727,927 08 | | |
| Dividends applied to shorten the endowment or premium-paying period | 22,989 05 | | |
| Surrender values applied to pay renewal premiums | 75,490 55 | | |
| Renewal premiums for deferred annuities | 36,695 05 | | |
| Renewal premiums | | 8,895,864 30 | |
| Premium income | | | $11,105,480 92 |
| Consideration for supplementary contracts involving life contingencies | | | 214,664 81 |
| Consideration for supplementary contracts not involving life contingencies | | | 64,063 81 |
| Dividends left with company to accumulate at interest | | | 680,288 32 |

## INCOME—Concluded.

| | | |
|---|---|---|
| Interest on mortgage loans | $1,720,397 89 | |
| Interest on bonds and dividends on stocks | 607,742 14 | |
| Interest on premium notes, policy loans or liens | 405,036 13 | |
| Interest on deposits | 32,837 64 | |
| Interest on other debts due the company | 1,738 41 | |
| Discount on claims paid in advance | 1,383 24 | |
| Rents—including $60,000.00 for company's occupancy of its own buildings | 148,158 63 | |
| Total interest and rents | | $2,917,294 08 |
| From other sources, viz: Guarantee of mortgage loans, $110.92; re-insurance reserve deposited with this company, $50,166.35 | | 50,277 27 |
| Agents' balances previously charged off | | 4,838 32 |
| Profit on sale or maturity of ledger assets | | 1,372 00 |
| Increase in book value of ledger assets | | 16,677 50 |
| Total income | | $15,054,957 03 |
| Total | | $70,090,557 02 |

## DISBURSEMENTS.

| | | |
|---|---|---|
| Death claims and additions | $2,303,800 42 | |
| Matured endowments and additions | 1,262,892 18 | |
| Total and permanent disability claims and additional accidental death benefits | 26,271 03 | |
| Total death claims and endowments | | $3,592,963 63 |
| Annuities involving life contingencies | | 300,106 48 |
| Surrender values paid in cash, or applied in liquidation of loans or notes | | 893,490 38 |
| Surrender values applied to pay new and renewal premiums | | 93,340 57 |
| Surrender values applied to purchase paid-up insurance and annuities | | 133,729 00 |
| Dividends paid policyholders in cash, or applied in liquidation of loans or notes | | 112,303 16 |
| Dividends applied to pay renewal premiums | | 727,927 08 |
| Dividends applied to shorten the endowment or premium-paying period | | 22,989 05 |
| Dividends applied to purchase paid-up additions and annuities | | 180,291 00 |
| Dividends left with the company to accumulate at interest | | 680,288 32 |
| (Total paid policyholders | $6,737,428 67) | |
| Expense of investigation and settlement of policy claims, including legal expenses | | 2,316 43 |
| Supplementary contracts not involving life contingencies | | 70,021 40 |
| Dividends with interest, held on deposit surrendered during the year | | 242,960 79 |
| Commissions to agents, first year, $688,623.97; renewal, $502,492.65; annuities (original), $9,809.30; (renewal), $2,135.38 | | 1,203,061 30 |
| Compensation of managers and agents not paid by commissions on new business | | 118,235 49 |
| Branch office expenses | | 263,422 28 |
| Medical examiners' fees and inspection of risks | | 81,122 34 |
| Salaries and all other compensation of officers and home office employees | | 462,620 05 |
| Rent | | 60,000 00 |
| Advertising, printing, stationery, postage, telegraph, telephone, express and exchange | | 113,176 40 |
| Legal expense | | 4,089 07 |
| Furniture, fixtures and safes | | 41,490 37 |
| Repairs and expenses (other than taxes) on real estate | | 82,084 92 |
| Taxes on real estate | | 40,658 45 |
| State taxes on premiums | | 145,913 31 |
| Insurance department licenses and fees | | 6,968 17 |
| Federal taxes | | 39,375 45 |
| All other licenses, fees and taxes | | 110,805 69 |
| Other disbursements, viz: Legislative expense, $498.24; home office travel expense, $13,134.86; miscellaneous expense, $56,458.36; mortgage loan expense, $8,247.89; foreclosure expense, $4,464.00; mortgage loan commissions, $21,842.71; company share expense investment bureau, $4,049.01 | | 108,695 07 |
| Interest on re-insurance reserve deposited with this company | | 8,910 40 |
| Loss on sale or maturity of ledger assets | | 1,612 00 |
| Decrease in book value of ledger assets | | 126,444 77 |
| Total disbursements | | $10,071,412 82 |
| Balance | | $60,019,144 20 |

## LEDGER ASSETS.

| | |
|---|---|
| Book value of real estate | $ 2,400,989 66 |
| Mortgage loans on real estate | 34,025,893 04 |
| Premiums advanced under Soldiers' and Sailors' Civil Relief Act | 27 00 |
| Loans on company's policies assigned as collateral | 9,347,124 35 |
| Premium notes on policies in force | 17,437 71 |
| Book value of bonds and stocks | 13,066,224 25 |
| Cash in office | 1,589 20 |
| Deposits in trust companies and banks on interest | 1,143,791 04 |
| Agents' balances (debit, $17,601.09; credit, $1,533.14) | 16,067 95 |
| Total ledger assets | $60,019,144 20 |

## LEDGER ASSETS—Concluded.

### NON-LEDGER ASSETS.

| | New business. | Renewals. | |
|---|---|---|---|
| Interest due and accrued on mortgages | | $998,690 41 | |
| Interest due and accrued on bonds | | 155,635 10 | |
| Interest due and accrued on premium notes, loans or liens | | 277,745 54 | |
| Interest due on other assets | | 77 24 | |
| | | | $1,432,148 29 |
| Market value of bonds and stocks over book value | | | 170,649 47 |
| Net uncollected and deferred premiums (paid for basis) | $110,688 27 | $1,026,396 78 | 1,137,085 05 |
| Gross assets | | | $62,759,027 01 |

### DEDUCT ASSETS NOT ADMITTED.

| | | |
|---|---|---|
| Agents' debit balances | $17,601 09 | |
| Overdue and accrued interest on bonds in default | 53,825 00 | |
| Total | | 71,426 09 |
| Admitted assets | | $62,687,600 92 |

## LIABILITIES.

| | | |
|---|---|---|
| Net present value of outstanding policies | $50,587,425 21 | |
| Same for dividend additions | 1,289,598 00 | |
| Same for annuities | 2,605,400 00 | |
| Total | $54,482,423 21 | |
| Deduct net value of risks re-insured | 558,379 00 | |
| Net reserve (paid for basis) | | $53,924,044 21 |
| Extra reserve for total and permanent disability benefits and for additional accidental death benefits included in life policies | | 237,045 00 |
| Present value of supplementary contracts not involving life contingencies | | 625,781 00 |
| Present value of amounts incurred but not yet due for total and permanent disability benefits | | 132,174 00 |
| Surrender values claimable on policies cancelled | | 5,737 43 |
| Death losses in process of adjustment | $16,018 33 | |
| Death losses reported for which no proofs have been received | 81,434 02 | |
| Reserve for net death losses incurred but unreported | 44,981 44 | |
| Matured endowments due and unpaid | 2,402 50 | |
| Death losses and other policy claims resisted | 23,607 73 | |
| Total and permanent disability benefits and additional accidental death benefits | 5,000 00 | |
| Total policy claims | | 173,444 02 |
| Dividends left with the company to accumulate at interest | | 2,684,373 83 |
| Gross premiums paid in advance, including surrender values so applied, less discount, if any | | 204,450 35 |
| Unearned interest and rent paid in advance | | 17,852 24 |
| Commissions to agents due or accrued | | 12,448 37 |
| Salaries, rents, office expenses, bills and accounts due or accrued | | 6,438 26 |
| Medical examiners' and legal fees due or accrued | | 6,586 00 |
| Estimated amount hereafter payable for federal, state and other taxes based upon the business of the year of this statement | | 330,051 00 |
| Dividends or other profits due policyholders | | 92,007 70 |
| Dividends declared and those provisionally held for annual dividend policies payable to policyholders during 1922 for period to December 31, 1922 | | 1,662,721 54 |
| Reserve for special paid-up option | | 4,000 00 |
| Reserve on policies re-insured, deposited and held by this company | | 226,891 21 |
| Accrued interest | | 5,672 28 |
| Other liabilities, viz: General equalization fund, $383,647.48; mortality fluctuation fund, $1,270,726.00; investment fluctuation fund, $550,003.00; disability and double indemnity fluctuation fund, $131,506.00 | | 2,335,882 48 |
| Total | | $62,687,600 92 |

## EXHIBIT OF POLICIES—ORDINARY.

### ALL BUSINESS PAID FOR.

| | Number. | Amount. | Number. | Amount. |
|---|---|---|---|---|
| Policies in force December 31, 1920 | | | 125,165 | $294,348,813 00 |
| Policies issued, revived and increased during the year | | | 14,157 | 50,462,274 00 |
| Total | | | 139,322 | $344,811,087 00 |
| Deduct policies which have ceased to be in force during the year— | | | | |
| By death | 1,009 | $2,345,287 00 | | |
| By maturity | 671 | 1,260,912 00 | | |
| By expiry | 1,125 | 2,173,739 00 | | |
| By surrender | 1,785 | 4,668,852 00 | | |

EXHIBIT OF POLICIES—ORDINARY—Concluded.

ALL BUSINESS PAID FOR.

| | Number. | Amount. | Number. | Amount. |
|---|---|---|---|---|
| Deduct policies which have ceased to be in force during the year— | | | | |
| By lapse | 3,473 | $10,659,236 00 | | |
| By decrease | -------- | 977,831 00 | | |
| Total | | | 8,063 | $22,085,857 00 |
| Total policies in force December 31, 1921 | | | 131,259 | $322,725,230 00 |
| Re-insured | | | 522 | $7,325,349 00 |

BUSINESS IN ILLINOIS—ORDINARY.

| | Number. | Amount. |
|---|---|---|
| Policies in force December 31, 1920 | 4,508 | $13,477,557 87 |
| Policies issued during the year | 472 | 2,698,059 05 |
| Total | 4,980 | $16,175,616 92 |
| Deduct policies ceased to be in force | 246 | 828,820 07 |
| Policies in force December 31, 1921 | 4,734 | $15,346,796 85 |
| Losses and claims unpaid December 31, 1920 | 2 | $4,000 00 |
| Losses and claims incurred during the year | 81 | 184,514 90 |
| Total | 83 | $188,514 90 |
| Losses and claims settled during the year | 80 | 181,514 90 |
| Losses and claims unpaid December 31, 1921 | 3 | $7,000 00 |
| Premiums received | | $531,717 73 |

GAIN AND LOSS EXHIBIT.

INSURANCE EXHIBIT.

| | | Gain in surplus. | Loss in surplus. |
|---|---|---|---|
| Loading on actual premiums of the year (averaging 20.8 per cent of the gross premiums) | $2,354,670 56 | | |
| Insurance expenses incurred during the year | 2,777,946 75 | | |
| Loss from loading | | -------------- | $ 423,276 19 |
| Interest earned during the year | $3,215,180 25 | | |
| Investment expenses incurred during the year | 251,220 06 | | |
| Net income from investments | $2,963,960 19 | | |
| Interest required to maintain reserve | 1,838,240 72 | | |
| Gain from interest | | $1,125,719 47 | |
| Expected mortality on net amount at risk | $3,114,865 00 | | |
| Actual mortality on net amount at risk | 1,533,881 84 | | |
| Gain from mortality | | 1,580,983 16 | |
| Expected disbursements to annuitants | $255,824 00 | | |
| Net actual annuity claims incurred | 268,432 48 | | |
| Loss from annuities | | -------------- | 12,608 48 |
| Total gain during the year from surrendered and lapsed policies | | 269,884 11 | |
| Decrease in surplus on dividend account | | -------------- | 1,932,159 61 |
| Increase in special funds and special reserves during the year | | -------------- | 543,895 86 |
| Net to profit account | | 4,838 32 | |

INVESTMENT EXHIBIT.

| | Gain in surplus. | Loss in surplus. |
|---|---|---|
| Total losses from real estate | -------------- | 118,043 97 |
| Total gains from stocks and bonds | 47,229 02 | |
| Total losses from stocks and bonds | -------------- | 1,612 00 |
| Gain from assets not admitted | 4,841 74 | |
| Net loss on account of total and permanent disability benefits or additional accidental death benefits included in life policies | -------------- | 1,899 71 |
| Total | $3,033,495 82 | $3,033,495 82 |

## THE PROVIDENT LIFE AND TRUST COMPANY OF PHILADELPHIA.

Located at Northwest Corner Fourth and Chestnut Streets, Philadelphia, Pennsylvania; incorporated March 22, 1865; commenced business in Illinois March 10, 1882.

ASA S. WING, President. LEONARD C. ASHTON, Secretary.

GEORGE M. HERRICK, Chicago, Attorney for service.

CAPITAL.

| | | |
|---|---|---|
| Capital paid up | $2,000,000 00 | |
| Amount of ledger assets December 31, of previous year | | $107,671,219 34 |

## INCOME.

| | | | |
|---|---|---|---|
| First year's premiums on original policies | | $2,699,981 31 | |
| Surrender values to pay first year's premiums | | 30,299 74 | |
| Dividends applied to purchase paid-up additions and annuities | | 341,545 32 | |
| Surrender values applied to purchase paid-up insurance and annuities | | 242,987 00 | |
| Consideration for original annuities involving life contingencies | | 42,937 66 | |
| New premiums | | $ 3,357,751 03 | |
| Renewal premiums | $14,965,116 00 | | |
| Dividends applied to pay renewal premiums | 2,166,844 69 | | |
| Renewal premiums for deferred annuities | 567 00 | | |
| Renewal premiums | | 17,132,527 69 | |
| Premium income | | | $20,490,278 72 |
| Consideration for supplementary contracts involving life contingencies | | | 16,025 10 |
| Consideration for supplementary contracts not involving life contingencies | | | 156,164 61 |
| Dividends left with company to accumulate at interest | | | 90,517 07 |
| Interest on mortgage loans | | $1,185,106 08 | |
| Interest on collateral loans | | 315,750 08 | |
| Interest on bonds and dividends on stocks | | 3,276,710 28 | |
| Interest on premium notes, policy loans or liens | | 830,135 87 | |
| Interest on deposits | | 18,466 89 | |
| Rents—including $20,500.00 for company's occupancy of its own buildings | | 88,241 87 | |
| Total interest and rents | | | 5,714,411 07 |
| From other sources, viz: Premiums received on collateral loans, $1,916.67; refund of expenses incurred in previous years, $254.85; deficiency judgment on mortgage, $25.70 | | | 2,197 22 |
| Profit on sale or maturity of ledger assets | | | 221,002 25 |
| Total income | | | $26,690,596 04 |
| Total | | | $134,361,815 38 |

## DISBURSEMENTS.

| | | |
|---|---|---|
| Death claims and additions | $4,228,163 14 | |
| Matured endowments and additions | 4,001,458 05 | |
| Total death claims and endowments | | $8,229,621 19 |
| Annuities involving life contingencies | | 150,568 62 |
| Surrender values paid in cash, or applied in liquidation of loans or notes | | 2,490,372 55 |
| Surrender values applied to pay new and renewal premiums | | 30,299 74 |
| Surrender values applied to purchase paid-up insurance and annuities | | 242,987 00 |
| Dividends paid policyholders in cash, or applied in liquidation of loans or notes | | 335,861 63 |
| Dividends applied to pay renewal premiums | | 2,166,844 69 |
| Dividends applied to purchase paid-up additions and annuities | | 341,545 32 |
| Dividends left with the company to accumulate at interest | | 90,517 07 |
| (Total paid policyholders | $14,078,617 81) | |
| Expense of investigation and settlement of policy claims, including legal expenses | | 2,034 27 |
| Supplementary contracts not involving life contingencies | | 174,957 60 |
| Dividends with interest, held on deposit surrendered during the year | | 27,976 49 |
| Commissions to agents, first year, $972,388.20; renewal, $1,124,461.54; annuities (original), $2,186.74; (renewal), $22.99 | | 2,099,059 47 |
| Compensation of managers and agents not paid by commissions on new business | | 33,833 26 |
| Agency supervision and traveling expenses of supervisors | | 16,332 36 |
| Branch office expenses | | 347,204 81 |
| Medical examiners' fees and inspection of risks | | 113,899 56 |
| Salaries and all other compensation of officers and home office employees | | 980,703 90 |
| Rent | | 20,980 00 |
| Advertising, printing, stationery, postage, telegraph, telephone, express and exchange | | 89,935 30 |
| Legal expense | | 13,612 80 |
| Furniture, fixtures and safes | | 26,052 25 |
| Repairs and expenses (other than taxes) on real estate | | 59,111 32 |
| Taxes on real estate | | 47,354 85 |
| Sundry investment expenses | | 1,258 08 |
| State taxes on premiums | | 300,768 62 |
| Insurance department licenses and fees | | 10,744 93 |
| Federal taxes | | 58,622 62 |
| All other licenses, fees and taxes | | 518,316 30 |
| Other disbursements, viz: Meals to office employees, $53,359.79; light, fuel, hauling, etc., home office, $16,466.40; expenses including $7,500.00 legal expense, in connection with mutualization plan, $13,159.70; insurance and surety bonds, $15,710.10; rent and services in connection with mechanical appliances, $2,735.29; burglar protection and detective service, $1,681.13; contribution to employees' activities, $3,244.66; dues and subscriptions, $4,211.64; uniforms, laundry, etc., $3,039.55; dictograph system, installation and equipment, $7,903.93; audits by agencies independent of company, $6,793.99; miscellaneous items less than $100.00 each, $2,488.55 | | 130,794 73 |
| Loss on sale or maturity of ledger assets | | 27,968 60 |
| Decrease in book value of ledger assets | | 57,012 13 |
| Total disbursements | | $19,237,152 06 |
| Balance | | $115,124,663 32 |

## LEDGER ASSETS.

| | |
|---|---|
| Book value of real estate | $ 807,215 85 |
| Mortgage loans on real estate | 22,042,100 84 |
| Loans secured by collaterals | 4,014,562 50 |
| Premiums advanced under Soldiers' and Sailors' Civil Relief Act | 633 80 |
| Loans on company's policies assigned as collateral | 16,092,504 87 |
| Book value of bonds and stocks | 71,841,580 46 |
| Deposits in trust companies and banks on interest | 281,673 34 |
| Agents' balances (debit, $53,693.89; credit, $9,302.23) net | 44,391 66 |
| Total ledger assets | $115,124,663 32 |

### NON-LEDGER ASSETS.

| | | | |
|---|---|---|---|
| Interest due and accrued on mortgages | | $ 369,155 66 | |
| Interest due and accrued on bonds | | 1,205,900 83 | |
| Interest accrued on collateral loans | | 30,951 68 | |
| Interest due and accrued on premium notes, loans or liens | | 365,149 98 | |
| Rents due on company's property | | 3,966 55 | |
| | | | 1,975,124 70 |
| Amortized value of bonds and stocks over book value | | | 8,558,725 46 |
| | New business. | Renewals. | |
| Net uncollected and deferred premiums (paid for basis) | $306,502 67 | $2,676,822 09 | 2,983,324 76 |
| All other assets, viz: Sundry payments made in advance; matured endowments, $34,038.00; annuities, $5,571.77; supplementary contracts, $978.02; dividends, $13,282.52 | | | 53,870 31 |
| Gross assets | | | $128,695,708 55 |

### DEDUCT ASSETS NOT ADMITTED.

| | | |
|---|---|---|
| Agents' debit balances | $ 53,693 89 | |
| Overdue and accrued interest on bonds in default | 242,496 89 | |
| Total | | 296,190 78 |
| Admitted assets | | $128,399,517 77 |

## LIABILITIES.

| | | |
|---|---|---|
| Net present value of outstanding policies computed by the Pennsylvania Insurance Department | $107,875,991 00 | |
| Same for dividend additions | 3,184,544 00 | |
| Same for annuities | 1,503,037 00 | |
| Total | | $112,563,572 00 |
| Present value of supplementary contracts not involving life contingencies | | 1,216,894 00 |
| Surrender values claimable on policies cancelled | | 56,516 17 |
| Death losses due and unpaid | $ 67,755 37 | |
| Death losses reported for which no proofs have been received | 108,035 00 | |
| Reserve for net death losses incurred but unreported | 75,000 00 | |
| Matured endowments due and unpaid | 29,913 00 | |
| Death losses and other policy claims resisted | 4,896 57 | |
| Annuity claims, involving life contingencies, due and unpaid | 2,591 54 | |
| Total policy claims | | 288,191 48 |
| Dividends left with the company to accumulate at interest | | 276,151 00 |
| Gross premiums paid in advance, including surrender values so applied, less discount, if any | | 625,942 75 |
| Unearned interest and rent paid in advance | | 3,723 00 |
| Commissions to agents due or accrued | | 2,258 34 |
| Salaries, rents, office expenses, bills and accounts due or accrued | | 4,363 30 |
| Medical examiners' fees due or accrued | | 8,747 50 |
| Estimated amount hereafter payable for federal, state and other taxes based upon the business of the year of this statement | | 574,615 00 |
| Dividends or other profits due policyholders | | 298,618 18 |
| Dividends declared on or apportioned to annual dividend policies payable to policyholders during 1922 for period to December 31, 1922 | | 3,296,000 00 |
| Reserve for purpose of mutualization of company | | 2,577,128 00 |
| Special reserves: Mortality fluctuation fund | | 2,109,091 00 |
| Asset depreciation fund | | 2,355,972 05 |
| Excess of reserve computed by company over reserve computed by insurance department | | 141,734 00 |
| Total | | $126,399,517 77 |
| Capital paid up | | 2,000,000 00 |
| Total | | $128,399,517 77 |

## EXHIBIT OF POLICIES—ORDINARY.

### ALL BUSINESS PAID FOR.

| | Number. | Amount. |
|---|---|---|
| Policies in force December 31, 1920 | 198,417 | $535,003,953 00 |
| Policies issued, revived and increased during the year | 27,225 | 87,607,287 00 |
| Total | 225,642 | $622,611,240 00 |

## EXHIBIT OF POLICIES—ORDINARY—Concluded.

ALL BUSINESS PAID FOR.

| | Number. | Amount. | Number. | Amount. |
|---|---|---|---|---|
| Deduct policies which have ceased to be in force during the year— | | | | |
| By death | 1,202 | $ 4,195,123 00 | | |
| By maturity | 1,657 | 4,011,400 00 | | |
| By expiry | 163 | 528,444 00 | | |
| By surrender | 3,963 | 12,599,301 00 | | |
| By lapse | 6,711 | 21,267,865 00 | | |
| By decrease | -------- | 5,285,250 00 | | |
| Total | | | 13,696 | $47,887,383 00 |
| Total policies in force December 31, 1921 | | | 211,946 | $574,723,857 00 |

## BUSINESS IN ILLINOIS—ORDINARY.

| | Number. | Amount. |
|---|---|---|
| Policies in force December 31, 1920 | 7,683 | $22,896,254 00 |
| Policies issued during the year | 1,606 | 5,234,698 00 |
| Total | 9,289 | $28,130,952 00 |
| Deduct policies ceased to be in force | 964 | 3,160,741 00 |
| Policies in force December 31, 1921 | 8,325 | $24,970,211 00 |
| Losses and claims unpaid December 31, 1920 | 2 | $ 2,766 00 |
| Losses and claims incurred during the year | 61 | 215,868 00 |
| Total | 63 | $218,634 00 |
| Losses and claims settled during the year | 54 | 204,566 00 |
| Losses and claims unpaid December 31, 1921 | 9 | $14,068 00 |
| Premiums received | | $825,518 58 |

## GAIN AND LOSS EXHIBIT.

INSURANCE EXHIBIT.

| | | Gain in surplus. | Loss in surplus. |
|---|---|---|---|
| Loading on actual premiums of the year (averaging 17.82 per cent of the gross premiums) | $3,729,383 17 | | |
| Insurance expenses incurred during the year | 4,746,755 10 | | |
| Loss from loading | | -------------- | $1,017,371 93 |
| Interest earned during the year | $5,918,453 81 | | |
| Investment expenses incurred during the year | 288,309 90 | | |
| Net income from investments | $5,630,143 91 | | |
| Interest required to maintain reserve | 3,876,562 00 | | |
| Gain from interest | | $1,753,581 91 | |
| Expected mortality on net amount at risk | $5,315,432 00 | | |
| Actual mortality on net amount at risk | 2,713,074 71 | | |
| Gain from mortality | | 2,602,357 29 | |
| Expected disbursements to annuitants | $ 86,492 00 | | |
| Net actual annuity claims incurred | 113,896 12 | | |
| Loss from annuities | | -------------- | 27,404 12 |
| Total gain during the year from surrendered and lapsed policies | | 258,509 61 | |
| Decrease in surplus on dividend account | | -------------- | 3,451,098 21 |
| Increase in special funds and special reserves during the year | | -------------- | 69,382 63 |
| Net to profit account | | 2,197 22 | |

INVESTMENT EXHIBIT.

| | Gain in surplus. | Loss in surplus. |
|---|---|---|
| Total gains from real estate | 3,890 00 | |
| Total losses from real estate | -------------- | 8,363 15 |
| Total gains from stocks and bonds | 217,112 25 | |
| Total losses from stocks and bonds | -------------- | 320,779 89 |
| Loss from assets not admitted | -------------- | 53,693 89 |
| Gain from use of reserve computed by insurance department of Pennsylvania | 110,538 00 | |
| Balance unaccounted for | -------------- | 92 46 |
| Total gains and losses in surplus during the year | $4,948,186 28 | $4,948,186 28 |

## THE PRUDENTIAL INSURANCE COMPANY OF AMERICA.

Located at No. 755-769 Broad Street, Newark, New Jersey; incorporated, 1873; commenced business in Illinois March 9, 1886.

FORREST F. DRYDEN, President.
WILLARD I. HAMILTON, 2d Vice President and Secretary.

A. A. HOFFMAN, Springfield, Attorney for service.

### CAPITAL.

| | | | |
|---|---|---|---|
| Capital paid up | | $2,000,000 00 | |
| Amount of ledger assets December 31, of previous year | | | $669,674,020 47 |

### INCOME.

| | | | |
|---|---|---|---|
| First year's premiums on original policies (ordinary) | | $12,518,318 39 | |
| First year's premiums for total and permanent disability benefits, (ordinary) | | 114,992 00 | |
| First year's premiums for additional accidental death benefits, (ordinary) | | 138,987 00 | |
| Dividends applied to purchase paid-up additions and annuities (ordinary) | | 187,377 88 | |
| Consideration for original annuities involving life contingencies (ordinary) | | 200,741 04 | |
| First premiums by disability claims (ordinary) | | 153 00 | |
| New premiums (ordinary) | | $13,160,569 31 | |
| Renewal premiums less re-insurance (ordinary) | $59,893,558 72 | | |
| Renewal premiums for total and permanent disability benefits (ordinary) | 218,949 00 | | |
| Renewal premiums for additional accidental death benefits (ordinary) | 284,395 00 | | |
| Dividends applied to pay renewal premiums (ordinary) | 2,936,636 26 | | |
| Renewal premiums by disability claims (ordinary) | 72,154 00 | | |
| Renewal premiums for deferred annuities (ordinary) | 3,551 79 | | |
| Renewal premiums (ordinary) | | 63,409,244 77 | |
| Premium income (ordinary) | | $76,569,814 08 | |
| Premium income (industrial) | | 111,156,132 84 | |
| Premiums advanced during year under Soldiers' and Sailors' Civil Relief Act (ordinary, $421.62; industrial, $7.95) | | 429 57 | |
| Total | | | $187,726,376 49 |
| Consideration for supplementary contracts involving life contingencies | | | 225,199 22 |
| Consideration for supplementary contracts not involving life contingencies | | | 1,618,246 12 |
| Dividends left with company to accumulate at interest | | | 59,695 80 |
| Interest on mortgage loans | | $11,793,403 88 | |
| Interest on collateral loans | | 53,685 62 | |
| Interest on bonds and dividends on stocks | | 18,220,867 82 | |
| Interest on premium notes, policy loans or liens | | 2,165,252 37 | |
| Interest on deposits | | 345,321 73 | |
| Interest on other debts due the company | | 65,318 25 | |
| Discount on payment for bonds purchased prior to date of issue | | 12,944 87 | |
| Rents—including $986,380.00 for company's occupancy of its own buildings | | 1,498,852 74 | |
| Total interest and rents | | | 34,155,647 28 |
| From other sources, viz: Dividend returned to company for distribution to policyholders on par value of capital stock of the company purchased pursuant to the provisions of Chapter 99 of the laws of New Jersey for the year 1913, and assigned to Austen Colgate, trustee for the policyholders of the company, $377,947.49; conscience fund, $1,534.00; exchange (premium on funds transferred to Canada, etc.), $17,684.76 | | | 397,166 25 |
| Profit on sale or maturity of ledger assets | | | 142,243 26 |
| Increase in book value of ledger assets | | | 515,152 28 |
| Total income | | | $224,839,726 70 |
| Total | | | $894,513,747 17 |

### DISBURSEMENTS.

| | | |
|---|---|---|
| Death claims and additions | $36,989,936 89 | |
| Matured endowments and additions | 4,667,017 34 | |
| Total and permanent disability claims and additional accidental death benefits | 986,675 54 | |
| Total death claims and endowments | | $42,643,629 77 |
| Annuities involving life contingencies | | 296,402 32 |
| Surrender values paid in cash, or applied in liquidation of loans or notes | | 9,492,658 50 |
| Dividends paid policyholders in cash, or applied in liquidation of loans or notes | | 6,278,743 69 |
| Dividends applied to pay renewal premiums | | 4,879,739 02 |
| Dividends applied to purchase paid-up additions and annuities | | 5,319,643 88 |
| Dividends left with the company to accumulate at interest | | 59,695 80 |
| (Total paid policyholders | $68,970,512 98) | |
| Expense of investigation and settlement of policy claims, including legal expenses | | 59,500 39 |
| Supplementary contracts not involving life contingencies | | 998,324 73 |

## DISBURSEMENTS—Concluded.

| | |
|---|---|
| Dividends with interest, held on deposit surrendered during the year | $ 7,399 77 |
| Dividends to stockholders | 400,000 00 |
| Commissions to agents, first year, $4,423,443.56; renewal, $2,547,348.25; annuities (original) $3,765.98; (renewal), $147.14; industrial, $20,901,177.83 | 27,875,882 76 |
| Agency supervision and traveling expenses of supervisors | 400,150 64 |
| Branch office expenses | 7,270,493 18 |
| Medical examiners' fees and inspection of risks | 912,020 13 |
| Salaries and all other compensation of officers and home office employees | 5,861,888 25 |
| Rent | 1,609,606 90 |
| Advertising, printing, stationery, postage, telegraph, telephone, express, exchange and customs duties | 1,114,939 99 |
| Legal expense | 56,597 52 |
| Furniture, fixtures and safes | 223,275 16 |
| Repairs and expenses (other than taxes) on real estate | 677,912 90 |
| Taxes on real estate | 577,367 70 |
| State and provincial taxes on premiums | 2,796,102 80 |
| Insurance department licenses and fees | 73,595 09 |
| Federal taxes | 1,155,065 63 |
| All other licenses, fees and taxes | 624,370 18 |
| Other disbursements, viz: Law library, $1,305.58; expense of annual audit by public accountants, $13,000.00; expense of examination by State Departments, $8,272.35; sundry general expenses (includes contribution of $15,654.92 toward expenses of The Association of Life Insurance Presidents, of which $744.06 was disbursed by them for legal expenses and $4,544.59 for legislative expenses), $316,661.60; premiums on surety bonds, $2,450.26; investment expense account, $220,035.57; legislative expenses, $4,158.64; service retirement and insurance allowances paid and payments made to disabled home office and field employees, $323,211.19; expenses on account of service disability allowances, $1,382.79; business conferences, $173,086.07; expenses in connection with mutualization of company, $2,501.76; premium paid on capital stock of the company purchased pursuant to the provisions of chapter 99 of the laws of New Jersey for the year 1913, and assigned to Austen Colgate, trustee for the policyholders of the company, $810.00 | 1,065,875 81 |
| Decrease in book value of ledger assets | 3,004,959 92 |
| Total disbursements | $125,735,842 43 |
| Balance | $768,777,904 74 |

## LEDGER ASSETS.

| | |
|---|---|
| Book value of real estate | $ 15,678,238 17 |
| Mortgage loans on real estate | 258,732,150 81 |
| Loans secured by collaterals | 932,000 00 |
| Premiums advanced under Soldiers' and Sailors' Civil Relief Act | 1,868 07 |
| Loans on company's policies assigned as collateral | 54,167,647 76 |
| Book value of bonds and stocks | 423,983,333 41 |
| Cash in office | 7,380 70 |
| Cash in transit from branch offices | 394,444 72 |
| Deposits in trust companies and banks not on interest | 823,377 99 |
| Deposits in trust companies and banks on interest | 12,160,110 07 |
| Agents' balances | 7,515 54 |
| Par value of capital stock of the company purchased pursuant to the provisions of chapter 99 of the laws of New Jersey for the year 1913, and assigned to Austen Colgate, trustee for the policyholders of the company | 1,889,837 50 |
| Total ledger assets | $768,777,904 74 |

### NON-LEDGER ASSETS.

| | | | |
|---|---|---|---|
| Interest due and accrued on mortgages | | $5,144,919 24 | |
| Interest due and accrued on bonds | | 7,002,186 93 | |
| Interest accrued on collateral loans | | 9,493 14 | |
| Interest due and accrued on premium notes, loans or liens | | 806,546 27 | |
| Interest accrued on premiums reported on U. S. monthly difference lists to war risk insurance bureau in accordance with the Soldiers' and Sailors' Civil Relief Act | | 206 59 | |
| Interest due on bank balances | | 26,152 51 | |
| Rents due and accrued on company's property | | 15,899 45 | |
| | | | 13,005,404 13 |
| Due from other companies for losses or claims on policies re-insured | | | 295 00 |
| Dividend, to be returned to company for distribution to policyholders, on par value of capital stock of the company purchased pursuant to the provisions of chapter 99 of the laws of New Jersey for the year 1913, and assigned to Austen Colgate, trustee for the policyholders of the company, (dividend declared December 12, 1921, payable and paid January 3, 1922, to stockholders of record December 31, 1921, and returned to company by trustee January 3, 1922) | | | 434,662 62 |
| | New business. | Renewals. | |
| Net uncollected and deferred premiums (paid for basis) (ordinary) | $1,800,258 94 | $10,395,353 35 | 12,195,612 29 |
| Net amount of uncollected premiums (industrial), (gross, $1,199,812.96; deduct loading, $425,541.26) | | | 774,271 70 |
| All other assets, viz: Supplies, stationery, printed matter, $10,000.00; furniture, fixtures, safes, $50,000.00; law library, $10,136.07 | | | 70,136 07 |
| Gross assets | | | $795,258,286 55 |

## LEDGER ASSETS—Concluded.

DEDUCT ASSETS NOT ADMITTED.

| | | |
|---|---|---|
| Par value of capital stock of the company purchased pursuant to the provisions of chapter 99 of the laws of New Jersey for the year 1913, and assigned to Austen Colgate, trustee for the policyholders of the company | $1,889,837 50 | |
| Supplies, printed matter and stationery | 10,000 00 | |
| Furniture, fixtures and safes, $50,000.00; law library, $10,136.07 | 60,136 07 | |
| Agents' debit balances | 7,515 54 | |
| Premium notes, policy loans and other policy assets in excess of net value and of other policy liabilities on individual policies | 698 84 | |
| Overdue and accrued interest on bonds in default | 1,260,850 00 | |
| Book value of bonds and stocks over market value | 2,521,024 82 | |
| Total | | $5,750,062 77 |
| Admitted assets | | $789,508,223 78 |

## LIABILITIES.

| | | |
|---|---|---|
| Net present value of outstanding policies computed by the Commissioner of Banking and Insurance of the State of New Jersey | $691,560,257 00 | |
| Same for dividend additions | 16,557,354 00 | |
| Same for annuities | 3,241,422 00 | |
| Total | $711,359,033 00 | |
| Deduct net value of risks re-insured | 997,222 00 | |
| Net reserve (paid for basis) | | $710,361,811 00 |
| Extra reserve for total and permanent disability benefits and for additional accidental death benefits included in life policies | | 3,203,395 00 |
| Present value of supplementary contracts not involving life contingencies | | 3,223,756 29 |
| Present value of amounts incurred but not yet due for total and permanent disability benefits | | 850,971 00 |
| Surrender values claimable on policies cancelled | | 147,981 00 |
| Death losses in process of adjustment | $ 642,781 15 | |
| Death losses reported for which no proofs have been received | 435,400 81 | |
| Reserve for net death losses incurred but unreported | 1,313,047 63 | |
| Matured endowments due and unpaid | 77,787 26 | |
| Death losses and other policy claims resisted | 170,317 08 | |
| Total and permanent disability benefits and additional accidental death benefits | 402,091 40 | |
| Total policy claims | | 3,041,425 33 |
| Due and unpaid on supplementary contracts not involving life contingencies | | 3,033 84 |
| Dividends left with the company to accumulate at interest | | 150,415 91 |
| Gross premiums paid in advance, including surrender values so applied less discount, if any | | 3,797,874 51 |
| Unearned interest and rent paid in advance | | 885,595 02 |
| Unearned interest not paid in advance | | 466,713 17 |
| Commissions to agents due or accrued | | 404,905 50 |
| Salaries, rents, office expenses, bills and accounts due or accrued | | 501,570 48 |
| Medical examiners' and legal fees due or accrued | | 123,350 12 |
| Estimated amount hereafter payable for federal, state and other taxes based upon the business of the year of this statement | | 5,875,350 69 |
| Unpaid dividends to stockholders | | 460,000 00 |
| Dividends or other profits due policyholders | | 897,527 84 |
| Dividends declared on or apportioned to annual dividend policies payable to policyholders to and including December 31, 1922, whether contingent upon the payment of renewal premiums or otherwise | | 6,899,457 00 |
| Dividends declared on or apportioned to deferred dividend policies payable to policyholders to and including December 31, 1922 | | 4,920,738 00 |
| Amounts set apart, apportioned, provisionally ascertained, calculated, declared or held awaiting apportionment upon deferred dividend policies | | 8,931,882 69 |
| Reserve for service insurance allowances home office and field employees | | 174,296 00 |
| Premium over the par value of the capital stock of the company not yet purchased for the policyholders | | 892,316 25 |
| Difference to bring state department computation of reserve up to company's figures | | 36,444 00 |
| Other liabilities, viz: Surrender values due and unpaid, $3,181.45; deposits to secure rent under lease and accrued interest thereon, $2,308.01; extra war premiums to be refunded, $260.81 | | 5,750 27 |
| Total | | $756,256,560 91 |
| *Capital paid up | | 2,000,000 00 |
| Unassigned funds (surplus) | | 31,251,662 87 |
| Total | | $789,508,223 78 |

* $1,889,837.50 par value of the capital stock of the company has been purchased pursuant to the provisions of chapter 99 of the laws of New Jersey for the year 1913, and assigned to Austen Colgate, trustee for the policyholders of the company.

## EXHIBIT OF POLICIES—ORDINARY.

PAID FOR BUSINESS ONLY.

| | Number. | Amount. | Number. | Amount. |
|---|---|---|---|---|
| Policies in force December 31, 1920 | | | 1,799,959 | $2,301,119,643 00 |
| Policies issued, revived and increased during the year | | | 296,954 | 453,330,553 00 |
| Total | | | 2,096,913 | $2,754,450,196 00 |
| Deduct policies which have ceased to be in force during the year— | | | | |
| By death | 11,179 | $14,692,686 00 | | |
| By maturity | 4,437 | 4,563,299 00 | | |
| By disability | 426 | 703,205 00 | | |
| By expiry | 71,441 | 88,621,644 00 | | |
| By surrender | 14,409 | 18,555,958 00 | | |
| By lapse | 65,516 | 99,092,200 00 | | |
| By decrease | -------- | 2,057,300 00 | | |
| By withdrawal | -------- | 12,775,588 00 | | |
| Total | | | 167,408 | 241,061,880 00 |
| Total policies in force December 31, 1921 | | | 1,929,505 | $2,513,388,316 00 |
| Re-insured | | | 87 | $3,046,197 00 |

## EXHIBIT OF POLICIES—GROUP INSURANCE.

PAID FOR BUSINESS ONLY.

| | Number. | Amount. | Number. | Amount. |
|---|---|---|---|---|
| Policies in force December 31, 1920 | | | 301 | $45,711,457 00 |
| Policies issued, revived and increased during the year | | | 40 | 16,934,161 00 |
| Total | | | 341 | $62,645,618 00 |
| Deduct policies which have ceased to be in force during the year— | | | | |
| By death | -------- | $ 303,060 00 | | |
| By disability | -------- | 30,000 00 | | |
| By lapse | 45 | 4,154,650 00 | | |
| By withdrawal | -------- | 12,775,588 00 | | |
| Total | | | 45 | 17,263,298 00 |
| Total policies in force December 31, 1921 | | | 296 | $45,382,320 00 |
| Distribution of business in force at end of year—One year term | | | 296 | $45,382,320 00 |

## EXHIBIT OF POLICIES—INDUSTRIAL.

PAID FOR BUSINESS ONLY.

| | Number. | Amount. | Number. | Amount. |
|---|---|---|---|---|
| Policies in force December 31, 1920 | | | 18,662,140 | $2,794,902,131 00 |
| Policies issued, revived and increased during the year | | | 3,081,543 | 686,453,679 00 |
| Total | | | 21,743,683 | $3,481,355,810 00 |
| Deduct policies which have ceased to be in force during the year— | | | | |
| By death | 163,708 | $ 21,886,893 00 | | |
| By maturity | 99 | 8,077 00 | | |
| By disability | -------- | 42,798 00 | | |
| By expiry | 50,430 | 25,691,096 00 | | |
| By surrender | 138,655 | 20,857,019 00 | | |
| By lapse | 1,177,063 | 254,276,889 00 | | |
| By decrease | -------- | 3,900,484 00 | | |
| Total | | | 1,529,955 | 326,663,256 00 |
| Total policies in force December 31, 1921 | | | 20,213,728 | $3,154,692,554 00 |

## BUSINESS IN ILLINOIS—ORDINARY.

| | Number. | Amount. |
|---|---|---|
| Policies in force December 31, 1920 | 161,468 | $182,540,593 00 |
| Policies issued and revived during the year | 28,979 | 36,979,805 00 |
| Total | 190,447 | $219,520,398 00 |
| Deduct policies ceased to be in force | 15,401 | 17,871,380 00 |
| Policies in force December 31, 1921 | 175,046 | $201,649,018 00 |
| Losses and claims unpaid December 31, 1920 | 104 | $ 112,660 68 |
| Losses and claims incurred during the year | 1,423 | 1,515,116 41 |
| Total | 1,527 | $1,627,777 09 |
| Losses and claims settled during the year | 1,409 | 1,495,216 55 |
| Losses and claims unpaid December 31, 1921 | 118 | $132,560 54 |
| Premiums received | | $5,296,316 42 |

## BUSINESS IN ILLINOIS—GROUP INSURANCE.

| | Number. | Amount. |
|---|---|---|
| Policies in force December 31, 1920 | 8 | $1,944,300 00 |
| Policies issued and increased during the year | 3 | 729,900 00 |
| Total | 11 | $2,674,200 00 |
| Deduct policies ceased to be in force | 2 | 596,100 00 |
| Policies in force December 31, 1921 | 9 | $2,078,100 00 |
| Losses and claims incurred during the year | 17 | $22,900 00 |
| Losses and claims settled during the year | 17 | 22,900 00 |
| Premiums received | | $19,210 17 |

## BUSINESS IN ILLINOIS—INDUSTRIAL.

| | Number. | Amount. |
|---|---|---|
| Policies in force December 31, 1920 | 1,593,250 | $227,628,943 00 |
| Policies issued and revived during the year | 246,949 | $51,017,520 00 |
| Total | 1,840,199 | $278,646,463 00 |
| Deduct policies ceased to be in force | 119,069 | 23,593,404 00 |
| Policies in force December 31, 1921 | 1,721,130 | $255,053,059 00 |
| Losses and claims unpaid December 31, 1920 | 451 | $ 61,908 56 |
| Losses and claims incurred during the year | 12,001 | 1,663,646 08 |
| Total | 12,452 | $1,725,554 64 |
| Losses and claims settled during the year | 11,994 | 1,658,382 39 |
| Losses and claims unpaid December 31, 1921 | 458 | $67,172 25 |
| Premiums received | | $8,259,181 62 |

## GAIN AND LOSS EXHIBIT.

### INSURANCE EXHIBIT.

| | | Gain in surplus. | Loss in surplus. |
|---|---|---|---|
| Loading on actual premiums of the year (averaging 24.90 per cent of the gross premiums) | $46,921,682 86 | | |
| Insurance expenses incurred during the year | 50,852,218 01 | | |
| Loss from loading | | | $ 3,930,535 15 |
| Interest earned during the year | $36,883,298 65 | | |
| Investment expenses incurred during the year | 2,877,950 39 | | |
| Net income from investments | $34,005,348 26 | | |
| Interest required to maintain reserve | 24,764,733 88 | | |
| Gain from interest | | $ 9,240,614 38 | |
| Expected mortality on net amount at risk | $51,201,570 94 | | |
| Actual mortality on net amount at risk | 29,056,266 00 | | |
| Gain from mortality | | 22,145,304 94 | |
| Expected disbursements to annuitants | $156,999 99 | | |
| Net actual annuity claims incurred | 216,586 23 | | |
| Loss from annuities | | | 59,586 24 |
| Total gain during the year from surrendered and lapsed policies | | 5,410,552 37 | |
| Dividends paid stockholders | | | 25,337 38 |
| Decrease in surplus on dividend account | | | 20,194,250 37 |

### INVESTMENT EXHIBIT.

| | | Gain in surplus. | Loss in surplus. |
|---|---|---|---|
| Total gains from real estate | | 46,212 02 | |
| Total losses from real estate | | | 2,000,000 00 |
| Total gains from stocks and bonds | | 96,031 24 | |
| Total losses from stocks and bonds | | | 640,084 37 |
| Gain from assets not admitted | | 1,714 37 | |
| Net gain on account of total and permanent disability benefits or additional accidental death benefits included in life policies | | 248,047 10 | |
| Loss from increase in reserve due to change to a more stringent valuation basis for certain industrial policies, $7,701,006.00 increase in reserve due to increase in benefits for certain industrial policies, $286,925.00 | | | 7,987,931 00 |
| Total gains and losses in surplus during the year | | $37,188,476 42 | $34,837,724 51 |
| Surplus December 31, 1920 | $28,900,910 96 | | |
| Surplus December 31, 1921 | 31,251,662 87 | | |
| Increase in surplus | | | 2,350,751 91 |
| Total | | $37,188,476 42 | $37,188,476 42 |

## REINSURANCE LIFE COMPANY OF AMERICA.

Located at Ninth and Walnut Streets, Des Moines, Iowa; incorporated June 15, 1917; commenced business in Illinois May 3, 1920.

H. B. HAWLEY, President. R. M. MALPAS, Secretary.

GEORGE A. BARR, Director of Trade and Commerce, Attorney for service at Springfield.

### CAPITAL.

| | | | |
|---|---|---|---|
| Capital paid up | | $500,000 00 | |
| Amount of ledger assets December 31, of previous year | | | $929,240 25 |

### INCOME.

| | | | |
|---|---|---|---|
| First year's premiums on original policies, less re-insurance | | $82,917 28 | |
| First year's premiums for total and permanent disability benefits, less re-insurance | | 3,711 32 | |
| First year's premiums for additional accidental death benefits, less re-insurance | | 30,509 99 | |
| New premiums | | $117,138 59 | |
| Renewal premiums less re-insurance | $126,472 42 | | |
| Renewal premiums for total and permanent disability benefits, less re-insurance | 1,748 88 | | |
| Renewal premiums for additional accidental death benefits, less re-insurance | 6,151 03 | | |
| Renewal premiums | | 134,372 33 | |
| Premium income | | | 251,510 92 |
| Interest on mortgage loans | | $31,464 36 | |
| Interest on bonds | | 4,416 59 | |
| Interest on deposits | | 22,874 28 | |
| Interest on other debts due the company | | 220 50 | |
| Total interest | | | 58,975 73 |
| Increase in book value of ledger assets | | | 525 00 |
| Total income | | | $311,011 65 |
| Total | | | $1,240,251 90 |

### DISBURSEMENTS.

| | | |
|---|---|---|
| Death claims | $74,005 42 | |
| Total and permanent disability claims and additional accidental death benefits | 11,293 33 | |
| Total death claims | | $85,298 75 |
| (Total paid policyholders | $85,298 75) | |
| Expense of investigation and settlement of policy claims, including legal expenses | | 751 65 |
| Supplementary contracts not involving life contingencies | | 889 00 |
| Dividends to stockholders | | 30,000 00 |
| Commissions to agents, first year, $15,467.05; renewal, $8,632.78 | | 24,099 83 |
| Compensation of managers and agents not paid by commissions on new business | | 1,859 06 |
| Agency supervision and traveling expenses of supervisors | | 3,301 98 |
| Medical examiners' fees and inspection of risks | | 54 80 |
| Salaries and all other compensation of officers and home office employees | | 30,676 72 |
| Rent | | 2,793 28 |
| Advertising, printing, stationery, postage, telegraph, telephone and express | | 5,860 13 |
| Legal expense | | 452 70 |
| Furniture, fixtures and safes | | 1,478 73 |
| State taxes on premiums | | 2,991 23 |
| Insurance department licenses and fees | | 1,103 51 |
| Federal taxes | | 4,386 92 |
| All other licenses fees and taxes | | 26 45 |
| Miscellaneous expense | | 1,356 32 |
| Decrease in book value of ledger assets | | 50 00 |
| Total disbursements | | $197,431 06 |
| Balance | | $1,042,820 84 |

### LEDGER ASSETS.

| | |
|---|---|
| Mortgage loans on real estate | $676,000 00 |
| Book value of bonds | 138,027 32 |
| Cash in office | 96 62 |
| Deposits in trust companies and banks not on interest | 30,342 54 |
| Deposits in trust companies and banks on interest | 197,404 96 |
| War savings stamps | 949 40 |
| Total ledger assets | $1,042,820 84 |

## LEDGER ASSETS—Concluded.

### NON-LEDGER ASSETS.

| | | |
|---|---|---|
| Interest accrued on mortgages | $17,499 33 | |
| Interest accrued on bonds | 4,168 25 | |
| Interest accrued on other assets | 4,617 48 | |
| | | $26,285 06 |
| Net uncollected and deferred premiums (paid for basis) renewals | | 21,472 75 |
| Gross assets | | $1,090,578 65 |

### DEDUCT ASSETS NOT ADMITTED.

| | | |
|---|---|---|
| Premium notes, policy loans and other policy assets in excess of net value and of other policy liabilities on individual policies | 8,272 91 | |
| Book value of bonds over market value | 2,674 31 | |
| Total | | 10,947 22 |
| Admitted assets | | $1,079,631 43 |

## LIABILITIES.

| | | |
|---|---|---|
| Net present value of outstanding policies computed by the Iowa Insurance Department | $143,669 73 | |
| Deduct net value of risks re-insured | 26,725 67 | |
| Net reserve (paid for basis) | | $116,944 06 |
| Extra reserve for total and permanent disability benefits and for additional accidental death benefits included in life policies, less re-insurance | | 22,241 20 |
| Present value of supplementary contracts not involving life contingencies | | 5,740 00 |
| Present value of amounts incurred but not yet due for total and permanent disability benefits | | 5,578 35 |
| Death losses reported for which no proofs have been received | $16,611 00 | |
| Death losses and other policy claims resisted | 5,000 00 | |
| Additional accidental death benefits | 2,000 00 | |
| Total policy claims | | 23,611 00 |
| Salaries, rents, office expenses, bills and accounts due or accrued | | 1,423 00 |
| Legal fees due or accrued | | 451 20 |
| Estimated amount hereafter payable for federal, state and other taxes based upon the business of the year of this statement | | 10,000 00 |
| Total | | $185,988 81 |
| Capital paid up | | 500,000 00 |
| Unassigned funds (surplus) | | 393,642 62 |
| Total | | $1,079,631 43 |

## EXHIBIT OF POLICIES—ORDINARY.

### ALL BUSINESS PAID FOR.

| | Number. | Amount. | Number. | Amount. |
|---|---|---|---|---|
| Policies in force December 31, 1920 | | | 4,718 | $21,969,076 00 |
| Policies issued, revived and increased during the year | | | 2,042 | 12,490,444 00 |
| Total | | | 6,760 | $34,459,520 00 |
| Deduct policies which have ceased to be in force during the year— | | | | |
| By death | 21 | $ 97,582 00 | | |
| By lapse | 1,993 | 9,196,560 00 | | |
| Total | | | 2,014 | 9,294,142 00 |
| Total policies in force December 31, 1921 | | | 4,746 | $25,165,378 00 |
| Re-insured | | | 485 | $4,849,955 00 |

## BUSINESS IN ILLINOIS—ORDINARY.

| | Number. | Amount. |
|---|---|---|
| Policies in force December 31, 1920 | 448 | $1,650,773 00 |
| Policies issued during the year | 328 | 1,560,187 00 |
| Total | 776 | $3,210,960 00 |
| Deduct policies ceased to be in force | 199 | 519,732 00 |
| Policies in force December 31, 1921 | 577 | $2,691,228 00 |
| Losses and claims incurred during the year | 1 | $475 00 |
| Losses and claims settled during the year | 1 | 475 00 |
| Premiums received | | $28,233 44 |

## GAIN AND LOSS EXHIBIT.

### INSURANCE EXHIBIT.

| | | Gain in surplus. | Loss in surplus. |
|---|---|---|---|
| Loading on actual premiums of the year | $—3,470 77 | | |
| Insurance expenses incurred during the year | 81,678 57 | | |
| Loss from loading | | | $85,149 34 |
| Interest earned during the year | $49,047 21 | | |
| Investment expenses incurred during the year | 2,427 03 | | |
| Net income from investments | $46,620 18 | | |
| Interest required to maintain reserve | 3,702 74 | | |
| Gain from interest | | $ 42,917 44 | |
| Expected mortality on net amount at risk | $197,071 62 | | |
| Actual mortality on net amount at risk | 95,584 97 | | |
| Gain from mortality | | 101,486 65 | |
| Total gain during the year from surrendered and lapsed policies | | 293 47 | |
| Dividends paid stockholders | | | 30,000 00 |

### INVESTMENT EXHIBIT.

| | | Gain in surplus. | Loss in surplus. |
|---|---|---|---|
| Total gains from bonds | | 525 00 | |
| Total losses from bonds | | | 166 17 |
| Loss from assets not admitted | | | 1,654 77 |
| Net gain on account of total and premanent disability benefits or additional accidental death benefits included in ife policies | | 5,829 59 | |
| Balance unaccounted for | | | 20 47 |
| Total gains and losses in surplus during the year | | $151,052 15 | $116,990 75 |
| Surplus December 31, 1920 | $359,581 22 | | |
| Surplus December 31, 1921 | 393,642 60 | | |
| Increase in surplus | | | 34,061 40 |
| Total | | $151,052 15 | $151,052 15 |

## RELIANCE LIFE INSURANCE COMPANY OF PITTSBURGH.

Located at Fifth Avenue and Wood Street, Pittsburgh, Pennsylvania; incorporated March 31, 1903; commenced business in Illinois, life, April 16, 1909; casualty, January 22, 1912.

J. H. REED, President. H. G. SCOTT, Secretary.

GEORGE A. BARR, Director of Trade and Commerce, Attorney for service at Springfield.

### CAPITAL.

| | | | |
|---|---|---|---|
| Capital paid up | | $1,000,000 00 | |
| Amount of ledger assets December 31, of previous year | | | $13,304,785 33 |

### INCOME.

| | | | |
|---|---|---|---|
| First year's premiums on original policies, less re-insurance | | $2,101,492 25 | |
| First year's premiums for total and permanent disability benefits | | 27,981 00 | |
| Dividends applied to purchase paid-up additions and annuities | | 179,918 22 | |
| Consideration for original annuities involving life contingencies | | 7,100 00 | |
| New premiums | | $2,316,491 47 | |
| Renewal premiums less re-insurance | $4,836,580 52 | | |
| Renewal premiums for total and permanent disability benefits | 32,228 00 | | |
| Renewal premiums | | 4,868,808 52 | |
| Total | | | $7,185,299 99 |
| Consideration for supplementary contracts involving life contingencies | | | 4,985 43 |
| Consideration for supplementary contracts not involving life contingencies | | | 27,000 00 |
| Dividends left with company to accumulate at interest | | | 76,269 54 |
| Interest on mortgage loans | | $ 65,240 88 | |
| Interest on bonds | | 487,826 96 | |
| Interest on premium notes, policy loans or liens | | 171,526 95 | |
| Interest on deposits | | 18,362 07 | |
| Interest on agents balances | | 4,201 98 | |
| Rents | | 9,625 00 | |
| Total interest and rents | | | 756,783 84 |

INCOME—Concluded.

| | | |
|---|---|---|
| Profit on sale or maturity of ledger assets | | $ 4,841 47 |
| Increase in book value of ledger assets | | 31,814 96 |
| Income, life department | | $8,086,995 23 |
| Income, casualty department | | 521,793 10 |
| Total income | | $8,608,788 33 |
| Total | | $21,913,573 66 |

DISBURSEMENTS.

| | | |
|---|---|---|
| Death claims and additions | $984,844 53 | |
| Matured endowments | 34,000 00 | |
| Total and permanent disability claims | 16,647 96 | |
| Total death claims and endowments | | $1,035,492 49 |
| Annuities involving life contingencies | | 6,322 03 |
| Premium notes and liens voided by lapse, less $4,100.68 restorations | | 32,270 88 |
| Surrender values paid in cash, or applied in liquidation of loans or notes | | 180,793 25 |
| Dividends paid policyholders in cash, or applied in liquidation of loans or notes | | 256,968 48 |
| Dividends applied to purchase paid-up additions and annuities | | 179,918 22 |
| Dividends left with the company to accumulate at interest | | 76,269 54 |
| (Total paid policyholders | $1,768,034 89) | |
| Expense of investigation and settlement of policy claims | | 100 41 |
| Supplementary contracts not involving life contingencies | | 7,090 13 |
| Dividends with interest, held on deposit surrendered during the year | | 6,872 29 |
| Dividends to stockholders | | 60,000 00 |
| Commissions to agents, first year, $1,329,391.46; renewal, $265,350.75; annuities (original), $1,367.99 | | 1,596,110 20 |
| Compensation of managers and agents not paid by commissions on new business | | 15,454 40 |
| Agency supervision and traveling expenses of supervisors | | 1,046 23 |
| Branch office expenses | | 279,056 16 |
| Medical examiners' fees and inspection of risks | | 156,720 50 |
| Salaries and all other compensation of officers and home office employees | | 211,018 52 |
| Rent | | 38,806 68 |
| Advertising, printing, stationery, postage, telegraph, telephone and express | | 79,257 57 |
| Legal expense | | 4,722 50 |
| Furniture, fixtures and safes | | 8,511 47 |
| Taxes on real estate | | 4,339 63 |
| State taxes on premiums | | 113,618 99 |
| Insurance department licenses and fees | | 4,530 84 |
| Federal taxes | | 39,064 87 |
| All other licenses, fees and taxes | | 20,461 44 |
| Other disbursements, viz: Library, $476.25; addressograph, $4,466.85; photographic, $2,668.64; Workmen's Compensation, $80.12; annual audit, $4,308.50; commissions on investments, $1.50; fire insurance, $335.17; office furniture charged off, vault rent, towel service, employees bonds and general expenses, $26,830.61 | | 39,167 64 |
| Interest on borrowed money | | 379,658 07 |
| Agents' balances charged off | | 9,595 77 |
| Loss on sale or maturity of ledger assets | | 3,813 14 |
| Decrease in book value of ledger assets | | 163,928 67 |
| Disbursements, life department | | $4,631,322 94 |
| Disbursements, casualty department | | 379,658 07 |
| Total disbursements | | $5,010,981 01 |
| Balance | | $16,902,592 65 |

LEDGER ASSETS.

| | | |
|---|---|---|
| Book value of real estate | | $ 158,743 86 |
| Mortgage loans on real estate | | 1,220,746 88 |
| Premiums advanced under Soldiers' and Sailors' Civil Relief Act | | 551 61 |
| Loans on company's policies assigned as collateral | | 2,351,031 51 |
| Premium notes on policies in force | | 1,049,464 26 |
| Book value of bonds | | 11,253,306 51 |
| Cash in office | | 14,495 00 |
| Deposits in trust companies and banks not on interest | | 7,986 92 |
| Deposits in trust companies and banks on interest | | 552,885 40 |
| Bills receivable | | 28,689 83 |
| Agents' balances (debit, $102,034.84; credit, $6,342.27) net | | 95,692 57 |
| Outstanding premiums, casualty department | | 168,998 30 |
| Total ledger assets | | $16,902,592 65 |

NON-LEDGER ASSETS.

| | | |
|---|---|---|
| Interest accrued on mortgages | $ 29,298 55 | |
| Interest due and accrued on bonds | 178,319 81 | |
| Interest accrued on premium notes, loans or liens | 38,334 61 | |
| Interest accrued on bank balances | 1,178 00 | |
| | | 247,130 97 |
| Market value of real estate over book value appraised value Pennsylvania Insurance Department | | 31,256 14 |

LEDGER ASSETS—Concluded.

NON-LEDGER ASSETS.

| | New business. | Renewals. | |
|---|---|---|---|
| Net uncollected and deferred premiums (paid for basis) | $67,015 13 | $846,779 77 | $913,794 90 |
| Office furniture and fixtures | | | 98,591 87 |
| Gross assets | | | $18,193,366 53 |

DEDUCT ASSETS NOT ADMITTED.

| | | |
|---|---|---|
| Furniture, fixtures and safes | $ 98,591 87 | |
| Agents' debit balances | 102,034 84 | |
| Bills receivable | 28,689 83 | |
| Premium notes, policy loans and other policy assets in excess of net value and of other liabilities on individual policies | 1,974 93 | |
| Overdue and accrued interest on bonds in default | 12,000 00 | |
| Certificate of deposit in banks and in default | 453 24 | |
| Total | | 243,744 71 |
| Admitted assets | | $17,949,621 82 |

LIABILITIES.

| | | |
|---|---|---|
| Net present value of outstanding policies computed by the Pennsylvania Insurance Department | $15,074,426 00 | |
| Same for dividend additions | 331,344 00 | |
| Same for annuities | 94,415 00 | |
| Total | $15,500,185 00 | |
| Deduct net value of risks re-insured | 200,487 00 | |
| Net reserve (paid for basis) | | $15,299,698 00 |
| Extra reserve for total and permanent disability benefits included in life policies | | 47,528 00 |
| Present value of supplementary contracts not involving life contingencies | | 118,642 57 |
| Present value of amounts incurred but not yet due for total and permanent disability benefits | | 28,263 96 |
| Death losses in process of adjustment | $61,300 46 | |
| Reserve for net death losses incurred but unreported | 7,457 87 | |
| Total policy claims | | 68,758 33 |
| Dividends left with the company to accumulate at interest | | 210,434 78 |
| Gross premiums paid in advance, including surrender values so applied, less discount, if any | | 9,261 42 |
| Unearned interest and rent paid in advance | | 58,775 07 |
| Commissions due agents on premium notes, when paid | | 5,273 28 |
| Commissions to agents due or accrued | | 27,781 79 |
| Salaries, rents, office expenses, bills and accounts due or accrued | | 2,989 85 |
| Medical examiners' fees due or accrued | | 9,926 00 |
| Estimated amount hereafter payable for federal, state and other taxes based upon the business of the year of this statement | | 75,626 00 |
| Dividends declared on or apportioned to annual dividend policies payable to policyholders during 1922 for period to February 28 | | 28,974 96 |
| Dividends declared on or apportioned to deferred dividend policies payable to policyholders during 1922 for period to December 31 | | 59,603 67 |
| Amounts set apart, apportioned, provisionally ascertained, calculated, declared or held awaiting apportionment upon deferred dividend policies | | 197,810 75 |
| Reserve, casualty department | | 197,438 91 |
| Other liabilities, viz: Casualty department, $38,657.88; special reserve fund for securities, etc., $109,000.00 | | 147,657 88 |
| Total | | $16,594,445 22 |
| Capital paid up | | 1,000,000 00 |
| Unassigned funds (surplus) | | 355,176 60 |
| Total | | $17,949,621 82 |

EXHIBIT OF POLICIES—ORDINARY.

ALL BUSINESS PAID FOR.

| | Number. | Amount. | Number. | Amount. |
|---|---|---|---|---|
| Policies in force December 31, 1920 | | | 90,427 | $196,272,085 00 |
| Policies issued, revived and increased during the year | | | 21,555 | 54,830,303 00 |
| Total | | | 111,982 | $251,102,388 00 |
| Deduct policies which have ceased to be in force during the year— | | | | |
| By death | 433 | $ 1,167,086 00 | | |
| By maturity | 16 | 30,248 00 | | |
| By expiry | 443 | 1,537,697 00 | | |
| By surrender | 461 | 864,703 00 | | |

## EXHIBIT OF POLICIES—ORDINARY—Concluded.

ALL BUSINESS PAID FOR.

| | Number. | Amount. | Number. | Amount. |
|---|---|---|---|---|
| Deduct policies which have ceased to be in force during the year— | | | | |
| By lapse | 12,684 | $28,359,647 00 | | |
| By decrease | 4 | 876,969 00 | | |
| Total | | | 14,041 | $32,836,350 00 |
| Total policies in force December 31, 1921 | | | 97,941 | $218,266,038 00 |
| Re-insured | | | 1,535 | $14,058,911 00 |

## BUSINESS IN ILLINOIS—ORDINARY.

| | Number. | Amount. |
|---|---|---|
| Policies in force December 31, 1920 | 2,967 | $7,541,921 00 |
| Policies issued during the year | 1,112 | 2,631,778 00 |
| Total | 4,079 | $10,173,699 00 |
| Deduct policies ceased to be in force | 408 | 1,192,217 00 |
| Policies in force December 31, 1921 | 3,671 | $8,981,482 00 |
| Losses and claims unpaid December 31, 1920 | 1 | $ 1,000 00 |
| Losses and claims incurred during the year | 11 | 35,984 16 |
| Total | 12 | $36,984 16 |
| Losses and claims settled during the year | 12 | 36,984 16 |
| Premiums received | | $312,273 82 |

## GAIN AND LOSS EXHIBIT.

INSURANCE EXHIBIT.

| | | Gain in surplus. | Loss in surplus. |
|---|---|---|---|
| Loading on actual premiums of the year (averaging 29.88 per cent of the gross premiums) | $2,208,451 23 | | |
| Insurance expenses incurred during the year | 2,649,385 01 | | |
| Loss from loading | | | $440,933 78 |
| Interest earned during the year | $793,108 22 | | |
| Investment expenses incurred during the year | 4,676 30 | | |
| Net income from investments | $788,431 92 | | |
| Interest required to maintain reserve | 470,981 52 | | |
| Gain from interest | | $317,450 40 | |
| Expected mortality on net amount at risk | $1,810,417 00 | | |
| Actual mortality on net amount at risk | 903,709 10 | | |
| Gain from mortality | | 906,707 90 | |
| Expected disbursements to annuitants | $3,794 61 | | |
| Net actual annuity claims incurred | 6,322 03 | | |
| Loss from annuities | | | 2,527 42 |
| Total gain during the year from surrendered and lapsed policies | | 111,567 23 | |
| Dividends paid stockholders | | | 60,000 00 |
| Decrease in surplus on dividend account | | | 605,148 57 |
| Increase in special funds and special reserves during the year | | | 109,000 00 |
| Net to loss account | | | 9,595 77 |

INVESTMENT EXHIBIT.

| | | Gain in surplus. | Loss in surplus. |
|---|---|---|---|
| Total gains from bonds | | 4,841 47 | |
| Total losses from bonds | | | 163,813 14 |
| Loss from assets not admitted | | | 17,264 46 |
| Net gain on account of total and permanent disability benefits included in life policies | | 2,730 31 | |
| Gain from casualty department | | 103,446 04 | |
| Total gains and losses in surplus during the year | | $1,446,743 35 | $1,408,283 14 |
| Surplus December 31, 1920 | $316,716 39 | | |
| Surplus December 31, 1921 | 355,176 60 | | |
| Increase in surplus | | | 38,460 21 |
| Total | | $1,446,743 35 | $1,446,743 35 |

## RESERVE LOAN LIFE INSURANCE COMPANY.

Located at No. 429 North Pennsylvania Street, Indianapolis, Indiana; incorporated as assessment association, March 2, 1897; re-incorporated as mutual legal reserve company, 1901; and as stock legal reserve company, December 14, 1909; commenced business in Illinois February 23, 1915.

CHALMERS BROWN, President. G. L. STAYMAN, Secretary.

GEORGE A. BARR, Director of Trade and Commerce, Attorney for service at Springfield.

### CAPITAL.

| | | | |
|---|---|---|---|
| Capital paid up | | $100,000 00 | |
| Amount of ledger assets December 31, of previous year | | | $5,085,676 01 |

### INCOME.

| | | | |
|---|---|---|---|
| First year's premiums on original policies, less re-insurance | | $493,926 73 | |
| First year's premiums for total and permanent disability benefits | | 5,184 93 | |
| First year's premiums for additional accidental death benefits, less re-insurance | | 4,801 24 | |
| Surrender values to pay first year's premiums | | 25,709 83 | |
| Dividends applied to purchase paid-up additions and annuities | | 1,413 59 | |
| Surrender values applied to purchase paid-up insurance and annuities | | 120,952 26 | |
| New premiums | | $ 651,988 58 | |
| Renewal premiums less re-insurance | $1,036,284 80 | | |
| Renewal premiums for total and permanent disability benefits | 9,149 82 | | |
| Renewal premiums for additional accidental death benefits | 8,543 69 | | |
| Dividends applied to pay renewal premiums | 2,436 25 | | |
| Surrender values applied to pay renewal premiums | 10,634 70 | | |
| Renewal premiums | | 1,067,049 26 | |
| Premium income | | | $1,719,037 84 |
| Dividends left with company to accumulate at interest | | | 480 83 |
| Interest on mortgage loans | | $206,011 72 | |
| Interest on bonds | | 10,924 43 | |
| Interest on premium notes, policy loans or liens | | 63,656 36 | |
| Interest on deposits | | 6,339 58 | |
| Interest on other debts due the company | | 1,673 63 | |
| Rents—including $12,000.00 for company's occupancy of its own buildings | | 12,151 59 | |
| Total interest and rents | | | 300,757 31 |
| From other sources, viz: Policy coupons, $35,995.04; profit from contingent survivorship, district fund on lapsed policies, $20.62; profit from liability on policies cancelled on lapsed policies, $127.73; suspense, $251.99; survivorship district fund, $2,132.39 | | | 38,527 77 |
| Increase in book value of ledger assets | | | 51 71 |
| Total income | | | $2,058,855 46 |
| Total | | | $7,144,531 47 |

### DISBURSEMENTS.

| | | |
|---|---|---|
| Death claims | $270,066 76 | |
| Additional accidental death benefits | 2,000 00 | |
| Total death claims and endowments | | $272,066 76 |
| Premium notes and liens voided by lapse | | 21,804 91 |
| Surrender values paid in cash, or applied in liquidation of loans or notes | | 373,554 70 |
| Surrender values applied to pay new and renewal premiums | | 36,344 53 |
| Surrender values applied to purchase paid-up insurance and annuities | | 120,952 26 |
| Dividends paid policyholders in cash, or applied in liquidation of loans or notes | | 6,454 48 |
| Dividends applied to pay renewal premiums | | 2,436 25 |
| Dividends applied to purchase paid-up additions and annuities | | 1,333 41 |
| Dividends left with the company to accumulate at interest | | 480 83 |
| (Total paid policyholders | $835,428 13) | |
| Expense of investigation and settlement of policy claims, including legal expenses | | 1,675 32 |
| Supplementary contracts not involving life contingencies | | 7,903 78 |
| Dividends with interest, held on deposit surrendered during the year | | 1,211 99 |
| Dividends to stockholders | | 8,000 00 |
| Commissions to agents, first year, $416,330.99; renewal, $43,792.97 | | 460,123 96 |
| Commuted renewal commissions | | 200 00 |
| Compensation of managers and agents not paid by commissions on new business | | 5,400 00 |
| Agency supervision and traveling expenses of supervisors | | 20,608 88 |
| Medical examiners' fees and inspection of risks | | 44,374 10 |
| Salaries and all other compensation of officers and home office employees | | 118,868 27 |
| Rent | | 12,000 00 |
| Advertising, printing, stationery, postage, telegraph, telephone and express | | 23,610 33 |
| Legal expense | | 1,306 3[illegible] |

DISBURSEMENTS—Concluded.

| | | |
|---|---|---|
| Furniture, fixtures and safes | | $ 6,525 77 |
| Repairs and expenses (other than taxes) on real estate | | 6,553 73 |
| Taxes on real estate | | 5,713 38 |
| State taxes on premiums | | 26,459 92 |
| Insurance department licenses and fees | | 4,174 38 |
| Federal taxes | | 20,659 36 |
| All other licenses, fees and taxes, franchise tax | | 100 00 |
| Other disbursements, viz: Survivorship surplus 1901 class applied to purchase paid-up additions, $30.18; interest paid on coupons, $418.50; accrued interest on survivorship district fund, $388.64; interest on survivorship surplus, $306.15; general traveling expense, $6,861.01; miscellaneous expense, $2,255.90; subscription, $445.00; office supplies, $4,642.05; survivorship surplus, $1,461.83; contingent survivorship district fund, $17.80 | | 16,877 06 |
| Agents' balances charged off | | 1,719 92 |
| Decrease in book value of ledger assets | | 144 50 |
| Total disbursements | | $1,629,639 30 |
| Balance | | $5,514,892 17 |

LEDGER ASSETS.

| | | |
|---|---|---|
| Book value of real estate | | $ 102,795 95 |
| Mortgage loans on real estate | | 3,895,889 00 |
| Loans on company's policies assigned as collateral | | 1,094,689 86 |
| Premium notes on policies in force | | 39,371 00 |
| Book value of bonds | | 220,301 07 |
| Cash in office | | 5,023 08 |
| Deposits in trust companies and banks on interest | | 119,712 05 |
| Agents' balances (debit, $42,690.67; credit, $5,580.51) net | | 37,110 16 |
| Total ledger assets | | $5,514,892 17 |

NON-LEDGER ASSETS.

| | | |
|---|---|---|
| Interest due and accrued on mortgages | $124,692 29 | |
| Interest accrued on bonds | 1,803 06 | |
| Interest due on premium notes, loans or liens | 2,172 13 | |
| Interest accrued on other assets | 402 93 | |
| | | 129,070 41 |
| Due from other companies for losses or claims on policies re-insured | | 8,000 00 |
| Net uncollected and deferred premiums (paid for basis) renewals | | 151,026 52 |
| All other assets, viz: Unearned fire insurance premiums, $373.03; amount due from other companies account refund re-insurance premiums, $158.70 | | 531 73 |
| Gross assets | | $5,803,520 83 |

DEDUCT ASSETS NOT ADMITTED.

| | | |
|---|---|---|
| Agents' debit balances | $42,690 67 | |
| Premium notes, policy loans and other policy assets in excess of net value and of other policy liabilities on individual policies | 6,425 93 | |
| Book value of bonds over market value | 1,733 79 | |
| Total | | 50,850 39 |
| Admitted assets | | $5,752,670 44 |

LIABILITIES.

| | | |
|---|---|---|
| Net present value of outstanding policies computed by the Indiana Insurance Department | $4,903,445 16 | |
| Deduct net value of risks re-insured | 25,627 00 | |
| Net reserve (paid for basis) | | $4,877,818 16 |
| Extra reserve for total and permanent disability benefits and for additional accidental death benefits included in life policies | | 13,953 93 |
| Present value of supplementary contracts not involving life contingencies | | 6,858 91 |
| Surrender values claimable on policies cancelled | | 567 01 |
| Death losses in process of adjustment | $ 1,000 00 | |
| Death losses reported for which no proofs have been received | 36,700 00 | |
| Death losses and other policy claims resisted | 27,866 98 | |
| Total policy claims | | 65,566 98 |
| Dividends left with the company to accumulate at interest | | 5,286 84 |
| Gross premiums paid in advance, including surrender values so applied, less discount, if any | | 7,821 34 |
| Unearned interest and rent paid in advance | | 30,669 41 |
| Commissions due agents on premium notes, when paid | | 2,190 72 |
| Salaries, rents, office expenses, bills and accounts due or accrued | | 29,145 41 |
| Medical examiners' and legal fees due or accrued | | 3,380 03 |
| Estimated amount hereafter payable for federal, state and other taxes based upon the business of the year of this statement | | 45,000 00 |
| Dividends or other profits due policyholders | | 243 90 |
| Dividends declared on or apportioned to annual dividend policies payable to policyholders during 1922 for period to December 31, 1922 | | 1,159 37 |

## LIABILITIES—Concluded.

| | |
|---|---|
| Dividends declared on or apportioned to deferred dividend policies payable to policyholders during 1922 for period to December 31, 1922 | $ 21,709 60 |
| Survivorship surplus | 9,478 37 |
| Survivorship distribution fund | 13,236 73 |
| Contingent survivorship distribution fund | 143 40 |
| Reserve for mortality fluctuations | 100,000 00 |
| Other liabilities, viz: Suspense account, $337.77; policy coupons, $201,736.27 and accrued interest, $23,030.74 | 225,104 78 |
| Total | $5,459,334 89 |
| Capital paid up | 100,000 00 |
| Unassigned funds (surplus) | 193,335 55 |
| Total | $5,752,670 44 |

## EXHIBIT OF POLICIES—ORDINARY.

ALL BUSINESS PAID FOR.

| | Number. | Amount. | Number. | Amount. |
|---|---|---|---|---|
| Policies in force December 31, 1920 | | | 25,600 | $47,178,238 00 |
| Policies issued, revived and increased during the year | | | 7,055 | 16,203,215 00 |
| Total | | | 32,655 | $63,381,453 00 |
| Deduct policies which have ceased to be in force during the year— | | | | |
| By death | 142 | $ 288,333 00 | | |
| By expiry | 97 | 161,295 00 | | |
| By surrender | 751 | 1,949,675 00 | | |
| By lapse | 5,088 | 10,512,049 00 | | |
| By decrease | | 154,750 00 | | |
| Total | | | 6,078 | 13,066,102 00 |
| Total policies in force December 31, 1921 | | | 26,577 | $50,315,351 00 |
| Re-insured | | | | $1,002,894 00 |

## BUSINESS IN ILLINOIS—ORDINARY.

| | Number. | Amount. |
|---|---|---|
| Policies in force December 31, 1920 | 304 | $943,818 00 |
| Policies issued during the year | 184 | 553,000 00 |
| Total | 488 | $1,496,818 00 |
| Deduct policies ceased to be in force | 173 | 585,810 00 |
| Policies in force December 31, 1921 | 315 | $911,008 00 |
| Losses and claims unpaid December 31, 1920 | 2 | $8,000 00 |
| Losses and claims incurred during the year | 3 | 8,500 00 |
| Total | 5 | $16,500 00 |
| Losses and claims settled during the year | 2 | 7,500 00 |
| Losses and claims unpaid December 31, 1921 | 3 | $9,000 00 |
| Premiums received | | $35,504 77 |

## GAIN AND LOSS EXHIBIT.

INSURANCE EXHIBIT.

| | | Gain in surplus. | Loss in surplus. |
|---|---|---|---|
| Loading on actual premiums of the year (averaging 27.3 per cent of the gross premiums) | $438,967 77 | | |
| Insurance expenses incurred during the year | 795,708 76 | | |
| Loss from loading | | | $356,740 99 |
| Interest earned during the year | $321,995 24 | | |
| Investment expenses incurred during the year | 19,599 09 | | |
| Net income from investments | $302,396 15 | | |
| Interest required to maintain reserve | 172,968 81 | | |
| Gain from interest | | $129,427 34 | |
| Expected mortality on net amount at risk | $476,012 06 | | |
| Actual mortality on net amount at risk | 232,480 13 | | |
| Gain from mortality | | 243,531 93 | |
| Total gain during the year from surrendered and lapsed policies | | 66,200 28 | |
| Dividends paid stockholders | | | 8,000 00 |
| Decrease in surplus on dividend account | | | 23,787 58 |
| Increase in special funds and special reserves during the year | | | 50,572 58 |
| Net to profit account | | 341 41 | |

GAIN AND LOSS EXHIBIT—Concluded.

INVESTMENT EXHIBIT.

| | | Gain in surplus. | Loss. in surplus. |
|---|---|---|---|
| Total gains from stocks and bonds | | $ 2,404 56 | |
| Total losses from stocks and bonds | | | $ 144 50 |
| Loss from assets not admitted | | | 8,646 43 |
| Net gain on account of total and permanent disability benefits or additional accidental death benefits included in life policies | | 26,211 89 | |
| Balance unaccounted for | | 2,615 88 | |
| Total gains and losses in surplus during the year | | $470,733 29 | $447,892 08 |
| Surplus December 31, 1920 | $170,494 34 | | |
| Surplus December 31, 1921 | 193,335 55 | | |
| Increase in surplus | | | 22,841 21 |
| Total | | $470,733 29 | $470,733 29 |

## SECURITY LIFE INSURANCE COMPANY OF AMERICA.

Located at Richmond, Virginia; executive offices, Rookery Building, Chicago, Illinois; incorporated March, 1902; commenced business in Illinois September 1, 1905.

O. W. JOHNSON, President. J. CHAS. SEITZ, Secretary.

W. M. JOHNSON, Chicago, Attorney for service.

### CAPITAL.

| | | | |
|---|---|---|---|
| Capital paid up | | $220,000 00 | |
| Amount of ledger assets December 31, of previous year | | | $3,860,396 45 |

### INCOME.

| | | | |
|---|---|---|---|
| First year's premiums on original policies, less re-insurance | | $229,975 64 | |
| First year's premiums for total and permanent disability benefits | | 6,279 77 | |
| First year's premiums for additional accidental death benefits, less re-insurance | | 608 04 | |
| New premiums | | $236,863 45 | |
| Renewal premiums less re-insurance | $841,922 33 | | |
| Renewal premiums for total and permanent disability benefits | 9,881 47 | | |
| Renewal premiums for additional accidental death benefits, less re-insurance | 806 48 | | |
| Surrender values applied to pay renewal premiums | 666 92 | | |
| Renewal premiums | | 853,277 20 | |
| Premium income | | | $1,090,140 65 |
| Guarantee reductions left with company to accumulate at interest | | | 356 32 |
| Interest on mortgage loans | | $80,980 22 | |
| Interest on collateral loans | | 4,209 03 | |
| Interest on bonds | | 76,862 81 | |
| Interest on premium notes, policy loans or liens | | 43,164 36 | |
| Interest on deposits | | 2,146 01 | |
| Interest on other debts due the company | | 1,198 67 | |
| Total interest | | | 208,561 10 |
| From other sources, viz: Discount on mortgages and bonds, $250.00; miscellaneous income, $2,517.71; collections on lapsed notes, $50.00 | | | 2,817 71 |
| Profit on sale or maturity of ledger assets | | | 2,788 87 |
| Total income | | | $1,304,664 65 |
| Total | | | $5,165,061 10 |

### DISBURSEMENTS.

| | | |
|---|---|---|
| Death claims | $230,983 29 | |
| Total and permanent disability claims | 3,900 00 | |
| Total death claims | | $234,883 29 |
| Annuities involving life contingencies | | 1,191 97 |
| Premium notes and liens voided by lapse, less $5,733.84 restorations | | 20,282 85 |
| Surrender values paid in cash, or applied in liquidation of loans or notes | | 142,520 76 |
| Surrender values applied to pay new and renewal premiums | | 666 92 |
| Guarantee reductions left with the company to accumulate at interest | | 356 32 |
| (Total paid policyholders | $399,902 11) | |
| Expense of investigation and settlement of policy claims, including legal expenses | | 2,882 46 |
| Supplementary contracts not involving life contingencies | | 9,147 79 |
| Guarantee reductions with interest, held on deposit surrendered during the year | | 140 75 |

## DISBURSEMENTS—Concluded.

|  |  |
|---|---|
| Commissions to agents, first year, $179,650.02; renewal, $35,734.36 | $215,384 38 |
| Compensation of managers and agents not paid by commissions on new business | 5,177 62 |
| Agency supervision and traveling expenses of supervisors | 9,363 05 |
| Branch office expenses | 1,057 94 |
| Medical examiners' fees and inspection of risks | 30,173 43 |
| Salaries and all other compensation of officers and home office employees | 72,193 88 |
| Rent | 14,533 12 |
| Advertising, printing, stationery, postage, telegraph, telephone, express and exchange | 23,805 74 |
| Legal expense | 1,922 01 |
| Furniture, fixtures and safes | 1,758 58 |
| State taxes on premiums | 21,864 40 |
| Insurance department licenses and fees | 2,608 03 |
| Federal taxes | 353 56 |
| All other licenses, fees and taxes | 372 27 |
| Other disbursements, viz: Officers traveling expense, $1,103.91; incidental office expense, $824.28; fidelity bonds, $943.05; miscellaneous disbursements, $1,496.93; bonus commissions, $6,336.84; board contract dividends, $6,417.41; agency expense, $9,766.53; health payments, $67.15 | 26,956 10 |
| Agents' balances charged off | 266 71 |
| Loss on sale or maturity of ledger assets | 95 39 |
| Total disbursements | $839,959 32 |
| Balance | $4,325,101 78 |

## LEDGER ASSETS.

|  |  |
|---|---|
| Book value of real estate | $ 32,681 43 |
| Mortgage loans on real estate | 1,239,600 00 |
| Loans secured by collaterals | 67,423 89 |
| Loans on company's policies assigned as collateral | 964,556 87 |
| Premium notes on policies in force | 38,088 35 |
| Book value of bonds | 1,761,242 35 |
| Cash in office | 600 00 |
| Deposits in trust companies and banks on interest | 175,230 55 |
| Bills receivable | 6,836 62 |
| Agents' balances (debit, $34,601.38; credit, $1,347.61) | 33,253 77 |
| Furniture and fixtures, $7,500.00; less war tax, $617.98; miscellaneous liability, $1,294.07 | 5,587 95 |
| Total ledger assets | $4,325,101 78 |

### NON-LEDGER ASSETS.

|  | | |  |
|---|---|---|---|
| Interest due and accrued on mortgages | | $29,460 33 | |
| Interest due and accrued on bonds | | 39,879 52 | |
| Interest due and accrued on collateral loans | | 722 21 | |
| Interest accrued on premium notes, loans or liens | | 5,500 00 | |
| | | | 75,562 06 |
| Due from other companies for losses or claims on policies re-insured | | | 5,000 00 |
| | New business. | Renewals. | |
| Net uncollected and deferred premiums (paid for basis) | $4,631 40 | $112,189 47 | 116,820 87 |
| Gross assets | | | $4,522,484 71 |

### DEDUCT ASSETS NOT ADMITTED.

|  | |  |
|---|---|---|
| Furniture, fixtures and safes | $ 7,500 00 | |
| Agents' debit balances | 34,601 38 | |
| Bills receivable | 6,836 62 | |
| Premium notes, policy loans and other policy assets in excess of net value and of other policy liabilities on individual policies | 3,366 20 | |
| Overdue and accrued interest on bonds in default | 4,485 30 | |
| Book value of bonds over market value | 23,625 85 | |
| Total | | 80,415 35 |
| Admitted assets | | $4,442,069 36 |

## LIABILITIES.

|  | |  |
|---|---|---|
| Net present value of outstanding policies computed by the Virginia Insurance Department | $3,854,113 00 | |
| Same for annuities | 13,998 00 | |
| Total | $3,868,111 00 | |
| Deduct net value of risks re-insured | 20,082 00 | |
| Net reserve (paid for basis) | | $3,848,029 00 |
| Extra reserve for total and permanent disability benefits included in life policies | | 23,284 85 |
| Present value of supplementary contracts not involving life contingencies | | 41,859 00 |
| Present value of amounts incurred but not yet due for total and permanent disability benefits | | 7,150 00 |
| Surrender values claimable on policies cancelled | | 1,427 02 |
| Death losses in process of adjustment | $10,500 00 | |
| Death losses reported for which no proofs have been received | 2,500 00 | |
| Reserve for net death losses incurred but unreported | 3,571 22 | |
| Death losses and other policy claims resisted | 22,833 00 | |
| Total policy claims | | $39,404 22 |

LIABILITIES—Concluded.

| | |
|---|---|
| Guarantee reductions left with the company to accumulate at interest | $ 3,359 19 |
| Gross premiums paid in advance, including surrender values so applied, less discount, if any | 3,949 99 |
| Unearned interest and rent paid in advance | 14,427 45 |
| Commissions due agents on premium notes, when paid | 757 74 |
| Salaries, rents, office expenses, bills and accounts due or accrued | 2,897 62 |
| Medical examiners' and inspection fees due or accrued | 2,846 00 |
| Estimated amount hereafter payable for federal, state and other taxes based upon the business of the year of this statement | 28,572 21 |
| Contingency reserve | 50,000 00 |
| Total | $4,067,964 29 |
| Capital paid up | 220,000 00 |
| Unassigned funds (surplus) | 154,105 07 |
| Total | $4,442,069 36 |

EXHIBIT OF POLICIES—ORDINARY.

ALL BUSINESS PAID FOR.

| | Number. | Amount. | Number. | Amount. |
|---|---|---|---|---|
| Policies in force December 31, 1920 | | | 19,896 | $35,675,435 00 |
| Policies issued, revived and increased during the year | | | 5,686 | 11,105,026 00 |
| Total | | | 25,582 | $46,780,461 00 |
| Deduct policies which have ceased to be in force during the year— | | | | |
| By death | 90 | $ 221,261 00 | | |
| By disability | 1 | 2,000 00 | | |
| By expiry | 96 | 127,588 00 | | |
| By surrender | 230 | 463,342 00 | | |
| By lapse | 3,627 | 6,671,887 00 | | |
| By decrease | 1,075 | 2,193,422 00 | | |
| Total | | | 5,119 | 9,679,500 00 |
| Total policies in force December 31, 1921 | | | 20,463 | $37,100,961 00 |
| Re-insured | | | 153 | $885,152 00 |

BUSINESS IN ILLINOIS—ORDINARY.

| | Number. | Amount. |
|---|---|---|
| Policies in force December 31, 1920 | 3,191 | $5,476,937 00 |
| Policies issued during the year | 1,053 | 2,063,135 00 |
| Total | 4,244 | $7,540,072 00 |
| Deduct policies ceased to be in force | 889 | 1,723,382 00 |
| Policies in force December 31, 1921 | 3,355 | $5,816,690 00 |
| Losses and claims unpaid December 31, 1920 | 1 | $ 1,000 00 |
| Losses and claims incurred during the year | 7 | 12,000 00 |
| Total | 8 | $13,000 00 |
| Losses and claims settled during the year | 8 | 13,000 00 |
| Premiums received | | $178,617 68 |

GAIN AND LOSS EXHIBIT.

INSURANCE EXHIBIT.

| | | Gain in surplus. | Loss in surplus. |
|---|---|---|---|
| Loading on actual premiums of the year (averaging 19 per cent of the gross premiums) | $210,568 52 | | |
| Insurance expenses incurred during the year | 424,839 26 | | |
| Loss from loading | | | $214,270 74 |
| Interest earned during the year | $213,366 28 | | |
| Investment expenses incurred during the year | 12,488 62 | | |
| Net income from investments | $200,877 66 | | |
| Interest required to maintain reserve | 126,965 00 | | |
| Gain from interest | | $ 73,912 66 | |
| Expected mortality on net amount at risk | $354,279 00 | | |
| Actual mortality on net amount at risk | 165,579 22 | | |
| Gain from mortality | | 188,699 78 | |
| Expected disbursements to annuitants | $ 875 00 | | |
| Net actual annuity claims incurred | 1,191 97 | | |
| Loss from annuities | | | 316 97 |
| Total gain during the year from surrendered and lapsed policies | | 43,770 84 | |
| Decrease in surplus on dividend account | | | 529 63 |
| Increase in special funds and special reserves during the year | | | 43,055 00 |
| Net to loss account | | | 24,466 41 |

GAIN AND LOSS EXHIBIT—Concluded.

INVESTMENT EXHIBIT.

| | | Gain in surplus. | Loss in surplus. |
|---|---|---|---|
| Total gains from bonds | | $22,570 48 | |
| Total losses from bonds | | | $ 95 39 |
| Gain from sale of mortgage, $500.00; discount on mortgage, $250.00 | | 750 00 | |
| Loss from assets not admitted | | | 8,413 07 |
| Net gain on account of total and permanent disability benefits or additional accidental death benefits included in life policies | | 8,307 91 | |
| Balance unaccounted for | | 3,098 16 | |
| Total gains and losses in surplus during the year | | $341,109 83 | $291,147 21 |
| Surplus December 31, 1920 | $104,142 45 | | |
| Surplus December 31, 1921 | 154,105 07 | | |
| Increase in surplus | | | 49,962 62 |
| Total | | $341,109 83 | $341,109 83 |

## SECURITY MUTUAL LIFE INSURANCE COMPANY.

Located at Security Mutual Life Building, Binghamton, New York; incorporated November 6, 1886; commenced business in Illinois July 5, 1899.

D. S. DICKENSON, President. C. A. LA DUE, Secretary.

R. P. HOLLETT, Chicago, Attorney for service.

| | | | |
|---|---|---|---|
| Amount of ledger assets December 31, of previous year | | | $10,750,717 29 |

### INCOME.

| | | | |
|---|---|---|---|
| First year's premiums on original policies, less re-insurance | | $324,420 10 | |
| First year's premiums for total and permanent disability benefits, less re-insurance | | 5,884 05 | |
| First year's premiums for additional accidental death benefits, less re-insurance | | 6,116 03 | |
| Dividends applied to purchase paid-up additions and annuities | | 13,713 20 | |
| Surrender values applied to purchase paid-up insurance and annuities | | 55,419 15 | |
| Consideration for original annuities involving life contingencies | | 1,000 00 | |
| New premiums | | $ 406,552 53 | |
| Renewal premiums less re-insurance | $1,853,619 74 | | |
| Renewal premiums for total and permanent disability benefits, less re-insurance | 3,977 01 | | |
| Renewal premiums for additional accidental death benefits, less re-insurance | 2,311 04 | | |
| Dividends applied to pay renewal premiums | 80,942 79 | | |
| Surrender values applied to pay renewal premiums | 13,993 74 | | |
| Renewal premiums | | 1,954,844 32 | |
| Premium income | | | $2,361,396 85 |
| Dividends left with company to accumulate at interest | | | 11,451 60 |
| Interest on mortgage loans | | $224,308 15 | |
| Interest on bonds and dividends on stocks | | 191,028 40 | |
| Interest on premium notes, policy loans or liens | | 127,414 13 | |
| Interest on deposits | | 5,486 60 | |
| Rents—including $21,000.00 for company's occupancy of its own buildings | | 72,408 09 | |
| Total interest and rents | | | 620,645 37 |
| Unclaimed checks | | | 5,182 40 |
| Profit on sale or maturity of ledger assets | | | 3,330 29 |
| Increase in book value of ledger assets | | | 6,299 81 |
| Total income | | | $3,008,306 32 |
| Total | | | $13,759,023 61 |

### DISBURSEMENTS.

| | | |
|---|---|---|
| Death claims and additions | $592,273 31 | |
| Matured endowments and additions | 156,251 00 | |
| Total and permanent disability claims and additional accidental death benefits | 6,232 68 | |
| Total death claims and endowments | | $754,756 99 |
| Annuities involving life contingencies | | 632 31 |
| Surrender values paid in cash, or applied in liquidation of loans or notes | | 389,958 35 |
| Surrender values applied to pay new and renewal premiums | | 13,993 74 |
| Surrender values applied to purchase paid-up insurance and annuities | | 55,419 15 |
| Dividends paid policyholders in cash, or applied in liquidation of loans or notes | | 33,671 55 |
| Dividends applied to pay renewal premiums | | 80,942 79 |
| Dividends applied to purchase paid-up additions and annuities | | 13,713 20 |

DISBURSEMENTS—Concluded.

|  | |  |
|---|---|---|
| Dividends left with the company to accumulate at interest | | $ 11,451 60 |
| (Total paid policyholders | $1,354,539 68) | |
| Expense of investigation and settlement of policy claims, including legal expenses | | 111 50 |
| Supplementary contracts not involving life contingencies | | 3,702 79 |
| Dividends with interest, held on deposit surrendered during the year | | 6,475 87 |
| Commissions to agents, first year, $135,601.99; renewal, $109,266.91; annuities (original), $50.00 | | 244,918 90 |
| Agency supervision and traveling expenses of supervisors | | 101,781 82 |
| Branch office expenses | | 46,429 41 |
| Medical examiners' fees and inspection of risks | | 33,840 09 |
| Salaries and all other compensation of officers and home office employees | | 174,534 85 |
| Rent | | 47,758 80 |
| Advertising, printing, stationery, postage, telegraph, telephone, express and exchange | | 32,608 25 |
| Legal expense | | 1,822 72 |
| Furniture, fixtures and safes | | 10,198 87 |
| Repairs and expenses (other than taxes) on real estate | | 38,794 10 |
| Taxes on real estate | | 19,005 00 |
| State taxes on premiums | | 33,844 52 |
| Insurance department licenses and fees | | 2,673 58 |
| Federal taxesp | | 8,477 98 |
| All other licenses, fees and taxes | | 1,143 71 |
| Other disbursements, viz: Decrease agents due bills, $7,411.94; library bureau, $3,199.93; books and subscriptions, $866.04; electric expense, $86.62; investment expense, $1,102.45; legislative expense, $110.73; home office travel, $13,536.86; agency and investment company, $7,875.00; Life Presidents Associations, $255.70; liability insurance, $592.99; employees bonds, $283.47; examination insurance department, $3,627.83; dues, $72.00; miscellaneous, $3,410.77 | | 42,432 33 |
| Agents' balances charged off | | 6,363 49 |
| Loss on sale or maturity of ledger assets | | 10,610 22 |
| Decrease in book value of ledger assets | | 1,170 30 |
| Total disbursements | | $2,223,238 78 |
| Balance | | $11,535,784 83 |

LEDGER ASSETS.

|  |  |
|---|---|
| Book value of real estate | $ 743,570 07 |
| Mortgage loans on real estate | 4,213,541 50 |
| Loans on company's policies assigned as collateral | 2,196,504 19 |
| Premium notes on policies in force | 71,478 83 |
| Book value of bonds and stocks | 4,068,573 27 |
| Cash in office | 6,779 06 |
| Deposits in trust companies and banks not on interest | 57,014 71 |
| Deposits in trust companies and banks on interest | 165,708 59 |
| Agents' balances (debit, $13,083.60; credit, $468.99) net | 12,614 61 |
| Total ledger assets | $11,535,784 83 |

NON-LEDGER ASSETS.

|  | New business. | Renewals. |  |
|---|---|---|---|
| Interest due and accrued on mortgages | | $98,542 71 | |
| Interest due and accrued on bonds | | 58,832 42 | |
| Interest due and accrued on premium notes, loans or liens | | 75,490 96 | |
| Interest due and accrued on other assets | | 1,309 03 | |
| Rents due and accrued on company's property | | 871 95 | |
| | | | 235,047 07 |
| Market value of real estate over book value | | | 118,429 93 |
| Net uncollected and deferred premiums (paid for basis) | $40,032 70 | $286,363 92 | 326,396 62 |
| Gross assets | | | $12,215,658 45 |

DEDUCT ASSETS NOT ADMITTED.

|  | |  |
|---|---|---|
| Agents' debit balances | $13,083 60 | |
| Premium notes, policy loans and other policy assets in excess of net value and of other policy liabilities on individual policies | 20,822 32 | |
| Overdue and accrued interest on bonds in default | 2,916 67 | |
| Book value of bonds and stocks over market value | 20,706 94 | |
| Deposit in bank | 2,000 00 | |
| Total | | 59,529 53 |
| Admitted assets | | $12,156,128 92 |

LIABILITIES.

|  | |  |
|---|---|---|
| Net present value of outstanding policies computed by the New York Insurance Department | $11,124,366 00 | |
| Same for dividend additions | 45,684 00 | |
| Same for annuities | 6,081 00 | |
| Total | $11,176,131 00 | |
| Deduct net value of risks re-insured | 33,997 00 | |
| Net reserve (paid for basis) | | $11,142,134 00 |

### LIABILITIES—Concluded.

| | | |
|---|---|---|
| Extra reserve for total and permanent disability benefits and for additional accidental death benefits included in life policies, less re-insurance | | $13,768 00 |
| Present value of supplementary contracts not involving life contingencies | | 43,904 60 |
| Present value of amounts incurred but not yet due for total and permanent disability benefits | | 1,859 47 |
| Surrender values claimable on policies cancelled | | 30,232 87 |
| Death losses in process of adjustment | $ 7,000 00 | |
| Death losses reported for which no proofs have been received | 39,236 00 | |
| Reserve for net death losses incurred but unreported | 9,601 00 | |
| Matured endowments due and unpaid | 6,600 00 | |
| Death losses and other policy claims resisted | 2,000 00 | |
| Total policy claims | | 64,437 00 |
| Dividends left with the company to accumulate at interest | | 44,996 22 |
| Gross premiums paid in advance, including surrender values so applied, less discount, if any | | 8,856 20 |
| Unearned interest and rent paid in advance | | 24,089 21 |
| Commissions to agents due or accrued | | 19,741 24 |
| Salaries, rents, office expenses, bills and accounts due or accrued | | 12,885 06 |
| Medical examiners' and legal fees due or accrued | | 3,194 15 |
| Estimated amount hereafter payable for federal, state and other taxes based upon the business of the year of this statement | | 55,000 00 |
| Dividends or other profits due policyholders | | 15,789 76 |
| Dividends declared on or apportioned to annual dividend policies payable to policyholders during 1922 for period to March 31, 1922 | | 25,817 47 |
| Dividends declared on or apportioned to deferred dividend policies payable to policyholders during 1922 for period to December 31, 1922 | | 57,000 00 |
| Amounts set apart, apportioned, provisionally ascertained, calculated, declared or held awaiting apportionment upon deferred dividend policies | | 75,109 57 |
| Total | | $11,638,814 82 |
| Unassigned funds (surplus) | | 517,314 10 |
| Total | | $12,156,128 92 |

### EXHIBIT OF POLICIES—ORDINARY.

ALL BUSINESS PAID FOR.

| | Number. | Amount. | Number. | Amount. |
|---|---|---|---|---|
| Policies in force December 31, 1920 | | | 42,943 | $67,252,413 00 |
| Policies issued, revived and increased during the year | | | 5,208 | 9,981,540 00 |
| Total | | | 48,151 | $77,233,953 00 |
| Deduct policies which have ceased to be in force during the year— | | | | |
| By death | 363 | $ 611,304 00 | | |
| By maturity | 125 | 158,851 00 | | |
| By expiry | 191 | 406,759 00 | | |
| By surrender | 660 | 1,058,025 00 | | |
| By lapse | 3,056 | 5,808,228 00 | | |
| By decrease | -------- | 99,677 00 | | |
| Total | | | 4,395 | 8,142,844 00 |
| Total policies in force December 31, 1921 | | | 43,756 | $69,091,109 00 |
| Re-insured | | | 101 | $735,788 00 |

### BUSINESS IN ILLINOIS—ORDINARY.

| | Number. | Amount. |
|---|---|---|
| Policies in force Decmber 31, 1920 | 1,967 | $2,939,019 12 |
| Policies issued during the year | 229 | 460,848 20 |
| Total | 2,196 | $3,399,867 32 |
| Deduct policies ceased to be in force | 145 | 288,298 20 |
| Policies in force December 31, 1921 | 2,051 | $3,111,569 12 |
| Losses and claims unpaid December 31, 1920 | 1 | $ 1,000 00 |
| Losses and claims incurred during the year | 8 | 10,012 20 |
| Total | 9 | $11,012 20 |
| Losses and claims settled during the year | 8 | 10,012 20 |
| Losses and claims unpaid December 31, 1921 | 1 | $1,000 00 |
| Premiums received | | $100,593 31 |

## GAIN AND LOSS EXHIBIT.

INSURANCE EXHIBIT.

| | | Gain in surplus. | Loss in surplus. |
|---|---|---|---|
| Loading on actual premiums of the year (averaging 21 per cent of the gross premiums) | $506,301 57 | | |
| Insurance expenses incurred during the year | 761,865 37 | | |
| Loss from loading | | | $255,563 80 |
| Interest earned during the year | $625,549 81 | | |
| Investment expenses incurred during the year | 85,408 49 | | |
| Net income from investments | $540,141 32 | | |
| Interest required to maintain reserve | 332,697 83 | | |
| Gain from interest | | $207,443 49 | |
| Expected mortality on net amount at risk | $768,038 97 | | |
| Actual mortality on net amount at risk | 477,020 39 | | |
| Gain from mortality | | 291,018 58 | |
| Expected disbursements to annuitants | $321 01 | | |
| Net actual annuity claims incurred | 534 54 | | |
| Loss from annuities | | | 213 53 |
| Total gain during the year from surrendered and lapsed policies | | 79,832 06 | |
| Decrease in surplus on dividend account | | | 178,060 13 |
| Decrease in special funds and special reserves during the year | | 297 85 | |
| Net to loss account | | | 1,181 09 |

INVESTMENT EXHIBIT.

| | | Gain in surplus. | Loss in surplus. |
|---|---|---|---|
| Total gains from stocks and bonds | | 3,330 29 | |
| Total losses from stocks and bonds | | | 16,261 88 |
| Loss on bank failure | | | 2,000 00 |
| Loss from assets not admitted | | | 4,687 64 |
| Net loss on account of total and permanent disability benefits or additional accidental death benefits included in life policies | | | 3,982 49 |
| Loss from all other sources: Examination by Insurance Department, $3,627.83; early policies, $5,103.82 | | | 8,731 65 |
| Total gains and losses in surplus during the year | | $581,922 27 | $470,682 21 |
| Surplus December 31, 1920 | $406,074 04 | | |
| Surplus December 31, 1921 | 517,314 10 | | |
| Increase in surplus | | | 111,240 06 |
| Total | | $581,922 27 | $581,922 27 |

## THE STATE LIFE INSURANCE COMPANY.

Located at The State Life Building, Indianapolis, Indiana; incorporated September 5, 1894; commenced business in Illinois July 19, 1904.

H. W. BENNETT, President. ALBERT SAHM. Secretary.

HARRY M. FISHER, Chicago, Attorney for service.

| | | | |
|---|---|---|---|
| Amount of ledger assets December 31, of previous year | | | $23,144,929 93 |

INCOME.

| | | | |
|---|---|---|---|
| First year's premiums on original policies, less re-insurance | | $829,450 24 | |
| First year's premiums for total and permanent disability benefits, less re-insurance | | 34,666 25 | |
| First year's premiums for additional accidental death benefits | | 24,189 85 | |
| Surrender values to pay first year's premiums | | 453 05 | |
| Dividends applied to purchase paid-up additions and annuities | | 19,602 76 | |
| Surrender values applied to purchase paid-up insurance and annuities | | 53,975 48 | |
| New premiums | | $ 962,337 63 | |
| Renewal premiums less re-insurance | $3,574,504 61 | | |
| Renewal premiums for total and permanent disability benefits, less re-insurance | 66,988 63 | | |
| Renewal premiums for additional accidental death benefits | 88,127 55 | | |
| Dividends applied to pay renewal premiums | 431,865 86 | | |
| Surrender values applied to pay renewal premiums | 8,271 41 | | |
| Renewal premiums | | 4,169,758 06 | |
| Premium income | | | $5,132,095 69 |

INCOME—Concluded.

| | | |
|---|---|---|
| Consideration for supplementary contracts not involving life contingencies | | $ 7,503 97 |
| Dividends left with company to accumulate at interest | | 59,581 54 |
| Interest on mortgage loans | $693,352 32 | |
| Interest on bonds | 236,254 45 | |
| Interest on premium notes, policy loans or liens | 326,327 59 | |
| Interest on deposits | 8,554 87 | |
| Interest on other debts due the company | 4,483 12 | |
| Rents—including $23,555.00 for company's occupancy of its own buildings | 125,384 81 | |
| Total interest and rents | | 1,394,357 16 |
| Partial payments on voided notes | | 5,610 74 |
| Profit on sale or maturity of ledger assets | | 1,200 26 |
| Total income | | $6,600,349 36 |
| Total | | $29,745,279 29 |

DISBURSEMENTS.

| | | |
|---|---|---|
| Death claims and additions | $985,493 25 | |
| Matured endowments | 86,047 00 | |
| Total and permanent disability claims and additional accidental death benefits, less re-insurance | 51,853 78 | |
| Total death claims and endowments | | $1,123,394 03 |
| Annuities involving life contingencies | | 1,656 48 |
| Premium notes, credits and liens voided by lapse | | 71,330 50 |
| Surrender values paid in cash, or applied in liquidation of loans or notes | | 432,587 00 |
| Surrender values applied to pay new and renewal premiums | | 8,724 46 |
| Surrender values applied to purchase paid-up insurance and annuities | | 53,975 48 |
| Dividends paid policyholders in cash, or applied in liquidation of loans or notes | | 259,956 62 |
| Dividends applied to pay renewal premiums | | 431,865 86 |
| Dividends applied to purchase paid-up additions and annuities | | 19,602 76 |
| Dividends left with the company to accumulate at interest | | 59,581 54 |
| (Total paid policyholders | $2,462,674 73) | |
| Expense of investigation and settlement of policy claims, including legal expenses | | 8,246 62 |
| Supplementary contracts not involving life contingencies | | 14,659 75 |
| Dividends with interest, held on deposit surrendered during the year | | 21,386 78 |
| Commissions to agents, first year, $726,611.39; renewal, $330,613.71 | | 1,057,225 10 |
| Compensation of managers and agents not paid by commissions on new business | | 3,000 00 |
| Agency supervision and traveling expenses of supervisors | | 16,510 16 |
| Branch office expenses | | 76,205 13 |
| Medical examiners' fees and inspection of risks | | 61,363 34 |
| Salaries and all other compensation of officers and home office employees | | 246,133 01 |
| Rent | | 29,527 60 |
| Advertising, printing, stationery, postage, telegraph, telephone, express and exchange | | 56,458 13 |
| Legal expense | | 924 91 |
| Furniture, fixtures and safes | | 15,228 53 |
| Repairs and expenses (other than taxes) on real estate | | 55,523 02 |
| Taxes on real estate | | 35,876 50 |
| State taxes on premiums | | 86,798 26 |
| Insurance department licenses and fees | | 5,265 01 |
| Federal taxes | | 4,442 60 |
| All other licenses, fees and taxes | | 24,618 08 |
| Other disbursements, viz: Investment expense, $18,986.19; miscellaneous expenses, $4,226.93; discount on premiums paid in advance, $1.00 | | 23,214 12 |
| Agents' balances charged off | | 6,712 79 |
| Total disbursements | | $4,311,994 17 |
| Balance | | $25,433.285 12 |

LEDGER ASSETS.

| | |
|---|---|
| Book value of real estate | $ 1,085,879 39 |
| Mortgage loans on real estate | 12,448,068 68 |
| Premiums advanced under Soldiers' and Sailors' Civil Relief Act | 900 00 |
| Loans on company's policies assigned as collateral | 6,419,555 65 |
| Premium notes on policies in force | 143,018 84 |
| Book value of bonds | 4,811,293 45 |
| Cash in office | 21,380 55 |
| Deposits in trust companies and banks on interest | 473,881 74 |
| Agents' balances (debit, $37,575.36; credit, $8,268.54) net | 29,306 82 |
| Total ledger assets | $25,433,285 12 |

NON-LEDGER ASSETS.

| | | |
|---|---|---|
| Interest due and accrued on mortgages | $267,768 06 | |
| Interest accrued on bonds | 42,050 30 | |
| Interest accrued on premium notes, loans or liens | 1,430 19 | |
| Interest due and accrued on other assets | 544 91 | |
| Rents due on company's property | 418 20 | |
| | | 312,211 66 |
| Market value of real estate over book value | | 152,652 34 |

## LEDGER ASSETS—Concluded.

### NON-LEDGER ASSETS.

| | New business. | Renewals. | |
|---|---|---|---|
| Net uncollected and deferred premiums (paid for basis) | $3,844 29 | $454,121 41 | $457,965 70 |
| All other assets, viz: Unearned premiums on fire insurance on home office building, $3,859.00 and unearned premiums from re-insurance companies, $433.47 | | | 4,292 47 |
| Gross assets | | | $26,360,407 29 |

### DEDUCT ASSETS NOT ADMITTED.

| | | |
|---|---|---|
| Agents' debit balances | $37,575 36 | |
| Premium notes, policy loans and other policy assets in excess of net value and of other policy liabilities on individual policies | 20,431 39 | |
| Book value of other ledger assets over market value | 80,844 83 | |
| Total | | 138,851 58 |
| Admitted assets | | $26,221,555 71 |

## LIABILITIES.

| | | |
|---|---|---|
| Net present value of outstanding policies computed by the Indiana Insurance Department | $22,122,068 77 | |
| Same for dividend additions | 54,817 57 | |
| Same for annuities | 10,789 19 | |
| Total | $22,187,675 53 | |
| Deduct net value of risks re-insured | 33,352 77 | |
| Net reserve (paid for basis) | | $22,154,322 76 |
| Extra reserve for total and permanent disability benefits and for additional accidental death benefits included in life policies | | 168,761 19 |
| Present value of supplementary contracts not involving life contingencies | | 127,674 61 |
| Present value of amounts incurred but not yet due for total and permanent disability benefits | | 39,196 88 |
| Death losses in process of adjustment | $9,018 46 | |
| Death losses reported for which no proofs have been received | 38,059 00 | |
| Reserve for net death losses incurred but unreported | 28,493 94 | |
| Death losses and other policy claims resisted | 26,504 85 | |
| Additional accidental death benefits | 11,000 00 | |
| Total policy claims | | $113,076 25 |
| Dividends left with the company to accumulate at interest | | 162,938 18 |
| Gross premiums paid in advance, including surrender values so applied, less discount, if any | | 24,222 11 |
| Unearned interest and rent paid in advance | | 163,212 48 |
| Commissions due agents on premium notes, when paid | | 9,391 17 |
| Commissions to agents due or accrued | | 79,746 17 |
| Salaries, rents, office expenses, bills and accounts due or accrued | | 9,014 78 |
| Medical examiners' fees due or accrued | | 4,666 50 |
| Estimated amount hereafter payable for federal, state and other taxes based upon the business of the year of this statement | | 201,985 30 |
| Dividends or other profits due policyholders | | 34,142 46 |
| Dividends declared on or apportioned to annual dividend policies payable to policyholders during 1922 for period to February 28, 1922 | | 96,420 07 |
| Dividends declared on or apportioned to deferred dividend policies payable to policyholders during 1922 for period to December 31, 1922 | | 245,735 16 |
| Special surplus on term policies | | 9,448 37 |
| Mortality and asset fluctuation fund and other contingent liabilities | | 511,701 27 |
| Soldiers and Sailors bonds | | 900 00 |
| Total | | $24,156,555 71 |
| Unassigned funds (surplus) | | 2,065,000 00 |
| Total | | $26,221,555 71 |

## EXHIBIT OF POLICIES—ORDINARY.

### ALL BUSINESS PAID FOR.

| | Number. | Amount. | Number. | Amount. |
|---|---|---|---|---|
| Policies in force December 31, 1920 | | | 64,199 | $146,425,137 00 |
| Policies issued, revived and increased during the year | | | 9,699 | 26,566,713 00 |
| Total | | | 73,898 | $172,991,850 00 |
| Deduct policies which have ceased to be in force during the year— | | | | |
| By death | 376 | $969,731 00 | | |
| By maturity | 35 | 82,797 00 | | |
| By disability | 1 | 5,000 00 | | |
| By expiry | 372 | 703,406 00 | | |
| By surrender | 881 | 2,168,196 00 | | |

## EXHIBIT OF POLICIES—ORDINARY—Concluded.

ALL BUSINESS PAID FOR.

| | Number. | Amount. | Number. | Amount. |
|---|---|---|---|---|
| Deduct policies which have ceased to be in force during the year— | | | | |
| By lapse | 6,634 | $17,148,680 00 | | |
| By decrease | 7 | 1,003,529 00 | | |
| Total | | | 8,306 | $22,081,339 00 |
| Total policies in force December 31, 1921 | | | 65,592 | $150,910,511 00 |
| Re-insured | | | | $5,629,709 00 |

## BUSINESS IN ILLINOIS—ORDINARY.

| | Number. | Amount. |
|---|---|---|
| Policies in force December 31, 1920 | 1,668 | $8,427,237 00 |
| Policies issued during the year | 247 | 2,170,259 00 |
| Total | 1,915 | $10,597,496 00 |
| Deduct policies ceased to be in force | 87 | 830,204 00 |
| Policies in force December 31, 1921 | 1,828 | $9,767,292 00 |
| Losses and claims incurred during the year | 7 | $36,500 00 |
| Losses and claims settled during the year | 5 | 34,000 00 |
| Losses and claims unpaid December 31, 1921 | 2 | $2,500 00 |
| Premiums received | | $295,496 72 |

## GAIN AND LOSS EXHIBIT.

INSURANCE EXHIBIT.

| | | Gain in surplus. | Loss in surplus. |
|---|---|---|---|
| Loading on actual premiums of the year (averaging 29.13 per cent of the gross premiums) | $1,474,868 03 | | |
| Insurance expenses incurred during the year | 1,750,759 91 | | |
| Loss from loading | | | $275,891 88 |
| Interest earned during the year | $1,413,528 79 | | |
| Investment expenses incurred during the year | 110,908 63 | | |
| Net income from investments | $1,302,620 16 | | |
| Interest required to maintain reserve | 702,645 44 | | |
| Gain from interest | | $599,974 72 | |
| Expected mortality on net amount at risk | $1,476,099 51 | | |
| Actual mortality on net amount at risk | 706,708 19 | | |
| Gain from mortality | | 769,391 32 | |
| Expected disbursements to annuitants | $1,259 77 | | |
| Net actual annuity claims incurred | 1,656 48 | | |
| Loss from annuities | | | 396 71 |
| Total gain during the year from surrendered and lapsed policies | | 37,451 78 | |
| Decrease in surplus on dividend account | | | 845,527 06 |
| Increase in special funds and special reserves during the year | | | 280,061 28 |
| Net to loss account | | | 41,393 57 |

INVESTMENT EXHIBIT.

| | | Gain in surplus. | Loss in surplus. |
|---|---|---|---|
| Total gains from real estate | | 1,200 26 | |
| Total losses from real estate | | | 1,768 00 |
| Total gains from bonds | | 21,190 77 | |
| Loss from soldiers' and sailors' relief bond | | | 900 00 |
| Net gain on account of total and permanent disability benefits or additional accidental death benefits included in life policies | | 77,573 71 | |
| Gain from all other sources | | 374 72 | |
| Balance unaccounted for | | 6,255 93 | |
| Total gains and losses in surplus during the year | | $1,513,413 21 | $1,460,830 45 |
| Surplus December 31, 1920 | $2,012,417 24 | | |
| Surplus December 31, 1921 | 2,065,000 00 | | |
| Increase in surplus | | | 52,582 76 |
| Total | | $1,513,413 21 | $1,513,413 21 |

## STATE MUTUAL LIFE ASSURANCE COMPANY.

Located at No. 340 Main Street, Worcester, Massachusetts; incorporated March 16, 1844; commenced business in Illinois January 16, 1862.

B. H. WRIGHT, President. D. W. CARTER, Secretary.

EDGAR H. CARMACK, Chicago, Attorney for service.

| | | | |
|---|---|---|---|
| Amount of ledger assets December 31, of previous year | | | $64,721,131 43 |

### INCOME.

| | | | |
|---|---|---|---|
| First year's premiums on original policies, less re-insurance | | $1,237,315 85 | |
| First year's premiums for total and permanent disability benefits | | 14,246 76 | |
| Dividends applied to purchase paid-up additions and annuities | | 142,093 41 | |
| Consideration for original annuities involving life contingencies | | 27,712 95 | |
| New premiums | | $1,421,368 97 | |
| Renewal premiums less re-insurance | $8,373,389 07 | | |
| Renewal premiums for total and permanent disability benefits | 23,060 34 | | |
| Dividends applied to pay renewal premiums | 963,474 30 | | |
| Renewal premiums | | 9,359,923 71 | |
| Premium income | | | $10,781,292 68 |
| Consideration for supplementary contracts involving life contingencies | | | 19,248 00 |
| Consideration for supplementary contracts not involving life contingencies | | | 140,688 37 |
| Dividends left with company to accumulate at interest | | | 290,245 80 |
| Interest on mortgage loans | | $1,197,530 37 | |
| Interest on collateral loans | | 1,968 75 | |
| Interest on bonds and dividends on stocks | | 1,469,084 88 | |
| Interest on premium notes, policy loans or liens | | 514,042 12 | |
| Interest on deposits | | 30,661 20 | |
| Interest on other debts due the company | | 6,991 13 | |
| Discount on claims paid in advance | | 154 99 | |
| Rents—including $54,206.44 for company's occupancy of its own buildings | | 198,755 89 | |
| Total interest and rents | | | 3,419,189 33 |
| From other sources, viz: Premium notes restored $490.00; interest on refund of federal excise tax, $2,804.03; exchange, $142.24 | | | 3,436 27 |
| Profit on sale or maturity of ledger assets | | | 10,628 04 |
| Increase in book value of ledger assets | | | 31,888 25 |
| Total income | | | $14,696,616 74 |
| Total | | | $79,417,748 17 |

### DISBURSEMENTS.

| | | | |
|---|---|---|---|
| Death claims and additions | | $2,873,658 68 | |
| Matured endowments and additions | | 1,037,572 10 | |
| Total and permanent disability claims | | 2,966 54 | |
| Total death claims and endowments | | | $3,914,197 32 |
| Annuities involving life contingencies | | | 46,180 65 |
| Surrender values paid in cash, or applied in liquidation of loans or notes | | | 1,334,670 88 |
| Dividends paid policyholders in cash, or applied in liquidation of loans or notes | | | 194,637 12 |
| Dividends applied to pay renewal premiums | | | 963,474 30 |
| Dividends applied to purchase paid-up additions and annuities | | | 142,093 41 |
| Dividends left with the company to accumulate at interest | | | 290,245 80 |
| (Total paid policyholders | | $6,885,499 48) | |
| Expense of investigation and settlement of policy claims, including legal expenses | | | 3,080 48 |
| Supplementary contracts not involving life contingencies | | | 72,904 23 |
| Dividends with interest, held on deposit surrendered during the year | | | 150,085 95 |
| Commissions to agents, first year, $563,162.87; renewal, $579,468.93; annuities (original), $831.39 | | | 1,143,463 19 |
| Commuted renewal commissions | | | 71,562 22 |
| Agency supervision and traveling expenses of supervisors | | | 13,633 90 |
| Branch office expenses | | | 125,529 31 |
| Medical examiners' fees and inspection of risks | | | 86,887 84 |
| Salaries and all other compensation of officers and home office employees | | | 290,039 15 |
| Rent | | | 104,530 09 |
| Advertising, printing, stationery, postage, telegraph, telephone and express | | | 114,379 35 |
| Legal expense | | | 100 22 |
| Furniture, fixtures and safes | | | 30,247 83 |
| Repairs and expenses (other than taxes) on real estate | | | 48,794 16 |
| Taxes on real estate | | | 47,420 10 |
| State taxes on premiums | | | 126,531 66 |
| Insurance department licenses and fees | | | 11,706 39 |

DISBURSEMENTS—Concluded.

| | |
|---|---|
| Federal taxes | $ 79,382 15 |
| All other licenses, fees and taxes | 50,127 14 |
| Other disbursements, viz: Lunches, $18,663.31; repairs and construction, $3,530.45; supplies and maintenance, $3,745.69; auditing, $3,400.00; lighting, $3,000.00; travel and entertainment, $5,577.92; newspapers and periodicals, $3,051.08; rent of machines, $2,172.38; appraising, $27.00; commission on bonds, $375.00; due to associations, $1,523.04 insurance and bonding, $1,164.70; legislative matters through Association of Life Insurance Presidents, $508.31; sundries, $210.91; refund of interest on Soldiers' and Sailors' bonds, $78.75 | 47,028 54 |
| Loss on sale or maturity of ledger assets | 6,162 09 |
| Decrease in book value of ledger assets | 200,171 09 |
| Total disbursements | $9,709,266 56 |
| Balance | $69,708,481 61 |

LEDGER ASSETS.

| | |
|---|---|
| Book value of real estate | $ 1,835,240 00 |
| Mortgage loans on real estate | 22,304,150 00 |
| Loans secured by collaterals | 25,000 00 |
| Premiums advanced under Soldiers' and Sailors' Civil Relief Act | 47 71 |
| Loans on company's policies assigned as collateral | 10,621,483 19 |
| Premium notes on policies in force | 7,183 00 |
| Book value of bonds and stocks | 33,996,010 04 |
| Cash in office | 3,138 07 |
| Deposits in trust companies and banks on interest | 916,229 60 |
| Total ledger assets | $69,708,481 61 |

NON-LEDGER ASSETS.

| | | | |
|---|---|---|---|
| Interest accrued on mortgages | | $392,449 16 | |
| Interest accrued on bonds | | 496,952 70 | |
| Interest accrued on collateral loans | | 712 50 | |
| Interest due and accrued on premium notes, loans or liens | | 206,029 25 | |
| Interest accrued on other assets | | 4,319 54 | |
| Rents due and accrued on company's property | | 22,506 89 | |
| | | | 1,122,970 04 |
| | New business. | Renewals. | |
| Net uncollected and deferred premiums (paid for basis) | $181,373 44 | $1,479,587 00 | 1,660,960 44 |
| Gross assets | | | $72,492,412 09 |

DEDUCT ASSETS NOT ADMITTED.

| | | |
|---|---|---|
| Overdue and accrued interest on bonds in default | $ 35,960 84 | |
| Book value of bonds and stocks over market value | 237,339 00 | |
| Total | | 273,299 84 |
| Admitted assets | | $72,219,112 25 |

LIABILITIES.

| | | |
|---|---|---|
| Net present value of outstanding policies computed by the Massachusetts Insurance Department | $61,025,940 00 | |
| Same for dividend additions | 1,819,081 00 | |
| Same for annuities | 506,421 00 | |
| Total | $63,351,442 00 | |
| Deduct net value of risks re-insured | 507,138 00 | |
| Net reserve (paid for basis) | | $62,844,304 00 |
| Extra reserve for total and permanent disability benefits and for additional accidental death benefits included in life policies | | 47,280 55 |
| Present value of supplementary contracts not involving life contingencies | | 799,495 78 |
| Present value of amounts incurred but not yet due for total and permanent disability benefits | | 16,287 58 |
| Surrender values claimable on policies cancelled | | 6,277 72 |
| Death losses reported for which no proofs have been received | $157,233 00 | |
| Reserve for net death losses incurred but unreported | 50,000 00 | |
| Matured endowments due and unpaid | 6,750 00 | |
| Death losses and other policy claims resisted | 10,000 00 | |
| Annuity claims, involving life contingencies, due and unpaid | 30 39 | |
| Total policy claims | | 224,013 39 |
| Dividends left with the company to accumulate at interest | | 1,300,597 87 |
| Gross premiums paid in advance, including surrender values so applied, less discount, if any | | 72,279 29 |
| Unearned interest and rent paid in advance | | 48 15 |
| Commissions to agents due or accrued | | 190 76 |
| Salaries, rents, office expenses, bills and accounts due or accrued | | 20,000 00 |
| Medical examiners' and legal fees due or accrued | | 6,750 00 |
| Estimated amount hereafter payable for federal, state and other taxes based upon the business of the year of this statement | | 350,000 00 |

## LIABILITIES—Concluded.

| | |
|---|---|
| Dividends or other profits due policyholders | $ 128,390 40 |
| Dividends declared on or apportioned to annual dividend policies payable to policyholders during 1922 for period to December 31, 1922 | 2,130,612 00 |
| Dividends declared on or apportioned to deferred dividend policies payable to policyholders during 1922 for period to December 31, 1922 | 63,062 00 |
| Amounts set apart, apportioned, provisionally ascertained, calculated, declared or held awaiting apportionment upon deferred dividend policies | 150,993 00 |
| Extra reserve on life annuities | 43,166 00 |
| Total | $68,203,748 49 |
| Unassigned funds (surplus) | 4,015,363 76 |
| Total | $72,219,112 25 |

## EXHIBIT OF POLICIES—ORDINARY.

ALL BUSINESS PAID FOR.

| | Number. | Amount. | Number. | Amount. |
|---|---|---|---|---|
| Policies in force December 31, 1920 | | | 112,977 | $315,156,687 00 |
| Policies issued, revived and increased during the year | | | 11,317 | 42,796,493 00 |
| Total | | | 124,294 | $357,953,180 00 |
| Deduct policies which have ceased to be in force during the year— | | | | |
| By death | 909 | $2,868,786 00 | | |
| By maturity | 472 | 1,036,177 00 | | |
| By disability | -------- | 2,400 00 | | |
| By expiry | 367 | 1,068,646 00 | | |
| By surrender | 1,638 | 4,508,560 00 | | |
| By lapse | 2,526 | 8,005,176 00 | | |
| By decrease | 85 | 2,186,840 00 | | |
| Total | | | 5,997 | 19,676,585 00 |
| Total policies in force December 31, 1921 | | | 118,297 | $338,276,595 00 |
| Re-insured | | | 252 | $5,789,758 00 |

## BUSINESS IN ILLINOIS—ORDINARY.

| | Number. | Amount. |
|---|---|---|
| Policies in force December 31, 1920 | 8,185 | $31,646,234 00 |
| Policies issued during the year | 938 | 5,010,308 00 |
| Total | 9,123 | $36,656,542 00 |
| Deduct policies ceased to be in force | 660 | 2,634,535 00 |
| Policies in force December 31, 1921 | 8,463 | $34,022,007 00 |
| Losses and claims unpaid December 31, 1920 | 4 | $ 20,060 00 |
| Losses and claims incurred during the year | 217 | 421,720 55 |
| Total | 221 | $441,780 55 |
| Losses and claims settled during the year | 217 | 440,532 55 |
| Losses and claims unpaid December 31, 1921 | 4 | $1,248 00 |
| Premiums received | | $1,145,554 51 |

## GAIN AND LOSS EXHIBIT.

INSURANCE EXHIBIT.

| | | Gain in surplus. | Loss in surplus. |
|---|---|---|---|
| Loading on actual premiums of the year (averaging 20.05 per cent of the gross premiums) | $2,200,766 12 | | |
| Insurance expenses incurred during the year | 2,363,478 73 | | |
| Loss from loading | | -------------- | $ 162,712 61 |
| Interest earned during the year | $3,582,933 50 | | |
| Investment expenses incurred during the year | 183,763 22 | | |
| Net income from investments | $3,399,170 28 | | |
| Interest required to maintain reserve | 2,102,241 63 | | |
| Gain from interest | | 1,296,928 65 | |
| Expected mortality on net amount at risk | $3,321,710 55 | | |
| Actual mortality on net amount at risk | 1,751,449 60 | | |
| Gain from mortality | | 1,570,260 95 | |
| Expected disbursements to annuitants | $23,142 41 | | |
| Net actual annuity claims incurred | 41,163 04 | | |
| Loss from annuities | | -------------- | 18,020 63 |
| Total gain during the year from surrendered and lapsed policies | | 161,399 49 | |
| Decrease in surplus on dividend account | | -------------- | 2,199,482 62 |

GAIN AND LOSS EXHIBIT—Concluded.

INVESTMENT EXHIBIT.

| | | Gain in surplus. | Loss in surplus. |
|---|---|---|---|
| Total gains from stocks and bonds | | $235,985 52 | |
| Total losses from stocks and bonds | | | $188,382 09 |
| Gain on interest on refund of federal excise tax | | 2,804 03 | |
| Net gain on account of total and permanent disability benefits or additional accidental death benefits included in life policies | | 9,432 15 | |
| Gain from profit on exchange | | 142 24 | |
| Balance unaccounted for | | 61 49 | |
| Total gains and losses in surplus during the year | | $3,277,014 52 | $2,568,597 95 |
| Surplus December 31, 1920 | $3,306,947 19 | | |
| Surplus December 31, 1921 | 4,015,363 76 | | |
| Increase in surplus | | | 708,416 57 |
| Total | | $3,277,014 52 | $3,277,014 52 |

## THE TRAVELERS INSURANCE COMPANY.

Located at No. 700 Main Street, Hartford, Connecticut; incorporated June 17, 1863; commenced business in Illinois, life, December 10, 1864; casualty, July 14, 1879.

LOUIS F. BUTLER, President. JAMES L. HOWARD, Secretary.

GEORGE A. BARR, Director of Trade and Commerce, Attorney for service at Springfield.

J. H. NOLAN, Chicago, Attorney for service.

CAPITAL.

| | | | |
|---|---|---|---|
| Capital paid up | | $7,500,000 00 | |
| Amount of ledger assets December 31, of previous year | | | $132,700,266 73 |

INCOME.

| | | | |
|---|---|---|---|
| First year's premiums on original policies, less re-insurance | | $7,593,754 96 | |
| First year's premiums for total and permanent disability benefits, less re-insurance | | 236,230 97 | |
| First year's premiums for additional accidental death benefits, less re-insurance | | 51,800 92 | |
| Dividends applied to purchase paid-up additions and annuities | | 27,696 17 | |
| Surrender values applied to purchase paid-up insurance and annuities | | 6,203 35 | |
| Consideration for original annuities involving life contingencies | | 547,854 65 | |
| New premiums | | $ 8,463,541 02 | |
| Renewal premiums less re-insurance | $31,544,252 93 | | |
| Renewal premiums for total and permanent disability, benefits, less re-insurance | 595,550 63 | | |
| Renewal premiums for additional accidental death benefits, less re-insurance | 86,820 52 | | |
| Dividends applied to pay renewal preminms | 38,501 26 | | |
| Surrender values applied to pay renewal premiums | 5,862 35 | | |
| Renewal premiums for deferred annuities | 17,332 43 | | |
| Renewal premiums | | 32,288,320 12 | |
| Premium income | | $40,751,861 14 | |
| Premiums advanced during year under Soldiers' and Sailors' Civil Relief Act | | 87 69 | |
| Total | | | $40,751,948 83 |
| Consideration for supplementary contracts involving life contingencies | | | 57,073 14 |
| Consideration for supplementary contracts not involving life contingencies | | | 1,213,676 72 |
| Interest on mortgage loans | | $2,704,309 89 | |
| Interest on bonds and dividends on stocks | | 2,848,917 20 | |
| Interest on premium notes, policy loans or liens | | 1,022,055 93 | |
| Interest on deposits | | 82,793 68 | |
| Interest on other debts due the company | | 4,840 63 | |
| Discount on claims paid in advance | | 463 26 | |
| Rents—including $460,318.68 for company's occupancy of its own buildings | | 513,130 56 | |
| Total interest and rents | | | 7,176,511 15 |
| From other sources, viz: Profit and loss, miscellaneous, $81.07; increase in liabilities on account of funds held under re-insurance treaties, $14,067.00 | | | 14,148 07 |
| Profit on sale or maturity of ledger assets | | | 26,321 83 |
| Increase in book value of ledger assets | | | 351,354 48 |
| Total income | | | $49,591,034 22 |
| Total | | | $182,291,300 95 |

## DISBURSEMENTS.

|  | | |
|---|---|---|
| Death claims and additions | $10,153,844 84 | |
| Matured endowments and additions | 1,617,437 89 | |
| Total and permanent disability claims and additional accidental death benefits | 309,551 78 | |
| Total death claims and endowments | | $12,080,834 51 |
| Annuities involving life contingencies | | 370,414 84 |
| Surrender values paid in cash, or applied in liquidation of loans or notes | | 2,385,877 85 |
| Surrender values applied to pay new and renewal premiums | | 5,862 35 |
| Surrender values applied to purchase paid-up insurance and annuities | | 6,203 35 |
| Dividends paid policyholders in cash, or applied in liquidation of loans or notes | | 30,964 66 |
| Dividends applied to pay renewal premiums | | 38,501 26 |
| Dividends applied to purchase paid-up additions and annuities | | 27,696 17 |
| (Total paid policyholders | $14,946,354 99) | |
| Expense of investigation and settlement of policy claims, including legal expenses | | 164,360 74 |
| Supplementary contracts not involving life contingencies | | 948,258 66 |
| Commissions to agents, first year, $3,313,705.75; renewal, $1,631,681.11; annuities (original), $23,148.41; (renewal), $551.25 | | 4,969,086 52 |
| Commuted renewal commissions | | 43,338 19 |
| Compensation of managers and agents not paid by commissions on new business | | 10,928 45 |
| Agency supervision and traveling expenses of supervisors | | 592,345 38 |
| Traveling expenses of home office employees | | 64,989 01 |
| Branch office expenses | | 863,183 28 |
| Medical examiners' fees and inspection of risks | | 455,645 10 |
| Salaries and all other compensation of officers and home office employees | | 1,625,007 76 |
| Rent | | 650,146 61 |
| Advertising, printing, stationery, postage, telegraph, telephone, express and exchange | | 275,277 74 |
| Legal expense | | 1,781 72 |
| Furniture, fixtures and safes | | 68,102 00 |
| Repairs and expenses (other than taxes) on real estate | | 79,382 65 |
| Taxes on real estate | | 117,533 51 |
| Mortgage loan expense | | 69,289 92 |
| State taxes on premiums | | 515,520 00 |
| Insurance department licenses and fees | | 28,413 84 |
| Federal taxes | | 258,763 05 |
| All other licenses, fees and taxes | | 220,114 24 |
| Other disbursements, viz: Heat, light and maintenance of offices, $86,273.43; dues fees, and expenses in connection with various associations, $12,082.96; insurance on companies employees, $10,979.32; newspapers, periodicals and books, $11,274.66; insurance, $4,719.20; miscellaneous expenses, $1,777.31; paid under protest to alien property custodian in re, Munich Re-insurance account, $253,029.58 | | 380,136 46 |
| Agents' balances charged off | | 334 55 |
| Loss on sale or maturity of ledger assets | | 139,364 50 |
| Decrease in book value of ledger assets | | 220,160 45 |
| Total disbursements | | $27,707,819 32 |
| Balance | | $154,583,481 63 |

## LEDGER ASSETS.

|  | |
|---|---|
| Home office real estate | $ 7,435,591 43 |
| Book value of real estate | 165,026 33 |
| Mortgage loans on real estate | 53,761,919 45 |
| Premiums advanced under Soldiers' and Sailors' Civil Relief Act | 663 18 |
| Loans on company's policies assigned as collateral | 21,384,243 19 |
| Book value of bonds and stocks | 67,751,557 50 |
| Deposits in trust companies and banks on interest | 3,915,187 97 |
| Agents' debit balances | 43,585 58 |
| Funds held under re-insurance treaties | 125,707 00 |
| Total ledger assets | $154,583,481 63 |

### NON-LEDGER ASSETS.

|  | | | |
|---|---|---|---|
| Interest due and accrued on mortgages | | $1,626,610 54 | |
| Interest due and accrued on bonds | | 1,088,740 12 | |
| Interest due on premium notes, loans or liens | | 13,268 06 | |
| | | | 2,728,618 72 |
| Market value of bonds and stocks over book value | | | 324,305 50 |
| Due from other companies for losses or claims on policies re-insured | | | 25,180 15 |
| | New business. | Renewals. | |
| Net uncollected and deferred premiums (paid for basis) | $664,608 89 | $4,974,886 20 | 5,639,495 09 |
| Amount due from alien property custodian in re Munich re-insurance account | | | 253,029 58 |
| Casualty department | | | 56,506,975 69 |
| Gross assets | | | $220,061,086 36 |

### DEDUCT ASSETS NOT ADMITTED.

|  | | |
|---|---|---|
| Agents' debit balances | $ 43,585 58 | |
| Overdue and accrued interest on bonds in default | 222,190 99 | |
| Casualty department | 789,627 55 | |
| Total | | 1,055,404 12 |
| Admitted assets | | $219,005,682 24 |

## LIABILITIES.

| | | |
|---|---|---|
| Net present value of outstanding policies | $145,485,728 00 | |
| Same for dividend additions | 291,365 00 | |
| Same for annuities | 4,139,713 00 | |
| Total | $149,916,806 00 | |
| Deduct net value of risks re-insured | 2,078,863 00 | |
| Net reserve (paid for basis) | | $147,837,943 00 |
| Extra reserve for total and permanent disability benefits and for additional accidental death benefits included in life policies, less re-insurance | | 1,354,316 00 |
| Present value of supplementary contracts not involving life contingencies | | 6,210,538 00 |
| Present value of amounts incurred but not yet due for total and permanent disability benefits | | 246,401 00 |
| Surrender values claimable on policies cancelled | | 18,402 44 |
| Death losses in process of adjustment | $116,016 97 | |
| Death losses reported for which no proofs have been received | 72,806 89 | |
| Reserve for net death losses incurred but unreported | 190,068 08 | |
| Matured endowments due and unpaid | 16,846 04 | |
| Death losses and other policy claims resisted | 157,246 00 | |
| Total and permanent disability benefits and additional accidental death benefits | 42,108 00 | |
| Annuity claims, involving life contingencies, due and unpaid | 150 00 | |
| Total policy claims | | 595,241 98 |
| Due and unpaid on supplementary contracts not involving life contingencies | | 867 30 |
| Gross premiums paid in advance, including surrender values so applied, less discount, if any | | 111,052 99 |
| Unearned interest and rent paid in advance | | 418,494 95 |
| Commissions to agents due or accrued | | 17,359 76 |
| Salaries, rents, office expenses, bills and accounts due or accrued | | 119,326 24 |
| Medical examiners' and legal fees due or accrued | | 51,786 03 |
| Estimated amount hereafter payable for federal, state and other taxes based upon the business of the year of this statement | | 1,038,481 00 |
| Dividends or other profits due policyholders | | 4,932 78 |
| Dividends declared on or apportioned to annual dividend policies payable to policyholders during 1922 for period to and including December 31, 1922 | | 64,216 45 |
| Amounts set apart, apportioned, provisionally ascertained, calculated, declared or held awaiting apportionment upon deferred dividend policies | | 503,297 00 |
| Additional reserve for pro-rata paid up insurance values and extra premiums | | 27,724 00 |
| Funds held under re-insurance treaties | | 125,707 00 |
| Casualty department | | 42,570,688 91 |
| Total | | $201,316,776 83 |
| Capital paid up | | 7,500,000 00 |
| Unassigned funds (surplus) | | 10,188,905 41 |
| Total | | $219,005,682 24 |

## EXHIBIT OF POLICIES—ORDINARY.

ALL BUSINESS PAID FOR.

| | Number. | Amount. | Number. | Amount. |
|---|---|---|---|---|
| Policies in force December 31, 1920 | | | 361,492 | $1,576,338,993 00 |
| Policies issued, revived and increased during the year | | | 76,186 | 477,123,176 00 |
| Total | | | 437,678 | $2,053,462,169 00 |
| Deduct policies which have ceased to be in force during the year— | | | | |
| By death | 2,279 | $ 10,608,309 00 | | |
| By maturity | 693 | 1,561,283 00 | | |
| By disability | 29 | 283,465 00 | | |
| By expiry | 2,181 | 4,387,493 00 | | |
| By surrender | 5,114 | 19,323,031 00 | | |
| By lapse | 17,940 | 108,307,993 00 | | |
| By decrease | 43 | 25,700 00 | | |
| By withdrawal | -------- | 152,475,069 00 | | |
| Total | | | 28,279 | 296,972,343 00 |
| Total policies in force December 31, 1921 | | | 409,399 | $1,756,489,826 00 |
| Re-insured | | | 2,409 | $40,571,549 00 |

## EXHIBIT OF POLICIES—GROUP INSURANCE.

ALL BUSINESS PAID FOR.

| | Number. | Amount. |
|---|---|---|
| Policies in force December 31, 1920 | 1,852 | $433,645,422 00 |
| Policies issued, revived and increased during the year | 173 | 183,746,914 00 |
| Total | 2,025 | $617,392,336 00 |
| Decrease by transfer | -------- | 2,750 00 |
| Total | 2,025 | $617,389,586 00 |

## EXHIBIT OF POLICIES—GROUP INSURANCE—Concluded.

ALL BUSINESS PAID FOR.

| | Number. | Amount. | Number. | Amount. |
|---|---|---|---|---|
| Deduct policies which have ceased to be in force during the year— | | | | |
| By death | -------- | $ 2,872,407 00 | | |
| By disability | -------- | 185,965 00 | | |
| By expiry | 2 | 195,500 00 | | |
| By surrender | -------- | 1,009,014 00 | | |
| By lapse | 228 | 36,208,004 00 | | |
| By withdrawal | -------- | 152,475,069 00 | | |
| Total | | | 230 | $192,945,959 00 |
| Total policies in force December 31, 1921 | | | 1,795 | $424,443,627 00 |
| Distribution of business in force at end of year— | | | | |
| One year term | | | 1,794 | $424,164,327 00 |
| All other | | | 1 | 279,300 00 |
| Total | | | 1,795 | $424,443,627 00 |

## BUSINESS IN ILLINOIS—ORDINARY.

| | Number. | Amount. |
|---|---|---|
| Policies in force December 31, 1920 | 17,634 | $68,361,172 00 |
| Policies issued during the year | 5,999 | 25,225,866 00 |
| Total | 23,633 | $93,587,038 00 |
| Deduct policies ceased to be in force | 1,322 | 6,058,138 00 |
| Policies in force December 31, 1921 | 22,311 | $87,528,900 00 |
| Losses and claims unpaid December 31, 1920 | 4 | $ 11,487 00 |
| Losses and claims incurred during the year | 163 | 630,332 15 |
| Total | 167 | $641,819 15 |
| Losses and claims settled during the year | 164 | 608,479 15 |
| Losses and claims unpaid December 31, 1921 | 3 | $33,340 00 |
| Premiums received | | $2,172,220 11 |

## BUSINESS IN ILLINOIS—GROUP INSURANCE.

| | Number. | Amount. |
|---|---|---|
| Policies in force December 31, 1920 | 112 | $35,859,502 00 |
| Policies issued during the year | 13 | 13,902,943 00 |
| Total | 125 | $49,762,445 00 |
| Deduct policies ceased to be in force | 20 | 17,399,198 00 |
| Policies in force December 31, 1921 | 105 | $32,363,247 00 |
| Losses and claims unpaid December 31, 1920 | 19 | $ 13,950 67 |
| Losses and claims incurred during the year | 199 | 201,300 00 |
| Total | 218 | $215,250 67 |
| Losses and claims settled during the year | 211 | 209,635 77 |
| Losses and claims unpaid December 31, 1921 | 7 | 5,614 90 |
| Premiums received | | $334,641 81 |

## GAIN AND LOSS EXHIBIT.

INSURANCE EXHIBIT.

| | | Gain in surplus. | Loss in surplus. |
|---|---|---|---|
| Loading on actual premiums of the year (averaging 6.36 per cent of the gross premiums) | $ 2,595,498 29 | | |
| Insurance expenses incurred during the year | 10,898,959 32 | | |
| Loss from loading | | ---- -------- | $8,303,461 03 |
| Interest earned during the year | $7,628,854 99 | | |
| Investment expenses incurred during the year | 454,329 00 | | |
| Net income from investments | $7,174,525 99 | | |
| Interest required to maintain reserve | 5,207,834 00 | | |
| Gain from interest | | $1,966,691 99 | |
| Expected mortality on net amount at risk | $16,562,192 00 | | |
| Actual mortality on net amount at risk | 8,373,474 50 | | |
| Gain from mortality | | 8,188,717 50 | |

## GAIN AND LOSS EXHIBIT—Concluded.

INSURANCE EXHIBIT.

| | | Gain in surplus. | Loss in surplus. |
|---|---|---|---|
| Expected disbursements to annuitants | $216,835 00 | | |
| Net actual annuity claims incurred | 284,857 84 | | |
| Loss from annuities | | | $ 68,022 84 |
| Total gain during the year from surrendered and lapsed policies | | $984,448 61 | |
| Decrease in surplus on dividend account | | | 113,512 66 |
| Decrease in special funds and special reserves during the year | | 17,276 00 | |
| Net to loss account | | | 253 48 |
| **INVESTMENT EXHIBIT.** | | | |
| Total gains from real estate | | 2,000 00 | |
| Total losses from real estate | | | 151,746 76 |
| Total gains from stocks and bonds | | 281,239 51 | |
| Total losses from stocks and bonds | | | 218,388 32 |
| Loss from assets not admitted | | | 43,448 02 |
| Net gain on account of total and permanent disability benefits or additional accidental death benefits included in life policies | | 202,429 26 | |
| Gain from all other sources | | 27,948 98 | |
| Loss from casualty department | | | 1,474,814 20 |
| Total gains and losses in surplus during the year | | $11,670,751 85 | $10,373,647 31 |
| Surplus December 31, 1920 | $ 8,891,800 87 | | |
| Surplus December 31, 1921 | 10,188,905 41 | | |
| Increase in surplus | | | 1,297,104 54 |
| Total | | $11,670,751 85 | $11,670,751 85 |

## UNION CENTRAL LIFE INSURANCE COMPANY.

Located at Nos. 1-7 West Fourth Street, Cincinnati, Ohio; incorporated, 1867; commenced business in Illinois July 26, 1867.

JOHN D. SAGE, President. R. FREDERICK RUST, Secretary.

FRANK Y. HAMILTON, Bloomington, Attorney for service.

### CAPITAL.

| | | |
|---|---|---|
| Capital paid up | $2,500,000 00 | |
| Amount of ledger assets December 31, of previous year | | $142,661,477 43 |

### INCOME.

| | | | |
|---|---|---|---|
| First year's premiums on original policies | | $3,393,238 92 | |
| First year's premiums for total and permanent disability benefits | | 41,196 77 | |
| First year's premiums for additional accidental death benefits | | 16,463 16 | |
| Surrender values to pay first year's premiums | | 13,276 26 | |
| Dividends applied to purchase paid-up additions and annuities | | 523,705 97 | |
| Surrender values applied to purchase paid-up insurance and annuities | | 76,021 26 | |
| Consideration for original annuities involving life contingencies | | 71,204 78 | |
| New premiums | | $ 4,135,107 12 | |
| Renewal premiums less re-insurance | $19,290,685 49 | | |
| Renewal premiums for total and permanent disability benefits | 117,528 24 | | |
| Renewal premiums for additional accidental death benefits | 861 21 | | |
| Dividends applied to pay renewal premiums | 3,622,168 73 | | |
| Surrender values applied to pay renewal premiums | 197,430 60 | | |
| Renewal premiums for deferred annuities | 48,774 25 | | |
| Renewal premiums | | 23,277,448 52 | |
| Premium income | | $27,412,555 64 | |
| Premiums advanced during year under Soldiers' and Sailors' Civil Relief Act | | 28 16 | |
| Total | | | $27,412,583 80 |
| Consideration for supplementary contracts not involving life contingencies | | | 257,660 18 |
| Dividends left with company to accumulate at interest | | | 87,691 86 |
| Interest on mortgage loans | | $6,322,941 87 | |
| Interest on bonds | | 316,654 20 | |
| Interest on premium notes, policy loans or liens | | 1,399,027 23 | |

## INCOME—Concluded.

| | | |
|---|---|---|
| Interest on deposits | $49,925 91 | |
| Interest on other debts due the company | 4,741 21 | |
| Discount on claims paid in advance | 3,496 60 | |
| Rents—including $148,473.50 for company's occupancy of its own buildings less $36,640.00 interest on incumbrances | 400,166 42 | |
| Total interest and rents | | $8,496,953 44 |
| From other sources, viz: Proceeds of policies left with the company to accumulate at interest, $760,590.30; deposits by policyholders on account of liberty bonds, $2,588.63; salary left by employees at interest, $61,630.47; judgment against U. S. Government collected, $40,257.47; refund of excise and income tax paid June, 1915, $2,581.97; gross profits from compromise and adjustments of mortgage loans, $40,557.86; gross profit on unlisted assets, $5,638.06 | | 913,844 76 |
| Borrowed money (gross) | | 350,000 00 |
| Agents' balances previously charged off | | 129 97 |
| Profit on sale or maturity of ledger assets | | 4,435 42 |
| Increase in book value of ledger assets | | 403 69 |
| Total income | | $37,523,703 12 |
| Total | | $180,185,180 55 |

## DISBURSEMENTS.

| | | |
|---|---|---|
| Death claims and additions | $6,132,583 11 | |
| Matured endowments and additions | 1,697,504 57 | |
| For matured life rate endowments (reserve, $1,286,717.67; surplus, $1,092,178.68 | 2,378,896 35 | |
| Total and permanent disability claims | 3,144 78 | |
| Total death claims and endowments | | $10,212,128 81 |
| Annuities involving life contingencies | | 36,627 72 |
| Premium notes and liens voided by lapse, less $37,700.52 restorations | | 159,017 62 |
| Surrender values paid in cash, or applied in liquidation of loans or notes | | 2,417,033 03 |
| Surrender values applied to pay new and renewal premiums | | 210,706 86 |
| Surrender values applied to purchase paid-up insurance and annuities | | 76,021 26 |
| Dividends paid policyholders in cash, or applied in liquidation of loans or notes | | 406,492 12 |
| Dividends applied to pay renewal premiums | | 3,622,168 73 |
| Dividends applied to purchase paid-up additions and annuities | | 523,705 97 |
| Dividends left with the company to accumulate at interest | | 87,691 86 |
| (Total paid policyholders | $17,751,593 98) | |
| Expense of investigation and settlement of policy claims, including legal expenses | | 20 00 |
| Supplementary contracts not involving life contingencies | | 233,326 02 |
| Dividends with interest, held on deposit surrendered during the year | | 28,187 47 |
| Dividends to stockholders | | 200,000 00 |
| Commissions to agents, first year, $1,639,344.93; renewal, $1,601,831.98; annuities (original), $9,337.26; (renewal), $2,528.79 | | 3,253,042 96 |
| Agency supervision and traveling expenses of supervisors | | 28,901 57 |
| Branch office expenses | | 88,969 32 |
| Medical examiners' fees and inspection of risks | | 141,166 18 |
| Salaries and all other compensation of officers and home office employees | | 1,015,463 06 |
| Rent | | 186,952 66 |
| Advertising, printing, stationery, postage, telegraph, telephone, express and exchange | | 124,540 98 |
| Legal expense | | 38,905 07 |
| Furniture, fixtures and safes | | 24,711 38 |
| Repairs and expenses (other than taxes) on real estate | | 180,920 59 |
| Taxes on real estate | | 72,566 37 |
| State taxes on premiums | | 481,032 97 |
| Insurance department licenses and fees | | 39,239 99 |
| Federal taxes | | 96,464 61 |
| All other licenses, fees and taxes | | 25,901 56 |
| Other disbursements, viz: Mortgage expense—expense of maintaining mortgage investments, $58,035.75; mortgage loan expense—expense of making new investments, $539,269.79; disability suspense, $24,000.00; liberty bonds paid for and delivered to policyholders, $2,951.87; interest on sundry small claims, $1,501.08; general expense home office, $33,549.92; traveling expense home office, $77,690.98; salary left by employees at interest withdrawn, $19,186.33; employees' benefit fund, $4,256.64; gross loss on unlisted assets, $6,331.69; gross loss on mortgage loans, $113.97; interest on policy claims, $19,964.06; surplus interest on installments, $13,724.59; policy deposits and interest thereon (contract, $28,008.13; surplus, $16,124.20) withdrawn, $692,070.92 | | 1,536,869 92 |
| Borrowed money repaid (gross) | | 850,000 00 |
| Interest on borrowed money | | 35,963 25 |
| Agents' balances charged off | | 17,296 23 |
| Loss on sale or maturity of ledger assets | | 1,414 73 |
| Decrease in book value of ledger assets | | 44,038 67 |
| Total disbursements | | $26,407,489 54 |
| Balance | | $153,687,691 01 |

## LEDGER ASSETS.

| | |
|---|---|
| Book value of real estate | $ 2,319,355 24 |
| Mortgage loans on real estate | 112,469,525 17 |
| Premiums advanced under Soldiers' and Sailors' Civil Relief Act | 120 51 |
| Loans on company's policies assigned as collateral | 27,293,387 85 |
| Premium notes on policies in force | 3,244,262 16 |
| Book value of bonds | 7,298,612 00 |
| Cash in office | 8,533 65 |
| Deposits in trust companies and banks not on interest | 394 54 |
| Deposits in trust companies and banks on interest | 894,404 82 |
| Proceeds of re-insurance policy left at interest with Confederation Life Association | 3,687 46 |
| Accounts collectible, debit, $207,840.09; credit, $52,432.48 net | 155,407 61 |
| Total ledger assets | $153,687,691 01 |

### NON-LEDGER ASSETS.

| | | | |
|---|---|---|---|
| Interest due and accrued on mortgages | | $4,866,606 13 | |
| Interest accrued on bonds | | 47,823 42 | |
| Interest due and accrued on premium notes, loans or liens | | 1,159,326 74 | |
| Rents due on company's property | | 2,822 31 | |
| | | | 6,076,578 60 |
| | New business. | Renewals. | |
| Net uncollected and deferred premiums (paid for basis) | $234,555 24 | $1,913,881 47 | 2,148,436 71 |
| Gross assets | | | $161,912,706 32 |

### DEDUCT ASSETS NOT ADMITTED.

| | | |
|---|---|---|
| Accounts collectible, debit balances, gross | $207,840 09 | |
| Premium notes, policy loans and other policy assets in excess of net value and of other policy liabilities on individual policies | 13,541 11 | |
| Book value of bonds over market value | 9,574 40 | |
| Total | | 230,955 60 |
| Admitted assets | | $161,681,750 72 |

## LIABILITIES.

| | | |
|---|---|---|
| Net present value of outstanding policies | $132,230,753 00 | |
| Same for dividend additions | 4,228,965 00 | |
| Same for annuities | 777,918 00 | |
| Total | $137,237,636 00 | |
| Deduct net value of risks re-insured | 25,928 00 | |
| Net reserve (paid for basis) | | $137,211,708 00 |
| Extra reserve for total and permanent disability benefits and for additional accidental death benefits included in life policies | | 216,739 00 |
| Present value of supplementary contracts not involving life contingencies | | 1,796,477 00 |
| Present value of amounts incurred but not yet due for total and permanent disability benefits | | 29,000 00 |
| Surrender values claimable on policies cancelled | | 5,063 70 |
| Death losses in process of adjustment | $100,397 88 | |
| Death losses reported for which no proofs have been received | 275,344 44 | |
| Reserve for net death losses incurred but unreported | 250,000 00 | |
| Matured endowments due and unpaid | 17,777 24 | |
| Death losses and other policy claims resisted | 74,200 00 | |
| Total and permanent disability benefits | 49,154 21 | |
| Total policy claims | | 766,873 77 |
| Due and unpaid on supplementary contracts not involving life contingencies | | 92 94 |
| Dividends left with the company to accumulate at interest | | 252,321 55 |
| Gross premiums paid in advance, including surrender values so applied, less discount, if any | | 205,951 86 |
| Unearned interest and rent paid in advance | | 125,852 47 |
| Commissions due agents on premium notes, when paid | | 507,388 22 |
| Cost of collection on uncollected and deferred premiums in excess of loading | | 41,043 78 |
| Salaries, rents, office expenses, bills, and accounts due or accrued | | 17,248 57 |
| Medical examiners' fees due or accrued | | 13,760 48 |
| Estimated amount hereafter payable for federal, state and other taxes based upon the business of the year of this statement | | 745,117 12 |
| Dividends or other profits due policyholders | | 427,807 42 |
| Dividends declared on or apportioned to annual dividend policies payable to policyholders during 1922 for period to December 31, 1922 | | 5,136,160 92 |
| Dividends declared on or apportioned to deferred dividend policies payable to policyholders during 1922 for period to December 31, 1922 | | 1,143,831 00 |
| Amounts set apart, apportioned, provisionally ascertained, calculated, declared or held awaiting apportionment upon deferred dividend policies | | 3,717,722 00 |
| Accrued interest on unpaid policy claims | | 6,082 57 |
| Deposited by policyholders on account of liberty bonds and interest | | 8,889 06 |

## LIABILITIES—Concluded.

| | |
|---|---|
| Surplus interest accrued in excess of contract rate allowed | $30,567 16 |
| Other liabilities, viz: Due upon individual accounts, $33,315.23; proceeds of policies left with the company at interest and accrued contract interest thereon, $874,041.02; salary left by employees with the company at interest, $51,967.84; surplus derived from non-participating policies, $83,776.35 | 1,043,100 44 |
| Total | $153,448,799 03 |
| Capital paid up | 2,500,000 00 |
| Unassigned funds (surplus) | 5,732,951 69 |
| Total | $161,681,750 72 |

## EXHIBIT OF POLICIES—ORDINARY.

ALL BUSINESS PAID FOR.

| | Number. | Amount. | Number. | Amount. |
|---|---|---|---|---|
| Policies in force December 31, 1920 | | | 283,343 | $778,917,578 00 |
| Policies issued, revived, and increased during the year | | | 28,869 | 112,465,017 00 |
| Total | | | 312,212 | $891,382,595 00 |
| Deduct policies which have ceased to be in force during the year— | | | | |
| By death | 2,100 | $6,275,650 00 | | |
| By maturity | 1,679 | 2,738,575 00 | | |
| By expiry | 1,646 | 3,730,650 00 | | |
| By surrender | 4,463 | 12,997,206 00 | | |
| By lapse | 9,973 | 32,220,793 00 | | |
| By decrease | | 1,547,709 00 | | |
| Total | | | 19,861 | 59,510,583 00 |
| Total policies in force December 31, 1921 | | | 292,351 | $831,872,012 00 |
| Re-insured | | | | $140,500 00 |

## BUSINESS IN ILLINOIS—ORDINARY.

| | Number. | Amount. |
|---|---|---|
| Policies in force December 31, 1920 | 22,954 | $65,223,748 00 |
| Policies issued during the year | 2,678 | 9,381,869 00 |
| Total | 25,632 | $74,605,617 00 |
| Deduct policies ceased to be in force | 2,251 | 6,922,296 00 |
| Policies in force December 31, 1921 | 23,381 | $67,683,321 00 |
| Losses and claims unpaid December 31, 1920 | 10 | $18,613 34 |
| Losses and claims incurred during the year | 343 | 979,611 42 |
| Total | 353 | $998,224 76 |
| Losses and claims settled during the year | 344 | 955,794 96 |
| Losses and claims unpaid December 31, 1921 | 9 | $42,429 80 |
| Premiums received | | $2,219,552 05 |

## GAIN AND LOSS EXHIBIT.

INSURANCE EXHIBIT.

| | | Gain in surplus. | Loss in surplus. |
|---|---|---|---|
| Loading on actual premiums of the year (averaging 18.92 per cent of the gross premiums) | $5,304,430 82 | | |
| Insurance expenses incurred during the year | 5,816,402 98 | | |
| Loss from loading | | | $511,972 16 |
| Interest earned during the year | $9,472,899 06 | | |
| Investment expenses incurred during the year | 876,694 06 | | |
| Net income from investments | $8,596,205 00 | | |
| Interest required to maintain reserve | 4,810,409 86 | | |
| Gain from interest | | $3,785,795 14 | |
| Expected mortality on net amount at risk | $8,427,272 00 | | |
| Actual mortality on net amount at risk | 4,441,474 43 | | |
| Gain from mortality | | 3,985,797 57 | |
| Expected disbursements to annuitants | $19,879 00 | | |
| Net actual annuity claims incurred | 33,315 72 | | |
| Loss from annuities | | | 13,436 72 |
| Total gain during the year from surrendered and lapsed policies | | 369,686 67 | |
| Dividends paid stockholders | | | 200,000 00 |
| Decrease in surplus on dividend account | | | 5,515,504 62 |
| Decrease in special funds, and special reserves during the year | | 31,063 11 | |
| Net to loss account | | | 17,166 26 |

GAIN AND LOSS EXHIBIT—Concluded.

INVESTMENT EXHIBIT.

| | | Gain in surplus. | Loss in surplus. |
|---|---|---|---|
| Total gains from real estate | | $ 4,435 42 | |
| Total losses from real estate | | | $45,453 40 |
| Total gains from bonds | | 1,806 38 | |
| Net gain from mortgage investments and unlisted assets | | 39,750 26 | |
| Loss from assets not admitted | | | 48,063 53 |
| Net loss on account of total and permanent disability benefits or additional accidental death benefits included in life policies | | | 24,138 68 |
| Loss from increase in policy claims other than death losses | | | 43,000 00 |
| Total gains and losses in surplus during the year | | $8,218,334 55 | $6,418,735 37 |
| Surplus December 31, 1920 | $3,933,352 51 | | |
| Surplus December 31, 1921 | 5,732,951 69 | | |
| Increase in surplus | | | 1,799,599 18 |
| Total | | $8,218,334 55 | $8,218,334 55 |

## UNION MUTUAL LIFE INSURANCE COMPANY.

Located at No. 396 Congress Street, Portland, Maine; incorporated July 17, 1848; commenced business in Illinois 1859.

ARTHUR L. BATES, President. SYLVAN B. PHILLIPS, Secretary.

GEORGE A. BARR, Director of Trade and Commerce, Attorney for service at Springfield.

| | | | |
|---|---|---|---|
| Amount of ledger assets December 31, of previous year | | | $19,470,627 05 |

INCOME.

| | | | |
|---|---|---|---|
| First year's premiums on original policies, less re-insurance | | $226,501 87 | |
| Dividends applied to purchase paid-up additions and annuities | | 54,156 48 | |
| Surrender values applied to purchase paid-up insurance and annuities | | 11,633 97 | |
| New premiums | | $ 292,292 32 | |
| Renewal premiums less re-insurance | $2,049,147 34 | | |
| Dividends applied to pay renewal premiums | 127,059 26 | | |
| Surrender values applied to pay renewal premiums | 4,410 32 | | |
| Renewal premiums | | 2,180,616 92 | |
| Premium income | | | $2,472,909 24 |
| Consideration for supplementary contracts not involving life contingencies | | | 22,324 58 |
| Dividends left with company to accumulate at interest | | | 10,583 35 |
| Interest on mortgage loans | | $ 33,105 16 | |
| Interest on collateral loans | | 6,062 69 | |
| Interest on bonds and dividends on stocks | | 627,811 60 | |
| Interest on premium notes, policy loans or liens | | 161,097 99 | |
| Interest on deposits | | 4,033 25 | |
| Interest on other debts due the company | | 4,304 13 | |
| Rents—including $14,400.00 for company's occupancy of its own buildings | | 50,019 32 | |
| Total interest and rents | | | 886,434 14 |
| Salaries retained | | | 125 83 |
| Profit on sale or maturity of ledger assets | | | 3,333 53 |
| Increase in book value of ledger assets | | | 25,128 45 |
| Total income | | | $3,420,839 12 |
| Total | | | $22,891,466 17 |

DISBURSEMENTS.

| | | |
|---|---|---|
| Death claims and additions | $954,504 63 | |
| Matured endowments and additions | 599,259 43 | |
| Total death claims and endowments | | $1,553,764 06 |
| Annuities involving life contingencies | | 6,549 09 |
| Premium notes and liens voided by lapse, less $851.91 restorations | | 17,951 28 |
| Loan to policyholders, this company's policies as collateral, notes voided by lapse, less $17,323.52 restorations | | 95,321 82 |
| Surrender values paid in cash, or applied in liquidation of loans or notes | | 634,304 57 |
| Surrender values applied to pay new and renewal premiums | | 4,410 32 |
| Surrender values applied to purchase paid-up insurance and annuities | | 11,633 97 |
| Dividends paid policyholders in cash, or applied in liquidation of loans or notes | | 204,446 86 |
| Dividends applied to pay renewal premiums | | 127,059 26 |
| Dividends applied to purchase paid-up additions and annuities | | 54,156 48 |
| Dividends left with the company to accumulate at interest | | 10,583 35 |
| (Total paid policyholders | $2,720,181 06) | |
| Expense of investigation and settlement of policy claims, including legal expenses | | 135 70 |
| Supplementary contracts not involving life contingencies | | 15,541 38 |

## DISBURSEMENTS—Concluded.

| | |
|---|---|
| Dividends with interest, held on deposit surrendered during the year | $ 6,240 10 |
| Commissions to agents, first-year, $104,399.22; renewal, $115,683.47 | 220,082 69 |
| Agency supervision and traveling expenses of supervisors | 18,691 15 |
| Branch office expenses | 75,161 51 |
| Medical examiners' fees and inspection of risks | 14,269 35 |
| Salaries and all other compensation of officers and home office employees | 101,090 24 |
| Rent | 36,012 67 |
| Advertising, printing, stationery, postage, telegraph, telephone, express and exchange | 13,490 93 |
| Legal expense | 3,441 78 |
| Furniture, fixtures and safes | 343 05 |
| Repairs and expenses (other than taxes) on real estate | 23,303 15 |
| Taxes on real estate | 11,666 11 |
| State taxes on premiums | 41,049 77 |
| Insurance department licenses and fees | 3,085 87 |
| Federal taxes | 627 00 |
| All other licenses, fees and taxes | 6,255 51 |
| Other disbursements, viz: Profit and loss, miscellaneous, $3.28; traveling expense officers and clerks, $219.59; salaries retained, $365.83; suspense account, $264.93; Library Bureau, $3,988.12; mercantile agencies, $125.00; Union Safe Deposit and Trust company for rental of boxes in safe deposit vault, $1,500.00; rubber stamps, translations, repairs and supplies for typewriting and adding machine, etc., $872.50 | 7,339 25 |
| Loss on sale or maturity of ledger assets | 7,954 01 |
| Decrease in book value of ledger assets | 20,166 23 |
| Total disbursements | $3,346,128 51 |
| Balance | $19,545,337 66 |

## LEDGER ASSETS.

| | |
|---|---|
| Book value of real estate | $ 516,168 95 |
| Mortgage loans on real estate | 705,885 97 |
| Loans secured by collaterals | 99,131 00 |
| Loans on company's policies assigned as collateral | 3,059,536 58 |
| Premium notes on policies in force | 98,283 45 |
| Book value of bonds and stocks | 14,878,411 77 |
| Cash in office | 434 61 |
| Deposits in trust companies and banks not on interest | 13,118 84 |
| Deposits in trust companies and banks on interest | 174,114 63 |
| Agents' debit balances | 251 86 |
| Total ledger assets | $19,545,337 66 |

### NON-LEDGER ASSETS.

| | | | |
|---|---|---|---|
| Interest due and accrued on mortgages | | $ 15,158 62 | |
| Interest due and accrued on bonds | | 194,318 90 | |
| Interest accrued on collateral loans | | 494 54 | |
| Interest due and accrued on premium notes, loans or liens | | 34,026 80 | |
| Rents due and accrued on company's property | | 1,492 21 | |
| | | | 245,491 07 |
| | New business. | Renewals. | |
| Net uncollected and deferred premiums (paid for basis) | $10,423 35 | $206,580 24 | 217,003 59 |
| Gross assets | | | $20,007,832 32 |

### DEDUCT ASSETS NOT ADMITTED.

| | | |
|---|---|---|
| Agents' debit balances | $ 251 86 | |
| Premium notes, policy loans and other policy assets in excess of net value and of other policy liabilities on individual policies | 5,157 11 | |
| Overdue and accrued interest on bonds in default | 10,461 34 | |
| Collateral loan and accrued interest thereon in excess of collateral | 380 00 | |
| Book value of stocks over market value | 970,882 68 | |
| Total | | 987,132 99 |
| Admitted assets | | $19,020,699 33 |

## LIABILITIES.

| | | |
|---|---|---|
| Net present value of outstanding policies | $17,514,228 00 | |
| Same for dividend additions | 566,350 00 | |
| Same for annuities | 42,605 00 | |
| Total | $18,123,183 00 | |
| Deduct net value of risks re-insured | 21,749 00 | |
| Net reserve (paid for basis) | | $18,101,434 00 |
| Present value of supplementary contracts not involving life contingencies | | 151,141 00 |
| Death losses in process of adjustment | $19,616 89 | |
| Death losses reported for which no proofs have been received | 34,937 86 | |
| Reserve for net death losses incurred but unreported | 5,000 00 | |
| Matured endowments due and unpaid | 8,419 23 | |
| Annuity claims, involving life contingencies, due and unpaid | 50 79 | |
| Total policy claims | | 68,024 77 |

LIABILITIES—Concluded.

| | |
|---|---|
| Dividends left with the company to accumulate at interest | $56,331 70 |
| Gross premiums paid in advance, including surrender values so applied, less discount, if any | 3,523 22 |
| Unearned interest and rent paid in advance | 41,490 92 |
| Commissions due agents on premium notes, when paid | 4,000 00 |
| Commissions to agents due or accrued | 1,700 00 |
| Cost of collection on uncollected and deferred premiums in excess of loading | 3,000 00 |
| Salaries, rents, office expenses, bills, and accounts due or accrued | 4,000 00 |
| Medical examiners' fees due or accrued | 7,300 00 |
| Estimated amount hereafter payable for federal, state and other taxes based upon the business of the year of this statement | 44,000 00 |
| Dividends or other profits due policyholders | 30,163 85 |
| Total | $18,516,109 46 |
| Unassigned funds (surplus) | 504,589 87 |
| Total | $19,020,699 33 |

## EXHIBIT OF POLICIES—ORDINARY.

ALL BUSINESS PAID FOR.

| | Number. | Amount. | Number. | Amount. |
|---|---|---|---|---|
| Policies in force December 31, 1920 | | | 41,576 | $72,248,892 00 |
| Policies issued, revived, and increased during the year | | | 2,691 | 7,162,832 00 |
| Total | | | 44,267 | $79,411,724 00 |
| Deduct policies which have ceased to be in force during the year— | | | | |
| By death | 454 | $ 882,618 00 | | |
| By maturity | 526 | 556,855 00 | | |
| By expiry | 495 | 1,037,996 00 | | |
| By surrender | 1,038 | 1,517,585 00 | | |
| By lapse | 961 | 2,234,682 00 | | |
| By decrease | 94 | 136,998 00 | | |
| Total | | | 3,568 | 6,366,734 00 |
| Total policies in force December 31, 1921 | | | 40,699 | $73,044,990 00 |
| Re-insured | | | 92 | $1,340,239 00 |

## BUSINESS IN ILLINOIS—ORDINARY.

| | Number. | Amount. |
|---|---|---|
| Policies in force December 31, 1920 | 1,899 | $4,086,615 63 |
| Policies issued during the year | 130 | 291,609 86 |
| Total | $2,029 | $4,378,225 49 |
| Deduct policies ceased to be in force | 139 | 303,491 74 |
| Policies in force December 31, 1921 | 1,890 | $4,074,733 75 |
| Losses and claims unpaid December 31, 1920 | 6 | $ 3,516 54 |
| Losses and claims incurred during the year | 39 | 72,437 64 |
| Total | 45 | $75,954 18 |
| Losses and claims settled during the year | 42 | 75,693 62 |
| Losses and claims unpaid December 31, 1921 | 3 | $260 56 |
| Premiums received | | $132,440 12 |

## GAIN AND LOSS EXHIBIT.

INSURANCE EXHIBIT.

| | | Gain in surplus. | Loss in surplus. |
|---|---|---|---|
| Loading on actual premiums of the year (averaging 20.44 per cent of the gross premiums) | $489,553 45 | | |
| Insurance expenses incurred during the year | 494,573 17 | | |
| Loss from loading | | | $ 5,019 72 |
| Interest earned during the year | $879,707 50 | | |
| Investment expenses incurred during the year | 83,320 89 | | |
| Net income from investments | $796,386 61 | | |
| Interest required to maintain reserve | 584,902 00 | | |
| Gain from interest | | $211,484 61 | |
| Expected mortality on net amount at risk | $713,304 00 | | |
| Actual mortality on net amount at risk | 501,312 61 | | |
| Gain from mortality | | 211,991 39 | |

GAIN AND LOSS EXHIBIT—Concluded.

INSURANCE EXHIBIT.

| | | Gain in surplus. | Loss in surplus. |
|---|---|---|---|
| Expected disbursements to annuitants | $2,341 87 | | |
| Net actual annuity claims incurred | 5,825 76 | | |
| Loss from annuities | | | $ 3,483 89 |
| Total gain during the year from surrendered and lapsed policies | | $36,430 60 | |
| Decrease in surplus on dividend account | | | 382,838 78 |
| Net to loss account | | | 3 28 |

INVESTMENT EXHIBIT.

| | | Gain in surplus. | Loss in surplus. |
|---|---|---|---|
| Total gains from stocks and bonds | | 19,475 53 | |
| Total losses from stocks and bonds | | | 195,999 01 |
| Loss from assets not admitted | | | 11,464 99 |
| Balance unaccounted for | | | 14,357 63 |
| Total gains and losses in surplus during the year | | $479,382 13 | $613,167 30 |
| Surplus December 31, 1920 | $638,375 04 | | |
| Surplus December 31, 1921 | 504,589 87 | | |
| Decrease in surplus | | 133,785 17 | |
| Total | | $613,167 30 | $613,167 30 |

## THE UNITED STATES LIFE INSURANCE COMPANY IN THE CITY OF NEW YORK.

Located at Nos. 105-107 Fifth Avenue, New York, New York; incorporated February, 1850; commenced business in Illinois November 2, 1855.

JOHN P. MUNN, President. A. WHEELWRIGHT, Secretary.

WM. G. BEALL, Chicago, Attorney for service.

CAPITAL.

| | | | |
|---|---|---|---|
| Capital paid up | | $264,000 00 | |
| Amount of ledger assets December 31, of previous year | | | $6,481,820 44 |

INCOME.

| | | | |
|---|---|---|---|
| First year's premiums on original policies, less re-insurance | | $52,161 68 | |
| First year's premiums for total and permanent disability benefits, less re-insurance | | 72 83 | |
| Surrender values to pay first year's premiums | | 170 15 | |
| Surrender values applied to purchase paid-up insurance and annuities | | 7,856 01 | |
| Consideration for original annuities involving life contingencies | | 5,000 00 | |
| New premiums | | $ 65,260 67 | |
| Renewal premiums less re-insurance | $550,445 53 | | |
| Renewal premiums for total and permanent disability benefits, less re-insurance | 213 49 | | |
| Surrender values applied to pay renewal premiums | 436 18 | | |
| Renewal premiums | | 551,095 20 | |
| Premium income | | | $616,355 87 |
| Consideration for supplementary contracts not involving life contingencies | | | 7,033 00 |
| Interest on mortgage loans | | $111,441 01 | |
| Interest on collateral loans | | 900 00 | |
| Interest on bonds | | 129,087 14 | |
| Interest on premium notes, policy loans or liens | | 57,574 21 | |
| Interest on deposits | | 1,596 51 | |
| Interest on other debts due the company | | 8 84 | |
| Rents | | 49,826 25 | |
| Total interest and rents | | | 350,433 96 |
| Exchange | | | 3,575 00 |
| Borrowed money (gross) | | | 175,000 00 |
| Agents' balances previously charged off | | | 2 50 |
| Profit on sale or maturity of ledger assets | | | 487 50 |
| Increase in book value of ledger assets | | | 861 64 |
| Total income | | | $1,153,749 47 |
| Total | | | $7,635,569 91 |

## DISBURSEMENTS.

| | | |
|---|---|---|
| Death claims and additions | $408,609 56 | |
| Matured endowments and additions | 230,024 90 | |
| Total death claims and endowments | | $638,634 46 |
| Annuities involving life contingencies | | 10,656 39 |
| Premium notes and liens voided by lapse, less $555.00 restorations | | 4,912 00 |
| Surrender values paid in cash, or applied in liquidation of loans or notes | | 381,301 28 |
| Surrender values applied to pay new and renewal premiums | | 606 33 |
| Surrender values applied to purchase paid-up insurance and annuities | | 7,856 01 |
| Dividends paid policyholders in cash, or applied in liquidation of loans or notes | | 93 62 |
| (Total paid policyholders $1,044,060 09) | | |
| Expense of investigation and settlement of policy claims, including legal expenses | | 989 85 |
| Supplementary contracts not involving life contingencies | | 6,047 11 |
| Commissions to agents, first year, $23,796.18; renewal, $24,120.97 | | 47,917 15 |
| Agency supervision and traveling expenses of supervisors | | 44,158 87 |
| Branch office expenses | | 16,341 15 |
| Medical examiners' fees and inspection of risks | | 6,544 13 |
| Salaries and all other compensation of officers and home office employees | | 74,141 79 |
| Rent | | 25,278 20 |
| Advertising, printing, stationery, postage, telegraph, telephone, express and exchange | | 13,983 18 |
| Legal expense | | 3,138 98 |
| Furniture, fixtures and safes | | 6,337 36 |
| Repairs and expenses (other than taxes) on real estate | | 22,158 21 |
| Taxes on real estate | | 10,114 94 |
| State taxes on premiums | | 8,741 76 |
| Insurance department licenses and fees | | 1,087 00 |
| Federal taxes | | 2,438 15 |
| All other licenses, fees and taxes | | 1,288 21 |
| Other disbursements, viz: Home office traveling expenses, $320.23; miscellaneous, $8,009.73; moving, $2,668.39; interest on death claim, $628.93 | | 11,627 28 |
| Borrowed money repaid (gross) | | 175,000 00 |
| Interest on borrowed money | | 1,835 97 |
| Agents' balances charged off | | 3 25 |
| Loss on sale or maturity of ledger assets | | 11 25 |
| Decrease in book value of ledger assets | | 1,465 20 |
| Total disbursements | | $1,524,709 08 |
| Balance | | $6,110,860 83 |

## LEDGER ASSETS.

| | |
|---|---|
| Book value of real estate | $ 333,579 55 |
| Mortgage loans on real estate | 1,831,100 00 |
| Loans secured by collaterals | 15,000 00 |
| Loans on company's policies assigned as collateral | 862,756 79 |
| Premium notes on policies in force | 60,568 00 |
| Book value of bonds | 2,939,995 03 |
| Cash in office | 1,524 29 |
| Deposits in trust companies and banks on interest | 65,561 17 |
| Agents' balances (debit, $776.24; credit, $0.24) net | 776 00 |
| Total ledger assets | $6,110,860 83 |

### NON-LEDGER ASSETS.

| | | |
|---|---|---|
| Interest accrued on mortgages | $26,538 24 | |
| Intereat due and accrued on bonds | 41,907 35 | |
| Interest accrued on collateral loans | 75 00 | |
| Interest due and accrued on premium notes, loans or liens | 14,130 23 | |
| Interest accrued on other assets | 108 53 | |
| Rents due on company's property | 71 00 | |
| | | 82,830 35 |
| Market value of real estate over book value | | 27,420 45 |
| Net uncollected and deferred premiums (paid for basis): Renewals | | 37,655 57 |
| Gross assets | | $6,258,767 20 |

### DEDUCT ASSETS NOT ADMITTED.

| | | |
|---|---|---|
| Agents' debit balances | $ 776 24 | |
| Premium notes, policy loans and other policy assets in excess of net value and of other policy liabilities on individual policies | 1,042 68 | |
| Overdue and accrued interest on bonds in default | 2,166 67 | |
| Book value of bonds not amortized over market value | 29,707 49 | |
| Total | | 33,693 08 |
| Admitted assets | | $6,225,074 12 |

## LIABILITIES.

| | | |
|---|---|---|
| Net present value of outstanding policies computed by the New York Insurance Department | $5,634,691 00 | |
| Same for dividend additions | 57,128 00 | |
| Same for annuities | 128,538 00 | |
| Total | $5,820,357 00 | |
| Deduct net value of risks re-insured | 93,315 00 | |
| Net reserve (paid for basis) | | $5,727,042 00 |
| Extra reserve for total and permanent disability benefits and for additional accidental death benefits included in life policies, less re-insurance | | 380 34 |
| Present value of supplementary contracts not involving life contingencies | | 68,380 00 |
| Surrender values claimable on policies cancelled | | 3,322 92 |
| Death losses in process of adjustment | $ 1,500 00 | |
| Death losses reported for which no proofs have been received | 33,149 60 | |
| Reserve for net death losses incurred but unreported | 1,445 00 | |
| Matured endowments due and unpaid | 13,992 00 | |
| Death losses and other policy claims resisted | 4,132 05 | |
| Total policy claims | | 54,218 65 |
| Gross premiums paid in advance, including surrender values so applied, less discount, if any | | 1,219 08 |
| Unearned interest and rent paid in advance | | 16,821 48 |
| Commissions due agents on premium notes, when paid | | 6,606 05 |
| Commissions to agents due or accrued | | 976 28 |
| Salaries, rents, office expenses, bills, and accounts due or accrued | | 2,840 00 |
| Medical examiners' and legal fees due or accrued | | 1,513 00 |
| Estimated amount hereafter payable for federal, state and other taxes based upon the business of the year of this statement | | 14,334 33 |
| Dividends or other profits due policyholders | | 3,757 80 |
| Real estate expenses | | 1,015 65 |
| Total | | $5,902,427 58 |
| Capital paid up | | 264,000 00 |
| Unassigned funds (surplus) | | 58,646 54 |
| Total | | $6,225,074 12 |

## EXHIBIT OF POLICIES—ORDINARY.

(Including group insurance.)

ALL BUSINESS PAID FOR.

| | Number. | Amount. | Number. | Amount. |
|---|---|---|---|---|
| Policies in force December 31, 1920 | | | 14,185 | $24,695,968 00 |
| Policies issued, revived, and increased during the year | | | 1,441 | 3,175,976 00 |
| Total | | | 15,626 | $27,871,944 00 |
| Deduct policies which have ceased to be in force during the year— | | | | |
| By death | 211 | $ 380,732 00 | | |
| By maturity | 177 | 231,547 00 | | |
| By expiry | 134 | 209,730 00 | | |
| By surrender | 587 | 1,157,867 00 | | |
| By lapse | 679 | 1,300,273 00 | | |
| By decrease | -------- | 162,691 00 | | |
| Total | | | 1,788 | 3,442,840 00 |
| Total policies in force December 31, 1921 | | | 13,838 | $24,429,104 00 |
| Re-insured | | | 142 | $1,021,069 00 |

## EXHIBIT OF POLICIES—GROUP INSURANCE.

(Included in Ordinary Exhibit above.)

ALL BUSINESS PAID FOR.

| | Number. | Amount. | Number. | Amount. |
|---|---|---|---|---|
| Policies in force December 31, 1920 | | | 82 | $150,350 00 |
| Policies issued, revived, and increased during the year | | | 2 | 31,234 00 |
| Total | | | 84 | $181,584 00 |
| Deduct policies which have ceased to be in force during the year— | | | | |
| By death | 2 | $5,140 00 | | |
| By expiry | 4 | 7,900 00 | | |
| Total | | | 6 | 13,040 00 |
| Total policies in force December 31, 1921 | | | 78 | $168,544 00 |
| Distribution of business in force at end of year—One year term | | | 78 | $168,544 00 |

BUSINESS IN ILLINOIS—ORDINARY.

| | Number. | Amount. |
|---|---|---|
| Policies in force December 31, 1920 | 1,260 | $2,337,543 00 |
| Policies issued during the year | 201 | 450,846 00 |
| Total | 1,461 | $2,788,389 00 |
| Deduct policies ceased to be in force | 189 | 363,515 00 |
| Policies in force December 31, 1921 | 1,272 | $2,424,874 00 |
| Losses and claims unpaid December 31, 1920 | 2 | $ 2,000 00 |
| Losses and claims incurred during the year | 14 | 39,033 33 |
| Total | 16 | $41,033 33 |
| Losses and claims settled during the year | 16 | 41,033 33 |
| Premiums received | | $58,860 05 |

GAIN AND LOSS EXHIBIT.

INSURANCE EXHIBIT.

| | | Gain in surplus. | Loss in surplus. |
|---|---|---|---|
| Loading on actual premiums of the year (averaging 16.01 per cent of the gross premiums) | $ 98,063 83 | | |
| Insurance expenses incurred during the year | 255,642 87 | | |
| Loss from loading | | | $157,579 04 |
| Interest earned during the year | $344,820 64 | | |
| Investment expenses incurred during the year | 47,963 22 | | |
| Net income from investments | $296,857 42 | | |
| Interest required to maintain reserve | 216,808 00 | | |
| Gain from interest | | $80,049 42 | |
| Expected mortality on net amount at risk | $270,137 00 | | |
| Actual mortality on net amount at risk | 212,229 33 | | |
| Gain from mortality | | 57,907 67 | |
| Expected disbursements to annuitants | 5,894 54 | | |
| Net actual annuity claims incurred | 10,656 39 | | |
| Loss from annuities | | | 4,761 85 |
| Total gain during the year from surrendered and lapsed policies | | 40,593 46 | |
| Increase in surplus on dividend account | | 114 97 | |
| Net to profit account | | 3,574 25 | |
| INVESTMENT EXHIBIT. | | | |
| Total gains from bonds | | 487 50 | |
| Total losses from bonds | | | 7,011 25 |
| Gain from assets not admitted | | 244 87 | |
| Net gain on account of total and permanent disability benefits or additional accidental death benefits included in life policies | | 193 05 | |
| Loss from increase in claims other than death claims | | | 1,503 00 |
| Balance unaccounted for | | | 4,193 64 |
| Total gains and losses in surplus during the year | | $183,165 19 | $175,048 78 |
| Surplus December 31, 1920 | $50,530 13 | | |
| Surplus December 31, 1921 | 58,646 54 | | |
| Increase in surplus | | | 8,116 41 |
| Total | | $183,165 19 | $183,165 19 |

## UNIVERSAL LIFE INSURANCE COMPANY.

Located at Nos. 623-629 Bank and Insurance Building, Dubuque, Iowa; incorporated August 8, 1919; commenced business in Illinois May 26, 1921.

D. J. MURPHY, President. F. W. COATES, Secretary.

GEORGE A. BARR, Director of Trade and Commerce, Attorney for service at Springfield.

CAPITAL.

| | | |
|---|---|---|
| Capital paid up | $326,300 00 | |
| Amount of ledger assets December 31, of previous year | $844,981 55 | |
| Increase of capital during year | 17,400 00 | |
| Total | $862,381 55 | |
| Decrease of subscribed capital during year | 68,900 00 | |
| Extended at | | $793,481 55 |

## INCOME.

| | | | |
|---|---|---|---|
| First year's premiums on original policies, less re-insurance | | $44,217 71 | |
| First year's premiums for total and permanent disability benefits, less re-insurance | | 610 65 | |
| First year's premiums for additional accidental death benefits, less re-surance | | 476 36 | |
| New premiums | | $45,304 72 | |
| Renewal premiums less re-insurance | $22,985 57 | | |
| Renewal premiums for total and permanent disability benefits | 280 24 | | |
| Renewal premiums for additional accidental death benefits, less re-insurance | 272 51 | | |
| Renewal premiums | | 23,538 32 | |
| Premium income | | | $68,843 04 |
| Interest on mortgage loans | | $17,747 46 | |
| Interest on bonds | | 4,479 89 | |
| Interest on premium notes, policy loans or liens | | 53 | |
| Interest on deposits | | 1,995 20 | |
| Interest on other debts due the company | | 7,709 88 | |
| Total | | | 31,932 96 |
| Premiums in suspense | | | 318 76 |
| Total income | | | $101,094 76 |
| Total | | | $894,576 31 |

## DISBURSEMENTS.

| | | |
|---|---|---|
| Death claims | | $5,533 59 |
| (Total paid policyholders | $5,533 59) | |
| Commissions to agents, first year, $33,901.26; renewal, $1,392.06 | | 35,293 32 |
| Agency supervision and traveling expenses of supervisors | | 4,698 46 |
| Medical examiners' fees and inspection of risks | | 3,573 35 |
| Salaries and all other compensation of officers and home office employees | | 11,976 00 |
| Rent | | 1,115 00 |
| Advertising, printing, stationery, postage, telegraph, telephone, express and exchange | | 7,221 45 |
| Legal expense | | 1,577 21 |
| Furniture, fixtures and safes | | 1,528 62 |
| State taxes on premiums | | 323 54 |
| Insurance department licenses and fees | | 769 93 |
| Federal taxes | | 1,533 18 |
| All other licenses, fees and taxes | | 505 00 |
| Other disbursements, viz: Traveling expense, $1,032.77; actuarial expense, $3,750.12; general expense and donations, $695.76; surplus portion stock notes charged off, $35,296.00 | | 40,774 65 |
| Total disbursements | | $116,423 30 |
| Balance | | $778,153 01 |

## LEDGER ASSETS.

| | |
|---|---|
| Mortgage loans on real estate | $364,800 00 |
| Premium notes on policies in force | 360 40 |
| Book value of bonds | 107,750 00 |
| Cash in office | 200 45 |
| Deposits in trust companies and banks not on interest | 17,235 33 |
| Deposits in trust companies and banks on interest | 45,980 83 |
| Bills receivable | 184 75 |
| Agents' balances (debit $5,136.10; credit, $410.60) | 4,725 50 |
| Stock notes | 236,915 75 |
| Total ledger assets | $778,153 01 |

### NON-LEDGER ASSETS.

| | | |
|---|---|---|
| Interest accrued on mortgages | $17,384 62 | |
| Interest accrued on bonds | 971 02 | |
| Interest accrued on other assets | 608 00 | |
| | | 18,963 64 |
| Net uncollected and deferred premiums (paid for basis): Renewals | | 4,799 07 |
| All other assets, viz: Double indemnity outstanding premiums less re-insurance thereon, $10.00; double indemnity deferred premiums less re-insurance thereon, $177.00; less $116.88; re-insurance, $70.12; net total disability premiums outstanding, $17.78; deferred, $15.19; less $40.84; re-insurance, $7.87 | | 62 25 |
| Gross assets | | $801,977 97 |

## LEDGER ASSETS—Concluded.

DEDUCT ASSETS NOT ADMITTED.

| | | |
|---|---|---|
| Agents' debit balances | $ 5,136 10 | |
| Bills receivable | 184 75 | |
| Premium notes, policy loans and other policy assets in excess of net value and of other policy liabilities on individual policies | 690 60 | |
| Book value of bonds over market value | 3,376 48 | |
| Book value of stock notes over market value | 236,915 75 | |
| Total | | $246,303 68 |
| Admitted assets | | $555,674 29 |

## LIABILITIES.

| | | |
|---|---|---|
| Net present value of outstanding policies computed by the Iowa Insurance Department | $33,968 72 | |
| Deduct net value of risks re-insured | 5,554 12 | |
| Net reserve (paid for basis) | | 28,414 60 |
| Extra reserve for total and permanent disability benefits and for additional accidental death benefits included in life policies, less re-insurance | | 199 59 |
| Salaries, rents, office expenses, bills, and accounts due or accrued | | 540 46 |
| Medical examiners' fees due or accrued | | 255 00 |
| Estimated amount hereafter payable for federal, state and other taxes based upon the business of the year of this statement | | 1,500 00 |
| Premiums in suspense | | 318 76 |
| Total | | $ 31,228 41 |
| Partial payments on capital stock | $ 43,142 13 | |
| Capital paid up | 326,300 00 | |
| | | 369,442 13 |
| Unassigned funds (surplus) | | 155,003 75 |
| Total | | $555,674 29 |

## EXHIBIT OF POLICIES—ORDINARY.

ALL BUSINESS PAID FOR.

| | Number. | Amount. | Number. | Amount. |
|---|---|---|---|---|
| Policies in force December 31, 1920 | | | 379 | $1,191,000 00 |
| Policies issued, revived, and increased during the year | | | 634 | 1,784,470 00 |
| Total | | | 1,013 | $2,975,470 00 |
| Deduct policies which have ceased to be in force during the year— | | | | |
| By death | 4 | $ 14,000 00 | | |
| By surrender | 1 | 5,000 00 | | |
| By lapse | 49 | 132,500 00 | | |
| By decrease | 5 | 17,000 00 | | |
| Total | | | 59 | 168,500 00 |
| Total policies in force December 31, 1921 | | | 954 | $2,806,970 00 |
| Re-insured | | | 212 | $842,970 00 |

## BUSINESS IN ILLINOIS—ORDINARY.

| | Number. | Amount. |
|---|---|---|
| Policies issued during the year | 23 | $63,500 00 |
| Policies in force December 31, 1921 | 23 | 63,500 00 |
| Premiums received | | $1,966 38 |

## GAIN AND LOSS EXHIBIT.

INSURANCE EXHIBIT.

| | | Gain in surplus. | Loss in surplus. |
|---|---|---|---|
| Loading on actual premiums of the year (averaging 45.52 per cent of the gross premiums) | $33,025 72 | | |
| Insurance expenses incurred during the year | 75,600 55 | | |
| Loss from loading | | | $42,574 83 |
| Interest earned during the year | $34,361 84 | | |
| Investment expenses incurred during the year | 2,019 92 | | |
| Net income from investments | $32,341 92 | | |
| Interest required to maintain reserve | 809 47 | | |
| Gain from interest | | $31,532 45 | |
| Expected mortality on net amount at risk | $15,258 56 | | |
| Actual mortality on net amount at risk | 5,509 92 | | |
| Gain from mortality | | 9,748 64 | |

GAIN AND LOSS EXHIBIT—Concluded.

INVESTMENT EXHIBIT.

| | | Gain in surplus. | Loss in surplus. |
|---|---|---|---|
| Total losses from stocks and bonds | | | $3,376 48 |
| Loss from assets not admitted | | | 5,594 29 |
| Net gain on account of total and permanent disability benefits or additional accidental death benefits included in life policies | | $ 1,903 45 | |
| Gain from increase in admitted stock surplus | | 28,196 12 | |
| Balance unaccounted for | | | 3 52 |
| Total gains and losses in surplus during the year | | $71,380 66 | $51,549 12 |
| Surplus December 31, 1920 | $135,172 21 | | |
| Surplus December 31, 1921 | 155,003 75 | | |
| Increase in surplus | | | 19,831 54 |
| Total | | $71,380 66 | $71,380 66 |

## WESTERN AND SOUTHERN LIFE INSURANCE COMPANY.

Located at Fourth and Broadway, Cincinnati, Ohio; incorporated February 23, 1888; commenced business in Illinois April 24, 1918.

W. J. WILLIAMS, President. JOHN F. RUEHLMANN, Secretary.

GEORGE A. BARR, Director of Trade and Commerce, Attorney for service at Springfield.

### CAPITAL.

| | | | |
|---|---|---|---|
| Capital paid up | | $1,250,000 00 | |
| Amount of ledger assets December 31, of previous year | | $22,168,923 73 | |
| Increase of paid-up capital during the year | | 500,000 00 | |
| Extended at | | | $22,668,923 73 |

### INCOME.

| | | | |
|---|---|---|---|
| First year's premiums on original policies | | $547,179 51 | |
| First year's premiums for total and permanent disability benefits | | 760 25 | |
| Surrender values applied to purchase paid-up insurance | | 23,577 04 | |
| New premiums | | $ 571,516 80 | |
| Renewal premiums | $1,472,821 20 | | |
| Renewal premiums for total and permanent disability benefits | 76 29 | | |
| Renewal premiums | | 1,472,897 49 | |
| Industrial premiums | | 8,049,580 68 | |
| Premium income | | | $10,093,994 97 |
| Interest on mortgage loans | | $897,205 93 | |
| Interest on bonds | | 290,129 38 | |
| Interest on premium notes, policy loans or liens | | 23,601 46 | |
| Interest on deposits | | 272 61 | |
| Interest on premiums past due | | 271 97 | |
| Rents—including $52,000.00 for company's occupancy of its own buildings | | 58,878 00 | |
| Total interest and rents | | | 1,270,359 35 |
| Profit on sale or maturity of ledger assets | | | 145 86 |
| Total income | | | $11,364,500 18 |
| Total | | | $34,033,423 91 |

### DISBURSEMENTS.

| | | | |
|---|---|---|---|
| Death claims and additions | | $1,789,428 56 | |
| Matured endowments and additions | | 364,492 00 | |
| Total death claims and endowments | | | $2,153,920 56 |
| Surrender values paid in cash, or applied in liquidation of loans or notes | | | 199,368 58 |
| Surrender values applied to purchase paid-up insurance | | | 23,577 04 |
| (Total paid policyholders | | $2,376,866 18) | |
| Expense of investigation and settlement of policy claims | | | 2 50 |
| Dividends to stockholders | | | 650,000 00 |
| Commissions to agents, first year, ordinary, $221,061.77; renewal, $65,086.90; industrial, $411,623.77; (renewal), $1,270,255.43 | | | 1,968,027 87 |
| Compensation of managers and agents not paid by commissions on new business | | | 685,180 94 |
| Agency supervision and traveling expenses of supervisors | | | 41,607 93 |
| Branch office expenses | | | 25,492 48 |
| Medical examiners' fees and inspection of risks | | | 80,668 54 |
| Salaries and all other compensation of officers and home office employees | | | 338,367 29 |
| Rent | | | 112,192 56 |

## DISBURSEMENTS—Concluded.

| | |
|---|---|
| Advertising, printing, stationery, postage, telegraph, telephone and express | $95,543 08 |
| Legal expense | 4,777 82 |
| Furniture, fixtures and safes | 32,705 87 |
| Repairs and expenses (other than taxes) on real estate | 4,913 20 |
| Taxes on real estate | 6,911 99 |
| State taxes on premiums | 89,223 53 |
| Insurance department licenses and fees | 9,258 14 |
| Federal taxes | 70,376 19 |
| All other licenses, fees and taxes | 3,414 41 |
| Other disbursements, viz: Office and general expenses, $22,310.85; lunch room, $14,655.91; investment expenses, $38,633.31; death benefit and casualty compensation paid to employees, $3,250.00; legislation expenses, $201.31 | 79,051 38 |
| Decrease in book value of ledger assets | 28,013 40 |
| Total disbursements | $6,702,595 30 |
| Balance | $27,330,828 61 |

## LEDGER ASSETS.

| | |
|---|---|
| Book value of real estate | $ 550,000 00 |
| Mortgage loans on real estate | 19,277,765 11 |
| Loans on company's policies assigned as collateral | 510,727 15 |
| Book value of bonds | 6,947,760 67 |
| Cash in office | 332 21 |
| Deposits in trust companies and banks on interest | 44,243 47 |
| Total ledger assets | $27,330,828 61 |

### NON-LEDGER ASSETS.

| | | | |
|---|---|---|---|
| Interest due and accrued on mortgages | | $416,410 57 | |
| Interest accrued on bonds | | 91,497 72 | |
| Interest due on premium notes, loans or liens | | 15,585 85 | |
| | | | 523,494 14 |
| | New business. | Renewals. | |
| Net uncollected and deferred premiums (paid for basis) | $79,012 66 | $308,370 89 | 387,383 55 |
| Industrial premiums due and uncollected, $83,423.08; deduct loading, 35 per cent, $29,198.08 | | | 54,225 00 |
| Admitted assets | | | $28,295,931 30 |

## LIABILITIES.

| | | |
|---|---|---|
| Net present value of outstanding policies computed by the Ohio Insurance Department | | $25,807,865 00 |
| Extra reserve for total and permanent disability benefits and for additional accidental death benefits included in life policies, less re-insurance | | 454 75 |
| Death losses in process of adjustment | $19,879 87 | |
| Death losses for which no proofs have been received | 30,000 00 | |
| Death losses and other policy claims resisted | 6,510 25 | |
| Total policy claims | | 56,390 12 |
| Gross premiums paid in advance, including surrender values so applied, less discount, if any | | 191,657 57 |
| Unearned interest paid in advance | | 9,476 59 |
| Salaries, rents, office expenses, bills and accounts due or accrued | | 8,354 34 |
| Medical examiners' fees due or accrued | | 2,345 16 |
| Estimated amount hereafter payable for federal, state and other taxes based upon the business of the year of this statement | | 93,000 00 |
| Total | | $26,169,543 53 |
| Capital paid up | | 1,250,000 00 |
| Unassigned funds (surplus) | | 876,387 77 |
| Total | | $28,295,931 30 |

## EXHIBIT OF POLICIES—ORDINARY.

ALL BUSINESS PAID FOR.

| | Number. | Amount. | Number. | Amount. |
|---|---|---|---|---|
| Policies in force December 31, 1920 | | | 53,859 | $52,983,835 00 |
| Policies issued, revived and increased during the year | | | 17,977 | 18,721,930 00 |
| Total | | | 71,836 | $71,705,765 00 |
| Deduct policies which have ceased to be in force during the year— | | | | |
| By death | 342 | $ 359,978 00 | | |
| By maturity | 13 | 7,638 00 | | |
| By expiry | 197 | 267,222 00 | | |
| By surrender | 388 | 359,800 00 | | |
| By lapse | 10,836 | 9,951,050 00 | | |
| By decrease | | 160,312 00 | | |
| Total | | | 11,776 | 11,106,000 00 |
| Total policies in force December 31, 1921 | | | 60,060 | $60,599,765 00 |

## EXHIBIT OF POLICIES—INDUSTRIAL.

ALL BUSINESS PAID FOR.

| | Number. | Amount. | Number. | Amount. |
|---|---|---|---|---|
| Policies in force December 31, 1920 | | | 1,223,418 | $198,610,529 00 |
| Policies issued, revived and increased during the year | | | 382,900 | 85,037,535 00 |
| Total | | | 1,606,318 | $283,648,064 00 |
| Deduct policies which have ceased to be in force during the year— | | | | |
| By death | 12,949 | $ 1,438,706 00 | | |
| By maturity | 3,820 | 358,070 00 | | |
| By expiry | 157 | 3,996 00 | | |
| By surrender | 4,148 | 390,903 00 | | |
| By lapse | 352,020 | 76,501,723 00 | | |
| By decrease | -------- | 473,347 00 | | |
| Total | | | 373,094 | 79,166,745 00 |
| Total policies in force December 31, 1921 | | | 1,233,224 | $204,481,319 00 |

## BUSINESS IN ILLINOIS—ORDINARY.

| | Number. | Amount. |
|---|---|---|
| Policies in force December 31, 1920 | 3,284 | $3,435,900 00 |
| Policies issued during the year | 2,400 | 2,593,250 00 |
| Total | 5,684 | $6,029,150 00 |
| Deduct policies ceased to be in force | 1,424 | 1,543,550 00 |
| Policies in force December 31, 1921 | 4,260 | $4,485,600 00 |
| Losses and claims incurred during the year | 21 | $20,635 00 |
| Losses and claims settled during the year | 20 | 18,635 00 |
| Losses and claims unpaid December 31, 1921 | 1 | $2,000 00 |
| Premiums received | | $86,996 20 |

## BUSINESS IN ILLINOIS—INDUSTRIAL.

| | Number. | Amount. |
|---|---|---|
| Policies in force December 31, 1920 | 30,441 | $6,544,550 00 |
| Policies issued during the year | 29,251 | 6,558,857 00 |
| Total | 59,692 | $13,103,407 00 |
| Deduct policies ceased to be in force | 24,337 | 5,281,129 00 |
| Policies in force December 31, 1921 | 35,355 | $7,822,278 00 |
| Losses and claims incurred during the year | 549 | $49,608 28 |
| Losses and claims settled during the year | 545 | 48,598 28 |
| Losses and claims unpaid December 31, 1921 | 4 | $1,010 00 |
| Premiums received | | $282,439 95 |

## GAIN AND LOSS EXHIBIT.

INSURANCE EXHIBIT.

| | | Gain in surplus. | Loss in surplus. |
|---|---|---|---|
| Loading on actual premiums of the year (averaging 35 per cent of the gross premiums) | $3,561,632 30 | | |
| Insurance expenses incurred during the year | 4,150,658 41 | | |
| Loss from loading | | -------------- | $589,026 11 |
| Interest earned during the year | $1,417,368 71 | | |
| Investment expenses incurred during the year | 50,458 50 | | |
| Net income from investment | $1,366,910 21 | | |
| Interest required to maintain reserve | 853,763 92 | | |
| Gain from interest | | 513,146 29 | |
| Expected mortality on net amount at risk | $2,337,215 00 | | |
| Actual mortality on net amount at risk | 1,613,663 19 | | |
| Gain from mortality | | 723,551 81 | |
| Total gain during the year from surrendered and lapsed policies | | 532,783 33 | |
| Dividends paid stockholders | | -------------- | 650,000 00 |

GAIN AND LOSS EXHIBIT—Concluded.

INVESTMENT EXHIBIT.

| | | Gain in surplus. | Loss in surplus. |
|---|---|---|---|
| Total losses from real estate | | | $9,025 38 |
| Total gains from bonds | | $145 86 | |
| Net gain on account of total and permanent disability benefits or additional accidental death benefits included in life policies | | 381 79 | |
| Total gains and losses in surplus during the year | | $1,770,009 08 | $1,248,051 49 |
| Surplus December 31, 1920 | $354,430 18 | | |
| Surplus December 31, 1921 | 876,387 77 | | |
| Increase in surplus | | | 521,957 59 |
| Total | | $1,770,009 08 | $1,770,009 08 |

## WESTERN UNION LIFE INSURANCE COMPANY.

Located at No. 1023 Riverside Avenue, Spokane, Washington; incorporated October 3, 1906; commenced business in Illinois August 12, 1920.

R. L. RUTTER, President. LEIGH H. MILLIKEN, Secretary.

GEORGE A. BARR, Director of Trade and Commerce, Attorney for service at Springfield.

CAPITAL.

| | | | |
|---|---|---|---|
| Capital paid up | | $200,000 00 | |
| Amount of ledger assets December 31, of previous year | | | $4,908,792 76 |

INCOME.

| | | | |
|---|---|---|---|
| First year's premiums on original policies, less re-insurance | | $234,553 17 | |
| First year's premiums for total and permanent disability benefits, less re-insurance | | 3,541 55 | |
| First year's premiums for additional accidental death benefits, less re-insurance | | 4,116 02 | |
| Coupons applied to purchase paid-up additions and annuities | | 671 96 | |
| Surrender values applied to purchase paid-up insurance and annuities | | 1,633 53 | |
| New premiums | | $ 244,516 23 | |
| Renewal premiums less re-insurance | $1,366,965 13 | | |
| Renewal premiums for total and permanent disability benefits, less re-insurance | 15,501 34 | | |
| Renewal premiums for additional accidental death benefits, less re-insurance | 17,069 78 | | |
| Coupons applied to pay renewal premiums | 9,832 93 | | |
| Accident and health premiums issued with life policies | 5,229 30 | | |
| Renewal premiums | | 1,414,598 48 | |
| Premium income | | | $1,659,114 71 |
| Coupons left with company to accumulate at interest | | | 86,435 21 |
| Interest on mortgage loans | | $147,084 01 | |
| Interest on collateral loans | | 2,180 12 | |
| Interest on bonds and dividends on stocks and warrants | | 71,171 55 | |
| Interest on premium notes, policy loans or liens | | 80,558 70 | |
| Interest on deposits | | 8,107 31 | |
| Interest on other debts due the company | | 581 62 | |
| Rents—including $6,000.00 for company's occupancy of its own buildings | | 6,386 85 | |
| Total interest and rents | | | 316,070 16 |
| From other sources, viz: Policy change fees, $247.25; commissions on mortgage bonds warrants, $2,979.10; refunded revenue tax, $125.02; refunded fire insurance premiums, $7.18 | | | 3,358 55 |
| Agents' balances previously charged off | | | 3,101 58 |
| Profit on sale or maturity of ledger assets | | | 1,465 80 |
| Increase in book value of ledger assets | | | 987 91 |
| Total income | | | $2,070,533 92 |
| Total | | | $6,979,326 68 |

DISBURSEMENTS.

| | | | |
|---|---|---|---|
| Death claims | | $239,177 12 | |
| Total and permanent disability claims and additional accidental death benefits, accident and health claims, less re-insurance | | 13,212 88 | |
| Total death claims | | | $252,390 00 |
| Premium notes and liens voided by lapse | | | 29,782 98 |
| Surrender values paid in cash, or applied in liquidation of loans or notes | | | 154,276 76 |

DISBURSEMENTS—Concluded.

| | | |
|---|---|---|
| Surrender values applied to purchase paid-up insurance and annuities | | $ 1,633 53 |
| Coupons paid policyholders in cash, or applied in liquidation of loans or notes | | 17,701 53 |
| Coupons applied to pay renewal premiums | | 9,832 93 |
| Coupons applied to purchase paid-up additions and annuities | | 671 96 |
| Coupons left with the company to accumulate at interest | | 86,435 21 |
| (Total paid policyholders | $552,724 90) | |
| Expense of investigation and settlement of policy claims, including legal expenses | | 4,750 33 |
| Supplementary contracts not involving life contingencies | | 600 00 |
| Dividends to stockholders | | 16,000 00 |
| Commissions to agents, first year, $165,048.25; renewal, $34,301.19 | | 199,349 44 |
| Compensation of managers and agents not paid by commissions on new business | | 40,850 93 |
| Agency supervision and traveling expenses of supervisors | | 48,295 13 |
| Branch office expenses | | 12,348 12 |
| Medical examiners' fees and inspection of risks | | 15,281 79 |
| Salaries and all other compensation of officers and home office employees | | 85,131 39 |
| Rent | | 6,000 00 |
| Advertising, printing, stationery, postage, telegraph, telephone, express and exchange | | 32,627 32 |
| Legal expense | | 1,153 72 |
| Furniture, fixtures and safes | | 14,409 26 |
| Repairs and expenses (other than taxes) on real estate | | 8,011 39 |
| Taxes on real estate | | 3,582 54 |
| State taxes on premiums | | 26,534 63 |
| Insurance department licenses and fees | | 3,920 53 |
| Federal taxes | | 1,425 54 |
| All other licenses, fees and taxes | | 324 26 |
| Other disbursements, viz: Premiums on fidelity bonds, $1,031.93; light, water and fuel, $1,606.80; entertainment, $328.10; library, $2,710.15; investment, $1,734.83; expense, $116.72; discount, $617.88; collection accounts, $118.91; miscellaneous, $421.29 | | 8,686 61 |
| Agents' balances charged off | | 12,362 32 |
| Loss on sale or maturity of ledger assets | | 15,248 24 |
| Decrease in book value of ledger assets | | 3,849 68 |
| Total disbursements | | $1,113,468 07 |
| Balance | | $5,865,858 61 |

LEDGER ASSETS.

| | |
|---|---|
| Book value of real estate | $ 141,820 25 |
| Mortgage loans on real estate | 2,283,415 38 |
| Loans secured by collaterals | 28,000 00 |
| Premiums advanced under Soldiers' and Sailors' Civil Relief Act | 22 21 |
| Loans on company's policies assigned as collateral | 1,269,253 63 |
| Premium notes on policies in force | 41,717 05 |
| Book value of bonds and stocks | 1,854,729 27 |
| Cash in office | 315 00 |
| Deposits in trust companies and banks not on interest | 28,109 00 |
| Deposits in trust companies and banks on interest | 217,008 17 |
| Taxes advanced on mortgages, $571.00; delinquent tax certificates, $96.96 | 667 96 |
| Due under re-insurance contracts | 800 69 |
| Total ledger assets | $5,865,858 61 |

NON-LEDGER ASSETS.

| | | |
|---|---|---|
| Interest due and accrued on mortgages | $65,694 94 | |
| Interest accrued on bonds | 21,899 98 | |
| Interest accrued on collateral loans | 122 08 | |
| Interest accrued on premium notes, loans or liens | 2,042 89 | |
| Interest accrued on other assets | 30 35 | |
| | | 89,790 24 |
| Net uncollected and deferred premiums (paid for basis) renewals | | 128,678 70 |
| Gross assets | | $6,084,327 55 |

DEDUCT ASSETS NOT ADMITTED.

| | |
|---|---|
| Premium notes, policy loans and other policy assets in excess of net value and of other policy liabilities on individual policies | 8,108 56 |
| Admitted assets | $6,076,218 99 |

LIABILITIES.

| | | |
|---|---|---|
| Net present value of outstanding policies computed by the Washington Insurance Department | $4,783,297 00 | |
| Same for annuities | 1,335 00 | |
| Total | $4,784,632 00 | |
| Deduct net value of risks re-insured | 12,507 00 | |
| Net reserve (paid for basis) | | $4,772,125 00 |
| Extra reserve for total and permanent disability benefits and for additional accidental death benefits included in life policies, less re-insurance | | 46,986 16 |

## LIABILITIES—Concluded.

| | | |
|---|---|---|
| Present value of supplementary contracts not involving life contingencies | | $ 5,565 29 |
| Present value of amounts incurred but not yet due for total and permanent disability benefits | | 32,106 35 |
| Death losses reported for which no proofs have been received | $12,926 79 | |
| Reserve for net death losses incurred but unreported | 2,000 00 | |
| Death losses and other policy claims resisted | 3,000 00 | |
| Total and permanent disability benefits | 600 00 | |
| Total policy claims | | 18,526 79 |
| Coupons left with the company to accumulate at interest | | 405,508 51 |
| Gross premiums paid in advance, including surrender values so applied, less discount, if any | | 9,458 31 |
| Unearned interest and rent paid in advance | | 33,568 91 |
| Salaries, rents, office expenses, bills and accounts due or accrued | | 3,494 75 |
| Estimated amount hereafter payable for federal, state and other taxes based upon the business of the year of this statement | | 40,000 00 |
| Judgment on appeal | | 8,000 00 |
| Total | | $5,375,340 07 |
| Capital paid up | | 200,000 00 |
| Unassigned funds (surplus) | | 500,878 92 |
| Total | | $6,076,218 99 |

## EXHIBIT OF POLICIES—ORDINARY.

ALL BUSINESS PAID FOR.

| | Number. | Amount. | Number. | Amount. |
|---|---|---|---|---|
| Policies in force December 31, 1920 | | | 24,855 | $61,057,337 00 |
| Policies issued, revived and increased during the year | | | 2,605 | 7,423,662 00 |
| Total | | | 27,460 | $68,480,999 00 |
| Deduct policies which have ceased to be in force during the year— | | | | |
| By death | 94 | $ 259,950 00 | | |
| By expiry | 24 | 166,020 00 | | |
| By surrender | 563 | 1,372,981 00 | | |
| By lapse | 4,076 | 13,227,002 00 | | |
| By decrease | -------- | 194,992 00 | | |
| Total | | | 4,757 | 15,220,945 00 |
| Total policies in force December 31, 1921 | | | 22,703 | $53,260,054 00 |
| Re-insured | | | 299 | $2,023,050 00 |

## BUSINESS IN ILLINOIS—ORDINARY.

| | Number. | Amount. |
|---|---|---|
| Policies in force December 31, 1920 | 92 | $151,885 00 |
| Policies issued during the year | 56 | 94,754 00 |
| Total | 148 | $246,639 00 |
| Deduct policies ceased to be in force | 17 | 30,500 00 |
| Policies in force December 31, 1921 | 131 | $216,139 00 |
| Losses and claims incurred during the year | 8 | 15,150 00 |
| Losses and claims settled during the year | 8 | 15,150 00 |
| Premiums received | | $6,564 88 |

## GAIN AND LOSS EXHIBIT.

INSURANCE EXHIBIT.

| | | Gain in surplus. | Loss in surplus. |
|---|---|---|---|
| Loading on actual premiums of the year (averaging 22.34 per cent of the gross premiums) | $368,895 26 | | |
| Insurance expenses incurred during the year | 503,688 92 | | |
| Loss from loading | | -------------- | $134,793 66 |
| Interest earned during the year | $324,641 69 | | |
| Investment expenses incurred during the year | 25,977 46 | | |
| Net income from investments | $298,664 23 | | |
| Interest required to maintain reserve | 165,994 95 | | |
| Gain from interest | | $132,669 28 | |
| Expected mortality on net amount at risk | $380,181 39 | | |
| Actual mortality on net amount at risk | 211,199 62 | | |
| Gain from mortality | | 168,981 77 | |
| Total gain during the year from surrendered and lapsed policies | | 10,308 21 | |
| Dividends paid stockholders | | -------------- | 16,000 00 |
| Net to loss account | | | 9,260 74 |

GAIN AND LOSS EXHIBIT—Concluded.

INVESTMENT EXHIBIT.

| | | Gain in surplus. | Loss in surplus. |
|---|---|---|---|
| Total losses from real estate | | | $6,035 11 |
| Total gains from stocks and bonds | | $1,465 80 | |
| Total losses from stocks and bonds | | | 458 08 |
| Loss on bank deposits | | | 225 36 |
| Loss from assets not admitted | | | 4,955 21 |
| Net loss on account of total and permanent disability benefits included in life policies | | | 7,988 25 |
| Gain from additional accidental death benefits | | 16,764 78 | |
| Gain from accident and health | | 812 27 | |
| Total gains and losses in surplus during the year | | $331,002 11 | $179,716 41 |
| Surplus December 31, 1920 | $349,593 22 | | |
| Surplus December 31, 1921 | 500,878 92 | | |
| Increase in surplus | | | 151,285 70 |
| Total | | $331,002 11 | $331,002 11 |

## WISCONSIN NATIONAL LIFE INSURANCE COMPANY.

Located at Nos. 14-16 Washington Boulevard, Oshkosh, Wisconsin; incorporated October 12, 1908; commenced business in Illinois August 4, 1914.

C. R. BOARDMANN, President. R. E. MARTIN, Secretary.

GEORGE A. BARR, Director of Trade and Commerce, Attorney for service at Springfield.

CAPITAL.

| | | | |
|---|---|---|---|
| Capital paid up | | $400,000 00 | |
| Amount of ledger assets December 31, of previous year | | | $1,828,395 67 |

INCOME.

| | | | |
|---|---|---|---|
| First year's premiums on original policies, less re-insurance | | $112,075 93 | |
| First year's premiums for total and permanent disability benefits | | 1,669 51 | |
| Surrender values to pay first year's premiums | | 174 55 | |
| New premiums | | $113,919 99 | |
| Renewal premiums less re-insurance | $465,557 81 | | |
| Renewal premiums for total and permanent disability benefits | 1,961 20 | | |
| Surrender values applied to pay renewal premiums | 119 22 | | |
| Renewal premiums | | 467,638 23 | |
| Total | | | $581,558 22 |
| Interest on mortgage loans | | $21,496 03 | |
| Interest on bonds | | 61,123 94 | |
| Interest on premium notes, policy loans or liens | | 6,786 71 | |
| Interest on deposits | | 2,389 01 | |
| General interest | | 81 58 | |
| Rents—including $1,200.00 for company's occupancy of its own buildings | | 4,213 88 | |
| Total interest and rents | | | 96,091 15 |
| From other sources, viz: War tax refunded by U. S. Government, $2.88; discount on mortgages purchased, $114.70; fees for stock exchange, $34.00; increase of premiums suspense items, $407.76; unpaid stock dividends transferred to suspense, $49.50 | | | 608 84 |
| Agents' balances previously charged off | | | 54 29 |
| Profit on sale or maturity of ledger assets | | | 125 00 |
| Increase in book value of ledger assets | | | 1,476 74 |
| Income, life department | | | $679,914 24 |
| Income, casualty department | | | 112,328 41 |
| Total income | | | $792,242 65 |
| Total | | | $2,620,638 32 |

DISBURSEMENTS.

| | | | |
|---|---|---|---|
| Death claims and additions | | $61,772 45 | |
| Matured endowments and additions | | 1,000 00 | |
| Total and permanent disability claims and additional accidental death benefits | | 244 93 | |
| Total death claims and endowments | | | 63,017 38 |

DISBURSEMENTS—Concluded.

| | | |
|---|---|---|
| Surrender values paid in cash, or applied in liquidation of loans or notes | | $ 20,040 93 |
| Surrender values applied to pay new and renewal premiums | | 293 77 |
| (Total paid policyholders | $83,352 08) | |
| Supplementary contracts not involving life contingencies | | 1,502 50 |
| Dividends to stockholders | | 24,000 00 |
| Commissions to agents, first year, $75,425.27; renewal, $24,660.57 | | 100,085 84 |
| Compensation of managers and agents not paid by commissions on new business | | 4,303 50 |
| Agency supervision and traveling expenses of supervisors | | 8,701 06 |
| Branch office expenses | | 2,960 25 |
| Medical examiners' fees and inspection of risks | | 13,971 50 |
| Salaries and all other compensation of officers and home office employees | | 40,858 88 |
| Rent | | 1,200 00 |
| Advertising, printing, stationery, postage, telegraph, telephone, express and exchange | | 10,154 05 |
| Furniture, fixtures and safes | | 704 67 |
| Repairs and expenses (other than taxes) on real estate | | 326 60 |
| Taxes on real estate | | 1,047 30 |
| State taxes on premiums | | 5,278 18 |
| Insurance department licenses and fees | | 622 84 |
| Federal taxes | | 604 89 |
| All other licenses, fees and taxes | | 1,436 84 |
| Other disbursements, viz: Special auditing, $485.27; actuarial fees, $185.00; settlement of stock sale commission claims, $272.45; premium collection fees, $1,179.34; dividends on profit sharing bonds, $2,563.86; fidelity bond premiums, $250.04 | | 4,935 96 |
| Agents' balances charged off | | 342 95 |
| Decrease in book value of ledger assets | | 1,918 07 |
| Disbursements, life department | | $308,307 96 |
| Disbursements, casualty department | | 98,168 15 |
| Total disbursements | | $406,476 11 |
| Balance | | $2,214,162 21 |

LEDGER ASSETS.

| | |
|---|---|
| Book value of real estate | $ 45,000 00 |
| Mortgage loans on real estate | 480,100 00 |
| Loans on company's policies assigned as collateral | 145,694 03 |
| Premium notes on policies in force | 3,860 96 |
| Book value of bonds | 1,311,848 10 |
| Cash in office | 150 00 |
| Deposits in trust companies and banks not on interest | 4,850 12 |
| Deposits in trust companies and banks on interest | 149,375 30 |
| Agents' balances (debit, $5,011.63; credit, $249.87) net | 4,761 76 |
| Casualty department | 68,521 94 |
| Total ledger assets | $2,214,162 21 |

NON-LEDGER ASSETS.

| | | | |
|---|---|---|---|
| Interest due and accrued on mortgages | | $14,255 60 | |
| Interest accrued on bonds | | 26,904 62 | |
| Interest accrued on premium notes, loans or liens | | 868 61 | |
| Interest accrued on bank deposits | | 1,604 57 | |
| Rents due on company's property | | 161 25 | |
| | | | 43,794 65 |
| Due from other companies for losses or claims on policies re-insured | | | 32,500 00 |
| | New business. | Renewals. | |
| Net uncollected and deferred premiums (paid for basis) | $2,519 23 | $50,652 61 | 53,171 84 |
| Casualty department | | | 1,071 19 |
| Gross assets | | | $2,344,699 89 |

DEDUCT ASSETS NOT ADMITTED.

| | | |
|---|---|---|
| Agents' debit balances | $5,011 63 | |
| Premium notes, policy loans and other policy assets in excess of net value and of other policy liabilities on individual policies | 852 71 | |
| Casualty department | 2,072 55 | |
| Total | | 7,936 89 |
| Admitted assets | | $2,336,763 00 |

LIABILITIES.

| | | |
|---|---|---|
| Net present value of outstanding policies | $1,617,308 81 | |
| Deduct net value of risks re-insured | 2,854 38 | |
| Net reserve (paid for basis) | | $1,614,454 43 |
| Extra reserve for total and permanent disability benefits | | 1,815 36 |
| Present value of supplementary contracts not involving life contingencies | | 13,433 41 |
| Death losses in process of adjustment | | 56,000 00 |
| Gross premiums paid in advance, including surrender values so applied, less discount, if any | | 2,309 37 |

LIABILITIES—Concluded.

| | |
|---|---|
| Unearned interest and rent paid in advance | $2,704 39 |
| Commissions to agents due or accrued | 1,015 85 |
| Cost of collection of uncollected and deferred premiums in excess of loading | 702 88 |
| Medical examiners' and legal fees due or accrued | 955 00 |
| Estimated amount hereafter payable for federal, state and other taxes based upon the business of the year of this statement | 4,162 06 |
| Unpaid dividends to stockholders | 49 50 |
| Emergency reserve to meet excess mortality if necessary | 20,000 00 |
| Suspense items | 1,944 91 |
| War service premiums subject to refund to policyholders | 85 70 |
| Accrued dividends on profit-sharing bonds | 695 46 |
| Casualty department | 20,092 45 |
| Total | $1,740,420 77 |
| Capital paid up | 400,000 00 |
| Unassigned funds (surplus) | 196,342 23 |
| Total | $2,336,763 00 |

## EXHIBIT OF POLICIES—ORDINARY.

ALL BUSINESS PAID FOR.

| | Number. | Amount. | Number. | Amount. |
|---|---|---|---|---|
| Policies in force December 31, 1920 | | | 12,434 | $18,794,125 46 |
| Policies issued, revived and increased during the year | | | 2,558 | 4,151,982 95 |
| Total | | | 14,992 | $22,946,108 41 |
| Deduct policies which have ceased to be in force during the year— | | | | |
| By death | 47 | $ 61,772 45 | | |
| By maturity | 1 | 1,000 00 | | |
| By expiry | 70 | 104,500 00 | | |
| By surrender | 102 | 137,016 50 | | |
| By lapse | 1,194 | 2,042,924 19 | | |
| By decrease | 4 | 4,878 55 | | |
| Total | | | 1,418 | 2,352,091 69 |
| Total policies in force December 31, 1921 | | | 13,574 | $20,594,016 72 |
| Re-insured | | | 123 | $476,261 00 |

## EXHIBIT OF POLICIES—INDUSTRIAL.

ALL BUSINESS PAID FOR.

| | Number. | Amount. | Number. | Amount. |
|---|---|---|---|---|
| Policies in force December 31, 1920 | | | 120 | $22,339 50 |
| Policies issued, revived and increased during the year | | | 1 | 549 00 |
| Total | | | 121 | $22,888 50 |
| Deduct policies which have ceased to be in force during the year— | | | | |
| By expiry | 5 | $983 00 | | |
| By surrender | 1 | 440 00 | | |
| By lapse | 2 | 591 00 | | |
| Total | | | 8 | 2,014 00 |
| Total policies in force December 31, 1921 | | | 113 | $20,874 50 |

## BUSINESS IN ILLINOIS—ORDINARY.

| | Number. | Amount. |
|---|---|---|
| Policies in force December 31, 1920 | 1,070 | $1,420,755 65 |
| Policies issued during the year | 402 | 523,498 80 |
| Total | 1,472 | $1,944,254 45 |
| Deduct policies ceased to be in force | 200 | 273,838 68 |
| Policies in force December 31, 1921 | 1,272 | $1,670,415 77 |
| Losses and claims incurred during the year | 4 | $6,000 00 |
| Losses and claims settled during the year | 4 | 6,000 00 |
| Premiums received | | 44,587 91 |

## BUSINESS IN ILLINOIS—INDUSTRIAL.

| | Number. | Amount. |
|---|---|---|
| Policies in force December 31, 1920 | 2 | $275 00 |
| Policies issued during the year | 1 | 549 00 |
| Policies in force December 31, 1921 | 3 | $824 00 |

## GAIN AND LOSS EXHIBIT.

### INSURANCE EXHIBIT.

| | | Gain in surplus. | Loss in surplus. |
|---|---|---|---|
| Loading on actual premiums of the year (averaging 21.5 per cent of the gross premiums) | $102,662 16 | | |
| Insurance expenses incurred during the year | 201,005 37 | | |
| Loss from loading | | | $98,343 21 |
| Interest earned during the year | $103,979 83 | | |
| Investment expenses incurred during the year | 1,373 90 | | |
| Net income from investments | $102,605 93 | | |
| Interest required to maintain reserve | 53,598 00 | | |
| Gain from interest | | $ 49,007 93 | |
| Expected mortality on net amount at risk | $180,987 00 | | |
| Actual mortality on net amount at risk | 75,634 82 | | |
| Gain from mortality | | 105,352 18 | |
| Total gain during the year from surrendered and lapsed policies | | 10,996 58 | |
| Dividends paid stockholders | | | 24,000 00 |
| Net to loss account | | | 288 66 |
| **INVESTMENT EXHIBIT.** | | | |
| Total gains from bonds | | 125 00 | |
| Loss from assets not admitted | | | 2,142 21 |
| Net gain on account of total and permanent disability benefits included in life policies | | 2,760 87 | |
| Gain from war tax refunded, $2.88; casualty department, $10,547.70; discount on mortgages, $114.70; stock transfer fees, $34.00; less stock sale commission claim, $272.45; and less supplementary contracts, $482.00 | | 9,944 83 | |
| Balance unaccounted for | | 212 35 | |
| Total gains and losses in surplus during the year | | $178,399 74 | $124,774 08 |
| Surplus December 31, 1920 | $142,716 57 | | |
| Surplus December 31, 1921 | 196,342 23 | | |
| Increase in surplus | | | 53,625 66 |
| Total | | $178,399 74 | $178,399 74 |

# LIFE INSURANCE COMPANIES OF FOREIGN GOVERNMENTS.

## CANADA LIFE ASSURANCE COMPANY.

Located at No. 46 King Street, West, Toronto, Ontario, Canada; organized August 21, 1847; incorporated April 25, 1849; commenced business in Illinois September 4, 1895.

H. C. COX, President. CHARLES R. ACRES, Secretary.

CHARLES F. BULLEN, Chicago, Attorney for service.

### CAPITAL.

| | | | |
|---|---|---|---|
| Capital paid up | | $1,000,000 00 | |
| Amount of ledger assets December 31, of previous year | | | $72,413,690.41 |

### ICOME.

| | | | |
|---|---|---|---|
| First year's premiums on original policies, less re-insurance | | $2,122,176 40 | |
| First year's premiums for total and permanent disability benefits, less re-insurance | | 16,330 15 | |
| Dividends applied to purchase paid-up additions and annuities | | 555,260 30 | |
| Consideration for original annuities involving life contingencies | | 205,142 41 | |
| New premiums | | $2,898,909 26 | |
| Renewal premiums less re-insurance | $8,036,247 11 | | |
| Renewal premiums for total and permanent disability benefits, less re-insurance | 52,090 18 | | |
| Dividends applied to pay renewal premiums | 152,654 49 | | |
| Renewal premiums for deferred annuities | 33,520 50 | | |
| Renewal premiums | | 8,274,512 28 | |
| Premium income | | | $11,173,421 54 |
| Consideration for supplementary contracts involving life contingencies | | | 26,805 97 |
| Consideration for supplementary contracts not involving life contingencies | | | 41,890 76 |
| Dividends left with company to accumulate at interest | | | 23,957 90 |
| Other amounts left with company to accumulate at interest | | | 1,839 28 |
| Interest on mortgage loans | | $1,690,232 65 | |
| Interest on collateral loans | | 66,937 23 | |
| Interest on bonds and dividends on stocks | | 1,752,676 87 | |
| Interest on premium notes, policy loans or liens | | 539,985 86 | |
| Interest on deposits | | 3,848 01 | |
| Rents—including $100,478.33 for company's occupancy of its own buildings less $18,051.70 interest on incumbrances | | 353,313 43 | |
| Total interest and rents | | | 4,406,994 05 |
| From other sources, viz: Amounts received and held in suspense, $46,591.35; staff savings and benefit fund contributions and grants, $50,304.95; gross profit on bank exchange, $12,291.58 | | | 109,187 88 |
| Profit on sale or maturity of ledger assets | | | 52,878 87 |
| Increase in book value of ledger assets | | | 51,965 40 |
| Total income | | | $15,888,941 65 |
| Total | | | $88,302,632 06 |

### DISBURSEMENTS.

| | | |
|---|---|---|
| Death claims and additions | $2,668,686 48 | |
| Matured endowments and additions | 832,434 47 | |
| Total and permanent disability claims | 3,445 60 | |
| Total death claims and endowments | | $3,504,566 55 |
| Annuities involving life contingencies | | 438,139 99 |
| Surrender values paid in cash, or applied in liquidation of loans or notes | | 1,071,091 78 |
| Surrender values claimable on policies subject to revival | | 5,204 48 |
| Dividends paid policyholders in cash, or applied in liquidation of loans or notes | | 780,890 18 |
| Dividends applied to pay renewal premiums | | 152,654 49 |

DISBURSEMENTS—Concluded.

| | | |
|---|---|---|
| Dividends applied to purchase paid-up additions and annuities | | $ 555,260 30 |
| Dividends left with the company to accumulate at interest | | 23,957 90 |
| (Total paid policyholders | $6,531,765 67) | |
| Supplementary contracts not involving life contingencies | | 34,800 12 |
| Supplementary contracts involving life contingencies | | 14,264 32 |
| Dividends with interest, held on deposit surrendered during the year | | 2,999 62 |
| Other amounts and interest thereon held on deposit surrendered during the year | | 2,035 77 |
| Dividends to stockholders | | 250,000 00 |
| Commissions to agents, first year, $929,525.53; renewal, $455.268.27; annuities (original), $3,442.44; (renewal), $959.25 | | 1,389,195 49 |
| Compensation of managers and agents not paid by commissions on new business | | 99,300 33 |
| Agency supervision and traveling expenses of supervisors | | 184,046 08 |
| Branch office expenses | | 236,432 14 |
| Medical examiners' fees and inspection of risks | | 116,638 01 |
| Salaries and all other compensation of officers and home office employees | | 449,893 19 |
| Rent | | 157,143 70 |
| Advertising, printing, stationery, postage, telegraph, telephone, express and exchange | | 180,990 91 |
| Legal expense | | 20,234 79 |
| Furniture, fixtures and safes | | 61,518 70 |
| Repairs and expenses (other than taxes) on real estate | | 170,745 59 |
| Taxes on real estate | | 86,061 27 |
| State taxes on premiums | | 112,926 58 |
| Insurance department licenses and fees | | 11,062 11 |
| Federal taxes | | 19,303 69 |
| All other licenses, fees and taxes | | 78,956 91 |
| Other disbursements, viz: Legislative expense, $130.85; books, $4,479.50; commission on loans, $26,674.98; light, fuel and water, $8,090.58; telephone rent, $7,906.09; company's grants to staff savings and benefit fund, $24,589.00; sundries, $43,781.63 | | 115,652 63 |
| Borrowed money repaid (gross) | | 2,000,000 00 |
| Interest on borrowed money | | 84,760 39 |
| Special expenditures charged to shareholders account | | 56,306 44 |
| Agents' balances charged off | | 73,808 71 |
| Staff savings and benefit fund, contributions, interest and death benefits paid | | 2,486 19 |
| Loss on sale or maturity of ledger assets | | 1,547 20 |
| Decrease in book value of ledger assets | | 17,328 29 |
| Total disbursements | | $12,567,204 84 |
| Balance | | $75,735,427 22 |

LEDGER ASSETS.

| | |
|---|---|
| Book value of real estate | $ 3,812,975 68 |
| Mortgage loans on real estate | 25,613,457 08 |
| Loans secured by collaterals | 1,115,000 00 |
| Loans on company's policies assigned as collateral | 11,339,328 07 |
| Book value of bonds and stocks | 33,553,228 52 |
| Cash in office | 1,569 17 |
| Deposits in trust companies and banks not on interest | 299,868 70 |
| Total ledger assets | $75,735,427 22 |

NON-LEDGER ASSETS.

| | | | |
|---|---|---|---|
| Interest due and accrued on mortgages | | $1,578,835 02 | |
| Interest due and accrued on bonds | | 433,083 56 | |
| Interest accrued on collateral loans | | 2,025 00 | |
| Interest due and accrued on premium notes, loans or liens | | 488,814 74 | |
| Rents due and accrued on company's property | | 20,140 28 | |
| | | | 2,522,898 60 |
| | New business. | Renewals. | |
| Net uncollected and deferred premiums (paid for basis) | $111,430 26 | $1,407,294 69 | 1,518,724 95 |
| Annuity considerations due and unreported | | | 2,227 88 |
| Admitted assets | | | $79,779,278 65 |

LIABILITIES.

| | | |
|---|---|---|
| Net present value of outstanding policies | $62,816,978 00 | |
| Same for dividend additions | 4,258,618 00 | |
| Same for annuities | 3,745,911 00 | |
| Total | $70,821,507 00 | |
| Deduct net value of risks re-insured | 2,575,977 00 | |
| Net reserve (paid for basis) | | $68,245,530 00 |
| Extra reserve for total and permanent disability benefits included in life policies, less re-insurance | | 101,266 00 |
| Present value of supplementary contracts not involving life contingencies | | 423,587 00 |
| Present value of amounts incurred but not yet due for total and permanent disability benefits | | 35,329 00 |
| Surrender values claimable on policies cancelled | | 2,395 25 |
| Death losses due and unpaid | $201,675 56 | |
| Death losses reported for which no proofs have been received | 202,348 53 | |

LIABILITIES—Concluded.

| | | |
|---|---|---|
| Reserve for net death losses incurred but unreported | $75,000 00 | |
| Matured endowments due and unpaid | 18,206 65 | |
| Annuity claims, involving life contingencies, due and unpaid | 42,375 18 | |
| Total policy claims | | $ 539,605 92 |
| Dividends left with the company to accumulate at interest | | 79,447 00 |
| Other amounts left with the company to accumulate at interest | | 2,048 00 |
| Gross premiums paid in advance, including surrender values so applied, less discount, if any | | 125,893 20 |
| Unearned interest and rent paid in advance | | 75,056 60 |
| Salaries, rents, office expenses, bills, and accounts due or accrued | | 22,127 75 |
| Medical examiners' fees due or accrued | | 6,268 00 |
| Estimated amount hereafter payable for federal, state and other taxes based upon the business of the year of this statement | | 140,605 47 |
| Dividends or other profits due policyholders | | 161,250 33 |
| Dividends declared on or apportioned to annual dividend policies payable to policyholders during 1922 for period to December 31, 1922 | | 300,340 00 |
| Dividends declared on or apportioned to deferred dividend policies payable to policyholders during 1922 for period to December 31, 1922 | | 1,549,750 00 |
| Amounts set apart, apportioned, provisionally ascertained, calculated, declared or held awaiting apportionment upon deferred dividend policies | | 5,145,716 00 |
| Investment reserve fund | | 284,263 00 |
| Contingent reserve | | 50,024 60 |
| Staff savings and benefit fund | | 293,948 91 |
| Shareholders' dividend reserve fund | | 400,887 89 |
| Items in suspense | | 5,978 28 |
| Total | | $77,991,318 20 |
| Capital paid up | | 1,000,000 00 |
| Unassigned funds (surplus) | | 787,960 45 |
| Total | | $79,779,278 65 |

## EXHIBIT OF POLICIES—ORDINARY.

(Including group insurance.)

ALL BUSINESS PAID FOR.

| | Number. | Amount. | Number. | Amount. |
|---|---|---|---|---|
| Policies in force December 31, 1920 | | | 109,784 | $272,968,749 99 |
| Policies issued, revived, and increased during the year | | | 18,002 | 64,728,947 77 |
| Total | | | 127,786 | $337,697,697 76 |
| Deduct policies which have ceased to be in force during the year— | | | | |
| By death | 1,028 | $ 2,865,802 61 | | |
| By maturity | 441 | 799,538 93 | | |
| By disability | 1 | 2,000 00 | | |
| By expiry | 80 | 336,875 00 | | |
| By surrender | 1,700 | 4,180,151 03 | | |
| By lapse | 4,464 | 12,539,970 00 | | |
| By decrease | -------- | 626,175 24 | | |
| By withdrawal | -------- | 799,150 00 | | |
| Total | | | 7,714 | 22,149,662 81 |
| Total policies in force December 31, 1921 | | | 120,072 | $315,548,034 95 |
| Re-insured | | | | $17,276,146 84 |

## EXHIBIT OF POLICIES—GROUP INSURANCE.

(Included in ordinary exhibit above.

ALL BUSINESS PAID FOR.

| | Number. | Amount. | Number. | Amount. |
|---|---|---|---|---|
| Policies in force December 31, 1920 | | | 18 | $2,322,950 00 |
| Policies issued, revived and increased during the year | | | 21 | 5,266,650 00 |
| Total | | | 39 | $7,589,600 00 |
| Deduct policies which have ceased to be in force during the year— | | | | |
| By death | ------- | $ 19,700 00 | | |
| By lapse | 5 | 381,050 00 | | |
| By withdrawal | ------- | 799,150 00 | | |
| Total | | ------- | 5 | 1,199,900 00 |
| Total policies in force December 31, 1921 | | | 34 | $6,389,700 00 |
| Distribution of business in force at end of year—One year term | | | 34 | $6,389,700 00 |

## BUSINESS IN ILLINOIS—ORDINARY.

(Excluding group insurance.)

| | Number. | Amount. |
|---|---|---|
| Policies in force December 31, 1920 | 1,674 | $9,159,940 00 |
| Policies issued during the year | 82 | 1,371,817 00 |
| Total | 1,756 | $10,531,757 00 |
| Deduct policies ceased to be in force | 64 | 379,796 00 |
| Policies in force December 31, 1921 | 1,692 | $10,151,961 00 |
| Losses and claims incurred during the year | 11 | $87,842 80 |
| Losses and claims settled during the year | 9 | 84,062 50 |
| Losses and claims unpaid December 31, 1921 | 2 | $3,780 30 |
| Premiums received | | $368,660 71 |

## BUSINESS IN ILLINOIS—GROUP INSURANCE.

| | Number. | Amount. |
|---|---|---|
| Policies issued during the year | 1 | $156,500 00 |
| Deduct policies ceased to be in force | -------- | 3,250 00 |
| Policies in force December 31, 1921 | 1 | $153,250 00 |
| Premiums received | | $1,493 00 |

## GAIN AND LOSS EXHIBIT.

### INSURANCE EXHIBIT.

| | | Gain in surplus. | Loss in surplus. |
|---|---|---|---|
| Loading on actual premiums of the year (averaging 17.7 per cent of the gross premiums) | $2,025,997 45 | | |
| Insurance expenses incurred during the year | 3,173,894 62 | | |
| Loss from loading | | ------------- | $1,147,897 17 |
| Interest earned during the year | $4,633,489 19 | | |
| Investment expenses incurred during the year | 441,993 26 | | |
| Net income from investments | $4,191,495 93 | | |
| Interest required to maintain reserve | 2,103,045 00 | | |
| Gain from interest | | $2,088,450 93 | |
| Expected mortality on net amount at risk | $2,885,827 00 | | |
| Actual mortality on net amount at risk | 1,427,006 61 | | |
| Gain from mortality | | 1,458,820 39 | |
| Expected disbursements to annuitants | $298,888 99 | | |
| Net actual annuity claims incurred | 349,100 99 | | |
| Loss from annuities | | ------------- | 50,212 00 |
| Total gain during the year from surrendered and lapsed policies | | 322,997 65 | |
| Dividends paid stockholders | | ------------- | 250,000 00 |
| Special expenditure charged to shareholders account | | ------------- | 56,306 44 |
| Decrease in surplus on dividend account | | ------------- | 2,252,426 87 |
| Increase in special funds, and special reserves during the year | | ------------- | 43,781 96 |

### INVESTMENT EXHIBIT.

| | | Gain in surplus. | Loss in surplus. |
|---|---|---|---|
| Total gains from real estate | | 1,000 00 | |
| Total gains from stocks and bonds | | 51,878 87 | |
| Total losses from stocks and bonds | | ------------- | 11,547 20 |
| Gain from staff savings and benefit fund (contributions from staff, net) | | 23,229 76 | |
| Net gain on account of total and permanent disability benefits or additional accidental death benefits included in life policies | | 13,020 17 | |
| Gain profit on bank exchange, $12,291.58; annuities surrendered for cash during the year, $262.22 | | 12,553 80 | |
| Balance unaccounted for | | 34,793 05 | |
| Total gains and losses in surplus during the year | | $4,006,744 62 | $3,812,171 64 |
| Surplus December 31, 1920 | $593,387 47 | | |
| Surplus December 31, 1921 | 787,960 45 | | |
| Increase in surplus | | ------------- | 194,572 98 |
| Total | | $4,006,744 62 | $4,006,744 62 |

## THE MANUFACTURERS LIFE INSURANCE COMPANY.

Located at Dominion Bank Building, Corner King and Yonge Streets, Toronto, Canada; incorporated June 23, 1887; commenced business in Illinois June 16, 1909.

W. G. GOODERHAM, President. E. S. MACFARLANE, Secretary.

HARRY GOODMAN, Chicago, Attorney for service.

### CAPITAL.

| | | | |
|---|---|---|---|
| Capital paid up | | $300,000 00 | |
| Amount of ledger assets December 31, of previous year | | | $31,433,332 99 |

### INCOME.

| | | | |
|---|---|---|---|
| First year's premiums on original policies, less re-insurance | | $1,715,742 91 | |
| First year's premiums for total and permanent disability benefits | | 12,602 39 | |
| Dividends applied to purchase paid-up additions and annuities | | 145,276 40 | |
| Surrender values applied to purchase paid-up insurance and annuities | | 9,632 00 | |
| Consideration for original annuities involving life contingencies | | 29,693 85 | |
| New premiums | | $1,912,947 55 | |
| Renewal premiums less re-insurance | $5,615,744 44 | | |
| Renewal premiums for total and permanent disability benefits, less re-insurance | 32,232 03 | | |
| Dividends applied to pay renewal premiums | 22,327 21 | | |
| Renewal premiums | | 5,670,303 68 | |
| Premium income | | | $7,583,251 23 |
| Consideration for supplementary contracts involving life contingencies | | | 21,731 72 |
| Consideration for supplementary contracts not involving life contingencies | | | 28,733 48 |
| Dividends left with company to accumulate at interest | | | 1,693 35 |
| Interest on mortgage loans | | $716,227 09 | |
| Interest on collateral loans | | 939 31 | |
| Interest on bonds and dividends on stocks | | 819,559 75 | |
| Interest on premium notes, policy loans or liens | | 273,217 38 | |
| Interest on deposits | | 9,561 11 | |
| Interest on other debts due the company | | 336 13 | |
| Total interest | | | 1,819,840 77 |
| From other sources, viz: Funds other than dividends left to accumulate at interest, $3,080.85; bonus on new mortgage advances, $750.00; profit on exchange, $58,132.71; agency balances, increase in liability, $16,428.36 | | | 78,391 92 |
| Profit on sale or maturity of ledger assets | | | 29,596 71 |
| Increase in book value of ledger assets | | | 18,216 02 |
| Total income | | | $9,581,455 20 |
| Total | | | $41,014,788 19 |

### DISBURSEMENTS.

| | | |
|---|---|---|
| Death claims and additions | $1,161,883 36 | |
| Matured endowments and additions | 656,118 07 | |
| Total and permanent disability claims | 2,265 65 | |
| Total death claims and endowments | | $1,820,267 08 |
| Annuities involving life contingencies | | 9,776 83 |
| Surrender values paid in cash, or applied in liquidation of loans or notes | | 665,646 25 |
| Surrender values applied to purchase paid-up insurance and annuities | | 9,632 00 |
| Dividends paid policyholders in cash, or applied in liquidation of loans or notes | | 320,327 08 |
| Dividends applied to pay renewal premiums | | 22,327 21 |
| Dividends applied to purchase paid-up additions and annuities | | 145,276 40 |
| Dividends left with the company to accumulate at interest | | 1,693 35 |
| (Total paid policyholders | $2,994,946 20) | |
| Expense of investigation and settlement of policy claims, including legal expenses | | 6,492 42 |
| Supplementary contracts not involving life contingencies | | 8,877 31 |
| Dividends with interest, held on deposit surrendered during the year | | 397 41 |
| Dividends to stockholders | | 24,000 00 |
| Commissions to agents, first year, $1,028,448.93; renewal, $378,203.83; annuities (original), $938.70 | | 1,407,591 46 |
| Compensation of managers and agents not paid by commissions on new business | | 35,474 19 |
| Agency supervision and traveling expenses of supervisors | | 22,385 53 |
| Branch office expenses | | 255,691 49 |
| Medical examiners' fees and inspections of risks | | 92,983 91 |
| Salaries and all other compensation of officers and home office employees | | 273,914 38 |
| Rent | | 64,245 23 |
| Advertising, printing, stationery, postage, telegraph, telephone and express | | 109,166 24 |
| Legal expense | | 4,176 09 |
| Furniture, fixtures and safes | | 27,859 75 |
| Taxes on real estate | | 5,890 02 |
| State taxes on premiums | | 79,973 32 |
| Insurance department licenses and fees | | 7,480 61 |

DISBURSEMENTS—Concluded.

| | |
|---|---|
| Federal taxes | $ 3,309 84 |
| All other licenses, fees and taxes | 39,033 25 |
| Other disbursements, viz: Interest account death claims, $2,080.57; funds on accumulation, $318.85; re-insurance, $31.39; suspense—reduction in liability, $615.61; premium paid in advance—reduction in liability, $3,131.47; audit and inspection, $11,950.21; agency conventions, $24,187.46; commissions on loans, $27,033.61; loan agents' expenses, $17,909.91; light, $1,738.33; insurance, books and papers, $1,836.52; employees' lunch room, $6,470.62; sundry expenses, $15,721.40 | 113,025 95 |
| Loss on sale or maturity of ledger assets | 320 55 |
| Decrease in book value of ledger assets | 98,019 05 |
| Total disbursements | $5,675,254 20 |
| Balance | $35,339,533 99 |

LEDGER ASSETS.

| | |
|---|---|
| Book value of real estate | $ 215,000 00 |
| Mortgage loans on real estate | 14,399,524 91 |
| Loans secured by collaterals | 9,064 83 |
| Loans on company's policies assigned as collateral | 5,012,452 93 |
| Book value of bonds and stocks | 15,230,920 50 |
| Deposits in trust companies and banks not on interest | 28,033 25 |
| Deposits in trust companies and banks on interest | 434,220 13 |
| Agents' balances (debit, $19,094.09; credit, $70,461.05; net, $51,366.96). | |
| School debenture collections, $7,489.69; life reversions, $2,827.75 | 10,317 44 |
| Total ledger assets | $35,339,533 99 |

NON-LEDGER ASSETS.

| | | | |
|---|---|---|---|
| Interest due and accrued on mortgages | | $904,000 35 | |
| Interest due and accrued on bonds | | 267,902 78 | |
| Interest accrued on collateral loans | | 73 61 | |
| Interest accrued on premium notes, loans or liens | | 182,400 50 | |
| Interest accrued on other assets | | 124 63 | |
| | | | 1,354,501 87 |
| Due from other companies for losses or claims on policies re-insured | | | 5,064 64 |
| | New business. | Renewals. | |
| Net uncollected and deferred premiums (paid for basis) | $198,486 42 | $929,794 45 | $1,128,280 87 |
| Agents' balances re advances against commissions—20 per cent of net debits | | | 4,156 24 |
| Gross assets | | | $37,831,537 61 |

DEDUCT ASSETS NOT ADMITTED.

| | |
|---|---|
| Agents' debit balances | 4,156 24 |
| Admitted assets | $37,827,381 37 |

LIABILITIES.

| | | |
|---|---|---|
| Net present value of outstanding policies | $31,486,325 00 | |
| Same for dividend additions | 520,364 00 | |
| Same for annuities | 212,785 00 | |
| Total | $32,219,474 00 | |
| Deduct net value of risks re-insured | 714,533 00 | |
| Net reserve (paid for basis) | | $31,504,941 00 |
| Extra reserve for total and permanent disability benefits included in life policies, less re-insurance | | 59,537 00 |
| Present value of supplementary contracts not involving life contingencies | | 67,365 00 |
| Present value of amounts incurred but not yet due for total and permanent disability benefits | | 43,100 00 |
| Death losses reported for which no proofs have been received | $236,380 41 | |
| Reserve for net death losses incurred but unreported | 75,000 00 | |
| Matured endowments due and unpaid | 46,078 00 | |
| Death losses and other policy claims resisted | 8,640 00 | |
| Annuity claims, involving life contingencies, due and unpaid | 1,501 18 | |
| Total policy claims | | 367,599 59 |
| Dividends left with the company to accumulate at interest | | 5,084 30 |
| Gross premiums paid in advance, including surrender values so applied, less discount, if any | | 16,128 11 |
| Commissions to agents due or accrued | | 5,514 50 |
| Salaries, rents, office expenses, bills, and accounts due or accrued | | 18,510 39 |
| Medical examiners' and legal fees due or accrued | | 8,074 98 |
| Estimated amount hereafter payable for federal, state and other taxes based upon the business of the year of this statement | | 105,000 00 |
| Unpaid dividends to stockholders | | 12,000 00 |
| Dividends or other profits due policyholders | | 64,191 00 |
| Dividends declared on or apportioned to annual dividend policies payable to policyholders during 1922 for period to December 31, 1922 | | 44,463 00 |

LIABILITIES—Concluded.

| | |
|---|---|
| Dividends declared on or apportioned to deferred dividend policies payable to policyholders during 1922 for period to December 31, 1922 | $ 600,613 00 |
| Amounts set apart, apportioned, provisionally ascertained, calculated, declared or held awaiting apportionment upon deferred dividend policies | 2,058,888 00 |
| Reserve for school debenture collections | 5,000 00 |
| Reserve for foreign exchange | 220,000 00 |
| Investment and contingency reserve | 530,000 00 |
| Other liabilities, viz: Agency balances, $70,461.05; balance of shareholders' funds, $397,145.69; amount other than dividends left with company to accumulate at interest with interest accrued thereon, $5,100.90 | 472,707 64 |
| Total | $36,208,717 51 |
| Capital paid up | 300,000 00 |
| Unassigned funds (surplus) | 1,318,663 86 |
| Total | $37,827,381 37 |

## EXHIBIT OF POLICIES—ORDINARY.

ALL BUSINESS PAID FOR.

| | Number. | Amount. | Number. | Amount. |
|---|---|---|---|---|
| Policies in force December 31, 1920 | | | 93,614 | $178,757,911 00 |
| Policies issued, revived and increased during the year | | | 18,916 | 42,096,015 00 |
| Total | | | 112,530 | $220,853,926 00 |
| Deduct policies which have ceased to be in force during the year— | | | | |
| By death | 602 | $ 1,180,313 00 | | |
| By maturity | 428 | 650,525 00 | | |
| By expiry | 40 | 150,292 00 | | |
| By surrender | 792 | 1,493,433 00 | | |
| By lapse | 6,590 | 16,498,169 00 | | |
| By decrease | -------- | 478,649 00 | | |
| Total | | | 8,452 | 20,451,381 00 |
| Total policies in force December 31, 1921 | | | 104,078 | $200,402,545 00 |
| Re-insured | | | | $5,258,990 00 |

## EXHIBIT OF POLICIES—GROUP INSURANCE.

(Included in ordinary exhibit above.)

ALL BUSINESS PAID FOR.

| | Number. | Amount. |
|---|---|---|
| Policies in force December 31, 1920 | 1 | $47,500 00 |
| Policies issued, revived and increased during the year | -------- | 10,800 00 |
| Total | 1 | $58,300 00 |
| Deduct policies which have ceased to be in force during the year: By decrease | -------- | 6,400 00 |
| Total policies in force December 31, 1921 | 1 | $51,900 00 |
| Distribution of business in force at end of year—One year term | 1 | $51,900 00 |

## BUSINESS IN ILLINOIS—ORDINARY.

| | Number. | Amount. |
|---|---|---|
| Policies in force December 31, 1920 | 199 | $913,657 00 |
| Policies issued during the year | 83 | 133,833 00 |
| Total | 282 | $1,047,490 00 |
| Deduct policies ceased to be in force | 29 | 50,000 00 |
| Policies in force December 31, 1921 | 253 | $997,490 00 |
| Premiums received | | $63,594 68 |

## GAIN AND LOSS EXHIBIT.

INSURANCE EXHIBIT.

| | | Gain in surplus. | Loss in surplus. |
|---|---|---|---|
| Loading on actual premiums of the year (averaging 19.76 per cent of the gross premiums) | $1,547,292 84 | | |
| Insurance expenses incurred during the year | 2,485,383 78 | | |
| Loss from loading | | -------------- | $938,090 94 |
| Interest earned during the year | $2,088,640 30 | | |
| Investment expenses incurred during the year | 124,265 17 | | |
| Net income from investments | $1,964,375 13 | | |
| Interest required to maintain reserve | 1,026,385 00 | | |
| Gain from interest | | $937,990 13 | |

## GAIN AND LOSS EXHIBIT—Concluded.

INSURANCE EXHIBIT.

| | | Gain in surplus. | Loss in surplus. |
|---|---|---|---|
| Expected mortality on net amount at risk | $1,655,601 00 | | |
| Actual mortality on net amount at risk | 804,521 43 | | |
| Gain from mortality | | $851,079 57 | |
| Expected disbursements to annuitants | $7,218 14 | | |
| Net actual annuity claims incurred | 9,441 83 | | |
| Loss from annuities | | | $ 2,223 69 |
| Total gain during the year from surrendered and lapsed policies | | 434,410 00 | |
| Dividends paid stockholders | | | 24,000 00 |
| Decrease in surplus on dividend account | | | 738,245 04 |
| Increase in special funds, and special reserves during the year | | | 144,485 20 |
| INVESTMENT EXHIBIT. | | | |
| Total gains from real estate | | 4,763 60 | |
| Total losses from real estate | | | 56,693 26 |
| Total gains from stocks and bonds | | 24,833 11 | |
| Total losses from stocks and bonds | | | 31,889 13 |
| Gain from assets not admitted | | 16,118 77 | |
| Net loss on account of total and permanent disability benefits or additional accidental death benefits included in life policies | | | 17,377 02 |
| Gain: Increase in amounts due from other companies on policies re-insured, $3,616.43; foreign exchange, $58,132.71 | | 61,749 14 | |
| Total gains and losses in surplus during the year | | $2,330,944 32 | $1,953,004 28 |
| Surplus December 31, 1920 | $ 940,723 76 | | |
| Surplus December 31, 1921 | 1,318,663 80 | | |
| Increase in surplus | | | 377,940 04 |
| Total | | $2,330,944 32 | $2,330,944 32 |

## NORTH AMERICAN LIFE ASSURANCE COMPANY.

Located at Nos. 112-118 King Street, West, Toronto, Canada; incorporated May 15, 1879; commenced business in Illinois February 7, 1900.

L. GOLDMAN, President. W. B. TAYLOR, Secretary.

GEORGE A. BARR, Director of Trade and Commerce, Attorney for service at Springfield.

### CAPITAL.

| | | | |
|---|---|---|---|
| Guarantee fund paid up | | $60,000 00 | |
| Amount of ledger assets December 31, of previous year | | | $19,550,048 48 |

### INCOME.

| | | | |
|---|---|---|---|
| First year's premiums on original policies, less re-insurance | | $607,670 87 | |
| First year's premiums for total and permanent disability benefits | | 5,979 30 | |
| Surrender values to pay first year's premiums | | 419 55 | |
| Dividends applied to purchase paid-up additions and annuities | | 32,204 73 | |
| New premiums | | $ 646,274 45 | |
| Renewal premiums less re-insurance | $2,792,411 15 | | |
| Renewal premiums for total and permanent disability benefits, less re-insurance | 15,175 05 | | |
| Dividends applied to pay renewal premiums | 40,546 36 | | |
| Surrender values applied to pay renewal premiums | 2,769 57 | | |
| Renewal premiums | | 2,850,902 13 | |
| Premium income | | | $3,497,176 58 |
| Consideration for supplementary contracts involving life contingencies | | | 10,929 00 |
| Consideration for supplementary contracts not involving life contingencies | | | 11,025 00 |
| Dividends left with the company to accumulate at interest | | | 7,934 25 |
| Interest on mortgage loans | | $309,037 00 | |
| Interest on bonds and dividends on stocks | | 693,400 72 | |
| Interest on premium notes, policy loans or liens | | 169,531 45 | |
| Interest on deposits | | 4,541 36 | |
| Rents—including $12,500.00 for company's occupancy of its own buildings | | 18,522 00 | |
| Total interest and rents | | | 1,195,032 53 |
| Exchange | | | 21,888 37 |
| Borrowed money (gross) | | | 50,000 00 |
| Profit on sale or maturity of ledger assets | | | 31,777 11 |
| Total income | | | $4,825,762 84 |
| Total | | | $24,375,811 32 |

## DISBURSEMENTS.

| | | |
|---|---|---|
| Death claims and additions | $520,424 59 | |
| Matured endowments | 431,471 25 | |
| Total and permanent disability claims | 209 85 | |
| Total death claims and endowments | | $952,105 69 |
| Annuities involving life contingencies | | 15,176 87 |
| Surrender values paid in cash, or applied in liquidation of loans or notes | | 538,164 50 |
| Surrender values applied to pay new and renewal premiums | | 3,189 12 |
| Dividends paid policyholders in cash, or applied in liquidation of loans or notes | | 376,313 37 |
| Dividends applied to pay renewal premiums | | 40,546 36 |
| Dividends applied to purchase paid-up additions and annuities | | 32,204 73 |
| Dividends left with the company to accumulate at interest | | 7,934 25 |
| (Total paid policyholders | $1,965,634 89) | |
| Supplementary contracts not involving life contingencies | | 6,459 25 |
| Dividends to stockholders | | 6,000 00 |
| Commissions to agents, first year, $359,918.11; renewal, $143,725.87 | | 503,643 98 |
| Agency supervision and traveling expenses of supervisors | | 11,730 93 |
| Branch office expenses | | 163,132 20 |
| Medical examiners' fees and inspection of risks | | 49,928 25 |
| Salaries and all other compensation of officers and home office employees | | 152,940 99 |
| Rent, fuel and light | | 39,415 56 |
| Advertising, printing, stationery, postage, telegraph, telephone, express and general expense | | 77,334 48 |
| Legal expense | | 646 01 |
| Furniture, fixtures and safes | | 6,998 30 |
| Repairs and expenses (other than taxes on real estate) | | 22,463 25 |
| Taxes on real estate | | 4,587 37 |
| State taxes on premiums | | 49,496 06 |
| Insurance department licenses and fees | | 1,517 16 |
| All other licenses, fees and taxes | | 11,516 18 |
| Other disbursements, viz: Suspense account, $2,067.86; investment expense Western Loan Department, $23,785.60; traveling expense home office, $5,268.83 | | 31,122 29 |
| Agents' balances charged off | | 17,339 21 |
| Decrease in book value of ledger assets | | 2,028 50 |
| Total disbursements | | $3,123,934 86 |
| Balance | | $21,251,876 46 |

## LEDGER ASSETS.

| | |
|---|---|
| Book value of real estate | $ 148,755 76 |
| Mortgage loans on real estate | 5,083,943 03 |
| Loans on company's policies assigned as collateral | 2,690,194 30 |
| Book value of bonds and stocks | 13,051,971 47 |
| Cash in office | 5,310 77 |
| Deposits in trust companies and banks not on interest | 15,148 80 |
| Deposits in trust companies and banks on interest | 254,523 61 |
| Fire insurance premiums paid on account of mortgagor | 2,028 72 |
| Total ledger assets | $21,251,876 46 |

### NON-LEDGER ASSETS.

| | | | |
|---|---|---|---|
| Interest due and accrued on mortgages | | $210,618 11 | |
| Interest due and accrued on bonds | | 111,244 90 | |
| Interest due and accrued on premium notes, loans or liens | | 30,503 63 | |
| Rents due on company's property | | 1,470 00 | |
| | | | 353,836 64 |
| Market value of real estate over book value | | | 54,820 72 |
| | New business. | Renewals. | |
| Net uncollected and deferred premiums (paid for basis) | $48,998 03 | $505,423 36 | 554,421 39 |
| Gross assets | | | $22,214,955 21 |

### DEDUCT ASSETS NOT ADMITTED.

| | |
|---|---|
| Book value of bonds and stocks over market value | 472,732 79 |
| Admitted assets | $21,742,222 42 |

## LIABILITIES.

| | | |
|---|---|---|
| Net present value of outstanding policies computed by the Pennsylvania Insurance Department | $18,106,849 00 | |
| Same for dividend additions | 121,900 00 | |
| Same for annuities | 85,049 00 | |
| Total | $18,313,843 00 | |
| Deduct net value of risks re-insured | 307,748 00 | |
| Net reserve (paid for basis) | | $18,006,095 00 |

LIABILITIES—Concluded.

| | | |
|---|---|---|
| Extra reserve for total and permanent disability benefits included in life policies, less re-insurance | | $ 22,409 00 |
| Present value of supplementary contracts not involving life contingencies | | 134,345 00 |
| Present value of amounts incurred but not yet due for total and permanent disability benefits | | 1,901 00 |
| Surrender values claimable on policies cancelled | | 3,000 00 |
| Death losses in process of adjustment | $100,600 58 | |
| Reserve for net death losses incurred but unreported | 30,000 00 | |
| Matured endowments due and unpaid | 21,106 50 | |
| Death losses and other policy claims resisted | 1,000 00 | |
| Annuity claims, involving life contingencies, due and unpaid | 276 15 | |
| Total policy claims | | 152,983 23 |
| Dividends left with the company to accumulate at interest | | 8,880 47 |
| Gross premiums paid in advance, including surrender values so applied, less discount, if any | | 7,051 96 |
| Unearned interest and rent paid in advance | | 70,945 49 |
| Commissions to agents due or accrued | | 21 17 |
| Salaries, rents, office expenses, bills and accounts due or accrued | | 20,930 90 |
| Medical examiners' and legal fees due or accrued | | 6,146 50 |
| Estimated amount hereafter payable for federal, state and other taxes based upon the business of the year of this statement | | 50,000 00 |
| Borrowed money and interest thereon | | 50,076 39 |
| Unpaid dividends to stockholders | | 3,000 00 |
| Dividends or other profits due policyholders | | 30,251 25 |
| Dividends declared on or apportioned to annual dividend policies payable to policyholders during 1922 for period to December 31, 1922 | | 890 00 |
| Dividends declared on or apportioned to deferred dividend policies payable to policyholders during 1922 for period to December 20, 1922 | | 508,811 28 |
| Amounts set apart, apportioned, provisionally ascertained, calculated, declared or held awaiting apportionment upon deferred dividend policies | | 1,559,471 00 |
| Amount apportioned to deferred dividend policies issued since January 1, 1911 | | 307,147 00 |
| Other liabilities, viz: Real estate contingent fund, $19,624.65; staff pension fund, $45,000.00; suspense account, $2,969.45 | | 67,594 10 |
| Total | | $21,011,950 74 |
| Guarantee fund | | 60,000 00 |
| Unassigned funds (surplus) | | 670,271 68 |
| Total | | $21,742,222 42 |

## EXHIBIT OF POLICIES—ORDINARY.

ALL BUSINESS PAID FOR.

| | Number. | Amount. | Number. | Amount. |
|---|---|---|---|---|
| Policies in force December 31, 1920 | | | 54,575 | $98,616,270 00 |
| Policies issued, revived and increased during the year | | | 9,188 | 19,302,840 00 |
| Total | | | 63,763 | $117,919,110 00 |
| Deduct policies which have ceased to be in force during the year— | | | | |
| By death | 290 | $ 547,973 00 | | |
| By maturity | 376 | 463,358 00 | | |
| By expiry | 105 | 245,323 00 | | |
| By surrender | 957 | 1,649,310 00 | | |
| By lapse | 4,571 | 9,506,245 00 | | |
| By decrease | 5 | 409,104 00 | | |
| Total | | | 6,304 | 12,821,313 00 |
| Total policies in force December 31, 1921 | | | 57,459 | $105,097,797 00 |
| Re-insured | | | | $1,874,728 00 |

## EXHIBIT OF POLICIES—INDUSTRIAL.

ALL BUSINESS PAID FOR.

| | Number. | Amount. | Number. | Amount. |
|---|---|---|---|---|
| Policies in force December 31, 1920 | | | 17 | $2,345 00 |
| Deduct policies which have ceased to be in force during the year— | | | | |
| By death | 1 | $200 00 | | |
| By surrender | 1 | 110 00 | | |
| Total | | | 2 | 310 00 |
| Total policies in force December 31, 1921 | | | 15 | $2,035 00 |

## BUSINESS IN ILLINOIS—ORDINARY.

| | Number. | Amount. |
|---|---|---|
| Policies in force December 31, 1920 | 1,303 | $2,008,002 00 |
| Policies issued during the year | 45 | 103,050 00 |
| Total | 1,348 | $2,111,052 00 |
| Deduct policies ceased to be in force | 78 | 129,335 00 |
| Policies in force December 31, 1921 | 1,270 | $1,981,717 00 |
| Losses and claims unpaid December 31, 1920 | 1 | $ 1,000 00 |
| Losses and claims incurred during the year | 7 | 10,500 00 |
| Total | 8 | $11,500 00 |
| Losses and claims settled during the year | 7 | 10,500 00 |
| Losses and claims unpaid December 31, 1921 | 1 | $1,000 00 |
| Premiums received | | $50,669 92 |

## GAIN AND LOSS EXHIBIT.

### INSURANCE EXHIBIT.

| | | Gain in surplus. | Loss in surplus. |
|---|---|---|---|
| Loading on actual premiums of the year (averaging 18.9 per cent of the gross premiums) | $ 676,131 78 | | |
| Insurance expenses incurred during the year | 1,062,924 48 | | |
| Loss from loading | | | $386,792 70 |
| Interest earned during the year | $1,240,576 58 | | |
| Investment expenses incurred during the year | 67,286 90 | | |
| Net income from investments | $1,173,289 68 | | |
| Interest required to maintain reserve | 598,393 00 | | |
| Gain from interest | | $574,896 68 | |
| Expected mortality on net amount at risk | $927,938 81 | | |
| Actual mortality on net amount at risk | 372,877 52 | | |
| Gain from mortality | | 555,061 29 | |
| Expected disbursements to annuitants | $10,720 00 | | |
| Net actual annuity claims incurred | 14,727 02 | | |
| Loss from annuities | | | 4,007 02 |
| Total gain during the year from surrendered and lapsed policies | | 161,949 38 | |
| Dividends paid stockholders | | | 6,000 00 |
| Decrease in surplus on dividend account | | | 478,443 48 |
| Increase in special funds and special reserves during the year | | | 171,910 86 |

### INVESTMENT EXHIBIT.

| | | Gain in surplus. | Loss in surplus. |
|---|---|---|---|
| Total gains from stocks and bonds | | 31,777 11 | |
| Total losses from stocks and bonds | | | 110,231 02 |
| Gain from exchange | | 21,888 37 | |
| Net gain on account of total and permanent disability benefits or additional accidental death benefits included in life policies | | 13,747 00 | |
| Total gains and losses in surplus during the year | | $1,359,319 83 | $1,157,385 08 |
| Surplus December 31, 1920 | $468,336 93 | | |
| Surplus December 31, 1921 | 670,271 68 | | |
| Increase in surplus | | | 201,934 75 |
| Total | | $1,359,319 83 | $1,359,319 83 |

# ASSESSMENT LIFE ASSOCIATIONS COMPLYING WITH THE INSURANCE LAWS OF ILLINOIS FOR THE YEAR 1922.

## Association Statements for the Year Ending December 31, 1921.

## ASSOCIATIONS OF THIS STATE.

### BANKERS MUTUAL LIFE COMPANY.

Articles approved September 12, 1907; home office, 3 East Stephenson Street, Freeport, Illinois.

W. B. ERFERT, President. J. C. PEASLEY, Secretary.

| | |
|---|---|
| Balance from previous year | $98,714 16 |
| **INCOME.** | |
| First year's assessments or premiums | $ 53,727 91 |
| Subsequent year's assessments or premiums | 124,533 95 |
| Total received from applicants and members | $178,261 86 |
| Deduct payments returned to applicants and members | 48 52 |
| Net amount received from applicants and members | $178,213 34 |
| Interest on mortgage loans | 229 83 |
| Interest on bonds | 3,531 24 |
| Interest on bank deposits | 187 07 |
| Increase in book value of ledger assets | 5,292 54 |
| Total income | $187,454 02 |
| Sum | $286,168 18 |
| **DISBURSEMENTS.** | |
| Death claims | $77,890 43 |
| Permanent disability claims | 2,400 00 |
| Total payments to members | $80,290 43 |
| Commissions and fees paid to agents on account of first year's fees, dues, assessments, or premiums | 42,786 48 |
| Commissions and fees paid to agents on account of subsequent year's fees, dues, assessments or premiums | 29,248 85 |
| Salaries of officers and trustees | 2,810 00 |
| Salaries of office employees | 4,630 82 |
| Salaries and fees paid to medical examiners | 9,177 50 |
| Traveling and other expenses of officers, trustees and committees | 78 65 |
| Insurance department's fees and licenses | 145 50 |
| Taxes on assessments or premiums | 738 23 |
| Other taxes, viz: Local federal income, $317.70; war tax on policies, $2,748.40 | 3,066 10 |
| Rent | 767 53 |
| Advertising, printing and stationery | 1,401 78 |
| Postage, express, telegraph and telephone | 879 23 |
| Legal expenses in litigating claims | 592 77 |
| Other legal expenses | 3 50 |
| Furniture and fixtures | 1,117 49 |
| Inspection of risks | 699 50 |
| Office sundries unclassified | 128 22 |
| Total disbursements | $178,562 58 |
| Balance | $107,605 60 |
| **LEDGER ASSETS.** | |
| Mortgage loans on real estate | $ 3,200 00 |
| Book value of bonds | 90,080 50 |
| Cash in association's office | 87 62 |
| Deposits in trust companies and banks not on interest | 9,986 38 |
| Deposits in trust companies and banks on interest | 4,251 10 |
| Total ledger assets | $107,605 60 |

## LEDGER ASSETS—Concluded.

### NON-LEDGER ASSETS.

| | |
|---|---|
| Interest accrued | $1,575 92 |
| Mortuary assessments due or unpaid on last call | 3,380 82 |
| Total admitted assets | $112,562 34 |

## LIABILITIES.

| | | |
|---|---|---|
| Death claims resisted | $ 7,065 40 | |
| Death claims reported during the year but not yet adjusted | 15,329 50 | |
| Total unpaid claims | | $22,394 90 |
| Salaries, rents, expenses, etc., due or accrued | | 1,185 73 |
| Taxes due or accrued | | 242 80 |
| Advance premiums or assessments | | 8,766 71 |
| Total | | $32,590 14 |

## EXHIBIT OF POLICIES OR CERTIFICATES.

| | Total business of the year. | | Business in Illinois during year. | |
|---|---|---|---|---|
| | Number. | Amount. | Number. | Amount. |
| Policies or certificates in force December 31, 1920, as per last statement | 7,043 | $10,356,500 00 | 4,060 | $6,024,500 00 |
| Policies or certificates written during the year | 2,455 | 3,679,500 00 | 1,306 | 1,827,000 00 |
| Total | 9,498 | $14,036,000 00 | 5,366 | $7,851,500 00 |
| Deduct terminated or decreased during the year | 1,834 | 2,576,500 00 | 665 | 1,062,500 00 |
| Total policies or certificates in force December 31, 1921 | 7,664 | $11,459,500 00 | 4,701 | $6,789,000 00 |

| | |
|---|---|
| Received during the year from members in Illinois: Mortuary, $54,753.74; expense, $52,422.61; total | $107,176 35 |

## EXHIBIT OF DEATH CLAIMS.

| | Total claims. | | Illinois claims. | |
|---|---|---|---|---|
| | Number. | Amount. | Number. | Amount. |
| Claims unpaid December 31, 1920, as per last statement | 12 | $21,135 33 | 5 | $ 6,000 00 |
| Claims reported during the year | 52 | 81,900 00 | 38 | 57,900 00 |
| Total | 64 | $103,035 33 | 43 | $63,900 00 |
| Claims paid during the year | 51 | 77,890 43 | 33 | 46,000 00 |
| Balance | 13 | $25,144 90 | 10 | $17,900 00 |
| Saved by compromising or scaling down claims during the year | -------- | 1,750 00 | -------- | 500 00 |
| Claims rejected during the year | 1 | 1,000 00 | -------- | ------------- |
| Claims unpaid December 31, 1921 | 12 | $22,394 90 | 10 | $17,400 00 |

## EXHIBIT OF PERMANENT DISABILITY CLAIMS.

| | Total claims. | | Illinois claims. | |
|---|---|---|---|---|
| | Number. | Amount. | Number. | Amount. |
| Claims unpaid December 31, 1920, as per last statement | 1 | $1,000 00 | 1 | $1,000 00 |
| Claims reported during the year and interest addition | 5 | 1,400 00 | 4 | 900 00 |
| Total | 6 | $2,400 00 | 5 | $1,900 00 |
| Claims paid during the year | 6 | 2,400 00 | 5 | 1,900 00 |

## SHOWING ALL BONDS OWNED BY THE ASSOCIATION, DECEMBER 31, 1921.

| Description. | Book value. | Par value. | Market value. |
|---|---|---|---|
| First Liberty Loan, 4s, 1947 | $ 1,000 00 | $ 1,000 00 | $ 1,000 00 |
| Second Liberty Loan, 4¼s, 1942 | 1,940 00 | 2,000 00 | 1,940 00 |
| Third Liberty Loan, 4¼s, 1928 | 21,315 00 | 21,750 00 | 21,315 00 |
| Fourth Liberty Loan, 4¼s, 1938 | 15,180 50 | 15,650 00 | 15,180 50 |
| Fifth Liberty Loan, 4¾s, 1923 | 1,500 00 | 1,500 00 | 1,500 00 |
| Federal Farm Loan, St. Paul, 5s, 1941 | 2,000 00 | 2,000 00 | 2,000 00 |
| Bear Lake, Idaho, funding bonds, 5s, 1931 | 1,960 00 | 2,000 00 | 1,960 00 |
| Bayard City, Neb., school district, 5¼s, 1944 | 2,000 00 | 2,000 00 | 2,000 00 |
| Fort Bend, County, Texas, road district, 5s, 1950 | 4,800 00 | 5,000 00 | 4,800 00 |
| Genoa Twp., Ill., high school district, 5s, 1931 | 1,010 00 | 1,000 00 | 1,010 00 |
| Geneva Twp., Ill., park district, 5s, 1928 | 505 00 | 500 00 | 505 00 |
| Goodfield, Ill., community high school district, 5½s, 1927 | 2,040 00 | 2,000 00 | 2,040 00 |
| Goodfield, Ill., community high school district, 5½s, 1928 | 2,060 00 | 2,000 00 | 2,060 00 |
| Jefferson Co., Tenn., road district, 5s, 1939 | 1,940 00 | 2,000 00 | 1,940 00 |
| Jacksonville, Ill., power plant, 5s, 1930 | 1,000 00 | 1,000 00 | 1,000 00 |

SHOWING ALL BONDS OWNED BY THE ASSOCIATION, DECEMBER 31, 1921—Concluded.

| Description. | Book value. | Par value. | Market value. |
|---|---|---|---|
| Jacksonville, Ill., filtration plant, 5s, 1928 | 1,000 00 | 1,000 00 | 1,000 00 |
| LaCrosse, Co., Wis., highway, 5s, 1926 | 1,020 00 | 1,000 00 | 1,020 00 |
| Monroe City, Mo., water works, 5s, 1933 | 1,000 00 | 1,000 00 | 1,000 00 |
| Marion Twp., Ill., high school, 4s, 1929 | 1,900 00 | 2,000 00 | 1,900 00 |
| Milledgeville, Ill., community high school, 5s, 1936 | 2,060 00 | 2,000 00 | 2,060 00 |
| Milledgeville, Ill., community high school, 5s, 1937 | 4,120 00 | 4,000 00 | 4,120 00 |
| Pennington Co., S. Dak., court house and jail, 6s, 1941 | 3,330 00 | 3,000 00 | 3,330 00 |
| Plum Bayou, Ark., levee district, 6s, 1945 | 1,030 00 | 1,000 00 | 1,030 00 |
| Savanna, Ill., water works, 5s, 1930 | 1,020 00 | 1,000 00 | 1,020 00 |
| Savanna, Ill., water works, 5s, 1931 | 1,020 00 | 1,000 00 | 1,020 00 |
| Savanna, Ill., water works, 5s, 1932 | 1,020 00 | 1,000 00 | 1,020 00 |
| Sherman, Tex., sewer, 5½s, 1947 | 2,050 00 | 2,000 00 | 2,050 00 |
| South Dakota Rural Credit, 5s, 1933 | 1,020 00 | 1,000 00 | 1,020 00 |
| Waukegan, Ill., park district, 5s, 1937 | 2,060 00 | 2,000 00 | 2,060 00 |
| Wapella, Ill., community high school, 5s, 1927 | 2,060 00 | 2,000 00 | 2,060 00 |
| Wapella, Ill., community high school, 5½s, 1939 | 1,030 00 | 1,000 00 | 1,030 00 |
| Yellowstone County, Mont., relief, 5½s, 1925 | 3,090 00 | 3,000 00 | 3,090 00 |
| Total | $90,080 50 | 90,400 00 | $90,080 50 |

## CHICAGO MUTUAL LIFE COMPANY.

Articles approved November 11, 1920; home office, 1530 Tribune Building, Chicago, Illinois.

ERNEST G. GEARHART, President. HARRY G. RICHARD, Secretary.

| | |
|---|---|
| Balance from previous year | $1,886 69 |

### INCOME.

| | |
|---|---|
| First year's assessments or premiums | $26,460 82 |
| Subsequent year's assessments or premiums | 8,224 35 |
| Net amount received from applicants and members | $34,685 17 |
| Interest on bank deposits | 198 26 |
| From all other sources, viz: Preferred agency corporation, $81,221.20; miscellaneous, income $1.00 | 81,222 20 |
| Total income | $116,105 63 |
| Sum | $117,992 32 |

### DISBURSEMENTS.

| | |
|---|---|
| Death claims | $ 1,000 00 |
| Commissions and fees paid to agents on account of first year's fees, dues, assessments, or premiums | 17,336 19 |
| Commissions and fees paid to agents on account of subsequent years' fees, dues, assessments or premiums | 751 70 |
| Salaries of officers and trustees | 9,837 00 |
| Salaries of office employees | 1,651 00 |
| Salaries and fees paid to medical examiners | 3,459 50 |
| Traveling and other expenses of officers, trustees and committees | 3,355 70 |
| Traveling and other expenses of managers and agents | 651 52 |
| Collection and remittance of assessments, etc | 9 62 |
| Insurance department's fees and licenses | 106 00 |
| Taxes on assessments or premiums | 1,117 44 |
| Rent | 1,350 00 |
| Advertising, printing and stationery | 2,658 18 |
| Postage, express, telegraph and telephone | 356 71 |
| Legal expenses | 637 00 |
| Furniture and fixtures | 1,266 73 |
| Other disbursements, viz: Directors' fees, $990.00; insurance, $90.00; light and heat, $52.05; actuarial and auditors' fees, $882.50; office expenses, $104.68 | 2,119 23 |
| Total disbursements | $47,663 52 |
| Balance | $70,328 80 |

### LEDGER ASSETS.

| | |
|---|---|
| Mortgage loans on real estate | $ 4,500 00 |
| Book value of stocks | 43,865 00 |
| Cash in association's office | 2,156 90 |
| Deposits in trust companies and banks on interest | 19,885 66 |
| Agents' balances (debit, $3,737.46; credit, $3,816.22) | —78 76 |
| Total ledger assets | $70,328 80 |

#### NON-LEDGER ASSETS.

| | |
|---|---|
| Interest accrued | 218 08 |
| Gross assets | $70,546 88 |

LEDGER ASSETS—Concluded.

DEDUCT ASSETS NOT ADMITTED.

| | |
|---|---|
| Miscellaneous stock | 43,865 00 |
| Total admitted assets | $26,681 88 |

LIABILITIES.

| | |
|---|---|
| Salaries, rents, expenses, etc., due or accrued | $1,285 26 |
| Advance premiums or assessments | 6,564 85 |
| Total | $7,850 11 |

EXHIBIT OF POLICIES OR CERTIFICATES.

| | Total business of the year. Number. | Amount. | Business in Illinois during year. Number. | Amount. |
|---|---|---|---|---|
| Policies or certificates in force December 31, 1920, as per last statement | 563 | $898,500 00 | 563 | $898,500 00 |
| Policies or certificates written during the year | 555 | 897,500 00 | 198 | 429,000 00 |
| Total | 1,118 | $1,796,000 00 | 761 | $1,327,500 00 |
| Deduct terminated or decreased during the year | 426 | 639,500 00 | 291 | 457,000 00 |
| Total policies or certificates in force December 31, 1921 | 692 | $1,156,500 00 | 470 | $870,500 00 |

| | |
|---|---|
| Received during the year from members in Illinois: Mortuary, $6,579.48; expense, $22,991.54; total | $29,571 02 |

EXHIBIT OF DEATH CLAIMS.

| | Total claims— Number. | Amount. |
|---|---|---|
| Claims reported during the year | 1 | $1,000 00 |
| Claims paid during the year | 1 | 1,000 00 |

SCHEDULE D—PART 2.

| Description. | Book value. | Par value. | Market value. |
|---|---|---|---|
| Preferred stock of the Preferred Agency Corporation, 8s | $43,865 00 | $43,865 00 | Not for sale |

---

## CLOVER LEAF MUTUAL LIFE INSURANCE COMPANY.

Articles approved December 6, 1915; home office, 306 East State Street, Jacksonville, Illinois.

F. H. ROWE, President. R. Y. ROWE, Secretary.

| | |
|---|---|
| Balance from previous year | $477 24 |

INCOME.

| | |
|---|---|
| First and subsequent year's assessments or premiums | $31,402 29 |
| Deduct payments returned to applicants and members | 13 19 |
| Total income | $31,389 10 |
| Sum | $31,866 34 |

DISBURSEMENTS.

| | |
|---|---|
| Death claims | $ 5,799 50 |
| Commissions and fees paid to agents on account of first and subsequent year's fees, dues, assessments, or premiums | 6,616 15 |
| Salaries of managers or agents | 11,215 51 |
| Salaries of officers and trustees | 6,000 00 |
| Salaries of office employees | 1,704 79 |
| Salaries and fees paid to medical examiners | 129 06 |
| Traveling and other expenses of officers, trustees and committees | 1,821 30 |
| Insurance department's fees and licenses | 10 00 |
| Federal taxes | 113 62 |
| Rent | 291 50 |
| Advertising, printing and stationery | 63 86 |
| Furniture and fixtures | 7 00 |
| Agents' balances charged off | 11 |
| Total disbursements | $33,772 38 |
| Balance, deficit | —$1,906 04 |

LEDGER ASSETS.

| | |
|---|---|
| Deposits in trust companies and banks not on interest | $ 781 16 |
| Agents' credit balances | —2,687 20 |
| Total ledger assets | —$1,906 04 |

EXHIBIT OF POLICIES OR CERTIFICATES.

| | Total business of the year—all in Illinois. Number. | Amount. |
|---|---|---|
| Policies or certificates in force December 31, 1920, as per last statement | 6,027 | $717,958 50 |
| Policies or certificates written during the year | 3,054 | 687,150 00 |
| Total | 9,081 | $1,405,108 50 |
| Deduct terminated or decreased during the year | 1,733 | 387,174 50 |
| Total policies or certificates in force December 31, 1921 | 7,348 | $1,017,934 00 |
| Received during the year from members in Illinois: Mortuary, $5,799.50; expense, $25,589.60; total | | $31,389.10 |

EXHIBIT OF DEATH CLAIMS.

| | Total claims—all in Illinois. Number. | Amount. |
|---|---|---|
| Claims reported during the year | 38 | $5,799 50 |
| Claims paid during the year | 38 | 5,799 50 |

---

## DREXEL MUTUAL LIFE INSURANCE COMPANY.

Articles approved August 1, 1921; home office, 208 North Wells Street, Chicago, Illinois.

SALVATORE D. REUDE, President. RICHARD REUDE, Secretary.

INCOME.

| | |
|---|---|
| Membership fees actually received | $1,020 00 |
| First year's assessments or premiums | 2,785 48 |
| Total received from applicants and members | $3,805 48 |
| Deduct payments returned to applicants and members | 10 00 |
| Total income | $3,795 48 |

DISBURSEMENTS.

| | |
|---|---|
| Commissions and fees paid to agents on account of first year's fees, dues, assessments, or premiums | $1,220 48 |
| Rent | 375 00 |
| Advertising, printing and stationery | 1,200 00 |
| Total disbursements | $2,795 48 |
| Balance | $1,000 00 |

LEDGER ASSETS.

| | |
|---|---|
| Cash in association's office | $1,000 00 |
| Total admitted assets | $1,000 00 |

EXHIBIT OF POLICIES OR CERTIFICATES.

| | Total business of the year—all in Illinois Number. | Amount. |
|---|---|---|
| Policies or certificates written during the year | 528 | $520,250 00 |
| Deduct terminated or decreased during the year | 247 | 243,000 00 |
| Total policies or certificates in force December 31, 1921 | 281 | $277,250 00 |
| Received during the year from members in Illinois: Mortuary, $1,573.10; expense, $2,222.38; total | | $3,795 48 |

## GLOBE MUTUAL LIFE INSURANCE COMPANY OF CHICAGO.

Articles approved March 23, 1895; home office, 431 South Dearborn Street, Chicago, Illinois.

T. F. BARRY, President. G. O. SANBORN, Assistant-Secretary.

| | |
|---|---|
| Balance from previous year | $226,919 94 |

### INCOME.

| | |
|---|---|
| Industrial premiums actually received | $261,478 85 |
| First year's assessments or premiums | 47,738 97 |
| Subsequent year's assessments or premiums | 106,307 63 |
| Total received from applicants and members | $415,525 45 |
| Deduct payments returned to applicants and members | 6,076 43 |
| Net amount received from applicants and members | $409,449 02 |
| Interest on mortgage loans | 2,886 75 |
| Interest on bonds and dividends on stocks | 11,052 37 |
| Interest on bank deposits | 96 27 |
| From all other sources, viz: Commission extending loan, $96.25; discounts, $130.75 | 227 00 |
| Total income | $423,711 41 |
| Sum | $650,631 35 |

### DISBURSEMENTS.

| | |
|---|---|
| Death claims | $89,650 30 |
| Permanent disability claims | 2,946 00 |
| Total payments to members | $92,596 30 |
| Commissions and fees paid to agents on account of first year's fees, dues, assessments, or premiums | 24,774 06 |
| Commissions and fees paid to agents on account of subsequent years' fees, dues, assessments or premiums | 142,683 35 |
| Salaries of managers or agents | 1,820 00 |
| Salaries of officers and trustees | 16,535 11 |
| Salaries of office employees | 12,346 98 |
| Salaries and fees paid to medical examiners | 6,662 20 |
| Traveling and other expenses of officers, trustees and committees | 180 74 |
| Insurance department's fees and licenses | 419 75 |
| Taxes on assessments or premiums | 2,416 42 |
| United States capital stock tax | 226 00 |
| Rent | 3,084 00 |
| Advertising, printing and stationery | 10,685 85 |
| Postage, express, telegraph and telephone | 1,850 92 |
| Legal expenses in litigating claims | 392 51 |
| Other legal expenses | 1,315 00 |
| Furniture and fixtures | 647 95 |
| Other disbursements, viz: Bonus, $1,008.00; miscellaneous, $1,790.24; exchange on checks, $4.65 | 2,802 89 |
| Total disbursements | $321,440 03 |
| Balance | $329,191 32 |

### LEDGER ASSETS.

| | |
|---|---|
| Mortgage loans on real estate | $ 30,600 00 |
| Book value of bonds and stocks | 289,621 57 |
| Cash in association's office | 73 22 |
| Deposits in trust companies and banks not on interest | 4,095 18 |
| Deposits in trust companies and banks on interest | 1,076 41 |
| Agents' debit balances | 1,263 34 |
| Bills receivable | 142 82 |
| Other ledger assets, viz: War saving stamps, $1,634.62; policy loans, $684.16 | 2,318 78 |
| Total ledger assets | $329,191 32 |

#### NON-LEDGER ASSETS.

| | |
|---|---|
| Interest accrued | 6,230 40 |
| Market value of bonds and stocks over book value | 20,282 43 |
| Mortuary assessments due or unpaid on last call | 69,254 24 |
| Gross assets | $424,958 39 |

#### DEDUCT ASSETS NOT ADMITTED.

| | | |
|---|---|---|
| Agents' debit balances | $ 1,263 34 | |
| Bills receivable | 142 82 | |
| Excess of mortuary assessments due or unpaid on last call over corresponding liability for unpaid claims | 60,062 24 | |
| Policy loans | 684 16 | |
| | | 62,152 56 |
| Total admitted assets | | $362,805 83 |

## LIABILITIES.

| | | |
|---|---|---|
| Death claims due and unpaid | $1,126 00 | |
| Death claims resisted | 2,666 00 | |
| Death claims reported during the year but not yet adjusted | 4,153 00 | |
| Present value of deferred death and disability claims payable in installments | 1,247 00 | |
| Total death claims | | $9,192 00 |
| Taxes due or accrued | | 542 20 |
| Advance premiums or assessments | | 12,153 69 |
| Total | | $21,887 89 |

## EXHIBIT OF POLICIES OR CERTIFICATES.

| | Total business of the year—all in Illinois. Number. | Amount. |
|---|---|---|
| Policies or certificates in force December 31, 1920, as per last statement | 59,969 | $15,428,771 00 |
| Policies or certificates written during the year | 19,432 | 4,833,323 00 |
| Total | 79,401 | $20,262,094 00 |
| Deduct terminated or decreased during the year | 13,600 | 3,558,855 00 |
| Total policies or certificates in force December 31, 1921 | 65,801 | $16,703,239 00 |
| Received during the year from members in Illinois | | $415,525 45 |

## EXHIBIT OF DEATH CLAIMS.

| | Total claims—all in Illinois. Number. | Amount. |
|---|---|---|
| Claims unpaid December 31, 1920, as per last statement | 15 | $5,770 00 |
| Claims reported during the year | 873 | 93,353 30 |
| Total | 888 | $99,123 30 |
| Claims paid during the year | 866 | 89,650 30 |
| Balance | 22 | $9,473 00 |
| Saved by compromising or scaling down claims during the year | -------- | 1,528 00 |
| Claims unpaid December 31, 1921 | 22 | $7,945 00 |

## EXHIBIT OF PERMANENT DISABILITY CLAIMS.

| | Total claims—all in Illinois. Number. | Amount. |
|---|---|---|
| Claims unpaid December 31, 1920, as per last statement | 6 | $750 00 |
| Claims reported during the year and interest addition | 21 | 3,518 00 |
| Total | 27 | $4,268 00 |
| Claims paid during the year | 17 | 2,946 00 |
| Claims unpaid December 31, 1921 | 10 | $1,322 00 |
| | -------- | —75 00 |
| | -------- | $1,247 00 |

## SCHEDULE D—PART 1.

| Description. | Book value. | Par value. | Market value. |
|---|---|---|---|
| First U. S. Liberty Loan, 4¼s, 1947, 1932 | $1,144 41 | $1,150 00 | $1,115 50 |
| Second U. S. Liberty Loan, 4¼s, 1942, 1927 | 11,248 00 | 11,750 00 | 11,397 50 |
| Third U. S. Liberty Loan, 4¼s, 1928 | 3,591 81 | 3,650 00 | 3,577 00 |
| Fourth U. S. Liberty Loan, 4¼s, 1938, 1933 | 23,856 82 | 25,200 00 | 24,444 00 |
| Fifth U. S. Liberty Loan, 4¾s, 1923 | 3,426 32 | 3,350 00 | 3,350 00 |
| Baltimore & Ohio R. R., secured gold, 6s, 1929 | 4,818 75 | 5,000 00 | 4,750 00 |
| Cleveland, Cin., Chi. R. R., refunding and imp., 6s, 1929 | 4,775 00 | 5,000 00 | 4,800 00 |
| Central of Georgia R. R., gold, 6s, 1929 | 9,700 00 | 10,000 00 | 9,600 00 |
| Chicago & Northwestern R. R., gold secured, 7s, 1930 | 4,987 50 | 5,000 00 | 5,300 00 |
| Chicago & Northwestern R. R., 15 yr. secured, 6½s, 1936 | 1,985 00 | 2,000 00 | 2,160 00 |
| Chicago & Northwestern R. R., 15 yr. secured, 6½s, 1936 | 990 00 | 1,000 00 | 1,080 00 |
| Chicago Union Station, 1st mort., gold, "Series C", 6½s, 1963 | 4,912 50 | 5,000 00 | 5,600 00 |
| Chicago Union Station, 1st mort. gold, "Series C", 6½s, 1963 | 5,037 50 | 5,000 00 | 5,600 00 |
| Great Northern R. R., gen'l mort. gold, 7s, 1936 | 4,800 00 | 5,000 00 | 5,400 00 |
| Illinois Central R. R., 15 yr. secured gold, 6½s, 1936 | 1,940 00 | 2,000 00 | 2,140 00 |
| Illinois Central R. R., 15 yr. secured gold, 6½s, 1936 | 2,910 00 | 3,000 00 | 3,210 00 |
| Illinois Central R. R., 15 yr. secured gold, 6½s, 1936 | 1,945 00 | 2,000 00 | 2,140 00 |
| Lake Shore & Mich. Southern, gold debenture, 4s, 1931 | 8,250 00 | 10,000 00 | 8,900 00 |
| New York Central R. R., conv. gold debenture, 6s, 1935 | 1,820 00 | 2,000 00 | 1,960 00 |
| New York Central R. R., collateral trust gold, 7s, 1930 | 4,987 50 | 5,000 00 | 5,300 00 |

SCHEDULE D—PART 1—Concluded.

| Description. | Book value. | Par value. | Market value. |
|---|---|---|---|
| New York Central R. R., equipment trust, 7s, 1935 | $ 4,987 50 | $ 5,000 00 | $ 5,500 00 |
| Northern Pacific & Great Northern Jt., convertible gold, 6½s, 1936 | 4,750 35 | 5,000 00 | 5,350 00 |
| Northern Pacific & Great Northern Jt., convertible gold, 6½s, 1936 | 4,800 00 | 5,000 00 | 5,350 00 |
| Northern Pacific & Great Northern Jt., convertible gold, 6½s, 1936 | 4,800 00 | 5,000 00 | 5,350 00 |
| Pennsylvania R. R., gen'l mort. gold notes "Series A", 4½s, 1965 | 4,062 50 | 5,000 00 | 4,350 00 |
| Pennsylvania R. R., gold notes, 7s, 1930 | 9,975 00 | 10,000 00 | 10,600 00 |
| Southern Pacific R. R., equipment trust "Series C", 7s, 1935 | 2,028 61 | 2,000 00 | 2,220 00 |
| Virginia R. R. Co., 1st mort., 5s, 1962 | 4,400 00 | 5,000 00 | 4,400 00 |
| Brooklyn Edison Co., gen'l mort. bond "D", 7s, 1940 | 12,593 75 | 13,000 00 | 13,910 00 |
| Commonwealth Edison Co., coll. gold notes, "Series A", 7s, 1925 | 9,675 00 | 10,000 00 | 10,200 00 |
| Commonwealth Edison Co., 1st mort. gold bond, 6s, 1943 | 4,562 50 | 5,000 00 | 5,150 00 |
| Commonwealth Edison Co., 1st mort. gold bond, 6s, 1943 | 4,562 50 | 5,000 00 | 5,150 00 |
| Commonwealth Edison Co., 1st mort. gold bond, 6s, 1943 | 2,737 50 | 3,000 00 | 3,090 00 |
| Commonwealth Edison Co., 1st mort. gold bond, 6s, 1943 | 1,825 00 | 2,000 00 | 2,060 00 |
| Commonwealth Edison Co., 1st mort. gold bond, 6s, 1943 | 4,562 50 | 5,000 00 | 5,150 00 |
| Consolidated Gas & Electric Light & Power of Baltimore, 1st ref. mort., 7s, 1931 | 4,900 00 | 5,000 00 | 5,150 00 |
| Consolidated Gas & Electric Light & Power of Baltimore, 1st ref. mort., 7s, 1931 | 4,912 50 | 5,000 00 | 5,150 00 |
| Duquesne Light & Power Co., 1st mort. coll. gold "Series A", 6s, 1949 | 4,250 00 | 5,000 00 | 5,000 00 |
| International Mercantile Marine, 1st mort. coll. trust, 6s, 1941 | 2,913 13 | 3,000 00 | 2,730 00 |
| Great Western Power of California, 1st and ref. mort., "Series A", 6s, 1949, 1939 | 9,400 00 | 10,000 00 | 10,700 00 |
| New York Edison Co., 1st and ref. mort. gold, 6½s, 1941 | 3,131 25 | 3,000 00 | 3,210 00 |
| New York Edison Co., 1st and ref. mort. gold, 6½s, 1941 | 1,043 75 | 1,000 00 | 1,070 00 |
| New York Edison Co., 1st and ref. mort. gold, 6½s, 1941 | 2,087 50 | 2,000 00 | 2,140 00 |
| New York Telephone Co., sinking fund gold deb., 6s, 1949 | 1,992 50 | 2,000 00 | 2,060 00 |
| New York Telephone Co., 20 yr. refunding, 6s, 1941 | 4,840 00 | 5,000 00 | 5,100 00 |
| North Western Bell Telephone Co., "Series A", 1st mort. gold, 7s, 1941, 1926 | 6,277 12 | 6,500 00 | 7,020 00 |
| Ohio Power Co., 1st and ref. mort. "Series A" sinking, 7s, 1951, 1926 | 18,950 00 | 20,000 00 | 20,000 00 |
| Pennsylvania Power & Light Co., 1st and ref. mort., 7s, 1951 | 4,575 00 | 5,000 00 | 5,150 00 |
| Public Service Co. of Northern Ill., 1st and ref. mort., 5s, 1956 | 3,750 00 | 5,000 00 | 4,300 00 |
| Puget Sound Power & Light Co., gen'l. ref. mort. gold, 7½s, 1941, 1926 | 4,850 00 | 5,000 00 | 5,250 00 |
| Southern California Edison Power Co., gen'l. ref. mort. gold, 6s, 1944 | 4,350 00 | 5,000 00 | 5,000 00 |
| Southern California Edison Power Co., gen'l. ref. mort. gold, 6s, 1944 | 1,885 00 | 2,000 00 | 2,000 00 |
| Union Tank Car Co., equipment trust gold notes, 7s, 1930 | 3,840 00 | 4,000 00 | 4,120 00 |
| West Penn Power Co., 1st mort., 7s, 1946 | 4,700 00 | 5,000 00 | 5,250 00 |
| West Penn Power Co., conv. gold debenture, 6s, 1924 | 4,587 50 | 5,000 00 | 4,850 00 |
| West Penn. Power Co., Series "C", 1st mort. gold bonds, 6s, 1958, 1923 | 4,437 50 | 5,000 00 | 5,000 00 |
| Total | $289,121 57 | $305,600 00 | $309,904 00 |

SCHEDULE D—PART 2.

| Description. | Book value. | Par value. | Market value. |
|---|---|---|---|
| Old Colony Trust | $500 00 | $500 00 | None |

---

## GUARANTEED EQUITY LIFE COMPANY.

Articles approved August 26, 1919; home office, 127 North Dearborn Street, Chicago, Illinois.

WILLIAM W. KREAMER, President. DONALD E. WEBSTER, Secretary.

| | |
|---|---|
| Balance from previous year | $8,448 77 |

INCOME.

| | |
|---|---|
| First year's assessments or premiums | $14,224 76 |
| Subsequent year's assessments or premiums | 5,015 01 |
| Advance payments | 7,944 81 |
| Total received from applicants and members | $27,184 58 |
| Deduct payments returned to applicants and members | 29 88 |
| Net amount received from applicants and members | $27,154 70 |

INCOME—Concluded.

| | |
|---|---|
| Interest on mortgage loans | $473 96 |
| Interest on bank deposits | 120 35 |
| War tax income | 392 00 |
| Total income | $28,141 01 |
| Sum | $36,589 78 |

DISBURSEMENTS.

| | |
|---|---|
| Death claims | $2,452 43 |
| Commissions and fees paid to agents on account of first year's fees, dues, assessments, or premiums | 9,879 70 |
| Commissions and fees paid to agents on account of subsequent year's fees, dues, assessments or premiums | 1,927 50 |
| Salaries of officers and trustees | 1,355 00 |
| Salaries and fees paid to medical examiners | 792 00 |
| Traveling and other expenses of officers, trustees and committees | 31 20 |
| Collection and remittance of assessments, etc | 22 49 |
| Insurance department's fees and licenses | 37 45 |
| War tax disbursements | 392 00 |
| Advertising, printing and stationery | 232 53 |
| Postage, express, telegraph and telephone | 158 37 |
| Other disbursements, viz: Miscellaneous expense, $24.50; inspections, $272.50; re-insurance premiums, $1,108.59; advance payment disbursements, $599.28 | 2,004 87 |
| Total disbursements | $19,285 54 |
| Balance | $17,304 24 |

LEDGER ASSETS.

| | |
|---|---|
| Mortgage loans on real estate | $10,600 00 |
| Cash in association's office | 25 00 |
| Deposits in trust companies and banks not on interest | 6,679 24 |
| Total ledger assets | $17,304 24 |

NON-LEDGER ASSETS.

| | |
|---|---|
| Mortuary assessments due or unpaid on last call | 2,042 17 |
| Gross assets | $19,346 41 |

DEDUCT ASSETS NOT ADMITTED.

| | |
|---|---|
| Excess of mortuary assessments due or unpaid on last call over corresponding liability for unpaid claims | 2,042 17 |
| Total admitted assets | $17,304 24 |

LIABILITIES.

| | |
|---|---|
| Advance premiums or assessments | $ 427 78 |
| Advance payment fund | 10,416 68 |
| Total | $10,844 46 |

EXHIBIT OF POLICIES OR CERTIFICATES.

| | Total business of the year—all in Illinois. Number. | Amount. |
|---|---|---|
| Policies or certificates in force December 31, 1920, as per last statement | 550 | $651,000 00 |
| Policies or certificates written during the year | 288 | 639,500 00 |
| Policies or certificates revived during the year | 17 | 28,500 00 |
| Total | 855 | $1,319,000 00 |
| Deduct terminated or decreased during the year | 149 | 273,000 00 |
| Total policies or certificates in force December 31, 1921 | 706 | $1,046,000 00 |

| | |
|---|---|
| Received during the year from members in Illinois: Mortuary, $3,589.92; expense, $15,619.97; total | $19,209 89 |

EXHIBIT OF DEATH CLAIMS.

| | Total claims—all in Illinois. Number. | Amount. |
|---|---|---|
| Claims reported during the year | 3 | $3,000 00 |
| Claims paid during the year | 3 | 2,452 43 |

| | |
|---|---|
| Saved by compromising or scaling down claims during the year | $547 57 |

## HOTEL MEN'S MUTUAL BENEFIT ASSOCIATION OF THE UNITED STATES AND CANADA.

Articles approved January 17, 1879; home office, Auditorium Tower, Chicago, Illinois.

F. HAROLD VAN ORMAN, President. J. K. BLATCHFORD, Secretary.

| | |
|---|---|
| Balance from previous year | $63,506 32 |

### INCOME.

| | |
|---|---|
| Suspense account | $ 10 00 |
| Advance payments | 5 25 |
| Mortuary fund | 25,838 00 |
| Reserve fund | 5,025 50 |
| Expense fund | 2,420 00 |
| Total received from applicants and members | $33,298 75 |
| Interest on bonds | 1,870 00 |
| Interest on bank deposits | 499 81 |
| From all other sources, viz: Associate memberships, $375.00; exchange on cheeks, $31.10; suspense account reinstatement, $6.00; outstanding checks, $2.00 | 414 10 |
| Total income | $36,082 66 |
| Sum | $99,588 98 |

### DISBURSEMENTS.

| | |
|---|---|
| Death claims | $26,178 00 |
| Salaries of officers and trustees | 3,000 00 |
| Salaries of office employees | 595 00 |
| Traveling and other expenses of officers, trustees and committees | 134 41 |
| Insurance department's fees and licenses | 249 71 |
| Rent | 501 00 |
| Printing and stationery | 806 28 |
| Postage, express, telegraph and telephone | 326 45 |
| Other disbursements, viz: Bank exchange, $130.62; suspense account applied, $32.50; rent of post office box and bank vault, $21.00; protested checks, $29.51; prize awarded, $250.00; premium on treasurer's bond, $37.50 | 501 13 |
| Total disbursements | $32,291 98 |
| Balance | $67,297 00 |

### LEDGER ASSETS.

| | |
|---|---|
| Book value of bonds | $42,600 48 |
| Deposits in trust companies and banks on interest | 24,696 52 |
| Total ledger assets | $67,297 00 |

#### NON-LEDGER ASSETS.

| | |
|---|---|
| Interest accrued | 478 95 |
| Market value of bonds over book value | 760 48 |
| Total admitted assets | $68,536 43 |

### LIABILITIES.

| | | |
|---|---|---|
| Death claims reported during the year but not yet adjusted | $9,000 00 | |
| Death claims incurred in 1921, not reported until 1922 | 2,400 00 | |
| Total unpaid claims | | $11,400 00 |
| Salaries, rents, expenses, etc., due or accrued | | 447 73 |
| Advance payments on assessments | | 223 25 |
| Applications in suspense | | 10 00 |
| Total | | $12,080 98 |

### EXHIBIT OF POLICIES OR CERTIFICATES.

| | Total business of the year. | | Business in Illinois during year. | |
|---|---|---|---|---|
| | Number. | Amount. | Number. | Amount. |
| Policies or certificates in force December 31, 1920, as per last statement | 1,216 | $1,185,000 00 | 131 | $127,800 00 |
| Policies or certificates written during the year | 118 | 70,800 00 | 12 | 7,200 00 |
| Policies or certificates revived during the year | 2 | 2,400 00 | | |
| Total | 1,336 | $1,258,200 00 | 143 | $135,000 00 |
| Deduct terminated or decreased during the year | 123 | 97,800 00 | 15 | 17,400 00 |
| Total policies or certificates in force December 31, 1921 | 1,213 | $1,160,400 00 | 128 | $117,600 00 |

| | |
|---|---|
| Received during the year from members in Illinois: Mortuary, $2,665.50; reserve, $542.50; expense, $256.00; total | $3,464 00 |

EXHIBIT OF DEATH CLAIMS.

| | Total claims. Number. | Total claims. Amount. | Illinois claims. Number. | Illinois claims. Amount. |
|---|---|---|---|---|
| Claims unpaid December 31, 1920, as per last statement | 4 | $ 4,800 00 | 1 | $1,200 00 |
| Claims reported during the year | 27 | 30,000 00 | 3 | 3,000 00 |
| Interest addition on account of installment claims | -------- | 378 00 | -------- | ------------- |
| Total | 31 | $35,178 00 | 4 | $4,200 00 |
| Claims paid during the year | 23 | 26,178 00 | 3 | 3,000 00 |
| Claims unpaid December 31, 1921 | 8 | $9,000 00 | 1 | $1,200 00 |

SCHEDULE D—PART 1.

| Description. | Book value. | Par value. | Market value. |
|---|---|---|---|
| Peoples Gas, Light & Coke Co., 5s, 1947 | $ 8,000 00 | $10,000 00 | $ 8,700 00 |
| U. S. Second Liberty Loan, 4s, 1942, 1927 | 30,000 00 | 30,000 00 | 30,000 00 |
| U. S. Fourth Liberty Loan, 4¼s, 1938, 1933 | 4,000 00 | 4,000 00 | 4,000 00 |
| U. S. War Savings Stamps of 1918, 1923 | 600 48 | 720 00 | 660 96 |
| Total | $42,600 48 | $44,720 00 | $43,360 96 |

---

## ILLINOIS BANKERS LIFE ASSOCIATION.

Articles approved November 3, 1897; home office, West First Avenue, Monmouth, Illinois.

W. H. WOODS, President. ROBT. M. WORK, Secretary.

| | |
|---|---|
| Balance from previous year | $1,505,825 90 |

### INCOME.

| | |
|---|---|
| Membership fees actually received | $ 275,228 50 |
| First year's assessments or premiums | 142,346 82 |
| Subsequent years' assessments or premiums | 1,391,419 59 |
| Deposits savings policy | 135 84 |
| Policy fees | 494 20 |
| Total received from applicants and members | $1,809,624 95 |
| Deduct payments returned to applicants and members | 3,193 20 |
| Net amount received from applicants and members | $1,806,431 75 |
| Interest on mortgage loans | 53,391 90 |
| Interest on bonds and dividends on stocks | 18,245 98 |
| Interest on bank deposits | 7,712 48 |
| Interest from all other sources | 336 21 |
| From all other sources, viz: Brokerage, $40,971.86; profit and loss, $687.61 | 41,659 47 |
| Total income | $1,927,777 79 |
| Sum | $3,433,603 69 |

### DISBURSEMENTS.

| | |
|---|---|
| Death claims | $584,418 85 |
| Permanent disability claims | 35,750 00 |
| Installment claims | 5,398 13 |
| Total payments to members | $625,566 98 |
| Commissions and fees paid to agents on account of first year's fees, dues, assessments, or premiums | 269,163 16 |
| Commissions and fees paid to agents on account of subsequent year's fees, dues, assessments or premiums | 18,686 00 |
| Salaries of managers or agents | 17,007 82 |
| Salaries of officers and trustees | 39,999 96 |
| Other compensation of officers and trustees | 6,749 57 |
| Salaries and other compensation of committees | 250 32 |
| Salaries of office employees | 48,099 65 |
| Other compensation of office employees | 246 00 |
| Salaries and fees paid to medical examiners | 38,316 00 |
| Traveling and other expenses of officers, trustees and committees | 2,744 55 |
| Traveling and other expenses of managers and agents | 2,071 48 |
| Collection and remittance of assessments, etc | 10,571 45 |
| Insurance department's fees and licenses | 3,427 80 |
| Other licenses and fees | 110 00 |
| Taxes on assessments or premiums | 15,784 27 |
| Other taxes | 26,741 71 |
| Rent | 7,902 73 |
| Advertising, printing and stationery | 42,731 79 |

DISBURSEMENTS—Concluded.

| | |
|---|---|
| Postage, express, telegraph and telephone | $18,942 49 |
| Legal expenses in litigating claims | 3,141 76 |
| Other legal expenses | 495 00 |
| Fire insurance premiums | 295 20 |
| Furniture and fixtures | 6,840 34 |
| Other disbursements, viz: Inspection of risks, $12,741.43; miscellaneous expenses, $4,967.35; investigation and settlement of claims, $2,515.11; contest prizes, $2,155.00; agents' convention expense, $3,106.73; profit and loss, $3,201.52 | 28,687 14 |
| Agents' balances charged off | 274 21 |
| Decrease in book value of ledger assets | 158 34 |
| Total disbursements | $1,235,005 72 |
| Balance | $2,198,597 97 |

## LEDGER ASSETS.

| | |
|---|---|
| Book value of real estate | $ 532 00 |
| Mortgage loans on real estate | 1,410,070 00 |
| Book value of bonds | 491,918 17 |
| Cash in association's office | 50 00 |
| Deposits in trust companies and banks on interest | 289,102 19 |
| Agents' debit balances | 6,478 35 |
| Premium notes | 447 26 |
| Total ledger assets | $2,198,597 97 |

NON-LEDGER ASSETS.

| | |
|---|---|
| Interest due and accrued | 47,973 27 |
| Market value of real estate over book value | 468 00 |
| Market value of bonds and stocks over book value | 4,606 83 |
| Gross assets | $2,251,646 07 |

DEDUCT ASSETS NOT ADMITTED.

| | | |
|---|---|---|
| Agents' debit balances | $6,478 35 | |
| Premium notes | 447 26 | |
| Appraised value loan not being twice loan value | 2,000 00 | |
| Certificate of deposit past due | 1,000 00 | |
| | | 9,925 61 |
| Total admitted assets | | $2,241,720 46 |

## LIABILITIES.

| | | |
|---|---|---|
| Death claims resisted | $28,000 00 | |
| Death claims reported during the year but not yet adjusted | 45,546 50 | |
| Death claims incurred in 1921, not reported until 1922 | 24,067 00 | |
| Present value of deferred death and disability claims payable in installments | 13,652 30 | |
| Total death claims | | $111,265 80 |
| Permanent disability claims reported during the year but not yet adjusted | | 12,000 00 |
| Total unpaid claims | | $123,265 80 |
| Salaries, rents, expenses, etc., due or accrued | | 4,499 44 |
| Taxes due or accrued | | 28,354 14 |
| Advance premiums or assessments | | 12,000 91 |
| 20 year savings policy, deposits, plus accrued interest | | 136 72 |
| Total | | $168,257 01 |

## EXHIBIT OF POLICIES OR CERTIFICATES.

| | Total business of the year. | | Business in Illinois during year. | |
|---|---|---|---|---|
| | Number. | Amount. | Number. | Amount. |
| Policies or certificates in force December 31, 1920, as per last statement | 66,830 | $108,021,587 98 | 27,775 | $45,355,595 85 |
| Policies or certificates written during the year | 9,328 | 19,041,750 00 | 2,294 | 3,764,000 00 |
| Policies or certificates revived during the year | 633 | 962,281 10 | 158 | 280,710 80 |
| Policies or certificates increased during the year | | 105,094 33 | | 56,594 33 |
| Total | 76,791 | $128,130,713 41 | 30,227 | $49,456,900 98 |
| Deduct terminated or decreased during the year | 14,549 | 25,929,535 50 | 3,946 | 6,960,760 80 |
| Total policies or certificates in force December 31, 1921 | 62,242 | $102,201,177 91 | 26,281 | $42,496,140 18 |

| | |
|---|---|
| Received during the year from members in Illinois: Mortuary, $546,022.14; expense, $136,505.54; total | $682,527 68 |

EXHIBIT OF DEATH CLAIMS.

| | Total claims. Number. | Amount. | Illinois claims. Number. | Amount. |
|---|---|---|---|---|
| Claims unpaid December 31, 1920, as per last statement | 54 | $ 94,012 06 | 25 | $ 40,572 50 |
| Claims reported during the year | 396 | 604,959 02 | 148 | 228,031 56 |
| Interest addition on account of installment claims | -------- | 2,093 97 | -------- | ------------ |
| Total | 450 | $701,065 05 | 173 | $268,604 06 |
| Claims paid during the year | 401 | 589,816 98 | 150 | 223,501 52 |
| Balance | 49 | $111,248 07 | 23 | $45,102 54 |
| Saved by compromising or scaling down claims during the year | -------- | 18,549 27 | -------- | 6,073 04 |
| Claims rejected during the year | 3 | 5,500 00 | 2 | 4,000 00 |
| Claims unpaid December 31, 1921 | 46 | $87,198 80 | 21 | $35,029 50 |

EXHIBIT OF PERMANENT DISABILITY CLAIMS.

| | Total claims. Number. | Amount. | Illinois claims. Number. | Amount. |
|---|---|---|---|---|
| Claims unpaid December 31, 1920, as per last statement | 9 | $ 6,500 00 | 3 | $ 2,000 00 |
| Claims reported during the year and interest addition | 62 | 46,250 00 | 31 | 25,000 00 |
| Total | 71 | $52,750 00 | 34 | $27,000 00 |
| Claims paid during the year | 49 | 35,750 00 | 27 | 21,000 00 |
| Balance | 22 | $17,000 00 | 7 | $6,000 00 |
| Claims rejected during the year | 7 | 5,000 00 | 2 | 1,500 00 |
| Claims unpaid December 31, 1921 | 15 | $12,000 00 | 5 | $4,500 00 |

SCHEDULE D—PART 1.

| Description. | Book value. | Par value. | Market value. |
|---|---|---|---|
| U. S. First Liberty Bonds, 4¼s, 1947- 1932 | $50,000 00 | $50,000 00 | $50,000 00 |
| U. S. Second Liberty Bonds, 4¼s, 1942, 1927 | 25,000 00 | 25,000 00 | 25,000 00 |
| U. S. Third Liberty Bonds, 4¼s, 1928 | 30,000 00 | 30,000 00 | 30,000 00 |
| U. S. Fourth Liberty Bonds, 4¼s, 1938 | 50,000 00 | 50,000 00 | 50,000 00 |
| Burnet Co., Tex., Road Dist. No. 2, 5½s, 1938, 1923 | 36,000 00 | 36,000 00 | 36,000 00 |
| Eastland, Tex., street improvement bonds, 6s, 1939 | 20,517 16 | 20,000 00 | 21,400 00 |
| Collins Co., Tex., road district, 5s, 1928-32 | 8,000 00 | 8,000 00 | 7,920 00 |
| Cooke Co., Tex., Road Dist. No. 2, 5½s, 1930-33 | 28,000 00 | 28,000 00 | 29,050 00 |
| Franklin Co., Tex., special road bonds, 5½s, 1931-34 | 25,000 00 | 25,000 00 | 25,870 00 |
| Freestone Co., Tex., Dist. No. 11, 5s, 1922-50 | 29,000 00 | 29,000 00 | 29,000 00 |
| Independent School District, Davenport, Iowa, 4½s, 1932 | 50,542 30 | 50,000 00 | 50,000 00 |
| Renwick, Iowa, funding bonds, 5½s, 1920-32 | 4,106 59 | 4,000 00 | 4,125 00 |
| School District No. 265, Serena, La Salle Co., Ill., 5s, 1921-24 | 15,023 08 | 15,000 00 | 15,000 00 |
| School District No. 13, Thurston Co., Nebr., 5½s, 1924-33 | 10,264 30 | 10,000 00 | 10,180 00 |
| Shelby Co., Tex., Road Dist. No. 4, 5s, 1937-40 | 40,000 00 | 40,000 00 | 39,600 00 |
| Upshur Co., Tex., special road bonds, 5½s, 1959 | 40,000 00 | 40,000 00 | 41,040 00 |
| Totals | $461,453 43 | $460,000 00 | $464,185 00 |

SCHEDULE D—PART 2.

| Description. | Book value. | Par value. | Market value. |
|---|---|---|---|
| Monmouth Trust & Savings Bank, Monmouth, Ill | $30,464 74 | $13,200 00 | $32,340 00 |

## MERCHANTS RESERVE LIFE INSURANCE COMPANY.

Articles approved October 19, 1907; home office, 10-12 East Pearson Street, Chicago, Illinois.

FLETCHER A. TINKHAM, President. I. M. MONTGOMERY, Secretary.

| | |
|---|---|
| Balance from previous year | $86,241 06 |

INCOME.

| | |
|---|---|
| Membership fees actually received | $10,716 02 |
| First year's assessments or premiums | 8,577 01 |
| Subsequent years' assessments or premiums | 92,596 74 |
| Medical examiners' fees actually received | 186 00 |
| Total received from applicants and members | $112,075 77 |
| Deduct payments returned to applicants and members | 213 89 |
| Net amount received from applicants and members | $111,861 88 |

## INCOME—Concluded.

| | |
|---|---|
| Interest on mortgage loans | $ 753 00 |
| Interest on bonds | 252 50 |
| Interest on bank deposits | 95 04 |
| Gross rents from association's property, including $1,000.00 for association's occupancy of its own buildings | 2,800 00 |
| Borrowed money (gross) | 3,000 00 |
| Federal policy tax | 220 80 |
| Founders' certificates | 5,400 00 |
| Increase in book value of ledger assets | 33,587 40 |
| Total income | $157,970 62 |
| Sum | $244,211 68 |

## DISBURSEMENTS.

| | |
|---|---|
| Death claims | $39,107 27 |
| Commissions and fees paid to agents on account of first year's fees, dues, assessments, or premiums | 10,700 07 |
| Commissions and fees paid to agents on account of subsequent years' fees, dues, assessments or premiums | 15,998 14 |
| Salaries of officers and trustees | 6,175 00 |
| Other compensation of officers and trustees | 135 81 |
| Salaries of office employees | 5,798 65 |
| Salaries and fees paid to medical examiners | 2,205 20 |
| Traveling and other expenses of officers, trustees and committees | 1,188 63 |
| Collection and remittance of assessments, etc | 219 42 |
| Insurance department's fees and licenses | 667 91 |
| Taxes on assessments or premiums | 108 77 |
| Other taxes | 1,618 35 |
| Rent, including $1,000.00 for association's occupancy of its own buildings | 1,670 00 |
| Advertising, printing and stationery | 5,062 50 |
| Postage, express, telegraph and telephone | 1,312 95 |
| Legal expenses in litigating claims | 3,010 28 |
| Other legal expenses | 917 50 |
| Repairs and expenses on real estate other than taxes | 1,131 61 |
| Furniture and fixtures | 194 78 |
| Other disbursements, viz: Office expenses, $647.14; re-insurance premiums, $1,248.41; coal account, $998.13 | 2,893 68 |
| Borrowed money repaid (gross) | 20,000 00 |
| Interest on borrowed money | 2,272 06 |
| Inspections | 1,141 40 |
| Commissions on mortgage loans | 2,056 35 |
| Commission on sale of founders' certificates | 540 00 |
| Gross decrease by adjustment of ledger assets | 12,449 58 |
| Total disbursements | $138,575 91 |
| Balance | $105,635 77 |

## LEDGER ASSETS.

| | |
|---|---|
| Book value of real estate | $43,550 42 |
| Mortgage loans on real estate | 11,800 00 |
| Book value of bonds | 9,055 33 |
| Cash in association's office | 235 69 |
| Deposits in trust companies and banks not on interest | 15,806 90 |
| Deposits in trust companies and banks on interest | 17,203 83 |
| Agents' debit balances | 1,983 60 |
| Bills receivable | 6,000 00 |
| Total ledger assets | $105,635 77 |

### NON-LEDGER ASSETS.

| | | |
|---|---|---|
| Interest due and accrued | | 1,528 49 |
| Mortuary assessments due or unpaid on last call | | 1,667 79 |
| Gross assets | | $108,832 05 |
| **DEDUCT ASSETS NOT ADMITTED.** | | |
| Agents' debit balances | $1,983 60 | |
| Bills receivable | 6,000 00 | |
| Book value of bonds over market value | 275 33 | |
| | | 8,258 93 |
| Total admitted assets | | $100,573 12 |

## LIABILITIES.

| | | |
|---|---|---|
| Death claims adjusted not yet due | $2,476 67 | |
| Death claims resisted | 488 12 | |
| Death claims reported during the year but not yet adjusted | 2,500 00 | |
| Death claims incurred in 1921, not reported until 1922 | 1,000 00 | |
| Total unpaid claims | | $6,464 79 |

LIABILITIES—Concluded.

| | |
|---|---|
| Salaries, rents, expenses, etc., due or accrued | $ 921 02 |
| Commissions to agents due or accrued | 3,833 35 |
| Taxes due or accrued | 800 00 |
| Advance premiums or assessments | 1,375 69 |
| All other liabilities, viz: Accrued interest on real estate incumbrances, $216.67; accrued interest on founders' certificates, $87.17; face amount of founders' certificates sold, $5,400.00; not a current liability | 303 84 |
| Total | $13,698 69 |

EXHIBIT OF POLICIES OR CERTIFICATES.

| | Total business of the year. | | Business in Illinois during year. | |
|---|---|---|---|---|
| | Number. | Amount. | Number. | Amount. |
| Policies or certificates in force December 31, 1920, as per last statement | 4,451 | $6,367,900 00 | 2,344 | $3,308,000 00 |
| Policies or certificates written during the year | 337 | 755,500 00 | 200 | 424,500 00 |
| Total | 4,788 | $7,123,400 00 | 2,544 | $3,732,500 00 |
| Deduct terminated or decreased during the year | 779 | 1,508,750 00 | 222 | 463,000 00 |
| Total policies or certificates in force December 31, 1921 | 4,009 | $5,614,650 00 | 2,322 | $3,269,500 00 |

| | |
|---|---|
| Received during the year from members in Illinois: Mortuary $25,363.39; expense, $11,909.50; total | $37,272 91 |

EXHIBIT OF DEATH CLAIMS.

| | Total claims. | | Illinois claims. | |
|---|---|---|---|---|
| | Number. | Amount. | Number. | Amount. |
| Claims unpaid December 31, 1920, as per last statement | 10 | $11,168 08 | 4 | $ 5,200 00 |
| Claims reported during the year | 29 | 35,750 00 | 10 | 16,000 00 |
| Interest addition on account of installment claims | | 1,133 94 | | 1,133 94 |
| Total | 39 | $48,052 02 | 14 | $22,333 94 |
| Claims paid during the year | 33 | 39,107 27 | 12 | 18,857 27 |
| Balance | 6 | $8,944 75 | 2 | $3,476 67 |
| Saved by compromising or scaling down claims during the year | | 1,500 00 | | |
| Claims rejected during the year | 1 | 979 96 | | |
| Claims unpaid December 31, 1921 | 5 | $6,464 79 | 2 | $3,476 67 |

SCHEDULE D.

| Description. | Book value. | Par value. | Market value. |
|---|---|---|---|
| U. S. Liberty Bonds, 4¼s, 1938, 1933 | $1,000 00 | $1,000 00 | $1,000 00 |
| Oklahoma School Bonds, Murray County, 6s, 1929 | 2,225 33 | 2,000 00 | 2,100 00 |
| Wisconsin Railroad, Light & Power, 5s, 1933 | 880 00 | 1,000 00 | 730 00 |
| Commonwealth Utility, Minnesota, 6s, 1933 | 4,950 00 | 5,500 00 | 4,950 00 |
| Totals | $9,055 33 | $9,500 00 | $8,780 00 |

---

## ROCHDALE LIFE INSURANCE COMPANY OF ILLINOIS.

Articles approved, January 1, 1918; home office, 130 North Wells Street, Chicago, Illinois.

N. A. HAWKINSON, President. GUSTAVE KOPP, Secretary.

| | |
|---|---|
| Balance from previous year | $1,476 02 |

INCOME.

| | |
|---|---|
| Subsequent years' assessments or premiums | $159 72 |
| Interest on bonds | 46 45 |
| Total income | $206 17 |
| Sum | $1,682 19 |

DISBURSEMENTS.

| | |
|---|---|
| Commissions and fees paid to agents on account of subsequent years' fees, dues, assessments or premiums | $31 84 |
| Total disbursements | $31 84 |
| Balance | $1,650 35 |

LEDGER ASSETS.

| | |
|---|---|
| Book value of bonds | $1,147 00 |
| Cash in association's office | 100 35 |
| Deposits in trust companies and banks not on interest | 403 00 |
| Total ledger assets | $1,650 35 |

NON-LEDGER ASSETS.

| | |
|---|---|
| Interest and rents due and accrued | 10 80 |
| Gross assets | $1,661 15 |

DEDUCT ASSETS NOT ADMITTED.

| | |
|---|---|
| Book value of bonds over market value | 17 72 |
| Total admitted assets | $1,643 43 |

LIABILITIES.

| | |
|---|---|
| Commissions to agents due or accrued | $8 09 |
| Total | $8 09 |

EXHIBIT OF POLICIES OR CERTIFICATES.

| | Total business of the year—all in Illinois. Number. | Amount. |
|---|---|---|
| Policies or certificates in force December 31, 1920, as per last statement | 5 | $5,000 00 |
| Received during the year from members in Illinois: Mortuary, $119.79; expense, $39.93; total | | $159 72 |

SCHEDULE D—PART 1.

| Description. | Book value. | Par value. | Market value. |
|---|---|---|---|
| Second converted Liberty Bonds, 4¼s, 1942, 1927 | $350 00 | $350 00 | $342 30 |
| Third converted Liberty Bonds, 4¼s, 1928 | 650 00 | 650 00 | 636 74 |
| Victory Liberty Bonds, 4¾s, 1923, 1922 | 147 00 | 150 00 | 150 24 |
| Totals | $1,147 00 | $1,150 00 | $1,129 28 |

---

## THE SWEDISH BAPTISTS' MUTUAL AID ASSOCIATION OF AMERICA.

Articles approved September 9, 1899; home office 82 West Washington Street, Chicago, Illinois.

JOHN E. SPANN, President. N. P. SEVERIN, Secretary.

| | |
|---|---|
| Balance from previous year | $158,695 39 |

INCOME.

| | |
|---|---|
| Membership fees actually received | $ 114 00 |
| First year's assessments or premiums | 566 69 |
| Subsequent years' assessments or premiums | 43,647 15 |
| Special trust fund | 912 82 |
| Net amount received from applicants and members | $45,240 66 |
| Interest on mortgage loans | 7,805 55 |
| Interest on bonds | 317 50 |
| Interest on bank deposits | 363 71 |
| Gross rents | 112 75 |
| Total income | $53,840 17 |
| Sum | $212,535 56 |

DISBURSEMENTS.

| | |
|---|---|
| Death claims | $20,500 00 |
| Salaries of officers and trustees | 1,900 00 |
| Other compensation of officers and trustees | 190 00 |
| Salaries of office employees | 1,600 00 |
| Salaries and fees paid to medical examiners | 105 00 |
| Collection and remittance of assessments, etc | 329 84 |
| Insurance department's fees and licenses | 145 36 |
| Real estate taxes | 180 45 |
| Rent | 450 00 |
| Advertising, printing and stationery | 852 81 |
| Postage, express, telegraph and telephone | 123 26 |
| Legal expenses in litigating claims | 100 00 |
| Premium on surety bond for secretary | 75 00 |
| Premium on John Berg Life Insurance | 264 00 |

DISBURSEMENTS—Concluded.

| | |
|---|---|
| Dues Mutual Life Underwriters | $ 25 00 |
| Sundry expense | 42 63 |
| Loss on sale or maturity of ledger assets | 2,000 00 |
| Total disbursements | $28,883 35 |
| Balance | $183,652 21 |

LEDGER ASSETS.

| | |
|---|---|
| Mortgage loans on real estate | $166,500 00 |
| Book value of bonds | 7,000 00 |
| Cash in association's office | 50 00 |
| Deposits in trust companies and banks on interest | 5,683 65 |
| Bills receivable | 4,418 56 |
| Total ledger assets | $183,652 21 |

NON-LEDGER ASSETS.

| | |
|---|---|
| Interest accrued | 2,227 62 |
| Gross assets | $185,879 83 |

DEDUCT ASSETS NOT ADMITTED.

| | |
|---|---|
| Bills receivable (John Berg notes) | 4,418 56 |
| Total admitted assets | $181,461 27 |

LIABILITIES.

| | |
|---|---|
| Death claims reported during the year but not yet adjusted | $3,500 00 |
| Advance premiums or assessments (special trust fund) | 3,651 77 |
| Total | $7,151 77 |

EXHIBIT OF POLICIES OR CERTIFICATES.

| | Total business of the year—all in Illinois. Number. | Amount. |
|---|---|---|
| Policies or certificates in force December 31, 1920, as per last statement | 2,174 | $2,207,500 00 |
| Policies or certificates written during the year | 24 | 28,000 00 |
| Total | 2,198 | $2,235,500 00 |
| Deduct terminated or decreased during the year | 35 | 36,500 00 |
| Total policies or certificates in force December 31, 1921 | 2,163 | $2,199,000 00 |

| | |
|---|---|
| Received during the year from members in Illinois: Mortuary, $27,854.72; reserve, $8,842.77; special trust fund, $912.82; expense, $7,630.35; total | $45,240 66 |

EXHIBIT OF DEATH CLAIMS.

| | Total claims—all in Illinois. Number. | Amount. |
|---|---|---|
| Claims unpaid December 31, 1920, as per last statement | 3 | $ 2,500 00 |
| Claims reported during the year | 20 | 21,500 00 |
| Total | 23 | $24,000 00 |
| Claims paid during the year | 20 | 20,500 00 |
| Claims unpaid December 31, 1921 | 3 | $3,500 00 |

SCHEDULE D.

| Description. | Book value. | Par value. | Market value. |
|---|---|---|---|
| United States of America, 3d Liberty Loan, Bond 4¼s, 1928 | $1,000 00 | $1,000 00 | $1,000 00 |
| United States of America, 4th Liberty Loan, 4¼s, 1938, 1933 | 2,000 00 | 2,000 00 | 2,000 00 |
| United States of America Victory Liberty Loan, 4¾s 1923, 1922 | 4,000 00 | 4,000 00 | 4,000 00 |
| Total | $7,000 00 | $7,000 00 | $7,000 00 |

---

## SWEDISH METHODISTS' AID ASSOCIATION.

Articles approved April 2, 1920; home office 69 West Washington Street, Chicago, Illinois.

ERU A. LARSON, President. ROY N. LENNSTRUM, Secretary.

| | |
|---|---|
| Balance from previous year | $202,806 52 |

## INCOME.

| | |
|---|---|
| Membership fees actually received | $ 2 00 |
| Subsequent year's assessments or premiums | 75,480 29 |
| Total received from applicants and members | $75,482 29 |
| Deduct payments returned to applicants and members | 23 31 |
| Net amount received from applicants and members | $75,458 98 |
| Interest on mortgage loans | 11,165 25 |
| Interest on bonds | 455 00 |
| Interest on bank deposits | 164 05 |
| Commission on mortgage loans | 179 50 |
| Total income | $87,422 78 |
| Sum | $290,229 30 |

## DISBURSEMENTS.

| | |
|---|---|
| Death claims | $59,090 00 |
| Salaries of officers and trustees | 3,221 63 |
| Salaries and other compensation of committees | 755 00 |
| Salaries of office employees | 2,290 81 |
| Traveling and other expenses of officers, trustees and committees | 500 00 |
| Collection and remittance of assessments, etc | 1,521 62 |
| Insurance department's fees and licenses | 156 01 |
| Rent | 600 00 |
| Advertising, printing and stationery | 1,007 50 |
| Postage, express, telegraph and telephone | 721 32 |
| Legal expenses | 194 38 |
| Other disbursements, viz: Special actuary service, $305.00; exchange, $18.08 | 323 08 |
| Total disbursements | $70,381 35 |
| Balance | $219,847 95 |

## LEDGER ASSETS.

| | |
|---|---|
| Mortgage loans on real estate | $202,000 00 |
| Loans secured by pledge of bonds | 11,000 00 |
| Cash in association's office | 75 00 |
| Deposits in trust companies and banks on interest | 5,394 51 |
| Furniture and fixtures | 1,378 44 |
| Total ledger assets | $219,847 95 |

### NON-LEDGER ASSETS.

| | |
|---|---|
| Interest accrued | 2,718 97 |
| Gross assets | $222,566 92 |

### DEDUCT ASSETS NOT ADMITTED.

| | |
|---|---|
| Furniture and fixtures | 1,378 44 |
| Total admitted assets | $221,187 48 |

## LIABILITIES.

| | |
|---|---|
| Advance premiums or assessments | $56 50 |
| Total | $56 50 |

## EXHIBIT OF POLICIES OR CERTIFICATES.

| | Total business of the year—all in Illinois. Number. | Amount. |
|---|---|---|
| Policies or certificates in force December 31, 1920, as per last statement | 3,817 | $3,525,000 00 |
| Policies or certificates written during the year | 2 | 2,000 00 |
| Total | 3,819 | $3,527,000 00 |
| Deduct terminated or decreased during the year | 637 | 613,380 00 |
| Total policies or certificates in force December 31, 1921 | 3,182 | $2,913,620 00 |

| | |
|---|---|
| Received during the year from members: Mortuary, $63,302.28; expense, $12,156.70; total | $75,458 98 |

## EXHIBIT OF DEATH CLAIMS.

| | Total claims—all in Illinois. Number. | Amount. |
|---|---|---|
| Claims unpaid December 31, 1920, as per last statement | 3 | $ 2,620 00 |
| Claims reported during the year | 67 | 56,470 00 |
| Total | 70 | $59,090 00 |
| Claims paid during the year | 70 | 59,090 00 |

SCHEDULE D—BONDS.

| Description. | Book value. | Par value. | Market value. |
|---|---|---|---|
| U. S. Liberty Bonds, 2d issue, 4¼s | $2,000 00 | $2,000 00 | $2,000 00 |
| U. S. Liberty Bonds, 3d issue, 4¼s | 2,000 00 | 2,000 00 | 2,000 00 |
| U. S. Liberty Bonds, 4th issue, 4¼s | 2,000 00 | 2,000 00 | 2,000 00 |
| W. F. Mosser, first mortgage lien real estate bonds, 8s, 1930 | 5,000 00 | 5,000 00 | 5,000 00 |
| Total | $11,000 00 | $11,000 00 | $11,000 00 |

## SWEDISH MISSION FRIENDS' AID ASSOCIATON.

Articles approved June 11, 1904; home office 30 North LaSalle Street, Chicago, Illinois.

OSCAR W. CARLSON, President. ANDREW SANDBERG, Secretary.

| | |
|---|---|
| Balance from previous year | $221,682 78 |

INCOME.

| | |
|---|---|
| First year's assessments or premiums | 610 48 |
| Subsequent year's assessments or premiums | 36,928 93 |
| Net amount received from applicants and members | $37,539 41 |
| Interest on mortgage loans | 13,313 90 |
| Interest on bonds | 13 09 |
| Interest on bank deposits | 104 49 |
| From all other sources, viz: Fees for exchange of beneficiary, $27.00; commissions on loans, $715.00 | 742 00 |
| Total income | $51,712 89 |
| Sum | $273,395 67 |

DISBURSEMENTS.

| | |
|---|---|
| Death claims | $13,000 00 |
| Solicitor's fees | 1,505 00 |
| Salaries of officers and trustees | 350 00 |
| Other compensation of officers and trustees | 525 00 |
| Salaries of office employees | 1,800 00 |
| Salaries and fees paid to medical examiners | 297 00 |
| Traveling and other expenses of officers, trustees and committees | 358 94 |
| Collection and remittance of assessments, etc | 874 90 |
| Insurance department's fees and licenses | 158 78 |
| Rent | 402 00 |
| Advertising, printing and stationery | 320 04 |
| Postage, express, telegraph and telephone | 136 07 |
| Furniture and fixtures | 190 00 |
| Other disbursements, viz: Exchange, $37.79; audit, $71.49; entertainment, $34.88; bonds, $50.00; miscellaneous, $77.37 | 271 53 |
| Total disbursements | $20,189 26 |
| Balance | $253,206 41 |

LEDGER ASSETS.

| | |
|---|---|
| Mortgage loans on real estate | $250,075 00 |
| Cash in association's office | 99 00 |
| Deposits in trust companies and banks not on interest | 3,032 41 |
| Total ledger assets | $253,206 41 |

NON-LEDGER ASSETS.

| | |
|---|---|
| Interest and rents due and accrued | 3,765 24 |
| Total admitted assets | $256,971 65 |

LIABILITIES.

| | | |
|---|---|---|
| Death claims adjusted not yet due | $4,500 00 | |
| Death claims reported during the year but not yet adjusted | 4,500 00 | |
| Total unpaid claims | | $9,000 00 |
| Advance premiums or assessments | | 918 79 |
| Total | | $9,918 79 |

EXHIBIT OF POLICIES OR CERTIFICATES.

| | Total business of the year—all in Illinois. Number. | Amount. |
|---|---|---|
| Policies or certificates in force December 31, 1920 as per last statement | 2,356 | $1,704,500 00 |
| Policies or certificates written during the year | 95 | 76,000 00 |
| Policies or certificates revived during the year | 12 | 9,000 00 |
| Total | 2,463 | $1,789,500 00 |
| Deduct terminated or decreased during the year | 82 | 60,500 00 |
| Total policies or certificates in force December 31, 1921 | 2,381 | $1,729,000 00 |
| Received during the year from members in Illinois: Mortuary, $24,400.54; reserve, $3,753.90; expense, $9,384.97; total | | $37,539 41 |

EXHIBIT OF DEATH CLAIMS.

| | Total claims—all in Illinois. Number. | Amount. |
|---|---|---|
| Claims unpaid December 31, 1920, as per last statement | 4 | $3,000 00 |
| Claims reported during the year | 28 | 19,000 00 |
| Total | 32 | $22,000 00 |
| Claims paid during the year | 19 | 13,000 00 |
| Claims unpaid December 31, 1921 | 13 | $9,000 00 |

## WESTERN LIFE INDEMNITY COMPANY.

Articles approved May 5, 1884; re-incorporated April 19, 1900 under 1893 assessment act; home office 159 North State Street, Chicago, Illinois.

GEO. M. MOULTON, President. A. M. RYAN, Secretary.

| | |
|---|---|
| Balance from previous year | $116,226 51 |

INCOME.

| | |
|---|---|
| Membership fees actually received | $ 286 60 |
| First year's assessments or premiums | 780 02 |
| Subsequent years' assessments or premiums | 258,651 51 |
| Industrial and monthly savings premiums | 48,472 17 |
| Total received from applicants and members | $308,190 30 |
| Deduct payments returned to applicants and members | 425 48 |
| Net amount received from applicants and members | $307,764 82 |
| Interest on bonds | 5,405 92 |
| Interest on bank deposits | 160 98 |
| Consideration for supplementary contract not involving life contingencies | 3,703 18 |
| Total income | $317,034 90 |
| Sum | $433,261 41 |

DISBURSEMENTS.

| | |
|---|---|
| Death claims | $180,054 22 |
| Permanent disability claims | 4,645 43 |
| Paid on supplementary contracts | 8,536 62 |
| Total payments to members | $193,236 27 |
| Commissions and fees paid to agents on account of subsequent years' fees, dues, assessments or premiums | 12,433 64 |
| Salaries of managers or agents | 8,505 00 |
| Salaries of officers and trustees | 12,200 00 |
| Salaries of office employees | 16,209 00 |
| Salaries and fees paid to medical examiners | 1,371 24 |
| Traveling and other expenses of officers, trustees and committees | 175 00 |
| Traveling and other expenses of managers and agents | 1,452 30 |
| Collection and remittance of assessments, etc | 7,044 81 |
| Insurance department's fees and licenses | 10 00 |
| Taxes on assessments or premiums | 65 79 |
| Other taxes | 26 95 |
| Rent | 4,800 00 |
| Advertising, printing and stationery | 3,015 75 |
| Postage, express, telegraph and telephone | 2,734 20 |
| Legal expenses in litigating claims | 1,776 51 |

## DISBURSEMENTS—Concluded.

| | |
|---|---|
| Other legal expenses | $1,200 00 |
| Other disbursements, viz: Office supplies, $869.47; rent and expense of agencies, $354.73; lien account, $19.99; dividend bond account, $9.66; suspense, $49.95 | 1,303 80 |
| Total disbursements | $267,560 26 |
| Balance | $165,701 15 |

## LEDGER ASSETS.

| | |
|---|---|
| Book value of bonds | $158,256 25 |
| Cash in association's office | 2,007 36 |
| Deposits in trust companies and banks not on interest | 193 25 |
| Deposits in trust companies and banks on interest | 4,972 29 |
| Policy loans | 172 00 |
| J. L. Phillips suspense account | 100 00 |
| Total ledger assets | $165,701 15 |

### NON-LEDGER ASSETS.

| | |
|---|---|
| Interest accrued | 2,239 82 |
| Mortuary assessments due or unpaid on last call | 4,375 89 |
| Gross assets | $172,316 86 |

### DEDUCT ASSETS NOT ADMITTED.

| | | |
|---|---|---|
| Book value of bonds over market value | $29,626 25 | |
| Other items, viz: Policy loans, $172.00; J. L. Phillips suspense account, $100.00; interest due and accrued (defaulted bond), $1,680.00 | 1,952 00 | |
| | | 31,578 25 |
| Total admitted assets | | $140,738 61 |

## LIABILITIES.

| | | |
|---|---|---|
| Death claims resisted | $ 1,182 06 | |
| Death claims reported during the year but not yet adjusted | 12,608 43 | |
| Death claims incurred in 1921, not reported until 1922 | 1,363 77 | |
| Present value of deferred death and disability claims payable in installments | 35,535 29 | |
| Total unpaid claims | | $50,689 55 |
| Salaries, rents, expenses, etc., due or accrued | | 372 37 |
| Advance premiums or assessments | | 4,315 67 |
| Total | | $55,377 59 |

## EXHIBIT OF POLICIES OR CERTIFICATES—ORDINARY.

| | Total business of the year. | | Business in Illinois during year. | |
|---|---|---|---|---|
| | Number. | Amount. | Number. | Amount. |
| Policies or certificates in force December 31, 1920, as per last statement | 9,658 | $8,137,922 00 | 3,317 | $2,742,856 00 |
| Policies or certificates written during the year | 101 | 64,906 00 | 60 | 38,783 00 |
| Policies or certificates revived during the year | 75 | 58,401 00 | 10 | 4,906 00 |
| Total | 9,834 | $8,261,229 00 | 3,387 | $2,786,545 00 |
| Deduct terminated or decreased during the year | 771 | 550,974 00 | 280 | 174,332 00 |
| Total policies or certificates in force December 31, 1921 | 9,063 | $7,710,255 00 | 3,107 | $2,612,213 00 |

| | |
|---|---|
| Received during the year from members in Illinois: Mortuary, $70,347.72; expense, $23,449.24; total | $93,796 96 |

## EXHIBIT OF DEATH CLAIMS—ORDINARY.

| | Total claims. | | Illinois claims. | |
|---|---|---|---|---|
| | Number. | Amount. | Number. | Amount. |
| Claims unpaid December 31, 1920, as per last statement | 25 | $ 20,520 81 | 5 | $ 4,598 92 |
| Claims reported during the year | 208 | 162,520 77 | 61 | 37,414 63 |
| Total | 233 | $183,041 58 | 66 | $42,013 55 |
| Claims paid during the year | 210 | 164,123 57 | 58 | 37,664 94 |
| Balance | 23 | $18,918 01 | 8 | $4,348 61 |
| Saved by compromising or scaling down claims during the year | | 4,250 52 | | 427 18 |
| Claims rejected during the year | 1 | 1,000 00 | | |
| Claims unpaid December 31, 1921 | 22 | $13,667 49 | 8 | $3,921 43 |

## EXHIBIT OF POLICIES OR CERTIFICATES—WEEKLY PREMIUM POLICIES.

| | Total business of the year. | | Business in Illinois during year. | |
|---|---|---|---|---|
| | Number. | Amount. | Number. | Amount. |
| Policies or certificates in force December 31, 1920, as per last statement | 7,711 | $1,479,191.00 | 3,896 | $821,269 00 |
| Policies or certificates written during the year | 388 | 78,321 00 | 343 | 62,125 00 |
| Policies or certificates revived during the year | 380 | 79,813 00 | 255 | 55,367 00 |
| Total | 8,479 | $1,637,325 00 | 4,494 | $938,761 00 |
| Deduct terminated or decreased during the year | 2,069 | 430,554 00 | 1,318 | 289,116 00 |
| Total policies or certificates in force December 31, 1921 | 6,410 | $1,206,771 00 | 3,176 | $649,645 00 |

## EXHIBIT OF DEATH CLAIMS—WEEKLY PREMIUM POLICIES.

| | Total claims. | | Illinois claims. | |
|---|---|---|---|---|
| | Number. | Amount. | Number. | Amount. |
| Claims unpaid December 31, 1920, as per last statement | 8 | $ 1,862 00 | 4 | $ 1,045 00 |
| Claims reported during the year | 102 | 17,812 90 | 68 | 11,317 50 |
| Total | 110 | $19,674 90 | 72 | $12,362 50 |
| Claims paid during the year | 102 | 15,930 65 | 67 | 10,140 25 |
| Balance | 8 | $3,744 25 | 5 | $2,222 25 |
| Saved by compromising or scaling down claims during the year | -------- | 2,465 25 | -------- | 1,394 25 |
| Claims rejected during the year | 7 | 1,156 00 | 4 | 705 00 |
| Claims unpaid December 31, 1921 | 1 | $123 00 | 1 | $123 00 |

## EXHIBIT OF PERMANENT DISABILITY CLAIMS.

| | Total claims. | | Illinois claims. | |
|---|---|---|---|---|
| | Number. | Amount. | Number. | Amount. |
| Claims adjusted by mutual consent during the year, of policies to the number and face value as follows | 29 | $14,478 00 | 5 | $2,750 00 |
| Claims paid during the year | 29 | 4,645 43 | 5 | 875 00 |
| Difference between face value of policies and amount paid | -------- | $9,832 57 | -------- | $1.875 00 |

## SCHEDULE D—PART 1.

| Description. | Book value. | Par value. | Market value. |
|---|---|---|---|
| Liberty Bonds— | | | |
| First, 3½s, 1932, 47 | $18,315 00 | $20,000 00 | $19,000 00 |
| First, 3½s, 1932, 1947 | 9,300 00 | 10,000 00 | 9,500 00 |
| First convertible, 4½s, 1932, 1947 | 890 00 | 1,000 00 | 970 00 |
| First, convertible, 4½s, 1932, 1947 | 907 50 | 1,000 00 | 970 00 |
| Second, 4¼s, 1927, 1942 | 435 00 | 500 00 | 485 00 |
| Second, 4¼s, 1927, 1942 | 4,400 00 | 5,000 00 | 4,850 00 |
| Second, 4¼s, 1927, 1942 | 1,305 00 | 1,500 00 | 1,455 00 |
| Second, 4¼s, 1927, 1942 | 2,625 00 | 3,000 00 | 2,910 00 |
| Third, 4¼s, 1928 | 4,540 00 | 5,000 00 | 4,900 00 |
| Third, 4¼s, 1928 | 9,113 00 | 10,000 00 | 9,800 00 |
| Third, 4¼s, 1928 | 9,210 00 | 10,000 00 | 9,800 00 |
| Fourth, 4¼s, 1933, 1938 | 500 00 | 500 00 | 485 00 |
| Fourth, 4¼s, 1933, 1938 | 3,948 75 | 4,500 00 | 4,365 00 |
| Fourth, 4¼s, 1933, 1938 | 4,625 00 | 5,000 00 | 4,850 00 |
| Fourth, 4¼s, 1933, 1938 | 4,900 00 | 5,000 00 | 4,850 00 |
| Victory, 4¾s, 1923, 1922 | 7,642 00 | 8,000 00 | 8,000 00 |
| Ft. Wayne, Bluffton & Marion Traction Co., 5s, 1935 | 11,400 00 | 12,000 00 | 5,400 00 |
| Ft. Wayne, Van Wert & Lima Traction Co., 5s, 1930 | 9,500 00 | 10,000 00 | 3,400 00 |
| Muncie, Hartford & Ft. Wayne, Ry., 5s, 1935, 1925 | 9,000 00 | 9,000 00 | 3,240 00 |
| Vicksburg Light & Traction Co., 5s, 1932 | 16,150 00 | 17,000 00 | 10,200 00 |
| Eastern Montana Light & Power Co., 6s, 1932 | 14,250 00 | 15,000 00 | 9,000 00 |
| Washington, Idaho Water, Light & Power Co., 6s, 1941 | 15,300 00 | 17,000 00 | 10,200 00 |
| Totals | $158,256 25 | $170,000 00 | $128,630 00 |

## EXPRESSMEN'S MUTUAL BENEFIT ASSOCIATION.

Incorporated January 12, 1897; commenced business in Illinois January 12, 1897; home office, 136 Liberty Street, New York, New York.

E. A. STEDMAN, President. W. E. SCOTT, Secretary.

| | |
|---|---|
| Balance from previous year | $910,840 85 |

INCOME.

| | |
|---|---|
| First year's assessments or premiums | $371,061 22 |
| Subsequent years' assessments or premiums | 137,623 25 |
| Interest and premium notes | 7,077 53 |
| Net amount received from applicants and members | $515,762 00 |
| Interest on bonds and dividends on stocks | 36,933 71 |
| Interest on bank deposits | 1,022 46 |
| Interest from all other sources | 2,192 88 |
| Total income | $555,911 05 |
| Sum | $1,466,751 90 |

DISBURSEMENTS.

| | |
|---|---|
| Death claims | $113,500 00 |
| Surrendered for cash | 14,140 88 |
| Total payments to members | $127,640 88 |
| Commissions and fees paid to agents on account of first year's fees, dues, assessments, or premiums | 103,464 53 |
| Salaries of officers and trustees | 4,600 00 |
| Other compensation of officers and trustees | 300 00 |
| Salaries of office employees | 13,751 61 |
| Salaries and fees paid to medical examiners | 52,988 40 |
| Collection and remittance of assessments, etc | 4,915 33 |
| Insurance department's fees and licenses | 10 00 |
| Federal taxes | 12,739 54 |
| Rent | 3,022 50 |
| Advertising, printing and stationery | 3,137 72 |
| Postage, express, telegraph and telephone | 1,566 45 |
| Legal expenses in litigating claims | 2,942 14 |
| Other legal expenses | 309 00 |
| Furniture and fixtures | 1,055 30 |
| Rent of vault | 138 55 |
| Miscellaneous | 587 52 |
| Loss on sale or maturity of ledger assets | 1,242 08 |
| Total disbursements | $334,411 55 |
| Balance | $1,132,340 35 |

LEDGER ASSETS.

| | |
|---|---|
| Book value of bonds and stocks | $991,982 98 |
| Deposits in trust companies and banks on interest | 13,544 26 |
| Other ledger assets, viz: Policy liens, $31,557.11; loans to members, $95,256.00 | 126,813 11 |
| Total ledger assets | $1,132,340 35 |

NON-LEDGER ASSETS.

| | |
|---|---|
| Interest accrued on bonds | 12,412 69 |
| Mortuary assessments due or unpaid on last call | 50,596 67 |
| Gross assets | $1,195,349 71 |

DEDUCT ASSETS NOT ADMITTED.

| | |
|---|---|
| Book value of bonds and stocks over market value | 17,323 56 |
| Total admitted assets | $1,178,026 15 |

LIABILITIES.

| | | |
|---|---|---|
| Death claims due and unpaid | | $5,500 00 |
| Commissions to agents due or accrued | | 2,120 00 |
| Taxes due or accrued | | 631 20 |
| Advance premiums or assessments | | 2,632 73 |
| Reserve or emergency fund | $1,012,189 00 | |
| Medical examinations | 4,724 30 | |
| Incidental expense | 90 50 | |
| | | 1,017,003 80 |
| Total | | $1,027,887 73 |

EXHIBIT OF POLICIES OR CERTIFICATES.

| | Total business of the year. Number. | Amount. | Business in Illinois during year. Number. | Amount. |
|---|---|---|---|---|
| Policies or certificates in force December 31, 1920, as per last statement | 11,593 | $13,465,341 00 | 1,913 | $2,222,091 00 |
| Policies or certificates written during the year | 12,337 | 13,750,500 00 | 1,473 | 1,502,409 00 |
| Total | 23,930 | $27,215,841 00 | 3,386 | $3,724,500 00 |
| Deduct terminated or decreased during the year | 2,939 | 3,731,950 00 | 459 | 528,000 00 |
| Total policies or certificates in force December 31, 1921 | 20,991 | $23,483,891 00 | 2,927 | $3,196,500 00 |

Received during the year from members in Illinois: Mortuary, $72,606.52; expense, $3,821.40; total — $76,427 92

EXHIBIT OF DEATH CLAIMS.

| | Total claims. Number. | Amount. | Illinois claims. Number. | Amount. |
|---|---|---|---|---|
| Claims unpaid December 31, 1920, as per last statement | 4 | $ 4,000 00 | 1 | $ 1,000 00 |
| Claims reported during the year | 85 | 115,000 00 | 14 | 17,500 00 |
| Total | 89 | $119,000 00 | 15 | $18,500 00 |
| Claims paid during the year | 83 | 113,500 00 | 13 | 16,500 00 |
| Claims unpaid December 31, 1921 | 6 | $5,500 00 | 2 | $2,000 00 |

---

## GUARANTEE FUND LIFE ASSOCIATION.

Incorporated December, 1901; commenced business in Illinois, July 5, 1912; home office, Brandeis Theatre Building, Omaha, Nebraska.

J. C. BUFFINGTON, President. R. E. LANGDON, Secretary.

| | |
|---|---|
| Balance from previous year | $4,061,153 33 |
| *Less memo suspense fund account advance premiums | 7,349 90 |
| Balance | $4,053,803 43 |

INCOME.

| | |
|---|---|
| First year's assessments or premiums | $ 537,199 98 |
| Subsequent year's assessments or premiums | 1,685,154 88 |
| Other payments by applicants and members, viz: Disability, $4,700.53; re-insurance, $62,613.62; double indemnity, $33,908.59 | 101,222 74 |
| Total received from applicants and members | $2,323,577 60 |
| Deduct payments returned to applicants and members declined and withdrawn | 33,874 03 |
| Net amount received from applicants and members | $2,289,703 57 |
| Interest on mortgage loans | 174,299 70 |
| Interest on bonds | 35,595 22 |
| Interest on bank deposits | 11,579 98 |
| Interest from all other sources | 1,319 11 |
| Gross rents from association's property | 2,031 30 |
| Bonus received on new loans | 13,934 00 |
| Total income | $2,528,462 88 |
| Sum | $6,582,266 31 |

## DISBURSEMENTS.

| | |
|---|---|
| Death claims | $621,479 60 |
| Old age benefits | 400 00 |
| Total payments to members | $621,879 60 |
| Commissions and fees paid to agents on account of first year's fees, dues, assessments, or premiums | 471,805 21 |
| Commissions and fees paid to agents on account of subsequent years' fees, dues, assessments or premiums | 60,477 10 |
| Salaries of officers and trustees | 66,533 67 |
| Salaries of office employees | 96,536 67 |
| Salaries and fees paid to medical examiners | 63,355 94 |
| Traveling and other expenses of officers, trustees and committees | 2,169 29 |
| Traveling and other expenses of managers and agents | 1,314 75 |
| Collection and remittance of assessments, etc | 7,965 26 |
| Insurance department's fees and licenses | 4,083 72 |
| Taxes on assessments or premiums | 32,275 77 |
| Other taxes, viz: City, county and other, $1,189.28; real estate, $1,341.96; war tax insurance issued, $23,262.20 | 25,793 44 |
| Rent | 15,843 80 |
| Advertising, printing and stationery | 34,932 12 |
| Postage, express, telegraph and telephone | 19,151 90 |
| Legal expenses | 923 78 |
| Furniture and fixtures | 10,510 76 |
| Miscellaneous | 15,087 22 |
| Office supplies | 10,903 49 |
| Organization | 6,900 00 |
| Interest on installment claims | 370 65 |
| Re-insurance premiums | 29,578 39 |
| Indemnity premiums | 25,516 26 |
| Investigation of risks and claims | 15,939 38 |
| Total disbursements | $1,639,848 17 |
| Balance | $4,942,418 14 |
| *Add memo suspense fund, advance premiums | 2,702 25 |
| Total | $4,945,120 39 |

## LEDGER ASSETS.

| | |
|---|---|
| Book value of real estate | $ 110,750 00 |
| Mortgage loans on real estate | 3,704,060 00 |
| Book value of bonds | 702,850 00 |
| Cash in association's office | 59 18 |
| Deposits in trust companies and banks not on interest | 386 85 |
| Deposits in trust companies and banks on interest | 293,244 44 |
| Agents' balances (debit, $84,047.83; credit, $269.18) | 83,778 65 |
| Bills receivable | 49,991 27 |
| Total ledger assets | $4,945,120 39 |

### NON-LEDGER ASSETS.

| | |
|---|---|
| Interest and rents due and accrued | 108,591 82 |
| Gross assets | $5,053,712 21 |

### DEDUCT ASSETS NOT ADMITTED.

| | | |
|---|---|---|
| Agents' debit balances | $84,047 83 | |
| Bills receivable | 49,991 27 | |
| | | 134,039 10 |
| Total admitted assets | | $4,919,673 11 |

## LIABILITIES.

| | | |
|---|---|---|
| Death claims reported during the year but not yet adjusted | $ 28,000 00 | |
| Present value of deferred death and disability claims payable in installments | 449,986 44 | |
| Total unpaid claims | | $477,986 44 |
| Salaries, rents, expenses, etc., due or accrued | | 15,000 00 |
| Taxes due or accrued | | 30,000 00 |
| Advance premiums or assessments | | 2,702 25 |
| Total | | $525,688 69 |

* This consists of advance policy payments received from members placed temporarily to their credit in this fund until properly distributed into the correct accounts or funds to which they apply.

EXHIBIT OF POLICIES OR CERTIFICATES.

| | Total business of the year. Number. | Amount. | Business in Illinois during year. Number. | Amount. |
|---|---|---|---|---|
| Policies or certificates in force December 31, 1920, as per last statement | 51,154 | $137,071,500 00 | 1,449 | $4,045,500 00 |
| Policies or certificates written during the year | 12,175 | 29,175,000 00 | 427 | 1,332,000 00 |
| Policies or certificates revived during the year | 1,546 | 3,587,500 00 | 35 | 93,500 00 |
| Policies or certificates increased during the year | | | 93 | 252,000 00 |
| Total | 64,875 | $169,834,000 00 | 2,004 | $5,723,000 00 |
| Deduct terminated or decreased during the year | 13,038 | 27,938,500 00 | 358 | 878,000 00 |
| Total policies or certificates in force December 31, 1921 | 51,837 | $141,895,500 00 | 1,646 | $4,845,000 00 |

Received during the year from members in Illinois: Mortuary, $40,576.28; re-insurance, $535.43; expense, $31,786.21; Total ........ $72,897 92

EXHIBIT OF DEATH CLAIMS.

| | Total claims. Number. | Amount. | Illinois claims. Number. | Amount. |
|---|---|---|---|---|
| Claims unpaid December 31, 1920, as per last statement | 187 | $423,306 79 | 2 | $ 6,000 00 |
| Claims reported during the year | 257 | 666,224 20 | 6 | 16,500 00 |
| Interest addition on account of installment claims | | 33,956 26 | | |
| Total | 444 | $1,123,487 25 | 8 | $22,500 00 |
| Claims paid during the year | 228 | 621,879 60 | 8 | 22,500 00 |
| Balance | 216 | $501,607 65 | | |
| Saved by compromising or scaling down claims during the year | | 23,621 21 | | |
| Claims unpaid December 31, 1921 | 216 | $477,986 44 | | |

EXHIBIT OF OLD AGE AND OTHER CLAIMS.

| | Total claims—all in Illinois. Number. | Amount. |
|---|---|---|
| Claims reported during the year and interest addition | 2 | $400 00 |
| Claims paid during the year | 2 | 400 00 |

## THE KNIGHTS TEMPLARS AND MASONIC MUTUAL AID ASSSOCIATION.

Incorporated October, 1877; commenced business in Illinois May 3, 1906; home office, No. 212 United Bank Building, Cincinnati, Ohio.

WM. B. MELISH, President. ARTHUR J. DAVIES, Secretary.

Balance from previous year ........ $436,566 92

INCOME.

| | |
|---|---|
| Membership fees actually received | $ 18 00 |
| First year's assessments or premiums | 3,016 86 |
| Subsequent years' assessments or premiums | 398,373 82 |
| Deduction, error of age | 16 72 |
| Net amount received from applicants and members | $401,425 40 |
| Interest on bonds | 17,960 00 |
| Gross rents from association's property | 2,275 00 |
| Ground rents | 330 00 |
| Total income | $421,990 40 |
| Sum | $858,557 32 |

DISBURSEMENTS.

| | |
|---|---|
| Death claims | $353,500 00 |
| Commissions and fees paid to agents on account of subsequent year's fees, dues, assessments or premiums | 6,109 50 |
| Salaries of managers or agents | 1,820 00 |
| Salaries of officers and trustees | 8,700 00 |
| Other compensation of officers and trustees | 50 00 |
| Salaries and other compensation of committees | 990 00 |
| Salaries of office employees | 3,514 50 |
| Salaries and fees paid to medical examiners | 684 00 |

DISBURSEMENTS—Concluded.

| | | |
|---|---|---|
| Traveling and other expenses of officers, trustees and committees | | $ 47 31 |
| Traveling and other expenses of managers and agents | | 3,522 80 |
| Collection and remittance of assessments, etc | | 1,695 43 |
| Insurance department's fees and licenses | | 178 60 |
| Other licenses and fees | | 102 09 |
| Taxes on assessments or premiums | | 1,949 96 |
| Internal revenue tax | | 25 00 |
| Real estate taxes | | 371 84 |
| Rent | | 900 00 |
| Advertising, printing and stationery | | 2,314 75 |
| Postage, express, telegraph and telephone | | 2,756 17 |
| Legal expenses in litigating claims | | 1,000 00 |
| Other legal expenses | | 129 40 |
| Repairs and expenses on real estate other than taxes | | 986 17 |
| Mutual life underwriters | | 125 00 |
| Advance assessments applied on balance and sums received during year | | 105 74 |
| Loss on sale or maturity of ledger assets | | 601 67 |
| Total disbursements | | $392,179 93 |
| Balance | | $466,377 39 |

LEDGER ASSETS.

| | | |
|---|---|---|
| Book value of real estate | | $ 7,773 90 |
| Mortgage loans on real estate | | 7,500 00 |
| Book value of bonds | | 369,000 00 |
| Cash in association's office | | 283 45 |
| Deposits in trust companies and banks not on interest | | 72,659 46 |
| Ground rents | | 5,500 00 |
| Furniture and fixtures | | 3,660 58 |
| Total ledger assets | | $466,377 39 |

NON-LEDGER ASSETS.

| | | |
|---|---|---|
| Interest and rents due and accrued | | 2,760 95 |
| Market value of real estate over book value | | 4,176 10 |
| Mortuary assessments due or unpaid on last call | | 92,000 00 |
| Gross assets | | $565,314 44 |

DEDUCT ASSETS NOT ADMITTED.

| | | |
|---|---|---|
| Book value of bonds over market value | $13,935 00 | |
| Furniture and fixtures | 3,660 58 | |
| | | 17,595 58 |
| Total admitted assets | | $547,718 86 |

LIABILITIES.

| | | |
|---|---|---|
| Death claims due and unpaid | $ 2,500 00 | |
| Death claims adjusted not yet due | 59,000 00 | |
| Death claims reported during the year but not yet adjusted | 1,000 00 | |
| Death claims incurred in 1921, not reported until 1922 | 13,000 00 | |
| Total unpaid claims | | $75,500 00 |
| Salaries, rents, expenses, etc., due or accrued | | 22 21 |
| Commissions to agents due or accrued | | 187 00 |
| Taxes due or accrued | | 130 50 |
| Advance premiums or assessments | | 689 47 |
| Total | | $76,529 18 |

EXHIBIT OF POLICIES OR CERTIFICATES.

| | Total business of the year. | | Business in Illinois during year. | |
|---|---|---|---|---|
| | Number. | Amount. | Number. | Amount. |
| Policies or certificates in force December 31, 1920, as per last statement | 5,086 | $10,209,000 00 | 480 | $785,000 00 |
| Policies or certificates written during the year | 227 | 561,000 00 | 17 | 44,000 00 |
| Policies or certificates increased during the year | | 5,000 00 | | |
| Total | 5,313 | $10,775,000 00 | 497 | 829,000 00 |
| Deduct terminated or decreased during the year | 339 | 804,000 00 | -39 | 71,000 00 |
| Total policies or certificates in force December 31, 1921 | 4,974 | $9,971,000 00 | 458 | $758,000 00 |

Received during the year from members in Illinois: Mortuary, $12,384.40; expense, $2,028.00; total $14,412 40

EXHIBIT OF DEATH CLAIMS.

| | Total claims. Number. | Amount. | Illinois claims. Number. | Amount. |
|---|---|---|---|---|
| Claims unpaid December 31, 1920, as per last statement | 47 | $111,000 00 | | |
| Claims reported during the year | 130 | 318,000 00 | 5 | $9,000 00 |
| Total | 177 | $429,000 00 | 5 | $9,000 00 |
| Claims paid during the year | 145 | 353,500 00 | 4 | 8,000 00 |
| Claims unpaid December 31, 1921 | 32 | $75,500 00 | 1 | $1,000 00 |

---

## NATIONAL LIFE ASSOCIATION.

Incorporated October 24, 1899; commenced business in Illinois August 8, 1905; home office, Des Moines, Iowa.

JAMES P. HEWITT, President. A. W. LAYMAN, Secretary.

| | |
|---|---|
| Balance from previous year | $1,176,809 60 |

INCOME.

| | |
|---|---|
| Membership fees actually received | $237,156 82 |
| Subsequent years' assessments or premiums | 945,835 21 |
| Advance premiums, accumulation payments, change of beneficiary and duplicate policy fees | 5,742 63 |
| Total received from applicants and members | $1,188,734 66 |
| Deduct payments returned to applicants and members | 23,352 50 |
| Net amount received from applicants and members | $1,165,382 16 |
| Interest on mortgage loans | 63,764 99 |
| Interest on bonds | 4,834 34 |
| Interest on bank deposits | 3,344 22 |
| Interest from all other sources | 72 96 |
| Re-insurance | 5,000 00 |
| Total income | $1,242,398 67 |
| Sum | $2,419,208 27 |

DISBURSEMENTS.

| | |
|---|---|
| Death claims | $450,618 85 |
| Permanent disability claims | 2,850 00 |
| Old age benefits | 3,450 00 |
| Advanced premiums applied and installment claims and interest | 6,761 77 |
| Total payments to members | $463,680 62 |
| Commissions and fees paid to agents on account of first year's fees, dues, assessments, or premiums | 188,795 69 |
| Commissions and fees paid to agents on account of subsequent years' fees, dues, assessments or premiums | 18,039 35 |
| Salaries of managers or agents | 7,694 58 |
| Salaries of officers and trustees | 31,750 00 |
| Salaries of office employees | 54,847 42 |
| Salaries and fees paid to medical examiners | 19,528 50 |
| Traveling and other expenses of managers and agents | 5,851 96 |
| Collection and remittance of assessments, etc | 4,038 70 |
| Insurance department's fees and licenses | 2,139 56 |
| Taxes on assessments or premiums | 20,000 17 |
| U. S. capital stock tax, government tax on insurance, real estate | 8,760 15 |
| Rent | 4,500 00 |
| Advertising, printing and stationery | 21,406 86 |
| Postage, express, telegraph and telephone | 10,784 67 |
| Legal expenses in litigating claims | 792 76 |
| Furniture and fixtures | 5,373 60 |
| Sundry items | 12,116 01 |
| Inspection service | 6,457 07 |
| Re-insurance premiums | 7,192 71 |
| Decrease in book value of ledger assets | 9 88 |
| Total disbursements | $893,760 26 |
| Balance | $1,525,448 01 |

## LEDGER ASSETS.

| | |
|---|---|
| Book value of real estate | $ 11,460 90 |
| Mortgage loans on real estate | 1,237,336 25 |
| Book value of bonds, less amount deducted in adjustment, $9.88 | 112,866 12 |
| Cash in association's office | 7,043 12 |
| Deposits in trust companies and banks not on interest | 120,872 39 |
| Deposits in trust companies and banks on interest | 16,885 76 |
| Agents' balances (debit, $19,197.92; credit, $214.45) | 18,983 47 |
| Total ledger assets | $1,525,448 01 |

### NON-LEDGER ASSETS.

| | | |
|---|---|---|
| Interest due and accrued | | 29,850 28 |
| Premiums or assessments actually collected by depository banks but not yet turned over to association | | 22,452 37 |
| Mortuary premiums or assessments due and unpaid | | 190,346 60 |
| Gross assets | | $1,768,097 26 |

### DEDUCT ASSETS NOT ADMITTED.

| | | |
|---|---|---|
| Agents' debit balances | $ 19,197 92 | |
| Excess of mortuary assessments due or unpaid on last call over corresponding liability for unpaid claims | 116,846 60 | |
| Mortgage loans in excess of 50 per cent of valuation of property | 16,595 50 | |
| | | 152,640 02 |
| Total admitted assets | | $1,615,457 24 |

## LIABILITIES.

| | | |
|---|---|---|
| Death claims resisted | $ 9,000 00 | |
| Death claims reported during the year but not yet adjusted | 64,500 00 | |
| Death claims incurred in 1921, not reported until 1922 | 1,000 00 | |
| Present value of deferred death and disability claims payable in installments | 7,166 07 | |
| Total death claims | | $81,666 07 |
| Salaries, rents, expenses, etc., due or accrued | | 3,063 64 |
| Taxes due or accrued | | 19,500 00 |
| Advance premiums or assessments | | 1,352 03 |
| Trust funds (accumulation account) | | 590 20 |
| Total | | $106,171 94 |

Valuation of outstanding benefit certificates or policies ascertained as provided by chapter 83, Acts of the Thirty-second General Assembly of Iowa (Actuaries combined experience table of mortality and four per cent interest), $493,604.22.

## EXHIBIT OF POLICIES OR CERTIFICATES.

| | Total business of the year. | | Business in Illinois during year. | |
|---|---|---|---|---|
| | Number. | Amount. | Number. | Amount. |
| Policies or certificates in force December 31, 1920, as per last statement | 35,094 | $72,382,500 00 | 2,347 | $5,555,000 00 |
| Policies or certificates written during the year | 4,937 | 11,235,500 00 | 330 | 878,500 00 |
| Policies or certificates revived during the year | 2,796 | 6,444,500 00 | 206 | 557,500 00 |
| Total | 42,827 | $90,062,500 00 | 2,883 | $6,991,000 00 |
| Deduct terminated or decreased during the year | 8,605 | 18,906,500 00 | 456 | 1,266,000 00 |
| Total policies or certificates in force December 31, 1921 | 34,222 | $71,156,000 00 | 2,427 | $5,725,000 00 |

Received during the year from members in Illinois: Benefit, $61,649.28; general, $34,695.78; total ..... $96,345 06

## EXHIBIT OF DEATH CLAIMS.

| | Total claims. | | Illinois claims. | |
|---|---|---|---|---|
| | Number. | Amount. | Number. | Amount. |
| Claims unpaid December 31, 1920, as per last statement | 27 | $ 52,500 00 | 3 | $ 4,000 00 |
| Claims reported during the year | 247 | 476,000 00 | 17 | 41,500 00 |
| Total | 274 | $528,500 00 | 20 | $45,500 00 |
| Claims paid during the year | 240 | 450,618 85 | 17 | 31,500 00 |
| Balance | 34 | $77,881 15 | 3 | $14,000 00 |
| Saved by compromising or scaling down claims during the year | | 4,381 15 | | |
| Claims unpaid December 31, 1921 | 34 | $73,500 00 | 3 | $14,000 00 |

## EXHIBIT OF PERMANENT DISABILITY CLAIMS.

| | Total claims. | |
|---|---|---|
| | Number. | Amount. |
| Claims reported during the year and interest addition | 4 | $2,850 00 |
| Claims paid during the year | 4 | 2,850 00 |

## EXHIBIT OF OLD AGE AND OTHER CLAIMS.

| | Total claims. | |
|---|---|---|
| | Number. | Amount. |
| Claims reported during the year and interest addition | 28 | $3,450 00 |
| Claims paid during the year | 28 | 3,450 00 |

# FRATERNAL BENEFICIARY SOCIETIES COMPLYING WITH THE LAWS OF ILLINOIS FOR THE YEAR 1922.

## Society Statements for the Year ending December 31, 1921.

## SOCIETIES OF THIS STATE.

### AMERICAN LITHUANIAN WOMENS ROMAN CATHOLIC ALLIANCE.

Located at No. 923 West Garfield Boulevard, Chicago, Illinois.

MARY JAKOBAITE, President. MARY VAICUINIENE, Secretary.

| | |
|---|---|
| Balance from previous year | $7,116 78 |
| **INCOME.** | |
| Membership fees actually received | $ 276 83 |
| Dues and per capita tax | 10,818 22 |
| Donation for expenses | 582 40 |
| Total received from members | $11,677 45 |
| Deduct payments returned to applicants and members | 21 40 |
| Net amount received from members | $11,656 05 |
| Gross interest on deposits in trust companies and banks | 271 09 |
| Total income | $11,927 14 |
| Sum | $19,043 92 |
| **DISBURSEMENTS.** | |
| Death claims | 300 00 |
| Sick and accident claims | 3,958 22 |
| Total benefits paid | $4,258 22 |
| Salaries of officers and trustees | 553 50 |
| Salaries and fees paid to supreme medical examiners | 22 00 |
| Traveling and other expenses of officers, trustees and committees | 84 95 |
| Insurance department fees | 5 00 |
| Advertising, printing and stationery | 82 17 |
| Postage, express, telegraph and telephone | 61 99 |
| Official publication | 2,783 65 |
| Charity | 39 35 |
| Auditing | 55 00 |
| Surety bond | 50 00 |
| Miscellaneous expenses | 122 22 |
| Total disbursements | $8,118 05 |
| Balance | $10,925 87 |
| **LEDGER ASSETS.** | |
| Cash in association's office | 403 01 |
| Deposits in trust companies and banks not on interest | 373 88 |
| Deposits in trust companies and banks on interest | 10,000 00 |
| Other ledger assets, viz: Interest on bank deposits | 148 98 |
| Total ledger assets | $10,925 87 |
| **NON-LEDGER ASSETS.** | |
| Society pins | 297 28 |
| Gross assets | $11,223 15 |
| **DEDUCT ASSETS NOT ADMITTED.** | |
| Society pins | 297 28 |
| Total admitted assets | $10,925 87 |

EXHIBIT OF CERTIFICATES.

| | Total business of the year. Number. | Amount. | Business in Illinois during year. Number. | Amount. |
|---|---|---|---|---|
| Benefit certificates in force December 31, 1920, as per last statement | 967 | $145,050 00 | 444 | $66,600 00 |
| Benefit certificates written and renewed during the year | 269 | 40,350 00 | 50 | 7,500 00 |
| Totals | 1,236 | $185,400 00 | 494 | $74,100 00 |
| Deduct terminated, decreased or transferred during the year by death | 2 | 300 00 | | |
| Deduct terminated or decreased during the year | | | 1 | 150 00 |
| Total benefit certificates in force December 31, 1921 | 1,234 | $185,100 00 | 493 | $73,950 00 |

Received during the year from members in Illinois: Mortuary, $591.60; reserve, $295.80; sick and accident, $950.00; expense, $825.50; total — $2,662 90

EXHIBIT OF DEATH CLAIMS.

| | Total claims. Number. | Amount. | Illinois claims. Number. | Amount. |
|---|---|---|---|---|
| Claims reported during the year and interest addition | 2 | $300 00 | 1 | $150 00 |
| Claims paid during the year | 2 | 300 00 | 1 | 150 00 |

EXHIBIT OF SICK AND ACCIDENT CLAIMS.

| | Total claims—amount. | Illinois claims—amount. |
|---|---|---|
| Claims reported during the year | $3,958 22 | $1,944 40 |
| Claims paid during the year | 3,958 22 | 1,944 40 |

## BANKER'S INSURANCE CORPORATION.

Located at No. 22 West Monroe Street, Chicago, Illinois.

W. BURTON, President. IRA J. BELL, Treasurer.

| | |
|---|---|
| Balance from previous year | $4,095 68 |

INCOME.

| | |
|---|---|
| Assessments or premiums during first 12 months of membership of which all or an extra percentage is used for expenses | $ 6,591 25 |
| All other assessments or premiums | 19,246 75 |
| Total received from members | $25,838 00 |
| Gross interest on bonds and dividends on stocks | 85 00 |
| For collecting Bankers Union special class | 1,957 15 |
| Rent of linoleum | 5 00 |
| Rent of telephone | 6 50 |
| Refund on insured check | 37 50 |
| Total income | $27,929 15 |
| Sum | $32,024 83 |

DISBURSEMENTS.

| | |
|---|---|
| Death claims | $ 494 00 |
| Sick and accident claims | 7,651 60 |
| Total benefits paid | $8,145 60 |
| Commissions and fees paid to deputies and organizers | 6,596 22 |
| Salaries of deputies and organizers | 640 00 |
| Salaries of officers and trustees | 4,385 00 |
| Salaries of office employees | 2,577 50 |
| Salaries and fees paid to supreme medical examiners | 1,200 00 |
| Salaries and fees paid to subordinate medical examiners | 1,076 00 |
| Insurance department fees | 5 00 |
| Rent | 2,417 40 |
| Advertising, printing and stationery | 503 42 |
| Postage, express, telegraph and telephone | 339 00 |
| Lodge supplies | 61 75 |
| Furniture and fixtures | 111 40 |
| All other disbursements | 103 66 |
| Total disbursements | $28,161 95 |
| Balance | $3,862 88 |

## LEDGER ASSETS.

| | | |
|---|---|---|
| Loans secured by pledge of bonds, stocks or other collateral | | $ 100 00 |
| Book value of bonds and stocks | | 2,000 00 |
| Cash in association's office | | 265 77 |
| Deposits in trust companies and banks not on interest | | 1,497 11 |
| Total ledger assets | | $3,862 88 |
| **NON-LEDGER ASSETS.** | | |
| Assessments actually collected by subordinate lodges not yet turned over to supreme lodge | | 2,324 75 |
| All other assets, viz— | | |
| Furniture and fixtures | $400 00 | |
| Supplies | 200 00 | |
| | | 600 00 |
| Gross assets | | $6,787 63 |
| **DEDUCT ASSETS NOT ADMITTED.** | | |
| Other items, viz— | | |
| Furniture and fixtures | $400 00 | |
| Supplies | 200 00 | |
| | | 600 00 |
| Total admitted assets | | $6,187 63 |

## EXHIBIT OF CERTIFICATES.

| | Total business of the year—all in Illinois Number. | Amount. |
|---|---|---|
| Benefit certificates in force December 31, 1920, as per last statement | 1,472 | $678,370 00 |
| Benefit certificates written and renewed during the year | 505 | 213,000 00 |
| Total | 1,977 | $891,370 00 |
| Deduct terminated, decreased or transferred during the year | 607 | 257,350 00 |
| Total benefit certificates in force December 31, 1921 | 1,370 | $634,020 00 |

Received during the year from members: Mortuary, $494.00; disability $7,863.82; expense, $17,480.18; total ........ $25,838 00

## EXHIBIT OF DEATH CLAIMS.

| | Total claims. Number. | Amount. |
|---|---|---|
| Claims reported during the year and interest addition | 3 | $494 00 |
| Claims paid during the year | 3 | 494 00 |

## EXHIBIT OF SICK AND ACCIDENT CLAIMS.

| | Total claims. Number. | Amount. |
|---|---|---|
| Claims reported during the year | 370 | $7,651 60 |
| Claims paid during the year | 370 | 7,651 60 |

## SCHEDULE D—BONDS.

| Description. | Book value. | Par value. |
|---|---|---|
| Third Liberty Loan, 4¼s | $500 00 | $500 00 |
| Third Liberty Loan, 4¼s | 500 00 | 500 00 |
| Third Liberty Loan, 4¼s | 500 00 | 500 00 |
| Third Liberty Loan, 4¼s | 100 00 | 100 00 |
| Third Liberty Loan, 4¼s | 100 00 | 100 00 |
| Second Liberty Loan, 4¼s | 100 00 | 100 00 |
| Second Liberty Loan, 4¼s | 100 00 | 100 00 |
| Second Liberty Loan, 4¼s | 100 00 | 100 00 |
| Total | $2,000 00 | $2,000 00 |

---

# BENEFIT ASSOCIATION OF RAILWAY EMPLOYEES.

Located at No. 190 North State Street, Chicago, Illinois.

R. A. LEITZ, President. G. M. CULVER, Secretary.

| | |
|---|---|
| Balance from previous year | $353,910 10 |

## INCOME.

| | |
|---|---|
| Assessments or premiums during first months of membership of which all or an extra percentage is used for expenses | $ 36,342 58 |
| All other assessments or premiums | 948,500 21 |
| Dues and per capita tax | 64,247 20 |
| Total received from members | $1,049,089 99 |
| Deduct payments returned to applicants and members | 10,087 67 |
| Net amount received from members | $1,039,002 32 |

INCOME—Concluded.

| | |
|---|---|
| Gross interest on bonds and dividends on stocks | 12,235 85 |
| Gross interest on deposits in trust companies and banks | 2,382 59 |
| Sale of lodge supplies | 104 43 |
| Return claim payments account of draft not presented | 637 42 |
| Total income | $1,054,362 61 |
| Sum | $1,408,272 71 |

DISBURSEMENTS.

| | |
|---|---|
| Death claims | $ 6,500 00 |
| Permanent disability claims | 428,880 52 |
| Total benefits paid | $435,380 52 |
| Salaries of deputies and organizers | 135,519 52 |
| Salaries of officers and trustees | 28,288 47 |
| Salaries of office employees | 62,418 70 |
| Salaries and fees paid to supreme medical examiners | 1,800 00 |
| Salaries and fees paid to subordinate medical examiners | 2,196 20 |
| Traveling and other expenses of officers, trustees and committees | 11,470 28 |
| For collection and remittance of assessments and dues | 27,354 78 |
| Insurance department fees | 1,933 12 |
| Rent | 8,762 42 |
| Advertising, printing and stationery | 14,090 24 |
| Postage, express, telegraph and telephone | 5,908 18 |
| Official publication | 54,996 00 |
| Expenses of supreme lodge meeting | 2,459 90 |
| Legal expense in litigating claims | 232 55 |
| Other legal expenses | 4,109 30 |
| Taxes, repairs and other expenses on real estate | 40 44 |
| Gross loss on sale or maturity of bond premiums of officers | 830 05 |
| Gross decrease in book value of expense of securing ded. privileges from railway companies | 6,185 85 |
| All other disbursements: Re-insurance | 51 57 |
| Per capita returned to lodge | 53,819 91 |
| Exchange on bank deposits | 726 12 |
| Fire insurance premiums | 31 81 |
| Audits | 2,129 15 |
| Total disbursements | $860,735 08 |
| Balance | $547,537 63 |

LEDGER ASSETS.

| | |
|---|---|
| Book value of bonds and stocks | $411,937 47 |
| Cash in association's office | 100 00 |
| Deposits in trust companies and banks on interest | 134,644 16 |
| Deposit state of Wisconsin war savings stamps | 832 00 |
| Note on life certificate loan | 24 00 |
| Total ledger assets | $547,537 63 |

NON-LEDGER ASSETS.

| | |
|---|---|
| Interest and rents due and accrued | 4,914 18 |
| Market value of bonds and stocks over book value | 19,484 03 |
| Assessments actually collected by subordinate lodges not yet turned over to supreme lodge | 85,500 00 |
| Due from organizers | 19,902 94 |
| Gross assets | $677,338 78 |

DEDUCT ASSETS NOT ADMITTED.

| | |
|---|---|
| Balance due from organizers not secured by bonds | 19,902 94 |
| Total admitted assets | $657,435 84 |

LIABILITIES.

| | |
|---|---|
| Death claims reported during the year but not yet adjusted | 1,000 00 |
| Sick and accident claims reported during the year but not yet adjusted | 51,170 40 |
| Total sick and accident claims | $52,170 40 |
| Salaries, rents, expenses, commissions, etc., due or accrued | 5,748 12 |
| Total | $57,918 52 |

## EXHIBIT OF CERTIFICATES.

| | Total business of the year. | | Business in Illinois during year. | |
|---|---|---|---|---|
| | Number. | Amount. | Number. | Amount. |
| Benefit certificates in force December 31, 1920, as per last statement | 57,047 | $2,827,500 00 | 8,353 | $265,500 00 |
| Benefit certificates written and renewed during the year | 26,507 | 864,000 00 | 3,376 | 99,500 00 |
| Benefit certificates increased during the year | -------- | 6,500 00 | -------- | 1,000 00 |
| Total | 83,554 | $3,698,000 00 | 11,729 | $366,000 00 |
| Deduct terminated, decreased or transferred during the year | 19,398 | 815,000 00 | -------- | ------------ |
| Deduct terminated or decreased during the year | -------- | ------------ | 2,677 | 38,500 00 |
| Total benefit certificates in force December 31, 1921 | 64,156 | $2,883,000 00 | 9,052 | $327,500 00 |

Received during the year from members in Illinois: Mortuary, $5,336.44; sick and accident, $77,187.87; expense, $54,579.86; total $137,104 17

## EXHIBIT OF DEATH CLAIMS.

| | Total claims. | | Illinois claims. | |
|---|---|---|---|---|
| | Number. | Amount. | Number. | Amount. |
| Claims reported during the year and interest addition | 8 | $7,500 00 | 2 | $1,500 00 |
| Claims paid during the year | 7 | 6,500 00 | 2 | 1,500 00 |
| Claims unpaid December 31, 1921 | 1 | $1,000 00 | -------- | ------------ |

## EXHIBIT OF SICK AND ACCIDENT CLAIMS.

| | Total claims. | | Illinois claims. | |
|---|---|---|---|---|
| | Number. | Amount. | Number. | Amount. |
| Claims unpaid December 31, 1920, as per last statement | 762 | $ 30,159 96 | 118 | $ 4,670 44 |
| Claims reported during the year | 9,309 | 449,890 96 | 1,232 | 28,079 13 |
| Total | 10,071 | $480,050 92 | 1,350 | $32,749 57 |
| Claims paid during the year | 8,633 | 428,880 52 | 1,185 | 26,042 77 |
| Claims rejected during the year | 408 | ------------ | 30 | ------------ |
| Claims unpaid December 31, 1921 | 1,030 | $51,170 40 | 135 | $6,706 80 |

## SCHEDULE D—BONDS.

| Description. | Book value. | Par value. | Market value. |
|---|---|---|---|
| Liberty Loan, 1st conv., 4¼s | $12,924 00 | $15,000 00 | $14,550 00 |
| Liberty Loan, 1st conv., 4¼s | 10,000 00 | 10,000 00 | 10,000 00 |
| Liberty Loan, 2d conv., 4¼s | 10,000 00 | 10,000 00 | 10,000 00 |
| Liberty Loan, 2d conv., 4¼s | 13,048 00 | 14,000 00 | 13,580 00 |
| Liberty Loan, 3d conv., 4¼s | 20,000 00 | 20,000 00 | 20,000 00 |
| Liberty Loan, 4th conv., 4¼s | 26,000 00 | 26,000 00 | 26,000 00 |
| Victory Loan, 5th conv., 4¾s | 15,000 00 | 15,000 00 | 15,000 00 |
| South Dakota, rural credit, 5s | 15,000 00 | 15,000 00 | 15,450 00 |
| South Dakota, rural credit, 5½s | 11,640 00 | 12,000 00 | 12,840 00 |
| State of Michigan, highway, 5½s | 7,332 50 | 7,000 00 | 8,120 00 |
| Arkansas County, Ark., road, 5s | 4,385 80 | 5,000 00 | 4,800 00 |
| Ada County, Idaho, road, 5s | 12,394 55 | 13,000 00 | 12,610 00 |
| Alberta City, Iowa, school, 6s | 15,324 00 | 15,000 00 | 15,324 00 |
| Brown County, Wis., road, 5s | 6,658 10 | 7,000 00 | 7,420 00 |
| Cleveland, Ohio, school, 6s | 31,161 00 | 30,000 00 | 32,700 00 |
| Clinton County, Iowa, 5s | 24,225 00 | 25,000 00 | 25,250 00 |
| Crawfordsville, Iowa, school, 6s | 15,322 50 | 15,000 00 | 15,322 50 |
| DeSota, Iowa, school, 6s | 10,215 00 | 10,000 00 | 10,215 00 |
| Douglass County, Neb., court house, 5s | 4,710 50 | 5,000 00 | 5,150 00 |
| Elmhurst, Ill., school, 5s | 9,599 10 | 10,000 00 | 10,200 00 |
| Egan, S. D., school, 6½s | 6,202 80 | 6,000 00 | 6,720 00 |
| Fallon County, Mont., road, 5½s | 4,689 62 | 5,000 00 | 5,300 00 |
| Green County, Iowa, funding, 5¾s | 15,000 00 | 15,000 00 | 15,000 00 |
| Indianapolis, Ind., school, 4¾s | 9,100 00 | 10,000 00 | 10,300 00 |
| Jackson, Tenn., school, 6s | 5,000 00 | 5,000 00 | 5,250 00 |
| Kalamazoo, Mich., 5s | 1,909 20 | 2,000 00 | 2,060 00 |
| Mahoning County, 6s | 10,000 00 | 10,000 00 | 10,900 00 |
| Mt. Airy, N. C., school, 5s | 5,000 00 | 5,000 00 | 5,000 00 |
| Napoleon, Ohio, 5s | 10,000 00 | 10,000 00 | 10,400 00 |
| Niles, Mich., 5s | 4,809 50 | 5,000 00 | 5,150 00 |
| Pocahontas County, Iowa, 6s | 2,049 50 | 2,000 00 | 2,120 00 |
| Sutter County, Cal., recl., 6s | 15,000 00 | 15,000 00 | 16,650 00 |
| Superior, Wis., school, 5s | 4,711 00 | 5,000 00 | 5,100 00 |
| Sac County, Iowa, 5¾s | 10,000 00 | 10,000 00 | 11,100 00 |
| Wood County, Wis., highway, 5s | 7,570 30 | 8,000 00 | 8,080 00 |
| Woodstock, Ill., H. S. D., 5s | 955 50 | 1,000 00 | 1,010 00 |
| Youngstown, Ohio, street, 6s | 25,000 00 | 25,000 00 | 26,750 00 |
| Total | $411,937 47 | $418,000 00 | $431,421 50 |

## BOHEMIAN AMERICAN FORESTERS.

Located at No. 3334 West Twenty-third Street, Chicago, Illinois.

ZIKMUND CHOBOTSKY, President. VACLAV T. HAJEK, Secretary.

| | |
|---|---|
| Balance from previous year | $64,468 69 |

### INCOME.

| | |
|---|---|
| All other assessments or premiums | $31,604 17 |
| Other payments by members, viz: Certificate fees | 78 50 |
| Net amount received from members | $31,682 67 |
| Gross interest on bonds | 2,622 23 |
| Gross interest from all other sources | 117 18 |
| Gross profit on sale or maturity of ledger assets | 395 80 |
| Annual celebration | 1,279 54 |
| Total income | $36,097 42 |
| Sum | $100,566 11 |

### DISBURSEMENTS.

| | |
|---|---|
| Death claims | $23,550 00 |
| Commissions and fees paid to members | 237 00 |
| Salaries of officers and trustees | 1,072 00 |
| Salaries and other compensation of committees | 45 00 |
| Insurance department fees | 5 00 |
| Rent | 21 00 |
| Advertising, printing and stationery | 269 85 |
| Postage, express, telegraph and telephone | 96 98 |
| Lodge supplies | 149 17 |
| Official publication | 882 65 |
| Expenses of convention | 55 95 |
| Bonding of officers | 20 00 |
| Insurance of treasurer | 12 50 |
| Donations to Bohemian free schools | 552 00 |
| Donations to organizations and charity | 80 00 |
| Total disbursements | $27,049 10 |
| Balance | $73,517 01 |

### LEDGER ASSETS.

| | |
|---|---|
| Book value of bonds | $64,500 00 |
| Deposits in banks on interest | 9,017 01 |
| Total ledger assets | $73,517 01 |

#### NON-LEDGER ASSETS.

| | |
|---|---|
| Interest accrued | 22 52 |
| Interest from bank | 8 10 |
| Gross assets | $73,547 63 |

#### DEDUCT ASSETS NOT ADMITTED.

| | |
|---|---|
| Book value of bonds and stocks over market value | 591 36 |
| Total admitted assets | $72,956 27 |

### LIABILITIES.

| | |
|---|---|
| Death claims adjusted not yet due | $3,000 00 |

### EXHIBIT OF CERTIFICATES.

| | Total business of the year—all in Illinois. Number. | Amount. |
|---|---|---|
| Benefit certificates in force December 31, 1920, as per last statement | 2,569 | $1,959,250 00 |
| Benefit certificates written and renewed during the year | 121 | 77,500 00 |
| Benefit certificates increased during the year | -------- | 4,500 00 |
| Total | 2,690 | $2,041,250 00 |
| Deduct terminated, decrease or transferred during the year | 89 | 59,500 00 |
| Total benefit certificates in force December 31, 1921 | 2,601 | $1,981,750 00 |

| | |
|---|---|
| Received during the year from members: Mortuary, $26,000.44; reserve, $3,541.33; expense, $2,140.90; total | $31,682 67 |

## EXHIBIT OF DEATH CLAIMS.

| | Total claims—all in Illinois. Number. | Amount. |
|---|---|---|
| Claims unpaid December 31, 1920, as per last statement | 3 | $ 2,500 00 |
| Claims reported during the year and interest addition | 27 | 24,500 00 |
| Total | 30 | $27,000 00 |
| Claims paid during the year | 27 | $23,550 00 |
| Balance | 3 | $3,450 00 |
| Saved by compromising or scaling down claims during the year | -------- | 450 00 |
| Claims unpaid December 31, 1921 | 3 | $3,000 00 |

## SCHEDULE D—BONDS.

| Description. | Book value. | Par value. | Market value. |
|---|---|---|---|
| Victory Liberty Loan, 4¾s | $1,000 00 | $1,000 00 | $1,000 00 |
| Victory Liberty Loan, 4¾s | 1,000 00 | 1,000 00 | 1,000 00 |
| Victory Liberty Loan, 4¾s | 1,000 00 | 1,000 00 | 1,000 00 |
| Victory Liberty Loan, 4¾s | 1,000 00 | 1,000 00 | 1,000 00 |
| Third Liberty Loan, 4¼s | 3,000 00 | 3,000 00 | 2,910 00 |
| Fourth Liberty Loan, 4¼s | 3,000 00 | 3,000 00 | 2,883 00 |
| Second Liberty Loan, 4¼s | 4,000 00 | 4,000 00 | 3,822 40 |
| First Liberty Loan, 4¼s | 1,000 00 | 1,000 00 | 932 40 |
| Sanitary District of Chicago, municipal bond, 4s | 1,000 00 | 1,000 00 | 1,000 00 |
| Sanitary District of Chicago, municipal bond, 4s | 1,000 00 | 1,000 00 | 997 10 |
| Sanitary District of Chicago, municipal bond, 4s | 983 80 | 1,000 00 | 984 90 |
| Sanitary District of Chicago, municipal bond, 4s | 990 00 | 1,000 00 | 947 40 |
| Sanitary District of Chicago, municipal bond, 4s | 1,000 00 | 1,000 00 | 977 90 |
| Sanitary District of Chicago, municipal bond, 4s | 990 00 | 1,000 00 | 971 20 |
| Sanitary District of Chicago, municipal bond, 4s | 922 40 | 1,000 00 | 971 20 |
| Sanitary District of Chicago, 4s | 1,990 00 | 2,000 00 | 1,942 40 |
| Sanitary District of Chicago, municipal bond, 4s | 2,970 00 | 3,000 00 | 2,913 60 |
| Sanitary District of Chicago, municipal bond, 4s | 995 88 | 1,000 00 | 964 80 |
| Sanitary District of Chicago, municipal bond, 4s | 2,998 75 | 3,000 00 | 2,876 10 |
| Sanitary District of Chicago, municipal bond, 4s | 3,997 50 | 4,000 00 | 3,811 60 |
| Sanitary District of Chicago, municipal bond, 4s | 3,992 50 | 4,000 00 | 3,827 10 |
| Sanitary District of Chicago, municipal bond, 4s | 3,000 00 | 3,000 00 | 2,811 30 |
| County of Cook, Ill., 3½s | 482 50 | 500 00 | 500 00 |
| The County of Cook, Ill., detention home, 4½s | 961 90 | 1,000 00 | 995 60 |
| City of Chicago, improvement bond, 4s | 942 50 | 1,000 00 | 983 50 |
| Thorton Township, high school dist., 4s | 993 75 | 1,000 00 | 1,000 00 |
| County of Champaign, Ill., school dist., 4½s | 904 80 | 1,000 00 | 964 10 |
| Lincoln Park, State Ill., Cook County bond, 5s | 979 40 | 1,000 00 | 1,007 20 |
| Board of Education of the City of Bloomington, Ill., 4½s | 951 90 | 1,000 00 | 982 30 |
| City of Decatur, Ill., school dist., 4s | 922 30 | 1,000 00 | 950 10 |
| School Dist. No. 37, Nampa, Idaho, 5s | 1,000 00 | 1,000 00 | 1,038 77 |
| City of Garnett, Kans., school dist., 5s | 2,870 70 | 3,000 00 | 3,000 00 |
| City of Garnett, Kans., school dist., 5s | 1,897 40 | 2,000 00 | 2,000 00 |
| Town of Beaver, Okla., electric light, 6s | 990 00 | 1,000 00 | 1,000 00 |
| City of Lubbock, Tex., sewer bond, 5s | 997 50 | 1,000 00 | 1,000 00 |
| Jackson County, Tex., drainage dist. No. 5, 5s | 2,000 00 | 2,000 00 | 2,000 00 |
| Halejax County, N. C., road and bridge bond, 5¼s | 951 40 | 1,000 00 | 998 50 |
| Halejax County, N. C., road and bridge bond, 5¼s | 942 90 | 1,000 00 | 997 35 |
| The Miami Conservancy Dist., Ohio, 5½s | 1,000 00 | 1,000 00 | 1,015 00 |
| Oxnard School Dist., Ventura County, Cal., 5s | 948 40 | 1,000 00 | 1,000 00 |
| County Sullivan, Ind., gravel road, 4½s | 1,000 00 | 1,000 00 | 1,000 00 |
| Totals | $63,568 18 | $64,500 00 | $62,976 82 |

# BOHEMIAN-AMERICAN UNION.

Located at No. 1870 Blue Island Avenue, Chicago, Illinois.

JOHN F. FOIT, President. FRANK VACLAVEK, Secretary.

| | |
|---|---|
| Balance from previous year | $59,588 35 |

## INCOME.

| | |
|---|---|
| All other assessments or premiums | $18,566 19 |
| Dues and per capita tax | 4,453 02 |
| Net amount received from members | $23,019 21 |
| Gross interest on mortgage loans | 2,148 38 |
| Gross interest on bonds and dividends on stocks | 553 24 |
| Gross interest on deposits in trust companies and banks | 86 08 |
| Sale of lodge supplies | 97 85 |
| Official publication | 198 36 |
| Change of certificates | 35 00 |

INCOME—Concluded.

| | |
|---|---|
| Bohemian free schools | $313 63 |
| Miscellaneous | 382 98 |
| Total income | $26,834 73 |
| Sum | $86,423 08 |

DISBURSEMENTS.

| | |
|---|---|
| Death claims | $9,375 00 |
| Salaries of deputies and organizers | 16 54 |
| Salaries of officers and trustees | 1,208 99 |
| Salaries and other compensation of committees | 50 00 |
| Salaries and fees paid to supreme medical examiners | 42 00 |
| Rent | 300 00 |
| Advertising, printing and stationery | 201 51 |
| Postage, express, telegraph and telephone | 78 40 |
| Lodge supplies | 92 35 |
| Official publication | 748 62 |
| Bohemian free schools | 485 80 |
| Bonding of officers | 137 64 |
| Miscellaneous expense | 899 41 |
| Total disbursements | $13,636 26 |
| Balance | $72,786 82 |

LEDGER ASSETS.

| | |
|---|---|
| Mortgage loans on real estate | $45,250 00 |
| Book value of bonds and stocks | 13,756 00 |
| Deposits in trust companies and banks on interest | 7,255 82 |
| Other ledger assets, viz: Shares in Labor Building and Loan Association | 6,525 00 |
| Total ledger assets | $72,786 82 |

NON-LEDGER ASSETS.

| | |
|---|---|
| Interest and rents due and accrued | 1,743 70 |
| Gross assets | $74,530 52 |

LIABILITIES.

| | |
|---|---|
| Death claims due and unpaid, No. 5 | $3,750 00 |

EXHIBIT OF CERTIFICATES.

| | Total business of the year. | | Business in Illinois during year. | |
|---|---|---|---|---|
| | Number. | Amount. | Number. | Amount. |
| Benefit certificates in force December 31, 1920, as per last statement | 1,679 | $1,291,750 00 | 1,582 | $1,221,250 00 |
| Benefit certificates written and renewed during the year | 100 | 70,500 00 | 96 | 68,500 00 |
| Totals | 1,779 | $1,362,250 00 | 1,678 | $1,289,750 00 |
| Deduct terminated, decreased or transferred during the year | 110 | 67,500 00 | | |
| Deduct terminated or decreased during the year | | | 101 | 60,750 00 |
| Total benefit certificates in force December 31, 1921 | 1,669 | $1,294,750 00 | 1,577 | $1,229,000 00 |

| | |
|---|---|
| Received during the year from members in Illinois: Mortuary, $16,059.72; reserve, $1,569.22; expense, $4,152.57; total | $21,781 51 |

EXHIBIT OF DEATH CLAIMS.

| | Total claims. | | Illinois claims. | |
|---|---|---|---|---|
| | Number. | Amount. | Number. | Amount. |
| Claims unpaid December 31, 1920, as per last statement | 4 | $4,000 00 | 4 | $4,000 00 |
| Claims reported during the year and interest addition | 13 | 9,250 00 | 11 | 8,000 00 |
| Totals | 17 | $13,250 00 | 15 | $12,000 00 |
| Claims paid during the year | 11 | 9,375 00 | 10 | 8,250 00 |
| Balance | 6 | $3,875 00 | 5 | $3,750 00 |
| Saved by compromising or scaling down claims during the year | 1 | 125 00 | | |
| Claims unpaid December 31, 1921 | 5 | $3,750 00 | 5 | $3,750 00 |

SCHEDULE D—BONDS AND STOCKS.

| Description. | Book value. | Par value. | Market value. |
|---|---|---|---|
| First U. S. Liberty Loan, 3½s | $3,000 00 | $3,000 00 | $3,000 00 |
| First U. S. Liberty Loan, 4s | 100 00 | 100 00 | 100 00 |
| Second U. S. Liberty Loan, 4s | 2,000 00 | 2,000 00 | 2,000 00 |
| Third U. S. Liberty Loan, 4¼s | 2,000 00 | 2,000 00 | 2,000 00 |
| Fourth U. S. Liberty Loan, 4¼s | 3,000 00 | 3,000 00 | 3,000 00 |
| Victory Loan, 4¾s | 2,000 00 | 2,000 00 | 2,000 00 |
| U. S. Thrift Stamps | 826 00 | | 965 20 |
| U. S. Thrift Stamps | 830 00 | | 932 00 |
| Total | $13,756 00 | $12,100 00 | $13,997 20 |

## BOHEMIAN SLAVONIAN BENEVOLENT SOCIETY OF UNITED STATES.

Located at No. 105 North Clark Street, Reaper Block, 720-722, Chicago, Illinois.

K. BERNUITER, President. J. V. LUNAK, Secretary.

| | |
|---|---|
| Balance from previous year | $566,604 77 |

### INCOME.

| | |
|---|---|
| Membership fees actually received | $337,599 44 |
| Dues and per capita tax | 17,896 46 |
| Other payments by members | 38 46 |
| Total received from members | $355,534 36 |
| Gross interest on bonds and dividends on stocks | 24,103 86 |
| Gross interest on deposits in trust companies and banks | 3,035 58 |
| Gross interest from all other sources | 164 85 |
| Sale of lodge supplies | 262 26 |
| Gross increase in book value of ledger assets | 2,061 82 |
| Death claims returned to supreme lodge | 1,647 00 |
| Loan returned from member | 200 00 |
| Certificates rewritten | 177 00 |
| Statutes and by-laws | 23 50 |
| 3 per cent dues from juvenile division | 167 94 |
| Diverse | 8 00 |
| Total income | $387,386 17 |
| Sum | $953,990 94 |

### DISBURSEMENTS.

| | |
|---|---|
| Death claims | $304,540 00 |
| Misfortunate members | 3,000 00 |
| Total benefits paid | $307,540 00 |
| Salaries of officers and trustees, No. 23 | 5,632 00 |
| Traveling and other expenses of officers, trustees and committees | 750 36 |
| Insurance department fees | 70 00 |
| Rent | 440 00 |
| Advertising, printing and stationery | 486 65 |
| Postage, express, telegraph and telephone | 474 49 |
| Lodge supplies | 424 50 |
| Official publication | 8,953 13 |
| Legal expense in litigating claims | 193 60 |
| Other legal expenses | 500 00 |
| Furniture and fixtures | 234 67 |
| 2 cents dues to secretaries of lodges monthly per capita | 111 94 |
| 3 cents dues, monthly per capita to supreme lodge | 167 94 |
| Premiums to lodges | 1,764 50 |
| Diverse (donations to charitable institutions and extras | 1,165 54 |
| Paid for premiums on bonds | 1,169 00 |
| Total disbursements | $330,078 32 |
| Balance | $623,912 62 |

### LEDGER ASSETS.

| | |
|---|---|
| Loans secured by pledge of bonds, stocks or other collateral | $542,315 00 |
| Deposits in trust companies and banks not on interest | 306 46 |
| Deposits in trust companies and banks on interest | 81,291 16 |
| Total ledger assets | $623,912 62 |

#### NON-LEDGER ASSETS.

| | |
|---|---|
| Interest and rents due and accrued | 8,090 63 |
| Assessments actually collected by subordinate lodges not yet turned over to supreme lodge, mortuary | 3,062 62 |
| Dues for reserve fund actually collected by subordinate lodges not yet turned over to supreme lodge | 3,142 41 |
| Gross assets | $638,208 28 |

## LEDGER ASSETS—Concluded.

DEDUCT ASSETS NOT ADMITTED.

| | |
|---|---|
| Book value of bonds and stocks over market value | $8,877 31 |
| Total admitted assets | $629,330 97 |

## LIABILITIES.

| | |
|---|---|
| Death claims reported during the year but not yet adjusted | $16,750 00 |

## EXHIBIT OF CERTIFICATES.

| | Total business of the year. | | Business in Illinois during year. | |
|---|---|---|---|---|
| | Number. | Amount. | Number. | Amount. |
| Benefit certificates in force December 31, 1920, as per last statement | 22,730 | $15,431,250 00 | 7,523 | $5,358,500 00 |
| Benefit certificates written and renewed during the year | 938 | 504,000 00 | 328 | 177,750 00 |
| Benefit certificates received by transfer during the year | | | 7 | 5,000 00 |
| Benefit certificates increased during the year | | 27,250 00 | | 5,750 00 |
| Totals | 23,668 | $15,962,500 00 | 7,858 | $5,547,000 00 |
| Deduct terminated, decreased or transferred during the year | 906 | 596,500 00 | | |
| Deduct terminated or decreased during the year | | | 306 | 210,000 00 |
| Total benefit certificates in force December 31, 1921 | 22,762 | $15,366,000 00 | 7,552 | $5,337,000 00 |

| | |
|---|---|
| Received during the year from members in Illinois: Mortuary, $105,593.08; reserve, $5,371.25; misfortunate members, $1,812.50; expense, $6,043.40; total | $118,820 23 |

## EXHIBIT OF DEATH CLAIMS.

| | Total claims. | | Illinois claims. | |
|---|---|---|---|---|
| | Number. | Amount. | Number. | Amount. |
| Claims unpaid December 31, 1920, as per last statement | 23 | $ 17,750 00 | 9 | $ 6,000 00 |
| Claims reported during the year and interest addition | 410 | 303,500 00 | 143 | 110,500 00 |
| Totals | 433 | $321,250 00 | 152 | $116,500 00 |
| Claims paid during the year | 412 | 304,500 00 | 147 | 111,500 00 |
| Claims unpaid December 31, 1921 | 21 | $16,750 00 | 5 | $5,000 00 |

## MISFORTUNATE MEMBERS.

| | Total claims. | | Illinois claims. | |
|---|---|---|---|---|
| | Number. | Amount. | Number. | Amount. |
| Claims paid during the year | 60 | $3,000 00 | 23 | $1,500 00 |

## SCHEDULE D—BONDS.

| Description. | Book value. | Market value. |
|---|---|---|
| Corporate stock, City of New York, 3½s | $6,000 00 | $6,000 00 |
| Corporate stock, City of New York, 3½s | 1,000 00 | 850 00 |
| Corporate stock, City of New York, 3½s | 1,500 00 | 1,275 00 |
| Corporate stock, City of New York, 3½s | 700 00 | 595 00 |
| Corporate stock, City of New York, 3½s | 1,300 00 | 1,105 00 |
| Corporate stock, City of New York, 3½s | 2,000 00 | 1,700 00 |
| Corporate stock, City of New York, 3½s | 600 00 | 510 00 |
| Corporate stock, City of New York, 3½s | 1,200 00 | 1,020 00 |
| Corporate stock, City of New York, 3½s | 1,000 00 | 850 00 |
| Corporate stock, City of New York, 3½s | 1,000 00 | 850 00 |
| Corporate stock, City of New York, 3½s | 1,000 00 | 850 00 |
| City of Lebanon, Mo., 5s | 250 00 | 250 00 |
| City of Lebanon, Mo., 5s | 250 00 | 250 00 |
| City of Buffalo, N. Y., 3½s | 1,000 00 | 995 00 |
| City of Plano, Tex., 4s | 500 00 | 450 00 |
| City of Clarksville, Tex., 4s | 500 00 | 450 00 |
| Corporate stock, City of New York, 3½s | 2,000 00 | 1,900 00 |
| Sulivan Hamilton Twp., Ind., gr. rd., 4½s | 500 00 | 490 00 |
| Sulivan Hamilton Twp., Ins., gr. rd., 4½s | 500 00 | 490 00 |
| Baker City, Ore., 5s | 500 00 | 500 00 |
| Nampa, Canyon County, Idaho, 5s | 1,000 00 | 985 00 |
| Nampa, Canyon County, Idaho, 5s | 1,000 00 | 985 00 |
| Newburgh, Ohio, water works, 4s | 1,000 00 | 960 00 |
| Wise Twp., Edgefield Co., S. C., 5s | 500 00 | 465 00 |
| Wise Twp., Edgefield Co., S. C., 5s | 500 00 | 465 00 |
| Wise Twp., Edgefield Co., S. C., 5s | 500 00 | 465 00 |
| Coahoma Co., Miss., road, bridge, 4½s | 500 00 | 450 00 |
| Corporate stock, City of New York, 3½s | 2,000 00 | 1,700 00 |
| Nottingham Village, Ohio, school district, 4½s | 1,000 00 | 910 00 |

SCHEDULE D—BONDS—Continued.

| Description. | Book value. | Market value. |
|---|---|---|
| City of Mariana, Ark., sewer impr. D., 6s | $1,000 00 | $1,000 00 |
| City of Mariana, Ark., sewer impr., D., 6s | 1,000 00 | 1,000 00 |
| City of Mariana, Ark., sewer impr., D., 6s | 1,000 00 | 1,000 00 |
| Chicago, Ill., sanitary district, 4s | 1,000 00 | 995 00 |
| Cleveland, Ohio, registered, 4s | 1,000 00 | 974 00 |
| Oklahoma City, Okla., refunding 1907, 5s | 500 00 | 480 00 |
| Corporate stock of New York, redem., 3½s | 2,000 00 | 1,990 00 |
| Cleveland, Ohio, registered, 4s | 1,000 00 | 960 00 |
| Web City, Mo., public sewer, 5s | 1,000 00 | 960 00 |
| St. Paul, Minn., school, 4s | 500 00 | 477 20 |
| Hector, Clay Co., Ark., special school district, 6s | 500 00 | 500 00 |
| St. Joseph, Mo., school district (building), 4s | 1,000 00 | 940 00 |
| Nampa, Canyon Co., Idaho, school district No. 37, 5s | 1,000 00 | 980 00 |
| Conway, Faulkner Co., Ark., school district, 6s | 500 00 | 500 00 |
| Sanitary district, Chicago, Ill., 4s | 1,000 00 | 980 00 |
| Corporate stock of New York, Rapid Transit, 3½s | 2,000 00 | 1,700 00 |
| Farnwood Park District, Chicago, Ill., impr., 4½s | 500 00 | 490 00 |
| Sanitary district, Chicago, Ill., 4s | 1,000 00 | 980 00 |
| Cleveland, Ohio, registered, 4½s | 2,000 00 | 1,970 00 |
| Litchfield, Ill., impr., 5s | 100 00 | 98 00 |
| Litchfield, Ill., impr., 5s | 100 00 | 98 00 |
| Litchfield, Ill., impr., 5s | 100 00 | 98 00 |
| Litchfield, Ill., impr., 5s | 100 00 | 98 00 |
| Litchfield, Ill., impr., 5s | 100 00 | 98 00 |
| Cuyahoga Co., Ohio., Dennison Harvard Bridge, 4s | 1,000 00 | 970 00 |
| Cuyahoga Co., Ohio, Dennison Harvard Bridge, 4s | 1,000 00 | 970 00 |
| Consard Bayon Drain Ditch, Jefferson Co., Ark., 6s | 500 00 | 505 00 |
| Consard Bayon Drain Ditch, Jefferson Co., Ark., 6s | 500 00 | 505 00 |
| Consard Bayon Drain Ditch, Jefferson Co., Ark., 6s | 500 00 | 505 00 |
| St. Paul, Minn., sewer, 4s | 1,000 00 | 930 00 |
| Corporate stock, City of New York, 3½s | 2,000 00 | 1,700 00 |
| Litchfield, Ill., impr., 5s | 100 00 | 98 00 |
| Litchfield, Ill., impr., 5s | 100 00 | 98 00 |
| Litchfield, Ill., impr., 5s | 100 00 | 98 00 |
| Litchfield, Ill., impr., 5s | 100 00 | 98 00 |
| Litchfield, Ill., impr., 5s | 100 00 | 98 00 |
| Cleveland, Ohio, Board of Education, 4½s | 1,000 00 | 985 00 |
| Corporate stock, City of New York, ERB, 3½s | 1,000 00 | 850 00 |
| Corporate stock, City of New York, ERB, 3½s | 1,000 00 | 850 00 |
| St. Paul, Minn., graded school, 4s | 1,000 00 | 950 00 |
| Cuyahoga Co., Ohio, county public building, 4s | 1,000 00 | 980 00 |
| Sanitary district, Chicago, Ill., 4s | 1,000 00 | 984 00 |
| Racine, Wis., school house, 4½s | 1,000 00 | 1,000 00 |
| West Chicago, park commission, Ill., 4s | 1,000 00 | 980 00 |
| Cleveland, Ohio, grade crossing road, 4s | 1,000 00 | 937 60 |
| Cleveland, Ohio, grade crossing road, 4s | 1,000 00 | 937 60 |
| Corporate stock of New York, school sites, 3½s | 1,000 00 | 850 00 |
| Sanitary district, Chicago, Ill., 4s | 1,000 00 | 979 80 |
| Cook County, Ill., 4s | 500 00 | 495 00 |
| Cleveland, Ohio, elevated road, 4s | 1,000 00 | 990 00 |
| West Chicago Park Commission, Ill., 4s | 1,000 00 | 984 00 |
| West Chicago Park Commission, Ill., 4s | 1,000 00 | 984 00 |
| West Chicago Park Commission, Ill., 4s | 1,000 00 | 984 00 |
| West Chicago Park Commission, Ill., 4s | 1,000 00 | 984 00 |
| West Chicago Park Commission, Ill., 4s | 1,000 00 | 984 00 |
| Corporate stock of New York, 3½s | 2,000 00 | 1,700 00 |
| West Chicago, Park Commission, Ill., 4s | 1,000 00 | 990 00 |
| West Chicago, Park Commission, Ill., 4s | 1,000 00 | 990 00 |
| South Milwaukee, Wis., water works, 5s | 500 00 | 500 00 |
| Cleveland, Ohio, Board of Education, 4s | 1,000 00 | 970 40 |
| West Chicago, Park Commission, Ill., 4s | 1,000 00 | 970 40 |
| Town of Ryan, Okla., water works, 6s | 1,000 00 | 1,030 00 |
| Town of Ryan, Okla., water works, 6s | 1,000 00 | 1,030 00 |
| Town of Ryan, Okla., water works, 6s | 1,000 00 | 1,030 00 |
| Town of Ryan, Okla., water works, 6s | 1,000 00 | 1,030 00 |
| Piney Drainage District, Monroe-Lee Counties, Ark., 6s | 500 00 | 510 00 |
| Piney Drainage District, Monroe-Lee Counties, Ark., 6s | 500 00 | 510 00 |
| Piney Drainage District, Monroe-Lee Counties, Ark., 6s | 500 00 | 510 00 |
| Cleveland, Ohio, registered, 4s | 2,000 00 | 1,875 20 |
| Corporate stock, New York, Rapid Transit R. R., 3½s | 3,000 00 | 2,550 00 |
| Erick, Okla., elec light, 6s | 1,000 00 | 1,060 00 |
| West Chicago, Park Commission, Ill., 4s | 1,000 00 | 990 00 |
| Erick, Okla., water works, 6s | 500 00 | 525 00 |
| County of Ward, Tex., Comm. school D.SH, 5s | 100 00 | 96 12 |
| Cleveland, Ohio, public hall impr., 4s | 1,000 00 | 920 00 |
| Village of Meridian, Idaho, 6s | 1,000 00 | 1,060 00 |
| Town of Marks, Miss, 6s | 500 00 | 525 00 |
| Oak Park, Cook County, Illinois, school buildings, 4½s | 1,000 00 | 990 00 |
| Town of Lake View, Chicago, Ill., L. Pk. Ex., 4s | 1,000 00 | 990 00 |
| Cleveland, Ohio, public hall impr., 4s | 1,000 00 | 920 00 |
| Cook County, Ill., hospital, 4s | 1,000 00 | 963 40 |
| Cleveland, Ohio, Cuyahoga River Purif, 4s | 1,000 00 | 934 00 |

SCHEDULE D—BONDS—Continued.

| Description. | Book value. | Market value. |
|---|---|---|
| Corporate stock of New York, Suppl of Wat., 3½s | $3,000 00 | $2,550 00 |
| Chicago, Ill., general corporate, 4s | 1,000 00 | 980 00 |
| Cleveland, Ohio, Board of Education, 4s | 1,000 00 | 960 00 |
| Cleveland, Ohio, Board of Education, 4s | 1,000 00 | 960 00 |
| Chicago, Ill., judgment funding, 4s | 1,000 00 | 980 00 |
| South Omaha, Neb., street impr., 5½s | 500 00 | 500 00 |
| Springfield, Ill., Sangamon County School District, 4½s | 1,000 00 | 950 00 |
| City of Auburn, Neb., electric light, 5s, Opt | 500 00 | 495 00 |
| Cleveland, Ohio, Clark Ave. Bridge, 4¼s | 1,000 00 | 967 12 |
| Cleveland, Ohio, Clark Av. Bridge, 4¼s | 1,000 00 | 967 12 |
| City of Auburn, Neb., electric light, 5s | 500 00 | 495 00 |
| City of Auburn, Neb., electric light, 5s | 500 00 | 495 00 |
| Cleveland, Ohio, Clark Ave, Bridge, 4¼s | 1,000 00 | 967 20 |
| Cleveland, Ohio, Clark Ave. Bridge, 4¼s | 1,000 00 | 967 20 |
| Fort Bend County, Tex., road district, 5s, Opt | 500 00 | 500 00 |
| Fort Bend County, Tex., road district, 5s, Opt | 500 00 | 500 00 |
| Corporate stock of New York, school sites, 3½s | 4,000 00 | 3,450 00 |
| City of Winchester, Scott County, Ill., water works, 5s | 500 00 | 495 00 |
| Cleveland, Ohio, registered grade crossing, 4s | 1,000 00 | 937 60 |
| Town of Beaver, Okia., water works, 6s | 1,000 00 | 1,050 00 |
| City of Madisonville, Tex., water works, 5s | 1,000 00 | 941 00 |
| Cleveland, Ohio, Sewer Dist. No. 9, 4s | 1,000 00 | 980 00 |
| County of Harris, Tex., common school district, 5s | 1,000 00 | 960 00 |
| Verda, Parish of Grand, La., school board, 5s | 500 00 | 500 00 |
| Cude Drainage District, Leflore County, Miss., 6s | 500 00 | 500 00 |
| Cude Drainage District, Leflore County, Miss., 6s | 500 00 | 500 00 |
| Cude Drainage District, Leflore County, Miss., 6s | 500 00 | 500 00 |
| Cude Drainage District, Leflore County, Miss., 6s | 500 00 | 500 00 |
| East Cleveland Village, Ohio, Board of Education, 4½s | 1,000 00 | 1,000 00 |
| City of Madisonville, Tex., water works, 5s | 1,000 00 | 941 00 |
| Gurthrie Center, Gurthrie County, Iowa, Ind. School, 5s | 500 00 | 490 00 |
| City of Madisonville, Tex., water works, 5s | 1,000 00 | 941 00 |
| Gurthrie Center, Gurthrie County, Iowa, Ind. S., 5s | 500 00 | 490 00 |
| Gurthrie Center, Gurthrie County, Iowa, Ind. S., 5s | 500 00 | 495 00 |
| Corporate stock of New York, Pub. Char. Bl., 3½s | 3,000 00 | 2,550 00 |
| Town of Baker, Fallon County, Mont , water works, 6s | 1,000 00 | 1,050 00 |
| Town of Baker, Fallon County, Mont., water work, 6s | 1,000 00 | 1,050 00 |
| City of Atlantic, Iowa, school building, 5s | 500 00 | 495 00 |
| County of Galveston, Tex., common school district, 5s | 1,000 00 | 960 00 |
| County of Smith, Miss, Board of Supp. Rd. D., 6s | 500 00 | 500 00 |
| City of Aransas Pass, Patricio County, Tex., water works, 5s | 1,000 00 | 960 00 |
| Hull, Iowa, school building, 5s | 1,000 00 | 990 00 |
| Bloomfield, Iowa, funding, 5½s | 500 00 | 500 00 |
| Montgomery County, Tex., Road Dist. No. 3, 5½s, Opt | 1,000 00 | 990 00 |
| Prairie Gregg, Drain. D. Par. of Vermilion, 5s | 500 00 | 500 00 |
| Prairie Gregg, Drain. D. Par. of Vermilion, 5s | 500 00 | 495 00 |
| Prairie Gregg, Drain. D. Par. of Vermilion, 5s | 500 00 | 495 00 |
| Iowa City, Iowa, funding, 5s, Opt | 1,000 00 | 980 00 |
| Iowa City, Iowa, funding, 5s, Opt | 1,000 00 | 980 00 |
| City of Chicago Heights, Ill., water works, 5s | 1,000 00 | 1,000 00 |
| City of Chicago Heights, Ill., water works, 5s | 1,000 00 | 1,000 00 |
| Chagrin Falls Village, Cuyahoga County, Ohio, street impr., 5s | 500 00 | 500 00 |
| Cleveland Heights Village, Ohio, Derbush Rd., 5s | 1,000 00 | 1,000 00 |
| City of Minneapolis, Minn., special improvement, 5s | 500 00 | 525 00 |
| Prairie Gregg, Drainage District, Paris of Vermilion, La., 5s | 500 00 | 485 00 |
| City of Pine Bluff, Ark., Paving Dist. No. 35, 5½s | 500 00 | 495 00 |
| Corporate stock of New York, repair of street, 3½s | 2,000 00 | 1,700 00 |
| City of Three Forks, Mont., water works, 5s, Opt | 500 00 | 497 50 |
| City of Three Forks, Mont., water works, 5s, Opt | 500 00 | 497 50 |
| Keota Town, Keokuk County, Iowa, water works, 5½s, Opt | 500 00 | 500 00 |
| Keota Town, Keokuk County, Iowa, water works, 5½s, Opt | 500 00 | 500 00 |
| Keota Town, Keokuk County, Iowa, water works, 5½s, Opt | 500 00 | 500 00 |
| County of Roscan, Minn., public drainage district, 6s | 1,000 00 | 1,050 00 |
| County of Roscan, Minn., public drainage district, 6s | 1,000 00 | 1,050 00 |
| Village of Euglid, Ohio, Chardon Road, 5½s | 1,000 00 | 1,000 00 |
| City of New Philadelphia, Ohio, street improvement, 5s | 500 00 | 480 00 |
| Parish of Laforche, La., Road Dist. No. 2, 5s | 500 00 | 475 00 |
| West Chicago, Park Commissions, Ill., 4s | 1,000 00 | 970 00 |
| Chicago, Ill., harbor construction, 4s | 1,000 00 | 970 00 |
| Corporate stock of New York, 3½s | 2,000 00 | 1,700 00 |
| Hidalgo County, Tex., Road District 1, 5½s | 500 00 | 515 00 |
| Hidalgo County, Tex., Road Dist. 1, 5½s | 500 00 | 515 00 |
| Hidalgo County, Tex., Road Dist. 1, 5½s | 500 00 | 515 00 |
| Hidalgo County, Tex., Road Dist. 1, 5½s | 500 00 | 515 00 |
| County of Pulaski, Ill., Mounds School Dist., 5s | 500 00 | 495 00 |
| County of Pulaski, Ill., Mounds School Dist., 5s | 500 00 | 495 00 |
| County of Pulaski, Ill., Mounds School Dist., 5s | 500 00 | 495 00 |
| Village of West Park, Cuyahoga County, Ohio, street improvement, 5s | 1,000 00 | 990 00 |
| County of Pulaski, Ill., Mounds School Dist., 5s | 500 00 | 495 00 |
| Jonesboro, Graighead County, Ark., special school, 5s, Opt | 500 00 | 495 00 |
| State Center, Iowa, sewer outlet, 6s | 500 00 | 510 00 |
| State Center, Iowa, sewer outlet, 6s | 500 00 | 510 00 |
| Little Yellow Drainage District, Juneau County, Wis., 6s | 500 00 | 510 00 |

SCHEDULE D—BONDS—Continued.

| Description. | Book value. | Market value. |
|---|---|---|
| Little Yellow Drainage District, Junean County, Wis., 6s | $ 500 00 | $ 510 00 |
| Little Yellow Drainage Dist., Junean County, Wis., 6s | 500 00 | 510 00 |
| Bordman Rural School Dist., Mahoning County, Ohio, 4½s | 500 00 | 450 75 |
| Bordman Rural School Dist., Mahoning County, Ohio, 4½s | 500 00 | 450 00 |
| Bordman Rural School Dist., Mahoning County, Ohio, 4½s | 500 00 | 450 00 |
| Palo Alto County, Iowa, Drainage Dist. No. 80, 5½s | 1,000 00 | 990 00 |
| Hillview Drainage Dist., Green Scott County, Ill., 6s | 1,000 00 | 1,040 00 |
| Hillview Drainage Dist., Green Scott County, Ill., 6½s | 1,000 00 | 1,040 00 |
| Cleveland, Ohio, registered, 4¼s | 1,000 00 | 980 00 |
| Hillview Drainage Levee Dist., Green Scott County, Ill., 6s | 1,000 00 | 1,040 00 |
| Hillview Drainage Levee Dist., Green Scott County, Ill., 6s | 1,000 00 | 1,040 00 |
| Hillview Drainage Levee Dist., Green Scott County, Ill., 6s | 1,000 00 | 1,040 00 |
| Wales Lincoln Center, Iowa, Cons. Ind. Sch., 5s | 500 00 | 485 00 |
| Wales Lincoln Center, Iowa, Cons. Ind. Sch., 5s | 500 00 | 485 00 |
| County of Cuyahoga, Ohio, Woodland Rd. Impr., 4½s | 1,000 00 | 1,000 00 |
| County of Simson, Miss., Supervisor D. R., 6s | 500 00 | 525 00 |
| County of Simson, Miss., Supervisor D. R., 6s | 500 00 | 525 00 |
| City of Fort Worth, Tex., school, 5s | 1,000 00 | 980 00 |
| City of Fort Worth, Tex., school, 5s | 1,000 00 | 980 00 |
| First Liberty Loan of 1917, converted, registered, 4s | 500 00 | 500 00 |
| First Liberty Loan of 1917, converted, registered, 4s | 100 00 | 100 00 |
| First Liberty Loan of 1917, converted, registered, 4s | 100 00 | 100 00 |
| First Liberty Loan of 1917, converted, registered, 4s | 100 00 | 100 00 |
| Second Liberty Loan 1917, registered, 4s | 1,000 00 | 1,000 00 |
| First Liberty Loan of 1917, converted, registered, 4s | 1,000 00 | 1,000 00 |
| First Liberty Loan of 1917, converted, registered, 4s | 1,000 00 | 1,000 00 |
| Third Liberty Loan, registered, 4¼s | 1,000 00 | 1,000 00 |
| Third Liberty Loan, registered, 4¼s | 1,000 00 | 1,000 00 |
| County of Sabine, Tex., road, 5½s | 1,000 00 | 980 00 |
| Village of Clayton, Union County, N. M., water works, 6s, Opt. | 1,000 00 | 1,050 00 |
| Village of Clayton, Union County, N. M., water works, 6s, Opt. | 1,000 00 | 1,050 00 |
| Big Creek Drainage Dist., No. 15, Graighead County, Ark., 5½s | 500 00 | 480 00 |
| Fourth Liberty Loan of U. S., 4¼s | 1,000 00 | 1,000 00 |
| Fourth Liberty Loan of U. S., 4¼s | 1,000 00 | 1,000 00 |
| Town of Williams, Coconino County, Ariz., water works, 6s, Opt. | 1,000 00 | 1,060 00 |
| Town of Williams, Coconino County, Ariz., water works, 6s, Opt. | 1,000 00 | 1,060 00 |
| Town of Williams, Coconino County, Ariz., water works, 6s, Opt. | 1,000 00 | 1,060 00 |
| Town of Williams, Coconino County, Ariz., water works, 6s, Opt. | 1,000 00 | 1,060 00 |
| Victory Liberty Loan of U. S., 4¾s | 50 00 | 50 00 |
| Victory Liberty Loan of U. S., 4¾s | 50 00 | 50 00 |
| Victory Liberty Loan of U. S., 4¾s | 50 00 | 50 00 |
| Victory Liberty Loan of U. S., 4¾s | 5,000 00 | 5,000 00 |
| Victory Liberty Loan of U. S., 4¾s | 5,000 00 | 5,000 00 |
| Monroe County , Ark., road improvement Dist., 6s | 500 00 | 500 00 |
| Monroe County, Ark., road improvement Dist., 6s | 500 00 | 500 00 |
| Monroe County, Ark., road improvement Dist., 6s | 500 00 | 500 00 |
| Village of Rittman, Wayne County, Ohio., street improvement, 5½s | 500 00 | 486 00 |
| Village of Rittman, Wayne County, Ohio, street improvement, 5½s | 500 00 | 486 00 |
| Village of Rittman, Wayne County, Ohio, street improvement, 5½s | 500 00 | 486 00 |
| Village of Rittman, Wayne County, Ohio, street improvement, 5½s | 500 00 | 486 00 |
| Village of Rittman, Wayne County, Ohio, street improvement, 5½s | 500 00 | 486 00 |
| Village of Rittman, Wayne County, Ohio, street improvement, 5½s | 500 00 | 486 00 |
| Village of Rittman, Wayne County, Ohio, street improvement, 5½s | 500 00 | 486 00 |
| Village of Newburgh Heights, Cuyahoga County, Ohio, water works, 5s | 500 00 | 460 00 |
| Village of Newburgh Heights, Cuyahoga County, Ohio, water works, 5s | 500 00 | 460 00 |
| Village of Newburgh Heights, Cuyahoga County, Ohio, water works, 5s | 500 00 | 460 00 |
| Village of Newburgh Heights, Cuyahoga County, Ohio, water works, 5s | 500 00 | 460 00 |
| Village of Roy, Mora County, N. Mex., water works, 6s | 1,000 00 | 1,020 00 |
| Village of Roy, Mora County, N. Mex., water works, 6s | 1,000 00 | 1,020 00 |
| Third Liberty Loan of U. S., 4¼s | 10,000 00 | 10,000 00 |
| Third Liberty Loan of U. S., 4¼s | 1,000 00 | 1,000 00 |
| Hennepin Drainage Levee Dist., Putnam County, Ill., 6s | 500 00 | 510 00 |
| Hennepin Drainage Levee Dist., Putnam County, Ill., 6s | 500 00 | 510 00 |
| Hennepin Drainage Levee Dist., Putnam County, Ill., 6s | 500 00 | 510 00 |
| Hennepin Drainage Levee Dist., Putnam County, Ill., 6s | 500 00 | 510 00 |
| Carrol Highway, Impr. Dist. No. 3, Carrol County, Ark., 5s | 1,000 00 | 890 00 |
| Carrol Highway, Impr. Dist. No. 3, Carrol County, Ark., 5s | 1,000 00 | 890 00 |
| Carrol Highway, Impr. Dist. No. 3, Carrol County, Ark., 5s | 1,000 00 | 890 00 |
| County of Falls, Tex., road and bridge fund, 6s | 1,000 00 | 1,000 00 |
| County of Falls, Tex., road and bridge fund, 6s | 1,000 00 | 1,000 00 |
| Third Liberty Loan of U. S., 4¼s | 10,000 00 | 10,000 00 |
| Third Liberty Loan of U. S., 4¼s | 5,000 00 | 5,000 00 |
| County of Nuecces, Tex., special road, series B, 5½s | 1,000 00 | 943 80 |
| County of Nuecces, Tex., special road, series B, 5½s | 1,000 00 | 943 80 |
| Second Liberty Loan of U. S., 4¼s | 1,000 00 | 1,000 00 |
| Second Liberty Loan of U. S., 4¼s | 1,000 00 | 1,000 00 |
| Belle Fourche, S. Dak., Ind. Sch. Dist. No. 1, Building, 6s | 500 00 | 500 00 |
| Belle Fourche, S. Dak., Ind. Sch. Dist. No. 1, Building, 6s | 500 00 | 500 00 |
| Belle Fourche, S. Dak., Ind. Sch. Dist. No. 1, Building, 6s | 500 00 | 500 00 |
| Belle Fourche, S. Dak., Ind. Sch. Dist. No. 1, Building, 6s | 500 00 | 515 00 |
| Belle Fourche, S. Dak., Ind. Sch. Dist. No. 1, Building, 6s | 500 00 | 515 00 |
| Belle Fourche, S. Dak., Ind. Sch. Dist. No. 1, Building, 6s | 500 00 | 515 00 |

SCHEDULE D—BONDS—Continued.

| Description. | Book value. | Market value. |
|---|---|---|
| First Liberty Loan of U. S., converted, 4¼s | $ 500 00 | $ 500 00 |
| West Matanzas, Drainage and Levee Dist., Fulton County, Ill., 6s | 1,000 00 | 1,040 00 |
| West Matanzas Drainage and Levee Dist., Fulton County, Ill., 6s | 1,000 00 | 1,040 00 |
| West Matanzas Drainage and Levee Dist., Fulton County, Ill., 6s | 1,000 00 | 1,040 00 |
| City of Knoxville, Tenn., refunding, 5s | 1,000 00 | 950 00 |
| City of Knoxville, Tenn., refunding, 5s | 1,000 00 | 940 00 |
| City of Knoxville, Tenn., refunding, 5s | 1,000 00 | 940 00 |
| Belle Fourche, Ind. School Dist. No. 1, Butte Co., S. Dak., 6s | 500 00 | 510 00 |
| Belle Fourche, Ind. School Dist. No. 1, Butte Co., S. Dak., 6s | 500 00 | 510 00 |
| Belle Fourche, Ind. School Dist. No. 1, Butte Co., S. Dak., 6s | 500 00 | 510 00 |
| Belle Fourche, Ind. School Dist. No. 1, Butte Co., S. Dak., 6s | 500 00 | 510 00 |
| City of Sidney, Cheeyene Co., Neb., water works, 6s | 1,000 00 | 1,010 00 |
| City of Sidney, Cheyene Co., Neb., water works, 6s | 1,000 00 | 1,010 00 |
| City of Sidney, Cheeyene Co., Neb., water works, 6s | 1,000 00 | 1,010 00 |
| City of Sidney, Cheeyene Co., Neb., water works, 6s | 1,000 00 | 1,010 00 |
| City of Sidney, Cheeyene Co., Neb., water works, 6s | 1,000 00 | 1,010 00 |
| Lindhurst Village, Cuyahoga Co., Ohio, School Dist., 6s | 1,000 00 | 1,030 00 |
| Lindhurst Village, Cuyahoga Co., Ohio, School Dist., 6s | 1,000 00 | 1,032 50 |
| Lindhurst Village, Cuyahoga Co., Ohio, School Dist., 6s | 1,000 00 | 1,032 50 |
| Lindhurst Village, Cuyahoga Co., Ohio, School Dist., 6s | 1,000 00 | 1,032 50 |
| Lindhurst Village, Cuyahoga Co., Ohio, School Dist., 6s | 1,000 00 | 1,032 75 |
| Lindhurst Village, Cuyahoga Co., Ohio, School Dist., 6s | 1,000 00 | 1,032 75 |
| Heyburn Paul Highway Dist., Minnedoka Co., Idaho, 6s | 1,000 00 | 1,012 50 |
| Heyburn Paul Highway Dist., Minnedoka Co., Idaho, 6s | 1,000 00 | 1,012 50 |
| Heyburn Paul Highway Dist., Minnedoka Co., Idaho, 6s | 1,000 00 | 1,012 50 |
| Hancock Co., W. Va., permanent road improvement, 5s | 1,000 00 | 900 00 |
| Hancock Co., W. Va., permanent road improvement, 5s | 1,000 00 | 900 00 |
| Hancock Co., W. Va., permanent road improvement, 5s | 1,000 00 | 900 00 |
| Bonne Co., Neb., Village of St. Edwards, No. 1, 7s | 1,000 00 | 1,070 00 |
| Bonne Co., Neb., Village of St. Edwards, Paving Dist., No. 2, 7s | 1,000 00 | 1,070 00 |
| Bonne Co., Neb., Village of St. Edwards, Paving Dist. No. 1, 7s | 1,000 00 | 1,087 10 |
| Bonne Co., Neb., Village of St. Edwards, Paving Dist., No. 2, 7s | 1,000 00 | 1,080 00 |
| Bonne Co., Neb., Village of St. Edwards, Paving Dist. No. 2, 7s | 1,000 00 | 1,080 00 |
| Fourth Liberty Loan, converted, 4¼s | 500 00 | 500 00 |
| Fourth Liberty Loan, converted, 4¼s | 10,000 00 | 10,000 00 |
| Fourth Liberty Loan, converted, 4¼s | 10,000 00 | 10,000 00 |
| Fourth Liberty Loan, converted, 4¼s | 10,000 00 | 10,000 00 |
| Trumbull Co., Ohio, McDonald School Dist., 5½s | 1,000 00 | 930 00 |
| Trumbull Co., Ohio, McDonald School Dist., 5½s | 1,000 00 | 930 00 |
| Trumbull Co., Ohio, McDonald School Dist., 5½s | 1,000 00 | 930 00 |
| Trumbull Co., Ohio, McDonald School Dist., 5½s | 1,000 00 | 930 00 |
| Marshall Co., Lake City, S. Dak., Ind. School Dist., 7s | 1,000 00 | 1,111 00 |
| Marshall Co., Lake City, S. Dak., Ind. School Dist., 7s | 1,000 00 | 1,111 00 |
| Marshall Co., Lake City, S. Dak., Ind. School Dist., 7s | 1,000 00 | 1,111 00 |
| Williams Co., Stryker, Ohio, street improvement, 6s | 1,000 00 | 1,000 00 |
| Eastland Co., Eastland, Tex., sewer, 6s | 1,000 00 | 1,000 00 |
| Eastland Co., Eastland, Tex., sewer, 6s | 1,000 00 | 1,000 00 |
| Eastland Co., Eastland, Tex., sewer, 6s | 1,000 00 | 1,000 00 |
| Eastland Co., Eastland, Tex., sewer, 6s | 1,000 00 | 1,000 00 |
| Eastland Co., Eastland, Tex., sewer, 6s | 1,000 00 | 1,000 00 |
| Eastland Co., Eastland, Tex., sewer, 6s | 1,000 00 | 1,000 00 |
| Eastland Co., Eastland, Tex., sewer, 6s | 1,000 00 | 1,000 00 |
| Sandusky Co., Clyde, Ohio, school, 6s | 1,000 00 | 1,020 00 |
| Millard Co., Utah, Drainage Dist., No. 1, 6s | 1,000 00 | 1,000 00 |
| Millard Co., Utah, Drainage Dist., No. 1, 6s | 1,000 00 | 1,000 00 |
| Millard Co., Utah, Drainage Dist. No. 1, 6s | 1,000 00 | 1,000 00 |
| Millard Co., Utah, Drainage Dist. No. 1, 6s | 1,000 00 | 1,000 00 |
| Millard Co., Utah, Drainage Dist. No. 1, 6s | 1,000 00 | 1,000 00 |
| City of Helena, Ark., refunding, 5s | 1,000 00 | 990 00 |
| City of Helena, Ark., refunding, 5s | 1,000 00 | 990 00 |
| St. Joseph, Mo., school dist. (building), 4s | 1,000 00 | 940 00 |
| Conway, Faulkner Co., Ark., school dist., 6s | 500 00 | 500 00 |
| Conway, Faulkner Co., Ark., school dist., 6s | 500 00 | 500 00 |
| Consart Bayon Drainage Dist., Jefferson Co., Ark., 6s | 500 00 | 500 00 |
| Consart Bayon Drainage Dist., Jefferson Co., Ark., 6s | 500 00 | 500 00 |
| County of Cook, Ill., infirmary, 4s | 500 00 | 488 75 |
| Sanitary Dist., Chicago, Ill., 4s | 1,000 00 | 995 00 |
| Town of North Chicago, Ill., 4s | 1,000 00 | 970 00 |
| West Chicago, Park Commission, Ill., 4s | 1,000 00 | 970 00 |
| West Chicago, Park Commission, Ill., 4s | 1,000 00 | 970 00 |
| West Chicago, Park Commission, Ill., 4s | 1,000 00 | 970 00 |
| West Chicago, Park Commission, Ill., (small park), 4s | 1,000 00 | 970 00 |
| West Chicago, Park Commission, Ill. (small park), 4s | 1,000 00 | 970 00 |
| Lincoln Park Commission, Chicago, Ill., 4s | 1,000 00 | 964 40 |
| West Chicago, Park Commission, Ill., small park, 4s | 1,000 00 | 964 40 |
| West Chicago, Park Commission, Ill., small park, 4s | 1,000 00 | 964 40 |
| Fulton, Gallaway Co., Mo., special road dist., 5s | 1,000 00 | 1,000 00 |
| Lincoln Park Commission, Chicago, Ill., 4s | 1,000 00 | 954 40 |
| Oak Park, Ill., School Dist. No. 97 (building), 4½s | 1,000 00 | 980 00 |
| Oak Park, Ill., School Dist. No. 97 (building), 4½s | 1,000 00 | 980 00 |
| Cook County, Ill., hospital, 4s | 1,000 00 | 970 00 |
| Springfield, Ill., School Dist. No. 186, 4½s | 1,000 00 | 950 00 |

SCHEDULE D—BONDS—Continued.

| Description. | Book value. | Par value. |
|---|---|---|
| Springfield, Ill., School Dist. No. 186, 4¼s | $1,000 00 | $ 950 00 |
| Omaha, Neb., Street Improvement Dist. No. 97, 5½s | 500 00 | 490 00 |
| Auburn, Neb., electric light, 5s | 500 00 | 480 00 |
| Auburn, Neb., electric light, 5s | 500 00 | 480 00 |
| Auburn, Neb., electric light, 5s | 500 00 | 480 00 |
| South Omaha, Neb., Street Improvement Dist. No. 9, 5½s | 500 00 | 490 00 |
| Town of Beaver, Beaver Co., Okla., water works, 6s | 1,000 00 | 1,050 00 |
| Parish of Acadia, La., 6 Ward, Crowley Dist., 5s | 500 00 | 480 00 |
| Town of Beaver, County of Beaver, Okla., water works, 6s | 1,000 00 | 1,050 00 |
| Town of Beaver, County of Beaver, Okla., water works, 6s | 1,000 00 | 1,050 00 |
| Town of Beaver, County of Beaver, Okla., water works, 6s | 1,000 00 | 1,050 00 |
| Town of Beaver, County of Beaver, Okla., water works, 6s | 1,000 00 | 1,050 00 |
| Parish of Morehouse, La., court house, 5s | 500 00 | 500 00 |
| Parish of Morehouse, La., court house, 5s | 500 00 | 500 00 |
| Cude Drainage Dist., Leflore Co., Miss., 6s | 500 00 | 500 00 |
| Cude Drainage Dist., Leflore Co., Miss., 6s | 500 00 | 500 00 |
| Cude Drainage Dist., Leflore Co., Miss., 6s | 500 00 | 500 00 |
| Cude Drainage Dist., Leflore Co., Miss., 6s | 500 00 | 510 00 |
| Cude Drainage Dist., Leflore Co., Miss., 6s | 500 00 | 510 00 |
| Town of Baker, Mont., water works, 6s | 1,000 00 | 1,050 00 |
| Town of Baker, Mont., water works, 6s | 1,000 00 | 1,050 00 |
| Town of Baker, Mont., water works, 6s | 1,000 00 | 1,050 00 |
| City of Canadian, Tex., water works, 5s | 1,000 00 | 970 00 |
| Forest Park Village, Cook Co., Ill., (Municipal Building), 5s | 500 00 | 500 00 |
| Forest Park Village, Cook Co., Ill. (Municipal Building), 5s | 500 00 | 500 00 |
| Forest Park Village, Cook Co., Ill. (Municipal Building), 5s | 500 00 | 500 00 |
| Forest Park Village, Cook Co., Ill. (Municipal Building), 5s | 500 00 | 500 00 |
| Forest Park Village, Cook Co., Ill. (Municipal Building), 5s | 500 00 | 500 00 |
| Atlantic, Iowa, school building, 5s | 500 00 | 495 00 |
| Atlantic, Iowa, school building, 5s | 500 00 | 495 00 |
| Atlantic, Iowa, school building, 5s | 500 00 | 495 00 |
| Forest City, Iowa, refunding, 5½s | 500 00 | 500 00 |
| Forest City, Iowa, refunding, 5½s | 500 00 | 500 00 |
| Teague, Freestone Co., Tex., Ind. School Dist., 5s | 500 00 | 500 00 |
| Teague, Freestone Co., Tex., Ind. School Dist., 5s | 500 00 | 500 00 |
| Teague, Freestone Co., Tex., Ind. School Dist., 5s | 500 00 | 500 00 |
| Teague, Freestone Co., Tex., Ind. School Dist., 5s | 500 00 | 500 00 |
| Iowa City, Iowa, funding, 5s, Opt | 1,000 00 | 980 00 |
| Onava, Iowa, 5s | 500 00 | 495 00 |
| City of Chicago Heights, Ill., water works, 5s | 1,000 00 | 1,000 00 |
| City of Chicago Heights, Ill., water works, 5s | 1,000 00 | 1,000 00 |
| Lime Creek, Cerro Cordo Co., Iowa, school building, 5s | 500 00 | 497 50 |
| Lime Creek, Cerro Cordo Co., Iowa, school building, 5s | 500 00 | 495 00 |
| Spencer, Iowa, funding, 5s | 500 00 | 495 00 |
| Bloomfield, Iowa, funding, 5½s | 500 00 | 500 00 |
| Bloomfield, Iowa, funding, 5½s | 500 00 | 500 00 |
| Bloomfield, Iowa, funding, 5½s | 500 00 | 500 00 |
| Three Forks, Gallatin Co., Mont., water works, 5s, Opt | 500 00 | 497 50 |
| Three Forks, Gallatin Co., Mont., water works, 5s, Opt | 500 00 | 497 50 |
| Three Forks, Gallatin Co., Mont., water works, 5s, Opt | 500 00 | 497 50 |
| Three Forks, Gallatin Co., Mont., water works, 5s, Opt | 500 00 | 497 50 |
| Three Forks, Gallatin Co., Mont., water works, 5s, Opt | 500 00 | 497 50 |
| Keota, Keokuk Co., Iowa, water works, 5½s, Opt | 500 00 | 495 00 |
| Keota, Keokuk Co., Iowa, water works, 5½s, Opt | 500 00 | 495 00 |
| Schaller, Iowa, school funding, 5s | 500 00 | 495 00 |
| Schaller, Iowa, school funding, 5s | 500 00 | 495 00 |
| Lime Creek, Cerro Cordo Co., Iowa, school building, 5s | 500 00 | 495 00 |
| Lime Creek, Cerro Cordo Co., Iowa, school building, 5s | 500 00 | 495 00 |
| County of Rosean, Minn., public drainage dist., 6s | 1,000 00 | 1,040 00 |
| County of Rosean, Minn., public drainage dist., 6s | 1,000 00 | 1,040 00 |
| County of Rosean, Minn., public drainage dist., 6s | 1,000 00 | 1,040 00 |
| Keota, Keokuk Co., Iowa, water works, 6s, Opt | 500 00 | 495 00 |
| Waren, Bradley Co., Ark., school dist., 6s | 1,000 00 | 1,070 00 |
| Waren, Bradley Co., Ark., school dist., 6s | 1,000 00 | 1,070 00 |
| Hidalgo Co., Tex., Road Dist. No. 1, 5½s, Opt | 500 00 | 515 00 |
| Hidalgo Co., Tex., Road Dist. No. 1, 5½s, Opt | 500 00 | 515 00 |
| Hidalgo Co., Tex., Road Dist. No. 1, 5½s, Opt | 500 00 | 515 00 |
| County of Cerro Cordo, Iowa, Drainage Dist., 5½s | 1,000 00 | 1,000 00 |
| County of Cerro Cordo, Iowa, Drainage Dist., 5½s | 1,000 00 | 1,000 00 |
| County of Cerro Cordo, Iowa, Drainage Dist., 5½s | 1,000 00 | 1,000 00 |
| Hamingway, Williamsburg Co., S. C., school, 6s | 1,000 00 | 1,050 00 |
| Hamingway, Williamsburg Co., S. C., school, 6s | 1,000 00 | 1,050 00 |
| Hamingway, Williamsburg Co., S. C., school, 6s | 1,000 00 | 1,050 00 |
| Hamingway, Williamsburg Co., S. C., school, 6s | 1,000 00 | 1,050 00 |
| Palo Alto Co., Iowa, Drainage Dist. No. 80, 5½s | 1,000 00 | 1,000 00 |
| Dunklin Co., Mo., Levee Dist. No. 4, 6s | 500 00 | 510 00 |
| Dunklin Co., Mo., Levee Dist. No. 4, 6s | 500 00 | 510 00 |
| Dunklin Co., Mo., Levee Dist. No. 4, 6s | 500 00 | 510 00 |
| Dunklin Co., Mo., Levee Dist. No. 4, 6s | 500 00 | 510 00 |
| Dunklin Co., Mo., Levee Dist. No. 4, 6s | 500 00 | 510 00 |
| Dunklin Co., Mo., Levee Dist. No. 4, 6s | 500 00 | 510 00 |
| County of Simpson, Miss., Supervisors Dist. Road, 6s | 500 00 | 525 00 |

SCHEDULE D—BONDS—Continued.

| Description. | Book value. | Par value. |
|---|---|---|
| County of Simpson, Miss., Supervisors Dist. Road, 6s | $ 500 00 | $ 525 00 |
| Second Liberty Loan of U. S., converted, 4¼s | 5,000 00 | 5,000 00 |
| County of Sabine, Tex., road, 5½s | 1,000 00 | 980 00 |
| County of Sabine, Tex., road, 5½s | 1,000 00 | 980 00 |
| First Liberty Loan of U. S., 3½s | 50 00 | 50 00 |
| Village of Clayton, Union Co., N. Mex., water works, 6s, Opt | 1,000 00 | 1,050 00 |
| Village of Clayton, Union Co., N. Mex., water works, 6s, Opt | 1,000 00 | 1,050 00 |
| Williams Town, Cocomimo Co., Ariz., water works, 6s | 1,000 00 | 1,050 00 |
| Monroe Co., Ark., road improvement dist., 6s | 500 00 | 500 00 |
| Monroe Co., Ark., road improvement dist., 6s | 500 00 | 500 00 |
| Monroe Co., Ark., road improvement dist., 6s | 500 00 | 500 00 |
| Monroe Co., Ark., road improvement dist., 6s | 500 00 | 500 00 |
| Monroe Co., Ark., road improvement dist., 6s | 500 00 | 500 00 |
| City of West Allis, Wis., school, 5s | 1,000 00 | 980 00 |
| City of West Allis, Wis., school, 5s | 1,000 00 | 980 00 |
| City of West Allis, Wis., school, 5s | 1,000 00 | 980 00 |
| Village of Newburgh Heights, Ohio, Cuyahoga Co., water works, 5s | 500 00 | 470 75 |
| Village of Newburgh Heights, Ohio, Cuyahoga Co., water works, 5s | 500 00 | 470 75 |
| Village of Newburgh Heights, Ohio, Cuyahoga Co., water works, 5s | 500 00 | 470 75 |
| Village of Newburgh Heights, Ohio, Cuyahoga Co., water works, 5s | 500 00 | 470 75 |
| Village of Newburgh Heights, Ohio, Cuyahoga Co., water works, 5s | 500 00 | 470 75 |
| Village of Newburgh Heights, Ohio, Cuyahoga Co., water works, 5s | 500 00 | 470 75 |
| U. S. of America, gold bond, 4¼s | 5,000 00 | 5,000 00 |
| County of Franklin, Ark., Road Improvement Dist. No. 1, 5s | 1,000 00 | 890 80 |
| County of Franklin, Ark., Road Improvement Dist. No. 1, 5s | 1,000 00 | 890 80 |
| County of Franklin, Ark., Road Improvement Dist. No. 1, 5s | 1,000 00 | 890 80 |
| Hennepin Drainage Levee Dist., Putnam Co., Ill., 6s | 500 00 | 510 00 |
| Hennepin Drainage Levee Dist., Putnam Co., Ill., 6s | 500 00 | 510 00 |
| Hennepin Drainage Levee Dist., Putnam Co., Ill., 6s | 500 00 | 510 00 |
| Hennepin Drainage Levee Dist., Putnam Co., Ill., 6s | 500 00 | 510 00 |
| Hennepin Drainage Levee Dist., Putnam Co., Ill., 6s | 500 00 | 510 00 |
| Hennepin Drainage Levee Dist., Putnam Co., Ill., 6s | 500 00 | 510 00 |
| Hennepin Drainage Levee Dist., Putnam Co., Ill., 6s | 457 50 | 468 94 |
| Hennepin Drainage Levee Dist., Putnam Co., Ill., 6s | 457 50 | 468 94 |
| Carrol Highway Improvement Dist. No. 3, Carrol Co., Ark., 5s | 1,000 00 | 890 80 |
| Carrol Highway Improvement Dist. No. 3, Carrol Co., Ark., 5s | 1,000 00 | 890 80 |
| Carrol Highway Improvement Dist. No. 3, Carrol Co., Ark., 5s | 1,000 00 | 890 80 |
| Hennepin Drainage Levee Dist., Putnam Co., Ill., 6s | 500 00 | 520 00 |
| Hennepin Drainage Levee Dist., Putnam Co., Ill., 6s | 500 00 | 520 00 |
| Hennepin Drainage Levee Dist., Putnam Co., Ill., 6s | 500 00 | 520 00 |
| Hennepin Drainage Levee Dist., Putnam Co., Ill., 6s | 500 00 | 520 00 |
| Wolf Point, Rosewelt Co., Mont., School Dist. No. 45, 6s, Opt. 29 | 1,000 00 | 1,050 00 |
| Wolf Point, Rosewelt Co., Mont., School Dist. No. 45, 6s, Opt. 29 | 1,000 00 | 1,050 00 |
| Hennepin Drainage Levee Dist., Putnam Co., Ill., ref., 6s | 500 00 | 515 00 |
| Hennepin Drainage Levee Dist., Putnam Co., Ill., ref., 6s | 500 00 | 515 00 |
| Third Liberty Loan of U. S., 4¼s | 10,000 00 | 10,000 00 |
| County of Pointsette, Ark., Drainage Dist. No. 7, 5s | 1,000 00 | 867 10 |
| County of Pointsette, Ark., Drainage Dist. No. 7, 5s | 1,000 00 | 867 10 |
| County of Poinsette, Ark., Drainage Dist. No. 7, 5s | 1,000 00 | 867 10 |
| County of Poinsette, Ark., Drainage Dist. No. 7, 5s | 1,000 00 | 867 10 |
| First Liberty Loan of U. S., converted, 4¼s | 1,000 00 | 1,000 00 |
| First Liberty Loan of U. S., converted, 4¼s | 1,000 00 | 1,000 00 |
| First Liberty Loan of U. S., converted, 4¼s | 1,000 00 | 1,000 00 |
| First Liberty Loan of U. S., converted, 4¼s | 1,000 00 | 1,000 00 |
| First Liberty Loan of U. S., converted, 4¼s | 1,000 00 | 1,000 00 |
| County of Poinsette, Ark., Drainage Dist. No. 7, 5s | 1,000 00 | 867 10 |
| County of Dunklin, Mo., Drainage Dist. No. 30, 6s | 500 00 | 500 00 |
| Village of Maple Heights, Cuyahoga Co., Ohio, Libbey Rd. Water, 6s | 500 00 | 510 00 |
| Village of Maple Heights, Cuyahoga Co., Ohio, Libbey Rd. Water, 6s | 500 00 | 510 00 |
| Village of Maple Heights, Cuyahoga Co., Ohio, Theodore St. Water, 6s | 500 00 | 510 00 |
| Village of Maple Heights, Cuyahoga Co., Ohio, Forest Ave. Impr., 6s | 500 00 | 510 00 |
| Village of Maple Heights, Cuyahoga Co., Ohio, Anthony St. Water, 6s | 500 00 | 510 00 |
| Village of Maple Heights, Cuyahoga Co., Ohio, Triend Ave., Impr., 6s | 500 00 | 510 00 |
| Village of Garfield Heights, Cuyahoga Co., Ohio, Drexel Ave. Water, 5½ | 1,000 00 | 1,000 00 |
| Village of Garfield Heights, Cuyahoga Co., Ohio, Drexel Ave. Water, 5½ | 1,000 00 | 1,000 00 |
| West Matanzas Drainage Levee Dist., Fulton Co., Ill., 6s | 1,000 00 | 1,040 00 |
| West Matanzas Drainage Levee Dist., Fulton Co., Ill., 6s | 1,000 00 | 1,040 00 |
| West Matanzas Drainage Levee Dist., Fulton Co., Ill., 6s | 1,000 00 | 1,040 00 |
| Village of Hubbard, Trumbull Co., Ohio, 6s | 500 00 | 510 00 |
| Village of Bedford, Cuyahoga Co., Ohio, Columbus St., Ext. S., 6s | 500 00 | 510 00 |
| Village of Bedford, Cuyahoga Co., Ohio, Columbus St. Ext. S., 6s | 500 00 | 510 00 |
| Village of Bedford, Cuyahoga Co., Ohio, Columbus St. Water, 6s | 500 00 | 510 00 |
| Village of Bedford, Cuyahoga Co., Ohio, Columbus St. Sewer, 6s | 500 00 | 512 50 |
| Village of Bedford, Cuyahoga Co., Ohio, Columbus St. Water, 6s | 500 00 | 512 50 |
| Village of Bedford, Cuyahoga Co., Ohio, Columbus St. Water, 6s | 500 00 | 512 50 |
| Village of Bedford, Cuyahoga Co., Ohio, Columbus St. Sewer, 6s | 500 00 | 513 75 |
| Village of Bedford, Cuyahoga Co., Ohio, Columbus St. Water, 6s | 500 00 | 513 75 |
| Village of Bedford, Cuyahoga Co., Ohio, Columbus St. Water, 6s | 500 00 | 513 75 |
| Village of Bedford, Cuyahoga Co., Ohio, Columbus St. Water, 6s | 500 00 | 513 75 |
| Village of Bedford, Cuyahoga Co., Ohio, Columbus St. Sewer, 6s | 500 00 | 515 00 |
| Village of Bedford, Cuyahoga Co., Ohio, Columbus St. Water, 6s | 500 00 | 515 00 |
| Village of Bedford, Cuyahoga Co., Ohio, Columbus St. Sewer, 6s | 500 00 | 515 00 |

SCHEDULE D—BONDS—Concluded.

| Description. | Book value. | Par value. |
|---|---|---|
| Hancock Co., W. Va., permanent road improvement, 5s, Opt. 1932 | 1,000 00 | 900 00 |
| Hancock Co., W. Va., permanent road improvement, 5s, Opt | 1,000 00 | 900 00 |
| Hancock Co., W. Va., permanent road improvement, 5s, Opt | 1,000 00 | 900 00 |
| Hancock Co., W. Va., permanent road improvement, 5s, Opt | 1,000 00 | 900 00 |
| Hancock Co., W. Va., permanent road improvement, 5s, Opt | 1,000 00 | 900 00 |
| Hancock Co., W. Va., permanent road improvement, 5s, Opt | 1,000 00 | 900 00 |
| Hancock Co., W. Va., permanent road improvements, 5s, Opt | 1,000 00 | 900 00 |
| Gallatine Co., Broadwater, Mont., school dist., 6s, Opt. 1945 | 1,000 00 | 1,030 00 |
| Gallatine Co., Broadwater, Mont., school dist., 6s, Opt. 1945 | 1,000 00 | 1,030 00 |
| Fourth Liberty Loan, converted, 4¼s | 1,000 00 | 1,000 00 |
| Fourth Liberty Loan, converted, 4¼s | 5,000 00 | 5,000 00 |
| Fourth Liberty Loan, converted, 4¼s | 10,000 00 | 10,000 00 |
| Auray Co., Colo., refunding series, 1921, 5s | 1,000 00 | 950 00 |
| Auray Co., Colo., refunding series, 1921, 5s | 1,000 00 | 950 00 |
| Auray Co., Colo., refunding series, 1921, 5s | 1,000 00 | 1,040 00 |
| Valley Co., Mont., School Dist. No. 2, 6s, Opt. 1935 | 1,000 00 | 1,040 00 |
| Valley Co , Mont., School Dist. No. 2, 6s, Opt | 1,000 00 | 1,040 00 |
| Valley Co., Mont., School Dist. No. 2, 6s, Opt | 1,000 00 | 1,040 00 |
| Valley Co., Mont., School Dist. No. 2, 6s, Opt | 1,000 00 | 1,040 00 |
| Valley Co., Mont., School Dist. No. 2, 6s, Opt | 1,000 00 | 1,040 00 |
| Valley Co., Mont., School Dist. No. 2, 6s, Opt | 1,000 00 | 1,040 00 |
| Marshall Co., Lake City, S. Dak., Ind. School, 7s | 1,000 00 | 1,110 00 |
| Marshall Co., Lake City, S. Dak., Ind. School, 7s | 500 00 | 555 00 |
| Marshall Co., Lake City, S. Dak., Ind. School, 7s | 1,000 00 | 1,110 00 |
| Marshall Co., Lake City, S. Dak., Ind. School, 7s | 1,000 00 | 1,110 00 |
| Cuyahoga Co., Maple Heights, Ohio, Thomas St., Water, 6s | 500 00 | 510 00 |
| Cuyahoga Co., Maple Heights, Ohio, Thomas St., Water, 6s | 500 00 | 510 00 |
| Eastland Co., Eastland, Tex., sewer, 6s, Opt. 1940 | 1,000 00 | 1,000 00 |
| Eastland Co., Eastland, Tex., sewer, 6s, Opt | 1,000 00 | 1,000 00 |
| Eastland Co., Eastland, Tex., sewer, 6s, Opt | 1,000 00 | 1,000 00 |
| Eastland Co., Eastland, Tex., sewer, 6s, Opt | 1,000 00 | 1,000 00 |
| Sandusky Co., Clyde, Ohio, school dist., 6s | 1,000 00 | 1,020 00 |
| Sandusky Co., Clyde, Ohio, school dist., 6s | 1,000 00 | 1,020 00 |
| Sandusky Co., Clyde, Ohio, school dist., 6s | 1,000 00 | 1,020 00 |
| Sandusky Co., Clyde, Ohio, school dist., 6s | 1,000 00 | 1,020 00 |
| Sandusky Co., Clyde, Ohio, school dist., 6s | 1,000 00 | 1,020 00 |
| Totals | $542,315 00 | $533,947 44 |

## BOHEMIAN SLAVONIAN UNION.

Located at No. 2309 South Millard Avenue, Chicago, Illinois.

DR. CHARLES NEUMANN, President. FRANK LUKES, Secretary.

| | |
|---|---|
| Balance from previous year | $109,589 49 |

### INCOME.

| | |
|---|---|
| All other assessments or premiums | $80,432 78 |
| Dues and per capita tax | 5,607 88 |
| Juvenile Department members | 694 92 |
| Total received from members | $86,735 58 |
| Gross interest on bonds and dividends on stocks | 4,662 22 |
| Gross interest from all other sources | 167 95 |
| Sale of lodge supplies | 102 90 |
| Benefit from entertainments | 765 03 |
| From certificates | 117 00 |
| Ads in publication | 104 89 |
| Returned old age benefit | 247 34 |
| Profit on purchasing bonds | 741 44 |
| Total income | $93,644 35 |
| Sum | $203,233 84 |

### DISBURSEMENTS.

| | |
|---|---|
| Death claims | $67,050 00 |
| Commissions and fees paid to members | 650 50 |
| Salaries of officers and trustees, No. 17 | 1,607 00 |
| Other compensation of officers and trustees | 65 00 |
| Salaries and other compensation of committees | 23 00 |
| Salaries and fees paid to supreme medical examiners | 149 50 |
| Salaries and fees paid to subordinate medical examiners | 561 75 |
| Traveling and other expenses of officers, trustees and committees | 422 70 |
| Insurance department fees | 5 00 |
| Rent | 89 50 |
| Advertising, printing and stationery | 577 71 |
| Postage, express, telegraph and telephone | 167 46 |
| Lodge supplies | 219 66 |
| Official publication | 2,228 83 |

DISBURSEMENTS—Concluded.

| | | |
|---|---|---|
| Other legal expenses | | $93 50 |
| Surety bond for officers | | 77 50 |
| Donations to organizations | | 79 00 |
| Total disbursements | | $74,067 61 |
| Balance | | $129,166 23 |

LEDGER ASSETS.

| | | |
|---|---|---|
| Book value of bonds and stocks | | $105,000 00 |
| Deposits in trust companies and banks not on interest | | 24,166 23 |
| Total ledger assets | | $129,166 23 |

NON-LEDGER ASSETS.

| | | |
|---|---|---|
| Interest and rents due and accrued | | 573 76 |
| Assessments actually collected by subordinate lodges not yet turned over to supreme lodge | | 6,129 75 |
| Reserve fund | $438 45 | |
| Per capita tax | 539 87 | |
| Juvenile department | 91 30 | |
| | | 1,069 62 |
| Gross assets | | $136,939 36 |

LIABILITIES.

| | | |
|---|---|---|
| Death claims reported during the year but not yet adjusted, No. 6 | $4,250 00 | |
| Death claims incurred in 1921, not reported, until 1922, No. 2 | 1,500 00 | |
| Total unpaid claims | | $5,750 00 |
| Salaries, rents, expenses, commissions, etc., due or accrued | | 835 86 |
| Total | | $6,585 86 |

EXHIBIT OF CERTIFICATES.

| | Total business of the year. | | Business in Illinois during year. | |
|---|---|---|---|---|
| | Number. | Amount. | Number. | Amount. |
| Benefit certificates in force December 31, 1920, as per last statement | 5,812 | $4,367,500 00 | 5,386 | $4,701,750 00 |
| Benefit certificates written and renewed during the year | 341 | 196,750 00 | 315 | 180,000 00 |
| Totals | 6,153 | $4,564,250 00 | 5,701 | $4,281,750 00 |
| Deduct terminated, decreased or transferred during the year | 311 | 194,250 00 | -------- | -------------- |
| Deduct terminated or decreased during the year | -------- | -------------- | 283 | 177,750 00 |
| Total benefit certificates in force December 31, 1921 | 5,842 | $4,370,000 00 | 5,418 | $4,104,000 00 |

Received during the year from members in Illinois: Mortuary, $69,158.16; reserve, $4,942.68; expense, $5,202.64; total — $79,303 48

EXHIBIT OF DEATH CLAIMS.

| | Total claims. | | Illinois claims. | |
|---|---|---|---|---|
| | Number. | Amount. | Number. | Amount. |
| Claims unpaid December 31, 1920, as per last statement | 6 | $ 5,250 00 | 5 | $ 4,250 00 |
| Claims reported during the year and interest addition | 81 | 66,050 00 | 77 | 63,300 00 |
| Totals | 87 | $71,300 00 | 82 | $67,550 00 |
| Claims paid during the year | 81 | 67,050 00 | 76 | 63,300 00 |
| Balance | 6 | $4,250 00 | 6 | $4,250 00 |
| Saved by compromising or scaling down claims during the year | -------- | 700 00 | -------- | 700 00 |
| Claims unpaid December 31, 1921 | 6 | $4,250 00 | 6 | $4,250 00 |

SCHEDULE D—BONDS.

| Description. | Book value. | Par value. |
|---|---|---|
| United States Liberty bonds, 1st, 4¼s | $1,000 00 | $1,000 00 |
| United States Liberty bonds, 2d, 4¼s | 2,150 00 | 2,150 00 |
| United States Liberty bonds, 3d, 4¼s | 4,100 00 | 4,100 00 |
| United States Liberty bonds, 4th, 4¼s | 9,150 00 | 9,150 00 |
| United States Liberty bonds, 5th, 4¾s | 3,100 00 | 3,100 00 |
| Counties of Arkansas and Prairie, Ark., road, 5½s | 3,000 00 | 3,000 00 |
| Counties of Ashe, North, Carolina, road bond, 6s | 2,000 00 | 2,000 00 |

SCHEDULE D—BONDS—Concluded.

| Description. | Book value. | Par value. |
|---|---|---|
| Counties of Anderson, Tenn., road bond, 5s | $3,000 00 | $3,000 00 |
| City of Astoria, Ore., municipal bond, 5s | 2,000 00 | 2,000 00 |
| County of Cook, Ill., detention home, 4½s | 2,000 00 | 2,000 00 |
| County of Collins, Tex., road District No. 7, 5s | 1,000 00 | 1,000 00 |
| Columbus Junction, Iowa, 4¼s | 1,000 00 | 1,000 00 |
| City of Bloomington, Ill., school, 4½s | 1,000 00 | 1,000 00 |
| City of Bronson, Iowa, school bond, 4¾s | 1,000 00 | 1,000 00 |
| City of Chicago, Ill., 4s | 1,000 00 | 1,000 00 |
| City of Chicago, Ill., city hall, 4s | 3,000 00 | 3,000 00 |
| City of Chicago, Ill., corporate bond, 4s | 2,000 00 | 2,000 00 |
| City of Chicago, Ill., Western Ave. improvement, 4s | 5,000 00 | 5,000 00 |
| City of Chicago, West Park Commission, 4s | 1,000 00 | 1,000 00 |
| City of Casper, Wyo., school bond, 6s | 1,000 00 | 1,000 00 |
| City of Detroit, Mich., school bond, 4s | 1,000 00 | 1,000 00 |
| City of DeKalb, Ill., water works ext., 4½s | 500 00 | 500 00 |
| City of Dallas, Tex., road bond, 4½s | 1,000 00 | 1,000 00 |
| City of Denver, Colo., water works, 4½s | 1,000 00 | 1,000 00 |
| State of S. Dak., rural credit, 5s | 1,000 00 | 1,000 00 |
| City of Forth Worth, Tex., imp. bond, 5s | 2,000 00 | 2,000 00 |
| City of Granite, Salt Lake Co., Utah, school, 4½s | 1,000 00 | 1,000 00 |
| City of Grangerville, school dist., King Co., Cal., 5½s | 1,000 00 | 1,000 00 |
| County of Halifax, N. C., 5¼s | 1,000 00 | 1,000 00 |
| County of Harris, Tex., special road, 4¾s | 1,000 00 | 1,000 00 |
| County of Hamilton, Ill., School Dist. No. 39, 4½s | 1,000 00 | 1,000 00 |
| City of Houston, Tex., paying, 4¾s | 1,000 00 | 1,000 00 |
| County of Jackson, Fla., road bond, 5s | 1,000 00 | 1,000 00 |
| City of Johnson, Tenn., road bond, 5s | 1,000 00 | 1,000 00 |
| City of Lewiston, Mont., water bond, 5s | 1,000 00 | 1,000 00 |
| City of Moline, Ill., School Dist. No. 40, 4½s | 1,000 00 | 1,000 00 |
| City of Miami, Conservancy Dist., Ohio, 5½s | 2,000 00 | 2,000 00 |
| County of Nawarro, Tex., Road Dist. No. 3, 5s | 1,000 00 | 1,000 00 |
| Newton, Iowa, gas works, 4½s | 1,000 00 | 1,000 00 |
| Oregon State Highway, 4½s | 2,000 00 | 2,000 00 |
| Omaha, Neb., sewer works, 4½s | 2,000 00 | 2,000 00 |
| Oxnard School Dist., Ventura Co., Cal., 5s | 1,000 00 | 1,000 00 |
| Oak Park, Ill., park dist., 4½s | 1,000 00 | 1,000 00 |
| Portland, Ore., 4½s | 1,000 00 | 1,000 00 |
| County of Piat, Ill., school bond, 4s | 1,000 00 | 1,000 00 |
| Phoenix, Ariz., 5s | 2,000 00 | 2,000 00 |
| Lincoln Park, 4s | 1,000 00 | 1,000 00 |
| Rapid City, S. Dak., school bond, 5s | 1,000 00 | 1,000 00 |
| Red River Co., Tex., road, 5s | 2,000 00 | 2,000 00 |
| County of Salt Lake, Utah, road bond, 5s | 3,000 00 | 3,000 00 |
| San Diego, Cal., water works, 4½s | 2,000 00 | 2,000 00 |
| South Park Commission, 4s | 4,000 00 | 4,000 00 |
| Sanitary Dist. of Chicago, 4s | 3,000 00 | 3,000 00 |
| County of Titus, Tex., road bond, 5½s | 2,000 00 | 2,000 00 |
| County of White, Ark., highway impr., 5½s | 4,000 00 | 4,000 00 |
| County of Wharton, Tex., road impr., 5s | 1,000 00 | 1,000 00 |
| County of W andotte, Kans., bridge and road, 4½s | 2,000 00 | 2,000 00 |
| West ChicagoPark Commission, 4s | 1,000 00 | 1,000 00 |
| Total | $105,000 00 | $105,000 00 |

## BUILDERS OF AMERICA.

Located at No. 26 East Forty-seventh Street, Chicago, Illinois.

A. HAMMOND, President. S. W. COLLINS, Secretary.

| | |
|---|---|
| Balance from previous year | $390 66 |

### INCOME.

| | |
|---|---|
| Membership fees actually received | $ 604 00 |
| Dues and per capita tax | 2,885 34 |
| Medical examiners' fees actually received | 302 00 |
| Total received from members | $3,791 34 |
| Deduct payments returned to applicants and members | 4 50 |
| Net amount received from members | $3,786 84 |
| Sale of lodge supplies | 31 00 |
| Borrowed money (gross) | 1,000 00 |
| Total income | $4,817 84 |
| Sum | $5,208 50 |

## DISBURSEMENTS.

| | |
|---|---|
| Death claims | $ 300 00 |
| Sick and accident claims | 1,150 30 |
| Total benefits paid | $1,450 30 |
| Commissions and fees paid to deputies and organizers | 604 00 |
| Salaries of office employees, No. 1 | 520 00 |
| Salaries and fees paid to supreme medical examiners | 302 00 |
| Insurance department fees | 5 00 |
| Rent | 298 00 |
| Advertising, printing and stationery | 247 65 |
| Postage, express, telegraph and telephone | 100 05 |
| Lodge supplies | 187 50 |
| Other legal expenses | 10 30 |
| Furniture and fixtures | 167 60 |
| Taxes, repairs and other expenses on real estate | 26 00 |
| Borrowed money repaid (gross) | 212 50 |
| Interest on borrowed money | 1 67 |
| Light | 66 52 |
| Total disbursements | $4,199 09 |
| Balance | $1,009 41 |

## LEDGER ASSETS.

| | |
|---|---|
| Cash in association's office | $ 55 20 |
| Deposits in trust companies and banks not on interest | 254 21 |
| Deposits in trust companies and banks on interest | 700 00 |
| Total ledger assets | $1,009 41 |

## LIABILITIES.

| | |
|---|---|
| Borrowed money | $1,000 00 |
| All other liabilities, viz: Balance on note to W. J. Reeves, $76.00; balance on note to Rev. Wm. Blackwell, $80.00; balance on note to Maggie Kimbers, $32.50; balance on note to Alice Carlton, $30.00; balance on note to Jos. C. Bess, $75.00 | 293 50 |
| Total | $1,293 50 |

## EXHIBIT OF CERTIFICATES.

| | Total business of the year—all in Illinois. Number. | Amount. |
|---|---|---|
| Benefit certificates in force December 31, 1920, as per last statement | 640 | $96,000 00 |
| Benefit certificates written and renewed during the year | 604 | 90,600 00 |
| Benefit certificates received by transfer during the year | 12 | 1,800 00 |
| Totals | 1,256 | $188,400 00 |
| Deduct terminated or decreased during the year | 731 | 109,650 00 |
| Total benefit certificates in force December 31, 1921 | 525 | $78,750 00 |

| | |
|---|---|
| Received during the year from members in Illinois: Mortuary, $865.60; reserve, $144.27; disability, $1,009.87; all other, $144.27; expense, $721.33; total | $2,885 34 |

## EXHIBIT OF DEATH CLAIMS.

| | Total claims—all in Illinois. Number. | Amount. |
|---|---|---|
| Claims paid during the year | 2 | $300 00 |

## EXHIBIT OF SICK AND ACCIDENT CLAIMS.

| | Total claims—all in Illinois. Number. | Amount. |
|---|---|---|
| Claims reported during the year | 124 | ---------- |
| Claims paid during the year | 116 | $1,150 30 |
| Claims rejected during the year | 8 | ---------- |

# CATHOLIC KNIGHTS AND LADIES OF ILLINOIS.

Located at No. 705 South Jackson, Belleville, Illinois.

DANIEL E. SWEENEY, President. WM. J. CLAUS, Secretary.

| | |
|---|---|
| Balance from previous year | $305,403 84 |

## INCOME.

| | |
|---|---|
| Membership fees actually received | $ 484 00 |
| All other assessments or premiums | 46,899 93 |
| Dues and per capita tax | 6,896 25 |
| Change of benefit certificates | 8 50 |
| Total received from members | $54,288 68 |

INCOME—Concluded.

| | |
|---|---|
| Gross interest on bonds and dividends on stocks | $16,270 61 |
| Sale of lodge supplies | 100 95 |
| Total income | $70,660 24 |
| Sum | $376,064 08 |

DISBURSEMENTS.

| | |
|---|---|
| Death claims | $31,858 35 |
| Old age benefits | 2,750 00 |
| Loans to members | 1,794 00 |
| Total benefits paid | $36,402 35 |
| Commissions and fees paid to deputies and organizers | 1,306 39 |
| Salaries of deputies and organizers | 3,170 00 |
| Salaries of officers and trustees | 2,693 46 |
| Salaries and fees paid to supreme medical examiners | 127 00 |
| Salaries and fees paid to subordinate medical examiners | 482 00 |
| Traveling and other expenses of officers, trustees and committees | 608 41 |
| Insurance department fees | 15 00 |
| Rent | 195 00 |
| Advertising, printing and stationery | 571 35 |
| Postage, express, telegraph and telephone | 144 72 |
| Lodge supplies | 568 00 |
| Official publication | 780 00 |
| Furniture and fixtures | 7 70 |
| All other disbursements | 331 83 |
| Total disbursements | $47,403 21 |
| Balance | $328,660 87 |

LEDGER ASSETS.

| | |
|---|---|
| Book value of bonds and stocks | $326,192 65 |
| Deposits in trust companies and banks not on interest | 2,468 22 |
| Total ledger assets | $328,660 87 |

NON-LEDGER ASSETS.

| | |
|---|---|
| Interest and rents due and accrued | 7,004 19 |
| Market value of bonds and stocks over book value | 1,689 30 |
| Assessments actually collected by subordinate lodges not yet turned over to supreme lodge | 4,767 15 |
| Total admitted assets | $342,121 51 |

LIABILITIES.

| | | |
|---|---|---|
| Death claims due and unpaid | $ 273 75 | |
| Death claims resisted | 1,000 00 | |
| Total death claims | | $1,273 75 |

EXHIBIT OF CERTIFICATES.

| | Total business of the year—all in Illinois. Number. | Amount. |
|---|---|---|
| Benefit certificates in force December 31, 1920, as per last statement | 515 | $ 283,550 00 |
| Benefit certificates written and renewed during the year | 378 | 385,900 00 |
| Benefit certificates received by transfer during the year | 2,784 | 2,087,200 00 |
| Total | 3,677 | $2,756,650 00 |
| Deduct terminated or decreased during the year | 797 | 560,200 00 |
| Total benefit certificates in force December 31, 1921 | 2,880 | $2,196,450 00 |

| | |
|---|---|
| Received during the year from members in Illinois: Mortuary, $46,899.93; expense, $7,380.25; total | $54,280 18 |

EXHIBIT OF DEATH CLAIMS.

| | Total claims—all in Illinois. Number. | Amount. |
|---|---|---|
| Claims unpaid December 31, 1920, as per last statement | 1 | $ 173 75 |
| Claims reported during the year and interest addition | 33 | 32,958 35 |
| Total | 34 | $33,132 10 |
| Claims paid during the year | 31 | 31,158 35 |
| Claims unpaid December 31, 1921 | 3 | $1,273 75 |

SCHEDULE D—BONDS.

| Description. | Book value. | Par value. | Market value. |
|---|---|---|---|
| Frisco Building Co., St. Louis | $17,750 00 | $18,000 00 | $18,000 00 |
| Star Building Co., St. Louis | 950 00 | 1,000 00 | 1,000 00 |
| East St. Louis & Sub. Co | 17,200 00 | 18,000 00 | 16,200 00 |
| Lincoln Place, East St. Louis, real estate | 12,500 00 | 12,500 00 | 12,500 00 |
| United Rys. Co., St. Louis | 6,000 00 | 8,000 00 | 6,180 00 |
| St. Joseph, Mo., school | 1,000 00 | 1,000 00 | 1,000 00 |
| Galatia, Ill., school | 1,700 00 | 1,700 00 | 1,700 00 |
| Chicago Ry. Co | 4,900 00 | 5,000 00 | 4,900 00 |
| City of Freeport, fire station | 2,748 95 | 3,000 00 | 2,958 75 |
| Texarkana, Ark., school | 3,000 00 | 3,000 00 | 3,000 00 |
| Ft. Smith, Ark., water dist | 5,770 00 | 6,000 00 | 6,000 00 |
| Granite City Gas, Light & Fuel | 2,800 00 | 3,000 00 | 2,872 50 |
| Jefferson City, Mo. Light, Heat & Power Co | 9,900 00 | 10,000 00 | 10,000 00 |
| Monroe & Lee Counties, Ark., drainage | 9,500 00 | 9,500 00 | 9,595 00 |
| Greene & Lawrence Co., Ark., drainage | 7,000 00 | 7,000 00 | 7,070 00 |
| Income Leashold Co., St. Louis | 2,895 00 | 3,000 00 | 2,895 00 |
| Cairo, Ill., drainage district | 4,000 00 | 4,000 00 | 4,080 00 |
| Villemont, Ark., drainage district | 5,000 00 | 5,000 00 | 5,050 00 |
| Lewistown, Ill., improvement | 193 00 | 200 00 | 200 00 |
| Flora, Ill., improvement | 4,850 00 | 5,000 00 | 5,000 00 |
| Carlyle, Ill., sewer | 2,340 00 | 2,400 00 | 2,400 00 |
| Sisters of St. Francis | 2,000 00 | 2,000 00 | 2,000 00 |
| DeSota County, Fla., road and bridge | 6,000 00 | 6,000 00 | 6,120 00 |
| Town of Smithfield, N. C., improvement | 3,000 00 | 3,000 00 | 3,075 00 |
| Fulton County, drainage and levee | 3,000 00 | 3,000 00 | 3,060 00 |
| Hildalgo County, Tex., road | 8,000 00 | 8,000 00 | 8,120 00 |
| Dubuque Electric Co | 6,000 00 | 6,000 00 | 5,820 00 |
| Indian Creek Drainage, Miss | 6,000 00 | 6,000 00 | 6,045 00 |
| Dunkin County, Mo., levee | 3,000 00 | 3,000 00 | 3,000 00 |
| Spring Lake Drainage and Levee, Tazewell County | 7,000 00 | 7,000 00 | 7,070 00 |
| Road Dist., Ft. Ouchita, La | 3,000 00 | 3,000 00 | 3,000 00 |
| Northern Iowa Gas & Electric Co | 3,000 00 | 3,000 00 | 3,000 00 |
| City Dubuque, Iowa, sewerage | 2,000 00 | 2,000 00 | 2,000 00 |
| U. S. Liberty Loan, 2nd | 1,500 00 | 1,500 00 | 1,500 00 |
| City of Kewanee, Ill., improvement | 2,500 00 | 2,500 00 | 2,500 00 |
| Rogersville, Tenn., improvement | 3,000 00 | 3,000 00 | 3,000 00 |
| Grassy Lake, Mississippi County, Ark., drainage | 3,000 00 | 3,000 00 | 3,000 00 |
| Henderson County, Tex., road | 5,000 00 | 5,000 00 | 5,025 00 |
| Village of Arlington Heights, Ill | 3,000 00 | 3,000 00 | 3,000 00 |
| Randolph County, Ark., road | 3,000 00 | 3,000 00 | 3,030 00 |
| Grant County, Ark., road No. 2 | 4,000 00 | 4,000 00 | 4,060 00 |
| Arkansas, La., highway improvement | 5,175 00 | 5,000 00 | 5,075 00 |
| Jefferson County, Ark., road | 3,500 00 | 3,500 00 | 3,500 00 |
| Mississippi County, Ark., drainage No. 17 | 2,985 00 | 3,000 00 | 2,985 00 |
| St. Francis County, Ark., road | 5,096 30 | 5,000 00 | 5,075 00 |
| Little River County, Ark., road | 4,912 00 | 5,000 00 | 4,912 00 |
| County of Crottenden, Ark., road No. 9 | 6,697 00 | 7,000 00 | 7,000 00 |
| Helena Improvement District | 2,000 00 | 2,000 00 | 2,030 00 |
| County of Grant, Ark., road dist. No. 3 | 2,970 00 | 3,000 00 | 3,000 00 |
| Helena-Ferguson Road District | 5,000 00 | 5,000 00 | 5,050 00 |
| County of Lawrence, road No. 4 | 1,980 00 | 2,000 00 | 2,020 00 |
| Marion County, Tex., refund | 4,950 00 | 5,000 00 | 5,050 00 |
| Rusk County Tex., road | 4,925 00 | 5,000 00 | 5,000 00 |
| County of Lubbuck, Tex., park | 4,000 00 | 4,000 00 | 4,000 00 |
| Stowlin Road District No. 2, Mississippi County, Ark | 10,000 00 | 10,000 00 | 10,100 00 |
| County of Shakey, Miss., school district | 5,910 00 | 6,000 00 | 6,120 00 |
| County of Jasper, Mo., special road | 2,880 00 | 3,000 00 | 3,000 00 |
| Town of Oneida, Tenn., improvement | 2,425 00 | 2,500 00 | 2,500 00 |
| County of Shelley, Mo., special road | 6,877 50 | 7,000 00 | 7,000 00 |
| Cache River, Ark., drainage | 4,700 00 | 5,000 00 | 5,000 00 |
| Craighend County, Ark., drainage | 900 00 | 1,000 00 | 1,050 00 |
| Crittenden County, road No. 7 | 1,860 00 | 2,000 00 | 2,010 00 |
| Greene County, N. C., road and bridge | 9,765 00 | 10,000 00 | 10,100 00 |
| County of Wichita, Tex., special road | 2,979 90 | 3,000 00 | 3,000 00 |
| Mississippi County, Ark., drainage | 900 00 | 1,000 00 | 1,000 00 |
| Grant County, Ark., road No. 5 | 4,000 00 | 4,000 00 | 4,060 00 |
| Cross County, Tyronza Road, Ark | 4,800 00 | 5,000 00 | 5,075 00 |
| Mississippi County, Ark., road No. 2 | 4,800 00 | 5,000 00 | 5,050 00 |
| Crittenden County, road No. 7 | 2,895 00 | 3,000 00 | 3,030 00 |
| County of Segnotyah, Okla., Gaus Township | 5,940 00 | 6,000 00 | 6,045 00 |
| Totals | $326,192 65 | $331,300 00 | $328,863 25 |

## CATHOLIC ORDER OF FORESTERS.

Located at No. 30 North LaSalle Street, Chicago, Illinois.

THOS. H. CANNON, High Chief Ranger. THOS. F. McDONALD, High Secretary.

| | |
|---|---|
| Balance from previous year | $9,379,614 15 |

## INCOME.

| | | |
|---|---|---|
| Membership fees actually received | | $2,503,512 49 |
| Certificate fees | | 5,871 00 |
| Total received from members | | $2,509,383 49 |
| Gross interest on deposits in trust companies and banks | | 478,450 98 |
| Gross interest from all other sources | | 2,404 49 |
| Sale of lodge supplies | | 5,251 28 |
| From all other sources, viz— | | |
| Advertising official journal | | 549 49 |
| Premium subordinate court officers' bonds | | 8,694 20 |
| Bonds | | 16,534 08 |
| Total income | | $3,021,268 01 |
| Sum | | $12,400,882 16 |

## DISBURSEMENTS.

| | | |
|---|---|---|
| Death claims | | $1,671,602 61 |
| Commissions and fees paid to deputies and organizers | | 24,726 89 |
| Salaries of deputies and organizers | | 10,281 00 |
| Salaries of managers or agents not deputies or organizers | | 15,500 00 |
| Salaries of officers and trustees | | 3,831 00 |
| Salaries of office employees | | 36,407 85 |
| Salaries and fees paid to supreme medical examiners | | 2,692 50 |
| Traveling and other expenses of officers, trustees and committees | | 7,770 45 |
| Insurance department fees | | 896 25 |
| Rent | | 10,810 92 |
| Advertising, printing and stationery | | 7,230 06 |
| Postage, express, telegraph and telephone | | 5,407 30 |
| Lodge supplies | | 6,910 67 |
| Official publication | | 33,246 30 |
| Bonds | | 6,461 70 |
| Expenses of supreme lodge meeting | | 24,945 31 |
| Legal expense in litigating claims | | 3,635 48 |
| Other legal expenses | | 539 90 |
| Furniture and fixtures | | 441 22 |
| Miscellaneous | | 682 93 |
| Depository | | 1,500 00 |
| Expenses bond purchases | | 258 80 |
| Audit | | 1,222 75 |
| Actuary | | 3,236 18 |
| All other disbursements, viz— | | |
| Premium T. bonds | | 500 00 |
| Subscriptions | | 284 97 |
| N. F. C. of A | | 934 18 |
| Premium subordinate court officers' bonds | | 8,694 20 |
| Total disbursements | | $1,890,651 42 |
| Balance | | $10,510,230 74 |

## LEDGER ASSETS.

| | | |
|---|---|---|
| Book value of bonds and stocks | | $10,435,213 91 |
| Deposits in trust companies and banks on interest | | 75,016 83 |
| Total ledger assets | | $10,510,230 74 |

### NON-LEDGER ASSETS.

| | | |
|---|---|---|
| Interest and rents due and accrued | | $173,479 06 |
| Assessments actually collected by subordinate lodges not yet turned over to supreme lodge | | 23,284 34 |
| All other assets, viz— | | |
| Due from advertising in official journal | $ 174 24 | |
| Lodge supplies | 3,500 00 | |
| Furniture and fixtures | 6,412 88 | |
| | | 10,087 12 |
| Gross assets | | $10,717,081 26 |

### DEDUCT ASSETS NOT ADMITTED.

| | | |
|---|---|---|
| Book value of bonds and stocks over market value | $248,387 56 | |
| Other items, viz— | | |
| Due from advertising in official journal | 174 24 | |
| Lodge supplies | 3,500 00 | |
| Furniture and fixtures | 6,412 88 | |
| | | 258,474 68 |
| Total admitted assets | | $10,458,606 58 |

## LIABILITIES.

| | | |
|---|---|---|
| Death claims due and unpaid—unpaid balances | $ 2,910 71 | |
| Death claims resisted | 5,000 00 | |
| Death claims reported during the year but not yet adjusted | 208,500 00 | |
| Death claims incurred in 1921, not reported until 1922 | 12,500 00 | |
| Total death claims | | $228,910 71 |
| Salaries, rents, expenses, commissions, etc., due or accrued | | 634 33 |
| Total | | $229,545 04 |

## EXHIBIT OF CERTIFICATES.

| | Total business of the year. Number. | Amount. | Business in Illinois during year. Number. | Amount. |
|---|---|---|---|---|
| Benefit certificates in force December 31, 1920, as per last statement | 161,008 | $160,534,250 00 | 38,702 | $39,961,500 00 |
| Benefit certificates written and renewed during the year | 7,030 | 6,062,000 00 | 1,325 | 1,014,000 00 |
| Benefit certificates received by transfer during the year | | | 8 | 7,500 00 |
| Benefit certificates increased during the year | | 79,500 00 | | 12,000 00 |
| Total | 168,038 | $166,675,750 00 | 40,035 | $40,995,000 00 |
| Deduct terminated, decreased or transferred during the year | 7,451 | 7,086,250 00 | | |
| Deduct terminated or decreased during the year | | | 1,599 | 1,493,000 00 |
| Total benefit certificates in force December 31, 1921 | 160,587 | $159,589,500 00 | 38,436 | $39,502,000 00 |

Received during the year from members in Illinois: Mortuary, $584,331.95; expense, $38,881.00; total ........ $623,212 95

## EXHIBIT OF DEATH CLAIMS.

| | Total claims—all in Illinois. Number. | Amount. |
|---|---|---|
| Reinstated | | $ 253 45 |
| Claims unpaid December 31, 1920, as per last statement | 225 | 230,151 19 |
| Claims reported during the year and interest addition | 1,594 | 1,683,500 00 |
| Total | 1,819 | $1,913,904 64 |
| Claims paid during the year | 1,593 | 1,671,602 61 |
| Balance | 226 | $242,302 03 |
| Saved by compromising or scaling down claims during the year | | 10,391 32 |
| Claims rejected during the year | 3 | 3,000 00 |
| Claims unpaid December 31, 1921 | 223 | $228,910 71 |

## SCHEDULE D—BONDS.

| Description. | Par value. | Book value. | Market value. |
|---|---|---|---|
| Dominion of Canada, The Government of, 20-yr., 5s | $ 20,000 00 | $ 20,016 96 | $ 19,400 00 |
| Dominion of Canada, The Government of, 20-yr., 5s | 80,000 00 | 80,000 00 | 77,600 00 |
| Dominion of Canada, 5th war loan, 5½s | 20,000 00 | 19,767 99 | 20,200 00 |
| Dominion of Canada, 5th war loan, 5½s | 80,000 00 | 78,526 48 | 80,800 00 |
| Dominion of Canada, The Government of, 15-yr., 5s | 25,000 00 | 24,833 63 | 24,250 00 |
| Dominion of Canada, The Government of, 15-yr., 5s | 25,000 00 | 24,833 63 | 24,250 00 |
| Dominion of Canada, The Government of, Public Service Loan Act, 5s | 25,000 00 | 25,000 00 | 24,250 00 |
| Dominion of Canada, The Government of, Public Service Loan Act, 5s | 30,000 00 | 30,000 00 | 29,100 00 |
| Dominion of Canada, 15-yr., Public Service Loan Act, 5s | 50,000 00 | 49,370 00 | 48,500 00 |
| Dominion of Canada, war loan, 20-yr., 5s | 100,000 00 | 96,343 90 | 101,000 00 |
| Dominion of Canada, war loan, 20-yr., 5s | 50,000 00 | 48,078 20 | 50,500 00 |
| Dominion of Canada, 15-yr., gold, 5½s | 3,000 00 | 2,752 50 | 2,970 00 |
| Dominion of Canada, 20-yr., war loan, 5s | 50,000 00 | 47,539 00 | 50,500 00 |
| Dominion of Canada, third war loan, 5s | 25,000 00 | 24,416 22 | 25,250 00 |
| United States of America, First Liberty Loan, converted, 1917, 4¼s | 60,000 00 | 60,000 00 | 60,000 00 |
| United States of America, Second Liberty Loan, converted, 1917, 4¼s | 40,000 00 | 40,000 00 | 40,000 00 |
| United States of America, First Liberty Loan, converted, 4¼s | 50,000 00 | 48,157 48 | 48,500 00 |
| United States of America, Fourth Liberty Loan, 4¼s | 250,000 00 | 250,000 00 | 250,000 00 |
| United States of America, Fourth Liberty Loan, 4¼s | 50,000 00 | 45,769 28 | 48,500 00 |
| Aberdeen, City of, Wash., water works, 5½s | 7,000 00 | 7,195 77 | 7,140 00 |
| Aberdeen, City of, Wash., water works, 5½s | 12,000 00 | 12,348 49 | 12,240 00 |
| Aberdeen, City of, Wash., water works, 5½s | 10,000 00 | 10,299 61 | 10,200 00 |
| Alberta, Prov. of, 10-yr., gold debentures, 6s | 50,000 00 | 45,666 24 | 50,000 00 |
| Alberta, Government of, Prov. of, 10-yr., gold deb., 5s | 50,000 00 | 49,523 84 | 48,500 00 |
| Alberta, Government of, Prov. of, 10-yr., gold deb., 5s | 25,000 00 | 24,763 39 | 24,250 00 |

SCHEDULE D—BONDS—Continued.

| Description. | Par value. | Book value. | Market value. |
|---|---|---|---|
| Alberta, Government of, Prov of, 10-yr. gold deb., 5s | $ 25,000 00 | $ 24,763 39 | $ 24,250 00 |
| Alberta, Government of, Prov. of, 10-yr., gold deb., 5s | 50,000 00 | 48,836 00 | 48,500 00 |
| Alberta, Government of, Prov. of, Canada deb., 4½s | 50,000 00 | 49,600 00 | 49,500 00 |
| Alberta, Government of, Prov. of, Canada deb., 4½s | 50,000 00 | 48,987 50 | 48,500 00 |
| Alberta, Government of, Prov. of, Canada deb., 4½s | 2,000 00 | 1,967 01 | 1,940 00 |
| Alberta, Government of, Prov. of, Canada deb., 4½s | 80,000 00 | 79,000 00 | 77,600 00 |
| Alberta, Government of, Prov. of, gold coupon deb., 4½s | 25,000 00 | 25,121 08 | 24,500 00 |
| Alberta, Government of, Prov. of, gold coupon deb., 4½s | 25,000 00 | 25,124 68 | 24,500 00 |
| Albuquerque, N. M., school, 5s | 25,000 00 | 25,564 38 | 23,750 00 |
| Albuquerque, N. M., water supply, 5s | 21,000 00 | 20,916 00 | 19,740 00 |
| Alpine High School Dist. No. 1, Utah County, Utah, high schools, 5s | 33,000 00 | 33,253 96 | 32,670 00 |
| Anderson County, Tenn., road, 4½s | 5,000 00 | 5,000 00 | 4,650 00 |
| Anderson County, Tenn., road, 4½s | 10,000 00 | 10,000 00 | 9,300 00 |
| Anderson County, Tenn., road, 4½s | 10,000 00 | 10,000 00 | 9,300 00 |
| Anderson County, Tex., court house, 5s | 25,000 00 | 24,996 26 | 24,500 00 |
| Austin, Tex., school, 5s | 10,000 00 | 10,285 12 | 9,700 00 |
| Austin, Tex., school, 5s | 10,000 00 | 10,355 20 | 9,700 00 |
| Baker City, Ore., water, 5s | 50,000 00 | 50,760 00 | 50,000 00 |
| Bartlesville, Okla., city hospital, 1917, 5s | 20,000 00 | 19,760 00 | 19,000 00 |
| Blackwell, Okla., electric light and improvement, 1918, 6s | 15,000 00 | 16,013 74 | 16,500 00 |
| Blackwell, Okla., fire equipment, 1918, 6s | 15,000 00 | 16,013 74 | 16,500 00 |
| Beaufort County, N. C., bridge, 5s | 50,000 00 | 50,968 00 | 50,000 00 |
| Bedford, Ohio, village school dist., 6s | 2,000 00 | 2,087 80 | 2,260 00 |
| Bedford, Ohio, village school dist., 6s | 1,000 00 | 1,045 30 | 1,113 00 |
| Bedford, Ohio, village school dist., 6s | 3,000 00 | 3,137 70 | 3,420 00 |
| Bedford, Ohio, village school dist., 6s | 3,000 00 | 3,139 50 | 3,420 00 |
| Bedford, Ohio, village school dist., 6s | 3,000 00 | 3,141 30 | 3,420 00 |
| Bedford, Ohio, village school dist., 6s | 3,000 00 | 3,144 90 | 3,420 00 |
| Bedford, Ohio, village school dist., 6s | 1,000 00 | 1,049 40 | 1,150 00 |
| Bedford, Ohio, village school dist., 6s | 2,000 00 | 2,108 20 | 2,300 00 |
| Bell County, Tex., special road, series M, 6s | 3,000 00 | 2,547 86 | 3,210 00 |
| Bell County, Tex., special road, series M, 6s | 18,000 00 | 15,258 32 | 19,260 00 |
| Bell County, Tex., special road, series M., 6s | 4,000 00 | 3,384 70 | 4,320 00 |
| Bon Homme County, S. D., court house and jail, 5s | 45,000 00 | 45,000 00 | 45,450 00 |
| Beaver, Borough of, Beaver County, Pa., series 9, borrowed money, 5s | 1,000 00 | 1,003 81 | 1,010 00 |
| Beaver, Borough of, Beaver County, Pa., series 9, borrowed money, 5s | 3,000 00 | 3,039 69 | 3,090 00 |
| Beaver, Borough of, Beaver County, Pa., series 9, borrowed money, 5s | 6,000 00 | 6,124 90 | 6,240 00 |
| Blackfoot, Idaho, water works, 6s | 86,000 00 | 80,722 40 | 91,160 00 |
| Brigham City, Utah, electric light, 6s | 20,000 00 | 19,810 00 | 22,000 00 |
| Birmingham, Ala., public schools, 5s | 25,000 00 | 21,744 47 | 25,000 00 |
| Brookings, S. D., Independent School Dist., building, 6¼s | 8,000 00 | 8,000 00 | 8,960 00 |
| Brownsville, Tex., Independent School Dist., schools, 6s | 60,000 00 | 59,100 00 | 64,800 00 |
| British Columbia, Prov. of, 5½s | 175,000 00 | 182,318 50 | 168,000 00 |
| British Columbia, Prov. of, 4½s | 25,000 00 | 22,629 87 | 21,000 00 |
| British Columbia, Prov. of, 4½s | 25,000 00 | 22,629 87 | 21,000 00 |
| British Columbia, Prov. of, 4½s | 25,000 00 | 22,629 87 | 21,000 00 |
| British Columbia, Prov. of, 4½s | 58,000 00 | 53,108 00 | 48,720 00 |
| British Columbia, Prov. of, 4½s | 25,000 00 | 22,629 87 | 21,000 00 |
| British Columbia, Prov. of, 5½s | 12,000 00 | 12,669 10 | 11,520 00 |
| Buchanan Village, Mich., water works, 5s | 10,000 00 | 10,730 07 | 10,000 00 |
| Burnet County, State of Texas, 4th series bridge, 5s | 17,000 00 | 17,000 00 | 17,000 00 |
| Cache County School District, Utah, 4½s | 25,000 00 | 24,906 43 | 24,250 00 |
| Calcasieu Parish, La., road, 5s | 25,000 00 | 25,374 42 | 25,000 00 |
| Calgary Public School Dist. No. 19, Alta., 5s | 5,000 00 | 4,989 83 | 5,000 00 |
| Calgary Public School Dist. No. 19, Alta., 5s | 4,750 00 | 4,725 86 | 4,607 50 |
| Calgary Public School Dist. No. 19, Alta., 5s | 4,000 00 | 3,967 92 | 3,800 00 |
| Calgary Public School Dist. No. 19, Alta., 5s | 4,000 00 | 3,958 33 | 3,760 00 |
| Calgary Public School Dist. No. 19, Alta., 5s | 4,000 00 | 3,947 34 | 3,680 00 |
| Calloway County, Ky., court house, 5s | 5,000 00 | 5,013 25 | 5,000 00 |
| Calloway County, Ky., court house, 5s | 5,000 00 | 5,025 63 | 5,000 00 |
| Callaway County, Ky., court house, 5s | 5,000 00 | 5,034 31 | 5,000 00 |
| Calloway County, Ky., court house, 5s | 15,000 00 | 15,107 90 | 15,150 00 |
| Cameron County, Tex., road, 5½s | 25,000 00 | 23,783 75 | 25,750 00 |
| Cameron County, Tex., road, 5½s | 35,000 00 | 33,300 31 | 36,050 00 |
| Canton, S, Dak., Independent School Dist. No. 1, building, 6s | 25,000 00 | 24,880 36 | 26,500 00 |
| Carter County, Okla., bridge 5s | 25,000 00 | 25,944 93 | 25,250 00 |
| Carter County, Tenn., pike road, 6s | 18,000 00 | 18,000 00 | 20,520 00 |
| Carter County, Tenn., pike road, 6s | 5,000 00 | 5,000 00 | 5,700 00 |
| Cartierville, P. Q. Deb., 5s | 10,000 00 | 9,811 51 | 8,800 00 |
| Casper, Wyo., water works and public buildings, 6s | 44,000 00 | 41,807 66 | 47,080 00 |
| Chattanooga, Tenn., public improvement, 4½s | 30,000 00 | 30,712 22 | 29,700 00 |
| Cherryville, Kan., water, 5½s | 30,000 00 | 31,080 00 | 31,200 00 |
| Chickasha, Okla, sewer, 5s | 50,000 00 | 51,147 50 | 50,500 00 |
| Crookston, Minn., independent school dist., 4½s | 25,000 00 | 25,000 00 | 24,750 00 |
| Cowlitz County, Wash., funding, 5s | 22,000 00 | 22,437 43 | 22,000 00 |

SCHEDULE D—BONDS—Continued.

| Description. | Par value. | Book value. | Market Value. |
|---|---|---|---|
| Columbus County, N. C., court house, 5s | $20,000 00 | $20,592 75 | $20,000 00 |
| Converse County, High School District, Wyo., high school, 5½s | 31,000 00 | 31,000 00 | 31,000 00 |
| Corvallis, Ore., sewers, 5s | 10,000 00 | 10,257 83 | 10,000 00 |
| Cottonwood County, Minn., public drainage ditch, 5s | 4,000 00 | 4,000 00 | 3,960 00 |
| Cottonwood County, Minn., public drainage ditch, 5s | 1,400 00 | 1,400 00 | 1,400 00 |
| Cottonwood County, Minn., public drainage ditch, 5s | 2,500 00 | 2,500 00 | 2,475 00 |
| Cottonwood County, Minn., public drainage ditch, 5s | 1,000 00 | 1,000 00 | 970 00 |
| Cottonwood County, Minn., public drainage ditch, 5s | 1,000 00 | 1,000 00 | 970 00 |
| Cottonwood County, Minn., public drainage ditch, 5s | 2,000 00 | 2,000 00 | 1,940 00 |
| Cottonwood County, Minn., public drainage ditch, 5s | 2,000 00 | 2,000 00 | 1,940 00 |
| Crystal Falls, Mich., school dist., buildings, 5s | 10,000 00 | 9,381 68 | 10,300 00 |
| Davidson County, Tenn., bridges, 4½s | 20,000 00 | 19,684 52 | 19,000 00 |
| Des Moines, City of, Ia., Court Ave., bridge, 4¼s | 4,000 00 | 4,004 00 | 4,000 00 |
| Des Moines, City of, Ia., Court Ave., bridge, 4¼s | 4,000 00 | 3,978 56 | 3,960 00 |
| Des Moines, City of, Ia., Court Ave., bridge, 4¼s | 4,000 00 | 3,959 44 | 3,960 00 |
| Des Moines, City of, Ia., Court Ave., bridge, 4¼s | 2,000 00 | 1,955 32 | 1,980 00 |
| Des Moines, City of, Ia., Court Ave., bridge, 4¼s | 5,000 00 | 4,870 40 | 4,900 00 |
| Des Moines, City of, Ia., Court Ave., bridge, 4¼s | 3,000 00 | 2,906 84 | 2,940 00 |
| Douglas County, Wis., court house and jail, 4½s | 1,500 00 | 1,490 61 | 1,470 00 |
| Douglas County, Wis., court house and jail, 4½s | 500 00 | 494 34 | 485 00 |
| Douglas County, Wis., court house and jail, 4½s | 19,000 00 | 18,783 62 | 18,430 00 |
| Douglas County, Wis., court house and jail, 4½s | 25,000 00 | 24,699 32 | 24,250 00 |
| Douglas County, Wis., court house and jail, 4½s | 20,000 00 | 19,746 48 | 19,200 00 |
| Douglas County, Wis., court house and jail, 4½s | 5,000 00 | 4,931 14 | 4,800 00 |
| Douglas County, Wis., court house and jail, 4½s | 5,000 00 | 4,954 59 | 4,800 00 |
| Douglas County, Wis., court house and jail, 4½s | 25,000 00 | 24,763 39 | 24,000 00 |
| Duluth, Minn., water and light, 4s | 20,000 00 | 19,277 26 | 19,000 00 |
| East St. Louis, Ill., funding, 4½s | 35,000 00 | 35,437 47 | 34,650 00 |
| Eastland County, Tex., special road, 5½s | 10,000 00 | 9,080 81 | 10,300 00 |
| Eastland County, Tex., special road, 5½s | 10,000 00 | 9,050 51 | 10,300 00 |
| Eastland County, Tex., special road, 5½s | 10,000 00 | 9,024 14 | 10,300 00 |
| Eastland County, Tex., special road, 5½s | 10,000 00 | 8,999 80 | 10,300 00 |
| Eastland County, Tex., special road, 5½s | 10,000 00 | 8,976 54 | 10,300 00 |
| Eastland County, Tex., special road, 5½s | 10,000 00 | 8,957 22 | 10,300 00 |
| Eastland, Tex., City of storm (sewers,) 6s | 25,000 00 | 22,345 79 | 26,750 00 |
| Edmonton, Prov. Alberta, Can., debentures, 4½s | 2,044 77 | 1,993 17 | 1,615 37 |
| Edmonton, Prov. Alberta, Can., debentures, 4½s | 4,753 25 | 4,629 35 | 3,422 34 |
| Edmonton, Prov. Alberta, Can., debentures, 4½s | 4,120 19 | 4,000 94 | 2,884 13 |
| Edmonton, Prov. Alberta, Can., debentures, 4½s | 2,000 00 | 1,949 16 | 1,580 00 |
| Edmonton, Prov. Alberta, Can., debentures, 4½s | 2,000 00 | 1,947 58 | 1,440 00 |
| Edmonton, Prov. Alberta, Can., debentures, 4½s | 2,000 00 | 1,946 08 | 1,440 00 |
| Edmonton, Prov. Alberta, Can., debentures, 4½s | 2,000 00 | 1,944 66 | 1,440 00 |
| Edmonton, Prov. Alberta, Can., debentures, 4½s | 1,084 25 | 1,053 56 | 769 82 |
| El Paso, Tex., school, 5s | 40,000 00 | 41,585 22 | 40,400 00 |
| El Paso, Tex., water works, 5s | 25,000 00 | 25,763 60 | 25,500 00 |
| El Paso, Tex., water works, 5s | 25,000 00 | 25,880 90 | 25,500 00 |
| El Paso, Tex., sewer, 5s | 25,000 00 | 25,584 26 | 25,500 00 |
| El Paso County, Tex., court and jail, series 1916, 4½s | 25,000 00 | 23,089 64 | 25,250 00 |
| El Paso County, Tex., special road, 5s | 35,000 00 | 34,929 99 | 35,700 00 |
| El Paso County, Tex., special road, 5s | 50,000 00 | 49,900 40 | 51,000 00 |
| El Paso County, Tex., poor farm, 5s | 30,000 00 | 30,000 00 | 30,000 00 |
| El Paso County, Tex., court house and jail, 5s | 50,000 00 | 50,383 14 | 50,500 00 |
| El Paso County, Tex., special road, 5s | 10,000 00 | 10,121 92 | 10,200 00 |
| El Paso County, Tex., court house and jail, series 1916, 4½s | 25,000 00 | 24,280 14 | 25,250 00 |
| Ennis, Tex., water works, 5s | 20,000 00 | 19,958 18 | 19,800 00 |
| Etowah County, Ala., public road and bridge, 5s | 23,000 00 | 23,000 00 | 22,310 00 |
| Fall River County, S. D., judgment fund., 1912, 5s | 15,000 00 | 15,290 59 | 15,000 00 |
| Fayetteville, N. C., graded school building, 6s | 50,000 00 | 52,755 00 | 56,000 00 |
| Fergus County, Mont., free high school, 5s | 5,000 00 | 5,000 00 | 4,950 00 |
| Fergus County, Mont., free high school, 5s | 10,000 00 | 10,000 00 | 9,900 00 |
| Fergus County, Mont., free high school, 5s | 10,000 00 | 10,000 00 | 9,900 00 |
| Flandreau, S. D., Independent School District building, series 1920, 6s | 10,000 00 | 10,191 70 | 10,900 00 |
| Flandreau, S. D., Independent School District building, series 1920, 6s | 10,000 00 | 10,204 55 | 11,000 00 |
| Flandreau, S. D., Independent School District building, series 1920, 6s | 5,000 00 | 5,106 20 | 5,550 00 |
| Florence, Neb., fund., 5s | 12,500 00 | 12,397 47 | 12,500 00 |
| Ft. Worth, Tex., series 20 and 28, fire hall and waterworks, 5s | 10,000 00 | 10,355 97 | 10,200 00 |
| Ft. Worth, Tex., waterworks, 5s | 25,000 00 | 25,665 90 | 25,500 00 |
| Fort William, Ont., debentures, 4½s | 24,820 00 | 23,806 20 | 20,600 60 |
| Gilmore City, Iowa, waterworks, 5½s | 8,000 00 | 8,350 36 | 8,320 00 |
| Guelph, Ont., bridges, 4½s | 2,810 00 | 2,763 93 | 2,472 80 |
| Guelph, Ont., collegiate institute, 4½s | 2,500 00 | 2,458 95 | 2,200 00 |
| Guelph, Ont., public schools, 4½s | 7,000 00 | 6,884 97 | 6,160 00 |
| Galion City, Dist. of Galion, Ohio, bldg. and site, 5s | 500 00 | 500 00 | 515 00 |
| Gallon City, Dist. of Galion, Ohio, bldg. and site, 5s | 500 00 | 500 00 | 515 00 |
| Galion City, Dist. of Gallon, Ohio, bldg. and site, 5s | 500 00 | 500 00 | 515 00 |
| Gallon City, Dist. of Gallon, Ohio, bldg. and site, 5s | 500 00 | 500 00 | 515 00 |

SCHEDULE D—BONDS—Continued.

| Description. | Par value. | Book value. | Market value. |
|---|---|---|---|
| Galion City, Dist. of Galion, Ohio, bldg. and site, 5s | $ 500 00 | $ 500 00 | $ 515 00 |
| Galion City, Dist. of Galion, Ohio, bldg. and site, 5s | 500 00 | 500 00 | 515 00 |
| Galion City, Dist. of Galion, Ohio, bldg. and site, 5s | 500 00 | 500 00 | 520 00 |
| Galion City, Dist. of Galion, Ohio, bldg. and site, 5s | 500 00 | 500 00 | 520 00 |
| Galion City, Dist. of Galion, Ohio, bldg. and site, 5s | 500 00 | 500 00 | 520 00 |
| Galion City, Dist. of Galion, Ohio, bldg. and site, 5s | 500 00 | 500 00 | 520 00 |
| Galion City, Dist. of Galion, Ohio, bldg. and site, 5s | 500 00 | 500 00 | 520 00 |
| Galion City, Dist. of Galion, Ohio, bldg. and site, 5s | 500 00 | 500 00 | 520 00 |
| Galion City, Dist. of Galion, Ohio, bldg. and site, 5s | 500 00 | 500 00 | 520 00 |
| Galion City, Dist. of Galion, Ohio, bldg. and site, 5s | 500 00 | 500 00 | 520 00 |
| Galion City, Dist. of Galion, Ohio, bldg. and site, 5s | 500 00 | 500 00 | 520 00 |
| Galion City, Dist. of Galion, Ohio, bldg. and site, 5s | 500 00 | 500 00 | 520 00 |
| Galion City, Dist. of Galion, Ohio, bldg. and site, 5s | 1,000 00 | 1,000 00 | 1,040 00 |
| Galion City, Dist. of Galion, Ohio, bldg. and site, 5s | 1,000 00 | 1,000 00 | 1,040 00 |
| Galion City, Dist. of Galion, Ohio, bldg. and site, 5s | 1,000 00 | 1,000 00 | 1,040 00 |
| Galion City, Dist. of Galion, Ohio, bldg. and site, 5s | 1,000 00 | 1,000 00 | 1,040 00 |
| Galion City, Dist. of Galion, Ohio, bldg. and site, 5s | 1,000 00 | 1,000 00 | 1,040 00 |
| Galion City, Dist. of Galion, Ohio, bldg. and site, 5s | 1,000 00 | 1,000 00 | 1,040 00 |
| Galion City, Dist. of Galion, Ohio, bldg. and site, 5s | 1,000 00 | 1,000 00 | 1 040 00 |
| Hamtramck, Mich., public sewers, 5s | 5,000 00 | 4,749 75 | 5,200 00 |
| Hamtramck, Mich., school and building site, 4½s | 5,000 00 | 4,555 87 | 4,950 00 |
| Harris County, Tex., road and bridge, 4½s | 25,000 00 | 24,955 60 | 23,250 00 |
| Harris County, Tex., special road, 4½s | 50,000 00 | 49,652 26 | 48,000 00 |
| Hastings County, Ont., 5s | 1,703 02 | 1,682 42 | 1,617 87 |
| Hastings County, Ont., 5s | 1,838 17 | 1,811 97 | 1,727 88 |
| Hastings County, Ont., 5s | 1,980 08 | 1,947 28 | 1,841 48 |
| Hastings County, Ont., 5s | 2,129 08 | 2,089 68 | 1,958 75 |
| Hastings County, Ont., 5s | 2,285 53 | 2,238 61 | 2,079 83 |
| Hastings County, Ont., 5s | 2,449 81 | 2,396 48 | 2,204 83 |
| Hastings County, Ont., 5s | 2,622 30 | 2,558 67 | 2,360 07 |
| Hastings County, Ont., 5s | 2,803 42 | 2,730 67 | 2,495 04 |
| Hochelaga School Commission of Montreal, P. Q., Deb., 5s | 25,000 00 | 24,460 28 | 23,000 00 |
| Hawkins County, Tenn., road and bridge, 5s | 1,000 00 | 1,018 70 | 1,000 00 |
| Hawkins County, Tenn., road and bridge, 5s | 1,000 00 | 1,031 82 | 1,000 00 |
| Hawkins County, Tenn., road and bridge, 5s | 3,000 00 | 3,096 94 | 3,000 00 |
| Hawkins County, Tenn., road and bridge, 5s | 3,000 00 | 3,097 72 | 3,000 00 |
| Hawkins County, Tenn., road and bridge, 5s | 3,000 00 | 3,098 40 | 3,000 00 |
| Hawkins County, Tenn., road and bridge, 5s | 3,000 00 | 3,101 73 | 3,000 00 |
| Hawkins County, Tenn., road and bridge, 5s | 3,000 00 | 3,102 27 | 3,000 00 |
| Hawkins County, Tenn., road and bridge, 5s | 2,000 00 | 2,068 61 | 2,000 00 |
| Henderson County, Tenn., road improvement, 6s | 48,000 00 | 46,300 86 | 53,760 00 |
| Henderson County, Tenn., road improvement, 6s | 27,000 00 | 26,917 60 | 30,780 00 |
| Hickman County, Tenn., road, 6s | 10,000 00 | 9,697 03 | 11,000 00 |
| Hickman County, Tenn., road, 6s | 10,000 00 | 9,682 11 | 11,100 00 |
| Houghton, Mich., water works, 5s | 10,000 00 | 10,000 00 | 10,200 00 |
| Houston, Tex., fire station market, 5s | 10,000 00 | 10,330 00 | 10,300 00 |
| Houston, Tex., water works, 5s | 10,000 00 | 10,678 66 | 10,400 00 |
| Houston, Tex., water works, 5s | 9,000 00 | 9,414 82 | 9,360 00 |
| Jackson County, Minn., public drainage ditch, 5s | 2,000 00 | 2,014 80 | 2,040 00 |
| Jackson County, Minn., public drainage ditch, 5s | 9,000 00 | 9,082 00 | 9,180 00 |
| Jackson County, Minn., public drainage ditch, 5s | 2,000 00 | 2,024 80 | 2,040 00 |
| Jackson County, Minn., public drainage ditch, 5s | 9,000 00 | 9,138 32 | 9,270 00 |
| Jackson County, Minn., public drainage ditch, 5s | 1,000 00 | 1,016 78 | 1,030 00 |
| Jackson County, Minn., public drainage ditch, 5s | 2,000 00 | 2,036 24 | 2,080 00 |
| Jackson County, Minn., public drainage ditch, 5s | 1,000 00 | 1,021 05 | 1,040 00 |
| Jackson County, Minn., public drainage ditch, 5s | 8,000 00 | 8,181 80 | 8,320 00 |
| Jackson County, Minn., public drainage ditch, 5s | 9,000 00 | 9,217 75 | 9,360 00 |
| Jackson County, Minn., public drainage ditch, 5s | 6,000 00 | 6,153 30 | 6,240 00 |
| Jackson County, Minn., public drainage ditch, 5s | 1,000 00 | 1,026 85 | 1,040 00 |
| Johnson County, Tenn., road improvement, 5s | 26,000 00 | 25,784 30 | 26,000 00 |
| Jackson, Miss., water works expense and imp., 5½s | 36,000 00 | 36,774 18 | 37,440 00 |
| Kenton, Ohio, city school district, school, 6s | 10,000 00 | 10,328 17 | 11,100 00 |
| Kenton, Ohio, city school district, school, 6s | 3,000 00 | 3,119 30 | 3,390 00 |
| Kenton, Ohio, city school district, school, 6s | 2,000 00 | 2,087 53 | 2,280 00 |
| King County, Wash., funding, 5s | 25,000 00 | 25,460 02 | 25,250 00 |
| Knoxville, Tenn., water works, 4½s | 25,000 00 | 25,440 55 | 23,500 00 |
| Knoxville, Tenn., refunding, 5s | 31,000 00 | 31,752 03 | 31,620 00 |
| Long Beach, Cal., 39th Place Pier, 5s | 625 00 | 623 97 | 631 25 |
| Long Beach, Cal., 39th Place Pier, 5s | 625 00 | 623 83 | 631 25 |
| Long Beach, Cal., 39th Place Pier, 5s | 625 00 | 623 62 | 631 25 |
| Long Beach, Cal., 39th Place Pier, 5s | 625 00 | 623 41 | 631 25 |
| Long Beach, Cal., 39th Place Pier, 5s | 625 00 | 623 34 | 637 50 |
| Long Beach, Cal., 39th Place Pier, 5s | 625 00 | 623 27 | 637 50 |
| Long Beach, Cal., 39th Place Pier, 5s | 625 00 | 623 20 | 637 50 |
| Long Beach, Cal., 39th Place Pier, 5s | 625 00 | 623 13 | 637 50 |
| Long Beach, Cal., 39th Place Pier, 5s | 625 00 | 623 06 | 637 50 |
| Long Beach, Cal., 39th Place Pier, 5s | 625 00 | 623 06 | 637 50 |
| Long Beach, Cal., 39th Place Pier, 5s | 625 00 | 622 92 | 637 50 |
| Long Beach, Cal., 39th Place Pier, 5s | 625 00 | 622 85 | 643 75 |
| Long Beach, Cal., 39th Place Pier, 5s | 625 00 | 622 78 | 643 75 |
| Long Beach, Cal., 39th Place Pier, 5s | 625 00 | 622 78 | 643 75 |
| Long Beach, Cal., 39th Place Pier, 5s | 625 00 | 622 78 | 643 75 |

SCHEDULE D—BONDS—Continued.

| Description. | Par value. | Book value. | Market value. |
|---|---|---|---|
| Long Beach, Cal., 39th Place Pier, 5s | $ 625 00 | $ 622 72 | $ 643 75 |
| Long Beach, Cal., 39th Place Pier, 5s | 625 00 | 622 72 | 643 75 |
| Long Beach, Cal., 39th Place Pier, 5s | 625 00 | 622 65 | 643 75 |
| Long Beach, Cal., 39th Place Pier, 5s | 625 00 | 622 65 | 643 75 |
| Long Beach, Cal., 39th Place Pier, 5s | 625 00 | 622 58 | 643 75 |
| Long Beach, Cal., 39th Place Pier, 5c | 625 00 | 622 51 | 650 00 |
| Long Beach, Cal., 39th Place Pier, 5s | 625 00 | 622 44 | 650 00 |
| Long Beach, Cal., 39th Place Pier, 5s | 625 00 | 622 44 | 650 00 |
| Long Beach, Cal., 39th Place Pier, 5s | 625 00 | 622 44 | 650 00 |
| Long Beach, Cal., 39th Place Pier, 5s | 625 00 | 622 44 | 650 00 |
| Long Beach, Cal., 39th Place Pier, 5s | 625 00 | 622 44 | 650 00 |
| Long Beach, Cal., 39th Place Pier, 5s | 625 00 | 622 44 | 650 00 |
| Long Beach, Cal., 39th Place Pier, 5s | 625 00 | 622 44 | 650 00 |
| Long Beach, Cal., 39th Place Pier, 5s | 625 00 | 622 44 | 650 00 |
| Long Beach, Cal., 39th Place Pier, 5s | 625 00 | 622 44 | 650 00 |
| Larksville, Pa., funding, 5½s | 9,000 00 | 9,407 76 | 9,720 00 |
| Larksville, Pa., funding, 5½s | 4,000 00 | 4,258 20 | 4,560 00 |
| Larksville, Pa., school dist., 5½s | 9,000 00 | 9,584 25 | 10,170 00 |
| Los Angeles, Cal., water, 4s | 12,500 00 | 12,923 54 | 11,250 00 |
| Los Angeles, Cal., water, 4s | 12,500 00 | 12,937 32 | 11,250 00 |
| Los Angeles, Cal., water, 4½s | 30,000 00 | 30,982 31 | 27,000 00 |
| Madison County, Idaho, road and bridge, 5½s | 2,000 00 | 2,022 00 | 2,020 00 |
| Madison County, Idaho, road and bridge, 5½s | 2,000 00 | 2,030 40 | 2,040 00 |
| Madison County, Idaho, road and bridge, 5½s | 2,000 00 | 2,029 90 | 2,060 00 |
| Madison County, Idaho, road and bridge, 5½s | 1,000 00 | 1,018 04 | 1,030 00 |
| Madison County, Idaho, road and bridge, 5½s | 2,000 00 | 2,041 24 | 2,060 00 |
| Madison County, Idaho, road and bridge, 5½s | 2,000 00 | 2,045 57 | 2,080 00 |
| Madison County, Idaho, road and bridge, 5½s | 1,000 00 | 1,024 66 | 1,040 00 |
| Madison County, Idaho, road and bridge, 5½s | 2,000 00 | 2,052 57 | 2,100 00 |
| Madison County, Idaho, road and bridge, 5½s | 2,000 00 | 2,055 20 | 2,100 00 |
| Madison County, Idaho, road and bridge, 5½s | 1,000 00 | 1,028 90 | 1,050 00 |
| Madison, Minn., water and light, 5s | 2,000 00 | 2,042 33 | 2,020 00 |
| Madison, Minn., water and light, 5s | 2,000 00 | 2,045 33 | 2,020 00 |
| Madison, Minn., water and light, 5s | 2,000 00 | 2,048 57 | 2,020 00 |
| Madison, Minn., water and light, 5s | 2,000 00 | 2,051 62 | 2,020 00 |
| Madison, Minn., water and light, 5s | 2,000 00 | 2,054 69 | 2,020 00 |
| Madison, Minn., water and light, 5s | 2,000 00 | 2,057 66 | 2,020 00 |
| Madison, Minn., water and light, 5s | 2,000 00 | 2,060 36 | 2,020 00 |
| Madison, Minn., water and light, 5s | 2,000 00 | 2,063 48 | 2,020 00 |
| Madison, Minn., water and light, 5s | 2,000 00 | 2,064 67 | 2,040 00 |
| Madison, Minn., water and light, 5s | 2,000 00 | 2,067 29 | 2,040 00 |
| Madison, Minn., water and light, 5s | 10,000 00 | 10,351 56 | 10,200 00 |
| Madison, S. D., electric light, 5s | 20,000 00 | 18,085 98 | 20,200 00 |
| Madison County, Tenn., road, series C, 4s | 25,000 00 | 24,316 63 | 21,250 00 |
| Maricopa County, Ariz., highways, 5½s | 25,000 00 | 23,334 62 | 26,500 00 |
| Maricopa County, Ariz., highways, 5½s | 15,000 00 | 13,976 63 | 15,900 00 |
| Maricopa County, Ariz., highways, 5½s | 19,000 00 | 17,677 00 | 20,330 00 |
| Maricopa County, Ariz., highways, 5½s | 40,000 00 | 38,469 21 | 42,800 00 |
| Marshall County, Minn., Pub. Drain. Ditch, No. 25, 5½s | 4,000 00 | 4,148 32 | 4,200 00 |
| Marshall County, Minn., Pub. Drain. Ditch, No. 25, 5½s | 4,000 00 | 4,154 60 | 4,240 00 |
| Marshall County, Minn., Pub. Drain. Ditch, No. 25, 5½s | 4,000 00 | 4,169 52 | 4,240 00 |
| Marshall County, Minn., Pub. Drain. Ditch, No. 25, 5½s | 4,000 00 | 4,179 20 | 4,240 00 |
| Marshall County, Minn., Pub. Drain. Ditch, No. 25, 5½s | 4,000 00 | 4,188 24 | 4,280 00 |
| Marshall County, Minn., Pub. Drain. Ditch, No. 25, 5½s | 7,000 00 | 7,345 42 | 7,490 00 |
| Marshall County, Minn., Pub. Drain. Ditch, No. 28, 5½s | 2,000 00 | 2,071 88 | 2,100 00 |
| Marshall County, Minn., Pub. Drain. Ditch, No. 28, 5½s | 2,000 00 | 2,077 40 | 2,120 00 |
| Marshall County, Minn., Pub. Drain. Ditch, No. 28, 5½s | 2,000 00 | 2,082 88 | 2,120 00 |
| Marshall County, Minn., Pub. Drain. Ditch, No. 28, 5½s | 2,000 00 | 2,087 92 | 2,120 00 |
| Marshall County, Minn., Pub. Drain. Ditch, No. 28, 5½s | 2,000 00 | 2,092 56 | 2,140 00 |
| Marshall County, Minn., Pub. Drain. Ditch, No. 28, 5½s | 13,000 00 | 13,631 94 | 13,910 00 |
| Maricopa County, Ariz., School District No. 40, 5s | 25,000 00 | 24,718 75 | 25,000 00 |
| Marion County, Ore., school building site, series A, B, C, 5s | 35,000 00 | 35,362 85 | 35,000 00 |
| Marion County, Ore., series D, 5s | 15,000 00 | 15,156 97 | 15,000 00 |
| Marion County, Ore., series D, 5s | 4,000 00 | 4,042 26 | 4,000 00 |
| Marion City School Dist., Ohio, 5½s | 1,000 00 | 1,022 78 | 1,040 00 |
| Marion City School Dist., Ohio, 5½s | 1,000 00 | 1,024 66 | 1,040 00 |
| Marion City School Dist., Ohio, 5½s | 1,000 00 | 1,024 66 | 1,050 00 |
| Marion City School Dist., Ohio, 5½s | 1,000 00 | 1,026 14 | 1,050 00 |
| Marion City School Dist., Ohio, 5½s | 1,000 00 | 1,026 14 | 1,050 00 |
| Marion City School Dist., Ohio, 5½s | 1,000 00 | 1,027 38 | 1,050 00 |
| Marion City School Dist., Ohio, 5½s | 1,000 00 | 1,027 38 | 1,060 00 |
| Marion City School Dist., Ohio, 5½s | 1,000 00 | 1,027 38 | 1,060 00 |
| Marion City School Dist., Ohio, 5½s | 1,000 00 | 1,029 34 | 1,060 00 |
| Marion City School Dist., Ohio, 5½s | 1,000 00 | 1,030 14 | 1,060 00 |
| Marion City School Dist., Ohio, 5½s | 1,000 00 | 1,030 14 | 1,070 00 |
| Marion City School Dist., Ohio, 5½s | 1,000 00 | 1,030 14 | 1,070 00 |
| Marion City School Dist., Ohio, 5½s | 1,000 00 | 1,030 14 | 1,070 00 |
| Marion City School Dist., Ohio, 5½s | 1,000 00 | 1,030 62 | 1,070 00 |
| Marion City School Dist., Ohio, 5½s | 1,000 00 | 1,030 62 | 1,070 00 |
| Marion City School Dist., Ohio, 5½s | 1,000 00 | 1,030 62 | 1,070 00 |
| Marion City School Dist., Ohio, 5½s | 1,000 00 | 1,031 38 | 1,080 00 |

SCHEDULE D—BONDS—Continued.

| Description. | Par value. | Book value. | Market value. |
|---|---|---|---|
| Marion City School Dist., Ohio, 5½s | $ 1,000 00 | $ 1,031 38 | $ 1,080 00 |
| Marion City School Dist., Ohio, 5½s | 1,000 00 | 1,031 94 | 1,080 00 |
| Marion City School Dist., Ohio, 5½s | 1,000 00 | 1,032 42 | 1,080 00 |
| Menominee City, Mich., public schools, 4½s | 5,000 00 | 4,883 14 | 4,950 00 |
| Menominee City, Mich., public schools, 4½s | 7,000 00 | 6,811 29 | 6,930 00 |
| Menominee City, Mich., public schools, 4½s | 7,000 00 | 6,787 37 | 6,930 00 |
| Memphis, Tenn., water, 4s | 25,000 00 | 25,196 75 | 23,000 00 |
| Memphis, Tenn., board of education, 4½s | 25,000 00 | 25,543 75 | 22,250 00 |
| Memphis, Tenn., Normal School, 4½s | 44,000 00 | 44,109 37 | 42,240 00 |
| Manitoba, Prov. of, 20-yr., gold coupon deb., 5½s | 20,000 00 | 20,623 90 | 19,800 00 |
| Mesa School District, Maricopa County, Ariz., building, 5½s | 43,000 00 | 40,602 00 | 45,580 00 |
| Manitoba, Prov. of, 20-yr. gold coupon deb., 5½s | 50,000 00 | 52,618 87 | 49,500 00 |
| Manitoba, Prov. of, 15-yr. gold coupon deb., 5½s | 175,000 00 | 182,238 02 | 173,250 00 |
| Manitoba, Prov. of, 15-yr. gold coupon deb., 5½s | 25,000 00 | 26,032 00 | 24,750 00 |
| Manitoba, Prov. of, 10-yr. gold coupon deb., 5s | 170,000 00 | 168,659 42 | 166,600 00 |
| Missoula County, Mont., School Dist. No. 28, building, 6s | 45,000 00 | 44,917 28 | 50,400 00 |
| Montgomery County, Ala., schools, 6s | 19,000 00 | 19,000 00 | 21,090 00 |
| Montreal, P. Q., St. Stanislaus School Commissioners, 5½s | 25,000 00 | 26,867 20 | 21,750 00 |
| Montreal, City of, P. Q., 5s | 138,000 00 | 138,000 00 | 118,680 00 |
| Montreal, City of, P. Q., 5s | 75,000 00 | 74,509 60 | 59,250 00 |
| Montreal, P. Q., municipal, 3½s | 30,000 00 | 30,104 00 | 20,700 00 |
| Montreal, P. Q., school, 4s | 25,000 00 | 25,516 83 | 17,500 00 |
| Montreal, City of, P. Q., 5s | 25,000 00 | 24,835 91 | 19,750 00 |
| Montreal, P. Q., Catholic School Commission, 5s | 50,000 00 | 49,270 88 | 40,500 00 |
| Montreal, P. Q., Catholic School Commission, 5s | 80,000 00 | 78,929 98 | 64,800 00 |
| Montreal, P. Q., Catholic School Commissioners of (bond loan), 5s | 50,000 00 | 48,196 20 | 41,000 00 |
| Mobile, Ala., refunding, 4½s | 29,000 00 | 28,446 63 | 27,840 00 |
| Mobile County, Ala., public roads, 5s | 35,000 00 | 35,000 00 | 35,700 00 |
| Mobile, Ala., school building, 5s | 34,000 00 | 34,497 74 | 34,680 00 |
| Mooresville, N. C., graded school dist., school, 6s | 25,000 00 | 24,637 93 | 27,750 00 |
| Murray City, Utah, water works and paving, 6s | 11,000 00 | 11,000 00 | 11,000 00 |
| Nash County, N. C., court house, 6s | 4,000 00 | 4,000 00 | 4,280 00 |
| Nash County, N. C., court house, 6s | 4,000 00 | 4,000 00 | 4,280 00 |
| Nash County, N. C., court house, 6s | 4,000 00 | 4,000 00 | 4,320 00 |
| Nash County, N. C., court house, 6s | 4,000 00 | 4,000 00 | 4,320 00 |
| Nash County, N. C., court house, 6s | 9,000 00 | 9,000 00 | 9,720 00 |
| Norwood, Ohio, Allison Street school building, 5s | 15,000 00 | 15,640 00 | 15,450 00 |
| Norwood, Ohio, Allison Street school building, 5s | 25,000 00 | 26,098 30 | 25,750 00 |
| New Brunswick, Province of, gold debentures, 5½s | 50,000 00 | 49,248 00 | 49,000 00 |
| New Brunswick, Prov. of, debentures, 6s | 50,000 00 | 49,159 84 | 50,500 00 |
| New Orleans, La., court house, 5s | 25,000 00 | 27,246 85 | 25,500 00 |
| New Orleans, La., court house, 5s | 25,000 00 | 27,524 83 | 25,500 00 |
| New York City stock, corp., 3½s | 25,000 00 | 25,000 00 | 21,500 00 |
| North Ft. Worth, Tex., water works, 4s | 10,000 00 | 9,283 03 | 8,900 00 |
| Nueces County, Tex., court house and jail, 5s | 16,000 00 | 16,129 44 | 16,000 00 |
| Nueces County, Tex., court house and jail, 5s | 50,000 00 | 50,752 68 | 50,000 00 |
| Nueces County, Tex., court house and jail, 5s | 5,000 00 | 4,998 52 | 5,000 00 |
| Ogden City, Utah, water, series 14, 4½s | 25,000 00 | 25,363 79 | 24,750 00 |
| Oklahoma City, water and sewer, 4½s | 25,000 00 | 25,715 30 | 23,000 00 |
| Oklahoma City, water and sewer, 4½s | 25,000 00 | 25,092 31 | 23,000 00 |
| Okmulgee, Okla., board of education building, 5s | 50,000 00 | 49,126 20 | 50,000 00 |
| Omaha, Neb., renewal, 4½s | 25,000 00 | 25,237 26 | 24,750 00 |
| Orange County, Tex., road, 5s | 50,000 00 | 50,954 00 | 49,000 00 |
| Ottawa, City of, Ont., debentures, 5½s | 10,000 00 | 10,500 92 | 9,700 00 |
| Ottawa, City of, Ont., debentures, 5½s | 20,000 00 | 21,024 48 | 19,400 00 |
| Ontario, Prov. of, 5-yr. gold debentures, 5½s | 100,000 00 | 98,900 00 | 99,000 00 |
| Ottawa, Ont., sewer, 3½s | 20,000 00 | 20,043 94 | 17,400 00 |
| Ottawa, City of, Ont., debentures, 5s | 4,000 00 | 3,992 57 | 3,680 00 |
| Ottawa, City of, Ont., debentures, 5s | 5,000 00 | 4,990 59 | 4,600 00 |
| Ottawa, City of, Ont., debentures, 5s | 5,000 00 | 4,990 43 | 4,600 00 |
| Ottawa, City of, Ont., debentures, 5s | 5,500 00 | 5,489 13 | 5,005 00 |
| Ottawa, City of, Ont., debentures, 5s | 5,000 00 | 4,990 17 | 4,550 00 |
| Ottawa, City of, Ont., debentures, 5s | 6,000 00 | 5,988 09 | 5,460 00 |
| Ottawa, City of, Ont., debentures, 5s | 6,500 00 | 6,486 99 | 5,915 00 |
| Ottawa, City of, Ont., debentures, 5s | 6,000 00 | 5,987 73 | 5,400 00 |
| Ottawa, City of, Ont., debentures, 5s | 57,000 00 | 56,883 95 | 51,300 00 |
| Ottawa, City of, Ont., debentures, 5s | 14,000 00 | 11,309 77 | 12,600 00 |
| Ottawa, City of, Ont., debentures, 5s | 15,000 00 | 12,094 88 | 13,500 00 |
| Ontario, Prov. of, debentures, 5½s | 400,000 00 | 377,382 24 | 392,000 00 |
| Ontario, Prov. of, consolidated revenue fund, 5s | 35,000 00 | 34,960 00 | 33,950 00 |
| Ontario, Prov. of, consolidated revenue loan, 5s | 100,000 00 | 99,868 45 | 97,000 00 |
| Ontario, Prov. of, consolidated revenue loan, 5s | 50,000 00 | 49,966 96 | 48,500 00 |
| Ontario, Prov. of, debentures, 4½s | 50,000 00 | 49,252 22 | 48,000 00 |
| Ontario, Prov. of, debentures, 5s | 50,000 00 | 50,070 29 | 48,500 00 |
| Pennington County, Minn., drainage, 5½s | 10,000 00 | 10,440 73 | 10,300 00 |
| Pennington County, Minn., drainage, 5½s | 10,000 00 | 10,465 86 | 10,300 00 |
| Pensacola, Fla., School Dist. No. 16, buildings, 6s | 9,000 00 | 8,895 37 | 10,350 00 |

SCHEDULE D—BONDS—Continued.

| Description. | Par value. | Book value. | Market value. |
| --- | --- | --- | --- |
| Pensacola, Fla., School Dist. No. 16, buildings, 6s | $ 7,000 00 | $ 6,916 81 | $ 8,120 00 |
| Pensacola, Fla., School Dist. No. 16, buildings, 6s | 9,000 00 | 8,891 01 | 10,440 00 |
| Pitt County, N. C., court house and jail, 5s | 25,000 00 | 26,100 43 | 24,250 00 |
| Pocatello, Idaho, water works, 6s | 25,000 00 | 22,290 95 | 25,000 00 |
| Polk County, Tenn., road, 5s | 30,000 00 | 29,562 08 | 29,400 00 |
| Port Arthur, Ont., local improvement deb., 5½s | 25,000 00 | 25,383 48 | 23,750 00 |
| Prince Edward Co., Ont., deb., 4½s | 1,359 93 | 1,358 59 | 1,359 93 |
| Prince Edward County, Ont., deb., 4½s | 1,421 10 | 1,414 25 | 1,392 68 |
| Prince Edward County, Ont., deb., 4½s | 1,485 06 | 1,472 46 | 1,425 66 |
| Prince Edward County, Ont., deb., 4½s | 1,551 90 | 1,533 28 | 1,474 31 |
| Prince Edward County, Ont., deb., 4½s | 1,621 74 | 1,596 84 | 1,524 44 |
| Prince Edward County, Ont., deb., 4½s | 1,694 70 | 1,663 25 | 1,576 07 |
| Prince Edward County, Ont., deb., 4½s | 1,770 96 | 1,732 71 | 1,611 59 |
| Prince Edward County, Ont., deb., 4½s | 1,850 67 | 1,805 29 | 1,665 60 |
| Prince Edward County, Ont., deb., 4½s | 1,933 95 | 1,881 07 | 1,721 22 |
| Prince Edward County, Ont., deb., 4½s | 2,020 98 | 1,960 30 | 1,778 46 |
| Prince Edward County, Ont., deb., 4½s | 2,111 91 | 2,043 13 | 1,858 48 |
| Quebec, P. Q., municipal, 3½s | 10,000 00 | 9,805 07 | 8,000 00 |
| Quebec, P. Q., Catholic School Commission, 4½s | 25,000 00 | 25,593 56 | 20,500 00 |
| Raton, City of, Colfax County, N. M., Raton water, 5s | 15,000 00 | 14,611 50 | 15,000 00 |
| Raton, City of, Colfax County, N. M., Raton water, 5s | 15,000 00 | 14,599 51 | 15,000 00 |
| Raton, City of, Colfax County, N. M., Raton water, 5s | 10,000 00 | 9,729 45 | 10,000 00 |
| Redwood County, Minn., public drainage ditch, 5s | 10,000 00 | 10,000 00 | 10,100 00 |
| Redwood County, Minn., public drainage ditch, 5s | 7,000 00 | 7,000 00 | 7,070 00 |
| Regina, Prov. of, Saskatchewan, debentures, 5s | 40,000 00 | 38,651 40 | 36,400 00 |
| Sacramento County, Cal., court house, 4½s | 12,500 00 | 12,845 58 | 12,125 00 |
| Sacramento County, Cal., road and highway, 4½s | 12,500 00 | 12,845 51 | 12,125 00 |
| San Antonio, Tex., Ind. School Dist., site and bldg., 5s | 26,000 00 | 26,000 00 | 26,000 00 |
| San Diego, Cal., municipal improvement, 5s | 1,000 00 | 1,000 00 | 1,030 00 |
| San Diego, Cal., municipal improvement, 5s | 2,000 00 | 2,000 00 | 2,060 00 |
| San Diego, Cal., municipal improvement, 5s | 5,000 00 | 5,000 00 | 5,200 00 |
| San Diego, Cal., municipal improvement, 5s | 6,000 00 | 6,000 00 | 6,240 00 |
| San Diego, Cal., municipal improvement, 5s | 5,000 00 | 5,000 00 | 5,250 00 |
| San Diego, Cal., municipal improvement, 5s | 6,000 00 | 6,000 00 | 6,300 00 |
| San Diego, Cal., municipal improvement, 5s | 1,000 00 | 1,000 00 | 1,050 00 |
| San Diego, Cal., municipal improvement, 5s | 1,000 00 | 1,000 00 | 1,060 00 |
| San Diego, Cal., municipal improvement, 5s | 3,000 00 | 3,000 00 | 3,180 00 |
| Saskatchewan, Prov. of, gold coupon debentures, 5s | 130,000 00 | 130,000 00 | 114,400 00 |
| Saskatchewan, Prov. of, gold coupon debentures, 5s | 80,000 00 | 79,499 98 | 77,600 00 |
| St. Boniface, Man., local improvement deb., 5s | 33,000 00 | 33,933 30 | 29,700 00 |
| St. Boniface, Man., public improvement, 5s | 20,000 00 | 20,826 76 | 16,400 00 |
| St. Boniface School District, Man., 5½s | 10,000 00 | 9,848 31 | 9,300 00 |
| St. Boniface School District, Man., 5½s | 10,000 00 | 9,831 08 | 9,300 00 |
| St. Boniface School District, Man., 5½s | 10,000 00 | 9,814 76 | 9,200 00 |
| St. Boniface School District, Man., 5½s | 10,000 00 | 9,799 46 | 9,200 00 |
| St. Boniface School District, Man., 5½s | 10,000 00 | 9,785 06 | 9,100 00 |
| St. Boniface School District, Man., 5½s | 10,000 00 | 9,947 30 | 9,700 00 |
| St. Boniface School District, Man., 5½s | 3,000 00 | 2,973 06 | 2,910 00 |
| St. Boniface School District, Man., 5½s | 4,000 00 | 3,953 27 | 3,840 00 |
| St. Boniface School District, Man., 5½s | 4,000 00 | 3,939 16 | 3,760 00 |
| St. Boniface School District, Man., deb., 5s | 25,000 00 | 24,170 96 | 19,250 00 |
| St. Cunegonde, P. Q., deb., 4½s | 10,000 00 | 10,101 35 | 9,200 00 |
| St. Edward County School Commissioners, Hochelaga, P. Q., schools, 5½s | 35,000 00 | 34,455 68 | 31,150 00 |
| St. Louis County, Minn., Independent School District No. 40, public school building, 5s | 25,000 00 | 25,000 00 | 25,000 00 |
| St. Thomas, Ont., 5s | 2,970 71 | 2,910 47 | 2,733 05 |
| St. Thomas, Ont., 5s | 3,119 24 | 3,049 85 | 2,838 50 |
| St. Thomas, Ont., 5s | 3,275 21 | 3,196 07 | 2,947 69 |
| St. Thomas, Ont., 5s | 3,438 97 | 3,349 87 | 3,095 07 |
| Sibley County, Minn., public drainage, 5¼s | 2,000 00 | 2,000 00 | 2,000 00 |
| Sibley County, Minn., public drainage, 5¼s | 1,000 00 | 1,002 60 | 1,000 00 |
| Sibley County, Minn., public drainage, 5½s | 7,000 00 | 7,269 00 | 7,210 00 |
| Sibley County, Minn., public drainage, 5½s | 8,000 00 | 8,346 68 | 8,240 00 |
| Silver Bow County, Mont., School Dist. No. 1, fund., 6s | 75,000 00 | 77,040 00 | 80,250 00 |
| Sarnia, Ont., 5s | 13,000 00 | 12,500 80 | 11,050 00 |
| Sarnia, Ont., 5s | 14,000 00 | 13,448 12 | 11,760 00 |
| Sault Ste. Marie, Ont., 5½s | 25,000 00 | 24,423 89 | 22,250 00 |
| Sault Ste. Marie, Ont., deb. public schools, 5s | 41,000 00 | 39,816 00 | 34,440 00 |
| Sault Ste. Marie, Ont., deb. sewers, 1911, 5s | 9,000 00 | 8,737 60 | 7,380 00 |
| Seattle, Wash., sewer, 4½s | 25,000 00 | 25,242 16 | 24,500 00 |
| Seattle, Wash., Ballard funding, 5s | 25,000 00 | 25,637 98 | 25,000 00 |
| Seattle, Port of, Wash., east waterway, 4½s | 20,000 00 | 19,346 92 | 18,800 00 |
| Seattle, Port of, Wash., east waterway, 4½s | 23,000 00 | 22,237 70 | 21,620 00 |
| Seattle, Port of, Wash., Salmon Bay, 4½s | 4,000 00 | 3,867 40 | 3,760 00 |
| Seattle, Port of, Wash., central water front, 4½s | 3,000 00 | 2,900 70 | 2,820 00 |
| Shelby County, Tenn., court house, 4s | 50,000 00 | 48,766 25 | 43,500 00 |
| Shelby County, Tenn., school house, 5s | 24,000 00 | 24,796 00 | 24,960 00 |
| San Francisco, City and County of, Cal., garbage system, 5s | 1,000 00 | 1,015 70 | 1,040 00 |
| San Francisco, City and County of, Cal., hospital, 5s | 4,000 00 | 4,062 66 | 4,160 00 |
| San Francisco, City and County of, Cal., fire protection, 5s | 20,000 00 | 20,499 84 | 21,200 00 |

SCHEDULE D—BONDS—Continued.

| Description. | Par value. | Book value. | Market value. |
|---|---|---|---|
| San Francisco, Cal., City and County of, municipal street railways, 5s | $ 11,000 00 | $ 11,007 21 | $11,000 00 |
| San Francisco, Cal., City and County of, municipal street railways, 5s | 11,000 00 | 11,014 37 | 11,110 00 |
| San Francisco, Cal., City and County of, municipal street railways, 5s | 5,000 00 | 5,009 97 | 5,050 00 |
| San Francisco, Cal., City and County of, municipal street railways, 5s | 4,000 00 | 4,015 29 | 4,080 00 |
| San Francisco, Cal., City and County of, municipal street railways, 5s | 1,000 00 | 1,004 41 | 1,030 00 |
| San Francisco, Cal., City and County of, municipal street railways, 5s | 3,500 00 | 3,517 25 | 3,605 00 |
| San Francisco, Cal., City and County of, municipal street railways, 5s | 4,000 00 | 4,040 44 | 4,240 00 |
| San Francisco, Cal., City and County of, municipal street railways, 5s | 2,000 00 | 2,022 04 | 2,140 00 |
| San Francisco, Cal., City and County of, municipal street railways, 5s | 3,000 00 | 3,033 94 | 3,210 00 |
| San Francisco, Cal., City and County of, municipal street railways, 5s | 9,000 00 | 9,106 62 | 9,720 00 |
| San Francisco, Cal., City and County of, municipal street railways, 5s | 1,000 00 | 1,012 75 | 1,080 00 |
| St. Henry, County of Hochelaga, P. Q., School Commissioners of, 5½s | 50,000 00 | 50,000 00 | 45,000 00 |
| St. Gregoire Le Thanaturge, P. Q., School Commissioners of, 6s | 100,000 00 | 106,916 60 | 95,000 00 |
| Sorel, City of, P. Q. School Commissioners of, 5½s | 50,000 00 | 49,864 60 | 45,500 00 |
| St. Hyacinthe, P. Q., School Commissioners for the Municipality of, 5½s | 500 00 | 502 44 | 475 00 |
| St. Hyancinthe, P. Q., School Commissioners for the Municipality of, 5½s | 2,500 00 | 2,515 48 | 2,375 00 |
| St. Hyacinthe, P. Q., School Commissioners for the Municipality of, 5½s | 2,500 00 | 2,516 80 | 2,350 00 |
| St. Hyacinthe, P. Q., School Commissioners for the Municipality of, 5½s | 2,500 00 | 2,518 15 | 2,350 00 |
| St. Hyacinthe, P. Q., School Commissioners for the Municipality of, 5½s | 3,000 00 | 3,023 28 | 2,820 00 |
| St. Hyacinthe, P. Q., School Commissioners for the Municipality of, 5½s | 3,000 00 | 3,024 57 | 2,790 00 |
| St. Hyacinthe, P. Q., School Commissioners for the Municipality of, 5½s | 3,000 00 | 3,025 90 | 2,790 00 |
| St. Hyacinthe, P. Q., School Commissioners for the Municipality of, 5½s | 3,500 00 | 3,531 65 | 3,255 00 |
| St. Hyacinthe, P. Q., School Commissioners for the Municipality of, 5½s | 3,500 00 | 3,533 12 | 3,220 00 |
| St. Hyacinthe, P. Q., School Commissioners for the Municipality of, 5½s | 3,500 00 | 3,534 20 | 3,220 00 |
| St. Hyacinthe, P. Q., School Commissioners for the Municipality of, 5½s | 4,000 00 | 4,040 68 | 3,680 00 |
| St. Hyacinthe, P. Q., School Commissioners for the Municipality of, 5½s | 4,000 00 | 4,042 18 | 3,680 00 |
| St. Hyacinthe, P. Q., School Commissioners for the Municipality of, 5½s | 4,500 00 | 4,548 80 | 4,095 00 |
| Shaker Heights, Ohio, Village School District, site and building, 6s | 5,000 00 | 5,099 07 | 5,450 00 |
| Shaker Heights, Ohio, Village School District, site and building, 6s | 5,000 00 | 5,107 55 | 5,450 00 |
| Shaker Heights, Ohio, Village School District, site and building, 6s | 5,000 00 | 5,115 90 | 5,500 00 |
| Shaker Heights, Ohio, Village School District, site and building, 6s | 5,000 00 | 5,123 52 | 5,550 00 |
| Shaker Heights, Ohio, Village School District, site and building, 6s | 3,000 00 | 3,078 50 | 3,360 00 |
| South St. Paul, Minn., City of, water works, 5½s | 25,000 00 | 25,433 40 | 27,250 00 |
| Stone County, Miss., court house and jail, 6s | 2,000 00 | 2,019 50 | 2,020 00 |
| Stone County, Miss., court house and jail, 6s | 2,000 00 | 2,031 44 | 2,040 00 |
| Stone County, Miss., court house and jail, 6s | 2,000 00 | 2,052 40 | 2,060 00 |
| Stone County, Miss., court house and jail, 6s | 2,000 00 | 2,067 24 | 2,080 00 |
| Stone County, Miss., court house and jail, 6s | 2,000 00 | 2,078 64 | 2,100 00 |
| Stone County, Miss., court house and jail, 6s | 2,000 00 | 2,079 36 | 2,100 00 |
| Stone County, Miss., court house and jail, 6s | 2,000 00 | 2,094 32 | 2,120 00 |
| Stone County, Miss., court house and jail, 6s | 2,000 00 | 2,100 00 | 2,140 00 |
| Stone County, Miss., court house and jail, 6s | 2,000 00 | 2,104 80 | 2,140 00 |
| Stone County, Miss., court house and jail, 6s | 2,000 00 | 2,108 84 | 2,160 00 |
| Stone County, Miss., court house and jail, 6s | 2,000 00 | 2,112 32 | 2,180 00 |
| Stone County, Miss., court house and jail, 6s | 2,000 00 | 2,115 28 | 2,180 00 |
| Stone County, Miss., court house and jail, 6s | 2,000 00 | 2,117 92 | 2,200 00 |
| Stone County, Miss., court house and jail, 6s | 2,000 00 | 2,120 24 | 2,200 00 |
| Stone County, Miss., court house and jail, 6s | 2,000 00 | 2,122 28 | 2,220 00 |
| Tarrant County, Tex., road and bridge, 5s | 50,000 00 | 49,903 20 | 50,000 00 |
| Texarkana, Tex., series E, schools, 5s | 6,000 00 | 6,000 00 | 6,000 00 |
| Three Rivers, City of, P. Q., debentures, 5s | 50,000 00 | 48,276 16 | 39,000 00 |

SCHEDULE D—BONDS—Concluded.

| Description. | Par value. | Book value. | Market value. |
|---|---|---|---|
| Three Rivers, P. Q., Can., debentures, 5s | $50,000 00 | $49,906 15 | $39,000 00 |
| Three Rivers, P. Q., cons. loan, 4½s | 25,000 00 | 25,175 10 | 17,000 00 |
| Toronto, City of, Ont., gen. cons. loan deb., 5s | 25,000 00 | 22,457 81 | 22,500 00 |
| Toronto, Ont., deb. gen., 3½s | 38,933 33 | 38,281 74 | 33,093 33 |
| Toronto, Ont., cons. loan, 3½s | 9,733 33 | 9,607 85 | 8,273 33 |
| Toronto, City of, Ont., 34-yr. gen. cons. loan deb., 4½s | 50,000 00 | 46,848 52 | 40,000 00 |
| Toronto, City of, Ont., gen. cons. loan deb., 5s | 50,000 00 | 50,000 00 | 44,500 00 |
| Toronto, City of, Ont., gen. cons. loan deb., 5s | 50,000 00 | 50,000 00 | 44,500 00 |
| Toronto, City of, Ont., gen. cons. loan deb., schools, 5½s | 6,000 00 | 6,170 30 | 5,640 00 |
| Toronto, City of, Ont., gen. cons. loan deb., schools, 5½s | 22,000 00 | 22,643 80 | 20,680 00 |
| Toronto, City of, Ont., gen. cons. loan deb., schools, 5½s | 23,000 00 | 23,692 37 | 21,620 00 |
| Toronto, City of, Ont., gen. cons. loan deb., schools, 5½s | 24,000 00 | 24,741 62 | 22,560 00 |
| Toronto, City of, Ont., gen. cons. loan deb., schools, 5½s | 25,000 00 | 25,791 43 | 23,500 00 |
| Toronto, City of, Ont., gen. cons. loan deb., schools, 5½s | 27,000 00 | 27,874 30 | 25,380 00 |
| Toronto, City of, Ont., gen. cons. loan deb., schools, 5½s | 28,000 00 | 28,925 82 | 26,320 00 |
| Toronto, City of, Ont., gen. cons. loan deb., schools, 5½s | 30,000 00 | 31,011 50 | 27,900 00 |
| Toronto, City of, Ont., gen. cons. loan deb., schools, 5½s | 32,000 00 | 33,098 78 | 29,760 00 |
| Toronto, City of, Ont., gen. cons. loan deb., schools, 5½s | 33,000 00 | 34,152 55 | 30,690 00 |
| Toronto, Ont., Harbor Commissioners, 6th series gold, 4½s | 30,000 00 | 25,159 00 | 23,700 00 |
| Toronto, Ont., Harbor Commissioners, 6th series gold, 4½s | 10,000 00 | 8,386 32 | 7,900 00 |
| Toronto, Ont., Harbor Commissioners, 6th series gold, 4½s | 35,000 00 | 29,377 80 | 27,650 00 |
| Toronto, Ont., Harbour Commissioners, 4½s | 63,000 00 | 53,852 19 | 49,770 00 |
| Tintic Jaub Co., Utah, school district, schools, 5s | 5,000 00 | 4,706 00 | 4,750 00 |
| Tintic Jaub Co., Utah, school district, schools, 5s | 5,000 00 | 4,676 95 | 4,750 00 |
| Tintic Jaub Co., Utah, school district, schools, 5s | 5,000 00 | 4,648 10 | 4,750 00 |
| Tintic Jaub Co., Utah, school district, schools, 5s | 5,000 00 | 4,621 00 | 4,750 00 |
| Thief River Falls, Minn., electric light, 5½s | 7,000 00 | 7,022 90 | 7,000 00 |
| Thief River Falls, Minn., electric light, 5½s | 2,000 00 | 2,041 01 | 2,080 00 |
| Thief River Falls, Minn., electric light, 5½s | 6,000 00 | 6,205 40 | 6,360 00 |
| Tucson, Ariz., street improvements, 6s | 13,000 00 | 13,191 92 | 13,000 00 |
| Tucson, Ariz., water works improvements, 6s | 2,000 00 | 2,029 53 | 2,000 00 |
| Twin Falls County, Idaho, Buhl Independent School District No. 3, 5½s | 20,000 00 | 20,490 83 | 20,000 00 |
| Twin Falls County, Idaho, court house and jail, 5s | 15,000 00 | 15,074 34 | 15,000 00 |
| Vermillion, S. D., Independent School District, building, 5½s | 25,000 00 | 24,763 25 | 26,500 00 |
| Vicksburg, Miss., sewer, 4½s | 20,000 00 | 20,177 52 | 19,800 00 |
| Victoria Prov., B. C., deb., 4½s | 65,000 00 | 61,980 51 | 54,600 00 |
| Wadena County, Minn., public drainage ditch, 5½s | 1,000 00 | 1,011 68 | 1,010 00 |
| Wadena County, Minn., public drainage ditch, 5½s | 4,000 00 | 4,067 54 | 4,040 00 |
| Wadena County, Minn., public drainage ditch, 5½s | 1,500 00 | 1,532 29 | 1,515 00 |
| Wadena County, Minn., public drainage ditch, 5½s | 4,000 00 | 4,104 00 | 4,040 00 |
| Wadena County, Minn., public drainage ditch, 5½s | 3,500 00 | 3,605 84 | 3,570 00 |
| Wadena County, Minn., public drainage ditch, 5½s | 1,500 00 | 1,551 38 | 1,530 00 |
| Wadena County, Minn., public drainage ditch, 5½s | 2,000 00 | 2,076 66 | 2,040 00 |
| Wadena County, Minn., public drainage ditch, 5½s | 2,500 00 | 2,601 05 | 2,550 00 |
| Wadena County, Minn., public drainage ditch, 5½s | 2,500 00 | 2,612 71 | 2,550 00 |
| Wadena County, Minn., public drainage ditch, 5½s | 2,500 00 | 2,620 83 | 2,550 00 |
| Warren County, Miss., bridge and road, 5s | 24,000 00 | 24,000 00 | 23,520 00 |
| Waukegan, Ill., City School Dist., school building, 4½s | 6,000 00 | 5,865 20 | 5,880 00 |
| Waukegan, Ill., City School Dist., 4½s | 12,000 00 | 11,697 28 | 11,640 00 |
| Watertown, S. D., City of, electric lighting, 5s | 46,000 00 | 41,114 72 | 46,000 00 |
| Watertown, S. D., City of, electric lighting, 5s | 39,000 00 | 34,865 22 | 39,000 00 |
| Waukegan, Ill., City of, School District, building, 5s | 5,000 00 | 4,909 15 | 5,100 00 |
| Waukegan, Ill., City of, School District, building, 5s | 10,000 00 | 9,803 70 | 10,200 00 |
| Weakley County, Tenn., highways, 6s | 25,000 00 | 25,000 00 | 27,500 00 |
| Wichita Falls, Tex., sanitary sewer, 6s | 23,000 00 | 22,944 48 | 25,990 00 |
| Wichita Falls, Tex., sanitary sewer, 6s | 1,000 00 | 995 17 | 1,130 00 |
| Wichita Falls, Tex., water works, 6s | 8,000 00 | 7,961 39 | 9,040 00 |
| Wilkes County, N. C., jail and county home, 6s | 1,500 00 | 1,581 96 | 1,605 00 |
| Wilkes County, N. C., jail and county home, 6s | 1,500 00 | 1,586 91 | 1,605 00 |
| Wilkes County, N. C., jail and county home, 6s | 1,500 00 | 1,590 27 | 1,620 00 |
| Wilkes County, N. C., jail and county home, 6s | 1,500 00 | 1,593 52 | 1,635 00 |
| Wilkes County, N. C., jail and county home, 6s | 2,000 00 | 2,128 85 | 2,180 00 |
| Wilkes County, N. C., jail and county home, 6s | 2,000 00 | 2,132 55 | 2,200 00 |
| Winnipeg, Man., deb. water works, 4s | 50,000 00 | 50,310 32 | 43,000 00 |
| Winnipeg, City of, Manitoba, 5½s | 60,000 00 | 60,000 00 | 58,800 00 |
| Totals | $10,524,637 56 | $10,435,213 91 | $10,186,826 35 |

## CHICAGO UNION OF BOHEMIAN LADIES.

Located at No. 1842 South May Street, Chicago, Illinois.

MARIE DUSICKA, President. MARIE SRAJBR, Secretary.

| | |
|---|---|
| Balance from previous year | $1,336 39 |

## INCOME.

| | |
|---|---|
| All other assessments or premiums | $9,192 55 |
| Other payments by members | 231 04 |
| Net amount received from members | $9,423 59 |
| Gross interest on deposits in trust companies and banks | 25 97 |
| Total income | $9,449 56 |
| Sum | $10,785 95 |

## DISBURSEMENTS.

| | |
|---|---|
| Death claims | $9,000 00 |
| Salaries of officers and trustees | 117 50 |
| Insurance department fees | 5 00 |
| Rent | 12 00 |
| Postage, express, telegraph and telephone | 12 75 |
| Lodge supplies | 18 25 |
| Miscellaneous donations | 17 65 |
| Total disbursements | $9,183 15 |
| Balance | $1,602 80 |

## LEDGER ASSETS.

| | |
|---|---|
| Deposits in trust companies and banks not on interest | $476 30 |
| Deposits in trust companies and banks on interest | 391 06 |
| Cash on hand in treasury | 735 44 |
| Total ledger assets | $1,602 80 |

## LIABILITIES.

| | |
|---|---|
| Death claims due and unpaid | $1,500 00 |

## EXHIBIT OF CERTIFICATES.

| | Total business of the year—all in Illinois. Number. | Amount. |
|---|---|---|
| Benefit certificates in force December 31, 1920, as per last statement | 1,011 | $303,300 00 |
| Benefit certificates increased during the year | 23 | 6,900 00 |
| Total | 1,034 | $310,200 00 |
| Deduct terminated or decreased during the year | 84 | 25,200 00 |
| Total benefit certificates in force December 31, 1921 | 950 | $285,000 00 |

## EXHIBIT OF DEATH CLAIMS.

| | Total claims—all in Illinois. Number. | Amount. |
|---|---|---|
| Claims unpaid December 31, 1920, as per last statement | 2 | $ 600 00 |
| Claims reported during the year and interest addition | 33 | 9,900 00 |
| Total | 35 | $10,500 00 |
| Claims paid during the year | 30 | 9,000 00 |
| Claims unpaid December 31, 1921 | 5 | $1,500 00 |

---

# COLUMBIAN CIRCLE.

Located at No. 69 West Washington Street, Chicago, Illinois.

W. C. J. MATTHIESEN, President. N. J. HEIN, Secretary.

| | |
|---|---|
| Balance from previous year | $578,275 65 |

## INCOME.

| | |
|---|---|
| Membership fees actually received | $ 3,046 50 |
| Assessments or premiums during first 12 months of membership of which all or an extra precentage is used for expenses | 193,993 78 |
| All other assessments or premiums | 496,551 36 |
| Dues and per capita tax | 29,913 24 |
| Change of benefit certificate fees | 264 75 |
| Total received from members | $723,769 63 |
| Deduct payments returned to applicants and members | 1,096 72 |
| Net amount received from members | $722,672 91 |
| Gross interest on mortgage loans | 1,202 78 |
| Gross interest on bonds and dividends on stocks | 25,353 22 |
| Gross interest on deposits in trust companies and banks | 1,150 40 |

INCOME—Concluded.

| | |
|---|---|
| Sale of lodge supplies | $ 933 98 |
| Borrowed money (gross) | 60,000 00 |
| Gross increase in book value of ledger assets | 8,419 06 |
| Exchange on checks received | 21 12 |
| Furniture sold | 157 00 |
| Surety bonds | 1,019 45 |
| Total income | $820,929 92 |
| Sum | $1,399,205 57 |

DISBURSEMENTS.

| | |
|---|---|
| Death claims | $550,483 25 |
| Permanent disability claims | 52,474 21 |
| Other benefits: Withdrawal equities | 477 17 |
| Total benefits paid | $603,434 63 |
| Commissions and fees paid to deputies and organizers | 168,510 54 |
| Salaries of deputies and organizers | 6,320 00 |
| Salaries of managers or agents not deputies or organizers | 8,324 75 |
| Salaries of officers and trustees | 19,400 00 |
| Other compensation of officers and trustees | 68 50 |
| Salaries and other compensation of committees | 209 50 |
| Salaries of office employees | 26,623 93 |
| Other compensation of office employees | 958 85 |
| Salaries and fees paid to supreme medical examiners | 2,528 50 |
| Salaries and fees paid to subordinate medical examiners | 4,228 75 |
| Traveling and other expenses of officers, trustees and committees | 4,546 31 |
| For collection and remittance of assessments and dues | 197 72 |
| Insurance department fees | 452 87 |
| Rent | 4,678 98 |
| Advertising, printing and stationery | 13,603 44 |
| Postage, express, telegraph and telephone | 2,607 24 |
| Lodge supplies | 2,409 48 |
| Official publication | 7,089 20 |
| Expenses of supreme lodge meeting | 283 80 |
| Legal expense in litigating claims | 907 01 |
| Other legal expenses | 3,310 75 |
| Furniture and fixtures | 475 14 |
| Taxes, repairs and other expenses on real estate | 576 70 |
| Gross decrease in book value of ledger assets | 1,260 50 |
| Interest on borrowed money | 2,165 82 |
| All other disbursements, viz— | |
| Actuarial expense, $1,980.00; office expense, $976.93 | 2,956 93 |
| Premium on surety bonds, $1,210.96; deputy superintendent president fees, $804.50 | 2,015 46 |
| Miscellaneous expense, $262.85; escrow trustee expense, $187.95 | 450 80 |
| Bills receivable charged off | 1,702 00 |
| Total disbursements | $892,298 10 |
| Balance | $506,907 47 |

LEDGER ASSETS.

| | |
|---|---|
| Book value of real estate | $ 15,269 82 |
| Mortgage loans on real estate | 25,122 20 |
| Book value of bonds and stocks | 436,868 00 |
| Deposits in trust companies and banks on interest | 29,447 45 |
| Contingent fund, Topeka, Kans. | 200 00 |
| Total ledger assets | $506,907 47 |

NON-LEDGER ASSETS.

| | |
|---|---|
| Interest and rents due and accrued | 11,388 79 |
| Assessments actually collected by subordinate lodges not yet turned over to supreme lodge | 65,581 42 |
| Total admitted assets | $583,877 68 |

LIABILITIES.

| | | |
|---|---|---|
| Death claims due and unpaid | $ 5,243 11 | |
| Death claims resisted | 6,000 00 | |
| Death claims reported during the year but not yet adjusted | 61,550 00 | |
| Total death claims | | $72,793 11 |
| Borrowed money | | 60,000 00 |
| All other liabilities, viz— | | |
| Present value of 7 outstanding paid up certificates | $ 1,425 89 | |
| Net reserve on American 4 per cent and N. F. C. business valued | 37,736 77 | |
| | | 39,162 66 |
| Total | | $183,417 03 |

## EXHIBIT OF CERTIFICATES.

| | Total business of the year. | | Business in Illinois during year. | |
|---|---|---|---|---|
| | Number. | Amount. | Number. | Amount. |
| Benefit certificates in force December 31, 1920, as per last statement | 27,600 | $29,738,250 00 | 14,106 | $14,923,000 00 |
| Benefit certificates written and renewed during the year | 2,072 | 1,775,000 00 | 1,587 | 1,260,250 00 |
| Benefit certificates received by transfer during the year | | | 991 | 1,089,750 00 |
| Benefit certificates increased during the year | | | | 12,361 00 |
| Total | 29,672 | $31,513,250 00 | 16,684 | $17,285,361 00 |
| Deduct terminated, decreased or transferred during the year | 5,242 | 5,583,138 39 | | |
| Deduct terminated or decreased during the year | | | 2,110 | 2,243,500 00 |
| Total benefit certificates in force December 31, 1921 | 24,430 | $25,930,111 61 | 14,574 | $15,041,861 00 |

Received during the year from members in Illinois: Mortuary, $248,577.79; expense, $87,277.67; juvenile, $830.89; total $336,686 35

## EXHIBIT OF DEATH CLAIMS.

| | Total claims. | | Illinois claims. | |
|---|---|---|---|---|
| | Number. | Amount. | Number. | Amount. |
| Claims unpaid December 31, 1920, as per last statement | 93 | $109,946 77 | 30 | $ 27,716 98 |
| Claims received during the year previously rejected or scaled | 3 | 4,122 12 | 2 | 2,500 00 |
| Claims reported during the year and interest addition | 431 | 541,500 00 | 208 | 258,250 00 |
| Total | 527 | $655,568 89 | 240 | $288,466 98 |
| Claims paid during the year | 457 | 550,049 25 | 208 | 254,706 50 |
| Balance | 70 | $105,519 64 | 32 | $33,760 48 |
| Saved by compromising or scaling down claims during the year | | 28,476 53 | | 3,393 50 |
| Claims rejected during the year | 3 | 4,250 00 | | |
| Claims unpaid December 31, 1921 | 67 | $72,793 11 | 32 | $30,366 98 |

## EXHIBIT OF PERMANENT DISABILITY CLAIMS.

| | Total claims. | | Illinois claims. | |
|---|---|---|---|---|
| | Number. | Amount. | Number. | Amount. |
| Claims reported during the year and interest addition | 76 | $110,000 00 | 49 | $75,500 00 |
| Claims paid during the year | 74 | 52,474 21 | 48 | 36,500 00 |
| Balance | 2 | $57,525 79 | 1 | $39,000 00 |
| Saved by compromising or scaling down claims during the year | | 53,525 79 | | 37,000 00 |
| Claims rejected during the year | 2 | 4,000 00 | 1 | 2,000 00 |

## EXHIBIT OF PARTIAL DISABILITY CLAIMS.

| | Total claims. | |
|---|---|---|
| | Number. | Amount. |
| Claims unpaid December 31, 1920, as per last statement | 8 | $1,552 90 |
| Increase in estimated liability | | 51 66 |
| Total | 8 | $1,604 56 |
| Claims paid during the year | 1 | 178 67 |
| Claims unpaid December 31, 1921 | 7 | $1,425 89 |

## EXHIBIT OF JUVENILE CLAIMS.

| | Total claims—all in Illinois. | |
|---|---|---|
| | Number. | Amount. |
| Claims unpaid December 31, 1920, as per last statement | 1 | $125 00 |
| Claims reported during the year and interest addition | 3 | 309 00 |
| Total | 4 | $434 00 |
| Claims paid during the year | 4 | 434 00 |

## SCHEDULE D—BONDS.

| Description. | Par value. | Book and market value. |
|---|---|---|
| U. S. Liberty Loan, 1st, converted, 4¼s | $ 50 00 | $ 48 50 |
| U. S. Liberty Loan, 2d, converted, 4¼s | 250 00 | 240 00 |
| U. S. Liberty Loan, 2d, converted, 4¼s | 5,600 00 | 5,376 00 |
| U. S. Liberty Loan, 3d, direct, 4¼s | 4,000 00 | 4,000 00 |
| U. S. Liberty Loan, 3d, direct, 4¼s | 3,500 00 | 3,430 00 |
| U. S. Liberty Loan, 4th, 4¼s | 450 00 | 436 50 |
| U. S. Victory Loan, 5th, direct, 4¾s | 10,000 00 | 10,000 00 |
| Alpha, Minn., water, 5s | 3,000 00 | 3,000 00 |
| Anadarko, Okla., electric light and water, 5½s | 7,000 00 | 7,140 00 |
| Banner Special Drainage District, Ill., 6s | 3,000 00 | 3,000 00 |
| Big Falls, Minn., refunding, 6s | 6,000 00 | 6,060 00 |
| Bokchito, Okla., water, 6s | 500 00 | 530 00 |
| Braggs, Okla., water, 6s | 5,000 00 | 5,400 00 |
| Burlington, N. C., water, 6s | 5,000 00 | 5,500 00 |
| Butte Falls, Ore., water, 6s | 12,000 00 | 12,600 00 |
| Callaway, Neb., water, 6s | 5,000 00 | 5,200 00 |
| Cameron County, Tex., Drainage District No. 1, 5s | 5,000 00 | 5,000 00 |
| Cameron County, Tex., Drainage District No. 1, 5s | 500 00 | 500 00 |
| Cameron County, Tex., Drainage District No. 5, 5s | 6,000 00 | 6,000 00 |
| Canal Bayou Drainage District, Madison Parish, La., 5s | 1,500 00 | 1,500 00 |
| Carmen, Okla., water, 6s | 8,000 00 | 8,560 00 |
| Central Point, Ore., water, 6s | 5,500 00 | 6,050 00 |
| Chester, Mont., water, 6s | 6,000 00 | 6,300 00 |
| Choctaw County, Okla., Sawyer School District No. 36, 5s | 500 00 | 500 00 |
| Choctaw County, Okla., Sawyer School District No. 36, 5s | 500 00 | 495 00 |
| Clear Lake, S. D., water, 4s | 9,000 00 | 8,820 00 |
| Clinton, N. C., street improvement, 6s | 7,000 00 | 7,280 00 |
| Coal Creek Drainage & Levee District, Ill., 6s | 6,000 00 | 6,060 00 |
| Coal Creek Drainage & Levee District, Ill., 6s | 6,000 00 | 6,120 00 |
| Colton, S. D., water, 6s | 3,000 00 | 3,150 00 |
| Coulee de Jou Drainage District, Vermillion Parish, La., 5s | 1,000 00 | 1,000 00 |
| Coweta, Okla., water, 6s | 1,000 00 | 1,070 00 |
| Crittendon County, Ark., road district, 6s | 10,000 00 | 10,500 00 |
| Crow Wing County, Minn., school, 5½s | 5,000 00 | 5,200 00 |
| Culbertson, Mont., water, 6s | 12,000 00 | 12,000 00 |
| Cutler Drainage District, Wis., 6s | 5,000 00 | 5,050 00 |
| Dundee, Neb., fire department, 6s | 7,000 00 | 7,000 00 |
| Erick, Okla., water, 6s | 4,500 00 | 4,815 00 |
| Frederick, Okla., water and sewer, 6s | 7,000 00 | 7,350 00 |
| Georgetown, Ill., sewer, 5s | 2,000 00 | 2,020 00 |
| Georgetown, Ill., sewer, 5s | 1,500 00 | 1,515 00 |
| Georgetown, Ill., sewer, 5s | 1,500 00 | 1,515 00 |
| Grand Junction, Colo., water, 5s | 3,000 00 | 3,000 00 |
| Granite, Okla., water and light, 5s | 12,500 00 | 12,250 00 |
| Hardy, Neb., water, 5s | 500 00 | 500 00 |
| Harlingen, Tex., water and light, 5s | 10,000 00 | 9,800 00 |
| Harlingen, Tex., street improvement, 5s | 5,500 00 | 5,390 00 |
| Harris County, Tex., Drainage District No. 5, 5s | 5,000 00 | 5,000 00 |
| Harrisburg, Tex., Independent School District, 5s | 1,000 00 | 990 00 |
| Harrisburg, Tex., Independent School District, 5s | 4,000 00 | 3,920 00 |
| Hennepin Drainage District, Ill., 6s | 3,000 00 | 3,060 00 |
| Hildalgo County, Tex., Drainage District No. 1, 5s | 4,000 00 | 4,000 00 |
| Independence County, Ark., road, 6s | 5,000 00 | 5,200 00 |
| International Falls, Minn., improvement, 6s | 8,000 00 | 8,800 00 |
| Kert Creek Drainage District, Wis., 6s | 1,000 00 | 1,000 00 |
| LaFlore County, Okla., School District No. 26, 6s | 6,000 00 | 6,300 00 |
| Lincoln County, Okla., Drainage District No. 1, 6s | 4,000 00 | 4,000 00 |
| Lincoln County, Okla., Drainage District No. 1, 6s | 4,000 00 | 4,040 00 |
| Lincoln County, Okla., Drainage District No. 1, 6s | 7,000 00 | 7,140 00 |
| Little River Drainage District, Mo., 5½s | 5,000 00 | 4,900 00 |
| Little Yellow Drainage District, Wis., 6s | 1,000 00 | 1,000 00 |
| Lynches River School District No. 24, Darlington, S. C., 6s | 300 00 | 318 00 |
| McGee Creek Drainage District, Ill., 6s | 800 00 | 800 00 |
| Memphis, Tenn., water, 4s | 5,000 00 | 4,600 00 |
| Merna, Neb., water, 5s | 3,000 00 | 3,000 00 |
| Monette, Ark., school, 6s | 2,000 00 | 2,020 00 |
| Montgomery County, Tex., Road District No. 1, 5s | 5,000 00 | 5,000 00 |
| Perry, Fla., sewer and street improvement, 5s | 5,000 00 | 4,950 00 |
| Petit Anse Coteau Drainage District, La., 5s | 2,750 00 | 2,750 00 |
| Poinsett County, Ark., Drainage District No. 5, 6s | 2,000 00 | 2,000 00 |
| Poinsett County, Ark., Drainage District No. 5, 6s | 1,000 00 | 1,000 00 |
| Pottawatomie County, Okla., Little River Drainage District No. 1, 6s | 10,000 00 | 10,000 00 |
| Pottawatomie County, Okla., Little River Drainage District No. 1, 6s | 4,000 00 | 4,040 00 |
| Remington Drainage District, Wis., 6s | 2,500 00 | 2,500 00 |
| Remington Drainage District, Wis., 6s | 2,500 00 | 2,525 00 |
| Roosevelt County, Mont., refunding, 6s | 15,000 00 | 15,900 00 |
| Roosevelt County, Mont., School District No. 45, 6s | 5,000 00 | 5,350 00 |
| Rowland, N. C., school, 6s | 4,000 00 | 4,280 00 |
| St. Petersburg, Fla., improvement, 6s | 10,000 00 | 11,000 00 |
| Sayre, Okla., electric light, 6s | 2,000 00 | 2,140 00 |

SCHEDULE D—BONDS—Concluded.

| Description. | Book and Par value. | Market value. |
|---|---|---|
| Seattle, Wash., School District No. 1, 4s | 5,000 00 | 5,000 00 |
| Sidney, Neb., water, 6s | 10,000 00 | 10,700 00 |
| Spring Lake Drainage and Levee District, Ill., 6s | 2,300 00 | 2,369 00 |
| Texarkana, Tex., street improvement, 6s | 6,000 00 | 6,180 00 |
| Toledo, Ore., Port of, river improvement, 6s | 10,000 00 | 10,500 00 |
| Ward County, Tex., School District No. 4, 5s | 400 00 | 400 00 |
| Waukegan, Ill., improvement, 5s | 3,000 00 | 3,030 00 |
| Waurika, Okla., water, 6s | 5,000 00 | 5,350 00 |
| West Matanzas Drainage and Levee District, Ill., 6s | 8,000 00 | 8,000 00 |
| West Matanzas Drainage and Levee District, Ill., 6s | 4,000 00 | 4,000 00 |
| Western Lawrence County, Ark., road, 6s | 5,000 00 | 5,000 00 |
| Wilmette, Ill., sewer, 5s | 4,500 00 | 4,545 00 |
| Totals | $426,900 00 | $436,868 00 |

## CONCORDIA MUTUAL BENEFIT LEAGUE.

Located at Room 33, No. 106 North LaSalle Street, Chicago, Illinois.

AUGUST FREUND, President. WILLIAM G. THIEL, Secretary.

| | |
|---|---|
| Balance from previous year | $138,020 09 |

### INCOME.

| | |
|---|---|
| Membership fees actually received | $ 73 55 |
| Assessments or premiums during first months of membership of which all or an extra percentage is used for expenses | 14,053 13 |
| All other assessments or premiums | 47,017 45 |
| Medical examiners' fees actually received | 24 00 |
| Sick benefit dues | 3,993 53 |
| Net amount received from members | $65,161 66 |
| Gross interest on mortgage loans | 6,938 03 |
| Gross interest on collateral loans | 160 00 |
| War saving stamps | 24 36 |
| Gross interest on bonds and dividends on stocks | 355 28 |
| Gross interest on deposits in trust companies and banks | 203 99 |
| Sale of lodge supplies | 124 98 |
| Miscellaneous | 2,894 40 |
| Paper | 5,498 45 |
| Returned check | 300 00 |
| Total income | $81,161 15 |
| Sum | $219,681 24 |

### DISBURSEMENTS.

| | |
|---|---|
| Death claims | $17,650 00 |
| Sick and accident claims | 2,564 70 |
| Cash surrender | 206 20 |
| Total benefits paid | $20,420 90 |
| Commissions and fees paid to deputies and organizers | 3,450 56 |
| Salaries of officers and trustees | 1,680 00 |
| Salaries of office employees | 2,889 35 |
| Salaries and fees paid to subordinate medical examiners | 150 00 |
| Traveling and other expenses of officers, trustees and committees | 615 74 |
| Insurance department fees | 284 14 |
| Rent | 600 00 |
| Advertising, printing and stationery | 1,140 77 |
| Postage, express, telegraph and telephone | 194 05 |
| Lodge supplies | 104 00 |
| Official publication | 4,018 65 |
| Furniture and fixtures | 226 93 |
| Actuary fees | 547 25 |
| Miscellaneous expenses | 2,437 31 |
| Total disbursements | $38,759 65 |
| Balance | $180,921 59 |

### LEDGER ASSETS.

| | |
|---|---|
| Mortgage loans on real estate | $161,300 00 |
| Loans secured by pledge of bonds, stocks or other collateral | 3,450 00 |
| Book value of bonds and stocks | 7,081 77 |

## LEDGER ASSETS—Concluded.

| | | |
|---|---|---|
| Deposits in trust companies and banks on interest | | $8,249 82 |
| Bills receivable | | 600 00 |
| Policy loans | | 240 00 |
| Total ledger assets | | $180,921 59 |

### NON-LEDGER ASSETS.

| | | |
|---|---|---|
| Interest and rents due and accrued | | 2,658 79 |
| Assessments actually collected by subordinate lodges not yet turned over to supreme lodge | | 1,054 85 |
| Other assets, cash due | $935 00 | |
| Furniture and fixtures, less 10 per cent | 855 00 | |
| Buttons and stationery | 250 00 | 2,040 00 |
| Gross assets | | $186,675 23 |

### DEDUCT ASSETS NOT ADMITTED.

| | | |
|---|---|---|
| Bills receivable | $600 00 | |
| Other items, viz— | | |
| Cash due | 935 00 | |
| Furniture and fixtures | 855 00 | |
| Buttons and stationery | 250 00 | 2,640 00 |
| Total admitted assets | | $184,035 23 |

## LIABILITIES.

| | | |
|---|---|---|
| Death claims due and unpaid | $ 725 00 | |
| Death claims reported during the year but not yet adjusted | 1,000 00 | |
| Total death claims | | $ 1,725 00 |
| Borrowed money | | 1,000 00 |
| Net reserve | | 162,834 00 |
| Sick benefit | | 4,953 41 |
| Total | | $170,512 41 |

## EXHIBIT OF CERTIFICATES.

| | Total business of the year. | | Business in Illinois during year. | |
|---|---|---|---|---|
| | Number. | Amount. | Number. | Amount. |
| Benefit certificates in force December 31, 1920, as per last statement | 4,123 | $2,086,885 00 | 3,738 | $1,921,385 00 |
| Benefit certificates written and renewed during the year | 444 | 366,400 00 | 310 | 216,800 00 |
| Benefit certificates increased during the year | 8 | 3,650 00 | 7 | 3,450 00 |
| Totals | 4,575 | $2,456,935 00 | 4,055 | $2,141,635 00 |
| Deduct terminated, decreased or transferred during the year | 158 | 82,410 00 | | |
| Deduct terminated or decreased during the year | | | 149 | 76,010 00 |
| Total benefit certificates in force December 31, 1921 | 4,417 | $2,374,525 00 | 3,906 | $2,065,625 00 |

Received during the year from members in Illinois: Mortuary, $44,313.69; sick benefit, $3,614.53; expense, $8,862.73; total — $56,790 95

## EXHIBIT OF DEATH CLAIMS.

| | Total claims—all in Illinois. | |
|---|---|---|
| | Number. | Amount. |
| Claims unpaid December 31, 1920, as per last statement | 1 | $ 500 00 |
| Claims reported during the year and interest addition | 38 | 17,475 00 |
| Totals | 39 | $17,975 00 |
| Claims paid during the year | 37 | 17,250 00 |
| Claims unpaid December 31, 1921 | 2 | $725 00 |

## EXHIBIT OF SICK AND ACCIDENT CLAIMS.

| | Total claims. | | Illinois claims. | |
|---|---|---|---|---|
| | Number. | Amount. | Number. | Amount. |
| Claims paid during the year | 337 | $2,337 00 | 303 | $2,031 00 |

SCHEDULE D—BONDS.

| Description. | Book value. | Par value. |
|---|---|---|
| Liberty Bonds— | | |
| Fifth, 4¾s | $100 00 | $100 00 |
| Fifth, 4¾s | 100 00 | 100 00 |
| Fifth, 4¾s | 100 00 | 100 00 |
| Fifth, 4¾s | 100 00 | 100 00 |
| First, 3½s | 100 00 | 100 00 |
| Second, 4¼s | 50 00 | 50 00 |
| Second, 4¼s | 50 00 | 50 00 |
| Second, 4¼s | 100 00 | 100 00 |
| Second, 4¼s | 100 00 | 100 00 |
| Third, 4¼s | 50 00 | 50 00 |
| Third, 4¼s | 50 00 | 50 00 |
| Third, 4¼s | 1,000 00 | 1,000 00 |
| Third, 4¼s | 1,000 00 | 1,000 00 |
| Third, 4¼s | 50 00 | 50 00 |
| Third, 4¼s | 50 00 | 50 00 |
| Fourth, 4¼s | 500 00 | 500 00 |
| Fourth, 4¼s | 1,000 00 | 1,000 00 |
| Fourth, 4¼s | 1,000 00 | 1,000 00 |
| Fourth, 4¼s | 500 00 | 500 00 |
| Fourth, 4¼s | 50 00 | 50 00 |
| Fourth, 4¼s | 50 00 | 50 00 |
| Fourth, 4¼s | 50 00 | 50 00 |
| War savings stamps | 931 77 | 931 77 |
| Total | $7,081 77 | $7,081 77 |

## CONFEDERATION OF BOHEMIAN AMERICAN LADIES.

Located at No. 2445 South St. Louis Avenue, Chicago, Illinois.

MRS. ANNA STOLFA, President. MRS. FRANCES SCHEJBAL, Secretary.

| | |
|---|---|
| Balance from previous year | $11,798 76 |
| **INCOME.** | |
| To reserve and expense funds | 335 85 |
| Total received from members | $31,459 02 |
| Gross interest on mortgage loans | 403 10 |
| Gross interest on bonds and dividends on stocks | 62 02 |
| Gross interest on deposits in trust companies and banks | 10 72 |
| Sale of lodge supplies | 11 35 |
| Collected for mortgages | 123 31 |
| Certificate fees | 33 50 |
| Proceeds of bazaar and miscellaneous | 125 60 |
| Total income | $32,228 62 |
| Sum | $44,027 38 |
| **DISBURSEMENTS.** | |
| Total benefits paid | $31,718 57 |
| Salaries of officers and trustees | 207 50 |
| Other compensation of officers and trustees | 3 00 |
| Other compensation of office employees | 25 00 |
| Insurance department fees | 5 00 |
| Rent | 12 00 |
| Postage, express, telegraph and telephone | 13 56 |
| Lodge supplies | 44 35 |
| Rent of box in vault and miscellaneous | 5 00 |
| Total disbursements | $32,033 98 |
| Balance | $11,993 40 |
| **LEDGER ASSETS.** | |
| Mortgage loans on real estate | $7,700 00 |
| Book value of bonds and stocks | 3,250 00 |
| Cash in association's office | 677 24 |
| Deposits in trust companies and banks on interest | 366 16 |
| Total ledger assets | $11,993 40 |
| **NON-LEDGER ASSETS.** | |
| Assessments actually collected by subordinate lodges not yet turned over to supreme lodge | 5,770 45 |
| Total admitted assets | $17,763 85 |

LIABILITIES.

| | | |
|---|---|---|
| Death claims due and unpaid | $3,510 93 | |
| Death claims adjusted not yet due | 5,500 00 | |
| Total death claims | | $9,010 93 |
| Borrowed money | | 123 31 |
| Total | | $9,134 24 |

EXHIBIT OF CERTIFICATES.

| | Total business of the year—all in Illinois. Number. | Amount. |
|---|---|---|
| Benefit certificates in force December 31, 1920, as per last statement | 1,718 | $859,000 00 |
| Benefit certificates written and renewed during the year | 3 | 1,500 00 |
| Totals | 1,721 | $860,500 00 |
| Deduct terminated or decreased during the year | 238 | 119,000 00 |
| Total benefit certificates in force December 31, 1921 | 1,483 | $741,500 00 |

Received during the year from members in Illinois: Mortuary, $31,070.52; reserve, $558.62; expense, $410.55; total ............ $32,039 69

EXHIBIT OF DEATH CLAIMS.

| | Total claims—all in Illinois. Number. | Amount. |
|---|---|---|
| Claims unpaid December 31, 1920, as per last statement | 23 | $ 5,729 50 |
| Claims reported during the year and interest addition | 70 | 35,000 00 |
| Totals | 93 | $40,729 50 |
| Claims paid during the year | 63 | 31,718 57 |
| Claims unpaid December 31, 1921 | 30 | $9,010 93 |

SCHEDULE D—BONDS.

| Description. | Book value. |
|---|---|
| Government— | |
| Third liberty loan, 4¼s | $100 00 |
| Third liberty loan, 4¼s | 50 00 |
| Fourth liberty loan, 4¼s | 100 00 |
| First mortgage, gold bonds secured by deed of trust— | |
| No. 27—Document No. 7135569, 6½s | 500 00 |
| No. 26—Document No. 7048882, 6½s | 500 00 |
| No. 30—Document No. 7048882, 6½s | 500 00 |
| No. 46—Document No. 7048882, 6½s | 500 00 |
| No. 47—Document No. 7048882, 6½s | 500 00 |
| No. 48—Document No. 7048882, 6½s | 500 00 |
| Total | $3,250 00 |

---

## COURT OF HONOR LIFE ASSOCIATION.

Located at No. 206 East Adams Street, Springfield, Illinois.

A. L. HEREFORD, President. L. M. DIXON, Secretary.

Balance from previous year ............ $2,601,333 35

INCOME.

| | |
|---|---|
| Assessments or premiums during first twelve months of membership of which all or an extra percentage is used for expenses | $ 314,870 27 |
| All other assessments or premiums | 1,462,316 66 |
| Dues and per capita tax | 117,116 84 |
| Certificate and transfer fees | 1,173 50 |
| Total received from members | $1,895,477 27 |
| Deduct payments returned to applicants and members | 744 11 |
| Net amount received from members | $1,894,733 16 |
| Gross interest on mortgage loans | 35,647 64 |
| Gross interest on bonds and dividends on stocks | 76,517 14 |
| Gross interest on deposits in trust companies and banks | 5,505 93 |
| Gross interest from all other sources | 56 47 |
| Gross rents from association's property, including $1,363.85 for association's occupancy of its own buildings | 2,083 85 |
| Sale of lodge supplies | 780 72 |
| Regalia | 1 02 |

INCOME—Concluded.

| | |
|---|---|
| Discount on bonds | $33,442 38 |
| Discount on mortgages | 284 00 |
| Advertising in official publication | 237 43 |
| Total income | $2,049,289 74 |
| Sum | $4,650,623 09 |

DISBURSEMENTS.

| | |
|---|---|
| Death claims | $1,005,148 03 |
| Permanent disability claims | 1,750 00 |
| Sick and accident claims | 5,817 49 |
| Old age benefits | 34,760 17 |
| Total benefits paid | $1,047,475 69 |
| Commissions and fees paid to deputies and organizers | 131,650 30 |
| Salaries of officers and trustees | 23,005 00 |
| Other compensation and expense of officers and trustees, and directors | 24,557 58 |
| Salaries and other compensation of committees | 1,504 93 |
| Salaries of office employees | 59,585 71 |
| Salaries and fees paid to supreme medical examiners | 4,750 00 |
| Traveling and other expenses of officers, trustees and committees | 2,309 96 |
| For collection and remittance of assessments and dues | 66,899 68 |
| Insurance department fees | 1,179 23 |
| Rent | 1,363 85 |
| Advertising, printing and stationery | 4,721 35 |
| Postage, express, telegraph and telephone | 5,124 53 |
| Official publication and editor's salary | 17,115 31 |
| Legal expense in litigating claims | 5,422 46 |
| Other legal expenses | 5,600 00 |
| Furniture and fixtures | 11,584 48 |
| Taxes, repairs and other expenses on real estate | 2,528 88 |
| Inspections | 764 76 |
| Actuarial expense | 540 61 |
| Office supplies | 9,748 68 |
| Commissions certificate exchange | 138,066 21 |
| Heat, light and janitor | 2,562 18 |
| Premium recorders' bond | 628 50 |
| Insurance and premium officials and deputies bonds | 821 50 |
| Fraternal Congress, $362.50; miscellaneous, $439.87 | 802 37 |
| Total disbursements | $1,570,313 75 |
| Balance | $3,080,309 34 |

LEDGER ASSETS.

| | |
|---|---|
| Book value of real estate | $ 43,562 99 |
| Mortgage loans on real estate | 939,155 00 |
| Book value of bonds and stocks | 1,966,710 96 |
| Deposits in trust companies and banks on interest | 129,826 75 |
| Extended insurance loans | 1,053 64 |
| Total ledger assets | $3,080,309 34 |

NON-LEDGER ASSETS.

| | |
|---|---|
| Interest and rents due and accrued | 55,033 30 |
| Market value of real estate over book value | 14,437 01 |
| Assessments actually collected by subordinate lodges not yet turned over to supreme lodge | 148,848 37 |
| Gross assets | $3,298,628 02 |

DEDUCT ASSETS NOT ADMITTED.

| | | |
|---|---|---|
| Book value of bonds and stocks over market value | $ 3,973 20 | |
| Other items, viz— | | |
| Book value of real estate, expense fund | 14,900 00 | |
| Deposited in banks and trust companies, relief and expense funds | 111,730 03 | |
| Assessments actually collected by subordinate lodges, not yet turned over to supreme lodge and relief and expense funds | 26,435 49 | |
| | | 157,038 72 |
| Total admitted assets | | $3,141,589 30 |

LIABILITIES.

| | | |
|---|---|---|
| Death claims due and unpaid | $ 1,908 34 | |
| Death claims resisted | 2,000 00 | |
| Death claims reported during the year but not yet adjusted | 64,000 00 | |
| Death claims incurred in 1921, not reported until 1922 | 28,000 00 | |
| Total unpaid claims | | $ 95,908 34 |

LIABILITIES—Concluded.

| | |
|---|---|
| Advance assessments | $ 1,668 81 |
| All other liabilities, viz: Net present value of outstanding certificates (less 1921 issues), $2,090,299.74; amount set apart provisionally ascertained and credited to Form A members over 60, $169,746.95; amount set apart provisionally ascertained and credited to members holding other than Form A certificates, $129,678.03; amount set apart and held for future apportionment to members as provided by the constitution of the society, $654,287.43 | 3,044,012 15 |
| Total | $3,141,589 30 |

EXHIBIT OF CERTIFICATES.

| | Total business of the year. | | Business in Illinois during year. | |
|---|---|---|---|---|
| | Number. | Amount. | Number. | Amount. |
| Benefit certificates in force December 31, 1920, as per last statement | 74,371 | $85,043,195 00 | 35,588 | $42,797,200 00 |
| Benefit certificates written and renewed during the year | 4,843 | 5,080,000 00 | 1,538 | 1,535,500 00 |
| Totals | 79,214 | $90,123,195 00 | 37,126 | $44,332,700 00 |
| Deduct terminated, decreased or transferred during the year | 11,413 | 10,379,667 00 | | |
| Deduct terminated or decreased during the year | | | 3,671 | 3,401,090 00 |
| Total benefit certificates in force December 31, 1921 | 67,801 | $79,743,528 00 | 33,455 | $40,931,090 00 |

| | |
|---|---|
| Received during the year from members in Illinois: Mortuary and disability, $920,639.68; all other, $2,903.60; expense, $58,116.36; total | $981,659 64 |

EXHIBIT OF DEATH CLAIMS.

| | Total claims. | | Illinois claims. | |
|---|---|---|---|---|
| | Number. | Amount. | Number. | Amount. |
| Claims unpaid December 31, 1920, as per last statement | 48 | $ 59,020 00 | 20 | $ 22,478 34 |
| Claims reported during the year and interest addition | 825 | 1,034,446 31 | 423 | 550,000 00 |
| Totals | 873 | $1,093,466 31 | 443 | $572,478 34 |
| Claims paid during the year | 820 | 1,005,148 03 | 418 | 532,315 45 |
| Balance | 53 | $88,318 28 | 25 | $40,162 89 |
| Saved by compromising or scaling down claims during the year | 2 | 20,409 94 | 1 | 7,004 55 |
| Claims unpaid December 31, 1921 | 51 | $67,908 34 | 24 | $33,158 34 |

EXHIBIT OF PERMANENT DISABILITY CLAIMS.

| | Total claims. | | Illinois claims. | |
|---|---|---|---|---|
| | Number. | Amount. | Number. | Amount. |
| Claims reported during the year and interest addition | 3 | $1,750 00 | 2 | $750 00 |
| Claims paid during the year | 3 | 1,750 00 | 2 | 750 00 |

EXHIBIT OF SICK AND ACCIDENT CLAIMS.

| | Total claims. | | Illinois claims. | |
|---|---|---|---|---|
| | Number. | Amount. | Number. | Amount. |
| Claims unpaid December 31, 1920, as per last statement | 6 | $ 354 35 | 2 | $ 94 85 |
| Claims reported during the year | 144 | 5,463 14 | 27 | 762 03 |
| Totals | 150 | $5,817 49 | 29 | $856 88 |
| Claims paid during the year | 150 | $5,817 49 | 29 | 856 88 |

EXHIBIT OF OLD AGE AND OTHER CLAIMS.

| | Total claims. | | Illinois claims. | |
|---|---|---|---|---|
| | Number. | Amount. | Number. | Amount. |
| Claims unpaid December 31, 1920, as per last statement | 1 | $ 400 00 | 1 | $ 400 00 |
| Claims reported during the year and interest addition | 113 | 34,360 17 | 86 | 26,222 61 |
| Totals | 114 | $34,760 17 | 87 | $26,622 61 |
| Claims paid during the year | 114 | 34,760 17 | 87 | 26,622 61 |

## SCHEDULE D—BONDS.

| Description. | Book and Par value. | Market value. |
|---|---|---|
| Seattle, Wash., School Dist. No. 1, 4s | $ 15,000 00 | $ 15,000 00 |
| Marshall Twp., Ill., high school, 5s | 4,000 00 | 4,000 00 |
| Burlington, Iowa, funding and refunding, 4s | 5,000 00 | 4,950 00 |
| East St. Louis, Ill., School Dist. No. 10, 5s | 13,000 00 | 13,130 00 |
| Chicago Heights, Ill., school dist., 4s | 18,000 00 | 17,640 00 |
| Duluth, Minn., school, 4s | 36,000 00 | 35,640 00 |
| Cook Co., Ill., School Dist. No. 95, 5s | 1,000 00 | 1,005 00 |
| Cook Co., Ill., School Dist. No. 95, 5s | 2,000 00 | 2,030 00 |
| Custer Co., school dist., funding, 4s | 9,710 96 | 9,710 96 |
| Ann Arbor, Mich., high school, 4s | 15,000 00 | 13,650 00 |
| Slater, Mo., high school, 5s | 3,000 00 | 3,015 00 |
| Sioux Falls, school dist., school, 5s | 20,000 00 | 20,000 00 |
| Hamtramck Twp., Mich., School Dist. No. 8, 5s | 12,000 00 | 12,480 00 |
| Oklahoma Co., Okla., jail, 4½s | 30,000 00 | 29,490 00 |
| Monroe City, Mo., school, 4s | 4,000 00 | 3,960 00 |
| Grosse Point, Mich., water, 4s | 10,000 00 | 9,500 00 |
| Cicero, Ill., water, 4½s | 9,000 00 | 8,910 00 |
| Macon, Mo., refunding, 4s | 12,500 00 | 12,250 00 |
| Corunna, Mich., water, 4½s | 5,000 00 | 4,950 00 |
| Corunna, Mich., water, 4½s | 5,000 00 | 4,900 00 |
| Corunna, Mich., water, 4½s | 2,000 00 | 1,940 00 |
| Owatonna, Minn., public city and fire hall, 5s | 2,000 00 | 2,000 00 |
| Clarion, Iowa, water, 5s | 5,500 00 | 5,500 00 |
| Manistique, Mich., water and sewer, 5s | 15,000 00 | 15,300 00 |
| Esterville, Iowa, water, 5s | 8,000 00 | 8,000 00 |
| Madison, Wis., high school, 4s | 20,000 00 | 19,600 00 |
| Topeka, Kans., refunding, 4½s | 20,000 00 | 20,000 00 |
| Osceola, Iowa, water and sewer, 4½s | 32,000 00 | 31,680 00 |
| Granite City, Ill., high school, 4½s | 10,000 00 | 9,876 00 |
| Mexico, Mo., high school, 4½s | 12,000 00 | 12,000 00 |
| Hutchinson, Kans., school, 5s | 22,500 00 | 22,725 00 |
| Belleville, Kans., electric light, 5s | 20,000 00 | 20,000 00 |
| Norfolk, Neb., general sewer, 4s | 15,000 00 | 13,950 00 |
| North Platte, Neb., sewer, 4s | 20,000 00 | 19,600 00 |
| Cheboygan, Mich., school, 5s | 24,000 00 | 24,000 00 |
| St. Cloud, Minn., funding, 5s | 50,000 00 | 50,000 00 |
| Dowagiac, Mich., sewer, 5s | 3,250 00 | 3,282 50 |
| Dowagiac, Mich., sewer, 5s | 50,000 00 | 50,500 00 |
| Two Harbors, Minn., sewer, 5s | 40,000 00 | 40,400 00 |
| Brookfield, Mo., water, 5s | 2,500 00 | 2,500 00 |
| Danville, Ill., school, 6s | 2,000 00 | 2,020 80 |
| Clayton, Mo., school, 5s | 10,000 00 | 10,200 00 |
| Oklahoma City, Okla., funding, 5s | 15,000 00 | 14,850 00 |
| Ft. Smith, Ark., sewer, 5s | 25,000 00 | 25,000 00 |
| Webster Grove, Mo., water, 5s | 3,000 00 | 3,060 00 |
| Waterloo, Iowa, park, 6s | 18,000 00 | 19,609 20 |
| Spirit Lake, Iowa, water works, 5s | 10,000 00 | 10,100 00 |
| Spirit Lake, Iowa, electric light, 5s | 1,000 00 | 1,000 00 |
| Madison, Ill., refunding, 5½s | 5,000 00 | 5,197 50 |
| Enid, Okla., water works, 5s | 30,000 00 | 30,000 00 |
| Ft. Worth, Tex., street improvement, 4½s | 20,000 00 | 19,200 00 |
| Bowie, Tex., water works, 6s | 8,000 00 | 8,400 00 |
| Birmingham, Ala., sewer, 5s | 15,000 00 | 15,000 00 |
| Lawton, Okla., 5s | 19,000 00 | 18,810 00 |
| Desota, Mo., road, 5s | 6,000 00 | 5,974 20 |
| Desota, Mo., road, 5s | 3,500 00 | 3,473 40 |
| Desota, Mo., road, 5s | 1,000 00 | 990 40 |
| Jefferson Co., Tex., 5s | 29,000 00 | 26,941 00 |
| Memphis, Tex., sewer, 6s | 500 00 | 520 00 |
| Ogle Co., Ill., road, 5s | 1,000 00 | 1,000 00 |
| Tazewell Co., School Dist. No. 136, 6s | 300 00 | 300 00 |
| Marion Twp., McDowell Co., N. C., 6s | 10,000 00 | 10,506 00 |
| Little River Drainage, 5½s | 10,000 00 | 9,800 00 |
| Central City of Ky., school, 6s | 5,000 00 | 5,000 00 |
| U. S. of America, Liberty Loan, 1st conv., 4½s | 39,500 00 | 39,500 00 |
| U. S. of America, Liberty Loan, 2d conv., 4½s | 41,050 00 | 41,050 00 |
| U. S. of America, Liberty Loan, 3d, 4½s | 142,000 00 | 142,000 00 |
| U. S. of America, Liberty Loan, 4th, 4½s | 148,900 00 | 148,900 00 |
| Texarkana, Tex., street improvement, 6s | 6,000 00 | 15,450 00 |
| Texarkana, Tex., street improvement, 6s | 9,000 00 | |
| Texarkana, Tex., street improvement, 6s | 20,000 00 | 36,050 00 |
| Texarkana, Tex., street improvement, 6s | 15,000 00 | |
| Limestone Co., Tex., Road Dist. No. 18, 5½s | 2,000 00 | 2,080 00 |
| Limestone Co., Tex., Road Dist. No. 18, 5½s | 3,000 00 | 3,120 00 |
| Limestone Co., Tex., Road Dist. No. 18, 5½s | 3,000 00 | 3,120 00 |
| Limestone Co., Tex., Road Dist. No. 18, 5½s | 1,000 00 | 1,040 00 |
| Limestone Co., Tex., Road Dist. No. 18, 5½s | 3,000 00 | 3,120 00 |
| Limestone Co., Tex., Road Dist. No. 18, 5½s | 2,000 00 | 2,080 00 |
| Limestone Co., Tex., Road Dist. No. 18, 5½s | 3,000 00 | 3,120 00 |
| Limestone Co., Tex., Road Dist. No. 18, 5½s | 3,000 00 | 3,120 00 |
| Limestone Co., Tex., Road Dist. No. 18, 5½s | 3,000 00 | 3,120 00 |
| Limestone Co., Tex., Road Dist. No. 18, 5½s | 4,000 00 | 4,160 00 |

SCHEDULE D—BONDS—Continued.

| Description. | Book and Par value. | Market value. |
|---|---|---|
| Limestone Co., Tex., Road Dist. No. 18, 5½s | $ 3,000 00 | $ 3,120 00 |
| Limestone Co., Tex., Road Dist. No. 18, 5½s | 2,000 00 | 2,080 00 |
| Collin County, Tex., Road Dist. No. 29, 5½s | 15,000 00 | 31,500 00 |
| Collin County, Tex., Road Dist. No. 29, 5½s | 15,000 00 | |
| Collin County, Tex., Road Dist. No. 7, 5½s | 4,000 00 | |
| Collin County, Tex., Road Dist. No. 7, 5½s | 5,000 00 | |
| Collin County, Tex., Road Dist. No. 7, 5½s | 5,000 00 | 21,000 00 |
| Collin County, Tex., Road Dist. No. 7, 5½s | 5,000 00 | |
| Collin County, Tex., Road Dist. No. 7, 5½s | 1,000 00 | |
| Monroe Co., Ark., Richland Twp., road improvement, 6s | 15,000 00 | 22,000 00 |
| Monroe Co., Ark., Richland Twp., road improvement, 6s | 7,000 00 | |
| Shelby Co., Tex., Road Dist. No. 3, 5s | 13,000 00 | 11,830 00 |
| Shelby Co., Tex., Road Dist. No. 3, 5s | 12,000 00 | 10,898 40 |
| Springfield, Ill., street department, 5s | 5,000 00 | 5,003 00 |
| Springfield, Ill., street department, 5s | 6,000 00 | 6,018 00 |
| Springfield, Ill., street department, 5s | 7,000 00 | 7,037 10 |
| Springfield, Ill., street department, 5s | 6,000 00 | 6,045 00 |
| Springfield, Ill., street department, 5s | 6,000 00 | 6,057 00 |
| Springfield, Ill., utility appraisal, 5s | 6,000 00 | 6,003 60 |
| Springfield, Ill., utility appraisal, 5s | 7,000 00 | 7,021 00 |
| Springfield, Ill., utility appraisal, 5s | 8,000 00 | 8,042 40 |
| Springfield, Ill., utility appraisal, 5s | 7,000 00 | 7,052 50 |
| Springfield, Ill., utility appraisal, 5s | 7,000 00 | 7,066 50 |
| Springfield, Ill., fire equipment, 5s | 6,000 00 | 6,003 60 |
| Springfield, Ill., fire equipment, 5s | 8,000 00 | 8,024 00 |
| Springfield, Ill., fire equipment, 5s | 10,000 00 | 10,053 00 |
| Springfield, Ill., fire equipment, 5s | 8,000 00 | 8,060 00 |
| Springfield, Ill., fire equipment, 5s | 8,000 00 | 8,076 00 |
| Shelby Co., Tex., Road Dist. No. 3, 5s | 1,000 00 | 926 60 |
| Shelby Co., Tex., Road Dist. No. 3, 5s | 2,000 00 | 1,846 80 |
| Shelby Co., Tex., Road Dist. No. 3, 5s | 11,000 00 | 10,125 50 |
| City of Casper, Wyo., water works, 5s | 15,000 00 | 14,337 00 |
| Upshur Co., Tex., special road, 5½s | 8,000 00 | 7,886 40 |
| Upshur Co., Tex., special road, 5½s | 7,000 00 | 6,899 20 |
| Upshur Co., Tex., special road, 5½s | 7,000 00 | 6,898 50 |
| Upshur Co., Tex., special road, 5½s | 1,000 00 | 985 20 |
| Upshur Co., Tex., special road, 5½s | 1,000 00 | 985 00 |
| Cherokee Co., Tex., Road Dist. No. 3, 5s | 5,000 00 | 4,686 00 |
| Cherokee Co., Tex., Road Dist. No. 3, 5s | 2,000 00 | 1,867 00 |
| Cherokee Co., Tex., Road Dist. No. 3, 5s | 3,000 00 | 2,789 70 |
| Cherokee Co., Tex., Road Dist. No. 3, 5s | 1,000 00 | 917 70 |
| Cherokee Co., Tex., Road Dist. No. 3, 5s | 2,000 00 | 1,852 80 |
| Cherokee Co., Tex., Road Dist. No. 3' 5s | 1,000 00 | 917 40 |
| Cherokee Co., Tex., Road Dist. No. 3, 5s | 2,000 00 | 1,831 80 |
| Cherokee Co., Tex., Road Dist. No. 3, 5s | 2,000 00 | 1,828 80 |
| Greene Co., N. C., 6s | 25,000 00 | 25,915 00 |
| Collin Co., Tex., Road Dist. No. 18, 5½s | 1,000 00 | 976 90 |
| Collin Co., Tex., Road Dist. No. 18, 5½s | 2,000 00 | 1,961 20 |
| Collin Co., Tex., Road Dist. No. 18, 5½s | 14,000 00 | 13,673 80 |
| Collin Co., Tex., Road Dist. No. 18, 5½s | 4,000 00 | 3,894 00 |
| Collin Co., Tex., Road Dist. No. 19, 5½s | 2,000 00 | 1,964 40 |
| Collin Co., Tex., Road Dist. No. 19, 5½s | 1,000 00 | 981 30 |
| Collin Co., Tex., Road Dist. No. 19, 5½s | 1,000 00 | 978 80 |
| Collin Co., Tex., Road Dist. No. 19, 5½s | 1,000 00 | 978 00 |
| Collin Co., Tex., Road Dist. No. 19, 5½s | 2,000 00 | 1,977 20 |
| Collin Co., Tex., Road Dist. No. 19, 5½s | 1,000 00 | 988 20 |
| Collin Co., Tex., Road Dist. No. 19, 5½s | 1,000 00 | 987 90 |
| Collin Co., Tex., Road Dist. No. 19, 5½s | 2,000 00 | 1,975 20 |
| Collin Co., Tex., Road Dist. No. 19, 5½s | 1,000 00 | 987 30 |
| Collin Co., Tex., Road Dist. No. 19, 5½s | 1,000 00 | 987 00 |
| Collin Co., Tex., Road Dist. No. 19, 5½s | 2,000 00 | 1,973 60 |
| Collin Co., Tex., Road Dist. No. 19, 5½s | 1,000 00 | 986 50 |
| Collin Co., Tex., Road Dist. No. 24, 5½s | 6,000 00 | 5,888 40 |
| Collin Co., Tex., Road Dist. No. 16, 5½s | 3,000 00 | 2,947 20 |
| Collin Co., Tex., Road Dist. No. 16, 5½s | 3,000 00 | 2,939 40 |
| Collin Co., Tex., Road Dist. No. 16, 5½s | 3,000 00 | 2,937 00 |
| Collin Co., Tex., Road Dist. No. 16, 5½s | 1,000 00 | 978 20 |
| Collin Co., Tex., Road Dist. No. 16, 5½s | 3,000 00 | 2,932 50 |
| Collin Co., Tex., Road Dist. No. 16, 5½s | 3,000 00 | 2,961 90 |
| Collin Co., Tex., Road Dist. No. 25, 5½s | 4,000 00 | 3,962 80 |
| Collin Co., Tex., Road Dist. No. 25, 5½s | 4,000 00 | 3,956 00 |
| Collin Co., Tex., Road Dist. No. 25, 5½s | 2,000 00 | 1,976 40 |
| Collin Co., Tex., Road Dist. No. 25, 5½s | 2,000 00 | 1,975 80 |
| Collin Co., Tex., Road Dist. No. 25, 5½s | 4,000 00 | 3,950 40 |
| Collin Co., Tex., Road Dist. No. 25, 5½s | 4,000 00 | 3,949 20 |
| Collin Co., Tex., Road Dist. No. 25, 5½s | 2,000 00 | 1,974 00 |
| Collin Co., Tex., Road Dist. No. 30, 5½s | 3,000 00 | 2,973 60 |
| Collin Co., Tex., Road Dist. No. 30, 5½s | 2,000 00 | 1,981 40 |
| Collin Co., Tex., Road Dist. No. 30, 5½s | 1,000 00 | 990 30 |
| Collin Co., Tex., Road Dist. No. 30, 5½s | 1,000 00 | 989 40 |
| Collin Co., Tex., Road Dist. No. 30, 5½s | 2,000 00 | 1,978 00 |

SCHEDULE D—BONDS—Continued.

| Description. | Book and Par value. | Market value. |
|---|---|---|
| Collin Co., Tex., Road Dist. No. 30, 5½s | $ 1,000 00 | $ 988 70 |
| Collin Co., Tex., Road Dist. No. 30, 5½s | 2,000 00 | 1,976 40 |
| Collin Co., Tex., Road Dist. No. 30, 5½s | 1,000 00 | 987 90 |
| Collin Co., Tex., Road Dist. No. 30, 5½s | 6,000 00 | 5,923 80 |
| Collin Co., Tex., Road Dist. No. 30, 5½s | 1,000 00 | 986 80 |
| Collin Co., Tex., Road Dist. No. 30, 5½s | 2,000 00 | 1,973 00 |
| Collin Co., Tex., Road Dist. No. 30, 5½s | 2,000 00 | 1,972 40 |
| Greene Co., N. C., road and bridge, 6s | 5,000 00 | 5,183 00 |
| Upshur Co., Tex., special road, series F, 5½s | 24,000 00 | 23,323 20 |
| Upshur Co., Tex., special road, series F, 5½s | 8,000 00 | 7,755 20 |
| Upshur Co., Tex., special road, series F, 5½s | 3,000 00 | 2,906 10 |
| Upshur Co., Tex., special road, series F, 5½s | 3,000 00 | 2,904 00 |
| Upshur Co., Tex., special road, series F, 5½s | 8,000 00 | 7,739 20 |
| Upshur Co., Tex., special road, series F, 5½s | 1,000 00 | 966 80 |
| Okeechobee Co., Fla., road, 6s | 14,000 00 | 14,000 00 |
| Okeechobee Co., Fla., road, 6s | 10,000 00 | 10,000 00 |
| Okeechobee Co., Fla., road, 6s | 9,000 00 | 9,000 00 |
| Okeechobee Co., Fla., road, 6s | 3,000 00 | 3,000 00 |
| Willcox, Ariz., Union High School Dist. No. 13, 6s | 3,000 00 | 3,000 00 |
| Willcox, Ariz., Union High School Dist. No. 13, 6s | 20,000 00 | 20,000 00 |
| Willcox, Ariz., Union High School Dist. No. 13, 6s | 20,000 00 | 20,000 00 |
| Golden Valley Co., Mont., funding, 6s | 17,000 00 | 17,312 80 |
| Golden Valley Co., Mont., funding, 6s | 18,000 00 | 18,356 40 |
| Golden Valley Co., Mont., funding, 6s | 18,000 00 | 18,379 80 |
| City of Miami, Okla., water works extention, 6s | 15,000 00 | 15,000 00 |
| City of Miami, Okla., water works extention, 6s | 9,000 00 | 9,145 80 |
| City of Miami, Okla., water works extention, 6s | 12,000 00 | 12,686 40 |
| City of Farmersville, Tex., 6s | 6,000 00 | 6,129 00 |
| City of Farmersville, Tex., 6s | 2,000 00 | 2,093 40 |
| City of Ferris, Tex., water works, 6s | 4,000 00 | 4,000 00 |
| City of Ferris, Tex., water works, 6s | 1,500 00 | 1,500 00 |
| City of Ferris, Tex., water works, 6s | 24,000 00 | 24,000 00 |
| City of Ferris, Tex., water works, 6s | 1,500 00 | 1,500 00 |
| City of Ferris, Tex., water works, 6s | 1,000 00 | 1,000 00 |
| Totals | $1,966,710 96 | $1,962,737 76 |

## CROATION LEAGUE OF ILLINOIS.

Located at No. 2552 Wentworth Avenue, Chicago, Illinois.

ANTON GAZDIC, President. MOTO L. MATANOVIC, Secretary.

| | |
|---|---|
| Balance from previous year | $231,312 80 |
| **INCOME.** | |
| All other assessments or premiums | $184,294 38 |
| Deduct payments returned to applicants and members | 140 25 |
| Net amount received from members | $184,154 13 |
| Gross interest on bonds and dividends on stocks | 6,438 48 |
| Gross interest on deposits in trust companies and banks | 3,048 15 |
| Gross rents from association's property, including $600.00 for association's occupancy of its own buildings | 1,080 00 |
| Sale of lodge supplies | 689 10 |
| Total income | $195,409 86 |
| Sum | $426,722 66 |
| **DISBURSEMENTS.** | |
| Death claims | $91,328 88 |
| Permanent disability claims | 16,550 00 |
| Sick and accident claims | 14,215 12 |
| Total benefits paid | $122,094 00 |
| Commissions and fees paid to deputies and organizers | 125 00 |
| Salaries of officers and trustees | 4,135 00 |
| Salaries and fees paid to supreme medical examiners | 600 00 |
| Salaries and fees paid to subordinate medical examiners | 135 00 |
| Traveling and other expenses of officers, trustees and committees | 121 23 |
| Insurance department fees | 194 34 |
| Rents | 600 00 |
| Advertising, printing and stationery | 1,569 46 |
| Postage, express, telegraph and telephone | 719 00 |
| Lodge supplies | 152 15 |
| Official publication | 3,692 28 |
| Expenses of supreme lodge meeting | 1,063 87 |
| Other legal expenses | 126 40 |

DISBURSEMENTS—Concluded.

| | |
|---|---|
| Furniture and fixtures | $ 174 75 |
| Taxes, repairs and other expenses on real estate | 827 09 |
| Convention expenses | 14,977 12 |
| Pueblo, Colorado, flood relief | 2,000 00 |
| Croation orphanage | 1,725 52 |
| Printing by-laws | 2,187 50 |
| Surety bonds for officers | 255 75 |
| Actuary | 30 75 |
| Miscellaneous | 192 33 |
| Total disbursements | $157,698 54 |
| Balance | $269,024 12 |

## LEDGER ASSETS.

| | | |
|---|---|---|
| Book value of real estate | | $ 13,000 00 |
| Book value of bonds and stocks | | 141,334 30 |
| Cash in association's office | | 1,224 99 |
| Deposits in trust companies and banks on interest | | 113,464 83 |
| Total ledger assets | | $269,024 12 |
| **NON-LEDGER ASSETS.** | | |
| Interest and rents due and accrued | | 2,638 64 |
| Assessments actually collected by subordinate lodges not yet turned over to supreme lodge | | 908 49 |
| All other assets, viz— | | |
| Furniture and fixtures | $1,867 28 | |
| Society books and emblems | 461 31 | |
| | | 2,328 59 |
| Gross assets | | $274,899 84 |
| **DEDUCT ASSETS NOT ADMITTED.** | | |
| Other items, viz— | | |
| Furniture and fixture | $1,867 28 | |
| Society books and emblems | 461 31 | |
| | | 2,328 59 |
| Total admitted assets | | $272,571 25 |

## LIABILITIES.

| | | |
|---|---|---|
| Death claims due and unpaid | $ 3,827 83 | |
| Death claims reported during the year but not yet adjusted | 11,000 00 | |
| Total death claims | | $14,827 83 |
| Permanent disability claims reported during the year but not yet adjusted | | 975 00 |
| Sick and accident claims due and unpaid | | 1,031 00 |
| Total | | $16,833 83 |

## EXHIBIT OF CERTIFICATES.

| | Total business of the year. | | Business in Illinois during year. | |
|---|---|---|---|---|
| | Number. | Amount. | Number. | Amount. |
| Benefit certificates in force December 31, 1920, as per last statement | 9,908 | $7,915,200 00 | 3,914 | $3,068,600 00 |
| Benefit certificates written and renewed during the year | 954 | 887,800 00 | 282 | 243,600 00 |
| Totals | 10,862 | $8,803,000 00 | 4,196 | $3,312,200 00 |
| Deduct terminated, decreased or transferred during the year | 972 | 742,800 00 | -------- | ------------- |
| Deduct terminated or decreased during the year | -------- | ------------- | 329 | 223,600 00 |
| Total benefit certificates in force December 31, 1921 | 9,890 | $8,060,200 00 | 3,867 | $3,088,600 00 |

Received during the year from members in Illinois: Mortuary, $46,058.21; reserve, $298.00; disability, $6,621.10; all other, $5,634.49; expense, $10,765.51; total ............ $69,377 31

## EXHIBIT OF DEATH CLAIMS.

| | Total claims. | | Illinois claims. | |
|---|---|---|---|---|
| | Number. | Amount. | Number. | Amount. |
| Claims unpaid December 31, 1920, as per last statement | 56 | $35,356 71 | 23 | $13,906 11 |
| Claims reported during the year and interest addition | 88 | 70,800 00 | 41 | 31,200 00 |
| Totals | 144 | $106,156 71 | 64 | $45,106 11 |
| Claims paid during the year | 120 | 91,328 88 | 55 | 39,231 11 |
| Claims unpaid December 31, 1921 | 24 | $14,827 83 | 9 | $5,875 00 |

EXHIBIT OF PERMANENT DISABILITY CLAIMS.

| | Total claims. Number. | Amount. | Illinois claims. Number. | Amount. |
|---|---|---|---|---|
| Claims unpaid December 31, 1920, as per last statement | 11 | $ 1,300 00 | 4 | $ 275 00 |
| Claims reported during the year and interest addition | 133 | 16,225 00 | 57 | 7,925 00 |
| Totals | 144 | $17,525 00 | 61 | $8,200 00 |
| Claims paid during the year | 134 | 16,550 00 | 57 | 7,800 00 |
| Claims unpaid December 31, 1921 | 10 | $975 00 | 4 | $400 00 |

EXHIBIT OF SICK AND ACCIDENT CLAIMS.

| | Total claims. Number. | Amount. | Illinois claims. Number. | Amount. |
|---|---|---|---|---|
| Claims unpaid December 31, 1920, as per last statement | 2 | $ 845 00 | 1 | $ 455 00 |
| Claims reported during the year | 115 | 14,401 12 | 47 | 5,815 52 |
| Totals | 117 | $15,246 12 | 48 | $6,270 52 |
| Claims paid during the year | 114 | 14,215 12 | 47 | 5,815 52 |
| Claims unpaid December 31, 1921 | 3 | $1,031 00 | 1 | $455 00 |

SCHEDULE D—BONDS.

| Description. | Book value. | Par value. |
|---|---|---|
| U. S. Liberty Bonds, 1st | $12,000 00 | $12,000 00 |
| U. S. Liberty Bonds, 2d | 25,000 00 | 25,000 00 |
| U. S. Liberty Bonds, 2d | 24,973 39 | 28,700 00 |
| U. S. Liberty Bonds, 3d | 8,000 00 | 8,000 00 |
| U. S. Liberty Bonds, 4th | 30,000 00 | 30,000 00 |
| U. S. Victory Bonds, 5th | 2,000 00 | 2,000 00 |
| U. S. Victory Bonds, 5th | 12,959 75 | 13,000 00 |
| State of California | 5,000 00 | 5,000 00 |
| Pulaski County, Ill., School Dist. No. 6 | 5,199 04 | 5,000 00 |
| Hillview Drainage and Levee Dist., Greene and Scott Counties, Ill | 5,167 12 | 5,000 00 |
| City of Chicago, general corporate | 5,000 00 | 5,000 00 |
| City of Chicago, 12th street improvement | 5,000 00 | 5,000 00 |
| City of Chicago, special assessment | 199 00 | 199 00 |
| War savings stamps | 836 00 | 836 00 |
| Total | $141,334 30 | $144,735 00 |

## FIREMENS MUTUAL AID AND BENEFIT ASSOCIATION.

Located at No. 209 North Dearborn Street, Chicago, Illinois.

JOHN F. CULLERTON, President. N. D. MURRAY, Secretary.

| | |
|---|---|
| Balance from previous year | $91,312 98 |

INCOME.

| | |
|---|---|
| Membership fees actually received | $ 236 00 |
| All other assessments or premiums | 64,544 00 |
| Dues and per capita tax | 4,148 00 |
| Medical examiners' fees actually received | 177 00 |
| Other payments by members, viz: Fines, certificates and cards | 15 80 |
| Total received from members | $69,120 80 |
| Deduct payments returned to applicants and members | 54 50 |
| Net amount received from members | $69,066 30 |
| Gross interest on bonds and dividends on stocks | 2,795 79 |
| Gross interest on deposits in trust companies and banks | 428 19 |
| Purchase of bonds | 324 95 |
| Donations | 600 00 |
| Benefit base ball games | 66,320 89 |
| Total income | $139,536 12 |
| Sum | $230,849 10 |

DISBURSEMENTS.

| | |
|---|---|
| Death claims | $82,000 00 |
| Salaries of officers and trustees | 3,066 70 |
| Paid district managers for applicants solicited year 1920 | 108 00 |
| Salaries and fees paid to supreme medical examiners | 177 00 |
| Insurance department fees | 7 50 |

DISBURSEMENTS—Concluded.

| | |
|---|---|
| Rent | $ 43 50 |
| Advertising, printing and stationery | 408 90 |
| Postage, express, telegraph and telephone | 339 76 |
| Office supplies | 15 80 |
| Furniture and fixtures | 407 00 |
| Gross loss on sale or maturity of ledger assets | 201 70 |
| All other disbursements, viz— | |
| Bonds of officers and trustees | 222 50 |
| Bands at funerals | 630 00 |
| Rent of vault | 9 10 |
| Exchange on checks | 6 83 |
| Repairing typewriter and numbering machine | 11 00 |
| Memorial | 35 00 |
| Total disbursements | $87,690 29 |
| Balance | $143,158 81 |

## LEDGER ASSETS.

| | |
|---|---|
| Book value of bonds and stocks | $120,520 00 |
| Deposits in trust companies and banks on interest | 22,638 81 |
| Total ledger assets | $143,158 81 |

NON-LEDGER ASSETS.

| | |
|---|---|
| Interest and rents due and accrued | 2,712 84 |
| Gross assets | $145,871 65 |

DEDUCT ASSETS NOT ADMITTED.

| | | |
|---|---|---|
| Overdue and accrued interest on bonds in default | $ 216 67 | |
| Book value of bonds and stocks over market value | 10,239 20 | |
| | | 10,455 87 |
| Total admitted assets | | $135,415 78 |

## LIABILITIES.

| | |
|---|---|
| Death claims due and unpaid | $6,000 00 |

## EXHIBIT OF CERTIFICATES.

| | Total business of the year—all in Illinois. Number. | Amount. |
|---|---|---|
| Benefit certificates in force December 31, 1920, as per last statement | 2,357 | $4,714,000 00 |
| Benefit certificates written and renewed during the year | 118 | 236,000 00 |
| Total | 2,475 | $4,950,000 00 |
| Deduct terminated, decreased or transferred during the year | 55 | 110,000 00 |
| Total benefit certificates in force December 31, 1921 | 2,420 | $4,840,000 00 |
| Received during the year from members in Illinois: Mortuary, $64,507.00; reserve, $226.00; expense, $4,333.30; total | | $69,066 30 |

## EXHIBIT OF DEATH CLAIMS.

| | Total claims—all in Illinois. Number. | Amount. |
|---|---|---|
| Claims unpaid December 31, 1920, as per last statement | 1 | $ 2,000 00 |
| Claims reported during the year and interest addition | 43 | 86,000 00 |
| Total | 44 | $88,000 00 |
| Claims paid during the year | 41 | 82,000 00 |
| Claims unpaid December 31, 1921 | 3 | $6,000 00 |

## SCHEDULE D—BONDS.

| Description. | Book value. | Par value. | Market value. |
|---|---|---|---|
| Dubuque Electric Co | $ 5,000 00 | $ 5,000 00 | $ 4,150 00 |
| Ind. Gas & Electric Co | 2,000 00 | 2,000 00 | ------------ |
| South West Gas & Electric | 5,000 00 | 5,000 00 | 4,750 00 |
| Defiance Gas & Electric Co | 3,000 00 | 3,000 00 | 2,040 00 |
| Northern Iowa Gas & Electric | 5,000 00 | 5,000 00 | 4,350 00 |
| Commonwealth Edison | 5,000 00 | 5,000 00 | 4,700 00 |
| P. G. L. & Coke Co | 4,000 00 | 4,000 00 | 3,480 00 |
| Chicago Ry. Co | 5,000 00 | 5,000 00 | 3,550 00 |
| Chicago City Rys | 5,000 00 | 5,000 00 | 3,550 00 |
| Inter. Bur. Rapid Transit | 2,000 00 | 2,000 00 | 1,160 00 |
| 4th Liberty Loan | 10,000 00 | 10,000 00 | 10,000 00 |
| Columbia Gas & Electric Co | 3,000 00 | 3,000 00 | 2,670 00 |
| Swift & Co., 7 per cent gold notes | 2,000 00 | 2,000 00 | 2,000 00 |

SCHEDULE D—BONDS—Concluded.

| Description. | Book value. | Par value. | Market value. |
|---|---|---|---|
| South West Bell Telephone Co | $2,000 00 | $2,000 00 | $2,000 00 |
| Pennsylvania R. R., collateral trust | 2,000 00 | 2,000 00 | 2,080 00 |
| New York City, postoffice station, serial, 7 per cent | 2,000 00 | 2,000 00 | 1,960 00 |
| Milwaukee Coke & Gas Co | 2,000 00 | 2,000 00 | 2,020 00 |
| John Deer Co., gold notes | 2,000 00 | 2,000 00 | 1,960 00 |
| Aluminum Goods Co of America | 2,000 00 | 2,000 00 | 2,040 00 |
| Libby, McNeill & Libby, 1st mortgage | 3,000 00 | 3,000 00 | 3,000 00 |
| W. F. Mosser Co., sinking fund gold notes | 1,000 00 | 1,000 00 | 1,020 00 |
| Ohio Light & Power, funding and refunding gold notes | 2,000 00 | 2,000 00 | 2,000 00 |
| Armour & Co., consolidated gold notes | 2,000 00 | 2,000 00 | 2,040 00 |
| By-Product Coke Co., 1st mortgage | 2,000 00 | 2,000 00 | 2,060 00 |
| G., T. & P. R. R. Co., 1st mortgage gold notes | 2,520 00 | 2,520 00 | 1,486 80 |
| Kansas City Terminal Rys | 1,000 00 | 1,000 00 | 1,030 00 |
| City of Toronto, Can., Harbor Commission | 2,000 00 | 2,000 00 | 1,690 00 |
| Duquesne Light Co., consolidated gold notes | 3,000 00 | 3,000 00 | 3,150 00 |
| Puget Sound Light & Power, 1st mortgage | 2,000 00 | 2,000 00 | 2,100 00 |
| Philadelphia Co., 1st refunding gold notes | 3,000 00 | 3,000 00 | 2,920 00 |
| C., B. & Q. R. R., equipment gold notes | 5,000 00 | 5,000 00 | 5,200 00 |
| Atchison, Topeka & Santa Fe, equipment trust notes | 2,000 00 | 2,000 00 | 2,040 00 |
| West Pen Power, 1st mortgage gold notes | 3,000 00 | 3,000 00 | 3,000 00 |
| State of Illinois, highway | 5,000 00 | 5,000 00 | 4,850 00 |
| Delaware & Hudson, equipment gold notes | 2,000 00 | 2,000 00 | 2,020 00 |
| C. & N. W., equipment gold notes | 2,000 00 | 2,000 00 | 2,022 00 |
| New York Central, equipment gold notes | 2,000 00 | 2,000 00 | 2,022 00 |
| Morris & Co., sinking fund gold notes | 3,000 00 | 3,000 00 | 3,090 00 |
| Armour & Co., 10-yr. sinking fund gold notes | 1,000 00 | 1,000 00 | 1,020 00 |
| Amer. Arg. Chem. Co., sinking fund gold notes | 2,000 00 | 2,000 00 | 2,020 00 |
| Swift & Co., 10-yr. gold notes | 2,000 00 | 2,000 00 | 2,040 00 |
| Totals | $120,520 00 | $120,520 00 | $110,280 80 |

## GERMAN ORDER OF HARUGARI OF THE STATE OF ILLINOIS.

Located at No, 1857 North Mozart Street, Chicago, Illinois.

JACOB KRAFT, President. CHARLES G. KAUTZ, Secretary.

| | |
|---|---|
| Balance from previous year | $80,209 41 |

### INCOME.

| | |
|---|---|
| All other assessments or premiums | $20,063 05 |
| Dues and per capita tax | 1,165 28 |
| Organization fund | 376 10 |
| Official publication | 291 32 |
| Net amount received from members | $21,895 75 |
| Gross interest on mortgage loans | 4,313 95 |
| Sale of lodge supplies | 32 30 |
| Total income | $26,242 00 |
| Sum | $106,451 41 |

### DISBURSEMENTS.

| | |
|---|---|
| Death claims | $21,000 00 |
| Salaries of officers and trustees | 875 84 |
| Salaries and other compensation of committees | 33 00 |
| Insurance department fees | 5 00 |
| Rent | 23 00 |
| Advertising, printing and stationery | 61 50 |
| Postage, express, telegraph and telephone | 111 05 |
| Official publication | 564 00 |
| Capita tax U. S. grand lodge | 48 44 |
| Officers' surety bond | 87 50 |
| Accrued interest | 137 00 |
| Donation to members in distress | 15 00 |
| Donation to Quaker relief | 100 00 |
| Medalion to all members Diamond Jubilee | 442 50 |
| Miscellaneous | 28 00 |
| Total disbursements | $23,531 83 |
| Balance | $82,919 58 |

### LEDGER ASSETS.

| | |
|---|---|
| Mortgage loans on real real estate | $78,900 00 |
| Cash in association's office | 1,175 58 |
| U. S. Liberty bonds | 2,000 00 |
| U. S. War Savings Stamps | 844 00 |
| Total ledger assets | $82,919 58 |

LEDGER ASSETS—Concluded.

NON-LEDGER ASSETS.

| | |
|---|---|
| Interest and rents due and accrued | $1,233 07 |
| Inventory | 400 00 |
| Gross assets | $84,552 65 |

DEDUCT ASSETS NOT ADMITTED.

| | |
|---|---|
| Inventory | 400 00 |
| Total admitted assets | $84,152 65 |

LIABILITIES.

| | |
|---|---|
| Death claims due and unpaid | $900 00 |
| All other liabilities, viz: Held in trust for minors | 200 00 |
| Total | $1,100 00 |

EXHIBIT OF CERTIFICATES.

| | Total business of the year—all in Illinois. Number. | Amount. |
|---|---|---|
| Benefit certificates in force December 31, 1920, as per last statement | 1,184 | $431,200 00 |
| Benefit certificates written and renewed during the year | 82 | 16,400 00 |
| Benefit certificates increased during the year | 18 | 3,900 00 |
| Total | 1,284 | $451,500 00 |
| Deduct terminated, decreased or transferred during the year | 103 | 33,800 00 |
| Total benefit certificates in force December 31, 1921 | 1,181 | $417,700 00 |

| | |
|---|---|
| Received during the year from members in Illinois: Mortuary, $18,476.45; reserve, $1,586.60; expense, $1,832.70; total | $21,895 75 |

EXHIBIT OF DEATH CLAIMS.

| | Total claims—all in Illinois. Number. | Amount. |
|---|---|---|
| Claims reported during the year and interest addition | 54 | $21,900 00 |
| Claims paid during the year | 51 | 21,000 00 |
| Claims unpaid December 31, 1921 | 3 | $900 00 |

SCHEDULE D—BONDS.

| Description. | Book value. | Par value. |
|---|---|---|
| Third U. S. Liberty Loan | $ 500 00 | $ 500 00 |
| Fourth U. S. Liberty Loan | 500 00 | 500 00 |
| U. S. Victory Loan | 1,000 00 | 1,000 00 |
| U. S. War Savings Stamps | 844 00 | 1,000 00 |
| Total | $2,844 00 | $3,000 00 |

---

## GRAND CARNIOLIAN SLOVENIAN CATHOLIC UNION.

Located at No. 1004 North Chicago Street, Joliet, Illinois.

JOSEPH SITAR, President. JOSEPH ZALAR, Secretary.

| | |
|---|---|
| Balance from previous year | $741,330 93 |

INCOME.

| | |
|---|---|
| Membership fees actually received | $ 403 50 |
| All other assessments or premiums | 248,660 38 |
| Medical examiners' fees actually received | 209 25 |
| Change of certificates | 249 50 |
| Net amount received from members | $249,522 63 |
| Gross interest on mortgage loans | 2,616 60 |
| Gross interest on bonds and dividends on stocks | 36,427 13 |
| Gross interest on deposits in trust companies and banks | 1,059 04 |
| Gross interest from all other sources | 278 25 |
| Gross rents from association's property, including $900.00 for association's occupancy of its own buildings | 1,017 50 |
| Sale of lodge supplies | 95 10 |
| Gross profit on sale or maturity of ledger assets | 3,417 57 |
| Juvenile department | 2,000 00 |
| Total income | $296,433 82 |
| Sum | $1,037,764 75 |

## DISBURSEMENTS.

| | | |
|---|---|---|
| Death claims | | $102,782 13 |
| Permanent disability claims | | 9,500 00 |
| Sick and accident claims | | 14,336 00 |
| Total benefits paid | | $126,618 13 |
| Commissions and fees paid to deputies and organizers | | 959 00 |
| Salaries of officers and trustees | | 5,680 00 |
| Other compensation of officers and trustees | | 1,176 00 |
| Salaries of office employees | | 2,203 00 |
| Other compensation of office employees | | 130 00 |
| Salaries and fees paid to supreme medical examiners | | 378 75 |
| Traveling and other expenses of officers, trustees and committees | | 707 95 |
| Insurance department fees | | 165 00 |
| Rent, including $900.00 for association's occupancy of its own buildings | | 900 00 |
| Advertising, printing and stationery | | 4,893 12 |
| Postage, express, telegraph and telephone | | 711 31 |
| Official publication | | 15,500 00 |
| Legal expense in litigating claims | | 50 00 |
| Other legal expenses | | 600 00 |
| Furniture and fixtures | | 390 00 |
| Taxes, repairs and other expenses on real estate | | 2,086 95 |
| Premium on surety bonds for officers and delegates | | 1,207 18 |
| Actuary | | 107 30 |
| Light | | 223 53 |
| Miscellaneous | | 151 65 |
| Total disbursements | | $164,838 87 |
| Balance | | $872,925 88 |

## LEDGER ASSETS.

| | | |
|---|---|---|
| Book value of real estate | | $ 9,750 00 |
| Mortgage loans on real estate | | 55,080 00 |
| Book value of bonds and stocks | | 780,287 50 |
| Deposits in trust companies and banks not on interest | | 6,443 40 |
| Deposits in trust companies and banks on interest | | 21,364 98 |
| Total ledger assets | | $872,925 88 |

### NON-LEDGER ASSETS.

| | | |
|---|---|---|
| Interest and rents due and accrued | | 9,652 57 |
| Market value of real estate over book value | | 4,000 00 |
| Market value of bonds and stocks over book value | | 9,627 50 |
| Assessments actually collected by subordinate lodges not yet turned over to supreme lodge | | 1,061 88 |
| Official organ | $1,668 80 | |
| Fixtures and supplies | 4,993 20 | |
| Advance real estate taxes, etc. (loan foreclosed) | 1,289 10 | |
| | | 7,951 10 |
| Gross assets | | $905,218 93 |

### DEDUCT ASSETS NOT ADMITTED.

| | | |
|---|---|---|
| Official organ | $1,668 80 | |
| Fixtures and supplies | 4,993 20 | |
| In hands of receiver—Mercantile National Bank, Pueblo, Colo | 1,000 00 | |
| | | 7,662 00 |
| Total admitted assets | | $897,556 93 |

## LIABILITIES.

| | | |
|---|---|---|
| Death claims due and unpaid | $16,807 99 | |
| Death claims reported during the year but not yet adjusted | 2,000 00 | |
| Death claims incurred in 1921, not reported until 1922 | 9,000 00 | |
| Total death claims | | $27,807 99 |
| Permanent disability claims due and unpaid | $ 50 00 | |
| Permanent disability claims reported during the year but not yet adjusted | 150 00 | |
| Permanent disability claims incurred in 1921, not reported until 1922 | 150 00 | |
| Total permanent disability claims | | 350 00 |
| Sick and accident claims reported during the year but not yet adjusted | $424 00 | |
| Sick and accident claims incurred in 1921, not reported until 1922 | 285 00 | |
| Total sick and accident claims | | 709 00 |
| Total unpaid claims | | $28,866 99 |
| Salaries, rents, expenses, commissions, etc., due or accrued | | 398 37 |
| Taxes due or accrued | | 142 20 |

LIABILITIES—Concluded.

| | |
|---|---|
| Advance assessments | $53 78 |
| Miscellaneous | 44 90 |
| Total | $29,506 24 |

## EXHIBIT OF CERTIFICATES.

| | Total business of the year. Number. | Amount. | Business in Illinois during year. Number. | Amount. |
|---|---|---|---|---|
| Benefit certificates in force December 31, 1920, as per last statement | 12,080 | $10,577,250 00 | 3,180 | $2,875,500 00 |
| Benefit certificates written and renewed during the year | 809 | 717,500 00 | 238 | 222,500 00 |
| Benefit certificates increased during the year | | 11,750 00 | | 3,500 00 |
| Total | 12,889 | $11,306,500 00 | 3,418 | $3,101,500 00 |
| Deduct terminated, decreased or transferred during the year | 600 | 520,750 00 | | |
| Deduct terminated or decreased during the year | | | 152 | 130,250 00 |
| Total benefit certificates in force December 31, 1921 | 12,289 | $10,785,750 00 | 3,266 | $2,971,250 00 |

Received during the year from members in Illinois: Mortuary, $52,300.86; reserve, $457.00; disability, $1,947.60; all other, $1,810.75; expense, $7,990.10; total $64,506 31

## EXHIBIT OF DEATH CLAIMS.

| | Total claims. Number. | Amount. | Illinois claims. Number. | Amount. |
|---|---|---|---|---|
| Claims unpaid December 31, 1920, as per last statement | 13 | $31,802 38 | 5 | $10,016 68 |
| Claims reported during the year and interest addition | 112 | 99,250 00 | 30 | 27,500 00 |
| Total | 125 | $131,052 38 | 35 | $37,516 68 |
| Claims paid during the year | 110 | 102,782 13 | 32 | 30,829 42 |
| Balance | 15 | $28,270 25 | 3 | $6,687 26 |
| Saved by compromising or scaling down claims during the year | | 462 26 | | 462 26 |
| Claims unpaid December 31, 1921 | 15 | $27,807 99 | 3 | $6,225 00 |

## EXHIBIT OF PERMANENT DISABILITY CLAIMS.

| | Total claims. Number. | Amount. | Illinois claims. Number. | Amount. |
|---|---|---|---|---|
| Claims unpaid December 31, 1920, as per last statement | 5 | $ 375 00 | 2 | $ 75 00 |
| Claims reported during the year and interest addition | 155 | 9,475 00 | 31 | 1,900 00 |
| Total | 160 | $9,850 00 | 33 | $1,975 00 |
| Claims paid during the year | 153 | 9,500 00 | 31 | 1,875 00 |
| Claims unpaid December 31, 1921 | 7 | $350 00 | 2 | $100 00 |

## EXHIBIT OF SICK AND ACCIDENT CLAIMS.

| | Total claims. Number. | Amount. | Illinois claims. Number. | Amount. |
|---|---|---|---|---|
| Claims reported during the year | 617 | $15,045 00 | 81 | $1,800 00 |
| Claims paid during the year | 588 | 14,336 00 | 79 | 1,736 00 |
| Claims unpaid December 31, 1921 | 29 | $709 00 | 2 | $64 00 |

## SCHEDULE D—BONDS.

| Description. | Book value. | Par value. | Market value. |
|---|---|---|---|
| U. S. Liberty Bonds, 1st, conv., 4¼s | $10,000 00 | $10,000 00 | $10,000 00 |
| U. S. Liberty Bonds, 3d, 4¼s | 20,000 00 | 20,000 00 | 20,000 00 |
| U. S. Liberty Bonds, 4th, 4¼s | 60,000 00 | 60,000 00 | 60,000 00 |
| City of New York, N. Y., 4½s | 10,000 00 | 10,000 00 | 10,400 00 |
| Louisiana Port Commission, 5s | 10,000 00 | 10,000 00 | 10,100 00 |
| Mineral Palace Paving District, Pueblo, Colo., 6s | 500 00 | 500 00 | 520 00 |
| Henderson County, Ill., drainage, 6s | 28,000 00 | 28,000 00 | 28,925 00 |
| City of Geneva, Ill., sanitary district, 5s | 900 00 | 900 00 | 900 00 |
| W. Matanzas, Fulton County, Ill., drainage and levee, 6s | 15,000 00 | 15,000 00 | 15,000 00 |
| Dade City, Fla., water and sewer, 5s | 8,500 00 | 8,500 00 | 8,500 00 |
| Lake County, Fla., road, 6s | 40,000 00 | 40,000 00 | 42,400 00 |
| Roseau County, Minn., drainage, 6s | 25,000 00 | 25,000 00 | 26,250 00 |
| Musselshell County, Mont., funding, 5s | 10,000 00 | 10,000 00 | 10,100 00 |

SCHEDULE D—BONDS—Concluded.

| Description. | Book value. | Par value. | Market value. |
|---|---|---|---|
| Hidalgo County, Tex., road, District No. 1, 5½s | $10,000 00 | $10,000 00 | $10,500 00 |
| Port Townsend, Wash., refunding, 5s | 10,000 00 | 10,000 00 | 10,000 00 |
| Joliet, Ill., improvement Collins Street, 5s | 2,000 00 | 2,000 00 | 2,000 00 |
| Fayetteville Magisterial District, Fayette County, W. Va., 5s | 20,000 00 | 20,000 00 | 20,400 00 |
| Tazewell County, Ill., drainage, 5½s | 20,000 00 | 20,000 00 | 20,000 00 |
| Iron County, Utah, school, 5s | 25,000 00 | 25,000 00 | 25,000 00 |
| City of Joliet, Ill., Marion Street pavement, 5s | 500 00 | 500 00 | 500 00 |
| City of Joliet, Ill., Comstock Street, pavement due 1923, 1925, 1926 and 1927, each year $500.00, 5s | 2,000 00 | 2,000 00 | 2,020 00 |
| Pinal County, Ariz., road, 5s | 35,000 00 | 35,000 00 | 35,000 00 |
| Jefferson County, Arkansas, Farelly Lake, 5½s | 10,000 00 | 10,000 00 | 10,000 00 |
| Supervisors Dist. No. 5, Simpson County, Miss., road, 6s | 5,000 00 | 5,000 00 | 5,000 00 |
| Forest City, Pa., school, 5s | 3,000 00 | 3,000 00 | 3,180 00 |
| Catholic School Commissioners, Montreal, Can., 5s | 18,000 00 | 18,000 00 | 14,800 00 |
| Minidoka County, Idaho, road, 6s | 10,000 00 | 10,000 00 | 11,100 00 |
| City of Price, Utah, water works, 6s | 15,000 00 | 15,000 00 | 16,200 00 |
| City of Price, Utah, water works, 6s | 5,000 00 | 5,000 00 | 5,400 00 |
| Tripp County, S. D., court house and jail, 5s | 5,000 00 | 5,000 00 | 5,000 00 |
| Town of Clinton, N. C., 6s | 10,000 00 | 10,000 00 | 10,550 00 |
| Hennepin Drainage, Putnam County, Ill., 6s | 9,787 50 | 9,787 50 | 10,000 00 |
| Hennepin Drainage, Putnam County, Ill., 6s | 2,000 00 | 2,000 00 | 2,040 00 |
| City of Pueblo, Colo., public improvement, 6s | 10,000 00 | 10,000 00 | 11,300 00 |
| Musselshell County, Mont., highway, 6s | 10,000 00 | 10,000 00 | 11,400 00 |
| Belle Fourche, Butte County, S. D., school district, 6s | 5,000 00 | 5,000 00 | 5,200 00 |
| Montgomery County, Ohio, 6s | 10,000 00 | 10,000 00 | 10,800 00 |
| Navajo County, Ariz., road, 6s | 5,000 00 | 5,000 00 | 5,550 00 |
| Mohave County, Ariz., road and hospital, 6s | 5,000 00 | 5,000 00 | 5,460 00 |
| Lake Bluff, Ill., water works, 6s | 10,000 00 | 10,000 00 | 10,900 00 |
| City of Leavenworth, Kans., water works, 6s | 10,000 00 | 10,000 00 | 11,200 00 |
| Gallatin and Broadwater Counties, Mont., Joint School District No. 24, payable from Jan. 1, 1936 to Jan. 1, 1941 each year, $2,000.00, 6s | 12,000 00 | 12,000 00 | 13,020 00 |
| Port of Astoria, Ore. (municipal gold bonds), 6s | 3,000 00 | 3,000 00 | 3,210 00 |
| Independent School District No. 13, school building, Aurora, Minn., 7s | 15,000 00 | 15,000 00 | 15,300 00 |
| Town of Ridgeway, Gallatin County, Ill., road, payable from July 1, 1922 to July 1, 1926, $4,000.00 each year, 5s | 20,000 00 | 20,000 00 | 20,040 00 |
| Howard County, Tex., special road, 5½s | 10,000 00 | 10,000 00 | 10,200 00 |
| Juab County, Utah, road, 6s | 10,000 00 | 10,000 00 | 11,100 00 |
| County of Yavapai, Ariz., road improvement, 6s | 10,000 00 | 10,000 00 | 10,550 00 |
| Greenlee County, Ariz., road, 6s | 10,000 00 | 10,000 00 | 10,500 00 |
| City of Joliet, Ill., local improvement, Pine Street, pavement warrant No. 804, 5s | 9,300 00 | 9,300 00 | 9,300 00 |
| City of Joliet, Ill., local improvement, Lime Street, pavement warrant No. 807, 5s | 700 00 | 700 00 | 700 00 |
| County of Phillips, funding, state of Montana, 6s | 10,000 00 | 10,000 00 | 10,000 00 |
| City of North Chicago, Lake County, Ill., improvement, payable from Oct. 2, 1923 to Oct. 2, 1930, $2,500.00 each year, 5s | 20,000 00 | 20,000 00 | 20,000 00 |
| City of North Chicago, Lake County, Ill., special assessment, 5s | 20,100 00 | 20,100 00 | 20,100 00 |
| Intermountain Ry., Light & Power Co., 6s | 10,000 00 | 10,000 00 | 7,300 00 |
| Commercial National Safe Deposit Co., 4½s | 15,000 00 | 15,000 00 | 14,100 00 |
| North American Light & Power Co., 6s | 10,000 00 | 10,000 00 | 8,500 00 |
| Northern Iowa Gas & Electric Co., 6s | 10,000 00 | 10,000 00 | 8,700 00 |
| Bohn Refrigerator Co., 7s | 15,000 00 | 15,000 00 | 14,700 00 |
| L. F. Beach Building Corporation, Joliet, Ill., 6s | 10,000 00 | 10,000 00 | 10,000 00 |
| Maynard Coal Co., 7s | 20,000 00 | 20,000 00 | 19,000 00 |
| Safe Cabinet Co., 7s | 10,000 00 | 10,000 00 | 10,000 00 |
| Safe Cabinet Co., 7s | 10,000 00 | 10,000 00 | 10,000 00 |
| Totals | $780,287 50 | $780,287 50 | $789,915 00 |

## GRAND GUILD OF AMERICA.

Located at No. 2326 North Sawyer Avenue, Chicago, Illinois, incorporated August 28, 1903; commenced business in Illinois August 28, 1903.

HENRY OVERHOFF, President. ANNA M. ENGEL, Secretary.

| | |
|---|---|
| Balance from previous year | $6,569 05 |

INCOME.

| | |
|---|---|
| All other assessments or premiums | $4,762 76 |
| Dues and per capita tax | 293 40 |
| Net amount received from members | $5,056 16 |

## INCOME—Concluded.

| | |
|---|---|
| Gross interest on mortgage loans | $129 00 |
| Gross interest on deposits in trust companies and banks | 83 57 |
| Gross interest from all other sources | 21 25 |
| Receipt book | 25 |
| Total income | $5,290 23 |
| Sum | $11,859 28 |

## DISBURSEMENTS.

| | |
|---|---|
| Death claims | $3,000 00 |
| Sick and accident claims | 228 43 |
| Total benefits paid | $3,228 43 |
| Salaries of officers and trustees | 143 00 |
| Insurance department fees | 5 00 |
| Rent | 12 00 |
| Advertising, printing and stationery | 6 50 |
| Postage, express, telegraph and telephone | 5 93 |
| Expenses of supreme lodge meeting | 5 00 |
| Other legal expenses—bonds for officers | 9 25 |
| All other disbursements, viz: Safety deposit box | 5 00 |
| Total disbursements | $3,420 11 |
| Balance | $5,918 02 |

## LEDGER ASSETS.

| | |
|---|---|
| Mortgage loans on real estate | $2,000 00 |
| Book value of bonds and stocks | 500 00 |
| Deposits in trust companies and banks on interest | 5,918 02 |
| Other ledger assets, viz: War stamps | 21 15 |
| Total ledger assets | $8,439 17 |

### NON-LEDGER ASSETS.

| | | |
|---|---|---|
| Interest and rents due and accrued | | 33 50 |
| All other assets, viz— | | |
| Color plate, $40.00; charters, $20.00; buttons and pins, $14.00 | $74 00 | |
| Certificates, $8.00; medical reports, $5.00; applications, $5.00 | 18 00 | |
| Constitutions, $20.00; quarterly reports, $4.00; seal, $2.00 | 26 00 | |
| Transfer cards, $1.00; gold seals, $0.50 | 1 50 | |
| Receipt books, $20.00; lodge books, $20.00 | 40 00 | 159 50 |
| Gross assets | | $8,632 17 |

### DEDUCT ASSETS NOT ADMITTED.

| | |
|---|---|
| Other items, viz: Items as shown above | 159 50 |
| Total admitted assets | $8,472 67 |

## LIABILITIES.

| | |
|---|---|
| Death claims due and unpaid | $857 25 |

## EXHIBIT OF CERTIFICATES.

| | Total business of the year—all in Illinois. Number. | Amount. |
|---|---|---|
| Benefit certificates in force December 31, 1920, as per last statement | 471 | $235,500 00 |
| Benefit certificates written and renewed during the year | 2 | 1,000 00 |
| Total | 473 | $236,500 00 |
| Deduct terminated or decreased during the year | 23 | 11,500 00 |
| Total benefit certificates in force December 31, 1921 | 450 | $225,000 00 |

## EXHIBIT OF DEATH CLAIMS.

| | Total claims—all in Illinois. Number. | Amount. |
|---|---|---|
| Claims unpaid December 31, 1920, as per last statement | 1 | $ 357 25 |
| Claims reported during the year and interest addition | 7 | 3,500 00 |
| Total | 8 | $3,857 25 |
| Claims paid during the year | 6 | 3,000 00 |
| Claims unpaid December 31, 1921 | 2 | $857 25 |

EXHIBIT OF SICK AND ACCIDENT CLAIMS.

| | Total claims—all in Illinois. Number. | Amount. |
|---|---|---|
| Claims reported during the year | 8 | $228 43 |
| Claims paid during the year | 8 | 228 43 |

## GUARDIAN INSURANCE CORPORATION.

Located at No. 440 Murphy Building, East St. Louis, Illinois.

J. C. KULP, President. J. H. FIEDLER, Secretary.

| | |
|---|---|
| Balance from previous year | $198 10 |

INCOME.

| | |
|---|---|
| Assessments or premiums | $1,028 51 |
| All other assessments | 7,932 12 |
| Net amount received from members | $8,960 63 |
| Sale of lodge supplies | 25 60 |
| Donated by officers | 190 00 |
| Rent for desk room | 90 00 |
| Total income | $9,266 23 |
| Sum | $9,464 33 |

DISBURSEMENTS.

| | |
|---|---|
| Death claims | $ 391 50 |
| Sick and accident claims | 1,988 67 |
| Total benefits paid | $2,380 17 |
| Commissions and fees paid to deputies and organizers | 736 58 |
| Salaries of officers and trustees | 4,249 50 |
| Salaries of office employees | 214 20 |
| Traveling and other expenses of officers, trustees and committees | 280 03 |
| For collection and remittance of assessments and dues | 784 38 |
| Insurance department fees | 5 00 |
| Rent | 324 00 |
| Advertising, printing and stationery | 171 86 |
| Postage, express, telegraph and telephone | 41 21 |
| Legal expense in litigating claims | 27 40 |
| Furniture, fixtures and miscellaneous | 46 30 |
| Total disbursements | $9,260 63 |
| Balance | $203 70 |

LEDGER ASSETS.

| | |
|---|---|
| Cash in association's office | $ 78 96 |
| Deposits in trust companies and banks not on interest | 124 74 |
| Total ledger assets | $203 70 |

LIABILITIES.

| | |
|---|---|
| Total sick and accident claims | $22 50 |

EXHIBIT OF CERTIFICATES.

| | Total business of the year—all in Illinois. Number. |
|---|---|
| Benefit certificates in force December 31, 1920, as per last statement | 1,125 |
| Benefit certificates written and renewed during the year | 705 |
| Total | 1,830 |
| Deduct terminated, decreased or transferred during the year | 1,229 |
| Total benefit certificates in force December 31, 1921 | 601 |

| | |
|---|---|
| Received during the year from members in Illinois: All other, $2,457.41; expense, $6,503.22; total | $8,960 63 |

EXHIBIT OF DEATH CLAIMS.

| | Total claims—all in Illinois. Number. | Amount. |
|---|---|---|
| Claims reported during the year and interest addition | 7 | $391 50 |
| Claims paid during the year | 7 | 391 50 |

EXHIBIT OF SICK AND ACCIDENT CLAIMS.

| | Total claims—all in Illinois. Number. | Amount. |
|---|---|---|
| Claims reported during the year | 324 | $2,011 10 |
| Claims paid during the year | 323 | 1,988 67 |
| Claims unpaid December 31, 1921 | 1 | $22 50 |

## HANCOCK COUNTY MUTUAL LIFE ASSOCIATION.

Located at Carthage, Illinois.

JAMES W. WESTFALL, President. LINUS CRUISE, Secretary.

| | |
|---|---|
| Balance from previous year | $6,689 37 |

### INCOME.

| | |
|---|---|
| Membership fees actually received | $ 245 00 |
| All other assessments or premiums | 31,851 20 |
| Dues and per capita tax | 2,585 50 |
| Overpay | 34 83 |
| Total received from members | $34,716 53 |
| Deduct payments returned to applicants and members | 34 83 |
| Net amount received from members | $34,681 70 |
| Change of policies | 26 50 |
| Total income | $34,708 20 |
| Sum | $41,397 57 |

### DISBURSEMENTS.

| | |
|---|---|
| Death claims | $33,083 34 |
| Commissions and fees paid to deputies and organizers | 330 50 |
| Salaries of officers and trustees | 600 00 |
| Other compensation of officers and trustees | 276 90 |
| Salaries and other compensation of committees | 116 90 |
| Insurance department fees | 5 00 |
| Rent | 84 00 |
| Postage, express, telegraph and telephone | 13 22 |
| Lodge supplies | 7 25 |
| Official publication | 550 73 |
| Expenses of supreme lodge meeting | 231 25 |
| Notary | 1 00 |
| Bonding | 42 70 |
| Premium on insurance | 6 48 |
| Total disbursements | $35,349 27 |
| Balance | $6,048 30 |

### LEDGER ASSETS.

| | | |
|---|---|---|
| Cash in association's office | | $6,048 30 |
| **NON-LEDGER ASSETS.** | | |
| All other assets, viz— | | |
| Files and desks | $150 00 | |
| Office supplies | 150 00 | |
| | | 300 00 |
| Gross assets | | $6,348 30 |
| **DEDUCT ASSETS NOT ADMITTED.** | | |
| Other items, viz— | | |
| Files and desks | $150 00 | |
| Office supplies | 150 00 | |
| | | 300 00 |
| Total admitted assets | | $6,048 30 |

### LIABILITIES.

| | | |
|---|---|---|
| Death claims due and unpaid | $2,000 00 | |
| Death claims reported during the year but not yet adjusted | 2,000 00 | |
| Total death claims unpaid | | $4,000 00 |

## EXHIBIT OF CERTIFICATES.

| | Total business of the year—all in Illinois. Number. | Amount. |
|---|---|---|
| Benefit certificates in force December 31, 1920, as per last statement | 2,578 | $4,265,500 00 |
| Benefit certificates written and renewed during the year | 68 | 107,000 00 |
| Benefit certificates increased during the year | | 1,500 00 |
| Totals | 2,646 | $4,374,000 00 |
| Deduct terminated or decreased during the year | 48 | 74,000 00 |
| Total benefit certificates in force December 31, 1921 | 2,598 | $4,300,000 00 |
| Received during the year from members in Illinois: Mortuary, $31,851.20; expense, $2,891.83; total | | $34,743 03 |

## EXHIBIT OF DEATH CLAIMS.

| | Total claims—all in Illinois. Number. | Amount. |
|---|---|---|
| Claims unpaid December 31, 1920, as per last statement | 3 | $ 4,083 34 |
| Claims reported during the year and interest addition | 22 | 33,000 00 |
| Totals | 25 | $37,083 34 |
| Claims paid during the year | 23 | 33,083 34 |
| Claims unpaid December 31, 1921 | 2 | $4,000 00 |

# HIBERNIAN LIFE INSURANCE ASSOCIATION.

Located at No. 155 North Clark Street, Chicago, Illinois.

JOHN J. MAHONEY, President. ELIZABETH A. LEAHY, Secretary.

| | |
|---|---|
| Balance from previous year | $80,188 75 |

## INCOME.

| | |
|---|---|
| Membership fees actually received | $36,401 67 |
| Dues and per capita tax | 3,582 20 |
| Net amount received from members | $39,983 87 |
| Gross interest on bonds and dividends on stocks | 3,305 01 |
| Gross interest on deposits in trust companies and banks | 296 63 |
| Gross interest from all other sources, reserve | 53 55 |
| Sale of lodge supplies | 86 85 |
| Office rent | 360 00 |
| Certificates changes | 25 50 |
| Interest on general fund bonds | 71 28 |
| Transferred to general fund | 280 49 |
| On account check | 6 00 |
| Total income | $44,469 18 |
| Sum | $124,657 93 |

## DISBURSEMENTS.

| | |
|---|---|
| Death claims | $26,500 00 |
| Refund on advanced assessments | 7 93 |
| Total benefits paid | $26,507 93 |
| Commissions and fees paid to deputies and organizers | 79 00 |
| Salaries of officers and trustees | 2,220 00 |
| Other compensation of officers and trustees, directors | 150 00 |
| Salaries and fees paid to supreme medical examiners | 40 50 |
| Insurance department fees | 5 00 |
| Rent for association's occupancy of its own buildings | 775 20 |
| Advertising, printing and stationery | 317 05 |
| Postage, express, telegraph and telephone | 121 27 |
| Lodge supplies | 63 10 |
| Official publication | 1 50 |
| Expenses of supreme lodge meeting national convention | 75 00 |
| Accrued interest on bonds purchased October 15, 1921 | 173 33 |
| Accrued interest on bonds purchased November 15, 1921 | 111 65 |
| Auditors | 30 00 |
| Division Auditors | 92 00 |
| Bonds secretary and treasurer | 49 50 |
| Rent of vault | 5 00 |
| Total disbursements | $30,817 03 |
| Balance | $93,840 90 |

LEDGER ASSETS.

| | |
|---|---|
| Book value of bonds and stocks | $71,116 00 |
| Cash in bank reserve fund | 6,262 33 |
| Deposits in trust companies and banks not on interest, general fund | 1,269 46 |
| Deposits in trust companies and banks on interest, benefit fund | 8,359 11 |
| Fourth liberty loan | 5,000 00 |
| Third liberty loan | 1,000 00 |
| War savings stamps | 834 00 |
| Total ledger assets | $93,840 90 |

LIABILITIES.

| | |
|---|---|
| Death claims due and unpaid | $401 53 |

EXHIBIT OF CERTIFICATES.

| | Total business of the year. | | Business in Illinois during year. | |
|---|---|---|---|---|
| | Number. | Amount. | Number. | Amount. |
| Benefit certificates in force December 31, 1920, as per last statement | 3,002 | $2,265,600 00 | 2,678 | $2,022,300 00 |
| Benefit certificates written and renewed during the year | 111 | 83,062 50 | 101 | 77,512 50 |
| Totals | 3,113 | $2,348,662 50 | 2,779 | $2,099,812 50 |
| Deduct terminated, decreased or transferred during the year | 230 | 195,312 50 | | |
| Deduct terminated or decreased during the year | | | 213 | 187,362 50 |
| Total benefit certificates in force December 31, 1921 | 2,883 | $2,153,350 00 | 2,566 | $1,912,450 00 |

| | |
|---|---|
| Received during the year from members in Illinois: Mortuary, $3,579.83; expense, $30,351.57; total | $33,931 40 |

EXHIBIT OF DEATH CLAIMS.

| | Total claims. | | Illinois claims. | |
|---|---|---|---|---|
| | Number. | Amount. | Number. | Amount. |
| Claims unpaid December 31, 1920, as per last statement | 1 | $ 401 53 | 1 | $ 401 53 |
| Claims reported during the year and interest addition | | | 32 | 25,350 00 |
| Totals | 1 | $ 401 53 | 33 | $25,751 53 |
| Claims paid during the year | 34 | 26,500 00 | 32 | 25,350 00 |
| Balance | 35 | $26,901 53 | 1 | $401 53 |

SCHEDULE D—BONDS.

| Description. | Par value. | Market value. |
|---|---|---|
| City of Chicago, water certificates, 6s | $10,000 00 | $10,000 00 |
| City of Chicago, water certificates, 6s | 5,000 00 | 5,000 00 |
| City of Chicago, bathing beach, 4s | 10,000 00 | 10,000 00 |
| City of Chicago, West Pullman Park, 5s | 4,000 00 | 4,000 00 |
| East St. Louis, school dist., 4s | 5,000 00 | 5,000 00 |
| Cook Co., Ill., Northwest Park Dist., 4½s | 5,000 00 | 5,000 00 |
| City of Chicago, bridge bonds, 4s | 10,000 00 | 10,000 00 |
| City of Chicago, Michigan Ave. improvement, 4s | 5,000 00 | 5,000 00 |
| City of Chicago, street lighting system, 4s | 5,000 00 | 5,000 00 |
| City of Chicago, street improvement bond, 4s | 1,000 00 | 1,000 00 |
| City of Chicago, city hall, 4s | 1,000 00 | 1,000 00 |
| City of Chicago, bathing beach, 4s | 3,000 00 | 3,000 00 |
| Cook Co., forest preserve, 4s | 8,000 00 | 8,000 00 |
| U. S. Third Liberty Loan, 4¼s | 1,000 00 | 1,000 00 |
| U. S. Fourth Liberty Loan, 4¼s | 5,000 00 | 5,000 00 |
| U. S. War Savings Stamps | 834 00 | 834 00 |
| Totals | $78,834 00 | $78,834 00 |

## HLAVNY TATRANSKA SLOVENSKA JEDNOTA.

Located at No. 4905 Henderson Street, Chicago, Illinois.

SAMUEL VRABLIK, President. JOHN DANKO, Secretary.

| | |
|---|---|
| Balance from previous year | $18,533 76 |

INCOME.

| | |
|---|---|
| Membership fees actually received | $ 84 00 |
| All other assessments or premiums | 10,890 45 |
| Total received from members | $10,974 45 |
| Deduct payments returned to applicants and members | 79 20 |
| Net amount received from members | $10,895 25 |

INCOME—Concluded.

| | |
|---|---|
| Gross interest on mortgage loans | $667 97 |
| Gross interest on deposits in trust companies and banks | 115 61 |
| Sale of lodge supplies | 134 45 |
| Advertisements in a special number of our monthly publication | 318 00 |
| Total income | $12,131 28 |
| Sum | $30,665 04 |

DISBURSEMENTS.

| | |
|---|---|
| Death claims | $4,825 00 |
| Commissions and fees paid to deputies and organizers | 30 00 |
| Salaries of officers and trustees | 564 50 |
| Other compensation of officers and trustees | 210 73 |
| Salaries and fees paid to subordinate medical examiners | 121 75 |
| Insurance department fees | 5 00 |
| Advertising, printing and stationery | 83 50 |
| Postage, express, telegraph and telephone | 44 46 |
| Lodge supplies | 569 03 |
| Official publication | 1,281 67 |
| Convention expenses | 863 71 |
| Bonds of the officers | 28 05 |
| Donation to Hoover's fund for children in Europe | 100 00 |
| Donations to schools | 20 00 |
| Total disbursements | $8,747 40 |
| Balance | $21,917 64 |

LEDGER ASSETS.

| | |
|---|---|
| Mortgage loans on real estate | $8,100 00 |
| Book value of bonds and stocks | 750 16 |
| Deposits in trust companies and banks on interest | 7,135 22 |
| Check account | 5,932 26 |
| Total ledger assets | $21,917 64 |

LIABILITIES.

| | |
|---|---|
| Death claims adjusted not yet due | $750 00 |

EXHIBIT OF CERTIFICATES.

| | Total business of the year. | | Business in Illinois during year. | |
|---|---|---|---|---|
| | Number. | Amount. | Number. | Amount. |
| Benefit certificates in force December 31, 1920, as per last statement | 928 | $780,850 00 | 834 | $656,850 00 |
| Benefit certificates written and renewed during the year | 112 | 85,650 00 | 97 | 75,100 00 |
| Totals | 1,040 | $866,500 00 | 931 | $731,950 00 |
| Deduct terminated, decreased or transferred during the year | 72 | 48,350 00 | -------- | ------------- |
| Deduct terminated or decreased during the year | -------- | ------------- | 58 | 43,450 00 |
| Total benefit certificates in force December 31, 1921 | 968 | $818,150 00 | 873 | $688,500 00 |

| | |
|---|---|
| Received during the year from members in Illinois: Mortuary, $7,941.00; reserve, $528.00; expense, $1,514.60; total | $9,983 60 |

EXHIBIT OF DEATH CLAIMS.

| | Total claims. | | Illinois claims. | |
|---|---|---|---|---|
| | Number. | Amount. | Number. | Amount. |
| Claims unpaid December 31, 1920, as per last statement | 4 | $1,725 00 | 3 | $1,525 00 |
| Claims reported during the year and interest addition | 9 | 3,850 00 | 8 | 3,500 00 |
| Totals | 13 | $5,575 00 | 11 | $5,025 00 |
| Claims paid during the year | 11 | 4,825 00 | 9 | 4,275 00 |
| Claims unpaid December 31, 1921 | 2 | $750 00 | 2 | $750 00 |

SCHEDULE D—BONDS.

| Description. | Book value. | Par value. | Market value. |
|---|---|---|---|
| U. S. Liberty Bond | $500 00 | $500 00 | $500 00 |
| U. S. War Saving Stamps | 250 16 | 250 16 | 250 16 |
| Totals | $750 16 | $750 16 | $750 16 |

## HOLY FAMILY SOCIETY OF THE U. S. OF A.

Located at No. 1006 North Chicago Street, Joliet, Illinois.

GEORGE STONICH, President. JOSEPH KLEPEC, Secretary.

| | |
|---|---|
| Balance from previous year | $12,507 47 |

### INCOME.

| | |
|---|---|
| Membership fees actually received | $ 172 00 |
| Assessments or premiums during first twelve months of membership of which all or an extra percentage is used for expenses | 1,157 00 |
| All other assessments or premiums | 5,804 21 |
| Net amount received from members | $7,133 21 |
| Gross interest from all sources | 561 05 |
| Profit on bonds purchased | 148 60 |
| Total income | $7,842 86 |
| Sum | $20,350 33 |

### DISBURSEMENTS.

| | |
|---|---|
| Death claims | $4,010 75 |
| Permanent disability claims | 650 00 |
| Total benefits paid | $4,660 75 |
| Commissions and fees paid to deputies and organizers | 129 00 |
| Salaries of officers and trustees | 514 42 |
| Insurance department fees | 5 00 |
| Rent | 60 00 |
| Advertising, printing and stationery | 292 40 |
| Lodge supplies | 199 43 |
| Flowers | 10 00 |
| Safety deposit vault | 3 00 |
| Total disbursements | $5,874 00 |
| Balance | $14,476 33 |

### LEDGER ASSETS.

| | |
|---|---|
| Book value of bonds | $11,000 00 |
| Deposits in trust companies and banks on interest | 3,476 33 |
| Total ledger assets | $14,476 33 |

### LIABILITIES.

| | |
|---|---|
| Total death claims | $2,602 75 |

### EXHIBIT OF CERTIFICATES.

| | Total business of the year. | | Business in Illinois during year. | |
|---|---|---|---|---|
| | Number. | Amount. | Number. | Amount. |
| Benefit certificates in force December 31, 1920, as per last statement | 821 | $337,000 00 | 694 | $288,500 00 |
| Benefit certificates written and renewed during the year | 110 | 55,000 00 | 83 | 41,500 00 |
| Totals | 931 | $392,000 00 | 777 | $330,000 00 |
| Deduct terminated, decreased or transferred during the year | 82 | 38,000 00 | | |
| Deduct terminated or decreased during the year | | | 54 | 26,000 00 |
| Total benefit certificates in force December 31, 1921 | 849 | $354,000 00 | 723 | $304,000 00 |

| | |
|---|---|
| Received during the year from members in Illinois: Mortuary $3,658.76; reserve, $698.80; disability, $433.30; all other, $140.00; expense, $989.20; total | $5,920 06 |

### EXHIBIT OF DEATH CLAIMS.

| | Total claims. | | Illinois claims. | |
|---|---|---|---|---|
| | Number. | Amount. | Number. | Amount. |
| Claims unpaid December 31, 1920, as per last statement | 5 | $1,812 50 | 2 | $ 962 50 |
| Claims reported during the year and interest addition | 13 | 4,800 00 | 12 | 4,550 00 |
| Totals | 18 | $6,612 50 | 14 | $5,512 50 |
| Claims paid during the year | 7 | 4,010 75 | 6 | 3,760 75 |
| Balance | 11 | $2,601 75 | 8 | $1,751 75 |

## EXHIBIT OF PERMANENT DISABILITY CLAIMS.

| | Total claims. Number. | Total claims. Amount. | Illinois claims. Number. | Illinois claims. Amount. |
|---|---|---|---|---|
| Claims reported during the year and interest addition | 12 | $650 00 | 11 | $600 00 |
| Claims paid during the year | 12 | 650 00 | 11 | 600 00 |

## SCHEDULE D—BONDS.

| Description. | Book value. |
|---|---|
| Joliet, Ill., municipal bonds, 5s | $10,000 00 |
| U. S. Liberty Bonds | 1,000 00 |
| Total | $11,000 00 |

# INDEPENDENT ORDER OF SVITHIOD.

Located at No. 139 North Clark Street, Chicago, Illinois.

JOHN G. CARSON, President. JOHN A. SANDGREN, Secretary.

| | |
|---|---|
| Balance from previous year | $397,518 62 |

## INCOME.

| | |
|---|---|
| Membership fees actually received | $ 971 75 |
| All other assessments or premiums | 107,956 20 |
| Dues and per capita tax | 10,604 60 |
| Net amount received from members | $119,532 55 |
| Gross interest on mortgage loans | 23,099 28 |
| Gross interest on bonds | 875 00 |
| Gross interest on deposits in trust companies and banks | 242 66 |
| Sale of lodge supplies | 384 38 |
| From all other sources, viz— | |
| Bonds for officers of subordinate lodges | 438 80 |
| Commission on loans made | 2,467 90 |
| Total income | $147,040 57 |
| Sum | $544,559 19 |

## DISBURSEMENTS.

| | |
|---|---|
| Death claims | $45,500 00 |
| Salaries of officers and trustees | 3,450 00 |
| Salaries and other compensation of committees | 426 00 |
| Salaries of office employees | 1,072 00 |
| Salaries and fees paid to supremem medical examiners | 367 80 |
| Traveling and other expenses of officers, trustees and committees | 246 47 |
| Insurance department fees | 143 08 |
| Rent | 968 72 |
| Advertising, printing and stationery | 423 66 |
| Postage, express, telegraph and telephone | 218 19 |
| Lodge supplies | 110 63 |
| Official publication | 2,491 78 |
| Expenses of supreme lodge meeting | 1,775 84 |
| Other legal expenses | 161 35 |
| All other disbursements, viz— | |
| Purchase of prizes | 104 75 |
| Organization expenses | 625 04 |
| Bonds for officers | 508 00 |
| Miscellaneous expenses | 325 23 |
| Total disbursements | $58,918 54 |
| Balance | $485,640 65 |

## LEDGER ASSETS.

| | |
|---|---|
| Mortgage loans on real estate | $443,700 00 |
| Book value of bonds | 20,830 00 |
| Cash in association's office | 392 25 |
| Deposits in trust companies and banks on interest | 20,718 40 |
| Total ledger assets | $485,640 65 |

## LEDGER ASSETS—Concluded.

### NON-LEDGER ASSETS.

| | | |
|---|---|---|
| Interest and rents due and accrued | | $6,937 75 |
| Assessments actually collected by subordinate lodges not yet turned over to supreme lodge | | 9,248 15 |
| All other assets, viz— | | |
| Registration fee collected by sub-lodges not yet turned over to the grand lodge | $507 50 | |
| Due from sub-lodges for supplies | 132 97 | |
| Furniture and supplies | 500 00 | |
| | | 1,140 47 |
| Gross assets | | $502,967 02 |

### DEDUCT ASSETS NOT ADMITTED.

| | | |
|---|---|---|
| Supplies | $132 97 | |
| Other items, viz— | | |
| Registration fee collected by sub-lodges not yet turned over to grand lodge | 507 50 | |
| Furniture and supplies | 500 00 | |
| | | 1,140 47 |
| Total admitted assets | | $501,826 55 |

## LIABILITIES.

| | | |
|---|---|---|
| Death claims due and unpaid | $ 250 00 | |
| Death claims reported during the year but not yet adjusted | 2,300 00 | |
| Total death claims | | $2,550 00 |
| Salaries, rents, expenses, commissions, etc., due or accrued | | 914 48 |
| Total | | $3,464 48 |

## EXHIBIT OF CERTIFICATES.

| | Total business of the year. | | Business in Illinois during year. | |
|---|---|---|---|---|
| | Number. | Amount. | Number. | Amount. |
| Benefit certificates in force December 31, 1920, as per last statement | 11,712 | $6,811,400 00 | 9,115 | $5,707,700 00 |
| Benefit certificates written and renewed during the year | 1,274 | 586,000 00 | 894 | 435,200 00 |
| Benefit certificates increased during the year | -------- | 17,800 00 | -------- | 10,200 00 |
| Total | 12,986 | $7,415,200 00 | 10,009 | $6,153,100 00 |
| Deduct terminated, decreased or transferred during the year | 667 | 296,300 00 | -------- | -------- |
| Deduct terminated or decreased during the year | -------- | -------- | 461 | 209,800 00 |
| Total benefit certificates in force December 31, 1921 | 12,319 | $7,118,900 00 | 9,548 | $5,943,300 00 |

| | |
|---|---|
| Received during the year from members in Illinois: Mortuary, $90,427.25; expense, $9,827.85; total | $100,255 10 |

## EXHIBIT OF DEATH CLAIMS.

| | Total claims. | | Illinois claims. | |
|---|---|---|---|---|
| | Number. | Amount. | Number. | Amount. |
| Claims unpaid December 31, 1920, as per last statement | 9 | $ 6,350 00 | 8 | $ 6,250 00 |
| Claims reported during the year and interest addition | 62 | 44,200 00 | 50 | 40,000 00 |
| Total | 71 | $50,550 00 | 58 | $46,250 00 |
| Claims paid during the year | 63 | 45,500 00 | 53 | 43,300 00 |
| Balance | 8 | $5,050 00 | 5 | $2,950 00 |
| Saved by compromising or scaling down claims during the year | -------- | 1,500 00 | -------- | 750 00 |
| Claims rejected during the year | 1 | 1,000 00 | 1 | 1,000 00 |
| Claims unpaid December 31, 1921 | 7 | $2,550 00 | 4 | $1,200 00 |

## SCHEDULE D—BONDS.

| Description. | Book value. | Par value. | Market value. |
|---|---|---|---|
| U. S. 2d Liberty Loan, 4¼s | $5,000 00 | $5,000 00 | $5,000 00 |
| U. S. 3d Liberty Loan, 4¼s | 5,000 00 | 5,000 00 | 5,000 00 |
| U. S. 4th Liberty Loan, 4¼s | 5,000 00 | 5,000 00 | 5,000 00 |
| U. S. Victory Loan, 4¾s | 5,000 00 | 5,000 00 | 5,000 00 |
| U. S. War Savings Stamps, 4s | 830 00 | 830 00 | 830 00 |
| Total | $20,830 00 | $20,830 00 | $20,830 00 |

## INDEPENDENT ORDER OF VIKINGS, GRAND LODGE.

Located at No. 80 West Washington Street, Chicago, Illinois.

CARL R. OLSON, President. ERIK THULIN, Secretary.

| | |
|---|---|
| Balance from previous year | $236,516 07 |

### INCOME.

| | |
|---|---|
| Membership fees actually received | $41,985 80 |
| All other assessments or premiums | 4,630 50 |
| Dues and per capita tax | 10,566 90 |
| Net amount received from members | $57,183 20 |
| Gross interest on mortgage loans | 12,710 43 |
| Gross interest on collateral loans | 30 00 |
| Gross interest on bonds and dividends on stocks | 478 12 |
| Gross interest on deposits in trust companies and banks | 26 43 |
| Sale of lodge supplies | 324 74 |
| Premium on bond | 166 66 |
| Traveling expenses from lodges | 1,516 19 |
| Rent of office | 20 00 |
| Advertisment in publication | 349 75 |
| From the directors of old peoples home | 136 06 |
| Commissions | 752 50 |
| Total income | $73,694 08 |
| Sum | $310,210 15 |

### DISBURSEMENTS.

| | |
|---|---|
| Death claims | $18,950 00 |
| Sick benefits to lodges | 997 00 |
| Total benefits paid | $19,947 00 |
| Returned assessments | 12 70 |
| Returned interest | 9 16 |
| Salaries of officers and trustees | 3,650 00 |
| Salaries and other compensation of committees | 105 00 |
| Salaries and fees paid to supreme medical examiners | 50 50 |
| Traveling and other expenses of officers, trustees and committees | 587 11 |
| For collection of assessments and dues and traveling expenses | 1,516 36 |
| Insurance department fees | 162 11 |
| Rent | 600 00 |
| Advertising, printing and stationery | 683 28 |
| Postage, express, telegraph and telephone | 276 52 |
| Lodge supplies | 444 58 |
| Official publication | 2,482 06 |
| To the directors of the old peoples home | 1,901 00 |
| Expenses of supreme lodge meeting | 514 60 |
| To the old peoples home | 775 09 |
| Prizes to lodges and members | 932 05 |
| Furniture and fixtures | 153 20 |
| Expenses for the ex-commission | 31 35 |
| A present to a past president | 50 90 |
| Premium on surety bond | 193 63 |
| Premiums on fire insurance | 350 62 |
| Valuation | 15 50 |
| All other disbursements, viz— | |
| Illinois Fraternal Congress | 10 00 |
| Light | 59 73 |
| Sundry expenses for the office | 216 05 |
| Campaign expenses to lodges | 96 65 |
| Total disbursements | $35,826 75 |
| Balance | $274,383 40 |

### LEDGER ASSETS.

| | |
|---|---|
| Mortgage loans on real estate | $257,300 00 |
| Loans secured by pledge of bonds, stocks or other collateral | 580 00 |
| Book value of bonds and stocks | 6,332 00 |
| Cash in association's office | 2,902 79 |
| Deposits in trust companies and banks on interest | 7,268 61 |
| Total ledger assets | $274,383 40 |

#### NON-LEDGER ASSETS.

| | |
|---|---|
| Interest and rents due and accrued | 3,974 05 |
| Gross assets | $278,357 45 |

LEDGER ASSETS—Concluded.

DEDUCT ASSETS NOT ADMITTED.

| | |
|---|---|
| 60-days judgment note | $80 00 |
| Total admitted assets | $278,277 45 |

LIABILITIES.

| | | |
|---|---|---|
| Death claims due and unpaid | $200 00 | |
| Death claims adjusted not yet due | 800 00 | |
| Total death claims | | $1,000 00 |
| Advance assessments | | 750 00 |
| Total | | $1,750 00 |

EXHIBIT OF CERTIFICATES.

| | Total business of the year. | | Business in Illinois during year. | |
|---|---|---|---|---|
| | Number. | Amount. | Number. | Amount. |
| Benefit certificates in force December 31, 1920, as per last statement | 8,854 | $2,559,250 00 | 8,010 | $2,317,850 00 |
| Benefit certificates written and renewed during the year | 1,040 | 342,550 00 | 768 | 264,150 00 |
| Benefit certificates increased during the year | 18 | 12,400 00 | | |
| Total | 9,912 | $2,914,200 00 | 8,778 | $2,582,000 00 |
| Deduct terminated, decreased or transferred during the year | 1,139 | 302,250 00 | | |
| Deduct terminated or decreased during the year | | | 1,010 | 269,100 00 |
| Total benefit certificates in force December 31, 1921 | 8,773 | $2,611,950 00 | 7,768 | $2,312,900 00 |

| | |
|---|---|
| Received during the year from members in Illinois: Mortuary, $37,039.63; expense, $15,076.88; total | $52,116 51 |

EXHIBIT OF DEATH CLAIMS.

| | Total claims. | | Illinois claims. | |
|---|---|---|---|---|
| | Number. | Amount. | Number. | Amount. |
| Claims unpaid December 31, 1920, as per last statement | 3 | $ 300 00 | 3 | $ 300 00 |
| Claims reported during the year and interest addition | 63 | $19,850 00 | 61 | 19,650 00 |
| Total | 66 | $20,150 00 | 64 | $19,950 00 |
| Claims paid during the year | 58 | 18,950 00 | 57 | 18,850 00 |
| Balance | 8 | $1,200 00 | 7 | $1,100 00 |
| Claims rejected during the year | 2 | 200 00 | 2 | 200 00 |
| Claims unpaid December 31, 1921 | 6 | $1,000 00 | 5 | $900 00 |

SCHEDULE D—BONDS.

| Description. | Book value. |
|---|---|
| Second U. S. Liberty Loan, 4s | $ 500 00 |
| Fourth U. S. Liberty Loan, 4¼s | 5,000 00 |
| Total | $5,500 00 |

## INDEPENDENT WESTERN STAR ORDER.

Located at No. 1127 Blue Island Avenue, Chicago, Illinois.

MAX LEVY, President. I. SHAPIRO, Secretary.

| | |
|---|---|
| Balance from previous year | $15,677 57 |

INCOME.

| | |
|---|---|
| All other assessments or premiums | $76,194 60 |
| Dues and per capita tax | 8,801 05 |
| Net amount received from members | $84,995 65 |
| Gross interest from all other sources | 23 05 |
| Sale of lodge supplies | 64 50 |
| American Bankers Insurance Company account claims | 12,000 00 |
| Liens deducted from paid claims | 2,364 71 |
| Total income | $99,447 91 |
| Sum | $115,125 48 |

## DISBURSEMENTS.

| | |
|---|---|
| Death claims | $93,625 00 |
| Permanent disability claims | 100 00 |
| Funeral expense | 50 00 |
| Total benefits paid | $93,775 00 |
| Commissions and fees paid to deputies and organizers | 65 00 |
| Salaries of deputies and organizers | 482 50 |
| Salaries of officers and trustees | 2,505 00 |
| Salaries of office employees | 1,310 00 |
| Salaries and fees paid to supreme medical examiners | 500 00 |
| Salaries and fees paid to subordinate medical examiners | 74 00 |
| Traveling and other expenses of officers, trustees and committees | 358 96 |
| Insurance department fees | 77 00 |
| Rent | 750 00 |
| Advertising, printing and stationery | 381 80 |
| Postage, express, telegraph and telephone | 595 64 |
| Legal expense in litigating claims | 160 00 |
| Furniture, fixtures and repairs | 5 00 |
| Borrowed money repaid (gross) | 924 51 |
| All other disbursements, viz— | |
| Indemnity bonds, fire insurance premiums | 291 20 |
| Gas and electric light bills | 171 44 |
| Office cleaning, clean towel supplies, water and ice | 175 50 |
| Donation, propaganda, etc | 38 00 |
| Total disbursements | $102,640 55 |
| Balance | $12,484 93 |

## LEDGER ASSETS.

| | |
|---|---|
| Deposits in trust companies and banks not on interest | 11,449 75 |
| Deposits in trust companies and banks on interest | 1,035 18 |
| Total ledger assets | $12,484 93 |

### NON-LEDGER ASSETS.

| | |
|---|---|
| Assessments actually collected by subordinate lodges not yet turned over to supreme lodges | 8,032 68 |
| Gross assets | $20,517 61 |

## LIABILITIES.

| | | |
|---|---|---|
| Death claims due and unpaid | $5,500 00 | |
| Death claims resisted | 500 00 | |
| Death claims reported during the year but not yet adjusted | 5,000 00 | |
| For tombstones on paid claims | 2,800 00 | |
| Total death claims | | $13,800 00 |
| Borrowed money | | 2,281 90 |
| Total | | $16,081 90 |

## EXHIBIT OF CERTIFICATES.

| | Total business of the year. | | Business in Illinois during year. | |
|---|---|---|---|---|
| | Number. | Amount. | Number. | Amount. |
| Benefit certificates in force December 31, 1920, as per last statement | 7,739 | $3,669,500 00 | 2,708 | $1,354,000 00 |
| Benefit certificates written and renewed during the year | 563 | 281,500 00 | 319 | 159,500 00 |
| Total | 7,902 | $3,951,000 00 | 3,027 | $1,513,500 00 |
| Deduct terminated, decreased or transferred during the year | 1,253 | 626,500 00 | | |
| Deduct terminated or decreased during the year | | | 499 | 249,500 00 |
| Total benefit certificates in force December 31, 1921 | 6,649 | $3,324,500 00 | 2,528 | $1,264,000 00 |

| | |
|---|---|
| Received during the year from members in Illinois: Mortuary, $30,007.04; expense, $3,332.40; total | $33,339 44 |

EXHIBIT OF DEATH CLAIMS.

| | Total claims. Number. | Total claims. Amount. | Illinois claims. Number. | Illinois claims. Amount. |
|---|---|---|---|---|
| Claims unpaid December 31, 1920, as per last statement | 62 | $33,175 00 | 15 | $ 7,200 00 |
| Claims reported during the year and interest addition | 150 | 75,000 00 | 54 | 27,000 00 |
| Total | 212 | $108,175 00 | 69 | $34,200 00 |
| Claims paid during the year | 190 | 93,625 00 | 63 | 31,200 00 |
| Balance | 22 | $14,550 00 | 6 | $3,000 00 |
| Saved by compromising or scaling down claims during the year | -------- | 750 00 | -------- | -------- |
| Claims unpaid December 31, 1921 | 22 | $13,800 00 | 6 | $3,000 00 |

EXHIBIT OF PERMANENT DISABILITY CLAIMS.

| | Total claims—all in Illinois. Number. | Total claims—all in Illinois. Amount. |
|---|---|---|
| Claims reported during the year and interest addition | 1 | $500 00 |
| Claims paid during the year | 1 | 100 00 |
| Claims unpaid December 31, 1921 | -------- | $400 00 |

## KNIGHTS OF PYTHIAS OF N. A. S. A. E. A. A. AND A.

Located at No. 3102 State Street, Chicago, Illinois.

ALLEN A. WESLEY, President. ALBERT B. GEORGE, Acting Secretary.

| | |
|---|---|
| Balance from previous year | $55,217 39 |

INCOME.

| | |
|---|---|
| Membership fees actually received | $ 483 00 |
| Dues | 31,134 90 |
| Certificate fees | 149 25 |
| Net amount received from members | $31,767 15 |
| Gross interest on bonds and dividends on stocks | 2,982 08 |
| Gross interest on deposits in trust companies and banks | 276 99 |
| Gross increase in book value of ledger assets | 1,038 50 |
| Voucher cancelled | 25 00 |
| Total income | $36,089 72 |
| Sum | $91,307 11 |

DISBURSEMENTS.

| | |
|---|---|
| Death claims | $10,900 00 |
| Salaries of officers and trustees | 1,645 00 |
| Other compensation of officers and trustees | 277 50 |
| Salaries of office employees | 120 00 |
| For collection and remittance of assessments and dues | 101 30 |
| Insurance department fees | 5 00 |
| Rent | 222 50 |
| Advertising, printing and stationery | 459 75 |
| Postage, express, telegraph and telephone | 228 20 |
| Lodge supplies | 13 00 |
| Rent of vault | 6 50 |
| Legal expense in litigating claims | 38 00 |
| Other legal expenses | 37 52 |
| Accrued interest on bonds purchased in 1921 | 149 20 |
| Insurance examiner | 36 51 |
| Bonds of treasurer | 15 00 |
| Bonds of secretary | 5 00 |
| Total disbursements | $14,259 98 |
| Balance | $77,047 13 |

LEDGER ASSETS.

| | |
|---|---|
| Book value of bonds and stocks | $46,000 00 |
| Cash in association's office | 15,254 40 |
| Deposits in trust companies and banks not on interest | 12,024 64 |
| Deposits in trust companies and banks on interest | 3,768 09 |
| Total ledger assets | $77,047 13 |

LIABILITIES.

| | |
|---|---|
| Death claims due and unpaid | $2,450 00 |

EXHIBIT OF CERTIFICATES.

| | Total business of the year—all in Illinois. Number. | Amount. |
|---|---|---|
| Benefit certificates in force December 31, 1920, as per last statement | 5,369 | $253,049 00 |
| Benefit certificates written and renewed during the year | 483 | 16,905 00 |
| Total | 5,852 | $269,954 00 |
| Deduct terminated, decreased or transferred during the year | 776 | 103,780 00 |
| Total benefit certificates in force December 31, 1921 | 5,076 | $166,174 00 |

Received during the year from members in Illinois: Mortuary, $25,945.76; expense, $5,821.39; total — $31,767 15

EXHIBIT OF DEATH CLAIMS.

| | Total claims—all in Illinois. Number. | Amount. |
|---|---|---|
| Claims unpaid December 31, 1920, as per last statement | 8 | $ 1,275 00 |
| Claims reported during the year and interest addition | 57 | 11,800 00 |
| Total | 65 | $13,075 00 |
| Claims paid during the year | 53 | 10,900 00 |
| Claims unpaid December 31, 1921 | 12 | $2,175 00 |

SCHEDULE D—BONDS.

| Description. | Book value. | Par value. |
|---|---|---|
| Ohio & Western Utilities, 6s | $5,000 00 | $5,000 00 |
| Minnesota Electric Light & Power, 6s | 4,000 00 | 4,000 00 |
| U. S. First Liberty Loan, 3½s | 2,000 00 | 2,000 00 |
| U. S. Third Liberty Loan, 4¼s | 1,000 00 | 1,000 00 |
| U. S. Fourth Liberty Loan, 4¼s | 7,000 00 | 7,000 00 |
| U. S. Victory Loan, 4¾s | 1,000 00 | 1,000 00 |
| Northern Iowa Gas & Electric, 6s | 6,000 00 | 6,000 00 |
| Minn. Gas & Electric Co., 6s | 9,000 00 | 9,000 00 |
| Binghamton Light, Heat & Power Co., 7s | 2,000 00 | 2,000 00 |
| Middle West Utilities Co., 8s | 4,000 00 | 4,000 00 |
| Lake Shore Motor Bus Corporation, 8s | 5,000 00 | 5,000 00 |
| Total | $46,000 00 | $46,000 00 |

## KNIGHTS OF TABOR AND DAUGHTERS OF TABERNACLE.

Located at No. 922 South Sixteenth Street, Springfield, Illinois.

J. H. FISHER, President. T. W. WARRICK, Secretary.

| | |
|---|---|
| Balance from previous year | $2,251 88 |

INCOME.

| | |
|---|---|
| Membership fees actually received | $5,086 68 |
| All other assessments or premiums | 295 52 |
| Total income | $5,384 20 |

DISBURSEMENTS.

| | |
|---|---|
| Total death benefits paid | $3,525 00 |
| Salaries of managers or agents not deputies or organizers | 158 53 |
| Other compensation of office employees | 48 00 |
| Traveling and other expenses of officers, trustees and committees | 14 52 |
| Insurance department fees | 5 00 |
| Advertising, printing and stationery | 53 00 |
| Postage, express, telegraph and telephone | 11 00 |
| Total disbursements | $3,815 03 |
| Balance | $3,821 05 |

LEDGER ASSETS.

| | |
|---|---|
| Deposits in trust companies and banks not on interest | $3,821 05 |

LIABILITIES.

| | | |
|---|---|---|
| Death claims adjusted not yet due | $550 00 | |
| Death claims reported during the year but not yet adjusted | 100 00 | |
| Total death claims | | $650 00 |

EXHIBIT OF CERTIFICATES.

| | Total business of the year—all in Illinois. Number. | Amount. |
|---|---|---|
| Benefit certificates in force December 31, 1920, as per last statement | 2,569 | $207,625 00 |
| Benefit certificates written and renewed during the year | 648 | 13,900 00 |
| Totals | 3,217 | $221,525 00 |
| Deduct terminated or decreased during the year | 641 | 10,500 00 |
| Total benefit certificates in force December 31, 1921 | 2,576 | $211,025 00 |
| Received during the year from members in Illinois: Mortuary, $5,088.68; expense, $295.52; total | | $5,384 20 |

EXHIBIT OF DEATH CLAIMS.

| | Total claims—all in Illinois. Number. | Amount. |
|---|---|---|
| Claims unpaid December 31, 1920, as per last statement | 3 | $ 150 00 |
| Claims reported during the year and interest addition | 44 | 4,025 00 |
| Totals | 47 | $4,175 00 |
| Claims paid during the year | 39 | 3,525 00 |
| Claims unpaid December 31, 1921 | 8 | $650 00 |

## LIBERTY LIFE AND CASUALTY INSURANCE COMPANY.

Located at No. 3202 Cottage Grove Avenue, Chicago, Illinois.

WM. H. KING, President. JOHN B. LEFTTEL, Treasurer.

| | |
|---|---|
| Balance from previous year | $2,016 66 |

INCOME.

| | |
|---|---|
| Assessments or premiums during first twelve months of membership of which all or an extra percentage is used for expenses | $ 451 01 |
| All other assessments or premiums | 1,295 50 |
| Net amount received from members | $1,746 51 |
| Sum | $3,763 17 |

DISBURSEMENTS.

| | |
|---|---|
| Death claims | $ 650 00 |
| Commissions and fees paid to deputies and organizers | 303 21 |
| Salaries of officers and trustees | 1,290 12 |
| Salaries of office employees | 402 51 |
| Other compensation of office employees | 100 00 |
| Salaries and fees paid to supreme medical examiners | 17 50 |
| Traveling and other expenses of officers, trustees and committees | 50 00 |
| Insurance department fees | 5 00 |
| Rent | 99 18 |
| Advertising, printing and stationery | 164 50 |
| Postage, express, telegraph and telephone | 5 03 |
| Other legal expenses | 75 00 |
| Miscellaneous expense | 6 86 |
| Total disbursements | $3,168 91 |
| Balance | $594 26 |

LEDGER ASSETS.

| | |
|---|---|
| Cash in association's office | $ 22 50 |
| Deposits in trust companies and banks not on interest | 571 76 |
| Total ledger assets | $594 26 |

LIABILITIES.

| | |
|---|---|
| Death claims adjusted not yet due | $400 00 |
| All other liabilities, viz: Mean reserve on new business written and old business written since December, 1920 | 76 58 |
| Total | $476 58 |

EXHIBIT OF CERTIFICATES.

| | Total business of the year. | | Business in Illinois during year. | |
|---|---|---|---|---|
| | Number. | Amount. | Number. | Amount. |
| Benefit certificates in force December 31, 1920, as per last statement | 390 | $117,800 00 | 277 | $95,950 00 |
| Benefit certificates written and renewed during the year | 40 | 10,000 00 | 40 | 10,000 00 |
| Total | 430 | $127,800 00 | 317 | $105,950 00 |
| Deduct terminated, decreased or transferred during the year | 90 | 17,800 00 | | |
| Deduct terminated or decreased during the year | | | 60 | 13,300 00 |
| Total benefit certificates in force December 31, 1921 | 340 | $110,000 00 | 257 | $92,650 00 |

Received during the year from members in Illinois: Reserve, $448.60; expense, $855.01; total $1,303 61

EXHIBIT OF DEATH CLAIMS.

| | Total claims. | | Illinois claims. | |
|---|---|---|---|---|
| | Number. | Amount. | Number. | Amount. |
| Claims unpaid December 31, 1920, as per last statement | 6 | $650 00 | 4 | $450 00 |
| Claims reported during the year and interest addition | 2 | 400 00 | | |
| Total | 8 | $1,050 00 | 4 | $450 00 |
| Claims paid during the year | 5 | 650 00 | 4 | 450 00 |
| Claims unpaid December 31, 1921 | 3 | $400 00 | | |

## LOW GERMAN GRAND GUILD OF THE U. S. A.

Located at No. 2040 West North Avenue, Chicago, Illinois.

FRANK DURSCHMID, President. FRANK VIGERSKE, Secretary.

| | |
|---|---|
| Balance from previous year | $259,787 58 |

INCOME.

| | |
|---|---|
| All other assessments or premiums | $78,458 10 |
| Dues and per capita tax | 5,216 85 |
| Net amount received from members | $83,674 95 |
| Gross interest on mortgage loans | 12,981 32 |
| Gross interest on bonds and dividends on stocks | 597 91 |
| Gross interest on deposits in trust companies and banks | 530 10 |
| Sale of lodge supplies | 63 30 |
| From official publication | 556 63 |
| Book from G. G. Agitation Committee | 50 00 |
| Book from Volksfest Committee | 25 00 |
| Total income | $98,479 21 |
| Sum | $358,266 79 |

DISBURSEMENTS.

| | |
|---|---|
| Death claims | $55,900 00 |
| Sick claims | 4,903 00 |
| Old age benefits | 2,427 00 |
| Total benefits paid | $63,230 00 |
| Salaries of officers and trustees | 2,835 00 |
| Other compensation of officers and trustees | 325 00 |
| Salaries and other compensation of committees | 832 25 |
| Salaries and fees paid to subordinate medical examiners | 5 00 |
| Traveling and other expenses of officers, trustees and committees | 28 53 |
| Insurance department fees | 60 00 |
| Rent, including office | 300 00 |
| Advertising, printing and stationery | 143 75 |
| Postage, express, telegraph and telephone and bank exchange | 164 85 |
| Lodge supplies | 20 95 |
| Official publication | 1,564 10 |
| Expenses of supreme lodge meeting | 36 00 |
| Legal expense in litigating claims | 11 75 |
| Furniture and fixtures and repairs | 27 00 |
| 29 convention expenses | 292 50 |
| Relief work | 100 00 |
| Fire insurance premium | 14 50 |
| Wisconsin Fraternal Congress dues | 25 00 |
| Bonds | 250 00 |

DISBURSEMENTS—Concluded.

| | |
|---|---|
| Electric light | $ 30 00 |
| Agitation | 429 25 |
| Total disbursements | $70,725 33 |
| Balance | $287,541 46 |

## LEDGER ASSETS.

| | |
|---|---|
| Mortgage loans on real estate | $239,850 00 |
| Loans secured by pledge of bonds, stocks or other collateral | 15,000 00 |
| Deposits in trust companies and banks on interest | 31,859 46 |
| War Savings Stamps | 832 00 |
| Total ledger assets | $287,541 46 |

NON-LEDGER ASSETS.

| | |
|---|---|
| Interest and rents due and accrued | 3,827 49 |
| Assessments actually collected by subordinate lodges not yet turned over to supreme lodge | 3,359 75 |
| Office fixtures, furniture, mailing list outfit | 2 313 00 |
| Gross assets | $297,041 70 |

DEDUCT ASSETS NOT ADMITTED.

| | |
|---|---|
| Office fixtures, furniture, mailing list outfit | 2,313 00 |
| Total admitted assets | $294,728 70 |

## LIABILITIES.

| | |
|---|---|
| Death claims adjusted not yet due | $6,900 00 |
| Sick claims due and unpaid | 847 00 |
| Old age and other benefits due and unpaid | 689 95 |
| Total unpaid claims | $8,436 95 |
| Salaries, rents, expenses, commissions, etc., due or accrued | 929 65 |
| Total | $9,366 60 |

## EXHIBIT OF CERTIFICATES.

| | Total business of the year. | | Business in Illinois during year. | |
|---|---|---|---|---|
| | Number. | Amount. | Number. | Amount. |
| Benefit certificates in force December 31, 1920, as per last statement | 6,602 | $3,301,000 00 | 6,087 | $3,043,500 00 |
| Benefit certificates written and renewed during the year | 108 | 54,000 00 | 106 | 53,000 00 |
| Total | 6,710 | $3,355,000 00 | 6,193 | $3,096,500 00 |
| Deduct terminated, decreased or transferred during the year | 257 | 128,500 00 | | |
| Deduct terminated or decreased during the year | | | 239 | 119,500 00 |
| Total benefit certificates in force December 31, 1921 | 6,453 | $3,226,500 00 | 5,954 | $2,977,000 00 |

Received during the year from members in Illinois: Mortuary, $57,360.20; sick, $15,626.00; expense, $4,831.25; total ........ $77,817 45

## EXHIBIT OF DEATH CLAIMS.

| | Total claims. | | Illinois claims. | |
|---|---|---|---|---|
| | Number. | Amount. | Number. | Amount. |
| Claims unpaid December 31, 1920, as per last statement | 10 | $ 4,800 00 | 9 | $ 4,500 00 |
| Claims reported during the year and interest addition | 116 | 58,000 00 | 108 | 54,000 00 |
| Total | 126 | $62,800 00 | 117 | $58,500 00 |
| Claims paid during the year | 112 | 55,900 00 | 105 | 52,500 00 |
| Claims unpaid December 31, 1921 | 14 | $6,900 00 | 12 | $6,000 00 |

EXHIBIT OF SICK CLAIMS.

| | Total claims. Number. | Amount. | Illinois claims. Number. | Amount. |
|---|---|---|---|---|
| Claims unpaid December 31, 1920, as per last statement | 122 | $1,480 00 | 121 | $1,471 00 |
| Claims reported during the year | 223 | 4,270 00 | 183 | 3,857 00 |
| Total | 345 | $5,750 00 | 304 | $5,328 00 |
| Claims paid during the year | 281 | 4,903 00 | 244 | 4,512 00 |
| Claims unpaid December 31, 1921 | 64 | $847 00 | 60 | $816 00 |

EXHIBIT OF OLD AGE CLAIMS.

| | Total claims. Number. | Amount. | Illinois claims. Number. | Amount. |
|---|---|---|---|---|
| Claims reported during the year and interest addition | 157 | $2,427 00 | 148 | $2,278 00 |
| Claims unpaid December 31, 1921 for the last quarter | 157 | $689 95 | 148 | $650 05 |

SCHEDULE D—BONDS.

| Description. | Book value. |
|---|---|
| Third Liberty Bond, 4¼s | $1,000 00 |
| Fourth Liberty Bond, 4¼s | 1,000 00 |
| Fourth Liberty Bond, 4¼s | 1,000 00 |
| Victory Liberty Bond, 4¾s | 1,000 00 |
| Victory Liberty Loan, 4¾s | 1,000 00 |
| War Saving Stamps | 1,000 00 |
| Argyle Building, gold, 7s | 5,000 00 |
| Argyle Building, gold, 7s | 2,000 00 |
| Argyle and Sheridan Road, Chicago, Ill., County Cook, 7s | 3,000 00 |
| Total | $16,000 00 |

## LOYAL AMERICAN LIFE ASSOCIATION.

Located at No. 3952 Ellis Avenue, Chicago, Illinois.

E. J. DUNN, President. H. D. COWAN, Secretary.

| | |
|---|---|
| Balance from previous year | $585,905 71 |

INCOME.

| | |
|---|---|
| All other assessments or premiums | $440,588 08 |
| Regular fees and social dues | 706 10 |
| Total received from members | $441,294 18 |
| Deduct payments returned to applicants and members | 1,486 64 |
| Net amount received from members | $439,807 54 |
| Gross interest on mortgage loans | 7,174 75 |
| Gross interest on bonds and dividends on stocks | 16,011 33 |
| Gross interest on deposits in trust companies and banks | 1,007 82 |
| Gross interest from all other sources | 372 57 |
| Gross rents from association's property, including $2,549.00 for association's occupancy of its own buildings | 3,831 72 |
| Sale of lodge supplies | 165 90 |
| Borrowed money (gross) | 20,000 00 |
| Gross profit on sale or maturity of ledger assets | 334 93 |
| Gross increase in book value of ledger assets | 407 75 |
| Bond premium, local secretary's | 169 19 |
| Total income | $489,283 50 |
| Sum | $1,075,189 21 |

DISBURSEMENTS.

| | |
|---|---|
| Death claims | $200,975 00 |
| Disability claims | 800 00 |
| Old age benefits | 3,863 66 |
| Broken bones | 825 00 |
| Total benefits paid | $206,463 66 |
| Commissions and fees paid to deputies and organizers | 50,165 26 |
| Salaries of officers and trustees | 24,941 55 |
| Salaries and other compensation of committees | 889 96 |
| Salaries of office employees | 21,083 31 |
| Salaries and fees paid to supreme medical examiners | 3,150 00 |
| Traveling and other expenses of officers, trustees and committees | 5,864 53 |
| Insurance department fees | 457 00 |

DISBURSEMENTS—Concluded.

| | | |
|---|---|---|
| Rent | | $2,549 00 |
| Advertising, printing and stationery | | 6,295 70 |
| Postage, express, telegraph and telephone | | 1,713 98 |
| Lodge supplies | | 969 64 |
| Official publication | | 6,526 55 |
| Expenses of supreme lodge meeting | | 7,112 87 |
| Legal expense in litigating claims | | 1,226 60 |
| Other legal expenses | | 23 80 |
| Furniture and fixtures | | 361 05 |
| Taxes, repairs and other expenses on real estate | | 1,200 22 |
| Gross loss on sale or maturity of ledger assets | | 49 27 |
| Borrowed money repaid (gross) | | 30,000 00 |
| All other disbursements, viz: Subscriptions, books, etc., $847.88; United Service Bureau and actuary, $858.89; custodian of securities and Fraternal Congress of America, $239.00; bond premiums, $283.30; sundry expenses, home office, $2,779.19; miscellaneous, $498.66 | | 5,506 92 |
| Total disbursements | | $376,550 87 |
| Balance | | $698,638 34 |

LEDGER ASSETS.

| | | |
|---|---|---|
| Book value of real estate | | $ 90,638 20 |
| Mortgage loans on real estate | | 243,000 00 |
| Book value of bonds and stocks | | 310,650 00 |
| Deposits in trust companies and banks on interest | | 54,350 14 |
| Total ledger assets | | $698,638 34 |

NON-LEDGER ASSETS.

| | | |
|---|---|---|
| Interest and rents due and accrued | | 16,709 72 |
| Market value of bonds and stocks over book value | | 3,420 00 |
| Assessments actually collected by subordinate lodges not yet turned over to supreme lodge | | 36,178 39 |
| Office furniture, fixtures, supplies | | 5,500 00 |
| Gross assets | | $760,446 45 |

DEDUCT ASSETS NOT ADMITTED.

| | | |
|---|---|---|
| Book value of bonds and stocks over market value | $ 380 00 | |
| Office furniture, fixtures, supplies, etc | 5,500 00 | |
| | | 5,880 00 |
| Total admitted assets | | $754,566 45 |

LIABILITIES.

| | | |
|---|---|---|
| Death claims reported during the year but not yet adjusted | $13,450 00 | |
| Death claims incurred in 1921, not reported until 1922 | 10,200 00 | |
| Present value of deferred death claims payable in installments | 2,340 00 | |
| Total death claims | | $25,990 00 |
| Accident claims reported during the year but not yet adjusted | $ 50 00 | |
| Accident claims incurred in 1921, not reported until 1922 | 150 00 | |
| Total sick and accident claims | | 200 00 |
| Old age and other benefits due and unpaid | | 41 36 |
| Total unpaid claims | | 26,231 36 |
| Salaries, rents, expenses, commissions, etc., due or accrued | | 1,925 78 |
| Borrowed money | | 20,000 00 |
| Special deposits | | 52 31 |
| Total | | $48,209 45 |

EXHIBIT OF CERTIFICATES.

| | Total business of the year. | | Business in Illinois during year. | |
|---|---|---|---|---|
| | Number. | Amount. | Number. | Amount. |
| Benefit certificates in force December 31, 1920, as per last statement | 15,952 | $16,721,304 00 | 10,464 | $11,355,635 00 |
| Benefit certificates written and renewed during the year | 2,129 | 2,486,900 00 | 809 | 971,908 00 |
| Total | 18,081 | $19,208,204 00 | 11,273 | $12,327,543 00 |
| Deduct terminated, decreased or transferred during the year | 1,919 | 2,355,339 00 | | |
| Deduct terminated or decreased during the year | | | 961 | 1,185,451 00 |
| Total benefit certificates in force December 31, 1921 | 16,162 | $16,852,865 00 | 10,312 | $11,142,092 00 |

| | |
|---|---|
| Received during the year from members in Illinois: Mortuary, $206,205.47; expense, $92,916.71; total | $299,122 18 |

EXHIBIT OF DEATH CLAIMS.

| | Total claims. Number. | Amount. | Illinois claims. Number. | Amount. |
|---|---|---|---|---|
| Claims unpaid December 31, 1920, as per last statement | 22 | $ 16,667 50 | 17 | $ 12,417 50 |
| Claims reported during the year and interest addition | 203 | 206,765 50 | 131 | 145,908 00 |
| Total | 225 | $223,433 00 | 148 | $158,325 50 |
| Claims paid during the year | 208 | 200,975 00 | 138 | 144,173 19 |
| Balance | 17 | $22,458 00 | 10 | $14,152 31 |
| Saved by compromising or scaling down claims during the year | -------- | 6,668 00 | -------- | 3,712 31 |
| Claims unpaid December 31, 1921 | 17 | $15,790 00 | 10 | $10,440 00 |

EXHIBIT OF ACCIDENT CLAIMS.

| | Total claims. Number. | Amount. | Illinois claims. Number. | Amount. |
|---|---|---|---|---|
| Claims unpaid December 31, 1920, as per last statement | 2 | $ 125 00 | 2 | $ 125 00 |
| Claims reported during the year | 25 | 1,550 00 | 20 | 1,400 00 |
| Total | 27 | $1,675 00 | 22 | $1,525 00 |
| Claims paid during the year | 26 | 1,625 00 | 21 | 1,475 00 |
| Claims unpaid December 31, 1921 | 1 | $50 00 | 1 | $50 00 |

EXHIBIT OF OLD AGE AND OTHER CLAIMS.

| | Total claims. Number. | Amount. | Illinois claims. Number. | Amount. |
|---|---|---|---|---|
| Claims unpaid December 31, 1920, as per last statement | 1 | $ 41 36 | 1 | $ 41 36 |
| Claims reported during the year and interest addition | 21 | 3,863 66 | 12 | 2,100 67 |
| Total | 22 | $3,905 02 | 13 | $2,142 03 |
| Claims paid during the year | 21 | 3,863 66 | 12 | 2,100 67 |
| Claims unpaid December 31, 1921 | 1 | $41 36 | 1 | $41 36 |

SCHEDULE D—BONDS.

| Description. | Book value. | Par value. | Market value. |
|---|---|---|---|
| Second Liberty Loan | $ 2,000 00 | $ 2,000 00 | $ 2,000 00 |
| Third Liberty Loan | 30,000 00 | 30,000 00 | 30,000 00 |
| Fourth Liberty Loan | 39,000 00 | 39,000 00 | 39,000 00 |
| Victory Loan | 10,000 00 | 10,000 00 | 10,000 00 |
| Allendale; S. C., school | 5,000 00 | 5,000 00 | 5,250 00 |
| Austin, Tex., school | 10,000 00 | 10,000 00 | 9,800 00 |
| Austin, Tex., school | 8,000 00 | 8,000 00 | 7,920 00 |
| Cranberry Creek, Wood and J. Co., Wis | 6,000 00 | 6,000 00 | 6,000 00 |
| Cranberry Creek, Wood and J. Co., Wis | 3,000 00 | 3,000 00 | 3,000 00 |
| City of Reno, Nev., street | 5,000 00 | 5,000 00 | 5,000 00 |
| City of Everett, Wash., water | 15,500 00 | 15,500 00 | 15,965 00 |
| City of Ironwood, Mich | 5,000 00 | 5,000 00 | 5,150 00 |
| Dancy, Wis., drainage | 9,500 00 | 9,500 00 | 9,500 00 |
| Dancy, Wis., drainage | 11,000 00 | 11,000 00 | 11,000 00 |
| Dorchester County, S. C., school | 5,000 00 | 5,000 00 | 5,350 00 |
| Indian Grove Drainage Dist | 55,000 00 | 55,000 00 | 55,550 00 |
| Jersey County, Ill., high school | 10,000 00 | 10,000 00 | 10,200 00 |
| Kart Creek Drainage, Wood and J. Co., Wis | 3,500 00 | 3,500 00 | 3,500 00 |
| Morehead City, N. C | 5,000 00 | 5,000 00 | 4,950 00 |
| Morehead City, N. C | 5,000 00 | 5,000 00 | 4,950 00 |
| Meadows Company | 3,000 00 | 3,000 00 | 3,000 00 |
| Marin County, Cal | 15,000 00 | 15,000 00 | 15,450 00 |
| Presho School Dist. No. 31, Lyman County, S. D | 7,000 00 | 7,000 00 | 7,490 00 |
| Poinsett County, Ark., Dist | 5,000 00 | 5,000 00 | 5,000 00 |
| Poinsett County, Ark., Dist | 6,500 00 | 6,500 00 | 6,565 00 |
| Spring Lake Drainage and Levee Dist., Ill | 5,000 00 | 5,000 00 | 5,150 00 |
| South Omaha, Neb., school | 5,000 00 | 5,000 00 | 5,000 00 |
| South Quincy Drainage and Levee Dist | 11,650 00 | 11,650 00 | 11,650 00 |
| Whiteville, N. C., street | 10,000 00 | 10,000 00 | 10,300 00 |
| Totals | $310,650 00 | $310,650 00 | $313,690 00 |

## LUXEMBURGER BROTHERHOOD OF AMERICA.

Located at No. 1833 Greenleaf Avenue, Chicago, Illinois.

HENRY C. GEIMER, President. NICHOLAS NILLES, Secretary.

| | |
|---|---|
| Balance from previous year | $43,172 79 |

### INCOME.

| | |
|---|---|
| Membership fees actually received | $ 85 50 |
| Assessments or premiums | 3,094 50 |
| Dues and per capita tax | 777 00 |
| Total received from members | $3,957 00 |
| Gross interest on mortgage loans | 2,167 35 |
| Gross interest on collateral loans | 158 75 |
| Sale of lodge supplies | 6 40 |
| Surety bonds | 173 50 |
| Total income | $6,463 00 |
| Sum | $49,635 79 |

### DISBURSEMENTS.

| | |
|---|---|
| Death claims | $1,400 00 |
| Salaries of officers and trustees | 437 50 |
| Traveling and other expenses of officers, trustees and committees | 136 36 |
| Insurance department fees | 33 75 |
| Rent | 32 50 |
| Advertising, printing and stationery | 95 50 |
| Postage, express, telegraph and telephone | 37 60 |
| Lodge supplies | 15 16 |
| Official publication | 200 00 |
| Expenses of supreme lodge meeting | 72 00 |
| All other disbursements, viz— | |
| Actuarial expenses | 87 05 |
| Surety bonds | 234 50 |
| Miscellaneous | 254 00 |
| Total disbursements | $3,052 92 |
| Balance | $46,599 87 |

### LEDGER ASSETS.

| | |
|---|---|
| Mortgage loans on real estate | $39,000 00 |
| Loans secured by pledge of bonds, stocks or other collateral | 4,500 00 |
| Cash in association's office | 3,099 87 |
| Total ledger assets | $46,599 87 |

### EXHIBIT OF CERTIFICATES.

| | Total business of the year. | | Business in Illinois during year. | |
|---|---|---|---|---|
| | Number. | Amount. | Number. | Amount. |
| Benefit certificates in force December 31, 1920, as per last statement | 1,581 | $158,100 00 | 1,425 | $142,500 00 |
| Benefit certificates written and renewed during the year | 66 | 6,600 00 | 66 | 6,600 00 |
| Total | 1,647 | $164,700 00 | 1,491 | $149,100 00 |
| Deduct terminated, decreased or transferred during the year | 85 | 8,500 00 | | |
| Deduct terminated or decreased during the year | | | 76 | 7,600 00 |
| Total benefit certificates in force December 31, 1921 | 1,562 | $156,200 00 | 1,415 | $141,500 00 |

| | |
|---|---|
| Received during the year from members in Illinois: Mortuary, $2,830.00; expense, $954.50; total | $3,784 50 |

### EXHIBIT OF DEATH CLAIMS.

| | Total claims. | | Illinois claims. | |
|---|---|---|---|---|
| | Number. | Amount. | Number. | Amount. |
| Claims reported during the year and interest addition | 14 | $1,400 00 | 12 | $1,200 00 |
| Claims paid during the year | 14 | 1,400 00 | 12 | 1,200 00 |

### SCHEDULE D—BONDS.

| Description. | Book value. |
|---|---|
| U. S. Liberty Loan, 4¼s | $1,500 00 |
| U. S. Liberty Loan, 4¼s | 2,000 00 |
| U. S. Liberty Loan, 4¼s | 1,000 00 |
| Total | $4,500 00 |

## MODERN WOODMEN OF AMERICA.

Located at Fifteenth Street and Third Avenue, Rock Island, Illinois.

A. R. TALBOT, Head Consul. J. G. RAY, Head Clerk.

| | |
|---|---|
| Balance from previous year | $19,382,117 41 |

### INCOME.

| | |
|---|---|
| Assessments or premiums during first twelve months of membership of which all or an extra percentage is used for expenses | $ 61,658 50 |
| All other assessments or premiums | 22,677,291 20 |
| Dues and per capita tax | 1,899,754 38 |
| Certificate fees | 16,267 75 |
| Total received from members | $24,654,971 83 |
| Deduct payments returned to applicants and members | 2,204 28 |
| Net amount received from members | $24,652,767 55 |
| Gross interest on mortgage loans | 68,147 06 |
| Gross interest on bonds and dividends on stocks | 675,779 92 |
| Gross interest on deposits in trust companies and banks | 98,834 32 |
| Gross rents from association's property, including $13,000.00 for association's occupancy of its own buildings | 13,673 34 |
| Sale of lodge supplies | 75,596 05 |
| Gross increase in book value of ledger assets: Bonds | 50,107 01 |
| Advertising official paper | 120,580 26 |
| Printing department | 3,222 68 |
| Refund death claim | 1,000 00 |
| Gross profit on purchase of real estate mortgages | 5,044 00 |
| Paper stock and material | 7,491 84 |
| Total income | $25,772,244 03 |
| Sum | $45,154,361 44 |

### DISBURSEMENTS.

| | |
|---|---|
| Death claims | $16,494,534 07 |
| 70-year benefits | 246,916 35 |
| Total benefits paid | $16,741,450 42 |
| Salaries of deputies and organizers | 702,148 56 |
| Salaries of officers and trustees | 75,016 65 |
| Salaries and other compensation of committees | 11,895 95 |
| Salaries of office employees | 208,691 20 |
| Salaries and fees paid to supreme medical examiners | 22,580 77 |
| Salaries and fees paid to subordinate medical examiners | 2,989 07 |
| Traveling and other expenses of officers, trustees and committees | 23,762 80 |
| Insurance department fees | 953 25 |
| Rent, including $13,000.00 for association's occupancy of its own buildings | 17,510 80 |
| Advertising, printing and stationery | 956 20 |
| Postage, express, telegraph and telephone | 23,284 71 |
| Lodge supplies | 59,430 64 |
| Official publication | 265,019 65 |
| Expenses of supreme lodge meeting | 182,771 47 |
| Legal expense in litigating claims | 35,643 69 |
| Other legal expenses—salary general attorney | 9,066 65 |
| Furniture, fixtures and library | 4,397 09 |
| Taxes, repairs and other expenses on real estate | 11,189 41 |
| Gross decrease in book value of ledger assets: (a) Real estate, $12,637.24; (b) bonds, $2,268.70 | 14,905 94 |
| All other disbursements, viz: Class adoptions, $4,161.65; salary editor, $5,625.00; executive council expense, $130.52; Foresters, $47,157.14; Fraternal Congresses, $209.54; American Fraternal Congress, $1,652.11; head consul's office expense, $20,799.40; head office expense, $5,936.57; head banker's office expense, $5,736.66; head camp committees, $18,922.45; inspectors expense, $32,568.40; interest contested claims, $3,204.54; investigating claims, $6,617.24; investments expense, $13,615.82; lecturers expense, $49,273.75; light, fuel and water meter, $6.092.53; local camps expense, $8,976.95; state camps expense, $71,138.36; motion picture department, $6,822.16; National Camp Clerk's Association, $766.15; office supplies, $70,896.19; official paper expense advertising, $14,169.91; prizes and free supplies, $11,564.02; publication building expense, $19,911.15; surety bonds, $17,290.89; special audit, $7,981.45; insurance premiums, $1,592.32 | 452,812 87 |
| Sanatorium chattel | 7,396 45 |
| Sanatorium maintenance and operation | 296,669 73 |
| Total disbursements | $19,170,543 97 |
| Balance | $25,983,817 47 |

## LEDGER ASSETS.

| | |
|---|---|
| Book value of real estate | $ 1,537,673 07 |
| Mortgage loans on real estate | 1,538,650 00 |
| Book value of bonds and stocks | 18,928,256 10 |
| Deposits in trust companies and banks on interest | 3,979,238 30 |
| Total ledger assets | $25,983,817 47 |

### NON-LEDGER ASSETS.

| | | |
|---|---|---|
| Interest and rents due and accrued | | 336,118 93 |
| Assessments actually collected by subordinate lodges not yet turned over to supreme lodge | | 1,915,000 00 |
| All other assets, viz— | | |
| Lodge, office and utility supplies inventory | $ 18,953 40 | |
| Furniture inventory | 109,948 01 | |
| Library inventory | 18,068 48 | |
| Sanatorium chattel and maintenance and operation inventory | 222,230 67 | |
| Printing plant inventory | 129,425 81 | |
| | | 498,626 37 |
| Gross assets | | $28,733,562 77 |

### DEDUCT ASSETS NOT ADMITTED.

| | |
|---|---|
| Other items, viz: Lodge, office, utility, furniture, library, printing, sanatorium chattel and maintenance and operation inventories | 498,626 37 |
| Total admitted assets | $28,234,936 40 |

## LIABILITIES.

| | | |
|---|---|---|
| Death claims due and unpaid | $ 250,552 73 | |
| Death claims resisted | 145,500 00 | |
| Death claims reported during the year but not yet adjusted | 1,347,850 00 | |
| Death claims incurred in 1921, not reported until 1922 | 483,000 00 | |
| Total death claims | | $2,226,902 73 |
| Salaries, rents, expenses, commissions, etc., due or accrued | | 98,612 75 |
| Total | | $2,325,515 48 |

## EXHIBIT OF CERTIFICATES.

| | Total business of the year. | | Business in Illinois during year. | |
|---|---|---|---|---|
| | Number. | Amount. | Number. | Amount. |
| Benefit certificates in force December 31, 1920, as per last statement | 1,059,344 | $1,627,671,000 00 | 173,502 | $289,292,500 00 |
| Benefit certificates written and renewed during the year | 73,837 | 89,874,000 00 | 7,105 | 9,033,500 00 |
| Benefit certificates received by transfer during the year | -------- | ---------------- | 2,581 | 4,025,000 00 |
| Benefit certificates increased during the year | -------- | 3,192,000 00 | -------- | 482,000 00 |
| Total | 1,133,181 | $1,720,737,000 00 | 183,188 | $302,833,000 00 |
| Deduct terminated, decreased or transferred during the year | 80,076 | 108,389,500 00 | -------- | -------------- |
| Deduct terminated or decreased during the year | -------- | -------------- | 10,327 | 15,915,000 00 |
| Total benefit certificates in force December 31, 1921 | 1,053,105 | $1,612,347,500 00 | 172,861 | $286,918,000 00 |

| | |
|---|---|
| Received during the year from members in Illinois: Mortuary, $4,016,591.10; expense, $330,123.28; total | $4,346,714 38 |

## EXHIBIT OF DEATH CLAIMS.

| | Total claims. | | Illinois claims. | |
|---|---|---|---|---|
| | Number. | Amount. | Number. | Amount. |
| Claims unpaid December 31, 1920, as per last statement | 1,102 | $ 1,828,245 15 | 190 | $ 366,241 70 |
| Claims reported during the year | 9,525 | 16,534,500 00 | 1,842 | 3,492,000 00 |
| Previously dropped reinstated | 1 | 2,000 00 | -------- | -------------- |
| Total | 10,628 | $18,364,745 15 | 2,032 | $3,858,241 70 |
| Claims paid during the year | 9,553 | 16,494,534 07 | 1,831 | 3,473,242 10 |
| Balance | 1,075 | $1,870,211 08 | 201 | $384,999 60 |
| Saved by compromising or scaling down claims during the year | -------- | 42,308 35 | -------- | 7,590 80 |
| Claims rejected during the year | 56 | 84,000 00 | 12 | 20,500 00 |
| Claims unpaid December 31, 1921 | 1,019 | $1,743,902 73 | 189 | $356,908 80 |

## EXHIBIT OF 70-YEAR BENEFITS.

| | Total claims. | | Illinois claims. | |
|---|---|---|---|---|
| | Number. | Amount. | Number. | Amount. |
| Claims reported during the year and interest addition | 476 | $946,000 00 | 118 | $245,500 00 |
| Claims paid during the year | 476 | 246,916 35 | 118 | 63,512 60 |
| Balance | -------- | $699,083 65 | -------- | $181,987 40 |
| Saved by compromising or scaling down claims during the year | -------- | 699,083 65 | -------- | 181,987 40 |

## SCHEDULE D—BONDS.

| Description. | Book value. | Par value. | Market value. |
|---|---|---|---|
| United States of America, 1st Liberty Loan, conv., 4¼s | $ 112,500 00 | $ 112,500 00 | $ 112,500 00 |
| United States of America, 2d Liberty Loan, conv., 4¼s | 545,000 00 | 545,000 00 | 545,000 00 |
| United States of America, 2d Liberty Loan, conv., 4½s | 1,440,614 97 | 1,536,100 00 | 1,490,017 00 |
| United States of America, 3d Liberty Loan, conv., 4¼s | 350,000 00 | 350,000 00 | 350,000 00 |
| United States of America, 3d Liberty Loan, conv., 4¼s | 2,739,007 86 | 3,030,150 00 | 2,969,547 00 |
| United States of America, 4th Liberty Loan, conv., 4¼s | 1,000,000 00 | 1,000,000 00 | 1,000,000 00 |
| United States of America, 4th Liberty Loan, conv., 4¼s | 3,150,975 48 | 3,381,100 00 | 3,279,667 00 |
| United States of America, Victory Liberty Loan, 4¾s | 250,000 00 | 250,000 00 | 250,000 00 |
| Soldiers and Sailors Civil Relief Insurance, 3½s | 2,900 00 | 2,900 00 | 2,900 00 |
| Dominion of Canada, Victory Loan, 5½s | 31,241 10 | 33,000 00 | 32,670 00 |
| Adams and Arapahoe Counties, Colo., School Dist No. 29, building, 6s | 15,500 00 | 15,500 00 | 15,965 00 |
| Ashland, Neb., School District No. 1, building, 6s | 5,094 07 | 5,000 00 | 5,000 00 |
| Ashland, Neb., School District No. 1, building, 6s | 5,100 87 | 5,000 00 | 5,000 00 |
| Ashland, Neb., School District No. 1, building, 6s | 5,107 29 | 5,000 00 | 5,000 00 |
| Ashland, Neb., School District No. 1, building, 6s | 5,113 36 | 5,000 00 | 5,000 00 |
| Ashland, Neb., School District No. 1, building, 6s | 5,119 09 | 5,000 00 | 5,000 00 |
| Ashland, Neb., School District No. 1, building, 6s | 5,124 51 | 5,000 00 | 5,000 00 |
| Ashland, Neb., School District No. 1, building, 6s | 5,129 63 | 5,000 00 | 5,000 00 |
| Ashland, Neb., School District No. 1, building, 6s | 5,134 46 | 5,000 00 | 5,000 00 |
| Ashland, Neb., School District No. 1, building, 6s | 5,139 04 | 5,000 00 | 5,000 00 |
| Ashland, Neb., School District No. 1, building, 6s | 5,143 35 | 5,000 00 | 5,000 00 |
| Ashland, Neb., School District No. 1, building, 6s | 5,147 43 | 5,000 00 | 5,000 00 |
| Ashland, Neb., School District No. 1, building, 6s | 5,151 29 | 5,000 00 | 5,000 00 |
| Ashland, Neb., School District No. 1, building, 6s | 5,154 93 | 5,000 00 | 5,000 00 |
| Ashland, Neb., School District No. 1, building, 6s | 5,158 38 | 5,000 00 | 5,000 00 |
| Ashland, Neb., School District No. 1, building, 6s | 5,161 63 | 5,000 00 | 5,000 00 |
| Ashland, Neb., School District No. 1, building, 6s | 5,164 70 | 5,000 00 | 5,000 00 |
| Ashland, Neb., School District No. 1, building, 6s | 5,167 61 | 5,000 00 | 5,000 00 |
| Ashland, Neb., School District No. 1, building, 6s | 5,170 35 | 5,000 00 | 5,000 00 |
| Ashland, Neb., School District No. 1, building, 6s | 5,172 94 | 5,000 00 | 5,000 00 |
| Ashland, Neb., School District No. 1, building, 6s | 5,175 39 | 5,000 00 | 5,000 00 |
| Atchison, Kan., internal improvement, 5s | 5,559 77 | 5,600 00 | 5,600 00 |
| Atchison, Kan., internal improvement, 5s | 5,520 67 | 5,600 00 | 5,600 00 |
| Atchison, Kan., internal improvement, 5s | 5,484 26 | 5,600 00 | 5,600 00 |
| Atchison, Kan., internal improvement, 5s | 5,449 86 | 5,600 00 | 5,600 00 |
| Atchison, Kan., internal improvement, 5s | 5,417 36 | 5,600 00 | 5,600 00 |
| Atchison, Kan., internal improvement, 5s | 5,386 66 | 5,600 00 | 5,600 00 |
| Atchison, Kan., internal improvement, 5s | 5,357 65 | 5,600 00 | 5,600 00 |
| Atchison, Kan., internal improvement, 5s | 5,329 68 | 5,600 00 | 5,600 00 |
| Atchison, Kan., internal improvement, 5s | 5,304 34 | 5,600 00 | 5,600 00 |
| Aurora, Neb., intersection paving, 6s | 57,000 00 | 57,000 00 | 57,570 00 |
| Aurora, Neb., intersection paving, 6s | 52,000 00 | 52,000 00 | 52,520 00 |
| Aurora, Neb., intersection paving, 6s | 18,000 00 | 18,000 00 | 18,180 00 |
| Avery County, N. C., road, 5½s | 48,639 60 | 45,000 00 | 45,900 00 |
| Beadle County, S. D., court house, 6s | 60,484 80 | 60,000 00 | 60,600 00 |
| Beadle County, S. D., court house, 6s | 71,120 00 | 70,000 00 | 71,400 00 |
| Beadle County, S. D., court house, 6s | 102,191 00 | 100,000 00 | 102,000 00 |
| Beadle County, S. D., court house, 6s | 123,157 20 | 120,000 00 | 123,600 00 |
| Blair, Neb., paving, 6s | 48,000 00 | 48,000 00 | 48,960 00 |
| Blair, Neb., intersection paving, 6s | 23,000 00 | 23,000 00 | 24,610 00 |
| Blair, Neb., intersection paving, 6s | 23,630 00 | 25,000 00 | 26,750 00 |
| Blair, Neb., intersection paving, 6s | 25,088 07 | 26,559 00 | 28,418 13 |
| Bogalusa School District, Washington Parish, La., 5s | 4,942 50 | 5,000 00 | 5,000 00 |
| Bogalusa School District, Washington Parish, La., 5s | 5,805 60 | 6,000 00 | 6,000 00 |
| Bogalusa School District, Washington Parish, La., 5s | 5,748 60 | 6,000 00 | 6,000 00 |
| Bogalusa School District, Washington Parish, La., 5s | 5,694 60 | 6,000 00 | 6,000 00 |
| Bogalusa School District, Washington Parish, La., 5s | 1,881 20 | 2,000 00 | 2,000 00 |
| Bogalusa School District, Washington Parish, La., 5s | 6,528 90 | 7,000 00 | 7,000 00 |
| Bogalusa School District, Washington Parish, La., 5s | 7,345 60 | 8,000 00 | 8,000 00 |
| Bogalusa School District, Washington Parish, La., 5s | 8,204 40 | 9,000 00 | 9,000 00 |
| Bogalusa School District, Washington Parish, La., 5s | 7,242 40 | 8,000 00 | 8,000 00 |
| Bogalusa School District, Washington Parish, La., 5s | 7,196 00 | 8,000 00 | 8,000 00 |
| Bogalusa School District, Washington Parish, La., 5s | 7,152 00 | 8,000 00 | 8,000 00 |
| Bogalusa School District, Washington Parish, La., 5s | 3,555 20 | 4,000 00 | 4,000 00 |
| Bogalusa School District, Washington Parish, La., 5s | 4,419 50 | 5,000 00 | 5,000 00 |
| Bogalusa School District, Washington Parish, La., 5s | 8,793 00 | 10,000 00 | 10,000 00 |
| Bogalusa School District, Washington Parish, La., 5s | 9,625 00 | 11,000 00 | 11,000 00 |
| Bogalusa School District, Washington Parish, La., 5s | 10,450 80 | 12,000 00 | 12,000 00 |

SCHEDULE D—BONDS—Continued.

| Description. | Book value. | Par value. | Market value. |
|---|---|---|---|
| Brookfield, Mo., waterworks, 6s | $142,073 55 | $140,000 00 | $151,200 00 |
| Bruceville, Tex., Independent School District, bldg., 5s | 5,000 00 | 5,000 00 | 4,800 00 |
| Canton, Ohio, school district, building, 6s | 36,460 68 | 36,000 00 | 39,240 00 |
| Canton, Ohio, school district, building, 6s | 46,650 14 | 46,000 00 | 50,140 00 |
| Canton, Ohio, school district, building, 6s | 46,711 36 | 46,000 00 | 50,600 00 |
| Canton, Ohio, school district, building, 6s | 46,773 35 | 46,000 00 | 51,060 00 |
| Canton, Ohio, school district, building, 6s | 37,663 37 | 37,000 00 | 41,440 00 |
| Canton, Ohio, school district, improvement, 6s | 10,323 71 | 10,000 00 | 10,500 00 |
| Canton, Ohio, school district, improvement, 6s | 5,187 56 | 5,000 00 | 5,300 00 |
| Canton, Ohio, school district, improvement, 6s | 10,423 84 | 10,000 00 | 10,700 00 |
| Canton, Ohio, school district, improvement, 6s | 10,595 16 | 10,000 00 | 11,000 00 |
| Canton, Ohio, school district, improvement, 6s | 5,305 19 | 5,000 00 | 5,600 00 |
| Canton, Ohio, school district, improvement, 6s | 10,733 93 | 10,000 00 | 11,300 00 |
| Canton, Ohio, school district, improvement, 6s | 10,764 32 | 10,000 00 | 11,400 00 |
| Canton, Ohio, school district, improvement, 6s | 10,793 17 | 10,000 00 | 11,400 00 |
| Canton, Ohio, school district, improvement, 6s | 7,574 21 | 7,000 00 | 8,050 00 |
| Canton, Ohio, school district, improvement, 6s | 10,871 13 | 10,000 00 | 11,600 00 |
| Canton, Ohio, school district improvement, 6s | 10,894 52 | 10,000 00 | 11,600 00 |
| Canton, Ohio, school district, improvement, 6s | 10,916 71 | 10,000 00 | 11,700 00 |
| Canton, Ohio, school district, improvement, 6s | 10,937 76 | 10,000 00 | 11,700 00 |
| Canton, Ohio, school district, improvement, 6s | 10,957 74 | 10,000 00 | 11,800 00 |
| Canton, Ohio, school district, improvement, 6s | 10,976 70 | 10,000 00 | 11,800 00 |
| Canton, Ohio, school district, improvement, 6s | 10,994 70 | 10,000 00 | 11,800 00 |
| Canton, Ohio, school district, improvement, 6s | 11,011 67 | 10,000 00 | 11,900 00 |
| Canton, Ohio, school district, improvement, 6s | 11,027 97 | 10,000 00 | 11,900 00 |
| Canton, Ohio, school district, improvement, 6s | 5,528 91 | 5,000 00 | 6,000 00 |
| Carter County, Okla., School Dist. No. 55, building, 6s | 53,039 40 | 54,500 00 | 61,040 00 |
| Casper, Wyo., public building, 6s | 16,175 27 | 17,000 00 | 19,210 00 |
| Casper, Wyo., public building, 5s | 24,245 28 | 29,500 00 | 29,500 00 |
| Casper, Wyo., sewer, 6s | 22,972 79 | 24,000 00 | 26,640 00 |
| Casper, Wyo., sewer, 5s | 46,064 51 | 54,000 00 | 54,000 00 |
| Casper, Wyo., water works, 6s | 47,574 34 | 50,000 00 | 54,500 00 |
| Casper, Wyo., water works, 5s | 13,971 86 | 17,000 00 | 17,000 00 |
| Casper, Wyo., cemetery, 6s | 8,563 38 | 9,000 00 | 9,630 00 |
| Caswell County, N. C., road, 6s | 1,989 40 | 2,000 00 | 2,100 00 |
| Caswell County, N. C., road, 6s | 1,988 20 | 2,000 00 | 2,120 00 |
| Caswell County, N. C., road, 6s | 1,986 80 | 2,000 00 | 2,140 00 |
| Caswell County, N. C., road, 6s | 3,971 60 | 4,000 00 | 4,280 00 |
| Caswell County, N. C., road, 6s | 1,984 60 | 2,000 00 | 2,160 00 |
| Caswell County, N. C., road, 6s | 1,983 60 | 2,000 00 | 2,180 00 |
| Caswell County, N. C., road, 6s | 1,982 60 | 2,000 00 | 2,180 00 |
| Caswell County, N. C., road, 6s | 1,981 80 | 2,000 00 | 2,200 00 |
| Caswell County, N. C., road, 6s | 1,981 00 | 2,000 00 | 2,200 00 |
| Caswell County, N. C., road, 6s | 3,960 40 | 4,000 00 | 4,440 00 |
| Caswell County, N. C., road, 6s | 3,958 80 | 4,000 00 | 4,440 00 |
| Caswell County, N. C., road, 6s | 3,957 20 | 4,000 00 | 4,480 00 |
| Caswell County, N. C., road, 6s | 3,956 00 | 4,000 00 | 4,480 00 |
| Caswell County, N. C., road, 6s | 3,954 80 | 4,000 00 | 4,480 00 |
| Caswell County, N. C., road, 6s | 3,953 60 | 4,000 00 | 4,520 00 |
| Caswell County, N. C., road, 6s | 3,952 40 | 4,000 00 | 4,520 00 |
| Caswell County, N. C., road, 6s | 3,951 20 | 4,000 00 | 4,520 00 |
| Caswell County, N. C., road, 6s | 3,950 40 | 4,000 00 | 4,560 00 |
| Caswell County, N. C., road, 6s | 3,949 60 | 4,000 00 | 4,560 00 |
| Caswell County, N. C., road, 6s | 4,935 50 | 5,000 00 | 5,700 00 |
| Caswell County, N. C., road, 6s | 4,934 50 | 5,000 00 | 5,750 00 |
| Caswell County, N. C., road, 6s | 5,000 00 | 5,000 00 | 5,750 00 |
| Caswell County, N. C., road, 6s | 5,000 00 | 5,000 00 | 5,750 00 |
| Cerro Gordo County, Iowa, road, 5s | 71,471 86 | 75,000 00 | 76,500 00 |
| Chadron, Neb., school district, 6s | 4,965 00 | 5,000 00 | 5,100 00 |
| Chadron, Neb., school district, 6s | 4,957 50 | 5,000 00 | 5,150 00 |
| Chadron, Neb., school district, 6s | 4,937 50 | 5,000 00 | 5,150 00 |
| Chadron, Neb., school district, 6s | 4,932 00 | 5,000 00 | 5,200 00 |
| Chadron, Neb., school district, 6s | 2,952 60 | 3,000 00 | 3,120 00 |
| Chadron, Neb., school district, 6s | 4,916 00 | 5,000 00 | 5,250 00 |
| Chadron, Neb., school district, 6s | 4,911 50 | 5,000 00 | 5,250 00 |
| Chadron, Neb., school district, 6s | 4,907 50 | 5,000 00 | 5,300 00 |
| Chadron, Neb., school district, 6s | 9,807 00 | 10,000 00 | 10,600 00 |
| Chadron, Neb., school district, 6s | 9,799 00 | 10,000 00 | 10,600 00 |
| Chadron, Neb., school district, 6s | 3,914 00 | 4,000 00 | 4,280 00 |
| Chadron, Neb., school district, 6s | 40,093 90 | 41,000 00 | 43,870 00 |
| Chariton, Iowa, school building, 6s | 190,854 33 | 185,000 00 | 190,854 33 |
| Cheyenne, Wyo., sewer, 6s | 149,258 61 | 150,000 00 | 163,500 00 |
| Clarendon, Tex., Independent School Dist., bldg., 5s | 626 49 | 625 00 | 625 00 |
| Clarendon, Tex., Independent School Dist., bldg., 5s | 627 92 | 625 00 | 625 00 |
| Clarendon, Tex., Independent School Dist., bldg., 5s | 629 28 | 625 00 | 618 75 |
| Clarendon, Tex., Independent School Dist., bldg., 5s | 630 58 | 625 00 | 618 75 |
| Clarendon, Tex., Independent School Dist., bldg., 5s | 631 81 | 625 00 | 618 75 |
| Clarendon, Tex., Independent School Dist., bldg., 5s | 632 99 | 625 00 | 618 75 |
| Clarendon, Tex., Independent School Dist., bldg., 5s | 634 13 | 625 00 | 618 75 |
| Clarendon, Tex., Independent School Dist., bldg., 5s | 635 20 | 625 00 | 612 50 |
| Clarendon, Tex., Independent School Dist., bldg., 5s | 636 23 | 625 00 | 612 50 |
| Clarendon, Tex., Independent School Dist., bldg., 5s | 637 21 | 625 00 | 612 50 |

SCHEDULE D—BONDS—Continued.

| Description. | Book value. | Par value. | Market value. |
|---|---|---|---|
| Clarendon, Tex., Independent School Dist., bldg., 5s | $ 638 15 | $ 625 00 | $ 612 50 |
| Clarendon, Tex., Independent School Dist , bldg., 5s | 639 04 | 625 00 | 612 50 |
| Clarendon, Tex., Independent School Dist., bldg., 5s | 639 90 | 625 00 | 612 50 |
| Clarendon, Tex., Independent School Dist., bldg., 5s | 640 72 | 625 00 | 612 50 |
| Clarendon, Tex., Independent School Dist., bldg., 5s | 641 49 | 625 00 | 606 25 |
| Clarendon, Tex., Independent School Dist., bldg., 5s | 642 24 | 625 00 | 606 25 |
| Clarendon, Tex., Independent School Dist., bldg., 5s | 642 95 | 625 00 | 606 25 |
| Clarendon, Tex., Independent School Dist., bldg., 5s | 643 63 | 625 00 | 606 25 |
| Clarendon, Tex., Independent School Dist., bldg., 5s | 644 28 | 625 00 | 606 25 |
| Clarendon, Tex., Independent School Dist., bldg., 5s | 644 89 | 625 00 | 606 25 |
| Clarendon, Tex., Independent School Dist., bldg., 5s | 645 48 | 625 00 | 606 25 |
| Clarendon, Tex., Inde endent School Dist., bldg., 5s | 646 04 | 625 00 | 606 25 |
| Clarendon, Tex., Independent School Dist., bldg., 5s | 646 58 | 625 00 | 606 25 |
| Clarendon, Tex., Independent School Dist., bldg., 5s | 647 09 | 625 00 | 606 25 |
| Clarendon, Tex., Independent School Dist., bldg., 5s | 647 58 | 625 00 | 606 25 |
| Clarendon, Tex., Independent School Dist., bldg., 5s | 648 05 | 625 00 | 606 25 |
| Clarendon, Tex., Independent School Dist., bldg., 5s | 648 50 | 625 00 | 600 00 |
| Clarendon, Tex., Independent School Dist., bldg., 5s | 648 93 | 625 00 | 600 00 |
| Clarendon, Tex., Independent School Dist., bldg., 5s | 649 33 | 625 00 | 600 00 |
| Clarendon, Tex., Inde endent School Dist., bldg., 5s | 649 72 | 625 00 | 600 00 |
| Clarendon, Tex., Independent School Dist., bldg., 5s | 650 09 | 625 00 | 600 00 |
| Clarendon, Tex., Independent School Dist., bldg., 5s | 650 44 | 625 00 | 600 00 |
| Cleveland Heights, Ohio, school district, series 22, 6s | 5,076 82 | 5,000 00 | 5,500 00 |
| Cleveland Heights, Ohio, school district, series 22, 6s | 18,298 73 | 18,000 00 | 19,980 00 |
| Cleveland Heights, Ohio, school district, series 22, 6s | 18,320 90 | 18,000 00 | 20,160 00 |
| Cleveland Heights, Ohio, school district, series 23, 6s | 29,481 28 | 29,000 00 | 32,190 00 |
| Cleveland Heights, Ohio, school district, series 23, 6s | 29,517 00 | 29,000 00 | 32,480 00 |
| Clinton, Mo., electric light extension, 6s | 35,000 00 | 35,000 00 | 36,400 00 |
| Community High School District No. 303, Hancock, Schuyler and Adams Counties, Ill., 5½s | 3,037 13 | 3,000 00 | 3,000 00 |
| Community High School District No. 303, Hancock, Schuyler and Adams Counties, Ill., 5½s | 3,048 50 | 3,000 00 | 3,000 00 |
| Community High School District No. 303, Hancock, Schuyler and Adams Counties, Ill., 5½s | 3,059 47 | 3,000 00 | 3,000 00 |
| Community High School District No. 303, Hancock, Schuyler and Adams Counties, Ill., 5½s | 3,070 08 | 3,000 00 | 3,000 00 |
| Community High School District No. 303, Hancock, Schuyler and Adams Counties, Ill., 5½s | 4,106 97 | 4,000 00 | 4,000 00 |
| Community High School District No. 303, Hancock, Schuyler and Adams Counties, Ill., 5½s | 4,119 87 | 4,000 00 | 4,000 00 |
| Community High School District No. 303, Hancock, Schuyler and Adams Counties, Ill., 5½s | 4,132 16 | 4,000 00 | 4,000 00 |
| Community High School District No. 303, Hancock, Schuyler and Adams Counties, Ill., 5½s | 4,144 07 | 4,000 00 | 4,000 00 |
| Community High School District No. 303, Hancock, Schuyler and Adams Counties, Ill., 5½s | 6,233 02 | 6,000 00 | 6,000 00 |
| Community High School District No. 303, Hancock, Schuyler and Adams Counties, Ill., 5½s | 6,250 57 | 6,000 00 | 6,000 00 |
| Community High School District No. 303, Hancock, Schuyler and Adams Counties, Ill., 5½s | 1,044 07 | 1,000 00 | 1,000 00 |
| Community High School District No. 303, Hancock, Schuyler and Adams Counties, Ill., 5½s | 1,046 48 | 1,000 00 | 1,000 00 |
| Community High School District No. 303, Hancock, Schuyler and Adams Counties, Ill., 5½s | 7,341 89 | 7,000 00 | 7,000 00 |
| Community High School District No. 303, Hancock, Schuyler and Adams Counties, Ill., 5½s | 7,357 36 | 7,000 00 | 7,000 00 |
| Community High School District No. 303, Hancock, Schuyler and Adams Counties, Ill., 5½ | 7,372 15 | 7,000 00 | 7,000 00 |
| Community High School District No. 303, Hancock, Schuyler and Adams Counties, Ill., 5½s | 7,386 19 | 7,000 00 | 7,000 00 |
| Crawford County, Iowa, funding, 4½s | 1,002 90 | 1,000 00 | 1,000 00 |
| Creek County, Okla., School Dist. No. 75, building, 7s | 108,270 00 | 100,000 00 | 109,000 00 |
| Curtis, Neb., school district, building, 6s | 4,077 32 | 4,000 00 | 4,077 32 |
| Curtis, Neb., school district, building, 6s | 4,082 54 | 4,000 00 | 4,082 54 |
| Curtis, Neb., school district, building, 6s | 4,087 72 | 4,000 00 | 4,087 72 |
| Curtis, Neb., school district, building, 6s | 4,092 54 | 4,000 00 | 4,092 54 |
| Curtis, Neb., school district, building, 6s | 3,072 69 | 3,000 00 | 3,072 69 |
| Curtis, Neb., school district, building, 6s | 4,115 72 | 4,000 00 | 4,115 72 |
| Curtis, Neb., school district, building, 6s | 4,118 94 | 4,000 00 | 4,118 94 |
| Curtis, Neb., school district, building, 6s | 4,121 74 | 4,000 00 | 4,121 74 |
| Curtis, Neb., school district, building, 6s | 4,124 54 | 4,000 00 | 4,124 54 |
| Curtis, Neb., school district, building, 6s | 3,095 52 | 3,000 00 | 3,095 52 |
| Del Rio, Tex., Independent School District, building, 5s | 20,000 00 | 20,000 00 | 18,600 00 |
| Delta County, Tex., road, series B, 5s | 15,922 34 | 16,000 00 | 16,000 00 |
| Delta County, Tex., road, series B, 5s | 15,773 71 | 16,000 00 | 16,000 00 |
| Delta County, Tex., road, series B, 5s | 15,633 62 | 16,000 00 | 16,000 00 |
| Delta County, Tex., road, series B, 5s | 16,470 43 | 17,000 00 | 17,000 00 |
| Delta County, Tex., road, series B, 5s | 16,338 17 | 17,000 00 | 17,000 00 |
| Delta County, Tex., road, series B, 5s | 16,213 53 | 17,000 00 | 17,000 00 |
| Delta County, Tex., road, series B, 5s | 16,096 03 | 17,000 00 | 17,000 00 |
| Delta County, Tex., road, series B, 5s | 15,985 27 | 17,000 00 | 17,000 00 |
| Delta County, Tex., road, series B, 5s | 15,880 87 | 17,000 00 | 17,000 00 |
| Delta County, Tex., road, series B, 5s | 15,782 47 | 17,000 00 | 17,000 00 |

SCHEDULE D—BONDS—Continued.

| Description. | Book value. | Par value. | Market value. |
|---|---|---|---|
| Delta County, Tex., road, series B, 5s | $15,689 73 | $17,000 00 | $17,000 00 |
| Delta County, Tex., road, series B, 5s | 15,602 29 | 17,000 00 | 17,000 00 |
| Delta County, Tex., road, series B, 5s | 15,519 88 | 17,000 00 | 17,000 00 |
| Delta County, Tex., road, series B, 5s | 14,533 84 | 16,000 00 | 16,000 00 |
| Delta County, Tex., road, series B, 5s | 14,464 93 | 16,000 00 | 16,000 00 |
| Delta County, Tex., road, series B, 5s | 14,399 97 | 16,000 00 | 16,000 00 |
| Delta County, Tex., road, series B, 5s | 14,338 74 | 16,000 00 | 16,000 00 |
| Delta County, Tex., road, series B, 5s | 14,281 02 | 16,000 00 | 16,000 00 |
| Delta County, Tex., road, series B, 5s | 15,115 79 | 17,000 00 | 17,000 00 |
| Delta County, Tex., road, series B, 5s | 15,061 30 | 17,000 00 | 17,000 00 |
| Delta County, Tex., road, series B, 5s | 15,009 95 | 17,000 00 | 17,000 00 |
| Delta County, Tex., road, series B, 5s | 14,961 53 | 17,000 00 | 17,000 00 |
| Delta County, Tex., road, series B, 5s | 14,915 90 | 17,000 00 | 17,000 00 |
| Delta County, Tex., road, series B, 5s | 14,872 89 | 17,000 00 | 17,000 00 |
| Delta County, Tex., road, series B, 5s | 14,832 36 | 17,000 00 | 17,000 00 |
| Delta County, Tex., road, series B, 5s | 14,794 15 | 17,000 00 | 17,000 00 |
| Delta County, Tex., road, series B, 5s | 14,758 13 | 17,000 00 | 17,000 00 |
| Delta County, Tex., road, series B, 5s | 14,724 18 | 17,000 00 | 17,000 00 |
| Delta County, Tex., road, series B, 5s | 13,827 82 | 16,000 00 | 16,000 00 |
| Eaton County, Walton Twp., Mich., school district, 6s | 2,004 10 | 2,000 00 | 2,000 00 |
| Eaton County, Walton Twp., Mich., school district, 6s | 2,008 50 | 2,000 00 | 2,020 00 |
| Eaton County, Walton Twp., Mich., school district, 6s | 2,012 80 | 2,000 00 | 2,020 00 |
| Eaton County, Walton Twp., Mich., school district, 6s | 2,016 91 | 2,000 00 | 2,040 00 |
| Eaton County, Walton Twp., Mich., school district, 6s | 303 12 | 300 00 | 306 00 |
| Eaton County, Walton Twp., Mich., school district, 6s | 2,530 50 | 2,500 00 | 2,550 00 |
| Eaton County, Walton Twp., Mich., school district, 6s | 2,534 83 | 2,500 00 | 2,575 00 |
| Eaton County, Walton Twp., Mich., school district, 6s | 3,046 65 | 3,000 00 | 3,090 00 |
| Eaton County, Walton Twp., Mich., school district, 6s | 3,559 83 | 3,500 00 | 3,605 00 |
| Eaton County, Walton Twp., Mich., school district, 6s | 3,564 93 | 3,500 00 | 3,640 00 |
| Eaton County, Walton Twp., Mich., school district, 6s | 4,079 70 | 4,000 00 | 4,160 00 |
| Eaton County, Walton Twp., Mich., school district, 6s | 4,084 87 | 4,000 00 | 4,160 00 |
| Eaton County, Walton Twp., Mich., school district, 6s | 4,600 98 | 4,500 00 | 4,680 00 |
| Eaton County, Walton Twp., Mich., school district, 6s | 5,629 83 | 5,500 00 | 5,775 00 |
| Eaton County, Walton Twp., Mich., school district, 6s | 5,635 88 | 5,500 00 | 5,775 00 |
| Edmonton, Alberta, Can., School Dist. No. 7, bldg., 5s | 20,753 83 | 22,000 00 | 16,500 00 |
| Fairfax, Okla., school district, building, 6½s | 52,086 53 | 50,000 00 | 56,500 00 |
| Faulk County, S. D., Cresbard Con. School Dist. No. 2, building, 7s | 10,363 00 | 10,000 00 | 10,700 00 |
| Faulk County, S. D., Cresbard Con. School Dist. No. 2, building, 7s | 10,389 00 | 10,000 00 | 10,800 00 |
| Faulk County, S. D., Cresbard Con. School Dist. No. 2, building, 7s | 10,412 00 | 10,000 00 | 10,800 00 |
| Faulk County, S. D., Cresbard Con. School Dist. No. 2, building, 7s | 5,217 00 | 5,000 00 | 5,450 00 |
| Faulk County, S. D., Cresbard Con. School Dist. No. 2, building, 7s | 3,137 73 | 3,000 00 | 3,300 00 |
| Faulk County, S. D., Cresbard Con. School Dist. No. 2, building, 7s | 10,478 31 | 10,000 00 | 11,100 00 |
| Faulk County, S. D., Cresbard Con. School Dist. No. 2, building, 7s | 5,217 16 | 5,000 00 | 5,450 00 |
| Faulk County, S. D., Cresbard Con. School Dist. No. 2, building, 7s | 5,227 54 | 5,000 00 | 5,450 00 |
| Faulk County, S. D., Cresbard Con. School Dist. No. 2, building, 7s | 5,237 27 | 5,000 00 | 5,500 00 |
| Faulk County, S. D., Cresbard Con. School Dist. No. 2, building, 7s | 5,246 41 | 5,000 00 | 5,500 00 |
| Faulk County, S. D., Cresbard Con. School Dist. No. 2, building, 7s | 2,101 99 | 2,000 00 | 2,200 00 |
| Flint, Mich., Civic Park School District, building, 6s | 10,243 49 | 10,000 00 | 11,400 00 |
| Flint, Mich., Civic Park School District, building, 6s | 10,234 00 | 10,000 00 | 11,400 00 |
| Flint, Mich., Missouri Avenue School Dist., bldg., 6s | 50,740 00 | 50,000 00 | 55,500 00 |
| Flint, Mich., Missouri Avenue School Dist., bldg., 6s | 3,056 43 | 3,000 00 | 3,300 00 |
| Flint, Mich., Missouri Avenue School Dist., bldg., 6s | 1,021 49 | 1,000 00 | 1,120 00 |
| Flint, Mich., Missouri Avenue School Dist., bldg., 6s | 10,249 68 | 10,000 00 | 11,300 00 |
| Flint, Mich., Union School District, building, 6s | 25,780 00 | 25,000 00 | 28,750 00 |
| Flint, Mich., Union School District, building, 6s | 1,016 27 | 1,000 00 | 1,100 00 |
| Flint, Mich., Union School District, building, 6s | 25,592 13 | 25,000 00 | 28,500 00 |
| Flint, Mich., Union School District, building, 6s | 15,312 03 | 15,000 00 | 16,800 00 |
| Flint, Mich., Union School District, building, 6s | 4,092 93 | 4,000 00 | 4,520 00 |
| Flint, Mich., Union School District, building, 6s | 15,365 24 | 15,000 00 | 17,100 00 |
| Fort Dodge, Ia., Independent School Dist., bldg., 5s | 16,738 51 | 18,000 00 | 18,720 00 |
| Fort Dodge, Ia., Independent School Dist., bldg., 5s | 3,688 73 | 4,000 00 | 4,160 00 |
| Fort Dodge, Ia., Independent School Dist., bldg., 5s | 919 23 | 1,000 00 | 1,040 00 |
| Fort Dodge, Ia., Independent School Dist., bldg., 5s | 1,833 37 | 2,000 00 | 2,080 00 |
| Gage County, Neb., School Dist. No. 165, building, 6s | 1,500 00 | 1,500 00 | 1,500 00 |
| Gage County, Neb., School Dist. No. 165, building, 6s | 1,500 00 | 1,500 00 | 1,515 00 |
| Gage County, Neb., School Dist. No. 165, building, 6s | 1,500 00 | 1,500 00 | 1,515 00 |
| Gage County, Neb., School Dist. No. 165, building, 6s | 1,500 00 | 1,500 00 | 1,530 00 |
| Cage County, Neb., School Dist. No. 165, building, 6s | 1,500 00 | 1,500 00 | 1,530 00 |
| Gage County, Neb., School Dist. No. 165, building, 6s | 1,500 00 | 1,500 00 | 1,530 00 |
| Gage County, Neb., School Dist. No. 165, building, 6s | 1,500 00 | 1,500 00 | 1,545 00 |
| Gage County, Neb., School Dist. No. 165, building, 6s | 1,500 00 | 1,500 00 | 1,545 00 |

SCHEDULE D—BONDS—Continued.

| Description. | Book value. | Par value. | Market value. |
|---|---|---|---|
| Gage County, Neb., School Dist. No. 165, building, 6s | $ 1,500 00 | $ 1,500 00 | $ 1,545 00 |
| Gage County, Neb., School Dist. No. 165, building, 6s | 1,500 00 | 1,500 00 | 1,560 00 |
| Gage County, Neb., School Dist. No. 165, building, 6s | 1,500 00 | 1,500 00 | 1,560 00 |
| Gage County, Neb., School Dist. No. 165, building, 6s | 1,500 00 | 1,500 00 | 1,560 00 |
| Gage County, Neb., School Dist. No. 165, building, 6s | 1,500 00 | 1,500 00 | 1,560 00 |
| Gage County, Neb., School Dist. No. 165, building, 6s | 1,500 00 | 1,500 00 | 1,575 00 |
| Gage County, Neb., School Dist. No. 165, building, 6s | 1,500 00 | 1,500 00 | 1,575 00 |
| Gage County, Neb., School Dist. No. 165, building, 6s | 1,500 00 | 1,500 00 | 1,575 00 |
| Gage County, Neb., School Dist. No. 165, building, 6s | 1,500 00 | 1,500 00 | 1,575 00 |
| Gage County, Neb., School Dist. No. 165, building, 6s | 1,500 00 | 1,500 00 | 1,590 00 |
| Gage County, Neb., School Dist. No. 165, building, 6s | 1,500 00 | 1,500 00 | 1,590 00 |
| Gage County, Neb., School Dist. No. 165, building, 6s | 1,500 00 | 1,500 00 | 1,590 00 |
| Gage County, Neb., School Dist. No. 165, building, 6s | 1,500 00 | 1,500 00 | 1,590 00 |
| Gage County, Neb., School Dist. No. 165, building, 6s | 1,500 00 | 1,500 00 | 1,590 00 |
| Gage County, Neb., School Dist. No. 165, building, 6s | 1,500 00 | 1,500 00 | 1,590 00 |
| Gage County, Neb., School Dist. No. 165, building, 6s | 1,500 00 | 1,500 00 | 1,605 00 |
| Gage County, Neb., School Dist. No. 165, building, 6s | 1,500 00 | 1,500 00 | 1,605 00 |
| Gage County, Neb., School Dist. No. 165, building, 6s | 1,500 00 | 1,500 00 | 1,605 00 |
| Gage County, Neb., School Dist. No. 165, building, 6s | 1,500 00 | 1,500 00 | 1,605 00 |
| Gage County, Neb., School Dist. No. 165, building, 6s | 1,500 00 | 1,500 00 | 1,605 00 |
| Georgetown, Ohio, school district, 6s | 508 31 | 500 00 | 555 00 |
| Georgetown, Ohio, school district, 6s | 508 56 | 500 00 | 555 00 |
| Georgetown, Ohio, school district, 6s | 508 80 | 500 00 | 555 00 |
| Georgetown, Ohio, school district, 6s | 509 04 | 500 00 | 555 00 |
| Georgetown, Ohio, school district, 6s | 509 27 | 500 00 | 555 00 |
| Georgetown, Ohio, school district, 6s | 509 50 | 500 00 | 555 00 |
| Georgetown, Ohio, school district, 6s | 509 72 | 500 00 | 555 00 |
| Georgetown, Ohio, school district, 6s | 509 93 | 500 00 | 555 00 |
| Georgetown, Ohio, school district, 6s | 510 13 | 500 00 | 555 00 |
| Georgetown, Ohio, school district, 6s | 510 33 | 500 00 | 555 00 |
| Georgetown, Ohio, school district, 6s | 510 53 | 500 00 | 555 00 |
| Georgetown, Ohio, school district, 6s | 510 72 | 500 00 | 555 00 |
| Georgetown, Ohio, school district, 6s | 510 90 | 500 00 | 555 00 |
| Georgetown, Ohio, school district, 6s | 511 08 | 500 00 | 555 00 |
| Georgetown, Ohio, school district, 6s | 511 25 | 500 00 | 555 00 |
| Georgetown, Ohio, school district, 6s | 511 42 | 500 00 | 555 00 |
| Georgetown, Ohio, school district, 6s | 511 59 | 500 00 | 555 00 |
| Georgetown, Ohio, school district, 6s | 511 75 | 500 00 | 555 00 |
| Georgetown, Ohio, school district, 6s | 511 90 | 500 00 | 555 00 |
| Georgetown, Ohio, school district, 6s | 512 05 | 500 00 | 555 00 |
| Georgetown, Ohio, school district, 6s | 512 20 | 500 00 | 555 00 |
| Georgetown, Ohio, school district, 6s | 512 34 | 500 00 | 555 00 |
| Georgetown, Ohio, school district, 6s | 512 48 | 500 00 | 555 00 |
| Georgetown, Ohio, school district, 6s | 512 61 | 500 00 | 555 00 |
| Georgetown, Ohio, school district, 6s | 512 74 | 500 00 | 555 00 |
| Georgetown, Ohio, school district, 6s | 512 87 | 500 00 | 555 00 |
| Georgetown, Ohio, school district, 6s | 512 99 | 500 00 | 555 00 |
| Georgetown, Ohio, school district, 6s | 513 11 | 500 00 | 555 00 |
| Georgetown, Ohio, school district, 6s | 513 23 | 500 00 | 555 00 |
| Georgetown, Ohio, school district, 6s | 513 34 | 500 00 | 555 00 |
| Georgetown, Ohio, school district, 6s | 513 45 | 500 00 | 555 00 |
| Georgetown, Ohio, school district, 6s | 513 56 | 500 00 | 555 00 |
| Georgetown, Ohio, school district, 6s | 513 66 | 500 00 | 555 00 |
| Georgetown, Ohio, school district, 6s | 513 76 | 500 00 | 555 00 |
| Georgetown, Ohio, school district, 6s | 513 86 | 500 00 | 555 00 |
| Georgetown, Ohio, school district, 6s | 513 96 | 500 00 | 555 00 |
| Georgetown, Ohio, school district, 6s | 514 05 | 500 00 | 555 00 |
| Georgetown, Ohio, school district, 6s | 514 14 | 500 00 | 555 00 |
| Georgetown, Ohio, school district, 6s | 514 23 | 500 00 | 555 00 |
| Georgetown, Ohio, school district, 6s | 514 31 | 500 00 | 555 00 |
| Georgetown, Ohio, school district, 6s | 514 39 | 500 00 | 555 00 |
| Gladstone, Mich., school building, 6s | 5,042 20 | 5,000 00 | 5,050 00 |
| Gladstone, Mich., school building, 6s | 13,126 23 | 13,000 00 | 13,130 00 |
| Gladstone, Mich., school building, 6s | 13,141 57 | 13,000 00 | 13,130 00 |
| Greene County, Tenn., road, 5s | 33,391 68 | 32,000 00 | 31,680 00 |
| Greene County, Tenn., road, 5s | 25,083 60 | 24,000 00 | 23,760 00 |
| Greenville, Miss., sewer, 5½s | 973 80 | 1,000 00 | 1,010 00 |
| Greenville, Miss., sewer refunding, 5½s | 1,460 70 | 1,500 00 | 1,515 00 |
| Greenville, Miss., storm sewer, 6s | 1,500 00 | 1,500 00 | 1,500 00 |
| Greenville, Miss., storm sewer, 6s | 1,500 00 | 1,500 00 | 1,515 00 |
| Greenville, Miss., storm sewer, 6s | 1,500 00 | 1,500 00 | 1,530 00 |
| Greenville, Miss., storm sewer, 6s | 1,500 00 | 1,500 00 | 1,530 00 |
| Greenville, Miss., storm sewer, 6s | 1,500 00 | 1,500 00 | 1,545 00 |
| Greenville, Miss., storm sewer, 6s | 1,500 00 | 1,500 00 | 1,560 00 |
| Greenville, Miss., storm sewer, 6s | 1,500 00 | 1,500 00 | 1,560 00 |
| Greenville, Miss., storm sewer, 6s | 1,500 00 | 1,500 00 | 1,575 00 |
| Greenville, Miss., storm sewer, 6s | 1,500 00 | 1,500 00 | 1,575 00 |
| Greenville, Miss., storm sewer, 6s | 1,500 00 | 1,500 00 | 1,590 00 |
| Greenville, Miss., storm sewer, 6s | 1,500 00 | 1,500 00 | 1,590 00 |
| Greenville, Miss., storm sewer, 6s | 1,500 00 | 1,500 00 | 1,590 00 |
| Greenville, Miss., storm sewer, 6s | 1,500 00 | 1,500 00 | 1,605 00 |
| Greenville, Miss., storm sewer, 6s | 1,500 00 | 1,500 00 | 1,605 00 |

SCHEDULE D—BONDS—Continued.

| Description. | Book value. | Par value. | Market value. |
|---|---|---|---|
| Greenville, Miss., storm sewer, 6s | $ 1,500 00 | $ 1,500 00 | $ 1,620 00 |
| Greenville, Miss., storm sewer, 6s | 1,500 00 | 1,500 00 | 1,620 00 |
| Greenville, Miss., storm sewer, 6s | 500 00 | 500 00 | 540 00 |
| Greenville, Miss., city hall, 6s | 1,500 00 | 1,500 00 | 1,500 00 |
| Greenville, Miss., city hall, 6s | 1,500 00 | 1,500 00 | 1,515 00 |
| Greenville, Miss., city hall, 6s | 1,500 00 | 1,500 00 | 1,530 00 |
| Greenville, Miss., city hall, 6s | 1,000 00 | 1,000 00 | 1,020 00 |
| Greenville, Miss., city hall, 6s | 1,000 00 | 1,000 00 | 1,030 00 |
| Greenville, Miss., city hall, 6s | 1,500 00 | 1,500 00 | 1,575 00 |
| Greenville, Miss., city hall, 6s | 1,500 00 | 1,500 00 | 1,590 00 |
| Greenville, Miss., city hall, 6s | 1,500 00 | 1,500 00 | 1,590 00 |
| Greenville, Miss., city hall, 6s | 1,500 00 | 1,500 00 | 1,590 00 |
| Greenville, Miss., city hall, 6s | 1,500 00 | 1,500 00 | 1,605 00 |
| Greenville, Miss., city hall, 6s | 1,500 00 | 1,500 00 | 1,605 00 |
| Greenville, Miss., city hall, 6s | 1,500 00 | 1,500 00 | 1,620 00 |
| Greenville, Miss., city hall, 6s | 1,500 00 | 1,500 00 | 1,620 00 |
| Greenville, Miss., city hall, 6s | 1,500 00 | 1,500 00 | 1,620 00 |
| Greenville, Miss., city hall, 6s | 1,500 00 | 1,500 00 | 1,635 00 |
| Greenville, Miss., city hall, 6s | 1,500 00 | 1,500 00 | 1,635 00 |
| Greer County, Okla., Con. School District No. 7, 7s | 21,967 34 | 20,000 00 | 21,967 34 |
| Hamilton, Mo., school district, 6s | 2,533 25 | 2,500 00 | 2,675 00 |
| Hamilton, Mo., school district, 6s | 2,536 25 | 2,500 00 | 2,675 00 |
| Hamilton, Mo., school district, 6s | 3,046 80 | 3,000 00 | 3,210 00 |
| Hamilton, Mo., school district, 6s | 3,049 80 | 3,000 00 | 3,210 00 |
| Hamilton, Mo., school district, 6s | 3,052 80 | 3,000 00 | 3,210 00 |
| Hamilton, Mo., school district, 6s | 3,564 75 | 3,500 00 | 3,745 00 |
| Hamilton, Mo., school district, 6s | 3,567 90 | 3,500 00 | 3,745 00 |
| Hamilton, Mo., school district, 6s | 3,571 05 | 3,500 00 | 3,745 00 |
| Hamilton, Mo., school district, 6s | 4,084 40 | 4,000 00 | 4,280 00 |
| Hamilton, Mo., school district, 6s | 4,087 20 | 4,000 00 | 4,280 00 |
| Hamilton, Mo., school district, 6s | 4,601 25 | 4,500 00 | 4,815 00 |
| Hamilton, Mo., school district, 6s | 5,116 00 | 5,000 00 | 5,350 00 |
| Hammond, Ind., school building, 6s | 20,447 15 | 20,000 00 | 21,000 00 |
| Hammond, Ind., school building, 6s | 18,435 57 | 18,000 00 | 19,080 00 |
| Hammond, Ind., school building, 6s | 23,596 82 | 23,000 00 | 24,610 00 |
| Hammond, Ind., school building, 6s | 19,525 18 | 19,000 00 | 20,520 00 |
| Hammond, Ind., school building, 6s | 16,533 14 | 16,000 00 | 17,600 00 |
| Hammond, Ind., school building, 6s | 4,138 74 | 4,000 00 | 17,760 00 |
| Hammond, Ind., school building, 6s | 18,355 81 | 18,000 00 | 18,900 00 |
| Hammond, Ind., school building, 6s | 25,793 55 | 25,000 00 | 27,000 00 |
| Hammond, Ind., school building, 6s | 3,100 18 | 3,000 00 | 3,300 00 |
| Hammond, Ind., school building, 6s | 19,717 73 | 19,000 00 | 21,090 00 |
| Hammond, Ind., school building, 6s | 2,078 18 | 2,000 00 | 2,240 00 |
| Harrison Co., Mo., Con. School Dist. No. 2, bldg., 6s | 25,000 00 | 25,000 00 | 25,000 00 |
| Hastings, Neb., auditorium, 5½s | 100,530 00 | 100,000 00 | 100,530 00 |
| Hasting, Neb., park, 5½s | 75,397 50 | 75,000 00 | 75,397 50 |
| Hoboken, N. J. Patterson Ave., temporary street improvement, 6s | 100,429 23 | 100,000 00 | 104,000 00 |
| Hood River County, Ore., road, 6s | 52,226 00 | 50,000 00 | 52,226 00 |
| Hugo, Okla., school district, building, 5s | 57,829 72 | 63,000 00 | 61,110 00 |
| Independence, Mo., electric light improvement, 6s | 26,000 00 | 26,000 00 | 29,640 00 |
| Independence, Mo., school district, building, 4½s | 32,052 99 | 36,500 00 | 36,135 00 |
| Independence, Mo., school district, building, 4½s | 21,822 45 | 25,000 00 | 24,750 00 |
| Ironton, Ohio, school district, building, series B, 6s | 36,015 00 | 35,000 00 | 41,200 00 |
| Ironton, Ohio, water works, 6s | 23,660 10 | 23,000 00 | 26,680 00 |
| Itasca County, Minn., Independent School Dist. No. 9, building, 6½s | 34,000 00 | 34,000 00 | 34,000 00 |
| Itasca County, Minn., Independent School Dist. No. 9, building, 6½s | 10,000 00 | 10,000 00 | 10,300 00 |
| Jackson County, Okla., Union Graded School District No. 1, 7s | 18,176 40 | 17,000 00 | 18,870 00 |
| Jersey City, N. J., temporary improvement, 6s | 201,960 92 | 200,000 00 | 208,000 00 |
| Johnston County, N. C., court house and jail, 6s | 107,358 75 | 103,000 00 | 107,120 00 |
| Kearney, Neb., School District No. 7, building, 6s | 69,139 56 | 70,000 00 | 77,700 00 |
| Kingston, Okla., school district, 7s | 13,185 60 | 12,000 00 | 13,185 60 |
| Lancaster County, Neb., School Dist. No. 145, bldg., 6s | 2,500 00 | 2,500 00 | 2,600 00 |
| Lancaster County, Neb., School Dist. No. 145, bldg., 6s | 2,500 00 | 2,500 00 | 2,600 00 |
| Lancaster County, Neb., School Dist. No. 145, bldg., 6s | 2,500 00 | 2,500 00 | 2,625 00 |
| Lancaster County, Neb., School Dist. No. 145, bldg., 6s | 2,500 00 | 2,500 00 | 2,625 00 |
| Lancaster County, Neb., School Dist. No. 145, bldg., 6s | 2,500 00 | 2,500 00 | 2,650 00 |
| Lancaster County, Neb., School Dist. No. 145, bldg., 6s | 2,500 00 | 2,500 00 | 2,650 00 |
| Lancaster County, Neb., School Dist. No. 145, bldg., 6s | 2,500 00 | 2,500 00 | 2,675 00 |
| Lancaster County, Neb., School Dist. No. 145, bldg., 6s | 2,500 00 | 2,500 00 | 2,675 00 |
| Lancaster County, Neb., School Dist. No. 145, bldg., 6s | 2,500 00 | 2,500 00 | 2,700 00 |
| Lancaster County, Neb., School Dist. No. 145, bldg., 6s | 2,500 00 | 2,500 00 | 2,700 00 |
| Lancaster County, Neb., School Dist. No. 145, bldg., 6s | 2,500 00 | 2,500 00 | 2,725 00 |
| Lancaster County, Neb., School Dist. No. 145, bldg., 6s | 2,500 00 | 2,500 00 | 2,750 00 |
| Lancaster County, Neb., School Dist. No. 145, bldg., 6s | 2,500 00 | 2,500 00 | 2,775 00 |
| Lancaster County, Neb., School Dist. No. 145, bldg., 6s | 2,500 00 | 2,500 00 | 2,775 00 |
| Lancaster County, Neb., School Dist. No. 145, bldg., 6s | 5,000 00 | 5,000 00 | 5,600 00 |
| Lancaster County, Neb., School Dist. No. 145, bldg., 5s | 140,000 00 | 140,000 00 | 141,400 00 |
| Leavenworth County, Kan., road, 5s | 9,963 55 | 10,000 00 | 10,000 00 |

SCHEDULE D—BONDS—Continued.

| Description. | Book value. | Par value. | Market value. |
|---|---|---|---|
| Leavenworth County, Kan., road, 5s | $ 9,893 67 | $ 10,000 00 | $ 10,100 00 |
| Leavenworth County, Kan., road, 5s | 9,827 65 | 10,000 00 | 10,100 00 |
| Leavenworth County, Kan., road, 5s | 9,765 26 | 10,000 00 | 10,100 00 |
| Leavenworth County, Kan., road, 5s | 9,706 31 | 10,000 00 | 10,000 00 |
| Leavenworth County, Kan., road, 5s | 9,650 61 | 10,000 00 | 10,000 00 |
| Leavenworth County, Kan., road, 5s | 9,597 98 | 10,000 00 | 10,000 00 |
| Leavenworth County, Kan., road, 5s | 9,548 25 | 10,000 00 | 10,000 00 |
| Leavenworth County, Kan., road, 5s | 9,501 26 | 10,000 00 | 10,000 00 |
| Leavenworth County, Kan., road, 5s | 9,456 87 | 10,000 00 | 10,000 00 |
| Leavenworth County, Kan., road, 5s | 9,414 91 | 10,000 00 | 10,000 00 |
| Leavenworth County, Kan., road, 5s | 9,375 27 | 10,000 00 | 10,000 00 |
| Leavenworth County, Kan., road, 5s | 9,337 82 | 10,000 00 | 10,000 00 |
| Leavenworth County, Kan., road, 5s | 9,302 43 | 10,000 00 | 10,000 00 |
| Leavenworth County, Kan., road, 5s | 9,268 99 | 10,000 00 | 10,000 00 |
| Leavenworth County, Kan., road, 5s | 6,817 11 | 7,000 00 | 7,070 00 |
| Leavenworth County, Kan., road, 5s | 6,771 27 | 7,000 00 | 7,000 00 |
| Leavenworth County, Kan., road, 5s | 6,728 00 | 7,000 00 | 7,000 00 |
| Leavenworth County, Kan., road, 5s | 6,687 14 | 7,000 00 | 7,000 00 |
| Leavenworth County, Kan., road, 5s | 6,648 64 | 7,000 00 | 7,000 00 |
| Leavenworth County, Kan., road, 5s | 4,722 97 | 5,000 00 | 5,000 00 |
| Leavenworth County, Kan., road, 5s | 6,577 77 | 7,000 00 | 7,000 00 |
| Leavenworth County, Kan., road, 5s | 6,545 31 | 7,000 00 | 7,000 00 |
| Leavenworth County, Kan., road, 5s | 6,514 67 | 7,000 00 | 7,000 00 |
| Lee County, Fla., School District No. 1, building, 6s | 2,999 22 | 3,000 00 | 3,000 00 |
| Lee County, Fla., School District No. 1, building, 6s | 2,997 83 | 3,000 00 | 3,030 00 |
| Lee County, Fla., School District No. 1, building, 6s | 2,996 43 | 3,000 00 | 3,060 00 |
| Lee County, Fla., School District No. 1, building, 6s | 2,995 19 | 3,000 00 | 3,060 00 |
| Lee County, Fla., School District No. 1, building, 6s | 2,993 95 | 3,000 00 | 3,090 00 |
| Lee County, Fla., School District No. 1, building, 6s | 2,992 87 | 3,000 00 | 3,120 00 |
| Lee County, Fla., School District No. 1, building, 6s | 2,991 77 | 3,000 00 | 3,120 00 |
| Lee County, Fla., School District No. 1, building, 6s | 2,990 84 | 3,000 00 | 3,150 00 |
| Lee County, Fla., School District No. 1, building, 6s | 2,989 76 | 3,000 00 | 3,150 00 |
| Lee County, Fla., School District No. 1, building, 6s | 2,988 98 | 3,000 00 | 3,180 00 |
| Lee County, Fla., School District No. 1, building, 6s | 2,988 05 | 3,000 00 | 3,180 00 |
| Lee County, Fla., School District No. 1, building, 6s | 2,987 27 | 3,000 00 | 3,180 00 |
| Lee County, Fla., School District No. 1, building, 6s | 2,986 50 | 3,000 00 | 3,210 00 |
| Lee County, Fla., School District No. 1, building, 6s | 2,985 88 | 3,000 00 | 3,210 00 |
| Lee County, Fla., School District No. 1, building, 6s | 2,985 27 | 3,000 00 | 3,240 00 |
| Lee County, Fla., School District No. 1, building, 6s | 2,984 64 | 3,000 00 | 3,240 00 |
| Lee County, Fla., School District No. 1, building, 6s | 2,984 01 | 3,000 00 | 3,240 00 |
| Lee County, Fla., School District No. 1, building, 6s | 2,983 39 | 3,000 00 | 3,270 00 |
| Lee County, Fla., School District No. 1, building, 6s | 2,982 93 | 3,000 00 | 3,270 00 |
| Lee County, Fla., School District No. 1, building, 6s | 2,982 46 | 3,000 00 | 3,270 00 |
| Lee County, Fla., School District No. 1, building, 6s | 3,976 00 | 4,000 00 | 4,360 00 |
| Lee County, Fla., School District No. 1, building, 6s | 3,975 36 | 4,000 00 | 4,400 00 |
| Lee County, Fla., School District No. 1, building, 6s | 3,974 76 | 4,000 00 | 4,400 00 |
| Lee County, Fla., School District No. 1, building, 6s | 3,974 34 | 4,000 00 | 4,400 00 |
| Lee County, Fla., School District No. 1, building, 6s | 3,973 93 | 4,000 00 | 4,400 00 |
| Lee County, Fla., School District No. 1, building, 6s | 3,973 31 | 4,000 00 | 4,400 00 |
| Lee County, Fla., School District No. 1, building, 6s | 3,972 89 | 4,000 00 | 4,440 00 |
| Lee County, Fla., School District No. 1, building, 6s | 3,972 43 | 4,000 00 | 4,440 00 |
| Lee County, Fla., School District No. 1, building, 6s | 3,972 27 | 4,000 00 | 4,440 00 |
| Lee County, Fla., School District No. 1, building, 6s | 3,971 86 | 4,000 00 | 4,440 00 |
| Lenior County, N. C., road, series A and B, 5½s | 97,720 00 | 100,000 00 | 100,000 00 |
| Lenior County, N. C., road, series A and B, 5½s | 29,070 00 | 30,000 00 | 30,000 00 |
| Lenior County, N. C., road, series A and B, 5½s | 4,806 50 | 5,000 00 | 5,000 00 |
| Lenior County, N. C., road, 6s | 59,705 32 | 60,000 00 | 65,400 00 |
| Lenior County, N. C., road, 6s | 79,608 40 | 80,000 00 | 87,200 00 |
| Lewis and Clark Counties, Mont., School Dist. No. 1, 6s | 20,671 74 | 20,000 00 | 21,400 00 |
| Lincoln, Neb., paving and fire, 6s | 13,974 00 | 13,974 00 | 13,974 00 |
| Lincoln, Neb., paving and fire, 6s | 13,974 00 | 13,974 00 | 14,113 74 |
| Lincoln, Neb., paving and fire, 6s | 13,974 00 | 13,974 00 | 14,393 22 |
| Lincoln, Neb., paving and fire, 6s | 13,974 00 | 13,974 00 | 14,532 96 |
| Lincoln, Neb., paving and fire, 6s | 13,974 00 | 13,974 00 | 14,672 70 |
| Lincoln, Neb., paving and fire, 6s | 13,974 00 | 13,974 00 | 14,952 18 |
| Lincoln, Neb., paving and fire, 6s | 13,974 00 | 13,974 00 | 15,091 92 |
| Lincoln, Neb., paving and fire, 6s | 13,974 00 | 13,974 00 | 15,231 66 |
| Lincoln, Neb., paving and fire, 6s | 13,974 00 | 13,974 00 | 15,371 40 |
| Lincoln, Neb., school district, building, 5s | 400,000 00 | 400,000 00 | 400,000 00 |
| Love County, Okla., Hickory Twp., road and bridge, 6s | 68,000 00 | 68,000 00 | 72,080 00 |
| Madison County, Neb., School District No. 12, bldg., 6s | 6,356 40 | 6,000 00 | 6,420 00 |
| Marshalltown, Iowa, bridge, 5s | 2,957 57 | 3,000 00 | 3,000 00 |
| Marshalltown, Iowa, bridge, 5s | 2,931 30 | 3,000 00 | 3,030 00 |
| Marshalltown, Iowa, bridge, 5s | 2,906 55 | 3,000 00 | 3,030 00 |
| Marshalltown, Iowa, bridge, 5s | 2,883 21 | 3,000 00 | 3,030 00 |
| Marshalltown, Iowa, bridge, 5s | 2,861 21 | 3,000 00 | 3,030 00 |
| Marshalltown, Iowa, bridge, 5s | 2,840 48 | 3,000 00 | 3,030 00 |
| Maumee, Ohio, school district, building, 6s | 4,168 76 | 4,000 00 | 4,184 72 |
| Maumee, Ohio, school district, building, 6s | 4,173 71 | 4,000 00 | 4,190 16 |
| Maumee, Ohio, school district, building, 6s | 4,178 36 | 4,000 00 | 4,195 29 |
| Maumee, Ohio, school district, building, 6s | 4,182 50 | 4,000 00 | 4,200 14 |
| Maumee, Ohio, school district, building, 6s | 4,186 98 | 4,000 00 | 4,204 74 |

SCHEDULE D—BONDS—Continued.

| Description. | Book value. | Par value. | Market value. |
|---|---|---|---|
| Maumee, Ohio, school district, building, 6s | $ 4,190 94 | $ 4,000 00 | $ 4,209 09 |
| Maumee, Ohio, school district, building, 6s | 4,194 67 | 4,000 00 | 4,213 21 |
| Maumee, Ohio, school district, building, 6s | 5,247 83 | 5,000 00 | 5,271 39 |
| Maumee, Ohio, school district, building, 6s | 5,251 95 | 5,000 00 | 5,276 00 |
| Maumee, Ohio, school district, building, 6s | 5,255 91 | 5,000 00 | 5,280 36 |
| Maumee, Ohio, school district, building, 6s | 5,259 65 | 5,000 00 | 5,284 48 |
| Maumee, Ohio, school district, building, 6s | 5,263 20 | 5,000 00 | 5,288 38 |
| Maumee, Ohio, school district, building, 6s | 5,266 54 | 5,000 00 | 5,292 08 |
| Maumee, Ohio, school district, building, 6s | 5,269 73 | 5,000 00 | 5,295 58 |
| Maumee, Ohio, school district, building, 6s | 6,327 25 | 6,000 00 | 6,358 67 |
| Maumee, Ohio, school district, building, 6s | 6,330 67 | 6,000 00 | 6,362 42 |
| Maumee, Ohio, school district, building, 6s | 6,333 88 | 6,000 00 | 6,365 97 |
| Maumee, Ohio, school district, building, 6s | 6,336 93 | 6,000 00 | 6,369 32 |
| Maumee, Ohio, school district, building, 6s | 6,339 80 | 6,000 00 | 6,372 52 |
| Maumee, Ohio, school district, building, 6s | 6,342 54 | 6,000 00 | 6,375 52 |
| Maumee, Ohio, school district, building, 6s | 6,345 11 | 6,000 00 | 6,378 37 |
| Maumee, Ohio, school district, building, 6s | 6,347 57 | 6,000 00 | 6,381 07 |
| Mitchell, S. D., Independent School Dist., building, 6s | 99,011 25 | 100,000 00 | 107,000 00 |
| Mooresville, N. C., Graded School Dist., building, 5s | 5,000 00 | 5,000 00 | 4,950 00 |
| Mullin, Tex., Independent School Dist., building, 5s | 7,800 00 | 7,800 00 | 7,644 00 |
| McIntosh County, Okla., School Dist. No. 20, bldg., 7s | 21,384 00 | 20,000 00 | 24,200 00 |
| Nash County, N. C., court house, 6s | 6,018 96 | 6,000 00 | 6,060 00 |
| Nash County, N. C., court house, 6s | 9,041 31 | 9,000 00 | 9,180 00 |
| Nash County, N. C., court house, 6s | 9,053 55 | 9,000 00 | 9,180 00 |
| Nash County, N. C., court house, 6s | 8,058 48 | 8,000 00 | 8,240 00 |
| Nash County, N. C., court house, 6s | 9,076 50 | 9,000 00 | 9,360 00 |
| Nash County, N. C., court house, 6s | 9,087 21 | 9,000 00 | 9,360 00 |
| Nash County, N. C., court house, 6s | 9,097 02 | 9,000 00 | 9,450 00 |
| Nash County, N. C., court house, 6s | 6,070 80 | 6,000 00 | 6,300 00 |
| Nash County, N. C., court house, 6s | 4,051 00 | 4,000 00 | 4,240 00 |
| Nash County, N. C., court house, 6s | 9,123 03 | 9,000 00 | 9,540 00 |
| Nash County, N. C., court house, 6s | 4,058 08 | 4,000 00 | 4,240 00 |
| Nash County, N. C., court house, 6s | 1,019 96 | 1,000 00 | 1,090 00 |
| Nash County, N. C., court house, 6s | 5,000 00 | 5,000 00 | 5,300 00 |
| Nash County, N. C., court house, 6s | 5,000 00 | 5,000 00 | 5,350 00 |
| Nash County, N. C., court house, 6s | 5,000 00 | 5,000 00 | 5,350 00 |
| Nash County, N. C., court house, 6s | 5,000 00 | 5,000 00 | 5,400 00 |
| Norfolk, Neb., Paving District No. 14, 6½s | 9,000 00 | 9,000 00 | 9,000 00 |
| Norfolk, Neb., Paving District No. 14, 6½s | 9,000 00 | 9,000 00 | 9,180 00 |
| Norfolk, Neb., Paving District No. 14, 6½s | 9,000 00 | 9,000 00 | 9,270 00 |
| Norfolk, Neb., Paving District No. 14, 6½s | 9,000 00 | 9,000 00 | 9,360 00 |
| Norfolk, Neb., Paving District No. 14, 6½s | 9,000 00 | 9,000 00 | 9,450 00 |
| Norfolk, Neb., Paving District No. 14, 6½s | 9,000 00 | 9,000 00 | 9,540 00 |
| Norfolk, Neb., Paving District No. 14, 6½s | 9,000 00 | 9,000 00 | 9,630 00 |
| Norfolk, Neb., Paving District No. 14, 6½s | 9,000 00 | 9,000 00 | 9,720 00 |
| Norfolk, Neb., Paving District No. 14, 6½s | 8,337 00 | 8,337 00 | 9,720 00 |
| Norfolk, Neb., school district, building, 5½s | 52,735 00 | 53,000 00 | 52,735 00 |
| Norfolk, Neb., Paving District No. 15, 7s | 13,057 31 | 13,000 00 | 13,000 00 |
| Norfolk, Neb., Paving District No. 15, 7s | 13,114 85 | 13,000 00 | 13,260 00 |
| Norfolk, Neb., Paving District No. 15, 7s | 13,168 89 | 13,000 00 | 13,390 00 |
| Norfolk, Neb., Paving District No. 15, 7s | 13,219 65 | 13,000 00 | 13,520 00 |
| Norfolk, Neb., Paving District No. 15, 7s | 13,267 29 | 13,000 00 | 13,650 00 |
| Norfolk, Neb., Paving District No. 15, 7s | 13,312 05 | 13,000 00 | 13,780 00 |
| Norfolk, Neb., Paving District No. 15, 7s | 13,352 12 | 13,000 00 | 13,910 00 |
| Norfolk, Neb., Paving District No. 15, 7s | 13,393 25 | 13,000 00 | 14,040 00 |
| Norfolk, Neb., Paving District No. 15, 7s | 13,946 98 | 13,500 00 | 14,580 00 |
| Oberlin, Ohio, school district, building, 6s | 4,010 08 | 4,000 00 | 4,010 08 |
| Oberlin, Ohio, school district, building, 6s | 4,021 04 | 4,000 00 | 4,021 04 |
| Oberlin, Ohio, school district, building, 6s | 4,031 40 | 4,000 00 | 4,031 40 |
| Oberlin, Ohio, school district, building, 6s | 4,041 20 | 4,000 00 | 4,041 20 |
| Oberlin, Ohio, school district, building, 6s | 4,050 40 | 4,000 00 | 4,050 40 |
| Oberlin, Ohio, school district, building, 6s | 4,059 20 | 4,000 00 | 4,059 20 |
| Oberlin, Ohio, school district, building, 6s | 4,067 60 | 4,000 00 | 4,067 60 |
| Oberlin, Ohio, school district, building, 6s | 4,075 28 | 4,000 00 | 4,075 28 |
| Oberlin, Ohio, school district, building, 6s | 4,082 64 | 4,000 00 | 4,082 64 |
| Oberlin, Ohio, school district, building, 6s | 4,089 60 | 4,000 00 | 4,089 60 |
| Oberlin, Ohio, school district, building, 6s | 4,096 24 | 4,000 00 | 4,096 24 |
| Oberlin, Ohio, school district, building, 6s | 4,102 48 | 4,000 00 | 4,102 48 |
| Oberlin, Ohio, school district, building, 6s | 4,108 40 | 4,000 00 | 4,108 40 |
| Oberlin, Ohio, school district, building, 6s | 4,114 00 | 4,000 00 | 4,114 00 |
| Oberlin, Ohio, school district, building, 6s | 4,119 20 | 4,000 00 | 4,119 20 |
| Oberlin, Ohio, school district, building, 6s | 4,124 64 | 4,000 00 | 4,124 64 |
| Oberlin, Ohio, school district, building, 6s | 4,128 96 | 4,000 00 | 4,128 96 |
| Oberlin, Ohio, school district, building, 6s | 4,132 64 | 4,000 00 | 4,132 64 |
| Oberlin, Ohio, school district, building, 6s | 4,137 60 | 4,000 00 | 4,137 60 |
| Oberlin, Ohio, school district, building, 6s | 4,141 60 | 4,000 00 | 4,141 60 |
| Oberlin, Ohio, school district, building, 6s | 4,145 40 | 4,000 00 | 4,145 40 |
| Oberlin, Ohio, school district, building, 6s | 4,148 80 | 4,000 00 | 4,148 80 |
| Oberlin, Ohio, school district, building, 6s | 4,152 32 | 4,000 00 | 4,152 32 |
| Oberlin, Ohio, school district, building, 6s | 4,155 40 | 4,000 00 | 4,155 40 |
| Oberlin, Ohio, school district, building, 6s | 4,158 40 | 4,000 00 | 4,158 40 |
| Oberlin, Ohio, school district, building, 6s | 5,201 50 | 5,000 00 | 5,201 50 |

SCHEDULE D—BONDS—Continued.

| Description. | Book value. | Par value. | Market value. |
|---|---|---|---|
| Oberlin, Ohio, school district, building, 6s | $ 5,205 00 | $ 5,000 00 | $ 5,205 00 |
| Oberlin, Ohio, school district, building, 6s | 5,208 20 | 5,000 00 | 5,208 20 |
| Oberlin, Ohio, school district, building, 6s | 5,211 20 | 5,000 00 | 5,211 20 |
| Oberlin, Ohio, school district, building, 6s | 5,214 00 | 5,000 00 | 5,214 00 |
| Oconee County, S. C., road and bridge, 6s | 2,000 00 | 2,000 00 | 2,020 00 |
| Oconee County, S. C., road and bridge, 6s | 2,000 00 | 2,000 00 | 2,040 00 |
| Oconee County, S. C., road and bridge, 6s | 2,000 00 | 2,000 00 | 2,060 00 |
| Oconee County, S. C., road and bridge, 6s | 4,000 00 | 4,000 00 | 4,160 00 |
| Oconee County, S. C., road and bridge, 6s | 4,000 00 | 4,000 00 | 4,200 00 |
| Oconee County, S. C., road and bridge, 6s | 4,000 00 | 4,000 00 | 4,240 00 |
| Oconee County, S. C., road and bridge, 6s | 4,000 00 | 4,000 00 | 4,280 00 |
| Oconee County, S. C., road and bridge, 6s | 4,000 00 | 4,000 00 | 4,320 00 |
| Oconee County, S. C., road and bridge, 6s | 4,000 00 | 4,000 00 | 4,320 00 |
| Oconee County, S. C., road and bridge, 6s | 4,000 00 | 4,000 00 | 4,360 00 |
| Oconee County, S. C., road and bridge, 6s | 4,000 00 | 4,000 00 | 4,360 00 |
| Oconee County, S. C., road and bridge, 6s | 4,000 00 | 4,000 00 | 4,400 00 |
| Oconee County, S. C., road and bridge, 6s | 4,000 00 | 4,000 00 | 4,400 00 |
| Oconee County, S. C., road and bridge, 6s | 4,000 00 | 4,000 00 | 4,440 00 |
| Okfuskee County, Okla., Okfuskee Twp., road and bridge, 6s | 40,000 00 | 40,000 00 | 44,000 00 |
| Okmulgee, Okla., school district, building, 5s | 21,080 40 | 22,000 00 | 22,000 00 |
| Okmulgee, Okla., school district, building, 5s | 20,999 00 | 22,000 00 | 22,000 00 |
| Okmulgee, Okla., school district, building, 5s | 20,919 80 | 22,000 00 | 22,000 00 |
| Okmulgee, Okla., school district, building, 5s | 20,847 20 | 22,000 00 | 22,000 00 |
| Okmulgee, Okla., school district, building, 5s | 20,776 80 | 22,000 00 | 22,000 00 |
| Okmulgee, Okla., school district, building, 5s | 20,710 80 | 22,000 00 | 22,000 00 |
| Okmulgee, Okla., school district, building, 5s | 20,649 20 | 22,000 00 | 22,000 00 |
| Okmulgee, Okla., school district, building, 5s | 19,653 90 | 21,000 00 | 21,000 00 |
| Okmulgee, Okla., school district, building, 5s | 19,601 40 | 21,000 00 | 21,000 00 |
| Okmulgee, Okla., school district, building, 5s | 19,551 00 | 21,000 00 | 21,000 00 |
| Okmulgee, Okla., school district, building, 5s | 19,502 70 | 21,000 00 | 21,000 00 |
| Ottawa County, Okla., School District No. 15, bldg., 7s | 41,142 60 | 38,000 00 | 41,155 52 |
| Pawnee City, Neb., electric light, 6s | 3,577 35 | 3,500 00 | 3,577 35 |
| Pawnee City, Neb., electric light, 6s | 5,126 50 | 5,000 00 | 5,126 50 |
| Pawnee City, Neb., electric light, 6s | 5,141 50 | 5,000 00 | 5,141 50 |
| Pawnee City, Neb., electric light, 6s | 5,155 50 | 5,000 00 | 5,155 50 |
| Pawnee City, Neb., electric light, 6s | 3,618 30 | 3,500 00 | 3,618 50 |
| Pawnee City, Neb., electric light, 6s | 5,181 50 | 5,000 00 | 5,181 50 |
| Pawnee City, Neb., electric light, 6s | 5,193 00 | 5,000 00 | 5,193 00 |
| Pawnee City, Neb., electric light, 6s | 5,204 50 | 5,000 00 | 5,204 50 |
| Pawnee City, Neb., electric light, 6s | 5,215 50 | 5,000 00 | 5,215 50 |
| Pawnee City, Neb., electric light, 6s | 5,225 50 | 5,000 00 | 5,225 50 |
| Pawnee City, Neb., electric light, 6s | 5,235 00 | 5,000 00 | 5,235 00 |
| Pawnee City, Neb., electric light, 6s | 5,244 00 | 5,000 00 | 5,244 00 |
| Pawnee City, Neb., electric light, 6s | 5,252 50 | 5,000 00 | 5,252 50 |
| Pawnee City, Neb., electric light, 6s | 5,260 50 | 5,000 00 | 5,260 50 |
| Pawnee City, Neb., electric light, 6s | 5,268 50 | 5,000 00 | 5,268 50 |
| Pierce County, Neb., School District No. 5, bldg., 5½s | 23,635 50 | 25,000 00 | 25,250 00 |
| Pima County, Ariz., road, 5½s | 3,872 80 | 4,000 00 | 4,040 00 |
| Pima County, Ariz., road, 5½s | 4,745 00 | 5,000 00 | 5,150 00 |
| Pima County, Ariz., road, 5½s | 6,613 60 | 7,000 00 | 7,210 00 |
| Pima County, Ariz., road, 5½s | 16,938 00 | 18,000 00 | 18,540 00 |
| Pima County, Ariz., road, 5½s | 1,874 60 | 2,000 00 | 2,060 00 |
| Polytechnic Heights, Tex., Independent School Dist., building, 6s | 96,348 10 | 100,000 00 | 96,348 10 |
| Pontiac, Mich., sewer extension, 6s | 5,055 77 | 5,000 00 | 5,350 00 |
| Pontiac, Mich., sewer extension, 6s | 1,013 68 | 1,000 00 | 1,090 00 |
| Pontiac, Mich., sewer extension, 6s | 5,074 16 | 5,000 00 | 5,500 00 |
| Pontiac, Mich., sewer extension, 6s | 5,084 77 | 5,000 00 | 5,600 00 |
| Pontiac, Mich., sewer extension, 6s | 2,035 86 | 2,000 00 | 2,260 00 |
| Pontiac, Mich., sewer disposal works, 5s | 1,924 19 | 2,000 00 | 1,921 75 |
| Pontiac, Mich., sewer disposal works, 5s | 1,893 10 | 2,000 00 | 1,890 60 |
| Pontiac, Mich., sewer disposal works, 5s | 1,883 87 | 2,000 00 | 1,881 35 |
| Pontiac, Mich., sewer disposal works, 5s | 1,875 12 | 2,000 00 | 1,872 61 |
| Pontiac, Mich., sewer disposal works, 5s | 1,866 86 | 2,000 00 | 1,864 36 |
| Pontiac, Mich., sewer disposal works, 5s | 1,859 21 | 2,000 00 | 1,856 57 |
| Pontiac, Mich., sewer disposal works, 5s | 1,851 75 | 2,000 00 | 1,849 21 |
| Pontiac, Mich., sewer disposal works, 5s | 1,844 90 | 2,000 00 | 1,851 64 |
| Pontiac, Mich., sewer disposal works, 5s | 1,838 24 | 2,000 00 | 1,845 44 |
| Pontiac, Mich., sewer disposal works, 5s | 916 09 | 1,000 00 | 919 79 |
| Rock Island, Ill., storm drain, 5s | 4,308 07 | 4,500 00 | 4,545 00 |
| Rock Island, Ill., storm drain, 5s | 3,800 92 | 4,000 00 | 4,040 00 |
| Rock Island, Ill., storm drain, 5s | 7,076 40 | 7,500 00 | 7,575 00 |
| Rock Island, Ill., storm drain, 5s | 7,028 96 | 7,500 00 | 7,650 00 |
| Rock Island, Ill., storm drain, 5s | 6,518 62 | 7,000 00 | 7,140 00 |
| Sanders County, Mont., School Dist. No. 2, bldg., 6s | 32,368 18 | 31,000 00 | 32,368 18 |
| San Francisco, Cal., city and county water works, 4½s | 21,942 81 | 25,000 00 | 25,000 00 |
| San Francisco, Cal., city and county water works, 4½s | 36,684 02 | 42,000 00 | 42,000 00 |
| San Francisco, Cal., city and county water works, 4½s | 26,143 56 | 30,000 00 | 30,000 00 |
| San Francisco, Cal., city and county water works, 4½s | 2,589 00 | 3,000 00 | 3,000 00 |
| Saunders County, Neb., School Dist. No. 72, bldg., 5½s | 29,546 98 | 30,000 00 | 30,000 00 |

SCHEDULE D—BONDS—Continued.

| Description. | Book value. | Par value. | Market value. |
|---|---|---|---|
| Sequoyah County, Okla., McKey Twp., road and bridge, 6s | $50,000 00 | $50,000 00 | $50,000 00 |
| Shawnee, Okla., school district, building, 5s | 11,602 20 | 12,000 00 | 11,880 00 |
| Shawnee, Okla., school district, building, 5s | 11,192 40 | 12,000 00 | 11,760 00 |
| Shawnee, Okla., school district, building, 5s | 10,887 60 | 12,000 00 | 11,760 00 |
| Shawnee, Okla., school district, building, 5s | 12,436 90 | 14,000 00 | 13,580 00 |
| Shawnee, Okla., school district, building, 5s | 5,801 10 | 6,000 00 | 5,940 00 |
| Shawnee, Okla., school district, building, 5s | 41,038 80 | 44,000 00 | 43,120 00 |
| Shawnee, Okla., school district, building, 5s | 48,994 20 | 54,000 00 | 52,920 00 |
| Shawnee, Okla., school district, building, 5s | 14,213 60 | 16,000 00 | 15,520 00 |
| Sidney, Ohio, sewer, 6s | 2,579 31 | 2,500 00 | 2,850 00 |
| Sidney, Ohio, sewer, 6s | 2,582 09 | 2,500 00 | 2,875 00 |
| Sidney, Ohio, sewer, 6s | 2,584 85 | 2,500 00 | 2,875 00 |
| Sidney, Ohio, sewer, 6s | 2,587 35 | 2,500 00 | 2,900 00 |
| Sidney, Ohio, sewer, 6s | 2,589 85 | 2,500 00 | 2,900 00 |
| Sidney, Ohio, water works, 6s | 2,579 31 | 2,500 00 | 2,850 00 |
| Sidney, Ohio, water works, 6s | 2,582 09 | 2,500 00 | 2,875 00 |
| Sidney, Ohio, water works, 6s | 2,584 85 | 2,500 00 | 2,875 00 |
| Sidney, Ohio, water works, 6s | 2,587 35 | 2,500 00 | 2,900 00 |
| Sidney, Ohio, water works, 6s | 2,589 85 | 2,500 00 | 2,900 00 |
| Springfield, Ohio, school district, building, 6s | 15,165 00 | 15,000 00 | 15,169 88 |
| Springfield, Ohio, school district, building, 6s | 15,317 25 | 15,000 00 | 15,321 57 |
| Springfield, Ohio, school district, building, 6s | 15,466 50 | 15,000 00 | 15,469 32 |
| Springfield, Ohio, school district, building, 6s | 31,158 00 | 30,000 00 | 31,162 27 |
| Springfield, Ohio, school district, building, 6s | 31,297 50 | 30,000 00 | 31,301 35 |
| Springfield, Ohio, school district, building, 6s | 20,941 00 | 20,000 00 | 20,941 76 |
| Titus County, Tex., road, 5½s | 23,850 00 | 25,000 00 | 25,750 00 |
| Titus County, Tex., road, 5½s | 23,772 50 | 25,000 00 | 25,750 00 |
| Titus County, Tex., road, 5½s | 18,962 00 | 20,000 00 | 20,600 00 |
| Titus County, Tex., road, 5½s | 22,687 20 | 24,000 00 | 24,960 00 |
| Titus County, Tex., road, 5½s | 942 80 | 1,000 00 | 1,040 00 |
| Tulsa County, Okla., School Dist. No. 23, bldg., 5½s | 12,331 25 | 12,500 00 | 12,625 00 |
| Tulsa County, Okla., School Dist. No. 23, bldg., 5½s | 12,107 50 | 12,500 00 | 12,750 00 |
| Tulsa County, Okla., School Dist. No. 23, bldg., 5½s | 11,941 25 | 12,500 00 | 12,750 00 |
| Tulsa County, Okla., School Dist. No. 23, bldg., 5½s | 11,817 50 | 12,500 00 | 12,875 00 |
| Tunica County, Miss., court house, 6s | 3,994 40 | 4,000 00 | 4,040 00 |
| Tunica County, Miss., court house, 6s | 3,987 60 | 4,000 00 | 4,080 00 |
| Tunica County, Miss., court house, 6s | 3,984 40 | 4,000 00 | 4,080 00 |
| Tunica County, Miss., court house, 6s | 7,957 60 | 8,000 00 | 8,240 00 |
| Tunica County, Miss., court house, 6s | 7,943 20 | 8,000 00 | 8,320 00 |
| Tunica County, Miss., court house, 6s | 7,938 40 | 8,000 00 | 8,320 00 |
| Tunica County, Miss., court house, 6s | 7,930 40 | 8,000 00 | 8,320 00 |
| Tunica County, Miss., court house, 6s | 7,924 00 | 8,000 00 | 8,400 00 |
| Tunica County, Miss., road, 6s | 3,032 61 | 3,000 00 | 3,090 00 |
| Tunica County, Miss., road, 6s | 6,072 26 | 6,000 00 | 6,240 00 |
| Tunica County, Miss., road, 6s | 6,078 83 | 6,000 00 | 6,240 00 |
| Tunica County, Miss., road, 6s | 6,084 95 | 6,000 00 | 6,240 00 |
| Tunica County, Miss., road, 6s | 6,090 95 | 6,000 00 | 6,240 00 |
| Tunica County, Miss., road, 6s | 6,097 20 | 6,000 00 | 6,300 00 |
| Tunica County, Miss., road, 6s | 6,101 73 | 6,000 00 | 6,300 00 |
| Tunica County, Miss., road, 6s | 10,178 32 | 10,000 00 | 10,500 00 |
| Tunica County, Miss., road, 6s | 10,186 30 | 10,000 00 | 10,500 00 |
| Tunica County, Miss., road, 6s | 6,116 11 | 6,000 00 | 6,360 00 |
| Twin Falls County, Idaho, Independent School District No. 1, building, 6s | 10,585 80 | 10,000 00 | 11,200 00 |
| Twin Falls County, Idaho, Independent School District No. 1, building, 6s | 5,314 20 | 5,000 00 | 5,600 00 |
| Tyler County, Tex., road, 5s | 3,736 40 | 4,000 00 | 4,000 00 |
| Tyler County, Tex., road, 5s | 4,493 00 | 5,000 00 | 5,000 00 |
| Tyler County, Tex., road, 5s | 4,463 50 | 5,000 00 | 5,000 00 |
| Tyler County, Tex., road, 5s | 4,409 50 | 5,000 00 | 5,000 00 |
| Tyler County, Tex., road, 5s | 2,617 20 | 3,000 00 | 3,000 00 |
| Tyler County, Tex., road, 5s | 1,736 20 | 2,000 00 | 2,000 00 |
| Tyrone, Tex., County, Okla., Con. School District No. 53, building, 7s | 7,729 69 | 7,500 00 | 7,751 88 |
| Tyrone, Tex., County, Okla., Con. School District No. 53, building, 7s | 7,948 88 | 7,500 00 | 7,965 05 |
| Tyrone, Tex., County, Okla., Con. School District No. 53, building, 7s | 8,110 88 | 7,500 00 | 8,123 10 |
| Tyrone, Tex., County, Okla., Con. School District No. 53, building, 7s | 8,230 88 | 7,500 00 | 8,239 81 |
| Union County, N. C., road and bridge, 6s | 5,000 00 | 5,000 00 | 5,000 00 |
| Union County, N. C., road and bridge, 6s | 5,000 00 | 5,000 00 | 5,000 00 |
| Union County, N. C., road and bridge, 6s | 5,000 00 | 5,000 00 | 5,050 00 |
| Union County, N. C., road and bridge, 6s | 5,000 00 | 5,000 00 | 5,050 00 |
| Union County, N. ., road and bridge, 6s | 5,000 00 | 5,000 00 | 5,100 00 |
| Union County, N. ., road and bridge, 6s | 5,000 00 | 5,000 00 | 5,100 00 |
| Union County, N. C., road and bridge, 6s | 5,000 00 | 5,000 00 | 5,050 00 |
| Union County, N. C., road and bridge, 6s | 5,000 00 | 5,000 00 | 5,050 00 |
| Union County, N. C., road and bridge, 6s | 5,000 00 | 5,000 00 | 5,050 00 |
| Union County, N. C., road and bridge, 6s | 5,000 00 | 5,000 00 | 5,050 00 |
| Union County, N. C., road and bridge, 6s | 5,000 00 | 5,000 00 | 5,050 00 |

SCHEDULE D—BONDS—Continued.

| Description. | Book value. | Par value. | Market value. |
|---|---|---|---|
| Union County, N. C., road and bridge, 6s | $ 5,000 00 | $ 5,000 00 | $ 5,050 00 |
| Union County, N. C., road and bridge, 6s | 5,000 00 | 5,000 00 | 5,050 00 |
| Union County, N. C., road and bridge, 6s | 5,000 00 | 5,000 00 | 5,150 00 |
| Union County, N. C., road and bridge, 6s | 5,000 00 | 5,000 00 | 5,100 00 |
| Union County, N. C., road and bridge, 6s | 5,000 00 | 5,000 00 | 5,100 00 |
| Union County, N. C., road and bridge, 6s | 5,000 00 | 5,000 00 | 5,100 00 |
| Union County, N. C., road and bridge, 6s | 5,000 00 | 5,000 00 | 5,100 00 |
| Union County, N. C., road and bridge, 6s | 5,000 00 | 5,000 00 | 5,100 00 |
| Urbana, Ohio, school district, building, 6s | 2,002 18 | 2,000 00 | 2,002 18 |
| Urbana, Ohio, school district, building, 6s | 2,005 04 | 2,000 00 | 2,005 04 |
| Urbana, Ohio, school district, building, 6s | 2,007 82 | 2,000 00 | 2,007 82 |
| Urbana, Ohio, school district, building, 6s | 2,010 52 | 2,000 00 | 2,010 52 |
| Urbana, Ohio, school district, building, 6s | 2,013 14 | 2,000 00 | 2,013 14 |
| Urbana, Ohio, school district, building, 6s | 2,015 70 | 2,000 00 | 2,015 70 |
| Urbana, Ohio, school district, building, 6s | 2,018 18 | 2,000 00 | 2,018 18 |
| Urbana, Ohio, school district, building, 6s | 2,020 60 | 2,000 00 | 2,020 60 |
| Urbana, Ohio, school district, building, 6s | 2,022 94 | 2,000 00 | 2,022 94 |
| Urbana, Ohio, school district, building, 6s | 2,025 22 | 2,000 00 | 2,025 22 |
| Urbana, Ohio, school district, building, 6s | 2,027 44 | 2,000 00 | 2,027 44 |
| Urbana, Ohio, school district, building, 6s | 2,029 60 | 2,000 00 | 2,029 60 |
| Urbana, Ohio, school district, building, 6s | 2,031 68 | 2,000 00 | 2,031 68 |
| Urbana, Ohio, school district, building, 6s | 2,033 72 | 2,000 00 | 2,033 72 |
| Urbana, Ohio, school district, building, 6s | 2,035 70 | 2,000 00 | 2,035 70 |
| Urbana, Ohio, school district, building, 6s | 2,037 64 | 2,000 00 | 2,037 64 |
| Urbana, Ohio, school district, building, 6s | 2,039 52 | 2,000 00 | 2,039 52 |
| Urbana, Ohio, school district, building, 6s | 2,041 32 | 2,000 00 | 2,041 32 |
| Urbana, Ohio, school district, building, 6s | 2,043 10 | 2,000 00 | 2,043 10 |
| Urbana, Ohio, school district, building, 6s | 2,044 82 | 2,000 00 | 2,044 82 |
| Urbana, Ohio, school district, building, 6s | 2,046 50 | 2,000 00 | 2,046 50 |
| Urbana, Ohio, school district, building, 6s | 2,048 12 | 2,000 00 | 2,048 12 |
| Urbana, Ohio, school district, building, 6s | 2,049 72 | 2,000 00 | 2,049 72 |
| Urbana, Ohio, school district, building, 6s | 2,051 26 | 2,000 00 | 2,051 26 |
| Urbana, Ohio, school district, building, 6s | 2,052 74 | 2,000 00 | 2,052 74 |
| Urbana, Ohio, school district, building, 6s | 2,054 20 | 2,000 00 | 2,054 20 |
| Urbana, Ohio, school district, building, 6s | 2,055 60 | 2,000 00 | 2,055 60 |
| Urbana, Ohio, school district, building, 6s | 2,057 00 | 2,000 00 | 2,057 00 |
| Urbana, Ohio, school district, building, 6s | 2,058 32 | 2,000 00 | 2,058 32 |
| Urbana, Ohio, school district, building, 6s | 2,059 64 | 2,000 00 | 2,059 64 |
| Urbana, Ohio, school district, building, 6s | 2,060 90 | 2,000 00 | 2,060 90 |
| Urbana, Ohio, school district, building, 6s | 2,062 12 | 2,000 00 | 2,062 12 |
| Urbana, Ohio, school district, building, 6s | 2,063 32 | 2,000 00 | 2,063 32 |
| Urbana, Ohio, school district, building, 6s | 2,064 58 | 2,000 00 | 2,064 58 |
| Urbana, Ohio, school district, building, 6s | 2,065 60 | 2,000 00 | 2,065 60 |
| Urbana, Ohio, school district, building, 6s | 2,066 70 | 2,000 00 | 2,066 70 |
| Urbana, Ohio, school district, building, 6s | 2,067 78 | 2,000 00 | 2,067 78 |
| Urbana, Ohio, school district, building, 6s | 2,068 80 | 2,000 00 | 2,068 80 |
| Urbana, Ohio, school district, building, 6s | 2,069 80 | 2,000 00 | 2,069 80 |
| Urbana, Ohio, school district, building, 6s | 2,070 80 | 2,000 00 | 2,070 80 |
| Urbana, Ohio, school district, building, 6s | 2,071 76 | 2,000 00 | 2,071 76 |
| Urbana, Ohio, school district, building, 6s | 2,072 70 | 2,000 00 | 2,072 70 |
| Urbana, Ohio, school district, building, 6s | 2,073 60 | 2,000 00 | 2,073 60 |
| Urbana, Ohio, school district, building, 6s | 2,074 46 | 2,000 00 | 2,074 46 |
| Urbana, Ohio, school district, building, 6s | 2,075 32 | 2,000 00 | 2,075 32 |
| Urbana, Ohio, school district, building, 6s | 2,076 16 | 2,000 00 | 2,076 16 |
| Urbana, Ohio, school district, building, 6s | 2,076 96 | 2,000 00 | 2,076 96 |
| Urbana, Ohio, school district, building, 6s | 2,077 74 | 2,000 00 | 2,077 74 |
| Urbana, Ohio, school district, building, 6s | 2,078 50 | 2,000 00 | 2,078 50 |
| Urbana, Ohio, school district, building, 6s | 2,079 20 | 2,000 00 | 2,079 20 |
| Urbana, Ohio, school district, building, 6s | 2,080 00 | 2,000 00 | 2,080 00 |
| Urbana, Ohio, school district, building, 6s | 2,080 66 | 2,000 00 | 2,080 66 |
| Urbana, Ohio, school district, building, 6s | 2,081 34 | 2,000 00 | 2,081 34 |
| Urbana, Ohio, school district, building, 6s | 2,082 00 | 2,000 00 | 2,082 00 |
| Urbana, Ohio, school district, building, 6s | 2,082 66 | 2,000 00 | 2,082 66 |
| Urbana, Ohio, school district, building, 6s | 2,083 28 | 2,000 00 | 2,083 28 |
| Urbana, Ohio, school district, building, 6s | 2,083 90 | 2,000 00 | 2,083 90 |
| Urbana, Ohio, school district, building, 6s | 2,084 50 | 2,000 00 | 2,084 50 |
| Urbana, Ohio, school district, building, 6s | 2,085 06 | 2,000 00 | 2,085 06 |
| Urbana, Ohio, school district, building, 6s | 2,085 60 | 2,000 00 | 2,085 60 |
| Urbana, Ohio, school district, building, 6s | 2,086 16 | 2,000 00 | 2,086 16 |
| Urbana, Ohio, school district, building, 6s | 2,086 70 | 2,000 00 | 2,086 70 |
| Urbana, Ohio, school district, building, 6s | 2,087 20 | 2,000 00 | 2,087 20 |
| Urbana, Ohio, school district, building, 6s | 2,087 70 | 2,000 00 | 2,087 70 |
| Urbana, Ohio, school district, building, 6s | 2,088 20 | 2,000 00 | 2,088 20 |
| Urbana, Ohio, school district, building, 6s | 2,088 66 | 2,000 00 | 2,088 66 |
| Urbana, Ohio, school district, building, 6s | 2,089 12 | 2,000 00 | 2,089 12 |
| Urbana, Ohio, school district, building, 6s | 2,089 60 | 2,000 00 | 2,089 60 |
| Urbana, Ohio, school district, building, 6s | 2,090 20 | 2,000 00 | 2,090 20 |
| Utah County, Utah, Alpine, school district, 5s | 1,883 65 | 2,000 00 | 1,883 65 |
| Utah County, Utah, Alpine, school district, 5s | 13,094 34 | 14,000 00 | 13,094 34 |
| Utah County, Utah, Alpine, school district, 5s | 13,008 37 | 14,000 00 | 13,008 37 |
| Utah County, Utah, Alpine, school district, 5s | 11,080 57 | 12,000 00 | 11,080 57 |
| Utah County, Utah, Alpine, school district, 5s | 11,933 03 | 13,000 00 | 11,933 03 |

SCHEDULE D—BONDS—Concluded.

| Description. | Book value. | Par value. | Market value. |
|---|---|---|---|
| Utah County, Utah, Alpine, school district, 5s | $11,866 17 | $ 13,000 00 | $ 11,866 17 |
| Utah County, Utah, Alpine, school district, 5s | 11,803 14 | 13,000 00 | 11,803 14 |
| Utah County, Utah, Alpine, school district, 5s | 884 16 | 1,000 00 | 884 16 |
| Vinita, Okla., school district, building, 5s | 9,114 50 | 10,000 00 | 9,800 00 |
| Vinita, Okla., school district, building, 5s | 8,819 50 | 10,000 00 | 9,700 00 |
| Vinita, Okla., school district, building, 5s | 8,602 50 | 10,000 00 | 9,700 00 |
| Washington County, Miss., road, 6s | 3,017 10 | 3,000 00 | 3,060 00 |
| Washington County, Miss., road, 6s | 17,166 60 | 17,000 00 | 17,510 00 |
| Washington County, Miss., road, 6s | 20,232 00 | 20,000 00 | 20,800 00 |
| Washington County, Miss., road, 6s | 13,174 20 | 13,000 00 | 13,520 00 |
| Washington County, Miss., road, 6s | 20,302 00 | 20,000 00 | 2,100 00 |
| Washington County, Miss., road, 6s | 15,249 00 | 15,000 00 | 15,750 00 |
| Washington County, Miss., road, 6s | 20,362 00 | 20,000 00 | 21,200 00 |
| Washington County, Miss., road, 6s | 20,390 00 | 20,000 00 | 21,200 00 |
| Washington County, Miss., road, 6s | 16,332 80 | 16,000 00 | 16,960 00 |
| Wayne County, Hamtramck Twp., Mich., School Dist. No. 8, building, 4½s | 26,689 08 | 30,000 00 | 29,700 00 |
| Wayne County, Mich., School Dist. No. 4, building, 5s | 92,854 70 | 100,000 00 | 105,000 00 |
| Wichita Falls, Tex., storm sewer, 6s | 99,752 95 | 100,000 00 | 113,000 00 |
| Winnebago County, Ill., School District No. 3, 6s | 1,024 97 | 1,000 00 | 1,024 97 |
| Winnebago County, Ill., School District No. 3, 6s | 2,052 24 | 2,000 00 | 2,052 24 |
| Winnebago County, Ill., School District No. 3, 6s | 2,054 39 | 2,000 00 | 2,054 39 |
| Winnebago County, Ill., School District No. 3, 6s | 2,056 52 | 2,000 00 | 2,056 52 |
| Winnebago County, Ill., School District No. 3, 6s | 1,029 25 | 1,000 00 | 1,029 25 |
| Winnebago County, Ill., School District No. 3, 6s | 2,060 32 | 2,000 00 | 2,060 32 |
| Winnebago County, Ill., School District No. 3, 6s | 2,577 64 | 2,500 00 | 2,577 64 |
| Wyandotte, Mich., water works, 4½s | 9,700 65 | 9,247 66 | 9,155 18 |
| Totals | $18,928,256 10 | $19,620,659 66 | $18,877,591 12 |

## MUTUAL BENEFIT AND AID SOCIETY.

Located at No. 155 North Clark Street, Chicago, Illinois.

JOHN CREMER, President. JOSEPH SIEBEN, Secretary.

| | |
|---|---|
| Balance from previous year | $84,262 92 |

### INCOME.

| | |
|---|---|
| Membership fees actually received | $ 540 00 |
| All other assessments or premiums | 24,091 15 |
| Dues and per capita tax | 39,388 05 |
| Medical examiners' fees actually received | 750 00 |
| Special dues | 2,148 75 |
| Section dues | 4,094 00 |
| Fines | 119 70 |
| Net amount received from members | $71,131 65 |
| Gross interest on bonds and dividends on stocks | 3,651 41 |
| Sale of lodge supplies | 113 40 |
| Local treasurer bond | 39 75 |
| War sufferers fund | 665 48 |
| Total income | $75,601 69 |
| Sum | $159,864 61 |

### DISBURSEMENTS.

| | |
|---|---|
| Death claims | $18,500 00 |
| Sick and accident claims | 19,551 75 |
| Total benefits paid | $38,051 75 |
| Commissions and fees paid to deputies and organizers | 938 00 |
| Salaries of officers and trustees | 4,110 00 |
| Salaries of office employees | 2,897 50 |
| Salaries and fees paid to subordinate medical examiners | 750 00 |
| Insurance department fees | 5 00 |
| Rent | 1,071 00 |
| Advertising, printing and stationery | 863 60 |
| Postage, express, telegraph and telephone | 557 30 |
| Official publication | 58 80 |
| Legal expense in litigating claims | 177 50 |
| Other legal expenses | 384 90 |
| War relief | 313 50 |
| Special benefit | 1,392 00 |
| Section dues | 4,110 00 |
| Total disbursements | $55,680 85 |
| Balance | $104,183 76 |

## LEDGER ASSETS.

| | |
|---|---|
| Book value of bonds and stocks | $97,800 00 |
| Cash in association's office | 338 48 |
| Deposits in trust companies and banks not on interest | 1,545 28 |
| Deposits in trust companies and banks on interest | 3,000 00 |
| Bills receivable | 1,500 00 |
| Total ledger assets | $104,183 76 |

### NON-LEDGER ASSETS.

| | |
|---|---|
| Furniture and fixtures | 421 75 |
| Gross assets | $104,605 51 |

### DEDUCT ASSETS NOT ADMITTED.

| | |
|---|---|
| Furniture and fixtures | 421 75 |
| Total admitted assets | $104,183 76 |

## LIABILITIES.

| | | |
|---|---|---|
| Death claims adjusted not yet due | $1,000 00 | |
| Death claims reported during the year but not yet adjusted | 1,750 00 | |
| Total death claims | | $2,750 00 |

## EXHIBIT OF CERTIFICATES.

| | Total business of the year—all in Illinois. Number. | Amount. |
|---|---|---|
| Benefit certificates in force December 31, 1920, as per last statement | 3,969 | $1,984,500 00 |
| Benefit certificates written and renewed during the year | 280 | 140,000 00 |
| Totals | 4,249 | $2,124,500 00 |
| Deduct terminated, decreased or transferred during the year | 150 | 75,000 00 |
| Total benefit certificates in force December 31, 1921 | 4,099 | $2,049,500 00 |

Received during the year from members in Illinois: Mortuary, $24,091.15; reserve, $11,630.80; disability, $19,551.75; expense, $9,615.20; total ---- $64,888 90

## EXHIBIT OF DEATH CLAIMS.

| | Total claims—all in Illinois. Number. | Amount. |
|---|---|---|
| Claims unpaid December 31, 1920, as per last statement | 4 | $1,750 00 |
| Claims reported during the year and interest addition | 39 | 19,500 00 |
| Totals | 43 | $21,500 00 |
| Claims paid during the year | 37 | 18,500 00 |
| Balance | 6 | $2,750 00 |

## EXHIBIT OF SICK AND ACCIDENT CLAIMS.

| | Total claims—all in Illinois. Number. | Amount. |
|---|---|---|
| Claims paid during the year | 498 | $19,551 75 |

## SCHEDULE D—BONDS.

| Description. | Book value. | Par value. |
|---|---|---|
| Cook County School | $ 500 00 | $ 500 00 |
| Bullet County, Ky., 5s | 1,000 00 | 1,000 00 |
| City of Sheboygan, Mich., 5s | 5,000 00 | 5,000 00 |
| City of Sheboygan, Mich., 5s | 2,000 00 | 2,000 00 |
| Sanitary Dist., 4s | 4,000 00 | 4,000 00 |
| Frederick, Okla., board of education, 5s | 3,000 00 | 3,000 00 |
| Bartlesville, Okla., city hall, 5s | 1,000 00 | 1,000 00 |
| City of Reno, Nev., 5s | 3,000 00 | 3,000 00 |
| Burrelson Co., Tex., 5s | 1,000 00 | 1,000 00 |
| West Allis, Wis., 5s | 1,000 00 | 1,000 00 |
| Hamilton Co., Tex., 4½s | 2,000 00 | 2,000 00 |
| San Francisco, Cal., 5s | 1,000 00 | 1,000 00 |
| Holvard, Okla., 5s | 3,000 00 | 3,000 00 |
| Koochishing Co., Minn., 5s | 2,000 00 | 2,000 00 |
| Kent Creek, Wis., 6s | 2,000 00 | 2,000 00 |
| Gary, Ind., improvement, 6s | 3,000 00 | 3,000 00 |
| Gary, Ind., improvement, 6s | 500 00 | 500 00 |
| Lake Arthur, N. Mex., 6s | 3,000 00 | 3,000 00 |
| Bettramy, Minn., 6s | 3,000 00 | 3,000 00 |
| Tiro, Ohio, school division, 5s | 500 00 | 500 00 |
| City of Pontiac, Mich., 5s | 1,000 00 | 1,000 00 |

SCHEDULE D—BONDS—Concluded.

| Description. | Book value. | Par value. | Market value. |
|---|---|---|---|
| City of Oplelouses, La., 6s | | $ 3,500 00 | $ 3,500 00 |
| City of Oplelouses, La., 6s | | 500 00 | 500 00 |
| Town of Greenville, N. C., 6s | | 1,000 00 | 1,000 00 |
| City of Miami, Fla., 6s | | 2,000 00 | 2,000 00 |
| Bendon Co., Ark., 5½s | | 3,000 00 | 3,000 00 |
| Bay Co., Fla., 5½s | | 3,000 00 | 3,000 00 |
| Harrimann, Tenn., 6s | | 4,000 00 | 4,000 00 |
| Franklin, N. C., 6s | | 1,000 00 | 1,000 00 |
| Franklin, N. C., 6s | | 3,000 00 | 3,000 00 |
| City of Kissimmee, Fla., 6s | | 4,000 00 | 4,000 00 |
| Palo Pinto Co., Tex., 5½s | | 2,000 00 | 2,000 00 |
| Palo Pinto Co., Tex., 5½s | | 2,000 00 | 2,000 00 |
| Palo Pinto Co., Tex., 5½s | | 2,000 00 | 2,000 00 |
| Red River Bayoudes, Glaizo, La | | 4,000 00 | 4,000 00 |
| Liberty bonds | | 20,300 00 | 20,300 00 |
| Totals | | $97,800 00 | $97,800 00 |

## MYSTIC WORKERS OF THE WORLD.

Located at Fulton, Illinois.

D. E. SMITH, President. O. HAMMERLUND, Secretary.

| | |
|---|---|
| Balance from previous year | $752,605 24 |

### INCOME.

| | |
|---|---|
| Assessments or premiums | $ 339,247 97 |
| All other assessments or premiums | 1,654,587 90 |
| Dues and per capita tax | 122,756 58 |
| Certificate fees | 1,640 76 |
| Total received from members | $2,118,233 21 |
| Deduct payments returned to applicants and members | 2,451 59 |
| Net amount received from members | $2,115,781 62 |
| Gross interest on mortgage loans | 20,057 60 |
| Gross interest on bonds and dividends on stocks | 22,537 91 |
| Gross interest on deposits in trust companies and banks | 2,707 31 |
| Gross interest from all other sources | 6 50 |
| Sale of lodge supplies | 2,272 73 |
| Gross increase in book value of ledger assets | 6,500 00 |
| Surety bond | 3,152 35 |
| Advertising | 1,213 61 |
| Miscellaneous | 1,755 69 |
| Total income | $2,175,985 32 |
| Sum | $2,928,590 56 |

### DISBURSEMENTS.

| | |
|---|---|
| Death claims | $835,733 74 |
| Permanent disability claims | 45 00 |
| Sick and accident claims | 30,525 00 |
| Old age benefits | 48,250 00 |
| Total benefits paid | $914,353 74 |
| Commissions and fees paid to deputies and organizers | 158,141 36 |
| Salaries of deputies and organizers | 17,034 69 |
| Salaries of officers and trustees | 11,645 00 |
| Salaries and other compensation of committees | 5,367 64 |
| Salaries of office employees | 29,101 45 |
| Salaries and fees paid to supreme medical examiners | 3,749 50 |
| Salaries and fees paid to subordinate medical examiners | 22,770 00 |
| Traveling and other expenses of officers, trustees and committees | 9,307 32 |
| For collection and remittance of assessments, dues and surety bond | 1,995 85 |
| Insurance department fees | 1,246 22 |
| Advertising, printing and stationery | 11,419 67 |
| Postage, express, telegraph and telephone | 4,820 91 |
| Lodge supplies and office supplies | 3,050 24 |
| Official publication and mailing list | 11,347 65 |
| Expenses of supreme lodge meeting | 770 01 |
| Legal expense in litigating claims | 511 27 |
| Other legal expenses | 473 49 |
| Furniture and fixtures and library | 1,356 92 |
| Taxes, repairs and other expenses on real estate and janitor | 3,297 33 |
| Gross loss on sale or maturity of ledger assets | 11,725 40 |
| Gross decrease in book value of ledger assets | 5,000 00 |
| Premiums on bonds | 50 80 |
| Special investigation | 56 62 |
| Valuation and actuary | 1,940 81 |

DISBURSEMENTS—Concluded.

| | | |
|---|---|---|
| Expenses— | | |
| Supreme master's office | | $ 593 30 |
| Supreme medical examiner | | 1,575 24 |
| Supreme attorney | | 939 36 |
| Supreme banker | | 395 15 |
| Fraternal congress | | 65 00 |
| Special compensation and suspense | | 9,780 39 |
| Total disbursements | | $1,245,735 44 |
| Balance | | $1,682,655 12 |

LEDGER ASSETS.

| | | |
|---|---|---|
| Book value of real estate | | $ 20,991 66 |
| Mortgage loans on real estate | | 1,123,700 00 |
| Book value of bonds and stocks | | 467,355 74 |
| Deposits in trust companies and banks on interest | | 70,607 72 |
| Total ledger assets | | $1,682,655 12 |

NON-LEDGER ASSETS.

| | | |
|---|---|---|
| Interest and rents due and accrued | | 39,342 55 |
| Market value of bonds and stocks over book value | | 15,488 26 |
| Assessments actually collected by subordinate lodges not yet turned over to supreme lodge | | 163,722 15 |
| All other assets, viz— | | |
| Furniture and fixtures | $10,154 55 | |
| Library inventory | 1,422 94 | |
| Supply inventory | 1,226 38 | |
| | | 12,803 87 |
| Gross assets | | $1,914,011 95 |

DEDUCT ASSETS NOT ADMITTED.

| | | |
|---|---|---|
| Other items, viz— | | |
| Furniture and fixtures | $10,154 55 | |
| Library inventory | 1,422 94 | |
| Supply inventory | 1,226 38 | |
| | | 12,803 87 |
| Total admitted assets | | $1,901,208 08 |

LIABILITIES.

| | | |
|---|---|---|
| Death claims due and unpaid | $ 440 05 | |
| Death claims resisted | 11,000 00 | |
| Death claims reported during the year but not yet adjusted | 78,050 00 | |
| Death claims incurred in 1921, not reported until 1922 | 18,450 00 | |
| Total death claims | | $107,940 05 |
| Sick and accident claims reported during the year but not yet adjusted | $3,200 00 | |
| Sick and accident claims incurred in 1921, not reported until 1922 | 2,100 00 | |
| Total sick and accident claims | | 5,300 00 |
| Total unpaid claims | | $113,240 05 |
| Salaries, rents, expenses, commissions, etc., due or accrued | | 580 34 |
| Taxes due or accrued | | 225 78 |
| Advance assessments | | 33,805 23 |
| All other liabilities, viz— | | |
| Reserve on American 4 per cent certificates | $55,529 12 | |
| Reserve on juvenile certificates | 1,474 49 | |
| | | 57,003 61 |
| Total | | $204,855 01 |

EXHIBIT OF CERTIFICATES.

| | Total business of the year. | | Business in Illinois during year. | |
|---|---|---|---|---|
| | Number. | Amount. | Number. | Amount. |
| Benefit certificates in force December 31, 1920, as per last statement | 95,711 | $1,142,698 99 | 48,833 | $605,501 66 |
| Benefit certificates written and renewed during the year | 23,543 | 257,731 74 | 10,479 | 118,563 22 |
| Benefit certificates received by transfer during the year | | | 486 | 5,875 00 |
| Benefit certificates increased during the year | | 197 50 | | 609 98 |
| Totals | 119,254 | $1,400,628 23 | 59,798 | $730,549 86 |
| Deduct terminated, decreased or transferred during the year | 41,477 | 481,730 33 | | |
| Deduct terminated or decreased during the year | | | 18,924 | 228,858 42 |
| Total benefit certificates in force December 31, 1921 | 77,777 | $918,897 90 | 40,874 | $501,691 44 |

Received during the year from members in Illinois: Mortuary, $1,061,999.23; expense, $64,685.90; total — $1,126,685 13

## EXHIBIT OF DEATH CLAIMS.

| | Total claims. Number. | Total claims. Amount. | Illinois claims. Number. | Illinois claims. Amount. |
|---|---|---|---|---|
| Claims unpaid December 31, 1920, as per last statement | 80 | $ 91,765 05 | 38 | $ 46,165 05 |
| Claims reported during the year and interest addition | 695 | 844,340 00 | 358 | 454,231 00 |
| Totals | 775 | $936,105 05 | 396 | $500,396 05 |
| Claims paid during the year | 700 | 835,733 74 | 363 | 453,425 36 |
| Balance | 75 | $100,371 31 | 33 | $46,970 69 |
| Saved by compromising or scaling down claims during the year | | 7,881 26 | | 4,530 64 |
| Claims rejected during the year | 2 | 3,000 00 | 1 | 1,000 00 |
| Claims unpaid December 31, 1921 | 73 | $89,490 05 | 32 | $41,440 05 |

## EXHIBIT OF PERMANENT DISABILITY CLAIMS.

| | Total claims—all in Illinois. Number. | Total claims—all in Illinois. Amount. |
|---|---|---|
| Claims reported during the year and interest addition | 1 | $45 00 |
| Claims paid during the year | 1 | 45 00 |

## EXHIBIT OF SICK AND ACCIDENT CLAIMS.

| | Total claims. Number. | Total claims. Amount. | Illinois claims. Number. | Illinois claims. Amount. |
|---|---|---|---|---|
| Claims unpaid December 31, 1920, as per last statement | 28 | $ 2,725 00 | 10 | $ 1,250 00 |
| Reopened in estimated liability | 1 | 200 00 | | |
| Increase in estimatued liability | | | 1 | 200 00 |
| Claims reported during the year | 324 | 34,225 00 | 149 | 16,225 00 |
| Totals | 353 | $37,150 00 | 160 | $17,675 00 |
| Claims paid during the year | 299 | 30,525 00 | 135 | 13,675 00 |
| Claims rejected during the year | 33 | 3,425 00 | 11 | 1,400 00 |
| Claims unpaid December 31, 1921 | 21 | $3,200 00 | 14 | $2,600 00 |

## EXHIBIT OF OLD AGE AND OTHER CLAIMS.

| | Total claims. Number. | Total claims. Amount. | Illinois claims. Number. | Illinois claims. Amount. |
|---|---|---|---|---|
| Claims unpaid December 31, 1920, as per last statement | 24 | $ 1,900 00 | 16 | $ 1,300 00 |
| Claims reported during the year and interest addition | 667 | 51,875 00 | 491 | 40,275 00 |
| Totals | 691 | $53,775 00 | 507 | $41,575 00 |
| Claims paid during the year | 620 | 48,250 00 | 469 | 38,075 00 |
| Balance | 71 | $5,525 00 | 38 | $3,500 00 |
| Claims rejected during the year | 37 | 3,325 00 | 18 | 2,150 00 |
| Claims unpaid December 31, 1921 | 34 | $2,200 00 | 20 | $1,350 00 |

## SCHEDULE D—BONDS.

| Description. | Book value. | Par value. | Market value. |
|---|---|---|---|
| Astoria, Ore., water works, 5s | $10,000 00 | $10,000 00 | $10,000 00 |
| Audubon, Iowa, sewer, 6s | 2,000 00 | 2,000 00 | 2,000 00 |
| Arenac County, Mich., road, 5¼s | 50 00 | 50 00 | 50 00 |
| Breckenridge, Minn., water works, 5s | 15,000 00 | 15,000 00 | 15,150 00 |
| Beaumont, Tex., navigation, 5s | 9,900 00 | 10,000 00 | 9,800 00 |
| Benson, Neb., school, 5s | 5,000 00 | 5,000 00 | 5,100 00 |
| Bend, Ore., sewer, 6s | 10,000 00 | 10,000 00 | 10,600 00 |
| Bessemer, Twp., Mich., school, 6½s | 2,000 00 | 2,000 00 | 2,140 00 |
| Bee County, Tex., court house, 5½s | 11,667 60 | 12,000 00 | 12,120 00 |
| Cook County, Tex., court house, 4s | 4,350 00 | 5,000 00 | 4,250 00 |
| Canova, S. Dak., water works, 6s | 4,000 00 | 4,000 00 | 4,240 00 |
| Clay County, Ill., school building, 6s | 1,600 00 | 1,600 00 | 1,600 00 |
| Clearwater, Minn., drainage, 6s | 15,000 00 | 15,000 00 | 15,600 00 |
| Cherokee & Buena Vista Co., Iowa., school, 5s | 14,325 00 | 15,000 00 | 15,000 00 |
| Casper, Wyo., drainage, 6s | 5,257 45 | 5,500 00 | 6,105 00 |
| Dunn County, N. Dak., seed, grain and feed, 6s | 5,000 00 | 5,000 00 | 5,000 00 |
| Fairfax, Okla., school building, 6s | 5,000 00 | 5,000 00 | 5,250 00 |
| Finchford, Iowa, school building, 5s | 9,523 34 | 10,000 00 | 10,200 00 |
| Gilman, Iowa, school, 5s | 2,879 50 | 3,000 00 | 3,000 00 |
| Gustavus Twp., Ohio, road, 5s | 2,000 00 | 2,000 00 | 2,000 00 |
| Gun Plains Twp., Mich., school, 6s | 1,972 80 | 2,000 00 | 2,100 00 |
| Henry County, Ill., school building, 5s | 1,500 00 | 1,500 00 | 1,500 00 |
| Henryetta, Okla., water works, 6s | 1,000 00 | 1,000 00 | 1,100 00 |
| Harding County, S. Dak., funding, 5s | 1,971 40 | 2,000 00 | 2,000 00 |

SCHEDULE D—BONDS—Concluded.

| Description. | Book value. | Par value. | Market value. |
|---|---|---|---|
| Houston County, Tex., road, 5½s | $ 9,135 40 | $10,000 00 | $10,500 00 |
| Harrison County, Tex., road, 5s | 16,150 00 | 17,000 00 | 17,340 00 |
| Harrison County, Tex., road, 5s | 4,685 00 | 5,000 00 | 5,100 00 |
| Ironwood, Mich., site and building, 5s | 9,657 00 | 10,000 00 | 10,100 00 |
| Jackson County, Tennessee, road and bridge, 5s | 10,000 00 | 10,000 00 | 9,800 00 |
| Kalamazoo County, Mich., road, 5½s | 100 00 | 100 00 | 100 00 |
| Lawton, Okla., school building, 5s | 5,000 00 | 5,000 00 | 4,950 00 |
| Leland Twp., Mich., school building, 6s | 600 00 | 600 00 | 600 00 |
| Litchfield Twp., Ohio, road, 5s | 2,500 00 | 2,500 00 | 2,525 00 |
| Lake County, S. Dak., school, 6½s | 10,264 00 | 10,000 00 | 10,000 00 |
| Lawton, Okla., funding, 5s | 10,000 00 | 10,000 00 | 9,900 00 |
| Lawton, Okla., dam and water works, 5s | 4,000 00 | 4,000 00 | 3,960 00 |
| Loudon Co., Tenn., road, 5s | 10,000 00 | 10,000 00 | 10,000 00 |
| Muskogee, Okla., school building, 5s | 5,000 00 | 5,000 00 | 4,850 00 |
| Marcus, Iowa, water works, 5½s | 5,000 00 | 5,000 00 | 5,000 00 |
| Marshall County, Minn., drainage, 6s | 2,000 00 | 2,000 00 | 2,200 00 |
| Montgomery County, Tex., road, 5½s | 10,000 00 | 10,000 00 | 10,100 00 |
| Montgomery and Macoupin Counties, Ill., school, 5½s | 2,978 70 | 3,000 00 | 3,000 00 |
| Nampa, Idaho, municipal, 6s | 8,000 00 | 8,000 00 | 8,000 00 |
| Nez Perce, Idaho, road, 5s | 15,000 00 | 15,000 00 | 15,900 00 |
| North Crandon, Wis., road, 5s | 11,000 00 | 11,000 00 | 11,220 00 |
| Pawhuska, Okla., public utility, 5s | 10,000 00 | 10,000 00 | 10,000 00 |
| Pittsburg, Kans., school, 4¾s | 4,000 00 | 4,000 00 | 4,000 00 |
| Pennington County, Minn., drainage, 6s | 5,000 00 | 5,000 00 | 5,160 00 |
| Robertson County, Tenn., road, 4s | 9,250 00 | 10,000 00 | 8,900 00 |
| Regina, Saskatchewan, Can., school, 5s | 7,710 40 | 8,000 00 | 7,040 00 |
| Rector, Ark., water works, 6s | 3,000 00 | 3,000 00 | 3,060 00 |
| Rock Island, Ill., school, 6s | 25,935 00 | 26,000 00 | 27,300 00 |
| Rector, Ark., sewer, 6s | 5,000 00 | 5,000 00 | 5,150 00 |
| San Angelo, Tex., street and bridge, 5s | 1,000 00 | 1,000 00 | 1,000 00 |
| St. Charles, La., road, 5s | 10,000 00 | 10,000 00 | 10,000 00 |
| Sisseton, S. Dak., sewer, 5s | 3,000 00 | 3,000 00 | 3,000 00 |
| Spencer Twp., Ohio, road, 5s | 5,000 00 | 5,000 00 | 5,000 00 |
| Second Liberty Loan, 4¼s | 11,000 00 | 11,000 00 | 10,560 00 |
| Shelby County, Tex., road, 5s | 12,327 30 | 15,000 00 | 14,850 00 |
| Shellsburg, Iowa, school, 6s | 4,975 00 | 5,000 00 | 5,100 00 |
| Sac City, Iowa, school, 6s | 2,958 60 | 3,000 00 | 3,060 00 |
| Temple, Tex., water works, 5s | 11,000 00 | 11,000 00 | 10,780 00 |
| Trinity River, Tex., irrigation, 5½s | 7,926 25 | 8,500 00 | 8,500 00 |
| Three Rivers, Mich., school, 5½s | 5,823 00 | 6,000 00 | 6,120 00 |
| U. S. War Saving Certificates, 4s | 824 00 | 824 00 | 824 00 |
| Upshur County, Tex., road, 5½s | 8,590 00 | 10,000 00 | 10,490 00 |
| West Hammond, Ill., general corporate, 5s | 1,500 00 | 1,500 00 | 1,500 00 |
| Frio County, Tex., road, 5½s | 19,469 00 | 20,000 00 | 20,400 00 |
| Totals | $467,355 74 | $478,674 00 | $482,844 00 |

## NATIONAL FRATERNAL SOCIETY OF THE DEAF.

Located at No. 21 North LaSalle Street, Chicago, Illinois.

HARRY C. ANDERSON, President. FRANCIS P. GIBSON, Secretary.

| | |
|---|---|
| Balance from previous year | $281,418 90 |

### INCOME.

| | |
|---|---|
| Membership fees actually received | $ 1,508 00 |
| All other assessments or premiums | 66,777 68 |
| Dues and per capita tax | 30,509 28 |
| Special assessment | 4,648 00 |
| Recording and registry fees | 78 75 |
| Total received from members | $103,521 71 |
| Deduct payments returned to applicants and members | 24 32 |
| Net amount received from members | $103,497 39 |
| Gross interest on mortgage loans | 10,796 83 |
| Gross interest on bonds | 4,963 33 |
| Gross interest on deposits in trust companies and banks | 119 79 |
| Sale of lodge supplies | 568 29 |
| Borrowed money (gross) | 24,000 00 |
| Gross profit on sale or maturity of ledger assets | 148 34 |
| Gross increase in book value of ledger assets | 813 90 |
| Sale of sundry supplies | 87 74 |
| Exchange on checks, etc | 136 36 |
| Rent for part use of office | 120 00 |
| For surety bond premiums | 110 60 |
| Total income | $145,362 57 |
| Sum | $426,781 47 |

## DISBURSEMENTS.

| | |
|---|---|
| Death claims | $13,739 30 |
| Sick and accident claims | 8,960 00 |
| Total benefits paid | $22,699 30 |
| Salaries of officers and trustees | 5,787 50 |
| Salaries of office employees | 3,798 33 |
| Salaries and fees paid to supreme medical examiners | 320 00 |
| Traveling and other expenses of officers, trustees and committees | 150 22 |
| Insurance department fees | 708 34 |
| Rent | 1,625 00 |
| Advertising, printing and stationery | 65 25 |
| Postage, express, telegraph and telephone | 219 99 |
| Lodge supplies | 565 19 |
| Official publication | 1,665 53 |
| Expenses of supreme lodge meeting | 10,955 79 |
| Legal expense in litigating claims | 25 00 |
| Furniture and fixtures | 170 75 |
| Borrowed money repaid (gross) | 24,000 00 |
| Interest on borrowed money | 96 25 |
| Office expenses | 694 30 |
| Surety bond premiums | 121 40 |
| Sundry supplies | 62 90 |
| Total disbursements | $73,731 04 |
| Balance | $353,050 43 |

## LEDGER ASSETS.

| | |
|---|---|
| Mortgage loans on real estate | $249,015 01 |
| Book value of bonds | 90,479 06 |
| Cash in association's office | 665 33 |
| Deposits in trust companies and banks not on interest | 168 24 |
| Deposits in trust companies and banks on interest | 12,422 79 |
| Secretary's contingent fund | 300 00 |
| Total ledger assets | $353,050 43 |

### NON-LEDGER ASSETS.

| | |
|---|---|
| Interest accrued | 5,277 75 |
| Market value of bonds and stocks over book value | 2,180 94 |
| Gross assets | $360,509 12 |

## LIABILITIES.

| | |
|---|---|
| Death claims reported during the year but not yet adjusted | $3,500 00 |
| Sick and accident claims reported during the year but not yet adjusted | 610 00 |
| Total unpaid claims | $4,110 00 |
| Salaries, rents, expenses, commissions, etc., due or accrued | 173 59 |
| Advance assessments | 882 51 |
| Total | $5,166 10 |

## EXHIBIT OF CERTIFICATES.

| | Total business of the year. | | Business in Illinois during year. | |
|---|---|---|---|---|
| | Number. | Amount. | Number. | Amount. |
| Benefit certificates in force December 31, 1920, as per last statement | 4,807 | $3,855,750 00 | 426 | $368,500 00 |
| Benefit certificates written and renewed during the year | 374 | 360,500 00 | 36 | 41,750 00 |
| Benefit certificates received by transfer during the year | | | 13 | 11,500 00 |
| Benefit certificates increased during the year | | 20,500 00 | | 1,500 00 |
| Totals | 5,181 | $4,236,750 00 | 475 | $423,250 00 |
| Deduct terminated, decreased or transferred during the year | 230 | 207,000 00 | | |
| Deduct terminated or decreased during the year | | | 26 | 23,250 00 |
| Total benefit certificates in force December 31, 1921 | 4,951 | $4,029,750 00 | 449 | $400,000 00 |

Received during the year from members in Illinois: Mortuary, $6,690.50; all other, $1,332.90; expense, $1,963.76; total ..... $9,987 16

## EXHIBIT OF DEATH CLAIMS.

| | Total claims. Number. | Amount. | Illinois claims. Number. | Amount. |
|---|---|---|---|---|
| Claims unpaid December 31, 1920, as per last statement | 1 | $ 1,000 00 | | |
| Claims reported during the year and interest addition | 27 | 21,250 00 | 5 | $5,500 00 |
| Totals | 28 | $22,250 00 | 5 | $5,500 00 |
| Claims paid during the year | 22 | 13,739 30 | 5 | 5,000 00 |
| Balance | 6 | $8,510 70 | | $500 00 |
| Saved by compromising or scaling down claims during the year | | 2,510 70 | | 500 00 |
| Claims rejected during the year | 2 | 2,500 00 | | |
| Claims unpaid December 31, 1921 | 4 | $3,500 00 | | |

## EXHIBIT OF SICK AND ACCIDENT CLAIMS.

| | Total claims. Number. | Amount. | Illinois claims. Number. | Amount. |
|---|---|---|---|---|
| Claims unpaid December 31, 1920, as per last statement | 17 | $ 450 00 | 2 | $20 00 |
| Increase in estimated liability | 56 | 1,565 00 | 3 | 95 00 |
| Claims reported during the year | 315 | 7,555 00 | 25 | 650 00 |
| Totals | 388 | $9,570 00 | 30 | $765 00 |
| Claims paid during the year | 366 | 8,960 00 | 27 | 730 00 |
| Claims unpaid December 31, 1921 | 22 | $610 00 | 3 | $35 00 |

## SCHEDULE D—BONDS.

| Description. | Book value. | Par value. | Market value. |
|---|---|---|---|
| U. S. First Liberty Loan, 4¼s | $ 5,100 00 | $ 5,100 00 | $ 5,100 00 |
| U. S. Second Liberty Loan, 4¼s | 100 00 | 100 00 | 100 00 |
| U. S. Third Liberty Loan, 4¼s | 5,000 00 | 5,000 00 | 5,000 00 |
| U. S. Third Liberty Loan, 4¼s | 13,537 92 | 10,000 00 | 9,800 00 |
| U. S. Third Liberty Loan, 4¼s | | 5,000 00 | 5,000 00 |
| U. S. Fourth Liberty Loan, 4¼s | 10,000 00 | 10,000 00 | 10,000 00 |
| U. S. Fourth Liberty Loan, 4¼s | 5,000 00 | 5,000 00 | 5,000 00 |
| U. S. Fourth Liberty Loan, 4¼s | 3,458 45 | 4,000 00 | 3,880 00 |
| U. S. Victory Loan, 4¾s | 5,000 00 | 5,000 00 | 5,000 00 |
| Dominion of Canada, Victory Loan, 5½s | | 5,000 00 | 4,950 00 |
| Dominion of Canada, Victory Loan, 5½s | (9,802 09) | 5,000 00 | 4,950 00 |
| Dominion of Canada, Vicotry Loan, 5½s | 495 44 | 500 00 | 500 00 |
| Province of Ontario, external, 5½s | 4,818 23 | 5,000 00 | 4,950 00 |
| Province of Ontario, debentures, 6s | 995 04 | 1,000 00 | 1,030 00 |
| Cecil Apartment Building (Chicago), 5½s | 2,000 00 | 2,000 00 | 2,000 00 |
| Fullerton Parkway Apartments, 5s | (9,671 89) | 5,000 00 | 5,000 00 |
| Fullerton Parkway Apartments, 5s | | 5,000 00 | 5,000 00 |
| Foslyn Apartment Buildings, 6s | 12,500 00 | 12,500 00 | 12,500 00 |
| Cecil Apartment Building, 5½s | 3,000 00 | 3,000 00 | 3,000 00 |
| Totals | $90,479 06 | $93,200 00 | $92,660 00 |

---

# NORTH AMERICAN UNION.

Located at No. 56 West Randolph Street, Chicago, Illinois.

HENRY J. BECKER, President. C. A. GILLESPIE, Secretary.

| | |
|---|---|
| Balance from previous year | $504,598 89 |

## INCOME.

| | |
|---|---|
| Membership fees actually received | $ 1,280 00 |
| All other assessments or premiums | 482,794 33 |
| Change of benefit certificates | 348 50 |
| Total received from members | $484,422 83 |
| Deduct payments returned to applicants and members | 126 82 |
| Net amount received from members | $484,296 01 |
| Gross interest on bonds and dividends on stocks | 23,257 55 |
| Gross interest on deposits in trust companies and banks | 1,720 99 |
| Sale of lodge supplies | 825 53 |

INCOME—Concluded.

| | | |
|---|---|---|
| Official publication | | $3,133 68 |
| Gross profit on sale or maturity of ledger assets | | 127 76 |
| Total income | | $513,361 52 |
| Sum | | $1,017,960 41 |

DISBURSEMENTS.

| | | |
|---|---|---|
| Death claims | | $310,793 66 |
| Permanent disability claims | | 5,841 62 |
| Old age benefits | | 2,525 00 |
| Total benefits paid | | $319,160 28 |
| Deputies and organizers expense | | 5,113 88 |
| Salaries of deputies and organizers | | 27,555 04 |
| Salaries of officers and trustees | | 4,025 00 |
| Salaries and other compensation of committees | | 1,072 64 |
| Salaries of office employees | | 19,984 32 |
| Other compensation of office employees, extra help | | 42 64 |
| Salaries and fees paid to supreme medical examiners | | 1,148 00 |
| Salaries and fees paid to subordinate medical examiners | | 2,509 00 |
| Traveling and other expenses of officers, trustees and committees | | 1,219 48 |
| Insurance department fees | | 330 55 |
| Rent | | 3,786 00 |
| Advertising, printing and stationery | | 2,766 58 |
| Postage, express, telegraph and telephone | | 2,478 39 |
| Official publication | | 4,800 94 |
| Legal expense in litigating claims | | 4,607 74 |
| Claim investigations | | 695 43 |
| Organization expense | | 5,113 88 |
| Gross loss on sale or maturity of ledger assets | | 80 56 |
| Office expense | | 2,057 78 |
| Bank exchanges | | 34 09 |
| Officers surety bonds | | 615 43 |
| Actuarial expense | | 1,300 00 |
| Branch office expense | | 781 26 |
| Prize account | | 376 92 |
| Miscellaneous expense | | 20 00 |
| Total disbursements | | $406,561 95 |
| Balance | | $611,398 46 |

LEDGER ASSETS.

| | | |
|---|---|---|
| Book value of bonds and stocks | | 552,363 94 |
| Cash in association's office | | 93 35 |
| Deposits in trust companies and banks on interest | | 48,941 17 |
| Loan to local council | | 200 00 |
| United States Fidelity and Guarantee Co. | | 8,800 00 |
| Union Trust Co., Baltimore | | 1,000 00 |
| Total ledger assets | | $611,398 46 |

NON-LEDGER ASSETS.

| | | |
|---|---|---|
| Interest and rents due and accrued | | 10,346 37 |
| Assessments actually collected by subordinate lodges not yet turned over to supreme lodge | | 40,000 00 |
| All other assets, viz— | | |
| December remittance deposited in Baltimore | $1,729 37 | |
| Furniture and fixtures | 7,000 00 | |
| | | 8,792 37 |
| Gross assets | | $670,537 20 |

DEDUCT ASSETS NOT ADMITTED.

| | | |
|---|---|---|
| Book value of bonds and stocks over market value | $10,700 28 | |
| Furniture and fixtures | 7,000 00 | |
| | | 17,700 28 |
| Total admitted assets | | $652,836 92 |

LIABILITIES.

| | | |
|---|---|---|
| Death claims due and unpaid | $3,500 00 | |
| Death claims resisted | 12,000 00 | |
| Death claims reported during the year but not yet adjusted | 29,000 00 | |
| Death claims incurred in 1921, not reported until 1922 | 1,500 00 | |
| Present value of deferred death claims payable in installments | 11,647 00 | |
| Total death claims | | $57,647 00 |
| Old age and other benefits due and unpaid | | 6,850 00 |
| Total unpaid claims | | $64,497 00 |

LIABILITIES—Concluded.

| | | |
|---|---|---|
| All other liabilities, viz— | | |
| Trust fund certificates | $75,500 00 | |
| Reserved for unknown contingencies | 5,000 00 | |
| | | 80,500 00 |
| Total | | $144,997 00 |

EXHIBIT OF CERTIFICATES.

| | Total business of the year. Number. | Amount. | Business in Illinois during year. Number. | Amount. |
|---|---|---|---|---|
| Benefit certificates in force December 31, 1920, as per last statement | 17,828 | $18,196,000 00 | 11,293 | $12,175,550 79 |
| Benefit certificates written and renewed during the year | 1,336 | 1,176,000 00 | 843 | 720,750 00 |
| Benefit certificates increased during the year | | 29,250 00 | | 29,250 00 |
| Totals | 19,164 | $19,401,250 00 | 12,136 | $12,925,550 79 |
| Deduct terminated, decreased or transferred during the year | 3,344 | 2,707,386 00 | | |
| Deduct terminated or decreased during the year | | | 2,155 | 2,386,267 75 |
| Total benefit certificates in force December 31, 1921 | 15,820 | $16,693,864 00 | 9,981 | $10,539,283 04 |

Received during the year from members in Illinois: Mortuary, $311,483.45; expense, $56,994.50; total ........ $370,225 27

EXHIBIT OF DEATH CLAIMS.

| | Total claims. Number. | Amount. | Illinois claims. Number. | Amount. |
|---|---|---|---|---|
| Claims unpaid December 31, 1920, as per last statement | 72 | $ 75,086 39 | 59 | $ 62,826 39 |
| Claims reported during the year and interest addition | 269 | 310,220 40 | 174 | 232,039 14 |
| Totals | 341 | $385,306 79 | 233 | $294,865 53 |
| Claims paid during the year | 276 | 310,793 66 | 187 | 243,430 46 |
| Balance | 65 | $74,513 13 | 46 | $51,435 07 |
| Saved by compromising or scaling down claims during the year | | 16,866 13 | | 13,288 07 |
| Claims unpaid December 31, 1921 | 65 | $57,647 00 | 46 | $38,147 00 |

EXHIBIT OF PERMANENT DISABILITY CLAIMS.

| | Total claims—all in Illinois. Number. | Amount. |
|---|---|---|
| Claims paid during the year | 11 | $5,841 62 |

EXHIBIT OF OLD AGE AND OTHER CLAIMS.

| | Total claims—all in Illinois. Number. | Amount. |
|---|---|---|
| Claims unpaid December 31, 1920, as per last statement | 12 | $6,102 13 |
| Claims reported during the year and interest addition | 2 | 4,000 00 |
| Total | 14 | $10,102 13 |
| Claims paid during the year | 5 | 2,525 00 |
| Balance | 9 | $7,577 13 |
| Saved by compromising or scaling down claims during the year | | 727 13 |
| Claims unpaid December 31, 1921 | 9 | $6,850 00 |

SCHEDULE D—BONDS.

| Description. | Book value. | Par value. | Market value. |
|---|---|---|---|
| Union Electric Ry. Co., 5s | $ 9,000 00 | $ 9,000 00 | $ 4,940 00 |
| City of Escanaba, Mich., city hall, 4½s | 25,000 00 | 25,000 00 | 24,500 00 |
| Metro. W. S. Electric Ry. Co., 4s | 25,000 00 | 25,000 00 | 11,500 00 |
| Grand Haven, Mich., school board, 4s | 2,000 00 | | 1,840 00 |
| Grand Haven, Mich., school board, 4s | 3,000 00 | | 2,670 00 |
| Grand Haven, Mich., school board, 4s | 2,000 00 | 7,000 00 | 1,780 00 |
| Henry, Ill., water works, 4s | 1,000 00 | 1,000 00 | 1,000 00 |
| Centralia, Ill., Twp. high schoool dist., 4½s | 3,000 00 | | 3 000 00 |
| Centralia, Ill., Twp. high school dist., 4½s | 2,000 00 | 5,000 00 | 1,980 00 |
| Henry, Ill., School Dist. No. 51, 5s | 6,500 00 | | |
| Henry, Ill., School Dist. No. 51, 5s | 6,500 00 | 13,000 00 | 13,000 00 |
| Fayette Co., Fairchance, Pa., 4½s | 4,000 00 | 4,000 00 | 3,960 00 |
| Wyandotte, Mich., sewer, 4½s | 13,000 00 | 13,000 00 | 12,870 00 |
| Herrington, Kans., 5s | 2,000 00 | 2,000 00 | 2,000 00 |

SCHEDULE D—BONDS—Continued.

| Description. | Book value. | Par value. | Market value. |
|---|---|---|---|
| Norway Dickinson Co., Mich., school board, 4½s | $ 6,000 00 | $ 6,000 00 | $ 6,000 00 |
| Wakefield, Gobebic Co., Mich., School Board No. 26, 5s. | 4,000 00 | 4,000 00 | 4,000 00 |
| Lawrenceville, Ill., School Dist. No. 14, 5½s | 3,000 00 | 3,000 00 | 3,030 00 |
| Industry McDonough Co., Ill., high school, 5s | 3,000 00 | 3,000 00 | 3,000 00 |
| Richmond, McHenry Co., Ill., School Dist. No. 29, 5s | 9,000 00 | 9,000 00 | 9,090 00 |
| Shermerville, Cook Co., Ill., School Dist. No. 28, 5s | 500 00 | | 500 00 |
| Shermerville, Cook Co., Ill., School Dist. No. 28, 5s | 1,500 00 | 2,000 00 | 1,515 00 |
| Cook Co., Ill., School Dist. No. 89, refunding, 5s | 500 00 | | 510 00 |
| Cook Co., Ill., School Dist. No. 89, refunding, 5s | 4,500 00 | 5,000 00 | 4,680 00 |
| Cook Co., Ill., School Dist. No. 157, refunding, 5s | 250 00 | 250 00 | 250 00 |
| Roseau Co., Minn., School Dist. No. 12, 6s | 12,000 00 | 12,000 00 | 12,360 00 |
| Livermore Humboldt Co., Iowa, Indpt. school dist., 5s. | 3,000 00 | 3,000 00 | 2,970 00 |
| Superior Twp., Dickinson Co., Iowa, school board, 5s | 7,000 00 | 7,000 00 | 7,070 00 |
| Keewatin, Minn., water works improvement board, 5s | 2,000 00 | 2,000 00 | 2,000 00 |
| Baltrami Co., Minn., School Dist. No. 4, 5s | 4,200 00 | 4,200 00 | 4,200 00 |
| Westfield, Ill., water works, 5s | 2,000 00 | 2,000 00 | 2,000 00 |
| Bethany, Ill., electric light, 5s | 1,000 00 | | |
| Bethany, Ill., electric light, 5s | 500 00 | 1,500 00 | 1,500 00 |
| Viola, Ill., water works, 6s | 1,000 00 | 1,000 00 | 1,000 00 |
| Scott Co., Ill., School Dist. No. 35, 5s | 1,750 00 | 1,750 00 | 1,750 00 |
| Pekin, Ill., street railway, 4½s | 1,500 00 | 1,500 00 | 1,500 00 |
| DuPage Co., Ill., School Dist. No. 2, 5s | 4,000 00 | 4,000 00 | 4,000 00 |
| DuPue, Ill., Park Board No. 6, 5s | 5,625 00 | 5,625 00 | 5,625 00 |
| Christian Co., Ill., School Dist. No. 182, 5s | 4,000 00 | 4,000 00 | 4,000 00 |
| Potomac Twp., Vermilion Co., Ill., High School No. 229, 6s | 8,000 00 | 8,000 00 | 8,000 00 |
| Valley Junction, Iowa, refunding, 6s | 3,000 00 | 3,000 00 | 3,000 00 |
| Valley Junction, Iowa., refunding, 6s | 2,000 00 | 2,000 00 | 2,000 00 |
| Valley Junction, Iowa, refunding, 6s | 2,000 00 | 2,000 00 | 2,000 00 |
| Phillips Twp., White Co., Ill., 5s | 5,000 00 | 5,000 00 | 5,000 00 |
| Hamilton Co., Ill., School Dist. No. 39, 4½s | 2,500 00 | 2,500 00 | 2,500 00 |
| Marshall Co., Ill., School Dist. No. 54, 5½s | 2,500 00 | 2,500 00 | 2,500 00 |
| Lake Co., Warren Twp., Ill., School Dists No. 121, 5s | 1,500 00 | 1,500 00 | 1,500 00 |
| Ironwood, Gogebic Co., Mich., 5s | 10,000 00 | 10,000 00 | 10,000 00 |
| Allison, Lawrence Co., Ill., 5s | 997 50 | 1,000 00 | 1,000 00 |
| Sandusky Co., Ohio, improvement bond, 5s | 5,000 00 | 5,000 00 | 5,000 00 |
| Clintonville, Wis., School Dist. No. 1, 5½s | 1,017 48 | | |
| Clintonville, Wis., School Dist. No. 1, 5½s | 4,100 96 | 5,000 00 | 5,000 00 |
| Hawarden, Sioux Co., Iowa, 5½s | 2,543 75 | | |
| Hawarden, Sioux Co., Iowa, 5½s | 2,062 91 | 4,500 00 | 4,500 00 |
| Staumbaugh, Iron Co., Mich., school board, 4½s | 4,836 50 | 5,000 00 | 4,950 00 |
| Beresford, Union Co., S. Dak., water works, 5s | 4,887 00 | 5,000 00 | 5,000 00 |
| Park Ridge, Ill., water works, 5½s | 1,022 30 | | |
| Park Ridge, Ill., water works, 5½s | 1,022 30 | | |
| Park Ridge, Ill., water works, 5½s | 1,022 30 | 3,000 00 | 3,000 00 |
| Summit Cook Co., Ill., electric light, 5s | 1,990 00 | 2,000 00 | 2,020 00 |
| Waukegan, Lake Co., Ill., park dist., 4½s | 864 00 | | |
| Waukegan, Lake Co., Ill., park dist., 4½s | 96 00 | | |
| Waukegan, Lake Co., Ill., park dist., 4½s | 960 00 | | |
| Waukegan, Lake Co., Ill., park dist., 4½s | 1,152 00 | | |
| Wauke an, Lake Co., Ill., park dist., 4½s | 768 00 | 4,000 00 | 3,920 00 |
| BureauCo., Ill., School Dist. No. 250, building, 5s | 2,000 00 | 2,000 00 | 2,000 00 |
| Sciotoville, Scioto Co., Ohio, school board, 5½s | 1,025 51 | | |
| Sciotoville, Scioto Co., Ohio, school board, 5½s | 1,029 97 | | |
| Sciotoville, Scioto Co., Ohio, school board, 5½s | 1,032 40 | 3,000 00 | 3,030 00 |
| Carroll, Iowa, sewage cert., 6s | 3,117 19 | 3,000 00 | 3,000 00 |
| Clinton, Iowa, main sewer, 6s | 2,045 80 | 2,000 00 | 2,000 00 |
| Clinton, Iowa, main sewer, 6s | 2,049 39 | | |
| Clinton, Iowa, main sewer, 6s | 363 19 | 2,354 44 | 2,354 44 |
| Oakland Co., Mich., highway improvement board, 6s | 2,595 50 | 2,500 00 | 2,500 00 |
| Kankakee, Ill., School Dist. No. 97, 6s | 510 65 | 500 00 | 500 00 |
| West Point, Cuming Co., Neb., school board, 6s | 1,950 00 | | |
| West Point, Cuming Co., Neb., school board, 6s | 5,850 00 | 8,000 00 | 8,000 00 |
| Johnston City, Williamson Co., Ill., School Dist. No. 13, 5½s | 2,924 60 | | |
| Johnston City, Williamson Co., Ill., School Dist. No. 13, 5½s | 945 50 | 4,000 00 | 4,000 00 |
| Monticello, Champaign & Pratt Co., Ill., Comm. High School Dist. No. 168, 5s | 4,798 75 | 5,000 00 | 5,000 00 |
| Franklin Co., Ill., School Dist. No. 48, 6s | 5,000 00 | 5,000 00 | 5,100 00 |
| Minnesota Soldiers Bonus, 5s | 1,957 36 | 2,000 00 | 2,000 00 |
| Eagle River, Vilas Co., Wis., school board, 6s | 4,016 00 | | |
| Eagle River, Vilas Co., Wis., school board, 6s | 1,004 00 | 5,000 00 | 5,000 00 |
| Independent School Dist., Clinton, Iowa, 5s | 2,939 94 | | |
| Independent School Dist., Clinton, Iowa, 5s | 1,948 74 | 5,000 00 | 5,000 00 |
| Brookfield, Ill., improvement board, Series No. 2, 5s | 1,380 00 | | |
| Brookfield, Ill., improvement board, Series No. 2, 5s | 3,220 00 | 5,000 00 | 5,000 00 |
| Pocahontas Co., Iowa, funding, 6s | 5,228 00 | 5,000 00 | 5,250 00 |
| Benton, Franklin Co., Ill., High School Dist. No. 103, 6s | 5,025 00 | 5,000 00 | 5,000 00 |
| Howard, S. Dak., Independent school dist., 7s | 2,048 47 | | |
| Howard, S. Dak., independent school dist., 7s | 1,027 50 | | |
| Howard, S. Dak., independent school dist., 7s | 2,061 12 | 5,000 00 | 5,000 00 |
| Wapella, DeWitt Co., Ill., high school dist., 6s | 1,008 40 | | |

SCHEDULE D—BONDS—Concluded.

| Description. | Book value. | Par value. | Market value. |
|---|---|---|---|
| Wapella, DeWitt Co., Ill., high school dist., 6s | $ 2,026 20 | | |
| Wapella, DeWitt Co., Ill., high school dist., 6s | 2,029 00 | $ 5,000 00 | $ 5,050 00 |
| Hillsdale, Ill., Comm., High School No. 215, 6s | 2,027 20 | | |
| Hillsdale, Ill., Comm., High School, No. 215, 6s | 3,045 00 | 5,000 00 | 5,000 00 |
| Napoleon, Henry Co., Ohio, school board, 5s | 4,602 20 | 5,000 00 | 5,000 00 |
| St. Paul, Howard Co., Neb., 6s | 5,000 00 | 5,000 00 | 5,300 00 |
| Ladd, Bureau Co., Ill., W. S., 6s | 2,000 00 | 2,000 00 | 2,000 00 |
| Homer, Champaign Co., Ill., 6s | 8,000 00 | 8,000 00 | 8,160 00 |
| Union Twp., Adair Co., Iowa, independent school dist., 5s | 4,637 35 | 5,000 00 | 5,100 00 |
| Will Co., Ill., School Dist. No. 84, 5s | 962 30 | 1,000 00 | 1,000 00 |
| West Park, Cuyahoga Co., Ohio, school dist., 6s | 5,101 00 | 5,000 00 | 5,400 00 |
| Woodford Co., Ill., School Dist. No. 122, 5s | 1,893 60 | | |
| Woodford Co., Ill., School Dist. No. 122, 5s | 934 20 | | |
| Woodford Co., Ill., School Dist. No. 122, 5s | 1,856 80 | 5,000 00 | 5,000 00 |
| Newton Falls, Trumbull Co., Ohio, school dist., 5s | 1,767 80 | | |
| Newton Falls, Trumbull Co., Ohio, school dist., 5s | 1,762 20 | | |
| Newton Falls, Trumbull Co., Ohio, school dist., 5s | 875 10 | 5,000 00 | 5,000 00 |
| Green Bay, Wis., water works, 6s | 4,987 50 | 5,000 00 | 5,200 00 |
| City of Chicago, sewer funding, 4s | 1,815 00 | 2,000 00 | 1,960 00 |
| Sanitary Dist. of Chicago, 4s | 1,792 00 | 2,000 00 | 1,960 00 |
| Sanitary Dist. of Chicago, Series No. 27, 4s | 883 50 | 1,000 00 | 980 00 |
| Chicago Bathing Beach, 4s | 469 25 | 500 00 | 490 00 |
| Jamesport, Daviess Co., Mo., 6s | 4,861 00 | 5,000 00 | 5,000 00 |
| Dallas City, Ill., water works, 6s | 6,000 00 | 6,000 00 | 6,000 00 |
| Henderson Co., Tenn., refunding, 6s | 2,935 20 | | |
| Henderson Co., Tenn., refunding, 6s | 1,953 60 | 5,000 00 | 5,000 00 |
| County of St. Joseph, Ind., Road No. X, 6s | 3,000 00 | | |
| County of St. Joseph, Ind., Road No. X, 6s | 2,000 00 | 5,000 00 | 5,000 00 |
| Elmhurst, DuPage Co., Ill., park, 5s | 2,832 00 | | |
| Elmhurst, DuPage Co., Ill., park, 5s | 1,852 20 | 5,000 00 | 5,000 00 |
| County of Pulaski, Ark., funding warrent, 7s | 4,663 75 | 5,000 00 | 5,000 00 |
| Watertown, S. Dak., electric light, 5s | 4,404 50 | 5,000 00 | 5,000 00 |
| Govt. of Phillipines, certificate of indebtedness, 4s | 4,901 88 | 5,000 00 | 5,000 00 |
| Billings, Yellowstone Co., Mont., School Dist. No. 2, Series B, 6s | 5,000 00 | 5,000 00 | 5,300 00 |
| Knignt, Iron Co., Wis., School Board, No. 2, 6s | 1,000 00 | | |
| Knight, Iron Co., Wis., School Board, No. 2, 6s | 4,000 00 | 5,000 00 | 5,100 00 |
| Linn Co., Iowa, funding, 5s | 4,905 03 | 5,000 00 | 5,000 00 |
| St. Louis Co., Minn., School Dist. No. 35, 6½s | 4,987 50 | 5,000 00 | 5,500 00 |
| Watertown, Codington Co., S. Dak., school board, 6s | 4,929 00 | 5,000 00 | 5,100 00 |
| Cumberland Co., N. C., roads and bridges, 6s | 4,892 82 | 5,000 00 | 5,000 00 |
| Maple Heights, Cuyahoga Co., Ohio, 6s | 4,908 00 | 5,000 00 | 5,050 00 |
| Garden Co., Neb., court house, 6s | 4,987 50 | 5,000 00 | 5,150 00 |
| Aurora, St. Louis Co., Minn., Indpt. School Dist. No. 13, 7s | 8,048 10 | 8,000 00 | 8,160 00 |
| State of New Mexico, highway debentures, 6s | 4,975 00 | 5,000 00 | 5,000 00 |
| Seattle, Wash., light and power plant, 5s | 2,918 74 | 3,000 00 | 3,000 00 |
| Blue Island, Ill., high school dist., Series A, 4½s | 992 72 | 1,000 00 | 1,000 00 |
| Kenosha, Wis., New Bain, school board, 5s | 964 90 | 1,000 00 | 1,000 00 |
| Malden, Mass., sewerage loan, 4s | 990 29 | 1,000 00 | 1,000 00 |
| Cook Co., Ill., Irving Park Dist., 4½s | 951 31 | 1,000 00 | 1,000 00 |
| Pennington Co., Minn., drainage ditch, 5½s | 994 00 | 1,000 00 | 1,000 00 |
| McDonald, Trumbull Co., Ohio, fire dept., 6s | 3,000 00 | | |
| McDonald, Trumbull Co., Ohio, fire dept., 6s | 2,000 00 | 5,000 00 | 5,100 00 |
| Grainger Co., Tenn., Road B, 6s | 4,987 50 | 5,000 00 | 5,100 00 |
| Municipality of Arecibo, Porto Rico, 5½s | 10,000 00 | 10,000 00 | 10,000 00 |
| City of Broken Bow, Neb., paving, 6s | 5,000 00 | 5,000 00 | 5,000 00 |
| Wellsburg, Iowa, 5s | 2,000 00 | 2,000 00 | 2,000 00 |
| Third Liberty Loan, 4¼s | 4,433 00 | 5,000 00 | |
| Third Liberty Loan, 4¼s | 4,411 00 | 5,000 00 | |
| Third Liberty Loan, 4¼s | 4,536 13 | 5,000 00 | |
| Third Liberty Loan, 4¼s | 4,411 12 | 5,000 00 | 17,791 25 |
| First LibertyyLoan, 4¼s | 10,500 00 | 10,500 00 | |
| Second Liberty Loan, 4¼s | 9,250 00 | 9,250 00 | |
| Third LibertyyLoan, 4¼s | 2,506 75 | 2,600 00 | |
| Fourth Liberty Loan, 4¼s | 241 22 | 250 00 | 22,497 97 |
| Totals | $552,363 94 | $559,279 44 | $541,663 66 |

## NORTH STAR BENEFIT ASSOCIATION.

Located at No. 509-511 Fifteenth Street, Moline, Illinois.

A. T. LARSON, President. JOHN A. SWANSON, Secretary.

| | |
|---|---|
| Balance from previous year | $351,124 56 |

## INCOME.

| | |
|---|---|
| All other assessments or premiums | $73,548 46 |
| Dues and per capita tax | 24,499 07 |
| Certificate fees | 331 25 |
| Net amount received from members | $98,378 78 |
| Gross interest on mortgage loans | 14,083 41 |
| Gross interest on bonds and dividends on stocks | 2,210 00 |
| Gross interest on deposits in trust companies and banks | 557 85 |
| Gross interest from all other sources | 1,230 00 |
| Sale of lodge supplies | 118 50 |
| Gross increase in book value of ledger assets | 2,372 06 |
| Bonding local officers | 99 75 |
| Investigating loans | 5 00 |
| Refund fire insurance premiums | 3 25 |
| Refund interest accrued on bonds to Class C | 104 13 |
| Total income | $119,162 73 |
| Sum | $470,287 29 |

## DISBURSEMENTS.

| | |
|---|---|
| Death claims | $50,885 41 |
| Old age benefits | 3,650 00 |
| Total benefits paid | $54,535 41 |
| Commissions and fees paid to deputies and organizers | 5,697 28 |
| Salaries of officers and trustees | 7,035 00 |
| Salaries and other compensation of committees | 358 17 |
| Salaries of office employees | 1,943 53 |
| Chief office expense | 346 88 |
| Salaries and fees paid to supreme medical examiners | 900 00 |
| Traveling and other expenses of officers, trustees and committees | 1,961 69 |
| Insurance department fees | 42 00 |
| Rent | 840 00 |
| Advertising, printing and stationery | 467 83 |
| Postage, express, telegraph and telephone | 434 21 |
| Official publication and editor | 1,666 16 |
| Other legal expenses | 1,500 00 |
| Furniture and fixtures | 105 55 |
| Taxes, repairs and other expenses on real estate | 16 34 |
| Interest refund to Class C | 104 13 |
| All other disbursements, viz: Bonding local officers, actuarial service, fire insurance premium, Iowa Fraternal Congress, refund to recorders and members | 476 78 |
| Total disbursements | $78,430 96 |
| Balance | $391,856 33 |

## LEDGER ASSETS.

| | |
|---|---|
| Book value of real estate | $ 19,500 00 |
| Mortgage loans on real estate | 275,700 00 |
| Book value of bonds and stocks | 47,042 50 |
| Cash in association's office | 1,000 00 |
| Deposits in trust companies and banks on interest | 48,613 83 |
| Total ledger assets | $391,856 33 |

### NON-LEDGER ASSETS.

| | |
|---|---|
| Interest and rents due and accrued | 10,035 35 |
| Assessments actually collected by subordinate lodges not yet turned over to supreme lodge | 6,090 75 |
| Office furniture and supplies | 1,400 00 |
| Gross assets | $409,382 43 |

### DEDUCT ASSETS NOT ADMITTED.

| | |
|---|---|
| Office furniture and supplies | 1,400 00 |
| Total admitted assets | $407,982 43 |

## LIABILITIES.

| | | |
|---|---|---|
| Death claims reported during the year but not yet adjusted | | $8,473 16 |
| Salaries, rents, expenses, commissions, etc., due or accrued | | 1,409 29 |
| All other liabilities, viz— | | |
| Present value of outstanding certificates N. F. C. | $68,251 34 | |
| Present value of juvenile certificates | 2,581 96 | |
| | | 70,833 30 |
| Total | | $80,715 75 |

## EXHIBIT OF CERTIFICATES.

| | Total business of the year. Number. | Amount. | Business in Illinois during year. Number. | Amount. |
|---|---|---|---|---|
| Benefit certificates in force December 31, 1920, as per last statement | 7,478 | $7,053,450 00 | 5,128 | $4,878,500 00 |
| Benefit certificates written and renewed during the year | 330 | 259,500 00 | 250 | 193,500 00 |
| Benefit certificates received by transfer during the year | | | 43 | 40,000 00 |
| Benefit certificates increased during the year | | 4,000 00 | | 4,000 00 |
| Totals | 7,808 | $7,316,950 00 | 5,421 | $5,116,000 00 |
| Deduct terminated, decreased or transferred during the year | 623 | 577,100 00 | | |
| Deduct terminated or decreased during the year | | | 442 | 432,900 00 |
| Total benefit certificates in force December 31, 1921 | 7,185 | $6,739,850 00 | 4,979 | $4,683,100 00 |

Received during the year from members in Illinois: Mortuary, $53,292.55; expense, $17,517.83; total $70,810 38

## EXHIBIT OF DEATH CLAIMS.

| | Total claims. Number. | Amount. | Illinois claims. Number. | Amount. |
|---|---|---|---|---|
| Claims unpaid December 31, 1920, as per last statement | 5 | $ 6,066 98 | 4 | $ 5,051 93 |
| Claims reported during the year and interest addition | 54 | 52,681 59 | 41 | 41,846 23 |
| Total | 59 | $58,748 57 | 45 | $46,898 16 |
| Claims paid during the year | 53 | 50,275 41 | 40 | 38,825 00 |
| Claims unpaid December 31, 1921 | 6 | $8,473 16 | 5 | $8,073 16 |

## EXHIBIT OF OLD AGE AND OTHER CLAIMS.

| | Total claims. Number. | Amount. | Illinois claims. Number. | Amount. |
|---|---|---|---|---|
| Claims reported during the year and interest addition | 32 | $3,650 00 | 27 | $3,050 00 |
| Claims paid during the year | 32 | 3,650 00 | 27 | 3,050 00 |

## SCHEDULE D—BONDS.

| Description. | Book value. | Par value. |
|---|---|---|
| Fourth U. S. Liberty bonds | $ 2,000 00 | $ 2,000 00 |
| Third U. S. Liberty bonds | 37,835 70 | 42,000 00 |
| Third U. S. Liberty bonds | 7,206 80 | 8,000 00 |
| Total | $47,042 50 | $52,000 00 |

---

# ORDER DER HERMANN SCHWESTERN.

Located at No. 2502 Ballou Street, Chicago, Illinois.

MINNA MEFFERT, President. LINDA SCHMIDT, Secretary.

Balance from previous year $58,728 91

## INCOME.

| | |
|---|---|
| Assessments or premiums during first twelve months of membership | $10,132 20 |
| All other assessments or premiums | 671 85 |
| Dues and per capita tax | 1,349 70 |
| Other payments by members, viz: Certificates | 284 00 |
| Net amount received from members | $12,437 75 |
| Gross interest on mortgage loans | 3,472 07 |
| Gross interest on deposits in trust companies and banks | 211 02 |
| Sale of lodge supplies | 325 78 |
| Refund on installation | 175 35 |
| Refund of rent advanced | 155 00 |
| Deputy fees | 140 00 |
| Total income | $16,916 97 |
| Sum | $75,645 88 |

DISBURSEMENTS.

| | |
|---|---|
| Death claims | $7,800 00 |
| Salaries of deputies and organizers | 277 50 |
| Salaries of officers and trustees | 1,154 20 |
| Other compensation of officers and trustees | 230 85 |
| Insurance department fees | 40 65 |
| Advertising, printing and stationery | 95 00 |
| Postage, express, telegraph and telephone | 71 99 |
| Lodge supplies | 144 85 |
| Expenses of supreme lodge meeting | 49 00 |
| Miscellaneous | 32 65 |
| Advance for rent | 155 00 |
| All other disbursements, viz— | |
| Safety deposit vault | 5 00 |
| Entertainment | 78 65 |
| Insurance premium | 4 88 |
| Surety bonds | 13 00 |
| Total disbursements | $10,153 22 |
| Balance | $65,492 66 |

LEDGER ASSETS.

| | |
|---|---|
| Mortgage loans on real estate | 63,200 00 |
| Book value of bonds and stocks | 1,000 00 |
| Deposits in trust companies and banks not on interest | 1,292 66 |
| Total ledger assets | $65,492 66 |

LIABILITIES.

| | |
|---|---|
| Death claims due and unpaid | $1,133 33 |

EXHIBIT OF CERTIFICATES.

| | Total business of the year—all in Illinois. Number. | Amount. |
|---|---|---|
| Benefit certificates in force December 31, 1920, as per last statement | 4,371 | $874,200 00 |
| Benefit certificates written and renewed during the year | 454 | 90,800 00 |
| Totals | 4,825 | $965,000 00 |
| Deduct terminated or decreased during the year | 270 | 54,000 00 |
| Total benefit certificates in force December 31, 1921 | 4,555 | $911,000 00 |

Received during the year from members in Illinois: Mortuary, $10,132.20; reserve, $671.85; expense, $1,633.70; total $12,437 75

EXHIBIT OF DEATH CLAIMS.

| | Total claims—all in Illinois. Number. | Amount. |
|---|---|---|
| Claims unpaid December 31, 1920, as per last statement | 7 | $1,133 33 |
| Claims reported during the year and interest addition | 42 | 8,400 00 |
| Totals | 49 | $9,533 33 |
| Claims paid during the year | 39 | 7,800 00 |
| Balance | 10 | $1,733 33 |
| Saved by compromising or scaling down claims during the year, dropped | 3 | 600 00 |
| Claims unpaid December 31, 1921 | 7 | $1,133 33 |

SCHEDULE D—BONDS.

| Description. | Book value. |
|---|---|
| U. S. Third Liberty Loan, 4¼s | $1,000 00 |

## ORDER OF MUTUAL PROTECTION, SUPREME LODGE.

Located at No. 159 North State Street, Chicago, Illinois.

SEB J. MUELLER, Jr., President. G. DEL VECCHIA, Secretary.

| | |
|---|---|
| Balance from previous year | $607,693 22 |

INCOME.

| | |
|---|---|
| Assessments or premiums during first 12 months of membership of which all or an extra percentage is used for expenses | $ 3,732 97 |
| All other assessments or premiums | 75,782 37 |
| Dues and per capita tax | 10,761 00 |
| Net amount received from members | $90,276 34 |

## INCOME—Concluded.

| | |
|---|---|
| Gross interest on mortgage loans | $35,845 65 |
| Gross interest on bonds and dividends on stocks | 212 50 |
| Gross interest on deposits in trust companies and banks | 140 64 |
| Sale of lodge supplies | 1,143 40 |
| Total income | $127,618 53 |
| Sum | $735,311 75 |

## DISBURSEMENTS.

| | |
|---|---|
| Death claims | $69,548 48 |
| Permanent disability claims | 925 00 |
| Total benefits paid | $70,473 48 |
| Commissions and fees paid to deputies and organizers | 721 03 |
| Salaries of officers and trustees | 4,625 00 |
| Other compensation of officers and trustees | 170 70 |
| Salaries of office employees | 4,680 00 |
| Salaries and fees paid to supreme medical examiners | 187 36 |
| Traveling and other expenses of officers, trustees and committees | 50 40 |
| Insurance department fees | 206 76 |
| Rent | 1,887 47 |
| Advertising, printing and stationery | 896 39 |
| Postage, express, telegraph and telephone | 310 93 |
| Lodge supplies | 1,036 72 |
| Official publication | 1,592 79 |
| Other legal expenses | 350 60 |
| Furniture and fixtures | 74 90 |
| All other disbursements, viz: Actuarial expense, $462.75; fidelity bonds, $65.50; dues Fraternal Congress, $65.00; safe deposit boxes, $20.00; propagation expense, $15.50; miscellaneous, $106.52 | 735 27 |
| Total disbursements | $87,999 80 |
| Balance | $647,311 95 |

## LEDGER ASSETS.

| | |
|---|---|
| Mortgage loans on real estate | $639,500 00 |
| Book value of bonds and stocks | 5,000 00 |
| Deposits in trust companies and banks not on interest | 677 85 |
| Deposits in trust companies and banks on interest | 2,134 10 |
| Total ledger assets | $647,311 95 |

### NON-LEDGER ASSETS.

| | |
|---|---|
| Interest and rents due and accrued | 8,813 57 |
| Assessments actually collected by subordinate lodges not yet turned over to supreme lodge | 5,927 76 |
| Gross assets | $662,053 28 |

## LIABILITIES.

| | | |
|---|---|---|
| Death claims reported during the year but not yet adjusted | $11,527 33 | |
| Held for 2 beneficiaries | 219 02 | |
| Total death claims unpaid | | $11,746 35 |

## EXHIBIT OF CERTIFICATES.

| | Total business of the year. | | Business in Illinois during year. | |
|---|---|---|---|---|
| | Number. | Amount. | Number. | Amount. |
| Benefit certificates in force December 31, 1920, as per last statement | 5,797 | $3,864,940 00 | 3,700 | $2,572,551 00 |
| Benefit certificates written and renewed during the year | 361 | 249,000 00 | 303 | 216,250 00 |
| Benefit certificates increased during the year | | 3,250 00 | | 1,500 00 |
| Total | 6,158 | $4,117,190 00 | 4,003 | $2,790,301 00 |
| Deduct terminated, decreased or transferred during the year | 356 | 210,744 00 | | |
| Deduct terminated or decreased during the year | | | 217 | 139,750 00 |
| Total benefit certificates in force December 31, 1921 | 5,802 | $3,906,446 00 | 3,786 | $2,650,551 00 |

| | |
|---|---|
| Received during the year from members in Illinois: Mortuary, $46,694.75; expense, $12,426.87; total | $59,121 62 |

EXHIBIT OF DEATH CLAIMS.

| | Total claims. Number. | Total claims. Amount. | Illinois claims. Number. | Illinois claims. Amount. |
|---|---|---|---|---|
| Claims unpaid December 31, 1920, as per last statement | 16 | $13,442 07 | 7 | $6,473 05 |
| Claims reported during the year and interest addition | 93 | 70,938 32 | 63 | 52,625 23 |
| Total | 109 | $84,380 39 | 70 | $59,098 28 |
| Claims paid during the year | 90 | 69,548 48 | 60 | 49,167 93 |
| Balance | 19 | $14,831 91 | 10 | $9,930 35 |
| Saved by compromising or scaling down claims during the year | -------- | 1,585 56 | -------- | 1,187 27 |
| Claims rejected during the year | *4 | 1,500 00 | *1 | 250 00 |
| Claims unpaid December 31, 1921 | 15 | $11,746 35 | 9 | $8,493 08 |

EXHIBIT OF PERMANENT DISABILITY CLAIMS.

| | Total claims. Number. | Total claims. Amount. | Illinois claims. Number. | Illinois claims. Amount. |
|---|---|---|---|---|
| Claims reported during the year and interest addition | 8 | 925 00 | 2 | $100 00 |
| Claims paid during the year | 8 | 925 00 | 2 | 100 00 |

SCHEDULE D—BONDS.

| Description. | Book value. | Par value. | Market value. |
|---|---|---|---|
| U. S. 3rd Liberty Loan, 4¼s | $5,000 00 | $5,000 00 | $5,000 00 |

---

## ORDER SONS OF ST. GEORGE, GRAND LODGE OF THE STATE OF ILLINOIS.

Located at No. 4638 Cottage Grove Avenue, Chicago, Illinois.

JOHN CHORLEY, President. CHAS. C. MEURISSE, Secretary.

| | |
|---|---|
| Balance from previous year | $76,737 32 |
| **INCOME.** | |
| Membership fees actually received | $ 87 50 |
| All other assessments or premiums | 28,185 36 |
| Dues and per capita tax | 4,635 00 |
| Medical examiners' fees actually received | 36 00 |
| Other payments by members, viz: Certificate fees | 71 00 |
| Net amount received from members | $33,014 86 |
| Gross interest on bonds and dividends on stocks less $161.98 | 2,862 02 |
| Gross interest on deposits in trust companies and banks | 242 49 |
| Sale of lodge supplies | 174 59 |
| Premium surety bonds | 37 85 |
| Ads in publications, etc | 117 10 |
| Total income | $36,448 91 |
| Sum | $113,186 23 |
| **DISBURSEMENTS.** | |
| Death claims | $17,500 00 |
| Salaries of officers and trustees | 2,350 00 |
| Salaries and fees paid to grand medical examiners | 58 00 |
| Salaries and fees paid to subordinate medical examiners | 45 00 |
| Traveling and other expenses of officers, trustees and committees | 101 81 |
| Insurance department fees | 70 97 |
| Rent | 74 00 |
| Advertising, printing and stationery | 368 80 |
| Postage, express, telegraph and telephone | 115 14 |
| Lodge supplies | 249 34 |
| Official publication | 1,528 71 |
| Legal expense in litigating claims | 25 00 |
| Per capita tax supreme lodge | 798 75 |
| Surety bonds | 114 60 |
| Actuarial services | 62 00 |
| Expenses account funerals, etc | 129 50 |
| Donations | 50 00 |
| Miscellaneous | 95 21 |
| Total disbursements | $23,736 83 |
| Balance | $89,449 40 |

* No claimants appeared and claims dropped.

## LEDGER ASSETS.

| | |
|---|---|
| Book value of bonds and stocks | $78,988 58 |
| Cash in association's office | 157 03 |
| Deposits in trust companies and banks on interest | 10,303 79 |
| Total ledger assets | $89,449 40 |

### NON-LEDGER ASSETS.

| | |
|---|---|
| Interest and rents due and accrued | 1,048 30 |
| Market value of bonds and stocks over book value | 1,407 42 |
| Assessments actually collected by subordinate lodges not yet turned over to supreme lodge | 3,092 14 |
| Gross assets | $94,997 26 |

## LIABILITIES.

| | |
|---|---|
| Death claims reported during the year but not yet adjusted | $3,500 00 |

## EXHIBIT OF CERTIFICATES.

| | Total business of the year. | | Business in Illinois during year. | |
|---|---|---|---|---|
| | Number. | Amount. | Number. | Amount. |
| Benefit certificates in force December 31, 1920, as per last statement | 2,553 | $1,789,000 00 | 2,503 | $1,759,750 00 |
| Benefit certificates written and renewed during the year | 72 | 43,500 00 | 69 | 42,000 00 |
| Benefit certificates increased during the year | -------- | 1,250 00 | -------- | 1,250 00 |
| Total | 2,625 | $1,833,750 00 | 2,572 | $1,803,000 00 |
| Deduct terminated, decreased or transferred during the year | 234 | 163,750 00 | -------- | -------------- |
| **Deduct terminated or decreased during the year** | -------- | -------------- | 232 | 163,000 00 |
| Total benefit certificates in force December 31, 1921 | 2,391 | $1,670,000 00 | 2,340 | $1,640,000 00 |

| | |
|---|---|
| Received during the year from members in Illinois: Mortuary, $27,695.75; expense, $4,629.57; total | $32,325 32 |

## EXHIBIT OF DEATH CLAIMS.

| | Total claims. | | Illinois claims. | |
|---|---|---|---|---|
| | Number. | Amount. | Number. | Amount. |
| Claims unpaid December 31, 1920, as per last statement | 5 | $3,500 00 | 5 | $3,500 00 |
| Claims reported during the year and interest addition | 29 | 17,500 00 | 28 | 17,000 00 |
| Total | 34 | $21,000 00 | 33 | $20,500 00 |
| Claims paid during the year | 27 | 17,500 00 | 26 | 17,000 00 |
| Claims unpaid December 31, 1921 | 7 | $3,500 00 | 7 | $3,500 00 |

## SCHEDULE D—BONDS.

| Description. | Book value. | Par value. | Market value. |
|---|---|---|---|
| First Liberty Loan | $9,000 00 | $9,000 00 | $9,000 00 |
| Third Liberty Loan | 5,000 00 | 5,000 00 | 5,000 00 |
| Fourth Liberty Loan | 6,000 00 | 6,000 00 | 6,000 00 |
| Fourth Liberty Loan | 3,637 60 | 4,000 00 | 3,880 00 |
| Fourth Liberty Loan | 2,043 78 | 2,300 00 | 2,231 00 |
| Fourth Liberty Loan | 3,946 50 | 4,500 00 | 4,365 00 |
| Napier County, Iowa, school | 968 75 | 1,000 00 | 990 00 |
| Sanitary District | 3,000 00 | 3,000 00 | 2,940 00 |
| Sanitary District | 1,990 00 | 2,000 00 | 1,960 00 |
| Sanitary District | 1,000 00 | 1,000 00 | 980 00 |
| Sanitary District | 1,000 00 | 1,000 00 | 970 00 |
| County of Cook | 495 00 | 500 00 | 490 00 |
| West Chicago Park | 1,985 00 | 2,000 00 | 1,920 00 |
| West Chicago Park | 2,000 00 | 2,000 00 | 1,900 00 |
| Lincoln Park | 3,980 00 | 4,000 00 | 3,920 00 |
| City of Chicago | 484 45 | 500 00 | 490 00 |
| City of Chicago, sewerage | 2,000 00 | 2,000 00 | 1,960 00 |
| City of Chicago, gen. corp | 1,997 50 | 2,000 00 | 2,000 00 |
| City of Chicago, city hall | 997 50 | 1,000 00 | 990 00 |
| City of Chicago, judg. funding | 975 00 | 1,000 00 | 980 00 |
| City of Chicago, bridge | 1,000 00 | 1,000 00 | 970 00 |

SCHEDULE D—BONDS—Concluded.

| Description. | Book value. | Par value. | Market value. |
|---|---|---|---|
| City of Chicago, bathing beach | $ 500 00 | $ 500 00 | $ 480 00 |
| Edison Electric App., 1st mort | 2,940 00 | 3,000 00 | 3,000 00 |
| Michigan Ave. Trust Building, 1st mort | 3,000 00 | 3,000 00 | 2,940 00 |
| Insurance Exchange Building, 1st mort | 970 00 | 1,000 00 | 980 00 |
| Insurance Exchange Building, 1st mort | 7,840 00 | 8,000 00 | 7,840 00 |
| Swift & Co., 1st mort | 5,092 50 | 6,000 00 | 5,580 00 |
| Commonwealth Edison, 1st mort | 5,145 00 | 6,000 00 | 5,640 00 |
| Totals | $78,988 58 | $82,300 00 | $80,396 00 |

## PIKE COUNTY MUTUAL LIFE ASSOCIATION.

Located at Perry, Illinois.

H. A. DOBER, President. HARVEY SIX, Secretary.

| | |
|---|---|
| Balance from previous year | $21,674 24 |

### INCOME.

| | |
|---|---|
| All other assessments or premiums | $46,301 63 |
| Dues and per capita tax | 4,378 15 |
| Total received from members | $50,679 78 |
| Deduct payments returned to applicants and members | 11 36 |
| Total income | $50,668 42 |
| Sum | $72,342 66 |

### DISBURSEMENTS.

| | |
|---|---|
| Death claims | $50,000 00 |
| Commissions and fees paid to deputies and organizers | 916 50 |
| Salaries of officers and trustees | 1,424 70 |
| Other compensation of officers and trustees | 288 00 |
| Salaries and other compensation of committees | 110 75 |
| Traveling and other expenses of officers, trustees and committees | 190 30 |
| Insurance department fees | 5 00 |
| Rent | 60 00 |
| Advertising, printing and stationery | 298 04 |
| Postage, express, telegraph and telephone | 172 32 |
| Official publication | 575 00 |
| Expenses of supreme lodge meeting | 483 04 |
| Office expense | 28 35 |
| Surety bonds | 28 70 |
| Total disbursements | $54,580 70 |
| Balance | $17,761 96 |

### LEDGER ASSETS.

| | |
|---|---|
| Cash in association's office | $17,761 96 |
| Total admitted assets | $17,761 96 |

### EXHIBIT OF CERTIFICATES.

| | Total business of the year—all in Illinois. Number. | Amount. |
|---|---|---|
| Benefit certificates in force December 31, 1920, as per last statement | 4,191 | $6,197,000 00 |
| Benefit certificates written and renewed during the year | 269 | 446,000 00 |
| Benefit certificates increased during the year | 37 | 45,500 00 |
| Total | 4,497 | $6,688,500 00 |
| Deduct terminated, decreased or transferred during the year | 142 | 174,000 00 |
| Total benefit certificates in force December 31, 1921 | 4,355 | $6,514,500 00 |

| | |
|---|---|
| Received during the year from members in Illinois: Mortuary, $46,290.27; expense, $4,378.15; total | $50,668 42 |

### EXHIBIT OF DEATH CLAIMS.

| | Total claims—all in Illinois. Number. | Amount. |
|---|---|---|
| Claims rejected during the year | 30 | $50,000 00 |

## POLISH ALMA MATER OF THE UNITED STATES OF NORTH AMERICA.

Located at No. 1457 West Division Street, Chicago, Illinois.

ALBERT F. SOSKA, President. THOMAS S. BLACHOWSKI, Secretary.

| | |
|---|---|
| Balance from previous year | $136,664 51 |

### INCOME.

| | |
|---|---|
| Membership fees actually received | $ 20 00 |
| All other assessments or premiums | 66,785 41 |
| Medical examiners' fees actually received | 78 25 |
| Total received from members | $66,883 66 |
| Deduct payments returned to applicants and members | 1,107 52 |
| Net amount received from members | $65,776 14 |
| Gross interest on mortgage loans | 8,165 63 |
| Gross interest on deposits in trust companies and banks | 147 89 |
| Gross interest from all other sources | 140 92 |
| Gross rents from association's property | 255 00 |
| Sale of lodge supplies | 566 97 |
| Borrowed money (gross) | 10,000 00 |
| Commissions on loans | 432 00 |
| Check cancelled and redeposited | 500 00 |
| Total income | $85,984 55 |
| Sum | $222,649 06 |

### DISBURSEMENTS.

| | |
|---|---|
| Death claims | $21,400 00 |
| Commissions and fees paid to deputies and organizers | 422 50 |
| Salaries of deputies and organizers | 487 82 |
| Salaries of officers and trustees | 4,209 00 |
| Salaries of office employees | 1,740 00 |
| Salaries and fees paid to supreme medical examiners | 74 25 |
| Traveling and other expenses of officers, trustees and committees | 342 70 |
| Insurance department fees | 35 00 |
| Rent | 964 30 |
| Advertising, printing and stationery | 1,455 00 |
| Postage, express, telegraph and telephone | 279 81 |
| Lodge supplies | 1,752 37 |
| Expenses of supreme lodge meeting | 26 75 |
| Legal expense in litigating claims | 70 00 |
| Other legal expenses | 26 00 |
| Educational fund expense | 1,509 42 |
| Interest on borrowed money | 152 00 |
| All other disbursements, viz: Janitor, $127.50; notary, $2.00; autos and office insurance, $181.74; bonds of officers, $32.50; check returned, N. S. F., $77.60; valuation fee, $101.32 | 522 66 |
| Total disbursements | $35,469 58 |
| Balance | $187,179 48 |

### LEDGER ASSETS.

| | |
|---|---|
| Mortgage loans on real estate | $177,700 00 |
| Book value of bonds and stocks | 8,000 00 |
| Cash in association's office | 2 15 |
| Deposits in trust companies and banks on interest | 1,477 33 |
| Total ledger assets | $187,179 48 |

#### NON-LEDGER ASSETS.

| | |
|---|---|
| Interest and rents due and accrued | 2,560 05 |
| Assessments actually collected by subordinate lodges not yet turned over to supreme lodge | 2,247 44 |
| Gross assets | $191,986 97 |

#### DEDUCT ASSETS NOT ADMITTED.

| | |
|---|---|
| Loan from Home Bank & Trust Co. | 10,000 00 |
| Total admitted assets | $181,986 97 |

## LIABILITIES.

| | | |
|---|---|---|
| Death claims due and unpaid | $ 500 00 | |
| Death claims resisted | 375 00 | |
| Death claims reported during the year but not yet adjusted | 2,550 00 | |
| Total death claims | | $3,425 00 |
| Borrowed money | | 10,000 00 |
| All other liabilities, viz: Telephone, $7.04; advertising, $25.00; medical examinations, $11.75; janitor, $1.50; office supplies, $5.10; organizer's expense, $6.00 | | 56 39 |
| Total | | $13,481 39 |

## EXHIBIT OF CERTIFICATES.

| | Total business of the year. | | Business in Illinois during year. | |
|---|---|---|---|---|
| | Number. | Amount. | Number. | Amount. |
| Benefit certificates in force December 31, 1920, as per last statement | 6,893 | $3,675,150 00 | 5,992 | $2,937,775 00 |
| Benefit certificates written and renewed during the year | 252 | 154,300 00 | 165 | 115,600 00 |
| Total | 7,145 | $3,829,450 00 | 6,157 | $3,053,375 00 |
| Deduct terminated, decreased or transferred during the year | 550 | 285,400 00 | | |
| Deduct terminated or decreased during the year | | | 454 | 134,420 00 |
| Total benefit certificates in force December 31, 1921 | 6,595 | $3,544,050 00 | 5,703 | $2,918,950 00 |

Received during the year from members in Illinois: Mortuary, $50,113.76; expense, $10,645.29; total — $60,759 05

## EXHIBIT OF DEATH CLAIMS.

| | Total claims. | | Illinois claims. | |
|---|---|---|---|---|
| | Number. | Amount. | Number. | Amount. |
| Claims unpaid December 31, 1920, as per last statement | 4 | $ 1,750 00 | 4 | $ 1,750 00 |
| Claims reported during the year and interest addition | 44 | 22,575 00 | 43 | 22,075 00 |
| Total | 48 | $24,325 00 | 47 | $23,825 00 |
| Claims paid during the year | 40 | 20,900 00 | 39 | 20,400 00 |
| Claims unpaid December 31, 1921 | 8 | $3,425 00 | 8 | $3,425 00 |

## SCHEDULE D—BONDS.

| Description. | Book value. |
|---|---|
| U. S. First Liberty Loan | $1,100 00 |
| U. S. Second Liberty Loan | 1,000 00 |
| U. S. Third Liberty Loan | 4,500 00 |
| U. S. Fourth Liberty Loan | 500 00 |
| U. S. Victory Loan | 900 00 |
| Total | $8,000 00 |

---

# POLISH NATIONAL ALLIANCE OF THE UNITED STATES OF NORTH AMERICA.

Located at No. 1406-1408 West Division Street, Chicago, Illinois.

K. ZYCHLINSKI, President. JOHN S. ZAWILINSKI, Secretary.

| | |
|---|---|
| Balance from previous year | $5,351,695 80 |

## INCOME.

| | |
|---|---|
| Membership fees actually received | $ 2,357 25 |
| All other assessments or premiums | 1,580,375 49 |
| Other payments by members, viz: Certificates, badges, etc | 1,494 60 |
| Total received from members | $1,584,227 34 |
| Deduct payments returned to applicants and members | 59 49 |
| Net amount received from members | $1,584,167 85 |

## INCOME—Concluded.

| | |
|---|---|
| Gross interest on mortgage loans | $242,857 18 |
| Gross interest on bonds and dividends on stocks | 52,168 75 |
| Gross interest on deposits in trust companies and banks | 3,706 14 |
| Gross interest from all other sources | 482 94 |
| Gross rents from association's property, including, $1,000.00 for association's occupancy of its own buildings | 2,978 12 |
| Sale of lodge supplies | 230 12 |
| From all other sources, viz— | |
| Appraisal fees | 14,147 50 |
| Taxes advanced and refunded | 3,953 71 |
| Non-ledger assets reported December 31, 1920 as such written up on the ledger: Furniture and fixtures, $16,391.50; printing plant, $57,879.43; library, $7,000.00; books and lodges supplies, $3,802.18 | 85,073 11 |
| Advanced to subsidiary institutions | 30,105 11 |
| Total income | $2,019,870 53 |
| Sum | $7,371,566 33 |

## DISBURSEMENTS.

| | |
|---|---|
| Death claims | $764,736 53 |
| Old age benefits | 7,724 16 |
| Total benefits paid | $772,460 69 |
| Salaries of deputies and organizers | 854 06 |
| Salaries of officers and trustees | 18,650 00 |
| Salaries of office employees | 42,279 30 |
| Other compensation of office employees | 549 60 |
| Salaries and fees paid to supreme medical examiners | 958 80 |
| Traveling and other expenses of officers, trustees and committees | 4,700 03 |
| For collection and remittance of assessments and dues | 4 94 |
| Insurance department fees | 382 50 |
| Rent | 1,000 00 |
| Advertising, printing and stationery | 6,640 29 |
| Postage, express, telegraph and telephone | 4,723 93 |
| Lodge supplies | 2,697 83 |
| Official publication | 43,288 07 |
| Expenses of supreme lodge meeting | 54,568 06 |
| Legal expense in litigating claims | 385 65 |
| Other legal expenses | 1,713 29 |
| Taxes, repairs and other expenses on real estate | 5,330 56 |
| All other disbursements, viz— | |
| P. N. A. College, $76,158.00; relief department, $15,212.57; imigration home, $2,300.00 | 93,670 57 |
| For war sufferers | 64,320 19 |
| Light, heat and miscellaneous office expenses | 4,054 18 |
| Educational department, $5,101.82; donations, $1,725.65 | 6,827 47 |
| Total disbursements | $1,130,060 01 |
| Balance | $6,241,506 32 |

## LEDGER ASSETS.

| | |
|---|---|
| Book value of real estate | $ 36,500 00 |
| Mortgage loans on real estate | 4,913,825 00 |
| Book value of bonds and stocks | 984,468 08 |
| Deposits in trust companies and banks on interest | 144,840 86 |
| Other ledger assets, viz: Furniture and fixtures, $16,745.11; printing plant, $57,879.43; library, $7,000.00; advance to subsid. inst., $77,105.11; books and lodge supplies, $3,142.73 | 161,872 38 |
| Total ledger assets | $6,241,506 32 |

### NON-LEDGER ASSETS.

| | |
|---|---|
| Interest and rents due and accrued | 91,436 46 |
| Market value of real estate over book value | 600 00 |
| Gross assets | $6,333,542 78 |

### DEDUCT ASSETS NOT ADMITTED.

| | | |
|---|---|---|
| Book value of bonds and stocks over market value | $ 11,520 88 | |
| Other items, viz: Furniture and fixtures, $16,745.11; printing plant, $57,879.43; library, $7,000.00; books and lodge supplies, $3,142.73; advance to subsidiary institutions, $77,105.11 | 161,872 38 | |
| | | 173,393 26 |
| Total admitted assets | | $6,160,149 52 |

## LIABILITIES.

| | | |
|---|---|---|
| Death claims due and unpaid | $133,153 61 | |
| Death claims adjusted not yet due | 29,100 00 | |
| Death claims reported during the year but not yet adjusted | 94,000 00 | |
| Death claims incurred in 1921, not reported until 1922 | 8,400 00 | |
| Total death claims | | $264,653 61 |
| Old age and other benefits due and unpaid | | 21,586 71 |
| Total unpaid claims | | $286,240 32 |
| Salaries, rents, expenses, commissions, etc., due or accrued | | 316 50 |
| Taxes due or accrued | | 452 00 |
| Total | | $287,008 82 |

## EXHIBIT OF CERTIFICATES.

| | Total business of the year. | | Business in Illinois during year. | |
|---|---|---|---|---|
| | Number. | Amount. | Number. | Amount. |
| Benefit certificates in force December 31, 1920, as per last statement | 124,225 | $72,830,800 00 | 26,368 | $15,176,300 00 |
| Benefit certificates written and renewed during the year | 14,223 | 8,924,800 00 | 1,196 | 765,100 00 |
| Benefit certificates received by transfer during the year | -------- | -------------- | 1,221 | 733,000 00 |
| Benefit certificates increased during the year | -------- | 128,600 00 | -------- | 21,200 00 |
| Total | 138,448 | $81,884,200 00 | 28,785 | $16,695,600 00 |
| Deduct terminated, decreased or transferred during the year | 16,809 | 9,716,900 00 | -------- | -------------- |
| Deduct terminated or decreased during the year | -------- | -------------- | 3,168 | 1,787,100 00 |
| Total benefit certificates in force December 31, 1921 | 121,639 | $72,167,300 00 | 25,617 | $14,908,500 00 |

Received during the year from members in Illinois: Mortuary, $259,608.71; benevolent, $25,169.61; war sufferers, $15,731.00; expense, $27,351.94; total ........ $327,861 26

## EXHIBIT OF DEATH CLAIMS.

| | Total claims. | | Illinois claims. | |
|---|---|---|---|---|
| | Number. | Amount. | Number. | Amount. |
| Claims unpaid December 31, 1920, as per last statement | 695 | $301,307 04 | 121 | $ 50,568 20 |
| Claims reported during the year and interest addition | 1,275 | 749,100 00 | 284 | 166,300 00 |
| Total | 1,970 | $1,050,407 04 | 405 | $216,868 20 |
| Claims paid during the year | 1,358 | 764,736 53 | 296 | 164,941 23 |
| Balance | 612 | $285,670 51 | 109 | $51,926 97 |
| Saved by compromising or scaling down claims during the year | -------- | 26,416 90 | -------- | 6,468 72 |
| Claims rejected during the year | 7 | 3,000 00 | 1 | 3,000 00 |
| Claims unpaid December 31, 1921 | 605 | $256,253 61 | 108 | $45,158 25 |

## EXHIBIT OF OLD AGE AND OTHER CLAIMS.

| | Total claims. | | Illinois claims. | |
|---|---|---|---|---|
| | Number. | Amount. | Number. | Amount. |
| Claims unpaid December 31, 1920, as per last statement | 68 | $30,689 10 | 14 | $5,510 80 |
| Claims paid during the year | 15 | 7,724 16 | 5 | 1,955 20 |
| Balance | 53 | $22,964 94 | 9 | $3,555 60 |
| Saved by compromising or scaling down claims during the year | -------- | 1,378 23 | -------- | -------------- |
| Claims unpaid December 31, 1921 | 53 | $21,586 71 | 9 | $3,555 60 |

## SCHEDULE D—BONDS.

| Description. | Book value. | Par value. | Market value. |
|---|---|---|---|
| U. S. Government Liberty Bonds, 1st, 4¼s | $ 50,000 00 | $ 50,000 00 | $ 50,000 00 |
| U. S. Government Liberty Bond, 2d, 4¼s | 50,000 00 | 50,000 00 | 50,000 00 |
| U. S. Government Liberty Bonds, 3d, 4¼s | 50,000 00 | 50,000 00 | 50,000 00 |
| U. S. Government Liberty Bonds, 4th, 4¼s | 300,000 00 | 300,000 00 | 300,000 00 |
| U. S. Government Liberty Bonds, 4th, 4¼s | 200,000 00 | 200,000 00 | 200,000 00 |
| U. S. Government Victory Bonds, 5th, 4¾s | 98,800 00 | 100,000 00 | 100,000 00 |
| U. S. Government Victory Bonds, 5th, 4¾s | 147,300 00 | 150,000 00 | 150,000 00 |
| U. S. Government Victory Bonds, 5th, 4¾s | 25,000 00 | 25,000 00 | 25,000 00 |
| War Savings Stamps, 4s | 830 00 | 1,000 00 | 918 00 |

SCHEDULE D—BONDS—Concluded.

| Description. | Book value. | Par value. | Market value. |
|---|---|---|---|
| War Savings Certificate, 4s | $ 844 00 | $ 1,000 00 | $ 894 00 |
| War Saving Thrift Stamps and War Stamps, 105 W. S. S., 1213 Thrift Stamps | 751 84 | 828 25 | 785 20 |
| Winnipeg School District, debentures, 4s | 9,975 00 | 10,000 00 | 9,400 00 |
| Dominion of Canada War Loan Bond, 5s | 967 24 | 1,000 00 | 950 00 |
| Polish Government Dollar Bonds, 6s | 50,000 00 | 50,000 00 | 35,000 00 |
| Totals | $984,468 08 | $988,828 25 | $972,947 20 |

## POLISH ROMAN CATHOLIC UNION.

Located at No. 984 Milwaukee Avenue, Chicago, Illinois.

N. L. PIOTROWSKI, President. STAN GODZICH, Secretary.

| | |
|---|---|
| Balance from previous year | $3,301,404 40 |

### INCOME.

| | |
|---|---|
| Membership fees actually received | $875,256 03 |
| All other assessments or premiums | 98,801 17 |
| Dues and per capita tax | 2,733 00 |
| Medical examiners' fees actually received | 441 00 |
| Other payments by members | 30,770 15 |
| Net amount received from members | $1,008,001 35 |
| Gross interest on mortgage loans | 152,910 75 |
| Gross interest on bonds and dividends on stocks | 19,225 00 |
| Gross interest on deposits in trust companies and banks | 1,318 32 |
| Gross interest from all other sources—miscellaneous | 20,630 21 |
| Gross rents from association's property, including $2,400.00 for association's occupancy of its own buildings | 14,120 65 |
| Sale of lodge supplies | 3,250 03 |
| Borrowed money (gross) | 130,000 00 |
| Total income | $1,349,456 31 |
| Sum | $4,650,860 71 |

### DISBURSEMENTS.

| | |
|---|---|
| Death claims | $474,638 20 |
| Permanent disability claims | 7,720 00 |
| Education | 7,445 00 |
| Total benefits paid | $489,803 20 |
| Commissions and fees paid to deputies and organizers | 3,065 50 |
| Salaries of deputies and organizers | 1,076 25 |
| Salaries of officers and trustees | 12,960 00 |
| Salaries and other compensation of committees | 500 00 |
| Salaries of office employees | 21,510 94 |
| Salaries and fees paid to supreme medical examiners | 2,499 96 |
| Traveling and other expenses of officers, trustees and committees | 5,025 59 |
| Insurance department fees | 166 38 |
| Rent | 2,400 00 |
| Advertising, printing and stationery | 5,752 50 |
| Postage, express, telegraph and telephone | 2,341 01 |
| Lodge supplies | 1,180 41 |
| Official publication | 41,575 30 |
| Gross decrease on ledger assets—real estate | 24,797 84 |
| Bonds | 2,086 38 |
| Furniture and fixtures | 1,700 91 |
| Legal expense in litigating claims | 135 00 |
| Other legal expenses | 832 34 |
| Auditing | 2,572 37 |
| Taxes, repairs and other expenses on real estate | 15,551 09 |
| Interest on borrowed money | 3,270 03 |
| Borrowed money repaid (gross) | 65,000 00 |
| Miscellaneous | 2,051 69 |
| Taxes and expenses, foreclosures | 1,135 67 |
| Interest on building loan | 6,750 00 |
| Disability and educational meetings | 1,214 50 |
| War victims | 20,000 00 |
| Library | 2,350 60 |
| Donations | 100 00 |
| Total disbursements | $739,455 46 |
| Balance | $3,911,405 25 |

## LEDGER ASSETS.

| | |
|---|---|
| Book value of real estate | $ 75,426 20 |
| Mortgage loans on real estate | 3,282,735 00 |
| Book value of bonds and stocks | 441,004 00 |
| Deposits in trust companies and banks on interest | 43,413 85 |
| War savings stamps | 1,674 00 |
| Library, furniture and fixtures | 12,152 20 |
| Printing plant | 55,000 00 |
| Total ledger assets | $3,911,405 25 |

### NON-LEDGER ASSETS.

| | |
|---|---|
| Interest and rents due and accrued | 33,427 25 |
| Interest on bonds | 4,230 92 |
| Rents | 915 00 |
| Assessments actually collected by subordinate lodges not yet turned over to supreme lodge | 13,215 05 |
| Lodge supplies | 1,500 00 |
| Gross assets | $3,964,693 47 |

### DEDUCT ASSETS NOT ADMITTED.

| | | |
|---|---|---|
| Printing plant | $55,000 00 | |
| Library, furniture and fixtures | 12,152 20 | |
| Lodge supplies | 1,500 00 | |
| Polish bonds | 19,000 00 | |
| | | 87,652 20 |
| Total admitted assets | | $3,877,041 27 |

## LIABILITIES.

| | | |
|---|---|---|
| Death claims due and unpaid | $119,612 16 | |
| Death claims adjusted not yet due | 16,500 00 | |
| Death claims resisted | 2,250 00 | |
| Total death claims | | $138,362 16 |
| Borrowed money, $65,000.00; interest due or accrued on same, $278.07 | | 65,278 07 |
| Beneficiaries trust | | 600 00 |
| Total | | $204,240 23 |

## EXHIBIT OF CERTIFICATES.

| | Total business of the year. | | Business in Illinois during year. | |
|---|---|---|---|---|
| | Number. | Amount. | Number. | Amount. |
| Benefit certificates in force December 31, 1920, as per last statement | 83,993 | $52,092,900 00 | 29,328 | $18,196,800 00 |
| Benefit certificates written and renewed during the year | 5,580 | 3,271,200 00 | 1,544 | 903,950 00 |
| Total | 89,573 | $55,364,100 00 | 30,872 | $19,100,750 00 |
| Deduct terminated, decreased or transferred during the year | 10,808 | 6,669,850 00 | -------- | -------------- |
| Deduct terminated or decreased during the year | -------- | -------------- | 2,979 | 1,320,200 00 |
| Total benefit certificates in force December 31, 1921 | 78,765 | $48,694,250 00 | 27,893 | $17,780,550 00 |

| | |
|---|---|
| Received during the year from members in Illinois: Mortuary, $304,950.00; disability, $342.00; expense, $47,025.00; total | $352,317 00 |

## EXHIBIT OF DEATH CLAIMS.

| | Total claims. | | Illinois claims. | |
|---|---|---|---|---|
| | Number. | Amount. | Number | Amount. |
| Claims unpaid December 31, 1920, as per last statement | 400 | $194,450 93 | 105 | $ 46,750 68 |
| Claims reported during the year and interest addition | 871 | 504,000 00 | 304 | 173,750 00 |
| Total | 1,271 | $698,450 93 | 409 | $220,500 68 |
| Claims paid during the year | 973 | 474,638 20 | 328 | 160,024 92 |
| Balance | 298 | $223,812 73 | 81 | $60,475 76 |
| Saved by compromising or scaling down claims during the year | -------- | 85,450 57 | -------- | 26,556 75 |
| Claims unpaid December 31, 1921 | 298 | $138,362 16 | 81 | $33,919 01 |

## EXHIBIT OF PERMANENT DISABILITY CLAIMS.

| | Total claims. | | Illinois claims. | |
|---|---|---|---|---|
| | Number. | Amount. | Number. | Amount. |
| Claims reported during the year and interest addition | 197 | $7,720 00 | 30 | $1,305 00 |
| Claims paid during the year | 197 | 7,720 00 | 30 | 1,305 00 |

## SCHEDULE D—BONDS.

| Description. | Book value. | Par value. | Market value. |
|---|---|---|---|
| U. S. First Liberty Loan, 4¼s | $10,000 00 | $10,000 00 | $10,000 00 |
| U. S. Second Liberty Loan, 4s | 30,000 00 | 30,000 00 | 30,000 00 |
| U. S. Liberty Loan, Second, 4¼s | 29,344 00 | 35,000 00 | 33,950 00 |
| U. S. Third Liberty Loan, 4¼s | 60,000 00 | 60,000 00 | 60,000 00 |
| U. S. Third Liberty Loan, 4¼s | 13,458 00 | 15,000 00 | 14,700 00 |
| U. S. Third Liberty Loan, 4¼s | 43,970 00 | 50,000 00 | 49,000 00 |
| U. S. Third Liberty Loan, 4¼s | 44,820 00 | 50,000 00 | 49,000 00 |
| U. S. Third Liberty Loan, 4¼s | 34,448 00 | 40,000 00 | 39,200 00 |
| U. S. Fourth Liberty Loan, 4¼s | 100,000 00 | 100,000 00 | 100,000 00 |
| U. S. Fourth Liberty Loan, 4¼s | 21,470 00 | 25,000 00 | 24,250 00 |
| U. S. Victory Loan, 4¾s | 25,000 00 | 25,000 00 | 25,000 00 |
| U. S. Victory Loan, 4¾s | 9,494 00 | 10,000 00 | 10,000 00 |
| Polish Government, 6s | 19,000 00 | 24,000 00 | 24,000 00 |
| Totals | $441,004 00 | $474,000 00 | $469,100 00 |

# POLISH WOMEN'S ALLIANCE OF AMERICA.

Located at No. 1309-1315 North Ashland Avenue, Chicago, Illinois.

A. EMILY NAPIERALSKI, President. VICTORIA M. LATWIS, Secretary.

| | |
|---|---|
| Balance from previous year | $479,163 96 |

## INCOME.

| | |
|---|---|
| Membership fees actually received | $ 964 50 |
| All other assessments or premiums | 140,024 75 |
| Dues and per capita tax | 13,710 59 |
| Medical examiners' fees actually received | 9 75 |
| Certificates and transfer fees | 668 55 |
| Other certificate fees | 196 20 |
| Total received from members | $155,574 34 |
| Deduct payments returned to applicants and members | 282 29 |
| Net amount received from members | $155,292 05 |
| Gross interest on mortgage loans | 11,361 47 |
| Gross interest on bonds and dividends on stocks | 5,117 42 |
| Gross interest on deposits in trust companies and banks | 2,958 89 |
| Gross rents from association's property, including $1,800.00 for association's occupancy of its own buildings | 7,063 00 |
| Sale of lodge supplies, pins, books and by-laws | 1,326 21 |
| Rental piano and dishes | 384 68 |
| Official publication | 13,694 15 |
| Convention fund | 3,097 63 |
| Educational fund | 2,739 08 |
| National relief fund | 10,951 68 |
| Miscellaneous | 1,239 40 |
| Total income | $215,225 66 |
| Sum | $694,389 62 |

## DISBURSEMENTS.

| | |
|---|---|
| Death claims | $69,072 51 |
| Commissions and fees paid to deputies and organizers | 61 04 |
| Premiums for new members | 1,103 00 |
| Salaries of officers and trustees | 4,886 65 |
| Salaries and other compensation of committees, auditing committee | 199 98 |
| Salaries of office employees | 3,445 25 |
| Other compensation of office employees, janitor service and supplies | 1,790 34 |
| Salaries and fees paid to supreme medical examiners | 396 35 |
| Traveling and other expenses of officers, trustees and committees | 1,118 48 |
| Insurance department fees | 236 82 |
| Rent | 1,800 00 |
| Advertising, printing and stationery | 850 17 |
| Postage, express, telegraph and telephone | 742 75 |
| Lodge supplies | 1,425 54 |
| Official publication | 13,705 02 |
| Other legal expenses | 351 00 |

DISBURSEMENTS—Concluded.

| | |
|---|---|
| Furniture and fixtures | $ 251 57 |
| Taxes, repairs and other expenses on real estate | 2,287 26 |
| Dishes | 301 19 |
| Light, fuel and water | 1,703 82 |
| Donations | 712 00 |
| Liability insurance | 311 62 |
| Fidelity bonds of officers | 32 50 |
| Office supplies | 150 83 |
| Educational fund | 1,279 06 |
| National relief fund | 5,160 03 |
| Miscellaneous | 871 56 |
| Convention fund | 6,596 00 |
| Total disbursements | $120,842 34 |
| Balance | $573,547 28 |

## LEDGER ASSETS.

| | |
|---|---|
| Book value of real estate | $ 64,341 41 |
| Mortgage loans on real estate | 290,100 00 |
| Book value of bonds and stocks | 80,626 00 |
| Cash in association's office | 1 00 |
| Deposits in trust companies and banks on interest | 138,478 87 |
| Total ledger assets | $573,547 28 |

NON-LEDGER ASSETS.

| | |
|---|---|
| Market value of real estate over book value | 10,658 59 |
| Gross assets | $584,205 87 |

DEDUCT ASSETS NOT ADMITTED.

| | |
|---|---|
| Book value of bonds and stocks over market value | 140 00 |
| Total admitted assets | $584,065 87 |

## LIABILITIES.

| | | |
|---|---|---|
| Death claims due and unpaid | $10,555 81 | |
| Death claims reported during the year but not yet adjusted | 20,300 00 | |
| Total death claims unpaid | | $30,855 81 |

## EXHIBIT OF CERTIFICATES.

| | Total business of the year. Number. | Amount. | Business in Illinois during year. Number. | Amount. |
|---|---|---|---|---|
| Benefit certificates in force December 31, 1920, as per last statement | 22,496 | $11,803,300 00 | 14,348 | $7,581,000 00 |
| Benefit certificates written and renewed during the year | 1,875 | 1,098,500 00 | 661 | 476,100 00 |
| Benefit certificates increased during the year | | 26,700 00 | | 11,300 00 |
| Totals | 24,371 | $12,928,500 00 | 15,009 | $8,068,400 00 |
| Deduct terminated, decreased or transferred during the year | 1,432 | 834,100 00 | | |
| Deduct terminated or decreased during the year | | | 780 | 506,200 00 |
| Total benefit certificates in force December 31, 1921 | 22,939 | $12,094,400 00 | 14,229 | $7,562,200 00 |

Received during the year from members in Illinois: Mortuary, $87,321.68; reserve, $68.10; educational, $1,715.26; convention, $1,715.26; national relief, $6,462.60; expense, $18,332.64; total $115,615 54

## EXHIBIT OF DEATH CLAIMS.

| | Total claims. Number. | Amount. | Illinois claims. Number. | Amount. |
|---|---|---|---|---|
| Claims unpaid December 31, 1920, as per last statement | 63 | $22,586 66 | 44 | $14,061 66 |
| Claims reported during the year and interest addition | 158 | 81,200 00 | 115 | 59,100 00 |
| Totals | 221 | $103,786 66 | 159 | $73,161 66 |
| Claims paid during the year | 141 | 69,072 51 | 97 | 48,830 85 |
| Balance | 80 | $34,714 15 | 62 | $24,330 81 |
| Saved by compromising or sealing down claims during the year | | 3,858 34 | | 750 00 |
| Claims unpaid December 31, 1921 | 80 | $30,855 81 | 62 | $23,580 81 |

SCHEDULE D—BONDS AND STOCKS.

| Description. | Book value. | Par value. | Market value. |
|---|---|---|---|
| First U. S. Government Liberty Bonds, 4½s | $ 5,000 00 | $ 5,000 00 | $ 5,000 00 |
| Second U. S. Government Liberty Loan, 4s | 100 00 | 100 00 | 100 00 |
| Third U. S. Government Liberty Loan, 4¼s | 5,000 00 | 5,000 00 | 5,000 00 |
| Fourth U. S. Government Liberty Loan, 4¼s | 50,000 00 | 50,000 00 | 50,000 00 |
| Fifth U. S. Government Liberty Loan Bonds, 4¾s | 5,000 00 | 5,000 00 | 5,000 00 |
| Polish Republic Liberty Bonds, 6s | 8,900 00 | 8,900 00 | 8,900 00 |
| Polish American Publishing Co | 140 00 | 140 00 | 140 00 |
| Totals | $74,140 00 | $74,140 00 | $74,140 00 |

## ROYAL LEAGUE.

Located at No. 1554 Ogden Avenue, Chicago, Illinois.

WM. E. HYDE, President. CHARLES E. PIPER, Secretary.

| | |
|---|---|
| Balance from previous year | $2,800,761 27 |

INCOME.

| | |
|---|---|
| Assessments or premiums during first twelve months of membership of which all or an extra percentage is used for expenses | $ 16,427 58 |
| All other assessments or premiums | 794,405 47 |
| Other payments by members, viz: Benefit certificate fees, reinstatement fees, social members dues, register fees, dues members at large | 803 16 |
| Net amount received from members | $811,636 21 |
| Gross interest on bonds and dividends on stocks | 137,586 79 |
| Gross interest on deposits in trust companies and banks | 2,899 32 |
| Gross rents, lodge halls | 1,269 00 |
| Sale of lodge supplies | 5,694 79 |
| Borrowed money (gross) | 8,500 00 |
| Gross increase in book value of ledger assets | 1,645 10 |
| Commissions on bonds purchased | 3,420 00 |
| Miscellaneous | 386 23 |
| Total income | $973,037 44 |
| Sum | $3,773,798 71 |

DISBURSEMENTS.

| | |
|---|---|
| Death claims | $495,916 73 |
| Permanent disability claims | 6,694 29 |
| Total benefits paid | $502,611 02 |
| Commissions and fees paid to deputies and organizers | 2,961 75 |
| Salaries of deputies and organizers | 29,314 15 |
| Salaries of officers and trustees | 15,900 00 |
| Salaries and other compensation of committees | 294 85 |
| Salaries of office employees | 16,814 85 |
| Salaries and fees paid to supreme medical examiners | 4,200 00 |
| Traveling and other expenses of officers, trustees and committees | 3,902 14 |
| Insurance department fees | 281 50 |
| Rent | 6,353 64 |
| Advertising, printing and stationery | 3,472 18 |
| Postage, express, telegraph and telephone | 2,505 08 |
| Lodge supplies | 6,383 33 |
| Expenses of supreme lodge meeting | 1,315 40 |
| Other legal expenses | 11 50 |
| Furniture and fixtures | 9,965 34 |
| Custody of securities | 2,000 00 |
| Gross decrease in book value of ledger assets | 3,399 79 |
| Borrowed money repaid (gross) | 6,000 00 |
| Interest on borrowed money | 304 69 |
| All other disbursements, viz: Prizes, councils and members, $2,334.47; per capita tax advisory councils, $8,388.88; bonds, officers and others, $256.00; actuarial expense, $283.34; taxes and insurance on office, $143.09; miscellaneous expenses, $2,200.63 | 13,606 41 |
| Total disbursements | $631,597 62 |
| Balance | $3,142,201 09 |

LEDGER ASSETS.

| | |
|---|---|
| Book value of bonds and stocks | $3,026,176 73 |
| Deposits in trust companies and banks on interest | 116,024 36 |
| Total ledger assets | $3,142,201 09 |

## LEDGER ASSETS—Concluded.

### NON-LEDGER ASSETS.

| | | |
|---|---|---|
| Interest and rents due and accrued | | $53,239 14 |
| Market value of bonds and stocks over book value | | 17,373 27 |
| Assessments actually collected by subordinate lodges not yet turned over to supreme lodge | | 63,612 39 |
| Due from councils, supplies, etc | $1,861 47 | |
| Inventory, furniture, fixtures and supplies | 9,758 57 | |
| | | 11,620 04 |
| Gross assets | | $3,288,045 93 |

### DEDUCT ASSETS NOT ADMITTED.

| | | |
|---|---|---|
| Due from councils, supplies, etc | $1,861 47 | |
| Inventory, furniture, fixtures and supplies | 9,758 57 | |
| | | 11,620 04 |
| Total admitted assets | | $3,276,425 89 |

## LIABILITIES.

| | | |
|---|---|---|
| Death claims reported during the year but not yet adjusted | | $77,177 80 |
| Salaries, rents, expenses, commissions, etc., due or accrued | | 7,692 17 |
| Taxes due or accrued | | 60 00 |
| Borrowed money | | 2,500 00 |
| All other liabilities, viz— | | |
| Premium subordinate officers, bonds paid in advance | $ 29 40 | |
| Bills payable, $4,250.00; interest accrued on same, $26.40 | 4,276 40 | |
| | | 4,305 80 |
| Total | | $91,735 77 |

## EXHIBIT OF CERTIFICATES.

| | Total business of the year. | | Business in Illinois during year. | |
|---|---|---|---|---|
| | Number. | Amount. | Number. | Amount. |
| Benefit certificates in force December 31, 1920, as per last statement | 23,093 | $30,278,750 00 | 16,089 | $19,844,500 00 |
| Benefit certificates written and renewed during the year | 1,479 | 1,383,000 00 | 943 | 871,000 00 |
| Benefit certificates increased during the year | -------- | 38,500 00 | -------- | 15,500 00 |
| Totals | 24,572 | $31,700,250 00 | 17,032 | $20,731,000 00 |
| Deduct terminated, decreased or transferred during the year | 2,230 | 2,463,500 00 | -------- | -------- |
| Deduct terminated or decreased during the year | -------- | -------- | 1,389 | 1,554,750 00 |
| Total benefit certificates in force December 31, 1921 | 22,342 | $29,236,750 00 | 15,643 | $19,176,250 00 |

Received during the year from members in Illinois: Mortuary, $382,551.34; reserve, $156,285.00; expense, $72,484.94; total — $611,321 48

## EXHIBIT OF DEATH CLAIMS.

| | Total claims. | | Illinois claims. | |
|---|---|---|---|---|
| | Number. | Amount. | Number. | Amount. |
| Claims unpaid December 31, 1920, as per last statement | 52 | $ 79,927 80 | 40 | $ 62,927 80 |
| Claims reported during the year and interest addition | 290 | 508,071 48 | 218 | 397,571 48 |
| Totals | 342 | $587,999 28 | 258 | $460,499 28 |
| Claims paid during the year | 292 | 495,916 73 | 214 | 380,635 09 |
| Balance | 50 | $92,082 55 | 44 | $79,864 19 |
| Saved by compromising or scaling down claims during the year | -------- | 14,904 75 | -------- | 11,186 39 |
| Claims unpaid December 31, 1921 | 50 | $77,177 80 | 44 | $68,677 80 |

## EXHIBIT OF PERMANENT DISABILITY CLAIMS.

| | Total claims. | | Illinois claims. | |
|---|---|---|---|---|
| | Number. | Amount. | Number. | Amount. |
| Claims unpaid December 31, 1920, as per last statement | 1 | $ 100 00 | 1 | $ 100 00 |
| Claims reported during the year and interest addition | 13 | 28,500 00 | 9 | 23,000 00 |
| Totals | 14 | $28,600 00 | 10 | $23,100 00 |
| Claims paid during the year | 14 | 6,694 29 | 10 | 4,845 81 |
| Balance | -------- | $21,905 71 | -------- | $18,254 19 |

## SCHEDULE D—BONDS.

| Description. | Book value. | Par value. | Market value. |
|---|---|---|---|
| City of Mobile, Ala., 4½s | $ 76,498 50 | $ 78,000 00 | $ 74,880 00 |
| Sacramento Co., Cal., 4½s | 78,127 69 | 76,500 00 | 74,970 00 |
| Oklahoma City, Okla., 5s | 26,272 00 | 25,000 00 | 24,250 00 |
| Ft. Worth, Tex., 4½s | 25,353 00 | 25,000 00 | 24,000 00 |
| Lawton, Okla., 5s | 20,438 75 | 20,000 00 | 19,800 00 |
| City of Enid, Okla., 5s | 20,475 00 | 20,000 00 | 20,000 00 |
| Fort Worth, Tex., 4½s | 20,223 00 | 20,000 00 | 19,200 00 |
| City of Birmingham, Ala., 5s | 78,297 48 | 75,000 00 | 75,000 00 |
| Chickasha, Okla., 5s | 51,300 00 | 50,000 00 | 50,000 00 |
| Birmingham, Ala., funding, 5s | 103,700 00 | 100,000 00 | 100,000 00 |
| City of Lawton, Okla., water, 5s | 50,280 00 | 50,000 00 | 49,500 00 |
| Rutherford Co., Tenn., school, 5s | 25,597 92 | 25,000 00 | 24,500 00 |
| Kaw Valley Drainage District, 5s | 50,797 45 | 50,000 00 | 48,000 00 |
| Ada, Okla., water works, 5s | 49,855 00 | 50,000 00 | 50,000 00 |
| Taylor Co., Tex., road, 5s | 50,365 39 | 50,000 00 | 50,000 00 |
| Kaw Valley Drainage District, 5s | 25,409 60 | 25,000 00 | 24,000 00 |
| Lake County, Tenn., 5s | 20,230 00 | 20,000 00 | 20,000 00 |
| Lake County, Tenn., 5s | 20,254 60 | 20,000 00 | 20,000 00 |
| Jefferson Co., Tex., 5s | 60,442 20 | 60,000 00 | 58,800 00 |
| Coffee Co., Ala., 5s | 77,870 00 | 75,000 00 | 73,500 00 |
| Grayson County, Tex., road, 5s | 40,867 01 | 40,000 00 | 40,000 00 |
| Smyth County, Va., 6s | 40,970 72 | 38,000 00 | 40,280 00 |
| Lee County, Ark., 5½s | 29,085 55 | 28,000 00 | 28,000 00 |
| Hale County, Ala., 5s | 52,100 00 | 50,000 00 | 49,000 00 |
| Hinds County, Miss., 5s | 25,440 00 | 25,000 00 | 24,250 00 |
| Astoria, Ore., water works, 5s | 25,016 26 | 25,000 00 | 25,000 00 |
| Pennington, Minn., ditch, 5½s | 10,080 00 | 10,000 00 | 10,300 00 |
| Thief River Falls, Minn., water works, 5s | 13,832 00 | 14,000 00 | 14,140 00 |
| For County, Miss., Supervisors Dist. No. 1 and No. 3, 6s | 44,905 20 | 46,000 00 | 45,540 00 |
| Harris Co., Tex., navigation dist., 5s | 102,876 25 | 100,000 00 | 100,000 00 |
| Scott County, Va., road improvement, 5¼s | 14,383 25 | 14,000 00 | 14,560 00 |
| Scott County, Va., road improvement, 5¼s | 20,695 80 | 20,000 00 | 20,800 00 |
| Scott County, Va., road improvement, 5¼s | 20,816 05 | 20,000 00 | 21,000 00 |
| Jefferson Parish, La., Road Dist. No. 2, 5s | 57,899 65 | 59,000 00 | 59,000 00 |
| Jefferson Parish, La., Road Dist. No. 1, 5s | 40,210 70 | 41,000 00 | 41,000 00 |
| Marion County, Ala., 5s | 19,771 12 | 20,000 00 | 19,400 00 |
| Navarro County, Tex., Road Dist. No. 1, 5s | 29,876 88 | 30,000 00 | 30,000 00 |
| Marion County, Ala., 5s | 29,767 21 | 30,000 00 | 29,100 00 |
| Navarro County, Tex., Road Dist. No. 1, 5s | 69,713 70 | 70,000 00 | 70,000 00 |
| Blount County, Ala., road, 5s | 40,156 71 | 40,000 00 | 38,000 00 |
| Corpus Christi, Tex., water works, 5s | 15,000 00 | 15,000 00 | 15,000 00 |
| Henryetta, Okla., water works, 6s | 42,900 16 | 40,000 00 | 44,000 00 |
| Gila County, Ariz., road and bridge, 5½s | 56,926 98 | 53,000 00 | 55,650 00 |
| Seminole County, Fla., road and bridge, 5½s | 10,708 72 | 10,000 00 | 10,200 00 |
| Putnam County, Fla., road and bridge, 5s | 25,612 50 | 25,000 00 | 25,000 00 |
| Daytona, Valusia County, Fla., school, 6s | 37,608 35 | 35,000 00 | 38,500 00 |
| Lee County, Miss., Supervisors Dist. No. 4, road, 5s | 44,220 90 | 43,000 00 | 43,000 00 |
| Lee County, Miss., Supervisors Dist. No. 5, road, 5s | 44,220 90 | 43,000 00 | 43,000 00 |
| Pinellas County, Fla., road and bridge, 5s | 25,692 18 | 25,000 00 | 25,000 00 |
| Pinellas County, Fla., road, 5s | 56,435 50 | 55,000 00 | 55,000 00 |
| Third Liberty Loan, U. S. A., 4¼s | 40,000 00 | 40,000 00 | 40,000 00 |
| Fourth Liberty Loan, U. S. A., 4¼s | 50,000 00 | 50,000 00 | 50,000 00 |
| Victory Liberty Loan, U. S. A., 4¾s | 40,000 00 | 40,000 00 | 40,000 00 |
| Marin, Cal., municipal water works, 5s | 29,861 30 | 30,000 00 | 31,200 00 |
| Wood Co., Tex., road, 5½s | 42,668 21 | 40,000 00 | 42,800 00 |
| City of Bisbee, Ariz., street imp., 5½s | 15,775 25 | 15,000 00 | 15,450 00 |
| Clifton, Ariz., sewer, 6s | 16,386 40 | 15,000 00 | 16,200 00 |
| Ellis Co., Tex., road, 5½s | 10,608 80 | 10,000 00 | 10,200 00 |
| Wood Co., Tex., road, 5½s | 13,697 46 | 13,000 00 | 13,780 00 |
| Escambia Co., Fla., school, 5½s | 31,626 32 | 30,000 00 | 30,900 00 |
| Adair County, Okla., refunding, 6s | 18,964 40 | 17,000 00 | 17,850 00 |
| Maricopa Co., Ariz., highway, 5½s | 23,480 62 | 22,000 00 | 23,540 00 |
| Greenlee Co., Ariz., highway, 6s | 10,585 12 | 10,000 00 | 10,500 00 |
| Grayson Co., Tex., Road Dist. No. 2, 5s | 4,691 04 | 5,000 00 | 5,000 00 |
| Pima Co., Ariz., road, 5½s | 30,938 01 | 30,000 00 | 31,500 00 |
| Robeson Co., N. C., road and bridge, 5½s | 20,645 98 | 20,000 00 | 20,600 00 |
| Port of Tacoma, Wash., 5s | 29,420 11 | 30,000 00 | 30,000 00 |
| Sampson Co., N. C., road, 5s | 15,779 64 | 16,500 00 | 16,170 00 |
| Musselshell Co., Mont., 6s | 20,969 40 | 20,000 00 | 22,800 00 |
| Pima Co., Ariz., 5½s | 25,000 00 | 25,000 00 | 26,250 00 |
| Port of Tacoma, Wash., 5s | 11,200 47 | 12,000 00 | 12,000 00 |
| Port of Tacoma, Wash., 5s | 12,128 62 | 13,000 00 | 13,000 00 |
| Port of Tacoma, Wash., 5s | 17,588 60 | 20,000 00 | 20,000 00 |
| Port of Tacoma, Wash., 5s | 4,407 06 | 5,000 00 | 5,000 00 |
| Franklin Co., Tex., road, 5½s | 31,225 04 | 35,000 00 | 36,750 00 |
| Franklin Co., Tex., road, 5½s | 23,005 26 | 26,000 00 | 27,300 00 |
| Upshur Co., Tex., road, 5½s | 23,314 37 | 25,000 00 | 26,000 00 |
| Upshur Co., Tex., road, 5½s | 13,705 08 | 15,000 00 | 15,600 00 |
| Ellis Co., Tex., road, 5½s | 28,490 56 | 30,000 00 | 30,600 00 |
| Ellis Co., Tex., road, 5½s | 22,626 80 | 24,000 00 | 24,480 00 |
| Casper, Wyo., water, 5s | 26,955 72 | 30,000 00 | 30,000 00 |
| Missoula Co., Mont., school, 5¼s | 19,115 89 | 20,000 00 | 21,600 00 |

SCHEDULE D—BONDS—Concluded.

| Description. | Book value. | Par value. | Market value |
|---|---|---|---|
| Pensacola, Fla., school, 6s | $20,195 92 | $20,000 00 | $23,140 00 |
| Lincoln Co., N. C., 5s | 17,825 54 | 20,000 00 | 20,000 00 |
| Pensacola, Fla., school, 6s | 26,979 39 | 27,000 00 | 29,790 00 |
| Casper, Wyo., water, 5s | 16,782 50 | 20,000 00 | 20,000 00 |
| St. Landry Parish, La., road, 5s | 8,077 00 | 10,000 00 | 10,000 00 |
| Maricopa Co., Ariz., 5½s | 23,452 91 | 25,000 00 | 26,750 00 |
| Sevier Co., Tenn., school, 6s | 10,000 00 | 10,000 00 | 10,600 00 |
| Seattle, Wash., school, 6s | 20,922 50 | 20,000 00 | 23,800 00 |
| Harris Co., Tex., road, 5s | 35,141 00 | 40,000 00 | 40,000 00 |
| City of Manistique, Mich., water works, 6s | 12,848 87 | 12,000 00 | 13,080 00 |
| Scott Co., Tenn., road, 5½s | 18,816 00 | 20,000 00 | 20,400 00 |
| Tarrant Co., Tex., road, 5s | 9,145 94 | 10,000 00 | 10,000 00 |
| Province of Ontario, 6s | 9,900 00 | 10,000 00 | 10,200 00 |
| State of Michigan, 5½s | 10,466 00 | 10,000 00 | 11,600 00 |
| Butte, Mont., school, 6s | 31,183 80 | 30,000 00 | 33,000 00 |
| Arlington Heights, Tex., school, 6s | 10,000 00 | 10,000 00 | 10,000 00 |
| Totals | $3,026,176 73 | $3,006,000 00 | $3,043,550 00 |

## ROYAL NEIGHBORS OF AMERICA.

Located at Rock Island, Illinois.

EVA CHILD, President. ALICE GILLILAND, Secretary.

| | |
|---|---|
| Balance from previous year | $5,670,011 68 |

### INCOME.

| | |
|---|---|
| Membership fees actually received | $ 26,553 00 |
| All other assessments or premiums | 5,634,725 91 |
| Dues and per capita tax | 466,440 38 |
| Change card and license fees | 22,753 15 |
| Total received from members | $6,150,472 44 |
| Deduct payments returned to applicants and members | 641 24 |
| Net amount received from members | $6,149,831 20 |
| Gross interest on bonds and dividends on stocks | 227,335 37 |
| Gross interest on deposits in trust companies and banks | 35,200 77 |
| Gross rents from association's property, including $1,350.00 for association's occupancy of its own buildings | 1,806 00 |
| Sale of lodge supplies | 39,126 66 |
| Gross increase in book value of ledger assets | 15,222 53 |
| Surety bond premiums | 5,580 81 |
| Surety losses recovered | 487 19 |
| Income official paper | 21,067 81 |
| Minors benefits held in trust | 1,233 08 |
| Reconstruction work | 668 75 |
| Total income | $6,497,560 17 |
| Sum | $12,167,571 85 |

### DISBURSEMENTS.

| | |
|---|---|
| Death claims | $2,639,987 66 |
| Old age benefits | 1,578 70 |
| Total benefits paid | $2,641,566 36 |
| Commissions and fees paid to deputies and organizers | 175,988 74 |
| Salaries of managers or agents not deputies or organizers | 1,325 00 |
| Salaries of officers and trustees | 26,533 56 |
| Salaries of office employees | 93,278 63 |
| Salaries and fees paid to supreme medical examiners | 46 00 |
| Salaries and fees paid to subordinate medical examiners | 98 75 |
| Traveling and other expenses of officers, trustees and committees | 15,392 77 |
| Insurance department fees | 903 00 |
| Rent, including $1,350.00 for association's occupancy of its own buildings | 11,221 25 |
| Advertising, printing and stationery | 40,063 82 |
| Postage, express, telegraph and telephone | 17,066 47 |
| Lodge supplies | 28,311 99 |
| Official publication | 72,913 44 |
| Expenses of supreme lodge meeting | 127,117 65 |
| Legal expense in litigating claims | 4,024 11 |
| Other legal expenses | 6,979 85 |
| Furniture and fixtures | 4,359 97 |
| Taxes, repairs and other expenses on real estate | 2,024 80 |
| Surety losses | 5,378 75 |
| Gross decrease in book value of ledger assets | 2,562 76 |
| Investigating claims | 2,308 58 |

DISBURSEMENTS—Concluded.

| | |
|---|---|
| Appeals for help | $ 415 95 |
| Supreme physicians office expense | 2,841 33 |
| Actuarial expense | 250 00 |
| Investment expense | 143 73 |
| Surety bond and employees liability insurance | 628 87 |
| Fire insurance, fuel, light and water | 947 85 |
| Fraternal associations | 844 64 |
| Total disbursements | $3,285,538 62 |
| Balance | $8,882,033 23 |

LEDGER ASSETS.

| | |
|---|---|
| Book value of real estate | $ 13,500 00 |
| Book value of bonds and stocks | 7,306,775 27 |
| Deposits in trust companies and banks on interest | 1,561,757 96 |
| Total ledger assets | $8,882,033 23 |

NON-LEDGER ASSETS.

| | |
|---|---|
| Interest due and accrued on bonds | 98,036 49 |
| Market value of real estate over book value | 11,500 00 |
| Market value of bonds and stocks over book value | 230,200 95 |
| Assessments actually collected by subordinate lodges not yet turned over to supreme lodge | 471,773 33 |
| Gross assets | $9,693,544 00 |

LIABILITIES.

| | | |
|---|---|---|
| Death claims due and unpaid | $ 23,977 11 | |
| Death claims resisted | 26,750 00 | |
| Death claims reported during the year but not yet adjusted | 328,750 00 | |
| Death claims incurred in 1921, not reported until 1922 | 42,500 00 | |
| Total unpaid claims | | $421,977 11 |
| Salaries, rents, expenses, commissions, etc., due or accrued | | 35,000 00 |
| Taxes due or accrued | | 800 00 |
| Total | | $457,777 11 |

EXHIBIT OF CERTIFICATES.

| | Total business of the year. | | Business in Illinois during year. | |
|---|---|---|---|---|
| | Number. | Amount. | Number. | Amount. |
| Benefit certificates in force December 31, 1920, as per last statement | 390,185 | $391,341,000 00 | 100,103 | $99,019,750 00 |
| Benefit certificates written and renewed during the year | 27,453 | 24,293,500 00 | 6,918 | 5,884,750 00 |
| Benefit certificates received by transfer during the year | | | 1,573 | 1,583,750 00 |
| Totals | 417,638 | $416,285,000 00 | 108,594 | $106,673,750 00 |
| Deduct terminated, decreased or transferred during the year | 22,205 | 21,877,750 00 | | |
| Deduct terminated or decreased during the year | | | 6,762 | 6,504,000 00 |
| Total benefit certificates in force December 31, 1921 | 395,433 | $394,407,250 00 | 101,832 | $100,169,750 00 |

Received during the year from members in Illinois: Mortuary, $1,409,886.94; surety, $943.15; expense, $135,130.23; total $1,545,960 32

EXHIBIT OF DEATH CLAIMS.

| | Total claims. | | Illinois claims. | |
|---|---|---|---|---|
| | Number. | Amount. | Number. | Amount. |
| Claims unpaid December 31, 1920, as per last statement | 451 | $ 403,335 26 | 111 | $ 94,984 88 |
| Claims reported during the year and interest addition | 2,672 | 2,649,000 00 | 660 | 656,500 00 |
| Reinstated | 2 | 1,000 00 | | |
| Totals | 3,125 | $3,053,335 26 | 771 | $751,484 88 |
| Claims paid during the year | 2,684 | 2,639,987 66 | 650 | 639,338 29 |
| Balance | 441 | $413,347 60 | 121 | $112,146 59 |
| Saved by compromising or scaling down claims during the year | | 17,370 49 | | 5,052 41 |
| Claims rejected during the year | 19 | 16,500 00 | 4 | 3,500 00 |
| Claims unpaid December 31, 1921 | 422 | $379,477 11 | 117 | $103,594 18 |

EXHIBIT OF 70 YEAR WITHDRAWALS.

| | Total claims. | | Illinois claims. | |
|---|---|---|---|---|
| | Number. | Amount. | Number. | Amount. |
| Claims reported during the year and interest addition | 7 | $1,578 70 | 2 | $457 35 |
| Claims paid during the year | 7 | 1,578 70 | 2 | 457 35 |

SCHEDULE D—BONDS.

| Description. | Book value. | Par value. | Market value. |
|---|---|---|---|
| U. S. of America, First Liberty, 3½s | $ 20,000 00 | $ 20,000 00 | $ 20,000 00 |
| U. S. of America, Second Liberty, 4s | 25,000 00 | 25,000 00 | 25,000 00 |
| U. S. of America, Second Liberty, 4s | 170,723 07 | 200,000 00 | 192,000 00 |
| U. S. of America, Second Liberty, 4s | 256,084 60 | 300,000 00 | 288,000 00 |
| U. S. of America, Second Liberty, 4s | 254,325 60 | 300,000 00 | 288,000 00 |
| U. S. of America, Third Liberty, 4¼s | 25,000 00 | 25,000 00 | 25,000 00 |
| U. S. of America, Third Liberty, 4¼s | 30,000 00 | 30,000 00 | 30,000 00 |
| U. S. of America, Third Liberty, 4¼s | 25,000 00 | 25,000 00 | 25,000 00 |
| U. S. of America, Third Liberty, 4¼s | 25,000 00 | 25,000 00 | 25,000 00 |
| U. S. of America, Third Liberty, 4¼s | 26,172 21 | 29,000 00 | 28,420 00 |
| U. S. of America, Third Liberty, 4¼s | 64,076 79 | 71,000 00 | 69,580 00 |
| U. S. of America, Third Liberty, 4¼s | 90,116 00 | 100,000 00 | 98,000 00 |
| U. S. of America, Third Liberty, 4¼s | 90,649 00 | 100,000 00 | 98,000 00 |
| U. S. of America, Fourth Liberty, 4¼s | 20,000 00 | 20,000 00 | 20,000 00 |
| U. S. of America, Fourth Liberty, 4¼s | 5,000 00 | 5,000 00 | 5,000 00 |
| U. S. of America, Fourth Liberty, 4¼s | 5,000 00 | 5,000 00 | 5,000 00 |
| U. S. of America, Fourth Liberty, 4¼s | 25,000 00 | 25,000 00 | 25,000 00 |
| U. S. of America, Fourth Liberty, 4¼s | 10,000 00 | 10,000 00 | 10,000 00 |
| U. S. of America, Fourth Liberty, 4¼s | 30,000 00 | 30,000 00 | 30,000 00 |
| U. S. of America, Fourth Liberty, 4¼s | 30,000 00 | 30,000 00 | 30,000 00 |
| U. S. of America, Fourth Liberty, 4¼s | 172,618 00 | 200,000 00 | 194,000 00 |
| U. S. of America, Fourth Liberty, 4¼s | 271,239 00 | 300,000 00 | 291,000 00 |
| U. S. of America, Fourth Liberty, 4¼s | 92,833 00 | 100,000 00 | 97,000 00 |
| U. S. of America, Fourth Liberty, 4¼s | 91,691 10 | 100,000 00 | 97,000 00 |
| U. S. of America, Fourth Liberty, 4¼s | 91,691 10 | 100,000 00 | 97,000 00 |
| U. S. of America, Fourth Liberty, 4¼s | 183,382 20 | 200,000 00 | 194,000 00 |
| U. S. of America, Fourth Liberty, 4¼s | 91,691 10 | 100,000 00 | 97,000 00 |
| U. S. of America, Fourth Liberty, 4¼s | 45,711 30 | 50,000 00 | 48,500 00 |
| U. S. of America, Fourth Liberty, 4¼s | 45,683 10 | 50,000 00 | 48,500 00 |
| U. S. of America, Fourth Liberty, 4¼s | 45,683 10 | 50,000 00 | 48,500 00 |
| U. S. of America, Fourth Liberty, 4¼s | 45,654 90 | 50,000 00 | 48,500 00 |
| U. S. of America, Fourth Liberty, 4¼s | 269,661 00 | 300,000 00 | 291,000 00 |
| U. S. of America, Fourth Liberty, 4¼s | 259,677 00 | 300,000 00 | 291,000 00 |
| U. S. of America, Fourth Liberty, 4¼s | 43,530 00 | 50,000 00 | 48,500 00 |
| U. S. of America, Fourth Liberty, 4¼s | 21,765 00 | 25,000 00 | 24,250 00 |
| U. S. of America, Fourth Liberty, 4¼s | 21,765 00 | 25,000 00 | 24,250 00 |
| U. S. of America, Victory Liberty, 4¾s | 97,883 63 | 100,000 00 | 100,000 00 |
| Aberdeen, S. D., independence school, 5½s | 25,000 00 | 25,000 00 | 26,000 00 |
| Aberdeen, S. D., independence school, 5½s | 25,000 00 | 25,000 00 | 26,250 00 |
| Aberdeen, S. D., independence school, 5½s | 5,000 00 | 5,000 00 | 5,250 00 |
| Anderson County, Tenn., school, 5s | 5,130 53 | 5,000 00 | 4,950 00 |
| Anderson County, Tenn., school, 5s | 10,272 23 | 10,000 00 | 9,900 00 |
| Anderson County, Tenn., school, 5s | 10,282 89 | 10,000 00 | 9,900 00 |
| Ashtabula County, Ohio, road, 6s | 22,984 49 | 23,000 00 | 23,230 00 |
| Ashtabula County, Ohio, road, 6s | 22,979 92 | 23,000 00 | 23,460 00 |
| Ashtabula County, Ohio, road, 6s | 22,975 63 | 23,000 00 | 23,460 00 |
| Ashtabula County, Ohio, road, 6s | 22,971 59 | 23,000 00 | 23,460 00 |
| Ashtabula County, Ohio, road, 6s | 7,988 80 | 8,000 00 | 8,240 00 |
| Belle Plaine, Iowa, school, 6s | 40,000 00 | 40,000 00 | 41,200 00 |
| Beltrami County, Minn., ditch, 5½s | 18,372 50 | 18,000 00 | 18,180 00 |
| Beltrami County, Minn., ditch, 5½s | 8,207 98 | 8,000 00 | 8,080 00 |
| Beltrami County, Minn., ditch, 5½s | 3,093 16 | 3,000 00 | 3,060 00 |
| Boyden, Iowa, school, 5s | 502 90 | 500 00 | 500 00 |
| Boyden, Iowa, school, 5s | 505 68 | 500 00 | 500 00 |
| Boyden, Iowa, school, 5s | 508 35 | 500 00 | 505 00 |
| Boyden, Iowa, school, 5s | 510 89 | 500 00 | 505 00 |
| Boyden, Iowa, school, 5s | 513 33 | 500 00 | 505 00 |
| Boyden, Iowa, school, 5s | 515 67 | 500 00 | 505 00 |
| Boyden, Iowa, school, 5s | 517 91 | 500 00 | 505 00 |
| Boyden, Iowa, school, 5s | 520 05 | 500 00 | 510 00 |
| Boyden, Iowa, school, 5s | 522 10 | 500 00 | 510 00 |
| Boyden, Iowa, school, 5s | 1,048 12 | 1,000 00 | 1,020 00 |
| Boyden, Iowa, school, 5s | 1,051 88 | 1,000 00 | 1,020 00 |
| Boyden, Iowa, school, 5s | 1,055 48 | 1,000 00 | 1,020 00 |
| Boyden, Iowa, school, 5s | 1,058 92 | 1,000 00 | 1,020 00 |
| Boyden, Iowa, school, 5s | 1,062 22 | 1,000 00 | 1,020 00 |
| Boyden, Iowa, school, 5s | 1,598 07 | 1,500 00 | 1,545 00 |
| Boyden, Iowa, school, 5s | 14,403 23 | 13,500 00 | 13,905 00 |
| Boynton, Okla., school, 6s | 64,083 50 | 65,000 00 | 64,083 50 |
| Bradford, Ohio, school, 6s | 1,004 14 | 1,000 00 | 1,000 00 |
| Bradford, Ohio, school, 6s | 1,012 12 | 1,000 00 | 1,020 00 |
| Bradford, Ohio, school, 6s | 1,019 70 | 1,000 00 | 1,030 00 |
| Bradford, Ohio, school, 6s | 1,026 91 | 1,000 00 | 1,030 00 |

SCHEDULE D—BONDS—Continued.

| Description. | Book value. | Par value. | Market value. |
|---|---|---|---|
| Bradford, Ohio, school, 6s | $ 1,033 77 | $ 1,000 00 | $ 1,050 00 |
| Bradford, Ohio, school, 6s | 1,040 28 | 1,000 00 | 1,060 00 |
| Bradford, Ohio, school, 6s | 1,046 47 | 1,000 00 | 1,070 00 |
| Bradford, Ohio, school, 6s | 1,052 36 | 1,000 00 | 1,080 00 |
| Bradford, Ohio, school, 6s | 1,057 96 | 1,000 00 | 1,090 00 |
| Bradford, Ohio, school, 6s | 1,063 28 | 1,000 00 | 1,090 00 |
| Bradford, Ohio, school, 6s | 1,068 33 | 1,000 00 | 1,100 00 |
| Bradford, Ohio, school, 6s | 1,073 14 | 1,000 00 | 1,110 00 |
| Bradford, Ohio, school, 6s | 1,077 71 | 1,000 00 | 1,120 00 |
| Bradford, Ohio, school, 6s | 1,082 06 | 1,000 00 | 1,120 00 |
| Bradford, Ohio, school, 6s | 1,086 19 | 1,000 00 | 1,130 00 |
| Bradford, Ohio, school, 6s | 1,090 11 | 1,000 00 | 1,140 00 |
| Bradford, Ohio, school, 6s | 1,093 84 | 1,000 00 | 1,140 00 |
| Bradford, Ohio, school, 6s | 1,097 39 | 1,000 00 | 1,150 00 |
| Bradford, Ohio, school, 6s | 3,302 28 | 3,000 00 | 3,450 00 |
| Bradford, Ohio, school, 6s | 3,311 91 | 3,000 00 | 3,480 00 |
| Bradford, Ohio, school, 6s | 3,321 06 | 3,000 00 | 3,480 00 |
| Bradford, Ohio, school, 6s | 3,329 75 | 3,000 00 | 3,510 00 |
| Bradford, Ohio, school, 6s | 3,338 01 | 3,000 00 | 3,510 00 |
| Bradford, Ohio, school, 6s | 3,345 86 | 3,000 00 | 3,540 00 |
| Bradford, Ohio, school, 6s | 3,353 32 | 3,000 00 | 3,540 00 |
| Bradford, Ohio, school, 6s | 3,360 38 | 3,000 00 | 3,540 00 |
| Bradford, Ohio, school, 6s | 3,367 01 | 3,000 00 | 3,570 00 |
| Butler Twp., Ohio, school, 6s | 1,000 00 | 1,000 00 | 1,030 00 |
| Butler Twp., Ohio, school, 6s | 1,000 00 | 1,000 00 | 1,040 00 |
| Butler Twp., Ohio, school, 6s | 1,000 00 | 1,000 00 | 1,040 00 |
| Butler Twp., Ohio, school, 6s | 1,000 00 | 1,000 00 | 1,050 00 |
| Butler Twp., Ohio, school, 6s | 1,000 00 | 1,000 00 | 1,050 00 |
| Butler Twp., Ohio, school, 6s | 2,000 00 | 2,000 00 | 2,160 00 |
| Butler Twp., Ohio, school, 6s | 3,000 00 | 3,000 00 | 3,330 00 |
| Butler Twp., Ohio, school, 6s | 3,000 00 | 3,000 00 | 3,330 00 |
| Butler Twp., Ohio, school, 6s | 3,000 00 | 3,000 00 | 3,360 00 |
| Butler Twp., Ohio, school, 6s | 3,000 00 | 3,000 00 | 3,360 00 |
| Butler Twp., Ohio, school, 6s | 1,000 00 | 1,000 00 | 1,120 00 |
| Butler Twp., Ohio, school, 6s | 3,000 00 | 3,000 00 | 3,420 00 |
| Butler Twp., Ohio, school, 6s | 3,000 00 | 3,000 00 | 3,420 00 |
| Butler Twp., Ohio, school, 6s | 3,000 00 | 3,000 00 | 3,420 00 |
| Butler Twp., Ohio, school, 6s | 3,000 00 | 3,000 00 | 3,420 00 |
| Butler Twp., Ohio, school, 6s | 4,000 00 | 4,000 00 | 4,600 00 |
| Butler Twp., Ohio, school, 6s | 4,000 00 | 4,000 00 | 4,600 00 |
| Butler Twp., Ohio, school, 6s | 4,000 00 | 4,000 00 | 4,600 00 |
| Butler Twp., Ohio, school, 6s | 4,000 00 | 4,000 00 | 4,640 00 |
| Butler Twp., Ohio, school, 6s | 4,000 00 | 4,000 00 | 4,640 00 |
| Butler Twp., Ohio, school, 6s | 4,000 00 | 4,000 00 | 4,680 00 |
| Butler Twp., Ohio, school, 6s | 4,000 00 | 4,000 00 | 4,680 00 |
| Butler Twp., Ohio, school, 6s | 4,000 00 | 4,000 00 | 4,680 00 |
| Butler Twp., Ohio, school, 6s | 1,000 00 | 1,000 00 | 1,170 00 |
| Central City, Iowa, school, 6s | 35,075 49 | 34,000 00 | 35,075 49 |
| Clark Co., Ohio, court house, 6s | 10,154 00 | 10,000 00 | 10,154 00 |
| Clark Co., Ohio, court house, 6s | 10,189 00 | 10,000 00 | 10,189 00 |
| Clark Co., Ohio, court house, 6s | 10,222 00 | 10,000 00 | 10,222 00 |
| Clark Co., Ohio, court house, 6s | 10,253 00 | 10,000 00 | 10,253 00 |
| Clark Co., Ohio, court house, 6s | 10,283 00 | 10,000 00 | 10,283 00 |
| Clark Co., Ohio, court house, 6s | 10,311 00 | 10,000 00 | 10,311 00 |
| Clark Co., Ohio, court house, 6s | 10,338 00 | 10,000 00 | 10,338 00 |
| Clark Co., Ohio, court house, 6s | 10,363 00 | 10,000 00 | 10,363 00 |
| Clark Co., Ohio, court house, 6s | 10,387 00 | 10,000 00 | 10,387 00 |
| Clark Co., Ohio, court house, 6s | 10,409 50 | 10,000 00 | 10,409 50 |
| Coal Twp., Jackson Co., Ohio, school, 5s | 511 67 | 500 00 | 515 00 |
| Coal Twp., Jackson Co., Ohio, school, 5s | 1,024 45 | 1,000 00 | 1,030 00 |
| Coal Twp., Jackson Co., Ohio, school, 5s | 1,538 25 | 1,500 00 | 1,545 00 |
| Coal Twp., Jackson Co., Ohio, school, 5s | 1,539 73 | 1,500 00 | 1,545 00 |
| Coal Twp., Jackson Co., Ohio, school, 5s | 1,541 16 | 1,500 00 | 1,545 00 |
| Coal Twp., Jackson Co., Ohio, school, 5s | 1,028 35 | 1,000 00 | 1,030 00 |
| Creek Co., Okla., road, 5s | 39,617 31 | 40,000 00 | 40,000 00 |
| Creek Co., Okla., road, 5s | 39,256 59 | 40,000 00 | 40,000 00 |
| Creek Co., Okla., road, 5s | 5,837 48 | 6,000 00 | 5,940 00 |
| East Cleveland, Ohio, school, 6s | 1,029 16 | 1,000 00 | 1,080 00 |
| East Cleveland, Ohio, school, 6s | 28,880 12 | 28,000 00 | 30,520 00 |
| East Cleveland, Ohio, school, 6s | 25,839 55 | 25,000 00 | 27,500 00 |
| East Cleveland, Ohio, school, 6s | 3,123 25 | 3,000 00 | 3,360 00 |
| East St. Louis, Ill., park dist., 4½s | 15,221 94 | 15,000 00 | 14,700 00 |
| Edenton, N. C., school, 5s | 1,001 22 | 1,000 00 | 1,000 00 |
| Edenton, N. C., school, 5s | 1,003 58 | 1,000 00 | 1,000 00 |
| Edenton, N. C., school, 5s | 1,005 83 | 1,000 00 | 990 00 |
| Edenton, N. C., school, 5s | 1,007 97 | 1,000 00 | 990 00 |
| Edenton, N. C., school, 5s | 1,010 02 | 1,000 00 | 990 00 |
| Edenton, N. C., school, 5s | 1,011 98 | 1,000 00 | 990 00 |
| Edenton, N. C., school, 5s | 1,013 84 | 1,000 00 | 990 00 |
| Edenton, N. C., school, 5s | 1,015 62 | 1,000 00 | 980 00 |
| Edenton, N. C., school, 5s | 1,017 32 | 1,000 00 | 980 00 |
| Edenton, N. C., school, 5s | 1,018 94 | 1,000 00 | 980 00 |

SCHEDULE D—BONDS—Continued.

| Description. | Book value. | Par value. | Market value. |
|---|---|---|---|
| Edenton, N. C., school, 5s | $ 1,020 48 | $ 1,000 00 | $ 980 00 |
| Edenton, N. C., school, 5s | 1,021 96 | 1,000 00 | 980 00 |
| Edenton, N. C., school, 5s | 1,023 36 | 1,000 00 | 980 00 |
| Edenton, N. C., school, 5s | 1,024 71 | 1,000 00 | 980 00 |
| Edenton, N. C., school, 5s | 1,025 99 | 1,000 00 | 970 00 |
| Edenton, N. C., school, 5s | 1,027 21 | 1,000 00 | 970 00 |
| Edenton, N. C., school, 5s | 1,028 37 | 1,000 00 | 970 00 |
| Edenton, N. C., school, 5s | 1,029 49 | 1,000 00 | 970 00 |
| Edenton, N. C., school, 5s | 2,061 10 | 2,000 00 | 970 00 |
| Elyria, Ohio, school, 6s | 5,077 49 | 5,000 00 | 5,077 49 |
| Elyria, Ohio, school, 6s | 25,426 05 | 25,000 00 | 25,426 05 |
| Elyria, Ohio, school, 6s | 20,444 96 | 20,000 00 | 20,444 96 |
| Elyria, Ohio, school, 6s | 10,239 08 | 10,000 00 | 10,239 08 |
| Elyria, Ohio, school, 6s | 25,636 95 | 25,000 00 | 25,636 95 |
| Elyria, Ohio, school, 6s | 25,674 05 | 25,000 00 | 25,674 05 |
| Elyria, Ohio, school, 6s | 15,425 46 | 15,000 00 | 15,425 46 |
| Euclid, Ohio, sewer, 6s | 10,597 44 | 10,000 00 | 10,597 44 |
| Euclid, Ohio, sewer, 6s | 10,613 80 | 10,000 00 | 10,613 80 |
| Euclid, Ohio, sewer, 6s | 10,629 31 | 10,000 00 | 10,629 31 |
| Euclid, Ohio, sewer, 6s | 10,644 00 | 10,000 00 | 10,644 00 |
| Euclid, Ohio, sewer, 6s | 8,531 78 | 8,000 00 | 8,531 78 |
| Euclid, Ohio, sewer, 6s | 2,138 67 | 2,000 00 | 2,138 67 |
| Excelsior Springs, Mo., 6s | 25,179 85 | 25,000 00 | 28,000 00 |
| Fairmont, Minn., 6s | 5,038 18 | 5,000 00 | 5,038 18 |
| Fairmont, Minn., 6s | 5,042 73 | 5,000 00 | 5,042 73 |
| Fairmont, Minn., 6s | 10,089 76 | 10,000 00 | 10,089 76 |
| Fairmont, Minn., 6s | 16,293 39 | 16,000 00 | 16,293 39 |
| Fairmont, Minn., 6s | 16,313 87 | 16,000 00 | 16,313 87 |
| Fairmont, Minn., 6s | 16,333 39 | 16,000 00 | 16,333 39 |
| Fairmont, Minn., 6s | 16,351 63 | 16,000 00 | 16,351 63 |
| Fairmont, Minn., 6s | 16,369 07 | 16,000 00 | 16,369 07 |
| Fairmont, W. Va., school, 5s | 25,519 15 | 25,000 00 | 25,519 15 |
| Franklin Co., Ohio, highway, 6s | 24,111 84 | 24,000 00 | 24,480 00 |
| Franklin Co., Ohio, highway, 6s | 29,197 17 | 29,000 00 | 29,870 00 |
| Franklin Co., Ohio, highway, 6s | 39,344 02 | 39,000 00 | 40,560 00 |
| Franklin Co., Ohio, highway, 6s | 22,236 08 | 22,000 00 | 22,880 00 |
| Fremont Co., Iowa, funding, 6s | 7,033 60 | 7,000 00 | 7,000 00 |
| Fremont Co., Iowa, funding, 6s | 2,018 69 | 2,000 00 | 2,020 00 |
| Fremont Co., Iowa, funding, 6s | 7,095 59 | 7,000 00 | 7,140 00 |
| Fremont Co., Iowa, funding, 6s | 6,106 41 | 6,000 00 | 6,180 00 |
| Fremont Co., Iowa, funding, 6s | 7,151 20 | 7,000 00 | 7,210 00 |
| Fremont Co., Iowa, funding, 6s | 2,050 52 | 2,000 00 | 2,080 00 |
| Fremont Co., Iowa, funding, 6s | 7,201 09 | 7,000 00 | 7,350 00 |
| Georgetown, Tex., water, 5s | 20,000 00 | 20,000 00 | 20,000 00 |
| Gettysburg, S. D., school, 6s | 987 12 | 1,000 00 | 987 12 |
| Gettysburg, S. D., school, 6s | 2,970 66 | 3,000 00 | 2,970 66 |
| Gettysburg, S. D., school, 6s | 2,966 01 | 3,000 00 | 2,966 01 |
| Gettysburg, S. D., school, 6s | 2,981 37 | 3,000 00 | 2,981 37 |
| Gettysburg, S. D., school, 6s | 2,979 60 | 3,000 00 | 2,979 60 |
| Gettysburg, S. D., school, 6s | 5,044 75 | 5,000 00 | 5,044 75 |
| Gettysburg, S. D., school, 6s | 5,047 00 | 5,000 00 | 5,047 00 |
| Gettysburg, S. D., school, 6s | 5,049 15 | 5,000 00 | 5,049 15 |
| Gettysburg, S. D., school, 6s | 7,107 80 | 7,000 00 | 7,107 80 |
| Gettysburg, S. D., school, 6s | 7,111 79 | 7,000 00 | 7,111 79 |
| Gettysburg, S. D., school, 6s | 7,154 70 | 7,000 00 | 7,154 70 |
| Gettysburg, S. D., school, 6s | 7,159 53 | 7,000 00 | 7,159 53 |
| Gettysburg, S. D., school, 6s | 20,588 40 | 20,000 00 | 20,588 40 |
| Hamilton Co., Iowa, funding, 6s | 63,311 80 | 62,000 00 | 66,960 00 |
| Hamilton Co., Tenn., school, 4½s | 25,097 10 | 25,000 00 | 23,750 00 |
| Haywood Co., Tenn., refunding, 5s | 2,553 06 | 2,500 00 | 2,450 00 |
| Haywood Co., Tenn., refunding, 5s | 9,204 01 | 9,000 00 | 8,820 00 |
| Haywood Co., Tenn., refunding, 5s | 13,824 56 | 13,500 00 | 13,230 00 |
| Hot Springs, Ark., school, 5s | 12,173 73 | 12,000 00 | 12,000 00 |
| Hot Springs, Ark., school, 5s | 13,204 58 | 13,000 00 | 13,000 00 |
| Hot Springs, Ark., school, 5s | 10,169 38 | 10,000 00 | 10,000 00 |
| Houston Heights, Tex., street, 5s | 35,219 39 | 34,000 00 | 34,680 00 |
| Huron Beadle Co., S. D., school, 6s | 25,270 38 | 25,000 00 | 26,750 00 |
| Huron Beadle Co., S. D., school, 6s | 25,485 80 | 25,000 00 | 27,250 00 |
| Huron Beadle Co., S. D., school, 6s | 20,581 68 | 20,000 00 | 22,200 00 |
| Huron, S. D., city hall and water, 6s | 73,951 75 | 75,000 00 | 83,250 00 |
| Kensett, Iowa, school, 6s | 25,500 00 | 25,500 00 | 26,265 00 |
| La Prairie, Ill., community high school, 5s | 3,940 39 | 4,000 00 | 4,000 00 |
| LaPrairie, Ill., community high school, 5s | 3,913 06 | 4,000 00 | 4,040 00 |
| LaPrairie, Ill., community high school, 5s | 3,887 23 | 4,000 00 | 4,040 00 |
| LaPrairie, Ill., community high school, 5s | 3,862 86 | 4,000 00 | 4,040 00 |
| LaPrairie, Ill., community high school, 5s | 3,839 83 | 4,000 00 | 4,040 00 |
| LaPrairie, Ill., community high school, 5s | 1,909 05 | 2,000 00 | 2,020 00 |
| LaPrairie, Ill., community high school, 5s | 949 39 | 1,000 00 | 1,020 00 |
| LaPrairie, Ill., community high school, 5s | 3,778 18 | 4,000 00 | 4,080 00 |
| Lacqui Parle Co., Minn., 5¾s | 2,600 00 | 2,600 00 | 2,600 00 |
| Lacqui Parle Co., Minn., 5¾s | 5,000 00 | 5,000 00 | 5,000 00 |
| Lacqui Parle Co., Minn., 5¾s | 5,416 79 | 5,400 00 | 5,416 79 |

SCHEDULE D—BONDS—Continued.

| Description. | Book value. | Par value. | Market value. |
|---|---|---|---|
| Lacqui Parle Co., Minn., 5¾s | $ 6,020 64 | $ 6,000 00 | $ 6,020 64 |
| Lacqui Parle Co., Minn., 5¾s | 6,067 32 | 6,000 00 | 6,067 32 |
| Lacqui Parle Co., Minn., 5¾s | 6,072 30 | 6,000 00 | 6,072 30 |
| Lacqui Parle Co., Minn., 5¾s | 6,077 16 | 6,000 00 | 6,077 16 |
| Lacqui Parle Co., Minn., 5¾s | 6,109 08 | 6,000 00 | 6,109 08 |
| Lacqui Parle Co., Minn., 5¾s | 7,133 91 | 7,000 00 | 7,133 91 |
| Lacqui Parle Co., Minn., 5¾s | 7,175 91 | 7,000 00 | 7,175 91 |
| Lacqui Parle Co., Minn., 5¾s | 7,183 33 | 7,000 00 | 7,183 33 |
| Lacqui Parle Co., Minn., 5¾s | 7,190 54 | 7,000 00 | 7,190 54 |
| Lacqui Parle Co., Minn., 5¾s | 8,225 36 | 8,000 00 | 8,225 36 |
| Lacqui Parle Co., Minn., 5¾s | 8,232 64 | 8,000 00 | 8,232 64 |
| Lacqni Parle Co., Minn., 5¾s | 8,239 60 | 8,000 00 | 8,239 60 |
| Lincoln Co., Minn., drainage, 5¾s | 3,991 43 | 4,000 00 | 4,080 00 |
| Lincoln Co., Minn., drainage, 5¾s | 2,991 47 | 3,000 00 | 3,090 00 |
| Lincoln Co., Minn., drainage, 5¾s | 2,989 60 | 3,000 00 | 3,120 00 |
| Lincoln Co., Minn., drainage, 5¾s | 2,987 93 | 3,000 00 | 3,120 00 |
| Lincoln Co., Minn., drainage, 5¾s | 2,983 92 | 3,000 00 | 3,180 00 |
| Lincoln Co., Minn., drainage, 5¾s | 2,983 38 | 3,000 00 | 3,180 00 |
| Lincoln Co., Minn., drainage, 5¾s | 2,982 86 | 3,000 00 | 3,180 00 |
| Mansfield, Ohio, school, 6s | 5,007 00 | 5,000 00 | 5,007 00 |
| Mansfield, Ohio, school, 6s | 5,015 50 | 5,000 00 | 5,015 50 |
| Mansfield, Ohio, school, 6s | 5,023 50 | 5,000 00 | 5,023 50 |
| Mansfield, Ohio, school, 6s | 5,031 50 | 5,000 00 | 5,031 50 |
| Mansfield, Ohio, school, 6s | 5,038 00 | 5,000 00 | 5,038 00 |
| Mansfield, Ohio, school, 6s | 5,046 50 | 5,000 00 | 5,046 50 |
| Mansfield, Ohio, school, 6s | 5,054 00 | 5,000 00 | 5,054 00 |
| Mansfield, Ohio, school, 6s | 5,061 00 | 5,000 00 | 5,061 00 |
| Mansfield, Ohio, school, 6s | 5,067 50 | 5,000 00 | 5,067 50 |
| Mansfield, Ohio, school, 6s | 5,074 50 | 5,000 00 | 5,074 50 |
| Mansfield, Ohio, school, 6s | 5,081 00 | 5,000 00 | 5,081 00 |
| Mansfield, Ohio, school, 6s | 5,087 00 | 5,000 00 | 5,087 00 |
| Mansfield, Ohio, school, 6s | 5,093 00 | 5,000 00 | 5,093 00 |
| Mansfield, Ohio, school, 6s | 5,099 00 | 5,000 00 | 5,099 00 |
| Mansfield, Ohio, school, 6s | 5,105 00 | 5,000 00 | 5,105 00 |
| Mansfield, Ohio, school, 6s | 5,110 50 | 5,000 00 | 5,110 50 |
| Mansfield, Ohio, school, 6s | 5,116 00 | 5,000 00 | 5,116 00 |
| Mansfield, Ohio, school, 6s | 5,121 50 | 5,000 00 | 5,121 50 |
| Mansfield, Ohio, school, 6s | 5,126 50 | 5,000 00 | 5,126 50 |
| Mansfield, Ohio, school, 6s | 5,131 50 | 5,000 00 | 5,131 50 |
| Mansfield, Ohio, school, 6s | 5,136 50 | 5,000 00 | 5,136 50 |
| Mansfield, Ohio, school, 6s | 5,141 00 | 5,000 00 | 5,141 00 |
| Mansfield, Ohio, school, 6s | 5,146 00 | 5,000 00 | 5,146 00 |
| Mansfield, Ohio, school, 6s | 5,150 50 | 5,000 00 | 5,150 00 |
| Mansfield, Ohio, school, 6s | 5,154 50 | 5,000 00 | 5,154 50 |
| Mansfield, Ohio, school, 6s | 5,159 00 | 5,000 00 | 5,159 00 |
| Mansfield, Ohio, school, 6s | 5,163 00 | 5,000 00 | 5,163 00 |
| Mansfield, Ohio, school, 6s | 5,167 00 | 5,000 00 | 5,167 00 |
| Mansfield, Ohio, school, 6s | 5,171 00 | 5,000 00 | 5,171 00 |
| Mansfield, Ohio, school, 6s | 5,174 50 | 5,000 00 | 5,174 50 |
| Mansfield, Ohio, school, 6s | 5,178 50 | 5,000 00 | 5,178 50 |
| Mansfield, Ohio, school, 6s | 5,182 00 | 5,000 00 | 5,182 00 |
| Mansfield, Ohio, school, 6s | 5,185 50 | 5,000 00 | 5,185 50 |
| Mansfield, Ohio, school, 6s | 5,189 00 | 5,000 00 | 5,189 00 |
| Mansfield, Ohio, school, 6s | 5,192 50 | 5,000 00 | 5,192 50 |
| Mansfield, Ohio, school, 6s | 5,195 50 | 5,000 00 | 5,195 00 |
| Mansfield, Ohio, school, 6s | 5,198 50 | 5,000 00 | 5,198 50 |
| Mansfield, Ohio, school, 6s | 5,201 50 | 5,000 00 | 5,201 50 |
| Marshall Co., Iowa, funding, 6s | 63,561 04 | 60,000 00 | 6,600 00 |
| Marshfield, Wis., water works, 4½s | 5,055 36 | 5,000 00 | 4,890 00 |
| Marshfield, Wis., water works, 4½s | 10,120 58 | 10,000 00 | 9,800 00 |
| Marshfield, Wis., water works, 4½s | 10,130 03 | 10,000 00 | 9,800 00 |
| McAlester, Okla., water, 5s | 25,680 20 | 25,000 00 | 25,000 00 |
| McCurtain Co., Okla., road, 5s | 6,346 33 | 7,000 00 | 6,860 00 |
| McCurtain Co., Okla., road, 5s | 6,303 32 | 7,000 00 | 6,860 00 |
| McCurtain Co., Okla., road, 5s | 6,262 86 | 7,000 00 | 6,860 00 |
| McCurtain Co., Okla., road, 5s | 6,224 82 | 7,000 00 | 6,860 00 |
| McCurtain Co., Okla., road, 5s | 6,189 04 | 7,000 00 | 6,860 00 |
| McCurtain Co., Okla., road, 5s | 6,155 38 | 7,000 00 | 6,860 00 |
| Monroe Co., Iowa, funding, 6s | 75,312 44 | 74,000 00 | 74,740 00 |
| Moorehead, Iowa, school, 6s | 50,000 00 | 50,000 00 | 59,474 00 |
| Moorland, Iowa, school, 6s | 69,000 00 | 69,000 00 | 69,000 00 |
| Murray Co., Minn., road, 6s | 41,018 56 | 40,000 00 | 42,800 00 |
| Murray City, Ohio, school, 5½s | 316 87 | 300 00 | 315 00 |
| Murray City, Ohio, school, 5½s | 317 74 | 300 00 | 315 00 |
| Murray City, Ohio, school, 5½s | 851 74 | 800 00 | 848 00 |
| Murray City, Ohio, school, 5½s | 853 89 | 800 00 | 848 00 |
| Murray City, Ohio, school, 5½s | 855 99 | 800 00 | 848 00 |
| Murray City, Ohio, school, 5½s | 858 04 | 800 00 | 848 00 |
| Murray City, Ohio, school, 5½s | 860 04 | 800 00 | 856 00 |
| Murray City, Ohio, school, 5½s | 862 00 | 800 00 | 856 00 |
| Murray City, Ohio, school, 5½s | 863 91 | 800 00 | 856 00 |
| Murray City, Ohio, school, 5½s | 865 79 | 800 00 | 856 00 |

SCHEDULE D—BONDS—Continued.

| Description. | Book value. | Par value. | Market value. |
|---|---|---|---|
| Murray City, Ohio, school, 5½s | $ 867 61 | $ 800 00 | $ 856 00 |
| Murray City, Ohio, school, 5½s | 869 40 | 800 00 | 856 00 |
| Murray City, Ohio, school, 5½s | 871 15 | 800 00 | 864 00 |
| Murray City, Ohio, school, 5½s | 872 85 | 800 00 | 864 00 |
| Murray City, Ohio, school, 5½s | 874 52 | 800 00 | 864 00 |
| Murray City, Ohio, school, 5½s | 876 15 | 800 00 | 864 00 |
| Murray City, Ohio, school, 5½s | 877 74 | 800 00 | 872 00 |
| Murray City, Ohio, school, 5½s | 879 30 | 800 00 | 872 00 |
| Murray City, Ohio, school, 5½s | 880 82 | 800 00 | 872 00 |
| Murray City, Ohio, school, 5½s | 882 30 | 800 00 | 872 00 |
| New Carlisle, Ohio, school, 6s | 1,033 59 | 1,000 00 | 1,090 00 |
| New Carlisle, Ohio, school, 6s | 1,035 12 | 1,000 00 | 1,090 00 |
| New Carlisle, Ohio, school, 6s | 1,036 62 | 1,000 00 | 1,090 00 |
| New Carlisle, Ohio, school, 6s | 1,038 07 | 1,000 00 | 1,090 00 |
| New Carlisle, Ohio, school, 6s | 1,039 48 | 1,000 00 | 1,100 00 |
| New Carlisle, Ohio, school, 6s | 1,040 86 | 1,000 00 | 1,100 00 |
| New Carlisle, Ohio, school, 6s | 1,042 20 | 1,000 00 | 1,110 00 |
| New Carlisle, Ohio, school, 6s | 1,043 50 | 1,000 00 | 1,110 00 |
| New Carlisle, Ohio, school, 6s | 1,044 77 | 1,000 00 | 1,120 00 |
| New Carlisle, Ohio, school, 6s | 1,046 00 | 1,000 00 | 1,120 00 |
| New Carlisle, Ohio, school, 6s | 1,047 21 | 1,000 00 | 1,120 00 |
| New Carlisle, Ohio, school, 6s | 1,048 38 | 1,000 00 | 1,120 00 |
| New Carlisle, Ohio, school, 6s | 1,049 52 | 1,000 00 | 1,130 00 |
| New Carlisle, Ohio, school, 6s | 1,050 63 | 1,000 00 | 1,130 00 |
| New Carlisle, Ohio, school, 6s | 1,051 70 | 1,000 00 | 1,140 00 |
| New Carlisle, Ohio, school, 6s | 1,052 75 | 1,000 00 | 1,140 00 |
| New Carlisle, Ohio, school, 6s | 1,053 77 | 1,000 00 | 1,140 00 |
| New Carlisle, Ohio, school, 6s | 1,054 77 | 1,000 00 | 1,140 00 |
| New Carlisle, Ohio, school, 6s | 1,055 73 | 1,000 00 | 1,150 00 |
| New Carlisle, Ohio, school, 6s | 1,056 67 | 1,000 00 | 1,150 00 |
| New Carlisle, Ohio, school, 6s | 1,057 59 | 1,000 00 | 1,150 00 |
| New Carlisle, Ohio, school, 6s | 1,058 48 | 1,000 00 | 1,150 00 |
| New Carlisle, Ohio, school, 6s | 1,059 35 | 1,000 00 | 1,160 00 |
| New Carlisle, Ohio, school, 6s | 1,060 20 | 1,000 00 | 1,160 00 |
| New Carlisle, Ohio, school, 6s | 1,061 02 | 1,000 00 | 1,160 00 |
| New Carlisle, Ohio, school, 6s | 1,061 82 | 1,000 00 | 1,160 00 |
| New Carlisle, Ohio, school, 6s | 1,062 60 | 1,000 00 | 1,170 00 |
| New Carlisle, Ohio, school, 6s | 1,063 35 | 1,000 00 | 1,170 00 |
| New Carlisle, Ohio, school, 6s | 1,064 09 | 1,000 00 | 1,170 00 |
| New Carlisle, Ohio, school, 6s | 1,064 81 | 1,000 00 | 1,170 00 |
| New Carlisle, Ohio, school, 6s | 1,065 51 | 1,000 00 | 1,180 00 |
| New Carlisle, Ohio, school, 6s | 1,066 19 | 1,000 00 | 1,180 00 |
| New Carlisle, Ohio, school, 6s | 1,066 80 | 1,000 00 | 1,180 00 |
| New Carlisle, Ohio, school, 6s | 1,067 50 | 1,000 00 | 1,180 00 |
| New Carlisle, Ohio, school, 6s | 1,068 10 | 1,000 00 | 1,180 00 |
| New Carlisle, Ohio, school, 6s | 1,068 70 | 1,000 00 | 1,180 00 |
| New Carlisle, Ohio, school, 6s | 1,069 30 | 1,000 00 | 1,190 00 |
| New Carlisle, Ohio, school, 6s | 1,069 90 | 1,000 00 | 1,190 00 |
| New Carlisle, Ohio, school, 6s | 1,070 50 | 1,000 00 | 1,190 00 |
| New Carlisle, Ohio, school, 6s | 1,071 00 | 1,000 00 | 1,190 00 |
| New Carlisle, Ohio, school, 6s | 1,071 50 | 1,000 00 | 1,190 00 |
| New Carlisle, Ohio, school, 6s | 1,072 10 | 1,000 00 | 1,190 00 |
| New Carlisle, Ohio, school, 6s | 1,072 60 | 1,000 00 | 1,200 00 |
| New Carlisle, Ohio, school, 6s | 1,073 10 | 1,000 00 | 1,200 00 |
| New Carlisle, Ohio, school, 6s | 1,074 00 | 1,000 00 | 1,200 00 |
| New Madrid, Mo., road, 5s | 22,608 00 | 24,000 00 | 24,480 00 |
| New Madrid, Mo., road, 5s | 24,388 00 | 26,000 00 | 26,520 00 |
| New Madrid, Mo., road, 5s | 26,157 60 | 28,000 00 | 28,560 00 |
| New Madrid, Mo., road, 5s | 20,473 20 | 22,000 00 | 22,440 00 |
| New Madrid, Mo., road, 5s | 31,528 20 | 34,000 00 | 35,020 00 |
| New Madrid, Mo., road, 5s | 30,495 30 | 33,000 00 | 33,990 00 |
| New Madrid, Mo., road, 5s | 30,396 30 | 33,000 00 | 33,990 00 |
| Nobles Co., Minn., funding, 6s | 8,181 03 | 8,000 00 | 8,640 00 |
| Nobles Co., Minn., funding, 6s | 8,194 15 | 8,000 00 | 8,800 00 |
| Nobles Co., Minn., funding, 6s | 7,180 73 | 7,000 00 | 7,700 00 |
| Nobles Co., Minn., funding, 6s | 3,081 85 | 3,000 00 | 3,330 00 |
| Nobles Co., Minn., funding, 6s | 3,086 01 | 3,000 00 | 3,360 00 |
| Nobles Co., Minn., funding, 6s | 3,089 94 | 3,000 00 | 3,360 00 |
| Nobles Co., Minn., funding, 6s | 3,093 65 | 3,000 00 | 3,390 00 |
| Nobles Co., Minn., funding, 6s | 5,161 94 | 5,000 00 | 5,650 00 |
| Olivia, Minn., school, 5½s | 51,910 00 | 50,000 00 | 51,910 00 |
| Omaha, Neb., school, 4½s | 25,718 21 | 25,000 00 | 24,750 00 |
| Parkersburg, W. Va., school, 5s | 30,433 90 | 30,000 00 | 30,300 00 |
| Portsmouth, Va., improvement, 5¼s | 99,639 15 | 100,000 00 | 112,000 00 |
| Pottawatomie Co., Okla., funding, 5s | 25,592 96 | 25,000 00 | 24,500 00 |
| Reinbeck, Iowa, school, 6s | 100,000 00 | 100,000 00 | 100,000 00 |
| Rice Co., Minn., funding, 5¾s | 8,069 12 | 8,000 00 | 8,240 00 |
| Rice Co., Minn., funding, 5¾s | 13,247 53 | 13,000 00 | 13,520 00 |
| Rice Co., Minn., funding, 5¾s | 11,238 36 | 11,000 00 | 11,440 00 |
| Rice Co., Minn., funding, 5¾s | 14,446 76 | 14,000 00 | 14,700 00 |
| Rice Co., Minn., funding, 5¾s | 14,484 68 | 14,000 00 | 14,840 00 |
| Rice Co., Minn., funding, 5¾s | 14,520 67 | 14,000 00 | 14,840 00 |

SCHEDULE D—BONDS—Continued.

| Description. | Book value. | Par value. | Market value. |
|---|---|---|---|
| Rice Co., Minn., funding, 5¾s | $ 4,158 52 | $ 4,000 00 | $ 4,280 00 |
| Rice Co., Minn., funding, 5¾s | 2,083 89 | 2,000 00 | 2,140 00 |
| Sacramento Co., Cal., court house and B., 4½s | 16,851 25 | 16,000 00 | 15,840 00 |
| Sacramento Co., Cal., court house and B., 4½s | 9,528 03 | 9,000 00 | 8,910 00 |
| Scott County, Iowa, road, 5s | 99,801 00 | 100,000 00 | 100,000 00 |
| St. Joseph Co., Ind., road, 6s | 40,100 00 | 40,100 00 | 40,100 00 |
| St. Joseph Co., Ind., road, 6s | 40,100 00 | 40,100 00 | 40,100 00 |
| St. Joseph Co., Ind., road, 6s | 40,100 00 | 40,100 00 | 40,100 00 |
| St. Marys, Ohio, school, 5s | 1,035 41 | 1,000 00 | 1,020 00 |
| St. Marys, Ohio, school, 5s | 1,036 57 | 1,000 00 | 1,020 00 |
| St. Marys, Ohio, school, 5s | 1,037 71 | 1,000 00 | 1,020 00 |
| St. Marys, Ohio, school, 5s | 1,038 81 | 1,000 00 | 1,020 00 |
| St. Marys, Ohio, school, 5s | 1,039 90 | 1,000 00 | 1,020 00 |
| St. Marys, Ohio, school, 5s | 1,040 95 | 1,000 00 | 1,020 00 |
| St. Marys, Ohio, school, 5s | 1,041 99 | 1,000 00 | 1,030 00 |
| St. Marys, Ohio, school, 5s | 1,043 00 | 1,000 00 | 1,030 00 |
| St. Marys, Ohio, school, 5s | 1,043 98 | 1,000 00 | 1,030 00 |
| St. Marys, Ohio, school, 5s | 1,044 95 | 1,000 00 | 1,030 00 |
| St. Marys, Ohio, school, 5s | 1,045 90 | 1,000 00 | 1,030 00 |
| St. Marys, Ohio, school, 5s | 1,046 82 | 1,000 00 | 1,030 00 |
| St. Marys, Ohio, school, 5s | 1,047 72 | 1,000 00 | 1,030 00 |
| St. Marys, Ohio, school, 5s | 1,048 60 | 1,000 00 | 1,030 00 |
| St. Marys, Ohio, school, 5s | 1,049 47 | 1,000 00 | 1,030 00 |
| St. Marys, Ohio, school, 5s | 1,050 31 | 1,000 00 | 1,030 00 |
| St. Marys, Ohio, school, 5s | 1,051 13 | 1,000 00 | 1,030 00 |
| St. Marys, Ohio, school, 5s | 1,051 94 | 1,000 00 | 1,030 00 |
| St. Marys, Ohio, school, 5s | 1,052 73 | 1,000 00 | 1,030 00 |
| St. Marys, Ohio, school, 5s | 1,053 50 | 1,000 00 | 1,030 00 |
| St. Marys, Ohio, school, 5s | 1,054 25 | 1,000 00 | 1,030 00 |
| St. Marys, Ohio, school, 5s | 1,054 98 | 1,000 00 | 1,030 00 |
| St. Marys, Ohio, school, 5s | 1,055 70 | 1,000 00 | 1,030 00 |
| St. Marys, Ohio, school, 5s | 1,056 40 | 1,000 00 | 1,030 00 |
| Shawano Co., Wis., insane asylum, 4s | 1,995 63 | 2,000 00 | 2,000 00 |
| Shawano Co., Wis., insane asylum, 4s | 1,991 45 | 2,000 00 | 1,980 00 |
| Shawano Co., Wis., insane asylum, 4s | 1,987 44 | 2,000 00 | 1,960 00 |
| Shawano Co., Wis., insane asylum, 4s | 1,983 59 | 2,000 00 | 1,960 00 |
| Shawano Co., Wis., insane asylum, 4s | 1,979 90 | 2,000 00 | 1,940 00 |
| Shawano Co., Wis., insane asylum, 4s | 1,976 37 | 2,000 00 | 1,920 00 |
| Shawano Co., Wis., insane asylum, 4s | 1,972 97 | 2,000 00 | 1,920 00 |
| Shawano Co., Wis., insane asylum, 4s | 1,969 72 | 2,000 00 | 1,900 00 |
| Shawano Co., Wis., insane asylum, 4s | 2,460 18 | 2,500 00 | 2,375 00 |
| Shawano Co., Wis., insane asylum, 4s | 1,966 60 | 2,000 00 | 1,900 00 |
| Shawano Co., Wis., insane asylum, 4s | 18,668 36 | 19.000 00 | 17,860 00 |
| Shawano Co., Wis., insane asylum, 4s | 16,690 68 | 17,000 00 | 15,980 00 |
| Sheffield Lake Village, Ohio, 6s | 1,019 84 | 1,000 00 | 1,019 84 |
| Sheffield Lake Village, Ohio, 6s | 1,024 31 | 1,000 00 | 1,024 31 |
| Sheffield Lake Village, Ohio, 6s | 1,028 58 | 1,000 00 | 1,028 58 |
| Sheffield Lake Village, Ohio, 6s | 1,032 58 | 1,000 00 | 1,032 58 |
| Sheffield Lake Village, Ohio, 6s | 1,036 40 | 1,000 00 | 1,036 40 |
| Sheffield Lake Village, Ohio, 6s | 1,038 23 | 1,000 00 | 1,038 23 |
| Sheffield Lake Village, Ohio, 6s | 1,040 02 | 1,000 00 | 1,040 02 |
| Sheffield Lake Village, Ohio, 6s | 1,041 75 | 1,000 00 | 1,041 75 |
| Sheffield Lake Village, Ohio, 6s | 1,043 45 | 1,000 00 | 1,043 45 |
| Sheffield Lake Village, Ohio, 6s | 1,045 09 | 1,000 00 | 1,045 09 |
| Sheffield Lake Village, Ohio, 6s | 1,046 70 | 1,000 00 | 1,046 70 |
| Sheffield Lake Village, Ohio, 6s | 1,048 26 | 1,000 00 | 1,048 26 |
| Sheffield Lake Village, Ohio, 6s | 1,049 78 | 1,000 00 | 1,049 78 |
| Sheffield Lake Village, Ohio, 6s | 1,051 26 | 1,000 00 | 1,051 26 |
| Sheffield Lake Village, Ohio, 6s | 1,052 70 | 1,000 00 | 1,052 70 |
| Sheffield Lake Village, Ohio, 6s | 1,054 11 | 1,000 00 | 1,054 11 |
| Sheffield Lake Village, Ohio, 6s | 1,055 47 | 1,000 00 | 1,055 47 |
| Sheffield Lake Village, Ohio, 6s | 1,056 81 | 1,000 00 | 1,056 81 |
| Sheffield Lake Village, Ohio, 6s | 1,058 10 | 1,000 00 | 1,058 10 |
| Sheffield Lake Village, Ohio, 6s | 1,059 36 | 1,000 00 | 1,059 36 |
| Sheffield Lake Village, Ohio, 6s | 1,060 59 | 1,000 00 | 1,060 59 |
| Sheffield Lake Village, Ohio, 6s | 1,061 79 | 1,000 00 | 1,061 79 |
| Sheffield Lake Village, Ohio, 6s | 1,062 95 | 1,000 00 | 1,062 95 |
| Sheffield Lake Village, Ohio, 6s | 1,064 09 | 1,000 00 | 1,064 09 |
| Sheffield Lake Village, Ohio, 6s | 1,065 19 | 1,000 00 | 1,065 19 |
| Sheffield Lake Village, Ohio, 6s | 1,066 27 | 1,000 00 | 1,066 27 |
| Sheffield Lake Village, Ohio, 6s | 1,067 32 | 1,000 00 | 1,067 32 |
| Sheffield Lake Village, Ohio, 6s | 1,068 34 | 1,000 00 | 1,068 34 |
| Sheffield Lake Village, Ohio, 6s | 1,069 33 | 1,000 00 | 1,069 33 |
| Sherman, Tex., street improvement, 5s | 2,584 73 | 2,500 00 | 2,500 00 |
| Sherman, Tex., street improvement, 5s | 2,586 88 | 2,500 00 | 2,500 00 |
| Sherman, Tex., street improvement, 5s | 2,588 93 | 2,500 00 | 2,500 00 |
| Sherman, Tex., street improvement, 5s | 2,590 88 | 2,500 00 | 2,500 00 |
| Sherman, Tex., street improvement, 5s | 2,592 75 | 2,500 00 | 2,500 00 |
| Sherman, Tex., street improvement, 5s | 2,594 53 | 2,500 00 | 2,500 00 |
| Sherman, Tex., street improvement, 5s | 2,596 23 | 2,500 00 | 2,500 00 |

SCHEDULE D—BONDS—Concluded.

| Description. | Book value. | Par value. | Market value. |
|---|---|---|---|
| Sherman, Tex., street improvement, 5s | $ 2,597 85 | $ 2,500 00 | $ 2,500 00 |
| Sherman, Tex., street improvement, 5s | 2,599 40 | 2,500 00 | 2,500 00 |
| Sherman, Tex., street improvement, 5s | 2,600 87 | 2,500 00 | 2,500 00 |
| South Dakota, State, 6s | 167,374 93 | 160,000 00 | 167,374 93 |
| Superior, Wis., school, 4s | 19,597 46 | 20,000 00 | 19,000 00 |
| Stearns Co., Minn., court house, 6s | 46,557 59 | 45,000 00 | 49,500 00 |
| Stearns Co., Minn., court house, 6s | 9,329 32 | 9,000 00 | 9,990 00 |
| Stearns Co., Minn., court house, 6s | 21,012 46 | 20,000 00 | 22,400 00 |
| Stearns Co., Minn., court house, 6s | 10,527 51 | 10,000 00 | 11,300 00 |
| Stearns Co., Minn., court house, 6s | 2,109 53 | 2,000 00 | 2,260 00 |
| Story Co., Iowa, funding, 6s | 10,171 38 | 10,000 00 | 1,050 00 |
| Story Co., Iowa, funding, 6s | 10,190 84 | 10,000 00 | 1,060 00 |
| Story Co., Iowa, funding, 6s | 3,062 77 | 3,000 00 | 3,210 00 |
| Swaledale, Iowa, school, 5s | 1,016 09 | 1,000 00 | 1,010 00 |
| Swaledale, Iowa, school, 5s | 1,019 24 | 1,000 00 | 1,010 00 |
| Swaledale, Iowa, school, 5s | 1,022 25 | 1,000 00 | 1,010 00 |
| Swaledale, Iowa, school, 5s | 1,025 13 | 1,000 00 | 1,020 00 |
| Swaledale, Iowa, school, 5s | 1,027 87 | 1,000 00 | 1,020 00 |
| Swaledale, Iowa, school, 5s | 1,030 50 | 1,000 00 | 1,020 00 |
| Swaledale, Iowa, school, 5s | 1,033 01 | 1,000 00 | 1,020 00 |
| Swaledale, Iowa, school, 5s | 1,035 41 | 1,000 00 | 1,020 00 |
| Swaledale, Iowa, school, 5s | 1,037 70 | 1,000 00 | 1,020 00 |
| Swaledale, Iowa, school, 5s | 1,039 89 | 1,000 00 | 1,020 00 |
| Swaledale, Iowa, school, 5s | 20,839 75 | 20,000 00 | 20,600 00 |
| Swift Co., Minn., drainage, ditch, 5¾s | 3,000 00 | 3,000 00 | 3,000 00 |
| Swift Co., Minn., drainage, ditch, 5¾s | 3,000 00 | 3,000 00 | 3,000 00 |
| Swift Co., Minn., drainage, ditch, 5¾s | 3,009 39 | 3,000 00 | 3,009 39 |
| Swift Co., Minn., drainage, ditch, 5¾s | 3,010 17 | 3,000 00 | 3,010 17 |
| Swift Co., Minn., drainage, ditch, 5¾s | 3,033 63 | 3,000 00 | 3,033 63 |
| Swift Co., Minn., drainage, ditch, 5¾s | 3,035 97 | 3,000 00 | 3,035 97 |
| Swift Co., Minn., drainage, ditch, 5¾s | 3,038 49 | 3,000 00 | 3,038 49 |
| Swift Co., Minn., drainage, ditch, 5¾s | 3,054 51 | 3,000 00 | 3,054 51 |
| Swift Co., Minn., drainage, ditch, 5¾s | 3,057 42 | 3,000 00 | 3,057 42 |
| Swift Co., Minn., drainage, ditch, 5¾s | 3,060 06 | 3,000 00 | 3,060 06 |
| Swift Co., Minn., drainage, dtich, 5¾s | 3,078 51 | 3,000 00 | 3,078 51 |
| Swift Co., Minn., drainage, ditch, 5¾s | 3,081 60 | 3,000 00 | 3,081 60 |
| Swift Co., Minn., drainage, ditch, 5¾s | 3,084 36 | 3,000 00 | 3,084 36 |
| Swift Co., Minn., drainage, ditch, 5¾s | 3,087 21 | 3,000 00 | 3,087 21 |
| Swift Co., Minn., drainage, ditch, 5¾s | 6,831 56 | 6,633 00 | 6,831 56 |
| Umatilla Co., Ore., school, 5s | 18,186 87 | 18,000 00 | 18,000 00 |
| Waseca Co., Minn., drainage, 6s | 4,003 60 | 4,000 00 | 4,003 60 |
| Waseca Co., Minn., drainage, 6s | 2,002 80 | 2,000 00 | 2,002 80 |
| Waseca Co., Minn., drainage, 6s | 2,007 10 | 2,000 00 | 2,007 10 |
| Waseca Co., Minn., drainage, 6s | 1,004 60 | 1,000 00 | 1,004 60 |
| Waseca Co., Minn., drainage, 6s | 4,026 48 | 4,000 00 | 4,026 48 |
| Waseca Co., Minn., drainage, 6s | 2,015 60 | 2,000 00 | 2,015 60 |
| Waseca Co., Minn., drainage, 6s | 3,031 20 | 3,000 00 | 3,031 20 |
| Waseca Co., Minn., drainage, 6s | 1,011 80 | 1,000 00 | 1,011 80 |
| Waseca Co., Minn., drainage, 6s | 4,050 80 | 4,000 00 | 4,050 80 |
| Waseca Co., Minn., drainage, 6s | 2,037 40 | 2,000 00 | 2,037 40 |
| Waseca Co., Minn., drainage, 6s | 3,059 70 | 3,000 00 | 3,059 70 |
| Watertown, S. D., school, 6s | 20,000 00 | 20,000 00 | 22,200 00 |
| Watertown, S. D., school, 6s | 22,500 00 | 22,500 00 | 25,200 00 |
| Watertown, S. D., school, 6s | 22,500 00 | 22,500 00 | 25,200 00 |
| Watertown, S. D., school, 6s | 2,500 00 | 2,500 00 | 2,800 00 |
| Wichita Falls, Tex., storm, sewer, 6s | 24,752 50 | 25,000 00 | 28,250 00 |
| Yellow Medicine Co., Minn., ditch, 5¾s | 27,223 29 | 27,000 00 | 29,160 00 |
| Yellow Medicine Co., Minn., dtich, 5¾s | 8,070 32 | 8,000 00 | 8,640 00 |
| Youngstown, Ohio, school district, 5s | 29,338 48 | 30,000 00 | 30,600 00 |
| Youngstown, Ohio, school district, 5s | 29,299 74 | 30,000 00 | 30,600 00 |
| Youngstown, Ohio, school district, 5s | 39,017 28 | 40,000 00 | 40,800 00 |
| Totals | $7,306,775 27 | $7,616,933 00 | $7,536,976 22 |

## SICILIAN UNION OF MUTUAL BENEFIT.

Located at No. 8 South Dearborn Street, Chicago, Illinois.

DOMENICO TINAGLIA, President. JOHN B. FONTANA, Secretary.

| | |
|---|---|
| Balance from previous year | $15,850 07 |

### INCOME.

| | |
|---|---|
| Membership fees actually received | $55,926 45 |
| Assessments or premiums | 1,218 25 |
| Net amount received from members | $57,144 70 |

INCOME—Concluded.

| | |
|---|---|
| Gross interest on U. S. Liberty bonds and dividends on stocks | $ 637 50 |
| Gross interest on deposits in trust companies and banks | 67 27 |
| Sale of lodge supplies | 815 10 |
| Received from subordinate lodges for general president's funeral expenses | 1,852 50 |
| Sale of furniture | 592 00 |
| Profit from a picnic | 2,581 35 |
| Total income | $63,690 42 |
| Sum | $79,540 49 |

DISBURSEMENTS.

| | |
|---|---|
| Death claims | $66,000 00 |
| Salaries of officers and trustees | 260 00 |
| Salaries of office employees | 2,080 00 |
| Salaries and fees paid to supreme medical examiners | 536 00 |
| Salaries and fees paid to subordinate medical examiners | 1,350 00 |
| Traveling and other expenses of officers, trustees and committees | 628 12 |
| Assistance to poor members | 25 00 |
| Insurance department fees | 5 00 |
| Rent, office | 1,100 00 |
| Advertising, printing and stationery | 260 90 |
| Postage, express, telegraph and telephone | 961 28 |
| Lodge supplies | 513 50 |
| Official publication | 240 50 |
| Expenses of supreme lodge meeting | 46 00 |
| Legal expense in litigating claims | 286 00 |
| Other legal expenses | 180 00 |
| Furniture and fixtures | 135 50 |
| Gross loss on sale of $10,000.00 U. S. Liberty bonds | 337 00 |
| Moving expense | 27 00 |
| Light, water, ice and towels | 158 15 |
| Reimbursed to lodges | 25 00 |
| General president and officers for funeral expenses | 2,243 00 |
| Total disbursements | $77,397 95 |
| Balance | $2,142 54 |

LEDGER ASSETS.

| | |
|---|---|
| Deposits in trust companies and banks on interest | $2,142 54 |

EXHIBIT OF CERTIFICATES.

| | Total business of the year—all in Illinois. Number. | Amount. |
|---|---|---|
| Benefit certificates in force December 31, 1920, as per last statement | 2,702 | $4,053,000 00 |
| Benefit certificates written and renewed during the year | 414 | 621,000 00 |
| Benefit certificates increased during the year | 405 | 607,000 00 |
| Totals | 3,521 | $5,281,500 00 |
| Deduct terminated, decreased or transferred during the year | 1,421 | 2,131,500 00 |
| Total benefit certificates in force December 31, 1921 | 2,100 | $3,150,000 00 |

| | |
|---|---|
| Received during the year from members in Illinois: Mortuary, $53,082.45; reserve, $800.00; expense, $3,262.25; total | $57,144 70 |

EXHIBIT OF DEATH CLAIMS.

| | Total claims—all in Illinois. Number. | Amount. |
|---|---|---|
| Claims reported during the year and interest addition | 44 | $66,000 00 |
| Claims paid during the year | 44 | 66,000 00 |

## SLOVAK EVANGELICAL SOCIETY.

Located at No. 927 West Nineteenth Place, Chicago, Illinois.

JOHN PODMAJERSKY, President. JOHN ZIDEK, Secretary.

| | |
|---|---|
| Balance from previous year | $13,618 85 |

INCOME.

| | |
|---|---|
| Membership fees actually received | $13,610 22 |
| Gross interest on deposits in trust companies and banks | 378 21 |
| Sale of lodge supplies | 241 13 |
| Postage | 1 22 |
| Deduct from orphan's fund | 232 91 |

INCOME—Concluded.

| | |
|---|---|
| Donations | $ 7 00 |
| Iniation fees | 14 50 |
| Total income | $14,485 19 |
| Sum | $28,104 04 |

DISBURSEMENTS.

| | |
|---|---|
| Death claims | $4,450 00 |
| Death benefits previously paid to orphan's fund | 452 91 |
| Total benefits paid | $4,902 91 |
| Salaries of officers and trustees | 575 00 |
| Other compensation of officers and trustees | 141 02 |
| Traveling and other expenses of officers, trustees and committees | 43 56 |
| Insurance department fees | 5 00 |
| Postage, express, telegraph and telephone | 41 00 |
| Lodge supplies | 390 25 |
| Official publication | 1,465 10 |
| Expenses of supreme lodge meeting | 172 00 |
| Interest on officers' bonds | 22 39 |
| Donations | 142 00 |
| Money loaned | 85 00 |
| Office supplies | 13 55 |
| Total disbursements | $7,998 78 |
| Balance | $20,105 26 |

LEDGER ASSETS.

| | |
|---|---|
| Book value of bonds and stocks | $ 100 00 |
| Cash in association's office | 763 65 |
| Deposits in trust companies and banks not on interest | 1,342 75 |
| Deposits in trust companies and banks on interest | 17,648 86 |
| War Savings Stamps | 250 00 |
| Total ledger assets | $20,105 26 |

NON-LEDGER ASSETS.

| | |
|---|---|
| Assessments actually collected by subordinate lodges not yet turned over to supreme lodge | 176 00 |
| Total admitted assets | $20,281 26 |

EXHIBIT OF CERTIFICATES.

| | Total business of the year. | | Business in Illinois during year. | |
|---|---|---|---|---|
| | Number. | Amount. | Number. | Amount. |
| Benefit certificates in force December 31, 1920, as per last statement | 1,194 | $768,825 00 | 1,122 | $701,900 00 |
| Benefit certificates written and renewed during the year | 1,271 | 914,850 00 | 217 | 172,800 00 |
| Total | 2,465 | $1,683,675 00 | 1,339 | $874,700 00 |
| Deduct terminated, decreased or transferred during the year | 1,277 | 815,175 00 | | |
| Deduct terminated or decreased during the year | | | 221 | 117,450 00 |
| Total benefit certificates in force December 31, 1921 | 1,188 | $868,500 00 | 1,118 | $874,700 00 |

| | |
|---|---|
| Received during the year from members in Illinois: Mortuary, $9,438.34; reserve, $481.04; disability, $340.50; expense, $2,425.89; total | $12,685 77 |

EXHIBIT OF DEATH CLAIMS.

| | Total claims—all in Illinois. | |
|---|---|---|
| | Number. | Amount. |
| Claims unpaid December 31, 1920, as per last statement | 1 | $ 850 00 |
| Claims reported during the year and interest addition | 5 | 3,600 00 |
| Total | 6 | $4,450 00 |
| Claims paid during the year | 6 | 4,450 00 |

SCHEDULE D—BONDS.

| Description. | Market value. |
|---|---|
| Second U. S. Liberty Bond | $100 00 |

## SLOVENIC NATIONAL BENEFIT SOCIETY.

Located at No. 2657-59 South Lawndale Avenue, Chicago, Illinois.

VINCENT CAINKAR, President. MATTHEW J. TURK, Secretary.

| | | |
|---|---|---|
| Balance from previous year | | $722,790 22 |
| **INCOME.** | | |
| Membership fees actually received | | $ 3,536 00 |
| All other assessments or premiums | | 696,217 24 |
| Net amount received from members | | $699,753 24 |
| Gross interest on mortgage loans | | 854 16 |
| Gross interest on bonds and dividends on stocks less $6,185.67 | | 28,618 88 |
| Gross interest on deposits in trust companies and banks | | 3,680 59 |
| Gross rents from association's property, including $900.00 for association's occupancy of its own buildings | | 1,854 50 |
| Sale of lodge supplies | | 1,073 61 |
| Gross profit on sale or maturity of ledger assets | | 4,978 20 |
| Juvenile department | | 3,506 90 |
| Refund—embezzled assessment | | 37 86 |
| Slovenic Workingmen's Benefit Union, consolidated with S, N, B, S, June 30, 1921 | | 218,266 90 |
| Total income | | $962,624 84 |
| Sum | | $1,685,415 06 |
| **DISBURSEMENTS.** | | |
| Death claims | | $119,660 03 |
| Permanent disability claims | | 36,383 00 |
| Sick and accident claims | | 313,601 50 |
| Total benefits paid | | $469,644 53 |
| Salaries of officers and trustees | | 9,220 20 |
| Wages extra help | | 2,979 67 |
| Salaries of office employees | | 3,825 47 |
| Salaries and fees paid to supreme medical examiners | | 600 00 |
| Traveling and other expenses of officers, trustees and committees, delegates and convention | | 36,719 60 |
| Rent | | 900 00 |
| Advertising, printing and stationery | | 8,776 65 |
| Postage, express, telegraph and telephone | | 1,583 74 |
| Lodge supplies | | 552 00 |
| Official publication | | 33,054 53 |
| Legal expense in litigating claims | | 3,325 20 |
| Furniture and fixtures | | 681 70 |
| Taxes, repairs and other expenses on real estate | | 1,641 65 |
| Educational board | | 1,600 00 |
| Office supplies | | 351 14 |
| Assessment, insane members | | 249 25 |
| Premium surety bonds | | 431 74 |
| Actuary and accountants' fees | | 1,143 28 |
| Students assessment | | 1,666 96 |
| Miscellaneous | | 3,033 22 |
| Donations | | 1,095 00 |
| Medical examination new members campaign | | 2,829 75 |
| Total disbursements | | $586,020 08 |
| Balance | | $1,099,394 98 |
| **LEDGER ASSETS.** | | |
| Book value of real estate | | $ 13,007 00 |
| Mortgage loans on real estate | | 15,000 00 |
| Loans secured by pledge of bonds, stocks or other collateral | | 1,030,191 39 |
| Deposits in trust companies and banks on interest | | 41,196 59 |
| Total ledger assets | | $1,099,394 98 |
| **NON-LEDGER ASSETS.** | | |
| Interest and rents due and accrued | | 19,326 01 |
| Market value of bonds and stocks over book value | | 18,489 86 |
| Assessments actually collected by subordinate lodges not yet turned over to supreme lodge | | 7,193 13 |
| Total admitted assets | | $1,144,403 98 |
| **LIABILITIES.** | | |
| Death claims due and unpaid | $53,261 95 | |
| Death claims adjusted not yet due | 9,800 00 | |
| Total unpaid claims | | $63,061 95 |

## EXHIBIT OF CERTIFICATES.

| | Total business of the year. Number. | Amount. | Business in Illinois during year. Number. | Amount. |
|---|---|---|---|---|
| Benefit certificates in force December 31, 1920, as per last statement | 18,981 | $13,172,250 00 | 2,535 | $1,717,550 00 |
| Benefit certificates written and renewed during the year | 3,473 | 2,647,400 00 | 701 | 504,600 00 |
| Slovenic Workingmen's Benefit Union | 5,125 | 3,302,650 00 | 259 | 132,300 00 |
| Increased | | 294,200 00 | | |
| Total | 27,579 | $19,416,500 00 | 3,495 | $2,354,450 00 |
| Deduct terminated, decreased or transferred during the year | 966 | 623,200 00 | | |
| Deduct terminated or decreased during the year | | | 178 | 91,600 00 |
| Total benefit certificates in force December 31, 1921 | 26,613 | $18,793,300 00 | 3,317 | $2,262,850 00 |

Received during the year from members in Illinois: Mortuary, $32,251.11; disability, $3,638.60; sick, $41,048.35; expense, $10,068.64; total $87,006 70

## EXHIBIT OF DEATH CLAIMS.

| | Total claims. Number. | Amount. | Illinois claims. Number. | Amount. |
|---|---|---|---|---|
| Slovenic Workingmen's Benefit Union | 35 | $ 12,578 75 | 4 | $ 1,587 50 |
| Claims unpaid December 31, 1920, as per last statement | 128 | 58,693 23 | 10 | 3,766 60 |
| Claims reported during the year and interest addition | 177 | 111,450 00 | 24 | 15,050 00 |
| Total | 340 | $182,721 98 | 38 | $20,404 10 |
| Claims paid during the year | 184 | 119,660 03 | 22 | 14,309 60 |
| Claims unpaid December 31, 1921 | 156 | $63,061 95 | 16 | $6,094 50 |

## EXHIBIT OF PERMANENT DISABILITY CLAIMS.

| | Total claims. Number. | Amount. | Illinois claims. Number. | Amount. |
|---|---|---|---|---|
| Claims reported during the year and interest addition | 413 | $36,383 00 | 51 | $5,010 00 |
| Claims paid during the year | 413 | 36,383 00 | 51 | 5,010 00 |

## EXHIBIT OF SICK AND ACCIDENT CLAIMS.

| | Total claims. Number. | Amount. | Illinois claims. Number. | Amount. |
|---|---|---|---|---|
| Increase in estimated liability | 9,567 | $313,601 50 | 1,268 | $38,183 50 |
| Claims paid during the year | 9,567 | 313,601 50 | 1,268 | 38,183 50 |

## SCHEDULE D—BONDS.

| Description. | Book value. | Par value. | Market value. |
|---|---|---|---|
| Health Department, Chicago, Ill., 4s | $ 5,970 00 | $ 6,000 00 | $ 5,760 00 |
| West Park, Chicago, Ill., 4s | 991 25 | 1,000 00 | 950 00 |
| Sanitary District, Chicago, Ill., 4s | 992 50 | 1,000 00 | 980 00 |
| Sanitary District, Chicago, Ill., 4s | 992 50 | 1,000 00 | 970 00 |
| Sanitary District, Chicago, Ill., 4s | 1,985 00 | 2,000 00 | 1,940 00 |
| Sanitary District, Chicago, Ill., 4s | 3,970 00 | 4,000 00 | 3,920 00 |
| City of Chicago, Ill., 4s | 960 00 | 1,000 00 | 970 00 |
| Sanitary District, Chicago, Ill., 4s | 3,910 00 | 4,000 00 | 3,960 00 |
| South Park Commission, Chicago, Ill., 4s | 14,906 25 | 15,000 00 | 14,400 00 |
| City of Chicago, Ill., 4s | 4,887 50 | 5,000 00 | 4,850 00 |
| Lincoln Park, Chicago, Ill., 4s | 34,868 75 | 35,000 00 | 32,550 00 |
| City of Chicago, Ill., 4s | 3,000 00 | 3,000 00 | 2,910 00 |
| City of Chicago, Ill., 4s | 600 00 | 600 00 | 582 00 |
| City of Chicago, Ill., 4s | 19,000 00 | 19,000 00 | 18,430 00 |
| City of Chicago, Ill., 4s | 2,400 00 | 2,400 00 | 2,328 00 |
| Sanitary District, Chicago, Ill., 4s | 4,000 00 | 4,000 00 | 3,920 00 |
| Sanitary District, Chicago, Ill., 4s | 1,000 00 | 1,000 00 | 980 00 |
| Sanitary District, Chicago, Ill., 4s | 2,000 00 | 2,000 00 | 1,960 00 |
| Cook County Forest Preserve, 4s | 30,000 00 | 30,000 00 | 28,800 00 |
| United States Liberty Bonds, 4¼s | 10,000 00 | 10,000 00 | 10,000 00 |
| Cook County Forest Preserve, 4s | 14,268 84 | 15,000 00 | 14,700 00 |
| Cook County Forest Preserve, 4s | 946 67 | 1,000 00 | 980 00 |
| United States Liberty Bonds, 4¼s | 10,000 00 | 10,000 00 | 10,000 00 |
| United States Liberty Bonds, 4¼s | 50,000 00 | 50,000 00 | 50,000 00 |
| United States Liberty Bonds, 4¼s | 30,000 00 | 30,000 00 | 30,000 00 |
| United States Liberty Bonds, 4¼s | 50,000 00 | 50,000 00 | 50,000 00 |
| United States Victory Bonds, 4¾s | 14,947 50 | 15,000 00 | 14,947 50 |
| United States Liberty Bonds, 4¼s | 45,350 00 | 50,000 00 | 45,350 00 |
| United States Liberty Bonds, 4¼s | 22,096 25 | 25,000 00 | 22,096 25 |

SCHEDULE D—BONDS—Concluded.

| Description. | Book value. | Par value. | Market value. |
|---|---|---|---|
| United States Liberty Bonds, 4¼s | $22,017 50 | $25,000 00 | $22,017 50 |
| North Dakota Real Estate Bonds, 5¾s | 49,750 00 | 50,000 00 | 54,000 00 |
| Howard County, Tex., 5½s | 13,275 22 | 14,000 00 | 14,420 00 |
| Howard County, Tex., 5½s | 6,637 61 | 7,000 00 | 7,210 00 |
| Howard County, Tex., 5½s | 8,534 07 | 9,000 00 | 9,360 00 |
| Howard County, Tex., 5½s | 4,741 15 | 5,000 00 | 5,200 00 |
| Howard County, Tex., 5½s | 4,741 15 | 5,000 00 | 5,250 00 |
| Chester County, Tenn., 5½s | 2,937 00 | 3,000 00 | 3,150 00 |
| Chester County, Tenn., 5½s | 2,898 60 | 3,000 00 | 3,240 00 |
| Chester County, Tenn., 5½s | 2,866 80 | 3,000 00 | 3,330 00 |
| Chester County, Tenn., 5½s | 2,857 20 | 3,000 00 | 3,360 00 |
| Chester County, Tenn., 5½s | 946 70 | 1,000 00 | 1,130 00 |
| Chester County, Tenn., 5½s | 2,817 60 | 3,000 00 | 3,480 00 |
| Chester County, Tenn., 5½s | 1,866 00 | 2,000 00 | 3,340 00 |
| Valley County, Mont., 6s | 2,955 00 | 3,000 00 | 3,210 00 |
| Valley County, Mont., 6s | 6,895 00 | 7,000 00 | 7,560 00 |
| Valley County, Mont., 6s | 4,925 00 | 5,000 00 | 5,400 00 |
| Vaugh School District, N. M., 6s | 19,073 60 | 20,000 00 | 20,800 00 |
| Jonesville School District, La., 5s | 428 68 | 500 00 | 500 00 |
| Jonesville School District, La., 5s | 2,558 85 | 3,000 00 | 3,000 00 |
| Jonesville School District, La., 5s | 2,546 40 | 3,000 00 | 3,000 00 |
| Jonesville School District, La., 5s | 2,956 98 | 3,500 00 | 3,500 00 |
| Jonesville School District, La., 5s | 2,944 20 | 3,500 00 | 3,500 00 |
| Jonesville School District, La., 5s | 2,931 95 | 3,500 00 | 3,500 00 |
| Jonesville School District, La., 5s | 3,293 20 | 4,000 00 | 4,000 00 |
| Jonesville School District, La., 5s | 3,283 80 | 4,000 00 | 4,000 00 |
| Juab County, Utah, 6s | 6,965 00 | 7,000 00 | 7,840 00 |
| Howard County, Ark., 5s | 4,073 80 | 5,000 00 | 5,000 00 |
| Howard County, Ark., 5s | 8,101 40 | 10,000 00 | 10,000 00 |
| Poinsett County, Ark., 5s | 9,972 60 | 12,000 00 | 12,000 00 |
| Peters Creek Twp., Stokes County, N. C., 6s | 4,681 40 | 5,000 00 | 5,000 00 |
| Juab County, Utah, 6s | 15,000 00 | 15,000 00 | 16,650 00 |
| Harlingen, Tex., 6s | 24,675 00 | 25,000 00 | 24,500 00 |
| Winnett, Mont., 6s | 35,000 00 | 35,000 00 | 35,000 00 |
| Winnett, Mont., 6s | 17,000 00 | 17,000 00 | 17,000 00 |
| Thermopolis, Wyo., 6s | 9,980 00 | 10,000 00 | 10,000 00 |
| Tarpon Springs, Fla., 6s | 4,950 00 | 5,000 00 | 5,000 00 |
| Tarpon Springs, Fla., 6s | 11,880 00 | 12,000 00 | 12,000 00 |
| Tarpon Springs, Fla., 6s | 11,880 00 | 12,000 00 | 12,000 00 |
| Tarpon Springs, Fla., 6s | 8,910 00 | 9,000 00 | 9,000 00 |
| Tarpon Springs, Fla., 6s | 8,910 00 | 9,000 00 | 9,000 00 |
| Tarpon Springs, Fla., 6s | 2,970 00 | 3,000 00 | 3,000 00 |
| Tangipahoa Parish, La., 5s | 12,420 00 | 13,500 00 | 13,500 00 |
| Tangipahoa Parish, La., 5s | 11,960 00 | 13,000 00 | 13,000 00 |
| Tangipahoa Parish, La., 5s | 3,220 00 | 3,500 00 | 3,500 00 |
| San Patrico, Tex., 5½s | 2,820 00 | 3,000 00 | 3,000 00 |
| San Patrico, Tex., 5½s | 2,820 00 | 3,000 00 | 3,000 00 |
| San Patrico, Tex., 5½s | 2,820 00 | 3,000 00 | 3,000 00 |
| San Patrico, Tex., 5½s | 2,820 00 | 3,000 00 | 3,000 00 |
| San Patrico, Tex., 5½s | 2,820 00 | 3,000 00 | 3,000 00 |
| San Patrico, Tex., 5½s | 2,820 00 | 3,000 00 | 3,000 00 |
| San Patrico, Tex., 5½s | 1,880 00 | 2,000 00 | 2,000 00 |
| Pinckney Twp., S. C., 6s | 25,437 50 | 25,000 00 | 25,000 00 |
| Brevard County, Fla., 6s | 7,820 00 | 8,000 00 | 8,000 00 |
| Brevard County, Fla., 6s | 11,730 00 | 12,000 00 | 12,000 00 |
| Brevard County, Fla., 6s | 14,662 50 | 15,000 00 | 15,000 00 |
| Sumter County, Fla., 6s | 20,200 00 | 20,000 00 | 20,000 00 |
| Sumter County, Fla., 6s | 5,050 00 | 5,000 00 | 5,000 00 |
| Claxton, Ga., 6s | 5,000 00 | 5,000 00 | 5,000 00 |
| Jonesville School District, La., 5s | 1,445 85 | 1,500 00 | 1,500 00 |
| Jonesville School District, La., 5s | 1,434 60 | 1,500 00 | 1,500 00 |
| Jonesville School District, La., 5s | 1,422 10 | 1,500 00 | 1,500 00 |
| Jonesville School District, La., 5s | 2,244 00 | 2,500 00 | 2,500 00 |
| Jonesville School District, La., 5s | 2,234 75 | 2,500 00 | 2,500 00 |
| Rosedale, school, S. D., 7s | 2,654 80 | 2,500 00 | 2,500 00 |
| Rosedale, school, S. D., 7s | 2,679 70 | 2,500 00 | 2,500 00 |
| Rosedale, school, S. D., 7s | 2,700 12 | 2,500 00 | 2,500 00 |
| United States Liberty Bonds, 4s | 5,000 00 | 5,000 00 | 5,000 00 |
| United States Liberty Bonds, 4¼s | 10,000 00 | 10,000 00 | 10,000 00 |
| United States Liberty Bonds, 4¼s | 24,000 00 | 24,000 00 | 24,000 00 |
| United States Victory Bonds, 4¾s | 5,000 00 | 5,000 00 | 5,000 00 |
| Catholic School Commission, Montreal, Can., 5s | 25,000 00 | 26,000 00 | 26,000 00 |
| West Matanzas Drainage and Water District, Fulton County, Ill., 6s | 9,900 00 | 10,000 00 | 10,000 00 |
| Town of Williams, Coramina County, Ariz., 6s | 5,312 50 | 5,000 00 | 5,000 00 |
| Village of Clayton, Union County, N. M., 6s | 10,675 00 | 10,000 00 | 10,000 00 |
| Hildalgo County, Tex., 5½s | 4,357 08 | 4,000 00 | 4,000 00 |
| Hidalgo County, Tex., 5½s | 6,510 62 | 6,000 00 | 6,000 00 |
| Hidalgo County, Tex., 5½s | 7,064 09 | 6,500 00 | 6,500 00 |
| Hidalgo County, Tex., 5½s | 6,520 62 | 6,000 00 | 6,000 00 |
| Hidalgo County, Tex., 5½s | 7,064 09 | 6,500 00 | 6,500 00 |
| Totals | $1,030,191 39 | $1,058,000 00 | $1,048,681 25 |

## SLOVENIC PROGRESSIVE BENEFIT SOCIETY.

Located at No. 1541 West Eighteenth Street, Chicago, Illinois.

FRANK SOMRAK, President. WILLIAM RUS, Secretary.

| | |
|---|---|
| Balance from previous year | $184,381 63 |

### INCOME.

| | |
|---|---|
| All other assessments or premiums | $111,477 26 |
| Entry fees | 465 00 |
| Total received from members | $111,942 26 |
| Deduct payments returned to applicants and members | 56 22 |
| Net amount received from members | $111,886 04 |
| Gross interest on mortgage loans | 7,424 05 |
| Gross interest on bonds and dividends on stocks | 2,680 36 |
| Gross interest on deposits in trust companies and banks | 364 60 |
| Gross interest from all other sources | 69 29 |
| Sale of lodge supplies | 455 41 |
| Returned sick benefit | 134 00 |
| Transfer from juvenile fund for administration expenses | 1,095 74 |
| Voluntary donations | 51 31 |
| Mortgage foreclosure expense refund | 3,264 02 |
| Commission on bonds bought | 50 00 |
| Deducted from death benefit for paying too low assessments | 2 44 |
| Total income | $127,507 26 |
| Sum | $311,888 89 |

### DISBURSEMENTS.

| | |
|---|---|
| Death claims | $35,108 17 |
| Permanent disability claims | 2,150 00 |
| Sick and accident claims | 57,368 70 |
| Compensation for operations | 3,100 00 |
| Benevolent benefits paid | 387 85 |
| Total benefits paid | $98,114 72 |
| Commissions and fees paid to deputies and organizers | 4 50 |
| Salaries of officers and trustees | 2,739 75 |
| Other compensation of officers and trustees | 1,494 50 |
| Salaries and other compensation of committees | 63 00 |
| Salaries of office employees | 1,800 00 |
| Other compensation of office employees | 194 00 |
| Salaries and fees paid to supreme medical examiners | 177 75 |
| Salaries and fees paid to subordinate medical examiners | 55 00 |
| Traveling and other expenses of officers, trustees and committees | 1,243 32 |
| Insurance department fees | 73 29 |
| Rent | 326 74 |
| Advertising, printing and stationery | 1,035 72 |
| Postage, express, telegraph and telephone | 322 04 |
| Official publication | 750 00 |
| Legal expense in litigating claims | 6,171 71 |
| Other legal expenses | 1,142 81 |
| Furniture and fixtures | 10 84 |
| All other disbursements, viz— | |
| Surety bonds | 191 30 |
| Actuary, public accountants and N. F. C. of A. fees | 308 50 |
| Rent of hall for meetings and compensation to minutes secretary | 32 00 |
| Exchange of checks, special medical examinations and translations of minutes | 147 10 |
| Total disbursements | $116,398 59 |
| Balance | $195,490 30 |

### LEDGER ASSETS.

| | |
|---|---|
| Book value of real estate | $5,600 00 |
| Mortgage loans on real estate | 77,550 00 |
| Book value of bonds and stocks | 94,850 50 |
| Cash in association's office | 3 00 |
| Deposits in trust companies and banks on interest | 17,486 80 |
| Total ledger assets | $195,490 30 |

LEDGER ASSETS—Concluded.

NON-LEDGER ASSETS.

| | | |
|---|---|---|
| Interest and rents due and accrued | | $4,965 77 |
| Market value of real estate over book value | | 3,400 00 |
| Assessments actually collected by subordinate lodges not yet turned over to supreme lodge | | 110 82 |
| All other assets, viz— | | |
| Lodge supplies sold not yet paid | $ 176 44 | |
| Inventory of office furniture and lodge supply | 2,508 81 | |
| | | 2,685 25 |
| Gross assets | | $206,652 14 |

DEDUCT ASSETS NOT ADMITTED.

| | | |
|---|---|---|
| Book value of bonds and stocks over market value | $3,215 50 | |
| Other items, viz— | | |
| Lodge supply sold not paid for | 176 44 | |
| Inventory of office furniture and lodge supply | 2,508 81 | |
| | | 5,900 75 |
| Total admitted assets | | $200,751 39 |

LIABILITIES.

| | | |
|---|---|---|
| Death claims due and unpaid | $8,897 12 | |
| Death claims adjusted not yet due | 4,100 00 | |
| Total death claims | | $12,997 12 |

EXHIBIT OF CERTIFICATES.

| | Total business of the year. | | Business in Illinois during year. | |
|---|---|---|---|---|
| | Number. | Amount. | Number. | Amount. |
| Benefit certificates in force December 31, 1920, as per last statement | 4,776 | $2,720,350 00 | 757 | $420,500 00 |
| Benefit certificates written and renewed during the year | 528 | 371,400 00 | 92 | 49,500 00 |
| Benefit certificates received by transfer during the year | | | 18 | 11,200 00 |
| Benefit certificates increased during the year | | 20,700 00 | | 1,800 00 |
| Total | 5,304 | $3,112,450 00 | 867 | $483,000 00 |
| Deduct terminated, decreased or transferred during the year | 372 | 215,700 00 | | |
| Deduct terminated or decreased during the year | | | 47 | 22,800 00 |
| Total benefit certificates in force December 31, 1921 | 4,932 | $2,896,750 00 | 820 | $460,200 00 |

Received during the year from members in Illinois: Mortuary, $7,054.23; reserve, $92.00; disability, $478.20; all other, $8,194.91; expense, $1,735.51; total $17,554 85

EXHIBIT OF DEATH CLAIMS.

| | Total claims. | | Illinois claims. | |
|---|---|---|---|---|
| | Number. | Amount. | Number. | Amount. |
| Claims unpaid December 31, 1920, as per last statement | 42 | $19,505 29 | 2 | $1,000 00 |
| Claims reported during the year and interest addition | 51 | 28,600 00 | 7 | 2,800 00 |
| Total | 93 | $48,105 29 | 9 | $3,800 00 |
| Claims paid during the year | 61 | 35,108 17 | 7 | 3,234 00 |
| Claims unpaid December 31, 1921 | 32 | $12,997 12 | 2 | $566 00 |

EXHIBIT OF PERMANENT DISABILITY CLAIMS.

| | Total claims. | | Illinois claims. | |
|---|---|---|---|---|
| | Number. | Amount. | Number. | Amount. |
| Claims reported during the year and interest addition | 13 | $2,150 00 | 7 | $1,200 00 |
| Claims paid during the year | 13 | 2,150 00 | 7 | 1,200 00 |

EXHIBIT OF SICK AND ACCIDENT CLAIMS.

| | Total claims. | | Illinois claims. | |
|---|---|---|---|---|
| | Number. | Amount. | Number. | Amount. |
| Claims reported during the year | 1,158 | $57,368 70 | 198 | $10,512 73 |
| Claims paid during the year | 1,158 | 57,368 70 | 198 | 10,512 73 |

SCHEDULE D—BONDS.

| Description. | Book value. | Par value. | Market value. |
|---|---|---|---|
| Second Liberty, U. S., 4¼s | $10,000 00 | $10,000 00 | $10,000 00 |
| Third Liberty, U. S., 4¼s | 15,000 00 | 15,000 00 | 15,000 00 |
| Fourth Liberty, U. S., 4¼s | 15,000 00 | 15,000 00 | 15,000 00 |
| State of North Dakota, real estate, series A, 5½s | 10,100 00 | 10,000 00 | 11,300 00 |
| County of Howard, Ark., Road Improvement District No. 7, 5s | 3,457 08 | 4,000 00 | 3,920 00 |
| County of Howard, Ark., Road Improvement District No. 7, 5s | 1,728 54 | 2,000 00 | 1,960 00 |
| County of Poinsett, Ark., Road District No. 5, 5s | 3,429 88 | 4,000 00 | 3,760 00 |
| Intermountain Railway, Light and Power Co., (Colorado-Wyoming Divisions), first mort. refund. gold, 8s | 21,285 00 | 21,500 00 | 15,695 00 |
| Blackhawk Hotel Co. and Miller Hotel Co. of Davenport-Des Moines, Iowa, real estate serial gold, 8s | 3,960 00 | 4,000 00 | 4,000 00 |
| Blackhawk Hotel Co. and Miller Hotel Co., of Davenport-Des Moines, Iowa, real estate serial gold, 8s | 4,950 00 | 5,000 00 | 5,000 00 |
| Blackhawk Hotel Co. and Miller Hotel Co., of Davenport-Des Moines, Iowa., real estate serial gold, 8s | 5,940 00 | 6,000 00 | 6,000 00 |
| Total | $94,850 50 | $96,500 00 | $91,635 00 |

---

## SUPREME ROYAL CIRCLE OF FRIENDS OF THE WORLD.

Located at No. 3517 Indiana Avenue, Chicago, Illinois.

DR. R. A. WILLIAMS, President. M. S. HUDSON, Secretary.

| | |
|---|---|
| Balance from previous year | $ 3,398 32 |

### INCOME.

| | |
|---|---|
| All other assessments or premiums | $31,124 22 |
| Medical examiners' fees actually received | 1,000 00 |
| Total received from members | $32,124 22 |
| Total income | $32,124 22 |
| Sum | $35,522 54 |

### DISBURSEMENTS.

| | |
|---|---|
| Death claims | $4,177 00 |
| Sick and accident claims | 5,287 75 |
| Total benefits paid | $9,464 75 |
| Salaries of officers and trustees | 1,400 00 |
| Salaries of office employees | 600 00 |
| Salaries and fees paid to supreme medical examiners | 200 00 |
| Salaries and fees paid to subordinate medical examiners | 800 00 |
| For collection and remittance of assessments and dues | 9,337 26 |
| Insurance department fees | 5 00 |
| Rent | 3,000 00 |
| Advertising, printing and stationery | 1,545 52 |
| Postage, express, telegraph and telephone and electric lights | 312 00 |
| Expenses of supreme lodge meeting | 960 65 |
| Furniture and fixtures | 1,200 00 |
| Total disbursements | $28,825 18 |
| Balance | $6,697 36 |

### LEDGER ASSETS.

| | |
|---|---|
| Cash in association's office | $6,697 36 |
| Total ledger assets | $6,697 36 |

NON-LEDGER ASSETS.

| | |
|---|---|
| Furniture and fixtures | 1,200 00 |
| Gross assets | $7,897 36 |

DEDUCT ASSETS NOT ADMITTED.

| | |
|---|---|
| Furniture and fixtures | 1,200 00 |
| Total admitted assets | $6,697 36 |

EXHIBIT OF CERTIFICATES.

| | Total business of the year—all in Illinois. Number. | Amount. |
|---|---|---|
| Benefit certificates in force December 31, 1920, as per last statement | 1,255 | $125,300 00 |
| Benefit certificates written and renewed during the year | 4,099 | 625,500 00 |
| Total | 5,354 | $750,800 00 |
| Deduct terminated or decreased during the year | 3,009 | 390,750 00 |
| Total benefit certificates in force December 31, 1921 | 2,345 | $360,050 00 |

Received during the year from members in Illinois: Mortuary, $6,224.84; reserve, $311.24; disability, $6,224.84; all other, $1,000.00; expense, $18,363.30; total — $3,124 22

EXHIBIT OF DEATH CLAIMS.

| | Total claims—all in Illinois. Number. | Amount. |
|---|---|---|
| Claims reported during the year and interest addition | 30 | $4,177 00 |
| Claims paid during the year | 30 | 4,177 00 |

EXHIBIT OF SICK AND ACCIDENT CLAIMS.

| | Total claims—all in Illinois. Number. | Amount. |
|---|---|---|
| Claims reported during the year | 1,386 | $5,287 75 |
| Claims paid during the year | 1,386 | 5,287 75 |

## TRI-STATE COUNTIES MUTUAL LIFE ASSOCIATION.

Located at Carthage, Illinois.

S. F. HUSTON, President. LINUS CRUISE, Secretary.

| | |
|---|---|
| Balance from previous year | $6,850 39 |

INCOME.

| | |
|---|---|
| All other assessments or premiums | $58,193 07 |
| Dues and per capita tax | 7,232 01 |
| Medical examiners' fees actually received | 235 00 |
| Total received from members | $65,660 08 |
| Deduct payments returned to applicants and members | 8 50 |
| Net amount received from members | $65,651 58 |
| Sale of lodge supplies | 182 95 |
| Change of policies | 111 75 |
| Total income | $65,946 28 |
| Sum | $72,796 67 |

DISBURSEMENTS.

| | |
|---|---|
| Death claims | $55,138 85 |
| Commissions and fees paid to deputies and organizers | 894 00 |
| Salaries of officers and trustees—secretary, president, vice president and treasurer | 2,436 47 |
| Other compensation of officers and trustees—board of directors | 844 95 |
| Salaries and other compensation of committees | 205 58 |
| Salaries and fees paid to supreme medical examiners | 220 25 |
| Traveling and other expenses of officers, trustees and committees | 14 44 |
| Insurance department fees | 7 00 |
| Rent | 112 56 |
| Advertising, printing and stationery | 361 59 |
| Postage, express, telegraph and telephone | 105 08 |
| Lodge supplies | 201 10 |
| Official publication | 1,169 97 |
| Expenses of supreme lodge meeting | 573 06 |
| Furniture and fixtures | 377 05 |
| All other disbursements, viz— | |
| Change of policies | 36 00 |
| Bonding company—premium on insurance | 157 20 |
| Light, janitor | 25 26 |
| Notary, donations and repairs | 39 00 |
| Total disbursements | $62,919 41 |
| Balance | $9,877 26 |

## LEDGER ASSETS.

| | |
|---|---|
| Cash in association's office | $9,877 26 |
| Furniture and supplies | 1,000 00 |
| Gross assets | $10,877 76 |
| DEDUCT ASSETS NOT ADMITTED. | |
| Furniture and supplies | 1,000 00 |
| Total admitted assets | $9,877 26 |

## LIABILITIES.

| | |
|---|---|
| Death claims reported during the year but not yet adjusted | $6,000 00 |

## EXHIBIT OF CERTIFICATES.

| | Total business of the year—all in Illinois. Number. | Amount. |
|---|---|---|
| Benefit certificates in force December 31, 1920, as per last statement | 6,608 | $9,808,500 00 |
| Benefit certificates written and renewed during the year | 851 | 1,116,000 00 |
| Benefit certificates increased during the year | -------- | 10,000 00 |
| Total | 7,459 | $10,934,500 00 |
| Deduct terminated or decreased during the year | 201 | 276,000 00 |
| Total benefit certificates in force December 31, 1921 | 7,258 | $10,658,500 00 |

| | |
|---|---|
| Received during the year from members in Illinois: Mortuary, $58,193.07; expense, $7,753.21; total | $65,946 28 |

## EXHIBIT OF DEATH CLAIMS.

| | Total claims—all in Illinois. Number. | Amount. |
|---|---|---|
| Claims unpaid December 31, 1920, as per last statement | 6 | $ 9,000 00 |
| Claims reported during the year and interest addition | 38 | 54,500 00 |
| Total | 44 | $63,500 00 |
| Claims paid during the year | 39 | 55,107 92 |
| Balance | 5 | $8,392 08 |
| Saved by compromising or scaling down claims during the year | -------- | 2,392 08 |
| Claims unpaid December 31, 1921 | 5 | $6,000 00 |

---

# UNITED BROTHERS OF FRIENDSHIP AND SISTERS OF MYSTERIOUS TEN.

Located at No. 400 West Williams Street, Springfield, Illinois.

JORDAN TUTT, President. ROBERT A. BYRD, Secretary.

| | |
|---|---|
| Balance from previous year | $4,599 18 |

## INCOME.

| | |
|---|---|
| Membership fees actually received | $7,650 43 |
| Total income | $7,650 43 |
| Sum | $12,249 61 |

## DISBURSEMENTS.

| | |
|---|---|
| Total death claims paid | $5,400 00 |
| Salaries and other compensation of committees | 40 00 |
| Traveling and other expenses of officers, trustees and committees | 379 28 |
| For collection and remittance of assessments and dues | 765 04 |
| Insurance department fees | 5 00 |
| Advertising, printing and stationery | 85 75 |
| Postage, express, telegraph and telephone | 43 45 |
| Official publication | 75 00 |
| Other legal expenses | 54 00 |
| Borrowed money—grand lodge | 55 00 |
| Total disbursements | $1,502 52 |
| Balance | $5,347 09 |

LEDGER ASSETS.

| | |
|---|---|
| Cash in association's office | $ 28 46 |
| Deposits in trust companies and banks not on interest | 3,818 53 |
| Deposits in trust companies and banks on interest | 1,500 00 |
| Total ledger assets | $5,347 09 |

LIABILITIES.

| | | |
|---|---|---|
| Death claims due and unpaid | $200 00 | |
| Death claims reported during the year but not yet adjusted | 750 00 | |
| Total death claims | | $950 00 |

EXHIBIT OF CERTIFICATES.

| | Total business of the year—all in Illinois. Number. | Amount. |
|---|---|---|
| Benefit certificates in force December 31, 1920, as per last statement | 3,706 | $370,000 00 |
| Benefit certificates written and renewed during the year | 830 | 83,000 00 |
| Total | 4,536 | $453,600 00 |
| Deduct terminated or decreased during the year | 531 | 53,100 00 |
| Total benefit certificates in force December 31, 1921 | 4,005 | $400,500 00 |

EXHIBIT OF DEATH CLAIMS.

| | Total claims—all in Illinois. Number. | Amount. |
|---|---|---|
| Claims unpaid December 31, 1920, as per last statement | 14 | $1,400 00 |
| Claims reported during the year and interest addition | 51 | 4,925 00 |
| Total | 65 | $6,325 00 |
| Claims paid during the year | 55 | 5,400 00 |
| Balance | 10 | $925 00 |

## WESTERN CATHOLIC UNION, SUPREME COUNCIL.

Located at No. 712-20 Illinois State Bank Building, Quincy, Illinois.

F. WM. HECKENKAMP, Jr., President. WILLIAM K. OTT, Secretary.

| | |
|---|---|
| Balance from previous year | $449,164 17 |

INCOME.

| | |
|---|---|
| All other assessments or premiums | $187,081 67 |
| Dues and per capita tax | 30,521 20 |
| Medical examiners' fees actually received | 2,556 00 |
| Net amount received from members | $220,158 87 |
| Gross interest on mortgage loans | 22,323 88 |
| Gross interest on bonds and dividends on stocks | 437 50 |
| Gross interest on deposits in trust companies and banks | 736 26 |
| Gross interest from all other sources | 203 75 |
| Sale of lodge supplies | 1,270 57 |
| Borrowed money (gross) | 10,000 00 |
| Benefit certificates | 121 50 |
| Bonding fees | 304 93 |
| Social members | 293 45 |
| From branches for securing new members | 69 25 |
| Charter fees | 25 00 |
| Suspension expense | 1 50 |
| Total income | $255,946 46 |
| Sum | $705,110 63 |

DISBURSEMENTS.

| | |
|---|---|
| Death claims | $147,205 23 |
| Old age installment | 506 00 |
| Total benefits paid | $147,711 23 |
| Commissions and fees paid to deputies and organizers | 5,208 96 |
| Salaries of deputies and organizers | 1,750 00 |
| Salaries of officers and trustees | 6,805 00 |
| Salaries of office employees | 1,760 00 |
| Salaries and fees paid to supreme medical examiners | 677 00 |
| Salaries and fees paid to subordinate medical examiners | 2,180 50 |
| Traveling and other expenses of officers, trustees and committees | 991 64 |
| Insurance department fees | 57 00 |
| Rent | 849 80 |

## DISBURSEMENTS—Concluded.

|  | |  |
|---|---|---|
| Advertising, printing and stationery | | $ 1,921 50 |
| Postage, express, telegraph and telephone | | 535 60 |
| Lodge supplies | | 2,723 63 |
| Official publication | | 2,545 76 |
| Expenses of supreme lodge meeting | | 670 29 |
| Furniture and fixtures | | 380 89 |
| Miscellaneous | | 378 27 |
| Borrowed money repaid (gross) | | 10,000 00 |
| Interest on borrowed money | | 150 00 |
| All other disbursements, viz— | | |
| Investigating of loans | | 54 95 |
| Actuary fees | | 330 55 |
| Audit fees | | 100 00 |
| Bonding fees, branch officers | | 297 75 |
| Bonding fees, supreme officers | | 127 50 |
| Premiums for securing new members | | 177 00 |
| Total disbursements | | $188,384 82 |
| Balance | | $516,725 81 |

## LEDGER ASSETS.

|  | |  |
|---|---|---|
| Mortgage loans on real estate | | $468,250 00 |
| Book value of bonds and stocks | | 10,000 00 |
| Deposits in trust companies and banks on interest | | 20,075 81 |
| 184 old age benefit notes | | 18,400 00 |
| Total ledger assets | | $516,725 81 |

### NON-LEDGER ASSETS.

|  | |  |
|---|---|---|
| Interest and rents due and accrued | | 13,534 82 |
| All other assets, viz— | | |
| Office furniture | $2,242 36 | |
| Stationery and supplies | 3,524 83 | |
| | | 5,767 19 |
| Gross assets | | $536,027 82 |

### DEDUCT ASSETS NOT ADMITTED.

|  | |  |
|---|---|---|
| Organizers balances | $ 681 13 | |
| Book value of bonds and stocks over market value | 746 00 | |
| Other items, viz— | | |
| Office furniture | 2,242 36 | |
| Stationery and supplies | 3,524 83 | |
| Old age benefit notes | 18,400 00 | |
| Accrued interest on above | 1,713 75 | |
| | | 27,308 07 |
| Total admitted assets | | $508,619 75 |

## LIABILITIES.

|  | |  |
|---|---|---|
| Death claims due and unpaid | $ 222 22 | |
| Death claims reported during the year but not yet adjusted | 5,000 00 | |
| Total death claims | | $5,222 22 |
| Advance assessments | | 830 02 |
| Total | | $6,052 24 |

## EXHIBIT OF CERTIFICATES.

| | Total business of the year. Number. | Amount. | Business in Illinois during year. Number. | Amount. |
|---|---|---|---|---|
| Benefit certificates in force December 31, 1920, as per last statement | 12,580 | $11,214,250 00 | 8,509 | $8,265,250 00 |
| Benefit certificates written and renewed during the year | 844 | 548,750 00 | 303 | 298,250 00 |
| Benefit certificates received by transfer during the year | -------- | -------------- | 1 | 1,000 00 |
| Benefit certificates increased during the year | -------- | 27,250 00 | -------- | 14,000 00 |
| Total | 13,424 | $11,790,250 00 | 8,903 | $8,478,500 00 |
| Deduct terminated, decreased or transferred during the year | 716 | 610,750 00 | -------- | -------------- |
| Deduct terminated or decreased during the year | -------- | -------------- | 515 | 484,500 00 |
| Total benefit certificates in force December 31, 1921 | 12,708 | $11,179,500 00 | 8,388 | $7,994,000 00 |

Received during the year from members in Illinois: Mortuary, $138,773.34; expense, $22,571.89; total — $161,345 23

EXHIBIT OF DEATH CLAIMS.

| | Total claims. Number. | Total claims. Amount. | Illinois claims. Number. | Illinois claims. Amount. |
|---|---|---|---|---|
| Claims unpaid December 31, 1920, as per last statement | 10 | $ 13,250 00 | 8 | $11,750 00 |
| Claims reported during the year and interest addition | 115 | 141,500 00 | 88 | 119,000 00 |
| Total | 125 | $154,750 00 | 96 | $130,750 00 |
| Claims paid during the year | 121 | 147,205 23 | 93 | 124,205 23 |
| Balance | 4 | 7,544 77 | 3 | $6,544 77 |
| Saved by compromising or scaling down claims during the year | | 2,322 55 | | 2,322 55 |
| Claims unpaid December 31, 1921 | 4 | $5,222 22 | 3 | $4,222 22 |

SCHEDULE D—BONDS.

| Description. | Book value. | Par value. |
|---|---|---|
| Western Union Telegraph Co., 4½s | $1,000 00 | $1,000 00 |
| Western Union Telegraph Co., 4½s | 1,000 00 | 1,000 00 |
| Western Union Telegraph Co., 4½s | 1,000 00 | 1,000 00 |
| Western Union Telegraph Co., 4½s | 1,000 00 | 1,000 00 |
| Western Union Telegraph Co., 4½s | 1,000 00 | 1,000 00 |
| Second U. S. Liberty Loan, 4s | 1,000 00 | 1,000 00 |
| Second U. S. Liberty Loan, 4s | 1,000 00 | 1,000 00 |
| Second U. S. Liberty Loan, 4s | 1,000 00 | 1,000 00 |
| Second U. S. Liberty Loan, 4s | 1,000 00 | 1,000 00 |
| Second U. S. Liberty Loan, 4s | 1,000 00 | 1,000 00 |
| Totals | $10,000 00 | $10,000 00 |

## WOMEN'S CATHOLIC ORDER OF FORESTERS.

Located at No. 140 North Dearborn Street, Chicago, Illinois.

MARY L. DOWNES, President. ANNA E. PHELAN, Secretary.

| | |
|---|---|
| Balance from previous year | $3,973,219 28 |

INCOME.

| | |
|---|---|
| Membership fees actually received | $1,415,451 35 |
| Dues and per capita tax | 104,231 60 |
| Other payments by members, viz: Convention, $20,574.17; church extension, $110.15; Pueblo flood, $2,107.32 | 22,791 64 |
| Total received from members | $1,542,474 59 |
| Deduct payments returned to applicants and members | 584 88 |
| Net amount received from members | $1,541,889 71 |
| Gross interest on bonds and dividends on stocks | 193,273 83 |
| Gross interest on deposits in trust companies and banks | 8,807 87 |
| Sale of lodge supplies | 6,861 03 |
| Gross profit on sale or maturity of ledger assets | 217 18 |
| Certificates | 4,156 65 |
| Reimbursed U. S. F. & G. Co | 233 48 |
| Advertisements in official publication | 250 00 |
| Bonds | 1,157 15 |
| Miscellaneous credit | 102 05 |
| Special discount bonds purchased | 200 00 |
| Total income | $1,757,148 95 |
| Sum | $5,730,368 33 |

DISBURSEMENTS.

| | |
|---|---|
| Death claims | $1,104,557 49 |
| Commissions and fees paid to deputies and organizers | 4,456 89 |
| Salaries of organizers | 7,728 50 |
| Organizers expense | 5,691 18 |
| Salaries of officers and trustees | 9,083 36 |
| Compensation of trustees | 1,814 50 |
| Salaries of office employees | 22,065 75 |
| Other compensation of office employes | 2,251 20 |
| Fees paid to supreme medical examiners | 84 90 |
| Fees paid to subordinate medical examiners | 359 00 |
| Traveling and other expenses of officers, trustees and committees | 4,298 11 |
| For collection and remittance of assessments and dues | 523 07 |
| Insurance department fees | 550 00 |
| Rent | 3,600 00 |
| Advertising, printing and stationery | 14,244 03 |

DISBURSEMENTS—Concluded.

| | |
|---|---|
| Postage, express, telegraph and telephone | $ 3,443 69 |
| Official publication | 12,899 95 |
| Expenses of supreme lodge meeting | 58,496 71 |
| Legal expense in litigating claims | 4,085 50 |
| Actuary report and conference | 1,310 81 |
| Pueblo flood sufferers | 2,097 32 |
| Gross loss on sale or maturity of ledger assets | 589 90 |
| Church extension | 117 04 |
| Miscellaneous | 3,105 90 |
| Rerating expense | 17,028 11 |
| Premium new members | 398 50 |
| Reimbursed by U. S. F. & G. Co | 233 48 |
| Bonds high court and subordinate court officers | 1,575 00 |
| Auditing | 500 00 |
| Total disbursements | $1,287,189 89 |
| Balance | $4,443,178 34 |

LEDGER ASSETS.

| | |
|---|---|
| Book value of bonds and stocks | $4,150,312 36 |
| Deposits in trust companies and banks not on interest | 292,865 98 |
| Total ledger assets | $4,443,178 34 |

NON-LEDGER ASSETS.

| | |
|---|---|
| Interest and rents due and accrued | 70,739 65 |
| Assessments actually collected by subordinate lodges not yet turned over to supreme lodge—estimated | 117,954 28 |
| Gross assets | $4,631,872 27 |

DEDUCT ASSETS NOT ADMITTED.

| | |
|---|---|
| Book value of bonds and stocks over market value | 10,371 81 |
| Total admitted assets | $4,621,500 46 |

LIABILITIES.

| | | |
|---|---|---|
| Death claims due and unpaid | $ 42,023 73 | |
| Death claims adjusted not yet due | 118,475 00 | |
| Death claims resisted | 1,450 00 | |
| Total unpaid claims | | $161,948 73 |

EXHIBIT OF CERTIFICATES.

| | Total business of the year. | | Business in Illinois during year. | |
|---|---|---|---|---|
| | Number. | Amount. | Number. | Amount. |
| Benefit certificates in force December 31, 1920, as per last statement | 81,251 | $77,363,300 00 | 41,245 | $4,782,600 00 |
| Benefit certificates written and renewed during the year | 4,705 | 3,704,750 00 | 1,308 | 1,109,750 00 |
| Benefit certificates increased during the year | -------- | 48,250 00 | -------- | 22,500 00 |
| Total | 85,956 | $81,116,300 00 | 42,553 | $5,914,850 00 |
| Deduct terminated, decreased or transferred during the year | 2,414 | 2,176,100 00 | -------- | ------------ |
| Deduct terminated or decreased during the year | -------- | ------------ | 1,141 | 1,103,500 00 |
| Total benefit certificates in force December 31, 1921 | 83,542 | $78,940,200 00 | 41,412 | $4,811,350 00 |

Received during the year from members in Illinois: Mortuary, $745,002.62; expense, $55,303.75; total — $800,306 37

EXHIBIT OF DEATH CLAIMS.

| | Total claims. | | Illinois claims. | |
|---|---|---|---|---|
| | Number. | Amount. | Number. | Amount. |
| Claims unpaid December 31, 1920, as per last statement | 164 | $ 143,781 22 | 103 | $ 86,581 22 |
| Claims reported during the year and interest addition | 1,090 | 1,125,125 00 | 698 | 733,100 00 |
| Total | 1,254 | $1,268,906 22 | 801 | $819,681 22 |
| Claims paid during the year | 1,077 | 1,104,557 49 | 686 | 710,744 99 |
| Balance | 177 | $164,348 73 | 115 | $108,936 23 |
| Saved by compromising or scaling down claims during the year | -------- | 2,400 00 | -------- | 2,400 00 |
| Claims unpaid December 31, 1921 | 177 | $161,948 73 | 115 | $106,536 23 |

SCHEDULE D—BONDS.

| Description. | Book value. | Par value. | Market value. |
|---|---|---|---|
| Albany, Ore., refunding, 5s | $20,367 40 | $20,000 00 | $19,600 00 |
| Albert Lea, Minn., permanent improvement, 4½s | 20,000 00 | 20,000 00 | 20,000 00 |
| Alberta Province, Can., 10-yr. gold, 5s | 24,517 50 | 25,000 00 | 24,000 00 |
| Alpine, Utah, high school, 5s | 15,217 50 | 15,000 00 | 14,850 00 |
| Altamont, Ill., sewer, 5s | 5,527 50 | 5,500 00 | 5,500 00 |
| Ashe County, N. C., road, 5½s | 24,299 50 | 25,000 00 | 25,250 00 |
| Ashland, Wis., refunding, 4½s | 10,130 00 | 10,000 00 | 9,600 00 |
| Astoria, Port of Oregon, municipal, 5s | 30,000 00 | 30,000 00 | 30,000 00 |
| Athens, Tex., water works, 5s | 5,000 00 | 5,000 00 | 4,900 00 |
| Austin, Tex., street sewer, bridge, 5s | 25,292 50 | 25,000 00 | 24,500 00 |
| Averyville, Ill., improvement, 5s | 5,673 50 | 5,000 00 | 5,000 00 |
| Ballard, Wash., funding, 4½s | 21,573 20 | 22,000 00 | 21,560 00 |
| Banner Township, N. C., road improvement, 6s | 44,620 00 | 40,000 00 | 43,200 00 |
| Bay City, Mich., park, 4s | 10,100 00 | 10,000 00 | 9,300 00 |
| Beaumont, Tex., sewer, 5s | 30,750 00 | 30,000 00 | 28,900 00 |
| Beggs, Okla., board of education, 6s | 21,802 00 | 20,000 00 | 21,800 00 |
| Belle Fourche, S. D., water works, 5s | 11,000 00 | 11,000 00 | 10,890 00 |
| Bellingham, Wash., funding, 5s | 5,264 00 | 5,000 00 | 4,950 00 |
| Benson, Neb., sewer, 5s | 20,000 00 | 20,000 00 | 20,200 00 |
| Bessemer, Mich., sewer, 5½s | 15,442 50 | 15,000 00 | 16,500 00 |
| Bessemer Township, Mich., school district, 6½s | 31,260 00 | 30,000 00 | 32,100 00 |
| Bingham County, Idaho, road and bridge, 5s | 15,150 00 | 15,000 00 | 15,150 00 |
| Birmingham, Ala., funding, 5s | 5,240 00 | 5,000 00 | 5,000 00 |
| Birmingham, Ala., refunding, 5s | 30,750 00 | 30,000 00 | 30,000 00 |
| Blue Earth County, Minn., public drain, 5s | 25,745 30 | 25,000 00 | 26,000 00 |
| Boliver County, Miss., special road, 5½s | 39,969 74 | 38,000 00 | 39,900 00 |
| Boone, Iowa, Independent School District, 4½s | 19,800 00 | 20,000 00 | 20,000 00 |
| Bossier Parish, La., Road District No. 2, 5s | 12,000 00 | 12,000 00 | 12,000 00 |
| Bureau County, Ill., School District 250, 5s | 20,347 20 | 20,000 00 | 20,400 00 |
| Butte County, S. D., funding, 5s | 51,245 00 | 50,000 00 | 50,000 00 |
| Box Elder County, Utah, road, 4½s | 23,812 50 | 25,000 00 | 24,500 00 |
| Bledosoe County, Tenn., school, 6s | 24,000 00 | 25,000 00 | 27,750 00 |
| Cache County, Utah, school district, 4½s | 19,850 00 | 20,000 00 | 19,400 00 |
| Caldwell, Idaho, water works extension, 6s | 5,350 00 | 5,000 00 | 5,000 00 |
| Calgary, Can., 5s | 24,630 00 | 25,000 00 | 21,000 00 |
| Caney, Kans., funding, 5s | 5,137 60 | 5,000 00 | 5,100 00 |
| Cass County, Minn., court house, 5s | 6,660 00 | 6,000 00 | 6,000 00 |
| Cassia County, Idaho, Burley Hyway, 5½s | 20,603 00 | 20,000 00 | 21,200 00 |
| Chattanooga, Tenn., funding, 4½s | 17,730 00 | 18,000 00 | 17,640 00 |
| Cherokee County, Tex., Road District No. 1, 5s | 25,000 00 | 25,000 00 | 25,000 00 |
| Cherokee County, Tex., Road District No. 1, 5s | 25,000 00 | 25,000 00 | 25,000 00 |
| Chicago Heights, Ill., sewer, 5s | 14,355 00 | 14,500 00 | 14,500 00 |
| Claiborne County, Miss., Spr. District 4, 5¾s | 34,010 50 | 35,000 00 | 35,000 00 |
| Claiborne County, Miss., Spr. Dist 4, 5¾s | 971 80 | 1,000 00 | 1,000 00 |
| Clarion, Iowa, Indepdndent School District, 5s | 20,300 00 | 20,000 00 | 20,000 00 |
| Clarksburg, W. Va., school district, 5s | 5,201 50 | 5,000 00 | 5,000 00 |
| Clearwater, Nez Perce County, Idaho Highway Dist., 6s | 15,822 00 | 15,000 00 | 15,600 00 |
| Cochise County, Ariz., School District No. 9, 5s | 45,000 00 | 45,000 00 | 45,000 00 |
| Coffeyville, Kans., water works, 5s | 10,488 00 | 10,000 00 | 10,000 00 |
| Community High School District No. 384, McDonough and Fulton Counties, Ill., 5½s | 10,890 00 | 11,000 00 | 11,000 00 |
| Cook County, Ill., high school district, 4½s | 4,869 16 | 5,000 00 | 5,000 00 |
| Cheyenne, Wyo., sewer and storm, 6s | 23,880 00 | 24,000 00 | 26,160 00 |
| Dade County, Fla., road, 5s | 25,000 00 | 25,000 00 | 25,000 00 |
| Dallas, Tex., water works, 4s | 19,900 00 | 20,000 00 | 17,800 00 |
| Danville, Ill., improvement, 5s | 3,483 90 | 3,500 00 | 3,500 00 |
| Daytona, Fla., school, 5s | 5,060 50 | 5,000 00 | 5,000 00 |
| DeKalb Township, S. C., road, 6s | 38,000 00 | 38,000 00 | 40,280 00 |
| Denton County, Tex., road District No. 3, 5s | 20,000 00 | 20,000 00 | 20,000 00 |
| Dinwiddie County, Va., road improvement, 6s | 5,525 00 | 5,000 00 | 5,350 00 |
| Durham County, N. C., court house, 4¾s | 20,508 40 | 20,000 00 | 19,600 00 |
| Eastland County, Tex., sewer, 6s | 22,907 50 | 25,000 00 | 26,750 00 |
| Eastland County, Tex., Independent School District, 5s | 19,800 00 | 20,000 00 | 19,200 00 |
| Edmonton, Alta., Can., school district, 5s | 18,700 00 | 20,000 00 | 15,000 00 |
| Elko County, Nev., jail bonds, 6s | 11,508 50 | 10,000 00 | 10,100 00 |
| East Cleveland, Ohio, school district building, 6s | 31,094 00 | 30,000 00 | 33,000 00 |
| Fairbury, Neb., water works, 5s | 5,050 00 | 5,000 00 | 5,000 00 |
| Farmington, Ill., water works, 5s | 15,260 60 | 15,000 00 | 15,000 00 |
| Fisher County, Tex., court house, 5s | 30,000 00 | 30,000 00 | 30,000 00 |
| Fort Smith, Ark., water works, 5s | 20,100 00 | 20,000 00 | 20,000 00 |
| Fort Worth, Tex., reservoir con., 5s | 14,814 00 | 15,000 00 | 15,300 00 |
| Galveston, Tex., public school, 5s | 25,613 50 | 25,000 00 | 26,000 00 |
| Gastonia, N. C., school, 5s | 21,284 00 | 20,000 00 | 19,200 00 |
| Gila County, Ariz., School District No. 26, 6s | 21,024 28 | 20,000 00 | 20,800 00 |
| Great Falls, Mont., refunding water works, 5s | 7,110 60 | 7 000 00 | 7,000 00 |
| Greenlee County, Ariz., road, 6s | 26,935 00 | 25,000 00 | 26,250 00 |
| Greenlee County, Ariz., road, 6s | 15,985 82 | 15,000 00 | 15,750 00 |
| Green Bay, Wis., paving B., 4s | 8,092 80 | 8,000 00 | 8,000 00 |
| Grinnell, Iowa, water works, 5s | 15,417 09 | 15,000 00 | 15,000 00 |
| Gladstone, Mich., board of education, 6s | 24,750 00 | 25,000 00 | 27,750 00 |
| Harding County, S. D., fundings, 5s | 10,254 00 | 10,000 00 | 10,100 00 |

SCHEDULE D—BONDS—Continued.

| Description. | Book value. | Par value. | Market value. |
|---|---|---|---|
| Harding County, S. D., fundings, 5s | $10,311 00 | $10,000 00 | $10,100 00 |
| Hawkins County, Tenn., road improvement, 5s | 25,578 00 | 25,000 00 | 25,000 00 |
| Hemphill County, Tex., bridge, 5s | 25,000 00 | 25,000 00 | 25,000 00 |
| Highland Park, Mich., police station, 4¾s | 40,516 00 | 40,000 00 | 40,000 00 |
| Hill County, Mont., road, 5¼s | 48,525 00 | 50,000 00 | 54,000 00 |
| Hinds County, Miss., bridge, 5¼s | 25,875 00 | 25,000 00 | 25,000 00 |
| Hochelaga, Can., school, 5½s | 50,768 50 | 50,000 00 | 47,500 00 |
| Hoopeston, Ill., water works, 5s | 4,520 00 | 4,000 00 | 4,000 00 |
| Houston, Tex., water works, 5s | 27,687 50 | 25,000 00 | 26,000 00 |
| Houston, Tex., high school, 4¾s | 24,468 75 | 25,000 00 | 25,000 00 |
| Houston, Tex., road and bridge, Municipal P. Pk., 4¾s | 24,568 33 | 25,000 00 | 25,000 00 |
| Hunt County, Tex., road improvement, 5s | 12,000 00 | 12,000 00 | 12,000 00 |
| Indianapolis, Ind., school, city, 4¾s | 18,150 00 | 20,000 00 | 20,600 00 |
| Independent School District, Humboldt, Iowa, 5s | 25,477 50 | 25,000 00 | 25,250 00 |
| Independence, Kans., water works extension, 4¾s | 11,857 86 | 11,600 00 | 11,484 00 |
| Iron County, Utah, school building, 5s | 8,859 23 | 9,000 00 | 9,000 00 |
| Ironwood, Mich., 5s | 27,678 70 | 30,000 00 | 30,600 00 |
| Isanti County, Minn., Independent School District No. 4, 6s | 16,564 50 | 15,000 00 | 16,500 00 |
| Iron County, Mich., road, 5s | 22,625 00 | 25,000 00 | 25,500 00 |
| Jefferson County, Ark., bridge, 5s | 24,500 00 | 25,000 00 | 25,000 00 |
| Jefferson Davis Parish, La., court house, 5s | 25,447 00 | 25,000 00 | 25,000 00 |
| Kansas City, Mo., school, 4s | 24,250 00 | 25,000 00 | 24,000 00 |
| Lafayette Parish, La., improvement, 5s | 19,700 00 | 20,000 00 | 20,000 00 |
| Lake Charles, La., funding certificate of indebtedness, 5s | 29,970 00 | 29,500 00 | 29,500 00 |
| Lamar, Colo., water works, 6s | 5,350 00 | 5,000 00 | 5,100 00 |
| Lawrence County, S. D., refunding, 5s | 5,125 00 | 5,000 00 | 5,000 00 |
| Lee County, Miss., road, 5s | 20,700 00 | 20,000 00 | 20,000 00 |
| Lee County, Miss., District No. 4 and 5, 5s | 12,344 75 | 12,000 00 | 12,000 00 |
| Lethbridge, Alta, Can., 5s | 23,371 36 | 24,820 00 | 19,607 80 |
| Llano County, Tex., Bridge No. 2, 5s | 15,156 00 | 15,000 00 | 14,850 00 |
| Los Angeles, Cal., school, 4½s | 18,877 79 | 19,000 00 | 18,430 00 |
| London County, Tenn., road and bridge, 5s | 19,950 00 | 20,000 00 | 20,000 00 |
| Lusk, Wyo., water works, 6s | 26,775 00 | 25,000 00 | 25,500 00 |
| Laurens County, S. C., road, 6s | 39,900 00 | 40,000 00 | 44,800 00 |
| Maywood, Ill., School District No. 89, 5s | 27,895 40 | 30,000 00 | 27,900 00 |
| Medford, Wis., water works, 5s | 5,321 50 | 5,000 00 | 5,050 00 |
| Meridian, Miss., water works, 4½s | 20,200 00 | 20,000 00 | 19,400 00 |
| Meridian, Miss., water works, 4½s | 17,000 00 | 17,000 00 | 16,660 00 |
| Middlesborough, Ky., refunding, 6s | 35,963 37 | 35,000 00 | 35,700 00 |
| Miles City, Mont., electric light, 5½s | 10,387 50 | 10,000 00 | 10,000 00 |
| Minnespolis, Minn., improvement, 4¾s | 20,634 00 | 20,000 00 | 20,200 00 |
| Montreal, Can., 5s | 20,000 00 | 20,000 00 | 17,200 00 |
| Montreal, Can., Catholic school, 5s | 4,975 00 | 5,000 00 | 4,100 00 |
| Montreal, Can., sinking fund, 5s | 34,737 50 | 35,000 00 | 26,650 00 |
| McCurtain County, Okla., road, 5s | 32,298 70 | 35,000 00 | 34,300 00 |
| New Canton Community, Pike County, Ill., high school district, 5½s | 30,000 00 | 30,000 00 | 30,000 00 |
| New Orleans, La., improvement, 5s | 25,000 00 | 25,000 00 | 25,000 00 |
| Newport News, Va., harbor, 4½s | 24,437 50 | 25,000 00 | 24,500 00 |
| Newton, Kans., water works extension, 5s | 5,200 00 | 5,000 00 | 5,000 00 |
| New York City, N. Y., reg., 4s | 25,468 75 | 25,000 00 | 23,750 00 |
| New York City, N. Y., reg., 4s | 25,468 75 | 25,000 00 | 23,750 00 |
| Nez Perce County, Idaho, refunding, 5s | 10,552 20 | 10,000 00 | 10,000 00 |
| Oklahoma, Okla., water and sewer, 4½s | 10,590 00 | 10,000 00 | 9,200 00 |
| Oklahoma County, Okla., court house, 4½s | 10,592 00 | 10,000 00 | 9,500 00 |
| Ontario Province, Can., debenture, 5s | 25,000 00 | 25,000 00 | 24,250 00 |
| Orange County, Fla., road, 5s | 25,192 50 | 25,000 00 | 25,000 00 |
| Oneida County, Idaho, road, 5s | 34,438 20 | 38,000 00 | 38,000 00 |
| Pasco, Franklin County, Wash., city hall, 5s | 20,640 00 | 20,000 00 | 20,200 00 |
| Pensacola, Fla., improvement, 4½s | 4,900 00 | 5,000 00 | 4,850 00 |
| Pinal, Ariz., road and bridge, 5s | 9,585 00 | 9,000 00 | 9,000 00 |
| Pocatello, Idaho, Independent School District, 5s | 12,222 00 | 12,000 00 | 12,000 00 |
| Polk County, Tenn., road improvement, 5s | 27,125 00 | 25,000 00 | 24,500 00 |
| Pontiac, Ill., improvement, 4½s | 5,342 00 | 5,000 00 | 5,000 00 |
| Portland, Ore., water, 4s | 23,875 00 | 25,000 00 | 22,750 00 |
| Pueblo, Colo., water works, 4½s | 9,512 50 | 10,000 00 | 9,700 00 |
| Putnam, Ill., No. 536 School Site and Building, 5½s | 4,585 47 | 4,500 00 | 4,590 00 |
| Phalia County of Bolivar, Miss., Sept. Road Dist., 5¼s | 30,520 80 | 29,000 00 | 31,320 00 |
| Quitman County, Miss., road, 6s | 23,681 70 | 25,000 00 | 27,250 00 |
| Raton, Colfax County, N. M., water, 5s | 24,150 00 | 25,000 00 | 25,000 00 |
| Roane County, Tenn., funding C., 5s | 26,185 00 | 25,000 00 | 25,000 00 |
| Robertson County, Tex., road, Prec. No. 2, 5s | 12,187 50 | 12,500 00 | 12,500 00 |
| Russell County, Ky., road and bridge, 5s | 24,450 95 | 23,500 00 | 23,735 00 |
| Salt Lake City, Utah, water works, 4¼s | 10,025 00 | 10,000 00 | 9,800 00 |
| Sandpoint, Idaho, municipal, 6s | 27,372 80 | 26,000 00 | 28,080 00 |
| Santa Barbara, Cal., school district, 4½s | 10,927 10 | 10,125 00 | 10,023 75 |
| Seattle, Wash., school district, 4s | 14,962 50 | 15,000 00 | 14,550 00 |
| Seattle, Wash., electric light extension, 4½s | 10,400 00 | 10,000 00 | 9,700 00 |
| Seattle Port, Wash., waterway improvement, 5s | 25,864 60 | 25,000 00 | 25,500 00 |
| Shreveport, La., water works and sewer, 4¾s | 21,478 92 | 20,000 00 | 19,600 00 |
| Sioux City, Ia., refunding, 4¾s | 17,219 30 | 17,000 00 | 17,000 00 |

SCHEDULE D—BONDS—Concluded.

| Description. | Book value. | Par value. | Market value. |
|---|---|---|---|
| Sioux Falls, S. D., sewer, 5s | $31,524 00 | $30,000 00 | $30,300 00 |
| Skamania County, Wash., road, 5½s | 26,099 88 | 25,000 00 | 26,250 00 |
| Spokane, Wash., bridge, 4½s | 21,550 00 | 20,000 00 | 19,800 00 |
| Spokane, Wash., school district, 4½s | 5,056 00 | 5,000 00 | 4,950 00 |
| State of South Dakota, rural credit S., 6s | 28,220 40 | 27,000 00 | 31,320 00 |
| Stillwater County, Mont., highway, 6s | 25,000 00 | 25,000 00 | 27,000 00 |
| St. Louis County, Minn., school district, 5s | ---------- | ---------- | ---------- |
| St. Petersburg, Fla., improvement, 6s | 5,500 00 | 5,000 00 | 5,450 00 |
| Strahan Dist., Iowa, Col. Ind. School Building, 5s | 20,508 20 | 20,000 00 | 20,000 00 |
| Superior, Wis., school, 4½s | 5,137 50 | 5,000 00 | 4,950 00 |
| Tacoma, Wash., light and power, 4½s | 10,650 00 | 10,000 00 | 9,700 00 |
| Tacoma, Wash., Spec. Green R. W. F., 5s | 5,094 67 | 5,000 00 | 5,000 00 |
| Tangipahoa Parish, La., Road District No. 3, 5s | 28,845 90 | 28,000 00 | 28,000 00 |
| Trinity County, Tex., Road District No. 1, 5s | 24,000 00 | 25,000 00 | 25,000 00 |
| Trinity County, Tex., road, 5½s | 25,778 00 | 25,000 00 | 25,000 00 |
| Tulsa, Okla., school district, 5s | 20,147 98 | 20,000 00 | 20,000 00 |
| Tuscaloosa, Ala., water works, 5s | 28,000 00 | 28,000 00 | 26,600 00 |
| Twin Falls, Idaho, parking and sewer, 5s | 6,211 60 | 6,000 00 | 6,000 00 |
| Twin Falls, Idaho, school, 5½s | 15,703 50 | 15,000 00 | 15,000 00 |
| Twin Falls, Idaho, School District So. 7, 6s | 32,000 00 | 32,000 00 | 33,280 00 |
| United States Liberty Loan, second cour., 4¼s | 10,000 00 | 10,000 00 | 10,000 00 |
| United States Liberty Loan, 4¼s | 50,000 00 | 50,000 00 | 50,000 00 |
| United States Liberty Loan, fourth, 4¼s | 50,000 00 | 50,000 00 | 50,000 00 |
| United States Liberty Loan, fourth, 4¼s | 50,000 00 | 50,000 00 | 50,000 00 |
| United States Liberty Loan, 4¾s | 35,000 00 | 35,000 00 | 35,000 00 |
| United States Liberty Loan, 4¾s | 40,000 00 | 40,000 00 | 40,000 00 |
| United States Liberty Loan, fourth, 4¼s | 42,900 00 | 50,000 00 | 48,500 00 |
| Valleytown, Cherokee County, N. C., township, 5½s | 19,900 00 | 20,000 00 | 20,400 00 |
| Van Wert County, Ohio, school building imp., 5½s | 42,446 00 | 40,000 00 | 40,400 00 |
| Victoria County, Tex., sewer disp. pl., 5s | 25,250 00 | 25,000 00 | 25,000 00 |
| Victoria, B. C., local improvement, 4s | 18,498 66 | 20,000 00 | 19,400 00 |
| Virginia, Minn., W. and L., 5s | 12,000 00 | 12,000 00 | 12,000 00 |
| Vermillion, S. D., independent school, 5¾s | 25,147 50 | 25,000 00 | 26,500 00 |
| Wadena, Minn., ditch, 5½s | 6,109 35 | 6,000 00 | 6,060 00 |
| Ward County, N. D., funding, 4½s | 16,014 00 | 15,000 00 | 14,850 00 |
| Washington County, Utah, school, 5s | 17,486 20 | 17,000 00 | 17,170 00 |
| Waterloo, Iowa, water works, 4½s | 5,125 00 | 5,000 00 | 4,900 00 |
| Watertown, S. D., sewer, 5s | 27,191 60 | 26,000 00 | 26,000 00 |
| West Point, Neb., school, 6s | 30,000 00 | 30,000 00 | 30,000 00 |
| Will County, Ill., school district, 5s | 1,035 35 | 1,000 00 | 1,000 00 |
| Wymore, Gage County, Neb., water, 5s | 5,000 00 | 5,000 00 | 5,050 00 |
| Watertown, S. D., electric light, 5s | 27,528 00 | 30,000 00 | 30,000 00 |
| West Park, County of Cuyahoga, Ohio, school, 6s | 32,236 40 | 30,000 00 | 36,000 00 |
| Wichita Falls, Tex., water works, 5s | 26,316 72 | 30,000 00 | 29,400 00 |
| Yavapai County, Ariz., road, 6s | 24,261 28 | 25,000 00 | 27,000 00 |
| Totals | $4,150,312 36 | $4,123,045 00 | $4,139,940 55 |

# SOCIETIES OF OTHER STATES.

## AID ASSOCIATION FOR LUTHERANS.

Located at First National Bank Building, Appleton, Wisconsin.

G. D. ZIEGLER, President. ALBERT VOECKS, Secretary.

| | |
|---|---|
| Balance from previous year | $1,320,471 54 |
| **INCOME.** | |
| Membership fees actually received | $ 1,741 92 |
| Assessments or premiums during first 12 months of membership of which all or an extra percentage is used for expenses | 122,200 13 |
| All other assessments or premiums | 337,780 64 |
| Dues and per capita tax | 463 50 |
| Surplus of 1920 applied on assessments | 52,533 19 |
| Principal of certificate loans | 26,063 84 |
| Interest on certificate loans | 13,782 83 |
| Change of beneficiary | 216 00 |
| Total received from members | $554,782 05 |
| Deduct payments returned to applicants and members | 221 54 |
| Net amount received from members | $554,560 51 |
| Gross interest on mortgage loans | 21,491 86 |
| Gross interest on bonds and dividends on stocks | 57,001 31 |
| Gross interest on deposits in banks | 795 35 |
| Sale of lodge supplies | 108 10 |
| Borrowed money (gross) | 12,100 00 |
| Gross profit on sale or maturity of ledger assets— | |
| Real estate | 240 65 |
| Bonds | 313 17 |
| Gross increase in book value of ledger assets—real estate | 1,161 63 |
| Official publication | 52 95 |
| Miscellaneous | 173 63 |
| Total income | $647,999 16 |
| Sum | $1,968,470 70 |
| **DISBURSEMENTS.** | |
| Death claims | $72,432 93 |
| Permanent disability claims | 1,500 00 |
| Sick and accident claims | 23,520 58 |
| Surplus of 1920 used for payments of assessments | 52,533 19 |
| Withdrawal equities | 20,326 11 |
| Total benefits paid | $170,312 81 |
| Commissions and fees paid to deputies and organizers, salaries and expenses | 81,851 46 |
| Salaries of officers and trustees | 8,540 00 |
| Salaries and other compensation of committees | 46 25 |
| Salaries of office employees | 10,567 58 |
| Salaries and fees paid to supreme medical examiners | 2,800 00 |
| Salaries and fees paid to subordinate medical examiners | 18,942 50 |
| Traveling and other expenses of officers, trustees and committees | 1,191 23 |
| Insurance department fees | 463 95 |
| Rent | 750 00 |
| Advertising, printing and stationery | 4,305 22 |
| Postage, express, telegraph and telephone | 1,232 22 |
| Lodge supplies | 2,941 62 |
| Official publication | 3,601 41 |
| Expenses of supreme lodge meeting | 68 90 |
| Furniture and fixtures | 972 33 |
| Taxes, repairs and other expenses on real estate | 441 83 |
| Gross loss on sale or maturity of ledger assets | 227 42 |
| Premium on surety bonds | 396 50 |
| Premium on compensation insurance | 62 95 |
| Valuation | 157 40 |
| Examination | 109 48 |
| Miscellaneous | 185 62 |
| Total disbursements | $310,258 68 |
| Balance | $1,658,212 02 |

## LEDGER ASSETS.

| | |
|---|---|
| Book value of real estate | $ 129,492 02 |
| Mortgage loans on real estate | 383,491 33 |
| Book value of bonds and stocks | 1,097,133 04 |
| Deposits in trust companies and banks on interest | 48,095 63 |
| Total ledger assets | $1,658,212 02 |

### NON-LEDGER ASSETS.

| | |
|---|---|
| Interest and rents due and accrued | 38,328 22 |
| Market value of real estate over book value | 338 37 |
| Market value of bonds and stocks over book value | 34,963 58 |
| Principal of certificate loans | 422,134 45 |
| Gross assets | $2,153,976 64 |

### DEDUCT ASSETS NOT ADMITTED.

| | | |
|---|---|---|
| Principal of certificate loans | $422,134 45 | |
| Interest due and accrued on certificate loans | 8,564 31 | |
| | | 430,698 76 |
| Total admitted assets | | $1,723,277 88 |

## LIABILITIES.

| | |
|---|---|
| Death claims reported during the year but not yet adjusted | $ 4,250 00 |
| Salaries, rents, expenses, commissions, etc., due or accrued | 13,372 13 |
| Taxes due or accrued | 420 35 |
| Borrowed money | 12,100 00 |
| Advance assessments | 8,739 47 |
| Total | $38,881 95 |

## EXHIBIT OF CERTIFICATES.

| | Total business of the year. | | Business in Illinois during year. | |
|---|---|---|---|---|
| | Number. | Amount. | Number. | Amount. |
| Benefit certificates in force December 31, 1920, as per last statement | 17,118 | $14,866,127 00 | 4,160 | $3,091,052 00 |
| Benefit certificates written and renewed during the year | 6,842 | 6,075,750 00 | 1,811 | 1,523,500 00 |
| Benefit certificates received by transfer during the year | | | 23 | 20,500 00 |
| Total | 23,960 | $20,941,877 00 | 5,994 | $4,635,052 00 |
| Deduct terminated, decreased or transferred during the year | 1,268 | 1,189,831 00 | | |
| Deduct terminated or decreased during the year | | | 348 | 293,023 00 |
| Total benefit certificates in force December 31, 1921 | 22,692 | $19,752,046 00 | 5,646 | $4,342,029 00 |

| | |
|---|---|
| Received during the year from members in Illinois: Mortuary, $69,370.07; sick and accident, $5,352.00; expense, $31,426.54; total | $106,148 61 |

## EXHIBIT OF DEATH CLAIMS.

| | Total claims. | | Illinois claims. | |
|---|---|---|---|---|
| | Number. | Amount. | Number. | Amount. |
| Claims unpaid December 31, 1920, as per last statement | 3 | $ 1,250 00 | | |
| Claims reported during the year and interest addition | 90 | 75,432 93 | 14 | $7,105 52 |
| Total | 93 | $76,682 93 | 14 | $7,105 52 |
| Claims paid during the year | 88 | 72,432 93 | 14 | 7,105 52 |
| Claims unpaid December 31, 1921 | 5 | 4,250 00 | | |

## EXHIBIT OF PERMANENT DISABILITY CLAIMS.

| | Total claims—all in Illinois. | |
|---|---|---|
| | Number. | Amount. |
| Claims reported during the year and interest addition | 2 | $1,500 00 |
| Claims paid during the year | 2 | 1,500 00 |

## EXHIBIT OF SICK AND ACCIDENT CLAIMS.

| | Total claims. | | Illinois claims. | |
|---|---|---|---|---|
| | Number. | Amount. | Number. | Amount. |
| Claims reported during the year | 591 | $23,520 58 | 79 | $3,170 48 |
| Claims paid during the year | 591 | 23,520 58 | 79 | 3,170 48 |

## AMERICAN INSURANCE UNION.

Located at No. 44 West Broad Street, Columbus, Ohio.

JOHN J. LENTZ, President. GEORGE W. HOGLAN, Secretary.

| | |
|---|---|
| Balance from previous year | $897,517 63 |

### INCOME.

| | |
|---|---|
| Membership fees actually received | $ 23,242 39 |
| Assessments or premiums during first 12 months of membership of which all or an extra percentage is used for expenses | 192,315 68 |
| All other assessments or premiums | 2,035,261 23 |
| Dues and per capita tax | 3,792 74 |
| Other payments by members, viz— | |
| Changed certificate fees | 1,704 65 |
| Reinstatement fees | 177 55 |
| Total received from members | $2,256,494 24 |
| Deduct payments returned to applicants and members | 4,008 93 |
| Net amount received from members | $2,252,485 31 |
| Gross interest on mortgage loans | 15,220 51 |
| Gross interest on collateral loans | 580 72 |
| Gross interest on bonds and dividends on stocks | 10,643 18 |
| Gross interest on deposits in trust companies and banks | 5,590 09 |
| Gross interest from all other sources | 24 65 |
| Gross rents from association's property, including $5,040.00 for association's occupancy of its own buildings | 97,857 47 |
| Sale of lodge supplies | 5,016 19 |
| Gross profit on sale or maturity of ledger assets—real estate | 14 88 |
| Gross increase in book value of ledger assets—bonds | 359 15 |
| Interest on certificate liens and loans | 1,321 90 |
| Income investigating investments | 1,380 00 |
| Total income | $2,390,494 05 |
| Sum | $3,288,011 68 |

### DISBURSEMENTS.

| | |
|---|---|
| Death claims | $1,367,324 55 |
| Permanent disability claims | 18,355 75 |
| Sick and accident claims | 46,248 87 |
| Old age benefits | 28,390 46 |
| Partial disability claims | 8,874 47 |
| Withdrawal equity claims | 4,604 50 |
| Liquidation payments | 71,397 24 |
| Total benefits paid | $1,545,195 84 |
| Commissions and fees paid to deputies and organizers | 119,232 57 |
| Salaries of deputies and organizers | 34,911 18 |
| Salaries of managers or agents not deputies or organizers | 29,381 02 |
| Salaries of officers and trustees | 45,499 93 |
| Other compensation of officers and trustees | 5,149 98 |
| Salaries and other compensation of committees | 5,755 00 |
| Salaries of office employees | 86,471 15 |
| Salaries and fees paid to supreme medical examiners | 8,124 99 |
| Salaries and fees paid to subordinate medical examiners | 20,019 00 |
| Traveling and other expenses of officers, trustees and committees | 4,379 66 |
| For collection and remittance of assessments and dues | 13,971 54 |
| Insurance department fees | 524 00 |
| Rent | 5,040 00 |
| Advertising, printing and stationery | 22,355 71 |
| Postage, express, telegraph and telephone | 7,807 53 |
| Lodge supplies | 3,403 05 |
| Official publication | 21,826 44 |
| Expenses of National Congress meeting | 10,040 39 |
| Legal expense in litigating claims | 1,352 90 |
| Other legal expenses | 6,090 29 |
| Furniture and fixtures | 4,537 68 |
| Taxes, repairs and other expenses on real estate | 94,550 88 |
| Gross loss on sale or maturity of ledger assets (real estate, bonds, collaterals) | 629 21 |
| Gross decrease in book value of ledger assets (bonds and collaterals) | 8,428 05 |
| Interest on borrowed money | 900 00 |
| Impairment and inspection | 2,075 54 |
| Office supplies and sundries | 12,464 11 |
| Branch office expenses | 16,821 53 |
| Fraternal associations | 888 37 |

DISBURSEMENTS—Concluded.

| | |
|---|---|
| Actuarial services | $9,394 81 |
| Bonds of officers, employees and representatives | 354 53 |
| Expenses investigating investments | 129 52 |
| Total disbursements | $2,147,706 40 |
| Balance | $1,140,305 28 |

## LEDGER ASSETS.

| | |
|---|---|
| Book value of real estate | $335,303 97 |
| Mortgage loans on real estate | 472,550 00 |
| Loans secured by pledge of bonds, stocks or other collateral | 1,500 00 |
| Book value of bonds and stocks | 255,576 48 |
| Cash in association's office | 13 04 |
| Deposits in trust companies and banks on interest | 75,130 79 |
| Loans to certificate holders | 231 00 |
| Total ledger assets | $1,140,305 28 |

NON-LEDGER ASSETS.

| | |
|---|---|
| Interest and rents due and accrued | 12,073 30 |
| Assessments actually collected by subordinate lodges not yet turned over to supreme lodge | 165,913 41 |
| Due from subordinate chapters for supplies | 1,455 37 |
| Total admitted assets | $1,319,747 36 |

## LIABILITIES.

| | | |
|---|---|---|
| Death claims resisted | $11,125 00 | |
| Death claims reported during the year but not yet adjusted | 114,380 94 | |
| Death claims incurred in 1921, not reported until 1922 | 32,102 00 | |
| Present value of deferred death claims payable in installments | 371 36 | |
| Total death claims | | $157,979 30 |
| Permanent disability claims resisted | $500 00 | |
| Permanent disability claims reported during the year but not yet adjusted | 2,750 00 | |
| Total permanent disability claims | | 3,250 00 |
| Sick and accident claims resisted | $511 70 | |
| Sick and accident claims reported during the year but not yet adjusted | 4,196 02 | |
| Total sick and accident claims | | 4,707 72 |
| Old age and other benefits due and unpaid | | 2,239 03 |
| Total unpaid claims | | $168,176 05 |
| Salaries, rents, expenses, commissions, etc., due or accrued | | 33,203 94 |
| Taxes due or accrued | | 18,426 02 |
| Advance assessments | | 6,138 59 |
| All other liabilities, viz— | | |
| Interest on mortgages paid in advance | $49 85 | |
| Reserve for expenses litigation | 733 10 | |
| | | 782 95 |
| Total | | $226,727 55 |

## EXHIBIT OF CERTIFICATES.

| | Total business of the year. Number. | Amount. | Business in Illinois during year. Number. | Amount. |
|---|---|---|---|---|
| Benefit certificates in force December 31, 1920, as per last statement | 110,249 | $114,837,559 01 | 11,226 | $11,056,324 00 |
| Benefit certificates written and renewed during the year | 14,687 | 15,830,891 75 | 1,813 | 1,833,830 00 |
| Benefit certificates received by transfer during the year | | | 23 | 21,657 31 |
| Benefit certificates increased during the year | | 337,940 00 | | 47,500 00 |
| Total | 124,936 | $131,006,390 76 | 13,062 | $12,959,311 31 |
| Deduct terminated, decreased or transferred during the year | 18,278 | 19,892,424 07 | | |
| Deduct terminated or decreased during the year | | | 1,584 | 1,784,583 00 |
| Total benefit certificates in force December 31, 1921 | 106,658 | $111,113,966 69 | 11,478 | $11,174,728 31 |

| | |
|---|---|
| Received during the year from members in Illinois: Mortuary, $118,036.79; reserve, $9,283.79; disability, $3,722.53; junior, $1,407.96; expense, $142,890.06; total | $175,341 13 |

## EXHIBIT OF DEATH CLAIMS.

| | Total claims. Number. | Total claims. Amount. | Illinois claims. Number. | Illinois claims. Amount. |
|---|---|---|---|---|
| Claims unpaid December 31, 1920, as per last statement | 156 | $ 154,369 40 | 9 | $ 8,053 33 |
| Claims reported during the year and interest addition | 1,279 | 1,369,881 26 | 89 | 90,281 78 |
| Total | 1,435 | $1,524,250 66 | 98 | $98,335 11 |
| Claims paid during the year | 1,297 | 1,367,324 55 | 92 | 92,335 11 |
| Balance | 138 | $156,926 11 | 6 | $6,000 00 |
| Saved by compromising or scaling down claims during the year | | 13,460 01 | | |
| Claims rejected during the year | 19 | 17,588 80 | | |
| Claims unpaid December 31, 1921 | 119 | $125,877 30 | 6 | $6,000 00 |

## EXHIBIT OF PERMANENT DISABILITY CLAIMS.

| | Total claims. Number. | Total claims. Amount. |
|---|---|---|
| Claims unpaid December 31, 1920, as per last statement | 1 | $ 1,000 00 |
| Claims reported during the year and interest addition | 35 | 20,950 00 |
| Total | 36 | $21,950 00 |
| Claims paid during the year | 31 | 18,355 75 |
| Balance | 5 | $3,594 25 |
| Saved by compromising or scaling down claims during the year | | 344 25 |
| Claims unpaid December 31, 1921 | 5 | $3,250 00 |

## EXHIBIT OF SICK AND ACCIDENT CLAIMS.

| | Total claims. Number. | Total claims. Amount. | Illinois claims. Number. | Illinois claims. Amount. |
|---|---|---|---|---|
| Claims unpaid December 31, 1920, as per last statement | 144 | $10,858 49 | 14 | $ 720 22 |
| Increase in estimated liability | | 1,396 14 | | |
| Decrease in estimated liability | | | | 28 50 |
| Claims reported during the year | 1,060 | 42,401 29 | 74 | 3,253 58 |
| Total | 1,204 | $54,655 92 | 88 | $3,945 30 |
| Claims paid during the year | 1,037 | 46,248 87 | 77 | 3,505 30 |
| Claims rejected during the year | 72 | 3,699 83 | 7 | 105 00 |
| Claims unpaid December 31, 1921 | 95 | $4,707 22 | 4 | $335 00 |

## EXHIBIT OF OLD AGE AND OTHER CLAIMS.

| | Total claims. Number. | Total claims. Amount. | Illinois claims. Number. | Illinois claims. Amount. |
|---|---|---|---|---|
| Claims unpaid December 31, 1920, as per last statement | 11 | $ 4,771 25 | | |
| Claims reported during the year and interest addition | 133 | 40,688 46 | 11 | $1,426 53 |
| Total | 144 | $45,459 71 | 11 | $1,426 53 |
| Claims paid during the year | 131 | 41,869 43 | 10 | 1,405 00 |
| Balance | 13 | $3,590 28 | 1 | $21 53 |
| Saved by compromising or scaling down claims during the year | | 343 75 | | |
| Claims rejected during the year | 7 | 1,007 50 | | |
| Claims unpaid December 31, 1921 | 6 | $2,239 03 | 1 | $21 53 |

---

## AMERICAN WOODMEN, SUPREME CAMP.

Located at No. 1022 Arapahoe Street, Denver, Colorado.

C. M. WHITE, Supreme Commander. L. H. LIGHTNER, Supreme Clerk.

| | |
|---|---|
| Balance from previous year | $601,605 59 |

## INCOME.

| | | |
|---|---|---|
| Membership fees actually received | | $ 1,282 45 |
| Assessments or premiums during first 12 months of membership of which all or an extra percentage is used for expenses | | 154,718 40 |
| All other assessments or premiums | | 262,721 25 |
| Dues and per capita tax | | 70,218 85 |
| Total received from members | | $488,940 95 |
| Deduct payments returned to applicants and members | | 1,480 71 |
| Net amount received from members | | $487,460 24 |
| Gross interest on mortgage loans | | 37,497 68 |
| Gross interest on bonds | | 1,551 11 |
| Gross interest on deposits in trust companies and banks | | 862 29 |
| Sale of lodge supplies | | 7,712 32 |
| Prizes | | 40 00 |
| Refund death claims | | 762 03 |
| Commission on loans | | 242 50 |
| Local camp dues | | 14 75 |
| Total income | | $536,142 92 |
| Sum | | $1,137,748 51 |

## DISBURSEMENTS.

| | | |
|---|---|---|
| Death claims | | $128,211 42 |
| Accident claims | | 3,330 00 |
| Claims compromised | | 346 00 |
| Total benefits paid | | $131,887 42 |
| Salaries of deputies and organizers | | 104,445 68 |
| Salaries of officers and trustees | | 14,028 00 |
| Salaries of office employees | | 22,865 48 |
| Salaries and fees paid to supreme medical examiners | | 1,090 01 |
| Traveling and other expenses of officers, trustees and committees | | 12,587 72 |
| For collection and remittance of assessments and dues | | 4,394 00 |
| Insurance department fees | | 786 00 |
| Rent supreme camp office and branch offices | | 7,201 01 |
| Advertising, printing and stationery | | 11,242 78 |
| Postage, express, telegraph and telephone | | 3,676 55 |
| Lodge supplies | | 8,507 08 |
| Official publication | | 1,167 97 |
| Expenses of supreme lodge meeting | | 7,447 31 |
| Other legal expenses | | 1,631 15 |
| Furniture and fixtures | | 2,932 12 |
| Taxes, personal | | 59 57 |
| Convention examination | | 4,751 68 |
| All other disbursements, viz— | | |
| Postoffice box, $16.00; Tulsa relief, $58.25; checks returned, $191.26 | | 265 51 |
| Bank exchange, $427.35; office supplies, $1,406.42; general expenses, $763.89 | | 2,597 66 |
| Supreme camp officers' bond, $400.00; janitor's services, $237.32 | | 637 32 |
| Actuarial expenses, $114.22; fire insurance, $112.00 | | 326 22 |
| Total disbursements | | $344,428 24 |
| Balance | | $793,320 27 |

## LEDGER ASSETS.

| | | |
|---|---|---|
| Mortgage loans on real estate | | $669,868 34 |
| Book value of bonds | | 37,973 12 |
| Cash in association's office | | 2,885 47 |
| Deposits in trust companies and banks on interest | | 81,392 45 |
| Bills receivable | | 950 89 |
| Other ledger assets, viz— | | |
| Deposit to secure office lease | $225 00 | |
| Petty cash | 25 00 | |
| | | 250 00 |
| Total ledger assets | | $793,320 27 |

### NON-LEDGER ASSETS.

| | | |
|---|---|---|
| Interest accrued | | 12,683 18 |
| Assessments actually collected by subordinate lodges not yet turned over to supreme lodge | | 30,000 00 |
| All other assets, viz— | | |
| Furniture and fixtures | $10,000 00 | |
| Stock and supplies | 5,000 00 | |
| | | 15,000 00 |
| Gross assets | | $851,003 45 |

## LEDGER ASSETS—Concluded.

DEDUCT ASSETS NOT ADMITTED.

| | | |
|---|---|---|
| Bills receivable | $ 950 89 | |
| Other items, viz— | | |
| Furniture and fixtures | 10,000 00 | |
| Stock and supplies | 5,000 00 | $15,950 89 |
| Total admitted assets | | $835,052 56 |

## LIABILITIES.

| | | |
|---|---|---|
| Death claims reported during the year but not yet adjusted | | $13,583 75 |
| Sick and accident claims adjusted, and not yet due | | 312 50 |
| All other liabilities, viz— | | |
| Trade accounts payable | $6,944 71 | |
| Local camp dues | 14 75 | 6,959 46 |
| Total | | $20,855 71 |

## EXHIBIT OF CERTIFICATES.

| | Total business of the year. | | Business in Illinois during year. | |
|---|---|---|---|---|
| | Number. | Amount. | Number. | Amount. |
| Benefit certificates in force December 31, 1920, as per last statement | 59,356 | $27,805,150 00 | 997 | $461,050 00 |
| Benefit certificates written and renewed during the year | 25,903 | 12,029,100 00 | 1,090 | 531,000 00 |
| Benefit certificates received by transfer during the year | | | 23 | 11,500 00 |
| Benefit certificates increased during the year | | 40,150 00 | | 500 00 |
| Total | 85,259 | $39,874,400 00 | 2,110 | $1,004,050 00 |
| Deduct terminated, decreased or transferred during the year | 32,627 | 15,154,550 00 | | |
| Deduct terminated or decreased during the year | | | 1,105 | 524,350 00 |
| Total benefit certificates in force December 31, 1921 | 52,632 | $24,719,850 00 | 1,005 | $479,700 00 |

Received during the year from members in Illinois: Mortuary, $2,725.46; expense, $4,558.56; total — $7,284 02

## EXHIBIT OF DEATH CLAIMS.

| | Total claims. | | Illinois claims. | |
|---|---|---|---|---|
| | Number. | Amount. | Number. | Amount. |
| Claims unpaid December 31, 1920, as per last statement | 39 | $ 15,783 93 | | |
| Claims reported during the year and interest addition | 516 | 231,650 00 | 7 | $3,000 00 |
| Total | 555 | $247,433 93 | 7 | $3,000 00 |
| Claims paid during the year | 498 | 128,211 42 | 7 | 1,000 00 |
| Balance | 57 | $119,222 51 | | $2,000 00 |
| Saved by compromising or scaling down claims during the year | | 94,860 01 | | 2,000 00 |
| Claims rejected during the year | 9 | 3,900 00 | | |
| Claims unpaid December 31, 1921 | 48 | $20,462 50 | | |
| Actual liability | 48 | $13,583 75 | | |

## EXHIBIT OF ACCIDENT CLAIMS.

| | Total claims. | | Illinois claims. | |
|---|---|---|---|---|
| | Number. | Amount. | Number. | Amount. |
| Claims unpaid December 31, 1920, as per last statement | 7 | $ 275 00 | | |
| Claims reported during the year | 137 | 6,387 50 | 1 | $25 00 |
| Total | 144 | $6,662 50 | 1 | $25 00 |
| Claims paid during the year | 126 | 3,330 00 | 1 | 5 00 |
| Saved by scaling | | 2,595 00 | | 20 00 |
| Claims rejected during the year | 10 | 325 00 | | |
| Claims unpaid December 31, 1921 | 8 | $412 50 | | |
| Actual liability | 8 | $312 50 | | |

## ANCIENT ORDER OF GLEANERS.

Located at No. 5705 Woodward Avenue, Detroit, Michigan.

GRANT SLOCUM, President. ROSS L. HOLLOWAY, Secretary.

| | |
|---|---|
| Balance from previous year | $1,315,269 13 |

### INCOME.

| | |
|---|---|
| Membership fees actually received | $ 1,136 95 |
| Assessments or premiums during first twelve months of membership of which all or an extra percentage is used for expenses | 19,468 52 |
| All other assessments or premiums | 568,276 24 |
| Dues and per capita tax | 133,119 88 |
| Medical examiners' fees actually received | 30 50 |
| Other payments by members, viz: Policy fees | 982 03 |
| Net amount received from members | $723,014 12 |
| Gross interest on mortgage loans | 39,507 24 |
| Gross interest on certificates of deposit | 2,647 21 |
| Gross interest on bonds | 6,275 00 |
| Gross interest from all other sources, daily balances | 5,326 34 |
| Gross rents from association's property | 500 00 |
| Sale of lodge supplies | 1,193 28 |
| Gross increase in book value of ledger assets | 500 00 |
| Refund | 5,025 56 |
| Total income | $783,988 75 |
| Sum | $2,099,257 88 |

### DISBURSEMENTS.

| | |
|---|---|
| Death claims | $460,449 85 |
| Assessments returned for cancellation of certificates | 293 42 |
| Benefits paid to members disabled and in need | 19,416 00 |
| Total benefits paid | $480,159 27 |
| Commissions and fees paid to deputies and organizers | 19,349 28 |
| Salaries of deputies and organizers | 57,198 42 |
| Salaries of managers or agents not deputies or organizers | 2,500 00 |
| Salaries of officers and trustees | 19,725 04 |
| Salaries of office employees | 50,948 42 |
| Traveling and other expenses of officers, trustees and committees | 895 04 |
| Insurance department fees | 124 75 |
| Advertising, printing and stationery | 5,739 45 |
| Postage, express, telegraph and telephone | 6,303 39 |
| Lodge supplies | 751 02 |
| Official publication | 16,075 42 |
| Expenses of supreme lodge meeting | 1,392 81 |
| Other legal expenses | 2,071 84 |
| Furniture and fixtures | 159 28 |
| Taxes, repairs and other expenses on real estate | 3,273 96 |
| Prizes for securing new members and local medical examiners fees | 10,876 28 |
| Light and fuel | 606 32 |
| Officers bonds | 755 53 |
| General office expense | 289 91 |
| Postcards | 100 00 |
| Appraisers expenses negotiating loans, etc | 1,842 38 |
| New equipment for office building | 1,700 00 |
| Public meetings | 1,517 40 |
| Miscellaneous | 2,395 21 |
| Total disbursements | $686,750 42 |
| Balance | $1,412,507 46 |

### LEDGER ASSETS.

| | |
|---|---|
| Book value of real estate | $164,725 65 |
| Mortgage loans on real estate | 802,607 96 |
| Book value of bonds and stocks | 155,875 00 |
| Deposits in trust companies and banks on interest | 288,256 35 |
| U. S. war savings stamps | 1,042 50 |
| Total ledger assets | $1,412,507 46 |

#### NON-LEDGER ASSETS.

| | |
|---|---|
| Interest and rents due and accrued | $28,943 38 |
| Assessments actually collected by subordinate lodges not yet turned over to supreme lodge | 48,978 73 |

LEDGER ASSETS—Concluded.

| | | |
|---|---|---|
| All other assets, viz— | | |
| Interest on Canadian Victory Loan, deposit in Merchants Bank of Canada exchanged for bonds of Canadian Victory Loan | $ 3,500 00 | |
| Unapportioned amount deposited in Merchants National Bank, Detroit, Mich., to the credit of local arbors | 10,970 34 | |
| Furniture and fixtures | 21,443 54 | |
| | | $35,913 88 |
| Gross assets | | $1,526,343 45 |

DEDUCT ASSETS NOT ADMITTED.

| | | |
|---|---|---|
| Other items, viz— | | |
| Interest on Canadian Victory bonds | $ 3,500 00 | |
| Unapportioned amount deposited in Merchant's National Bank, Detroit, Mich., to credit of local arbors | 10,970 34 | |
| Furniture and fixtures | 21,443 54 | |
| | | 35,913 88 |
| Total admitted assets | | $1,490,429 61 |

LIABILITIES.

| | | |
|---|---|---|
| Death claims reported during the year but not yet adjusted | | $61,188 34 |
| All other liabilities, viz— | | |
| Salaries, expenses and commissions due organizers | 2,400 51 | |
| Miscellaneous bills | 1,065 40 | |
| | | 3,471 91 |
| Total | | $64,660 25 |

EXHIBIT OF CERTIFICATES.

| | Total business of the year. | | Business in Illinois during year. | |
|---|---|---|---|---|
| | Number. | Amount. | Number. | Amount. |
| Benefit certificates in force December 31, 1920, as per last statement | 63,427 | $54,701,505 00 | 3,237 | $2,746,485 00 |
| Benefit certificates written and renewed during the year | 5,916 | 5,503,400 00 | 309 | 282,500 00 |
| Benefit certificates increased during the year | | 159,500 00 | | 9,000 00 |
| Totals | 69,343 | $60,364,405 00 | 3,546 | $3,037,985 00 |
| Deduct terminated, decreased or transferred during the year | 4,970 | 4,203,935 00 | | |
| Deduct terminated or decreased during the year | | | 440 | 371,000 00 |
| Total benefit certificates in force December 31, 1921 | 64,373 | $56,160,470 00 | 3,106 | $2,666,985 00 |

Received during the year from members in Illinois: Mortuary, $28,652.91; general, $6,862.26; total — $35,515 17

EXHIBIT OF DEATH CLAIMS.

| | Total claims. | | Illinois claims. | |
|---|---|---|---|---|
| | Number. | Amount. | Number. | Amount. |
| Claims unpaid December 31, 1920, as per last statement | 89 | $ 77,639 00 | | |
| Two 1920 claims revived | 2 | 400 00 | | |
| Claims reported during the year | 553 | 460,135 00 | 6 | $5,000 00 |
| Totals | 644 | $538,174 00 | 6 | $5,000 00 |
| Claims paid during the year | 565 | 458,449 85 | 5 | 4,000 00 |
| Balance | 79 | $79,724 15 | 1 | $1,000 00 |
| Saved by compromising or scaling down claims during the year | | 13,555 81 | | |
| Claims rejected during the year | 5 | 4,980 00 | | |
| Claims unpaid December 31, 1921 | 74 | $61,188 34 | 1 | $1,000 00 |

EXHIBIT OF SICK AND ACCIDENT CLAIMS.

| | Total claims. | | Illinois claims. | |
|---|---|---|---|---|
| | Number. | Amount. | Number. | Amount. |
| Claims reported during the year | 794 | $19,416 00 | 1 | $10 00 |
| Claims paid during the year | 794 | 19,416 00 | 1 | 10 00 |

## ANCIENT ORDER UNITED WORKMEN OF IOWA.

Located at No. 2100 Grand Avenue, Des Moines, Iowa.

J. A. LOWENBERG, President. W. H. STOWELL, Secretary.

| | |
|---|---|
| Balance from previous year | $1,376,301 14 |

### INCOME.

| | |
|---|---|
| Certificate fees actually received | $ 655 50 |
| Assessments or premiums during first twelve months of membership of which all or an extra percentage is used for expenses | 39,130 10 |
| All other assessments or premiums | 470,548 72 |
| Dues and per capita tax | 29,020 00 |
| Transfer to limited payment plan | 260 08 |
| Net amount received from members | $539,614 40 |
| Gross interest on mortgage loans | 53,001 91 |
| Gross interest on certificate loans | 5,514 66 |
| Gross interest on bonds | 46 75 |
| Gross interest on deposits in trust companies and banks | 2,756 32 |
| Gross rents from association's property, including $36.00 for association's occupancy of its own buildings | 7 207 43 |
| Sale of lodge supplies | 104 61 |
| Bond premium | 437 46 |
| Miscellaneous | 2,032 92 |
| Commissions and abstract fees and discount | 8,059 43 |
| Total income | $618,775 89 |
| Sum | $1,995,077 03 |

### DISBURSEMENTS.

| | |
|---|---|
| Death claims | $233,299 35 |
| Commissions and fees paid to deputies and organizers | 26,000 41 |
| Salaries of managers or agents not deputies or organizers | 1,734 06 |
| Salaries of officers | 6,488 33 |
| Salaries and other compensation of committees | 1,619 82 |
| Salaries of office employees | 11,258 47 |
| Traveling and other expenses of officers, trustees and committees | 1,173 79 |
| Insurance department fees | 652 66 |
| Rent | 3,600 00 |
| Advertising, printing and stationery | 4,236 34 |
| Postage, express, telegraph and telephone | 2,006 31 |
| Lodge supplies | 348 65 |
| Official publication | 3,868 66 |
| Expenses of grand lodge meeting | 3,977 78 |
| Legal expense in litigating claims | 9,344 84 |
| Other legal expenses | 2,500 00 |
| Furniture and fixtures | 351 75 |
| Taxes, repairs and other expenses on real estate | 4,992 79 |
| Gross loss on sale or maturity of ledger assets | 23,181 46 |
| Supreme lodge, per capita tax | 1,891 28 |
| Miscellaneous | 4,370 24 |
| Total disbursements | $346,896 99 |
| Balance | $1,648,180 04 |

### LEDGER ASSETS.

| | |
|---|---|
| Book value of real estate | $ 89,631 79 |
| Mortgage loans on real estate | 1,285,974 60 |
| Loans secured by pledge of bonds, stocks or other collateral | 116,038 77 |
| Book value of bonds and stocks | 1,924 00 |
| Deposits in trust companies and banks not on interest | 44,161 57 |
| Bills receivable | 3,389 31 |
| Leins on certificates | 107,060 00 |
| Total ledger assets | $1,648,180 04 |

#### NON-LEDGER ASSETS.

| | |
|---|---|
| Interest and rents due and accrued | 81,711 73 |
| Assessments actually collected by subordinate lodges not yet turned over to supreme lodge | 43,452 73 |
| Gross assets | $1,773,344 50 |

#### DEDUCT ASSETS NOT ADMITTED.

| | |
|---|---|
| Bills receivable | 3,389 31 |
| Total admitted assets | $1,769,955 19 |

LIABILITIES.

| | |
|---|---|
| Death claims reported during the year but not yet adjusted | $33,880 77 |

EXHIBIT OF CERTIFICATES.

| | Total business of the year. Number. | Amount. | Business in Illinois during year. Number. | Amount. |
|---|---|---|---|---|
| Benefit certificates in force December 31, 1920, as per last statement | 12,996 | $18,094,694 00 | 782 | $948,937 00 |
| Benefit certificates written and renewed during the year | 2,512 | 3,635,560 58 | 126 | 178,500 00 |
| Totals | 15,508 | $21,730,254 58 | 908 | $1,127,437 00 |
| Deduct terminated, decreased or transferred during the year | 2,198 | 3,304,929 00 | | |
| Deduct terminated or decreased during the year | | | 162 | 226,000 00 |
| Total benefit certificates in force December 31, 1921 | 13,310 | $18,425,325 58 | 746 | $901,437 00 |

| | |
|---|---|
| Received during the year from members in Illinois: Mortuary, $27,496.98; children, $76.25; expense, $4,584.96; total | $32,158 19 |

EXHIBIT OF DEATH CLAIMS.

| | Total claims. Number. | Amount. | Illinois claims. Number. | Amount. |
|---|---|---|---|---|
| Claims unpaid December 31, 1920, as per last statement | 22 | $ 25,524 89 | | |
| Claims reported during the year and interest addition | 176 | 252,149 00 | 12 | $12,500 00 |
| Totals | 198 | $277,673 89 | 12 | $12,500 00 |
| Claims paid during the year | 174 | 233,225 35 | 8 | 10,159 87 |
| Balance | 24 | $44,448 54 | 4 | $2,340 13 |
| Saved by compromising or scaling down claims during the year | | 10,567 77 | | 840 13 |
| Claims unpaid December 31, 1921 | 24 | $33,880 77 | 4 | $1,500 00 |

## ASSOCIATION CANADO-AMERICAINE.

Located at No. 1034 Elm Street, Manchester, New Hampshire.

A. A. E. BRIEN, M. D., President. ADOLPH ROBERT, Secretary.

| | |
|---|---|
| Balance from previous year | $595,806 68 |

INCOME.

| | |
|---|---|
| All other assessments or premiums | $261,182 27 |
| Dues and per capita tax | 39,746 65 |
| Medical examiners' fees actually received | 142 75 |
| Other payments by members, viz: Certificates | 112 75 |
| Total received from members | $301,184 42 |
| Deduct payments returned to applicants and members | 964 84 |
| Net amount received from members | $300,219 58 |
| Gross interest on bonds and dividends on stocks | 30,855 57 |
| Gross interest on deposits in trust companies and banks | 745 20 |
| Gross interest from all other sources | 83 70 |
| Sale of lodge supplies | 564 61 |
| Gross profit on sale or maturity of ledger assets | 1,482 06 |
| Gross increase in book value of ledger assets | 2,144 25 |
| Officers bonds | 352 72 |
| Exchange | 12 46 |
| Jubilee | 671 01 |
| Total income | $337,131 16 |
| Sum | $932,937 84 |

## DISBURSEMENTS.

| | | |
|---|---|---|
| Death claims | | $100,849 00 |
| Sick and accident claims | | 28,194 43 |
| Benefits surrendered | | 4,250 11 |
| Total benefits paid | | $133,293 54 |
| Commissions and fees paid to deputies and organizers | | 1,386 46 |
| Salaries of deputies and organizers | | 2,640 00 |
| Salaries of officers and trustees | | 10,059 52 |
| Other compensation of officers and trustees | | 386 00 |
| Salaries and other compensation of committees | | 25 00 |
| Salaries of office employees | | 9,357 00 |
| Other compensation of office employees | | 167 03 |
| Salaries and fees paid to supreme medical examiners | | 1,500 00 |
| Salaries and fees paid to subordinate medical examiners | | 1 50 |
| Traveling and other expenses of officers, trustees and committees | | 2,070 61 |
| For collection and remittance of assessments and dues | | 654 51 |
| Insurance department fees | | 1,459 22 |
| Rent | | 1,854 13 |
| Advertising, printing and stationery | | 1,902 67 |
| Postage, express, telegraph and telephone | | 689 10 |
| Lodge supplies | | 883 65 |
| Official publication | | 2,783 45 |
| Legal expense in litigating claims | | 75 00 |
| Other legal expenses | | 128 14 |
| Furniture and fixtures | | 197 80 |
| Gross loss on sale or maturity of ledger assets | | 290 38 |
| Gross decrease in book value of ledger assets | | 8 93 |
| All other disbursements, viz— | | |
| Officers bonds, $121.25; insurance on furniture, $61.00; jubilee, $2,198.19 | | 2,380 44 |
| National fraternal congress and federation, $558.40; exchange and commission, $54.67; petty expenses, $193.12 | | 806 19 |
| Library, $513.65; local officers bonds, $723.12 | | 1,236 77 |
| Industrial insurance, $7.75; re-adjustment, $3,548.50 | | 3,556 25 |
| Total disbursements | | $179,846 24 |
| Balance | | $753,091 60 |

## LEDGER ASSETS.

| | | |
|---|---|---|
| Book value of bonds and stocks | | $730,391 56 |
| Cash in association's office | | 59 30 |
| Deposits in trust companies and banks on interest | | 22,640 74 |
| Total ledger assets | | $753,091 60 |

### NON-LEDGER ASSETS.

| | | |
|---|---|---|
| Interest and rents due and accrued | | 13,344 79 |
| Assessments actually collected by subordinate lodges not yet turned over to supreme lodge | | 25,231 00 |
| All other assets, viz— | | |
| Furniture and fixtures | $5,677 25 | |
| Lodge supplies | 976 10 | |
| Library | 4,100 00 | |
| | | 10,753 45 |
| Gross assets | | $802,420 84 |

### DEDUCT ASSETS NOT ADMITTED.

| | | |
|---|---|---|
| Book value of bonds and stocks over market value | $1,375 00 | |
| Other items, viz— | | |
| Furniture and fixtures | 5,677 25 | |
| Lodge supplies | 976 20 | |
| Library | 4,100 00 | |
| | | 12,128 45 |
| Total admitted assets | | $790,292 39 |

## LIABILITIES.

| | | |
|---|---|---|
| Death claims reported during the year but not yet adjusted | | $3,465 00 |
| Sick and accident claims reported during the year but not yet adjusted | | 105 00 |
| Total unpaid claims | | $3,570 00 |
| Advance assessments | | 164 30 |
| Library | | 1,000 00 |
| Total | | $4,734 30 |

## EXHIBIT OF CERTIFICATES.

| | Total business of the year. | | Business in Illinois during year. | |
|---|---|---|---|---|
| | Number. | Amount. | Number. | Amount. |
| Benefit certificates in force December 31, 1920, as per last statement | 15,674 | $11,514,800 00 | 10 | $3,000 00 |
| Benefit certificates written and renewed during the year | 438 | 289,400 00 | 1 | 1,000 00 |
| Benefit certificates increased during the year | | 13,550 00 | | |
| Totals | 16,112 | $11,817,750 00 | 11 | $4,000 00 |
| Deduct terminated, decreased or transferred during the year | 1,935 | 1,754,173 42 | | |
| Total benefit certificates in force December 31, 1921 | 14,177 | $10,063,576 58 | 11 | $4,000 00 |

Received during the year from members in Illinois: Mortuary, $112.92; all other, $5.40; expense, $32.15; total ........ $150 47

## EXHIBIT OF DEATH CLAIMS.

| | Total claims—all in Illinois. | |
|---|---|---|
| | Number. | Amount. |
| Claims unpaid December 31, 1920, as per last statement | 14 | $11,800 00 |
| Claims reported during the year and interest addition | 123 | 93,314 00 |
| Totals | 137 | $105,114 00 |
| Claims paid during the year | 130 | 100,849 00 |
| Balance | 7 | $4,265 00 |
| Claims rejected during the year | 1 | 800 00 |
| Claims unpaid December 31, 1921 | 6 | $3,465 00 |

## EXHIBIT OF SICK AND ACCIDENT CLAIMS.

| | Total claims—all in Illinois. | |
|---|---|---|
| | Number. | Amount. |
| Claims unpaid December 31, 1920, as per last statement | 10 | $ 202 83 |
| Claims reported during the year | 1,348 | 28,096 60 |
| Totals | 1,358 | $28,299 43 |
| Claims paid during the year | 1,356 | 28,194 43 |
| Claims unpaid December 31, 1921 | 2 | $105 00 |

# BEAVERS NATIONAL MUTUAL BENEFIT.

Located at Gay Building, Madison, Wisconsin.

J. W. PARSONS, President. S. A. OSCAR, Secretary.

| | |
|---|---|
| Balance from previous year | $86,394 82 |

## INCOME.

| | |
|---|---|
| Membership fees actually received | $54,921 87 |
| Assessments or premiums during first twelve months of membership of which all or an extra percentage is used for expenses | 84,488 73 |
| Medical examiners' fees actually received | 72 00 |
| Total received from members | $139,482 60 |
| Deduct payments returned to applicants and members | 40 47 |
| Net amount received from members | $139,442 13 |
| Gross interest on mortgage loans | 544 26 |
| Gross interest on bonds and dividends on stocks | 2,280 83 |
| Gross interest on deposits in trust companies and banks | 555 70 |
| Gross interest from all other sources | 48 46 |
| Gross increase in book value of ledger assets | 270 33 |
| Total income | $143,141 71 |
| Sum | $229,536 53 |

## DISBURSEMENTS.

| | |
|---|---|
| Death claims | $29,000 00 |
| Premium loans expirations | 171 47 |
| Total benefits paid | $29,171 47 |
| Commissions and fees paid to deputies and organizers | 20,460 96 |
| Salaries of deputies and organizers | 10,000 00 |

DISBURSEMENTS—Concluded.

| | |
|---|---|
| Other compensation of officers and trustees | $1,560 00 |
| Salaries of office employees | 3,112 20 |
| Salaries and fees paid to supreme medical examiners | 992 42 |
| Salaries and fees paid to subordinate medical examiners | 6,178 30 |
| Traveling and other expenses of officers, trustees and committees | 506 29 |
| For collection and remittance of assessments and dues | 1,511 20 |
| Insurance department fees | 40 00 |
| Rent | 232 04 |
| Advertising, printing and stationery | 207 04 |
| Postage, express, telegraph and telephone | 256 63 |
| Other legal expenses | 200 00 |
| Deputy expenses | 4,666 28 |
| Office supplies | 78 20 |
| Actuarial expenses | 3,348 08 |
| Bonds of officers | 90 00 |
| Total disbursements | $82,611 11 |
| Balance | $148,016 42 |

LEDGER ASSETS.

| | |
|---|---|
| Mortgage loans on real estate | $81,000 00 |
| Book value of bonds and stocks | 41,235 55 |
| Deposits in trust companies and banks not on interest | 146 34 |
| Deposits in trust companies and banks on interest | 23,120 03 |
| Premium loans to members | 2,514 50 |
| Total ledger assets | $148,016 42 |

NON-LEDGER ASSETS.

| | |
|---|---|
| Interest and rents due and accrued | 3,914 33 |
| Furniture and fixtures | 500 00 |
| Gross assets | $152,430 75 |

DEDUCT ASSETS NOT ADMITTED.

| | |
|---|---|
| Furniture and fixtures | 500 00 |
| Total admitted assets | $151,930 75 |

LIABILITIES.

| | | |
|---|---|---|
| Death claims reported during the year but not yet adjusted | | $2,000 00 |
| Salaries, rents, expenses, commissions, etc., due or accrued | | 300 00 |
| Advance assessments | | 6,596 78 |
| All other liabilities, viz— | | |
| Amount due general fund for medical examinations | $ 7,170 72 | |
| Reserve on outstanding certificates | 91,554 14 | |
| General fund surplus | 1,763 29 | |
| Mortuary fund surplus | 42,545 82 | |
| | | 143,033 97 |
| Total | | $151,930 75 |

EXHIBIT OF CERTIFICATES.

| | Total business of the year. | | Business in Illinois during year. | |
|---|---|---|---|---|
| | Number. | Amount. | Number. | Amount. |
| Benefit certificates in force December 31, 1920, as per last statement | 5,212 | $5,457,613 41 | 49 | $50,500 00 |
| Benefit certificates written and renewed during the year | 2,926 | 3,263,450 00 | 8 | 8,000 00 |
| Totals | 8,138 | $8,721,063 41 | 57 | $58,500 00 |
| Deduct terminated, decreased or transferred during the year | 1,064 | 1,297,983 61 | | |
| Total benefit certificates in force December 31, 1921 | 7,074 | $7,423,079 80 | 57 | $58,500 00 |

EXHIBIT OF DEATH CLAIMS.

| | Total claims—all in Illinois. | |
|---|---|---|
| | Number. | Amount. |
| Claims unpaid December 31, 1920, as per last statement | 4 | $ 3,250 00 |
| Claims reported during the year and interest addition | 27 | 27,750 00 |
| Totals | 31 | $31,000 00 |
| Claims paid during the year | 30 | 29,000 00 |
| Claims unpaid December 31, 1921 | 1 | $2,000 00 |

## BEN HUR, SUPREME TRIBE.

Located at Corner Main and Water Streets, Crawfordsville, Indiana.

R. H. GERARD, President. JNO. C. SNYDER, Secretary.

| | |
|---|---|
| Balance from previous year | $2,559,805 89 |

### INCOME.

| | |
|---|---|
| Assessments or premiums during first twelve months of membership of which all or an extra percentage is used for expenses | $ 155,245 69 |
| All other assessments or premiums | 1,544,610 81 |
| Dues and per capita tax | 439 58 |
| Medical examiners' fees actually received | 1 50 |
| Other payments by members, viz: Certificate fees and change of beneficiary | 1,036 00 |
| Total received from members | $1,701,333 58 |
| Deduct payments returned to applicants and members | 1,557 98 |
| Net amount received from members | $1,699,775 60 |
| Gross interest on mortgage loans | 6,078 28 |
| Gross interest on bonds and dividends on stocks | 127,240 33 |
| Gross interest on deposits in trust companies and banks | 4,505 98 |
| Gross interest from all other sources | 2,845 71 |
| Gross rents from association's property, including $5,400.00 for association's occupancy of its own buildings | 25,861 84 |
| Sale of lodge supplies | 2,980 72 |
| Total income | $1,869,288 46 |
| Sum | $4,429,094 35 |

### DISBURSEMENTS.

| | |
|---|---|
| Death claims | $872,216 66 |
| Permanent disability claims | 10,584 82 |
| Old age benefits | 15,149 75 |
| Partial disability | 1,325 00 |
| Total benefits paid | $899,276 23 |
| Commissions and fees paid to deputies and organizers | 88,237 66 |
| Salaries of deputies and organizers | 48,919 83 |
| Salaries of officers and trustees | 25,916 61 |
| Salaries and other compensation of committees | 2,600 00 |
| Salaries of office employees | 54,797 91 |
| Salaries and fees paid to supreme medical examiners | 11,708 34 |
| Salaries and fees paid to subordinate medical examiners | 7 00 |
| Traveling and other expenses of officers, trustees and committees | 5,421 61 |
| Insurance department fees | 2,046 79 |
| Rent, including $5,400.00 for association's occupancy of its own buildings | 7,228 25 |
| Advertising, printing and stationery | 19,151 83 |
| Postage, express, telegraph and telephone | 4,943 57 |
| Lodge supplies | 3,204 70 |
| Official publication | 20,836 67 |
| Legal expense in litigating claims | 3,733 37 |
| Other legal expenses | 5,142 40 |
| Furniture and fixtures | 883 51 |
| Taxes, repairs and other expenses on real estate | 24,207 26 |
| Gross decrease in book value of ledger assets | 3,854 95 |
| All other disbursements, viz: Investigation of claims, $6,427.42; investment expense, $268.25; traveling expense, field, $26,018.43; surety bonds, $2,334.08; miscellaneous expense, $3,356.66; medical inspection, $435.52 | 38,840 36 |
| Total disbursements | $1,270,958 85 |
| Balance | $3,158,135 50 |

### LEDGER ASSETS.

| | |
|---|---|
| Book value of real estate | $ 227,319 43 |
| Mortgage loans on real estate | 97,150 00 |
| Book value of bonds and stocks | 2,677,547 54 |
| Cash in association's office | 250 00 |
| Deposits in trust companies and banks on interest | 155,868 53 |
| Total ledger assets | $3,158,135 50 |

#### NON-LEDGER ASSETS.

| | |
|---|---|
| Interest and rents due and accrued | $30,927 04 |
| Market value of real estate over book value | 43,643 10 |
| Market value of bonds and stocks over book value | 48,296 60 |
| Assessments actually collected by subordinate lodges not yet turned over to supreme lodge | 10,863 43 |
| Total admitted assets | $3,291,865 67 |

## LIABILITIES.

| | | |
|---|---|---|
| Death claims due and unpaid | $ 8,050 00 | |
| Death claims resisted | 7,000 00 | |
| Death claims reported during the year but not yet adjusted | 71,010 00 | |
| Death claims incurred in 1921, not reported until 1922 | 3,450 00 | |
| Present value of deferred death claims payable in installments | 11,009 95 | |
| Total unpaid claims | | $100,519 95 |
| Salaries, rents, expenses, commissions, etc., due or accrued | | 4,556 17 |
| Taxes due or accrued | | 3,201 12 |
| Advance assessments | | 11,715 20 |
| Total | | $119,992 44 |

## EXHIBIT OF CERTIFICATES.

| | Total business of the year. | | Business in Illinois during year. | |
|---|---|---|---|---|
| | Number. | Amount. | Number. | Amount. |
| Benefit certificates in force December 31, 1920, as per last statement | 75,624 | $77,479,233 00 | 15,975 | $16,506,489 00 |
| Benefit certificates written and renewed during the year | 7,311 | 9,449,415 00 | 1,736 | 2,191,409 00 |
| Benefit certificates received by transfer during the year | | | 18 | 19,250 00 |
| Totals | 82,935 | $86,928,648 00 | 17,729 | $18,717,148 00 |
| Deduct terminated, decreased or transferred during the year | 12,565 | 14,187,918 00 | | |
| Deduct terminated or decreased during the year | | | 2,459 | 2,790,177 00 |
| Total benefit certificates in force December 31, 1921 | 70,370 | $72,740,730 00 | 15,270 | $15,926,971 00 |

Received during the year from members in Illinois: Mortuary, $277,508.17; expense, $72,281.01; total $349,789 18

## EXHIBIT OF DEATH CLAIMS.

| | Total claims. | | Illinois claims. | |
|---|---|---|---|---|
| | Number. | Amount. | Number. | Amount. |
| Claims unpaid December 31, 1920, as per last statement | 118 | $120,185 68 | 24 | $ 23,800 00 |
| Claims reported during the year and interest addition | 844 | 869,823 94 | 174 | 182,549 00 |
| Totals | 962 | $990,009 62 | 198 | $206,349 00 |
| Claims paid during the year | 868 | 872,216 66 | 177 | 180,303 04 |
| Balance | 94 | $117,792 96 | 21 | $26,045 96 |
| Saved by compromising or scaling down claims during the year | | 17,723 01 | | 6,870 96 |
| Claims rejected during the year | 3 | 3,000 00 | 3 | 3,000 00 |
| Claims unpaid December 31, 1921 | 91 | $97,069 95 | 18 | $16,175 00 |

## EXHIBIT OF PERMANENT DISABILITY CLAIMS.

| | Total claims. | | Illinois claims. | |
|---|---|---|---|---|
| | Number. | Amount. | Number. | Amount. |
| Claims reported during the year and interest addition | 37 | $10,584 82 | 1 | $708 51 |
| Claims paid during the year | 37 | 10,584 82 | 1 | 708 51 |

## EXHIBIT OF PARTIAL DISABILITY CLAIMS (LOSS OF LIMB OR EYESIGHT).

| | Total claims. | | Illinois claims. | |
|---|---|---|---|---|
| | Number. | Amount. | Number. | Amount. |
| Claims reported during the year | 3 | $1,325 00 | 1 | $375 00 |
| Claims paid during the year | 3 | 1,325 00 | 1 | 375 00 |

## EXHIBIT OF OLD AGE AND OTHER CLAIMS.

| | Total claims. | | Illinois claims. | |
|---|---|---|---|---|
| | Number. | Amount. | Number. | Amount. |
| Claims reported during the year and interest addition | 42 | $15,149 75 | 11 | $5,716 50 |
| Claims paid during the year | 42 | 15,149 75 | 11 | 5,716 50 |

## BOHEMIAN ROMAN CATHOLIC FIRST CENTRAL UNION.

Located at No. 1436 West Eighteenth Street, Chicago, Illinois.

VINCENT KOLDA, Grand President. JOSEPH J. MOUDRY, Grand Secretary.

| | |
|---|---|
| Balance from previous year | $373,518 17 |

### INCOME.

| | |
|---|---|
| Assessments or premiums | $94,102 81 |
| Dues and per capita tax | 5,778 53 |
| Age adjustment | 1,149 90 |
| Net amount received from members | $101,031 24 |
| Gross interest on mortgage loans | 15,011 25 |
| Gross interest on bonds and dividends on stocks | 2,870 88 |
| Gross interest on deposits in trust companies and banks | 2,167 34 |
| Sale of lodge supplies | 378 40 |
| Official publications | 194 50 |
| Appraisal fees | 4 00 |
| Discount on loans | 4,472 50 |
| Registering bonds | 7 50 |
| Insurance department fee (refund) | 25 00 |
| Total income | $126,162 61 |
| Sum | $499,680 78 |

### DISBURSEMENTS.

| | |
|---|---|
| Death claims | $74,900 00 |
| Commissions and fees paid to deputies and organizers | 319 00 |
| Salaries of officers and trustees | 3,770 00 |
| Salaries and fees paid to supreme medical examiners | 75 00 |
| Traveling and other expenses of officers, trustees and committees | 172 59 |
| Insurance department fees | 11 00 |
| Rent | 235 00 |
| Advertising, printing and stationery | 626 05 |
| Postage, express, telegraph and telephone | 149 85 |
| Official publication | 1,165 87 |
| Expenses of supreme lodge meeting | 3 69 |
| Other legal expenses | 205 96 |
| Furniture and fixtures | 31 50 |
| Office expense | 45 14 |
| Registering bonds | 7 50 |
| Total disbursements | $81,718 15 |
| Balance | $417,962 63 |

### LEDGER ASSETS.

| | |
|---|---|
| Mortgage loans on real estate | $277,450 00 |
| Loans secured by pledge of bonds, stocks or other collateral | 100,001 85 |
| Total ledger assets | $417,962 63 |

#### NON-LEDGER ASSETS.

| | |
|---|---|
| Interest and rents due and accrued | $7,114 05 |
| Market value of real estate over book value | 2,006 95 |
| Assessments actually collected by subordinate lodges not yet turned over to supreme lodge | 37 20 |
| Dues | 1 20 |
| Gross assets | $427,122 03 |

### LIABILITIES.

| | |
|---|---|
| Death claims due and unpaid | $11,400 00 |

### EXHIBIT OF CERTIFICATES.

| | Total business of the year. | | Business in Illinois during year. | |
|---|---|---|---|---|
| | Number. | Amount. | Number. | Amount. |
| Benefit certificates in force December 31, 1920, as per last statement | 5,002 | $3,975,150 00 | 1,829 | $1,525,550 00 |
| Benefit certificates written and renewed during the year | 216 | 187,200 00 | 50 | 107,500 00 |
| Total | 5,218 | $4,162,350 00 | 1,879 | $1,633,050 00 |
| Deduct terminated, decreased or transferred during the year | 192 | 142,000 00 | | |
| Deduct terminated or decreased during the year | | | 71 | 57,100 00 |
| Total benefit certificates in force December 31, 1921 | 5,126 | $4,020,350 00 | 1,808 | $1,575,950 00 |

| | |
|---|---|
| Received during the year from members in Illinois: Mortuary, $35,944.22; expense, $2,219.05; total | $38,163 27 |

EXHIBIT OF DEATH CLAIMS.

| | Total claims. Number. | Amount. | Illinois claims. Number. | Amount. |
|---|---|---|---|---|
| Claims unpaid December 31, 1920, as per last statement | 28 | $18,800 00 | 6 | $ 3,900 00 |
| Claims reported during the year and interest addition | 90 | 67,500 00 | 36 | 29,100 00 |
| Total | 118 | $86,300 00 | 42 | $33,000 00 |
| Claims paid during the year | 103 | 74,900 00 | 38 | 31,700 00 |
| Claims unpaid December 31, 1921 | 15 | $11,400 00 | 4 | $4,300 00 |

---

## BOHEMIAN SLAVONIAN FRATERNAL BENEFICIARY UNION.

Located at No. 321 East Seventy-Third Street, New York, New York.

AUGUST RUDOLF ZIDIA, President. JAN JIRI KARNIK, Secretary.

| | |
|---|---|
| Balance from previous year | $60,583 38 |

INCOME.

| | |
|---|---|
| Membership fees actually received | $48,191 82 |
| Assessments or premiums | 2,647 63 |
| All other assessments or premiums | 396 63 |
| Dues and per capita tax | 3,986 64 |
| New members | 111 00 |
| Net amount received from members | $55,333 72 |
| Gross interest on bonds and dividends on stocks | 2,817 89 |
| Sale of lodge supplies | 549 76 |
| Official organ | 877 00 |
| Interest on daily deposits | 380 20 |
| Total income | $ 59,958 57 |
| Sum | $120,541 95 |

DISBURSEMENTS.

| | |
|---|---|
| Death claims | $39,591 43 |
| Sick and accident claims | 466 91 |
| Total benefits paid | $40,058 34 |
| Commissions and fees paid to deputies and organizers | 713 37 |
| Salaries of officers and trustees | 728 00 |
| Other compensation of officers and trustees | 111 00 |
| Salaries and other compensation of committees | 106 00 |
| Insurance department fees | 81 68 |
| Rent | 171 00 |
| Advertising, printing and stationery | 568 91 |
| Postage, express, telegraph and telephone | 104 77 |
| Official publication | 1,917 35 |
| Expenses of supreme lodge meeting | 70 40 |
| Legal expense in litigating claims | 9 21 |
| Furniture and fixtures | 155 45 |
| Bohemian Freeth Federation | 35 07 |
| Total disbursements | $44,830 55 |
| Balance | $75,711 40 |

LEDGER ASSETS.

| | |
|---|---|
| Book value of bonds and stocks | $48,800 00 |
| Cash in association's office | 26,911 40 |
| Total ledger assets | $75,711 40 |

LIABILITIES.

| | |
|---|---|
| Death claims due and unpaid | $230 00 |

EXHIBIT OF CERTIFICATES.

| | Total business of the year. Number. | Amount. | Business in Illinois during year. Number. | Amount. |
|---|---|---|---|---|
| Benefit certificates in force December 31, 1920, as per last statement | 3,465 | $2,319,300 00 | 1,171 | $833,800 00 |
| Benefit certificates written and renewed during the year | 147 | 73,200 00 | 51 | 28,000 00 |
| Total | 3,612 | $2,392,500 00 | 1,222 | $861,800 00 |
| Deduct terminated, decreased or transferred during the year | 205 | 130,000 00 | | |
| Deduct terminated or decreased during the year | | | 77 | 51,500 00 |
| Total benefit certificates in force December 31, 1921 | 3,407 | $2,262,500 00 | 1,145 | $810,300 00 |

Received during the year from members in Illinois: Mortuary, $16,190.67; reserve, $1,858.84; disability, $131.21; expense, $1,804.46; total ........ $19,985 18

EXHIBIT OF DEATH CLAIMS.

| | Total claims. Number. | Amount. | Illinois claims. Number. | Amount. |
|---|---|---|---|---|
| Claims unpaid December 31, 1920, as per last statement | 6 | $ 580 00 | 3 | $ 400 00 |
| Claims reported during the year and interest addition | 50 | 39,200 00 | 22 | 17,200 00 |
| Total | 56 | $39,780 00 | 25 | $17,600 00 |
| Claims paid during the year | 53 | 39,550 00 | 24 | 17,500 00 |
| Claims unpaid December 31, 1921 | 3 | $230 00 | 1 | $100 00 |

EXHIBIT OF SICK AND ACCIDENT CLAIMS.

| | Total claims. Number. | Amount. | Illinois claims. Number. | Amount. |
|---|---|---|---|---|
| Claims paid during the year | 12 | $46,691 00 | 4 | $150 00 |

## BROTHERHOOD OF AMERICAN YEOMEN.

Located at Fifth and Park Streets, Des Moines, Iowa.

GEO. N. FRINK, President. W. E. DAVY, Secretary.

| | |
|---|---|
| Balance from previous year | $4,325,748 43 |

INCOME.

| | |
|---|---|
| Membership fees actually received | $ 5,800 45 |
| Assessments or premiums during first 12 months of membership of which all or an extra percentage is used for expenses | 647,684 82 |
| All other assessments or premiums | 3,186,802 27 |
| Dues and per capita tax | 586,346 19 |
| Medical examiners' fees actually received | 21,020 50 |
| Total received from members | $4,447,654 23 |
| Deduct payments returned to applicants and members | 1,892 99 |
| Net amount received from members | $4,445,761 24 |
| Gross interest on mortgage loans | 174,772 03 |
| Gross interest on bonds and dividends on stocks | 11,779 14 |
| Gross interest on deposits in trust companies and banks | 22,968 38 |
| Gross interest from all other sources—taxes | 7 68 |
| Gross rents from association's property, including $9,000.00 for association's occupancy of its own buildings | 9,392 50 |
| Sale of lodge supplies | 20,495 33 |
| Surety bonds | 8,495 90 |
| Shield advertising | 11,806 10 |
| War risk | 30 15 |
| Protested checks | 1,367 93 |
| Unaudited reports | 99,898 22 |
| Gross increase by adjustment in book value of real estate | 77,500 00 |
| Total income | $4,884,274 60 |
| Sum | $9,210,023 03 |

DISBURSEMENTS.

| | |
|---|---|
| Death claims | $1,984,853 66 |
| Permanent disability claims | 172,313 91 |
| Sick and accident claims | 45,903 17 |
| Old age benefits | 272,868 75 |

DISBURSEMENTS—Concluded.

| | |
|---|---|
| Surgical benefits | $54,450 00 |
| Maternity benefits | 90,400 00 |
| Total benefits paid | $2,620,789 49 |
| Commissions and fees paid to deputies and organizers | 681,303 61 |
| Salaries of officers and trustees | 29,516 66 |
| Other compensation of officers and trustees | 26,250 00 |
| Salaries and other compensation of committees | 1,575 00 |
| Salaries of office employees | 161,921 61 |
| Other compensation of office employees | 8,889 06 |
| Salaries and fees paid to supreme medical examiners | 7,500 00 |
| Salaries and fees paid to subordinate medical examiners | 6,090 00 |
| Traveling and other expenses of officers, trustees and committees | 14,684 22 |
| Insurance department fees | 1,386 80 |
| Rent, including $9,000.00 for association's occupancy of its own buildings | 9,720 00 |
| Advertising, printing and stationery | 40,413 80 |
| Postage, express, telegraph and telephone | 21,190 89 |
| Lodge supplies | 13,896 48 |
| Official publication | 65,422 16 |
| Expenses of supreme lodge meeting | 75,708 67 |
| Legal expense in litigating claims | 5,647 72 |
| Other legal expenses | 11,956 16 |
| Furniture and fixtures | 12,882 99 |
| Taxes, repairs and other expenses on real estate | 20,303 71 |
| All other disbursements | 82,060 73 |
| Juvenile prizes | 40 00 |
| Total disbursements | $3,919,149 76 |
| Balance | $5,290,873 27 |

LEDGER ASSETS.

| | |
|---|---|
| Book value of real estate | $ 188,455 68 |
| Mortgage loans on real estate | 3,702,056 50 |
| Book value of bonds and stocks | 192,958 42 |
| Cash in association's office | 1,500 00 |
| Deposits in trust companies and banks on interest | 1,121,315 79 |
| War Savings Stamps | 826 00 |
| Certificate of indebtedness | 72,803 00 |
| Tax sale certificates | 7,898 70 |
| Loan foreclosures | 3,059 18 |
| Total ledger assets | $5,290,873 27 |

NON-LEDGER ASSETS.

| | | |
|---|---|---|
| Interest and rents due and accrued | | 113,735 66 |
| Market value of bonds and stocks over book value | | 1,042 00 |
| Assessments actually collected by subordinate lodges not yet turned over to supreme lodge | | 415,502 07 |
| All other assets, viz— | | |
| Furniture and fixtures | $55,285 14 | |
| Lodge supply inventory | 28,317 07 | |
| Supply invoices unpaid | 537 75 | |
| Postage | 1,592 94 | |
| Expectancy reserve—unpaid claims | 51,507 76 | |
| | | 137,240 66 |
| Gross assets | | $5,958,393 66 |

DEDUCT ASSETS NOT ADMITTED.

| | | |
|---|---|---|
| Overdue and accrued interest on bonds in default | $ 1,267 24 | |
| Other items, viz— | | |
| Furniture and fixtures | 55,285 14 | |
| Lodge supply inventory | 28,317 07 | |
| Supply invoices unpaid | 537 75 | |
| | | 85,407 20 |
| Total admitted assets | | $5,872,986 46 |

LIABILITIES.

| | | |
|---|---|---|
| Death claims due and unpaid | $ 27,465 38 | |
| Death claims resisted | 66,050 00 | |
| Death claims reported during the year but not yet adjusted | 263,651 20 | |
| Death claims incurred in 1921, not reported until 1922 | 81,600 00 | |
| Total death claims | | $438,766 58 |

LIABILITIES—Concluded.

| | | |
|---|---|---|
| Permanent disability claims due and unpaid | $ 1,500 00 | |
| Permanent disability claims resisted | 46,337 50 | |
| Permanent disability claims reported during the year but not yet adjusted | 47,902 50 | |
| Permanent disability claims incurred in 1921, not reported until 1922 | 45,562 50 | |
| Total permanent disability claims | | $ 141,302 50 |
| Sick and accident claims resisted | $ 7,613 75 | |
| Sick and accident claims reported during the year but not yet adjusted | 3,435 00 | |
| Sick and accident claims incurred in 1921, not reported until 1922 | 15,375 00 | |
| Total sick and accident claims | | 26,423 75 |
| Old age and other benefits due and unpaid | | 1,173,948 18 |
| Total unpaid claims | | $1,780,441 01 |
| Salaries, rents, expenses, commissions, etc., due or accrued | | 9,643 79 |
| Advance assessments | | 15,000 00 |
| All other liabilities, viz— | | |
| Legal reserve | $694,408 59 | |
| Juvenile legal reserve | 10,435 95 | |
| | | 704,844 54 |
| Total | | $2,509,929 34 |

EXHIBIT OF CERTIFICATES.

| | Total business of the year. Number. | Amount. | Business in Illinois during year. Number. | Amount. |
|---|---|---|---|---|
| Benefit certificates in force December 31, 1920, as per last statement | 285,948 | $367,882,000 00 | 9,442 | $10,666,500 00 |
| Benefit certificates written and renewed during the year | 43,643 | 50,034,000 00 | 2,859 | 3,226,000 00 |
| Benefit certificates increased during the year | -------- | 963,000 00 | 9 | 42,000 00 |
| Total | 329,591 | $418,879,000 00 | 12,301 | $13,934,500 00 |
| Deduct terminated, decreased or transferred during the year | 62,402 | 75,122,500 00 | -------- | ------------- |
| Deduct terminated or decreased during the year | -------- | ------------- | 3,917 | 4,309,000 00 |
| Total benefit certificates in force December 31, 1921 | 267,189 | $343,756,500 00 | 8,384 | $9,625,500 00 |

Received during the year from members in Illinois: Mortuary, $97,323.40; expense, $35,526.16; total $132,849 56

EXHIBIT OF DEATH CLAIMS.

| | Total claims. Number. | Amount. | Illinois claims. Number. | Amount. |
|---|---|---|---|---|
| Claims unpaid December 31, 1920, as per last statement | 250 | $ 304,720 31 | 7 | $ 9,208 36 |
| Claims reported during the year and interest addition | 1,881 | 2,500,000 00 | 51 | 51,250 00 |
| Total | 2,131 | $2,804,720 31 | 58 | $60,458 36 |
| Claims paid during the year | 1,783 | 1,984,853 66 | 49 | 48,647 30 |
| Balance | 348 | $819,866 65 | 9 | $11,811 06 |
| Saved by compromising or scaling down claims during the year | -------- | 396,650 07 | -------- | 787 06 |
| Claims rejected during the year | 48 | 66,050 00 | -------- | ------------- |
| Claims unpaid December 31, 1921 | 300 | $357,166 58 | 9 | $11,024 00 |

EXHIBIT OF PERMANENT DISABILITY CLAIMS.

| | Total claims. Number. | Amount. | Illinois claims. Number. | Amount. |
|---|---|---|---|---|
| Claims unpaid December 31, 1920, as per last statement | 73 | $ 49,500 00 | 1 | $500 00 |
| Claims reported during the year and interest addition | 388 | 269,175 00 | 2 | 750 00 |
| Total | 461 | $318,675 20 | 3 | $1,250 00 |
| Claims paid during the year | 294 | 172,313 91 | 1 | 250 00 |
| Balance | 167 | $146,361 29 | 2 | $1,000 00 |
| Saved by compromising or scaling down claims during the year | -------- | 28,433 79 | -------- | ------------- |
| Claims rejected during the year | 34 | 22,187 50 | -------- | ------------- |
| Claims unpaid December 31, 1921 | 133 | $95,740 00 | 2 | $100 00 |

EXHIBIT OF SICK AND ACCIDENT CLAIMS.

| | Total claims. Number. | Amount. | Illinois claims. Number. | Amount. |
|---|---|---|---|---|
| Claims unpaid December 31, 1920, as per last statement | 145 | 11,870 00 | 6 | $ 520 00 |
| Claims reported during the year | 2,858 | $201,486 37 | 105 | 6,605 00 |
| Total | 3,003 | $213,356 37 | 111 | $7,125 00 |
| Claims paid during the year | 2,883 | 190,753 17 | 105 | 6,675 00 |
| Claims rejected during the year | 37 | 11,554 45 | | |
| Claims unpaid December 31, 1921 | 83 | 11,048 75 | 6 | $450 00 |

EXHIBIT OF OLD AGE AND OTHER CLAIMS.

| | Total claims. Amount. |
|---|---|
| Claims unpaid December 31, 1920, as per last statement | $878,162 40 |
| Claims reported during the year and interest addition | 568,654 53 |
| Total | $1,446,816 93 |
| Claims paid during the year | 272,868 75 |
| Claims unpaid December 31, 1921 | $1,173,948 18 |

## CATHOLIC BENEVOLENT LEGION, SUPREME COUNCIL.

Located at No. 186 Remsen Street, Brooklyn, New York.

CHRISTOPHER C. KEENAN, President. JOHN E. DUNN, Secretary.

| | |
|---|---|
| Balance from previous year | $769,229 42 |

INCOME.

| | |
|---|---|
| All other assessments or premiums | $314,977 49 |
| Dues and per capita tax | 11,201 10 |
| Other payments by members, viz: Extension tax, $3,520.79; benefit certificates and changes, $259.00 | 3,779 79 |
| Net amount received from members | $329,958 38 |
| Gross interest on bonds and dividends on stocks | 28,260 62 |
| Gross interest on deposits in trust companies and banks | 7,286 30 |
| Sale of lodge supplies | 285 28 |
| From all other sources, viz— | |
| Bulletins | 5,695 76 |
| Advertisements | 49 50 |
| Member at large cards | 12 00 |
| Clearing house charges | 1 60 |
| Total income | $371,549 44 |
| Sum | $1,140,778 86 |

DISBURSEMENTS.

| | |
|---|---|
| Death claims | $236,626 88 |
| Salaries of officers and trustees | 5,000 00 |
| Other compensation of officers and trustees | 102 50 |
| Salaries and other compensation of committees | 52 00 |
| Salaries of office employees | 4,650 00 |
| Traveling and other expenses of officers, trustees and committees | 197 03 |
| For collection and remittance of assessments and dues | 34 05 |
| Insurance department fees | 35 00 |
| Rent | 1,600 08 |
| Advertising, printing and stationery | 1,290 18 |
| Postage, express, telegraph and telephone | 430 97 |
| Lodge supplies | 166 00 |
| Official publication | 2,822 00 |
| Expenses of supreme lodge meeting | 642 44 |
| Legal expense in litigating claims | 4,175 90 |
| Furniture and fixtures | 74 60 |
| All other disbursements, viz— | |
| Miles M. Dawson, actuary | 300 00 |
| Fraternal Monitor, $11.50; fire insurance premium, $25.48 | 36 98 |
| National Catholic Welfare Council, $100.00; safe deposit box, $10.00; office expenses, petty accounts, $134.90 | 244 90 |
| Total disbursements | $258,481 51 |
| Balance | $882,297 35 |

## LEDGER ASSETS.

| | | |
|---|---|---|
| Book value of bonds and stocks | | $685,913 71 |
| Deposits in trust companies and banks on interest | | 196,383 64 |
| Total ledger assets | | $882,297 35 |
| **NON-LEDGER ASSETS.** | | |
| Interest and rents due and accrued | | 4,536 79 |
| Assessments actually collected by subordinate lodges not yet turned over to supreme lodge | | 9,286 33 |
| All other assets, viz— | | |
| Optional reserve | $ 106,896 46 | |
| Terminal reserve | 9,519 50 | |
| Deficiency reserve lien | 3,047,464 00 | |
| | | 3,163,879 96 |
| Gross assets | | $4,060,000 43 |
| **DEDUCT ASSETS NOT ADMITTED.** | | |
| Balance due from organizers not secured by bonds | | 16,843 71 |
| Total admitted assets | | $4,043,156 72 |

## LIABILITIES.

| | | |
|---|---|---|
| Death claims resisted | $ 5,000 00 | |
| Death claims reported during the year but not yet adjusted | 24,915 93 | |
| Total unpaid claims | | $29,915 93 |
| Advance assessments | | 140 52 |
| All other liabilities, viz— | | |
| Reserve on outstanding certificates— | | |
| Members admitted since Sept. 1, 1904 | $ 181,338 00 | |
| Members admitted prior to Sept. 1, 1904 | 3,736,430 00 | |
| | | 3,917,768 00 |
| Total | | $3,947,824 45 |

## EXHIBIT OF CERTIFICATES.

| | Total business of the year. | | Business in Illinois during year. | |
|---|---|---|---|---|
| | Number. | Amount. | Number. | Amount. |
| Benefit certificates in force December 31, 1920, as per last statement | 11,008 | $11,383,750 00 | 214 | $297,250 00 |
| Benefit certificates written and renewed during the year | 145 | 86,000 00 | | |
| Benefit certificates increased during the year | | 1,500 00 | | |
| Total | 11,153 | $11,471,250 00 | 214 | $297,250 00 |
| Deduct terminated, decreased or transferred during the year | 647 | 679,750 00 | | |
| Deduct terminated or decreased during the year | | | 9 | 8,500 00 |
| Total benefit certificates in force December 31, 1921 | 10,506 | $10,791,500 00 | 205 | $288,750 00 |

Received during the year from members in Illinois: Mortuary, $9,636.73; all other, $92.40; expense, $209.50; total ........ $9,938 63

## EXHIBIT OF DEATH CLAIMS.

| | Total claims. | | Illinois claims. | |
|---|---|---|---|---|
| | Number. | Amount. | Number. | Amount. |
| Claims unpaid December 31, 1920, as per last statement | 36 | $ 28,881 06 | | |
| Claims reported during the year and interest addition | 300 | 387,250 00 | 7 | $7,000 00 |
| Total | 336 | $416,131 06 | 7 | $7,000 00 |
| Claims paid during the year | 295 | 236,626 88 | 6 | 4,298 30 |
| Balance | 41 | $179,504 18 | 1 | $2,701 70 |
| Saved by compromising or scaling down claims during the year | | 149,588 25 | | 2,165 07 |
| Claims unpaid December 31, 1921 | 41 | $29,915 93 | 1 | $536 63 |

---

## CATHOLIC FRATERNAL LEAGUE.

Located at No. 185 Summer Street, Boston, Massachusetts.

JOHN MERRILL, President. J. F. REYNOLDS, Secretary.

| | |
|---|---|
| Balance from previous year | $50,043 23 |

## INCOME.

| | | |
|---|---|---|
| Assessments or premiums during first twelve months of membership of which all or an extra percentage is used for expenses | | $ 2,430 25 |
| All other assessments or premiums | | 32,989 90 |
| Certificate fees | | 12 50 |
| Net amount received from members | | $35,432 65 |
| Gross interest on bonds and dividends on stocks | | 1,716 75 |
| Gross interest on deposits in trust companies and banks | | 201 13 |
| Sale of lodge supplies | | 9 25 |
| Canadian exchange | | 3 47 |
| Notes of members | | 117 00 |
| Total income | | $37,480 25 |
| Sum | | $87,523 48 |

## DISBURSEMENTS.

| | | |
|---|---|---|
| Death claims | | $13,183 33 |
| Permanent disability claims | | 350 00 |
| Sick and accident claims | | 5,640 00 |
| Old age benefits | | 519 00 |
| Total benefits paid | | $19,692 33 |
| Commissions and fees paid to deputies and organizers | | 1,621 13 |
| Salaries of officers and trustees | | 4,966 64 |
| Salaries of office employees | | 1,471 00 |
| Salaries and fees paid to supreme medical examiners | | 816 64 |
| Traveling and other expenses of officers, trustees and committees | | 385 98 |
| For collection and remittance of assessments and dues | | 589 73 |
| Insurance department fees | | 209 00 |
| Rent | | 840 00 |
| Advertising, printing and stationery | | 347 83 |
| Postage, express, telegraph and telephone | | 210 76 |
| Lodge supplies | | 41 90 |
| Official publication | | 54 00 |
| Legal expense in litigating claims | | 36 00 |
| Other legal expenses | | 35 00 |
| Office expenses and incidentals | | 128 17 |
| Canadian exchange | | 107 34 |
| Actuarial services | | 100 00 |
| Officers' bonds | | 37 20 |
| Commission on purchase of bonds | | 3 75 |
| Total disbursements | | $31,694 40 |
| Balance | | $55,829 08 |

## LEDGER ASSETS.

| | | |
|---|---|---|
| Book value of bonds and stocks | | $47,168 06 |
| Cash in association's office | | 17 14 |
| Deposits in trust companies and banks on interest | | 7,463 58 |
| Other ledger assets, viz: Notes of members | | 1,180 30 |
| Total ledger assets | | $55,829 08 |

### NON-LEDGER ASSETS.

| | | |
|---|---|---|
| Interest and rents due and accrued | | 409 43 |
| Assessments actually collected by subordinate lodges not yet turned over to supreme lodge | | 3,139 15 |
| All other assets, viz— | | |
| Furniture, fixtures and safe | $700 00 | |
| Supplies, printed matter and stationery | 500 00 | |
| Money advanced to organizers | 329 31 | |
| Accrued interest on notes of members | 91 45 | |
| | | 1,620 76 |
| Gross assets | | $60,998 42 |

### DEDUCT ASSETS NOT ADMITTED.

| | | |
|---|---|---|
| Overdue and accrued interest on bonds in default | $ 198 00 | |
| Book value of bonds and stocks over market value | 11,184 06 | |
| Other items, viz— | | |
| Furniture, fixtures and safe | 700 00 | |
| Supplies, printed matter and stationery | 500 00 | |
| Money advanced to organizers | 329 31 | |
| Accrued interest on notes of members and notes of members | 1,271 75 | |
| | | 14,183 12 |
| Total admitted assets | | $46,815 30 |

## LIABILITIES.

| | | |
|---|---|---|
| Death claims reported during the year but not yet adjusted | | $5,000 00 |
| Sick and accident claims reported during the year but not yet adjusted | $960 00 | |
| Sick and accident claims incurred in 1921, not reported until 1922 | 535 00 | |
| Total sick and accident claims | | 1,495 00 |
| Total unpaid claims | | 6,495 00 |
| Salaries, rents, expenses, commissions, etc., due or accrued | | 1,016 72 |
| Total | | $7,511 72 |

## EXHIBIT OF CERTIFICATES.

| | Total business of the year. | | Business in Illinois during year. | |
|---|---|---|---|---|
| | Number. | Amount. | Number. | Amount. |
| Benefit certificates in force December 31, 1920, as per last statement | 2,188 | $1,288,450 00 | 104 | $79,750 00 |
| Benefit certificates written and renewed during the year | 302 | 134,250 00 | 27 | 23,250 00 |
| Benefit certificates increased during the year | | 2,250 00 | | 1,500 00 |
| Totals | 2,490 | $1,424,950 00 | 131 | $104,500 00 |
| Deduct terminated, decreased or transferred during the year | 336 | 183,650 00 | | |
| Deduct terminated or decreased during the year | | | 24 | 19,000 00 |
| Total benefit certificates in force December 31, 1921 | 2,154 | $1,241,300 00 | 107 | $85,500 00 |

Received during the year from members in Illinois: Mortuary, $998.16; disability, $77.41; expense, $777.83; total $1,853 40

## EXHIBIT OF DEATH CLAIMS.

| | Total claims. | | Illinois claims. | |
|---|---|---|---|---|
| | Number. | Amount. | Number. | Amount. |
| Claims unpaid December 31, 1920, as per last statement | 4 | $ 3,000 00 | | |
| Claims reported during the year and interest addition | 25 | 16,500 00 | 2 | $1,500 00 |
| Totals | 29 | $19,500 00 | 2 | $1,500 00 |
| Claims paid during the year | 22 | 13,183 33 | 2 | 833 33 |
| Balance | 7 | $6,316 67 | | $666 67 |
| Saved by compromising or scaling down claims during the year | | 1,316 67 | | 666 67 |
| Claims unpaid December 31, 1921 | 7 | $5,000 00 | | |

## EXHIBIT OF PERMANENT DISABILITY CLAIMS.

| | Total claims—all in Illinois. | |
|---|---|---|
| | Number. | Amount. |
| Claims reported during the year and interest addition | 2 | $350 00 |
| Claims paid during the year | 2 | 350 00 |

## EXHIBIT OF SICK AND ACCIDENT CLAIMS.

| | Total claims—all in Illinois. | |
|---|---|---|
| | Number. | Amount. |
| Claims unpaid December 31, 1920, as per last statement | 19 | $ 530 00 |
| Decrease in estimated liability | | 30 00 |
| Claims reported during the year | 245 | 6,100 00 |
| Totals | 264 | $6,600 00 |
| Claims paid during the year | 221 | 5,640 00 |
| Claims uncompleted, dropped | 13 | |
| Claims unpaid December 31, 1921 | 30 | $960 00 |

## EXHIBIT OF OLD AGE AND OTHER CLAIMS.

| | Total claims—all in Illinois. | |
|---|---|---|
| | Number. | Amount. |
| Claims reported during the year and interest addition | 3 | $519 00 |
| Claims paid during the year | 3 | 519 00 |

## CATHOLIC KNIGHTS OF AMERICA, SUPREME COUNCIL.

Located at No. 211 North Seventh Street, St. Louis, Missouri.

DR. FELIX GANDIN, President. HENRY SIEMER, Secretary.

| | |
|---|---|
| Balance from previous year | $1,077,381 19 |

### INCOME.

| | |
|---|---|
| Assessments or premiums during first twelve months of membership of which all or an extra percentage is used for expenses | $ 23,926 45 |
| All other assessments or premiums | 410,366 40 |
| Dues and per capita tax | 35,008 30 |
| Medical examiners' fees actually received | 24 50 |
| Other payments by members, viz— | |
| Fines | 108 00 |
| Benefit certificates | 210 50 |
| Net amount received from members | $469,644 15 |
| Gross interest on bonds and dividends on stocks | 48,971 81 |
| Gross interest on deposits in trust companies and banks | 3,656 69 |
| Sale of lodge supplies | 458 87 |
| Refund interest overpaid | 36 00 |
| Postage returned | 4 93 |
| Cancelled warrants | 9 50 |
| Charter fees | 25 00 |
| Refund insurance department | 46 00 |
| Total income | $522,852 95 |
| Sum | $1,600,234 14 |

### DISBURSEMENTS.

| | |
|---|---|
| Death claims | $400,201 28 |
| Old age benefits | 105 00 |
| Total benefits paid | $400,306 28 |
| Commissions and fees paid to deputies and organizers | 2,463 86 |
| Salaries of deputies and organizers | 1,500 00 |
| Salaries of officers and trustees | 9,299 96 |
| Salaries of office employees | 315 00 |
| Salaries and fees paid to supreme medical examiners | 641 50 |
| Salaries and fees paid to subordinate medical examiners | 2,632 50 |
| Traveling and other expenses of officers, trustees and committees | 1,663 81 |
| Insurance department fees | 702 74 |
| Rent | 1,590 00 |
| Advertising, printing and stationery | 4,027 71 |
| Postage, express, telegraph and telephone | 1,046 27 |
| Official publication | 4,350 00 |
| Legal expense in litigating claims | 290 25 |
| Other legal expenses | 28 50 |
| Furniture and fixtures | 373 05 |
| Taxes, repairs and other expenses on real estate | 34 08 |
| Gross loss on sale or maturity of ledger assets | 986 65 |
| Borrowed money repaid (gross) | 55,000 00 |
| Interest on borrowed money | 3,571 45 |
| Members premiums | 3,843 03 |
| Membership fees N. F. C. & C. P. A | 92 00 |
| Refund to branches | 30 63 |
| Actuarial service | 160 70 |
| Surety bonds | 494 49 |
| Accrued interest bonds bought | 28 33 |
| Total disbursements | $495,472 79 |
| Balance | $1,104,761 35 |

### LEDGER ASSETS.

| | |
|---|---|
| Book value of bonds and stocks | $1,044,907 25 |
| Deposits in trust companies and banks on interest | 59,854 10 |
| Total ledger assets | $1,104,761 35 |

#### NON-LEDGER ASSETS.

| | |
|---|---|
| Interest and rents due and accrued | 16,883 86 |
| Assessments actually collected by subordinate lodges not yet turned over to supreme lodge | 12,019 72 |
| Furniture and fixtures | 2,000 00 |
| Gross assets | $1,135,644 93 |

LEDGER ASSETS—Concluded.

DEDUCT ASSETS NOT ADMITTED.

| | | |
|---|---|---|
| Book value of bonds and stocks over market value | $36,886 25 | |
| Other items, viz: Furniture and fixtures | 2,000 00 | |
| | | 38,886 25 |
| Total admitted assets | | $1,096,778 68 |

LIABILITIES.

| | | |
|---|---|---|
| Death claims due and unpaid | $10,830 97 | |
| Death claims reported during the year but not yet adjusted | 23,500 00 | |
| Death claims incurred in 1921, not reported until 1922 | 4,000 00 | |
| Total death claims | | $38,330 97 |
| Total unpaid claims | | 1,148 13 |
| Borrowed money | | 20,000 00 |
| Advance assessments | | 15 41 |
| Total | | $59,494 51 |

EXHIBIT OF CERTIFICATES.

| | Total business of the year. | | Business in Illinois during year. | |
|---|---|---|---|---|
| | Number. | Amount. | Number. | Amount. |
| Benefit certificates in force December 31, 1920, as per last statement | 18,940 | $19,314,426 04 | 1,736 | $1,564,354 11 |
| Benefit certificates written and renewed during the year | 972 | 738,500 00 | 108 | 79,000 00 |
| Benefit certificates received by transfer during the year | -------- | ------------- | 1 | 1,000 00 |
| Benefit certificates increased during the year | -------- | 23,750 00 | -------- | 6,500 00 |
| Totals | 19,912 | $20,076,676 04 | 1,845 | $1,650,854 11 |
| Deduct terminated, decreased or transferred during the year | 984 | 958,138 05 | -------- | ------------- |
| Deduct terminated or decreased during the year | -------- | ------------- | 60 | 56,677 04 |
| Total benefit certificates in force December 31, 1921 | 18,928 | $19,118,537 99 | 1,785 | $1,594,177 07 |

| | |
|---|---|
| Received during the year from members in Illinois: Mortuary, $29,840.99; reserve, $1,027.80; expense, $4,507.86; total | $35,376 65 |

EXHIBIT OF DEATH CLAIMS.

| | Total claims. | | Illinois claims. | |
|---|---|---|---|---|
| | Number. | Amount. | Number. | Amount. |
| Claims unpaid December 31, 1920, as per last statement | 49 | $ 56,720 37 | 7 | $ 6,417 00 |
| Claims reported during the year and interest addition | 319 | 432,768 73 | 21 | 23,677 04 |
| Totals | 368 | $489,489 10 | 28 | $30,094 04 |
| Claims paid during the year | 336 | 400,201 28 | 26 | 27,042 45 |
| Balance | 32 | $89,287 82 | 2 | $3,051 59 |
| Saved by compromising or scaling down claims during the year, liens deducted | -------- | 52,986 60 | -------- | 2,134 59 |
| Claims dropped during the year | 5 | 1,970 25 | 2 | 917 00 |
| Claims unpaid December 31, 1921 | 27 | $34,330 97 | -------- | ------------- |

EXHIBIT OF OLD AGE AND OTHER CLAIMS.

| | Total claims. | |
|---|---|---|
| | Number. | Amount. |
| Balance | 1 | 105 00 |

## CATHOLIC WORKMAN.

Located at New Prague, Minnesota.

JOSEPH F. REZNICEK, President. THOS. G. HOVORKA, Secretary.

| | |
|---|---|
| Balance from previous year | $461,317 40 |

## INCOME.

| | | |
|---|---|---|
| All other assessments or premiums | | $71,310 70 |
| Dues and per capita tax | | 7,865 30 |
| Member certificate | | 66 50 |
| Net amount received from members | | $79,242 50 |
| Gross interest on mortgage loans | | 17,306 59 |
| Gross interest on bonds and dividends on stocks | | 2,362 50 |
| Gross interest on deposits in trust companies and banks | | 2,631 69 |
| Sale of lodge supplies | | 64 00 |
| Total income | | $101,607 28 |
| Sum | | $562,924 68 |

## DISBURSEMENTS.

| | | |
|---|---|---|
| Death claims | | $35,890 67 |
| Commissions and fees paid to deputies and organizers | | 364 50 |
| Salaries of officers and trustees | | 3,112 50 |
| Other compensation of office employees | | 20 00 |
| For collection and remittance of assessments and dues | | 39 65 |
| Insurance department fees | | 123 00 |
| Rent | | 180 00 |
| Advertising, printing and stationery | | 988 85 |
| Postage, express, telegraph and telephone | | 252 05 |
| Lodge supplies | | 53 00 |
| Official publication | | 1,026 86 |
| Expenses of supreme lodge meeting | | 3,367 61 |
| All other disbursements, viz— | | |
| Officers' bonds, $37.00; insurance premium, office contents, $12.50 | | 49 50 |
| Incidentals | | 176 60 |
| Rent safety deposit box | | 30 00 |
| Interest refunded | | 47 35 |
| Total disbursements | | $45,722 14 |
| Balance | | $517,202 54 |

## LEDGER ASSETS.

| | | |
|---|---|---|
| Mortgage loans on real estate | | $394,700 99 |
| Book value of bonds and stocks | | 55,836 00 |
| Deposits in trust companies and banks not on interest | | 66,665 55 |
| Total ledger assets | | $517,202 54 |

### NON-LEDGER ASSETS.

| | | |
|---|---|---|
| Interest and rents due and accrued | | 18,940 37 |
| All other assets, viz— | | |
| Liens on certificates | $9,393 84 | |
| Office contents | 1,300 00 | |
| | | 10,693 84 |
| Gross assets | | $546,836 75 |

### DEDUCT ASSETS NOT ADMITTED.

| | | |
|---|---|---|
| Other items, viz— | | |
| Liens on certificates | $9,393 84 | |
| Office contents | 1,300 00 | |
| | | 10,693 84 |
| Total admitted assets | | $536,142 91 |

## LIABILITIES.

| | | |
|---|---|---|
| Death claims due and unpaid | $3,060 75 | |
| Death claims adjusted not yet due | 5,000 00 | |
| Death claims reported during the year but not yet adjusted | 1,000 00 | |
| Total unpaid claims | | $9,060 75 |
| All other liabilities, viz— | | |
| Official monthly | $135 00 | |
| Supreme counselor's fees | 300 00 | |
| | | 435 00 |
| Total | | $9,495 75 |

EXHIBIT OF CERTIFICATES.

| | Total business of the year. | | Business in Illinois during year. | |
|---|---|---|---|---|
| | Number. | Amount. | Number. | Amount. |
| Benefit certificates in force December 31, 1920, as per last statement | 4,273 | $4,708,500 00 | 443 | $427,500 00 |
| Benefit certificates written and renewed during the year | 365 | 349,500 00 | 37 | 30,500 00 |
| Benefit certificates increased during the year | -------- | 3,000 00 | -------- | 500 00 |
| Totals | 4,638 | $5,061,000 00 | 480 | $458,500 00 |
| Deduct terminated, decreased or transferred during the year | 93 | 102,500 00 | -------- | -------------- |
| Deduct terminated or decreased during the year | -------- | -------------- | 15 | 16,000 00 |
| Total benefit certificates in force December 31, 1921 | 4,545 | $4,958,500 00 | 465 | $442,500 00 |

Received during the year from members in Illinois: Mortuary, $6,554.70; expense, $832.85; total $7,387 55

EXHIBIT OF DEATH CLAIMS.

| | Total claims. | | Illinois claims. | |
|---|---|---|---|---|
| | Number. | Amount. | Number. | Amount. |
| Claims unpaid December 31, 1920, as per last statement | 14 | $10,855 75 | -------- | -------------- |
| Claims reported during the year and interest addition | 29 | 36,000 00 | 2 | $1,500 00 |
| Totals | 43 | $46,855 75 | 2 | $1,500 00 |
| Claims paid during the year | 31 | 35,890 67 | 2 | 1,500 00 |
| Balance | 12 | $10,965 08 | -------- | -------------- |
| Saved by compromising or scaling down claims during the year | -------- | 1,904 33 | -------- | -------------- |
| Claims unpaid December 31, 1921 | 12 | $9,060 75 | -------- | -------------- |

## COLUMBIAN MUTUAL LIFE ASSURANCE SOCIETY.

Located at Hurt Building, Atlanta, Georgia.

LLOYD T. BINFORD, President. GEO W. CLAYTON, Secretary.

| | |
|---|---|
| Balance from previous year | $1,926,459 98 |

INCOME.

| | |
|---|---|
| All assessments or premiums | $803,356 08 |
| Dues and per capita tax | 13 10 |
| Medical examiners' fees actually received | 5,907 00 |
| Other payments by members, viz: Overages and advances | 64,744 86 |
| Total received from members | $874,021 04 |
| Deduct payments returned to applicants and members and credits | 69,636 80 |
| Net amount received from members | $804,384 24 |
| Gross interest on mortgage loans | 28,745 23 |
| Gross interest on collateral loans | 2,075 55 |
| Gross interest on bonds and dividends on stocks | 32,259 53 |
| Gross interest on deposits in trust companies and banks | 3,731 71 |
| Gross interest from all other sources | 38,433 81 |
| Gross profit on sale or maturity of ledger assets | 16,999 47 |
| Gross increase in book value of ledger assets | 682 62 |
| Liens re-instated | 1,244 03 |
| Miscellaneous dues, etc | 2,045 91 |
| Dividends left to accumulate | 13 55 |
| Sale of premiums | 1,612 49 |
| Sale of buttons | 12 10 |
| Organizers bond fees | 643 00 |
| Change covenant fees | 191 70 |
| Recording fees | 153 50 |
| Total income | $933,228 44 |
| Sum | $2,859,688 42 |

## DISBURSEMENTS.

| | |
|---|---|
| Death claims | $267,116 01 |
| Permanent disability claims | 38,918 00 |
| Sick and accident claims | 3,266 84 |
| Old age benefits | 2,848 57 |
| All other | 82,778 41 |
| Total benefits paid | $394,927 83 |
| Commissions and fees paid to deputies and organizers | 94,738 40 |
| Salaries, expenses of deputies and organizers | 6,554 18 |
| Salaries of managers or agents not deputies or organizers and expenses | 4,971 29 |
| Salaries of officers and trustees | 19,245 00 |
| Salaries and other compensation of committees and expenses | 1,156 78 |
| Salaries of office employees | 50,070 98 |
| Other compensation of office employees | 2,670 35 |
| Salaries and fees paid to supreme medical examiners | 5,000 00 |
| Salaries and fees paid to subordinate medical examiners | 14,563 11 |
| Traveling and other expenses of officers, trustees and committees | 2,215 59 |
| Insurance department fees | 751 00 |
| Rent | 10,639 48 |
| Advertising, printing and stationery | 14,892 71 |
| Postage, express, telegraph and telephone | 8,245 58 |
| Lodge supplies | 292 76 |
| Official publication | 8,533 89 |
| Expenses of supreme lodge meeting | 13,384 67 |
| Legal expense in litigating claims | 1,629 49 |
| Other legal expenses | 4,100 00 |
| Taxes on assets | 16,100 67 |
| Gross loss on sale or maturity of ledger assets | 997 76 |
| Gross decrease in book value of ledger assets | 166 25 |
| All other disbursements, viz: Bonus field men, $187.50; inspection fees and commercial agencies, $8,016.25; field lecturers, $4,774.48; field men's supplies, $206.95; office expense sundry, $582.68; premium officers' bonds, $260.00; premium bonds; branch secretarys, $45.80; ice, towel and electric service, $368.30; books, insurance papers and publications, $572.22; X-ray and special examinations, $329.75; expense settlement claims and losses, $438.45; premiums or prizes, $1,087.50; actuary, $900.00; auditor, $900.00; donations, $196.50; expense examination, $512.11; subscriptions, dues, etc., $213.50; souvenir card cases and bill folders, $1,339.40; buttons and pins, $478.69; parcel post insurance, $101.70; actuarial expense, $750.00; protested checks, $6.84; expense moving, $1,300.89; expense merger, $6,047.03; expense royal household meetings (grand lodge) 11,737.99; investment expense, $243.36; relief payments, $300.00 | 41,897 89 |
| Total disbursements | $717,745 66 |
| Balance | $2,141,942 76 |

## LEDGER ASSETS.

| | |
|---|---|
| Mortgage loans on real estate | $301,185 00 |
| Loans secured by pledge of bonds, stocks or other collateral | 26,650 00 |
| Book value of bonds | 828,969 73 |
| Cash in association's office | 104 00 |
| Premium liens and loans to covenant holders | 837,673 35 |
| Deposits in trust companies and banks on interest | 44,258 46 |
| Bills receivable, $24,379.90; organizers' balances, $44,758.78 | 69,138 68 |
| Other ledger assets, viz— | |
| Automobiles and field equipment | 1,951 09 |
| Furniture and fixtures, home office and club rooms | 32,012 45 |
| Total ledger assets | $2,141,942 76 |

### NON-LEDGER ASSETS.

| | |
|---|---|
| Interest due and accrued | 20,018 61 |
| Market value of bonds and stocks over book value | 6,410 27 |
| Gross assets | $2,168,371 64 |

### DEDUCT ASSETS NOT ADMITTED.

| | | |
|---|---|---|
| Balance due from organizers not secured by bonds | $35,694 45 | |
| Bills receivable | 13,481 94 | |
| Other items, viz— | | |
| Automobile and field equipment | 1,951 09 | |
| Furniture and fixtures | 32,012 45 | |
| | | 83,139 93 |
| Total admitted assets | | $2,085,231 71 |

## LIABILITIES.

| | | |
|---|---|---|
| Death claims resisted | $8,671 05 | |
| Death claims reported during the year but not yet adjusted | 16,000 00 | |
| Present value of deferred death claims payable in installments | 5,464 74 | |
| Total death claims | | $30,135 79 |

LIABILITIES—Concluded.

| | | |
|---|---|---|
| Permanent disability claims adjusted not yet due | $ 1,870 00 | |
| Permanent disability claims reported during the year but not yet adjusted | 1,000 00 | |
| Present value of disability claims payable in installments | 22,567 53 | |
| Total permanent disability claims | | $25,437 53 |
| Old age and other benefits due and unpaid | | 1,000 00 |
| Total unpaid claims | | $56,573 32 |
| Salaries, rents, expenses, commissions, etc., due or accrued, expenses, $6,617.91; examiners, $1,843.50; commissions, $6,975.13 | | 15,436 54 |
| Advance assessments | | 37,713 18 |
| All other liabilities, viz— | | |
| Overages | $ 380 52 | |
| Advances applications, suspense | 6,187 40 | |
| Dividends unpaid and left to accumulate | 1,457 14 | |
| Net reserve on all outstanding covenants, December 31, 1921, American experience, 3½ per cent | 1,916,062 62 | |
| | | 1,924,087 68 |
| Total | | $2,033,810 72 |

EXHIBIT OF CERTIFICATES.

| | Total business of the year—all in Illinois. Number. | Amount. |
|---|---|---|
| Benefit certificates in force December 31, 1920, as per last statement | 20,802 | $28,054,409 00 |
| By merger | 1,893 | 2,250,500 00 |
| Benefit certificates written and renewed during the year | 5,403 | 6,598,500 00 |
| Extended lapsed 1921 | 107 | 125,000 00 |
| Benefit certificates increased during the year | 250 | 291,508 00 |
| Totals | 28,455 | $37,320,917 00 |
| Deduct terminated, decreased or transferred during the year | 5,326 | 6,317,586 00 |
| Total benefit certificates in force December 31, 1921 | 23,129 | $31,003,331 00 |

EXHIBIT OF DEATH CLAIMS.

| | Total claims—all in Illinois. Number. | Amount. |
|---|---|---|
| Claims unpaid December 31, 1920, as per last statement | 34 | $ 40,801 05 |
| Claims reported during the year and interest addition | 191 | 262,592 00 |
| Totals | 225 | $303,393 05 |
| Claims paid during the year | 197 | 267,116 01 |
| Balance | 28 | $36,277 04 |
| Saved by compromising or scaling down claims during the year | -------- | 3,112 33 |
| Adjustment age or occupation | -------- | 1,159 16 |
| Claims rejected during the year | 2 | 2,000 00 |
| Claims unpaid December 31, 1921 | 26 | $30,005 55 |

EXHIBIT OF PERMANENT DISABILITY CLAIMS.

| | Total claims—all in Illinois. Number. | Amount. |
|---|---|---|
| Claims unpaid December 31, 1920, as per last statement | 47 | $27,744 52 |
| Claims reported during the year and interest addition | 78 | 91,438 00 |
| Totals | 125 | $119,182 52 |
| Claims paid during the year | 60 | 38,918 00 |
| Balance | 65 | $80,264 52 |
| Saved by compromising or scaling down claims during the year | -------- | 37,355 62 |
| Transferred to death claims | 3 | 2,100 00 |
| Claims rejected during the year | 12 | 12,250 00 |
| Claims unpaid December 31, 1921 | 50 | $28,558 90 |

EXHIBIT OF SICK AND ACCIDENT CLAIMS.

| | Total claims—all in Illinois. Number. | Amount. |
|---|---|---|
| Claims unpaid December 31, 1920, as per last statement | 8 | $ 650 00 |
| Increase in estimated liability | 38 | 3,350 00 |
| Totals | 46 | $4,000 00 |
| Claims paid during the year | 38 | 3,266 84 |
| Adjustment | -------- | 33 16 |
| Claims rejected during the year | 8 | 700 00 |

## EXHIBIT OF OLD AGE AND OTHER CLAIMS.

| | Total claims—all in Illinois. Number. | Amount. |
|---|---|---|
| Claims unpaid December 31, 1920, as per last statement | 1 | $ 50 00 |
| Claims reported during the year and interest addition | 38 | 7,200 00 |
| Totals | 39 | $7,250 00 |
| Claims paid during the year | 38 | 4,598 57 |
| Balance | 1 | $2,651 43 |
| Saved by compromising or scaling down claims during the year | | 1,651 43 |
| Claims unpaid December 31, 1921 | 1 | $1,000 00 |

## DANISH BROTHERHOOD IN AMERICA.

Located at No. 927 Omaha National Bank Building, Omaha, Nebraska.

S. IVERSEN, President. FRANK V. LAWSON, Secretary.

| | |
|---|---|
| Balance from previous year | $896,855 66 |

### INCOME.

| | |
|---|---|
| Membership fees actually received | $ 981 00 |
| All other assessments or premiums | 229,012 45 |
| Dues and per capita tax | 28,718 00 |
| Changing certificates | 114 00 |
| Net amount received from members | $258,825 45 |
| Gross interest on bank deposits | 1,501 42 |
| Gross interest on bonds and dividends on stocks | 44,006 78 |
| Sale of lodge supplies | 644 26 |
| Gross increase in book value of ledger assets | 7,601 60 |
| Advertising official paper | 204 00 |
| Total income | $312,783 51 |
| Sum | $1,209,639 17 |

### DISBURSEMENTS.

| | |
|---|---|
| Death claims | $86,626 50 |
| Sick and accident claims | 2,210 00 |
| Old age benefits | 1,550 14 |
| Funeral expenses | 5,450 00 |
| Total benefits paid | $95,836 64 |
| Salaries of officers and trustees | 4,617 44 |
| Salaries of office employees | 3,257 50 |
| Traveling and other expenses of officers, trustees and committees | 1,818 37 |
| Insurance department fees | 115 00 |
| Rent | 1,109 80 |
| Advertising, printing and stationery | 1,359 08 |
| Postage, express, telegraph and telephone | 918 05 |
| Lodge supplies | 379 70 |
| Official publication | 6,211 50 |
| Other legal expenses | 982 00 |
| Furniture and fixtures | 782 50 |
| All other disbursements, viz— | |
| Insurance department examination | 2,154 47 |
| Auditing books | 216 25 |
| Miscellaneous, $60.64; Denmark Lodge expense, $69.99; coupon collections, $38.40 | 169 03 |
| Safety box, $50.00; prizes to members, $120.00 | 170 00 |
| Total disbursements | $120,097 33 |
| Balance | $10,895,541 84 |

### LEDGER ASSETS.

| | |
|---|---|
| Book value of bonds and stocks | $1,030,000 00 |
| Deposits in trust companies and banks not on interest | 59,541 84 |
| Total ledger assets | $1,089,541 84 |
| NON-LEDGER ASSETS. | |
| Interest and rents due and accrued | 18,423 24 |
| Market value of bonds and stocks over book value | 4,014 20 |
| Assessments actually collected by subordinate lodges not yet turned over to supreme lodge | 19,001 17 |
| Gross assets | $1,131,980 45 |

LIABILITIES.

| | | |
|---|---|---|
| Death claims reported during the year but not yet adjusted | $ 1,000 00 | |
| Death claims incurred in 1921, not reported until 1922 | 11,000 00 | |
| Total death claims | | $12,000 00 |
| Salaries, rents, expenses, commissions, etc., due or accrued | | 729 78 |
| Total | | $12,729 78 |

EXHIBIT OF CERTIFICATES.

| | Total business of the year. | | Business in Illinois during year. | |
|---|---|---|---|---|
| | Number. | Amount. | Number. | Amount. |
| Benefit certificates in force December 31, 1920, as per last statement | 19,889 | $13,606,500 00 | 2,258 | $1,683,500 00 |
| Benefit certificates written and renewed during the year | 823 | 470,250 00 | 80 | 44,000 00 |
| Benefit certificates received by transfer during the year | -------- | -------------- | 4 | 2,750 00 |
| Benefit certificates increased during the year | -------- | 12,750 00 | -------- | -------------- |
| Total | 20,712 | $14,089,500 00 | 2,342 | $1,730,250 00 |
| Deduct terminated, decreased or transferred during the year | 1,270 | 772,500 00 | -------- | -------------- |
| Deduct terminated or decreased during the year | -------- | -------------- | 81 | 50,250 00 |
| Total benefit certificates in force December 31, 1921 | 19,442 | $13,317,000 00 | 2,261 | $1,680,000 00 |

Received during the year from members in Illinois: Mortuary, $17,602.39; expense, $3,392.00; total ........ $20,994 39

EXHIBIT OF DEATH CLAIMS.

| | Total claims. | | Illinois claims. | |
|---|---|---|---|---|
| | Number. | Amount. | Number. | Amount. |
| Claims unpaid December 31, 1920, as per last statement | 2 | $ 1,000 00 | -------- | -------------- |
| Claims reported during the year and interest addition | 174 | 125,750 00 | 21 | $15,000 00 |
| Total | 176 | $126,750 00 | 21 | $15,000 00 |
| Claims paid during the year | 174 | 125,750 00 | 21 | 15,000 00 |
| Claims unpaid December 31, 1921 | 2 | 1,000 00 | -------- | -------------- |

## DAUGHTERS OF NORWAY.

Located at No. 1919 South Fourth Street, Minneapolis, Minnesota.

SOPHIA WETTELAND, President. AUGUSTA SWAN, Secretary.

| | |
|---|---|
| Balance from previous year | $28,477 87 |

INCOME.

| | |
|---|---|
| Membership fees actually received | $ 165 25 |
| All other assessments or premiums | 7,114 50 |
| Dues and per capita tax | 2,208 65 |
| Certificate fees | 18 50 |
| Net amount received from members | $9,506 90 |
| Gross interest on mortgage loans | 404 00 |
| Gross interest on bonds and dividends on stocks | 108 75 |
| Gross interest on deposits in trust companies and banks | 729 46 |
| Sale of lodge supplies | 758 71 |
| Fines | 75 |
| Relief fund | 148 00 |
| Advertisement | 13 00 |
| Total income | $11,669 57 |
| Sum | $40,147 44 |

## DISBURSEMENTS.

| | |
|---|---|
| Death claims | $2,300 00 |
| Salaries of officers and trustees | 910 00 |
| Traveling and other expenses of officers, trustees and committees | 141 26 |
| Insurance department fees | 70 00 |
| Postage, express, telegraph and telephone | 86 01 |
| Lodge supplies | 508 14 |
| Official publication | 966 89 |
| Expenses of supreme lodge meeting | 447 44 |
| Other legal expenses | 5 00 |
| Premium on bonds and insurance | 18 66 |
| Safety deposit box | 2 50 |
| Bank exchange | 3 58 |
| Premiums to members | 204 50 |
| Total disbursements | $5,663 98 |
| Balance | $34,483 46 |

## LEDGER ASSETS.

| | |
|---|---|
| Mortgage loans on real estate | $ 9,900 00 |
| Book value of bonds and stocks | 2,500 00 |
| Deposits in trust companies and banks not on interest | 55 30 |
| Deposits in trust companies and banks on interest | 22,028 16 |
| Total ledger assets | $34,483 46 |

### NON-LEDGER ASSETS.

| | |
|---|---|
| Market value of real estate over book value | 149 87 |
| Books and furniture | 500 00 |
| Gross assets | $35,133 33 |

### DEDUCT ASSETS NOT ADMITTED.

| | |
|---|---|
| Books and furniture | 500 00 |
| Total admitted assets | $34,633 33 |

## LIABILITIES.

| | |
|---|---|
| Total death claims | $100 00 |

## EXHIBIT OF CERTIFICATES.

| | Total business of the year. | | Business in Illinois during year. | |
|---|---|---|---|---|
| | Number. | Amount. | Number. | Amount. |
| Benefit certificates in force December 31, 1920, as per last statement | 4,346 | $434,600 00 | 698 | 69,800 00 |
| Benefit certificates written and renewed during the year | 642 | 64,200 00 | 122 | 12,200 00 |
| Total | 4,988 | $498,800 00 | 820 | $82,000 00 |
| Deduct terminated, decreased or transferred during the year | 299 | 29,900 00 | | |
| Deduct terminated or decreased during the year | | | 41 | 4,100 00 |
| Total benefit certificates in force December 31, 1921 | 4,689 | $468,900 00 | 779 | $77,900 00 |

Received during the year from members in Illinois: Mortuary, $1,027.80; reserve, $114.20; expense, $460.82; total $1,602 82

## EXHIBIT OF DEATH CLAIMS.

| | Total claims. | | Illinois claims. | |
|---|---|---|---|---|
| | Number. | Amount. | Number. | Amount. |
| Claims unpaid December 31, 1920, as per last statement | 1 | $ 100 00 | | |
| Claims reported during the year and interest addition | 26 | 2,600 00 | 4 | $400 00 |
| Total | 27 | $2,700 00 | 4 | $400 00 |
| Claims paid during the year | 24 | 2,300 00 | 4 | 350 00 |
| Balance | 3 | $400 00 | | $50 00 |
| Saved by compromising or scaling down claims during the year | | 100 00 | | 50 00 |
| Claims unpaid December 31, 1921 | 3 | $300 00 | | |

## DEGREE OF HONOR, PROTECTIVE ASSOCIATION.

Located at No. 580 Shubert Building, St. Paul, Minnesota.

FRANCES BUELL OLSON, President. KATE S. HOLMES, Secretary.

| | |
|---|---|
| Balance from previous year | $1,786,446 46 |

### INCOME.

| | |
|---|---|
| Assessments or premiums during first 12 months of membership of which all or an extra percentage is used for expenses | $112,677 01 |
| All other assessments or premiums | 436,087 49 |
| Dues and per capita tax | 13,546 00 |
| Certificate fees | 331 25 |
| Net amount received from members | $526,641 75 |
| Gross interest on bonds and dividends on stocks | 94,546 92 |
| Gross interest on deposits in trust companies and banks | 100 00 |
| Gross interest from all other sources— | |
| Interest on building | 547 43 |
| Interest on daily balance | 1,281 51 |
| Gross rents from association's property | 452 57 |
| Sale of lodge supplies | 2,859 01 |
| Gross increase in book value of ledger assets | 6,523 90 |
| Contributions | 8,417 27 |
| Miscellaneous | 498 45 |
| Michigan grand lodge | 7,757 55 |
| Michigan grand lodge, real estate | 36,495 51 |
| Michigan grand lodge, bonds | 160,234 00 |
| Total income | $882,355 87 |
| Sum | $2,668,802 33 |

### DISBURSEMENTS.

| | |
|---|---|
| Death claims | $280,066 70 |
| Permanent disability claims | 500 00 |
| Old age benefits | 5,835 00 |
| Settlement of claim | 41 63 |
| Total benefits paid | $286,443 33 |
| Commissions and fees paid to deputies and organizers | 11,003 42 |
| Salaries of deputies and organizers | 26,569 47 |
| Salaries of officers and trustees | 6,900 00 |
| Salaries and other compensation of committees | 395 25 |
| Salaries of office employees | 10,337 70 |
| Salaries and fees paid to supreme medical examiners | 1,066 95 |
| Traveling and other expenses of officers, trustees and committees | 3,112 52 |
| Insurance department fees | 731 00 |
| Rent | 1,468 89 |
| Advertising, printing and stationery | 1,868 06 |
| Postage, express, telegraph and telephone | 1,989 16 |
| Lodge supplies | 7,809 26 |
| Official publication | 8,345 98 |
| Expenses of supreme lodge meeting | 2,856 35 |
| Other legal expenses | 474 02 |
| Furniture and fixtures | 113 40 |
| Taxes, repairs and other expenses on real estate | 52 14 |
| Gross loss on sale or maturity of ledger assets | 2,326 90 |
| Gross decrease in book value of ledger assets | 4,490 93 |
| Actuary service | 560 44 |
| All other disbursements, viz— | |
| Surety bonds | 479 12 |
| N. F. C. dues and expenses | 362 50 |
| Five-sixths of 60 per cent of new members first 12 assessments returned to Minnesota, Missouri, Michigan; one-half monthly tax, one-half W. L. & Dis. first 12 assessments, S. & S. D. for extension work | 31,231 45 |
| Miscellaneous | 255 78 |
| Total disbursements | $411,244 02 |
| Balance | $2,257,558 31 |

### LEDGER ASSETS.

| | |
|---|---|
| Book value of real estate | $ 36,042 94 |
| Book value of bonds | 2,144,501 32 |
| Deposits in trust companies and banks on interest | 77,014 05 |
| Total ledger assets | $2,257,558 31 |

## LEDGER ASSETS—Concluded.

### NON-LEDGER ASSETS.

| | | |
|---|---|---|
| Interest and rents due and accrued | | $41,117 87 |
| Market value of bonds and stocks over book value | | 14,090 68 |
| Assessments actually collected by subordinate lodges not yet turned over to supreme lodge | | 40,040 98 |
| Monthly tax | | 3,415 30 |
| All other assets, viz— | | |
| Due from grand and subordinate lodges for supplies | $1,483 48 | |
| Inventory of supplies for re-sale | 5,765 30 | |
| Furniture and fixtures in national office | 2,872 36 | |
| | | 10,121 14 |
| Gross assets | | $2,366,344 28 |

### DEDUCT ASSETS NOT ADMITTED.

| | | |
|---|---|---|
| Inventory of supplies for re-sale | 5,765 30 | |
| Furniture and fixtures in national office | 2,872 36 | |
| | | 8,637 66 |
| Total admitted assets | | $2,357,606 62 |

## LIABILITIES.

| | | |
|---|---|---|
| Death claims due and unpaid | | $10,100 00 |
| Salaries, rents, expenses, commissions, etc., due or accrued | | 1,758 35 |
| All other liabilities, viz— | | |
| Official publication (paid in January) | $ 689 77 | |
| Minnesota, Missouri, Michigan and South Dakota expense tax (paid in January) | 1,093 95 | |
| Minnesota, Missouri, Michigan and South Dakota share of new members first 12 assessments (paid in January) | 1,374 25 | |
| | | 3,157 97 |
| Total | | $15,016 32 |

## EXHIBIT OF CERTIFICATES.

| | Total business of the year. | | Business in Illinois during year. | |
|---|---|---|---|---|
| | Number. | Amount. | Number. | Amount. |
| Benefit certificates in force December 31, 1920, as per last statement | 30,999 | $27,422,001 75 | 1,019 | $763,500 00 |
| Benefit certificates written and renewed during the year | 9,889 | 9,911,828 25 | 156 | 118,000 00 |
| Total | 40,888 | $37,333,830 00 | 1,175 | $881,500 00 |
| Deduct terminated, decreased or transferred during the year | 5,050 | 5,731,657 00 | | |
| Deduct terminated or decreased during the year | | | 205 | 142,950 00 |
| Total benefit certificates in force December 31, 1921 | 35,838 | $31,602,173 00 | 970 | $738,550 00 |

Received during the year from members in Illinois: Mortuary, $11,915.57; home relief, $244.80; expense, $2,007.79; total — $14,168 16

## EXHIBIT OF DEATH CLAIMS.

| | Total claims. | | Illinois claims. | |
|---|---|---|---|---|
| | Number. | Amount. | Number. | Amount. |
| Claims unpaid December 31, 1920, as per last statement | 27 | $ 23,166 67 | | |
| Claims reported during the year and interest addition | 288 | 267,000 03 | 15 | $11,000 00 |
| Total | 315 | $290,166 70 | 15 | $11,000 00 |
| Claims paid during the year | 303 | 280,066 70 | 14 | 10,500 00 |
| Claims unpaid December 31, 1921 | 12 | $10,100 00 | 1 | $500 00 |

## EXHIBIT OF PERMANENT DISABILITY CLAIMS.

| | Total claims. | |
|---|---|---|
| | Number. | Amount. |
| Claims reported during the year and interest addition | 2 | $500 00 |

## EXHIBIT OF OLD AGE AND OTHER CLAIMS.

| | Total claims. | | Illinois claims. | |
|---|---|---|---|---|
| | Number. | Amount. | Number. | Amount. |
| Claims paid during the year | 30 | $5,876 63 | 3 | $700 00 |

## EQUITABLE FRATERNAL UNION, SUPREME ASSEMBLY.

Located at South Commercial Street, Neenah, Wisconsin.

J. C. KAREL, President. ORRIN THOMPSON, Secretary.

| | |
|---|---|
| Balance from previous year | $3,201,615 66 |

### INCOME.

| | |
|---|---|
| Assessments or premiums during first 12 months of membership of which all or an extra percentage is used for expenses | $ 63,062 23 |
| All other assessments or premiums | 439,560 58 |
| Dues and per capita tax | 36,757 91 |
| Fines and fees | 192 25 |
| Total received from members | $539,572 97 |
| Deduct payments returned to applicants and members | 55 67 |
| Net amount received from members | $539,517 30 |
| Gross interest on mortgage loans | 94,212 00 |
| Gross interest on bonds and dividends on stocks | 75,175 54 |
| Gross interest on deposits in trust companies and banks | 1,116 20 |
| Gross rents from association's property, including $3,000.00 for association's occupancy of its own buildings | 6,131 39 |
| Sale of lodge supplies | 755 61 |
| Gross profit on sale or maturity of ledger assets | 1,400 33 |
| Gross increase in book value of ledger assets | 143 74 |
| Received on bonds charged off | 1,096 50 |
| Sale society emblems | 86 00 |
| Advertising in official publication | 951 32 |
| Miscellaneous | 13 88 |
| Total income | $720,599 81 |
| Sum | $3,922,215 47 |

### DISBURSEMENTS.

| | |
|---|---|
| Death claims | $322,726 55 |
| Permanent disability claims | 500 00 |
| Accident claims | 1,450 00 |
| Old age benefits | 41,538 33 |
| Contracts retired | 13,250 96 |
| Total benefits paid | $379,465 84 |
| Commissions and fees paid to deputies and organizers | 36,711 63 |
| Salaries of deputies and organizers | 41,579 82 |
| Salaries of officers and trustees | 19,600 00 |
| Salaries and other compensation of committees | 1,268 23 |
| Salaries of office employees | 10,305 50 |
| Salaries and fees paid to supreme medical examiners | 637 00 |
| Salaries and fees paid to subordinate medical examiners | 12 75 |
| Traveling and other expenses of officers and trustees | 3,731 11 |
| Insurance department fees | 359 35 |
| Rent | 3,000 00 |
| Advertising, printing and stationery | 1,414 85 |
| Postage, express, telegraph and telephone | 1,356 81 |
| Lodge supplies | 1,051 79 |
| Official publication | 9,004 86 |
| Legal expense in litigating claims | 95 00 |
| Other legal expenses | 1,385 77 |
| Furniture and fixtures | 62 25 |
| Taxes, repairs and other expenses on real estate | 4,167 06 |
| Gross loss on sale or maturity of ledger assets | 220 60 |
| Gross decrease in book value of ledger assets | 3,343 73 |
| All other disbursements, viz— | |
| Actuary, $600.00; janitor, $1,673.00; bonds of officers, $791.26 | 3,064 26 |
| Fuel, $1,756.95; water, $80.16; fire insurance, $161.48; N. F. C., $210.00 | 2,208 59 |
| Wis. F. C., $5.00; library, $52.00; expense account loans, $155.89; liability insurance, $119.39 | 332 28 |
| Light and power, $187.79; miscellaneous, $1,158.20 | 1,345 99 |
| Total disbursements | $525,725 07 |
| Balance | $3,396,490 40 |

### LEDGER ASSETS.

| | |
|---|---|
| Book value of real estate | $ 70,000 00 |
| Mortgage loans on real estate | 1,746,839 00 |
| Book value of bonds and stocks | 1,511,624 11 |
| Deposits in trust companies and banks not on interest | 300 00 |
| Deposits in trust companies and banks on interest | 67,727 29 |
| Total ledger assets | $3,396,490 40 |

## LEDGER ASSETS—Concluded.

NON-LEDGER ASSETS.

| | |
|---|---|
| Interest and rents due and accrued | $95,033 21 |
| Assessments actually collected by subordinate lodges not yet turned over to supreme lodge | 41,659 00 |
| Gross assets | $3,533,182 61 |

DEDUCT ASSETS NOT ADMITTED.

| | |
|---|---|
| Overdue and accrued interest on bonds in default | 120 00 |
| Total admitted assets | $3,533,062 61 |

## LIABILITIES.

| | | |
|---|---|---|
| Death claims reported during the year but not yet adjusted | $33,500 00 | |
| Death claims incurred in 1921, not reported until 1922 | 2,618 24 | |
| Total death claims | | $36,118 24 |
| Accident claims reported during the year but not yet adjusted | $125 00 | |
| Accident claims incurred in 1921, not reported until 1922 | 40 00 | |
| Total sick and accident claims | | 165 00 |
| Old age and other benefits due and unpaid | | 36,283 24 |
| Total | | $36,283 24 |

## EXHIBIT OF CERTIFICATES.

| | Total business of the year. | | Business in Illinois during year. | |
|---|---|---|---|---|
| | Number. | Amount. | Number. | Amount. |
| Benefit certificates in force December 31, 1920, as per last statement | 30,143 | $38,540,033 08 | 977 | $1,106,500 00 |
| Benefit certificates written and renewed during the year | 2,313 | 2,567,000 00 | 339 | 354,500 00 |
| Benefit certificates received by transfer during the year | | | 1 | 1,000 00 |
| Benefit certificates increased during the year | | 31,500 00 | | 4,000 00 |
| Total | 32,456 | $41,138,533 08 | 1,317 | $1,466,000 00 |
| Deduct terminated, decreased or transferred during the year | 2,408 | 2,837,582 79 | | |
| Deduct terminated or decreased during the year | | | 296 | 308,723 00 |
| Total benefit certificates in force December 31, 1921 | 30,048 | $38,300,950 29 | 1,021 | $1,157,277 00 |

| | |
|---|---|
| Received during the year from members in Illinois: Mortuary, $11,508.34; accident, $267.15; expense, $6,155.72; total | $17,931 21 |

## EXHIBIT OF DEATH CLAIMS.

| | Total claims. | | Illinois claims. | |
|---|---|---|---|---|
| | Number. | Amount. | Number. | Amount. |
| Claims unpaid December 31, 1920, as per last statement | 23 | $31,822 05 | 1 | $1,000 00 |
| Claims reported during the year and interest addition | 252 | 359,542 66 | 12 | 10,500 00 |
| Total | 275 | $391,364 71 | 13 | $11,500 00 |
| Unearned insurance—beneficiaries | | 35,138 16 | | 1,727 32 |
| Claims paid during the year | 251 | 322,726 55 | 12 | 9,272 68 |
| Claims unpaid December 31, 1921 | 24 | $33,500 00 | 1 | $500 00 |

## EXHIBIT OF PERMANENT DISABILITY CLAIMS.

| | Total claims. | |
|---|---|---|
| | Number. | Amount. |
| Claims unpaid December 31, 1920, as per last statement | 1 | $500 00 |
| Claims paid during the year | 1 | 500 00 |

## EXHIBIT OF ACCIDENT CLAIMS.

| | Total claims. | | Illinois claims. | |
|---|---|---|---|---|
| | Number. | Amount. | Number. | Amount. |
| Claims unpaid December 31, 1920, as per last statement | 1 | $50 00 | | |
| Claims reported during the year | 21 | 1,615 00 | 3 | $180 00 |
| Total | 22 | $1,665 00 | 3 | $180 00 |
| Claims paid during the year | 19 | 1,450 00 | 3 | 180 00 |
| Claims rejected during the year | 2 | 90 00 | | |
| Claims unpaid December 31, 1921 | 1 | $125 00 | | |

EXHIBIT OF OLD AGE AND OTHER CLAIMS.

| | Total claims. Number. | Amount. |
|---|---|---|
| Claims reported during the year and interest addition | 232 | $41,538 33 |
| Claims paid during the year | 232 | 41,538 33 |

## FIRST CATHOLIC SLOVAK UNION.

Located at No. 3289 East Fifty-fifth Street, Cleveland, Ohio.

ANDREW H. DORKO, President. MICHAEL SENKO, Secretary.

| | |
|---|---|
| Balance from previous year | $2,172,573 47 |

### INCOME.

| | |
|---|---|
| Membership fees actually received | $ 710 00 |
| All other assessments or premiums | 689,642 62 |
| For changes of beneficiaries | 346 75 |
| Net amount received from members | $690,699 37 |
| Gross interest on mortgage loans | 3,271 15 |
| Gross interest on bonds and dividends on stocks | 46,433 61 |
| Gross interest on deposits in trust companies and banks | 29,536 92 |
| Gross rents from association's property | 2,016 00 |
| Transferred from indigent fund | 10,000 00 |
| Gross increase in book value of ledger assets | 12,576 31 |
| From printing plant | 37,980 46 |
| Compensation from U. S. War Department | 460 46 |
| Tuition and board from orphans | 1,713 00 |
| Credit given to applicants from junior branch refunded by junior branch | 876 00 |
| Transferred from national fund | 9,573 77 |
| Sundry income | 40 00 |
| Total income | $ 845,177 05 |
| Balance from 1920 | 2,172,573 47 |
| Sum | $3,017,750 52 |

### DISBURSEMENTS.

| | |
|---|---|
| Death claims | $374,850 00 |
| Indigent donations | 9,657 54 |
| Total benefits paid | $384,507 54 |
| Salaries of officers and trustees | 9,523 62 |
| Salaries of office employees | 4,778 60 |
| Traveling and other expenses of officers, trustees and committees | 4,542 99 |
| Insurance department fees | 35 00 |
| Rent, including $1,830.00 for association's occupancy of its own buildings | 2,010 00 |
| Advertising, printing and stationery | 8,542 06 |
| Postage, express, telegraph and telephone | 1,058 88 |
| Official publication | 41,844 99 |
| Expenses of supreme lodge meeting | 59 80 |
| Transfer A. D. F. | 10,573 77 |
| Legal expense | 1,501 24 |
| Operation of farm (net loss) | 573 86 |
| Taxes, repairs and other expenses on real estate | 1,716 33 |
| Operation of printing plant | 33,016 35 |
| Premium on depository bonds | 1,755 50 |
| Actuary's fee | 1,400 00 |
| Miscellaneous expenses | 215 02 |
| Expenses in orphanage | 18,283 13 |
| Depreciation on furniture and fixtures | 4,718 35 |
| Premium on insurance | 206 00 |
| Returned donation | 550 00 |
| Total disbursements | $540,413 03 |
| Balance | $2,477,337 49 |

### LEDGER ASSETS.

| | |
|---|---|
| Book value of real estate | $ 236,111 21 |
| Mortgage loans on real estate | 91,116 94 |
| Book value of bonds and stocks | 1,202,800 00 |
| Cash in association's office | 3,149 94 |
| Deposits in trust companies and banks on interest | 872,108 47 |
| Bills receivable, $12,307.34; prepaid insurance, $514.99 | 12,822 33 |
| Other ledger assets, viz— | |
| Machinery and equipment | 32,397 78 |
| Inventory of farm and printery, $19,146.10; furniture and fixtures, $7,684.72 | 26,830 82 |
| Total ledger assets | $2,477,337 49 |

## LEDGER ASSETS—Concluded.

### NON-LEDGER ASSETS.

| | | |
|---|---|---|
| Interest and rents due and accrued | | $12,737 34 |
| Market value of real estate over book value | | 15,900 60 |
| Gross assets | | $2,505,975 43 |

### DEDUCT ASSETS NOT ADMITTED.

| | | |
|---|---|---|
| Bills receivable | $12,307 34 | |
| Book value of bonds and stocks over market value | 17,734 45 | |
| Other items, viz— | | |
| Furniture and fixtures | 7,684 72 | |
| Machinery and equipment | 32,397 78 | |
| Inventory of farm and printery | 19,146 10 | |
| | | 89,270 39 |
| Total admitted assets | | $2,416,705 04 |

## LIABILITIES.

| | | |
|---|---|---|
| Death claims due and unpaid | $ 4,900 00 | |
| Death claims adjusted not yet due | 37,250 00 | |
| Death claims resisted | 500 00 | |
| Total death claims | | 42,650 00 |
| Total unpaid claims | | $42,650 00 |

## EXHIBIT OF CERTIFICATES.

| | Total business of the year. | | Business in Illinois during year. | |
|---|---|---|---|---|
| | Number. | Amount. | Number. | Amount. |
| Benefit certificates in force December 31, 1920, as per last statement | 50,567 | $41,219,500 00 | 4,080 | $3,556,650 00 |
| Benefit certificates written and renewed during the year | 2,376 | 2,184,000 00 | 304 | 170,500 00 |
| Benefit certificates received by transfer during the year | | | 82 | 50,750 00 |
| Total | 52,943 | $43,403,500 00 | 4,466 | $3,777,900 00 |
| Deduct terminated, decreased or transferred during the year | 2,536 | 2,054,750 00 | | |
| Deduct terminated or decreased during the year | | | 289 | 234,500 00 |
| Total benefit certificates in force December 31, 1921 | 50,407 | $41,348,750 00 | 4,177 | $3,543,400 00 |

Received during the year from members in Illinois: Mortuary, $45,007.20; reserve, $2,368.70; disability, $1,440.00; all other, $2,400.00; expense, $5,760.00; total — $56,975 90

## EXHIBIT OF DEATH CLAIMS.

| | Total claims. | | Illinois claims. | |
|---|---|---|---|---|
| | Number. | Amount. | Number. | Amount. |
| Claims unpaid December 31, 1920, as per last statement | 48 | $ 39,300 00 | 5 | $ 5,000 00 |
| Claims reported during the year and interest addition | 475 | 386,500 00 | 38 | 31,250 00 |
| Total | 523 | $425,800 00 | 43 | $36,250 00 |
| Claims paid during the year | 472 | 374,850 00 | 37 | 31,350 00 |
| Balance | 51 | $42,650 00 | 6 | $4,900 00 |
| Saved by compromising or scaling down claims during the year | | 8,300 00 | | 650 00 |
| Claims unpaid December 31, 1921 | 51 | $42,650 00 | 6 | $4,250 00 |

---

# FRATERNAL AID UNION.

Located at Eighth and Vermont Street, Lawrence, Kansas.

V. A. YOUNG, President. SAMUEL S. BATY, Secretary.

| | |
|---|---|
| Balance from previous year | $2,723,046 72 |

## INCOME.

| | |
|---|---|
| Assessments or premiums during first months of membership of which all or an extra percentage is used for expenses | $ 391,686 87 |
| All other assessments or premiums | 3,091,433 10 |

INCOME—Concluded.

| | |
|---|---|
| Dues and per capita tax | $553 25 |
| Other payments by members | 128 97 |
| Total received from members | $3,483,802 19 |
| Deduct payments returned to applicants and members | 4,458 61 |
| Net amount received from members | $3,479,343 58 |
| Gross interest on mortgage loans | 82,122 01 |
| Gross interest on bonds and dividends on stocks | 44,105 33 |
| Gross interest on deposits in trust companies and banks | 8,155 88 |
| Gross interest from all other sources | 4,738 57 |
| Gross rents from association's property, including $3,600.00 for association's occupancy of its own buildings | 8,024 95 |
| Sale of lodge supplies | 2,227 35 |
| Gross profit on sale or maturity of ledger assets | 451 70 |
| Surety bond premium | 3,082 28 |
| Collection and exchange | 7 85 |
| Total income | $3,632,259 50 |
| Sum | $6,355,306 22 |

DISBURSEMENTS.

| | |
|---|---|
| Death claims | $1,788,066 88 |
| Permanent disability claims | 2,655 97 |
| Sick and accident claims | 290 00 |
| Old age benefits | 133,243 24 |
| Annuity | 300 00 |
| Surrenders | 238 15 |
| Return of payment | 48,582 30 |
| Total benefits paid | $1,973,376 54 |
| Commissions and fees paid to deputies and organizers | 251,540 18 |
| Salaries of deputies and organizers | 69,383 01 |
| Salaries of officers and trustees | 27,666 58 |
| Salaries of office employees | 84,599 61 |
| Salaries and fees paid to supreme medical examiners | 5,000 04 |
| Salaries and fees paid to subordinate medical examiners | 16,755 00 |
| Traveling and other expenses of officers, trustees and committees | 17,293 74 |
| For collection and remittance of assessments and dues | 21,870 38 |
| Insurance department fees | 897 05 |
| Rent, including $3,600.00 for association's occupancy of its own buildings | 7,350 50 |
| Advertising, printing and stationery | 29,081 32 |
| Postage, express, telegraph and telephone | 14,553 07 |
| Lodge supplies | 2,563 47 |
| Official publication | 18,509 85 |
| Expenses of supreme lodge meeting | 20,783 65 |
| Legal expense in litigating claims | 8,386 33 |
| Other legal expenses | 11,799 30 |
| Furniture and fixtures | 2,655 35 |
| Taxes, repairs and other expenses on real estate | 12,659 50 |
| Gross loss on sale or maturity of ledger assets | 23,281 30 |
| All other disbursements, viz: Suspense, $307.76; sundries, $290.30; actuarial expense, $4,064.31; mortality fund, surety bond premiums, $2,595.38; petty, $20.00; liens on exchange certificates terminated, $7,481.45; provisional, $649.73; expense mortgage loans, $31.45; adjustments and investigations, $729.09; internal revenue tax, $75.30; National Fraternal Congress of America and auxiliary societies, $294.33; fire insurance policy premiums, $223.21; inspection of risks, $6,242.00 | 23,004 31 |
| Total disbursements | $2,622,056 91 |
| Balance | $3,733,249 31 |

LEDGER ASSETS.

| | |
|---|---|
| Book value of real estate | $ 93,738 16 |
| Mortgage loans on real estate | 2,448,775 75 |
| Book value of bonds and stocks | 872,843 15 |
| Deposits in trust companies and banks on interest | 137,390 18 |
| Other ledger assets, viz— | |
| Liens on exchange certificates | 175,257 33 |
| Policy loans | 5,244 74 |
| Total ledger assets | $3,733,249 31 |

NON-LEDGER ASSETS.

| | |
|---|---|
| Interest and rents due and accrued | 60,315 19 |
| Market value of bonds and stocks over book value | 21,270 57 |
| Assessments actually collected by subordinate lodges not yet turned over to supreme lodge | 290,272 32 |
| Gross assets | $4,114,107 39 |

## LEDGER ASSETS—Concluded.

DEDUCT ASSETS NOT ADMITTED.

| | | |
|---|---|---|
| Book value of real estate over market value | | $3,181 76 |
| Total admitted assets | | $4,110,925 63 |

## LIABILITIES.

| | | |
|---|---|---|
| Death claims resisted | $ 38,129 60 | |
| Death claims reported during the year and prior but not yet adjusted | 207,482 69 | |
| Death claims incurred in 1921, not reported until 1922 | 36,926 19 | |
| Total death claims | | $282,538 48 |
| Permanent disability claims adjusted not yet due | $ 177 50 | |
| Perman nt disability claims resisted | 1,000 00 | |
| Total permanent disability claims | | 1,177 50 |
| Old age and other benefits due and unpaid | | 16,138 13 |
| Total unpaid claims | | $299,854 11 |
| Taxes due or accrued | | 3 68 |
| Advance assessments | | 165,632 13 |
| All other liabilities, viz: Reserves on American Express 4 per cent certificates | | 1,984,200 28 |
| Total | | $2,449,690 20 |

## EXHIBIT OF CERTIFICATES.

| | Total business of the year. Number. | Amount. | Business in Illinois during year. Number. | Amount. |
|---|---|---|---|---|
| Benefit certificates in force December 31, 1920, as per last statement | 81,147 | $90,796,320 00 | 3,377 | $3,154,664 00 |
| Benefit certificates written during the year | 6,662 | 6,934,277 00 | 292 | 262,500 00 |
| Benefit certificates exchanged during the year | 2,487 | 2,820,050 00 | 89 | 97,200 00 |
| Benefit certificates revived during the year | 7,189 | 7,932,411 00 | 252 | 260,609 00 |
| Benefit certificates received by transfer during the year | 860 | 1,022,764 00 | 18 | 17,621 00 |
| Benefit certificates received by miscellaneous during the year | 408 | 418,899 00 | 35 | 39,073 00 |
| Benefit certificates increased during the year | -------- | 37,204 00 | -------- | 2,079 00 |
| Total | 98,753 | $109,961,925 00 | 4,063 | $3,833,746 00 |
| Deduct terminated, decreased or transferred during the year | 21,288 | 24,725,358 00 | 861 | 886,406 00 |
| Total benefit certificates in force December 31, 1921 | 77,465 | $85,236,567 00 | 3,202 | $2,947,340 00 |
| Benefit certificates terminated by death reported during the year | 1,582 | $ 1,756,083 00 | 63 | $ 61,308 00 |
| Benefit certificates terminated by expiry reported during the year | 41 | 43,000 00 | -------- | -------------- |
| Benefit certificates terminated by lapse reported during the year | 14,401 | 16,095,554 00 | 678 | 665,034 00 |
| Benefit certificates terminated by old age and disability during the year | 109 | 129,160 00 | -------- | -------------- |
| Benefit certificates reported transferred during the year | 860 | 1,022,764 00 | 13 | 15,250 00 |
| Benefit certificates exchanged during the year | 2,480 | 3,176,109 00 | 90 | 110,528 00 |
| Benefit certificates terminated by miscellaneous reported during the year | 1,815 | 2,150,164 00 | 17 | 23,111 00 |
| Benefit certificates decreased during the year | -------- | 352,524 00 | -------- | 11,175 00 |

| | |
|---|---|
| Received during the year from members in Illinois: Mortuary, $124,200.27; expense, $4,821.81; total | $129,022 08 |

## EXHIBIT OF DEATH CLAIMS.

| | Total claims. Number. | Amount. | Illinois claims. Number. | Amount. |
|---|---|---|---|---|
| Claims unpaid December 31, 1920, as per last statement | 339 | $ 378,806 98 | 11 | $11,939 57 |
| Claims reported during the year and interest addition | 1,582 | 1,756,083 03 | 63 | 61,307 74 |
| Total | 1,921 | $2,134,890 01 | 74 | $73,247 31 |
| Claims paid during the year | 1,669 | 1,788,066 88 | 66 | 59,007 25 |
| Balance | 252 | $346,823 13 | 8 | $14,240 06 |
| Saved by compromising or scaling down claims during the year | -------- | 48,984 27 | -------- | 5,816 06 |
| Claims rejected during the year | 15 | 15,300 38 | -------- | -------------- |
| Claims unpaid December 31, 1921 | 237 | $282,538 48 | 8 | $8,424 00 |

## EXHIBIT OF PERMANENT DISABILITY CLAIMS.

| | Total claims. Number. | Total claims. Amount. |
|---|---|---|
| Claims unpaid December 31, 1920, as per last statement | 2 | $216 00 |
| Claims reported during the year and interest addition | 28 | 4,167 47 |
| Total | 30 | $4,383 47 |
| Claims paid during the year | 27 | 2,655 97 |
| Balance | 3 | $1,727 50 |
| Saved by compromising or scaling down claims during the year | -------- | 550 00 |
| Claims unpaid December 31, 1921 | 3 | $1,177 50 |

## EXHIBIT OF SICK AND ACCIDENT CLAIMS.

| | Total claims. Number. | Total claims. Amount. |
|---|---|---|
| Claims unpaid December 31, 1920, as per last statement | 1 | $240 00 |
| Claims reported during the year | 1 | 50 00 |
| Total | 2 | $290 00 |
| Claims paid during the year | 2 | 290 00 |

## EXHIBIT OF OLD AGE AND OTHER CLAIMS.

| | Total claims. Number. | Total claims. Amount. | Illinois claims. Number. | Illinois claims. Amount. |
|---|---|---|---|---|
| Claims unpaid December 31, 1920, as per last statement | 97 | $ 30,528 82 | 1 | $100 00 |
| Claims reported during the year and interest addition | 809 | 224,427 16 | 5 | 775 00 |
| Total | 906 | $254,955 98 | 6 | $875 00 |
| Claims paid during the year | 819 | 133,243 24 | 5 | 775 00 |
| Balance | 87 | $121,712 74 | 1 | $100 00 |
| Saved by compromising or scaling down claims during the year | -------- | 103,132 58 | -------- | ------------- |
| Claims rejected during the year | 14 | 2,442 03 | -------- | ------------- |
| Claims unpaid December 31, 1921 | 73 | $16,138 13 | 1 | $100 00 |

---

# FRATERNAL BROTHERHOOD, SUPREME LODGE.

Located at No. 845 South Figueroa Street, Los Angeles, California.

J. A. BATCHELOR, Supreme President. H. V. DAVIS, Supreme Secretary.

| | |
|---|---|
| Balance from previous year | $1,910,327 11 |

## INCOME.

| | |
|---|---|
| Assessments or premiums during first 12 months of membership of which all or an extra percentage is used for expenses | 45,664 30 |
| All other assessments or premiums | 479,325 21 |
| Dues and per capita tax | 39,758 00 |
| Re-issue fees | 368 00 |
| Total received from members | $565,115 51 |
| Deduct payments returned to applicants and members | 212 59 |
| Net amount received from members | $564,902 92 |
| Gross interest on mortgage loans | 23,321 49 |
| Gross interest on bonds and dividends on stocks | 33,059 64 |
| Gross interest on deposits in trust companies and banks | 1,331 81 |
| Gross interest from all other sources | 6,594 81 |
| Gross rents from association's property, including $4,000.00 for association's occupancy of its own buildings | 9,871 50 |
| Sale of lodge supplies | 11,679 57 |
| Gross increase in book value of ledger assets | 792 37 |
| From all other sources, viz— | |
| Rent Tulare County property, $709.16; disbanded lodges, $22.14 | 731 30 |
| Excess premium on treasurer's bonds, $36.55; refund Washington Park, $137.31 receipts | 173 86 |
| Printing machine sold, $900.00; members subscriptions liberty loan, $112.50 | 1,012 50 |
| Accounts payable, $24.88; promotion tax, $56.00 | 80 88 |
| Over paid on taxes Washington Park, $179.06; Commission Mead & Clemants, $568.12 | 747 18 |
| Certificate liens—assessment and interest charged during year of 1921, as a first lien against certificates affected by adjustment of rates | 83,367 26 |
| Total income | $737,667 09 |
| Sum | $2,647,994 20 |

## DISBURSEMENTS.

| | | |
|---|---|---|
| Death claims | | $229,805 90 |
| Permanent disability claims | | 47,067 29 |
| Sick and accident claims | | 79,196 61 |
| Old age benefits | | 105,562 82 |
| Surplus account American Experience Valuation | | 1,815 55 |
| Total benefits paid | | $463,448 17 |
| Commissions and fees paid to deputies and organizers | | 51,371 23 |
| Salaries of deputies and organizers | | 27,163 11 |
| Salaries of officers and trustees | | 10,826 25 |
| Salaries of office employees | | 33,120 24 |
| Salaries and fees paid to supreme medical examiners | | 2,400 00 |
| Salaries and fees paid to subordinate medical examiners | | 827 50 |
| Traveling and other expenses of officers, trustees and committees | | 2,671 03 |
| For collection and remittance of assessments and dues | | 125 54 |
| Insurance department fees | | 282 00 |
| Rent | | 4,000 00 |
| Advertising, printing and stationery | | 9,947 73 |
| Postage, express, telegraph and telephone | | 2,449 25 |
| Lodge supplies | | 8,989 92 |
| Official publication | | 3,566 72 |
| Expenses of supreme lodge meeting | | 7,476 93 |
| Other legal expenses | | 1,094 00 |
| Furniture and fixtures | | 699 43 |
| Taxes, repairs and other expenses on real estate | | 7,374 91 |
| Gross decrease in book value of ledger assets | | 460 12 |
| All other disbursements, viz— | | |
| Subscription liberty loan bonds, $398.00; accounts payable, $438.46 | | 836 46 |
| Expense home office building | | 4,373 97 |
| Re-insurance | | 2,791 23 |
| Discount sale of lots, $176.15; other expenses, general, $1,724.18 | | 1,900 33 |
| Total disbursements | | $648,196 07 |
| Balance | | $2,002,017 29 |

## LEDGER ASSETS.

| | | |
|---|---|---|
| Book value of real estate | | $ 83,306 41 |
| Mortgage loans on real estate | | 368,265 00 |
| Loans secured by pledge of bonds, stocks or other collateral | | 723,927 21 |
| Book value of bonds and stocks | | 300 00 |
| Deposits in trust companies and banks not on interest | | 44,061 60 |
| Bills receivable | | 613 54 |
| Other ledger assets, viz— | | |
| Bonds of individuals, liberty loan | $ 50 00 | |
| Agreement sale of lots Washington Park | 81,670 29 | |
| Certificate liens | 699,823 24 | |
| | | 781,543 53 |
| Total ledger assets | | 2,002,017 29 |

### NON-LEDGER ASSETS.

| | | |
|---|---|---|
| Market value of real estate over book value | | 17,675 85 |
| Market value of bonds and stocks over book value | | 91,105 00 |
| Assessments actually collected by subordinate lodges not yet turned over to supreme lodge | | 45,755 56 |
| All other assets, viz— | | |
| Safes and lodge supplies | $2,100 00 | |
| Furniture and fixtures | 4,859 72 | |
| Printing plant | 1,965 50 | |
| | | 8,925 22 |
| Gross assets | | $2,165,478 92 |

### DEDUCT ASSETS NOT ADMITTED.

| | | |
|---|---|---|
| Bills receivable | 613 54 | |
| Overdue and accrued interest on bonds in default | 1,921 00 | |
| Other items, viz— | | |
| Safes and lodge supplies | 2,100 00 | |
| Furniture and fixtures | 4,859 72 | |
| Printing plant | 1,965 50 | |
| | | 11,459 76 |
| Total admitted assets | | $2,154,019 16 |

## LIABILITIES.

| | | |
|---|---|---|
| Death claims reported during the year but not yet adjusted | | $ 43,137 37 |
| Permanent disability claims incurred in 1921, not reported until 1922 | | 90,241 00 |
| Sick and accident claims due and unpaid | $5,098 26 | |
| Sick and accident claims reported during the year but not yet adjusted | 4,300 00 | |
| Total sick and accident claims | | 9,398 26 |
| Old age and other benefits due and unpaid | | 432,557 00 |
| Total unpaid claims | | $575,333 63 |

LIABILITIES—Concluded.

| | | |
|---|---|---|
| Salaries, rents, expenses, commissions, etc., due or accrued | | $ 4,707 16 |
| Taxes due or accrued | | 880 08 |
| Advance assessments | | 11,219 96 |
| All other liabilities, viz— | | |
| Accounts payable | $ 24 88 | |
| Surplus account American Experience Valuation | 1,905 66 | |
| | | 1,930 54 |
| Total | | $594,071 37 |

EXHIBIT OF CERTIFICATES.

| | Total business of the year. Number. | Amount. | Business in Illinois during year. Number. | Amount. |
|---|---|---|---|---|
| Benefit certificates in force December 31, 1920, as per last statement | 25,346 | $24,595,957 00 | 56 | $55,480 00 |
| Benefit certificates written and renewed during the year | 3,140 | 1,570,000 00 | -------- | ------------- |
| Total | 28,486 | $26,165,957 00 | 56 | $55,480 00 |
| Deduct terminated, decreased or transferred during the year | 3,687 | 3,084,868 00 | -------- | ------------- |
| Deduct terminated or decreased during the year | -------- | ------------- | 4 | 4,244 00 |
| Total benefit certificates in force December 31, 1921 | 24,799 | $23,081,089 00 | 52 | $51,236 00 |

Received during the year from members in Illinois: Mortuary, $788.99; sickness and accident, $66.05; expense, $242.26; total 1,097 30

EXHIBIT OF DEATH CLAIMS.

| | Total claims. Numbr. | Amount. |
|---|---|---|
| Claims unpaid December 31, 1920, as per last statement | 29 | $ 39,900 00 |
| Claims reported during the year and interest addition | 173 | 225,231 00 |
| Total | 202 | $265,131 00 |
| Claims paid during the year | 175 | 229,805 90 |
| Balance | 27 | $35,325 10 |
| Saved by compromising or scaling down claims during the year | -------- | 3,338 10 |
| Claims rejected during the year—dropped | 2 | 1,550 00 |
| Claims unpaid December, 31 1921 | 25 | $30,437 00 |

EXHIBIT OF PERMANENT DISABILITY CLAIMS.

| | Total claims. Number. | Amount. |
|---|---|---|
| Claims unpaid December 31, 1920, as per last statement | 150 | $99,259 00 |
| Claims reported during the year and interest addition | 156 | 38,849 29 |
| Total | 306 | $138,108 29 |
| Claims paid during the year | 165 | 47,067 29 |
| Balance | 141 | $91,041 00 |
| Claims rejected during the year—dropped | 1 | 800 00 |
| Claims unpaid December 31, 1921 | 140 | $90,241 00 |

EXHIBIT OF SICK AND ACCIDENT CLAIMS.

| | Total claims. Number. | Amount. | Illinois claims. Number. | Amount. |
|---|---|---|---|---|
| Claims unpaid December 31, 1920, as per last statement | 21 | $ 1,983 21 | -------- | ------------- |
| Decrease in estimated liability | 1,186 | 85,731 44 | -------- | ------------- |
| Claims reported during the year | 1,207 | 87,714 65 | 1 | $37 14 |
| Total | 1,101 | $79,196 61 | 1 | $37 14 |
| Claims paid during the year | 40 | 3,419 78 | 1 | 37 14 |
| Claims rejected during the year | 66 | 5,098 26 | -------- | ------------- |
| Claims unpaid December 31, 1921 | 995 | $70,687 55 | -------- | ------------- |

EXHIBIT OF OLD AGE AND OTHER CLAIMS.

| | Total claims. Number. | Amount. |
|---|---|---|
| Claims unpaid December 31, 1920, as per last statement | 488 | $401,834 00 |
| Claims reported during the year and interest addition | 663 | 136,285 82 |
| Total | 1,151 | $538,119 82 |
| Claims paid during the year | 595 | 105,562 82 |
| Claims unpaid December 31, 1921 | 556 | $432,557 00 |

## FRATERNAL HOME INSURANCE SOCIETY, SUPREME LODGE.

Located at No. 1913 Arch Street, Philadelphia, Pennsylvania.

WILLIAM C. PAUL, President. W. R. BUFFINGTON, Secretary.

| | |
|---|---|
| Balance from previous year | $548,707 44 |

### INCOME.

| | |
|---|---|
| All other assessments or premiums | $468,740 87 |
| Medical examiners' fees actually received | 12 50 |
| Changing certificates | 154 50 |
| Total received from members | $468,907 87 |
| Deduct payments returned to applicants and members | 166 86 |
| Net amount received from members | $468,741 01 |
| Gross interest on mortgage loans | 20,468 90 |
| Gross interest on bonds and dividends on stocks | 7,628 27 |
| Gross interest on deposits in trust companies and banks | 910 70 |
| Gross rents from association's property, including $2,400.00 for association's occupancy of its own buildings | 5,571 84 |
| Sale of lodge supplies | 297 64 |
| Miscellaneous | 53 51 |
| Total income | $503,671 87 |
| Sum | $1,052,379 31 |

### DISBURSEMENTS.

| | |
|---|---|
| Death claims | $218,111 15 |
| Permanent disability claims | 9,525 00 |
| Sick and accident claims | 25,087 15 |
| Old age benefits | 6,838 94 |
| Total benefits paid | $259,562 24 |
| Commissions and fees paid to deputies and organizers and expenses | 38,700 73 |
| Salaries of deputies and organizers | 21,675 68 |
| Salaries of managers or agents not deputies or organizers | 4,250 00 |
| Salaries of officers and trustees | 11,840 03 |
| Salaries of office employees | 19,414 28 |
| Salaries and fees paid to supreme medical examiners | 2,111 67 |
| Salaries and fees paid to subordinate medical examiners | 4,862 13 |
| Traveling and other expenses of officers, trustees and committees | 880 95 |
| For collection and remittance of assessments and dues | 755 00 |
| Insurance department fees | 498 28 |
| Rent, including $2,400.00 for association's occupancy of its own buildings | 2,565 00 |
| Advertising, printing and stationery | 1,694 91 |
| Postage, express, telegraph and telephone | 1,714 58 |
| Lodge supplies | 1,841 82 |
| Official publication | 5,547 82 |
| Expenses of supreme lodge meeting | 4,494 39 |
| Legal expense in litigating claims | 138 95 |
| Other legal expenses | 1,206 00 |
| Furniture and fixtures | 178 45 |
| Taxes, repairs and other expenses on real estate | 3,526 96 |
| Gross loss on sale or maturity of ledger assets | 231 64 |
| Gross decrease in book value of ledger assets | 1,177 15 |
| Fraternal Congress | 108 50 |
| Official bonds | 407 60 |
| Membership prizes | 393 47 |
| Actuarial work | 2,125 00 |
| Miscellaneous | 1,063 76 |
| Distribution surplus A. E. Division | 7,175 47 |
| Total disbursements | $400,142 46 |
| Balance | $652,236 85 |

### LEDGER ASSETS.

| | |
|---|---|
| Book value of real estate | $ 53,924 41 |
| Mortgage loans on real estate | 339,730 00 |
| Book value of bonds and stocks | 203,994 00 |
| Cash in association's office | 915 29 |
| Deposits in trust companies and banks on interest | 52,749 73 |
| Loans on A. E. Certificates | 923 42 |
| Total ledger assets | $652,236 85 |

LEDGER ASSETS—Concluded.

NON-LEDGER ASSETS.

| | | |
|---|---|---|
| Interest and rents due and accrued | | $ 7,622 96 |
| Assessments actually collected by subordinate lodges not yet turned over to supreme lodge | | 37,394 42 |
| All other assets, viz— | | |
| Furniture and fixtures and supplies | $ 7,949 16 | |
| Personal and lodge balances | 2,915 20 | |
| Liens and interest on certificate A. E. Division | 91,262 01 | |
| | | 102,126 37 |
| Gross assets | | $799,380 60 |

DEDUCT ASSETS NOT ADMITTED.

| | | |
|---|---|---|
| Book value of bonds and stocks over market value | $2,150 00 | |
| Other items, viz— | | |
| Furniture, fixtures and supplies | 7,949 16 | |
| Personal and lodge balances | 2,915 20 | |
| | | 13,014 36 |
| Total admitted assets | | $786,366 24 |

LIABILITIES.

| | | |
|---|---|---|
| Death claims reported during the year but not yet adjusted | 26,268 37 | |
| Present value of deferred death claims payable in installments | 24,358 11 | |
| Total death claims | | $50,626 48 |
| Salaries, rents, expenses, commissions, etc., due or accrued | | 5,825 20 |
| Advance assessments | | 8,051 82 |
| All other liabilities, viz— | | |
| Funds sick and accident division | $ 9,078 39 | |
| Reserves on certificates A. E. Division 3½ per cent American Experience | 569,198 17 | |
| | | 592,153 58 |
| Total | | $642,780 06 |

EXHIBIT OF CERTIFICATES.

| | Total business of the year. | | Business in Illinois during year. | |
|---|---|---|---|---|
| | Number. | Amount. | Number. | Amount. |
| Benefit certificates in force December 31, 1920, as per last statement | 19,087 | $12,737,900 00 | 454 | $343,764 00 |
| Benefit certificates written and renewed during the year | 4,383 | 1,982,650 00 | 41 | 23,200 00 |
| Total | 23,470 | $14,720,550 00 | 495 | $366,964 00 |
| Deduct terminated, decreased or transferred during the year | 4,296 | 2,340,722 00 | | |
| Deduct terminated or decreased during the year | | | 60 | 33,829 00 |
| Total benefit certificates in force December 31, 1921 | 19,174 | $12,379,828 00 | 435 | $333,135 00 |

Received during the year from members in Illinois: Mortuary disability, $8,445.04; expense, $3,261.32; total — $11,706 36

EXHIBIT OF DEATH CLAIMS.

| | Total claims. | | Illinois claims. | |
|---|---|---|---|---|
| | Number. | Amount. | Number. | Amount. |
| Claims unpaid December 31, 1920, as per last statement | 52 | $ 71,609 73 | 1 | $ 274 33 |
| Claims reported during the year and interest addition | 191 | 203,497 44 | 9 | 8,129 00 |
| Interest addition | | 1,474 74 | | |
| Total | 243 | $276,581 91 | 10 | $8,403 33 |
| Claims paid during the year | 198 | 218,111 15 | 8 | 6,903 33 |
| Balance | 45 | $58,470 76 | 2 | $1,500 00 |
| Saved by compromising or scaling down claims during the year | | 6,844 28 | | |
| Claims dropped during the year | 1 | 1,000 00 | | |
| Claims unpaid December 31, 1921 | 44 | $50,626 48 | 2 | $1,500 00 |

EXHIBIT OF PERMANENT DISABILITY CLAIMS.

| | Total claims. | |
|---|---|---|
| | Number. | Amount. |
| Claims reported during the year and interest addition | 19 | $9,525 00 |
| Claims paid during the year | 19 | 9,525 00 |

EXHIBIT OF SICK AND ACCIDENT CLAIMS.

| | Total claims. | | Illinois claims. | |
|---|---|---|---|---|
| | Number. | Amount. | Number. | Amount. |
| Claims reported during the year | 769 | $25,087 15 | 4 | $97 14 |
| Claims paid during the year | 769 | 25,087 15 | 4 | 97 14 |

EXHIBIT OF OLD AGE AND OTHER CLAIMS.

| | Total claims. | |
|---|---|---|
| | Number. | Amount. |
| Claims reported during the year and interest addition | 12 | $6,838 94 |
| Claims paid during the year | 12 | 6,838 94 |

## FRATERNAL ORDER OF EAGLES, GRAND AERIE.

Located at No. 200 Gumbel Building, Kansas City, Missouri.

CONRAD H. MANN, Chairman Board of Insurance Directors. J. S. PARRY, Secretary.

| | |
|---|---|
| Balance from previous year | $21,720 45 |

INCOME.

| | |
|---|---|
| Membership fees actually received | $50,868 84 |
| Certificate fees | 20 30 |
| Total received from members | $50,889 14 |
| Deduct payments returned to applicants and members | 4 82 |
| Net amount received from members | $50,884 32 |
| Gross interest on bonds and dividends on stocks | 643 08 |
| Gross interest on deposits in trust companies and banks | 186 88 |
| Total income | $51,714 28 |
| Sum | $73,434 73 |

DISBURSEMENTS.

| | |
|---|---|
| Death claims | $5,000 00 |
| Commissions and fees paid to deputies and organizers | 9,789 31 |
| Salaries of officers and trustees | 2,466 66 |
| Salaries of office employees | 3,255 00 |
| Salaries and fees paid to supreme medical examiners | 396 50 |
| Salaries and fees paid to subordinate medical examiners | 1,710 00 |
| Traveling and other expenses of officers, trustees and committees | 725 59 |
| For collection and remittance of assessments and dues | 2,101 71 |
| Insurance department fees | 617 31 |
| Rent | 489 00 |
| Advertising, printing and stationery | 1,056 53 |
| Postage, express, telegraph and telephone | 361 04 |
| Furniture and fixtures | 70 00 |
| Audit of records | 80 00 |
| Total disbursements | $28,118 65 |
| Balance | $45,316 08 |

LEDGER ASSETS.

| | |
|---|---|
| Book value of bonds | $35,879 35 |
| Deposits in trust companies and banks on interest | 9,436 73 |
| Total ledger assets | $45,316 08 |

NON-LEDGER ASSETS.

| | |
|---|---|
| Interest due | 646 25 |
| Market value of bonds and stocks over book value | 120 65 |
| Assessments actually collected by subordinate lodges not yet turned over to supreme lodge approximately | 3,500 00 |
| Gross assets | $49,582 98 |

LIABILITIES.

| | |
|---|---|
| Death claims reported during the year but not yet adjusted | $3,000 00 |
| Salaries, rents, expenses, commissions, etc., due or accrued | 2,696 43 |
| Advance assessments | 4,082 12 |
| Total | $9,778 55 |

EXHIBIT OF CERTIFICATES.

| | Total business of the year. Number. | Amount. | Business in Illinois during year. Number. | Amount. |
|---|---|---|---|---|
| Benefit certificates in force December 31, 1920, as per last statement | 1,390 | $1,656,500 00 | 295 | $316,500 00 |
| Benefit certificates written and renewed during the year | 768 | 951,500 00 | 220 | 227,000 00 |
| Totals | 2,158 | $2,608,000 00 | 515 | $543,500 00 |
| Deduct terminated, decreased or transferred during the year | 420 | 522,500 00 | | |
| Deduct terminated or decreased during the year | | | 123 | 133,000 00 |
| Total benefit certificates in force December 31, 1921 | 1,738 | $2,085,500 00 | 392 | $410,500 00 |

Received during the year from members in Illinois: Mortuary, $3,068.04; all other, $1,308.33; expense, $3,629.08; total ........ $8,005 45

EXHIBIT OF DEATH CLAIMS.

| | Total claims. Number. | Amount. | Illinois claims. Number. | Amount. |
|---|---|---|---|---|
| Claims unpaid December 31, 1920, as per last statement | 2 | $2,000 00 | | |
| Claims reported during the year and interest addition | 5 | 6,000 00 | 1 | $2,000 00 |
| Totals | 7 | $8,000 00 | 1 | $2,000 00 |
| Claims paid during the year | 5 | 5,000 00 | | |
| Claims unpaid December 31, 1921 | 2 | $3,000 00 | 1 | $2,000 00 |

---

## FRATERNAL RESERVE ASSOCIATION.

Located at Washington Boulevard and State Street, Oshkosh, Wisconsin.

E. R. HICKS, President. C. M. ROBINSON, Secretary.

| | |
|---|---|
| Balance from previous year | $475,688 73 |

INCOME.

| | |
|---|---|
| Assessments or premiums during first twelve months of membership of which all or an extra percentage is used for expenses | $93,308 41 |
| All other assessments or premiums | 300,461 73 |
| Dues and per capita tax | 20,265 76 |
| Certificate fees | 191 00 |
| Total received from members | $414,226 90 |
| Deduct payments returned to applicants and members | 929 44 |
| Net amount received from members | $413,297 46 |
| Gross interest on mortgage loans | 9,737 38 |
| Gross interest on bonds and dividends on stocks | 6,805 38 |
| Gross interest on deposits in trust companies and banks | 1,010 20 |
| Gross interest from all other sources | 5 75 |
| Gross rents from association's property | 12,280 30 |
| Sale of lodge supplies | 639 79 |
| Miscellaneous | 383 12 |
| Surety bonds | 172 97 |
| Total income | $444,332 35 |
| Sum | $920,021 08 |

DISBURSEMENTS.

| | |
|---|---|
| Death claims | $94,050 99 |
| Sick and accident claims | 4,469 48 |
| Old age settlements | 15,141 27 |
| Credit on class A transfer value | 158,021 47 |
| Total benefits paid | $271,683 21 |
| Commissions and fees paid to deputies and organizers | 80,869 00 |
| Salaries of deputies and organizers | 13,945 32 |
| Salaries of officers and trustees | 13,733 54 |

DISBURSEMENTS—Concluded.

| | | |
|---|---|---|
| Other compensation of officers and trustees | | $ 1,690 00 |
| Salaries and other compensation of committees | | 100 80 |
| Salaries of office employees | | 10,466 48 |
| Salaries and fees paid to supreme medical examiners | | 2,969 10 |
| Salaries and fees paid to subordinate medical examiners | | 1,564 50 |
| Traveling and other expenses of officers, trustees and committees | | 1,397 43 |
| Insurance department fees | | 188 86 |
| Rent, including $1,800.00 for association's occupancy of its own buildings | | 1,812 50 |
| Advertising, printing and stationery | | 3,074 71 |
| Postage, express, telegraph and telephone | | 1,510 97 |
| Lodge supplies | | 586 13 |
| Official publication | | 2,245 99 |
| Expenses of supreme lodge meeting | | 1,764 90 |
| Legal expense in litigating claims | | 541 98 |
| Furniture and fixtures | | 738 20 |
| Taxes, repairs and other expenses on real estate | | 6,463 12 |
| All other disbursements, viz— | | |
| Real estate | | 259 90 |
| Miscellaneous, $649.52; surety bonds, $200.00 | | 849 52 |
| Agents traveling expenses, $6,065.69; services of actuary, $566.37 | | 6,632 06 |
| Office expense, $831.44; state council dues, $1,915.44 | | 2,746 88 |
| Total disbursements | | $427,835 20 |
| Balance | | $492,185 88 |

LEDGER ASSETS.

| | | |
|---|---|---|
| Book value of real estate | | $122,337 16 |
| Mortgage loans on real estate | | 174,324 04 |
| Book value of bonds and stocks | | 140,576 74 |
| Cash in association's office | | 15 00 |
| Deposits in trust companies and banks not on interest | | 2,925 00 |
| Deposits in trust companies and banks on interest | | 48,000 00 |
| Furniture and fixtures | | 4,007 86 |
| Total ledger assets | | $492,185 88 |

NON-LEDGER ASSETS.

| | | |
|---|---|---|
| Interest and rents due and accrued | | $ 9,214 72 |
| Market value of real estate over book value | | 600 00 |
| Market value of bonds and stocks over book value | | 1,326 47 |
| Assessments actually collected by subordinate lodges not yet turned over to supreme lodge | | 22,592 76 |
| All other assets, viz— | | |
| Monthly dues actually collected by subordinate lodges not yet turned over to supreme council | $1,241 94 | |
| Office furniture, fixtures and supplies | 4,835 41 | |
| Premium loan | 9,417 03 | |
| | | 15,494 30 |
| Gross assets | | $541,414 21 |

DEDUCT ASSETS NOT ADMITTED.

| | | |
|---|---|---|
| Other items, viz— | | |
| Office furniture, fixtures and supplies | $4,835 41 | |
| Furniture and fixtures of home office building | 4,007 86 | |
| | | 8,843 27 |
| Total admitted assets | | $532,570 94 |

LIABILITIES.

| | | |
|---|---|---|
| Death claims due and unpaid | $3,669 30 | |
| Death claims adjusted not yet due | 5,900 00 | |
| Death claims incurred in 1921, not reported until 1922 | 3,000 00 | |
| Total death claims | | $12,569 30 |
| Sick and accident claims resisted | $250 00 | |
| Sick and accident claims reported during the year but not yet adjusted | 700 00 | |
| Sick and accident claims incurred in 1921, not reported until 1922 | 350 00 | |
| Total sick and accident claims | | 1,300 00 |
| Total unpaid claims | | $18,369 30 |
| Salaries, rents, expenses, commissions, etc., due or accrued | | 2,910 92 |
| Taxes due or accrued | | 1,810 10 |
| Advance assessments | | 44,207 40 |
| Advance dues | | 1,707 50 |
| Total | | $65,505 22 |

## EXHIBIT OF CERTIFICATES.

| | Total business of the year. Number. | Amount. | Business in Illinois during year. Number. | Amount. |
|---|---|---|---|---|
| Benefit certificates in force December 31, 1920, as per last statement | 15,571 | $17,608,750 00 | 841 | $903,250 00 |
| Benefit certificates written and renewed during the year | 4,747 | 5,585,250 00 | 313 | 443,000 00 |
| Benefit certificates received by transfer during the year | -------- | ------------- | 7 | 5,500 00 |
| Benefit certificates increased during the year | 142 | 235,750 00 | -------- | ------------- |
| Totals | 20,460 | $23,429,750 00 | 1,161 | $1,351,750 00 |
| Deduct terminated, decreased or transferred during the year | 5,306 | 6,472,250 00 | -------- | ------------- |
| Deduct terminated or decreased during the year | -------- | ------------- | 432 | 555,750 00 |
| Total benefit certificates in force December 31, 1921 | 15,154 | $16,957,500 00 | 729 | $796,000 00 |

Received during the year from members in Illinois: Mortuary, $9,074.32; disability, $189.14; expense, $6,712.32; total $15,975 78

## EXHIBIT OF DEATH CLAIMS.

| | Total claims—all in Illinois. Number. | Amount. |
|---|---|---|
| Claims unpaid December 31, 1920, as per last statement | 6 | $ 6,767 26 |
| Claims reported during the year and interest addition | 84 | 93,153 03 |
| Rejected last year reconsidered and paid in 1921 | 2 | 3,700 00 |
| Totals | 92 | $103,620 29 |
| Claims paid during the year | 85 | 94,050 99 |
| Claims unpaid December 31, 1921 | 7 | $9,569 30 |

## EXHIBIT OF PERMANENT DISABILITY CLAIMS.

| | Illinois claims. Number. | Amount. |
|---|---|---|
| Claims unpaid December 31, 1920, as per last statement | 2 | $1,500 00 |
| Claims reported during the year and interest addition | 2 | 3,000 00 |
| Totals | 4 | $4,500 00 |
| Claims paid during the year | -------- | ------------- |
| Balance | -------- | ------------- |
| Claims unpaid December 31, 1921 | 4 | $4,500 00 |

## EXHIBIT OF SICK AND ACCIDENT CLAIMS.

| | Total claims. Number. | Amount. | Illinois claims. Number. | Amount. |
|---|---|---|---|---|
| Claims unpaid December 31, 1920, as per last statement | 2 | $ 93 28 | -------- | ------------- |
| Claims reported during the year | 54 | 5,326 20 | -------- | ------------- |
| Totals | 56 | $5,419 48 | -------- | ------------- |
| Claims paid during the year | 51 | 4,469 48 | 2 | $75 00 |
| Claims rejected during the year | 3 | 250 00 | -------- | ------------- |
| Claims unpaid December 31, 1921 | 2 | $700 00 | -------- | ------------- |

---

# GERMAN BENEFICIAL UNION.

Located at No. 1505-1507 Carson Street, Pittsburgh, Pennsylvania.

LOUIS VOLZ, President. ERNEST HERKLOTZ, Secretary.

| | |
|---|---|
| Balance from previous year | $2,159,278 99 |

## INCOME.

| | |
|---|---|
| Membership fees actually received | $ 4,828 00 |
| All other assessments or premiums | 913,939 85 |
| Dues and per capita tax | 27,146 40 |
| Net amount received from members | $945,914 25 |

INCOME—Concluded.

| | |
|---|---|
| Gross interest on mortgage loans | $35,938 23 |
| Gross interest on bonds and dividends on stocks | 72,493 31 |
| Gross interest on deposits in trust companies and banks | 5,277 50 |
| Gross interest from all other sources | 235 00 |
| Gross rents from association's property, including $3,600.00 for association's occupancy of its own buildings | 6,526 74 |
| Sale of lodge supplies | 2,370 24 |
| Gross profit on sale or maturity of ledger assets | 285 00 |
| Gross increase in book value of ledger assets | 548 05 |
| Certificate changes | 497 50 |
| Surety bond premiums | 827 72 |
| Benefit refunds | 2,256 25 |
| Total income | $1,073,169 79 |
| Sum | $3,232,448 78 |

DISBURSEMENTS.

| | |
|---|---|
| Death claims | $120,645 37 |
| Sick and accident claims | 18,618 50 |
| Matured certificates | 338,767 08 |
| Cancelled certificates | 33,709 20 |
| Certificate loans | 64,485 25 |
| Total benefits paid | $576,225 40 |
| Commissions and fees paid to deputies and organizers | 45,885 54 |
| Salaries of deputies and organizers | 4,500 00 |
| Salaries of officers and trustees | 15,920 83 |
| Salaries and other compensation of committees | 2,171 68 |
| Salaries of office employees | 20,800 00 |
| Salaries and fees paid to supreme medical examiners | 2,666 67 |
| Salaries and fees paid to subordinate medical examiners | 118 00 |
| Traveling and other expenses of officers, trustees and committees | 1,122 99 |
| Insurance department fees | 117 00 |
| Rents, including $3,600.00 for association's occupancy of its own buildings | 3,600 00 |
| Advertising, printing and stationery | 7,518 19 |
| Postage, express, telegraph and telephone | 2,572 35 |
| Lodge supplies | 2,620 71 |
| Official publication | 8,887 85 |
| Expenses of supreme lodge meeting | 9,670 83 |
| Legal expense in litigating claims | 52 65 |
| Other legal expenses | 1,497 45 |
| Furniture and fixtures | 248 90 |
| Taxes, repairs and other expenses on real estate | 4,093 70 |
| Gross decrease in book value of ledger assets | 2,442 99 |
| All other disbursements, viz— | |
| National Fraternal Congress | 197 50 |
| Miscellaneous | 349 00 |
| Surety bond premium | 740 47 |
| Safe deposit box rental | 50 00 |
| Auditor and actuary | 250 94 |
| Examination by Pennsylvania Insurance Department | 428 39 |
| Total disbursements | $714,750 03 |
| Balance | $2,517,698 75 |

LEDGER ASSETS.

| | |
|---|---|
| Book value of real estate | $ 67,537 79 |
| Mortgage loans on real estate | 651,670 00 |
| Book value of bonds and stocks | 1,610,457 90 |
| Cash in association's office | 100 00 |
| Deposits in trust companies and banks not on interest | 88,769 06 |
| Deposits in trust companies and banks on interest | 90,000 00 |
| U. S. war saving certificate stamps | 9,164 00 |
| Total ledger assets | $2,517,698 75 |

NON-LEDGER ASSETS.

| | |
|---|---|
| Interest and rents due and accrued | 24,957 48 |
| Market value of real estate over book value | 12,400 00 |
| Market value of bonds and stocks over book value | 34,857 10 |
| Total admitted assets | $2,589,913 33 |

LIABILITIES.

| | | |
|---|---|---|
| Death claims due and unpaid | $8,554 52 | |
| Death claims reported during the year but not yet adjusted | 10,588 90 | |
| Total death claims | | $19,143 42 |
| Sick and accident claims reported during the year but not yet adjusted | | 1,800 00 |
| Total unpaid claims | | $20,943 42 |
| Salaries, rents, expenses, commissions, etc., due or accrued | | 5,000 00 |
| Total | | $25,943 42 |

EXHIBIT OF CERTIFICATES.

| | Total business of the year. | | Business in Illinois during year. | |
|---|---|---|---|---|
| | Number. | Amount. | Number. | Amount. |
| Benefit certificates in force December 31, 1920, as per last statement | 45,178 | $30,400,650 00 | 2,343 | $1,563,350 00 |
| Benefit certificates written and renewed during the year | 9,941 | 7,034,050 00 | 507 | 408,200 00 |
| Totals | 55,119 | $37,434,700 00 | 2,850 | $1,971,550 00 |
| Deduct terminated, decreased or transferred during the year | 7,054 | 4,703,650 00 | | |
| Deduct terminated or decreased during the year | | | 109 | 66,000 00 |
| Total benefit certificates in force December 31, 1921 | 48,065 | $32,731,050 00 | 2,741 | $1,905,550 00 |

Received during the year from members in Illinois: Mortuary, $46,058.37; sick and accident, $1,029.28; expense, $6,478.80; total $53,566 45

EXHIBIT OF DEATH CLAIMS.

| | Total claims. | | Illinois claims. | |
|---|---|---|---|---|
| | Number. | Amount. | Number. | Amount. |
| Claims unpaid December 31, 1920, as per last statement | 85 | $19,649 26 | 3 | $835 42 |
| Claims reported during the year and interest addition | 376 | 120,544 13 | 17 | 3,914 26 |
| Totals | 461 | $140,193 39 | 20 | $4,749 68 |
| Claims paid during the year | 369 | 120,645 37 | 15 | 3,431 76 |
| Balance | 92 | $19,548 02 | 5 | $1,317 92 |
| Saved by compromising or scaling down claims during the year | | 264 60 | | 113 60 |
| Claims rejected during the year | 1 | 140 00 | 1 | 140 00 |
| Claims unpaid December 31, 1921 | 91 | $19,143 42 | 4 | $1,064 32 |

EXHIBIT OF SICK AND ACCIDENT CLAIMS.

| | Total claims. | | Illinois claims. | |
|---|---|---|---|---|
| | Number. | Amount. | Number. | Amount. |
| Claims unpaid December 31, 1920, as per last statement | 50 | $1,600 00 | 5 | $180 00 |
| Increase in estimated liability | 10 | 200 00 | | |
| Claims reported during the year | 575 | 18,618 50 | 40 | 1,388 00 |
| Totals | 635 | $20,418 50 | 45 | $1,568 00 |
| Claims paid during the year | 575 | 18,618 50 | 40 | 1,388 00 |
| Claims unpaid December 31, 1921 | 60 | $1,800 00 | 5 | $180 00 |

## HOMESTEADERS.

Located at Securities Building, Des Moines, Iowa.

HARRY J. GREEN, President. A. H. COREY, Secretary.

| | |
|---|---|
| Balance from previous year | $406,904 13 |

INCOME.

| | |
|---|---|
| Assessments or premiums during first twelve months of membership of which all or an extra percentage is used for expenses | $158,769 93 |
| All other assessments or premiums | 457,107 87 |
| Dues and per capita tax | 2,770 46 |

INCOME—Concluded.

| | | |
|---|---|---|
| Medical examiners' fees actually received | | $ 89 00 |
| Other payments by members, viz: Expense benefit fee | | 53,039 15 |
| Total received from members | | $671,776 41 |
| Deduct payments returned to applicants and members | | 799 39 |
| Net amount received from members | | $670,977 02 |
| Gross interest on mortgage loans | | 11,629 65 |
| Gross interest on bonds and dividends on stocks | | 3,109 28 |
| Gross interest on deposits in trust companies and banks | | 2,672 06 |
| Sale of lodge supplies | | 654 53 |
| Bond premium | | 986 50 |
| Change of certificates | | 197 90 |
| Miscellaneous | | 2,040 44 |
| Total income | | $692,267 38 |
| Sum | | $1,099,171 51 |

DISBURSEMENTS.

| | | |
|---|---|---|
| Death claims | | $273,982 23 |
| Permanent disability claims | | 2,591 00 |
| Accident claims | | 13,443 04 |
| Old age benefits | | 275 00 |
| Total benefits paid | | $290,291 27 |
| Commissions and fees paid to deputies and organizers | | 124,792 36 |
| Salaries of deputies and organizers | | 25,101 68 |
| Salaries of managers or agents not deputies or organizers | | 4,300 00 |
| Salaries of officers and trustees | | 19,371 00 |
| Salaries and other compensation of committees | | 1,400 00 |
| Salaries of office employees | | 34,708 29 |
| Salaries and fees paid to supreme medical examiners | | 5,875 00 |
| Salaries and fees paid to subordinate medical examiners | | 7,595 00 |
| Traveling and other expenses of officers, trustees and committees | | 4,427 94 |
| Insurance department fees | | 1,023 90 |
| Rent | | 6,000 00 |
| Advertising, printing and stationery | | 11,112 28 |
| Postage, express, telegraph and telephone | | 4,090 81 |
| Lodge supplies | | 429 75 |
| Official publication | | 11,064 59 |
| Legal expense in litigating claims | | 156 62 |
| Other legal expenses | | 2,500 00 |
| Furniture and fixtures | | 305 60 |
| All other disbursements, viz: Fraternal Congress, $167.50; actuary expense, $200.25; expense deputies, $5,386.80; expense managers and agents, $2,639.07; field and expense, $9,441.74; bond and fire insurance premiums, $1,257.28; impairment service, $980.75,; miscellaneous expense, $1,307.63; unpaid check less repaid, $406.58 | | 21,787 60 |
| Total disbursements | | $576,333 69 |
| Balance | | $522,837 82 |

LEDGER ASSETS.

| | | |
|---|---|---|
| Mortgage loans on real estate | | $355,450 00 |
| Book value of bonds and stocks | | 46,178 17 |
| Cash in association's office | | 1,836 00 |
| Deposits in trust companies and banks on interest | | 119,373 65 |
| Total ledger assets | | $522,837 82 |

NON-LEDGER ASSETS.

| | | |
|---|---|---|
| Interest and rents due and accrued | | 13,579 04 |
| Assessments actually collected by subordinate lodges not yet turned over to supreme lodge | | 55,350 00 |
| All other assets, viz— | | |
| Organizers balance | $16,355 43 | |
| Furniture and fixtures | 5,770 39 | |
| Stationery and supplies | 6,737 27 | |
| Due from homesteads on account | 221 07 | |
| | | 29,084 16 |
| Gross assets | | $620,851 02 |

DEDUCT ASSETS NOT ADMITTED.

| | | |
|---|---|---|
| Balance due from organizers not secured by bonds | $16,355 43 | |
| Other items, viz— | | |
| Furniture and fixtures | 5,770 39 | |
| Stationery and supplies | 6,737 27 | |
| Due from homesteads on account | 221 07 | |
| | | 29,084 16 |
| Total admitted assets | | $591,766 86 |

## LIABILITIES.

| | | |
|---|---|---|
| Death claims reported during the year but not yet adjusted | $54,685 50 | |
| Death claims incurred in 1921, not reported until 1922 | 1,697 00 | |
| Total death claims | | $56,382 50 |
| Permanent disability claims adjusted not yet due | | 400 00 |
| Sick and accident claims reported during the year but not yet adjusted | | 700 00 |
| Old age and other benefits due and unpaid, including $1,212.22 present value of such benefits payable in installments | | 1,212 22 |
| Total unpaid claims | | $58,694 72 |
| Salaries, rents, expenses, commissions, etc., due or accrued | | 8,363 31 |
| Advance assessments | | 27,053 67 |
| Total | | $94,111 70 |

## EXHIBIT OF CERTIFICATES.

| | Total business of the year. Number. | Amount. | Business in Illinois during year. Number. | Amount. |
|---|---|---|---|---|
| Benefit certificates in force December 31, 1920, as per last statement | 27,018 | $37,587,000 00 | 552 | $674,500 00 |
| Benefit certificates written and renewed during the year | 5,174 | 6,432,500 00 | 235 | 272,500 00 |
| Benefit certificates increased during the year | -------- | 6,500 00 | -------- | ------------- |
| Totals | 32,192 | $44,026,000 00 | 787 | $947,000 00 |
| Deduct terminated, decreased or transferred during the year | 7,441 | 10,077,000 00 | -------- | ------------- |
| Deduct terminated or decreased during the year | -------- | ------------- | 230 | 254,500 00 |
| Total benefit certificates in force December 31, 1921 | 24,751 | $33,949,000 00 | 557 | $692,500 00 |

Received during the year from members in Illinois: Mortuary, $7,060.44; all other, $166.61; expense, $5,563.79; total ........ $12,790 84

## EXHIBIT OF DEATH CLAIMS.

| | Total claims. Number. | Amount. | Illinois claims. Number. | Amount. |
|---|---|---|---|---|
| Claims unpaid December 31, 1920, as per last statement | 40 | $ 45,209 73 | 1 | $ 500 00 |
| Increase change in classification | -------- | 1,342 25 | -------- | ------------- |
| Claims reported during the year and interest addition | 237 | 286,633 96 | 7 | 6,666 00 |
| Totals | 277 | $333,185 94 | 8 | $7,166 00 |
| Claims paid during the year | 233 | 273,982 23 | 7 | 6,268 00 |
| Balance | 44 | $59,203 71 | 1 | $898 00 |
| Saved by compromising or scaling down claims during the year | -------- | 2,821 21 | -------- | ------------- |
| Claims unpaid December 31, 1921 | 44 | $56,382 50 | 1 | $898 00 |

## EXHIBIT OF PERMANENT DISABILITY CLAIMS.

| | Total claims. Number. | Amount. |
|---|---|---|
| Claims reported during the year and interest addition | 4 | $1,791 00 |
| Claims paid during the year | 2 | 1,391 00 |
| Claims unpaid December 31, 1921 | 2 | $400 00 |

## EXHIBIT OF ACCIDENT CLAIMS.

| | Total claims. Number. | Amount. | Illinois claims. Number. | Amount. |
|---|---|---|---|---|
| Claims unpaid December 31, 1920, as per last statement | 5 | $ 277 97 | -------- | ------------- |
| Increase in estimated liability | -------- | 31 58 | -------- | ------------- |
| Claims reported during the year | 210 | 13,920 09 | 7 | $612 88 |
| Totals | 215 | $14,229 64 | 7 | $612 88 |
| Claims paid during the year | 203 | 13,443 04 | 7 | 612 88 |
| Claims rejected during the year | 6 | 86 60 | -------- | ------------- |
| Claims unpaid December 31, 1921 | 6 | $700 00 | -------- | ------------- |

## EXHIBIT OF OLD AGE AND OTHER CLAIMS.

| | Total claims—all in Illinois. Number. | Amount. |
|---|---|---|
| Claims reported during the year and interest addition | 4 | $225 00 |
| Claims paid during the year | 4 | 225 00 |

## INDEPENDENT ORDER BRITH ABRAHAM OF U. S. OF A.

Located at No. 37 Seventh Street, New York, New York.

HON. AARON J. LEVY, President. MAX L. HOLLANDER, Secretary.

| | |
|---|---|
| Balance from previous year | $1,522,932 68 |

### INCOME.

| | |
|---|---|
| All other assessments or premiums | $1,153,250 95 |
| Dues and per capita tax | 67,629 15 |
| Net amount received from members | $1,220,880 10 |
| Gross interest on mortgage loans | 4,806 38 |
| Gross interest on bonds and dividends on stocks | 44,378 93 |
| Gross interest on deposits in trust companies and banks | 14,314 48 |
| Gross rents from association's property, including $3,248.00 for association's occupancy of its own buildings | 3,802 00 |
| Sale of lodge supplies | 229 52 |
| Gross increase in book value of ledger assets | 17,480 00 |
| Headstone deposits | 1,367 00 |
| Permits and reserved graves | 828 00 |
| Membership certificates | 714 79 |
| Ball tickets | 7,454 75 |
| Lodge officers bonds | 1,070 69 |
| Withdrawal cards deposits | 110 00 |
| Propaganda tax | 4,480 46 |
| Donations to Pueblo flood sufferers | 880 00 |
| Total income | $1,322,797 10 |
| Sum | $2,845,729 78 |

### DISBURSEMENTS.

| | |
|---|---|
| Death claims | $879,350 00 |
| Permanent disability claims | 14,000 00 |
| Total benefits paid | $893,350 00 |
| Organization expenses | 225 65 |
| District deputies expenses | 151 65 |
| Salaries of officers and trustees | 6,500 00 |
| Other compensation of officers and trustees | 400 00 |
| Committees expenses | 621 25 |
| Salaries of office employees | 11,479 25 |
| Other compensation of office employees | 279 00 |
| Salaries and fees paid to medical examiners | 166 00 |
| Bonding of grand and lodge officers | 1,071 38 |
| Traveling and other expenses of officers, trustees and committees | 4,123 70 |
| For collection fees | 49 07 |
| Insurance department fees | 211 02 |
| Rent, including $3,248.00 for association's occupancy of its own buildings | 3,348 00 |
| Advertising, printing and stationery | 7,247 24 |
| Postage, express, telegraph and telephone | 2,820 19 |
| Light and heat | 965 25 |
| Withdrawal cards deposits returned | 45 00 |
| Expenses of supreme lodge meeting | 1,828 21 |
| Legal expense | 185 62 |
| Office expenses | 666 97 |
| Ball and relief committee expenses | 3,805 90 |
| Taxes, repairs and other expenses on real estate | 3,942 07 |
| Commission on purchased bonds | 153 13 |
| Donations to Pueblo flood sufferers | 1,000 00 |
| Resolutions and testimonials | 244 00 |
| All other disbursements, viz— | |
| Auditing books, $1,000; maintenance of cemetery, $676.00 | 1,676 00 |
| Headstone deposits returned, $1,369.00; repairs and renewals, $287.62 | 1,656 62 |
| Donations for relief of members, $19,231.00; donations to charitable institutions, $13,395.00 | 32,626 00 |
| Office and window cleaning, $855.00; propaganda expense, $3,854.95; actuary expenses, $50.00 | 4,759 95 |
| Total disbursements | $985,598 12 |
| Balance | $1,860,131 66 |

### LEDGER ASSETS.

| | |
|---|---|
| Book value of real estate | $ 29,373 90 |
| Mortgage loans on real estate | 88,600 00 |
| Book value of bonds and stocks | 1,199,400 00 |
| Deposits in trust companies and banks not on interest | 600 00 |
| Deposits in trust companies and banks on interest | 542,157 76 |
| Total ledger assets | $1,860,131 66 |

## LEDGER ASSETS—Concluded.

NON-LEDGER ASSETS.

| | | |
|---|---|---|
| Interest accrued on mortgages | $ 1,369 94 | |
| Interest accrued on bonds | 11,648 25 | |
| | | $13,018 19 |
| Gross assets | | $1,873,149 85 |

DEDUCT ASSETS NOT ADMITTED.

| | |
|---|---|
| Book value of bonds and stocks over market value | 29,941 00 |
| Total admitted assets | $1,843,208 85 |

## LIABILITIES.

| | | |
|---|---|---|
| Death claims adjusted not yet due | $152,500 00 | |
| Death claims incurred in 1921, not reported until 1922 | 63,500 00 | |
| Total death claims | | $216,000 00 |
| Permanent disability claims adjusted not yet due | | 4,250 00 |
| Total unpaid claims | | $220,250 00 |
| All other liabilities, viz— | | |
| Withdrawal cards deposits | $ 675 85 | |
| Headstone deposits | 3,835 00 | |
| | | 4,510 85 |
| Total | | $224,760 85 |

## EXHIBIT OF CERTIFICATES.

| | Total business of the year. | | Business in Illinois during year. | |
|---|---|---|---|---|
| | Number. | Amount. | Number. | Amount. |
| Benefit certificates in force December 31, 1920, as per last statement | 152,289 | $76,144,500 00 | 5,656 | $2,828,000 00 |
| Benefit certificates written and renewed during the year | 6,536 | 3,268,000 00 | 217 | 108,500 00 |
| Total | 158,825 | $79,412,500 00 | 5,873 | $2,936,500 00 |
| Deduct terminated, decreased or transferred during the year | 12,256 | 6,128,000 00 | | |
| Deduct terminated or decreased during the year | | | 501 | 250,500 00 |
| Total benefit certificates in force December 31, 1921 | 146,569 | $73,284,500 00 | 5,372 | $2,686,000 00 |

| | |
|---|---|
| Received during the year from members in Illinois: Mortuary, $34,619.25; endowment, $9,877.40; disability, $596.53; expense, $2,922.08; total | $48,015 26 |

## EXHIBIT OF DEATH CLAIMS.

| | Total claims. | | Illinois claims. | |
|---|---|---|---|---|
| | Number. | Amount. | Number. | Amount. |
| Claims unpaid December 31, 1920, as per last statement | 429 | $214,500 00 | 24 | $12,000 00 |
| Claims reported during the year and interest addition | 1,763 | 881,500 00 | 69 | 34,500 00 |
| Total | 2,192 | $1,096,000 00 | 93 | $46,500 00 |
| Claims paid during the year | 1,760 | 879,350 00 | 77 | 38,500 00 |
| Balance | 432 | $216,650 00 | 16 | $8,000 00 |
| Saved by compromising or scaling down claims during the year | | 650 00 | | |
| Claims unpaid December 31, 1921 | 432 | $216,000 00 | 16 | $8,000 00 |

## EXHIBIT OF PERMANENT DISABILITY CLAIMS.

| | Total claims. | | Illinois claims. | |
|---|---|---|---|---|
| | Number. | Amount. | Number. | Amount. |
| Claims unpaid December 31, 1920, as per last statement | 15 | $ 4,000 00 | | |
| Claims reported during the year and interest addition | 58 | 15,500 00 | 3 | $750 00 |
| Total | 73 | $19,500 00 | 3 | $750 00 |
| Claims paid during the year | 52 | 14,000 00 | 2 | 500 00 |
| Balance | 21 | $5,500 00 | 1 | $250 00 |
| Claims rejected during the year | 5 | 1,250 00 | | |
| Claims unpaid December 31, 1921 | 16 | $4,250 00 | 1 | $250 00 |

## INDEPENDENT ORDER OF BRITISH SHOLOM.

Located at Nos. 506-508 Pine Street, Philadelphia, Pennsylvania.

SOLOMON C. KRAUS, President. MARTIN B. LEVY, Secretary.

| | | |
|---|---|---|
| Balance from previous year | | $422,542 90 |

### INCOME.

| | | |
|---|---|---|
| All other assessments or premiums | | $375,937 23 |
| Gross interest on mortgage loans | | 16,138 15 |
| Gross interest on bonds and dividends on stocks | | 980 96 |
| Gross interest on deposits in trust companies and banks | | 265 26 |
| Sale of lodge supplies | | 197 90 |
| Borrowed money (gross) | | 35,000 00 |
| From all other sources, viz— | | |
| Membership certificate | | 643 00 |
| Bonding of officers | | 766 25 |
| Miscellaneous | | 111 88 |
| Checks voided | | 500 00 |
| Suspended member | | 3 75 |
| Total income | | $430,544 38 |
| Sum | | $853,087 28 |

### DISBURSEMENTS.

| | | |
|---|---|---|
| Death claims | | $225,250 00 |
| Permanent disability claims | | 3,550 00 |
| Other benefits: Refund to members | | 26,264 37 |
| Total benefits paid | | $255,064 37 |
| Commissions and fees paid to deputies and organizers | | 50 00 |
| Salaries of officers and trustees | | 8,999 50 |
| Salaries of office employees | | 4,324 00 |
| Salaries and fees paid to subordinate medical examiners | | 232 50 |
| Traveling and other expenses of officers, trustees and committees | | 2,891 22 |
| Insurance department fees | | 173 00 |
| Rent | | 2,000 00 |
| Advertising, printing and stationery | | 5,218 34 |
| Postage, express, telegraph and telephone | | 2,472 32 |
| Official publication | | 3,602 87 |
| Expenses of supreme lodge meeting | | 272 85 |
| Furniture and fixtures | | 1,736 46 |
| Gross loss on sale or maturity of ledger assets | | 9,340 87 |
| Borrowed money repaid (gross) | | 45,000 00 |
| Interest on borrowed money | | 1,290 00 |
| All other disbursements | | 20,840 58 |
| Total disbursements | | $363,508 88 |
| Balance | | $489,578 40 |

### LEDGER ASSETS.

| | | |
|---|---|---|
| Mortgage loans on real estate | | $438,100 00 |
| Book value of bonds and stocks | | 25,530 00 |
| Deposits in trust companies and banks not on interest | | 2,276 70 |
| Deposits in trust companies and banks on interest | | 22,961 88 |
| Other ledger assets, viz: War Savings Stamps | | 708 82 |
| Total ledger assets | | $489,578 40 |

#### NON-LEDGER ASSETS.

| | | |
|---|---|---|
| Interest and rents due and accrued | | 5,023 98 |
| Assessments actually collected by subordinate lodges not yet turned over to supreme lodge | | 41,706 78 |
| Total admitted assets | | $536,309 16 |

### LIABILITIES.

| | | |
|---|---|---|
| Death claims due and unpaid | $ 2,750 00 | |
| Death claims adjusted not yet due | 42,050 00 | |
| Death claims resisted | 500 00 | |
| Death claims reported during the year not yet adjusted | 6,750 00 | |
| Total death claims | | $52,050 00 |
| Permanent disability claims due and unpaid | | 1,500 00 |
| Total unpaid claims | | $53,550 00 |
| Borrowed money | | 15,000 00 |
| Total | | $68,550 00 |

### EXHIBIT OF CERTIFICATES.

| | Total business of the year. Number. | Amount. |
|---|---|---|
| Benefit certificates in force December 31, 1920, as per last statement | 45,804 | $22,494,500 00 |
| Benefit certificates written and renewed during the year | 2,711 | 1,284,500 00 |
| Total | 48,515 | $23,779,000 00 |
| Deduct terminated, decreased or transferred during the year | 5,535 | 2,736,750 00 |
| Total benefit certificates in force December 31, 1921 | 42,980 | $21,042,250 00 |
| Received during the year from members in Illinois: Mortuary, $5,666.62; reserve, $1,126.86; disability, $89.16; all other, $1,533.24; expense, $877.39; total | | $9,293 27 |

### EXHIBIT OF DEATH CLAIMS.

| | Total claims. Number. | Amount. |
|---|---|---|
| Claims unpaid December 31, 1920, as per last statement | 125 | $57,100 00 |
| Claims reported during the year and interest addition | 467 | 221,500 00 |
| Total | 592 | $278,600 00 |
| Claims paid during the year | 481 | 225,250 00 |
| Balance | 111 | $53,350 00 |
| Saved by compromising or scaling down claims during the year | -------- | 1,300 00 |
| Claims unpaid December 31, 1921 | 111 | $52,050 00 |

### EXHIBIT OF PERMANENT DISABILITY CLAIMS.

| | Total claims. Number. | Amount. |
|---|---|---|
| Claims reported during the year and interest addition | 16 | $5,050 00 |
| Claims paid during the year | 12 | 3,550 00 |
| Claims unpaid December 31, 1921 | 4 | $1,500 00 |

## INDEPENDENT ORDER FREE SONS OF ISRAEL, GRAND LODGE, U. S. A.

Located at No. 21 West One Hundred and Twenty-fourth Street, New York, New York.

SOLON J. LIEBESKIND, President. HENRY J. HYMON, Secretary.

| | |
|---|---|
| Balance from previous year | $1,390,851 41 |

### INCOME.

| | |
|---|---|
| Membership fees actually received | $266,654 92 |
| Dues and per capita tax | 17,846 56 |
| Other payments by members, viz: Refund of mileage and miscellaneous expense paid by order | 2,564 22 |
| Net amount received from members | $287,065 70 |
| Gross interest on mortgage loans | 38,266 17 |
| Gross interest on bonds and dividends on stocks | 22,920 31 |
| Gross interest on deposits in trust companies and banks | 3,333 95 |
| Gross rents from association's property | 11,870 78 |
| Refund of surety bonds paid by order | 209 60 |
| From rents of lodge rooms | 579 42 |
| Gross profits on sale of real estate | 1,369 49 |
| Total income | $365,615 42 |
| Sum | $1,756,466 83 |

### DISBURSEMENTS.

| | |
|---|---|
| Death claims | $231,803 21 |
| Commissions and fees paid to deputies and organizers | 726 48 |
| Salaries of officers and trustees | 6,058 27 |
| Other compensation of officers and trustees | 1,129 50 |
| Salaries of office employees | 3,170 01 |
| Traveling and other expenses of officers, trustees and committees | 1,389 86 |
| For collection and remittance of assessments and dues | 21 29 |
| Insurance department fees | 255 62 |
| Rent | 7,429 17 |
| Advertising, printing and stationery | 1,463 14 |
| Postage, express, telegraph and telephone | 718 58 |
| Lodge supplies | 263 00 |
| Expenses of supreme lodge meeting | 4,191 33 |
| Other legal expenses | 162 20 |
| Taxes, repairs and other expenses on real estate | 3,820 43 |
| Gross loss on sale or maturity of ledger assets | 4,572 92 |
| Sums paid to members and lodges to secure new business | 2,16[illegible] 50 |

DISBURSEMENTS—Concluded.

| | |
|---|---|
| Auditing books | $1,000 00 |
| Actuarial fees | 125 00 |
| Donations | 697 50 |
| Surety bonds | 184 50 |
| Miscellaneous | 598 21 |
| Trust funds paid | 547 91 |
| Total disbursements | $272,451 63 |
| Balance | $1,484,015 20 |

## LEDGER ASSETS.

| | | |
|---|---|---|
| Book value of real estate | | $ 50,633 34 |
| Mortgage loans on real estate | | 685,125 00 |
| Book value of bonds and stocks | | 644,161 87 |
| Deposits in trust companies and banks not on interest | | 104,094 99 |
| Total ledger assets | | $1,484,015 20 |

NON-LEDGER ASSETS.

| | | |
|---|---|---|
| Interest and rents due and accrued | | 13,219 21 |
| Market value of real estate over book value | | 18,366 66 |
| Market value of bonds and stocks over book value | | 22,888 13 |
| Assessments levied and uncollected | $11,322 12 | |
| Expense items levied and uncollected | 1,334 45 | |
| Furniture and fixtures | 1,400 00 | |
| | | 14,056 57 |
| Gross assets | | $1,552,545 77 |

DEDUCT ASSETS NOT ADMITTED.

| | | |
|---|---|---|
| Assessments levied and uncollected | $11,322 12 | |
| Expense items levied and uncollected | 1,334 45 | |
| Furniture and fixtures | 1,400 00 | |
| | | 14,056 57 |
| Total admitted assets | | $1,538,489 20 |

## LIABILITIES.

| | | |
|---|---|---|
| Death claims due and unpaid | | $46,409 55 |
| All other liabilities, viz— | | |
| Moneys held in trust | $1,064 16 | |
| Surety bonds paid by lodges not yet disbursed by order | 25 10 | |
| | | 1,089 26 |
| Total | | $47,498 81 |

## EXHIBIT OF CERTIFICATES.

| | Total business of the year. | | Business in Illinois during year. | |
|---|---|---|---|---|
| | Number. | Amount. | Number. | Amount. |
| Benefit certificates in force December 31, 1920, as per last statement | 7,218 | $6,417,000 00 | 1,961 | $1,527,250 00 |
| Benefit certificates written and renewed during the year | 275 | 164,250 00 | 193 | 123,250 00 |
| Benefit certificates increased during the year | 50 | 39,000 00 | | |
| Total | 7,543 | $6,620,250 00 | 2,154 | $1,650,500 00 |
| Deduct terminated, decreased or transferred during the year | 651 | 512,500 00 | | |
| Deduct terminated or decreased during the year | | | 229 | 127,000 00 |
| Total benefit certificates in force December 31, 1921 | 6,892 | $6,107,750 00 | 1,925 | $1,523,500 00 |

Received during the year from members in Illinois: Mortuary, $41,180.26; expense, $3,864.52; total $45,044 78

## EXHIBIT OF DEATH CLAIMS.

| | Total claims. | | Illinois claims. | |
|---|---|---|---|---|
| | Number. | Amount. | Number. | Amount. |
| Claims unpaid December 31, 1920, as per last statement | 54 | $ 48,462 76 | 4 | $ 3,100 00 |
| Claims reported during the year and interest addition | 235 | 229,750 00 | 20 | 17,500 00 |
| Total | 289 | $278,212 76 | 24 | $20,600 00 |
| Claims paid during the year | 238 | 231,803 21 | 19 | 16,500 00 |
| Claims unpaid December 31, 1921 | 51 | $46,409 55 | 5 | $4,100 00 |

## JEWISH NATIONAL WORKERS' ALLIANCE OF AMERICA.

Located at No. 153 East Broadway, New York, New York.

DAVID PINSKI, President. MEYER L. BROWN, Secretary.

| | |
|---|---|
| Balance from previous year | $135,447 28 |

### INCOME.

| | |
|---|---|
| Assessments or premiums during first 12 months of membership of which all or an extra percentage is used for expenses | 10,309 30 |
| All other assessments or premiums | 37,646 43 |
| Dues and per capita tax | 14,423 89 |
| Total received from members | $62,379 62 |
| Deduct payments returned to applicants and members | 109 30 |
| Net amount received from members | $62,270 32 |
| Gross interest on mortgage loans | 1,100 00 |
| Gross interest on bonds and dividends on stocks | 3,452 50 |
| Gross interest on deposits in trust companies and banks | 197 21 |
| Borrowed money (gross) | 10,000 00 |
| Contribution funds received | 4,611 99 |
| Literature | 51 45 |
| Alliance organization funds | 186 21 |
| Total income | $81,869 68 |
| Sum | $217,316 96 |

### DISBURSEMENTS.

| | |
|---|---|
| Death claims | $ 5,750 00 |
| Sick and accident claims | 15,281 00 |
| Total benefits paid | $21,031 00 |
| Salaries of deputies and organizers | 2,745 60 |
| Salaries of officers and trustees | 3,920 00 |
| Salaries and other compensation of committees | 2,154 31 |
| Salaries of office employees | 5,904 50 |
| Traveling and other expenses of officers, trustees and committees | 1,192 08 |
| For collection and remittance of assessments and dues | 36 53 |
| Insurance department fees | 498 35 |
| Rent | 1,052 00 |
| Advertising, printing and stationery | 3,110 86 |
| Postage, express, telegraph and telephone | 1,310 37 |
| Expenses of supreme lodge meeting | 4,115 07 |
| Exchange Canadian money | 36 65 |
| Other legal expenses | 1,268 66 |
| Furniture and fixtures | 903 30 |
| Preliminary organization expense (new branches) | 1,043 08 |
| Literature | 380 00 |
| N. G. checks | 257 07 |
| Bonds for local officers | 240 00 |
| Interest on borrowed money | 200 00 |
| Contribution funds forwarded | 17,272 55 |
| General office expense | 1,136 03 |
| Entertainment for branches | 1,117 98 |
| Publication and educational activities | 1,555 72 |
| Total disbursements | $72,481 71 |
| Balance | $144,835 25 |

### LEDGER ASSETS.

| | |
|---|---|
| Mortgage loans on real estate | $25,000 00 |
| Book value of bonds and stocks | 87,264 79 |
| Deposits in trust companies and banks not on interest | 10,378 00 |
| Deposits in trust companies and banks on interest | 22,164 96 |
| Advanced to branch No. 14 | 27 50 |
| Total ledger assets | $144,835 25 |

#### NON-LEDGER ASSETS.

| | | |
|---|---|---|
| Interest and rents due and accrued | | 2,000 42 |
| Market value of bonds and stocks over book value | | 3,551 67 |
| All other assets, viz— | | |
| Stationery (buttons, ledgers, etc.) | $1,000 00 | |
| Books and publications (educational) | 1,500 00 | |
| | | 2,500 00 |
| Gross assets | | $152,887 34 |

## LEDGER ASSETS—Concluded.

DEDUCT ASSETS NOT ADMITTED.

| | | |
|---|---|---|
| Book value of bonds and stocks over market value | $770 79 | |
| Other items, viz: Advanced to branch No. 14 | 27 50 | |
| | | $798 29 |
| Total admitted assets | | $152,089 05 |

## LIABILITIES.

| | | |
|---|---|---|
| Death claims due and unpaid | $1,850 00 | |
| Death claims reported during the year but not yet adjusted | 1,250 00 | |
| Total death claims | | $3,100 00 |
| Sick and accident claims reported during the year but not yet adjusted | | 758 00 |
| Total unpaid claims | | $ 3,858 00 |
| Borrowed money | | 10,000 00 |
| All other liabilities, viz— | | |
| Actuarial salaries | $ 75 00 | |
| Printing and stationery | 589 50 | |
| | | 664 50 |
| Total | | $14,522 50 |

## EXHIBIT OF CERTIFICATES.

| | Total business of the year. | | Business in Illinois during year. | |
|---|---|---|---|---|
| | Number. | Amount. | Number. | Amount. |
| Benefit certificates in force December 31, 1920, as per last statement | 5,705 | $1,952,850 00 | 302 | $107,200 00 |
| Benefit certificates written and renewed during the year | 1,558 | 463,800 00 | 32 | 15,700 00 |
| Total | 7,263 | $2,416,650 00 | 334 | $122,900 00 |
| Deduct terminated, decreased or transferred during the year | 1,492 | 479,950 00 | | |
| Deduct terminated or decreased during the year | | | 79 | 22,150 00 |
| Total benefit certificates in force December 31, 1921 | 5,771 | $1,936,700 00 | 255 | $100,750 00 |

Received during the year from members in Illinois: Mortuary, $1,461.53; disability, 1,082.10; expense, $965.66; total $3,509 29

## EXHIBIT OF DEATH CLAIMS.

| | Total claims. | | Illinois claims. | |
|---|---|---|---|---|
| | Number. | Amount. | Number. | Amount. |
| Claims unpaid December 31, 1920, as per last statement | 8 | $2,600 00 | 1 | $ 250 00 |
| Claims reported during the year and interest addition | 13 | 6,250 00 | 2 | 1,500 00 |
| Total | 21 | $8,850 00 | 3 | $1,750 00 |
| Claims paid during the year | 14 | 5,750 00 | 3 | 1,750 00 |
| Claims unpaid December 31, 1921 | 7 | $3,100 00 | | |

## EXHIBIT OF SICK AND ACCIDENT CLAIMS.

| | Total claims. | | Illinois claims. | |
|---|---|---|---|---|
| | Number. | Amount. | Number. | Amount. |
| Claims unpaid December 31, 1920, as per last statement | 43 | $ 678 00 | 1 | $ 36 00 |
| Increase in estimated liability | | | 44 | 1,053 00 |
| Claims reported during the year | 757 | 15,643 00 | | |
| Total | 800 | $16,321 00 | 45 | $1,089 00 |
| Claims paid during the year | 736 | 15,281 00 | 40 | 975 00 |
| Claims rejected during the year | 14 | 282 00 | | |
| Claims unpaid December 31, 1921 | 50 | $758 00 | 5 | $114 00 |

---

## JUNIOR ORDER UNITED AMERICAN MECHANICS, NATIONAL COUNCIL.

Located at Rooms 733 to 749 Wabash Building, 410 Liberty Street, Pittsburgh, Pennsylvania.

E. C. LAFEAN, President. ARTHUR M. FORDING, Secretary.

| | |
|---|---|
| Balance from previous year | $733,506 72 |

## INCOME.

| | |
|---|---|
| Membership fees actually received | $ 368 50 |
| Assessments or premiums during first twelve months of membership of which all or an extra percentage is used for expenses | 139,781 79 |
| All other assessments or premiums | 339,270 25 |
| Total received from members | $479,420 54 |
| Deduct payments returned to applicants and members | 2,260 22 |
| Net amount received from members | $477,160 32 |
| Gross interest on mortgage loans | 43,891 28 |
| Gross interest on bonds and dividends on stocks | 1,399 92 |
| Gross interest on deposits in trust companies and banks | 1,207 45 |
| Gross interest from all other sources | 841 51 |
| Gross profit on sale or maturity of ledger assets | 35 45 |
| Real estate appraisal fees | 260 00 |
| Commission on mortgage loans | 2,592 00 |
| Total income | $527,387 93 |
| Sum | $1,260,894 65 |

## DISBURSEMENTS.

| | |
|---|---|
| Death claims | $125,306 91 |
| Permanent disability claims | 15,670 79 |
| Total benefits paid | $140,977 70 |
| Commissions and fees paid to deputies and organizers | 63,132 77 |
| Salaries of deputies and organizers | 2,000 00 |
| Salaries of officers and trustees | 3,162 49 |
| Salaries of office employees | 7,377 99 |
| Other compensation of office employees | 47 16 |
| Salaries and fees paid to supreme medical examiners | 150 00 |
| Traveling and other expenses of officers, trustees and committees | 1,539 52 |
| For collection and remittance of assessments and dues | 25,888 43 |
| Insurance department | 522 68 |
| Rent | 1,634 32 |
| Advertising, printing and stationery | 4,583 88 |
| Postage, express, telegraph and telephone | 1,924 63 |
| Legal expense in litigating claims | 705 29 |
| Other legal expenses | 624 97 |
| Furniture and fixtures | 39 00 |
| Interest on advance assessments | 782 10 |
| Actuary's fees | 990 00 |
| Lapel buttons | 790 00 |
| Actuary's expenses | 300 76 |
| National fraternal congress | 193 81 |
| Audit of books | 151 25 |
| Sundry expenses | 358 31 |
| Total disbursements | $257,877 06 |
| Balance | $1,003,017 59 |

## LEDGER ASSETS.

| | |
|---|---|
| Book value of real estate | $ 1,983 90 |
| Mortgage loans on real estate | 924,200 00 |
| Book value of bonds and stocks | 45,000 00 |
| Deposits in trust companies and banks on interest | 31,833 69 |
| Total ledger assets | $1,003,017 59 |

### NON-LEDGER ASSETS.

| | |
|---|---|
| Interest and rents due and accrued | 15,378 34 |
| Assessments actually collected by subordinate lodges not yet turned over to supreme lodge | 12,024 70 |
| All other assets, viz: Liens on old class certificates | 40,220 46 |
| Total admitted assets | $1,070,641 09 |

## LIABILITIES.

| | | |
|---|---|---|
| Death claims resisted | $ 2,000 00 | |
| Death claims reported during the year but not yet adjusted | 20,500 00 | |
| Total death claims | | $22,500 00 |
| Permanent disability claims reported during the year but not yet adjusted | | 12,500 00 |
| Total unpaid claims | | $35,000 00 |
| Advance assessments | | 16,603 46 |
| Total | | $51,603 46 |

EXHIBIT OF CERTIFICATES.

| | Total business of the year. Number. | Amount. | Business in Illinois during year. Number. | Amount. |
|---|---|---|---|---|
| Benefit certificates in force December 31, 1920, as per last statement | 23,023 | $27,675,500 00 | 26 | $38,500 00 |
| Benefit certificates written and renewed during the year | 5,551 | 7,378,500 00 | | |
| Benefit certificates increased during the year | | 159,500 00 | | |
| Totals | 28,574 | $35,213,500 00 | 26 | $38,500 00 |
| Deduct terminated, decreased or transferred during the year | 4,364 | 6,085,500 00 | | |
| Deduct terminated or decreased during the year | | | | 500 00 |
| Total benefit certificates in force December 31, 1921 | 24,210 | $29,128,000 00 | 26 | $38,000 00 |

Received during the year from members in Illinois: Mortuary $859 90

EXHIBIT OF DEATH CLAIMS.

| | Total claims—all in Illinois. Number. | Amount. |
|---|---|---|
| Claims unpaid December 31, 1920, as per last statement | 23 | $ 31,500 00 |
| Claims reported during the year and interest addition | 130 | 160,155 24 |
| Totals | 153 | $191,655 24 |
| Claims paid during the year | 124 | 125,306 91 |
| Balance | 29 | $66,348 33 |
| Saved by compromising or scaling down claims during the year | | 28,848 33 |
| Claims rejected during the year | 11 | 15,000 00 |
| Claims unpaid December 31, 1921 | 18 | $22,500 00 |

EXHIBIT OF PERMANENT DISABILITY CLAIMS.

| | Total claims—all in Illinois. Number. | Amount. |
|---|---|---|
| Claims unpaid December 31, 1920, as per last statement | 2 | $ 3,000 00 |
| Claims reported during the year and interest addition | 38 | 42,700 00 |
| Totals | 40 | $45,700 00 |
| Claims paid during the year | 15 | 15,670 79 |
| Balance | 25 | $30,029 21 |
| Saved by compromising or scaling down claims during the year | | 3,029 21 |
| Claims rejected during the year | 15 | 14,500 00 |
| Claims unpaid December 31, 1921 | 10 | $12,500 00 |

---

## KNIGHTS AND LADIES OF FATHER MATHEW.

Located at No. 4053 Lindell Boulevard, St. Louis, Missouri.

JOHN P. SHELLY, President. JOSEPH M. McCORMACK, Secretary.

| | |
|---|---|
| Balance from previous year | $47,285 41 |

INCOME.

| | |
|---|---|
| All other assessments or premiums | $42,004 52 |
| Dues and per capita tax | 3,952 90 |
| Net amount received from members | $45,957 42 |
| Gross interest on bonds and dividends on stocks | 1,805 50 |
| Gross interest on deposits in trust companies and banks | 160 88 |
| Sale of lodge supplies | 23 40 |
| Benefit certificates | 18 00 |
| Official publication | 330 53 |
| Initiation fees | 3 00 |
| Sundries | 126 00 |
| Total income | $48,424 73 |
| Sum | $95,710 14 |

## DISBURSEMENTS.

| | |
|---|---|
| Death claims | $3,375 00 |
| Salaries of officers and trustees | 2,500 00 |
| Salaries and other compensation of committees | 70 00 |
| Traveling and other expenses of officers, trustees and committees | 226 64 |
| Insurance department fees | 30 00 |
| Rent | 480 00 |
| Advertising, printing and stationery | 92 80 |
| Postage, express, telegraph and telephone | 597 70 |
| Lodge supplies | 310 00 |
| Official publication | 1,085 85 |
| Borrowed money repaid (gross) | 3,000 00 |
| Interest on borrowed money | 254 74 |
| All other disbursements, viz— | |
| Actuary | 75 00 |
| Examination of books | 48 00 |
| Premium on bonds | 172 00 |
| Uniform rank | 58 00 |
| Sundries | 399 55 |
| Total disbursements | $43,150 28 |
| Balance | $52,559 86 |

## LEDGER ASSETS.

| | |
|---|---|
| Book value of bonds and stocks | $44,600 00 |
| Deposits in trust companies and banks on interest | 7,959 86 |
| Total ledger assets | $52,559 86 |

### NON-LEDGER ASSETS.

| | |
|---|---|
| Interest and rents due and accrued | 669 19 |
| Assessments actually collected by subordinate lodges not yet turned over to supreme lodge | 7,000 00 |
| Gross assets | $60,229 05 |

### DEDUCT ASSETS NOT ADMITTED.

| | |
|---|---|
| Book value of bonds and stocks over market value | 2,431 00 |
| Total admitted assets | $57,798 05 |

## LIABILITIES.

| | |
|---|---|
| Death claims reported during the year but not yet adjusted | $1,000 00 |
| Borrowed money | 2,000 00 |
| Total | $3,000 00 |

## EXHIBIT OF CERTIFICATES.

| | Total business of the year. | | Business in Illinois during year. | |
|---|---|---|---|---|
| | Number. | Amount. | Number. | Amount. |
| Benefit certificates in force December 31, 1920, as per last statement | 1,430 | $1,344,050 00 | 22 | $31,350 00 |
| Benefit certificates written and renewed during the year | 8 | 3,000 00 | | |
| Totals | 1,438 | $1,347,050 00 | | |
| Deduct terminated, decreased or transferred during the year | 121 | 75,400 00 | | |
| Total benefit certificates in force December 31, 1921 | 1,317 | $1,271,650 00 | | |

Received during the year from members in Illinois: Mortuary, $855.32; expense, $63.12; total — $918 44

## EXHIBIT OF DEATH CLAIMS.

| | Total claims—all in Illinois. Number. | Amount. |
|---|---|---|
| Claims unpaid December 31, 1920, as per last statement | 4 | $ 4,500 00 |
| Claims reported during the year and interest addition | 21 | 30,250 00 |
| Totals | 25 | $34,750 00 |
| Claims paid during the year | 24 | 33,750 00 |
| Claims unpaid December 31, 1921 | 1 | $1,000 00 |

## KNIGHTS OF COLUMBUS.

Located at No. 956 Chapel Street, New Haven, Connecticut.

JAMES A. FLAHERTY, President. WM. J. McGINLEY, Secretary.

| | |
|---|---|
| Balance from previous year | $11,398,892 08 |

### INCOME.

| | |
|---|---|
| All other assessments or premiums | $2,804 967 81 |
| Dues and per capita tax | 991,389 29 |
| Other payments by members, viz: Interest on account credit liens, $956.98; final withdrawal card fees, $2,917.06 | 3,874 04 |
| Net amount received from members | $3,800,231 14 |
| Gross interest on mortgage loans | 26,371 38 |
| Gross interest on bonds | 473,397 15 |
| Gross interest on deposits in trust companies and banks | 14,168 48 |
| Gross interest from all other sources | 29 98 |
| Gross rents from association's property | 1,799 50 |
| Sale of lodge supplies | 59,357 84 |
| Gross increase in book value of ledger assets | 28,594 65 |
| Premium earned in Canada on U. S. of A. funds | 15 11 |
| Transferred from war camp fund | 65,596 40 |
| Total income | $4,469,561 63 |
| Sum | $15,868,453 71 |

### DISBURSEMENTS.

| | |
|---|---|
| Death claims | $1,217,933 41 |
| Salaries of officers | 39,500 00 |
| Other compensation of officers and trustees | 8,075 00 |
| Salaries and other compensation of committees | 2,834 96 |
| Salaries of office employees | 100,829 21 |
| Salaries paid to supreme medical examiners | 10,000 00 |
| Traveling and other expenses of officers, trustees and committees | 35,196 33 |
| Insurance department fees | 1,462 00 |
| Rent | 5,754 92 |
| Advertising, printing and stationery | 15,204 11 |
| Postage, express, telegraph and telephone | 14,807 86 |
| Lodge supplies | 50,298 87 |
| Official publication | 207,348 84 |
| Expenses of supreme lodge meeting | 180,667 72 |
| Legal expense in litigating claims | 399 67 |
| Other legal expenses | 10,313 26 |
| Furniture and fixtures | 1,257 67 |
| Taxes, repairs and other expenses on real estate | 2,792 14 |
| Gross decrease in book value of ledger assets | 3,996 15 |
| All other disbursements, viz:— | |
| Expenses supreme office, $1,335.54; organization and institution of new councils, $24,637.70; deputies traveling expenses, $59,890.86 | 85,864 10 |
| Deputies robes and degree sets, $4,788.84; bonding supreme and subordinate council officers, $2,639.30; actuaries fees and expenses, $3,324.60 | 10,752 74 |
| Supreme audit, $4,333.34; special lecturers compensation and expenses, $4,885.39; Pueblo, Colo., flood sufferers, $7,500.00 | 16,718 73 |
| Tulsa, Okla., riot sufferers, $346.38; general expense, $34,231.05 | 34,577 43 |
| Total disbursements | $2,056,585 12 |
| Balance | $13,811,868 59 |

### LEDGER ASSETS.

| | |
|---|---|
| Book value of real estate | $ 424,604 29 |
| Mortgage loans on real estate | 546,400 00 |
| Book value of bonds | 12,565,171 63 |
| Deposits in trust companies and banks not on interest | 2,308 93 |
| Deposits in trust companies and banks on interest | 265,383 74 |
| Revolving fund in hands of manager of official publication | 7,000 00 |
| Revolving fund in hands of special supreme agents | 1,000 00 |
| Total ledger assets | $13,811,868 59 |

#### NON-LEDGER ASSETS.

| | |
|---|---|
| Interest and rents due and accrued | $176,385 81 |
| Assessments actually collected by subordinate lodges not yet turned over to supreme lodge (ledger) | 2,212 51 |

## LEDGER ASSETS—Concluded.

| | | |
|---|---|---|
| All other assets, viz— | | |
| Assessment credit liens (ledger) | $26,984 64 | |
| Due from subordinate councils for interest on assessment credit liens (ledger) | 541 70 | |
| Due from subordinate councils for per capita tax (ledger) | 24,118 81 | |
| Due from subordinate councils for supplies (ledger) | 9,379 03 | |
| Due from subordinate councils for F. W. card fees (ledger) | 408 39 | |
| Due from advertisers in official publication (ledger) | 19,310 52 | |
| | | 80,743 09 |
| Gross assets | | $14,071,210 00 |

### DEDUCT ASSETS NOT ADMITTED.

| | | |
|---|---|---|
| Bills receivable | $53,216 75 | |
| Overdue and accrued interest on bonds in default | 14,333 33 | |
| Book value of bonds not amortized over market value (Chicago & Eastern Ill. R. R.) | 346 43 | |
| | | 67,896 51 |
| Total admitted assets | | $14,003,313 49 |

## LIABILITIES.

| | | |
|---|---|---|
| Death claims due and unpaid | $ 47,771 86 | |
| Death claims resisted | 4,000 00 | |
| Death claims reported during the year but not yet adjusted | 130,501 00 | |
| Death claims incurred in 1921, not reported until 1922 | 22,000 00 | |
| Total unpaid claims | | $204,272 86 |
| Salaries, rents, expenses, commissions, etc., due or accrued | | 25,000 00 |
| Total | | $229,272 86 |

## EXHIBIT OF CERTIFICATES.

| | Total business of the year. | | Business in Illinois during year. | |
|---|---|---|---|---|
| | Number. | Amount. | Number. | Amount. |
| Benefit certificates in force December 31, 1920, as per last statement | 202,359 | $217,224,510 33 | 32,251 | $33,993,521 00 |
| Benefit certificates written and renewed during the year | 28,877 | 32,118,000 00 | 5,124 | 5,473,000 00 |
| Benefit certificates increased during the year (reinstatements) | 131 | 140,000 00 | | |
| Totals | 231,367 | $249,482,510 33 | 37,375 | $39,466,521 00 |
| Deduct terminated, decreased or transferred during the year | 11,864 | 12,868,648 00 | | |
| Deduct terminated or decreased during the year | | | 1,450 | 1,597,200 00 |
| Total benefit certificates in force December 31, 1921 | 219,503 | $236,613,862 33 | 35,925 | $37,869,321 00 |

Received during the year from members in Illinois: Mortuary, $400,822.48; expense, $99,422.26; total ..... $500,244 74

## EXHIBIT OF DEATH CLAIMS.

| | Total claims. | | Illinois claims. | |
|---|---|---|---|---|
| | Number. | Amount. | Number. | Amount. |
| Claims unpaid December 31, 1920, as per last statement | 168 | $ 171,762 86 | 27 | $ 28,000 00 |
| Claims reported during the year and interest addition | 1,137 | 1,230,423 03 | 140 | 155,065 50 |
| Totals | 1,305 | $1,402,185 89 | 167 | $183,065 50 |
| Claims paid during the year | 1,133 | 1,217,933 41 | 148 | 161,852 50 |
| Balance | 172 | $184,252 48 | 19 | $21,213 00 |
| Saved by compromising or scaling down claims during the year | | 1,084 39 | | |
| Liens and interest deducted | | 895 23 | | |
| Deducted account liens and interest | | | | 213 00 |
| Claims unpaid December 31, 1921 | 172 | $182,272 86 | 19 | $21,000 00 |

## KNIGHTS OF PYTHIAS, SUPREME LODGE.

Located at 900 Pythian Building, Indianapolis, Indiana.

HARRY WADE, President. W. O. POWERS, Secretary.

| | |
|---|---|
| Balance from previous year | $12,182,338 48 |

### INCOME.

| | |
|---|---|
| Membership fees actually received | $ 13,506 50 |
| All other assessments or premiums | 2,849,396 06 |
| Total received from members | $2,862,902 56 |
| Deduct payments returned to applicants and members | 16,514 08 |
| Net amount received from members | $2,856,388 48 |
| Gross interest on mortgage loans | 6,999 96 |
| Gross interest on collateral loans | 16,748 17 |
| Gross interest on bonds and dividends on stocks | 623,578 34 |
| Gross interest on deposits in trust companies and banks | 2,420 58 |
| Gross profit on sale or maturity of ledger assets | 9,615 25 |
| Gross increase in book value of ledger assets | 6,928 07 |
| Miscellaneous fees | 82 32 |
| Total income | $3,522,761 17 |
| Sum | $15,705,099 65 |

### DISBURSEMENTS.

| | |
|---|---|
| Death claims | $1,774,915 98 |
| Commissions and fees paid to deputies and organizers | 186,887 46 |
| Salaries of deputies and organizers | 5,253 67 |
| Premiums on fidelity | 2,576 84 |
| Salaries of officers and trustees | 15,666 80 |
| Mileage and per diem | 9,516 30 |
| Actuarial expense | 10,077 66 |
| Salaries of office employees | 62,382 82 |
| Salaries and fees paid to supreme medical examiners | 4,933 60 |
| Salaries and fees paid to subordinate medical examiners | 19,681 50 |
| Traveling and other expenses of officers, trustees and committees | 10,078 79 |
| For collection and remittance of assessments and dues | 132,090 29 |
| Insurance department fees | 1,637 07 |
| Rent | 7,143 60 |
| Advertising, printing and stationery | 19,954 00 |
| Postage, express, telegraph and telephone | 10,431 70 |
| Office supplies | 988 76 |
| Official publication | 52,549 61 |
| Expenses of supreme lodge meeting | 572 27 |
| Legal expense in litigating claims | 3,330 00 |
| Miscellaneous expenses | 915 26 |
| Furniture and fixtures | 1,769 07 |
| Audit expense | 2,616 83 |
| Gross loss on sale or maturity of ledger assets | 591 35 |
| Gross decrease in book value of ledger assets | 13,273 08 |
| Discount on advance payments | 15,139 76 |
| Rent on tabulating machines | 811 62 |
| Investment expense | 597 78 |
| Office improvement | 350 88 |
| Insurance and exchange | 128 39 |
| Total disbursements | $2,366,907 80 |
| Balance | $13,338,191 85 |

### LEDGER ASSETS.

| | |
|---|---|
| Mortgage loans on real estate | $ 200,000 00 |
| Book value of bonds and stocks | 12,412,638 76 |
| Cash in association's office | 1,200 00 |
| Deposits in trust companies and banks on interest | 76,738 11 |
| Organizers' balances | 567 92 |
| Certificate loans, 4th and 5th classes | 474,845 65 |
| Certificate liens | 172,201 41 |
| Total ledger assets | $13,338,191 85 |

#### NON-LEDGER ASSETS.

| | |
|---|---|
| Interest and rents due and accrued | $269,268 27 |
| Market value of bonds and stocks over book value | 239,250 58 |
| Assessments actually collected by subordinate lodges not yet turned over to supreme lodge | 57,068 04 |
| Postage | 287 50 |
| Gross assets | $13,904,066 24 |

LEDGER ASSETS—Concluded.

DEDUCT ASSETS NOT ADMITTED.

| | | |
|---|---|---|
| Balance due from organizers not secured by bonds | $ 567 92 | |
| Overdue and accrued interest on bonds in default | 7,973 31 | $8,541 23 |
| Total admitted assets | | $13,895,525 01 |

LIABILITIES.

| | | |
|---|---|---|
| Death claims resisted | $ 1,000 00 | |
| Death claims reported during the year but not yet adjusted | 116,534 00 | |
| Death claims incurred in 1921, not reported until 1922 | 7,508 84 | |
| Present value of deferred death claims payable in installments | 57,065 21 | |
| Total unpaid claims | | $ 182,108 05 |
| Salaries, rents, expenses, commissions, etc., due or accrued | | 34,549 34 |
| Advance assessments | | 119,131 46 |
| All other liabilities, viz— | | |
| Unpaid bills, $328.03; medical examiners fees, $756.00 | $ 1,084 03 | |
| Reserve on certificates transferred from plan D to A | 3,345 39 | |
| Reserve on certificates, 4th class | 419,644 00 | |
| Reserve on 5th class certificates in plans A, B, D, E, G and H | 11,671,166 89 | |
| Disability fund | 5,622 94 | 12,100,863 25 |
| Total | | $12,436,652 10 |

EXHIBIT OF CERTIFICATES.

| | Total business of the year. Number. | Amount. | Business in Illinois during year. Number. | Amount. |
|---|---|---|---|---|
| Benefit certificates in force December 31, 1920, as per last statement | 81,119 | $108,865,799 00 | 5,508 | $6,319,726 00 |
| Benefit certificates written and renewed during the year | 9,127 | 13,336,500 00 | 921 | 1,115,750 00 |
| Benefit certificates received by transfer during the year | | | 16 | 19,500 00 |
| Benefit certificates increased during the year | 1,665 | 2,351,562 00 | | |
| Totals | 91,911 | $124,553,861 00 | 6,445 | $7,454,976 00 |
| Deduct terminated, decreased or transferred during the year | 8,187 | 12,404,918 00 | | |
| Deduct terminated or decreased during the year | | | 527 | 636,479 00 |
| Total benefit certificates in force December 31, 1921 | 83,724 | $112,148,943 00 | 5,918 | $6,818,497 00 |

Received during the year from members in Illinois: Mortuary, $142,627.60; disability, $413.81; expense, $24,479.72; total — $167,521 13

EXHIBIT OF DEATH CLAIMS.

| | Total claims. Number. | Amount. | Illinois claims. Number. | Amount. |
|---|---|---|---|---|
| Claims unpaid December 31, 1920, as per last statement | 67 | $ 148,546 51 | 1 | $ 245 00 |
| Claims reported during the year and interest addition | 1,164 | 1,811,836 40 | 82 | 100,174 00 |
| Totals | 1,231 | $1,960,382 91 | 83 | $100,419 00 |
| Claims paid during the year | 1,142 | 1,774,322 93 | 77 | 93,919 00 |
| Balance | 89 | $186,059 98 | 6 | $6,500 00 |
| Saved by compromising | | 11,460 77 | | |
| Claims unpaid December 31, 1921 | 89 | $174,599 21 | 6 | $6,500 00 |

## LADIES' CATHOLIC BENEVOLENT ASSOCIATION.

Located at No. 443 West Eleventh Street, Erie, Pennsylvania.

MISS KATE MAHONEY, Supreme President. MRS. J. A. ROYER, Supreme Recorder.

Balance from previous year — $5,341,951 52

## INCOME.

| | | |
|---|---|---|
| Membership fees actually received | | $ 2,370 00 |
| Assessments or premiums during first 12 months of membership of which all or an extra percentage is used for expenses | | 1,103,645 16 |
| All other assessments or premiums | | 1,134,227 17 |
| Net amount received from members | | $2,307,552 33 |
| Gross interest on mortgage loans | | 51,837 32 |
| Gross interest on bonds and dividends on stocks | | 168,945 83 |
| Gross interest on deposits in trust companies and banks | | 33,800 98 |
| Sale of lodge supplies | | 9,718 62 |
| Official publication | | 23,780 20 |
| Total income | | $2,595,635 28 |
| Sum | | $7,937,586 80 |

## DISBURSEMENTS.

| | | |
|---|---|---|
| Death claims | | $1,395,683 96 |
| Commissions and fees paid to deputies and organizers | | 23,133 26 |
| Salaries of officers and trustees | | 12,700 00 |
| Salaries of office employees | | 43,237 81 |
| Traveling and other expenses of officers, trustees and committees | | 10,872 16 |
| Insurance department fees | | 2,778 46 |
| Rent | | 1,470 00 |
| Advertising, printing and stationery | | 18,486 55 |
| Postage, express, telegraph and telephone | | 10,190 96 |
| Lodge supplies | | 2,181 51 |
| Official publication | | 20,727 52 |
| Expenses of supreme lodge meeting | | 83,602 78 |
| Other legal expenses | | 948 09 |
| Premium on bonds purchased for other funds | | 1,732 22 |
| Insurance on deposits | | 25 50 |
| Gross loss on sale or maturity of ledger assets | | 1,242 08 |
| State examiners | | 102 32 |
| Settlement claims | | 2,628 00 |
| Exchange on Canadian checks | | 1,035 05 |
| All other disbursements, viz— | | |
| Vault rental | | 260 35 |
| Actuary | | 483 32 |
| National Fraternal Congress | | 520 94 |
| Bonding supreme officers | | 1,915 69 |
| Total disbursements | | $1,635,958 53 |
| Balance | | $6,301,628 27 |

## LEDGER ASSETS.

| | | |
|---|---|---|
| Mortgage loans on real estate | | $1,005,705 00 |
| Book value of bonds and stocks | | 4,077,190 02 |
| Deposits in trust companies and banks not on interest | | 20,943 89 |
| Deposits in trust companies and banks on interest | | 1,197,789 36 |
| Total ledger assets | | $6,301,628 27 |

### NON-LEDGER ASSETS.

| | | |
|---|---|---|
| Interest and rents due and accrued | | 70,333 13 |
| Market value of real estate over book value | | 5,730 98 |
| Market value of bonds and stocks over book value | | 202,590 52 |
| All other assets, viz— | | |
| Per capita tax | $63,500 00 | |
| Furniture and fixtures | 10,500 00 | |
| | | 74,000 00 |
| Gross assets | | $6,654,282 90 |

### DEDUCT ASSETS NOT ADMITTED.

| | | |
|---|---|---|
| Furniture and fixtures | | 10,500 00 |
| Total admitted assets | | $6,643,782 90 |

## LIABILITIES.

| | | |
|---|---|---|
| Death claims due and unpaid | $15,501 90 | |
| Death claims reported during the year but not yet adjusted | 88,550 00 | |
| Death claims incurred in 1921, not reported until 1922 | 48,500 00 | |
| Total death claims | | $152,551 90 |
| Salaries, rents, expenses, commissions, etc., due or accrued | | 4,748 54 |
| Total | | $157,300 44 |

EXHIBIT OF CERTIFICATES.

| | Total business of the year. Number. | Amount. | Business in Illinois during year. Number. | Amount. |
|---|---|---|---|---|
| Benefit certificates in force December 31, 1920, as per last statement | 121,023 | $97,811,500 00 | 10,683 | $9,151,750 00 |
| Benefit certificates written and renewed during the year | 2,542 | 1,609,500 00 | 277 | 187,750 00 |
| Benefit certificates increased during the year | | 1,274,250 00 | | 59,500 00 |
| Total | 123,565 | $100,695,250 00 | 10,960 | $9,399,000 00 |
| Deduct terminated, decreased or transferred during the year | 4,389 | 6,332,347 50 | | |
| Deduct terminated or decreased during the year | | | 254 | 353,317 50 |
| Total benefit certificates in force December 31, 1921 | 119,176 | $94,362,902 50 | 10,706 | $9,045,682 50 |

Received during the year from members in Illinois: Mortuary, $82,468.50; reserve, $4,340.44; expense, $199.668.51; total $286,477 45

EXHIBIT OF DEATH CLAIMS.

| | Total claims. Number. | Amount. | Illinois business. Number. | Amount. |
|---|---|---|---|---|
| Claims unpaid December 31, 1920, as per last statement | 208 | $ 159,285 73 | 14 | $10,800 00 |
| Claims reported during the year and interest addition | 1,551 | 1,342,500 00 | 109 | 97,750 00 |
| Total | 1,759 | $1,501,785 73 | 123 | $108,550 00 |
| Claims paid during the year | 1,612 | 1,395,683 96 | 114 | 102,150 00 |
| Balance | 147 | $106,101 77 | 9 | $6,400 00 |
| Saved by compromising or scaling down claims during the year | | 2,049 87 | | |
| Claims unpaid December 31, 1921 | 147 | $104,051 90 | 9 | $6,400 00 |

## LADIES OF THE MACCABEES.

Located at Pine Grove Avenue and Stanton Street, Port Huron, Michigan.

FRANCES E. BURNS, President. EMMA E. BOWER, Secretary.

| | |
|---|---|
| Balance from previous year | $1,727,389 32 |

INCOME.

| | |
|---|---|
| Membership fees actually received | $ 1,456 25 |
| Assessments or premiums during first 12 months of membership of which all or an extra percentage is used for expense | 38,705 67 |
| All other assessments or premiums | 526,009 37 |
| Dues and per capita tax | 100,161 01 |
| Medical examiners' fees actually received | 1 50 |
| Other payments by members, viz: Certificate fees and card fees | 599 50 |
| Total received from members | $666,933 30 |
| Deduct payments returned to applicants and members | 2,378 29 |
| Net amount received from members | $664,555 01 |
| Gross interest on bonds and dividends on stocks | 86,801 16 |
| Gross interest on deposits in trust companies and banks | 3,913 05 |
| Gross rents from association's property | 1,415 19 |
| Sale of lodge supplies | 3,070 82 |
| Gross increase in book value of ledger assets | 2,145 32 |
| Advertising | 121 68 |
| Returns on remittances | 1 63 |
| Contribution of bed fund | 180 65 |
| Susie S. Graves memorial | 218 96 |
| Total income | $762,423 47 |
| Sum | $2,489,812 79 |

## DISBURSEMENTS.

|  |  |
|---|---|
| Death claims | $336,563 45 |
| Permanent disability claims | 4,167 29 |
| Old age benefits | 18,552 32 |
| Maternity | 8,400 00 |
| Hospital and relief | 7,893 31 |
| Total benefits paid | $375,576 37 |
| Commissions and fees paid to deputies and organizers | 6,585 00 |
| Salaries of deputies and organizers | 57,514 61 |
| Salaries of officers and trustees | 14,800 00 |
| Salaries and other compensation of committees | 774 16 |
| Salaries of office employees | 27,594 70 |
| Salaries and fees paid to supreme medical examiners | 4,020 75 |
| Salaries and fees paid to subordinate medical examiners | 1 06 |
| Traveling and other expenses of officers, trustees and committees | 3,519 64 |
| Insurance department fees | 412 70 |
| Rent | 3,350 00 |
| Advertising, printing and stationery | 2,864 02 |
| Postage, express, telegraph and telephone | 2,514 18 |
| Lodge supplies | 1,153 56 |
| Official publication | 974 03 |
| Expenses of supreme lodge meeting and deputy school | 136 06 |
| Legal expense in litigating claims | 16 32 |
| Other legal expenses | 2,437 39 |
| Furniture and fixtures | 1,204 41 |
| Taxes, repairs and other expenses on real estate | 2,842 14 |
| Gross decrease in book value of ledger assets | 2,410 77 |
| All other disbursements, viz— | |
| Office supplies, $409.08; office expense, $1,233.37 | 1,642 45 |
| Schedule bond, $122.76; fraternal association dues, $382.00 | 504 76 |
| Public initiation, $466.60; books and periodicals, $93.22 | 559 82 |
| Miscellaneous | 1,004 55 |
| Total disbursements | $514,413 45 |
| Balance | $1,975,399 34 |

## LEDGER ASSETS.

|  |  |
|---|---|
| Book value of real estate | $ 60,000 00 |
| Book value of bonds | 1,815,285 52 |
| Deposits in trust companies and banks on interest | 100,113 82 |
| Total ledger assets | $1,975,399 34 |

### NON-LEDGER ASSETS.

|  | |  |
|---|---|---|
| Interest and rents due and accrued | | 21,703 69 |
| Market value of bonds and stocks over book value | | 21,496 46 |
| Assessments actually collected by subordinate lodges not yet turned over to supreme lodge | | 42,632 07 |
| All other assets, viz— | | |
| Great commander's special fund | $ 366 01 | |
| Great record keeper's special fund | 1,239 16 | |
| Tax actually collected by subordinate lodge not turned over to supreme lodge | 8,009 86 | |
| Membership fee actually collected by subordinate lodge not turned over to supreme lodge | 116 00 | |
| | | 9,731 03 |
| Gross assets | | $2,070,962 59 |

## LIABILITIES.

|  | |  |
|---|---|---|
| Death claims due and unpaid | $ 1,063 89 | |
| Death claims reported during the year but not yet adjusted | 15,211 08 | |
| Total death claims | | $16,274 97 |
| Permanent disability claims reported during the year but not yet adjusted | $ 50 00 | |
| Present value of disability claims payable in installments | 13,370 07 | |
| Total permanent disability claims | | 13,420 07 |
| Maternity claims reported during the year but not yet adjusted | | 100 00 |
| Old age and other benefits due and unpaid | | 52,289 27 |
| Total unpaid claims | | $82,084 31 |
| Salaries, rents, expenses, commissions, etc., due or accrued | | 5,684 35 |
| Advance assessments, $8,080.36; advance tax, $1,817.05 | | 9,897 41 |
| Total | | $97,666 07 |

## EXHIBIT OF CERTIFICATES.

| | Total business of the year. | | Business in Illinois during year. | |
|---|---|---|---|---|
| | Number. | Amount. | Number. | Amount. |
| Benefit certificates in force December 31, 1920, as per last statement | 46,300 | $34,042,750 00 | 2,266 | $1,622,750 00 |
| Benefit certificates written and renewed during the year | 3,198 | 2,277,250 00 | 247 | 180,500 00 |
| Benefit certificates received by transfer during the year | | | 29 | 22,000 00 |
| Benefit certificates increased during the year | | 31,500 00 | | 500 00 |
| Total | 49,498 | $36,351,500 00 | 2,542 | $1,825,750 00 |
| Deduct terminated, decreased or transferred during the year | 3,723 | 2,590,750 00 | | |
| Deduct terminated or decreased during the year | | | 260 | 184,750 00 |
| Total benefit certificates in force December 31, 1921 | 45,775 | $33,760,750 00 | 2,282 | $1,641,000 00 |

Received during the year from members in Illinois: Mortuary, $22,936.34; relief, $297.57; general, $6,367.29; total $29,601 20

## EXHIBIT OF DEATH CLAIMS.

| | Total claims. | | Illinois claims. | |
|---|---|---|---|---|
| | Number. | Amount. | Number. | Amount. |
| Claims unpaid December 31, 1920, as per last statement | 18 | $ 13,377 91 | | |
| Claims reported during the year and interest addition | 464 | 357,250 00 | 19 | $12,250 00 |
| Total | 482 | $370,627 91 | 19 | $12,250 00 |
| Claims paid during the year | 460 | 336,563 45 | 17 | 10,394 87 |
| Balance | 22 | $34,064 46 | 2 | $1,855 13 |
| Liens | | 13,583 96 | | 320 70 |
| Saved by compromising or scaling down claims during the year | | 103 59 | | 34 43 |
| Disability already paid | | 2,665 10 | | |
| Claims rejected during the year | | 1,436 84 | | |
| Claims unpaid December 31, 1921 | 22 | $16,274 97 | 2 | $1,500 00 |

## EXHIBIT OF PERMANENT DISABILITY CLAIMS.

| | Total claims. | |
|---|---|---|
| | Number. | Amount. |
| Claims unpaid December 31, 1920, as per last statement | 50 | $15,348 87 |
| Claims reported during the year and interest addition | 7 | 4,546 51 |
| Total | 57 | $19,895 38 |
| Claims paid during the year | 7 | 4,167 29 |
| Balance | 50 | $15,728 09 |
| Transferred to death and old age | 6 | 1,918 99 |
| Claims rejected during the year | 1 | 389 03 |
| Claims unpaid December 31, 1921 | 43 | $13,420 07 |

## EXHIBIT OF MATERNITY CLAIMS.

| | Total claims. | | Illinois claims. | |
|---|---|---|---|---|
| | Number. | Amount. | Number. | Amount. |
| Claims reported during the year | 165 | $8,500 00 | 7 | $350 00 |
| Claims paid during the year | 163 | 8,400 00 | 7 | 350 00 |
| Claims unpaid December 31, 1921 | 2 | $100 00 | | |

## EXHIBIT OF OLD AGE AND OTHER CLAIMS.

| | Total claims. | | Illinois claims. | |
|---|---|---|---|---|
| | Number. | Amount. | Number. | Amount. |
| Claims unpaid December 31, 1920, as per last statement | 136 | $47,882 37 | 2 | $381 75 |
| Claims reported during the year and interest addition | 42 | 23,517 89 | | 95 31 |
| Total | 178 | $71,400 26 | 2 | $477 06 |
| Claims paid during the year | 41 | 18,552 32 | 1 | 200 00 |
| Balance | 137 | $52,847 94 | 1 | $277 06 |
| Transferred to death | 2 | 558 67 | | |
| Claims unpaid December 31, 1921 | 135 | $52,289 27 | 1 | $277 06 |

## LITHUANIAN ALLIANCE OF AMERICA.

Located at Coal Exchange Building, Wilkes Barre, Pennsylvania.

ST. GEGUZIS, President. P. JURGELIUTE, Secretary.

| | | |
|---|---|---|
| Balance from previous year | | $300,337 03 |
| **INCOME.** | | |
| Membership fees actually received | | $ 4,536 07 |
| Widows and orphans | | 1,233 70 |
| All other assessments or premiums | | 124,954 46 |
| Dues and per capita tax | | 13,113 02 |
| Philanthropy | | 1,450 57 |
| Official publication | | 13,113 06 |
| Total received from members | | $158,400 88 |
| Deduct payments returned to applicants and members | | 172 19 |
| Net amount received from members | | $158,228 69 |
| Gross interest on mortgage loans | | 2,680 00 |
| Gross interest on bonds | | 6,389 47 |
| Gross interest on deposits in trust companies and banks | | 2,132 10 |
| Gross rents from association's property, including $1,680.00 for association's occupancy of its own buildings | | 2,680 00 |
| Sale of lodge supplies—books | | 46 15 |
| From all other sources, viz: Advertisements, subscriptions, job printing, literature, badges, home for aged, sub-lodges bonds, sundries | | 7,592 28 |
| Total income | | $179,748 69 |
| Sum | | $480,085 72 |
| **DISBURSEMENTS.** | | |
| Death claims | | $36,075 00 |
| Sick and accident claims | | 46,967 45 |
| Child burial | | 150 00 |
| Total benefits paid | | $83,192 45 |
| Commissions and fees paid to deputies and organizers | | 1,221 50 |
| Salaries of officers and trustees | | 3,790 00 |
| Salaries of office employees | | 10,466 03 |
| Salaries and fees paid to supreme medical examiners | | 436 00 |
| Salaries and fees paid to subordinate medical examiners | | 13 00 |
| Traveling and other expenses of officers, trustees and committees | | 828 90 |
| Insurance department fees | | 473 31 |
| Rent | | 1,680 00 |
| Advertising, printing and stationery | | 861 47 |
| Postage, express, telegraph and telephone | | 963 06 |
| Salaries, printing est. employees | | 5,059 00 |
| Official publication | | 5,653 02 |
| Job printing | | 826 15 |
| Furniture and fixtures | | 1,058 85 |
| Taxes, repairs and other expenses on real estate | | 2,566 37 |
| All other disbursements, viz: Widows and orphans, home for aged, literature, actuary fees and sundries | | 3,741 11 |
| Total disbursements | | $122,830 22 |
| Balance | | $357,255 50 |
| **LEDGER ASSETS.** | | |
| Book value of real estate | | $ 30,000 00 |
| Mortgage loans on real estate | | 70,000 00 |
| Book value of bonds | | 174,736 50 |
| Cash in association's office | | 500 00 |
| Deposits in trust companies and banks not on interest | | 17,791 06 |
| Deposits in trust companies and banks on interest | | 62,777 94 |
| Loan to students | | 1,450 00 |
| Total ledger assets | | $357,255 50 |
| **NON-LEDGER ASSETS.** | | |
| Market value of bonds and stocks over book value | | 1,763 50 |
| All other assets, viz— | | |
| Office inventory | $2,432 64 | |
| Printing plant | 9,884 30 | |
| Literature | 2,218 76 | |
| Lodge supplies | 309 90 | |
| | | 14,845 60 |
| Gross assets | | $373,864 60 |

LEDGER ASSETS—Concluded.

DEDUCT ASSETS NOT ADMITTED.

| | |
|---|---|
| Book value of bonds and stocks over market value | $ 1,763 50 |
| Office inventory, printing plant, literature and lodge supplies | 14,845 60 |
| Total admitted assets | $357,255 50 |

LIABILITIES.

| | | |
|---|---|---|
| Death claims due and unpaid | $10,577 50 | |
| Death claims reported during the year but not yet adjusted | 2,500 00 | |
| Total death claims | | $13,077 50 |

EXHIBIT OF CERTIFICATES.

| | Total business of the year. Number. | Amount. | Business in Illinois during year. Number. | Amount. |
|---|---|---|---|---|
| Benefit certificates in force December 31, 1920, as per last statement | 12,287 | $4,101,880 00 | 3,114 | $1,104,050 00 |
| Benefit certificates written and renewed during the year | 1,598 | 705,200 00 | 620 | 255,800 00 |
| Benefit certificates received by transfer during the year | | | 195 | 58,900 00 |
| Benefit certificates increased during the year | | 14,600 00 | | 4,550 00 |
| Total | 13,885 | $4,821,680 00 | 3,929 | $1,423,300 00 |
| Deduct terminated, decreased or transferred during the year | 1,299 | 389,350 00 | | |
| Deduct terminated or decreased during the year | | | 475 | 166,000 00 |
| Total benefit certificates in force December 31, 1921 | 12,586 | $4,432,330 00 | 3,454 | $1,257,300 00 |

| | |
|---|---|
| Received during the year from members in Illinois: Mortuary, $19,944.17; disability, $15,355.38; expense, $7,476.58; total | $42,776 13 |

EXHIBIT OF DEATH CLAIMS.

| | Total claims. Number. | Amount. | Illinois claims. Number. | Amount. |
|---|---|---|---|---|
| Claims unpaid December 31, 1920, as per last statement | 64 | $12,652 00 | 18 | $ 4,125 00 |
| Claims reported during the year and interest addition | 117 | 43,550 00 | 31 | 11,350 00 |
| Total | 181 | $56,202 00 | 49 | $15,475 00 |
| Claims paid during the year | 114 | 36,075 00 | 33 | 9,075 00 |
| Balance | 67 | $20,127 00 | 16 | $6,400 00 |
| Saved by compromising or scaling down claims during the year | | 7,049 50 | | 2,950 00 |
| Claims unpaid December 31, 1921 | 67 | $13,077 50 | 16 | $3,450 00 |

EXHIBIT OF SICK AND ACCIDENT CLAIMS.

| | Total claims. Number. | Amount. | Illinois claims. Number. | Amount. |
|---|---|---|---|---|
| Claims reported during the year | 1,831 | $46,967 45 | 374 | $17,197 00 |
| Claims paid during the year | 1,831 | 46,967 45 | 374 | 17,197 00 |

---

## LITHUANIAN ROMAN CATHOLIC ALLIANCE OF AMERICA.

Located at No. 222 South Ninth Street, Brooklyn, New York.

J. S. VASILISUSKAS, President. G. TUMASONES, Secretary.

| | |
|---|---|
| Balance from previous year | $227,753 13 |

INCOME.

| | |
|---|---|
| Membership fees actually received | $ 1,787 50 |
| All other assessments or premiums | 156,311 36 |
| Dues and per capita tax | 20,273 14 |
| Extra "Flu" 1918 assessment | 1,310 26 |
| Total received from members | $179,682 26 |
| Deduct payments returned to applicants and members | 163 84 |
| Net amount received from members | $179,518 42 |

INCOME—Concluded.

| | |
|---|---|
| Gross interest on mortgage loans | $3,080 00 |
| Gross interest on bonds and dividends on stocks | 2,952 09 |
| Gross interest on deposits in trust companies and banks | 1,470 37 |
| Gross interest from all other sources | 220 85 |
| Gross rents from association's property, including $980.00 for association's occupancy of its own buildings | 2,835 10 |
| Total income | $190,076 83 |
| Sum | $417,829 96 |

## DISBURSEMENTS.

| | |
|---|---|
| Death claims | $48,566 66 |
| Minor heir claims | 400 00 |
| Sick and accident claims | 59,948 25 |
| Donation to orphans | 35 00 |
| Total benefits paid | $108,949 91 |
| Commissions and fees paid to deputies and organizers | 540 00 |
| Salaries of officeres and trustees | 3,950 00 |
| Salaries of office employees | 2,450 00 |
| Traveling and other expenses of officers, trustees and committees | 1,301 72 |
| Rent | 980 00 |
| Advertising, printing and stationery | 2,649 86 |
| Postage, express, telegraph and telephone | 632 99 |
| Official publication | 12,469 95 |
| Other legal expenses | 40 25 |
| Taxes, repairs and other expenses on real estate | 2,660 77 |
| Federation dues | 727 08 |
| Bonds for secretary and treasurer | 42 50 |
| Safe deposit vaults | 25 00 |
| Actuary's services | 1,101 52 |
| Office expenses | 1,260 63 |
| Total disbursements | $139,782 18 |
| Balance | $278,047 78 |

## LEDGER ASSETS.

| | |
|---|---|
| Book value of real estate | $43,500 00 |
| Mortgage loans on real estate | 80,000 00 |
| Loans secured by pledge of bonds, stocks or other collateral | 7,503 40 |
| Book value of bonds and stocks | 93,290 34 |
| Deposits in trust companies and banks not on interest | 16,962 08 |
| Deposits in trust companies and banks on interest | 36,791 96 |
| Total ledger assets | $278,047 78 |

### NON-LEDGER ASSETS.

| | | |
|---|---|---|
| Interest and rents due and accrued | | 4,897 38 |
| Market value of real estate over book value | | 1,500 00 |
| Assessments actually collected by subordinate lodges not yet turned over to supreme lodge | | 5,393 59 |
| All other assets, viz— | | |
| Office furniture | $1,975 00 | |
| Assessments due not collected | 4,324 71 | |
| | | 6,299 71 |
| Gross assets | | $296,138 46 |

### DEDUCT ASSETS NOT ADMITTED.

| | | |
|---|---|---|
| Other items, viz— | | |
| Office furniture | $1,975 00 | |
| Assessment dues not collected | 4,324 71 | |
| | | 6,299 71 |
| Total admitted assets | | $289,838 75 |

## LIABILITIES.

| | | |
|---|---|---|
| Death claims due and unpaid | $4,500 00 | |
| Death claims incurred in 1921, not reported until 1922 | 1,400 00 | |
| Total death claims | | $5,950 00 |

## EXHIBIT OF CERTIFICATES.

| | Total business of the year. | | Business in Illinois during year. | |
|---|---|---|---|---|
| | Number. | Amount. | Number. | Amount. |
| Benefit certificates in force December 31, 1920, as per last statement | 12,118 | $4,399,300 00 | 1,481 | $554,000 00 |
| Benefit certificates written and renewed during the year | 1,528 | 810,700 00 | 214 | 104,200 00 |
| Benefit certificates received by transfer during the year | | | 56 | 24,000 00 |
| Benefit certificates increased during the year | | 95,250 00 | | 10,450 00 |
| Total | 13,646 | $5,305,250 00 | 1,751 | $692,650 00 |
| Deduct terminated, decreased or transferred during the year | 1,206 | 416,500 00 | | |
| Deduct terminated or decreased during the year | | | 198 | 68,850 00 |
| Total benefit certificates in force December 31, 1921 | 12,440 | $4,888,750 00 | 1,553 | $623,800 00 |

Received during the year from members in Illinois: Mortuary, $11,900.82; minor heirs, $263.51; sick and accident, $9,417.00; expense, $2,912.36; total $24,493 69

## EXHIBIT OF DEATH CLAIMS.

| | Total claims. | | Illinois claims. | |
|---|---|---|---|---|
| | Number. | Amount. | Number. | Amount. |
| Claims unpaid December 31, 1920, as per last statement | 23 | $ 7,150 00 | 1 | $ 500 00 |
| Claims reported during the year and interest addition | 137 | 48,550 00 | 19 | 8,300 00 |
| Total | 160 | $55,700 00 | 20 | $8,800 00 |
| Claims paid during the year | 137 | 48,566 66 | 18 | 7,983 33 |
| Balance | 23 | $7,133 34 | 2 | $816 67 |
| Saved by compromising or scaling down claims during the year | | 683 34 | | 516 67 |
| Claims rejected during the year | 5 | 1,900 00 | 1 | 150 00 |
| Claims unpaid December 31, 1921 | 18 | $4,550 00 | 1 | $150 00 |

## EXHIBIT OF SICK AND ACCIDENT CLAIMS.

| | Total claims. | | Illinois claims. | |
|---|---|---|---|---|
| | Number. | Amount. | Number. | Amount. |
| Claims paid during the year | 1,018 | $59,948 25 | 43 | $9,135 50 |

---

# L' UNION ST. JEAN BAPTISTE D' AMERIQUE.

Located at No. 231 Main Street, Woonsocket, Rhode Island

HENRI T. LEDOUX, President. ELIE VEZINA, Secretary.

| | |
|---|---|
| Balance from previous year | $1,577,114 73 |

## INCOME.

| | |
|---|---|
| Assessments or premiums during first twelve months of membership of which all or an extra percentage is used for expenses | 19,431 20 |
| All other assessments or premiums | 420,674 34 |
| Medical examiners' fees actually received | 1,100 04 |
| Other payments by members, viz: Changes of certificates and transfers | 605 75 |
| Total received from members | $441,811 33 |
| Deduct payments returned to applicants and members | 55 46 |
| Net amount received from members | $441,755 87 |
| Gross interest on mortgage loans | 3,622 75 |
| Gross interest on bonds and dividends on stocks | 65,307 63 |
| Gross interest on deposits in trust companies and banks | 2,748 24 |
| Gross rents from association's property, including $2,050.00 for association's occupancy of its own buildings | 7,354 00 |
| Sale of lodge supplies | 2,290 90 |
| Borrowed money (gross) | 8,000 00 |
| Gross profit on sale or maturity of ledger assets | 169 60 |
| Gross increase in book value of ledger assets | 2,109 73 |
| Official publication | 86 55 |
| Gifts from members | 676 00 |
| Total income | $534,121 27 |
| Sum | $2,111,236 00 |

DISBURSEMENTS.

| | |
|---|---|
| Death claims | $133,304 48 |
| Sick and accident claims | 25,789 00 |
| Old age benefits | 12,262 86 |
| Death benefit paid twice through fraud | 1,000 00 |
| Total benefits paid | $172,356 34 |
| Commissions and fees paid to deputies and organizers | 835 31 |
| Salaries of deputies and organizers | 4,785 00 |
| Salaries of officers and trustees | 13,757 41 |
| Salaries and other compensation of committees | 270 00 |
| Salaries of office employees | 20,388 70 |
| Salaries and fees paid to supreme medical examiners | 1,431 75 |
| Salaries and fees paid to subordinate medical examiners | 28 25 |
| Traveling and other expenses of officers, trustees and committees | 7,696 54 |
| Insurance department fees | 190 00 |
| Rent | 2,050 00 |
| Advertising, printing and stationery | 3,003 83 |
| Postage, express, telegraph and telephone | 2,353 10 |
| Lodge supplies | 1,594 84 |
| Official publication | 10,603 48 |
| Expenses of supreme lodge meeting | 14,104 40 |
| Furniture and fixtures | 962 87 |
| Taxes, repairs and other expenses on real estate | 9,000 42 |
| Gross loss on sale or maturity of ledger assets | 150 00 |
| Scholarships | 4,083 45 |
| Audit of books of association | 350 00 |
| Borrowed money repaid (gross) | 5,000 00 |
| Major Mallet library | 27 30 |
| Interest on borrowed money | 113 17 |
| Insurance and other sundry expenses | 440 17 |
| Bonding of officers, employees and officers of lodges | 534 20 |
| Membership contests and other organization expenses | 7,522 62 |
| Valuation of insurance certificates | 160 00 |
| Total disbursements | $283,793 15 |
| Balance | $1,827,442 85 |

LEDGER ASSETS.

| | |
|---|---|
| Book value of real estate | $ 47,340 73 |
| Mortgage loans on real estate | 54,250 00 |
| Book value of bonds and stocks | 1,649,505 70 |
| Cash in association's office | 100 00 |
| Deposits in trust companies and banks on interest | 76,246 42 |
| Total ledger assets | $1,827,442 85 |

NON-LEDGER ASSETS.

| | | |
|---|---|---|
| Interest and rents due and accrued | | 24,008 43 |
| Assessments actually collected by subordinate lodges not yet turned over to supreme lodge | | 33,057 78 |
| All other assets, viz— | | |
| Office furniture and fixtures | $11,477 01 | |
| Lodge supplies | 4,376 24 | |
| Balance due from lodges for supplies and medical examiners' fees | 734 84 | |
| Major Mallet library | 2,471 21 | |
| | | 19,059 30 |
| Gross assets | | $1,903,568 36 |

DEDUCT ASSETS NOT ADMITTED.

| | | |
|---|---|---|
| Overdue and accrued interest on bonds in default | $ 4,893 33 | |
| Book value of real estate over market value | 2,500 00 | |
| Book value of bonds and stocks over amortized value | 24,995 76 | |
| Other items, viz— | | |
| Office furniture and fixtures | 11,477 01 | |
| Lodge supplies | 4,376 24 | |
| Balance due from lodges for supplies and medical examiners' fees | 734 84 | |
| Major Mallet library | 2,471 21 | |
| | | 51,448 39 |
| Total admitted assets | | $1,852,119 97 |

## LIABILITIES.

| | | |
|---|---|---|
| Death claims due and unpaid | $ 500 00 | |
| Death claims reported during the year but not yet adjusted | 2,850 00 | |
| Death claims incurred in 1921, not reported until 1922 | 3,400 00 | |
| Total death claims | | $6,750 00 |
| Sick and accident claims reported during the year but not yet adjusted | $ 469 79 | |
| Sick and accident claims incurred in 1921, not reported until 1922 | 2,149 55 | |
| Total sick and accident claims | | 2,619 34 |
| Total unpaid claims | | $9,369 34 |
| Salaries, rents, expenses, commissions, etc., due or accrued | | 1,265 86 |
| Borrowed money | | 8,000 00 |
| Advance assessments | | 4,361 65 |
| Total | | $22,996 85 |

## EXHIBIT OF CERTIFICATES.

| | Total business of the year. | | Business in Illinois during year. | |
|---|---|---|---|---|
| | Number. | Amount. | Number. | Amount. |
| Benefit certificates in force December 31, 1920, as per last statement | 40,164 | $18,516,075 00 | 1,053 | $681,200 00 |
| Benefit certificates written and renewed during the year | 5,128 | 2,002,350 00 | 45 | 30,000 00 |
| Benefit certificates received by transfer during the year | | | 2 | 1,500 00 |
| Benefit certificates increased during the year | | 74,650 00 | | 1,500 00 |
| Totals | 45,292 | $20,593,075 00 | 1,100 | $714,200 00 |
| Deduct terminated, decreased or transferred during the year | 3,766 | 1,755,200 00 | | |
| Deduct terminated or decreased during the year | | | 61 | 39,950 00 |
| Total benefit certificates in force December 31, 1921 | 41,526 | $18,837,875 00 | 1,039 | $674,250 00 |

Received during the year from members in Illinois: Mortuary, $11,377.20; aged, crippled incurables fund, $521.50; sick and accident, $385.21; expense, $2,239.23; total ........ $14,523 14

## EXHIBIT OF DEATH CLAIMS.

| | Total claims. | | Illinois claims. | |
|---|---|---|---|---|
| | Number. | Amount. | Number. | Amount. |
| Claims unpaid December 31, 1920, as per last statement (including 2 partially paid) | 12 | $ 5,000 00 | | |
| Claims reported during the year and interest addition | 311 | 132,600 00 | | |
| Totals | 323 | $137,600 00 | | |
| Claims paid during the year | 313 | 133,304 48 | 14 | $9,850 00 |
| Balance | 10 | $4,295 52 | | |
| Saved by compromising or scaling down claims during the year | | 595 52 | | |
| Claims rejected during the year | 2 | 350 00 | | |
| Claims unpaid December 31, 1921 | 8 | $3,350 00 | | |

## EXHIBIT OF SICK AND ACCIDENT CLAIMS.

| | Total claims. | | Illinois claims. | |
|---|---|---|---|---|
| | Number. | Amount. | Number. | Amount. |
| Claims unpaid December 31, 1920, as per last statement | 22 | $ 354 73 | | |
| Claims reported during the year | 1,156 | 26,183 14 | | |
| Totals | 1,178 | $26,537 87 | | |
| Claims paid during the year | 1,148 | 25,789 00 | 4 | $119 97 |
| Claims rejected during the year | 15 | 279 08 | | |
| Claims unpaid December 31, 1921 | 15 | $469 79 | | |

---

## LUTHERAN BROTHERHOOD.

Located at No. 938 Security Building, Minneapolis, Minnesota.

TH. EGGEN, President. J. A. O. PREUS, Secretary.

| | |
|---|---|
| Balance from previous year | $42,832 63 |

## INCOME.

| | |
|---|---|
| Assessments or premiums during first twelve months of membership of which all or an extra percentage is used for expenses | $32,810 04 |
| All other assessments or premiums | 49,732 26 |
| Double indemnity | 512 52 |
| Total received from members | $83,054 82 |
| Deduct payments returned to applicants and members | 2,233 10 |
| Net amount received from members | $80,821 72 |
| Gross interest on mortgage loans | 2,365 50 |
| Gross interest on bonds and dividends on stocks | 20 64 |
| Gross interest on deposits in trust companies and banks | 88 94 |
| Gross interest from all other sources | 49 35 |
| Borrowed money (gross) | 7,000 00 |
| Rent and light | 830 75 |
| Re-insurance commissions | 788 65 |
| Applications written, pending approval | 7,731 84 |
| Protested checks paid | 99 08 |
| Total income | $99,796 47 |
| Sum | $142,629 10 |

## DISBURSEMENTS.

| | |
|---|---|
| Death claims | $4,000 00 |
| Commissions and fees paid to deputies and organizers | 14,546 96 |
| Salaries of officers and trustees | 5,700 00 |
| Salaries of office employees | 4,180 69 |
| Salaries and fees paid to supreme medical examiners | 469 75 |
| Salaries and fees paid to subordinate medical examiners | 2,907 00 |
| Traveling and other expenses of officers, trustees and committees | 905 32 |
| For collection and remittance of assessments and dues | 66 08 |
| Insurance department fees | 197 53 |
| Rent | 1,417 00 |
| Advertising, printing and stationery | 2,512 16 |
| Postage, express, telegraph and telephone | 749 30 |
| Official publication | 318 89 |
| Other legal expenses | 37 50 |
| Furniture and fixtures | 311 05 |
| Borrowed money repaid (gross) | 5,000 00 |
| Interest on borrowed money | 137 70 |
| Re-insurance premiums | 5,145 23 |
| Surrender values | 136 77 |
| Application pending, approved | 8,065 81 |
| Protested checks returned | 221 23 |
| Inspection fees | 106 90 |
| Miscellaneous expenses | 337 39 |
| Total disbursements | $57,470 26 |
| Balance | $85,158 84 |

## LEDGER ASSETS.

| | |
|---|---|
| Mortgage loans on real estate | $77,360 00 |
| Book value of bonds and stocks | 350 00 |
| Cash in association's office | 804 67 |
| Deposits in trust companies and banks on interest | 1,635 12 |
| Bills receivable, $95.46; organizers' balances, $1,496.50 | 2,439 79 |
| Other ledger assets, viz— | |
| Premium notes | 784 48 |
| Certificate loans, $99.18; automatic premium loans | 2,632 61 |
| Total ledger assets | $85,158 84 |

### NON-LEDGER ASSETS.

| | |
|---|---|
| Interest and rents due and accrued | 2,255 21 |
| Premiums due and deferred, net | 11,049 29 |
| Furniture, fixtures and supplies | 2,000 00 |
| Gross assets | $100,463 34 |

### DEDUCT ASSETS NOT ADMITTED.

| | | |
|---|---|---|
| Balance due from organizers not secured by bonds | $1,496 50 | |
| Bills receivable | 95 46 | |
| Other items, viz— | | |
| Premium notes | 569 15 | |
| Furniture, fixtures and supplies | 2,000 00 | |
| | | 4,161 11 |
| Total admitted assets | | $96,302 23 |

LIABILITIES.

| | | |
|---|---|---|
| Advance assessments | | $ 158 95 |
| All other liabilities, viz: Mean reserve American Exp. C, 4 per cent, $69,778.00 less re-insurance, $2,345.50 | | 67,432 50 |
| Reserve for disability provisions | $ 233 75 | |
| Re-insurance due other companies | 698 31 | |
| Refunds due policyholders | 16 53 | |
| Expense fund | 1,115 55 | |
| Suspense fund | 229 00 | |
| | | 2,293 14 |
| Surplus (unassigned funds) | | 26,417 64 |
| Total | | $96,302 23 |

EXHIBIT OF CERTIFICATES.

| | Total business of the year. Number. | Amount. | Business in Illinois during year. Number. | Amount. |
|---|---|---|---|---|
| Benefit certificates in force December 31, 1920, as per last statement | 1,329 | $2,193,500 00 | 41 | $59,000 00 |
| Benefit certificates written and renewed during the year | 816 | 1,374,000 00 | 43 | 94,000 00 |
| Benefit certificates received by transfer during the year | | | 4 | 5,000 00 |
| Benefit certificates increased during the year | | 6,874 00 | | 220 00 |
| Totals | 2,145 | $3,574,374 00 | 88 | $158,220 00 |
| Deduct terminated, decreased or transferred during the year | 259 | 450,500 00 | | |
| Deduct terminated or decreased during the year | | | 19 | 34,000 00 |
| Total benefit certificates in force December 31, 1921 | 1,886 | $3,123,874 00 | 69 | $124,220 00 |

| | |
|---|---|
| Received during the year from members in Illinois: Mortuary, $2,104.68; disability, $10.69; expense, $1,404.09; total | $3,519 46 |

EXHIBIT OF DEATH CLAIMS.

| | Total claims—all in Illinois. Number. | Amount. |
|---|---|---|
| Claims paid during the year | 4 | $4,000 00 |

## LUTHERAN MUTUAL AID SOCIETY.

Located at Waverly, Iowa.

O. HARDWIG, President. G. A. GROSSMANN, Secretary.

| | |
|---|---|
| Balance from previous year | $339,480 83 |

INCOME.

| | |
|---|---|
| Membership fees actually received | $ 1,505 00 |
| Assessments or premiums during first months of membership of which all or an extra percentage is used for expenses | 2,010 25 |
| All other assessments or premiums | 152,004 98 |
| Dues and per capita tax | 16,100 70 |
| Net amount received from members | $171,620 93 |
| Gross interest on mortgage loans | 15,869 32 |
| Gross interest on bonds and dividends on stocks | 255 00 |
| Gross interest on deposits in trust companies and banks | 301 82 |
| Gross rents from association's property, including $315.00; for association's occupancy of its own buildings | 675 00 |
| Total income | $188,722 07 |
| Sum | $528,202 90 |

DISBURSEMENTS.

| | |
|---|---|
| Death claims | $133,545 60 |
| Commissions and fees paid to deputies and organizers | 552 50 |
| Salaries of deputies and organizers | 2,099 00 |
| Salaries of officers and trustees | 4,200 00 |
| Other compensation of officers and trustees | 92 50 |
| Salaries of office employees | 3,420 00 |
| Salaries and fees paid to supreme medical examiners | 200 25 |
| Traveling and other expenses of officers, trustees and committees | 1.509 31 |

DISBURSEMENTS—Concluded.

| | |
|---|---|
| Insurance department fees | $ 93 00 |
| Rent | 315 00 |
| Advertising, printing and stationery | 2,257 42 |
| Postage, express, telegraph and telephone | 384 49 |
| Other legal expenses | 1,041 26 |
| Taxes, repairs and other expenses on real estate | 72 10 |
| All other disbursements | 3,494 68 |
| Total disbursements | $153,277 11 |
| Balance | $378,167 59 |

LEDGER ASSETS.

| | |
|---|---|
| Book value of real estate | $ 13,500 00 |
| Mortgage loans on real estate | 340,430 00 |
| Book value of bonds and stocks | 4,000 00 |
| Deposits in trust companies and banks on interest | 16,995 79 |
| Total ledger assets | $374,925 79 |

NON-LEDGER ASSETS.

| | |
|---|---|
| Interest and rents due and accrued | 12,588 11 |
| Gross assets | $387,513 90 |

LIABILITIES.

| | | |
|---|---|---|
| Death claims adjusted not yet due | $20,500 00 | |
| Death claims reported during the year but not yet adjusted | 10,500 00 | |
| Total death claims | | $31,000 00 |
| Advance assessments | | 48 01 |
| Total | | $31,048 01 |

EXHIBIT OF CERTIFICATES.

| | Total business of the year. | | Business in Illinois during year. | |
|---|---|---|---|---|
| | Number. | Amount. | Number. | Amount. |
| Benefit certificates in force December 31, 1920, as per last statement | 8,296 | $8,966,000 00 | 752 | $816,500 00 |
| Benefit certificates written and renewed during the year | 279 | 275,500 00 | 58 | 60,000 00 |
| Benefit certificates received by transfer during the year | | | 8 | 8,000 00 |
| Totals | 8,575 | $9,241,500 00 | 818 | $884,500 00 |
| Deduct terminated, decreased or transferred during the year | 279 | 297,000 00 | | |
| Deduct terminated or decreased during the year | | | 23 | 24,000 00 |
| Total benefit certificates in force December 31, 1921 | 8,296 | $8,944,500 00 | 795 | $860,500 00 |

Received during the year from members in Illinois: Mortuary, $11,763.05; reserve, $2,299.06; expense, $1,926.00; total $15,988 11

EXHIBIT OF DEATH CLAIMS.

| | Total claims. | | Illinois claims. | |
|---|---|---|---|---|
| | Number. | Amount. | Number. | Amount. |
| Claims unpaid December 31, 1920, as per last statement | 19 | $ 20,000 00 | 1 | $1,000 00 |
| Claims reported during the year and interest addition | 138 | 143,500 00 | 5 | 6,000 00 |
| Totals | 157 | $163,500 00 | 6 | $7,000 00 |
| Claims paid during the year | 128 | 133,500 00 | 6 | 7,000 00 |
| Claims unpaid December 31, 1921 | 29 | $30,000 00 | | |

---

## THE MACCABEES.

Located at No. 5065 Woodward Avenue, Detroit, Michigan.

D. P. MARKEY, Supreme Commander. THOMAS WATSON, Supreme Record Keeper.

| | |
|---|---|
| Balance from previous year | $14,465,800 45 |

## INCOME.

| | |
|---|---|
| Assessments or premiums during first twelve months of membership of which all or an extra percentage is used for expenses | $1,961,406 02 |
| All other assessments or premiums | 5,519,142 06 |
| Dues and per capita tax | 367,406 03 |
| Total received from members | $7,847,954 11 |
| Deduct payments returned to applicants and members | 22,325 50 |
| Net amount received from members | $7,825,628 61 |
| Gross interest on bonds and dividends on stocks | 740,532 40 |
| Gross interest on deposits in trust companies and banks | 18,766 65 |
| Gross interest from all other sources | 3,827 07 |
| Gross rents from association's property | 2,025 00 |
| Sale of lodge supplies | 3,306 78 |
| Relief fund fees | 31,031 75 |
| Received from beneficiaries held in trust | 5,332 74 |
| Bonds, profit | 10,550 29 |
| Bonds, discount | 16,511 43 |
| Total income | $8,657,512 72 |
| Sum | $23,123,313 17 |

## DISBURSEMENTS.

| | |
|---|---|
| Death claims | $5,067,169 03 |
| Permanent disability claims | 782,885 74 |
| Sick and accident claims | 106,872 04 |
| Relief of members in distress | 13,510 48 |
| Specific benefit, loss of eye | 2,800 00 |
| War claims | 1,965 50 |
| Total benefits paid | $5,975,202 79 |
| Commissions and fees paid to deputies and organizers | 941,646 13 |
| Salaries of managers or agents not deputies or organizers, great camps | 390,858 50 |
| Salaries of officers and trustees | 21,207 26 |
| Salaries of office employees | 162,131 92 |
| Other compensation of office employees | 6,333 49 |
| Salaries and fees paid to supreme medical examiners | 36,509 00 |
| Salaries and fees paid to subordinate medical examiners | 6,315 38 |
| Insurance department fees | 2,272 43 |
| Advertising, printing and stationery | 41,714 27 |
| Postage, express, telegraph and telephone | 15,649 80 |
| Lodge supplies | 14,859 93 |
| Official publication | 34,933 50 |
| Legal expense in litigating claims | 4,197 91 |
| Other legal expenses | 7,264 14 |
| Furniture and fixtures | 8,152 07 |
| Taxes, repairs and other expenses on real estate | 6,278 39 |
| Gross loss on sale or maturity of ledger assets | 2,357 55 |
| Gross decrease in book value of ledger assets | 15,387 09 |
| Trust claims paid | 4,069 26 |
| Home and relief | 31,493 90 |
| Miscellaneous | 12,196 62 |
| Total disbursements | $7,741,031 33 |
| Balance | $15,382,281 84 |

## LEDGER ASSETS.

| | |
|---|---|
| Book value of real estate | $ 189,471 50 |
| Book value of bonds and stocks | 14,711,009 33 |
| Cash in association's office | 1,200 00 |
| Deposits in trust companies and banks on interest | 478,508 21 |
| Bills receivable | 2,092 80 |
| Total ledger assets | $15,382,281 84 |

### NON-LEDGER ASSETS.

| | |
|---|---|
| Interest and rents due and accrued | 402,347 61 |
| Market value of bonds and stocks over book value | 66,082 23 |
| Assessments actually collected by subordinate lodges not yet turned over to supreme lodge | 618,750 00 |
| Liens charges and interest | 4,297,790 91 |
| Gross assets | $20,767,252 59 |

### DEDUCT ASSETS NOT ADMITTED.

| | | |
|---|---|---|
| Overdue and accrued interest on bonds in default | $ 82,760 96 | |
| Book value of bonds and stocks over market value | 103,366 58 | |
| | | 186,127 54 |
| Total admitted assets | | $20,581,125 05 |

## LIABILITIES.

| | | |
|---|---|---|
| Death claims due and unpaid | $121,798 88 | |
| Death claims resisted | 8,624 40 | |
| Death claims incurred in 1921, not reported until 1922 | 256,018 57 | |
| Total death claims | | $ 386,441 85 |
| Present value of disability claims payable in installments | | 2,162,731 00 |
| Sick and accident claims reported during the year but not yet adjusted | $8,296 48 | |
| Sick and accident claims incurred in 1921, not reported until 1922 | 3,971 09 | |
| Total sick and accident claims | | 12,267 57 |
| Total unpaid claims | | $2,561,440 42 |
| Salaries, rents, expenses, commissions, etc., due or accrued | | 98,163 37 |
| Advance assessments | | 258,876 43 |
| All other liabilities, viz— | | |
| Trust funds | $ 14,346 04 | |
| Reserve on 20 pay life, special and whole life transfer American Experience, 4 per cent | 1,776,811 00 | |
| Reserve on straight whole life, fraternal combined experience 4 per cent | 153,523 00 | |
| Reserve on term to 45 national fraternal congress, 4 per cent | 1,360 00 | |
| Contingency reserve and reserve for mortality fluctuation | 475,000 00 | |
| Unassigned funds, life benefit fund No. 2 | 381,714 52 | |
| | | 2,802,754 56 |
| Total | | $5,721,234 78 |

## EXHIBIT OF CERTIFICATES.

| | Total business of the year. | | Business in Illinois during year. | |
|---|---|---|---|---|
| | Number. | Amount. | Number. | Amount. |
| Benefit certificates in force December 31, 1920, as per last statement | 293,249 | $349,010,268 42 | 20,215 | $23,260,000 00 |
| Benefit certificates written and renewed during the year | 14,418 | 15,544,500 00 | 522 | 514,500 00 |
| Benefit certificates increased during the year | -------- | 1,077,100 00 | -------- | 44,500 00 |
| Totals | 307,667 | $365,631,868 42 | 20,737 | $23,819,000 00 |
| Deduct terminated, decreased or transferred during the year | 32,246 | 38,402,686 49 | -------- | ------------- |
| Total benefit certificates in force December 31, 1921 | 275,421 | $327,229,181 93 | 20,737 | $23,819,000 00 |

Received during the year from members in Illinois: Mortuary, $397,819.74; expense, $25,354.28; total ........ $423,174 02

## EXHIBIT OF DEATH CLAIMS.

| | Total claims. | | Illinois claims. | |
|---|---|---|---|---|
| | Number. | Amount. | Number. | Amount. |
| Claims unpaid December 31, 1920, as per last statement | 125 | $ 144,498 40 | 6 | $ 11,000 00 |
| Claims reported during the year and interest addition | 3,944 | 5,206,920 51 | 329 | 419,123 20 |
| Totals | 4,069 | $5,351,418 91 | 335 | $430,123 20 |
| Claims paid during the year | 3,952 | 5,067,169 03 | 327 | 406,636 56 |
| Balance | 117 | $284,249 88 | 8 | $23,486 64 |
| Saved by compromising or scaling down claims during the year | -------- | 142,926 60 | -------- | 12,319 97 |
| Claims rejected during the year | 9 | 10,900 00 | 1 | 3,000 00 |
| Claims unpaid December 31, 1921 | 108 | $130,423 28 | 7 | $8,166 67 |

## EXHIBIT OF PERMANENT DISABILITY CLAIMS.

| | Total claims. | | Illinois claims. | |
|---|---|---|---|---|
| | Number. | Amount. | Number. | Amount. |
| Claims unpaid December 31, 1920, as per last statement | 3,618 | $2,889,291 45 | 158 | $160,113 54 |
| Claims reported during the year and interest addition | 981 | 1,468,271 65 | 38 | 56,976 00 |
| Totals | 4,599 | $4,357,563 10 | 196 | $217,089 54 |
| Claims paid during the year | 506 | 782,885 74 | 12 | 31,137 65 |
| Balance | 4,093 | $3,574,677 36 | 184 | $185,951 89 |
| Saved by compromising or scaling down claims during the year | -------- | 225,674 15 | -------- | 7,636 69 |
| Claims rejected during the year | 880 | 543,453 55 | 52 | 38,841 54 |
| Claims unpaid December 31, 1921 | 3,213 | $2,805,549 66 | 132 | $139,473 66 |

EXHIBIT OF SICK AND ACCIDENT CLAIMS.

| | Total claims—all in Illinois. Number. | Amount. |
|---|---|---|
| Claims unpaid December 31, 1920, as per last statement | 345 | $ 11,409 61 |
| Claims reported during the year | 3,134 | 104,108 22 |
| Totals | 3,479 | $115,517 83 |
| Claims paid during the year | 3,191 | 106,872 04 |
| Claims rejected during the year | 17 | 349 31 |
| Claims unpaid December 31, 1921 | 271 | $8,296 48 |

EXHIBIT OF RELIEF NO. 1 AND OTHER CLAIMS.

| | Total claims. Number. | Amount. | Illinois claims. Number. | Amount. |
|---|---|---|---|---|
| Claims paid during the year | 216 | $13,510 48 | 10 | $965 28 |

---

## MASONIC MUTUAL LIFE ASSOCIATION.

Located at Homer Building, Thirteenth and F Streets, North West, Washington, D. C.

WILLIAM MONTGOMERY, President. J. P. YOST, Secretary.

| | |
|---|---|
| Balance from previous year | $2,474,165 94 |

INCOME.

| | |
|---|---|
| Assessments or premiums | $1,052,877 35 |
| All other assessments or premiums | 1,547,758 46 |
| Net amount received from members | $2,600,635 81 |
| Gross interest on mortgage loans | 73,001 97 |
| Gross interest on collateral loans | 225 00 |
| Gross interest on bonds and dividends on stocks | 43,148 63 |
| Gross interest on deposits in trust companies and banks | 1,679 00 |
| Gross interest from all other sources | 22,956 33 |
| Gross rents from association's property including $7,499.99 for association's occupancy of its own buildings | 10,341 62 |
| Borrowed money (gross) | 50,000 00 |
| Gross profit on sale or maturity of ledger assets | 231 25 |
| Policy loans, reinstated policies | 3,819 95 |
| Premium on surety bonds—refunded | 196 55 |
| Investment expense account (net balance) | 56 66 |
| Suspense (net) | 880 93 |
| Rent refunded | 300 00 |
| Total income | $2,807,473 70 |
| Sum | $5,281,639 64 |

DISBURSEMENTS.

| | |
|---|---|
| Death claims | $318,432 22 |
| Permanent disability claims | 492 05 |
| Policy loans and liens charged off by lapse | 44,861 65 |
| Return of savings through reduction of premiums | 48,647 11 |
| Total benefits paid | $412,433 03 |
| Commissions and fees paid to deputies and organizers | 543,373 52 |
| Salaries of deputies and organizers | 4,181 92 |
| Salaries of officers and trustees | 23,601 58 |
| Salaries and other compensation of committees | 3,638 00 |
| Salaries of office employees | 165,002 63 |
| Salaries and fees paid to supreme medical examiners | 6,300 00 |
| Salaries and fees paid to subordinate medical examiners | 72,826 27 |
| Traveling and other expenses of officers, trustees and committees | 7,750 24 |
| For collection and remittance of assessments and dues | 93,837 64 |
| Insurance department fees | 946 25 |
| Rent, including $7,499.99 for association's occupancy of its own buildings | 12,713 28 |
| Advertising, printing and stationery | 40,889 92 |
| Postage, express, telegraph and telephone | 18,404 11 |
| Legal expense in litigating claims | 717 80 |
| Other legal expenses | 2,043 50 |
| Furniture and fixtures | 15,489 78 |
| Incidentals | 816 00 |
| Taxes, repairs and other expenses on real estate | 3,720 52 |
| Fraternal Congress dues | 202 00 |

DISBURSEMENTS—Concluded.

| | |
|---|---|
| Moving offices | $ 329 15 |
| Borrowed money repaid (gross) | 50,000 00 |
| Interest on borrowed money | 758 33 |
| Branch office expense | 86,516 92 |
| Auditing | 387 50 |
| Miscellaneous office supplies and sundries | 2,603 53 |
| Examination expense | 2,209 93 |
| Inspection fees | 16,163 11 |
| Robbery and fire insurance premiums | 511 55 |
| Deputies' convention | 13,886 16 |
| Alterations and new office | 2,582 55 |
| Total disbursements | $1,604,836 72 |
| Balance | $3,676,802 92 |

LEDGER ASSETS.

| | | |
|---|---|---|
| Book value of real estate | | $ 123,780 64 |
| Mortgage loans on real estate | | 1,578,654 85 |
| War savings stamps | | 1,000 00 |
| Loans secured by pledge of bonds, stocks or other collateral | | 5,000 00 |
| Book value of bonds and stocks | | 1,139,419 43 |
| Due association from re-insurance company | | 76 48 |
| Cash in association's office | | 5,073 54 |
| Deposits in trust companies and banks not on interest | | 225,701 44 |
| Deposits in trust companies and banks on interest | | 36,275 86 |
| Organizers' balances | | 16,436 74 |
| Other ledger assets, viz— | | |
| Policy loans, automatic policy loans, disability loans and premiums liens secured by reserve | | 535,952 80 |
| Premium notes | | 9,431 14 |
| Total ledger assets | | $3,676,802 92 |
| **NON-LEDGER ASSETS.** | | |
| Interest and rents due and accrued | | 50,871 52 |
| Market value of real estate over book value | | 53,630 33 |
| Market value of bonds and stocks over book value | | 27,052 07 |
| All other assets, viz— | | |
| Net due and deferred premiums on all contracts (reserve charged in liabilities) | $762,686 55 | |
| Office furniture and fixtures | 42,451 18 | |
| | | 805,137 73 |
| Gross assets | | $4,613,494 57 |
| **DEDUCT ASSETS NOT ADMITTED.** | | |
| Balance due from organizers not secured by bonds | $32,506 50 | |
| Other items, viz— | | |
| Office furniture and fixtures | 42,451 18 | |
| Premium notes not secured | 3,488 94 | |
| Excess of policy indebtedness over reserve | 2,349 72 | |
| | | 80,796 34 |
| Total admitted assets | | $4,532,698 23 |

LIABILITIES.

| | | |
|---|---|---|
| Death claims reported during the year but not yet adjusted | $20,500 00 | |
| Death claims incurred in 1921, not reported until 1922 | 11,000 00 | |
| Present value of deferred death claims payable in installments | 23,692 56 | |
| Total death claims | | $55,192 56 |
| Present value of disability claims payable in installments | | 834 00 |
| Total unpaid claims | | $56,026 56 |
| Salaries, rents, expenses, commissions, etc., due or accrued | | 3,941 63 |
| Interest paid in advance on policy loans and liens | | 3,457 10 |
| Advance assessments | | 6,627 36 |
| All other liabilities, viz— | | |
| Reserve at $3\frac{1}{2}$ per cent American Experience Table of Mortality on all contracts | $4,189,777 00 | |
| Reserve disability benefits | 24,184 00 | |
| Suspense account, deposits made with applications for membership and re-instatement | 12,497 24 | |
| U. S. Treasury Department—Soldiers and Sailors Civil Relief Act | 22 41 | |
| | | 4,226,480 65 |
| Total | | $4,296,533 30 |

EXHIBIT OF CERTIFICATES.

| | Total business of the year. | | Business in Illinois during year. | |
|---|---|---|---|---|
| | Number. | Amount. | Number. | Amount. |
| Benefit certificates in force December 31, 1920, as per last statement | 39,047 | $71,097,545 00 | 5,918 | $11,196,000 00 |
| Benefit certificates written and renewed during the year | 23,689 | 46,737,250 00 | 2,561 | 5,217,500 00 |
| Benefit certificates increased during the year | -------- | 2,000 00 | -------- | ------------- |
| Total | 62,736 | $117,836,795 00 | 8,479 | $16,413,500 00 |
| Deduct terminated, decreased or transferred during the year | 7,588 | 16,614,500 00 | -------- | ------------- |
| Deduct terminated or decreased during the year | -------- | ------------- | 1,127 | 2,540,750 00 |
| Total benefit certificates in force December 31, 1921 | 55,148 | $101,222,295 00 | 7,352 | $13,872,750 00 |

Received during the year from members in Illinois: Mortuary and reserve, $214,855.33; expense, $149,201.97; total ........ $364,057 30

EXHIBIT OF DEATH CLAIMS.

| | Total claims. | | Illinois claims. | |
|---|---|---|---|---|
| | Number. | Amount. | Number. | Amount. |
| Claims unpaid December 31, 1920, as per last statement | 34 | $ 51,345 30 | 6 | $10,000 00 |
| Claims reported during the year and interest addition | 209 | 353,279 48 | 29 | 55,843 00 |
| Total | 243 | $404,624 78 | 35 | $65,843 00 |
| Claims paid during the year | 210 | 344,932 22 | 31 | 58,343 00 |
| Balance | 33 | $59,692 56 | 4 | $7,500 00 |
| Saved by compromising or scaling down claims during the year | -------- | 4,500 00 | -------- | 2,500 00 |
| Claims unpaid December 31, 1921 | 33 | $55,192 56 | 4 | $5,000 00 |

EXHIBIT OF PERMANENT DISABILITY CLAIMS.

| | Total claims. Amount. |
|---|---|
| Claims paid during the year | $492 05 |

## MODERN BROTHERHOOD OF AMERICA.

Located at No. 101-107 East State Street, Mason City, Iowa.

ALBERT HASS, President. E. L. BALZ, Secretary.

| | |
|---|---|
| Balance from previous year | $4,743,781 90 |

INCOME.

| | |
|---|---|
| Membership fees actually received | $ 29,497 67 |
| Assessments or premiums during first 12 months of membership of which all or an extra percentage is used for expenses | 35,131 16 |
| All other assessments or premiums | 1,066,250 86 |
| Dues and per capita tax | 110,967 64 |
| Other payments by members | 8,623 72 |
| Total received from members | $1,250,471 05 |
| Deduct payments returned to applicants and members | 14,451 17 |
| Net amount received from members | $1,236,019 88 |
| Gross interest on mortgage loans | 160,718 01 |
| Gross interest on bonds and dividends on stocks | 75,587 84 |
| Gross interest on deposits in trust companies and banks | 6,043 30 |
| Gross rents and heating from association's property, including $5,000.00 for association's occupancy of its own buildings | 50,397 38 |
| Sale of lodge supplies | 1,504 96 |
| Gross profit on sale or maturity of ledger assets | 437 50 |
| Field work and expense | 15,985 36 |
| Premium surety bonds | 1,583 64 |
| License fees South Dakota lodges | 31 00 |
| Advertising official paper | 1,457 62 |
| Deputy bond fund | 142 50 |
| Furniture sold | 37 50 |
| Refunds account field expense | 18 74 |
| Refund expenses investigating loans | 1,785 70 |
| Miscellaneous | 1 24 |
| Total income | $1,551,752 17 |
| Sum | $6,295,534 07 |

## DISBURSEMENTS.

| | |
|---|---|
| Death claims | $575,796 18 |
| Permanent disability claims | 4,500 00 |
| Sick and accident claims | 9,400 00 |
| Old age benefits | 204,210 67 |
| Total benefits paid | $793,906 85 |
| Commissions and fees paid to deputies and organizers | 72,795 61 |
| Salaries of deputies and organizers | 2,100 00 |
| Salaries of officers and directors | 22,400 00 |
| Other compensation of officers and directors—expense of directors | 3,532 09 |
| Salaries and other compensation of committees—auditing committee | 1,055 16 |
| Salaries of office employees | 37,752 34 |
| Traveling and other expenses of officers | 1,894 81 |
| Insurance department fees | 787 50 |
| Rent and light, including $5,000.00 for association's occupancy of its own buildings | 5,174 64 |
| Advertising, printing and stationery | 6,952 88 |
| Postage, express, telegraph and telephone | 4,946 30 |
| Lodge supplies | 2,638 85 |
| Official publication | 6,758 24 |
| Legal expense in litigating claims | 5,665 55 |
| Other legal expenses | 198 33 |
| Furniture and fixtures | 282 79 |
| Taxes, repairs and other expenses on real estate | 31,029 94 |
| Premium surety bonds | 874 66 |
| Gross loss on sale or maturity of ledger assets | 1,775 00 |
| Reports impaired risks | 655 27 |
| Investigating claims | 238 50 |
| Investigating loans | 1,670 95 |
| Actuarial work | 976 31 |
| All other disbursements, viz— | |
| Bonds supreme officers and employees | 148 50 |
| Dues and assessments National Fraternal Congress and subscriptions | 387 30 |
| Repairing typewriters and adding machines | 118 40 |
| Insurance, clock service, box rent, notary fees | 79 00 |
| Repairing furniture and publishing expense | 38 00 |
| Miscellaneous | 29 07 |
| Total disbursements | $1,006,862 84 |
| Balance | $5,288,671 23 |

## LEDGER ASSETS.

| | |
|---|---|
| Book value of real estate | $ 305,349 64 |
| Mortgage loans on real estate | 3,468,833 00 |
| Book value of bonds and stocks | 1,389,300 00 |
| Deposits in trust companies and banks on interest | 125,188 59 |
| Total ledger assets | $5,288,671 23 |

### NON-LEDGER ASSETS.

| | |
|---|---|
| Interest and rents due and accrued | 147,910 49 |
| Assessments actually collected by subordinate lodges not yet turned over to supreme lodge | 104,375 00 |
| Suspense account deposited but not yet distributed to regular accounts | 18,168 19 |
| Gross assets | $5,559,124 91 |

### DEDUCT ASSETS NOT ADMITTED.

| | |
|---|---|
| Book value of bonds and stocks over market value | 22,987 50 |
| Total admitted assets | $5,536,137 41 |

## LIABILITIES.

| | | |
|---|---|---|
| Death claims resisted | $ 9,303 25 | |
| Death claims reported during the year but not yet adjusted | 97,234 01 | |
| Death claims incurred in 1921, not reported until 1922 | 8,377 51 | |
| Total death claims | | $114,914 77 |
| Permanent disability claims reported during the year but not yet adjusted | | 4,500 00 |
| Sick and accident claims resisted | $ 200 00 | |
| Sick and accident claims reported during the year but not yet adjusted | 1,325 00 | |
| Sick and accident claims incurred in 1921, not reported until 1922 | 675 00 | |
| Total sick and accident claims | | 2,200 00 |
| Old age benefits reported but not due or adjusted (present worth) | | 153,245 87 |
| Total unpaid claims | | $274,860 64 |
| Salaries, rents, expenses, commissions, etc., due or accrued | | 5,253 38 |
| Advance assessments | | 17,602 28 |
| Total | | $297,716 30 |

## EXHIBIT OF CERTIFICATES.

| | Total business of the year. Number. | Amount. | Business in Illinois during year. Number. | Amount. |
|---|---|---|---|---|
| Benefit certificates in force December 31, 1920, as per last statement | 50,872 | $58,792,576 48 | 2,320 | $2,249,438 70 |
| Benefit certificates written and renewed during the year | 4,322 | 4,635,905 07 | 292 | 258,500 00 |
| Benefit certificates received by transfer during the year | | | 6 | 6,000 00 |
| Benefit certificates increased during the year | | 227,801 69 | | 6,556 67 |
| Total | 55,194 | $63,656,283 24 | 2,618 | $2,520,495 37 |
| Deduct terminated, decreased or transferred during the year | 5,509 | 6,381,832 72 | | |
| Deduct terminated or decreased during the year | | | 181 | 165,337 32 |
| Total benefit certificates in force December 31, 1921 | 49,685 | $57,274,450 52 | 2,437 | $2,355,158 05 |

Received during the year from members in Illinois: Mortuary, $38,147.67; expense, $7,356.49; total $45,504 16

## EXHIBIT OF DEATH CLAIMS.

| | Total claims. Number. | Amount. | Illinois claims. Number. | Amount. |
|---|---|---|---|---|
| Claims unpaid December 31, 1920, as per last statement | 86 | $108,481 35 | 4 | $ 3,500 00 |
| Claims reported during the year and interest addition | 531 | 594,331 85 | 18 | 20,311 52 |
| Total | 617 | $702,813 20 | 22 | $23,811 52 |
| Claims paid during the year | 524 | 575,796 18 | 19 | 21,311 52 |
| Balance | 93 | $127,017 02 | 3 | $2,500 00 |
| Saved by compromising or scaling down claims during the year | | 16,979 76 | | |
| Claims withdrawn during the year | 1 | 1,000 00 | | |
| Claims rejected during the year | 3 | 2,500 00 | | |
| Claims unpaid December 31, 1921 | 89 | $106,537 26 | 3 | $2,500 00 |

## EXHIBIT OF PERMANENT DISABILITY CLAIMS.

| | Total claims. Number. | Amount. |
|---|---|---|
| Claims unpaid December 31, 1920, as per last statement | 4 | $2,000 00 |
| Claims reported during the year and interest addition | 12 | 8,000 00 |
| Total | 16 | $10,000 00 |
| Claims paid during the year | 8 | 4,500 00 |
| Balance | 8 | $5,500 00 |
| Claims withdrawn during the year | 1 | 500 00 |
| Claims rejected during the year | 1 | 500 00 |
| Claims unpaid December 31, 1921 | 6 | $4,500 00 |

## EXHIBIT OF SICK AND ACCIDENT CLAIMS.

| | Total claims. Number. | Amount. | Illinois claims. Number. | Amount. |
|---|---|---|---|---|
| Claims unpaid December 31, 1920, as per last statement | 15 | $ 2,425 00 | | |
| Claims reported during the year | 109 | 10,100 00 | 4 | $275 00 |
| Total | 124 | $12,525 00 | 4 | $275 00 |
| Claims paid during the year | 103 | 9,400 00 | 2 | 50 00 |
| Saved by compromise | | 275 00 | | |
| Claims rejected during the year | 4 | 725 00 | | |
| Claims withdrawn during the year | 2 | 600 00 | | |
| Claims unpaid December 31, 1921 | 15 | $1,525 00 | 2 | $225 00 |

EXHIBIT OF OLD AGE AND OTHER CLAIMS.

| | Total claims. Number. | Amount. |
|---|---|---|
| Claims unpaid December 31, 1920, as per last statement | 211 | $151,285 29 |
| Claims reported during the year and interest addition | 400 | 221,137 79 |
| Total | 611 | $372,423 08 |
| Claims paid during the year | 376 | 204,210 67 |
| Balance | 235 | $168,212 41 |
| Saved by compromising or scaling down claims during the year | | 5,083 58 |
| Claims withdrawn during the year | 14 | 9,882 96 |
| Claims unpaid December 31, 1921 | 221 | $153,245 87 |

## MODERN ORDER OF PRAETORIANS.

Located at Praetorian Building, Dallas, Texas.

C. B. GARDNER, President. J. W. ALLEN, Secretary.

| | |
|---|---|
| Balance from previous year | $2,496,487 72 |

INCOME.

| | |
|---|---|
| Assessments or premiums during first months of membership of which all or an extra percentage is used for expenses | $226,781 81 |
| All other assessments or premiums | 762,931 29 |
| Dues and per capita tax | 55,997 48 |
| Total received from members | $1,045,710 58 |
| Deduct payments returned to applicants and members | 4,132 78 |
| Net amount received from members | $1,041,577 80 |
| Gross interest on mortgage loans | 112,901 65 |
| Gross interest on bonds and dividends on stocks | 11,942 38 |
| Gross interest from all other sources | 8,335 04 |
| Gross rents from association's property, including $5,160.00 for association's occupancy of its own buildings | 105,939 62 |
| Sale of lodge supplies | 648 35 |
| Exchange | 20 |
| Total income | $1,281,345 04 |
| Sum | $3,777,832 76 |

DISBURSEMENTS.

| | |
|---|---|
| Death claims | $261,720 46 |
| Permanent disability claims | 659 90 |
| Sick and accident claims | 1,000 00 |
| Old age benefits | 733 30 |
| Interest | 586 59 |
| Surrender values | 190,074 15 |
| Total benefits paid | $454,774 40 |
| Commissions and fees paid to deputies and organizers | 161,042 39 |
| Salaries of deputies and organizers | 23,020 85 |
| Salaries of officers and trustees | 25,279 80 |
| Salaries and other compensation of committees | 4,795 20 |
| Salaries of office employees | 28,993 00 |
| Salaries and fees paid to supreme medical examiners | 6,162 30 |
| Salaries and fees paid to subordinate medical examiners | 47 00 |
| Traveling and other expenses of officers, trustees and committees | 291 15 |
| For collection and remittance of assessments and dues | 393 36 |
| Insurance department fees | 641 00 |
| Rent, including $5,160.00 for association's occupancy of its own buildings | 7,968 75 |
| Advertising, printing and stationery | 14,569 10 |
| Postage, express, telegraph and telephone | 6,261 61 |
| Lodge supplies | 1,254 23 |
| Official publication | 8,498 45 |
| Legal expense in litigating claims | 1,238 19 |
| Furniture and fixtures | 754 20 |
| Taxes, repairs and other expenses on real estate | 60,584 78 |
| All other disbursements, viz— | |
| Bond premium, $610.79; traveling expense, general, $11,814.38; prize, $2,350.50; inspections, $1,468.25 | 16,243 92 |
| Actuary, $510.00; auditor, $635.00; Fraternal Congress, $90.00; insurance, $78.53 | 1,313 53 |
| Charity, $396.00; interest and dividends, $267.28; over age deducted by councils, $1,076.23 | 1,739 51 |
| Total disbursements | $825,836 72 |
| Balance | $2,951,996 04 |

## LEDGER ASSETS.

| | | |
|---|---|---|
| Book value of real estate | | $ 605,542 02 |
| Mortgage loans on real estate | | 1,804,840 00 |
| Book value of bonds and stocks | | 234,034 00 |
| Cash in association's office | | 25 00 |
| Deposits in trust companies and banks not on interest | | 59,269 20 |
| Organizers' balances | | 70,665 23 |
| Other ledger assets, viz— | | |
| Loans on certificates | $ 27,620 59 | |
| First lien on sale of Waco property | 150,000 00 | |
| | | 177,620 59 |
| Total ledger assets | | $2,951,996 04 |

### NON-LEDGER ASSETS.

| | |
|---|---|
| Interest and rents due and accrued | 42,066 01 |
| Market value of real estate over book value | 594,457 98 |
| Assessments actually collected by subordinate lodges not yet turned over to supreme lodge | 4,175 25 |
| Gross assets | $3,592,695 28 |

### DEDUCT ASSETS NOT ADMITTED.

| | |
|---|---|
| Balance due from organizers not secured by bonds | 70,665 23 |
| Total admitted assets | $3,522,030 05 |

## LIABILITIES.

| | | |
|---|---|---|
| Death claims due and unpaid | $2,167 00 | |
| Death claims resisted | 1,000 00 | |
| Death claims reported during the year but not yet adjusted | 14,520 00 | |
| Present value of deferred death claims payable in installments | 29,544 98 | |
| Total death claims | | $47,231 98 |
| Present value of disability claims payable in installments | | 2,595 90 |
| Old age and other benefits due and unpaid | | 4,549 72 |
| Total unpaid claims | | $54,377 60 |
| Salaries, rents, expenses, commissions, etc., due or accrued | | 9,433 68 |
| Advance assessments | | 7,123 10 |
| Total | | $70,934 38 |

## EXHIBIT OF CERTIFICATES.

| | Total business of the year. | | Business in Illinois during year. | |
|---|---|---|---|---|
| | Number. | Amount. | Number. | Amount. |
| Benefit certificates in force December 31, 1920, as per last statement | 36,020 | $44,284,984 00 | 7 | $7,000 00 |
| Benefit certificates written and renewed during the year | 9,880 | 12,676,750 00 | | |
| Total | 45,900 | $56,961,734 00 | 7 | $7,000 00 |
| Deduct terminated, decreased or transferred during year | 9,296 | 12,255,992 00 | | |
| Total benefit certificates in force December 31, 1921 | 36,604 | $44,705,742 00 | 7 | $7,000 00 |

Received during the year from members in Illinois: Mortuary, $116.29; expense, $24.96; total ..... $141 25

## EXHIBIT OF DEATH CLAIMS.

| | Total claims. | |
|---|---|---|
| | Number. | Amount. |
| Claims unpaid December 31, 1920, as per last statement | 21 | $ 62,917 56 |
| Claims reported during the year and interest addition | 198 | 256,323 00 |
| Total | 219 | 319,240 56 |
| Claims paid during the year | 200 | 264,700 25 |
| Balance | 19 | $54,540 31 |
| Saved by compromising or scaling down claims during the year | | 6,308 31 |
| Claims rejected during the year | 1 | 1,000 00 |
| Claims unpaid December 31, 1921 | 18 | $47,231 98 |

### EXHIBIT OF PERMANENT DISABILITY CLAIMS.

| | Total claims. Amount. |
|---|---|
| Claims unpaid December 31, 1920, as per last statement | $3,255 80 |
| Claims paid during the year | 659 90 |
| Claims unpaid December 31, 1921 | $2,595 90 |

### EXHIBIT OF SICK AND ACCIDENT CLAIMS.

| | Total claims. Number. | Amount. |
|---|---|---|
| Claims reported and paid during the year | 3 | $1,000 00 |

### EXHIBIT OF OLD AGE AND OTHER CLAIMS.

| | Total claims. Amount. |
|---|---|
| Claims unpaid December 31, 1920, as per last statement | $5,283 02 |
| Claims paid during the year | 733 30 |
| Claims unpaid December 31, 1921 | $4,549 72 |

## MOSAIC TEMPLARS OF AMERICA.

Located at No. 904 Broadway Street, Little Rock, Arkansas.

S. J. ELLIOTT, President. C. E. BUSH, Secretary.

| | |
|---|---|
| Balance from previous year | $664,573 41 |

### INCOME.

| | |
|---|---|
| All other assessments or premiums | $401,905 04 |
| Dues and per capita tax | 28,886 68 |
| Medical examiners' fees actually received | 1,095 85 |
| Total received from members | $431,887 57 |
| Deduct payments returned to applicants and members | 6,790 20 |
| Net amount received from members | $425,097 37 |
| Gross interest on mortgage loans | 1,457 61 |
| Gross interest on bonds and dividends on stocks | 7,090 00 |
| Gross interest on deposits in trust companies and banks | 5,863 55 |
| Gross rents from association's property, including $3,967.00 for association's occupancy of its own buildings | 8,585 70 |
| Sale of fixtures | 97 00 |
| Total income | $448,191 23 |
| Sum | $1,112,764 64 |

### DISBURSEMENTS.

| | |
|---|---|
| Death claims | $272,754 44 |
| Monuments | 47,613 00 |
| Total benefits paid | $320,367 44 |
| Salaries of deputies and organizers | 1,250 00 |
| Salaries of officers and trustees | 38,125 00 |
| Salaries and other compensation of committees | 4,505 24 |
| Salaries of office employees | 28,127 51 |
| Salaries and fees paid to supreme medical examiners | 3,100 00 |
| Traveling and other expenses of officers, trustees and committees | 5,559 05 |
| Insurance department fees | 455 40 |
| Rent | 3,967 00 |
| Advertising, printing and stationery | 8,467 67 |
| Postage, express, telegraph and telephone | 4,018 79 |
| Expenses of supreme lodge meeting | 2,489 01 |
| Legal expense in litigating claims | 328 10 |
| Other legal expenses | 1,708 45 |
| Furniture and fixtures | 265 88 |
| Taxes, repairs and other expenses on real estate | 20,365 68 |
| Auditing and actuary | 915 37 |
| Premium bonds | 37 50 |
| Miscellaneous | 106 02 |
| Uniforms, regalia and prizes | 6,056 68 |
| Total disbursements | $450,215 79 |
| Balance | $662,548 85 |

## LEDGER ASSETS.

| | |
|---|---|
| Book value of real estate | $150,000 00 |
| Mortgage loans on real estate | 142,150 00 |
| Book value of bonds and stocks | 162,739 06 |
| Cash in association's office | 43,988 71 |
| Deposits in trust companies and banks on interest | 157,671 08 |
| Bills receivable | 4,000 00 |
| Printing outfit | 2,000 00 |
| Total ledger assets | $662,548 85 |

### NON-LEDGER ASSETS.

| | |
|---|---|
| Interest and rents due and accrued | 9,355 68 |
| Gross assets | $671,904 53 |

### DEDUCT ASSETS NOT ADMITTED.

| | | |
|---|---|---|
| Bills receivable | $4,000 00 | |
| Printing outfit | 2,000 00 | |
| | | 6,000 00 |
| Total admitted assets | | $665,904 53 |

## LIABILITIES.

| | |
|---|---|
| Death claims reported during the year but not yet adjusted | $82,018 67 |

## EXHIBIT OF CERTIFICATES.

| | Total business of the year. | | Business in Illinois during year. | |
|---|---|---|---|---|
| | Number. | Amount. | Number. | Amount. |
| Benefit certificates in force December 31, 1920, as per last statement | 127,958 | $38,387,400 00 | 748 | $224,400 00 |
| Benefit certificates written and renewed during the year | 12,079 | 3,623,700 00 | 224 | 67,200 00 |
| Total | 140,037 | $42,011,100 00 | 972 | $291,600 00 |
| Deduct terminated, decreased or transferred during the year | 6,722 | 2,016,600 00 | -------- | ------------- |
| Deduct terminated or decreased during the year | -------- | ------------- | 69 | 20,700 00 |
| Total benefit certificates in force December 31, 1921 | 133,315 | $39,994,500 00 | 903 | $270,900 00 |

Received during the year from members in Illinois: Mortuary, $2,637.55; expense, $184.15; total — $2,821 70

## EXHIBIT OF DEATH CLAIMS.

| | Total claims. | | Illinois claims. | |
|---|---|---|---|---|
| | Number. | Amount. | Number. | Amount. |
| Claims unpaid December 31, 1920, as per last statement | 592 | $ 90,452 54 | 5 | $350 00 |
| Claims reported during the year and interest addition | 1,334 | 285,179 98 | 7 | 925 00 |
| Total | 1,926 | $375,632 52 | 12 | $1,275 00 |
| Claims paid during the year | 1,295 | 271,954 44 | 8 | 1,125 00 |
| Balance | 631 | $103,678 08 | 4 | $150 00 |
| Saved by compromising or scaling down claims during the year | -------- | 2,279 41 | -------- | ------------- |
| Claims rejected during the year | 183 | 19,380 00 | 1 | 100 00 |
| Claims unpaid December 31, 1921 | 448 | $82,018 67 | 3 | $50 00 |

---

# MUTUAL BENEFICIAL ASSOCIATION OF PENNSYLVANIA RAILROAD EMPLOYEES, INC.

Located at No. 1841 Filbert Street, Philadelphia, Pennsylvania.

GEORGE W. BROWN, President. CURTIS M. BRINKER, Secretary.

| | |
|---|---|
| Balance from previous year | $194,714 92 |

## INCOME.

| | |
|---|---|
| Membership fees actually received | $ 3,933 00 |
| All other assessments or premiums | 73,973 46 |

## INCOME—Concluded.

| | |
|---|---|
| Dues and per capita tax | $12,195 57 |
| Medical examiners' fees actually received | 3,742 00 |
| Net amount received from members | $93,844 03 |
| Gross interest on mortgage loans | 185 00 |
| Gross interest on bonds and dividends on stocks | 8,415 14 |
| Gross interest on deposits in trust companies and banks | 244 68 |
| Gross interest from all other sources | 1 52 |
| Sale of lodge supplies | 58 25 |
| Official publication | 2,359 72 |
| Local assembly dues collected | 153 83 |
| Total income | $105,262 17 |
| Sum | $299,977 09 |

## DISBURSEMENTS.

| | |
|---|---|
| Death claims | $31,975 00 |
| Traveling and other expenses of officers, trustees and committees | 3,065 97 |
| Insurance department fees | 53 30 |
| Advertising, printing and stationery | 3,504 58 |
| Lodge supplies | 1,233 06 |
| Official publication | 1,575 49 |
| Expenses of supreme lodge meeting | 431 29 |
| Other legal expenses | 300 00 |
| Gross loss on sale or maturity of ledger assets | 100 00 |
| Medical examiners paid | 3,471 00 |
| Local assembly dues returned | 153 83 |
| Total disbursements | $45,863 52 |
| Balance | $254,113 57 |

## LEDGER ASSETS.

| | |
|---|---|
| Mortgage loans on real estate | $ 5,500 00 |
| Loans secured by pledge of bonds, stocks or other collateral | 6,050 00 |
| Book value of bonds and stocks | 232,735 00 |
| Deposits in trust companies and banks on interest | 9,827 77 |
| Total ledger assets | $254,113 57 |

### NON-LEDGER ASSETS.

| | |
|---|---|
| Interest and rents due and accrued | 5,150 05 |
| Gross assets | $259,263 62 |

## LIABILITIES.

| | |
|---|---|
| Death claims reported during the year but not yet adjusted | $1,000 00 |
| Advance assessments | 1,653 41 |
| Due medical examiners | 1,560 50 |
| Total | $4,213 91 |

## EXHIBIT OF CERTIFICATES.

| | Total business of the year—all in Illinois. Number. | Amount. |
|---|---|---|
| Benefit certificates in force December 31, 1920, as per last statement | 5,261 | $3,238,750 00 |
| Benefit certificates written and renewed during the year | 3,669 | 1,986,750 00 |
| Benefit certificates increased during the year | -------- | 21,250 00 |
| Totals | 9,430 | $5,246,750 00 |
| Deduct terminated, decreased or transferred during the year | 2,328 | 1,235,250 00 |
| Total benefit certificates in force December 31, 1921 | 7,102 | $4,011,500 00 |

## EXHIBIT OF DEATH CLAIMS.

| | Total claims—all in Illinois. Number. | Amount. |
|---|---|---|
| Claims unpaid December 31, 1920, as per last statement | 5 | $ 3,475 00 |
| Claims reported during the year and interest addition | 47 | 29,500 00 |
| Totals | 52 | $32,975 00 |
| Claims paid during the year | 49 | 31,975 00 |
| Claims unpaid December 31, 1921 | 3 | $1,000 00 |

## NATIONAL BENEVOLENT SOCIETY.

Located at No. 3101-3 Troost Avenue, Kansas City, Missouri.

GEORGE R. COLLINS, President. FRANK E. LOTT, Secretary.

| | | |
|---|---|---|
| Balance from previous year | | $12,882 43 |
| **INCOME.** | | |
| Membership fees actually received | | $1,722 50 |
| All other assessments or premiums | | 48,025 14 |
| Medical examiners' fees actually received | | 360 50 |
| Total received from members | | $50,108 14 |
| Deduct payments returned to applicants and members | | 355 28 |
| Net amount received from members | | $49,752 86 |
| Gross interest on mortgage loans | | 130 00 |
| Gross interest on deposits in trust companies and banks | | 112 52 |
| Gross rents from association's property | | 144 00 |
| Sale of lodge supplies | | 638 74 |
| Returned checks | | 397 89 |
| Total income | | $51,176 01 |
| Sum | | $64,058 44 |
| **DISBURSEMENTS.** | | |
| Death claims | | $2,568 40 |
| Permanent disability claims | | 16,744 90 |
| Total benefits paid | | $19,313 30 |
| Salaries of lecturers and organizers | | 10,268 74 |
| Salaries of officers and trustees | | 3,900 00 |
| Salaries of office employees | | 8,164 96 |
| Salaries and fees paid to supreme medical examiners | | 10 00 |
| Salaries and fees paid to subordinate medical examiners | | 37 00 |
| Traveling and other expenses of officers, trustees and committees | | 696 34 |
| Insurance department fees | | 633 93 |
| Rent | | 1,303 87 |
| Advertising, printing and stationery | | 2,010 32 |
| Postage, express, telegraph and telephone | | 2,789 42 |
| Lodge supplies | | 871 83 |
| Official publication | | 1,251 80 |
| Expenses of supreme lodge meeting | | 106 65 |
| Other legal expenses | | 275 00 |
| Furniture and fixtures | | 44 36 |
| Taxes, repairs and other expenses on real estate | | 78 52 |
| Sundry office expenses | | 94 43 |
| Electrotypes | | 54 97 |
| Fraternal Congress expense | | 5 00 |
| Total disbursements | | $51,910 44 |
| Balance | | $12,148 00 |
| **LEDGER ASSETS.** | | |
| Book value of real estate | | $1,750 00 |
| Mortgage loans on real estate | | 3,750 00 |
| Cash in association's office | | 632 54 |
| Deposits in trust companies and banks not on interest | | 3,071 00 |
| Deposits in trust companies and banks on interest | | 2,944 46 |
| Total ledger assets | | $12,148 00 |
| **NON-LEDGER ASSETS.** | | |
| Interest and rents due and accrued | | 95 70 |
| Assessments actually collected by subordinate lodges not yet turned over to supreme lodge | | 140 00 |
| All other assets, viz— | | |
| Organizers balances | $749 23 | |
| Furniture, safes, etc., $1,919.10; electrotypes, $637.47 | 2,556 57 | |
| Lien notes | 21,700 75 | |
| Premium notes | 1,413 00 | |
| Cash lions | 14,401 27 | |
| Assessments in process of collection | 410 00 | |
| | | 44,260 82 |
| Gross assets | | $56,644 52 |

LEDGER ASSETS—Concluded.

DEDUCT ASSETS NOT ADMITTED.

| | | |
|---|---|---|
| Total amount of non-ledger assets | | $44,496 52 |
| Total admitted assets | | $12,148 00 |

LIABILITIES.

| | | |
|---|---|---|
| Death claims reported during the year but not yet adjusted | | $225 00 |
| Sick and accident claims reported during the year but not yet adjusted. | $308 00 | |
| Sick and accident claims incurred in 1921, not reported until 1922 | 84 00 | |
| Total sick and accident claims | | 392 00 |
| Total unpaid claims | | $617 00 |
| Advance assessments | | 131 00 |
| Total | | $748 00 |

EXHIBIT OF CERTIFICATES.

| | Total business of the year. | | Business in Illinois during year. | |
|---|---|---|---|---|
| | Number. | Amount. | Number. | Amount. |
| Benefit certificates in force December 31, 1920, as per last statement | 5,558 | $238,575 00 | 77 | $1,925 00 |
| Benefit certificates written and renewed during the year | 4,810 | 120,250 00 | 120 | 3,000 00 |
| Benefit certificates increased during the year | | 26,750 00 | | 1,550 00 |
| Totals | 10,368 | $385,575 00 | 197 | $6,475 00 |
| Deduct terminated, decreased or transferred during the year | 5,528 | 157,750 00 | | |
| Deduct terminated or decreased during the year | | | 38 | 950 00 |
| Total benefit certificates in force December 31, 1921 | 4,840 | $227,825 00 | 159 | $5,525 00 |

| | |
|---|---|
| Received during the year from members in Illinois: Expense | $1,858 20 |

EXHIBIT OF DEATH CLAIMS.

| | Total claims—all in Illinois. | |
|---|---|---|
| | Number. | Amount. |
| Claims unpaid December 31, 1920, as per last statement | 4 | $ 150 00 |
| Claims reported during the year and interest addition | 66 | 2,643 40 |
| Totals | 70 | $2,793 40 |
| Claims paid during the year | 63 | 2,568 40 |
| Claims unpaid December 31, 1921 | 7 | $225 00 |

EXHIBIT OF SICK AND ACCIDENT CLAIMS.

| | Total claims. | | Illinois claims. | |
|---|---|---|---|---|
| | Number. | Amount. | Number. | Amount. |
| Claims unpaid December 31, 1920, as per last statement | 65 | $ 390 00 | | |
| Claims reported during the year | 2,286 | 16,618 90 | 92 | $568 49 |
| Totals | 2,351 | $17,008 90 | 92 | $568 49 |
| Claims paid during the year | 2,307 | 16,744 90 | 91 | 561 49 |
| Claims unpaid December 31, 1921 | 44 | $264 00 | 1 | $7 00 |

---

## NATIONAL CROATION SOCIETY OF THE U. S. A.

Located at No. 1012 Peralta Street, N. S. Pittsburgh, Pennsylvania.

THOMAS BESENIC, President. VINKO SOLIC, Secretary.

| | |
|---|---|
| Balance from previous year | $1,092,871 05 |

INCOME.

| | |
|---|---|
| Membership fees actually received | $605,306 16 |
| Assessments or premiums during first months of membership of which all or an extra percentage is used for expenses | 2,832 00 |
| All other assessments or premiums | 55,110 31 |
| Dues and per capita tax | 35,844 76 |
| Changing of beneficiaries | 544 75 |
| Net amount received from members | $699,637 98 |

INCOME—Concluded.

| | | |
|---|---|---|
| Gross interest on bonds and dividends on stocks | | $35,998 55 |
| Gross interest on deposits in trust companies and banks | | 10,730 47 |
| Sale of lodge supplies | | 3,346 71 |
| Official publication | | 24,424 62 |
| Refund sick benefit paid on account of policies | | 9,490 00 |
| Return cash | | 661 75 |
| Return check | | 2,033 60 |
| Official organ subscriptions | | 81 60 |
| All other income | | 6,384 19 |
| Total income | | $792,789 47 |
| Sum | | $1,885,660 52 |

DISBURSEMENTS.

| | | |
|---|---|---|
| Death claims | | $315,455 47 |
| Permanent disability claims | | 62,075 00 |
| Sick and accident claims | | 117,604 30 |
| Sick benefit paid on account of policies | | 12,695 00 |
| Total benefits paid | | $507,829 77 |
| Salaries of officers and trustees | | 8,640 00 |
| Salaries and other compensation of supreme counselor | | 1,800 00 |
| Salaries of office employees | | 8,232 00 |
| Salaries and fees paid to supreme medical examiners | | 1,800 00 |
| Traveling and other expenses of officers, trustees and committees | | 1,568 74 |
| Insurance department fees | | 292 00 |
| Advertising, printing and stationery | | 4,336 26 |
| Postage, express, telegraph and telephone | | 1,610 57 |
| Lodge supplies | | 3,476 85 |
| Official publication | | 20,921 63 |
| Expenses of supreme lodge meeting | | 620 00 |
| Legal expense in litigating claims | | 480 00 |
| Other legal expenses with 14th convention | | 45,236 90 |
| Furniture and fixtures | | 550 32 |
| Taxes, repairs and other expenses on real estate | | 810 44 |
| Gross loss on sale or maturity of ledger assets | | 80 00 |
| Loss on savings account | | 2,937 66 |
| Donations by 14th convention | | 34,376 25 |
| Croation war orphans collected 1920 and carried in mortuary fund | | 34,816 00 |
| Interest on transfer fund, orphans fund | | 1,250 00 |
| Total disbursements | | $681,665 39 |
| Balance | | $1,203,995 13 |

LEDGER ASSETS.

| | | |
|---|---|---|
| Book value of real estate | | $ 17,000 00 |
| Book value of bonds and stocks | | 836,789 18 |
| Cash in association's office | | 500 00 |
| Deposits in trust companies and banks on interest | | 349,705 95 |
| Total ledger assets | | $1,203,995 13 |

NON-LEDGER ASSETS.

| | | |
|---|---|---|
| Interest and rents due and accrued | | 9,550 38 |
| Assessments actually collected by subordinate lodges not yet turned over to supreme lodge | | 16,172 38 |
| All other assets, viz— | | |
| Furniture and fixtures | $ 8,640 67 | |
| Book and emblems | 1,596 75 | |
| Deposit for gas | 15 00 | |
| Due on policies paid to members as sick benefit | 19,149 00 | |
| | | 29,401 42 |
| Gross assets | | $1,259,119 31 |

DEDUCT ASSETS NOT ADMITTED.

| | | |
|---|---|---|
| Interest not transferred to orphanage | $ 593 75 | |
| Book value of bonds and stocks over market value | 17,491 98 | |
| Books and emblems | 1,596 75 | |
| Due on policies paid to members on sick benefit | 19,149 00 | |
| Furniture and fixtures | 8,640 67 | |
| | | 47,472 15 |
| Total admitted assets | | $1,248,288 14 |

LIABILITIES.

| | | |
|---|---|---|
| Death claims due and unpaid | $31,018 10 | |
| Death claims reported during the year but not yet adjusted | 14,600 00 | |
| Total death claims | | $45,618 10 |

LIABILITIES—Concluded.

| | | |
|---|---|---|
| Permanent disability claims due and unpaid | $ 200 00 | |
| Permanent disability claims reported during the year but not yet adjusted | 5,000 00 | |
| Total permanent disability claims | | $5,200 00 |
| Sick and accident claims due and unpaid | | 4,178 04 |
| Total unpaid claims | | $54,996 14 |
| All other liabilities, viz— | | |
| Unpaid bills | $ 157 25 | |
| Balance due to lodges | 1,812 99 | |
| | | 1,970 24 |
| Total | | $56,966 38 |

EXHIBIT OF CERTIFICATES.

| | Total business of the year. | | Business in Illinois during year. | |
|---|---|---|---|---|
| | Number. | Amount. | Number. | Amount. |
| Benefit certificates in force December 31, 1920, as per last statement | 38,034 | $29,393,400 00 | 4,549 | $3,458,800 00 |
| Benefit certificates written and renewed during the year | 3,057 | 2,706,400 00 | 435 | 286,600 00 |
| Benefit certificates received by transfer during the year | | | | 90,200 00 |
| Benefit certificates increased during the year | | 107,600 00 | | |
| Totals | 41,091 | $32,207,400 00 | 4,984 | $3,835,600 00 |
| Deduct terminated, decreased or transferred during the year | 3,273 | 2,696,600 00 | | |
| Deduct terminated or decreased during the year | | | 1,139 | 772,400 00 |
| Total benefit certificates in force December 31, 1921 | 37,818 | $29,510,800 00 | 3,845 | $3,063,200 00 |

Received during the year from members in Illinois: Mortuary, $56,896.68; disability, $6,019.20; all other, $12,038.40; expense, $8,025.60; total $82,979 88

EXHIBIT OF DEATH CLAIMS.

| | Total claims. | | Illinois claims. | |
|---|---|---|---|---|
| | Number. | Amount. | Number. | Amount. |
| Claims unpaid December 31, 1920, as per last statement | 85 | $ 48,549 60 | 6 | $ 3,590 00 |
| Claims reported during the year and interest addition | 370 | 296,600 00 | 32 | 34,800 00 |
| Totals | 455 | $345,149 60 | 38 | $38,390 00 |
| Claims paid during the year | 397 | 314,131 50 | 30 | 34,257 00 |
| Balance | 58 | $31,018 10 | 8 | $4,133 00 |
| Claims unpaid December 31, 1921 | 77 | $45,618 10 | | |

EXHIBIT OF PERMANENT DISABILITY CLAIMS.

| | Total claims. | | Illinois claims. | |
|---|---|---|---|---|
| | Number. | Amount. | Number. | Amount. |
| Claims unpaid December 31, 1920, as per last statement | 2 | $ 500 00 | 68 | $8,925 00 |
| Claims reported during the year and interest addition | 526 | 61,575 00 | | |
| Totals | 528 | $62,075 00 | | |
| Claims paid during the year | 526 | 61,875 00 | | |
| Balance | 2 | $200 00 | | |
| Claims unpaid December 31, 1921 | 52 | $5,200 00 | | |

EXHIBIT OF SICK AND ACCIDENT CLAIMS

| | Total claims. | | Illinois claims. | |
|---|---|---|---|---|
| | Number. | Amount. | Number. | Amount. |
| Claims unpaid December 31, 1920, as per last statemen | 9 | $ 1,535 74 | 1 | $ 54 00 |
| Increase in estimated liability | 445 | 119,156 00 | | 14,484 00 |
| Totals | 454 | $120,691 74 | | $14,538 00 |
| Claims paid during the year | 441 | 116,513 70 | | 14,253 00 |
| Claims rejected during the year | 13 | 4,178 04 | | 285 00 |

## NATIONAL PROTECTIVE LEGION.

Located at No. 433-439 Fulton Street, Waverly, New York.

GEORGE A. SCOTT, President. H. C. LOCKWOOD, Secretary.

| | |
|---|---|
| Balance from previous year | $124,375 87 |

### INCOME.

| | |
|---|---|
| Membership fees actually received | $ 2,357 01 |
| Assessments or premiums during first twelve months of membership of which all or an extra percentage is used for expenses | 127,229 62 |
| All other assessments or premiums | 152,976 84 |
| Dues and per capita tax | 755 18 |
| Expense revenue from juvenile | 166 10 |
| Net amount received from members | $283,484 75 |
| Gross interest on mortgage loans | 825 00 |
| Gross interest on bonds and dividends on stocks | 3,160 00 |
| Gross rents from association's property | 3,430 08 |
| Sale of lodge supplies | 2,111 54 |
| Interest on Class A balances | 1,039 43 |
| Checks returned | 137 40 |
| Limited term levy | 17 00 |
| Borrowed money | 42,300 00 |
| Expense levy | 25,497 12 |
| Other items | 232 24 |
| Total income | $362,234 56 |
| Sum | $486,610 43 |

### DISBURSEMENTS.

| | |
|---|---|
| Death claims | $112,526 54 |
| Sick and accident claims | 71,984 69 |
| Old age benefits | 4,866 62 |
| Total benefits paid | $189,377 85 |
| Commissions and fees paid to deputies and organizers | 11,220 80 |
| Salaries of deputies and organizers | 36,943 41 |
| Salaries of officers and trustees | 10,559 88 |
| Salaries of office employees | 13,199 25 |
| Salaries and fees paid to supreme medical examiners | 1,599 96 |
| Salaries and fees paid to subordinate medical examiners | 3,893 26 |
| Traveling and other expenses of officers, trustees and committees | 8,105 76 |
| Insurance department fees | 428 00 |
| Rent | 7,037 35 |
| Advertising, printing and stationery | 7,828 78 |
| Postage, express, telegraph, telephone, freight and dray | 6,856 19 |
| Lodge supplies | 802 28 |
| Official publication | 4,000 00 |
| Expenses of supreme lodge meeting | 1,220 32 |
| Other legal expenses | 1,476 20 |
| Taxes, repairs and other expenses on real estate | 1,844 51 |
| Borrowed money repaid (gross) | 15,800 00 |
| Interest on borrowed money | 300 00 |
| All other disbursements, viz— | |
| Fees returned, $478.81; organizers travel expense, $12,640.78; actuary, $682.40 | 13,801 99 |
| Janitor and cleaning, $966.40; fuel, $2,004.75; water, light and power, $1,718.69 | 4,689 84 |
| Office supplies, $710.24; subscriptions and dues, $720.58; books for home office, $481.13 | 1,911 95 |
| Other items, $1,873.67; interest, $2,674.43; repairs, $355.81; incurred by transfer, $48.10 | 4,952 01 |
| Total disbursements | $347,849 59 |
| Balance | $138,760 84 |

### LEDGER ASSETS.

| | |
|---|---|
| Book value of real estate | $34,000 00 |
| Mortgage loans on real estate | 15,000 00 |
| Book value of bonds and stocks | 67,546 00 |
| Deposits in trust companies and banks not on interest | 22,214 84 |
| Total ledger assets | $138,760 84 |

#### NON-LEDGER ASSETS.

| | | |
|---|---|---|
| Interest and rents due and accrued | | 3,912 76 |
| Market value of real estate over book value | | 10,000 00 |
| Assessments actually collected by subordinate lodges not yet turned over to supreme lodge | | 24,627 86 |
| All other assets, viz— | | |
| Office fixtures and printing plant in Legion Temple | $30,025 00 | |
| Supplies and paper stock on hand in Legion Temple | 11,396 82 | |

LEDGER ASSETS—Concluded.

| | | |
|---|---|---|
| All other assets, viz: | | |
| Office fixtures and supplies in hands of organizers | $3,000 00 | |
| Due for supplies from district managers and local legions | 5,480 22 | |
| | | $49,902 04 |
| Gross assets | | $227,203 50 |

DEDUCT ASSETS NOT ADMITTED.

| | | |
|---|---|---|
| Bills receivable | $ 5,480 22 | |
| Other items, viz— | | |
| Office fixtures and printing plant in Legion Temple | 30,025 00 | |
| Supplies and paper stock in hand in Legion Temple | 11,396 82 | |
| Office fixtures in hands of organizers | 3,000 00 | |
| | | 49,902 04 |
| Total admitted assets | | $177,301 46 |

LIABILITIES.

| | | |
|---|---|---|
| Death claims due and unpaid | | $7,590 00 |
| Sick and accident claims due and unpaid | | 1,083 20 |
| Total unpaid claims | | $ 8,673 20 |
| Borrowed money | | 57,450 00 |
| Advance assessments | | 418 78 |
| All other liabilities, viz— | | |
| Geo. A. Scott, miscellaneous bills paid by him | $2,278 54 | |
| J. and F. B. Garrett paper stock in hand | 411 90 | |
| Fraternal Monitor advertising | 469 55 | |
| Miscellaneous bills, insurance and etc | 435 50 | |
| | | 3,595 49 |
| Total | | $70,137 47 |

EXHIBIT OF CERTIFICATES.

| | Total business of the year. | | Business in Illinois during year. | |
|---|---|---|---|---|
| | Number. | Amount. | Number. | Amount. |
| Benefit certificates in force December 31, 1920, as per last statement | 22,638 | $12,864,385 00 | 4,800 | $3,539,825 00 |
| Benefit certificates written and renewed during the year | 3 789 | 2,431,987 50 | 1,069 | 910,187 50 |
| Totals | 26,427 | $15,296,372 50 | 5,869 | $4,450,012 50 |
| Deduct terminated, decreased or transferred during the year | 7,125 | 3,526,010 00 | | |
| Deduct terminated or decreased during the year | | | 1,751 | 1,277,550 00 |
| Total benefit certificates in force December 31, 1921 | 19,302 | $11,770,362 50 | 4,118 | $3,172,462 50 |

Received during the year from members in Illinois: Mortuary, $26,248.34; extra, $4,659.48; new benefits, $4,752.63; Class C, $3,732.05; expense, $18,215.39; total ........ $57,607 89

EXHIBIT OF DEATH CLAIMS.

| | Total claims. | | Illinois claims. | |
|---|---|---|---|---|
| | Number. | Amount. | Number. | Amount. |
| Claims unpaid December 31, 1920, as per last statement | 10 | $ 7,705 65 | 3 | $ 3,500 00 |
| Claims reported during the year and interest addition | 186 | 113,010 89 | 37 | 29,564 49 |
| Totals | 196 | $120,716 54 | 40 | $33,064 49 |
| Claims paid during the year | 183 | 112,526 54 | 40 | 32,464 49 |
| Balance | 13 | $8,190 00 | | |
| Saved by compromising or scaling down claims during the year | | 600 00 | | $600 00 |
| Claims unpaid December 31, 1921 | 13 | $7,590 00 | | |

EXHIBIT OF SICK AND ACCIDENT CLAIMS.

| | Total claims. | | Illinois claims. | |
|---|---|---|---|---|
| | Number. | Amount. | Number. | Amount. |
| Claims unpaid December 31, 1920, as per last statement | 66 | $ 2,331 15 | 9 | $ 557 65 |
| Claims reported during the year | 2,024 | 72,310 88 | 270 | 10,432 60 |
| Totals | 2,090 | $74,642 03 | 279 | $10,990 25 |
| Claims paid during the year | 2,005 | 71,984 69 | 267 | 10,532 83 |
| Claims rejected during the year | 53 | 1,574 14 | 9 | 390 92 |
| Claims unpaid December 31, 1921 | 32 | $1,083 20 | 3 | $66 50 |

EXHIBIT OF OLD AGE AND OTHER CLAIMS.

| | Total claims. Number. | Total claims. Amount. | Illinois claims. Number. | Illinois claims. Amount. |
|---|---|---|---|---|
| Claims paid during the year | 13 | $4,866 62 | 2 | $1,333 33 |

## NATIONAL SLOVAK SOCIETY, U. S. A.

Located at Corner Hooper and Ivanhoe Streets, Pittsburgh, Pennsylvania.

ALBERT MAMATEY, President. JOSEPH DURISH, Secretary.

| | |
|---|---|
| Balance from previous year | $1,724,104 96 |

INCOME.

| | |
|---|---|
| Net amount received from members | $496,861 45 |
| Gross interest on mortgage loans | 1,722 90 |
| Gross interest on bonds and dividends on stocks | 66,410 79 |
| Gross interest on deposits in trust companies and banks | 8,753 05 |
| Gross rents from association's property, including $1,200.00 for association's occupancy of its own buildings | 6,328 42 |
| Sale of lodge supplies | 857 78 |
| Gross profit on sale or maturity of ledger assets | 17,413 21 |
| Gross increase in book value of ledger assets | 800 65 |
| Returned recording fee | 6 00 |
| One per cent orphans' cash | 1,355 86 |
| Compensation insurance | 2 94 |
| Returned insane dues | 124 66 |
| Total income | $600,637 71 |
| Sum | $2,324,742 67 |

DISBURSEMENTS.

| | |
|---|---|
| Death claims | $283,725 52 |
| Sick and accident claims | 10,807 81 |
| Total benefits paid | $294,533 33 |
| Salaries of officers and trustees | 8,345 00 |
| Salaries of office employees | 7,643 12 |
| Salaries and fees paid to supreme medical examiners | 23 50 |
| Traveling and other expenses of officers, trustees and committees | 1,528 34 |
| Insurance department fees | 628 95 |
| Rent | 1,200 00 |
| Advertising, printing and stationery | 5,565 44 |
| Postage, express, telegraph and telephone | 935 98 |
| Lodge supplies | 767 56 |
| Official publication | 24,000 00 |
| Expenses of supreme lodge meeting | 2,863 67 |
| Legal expense in litigating claims | 220 33 |
| Other legal expenses | 70 00 |
| Furniture and fixtures | 360 91 |
| Taxes, repairs and other expenses on real estate | 8,248 99 |
| Gross decrease in book value of ledger assets | 2,108 58 |
| All other disbursements, viz— | |
| Educational work | 2,806 29 |
| Sundry expense, $4,051.29; deposit for gas, $10.00 | 4,061 29 |
| Bonding supreme officers, $512.50; supreme court session, $264.95 | 777 45 |
| Preparing state reports | 1,097 02 |
| Total disbursements | $367,785 75 |
| Balance | $1,956,956 92 |

LEDGER ASSETS.

| | |
|---|---|
| Book value of real estate | $ 91,947 43 |
| Mortgage loans on real estate | 33,183 83 |
| Book value of bonds and stocks | 1,484,751 79 |
| Deposits in trust companies and banks on interest | 347,073 87 |
| Total ledger assets | $1,956,956 92 |

NON-LEDGER ASSETS.

| | | |
|---|---|---|
| Interest and rents due and accrued | | 25,363 64 |
| Assessments actually collected by subordinate lodges not yet turned over to supreme lodge | | 9,746 38 |
| All other assets, viz— | | |
| Furniture, fixtures and machinery | $ 15,075 81 | |
| Dues advanced to insane members | 8,696 53 | |
| Lodge supplies | 2,674 65 | |
| Miscellaneous | 86 90 | |
| Orphans cash deposited in banks | 161,659 04 | |
| | | 188,192 93 |
| Gross assets | | $2,180,259 87 |

## LEDGER ASSETS—Concluded.

DEDUCT ASSETS NOT ADMITTED.

| | | |
|---|---|---|
| Book value of bonds and stocks over market value | $ 9,651 29 | |
| Other items, viz— | | |
| Furniture, fixtures and machinery | 15,075 81 | |
| Dues advanced to insane members | 8,696 53 | |
| Lodge supplies | 2,674 65 | |
| Miscellaneous | 86 90 | |
| | | $36,185 18 |
| Total admitted assets | | $2,144,074 69 |

## LIABILITIES.

| | | |
|---|---|---|
| Death claims due and unpaid | $24,464 71 | |
| Death claims adjusted not yet due | 26,950 00 | |
| Death claims reported during the year but not yet adjusted | 17,950 00 | |
| Total death claims | | $69,364 71 |
| Sick and accident claims adjusted, and not yet due | | 785 00 |
| Total unpaid claims | | $70,149 71 |
| Salaries, rents, expenses, commissions, etc., due or accrued | | 981 35 |
| Advance assessments | | 1,209 68 |
| All other liabilities, viz— | | |
| Bonds for appeal for supreme court session | $ 75 00 | |
| Orphans' cash deposited in banks | 161,659 04 | |
| | | 161,734 04 |
| Total | | $234,074 78 |

## EXHIBIT OF CERTIFICATES.

| | Total business of the year. | | Business in Illinois during year. | |
|---|---|---|---|---|
| | Number. | Amount. | Number. | Amount. |
| Benefit certificates in force December 31, 1920, as per last statement | 39,473 | $29,439,250 00 | 3,838 | $2,853,950 00 |
| Benefit certificates written and renewed during the year | 1,265 | 1,058,250 00 | 138 | 114,000 00 |
| Benefit certificates received by transfer during the year | | | 46 | 36,250 00 |
| Benefit certificates increased during the year | | 20,500 00 | | 1,750 00 |
| Total | 40,738 | $30,518,000 00 | 4,022 | $3,005,950 00 |
| Deduct terminated, decreased or transferred during the year | 1,783 | 1,358,500 00 | | |
| Deduct terminated or decreased during the year | | | 212 | 158,000 00 |
| Total benefit certificates in force December 31, 1921 | 38,955 | $29,159,500 00 | 3,810 | $2,847,950 00 |

Received during the year from members in Illinois: Mortuary, $38,905.37; national, $678.46; aged and orphans' home, $1,356.92; sick and accident, $1,319.38; expense, $5,434.25; total ........ $47,694 38

## EXHIBIT OF DEATH CLAIMS.

| | Total claims. | | Illinois claims. | |
|---|---|---|---|---|
| | Number. | Amount. | Number. | Amount. |
| Claims unpaid December 31, 1920, as per last statement | 114 | $ 66,115 23 | 6 | $ 2,244 52 |
| Claims reported during the year and interest addition | 375 | 286,975 00 | 32 | 23,000 00 |
| Total | 489 | $353,090 23 | 38 | $25,244 52 |
| Claims paid during the year | 374 | 283,725 52 | 32 | 22,834 00 |
| Claims unpaid December 31, 1921 | 115 | $69,364 71 | 6 | $2,410 52 |

## EXHIBIT OF SICK AND ACCIDENT CLAIMS.

| | Total claims. | | Illinois claims. | |
|---|---|---|---|---|
| | Number. | Amount. | Number. | Amount. |
| Claims unpaid December 31, 1920, as per last statement | 17 | $ 742 32 | | |
| Claims reported during the year | 264 | 10,875 40 | | |
| Total | 281 | $11,617 81 | | |
| Claims paid during the year | 258 | 10,807 81 | 37 | $910 00 |
| Claims rejected during the year | 1 | 25 00 | | |
| Claims unpaid December 31, 1921 | 22 | $785 00 | | |

## NATIONAL UNION ASSURANCE SOCIETY.

Located at No. 437 Michigan Street, Toledo, Ohio.

D. A. HELPMAN, President. E. A. MYERS, Secretary.

| | |
|---|---|
| Balance from previous year | $1,751,158 28 |

### INCOME.

| | |
|---|---|
| Membership fees actually received | $ 33 00 |
| All other assessments or premiums | 3,268,205 13 |
| Dues and per capita tax | 4,607 00 |
| Other payments by members, viz: Changing certificates, $95.35; reg. socials, $4.00 | 99 35 |
| Net amount received from members | $3,272,944 48 |
| Gross interest on bonds and dividends on stocks | 68,432 16 |
| Gross interest on deposits in trust companies and banks | 10,604 02 |
| Gross interest from all other sources | 226 41 |
| Gross rents from association's property | 2,625 00 |
| Sale of lodge supplies | 1,314 77 |
| Gross increase in book value of ledger assets | 6,585 26 |
| Fines | 107 80 |
| Premiums council bonds | 1,686 22 |
| Accounts overpaid returned | 13 00 |
| Sale of photo supplies | 85 75 |
| Total income | $3,364,624 87 |
| Sum | 5,115,783 15 |

### DISBURSEMENTS.

| | |
|---|---|
| Death claims | $1,886,873 35 |
| Old age benefits | 156,500 00 |
| Withdrawal | 1,239 56 |
| Total benefits paid | $2,044,612 91 |
| Commissions and fees paid to deputies and organizers | 347,471 94 |
| Salaries of deputies and organizers | 29,685 00 |
| Salaries of managers or agents not deputies or organizers | 5,500 00 |
| Salaries of officers and trustees | 23,100 00 |
| Salaries and other compensation of committees | 3,285 00 |
| Salaries of office employees | 69,434 42 |
| Other compensation of office employees | 50 00 |
| Salaries and fees paid to supreme medical examiners | 5,500 00 |
| Salaries and fees paid to subordinate medical examiners | 3,998 00 |
| Traveling and other expenses of officers, trustees and committees | 12,341 75 |
| For collection and remittance of assessments and dues | 12,843 29 |
| Insurance department fees | 689 15 |
| Rent, including $2,625.00 for association's occupancy of its own buildings | 15,143 75 |
| Advertising, printing and stationery | 14,506 33 |
| Postage, express, telegraph and telephone | 6,732 82 |
| Legal expense in litigating claims | 973 49 |
| Furniture and fixtures | 9,449 10 |
| Taxes, repairs and other expenses on real estate | 13,769 63 |
| Gross loss on sale or maturity of ledger assets | 24,772 72 |
| Gross decrease in book value of ledger assets | 1,166 96 |
| Borrowed money repaid (gross) | 150,000 00 |
| Interest on borrowed money | 3,104 83 |
| All other disbursements, viz— | |
| Expense field department | 21,278 83 |
| Premium surety bonds, inspections, per capita to local bodies, special organization expense, Fraternal Congress, expense city headquarters | 13,111 15 |
| Total disbursements | $2,832,521 08 |
| Balance | $2,283,262 07 |

### LEDGER ASSETS.

| | |
|---|---|
| Book value of real estate | $ 130,405 34 |
| Book value of bonds and stocks | 1,833,994 11 |
| Deposits in trust companies and banks on interest | 318,369 37 |
| Premium loans | 493 25 |
| Total ledger assets | $2,283,262 07 |

#### NON-LEDGER ASSETS.

| | |
|---|---|
| Interest and rents due and accrued | 23,111 77 |
| Market value of real estate over book value | 15,000 00 |
| Assessments actually collected by subordinate lodges not yet turned over to supreme lodge | 213,144 70 |
| Net deferred premiums | 686,730 20 |
| Gross assets | $3,317,847 63 |

## LIABILITIES.

| | | |
|---|---|---|
| Death claims reported during the year but not yet adjusted | $309,178 00 | |
| Death claims incurred in 1921, not reported until 1922 | 19,000 00 | |
| Total death claims | | $328,178 00 |
| Salaries, rents, expenses, commissions, etc., due or accrued | | 10,634 44 |
| Taxes due or accrued | | 633 81 |
| All other liabilities, viz— | | |
| Reserve liability American, 3½ per cent interest | $ 757,604 69 | |
| Reserve liability American, 4 per cent interest | 1,179,112 70 | |
| Reserve liability, special for dividends | 100,000 00 | |
| Reserve liability, special for contingencies | 200,000 00 | |
| | | 2,236,717 39 |
| Total | | $2,576,213 64 |

## EXHIBIT OF CERTIFICATES.

| | Total business of the year. | | Business in Illinois during year. | |
|---|---|---|---|---|
| | Number. | Amount. | Number. | Amount. |
| Benefit certificates in force December 31, 1920, as per last statement | 42,121 | $71,374,580 00 | 12,220 | $19,494,412 00 |
| Benefit certificates written and renewed during the year | 1,011 | 1,126,646 06 | 369 | 377,500 00 |
| Benefit certificates received by transfer during the year | | | 338 | 540,500 00 |
| Benefit certificates increased during the year | | 169,997 00 | | 54,743 00 |
| Total | 43,132 | $72,671,223 06 | 12,927 | $20,467,155 00 |
| Deduct terminated, decreased or transferred during the year | 4,789 | 8,771,643 06 | | |
| Deduct terminated or decreased during the year | | | 1,678 | 2,921,775 00 |
| Total benefit certificates in force December 31, 1921 | 38,343 | $63,899,580 00 | 11,249 | $17,545,380 00 |

Received during the year from members in Illinois: Mortuary, $692,083.84; expense, $173,290.72; total $865,374 56

## EXHIBIT OF DEATH CLAIMS.

| | Total claims. | | Illinois claims. | |
|---|---|---|---|---|
| | Number. | Amount. | Number. | Amount. |
| Claims unpaid December 31, 1920, as per last statement | 114 | $ 240,500 00 | 25 | $ 39,000 00 |
| Claims reported during the year and interest addition | 883 | 1,959,827 55 | 201 | 402,775 00 |
| Total | 997 | $2,200,327 55 | 226 | $441,775 00 |
| Claims paid during the year | 855 | 1,886,873 35 | 189 | 361,680 00 |
| Balance | 142 | $313,454 20 | 37 | $80,095 00 |
| Saved by compromising or scaling down claims during the year | | 4,276 20 | | |
| Claims unpaid December 31, 1921 | 142 | $309,178 00 | 37 | $80,095 00 |

## EXHIBIT OF OLD AGE AND OTHER CLAIMS.

| | Total claims. | | Illinois claims. | |
|---|---|---|---|---|
| | Number. | Amount. | Number. | Amount. |
| Claims paid during the year | 224 | $156,500 00 | 41 | $137,500 00 |

# NEW ERA ASSOCIATION.

Located at Grand Rapids Savings Bank Building, Grand Rapids, Michigan.

CHARLES D. SHARROW, President. CORNELIUS L. HARVEY, General Secretary.

| | |
|---|---|
| Balance from previous year | $162,937 41 |

## INCOME.

| | |
|---|---|
| Membership fees actually received | $490,269 89 |
| All other assessments or premiums | 2,979 65 |
| Other payments by members, viz: Protection fees, certificate and transfers | 5,639 21 |
| Total received from members | $498,888 75 |
| Deduct payments returned to applicants and members | 543 20 |
| Net amount received from members | $498,345 55 |

INCOME—Concluded.

| | |
|---|---|
| Gross interest on bonds | $4,770 83 |
| Gross interest on deposits in trust companies and banks | 1,565 45 |
| Reimbursed premiums | 117 40 |
| Reinstatements | 49 75 |
| Litigation claims | 550 00 |
| Reports pending | 816 73 |
| Reimbursement on rent | 2,100 00 |
| Miscellaneous receipts | 2,760 10 |
| Total income | $511,619 01 |
| Sum | $674,556 42 |

DISBURSEMENTS.

| | |
|---|---|
| Death claims | $372,994 60 |
| Cash surrenders | 666 74 |
| Total benefits paid | $373,661 34 |
| Commissions and fees paid to deputies and organizers | 24,967 59 |
| Salaries of deputies and organizers | 706 20 |
| Salaries of managers or agents not deputies or organizers | 13,837 92 |
| Salaries of officers and trustees | 7,865 00 |
| Other compensation of officers and trustees | 2,325 00 |
| Salaries and other compensation of committees—governing body | 150 00 |
| Salaries of office employees | 33,180 95 |
| Salaries and fees paid to supreme medical examiners | 2,426 67 |
| Traveling and other expenses of officers, trustees and committees | 5,499 42 |
| For collection and remittance of assessments and dues | 16,889 62 |
| Insurance department fees | 10 00 |
| Rent | 4,089 94 |
| Advertising, printing and stationery | 5,571 80 |
| Postage, express, telegraph and telephone | 2,907 01 |
| Supplies for office | 1,122 52 |
| Official publication and periodicals | 5,941 84 |
| Legal expense in litigating claims | 1,418 98 |
| Furniture and fixtures | 4,511 27 |
| Taxes, repairs and other expenses on real estate, repairs and electricity | 417 80 |
| Miscellaneous | 4,864 37 |
| Total disbursements | $522,286 19 |
| Balance | $152,270 23 |

LEDGER ASSETS.

| | |
|---|---|
| Book value of bonds and stocks | $111,452 00 |
| Cash in association's office | 250 00 |
| Deposits in trust companies and banks not on interest | 3,935 67 |
| Deposits in trust companies and banks on interest | 52,084 70 |
| Bills receivable, $7,584.21; due field department, $514.10 | 8,098 31 |
| Reports pending | 7,353 83 |
| Total ledger assets | $152,270 23 |

NON-LEDGER ASSETS.

| | |
|---|---|
| Interest and rents due and accrued | 1,657 88 |
| Assessments actually collected by subordinate lodges not yet turned over to supreme lodge | 41,348 45 |
| All other assets, viz: Book value of bonds in excess of cost value | 10,738 50 |
| Gross assets | $206,015 06 |

DEDUCT ASSETS NOT ADMITTED.

| | |
|---|---|
| Book value of bonds and stocks over market value | 2,497 62 |
| Total admitted assets | $203,517 44 |

LIABILITIES.

| | | |
|---|---|---|
| Death claims adjusted not yet due | $31,000 00 | |
| Death claims incurred in 1921, not reported until 1922 | 5,000 00 | |
| Total death claims | | $36,000 00 |
| Advance assessments | | 6,480 85 |
| All other liabilities, viz— | | |
| Accounts payable current bills | $5,167 51 | |
| Cost of collection December premiums | 2,103 28 | |
| | | 7,270 79 |
| Total | | $49,751 64 |

EXHIBIT OF CERTIFICATES.

| | Total business of the year. Number. | Amount. | Business in Illinois during year. Number. | Amount. |
|---|---|---|---|---|
| Benefit certificates in force December 31, 1920, as per last statement | 37,372 | $42,306,500 00 | 2,385 | $2,444,500 00 |
| Benefit certificates written and renewed during the year | 4,146 | 4,910,500 00 | 570 | 625,000 00 |
| Benefit certificates increased during the year | -------- | 196,500 00 | -------- | 21,000 00 |
| Total | 41,518 | $47,413,500 00 | 2,955 | $3,090,500 00 |
| Deduct terminated, decreased or transferred during the year | 3,891 | 4,294,000 00 | -------- | ------------ |
| Deduct terminated or decreased during the year | -------- | ------------ | 410 | 386,500 00 |
| Total benefit certificates in force December 31, 1921 | 37,627 | $43,119,500 00 | 2,545 | $2,704,000 00 |

Received during the year from members in Illinois: Benefit, $15,439.58; guaranty, $14,478.75; field, $12,046.85; I. and I., $133.20; expense, $4,338.79; total $36,437 17

EXHIBIT OF DEATH CLAIMS.

| | Total claims. Number. | Amount. | Illinois claims. Number. | Amount. |
|---|---|---|---|---|
| Claims unpaid December 31, 1920, as per last statement | 44 | $ 55,000 00 | 15 | $20,500 00 |
| Claims reported during the year and interest addition with extra assessments returned | 319 | 368,883 94 | 31 | 39,196 75 |
| Total | 363 | $423,883 94 | 46 | $59,696 75 |
| Claims paid during the year | 328 | 372,994 60 | 35 | 35,780 25 |
| Balance | 35 | $50,889 34 | 11 | $23,916 50 |
| Saved by compromising or scaling down claims during the year | -------- | 11,889 34 | -------- | 8,976 50 |
| Claims rejected during the year | 7 | 8,000 00 | 1 | 2,000 00 |
| Claims unpaid December 31, 1921 | 28 | $31,000 00 | 10 | $13,000 00 |

EXHIBIT OF CASH SURRENDERS IN ILLINOIS.

| | Total claims. Number. | Amount. |
|---|---|---|
| Claims reported during the year and interest addition—cash surrenders in Michigan | 7 | $7,500 00 |
| Saved by compromising or scaling down claims during the year | | $6,833 26 |

## ORDER BRITH ABRAHAM, U. S. GRAND LODGE.

Located at Nos. 266 and 268 Grand Street, New York, New York.

SAMUEL DORT, Grand Master. GEO. W. LEISERSOHN, Grand Secretary.

| | |
|---|---|
| Balance from previous year | $98,535 20 |

INCOME.

| | |
|---|---|
| All other assessments or premiums | $310,304 83 |
| Dues and per capita tax | 24,622 75 |
| Head stones | 90 00 |
| Certificate fees | 98 67 |
| Net amount received from members | $335,116 25 |
| Gross interest on bonds and dividends on stocks | 2,743 75 |
| Gross interest on deposits in trust companies and banks | 1,059 26 |
| Sale of lodge supplies | 17 25 |
| Borrowed money (gross) | 6,000 00 |
| Withdrawal and traveling cards | 56 27 |
| Dissolved lodges | 3,470 32 |
| Reimbursement for advances | 302 62 |
| Orphan adoption contribution | 1,761 27 |
| Total income | $350,526 99 |
| Sum | $449,062 19 |

DISBURSEMENTS.

| | |
|---|---|
| Death claims | $297,066 00 |
| Permanent disability claims | 1,755 00 |
| Head stones | 30 00 |
| Total benefits paid | $298,851 00 |
| Commissions and fees paid to deputies and organizers | 236 07 |
| Salaries of officers and trustees | 5,225 00 |

DISBURSEMENTS—Concluded.

| | |
|---|---|
| Compensation of grand master | $2,800 00 |
| Salaries and other compensation of committees | 69 50 |
| Salaries of office employees | 7,065 92 |
| Traveling and other expenses of officers, trustees and committees | 119 81 |
| Insurance department fees | 849 53 |
| Rent | 2,400 00 |
| Advertising, printing and stationery | 1,315 78 |
| Postage, express, telegraph and telephone | 607 86 |
| Expenses of supreme lodge meeting | 6,143 29 |
| Legal expense in litigating claims | 710 00 |
| Other legal expenses | 82 00 |
| Furniture and fixtures | 1,043 45 |
| Borrowed money repaid (gross) | 3,300 00 |
| Interest on borrowed money | 572 22 |
| All other disbursements, viz— | |
| Propaganda, $1,421.49; bonds, $526.18 | 1,947 67 |
| Testimonials and funerals, $566.65; returned overpayments, $2.58 | 569 23 |
| Office sundries | 448 45 |
| Relief donations | 202 69 |
| Total disbursements | $336,659 47 |
| Balance | $112,402 72 |

LEDGER ASSETS.

| | |
|---|---|
| Book value of bonds and stocks | $78,000 17 |
| Cash in association's office | 120 71 |
| Deposits in trust companies and banks not on interest | 4,157 66 |
| Deposits in trust companies and banks on interest | 30,124 18 |
| Total ledger assets | $112,402 72 |

NON-LEDGER ASSETS.

| | |
|---|---|
| Interest and rents due and accrued | 521 03 |
| Assessments actually collected by subordinate lodges not yet turned over to supreme lodge | 57,880 88 |
| Gross assets | $170,804 63 |

DEDUCT ASSETS NOT ADMITTED.

| | |
|---|---|
| Book value of bonds and stocks over market value | 5,428 07 |
| Total admitted assets | $165,376 56 |

LIABILITIES.

| | | |
|---|---|---|
| Death claims due and unpaid | $14,300 00 | |
| Death claims adjusted not yet due | 45,000 00 | |
| Death claims reported during the year but not yet adjusted | 6,000 00 | |
| Death claims incurred in 1921, not reported until 1922 | 5,000 00 | |
| Total death claims | | $70,300 00 |
| Salaries, rents, expenses, commissions, etc., due or accrued | | 666 67 |
| Borrowed money, $11,900.00; interest due or accrued on same, $178.30 | | 12,078 30 |
| All other liabilities, viz— | | |
| Orphan adoption fund | $1,761 27 | |
| Old home fund | 424 63 | |
| Head stone deposit balance | 385 00 | |
| Bonds subordinate lodge officers | 72 00 | |
| | | 2,642 90 |
| Total | | $85,687 87 |

EXHIBIT OF CERTIFICATES.

| | Total business of the year. Number. | Amount. | Business in Illinois during year. Number. | Amount. |
|---|---|---|---|---|
| Benefit certificates in force December 31, 1920, as per last statement | 22,910 | $11,388,750 00 | 2,432 | $1,215,750 00 |
| Benefit certificates written and renewed during the year | 468 | 225,750 00 | 77 | 38,500 00 |
| Total | 23,378 | $11,614,500 00 | 2,509 | $1,254,250 00 |
| Deduct terminated, decreased or transferred during the year | 5,944 | 2,972,000 00 | | |
| Deduct terminated or decreased during the year | | | 707 | 353,500 00 |
| Total benefit certificates in force December 31, 1921 | 17,434 | $8,642,500 00 | 1,802 | $900,750 00 |

Received during the year from members in Illinois: Mortuary, $36,259.09; disability, $124.70; expense, $2,584.88; total ........ $38,968 67

EXHIBIT OF DEATH CLAIMS.

| | Total claims. Number. | Total claims. Amount. | Illinois claims. Number. | Illinois claims. Amount. |
|---|---|---|---|---|
| Claims unpaid December 31, 1920, as per last statement | 144 | $ 71,179 00 | 13 | $ 6,500 00 |
| Claims reported during the year and interest addition | 593 | 296,043 00 | 73 | 36,150 00 |
| Total | 737 | $367,222 00 | 86 | $42,650 00 |
| Claims paid during the year | 605 | 297,066 00 | 62 | 30,750 00 |
| Balance | 132 | $70,156 00 | 24 | $11,900 00 |
| Saved by compromising or scaling down claims during the year | | 4,856 00 | | 250 00 |
| Claims unpaid December 31, 1921 | 132 | $65,300 00 | 24 | $11,650 00 |

EXHIBIT OF PERMANENT DISABILITY CLAIMS.

| | Total claims. Number. | Total claims. Amount. |
|---|---|---|
| Claims unpaid December 31, 1920, as per last statement | 1 | $ 500 00 |
| Claims reported during the year and interest addition | 5 | 2,500 00 |
| Total | 6 | $3,000 00 |
| Claims paid during the year | 6 | 1,750 00 |
| Balance | | $1,250 00 |
| Saved by compromising or scaling down claims during the year | | 1,250 00 |

EXHIBIT OF TRUSTEE DEPOSITS FOR UNSETTLED CLAIMS.

| | Total claims. Number. | Total claims. Amount. | Illinois claims. Number. | Illinois claims. Amount. |
|---|---|---|---|---|
| Claims unpaid December 31, 1920, as per last statement | 198 | $20,789 90 | 7 | $1,157 98 |
| Claims reported during the year | 50 | 4,503 55 | 4 | 252 49 |
| Total | 248 | $25,293 45 | 11 | $1,410 47 |
| Claims paid during the year | 29 | 4,465 53 | 1 | 163 17 |
| Claims unpaid December 31, 1921 | 219 | $20,887 92 | 10 | $1,247 30 |

## ORDER KNIGHTS OF JOSEPH.

Located at No. 312 Society for Savings Building, Cleveland, Ohio.

MAX ABRAMOFF, President. D. J. ZINNER, Secretary.

| | |
|---|---|
| Balance from previous year | $71,610 38 |

INCOME.

| | |
|---|---|
| All other assessments or premiums | $92,712 19 |
| Dues and per capita tax | 8,384 49 |
| Net amount received from members | $101,096 68 |
| Gross interest on mortgage loans | 1,285 60 |
| Gross interest on bonds and dividends on stocks | 475 00 |
| Gross interest on deposits in trust companies and banks | 1,030 12 |
| Total income | $103,887 40 |
| Sum | $175,497 78 |

DISBURSEMENTS.

| | |
|---|---|
| Death claims | $98,772 79 |
| Disability | 500 00 |
| Total benefits paid | $99,272 79 |
| Salaries of officers and trustees | 3,000 00 |
| Salaries and fees paid to supreme medical examiners | 414 00 |
| Traveling and other expenses of officers, trustees and committees | 353 15 |
| Insurance department fees | 85 00 |
| Rent | 1,200 00 |
| Advertising, printing and stationery | 692 04 |
| Postage, express, telegraph and telephone | 2,097 53 |
| Supreme meetings | 310 00 |
| Total disbursements | $107,424 51 |
| Balance | $68,073 27 |

LEDGER ASSETS.

| | | |
|---|---|---|
| Book value of real estate | $24,580 00 | |
| Book value bonds | 10,000 00 | |
| Cash in association's office, $370.37; deposited in banks (not on interest), $32,272.90 | 32,643 27 | |
| War saving stamps | 850 00 | |
| Total ledger assets | | $68,073 27 |

NON-LEDGER ASSETS.

| | | |
|---|---|---|
| Interest due, $90.00 and accrued, $216.80 on mortgages | $306 80 | |
| Banks | 317 05 | |
| Total interest and rents due and accrued | | 623 05 |
| Assessments actually collected by subordinate lodges not yet turned over to supreme lodge | | 8,294 50 |
| Gross assets | | $76,991 62 |

EXHIBIT OF CERTIFICATES.

| | Total business of the year. | | Business in Illinois during year. | |
|---|---|---|---|---|
| | Number. | Amount. | Number. | Amount. |
| Benefit certificates in force December 31, 1920 | 14,384 | $7,192,000 00 | 3,689 | $1,844,500 00 |
| Benefit certificates written during the year | 667 | 333,500 00 | 203 | 101,500 00 |
| Totals | 15,051 | $7,525,500 00 | 3,892 | $1,946,000 00 |
| Deduct terminated, decreased or transferred during the year | 948 | 474,000 00 | 262 | 131,000 00 |
| Total benefit certificates in force December 31, 1921 | 14,103 | $7,051,500 00 | 3,630 | $1,815,000 00 |
| Benefit certificates terminated by death reported during the year | 150 | 75,000 00 | 34 | 17,000 00 |
| Benefit certificates terminated by lapse reported during the year | 798 | 399,000 00 | 228 | 114,000 00 |

| | |
|---|---|
| Received during the year from members in Illinois: Mortuary, $21,823.70; reserve, $1,377.14; disability, $418.65; expense, $2,122.61; total | $25,742 10 |

EXHIBIT OF DEATH CLAIMS.

| | Total claims—all in Illinois. | |
|---|---|---|
| | Number. | Amount. |
| Claims paid during the year | 34 | $17,000 00 |

EXHIBIT OF PERMANENT DISABILITY CLAIMS.

| | Total claims—all in Illinois. | |
|---|---|---|
| | Number. | Amount. |
| Claims paid during the year | 1 | $250 00 |

## ORDER KNIGHTS OF THE WHITE CROSS.

Located at No. 434½ Seventeenth Avenue, Milwaukee, Wisconsin.

MAGNUS KYLLINGSTAD, President. T. M. HOLDERY, Financial Secretary.

| | |
|---|---|
| Balance from previous year, December 31, 1920 | $4,442 36 |

INCOME.

| | |
|---|---|
| Membership fees actually received | $ 35 00 |
| All other assessments or premiums | 7,277 62 |
| Dues and per capita tax | 986 00 |
| Medical examiners' fees actually received | 8 75 |
| Net amount received from members | $12,749 73 |
| Gross interest on bonds and dividends on stocks | 103 62 |
| Gross interest on deposits in trust companies and banks | 29 00 |
| Sale of lodge supplies, emblems | 9 00 |
| Change of certificates | 6 50 |
| Sum | $12,897 85 |

DISBURSEMENTS.

| | |
|---|---|
| Death claims | $3,000 00 |
| Burial claims | 300 00 |
| Total benefits paid | $3,300 00 |

DISBURSEMENTS—Concluded.

| | |
|---|---|
| Salaries of officers | $475 00 |
| For remittance of assessments | 1 16 |
| Insurance department fees | 55 00 |
| Advertising, printing and stationery | 36 00 |
| Postage, express, telegraph and telephone | 39 34 |
| Lodge supplies | 331 25 |
| Official publication | 10 50 |
| Legal expense in litigating claims, attorney fees | 35 00 |
| Other legal expenses, grand lodge officials, attending funeral | 29 25 |
| Furniture and fixtures | 15 75 |
| Financial secretary's bond | 5 00 |
| Treasurer's bond | 25 00 |
| State treasurer, clip coupons, U. S. Govt. bonds | 1 75 |
| Valuation report statement | 5 00 |
| Total disbursements | $4,365 00 |
| Balance | $8,532 85 |

LEDGER ASSETS.

| | |
|---|---|
| Book value of bonds and stocks | $3,100 00 |
| Cash in association's office | 522 57 |
| Deposits in trust companies and banks on interest | 4,910 28 |
| Total ledger assets | $8,532 85 |

NON-LEDGER ASSETS.

| | |
|---|---|
| Assessments actually collected by subordinate lodges not yet turned over to supreme lodge | 785 97 |
| Gross assets | $9,318 82 |

EXHIBIT OF CERTIFICATES.

| | Total business of the year. | | Business in Illinois during year. | |
|---|---|---|---|---|
| | Number. | Amount. | Number. | Amount. |
| Benefit certificates in force December 31, 1920, as per last statement | 547 | $262,625 00 | 390 | $186,125 00 |
| Benefit certificates written and renewed during the year | 32 | 10,625 00 | 19 | 7,875 00 |
| Totals | 579 | $273,250 00 | 409 | $194,000 00 |
| Deduct terminated, decreased or transferred during the year | 48 | 22,875 00 | | |
| Deduct terminated or decreased during the year | | | 38 | 17,875 00 |
| Total benefit certificates in force December 31, 1921 | 531 | $250,375 00 | 371 | $176,125 00 |

Received during the year from members in Illinois: Mortuary, $4,059.61; reserve, $451.07; burial, $164.00; expense, $748.00; total — $5,422 68

EXHIBIT OF DEATH CLAIMS.

| | Total claims. | | Illinois claims. | |
|---|---|---|---|---|
| | Number. | Amount. | Number. | Amount. |
| Claims paid during the year | 6 | $3,000 00 | 5 | $2,500 00 |

EXHIBIT OF BURIAL CLAIMS.

| | Total claims—all in Illinois. | |
|---|---|---|
| | Number. | Amount. |
| Claims paid during the year | 3 | $300 00 |

## ORDER OF SCOTTISH CLANS.

Located at No. 248 Boylston Street, Boston, Massachusetts.

THOMAS R. P. GIBB, President. ALEXANDER G. FINDLAY, Secretary.

| | |
|---|---|
| Balance from previous year | $477,071 83 |

INCOME.

| | |
|---|---|
| All other assessments or premiums | $181,217 85 |
| Dues and per capita tax | 24,324 73 |
| Benefit certificates | 1,689 00 |
| Net amount received from members | $207,231 48 |

## INCOME—Concluded.

| | |
|---|---|
| Gross interest on bonds and dividends on stocks | $20,927 85 |
| Gross interest on deposits in trust companies and banks | 1,049 10 |
| Gross interest from all other sources | 1,258 00 |
| Sale of lodge supplies | 806 45 |
| Charter fees | 125 00 |
| Contribution to publicity fund | 13,673 58 |
| Deductions from death claims | 850 46 |
| Total income | $245,921 92 |
| Sum | $772,993 75 |

## DISBURSEMENTS.

| | |
|---|---|
| Death claims | $149,016 00 |
| Old age benefits | 7,750 00 |
| Total benefits paid | $156,766 00 |
| Commissions and fees paid to deputies and organizers | 164 42 |
| Salaries of officers and trustees | 3,600 00 |
| Other compensation of officers and trustees | 500 00 |
| Salaries and other compensation of committees | 350 00 |
| Salaries of office employees | 4,622 75 |
| Salaries and fees paid to supreme medical examiners | 767 50 |
| Traveling and other expenses of officers, trustees and committees | 220 34 |
| Insurance department fees | 165 00 |
| Rent | 1,800 00 |
| Advertising, printing and stationery | 1,723 58 |
| Postage, express, telegraph and telephone | 800 86 |
| Official publication | 8,010 29 |
| Expenses of supreme lodge meeting | 9,740 88 |
| Other legal expenses | 100 00 |
| Furniture and fixtures | 15 00 |
| Auditors fees | 200 00 |
| Sundry office expenses | 725 89 |
| Rent, safe, deposit vault | 20 00 |
| Bank charges | 89 68 |
| Surety bond premiums | 247 02 |
| Actuary's fees | 1,046 00 |
| Total disbursements | $191,675 21 |
| Balance | $531,318 54 |

## LEDGER ASSETS.

| | |
|---|---|
| Book value of bonds and stocks | $508,377 50 |
| Cash, Insurance Department, Quebec | 5,000 00 |
| Deposits in trust companies and banks on interest | 17,941 04 |
| Total ledger assets | $531,318 54 |

### NON-LEDGER ASSETS.

| | |
|---|---|
| Interest due | 8,634 07 |
| Assessments actually collected by subordinate lodges not yet turned over to supreme lodge | 14,616 45 |
| Old age benefit paid to members and upon which said members are paying 4 per cent | 47,460 00 |
| Gross assets | $602,029 06 |

### DEDUCT ASSETS NOT ADMITTED.

| | | |
|---|---|---|
| Overdue and accrued interest on bonds in default | $ 6,375 00 | |
| Book value of bonds and stocks over market value | 23,172 50 | |
| Other items, viz: Old age benefit paid to members and upon which said members are paying 4 per cent | 47,460 00 | 77,007 50 |
| Total admitted assets | | $525,021 56 |

## LIABILITIES.

| | | |
|---|---|---|
| Death claims due and unpaid | $5,050 00 | |
| Death claims reported but not yet adjusted | 7,750 00 | |
| Death claims incurred in 1921, not reported until 1922 | 2,750 00 | |
| Total unpaid claims | | $15,550 00 |
| Salaries, rents, expenses, due or accrued | | 1,001 35 |
| Publicity fund not disposed of | | 14,158 83 |
| Total | | $30,709 18 |

EXHIBIT OF CERTIFICATES.

| | Total business of the year. Number. | Amount. | Business in Illinois during year. Number. | Amount. |
|---|---|---|---|---|
| Benefit certificates in force December 31, 1920, as per last statement | 19,280 | $10,867,050 00 | 1,161 | $719,250 00 |
| Benefit certificates written and renewed during the year | 1,605 | 848,500 00 | 103 | 55,750 00 |
| Benefit certificates received by transfer during the year | | | 4 | 3,000 00 |
| Benefit certificates increased during the year | | 43,500 00 | | 250 00 |
| Totals | 20,885 | $11,759,050 00 | 1,268 | $778,250 00 |
| Deduct terminated, decreased or transferred during the year | 1,863 | 986,200 00 | | |
| Deduct terminated or decreased during the year | | | 101 | 70,400 00 |
| Total benefit certificates in force December 31, 1921 | 19,022 | $10,772,850 00 | 1,167 | $707,850 00 |

Received during the year from members in Illinois: Mortuary, $12,019.00; expense, $1,619.60; total — 13,638 60

EXHIBIT OF DEATH CLAIMS.

| | Total claims. Number. | Amount. | Illinois claims. Number. | Amount. |
|---|---|---|---|---|
| Claims unpaid December 31, 1920, as per last statement | 16 | $ 9,800 00 | 2 | $1,800 00 |
| Claims reported during the year and interest addition | 198 | 152,200 00 | 9 | 8,250 00 |
| Totals | 214 | $162,000 00 | 11 | $10,050 00 |
| Claims paid during the year | 198 | 149,200 00 | 9 | 9,250 00 |
| Saved by compromising or scaling down claims during the year | | 850 46 | | |
| Claims unpaid December 31, 1921 | 16 | $12,800 00 | 2 | $2,800 00 |

EXHIBIT OF OLD AGE AND OTHER CLAIMS.

| | Total claims. Number. | Amount. | Illinois claims. Number. | Amount. |
|---|---|---|---|---|
| Claims paid during the year | 53 | $7,750 00 | 2 | $400 00 |

## ORDER SONS OF ZION.

Located at No. 44 East Twenty-third Street, New York, New York.

JACOB S. STRAHL, President. JACOB ISH KISHOAR, Secretary.

| | |
|---|---|
| Balance from previous year | $133,313 25 |

INCOME.

| | |
|---|---|
| Membership fees actually received | $ 57 00 |
| Assessments or premiums during first twelve months of membership of which all or an extra percentage is used for expenses | 1,952 28 |
| All other assessments or premiums | 23,877 59 |
| Dues and per capita tax | 10,783 98 |
| Special Zionist tax | 5,393 10 |
| Total received from members | $42,063 95 |
| Deduct payments returned to applicants and members | 70 04 |
| Net amount received from members | $41,993 91 |
| Reserve for overpayment | 81 77 |
| Suspense | 68 13 |
| Gross interest on bonds | 5,188 10 |
| Advertising and stationery | 11 10 |
| General expense | 364 08 |
| Policy certificate | 285 75 |
| Indemnity fees | 111 00 |
| Borrowed money (gross) | 27,080 00 |
| Camp supplies | 277 08 |
| Due camps | 1,341 58 |
| From all other sources, viz— | |
| Cholutzem fund | 632 67 |
| J. S. Strahl propaganda | 475 00 |
| Nasi's present | 460 00 |
| Insurance department fees | 10 00 |

INCOME—Concluded.

| | | |
|---|---|---|
| From all other sources, viz— | | |
| Shokolim fund | | $741 00 |
| Keren Hayesod (Palestine Foundation Fund) | | 718 00 |
| Salaries returned | | 12 00 |
| Surety bond | | 12 00 |
| Total income | | $79,863 17 |
| Sum | | $213,176 42 |

## DISBURSEMENTS.

| | | |
|---|---|---|
| Death claims | | $8,000 00 |
| Sick and accident claims | | 192 73 |
| Total benefits paid | | $8,192 73 |
| Convention expense | | 351 80 |
| Salaries of deputies and organizers | | 1,089 85 |
| Salaries of managers or agents not deputies or organizers | | 3,120 00 |
| Indemnity fees | | 102 72 |
| Salaries of office employees | | 3,840 00 |
| Salaries and fees paid to supreme medical examiners | | 600 00 |
| Traveling and other expenses of officers, trustees and committees | | 586 71 |
| Auxiliary organizations | | 180 00 |
| Insurance department fees | | 185 00 |
| Rent | | 1,060 46 |
| Advertising, printing and stationery | | 1,922 58 |
| Postage, express, telegraph and telephone | | 1,092 37 |
| Due camps | | 1,566 66 |
| J. S. Strahl propaganda | | 1,000 00 |
| Shokolim to World Zionist Organization | | 4,705 00 |
| Chalutzem fund | | 632 67 |
| Bonding | | 50 00 |
| Furniture and fixtures | | 63 88 |
| Delegation to Zion Congress | | 500 00 |
| Accounts payable | | 137 81 |
| Reserve for overpayment | | 42 44 |
| Borrowed money repaid (gross) | | 19,200 00 |
| Interest on borrowed money | | 655 42 |
| All other disbursements, viz— | | |
| Suspense | | 1 50 |
| Accounting | | 300 00 |
| General expense | | 1,000 77 |
| Per capita tax | | 9 95 |
| Total disbursements | | $52,190 32 |
| Balance | | $160,986 10 |

## LEDGER ASSETS.

| | | |
|---|---|---|
| Book value of bonds | | $151,072 98 |
| Cash in association's office | | 241 48 |
| Deposits in trust companies and banks not on interest | | 9,671 64 |
| Total ledger assets | | $160,986 10 |

### NON-LEDGER ASSETS.

| | | |
|---|---|---|
| Interest accrued | | 1,427 34 |
| Market value of bonds and stocks over book value | | 1,949 52 |
| All other assets, viz— | | |
| Furniture and fixtures | $2,209 98 | |
| Stationery, printing and supplies | 335 00 | 2,544 90 |
| Gross assets | | $166,907 94 |

### DEDUCT ASSETS NOT ADMITTED.

| | | |
|---|---|---|
| Furniture and fixtures | $2,209 98 | |
| Stationery, printing and supplies | 335 00 | 1,875 98 |
| Total admitted assets | | $165,031 96 |

## LIABILITIES.

| | | |
|---|---|---|
| Death claims due and unpaid | $1,650 00 | |
| Death claims reported during the year but not yet adjusted | 900 00 | |
| Total unpaid claims | | $ 2,550 00 |
| Taxes due or accrued | | 33 10 |
| Borrowed money | | 25,580 00 |
| Total | | $28,163 10 |

EXHIBIT OF CERTIFICATES.

| | Total business of the year. Number. | Amount. | Business in Illinois during year. Number. | Amount. |
|---|---|---|---|---|
| Benefit certificates in force December 31, 1920, as per last statement | 4,186 | $1,250,300 00 | 47 | $20,500 00 |
| Benefit certificates written and renewed during the year | 208 | 78,900 00 | 5 | 1,850 00 |
| Totals | 4,394 | $1,329,200 00 | 52 | $22,350 00 |
| Deduct terminated, decreased or transferred during the year | 434 | 129,550 00 | | |
| Deduct terminated or decreased during the year | | | 12 | 5,950 00 |
| Total benefit certificates in force December 31, 1921 | 3,960 | $1,199,650 00 | 40 | $16,400 00 |

Received during the year from members in Illinois: Mortuary, $415.79; sick and accident, $112.44; expense, $121.04; total ........ 649 27

EXHIBIT OF DEATH CLAIMS.

| | Total claims. Number. | Amount. | Illinois claims. Number. | Amount. |
|---|---|---|---|---|
| Claims unpaid December 31, 1920, as per last statement | 12 | $3,350 00 | | |
| Claims reported during the year and interest addition | 29 | 7,200 00 | 1 | $250 00 |
| Totals | 41 | $10,550 00 | 1 | $250 00 |
| Claims paid during the year | 27 | 8,000 00 | 1 | 250 00 |
| Claims unpaid December 31, 1921 | 14 | $2,550 00 | | |

EXHIBIT OF SICK AND ACCIDENT CLAIMS.

| | Total claims. Number. | Amount. | Illinois claims. Number. | Amount. |
|---|---|---|---|---|
| Claims paid during the year | 6 | $192 73 | 5 | $172 73 |

## ORDER OF UNITED COMMERCIAL TRAVELERS OF AMERICA.

Located at No. 638 North Park Street, Columbus, Ohio.

C. V. HOLDERMAN, President. WALTER D. MURPHY, Secretary.

| | |
|---|---|
| Balance from previous year | $1,180,466 53 |

INCOME.

| | |
|---|---|
| Membership fees actually received | $ 38,514 00 |
| All other assessments or premiums | 1,197,647 00 |
| Dues and per capita tax | 49,776 50 |
| Total received from members | $1,285,937 50 |
| Deduct payments returned to applicants and members | 798 50 |
| Net amount received from members | $1,285,139 00 |
| Gross interest on bonds and dividends on stocks | 37,265 51 |
| Gross interest on deposits in trust companies and banks | 11,064 18 |
| Gross rents from association's property, including $5,000.00 for association's occupancy of its own buildings | 5,351 00 |
| Sale of lodge supplies | 4,260 90 |
| Suspense account | 9,456 92 |
| Official publication | 20,345 41 |
| Gross increase in book value of ledger assets | 7,800 86 |
| From all other sources, viz— | |
| Miscellaneous receipts | 84 56 |
| Fines | 582 20 |
| Donations | 220 92 |
| Ladies pins, $85.00; Ray of Hope (pictures), $12.00 | 97 00 |
| War Savings Stamps, $100.00; Fourth Liberty Loan, $50.00 donated | 150 00 |
| Vouchers not cashed, refunded | 60 00 |
| Total income | $1,381,878 46 |
| Sum | $2,562,344 99 |

DISBURSEMENTS.

| | |
|---|---|
| Death claims | $322,104 40 |
| Weekly payments | 70,612 50 |
| Accident claims | 448,575 03 |
| Widows' and orphans' | 69,800 16 |
| Total benefits paid | $911,092 09 |

DISBURSEMENTS—Concluded.

| | | |
|---|---|---|
| Salary of chief agent of Canada | | $ 1,500 00 |
| Salaries of officers and trustees | | 15,800 00 |
| Other compensation of officers and trustees—ex-supreme counselor | | 1,080 33 |
| Salaries of office employees | | 46,161 95 |
| Salaries and fees paid to supreme medical examiners | | 5,500 00 |
| Salaries and fees paid to subordinate medical examiners | | 3,686 00 |
| Traveling and other expenses of officers, trustees and committees | | 3,643 28 |
| Insurance department fees | | 1,463 82 |
| Rent, including $5,000.00 for association's occupancy of its own buildings | | 5,000 00 |
| Advertising, printing and stationery | | 19,013 42 |
| Postage, express, telegraph and telephone | | 19,251 29 |
| Lodge supplies | | 4,087 52 |
| Official publication | | 68,684 71 |
| Expenses of supreme lodge meeting | | 51,261 37 |
| Legal expense in litigating claims | | 7,558 67 |
| Other legal expenses | | 6,500 00 |
| Furniture and fixtures | | 2,525 07 |
| Taxes, repairs and other expenses on real estate | | 780 01 |
| Expense investigating claims | | 7,365 81 |
| Exchange account | | 626 61 |
| Office expense | | 1,337 54 |
| House account | | 2,259 24 |
| Bonds officers | | 514 67 |
| Information bureau | | 776 66 |
| Federation membership | | 1,342 47 |
| Refund to secretaries | | 9,522 00 |
| Expense W. and O | | 88 10 |
| Total disbursements | | $1,198,422 63 |
| Balance | | $1,363,922 36 |

LEDGER ASSETS.

| | | |
|---|---|---|
| Book value of real estate | | $39,166 00 |
| Book value of bonds and stocks | | 943,550 00 |
| Cash in association's office | | 48,228 05 |
| Deposits in trust companies and banks not on interest | | 43,460 05 |
| Deposits in trust companies and banks on interest | | 285,851 50 |
| War Savings Stamps | | 3,666 76 |
| Total ledger assets | | $1,363,922 36 |

NON-LEDGER ASSETS.

| | | |
|---|---|---|
| Interest and rents due and accrued | | $ 15,532 76 |
| Market value of real estate over book value | | 35,129 00 |
| Market value of bonds and stocks over book value | | 518 00 |
| Assessments actually collected by subordinate lodges not yet turned over to supreme lodge | | 206,216 00 |
| All other assets, viz— | | |
| Due from subordinate grand councils | $27,301 20 | |
| Furniture and fixtures | 13,514 72 | |
| Stationery supplies | 7,427 66 | |
| | | 48,243 58 |
| Gross assets | | $1,669,561 70 |

DEDUCT ASSETS NOT ADMITTED.

| | | |
|---|---|---|
| Bills receivable | $27,301 20 | |
| Other items, viz— | | |
| Furniture and fixtures | $13,514 72 | |
| Stationery and supplies | 7,427 66 | |
| | | 48,243 58 |
| Total admitted assets | | $1,621,318 12 |

LIABILITIES.

| | | |
|---|---|---|
| Death claims resisted | $81,900 00 | |
| Death claims reported during the year but not yet adjusted | 63,000 00 | |
| Present value of deferred death claims payable in installments—death weekly | 43,137 50 | |
| Total death claims | | $188,037 50 |
| Accident claims resisted | $ 5,302 50 | |
| Accident claims reported during the year but not yet adjusted | 61,735 68 | |
| Total sick and accident claims | | 67,038 18 |
| Total unpaid claims | | $255,075 68 |
| Salaries, rents, expenses, commissions, etc., due or accrued | | 579 31 |
| Suspense fund | | 322 55 |
| Total | | $255,977 54 |

## EXHIBIT OF CERTIFICATES.

| | Total business of the year. Number. | Amount. | Business in Illinois during year. Number. | Amount. |
|---|---|---|---|---|
| Benefit certificates in force December 31, 1920, as per last statement | 99,737 | $498,685,000 00 | 5,381 | $26,905,000 00 |
| Benefit certificates written and renewed during the year | 12,807 | 64,035,000 00 | 629 | 3,145,000 00 |
| Benefit certificates received by transfer during the year | | | 54 | 270,000 00 |
| Benefit certificates increased during the year | 1,966 | 9,830,000 00 | | |
| Total | 114,510 | $572,550,000 00 | 6,064 | $30,320,000 00 |
| Deduct terminated, decreased or transferred during the year | 10,374 | 51,870,000 00 | | |
| Deduct terminated or decreased during the year | | | 612 | 3,060,000 00 |
| Total benefit certificates in force December 31, 1921 | 104,136 | $520,680,000 00 | 5,452 | $27,260,000 00 |

Received during the year from members in Illinois: Mortuary, $17,484.74; reserve, $5,318.80; disability, $24,747.96; expense, $15,850.50; total — $63,402 00

## EXHIBIT OF DEATH CLAIMS.

| | Total claims. Number. | Amount. | Illinois claims. Number. | Amount. |
|---|---|---|---|---|
| Claims unpaid December 31, 1920, as per last statement | 21 | $176,500 00 | 1 | $ 8,325 00 |
| Claims reported during the year and interest addition | 92 | 573,299 40 | 9 | 59,850 00 |
| Total | 113 | $749,799 40 | 10 | $68,175 00 |
| Claims paid during the year — Death weekly | | 70,612 50 | | |
| Claims paid during the year — Deaths | 78 | 322,104 40 | | |
| Claims paid during the year | | | 7 | 38,724 90 |
| Balance | 35 | $357,082 50 | 3 | $29,450 10 |
| Saved by compromising or scaling down claims during the year | | 96,595 00 | | 6,587 60 |
| Claims rejected during the year | 10 | 59,850 00 | | |
| Claims dropped during the year | 2 | 12,600 00 | | |
| Claims unpaid December 31, 1921 | 23 | $188,037 50 | 3 | $22,862 50 |

## EXHIBIT OF ACCIDENT CLAIMS.

| | Total claims. Number. | Amount. | Illinois claims. Number. | Amount. |
|---|---|---|---|---|
| Claims unpaid December 31, 1920, as per last statement | 752 | $ 63,869 64 | 43 | $ 3,555 64 |
| Claims reported during the year | 5,188 | 456,063 51 | 345 | 26,483 95 |
| Total | 5,940 | $519,933 15 | 388 | $30,039 59 |
| Claims paid during the year | 5,181 | 448,575 03 | 344 | 26,259 60 |
| Compromised and scaled down | | 2,889 62 | | |
| Claims rejected during the year | 17 | 1,430 32 | | 89 27 |
| Claims unpaid December 31, 1921 | 742 | $67,038 18 | 44 | $3.690 72 |

# PILGRIM KNIGHTS OF THE WORLD, SUPREME LODGE.

Located at No. 410 Ferry Street, LaFayette, Indiana.

FREDERICK O. EVANS, Supreme Master. GEORGE C. PARKER, Supreme Secretary.

| | |
|---|---|
| Balance from previous year | $953 08 |

## INCOME.

| | |
|---|---|
| Membership fees actually received | $ 168 00 |
| All other assessments or premiums | 1,276 60 |
| Dues and per capita tax | 96 50 |
| Medical examiners' fees actually received | 336 00 |
| Total received from members | $1,877 10 |
| Deduct payments returned to applicants and members | 369 10 |
| Net amount received from members | $1,508 00 |
| Gross interest on deposits in trust companies and banks | 5 36 |
| Sale of lodge supplies | 36 10 |
| Total income | $1,549 46 |
| Sum | $2,502 54 |

## DISBURSEMENTS.

| | |
|---|---|
| Death claims | $550 00 |
| Monument | 235 00 |
| Burial | 235 00 |
| Total benefits paid | $1,020 00 |
| Salaries and fees paid to supreme medical examiners | 84 00 |
| Salaries and fees paid to subordinate medical examiners | 252 00 |
| Insurance department fees | 30 00 |
| Rent | 63 00 |
| Advertising, printing and stationery | 168 00 |
| Postage, express, telegraph and telephone | 25 44 |
| Lodge supplies | 20 00 |
| Official publication | 50 00 |
| Other legal expenses | 25 00 |
| Insurance department fees | 5 00 |
| Total disbursements | $1,742 44 |
| Balance | $750 10 |

## LEDGER ASSETS.

| | |
|---|---|
| Cash in association's office | $160 11 |
| Deposits in trust companies and banks not on interest | 192 09 |
| Deposits in trust companies and banks on interest | 252 78 |
| Cash in office of supreme endowment committee | 155 12 |
| Total ledger assets | $760 10 |

### NON-LEDGER ASSETS.

| | | |
|---|---|---|
| Assessments actually collected by subordinate lodges not yet turned over to supreme lodge | | 112 15 |
| All other assets, viz— | | |
| Lodge supplies, furniture, blanks, rituals, etc | $436 25 | |
| Printing outfit and plant | 100 00 | |
| Due from lodges per capita tax | 160 65 | |
| | | 696 90 |
| Gross assets | | $1,569 15 |

### DEDUCT ASSETS NOT ADMITTED.

| | | |
|---|---|---|
| Other items, viz— | | |
| Lodge supplies, etc | $436 25 | |
| Printing outfit and plant | 100 00 | |
| | | 536 25 |
| Total admitted assets | | $1,032 90 |

## LIABILITIES.

| | |
|---|---|
| Salaries, rents, expenses, commissions, etc., due or accrued | 7 00 |
| Advance assessments | 18 36 |
| Total | $25 36 |

## EXHIBIT OF CERTIFICATES.

| | Total business of the year. | | Business in Illinois during year. | |
|---|---|---|---|---|
| | Number. | Amount. | Number. | Amount. |
| Benefit certificates in force December 31, 1920, as per last statement | 660 | $108,000 00 | 151 | $32,500 00 |
| Benefit certificates written and renewed during the year | 168 | 41,700 00 | 69 | 18,700 00 |
| Total | 828 | $149,700 00 | 220 | $51,200 00 |
| Deduct terminated, decreased or transferred during the year | 156 | 38,800 00 | | |
| Deduct terminated or decreased during the year | | | 55 | 17,100 00 |
| Total benefit certificates in force December 31, 1921 | 672 | $110,900 00 | 165 | $34,100 00 |

| | |
|---|---|
| Received during the year from members in Illinois: Mortuary, $319.80; reserve, $41.00; expense, $49.20; total | $410 00 |

## EXHIBIT OF DEATH CLAIMS.

| | Total claims. | | Illinois claims. | |
|---|---|---|---|---|
| | Number. | Amount. | Number. | Amount. |
| Claims paid during the year | 2 | $550 00 | 1 | $300 00 |

## EXHIBIT OF MONUMENT AND BURIAL CLAIMS.

| | Total claims. | | Illinois claims. | |
|---|---|---|---|---|
| | Number. | Amount. | Number. | Amount. |
| Claims paid during the year | 2 | $470 00 | 1 | $235 00 |

## POLISH ASSOCIATION OF AMERICA.

Located at No. 451 Mitchell Street, Milwaukee, Wisconsin.

JOSEPH A. DOMACHOWSKI, President. JOHN KANTAK, Secretary.

| | |
|---|---|
| Balance from previous year | $165,897 11 |

### INCOME.

| | |
|---|---|
| Membership fees actually received | $ 282 91 |
| All other assessments or premiums | 111,954 40 |
| Medical examiners' fees actually received | 125 70 |
| Expense fund | 10,821 36 |
| Net amount received from members | $123,184 37 |
| Gross interest on mortgage loans | 8,803 82 |
| Gross interest on bonds and dividends on stocks | 407 51 |
| Gross rents from association's property | 162 00 |
| Sale of lodge supplies | 196 55 |
| Official publication | 3,337 50 |
| Polish relief dues | 4,199 21 |
| Fines | 62 75 |
| Advertisements | 107 45 |
| Commission on loans | 75 00 |
| Miscellaneous | 436 63 |
| Total income | $140,972 79 |
| Sum | $306,869 90 |

### DISBURSEMENTS.

| | |
|---|---|
| Death claims | $69,075 00 |
| Commissions and fees paid to deputies and organizers | 654 00 |
| Salaries of officers and trustees | 2,900 00 |
| Salaries and other compensation of committees | 30 00 |
| Salaries of office employees | 1,686 90 |
| Salaries and fees paid to supreme medical examiners | 124 75 |
| Salaries and fees paid to subordinate medical examiners | 317 00 |
| Traveling and other expenses of officers, trustees and committees | 540 48 |
| Insurance department fees | 118 16 |
| Rent | 840 00 |
| Advertising, printing and stationery | 1,022 83 |
| Postage, express, telegraph and telephone | 846 78 |
| Lodge supplies | 36 90 |
| Official publication | 5,347 46 |
| Expenses of supreme lodge meeting | 2,743 80 |
| Other legal expenses | 358 30 |
| Furniture and fixtures | 893 25 |
| Polish relief expense | 532 10 |
| Officers' bonds | 57 50 |
| Report on valuation of our society | 500 00 |
| Miscellaneous | 406 22 |
| Total disbursements | $89,031 43 |
| Balance | $217,838 47 |

### LEDGER ASSETS.

| | |
|---|---|
| Mortgage loans on real estate | $207,350 00 |
| Book value of bonds and stocks | 9,415 00 |
| Deposits in trust companies and banks not on interest | 1,073 47 |
| Total ledger assets | $217,838 47 |

#### NON-LEDGER ASSETS.

| | |
|---|---|
| Interest and rents due and accrued | 3,998 96 |
| Gross assets | $221,837 43 |

### LIABILITIES.

| | |
|---|---|
| Death claims due and unpaid | $4,500 00 |

EXHIBIT OF CERTIFICATES.

| | Total business of the year. Number. | Amount. | Business in Illinois during year. Number. | Amount. |
|---|---|---|---|---|
| Benefit certificates in force December 31, 1920, as per last statement | 10,657 | $6,205,050 00 | 2,404 | $1,362,650 00 |
| Benefit certificates written and renewed during the year | 478 | 272,100 00 | 58 | 31,500 00 |
| Total | 11,135 | $6,477,150 00 | 2,462 | $1,394,150 00 |
| Deduct terminated, decreased or transferred during the year | 861 | 506,100 00 | | |
| Deduct terminated or decreased during the year | | | 272 | 84,350 00 |
| Total benefit certificates in force December 31, 1921 | 10,274 | $5,971,050 00 | 2,190 | $1,309,800 00 |

Received during the year from members in Illinois: Mortuary, $25,256.95; expense, $3,942.00; total ........ $29,198 95

EXHIBIT OF DEATH CLAIMS.

| | Total claims. Number. | Amount. | Illinois claims. Number. | Amount. |
|---|---|---|---|---|
| Claims unpaid December 31, 1920, as per last statement | 13 | $ 3,900 00 | 2 | $ 500 00 |
| Claims reported during the year and interest addition | 114 | 70,950 00 | 29 | 15,850 00 |
| Total | 127 | $74,850 00 | 31 | $16,350 00 |
| Claims paid during the year | 114 | 69,075 00 | 29 | 15,125 00 |
| Balance | 13 | $5,775 00 | 2 | $1,225 00 |
| Saved by compromising or scaling down claims during the year | | 1,275 00 | | 725 00 |
| Claims unpaid December 31, 1921 | 13 | $4,500 00 | 2 | $500 00 |

## POLISH FEDERATION OF AMERICA.

Located at Nos. 425-27 Mitchell Street, Milwaukee, Wisconsin.

HARRY H. OLSZEWSKI, President. PETER P. MARKOWSKI, Secretary.

| | |
|---|---|
| Balance from previous year | $28,650 09 |

INCOME.

| | |
|---|---|
| All other assessments or premiums | $10,015 75 |
| Dues and per capita tax | 2,307 02 |
| Total received from members | $12,322 77 |
| Deduct payments returned to applicants and members | 63 |
| Net amount received from members | $12,322 14 |
| Gross interest on mortgage loans | 1,641 81 |
| Gross interest on deposits in trust companies and banks | 6 45 |
| Gross interest from all other sources | 120 03 |
| Sale of lodge supplies | 44 85 |
| Borrowed money from seniors | 500 00 |
| Borrowed money from juniors | 500 00 |
| From all other sources, viz— | |
| Auto premium loan interest | 6 63 |
| Policy loan interest | 24 62 |
| Application fees | 86 75 |
| Policy change fees | 5 35 |
| Premium from juvenile department | 533 76 |
| Sale of furniture | 76 90 |
| Miscellaneous | 18 39 |
| Bond premiums | 21 90 |
| Total income | $15,909 58 |
| Sum | $44,559 67 |

DISBURSEMENTS.

| | |
|---|---|
| Death claims | $2,643 00 |
| Surrender value | 628 17 |
| Total benefits paid | $3,271 17 |
| Commissions and fees paid to deputies and organizers | 235 00 |
| Salaries of officers and trustees | 1,500 00 |

## DISBURSEMENTS—Concluded.

| | |
|---|---|
| Salaries of office employees | $156 00 |
| Other compensation of office employees | 567 00 |
| Salaries and fees paid to supreme medical examiners | 35 25 |
| Salaries and fees paid to subordinate medical examiners | 86 75 |
| Traveling and other expenses of officers, trustees and committees | 29 64 |
| For collection and remittance of assessments and dues | 82 68 |
| Insurance department fees | 115 00 |
| Rent | 445 00 |
| Advertising, printing and stationery | 681 24 |
| Postage, express, telegraph and telephone | 152 48 |
| Official publication | 225 00 |
| Legal expense in litigating claims | 1 90 |
| Furniture and fixtures | 219 56 |
| Borrowed money to junior mortuary fund | 500 00 |
| All other disbursements, viz— | |
| State examination | 37 77 |
| Premium from juvenile department | 533 76 |
| Light | 18 12 |
| Fire insurance | 25 00 |
| Miscellaneous | 128 79 |
| Officers' bonds and bond expense | 135 35 |
| Cuts and drawings | 54 92 |
| Total disbursements | $8,887 38 |
| Balance | $35,672 29 |

## LEDGER ASSETS.

| | |
|---|---|
| Mortgage loans on real estate | $29,791 65 |
| Cash in association's office | 970 18 |
| Deposits in trust companies and banks not on interest | 1,071 02 |
| Loan juvenile department | 500 00 |
| Other ledger assets, viz— | |
| Policy loans | 872 00 |
| Certificate loans and War Savings Stamps | 2,467 44 |
| Total ledger assets | $35,672 29 |

### NON-LEDGER ASSETS.

| | | |
|---|---|---|
| Interest and rents due and accrued | | 13 75 |
| Market value of bonds and stocks over book value | | 137 59 |
| Assessments actually collected by subordinate lodges not yet turned over to supreme lodge | | 1,294 27 |
| All other assets, viz— | | |
| Interest due War Savings Stamps | $ 7 16 | |
| Interest due policy loans | 15 31 | |
| Furniture and fixtures | 1,459 38 | |
| Lodge supplies | 1,148 76 | |
| | | 2,630 61 |
| Gross assets | | $39,748 51 |

### DEDUCT ASSETS NOT ADMITTED.

| | | |
|---|---|---|
| Furniture and fixtures | $1,459 38 | |
| Lodge supplies | 1,148 76 | |
| | | 2,608 14 |
| Total admitted assets | | $37,140 37 |

## LIABILITIES.

| | |
|---|---|
| Death claims due and unpaid | $300 00 |

## EXHIBIT OF CERTIFICATES.

| | Total business of the year. Number. | Amount. | Business in Illinois during year. Number. | Amount. |
|---|---|---|---|---|
| Benefit certificates in force December 31, 1920, as per last statement | 1,102 | $541,600 00 | 43 | $20,900 00 |
| Benefit certificates written and renewed during the year | 306 | 182,900 00 | 5 | 3,200 00 |
| Benefit certificates increased during the year | | 5,200 00 | | |
| Total | 1,408 | $729,700 00 | 48 | $24,100 00 |
| Deduct terminated, decreased or transferred during the year | 122 | 64,400 00 | | |
| Deduct terminated or decreased during the year | | | 9 | 3,900 00 |
| Total benefit certificates in force December 31, 1921 | 1,286 | $665,300 00 | 39 | $20,200 00 |

Received during the year from members in Illinois: Mortuary, $368.98; expense, $63.50; total — $432 48

EXHIBIT OF DEATH CLAIMS.

| | Total claims. Number. | Amount. |
|---|---|---|
| Claims reported during the year and interest addition | 5 | $2,600 00 |
| Claims paid during the year | 4 | 2,200 00 |
| Balance | 1 | $400 00 |
| Saved by compromising or scaling down claims during the year | | 100 00 |
| Claims unpaid December 31, 1921 | 1 | $300 00 |

EXHIBIT OF JUVENILE DEPARTMENT.

| | Total claims. Number. |
|---|---|
| Claims unpaid December 31, 1920, as per last statement | 527 |
| Claims reported during the year and interest addition | 236 |
| Total | 763 |
| Claims paid during the year | 116 |
| Balance | 647 |
| Claims rejected during the year | 4 |
| Claims unpaid December 31, 1921 | 112 |

EXHIBIT OF SICK AND ACCIDENT CLAIMS.

| | Total claims. Number. | Amount. |
|---|---|---|
| Claims paid during the year | 4 | $443 00 |

## POLISH UNION OF AMERICA.

Located at No. 761-65 Fillmore Avenue, Buffalo, New York.

STANESLAW CZASTER, President. FRANK ZANDRAWICZ, Secretary.

| | |
|---|---|
| Balance from previous year | $307,919 52 |

INCOME.

| | |
|---|---|
| All other assessments or premiums | $140,830 31 |
| Other payments by members, viz: Interest on option "B" liens, $707.10; transfer card fees, $4.50; certificate fees, $105.75; initiation fees, $590.00 | 1,407 35 |
| Net amount received from members | $142,237 66 |
| Gross interest on mortgage loans | 7,731 55 |
| Gross interest on collateral loans | 203 70 |
| Gross interest on bonds and dividends on stocks | 1,225 00 |
| Gross interest on deposits in trust companies and banks | 1,578 97 |
| Gross rents from association's property | 4,000 00 |
| Sale of lodge supplies | 400 35 |
| Receipts for official paper | 3,756 45 |
| Protested check re-deposited | 22 52 |
| Premiums on secretaries bond | 227 00 |
| Payments received on policy liens, option "B" | 701 93 |
| Total income | $162,085 13 |
| Sum | $470,004 65 |

DISBURSEMENTS.

| | |
|---|---|
| Death claims | $62,271 35 |
| Sick and accident claims | 3,375 00 |
| Total benefits paid | $65,646 35 |
| Commissions and fees paid to deputies and organizers | 221 50 |
| Salaries of officers and trustees | 6,925 00 |
| Other compensation of officers and trustees | 480 00 |
| Salaries of office employees | 4,394 13 |
| Salaries and fees paid to supreme medical examiners | 66 50 |
| Traveling and other expenses of officers, trustees and committees | 1,769 32 |
| Insurance department fees | 5 00 |
| Advertising, printing and stationery | 1,201 81 |
| Postage, express, telegraph and telephone | 458 37 |
| Lodge supplies | 17 00 |
| Official publication | 4,994 18 |
| Other legal expenses | 4,577 37 |
| Furniture and fixtures | 150 29 |
| Premiums on bonds of officers and secretary | 277 40 |
| Commission on new members | 287 00 |

DISBURSEMENTS—Concluded.

| | |
|---|---|
| Miscellaneous general expense | $84 50 |
| Donations | 10 00 |
| Total disbursements | $91,565 72 |
| Balance | $378,438 93 |

LEDGER ASSETS.

| | |
|---|---|
| Book value of real estate | $100,000 00 |
| Mortgage loans on real estate | 194,538 00 |
| Loans secured by pledge of bonds, stocks or other collateral | 1,190 00 |
| Book value of bonds and stocks | 30,000 00 |
| Deposits in trust companies and banks on interest | 52,710 93 |
| Total ledger assets | $378,438 93 |

NON-LEDGER ASSETS.

| | | |
|---|---|---|
| Interest and rents due and accrued | | 6,841 61 |
| Assessments actually collected by subordinate lodges not yet turned over to supreme lodge | | 12,917 87 |
| All other assets, viz— | | |
| Due from New York State Insurance Department | $48,305 36 | |
| Liens on policies | 18,530 93 | |
| | | 66,836 29 |
| Gross assets | | $465,034 70 |

DEDUCT ASSETS NOT ADMITTED.

| | |
|---|---|
| Book value of bonds and stocks over market value | 958 00 |
| Total admitted assets | $464,076 70 |

LIABILITIES.

| | | |
|---|---|---|
| Death claims due and unpaid | | $4,000 00 |
| Sick and accident claims due and unpaid | | 300 00 |
| Total unpaid claims | | $4,300 00 |
| Salaries, rents, expenses, commissions, etc., due or accrued | | 521 14 |
| All other liabilities, viz— | | |
| Estimated claims in hands of New York State Insurance Dept | $48,305 36 | |
| Note payable | 14,688 00 | |
| Option D, distributive share held to apply on mortuary assessments | 143 10 | |
| | | 63,136 46 |
| Total | | $67,957 60 |

EXHIBIT OF DEATH CLAIMS.

| | Total claims. | | Illinois claims. | |
|---|---|---|---|---|
| | Number. | Amount. | Number. | Amount. |
| Claims unpaid December 31, 1920, as per last statement | 12 | $ 5,750 00 | -------- | -------------- |
| Claims reported during the year and interest addition | 107 | 61,014 75 | 3 | $2,000 00 |
| Totals | 119 | $66,764 75 | 3 | $2,000 00 |
| Claims paid during the year | 111 | 62,271 35 | 2 | 1,500 00 |
| Balance | 8 | $4,493 40 | 1 | $500 00 |
| Saved by compromising or scaling down claims during the year | -------- | 493 40 | -------- | -------------- |
| Claims unpaid December 31, 1921 | 8 | $4,000 00 | 1 | $500 00 |

EXHIBIT OF SICK AND ACCIDENT CLAIMS.

| | Total claims—all in Illinois. | |
|---|---|---|
| | Number. | Amount. |
| Claims unpaid December 31, 1920, as per last statement | 1 | $ 250 00 |
| Decrease in estimated liability | -------- | 50 00 |
| Claims reported during the year | 18 | 3,675 00 |
| Totals | 19 | $3,875 00 |
| Claims paid during the year | 16 | 3,375 00 |
| Claims rejected during the year | 1 | 200 00 |
| Claims unpaid December 31, 1921 | 2 | $300 00 |

## POLISH UNION OF U. S. OF NORTH AMERICA.

Located at No. 828-830 Miners Bank Building, Wilkes-Barre, Pennsylvania.

JACOB DEMBIEC, President. S. W. WARAKOMSKI, Secretary.

| | |
|---|---|
| Balance from previous year | $389,282 04 |

### INCOME.

| | |
|---|---|
| Membership fees actually received | $ 713 00 |
| All other assessments or premiums | 25,570 22 |
| Dues and per capita tax | 191,343 19 |
| Official publication | 13,069 33 |
| Net amount received from members | $230,695 74 |
| Gross interest on mortgage loans | 15,266 29 |
| Gross interest from all other sources | 2,751 18 |
| Sale of lodge supplies | 19 60 |
| Benefit certificate | 92 25 |
| Total income | $248,825 06 |
| Sum | $638,107 10 |

### DISBURSEMENTS.

| | |
|---|---|
| Death claims | $108,934 53 |
| Permanent disability claims | 3,700 00 |
| Old age benefits | 4,450 00 |
| Death benefit account | 1,833 33 |
| Scholarship account | 1,500 00 |
| Total benefits paid | $120,417 86 |
| Salaries of officers and trustees | 5,912 27 |
| Other compensation of officers and trustees | 250 03 |
| Salaries and fees paid to supreme medical examiners | 395 00 |
| Traveling and other expenses of officers, trustees and committees | 3,272 68 |
| Rent | 1,164 00 |
| Advertising, printing and stationery | 1,296 42 |
| Postage, express, telegraph and telephone | 375 25 |
| Official publication | 14,242 74 |
| Legal expense in litigating claims | 397 50 |
| Furniture and fixtures | 575 40 |
| Office help | 695 00 |
| State auditors | 144 25 |
| Bonds for officers, auditors, trustees and lodges | 1,001 25 |
| Donations to various charities | 4,250 00 |
| Office expenses | 189 13 |
| Dues National Fraternal Congress and C. C | 137 50 |
| Light | 19 71 |
| Convention expenses | 1,431 18 |
| Total disbursements | $156,167 17 |
| Balance | $481,939 93 |

### LEDGER ASSETS.

| | |
|---|---|
| Mortgage loans o n real estate | $189,496 91 |
| Liberty bonds | 126,000 00 |
| Deposits in trust companics and banks not on interest | 40,581 09 |
| Deposits in trust companies and banks on interest | 125,861 93 |
| Other ledger assets | 292,443 02 |
| Total ledger assets | $481,939 93 |

#### NON-LEDGER ASSETS.

| | |
|---|---|
| Interest and rents due and accrued | 1,986 84 |
| Cross assets | $483,926 77 |

### LIABILITIES.

| | |
|---|---|
| Death claims due and unpaid | $22,972 92 |
| Permanent disability claims due and unpaid | 1,200 00 |
| Total | $24,172 92 |

## EXHIBIT OF CERTIFICATES.

| | Total business of the year. Number. | Amount. | Business in Illinois during year. Number. | Amount. |
|---|---|---|---|---|
| Benefit certificates in force December 31, 1920, as per last statement | 20,963 | $14,166,835 00 | 2,354 | $625,600 00 |
| Benefit certificates written and renewed during the year | 919 | 744,150 00 | 49 | 36,250 00 |
| Totals | 21,882 | $14,910,985 00 | 2,403 | $661,850 00 |
| Deduct terminated, decreased or transferred during the year | 1,284 | 801,875 00 | | |
| Deduct terminated or decreased during the year | | | 268 | 134,000 00 |
| Total benefit certificates in force December 31, 1921 | 20,598 | $14,109,110 00 | 2,135 | $527,850 00 |

Received during the year from members in Illinois: Mortuary, $17,670.70; sinking, $511.00; disability, $584.09; educational, $255.50; expense, $1,788.50; total $20,809 79

## EXHIBIT OF DEATH CLAIMS.

| | Total claims. Number. | Amount. | Illinois claims. Number. | Amount. |
|---|---|---|---|---|
| Claims unpaid December 31, 1920, as per last statement | 68 | $35,507 87 | 5 | $2,309 56 |
| Claims reported during the year and interest addition | 132 | 80,550 00 | 9 | 5,000 00 |
| Totals | 200 | $116,057 87 | 14 | $7,309 56 |
| Claims paid during the year | 145 | 93,084 95 | 10 | 6,126 23 |
| Claims unpaid December 31, 1921 | 55 | $22,972 92 | 4 | $1,183 33 |

## EXHIBIT OF PERMANENT DISABILITY CLAIMS.

| | Total claims—all in Illinois. Number. | Amount. |
|---|---|---|
| Claims reported during the year and interest addition | 24 | $6,100 00 |
| Claims paid during the year | 19 | 4,900 00 |
| Claims unpaid December 31, 1921 | 5 | $1,200 00 |

## EXHIBIT OF OLD AGE AND OTHER CLAIMS.

| | Total claims—all in Illinois. Number. | Amount. |
|---|---|---|
| Claims reported during the year and interest addition | 13 | $4,450 00 |

# PROGRESSIVE ORDER OF THE WEST.

Located at No. 406 Frisco Building, St. Louis, Missouri.

SAMUEL EPSTEIN, Grand Master. MORRIS SHAPIRO, Grand Secretary.

Balance from previous year $190,968 34

## INCOME.

| | |
|---|---|
| All other assessments or premiums | $137,628 25 |
| Dues and per capita tax | 8,273 96 |
| Membership certificates | 182 50 |
| Net amount received from members | $147,084 81 |
| Gross interest on bonds and dividends on stocks | 5,142 50 |
| Gross interest on deposits in trust companies and banks | 689 60 |
| Gross interest from all other sources | 552 20 |
| Sale of lodge supplies | 46 80 |
| Profits on purchase of U. S. liberty bonds | 6,163 42 |
| Relief returned | 25 00 |
| Returned by the convention committee | 57 12 |
| Total income | $159,761 25 |
| Sum | $350,729 59 |

## DISBURSEMENTS.

| | |
|---|---|
| Death claims | $68,640 56 |
| Permanent disability claims | 2,250 00 |
| Funeral benefits | 5,700 00 |
| Total benefits paid | $76,590 56 |

DISBURSEMENTS—Concluded.

| | |
|---|---|
| Commissions and fees paid to deputies and organizers | $ 941 00 |
| Salaries of officers and trustees | 3,702 65 |
| Salaries of office employees | 1,200 00 |
| Salaries and fees paid to subordinate medical examiners | 543 00 |
| Traveling and other expenses of officers, trustees and committees | 1,432 10 |
| Insurance department fees | 97 50 |
| Rent | 1,095 00 |
| Advertising, printing and stationery | 1,747 34 |
| Postage, express, telegraph and telephone | 647 66 |
| Lodge supplies | 139 29 |
| Other legal expenses | 6,048 12 |
| Donations to charitable institutions | 2,230 00 |
| Relief to sick and distressed members | 760 00 |
| Total disbursements | $97,175 22 |
| Balance | $253,554 37 |

LEDGER ASSETS.

| | |
|---|---|
| Book value of bonds | $201,000 00 |
| Deposits in trust companies and banks not on interest | 31,624 77 |
| Deposits in trust companies and banks on interest | 20,929 60 |
| Total ledger assets | $253,554 37 |

NON-LEDGER ASSETS.

| | |
|---|---|
| Assessments actually collected by subordinate lodges not yet turned over to supreme lodge | 12,569 60 |
| Gross assets | $266,123 97 |

DEDUCT ASSETS NOT ADMITTED.

| | |
|---|---|
| Profits on purchase of liberty bonds | 6'163 42 |
| Total admitted assets | $259,960 55 |

LIABILITIES.

| | | |
|---|---|---|
| Death claims due and unpaid | $ 5,994 57 | |
| Death claims adjusted not yet due | 12,500 00 | |
| Total death claims | | $18,494 57 |
| Funeral benefits | | 100 00 |
| Total | | $18,594 57 |

EXHIBIT OF CERTIFICATES.

| | Total business of the year. | | Business in Illinois during year. | |
|---|---|---|---|---|
| | Number. | Amount. | Number. | Amount. |
| Benefit certificates in force December 31, 1920, as per last statement | 12,820 | $6,410,500 00 | 4,856 | $2,428,000 00 |
| Benefit certificates written and renewed during the year | 1,828 | 914,000 00 | 888 | 444,000 00 |
| Totals | 14,648 | $7,324,000 00 | 5,744 | $2,872,000 00 |
| Deduct terminated, decreased or transferred during the year | 1,873 | 936,500 00 | | |
| Deduct terminated or decreased during the year | | | 859 | 429,500 00 |
| Total benefit certificates in force December 31, 1921 | 12,775 | $6,387,500 00 | 4,885 | $2,442,500 00 |

| | |
|---|---|
| Received during the year from members in Illinois: Mortuary, $47,157.49; disability, $1,223.35; funeral, $2,204.70; expense, $3,288.60; total | $53,874 14 |

EXHIBIT OF DEATH CLAIMS.

| | Total claims. | | Illinois claims. | |
|---|---|---|---|---|
| | Number. | Amount. | Number. | Amount. |
| Claims unpaid December 31, 1920, as per last statement | 26 | $13,000 00 | 11 | $ 5,500 00 |
| Claims reported during the year and interest addition | 149 | 74,500 00 | 47 | 23,500 00 |
| Totals | 175 | $87,500 00 | 58 | $29,000 00 |
| Claims paid during the year | 137 | 68,640 56 | 43 | 21,500 00 |
| Claims unpaid December 31, 1921 | 38 | $18,000 00 | 15 | $7,500 00 |

EXHIBIT OF PERMANENT DISABILITY CLAIMS.

| | Total claims. Number. | Total claims. Amount. | Illinois claims. Number. | Illinois claims. Amount. |
|---|---|---|---|---|
| Claims reported during the year and interest addition | 5 | $2,500 00 | 2 | $1,000 00 |
| Claims paid during the year | 5 | 2,250 00 | 2 | 750 00 |
| Saved by compromising or scaling down claims during the year | | 250 00 | | |

EXHIBIT OF OLD AGE AND OTHER CLAIMS.

| | Total claims. Number. | Total claims. Amount. | Illinois claims. Number. | Illinois claims. Amount. |
|---|---|---|---|---|
| Claims unpaid December 31, 1920, as per last statement | 17 | $ 850 00 | 7 | $ 350 00 |
| Claims reported during the year and interest addition | 99 | 4,950 00 | 30 | 1,500 00 |
| Totals | 116 | $5,800 00 | 37 | $1,850 00 |
| Claims paid during the year | 114 | 5,700 00 | 36 | 1,800 00 |
| Balance | 2 | $100 00 | 1 | $50 00 |

## PROTECTED HOME CIRCLE.

Located at No. 30 East State Street, Sharon, Pennsylvania.

A. C. McLEAN, President. W. S. PALMER, Secretary.

| | |
|---|---|
| Balance from previous year | $814,160 05 |

### INCOME.

| | |
|---|---|
| Assessments or premiums during first ten months of membership of which all or an extra percentage is used for expenses | $ 163,419 40 |
| All other assessments or premiums | 1,183,420 55 |
| Dues and per capita tax | 182,826 78 |
| Medical examiners' fees actually received | 1,894 00 |
| Net amount received from members | $1,531,560 73 |
| Gross interest on mortgage loans | 7,374 83 |
| Gross interest on collateral loans | 18 00 |
| Gross interest on bonds and dividends on stocks | 24,754 99 |
| Gross rents from association's property, including $1,500.00 for association's occupancy of its own buildings | 6,417 50 |
| Sale of lodge supplies | 4,356 06 |
| Total income | $1,574,482 11 |
| Sum | $2,388,642 16 |

### DISBURSEMENTS.

| | |
|---|---|
| Death claims | $1,067,238 11 |
| Permanent disability claims | 11,559 09 |
| Old age benefits | 93,098 75 |
| Total benefits paid | $1,171,895 95 |
| Commissions and fees paid to deputies and organizers | 213,673 68 |
| Salaries of officers and trustees | 33,187 60 |
| Salaries and other compensation of committees | 1,303 65 |
| Salaries of office employees | 33,337 73 |
| Other compensation of office employees | 600 00 |
| Salaries and fees paid to subordinate medical examiners | 104 50 |
| Traveling and other expenses of officers, trustees and committees | 2,776 92 |
| Insurance department fees | 879 00 |
| Rent | 1,500 00 |
| Advertising, printing and stationery | 8,493 14 |
| Postage, express, telegraph and telephone | 4,340 85 |
| Lodge supplies | 7,381 90 |
| Official publication | 14,550 61 |
| Expenses of supreme lodge meeting | 5,440 10 |
| Legal expense in litigating claims | 1,181 99 |
| Furniture and fixtures | 846 20 |
| Taxes, repairs and other expenses on real estate | 2,916 17 |
| Gross loss on sale or maturity of ledger assets | 2,500 00 |
| Borrowed money repaid (gross) | 68,000 00 |
| Interest on borrowed money | 3,939 18 |
| Fuel and light | 1,074 36 |

DISBURSEMENTS—Concluded.

| | |
|---|---|
| Premium on officer's bonds | $1,531 84 |
| Fraternal Congress dues | 256 00 |
| Insurance federation | 200 00 |
| Incidentals | 1,283 50 |
| Hallerith system | 1,468 45 |
| Total disbursements | $1,584,663 32 |
| Balance | $803,978 84 |

## LEDGER ASSETS.

| | |
|---|---|
| Book value of real estate | $ 81,896 89 |
| Mortgage loans on real estate | 86,486 63 |
| Loans secured by pledge of bonds, stocks or other collateral | 1,550 00 |
| Book value of bonds and stocks | 560,732 30 |
| Deposits in trust companies and banks not on interest | 73,313 02 |
| Total ledger assets | $803,978 84 |

NON-LEDGER ASSETS.

| | |
|---|---|
| Interest and rents due and accrued | 9,604 58 |
| Market value of real estate over book value | 18,103 11 |
| Gross assets | $831,686 53 |

DEDUCT ASSETS NOT ADMITTED.

| | |
|---|---|
| Book value of bonds and stocks over market value | 29,901 22 |
| Total admitted assets | $801,785 31 |

## LIABILITIES.

| | | |
|---|---|---|
| Death claims due and unpaid | $ 17,500 00 | |
| Death claims resisted | 32,000 00 | |
| Death claims reported during the year but not yet adjusted | 23,000 00 | |
| Death claims incurred in 1921, not reported until 1922 | 105,000 00 | |
| Total unpaid claims | | $177,500 00 |
| Borrowed money, $50,000.00; interest due or accrued on same, $750.00 | | 50,750 00 |
| Total | | $228,250 00 |

## EXHIBIT OF CERTIFICATES.

| | Total business of the year. | | Business in Illinois during year. | |
|---|---|---|---|---|
| | Number. | Amount. | Number. | Amount. |
| Benefit certificates in force December 31, 1920, as per last statement | 119,743 | $101,769,500 00 | 1,436 | $1,215,750 00 |
| Benefit certificates written and renewed during the year | 19,642 | 17,543,750 00 | 232 | 221,500 00 |
| Benefit certificates received by transfer during the year | -------- | ------------- | 94 | 74,750 00 |
| Totals | 139,385 | $119,313,250 00 | 1,762 | $1,512,000 00 |
| Deduct terminated, decreased or transferred during the year | 17,845 | 15,049,170 00 | -------- | ------------- |
| Deduct terminated or decreased during the year | -------- | ------------- | 384 | 346,500 00 |
| Total benefit certificates in force December 31, 1921 | 121,540 | $104,264,080 00 | 1,378 | $1,165,500 00 |

| | |
|---|---|
| Received during the year from members in Illinois: Mortuary, $10,354.17; reserve, $3,451.38; expense, $5,975.94; total | $19,781 49 |

## EXHIBIT OF DEATH CLAIMS.

| | Total claims. | | Illinois claims. | |
|---|---|---|---|---|
| | Number. | Amount. | Number. | Amount. |
| Claims unpaid December 31, 1920, as per last statement | 74 | $ 73,000 00 | 1 | $ 500 00 |
| Claims reported during the year and interest addition | 1,181 | 1,082,770 37 | 21 | 19,000 00 |
| Totals | 1,255 | $1,155,770 37 | 22 | $19,500 00 |
| Claims paid during the year | 1,186 | 1,067,238 11 | 21 | 17,918 06 |
| Balance | 69 | $88,532 26 | 1 | $1,581 94 |
| Saved by compromising or scaling down claims during the year | -------- | 16,032 26 | -------- | 581 94 |
| Claims unpaid December 31, 1921 | 69 | $72,500 00 | 1 | $1,000 00 |

EXHIBIT OF PERMANENT DISABILITY CLAIMS.

| | Total claims—all in Illinois. Number. | Amount. |
|---|---|---|
| Claims paid during the year | 21 | $11,559 09 |

EXHIBIT OF OLD AGE AND OTHER CLAIMS.

| | Total claims. Number. | Amount. | Illinois claims. Number. | Amount. |
|---|---|---|---|---|
| Claims paid during the year | 1,252 | $93,098 75 | 4 | $350 00 |

## RAILWAY MAIL ASSOCIATION.

Located at No. 10 Congress Street, Portsmouth, New Hampshire.

W. M. COLLINS, President. R. E. ROSS, Secretary.

| | |
|---|---|
| Balance from previous year | $154,921 60 |

### INCOME.

| | |
|---|---|
| Membership fees actually received | $ 1,392 50 |
| All other assessments or premiums | 125,583 25 |
| Dues and per capita tax | 23,548 50 |
| Changes of beneficiary | 346 00 |
| Net amount received from members | $150,870 25 |
| Gross interest on bonds and dividends on stocks | 6,159 55 |
| Gross interest on deposits in trust companies and banks | 458 33 |
| Return of benefits refused | 795 00 |
| Miscellaneous | 107 98 |
| Total income | $158,391 11 |
| Sum | $313,312 71 |

### DISBURSEMENTS.

| | |
|---|---|
| Death claims | $39,050 00 |
| Permanent disability claims | 4,462 15 |
| Accident claims | 67,785 00 |
| Total benefits paid | $111,297 15 |
| Salaries of officers and trustees | 2,625 00 |
| Salaries of office employees | 3,881 50 |
| Traveling and other expenses of officers, trustees and committees | 119 78 |
| For collection and remittance of assessments and dues | 4,146 08 |
| Insurance department fees | 470 59 |
| Rent | 836 48 |
| Advertising, printing and stationery | 2,027 74 |
| Postage, express, telegraph and telephone | 1,861 55 |
| Official publication | 1,500 00 |
| Expenses of supreme lodge meeting | 4,000 00 |
| Legal expense in litigating claims | 3,786 27 |
| Furniture and fixtures | 304 68 |
| Gross loss on sale or maturity of ledger assets | 1,221 30 |
| Premium on bonds of officers | 209 27 |
| Insurance on office equipment | 77 15 |
| Expenses of audit | 518 76 |
| Miscellaneous | 6 50 |
| Total disbursements | $138,889 80 |
| Balance | $174,422 91 |

### LEDGER ASSETS.

| | |
|---|---|
| Book value of bonds and stocks | $147,146 85 |
| Deposits in trust companies and banks not on interest | 7,276 06 |
| Deposits in trust companies and banks on interest | 20,000 00 |
| Total ledger assets | $174,422 91 |

#### NON-LEDGER ASSETS.

| | |
|---|---|
| Interest and rents due and accrued | 1,473 33 |
| Market value of bonds and stocks over book value | 7,143 15 |
| Gross assets | $183,039 39 |

LIABILITIES.

| | | |
|---|---|---|
| Death claims resisted | | $8,000 00 |
| Accident claims resisted | $789 00 | |
| Accident claims reported during the year but not yet adjusted | 459 00 | |
| Total accident claims | | 1,248 00 |
| Total unpaid claims | | $9,248 00 |
| Salaries, rents, expenses, commissions, etc., due or accrued | | 75 00 |
| Total | | $9,323 00 |

EXHIBIT OF CERTIFICATES.

| | Total business of the year. | | Business in Illinois during year. | |
|---|---|---|---|---|
| | Number. | Amount. | Number. | Amount. |
| Benefit certificates in force December 31, 1920, as per last statement | 14,372 | $57,488,000 00 | 1,304 | $5,216,000 00 |
| Benefit certificates written and renewed during the year | 2,829 | 11,316,000 00 | 262 | 1,048,000 00 |
| Benefit certificates received by transfer during the year | | | 70 | 280,000 00 |
| Total | 17,201 | $68,804,000 00 | 1,636 | $6,544,000 00 |
| Deduct terminated, decreased or transferred during the year | 963 | 3,852,000 00 | | |
| Deduct terminated or decreased during the year | | | 182 | 728,000 00 |
| Total benefit certificates in force December 31, 1921 | 16,238 | $64,952,000 00 | 1,454 | $5,816,000 00 |

Received during the year from members in Illinois: Mortuary and disability, $12,357.75; expense, $1,827.75; total ... $14,185 50

EXHIBIT OF DEATH CLAIMS.

| | Total claims. | |
|---|---|---|
| | Number. | Amount. |
| Claims unpaid December 31, 1920, as per last statement | 3 | $12,000 00 |
| Claims reported during the year and interest addition | 12 | 47,895 00 |
| Interest addition | | 1,155 00 |
| Total | 15 | $61,050 00 |
| Claims paid during the year | 10 | 39,050 00 |
| Balance | 5 | $22,000 00 |
| Saved by compromising or scaling down claims during the year | | 2,000 00 |
| Claims rejected during the year | 3 | 12,000 00 |
| Claims unpaid December 31, 1921 | 2 | $8,000 00 |

EXHIBIT OF PERMANENT DISABILITY CLAIMS.

| | Total claims. | |
|---|---|---|
| | Number. | Amount. |
| Claims paid during the year | 5 | $4,462 15 |

EXHIBIT OF ACCIDENT CLAIMS.

| | Total claims. | | Illinois claims. | |
|---|---|---|---|---|
| | Number. | Amount. | Number. | Amount. |
| Claims unpaid December 31, 1920, as per last statement | 13 | $1,554 00 | | |
| Claims reported during the year | 874 | 70,000 50 | 83 | $4,951 00 |
| Total | 887 | $71,554 50 | 83 | $4,951 00 |
| Claims paid during the year | 857 | 67,785 00 | 77 | 4,651 00 |
| Claims rejected during the year | 19 | 2,521 50 | 4 | 255 00 |
| Claims unpaid December 31, 1921 | 11 | $1,248 00 | 2 | $45 00 |

---

## ROYAL ARCANUM, SUPREME COUNCIL.

Located at Nos. 407-409 Shawmut Avenue, Boston, Massachusetts.

CARLETON E. HOADLEY, Supreme Regent. SAM'L N. HOAG, Supreme Secretary.

Balance from previous year ... $9,992,765 54

## INCOME.

| | |
|---|---|
| Half cash liens in 1921 (assets) | $ 89,962 15 |
| All other assessments or premiums | 5,955,360 07 |
| Accumulated interest on liens | 29,928 12 |
| Dues and per capita tax | 290,898 21 |
| Interest half cash payments | 40 87 |
| Other payments by members, viz: Cards members at large, $4.00; R. A. Bulletin, $0.30; changes of benefit certificates, $1,394.00 | 1,398 30 |
| Total received from members | $6,367,587 72 |
| Deduct payments returned to applicants and members | 7 50 |
| Net amount received from members | $6,367,580 22 |
| Gross interest on bonds and dividends on stocks | 402,878 69 |
| Gross interest on deposits in trust companies and banks | 24,439 78 |
| Gross rents from association's property, including $2,600.00 for association's occupancy of its own buildings | 2,600 00 |
| Sale of lodge supplies | 1,439 54 |
| Gross increase in book value of ledger assets | 37,267 82 |
| Fines | 511 80 |
| R. A. Bulletin advertisements | 279 84 |
| Sale of old paper | 25 95 |
| Total income | $6,837,023 64 |
| Sum | $16,829,789 18 |

## DISBURSEMENTS.

| | | |
|---|---|---|
| Actual cash payments | $4,420,236 27 | |
| Recovered account liens on certificates — Principal | 111,624 36 | |
| Recovered account liens on certificates — interest | 24,450 70 | |
| | | $4,556,311 33 |
| Permanent disability claims | | 34,269 60 |
| Old age benefits | | 30,767 61 |
| Total benefits paid | | $4,621,348 54 |
| Salaries of deputies and organizers | | 39,904 24 |
| Salaries of officers and trustees | | 28,500 02 |
| Other compensation of officers and trustees | | 700 00 |
| Salaries and other compensation of committees | | 12,766 60 |
| Salaries of office employees | | 51,856 68 |
| Salaries and fees paid to supreme medical examiners | | 4,500 00 |
| Salaries and fees paid to subordinate medical examiners | | 8 00 |
| Traveling and other expenses of officers, trustees and committees | | 9,822 26 |
| Insurance department fees | | 1,248 14 |
| Rent, including $2,600.00 for association's occupancy of its own buildings | | 5,075 00 |
| Advertising, printing and stationery | | 19,039 22 |
| Postage, express, telegraph and telephone | | 5,280 44 |
| Lodge supplies | | 1,883 84 |
| Official publication | | 14,321 54 |
| Expenses of supreme lodge meeting | | 23,627 21 |
| Legal expense in litigating claims | | 1,697 19 |
| Other legal expenses | | 592 79 |
| Furniture and fixtures | | 476 69 |
| Taxes, repairs and other expenses on real estate | | 6,579 99 |
| Gross loss on sale or maturity of ledger assets—bonds | | 8,025 18 |
| Gross decrease in book value of ledger assets—bonds | | 29,592 59 |
| All other disbursements, viz— | | |
| Deduct account half cash lapses | | 94,943 15 |
| Deduct account of selection of half cash option | | 591 43 |
| Custody of securities, $675.00; bonding supreme council officers, $600.27; actuarial services, $1,628.65; investigating of death claims, $196.49; printing plant, $851.82; Fraternal Congress, $924.44; prizes, membership contests, $7,450.00; prizes for initiates, $34,495.00; floral tributes, $30.00; special investigation of applicants, $397.85; law books, $181.00; deputies' jewels, $89.25; liability and other insurance, $68.19; notary fees, $20.50; renting and care of typewriters and adding machines, $111.96; soap, towels and spring water, $568.62; sundries, $808.02 | | 49,097 06 |
| Total disbursements | | $5,029,777 80 |
| Balance | | $11,800,011 38 |

## LEDGER ASSETS.

| | |
|---|---|
| Book value of real estate | $ 71,866 55 |
| Loans secured by benefit certificates in force December 31, 1921: Principal, $719,118.15; interest, $148,943.90 | 868,062 05 |
| Loans secured by benefit certificates matured by death, unpaid December 31, 1921: Principal, $7,143.22; interest, $1,446.23 | 8,589 45 |
| Book value of bonds and stocks | 9,864,726 71 |
| Deposits in trust companies and banks on interest | 986,534 39 |
| Total ledger assets | $11,800,011 38 |

## LEDGER ASSETS—Concluded.

### NON-LEDGER ASSETS.

| | | |
|---|---|---|
| Interest accrued | | $157,576 62 |
| Assessments actually collected by subordinate lodges not yet turned over to supreme lodge | | 485,000 00 |
| Supreme council dues collected by subordinate lodges not yet turned over to supreme lodge | | 78,000 00 |
| All other assets, viz— | | |
| Due from councils and grand councils | $ 1,884 84 | |
| Printing plant, $19,206.59; printing material, $2,326.98 | 21,533 57 | |
| Supplies for sale, $1,286.40; office furniture, $7,230.11 | 8,516 51 | |
| | | 31,934 92 |
| Gross assets | | $12,552,522 92 |

### DEDUCT ASSETS NOT ADMITTED.

| | | |
|---|---|---|
| Bills receivable | $ 1,884 84 | |
| Book value of real estate over market value | 20,471 55 | |
| Other items, viz— | | |
| Printing plant, $19,206.59; printing material, $2,326.98 | 21,533 57 | |
| Supplies for sale, $1,286.40; office furniture, $7,230.11 | 8,516 51 | |
| Amount of liens under half cash plan: Principal, $719,118.15; interest, $148,943.90 | 868,062 05 | |
| | | 920,468 52 |
| Total admitted assets | | $11,632,054 40 |

## LIABILITIES.

| | | |
|---|---|---|
| Death claims due and unpaid | $ 25,990 86 | |
| Death claims resisted | 27,000 00 | |
| Death claims reported during the year but not yet adjusted | 396,334 66 | |
| Death claims incurred in 1921, not reported until 1922 | 45,365 00 | |
| Total death claims | | $494,690 52 |
| Salaries, rents, expenses, commissions, etc., due or accrued | | 3,085 82 |
| Due councils | | 314 61 |
| Total | | $498,090 95 |

## EXHIBIT OF CERTIFICATES.

| | Total business of the year. | | Business in Illinois during year. | |
|---|---|---|---|---|
| | Number. | Amount. | Number. | Amount. |
| Benefit certificates in force December 31, 1920, as per last statement | 135,567 | $220,142,142 01 | 14,193 | $21,364,959 00 |
| Benefit certificates written and renewed during the year | 6,362 | 7,312,447 00 | 884 | 965,000 00 |
| Benefit certificates received by transfer during the year | -------- | ------------- | 41 | 56,500 00 |
| Benefit certificates increased during the year | -------- | 811,371 00 | -------- | 49,243 00 |
| Total | 141,929 | $228,265,960 01 | 15,118 | $22,435,702 00 |
| Deduct terminated, decreased or transferred during the year | 11,114 | 16,976,126 01 | -------- | ------------- |
| Deduct terminated or decreased during the year | -------- | ------------- | 1,393 | 1,958,616 00 |
| Total benefit certificates in force December 31, 1921 | 130,815 | $211,289,834 00 | 13,725 | $20,477,086 00 |

| | |
|---|---|
| Received during the year from members in Illinois: Mortuary, $535,659.27; expense, $30,603.80; total | $566,263 07 |

## EXHIBIT OF DEATH CLAIMS.

| | Total claims. | | Illinois claims. | |
|---|---|---|---|---|
| | Number. | Amount. | Number. | Amount. |
| Claims unpaid December 31, 1920, as per last statement | 237 | $ 444,961 39 | 24½ | $ 38,500 02 |
| Claims reported during the year and interest addition | 2,464 | 4,584,706 66 | 228 | 425,780 67 |
| Total | 2,701 | $5,029,668 05 | 252½ | $464,280 69 |
| Claims paid during the year | 2,462 | 4,556,311 33 | 227 | 423,066 10 |
| Balance | 239 | $473,356 72 | 25½ | $41,214 59 |
| Saved by compromising or scaling down claims during the year | -------- | 6,781 20 | -------- | 214 57 |
| Claims rejected during the year | 12 | 17,250 00 | 3 | 4,000 00 |
| Claims unpaid December 31, 1921 | 227 | $449,325 52 | 22½ | $37,000 00 |

## EXHIBIT OF PERMANENT DISABILITY CLAIMS.

| | Total claims. Number. | Amount. | Illinois claims. Number. | Amount. |
|---|---|---|---|---|
| Claims unpaid December 31, 1920, as per last statement | 2 | $ 1,000 00 | | |
| Claims reported during the year and interest addition | 37 | 33,269 60 | | |
| Claims paid during the year | 39 | 34,269 60 | 3 | $2,750 00 |

## EXHIBIT OF OLD AGE AND OTHER CLAIMS.

| | Total claims. Number. | Amount. | Illinois claims. Number. | Amount. |
|---|---|---|---|---|
| Claims unpaid December 31, 1920, as per last statement | 8 | $ 2,697 10 | | |
| Claims reported during the year and interest addition | 106 | 28,070 57 | | |
| Total | 114 | $30,767 67 | | |
| Claims paid during the year | 114 | $30,767 61 | 9 | $3,349 08 |
| Balance | | $0 06 | | |
| Saved by compromising or scaling down claims during the year | | 06 | | |

## THE ROYAL HIGHLANDERS.

Located at No. 422 Terminal Building, Lincoln, Nebraska.

W. E. SHARP, President. F. J. SHARP, Chief Secretary.

| | |
|---|---|
| Balance from previous year | $1,812,827 50 |

### INCOME.

| | |
|---|---|
| Membership fees actually received | $ 539 00 |
| All other assessments or premiums | 675,552 45 |
| Dues and per capita tax | 22,463 00 |
| Net amount received from members | $698,554 45 |
| Gross interest on mortgage loans | 86,376 98 |
| Gross interest on bonds and dividends on stocks | 637 50 |
| Gross interest on deposits in trust companies and banks | 5,888 84 |
| Gross rents from association's property | 3,200 00 |
| Sale of lodge supplies | 542 44 |
| Commissions on loans | 25,706 00 |
| Sale of shelving in building at Aurora | 350 00 |
| Total income | $821,256 21 |
| Sum | $2,634,083 71 |

### DISBURSEMENTS.

| | |
|---|---|
| Death claims | $253,967 72 |
| Permanent disability claims | 9,450 00 |
| Old age benefits | 61,050 00 |
| Other benefits | 64,464 81 |
| Total benefits paid | $388,932 53 |
| Commissions and fees paid to deputies and organizers | 5,531 74 |
| Salaries of deputies and organizers | 9,573 70 |
| Salaries of officers and trustees | 27,562 46 |
| Salaries of office employees | 19,625 00 |
| Salaries and fees paid to supreme medical examiners | 147 00 |
| Traveling and other expenses of officers, trustees and committees | 732 65 |
| Insurance department fees | 289 00 |
| Rent | 2,996 00 |
| Advertising, printing and stationery | 4,845 39 |
| Postage, express, telegraph and telephone | 1,681 69 |
| Lodge supplies | 1,021 94 |
| Official publication | 9,529 27 |
| Expenses of supreme lodge meeting September, 1921 | 17,674 87 |
| Legal expense in litigating claims and other legal expenses | 7,393 70 |
| Furniture and fixtures | 278 92 |
| Taxes, repairs and other expenses on real estate | 1,365 06 |
| Gross decrease in book value of ledger assets—by sale of shelving | 350 00 |
| Fuel, light and water | 1,024 09 |
| Officers' bonds | 1,049 87 |
| Miscellaneous items | 340 19 |
| Total disbursements | $501,945 07 |
| Balance | $2,132,138 64 |

## LEDGER ASSETS.

| | |
|---|---|
| Book value of real estate | $ 44,907 87 |
| Mortgage loans on real estate | 2,002,700 00 |
| Book value of bonds and stocks | 16,000 00 |
| Deposits in trust companies and banks on interest | 68,530 77 |
| Total ledger assets | $2,132,138 64 |

### NON-LEDGER ASSETS.

| | |
|---|---|
| Interest and rents due and accrued | 68,979 93 |
| Assessments actually collected by subordinate lodges not yet turned over to supreme lodge | 65,248 00 |
| Total admitted assets | $2,266,366 57 |

## LIABILITIES.

| | | |
|---|---|---|
| Death claims resisted | $ 1,000 00 | |
| Death claims reported during the year but not yet adjusted | 15,800 00 | |
| Death claims incurred in 1921, not reported until 1922 | 3,000 00 | |
| Total death claims | | $19,800 00 |
| Old age and other benefits due and unpaid | | 700 00 |
| Total unpaid claims | | $20,500 00 |

## EXHIBIT OF CERTIFICATES.

| | Total business of the year. | | Business in Illinois during year. | |
|---|---|---|---|---|
| | Number. | Amount. | Number. | Amount. |
| Benefit certificates in force December 31, 1920, as per last statement | 23,412 | $32,221,150 00 | 6 | $6,000 00 |
| Benefit certificates written and renewed during the year | 370 | 419,000 00 | 1 | 1,000 00 |
| Total | 23,782 | $32,640,150 00 | 7 | $7,000 00 |
| Deduct terminated, decreased or transferred during the year | 1,854 | 2,563,150 00 | -------- | ------------- |
| Total benefit certificates in force December 31, 1921 | 21,928 | $30,077,000 00 | 7 | $7,000 00 |

Received during the year from members in Illinois: Disability, $110.02; expense, $25.38; total $135 40

## EXHIBIT OF DEATH CLAIMS.

| | Total claims. Number. | Amount. |
|---|---|---|
| Claims unpaid December 31, 1920, as per last statement | 15 | $ 26,700 00 |
| Claims reported during the year and interest addition | 181 | 246,067 72 |
| Total | 196 | $272,767 72 |
| Claims paid during the year | 181 | 253,967 72 |
| Balance | 15 | $18,800 00 |
| Saved by compromising or scaling down claims during the year | -------- | 2,000 00 |
| Claims unpaid December 31, 1921 | 15 | $16,800 00 |

## EXHIBIT OF PERMANENT DISABILITY CLAIMS.

| | Total claims. Number. | Amount. |
|---|---|---|
| Claims paid during the year | 52 | $9,450 00 |

## EXHIBIT OF OLD AGE AND OTHER CLAIMS.

| | Total claims. Number. | Amount. |
|---|---|---|
| Claims reported during the year and interest addition | 553 | $126,214 81 |
| Claims paid during the year | 550 | 125,514 81 |
| Claims unpaid December 31, 1921 | 3 | $700 00 |

---

# SCANDINAVIAN-AMERICAN FRATERNITY.

Located at Union Savings Bank Building, Eau Claire, Wisconsin.

ALBERT NELSON, President. PETER J. SMITH, Secretary.

| | |
|---|---|
| Balance from previous year | $227,624 53 |

## INCOME.

| | |
|---|---|
| Membership fees actually received | $ 406 50 |
| All other assessments or premiums | 76,274 70 |
| Dues and per capita tax | 14,673 40 |
| Net amount received from members | $91,354 60 |
| Gross interest on bonds and dividends on stocks | 10,960 63 |
| Gross interest on deposits in trust companies and banks | 616 38 |
| Sale of lodge supplies | 277 89 |
| Gross increase in book value of ledger assets | 379 41 |
| Surplus mortality transferred by Wisconsin Insurance Department | 1,376 62 |
| Total income | $104,965 53 |
| Sum | $332,590 06 |

## DISBURSEMENTS.

| | |
|---|---|
| Death claims | $34,465 00 |
| Sick and accident claims | 4,053 74 |
| Old age benefits | 2,500 00 |
| Emergency assistance | 100 00 |
| Total benefits paid | $41,118 74 |
| Commissions and fees paid to deputies and organizers | 5,563 26 |
| Salaries of deputies and organizers | 1,721 83 |
| Salaries of officers and trustees | 2,385 00 |
| Salaries and other compensation of committees | 478 12 |
| Salaries of office employees | 647 00 |
| Salaries and fees paid to supreme medical examiners | 742 00 |
| Traveling and other expenses of officers, trustees and committees | 141 93 |
| Insurance department fees | 158 02 |
| Rent | 345 00 |
| Advertising, printing and stationery | 449 44 |
| Postage, express, telegraph and telephone | 340 14 |
| Lodge supplies | 234 98 |
| Official publication | 1,512 06 |
| Expenses of supreme lodge meeting | 3,899 43 |
| Furniture and fixtures | 195 01 |
| Gross decrease in book value of ledger assets | 2,002 51 |
| Surplus mortality transferred by Wisconsin Insurance Department | 1,376 62 |
| Actuary expense | 195 00 |
| Audit, surety bonds, janitor, etc. | 222 71 |
| Box rents, safety | 6 00 |
| Total disbursements | $63,740 80 |
| Balance | $268,849 26 |

## LEDGER ASSETS.

| | |
|---|---|
| Book value of bonds and stocks | $234,607 00 |
| Deposits in trust companies and banks not on interest | 34,242 26 |
| Total ledger assets | $268,849 26 |

### NON-LEDGER ASSETS.

| | |
|---|---|
| Interest and rents due and accrued | 4,045 84 |
| Assessments actually collected by subordinate lodges not yet turned over to supreme lodge | 7,000 00 |
| Gross assets | $279,894 50 |

### DEDUCT ASSETS NOT ADMITTED.

| | |
|---|---|
| Book value of bonds and stocks over market value | 2,129 00 |
| Total admitted assets | $277,765 50 |

## LIABILITIES.

| | | |
|---|---|---|
| Death claims due and unpaid | $ 400 00 | |
| Death claims reported during the year but not yet adjusted | 4,300 00 | |
| Total death claims | | $4,700 00 |

## EXHIBIT OF CERTIFICATES.

| | Total business of the year. | |
|---|---|---|
| | Number. | Amount. |
| Benefit certificates in force December 31, 1920, as per last statement | 7,840 | $5,844,025 00 |
| Benefit certificates written and renewed during the year | 1,281 | 792,125 00 |
| Total | 9,221 | $6,636,150 00 |
| Deduct terminated, decreased or transferred during the year | 898 | 516,500 00 |
| Total benefit certificates in force December 31, 1921 | 8,223 | $6,119,650 00 |

## EXHIBIT OF DEATH CLAIMS.

| | Total claims. Number. | Amount. |
|---|---|---|
| Claims unpaid December 31, 1920, as per last statement | 7 | $ 3,470 00 |
| Claims reported during the year and interest addition | 56 | 35,695 00 |
| Total | 63 | $39,165 00 |
| Claims paid during the year | 56 | 34,465 00 |
| Claims unpaid December 31, 1921 | 7 | $4,700 00 |

## EXHIBIT OF SICK AND ACCIDENT CLAIMS.

| | Total claims. Number. | Amount. |
|---|---|---|
| Claims paid during the year | 100 | $4,053 74 |

## EXHIBIT OF OLD AGE AND OTHER CLAIMS.

| | Total claims. Number. | Amount. |
|---|---|---|
| Claims paid during the year | 25 | $2,500 00 |

# SLAVONIC EVANGELICAL UNION OF AMERICA.

Located at No. 1601 Beaver Avenue, Pittsburgh, Pennsylvania.

JOHN BIBZA, President. PETER H. JURISH, Secretary.

| | |
|---|---|
| Balance from previous year | $374,392 80 |

## INCOME.

| | |
|---|---|
| Membership fees actually received | $129,172 44 |
| Gross interest on bonds and dividends on stocks | 11,983 75 |
| Gross interest on deposits in trust companies and banks | 3,923 98 |
| Gross rents from association's property, including $900.00 for association's occupancy of its own buildings | 2,388 15 |
| Sale of lodge supplies | 571 50 |
| Total income | $148,039 82 |
| Sum | $522,432 62 |

## DISBURSEMENTS.

| | |
|---|---|
| Death claims | $59,235 00 |
| Permanent disability claims | 3,962 65 |
| Other compensation of officers and trustees | 4,297 33 |
| Salaries and other compensation of committees | 6,290 43 |
| Salaries of office employees | 805 00 |
| Traveling and other expenses of officers, trustees and committees | 2,300 87 |
| Rent | 900 00 |
| Advertising, printing and stationery | 2,261 41 |
| Postage, express, telegraph and telephone | 549 12 |
| Lodge supplies | 439 10 |
| Official publication | 7,046 10 |
| Taxes, repairs and other expenses on real estate | 2,286 43 |
| National fund | 335 00 |
| Bonds for officers | 120 00 |
| Office expense | 1,624 99 |
| Total disbursements | $92,453 43 |
| Balance | $429,979 19 |

## LEDGER ASSETS.

| | |
|---|---|
| Book value of real estate | $ 14,000 00 |
| Book value of bonds and stocks | 288,755 75 |
| Deposits in trust companies and banks not on interest | 122,583 79 |
| Loan to printing department | 3,000 00 |
| Loan to orphans fund | 1,639 65 |
| Total ledger assets | $429,979 19 |

### NON-LEDGER ASSETS.

| | | |
|---|---|---|
| Interest and rents due and accrued | | 5,622 98 |
| All other assets, viz— | | |
| Furniture and fixtures | $ 500 00 | |
| Presses, machinery and supplies | 7,800 00 | |
| Lodge supplies | 150 00 | |
| | | 8,450 00 |
| Orphans cash depository | | 54,936 00 |
| Gross assets | | $498,988 17 |

LEDGER ASSETS—Concluded.

DEDUCT ASSETS NOT ADMITTED.

| | | |
|---|---|---|
| Furniture and fixtures | $ 500 00 | |
| Presses, machinery and supplies | 7,800 00 | |
| Lodge supplies | 150 00 | |
| Loan to printing department | 3,000 00 | |
| | | $11,450 00 |
| Total admitted assets | | $487,538 17 |

LIABILITIES.

| | | |
|---|---|---|
| Death claims due and unpaid | $2,325 00 | |
| Death claims adjusted not yet due | 7,450 00 | |
| Total death claims | | $ 9,775 00 |
| Funds due orphans offset by orphans cash depository | | 54,936 00 |
| Total | | $64,711 00 |

EXHIBIT OF CERTIFICATES.

| | Total business of the year. Number. | Amount. | Business in Illinois during year. Number. | Amount. |
|---|---|---|---|---|
| Benefit certificates in force December 31, 1920, as per last statement | 7,675 | $6,960,275 00 | 683 | $603,650 00 |
| Benefit certificates written and renewed during the year | 594 | 542,000 00 | 48 | 42,500 00 |
| Totals | 8,269 | $7,502,275 00 | 731 | $646,150 00 |
| Deduct terminated, decreased or transferred during the year | 516 | 441,250 00 | | |
| Deduct terminated or decreased during the year | | | 32 | 26,000 00 |
| Total benefit certificates in force December 31, 1921 | 7,753 | $7,061,025 00 | 699 | $620,150 00 |

| | |
|---|---|
| Received during the year from members in Illinois: Mortuary, $8,107.00; disability, $1,329.28; all other, $118.26; expense, $1,976.54; total | $10,531 08 |

EXHIBIT OF DEATH CLAIMS.

| | Total claims. Number. | Amount. | Illinois claims. Number. | Amount. |
|---|---|---|---|---|
| Claims unpaid December 31, 1920, as per last statement | 16 | $11,285 00 | | |
| Claims reported during the year and interest addition | 66 | 57,725 00 | | |
| Totals | 82 | $69,010 00 | | |
| Claims paid during the year | 69 | 59,235 00 | 8 | $7,250 00 |
| Claims unpaid December 31, 1921 | 13 | $9,775 00 | | |

EXHIBIT OF SICK AND ACCIDENT CLAIMS.

| | Total claims. Number. | Amount. | Illinois claims. Number. | Amount. |
|---|---|---|---|---|
| Claims paid during the year | 76 | $3,962 65 | 6 | $315 36 |

## SECURITY BENEFIT ASSOCIATION.

Located at No. 701 Kansas Avenue, Topeka, Kansas.

J. M. KIRKPATRICK, President. J. V. ABRAHAMS, Secretary.

| | |
|---|---|
| Balance from previous year | $1,886,772 14 |

INCOME.

| | |
|---|---|
| Assessments or premiums during first twelve months of membership of which all or an extra percentage is used for expenses | $ 461,138 94 |
| All other assessments or premiums | 3,472,444 80 |
| Dues and per capita tax | 2,363 64 |
| Certificate fees | 3,361 80 |
| Total received from members | $3,939,309 18 |
| Deduct payments returned to applicants and members | 486 10 |
| Net amount received from members | $3,938,823 08 |

## INCOME—Concluded.

| | |
|---|---|
| Gross interest on mortgage loans | $51,182 50 |
| Gross interest on bonds and dividends on stocks | 17,603 13 |
| Gross interest from all other sources | 12,012 06 |
| Gross rents from association's property | 16,500 00 |
| Sale of lodge supplies | 8,833 70 |
| Refund account of bank failures | 137 83 |
| Conscience fund | 36 00 |
| General fund from disbanded councils | 39 68 |
| Commission account | 237 35 |
| Total income | $4,045,394 33 |
| Sum | $5,932,166 47 |

## DISBURSEMENTS.

| | |
|---|---|
| Death claims | $2,446,905 00 |
| Permanent disability claims | 8,640 63 |
| Old age benefits | 261,030 29 |
| Partial disability | 8,056 25 |
| Compromised | 39,496 84 |
| Total benefits paid | $2,764,129 01 |
| Commissions and fees paid to deputies and organizers | 452,067 99 |
| Actuarial services | 1,278 31 |
| Salaries of managers or agents not deputies or organizers | 736 58 |
| Salaries of officers and trustees | 23,600 00 |
| Compensation of other officers and trustees | 25,055 57 |
| Salaries and other compensation of committees | 6,159 58 |
| Salaries of office employees | 101,062 52 |
| Other compensation of office employees, janitor | 917 55 |
| Salaries and fees paid to supreme medical examiners | 6,000 00 |
| Salaries and fees paid to subordinate medical examiners | 192 00 |
| Traveling and other expenses of officers, trustees and committees | 3,065 05 |
| State and National Fraternal Congress | 50 00 |
| Expenses of examination | 7,815 04 |
| Insurance department fees | 891 34 |
| Rent | 5,525 00 |
| Advertising, printing and stationery | 51,007 73 |
| Postage, express, telegraph and telephone | 13,140 46 |
| Lodge supplies | 7,733 33 |
| Official publication | 49,803 23 |
| Assurity bonds | 5,190 68 |
| Legal expense in litigating claims | 8,688 01 |
| Other legal expenses | 26,569 14 |
| Furniture and fixtures | 570 40 |
| Taxes, repairs and other expenses on real estate | 6,095 15 |
| Gross loss on sale or maturity of ledger assets | 672 59 |
| Gross decrease in book value of ledger assets | 532 62 |
| Home and hospital | 190,000 00 |
| Light, heat, water, gas and towels | 2,099 82 |
| Supplies and repairs | 971 83 |
| Insurance | 934 31 |
| Rent and expense of tabulating machine | 793 60 |
| National council band | 446 90 |
| Miscellaneous | 659 66 |
| Total disbursements | $3,764,455 00 |
| Balance | $2,167,711 47 |

## LEDGER ASSETS.

| | |
|---|---|
| Book value of real estate | $164,894 03 |
| Mortgage loans on real estate | 952,291 67 |
| Book value of bonds and stocks | 601,851 38 |
| Deposits in trust companies and banks on interest | 448,674 39 |
| Total ledger assets | $2,167,711 47 |

### NON-LEDGER ASSETS.

| | |
|---|---|
| Interest and rents due and accrued | 31,666 80 |
| Assessments actually collected by subordinate lodges not yet turned over to supreme lodge | 322,940 40 |
| Total admitted assets | $2,522,318 67 |

## LIABILITIES.

| | | |
|---|---|---|
| Death claims due and unpaid | $ 29,480 33 | |
| Death claims reported during the year but not yet adjusted | 381,354 85 | |
| Death claims incurred in 1921, not reported until 1922 | 56,968 00 | |
| Present value of deferred death claims payable in installments, N. A. annuities | 39,325 38 | |
| Total death claims | | $507,128 76 |

LIABILITIES—Concluded.

| | | |
|---|---|---|
| Permanent disability claims reported during the year but not yet adjusted | | $11,262 50 |
| Juvenile claims due and unpaid | $360 00 | |
| Juvenile claims incurred in 1921, not reported until 1922 | 268 00 | |
| Total juvenile claims | | 628 00 |
| Old age and other benefits due and unpaid | | 2,150 00 |
| Total unpaid claims | | $521,169 26 |
| Due or accrued expense, $7,526.05; commissions, $26,555.79 | | 34,081 84 |
| Legal reserves | | 65,105 16 |
| Advance assessments | | 19,613 92 |
| All other liabilities, viz: Salary contracts with former officers of National American for services rendered expiring Sept. 23, 1923, $1,458.33; salary contract with W. A. Biby for National lecturer and in such other capacity as the society may direct, expiring September, 1922, $416.66 | | 34,374 87 |
| Total | | $674,345 05 |

There are 65 claims on which suit has been brought and are now in litigation amounting to $875.00. These claims were reported rejected or outstanding in year death took place. Many of them cannot possibly be a liability on the society.

EXHIBIT OF CERTIFICATES.

| | Total business of the year. | | Business in Illinois during year. | |
|---|---|---|---|---|
| | Number. | Amount. | Number. | Amount. |
| Benefit certificates in force December 31, 1920, as per last statement | 233,682 | $277,875,019 00 | 32,944 | $36,023,516 00 |
| Benefit certificates written and renewed during the year | 76,304 | 83,998,028 00 | 10,097 | 10,759,504 00 |
| Benefit certificates received by transfer during the year | | | 60 | 61,500 00 |
| Benefit certificates increased during the year | | 472,450 00 | | 55,000 00 |
| Totals | 309,986 | $362,345,497 00 | 43,101 | $46,899,520 00 |
| Deduct terminated, decreased or transferred during the year | 74,503 | 85,325,226 00 | | |
| Deduct terminated or decreased during the year | | | 8,566 | 9,324,216 00 |
| Total benefit certificates in force December 31, 1921 | 235,483 | $277,020,271 00 | 34,535 | $37,575,304 00 |

| | |
|---|---|
| Received during the year from members in Illinois: Mortuary, $384,210.22; expense, $126,404.01; total | $510,614 23 |

EXHIBIT OF DEATH CLAIMS.

| | Total claims. | | Illinois claims. | |
|---|---|---|---|---|
| | Number. | Amount. | Number. | Amount. |
| Claims unpaid December 31, 1920, as per last statement | 489 | $ 577,500 00 | 75 | $ 84,000 00 |
| Claims reported during the year and interest addition | 2,311 | 2,625,068 69 | 340 | 342,051 00 |
| Totals | 2,800 | $3,202,568 69 | 415 | $426,051 00 |
| Claims paid during the year | 2,320 | 2,481,534 84 | 354 | 351,789 47 |
| Balance | 480 | $721,033 85 | 61 | $74,261 53 |
| Saved by compromising or scaling down claims during the year | | 156,033 85 | | 8,761 53 |
| Claims rejected during the year | 39 | 52,000 00 | 7 | 10,000 00 |
| Claims unpaid December 31, 1921 | 441 | $513,000 00 | 54 | $55,500 00 |

EXHIBIT OF PERMANENT DISABILITY CLAIMS.

| | Total claims. | | Illinois claims. | |
|---|---|---|---|---|
| | Number. | Amount. | Number. | Amount. |
| Claims unpaid December 31, 1920, as per last statement | 14 | $ 9,250 00 | 1 | $ 250 00 |
| Claims reported during the year and interest addition | 52 | 21,459 38 | 2 | 1,787 50 |
| Totals | 66 | $30,709 38 | 3 | $2,037 50 |
| Claims paid during the year | 40 | 16,696 88 | 1 | 237 50 |
| Balance | 26 | $14,012 50 | 2 | $1,800 00 |
| Claims rejected during the year | 7 | 2,750 00 | | |
| Claims unpaid December 31, 1921 | 19 | $11,262 50 | 2 | $1,800 00 |

EXHIBIT OF JUVENILE CLAIMS.

| | Total claims. Number. | Total claims. Amount. | Illinois claims. Number. | Illinois claims. Amount. |
|---|---|---|---|---|
| Claims reported during the year | 39 | $5,227 00 | 10 | $1,575 00 |
| Claims paid during the year | 36 | 4,867 00 | 9 | 1,470 00 |
| Claims unpaid December 31, 1921 | 3 | $360 00 | 1 | $105 00 |

EXHIBIT OF OLD AGE AND OTHER CLAIMS.

| | Total claims. Number. | Total claims. Amount. | Illinois claims. Number. | Illinois claims. Amount. |
|---|---|---|---|---|
| Claims unpaid December 31, 1920, as per last statement | 16 | $ 2,250 00 | | |
| Claims reported during the year and interest addition | 1,962 | 260,930 29 | 61 | $6,460 75 |
| Totals | 1,978 | $263,180 29 | 61 | $6,460 75 |
| Claims paid during the year | 1,962 | 261,030 29 | 60 | 6,410 75 |
| Claims unpaid December 31, 1921 | 16 | $2,150 00 | 1 | $50 00 |

## SOCIETY OF THE TABORITES, NATIONAL SUPREME LODGE.

Located at No. 3416 East Fifty-third Street, Cleveland, Ohio.

FERDINAND PRUSA, President. FRANK CERNOHORSKY, Secretary.

| | |
|---|---|
| Balance from previous year | $43,603 84 |

INCOME.

| | |
|---|---|
| All other assessments or premiums | $22,232 02 |
| Dues and per capita tax | 1,455 60 |
| Total received from members | $23,687 62 |
| Gross interest on bonds and dividends on stocks | 2,254 99 |
| Gross interest on deposits in trust companies and banks | 262 16 |
| Sale of lodge supplies and emblems | 79 07 |
| Gross increase in book value of ledger assets | 789 97 |
| From all other sources, viz— | |
| Certificates rewritten | 32 25 |
| Juvenile department 5 cents per quarter per child insured for expense fund | 98 68 |
| Agitation fund | 697 90 |
| Admission fee of 2 new lodges | 10 00 |
| All other payments | 1 00 |
| Total income | $27,913 64 |
| Sum | $71,517 48 |

DISBURSEMENTS.

| | |
|---|---|
| Death claims | $16,220 00 |
| Salaries of officers and trustees | 1,166 04 |
| Other compensation of officers and trustees | 101 00 |
| Traveling and other expenses of officers, trustees and committees | 145 00 |
| Insurance department fees | 5 00 |
| Rent | 117 00 |
| Advertising, printing and stationery | 155 29 |
| Postage, express, telegraph and telephone | 118 09 |
| Lodge supplies and emblems | 61 25 |
| Official publication | 1,429 02 |
| Expenses of supreme lodge meeting | 15 00 |
| Schools and charity | 235 00 |
| All other disbursements, viz— | |
| Contributions to grand lodges | 343 25 |
| Bonds for officers and trustees | 40 00 |
| Donations to new lodges (2) | 40 00 |
| All other disbursements | 1 00 |
| Total disbursements | $20,191 94 |
| Balance | $51,325 54 |

LEDGER ASSETS.

| | |
|---|---|
| Book value of bonds | $45,348 40 |
| Deposits in trust companies and banks on interest | 5,977 14 |
| Total ledger assets | $51,325 54 |

LEDGER ASSETS—Concluded.

NON-LEDGER ASSETS.

| | |
|---|---|
| Interest and rents due and accrued on bonds | $866 72 |
| Total admitted assets | $52,192 26 |

EXHIBIT OF CERTIFICATES.

| | Total business of the year. Number. | Amount. | Business in Illinois during year. Number. | Amount. |
|---|---|---|---|---|
| Benefit certificates in force December 31, 1920, as per last statement | 2,980 | $1,051,500 00 | 1,914 | $685,400 00 |
| Benefit certificates written and renewed during the year | 308 | 111,300 00 | 198 | 71,800 00 |
| Totals | 3,288 | $1,162,800 00 | 2,112 | $757,200 00 |
| Deduct terminated, decreased or transferred during the year | 160 | 55,300 00 | | |
| Deduct terminated or decreased during the year | | | 98 | 36,500 00 |
| Total benefit certificates in force December 31, 1921 | 3,128 | $1,107,500 00 | 2,014 | $720,700 00 |

| | |
|---|---|
| Received during the year from members in Illinois: Mortuary, $11,228.44; reserve, $1,708.04; official publication, $950.70; charity and schools, $232.59; agitation, $1,439.13; convention, $232.59; total | $15,791 49 |

EXHIBIT OF DEATH CLAIMS.

| | Total claims. Number. | Amount. | Illinois claims. Number. | Amount. |
|---|---|---|---|---|
| Claims reported during the year and interest addition | 48 | $16,220 00 | 38 | $13,420 00 |
| Claims paid during the year | 48 | 16,220 00 | 38 | 13,420 00 |

## SONS OF NORWAY.

Located at No. 903-7 New York Life Building, Minneapolis, Minnesota.

T. O. GILBERT, President. L. STAVNHEIM, Secretary.

| | |
|---|---|
| Balance from previous year | $350,740 43 |

INCOME.

| | |
|---|---|
| Membership fees actually received | $ 2,500 00 |
| Assessments or premiums during first twelve months of membership of which all or an extra percentage is used for expenses | 40,303 74 |
| All other assessments or premiums | 47,242 88 |
| Dues and per capita tax | 12,256 95 |
| Medical examiners' fees actually received | 265 75 |
| Other payments by members, viz— | |
| Extra assessment for organization work | 4,990 00 |
| Certificate fees | 51 50 |
| Net amount received from members | $107,610 82 |
| Gross interest on mortgage loans | 13,885 45 |
| Gross interest on collateral loans | 23 00 |
| Gross interest on bonds and dividends on stocks | 2,750 92 |
| Gross interest on deposits in trust companies and banks | 520 85 |
| Gross rents from association's property | 180 00 |
| Sale of lodge supplies | 982 97 |
| Commission | 60 78 |
| Charter fees | 160 00 |
| Official publication | 5,397 54 |
| Telephone | 13 80 |
| Total income | $131,586 13 |
| Sum | $482,326 56 |

DISBURSEMENTS.

| | |
|---|---|
| Death claims | $31,190 49 |
| Commissions and fees paid to deputies and organizers | 10,530 64 |
| Salaries of deputies and organizers | 775 00 |
| Salaries of officers and trustees | 2,700 00 |
| Salaries of office employees | 2,855 00 |
| Salaries and fees paid to supreme medical examiners | 626 00 |
| Traveling and other expenses of officers, trustees and committees | 1,616 93 |
| Insurance department fees | 213 74 |
| Rent | 1,170 00 |
| Advertising, printing and stationery | 594 91 |

## DISBURSEMENTS—Concluded.

| | |
|---|---|
| Postage, express, telegraph and telephone | $ 789 19 |
| Lodge supplies | 1,335 76 |
| Official publication | 7,232 52 |
| Other legal expenses | 213 00 |
| Furniture and fixtures | 81 00 |
| Paid premiums on bonds acquired | 606 53 |
| Paid for re-insurance | 91 91 |
| Bank exchange | 96 74 |
| Audits | 100 00 |
| Actuary service | 200 00 |
| Bonds and insurance | 69 60 |
| Sundries | 570 58 |
| Total disbursements | $63,659 54 |
| Balance | $418,667 02 |

## LEDGER ASSETS.

| | |
|---|---|
| Mortgage loans on real estate | $312,600 00 |
| Loans secured by pledge of bonds, stocks or other collateral | 200 00 |
| Book value of bonds and stocks | 72,000 00 |
| Deposits in trust companies and banks not on interest | 33,867 02 |
| Total ledger assets | $418,667 02 |

### NON-LEDGER ASSETS.

| | | |
|---|---|---|
| Interest and rents due and accrued | | 12,592 03 |
| Market value of bonds and stocks over book value | | 4,685 00 |
| All other assets, viz— | | |
| Furniture and fixtures | $1,411 00 | |
| Supplies | 587 50 | |
| | | 1,998 50 |
| Gross assets | | $437,942 55 |

### DEDUCT ASSETS NOT ADMITTED.

| | | |
|---|---|---|
| Furniture and fixtures | $1,411 00 | |
| Supplies | 587 50 | |
| | | 1,998 50 |
| Total admitted assets | | $435,944 05 |

## LIABILITIES.

| | |
|---|---|
| Death claims due and unpaid | $500 00 |

## EXHIBIT OF CERTIFICATES.

| | Total business of the year. Number. | Amount. | Business in Illinois during year. Number. | Amount. |
|---|---|---|---|---|
| Benefit certificates in force December 31, 1920, as per last statement | 6,689 | $4,070,600 00 | 183 | $107,500 00 |
| Benefit certificates written and renewed during the year | 1,008 | 928,500 00 | 40 | 37,250 00 |
| Benefit certificates increased during the year | | 12,200 00 | | |
| Totals | 7,697 | $5,011,300 00 | 223 | $144,750 00 |
| Deduct terminated, decreased or transferred during the year | 534 | 371,400 00 | | |
| Deduct terminated or decreased during the year | | | 18 | 6,900 00 |
| Total benefit certificates in force December 31, 1921 | 7,163 | $4,639,900 00 | 205 | $137,850 00 |

| | |
|---|---|
| Received during the year from members in Illinois: Mortuary, $1,859.52; expense, $2,169.99; total | $4,029 51 |

## EXHIBIT OF DEATH CLAIMS.

| | Total claims—all in Illinois. Number. | Amount. |
|---|---|---|
| Claims unpaid December 31, 1920, as per last statement | 2 | $ 600 00 |
| Claims reported during the year and interest addition | 58 | 32,800 00 |
| Totals | 60 | $33,400 00 |
| Claims paid during the year | 59 | 31,190 49 |
| Balance | 1 | $2,209 51 |
| Saved by compromising or scaling down claims during the year | | 1,709 51 |
| Claims unpaid December 31, 1921 | 1 | $500 00 |

## SOUTH SLAVONIC CATHOLIC UNION.

Located at Ely, Minnesota.

RUDOLPH PERDAN, President. JOSEPH PISHLER, Secretary.

| | |
|---|---|
| Balance from previous year | $381,209 03 |

### INCOME.

| | |
|---|---|
| Membership fees actually received | $ 777 00 |
| All other assessments or premiums | 219,624 17 |
| Payments to unpaid claims fund | 16,673 43 |
| Net amount received from members | $237,074 60 |
| Gross interest on bonds and dividends on stocks | 14,597 08 |
| Gross interest on deposits in trust companies and banks | 5,058 32 |
| Sale of lodge supplies | 361 10 |
| Refunds | 560 14 |
| Gross increase by adjustment in book value of ledger assets of bonds | 4,933 60 |
| Total income | $262,584 84 |
| Sum | $643,793 87 |

### DISBURSEMENTS.

| | |
|---|---|
| Death claims | $61,250 00 |
| Permanent disability claims | 1,000 00 |
| Sick and accident claims | 70,525 28 |
| Payments from unpaid claims fund | 24,128 71 |
| Compromised claim | 800 00 |
| Total benefits paid | $157,703 99 |
| Commissions and fees paid to deputies and organizers | 1,116 00 |
| Salaries of officers and trustees | 4,220 00 |
| Other compensation of officers and trustees | 421 00 |
| Salaries and other compensation of committees | 75 35 |
| Salaries of office employees | 1,200 00 |
| Other compensation of office employees | 110 00 |
| Salaries and fees paid to supreme medical examiners | 1,095 64 |
| Salaries and fees paid to subordinate medical examiners | 35 00 |
| Traveling and other expenses of officers, trustees and committees | 2,926 55 |
| Insurance department fees | 295 50 |
| Rent | 360 00 |
| Advertising, printing and stationery | 2,450 71 |
| Postage, express, telegraph and telephone | 593 09 |
| Lodge supplies | 319 82 |
| Official publication | 4,592 92 |
| Other legal expenses | 86 00 |
| Furniture and fixtures | 27 30 |
| Gross decrease in book value of ledger assets | 298 00 |
| Rent safety deposit box | 25 00 |
| Fuel, light and water | 390 40 |
| Minnesota and National Fraternal Congress dues | 80 00 |
| Fire insurance | 20 20 |
| Premium on surety bonds | 755 38 |
| Total disbursements | $179,197 85 |
| Balance | $464,596 02 |

### LEDGER ASSETS.

| | |
|---|---|
| Book value of bonds and stocks | 345,900 00 |
| Deposits in trust companies and banks not on interest | 521 00 |
| Deposits in trust companies and banks on interest | 118,175 02 |
| Total ledger assets | $464,596 02 |

#### NON-LEDGER ASSETS.

| | |
|---|---|
| Interest and rents due and accrued | 3,653 06 |
| Market value of bonds and stocks over book value | 1,831 40 |
| Assessments actually collected by subordinate lodges not yet turned over to supreme lodge | 50 13 |
| Office fixtures and supplies | 1,859 30 |
| Gross assets | $471,989 91 |

## LIABILITIES.

| | | |
|---|---|---|
| Salaries, rents, expenses, commissions, etc., due or accrued | | $ 383 00 |
| Advance assessments | | 17 27 |
| All other liabilities, viz— | | |
| Official publication | $ 3,419 41 | |
| Unpaid death benefits held in escrow as per Article XVI, Section 36 and 37 By-Laws | 46,504 59 | |
| | | 49,924 00 |
| Total | | $50,324 27 |

## EXHIBIT OF CERTIFICATES.

| | Total business of the year. Number. | Amount. | Business in Illinois during year. Number. | Amount. |
|---|---|---|---|---|
| Benefit certificates in force December 31, 1920, as per last statement | 7,879 | $6,538,250 00 | 652 | $517,000 00 |
| Benefit certificates written and renewed during the year | 877 | 676,500 00 | 19 | 15,750 00 |
| Benefit certificates received by transfer during the year | 295 | 250,750 00 | -------- | -------------- |
| Benefit certificates increased during the year | -------- | 40,750 00 | -------- | 1,000 00 |
| Total | 9,051 | $7,506,750 00 | 671 | $533,750 00 |
| Deduct terminated, decreased or transferred during the year | 778 | 644,000 00 | -------- | -------------- |
| Deduct terminated or decreased during the year | -------- | -------------- | 7 | 5,000 00 |
| Total benefit certificates in force December 31, 1921 | 8,273 | $6,862,250 00 | 664 | $528,750 00 |

Received during the year from members in Illinois: Mortuary, $8,092.17; reserve, $1,780.59; disability, $159.48; sick and accident, $5,844.40; expense, $1,571.85; total ----- $17,448 49

## EXHIBIT OF DEATH CLAIMS.

| | Total claims. Number. | Amount. | Illinois claims. Number. | Amount. |
|---|---|---|---|---|
| Claims paid during the year | 74 | $61,250 00 | 3 | $225 00 |

## EXHIBIT OF PERMANENT DISABILITY CLAIMS.

| | Total claims. Number. | Amount. | Illinois claims. Number. | Amount. |
|---|---|---|---|---|
| Claims paid during the year | 25 | $1,000 00 | 3 | $90 00 |

## EXHIBIT OF SICK AND ACCIDENT CLAIMS.

| | Total claims. Number. | Amount. | Illinois claims. Number. | Amount. |
|---|---|---|---|---|
| Claims paid during the year | 2,160 | $70,525 28 | 170 | $5,747 33 |
| Claims rejected during the year | 3 | 90 00 | -------- | -------------- |

---

# SWITCHMEN'S UNION OF NORTH AMERICA.

Located at No. 39 North Street, Buffalo, New York.

T. C. CASHEN, President. M. R. WELCH, Secretary.

| | |
|---|---|
| Balance from previous year | $703,087 28 |

## INCOME.

| | |
|---|---|
| Membership fees actually received | $ 792 00 |
| All other assessments or premiums | 213,106 39 |
| Dues and per capita tax | 55,827 03 |
| Medical examiners' fees actually received | 29 00 |
| Other payments by members, viz: General grievance, $7,154.66; change certificate fees, $218.50; assessment 173, $7,988.50 | 15,361 66 |
| Total received from members | $285,116 08 |
| Deduct payments returned to applicants and members | 556 35 |
| Net amount received from members | $284,559 73 |
| Gross interest on bonds and dividends on stocks | 28,868 87 |
| Gross interest on deposits in trust companies and banks | 4,102 35 |
| Gross rents from association's property | 240 00 |
| Sale of lodge supplies | 2,174 88 |
| Gross increase in book value of ledger assets | 2,245 00 |
| Journal | 11,186 10 |

INCOME—Concluded.

| | |
|---|---|
| Local lodge fines | $ 23 80 |
| Local lodge bonds | 837 50 |
| Officers' balances | 1,610 93 |
| Total income | $335,849 16 |
| Sum | $1,038,936 44 |

DISBURSEMENTS.

| | |
|---|---|
| Death claims | $114,769 65 |
| Permanent disability claims | 17,250 00 |
| Burial claims | 1,350 00 |
| Benevolent donations | 9,750 00 |
| Total benefits paid | $143,119 65 |
| Salaries of deputies and organizers | 5,122 82 |
| Salaries of officers and trustees | 34,822 11 |
| Salaries and other compensation of committees | 8,279 99 |
| Salaries of office employees | 8,721 59 |
| Salaries and fees paid to supreme medical examiners | 112 75 |
| Traveling and other expenses of officers, trustees and committees | 6,970 75 |
| Insurance department fees | 45 00 |
| Rent | 150 00 |
| Advertising, printing and stationery | 698 37 |
| Postage, express, telegraph and telephone | 761 84 |
| Lodge supplies | 1,494 12 |
| Official publication | 9,278 08 |
| Expenses of supreme lodge meeting | 32,121 93 |
| Legal expense in litigating claims | 1,102 37 |
| Other legal expenses | 500 00 |
| Furniture and fixtures | 60 20 |
| Taxes, repairs and other expenses on real estate | 2,427 04 |
| Gross decrease in book value of ledger assets | 200 00 |
| Protested draft | 84 95 |
| All other disbursements, viz— | |
| Assessment No. 173, $5,519.81; American Federation of Labor, $3,881.29 | 9,401 10 |
| American Association, labor legislation, $25.00; National Fraternal Congress of America, $97.50 | 122 50 |
| Plumb Plan League, $200.00; bonds local treasurers, $870.89; bonds of grand secretary and treasurer, $375.00 | 1,445 89 |
| Miscellaneous expense, $143.13; police bond, $5.00; A., B. & A. R. R. strikers' donation, $217.88 | 366 01 |
| Total disbursements | $267,409 06 |
| Balance | $771,527 38 |

LEDGER ASSETS.

| | |
|---|---|
| Book value of real estate | $ 29,500 00 |
| Book value of bonds and stocks | 623,450 00 |
| Cash in association's office | 200 34 |
| Deposits in trust companies and banks on interest | 116,766 11 |
| Officers' balances | 1,610 93 |
| Total ledger assets | $771,527 38 |

NON-LEDGER ASSETS.

| | | |
|---|---|---|
| Interest and rents due and accrued | | 12,102 17 |
| Assessments actually collected by subordinate lodges not yet turned over to supreme lodge | | 21,221 62 |
| All other assets, viz— | | |
| Furniture | $5,000 00 | |
| General grievance account, $480.00; convention account, $32.00 | 512 00 | |
| Supplies, $28.70; assessment No. 173, $262.50 | 291 20 | |
| Benevolent assessment, $11.00; local lodge bonds, $10.00 | 21 00 | |
| | | 5,824 20 |
| Gross assets | | $810,675 37 |

DEDUCT ASSETS NOT ADMITTED.

| | | |
|---|---|---|
| Balance due from officers not secured by bonds | $ 1,610 93 | |
| Book value of bonds and stocks over market value | 33,004 00 | |
| Other items, viz— | | |
| Furniture | 5,000 00 | |
| General grievance account, $480.00; convention account, $32.00 | 512 00 | |
| Supplies, $28.70; assessment No. 173, $262.50 | 291 20 | |
| Benevolent assessment, $11.00; local lodge bonds, $10.00 | 21 00 | |
| | | 40,439 13 |
| Total admitted assets | | $770,236 24 |

LIABILITIES.

| | | |
|---|---|---|
| Death claims due and unpaid | $ 2,508 30 | |
| Death claims resisted | 6,825 00 | |
| Death claims reported during the year but not yet adjusted | 12,000 00 | |
| Total death claims | | $21,333 30 |
| Permanent disability claims adjusted not yet due | 5,250 00 | |
| Permanent disability claims resisted | 1,200 00 | |
| Total permanent disability claims | | 6,450 00 |
| Total unpaid claims | | $27,783 30 |

EXHIBIT OF CERTIFICATES.

| | Total business of the year. | | Business in Illinois during year. | |
|---|---|---|---|---|
| | Number. | Amount. | Number. | Amount. |
| Benefit certificates in force December 31, 1920, as per per last statement | 9,143 | $11,268,750 00 | 1,080 | $1,457,250 00 |
| Benefit certificates written and renewed during the year | 2,027 | 2,349,375 00 | 203 | 249,000 00 |
| Total | 11,170 | $13,618,125 00 | 1,283 | $1,706,250 00 |
| Deduct terminated, decreased or transferred during year | 3,108 | 3,662,625 00 | | |
| Deduct terminated or decreased during the year | | | 265 | 342,000 00 |
| Total benefit certificates in force December 31, 1921 | 8,062 | $9,955,500 00 | 1,018 | $1,364,250 00 |

Received during the year from members in Illinois: Disability, $28,436.15; reserve, $74.00; expense, $10,769.92; total ........ $39,280 07

EXHIBIT OF DEATH CLAIMS.

| | Total claims. | | Illinois claims. | |
|---|---|---|---|---|
| | Number. | Amount. | Number. | Amount. |
| Claims unpaid December 31, 1920, as per last statement | 26 | $ 25,507 40 | 3 | $ 3,300 00 |
| Claims reported during the year and interest addition | 90 | 110,625 00 | 14 | 18,000 00 |
| Total | 116 | $136,132 40 | 17 | $21,300 00 |
| Claims paid during the year | 94 | 114,769 65 | 14 | 18,000 00 |
| Balance | 22 | $21,362 75 | 3 | $3,300 00 |
| Saved by compromising or scaling down claims during the year | | 29 45 | | |
| Claims unpaid December 31, 1921 | 22 | $21,333 30 | 3 | $3,300 00 |

EXHIBIT OF PERMANENT DISABILITY CLAIMS.

| | Total claims. | | Illinois claims. | |
|---|---|---|---|---|
| | Number. | Amount. | Number. | Amount. |
| Claims unpaid December 31, 1920, as per last statement | 1 | $ 1,200 00 | | |
| Claims reported during the year and interest addition | 17 | 22,500 00 | | |
| Total | 18 | $23,700 00 | | |
| Claims paid during the year | 13 | 17,250 00 | | |
| Claims unpaid December 31, 1921 | 5 | $6,450 00 | 1 | $1,200 00 |

---

## TRAVELERS PROTECTIVE ASSOCIATION OF AMERICA.

Located at 915 Olive Street, St. Louis, Missouri.

WILLIAM O'NEILL, President. T. S. LOGAN, Secretary.

| | |
|---|---|
| Balance from previous year | $715,831 01 |

INCOME.

| | |
|---|---|
| Membership fees actually received | $ 33,582 00 |
| All other assessments or premiums | 800,891 11 |
| Transfers and changes | 308 00 |
| Total received from members | $834,871 11 |
| Deduct payments returned to applicants and members | 7,426 87 |
| Net amount received from members | $827,444 24 |

INCOME—Concluded.

| | |
|---|---|
| Gross interest on bonds and dividends on stocks | $34,231 11 |
| Gross interest on deposits in trust companies and banks | 4,599 20 |
| Sale of lodge supplies | 140 50 |
| Credit on outstanding check | 25 00 |
| Total income | $866,440 05 |
| Sum | $1,582,271 06 |

DISBURSEMENTS.

| | |
|---|---|
| Death claims | $269,497 27 |
| Permanent disability claims | 19,228 58 |
| Accident claims | 333,791 40 |
| Total benefits id | $622,517 25 |
| Commissions and fees paid to deputies and organizers | 12,642 79 |
| Salaries of deputies and organizers | 35 00 |
| Salaries of officers and trustees | 9,500 00 |
| Other compensation of officers and trustees | 11,345 84 |
| Salaries and other compensation of committees | 827 08 |
| Salaries of office employees | 26,115 70 |
| Other compensation of state employees | 619 52 |
| Salaries and fees paid to supreme medical examiners | 2,400 00 |
| Salaries and fees paid to subordinate medical examiners | 2,912 00 |
| Traveling and other expenses of officers, trustees and committees | 1,891 42 |
| For collection and remittance of assessments and dues | 386 41 |
| Insurance department fees | 1,970 66 |
| Rent | 4,440 00 |
| Advertising, printing and stationery | 6,219 36 |
| Postage, express, telegraph and telephone | 10,004 00 |
| Lodge supplies | 2,376 59 |
| Official publication | 37,468 63 |
| Expenses of supreme lodge meeting | 3,495 13 |
| Legal expense in litigating claims | 9,418 05 |
| Other legal expenses | 3,900 00 |
| Taxes, repairs and other expenses on real estate | 309 17 |
| Gross loss on sale or maturity of ledger assets | 281 70 |
| Depreciation on office fixtures | 1,285 32 |
| Insuring supreme delegates | 250 00 |
| Difference in state secretary's remittances | 265 73 |
| Audit | 650 00 |
| Premium on officers' bonds | 226 00 |
| Dues in organizations | 1,106 17 |
| Petty office expense | 819 10 |
| Total disbursements | $775,678 62 |
| Balance | $806,592 44 |

LEDGER ASSETS.

| | |
|---|---|
| Book value of bonds | $662,310 06 |
| Deposits in trust companies and banks not on interest | 140,130 40 |
| Furniture and office fixtures | 4,151 98 |
| Total ledger assets | $806,592 44 |

NON-LEDGER ASSETS.

| | |
|---|---|
| Interest due and accrued on bonds | 9,425 77 |
| Market value of bonds and stocks over book value | 6,764 94 |
| Assessments actually collected by subordinate lodges not yet turned over to supreme lodge | 265 73 |
| Gross assets | $823,048 88 |

DEDUCT ASSETS NOT ADMITTED.

| | |
|---|---|
| Furniture and office fixtures | 4,151 98 |
| Total admitted assets | $818,896 90 |

LIABILITIES.

| | | |
|---|---|---|
| Death claims resisted | $30,450 00 | |
| Death claims reported during the year but not yet adjusted | 25,000 00 | |
| Total death claims | | $55,450 00 |
| Accident claims reported during the year but not yet adjusted | $56,949 75 | |
| Accident claims incurred in 1921, not reported until 1922 | 1,548 12 | |
| Total accident claims | | 58,497 87 |
| Total unpaid claims | | $113,947 87 |
| Advance dues | | 28,208 00 |

LIABILITIES—Concluded.

| | | |
|---|---|---|
| All other liabilities, viz— | | |
| Bills payable | $2,820 97 | |
| Excess liability, market over value of special deposits | 5,800 50 | |
| | | $8,621 47 |
| Total | | $150,777 34 |

EXHIBIT OF CERTIFICATES.

| | Total business of the year. Number. | Amount. | Business in Illinois during year. Number. | Amount. |
|---|---|---|---|---|
| Benefit certificates in force December 31, 1920, as per last statement | 95,588 | $477,940,000 00 | 7,034 | $35,170,000 00 |
| Benefit certificates written and renewed during the year | 21,426 | 107,130,000 00 | 1,273 | 6,365,000 00 |
| Benefit certificates received by transfer during the year | -------- | ------------- | 35 | 175,000 00 |
| Total | 117,014 | $585,070,000 00 | 8,342 | $41,710,000 00 |
| Deduct terminated, decreased or transferred during the year | 16,610 | 83,050,000 00 | -------- | ------------- |
| Deduct terminated or decreased during the year | -------- | ------------- | 943 | 4,715,000 00 |
| Total benefit certificates in force December 31, 1921 | 100,404 | $502,020,000 00 | 7,399 | $36,995,000 00 |

Received during the year from members in Illinois: Mortuary, $43,464.00; state proportion, $21,732.00; expense, $14,488.00; total ... $79,684 00

EXHIBIT OF DEATH CLAIMS.

| | Total claims. Number. | Amount. | Illinois claims. Number. | Amount. |
|---|---|---|---|---|
| Claims unpaid December 31, 1920, as per last statement | 13 | $ 51,500 00 | 1 | $ 5,000 00 |
| Claims reported during the year and interest addition | 77 | 376,359 68 | 8 | 40,569 47 |
| Total | 90 | $427,859 68 | 9 | $45,569 47 |
| Claims paid during the year | 72 | 269,497 27 | 8 | 29,857 07 |
| Balance | 18 | $158,362 41 | 1 | $15,712 40 |
| Saved by compromising or scaling down claims during the year | -------- | 102,912 41 | -------- | 10,712 40 |
| Claims unpaid December 31, 1921 | 18 | $55,450 00 | 1 | $5,000 00 |

EXHIBIT OF PERMANENT DISABILITY CLAIMS.

| | Total claims. Number. | Amount. | Illinois claims. Number. | Amount. |
|---|---|---|---|---|
| Claims paid during the year | 14 | $19,228 58 | 2 | $3,250 00 |

EXHIBIT OF ACCIDENT CLAIMS.

| | Total claims. Number. | Amount. | Illinois claims. Number. | Amount. |
|---|---|---|---|---|
| Claims unpaid December 31, 1920, as per last statement | 672 | $ 56,768 00 | 61 | $ 4,971 50 |
| Claims reported during the year | 4,234 | 335,973 15 | 368 | 25,781 56 |
| Total | 4,906 | $390,741 15 | 429 | $30,753 06 |
| Claims paid during the year | 4,191 | 333,791 40 | 364 | 25,575 81 |
| Claims unpaid December 31, 1921 | 715 | $56,949 75 | 65 | $5,177 25 |

## UKRAINIAN WORKINGMEN'S ASSOCIATION.

Located at Nos. 524-530 Olive Street, Scranton, Pennsylvania.

GEORGE KREKEVSKY, President. JOSEPH LENCHITSKY, Secretary.

| | |
|---|---|
| Balance from previous year | $103,627 92 |

## INCOME.

|  |  |
|---|---|
| Membership fees actually received | $101,772 99 |
| Assessments or premiums during first initiation months of membership of which all or an extra percentage is used for expenses | 298 00 |
| All other assessments or premiums | 3,279 90 |
| Net amount received from members | $105,350 89 |
| Gross interest on bonds and dividends on stocks | 2,932 22 |
| Gross interest on deposits in trust companies and banks | 3,084 22 |
| Gross rents from association's property, including $245.00 for association's occupancy of its own buildings | 2,869 00 |
| Sale of lodge supplies | 527 25 |
| From all other sources | 1,668 98 |
| Total income | $116,432 56 |
| Sum | $310,060 48 |

## DISBURSEMENTS.

|  |  |
|---|---|
| Death claims | $32,173 53 |
| Permanent disability claims | 2,095 00 |
| Total benefits paid | $34,268 53 |
| Commissions and fees paid to deputies and organizers | 600 00 |
| Salaries of officers and trustees | 4,140 00 |
| Fees paid to supreme medical examiners | 79 95 |
| Traveling and other expenses of officers, trustees and committees | 657 81 |
| Insurance department fees | 100 00 |
| Rent, including $25.00 for association's occupancy of its own buildings | 300 00 |
| Advertising, printing and stationery | 2,842 34 |
| Postage, express, telegraph and telephone | 386 50 |
| Lodge supplies | 155 86 |
| Official publication | 9,228 45 |
| Expenses of supreme lodge meeting | 635 57 |
| Other legal expenses | 587 50 |
| Taxes, repairs and other expenses on real estate | 2,690 41 |
| Interest on borrowed money | 500 00 |
| All other disbursements | 576 68 |
| Total disbursements | $57,749 60 |
| Balance | $252,310 88 |

## LEDGER ASSETS.

|  |  |
|---|---|
| Book value of real estate | $ 20,700 00 |
| Book value of bonds and stocks | 59,230 92 |
| Deposits in trust companies and banks on interest | 147,696 01 |
| Other ledger assets, viz— | |
| War Saving Stamps | 720 86 |
| Furniture and fixtures, $2,993.83; printing press and equipments, $20,969.26 | 23,963 09 |
| Total ledger assets | $252,310 88 |

DEDUCT ASSETS NOT ADMITTED.

|  |  |
|---|---|
| Book value of bonds and stocks over market value | 896 09 |
| Total admitted assets | $251,414 79 |

## LIABILITIES.

|  |  |
|---|---|
| Total death claims reported during the year but not yet adjusted | $10,350 00 |

## EXHIBIT OF CERTIFICATES.

| | Total business of the year. | | Business in Illinois during year. | |
|---|---|---|---|---|
| | Number. | Amount. | Number. | Amount. |
| Benefit certificates in force December 31,1920, as per last statement | 5,616 | $4,671,150 00 | 183 | $127,200 00 |
| Benefit certificates written and renewed during the year | 654 | 561,000 00 | 5 | 3,200 00 |
| Total | 6,270 | $5,232,150 00 | 188 | $130,400 00 |
| Deduct terminated, decreased or transferred during the year | 550 | 427,900 00 | | |
| Deduct terminated or decreased during the year | | | 24 | 13,200 00 |
| Total benefit certificates in force December 31, 1921 | 5,720 | $4,804,250 00 | 164 | $117,200 00 |

EXHIBIT OF DEATH CLAIMS.

| | Total claims. Number. | Total claims. Amount. | Illinois claims. Number. | Illinois claims. Amount. |
|---|---|---|---|---|
| Claims unpaid December 31, 1920, as per last statement | 12 | $ 8,850 00 | | |
| Claims reported during the year and interest addition | 42 | 33,900 00 | 2 | $1,000 00 |
| Total | 54 | $42,750 00 | 2 | $1,000 00 |
| Claims paid during the year | 41 | 32,173 53 | 2 | 1,000 00 |
| Balance | 13 | $10,576 47 | | |
| Saved by liens or scaling down claims during the year | | 226 47 | | |
| Claims unpaid December 31, 1921 | 13 | $10,350 00 | | |

EXHIBIT OF PERMANENT DISABILITY CLAIMS.

| | Total claims. Amount. | Illinois claims. Amount. |
|---|---|---|
| Claims reported during the year and interest addition | $2,095 00 | $20 00 |

---

## UNITED ORDER OF FORESTERS.

Located at Colby-Abbott Building, Milwaukee, Wisconsin.

R. C. SHERRARD, Supreme Ranger. GEO W. BLANN, Supreme Secretary.

| | |
|---|---|
| Balance from previous year | $418,161 22 |

INCOME.

| | |
|---|---|
| Membership fees actually received | $ 2,233 50 |
| Assessments or premiums during first twelve months of membership of which all or an extra percentage is used for expenses | 18,570 18 |
| All other assessments or premiums | 185,105 52 |
| Dues and per capita tax | 29,883 16 |
| Junior dues | 315 75 |
| Miscellaneous receipts | 509 59 |
| Total received from members | $236,617 70 |
| Deduct payments returned to applicants and members | 407 74 |
| Net amount received from members | $236,209 96 |
| Gross interest on bonds and dividends on stocks | 21,243 70 |
| Gross interest on deposits in trust companies and banks | 444 72 |
| Sale of lodge supplies | 659 39 |
| Contingent fund | 250 00 |
| Total income | $258,807 77 |
| Sum | $676,968 99 |

DISBURSEMENTS.

| | |
|---|---|
| Death claims | $148,000 00 |
| Permanent disability claims | 1,000 00 |
| Old age benefits | 1,300 00 |
| Deferred payments, interest paid | 2,112 50 |
| Total benefits paid | $152,412 50 |
| Commissions and fees paid to deputies and organizers | 10,598 56 |
| Salaries of deputies and organizers | 7,552 00 |
| Salaries of officers and trustees | 8,050 00 |
| Salaries of office employees | 3,796 66 |
| Salaries and fees paid to supreme medical examiners | 900 00 |
| Salaries and fees paid to subordinate medical examiners | 1,921 00 |
| Traveling and other expenses of officers, trustees and committees | 447 54 |
| Insurance department fees | 165 50 |
| Rent | 1,632 00 |
| Advertising, printing and stationery | 1,395 34 |
| Postage, express, telegraph and telephone | 579 29 |
| Lodge supplies | 567 81 |
| Official publication | 3,075 18 |
| Legal expense in litigating claims | 1,176 63 |
| Furniture and fixtures | 75 00 |

DISBURSEMENTS—Concluded.

| | |
|---|---|
| Bonds | $1,023 70 |
| Expense of organizers | 580 42 |
| Capitation tax to high courts | 5,300 00 |
| General expense | 361 77 |
| Expense of examination | 35 61 |
| Expense of valuing benefit certificates | 116 08 |
| Premium on surety bonds | 520 36 |
| Total disbursements | $202,282 95 |
| Balance | $474,686 04 |

## LEDGER ASSETS.

| | |
|---|---|
| Book value of bonds and stocks | $447,387 69 |
| Deposits in trust companies and banks not on interest | 8,123 10 |
| Deposits in trust companies and banks on interest | 18,825 94 |
| Bills receivable | 349 31 |
| Total ledger assets | $474,686 04 |

NON-LEDGER ASSETS.

| | | |
|---|---|---|
| Interest and rents due and accrued | | $9,912 33 |
| Market value of bonds and stocks over book value | | 7,783 70 |
| Assessments actually collected by subordinate lodges not yet turned over to supreme lodge | | 1,393 59 |
| All other assets, viz— | | |
| Furniture, fixtures and supplies, estimated | $2,500 00 | |
| Emergency funds in hands of supreme ranger | 150 00 | |
| | | 2,650 00 |
| Gross assets | | $496,425 86 |

DEDUCT ASSETS NOT ADMITTED:

| | | |
|---|---|---|
| Furniture, fixtures and supplies, estimated | $2,500 00 | |
| Emergency fund in hands of supreme ranger | 150 00 | |
| | | 2,650 00 |
| Total admitted assets | | $493,775 86 |

## LIABILITIES.

| | | |
|---|---|---|
| Death claims resisted | $ 500 00 | |
| Death claims reported during the year but not yet adjusted | 13,500 00 | |
| Total death claims | | $14,000 00 |
| Permanent disability claims adjusted not yet due | | 750 00 |
| Old age and other benefits due and unpaid | | 20,250 00 |
| Total unpaid claims | | $35,000 00 |
| Salaries, rents, expenses, commissions, etc., due or accrued, class 1, $1,463.50; class 2, $1,809.54 | | 3,273 04 |
| Advance assessments, class 1, $334.51; class 2, $1,704.20 | | 2,038 71 |
| Total | | $40,311 75 |

## EXHIBIT OF CERTIFICATES.

| | Total business of the year. | | Business in Illinois during year. | |
|---|---|---|---|---|
| | Number. | Amount. | Number. | Amount. |
| Benefit certificates in force December 31, 1920, as per last statement | 10,988 | $10,332,300 00 | 3,166 | $2,987,250 00 |
| Benefit certificates written and renewed during the year | 1,646 | 1,272,000 00 | 200 | 149,250 00 |
| Benefit certificates increased during the year | | 1,500 00 | | 1,000 00 |
| Totals | 12,634 | $11,605,800 00 | 3,366 | $3,137,500 00 |
| Deduct terminated, decreased or transferred during the year | 1,745 | 1,453,050 00 | | |
| Deduct terminated or decreased during the year | | | 214 | 268,200 00 |
| Total benefit certificates in force December 31, 1921 | 10,889 | $10,152,750 00 | 3,152 | $2,869,300 00 |

| | |
|---|---|
| Received during the year from members in Illinois: Mortuary, $51,444.58; expense, $10,162.24; total | $61,606 82 |

EXHIBIT OF DEATH CLAIMS.

| | Total claims. Number. | Amount. | Illinois claims. Number. | Amount. |
|---|---|---|---|---|
| Claims unpaid December 31, 1920, as per last statement | 25 | $ 28,250 00 | 8 | $ 6,500 00 |
| Claims reported during the year and interest addition | 136 | 137,612 50 | 42 | 40,250 00 |
| Totals | 161 | $165,862 50 | 50 | $46,750 00 |
| Claims paid during the year | 145 | 150,112 50 | 45 | 41,000 00 |
| Balance | 16 | $15,750 00 | 5 | $5,750 00 |
| Saved by compromising or scaling down claims during the year | -------- | 1,750 00 | -------- | 1,750 00 |
| Claims unpaid December 31, 1921 | 16 | $14,000 00 | 5 | $4,000 00 |

EXHIBIT OF PERMANENT DISABILITY CLAIMS.

| | Total claims. Number. | Amount. | Illinois claims Number. | Amount. |
|---|---|---|---|---|
| Claims unpaid December 31, 1920, as per last statement | 1 | $ 250 00 | -------- | -------- |
| Claims reported during the year and interest addition | 6 | 2,500 00 | 1 | $500 00 |
| Totals | 7 | $2,750 00 | 1 | $500 00 |
| Claims paid during the year | 4 | 1,000 00 | -------- | -------- |
| Balance | 3 | $1,750 00 | 1 | $500 00 |
| Claims rejected during the year | 1 | 1,000 00 | -------- | -------- |
| Claims unpaid December 31, 1921 | 2 | $750 00 | 1 | $500 00 |

EXHIBIT OF OLD AGE AND OTHER CLAIMS.

| | Total claims. Number. | Amount. | Illinois claims. Number. | Amount. |
|---|---|---|---|---|
| Claims unpaid December 31, 1920, as per last statement | 19 | $21,050 00 | 6 | $4,900 00 |
| Claims reported during the year and interest addition | 1 | 1,000 00 | -------- | -------- |
| Totals | 20 | $22,050 00 | 6 | $4,900 00 |
| Claims paid during the year | 1 | 1,300 00 | 1 | 900 00 |
| Balance | 19 | $20,750 00 | 5 | $4,000 00 |
| Saved by compromising or scaling down claims during the year | -------- | 500 00 | -------- | 500 00 |
| Claims unpaid December 31, 1921 | 19 | $20,250 00 | 5 | $3,500 00 |

---

## UNITED ORDER OF THE GOLDEN CROSS.

Located at No. 412 Empire Building, Knoxville, Tennessee.

JOS. P. BURLINGAME, President. W. R. COOPER, Secretary.

| | |
|---|---|
| Balance from previous year | $113,208 31 |

INCOME.

| | |
|---|---|
| Assessments or premiums during first twelve months of membership of which all or an extra percentage is used for expenses | $ 17,481 10 |
| All other assessments or premiums | 413,535 09 |
| Dues and per capita tax | 220 50 |
| Certificate fees | 197 50 |
| Net amount received from members | $431,434 19 |
| Gross interest on bonds and dividends on stocks | 2,927 50 |
| Gross interest on deposits in trust companies and banks | 1,761 58 |
| Gross interest from all other sources | 408 00 |
| Sale of lodge supplies | 114 42 |
| Fines | 57 55 |
| Total income | $436,703 24 |
| Sum | $549,911 55 |

DISBURSEMENTS.

| | |
|---|---|
| Death claims | $361,743 28 |
| Commissions and fees paid to deputies and organizers | 6,074 50 |
| Salaries of deputies and organizers | 14,187 50 |

DISBURSEMENTS—Concluded.

| | |
|---|---|
| Salaries of officers and trustees | $8,616 68 |
| Salaries and other compensation of committees | 250 00 |
| Salaries of office employees | 7,183 28 |
| Other compensation of office employees | 75 46 |
| Salaries and fees paid to supreme medical examiners | 674 00 |
| Traveling and other expenses of officers, trustees and committees | 382 49 |
| For collection and remittance of assessments and dues | 14 37 |
| Insurance department fees | 1,551 00 |
| Rent | 1,297 50 |
| Advertising, printing and stationery | 2,604 39 |
| Postage, express, telegraph and telephone | 611 42 |
| Lodge supplies | 107 88 |
| Official publication | 4,678 45 |
| Expenses of supreme lodge meeting | 3,490 50 |
| Legal expense in litigating claims | 2,911 38 |
| Other legal expenses | 167 80 |
| Furniture and fixtures | 309 60 |
| Taxes, repairs and other expenses on real estate | 295 69 |
| All other disbursements, viz— | |
| Bond and insurance premium | 465 93 |
| Valuation expense | 141 81 |
| Fraternal societies | 116 00 |
| Representative to N. F. C., $9.00; war tax, $1.07 | 10 07 |
| Total disbursements | $417,960 98 |
| Balance | $131,950 57 |

LEDGER ASSETS.

| | |
|---|---|
| Book value of real estate | $ 8,800 00 |
| Book value of bonds and stocks | 79,429 32 |
| Cash in association's office | 1,932 10 |
| Deposits in trust companies and banks on interest | 36,689 15 |
| Three notes secured by vendors lien on real estate sold—$1,700.00 each | 5,100 00 |
| Total ledger assets | $131,950 57 |

NON-LEDGER ASSETS.

| | |
|---|---|
| Interest and rents due and accrued | 1,323 83 |
| Assessments actually collected by subordinate lodges not yet turned over to supreme lodge | 35,012 46 |
| Gross assets | $168,286 86 |

DEDUCT ASSETS NOT ADMITTED.

| | | |
|---|---|---|
| Book value of real estate over market value | $2,500 00 | |
| Book value of bonds and stocks over market value | 9,689 32 | |
| | | 12,189 32 |
| Total admitted assets | | $156,097 54 |

LIABILITIES.

| | | |
|---|---|---|
| Death claims due and unpaid | $ 4,433 34 | |
| Death claims resisted | 8,000 00 | |
| Death claims reported during the year but not yet adjusted | 26,100 00 | |
| Death claims incurred in 1921, not reported until 1922 | 17,750 00 | |
| Total unpaid claims | | $56,283 34 |
| Salaries, rents, expenses, commissions, etc., due or accrued | | 653 96 |
| Total | | $56,937 30 |

EXHIBIT OF CERTIFICATES.

| | Total business of the year. | | Business in Illinois during year. | |
|---|---|---|---|---|
| | Number. | Amount. | Number. | Amount. |
| Benefit certificates in force December 31, 1920, as per last statement | 15,355 | $14,259,975 00 | 85 | $93,350 00 |
| Benefit certificates written and renewed during the year | 1,191 | 857,000 00 | | |
| Benefit certificates increased during the year | | 22,500 00 | | |
| Totals | 16,546 | $15,139,475 00 | 85 | $93,350 00 |
| Deduct terminated, decreased or transferred during the year | 1,770 | 1,520,100 00 | | |
| Deduct terminated or decreased during the year | | | 8 | 9,000 00 |
| Total benefit certificates in force December 31, 1921 | 14,776 | $13,619,375 00 | 77 | $84,350 00 |

| | |
|---|---|
| Received during the year from members in Illinois: Mortuary, $3,245.13; expense, $360.57; total | $3,605 70 |

EXHIBIT OF DEATH CLAIMS.

| | Total claims. Number. | Total claims. Amount. | Illinois claims. Number. | Illinois claims. Amount. |
|---|---|---|---|---|
| Claims unpaid December 31, 1920, as per last statement | 34 | $ 38,933 34 | | |
| Claims reported during the year and interest addition | 308 | 362,075 00 | | |
| Totals | 342 | $401,008 34 | | |
| Claims paid during the year | 306 | 361,743 28 | 6 | $7,500 00 |
| Balance | 36 | $39,265 06 | | |
| Saved by compromising or scaling down claims during the year | | 731 72 | | |
| Claims unpaid December 31, 1921 | 36 | $38,533 34 | | |

## WOMAN'S BENEFIT ASSOCIATION OF THE MACCABEES.

Located at Port Huron, Michigan.

MISS BINA M. WEST, President. MISS FRANCES D. PARTRIDGE, Secretary.

| | |
|---|---|
| Balance from previous year | $14,198,529 84 |

### INCOME.

| | |
|---|---|
| Membership fees actually received | $ 8,306 00 |
| Assessments or premiums during first twelve months of membership of which all or an extra percentage is used for expenses | 399,589 77 |
| All other assessments or premiums | 2,327,075 01 |
| Dues and per capita tax | 439,075 80 |
| Medical examiners' fees actually received | 8,800 93 |
| Junior | 25,640 61 |
| Patriotic, hospital | 140,366 16 |
| Total received from members | $3,348,854 28 |
| Deduct payments returned to applicants and members | 2,955 71 |
| Net amount received from members | $3,345,898 57 |
| Gross interest on bonds and dividends on stocks | 597,701 05 |
| Gross interest on deposits in trust companies and banks | 11,383 14 |
| Gross rents from association's property, including $21,339.06; for association's occupancy of its own buildings | 29,161 56 |
| Gross increase in book value of ledger assets | 4,298 99 |
| Defunct review funds | 53 23 |
| Hooper memorial | 1,985 78 |
| Total income | $3,990,482 32 |
| Sum | $18,189,012 16 |

### DISBURSEMENTS.

| | |
|---|---|
| Death claims | $1,583,283 24 |
| Permanent disability claims | 3,165 17 |
| Sick and accident claims | 1,440 00 |
| Maternity benefit claims | 1,150 00 |
| Junior | 4,514 00 |
| Hospital service | 82,835 78 |
| Relief | 749 60 |
| Total benefits paid | $1,677,137 79 |
| Commissions and fees paid to deputies and organizers | 42,579 84 |
| Salaries of deputies and organizers | 388,829 12 |
| Salaries of officers and trustees | 21,200 00 |
| Salaries of office employees | 139,593 24 |
| Salaries and fees paid to supreme medical examiners | 10,800 00 |
| Salaries and fees paid to subordinate medical examiners | 1,048 15 |
| Traveling and other expenses of officers, trustees and committees | 9,227 60 |
| Insurance department fees | 2,140 82 |
| Rent, including $21,339.06 for association's occupancy of its own buildings | 21,339 06 |
| Advertising, printing and stationery | 51,885 75 |
| Postage, express, telegraph and telephone | 21,583 47 |
| Lodge supplies | 24,447 02 |
| Official publication | 3,820 76 |
| Legal expense in litigating claims | 23,817 50 |
| Other legal expenses | 3,007 18 |
| Furniture and fixtures | 4,321 74 |

DISBURSEMENTS—Concluded.

| | |
|---|---|
| Taxes, repairs and other expenses on real estate | $22,228 00 |
| Gross decrease in book value of ledger assets | 28,285 71 |
| Class work | 10,539 33 |
| Affiliated societies | 759 36 |
| Light, $1,154.28; janitor, $6,480.75 | 7,635 03 |
| Insurance, accident and fire | 1,360 13 |
| Bonds, sub. review officers | 1,919 37 |
| Miscellaneous | 5,602 19 |
| Total disbursements | $2,525,108 16 |
| Balance | $15,663,904 00 |

## LEDGER ASSETS.

| | | |
|---|---|---|
| Book value of real estate | | $ 715,407 80 |
| Book value of bonds and stocks | | 14,653,135 48 |
| Cash in association's office | | 35,856 22 |
| Deposits in trust companies and banks on interest | | 259,504 50 |
| Total ledger assets | | $15,663,904 00 |
| **NON-LEDGER ASSETS.** | | |
| Interest and rents due and accrued | | 272,915 59 |
| Assessments actually collected by subordinate lodges not yet turned over to supreme lodge | | 225,000 00 |
| All other assets, viz— | | |
| Per capita tax on benefit members now in hands of collectors | $ 34,759 35 | |
| Per capita tax on social members now in hands of collectors | 1,649 10 | |
| Furniture and office equipment | 119,084 73 | |
| Supplies, printed matter and stationery | 49,658 81 | |
| | | 205,151 99 |
| Gross assets | | $19,366,971 58 |
| **DEDUCT ASSETS NOT ADMITTED.** | | |
| Furniture and office equipment | $119,084 73 | |
| Supplies, printed matter and stationery | 49,658 81 | |
| | | 168,743 54 |
| Total admitted assets | | $19,198,228 04 |

## LIABILITIES.

| | | |
|---|---|---|
| Death claims resisted | $ 2,000 00 | |
| Death claims reported during the year but not yet adjusted | 141,913 23 | |
| Death claims reported prior to 1921 but not yet adjusted | 7,321 94 | |
| Death claims incurred in 1921, not reported until 1922 | 33,750 00 | |
| Total death claims | | $184,985 17 |
| Present value of disability claims payable in installments | | 9,499 97 |
| Total unpaid claims | | $194,485 14 |
| Salaries, rents, expenses, commissions, etc., due or accrued | | 61,330 63 |
| Taxes due or accrued | | 981 00 |
| Advance assessments | | 17,297 03 |
| Total | | $274,093 80 |

## EXHIBIT OF CERTIFICATES.

| | Total business of the year. | | Business in Illinois during year. | |
|---|---|---|---|---|
| | Number. | Amount. | Number. | Amount. |
| Benefit certificates in force December 31, 1920, as per last statement | 223,108 | $174,780,256 81 | 22,294 | $17,387,662 26 |
| Benefit certificates written and renewed during the year | 31,833 | 27,560,350 00 | 3,808 | 3,190,050 00 |
| Totals | 254,941 | $202,340,606 81 | 26,102 | $20,577,712 26 |
| Deduct terminated, decreased or transferred during the year | 21,827 | 17,566,723 01 | | |
| Deduct terminated or decreased during the year | | | 1,797 | 1,572,599 28 |
| Total benefit certificates in force December 31, 1921 | 233,114 | $184,773,883 80 | 24,305 | $19,005,112 98 |

| | |
|---|---|
| Received during the year from members in Illinois: Mortuary, $150,731.91; reserve, $76,931.11; expense, $84,534.65; total | $312,197 67 |

EXHIBIT OF DEATH CLAIMS.

| | Total claims. Number. | Total claims. Amount. | Illinois claims. Number. | Illinois claims. Amount. |
|---|---|---|---|---|
| Claims unpaid December 31, 1920, as per last statement | 207 | $ 172,746 94 | 19 | $ 14,250 00 |
| Claims reported during the year and interest addition | 1,970 | 1,602,016 88 | 243 | 200,354 92 |
| Claims appealed | 2 | 2,000 00 | | |
| Totals | 2,179 | $1,776,763 82 | 262 | $214,604 92 |
| Claims paid during the year | 2,003 | 1,583,283 24 | 245 | 192,575 57 |
| Balance | 176 | $193,480 58 | 17 | $22,029 35 |
| Saved by compromising or scaling down claims during the year | | 42,495 41 | | 4,666 12 |
| Claims rejected during the year | 3 | 1,750 00 | | |
| Claims unpaid December 31, 1921 | 173 | $149,235 17 | 17 | $17,363 23 |

EXHIBIT OF PERMANENT DISABILITY CLAIMS.

| | Total claims. Number. | Total claims. Amount. | Illinois claims. Number. | Illinois claims. Amount. |
|---|---|---|---|---|
| Claims paid during the year | 25 | $3,165 17 | 4 | $345 17 |

EXHIBIT OF SICK AND ACCIDENT CLAIMS.

| | Total claims. Number. | Total claims. Amount. | Illinois claims. Number. | Illinois claims. Amount. |
|---|---|---|---|---|
| Claims paid during the year | 35 | $1,440 00 | 1 | $31 00 |

EXHIBIT OF MATERNITY BENEFIT CLAIMS.

| | Total claims—all in Illinois. Number. | Amount. |
|---|---|---|
| Claims paid during the year | 23 | $1,150 00 |

## WOMEN'S BOHEMIAN ROMAN CATHOLIC CENTRAL UNION OF U. S. OF A.

Located at No. 3226 East One hundred Eighteenth Street, Cleveland, Ohio.

ROZALIE NEDVED, President. ANNA BILEK, Secretary.

| | |
|---|---|
| Balance from previous year | $307,671 03 |

INCOME.

| | |
|---|---|
| All other assessments or premiums | $107,761 01 |
| Dues and per capita tax | 6,953 35 |
| Reserve fund | 12,451 80 |
| Net amount received from members | $127,166 16 |
| Gross interest on mortgage loans | 8,848 04 |
| Gross interest on bonds and dividends on stocks | 1,273 75 |
| Gross interest on deposits in trust companies and banks | 1,192 60 |
| Total income | $138,480 55 |
| Sum | $446,151 58 |

DISBURSEMENTS.

| | |
|---|---|
| Death claims | $104,400 00 |
| Commissions and fees paid to deputies and organizers | 47 50 |
| Salaries of officers and trustees | 3,149 96 |
| Salaries and other compensation of committees | 100 00 |
| Traveling and other expenses of officers, trustees and committees | 375 43 |
| Insurance department fees | 30 00 |
| Advertising, printing and stationery | 1,842 66 |
| Postage, express, telegraph and telephone | 360 73 |
| Official publication | 324 75 |
| Furniture and fixtures | 150 00 |
| Bonds of officers and representatives | 913 72 |
| Attorney and actuary | 299 00 |
| Total disbursements | $111,993 75 |
| Balance | $334,157 83 |

LEDGER ASSETS.

| | |
|---|---|
| Mortgage loans on real estate | $259,000 00 |
| Book value of bonds and stocks | 29,000 00 |
| Cash in association's office | 56,157 83 |
| Total ledger assets | $344,157 83 |

## EXHIBIT OF CERTIFICATES.

| | Total business of the year. Number. | Amount. | Business in Illinois during year. Number. | Amount. |
|---|---|---|---|---|
| Benefit certificates in force December 31, 1920, as per last statement | 10,210 | $7,383,200 00 | 4,191 | $3,355,300 00 |
| Benefit certificates written and renewed during the year | 504 | 428,100 00 | 130 | 96,800 00 |
| Totals | 10,714 | $7,811,300 00 | 4,321 | $3,452,100 00 |
| Deduct terminated, decreased or transferred during the year | 248 | 192,600 00 | | |
| Deduct terminated or decreased during the year | | | 97 | 73,800 00 |
| Total benefit certificates in force December 31, 1921 | 10,466 | $7,618,700 00 | 4,224 | $3,378,300 00 |

## EXHIBIT OF DEATH CLAIMS.

| | Total claims. Number. | Amount. | Illinois claims. Number. | Amount. |
|---|---|---|---|---|
| Claims paid during the year | 142 | $104,400 00 | 73 | $57,800 00 |

---

# WOODMEN CIRCLE, SUPREME FOREST.

Located at Fourteenth and Farnam Streets, Omaha, Nebraska.

MARY E. LA ROCCA, President. DORA ALEXANDER TALLEY, Secretary.

| | |
|---|---|
| Balance from previous year | $9,109,949 95 |

## INCOME.

| | |
|---|---|
| Assessments or premiums during first 12 months of membership of which all or an extra percentage is used for expenses | $ 367,488 99 |
| All other assessments or premiums | 2,310,850 01 |
| Dues and per capita tax | 7,362 75 |
| Certificate fees | 9,795 75 |
| Other payments by members, viz: Subscriptions to official organ | 77,900 92 |
| Total received from members | $2,773,398 42 |
| Deduct payments returned to applicants and members | 17,273 25 |
| Net amount received from members | $2,756,125 17 |
| Gross interest on mortgage loans | 2,500 00 |
| Gross interest on bonds | 440,421 91 |
| Gross interest on deposits in trust companies and banks | 8,254 23 |
| Gross interest from all other sources | 20,096 66 |
| Sale of lodge supplies | 3,862 35 |
| Gross profit on sale or maturity of ledger assets | 238 18 |
| Gross increase in book value of ledger assets | 2,862 49 |
| Payment on liens | 2,186 07 |
| Cancelled warrants | 604 50 |
| Surety bonds | 7,560 14 |
| Advertising | 13,761 08 |
| Sale of premiums | 455 65 |
| Sale of patterns and paper | 252 56 |
| Total income | $3,259,180 99 |
| Sum | $12,369,130 94 |

## DISBURSEMENTS.

| | |
|---|---|
| Death claims | $1,125,655 82 |
| Permanent disability claims | 11,578 80 |
| Old age benefits | 11,532 52 |
| Monuments | 69,953 00 |
| Funeral benefits | 19,747 77 |
| Total benefits paid | $1,238,467 91 |
| Commissions and fees paid to deputies and organizers | 207,705 61 |
| Salaries of deputies and organizers | 60,075 60 |
| Salaries of officers and trustees | 21,300 00 |
| Salaries and other compensation of committees | 2,380 00 |
| Salaries of office employees | 147,473 15 |
| Salaries and fees paid to supreme medical examiners | 5,000 05 |
| Salaries and fees paid to subordinate medical examiners | 63 20 |
| Traveling and other expenses of officers, trustees and committees | 7,126 44 |
| Insurance department fees | 806 50 |
| Rent | 13,444 00 |
| Advertising, printing and stationery | 46,272 98 |
| Postage, express, telegraph and telephone | 22,265 36 |

DISBURSEMENTS—Concluded.

| | |
|---|---|
| Lodge supplies | $ 6,878 17 |
| Official publication | 47,344 01 |
| Expenses of supreme lodge meeting | 165,406 28 |
| Legal expense in litigating claims | 761 52 |
| Other legal expenses | 12,478 67 |
| Furniture and fixtures | 5,636 74 |
| Gross decrease in book value of ledger assets—bonds | 13,271 28 |
| Executive council meetings | 14,708 56 |
| Annual receipt card cases | 5,886 00 |
| Surety bonds | 4,524 69 |
| Office expense | 5,125 08 |
| Miscellaneous expense | 2,052 14 |
| Prizes for new members | 511 25 |
| Total disbursements | $2,056,965 19 |
| Balance | $10,312,165 75 |

## LEDGER ASSETS.

| | |
|---|---|
| Mortgage loans on real estate | $ 50,000 00 |
| Book value of bonds | 10,013,928 57 |
| Cash in association's office | 13,177 19 |
| Deposits in trust companies and banks on interest | 234,231 99 |
| War Savings Stamps | 828 00 |
| Total ledger assets | $10,312,165 75 |

NON-LEDGER ASSETS.

| | |
|---|---|
| Interest and rents due and accrued | $188,354 02 |
| Assessments actually collected by subordinate lodges not yet turned over to supreme lodge | 240,000 00 |
| All other assets, viz: Furniture, supplies, etc., inventory | 64,844 93 |
| Gross assets | $10,805,364 70 |

DEDUCT ASSETS NOT ADMITTED.

| | |
|---|---|
| Furniture, supplies, etc., inventories | 64,844 93 |
| Total admitted assets | $10,740,519 77 |

## LIABILITIES.

| | | |
|---|---|---|
| Death claims due and unpaid | $ 15,180 81 | |
| Death claims reported during the year but not yet adjusted | 196,399 40 | |
| Death claims incurred in 1921, not reported until 1922 | 3,200 00 | |
| Total death claims | | $214,780 21 |
| Present value of disability claims payable in installments | | 62,409 86 |
| Total unpaid claims | | $277,190 07 |
| Salaries, rents, expenses, commissions, etc., due or accrued | | 24,479 76 |
| Advance assessments | | 17,590 10 |
| Protested remittances in process of adjustment | | 1,487 69 |
| Total | | $320,747 62 |

## EXHIBIT OF CERTIFICATES.

| | Total business of the year. | | Business in Illinois during year. | |
|---|---|---|---|---|
| | Number. | Amount. | Number. | Amount. |
| Benefit certificates in force December 31, 1920, as per last statement | 163,969 | $162,040,999 00 | 2,639 | $2,458,155 00 |
| Benefit certificates written and renewed during the year | 12,224 | 12,453,610 00 | 494 | 491,000 00 |
| Benefit certificates received by transfer during the year | | | 5 | 4,300 00 |
| Benefit certificates increased during the year | | 988,700 50 | | 23,300 00 |
| Total | 176,193 | $175,483,309 50 | 3,138 | $2,976,755 00 |
| Deduct terminated, decreased or transferred during the year | 33,068 | 32,632,874 50 | | |
| Deduct terminated or decreased during the year | | | 592 | 564,100 00 |
| Total benefit certificates in force December 31, 1921 | 143,125 | $142,850,435 00 | 2,546 | $2,412,655 00 |

| | |
|---|---|
| Received during the year from members in Illinois: Mortuary, $37,769.52; expense, $10,187.85; total | $47,957 38 |

EXHIBIT OF DEATH CLAIMS.

| | Total claims. Number. | Total claims. Amount. | Illinois claims. Number. | Illinois claims. Amount. |
|---|---|---|---|---|
| Claims unpaid December 31, 1920, as per last statement | 293 | $ 301,796 09 | 7 | $ 6,956 19 |
| Claims reported during the year and interest addition | 1,303 | 1,156,226 43 | 23 | 19,971 38 |
| Total | 1,596 | $1,458,022 52 | 30 | $26,927 57 |
| Claims paid during the year | 1,363 | 1,215,356 59 | 26 | 22,383 27 |
| Balance | 233 | $242,665 93 | 4 | $4,544 30 |
| Saved by compromising or scaling down claims during the year | | 12,973 69 | | |
| Claims rejected during the year | 36 | 18,112 03 | 1 | 1,100 00 |
| Claims unpaid December 31, 1921 | 197 | $211,580 21 | 3 | $3,444 30 |

EXHIBIT OF PERMANENT DISABILITY CLAIMS.

| | Total claims. Number. | Total claims. Amount. | Illinois claims. Number. | Illinois claims. Amount. |
|---|---|---|---|---|
| Claims unpaid December 31, 1920, as per last statement | 108 | $60,879 09 | | |
| Claims reported during the year and interest addition | 24 | 16,109 57 | | |
| Total | 132 | $76,988 66 | | |
| Claims paid during the year | 1 | 11,578 80 | | |
| Balance | 131 | $65,409 86 | | |
| Claims died during the year | 4 | 3,000 00 | | |
| Claims unpaid December 31, 1921 | 127 | $62,409 86 | 1 | $402 01 |

EXHIBIT OF OLD AGE AND OTHER CLAIMS.

| | Total claims. Number. | Total claims. Amount. |
|---|---|---|
| Claims paid during the year | 33 | $11,532 52 |

## WOODMEN OF THE WORLD, SOVEREIGN CAMP.

Located at Omaha, Nebraska.

W. A. FRASER, President. JNO. T. YATES, Secretary.

| | |
|---|---|
| Balance from previous year | $41,452,252 75 |

INCOME.

| | |
|---|---|
| Membership fees actually received | $ 33,548 26 |
| Assessments or premiums during first months of membership of which all or an extra percentage is used for expenses | 1,011,693 95 |
| All other assessments or premiums | 13,127,356 93 |
| Dues and per capita tax | 11,554 57 |
| Infantile certificates | 117,025 17 |
| Total received from members | $14,301,178 88 |
| Deduct payments returned to applicants and members | 28,706 91 |
| Net amount received from members | $14,272,471 97 |
| Gross interest on mortgage loans | 5,894 99 |
| Gross interest on bonds and dividends on stocks | 2,002,617 42 |
| Gross interest on deposits in trust companies and banks | 31,659 74 |
| Gross interest from all other sources | 7 00 |
| Gross rents from association's property, including $85,754.80 for association's occupancy of its own buildings | 302,439 08 |
| Sale of lodge supplies | 12,126 96 |
| Gross profit on sale or maturity of ledger assets | 2,884 28 |
| Gross increase in book value of ledger assets | 20,389 33 |
| Boys of Woodcraft | 17 00 |
| Official publication Sovereign Visitor Advertising | 137,526 82 |
| Surety bonds of camp officers and deputies | 17,285 97 |
| Official publication Sovereign Visitor subscriptions | 148,625 00 |
| Cancelled warrants, death claims | 5,218 73 |
| Cancelled warrants, disability claims | 259 65 |
| Miscellaneous income | 65 81 |
| Total income | $16,959,489 75 |
| Sum | $58,411,742 50 |

## DISBURSEMENTS.

| | | |
|---|---|---|
| Death claims | | $7,231,588 37 |
| Permanent disability claims | | 541,379 46 |
| Monument claims | | 307,375 00 |
| Total benefits paid | | $8,080,342 83 |
| Commissions and fees paid to deputies and organizers | | 264,209 42 |
| Salaries and expenses of deputies and organizers | | 183,940 32 |
| Salaries of officers and trustees | | 67,755 00 |
| Salaries of office employees | | 486,046 92 |
| Salaries and fees paid to supreme medical examiners | | 7,500 00 |
| Salaries and fees paid to subordinate medical examiners | | 2,436 50 |
| Traveling and other expenses of officers, trustees and committees | | 30,105 66 |
| Insurance department fees | | 952 00 |
| Rent, including, $85,754.80 for association's occupancy of its own buildings | | 87,254 80 |
| Advertising, printing and stationery | | 178,945 52 |
| Postage, express, telegraph and telephone | | 43,984 80 |
| Lodge supplies | | 20,124 89 |
| Official publication | | 354,727 24 |
| Expenses of supreme lodge meeting | | 301,008 54 |
| Legal expense in litigating claims | | 46,430 29 |
| Other legal expenses | | 11,612 20 |
| Furniture and fixtures | | 24,785 03 |
| Taxes, repairs and other expenses on real estate | | 184,599 03 |
| Gross decrease in book value of ledger assets | | 55,088 42 |
| Distribution of savings | | 604,505 04 |
| Miscellaneous disbursements | | 44,211 62 |
| Personal injury suit, Dailey vs. W. O. W | | 45,620 01 |
| Special compensation to clerks for rerating members | | 42,100 00 |
| Surety bonds of Sov. camp officers, camp officers and deputies | | 20,213 80 |
| Special prizes to clerks | | 443 00 |
| Mailing equipment for official publication | | 31,362 68 |
| Office supplies | | 17,523 74 |
| Total disbursements | | $11,237,829 30 |
| Balance | | $47,173,913 20 |

## LEDGER ASSETS.

| | | |
|---|---|---|
| Book value of real estate | | $ 1,951,123 78 |
| Mortgage loans on real estate | | 123,000 00 |
| Book value of bonds and stocks | | 43,666,562 37 |
| Cash in association's office | | 35,391 48 |
| Deposits in trust companies and banks on interest | | 1,397,835 57 |
| Total ledger assets | | $47,173,913 20 |

### NON-LEDGER ASSETS.

| | | |
|---|---|---|
| Interest and rents due and accrued | | $ 510,888 89 |
| Assessments actually collected by subordinate lodges not yet turned over to supreme lodge | | 1,150,000 00 |
| All other assets, viz— | | |
| Due from camps secured by bonds | $ 129,475 50 | |
| Inventory—supplies, blanks and printing, furniture, equipment, etc. | 352,648 46 | |
| Liens on certificates in force | 2,379,259 69 | |
| Accounts receivable | 1,311 61 | |
| | | 2,862,695 26 |
| Gross assets | | $51,697,497 35 |

### DEDUCT ASSETS NOT ADMITTED.

| | | |
|---|---|---|
| Other items, viz— | | |
| Accounts receivable | $ 1,311 61 | |
| Inventory—supplies, blanks and printing, furniture, equipment, etc. | 352,648 46 | |
| Liens on certificates in force | 2,379,259 69 | |
| | | 2,733,219 76 |
| Total admitted assets | | $48,964,277 59 |

## LIABILITIES.

| | | |
|---|---|---|
| Death claims due and unpaid | $ 16,806 46 | |
| Death claims resisted | 208,008 58 | |
| Death claims reported during the year but not yet adjusted | 944,599 97 | |
| Death claims incurred in 1921, not reported until 1922 | 184,678 00 | |
| Unpaid monuments | 248,300 00 | |
| Total death claims | | $1,602,393 01 |
| Permanent disability claims resisted | | 1,250 00 |
| Fraternal disability experience and 4 per cent | | 61,103 12 |
| Total unpaid claims | | $1,664,746 13 |
| Salaries, rents, expenses, commissions, etc., due or accrued | | 71,966 70 |

LIABILITIES—Concluded.

| | | |
|---|---|---|
| All other liabilities, viz— | | |
| Boys of Woodcraft | $5,254 01 | |
| General relief fund | 1,276 13 | |
| Infantile death claims | 719 00 | |
| Miscellaneous | 77 56 | |
| | | 7,326 70 |
| Total | | $1,744,039 53 |

## EXHIBIT OF CERTIFICATES.

| | Total business of the year. Number. | Amount. | Business in Illinois during year. Number. | Amount. |
|---|---|---|---|---|
| Benefit certificates in force December 31, 1920, as per last statement | 646,719 | $822,552,903 00 | 11,822 | $13,277,768 00 |
| Benefit certificates written and renewed during the year | 52,228 | 60,788,696 00 | 1,385 | 1,475,550 00 |
| Benefit certificates received by transfer during the year | | | 61 | 72,100 00 |
| Benefit certificates increased during the year | | 560,314 00 | | 3,300 00 |
| Total | 698,947 | $883,901,913 00 | 13,268 | $14,828,718 00 |
| Deduct terminated, decreased or transferred during the year | 156,437 | 190,830,742 00 | | |
| Deduct terminated or decreased during the year | | | 3,119 | 3,252,151 00 |
| Total benefit certificates in force December 31, 1921 | 542,510 | $693,071,171 00 | 10,149 | $11,576,567 00 |

Received during the year from members in Illinois: Mortuary, $232,514.84; expense, $60,629.60; total $293,144 44

## EXHIBIT OF DEATH CLAIMS.

| | Total claims. Number. | Amount. | Illinois claims. Number. | Amount. |
|---|---|---|---|---|
| Claims unpaid December 31, 1920, as per last statement | 1,619 | $2,240,934 43 | 23 | $ 33,615 00 |
| Claims reported during the year and interest addition | 5,913 | 6,947,939 13 | 121 | 124,985 00 |
| Claims reinstated during the year | 137 | 200,155 43 | 8 | 7,747 08 |
| Total | 7,669 | $9'389,028 99 | 152 | $166,347 08 |
| Claims paid during the year | 6,417 | 7,525,683 37 | 117 | 124,853 56 |
| Balance | 1,252 | $1,863,345 62 | 35 | $41,493 52 |
| Saved by compromising or scaling down claims during the year | | 207,014 19 | | 5,903 86 |
| Claims rejected during the year | 206 | 238,616 42 | 8 | 7,635 00 |
| Claims unpaid December 31, 1921 | 1,046 | $1,417,715 01 | 27 | $27,954 66 |

## EXHIBIT OF PERMANENT DISABILITY CLAIMS.

| | Total claims. Number. | Amount. | Illinois claims. Number. | Amount. |
|---|---|---|---|---|
| Claims reported during the year and interest addition | 402 | $116,136 05 | | |
| Claims paid during the year | 400 | 114,886 05 | 2 | $1,000 00 |
| Claims unpaid December 31, 1921 | 2 | $1,250 00 | | |

## EXHIBIT OF OLD AGE AND OTHER CLAIMS.

| | Total claims. Number. | Amount. | Illinois claims. Number. | Amount. |
|---|---|---|---|---|
| Claims unpaid December 31, 1920, as per last statement | 97 | $103,400 00 | 2 | $1,400 00 |
| Claims reported during the year and interest addition | 1,312 | 473,476 24 | 4 | 662 89 |
| Total | 1,409 | $576,876 24 | 6 | $2,062 89 |
| Claims paid during the year | 1,251 | 426,793 41 | 4 | 962 89 |
| Balance | 158 | $150,082 83 | 2 | $1,100 00 |
| Claims paid in full and deceased | 14 | 11,500 00 | | |
| Claims rejected during the year | 14 | 15,701 00 | | |
| Claims unpaid December 31, 1921 | 130 | $122,881 83 | 2 | $1,100 00 |

## WOODMEN OF UNION.

Located at Hot Springs, Arkansas.

DR. E. A. KENDALL, President. JNO. L. WEBB, Secretary and Custodian.

| | |
|---|---|
| Balance from previous year | $106,513 89 |

## INCOME.

| | |
|---|---|
| Membership fees actually received | $ 7,130 68 |
| All other assessments or premiums | 183,668 28 |
| Total received from members | $190,798 96 |
| Deduct payments returned to applicants and members | 463 85 |
| Net amount received from members | $190,335 11 |
| Gross interest on mortgage loans | 216 00 |
| Gross interest on bonds and dividends on stocks | 220 00 |
| Gross rents from association's property | 1,060 75 |
| Sale of lodge supplies | 2,352 65 |
| Gross increase in book value of ledger assets | 651 48 |
| Charters and dispensations | 46,566 17 |
| Quarterly tax | 4,184 14 |
| Annual tax | 5,205 25 |
| Educational tax | 2,022 05 |
| Subscription to journal | 4,907 30 |
| Supreme lodge tax | 32 50 |
| Total income | $257,753 40 |
| Sum | $364,267 29 |

## DISBURSEMENTS.

| | |
|---|---|
| Death claims | $50,596 14 |
| Sick and accident claims | 74,258 10 |
| Total benefits paid | $124,854 24 |
| Commissions and fees paid to deputies and organizers | 29,000 00 |
| Salaries of deputies and organizers | 4,946 00 |
| Salaries of managers or agents not deputies or organizers | 675 00 |
| Salaries of officers and trustees | 1,335 00 |
| Salaries of office employees | 17,980 21 |
| Salaries and fees paid to supreme medical examiners | 3,075 00 |
| Traveling and other expenses of officers, trustees and committees | 643 50 |
| Insurance department fees | 373 08 |
| Advertising, printing and stationery | 3,865 37 |
| Postage, express, telegraph and telephone | 2,393 13 |
| Lodge supplies | 2,822 68 |
| Official publication | 2,785 36 |
| Expenses of supreme lodge meeting | 2,213 54 |
| Actuarial fee | 101 07 |
| Other legal expenses | 415 00 |
| Furniture and fixtures | 1,281 75 |
| Taxes, repairs and other expenses on real estate | 484 76 |
| All other disbursements, viz— | |
| Office expense, $1,153.94; investment expense, $4.00; fire insurance premium, $938.90 | 2,096 84 |
| Light and fuel, $90.50; examination fee, $662.91; donation charitable purpose, $81.00 | 834 41 |
| Rejected checks | 611 40 |
| Total disbursements | $204,378 10 |
| Balance | $159,889 19 |

## LEDGER ASSETS.

| | |
|---|---|
| Book value of real estate | $125,045 41 |
| Mortgage loans on real estate | 11,550 52 |
| Book value of bonds and stocks | 10,000 00 |
| Deposits in trust companies and banks not on interest | 13,059 76 |
| War Savings Stamps | 233 50 |
| Gross assets | $159,889 19 |

## EXHIBIT OF CERTIFICATES.

| | Total business of the year. | | Business in Illinois during year. | |
|---|---|---|---|---|
| | Number. | Amount. | Number. | Amount. |
| Benefit certificates in force December 31, 1920, as per last statement | 26,757 | $2,791,940 00 | | |
| Benefit certificates written and renewed during the year | 14,728 | 989,120 00 | 189 | $17,460 00 |
| Total | 41,485 | $3,781,060 00 | 189 | $17,460 00 |
| Deduct terminated or decreased during the year | | | 14 | 1,160 00 |
| Total benefit certificates in force December 31, 1921 | 41,485 | $3,781,060 00 | 175 | $16,300 00 |

Received during the year from members in Illinois: Mortuary, $605.54; expense, $83.46; total ........ $689 00

EXHIBIT OF DEATH CLAIMS.

| | Total claims. Number. | Total claims. Amount. | Illinois claims. Number. | Illinois claims. Amount. |
|---|---|---|---|---|
| Claims paid during the year | 354 | $50,596 14 | 1 | $15 00 |

## WORKMEN'S CIRCLE.

Located at 175 East Broadway, New York, New York.

R. GUSKIN, President. JOSEPH BASKIN, Secretary.

| | |
|---|---|
| Balance from previous year | $1,535,998 57 |

INCOME.

| | |
|---|---|
| Membership fees actually received | $ 20,162 00 |
| All other assessments or premiums | 917,289 53 |
| Constitution fees and M. C. | 526 70 |
| For transfers received | 445 50 |
| For charitable purposes | 79,501 89 |
| Special assessments | 38,686 15 |
| Total received from members | $1,056,611 77 |
| Deduct payments returned to applicants and members | 22,044 46 |
| Net amount received from members | $1,034,567 31 |
| Gross interest on mortgage loans | 5,183 70 |
| Gross interest on bonds and dividends on stocks less $3,291.05 | 50,604 95 |
| Gross interest on deposits in trust companies and banks | 3,626 82 |
| Gross interest from all other sources | 4 60 |
| Sale of lodge supplies | 355 13 |
| Gross increase in book value of ledger assets—bonds | 2,891 50 |
| From all other sources, viz— | |
| N. Portnoy, $90.00; sale of farm products, food, etc., $493.06; compensation for auto accident, $479.77 | 1,062 83 |
| Labor League patients, $702.87; consumptive patients, $23,701.94; anniversary celebration, $1,903.42 | 26,308 23 |
| Donations, $20.00; deposits, $695.30; flag rent, $111.00; notary public, $15.45 | 841 75 |
| Applications for approval, $19,898.08; for Rubin Star, $23.04; Denver Sanitarium deposit, $50.00 | 19,971 12 |
| From unknown remitter, $0.25; Canadian exahange, $45.94 | 46 19 |
| Total income | $1,179,308 11 |
| Sum | $2,715,306 68 |

DISBURSEMENTS.

| | |
|---|---|
| Death claims | $ 82,029 50 |
| Sick and accident claims | 183,723 00 |
| Consumptive benefit | 19,854 92 |
| Total benefits paid | $285,607 42 |
| Salaries of officers and trustees | 5,250 00 |
| Salaries and other compensation of committees | 6,912 20 |
| Salaries of office employees | 32,626 70 |
| Other compensation of office employees | 596 52 |
| Salaries and fees paid to supreme medical examiners | 29 50 |
| Traveling and other expenses of officers, trustees and committees | 560 28 |
| For collection and exchange | 455 00 |
| Insurance department fees | 1,170 00 |
| Rent, excluding $840.00 for subleting part of office | 2,559 96 |
| Advertising, printing and stationery | 5,530 54 |
| Postage, express, telegraph and telephone | 3,282 19 |
| Official publication | 26,352 76 |
| Expenses of supreme lodge meeting | 57,563 00 |
| Other legal expenses | 7,417 85 |
| Furniture and fixtures | 2,610 28 |
| Taxes, repairs and other expenses on real estate | 784 04 |
| Gross decrease in book value of ledger assets | 35,981 70 |
| All other disbursements, viz— | |
| Educational work, $36,902.05; return of L. L. deposit, $500.00; maintenance of sanitorium, $103,891.42 | 141,293 47 |
| Refunds to patients, $116.78; cost of anniversary celebration, $1,817.73; for charitable purposes, $84,218.29 | 86,152 80 |
| Organization work, $12,378.15; applications for approval, $20,017.72; balance of collections for cemetery department, $207.76; H. Horn, $41.00 | 32,644 63 |
| Sundry expenses | 9,476 71 |
| Total disbursements | $744,857 55 |
| Balance | $1,970,449 13 |

## LEDGER ASSETS.

| | | |
|---|---|---|
| Book value of real estate | | $ 96,693 19 |
| Mortgage loans on real estate | | 158,500 00 |
| Book value of bonds and stocks | | 1,502,696 87 |
| Cash in association's office, $5,600.00 sanitorium department, $2,500.00 | | 9,100 00 |
| Deposits in trust companies and banks on interest | | 101,889 49 |
| Other ledger assets, viz: P. O. Passaic, $216.82; branches, $52,241.76; members at large, $1,292.03; branch supplies, $4,261.86; machinery F. and F. Friendship department, $1,011.01, plates, $3,000.00; F. and F., $5,831.81; sanitarium F. and F., $17,660.71; live stock, $739.66; postage, $49.32; books, $14,184.16; special re-imbursement, $917.03; paper, $983.41 | | 102,569 58 |
| Total ledger assets | | $1,970,449 13 |

### NON-LEDGER ASSETS.

| | | |
|---|---|---|
| Interest and rents due and accrued | | 21,420 34 |
| Market value of bonds and stocks over book value | | 69,461 13 |
| Administration fund | $18,974 25 | |
| Friend fund | 3,431 70 | |
| Publications | 12,510 60 | |
| | | 34,916 55 |
| Gross assets | | $2,096,247 15 |

### DEDUCT ASSETS NOT ADMITTED.

| | | |
|---|---|---|
| Other items, viz— | | |
| P. O. Passaic, $216.82; branches, $52,421.76; members at large, $1,292.03; branch supplies, $4,261.86; machinery F. and F. Friend Department, $1,011.01; plates, $3,000.00; F. and F., $5,831.81; sanitarium F. and F., $17,660.71; live stock, $739.66; postage, $49.32; books, $14,184.16; special re-imbursement, $917.03; paper, $983.41 | $102,569 58 | |
| Administrative fund, $18,974.25; friend fund, $3,431.70; publications, $12,510.60 | 34,916 55 | |
| | | 137,486 13 |
| Total admitted assets | | $1,958,761 02 |

## LIABILITIES.

| | | |
|---|---|---|
| Death claims due and unpaid | $59,233 92 | |
| Death claims incurred in 1921, not reported until 1922 | 4,900 00 | |
| Total death claims | | $64,133 92 |
| Permanent disability claims due and unpaid | | 111 39 |
| Sick and accident claims due and unpaid | | 97 88 |
| Total unpaid claims | | $64,343 19 |
| All other liabilities, viz: Applications for approval, $563.36; sanitarium deposits, $1,092.38; Canadian exchange, $79.05; Denver sanitarium deposit, $50.00; H. Klipper, $41.00; suspense, $387.40; Rubin Star, $23.04; voluntary contributions, $20,420.38; uncollected checks, $606.92; special fund for drafted members, $8,042.85 | | 31,306 38 |
| Total | | $95,649 57 |

## EXHIBIT OF CERTIFICATES.

| | Total business of the year. | | Business in Illinois during year. | |
|---|---|---|---|---|
| | Number. | Amount. | Number. | Amount. |
| Benefit certificates in force December 31, 1920, as per last statement | 81,571 | $21,870,900 00 | 5,744 | $1,547,100 00 |
| Benefit certificates written and renewed during the year | 13,338 | 3,249,600 00 | 653 | 181,100 00 |
| Benefit certificates received by transfer during the year | -------- | ------------- | 145 | 37,000 00 |
| Benefit certificates increased during the year | -------- | 15,700 00 | -------- | 1,500 00 |
| Total | 94,909 | $25,136,200 00 | 6,542 | $1,766,700 00 |
| Deduct terminated, decreased or transferred during the year | 11,803 | 2,999,600 00 | -------- | ------------- |
| Deduct terminated or decreased during the year | -------- | ------------- | 1,434 | 368,600 00 |
| Total benefit certificates in force December 31, 1921 | 83,106 | $22,136,600 00 | 5,108 | $1,398,100 00 |

| | |
|---|---|
| Received during the year from members in Illinois: Mortuary, $14,554.10; reserve, $7,315.43; disability, $1,797.05; all other, $16,194.40; expense, $12,789.85; total | $52,650 78 |

## EXHIBIT OF DEATH CLAIMS.

| | Total claims. Number. | Amount. | Illinois claims. Number. | Amount. |
|---|---|---|---|---|
| Claims unpaid December 31, 1920, as per last statement | 237 | $57,577 18 | 15 | $3,690 16 |
| Claims reported during the year and interest addition | 297 | 83,886 24 | 16 | 4,708 48 |
| Total | 534 | $141,463 42 | 31 | $8,398 64 |
| Claims paid during the year | 288 | 82,029 50 | 17 | 4,633 33 |
| Balance | 246 | $59,433 92 | 14 | $3,765 31 |
| Claims rejected during the year | 1 | 200 00 | | |
| Claims unpaid December 31, 1921 | 245 | $59,233 92 | 14 | $3,765 31 |

## EXHIBIT OF CONSUMPTION BENEFIT CLAIMS.

| | Total claims. Number. | Amount. | Illinois claims. Number. | Amount. |
|---|---|---|---|---|
| Claims unpaid December 31, 1920, as per last statement | 1 | $ 107 07 | | |
| Claims reported during the year and interest addition | 160 | 19,859 24 | | |
| Total | 161 | $19,966 31 | | |
| Claims paid during the year | 160 | $19,854 92 | 18 | $2,144 66 |
| Claims unpaid December 31, 1921 | 1 | $111 39 | | |

## EXHIBIT OF SICK AND ACCIDENT CLAIMS.

| | Total claims. Number. | Amount. | Illinois claims. Number. | Amount. |
|---|---|---|---|---|
| Claims unpaid December 31, 1920, as per last statement | 1 | $ 7 60 | | |
| Increase by interest | | 28 | | |
| Claims reported during the year | 9,012 | 183,813 00 | | |
| Total | 9,013 | $183,820 88 | | |
| Claims paid during the year | 9,011 | 183,723 00 | 653 | $13,234 00 |
| Claims unpaid December 31, 1921 | 2 | $97 88 | | |

---

# WORKMEN'S SICK AND DEATH BENEFIT FUND.

Located at No. 9 Seventh Street, New York, New York.

PAUL FLASHEL, President. WM. MEYER, Secretary.

| | |
|---|---|
| Balance from previous year | $1,458,557 90 |

## INCOME.

| | |
|---|---|
| Membership fees actually received | $ 9,492 00 |
| All other assessments or premiums | 620,663 60 |
| Fines | 122 75 |
| Total received from members | $630,278 35 |
| Deduct payments returned to applicants and members | 68 00 |
| Net amount received from members | $630,210 35 |
| Gross interest on mortgage loans | 70,059 84 |
| Gross interest on deposits in trust companies and banks | 2,754 86 |
| Gross rents from association's property | 2,646 50 |
| Constitutions and branch seals | 3 10 |
| Sale of society emblems | 241 25 |
| Mortgage appraisal deposits | 330 00 |
| Refund of expenses for mortgage committees | 27 15 |
| Premium on surety bond refunded | 12 50 |
| Premium on fire insurance refunded | 7 63 |
| From sale of pictures | 15 95 |
| From sale of official publication | 1 60 |
| Spoiled portals exchanged | 2 46 |
| Total income | $706,313 19 |
| Sum | $2,164,871 09 |

## DISBURSEMENTS.

| | | |
|---|---|---|
| Death claims | | $150,255 45 |
| Sick and accident claims | | 310,014 05 |
| Total benefits paid | | $460,269 50 |
| Salaries of officers | | 3,553 89 |
| Other compensation of trustees | | 132 43 |
| Salaries and other compensation of committees | | 31 20 |
| Salaries of office employees | | 12,319 27 |
| Insurance department fees | | 80 00 |
| Rent | | 1,400 00 |
| Advertising, printing and stationery | | 2,186 69 |
| Postage, express, telegraph and telephone | | 547 51 |
| Official publication | | 19,465 60 |
| Expenses of supreme lodge meeting | | 824 10 |
| Legal expenses in litigating claims | | 750 00 |
| Other legal expenses | | 409 28 |
| Furniture and fixtures | | 182 70 |
| Taxes, repairs and other expenses on real estate | | 1,174 16 |
| Society emblems | | 267 98 |
| Fire insurance premium | | 23 90 |
| Auditing | | 263 70 |
| Actuary's fees valuing certificates | | 100 00 |
| Membership fee, N. F. Congress, N. Y | | 7 50 |
| Bonding officers | | 37 85 |
| Interest paid minor beneficiaries | | 83 66 |
| Special, sick, control | | 45 68 |
| Office, lighting | | 44 43 |
| Office, cleaning | | 260 00 |
| Mortgage appraisals | | 265 00 |
| Refund of appraisal, deposits | | 80 00 |
| Office and branch seals | | 22 60 |
| Collection fee on checks | | 16 43 |
| Tax, searches on mortgaged properties | | 208 00 |
| Sundries | | 70 05 |
| Total disbursements | | $505,123 11 |
| Balance | | $1,659,747 98 |

## LEDGER ASSETS.

| | | |
|---|---|---|
| Book value of real estate | | $ 16,000 00 |
| Mortgage loans on real estate | | 1,464,550 00 |
| Cash in association's office | | 87 68 |
| Deposits in trust companies and banks on interest | | 52,052 12 |
| In treasuries of subordinate bodies or deposited in banks by them | | 127,058 18 |
| Total ledger assets | | $1,659,747 98 |

### NON-LEDGER ASSETS.

| | | |
|---|---|---|
| Interest and rents due and accrued | | 23,914 21 |
| Market value of real estate over book value | | 2,000 00 |
| All other assessments, viz— | | |
| Assessments due and unpaid | $40,927 02 | |
| Office fixtures, safes, etc | 1,300 00 | |
| Society emblems and advertising pictures | 170 00 | |
| Supplies, blank books, stationery | 1,200 00 | |
| | | 43,597 02 |
| Gross assets | | $1,729,259 21 |

### DEDUCT ASSETS NOT ADMITTED.

| | | |
|---|---|---|
| Assessments due and unpaid | $40,927 02 | |
| Office fixtures, safes, etc | 1,300 00 | |
| Supplies, blank books, stationery | 1,200 00 | |
| Society emblems and advertising pictures | 170 00 | |
| | | 43,597 02 |
| Total admitted assets | | $1,685,662 19 |

## LIABILITIES.

| | | |
|---|---|---|
| Death claims due and unpaid | $29,716 02 | |
| Death claims resisted | 2,150 00 | |
| Death claims reported during the year but not yet adjusted | 6,312 50 | |
| Death claims incurred in 1921, not reported until 1922 | 1,500 00 | |
| Total death claims | | $39,678 52 |
| Sick and accident claims due and unpaid | | 11,663 52 |
| Total unpaid claims | | $51,342 04 |
| Advance assessments | | 1,183 90 |

LIABILITIES—Concluded.

| | | |
|---|---|---|
| All other liabilities, viz— | | |
| Interest accrued on death benefit due minor beneficiaries | $981 80 | |
| Bills due and unpaid | 155 84 | |
| | | $1,137 64 |
| Total | | $53,663 58 |

## EXHIBIT OF CERTIFICATES.

| | Total business of the year. | | Business in Illinois during year. | |
|---|---|---|---|---|
| | Number. | Amount. | Number. | Amount. |
| Benefit certificates in force December 31, 1920, as per last statement | 53,738 | $13,434,500 00 | 2,973 | $743,250 00 |
| Benefit certificates written and renewed during the year | 2,238 | 559,500 00 | 202 | 50,500 00 |
| Benefit certificates received by transfer during the year | | | 15 | 3,750 00 |
| Totals | 55,976 | $13,994,000 00 | 3,190 | $797,500 00 |
| Deduct terminated, decreased or transferred during the year | 2,455 | 613,750 00 | | |
| Deduct terminated or decreased during the year | | | 156 | 39,000 00 |
| Total benefit certificates in force December 31, 1921 | 53,521 | $13,380,250 00 | 3,034 | $758,500 00 |

Received during the year from members in Illinois: Mortuary, $10,374.47; reserve, $924.00; sick and accident, $24,539.60; expense, $1,958.88; total $37,796 95

## EXHIBIT OF DEATH CLAIMS.

| | Total claims. | | Illinois claims. | |
|---|---|---|---|---|
| | Number. | Amount. | Number. | Amount. |
| Claims unpaid December 31, 1920, as per last statement | 175 | $ 35,016 12 | 9 | $1,844 62 |
| Claims reported during the year and interest addition | 619 | 154,750 00 | 23 | 5,750 00 |
| Totals | 794 | $189,766 12 | 32 | $7,594 62 |
| Claims paid during the year | 597 | 150,255 45 | 25 | 6,452 37 |
| Balance | 197 | $39,510 67 | 7 | $1,144 25 |
| Saved by not having been in benefit claims during the year | 1 | 250 00 | | |
| Balance | 196 | $39,260 67 | 7 | $1,144 25 |
| Saved by compromising or scaling down claims during the year, dropped | | | 1 | 151 65 |
| Claims during the year dropped | 7 | 1,082 15 | | |
| Claims rejected during the year | | | 6 | 990 60 |
| Claims unpaid December 31, 1921 | 189 | $38,178 52 | | |

## EXHIBIT OF SICK AND ACCIDENT CLAIMS.

| | Total claims. | | Illinois claims. | |
|---|---|---|---|---|
| | Number. | Amount. | Number. | Amount. |
| Claims unpaid December 31, 1920, as per last statement | 643 | $ 9,664 52 | 50 | $ 1,142 25 |
| Claims reported during the year | 8,250 | 312,170 55 | 631 | 24,056 25 |
| Totals | 8,893 | $321,835 07 | 681 | $25,198 50 |
| Claims paid during the year | 8,158 | 310,171 55 | 628 | 23,853 95 |
| Claims unpaid December 31, 1921 | 735 | $11,663 52 | 53 | $1,344 55 |

# SOCIETIES OF FOREIGN GOVERNMENTS.

## INDEPENDENT ORDER OF FORESTERS, SUPREME COURT.

Located at Bay and Richmond Streets, Toronto, Canada.

W. H. HUNTER, President. G. E. BAILEY, Secretary.

| | |
|---|---|
| Balance from previous year | $46,267,365 45 |

### INCOME.

| | |
|---|---|
| All other assessments or premiums | $3,389,531 87 |
| Deduct payments returned to applicants and members | 10,264 74 |
| Net amount received from members | $3,379,267 13 |
| Gross interest on mortgage loans | 216,370 56 |
| Gross interest on collateral loans | 201,115 51 |
| Gross interest on bonds and dividends on stocks | 606,664 70 |
| Gross interest on deposits in trust companies and banks | 9,942 71 |
| Gross interest from all other sources | 170 40 |
| Gross rents from association's property | 125,138 34 |
| Interest policy loans | 885,194 00 |
| Gross profit on sale or maturity of ledger assets | 7,208 67 |
| Re-deposited checks | 771 58 |
| Special donation account orphan home | 1,795 83 |
| Re-payment accrued interest | 1,188 70 |
| Business tax refund | 1,140 97 |
| Total income | $5,435,969 10 |
| Sum | $51,703,334 55 |

### DISBURSEMENTS.

| | |
|---|---|
| Death claims | $2,042,320 28 |
| Permanent disability claims | 109,070 78 |
| Sick and accident claims | 229,632 26 |
| Old age benefits | 1,079,724 99 |
| Other benefits, funeral claims | 17,931 21 |
| Expectation of life claims | 44,559 89 |
| Grants from surplus | 159,793 94 |
| Total benefits paid | $3,683,033 35 |
| Commissions and fees paid to deputies and organizers | 164,219 70 |
| Salaries of deputies and organizers | 94,351 05 |
| Salaries of managers or agents not deputies or organizers | 100,262 15 |
| Salaries of officers and trustees | 35,399 80 |
| Other compensation of officers and trustees | 10,499 96 |
| Books and periodicals | 1,100 15 |
| Salaries of office employees | 144,209 58 |
| Auditors fees | 4,145 00 |
| Inspection and substitution of risks | 1,009 05 |
| Salaries and fees paid to subordinate medical examiners | 35,972 92 |
| Traveling and other expenses of officers, trustees and committees | 9,812 58 |
| Printing and stationery | 13,380 58 |
| Insurance department fees | 2,154 97 |
| Rent | 17,805 16 |
| Advertising, printing and stationery | 4,593 26 |
| Postage, express, telegraph and telephone | 5,079 22 |
| Lodge supplies | 371 54 |
| Official publication | 21,387 64 |
| Expenses of supreme lodge meeting | 52,588 50 |
| Legal expense in litigating claims | 161 45 |
| Other legal expenses | 19,637 07 |
| Furniture and fixtures | 2,345 89 |
| Taxes, repairs and other expenses on real estate | 94,572 63 |

DISBURSEMENTS—Concluded.

| | |
|---|---|
| Gross loss on sale or maturity of ledger assets | $1,282,274 74 |
| Gross decrease in book value of ledger assets, policy liens cancelled by lapse | 476,620 84 |
| Borrowed money repaid (gross) | 100,000 00 |
| Interest on borrowed money | 16,573 70 |
| All other disbursements, viz— | |
| General expense | 2,698 80 |
| Donation and fraternal societies | 1,914 04 |
| Orphans home and sanitorium | 83,737 39 |
| Orphans grants | 18,025 43 |
| Valuation fees | 581 64 |
| Total disbursements | $6,500,609 78 |
| Balance | $45,202,724 77 |

LEDGER ASSETS.

| | |
|---|---|
| Book value of real estate | $ 1,207,230 34 |
| Mortgage loans on real estate | 3,516,586 24 |
| Loans secured by pledge of bonds, stocks or other collateral | 4,036,243 09 |
| Book value of bonds and stocks | 13,970,351 33 |
| Deposits in trust companies and banks not on interest | 59,363 20 |
| Deposits in trust companies and banks on interest | 525,327 68 |
| Organizers' balances | 7,202 08 |
| Special donation re orphans home endowment, etc | 4,357 50 |
| Other ledger assets, viz— | |
| Temporary advances re mortgage loans, fire insurance, etc | 15,523 31 |
| Policy loans | 21,860,540 00 |
| Total ledger assets | $45,202,724 77 |

NON-LEDGER ASSETS.

| | |
|---|---|
| Interest and rents due and accrued | 686,613 67 |
| Market value of real estate over book value | 195,820 72 |
| Assessments actually collected by subordinate lodges not yet turned over to supreme lodge, inclusive premiums, $31,292.43; sick benefit premiums, $2,745.30 | 34,037 73 |
| All other assets, viz: Furniture and fixtures, $28,418.53; supplies, $19,270.45 | 47,688 98 |
| Gross assets | $46,166,885 87 |

DEDUCT ASSETS NOT ADMITTED.

| | | |
|---|---|---|
| Overdue and accrued interest on bonds in default | $ 89,176 53 | |
| Book value of bonds and stocks over market value | 2,276,692 57 | |
| Other items, viz: Furniture and fixtures, $28,418.53; supplies, $19,270.45 | 47,688 98 | |
| | | 2,413,558 08 |
| Total admitted assets | | $43,753,327 79 |

LIABILITIES.

| | | |
|---|---|---|
| Death claims adjusted not yet due | $ 13,835 93 | |
| Death claims resisted | 4,000 00 | |
| Death claims reported during the year but not yet adjusted | 105,090 50 | |
| Death claims incurred in 1921, not reported until 1922 | 142,402 54 | |
| Present value of deferred death claims payable in installments | 1,144 00 | |
| Total death claims | | $266,472 97 |
| Sick claims due and unpaid | $ 1,642 73 | |
| Funeral | 50 00 | |
| Sick claims reported during the year but not yet adjusted | 8,200 32 | |
| Funeral | 821 76 | |
| Sick and accident claims incurred in 1921, not reported until 1922 | 34,129 76 | |
| Total sick and accident claims | | 44,844 57 |
| Old age and other benefits due and unpaid, $15,500.00 including $3,623.00 present value of such benefits payable in installments | | 19,123 00 |
| Total unpaid claims | | $ 330,440 54 |
| Accounts due or accrued, $3,264.88; medical fees, $4,377.86 | | 7,642 74 |
| Borrowed money, $100,000.00; interest due or accrued on same, $66.66 | | 100,066 66 |
| Advance assessments, inclusive premiums, $15,481.43; sick benefit premiums, $770.32 | | 16,251 75 |
| All other liabilities, viz— | | |
| Reserves for investment fluctuation | | 500,000 00 |
| Reserves on unmatured policies | | 42,123,882 00 |
| Total | | $43,078,283 69 |

## EXHIBIT OF CERTIFICATES.

| | Total business of the year. Number. | Amount. | Business in Illinois during year. Number. | Amount. |
|---|---|---|---|---|
| Benefit certificates in force December 31, 1920, as per last statement | 176,265 | $172,134,894 00 | 9,321 | $9,260,817 00 |
| Benefit certificates written and renewed during the year | 17,771 | 18,654,972 00 | 930 | 1,040,250 00 |
| Benefit certificates increased during the year | -------- | 545,890 00 | -------- | 59,656 00 |
| Totals | 194,036 | $191,335,756 00 | 10,251 | $10,360,723 00 |
| Deduct terminated, decreased or transferred during the year | 20,382 | 21,677,681 00 | -------- | -------------- |
| Deduct terminated or decreased during the year | -------- | -------------- | 1,058 | 1,166,292 00 |
| Total benefit certificates in force December 31, 1921 | 173,654 | $169,658,075 00 | 9,193 | $9,194,431 00 |

Received during the year from members in Illinois: Mortuary, $168,408.82; sick and funeral, $312.21; total ........ $168,721 03

## EXHIBIT OF DEATH CLAIMS.

| | Total claims. Number. | Amount. | Illinois claims. Number. | Amount. |
|---|---|---|---|---|
| Claims unpaid December 31, 1920, as per last statement | 126 | $ 115,655 62 | 6 | $ 4,256 85 |
| Claims reported during the year and interest addition | 1,936 | 2,065,078 59 | 129 | 129,416 06 |
| Totals | 2,062 | $2,180,734 21 | 135 | $133,672 91 |
| Claims paid during the year | 1,931 | 2,042,320 28 | 127 | 125,666 06 |
| Balance | 131 | $138,413 93 | 8 | $8,006 85 |
| Saved by compromising or scaling down claims during the year | -------- | 10,500 84 | -------- | -------------- |
| Claims rejected during the year | 6 | 4,986 66 | -------- | -------------- |
| Claims unpaid December 31, 1921 | 125 | $122,926 43 | 8 | $8,006 85 |

## EXHIBIT OF PERMANENT DISABILITY CLAIMS.

| | Total claims. Number. | Amount. | Illinois claims. Number. | Amount. |
|---|---|---|---|---|
| Claims paid during the year | 128 | 109,070 78 | 6 | $5,586 00 |

## EXHIBIT OF SICK AND FUNERAL CLAIMS.

| | Total claims. Number. | Amount. | Illinois claims. Number. | Amount. |
|---|---|---|---|---|
| Claims unpaid December 31, 1920, as per last statement | 184 | $ 7,729 29 | 1 | $ 29 00 |
| Increase in estimated liability, incurred | 8,100 | 256,413 94 | 9 | 220 38 |
| Claims reported during the year, revived | 2 | 128 34 | -------- | -------------- |
| Totals | 8,286 | $264,271 57 | 10 | $249 38 |
| Claims paid during the year | 7,873 | $247,563 47 | 10 | 224 67 |
| Claims rejected during the year and compromised | 139 | 5,993 29 | -------- | 24 71 |
| Claims unpaid December 31, 1921 | 274 | $10,714 81 | -------- | -------------- |

## EXHIBIT OF OLD AGE AND EXPECTATION OF LIFE.

| | Total claims. Number. | Amount. | Illinois claims. Number. | Amount. |
|---|---|---|---|---|
| Claims unpaid December 31, 1920, as per last statement | 1 | $ 100 00 | -------- | -------------- |
| Expectation of life claims reported during the year and interest addition | 1,237 | 1,139,684 88 | -------- | -------------- |
| Totals | 1,238 | $1,139,784 88 | -------- | -------------- |
| Expectation of life claims paid during the year | 1,221 | 1,124,284 88 | -------- | -------------- |
| Claims paid during the year | -------- | -------------- | 29 | $23,977 53 |
| Claims unpaid December 31, 1921 | 17 | $15,500 00 | -------- | -------------- |

# RECEIVERS' REPORTS.

## REPORT ON AMERICAN LIFE INSURANCE COMPANY OF ILLINOIS.

American Life Insurance Company of Illinois—No report.

## REPORT ON GERMAN NATIONAL LIFE INSURANCE COMPANY.

Simon P. Gary, Attorney at Law, Suite 1214 Ashland Block.

CHICAGO, ILLINOIS, *March 4, 1922.*

*Department of Trade and Commerce, Springfield, Illinois:*

Attention Mr. T. J. Houston, Superintendent of Insurance.

MY DEAR SIR: Yours of January 18, 1922 received. I note your request for a report covering operation during 1921, and I am pleased to submit it. It is as follows:

No receipts.

Disbursed the sum of $58.80, having paid the same to August Rhode, a stockholder of said German National Life Insurance Company, and balance in the bank December 31, 1921 of $2,321.74.

SIMON P. GARY,

*Receiver for German National Life Insurance Company.*

Since receiving your letter I have again gone over my files inspecting the checks which I have executed and on file ready to be delivered to the stockholders who have not responded to my correspondence and requests to send in their certificate or receipts. I recently received one response from a stockholder stating that he had sold his certificate but he did not know who bought it.

I am again preparing letters sending them to the last known addresses of the stockholders who have not received their distributions in hopes that I can wake up some of them and get this matter in shape that it may be closed.

Trusting that the above gives you, together with my previous letter, full information concerning the above matter and assuring you that we shall be pleased to give you any further information within our ability which you may desire, we remain

Yours very truly,

SIMON P. GARY.

## REPORT OF INDEPENDENT ORDER OF TREU BUND.

CENTRALIA, ILLINOIS, *January 24, 1922.*

*Department of Trade and Commerce, Mr. T. J. Houston, Superintendent of Insurance.*

DEAR SIR: In compliance with your request wish to state that nothing new has transpired regarding the Receivership of the Grand Lodge of the Independent Order of Treu Bund. All the Mexican bonds are securely placed in a safety box and we are waiting for the Mexican Government to redeem same. I have tried to sell these bonds, but there is no use of trying to dispose of same now, as there is hardly any value to them at present.

I have been requested by the old members to hold the bonds until such time that we will realize something for same.

Hoping this information will be satisfactory,

Yours very truly,

MAX PRILL,

*Receiver, Independent Order of Treu Bund.*

---

## REPORT OF NORTHERN LIFE INSURANCE COMPANY—FIRST STATE TRUST AND SAVINGS BANK.

SPRINGFIELD, ILLINOIS, *January 30, 1922.*

*Department of Trade and Commerce, T. J. Houston, Superintendent of Insurance, Springfield, Illinois.*

DEAR SIR: Referring to your letter of January 14th relative to the Receivership of the Northern Life Insurance Company, I beg to say that there has been no change in this account since our report to you of January 1, 1921, at which time we showed the sum of $969.95 on hand represented the amount of claims filed against the estate and which were not in shape for the approval of the court.

It is our intention to at once ask the court for an order discharging us as Receiver and directing the disposal of this sum.

Yours very truly,

FIRST STATE TRUST AND SAVINGS BANK,

Formerly Sangamon Loan and Trust Company,
*Receiver for the Northern Life Insurance Company.*

L. T. SOUTHER, *Trust Officer.*

---

## REPORT OF PIONEER LIFE INSURANCE COMPANY.

Pioneer Life Insurance Company—No report.

# INDEX TO PART II.

LIFE INSURANCE COMPANIES—MISCELLANEOUS.



LIFE INSURANCE COMPANIES OF ILLINOIS.



LIFE INSURANCE COMPANIES OF OTHER STATES.

## LIFE INSURANCE COMPANIES OF FOREIGN GOVERNMENTS.



## ASSESSMENT LIFE ASSOCIATIONS—MISCELLANEOUS.

## ASSESSMENT LIFE ASSOCIATIONS OF ILLINOIS.



## ASSESSMENT LIFE ASSOCIATIONS OF OTHER STATES.



## FRATERNAL BENEFICIARY SOCIETIES—MISCELLANEOUS.



## FRATERNAL BENEFICIARY SOCIETIES OF ILLINOIS.

## FRATERNAL BENEFICIARY SOCIETIES OF OTHER STATES.

## FRATERNAL BENEFICIARY SOCIETIES OF FOREIGN GOVERNMENTS.



## FINANCIAL REPORT.



## RECEIVERS' REPORTS.

Lightning Source UK Ltd.
Milton Keynes UK
UKHW012302301218
334781UK00009B/594/P

9 780260 964991